Webster's
American
&
Spanish–English
Dictionary

RANDOM HOUSE
NEW YORK

Typeset and printed in the United States of America

0 9 8 7 6 5 4 3 2 1

0-375-72013-8

New York   Toronto   London   Sydney   Auckland

Webster's
American
Dictionary

Contents

Pronunciation Key

The symbol (′), as in **moth′er,** is used to mark primary stress; the syllable preceding it is pronounced with greater prominence than the other syllables in the word. The symbol (′), as in **grand′moth′er,** is used to mark secondary stress; a syllable marked for secondary stress is pronounced with less prominence than one marked (′) but with more prominence than those bearing no stress mark at all.

a	act, bat	**o͝o**	book, put
ā	able, cape	**o͞o**	ooze, rule
â	air, dare	**ou**	out, loud
ä(r)	art, calm		
		p	page, stop
b	back, rub	**r**	read, cry
ch	chief, beach	**s**	see, miss
d	do, bed	**sh**	shoe, push
		t	ten, bit
e	ebb, set	**th**	thin, path
ē	equal, bee	**t͟h**	that, other
f	fit, puff	**u**	up, love
g	give, beg	**û**	urge, burn
h	hit, hear		
		v	voice, live
i	if, big	**w**	west, away
ī	ice, bite	**y**	yes, young
		z	zeal, lazy, those
j	just, edge	**zh**	vision, measure
k	kept, make		
l	low, all	**ə**	occurs only in unaccented syllables and indicates the sound of
			a *in* along
m	my, him		e *in* system
n	now, on		i *in* easily
ng	sing, England		o *in* gallop
			u *in* circus
o	box, hot		
ō	over, no		
ô	order, ball		
oi	oil, joy		

Abbreviations Commonly Used in This Book

adj.	adjective	*Math.*	mathematics
adv.	adverb	*n.*	noun
art.	article	*pp.*	past participle
aux.	auxiliary	*pl.*	plural
Brit.	British	*prep.*	preposition
cap.	capital	*pron.*	pronoun
conj.	conjunction	*pt.*	past tense
def.	definition	*sing.*	singular
esp.	especially	*usu.*	usually
fem.	feminine	*v.*	verb
Gram.	grammar	*v.i.*	intransitive verb
interj.	interjection	*v.t.*	transitive verb
l.c.	lower case		

A

A, a (ā) *n.* the first letter of the English alphabet.

a (ə; *when stressed* ā) *adj. or indef. art. before initial consonant sounds.* **1.** one. **2.** any; any one.

a- a prefix indicating: **1.** not. **2.** without.

AA Alcoholics Anonymous.

A.A. Associate of Arts.

aard′vark′ (ärd′värk′) *n.* an African ant-eating mammal.

A.B. Bachelor of Arts.

A.B.A. American Bar Association.

a·back′ (ə bak′) *adv.* —*Idiom.* **taken aback,** disconcerted.

ab′a·cus (ab′ə kəs) *n.* a counting device using rows of sliding beads.

ab′a·lo′ne (ab′ə lō′nē) *n.* an edible mollusk having a shell lined with mother-of-pearl.

a·ban′don (ə ban′dən) *v.t.* **1.** to leave completely. **2.** to give up. —*n.* **3.** a surrender to natural impulses. —**a·ban′don·ment,** *n.*

a·ban′doned *adj.* **1.** forsaken or deserted. **2.** unrestrained or uninhibited.

a·base′ (ə bās′) *v.t.*, **abased, abasing.** to humiliate or degrade. —**a·base′ment,** *n.*

a·bate′ (ə bāt′) *v.t.*, *v.i.*, **abated, abating.** to make or become less intense. —**a·bate′ment,** *n.*

ab′at·toir′ (ab′ə twär′, ab′ə twär′) *n.* a slaughterhouse.

ab′bess (ab′is) *n.* a woman who is head of a convent.

ab′bey (ab′ē) *n.* a monastery or convent.

ab′bot (ab′ət) *n.* a man who is head of a monastery.

abbr. abbreviation.

ab·bre′vi·ate′ (ə brē′vē āt′) *v.t.*, **-ated, -ating.** to shorten. —**ab·bre′vi·a′tion,** *n.*

ABC *n.*, *pl.* **ABC's, ABCs. 1.** the alphabet. **2.** **ABCs,** the basics.

ab′di·cate′ (ab′di kāt′) *v.t.*, *v.i.*, **-cated, -cating.** to give up (power or office). —**ab′di·ca′tion,** *n.*

ab′do·men (ab′də mən) *n.* the part of the body between the thorax and the pelvis; belly. —**ab·dom′i·nal** (ab dom′ə nl) *adj.*

ab·dom′i·nals *n.pl.* the muscles of the abdomen. Also, **abs.**

ab·duct′ (ab dukt′) *v.t.* to kidnap. —**ab·duc′tion,** *n.* —**ab·duc′tor,** *n.*

ab′er·ra′tion (ab′ə rā′shən) *n.* **1.** deviation from what is usual or normal. **2.** mental unsoundness. —**ab·er′rant** (ə ber′ənt, ab′ər-) *adj.*

a·bet′ (ə bet′) *v.t.*, **abetted, abetting.** to encourage in wrongdoing. —**a·bet′tor, a·bet′ter,** *n.*

a·bey′ance (ə bā′əns) *n.* **in abeyance,** temporarily inactive.

ab·hor′ (ab hôr′) *v.t.*, **-horred, -horring.** to loathe. —**ab·hor′rence,** *n.* —**ab·hor′rent,** *adj.*

a·bide′ (ə bīd′) *v.*, **abode** (ə bōd′) **or abided, abiding.** —*v.t.* **1.** to tolerate. —*v.i.* **2.** to remain. **3.** to reside. **4. abide by, a.** to comply with. **b.** to keep, as a promise.

a·bid′ing *adj.* steadfast; lasting.

a·bil′i·ty (ə bil′i tē) *n.*, *pl.* **-ties. 1.** the power to do something. **2.** competence.

ab′ject (ab′jekt, ab jekt′) *adj.* **1.** wretched. **2.** despicable. **3.** servile. —**ab′ject·ly,** *adv.* —**ab·jec′tion,** *n.*

ab·jure′ (ab joŏr′) *v.t.*, **-jured, -juring.** to repudiate or renounce. —**ab′ju·ra′tion,** *n.*

a·blaze′ (ə blāz′) *adj.* **1.** on fire. **2.** gleaming. **3.** excited.

a′ble (ā′bəl) *adj.*, **abler, ablest. 1.** having sufficient power or qualification. **2.** competent. —**a′bly,** *adv.*

-able a suffix indicating: **1.** able to be. **2.** tending to.

a′ble-bod′ied *adj.* physically fit.

ab·lu′tions (ə bloō′shənz) *n.pl.* the washing of one's body, esp. as a ritual.

ab′ne·gate′ (ab′ni gāt′) *v.t.*, **-gated, -gating.** to renounce. —**ab′ne·ga′tion,** *n.*

ab·nor′mal (ab nôr′məl) *adj.* not normal; not usual or typical. —**ab′nor·mal′i·ty** (-mal′i tē) *n.* —**ab·nor′mal·ly,** *adv.*

a·board′ (ə bôrd′) *adv.* **1.** on a ship, train, etc. —*prep.* **2.** on.

a·bode′ (ə bōd′) *n.* a dwelling.

a·bol′ish (ə bol′ish) *v.t.* to do away with.

ab′o·li′tion (ab′ə lish′ən) *n.* **1.** an abolishing or being abolished. **2.** (*sometimes cap.*) the end of slavery in the U.S. —**ab′o·li′tion·ist,** *n.*

a·bom′i·na·ble (ə bom′ə nə bəl) *adj.* **1.** very bad. **2.** detestable. —**a·bom′i·na·bly,** *adv.*

a·bom′i·nate′ (-nāt′) *v.t.*, **-nated, -nating.** to hate or detest. —**a·bom′i·na′tion,** *n.*

ab′o·rig′i·nal (ab′ə rij′ə nl) *adj.* **1.** having existed in a place from the beginning. —*n.* **2.** an aborigine.

ab′o·rig′i·ne (-rij′ə nē) *n.* an original inhabitant of a land.

a·bort′ (ə bôrt′) *v.i.*, *v.t.* **1.** to undergo or cause abortion. **2.** to end prematurely. —**a·bor′tive,** *adj.*

a·bor′tion *n.* the induced or spontaneous expulsion of a fetus before it is viable.

a·bound′ (ə bound′) *v.i.* **1.** to exist in large quantities. **2. abound in,** to be well supplied with.

a·bout′ (ə bout′) *prep.* **1.** concerning. **2.** near or around. **3.** on every side of. **4.** on the verge of. —*adv.* **5.** approximately. **6.** almost. **7.** nearby. **8.** on all sides. **9.** in the opposite direction. —**Usage.** Both ON and ABOUT mean "concerning"; ABOUT is used when the information given is general and not too technical: *a novel* ABOUT *the Civil War.* ON is used when the information is particular, as by being scholarly or technical: *an important article* ON *the Civil War.*

a·bove′ (ə buv′) *adv.* **1.** in or to a higher place. **2.** overhead. **3.** earlier in a text. —*prep.* **4.** over. **5.** higher or greater than. **6.** beyond the reach or level of. —*adj.* **7.** preceding. —**Idiom. 8. above all,** most importantly.

a·bove′board′ *adv., adj.* without deception.

a·bra′sion (ə brā′zhən) *n.* **1.** a wearing or rubbing away. **2.** a scraped area on the skin. —**a·brade′,** *v.t., v.i.*

a·bra′sive (ə brā′siv, -ziv) *adj.* **1.** tending to wear down. **2.** harsh. —*n.* **3.** material used to grind or smooth. —**a·bra′sive·ly,** *adv.*

a·breast′ (ə brest′) *adv.* **1.** side by side. **2. abreast of, a.** level with. **b.** informed or aware of.

a·bridge′ *v.t.,* **abridged, abridging.** to shorten. —**a·bridg′ment,** *n.*

a·broad′ (ə brôd′) *adv., adj.* **1.** away from one's own country. **2.** over a large area.

ab′ro·gate′ (ab′rə gāt′) *v.t.,* **-gated, -gating.** to abolish or repeal. —**ab′ro·ga′tion,** *n.*

ab·rupt′ (ə brupt′) *adj.* **1.** sudden. **2.** curt. **3.** steep. —**ab·rupt′ly,** *adv.* —**ab·rupt′ness,** *n.*

ab′scess (ab′ses) *n.* an infected, pus-filled place on the body.

ab·scond′ (-skond′) *v.i.* to depart suddenly and secretly.

ab′sent *adj.* (-sənt) **1.** not present. **2.** lacking. **3.** preoccupied. —*v.t.* (ab sent′) **4.** to keep (oneself) away. —**ab′sence,** *n.*

ab′sen·tee′ (-sən tē′) *n.* a person who is absent.

ab′sent-mind′ed *adj.* preoccupied; forgetful. —**ab′sent-mind′ed·ly,** *adv.* —**ab′sent-mind′ed·ness,** *n.*

ab′so·lute′ (-sə lōōt′) *adj.* **1.** complete; perfect. **2.** unrestricted. **3.** definite. **4.** pure. —**ab′so·lute′ly,** *adv.*

ab′solute ze′ro *n.* the temperature (−273.16° C or −459.69° F) at which molecular activity ceases.

ab·solve′ (- zolv′) *v.t.,* **-solved, -solving. 1.** to declare free from guilt. **2.** to release from a duty. —**ab′so·lu′tion** (-sə lōō′shən) *n.*

ab·sorb′ (-sôrb′, -zôrb′) *v.t.* **1.** to take in or soak up. **2.** to occupy completely; fascinate. —**ab·sorb′ing,** *adj.* —**ab·sorp′tion,** *n.* —**ab·sorp′tive,** *adj.*

ab·stain′ (-stān′) *v.i.* **1.** to refrain. **2.** to refrain from casting one's vote. —**ab·sten′tion** (-sten′shən) *n.*

ab·ste′mi·ous (-stē′mē əs) *adj.* moderate in eating, drinking, etc.

ab′sti·nence (-stə nəns) *n.* abstaining, as from food, alcohol, or sexual activity. —**ab′sti·nent,** *adj.*

ab′stract *adj.* (ab strakt′, ab′strakt) **1.** considered apart from specific objects. **2.** theoretical. **3.** (of art) not representing natural objects or forms. —*n.* (ab′strakt) **4.** a summary. **5.** an abstract idea. —*v.t.* (ab strakt′) **6.** to remove. **7.** to summarize. —**ab·strac′tion,** *n.*

ab·stract′ed *adj.* preoccupied; absent-minded.

ab·struse′ (-strōōs′) *adj.* hard to understand.

ab·surd′ (-sûrd′, -zûrd′) *adj.* contrary to common sense; ridiculous. —**ab·surd′i·ty,** *n.*

a·bun′dance (ə bun′dəns) *n.* a plentiful supply. —**a·bun′dant,** *adj.* —**a·bun′dant·ly,** *adv.*

a·buse′ *v.,* **abused, abusing,** *n.* —*v.t.* (-byōōz′) **1.** to use wrongly. **2.** to treat badly. **3.** to insult. —*n.* (-byōōs′) **4.** wrong use. **5.** mistreatment. **6.** insulting language. —**a·bu′sive,** *adj.*

a·but′ (-but′) *v.i., v.t.,* **abutted, abutting.** to be adjacent (to); border (on).

a·bys′mal (ə biz′məl) *adj.* **1.** extremely bad. **2.** very deep.

a·byss′ (ə bis′) *n.* **1.** a very deep chasm. **2.** hell.

AC 1. air conditioning. **2.** Also, **ac., a.c., A.C.** alternating current.

a·ca′cia (ə kā′shə) *n.* a small tree or shrub with yellow flowers.

ac′a·dem′ic (ak′ə dem′ik) *adj.* **1.** of a school, college, etc. **2.** theoretical. —*n.* **3.** a college teacher. —**ac′a·dem′i·cal·ly,** *adv.*

a·cad′e·my (ə kad′ə mē) *n., pl.* **-mies. 1.** a private secondary school. **2.** a school for specialized study. **3.** a society of scholars, artists, etc.

a′ cap·pel′la (ä′ kə pel′ə) *adv., adj.*

Music. without instrumental accompaniment.

ac·cede′ (ak sēd′) v. -ceded, -ceding. accede to, 1. to agree to. 2. to assume (an office or title).

ac·cel′er·ate′ (ak sel′ə rāt′) v., -ated, -ating. —v.t. 1. to increase the speed of. —v.i. 2. to speed up; hasten. —ac·cel′er·a′tion, n.

ac·cel′er·a′tor n. a pedal that controls a vehicle's speed.

ac′cent (ak′sent) n. 1. emphasis on a syllable or word. 2. a distinctive way of pronouncing. 3. a mark showing stress or vowel quality. —v.t. 4. to emphasize.

ac·cen′tu·ate′ (ak sen′chŏŏ āt′) v.t., -ated, -ating. to stress or emphasize. —ac·cen′tu·a′tion, n.

ac·cept′ (ak sept′) v.t. 1. to receive willingly. 2. to answer yes to (an invitation, offer, etc.). 3. to agree to. 4. to admit formally, as to a college. 5. to regard as true. —ac·cept′a·ble, adj. —ac·cept′ed, adj. —ac·cept′a·bil′i·ty, n. —ac·cept′a·bly, adv. —ac·cept′ance, n. —Usage. Because of similarity in pronunciation, ACCEPT and EXCEPT are sometimes confused in writing. ACCEPT is a verb meaning "to receive willingly": *Please accept my gift.* EXCEPT is usually a preposition meaning "other than": *Everybody came except you.* When EXCEPT is used as a verb, it means "to leave out": *Some students were excepted from taking the exam.*

ac′cess (ak′ses) n. 1. the right to enter or use. 2. a means of approach. —v.t. 3. to gain access to. 4. to gain access to (data, files, etc.) in a computer.

ac·ces′si·ble (-ses′ə bəl) adj. easy to reach or use. —ac·ces′si·bil′i·ty, n.

ac·ces′sion (-sesh′ən) n. 1. the attainment of a rank, an office, etc. 2. something added.

ac·ces′so·ry (-ses′ə rē) n., pl. -ries. 1. something added for convenience, decoration, etc. 2. a person who has knowledge of or helps another commit a felony.

ac′ci·dent (ak′si dənt) n. 1. an unexpected event, esp. one resulting in damage. 2. chance. —ac′ci·den′tal, adj.

ac·claim′ (ə klām′) v.t. 1. to greet with enthusiastic approval. —n. 2. enthusiastic approval. —ac′cla·ma′tion (ak′lə mā′shən) n.

ac′cli·mate′ (ak′lə māt′, ə klī′mit) v.t., v.i., -ated, -ating. to accustom or become accustomed to new conditions. Also, **ac·cli′ma·tize′**.

ac′co·lade′ (ak′ə lād′, -läd′) n. 1. an award. 2. high praise.

ac·com′mo·date′ (ə kom′ə dāt′) v.t., -dated, -dating. 1. to supply with something needed. 2. to do a favor for. 3. to provide with lodging, food, etc. 4. to adapt.

ac·com′mo·dat′ing adj. helpful; obliging.

ac·com′mo·da′tion n. 1. the act of accommodating. 2. **accommodations**, lodgings.

ac·com′pa·ni·ment (ə kum′pə nimənt, ə kump′ni-) n. 1. something added, as for decoration. 2. a musical part supporting the main part.

ac·com′pa·ny v.t., -nied, -nying. 1. to go or be with. 2. to provide musical support for (a soloist). —ac·com′pa·nist, n.

ac·com′plice (ə kom′plis) n. a partner in crime.

ac·com′plish (ə kom′plish) v.t. to complete successfully.

ac·com′plished adj. highly skilled.

ac·com′plish·ment n. 1. successful completion. 2. an achievement. 3. an acquired skill.

ac·cord′ (ə kôrd′) v.i. 1. to agree; be in harmony. —v.t. 2. to cause to agree. 3. to grant. —n. 4. agreement. —*Idiom.* 5. of one's own accord, voluntarily. —ac·cord′ance, n. —ac·cord′ant, adj.

ac·cord′ing·ly adv. therefore.

according to prep. 1. in keeping with. 2. as stated by.

ac·cor′di·on (ə kôr′dē ən) n. 1. a portable musical instrument with a keyboard and bellows. —adj. 2. having folds like an accordion bellows.

ac·cost′ (ə kôst′) v.t. 1. to approach and speak to. 2. to confront.

ac·count′ (ə kount′) n. 1. a report or narration. 2. importance. 3. a sum of money deposited in a bank. 4. a credit arrangement. 5. a record of business transactions. —v. 6. **account for,** to explain the reason for. —*Idiom.* 7. **on account of,** because of. 8. **on no account,** absolutely not. 9. **take into account,** to consider.

ac·count′a·ble adj. responsible.

ac·count′ant n. a person trained in accounting.

ac·count′ing n. the organization and maintenance of financial records. —ac·count′an·cy, n.

ac·cred′it (ə kred′it) v.t. 1. to certify as meeting requirements. 2. to attribute. —ac·cred′i·ta′tion, n.

ac·cre′tion (ə krē′shən) n. 1. an increase by growth or addition. 2. an addition.

ac·crue′ (ə krōō′) v.i., -crued, -cruing. to accumulate. —ac·cru′al, n.

ac·cu′mu·late′ (ə kyōō′myə lāt′)

v.t., v.i., **-lated, -lating. 1.** to gather; collect. **2.** to increase in quantity. —**ac•cu′mu•la′tion,** *n.* —**ac•cu′mu•la•tive** (-lə tiv) *adj.*

ac′cu•rate (ak′yər it) *adj.* exact; correct. —**ac′cu•rate•ly,** *adv.* —**ac′cu•ra•cy,** *n.*

ac•curs′ed (ə kûr′sid, ə kûrst′) *adj.* **1.** under a curse. **2.** hateful.

ac•cuse′ (ə kyōoz′) *v.t.,* **-cused, -cusing. 1.** to blame. **2.** to charge with an offense. —**ac′cu•sa′tion** (ak/yōo-zā′shən) *n.* —**ac•cus′er,** *n.* —**ac•cus′a•to′ry,** *adj.*

ac•cused′ *n.* a person charged with a crime.

ac•cus′tom (ə kus′təm) *v.t.* to make familiar by use.

ac•cus′tomed *adj.* usual; habitual.

ace (ās) *n., v.,* **aced, acing.** —*n.* **1.** a playing card with one spot. **2.** an expert. —*v.t.* **3.** to do very well on.

a•cer′bic (ə sûr′bik) *adj.* **1.** sharp, as in manner. **2.** sour.

a•ce′ta•min′o•phen (ə sē′tə min′ə-fən) *n.* a crystalline substance used to reduce pain or fever.

ac′e•tate′ (as′i tāt′) *n.* **1.** a salt or ester of acetic acid. **2.** a synthetic fiber derived from cellulose.

a•ce′tic (ə sē′tik) *adj.* of or producing vinegar.

ace′tic ac′id *n.* a sharp-tasting acid in vinegar.

ac′e•tone′ (as′i tōn′) *n.* a flammable liquid used as a solvent.

a•cet′y•lene′ (ə set′l ēn′) *n.* a gas used in welding, etc.

ache (āk) *v.,* **ached, aching,** *n.* —*v.i.* **1.** to suffer a continuous dull pain. **2.** to yearn. —*n.* **3.** a continuous dull pain.

a•chieve′ (ə chēv′) *v.t.,* **achieved, achieving.** to accomplish; bring about. —**a•chieve′ment,** *n.*

A•chil′les heel′ (ə kil′ēz) *n.* a vulnerable spot.

ac′id (as′id) *n.* **1.** a chemical that can react with a base to form a salt. **2.** a sour substance. —*adj.* **3.** of acids. **4.** sour or sharp. —**a•cid′ic,** *adj.* —**a•cid′i•ty,** *n.*

ac′id rain′ *n.* rain containing chemicals from pollution.

ac•knowl′edge (ak nol′ij) *v.t.,* **-edged, -edging. 1.** to admit. **2.** to show recognition of. **3.** to show appreciation for. —**ac•knowl′edg•ment,** *n.*

ac′me (ak′mē) *n.* the highest point.

ac′ne (ak′nē) *n.* a skin disorder characterized by pimples.

ac′o•lyte′ (ak′ə līt′) *n.* **1.** an altar attendant. **2.** a follower.

a′corn (ā′kôrn, ā′kərn) *n.* the nut of the oak tree.

a•cous′tic (ə kōō′stik) *adj.* of sound or hearing. —**a•cous′ti•cal•ly,** *adv.*

a•cous′tics *n.* **1.** the science of sound. **2.** the qualities of a space that affect sound.

ac•quaint′ (ə kwānt′) *v.t.* to make known or familiar.

ac•quaint′ance *n.* **1.** a person one knows casually. **2.** personal knowledge.

ac′qui•esce′ (ak′wē es′) *v.i.,* **-esced, -escing.** to agree or comply without protest. —**ac′qui•es′cence,** *n.* —**ac′qui•es′cent,** *adj.*

ac•quire′ (ə kwīᵊr′) *v.t.,* **-quired, -quiring.** to get; obtain.

ac′qui•si′tion (ak′wə zish′ən) *n.* **1.** an acquiring. **2.** something acquired.

ac•quis′i•tive (ə kwiz′i tiv) *adj.* eager to acquire things. —**ac•quis′i•tive•ness,** *n.*

ac•quit′ (ə kwit′) *v.t.,* **-quitted, -quitting. 1.** to declare free of blame or guilt. **2.** to behave or conduct (oneself). —**ac•quit′tal,** *n.*

a′cre (ā′kər) *n.* a unit of land measurement (1/640 sq. mi. or 43,560 sq. ft.). —**a′cre•age,** *n.*

ac′rid (ak′rid) *adj.* sharp; biting.

ac′ri•mo′ny (ak′rə mō′nē) *n.* bitterness of manner or speech.

ac′ro•bat′ (ak′rə bat′) *n.* a performer on the trapeze, tightrope, etc. —**ac′ro•bat′ic,** *adj.*

ac′ro•bat′ics *n. (used with a pl. v.)* **1.** an acrobat's feats. **2.** any feats requiring agility.

ac′ro•nym (-nim) *n.* a word formed from successive initials or groups of letters, as NATO or UNICEF.

ac′ro•pho′bi•a (ak′rə fō′bē ə) *n.* a fear of heights.

a•cross′ (ə krôs′) *prep.* **1.** from one side to the other of. **2.** on the other side of. —*adv.* **3.** from one side to another.

across′-the-board′ *adj.* applying to all members or categories.

a•cryl′ic (ə kril′ik) *n.* a chemical substance used to make textile fibers and paints.

act (akt) *n.* **1.** something done. **2.** a law or decree. **3.** a division of a play or opera. —*v.i.* **4.** to do something. **5.** to behave. **6.** to pretend. **7.** to perform in a play, movie, etc.

act′ing *adj.* substitute.

ac′tion (ak′shən) *n.* **1.** the process of doing something. **2.** something done. **3.** behavior. **4.** combat. **5.** a lawsuit.

ac′tion•a•ble *adj.* providing grounds for a lawsuit.

ac′ti•vate′ (ak′tə vāt′) *v.t.,* **-vated, -vating.** to make active; start. —**ac′ti•va′tion,** *n.*

ac′tive (ak′tiv) adj. **1.** doing something. **2.** energetic. **3.** currently in progress. —**ac′tive•ly,** adv.

ac′tiv•ism n. vigorous action in pursuit of social or political goals. —**ac′tiv•ist,** n.

ac•tiv/i•ty (ak tiv′i tē) n., pl. **-ties. 1.** the state or quality of being active. **2.** a specific occupation or pursuit.

ac′tor (ak′tər) n. a person who performs in plays or movies. —**ac′tress,** n.fem.

ac′tu•al (ak′chōō əl) adj. existing in reality. —**ac′tu•al/i•ty** (-al′i tē) n.

ac′tu•ar/y (ak′chōō er′ē) n., pl. **-aries.** a person who calculates insurance rates and risks. —**ac′tu•ar/i•al,** adj.

ac′tu•ate/ (ak′chōō āt′) v.t., **-ated, -ating.** to put into action.

a•cu/i•ty (ə kyōō′i tē) n. sharpness of perception.

a•cu/men (ə kyōō′mən) n. mental keenness.

ac′u•punc/ture (ak′yōō pungk′chər) n. the Chinese art of healing by inserting needles into the skin. —**ac′u•punc/tur•ist,** n.

a•cute/ (ə kyōōt′) adj. **1.** sharp; pointed. **2.** severe. **3.** keen. **4.** (of an angle) less than 90 degrees. —**a•cute/ly,** adv. —**a•cute/ness,** n.

ad (ad) an advertisement.

A.D. anno Domini: in the year of our Lord.

ad′age (ad′ij) n. a proverb.

a•da/gio (ə dä′jō, -zhē ō′) adj., adv. *Music.* slow.

ad/a•mant (ad′ə mənt) adj. unyielding.

Ad/am′s ap/ple (ad′əmz) n. the projection of thyroid cartilage in front of the neck.

a•dapt/ (ə dapt′) v.t. **1.** to make suitable to requirements or conditions. —v.i. **2.** to adjust oneself to new conditions, environment, etc.

a•dapt/a•ble adj. able to adjust easily to new conditions. —**a•dapt/a•bil/i•ty,**

ad/ap•ta/tion (ad′ap ta′shən) n. **1.** an adapting or being adapted. **2.** the result of adapting.

a•dapt/er or **a•dap/tor** n. **1.** a connector for parts of different size or design. **2.** a device for adapting a tool or machine to a new use.

add (ad) v.t. **1.** to join so as to increase. **2.** to find the sum of. **3.** to say further. —v.i. **4.** to be an addition. **5. add up,** to seem reasonable. **6. ~ up to,** to amount to.

ad•den/dum (ə den′dəm) n., pl. **-da** (-də). **1.** an addition. **2.** an appendix to a book.

ad/der (ad′ər) n. a small venomous snake.

ad/dict n. (ad′ikt) **1.** a person who is dependent on a substance, as a drug. —v.t. (ə dikt′) **2.** to make dependent on a drug. —**ad•dic/tion,** n. —**ad•dic/tive,** adj.

ad•di/tion (ə dish′ən) n. **1.** the act of adding. **2.** anything added. —**Idiom. 3. in addition to,** besides. —**ad•di/tion•al,** adj.

ad/di•tive (ad′i tiv) n. an added ingredient.

ad/dle (ad′l) v.t., **-dled, -dling.** to confuse.

ad•dress/ (ə dres′) n. **1.** the place where one lives or where mail may be delivered. **2.** a formal speech. —v.t. **3.** to write an address on. **4.** to speak to. **5.** to apply (oneself) to a task. —**ad/dress•ee/** (ad′re sē′) n.

ad•duce/ (ə dōōs′, ə dyōōs′) v.t., **-duced, -ducing.** to present or cite as evidence.

a•dept/ adj. (ə dept′) **1.** skilled. —n. (ad′ ept, ə dept′) **2.** expert.

ad/e•quate (ad′i kwit) adj. **1.** sufficient. **2.** just good enough. —**ad/e•quate•ly,** adv. —**ad/e•qua•cy,** n.

ad•here/ (ad hēr′) v.i., **-hered, -hering. 1.** to stick or cling. **2.** to be faithful or loyal. —**ad•her/ence,** n. —**ad•her/ent,** n., adj.

ad•he/sive (ad hē′siv, -ziv) adj. **1.** coated with a sticky substance. **2.** sticky. —n. **3.** a sticky substance.

ad hoc (ad hok′, hōk′) adj., adv. for a specified purpose.

a•dieu/ (ə dōō′, ə dyōō′) interj., n. *French.* good-by; farewell.

ad in/fi•ni/tum (ad in/fə nī′təm) adv. endlessly.

adj. adjective.

ad•ja/cent (ə jā′sənt) adj. lying near; adjoining.

ad/jec•tive (aj′ik tiv) n. a word describing a noun or pronoun. —**ad/jec•ti/val** (-tī′vəl) adj.

ad•join/ (ə join′) v.t. to be next to.

ad•journ/ (ə jûrn′) v.t., v.i. to suspend (a proceeding) to a future time or place. —**ad•journ/ment,** n.

ad•judge/ (ə juj′) v.t., **-judged, -judging. 1.** to decree or decide. **2.** to award judicially.

ad•ju/di•cate/ (ə jōō′di kāt′) v.t., **-cated, -cating.** to settle (a dispute) judicially. —**ad•ju/di•ca/tion,** n.

ad/junct (aj′ungkt) n. **1.** something added but not essential. **2.** an assistant. **3.** a person teaching at a college without full status.

ad•just/ (ə just′) v.t. **1.** to change slightly to make fit; adapt. **2.** to regulate. —v.i. **3.** to adapt oneself. —**ad•just/a•ble,** adj. —**ad•just/er, ad•jus/tor,** n. —**ad•just/ment,** n.

ad'ju·tant (aj'ə tənt) *n.* an assistant to a commanding officer.

ad-lib' *v.,* **-libbed, -libbing,** *adj.* —*v.t., v.i.* **1.** to improvise (speech, music, etc.). —*adj.* **2.** improvised. —**ad lib'**, *n., adv.*

Adm. admiral.

ad·min'is·ter (ad min'ə stər) *v.t.* **1.** to manage or direct. **2.** to give.

ad·min·is·tra'tion (-ə strā'shən) *n.* **1.** the management of an office or business. **2.** the act of dispensing. **3.** the executive branch of a government. —**ad·min'is·tra'tive,** *adj.*

ad·min'is·tra'tor *n.* a manager.

ad'mi·ra·ble (ad'mər ə bəl) *adj.* worthy of admiration.

ad'mi·ral (ad'mər əl) *n.* a high-ranking navy officer.

ad·mire' (ad mī^ər') *v.t.* **1.** to regard with pleasure or approval. **2.** to respect. —**ad'mi·ra'tion** (-mə rā'-shən) *n.* —**ad·mir'er,** *n.*

ad·mis'si·ble (ad mis'ə bəl) *adj.* able to be admitted or allowed.

ad·mis'sion (-mish'ən) *n.* **1.** the act of admitting. **2.** permission to enter. **3.** an entrance price. **4.** a confession or acknowledgment.

ad·mit' (-mit') *v.t.,* **-mitted, -mitting.** **1.** to allow to enter. **2.** to permit. **3.** to confess or acknowledge. —**ad·mit'tance,** *n.*

ad·mit'ted·ly *adv.* as must be acknowledged.

ad·mon'ish (ad mon'ish) *v.t.* **1.** to advise against something. **2.** to reprove mildly. —**ad'mo·ni'tion** (ad'mə nish'ən) *n.*

ad nau'se·am (ad nô'zē əm) *adv.* to a sickening degree.

a·do' (ə dōō') *n.* fuss; bother.

a·do'be (ə dō'bē) *n.* sun-dried brick.

ad'o·les'cence (ad'l es'əns) *n.* the period between childhood and adulthood. —**ad'o·les'cent,** *adj., n.*

a·dopt' (ə dopt') *v.t.* **1.** to accept as one's own. **2.** to become the legal parent of (the child of another). —**a·dop'tion,** *n.* —**a·dopt'ive,** *adj.*

a·dore' (ə dôr') *v.t.,* **adored, adoring.** **1.** to love greatly. **2.** to worship. **3.** to like very much. —**a·dor'a·ble,** *adj.* —**ad'o·ra'tion** (ad'ə rā'shən) *n.*

a·dorn' (-dôrn') *v.t.* to decorate with ornaments. —**a·dorn'ment,** *n.*

ad·re'nal (ə drēn'l) *adj.* of a pair of glands near the kidneys.

ad·ren'al·in (ə dren'l in) *n.* a hormone that stimulates the central nervous system.

a·drift' (ə drift') *adv., adj.* **1.** floating without anchor. **2.** without direction.

a·droit' (-droit') *adj.* expert; deft. —**a·droit'ly,** *adv.* —**a·droit'ness,** *n.*

ad'u·la'tion (aj'ə lā'shən) *n.* excessive praise.

a·dult' (-dult') *adj.* **1.** full-grown; mature. **2.** of, befitting, or for adults. —*n.* **3.** a full-grown person. —**a·dult'hood,** *n.*

a·dul'ter·ate' *v.t.,* **-ated, -ating.** to make impure. —**a·dul'ter·a'tion,** *n.* —**a·dul'ter·ant,** *n.*

a·dul'ter·y *n., pl.* **-teries.** marital infidelity. —**a·dul'ter·er,** *n.* —**a·dul'ter·ess,** *n.* —**a·dul'ter·ous,** *adj.*

adv. **1.** adverb. **2.** advertisement.

ad·vance' (ad vans') *v.,* **-vanced, -vancing.** —*v.t.* **1.** to move forward. **2.** to propose. **3.** to raise in rank, price, etc. **4.** to supply beforehand. —*v.i.* **5.** to go forward. **6.** to rise in rank or status. —*n.* **7.** a forward move. **8.** a promotion. **9.** an increase. **10.** a loan. **11.** a friendly gesture. —*adj.* **12.** early. —**Idiom. 13. in advance,** beforehand. —**ad·vance'ment,** *n.*

ad·vanced' *adj.* **1.** ahead in knowledge, skill, etc. **2.** far along, as in age. **3.** progressive.

ad·van'tage (ad van'tij) *n.* **1.** a circumstance or condition favorable to success. **2.** a benefit or gain. —**Idiom. 3. take advantage of, a.** to make use of. **b.** to impose upon by exploiting a weakness. —**ad'van·ta'geous** (-tā'jəs) *adj.*

ad·vent' (-vent) *n.* **1.** an arrival. **2. Advent,** the season beginning four Sundays before Christmas.

ad·ven·ti'tious (-vən tish'əs) *adj.* accidental.

ad·ven'ture (-yven'chər) *n., v.,* **-tured, -turing.** —*n.* **1.** a risky undertaking. **2.** an exciting experience. —**ad·ven'tur·er,** *n.* —**ad·ven'tur·ous,** *adj.*

ad'verb (-vûrb) *n.* a word modifying a verb, adjective, or other adverb. —**ad·ver'bi·al,** *adj.*

ad'ver·sar'y (-vər ser'ē) *n., pl.* **-saries.** an opponent.

ad·verse' (-vûrs') *adj.* opposing; unfavorable. —**ad·verse'ly,** *adv.*

ad·ver'si·ty (-vûr'si tē) *n., pl.* **-ties.** misfortune.

ad'ver·tise' (-vər tīz') *v.,* **-tised, -tising.** —*v.t.* **1.** to describe or praise publicly. **2.** to call public attention to. —*v.i.* **3.** to seek or offer goods or services in the news media. —**ad'ver·tis'er,** *n.* —**ad'ver·tise'ment,** *n.* —**ad'ver·tis'ing,** *n.*

ad·vice' (-vīs') *n.* a recommendation concerning action.

ad·vis'a·ble (-vī'zə bəl) *adj.* wise or prudent. —**ad·vis'a·bil'i·ty,** *n.*

ad·vise′ (-vīz′) *v.t.*, **-vised, -vising.**
1. to give advice to. **2.** to recommend. **3.** to give information to.
—**ad·vis′er, ad·vi′sor,** *n.*
ad·vis′ed·ly *adv.* deliberately.
ad·vi′so·ry *adj.* **1.** giving advice.
—*n.* **2.** a report on existing or predicted conditions.
ad′vo·cate′ *v.*, **-cated, -cating,** *n.*
—*v.t.* (ad′və kāt′) **1.** to urge or support by argument; recommend.
—*n.* (-kit) **2.** a supporter of a cause.
—**ad′vo·ca·cy** (-kə sē) *n.*
adz (adz) *n.* an axlike tool.
ae′gis (ē′jis) *n.* sponsorship.
ae′on (ē′ən, ē′on) *n.* an eon.
aer′ate (âr′āt) *v.t.*, **-ated, -ating.** to expose to or supply with air.
aer′i·al (âr′ē əl) *adj.* **1.** of or like the air. **2.** frequenting or growing in the air. —*n.* **3.** a radio or television antenna.
aer′ie (âr′ē, ēr′ē) *n*, *pl.* **-ies.** an eagle's nest.
aer·o′bic (â rō′bik) *adj.* **1.** needing oxygen to live. **2.** of aerobics.
aer·o′bics *n.pl.* exercises designed to strengthen the heart and lungs.
aer′o·dy·nam′ics (âr′ō dī nam′iks) *n.* the study of the action of air against solids. —**aer′o·dy·nam′ic,** *adj.*
aer′o·nau′tics *n.* the science of flight. —**aer′o·naut′i·cal,** *adj.*
aer′o·sol′ (âr′ə sôl′) *n.* **1.** liquid particles distributed through a gas.
2. a spray of such liquid.
aer′o·space′ (âr′ō spās′) *n.* **1.** the earth's atmosphere and the space beyond. —*adj.* **2.** of missiles, spacecraft, etc., used in aerospace.
aes·thet′ic (es thet′ik) *adj.* **1.** of or appreciating beauty. **2.** artistic.
—**aes′thete** (-thēt) *n.*
aes·thet′ics *n.* the branch of philosophy dealing with beauty.
a·far′ (ə fär′) *adv.* at a distance.
af′fa·ble (af′ə bəl) *adj.* warm and friendly. —**af′fa·bil′i·ty,** *n.*
af·fair′ (ə fâr′) *n.* **1.** anything requiring action; matter. **2. affairs,** business or public matters. **3.** a private concern. **4.** a sexual relationship. **5.** an incident causing public scandal. **6.** a social event.
af·fect′[1] (ə fekt′) *v.t.* to produce an effect on; act on; move. —**Usage.** Because of similarity in pronunciation, AFFECT and EFFECT are sometimes confused in writing. The verb AFFECT means "to act on" or "to move": *His words affected the crowd so deeply that many wept.* The verb EFFECT means "to bring about, accomplish": *The new taxes effected many changes in people's lives.* The noun EFFECT means "result, consequence": *the tragic effect of the hurricane.*

af·fect′[2] (ə fekt′) *v.t.* **1.** to pretend. **2.** to assume pretentiously.
af′fec·ta′tion (af′ek tā′shən) *n.* **1.** pretense. **2.** artificiality of manner or appearance.
af·fect′ed (ə fek′tid) *adj.* **1.** full of affectation. **2.** assumed artificially.
—**af·fect′ed·ly,** *adv.*
af·fec′tion (ə fek′shən) *n.* love; liking.
af·fec′tion·ate *adj.* fondly tender; loving. —**af·fec′tion·ate·ly,** *adv.*
af′fi·da′vit (af′i dā′vit) *n.* a written statement under oath.
af·fil′i·ate′ *v.*, **-ated, -ating,** *n.*
—*v.t.* (ə fil′ē āt′) **1.** to associate or connect. —*v.i.* **2.** to associate oneself; unite. —*n.* (-ē it) **3.** an associate. —**af·fil′i·a′tion,** *n.*
af·fin′i·ty (ə fin′i tē) *n.*, *pl.* **-ties. 1.** an attraction. **2.** a close similarity.
af·firm′ (ə fûrm′) *v.t.* **1.** to declare formally. **2.** to confirm. —*v.i.* **3.** to state something solemnly. —**af′fir·ma′tion** (af′ər mā′shən) *n.*
af·firm′a·tive *adj.* saying yes; affirming.
affirm′ative ac′tion *n.* a policy to increase opportunities for women and minorities.
af·fix′ *v.t.* (ə fiks′) **1.** to add on; attach. —*n.* (af′iks) **2.** an added part.
af·flict′ (ə flikt′) *v.t.* to distress physically or mentally. —**af·flic′tion,** *n.*
af′flu·ent (af′loo ənt) *adj.* rich; abundant. —**af′flu·ence,** *n.*
af·ford′ (ə fôrd′) *v.t.* **1.** to have resources enough for. **2.** to provide.
af·front′ (ə frunt′) *n.* **1.** an insult.
—*v.t.* **2.** to offend.
af′ghan (af′gan) *n.* a knitted blanket.
a·field′ (ə fēld′) *adv.* **1.** at a distance. **2.** off the mark.
a·fire′ (ə fīʳr′) *adv.*, *adj.* on fire.
a·flame′ (ə flām′) *adv.*, *adj.* in flames.
AFL-CIO American Federation of Labor and Congress of Industrial Organizations.
a·float′ (ə flōt′) *adv.*, *adj.* **1.** floating. **2.** at sea. **3.** out of debt.
a·foot′ (ə foŏt′) *adv.*, *adj.* **1.** in progress. **2.** on foot.
a·fore′said′ (ə fôr′sed′) *adj.* mentioned before. Also, **a·fore′men′tioned** (-men′shənd).
a·fraid′ (ə frād′) *adj.* **1.** frightened. **2.** regretful.
a·fresh′ (ə fresh′) *adv.* anew.
aft (aft) *adv.* Naut. at or toward the stern.
af′ter (af′tər) *prep.* **1.** behind. **2.**

afterbirth

8

about. **3.** later than. **4.** in imitation of. —*adv.* **5.** behind. **6.** later.

af·ter·birth/ *n.* the placenta expelled from the uterus after childbirth.

af·ter·ef·fect/ *n.* a delayed or secondary effect.

af·ter·glow/ *n.* **1.** a glow after sunset. **2.** a pleasant memory.

af·ter·life/ *n.* life after death.

af·ter·math/ *n.* consequences.

af·ter·noon/ *n.* the period between noon and evening.

af·ter·thought/ *n.* a later thought.

af·ter·ward (-wərd) *adv.* later. Also, **af·ter·wards**.

a·gain/ (ə gen/) *adv.* **1.** once more. **2.** besides.

a·gainst/ (ə genst/) *prep.* **1.** opposed to. **2.** in or into contact with.

a·gape/ (ə gāp/) *adv., adj.* wide open.

ag·ate (ag/it) *n.* a kind of quartz with colored bands.

age (āj) *n., v.,* **aged, aging** or **ag·ing.** —*n.* **1.** the length of time in existence. **2.** a period of human life. **3.** a historical or geological period. **4.** the later part of life. —*v.i., v.t.* **5.** to grow or cause to grow old. **6.** to mature, as wine. —*Idiom.* **7. of age,** having reached adulthood.

ag·ed *adj.* **1.** (ā/jid) having lived long. **2.** (ājd) matured. —*n.pl.* (ā/jid) **3.** elderly people.

age·less *adj.* **1.** apparently not aging. **2.** not outdated.

a/gen·cy (ā/jən sē) *n., pl.* **-cies.** **1.** the function or office of an agent. **2.** a government bureau. **3.** the means of doing something.

a·gen·da (ə jen/də) *n.* a list of matters to be dealt with.

a/gent (ā/jənt) *n.* **1.** one acting for another. **2.** a means. **3.** an official.

ag·glom/er·a/tion (ə glom/ə rā/shən) *n.* a mass of varied parts.

ag·gran·dize (ə gran/dīz, ag/rən-dīz/) *v.t.,* **-dized, -dizing. 1.** to make great or greater in power, honor, etc. **2.** to make (something) seem greater. —**ag·gran/dize·ment** (-diz mənt) *n.*

ag/gra·vate/ (ag/rə vāt/) *v.t.,* **-vated, -vating. 1.** to make worse. **2.** to annoy. —**ag/gra·va/tion,** *n.* —*Usage.* In formal speech and writing, the meaning "to annoy" (*Stop aggravating me!*) is sometimes criticized and is used less often than the meaning "to make worse" (*His insulting words aggravated the tense situation*).

ag/gre·gate *adj., n., v.,* **-gated, -gating.** —*adj.* (ag/ri git) **1.** total.

—*n.* (-git) **2.** a mass. —*v.t., v.i.* (-gāt/) **3.** to gather into a mass.

ag·gres/sion (ə gresh/ən) *n.* **1.** a hostile act; attack. **2.** hostile behavior. —**ag·gres/sor,** *n.*

ag·gres/sive (ə gres/iv) *adj.* **1.** hostile. **2.** vigorously energetic.

ag·grieve/ (ə grēv/) *v.t.,* **-grieved, -grieving.** to wrong severely.

a·ghast/ (ə gast/) *adj.* horrified.

ag·ile (aj/əl) *adj.* quick; nimble. —**a·gil/i·ty** (ə jil/i tē) *n.*

ag/i·ta (aj/i tə) *n.* **1.** indigestion. **2.** anxiety.

ag/i·tate/ (aj/i tāt/) *v.,* **-tated, -tating.** —*v.t.* **1.** to shake. **2.** to disturb; excite. —*v.i.* **3.** to try to arouse public feeling. —**ag/i·ta/tion,** *n.* —**ag/i·ta/tor,** *n.*

ag·nos/tic (ag nos/tik) *n.* a person who believes that the existence of God is unknown and unknowable. —**ag·nos/ti·cism** (-tə siz/əm) *n.*

a·go/ (ə gō/) *adj., adv.* in the past.

a·gog/ (ə gog/) *adj.* eagerly excited.

ag/o·nize/ (ag/ə nīz/) *v.i., v.t.,* **-nized, -nizing.** to suffer or cause to suffer pain or anguish.

ag/o·ny (-nē) *n., pl.* **-nies.** intense pain or suffering.

ag/o·ra·pho/bi·a (ag/ər ə fō/bē ə) *n.* a fear of open spaces.

a·grar/i·an (ə grâr/ē ən) *adj.* of the land.

a·gree/ (ə grē/) *v.i.,* **agreed, agreeing. 1.** to consent or promise. **2.** to have a similar opinion. **3.** to arrive at an understanding. **4.** to be beneficial. —**a·gree/ment,** *n.*

a·gree/a·ble *adj.* **1.** pleasant. **2.** willing. —**a·gree/a·bly,** *adv.*

ag/ri·busi/ness (ag/rə biz/nis) *n.* the large-scale business of growing, processing, and distributing farm products.

ag/ri·cul/ture *n.* farming. —**ag/ri·cul/tur·al,** *adj.*

a·gron/o·my (ə gron/ə mē) *n.* the science of farm management.

a·ground/ (ə ground/) *adv., adj.* (of a ship) on or onto the shore.

ah (ä) *interj.* (an exclamation of pain, surprise, or satisfaction)

a·head/ (ə hed/) *adv.* **1.** in or at the front. **2.** forward. **3.** into or for the future.

a·hoy/ (ə hoi/) *interj. Naut.* (hey there!)

aid (ād) *v.t., v.i.* **1.** to help. —*n.* **2.** help; assistance.

aide (ād) *n.* an assistant.

aide-de-camp (ād/də kamp/) *n., pl.* **aides-de-camp.** a military assistant.

AIDS (ādz) *n.* acquired immune deficiency syndrome: a disease making one increasingly susceptible to infections and other diseases.

ail (āl) *v.t.* **1.** to trouble. —*v.i.* **2.** to be sick.

ai·ler·on (ā′lə ron′) *n.* a flap on an airplane wing.

ail′ment *n.* an illness.

aim (ām) *v.t.* **1.** to point or direct at a target. —*v.i.* **2.** to direct a gun, punch, etc. **3.** to intend. **4.** to direct one's efforts. —*n.* **5.** the act of aiming. **6.** a target. **7.** a purpose. —**aim′less,** *adj.*

ain't (ānt) *Nonstandard or Dial.* am not; are not; is not. —**Usage.** AIN'T is more common in uneducated speech, though it occurs in the informal speech of the educated: *I ain't going. He ain't so young anymore.* The question form "Ain't I...?" is sometimes substituted for "Aren't I...?", which is usually considered to be ungrammatical. AIN'T also occurs in some humorous or set phrases, and it is sometimes used to give emphasis: *Ain't it the truth! It just ain't so!*

air (âr) *n.* **1.** the mixture of gases forming the earth's atmosphere. **2.** appearance; manner. **3.** a tune. —*v.t.* **4.** to expose to air. **5.** to broadcast. —**Idiom. 6. in the air,** current. **7. on the air,** broadcasting. **8. up in the air,** not decided.

air′ bag′ *n.* a bag that inflates automatically to protect passengers in a car collision.

air′borne′ (-bôrn) *adj.* carried by air; flying.

air′brush′ *n.* **1.** an atomizer for spraying paint or other liquid. —*v.t.* **2.** to paint with an airbrush.

air′ condi′tioning *n.* a system for controlling the temperature and humidity of air. —**air′-condi′-tioned,** *adj.*

air′craft′ *n.* a vehicle or vehicles for flight.

air′field′ *n.* a ground area on which airplanes land and take off.

air′ force′ *n.* the military branch that carries out air operations.

air′lift′ *n.* **1.** major transport of supplies by aircraft in an emergency. —*v.t.* **2.** to move by airlift.

air′line′ *n.* an air transport company.

air′lin′er *n.* a large passenger airplane operated by an airline.

air′mail′ *n.* **1.** the system of sending mail by airplane. **2.** mail sent by airplane. —*v.t.* **3.** to send by airplane. Also, **air′ mail′.**

air′plane′ *n.* a powered heavier-than-air craft with fixed wings.

air′port′ *n.* a place where aircraft pick up passengers and cargo.

air′ raid′ *n.* an attack by aircraft.

air′ship′ *n.* a lighter-than-air aircraft.

air′space′ *n.* the space above a nation, city, etc., over which it has control.

air′tight′ *adj.* **1.** impermeable to air. **2.** having no weak points.

air′waves′ *n.pl.* the medium of radio and television broadcasting.

air′y *adj.,* **-ier, -iest. 1.** of or like air. **2.** delicate. **3.** well ventilated. **4.** light; lively. —**air′i·ly,** *adv.*

aisle (īl) *n.* a passage between seats or shelves.

a·jar′ (ə jär′) *adj., adv.* partly open.

AK Alaska.

a.k.a. also known as.

a·kim·bo (ə kim′bō) *adj., adv.* with hands on hips.

a·kin′ (ə kin′) *adj.* alike.

AL Alabama.

à la or **a la** (ä′ lä, ä′ lə) *prep.* in the manner or style of.

Ala. Alabama.

al′a·bas′ter (al′ə bas′tər) *n.* a translucent white gypsum.

à la carte (ä′ lə kärt′) *adv., adj.* with each dish on a menu separately priced.

a·lac′ri·ty (ə lak′ri tē) *n.* cheerful readiness.

à la mode (ä′ lə mōd′) *adv., adj.* **1.** in the fashion. **2.** with ice cream.

a·larm′ (ə lärm′) *n.* **1.** sudden fear caused by danger. **2.** a warning signal. —*v.t.* **3.** to fill with fear.

alarm′ clock′ *n.* a clock with a device to awaken a sleeper.

a·las′ (ə las′) *interj.* (an expression of dismay)

al′ba·tross′ (al′bə trôs′) *n.* **1.** a large white sea bird. **2.** a burden.

al·be·it (ôl bē′it) *conj.* although.

al·bi·no (al bī′nō) *n., pl.* **-nos.** a person or animal lacking in pigmentation in the skin or hair.

al′bum (al′bəm) *n.* **1.** a blank book for pictures, stamps, etc. **2.** a collection of recordings.

al·bu′men (-byoo′mən) *n.* egg white.

al·bu′min *n.* a water-soluble protein found in egg white, milk, blood, etc.

al′che·my (al′kə mē) *n.* medieval chemistry. —**al′che·mist,** *n.*

al′co·hol′ (al′kə hôl′) *n.* **1.** a colorless flammable liquid produced by fermentation. **2.** an intoxicating liquor containing alcohol.

al′co·hol′ic *adj.* **1.** of or containing alcohol. —*n.* **2.** a person addicted to alcohol. —**al′co·hol·ism,** *n.*

al′cove (al′kōv) *n.* a recessed space.

al′der (ôl′dər) *n.* a small tree of the birch family.

al′der·man (-dər mən) *n.*, *pl.* **-men.** a city official.

ale (āl) *n.* a kind of beer.

a·lert′ (ə lûrt′) *adj.* **1.** observant. **2.** vigilant. —*n.* **3.** a warning or alarm. —*v.t.* **4.** to warn. —**a·lert′ly**, *adv.* —**a·lert′ness**, *n.*

al·fal′fa (al fal′fə) *n.* a clover-like forage plant.

al·fres′co (al fres′kō) *adv.*, *adj.* in the open air. Also, **al fres′co.**

al′gae (al′jē) *n.pl.*, *sing.* **-ga** (-gə). one-celled water plants.

al′ge·bra (al′jə brə) *n.* a branch of mathematics using symbols rather than specific numbers. —**al′ge·bra′ic** (-jə brā′ik) *adj.*

al′go·rithm (al′gə rith′əm) *n.* a set of rules or steps to solve mathematical problems, program a computer, etc. —**al′go·rith′mic**, *adj.*

a′li·as (ā′lē əs) *adv.* **1.** otherwise known as. —*n.* **2.** an assumed name.

al′i·bi (al′ə bī′) *n.* **1.** the defense by an accused person of having been elsewhere when a crime was committed. **2.** an excuse.

al′ien (āl′yən) *n.* **1.** a foreign-born resident. **2.** a creature from outer space. —*adj.* **3.** foreign.

al′ien·ate′ (-yə nāt′) *v.t.*, **-ated, -ating.** to cause to become unfriendly or hostile. —**al′ien·a′tion**, *n.*

a·light′¹ (ə līt′) *v.i.* **1.** to dismount. **2.** to descend to perch or sit.

a·light′² (ə līt′) *adv.*, *adj.* lighted up.

a·lign′ (ə līn′) *v.t.* **1.** to bring into line. **2.** to ally (oneself) with a group or cause. —**a·lign′ment**, *n.*

a·like′ (ə līk′) *adv.* **1.** similarly. —*adj.* **2.** similar.

al′i·men′ta·ry (al′ə men′tə rē) *adj.* of or for nourishment.

alimen′tary canal′ *n.* a tube in the body through which food passes.

al′i·mo′ny (al′ə mō′nē) *n.* money paid for the support of a spouse after separation or divorce.

a·live′ (ə līv′) *adj.* **1.** living. **2.** active. **3.** lively. **4.** teeming.

al′ka·li′ (al′kə lī′) *n.* a chemical that neutralizes acids. —**al′ka·line′**, *adj.*

al′ka·loid′ (-loid′) *n.* a bitter, nitrogen-containing compound in plants.

all (ôl) *adj.* **1.** the whole amount or number of. —*pron.* **2.** the whole quantity; everything. —*n.* **3.** one's whole energy or property. —*adv.* **4.** entirely. —*Idiom.* **5. all but,** almost. **6. all in all,** everything considered. **7. at all,** to any degree or in any way.

Al′lah (al′ə, ä′lə) *n.* the Muslim name for God.

all′-around′ *adj.* versatile.

al·lay′ (ə lā′) *v.t.* to quiet or lessen.

al·lege′ (ə lej′) *v.t.*, **-leged, -leging.** to state without proof. —**al′le·ga′·tion** (al′i gā′shən) *n.*

al·leged′ *adj.* **1.** declared to be so, but without proof. **2.** supposed. —**al·leg′ed·ly** (-lej′id-) *adv.*

al·le′giance (ə lē′jəns) *n.* loyalty to a government, group, cause, etc.

al′le·go′ry (al′ə gôr′ē) *n.*, *pl.* **-ries.** a story in which characters and actions are symbols for ideas. —**al′le·gor′i·cal**, *adj.*

al·le′gro (ə lā′grō, ə leg′rō) *adv. Music.* fast.

al′le·lu′ia (al′ə lōō′yə) *interj.* (hallelujah)

al′ler·gen (al′ər jən) *n.* a substance that causes an allergic reaction. —**al′ler·gen′ic** (-jen′ik) *adj.*

al·ler′gic (ə lûr′jik) *adj.* **1.** caused by an allergy. **2.** having an allergy. **3.** *Informal.* having a dislike.

al′ler·gy (-jē) *n.*, *pl.* **-gies.** **1.** a physical sensitivity to a substance. **2.** *Informal.* a strong dislike.

al·le′vi·ate′ (ə lē′vē āt′) *v.t.*, **-ated, -ating.** to lessen or relieve (pain).

al′ley (al′ē) *n.*, *pl.* **-leys.** a narrow street.

al′ley cat′ *n.* a domestic cat of unknown parentage.

al·li′ance (ə lī′əns) *n.* **1.** a formal union for mutual benefit. **2.** a close relationship.

al·lied′ (ə līd′, al′īd) *adj.* **1.** joined by common cause. **2.** related.

al′li·ga′tor (al′i gā′tər) *n.* a broadsnouted type of crocodile.

all′-in·clu′sive *adj.* comprehensive.

al·lit′er·a′tion (ə lit′ə rā′shən) *n.* repetition of the same sound at the beginning of two or more words.

al′lo·cate′ (al′ə kāt′) *v.t.*, **-cated, -cating.** to set apart for a special purpose. —**al′lo·ca′tion**, *n.*

al·lot′ (ə lot′) *v.t.*, **-lotted, -lotting.** to divide; distribute as a portion. —**al·lot′ment**, *n.*

all′-out′ *adj.* total; unrestricted.

al·low′ (ə lou′) *v.t.* **1.** to permit. **2.** to give. **3.** to concede. —*v.i.* **4.** to permit as a possibility. **5. allow for,** to make provision for. —**al·low′a·ble**, *adj.*

al·low′ance (ə lou′əns) *n.* **1.** an amount granted. **2.** a sum of money given regularly, as for expenses. —*Idiom.* **3. make allowance for,** to excuse.

al′loy *n.* (al′oi) **1.** a mixture of metals. —*v.t.* (ə loi′) **2.** to mix (metals).

all′ right′ *adv.* **1.** yes. **2.** satisfactorily. **3.** certainly. —*adj.* **4.** safe; sound. **5.** acceptable; satisfactory. —**Usage.** The spelling ALRIGHT is used in informal writing. However, the phrase ALL RIGHT is preferred in formal, edited writing.

All′ Saints′′ Day′ *n.* a Christian festival Nov. 1 in honor of the saints.

all′spice′ *n.* a sharp, fragrant spice from a tropical American tree.

all′-time′ *adj.* never equaled or surpassed.

al.lude′ (ə lood′) *v.i.,* **-luded, -luding.** to refer to casually or indirectly. —**al.lu′sion,** *n.*

al.lure′ (ə loor′) *n., v.,* **-lured, -luring.** —*n.* **1.** fascination. —*v.t.* **2.** to attract; tempt. —**al.lur′ing,** *adj.*

al.lu′vi.um (ə loo′vē əm) *n.* sediment deposited by flowing water. —**al.lu′vi.al,** *adj.*

al.ly′ *v.,* **-lied, -lying,** *n., pl.* **-lies.** —*v.t., v.i.* (ə lī′) **1.** to unite or become united in an alliance. —*n.* (al′ī) **2.** a person, nation, etc., bound to another, as by a treaty.

al′ma ma′ter (äl′mə mä′tər; al′mə mä′tər) *n.* one's school or college.

al′ma.nac′ (ôl′mə nak′) *n.* an annual publication containing statistical information, meteorological data, etc.

al.might′y (ôl mī′tē) *adj.* **1.** having unlimited power. —*n.* **2. the Almighty,** God.

al′mond (ä′mənd) *n.* the oval-shaped edible nut of a tree of the rose family.

al′most (ôl′mōst, ôl mōst′) *adv.* nearly.

alms (ämz) *n.pl.* money or food given to the poor.

a.loft′ (ə lôft′) *adv., adj.* high up.

a.lo′ha (ə lō′ə, ä lō′hä) *n., interj.* **1.** hello. **2.** farewell.

a.lone′ (ə lōn′) *adj., adv.* **1.** apart from others. **2.** without another person. **3.** only.

a.long′ (ə lông′) *prep.* **1.** through the length of. —*adv.* **2.** parallel in the same direction. **3.** onward. **4.** in company; together.

a.long′side′ *adv.* **1.** to one's side. —*prep.* **2.** beside.

a.loof′ (ə loof′) *adv.* **1.** at a distance. —*adj.* **2.** reserved; indifferent. —**a.loof′ness,** *n.*

a.lot′ (ə lot′) *n.* LOT (def. 4). —**Usage.** The spelling ALOT, though fairly common in informal writing, is usually considered an error. The two-word spelling A LOT is the accepted form: *He has a lot of money. I like her a lot.* A LOT is itself considered informal; in formal speech or writing, the phrases "a

great number," "a great amount," or "a great deal" are usually substituted for A LOT.

a.loud′ (ə loud′) *adv.* in a voice that can be heard.

al.pac′a (al pak′ə) *n.* a South American mammal related to the llama and having soft silky wool.

al′pha (al′fə) *n.* the first letter of the Greek alphabet.

al′pha.bet′ (al′fə bet′, -bit) *n.* the letters of a language in order. —**al′pha.bet′i.cal,** *adj.* —**al′pha.bet.ize′,** *v.t.*

al′pha.nu.mer′ic *adj.* using both letters and numbers. —**al′pha.nu.mer′i.cal.ly,** *adv.*

al′pine (al′pīn, -pin) *adj.* growing or found in high mountains.

al.read′y (ôl red′ē) *adv.* **1.** prior to a certain time. **2.** so soon.

al.right′ (ôl rīt′) *adv., adj.* ALL RIGHT. —**Usage.** See ALL RIGHT.

al′so (ôl′sō) *adv.* in addition.

alt. 1. alternate. **2.** altitude. **3.** alto.

al′tar (ôl′tər) *n.* a table used for religious rites.

al′ter *v.t., v.i.* to make or become different. —**al′ter.a′tion,** *n.*

al.ter.ca′tion (-kā′shən) *n.* an angry dispute.

al′ter e′go *n.* **1.** the other side of one's personality. **2.** a close friend.

al′ter.nate′ *v.,* **-nated, -nating,** *adj., n.* —*v.i., v.t.* (-nāt′) **1.** to occur or cause to occur in turns. —*adj.* (-nit) **2.** being every second one. —*n.* (-nit) **3.** a substitute. —**al′ter.na′tion,** *n.*

al′ternating cur′rent *n.* an electric current that regularly reverses its direction.

al.ter′na.tive (-tûr′nə tiv) *n.* **1.** another possible choice. —*adj.* **2.** offering a choice.

al′ter.na.tor (-tər nā′tər) *n.* a generator of alternating current.

al.though′ (ôl thō′) *conj.* even though.

al.tim′e.ter (al tim′i tər, al′tə mē′tər) *n.* a device for measuring altitude.

al′ti.tude′ (al′ti tood′, -tyood′) *n.* the height of a thing above a reference point, as sea level.

al′to (al′tō) *n., pl.* **-tos. 1.** the lowest female singing voice. **2.** a singer with this voice. —*adj.* **3.** of this pitch.

al′to.geth′er (ôl′tə geth′ər) *adv.* entirely.

al′tru.ism′ (al′troo iz′əm) *n.* unselfish concern for others. —**al′tru.ist,** *n.* —**al′tru.is′tic,** *adj.*

al′um (al′əm) *n.* an astringent substance containing aluminum and potassium.

a·lu'mi·num (ə lōō'mə nəm) *n.* a light, silvery metal. Also, *Brit.*, **al'u·min'i·um** (al'yə min'ē əm).

a·lum'na (ə lum'nə) *n., pl.* **-nae** (-nē). a female graduate.

a·lum'nus (-nəs) *n., pl.* **-ni** (-nī). a male graduate.

al'ways (ôl'wāz, -wēz) *adv.* **1.** all the time. **2.** every time.

Alz'hei·mer's disease' (älts'hī-mərz, ôlts'-) *n.* a disease marked by increasing memory loss and mental deterioration, usu. in old age.

am (am; *unstressed* əm, m) *v.* 1st pers. sing. pres. indic. of **be.**

a.m. the period before noon. Also, **A.M.**

A.M.A. American Medical Association.

a·mal'gam (ə mal'gəm) *n.* a mixture, esp. one with mercury.

a·mal'ga·mate' (-gə māt') *v.t., v.i.,* **-mated, -mating.** to combine. —**a·mal'ga·ma'tion,** *n.*

am'a·ryl'lis (am'ə ril'is) *n.* a plant with large red or pink lilylike flowers.

a·mass' (ə mas') *v.t.* to collect.

am'a·teur' (am'ə chōōr', -chər, -tər) *n.* a nonprofessional artist, athlete, etc. —**am'a·teur·ish,** *adj.* —**am'a·teur·ism,** *n.*

am'a·to'ry (-tôr'ē) *adj.* of love.

a·maze' (ə māz') *v.t.,* **amazed, amazing.** to astonish greatly. —**a·maze'ment,** *n.*

am'a·zon' (am'ə zon', -zən) *n.* **1.** a female warrior of Greek legend. **2.** a tall, powerful woman.

am·bas'sa·dor (am bas'ə dər, -dôr') *n.* a diplomat of the highest rank.

am'ber (am'bər) *n.* **1.** a yellowish brown fossil resin. **2.** yellowish brown.

am'ber·gris' (-grēs') *n.* a secretion of the sperm whale, used in perfumes.

am'bi·dex'trous (am'bi dek'strəs) *adj.* using both hands equally well.

am'bi·ence (am'bē əns) *n.* surroundings; atmosphere. Also, **am'bi·ance.** —**am'bi·ent,** *adj.*

am·big'u·ous (-big'yōō əs) *adj.* **1.** uncertain. **2.** having several possible interpretations. —**am'bi·gu'i·ty,** *n.*

am·bi'tion (-bish'ən) *n.* **1.** a desire for success, power, etc. **2.** the object so desired. —**am·bi'tious,** *adj.*

am·biv'a·lent (-biv'ə lənt) *adj.* with conflicting feelings. —**am·biv'a·lence,** *n.*

am'ble (am'bəl) *v.,* **-bled, -bling,** *n.* —*v.i.* **1.** to go at an easy pace. —*n.* **2.** a slow, easy pace.

am·bro'sia (am brō'zhə) *n.* the food of the Greek gods.

am'bu·lance (am'byə ləns) *n.* a vehicle for transporting the sick or wounded.

am'bu·la·to'ry (-lə tôr'ē) *adj.* able to walk.

am'bush (-bŏŏsh) *n.* **1.** concealment for a surprise attack. **2.** a place of such concealment. **3.** an attack from concealment. —*v.t., v.i.* **4.** to attack from ambush.

a·me'ba (ə mē'bə) *n., pl.* **-bas** or **-bae** (-bē). a microscopic one-celled animal. Also, **a·moe'ba.**

a·mel'io·rate' (ə mēl'yə rāt') *v.t., v.i.,* **-rated, -rating.** to improve. —**a·mel'io·ra'tion,** *n.*

a'men' (ā'men', ä'men') *interj.* (so be it!)

a·me'na·ble (ə mē'nə bəl, ə men'ə-) *adj.* willing; agreeable.

a·mend' (ə mend') *v.t.* **1.** to modify (a bill, law, etc.). **2.** to improve. **3.** to correct. —*Idiom.* **4.** make **amends,** to compensate, as for an injury, loss, etc.

a·mend'ment *n.* a change in a formal text, as a law.

a·men'i·ty (ə men'i tē) *n., pl.* **-ties.** a feature that provides comfort or pleasure.

am'e·thyst (am'ə thist) *n.* a violet quartz used in jewelry.

a'mi·a·ble (ā'mē ə bəl) *adj.* pleasantly kind or friendly. —**a'mi·a·bil'i·ty,** *n.* —**a'mi·a·bly,** *adv.*

am'i·ca·ble (am'i kə bəl) *adj.* friendly. —**am'i·ca·bly,** *adv.*

a·mid' (ə mid') *prep.* among. Also, **a·midst'.**

a·mi'no ac'id (ə mē'nō, am'ə nō) *n.* a type of organic compound from which proteins are made.

a·miss' (ə mis') *adv.* **1.** wrongly. —*adj.* **2.** wrong.

am'i·ty (am'i tē) *n.* friendship.

am'me'ter (am'mē'tər) *n.* an instrument for measuring amperes.

am·mo'nia (ə mōn'yə) *n.* **1.** a colorless, pungent, water-soluble gas. **2.** this gas dissolved in water.

am'mu·ni'tion (am'yə nish'ən) *n.* bullets or shells fired by guns.

am·ne'sia (am nē'zhə) *n.* loss of memory. —**am·ne'si·ac'** (-zhē ak'), *adj., n.*

am'nes·ty (am'nə stē) *n.* a general pardon for political crimes.

am'ni·o·cen·te'sis (am'nē ō sen tē'sis) *n., pl.* **-ses** (-sēz). a procedure in which fluid is withdrawn from the uterus of a pregnant woman for genetic diagnosis of the fetus.

a·muck' (ə muk', ə mok') *adv.* amuck.

a·mong' (ə mung') *prep.* **1.** in the midst of. **2.** in the group of. **3.** for each of. Also, **a·mongst'.**

—**Usage.** Traditionally, BETWEEN is used to show relationship involving two people or things (*to decide between tea and coffee*), while AMONG expresses more than two (*The four brothers quarrelled among themselves*). BETWEEN, *however, is also used to express relationship of persons or things considered individually, no matter how many:* Between holding public office, teaching, and raising a family, she has little free time.

a·mor′al (ā môr′əl) *adj.* indifferent to moral standards.

am′o·rous (am′ər əs) *adj.* inclined to or expressing sexual love.

a·mor′phous (ə môr′fəs) *adj.* **1.** formless. **2.** indeterminate.

am′or·tize′ (am′ər tīz′, ə môr′tīz) *v.t.,* **-tized, -tizing.** to pay off gradually. —**am′or·ti·za′tion,** *n.*

a·mount′ (ə mount′) *n.* **1.** the sum total. **2.** quantity. —*v.i.* **3. amount to, a.** to add up to. **b.** to be equal to. —**Usage.** AMOUNT refers to quantity that cannot be counted (*the amount of energy*), while NUMBER refers to things that can be counted (*a number of days*).

am′per·age (am′pər ij, am pēr′-) *n.* the strength of an electric current.

am′pere (am′pēr) *n.* a unit measuring electric current.

am′per·sand′ (am′pər sand′) *n.* a sign (&) meaning "and."

am·phet′a·mine (am fet′ə mēn′, -min) *n.* a drug that stimulates the central nervous system.

am·phib′i·an (-fib′ē ən) *n.* **1.** an animal living both in water and on land. —*adj.* **2.** Also, **am·phib′i·ous.** operating on land or water.

am·phi·the′a·ter (am′fə thē′ə tər, -thē′ə′-) *n.* a theater with seats arranged in tiers around an open area.

am′ple (am′pəl) *adj.,* **-pler, -plest. 1.** sufficient. **2.** abundant. —**am′ply,** *adv.*

am′pli·fy′ (am′plə fī′) *v.t.,* **-fied, -fying.** to make larger, stronger, or louder. —**am′pli·fi·ca′tion,** *n.* —**am′pli·fi′er,** *n.*

am′pli·tude (-tōōd′, -tyōōd′) *n.* **1.** extent. **2.** abundance.

am′pule (am′pyōōl, -pōōl) *n.* a sealed glass or plastic vial containing a solution for hypodermic injection. Also, **am′pul, am′poule.**

am′pu·tate′ (am′pyōō tāt′) *v.t.,* **-tated, -tating.** to cut off (a limb) by surgery. —**am′pu·ta′tion,** *n.* —**am′pu·tee′,** *n.*

a·muck′ (ə muk′) *adv.* —**Idiom. run** or **go amuck,** to be out of control.

am′u·let (am′yə lit) *n.* a charm worn to protect against evil.

a·muse′ (ə myōōz′) *v.t.,* **amused, amusing. 1.** to occupy pleasantly. **2.** to cause to laugh. —**a·muse′ment,** *n.*

amuse′ment park′ *n.* a park with recreational rides.

an (ən; *when stressed* an) *adj.* or *indef. art.* before initial vowel sounds. See **a.**

a·nach′ro·nism (ə nak′rə niz′əm) *n.* a thing that belongs to a time period other than that in which it is placed. —**a·nach′ro·nis′tic,** *adj.*

an′a·con′da (an′ə kon′də) *n.* a very large South American snake.

an′a·gram′ (an′ə gram′) *n.* a word formed from the rearranged letters of another.

a′nal (ān′l) *adj.* of the anus.

an′al·ge′sic (an′əl jē′zik) *n.* a drug that relieves pain.

an′alog comput′er *n.* a computer that represents data by measurable quantities rather than numbers.

a·nal′o·gy (ə nal′ə jē) *n., pl.* **-gies.** a similarity in some respects. —**a·nal′o·gous** (-gəs) *adj.*

a·nal′y·sis (-sis) *n., pl.* **-ses** (-sēz′). **1.** the separation of an entity into parts for close examination. **2.** psychoanalysis. —**an′a·lyst** (an′l ist) *n.* —**an′a·lyt′ic, an′a·lyt′i·cal,** *adj.*

an′a·lyze′ (-īz′) *v.t.,* **-lyzed, -lyzing. 1.** to subject to analysis. **2.** to psychoanalyze.

an′ar·chy (an′ər kē) *n.* **1.** a state of society without laws or government. **2.** chaos. —**an′ar·chist,** *n.*

a·nath′e·ma (ə nath′ə mə) *n.* **1.** a solemn curse. **2.** a thing or person detested.

a·nat′o·my (ə nat′ə mē) *n., pl.* **-mies. 1.** the structure of an animal or plant. **2.** the science dealing with such structure. —**an′a·tom′i·cal** (an′ə tom′i kəl) *adj.*

an′ces·tor (an′ses tər) *n.* a person from whom one is descended. —**an·ces′tral,** *adj.* —**an′ces·try,** *n.*

an′chor (ang′kər) *n.* **1.** a heavy device lowered from a ship to keep it in place. **2.** the main broadcaster who coordinates a TV or radio newscast. —*v.t.* **3.** to fasten by an anchor. **4.** to serve as anchor for (a newscast). —**an′chor·age,** *n.*

an′chor·man′ or **an′chor·wom′an** or **an′chor·per′son,** *n., pl.* **-men.** a person who anchors a program of news, sports, etc.

an′cho·vy (an′chō vē) *n., pl.* **-vies.** a small strongly flavored fish.

an′cient (ān′shənt) *adj.* **1.** of times long past. **2.** very old.

an′cil•lar′y (an′sə ler′ē) *adj.* **1.** subordinate. **2.** helping.

and (and; *unstressed* ənd, ən, n) *conj.* **1.** with; also. **2.** plus. **3.** *Informal.* (used in place of **to** in infinitive): *Try and stop me.*

an•dan′te (än dän′tā) *adv. Music.* at moderate speed.

and′i′ron (and′ī′ərn) *n.* one of a pair of metal supports for logs in a fireplace.

an′dro•gen (an′drə jən) *n.* a male sex hormone, as testosterone.

an•drog′y•nous (an droj′ə nəs) *adj.* having both masculine and feminine characteristics.

an′droid (an′droid) *n.* an automaton in human form.

an′ec•dote′ (an′ik dōt′) *n.* a short true story.

a•ne′mi•a (ə nē′mē ə) *n.* an inadequate supply of hemoglobin in the red blood cells. —**a•ne′mic,** *adj.*

a•nem′o•ne′ (ə nem′ə nē′) *n.* a plant with white, purple, or red flowers.

an′es•the′sia (an′əs thē′zhə) *n.* insensibility to pain. —**an′es•thet′ic** (-thet′ik) *n., adj.* —**an•es′the•tist** (ə nes′thi-) *n.* —**an•es′the•tize′,** *v.t.*

a•new′ (ə noō′, ə nyoō′) *adv.* **1.** again. **2.** in a new way.

an′gel (ān′jəl) *n.* **1.** a spiritual being who is a messenger of God. **2.** a very kind and helpful person. —**an•gel′ic,** *adj.*

an′ger (ang′gər) *n.* **1.** strong displeasure; outrage. —*v.t.* **2.** to make angry.

an•gi′na pec′to•ris (an jī′nə pek′tə-ris) *n.* chest pain caused by inadequate blood flow to the heart.

an′gi•o•plas′ty (an′jē ə plas′tē) *n., pl.* **-ties.** the surgical repair of a blood vessel.

an′gle¹ (ang′gəl) *n., v.,* **-gled, -gling.** —*n.* **1.** the space between converging lines or surfaces. **2.** a point of view. —*v.t., v.i.* **3.** to move or bend at an angle. **4.** to write from a certain viewpoint.

an′gle² (ang′gəl) *v.i.,* **-gled, -gling.** **1.** to fish with a hook on a line. **2.** to try for something by artful means. —**an′gler,** *n.*

An′gli•cize′ (ang′glə sīz′) *v.t., v.i.,* **-cized, -cizing.** to make or become English in form or character.

An•go′ra (ang gôr′ə) *n.* **1.** a cat, goat, or rabbit with long, silky hair. **2. angora,** yarn or fabric from an Angora goat or rabbit.

an′gry (ang′grē) *adj.,* **-grier, -griest.** **1.** full of anger. **2.** inflamed. —**an′gri•ly,** *adv.*

angst (ängkst) *n.* a feeling of dread or anxiety.

an′guish (ang′gwish) *n.* extreme pain or grief.

an′gu•lar (ang′gyə lər) *adj.* **1.** having angles. **2.** measured by an angle. **3.** lean and bony. —**an•gu•lar′i•ty,** *n.*

an′i•mad•ver′sion (an′ə mad vûr′-zhən) *n.* criticism. —**an′i•mad•vert′,** *v.i.*

an′i•mal (an′ə məl) *n.* **1.** a living thing that can move voluntarily. **2.** a beast. —*adj.* **3.** of animals.

an′i•mate′ *v.,* **-mated, -mating,** *adj.* —*v.t.* (-māt′) **1.** to give life to. **2.** to make lively. —*adj.* (-mit) **3.** alive.

an′i•ma′tion *n.* **1.** liveliness. **2.** an animated cartoon.

an′i•me′ (an′ə mā′) *n.* a Japanese style of animation, marked by highly stylized art and sexuality and violence.

an′i•mism (-miz′əm) *n.* the belief that animals and natural objects have souls.

an′i•mos′i•ty (an′ə mos′i tē) *n.* strong dislike or hostility.

an′i•mus (-məs) *n.* strong dislike; animosity.

an′ise (an′is) *n.* a plant yielding an aromatic seed (**an′i•seed′**) used in cooking.

an′kle (ang′kəl) *n.* the joint between the foot and the leg.

an′klet (-klit) *n.* **1.** a short, ankle-length sock. **2.** an ornament for the ankle.

an′nals (an′lz) *n.pl.* a historical record of events.

an•neal′ (ə nēl′) *v.t.* to toughen or temper (metal or glass).

an•nex′ *v.t.* (ə neks′) **1.** to attach to something larger. —*n.* (an′ eks) **2.** a thing annexed. **3.** an attached building. —**an′nex•a′tion,** *n.*

an•ni′hi•late′ (ə nī′ə lāt′) *v.t.,* **-lated, -lating.** to destroy completely. —**an•ni′hi•la′tion,** *n.*

an′ni•ver′sa•ry (an′ə vûr′sə rē) *n., pl.* **-ries.** the yearly recurrence of the date of a past event.

an′no•tate′ (an′ə tāt′) *v.t.,* **-tated, -tating** to supply (a text) with notes. —**an′no•ta′tion,** *n.*

an•nounce′ (ə nouns′) *v.t.,* **-nounced, -nouncing.** to make known publicly. —**an•nounce′-ment,** *n.* —**an•nounc′er,** *n.*

an•noy′ (ə noi′) *v.t.* to irritate or trouble. —**an•noy′ance,** *n.*

an′nu•al (an′yoō əl) *adj.* **1.** yearly. **2.** (of a plant) living only one season. —*n.* **3.** an annual plant. **4.** a yearbook. —**an′nu•al•ly,** *adv.*

an•nu′i•ty *n., pl.* **-ties.** the income from an investment, paid yearly.

an•nul′ (ə nul′) *v.t.,* **-nulled, -nul-**

ling. to declare void. —**an·nul'·ment,** *n.*

An·nun'ci·a'tion (ə nun'sē ā'shən) *n.* the announcement by the angel Gabriel to the Virgin Mary that she would become the mother of Christ (celebrated March 25).

an'ode (an'ōd) *n.* **1.** an electrode with a positive charge. **2.** the negative terminal of a battery.

a·noint' (ə noint') *v.t.* to put oil on, as in a religious consecration.

a·nom'a·ly (ə nom'ə lē) *n., pl.* **-lies.** something irregular or abnormal. —**a·nom'a·lous,** *adj.*

a·non' (ə non') *adv. Archaic.* soon.

anon. anonymous.

a·non'y·mous (ə non'ə məs) *adj.* of unknown or undisclosed origin. —**an'o·nym'i·ty** (an'ə nim'i tē) *n.*

an'o·rak' (an'ə rak') *n.* a hooded jacket; parka.

an'o·rex'i·a (an'ə rek'sē ə) *n.* Also, **anorexia ner·vo'sa** (nûr vō'sə). an eating disorder marked by excessive dieting. —**an'o·rex'ic,** *adj., n.*

an·oth'er (ə nuth'ər) *adj.* **1.** additional. **2.** different. —*n.* **3.** one more. **4.** a different one.

an'swer (an'sər) *n.* **1.** a reply, as to a question. **2.** a solution to a problem. —*v.i.* **3.** to speak, write, or act in response. **4.** to be responsible. **5.** to be satisfactory. **6.** to conform. —*v.t.* **7.** to reply to. **8.** to fulfill. **9.** to correspond to.

an'swer·a·ble *adj.* **1.** able to be answered. **2.** responsible.

an'swering machine' *n.* a device that answers telephone calls with a recorded message and records messages from callers.

ant (ant) *n.* a common small insect that lives in organized groups.

ant·ac'id (ant as'id) *n.* a medicine to counteract acids.

an·tag'o·nism' (an tag'ə niz'əm) *n.* hostility. —**an·tag'o·nist,** *n.* —**an·tag'o·nis'tic,** *adj.* —**an·tag'o·nize',** *v.t.*

ant·arc'tic (ant ärk'tik, -är'tik) *adj.* (*often cap.*) of or at the South Pole.

ante- a prefix indicating: **1.** happening before. **2.** in front of.

ant'eat'er *n.* a tropical American mammal having a long snout and feeding on ants and termites.

an'te·bel'lum (an'tē bel'əm) *adj.* before a war, esp. the American Civil War.

an'te·ced'ent (an'tə sēd'nt) *adj.* **1.** prior. —*n.* **2.** anything that precedes.

an'te·date' (an'ti dāt') *v.t.,* **-dated, -dating. 1.** to be of earlier date than. **2.** to predate.

an'te·di·lu'vi·an (an'tē di lōō'vē ən) *adj.* before the Biblical Flood.

an'te·lope' (an'tl ōp') *n.* a deerlike animal.

an·ten'na (an ten'ə) *n., pl.* **antennae** (-nē) *for 1.* **1.** a feeler on the head of an insect. **2.** wires for transmitting radio waves, TV pictures, etc.

an·te'ri·or (an tēr'ē ər) *adj.* **1.** earlier. **2.** situated in front of.

an'te·room' (an'tē rōōm', -rŏŏm') *n.* a room serving as an entrance to the main room.

an'them (an'thəm) *n.* a patriotic or sacred hymn.

an'ther (an'thər) *n.* the pollen-bearing part of a stamen.

an·thol'o·gy (an thol'ə jē) *n., pl.* **-gies.** a collection of writings.

an'thra·cite' (an'thrə sīt') *n.* hard coal.

an'thrax (an'thraks) *n.* a disease of cattle and sheep that is transmittable to humans.

an'thro·poid' (an'thrə poid') *adj.* resembling a human or an ape.

an'thro·pol'o·gy (-pol'ə jē) *n.* the study of the origins, development, customs, etc., of humans. —**an'thro·pol'o·gist,** *n.*

an'thro·po·mor'phic (-pə môr'fik) *adj.* ascribing human qualities to a nonhuman thing or being. —**an'thro·po·mor'phism** (-fiz əm) *n.*

anti- a prefix indicating: **1.** against or opposed to. **2.** acting against.

an'ti·bi·ot'ic (an'ti bī ot'ik) *n.* a substance used to kill bacteria.

an'ti·bod'y *n., pl.* **-bodies.** a substance produced by the body that destroys bacteria and viruses.

an'tic (an'tik) *n.* **1.** Usu. **antics.** a playful prank or a ridiculous act or gesture. —*adj.* **2.** ludicrous.

an·tic'i·pate' (an tis'ə pāt') *v.t.,* **-pated, -pating. 1.** to expect and prepare for. **2.** to look forward to. **3.** to forestall. —**an·tic'i·pa'tion,** *n.*

an'ti·cli'max (an'tē klī'maks, an'tī-) *n.* a disappointing or undramatic outcome.

an'ti·de·pres'sant (an'tē di pres'ənt, an'tī-) *n.* a drug for relieving depression.

an'ti·dote' (an'ti dōt') *n.* a medicine that counteracts poison.

an'ti·freeze' (an'ti frēz', an'tē-) *n.* a liquid used in an engine's radiator to prevent the cooling fluid from freezing.

an'ti·his'ta·mine' (an'tē his'tə mēn', -min) *n.* a substance used against allergic reactions.

an'ti·mat'ter (an'tē mat'ər, an'tī-) *n.* matter with charges opposite to those of common particles.

an′ti•mo′ny (an′tə mō′nē) *n.* a brittle white metallic element.

an′ti•ox′i•dant (an′tē ok′si dənt, an′tī-) *n.* an organic substance counteracting oxidation damage in animal tissues.

an′ti•pas′to (an′ti pä′stō) *n., pl.* **-pastos, -pasti** (-pä′stē). an Italian appetizer.

an•tip′a•thy (an tip′ə thē) *n.* dislike; aversion.

an′ti•per′spi•rant (an′ti pûr′spər-ənt) *n.* an astringent product for reducing perspiration.

an•tip′o•des (an tip′ə dēz′) *n.pl.* places opposite each other on the globe.

an′ti•quar′i•an (an′ti kwâr′ē ən) *adj.* **1.** relating to antiquities. —*n.* **2.** an antiquary.

an′ti•quar′y (-kwer′ē) *n., pl.* **-ries.** a collector of antiquities.

an′ti•quat′ed (-kwā′tid) *adj.* old or obsolete.

an•tique′ (an tēk′) *adj.* **1.** old or old-fashioned. —*n.* **2.** a valuable old object.

an•tiq′ui•ty (-tik′wi tē) *n.* **1.** ancient times. **2. antiquities,** things from ancient times.

an′ti-Sem′ite (an′tē sem′īt, an′tī-) *n.* a person hostile to Jews. —**an′-ti-Se•mit′ic** (-sə mit′ik) *adj.* —**an′-ti-Sem′i•tism** (-sem′i tiz′əm) *n.*

an′ti•sep′tic (an′tə sep′tik) *adj.* **1.** destroying certain germs. —*n.* **2.** an antiseptic substance.

an′ti•so′cial (an′tē sō′shəl, an′tī-) *adj.* **1.** not associating with others in a friendly way. **2.** hostile to society.

an•tith′e•sis (an tith′ə sis) *n., pl.* **-ses. 1.** contrast. **2.** the direct opposite.

an′ti•tox′in (an′ti tok′sin) *n.* a substance counteracting germ-produced poisons in the body.

ant′ler (ant′lər) *n.* one of the horns on an animal of the deer family.

an′to•nym (an′tə nim) *n.* a word of opposite meaning.

a′nus (ā′nəs) *n.* the opening at the lower end of the alimentary canal.

an′vil (an′vil) *n.* an iron block on which hot metals are hammered into shape.

anx•i′e•ty (ang zī′i tē) *n.* mental distress caused by fear. —**anx′ious** (angk′shəs) *adj.*

an′y (en′ē) *adj.* **1.** one or more. **2.** some. **3.** every. —*pron.* **4.** any person, thing, etc. —*adv.* **5.** at all. —**Usage.** See SOME.

an′y•bod′y *pron.* any person.

an′y•how′ *adv.* in any way, case, etc. Also, **an′y•way′.**

an′y•one′ *pron.* anybody.

an′y•place′ *adv.* anywhere.

an′y•thing′ *pron.* any thing whatever.

an′y•time′ *adv.* at any time.

an′y•where′ *adv.* **1.** in, at, or to any place. —*Idiom.* **2. get any-where,** to succeed.

A′ one′ (ā′ wun′) *adj.* excellent. Also, **A′ 1′, A′-1′.**

a•or′ta (ā ôr′tə) *n., pl.* **-tas, -tae** (-tē). the main artery from the heart.

a•pace′ (ə pās′) *adv.* quickly.

a•part′ (ə pärt′) *adv.* **1.** into pieces. **2.** separately. **3.** aside.

a•part′heid (-hāt, -hīt) *n.* (formerly, in South Africa) separation of and discrimination against blacks.

a•part′ment (-mənt) *n.* a set of rooms used as a residence.

ap′a•thy (ap′ə thē) *n.* lack of emotion or interest. —**ap′a•thet′ic** (-thet′ik) *adj.*

ape (āp) *n., v.,* **aped, aping.** —*n.* **1.** a large, tailless monkeylike animal. —*v.t.* **2.** to imitate stupidly.

a•pé•ri•tif′ (ə per′i tēf′) *n.* liquor served before a meal.

ap′er•ture (ap′ər chər) *n.* an opening.

a′pex (ā′peks) *n.* the tip; summit.

a′phid (ā′fid, af′id) *n.* a tiny insect that sucks sap from plants.

aph′o•rism′ (af′ə riz′əm) *n.* a brief maxim.

aph′ro•dis′i•ac′ (af′rə dē′ze ak′, -diz′ē ak′) *adj.* **1.** arousing sexual desire. —*n.* **2.** an aphrodisiac food, drug, etc.

a′pi•ar′y (ā′pē er′ē) *n., pl.* **-ries.** a place where bees are kept.

a•piece′ (ə pēs′) *adv.* for each.

a•plen′ty (ə plen′tē) *adj., adv.* in generous amounts.

a•plomb′ (ə plom′, ə plum′) *n.* poise; self-possession.

a•poc′a•lypse (ə pok′ə lips) *n.* **1.** a prophesy of a violent upheaval in which evil is defeated. **2. Apoca-lypse,** the last book of the New Testament. —**a•poc′a•lyp′tic,** *adj.*

A•poc′ry•pha (ə pok′rə fə) *n.* the Old Testament books not found in Jewish or Protestant scriptures.

a•poc′ry•phal *adj.* not verified; of doubtful authenticity.

ap′o•gee′ (ap′ə jē′) *n.* **1.** the remotest point of the orbit of the moon or a satellite. **2.** the highest point.

a′po•lit′i•cal (ā′pə lit′i kəl) *adj.* not interested in politics.

a•pol′o•gist (ə pol′ə jist) *n.* a person who defends a faith, idea, etc.

a•pol′o•gize′ *v.i.,* **-gized, -gizing.** to offer an apology.

a•pol′o•gy *n., pl.* **-gies. 1.** a statement of regret for one's act. **2.** a stated defense. —**a·pol′o·get′ic** (-jet′ik) *adj.*

ap′o·plex′y (ap′ə plek′sē) *n.* the sudden loss of bodily functions due to the bursting of a blood vessel. —**ap′o·plec′tic** (-plek′tik) *adj.*

a·pos′tate (ə pos′tāt, -tit) *n.* a deserter of one's faith, cause, etc. —**a·pos′ta·sy** (-tə sē) *n.*

a·pos′tle (ə pos′əl) *n.* **1.** a disciple sent by Jesus to preach the gospel. **2.** a moral reformer. —**ap′os·tol′ic** (ap′ə stol′ik) *adj.*

a·pos′tro·phe (ə pos′trə fē) *n.* a sign (′) indicating an omitted letter, the possessive, or certain plurals.

a·poth′e·car′y (ə poth′ə ker′ē) *n.,* *pl.* **-ries.** a pharmacist.

a·poth′e·o′sis (ə poth′ē ō′sis) *n., pl.* **-ses** (-sēz). **1.** elevation to the rank of a god. **2.** the ideal example.

ap·pall′ (ə pôl′) *v.t.* to fill with dismay. —**ap·pall′ing,** *adj.*

ap′pa·ra′tus (ap′ə rat′əs, -rā′təs) *n.* equipment for a specific task.

ap·par′el (ə par′əl) *n.* clothing.

ap·par′ent (ə par′ənt, ə pâr′-) *adj.* **1.** obvious. **2.** seeming but not real. —**ap·par′ent·ly,** *adv.*

ap′pa·ri′tion (ap′ə rish′ən) *n.* a ghost.

ap·peal′ (ə pēl′) *n.* **1.** a call for aid, mercy, etc. **2.** a request for a review of a court verdict. **3.** attractiveness. —*v.i.* **4.** to make an earnest plea. **5.** to be attractive.

ap·pear′ (ə pēr′) *v.i.* **1.** to come into sight. **2.** to come before the public. **3.** to seem.

ap·pear′ance (-əns) *n.* **1.** the act of appearing. **2.** outward look.

ap·pease′ (ə pēz′) *v.t.,* **-peased, -peasing. 1.** to pacify; soothe. **2.** to yield to the demands of. —**ap· pease′ment,** *n.*

ap·pel′late (ə pel′it) *adj.* (of a court) dealing with appeals.

ap·pend′ (ə pend′) *v.t.* to add or attach. —**ap·pend′age,** *n.*

ap′pen·dec′to·my (ap′ən dek′tə-mē) *n., pl.* **-mies.** removal of the appendix.

ap·pen·di·ci′tis (ə pen′də sī′tis) *n.* inflammation of the appendix.

ap·pen′dix (ə pen′diks) *n., pl.* **-dixes, -dices** (-də sēz′). **1.** a supplement. **2.** a closed tube attached to the large intestine.

ap′per·tain′ (ap′ər tān′) *v.i.* to belong or pertain.

ap′pe·tite′ (ap′i tīt′) *n.* a desire, esp. for food.

ap′pe·tiz′er (-tī′zər) *n.* a portion of food or drink served before a meal

to stimulate the appetite. —**ap′pe· tiz′ing,** *adj.*

ap·plaud′ (ə plôd′) *v.i., v.t.* **1.** to clap the hands in approval or praise (of). **2.** to praise.

ap′ple (ap′əl) *n.* a round fruit with firm, white flesh.

ap′ple·sauce′ *n.* apples stewed to a pulp.

ap·pli′ance (ə plī′əns) *n.* a device or instrument.

ap′pli·ca·ble (ap′li kə bəl) *adj.* relevant; appropriate.

ap′pli·cant (-kənt) *n.* a person who applies, as for a job.

ap′pli·ca′tion (-kā′shən) *n.* **1.** the act of applying. **2.** the use to which something is put. **3.** a form filled out by an applicant. **4.** relevance. **5.** a request. **6.** persistent attention.

ap′pli·ca′tor *n.* a device for applying a substance, as medication.

ap′pli·qué′ (ap′li kā′) *n., v.,* **-quéd, -quéing.** —*n.* **1.** a cutout design of one material applied to another. —*v.t.* **2.** to decorate with appliqué.

ap·ply′ (ə plī′) *v.,* **-plied, -plying.** —*v.i.* **1.** to make a formal request, as for a job. **2.** to be relevant. —*v.t.* **3.** to put to use. **4.** to assign to a purpose. **5.** to spread on. **6.** to employ (oneself) diligently.

ap·point′ (ə point′) *v.t.* **1.** to choose or assign officially. **2.** to fix or set. —**ap·point·ee′,** *n.* —**ap· poin′tive,** *adj.*

ap·point′ment *n.* **1.** the act of appointing. **2.** a prearranged meeting. **3.** a position to which a person is appointed.

ap·por′tion (ə pôr′shən) *v.t.* to divide into shares. —**ap·por′tion· ment,** *n.*

ap′po·site (ap′ə zit) *adj.* suitable.

ap·praise′ (ə prāz′) *v.t.,* **-praised, -praising.** to estimate the value or quality of. —**ap·prais′al,** *n.*

ap·pre·ci·a·ble (ə prē′shē ə bəl) *adj.* noticeable; considerable.

ap·pre′ci·ate′ (-shē āt′) *v.,* **-ated, -ating.** —*v.t.* **1.** to be grateful for. **2.** to value highly. —*v.i.* **3.** to increase in value. —**ap·pre′ci·a′tion,** *n.* —**ap·pre′cia·tive** (-shə tiv) *adj.*

ap·pre·hend′ (ap′ri hend′) *v.t.* **1.** to take into custody. **2.** to understand.

ap′pre·hen′sion (-hen′shən) *n.* **1.** anxiety. **2.** the act of understanding. **3.** the act of arresting.

ap′pre·hen′sive (-siv) *adj.* worried.

ap·pren′tice (ə pren′tis) *n., v.,* **-ticed, -ticing.** —*n.* **1.** a person learning a trade. —*v.t., v.i.* **2.** to employ or serve as an apprentice. —**ap·pren′tice·ship′,** *n.*

ap·prise′ (ə prīz′) v.t., **-prised, -prising.** to notify. Also, **ap·prize′.**

ap·proach′ (ə prōch′) v.t. **1.** to come nearer to. **2.** to begin work on. **3.** to make a proposal to. —v.i. **4.** to come nearer. —n. **5.** a coming near. **6.** a means of access. **7.** a method.

ap·pro·ba′tion (ap′rə bā′shən) n. approval.

ap·pro′pri·ate adj., v., **-ated, -ating.** —adj. (ə prō′prē it) **1.** suitable; proper. —v.t. (-prē āt′) **2.** to take possession of. **3.** to designate for a use. —**ap·pro′pri·ate·ly,** adv.

ap·pro′pri·a′tion n. **1.** the act of appropriating. **2.** money authorized to be paid from public funds.

ap·prov′al (ə prōō′vəl) n. **1.** the act of approving. **2.** permission. —*Idiom.* **3. on approval,** subject to rejection if not satisfactory.

ap·prove′ (ə prōōv′) v., **-proved, -proving.** —v.t. **1.** to think or speak well of. **2.** to agree to. **3.** to confirm formally. —v.i. **4.** to have a favorable view.

ap·prox′i·mate adj., v., **-mated, -mating.** —adj. (ə prok′sə mit) **1.** nearly exact. **2.** similar. —v.t. (-māt′) **3.** to be about the same as. —**ap·prox′i·mate′ly,** adv. —**ap·prox′i·ma′tion,** n.

ap·pur′te·nance (ə pûr′tn əns) n. something subordinate to something else.

Apr. April.

a′pri·cot′ (ap′ri kot′, ā′pri-) n. a small peachlike fruit.

A′pril (ā′prəl) n. the fourth month of the year.

a′ pri·o′ri (ā′ prē ôr′ī, -ôr′ē) adj. **1.** from a general law to a particular instance. **2.** existing in the mind independent of experience.

a′pron (ā′prən) n. a protective garment for the front of one's clothes.

ap′ro·pos′ (ap′rə pō′) adv. **1.** at the right time. **2.** by the way —adj. **3.** appropriate and timely.

apse (aps) n. a vaulted recess in a church.

apt (apt) adj. **1.** prone; disposed. **2.** likely. **3.** being quick to learn. **4.** suited to the occasion. —**apt′ly,** adv. —**apt′ness,** n.

apt. apartment.

ap′ti·tude′ (ap′ti tōōd′, -tyōōd′) n. **1.** skill; talent. **2.** quickness in learning.

aq′ua·ma·rine′ n. **1.** a light greenish blue. **2.** a gemstone of this color.

a·quar′i·um (ə kwâr′ē əm) n., pl. **-iums, -ia** (-ē ə). a place for exhibiting aquatic animals and plants.

a·quat′ic (ə kwat′ik, ə kwot′-) adj. of or living in water.

aq′ue·duct′ (ak′wi dukt′) n. an artificial channel for conducting water from a distance.

a′que·ous (ā′kwē əs, ak′wē-) adj. of or like water.

aq′ui·line′ (ak′wə līn′, -lin) adj. (of a nose) curved like a beak.

AR Arkansas.

Ar′abic nu′meral n. any of the numerals 0, 1, 2, 3, 4, 5, 6, 7, 8, or 9.

ar′a·ble (ar′ə bəl) adj. (of land) capable of producing crops.

a·rach′nid (ə rak′nid) n. a small eight-legged animal, as the spider.

ar′bit·er (är′bi tər) n. a person empowered to decide or judge.

ar′bi·trage (-träzh′) n. the simultaneous sale of the same security in different markets to profit from unequal prices. —**ar′bi·trag′er,** n.

ar′bi·trar′y (är′bi trer′ē) adj. **1.** based on random choice. **2.** capricious. **3.** despotic. —**ar′bi·trar′i·ly,** adv.

ar′bi·trate′ (-trāt′) v., **-trated, -trating.** —v.t. **1.** to settle as, or submit to, an arbitrator. —v.i. **2.** to act as arbitrator. —**ar′bi·tra′tion,** n.

ar′bi·tra′tor n. a person empowered to settle a dispute.

ar′bor (är′bər) n. a place shaded by vines or trees.

ar·bo′re·al (-bôr′ē əl) adj. of or living in trees.

ar′bo·re′tum (är′bə rē′təm) n., pl. **-tums, -ta** (-tə). a parklike area with different kinds of trees for study or display.

arc (ärk) n. **1.** part of a circle. **2.** a luminous current between two electric conductors.

ar·cade′ (är kād′) n. **1.** a row of archways. **2.** a covered passage with stores.

ar·cane′ (är kān′) adj. mysterious.

arch¹ (ärch) n. **1.** a curved structure spanning an opening. —v.i., v.t. **2.** to form (into) an arch.

arch² (ärch) adj. consciously playful. —**arch′ly,** adv.

ar′chae·ol′o·gy (är′kē ol′ə jē) n. the study of past cultures through objects or their remains. Also, **ar′che·ol′o·gy.** —**ar′chae·o·log′i·cal** (-ə loj′i kəl) adj. —**ar′chae·ol′o·gist,** n.

ar·cha′ic (är kā′ik) adj. belonging to an earlier period; ancient.

arch′an′gel (ärk′ān′jəl) n. a chief angel.

arch′bish′op (ärch′bish′əp) n. a bishop of the highest rank.

arch′di′o·cese (-dī′ə sis, -sēz′) n. the diocese of an archbishop. —**arch′di·oc′e·san** (-os′ə sən) adj.

arch′duke′ n. a prince of the former ruling house of Austria.

arch′en′e•my n., pl. **-mies.** a chief enemy.

arch′er (är′chər) n. one who shoots a bow and arrow. —**arch′er•y,** n.

ar′che•type′ (är′ki tīp′) n. an original pattern or model.

ar′chi•pel′a•go′ (är′kə pel′ə gō′) n., pl. **-gos, -goes. 1.** a large group of islands. **2.** the body of water surrounding such a group.

ar′chi•tect′ (är′ki tekt′) n. a person who designs buildings. —**ar′chi•tec′ture,** n. —**ar′chi•tec′tur•al,** adj.

ar′chives (är′kīvz) n.pl. **1.** historical documents. **2.** a place for such documents.

arch′way′ (ärch′wā′) n. an entrance covered by an arch.

arc′tic (ärk′tik, är′tik) adj. **1.** (often cap.) of or at the North Pole. **2.** extremely cold.

ar′dent (är′dnt) adj. passionate; zealous. —**ar′dent•ly,** adv.

ar′dor (är′dər) n. intensity of feeling; enthusiasm.

ar′du•ous (är′jŏŏ əs) adj. very difficult.

are (är; unstressed ər) v. pres. indic. pl. of **be.**

ar′e•a (âr′ē ə) n. **1.** the extent of a surface. **2.** a region. **3.** scope.

ar′ea code′ n. a three-digit number used in long-distance telephone dialing.

a•re′na (ə rē′nə) n. **1.** a space used for sports or other entertainments. **2.** a field of activity.

aren′t (ärnt, är′ənt) contraction of **are not.**

ar′got (är′gət, -gō) n. a special vocabulary used by a particular group of people.

ar′gu•a•ble (är′gyŏŏ ə bəl) adj. **1.** doubtful; questionable. **2.** capable of being supported by persuasive argument; possible.

ar′gu•a•bly (är′gyŏŏ ə blē) adv. as can be supported by persuasive argument.

ar′gue (är′gyŏŏ) v., **-gued, -guing.** —v.i. **1.** to present reasons for or against something. **2.** to dispute. —v.t. **3.** to give reasons for or against. **4.** to persuade. —**ar′gu•ment,** n. —**ar′gu•men•ta′tion,** n.

ar′gu•men′ta•tive (-men′tə tiv) adj. fond of argument.

a′ri•a (är′ē ə) n. an operatic solo.

ar′id (ar′id) adj. dry. —**a•rid′i•ty** (ə rid′i tē) n.

a•right′ (ə rīt′) adv. rightly.

a•rise′ (ə rīz′) v.i., **arose** (ə rōz′), **arisen** (ə riz′ən), **arising. 1.** to come into being. **2.** to get up. **3.** to move upward.

ar′is•toc′ra•cy (ar′ə stok′rə sē) n., pl. **-cies. 1.** the nobility. **2.** a class governed by the nobility. —**a•ris′to•crat′** (ə ris′tə krat′) n. —**a•ris′to•crat′ic,** adj.

a•rith′me•tic (ə rith′mə tik) n. computation by numbers. —**ar′ith•met′i•cal** (ar′ith met′i kəl) adj. —**ar′ith•met′i•cal•ly,** adv.

Ariz. Arizona.

ark (ärk) n. Archaic. a large ship.

Ark. Arkansas.

arm¹ (ärm) n. **1.** an upper limb of the human body. **2.** an armlike part. **3.** a projecting support at the side of a chair, sofa, etc.

arm² (ärm) n. **1.** a weapon. **2.** a branch of the military. —v.t. **3.** to equip with weapons. —v.i. **4.** to prepare for war. —Idiom. **5. up in arms,** indignant.

ar•ma′da (är mä′də) n. a fleet of warships.

ar′ma•dil′lo (är′mə dil′ō) n. a burrowing mammal covered with bony plates.

ar′ma•ged′don (är′mə ged′n) n. a crucial or final conflict.

ar′ma•ment (-mənt) n. **1.** military weapons. **2.** equipping for war.

arm′chair′ n. a chair with supports for the arms.

armed′ for′ces n.pl. military, naval, and air forces.

ar′mi•stice (är′mə stis) n. a truce.

ar′mor (är′mər) n. a protective metal covering, as against weapons.

ar′mor•y (-mə rē) n., pl. **-ries.** a storage place for weapons.

arm′pit′ n. the hollow under the arm at the shoulder.

ar′my (är′mē) n., pl. **-mies. 1.** a military force for land combat. **2.** a large group.

a•ro′ma (ə rō′mə) n. a pleasant odor. —**ar′o•mat′ic** (ar′ə mat′ik) adj.

a•ro•ma•ther′a•py n. the use of fragrances to alter a person's mood.

a•rose′ (ə rōz′) v. pt. of **arise.**

a•round′ (ə round′) adv. **1.** on all sides. **2.** in a circle. **3.** nearby. —prep. **4.** on all sides of. **5.** near. **6.** approximately.

a•rouse′ (ə rouz′) v.t., **aroused, arousing. 1.** to awaken. **2.** to excite. —**a•rous′al,** n.

ar•raign′ (ə rān′) v.t. **1.** to bring before a court. **2.** to accuse. —**ar•raign′ment,** n.

ar•range′ (ə rānj′) v.t., **-ranged, -ranging. 1.** to put in order. **2.** to plan or prepare. **3.** to adapt. —**ar•range′ment,** n.

ar•ray′ (ə rā′) v.t. **1.** to arrange in

order. **2.** to clothe. —*n.* **3.** an arrangement, as for battle. **4.** an impressive group. **5.** fine clothes.

ar•rears' (ə rērz') *n.pl.* **1.** the state of being late in repaying a debt. **2.** an overdue debt.

ar•rest' (ə rest') *v.t.* **1.** to take (a person) into legal custody. **2.** to stop or check. **3.** to catch and hold. —*n.* **4.** the taking of a person into legal custody. **5.** a stopping or being stopped.

ar•rest'ing *adj.* attracting attention; engaging.

ar•rive' (ə rīv') *v.i.*, **-rived, -riv•ing.** **1.** to reach one's destination. **2.** to come. **3.** to achieve success.

ar'ro•gant (ar'ə gənt) *adj.* insolently proud. —**ar'ro•gance,** *n.*

ar'ro•gate' (-gāt') *v.t.*, **-gated, -gating.** to claim or appropriate without right. —**ar'ro•ga'tion,** *n.*

ar'row (ar'ō) *n.* **1.** a pointed stick shot by a bow. **2.** a figure with a wedge-shaped end.

ar'row•head' *n.* the pointed tip of an arrow.

ar'row•root' *n.* the edible starch from the root of a tropical plant.

ar•roy'o (ə roi'ō) *n., pl.* **-os.** a steep, dry gulch that fills with water after a heavy rain.

ar'se•nal (är'sə nl) *n.* a military storehouse or factory.

ar'se•nic (är'sə nik) *n.* a grayish white element forming poisonous compounds.

ar'son (är'sən) *n.* the intentional and illegal burning of a building.

art (ärt) *n.* **1.** the production of something beautiful or extraordinary. **2.** paintings, drawings, sculptures, etc. **3.** skill; ability. **4. arts,** subjects other than the sciences. —**art'ful,** *adj.*

art dec'o (dek'ō) *n.* (*often caps.*) 1920s decorative art with geometric designs.

ar•te/ri•o•scle•ro'sis (är tēr'ē ō sklə rō'sis) *n.* hardening of the arteries.

ar'ter•y (är'tə rē) *n., pl.* **-ries. 1.** a blood vessel carrying blood from the heart. **2.** a main highway. —**ar•te'ri•al** (-tēr'ē əl) *adj.*

ar•thri'tis (är thrī'tis) *n.* inflammation of one or more joints. —**ar•thrit'ic** (-thrit'ik) *adj.*

ar'thro•pod' (är'thrə pod') *n.* an invertebrate with a segmented body and jointed legs.

ar'ti•choke' (är'ti chōk') *n.* a thistlelike plant with an edible flower head.

ar'ti•cle (är'ti kəl) *n.* **1.** a factual published piece of writing. **2.** a particular thing; item. **3.** the words *a, an,* or *the.*

ar•tic'u•late *adj., v.,* **-lated, -lating.** —*adj.* (är tik'yə lit) **1.** clear. **2.** able to express one's thoughts clearly. **3.** jointed. —*v.t.* (-lāt') **4.** to pronounce clearly. **5.** to give clarity to. **6.** to unite by joints. —*v.i.* **7.** to speak clearly. **8.** to form a joint. —**ar•tic'u•la'tion,** *n.*

ar'ti•fact' (är'tə fakt') *n.* an object made by humans, esp. one belonging to an earlier time.

ar'ti•fice (är'tə fis) *n.* **1.** a clever trick. **2.** cleverness. **3.** trickery.

ar'ti•fi'cial (-tə fish'əl) *adj.* **1.** made by humans. **2.** not genuine. **3.** not natural; forced. —**ar'ti•fi'cial•ly,** *adv.* —**ar'ti•fi'ci•al'i•ty** (-fish'ē al'i-tē) *n.*

ar'tifi'cial life' *n.* the simulation of any aspect of life, as through computers or biochemistry.

artifi'cial respira'tion *n.* the forcing of air into and out of the lungs of a nonbreathing person.

ar•til'ler•y (är til'ə rē) *n.* big guns.

ar'ti•san (är'tə zən) *n.* a person skilled in a practical art.

art'ist (är'tist) *n.* a practitioner of one of the fine arts. —**ar•tis'tic,** *adj.* —**art'ist•ry,** *n.*

art'less *adj.* natural.

art'y *adj.,* **-ier, -iest.** *Informal.* self-consciously artistic.

as (az; *unstressed* əz) *adv.* **1.** to the same extent. **2.** for example. —*conj.* **3.** to the same degree. **4.** in the same manner that. **5.** while. **6.** because. —*pron.* **7.** that. —*Idiom.* **8. as for** *or* **to,** with respect to. **9. as is,** the way it appears. **10. as well,** in addition.

ASAP (ā'es'ā'pē', ā'sap) **1.** as soon as possible. **2.** without delay. Also, **A.S.A.P., a.s.a.p.**

as•bes'tos (as bes'təs, az-) *n.* a fibrous mineral formerly used in fireproofing.

as•cend' (ə send') *v.i.* to climb; move upward. —**as•cent',** *n.*

as•cend'an•cy *n.* domination; power. —**as•cend'ant,** *adj., n.*

As•cen'sion (ə sen'shən) *n.* the bodily passing of Christ to heaven.

as'cer•tain' (as'ər tān') *v.t.* to find out.

as•cet'ic (ə set'ik) *adj.* **1.** not allowing oneself luxuries or pleasures. —*n.* **2.** a person who is ascetic. —**as•cet'i•cism** (-ə siz'əm) *n.*

ASCII (as'kē) *n.* American Standard Code for Information Interchange: a standardized code for computer storage and transmission.

as•cor'bic ac'id (ə skôr'bik) *n.* vitamin C.

as'cot (as'kət, -kot) *n.* a tie or scarf with broad ends.

as·cribe′ (ə skrīb′) *v.t.*, **-cribed, -cribing.** to credit to a cause or source; attribute. —**as·crip′tion** (ə-skrip′shən) *n.*

a·sex′u·al (ā sek′shōo əl) *adj.* **1.** without sex; sexless. **2.** having no sex organs.

ash¹ (ash) *n.*, *pl.* **ashes.** the powdery residue of burned matter.

ash² (ash) *n.* a tree having tough, straight-grained wood.

a·shamed′ (ə shāmd′) *adj.* feeling shame.

ash′en (ash′ən) *adj.* **1.** extremely pale. **2.** ash-colored.

a·shore′ (ə shôr′) *adv., adj.* on or to shore.

ash′tray′ *n.* a small dish for tobacco ashes.

a·side′ (ə sīd′) *adv.* **1.** on or to one side. **2.** away from a present group or area or from one's thoughts. **3.** in reserve. —*n.* **4.** words spoken so as not to be heard by certain people. —*Idiom.* **5. aside from,** except for.

as′i·nine′ (as′ə nīn′) *adj.* silly.

ask (ask, äsk) *v.t.* **1.** to address a question to. **2.** to request information about. **3.** to request or request of. **4.** to invite. —*v.i.* **5.** to inquire. **6.** to make a request.

a·skance′ (ə skans′) *adv.* **1.** with a side glance. **2.** skeptically.

a·skew′ (ə skyōo′) *adv., adj.* crooked(ly).

a·sleep′ (ə slēp′) *adj., adv.* sleeping.

a·so′cial (ā sō′shəl) *adj.* **1.** not sociable. **2.** selfish.

asp (asp) *n.* a small poisonous snake.

as·par′a·gus (ə spar′ə gəs) *n.* a plant of the lily family having edible shoots.

as′pect (as′pekt) *n.* **1.** appearance to the mind or eye. **2.** part; feature. **3.** the direction faced.

as′pen (as′pən) *n.* a kind of poplar.

as·per′i·ty (ə sper′i tē) *n.* **1.** sharpness. **2.** roughness.

as·per′sion (ə spûr′zhən, -shən) *n.* a derogatory remark.

as′phalt (as′fôlt) *n.* a hard black material used for pavements.

as·phyx′i·ate′ (as fik′sē āt′) *v.t., v.i.*, **-ated, -ating.** to suffocate. —**as·phyx′i·a′tion,** *n.*

as′pi·ra′tion *n.* **1.** a strong desire to achieve an objective. **2.** the removal of a fluid from a body cavity with a syringe. **3.** the act of inhaling a foreign body.

as·pire′ (ə spī°r′) *v.i.*, **-pired, -piring.** to long, aim, or seek for. —**as·pir′ant,** *n.*

as′pi·rin (as′pər in, -prin) *n.* a de-

rivative of salicylic acid used to reduce pain and fever.

ass (as) *n.* **1.** a donkey. **2.** a foolish person.

as·sail′ (ə sāl′) *v.t.* to attack violently. —**as·sail′ant,** *n.*

as·sas′si·nate′ (ə sas′ə nāt′) *v.t.*, **-nated, -nating. 1.** to kill a prominent person, usu. for political motives. **2.** to destroy viciously. —**as·sas′sin,** *n.* —**as·sas′si·na′tion,** *n.*

as·sault′ (ə sôlt′) *n.* **1.** a violent attack. —*v.t.* **2.** to attack violently.

as·say′ (a sā′) *v.t.* **1.** to analyze or evaluate. —*n.* **2.** an analysis of the composition of a substance.

as·sem′blage (ə sem′blij) *n.* **1.** a group. **2.** an assembling.

as·sem′ble (ə sem′bəl) *v.* **-bled, -bling.** —*v.i.* **1.** to come together. —*v.t.* **2.** to bring or put together.

as·sem′bly *n.*, *pl.* **-blies. 1.** a group gathered together. **2.** a legislative body. **3.** the putting together of parts.

as·sent′ (ə sent′) *v.i.* **1.** to agree. —*n.* **2.** agreement.

as·sert′ (ə sûrt′) *v.t.* **1.** to declare to be true. **2.** to defend, as rights or claims. —*Idiom.* **3. assert oneself,** to claim one's rights insistently. —**as·ser′tion,** *n.* —**as·ser′tive,** *adj.* —**as·ser′tive·ly,** *adv.*

as·sess′ (ə ses′) *v.t.* **1.** to estimate the value of. **2.** to determine the amount of. **3.** to impose a charge on. **4.** to judge the nature of. —**as·sess′ment,** *n.* —**as·ses′sor,** *n.*

as′set (as′et) *n.* **1.** property having monetary value. **2.** a useful quality.

as·sid′u·ous (ə sij′ōo əs) *adj.* persistent; diligent. —**as·sid′u·ous·ly,** *adv.* —**as′si·du′i·ty,** *n.*

as·sign′ (ə sīn′) *v.t.* **1.** to allot. **2.** to give as a task. **3.** to appoint. **4.** to ascribe. —**as·sign′a·ble,** *adj.* —**as·sign′ment,** *n.*

as′sig·na′tion (as′ig nā′shən) *n.* an appointment; rendezvous.

as·sim′i·late′ (ə sim′ə lāt′) *v.t., v.i.*, **-lated, -lating.** to absorb or become absorbed into the body, a group, the mind, etc. —**as·sim′i·la′tion,** *n.*

as·sist′ (ə sist′) *v.t., v.i.* to help; aid. —**as·sist′ance,** *n.* —**as·sist′ant,** *n., adj.*

assist′ed liv′ing *n.* housing for the elderly or infirm in which meals, medical care, and other assistance is available to residents.

assn. association.

as·so′ci·ate′ *v.*, **-ated, -ating,** *n., adj.* —*v.t.* (ə sō′shē āt′, -sē-) **1.** to join together; combine. **2.** to connect in the mind. —*v.i.* **3.** to join together as partners, colleagues, etc. —*n.* (-it) **4.** a partner; colleague. —*adj.* (-it) **5.** allied. —**as•so'ci•a'tion,** *n.*

as'so•nance (as'ə nəns) *n.* similarity of sound in words or syllables.

as•sort'ed (ə sôr'tid) *adj.* of various kinds.

as•sort'ment *n.* a mixed collection.

asst. assistant.

as•suage' (ə swāj') *v.t.,* **-suaged, -suaging.** to lessen (pain, grief, etc.).

as•sume' (ə sōōm') *v.t.,* **-sumed, -suming. 1.** to accept without proof. **2.** to take upon oneself. **3.** to pretend to be.

as•sump'tion (ə sump'shən) *n.* **1.** the act of assuming. **2.** an unverified belief.

as•sure' (ə shŏŏr') *v.t.,* **-sured, -suring. 1.** to declare positively to; promise. **2.** to make certain. —**as•sur'ance,** *n.* —**as•sured',** *adj., n.*

as'ter (as'tər) *n.* a flower with many petals around a yellow center disk.

as'ter•isk (as'tə risk) *n.* a star (*) symbol used in writing as a reference mark.   —**Pronunciation.** The word ASTERISK is pronounced (as'tə risk). Note that the final syllable is pronounced (-risk) with the (s) before the (k). Both (as'tə riks) and (as'tə rik) are considered nonstandard pronunciations.

a•stern' (ə stûrn') *adv., adj.* Naut. toward or at the rear.

as'ter•oid' (as'tə roid') *n.* any of the small solid bodies revolving around the sun.

asth'ma (az'mə) *n.* a chronic respiratory disorder causing difficulty in breathing. —**asth•mat'ic** (az mat'ik) *adj., n.*

a•stig'ma•tism (ə stig'mə tiz'əm) *n.* an eye defect in which light rays do not focus on a single point. —**as'tig•mat'ic** (as'tig mat'ik) *adj.*

a•stir' (ə stûr') *adj., adv.* moving.

as•ton'ish (ə ston'ish) *v.t.* to surprise greatly; amaze. —**as•ton'ish•ing,** *adj.* —**as•ton'ish•ment,** *n.*

as•tound' (ə stound') *v.t.* to overwhelm with amazement.

as'tral (as'trəl) *adj.* of the stars.

a•stray' (ə strā') *adj., adv.* straying.

a•stride' (ə strīd') *adv.* **1.** with a leg on either side. **2.** with legs apart. —*prep.* **3.** with a leg on each side of. **4.** on both sides of.

as•trin'gent (ə strin'jənt) *adj.* **1.** causing constriction of skin tissue. **2.** harsh. —*n.* **3.** an astringent substance.

as•trol'o•gy (ə strol'ə jē) *n.* the study of the assumed influence of the stars on human affairs. —**as'tro•log'i•cal** (as'trə loj'i kəl) *adj.* —**as•trol'o•ger,** *n.*

as'tro•naut (as'trə nôt') *n.* a person trained for space travel.

as'tro•nau'tics *n.* the science and technology of space travel.

as•tro•nom'i•cal (-nom'i kəl) *adj.* **1.** of astronomy. **2.** enormous. —**as'tro•nom'i•cal•ly,** *adv.*

as•tron'o•my (ə stron'ə mē) *n.* the study of all the celestial bodies. —**as•tron'o•mer,** *n.*

as'tro•phys'ics (as'trō fiz'iks) *n.* the branch of astronomy dealing with the physical properties of celestial bodies. —**as'tro•phys'i•cist,** *n.*

as•tute' (ə stōōt', ə styōōt') *adj.* keenly perceptive; clever. —**as•tute'ly,** *adv.* —**as•tute'ness,** *n.*

a•sun'der (ə sun'dər) *adv.* apart.

a•sy'lum (ə sī'ləm) *n.* **1.** an institution for the care of ill or needy persons. **2.** a place of refuge.

a•sym'me•try (ā sim'i trē) *n.* a lack of symmetry. —**a'sym•met'ric** (ā'sə me'trik), **a'sym•met'ri•cal,** *adj.*

at (at; *unstressed* ət, it) *prep.* **1.** (used to indicate a point in space or time). **2.** (used to indicate amount, degree, or rate). **3.** (used to indicate an objective). **4.** (used to indicate a condition). **5.** (used to indicate a cause).

at'a•vism (at'ə viz'əm) *n.* the reappearance of remote ancestral traits. —**at'a•vis'tic** (-vis'tik) *adj.*

ate (āt; *Brit.* et) *v.* pt. of **eat.**

at•el•ier' (at'l yā') *n.* a studio, esp. of an artist.

a'the•ism (ā'thē iz'əm) *n.* the belief that there is no God. —**a'the•ist,** *n.* —**a'the•is'tic** (-is'tik) *adj.*

ath'lete (ath'lēt) *n.* a person trained or gifted in sports or physical exercises. —**ath•let'ic** (-let'ik) *adj.* —**ath•let'ics,** *n.*   —**Pronunciation.** The word ATHLETE is normally pronounced as a two-syllable word: (ath'lēt). Similarly, ATHLETIC has only three syllables: (ath let'ik). Pronunciations of these words that add an extra syllable, with a weak vowel sound inserted between the (th) and the (l) are not considered standard.

ath'lete's foot' *n.* ringworm of the feet.

athlet'ic shoe' *n.* a shoe for exercise or sport; sneaker.

at'las (at'ləs) *n.* a book of maps.

ATM automated-teller machine: a machine that provides certain bank services when an electronic card is inserted.

at'mos•phere' (at'məs fēr') *n.* **1.** the air surrounding the earth. **2.** a pervading mood. —**at′mos•pher′ic** (-fer′ik) adj.

at′oll (at′ôl) n. a ring-shaped coral island.

at′om (at′əm) n. **1.** the smallest unit of an element having the properties of that element. **2.** something extremely small.

atom′ic bomb′ n. a bomb whose force is derived from the nuclear fission of certain atoms, causing the conversion of some mass to energy (**atomic energy**). Also, **atom bomb.**

at′om•iz′er (at′ə mī′zər) n. a device for making liquids into a fine spray.

a•ton′al (ā tōn′l) adj. lacking tonality. —**a′to•nal′i•ty** (-nal′i tē) n.

a•tone′ (ə tōn′) v.i., atoned, atoning. to make amends for a wrong. —**a•tone′ment,** n.

a•top′ (ə top′) adj., adv. **1.** on or at the top. —prep. **2.** on the top of.

a′tri•um (ā′trē əm) n., pl. atria, atriums. **1.** an enclosed court in a building. **2.** either of two upper chambers of the heart.

a•tro′cious (ə trō′shəs) adj. **1.** very bad. **2.** wicked. —**a•troc′i•ty** (ə tros′i tē) n.

at′ro•phy (a′trə fē) n., v., -phied, -phying. —n. **1.** a wasting away of a body part. —v.t., v.i. **2.** to cause or undergo atrophy.

at•tach′ (ə tach′) v.t. **1.** to fasten or join. **2.** to bind by emotion. **3.** to take by legal authority.

at′ta•ché′ (at′ə shā′) n. an embassy official.

at•tach′ment (ə tach′mənt) n. **1.** an attaching or being attached. **2.** something fastened on. **3.** an emotional tie.

at•tack′ (ə tak′) v.t. **1.** to act against in a violent or hostile way. **2.** to set to work on vigorously. —v.i. **3.** to make an attack. —n. **4.** the act of attacking. **5.** the onset of illness. —**at•tack′er,** n.

at•tain′ (ə tān′) v.t. to achieve or accomplish. —**at•tain′a•ble,** adj. —**at•tain′ment,** n.

at•tempt′ (ə tempt′) v.t. **1.** to make an effort to accomplish. —n. **2.** an effort to accomplish something.

at•tend′ (ə tend′) v.t. **1.** to be present at. **2.** to go with. **3.** to take care of. —v.i. **4.** to be present. **5.** to take charge. **6.** to pay attention. —**at•tend′ance,** n. —**at•tend′ant,** n., adj.

at•ten′tion (ə ten′shən) n. **1.** the act of concentrating the mind on something. **2.** consideration; care.

at•ten′u•ate′ (-yōō āt′) v.t., v.i.

-ated, -ating. to make or become weak or thin. —**at•ten′u•a′tion,** n.

at•test′ (ə test′) v.t. **1.** to certify as true, genuine, etc. **2.** to give proof of. —v.i. **3.** to testify. —**at′tes•ta′tion** (at′e stā′shən) n.

at′tic (at′ik) n. a room directly under the roof.

at•tire′ (ə tī°r′) v., -tired, -tiring, n. —v.t. **1.** to dress; adorn. —n. **2.** clothes.

at′ti•tude′ (at′i tōōd′, -tyōōd′) n. **1.** manner or feeling with regard to a person or thing. **2.** a position of the body.

attn. attention.

at•tor′ney (ə tûr′nē) n. a lawyer.

attor′ney gen′eral n., pl. attorneys general, attorney generals. the chief law officer of a country or state.

at•tract′ (ə trakt′) v.t. **1.** to draw by a physical force. **2.** to draw by appealing to the senses or by arousing the interest of a.

at•trac′tion n. **1.** the act or power of attracting. **2.** an attractive quality. **3.** one that attracts.

at•trac′tive (-tiv) adj. **1.** having the power to attract. **2.** pleasing. **3.** arousing interest. —**at•trac′tive•ly,** adv. —**at•trac′tive•ness,** n.

at•trib′ute v., -uted, -uting. —v.t. (ə trib′yōōt) **1.** to regard as caused by or belonging to. —n. (at′rə byōōt′) **2.** a special quality or characteristic. —**at′tri•bu′tion,** n.

at•tri′tion (ə trish′ən) n. a wearing away.

at•tune′ (ə tōōn′, ə tyōōn′) v.t., -tuned, -tuning. to bring into accord or harmony.

atty. attorney.

ATV n. all-terrain vehicle: a small motor vehicle with treads or wheels for nonroad travel.

a•typ′i•cal (ā tip′i kəl) adj. not typical; irregular. —**a•typ′i•cal•ly,** adv.

au′burn (ô′bərn) n. a reddish brown.

auc′tion (ôk′shən) n. **1.** the sale of goods to the highest bidders. —v.t. **2.** to sell by auction. —**auc′tion•eer′,** n.

au•da′cious (ô dā′shəs) adj. bold; daring. —**au•dac′i•ty** (-das′i tē) n.

au′di•ble (ô′də bəl) adj. capable of being heard. —**au′di•bil′i•ty,** n. —**au′di•bly,** adv.

au′di•ence (ô′dē əns) n. **1.** a group of hearers or spectators. **2.** a formal hearing or interview.

au′di•o′ (ô′dē ō′) adj. **1.** of sound reception or reproduction. —n. **2.** the audible part of TV.

au′dio book′ n. an audio recording of a book.

au•di•ol′o•gy (-ol′ə jē) *n.* the study and treatment of hearing disorders. —**au′di•ol′o•gist,** *n.*

au•di•om′e•ter (-om′i tər) *n.* an instrument for testing hearing.

au′di•o•tape′ (ô′dē ō-) *n.* a magnetic tape for recording sound.

au′di•o•vis′u•al *adj.* using films, TV, and recordings, as for education.

au′dit (ô′dit) *n.* 1. an official examination of financial records. —*v.t.* 2. to conduct an audit of.

au•di′tion (ô dish′ən) *n.* 1. a trial performance. —*v.t., v.i.* 2. to give an audition (to).

au′di•to′ri•um (-tôr′ē əm) *n.* a large room for an audience.

au′di•to′ry *adj.* of hearing.

Aug. August.

au′ger (ô′gər) *n.* a tool for boring holes.

aught[1] (ôt) *n.* anything whatever.

aught[2] (ôt) *n.* a cipher (0); zero.

aug•ment′ (ôg ment′) *v.t.* to increase. —**aug′men•ta′tion,** *n.*

au′gur (ô′gər) *v.t.* 1. to predict. —*v.i.* 2. to be a sign. —**au′gu•ry** (-gyə-) *n.*

Au′gust (ô′gəst) *n.* the eighth month of the year.

au•gust′ (ô gust′) *adj.* majestic.

auk (ôk) *n.* a northern diving bird.

auld′ lang syne′ (ôld′ lang zīn′) *n.* fondly remembered times.

aunt (ant, änt) *n.* 1. the sister of a parent. 2. the wife of an uncle.

au pair′ (ō pâr′) *n.* a young foreign visitor who does household tasks or cares for children in exchange for room and board.

au′ra (ôr′ə) *n.* 1. an atmosphere, quality, etc. 2. a radiance coming from the body.

au′ral (ôr′əl) *adj.* of or by hearing.

au′re•ole′ (ôr′ē ōl′) *n.* a halo.

au′ re•voir′ (ō′ rə vwär′) *interj.* *French.* good-by.

au′ri•cle (ôr′i kəl) *n.* 1. the outer part of the ear. 2. a chamber in the heart. —**au•ric′u•lar** (ô rik′yə lər) *adj.*

au•ror′a (ə rôr′ə) *n.* a display of bands of light in the night sky.

aus•pi′cious (ô spish′əs) *adj.* 1. promising success. 2. fortunate. —**aus•pi′cious•ly,** *adv.*

aus•tere′ (ô stēr′) *adj.* 1. severe, as in manner. 2. severely simple or plain. —**aus•ter′i•ty** (-ster′i tē) *n.*

au•then′tic (ô then′tik) *adj.* genuine; real. —**au•then′ti•cal•ly,** *adv.* —**au•then′ti•cate′,** *v.t.* —**au′then•tic′i•ty** (-tis′i tē) *n.*

au′thor (ô′thər) *n.* a writer or creator. —**au′thor•ship′,** *n.*

au•thor′i•tar′i•an (ə thôr′i târ′ē ən) *adj.* requiring total obedience.

au•thor′i•ta′tive (-tā′tiv) *adj.* 1. having authority. 2. accepted as true.

au•thor′i•ty *n., pl.* **-ties.** 1. the right to order or decide. 2. one with such a right. 3. a respected source of information.

au′thor•ize′ (ô′thə rīz′) *v.t.,* **-ized, -izing.** 1. to give authority to. 2. to give permission for. —**auth′or•i•za′tion,** *n.*

au′tism (ô′tiz əm) *n.* a disorder characterized by extreme self-absorption and detachment from one's environment. —**au•tis′tic** (ô-tis′tik) *adj.*

au′to (ô′tō) *n.* automobile.

auto- a prefix meaning self or same.

au′to•bi•og′ra•phy *n., pl.* **-phies.** the story of one's own life.

au•toc′ra•cy (ô tok′rə sē) *n., pl.* **-cies.** government in which one person has unlimited power. —**au′to•crat′** (ô′tə krat′) *n.* —**au′to•crat′ic,** *adj.*

au′to•graph′ (ô′tə graf′) *n.* 1. a signature. —*v.t.* 2. to write one's signature on.

au′to•im•mune′ (ô′tō i myoōn′) *adj.* of or relating to the body's immune response to its own components.

au′to•mat′ (ô′tə mat′) *n.* a restaurant with coin-operated service.

au′to•mate′ (-māt′) *v.t., v.i.,* **-mated, -mating.** to operate by or undergo automation.

au′to•mat′ic (-mat′ik) *adj.* 1. able to operate without human intervention. 2. involuntary. 3. done without thinking. —**au′to•mat′i•cal•ly,** *adv.*

au′tomat′ic pi′lot *n.* an electronic control system for piloting aircraft.

au′to•ma′tion (-mā′shən) *n.* the use of automatic devices to control mechanical processes.

au•tom′a•ton (ô tom′ə ton′) *n.* a robot.

au′to•mo•bile′ (ô′tə mə bēl′) *n.* a four-wheeled passenger vehicle with an internal-combustion engine.

au•ton′o•my (ô ton′ə mē) *n.* self-government.

au′top•sy (ô′top sē) *n., pl.* **-sies.** an examination of a corpse for causes of death.

au′tumn (ô′təm) *n.* the season before winter; fall. —**au•tum′nal** (ô tum′nl) *adj.*

aux•il′ia•ry (ôg zil′yə rē) *adj., n., pl.* **-ries.** —*adj.* 1. helping. 2. additional. 3. secondary. —*n.* 4. an auxiliary person, thing, or group. **5.** a verb preceding other verbs to express tense, voice, etc.

a.vail' (ə vāl') *v.t., v.i.* **1.** to be of use, value, or advantage (to). —*Idiom.* **2. avail oneself of,** to make use of. —*n.* **3.** use; help.

a.vail/a.ble *adj.* ready for use; accessible. —**a.vail/a.bil/i.ty,** *n.*

av/a.lanche' (av/ə lanch') *n.* a large mass of falling snow, ice, etc.

a.vant'-garde' (ä vänt/gärd', av/-änt-) *adj.* **1.** progressive, esp. in the arts. —*n.* **2.** the advance group in a field, esp. in the arts.

av/a.rice (av/ər is) *n.* greed. —**av/a.ri/cious** (-rish/əs) *adj.*

ave. avenue.

a.venge' (ə venj') *v.t.,* **avenged, avenging.** to take vengeance for. —**a.veng/er,** *n.*

av/e.nue' (av/ə nyōō') *n.* **1.** a broad street. **2.** an approach.

a.ver' (ə vûr') *v.t.,* **averred, averring.** to declare to be true; assert confidently.

av/er.age (av/ər ij) *n., adj., v.,* **-aged, -aging.** —*n.* **1.** a value arrived at by adding a series of quantities and dividing by the number of quantities in the series. **2.** a usual amount or level. —*adj.* **3.** of or like an average. **4.** common. —*v.t.* **5.** to find the average of. —*v.i.* **6.** to amount to an average.

a.verse' (ə vûrs') *adj.* unwilling.

a.ver/sion (ə vûr/zhən) *n.* strong dislike.

a.vert' (ə vûrt') *v.t.* **1.** to turn away. **2.** to prevent.

a/vi.ar/y (ā/vē er/ē) *n., pl.* **-aries.** a place in which birds are kept.

a/vi.a/tion (ā/vē ā/shən) *n.* the production or operation of aircraft. —**a/vi.a/tor,** *n.*

av/id (av/id) *adj.* eager; greedy. —**a.vid/i.ty,** *n.* —**av/id.ly,** *adv.*

av/o.ca/do (av/ə kä/dō, ä/və-) *n., pl.* **-dos.** a pear-shaped tropical fruit.

av/o.ca/tion (av/ə kā/shən) *n.* a hobby.

a.void' (ə void') *v.t.* to keep away from. —**a.void/a.ble,** *adj.* —**a.void/ance,** *n.*

av/oir.du.pois' (av/ər də poiz') *n.* a system of weights based on 16-ounce pounds.

a.vow' (ə vou') *v.t.* to declare. —**a.vow/al,** *n.* —**a.vowed',** *adj.*

a.wait' (ə wāt') *v.t.* to wait for.

a.wake' (ə wāk') *v.,* **awoke** (ə-wōk') or **awaked, awaking,** *adj.* —*v.t., v.i.* **1.** to rouse or emerge from sleep. —*adj.* **2.** not asleep. **3.** alert.

a.wak/en *v.t., v.i.* to waken. —**a.wak/en.ing,** *n., adj.*

a.ward' (ə wôrd') *v.t.* **1.** to give as deserved or merited. **2.** to give by the decision of a court. —*n.* **3.** something awarded.

a.ware' (ə wâr') *adj.* having knowledge or realization; conscious. —**a.ware/ness,** *n.*

a.wash' (ə wosh') *adj.* flooded.

a.way' (ə wā') *adv.* **1.** from this or that place. **2.** to or at a distance. **3.** out of one's possession. **4.** out of existence. **5.** persistently. —*adj.* **6.** absent. **7.** distant.

awe (ô) *n., v.,* **awed, awing.** —*n.* **1.** respectful fear and wonder. —*v.t.* **2.** to fill with awe.

awe/some (ô/səm) *adj.* **1.** inspiring or characterized by awe. **2.** *Slang.* very impressive.

awe/struck' *adj.* filled with awe.

aw/ful (ô/fəl) *adj.* **1.** very bad or unpleasant. **2.** inspiring fear.

aw/ful.ly *adv.* **1.** very badly. **2.** *Informal.* very.

a.while' (ə hwīl') *adv.* for a short time. —**Usage.** The adverb AWHILE is always spelled as one word: *We rested awhile.* A WHILE is a noun phrase (an article and a noun) and is used after a preposition: *We rested for a while.*

awk/ward (ôk/wərd) *adj.* **1.** lacking skill; clumsy. **2.** hard to use or deal with. **3.** inconvenient. **4.** embarrassing. —**awk/ward.ly,** *adv.* —**awk/ward.ness,** *n.*

awl (ôl) *n.* a pointed tool for making holes.

awn/ing (ô/ning) *n.* a rooflike shelter, as of canvas.

AWOL (*pronounced as initials or* ā/-wôl) *adj., adv.* absent without leave.

a.wry' (ə rī') *adv., adj.* **1.** crooked. **2.** wrong.

ax (aks) *n.* a small chopping tool. Also, **axe.**

ax/i.om (ak/sē əm) *n.* an accepted truth. —**ax/i.o.mat/ic** (-ə mat/ik) *adj.*

ax/is (ak/sis) *n., pl.* **axes** (ak/sēz). the line about which something turns. —**ax/i.al,** *adj.*

ax/le (ak/səl) *n.* a shaft on which a wheel rotates.

a/ya.tol/lah (ä/yə tō/lə) *n.* a senior Islamic religious leader.

aye (ī) *adv., n.* yes.

a.zal/ea (ə zāl/yə) *n.* a shrub with variously colored funnel-shaped flowers.

az/ure (azh/ər) *n.* a sky-blue.

B

B, b (bē) *n.* the second letter of the English alphabet.

B.A. Bachelor of Arts.

bab′ble (bab′əl) *v.i.,* **-bled, -bling. 1.** to talk indistinctly or foolishly. **2.** (of a stream) to murmur. —*n.* **3.** babbling speech or sound.

babe (bāb) *n.* **1.** a baby. **2.** a naive person.

ba·boon′ (ba bōōn′, bə-) *n.* a large monkey of Africa and Arabia.

ba′by (bā′bē) *n., pl.* **-bies,** *v.,* **-bied, -bying.** —*n.* **1.** an infant. **2.** a childish person. —*v.t.* **3.** to pamper. —**ba′by·ish,** *adj.*

ba′by boom′ *n.* a period of increase in the rate of births, esp. that following World War II. —**ba′by boom′er,** *n.*

ba′by-sit′ *v.,* **-sat** (-sat′) **-sitting.** —*v.i.* **1.** to care for a child while the parents are away. —*v.t.* **2.** to baby-sit for (a child). —**ba′by-sit′ter,** *n.*

bac·ca·lau′re·ate (bak′ə lôr′ē it) *n.* **1.** a bachelor's degree. **2.** a religious service for a graduating class.

bac′cha·nal′ (bak′ə nal′) *n.* an occasion of drunken revelry. —**bac′cha·na′li·an** (-nā′lē ən) *adj.*

bach′e·lor (bach′ə lər) *n.* **1.** an unmarried man. **2.** a person holding a degree from a 4-year college.

ba·cil′lus (bə sil′əs) *n., pl.* **-cilli** (-sil′-ī). a type of rod-shaped bacteria.

back (bak) *n.* **1.** the rear part of the human and animal body. **2.** the rear of an object or structure. **3.** the spine. —*v.t.* **4.** to sponsor. **5.** to cause to move backward. **6.** to bet in favor of. **7.** to furnish or form a back. —*v.i.* **8.** to move backward. **9. back down,** to abandon a claim or argument. **10. ~ off,** to retreat. —*adj.* **11.** situated in the rear. **12.** of a past time. **13.** overdue. —*adv.* **14.** at or toward the rear. **15.** toward the original point or condition. **16.** in return. —*Idiom.* **17. behind one's back,** without one's knowledge. —**back′er,** *n.* —**back′ing,** *n.*

back′board′ *n.* in basketball, a vertical board behind the basket.

back′bone′ *n.* **1.** a connected series of bones down the back; spine. **2.** strength of character.

back′break′ing *adj.* demanding great effort.

back′drop′ *n.* **1.** the curtain at the back of a stage. **2.** the background of an event; setting.

back′fire′ *v.i.,* **-fired, -firing. 1.** (of an engine) to make an explosive sound because of a wrongly timed ignition. **2.** to bring a result opposite to that planned. —*n.* **3.** an explosive ignition in an engine.

back′gam′mon (-gam′ən) *n.* a board game for two persons.

back′ground′ *n.* **1.** the back part of a picture. **2.** the causes of an event or condition. **3.** a person's origin, education, experience, etc.

back′hand′ *n.* **1.** in tennis and other sports, a stroke made with the back of the hand facing the direction of movement. —*v.t.* **2.** to hit with a backhand.

back′hand′ed *adj.* **1.** performed with the back of the hand forward. **2.** said in a sarcastic way; insincere.

back′lash′ *n.* a strong negative reaction.

back′log′ *n.* an accumulation.

back′pack′ *n.* **1.** a pack for supplies, carried on one's back. —*v.i.* **2.** to travel using a backpack.

back′-ped′al *v.i.,* **-pedaled, -pedaling. 1.** to slow a bicycle by pressing backward on the pedals. **2.** to retreat from a previous stand.

back′side′ *n.* the buttocks.

back′slide′ *v.i.,* **-slid** (-slid′) **-slid** or **-slidden, -sliding.** to fall back into bad habits.

back′stage′ *adv.* **1.** in the theater wings or dressing rooms. —*adj.* **2.** of the area behind the stage.

back′stroke′ *n.* a swimming stroke done while lying on one's back.

back′ talk′ *n.* impertinent replies.

back′track′ *v.i.* **1.** to retreat. **2.** to change one's opinion.

back′up′ *n.* **1.** a person or thing that supports or reinforces another. **2.** an accumulation caused by a stoppage. **3.** an alternate kept in reserve. **4.** a copy of a computer file kept in case the original is lost.

back′ward (-wərd) *adv.* Also, **back′wards. 1.** toward the rear. **2.** with the back foremost. **3.** in the reverse of the usual way. **4.** toward the past. —*adj.* **5.** directed toward the back or past. **6.** behind in development. **7.** reversed.

back′wa′ter *n.* a place that is backward or stagnant.

back′woods′ *n.pl.* wooded or unsettled districts.

ba′con (bā′kən) *n.* salted or smoked meat from a hog.

bac·te′ri·a (bak tēr′ē ə) *n.pl., sing.* **-um** (-əm). any group of one-celled organisms, involved in fermentation, infectious disease, etc. —**bac·te′ri·al,** *adj.*

bac·te/ri·ol/o·gy (-ol/ə jē) *n.* the study of bacteria. —**bac·te/ri·o·log/i·cal** (-ə loj/i kəl) *adj.* —**bac·te/ri·ol/o·gist,** *n.*

bad (bad) *adj.,* **worse** (wûrs) **worst** (wûrst) *n.* —*adj.* **1.** not good. —*n.* **2.** a bad thing, condition, or quality. —**bad/ly,** *adv.* —**bad/ness,** *n.* —*Usage.* The adjective BAD, meaning "unpleasant, unattractive, unfavorable, spoiled, etc.," is the usual form after such verbs as *sound, smell, look, feel,* and *taste: The music sounds bad. Are you feeling bad? The water tasted bad.* BAD as an adverb appears mainly in informal situations: *He wanted to win pretty bad.*

bad/ blood/ *n.* hostility.

badge (baj) *n.* an emblem or insignia worn as a sign of membership, authority, etc.

badg/er (baj/ər) *n.* **1.** a burrowing, flesh-eating mammal. —*v.t.* **2.** to pester.

bad/min·ton (bad/min tn) *n.* a game in which a shuttlecock is hit over a net with light rackets.

bad/-mouth/ (-mouth/, -mouᵗʰ/) *v.t.* to criticize. Also, **bad/mouth/.**

baf/fle (baf/əl) *v.,* **-fled, -fling,** *n.* —*v.t.* **1.** to bewilder. **2.** to frustrate. —*n.* **3.** an obstruction.

bag (bag) *n., v.,* **bagged, bagging.** —*n.* **1.** a sack or container of flexible material. **2.** a purse. —*v.i.* **3.** to bulge. **4.** to hang loosely. —*v.t.* **5.** to put into a bag. **6.** to kill or catch. —**bag/gy,** *adj.* —**bag/gi·ness,** *n.*

bag/a·telle/ (bag/ə tel/) *n.* something of little value.

ba/gel (bā/gəl) *n.* a hard ring-shaped bread roll.

bag/gage (bag/ij) *n.* trunks, suitcases, etc., for travel.

bag/pipe/ *n.* (*often pl.*) a musical instrument with a windbag and two or more pipes.

bail¹ (bāl) *n.* **1.** money given as security that an accused person will return for trial. **2.** the state of release following the payment of security. —*v.t.* **3.** to obtain the release of (an arrested person) by providing bail.

bail² (bāl) *v.t., v.i.* **1.** to dip (water) out of a boat. **2. bail out,** to make a parachute jump.

bail/iff (bā/lif) *n.* a public officer who keeps order in a courtroom.

bail/i·wick (bā/lə wik/) *n.* a person's area of authority, skill, etc.

bail/out/ *n.* a rescue from financial problems.

bait (bāt) *n.* **1.** food used as a lure in fishing or hunting. **2.** anything that lures. —*v.t.* **3.** to prepare (a hook or trap) with bait. **4.** to torment.

bake (bāk) *v.,* **baked, bak·ing.** —*v.t.* **1.** to cook by dry heat, as in an oven. **2.** to harden by heat. —*v.i.* **3.** to prepare food by baking it. **4.** to become baked.

bak/er's doz/en *n.* a dozen plus one; 13.

bak/er·y *n., pl.* **-eries.** a place for baking; baker's shop.

bak/ing pow/der *n.* a white powder used as a leavening agent.

bak/ing so/da *n.* sodium bicarbonate, a white powder used as an antacid and in baking.

bal/ance (bal/əns) *n., v.,* **-anced, -ancing.** —*n.* **1.** a state of even distribution of weight or amount. **2.** an instrument for weighing. **3.** steadiness, as of the body. **4.** the difference between debits and credits. **5.** the remainder. —*v.t.* **6.** to bring to or hold in a state of balance. **7.** to be equal to. **8.** to add up the two sides of (an account) and determine the difference. **9.** to counteract. —*v.i.* **10.** to be equal. **11.** to be in a state of balance. **12.** to be in a state in which debits equal credits.

bal/co·ny (bal/kə nē) *n., pl.* **-nies. 1.** a railed platform projecting from the wall of a building. **2.** the upper floor of seats in a theater.

bald (bôld) *adj.* **1.** lacking hair on the scalp. **2.** plain; undisguised.

bal/der·dash/ (bôl/dər dash/) *n.* nonsense.

bale (bāl) *n., v.,* **baled, baling.** —*n.* **1.** a large bundle, esp. one compressed and bound. —*v.t.* **2.** to make into bales.

bale/ful *adj.* evil; menacing. —**bale/ful·ly,** *adv.*

balk (bôk) *v.t.* **1.** to stop or stop short. —*v.t.* **2.** to hinder; thwart. **3. balk at,** to refuse firmly. —*n.* **4.** a hindrance. —**balk/y,** *adj.*

ball¹ (bôl) *n.* **1.** a round or roundish object. **2.** a game played with a ball. —*v.t., v.i.* **3.** to make or form into a ball.

ball² (bôl) *n.* **1.** a large formal party for dancing. **2.** *Informal.* a very good time.

bal/lad (bal/əd) *n.* **1.** a narrative folk song or poem. **2.** a slow, romantic song.

bal/last (bal/əst) *n.* **1.** heavy material carried to ensure stability. —*v.t.* **2.** to furnish with ballast.

ball/ bear/ing *n.* **1.** a bearing in which a moving part turns on steel balls. **2.** one of these balls.

bal/le•ri/na (bal/ə rē/nə) *n.* a female
ballet dancer.

bal•let/ (ba lā/) *n.* **1.** a dance form
having intricate, formalized
movements. **2.** a theatrical performance of such dancing.

ballis/tic mis/sile (bə lis/tik) *n.* a
guided missile that completes its
trajectory in free fall.

bal•lis/tics *n.* the study of the motion of projectiles.

bal•loon/ (bə lōōn/) *n.* **1.** a bag
filled with a gas lighter than air.
—*v.i.* **2.** to go up in a balloon. **3.**
to increase rapidly.

bal/lot (bal/ət) *n., v.,* **-loted, -loting.**
—*n.* **1.** a piece of paper or the like
used in voting. **2.** the method or
act of voting. **3.** the right to vote.
—*v.i.* **4.** to vote by ballot.

ball/park/ *n.* a stadium for baseball
games.

ball/point pen/ *n.* a pen that has a
small ball bearing as a point.

ball/room/ *n.* a large room for
dancing.

bal/ly•hoo/ (bal/ē hōō/) *n. Informal.*
exaggerated publicity.

balm (bäm) *n.* **1.** anything that
heals or soothes pain. **2.** an aromatic ointment or fragrance.

balm/y *adj.,* **-ier, -iest. 1.** mild; refreshing. **2.** fragrant.

bal/sa (bôl/sə, bäl/-) *n.* a tropical
tree with light wood.

bal/sam (bôl/səm) *n.* **1.** a fragrant
substance given off by certain
trees. **2.** any of these trees. **3.** an
aromatic ointment. —**bal•sam/ic**
(bôl sam/ik) *adj.*

bal/us•ter (bal/ə stər) *n.* a pillarlike
support for a railing.

bal/us•trade/ (-ə strād/) *n.* a series
of balusters supporting a railing.

bam•boo/ (bam bōō/) *n., pl.* **-boos.**
a treelike tropical grass having a
hollow woody stem.

bam•boo/zle (bam bōō/zəl) *v.t.,*
-zled, -zling. *Informal.* to trick.

ban (ban) *v.,* **banned, banning,** *n.*
—*v.t.* **1.** to prohibit. —*n.* **2.** a prohibition.

ba•nal/ (bə nal/, -näl/, bān/l) *adj.*
commonplace; uninteresting.
—**ba•nal/i•ty,** *n.*

ba•nan/a (bə nan/ə) *n.* the yellow,
finger-shaped fruit of a tropical
tree.

band¹ (band) *n.* **1.** a strip of material for binding. **2.** a stripe. **3.** a
range of frequencies, as in radio.
—*v.t.* **4.** to mark with bands.

band² (band) *n.* **1.** a company of
persons acting together. **2.** a group
of musicians. —*v.t., v.i.* **3.** to unite.

band/age (ban/dij) *n., v.,* **-aged,
-aging.** —*n.* **1.** a strip of cloth for
binding a wound. —*v.t.* **2.** to bind
with a bandage.

Band/-Aid/ *Trademark.* a small adhesive bandage with a gauze center.

ban•dan/na (ban dan/ə) *n.* a colored handkerchief worn on the
head. Also, **ban•dan/a.**

ban/dit (-dit) *n.* a robber; outlaw.

band/stand/ *n.* the platform on
which a band performs.

band/wag/on *n.* —*Idiom.* **jump
on the bandwagon,** to join a
cause or movement that appears
popular and successful.

ban/dy (ban/dē) *v.,* **-died, -dying,**
adj. —*v.t.* **1.** to exchange (words)
back and forth rapidly. —*adj.* **2.** (of
legs) bent outward. —**ban/dy-leg/-
ged** (-leg/id, -legd/) *adj.*

bane (bān) *n.* a thing causing ruin.
—**bane/ful** *adj.* destructive.

bang¹ (bang) *n.* **1.** a sudden loud
noise. —*v.i.* **2.** to make a loud
noise. —*v.t.* **3.** to strike noisily.

bang² (bang) *n.* Often, **bangs.** a
fringe of hair across the forehead.

ban/gle (bang/gəl) *n.* a rigid bracelet.

bang/-up/ *adj. Informal.* excellent.

ban/ish (ban/ish) *v.t.* **1.** to exile. **2.**
to drive or put away. —**ban/ish•
ment,** *n.*

ban/is•ter (ban/ə stər) *n.* a handrail, esp. on a staircase.

ban/jo (ban/jō) *n., pl.* **-jos, -joes.** a
stringed musical instrument with a
circular body. —**ban/jo•ist,** *n.*

bank¹ (bangk) *n.* **1.** a slope bordering a stream. **2.** a pile; heap. —*v.t.*
3. to border with or make into a
bank. **4.** to cover (a fire) to make it
burn slowly. —*v.i.* **5.** to slope upward.

bank² (bangk) *n.* **1.** an institution
for receiving, lending, or safeguard-
ing money. **2.** a store of something, as blood, for future use.
—*v.i., v.t.* **3.** to deposit in a bank.
4. bank on, to rely on. —**bank/er,**
n. —**bank/ing,** *n.*

bank/roll/ *n.* **1.** money possessed.
—*v.t.* **2.** to pay for; fund.

bank/rupt (-rupt) *adj.* **1.** unable to
pay one's debts. **2.** lacking. —*n.* **3.**
one who is bankrupt. —*v.t.* **4.** to
make bankrupt. —**bank/rupt•cy,** *n.*

ban/ner (ban/ər) *n.* **1.** a flag. —*adj.*
2. excellent.

banns (banz) *n.pl.* notice of intended marriage. Also, **bans.**

ban/quet (bang/kwit) *n.* **1.** a lavish
meal. **2.** a ceremonious public dinner. —*v.t.* **3.** to entertain with a
banquet.

ban/shee (ban/shē) *n.* a female

spirit of folklore whose wailing means a loved one is about to die.

ban′tam (ban′təm) *n.* **1.** a breed of small domestic fowl. —*adj.* **2.** tiny.

ban′ter (ban′tər) *n.* **1.** good-natured teasing. —*v.i.* **2.** to use banter.

ban′yan (ban′yən) *n.* an East Indian fig tree that grows new trunks from its branches.

bap′tism (bap′tiz əm) *n.* an immersion in or application of water as a rite of purification and admission to the Christian Church. —**bap•tis′mal,** *adj.*

bap•tize′ (bap tīz′, bap′tīz) *v.t.,* **-tized, -tizing.** to administer baptism to.

bar (bär) *n., v.,* **barred, barring,** *prep.* —*n.* **1.** a long, evenly shaped piece, esp. of wood or metal. **2.** a band; stripe. **3.** a long ridge in shallow waters. **4.** an obstruction; hindrance. **5.** a place where liquor is served. **6.** the legal profession or its members. **7.** a line marking the division between two measures of music. —*v.t.* **8.** to provide or fasten with a bar. **9.** to block; hinder. —*prep.* **10.** except for. —**barred,** *adj.*

barb (bärb) *n.* **1.** a point projecting backward. **2.** a nasty remark.

bar•bar′i•an (bär bâr′ē ən) *n.* **1.** a savage or uncivilized person. —*adj.* **2.** uncivilized. —**bar•bar′ic,** *adj.* —**bar•bar′i•cal•ly,** *adv.*

bar•ba′rism (-bə riz′əm) *n.* **1.** an uncivilized condition. **2.** a barbarous act.

bar•bar′i•ty (-bar′i tē) *n.* savage cruelty.

bar′ba•rous (-bər əs) *adj.* **1.** wild. **2.** savagely cruel. **3.** harsh.

bar•be•cue′ (bär′bi kyōō′) *n., v.,* **-cued, -cuing.** —*n.* **1.** meat or poultry roasted over an open fire. **2.** an outdoor meal at which foods are so cooked. —*v.t.* **3.** to cook over an open fire. Also, **bar′be•que′.**

bar′ber (bär′bər) *n.* **1.** a person who gives haircuts, shaves, etc. —*v.t.* **2.** to shave or cut the hair of.

bar•bi′tu•rate (bär bich′ər it) *n.* a sedative drug.

bar′ code′ *n.* a series of lines of different widths placed on an item for identification by a computer scanner.

bard (bärd) *n.* a poet.

bare (bâr) *adj.,* **barer, barest,** *v.,* **bared, baring.** —*adj.* **1.** uncovered; unclothed. **2.** unfurnished. **3.** plain. **4.** scarcely sufficient. —*v.t.* **5.** to reveal.

bare′back′ *adv., adj.* without a saddle.

bare′faced′ *adj.* **1.** undisguised. **2.** shameless.

bare′foot′ *adj., adv.* with the feet bare.

bare′ly *adv.* no more than; only just.

bar′gain (bär′gən) *n.* **1.** an agreement. **2.** something bought cheaply. —*v.i.* **3.** to discuss or arrive at an agreement. **4. bargain on** or **for,** to expect.

barge (bärj) *n., v.,* **barged, barging.** —*n.* **1.** an unpowered vessel for freight. —*v.t.* **2.** to carry by barge. —*v.i.* **3.** to move clumsily. **4. barge in,** to intrude.

bar′i•tone′ (bar′i tōn′) *n.* **1.** a male voice or part between tenor and bass. **2.** a baritone singer, instrument, etc.

bar′i•um (bâr′ē əm, bar′-) *n.* an active metallic element.

bark¹ (bärk) *n.* **1.** the short, sharp cry of a dog. **2.** a short, sharp sound. —*v.i.* **3.** to sound a bark. **4.** to speak sharply. —*v.t.* **5.** to utter gruffly.

bark² (bärk) *n.* **1.** the external covering of woody plants. —*v.t.* **2.** to scrape the skin of. **3.** to strip the bark from.

bark′er (bär′kər) *n.* a person who stands at the entrance to a show and shouts out its attractions.

bar′ley (bär′lē) *n.* an edible cereal plant.

bar mitz′vah (bär mits′və) *n.* a religious ceremony admitting a boy to the Jewish community as an adult.

barn (bärn) *n.* a farm building for storing hay, grain, etc., and for housing animals.

bar′na•cle (bär′nə kəl) *n.* a type of shellfish that clings to ship bottoms and timber.

barn′storm′ *v.i., v.t.* to tour (rural areas) giving speeches or performing plays.

barn′yard′ *n.* a fenced area next to a barn.

ba•rom′e•ter (bə rom′i tər) *n.* **1.** an instrument for measuring atmospheric pressure. **2.** anything that indicates changes. —**bar′o•met′ric** (bar′ə me′trik) *adj.*

bar′on (bar′ən) *n.* a member of the lowest rank of the nobility. —**ba•ro′ni•al** (bə rō′ nē əl) *adj.*

bar′on•et (-ə nit, -net′) *n.* a member of a British hereditary order of honor. —**bar′on•et•cy,** *n.*

Ba•roque′ (bə rōk′) *adj.* **1.** of an architectural style of the 17th and 18th centuries, marked by elaborate ornamentation and grotesque effects. **2.** of the musical period of the 17th and 18th centuries.

bar′racks (bar′əks) *n.* (*used with a sing. or pl. v.*) a building for lodging soldiers.

bar′ra•cu•da (bar′ə kōō′də) *n.* a long, predatory marine fish.

bar•rage′ (bə räzh′) *n.* **1.** concentrated artillery fire. **2.** an overwhelming quantity.

bar′rel (bar′əl) *n.*, *v.*, **-reled, -reling.** —*n.* **1.** a cylindrical wooden vessel with bulging sides. **2.** the quantity held in such a vessel. **3.** the tube-like part of a gun. —*v.i.* **4.** to travel very fast.

bar′ren (bar′ən) *adj.* **1.** sterile; unfruitful. **2.** dull. —**bar′ren•ness,** *n.*

bar•rette′ (bə ret′) *n.* a clasp for the hair.

bar′ri•cade′ (bar′i kād′, bar′i kād′) *n.*, *v.*, **-caded, -cading.** —*n.* **1.** a defensive barrier. —*v.t.* **2.** to block or defend with a barricade.

bar′ri•er (bar′ē ər) *n.* anything that obstructs or limits entrance or access.

bar′ring (bär′ing) *prep.* excepting.

bar′ris•ter (bar′ə stər) *n.* in Britain, a trial lawyer.

bar′row (bar′ō) *n.* **1.** a wheelbarrow. **2.** an artificial mound.

bar′tend′er (bär′-) *n.* a person who mixes and serves drinks at a bar.

bar′ter (bär′tər) *v.i.* **1.** to trade by exchange of goods rather than money. —*n.* **2.** the act of bartering.

ba•salt′ (bə sôlt′, bā′sôlt) *n.* the dark, hard rock from a volcano. —**ba•sal′tic,** *adj.*

base¹ (bās) *n.*, *v.*, **based, basing.** —*n.* **1.** the bottom or foundation of something. **2.** a fundamental principle. **3.** a starting point. **4.** a military headquarters or supply installation. **5.** a chemical compound that unites with an acid to form a salt. —*v.t.* **6.** to form a base for. **7.** to establish. —*Idiom.* **8. off base,** badly mistaken.

base² (bās) *adj.*, **baser, basest. 1.** deserving contempt; despicable. **2.** inferior.

base′ball′ *n.* **1.** a ball game involving the batting of a ball, played by two teams on a diamond-shaped field. **2.** the ball used.

base′board′ *n.* the board forming the foot of an inside wall.

base′less *adj.* having no foundation; unfounded.

base′line′ *n.* **1.** the line between the bases on a baseball diamond. **2.** the line at each end of a tennis court. **3.** a basic standard or level; guideline. Also, **base line.**

base′ment *n.* the story of a building below the ground floor.

bash (bash) *v.t.* **1.** to strike violently. **2.** to attack with blows or words. —*n.* **3.** a hard blow. **4.** a lively party.

bash′ful *adj.* shy; easily embarrassed.

ba′sic (bā′sik) *adj.* **1.** forming a base or basis; fundamental. —*n.* **2. basics,** essential ingredients, procedures, etc. —**ba′si•cal•ly,** *adv.*

bas′il (baz′əl, bā′zəl) *n.* an aromatic mintlike herb used in cooking.

ba•sil′i•ca (bə sil′i kə) *n.* an early Christian church with an apse at one end.

ba′sin (bā′sən) *n.* **1.** a round open container for liquids. **2.** an area drained by a river.

ba′sis (bā′sis) *n.*, *pl.* **-ses** (-sēz). **1.** a foundation. **2.** a fundamental principle. **3.** the main ingredient.

bask (bask) *v.i.* **1.** to lie in pleasant warmth. **2.** to take pleasure in.

bas′ket (bas′kit) *n.* a container woven of straw, strips of wood, etc.

bas′ket•ball′ *n.* **1.** a game played by two teams who score points by tossing a ball through a goal on the opponents' side of the court. **2.** the ball used.

bas′-re•lief′ (bä′ri lēf′) *n.* a sculpture in which the figures are raised slightly.

bass¹ (bās) *n.* **1.** the lowest pitch in music. **2.** the lowest male singing voice. **3.** a singer with this voice. —*adj.* **4.** of the lowest pitch.

bass² (bas) *n.*, *pl.* **basses, bass.** any of numerous edible, spiny fishes.

bas′set hound′ (bas′it) *n.* a short-legged hound with a long body and long, drooping ears.

bas′si•net′ (bas′ə net′) *n.* a hooded basket, used as a baby's cradle.

bas•soon′ (ba sōōn′, bə-) *n.* a large woodwind instrument of low range.

bas′tard (bas′tərd) *n.* **1.** an illegitimate child. **2.** a mean, unpleasant person. —*adj.* **3.** illegitimate in birth. **4.** not genuine; false. —**bas′tard•ize′,** *v.t.*

baste¹ (bāst) *v.t.*, **basted, basting.** to sew with long, loose, temporary stitches.

baste² (bāst) *v.t.*, **basted, basting.** to moisten (meat, poultry, etc.) while cooking.

bas′tion (bas′chən) *n.* **1.** the projecting part of a fortified place. **2.** a fortified place. **3.** anything seen as protecting some quality, condition, etc.

bat¹ (bat) *n.*, *v.*, **batted, batting.** —*n.* **1.** the wooden club used in certain games to strike the ball. **2.** a heavy stick or club. **3.** a blow, as with a bat. —*v.t.* **4.** to hit with a bat. —*v.i.* **5.** to take one's turn as a batter.

bat² (bat) *n.* a nocturnal flying mammal.

bat³ (bat) *v.t.*, **batted, batting. 1.** to blink; flutter. —*Idiom.* **2. not bat an eye,** to show no emotion.

batch (bach) *n.* a quantity produced at one time or taken together.

bat′ed (bā′tid) *adj.* —*Idiom.* **with bated breath,** in a state of suspenseful anticipation.

bath (bath) *n.*, *pl.* **baths. 1.** a washing of the entire body. **2.** the water used.

bathe (bāth) *v.*, **bathed, bathing.** —*v.i.* **1.** to take a bath. **2.** to swim for pleasure. —*v.t.* **3.** to immerse in water or other liquid. **4.** to give a bath to. **5.** to apply water or other liquid to. —**bath′er,** *n.*

bath′ing suit′ *n.* a garment worn for swimming; swimsuit.

ba′thos (bā′thos, -thōs) *n.* **1.** a change in tone from the important to the trivial. **2.** sentimentality; triteness. —**ba·thet′ic** (bə thet′ik) *adj.*

bath′robe′ *n.* a loose robe worn to and from the bath.

bath′room′ *n.* a room with a bathtub or shower and usu. a sink and toilet.

bath′tub′ *n.* a tub to bathe in.

bat mitz′vah (bät mits′və) *n.* a religious ceremony admitting a girl to the Jewish community as an adult.

ba·ton′ (bə ton′, ba-) *n.* **1.** a wand with which a conductor directs an orchestra. **2.** a staff serving as a mark of office.

bat·tal′ion (bə tal′yən) *n.* a military unit of at least three companies.

bat′ten (bat′n) *n.* **1.** a strip of wood holding something in place. —*v.t.* **2.** to fasten with this.

bat′ter¹ (bat′ər) *v.t.* **1.** to beat repeatedly. **2.** to subject (a person) to repeated abuse. **3.** to damage by rough usage.

batter² (bat′ər) *n.* a mixture of flour, milk, and eggs.

bat′ter³ (bat′ər) *n.* a player whose turn it is to bat.

bat′ter·y *n.*, *pl.* **-teries. 1.** a cell or cells for producing electricity. **2.** a group of artillery pieces. **3.** any group or series of similar or related things. **4.** an unlawful attack on a person by beating or wounding.

bat′tle (bat′l) *n.*, *v.*, **-tled, -tling.** —*n.* **1.** a hostile encounter. —*v.t.*, *v.i.* **2.** to fight.

bat′tle·field′ *n.* **1.** the ground on which a battle is fought. **2.** an area of conflict.

bat′tle·ment *n.* a low wall on a tower with spaces for shooting.

bat′tle·ship′ *n.* a heavily armed warship.

bat′ty (bat′ē) *adj.*, **-tier, -tiest.** *Slang.* crazy or eccentric.

bau′ble (bô′bəl) *n.* a cheap, showy trinket.

baud (bôd) *n.* a unit used to measure the speed of data transfer on a computer.

baux′ite (bôk′sīt, bō′zīt) *n.* the principal ore of aluminum.

bawd′y (bô′dē) *adj.*, **-ier, -iest.** indecent.

bawl (bôl) *v.i.* **1.** to cry lustily. —*v.t.* **2.** to shout out. —*n.* **3.** a loud shout.

bay¹ (bā) *n.* a wide inlet of the sea.

bay² (bā) *n.* **1.** a compartment or recess in a building. **2.** a compartment, as in an aircraft or ship.

bay³ (bā) *n.* **1.** a deep, prolonged howl. **2.** the stand made by a hunted animal or person. —*v.i.* **3.** to howl.

bay⁴ (bā) *n.* the laurel.

bay⁵ (bā) *n.* **1.** a reddish brown horse or other animal. **2.** a reddish brown.

bay′ber′ry *n.*, *pl.* **-ries.** a fragrant shrub with waxy berries.

bay′ leaf′ *n.* the dried leaf of the laurel, used in cooking.

bay′o·net (bā′ə net′, bā′ə nit) *n.*, *v.*, **-neted, -neting.** —*n.* **1.** a dagger attached to the muzzle of a gun. —*v.t.* **2.** to kill or wound with a bayonet.

bay′ou (bī′ōō) *n.*, *pl.* **bayous.** a marshy arm of a lake, river, etc.

ba·zaar′ (bə zär′) *n.* **1.** a marketplace. **2.** a sale to benefit a charity.

ba·zoo′ka (bə zōō′kə) *n.* a portable weapon that fires an armor-piercing missile.

BB (bē′bē′) *n.*, *pl.* **BB's.** small metal shot fired from an air rifle **(BB gun).**

B.C. before Christ.

B.C.E. before the Common (or Christian) Era.

be (bē; *unstressed* bē, bi) *v.* and *auxiliary v.*, *pres. sing. 1st pers.* **am,** *2nd* **are,** *3rd* **is,** *pres. pl.* **are;** *past sing. 1st pers.* **was,** *2nd* **were,** *3rd* **was,** *past pl.* **were;** *pres. subj.* **be;** *past subj. sing. 1st, 2nd, and 3rd pers.* **were;** *past subj. pl.* **were;** *past part.* **been;** *pres. part.* **be·ing.** —*v.i.* **1.** to exist or live. **2.** to occur. **3.** to occupy a certain place. **4.** to continue as before. **5.** (used to connect the subject with its predicate adjective or nominative). **6.** (used to form interrogative or imperative sentences). —*auxiliary verb.* **7.** (used with other verbs to form progressive tenses, the passive voice, etc.)

beach (bēch) *n.* **1.** an expanse of sand or pebbles along a shore. —*v.t.* **2.** to run or pull onto a beach.

beach′comb′er *n.* a person who gathers various objects on a beach.

beach′head′ *n.* the area that is the first objective of an invading army landing on a beach.

bea′con (bē′kən) *n.* a signal, as a light or fire.

bead (bēd) *n.* **1.** a small ball of glass, pearl, etc., designed to be strung. **2. beads,** a necklace of beads. **3.** any small globular body. —*v.t.* **4.** to ornament with beads. —*v.i.* **5.** to form in beads.

bea′gle (bē′gəl) *n.* a small hound with drooping ears.

beak (bēk) *n.* **1.** the bill of a bird. **2.** any similar projecting part.

beak′er *n.* **1.** a large drinking cup. **2.** a glass container with a pouring lip, used in a laboratory.

beam (bēm) *n.* **1.** a long piece of metal or wood that supports a structure or a machine. **2.** the breadth of a ship. **3.** a ray of light or other radiation. **4.** a radio signal. —*v.i.* **5.** to emit beams. **6.** to smile radiantly.

bean (bēn) *n.* **1.** the edible seed or pod of plants of the legume family. **2.** a plant producing beans. **3.** any other beanlike seed or plant. —*Idiom.* **4. spill the beans,** *Informal.* to reveal a secret.

bear[1] (bâr) *v.,* **bore** (bôr) **borne** (bôrn) **bearing.** —*v.t.* **1.** to support. **2.** to carry. **3.** to undergo; endure. **4.** to give birth to. —*v.i.* **5.** to go in a direction. **6. bear on,** to be relevant to. **7. ~ out,** to confirm. **8. ~ with,** to be patient with.

bear[2] (bâr) *n.* **1.** a large, stocky, omnivorous mammal. **2.** a clumsy or rude person. **3.** a person who believes that stock prices will fall. —*adj.* **4.** marked by falling prices, esp. of stocks.

beard (bērd) *n.* **1.** hair growing on the lower part of a man's face. **2.** a similar growth on an animal or plant. —*v.t.* **3.** to confront boldly.

bear′ hug′ *n.* a tight embrace.

bear′ing *n.* **1.** the manner in which one conducts or carries oneself. **2.** reference or relation. **3.** the support and guide for a rotating or sliding shaft, pivot, or wheel. **4. bearings,** position; direction.

beast (bēst) *n.* **1.** an animal. **2.** a coarse or inhuman person.

beast′ly *adj.,* **-lier, -liest. 1.** brutish. **2.** nasty.

beat (bēt) *v.,* **beat, beaten** or **beat, beating,** *n.* —*v.t.* **1.** to strike repeatedly. **2.** to dash against. **3.** to mark (time) in music. **4.** to flap. **5.** to stir vigorously. **6.** to defeat. —*v.i.* **7.** to pound. **8.** to throb. —*n.* **9.** a blow. **10.** the sound of a blow. **11.** one's regular path. **12.** musical rhythm.

be′a·tif′ic (bē′ə tif′ik) *adj.* blissful.

be·at′i·tude′ (bē at′i tōōd′, -tyōōd′) *n.* **1.** blessedness. **2.** (*often cap.*) any of the declarations of blessedness made by Jesus (Matthew 5).

beat′nik (bēt′nik) *n.* a disillusioned, unconventional person, esp. of the 1950s.

beau (bō) *n., pl.* **beaus, beaux.** a suitor.

beau′te·ous (byōō′tē əs) *adj.* beautiful.

beau·ti′cian (-tish′ən) *n.* a person who works in a beauty parlor.

beau′ti·ful (-tə fəl) *adj.* **1.** having beauty; delighting the senses or mind. **2.** wonderful.

beau′ti·fy′ (-fī′) *v.t.,* **-fied, -fying.** to make beautiful.

beau′ty *n., pl.* **-ties. 1.** the quality that gives intense pleasure to the sight or other senses. **2.** a beautiful thing or person.

beau′ty par′lor *n.* an establishment where women go for haircuts, manicures, etc.

bea′ver (bē′vər) *n.* a large amphibious rodent with sharp teeth and a flattened tail.

be·cause (bi kôz′, -koz′, -kuz′) *conj.* **1.** for the reason that. —*Idiom.* **2. because of,** on account of.

beck (bek) *n.* **1.** a beckoning gesture. —*Idiom.* **2. at someone's beck and call,** subject to someone's demands.

beck′on (-ən) *v.t., v.i.* to summon by a gesture.

be·cloud′ (bi kloud′) *v.t.* **1.** to darken with clouds. **2.** to make confused.

be·come′ (bi kum′) *v.,* **became** (-kām′) **become, becoming.** —*v.i.* **1.** to come, change, or grow to be. —*v.t.* **2.** to suit.

be·com′ing *adj.* **1.** attractive. **2.** suitable.

bed (bed) *n.* **1.** a piece of furniture on which a person sleeps. **2.** an area of ground on which plants are grown. **3.** the bottom of a lake, river, etc. **4.** a base.

bed′bug′ *n.* a wingless, bloodsucking insect.

bed′ding *n.* blankets, sheets, etc., for a bed.
be•dev′il (bi dev′əl) *v.t.*, **-iled, -il-ing. 1.** to torment maliciously. **2.** to confuse; confound.
bed′fel′low *n.* **1.** a person sharing one's bed. **2.** an ally.
bed′lam (bed′ləm) *n.* a scene of loud confusion.
bed′pan′ *n.* a shallow pan used as a toilet for a bedridden person.
be•drag′gled (bi drag′əld) *adj.* soiled and wet.
bed′rid•den (-rid′n) *adj.* confined to bed by illness.
bed′rock′ *n.* **1.** continuous solid rock under soil. **2.** any firm foundation.
bed′room′ *n.* a room for sleeping.
bed′sore′ *n.* a skin ulcer caused by long confinement in bed.
bed′spread′ *n.* a decorative cover for a bed.
bed′stead′ (-sted′, -stid) *n.* a frame for a bed.
bed′time′ *n.* the time a person goes to bed.
bee (bē) *n.* **1.** a four-winged, honey-producing insect. **2.** a social gathering for work or competition.
beech (bēch) *n.* a tree with smooth gray bark and small edible nuts (**beech′nuts′**).
beef (bēf) *n., pl.* **beeves** (bēvz) for 1; **beefs** for 4, *v.* —*n.* **1.** an adult cow, steer, or bull raised for its meat. **2.** its meat. **3.** *Informal.* muscular strength. **4.** *Slang.* a complaint. —*v.i.* **5.** *Slang.* to complain. **6. beef up,** to strengthen.
bee′hive′ *n.* **1.** a shelter for bees. **2.** a busy place.
bee′keep′er *n.* a person who raises bees.
bee′line′ *n.* a direct course.
been (bin) *v.* pp. of **be.**
beep (bēp) *n.* **1.** a short tone, usu. high in pitch, as from an electronic device. —*v.i.* **2.** to make a beep.
beep′er *n.* a small electronic device whose signal notifies the person carrying it of a message.
beer (bēr) *n.* a fermented beverage made from malt and hops.
beet (bēt) *n.* a plant with an edible red or white root.
bee•tle¹ (bēt′l) *n.* an insect with hard, horny forewings.
bee•tle² (bēt′l) *adj., v.,* **-tled, -tling.** —*adj.* **1.** projecting; overhanging. —*v.i.* **2.** to project or overhang.
be•fall′ (bi fôl′) *v.t., v.i.,* **-fell, -fallen, -falling.** to happen (to).
be•fit′ (bi fit′) *v.t.,* **-fitted, -fitting.** to be appropriate for.
be•fore′ (bi fôr′) *adv.* **1.** in front.

2. earlier. —*prep.* **3.** in front of. **4.** previously to. **5.** in preference to. —*conj.* **6.** earlier than.
be•fore′hand′ *adv.* in advance; ahead of time.
be•friend′ (bi frend′) *v.t.* to act as a friend to.
be•fud′dle (bi fud′l) *v.t.,* **-dled, -dl-ing.** to confuse thoroughly.
beg (beg) *v.t, v.i.,* **begged, beg-ging. 1.** to ask for (charity). **2.** to ask humbly. **3. beg off,** to ask release from an obligation.
be•gan′ (bi gan′) *v.* pt. of **begin.**
be•get′ (bi get′) *v.t.,* **begot** (bi got′) **begotten** or **begot, begetting. 1.** to be the father of. **2.** to cause.
beg′gar (beg′ər) *n.* **1.** a person who lives by begging. **2.** a very poor person. —*v.t.* **3.** to reduce to poverty.
beg′gar•ly *adj.* **1.** inadequate. **2.** mean.
be•gin′ (bi gin′) *v.i., v.t.,* **be•gan, be•gun, be•gin•ning. 1.** to perform the first part of (something). **2.** to come or bring into existence.
be•gin′ner (bi gin′ər) *n.* a person who is just starting to learn something.
be•gin′ning *n.* **1.** the time or place at which anything starts. **2.** origin.
be•gone′ (bi gôn′) *interj.* depart!
be•gon′ia (bi gōn′yə) *n.* a plant with bright flowers and waxy leaves.
be•grudge′ (bi gruj′) *v.t.,* **-grudged, -grudging. 1.** to envy the good fortune or pleasure of. **2.** to give or allow reluctantly.
be•guile′ (bi gīl′) *v.t.,* **-guiled, -guil-ing. 1.** to deceive. **2.** to charm or delight.
be•gun′ (bi gun′) *v.* pp. of **begin.**
be•half′ (bi haf′, -häf′) *n.* **1.** interest; support. —*Idiom.* **2. in** or **on behalf of,** as a representative of.
be•have′ (bi hāv′) *v.i.,* **-haved, -having. 1.** to act or react in a certain way. **2.** to act properly. —*v.t.* **3.** to conduct (oneself) in a proper manner.
be•hav′ior (-yər) *n.* a way of behaving.
be•head′ (bi hed′) *v.t.* to cut off the head of.
be•hest′ (bi hest′) *n.* **1.** a command. **2.** an earnest request.
be•hind′ (bi hīnd′) *prep.* **1.** at or toward the rear of. **2.** later than. **3.** in the state of making less progress than. **4.** supporting. **5.** hidden by. —*adv.* **6.** at or toward the rear. **7.** in arrears. **8.** slow; late. —*n.* **9.** *Informal.* the buttocks.
be•hold′ (bi hōld′) *v.,* **-held, -hold-**

ing, *interj.* —*v.t.* **1.** to look at; see. —*interj.* **2.** look! —**be•hold′er,** *n.*

be•hold′en *adj.* obliged.

be•hoove′ (bi hōōv′) *v.t.,* **-hooved, -hooving.** to be necessary or proper for.

beige (bāzh) *n.* a light brown.

be′ing (bē′ing) *n.* **1.** existence. **2.** a living person or thing.

be•la′bor (bi lā′bər) *v.t.* to discuss or explain excessively.

be•lat′ed (bi lā′tid) *adj.* late.

belch (belch) *v.i., v.t.* **1.** to expel (gas) from the stomach. **2.** to gush forth. —*n.* **3.** an act of belching.

be•lea′guer (bi lē′gər) *v.t.* to beset, as with difficulties.

bel′fry (bel′frē) *n., pl.* **-fries.** a bell tower.

be•lie′ (bi lī′) *v.t.,* **-lied, -lying. 1.** to misrepresent. **2.** to show to be false.

be•lief′ (bi lēf′) *n.* **1.** something believed. **2.** confidence; trust. **3.** a religious faith.

be•lieve′ (bi lēv′) *v.,* **-lieved, -lieving.** —*v.t.* **1.** to accept as true or as speaking the truth. **2.** to think; suppose. —*v.i.* **3.** to accept the truth of something. —**be•liev′a•ble,** *adj.* —**be•liev′er,** *n.*

be•lit′tle (bi lit′l) *v.t.,* **-littled, -littling.** to view or represent as less important.

bell (bel) *n.* **1.** a hollow, cup-shaped metal instrument producing a ringing sound when struck. —*v.t.* **2.** to put a bell on. —*v.i.* **3.** to have the shape of a bell.

bel′la•don′na (bel′ə don′ə) *n.* **1.** a poisonous plant having black berries and purplish red flowers. **2.** the drug obtained from this.

belle (bel) *n.* a beautiful woman.

bell′hop′ *n.* a person who carries luggage and runs errands in a hotel.

bel′li•cose′ (bel′i kōs′) *adj.* eager to fight.

bel•lig′er•ent (bə lij′ər ənt) *adj.* **1.** aggressively hostile. —*n.* **2.** a nation at war. —**bel•lig′er•ence,** *n.* —**bel•lig′er•ent•ly,** *adv.*

bel′low (bel′ō) *v.i.* **1.** to make the loud, deep sound of a bull. —*v.t.* **2.** to utter in a loud, deep voice. —*n.* **3.** an act or sound of bellowing.

bel′lows (bel′ōz, -əz) *n.* (*used with a sing. or pl. v.*) a device for producing a strong current of air, consisting of a chamber that can be expanded and contracted.

bell′ pep′per *n.* a mild, bell-shaped pepper.

bell′weth′er (bel′weth′ər) *n.* **1.** one that leads or marks a trend. **2.** a

male sheep wearing a bell and leading a flock.

bel′ly (bel′ē) *n., pl.* **-lies,** *v.,* **-lied, -lying.** —*n.* **1.** the abdomen. **2.** the stomach. **3.** a rounded part. —*v.t., v.i.* **4.** to swell out.

bel′ly•ache′ *n., v.,* **-ached, -aching.** —*n.* **1.** a pain in the abdomen. —*v.i.* **2.** *Informal.* to complain.

be•long′ (bi lông′) *v.i.* **1.** to be properly placed. **2.** to be suitable. **3. belong to, a.** to be the property of. **b.** to be part of. **c.** to be a member of.

be•long′ings *n.pl.* one's personal possessions.

be•lov′ed (bi luv′id, -luvd′) *adj.* **1.** greatly loved. —*n.* **2.** a person who is beloved.

be•low′ (bi lō′) *adv.* **1.** in or toward a lower place. **2.** in a lower rank or grade. **3.** later in a text. —*prep.* **4.** lower down than.

belt (belt) *n.* **1.** an encircling band, esp. for the waist. **2.** an endless band to transmit motion or carry objects. **3.** a region. **4.** *Slang.* a hard blow. —*v.t.* **5.** to put a belt around. **6.** *Slang.* to hit hard. —*Idiom.* **7. below the belt,** unfairly.

be•moan′ (bi mōn′) *v.t.* to express grief over.

be•mused′ (bi myōōzd′) *adj.* **1.** bewildered. **2.** lost in thought.

bench (bench) *n.* **1.** a long, hard seat. **2.** a work table. **3.** a judge's seat. **4.** judges collectively. **5.** the seat on which team members sit while not playing in a game.

bench′mark′ *n.* a standard against which others can be measured.

bend (bend) *v.,* **bent, bending,** *n.* —*v.t.* **1.** to curve. **2.** to shape into a curve. **3.** to guide in a certain direction. —*v.i.* **4.** to become curved. **5.** to turn or incline. —*n.* **6.** the act of bending. **7.** something bent.

be•neath′ (bi nēth′) *adv.* **1.** in or to a lower position; below. —*prep.* **2.** below; under. **3.** below the level or dignity of.

ben′e•dic′tion (ben′i dik′shən) *n.* a spoken blessing.

ben′e•fac′tor (-fak′tər) *n.* a person who gives financial or other help.

be•nef′i•cent (bə nef′ə sənt) *adj.* doing good. —**be•nef′i•cence,** *n.*

ben•e•fi′cial (ben′ə fish′əl) *adj.* having a helpful effect. —**ben′e•fi′cial•ly,** *adv.*

ben′e•fi′ci•ar•y (-fish′ē er′ē, -fish′ə rē) *n., pl.* **-aries.** a person who receives benefits or funds.

ben′e•fit (-fit) *n., v.,* **-fited, -fiting.** —*n.* **1.** something helpful or advantageous. **2.** money from insurance, a public agency, etc. **3.** entertainment for a worthy cause. —*v.t.* **4.** to do good to. —*v.i.* **5.** to gain an advantage.

be·nev/o·lent (bə nev/ə lənt) *adj.* kind and charitable. —**be·nev/o·lence,** *n.*

be·night/ed (bi nī/tid) *adj.* intellectually or morally ignorant.

be·nign/ (bi nīn/) *adj.* **1.** kind. **2.** favorable. **3.** not malignant. —**be·nign/ly,** *adv.*

be·nig/nant (-nig/nənt) *adj.* **1.** kind. **2.** beneficial.

bent (bent) *adj.* **1.** curved. **2.** determined. —*n.* **3.** a natural talent.

be·numb/ (bi num/) *v.t.* **1.** to make numb. **2.** to make inactive.

ben/zene (ben/zēn, ben zēn/) *n.* a flammable liquid, used as a solvent.

be·queath/ (bi kwēth/, -kwēth/) *v.t.* **1.** to give (property or money) in a will. **2.** to hand down.

be·quest/ (-kwest/) *n.* **1.** a bequeathing. **2.** something bequeathed.

be·rate/ (bi rāt/) *v.t.,* **-rated, -rating.** to scold.

be·reaved/ (bi revd/) *adj.* suffering a loved one's death. —**be·reave/,** *v.t.* —**be·reave/ment,** *n.*

be·reft/ (-reft/) *adj.* deprived.

be·ret/ (bə rā/) *n.* a soft, visorless cap.

ber/i·ber/i (ber/ē ber/ē) *n.* a disease caused by lack of vitamin B_1.

ber/ry (ber/ē) *n., pl.* **-ries,** *v.,* **-ried, -rying.** —*n.* **1.** a small, juicy, stoneless fruit. —*v.i.* **2.** to gather berries.

ber·serk/ (bər sûrk/, -zûrk/) *adj.* —*Idiom.* **go berserk,** to become violently enraged.

berth (bûrth) *n.* **1.** a sleeping space on a ship or train. **2.** a place for a ship to dock. —*v.t.* **3.** to provide with a berth.

ber/yl (ber/əl) *n.* a mineral, varieties of which are the gems emerald and aquamarine.

be·seech/ (bi sēch/) *v.t., v.i.,* **-sought, -seeching.** to implore; beg (for).

be·set/ (bi set/) *v.t.,* **-set, -setting. 1.** to attack on all sides. **2.** to surround.

be·side/ (bi sīd/) *prep.* **1.** at the side of. **2.** compared with. **3.** apart from. —*Idiom.* **4. beside oneself,** distraught.

be·sides/ *adv.* **1.** moreover; furthermore. **2.** in addition. —*prep.* **3.** in addition to. **4.** other than.

be·siege/ (bi sēj/) *v.t.,* **-sieged, -sieging. 1.** to lay siege to. **2.** to crowd around.

be·smirch/ (-smûrch/) *v.t.* to soil.

be·sot/ted (-sot/id) *adj.* infatuated.

be·speak/ (-spēk/) *v.t.,* **-spoke** (-spōk) **-spoken** or **-spoke, -speaking. 1.** to reserve. **2.** to show.

best (best) *adj.* **1.** of highest quality. **2.** most suitable. —*adv.* **3.** most excellently. **4.** in or to the highest degree. —*n.* **5.** someone or something that is best. —*v.t.* **6.** to defeat. —*Idiom.* **7. get the best of,** to defeat. **8. make the best of,** to accept.

bes/tial (bes/chəl, bēs/-) *adj.* **1.** beastlike. **2.** brutal.

be·stir/ (bi stûr/) *v.t.,* **-stirred, -stirring.** to rouse to action.

best/ man/ *n.* the chief attendant of the bridegroom.

be·stow/ (bi stō/) *v.t.* to present as a gift.

bet (bet) *v.,* **bet** or **betted, betting,** *n.* —*v.t.* **1.** to risk or pledge (something, esp. money) on the outcome of a future event. —*v.i.* **2.** to make a bet. —*n.* **3.** a pledge made in betting. **4.** a thing or amount bet.

bête/ noire/ (bāt/ nwär/, bet/) *n.* a dreaded person or thing.

be·tide/ (bi tīd/) *v.t., v.i.,* **-tided, -tiding.** to happen (to).

be·to/ken (bi tō/kən) *v.t.* to be a sign of.

be·tray/ (bi trā/) *v.t.* **1.** to deliver or reveal to an enemy by treachery. **2.** to be disloyal to. **3.** to reveal unintentionally. —**be·tray/al,** *n.* —**be·tray/er,** *n.*

be·troth/ (bi trōth/, -trôth/) *v.t.* to promise to marry. —**be·troth/al,** *n.* —**be·trothed/,** *adj., n.*

bet/ter (bet/ər) *adj.* **1.** of superior quality. **2.** preferable. **3.** greater. **4.** improved in health. —*adv.* **5.** in a more excellent manner. **6.** more completely. —*v.t.* **7.** to improve. **8.** to surpass. —*n.* **9.** something preferable. **10. betters.** those superior to oneself. —*Idiom.* **11. get the better of,** to prevail against.

be·tween/ (bi twēn/) *prep.* **1.** in the space separating. **2.** intermediate to. **3.** connecting. **4.** by the combined effort of. —*adv.* **5.** in the intervening space or time. —*Usage.* *Between you and I,* though occasionally heard in the speech of educated persons, is not the commonly accepted form. Since the pronouns are objects of the preposition BETWEEN, the correct form is *between you and me.* See also AMONG.

be·twixt/ (bi twikst/) *prep., adv.* between.

bev/el (bev/əl) *n., v.,* **-eled, -eling.** —*n.* **1.** a sloping edge. —*v.t.* **2.** to cut at a bevel. —*v.i.* **3.** to slant at a bevel.

bev·er·age (bev′ər ij) *n.* any drink.

bev′y (bev′ē) *n., pl.* **bevies. 1.** a flock of birds. **2.** a large group.

be·wail′ (bi wāl′) *v.t.* to lament.

be·ware′ (-wâr′) *v.t., v.i.,* **-wared, -waring.** to be cautious (of).

be·wil′der (-wil′dər) *v.t.* to confuse. —**be·wil′der·ment,** *n.*

be·witch′ (-wich′) *v.t.* **1.** to put under a magic spell. **2.** to charm.

be·yond′ (bē ond′) *prep.* **1.** on the farther side of. **2.** farther, more, or later on. —*adv.* **3.** farther on.

bi- a prefix meaning twice or two.

bi·an′nu·al (bī an′yōō əl) *adj.* occurring twice a year.

bi·as (bī′əs) *n.* **1.** a diagonal line running across a woven fabric. **2.** prejudice. —*adv.* **3.** in a diagonal manner. —*v.t.* **4.** to prejudice.

bi·ath′lon (bī ath′lon) *n.* an athletic contest comprising two consecutive events.

bib (bib) *n.* a covering tied under the chin to protect the clothing while eating.

Bi·ble (bī′bəl) *n.* the sacred writings of the Christian or the Jewish religion. —**Bib·li·cal, bib·li·cal** (bib′li-kəl) *adj.*

bib·li·og′ra·phy (bib′lē og′rə fē) *n., pl.* **-phies.** a list of writings on a subject or by an author.

bi·cam′er·al (bī kam′ər əl) *adj.* composed of two legislative bodies.

bi·car′bo·nate of so′da (bī kär′-bə nit, -nāt′) baking soda.

bi·cen·ten′ni·al *n.* a 200th anniversary. Also, **bi′cen·ten′a·ry.**

bi′ceps (-seps) *n.* a muscle of the upper arm.

bick′er (bik′ər) *v.i.* to quarrel about trivial things.

bi·cus′pid *n.* a tooth having two cusps or points.

bi·cy·cle (bī′si kəl) *n., v.,* **-cled, -cling.** —*n.* **1.** a two-wheeled vehicle propelled by pedals. —*v.i.* **2.** to ride a bicycle. —**bi′cy·clist,** *n.*

bid (bid) *v.,* **bade** (bad, bād) or **bid, bidden** or **bid, bidding.** —*v.t.* **1.** to command. **2.** to say as a greeting. **3.** to offer (a sum) as the price one will charge or pay. **4.** (in card games) to enter a bid of. —*v.i.* **5.** to make a bid. —*n.* **6.** the act of bidding. **7.** (in card games) a statement of the number of tricks a player expects to win. **8.** an offer of a price. **9.** an attempt.

bid′der *n.* a person who bids.

bide (bīd) *v.i.i.,* **bided, biding.** —*Idiom.* **bide one's time,** to wait for a favorable opportunity.

bi·det′ (bē dā′) *n.* a low tub for bathing the genital area.

bi·en′ni·al (bī en′ē əl) *adj.* occurring every two years.

bier (bēr) *n.* a stand for a coffin.

bi′fo·cal (bī′fō′kəl) *adj.* **1.** having two focuses. **2.** (of an eyeglass lens) having separate areas for near and far vision. —*n.* **3.** bifocals, eyeglasses with bifocal lenses.

big (big) *adj.,* **bigger, biggest. 1.** large in size, amount, etc. **2.** important.

big′a·my (big′ə mē) *n., pl.* **-mies.** the crime of marrying again while legally married. —**big′a·mist,** *n.*

big′ bang′ the′ory *n.* the theory that the universe began with an explosion of a dense mass of matter and is still expanding.

big′horn′ (big′hôrn′) *n.* a wild sheep of the Rocky Mountains with large, curving horns.

bight (bīt) *n.* **1.** a loop of rope. **2.** a deep bend in a coast; bay.

big′ot (big′ət) *n.* an intolerant person. —**big′ot·ed,** *adj.* —**big′ot·ry,** *n.*

bike (bīk) *n., v.,* **biked, biking.** —*n.* **1.** a bicycle or motorcycle. —*v.i.* **2.** to ride a bike. —**bik′er,** *n.*

bi·ki′ni (bi kē′nē) *n.* **1.** a very brief two-piece bathing suit for women. **2.** a very brief bathing suit for men.

bi·lat′er·al (bī lat′ər əl) *adj.* on or affecting two sides.

bile (bīl) *n.* **1.** a digestive secretion of the liver. **2.** ill temper.

bilge (bilj) **1.** the lowest inner part of a ship's hull. **2.** water collected in bilges. **3.** *Slang.* foolish talk.

bi·lin′gual (bī ling′gwəl) *adj.* speaking or expressed in two languages.

bil′ious (bil′yəs) *adj.* **1.** of bile. **2.** suffering from liver trouble. **3.** irritable.

bilk (bilk) *v.t.* to cheat; defraud.

bill¹ (bil) *n.* **1.** an account of money owed. **2.** a piece of paper money. **3.** a draft of a proposed law. **4.** a poster. —*v.t.* **5.** to charge.

bill² (bil) *n.* the horny part of a bird's jaw.

bill′board′ *n.* a large outdoor advertising display panel.

bil′let (bil′it) *n., v.,* **-leted, -leting.** —*n.* **1.** lodging for a soldier. —*v.t.* **2.** to provide lodging for.

bill′fold′ *n.* a wallet.

bil′liards (bil′yərdz) *n.* a game played with hard balls driven by a cue on a table.

bil′lion (bil′yən) *n.* a number represented in the U.S. by 1 followed by 9 zeros, and in Great Britain by 1 followed by 12 zeros.

bil′lion·aire′ (-âr′) *n.* a person whose assets are worth a billion dollars or more.

bill′ of sale′ *n.* a document transferring personal property from seller to buyer.

bil′low (bil′ō) *n.* **1.** a great wave or surge. —*v.i.* **2.** to swell out.

bil′ly goat′ *n.* a male goat.

bim′bo (bim′bō) *n., pl.* **-bos, -boes.** *Slang.* an attractive but stupid young woman.

bi·month′ly (bī munth′lē) *adv., adj.* every two months.

bin (bin) *n.* a box for storing grain, coal, etc.

bi′na·ry (bī′nə rē) *adj.* **1.** involving two parts, choices, etc. **2.** of a numerical system in which each place of a number is expressed as 0 or 1.

bind (bīnd) *v.t.,* **bound, binding. 1.** to tie or encircle with a band. **2.** to bandage. **3.** to unite. **4.** to fasten (a book) in its cover. **5.** to obligate.

bind′ing *n.* **1.** something that binds. —*adj.* **2.** obligatory.

binge (binj) *n., v.,* **binged, binging.** —*n.* **1.** a bout of excessive indulgence, as in eating. —*v.i.* **2.** to go on a binge.

bin′go (bing′gō) *n.* a game of chance using cards with numbered squares.

bin′na·cle (bin′ə kəl) *n.* a stand for a ship's compass.

bin·oc′u·lars (bə nok′yə lərz, bī-) *n.pl.* an instrument with two lenses that makes objects in the distance appear larger.

bio- a prefix meaning life or living organisms.

bi′o·chem′is·try (bī′ō kem′ə strē) *n.* the chemistry of living matter. —**bi′o·chem′ist,** *n.*

bi′o·de·grad′a·ble *adj.* capable of decaying and being absorbed harmlessly into the environment.

bi′o·di·ver′si·ty *n.* diversity of plant and animal species in an environment.

bi′o·eth′ics *n.* the study of the ethical implications of medical or biological procedures.

bi·og′ra·phy (bī og′rə fē) *n., pl.* **-phies.** a written account of a person's life. —**bi·og′ra·pher,** *n.* —**bi′o·graph′i·cal** (-ə graf′i kəl) *adj.*

bi′o·haz′ard *n.* anything used in or produced in biological research that poses a health hazard.

biolog′ical clock′ *n.* a natural mechanism regulating bodily cycles.

biolog′ical war′fare *n.* the use of toxic organisms as weapons.

bi·ol′o·gy (bī ol′ə jē) *n.* the scientific study of living organisms.

—**bi′o·log′i·cal** (-ə loj′i kəl) *adj.* —**bi·ol′o·gist,** *n.*

bi·on′ics (bī on′iks) *n.* the srudy of electronic devices that function like living organisms. —**bi·on′ic,** *adj.*

bi′op·sy (bī′op sē) *n., pl.* **-sies.** the removal of a piece of living tissue for diagnostic study.

bi′o·rhythm (bī′ō-) *n.* a natural, periodic bodily cycle, as sleeping and waking.

bi′o·sphere′ (bī′ə-) *n.* the part of the earth's surface and atmosphere that supports life.

bi′o·tech·nol′o·gy (bī′ō-) *n.* the use of living organisms in making products or to manage the environment.

bi·par′ti·san (bī pär′tə zən) *adj.* representing two parties.

bi·par′tite (-pär′tīt) *adj.* **1.** having two parts. **2.** shared by two; joint.

bi′ped (-ped) *n.* **1.** a two-footed animal. —*adj.* **2.** having two feet.

birch (bûrch) *n.* a tree with smooth light bark.

bird (bûrd) *n.* an egg-laying vertebrate with feathers and wings.

bird′s-eye′ (bûrdz′ī′) *adj.* seen from above.

birth (bûrth) *n.* **1.** an act or instance of being born. **2.** the act of bringing forth offspring. **3.** descent.

birth′ control′ *n.* the prevention of unwanted pregnancy.

birth′mark′ *n.* a blemish on the skin at birth.

birth′rate′ *n.* the number of births in a given time and place.

birth′right′ *n.* a hereditary right.

bis′cuit (bis′kit) *n.* a small, soft, raised bread.

bi·sect′ (bī sekt′) *v.t.* **1.** to cut into two parts. —*v.i.* **2.** to split into two parts.

bi·sex′u·al *adj.* **1.** sexually responsive to both sexes. —*n.* **2.** a bisexual person. —**bi·sex′u·al·i·ty,** *n.*

bish′op (bish′əp) *n.* **1.** a clergyman who supervises a number of local churches or a diocese. **2.** a chess piece that moves diagonally.

bish′op·ric (-rik) *n.* the diocese or office of a bishop.

bi′son (bī′sən) *n., pl.* **bisons, bison.** a North American buffalo having high, humped shoulders.

bis′tro (bis′trō, bē′strō) *n.* a small restaurant or café.

bit¹ (bit) *n.* **1.** the mouthpiece of a bridle. **2.** a part of a tool that drills or bores or grips when twisted.

bit² (bit) *n.* **1.** a small piece or quantity. **2.** a short time.

bit³ (bit) *n.* a single, basic unit of computer information.

bitch (bich) *n.* **1.** a female dog. **2.** *Slang.* a malicious, unpleasant woman. —*v.i.* **3.** *Slang.* to complain.

bite (bīt) *v.,* **bit, bitten** or **bit, biting,** *n.* —*v.t.* **1.** to cut or grip with the teeth. **2.** to sting. —*v.i.* **3.** to attack with the jaws. **4.** (of fish) to take bait. **5.** to take a firm hold. —*n.* **6.** the act of biting. **7.** a wound from biting. **8.** a sting. **9.** a morsel of food. **10.** a small meal.

bit′ing *adj.* **1.** sharp; harsh. **2.** severely critical.

bit′ter (bit′ər) *adj.* **1.** having a harsh taste. **2.** hard to bear. **3.** causing sharp pain. **4.** intensely hostile or resentful. —**bit′ter•ly,** *adv.* —**bit′ter•ness,** *n.*

bit′tern (bit′ərn) *n.* a type of wading bird.

bit′ter•sweet′ *adj.* **1.** tasting both bitter and sweet. **2.** being both painful and pleasant.

bi•tu′men (bī tōō′mən, -tyōō′-) *n.* asphalt or an asphaltlike substance.

bitu′minous coal′ *n.* soft coal.

bi′valve′ *n.* a mollusk with two shells hinged together.

biv•ou•ac′ (biv′ōō ak′) *n., v.,* **-acked, -acking.** —*n.* **1.** a temporary resting or assembly place for troops. —*v.i.* **2.** to assemble in a bivouac.

bi•week′ly (bī-) *adv., adj.* **1.** every two weeks. **2.** twice a week.

bi•zarre′ (bi zär′) *adj.* strange.

blab (blab) *v.,* **blabbed, blabbing.** —*v.i.* **1.** to talk idly. —*v.t.* **2.** to reveal (secrets).

black (blak) *adj.* **1.** lacking brightness or color. **2.** having dark skin color. **3.** without light. **4.** gloomy. **5.** wicked. —*n.* **6.** the color opposite to white. **7.** a member of a dark-skinned people, esp. of Africa or African ancestry. **8.** black clothing. —*v.t., v.i.* **9.** to make or become black. **10. black out,** to lose consciousness. —*Idiom.* **11. in the black,** earning a profit.

black′-and-blue′ *adj.* discolored, as by bruising.

black′ball′ *n.* **1.** an adverse vote. —*v.t.* **2.** to exclude; banish.

black′ber′ry *n., pl.* **-ries.** the dark purple fruit of certain brambles.

black′bird′ *n.* a black-feathered American bird.

black′board′ *n.* a smooth, dark board for writing on with chalk.

black′en *v.t.* **1.** to make black. **2.** to defame. —*v.i.* **3.** to grow black.

black′guard (blag′ärd, -ərd) *n.* a despicable person.

black′head′ *n.* a small, dark fatty mass in a skin follicle.

black′ hole′ *n.* an area in outer space whose great density prevents the escape of light.

black′jack′ *n.* **1.** a short, flexible, leather-covered club. **2.** a game of cards; twenty-one.

black′list′ *n.* **1.** a list of persons in disfavor. —*v.t.* **2.** to put on a blacklist.

black′ mag′ic *n.* sorcery.

black′mail′ *n.* **1.** payment demanded from a person by threats to disclose damaging information. —*v.t.* **2.** to subject (a person) to blackmail. —**black′mail′•er,** *n.*

black′ mar′ket *n.* the buying and selling of goods in violation of rationing, price controls, etc.

black′out′ *n.* **1.** the extinguishing or concealment of lights. **2.** a brief loss of consciousness.

black′ sheep′ *n.* a person who causes embarrassment or shame to his or her family.

black′smith′ *n.* a person who shoes horses or forges iron objects.

black′thorn′ *n.* a thorny shrub with plumlike fruit.

black′top′ *n., v.,* **-topped, -topping.** —*n.* **1.** a bituminous paving substance, as asphalt. —*v.t.* **2.** to pave with blacktop.

black′ wid′ow *n.* a poisonous spider.

blad′der (blad′ər) *n.* **1.** a sac in the body that holds urine. **2.** an inflatable bag.

blade (blād) *n.* **1.** the flat cutting part of a knife, sword, etc. **2.** a leaf, esp. of grass. **3.** the thin, flat part of something.

blame (blām) *v.,* **blamed, blaming,** *n.* —*v.t.* **1.** to hold responsible. **2.** to find fault with. —*n.* **3.** condemnation. **4.** responsibility for a fault. —**blame′less,** *adj.*

blanch (blanch) *v.t.* **1.** to whiten. **2.** to boil (food) briefly. —*v.i.* **3.** to turn pale.

bland (bland) *adj.* **1.** gentle; mild. **2.** not highly seasoned. **3.** dull.

blan′dish•ment (blan′dish mənt) *n.* coaxing or flattering words.

blank (blangk) *adj.* **1.** not written or printed on. **2.** without interest or expression. —*n.* **3.** a place or space where something is lacking. **4.** a printed form containing such spaces. **5.** a cartridge lacking a bullet. —**blank′ness,** *n.*

blan′ket (blang′kit) *n.* **1.** a warm bed covering. **2.** any extended covering. —*v.t.* **3.** to cover.

blare (blâr) *v.,* **blared, blaring,** *n.*

—*v.i.* **1.** to sound loudly. —*n.* **2.** a loud, raucous noise.

blar′ney (blär′nē) *n.* flattery.

bla·sé′ (blä zā′) *adj.* bored.

blas′phe·my (blas′fə mē) *n., pl.* **-mies.** irreverent speech or action concerning sacred things. —**blas· pheme′**, *v.t., v.i.* —**blas′phe·mous** *adj.*

blast (blast) *n.* **1.** a gust of wind. **2.** a loud trumpet tone. **3.** an explosion. **4.** *Slang.* a very good time. —*v.i.* **5.** to explode. **6.** to produce a loud sound. —*v.t.* **7.** to blow. **8.** to destroy.

blast′ fur′nace *n.* a forced-air furnace for smelting iron ore.

blast′off′ *n.* the launching of a rocket, spacecraft, etc.

bla′tant (blāt′nt) *adj.* very obvious. —**bla′tan·cy,** *n.* —**bla′tant·ly,** *adv.*

blaze¹ (blāz) *n., v.,* **blazed, blazing.** —*n.* **1.** a bright fire. **2.** a bright, hot glow. **3.** a vivid display. **4.** an outburst. —*v.i.* **5.** to burn or shine brightly.

blaze² (blāz) *n., v.,* **blazed, blazing.** —*n.* **1.** a mark made on a tree to indicate a trail. **2.** a white spot on an animal's face. —*v.t.* **3.** to mark with blazes.

blaz′er *n.* a solid color or striped sports jacket.

bldg. building.

bleach (blēch) *v.t., v.i.* **1.** to make or become whiter. —*n.* **2.** a bleaching agent.

bleach′ers *n.pl.* tiers of spectators' seats.

bleak (blēk) *adj.* **1.** bare. **2.** cold and raw. **3.** dreary; depressing. —**bleak′ly,** *adv.* —**bleak′ness,** *n.*

blear′y (blēr′ē) *adj.* (of the eyesight) blurred or dimmed.

bleat (blēt) *n.* **1.** the cry of a sheep or goat. —*v.i.* **2.** to make such a cry.

bleed (blēd) *v.,* **bled** (bled) **bleeding.** —*v.i.* **1.** to lose blood. **2.** to leak fluid. **3.** to run, as a dye. —*v.t.* **4.** to cause to lose blood. **5.** to drain fluid from. **6.** to extort money from.

bleep (blēp) *v.t.* to delete (sound, esp. speech) from a broadcast.

blem′ish (blem′ish) *v.t.* **1.** to spoil the perfection of. —*n.* **2.** a defect.

blend (blend) *v.t.* **1.** to mix smoothly so that the parts are no longer distinct. **2.** to mix, as tea or coffee, to produce a desired flavor. —*v.i.* **3.** to fit harmoniously. **4.** to have no visible separation. —*n.* **5.** something made by blending.

blend′er *n.* an electric appliance that purées or mixes food.

bless (bles) *v.t.,* **blessed** or **blest,**

blessing. 1. to make holy. **2.** to request divine favor on. **3.** to make happy.

blew (bloo) *v.* pt. of **blow.**

blight (blīt) *n.* **1.** a plant disease. **2.** a harmful influence. —*v.t.* **3.** to cause to wither. **4.** to ruin.

blimp (blimp) *n.* a small nonrigid airship.

blind (blīnd) *adj.* **1.** unable to see. **2.** uncontrolled. **3.** not based on reason or judgment. **4.** hidden. **5.** having no outlets. —*v.t.* **6.** to make blind. —*n.* **7.** a window covering. **8.** a decoy or disguise. —**blind′ly,** *adv.* —**blind′ness,** *n.*

blind′ date′ *n.* an arranged date between two strangers.

blind′fold′ *v.t.* **1.** to cover the eyes. —*n.* **2.** a covering over the eyes. —*adj.* **3.** with covered eyes.

blind′side′ *v.t.,* **-sided, -siding.** to hit someone unawares.

blink (blingk) *v.i.* **1.** to open and close the eyes rapidly. **2. blink at,** to ignore. —*n.* **3.** the act of blinking. **4.** a gleam. —*Idiom.* **5. on the blink,** not working properly.

blip (blip) *n.* a spot of light on a radar screen.

bliss (blis) *n.* supreme happiness. —**bliss′ful,** *adj.*

blis′ter (blis′tər) *n.* **1.** a swelling on the skin containing watery liquid. —*v.t.* **2.** to raise blisters on.

blithe (blīth, blīth) *adj.* lighthearted; carefree. —**blithe′ly,** *adv.*

blitz (blits) *n.* **1.** a sudden and overwhelming military attack. **2.** any swift, vigorous attack. —*v.t.* **3.** to attack with a blitz.

bliz′zard (bliz′ərd) *n.* a severe snowstorm with high wind.

bloat (blōt) *v.t.* **1.** to expand or distend. —*v.i.* **2.** to become swollen.

blob (blob) *n.* **1.** a small lump or drop. **2.** a shapeless mass.

bloc (blok) *n.* a group, as of nations or legislators, united for a common purpose.

block (blok) *n.* **1.** a solid mass of wood, stone, etc. **2.** a quantity taken as a unit. **3.** an obstacle. **4.** an obstruction in a physical or mental process. **5.** a frame enclosing a pulley. **6.** a city section enclosed by intersecting streets or the length of one side of such a section. —*v.t.* **7.** to obstruct. **8. block out,** to outline roughly.

block·ade′ (blo kād′) *n., v.,* **-aded, -ading.** —*n.* **1.** the closing off of a place by armed force. **2.** any obstruction. —*v.t.* **3.** to subject to a blockade.

block′age *n.* an obstruction.

block′bust′er *n.* a highly successful movie, novel, etc.

block′head′ *n.* a stupid person.

blond (blond) *adj.* **1.** having light-colored hair, skin, etc. **2.** light-colored. —*n.* **3.** a blond person.

blood (blud) *n.* **1.** the red fluid that circulates through the heart, veins, and arteries of animals. **2.** life. **3.** temperament. **4.** bloodshed. **5.** descent. **6.** kinship.

blood′ count′ *n.* the number of red and white blood cells in a specific volume of blood.

blood′cur′dling *adj.* causing terror.

blood′hound′ *n.* a large dog with an acute sense of smell.

blood′mo•bile′ (-mə bēl′) *n.* a truck with equipment for receiving blood donations.

blood′ pres′sure *n.* the pressure of the blood against the inner walls of the blood vessels.

blood′shed′ *n.* killing or wounding.

blood′shot′ *adj.* (of the eyes) red from dilated veins.

blood′stream′ *n.* the blood flowing through the circulatory system.

blood′suck′er *n.* **1.** any creature that sucks blood. **2.** a person who extorts money.

blood′thirst′y *adj.* eager to shed blood.

blood′ ves′sel *n.* an artery, vein, or capillary.

bloom (blōōm) *n.* **1.** a flower. **2.** the state of flowering. **3.** a healthy glow. —*v.i.* **4.** to bear flowers. **5.** to flourish. —**bloom′ing,** *adj.*

bloom′ers (blōō′mərz) *n.pl.* short loose trousers formerly worn as underwear by women.

bloop′er (blōō′pər) *n.* an embarrassing mistake.

blos′som (blos′əm) *n.* **1.** a flower. —*v.i.* **2.** to produce blossoms. **3.** to develop.

blot (blot) *n., v.,* **blotted, blotting.** —*n.* **1.** a spot or stain. —*v.t.* **2.** to spot or stain. **3.** to dry with absorbent material. —*v.i.* **4.** to become blotted. **5. blot out,** to destroy.

blotch (bloch) *n.* **1.** a large spot. **2.** a skin blemish. —*v.t.* **3.** to mark with blotches. —**blotch′y,** *adj.*

blot′ter *n.* a piece of paper for blotting.

blouse (blous, blouz) *n.* a loose garment covering the upper body.

blow¹ (blō) *n.* **1.** a sudden, hard stroke. **2.** a sudden shock, calamity, etc.

blow² (blō) *v.,* **blew, blown, blow•ing,** *n.* —*v.i.* **1.** (of the wind or air) to be in motion. **2.** to move along,

carried by the wind. **3.** to produce a current of air. **4.** to give out sound by blowing or being blown. **5.** (of a fuse, tire, etc.) to be destroyed. —*v.t.* **6.** to drive by a current of air. **7.** to shape (glass, smoke, etc.) with a current of air. **8.** to cause to sound by blowing. **9.** to cause to explode. **10.** to melt (a fuse). **11.** *Informal.* to squander (money). **12.** *Informal.* to bungle. **13. blow over,** to subside. **14. ~ up, a.** to explode. **b.** to lose one's temper. —*n.* **15.** a blast of air or wind.

blow′-by-blow′ *adj.* detailed.

blow′out′ *n.* a sudden rupture of a tire.

blow′torch′ *n.* a device producing a hot flame.

blow′up′ *n.* **1.** an explosion. **2.** a violent outburst of temper. **3.** a photographic enlargement.

blub′ber (blub′ər) *n.* **1.** the fat of whales. —*v.i.* **2.** to weep noisily.

bludg′eon (bluj′ən) *n.* **1.** a heavy club. —*v.t.* **2.** to strike with a bludgeon.

blue (blōō) *n., adj.,* **bluer, bluest,** *v.,* **blued, bluing** or **blueing.** —*n.* **1.** the color of a clear sky. —*adj.* **2.** (of skin) discolored as by cold. **3.** depressed or unhappy. **4.** indecent. —*v.t.* **5.** to make blue. —**Idiom. 6. out of the blue,** unexpectedly.

blue′ber′ry *n., pl.* **-ries.** the edible, usu. bluish, berry of certain shrubs.

blue′bird′ *n.* a small, blue North American songbird.

blue′ blood′ *n.* an aristocrat.

blue′ chip′ *n.* a high-priced stock issued by a company known for its financial strength and the regular payment of dividends.

blue′-col′lar *adj.* of or designating manual laborers.

blue′jay′ *n.* a crested jay with a bright blue back and gray breast.

blue′ jeans′ *n.pl.* trousers of blue denim.

blue′ law′ *n.* any law forbidding certain practices, as doing business, on Sunday.

blue′print′ *n.* **1.** a white-on-blue photographic print of an architectural drawing. **2.** a plan of action.

blue′ rib′bon *n.* the highest award.

blues *n.pl.* **1.** depression. **2.** a melancholy kind of jazz.

bluff¹ (bluf) *adj.* **1.** good-naturedly frank. —*n.* **2.** a steep cliff or hill.

bluff² (bluf) *v.t., v.i.* **1.** to mislead (someone) by a show of confidence. —*n.* **2.** the act of bluffing. **3.** one who bluffs. —**Idiom. 4. call someone's bluff,** to challenge someone to carry out a threat.

blu'ing *n.* a bleaching agent.

blun'der (blun'dər) *n.* **1.** a mistake. —*v.i.* **2.** to make a mistake. **3.** to move clumsily.

blunt (blunt) *adj.* **1.** having a dull edge or point. **2.** abrupt in manner. —*v.t., v.i.* **3.** to make or become blunt. —**blunt'ly,** *adv.*

blur (blûr) *v.,* **blurred, blurring,** *n.* —*v.t., v.i.* **1.** to make or become indistinct. —*n.* **2.** a smudge. **3.** a blurred condition or thing. —**blur'ry,** *adj.*

blurb (blûrb) *n.* a brief advertisement.

blurt (blûrt) *v.t.* to utter suddenly or tactlessly.

blush (blush) *v.i.* **1.** to redden. **2.** to feel embarrassment. —*n.* **3.** a reddening. **4.** a reddish tinge.

blus'ter (blus'tər) *v.i.* **1.** to blow stormily. **2.** to talk in an aggressive, swaggering manner. —*n.* **3.** boisterous noise and violence. **4.** noisy, empty threats.

blvd. boulevard.

bo'a (bō'ə) *n.* **1.** a large snake that crushes its prey. **2.** a long scarf of silk or feathers.

boar (bôr) *n.* a male swine.

board (bôrd) *n.* **1.** a thin flat piece of timber or stiff material. **2.** daily meals provided for a fixed price. **3.** an official controlling body. —*v.t.* **4.** to cover with boards. **5.** to enter (a ship, train, etc.). —*v.i.* **6.** to take one's meals for a fixed price. —**board'er,** *n.*

board'ing•house' *n.* a house where one can get room and board for payment.

board'walk' *n.* a wooden walk along a beach.

boast (bōst) *v.i.* **1.** to speak with excessive pride; brag. —*v.t.* **2.** to speak of with excessive pride. **3.** to be proud to own. —*n.* **4.** a thing boasted (of). **5.** bragging.

boat (bōt) *n.* **1.** a vessel for transport by water. —*v.i.* **2.** to go or move in a boat. —*Idiom.* **3. in the same boat,** in a similar difficult situation. —**boat'ing,** *n.* —**boat'man,** *n.*

boat'house' (bōt'hous') *n., pl.* **-houses** (-hou'ziz). a shed for sheltering boats at the water's edge.

boat'swain (bō'sən) *n.* a ship's officer in charge of deck work.

bob¹ (bob) *n., v.,* **bobbed, bob•bing.** —*n.* **1.** a short, jerky motion. —*v.t., v.i.* **2.** to move quickly down and up.

bob² (bob) *n., v.,* **bobbed, bob•bing.** —*n.* **1.** a short haircut. —*v.t.* **2.** to cut short.

bob'bin (bob'in) *n.* a reel or spool for thread.

bob'by pin *n.* a flat metal hairpin.

bob'cat' *n., pl.* **-cats, -cat.** a North American lynx.

bob'o•link' (-ə lingk') *n.* a meadow-dwelling songbird.

bob'sled' *n., v.,* **-sledded, -sledding.** —*n.* **1.** a long sled with two pairs of runners and a steering mechanism. —*v.i.* **2.** to ride on a bobsled.

bob'tail' *n.* **1.** a short tail. **2.** an animal with such a tail.

bob'white' *n.* a North American quail.

bode (bōd) *v.t., v.i.,* **boded, boding.** to be a sign of.

bod'ice (bod'is) *n.* the top part of a dress.

bod'y (bod'ē) *n., pl.* **bodies. 1.** the physical structure and substance of an animal. **2.** the torso. **3.** a corpse. **4.** the main or central part of a thing. **5.** a separate physical mass, as of land or water. **6.** a group regarded as a unit. **7.** substance; density.

bod'y•guard' *n.* a person employed to protect someone.

bo'dy lang'uage *n.* communication through gestures or attitudes.

bo'dy pierc'ing *n.* the piercing of a body part, as the navel, to insert an ornamental ring or stud.

bog (bog) *n., v.,* **bogged, bogging.** —*n.* **1.** swampy ground. —*v.* **2. bog down,** to sink in or as if in a bog. —**bog'gy,** *adj.*

bog'gle (bog'əl) *v.,* **-gled, -gling.** —*v.t., v.i.* to bewilder or be bewildered.

bo'gus (bō'gəs) *adj.* fake.

bo'gy (bō'gē, bŏŏg'ē, bŏŏ'gē) *n., pl.* **-gies.** anything that frightens. Also, **bo'gey, bo'gie.**

bo•he'mi•an (bō hē'mē ən) *n.* **1.** one who leads an unconventional life. —*adj.* **2.** unconventional.

boil¹ (boil) *v.i.* **1.** to bubble up and change into a gas as the result of heating. **2.** to be very angry. —*v.t.* **3.** to cause to boil. **4.** to cook in boiling liquid. —*n.* **5.** the act or state of boiling.

boil² (boil) *n.* an inflamed sore.

bois'ter•ous (boi'stər əs) *adj.* rough; noisy.

bok' choy' (bok' choy') *n.* an Asian plant whose leaves are used as a vegetable. Also, **bok'-choy'.**

bold (bōld) *adj.* **1.** courageous and daring. **2.** vivid; prominent. —**bold'ly,** *adv.*

bo•le'ro (bə lâr'ō, bō-) *n., pl.* **-ros. 1.** a lively Spanish dance. **2.** a waist-length, open jacket.

boll (bōl) *n.* a rounded seed pod of a plant.

boll′ wee′vil *n.* a beetle that attacks bolls of cotton.

bol′ster (bōl′stər) *n.* **1.** a long pillow. —*v.t.* **2.** to support.

bolt (bōlt) *n.* **1.** a bar fastening a door. **2.** a similar part in a lock. **3.** a threaded metal pin. **4.** a sudden flight. **5.** a roll of cloth. **6.** a thunderbolt. —*v.t.* **7.** to fasten with a bolt. **8.** to swallow hurriedly. —*v.i.* **9.** to move or leave suddenly.

bomb (bom) *n.* **1.** a case filled with explosive material and set off by a detonating device or by impact. **2.** *Slang.* a total failure. —*v.t.* **3.** to attack with bombs. —*v.i.* **4.** *Slang.* to fail totally. —**bomb′proof′**, *adj.*

bom·bard′ (bom bärd′) *v.t.* **1.** to attack with artillery or bombs. **2.** to attack with questions, suggestions, etc. **3.** to direct particles or radiation against. —**bom·bar·dier′** (-bər dēr′) *n.* —**bom·bard′ment**, *n.*

bom′bast (bom′bast) *n.* pompous words. —**bom·bas′tic**, *adj.*

bomb′er (bom′ər) *n.* **1.** an airplane that drops bombs. **2.** a person who drops or sets bombs.

bomb′shell′ *n.* something or someone having a sensational effect.

bo′na fide′ (bō′nə fīd′) *adj.* **1.** made or done in good faith. **2.** genuine.

bo·nan′za (bə nan′zə) *n.* **1.** a rich mass of ore. **2.** a source of riches.

bon′bon′ (bon′bon′) *n.* a piece of candy.

bond (bond) *n.* **1.** something that binds, confines, or unites. **2.** a written contractual obligation. **3.** an interest-bearing certificate of debt due to be paid to an individual. —*v.t.* **4.** to put on or under bond. **5.** to connect.

bond′age (bon′dij) *n.* slavery.

bonds′man *n., pl.* **-men.** a person who gives surety for another.

bone (bōn) *n., v.,* **boned, boning.** —*n.* **1.** one of the structures composing the skeleton. **2.** the hard substance forming it. —*v.t.* **3.** to remove the bones of. —*Idiom.* **4. to have a bone to pick with,** to have a reason to reproach. **5. make no bones about,** to speak openly about. —**bon′y**, *adj.*

bon′fire′ (bon′-) *n.* a large outdoor fire.

bon′go (bong′gō) *n., pl.* **-gos, -goes.** a small hand drum.

bon′kers (bong′kərz) *adj. Slang.* crazy.

bon′net (bon′it) *n.* a hat with strings tied under the chin.

bo′nus (bō′nəs) *n.* something given or paid beyond what is due.

boo (boo) *interj.* (an exclamation used to frighten or express contempt.)

boo′by (boo′bē) *n., pl.* **-bies.** *Informal.* a fool. Also, **boob.**

boo′by prize′ *n.* a prize given to the worst player in a contest.

boo′by trap′ *n.* a trap set for an unsuspecting person.

book (book) *n.* **1.** printed or blank sheets bound together. **2.** a long literary work or a division of one. **3. books,** accounts. —*v.t.* **4.** to enter in a book. **5.** to reserve. **6.** to enter a charge against (an arrested person).

book′bind′ing (book′bīn′ding) *n.* the process of binding books. —**book′bind′er**, *n.*

book′case′ *n.* a set of shelves for books.

book′end′ *n.* a support for holding up a row of books.

book′ie *n.* a bookmaker.

book′ish *adj.* fond of reading.

book′keep′ing *n.* the system of keeping records of business transactions. —**book′keep′er**, *n.*

book′let (-lit) *n.* a pamphlet.

book′mak′er *n.* a person whose business is taking bets.

book′mark′ *n.* something used to mark one's place in a book.

book′store (book′stôr′) *n.* a store where books are sold. Also, **book′-shop.**

book′worm′ *n.* a person who likes to read.

boom¹ (boom) *v.i.* **1.** to make a loud hollow sound. **2.** to flourish vigorously. —*n.* **3.** a loud hollow sound. **4.** rapid economic development.

boom² (boom) *n.* **1.** a long pole on a ship's mast, used to extend a sail. **2.** a beam on a derrick, used to support objects to be lifted.

boom′er·ang′ (boo′mə rang′) *n.* **1.** a curved piece of wood that returns when thrown. —*v.i.* **2.** to cause harm to the originator.

boon¹ (boon) *n.* a benefit.

boon² (boon) *adj.* **boon companion,** a jolly, pleasant companion.

boon′docks′ *n.pl.* **1.** a backwoods. **2.** a remote rural area.

boon′dog′gle (-dog′əl) *n. Informal.* useless work paid for with public money.

boor (boor) *n.* an unmannerly, rude person. —**boor′ish**, *adj.*

boost (boost) *v.t.* **1.** to lift by pushing. **2.** to aid by speaking well of. **3.** to increase. —*n.* **4.** an upward push. **5.** an act or comment that

helps someone. **6.** an increase.
—**boost′er,** *n.*

boot (bo͞ot) *n.* **1.** a covering for the foot and leg. **2.** a kick. —*v.t.* **3.** to kick. —***Idiom.* 4. to boot,** in addition.

booth (bo͞oth) *n.* **1.** a light structure for the sale or display of goods. **2.** a small compartment.

boot′leg′ *n., v.,* **-legged, -legging,** *adj.* —*n.* **1.** something, esp. liquor, that is made or sold illegally. —*v.t., v.i.* **2.** to deal in (liquor or other goods) illegally. —*adj.* **3.** made or sold illegally. —**boot′leg′-ger,** *n.*

boo′ty (bo͞o′tē) *n.* loot.

booze (bo͞oz) *n., v.,* **boozed, boozing.** *Informal.* —*n.* **1.** liquor. —*v.i.* **2.** to drink liquor excessively.

bo′rax (bôr′aks) *n.* a white crystalline substance used as a cleanser, in glassmaking, etc.

bor′der (bôr′dər) *n.* **1.** an edge or boundary. **2.** the dividing line between one country, state, etc., and another. **3.** an ornamental design around an edge. —*v.t.* **4.** to make a border around. **5.** to form a border to. **6.** to adjoin. **7. border on, a.** to come close to being. **b.** to be next to.

bor′der.line′ *n.* **1.** a boundary. —*adj.* **2.** not definite.

bore[1] (bôr) *v.,* **bored, bor.ing,** *n.* —*v.t.* **1.** to drill into. **2.** to make (a hole) by drilling or digging. —*v.i.* **3.** to make a hole. —*n.* **4.** a bored hole. **5.** the inside diameter of a hole or cylinder.

bore[2] (bôr) *v.,* **bored, bor.ing,** *n.* —*v.t.* **1.** to weary by dullness. —*n.* **2.** a dull person or thing. —**bore′-dom,** *n.*

born (bôrn) *adj.* **1.** brought forth by birth. **2.** having a certain quality from birth.

born′-a.gain′ *adj.* recommitted to faith through an intense religious experience.

bor′ough (bûr′ō, bur′ō) *n.* **1.** a small incorporated town. **2.** one of the five divisions of New York City.

bor′row (bor′ō) *v.t., v.i.* **1.** to take or obtain on loan. **2.** to appropriate. —**Usage.** Do not confuse BORROW and LEND. Think of BOR-ROW as "take," while LEND is "give." So you can *borrow* something you don't have, and you can *lend* something you do have.

bos′om (bo͞oz′əm, bo͞o′zəm) *n.* the breast.

boss (bôs) *n.* **1.** an employer. **2.** a politician who controls the party organization. **3.** a person who is in charge. —*v.t.* **4.** to control; manage. **5.** to order about. —**boss′y,** *adj.*

bot (bot) *n.* a piece of software that can execute commands without user intervention.

bot′a.ny (bot′n ē) *n.* the science that deals with plant life. —**bo.tan′i.cal** (bə tan′i kəl) *adj.* —**bot′a.nist,** *n.*

botch (boch) *v.t.* **1.** to bungle. **2.** to patch clumsily. —*n.* **3.** a poor piece of work.

both (bōth) *adj., pron.* **1.** one and the other; the two. —*conj.* **2.** (used before words or phrases joined by *and* to indicate that each of the joined elements is included).

both′er (both′ər) *v.t., v.i.* **1.** to annoy (someone). **2.** to trouble or inconvenience (oneself). —*n.* **3.** trouble.

both′er.some (-səm) *adj.* causing annoyance or worry.

bot′tle (bot′l) *n., v.,* **-tled, -tling.** —*n.* **1.** a narrow-necked glass or plastic container for liquids. —*v.t.* **2.** to put into a bottle.

bot′tle.neck′ *n.* **1.** a narrow passage. **2.** a place at which progress is obstructed.

bot′tom (bot′əm) *n.* **1.** the lowest part. **2.** the underside. **3.** the ground under a body of water. **4.** the seat of a chair. **5.** *Informal.* the buttocks. —*adj.* **6.** lowest. —*v.* **7. bottom out,** to reach the lowest level. —***Idiom.* 8. at bottom,** fundamentally.

bot′tom.less *adj.* **1.** without bottom. **2.** without limit.

bot′tom line′ *n.* **1.** the line of a financial statement that shows profit and loss. **2.** the final outcome.

bot′u.lism′ (boch′ə liz′əm) *n.* a sometimes fatal disease caused by eating spoiled foods.

bou′doir (bo͞o′dwär, -dwôr) *n.* a woman's bedroom or private room.

bouf.fant′ (bo͞o fänt′) *adj.* puffed out, as a hairdo.

bough (bou) *n.* a branch of a tree.

bouil′lon (bo͞ol′yon, -yən, bo͞o′-) *n.* a clear broth.

boul′der (bōl′dər) *n.* a large rock.

boul′e.vard′ (bo͞ol′ə värd′) *n.* a broad avenue.

bounce (bouns) *v.,* **bounced, bouncing,** *n.* —*v.i.* **1.** to strike a surface and rebound. **2.** to move in a lively manner. **3.** (of a check) to be refused because of insufficient funds in the account. —*v.t.* **4.** to cause to bounce. —*n.* **5.** a bound or rebound. **6.** a sudden leap. **7.** liveliness. —**bounc′y,** *adj.*

bounc′ing *adj.* healthy.

bound¹ (bound) *v.* **1.** pt. and pp. of **bind.** —*adj.* **2.** tied. **3.** made into a book. **4.** obligated. **5.** certain.

bound² (bound) *v.i.* **1.** to move by leaps. —*n.* **2.** a jump or bounce.

bound³ (bound) *n.* **1.** bounds, boundary. —*v.t.* **2.** to limit. **3.** to form the boundary of. —*Idiom.* **4.** out of bounds, beyond the permitted limits.

bound⁴ (bound) *adj.* going.

bound′a·ry (boun′də rē, -drē) *n., pl.* **-ries.** something marking limits.

bound′less *adj.* unlimited.

boun′te·ous (boun′tē əs) *adj.* generous. Also, **boun′ti·ful.**

boun′ty *n., pl.* **-ties. 1.** generosity. **2.** a generous gift. **3.** a reward.

bou·quet′ (bō kā′, bōō-) *n.* **1.** a bunch of flowers. **2.** an aroma.

bour′bon (bûr′bən) *n.* corn whiskey.

bour·geois′ (bŏŏr zhwä′) *n., pl.* **-geois,** *adj.* —*n.* **1.** a member of the middle class. —*adj.* **2.** of the middle class. **3.** overly concerned with respectability.

bour′geoi·sie′ (-zē′) *n.* the middle class.

bout (bout) *n.* **1.** a contest. **2.** a period; spell.

bou·tique′ (bōō tēk′) *n.* a small shop with fashionable items.

bo′vine (bō′vīn, -vēn) *adj.* **1.** of or resembling an ox or cow. **2.** dull.

bow¹ (bou) *v.i.* **1.** to bend the body or head, as in respect or greeting. **2.** to submit. —*v.t.* **3.** to bend (the body or head). **4.** to subdue. —*n.* **5.** a bending of the body or head in respect, greeting, etc.

bow² (bō) *n.* **1.** a strip of bent wood for shooting arrows. **2.** a bend or curve. **3.** a looped knot. **4.** a rod strung with horsehairs, for playing the violin, cello, etc. —*v.t., v.i.* **5.** to bend; curve.

bow³ (bou) *n.* the forward end of a ship or boat.

bow′el (bou′əl, boul) *n.* **1.** the intestine. Also, **bow′els. 2. bowels,** the innermost parts.

bow′er (bou′ər) *n.* a leafy shelter.

bowl¹ (bōl) *n.* **1.** a deep, round dish. **2.** a rounded, hollow part. **3.** a stadium.

bowl² (bōl) *n.* **1.** a delivery of the ball in bowling. —*v.i.* **2.** to play at bowling. **3.** to move along smoothly and rapidly. —*v.t.* **4.** to roll (a ball) in bowling. **5. bowl over,** to surprise greatly.

bow′leg·ged (bō′leg′id) *adj.* having legs curved outward.

bow′man (bō′mən) *n., pl.* **-men.** an archer.

box (boks) *n.* **1.** a container or

case, usu. having a lid. **2.** a compartment. **3.** a blow with the fist. **4.** Also, **box′wood′.** an evergreen tree or shrub. —*v.t.* **5.** to put into a box. —*v.i.* **6.** to fight with the fists. —**box′er,** *n.* —**box′ing,** *n.*

box′car′ *n.* a railroad freight car that is completely enclosed.

box′ of′fice *n.* an office at which tickets for a performance are sold.

boy (boi) *n.* a male child. —**boy′· hood,** *n.* —**boy′ish,** *adj.*

boy′cott (-kot) *v.t.* **1.** to refuse to deal with or buy from. —*n.* **2.** the act of boycotting.

boy′friend′ *n.* **1.** a male sweetheart or lover. **2.** a male friend.

bra (brä) *n.* a woman's undergarment for supporting the breasts.

brace (brās) *n., v.,* **braced, bracing.** —*n.* **1.** a device that holds parts together or in place. **2.** anything that stiffens or steadies. **3.** a character, {or}, used to connect words or lines to be considered together. **4. braces,** a device for straightening the teeth. **5.** a pair. —*v.t.* **6.** to fasten or strengthen with a brace. **7.** to steady (oneself).

brace′let (brās′lit) *n.* an ornamental band for the wrist.

brack′et (brak′it) *n.* **1.** a supporting piece projecting from a wall. **2.** either of two marks, [or], for enclosing parenthetical words. —*v.t.* **3.** to place within brackets.

brack′ish (brak′ish) *adj.* salty.

brad (brad) *n.* a small wire nail.

brag (brag) *v.i., v.t.,* **bragged, bragging.** to boast.

brag′gart (brag′ərt) *n.* a person who brags a lot.

braid (brād) *v.t.* **1.** to weave together three or more strands of. —*n.* **2.** something braided.

Braille (brāl) *n.* a system of writing for the blind, using combinations of raised dots.

brain (brān) *n.* **1.** the part of the central nervous system enclosed in the skull of vertebrates. **2.** Sometimes, **brains.** intelligence. —*v.t.* **3.** to smash the skull of.

brain′ death′ *n.* the complete ending of brain function: used as a legal definition of death. —**brain′-dead′,** *adj.*

brain′storm′ *n.* a sudden idea.

brain′wash′ *v.t.* to subject to brainwashing.

braise (brāz) *v.t.,* **braised, braising.** to cook slowly in a small amount of liquid in a closed container.

brake (brāk) *n., v.,* **braked, braking.** —*n.* **1.** a device for stopping a vehicle. —*v.t., v.i.* **2.** to slow or stop with a brake.

bram′ble (bram′bəl) *n.* a prickly shrub.

bran (bran) *n.* the partly ground husk of grain.

branch (branch) *n.* **1.** a division of the stem of a tree or shrub. **2.** a local office or store of a large organization. **3.** a section of a body or system. **4.** a division of a family. —*v.i.* **5.** to put out or divide into branches. **6. branch off,** to divide into separate parts. **7. branch out,** to expand or extend.

brand (brand) *n.* **1.** kind or make. **2.** a mark of ownership made by burning. **3.** a burning piece of wood. **4.** a mark of disgrace. —*v.t.* **5.** to mark with a brand. **6.** to put a mark of disgrace on.

brand′ish (bran′dish) *v.t.* to wave or flourish.

brand′-new′ (bran′-, brand′-) *adj.* extremely new.

bran′dy (bran′dē) *n., pl.* **-dies.** a spirit distilled from wine.

brash (brash) *adj.* **1.** impudent; tactless. **2.** rash; impetuous.

brass (bras) *n.* **1.** an alloy of copper and zinc. **2.** the brass instruments of a band or orchestra. **3.** high-ranking officials. **4.** bold impudence. —**brass′y,** *adj.*

bras•siere′ (brə zēr′) *n.* a bra.

brat (brat) *n.* a spoiled or rude child.

bra•va′do (brə vä′dō) *n.* boasting; swaggering.

brave (brāv) *adj.,* **braver, bravest,** *n., v.,* **braved, braving.** —*adj.* **1.** courageous. —*n.* **2.** a North American Indian warrior. —*v.t.* **3.** to meet courageously. **4.** to defy. —**brave′ly,** *adv.*

bra′vo (brä′vō, brä vō′) *interj.* well done!

brawl (brôl) *n.* **1.** a noisy quarrel. —*v.i.* **2.** to quarrel noisily.

brawn (brôn) *n.* **1.** muscles. **2.** muscular strength. —**brawn′y,** *adj.*

bray (brā) *n.* **1.** a harsh cry, as of a donkey. —*v.i.* **2.** to sound a bray.

bra′zen (brā′zən) *adj.* **1.** of or like brass. **2.** shameless; impudent.

bra′zier (brā′zhər) *n.* a metal stand for holding burning coals.

Bra•zil′ nut (brə zil′) *n.* the three-sided edible seed of a South American tree.

breach (brēch) *n.* **1.** a gap. **2.** a violation, as of a law. **3.** a severance of friendly relations. —*v.t.* **4.** to make a breach in.

bread (bred) *n.* **1.** a baked food made of dough. **2.** livelihood. —*v.t.* **3.** to cover with bread-crumbs.

bread′crumb′ *n.* a crumb of bread.

breadth (bredth, bretth) *n.* **1.** width. **2.** extent.

bread′win′ner *n.* a person who earns a livelihood to support dependents.

break (brāk) *v.,* **broke** (brōk) **broken, breaking,** *n.* —*v.t.* **1.** to split into pieces. **2.** to make useless. **3.** to fracture. **4.** to fail to keep (a promise, law, etc.) **5.** to reveal, as news. **6.** to ruin financially. **7.** to wear down the spirit of. —*v.i.* **8.** to split into fragments. **9.** to become useless. **10.** to become disconnected. **11.** to interrupt an activity. **12. break down,** to cease to function. **13. ~ out, a.** to begin abruptly. **b.** to become visible. **c.** to escape. —*n.* **14.** an opening made by breaking. **15.** the act of breaking. **16.** an interruption. **17.** a brief rest. **18.** an abrupt change. **19.** an opportunity. —**break′a•ble,** *adj.* —**break′age,** *n.*

break′down′ *n.* **1.** a mechanical failure. **2.** a mental or physical collapse. **3.** an analysis.

break′er *n.* a wave breaking on land.

break′fast (brek′fəst) *n.* **1.** the first meal of the day. —*v.i.* **2.** to eat breakfast.

break′-in′ (brāk′-) *n.* illegal forcible entry into a home, office, etc.

break′neck′ *adj.* reckless or dangerous.

break′through′ *n.* an important discovery.

break′up′ *n.* **1.** a separation or scattering of the parts of something. **2.** the ending of a personal relationship.

break′wa′ter *n.* a barrier that breaks the force of waves.

breast (brest) *n.* **1.** the chest. **2.** a milk-producing gland on a woman's body. —*v.t.* **3.** to meet or oppose boldly.

breast′bone′ *n.* the sternum.

breast′stroke′ *n.* a swimming stroke in which the arms are swept to the sides while the legs kick outward.

breath (breth) *n.* **1.** the air taken into the lungs and then let out. **2.** the act of breathing. **3.** life. **4.** a slight breeze. —**breath′less,** *adj.*

breathe (brēth) *v.,* **breathed, breathing.** —*v.t.* **1.** to take (air) into the lungs and let it out again. **2.** to whisper. —*v.i.* **3.** to inhale and exhale. **4.** to live.

breath′er (brē′thər) *n.* a pause for rest.

breath′tak′ing (breth′-) *adj.* astonishingly beautiful or exciting.

breech′es (brich′iz) *n.pl.* trousers.

breed

breed (brēd) *v.*, **bred** (bred) **breeding,** *n.* —*v.t.* **1.** to produce (offspring). **2.** to give rise to. **3.** to bring up. **4.** to raise (animals). —*v.i.* **5.** to produce offspring. **6.** to be produced. —*n.* **7.** a stock; strain. **8.** sort or kind.

breed′ing *n.* **1.** ancestry. **2.** training. **3.** manners.

breeze (brēz) *n.* a light current of air.

breeze′way′ *n.* an open-sided roofed passageway joining two buildings.

breth•ren (breth′rin) *n.pl.* **1.** fellow members. **2.** *Old use.* brothers.

bre′vi•ar′y (brē′vē er′ē, brev′ē-) *n.*, *pl.* **-aries.** a book of daily prayers and readings.

brev′i•ty (brev′i tē) *n.* shortness.

brew (brōō) *v.t.* **1.** to make (beer) by boiling and fermenting the ingredients. **2.** to prepare (tea or coffee) by boiling and steeping. **3.** to bring about. —*v.i.* **4.** to make beer. **5.** to begin to form. —*n.* **6.** a brewed beverage. —**brew′er•y,** *n.*

bri′ar (brī′ər) *n.* a brier.

bribe (brīb) *n.*, *v.*, **bribed, bribing.** —*n.* **1.** anything given to persuade or influence. —*v.t.* **2.** to give or influence by a bribe. —**brib′er•y,** *n.*

bric′-a-brac′ (brik′ə brak′) *n.* trinkets.

brick (brik) *n.* **1.** a building block of baked clay. —*v.t.* **2.** to pave or build with brick.

brick′bat′ *n.* **1.** a fragment of brick. **2.** a caustic criticism.

brid′al (brīd′l) *adj.* of or for a bride or a wedding.

bride (brīd) *n.* a woman newly married or about to be married.

bride′groom′ *n.* a man newly married or about to be married.

brides′maid′ *n.* a bride's wedding attendant.

bridge¹ (brij) *n.*, *v.*, **bridged, bridging.** —*n.* **1.** a structure spanning a river, road, etc. **2.** a raised platform from which a ship is navigated. **3.** the bony ridge of the nose. **4.** an artificial replacement for a missing tooth. —*v.t.* **5.** to make a bridge or passage over.

bridge² (brij) *n.* a card game for two pairs of players.

bridge′work′ *n.* a dental bridge.

bri′dle (brīd′l) *n.*, *v.*, **-dled, -dling.** —*n.* **1.** the head harness of a horse. **2.** anything that restrains. —*v.t.* **3.** to put a bridle on. **4.** to restrain.

brief (brēf) *adj.* **1.** short. **2.** concise. —*n.* **3.** a summary. **4.** a concise statement of the facts of a legal case. **5. briefs,** close-fitting legless underpants. —*v.t.* **6.** to make a summary of. **7.** to instruct by a brief. —**brief′ly,** *adv.*

brief′case′ *n.* a flat case for carrying papers.

bri′er (brī′ər) *n.* a prickly plant.

brig (brig) *n.* **1.** a two-masted square-rigged ship. **2.** a military prison.

bri•gade′ (bri gād′) *n.* **1.** a military unit forming part of a division. **2.** a group organized for a specific purpose.

brig′a•dier′ (brig′ə dēr′) *n.* an army officer ranking between a colonel and a major general. Also, **brig′adier gen′eral.**

brig′and (brig′ənd) *n.* a bandit.

bright (brīt) *adj.* **1.** giving out much light. **2.** brilliant. **3.** intelligent. **4.** cheerful; lively. —**bright′en,** *v.i.*, *v.t.*

bril′liant (bril′yənt) *adj.* **1.** shining brightly. **2.** outstanding. **3.** highly intelligent. —**bril′liance,** *n.*

brim (brim) *n.*, *v.*, **brimmed, brimming.** —*n.* **1.** the upper edge; rim. —*v.i.*, *v.t.* **2.** to fill or be full to the brim. —**brim′ful,** *adj.*

brim′stone′ *n.* sulfur.

brin′dled *adj.* gray or brown with darker streaks.

brine (brīn) *n.* **1.** salt water. **2.** the sea. —**brin′y,** *adj.*

bring (bring) *v.t.*, **brought** (brôt) **bringing. 1.** to carry. **2.** to cause to come. **3.** to cause to occur. **4. bring about,** to cause. **5. ~ forth,** to produce. **6. ~ off,** to accomplish. **7. ~ up, a.** to rear, as a child. **b.** to mention. **c.** to vomit.

brink (bringk) *n.* **1.** the edge of a steep place. **2.** any extreme edge.

bri•quette′ (bri ket′) *n.* a small block of charcoal. Also, **bri•quet′.**

brisk (brisk) *adj.* **1.** lively. **2.** stimulating. —**brisk′ly,** *adv.*

bris′ket (bris′kit) *n.* the meat from an animal's breast.

bris′tle (bris′əl) *n.*, *v.*, **-tled, -tling.** —*n.* **1.** a short, stiff, coarse hair. —*v.i.* **2.** to raise bristles, as in anger. **3.** to show indignation. **4.** to be thickly filled.

britch′es (brich′iz) *n.* (*used with a pl. v.*) breeches.

Brit′ish ther′mal u′nit *n.* the amount of heat needed to raise the temperature of 1 lb. (0.4 kg) water 1°F. *Abbr.:* Btu, BTU

brit′tle (brit′l) *adj.* hard but breaking easily.

broach (brōch) *v.t.* **1.** to mention for the first time. **2.** to pierce.

broad (brôd) *adj.* **1.** large from side to side; wide. **2.** having great extent. **3.** not limited. **4.** tolerant. **5.**

general. 6. plain or clear.
—**broad'ly,** *adv.*
broad'cast' *v.,* **-cast** or **-casted,**
-casting, *n.* —*v.t., v.i.* **1.** to send
(programs) by radio or television.
2. to scatter. —*n.* **3.** something
broadcast. **4.** a radio or television
program. —**broad'cast'er,** *n.*
broad'cloth' *n.* fine cotton material.
broad'en *v.i., v.t.* to make wider.
broad' jump' *n.* long jump.
broad'loom' *n.* any carpet woven
on a wide loom.
broad'-mind'ed *adj.* tolerant.
broad'side' *n., adv., v.,* **-sided, -sid-
ing.** —*n.* **1.** the simultaneous firing
of all guns on one side of a warship. **2.** a verbal attack. —*adv.* **3.**
directly on the side. —*v.t.* **4.** to hit
broadside.
broad'-spec'trum *adj.* (of antibiot-
ics) effective against a wide range
of organisms.
bro•cade' (brō kād') *n.* a woven
fabric with a raised design.
broc'co•li (brok'ə lē) *n.* a green
plant with edible flower heads.
bro•chure' (brō shŏŏr') *n.* a pamphlet; booklet.
brogue (brōg) *n.* an Irish accent.
broil (broil) *v.t., v.i.* to cook by direct heat. —**broil'er,** *n.*
broke (brōk) *v.* **1.** pt. of **break.**
—*adj.* **2.** without money.
bro'ken (brō'kən) *v.* **1.** pp. of
break. —*adj.* **2.** fragmented or frac-
tured. **3.** not functioning. **4.** inter-
rupted. **5.** violated. **6.** imperfectly
spoken.
bro'ken•heart'ed *adj.* sorrowing
deeply.
bro'ker *n.* an agent who buys and
sells for a fee.
bro'mide (brō'mīd, -mid) *n.* **1.** a
chemical compound used as a sedative. **2.** a trite saying.
bro'mine (brō'mēn, -min) *n.* a reddish, toxic liquid element.
bron'chi•al (brong'kē əl) *adj.* of the
bronchi, the two branches of the
windpipe.
bron•chi'tis (-kī'tis) *n.* an inflammation of the lining of the bronchial tubes.
bron'co (brong'kō) *n., pl.* **-cos.** a
wild pony or small horse of the
western U.S.
bronze (bronz) *n.* **1.** an alloy of
copper and tin. **2.** a brownish
color.
brooch (brōch) *n.* an ornamental
clasp or pin.
brood (brōōd) *n.* **1.** young born or
hatched at one time. —*v.i.* **2.** to sit
on eggs to be hatched. **3.** to think
in a troubled or morbid way.

brook¹ (brŏŏk) *n.* a small natural
stream of fresh water.
brook² (brŏŏk) *v.t.* to bear; tolerate.
broom (brōōm, brŏŏm) *n.* **1.** a long-
handled sweeping implement. **2.** a
shrub bearing yellow flowers.
broom'stick *n.* the handle of a
broom.
bros. brothers.
broth (brôth) *n.* a thin soup made
by simmering meat, fish, etc.
broth'el (broth'əl) *n.* a house
where women work as prostitutes.
broth'er (bru͝th'ər) *n.* **1.** a male
child of the same parents as another person. **2.** a male in the
same group as another. **3.** a male
member of a religious order.
—**broth'er•ly,** *adv.*
broth'er•hood' *n.* **1.** the condition
or quality of being a brother or
brothers. **2.** fellowship. **3.** those
engaged in a given trade.
broth'er-in-law' *n., pl.* **brothers-in-
law. 1.** one's husband's or wife's
brother. **2.** one's sister's husband.
brought (brôt) *v.* pt. and pp. of
bring.
brou'ha•ha' (brōō'hä hä') *n., pl.*
-has. an uproar.
brow (brou) *n.* **1.** an eyebrow. **2.**
the forehead. **3.** the edge of a
steep place.
brow'beat' *v.t.,* **-beat, -beaten,
-beating.** to intimidate.
brown (broun) *n.* **1.** a dark reddish
or yellowish color. —*v.t., v.i.* **2.** to
make or become brown.
brown'-bag' *v.t.,* **-bagged, -bag-
ging.** to bring (one's lunch) to
work or school.
brown'ie (brou'nē) *n.* a small,
chewy chocolate cake.
brown'out' *n.* a reduction of electric power to prevent a blackout.
browse (brouz) *v.t., v.i.,* **browsed,
browsing. 1.** to graze or feed (on).
2. to look through casually.
brows'er *n.* **1.** one that
browses. **2.** a computer program
that allows users to read World
Wide Web documents.
bruise (brōōz) *v.,* **bruised, bruising,**
n. —*v.t.* **1.** to injure without breaking the skin. —*n.* **2.** an injury due
to bruising.
bruis'er *n. Informal.* a strong,
tough man.
brunch (brunch) *n.* a meal that
serves as both breakfast and lunch.
bru•nette' (brōō net') *n.* a woman
with dark hair and, often, dark
skin and eyes.
brunt (brunt) *n.* the main force or
impact.
brush (brush) *n.* **1.** an instrument
with bristles. **2.** a bushy tail. **3.** a

close encounter. **4.** a light touch. **5.** dense bushes, shrubs, etc. —*v.t.* **6.** to sweep, paint, etc., with a brush. **7.** to touch lightly. **8. brush off,** to reject bluntly. **9. ~ up on,** to review, as a skill.

brush′-off′ *n.* a blunt rejection.

brusque (brusk) *adj.* abrupt in speech or manner. —**brusque′ly,** *adv.*

Brus′sels sprouts′ (brus′əlz) *n.* a kind of cabbage with small heads.

bru′tal (broot′l) *adj.* **1.** cruel. **2.** severe. —**bru·tal′i·ty,** *n.*

bru′tal·ize′ (broot′l īz′) *v.t.,* **-ized, -izing. 1.** to make brutal. **2.** to treat brutally.

brute (broot) *n.* **1.** a beast. **2.** a brutal person. —*adj.* **3.** animallike. **4.** irrational. **5.** savage; cruel. —**brut′·ish,** *adj.*

B.S. Bachelor of Science.

Btu British thermal unit. Also, **BTU.**

bu. bushel.

bub′ble (bub′əl) *n., v.,* **-bled, -bling.** —*n.* **1.** a transparent ball of gas, esp. in a liquid. —*v.i.* **2.** to form or produce bubbles. —**bub′·bly,** *adj.*

buc′ca·neer′ (buk′ə nēr′) *n.* a pirate.

buck¹ (buk) *n.* the male of the deer, rabbit, goat, etc.

buck² (buk) *v.i.* **1.** (of a horse) to leap with arched back. **2.** to resist something obstinately. —*v.t.* **3.** to throw (a rider) by bucking. **4.** to resist obstinately.

buck³ (buk) *n.* —*Idiom.* **pass the buck,** to shift responsibility.

buck′et (buk′it) *n.* **1.** a deep, open-topped container; pail. —*Idiom.* **2. drop in the bucket,** a small, inadequate amount.

buck′le (buk′əl) *n., v.,* **-led, -ling.** —*n.* **1.** a clasp for two loose ends. —*v.t., v.i.* **2.** to fasten with a buckle. **3.** to bend. **4. buckle down,** to set to work.

buck′ler *n.* a shield.

buck′ram (buk′rəm) *n.* a stiff cotton fabric.

buck′shot′ *n.* large lead shot.

buck′skin′ *n.* a strong, soft leather.

buck′tooth′ *n., pl.* **-teeth.** a projecting front tooth.

buck′wheat′ *n.* a plant with edible triangular seeds.

bu·col′ic (byoo kol′ik) *adj.* of or suggesting an idyllic rural life.

bud (bud) *n., v.,* **budded, budding.** —*n.* **1.** a small bulge on a plant stem from which leaves or flowers develop. —*v.i.* **2.** to put forth buds. **3.** to begin to develop.

bud′dy (bud′ē) *n., pl.* **-dies.** *Informal.* a friend; comrade.

budge (buj) *v.t., v.i.,* **budged, budging.** to move slightly.

budg′et (buj′it) *n.* **1.** an estimate of expected income and expenses. —*v.t.* **2.** to allot (money, time, etc.).

buff (buf) *n.* **1.** a soft, thick, light-yellow leather. **2.** a yellowish brown. **3.** an enthusiast. —*adj.* **4.** made or colored like buff. —*v.t.* **5.** to polish with a buffer.

buf′fa·lo′ (buf′ə lō′) *n., pl.* **-loes, -los, -lo.** any of several large, wild oxen, as the bison or the water buffalo.

buff′er¹ *n.* **1.** anything used for absorbing shock. —*v.t.* **2.** to act as a buffer to.

buff′er² *n.* a leather-covered polishing device.

buf·fet¹ (buf′it) *n.* **1.** a blow or violent shock. —*v.t.* **2.** to strike repeatedly.

buf·fet² (bə fā′, boo-) *n.* **1.** a cabinet for china, glassware, etc. **2.** a meal where guests serve themselves.

buf·foon′ (bə foon′) *n.* a clown.

bug (bug) *n., v.,* **bugged, bugging.** —*n.* **1.** an insect. **2.** a microorganism. **3.** a defect or imperfection. **4.** a hidden microphone. —*v.t.* **5.** to install a secret listening device in. **6.** *Informal.* to annoy.

bug′gy (bug′ē) *n., pl.* **-gies.** a carriage.

bu′gle (byoo′gəl) *n., v.,* **-gled, -gling.** —*n.* **1.** a brass wind instrument without valves. —*v.i.* **2.** to sound a bugle.

build (bild) *v.,* **built, building,** *n.* —*v.t.* **1.** to construct. **2.** to form. **3.** to establish. —*v.i.* **4.** to increase in intensity, tempo, etc. —*n.* **5.** bodily shape. —**build′er,** *n.*

build′ing *n.* a structure with a roof and walls.

build′up′ *n. Informal.* **1.** a steady increase. **2.** publicity.

built′-in′ *adj.* **1.** built as part of a structure. **2.** an inseparable part of.

built′-up′ *adj.* **1.** made bigger or higher by adding something. **2.** filled in with buildings.

bulb (bulb) *n.* **1.** a swollen, underground stem with fleshy leaves, as in the onion or daffodil. **2.** any round, enlarged part. **3.** an incandescent lamp or its glass housing.

bulge (bulj) *n., v.,* **bulged, bulging.** —*n.* **1.** a rounded projection. —*v.i.* **2.** to swell out. —**bulg′y,** *adj.*

bu·lim′i·a (byoo lim′ē ə, -lē′mē ə, boo-) *n.* a disorder marked by eating binges followed by self-induced vomiting.

bulk (bulk) *n.* **1.** size, esp. when

great. **2.** the main mass. —*v.i.* **3.** to increase in size or importance. —**bulk′y,** *adj.*

bulk′head′ *n.* a wall-like partition in a ship.

bull¹ (bŏŏl) *n.* **1.** the male of a bovine animal or of certain other animals, as the elephant, whale, and moose. **2.** a person who believes that stock prices will rise. —*adj.* **3.** male. **4.** marked by rising prices, esp. of stocks.

bull² (bŏŏl) *n.* an official document from the pope.

bull³ (bŏŏl) *n.* lies; nonsense.

bull′dog′ *n.* a breed of shorthaired, muscular dog.

bull′doz′er *n.* a powerful earth-moving tractor.

bul′let (bŏŏl′it) *n.* a small projectile for firing from small guns.

bul′le•tin (bŏŏl′i tn, -tin) *n.* **1.** a brief public statement, esp. late news. **2.** a periodical publication.

bull′fight′ *n.* a traditional spectacle in which a bull is fought and killed by a matador.

bull′frog′ *n.* a large frog with a deep voice.

bull′head′ed *adj.* stubborn.

bul′lion (bŏŏl′yən) *n.* gold or silver in bars.

bull′ock (bŏŏl′ək) *n.* a castrated bull.

bull′pen′ *n.* the place where relief pitchers warm up.

bull′s′-eye′ *n.* the center of a target.

bul′ly (bŏŏl′ē) *n., pl.* **-lies,** *v.,* **-lied, -lying.** —*n.* **1.** an overbearing person who intimidates weaker people. —*v.t.* **2.** to intimidate.

bul′rush′ (bŏŏl′rush′) *n.* a tall, rushlike plant.

bul′wark (bŏŏl′wərk, -wôrk) *n.* **1.** a defense wall. **2.** a protection.

bum (bum) *n. Informal.* **1.** a tramp or hobo. **2.** a loafer or idler. —*v.t.* **3.** *Informal.* to borrow without planning to return. —*adj.* **4.** of poor quality.

bum′ble (bum′bəl) *v.,* **-bled, -bling.** —*v.i.* **1.** to blunder. —*v.t.* **2.** to bungle or botch.

bum′ble•bee′ *n.* a large, hairy bee.

bum′mer (bum′ər) *n. Slang.* any unpleasant experience.

bump (bump) *v.t., v.i.* **1.** to strike or collide (with). **2.** to bounce along. —*n.* **3.** a collision; blow. **4.** a swelling from a blow. **5.** a small area higher than the surrounding surface. —**bump′y,** *adj.*

bump′er *n.* **1.** a guard for protecting the front or rear of an automobile in a collision. —*adj.* **2.** unusually abundant.

bump′kin *n.* an awkward, simple person from a rural area.

bun (bun) *n.* a kind of bread roll.

bunch (bunch) *n.* **1.** a cluster. **2.** a group. —*v.t., v.i.* **3.** to gather into a group.

bun′dle (bun′dl) *n., v.,* **-dled, -dling.** —*n.* **1.** several things loosely bound together. **2.** a package. —*v.t.* **3.** to wrap in a bundle. **4. bundle up,** to dress warmly.

bun′ga•low′ (bung′gə lō′) *n.* a small house.

bun′gle (bung′gəl) *v.,* **-gled, -gling,** *n.* —*v.t., v.i.* **1.** to do badly. —*n.* **2.** something bungled.

bun′ion (bun′yən) *n.* an inflamed swelling at the base of the big toe.

bunk¹ (bungk) *n.* a built-in bed.

bunk² (bungk) *n.* bunkum.

bunk′er (bung′kər) *n.* **1.** a large bin. **2.** an underground refuge.

bun′kum (bung′kəm) *n.* nonsense. Also, **bunk.**

bun′ny (bun′ē) *n., pl.* **-nies.** a rabbit.

bunt (bunt) *v.t., v.i.* to push or tap (something) forward.

bun′ting¹ (bun′ting) *n.* fabric for flags, signals, etc.

bun′ting² (bun′ting) *n.* a small, seed-eating songbird.

buoy (bŏŏ′ē, boi) *n.* **1.** an anchored floating marker. —*v.t.* **2.** to keep afloat. **3.** to mark with a buoy. **4.** to sustain or encourage.

buoy′ant (boi′ənt, bŏŏ′yənt) *adj.* **1.** able to float. **2.** cheerful. —**buoy′an•cy,** *n.*

bur (bûr) *n.* a prickly seed case.

bur′den (bûr′dn) *n.* **1.** a load. **2.** something borne with difficulty. —*v.t.* **3.** to load heavily or oppressively. —**bur′den•some,** *adj.*

bur′dock (bûr′dok) *n.* a broad-leaved weed bearing prickly burs.

bu′reau (byŏŏr′ō) *n., pl.* **-eaus, -eaux. 1.** a chest of drawers. **2.** a government department.

bu•reauc′ra•cy (byŏŏ rok′rə sē) *n., pl.* **-cies. 1.** government by a rigid hierarchy of officials. **2.** a group of officials. **3.** excessive administrative routine. —**bur′eau•crat′,** *n.* —**bur′eau•crat′ic,** *adj.*

bur′geon (bûr′jən) *v.i.* **1.** to grow quickly. **2.** to begin to grow.

burg′er (bûr′gər) *n.* a hamburger.

bur′glar (bûr′glər) *n.* a thief who breaks and enters. —**bur′glar•ize′,** *v.t., v.i.* —**bur′gla•ry,** *n.*

bur′i•al (ber′ē əl) *n.* the act of burying.

bur′lap (bûr′lap) *n.* a coarse fabric of hemp or jute.

bur•lesque′ (bər lesk′) *n., v.,* **-lesqued, -lesquing.** —*n.* **1.** a par-

ody. **2.** a bawdy stage show. —*v.t.,
v.i.* **3.** to mock by burlesque.

bur′ly (bûr′lē) *adj.,* **-lier, -liest. 1.**
of great bodily size. **2.** sturdy.

burn (bûrn) *v.,* **burned** or **burnt,
burning,** *n.* —*v.i.* **1.** to be on fire.
2. to give off light. **3.** to be hot. **4.**
to be injured, damaged, or de-
stroyed by fire or heat. **5.** to feel
strong emotion. —*v.t.* **6.** to damage or destroy by fire. **7.** to use as
fuel. **8.** to cause a stinging sensation in. **9. burn out,** to exhaust or
become exhausted. —*n.* **10.** an injury caused by burning.

bur′nish (bûr′nish) *v.t.* to polish by
friction.

burn′out′ *n.* **1.** the point at which
a rocket engine stops because it
runs out of fuel. **2.** fatigue and
frustration from too much work
and stress.

burp (bûrp) *n.* **1.** a belch. —*v.i.* **2.**
to belch. —*v.t.* **3.** to cause (a baby)
to belch.

burr (bûr) *n.* a bur.

bur′ro (bûr′ō, bŏŏr′ō, bur′ō) *n., pl.*
-ros. a donkey.

bur′row (bûr′ō, bur′ō) *n.* **1.** an animal's hole in the ground. —*v.i.* **2.**
to dig or hide in a burrow. **3.** to
proceed by digging. —*v.t.* **4.** to dig
a burrow into. **5.** to make by burrowing.

bur′sa (bûr′sə) *n., pl.* **-sae** (-sē) **-sas.**
a sac containing fluid, as between
a tendon and a bone.

bur′sar (bûr′sər, -sär) *n.* a treasurer,
esp. of a college.

bur·si′tis (bər sī′tis) *n.* inflammation of a bursa in a joint.

burst (bûrst) *v.,* **burst, bursting,** *n.*
—*v.i.* **1.** to break open or issue
forth violently. **2.** to rupture. —*v.t.*
3. to cause to burst. —*n.* **4.** an act
or result of bursting. **5.** a sudden
display of activity or emotion.

bur′y (ber′ē) *v.t.,* **buried, burying.
1.** to put in the ground and cover
with earth. **2.** to put (a dead body)
in the ground or a tomb or the
sea. **3.** to conceal. **4.** to involve
(oneself) deeply.

bus (bus) *n., pl.* **buses, busses,** *v.,*
bused or **bussed, busing** or **buss-
ing.** —*n.* **1.** a large motor vehicle
for many passengers. —*v.t.* **2.** to
move by bus. —*v.i.* **3.** to travel by
bus.

bus′boy′ *n.* a waiter's helper.

bush (bŏŏsh) *n.* **1.** a low plant with
many branches. **2.** land covered by
bushes. —**Idiom. 3. beat around
the bush,** to avoid talking about
something directly.

bushed *adj. Informal.* exhausted.

bush′el (bŏŏsh′əl) *n.* a unit of four
pecks.

bush′ league′ *n.* a secondary baseball league.

busi′ness (biz′nis) *n.* **1.** an occupation, profession, or trade. **2.** a prof-
it-seeking enterprise. **3.** patronage.
4. affair; matter.

busi′ness·like′ *adj.* practical and
efficient.

busi′ness·man′ or **-wo′man** or
-per′son, *n., pl.* **-men** or **-wo·men**
or **-per·sons.** a person engaged in
business.

bus′ing (bus′ing) *n.* the moving of
pupils by bus to achieve racially
balanced classes. Also, **bus′sing.**

bust¹ (bust) *n.* **1.** a sculpture of the
head and shoulders. **2.** a woman's
bosom.

bust² (bust) *Informal.* —*v.i.* **1.** to
burst or break. **2.** to go bankrupt.
—*v.t.* **3.** to break. **4.** to arrest. **5.** to
hit. —*n.* **6.** a failure. **7.** an arrest.

bus′tle (bus′əl) *v.,* **-tled, -tling,** *n.*
—*v.i.* **1.** to move or act energetically. —*n.* **2.** energetic activity.

bus′y (biz′ē) *adj.,* **-ier, -iest,** *v.,* **-ied,
-ing.** —*adj.* **1.** actively employed.
2. full of activity. —*v.t.* **3.** to make
or keep busy.

bus′y·bod′y *n., pl.* **-bodies.** one
who meddles in others' affairs.

but (but; *unstressed* bət) *conj.* **1.** on
the contrary. **2.** except. **3.** and yet.
—*prep.* **4.** other than. —*adv.* **5.**
only.

bu′tane (byŏŏ′tān) *n.* a colorless
gas used as fuel.

butch (bŏŏch) *adj. Slang.* **1.** (of a
woman) having traits usu. associated with men. **2.** (of a man) having exaggerated masculine traits.

butch′er (bŏŏch′ər) *n.* **1.** a dealer in
meat. **2.** a person who slaughters
or dresses animals for food. —*v.t.*
3. to slaughter or dress (animals).
4. to kill brutally. **5.** to bungle.
—**butch′er·y,** *n.*

but′ler (but′lər) *n.* the chief male
servant in a household.

butt¹ (but) *n.* **1.** the thicker or
blunter end of anything. **2.** an unused end of something. **3.** *Slang.*
the buttocks.

butt² (but) *n.* **1.** an object of ridicule. —*v.t., v.i.* **2.** to place or be
placed end to end.

butt³ (but) *v.t., v.i.* **1.** to strike with
the head or horns. **2. butt in,** to
intrude.

but′ter (but′ər) *n.* **1.** the solid fatty
part of milk. —*v.t.* **2.** to put butter
on. **3. butter up,** to flatter.

but′ter·cup′ *n.* a plant with yellow
cup-shaped flowers.

but′ter·fly′ *n., pl.* **-flies.** an insect with broad, colorful wings.

but′ter·milk′ *n.* the liquid remaining after butter has been separated from milk.

but′ter·nut′ *n.* the edible oily nut of a tree of the walnut family.

but′ter·scotch′ *n.* a kind of taffy.

but′tock (but′ək) *n.* either of the two fleshy rounded parts forming the rump of the human body.

but′ton (but′n) *n.* **1.** a disk or knob for fastening. **2.** a buttonlike object. —*v.t., v.i.* **3.** to fasten or be fastened with a button.

but′ton·down′ *adj.* **1.** (of a collar) having buttonholes for attaching it to a shirt. **2.** conventional.

but′ton·hole′ *n., v.,* **-holed, -holing.** —*n.* **1.** the slit through which a button is passed. —*v.t.* **2.** to approach and keep talking to.

but′tress (bu′tris) *n.* **1.** a projecting support built into or against a wall. **2.** any support. —*v.t.* **3.** to support.

bux′om (buk′səm) *adj.* (of a woman) full-bosomed.

buy (bī) *v.,* **bought** (bôt), **buying,** *n.* —*v.t.* **1.** to acquire by payment. **2. buy off,** to bribe. —*n.* **3.** a bargain.

buy′out′ *n.* the purchase of a majority of shares in a company.

buzz (buz) *n.* **1.** a low humming sound. —*v.i.* **2.** to make a low humming sound.

buz′zard (buz′ərd) *n.* a large carnivorous bird.

buzz′word′ *n. Informal.* a word or phrase that has come into fashion in a particular profession.

by (bī) *prep.* **1.** near to. **2.** through. **3.** not later than. **4.** past. **5.** by way of. —*adv.* **6.** during. **7.** near. **8.** past.

by′-elec′tion *n.* a special election to fill a vacancy.

by′gone′ *adj.* **1.** past. —*n.* **2.** something in the past.

by′law′ *n.* a rule governing matters within a corporation.

by′line′ *n.* a line, as in a newspaper, giving the writer's name.

by′pass′ *n.* **1.** a route going around a city or obstruction. **2.** a surgical procedure to provide passage around a diseased or blocked organ. —*v.t.* **3.** to avoid by means of a bypass.

by′-prod′uct *n.* a secondary product.

by′road′ *n.* a side road; byway.

by′stand′er *n.* a person present but not involved.

byte (bīt) *n.* a unit of computer information, larger than a bit.

by′way′ *n.* a little-used road.

by′word′ *n.* **1.** a favorite word or phrase. **2.** a person regarded as the embodiment of some quality.

Byz′an·tine′ (biz′ən tēn′, -tīn′) *adj. (sometimes l.c.)* **1.** complex; intricate. **2.** marked by intrigue.

C

C, c (sē) *n.* the third letter of the English alphabet.

C Celsius, Centigrade.

c. **1.** centimeter. **2.** century. **3.** copyright.

CA California.

ca. circa.

cab (kab) *n.* **1.** a taxicab. **2.** the part of a locomotive, truck, etc., where the driver sits.

ca·bal′ (kə bal′) *n.* a small group of secret plotters.

ca·ban′a (kə ban′ə, -ban′yə) *n.* a small shelter at a beach or pool.

cab′a·ret′ (kab′ə rā′) *n.* a restaurant providing entertainment.

cab′bage (kab′ij) *n.* a vegetable with a dense round head of leaves.

cab′in (kab′in) *n.* **1.** a small house. **2.** a room in a ship or plane.

cab′i·net (kab′ə nit) *n.* **1.** a chief executive's advisory council. **2.** a cupboard with shelves or drawers.

ca′ble (kā′bəl) *n., v.,* **-bled, -bling.** —*n.* **1.** a heavy, strong rope of fiber or metal wires. **2.** an insulated bundle of electrical wires. **3.** cable TV. **4.** a cablegram. —*v.t., v.i.* **5.** to send a cablegram (to).

ca′ble·gram′ *n.* a telegram sent by underwater wires.

ca′ble TV′ *n.* a system of distributing television programs to subscribers over coaxial cables.

ca·boose′ (kə bōōs′) *n.* a car for the crew at the rear of a train.

ca·ca′o (-kā′ō) *n., pl.* **-caos.** a tropical tree yielding cocoa.

cache (kash) *n., v.,* **cached, caching.** —*n.* **1.** a hiding place for treasure, food, etc. **2.** anything hidden in a cache. —*v.t.* **3.** to hide.

ca·chet′ (ka shā′) *n.* **1.** an official seal. **2.** superior status; prestige.

cack′le (kak′əl) *v.,* **-led, -ling,** *n.* —*v.i.* **1.** to utter a shrill, broken cry, as of a hen. —*n.* **2.** the act or sound of cackling.

ca·coph′o·ny (kə kof′ə nē) *n.* harsh, discordant sound.

cac′tus (kak′təs) *n., pl.* **-tuses, -ti** (-tī). a leafless, spiny desert plant.

cad (kad) *n.* a dishonorable man.
ca•dav′er (kə dav′ər) *n.* a corpse.
cad′die (kad′ē) *n.*, *v.*, **-died, -dying.** —*n.* **1.** a person who carries a golfer's clubs. —*v.i.* **2.** to work as a caddie. Also, **cad′dy.**
ca′dence (kād′ns) *n.* **1.** rhythmic flow, as of sounds. **2.** the rise and fall of the voice.
ca•det′ (kə det′) *n.* a student at a military academy.
cadge (kaj) *v.t.*, *v.i.*, **cadged, cadging.** to obtain (a thing) by begging.
cad′mi•um (kad′mē əm) *n.* a white metallic element used in plating.
ca′dre (kä′drā, kad′rē) *n.* a highly trained group in an organization.
Cae•sar′e•an (si zâr′ē ən) *n.* a Cesarean.
ca•fé′ (ka fā′) *n.* a small informal restaurant.
caf′e•te′ri•a (kaf′i tēr′ē ə) *n.* a self-service restaurant.
caf′feine (ka fēn′) *n.* a stimulant found in coffee, tea, etc.
caf′tan (kaf′tan) *n.* a long wide-sleeved garment.
cage (kāj) *n.*, *v.*, **caged, caging.** —*n.* **1.** a barred box or room. —*v.t.* **2.** to put in a cage.
cag′ey *adj.*, **-ier, -iest.** shrewd; cautious. Also, **cag′y.** —**cag′i•ly,** *adv.*
cais′son (kā′son, -sən) *n.* **1.** a two-wheeled ammunition wagon. **2.** a watertight chamber for underwater construction.
ca•jole′ (kə jōl′) *v.t.*, *v.i.*, **-joled, -joling.** to coax.
cake (kāk) *n.*, *v.*, **caked, caking.** —*n.* **1.** a sweet, baked breadlike food. **2.** a flat hard mass. —*v.t.*, *v.i.* **3.** to form into a compact mass. —*Idiom.* **4. piece of cake,** something that can be done easily.
Cal. California. Also, **Calif.**
cal. **1.** caliber. **2.** calorie.
cal′a•bash′ (kal′ə bash′) *n.* a kind of gourd.
cal′a•mine′ (kal′ə mīn′) *n.* a pink powder containing zinc oxide, used in skin lotions.
ca•lam′i•ty (kə lam′i tē) *n.*, *pl.* **-ties.** a disaster. —**ca•lam′i•tous,** *adj.*
cal′ci•fy′ (kal′sə fī′) *v.t.*, *v.i.*, **-fied, -fying.** to harden by the deposit of calcium salts.
cal′ci•um (kal′sē əm) *n.* a white metallic element.
cal′cu•late′ (kal′kyə lāt′) *v.t.*, **-lated, -lating. 1.** to determine by using mathematics. **2.** to estimate. —**cal′cu•la′tion,** *n.*
cal′cu•lat′ing *adj.* shrewd.
cal′cu•la′tor *n.* a small electronic or mechanical device for making mathematical calculations.
cal′cu•lus (kal′kyə ləs) *n.* a method

of calculation by a system of algebraic notations.
cal′dron (kôl′drən) *n.* a cauldron.
cal′en•dar (kal′ən dər) *n.* **1.** a table of the days, weeks, and months in a year. **2.** a list of events.
calf¹ (kaf) *n.*, *pl.* **calves.** the young of the cow and certain other mammals, as the elephant, whale, etc.
calf² (kaf) *n.*, *pl.* **calves.** the back part of the leg below the knee.
cal′i•ber (kal′ə bər) *n.* **1.** the diameter of a circular section. **2.** the diameter of a gun bore. **3.** degree of ability. Also, **cal′i•bre.**
cal′i•brate′ (-brāt′) *v.t.*, **-brated, -brating.** to mark (an instrument) for measuring purposes. —**cal′i•bra′tion,** *n.*
cal′i•co′ (kal′i kō′) *n.*, *pl.* **-coes, -cos. 1.** a printed cotton cloth. —*adj.* **2.** having blotches of a different color.
cal′i•pers (kal′ə pərz) *n.pl.* an instrument for measuring, consisting of two adjustable legs.
cal′is•then′ics (kal′əs then′iks) *n.pl.* physical exercises.
calk (kôk) *v.t.*, *n.* caulk.
call (kôl) *v.t.* **1.** to cry out loudly. **2.** to summon; invite. **3.** to telephone. **4.** to name. —*v.i.* **5.** to speak loudly. **6.** to make a brief visit. **7.** (of a bird) to utter a characteristic cry. **8. call off,** to cancel. —*n.* **9.** a cry or shout. **10.** a summons. **11.** a brief visit. **12.** a need; demand. —**call′er,** *n.*
cal•lig′ra•phy (kə lig′rə fē) *n.* beautiful handwriting.
call′ing *n.* a vocation or profession.
cal′lous (kal′əs) *adj.* insensitive.
cal′low (kal′ō) *adj.* immature.
cal′lus (kal′əs) *n.* a hardened part of the skin.
calm (käm) *adj.* **1.** not excited; tranquil. **2.** still; not windy. —*n.* **3.** freedom from disturbance. **4.** absence of wind. **5.** serenity. —*v.t.*, *v.i.* **6.** to make or become calm. —**calm′ly,** *adv.*
ca•lor′ic (kə lôr′ik) *adj.* **1.** of heat or calories. **2.** high in calories.
cal′o•rie (kal′ə rē) *n.* a unit used to express heat and the energy value of food.
ca•lum′ni•ate′ (kə lum′nē āt′) *v.t.*, **-ated, -ating.** to slander. —**cal′um•ny** (kal′əm nē) *n.*
calve (kav, käv) *v.i.*, *v.t.* **calved, calving.** to give birth to (a calf).
ca•lyx (kā′liks, kal′iks) *n.*, *pl.* **calyxes, calyces** (kal′ə sēz′, kā′lə-). the small leaflike parts around the petals of a flower.
cam (kam) *n.* a machine part that

gives a rocking motion to another part.

ca′ma•ra•de•rie (kä′mə rä′də rē) *n.* comradeship; fellowship.

cam′ber (kam′bər) *v.t., v.i.* **1.** to curve upward in the middle. —*n.* **2.** a slight upward curve.

cam′bric (kām′brik) *n.* a thin cotton or linen fabric.

cam′cord′er (kam′kôr′dər) *n.* a hand-held television camera that has a VCR.

came (kām) *v.* pt. of **come.**

cam′el (kam′əl) *n.* a large humped mammal living in the desert.

ca•mel′lia (kə mēl′yə) *n.* a shrub with glossy leaves and roselike flowers.

cam′e•o′ (kam′ē ō′) *n., pl.* **-eos. 1.** a gem with a head carved in a raised design. **2.** a brief appearance by a famous person in a film or play.

cam′er•a (kam′ər ə) *n.* **1.** a device for making photographs. —*Idiom.* **2. in camera,** privately.

cam′i•sole′ (kam′ə sōl′) *n.* a woman's sleeveless undershirt.

cam′o•mile′ (kam′ə mīl′) *n.* chamomile.

cam′ou•flage′ (kam′ə fläzh′) *n., v.,* **-flaged, -flaging.** —*n.* **1.** deceptive covering. —*v.t.* **2.** to disguise.

camp[1] (kamp) *n.* **1.** a place of temporary lodging, esp. in tents, for soldiers or vacationers. **2.** a faction. —*v.i.* **3.** to form or live in a camp. —**camp′er,** *n.*

camp[2] (kamp) *n.* **1.** something that amuses by being overdone or tasteless. —*adj.* **2.** Also, **camp′y.** amusing as camp.

cam•paign′ (kam pān′) *n.* **1.** a military operation. **2.** a course of organized activity in pursuit of a goal, as political office, sales, etc. —*v.i.* **3.** to engage in a campaign.

cam′phor (kam′fər) *n.* a white crystalline substance used as a moth repellent, medicine, etc.

camp′site *n.* a place for camping.

cam′pus (kam′pəs) *n.* the grounds of a school, college, etc.

cam′shaft′ *n.* an engine shaft fitted with cams.

can[1] (kan; *unstressed* kən) *auxiliary v., pres.* **can;** *past* **could.** to be able or know how to.

can[2] (kan) *v.,* **canned, canning.** —*n.* **1.** a sealed metal container for food, beverages, etc. **2.** a container for garbage. —*v.t.* **3.** to put in an airtight metal or glass container.

ca•nal′ (kə nal′) *n.* **1.** an artificial waterway. **2.** a tube for food, air, etc., in an animal or plant.

can′a•pé (kan′ə pē, -pā′) *n.* a cracker or piece of bread topped with meat, fish, etc., and served as an appetizer.

ca•nar′y (kə nâr′ē) *n., pl.* **-ries.** a yellow finch bred as a cage bird.

can′cel (kan′səl) *v.t.,* **-celed, -celing. 1.** to make void. **2.** to call off. **3.** to cross out. —**can′cel•la′tion,** *n.*

can′cer (kan′sər) *n.* a malignant growth that tends to spread. —**can′cer•ous,** *adj.*

can′de•la′brum (kan′dl ä′brəm) *n., pl.* **-bra** (-brə). a branched candlestick. Also, **can′de•la′bra,** *pl.* **-bras.**

can′did (kan′did) *adj.* **1.** frank or honest. **2.** unposed, as a photograph. —**can′did•ly,** *adv.*

can′di•da (kan′di də) *n.* a disease-causing fungus.

can′di•date′ (kan′di dāt′, -dit) *n.* one seeking to be elected or chosen. —**can′di•da•cy,** *n.*

can′dle (kan′dl) *n.* a wax cylinder with a wick for burning.

can′dor (kan′dər) *n.* frankness.

can′dy (kan′dē) *n., pl.* **-dies,** *v.,* **-died, -dying.** —*n.* **1.** a sweet food made from sugar and flavoring. —*v.t.* **2.** to cook with sugar or syrup.

cane (kān) *n., v.,* **caned, caning.** —*n.* **1.** a stick used for support in walking. **2.** a long, woody stem. **3.** a rod used for beating. —*v.t.* **4.** to beat with a cane.

ca′nine (kā′nīn) *adj.* **1.** of dogs. —*n.* **2.** an animal of the dog family. **3.** one of the four pointed teeth next to the incisors.

ca′nine tooth′ *n.* one of the four pointed teeth next to the incisors.

can′is•ter (kan′ə stər) *n.* a small box or can.

can′ker (kang′kər) *n.* an ulcerous sore, esp. in the mouth.

can′na•bis (kan′ə bis) *n.* the hemp plant.

canned (kand) *adj.* **1.** preserved in cans or sealed jars. **2.** *Informal.* recorded.

can′ner•y *n., pl.* **-ies.** a factory where foods are canned.

can′ni•bal (kan′ə bəl) *n.* **1.** a person who eats human flesh. **2.** an animal that eats its own kind.

can′ni•bal•ize′ *v.t., v.i.,* **-ized, -izing.** to take from one thing, as a part from a machine, for use in another.

can′non (kan′ən) *n.* a large mounted gun.

can′non•ade′ (-ə nād′) *n.* a long burst of cannon fire.

can′not (kan′ot, ka not′, kə-) *v.* a form of can not.

can′ny (kan′ē) *adj.,* **-nier, -niest. 1.** careful. **2.** shrewd.

ca·noe′ (kə nōō′) *n.* a slender, light boat propelled by paddles.

can′on¹ (kan′ən) *n.* 1. a rule enacted by a church body. 2. a group of writings accepted as authentic.

can′on² (kan′ən) *n.* a member of the clergy of a cathedral.

can′on·ize′ *v.t.,* **-ized, -izing.** to declare officially as a saint.

can′o·py (kan′ə pē) *n., pl.* **-pies.** 1. a covering hung over a bed, throne, etc. 2. an awning stretching from a doorway to a curb.

cant (kant) *n.* 1. insincere statements of a pious nature. 2. the vocabulary of a particular group.

can′t (kant) a contraction of **cannot.**

can′ta·loupe′ (kan′tl ōp′) *n.* a melon having a rough rind and orange flesh.

can·tan′ker·ous (kan tang′kər əs) *adj.* ill-natured.

can·ta′ta (kən tä′tə) *n.* a choral composition.

can·teen′ (kan tēn′) *n.* 1. a small container for carrying water. 2. a cafeteria or entertainment place for military personnel.

can′ter (kan′tər) *n.* 1. an easy gallop. —*v.i.* 2. to go at this pace.

can′ti·cle (kan′ti kəl) *n.* a hymn.

can′ti·le′ver (kan′tl ē′vər) *n.* a structure supported at one end only.

can′to (kan′tō) *n., pl.* **-tos.** a section of a long poem.

can′ton (kan′tn, kan ton′) *n.* a small district in Switzerland.

can′tor (kan′tər) *n.* a synagogue official who sings certain prayers.

can′vas (kan′vəs) *n.* 1. a heavy, coarse cloth used for sails, tents, etc. 2. a painting on canvas.

can′vas·back′ *n., pl.* **-backs, -back.** a wild duck with a whitish or grayish back.

can′vass (kan′vəs) *v.t., v.i.* 1. to solicit votes, opinions, etc., from a group. —*n.* 2. a soliciting of votes, opinions, etc. —**can′vass·er,** *n.*

can′yon (kan′yən) *n.* a deep, narrow valley.

cap (kap) *n., v.,* **capped, capping.** —*n.* 1. a tight-fitting hat with a visor. 2. a cover. 3. a maximum limit. —*v.t.* 4. to cover. 5. to outdo.

cap. 1. capacity. 2. capital(ize).

ca′pa·ble (kā′pə bəl) *adj.* able; qualified. —**ca′pa·bil′i·ty,** *n.*

ca·pa′cious (kə pā′shəs) *adj.* roomy.

ca·pac′i·tor (kə pas′i tər) *n.* a device for collecting and holding an electrical charge.

ca·pac′i·ty *n., pl.* **-ties.** 1. the abil-

ity to contain. 2. volume. 3. the ability to do. 4. a function.

cape (kāp) *n.* 1. a sleeveless coat. 2. a projecting point of land.

ca′per¹ (kā′pər) *v.i.* 1. to leap playfully. —*n.* 2. a playful leap. 3. a prank.

ca′per² (kā′pər) *n.* the pickled flower bud of a shrub, used as seasoning.

cap′il·lar′y (kap′ə ler′ē) *n., pl.* **-laries.** a tiny blood vessel or thin tube.

cap′i·tal (kap′i tl) *n.* 1. a city in which the seat of government is located. 2. a letter different from and larger than its corresponding lowercase letter. 3. money available for business use. —*adj.* 4. important or chief. 5. excellent. 6. uppercase. 7. punishable by death.

cap′ital gain′ *n.* profit from the sale of an asset.

cap′ital goods′ *n.pl.* machines for the production of goods.

cap′i·tal·ism *n.* an economic system in which industry is privately owned. —**cap′i·tal·ist,** *n.*

cap′i·tal·ize′ *v.t.,* **-ized, -izing.** 1. to put in capital letters. 2. to use as capital. 3. **capitalize on,** to take advantage of.

cap′i·tal·ly *adv.* excellently.

Cap′i·tol (kap′i tl) *n.* 1. the building in Washington, D.C., in which the U.S. Congress meets. 2. *(often l.c.)* the building used by a state legislature.

ca·pit′u·late′ (kə pich′ə lāt′) *v.i.,* **-lated, -lating.** to surrender or yield.

cap′let (kap′lit) *n.* an oval pill, coated for easy swallowing.

ca′pon (kā′pon, -pən) *n.* a castrated rooster.

ca·price′ (kə prēs′) *n.* a whim.

cap′size′ (kap′sīz) *v.t., v.i.,* **-sized, -sizing.** to overturn; upset.

cap′stan (-stən, -stan) *n.* a device for winding in cables, ropes, etc.

cap′sule (-səl) *n.* 1. a gelatin case enclosing medicine. 2. a cabin in a spacecraft. 3. a small sealed container. —**cap′su·lar,** *adj.*

capt. captain.

cap′tain (-tən) *n.* 1. an officer below major or rear admiral. 2. a ship's master. 3. the leader of a sports team. —**cap′tain·cy,** *n.*

cap′tion (-shən) *n.* an explanation for a picture.

cap′tious (-shəs) *adj.* fault-finding, esp. about trivial matters.

cap′ti·vate′ (-tə vāt′) *v.t.,* **-vated, -vating.** to charm.

cap′tive (-tiv) *n.* 1. a prisoner.

—*adj.* **2.** unable to escape.
—**cap•tiv′i•ty,** *n.*

cap′ture (-chər) *v.,* **-tured, -turing,** *n.* —*v.t.* **1.** to take prisoner. **2.** to record in lasting form. —*n.* **3.** the act of capturing. —**cap′tor,** *n.*

car (kär) *n.* **1.** an automobile. **2.** the cage of an elevator.

ca•rafe′ (kə raf′) *n.* a wide-mouthed bottle for wine, water, etc.

car′a•mel (kar′ə məl, kär′məl) *n.* a confection made of burnt sugar.

car′at (kar′ət) *n.* **1.** a unit of weight for gems. **2.** a karat.

car′a•van′ (kar′ə van′) *n.* a group traveling together.

car′a•way′ (kar′ə wā′) *n.* an herb with spicy seeds, used in cooking.

car′bide (kär′bīd) *n.* a carbon compound.

car′bine (kär′bēn, -bīn) *n.* a short rifle.

car′bo•hy′drate (kär′bō hī′drāt, -bə-) *n.* an organic compound group including starches and sugars.

car•bol′ic ac′id (kär bol′ik) *n.* a brown germicidal liquid.

car′bon (kär′bən) *n.* a nonmetallic element occurring as diamonds, charcoal, etc., and present in all living matter. —**car•bon•if′er•ous,** *adj.*

car′bon•ate′ (kär′bə nāt′) *v.t.,* **-ated, -ating.** to charge with carbon dioxide.

car′bon diox′ide *n.* a chemical compound of carbon and oxygen: a gas produced esp. by animal respiration.

car′bon monox′ide *n.* a chemical compound of carbon and oxygen: a poisonous gas produced esp. by automobile engines.

car′bon pa′per *n.* paper coated with a carbon pigment, used to make copies.

Car′bo•run′dum (kär′bə run′dəm) *Trademark.* an abrasive of carbon, silicon, etc.

car′bun•cle (kär′bung kəl) *n.* a painful sore under the skin.

car′bu•re′tor (kär′bə rā′tər, -byə-) *n.* a device that mixes fuel and air in an engine.

car′cass (kär′kəs) *n.* the dead body of an animal.

car•cin′o•gen (kär sin′ə jən) *n.* a cancer-producing substance. —**car′cin•o•gen′ic** (-sə nə jen′ik) *adj.*

car•ci•no′ma (kär′sə nō′mə) *n., pl.* **-mas, -mata.** a malignant tumor.

card¹ (kärd) *n.* **1.** a piece of stiff paper or plastic containing information. **2.** a folded piece of stiff paper printed with a greeting. **3.** a thin piece of cardboard used in playing various games. —*v.t.* **4.** to ask for proof of age.

card² (kärd) *n.* **1.** a comb for wool, flax, etc. —*v.t.* **2.** to dress (wool or flax) with a card.

card′board′ *n.* **1.** thin, stiff pasteboard. —*adj.* **2.** flimsy.

car′di•ac′ (kär′dē ak′) *adj.* of the heart.

car′diac arrest′ *n.* abrupt stopping of the heartbeat.

car′di•gan (kär′di gən) *n.* a sweater that buttons down the front.

car′di•nal (kär′dn l) *adj.* **1.** main; chief. **2.** (of numbers) used to express quantities or positions in series, e.g., 3, 15, 45. —*n.* **3.** a red songbird. **4.** a deep red. **5.** a high official of the Roman Catholic Church.

cardio- a prefix meaning heart.

car′di•o•graph′ (kär′dē ə graf′) *n.* an electrocardiograph. —**car′di•o•gram′,** *n.*

car′di•ol′o•gy (-ol′ə jē) *n.* the study of the heart and its functions.

car′di•o•pul′mo•nar′y *adj.* of the heart and lungs.

car′di•o•vas′cu•lar *adj.* of the heart and blood vessels.

card′sharp′ *n.* a person who cheats at card games. Also, **card′ shark′.**

care (kâr) *n., v.,* **cared, caring.** —*n.* **1.** worry. **2.** caution. **3.** serious attention. **4.** protection. —*v.i.* **5.** to be concerned. **6.** to make provision. —*v.t.* **7.** to feel concern about. —**care′free′,** *adj.*

ca•reen′ (kə rēn′) *v.i., v.t.* to lean or cause to lean to one side.

ca•reer′ (-rēr′) *n.* **1.** a profession followed as one's lifework. **2.** one's course through life. —*v.i.* **3.** to speed.

care′ful *adj.* **1.** cautious. **2.** done with accuracy. —**care′full•y,** *adv.*

care′giv′er *n.* a person who cares for a child or an invalid.

care′less *adj.* **1.** not paying attention. **2.** not accurate. **3.** unconcerned.

ca•ress′ (kə res′) *n.* **1.** a light touch expressing affection. —*v.t.* **2.** to stroke lightly and affectionately.

car′et (kar′it) *n.* a mark (^) indicating where something is to be inserted.

care′tak′er (kâr′-) *n.* **1.** a person who looks after a building, estate, etc. **2.** a caregiver.

car′fare′ (kär′fâr′) *n.* the cost of a ride.

car′go (kär′gō) *n., pl.* **-goes, -gos.** goods carried by vessel; freight.

car′i•bou′ (kar′ə boo′) *n.* the North American reindeer.

car′i•ca•ture (kar′i kə chər) *n., v.,*

-tured, -turing. —*n.* 1. a mocking, exaggerated portrait. —*v.t.* 2. to make a caricature of.

car′ies (kâr′ēz) *n., pl.* -ies. tooth decay.

car′il•lon′ (kar′ə lon′, -lən) *n.* a set of bells in a tower.

car′jack′ing (kär′jak′ing) *n.* the forcible theft of a car from its driver.

car′mine (-min) *n.* a crimson or purplish red.

car′nage (-nij) *n.* great slaughter.

car′nal (-nl) *adj.* of the body.

car•na′tion (kär nā′shən) *n.* a cultivated fragrant flower.

car′ni•val (kär′nə vəl) *n.* 1. an amusement fair. 2. the festival before Lent.

car′ni•vore′ (-vôr′) *n.* a flesh-eating mammal. —car•niv′o•rous (-niv′ə-rəs) *adj.*

car′ob (kar′əb) *n.* the pulp from the long pods of a Mediterranean tree, used as a chocolate substitute.

car′ol (-əl) *n., v.,* -oled, -oling. —*n.* 1. a Christmas hymn. —*v.i., v.t.* 2. to sing joyously. —car′ol•er, *n.*

car′om (-əm) *v.t.* 1. to hit and rebound. —*n.* 2. a hit and rebound.

ca•rot′id (kə rot′id) *n.* either of two large arteries in the neck.

ca•rouse′ (kə rouz′) *v.i.,* -roused, -rousing. to take part in a noisy or drunken gathering.

carp¹ (kärp) *v.i.* to find fault.

carp² (kärp) *n.* a large fresh-water fish.

car′pal (kär′pəl) *adj.* 1. of the carpus. —*n.* 2. a wrist bone.

car′pal tun′nel syn′drome *n.* chronic wrist and hand pain associated esp. with repetitive movements, as at a keyboard.

car′pel (kär′pəl) *n.* a seed-bearing leaf.

car′pen•ter (-pən tər) *n.* a person who builds or repairs wooden structures. —car′pen•try, *n.*

car′pet (-pit) *n.* 1. a fabric covering for floors. 2. any covering like a carpet. —*v.t.* 3. to cover with a carpet. —*Idiom.* 4. call on the carpet, to reprimand.

car′pool′ *n.* 1. an arrangement by automobile owners who take turns driving their cars to a destination, as to work. —*v.i.* 2. to take part in a carpool.

car′port′ *n.* a roof that provides shelter for a car.

car′pus (kär′pəs) *n., pl.* -pi (pī). 1. the wrist. 2. the wrist bones as a group.

car′rel (kar′əl) *n.* a small study space in a library. Also, car′rell.

car′riage (-ij) *n.* 1. a wheeled vehi-cle. 2. a movable part for carrying something. 3. posture.

car′ri•on (-ē ən) *n.* dead flesh.

car′rot (-ət) *n.* an orange root vegetable.

car′ry (kar′ē) *v.t.,* -ried, -rying. 1. to transport. 2. to support; bear the weight of. 3. to serve as a medium for the transmission of. 4. to win a majority of votes in. 5. to have as a consequence. 6. to have in stock. 7. carry on, a. to manage. b. to persevere. c. to be disruptive. 8. ~ out, to accomplish.

car′ry-out′ *adj., n.* takeout.

car′sick′ (kär′-) *adj.* nauseated and dizzy from car travel.

cart (kärt) *n.* a small wagon.

carte′ blanche′ (kärt′ blänch′, blän-sh′) *n.* authority to do as one thinks best.

car•tel′ (kär tel′) *n.* a syndicate controlling prices and production.

car′ti•lage (kär′tl ij) *n.* a firm, elastic type of body tissue.

car•tog′ra•phy (kär tog′rə fē) *n.* the production of maps.

car′ton (kär′tn) *n.* a cardboard box.

car•toon′ (kär tōōn′) *n.* 1. a comic drawing. 2. a sketch for a painting.

car′tridge (-trij) *n.* 1. a case containing a bullet and explosive for a gun. 2. a compact case, as for film.

cart′wheel′ *n.* 1. a sideways handspring. —*v.i.* 2. to roll forward end over end.

carve (kärv) *v.,* carved, carving. —*v.t.* 1. to cut in order to form a shape or design. 2. to cut into slices, as meat. —*v.i.* 3. to form designs by carving. 4. to carve meat. —carv′er, *n.*

cas•cade′ (kas kād′) *n.* 1. a waterfall. 2. anything falling like a waterfall. —*v.i.* 3. to fall in a cascade.

case¹ (kās) *n.* 1. an example. 2. the state of things. 3. a matter requiring investigation. 4. a statement of arguments. 5. a patient or client. 6. a lawsuit. 7. a category in the inflection of nouns, adjectives, and pronouns. —*Idiom.* 8. in case, if. 9. in case of, in the event of.

case² (kās) *n., v.,* cased, casing. —*n.* 1. a container. —*v.t.* 2. to put in a case.

ca′sein (kā′sēn) *n.* a protein derived from milk.

case′ment (kās′mənt) *n.* a window opening on side hinges.

cash (kash) *n.* 1. money in the form of coins or banknotes. —*v.t.* 2. to give or get cash for (a check, money order, etc.).

cash′ew (kash′ōō) *n.* a small curved nut.

cash•ier′ (ka shēr′) *n.* a person employed to collect money for purchases, as in a store.

cash′mere (kazh′mēr, kash′-) *n.* a soft wool fabric.

cas′ing (kā′sing) *n.* **1.** an outer covering. **2.** a framework, as of a door.

ca·si′no (kə sē′nō) *n., pl.* **-nos.** a place for gambling.

cask (kask) *n.* a barrel for liquids.

cas′ket (kas′kit) *n.* a coffin.

cas·sa′va (kə sä′və) *n.* a tropical plant with starchy roots.

cas′se·role′ (kas′ə rōl′) *n.* **1.** a covered baking dish. **2.** food baked in such a dish.

cas·sette′ (kə set′) *n.* a compact case for film or recording tape.

cas′sock (kas′ək) *n.* a long, close-fitting garment worn by the clergy.

cast (kast) *v.,* **cast, casting,** *n.* —*v.t.* **1.** to throw. **2.** to send forth. **3.** to deposit (a ballot or vote). **4.** to form (an object) by pouring into a mold. **5.** to choose (actors) for (a play). —*n.* **6.** the act of throwing. **7.** something made in a mold. **8.** the actors in a play. **9.** a rigid surgical dressing. **10.** a hue; shade.

cas′ta·net′ (kas′tə net′) *n.* one of a pair of wooden shells held in the palm and clicked together to accompany dancing.

cast′a·way′ *n.* a shipwrecked person.

caste (kast) *n.* a rigid system of social divisions.

cast′er *n.* a small swivel-mounted wheel. Also, **cast′or.**

cas′ti·gate′ (kas′ti gāt′) *v.t.,* **-gated, -gating.** to scold severely.

cast i′ron *n.* a hard, brittle alloy of carbon, iron, and silicon.

cas′tle (kas′əl) *n.* **1.** a royal or noble residence, usu. fortified. **2.** the rook in chess.

cas′tor oil (kas′tər) *n.* a strongly laxative oil.

cas′trate (kas′trāt) *v.t.,* **-trated, -trating.** to remove the testicles of.

cas′u·al (kazh′ōō əl) *adj.* **1.** accidental; not planned. **2.** not caring. **3.** informal.

cas′u·al·ty *n., pl.* **-ties.** a person injured or killed in an accident or in a war.

cas′u·ist·ry (kazh′ōō ə strē) *n.* overly subtle argument.

cat (kat) *n.* **1.** a small, furry domestic animal. —*Idiom.* **2. let the cat out of the bag,** to reveal a secret. —**cat′like′,** *adj.*

cat′a·clysm′ (-ə kliz′əm) *n.* a violent upheaval or disaster. —**cat′a·clys′mic,** *adj.*

cat′a·comb′ (-kōm′) *n.* an underground cemetery.

cat′a·logue′ (kat′l ôg′) *n., v.,* **-logued, -loguing.** —*n.* **1.** an organized list. **2.** a book or brochure containing descriptive information about items, courses, artworks, etc. —*v.t., v.i.* **3.** to make a catalogue (of). Also, **cat′a·log′.**

ca·tal′pa (kə tal′pə) *n.* a tree with bell-shaped white flowers.

cat′a·lyst (kat′l ist) *n.* **1.** a substance causing a chemical reaction without itself being affected. **2.** anything precipitating an event.

cat′a·ma·ran′ (kat′ə mə ran′) *n.* a two-hulled boat.

cat′a·mount′ *n.* a cougar.

cat′a·pult′ (-pult′, -pŏŏlt′) *n.* **1.** a device for hurling or launching (stones). —*v.t., v.i.* **2.** to hurl or be hurled from in this way.

cat′a·ract′ (-rakt′) *n.* **1.** a waterfall. **2.** an opaque area in the lens of the eye.

ca·tarrh′ (kə tär′) *n.* an inflammation of a mucous membrane, esp. of the respiratory tract.

ca·tas′tro·phe (kə tas′trə fē) *n.* a sudden great disaster. —**cat′a·stroph′ic** (kat′ə strof′ik) *adj.*

cat′bird′ *n.* a songbird with a cat-like call.

cat′call′ *n.* a jeer.

catch (kach) *v.,* **caught** (kôt) **catching,** *n.* —*v.t.* **1.** to capture. **2.** to trap. **3.** to surprise. **4.** to seize and hold. **5.** to be in time for. **6.** to get or contract, as an illness. —*v.i.* **7.** to become entangled. **8. catch on, a.** to become popular. **b.** to understand. **9. ~ up, a.** to overtake something moving. **b.** to do extra work so one is no longer behind. —*n.* **10.** the act of catching. **11.** anything that catches. **12.** something caught. **13.** a snag.

Catch-22 (katch′twen′tē tōō′) *n.* a frustrating situation in which one is trapped by contradictory conditions.

catch′ing *adj.* contagious.

catch′word′ *n.* a slogan.

catch′y *adj.,* **-ier, -iest.** memorable and pleasing.

cat′e·chism (kat′i kiz′əm) *n.* a set of questions and answers on the principles of a religion.

cat′e·gor′i·cal (-gôr′i kəl) *adj.* unconditional.

cat′e·go′ry (-gôr′ē) *n., pl.* **-ries.** a division; class. —**cat′e·go·rize′** (-gə rīz′) *v.t.*

ca′ter (kā′tər) *v.i.* **1.** to provide food and service for a party. **2.** to provide what is needed. —*v.t.* **3.** to provide food and service for. —**ca′ter·er,** *n.*

cat′er-cor′nered (kat′i-, kat′ē-, kat′ər-) *adj.* **1.** diagonal. —*adv.* **2.** diagonally.

cat′er·pil′lar (kat′ə pil′ər) *n.* the wormlike larva of a butterfly or moth.

cat′er·waul′ (kat′ər wôl′) *v.i.* 1. to utter long wailing cries. —*n.* 2. such a cry.

cat′fish′ *n.* a scaleless fresh-water fish.

cat′gut′ *n.* string made from animal intestines.

ca·thar′sis (kə thär′sis) *n.* 1. the release of the emotions, as through art. 2. purgation of the bowels.

ca·thar′tic *adj.* 1. causing a catharsis. —*n.* 2. a strong laxative.

ca·the′dral (kə thē′drəl) *n.* the main church of a diocese.

cath′e·ter (kath′i tər) *n.* a thin tube inserted into a body passage.

cath′ode (kath′ōd) *n.* 1. an electrode with a negative charge. 2. the positive terminal of a battery.

cath′ode ray′ *n.* a beam of electrons coming from a cathode.

cath′ode-ray′ tube′ *n.* a vacuum tube generating cathode rays directed at a screen, used to display images on a receiver or monitor. *Abbr.*: CRT.

cath′o·lic (kath′ə lik) *adj.* 1. universal. 2. broad-minded.

Cath′o·lic (kath′ə lik) *adj.* 1. of the Roman Catholic Church. 2. of any orthodox Christian church. 3. of the Christian church as a whole. —*n.* 4. a member of a Catholic church. —**Ca·thol′i·cism** (kə thol′ə-siz′əm) *n.*

cat′kin (kat′kin) *n.* a spike of bunched small petal-less flowers.

cat′nap′ *n., v.,* **-napped, -napping.** —*n.* 1. a short, light sleep. —*v.i.* 2. to sleep briefly.

cat′nip *n.* a plant with strong-smelling leaves attractive to cats.

CAT′ scan′ (kat) *n.* 1. an examination using x-rays at various angles to show a cross section of the body. 2. an image so produced.

cat's′-paw′ *n.* a person used by another to do unpleasant work.

cat′sup (kat′səp, kech′əp, kach′-) *n.* ketchup.

cat′tail′ *n.* a tall, spiky marsh plant.

cat′tle (kat′l) *n.* bovine animals, as cows and steers.

cat′ty (kat′ē) *adj.,* **-tier, -tiest.** slyly malicious.

cat′walk′ *n.* a high, narrow walkway.

cau′cus (kô′kəs) *n.* a political meeting.

caught (kôt) *v.* pt. and pp. of **catch.**

caul′dron (kôl′drən) *n.* a big kettle.

cau′li·flow′er (kô′lə flou′ər) *n.* a kind of cabbage with a head of white florets.

caulk (kôk) *v.t.* 1. to fill the seams of to keep water or air out. —*n.* 2. Also, **caulk′ing.** material used to caulk.

cause (kôz) *n., v.,* **caused, causing.** —*n.* 1. a person or thing producing a result. 2. a reason. 3. an ideal or goal. —*v.t.* 4. to bring about. —**caus′al,** *adj.* —**caus·al′i·ty,** *n.*

cause′way′ *n.* a raised road across wet ground.

caus′tic (kô′stik) *adj.* 1. corroding. 2. sharply critical or sarcastic.

cau′ter·ize′ (kô′tə rīz′) *v.t.,* **-ized, -izing.** to burn (tissue) to stop bleeding or kill infection.

cau′tion (kô′shən) *n.* 1. carefulness. 2. a warning. —*v.t., v.i.* 3. to warn. —**cau′tious,** *adj.*

cav′al·cade′ (kav′əl kād′) *n.* a procession, esp. on horseback.

cav′a·lier′ (kav′ə lēr′) *n.* 1. a knight or horseman. 2. a courtly gentleman. —*adj.* 3. haughty; indifferent. 4. casual.

cav′al·ry (kav′əl rē) *n., pl.* **-ries.** troops on horseback or in armored vehicles. —**cav′al·ry·man,** *n.*

cave (kāv) *n., v.,* **caved, caving.** —*n.* 1. a hollow space in the earth. —*v.* 2. **cave in, a.** to collapse or cause to collapse. **b.** to yield.

ca′ve·at′ (kav′ē ät′) *n.* a warning.

cave′ man′ *n.* 1. a Stone Age cave dweller. 2. a rough, brutal man.

cav′ern (kav′ərn) *n.* a large cave.

cav′i·ar′ (-ē är′) *n.* the roe of sturgeon, salmon, etc.

cav′il (-əl) *v.,* **-iled, -iling,** *n.* —*v.i.* 1. to raise trivial objections. —*n.* 2. a trivial objection.

cav′i·ty (-i tē) *n., pl.* **-ties.** 1. a hollow place. 2. a decayed place in a tooth.

ca·vort′ (kə vôrt′) *v.i.* to prance.

caw (kô) *n.* 1. the harsh call of a crow. —*v.i.* 2. to make a caw.

cay·enne′ (kī en′) *n.* hot pepper.

CB citizens band: a private two-way radio.

cc. 1. carbon copy. **2.** cubic centimeter.

CCU coronary-care unit.

CD 1. certificate of deposit. **2.** Civil Defense. **3.** compact disc.

CD-ROM (sē′dē′rom′) *n.* a compact disc for storing digitized read-only data.

cease (sēs) *v.,* **ceased, ceasing,** *n.* —*v.i., v.t.* 1. to stop; end. —*n.* 2. a stopping. —**cease′less,** *adj.*

cease′-fire′ *n.* a truce.

ce′dar (sē′dər) *n.* an evergreen tree having fragrant wood.

cede (sēd) *v.t.,* **ceded, ceding.** 1. to

yield or give up. **2.** to transfer by legal document.

ceil′ing (sē′ling) *n.* **1.** the overhead surface of a room. **2.** an upper limit.

cel′e•brate′ (sel′ə brāt′) *v.*, **-brated, -brating.** —*v.t.* **1.** to observe with festivities. **2.** to perform with appropriate rites. —*v.i.* **3.** to have a good time. —**cel′e•bra′tion,** *n.*

ce•leb′ri•ty (sə leb′ri tē) *n., pl.* **-ties. 1.** a famous person. **2.** fame.

ce•ler′i•ty (sə ler′i tē) *n.* speed.

cel′er•y (sel′ə rē) *n.* a plant with edible leaf stalks.

ce•les′tial (sə les′chəl) *adj.* of heaven or the sky.

cel′i•ba•cy (sel′ə bə sē) *n.* **1.** sexual abstinence. **2.** the state of being unmarried.

cell (sel) *n.* **1.** a small room. **2.** a microscopic biological structure containing nuclear material. **3.** a device for converting chemical energy into electricity. **4.** a unit of an organization. —**cel′lu•lar,** *adj.*

cel′lar (sel′ər) *n.* an underground room.

cel′lo (chel′ō) *n., pl.* **-los.** a large violinlike instrument. —**cel′list,** *n.*

cel′lo•phane′ (sel′ə fān′) *n.* transparent wrapping material.

cel′lular phone′ *n.* a mobile telephone. Also, **cell′ phone′.**

cel′lu•lite′ (sel′yə līt′, -lēt′) *n.* lumpy fat deposits, esp. in the thighs.

cel′lu•loid′ (-loid′) *n.* a tough flammable substance.

cel′lu•lose′ (-lōs′) *n.* a carbohydrate of plant origin.

Cel′si•us (sel′sē əs) *adj.* of a temperature scale in which water freezes at 0° and boils at 100°.

ce•ment′ (si ment′) *n.* **1.** a clay-lime mixture that hardens into a stonelike mass. **2.** a binding material. —*v.t.* **3.** to unite by or cover with cement.

cem′e•ter′y (sem′i ter′ē) *n., pl.* **-ries.** a burial ground.

cen′o•taph′ (sen′ə taf′) *n.* a monument for someone buried elsewhere.

cen′ser (sen′sər) *n.* an incense burner, swung on a chain.

cen′sor (sen′sər) *n.* **1.** an official who examines books, films, etc., to eliminate anything objectionable. —*v.t.* **2.** to act upon as a censor. —**cen′sor•ship′,** *n.*

cen•so′ri•ous (-sôr′ē əs) *adj.* severely critical.

cen′sure (-shər) *n., v.,* **-sured, -suring.** —*n.* **1.** strong disapproval. —*v.t.* **2.** to rebuke strongly.

cen′sus (sen′səs) *n.* an official count of inhabitants.

cent (sent) *n.* $\frac{1}{100}$ of a dollar; penny.

cent. century.

cen′taur (sen′tôr) *n.* a mythological creature that is half horse and half man.

cen•ten′ar•y (sen ten′ə rē, sen′tn er′ē) *n., pl.* **-aries.** a 100th anniversary.

cen•ten′ni•al (-ten′ē əl) *n.* **1.** a 100th anniversary. —*adj.* **2.** of 100 years.

cen′ter (sen′tər) *n.* **1.** the middle point, part, or person. —*v.t., v.i.* **2.** to place or gather at the center. **3.** to concentrate. Also, **cen′tre.**

cen′ter•fold′ *n.* the facing pages in the center of a magazine.

cen′ter•piece′ *n.* a decoration for the center of a table.

cen′ti•grade′ (sen′ti grād′) *adj.* Celsius.

cen′ti•gram′ *n.* $\frac{1}{100}$ of a gram.

cen′ti•li′ter (-lē′tər) *n.* $\frac{1}{100}$ of a liter.

cen′ti•me′ter *n.* $\frac{1}{100}$ of a meter.

cen′ti•pede′ (-pēd′) *n.* an insect with many legs.

cen′tral (sen′trəl) *adj.* **1.** in, of, at, or forming the center. **2.** main; principal. —**cen′tral•ly,** *adv.*

cen′tral•ize′ *v.,* **-ized, -izing.** —*v.t.* **1.** to gather about a center. **2.** to bring under one control. —*v.i.* **3.** to come together at or form a center. —**cen′tral•i•za′tion,** *n.*

cen•trif′u•gal (-trif′yə gəl, -ə gəl) *adj.* moving away from the center.

cen′tri•fuge′ (-fyo͞oj′) *n.* a high-speed rotating machine for separating substances.

cen′trist (sen′trist) *n.* a person with moderate political views.

cen′tu•ry (sen′chə rē) *n., pl.* **-ries.** a period of one hundred years.

CEO chief executive officer.

ce•ram′ic (sə ram′ik) *adj.* of clay and similar materials.

ce′re•al (sēr′ē əl) *n.* **1.** a grass plant yielding edible grain. **2.** a food made from such a grain.

cer′e•bel′lum (ser′ə bel′əm) *n.* the rear part of the brain, controlling movement and balance.

cer′e•bral (ser′ə brəl, sə rē′-) *adj.* **1.** of the brain. **2.** intellectual.

cere′bral pal′sy *n.* a condition marked by difficulty in coordinating movement, due to brain injury.

cer′e•brum (sə rē′brəm, ser′ə-) *n., pl.* **-brums, -bra** (-brə). the front part of the brain, controlling voluntary movement and conscious processes.

cer′e•mo′ny (ser′ə mō′nē) *n., pl.*

-nies. a formal act or ritual. —cer'-
e•mo'ni•al, *adj., n.*

ce•rise' (sə rēs', -rēz') *n.* a medium
to deep red.

cer'tain (sûr'tn) *adj.* 1. free from
doubt; sure. 2. inevitable. 3.
agreed upon. 4. definite but unspecified. —cer'tain•ly, *adv.*
—cer'tain•ty, *n.*

cer•tif'i•cate (sər tif'i kit) *n.* an official document affirming some-
thing.

cer'ti•fy' (sûr'tə fī') *v.t.,* -fied, -fy-
ing. 1. to attest as certain. 2. to
guarantee. 3. to vouch for in writing. —cer'ti•fi•ca'tion, *n.*

cer'ti•tude' (-tōod', -tyōod') *n.* sure-
ness.

ce•ru'le•an (sə rōo'lē ən) *n.* a deep
blue.

cer'vix (sûr'viks) *n., pl.* cervixes,
cervices (sûr'və sēz'). a necklike
part, esp. the lower end of the
uterus. —cer'vi•cal (-vi kəl) *adj.*

Ce•sar'e•an (si zâr'ē ən) *n.* the delivery of a baby by cutting through
the abdomen and uterus. Also, Cesarean section, C-section, Cae•sar'-
e•an.

ces•sa'tion (se sā'shən) *n.* a temporary or complete stopping.

ces'sion (sesh'ən) *n.* 1. the act of
ceding. 2. something ceded.

cess'pool' (ses'pōol') *n.* a receptacle for sewage from a house.

cf. compare.

cg. centigram.

ch. 1. chapter. 2. church.

chafe (chāf) *v.,* chafed, chafing.
—v.t. 1. to wear away or make sore
by rubbing. 2. to warm by rubbing. 3. to irritate. —v.i. 4. to rub.
5. to become irritated.

chaff (chaf) *n.* 1. the husks of grain
separated from the seeds. 2. worthless matter.

chaf'ing dish' (chā'fing) *n.* a device
for cooking or warming food at the
table.

cha•grin' (shə grin') *n.* 1. embarrassment or humiliation. —v.t. 2.
to cause chagrin to.

chain (chān) *n.* 1. a connected series of links. 2. any connected series. 3. a mountain range. —v.t. 4.
to fasten with a chain.

chain' reac'tion *n.* a series of
events, each causing the following.

chain' saw' *n.* a power saw with
teeth set on an endless chain.

chair (châr) *n.* 1. a seat, usu. with a
back and four legs, for one person.
2. a position of authority. 3. a
chairman, chairwoman, or chairperson. —v.t. 4. to preside over.

chair'man or -wom'an or -per'-
son, *n., pl.* -men or -women or

-persons. a presiding officer or
head of a board or department.

chaise' longue' (shāz' lông') *n.* a
chair with a long seat.

cha•let' (sha lā') *n.* a mountain
house with wide eaves.

chal'ice (chal'is) *n.* a large goblet.

chalk (chôk) *n.* 1. a soft, powdery
white limestone. 2. a piece of
chalk, used to write on black-
boards. —v.t. 3. to mark with
chalk. 4. chalk up, to score or
earn.

chal'lenge (chal'inj) *n., v.,* -lenged,
-lenging. —n. 1. a summons to engage in a contest. 2. a demand for
an explanation. 3. a demanding
task. 4. a formal objection. —v.t.
5. to issue a challenge to.

challenged *adj.* (as a euphemism)
disabled, handicapped, or deficient
(preceded by an adverb).

cham'ber (chām'bər) *n.* 1. a room,
esp. a bedroom. 2. an assembly
hall. 3. a legislative body. 4. chambers, a judge's office. 5. an enclosed space.

cham'ber•maid' *n.* a maid who
cleans hotel rooms.

cham'ber mu'sic *n.* music for performance by a small ensemble.

cha•me'le•on (kə mēl'ē ən) *n.* a lizard that is able to change color.

cham'ois (sham'ē) *n.* 1. a European
antelope. 2. the soft leather from
its skin.

cham'o•mile' (kam'ə mīl', -mēl') *n.*
a plant whose flowers are used as a
tea. Also, cam'o•mile'.

champ¹ (champ) *n. Informal.* a
champion.

champ² (chomp, champ) *v.t., v.i.* to
bite noisily.

cham•pagne' (sham pān') *n.* a
sparkling white wine.

cham'pi•on (cham'pē ən) *n.* 1. the
best competitor. 2. a supporter.
—v.t. 3. to support. —adj. 4. best.
—cham'pi•on•ship', *n.*

chance (chans) *n., v.,* chanced,
chancing, *adj.* —n. 1. fate; luck. 2.
a possibility. 3. an opportunity. 4.
a risk. —v.i. 5. to occur by chance.
—v.t. 6. to risk. —adj. 7. accidental.
—*Idiom.* 8. on the (off) chance,
relying on the (slight) possibility.

chan'cel (chan'səl) *n.* the space
around the altar in a church.

chan'cel•ler•y (-sə lə rē, -səl rē) *n.,*
pl. -leries. the position or offices of
a chancellor.

chan'cel•lor (-sə lər) *n.* 1. a chief or
high government official. 2. a university head.

chan'cre (shang'kər) *n.* a lesion.

chanc'y (chan'sē) *adj.,* -cier, -ciest.
risky; uncertain.

chan′de.lier′ (shan/dl ēr/) *n.* a decorative hanging lighting fixture.

change (chānj) *v.*, **changed, changing**, *n.* —*v.t.* **1.** to make different. **2.** to exchange. —*v.i.* **3.** to become different. **4.** to transfer between means of transportation. **5.** to put on different clothes. —*n.* **6.** an alteration. **7.** a substitution. **8.** coins. —**change′a.ble,** *adj.*

change′ of life′ *n.* menopause.

change′o′ver *n.* a change from one system to another.

chan′nel (chan/l) *n.*, *v.*, **-neled, -neling.** —*n.* **1.** the bed of a stream. **2.** a wide strait. **3.** a route. **4.** a frequency band used by radio or television. —*v.t.* **5.** to convey or direct in a channel.

chant (chant) *n.* **1.** a simple melody. **2.** a phrase repeated rhythmically. —*v.i.* **3.** to sing in a chant. **4.** to shout rhythmically.

chant′ey (shan/tē) *n.*, *pl.* **-eys, -ies.** a sailors' song. Also, **chant′y.**

Cha′nu.kah (кнä′nə kə, hä/-) *n.* Hanukkah.

cha′os (kā/os) *n.* complete disorder. —**cha.ot′ic** (-ot/ik) *adj.*

chap¹ (chap) *v.i.*, **chapped, chapping.** to burn slightly. (of the skin) to become rough and red.

chap² (chap) *n. Informal.* a fellow.

chap. chapter.

chap′el (chap/əl) *n.* a private or subordinate place of worship.

chap′er.on′ (shap/ə rōn′) *n.*, *v.*, **-oned, -oning.** —*n.* **1.** an older person who accompanies younger persons at a social gathering. —*v.t.*, *v.i.* **2.** to be a chaperon (for). Also, **chap′er.one′.**

chap′lain (chap/lin) *n.* a member of the clergy associated with a college, hospital, etc.

chaps (chaps, shaps) *n.pl.* leather leg protectors worn by cowboys.

chap′ter (chap/tər) *n.* **1.** a division of a book. **2.** a branch of an organization.

char (chär) *v.t.*, *v.i.*, **charred, charring.** to burn slightly.

char′ac.ter (kar/ik tər) *n.* **1.** the qualities that form the individual nature of a person or thing. **2.** moral quality. **3.** reputation. **4.** a person in a novel, play, etc. **5.** a written or printed symbol.

char′ac.ter.is′tic (-tə ris/tik) *adj.* **1.** typical. —*n.* **2.** a special feature.

char′ac.ter.ize′ *v.t.*, **-ized, -izing. 1.** to be a characteristic of. **2.** to describe the character of. —**char/ac.ter.i.za′tion,** *n.*

cha.rades′ (shə rādz/) *n.* a guessing game in which players act out a word or phrase.

char′coal′ *n.* a black material made by burning wood without air.

chard (chärd) *n.* a plant with edible leafy green stalks.

charge (chärj) *v.*, **charged, charging**, *n.* —*v.t.* **1.** to ask as a price. **2.** to defer payment for. **3.** to attack by rushing violently at. **4.** to accuse. **5.** to command. **6.** to fill. **7.** to supply with electrical energy. —*v.i.* **8.** to rush violently. **9.** to require payment. —*n.* **10.** an expense or cost. **11.** an attack. **12.** a duty. **13.** a command. **14.** an accusation. —*Idiom.* **15.** in charge, in command. —**charge′a.ble,** *adj.*

charg′er *n.* a battle horse.

char′i.ot (char/ē ət) *n.* a horse-drawn two-wheeled vehicle of the ancient world. —**char/i.ot.eer′,** *n.*

cha.ris′ma (kə riz/mə) *n.* the power to charm and inspire people. —**char/is.mat′ic** (kar/iz mat/ik) *adj.*

char′i.ty (char/i tē) *n.*, *pl.* **-ties. 1.** generosity toward the needy. **2.** a fund or institution that benefits the needy. **3.** kindness in judging others. —**char/i.ta.ble,** *adj.*

char′la.tan (shär/lə tn) *n.* a quack; fraud.

charm (chärm) *n.* **1.** the power to attract. **2.** a magical object, verse, etc. **3.** a trinket on a bracelet or necklace. —*v.t.*, *v.i.* **4.** to attract; enchant. —**charm′ing,** *adj.*

char′nel house′ (chär/nl) *n.* a place for dead bodies.

chart (chärt) *n.* **1.** a sheet displaying data in tabular form. **2.** a map. —*v.t.* **3.** to make a chart of.

char′ter *n.* **1.** a governmental document outlining the conditions under which a corporate body is organized. **2.** a temporary lease of a bus, aircraft, etc. —*v.t.* **3.** to establish by charter. **4.** to hire; lease.

char′ter mem′ber *n.* an original member of an organization.

char.treuse′ (shär trōōz′) *n.* a yellowish green.

char′y (châr/ē) *adj.*, **charier, chariest.** careful.

chase (chās) *v.*, **chased, chasing**, *n.* —*v.t.* **1.** to follow in order to seize. **2.** to drive away. —*n.* **3.** an instance of chasing.

chasm (kaz/əm) *n.* **1.** a deep cleft in the earth. **2.** any gap.

chas′sis (chas/ē, shas/ē) *n.* the frame, wheels, and motor of a vehicle.

chaste (chāst) *adj.*, **chaster, chastest. 1.** refraining from unlawful sexual activity. **2.** celibate. **3.** simple. —**chas/ti.ty** (chas/ti tē) *n.*

chas′ten (chā/sən) *v.t.* to discipline by punishing.

chas·tise/ (chas tīz/, chas/tīz) v.t., **-tised, -tising. 1.** to punish; beat. **2.** to criticize severely.

chat (chat) v., **chatted, chatting,** n. —v.i. **1.** to talk informally. —n. **2.** an informal conversation.

cha·teau/ (sha tō/) n., pl. **-teaux** (-tōz/). a stately residence.

chat/ room/ n. a branch of a computer system in which participants can have live discussions.

chat/tel (chat/l) n. a movable article of personal property.

chat/ter (chat/ər) v.i. **1.** to talk rapidly or foolishly. **2.** to click rapidly. —n. **3.** rapid or foolish talk.

chat/ty (chat/ē) adj., **-tier, -tiest. 1.** given to chatting. **2.** having a friendly, informal style.

chauf/feur (shō/fər, shō fûr/) n. a hired driver.

chau/vin·ism/ (shō/və niz/əm) n. **1.** excessive patriotism. **2.** fanatic devotion to any group, cause, etc. —**chau/vin·ist** (-və nist) n., adj.

cheap (chēp) adj. **1.** inexpensive. **2.** shoddy. **3.** stingy. —**cheap/en,** v.t., v.i.

cheap/skate/ n. a stingy person.

cheat (chēt) v.t. **1.** to defraud; swindle. —v.i. **2.** to practice deceit. **3.** to violate rules. —n. **4.** a person who cheats. **5.** a fraud.

check (chek) v.t. **1.** to stop or restrain. **2.** to investigate; verify. **3.** to note with a mark. **4.** to leave or receive for temporary custody. —v.i. **5.** to make an inquiry. **6. check in,** to report one's arrival. **7.** ~ **out,** to leave a hotel, hospital, etc., officially. —n. **8.** a stop; restraint. **9.** a written order for a bank to pay money. **10.** an inquiry. **11.** a mark (✓) to indicate approval, verification, etc. **12.** a restaurant bill. **13.** an identification tag. **14.** a square pattern. **15.** Chess. a direct attack on the king.

check/er n. **1.** a piece used in checkers. **2. checkers,** a game played on a checkerboard by two persons, each with 12 playing pieces.

check/er·board/ n. a board with 64 squares on which checkers is played.

check/ered adj. **1.** marked with squares. **2.** varied. **3.** dubious.

check/list/ n. a list of items for comparison, verification, etc.

check/mate/ (-māt/) n., v., **-mated, -mating.** —n. **1.** Chess. an inescapable check. **2.** a defeat. —v.t. **3.** Chess. to put into inescapable check. **4.** to defeat.

check/out/ n. **1.** the act of leaving and paying for a hotel room. **2.** a counter where customers pay for purchases.

check/point/ n. a place where travelers are stopped for inspection.

check/up/ n. a physical examination.

ched/dar (ched/ər) n. a sharp cheese.

cheek (chēk) n. **1.** the soft side of the face. **2.** Informal. a cheerful lack of respect. —**cheek/i·ly,** adv. —**cheek/y,** adj.

cheer (chēr) n. **1.** a shout of support. **2.** gladness. —v.t. **3.** to shout encouragement to. **4.** to raise the spirits of. —v.i. **5.** to utter cheers. **6.** to become cheerful.

cheer/ful adj. **1.** full of cheer. **2.** pleasant and bright.

cheer/less adj. gloomy.

cheese (chēz) n. a food made from pressed milk curds.

cheese/burg/er n. a hamburger with melted cheese.

cheese/cloth/ n. a cotton fabric of loose weave.

chee/tah (chē/tə) n. a wild cat resembling the leopard.

chef (shef) n. a professional cook.

chem/i·cal (kem/i kəl) adj. **1.** of chemistry. —n. **2.** a substance produced by or used in chemistry. —**chem/i·cal·ly,** adv.

chem/ical war/fare n. warfare using chemicals as weapons.

che·mise/ (shə mēz/) n. a woman's shirtlike undergarment.

chem/is·try (kem/ə strē) n. **1.** the study of the composition and activity of substances. **2.** rapport. —**chem/ist,** n.

che/mo·ther/a·py (kē/mō ther/ə pē) n. the treatment of disease, esp. cancer, with chemicals.

cheque (chek) n. Brit. a bank check.

cher/ish (cher/ish) v.t. to treat as dear.

cher/ry (cher/ē) n., pl. **-ries.** a small, pulpy red fruit of certain trees.

cher/ub (cher/əb) n. **1.** pl. **cherubim** (-ə bim). a celestial being. **2.** pl. **cherubs.** a chubby child with wings.

chess (ches) n. a board game for two players, each using 16 pieces.

chest (chest) n. **1.** the part of the body between the neck and the abdomen. **2.** a large box with a lid. **3.** a set of drawers for clothes.

chest/nut/ (ches/nut/) n. **1.** an edible nut. **2.** a reddish brown.

chev/ron (shev/rən) n. a set of V-shaped stripes.

chew (chōō) v.t., v.i. to crush with the teeth.

chew/y adj., **-ier, -iest.** not easily chewed.

chic (shēk) *adj.* stylish.
—**Pronunciation.** The pronunciation (chik) for the word CHIC is
considered nonstandard except
when used jokingly.

chi·can·er·y (shi kā′nə rē, chi-) *n.,
pl.* **-ies. 1.** deception. **2.** a trick.

chick (chik) *n.* **1.** a young chicken.
2. *Slang: Usu. Offensive.* a young
woman.

chick′a·dee′ (chik′ə dē′) *n.* a small
gray bird with a dark cap.

chick′en (chik′ən) *n.* **1.** a common
domestic fowl. **2.** *Slang.* a coward.

chick′en·pox′ *n.* a viral disease
marked by the eruption of blisters.

chick′pea′ *n.* a legume with pealike seeds.

chic′o·ry (-ə rē) *n., pl.* **-ries. 1.** a
plant with toothed edible leaves.
2. its root, ground and used with
coffee.

chide (chīd) *v.t., v.i.,* **chided, chid-
ing.** to scold.

chief (chēf) *n.* **1.** a leader. —*adj.* **2.**
main; principal. —**chief′ly,** *adv.*

chief′tain (-tən) *n.* the chief of a
clan or tribe.

chif·fon′ (shi fon′) *n.* a sheer silk or
rayon fabric.

chig′ger (chig′ər) *n.* the larva of
certain parasite mites.

chil·blain (chil′blān) *n.* an inflammation caused by overexposure to
cold.

child (chīld) *n., pl.* **children** (chil′-
drən). **1.** a boy or girl. **2.** a son or
daughter. —**child′hood,** *n.*
—**child′ish,** *adj.* —**child′less,** *adj.*
—**child′like′,** *adj.*

child′bear′ing *n.* **1.** the act of
bringing forth children. —*adj.* **2.**
capable of or relating to the bearing of children.

child′birth *n.* an act or instance of
bringing forth a child.

child′proof′ *adj.* designed to prevent children from being hurt.

chil′i (chil′ē) *n., pl.* **-ies. 1.** the pungent pod of a red pepper. **2.** a dish
made with these peppers.

chill (chil) *n.* **1.** coldness. **2.** a cold
feeling with shivering. —*adj.* **3.**
cold. **4.** not cordial. —*v.t., v.i.* **5.** to
make or become cold. —**chill′ly,** *adj.*

chime (chīm) *n., v.,* **chimed, chiming.** —*n.* **1.** a set of musical tubes,
bells, etc. —*v.i.* **2.** to sound
chimes. —*v.t.* **3.** to announce by
chiming. **4. chime in,** to interrupt.

chi·me′ra (ki mēr′ə, kī-) *n.* **1.** (*often
cap.*) a mythical monster with a
lion's head, goat's body, and serpent's tail. **2.** an illusion.

chim′ney (chim′nē) *n., pl.* **-neys.** a
structure for carrying off smoke.

chim′pan·zee′ (chim′pan zē′, chim-

pan′zē) *n.* a large, intelligent African ape.

chin (chin) *n.* the part of the face
below the mouth.

chi′na (chī′nə) *n.* **1.** porcelain or
ceramic material. **2.** tableware
made of this.

chin·chil′la (chin chil′ə) *n.* a small
rodent valued for its fur.

chink¹ (chingk) *n.* a crack, as in a
wall.

chink² (chingk) *n.* **1.** a short, sharp
ringing sound. —*v.i.* **2.** to make
such a sound.

chintz (chints) *n.* a printed cotton
fabric.

chintz′y *adj.,* **-ier, -iest.** cheap-
looking.

chip (chip) *n., v.,* **chipped, chip-
ping.** —*n.* **1.** a small, thin, flat
piece, as of wood. **2.** a small piece
of food. **3.** a flaw where something
has broken off. **4.** a disk used in
games. **5.** a tiny slice of semicon-
ducting material carrying an electric circuit. —*v.t.* **6.** to break a fragment from. —*v.i.* **7.** to break off in
small bits. **8. chip in,** to contribute. —*Idiom.* **9. chip on one's
shoulder,** a readiness to quarrel.

chip′munk (-mungk) *n.* a small,
striped squirrel-like animal.

chip′per *adj. Informal.* lively.

chi·rop′o·dy (ki rop′ə dē, kī-) *n.*
podiatry.

chi′ro·prac′tor (kī′rə prak′tər) *n.*
one who treats pain by manipulating body structures.

chirp (chûrp) *n.* **1.** the short, sharp
sound made by small birds. —*v.i.*
2. to make such a sound. Also,
chir′rup (chēr′əp, chûr′-).

chis′el (chiz′əl) *n.* **1.** a tool with a
broad cutting tip. —*v.t., v.i.* **2.** to
cut with such a tool. **3.** *Informal.*
to cheat.

chit′chat′ (chit′chat′) *n.* light talk.

chiv′al·ry (shiv′əl rē) *n.* **1.** qualities
such as courtesy and courage. **2.**
medieval knighthood. —**chiv′-
al·rous,** *adj.*

chive (chīv) *n.* an onionlike plant
with slender leaves.

chlo′rine (klôr′ēn, -in) *n.* a green
gaseous element.

chlo′ro·form′ (klôr′ə fôrm′) *n.* **1.** a
colorless liquid whose gas causes
unconsciousness. —*v.t.* **2.** to administer chloroform to.

chlo′ro·phyll (-fil) *n.* the green coloring matter of plants.

chock (chok) *n.* a wedge; block.

choc′o·late (chô′kə lit) *n.* **1.** a product made from cacao seeds, usu.
sweetened. **2.** a candy or beverage
made from this. **3.** a dark brown.

choice (chois) *n.* **1.** the act of

choosing. **2.** the right to choose. **3.** a person or thing chosen. —*adj.* **4.** excellent.

choir (kwīⁱr) *n.* a group of singers, esp. in a church.

choke (chōk) *v.*, **choked, choking,** *n.* —*v.t.* **1.** to stop the breath of. **2.** to obstruct. —*v.i.* **3.** to be unable to breathe. **4.** to be obstructed. —*n.* **5.** the act of choking. **6.** a device that controls the flow of air in an automobile engine.

chol·er·a (kol′ər ə) *n.* a severe, contagious infection of the small intestine.

cho·les·te·rol′ (kə les′tə rôl′) *n.* a fatty, crystalline substance in animal products.

chomp (chomp) *v.t., v.i.* to chew noisily.

choose (chōōz) *v.*, **chose** (chōz), **chosen, choosing.** —*v.t.* **1.** to select from a number of things. **2.** to desire. —*v.i.* **3.** to make a choice.

choos′y *adj.*, **-ier, -iest.** hard to please; particular.

chop¹ (chop) *v.*, **chopped, chopping,** *n.* —*v.t.* **1.** to cut with blows. **2.** to cut in pieces. —*n.* **3.** a sharp blow. **4.** a thick slice of meat with the rib.

chop² (chop) *n.* Usu., **chops,** the jaw.

chop′per *n.* **1.** a thing that chops. **2.** *Informal.* a helicopter.

chop′py *adj.*, **-pier, -piest. 1.** (of a body of water) forming short waves. **2.** uneven.

chop′sticks′ *n.pl.* sticks used in eating in some Asian countries.

cho′ral (kôr′əl) *adj.* of or for a chorus or choir.

cho·rale′ (kə ral′, -räl′) *n.* **1.** a type of hymn. **2.** a choir.

chord¹ (kôrd) *n.* a combination of notes sounded together.

chord² (kôrd) *n.* the line segment between two points on a curve.

chore (chôr) *n.* a routine job.

cho′re·og′ra·phy (kôr′ē og′rə fē) *n.* **1.** the art of composing dances. **2.** the movements composed for a dance, show, etc. —**cho′re·o· graph′** (-ə graf′) *v.t., v.i.*

chor·is·ter (-ə stər) *n.* a singer in a choir.

chor′tle (chôr′tl) *v.*, **-tled, -tling,** *n.* —*v.i.* **1.** to chuckle gleefully. —*n.* **2.** a gleeful chuckle.

cho′rus (kôr′əs) *n.* **1.** a group of singers. **2.** a refrain. **3.** something said or sung by many people, birds, etc. —*v.t., v.i.* **4.** to sing or speak simultaneously.

chose (chōz) *v.* pt. of **choose.**

chow (chou) *n. Slang.* food.

chow′der (chou′dər) *n.* a thick soup of vegetables, clams, etc.

Christ (krīst) *n.* Jesus Christ; (in Christian belief) the Messiah.

chris′ten (kris′ən) *v.t.* **1.** to baptize; name. **2.** to name at baptism.

Chris′ten·dom (-dəm) *n.* all Christians.

Chris′tian (kris′chən) *adj.* **1.** of Jesus Christ, His teachings, etc. —*n.* **2.** a believer in Christianity.

Chris′ti·an′i·ty (-chē an′i tē) *n.* the religion based on the teachings of Jesus Christ.

Christ′mas (-məs) *n.* an annual Christian festival honoring the birth of Jesus, celebrated on December 25.

chro·mat′ic (krō mat′ik, krə-) *adj.* **1.** of color. **2.** progressing by semitones.

chro′mi·um (krō′mē əm) *n.* a lustrous metallic element. Also, **chrome.**

chro·mo·some′ (krō′mə sōm′) *n.* the threadlike part of a cell that carries the genes.

chron′ic (kron′ik) *adj.* constant; long-lasting; habitual.

chron′i·cle (kron′i kəl) *n., v.*, **-cled, -cling.** —*n.* **1.** a record of events in order. —*v.t.* **2.** to record in a chronicle.

chrono- a prefix meaning time.

chro·nol·o·gy (krə nol′ə jē) *n., pl.* **-gies.** an arrangement of things in the order in which they occurred. —**chron′o·log′i·cal** (kron′l oj′i kəl) *adj.*

chro·nom′e·ter (krə nom′i tər) *n.* a very precise clock.

chrys′a·lis (kris′ə lis) *n.* the pupa of a moth or butterfly.

chry·san′the·mum (kri san′thə- məm) *n.* a plant that produces colorful flowers in the autumn.

chub′by *adj.*, **-bier, -biest.** plump.

chuck¹ (chuk) *v.t.* **1.** to toss. **2.** to pat lightly. —*n.* **3.** a light pat.

chuck² (chuk) *n.* the cut of beef between the neck and the shoulder blade.

chuck′le (chuk′əl) *v.*, **-led, -ling,** *n.* —*v.i.* **1.** to laugh softly. —*n.* **2.** a soft laugh.

chum (chum) *n.* a close friend.

chump (chump) *n. Informal.* a fool.

chunk (chungk) *n.* a thick piece.

chunk′y *adj.*, **-ier, -iest. 1.** thick or stocky. **2.** full of chunks.

church (chûrch) *n.* **1.** a place of Christian worship. **2.** a religious service. **3.** (*sometimes cap.*) a Christian denomination.

churl′ish (chûr′lish) *adj.* boorish.

churn (chûrn) *n.* **1.** a container in which cream or milk is beaten to make butter. —*v.t.* **2.** to agitate (cream or milk) or make (butter) in a churn. **3.** to shake briskly. —*v.i.* **4.** to move or shake in agitation.

chute (sho͞ot) *n.* a sloping slide.

chut′ney (chut′nē) *n.* an East Indian relish.

chutz′pah (KHo͞ot′spə, ho͞ot′-) *n. Slang.* nerve; gall. Also, **chutz′pa.**

CIA Central Intelligence Agency.

ci·ca′da (si kā′də) *n.* a large insect with a shrill call.

-cide a suffix indicating: **1.** a killer. **2.** the act of killing.

ci′der (sī′dər) *n.* apple juice.

ci·gar′ (si gär′) *n.* a roll of tobacco leaves for smoking.

cig′a·rette′ (sig′ə ret′) *n.* tobacco rolled in paper for smoking.

cinch (sinch) *n.* **1.** a strap for securing a saddle. **2.** *Informal.* a sure or easy thing.

cin′der (sin′dər) *n.* a partially burned piece; ash.

cin′e·ma (sin′ə mə) *n.* **1.** motion pictures. **2.** a movie theater.

cin′e·ma·tog′ra·phy (-tog′rə fē) *n.* the art or technique of motion-picture photography.

cin′na·mon (sin′ə mən) *n.* a brown spice from the bark of an Asian tree.

ci′pher (sī′fər) *n.* **1.** the symbol (0) for zero. **2.** secret writing.

cir′ca (sûr′kə) *prep.* approximately.

cir′cle (sûr′kəl) *n., v.,* **-cled, -cling.** —*n.* **1.** a closed plane curve with all points at a uniform distance from its center. **2.** a range; scope. **3.** a group of friends or associates. —*v.t.* **4.** to enclose in a circle. **5.** to revolve around. —*v.i.* **6.** to move in a circle.

cir′cuit (-kit) *n.* **1.** a line or route around an area or object. **2.** a tour, esp. in connection with duties. **3.** an electrical path. —**cir′cuit·ry,** *n.*

cir′cuit break′er *n.* a device that interrupts an electrical circuit to prevent excessive current.

cir·cu′i·tous (sər kyo͞o′i təs) *adj.* roundabout. —**cir·cu′i·tous·ly,** *adv.*

cir′cu·lar (-kyə lər) *adj.* **1.** of or in a circle. —*n.* **2.** a letter or advertisement for general circulation.

cir′cu·late′ (-lāt′) *v.,* **-lated, -lating.** —*v.i.* **1.** to move around. —*v.t.* **2.** to distribute. —**cir′cu·la·to′ry** (-lə-tôr′ē) *adj.*

circum- a prefix indicating around or about.

cir′cum·cise′ (sûr′kəm sīz′) *v.t.,* **-cised, -cising.** to remove the foreskin of. —**cir′cum·ci′sion** (-sizh′ən) *n.*

cir·cum′fer·ence (sər kum′fər əns) *n.* the outer boundary of a circle.

cir′cum·flex′ (sûr′kəm fleks′) *n.* a diacritical mark (^).

cir′cum·lo·cu′tion (-lō kyo͞o′shən) *n.* a roundabout expression.

cir′cum·nav′i·gate′ *v.t.,* **-gated, -gating.** to sail around.

cir′cum·scribe′ *v.t.,* **-scribed, -scribing.** **1.** to encircle. **2.** to confine.

cir′cum·spect′ (-spekt′) *adj.* cautious; watchful. —**cir′cum·spec′tion** (-spek′shən) *n.*

cir′cum·stance′ (-stans′) *n.* **1.** a condition accompanying or affecting a fact or event. **2.** Usu., **circumstances.** the existing conditions. **3. circumstances,** a person's condition with respect to material welfare. **4.** ceremony.

cir′cum·stan′tial (-stan′shəl) *adj.* **1.** of or from circumstances. **2.** incidental.

cir′cum·vent′ (-vent′) *v.t.* to outwit or evade. —**cir′cum·ven′tion,** *n.*

cir′cus (sûr′kəs) *n.* a show with animals, acrobats, etc.

cir·rho′sis (si rō′sis) *n.* a chronic liver disease.

cir′rus (sir′əs) *n.* a fleecy cloud.

cis′tern (sis′tərn) *n.* a water tank.

cit′a·del (sit′ə dl, -ə del′) *n.* a fortress.

cite (sīt) *v.t.,* **cited, citing. 1.** to quote as an authority or example. **2.** to summon to appear in court. **3.** to commend. —**ci·ta′tion,** *n.*

cit′i·zen (sit′ə zən, -sən) *n.* a native or naturalized inhabitant of a country. —**cit′i·zen·ship′,** *n.*

cit′ric ac′id (si′trik) *n.* a white powder found in citrus fruits.

cit′ron (si′trən) *n.* a lemonlike fruit.

cit′ro·nel′la (si′trə nel′ə) *n.* a pungent oil that repels insects.

cit′rus (si′trəs) *n.* a fruit such as the orange, lemon, etc.

cit′y (sit′ē) *n., pl.* **-ies.** a large town.

civ′ic (siv′ik) *adj.* of a city or citizens.

civ′ics *n.* the study of civic affairs.

civ′il (-əl) *adj.* **1.** of citizens. **2.** civilized. **3.** polite. —**ci·vil′i·ty** (-vil′i-tē) *n.*

ci·vil′ian (si vil′yən) *n.* **1.** a person not on active duty with the military, police, etc. —*adj.* **2.** of such persons.

civ′i·li·za′tion (siv′ə lə zā′shən) *n.* **1.** the act or process of civilizing. **2.** the culture of a people or period. **3.** civilized conditions.

civ′i·lize (-līz′) *v.t.,* **-lized, -lizing.** to bring out of a savage state.

civ′il lib′erty *n.* a fundamental right guaranteed by law.

civ′il rights′ *n.pl.* the rights of all people to freedom and equality.

civ′il ser′vant *n.* an employee of the civil service.

civ′il ser′vice *n.* the branches of governmental administration outside the armed services.

civ′il war′ *n.* a war between citizens of the same country.

cl. centiliter.

claim (klām) *v.t.* **1.** to demand as one's right, property, etc. **2.** to assert. —*n.* **3.** a demand. **4.** an assertion. **5.** something claimed. —**claim′ant,** *n.*

clair•voy′ant (klâr voi′ənt) *adj.* **1.** seeing beyond physical vision. —*n.* **2.** a person who has the ability to see beyond physical vision.

clam (klam) *n.* a hard-shelled, edible bivalve mollusk.

clam′ber (klam′bər, klam′ər) *v.t., v.i.* to climb awkwardly.

clam′my *adj.,* -**mier,** -**miest.** cold and damp. —**clam′mi•ness,** *n.*

clam′or (klam′ər) *n.* **1.** a loud outcry or noise. —*v.i.* **2.** to raise a clamor. —**clam′or•ous,** *adj.*

clamp (klamp) *n.* **1.** a device for holding objects together. —*v.t.* **2.** to fasten with a clamp.

clan (klan) *n.* a group of related families.

clan•des′tine (klan des′tin) *adj.* done in secret.

clang (klang) *v.i., v.t.* **1.** to ring harshly. —*n.* **2.** Also, **clang′or.** a harsh ring.

clank (klangk) *n.* **1.** a sharp, hard, nonvibrating sound. —*v.i., v.t.* **2.** to make or cause to make such a sound.

clap (klap) *v.,* **clapped, clapping,** *n.* —*v.t.* **1.** to hit together, as hands. —*v.i.* **2.** to applaud. —*n.* **3.** the act or sound of clapping.

clap′board (klab′ərd) *n.* overlapping boards on exterior walls.

clap′trap′ (klap′-) *n.* insincere speech.

clar′i•fy′ (klar′ə fī′) *v.t., v.i.,* -**fied,** -**fying.** to make or become clear. —**clar′i•fi•ca′tion,** *n.*

clar′i•net′ (-ə net′) *n.* a single-reed woodwind instrument.

clar′i•on (-ē ən) *adj.* clear and shrill.

clar′i•ty (-i tē) *n.* clearness.

clash (klash) *v.i.* **1.** to conflict. **2.** to collide loudly. —*v.t.* **3.** to strike with a loud sound. —*n.* **4.** a collision. **5.** a conflict.

clasp (klasp) *n.* **1.** a fastening device. **2.** a firm grasp. **3.** a hug. —*v.t.* **4.** to fasten. **5.** to grasp with the hand. **6.** to hug.

class (klas) *n.* **1.** a group of similar persons or things. **2.** social rank. **3.** a group of students. **4.** a divi-

sion. **5.** *Informal.* elegance, grace, or dignity. —*v.t.* **6.** to classify.

class′ action′ *n.* a lawsuit on behalf of persons with a complaint in common.

clas′sic (klas′ik) *adj.* Also, **clas′si•cal.** **1.** of the finest type. **2.** serving as a standard. **3.** in the Greek or Roman manner. —*n.* **4.** an author, book, etc., of acknowledged superiority. —**clas′si•cism′** (klas′ə-siz′əm) *n.*

clas′si•fied′ (klas′ə fīd′) *adj.* limited to authorized persons.

clas′si•fy′ *v.t.,* -**fied,** -**fying.** to arrange in classes. —**clas′si•fi•ca′tion,** *n.*

class′mate′ *n.* a member of the same class at school or college.

class′room′ *n.* a room in which classes are held.

class′y *adj.,* -**ier,** -**iest.** *Informal.* stylish; elegant.

clat′ter (klat′ər) *v.t., v.i.* **1.** to make or cause to make a rattling sound. —*n.* **2.** such a sound.

clause (klôz) *n.* **1.** a part of a sentence with its own subject and predicate. **2.** a part of a document.

claus′tro•pho′bi•a (klô′strə fō′bē ə) *n.* a fear of being in closed places. —**claus′tro•pho′bic,** *adj., n.*

clav′i•chord′ (klav′i kôrd′) *n.* an early keyboard instrument.

clav′i•cle (klav′i kəl) *n.* the slender bone connecting the scapula and the sternum.

claw (klô) *n.* **1.** a sharp, curved nail on an animal's paw. —*v.t.* **2.** to tear or scratch roughly.

clay (klā) *n.* a soft earthy material, flexible when wet, used in making bricks, pottery, etc.

clean (klēn) *adj.* **1.** free from dirt or foreign matter. **2.** pure. —*adv.* **3.** completely. —*v.t., v.i.* **4.** to make or become clean. **5. clean up, a.** to tidy up. **b.** to finish. **c.** to make a large profit. —**clean′er,** *n.*

clean•ly (klen′lē) *adj.* **1.** keeping or kept clean. —*adv.* **2.** in a clean manner. —**clean′li•ness,** *n.*

cleanse (klenz) *v.t.,* **cleansed, cleansing.** to clean or purify.

clear (klēr) *adj.* **1.** transparent. **2.** easily seen, heard, or understood. **3.** evident. **4.** unobstructed. **5.** free of obligations. **6.** blameless. —*adv.* **7.** in a clear manner. —*v.t., v.i.* **8.** to make or become clear. **9.** to pay in full. **10.** to pass beyond. **11. clear up,** to explain. —**clear′ly,** *adv.*

clear′ance *n.* **1.** the space between two objects. **2.** an authorization. **3.** Also called **clearance sale.** the sale of goods at very low prices to make room for new merchandise.

clear′-cut′ *adj.* **1.** having clear outlines. **2.** definite.

clear′ing *n.* a treeless space, as in a forest.

cleat (klēt) *n.* a metal piece fastened to a surface to give support or prevent slipping.

cleav′age (klē′vij) *n.* **1.** a split or division. **2.** the space between a woman's breasts.

cleave¹ (klēv) *v.t., v.i.,* **cleft** (kleft) or **cleaved, cleaving.** to split or divide.

cleave² (klēv) *v.i.,* **cleaved, cleaving.** **1.** to cling. **2.** to remain faithful.

cleav′er *n.* a heavy knife.

clef (klef) *n.* a sign on a musical staff that indicates pitch.

cleft (kleft) *n.* a split.

cleft′ lip′ *n.* a birth defect in which there is a vertical fissure in the upper lip.

cleft′ pal′ate *n.* a birth defect in which there is a fissure in the roof of the mouth.

clem•a•tis (klem′ə tis) *n.* a climbing vine having showy flowers.

clem′ent (klem′ənt) *adj.* **1.** merciful. **2.** (of the weather) mild. **—clem′en•cy,** *n.*

clench (klench) *v.t.* to close tightly.

cler′gy (klûr′jē) *n., pl.* **-gies.** the body of ordained persons in a religious denomination.

cler′ic (kler′ik) *n.* a member of the clergy.

cler′i•cal *adj.* **1.** of clerks. **2.** of the clergy.

clerk (klûrk) *n.* **1.** a person who does office tasks, keeps records, etc. **2.** a salesperson in a store.

clev′er (klev′ər) *adj.* bright, witty, or creative. **—clev′er•ly,** *adv.*

cli•ché′ (klē shā′) *n.* a trite expression.

click (klik) *n.* **1.** a slight, sharp sound. **—v.i. 2.** to make a click. **3.** *Informal.* to succeed. **—v.t. 4.** to cause to click.

cli′ent (klī′ənt) *n.* **1.** a person who uses the services of a professional. **2.** a customer.

cli′en•tele′ (-ən tel′) *n.* clients.

cliff (klif) *n.* a high, steep rock face.

cliff′-hang′er *n.* a suspenseful situation.

cli′mate (klī′mit) *n.* the prevailing weather conditions of an area. **—cli•mat′ic** (-mat′ik) *adj.*

cli′max (klī′maks) *n.* **1.** the highest point. **2.** a decisive moment in a plot. **3.** an orgasm. **—cli•mac′tic** (-mak′tik) *adj.*

climb (klīm) *v.i.* **1.** to move upward or toward the top. **—v.t. 2.** to get

to the top of. **—n. 3.** an ascent made by climbing.

clinch (klinch) *v.t.* **1.** to settle (a matter) decisively. **2.** to fasten (a nail) by bending the point. **—n. 3.** the act of clinching. **—clinch′er,** *n.*

cling (kling) *v.i.,* **clung** (klung), **clinging.** to hold firmly to a person, idea, etc.

clin′ic (klin′ik) *n.* a place for the medical treatment of outpatients.

clink (klingk) *v.i., v.t.* **1.** to make a light, ringing sound. **—n. 2.** such a sound.

clink′er (kling′kər) *n.* a fused stony mass, esp. in a furnace.

clip (klip) *v.,* **clipped, clipping,** *n.* **—v.t. 1.** to cut or cut off with short snips. **2.** *Informal.* to hit sharply. **—n. 3.** an act of clipping. **4.** a clasp. **5.** a cartridge holder.

clip′per (klip′ər) *n.* **1.** a cutting device. **2.** a fast sailing ship.

clique (klēk) *n.* a small, exclusive group.

clit•o•ris (klit′ər is) *n., pl.* **clitorises** or **clitorides** (kli tôr′i dēz′). the erectile organ of the vulva.

cloak (klōk) *n.* **1.** a loose outer garment. **—v.t. 2.** to cover with a cloak. **3.** to conceal.

cloak′-and-dag′ger *adj.* of espionage or intrigue.

clob′ber (klob′ər) *v.t. Informal.* **1.** to batter. **2.** to defeat decisively.

clock (klok) *n.* a device for telling time.

clock′wise′ *adv., adj.* in the direction that clock hands turn.

clock′work′ *n.* the mechanism of a clock.

clod (klod) *n.* a piece of earth.

clog (klog) *v.,* **clogged, clogging,** *n.* **—v.t. 1.** to obstruct. **—n. 2.** anything that obstructs. **3.** a shoe with a thick rubber or wooden sole.

clois′ter (kloi′stər) *n.* **1.** a covered walk. **2.** a monastery or nunnery.

clone (klōn) *n., v.,* **cloned, cloning.** **—n. 1.** an organism created by asexual reproduction. **2.** *Informal.* a duplicate. **—v.i., v.t. 3.** to grow or cause to grow as a clone.

close *v.,* **closed, closing,** *adj.,* **closer, closest,** *adv., n.* **—v.t.** (klōz) **1.** to shut or obstruct. **2.** to bring to an end. **3.** to bring together. **—v.i. 4.** to become closed. **5.** to reach an agreement. **6. close in on,** to approach stealthily. **—adj.** (klōs) **7.** near. **8.** intimate. **9.** compact. **10.** lacking fresh air. **11.** secretive. **12.** nearly equal. **—adv.** (klōs) **13.** in a close manner. **14.** near. **—n.** (klōz) **15.** the end. **—close′ly,** *adv.*

close′ call′ (klōs) n. a narrow escape.

closed′-cap′tioned adj. broadcast with captions visible only with a decoding device.

close′out′ (klōz′-) n. a sale on goods at greatly reduced prices.

clos′et (kloz′it) n. 1. a small room or cabinet for clothes, utensils, etc. —adj. 2. secret. —v.t. 3. to shut up in a private room for a talk.

close′up′ (klōs′-) n. a photograph taken at close range.

clo′sure n. 1. closing or being closed. 2. a conclusion. 3. something that closes.

clot (klot) n., v., **clotted, clotting.** —n. 1. a mass, esp. of dried blood. —v.i., v.t. 2. to form a clot.

cloth (klôth) n. 1. a fabric of woven or knitted threads. 2. a piece of such a fabric. 3. **the cloth,** the clergy. —adj. 4. made of cloth.

clothe (klōth) v.t., **clothed** or **clad** (klad) **clothing.** to dress or cover.

clothes (klōz, klōth̲z) n.pl. garments; apparel. Also, **cloth′ing.**

cloud (kloud) n. 1. a visible mass of water or ice in the air. 2. a mass of smoke or dust. 3. anything causing gloom. —v.t. 4. to cover with clouds or gloom. —v.i. 5. to become cloudy. —Idiom. 6. **under a cloud,** in disgrace.

clout (klout) n. 1. a blow with the hand. 2. Informal. influence. —v.t. 3. to hit with the hand.

clove[1] (klōv) n. a tropical spice.

clove[2] (klōv) n. a section of a plant bulb, as of garlic.

clo′ver (klō′vər) n. a plant with three-part leaves and dense flower heads.

clown (kloun) n. 1. a comic performer. 2. a prankster. 3. a fool. —v.i. 4. to act like a clown.

cloy (kloi) v.t., v.i. to weary by excess, as of sweetness.

club (klub) n., v., **clubbed, clubbing.** —n. 1. a heavy stick or bat. 2. an organized group. 3. **clubs,** a suit of playing cards. —v.t. 4. to beat with a club. —v.i. 5. to unite.

club′foot′ n. a deformed foot.

club′ so′da n. soda water.

cluck (kluk) n. 1. the call of a hen. —v.i. 2. to utter such a call.

clue (kloo) n. a guide in solving a problem, mystery, etc.

clump (klump) n. 1. a cluster. 2. a mass. —v.i. 3. to walk heavily. 4. to gather into clumps.

clum′sy (klum′zē) adj., **-sier, -siest.** awkward. —**clum′si•ly,** adv.

clung (klung) v. pt. and pp. of **cling.**

clus′ter (klus′tər) n. 1. a group; bunch. —v.t., v.i. 2. to gather into or form a cluster.

clutch (kluch) v.t. 1. to grasp tightly. —n. 2. a tight grip. 3. **clutches,** control. 4. a device for engaging or disengaging machinery.

clut′ter (klut′ər) v.t. 1. to litter with things in a disorderly way. —n. 2. things scattered in disorder.

cm centimeter.

CO 1. Colorado. 2. Commanding Officer.

co- a prefix indicating: 1. together. 2. joint.

Co. 1. Company. 2. County.

c/o care of.

coach (kōch) n. 1. an enclosed carriage, bus, etc. 2. an athletic trainer or a private tutor. 3. the least expensive class of air travel. —v.t. 4. to instruct.

co•ag′u•late′ (kō ag′yə lāt′) v.i., v.t., **-lated, -lating.** to thicken or clot.

coal (kōl) n. a black mineral burned as fuel.

co•a•lesce′ (kō′ə les′) v.i., **-lesced, -lescing.** to unite or grow together.

co•a•li′tion (-lish′ən) n. an alliance.

coarse (kôrs) adj., **coarser, coarsest.** 1. composed of large particles. 2. rough. 3. vulgar. —**coarse′ly,** adv. —**coars′en,** v.t., v.i.

coast (kōst) n. 1. the seashore. —v.i. 2. to drift easily. —**coast′al,** adj.

coast′er n. a small dish or mat for placing under a glass.

coast′ guard′ n. the military service that enforces maritime laws, saves lives at sea, etc.

coat (kōt) n. 1. an outer garment. 2. a covering, as fur or bark. 3. a layer of anything that covers. —v.t. 4. to cover with a coat.

coat′ing n. an outer layer.

coat′ of arms′ n. the emblems, motto, etc., of one's family.

co•au′thor (kō ô′thər, kō′ô′-) n. 1. one of two or more joint authors. —v.t. 2. to be a coauthor of.

coax (kōks) v.t., v.i. to urge by persuasion, flattery, etc.

co•ax′i•al (kō ak′sē əl) adj. having a common axis, as **coaxial cables** for simultaneous long-distance transmission of television signals.

cob (kob) n. a corncob.

co′balt (kō′bôlt) n. 1. a silvery metallic element. 2. a deep blue.

cob′ble (kob′əl) v.t., **-bled, -bling.** 1. to mend (shoes). 2. to put together clumsily. —**cob′bler,** n.

co′bra (kō′brə) n. a poisonous snake of India and Africa.

cob′web′ (kob′-) n. a spider web.

co•caine/ (kō kān/, kō/kān) *n.* a narcotic drug obtained from a South American shrub.

cock¹ (kok) *n.* **1.** a rooster. **2.** a male bird. **3.** a valve. **4.** the hammer in a gun. —*v.t.* **5.** to set the cock of (a gun).

cock² (kok) *v.t.* to turn up or to one side.

cock/a•too/ (kok/ə tōō/, kok/ə tōō/) *n.* a crested parrot.

cock/eyed/ *adj.* **1.** tilted to one side. **2.** ridiculous.

cock/le (kok/əl) *n.* **1.** a mollusk with heart-shaped valves. —*Idiom.* **2.** cockles of one's heart, the place of one's deepest feelings.

cock/pit/ *n.* a place for a pilot.

cock/roach/ *n.* a rapid crawling insect with a flat body.

cock/tail/ *n.* a drink containing chilled liquors and flavoring.

cock/y *adj.*, **-ier, -iest.** arrogant; conceited. —**cock/i•ness,** *n.*

co/coa (kō/kō) *n.* **1.** the powdered seeds of cacao. **2.** a beverage made from this. **3.** a shade of brown.

co/co•nut/ (kō/kə nut/, -nət) *n.* the large, hard-shelled seed of the **co/co palm.**

co•coon/ (kə kōōn/) *n.* the silky covering spun by insect larvae.

cod (kod) *n.* an edible N Atlantic fish.

C.O.D. cash, or collect, on delivery.

co/da (kō/də) *n.* the final passage of a musical movement.

cod/dle (kod/l) *v.t.*, **-dled, -dling. 1.** to pamper. **2.** to cook in water just below the boiling point.

code (kōd) *n.*, *v.*, **coded, coding.** —*n.* **1.** a system of laws or rules. **2.** a system of signals or secret words. —*v.t.* **3.** to put into code.

co/deine (kō/dēn) *n.* a drug derived from opium, used to relieve pain.

codg/er (koj/ər) *n.* an eccentric elderly man.

cod/i•cil (kod/ə səl) *n.* a supplement to a will.

cod/i•fy/ (kod/ə fī/, kō/də-) *v.t.*, **-fied, -fying.** to organize into a formal code. —**cod/i•fi•ca/tion,** *n.*

co/ed/ (kō/ed/, -ed/) *adj.* **1.** serving both men and woman; coeducational. —*n.* **2.** a female student, esp. in a coeducational school.

co/ed•u•ca/tion *n.* education of both sexes in the same classes.

co/ef•fi/cient (kō/ə fish/ənt) *n.* a number by which another is multiplied.

co•erce/ (kō ûrs/) *v.t.*, **-erced, -ercing.** to compel or bring about by force or threats. —**co•er/cion** (-ûr/-shən) *n.* —**co•er/cive,** *adj.*

co/ex•ist/ *v.i.* **1.** to exist at the same time. **2.** to exist together peacefully. —**co/ex•ist/ence,** *n.*

cof/fee (kô/fē) *n.* a beverage made from the roasted and ground seeds of a tropical tree.

cof/fer (kô/fər, kof/ər) *n.* **1.** a box for valuables. **2. coffers,** the treasury of an organization.

cof/fin (kô/fin) *n.* a box for a corpse.

cog (kog) *n.* a tooth on a wheel (**cog/wheel/**), connecting with another such wheel.

co/gent (kō/jənt) *adj.* convincing. —**co/gen•cy,** *n.* —**co/gent•ly,** *adv.*

cog/i•tate/ (koj/i tāt/) *v.i.*, *v.t.*, **-tated, -tating.** to think deeply (about). —**cog/i•ta/tion,** *n.*

co/gnac (kōn/yak) *n.* brandy.

cog/nate (kog/nāt) *adj.* **1.** related or similar. —*n.* **2.** a related word.

cog•ni/tion (-nish/ən) *n.* **1.** the act or process of knowing. **2.** something known.

cog/ni•zance (-nə zəns) *n.* awareness. —**cog/ni•zant,** *adj.*

co/gno•scen/ti (kon/yə shen/tē, kog/nə-) *n.pl., sing.* **-te** (-tā, -tē). those having superior knowledge of a particular field.

co•hab/it (kō hab/it) *v.i.* to live together, esp. as husband and wife, without being married. —**co•hab/i•ta/tion,** *n.*

co•here/ (kō hēr/) *v.i.*, **-hered, -hering.** to stick together.

co•her/ent (-hēr/ənt, -her/-) *adj.* logically connected. —**co•her/ence,** *n.*

co•he/sion (-hē/zhən) *n.* the act or state of cohering, uniting, or sticking together. —**co•he/sive,** *adj.*

co/hort (kō/hôrt) *n.* **1.** a companion. **2.** a group, esp. of soldiers.

coif•fure/ (kwä fyŏŏr/) *n.* a hairstyle.

coil (koil) *v.t.*, *v.i.* **1.** to wind in rings. —*n.* **2.** a series of spirals or rings. **3.** one such ring.

coin (koin) *n.* **1.** a piece of metal used as money. —*v.t.* **2.** to make metal into money. **3.** to invent (a word). —**coin/age,** *n.*

co/in•cide/ (kō/in sīd/) *v.i.*, **-cided, -ciding. 1.** to occur at the same time, place, etc. **2.** to match.

co/i•tus (kō/i təs) *n.* sexual intercourse. —**co/i•tal,** *adj.*

coke¹ (kōk) *n.* the solid carbon produced from coal.

coke² (kōk) *n. Slang.* cocaine.

Col. 1. Colonel. **2.** Colorado.

co/la (kō/lə) *n.* a soft drink containing an extract from kola nuts.

col/an•der (kul/ən dər, kol/-) *n.* a perforated container for draining foods.

cold (kōld) *adj.* **1.** having a low temperature. **2.** not affectionate or cordial. —*n.* **3.** the absence of heat. **4.** a common illness marked by sneezing, coughing, etc. —*Idiom.* **5.** out in the cold, neglected. —**cold′ly,** *adv.*

cold′-blood′ed *adj.* **1.** having blood at the same temperature as the environment. **2.** without feeling.

cold′ cream′ *n.* a preparation for cleansing or soothing the skin.

cold′ feet′ *n. Informal.* a lack of courage.

cold′ shoul′der *n.* a deliberate show of indifference.

cold′ tur′key *Informal.* —*n.* **1.** abrupt withdrawal from an addictive substance. —*adv.* **2.** impromptu.

cold′ war′ *n.* rivalry between nations just short of armed conflict.

cole•slaw′ (kōl′slô′) *n.* a salad of sliced raw cabbage.

col′ic (kol′ik) *n.* acute pain in the abdomen. —**col′ick•y,** *adj.*

col•i•se′um (kol′i sē′əm) *n.* a large stadium.

co•li′tis (kə lī′tis, kō-) *n.* inflammation of the colon.

col•lab′o•rate′ (kə lab′ə rāt′) *v.i.,* **-rated, -rating. 1.** to work with another. **2.** to cooperate with the enemy. —**col•lab′o•ra′tion,** *n.* —**col•lab′o•ra′tor,** *n.*

col•lage′ (kə läzh′) *n.* a work of art made by pasting various materials on a surface.

col•lapse′ (kə laps′) *v.,* **-lapsed, -lapsing,** *n.* —*v.i.* **1.** to fall in or together. **2.** to fail abruptly. —*v.t.* **3.** to cause to collapse. —*n.* **4.** a falling in or down. **5.** a sudden failure. —**col•laps′i•ble,** *adj.*

col′lar (kol′ər) *n.* **1.** the part of a garment around the neck. —*v.t.* **2.** to seize by the collar.

col′lar•bone′ *n.* the clavicle.

col•lat′er•al (kə lat′ər əl) *n.* **1.** security pledged on loan. —*adj.* **2.** additional. **3.** secondary.

col′league (kol′ēg) *n.* a fellow worker.

col•lect′ (kə lekt′) *v.t.* **1.** to gather together. **2.** to take payment of. —*v.i.* **3.** to accumulate. —*adj., adv.* **4.** payable on delivery. —**col•lec′tion,** *n.* —**col•lec′tor,** *n.*

col•lect′i•ble *n.* **1.** an object collected. —*adj.* **2.** able to be collected.

col•lec′tive *adj.* **1.** combined. **2.** of a group.

collec′tive bar′gaining *n.* negotiation between a union and employer.

col′lege (kol′ij) *n.* a degree-granting school of higher learning. —**col•le′giate** (kə lē′jit) *adj.*

col•lide′ (kə līd′) *v.i.,* **-lided, -liding. 1.** to strike one another violently; crash. **2.** to conflict.

col′lie (kol′ē) *n.* a kind of large, long-haired dog.

col′lier (kol′yər) *n.* a coal miner.

col•li′sion (kə lizh′ən) *n.* **1.** a crash. **2.** a conflict.

col•lo′qui•al (kə lō′kwē əl) *adj.* appropriate to casual rather than formal speech or writing.

col•lo′qui•um (-kwē əm) *n., pl.* **-qui•ums, -quia** (-kwē ə). a conference of experts in a field.

col′lo•quy (kol′ə kwē) *n., pl.* **-quies.** a discussion.

col•lu′sion (kə lōō′zhən) *n.* a conspiracy for illegal purposes.

Colo. Colorado.

co•logne′ (kə lōn′) *n.* a mildly perfumed liquid.

co′lon[1] (kō′lən) *n.* a punctuation mark (:).

co′lon[2] (kō′lən) *n.* the lower part of the large intestine.

colo′nel (kûr′nl) *n.* a military officer ranking below a general.

co•lo′ni•al•ism (kə lō′nē ə liz′əm) *n.* the policy of extending national authority over foreign territories.

col′on•nade′ (kol′ə nād′) *n.* a series of columns.

col′o•ny (kol′ə nē) *n., pl.* **-nies. 1.** a group of people settling in another land. **2.** a territory subject to an outside ruling power. **3.** a community. —**co•lo′ni•al** (kə lō′nē əl) *adj., n.* —**co′lo•nist,** *n.* —**col′o•nize′,** *v.t., v.i.*

col′or (kul′ər) *n.* **1.** the quality of an object with respect to the light reflected by it. **2.** pigment. **3.** complexion. **4.** a vivid quality. **5. colors,** a flag. —*v.t.* **6.** to apply color to. **7.** to give a special character to. Also, *Brit.,* **col′our.** —**col′or•ing,** *n.*

col′o•ra•tu′ra (kul′ər ə tŏŏr′ə, -tyŏŏr′ə, kol′-) *n.* a soprano specializing in music containing ornamental trills.

col′or-blind′ *adj.* **1.** unable to distinguish certain colors. **2.** without racial bias.

col′or•ful *adj.* **1.** full of color. **2.** vivid; interesting.

col′or•less *adj.* **1.** without color. **2.** drab.

co•los′sal (kə los′əl) *adj.* huge.

co•los′sus (-los′əs) *n.* **1.** a huge statue. **2.** anything huge.

colt (kōlt) *n.* a young male horse.

col′umn (kol′əm) *n.* **1.** an upright shaft or support. **2.** a long area of print. **3.** a regular journalistic piece. **4.** a long group of troops, ships, etc.

col′um•nist (-əm nist) *n.* a journalist who writes a regular column.

com- a prefix indicating: **1.** with or together. **2.** completely.

co′ma (kō/mə) *n.* a state of prolonged unconsciousness. —**com′a•tose′** (-tōs′) *adj.*

comb (kōm) *n.* **1.** a toothed object for straightening hair. **2.** the growth on a cock's head. —*v.t.* **3.** to tidy with a comb. **4.** to search.

com•bat′ *v.,* **-bated, -bating,** *n.* —*v.t., v.i.* (kəm bat′, kom′bat) **1.** to fight (against). —*n.* (kom′bat) **2.** battle. —**com•bat′ant,** *n.* —**com•bat′ive,** *adj.*

com′bi•na′tion (kom′bə nā′shən) *n.* **1.** the act of combining. **2.** a mixture. **3.** an alliance. **4.** the set of figures dialed to operate a lock.

com•bine′ *v.,* **-bined, -bining,** *n.* —*v.t., v.i.* (kəm bīn′) **1.** to unite; join. —*n.* (kom′bīn) **2.** a combination of persons for a common interest. **3.** a machine that cuts and threshes grain.

com′bo (kom′bō) *n., pl.* **-bos.** *Informal.* a small jazz band.

com•bus′ti•ble (kəm bus′tə bəl) *adj.* **1.** capable of burning. —*n.* **2.** a combustible substance.

com•bus′tion (-chən) *n.* **1.** the act or process of burning. **2.** the process in which substances combine with oxygen and produce heat.

come (kum) *v.i.,* **came, come, coming.** **1.** to move toward someone or something. **2.** to arrive. **3.** to occur. **4. come across** *or* **upon,** to encounter by chance. **5. ~ through, a.** to endure successfully. **b.** to fulfill requirements.

come′back′ *n.* **1.** a return to a former, higher status. **2.** a retort.

co•me′di•an (kə mē/dē ən) *n.* a humorous actor or performer.

com′e•dy (kom′i dē) *n., pl.* **-dies.** a humorous play, movie, etc.

come′ly (kum/lē) *adj.,* **-lier, -liest.** attractive. —**come′li•ness,** *n.*

com′et (kom′it) *n.* a small bright celestial body with a tail of dust and gas.

com′fort (kum/fərt) *v.t.* **1.** to console or soothe. —*n.* **2.** consolation. **3.** a person or thing giving consolation. **4.** a state of ease and satisfaction.

com′fort•er *n.* **1.** one who comforts. **2.** a warm quilt.

com′ic (kom′ik) *adj.* **1.** of comedy. **2.** Also, **com′i•cal.** funny. —*n.* **3.** a comedian. **4. comics,** comic strips.

com′ic strip′ *n.* a sequence of drawings relating a comic story.

com′ma (kom′ə) *n.* a punctuation mark (,).

com•mand′ (kə mand′) *v.t.* **1.** to order. **2.** to control. —*v.i.* **3.** to have authority. —*n.* **4.** an order. **5.** control. **6.** expertise. **7.** troops, a ship, etc., under a commander.

com′man•dant′ (kom′ən dant′, -dänt′) *n.* a commanding officer.

com′man•deer′ (-dēr′) *v.t.* to seize for official use.

com•mand′er *n.* **1.** a person who commands. **2.** a naval officer below a captain.

com•mand′ment *n.* a command.

com•man′do (kə man/dō) *n., pl.* **-dos, -does.** a member of a military unit trained for surprise raids.

com•mem′o•rate′ (kə mem/ə rāt′) *v.t.,* **-rated, -rating.** to honor the memory of. —**com•mem′o•ra•tive** (-rə tiv) *adj.*

com•mence′ (kə mens′) *v.i., v.t.,* **-menced, -mencing.** to start.

com•mence′ment *n.* **1.** a beginning. **2.** the ceremony of awarding degrees or diplomas at a school.

com•mend′ (kə mend′) *v.t.* **1.** to recommend. **2.** to entrust. **3.** to praise. —**com•mend′a•ble,** *adj.* —**com′men•da′tion** (kom′ən dā/-shən) *n.* —**com•mend′a•to′ry,** *adj.*

com•men′su•rate (-men/shə rit, -sə-) *adj.* **1.** of the same size. **2.** corresponding in size or degree.

com′ment (kom′ent) *n.* **1.** a remark. **2.** an interpretation. —*v.i.* **3.** to make remarks.

com′men•tar′y (-ən ter′ē) *n., pl.* **-taries.** explanatory comments.

com′men•ta′tor (-tā/tər) *n.* a person who discusses news or other topics on radio or television.

com′merce (kom′ərs) *n.* trade.

com•mer′cial (kə mûr/shəl) *adj.* **1.** of or in commerce. —*n.* **2.** a radio or television advertisement.

com•mer′cial•ize′ *v.t.,* **-ized, -izing.** to treat as a business.

com•min′gle (kə ming/gəl) *v.t., v.i.,* **-gled, -gling.** to blend.

com•mis′er•ate′ (kə miz/ə rāt′) *v.i.,* **-ated, -ating.** to sympathize.

com′mis•sar′y (kom′ə ser′ē) *n., pl.* **-ies.** a store selling food and supplies on a military post.

com•mis′sion (kə mish/ən) *n.* **1.** the act of committing. **2.** an order or document granting authority, esp. one granted to military officers. **3.** authority granted for an action. **4.** a group of persons with a special task. **5.** a sum paid to an agent, salesperson, etc. —*v.t.* **6.** to give a commission to. **7.** to authorize. **8.** to put into service.

commis′sioned of′ficer *n.* a military officer holding rank by commission.

com·mis′sion·er *n.* a government official in charge of a department.

com·mit′ (kə mit′) *v.t.,* **-mitted, -mitting. 1.** to give in trust or charge. **2.** to do. **3.** to obligate. —**com·mit′ment,** *n.*

com·mit′tee *n.* a group assigned to investigate or act on a matter.

com·mode′ (kə mōd′) *n.* **1.** a chest of drawers. **2.** a stand with a washbasin. **3.** a toilet.

com·mo′di·ous (kə mō′dē əs) *adj.* roomy.

com·mod′i·ty (kə mod′i tē) *n., pl.* **-ties. 1.** an article of trade. **2.** any unprocessed good.

com′mo·dore′ (kom′ə dôr′) *n.* an officer below a rear admiral.

com′mon (kom′ən) *adj.* **1.** belonging to or shared by all. **2.** widespread. **3.** ordinary. **4.** vulgar. —*n.* **5.** an area of public land. —*Idiom.* **6. in common,** shared equally. —**com′mon·ly,** *adv.*

com′mon·er *n.* one of the common people.

com′mon law′ *n.* the system of law based on custom and court decisions.

com′mon·place′ *adj.* **1.** ordinary; trite. —*n.* **2.** such a remark.

com′mons *n.* **1. Commons,** the elective house of certain legislatures. **2.** a large dining room, as in a college.

com′mon sense′ *n.* sound practical judgment. —**com′mon·sense′,** *adj.*

com′mon·weal′ (-wēl′) *n.* the common welfare.

com′mon·wealth′ (-welth′) *n.* **1.** a state. **2.** the people of a state.

com·mo′tion (kə mō′shən) *n.* disturbance.

com·mu′nal (kə myōōn′l, kom′yə nl) *adj.* of or belonging to a community.

com·mune′[1] (kə myōōn′) *v.i.,* **-muned, -muning.** to talk together.

com′mune[2] (kom′yōōn) *n.* a small community with shared property.

com·mu′ni·ca·ble (-ni kə bəl) *adj.* capable of being communicated.

com·mu′ni·cate′ *v.,* **-cated, -cating.** —*v.t.* **1.** to make known. **2.** to transmit. —*v.i.* **3.** to exchange thoughts, information, etc.

com·mu′ni·ca′tion *n.* **1.** the act of communicating. **2.** something communicated, as a letter.

com·mu′ni·ca′tive (-kā′tiv, -kə-) *adj.* inclined to communicate.

com·mun′ion (kə myōōn′yən) *n.* **1.** an act of sharing. **2.** a group with the same religion. **3. Holy Communion.**

com·mu′ni·qué′ (kə myōō′ni kā′) *n.* an official bulletin.

com′mu·nism (kom′yə niz′əm) *n.* **1.** a social system based on the collective ownership of property. **2. Communism,** a political doctrine advocating this. —**com′mu·nist** (-nist) *n., adj.*

com·mu′ni·ty (kə myōō′ni tē) *n., pl.* **-ties.** a group of people having common interests or living in one locality.

com·mute′ (kə myōōt′) *v.,* **-muted, -muting.** —*v.i.* **1.** to travel regularly between home and work. —*v.t.* **2.** to reduce (a punishment). —*n.* **3.** a trip made by commuting.

com·pact′ *adj.* (kəm pakt′, kom′-pakt) **1.** packed together. **2.** small. —*v.t.* (kəm pakt′) **3.** to pack tightly together. —*n.* (kom′pakt) **4.** a small cosmetic case. **5.** an agreement.

com′pact disc′ *n.* an optical disc on which music, data, or images are digitally recorded. Also, **CD.**

com·pac′tor (kəm pak′tər, kom′-pak-) *n.* an appliance that compresses trash into small bundles.

com·pan′ion (kəm pan′yən) *n.* **1.** an associate. **2.** a person in a close relationship with another. —**com·pan′ion·a·ble,** *adj.* —**com·pan′ion·ship′,** *n.*

com′pa·ny (kum′pə nē) *n., pl.* **-nies. 1.** a business organization. **2.** companionship. **3.** guests. **4.** a basic unit of troops. —*Idiom.* **5. part company,** to cease association.

com·par′a·tive (kəm par′ə tiv) *adj.* **1.** of or based on comparison. **2.** relative. **3.** designating the intermediate degree of comparison of adjectives and adverbs.

com·pare′ (kəm pâr′) *v.,* **-pared, -paring.** —*v.t.* **1.** to examine for similarities. **2.** to liken. —*v.i.* **3.** to be worthy of comparison. **4.** to make comparisons. —**com′-pa·ra·ble** (kom′pər ə bəl) *adj.*

com·par′i·son (kəm par′ə sən) *n.* **1.** a comparing or being compared. **2.** a likening.

com·part′ment (kəm pärt′mənt) *n.* a separate room, space, etc. —**com·part·men′tal·ize′,** *v.t.*

com′pass (kum′pəs) *n.* **1.** an instrument for determining direction. **2.** extent. **3.** a tool for drawing circles.

com·pas′sion (kəm pash′ən) *n.* sympathy. —**com·pas′sion·ate,** *adj.* —**com·pas′sion·ate·ly,** *adv.*

com·pat′i·ble (kəm pat′ə bəl) *adj.* able to exist or work together. —**com·pat′i·bil′i·ty,** *n.*

com·pa′tri·ot (kəm pā′trē ət) *n.* a person from one's own country.

com·pel′ (kəm pel′) *v.t.,* **-pelled, -pelling.** to force.

com·pen′di·um (-dē əm) *n., pl.,* **-diums, -dia** (-dē ə). a summary.

com′pen·sate′ (kom′pən sāt′) *v.t.,* **-sated, -sating. 1.** to counterbalance; offset. **2.** to pay. —**com′pen·sa′tion,** *n.*

com·pete′ (kəm pēt′) *v.i.,* **-peted, -peting.** to take part in a contest.

com′pe·tent (kom′pi tənt) *adj.* **1.** having suitable ability for some purpose. **2.** adequate. **3.** legally qualified. —**com′pe·tence, com′pe·ten·cy,** *n.*

com′pe·ti′tion (kom′pi tish′ən) *n.* **1.** the act of competing. **2.** contest. **3.** rivalry. —**com·pet′i·tive** (kəm·pet′i tiv) *adj.* —**com·pet′i·tor,** *n.*

com·pile′ (kəm pīl′) *v.t.,* **-piled, -piling. 1.** to put together (material from various sources) into a book, list, etc. **2.** to gather together. —**com·pil′er,** *n.* —**com′pi·la′tion** (kom′pə lā′shən) *n.*

com·pla′cen·cy (kəm plā′sən sē) *n., pl.* **-cies.** a feeling of quiet pleasure or security. Also, **com·pla′cence.** —**com·pla′cent,** *adj.*

com·plain′ (kəm plān′) *v.i.* **1.** to express pain, dissatisfaction, etc. **2.** to accuse formally in a law court.

com·plain′ant *n.* one who makes a complaint, as in a legal action.

com·plaint *n.* **1.** an expression of pain, discontent, etc. **2.** a cause of pain, discontent, etc. **3.** a formal accusation in a law court.

com·plai′sant (kəm plā′sənt) *adj.* inclined to please.

com′ple·ment *n.* (kom′plə mənt) **1.** that which completes. **2.** the amount that completes. —*v.t.* (-mənt′) **3.** to form a complement to. —**com′ple·men′ta·ry,** *adj.*

com·plete′ (kəm plēt′) *adj., v.,* **-pleted, -pleting.** —*adj.* **1.** entire. **2.** finished. **3.** thorough. —*v.t.* **4.** to make complete. —**com·plete′ly,** *adv.* —**com·ple′tion,** *n.*

com·plex′ *adj.* (kəm pleks′, kom′pleks) **1.** having many parts; intricate. —*n.* (kom′pleks) **2.** an assemblage of related parts. **3.** a group of feelings that influences behavior. —**com·plex′i·ty,** *n.*

com·plex′ion (kəm plek′shən) *n.* the color of the skin.

com′pli·ca′ted (kom′pli kā′tid) *adj.* complex or difficult. —**com′pli·cate′,** *v.t.*

com·plic′i·ty (kəm plis′i tē) *n., pl.* **-ties.** partnership in guilt.

com′pli·ment *n.* (kom′plə mənt) **1.** an expression of praise. —*v.t.*

(-mənt′) **2.** to pay a compliment to.

com′pli·men′ta·ry *adj.* **1.** praising. **2.** given free.

com·ply′ (kəm plī′) *v.i.,* **-plied, -plying.** to conform. —**com·pli′ance,** *n.* —**com·pli′ant,** *adj.*

com·po′nent (kəm pō′nənt) *n.* **1.** a part of a whole. —*adj.* **2.** serving as part of something larger.

com·port′ (kəm pôrt′) *v.t.* to conduct (oneself); behave.

com·pose′ (kəm pōz′) *v.t.,* **-posed, -posing. 1.** to make by combining. **2.** to constitute. **3.** to calm. **4.** to create (a musical work). —**com′po·si′tion** (kom′pə zish′ən) *n.*

com·posed′ *adj.* calm.

com·pos′er *n.* a writer, esp. of music.

com·pos′ite (kəm poz′it) *adj.* made of many parts.

com′post (kom′pōst) *n.* a decaying mixture of organic matter.

com·po′sure (kəm pō′zhər) *n.* calmness.

com′pote (kom′pōt) *n.* stewed fruit in syrup.

com′pound *adj.* (kom′pound) **1.** having two or more parts, functions, etc. —*n.* (kom′pound) **2.** something made by combining parts. **3.** an enclosure with buildings. —*v.t.* (kəm pound′) **4.** to combine. **5.** to make worse by adding to.

com′pre·hend′ (kom′pri hend′) *v.t.* **1.** to understand. **2.** to include. —**com′pre·hen′si·ble,** *adj.* —**com′pre·hen′sion,** *n.*

com′pre·hen′sive (-hen′siv) *adj.* including much or all.

com·press′ *v.t.* (kəm pres′) **1.** to press together into less space. **2.** to shorten. —*n.* (kom′pres) **3.** a pad applied to an injured or inflamed part of the body. —**com·pres′sion,** *n.* —**com·pres′sor,** *n.*

com·prise′ (kəm prīz′) *v.t.,* **-prised, -prising. 1.** to consist of. **2.** to include.

com′pro·mise′ (kom′prə mīz′) *n., v.,* **-mised, -mising.** —*n.* **1.** an agreement reached by mutual concessions. **2.** something intermediate. —*v.t.* **3.** to settle by compromise. **4.** to make vulnerable. —*v.i.* **5.** to make a compromise.

comp′ time′ (komp) *n.* time off from work granted to an employee in place of overtime pay.

comp·trol′ler (kən trō′lər) *n.* a government or corporate officer in charge of finances; controller.

com·pul′sion (kəm pul′shən) *n.* **1.** the act of compelling or the state of being compelled. **2.** an irresistible impulse.

com·pul′sive adj. due to or acting on inner compulsion.

com·punc′tion (-pungk′shən) n. regret.

com·pute′ (-pyo͞ot′) v., **-puted, -puting.** —v.i. **1.** to calculate. —v.t. **2.** to determine by arithmetical calculation. —**com′pu·ta′tion** (kom′-) n.

com·put′er n. a programmable electronic apparatus for processing data at high speed. —**com·pu′ter·ize′**, v.t.

com′rade (kom′rad) n. a companion or associate.

con[1] (kon) adv. **1.** against. —n. **2.** the argument or vote against something.

con[2] (kon) adj., v., **conned, conning.** —adj. **1.** involving abuse of trust. —v.t. **2.** to cheat.

con·cave′ (kon kāv′) adj. curved inward.

con·ceal′ (kən sēl′) v.t. to hide or keep secret. —**con·ceal′ment,** n.

con·cede′ (kən sēd′) v., **-ceded, -ceding.** —v.t. **1.** to acknowledge as true. **2.** to grant. —v.i. **3.** to make a concession.

con·ceit′ (kən sēt′) n. **1.** excess self-esteem. **2.** a fanciful idea.

con·ceive′ (kən sēv′) v., **-ceived, -ceiving.** —v.t. **1.** to form (a plan or idea). **2.** to imagine. **3.** to become pregnant with. —v.i. **4.** to think. **5.** to become pregnant.

con′cen·trate′ (kon′sən trāt′) v., **-trated, -trating,** n. —v.t. **1.** to direct toward one point. **2.** to intensify. —v.i. **3.** to give one's full attention. —n. **4.** a concentrated product. —**con′cen·tra′tion,** n.

concentra′tion camp′ n. a guarded compound for the confinement of political prisoners, minorities, etc.

con·cen′tric (kən sen′trik) adj. having the same center.

con′cept (kon′sept) n. a general idea.

con·cep′tion (kən sep′shən) n. **1.** the act of conceiving or the state of being conceived. **2.** an idea.

con·cep′tu·a·lize′ (-cho͞o ə līz′) v., **-lized, -lizing.** —v.t. **1.** to form a concept of. —v.i. **2.** to think in concepts.

con·cern′ (kən sûrn′) v.t. **1.** to relate to. **2.** to involve. **3.** to trouble. —n. **4.** something that relates to or affects a person. **5.** anxiety.

con·cerned′ adj. **1.** interested or affected. **2.** troubled; anxious.

con·cern′ing prep. about.

con′cert (kon′sûrt) n. **1.** a musical performance. **2.** accord. —**Idiom. 3. in concert,** jointly.

con·cert′ed (kən sûr′tid) adj. **1.** planned together. **2.** performed together or in cooperation.

con′cer·ti′na (kon′sər tē′nə) n. a small accordion.

con·cer′to (kən cher′tō) n., pl. **-tos** or **-ti** (-tē). a musical piece for solo instrument and orchestra.

con·ces′sion (kən sesh′ən) n. **1.** the act of conceding. **2.** the thing or point conceded.

conch (kongk, konch) n. a marine mollusk with a spiral shell.

con·cil′i·ate′ (kən sil′ē āt′) v.t., **-ated, -ating. 1.** to overcome the distrust of; win over. **2.** to reconcile. —**con·cil′i·a′tion,** n. —**con·cil′i·a·to′ry** (-ə tôr′ē) adj.

con·cise′ (kən sīs′) adj. brief; succinct. —**con·cise′ly,** adv.

con′clave (kon′klāv) n. a private meeting.

con·clude′ (kən klo͞od′) v., **-cluded, -cluding.** —v.t. **1.** to finish. **2.** to settle. **3.** to deduce. —v.i. **4.** to end. —**con·clu′sive,** adj.

con·clu′sion (-klo͞o′zhən) n. **1.** the end. **2.** a result. **3.** a deduction. **4.** a final decision.

con·coct′ (kon kokt′, kən-) v.t. **1.** to make by combining ingredients. **2.** to devise. —**con·coc′tion,** n.

con·com′i·tant (kon kom′i tənt, kən-) adj. accompanying. —n. **2.** anything concomitant.

con′cord (kon′kôrd, kong′-) n. **1.** an agreement. **2.** peace.

con·cord′ance (kon kôr′dns, kən-) n. **1.** concord. **2.** an index of the key words of a book.

con·cor′dat (kon kôr′dat) n. an official agreement.

con′course (kon′kôrs, kong′-) n. a large open space for crowds.

con′crete adj., n., v., **-creted, -creting.** —adj. (kon′krēt, kon krēt′) **1.** constituting an actual thing; real. **2.** made of concrete. —n. (kon′krēt) **3.** a building material of cement and hard matter. —v.t. (kon krēt′) **4.** to cover with concrete.

con′cu·bine′ (kong′kyə bīn′) n. **1.** a woman living with but not married to a man, esp. a woman regarded as subservient. **2.** a secondary wife.

con·cur′ (kən kûr′) v.i., **-curred, -curring. 1.** to agree. **2.** to occur at the same time. —**con·cur′rence,** n. —**con·cur′rent,** adj.

con·cus′sion (kən kush′ən) n. an injury to the brain from a blow, fall, etc.

con·demn′ (kən dem′) v.t. **1.** to express strong disapproval of. **2.** to pronounce guilty. **3.** to pronounce unfit for use. **—con·dem·na′tion** (kon′dem nā′shən, -dəm-) *n.*

con·dense′ (kən dens′) *v.,* **-densed, -densing.** *—v.t.* **1.** to make more dense or compact. **2.** to reduce from gas or vapor to liquid. *—v.i.* **3.** to become condensed. **—con′-den·sa′tion** (kon′den sā′shən) *n.*

condensed′ milk′ *n.* thick, sweetened milk.

con′de·scend′ (-də send′) *v.i.* to act as if one is doing something that is beneath one's dignity. **—con′de·scen′sion,** *n.*

con′di·ment (kon′də mənt) *n.* a seasoning.

con·di′tion (kən dish′ən) *n.* **1.** a state of being. **2.** a restricting circumstance; prerequisite. *—v.t.* **3.** to put in a proper state. **4.** to accustom. **—con·di′tion·al,** *adj.*

con·di′tion·er *n.* something that conditions, as a preparation applied to the hair or skin.

con·dole′ (kən dōl′) *v.i.,* **-doled, -doling.** to express sympathy. **—con·do′lence,** *n.*

con′dom (kon′dəm, kun′-) *n.* a contraceptive device worn over the penis.

con·do·min′i·um (kon′də min′ē-əm) *n.* an apartment house in which each unit is individually owned. Also, *Informal.* **con′do** (-dō).

con·done′ (kən dōn′) *v.t.,* **-doned, -doning.** to disregard or overlook.

con′dor (kon′dər, -dôr) *n.* a kind of vulture.

con·du′cive (kən dōō′siv, -dyōō′–) *adj.* tending to produce.

con′duct *n.* (kon′dukt) **1.** behavior. **2.** management. *—v.t.* (kən dukt′) **3.** to behave (oneself). **4.** to manage. **5.** to lead or carry. **6.** to direct, as an orchestra. **7.** to transmit. **—con·duc′tion,** *n.*

con·duc′tor (kən duk′tər) *n.* **1.** a guide. **2.** a person who conducts an orchestra or chorus. **3.** an official on a train. **4.** a substance that conveys electricity, heat, etc.

con′duit (kon′dwit) *n.* a pipe for water or other fluid.

cone (kōn) *n.* **1.** a form tapering from a round base to a single point. **2.** the fruit of the fir, pine, etc.

con·fec′tion (kən fek′shən) *n.* candy or another sweet preparation. **—con·fec′tion·er,** *n.* **—con·fec′tion·er′y,** *n.*

con·fed′er·a·cy (kən fed′ər ə sē) *n., pl.* **-cies. 1.** a league. **2. the Confederacy,** the eleven states that seceded from the U.S. in 1860–61.

con·fed′er·ate *adj.* (kən fed′ər it) **1.** in league. **2.** of the Confederacy. *—n.* (-ər it) **3.** an ally. **4.** an accomplice. **5. Confederate,** a supporter of the Confederacy.

con·fer′ (kən fûr′) *v.,* **-ferred, -ferring.** *—v.t.* **1.** to bestow. *—v.i.* **2.** to consult. **—con·fer′ment,** *n.*

con′fer·ence (kon′fər əns) *n.* a meeting for discussion.

con·fess′ (kən fes′) *v.t., v.i.* **1.** to admit or acknowledge. **2.** to declare (one's sins) to a priest. **—con·fes′sion,** *n.*

con·fes′sion·al *adj.* **1.** characteristic of confession. *—n.* **2.** a place in a church set apart for confession.

con·fes′sor *n.* **1.** one who confesses. **2.** one who hears confessions.

con·fet′ti (kən fet′ē) *n.* bits of colored paper thrown at festive events.

con′fi·dant′ or **con′fi·dante′** (kon′fi dant′, -dänt′) *n.* a person to whom secrets are told.

con·fide′ (kən fīd′) *v.,* **-fided, -fiding.** *—v.t.* **1.** to tell in secret. **2.** to entrust. **3. confide in,** to discuss private matters with.

con′fi·dence (kon′fi dəns) *n.* **1.** full trust. **2.** assurance. **3.** a secret communication. **—con′fi·dent,** *adj.*

con′fi·den′tial (-den′shəl) *adj.* **1.** secret or private. **2.** entrusted with secrets. **—con′fi·den′tial·ly,** *adv.*

con·fig′u·ra′tion (kən fig′yə rā′shən) *n.* shape; external form.

con·fine′ *v.,* **-fined, -fining.** *n.* *—v.t.* (kən fīn′) **1.** to keep within bounds. **2.** to shut or lock up. *—n.* **3. confines,** (kon′fīnz) a boundary.

con·fine′ment *n.* **1.** imprisonment. **2.** childbirth.

con·firm′ (kən fûrm′) *v.t.* **1.** to make definite. **2.** to make valid. **3.** to administer confirmation to.

con′fir·ma′tion (kon′fər-) *n.* **1.** a confirming or being confirmed. **2.** a ceremony of admission to membership in a church.

con·firmed′ *adj.* **1.** made definite. **2.** habitual.

con′fis·cate′ (kon′fə skāt′) *v.t.,* **-cated, -cating.** to seize by authority. **—con′fis·ca′tion,** *n.*

con′fla·gra′tion (kon′flə grā′shən) *n.* a fierce fire.

con·flict′ *v.t.* (kən flikt′) **1.** to clash; disagree. *—n.* (kon′flikt) **2.** a fight. **3.** a disagreement.

con′flu·ence (kon′flōō əns) *n.* an act or place of flowing together. **—con′flu·ent,** *adj.*

con·form′ (kən fôrm′) *v.i.* **1.** to comply. **2.** to act in accord with prevailing custom. **3.** to be similar.

—*v.t.* **4.** to make similar. **5.** to bring into accord. —**con•form′ist,** *n.* —**con•form′i•ty,** *n.*

con•found′ (kon found′) *v.t.* **1.** to confuse. **2.** to astonish.

con•found′ed *adj.* bewildered.

con•front′ (kən frunt′) *v.t.* **1.** to face in a hostile way. **2.** to stand or come in front of. —**con′fron•ta′tion** (kon′frən tā′shən) *n.* —**con′fron•ta′tion•al,** *adj.*

con•fuse′ (kən fyōōz′) *v.t.,* **-fused, -fusing. 1.** to bewilder. **2.** to make unclear. **3.** to throw into disorder. —**con•fu′sion,** *n.*

con•fute′ (-fyōōt′) *v.t.,* **-futed, -futing.** to prove wrong.

con•geal′ (kən jēl′) *v.t., v.i.* to make or become solid or thick.

con•gen′ial (kən jēn′yəl) *adj.* **1.** agreeable in nature. **2.** suited in tastes, temperament, etc. —**con•ge′ni•al′i•ty** (-jē′nē al′i tē) *n.*

con•gen′i•tal (kən jen′i tl) *adj.* present from birth.

con•gest′ (kən jest′) *v.t.* **1.** to fill to excess; clog. **2.** to make (a body part) abnormally full of blood or other fluid. —**con•ges′tion,** *n.*

con•glom′er•ate *n., adj., v.,* **-ated, -ating.** —*n.* (kən glom′ər it) **1.** something composed of heterogeneous elements. **2.** a company owning a variety of other companies. —*adj.* (-ər it) **3.** mixed. —*v.t.* (-ə rāt′) **4.** to gather into a coherent mass. —**con•glom′er•a′tion,** *n.*

con•grat′u•late′ (kən grach′ə lāt′) *v.t.,* **-lated, -lating.** to express pleasure to (a person) for an accomplishment or good fortune. —**con•grat′u•la′tions,** *n.pl.*

con′gre•gate′ (kong′gri gāt′) *v.i.,* **-gated, -gating.** to assemble. —**con′gre•ga′tion,** *n.* —**con′gre•ga′tion•al,** *adj.*

con′gress (kong′gris) *n.* **1. Congress,** the national legislative body of the U.S. **2.** a formal meeting. —**con•gres′sion•al** (kəng gresh′ə-nl) *adj.*

con•gru•ent (kong′grōō ənt) *adj.* **1.** agreeing. **2.** (of geometric figures) being exactly the same size and shape. —**con′gru•ence,** *n.*

con•gru′i•ty (kən grōō′i tē) *n., pl.* **-ties.** agreement; harmony. —**con′-gru•ous** (kong′grōō əs) *adj.*

con•ic (kon′ik) *adj.* of or like a cone. Also, **con′i•cal.**

co′ni•fer (kō′nə fər, kon′ə-) *n.* an evergreen tree bearing cones. —**co•nif′er•ous** (-nif′ər əs) *adj.*

con•jec′ture (kən jek′chər) *n., v.,* **-tured, -turing.** —*n.* **1.** a guess. —*v.t., v.i.* **2.** to conclude from insufficient evidence; guess.

con•join′ (kən join′) *v.t., v.i.* to join together.

con′ju•gal (kon′jə gəl) *adj.* of marriage.

con′ju•gate′ (-gāt′) *v.t.,* **-gated, -gating.** to give the inflected forms of (a verb). —**con′ju•ga′tion,** *n.*

con•junc′tion (kən jungk′shən) *n.* **1.** a union; combination. **2.** a word that joins words, phrases, clauses, or sentences.

con•junc′ti•vi′tis (kən jungk′tə vī′-tis) *n.* inflammation of the mucous membrane of the eye.

con′jure (kon′jər, kun′-) *v.,* **-jured, -juring.** —*v.i.* **1.** to invoke or produce by magic. —*v.i.* **2.** to practice magic. —**con′jur•er,** *n.*

conk (kongk) *Slang.* —*v.t.* **1.** to strike on the head. **2. conk out. a.** to break down. **b.** to go to sleep. —*n.* **3.** a blow on the head.

Conn. Connecticut.

con•nect′ (kə nekt′) *v.t., v.i.* **1.** to join together. **2.** to associate mentally. —**con•nec′tive,** *adj., n.*

con•nec′tion *n.* **1.** a connecting or being connected. **2.** anything that connects. **3.** relationship. **4.** a transfer by a passenger from one airplane, train, etc., to another.

con•nive′ (kə nīv′) *v.i.,* **-nived, -niving. 1.** to cooperate secretly; conspire. **2.** to give unspoken consent to. —**con•niv′ance,** *n.*

con′nois•seur′ (kon′ə sûr′) *n.* an expert judge in matters of taste.

con•note′ (kə nōt′) *v.t.,* **-noted, -noting.** to suggest in addition to the explicit meaning; imply. —**con′no•ta′tion** (kon′ə tā′shən) *n.*

con•nu′bi•al (kə nōō′bē əl, -nyōō′-) *adj.* matrimonial.

con′quer (kong′kər) *v.t.* **1.** to overcome by force. **2.** to win by effort. —**con′quer•or,** *n.* —**con′quest,** *n.*

con′science (kon′shəns) *n.* one's sense of right and wrong.

con′sci•en′tious (-shē en′shəs) *adj.* careful and hardworking.

conscien′tious objec′tor *n.* a person who refuses to serve in the military for moral reasons.

con′scious (kon′shəs) *adj.* **1.** aware of one's own existence, sensations, etc. **2.** having the mental faculties awake. **3.** intentional. —**con′-scious•ness,** *n.*

con′script *n.* (kon′skript) **1.** one drafted for military service. —*v.t.* (kən skript′) **2.** to draft for military service. —**con•scrip′tion,** *n.*

con′se•crate′ (kon′si krāt′) *v.t.,* **-crated, -crating. 1.** to make sacred. **2.** to dedicate to some purpose. —**con′se•cra′tion,** *n.*

con•sec′u•tive (kən sek′yə tiv) *adj.*

following in uninterrupted order.
—**con•sec′u•tive•ly,** adv.

con•sen′sus (kən sen′səs) n. general agreement.

con•sent′ (kən sent′) v.i. **1.** to agree to or comply with another's proposal. —n. **2.** agreement.

con′se•quence′ (kon′si kwens′) n. **1.** a result. **2.** importance.

con′se•quent′ adj. following; resulting. —**con′se•quent•ly,** adv.

con′ser•va′tion (kon′sər vā′shən) n. **1.** the act of conserving. **2.** the preservation of resources.

con•serv′a•tive (kən sûr′və tiv) adj. **1.** in favor of preserving existing conditions. **2.** cautious. **3.** traditional. —n. **4.** a conservative person. —**con•serv′a•tism,** n.

con•serv′a•to′ry (-tôr′ē) n., pl. **-ries. 1.** a school of music or drama. **2.** a greenhouse.

con•serve′ v., **-served, -serving,** n. —v.t. (kən sûrv′) **1.** to prevent injury, decay, or loss of. —n. (kon′sûrv) **2.** a kind of jam.

con•sid′er (kən sid′ər) v.t. **1.** to think about carefully. **2.** to believe or suppose. **3.** to respect. —**con•sid′er•ate,** adj.

con•sid′er•a•ble adj. important or sizable. —**con•sid′er•a•bly,** adv.

con•sid′er•a′tion (-ə rā′shən) n. **1.** careful thought. **2.** a fact kept in mind. **3.** regard. **4.** a payment.

con•sid′er•ing prep. in view of.

con•sign′ (kən sīn′) v.t. **1.** to deliver. **2.** to entrust. **3.** to ship (goods) for sale.

con•sist′ (kən sist′) v. **1. consist in,** to be contained or inherent in. **2. consist of,** to be composed of.

con•sist′en•cy (-sis′tən sē) n., pl. **-cies. 1.** degree of firmness or density. **2.** adherence to the same principles, behavior, etc.

con•sole′¹ (kən sōl′) v.t., **-soled, -soling.** to comfort. —**con′so•la′tion,** n. —**con•sol′a•ble,** adj.

con′sole² (kon′sōl) n. a cabinet or unit containing controls.

con•sol′i•date′ (kən sol′i dāt′) v.t., v.i., **-dated, -dating. 1.** to combine into a single whole. **2.** to make or become secure. —**con•sol′i•da′tion,** n.

con•som•mé′ (kon′sə mā′) n. a clear soup.

con′so•nant (kon′sə nənt) n. **1.** a letter other than a vowel or the sound it represents. —adj. **2.** consistent.

con′sort n. (kon′sôrt) **1.** a spouse, esp. of a ruler. —v.i. (kən sôrt′) **2.** to associate.

con•sor′ti•um (kən sôr′shē əm, -tē-) n., pl. **-tia** (-shē ə, -tē ə). a combination, as of corporations, for carrying out a purpose.

con•spic′u•ous (kən spik′yōō əs) adj. **1.** easily seen. **2.** attracting attention. —**con•spic′u•ous•ly,** adv.

con•spire′ (kən spīʳr′) v.i., **-spired, -spiring.** to plan secretly, usu. to do something unlawful. —**con•spir′a•cy** (-spir′ə sē) n. —**con•spir′a•tor,** n.

con•sta•ble (kon′stə bəl) n. a police officer.

con′stant (kon′stənt) adj. **1.** not changing. **2.** uninterrupted. **3.** faithful. —n. **4.** something unchanging. —**con′stan•cy,** n.

con•stel•la′tion (kon′stə lā′shən) n. a group of stars.

con′ster•na′tion (kon′stər nā′shən) n. sudden great dismay.

con′sti•pate′ (kon′stə pāt′) v.t., **-pated, -pating.** to cause difficult evacuation of the bowels.

con•stit′u•ent (kən stich′ōō ənt) adj. **1.** serving to make up something; component. —n. **2.** an ingredient. **3.** a voter in a given district. —**con•stit′u•en•cy,** n.

con′sti•tute′ (kon′sti tōōt′, -tyōōt′) v.t., **-tuted, -tuting. 1.** to compose or form. **2.** to establish.

con′sti•tu′tion n. **1.** a system of governmental principles or the document embodying these principles. **2.** composition. **3.** physical condition. —**con′sti•tu′tion•al,** adj.

con•strain′ (kən strān′) v.t. **1.** to force or oblige. **2.** to restrict. —**con•straint′,** n.

con•strict′ (kən strikt′) v.t. to make narrow, as by squeezing. —**con•stric′tion,** n.

con•struct′ (kən strukt′) v.t. to build by putting parts together. —**con•struc′tion,** n.

con•struc′tive adj. **1.** helping to improve. **2.** of construction.

con•strue′ (kən strōō′) v.t., **-strued, -struing.** to interpret.

con′sul (kon′səl) n. an official appointed by a government to look after its business interests and its citizens in a foreign country. —**con′su•lar,** adj. —**con′su•late** (-sə lit) n.

con•sult′ (kən sult′) v.t. **1.** to ask information or advice of. —v.i. **2.** to confer. —**con•sult′ant,** n.

con•sume′ (kən sōōm′) v.t., **-sumed, -suming. 1.** to use up. **2.** to devour. **3.** to destroy. **4.** to engross.

con•sum′er n. a person who uses goods or services.

con′sum•mate′ v., **-mated, -mating,** adj. —v.t. (kon′sə māt′) **1.** to make complete. **2.** to complete (a marriage) by sexual intercourse. —*adj.* (kən sum′it, kon′sə mit) **3.** perfect. —**con′sum·ma′tion,** *n.*

con·sump′tion (kən sump′shən) *n.* **1.** a consuming. **2.** the amount consumed. **3.** *Older Use.* tuberculosis. —**con·sump′tive,** *adj., n.*

cont. continued.

con′tact (kon′takt) *n.* **1.** a touching or meeting. **2.** close association. **3.** a person through whom one can gain access to information. **4.** an electrical connection. —*v.t.* **5.** to put into contact. **6.** to communicate with. —*v.i.* **7.** to enter into contact.

con′tact lens′ *n.* a corrective lens put directly on the eye.

con·ta′gion (kən tā′jən) *n.* **1.** the spread of disease by contact. **2.** a disease spread by contact. —**con·ta′gious,** *adj.*

con·tain′ (kən tān′) *v.t.* **1.** to have within itself. **2.** to include. **3.** to limit. —**con·tain′er,** *n.*

con·tam′i·nate′ (kən tam′ə nāt′) *v.t.,* **-nated, -nating.** to pollute.

con′tem·plate′ (kon′təm plāt′, -tem-) *v.,* **-plated, -plating.** —*v.t.* **1.** to observe thoughtfully. **2.** to consider. **3.** to intend. —*v.i.* **4.** to meditate. —**con′tem·pla′tion,** *n.*

con·tem′po·rar′y (kən tem′pə rer′ē) *adj., n., pl.* **-raries.** —*adj.* **1.** Also, **con·tem′po·ra′ne·ous** (-rā′nē əs). of the same age or date. **2.** of the present time. —*n.* **3.** a person or thing of the same date or age as another.

con·tempt′ (kən tempt′) *n.* **1.** scorn. **2.** the state of being despised. **3.** open disrespect.

con·tempt′i·ble *adj.* deserving contempt.

con·temp′tu·ous *adj.* showing contempt.

con·tend′ (kən tend′) *v.i.* **1.** to compete. —*v.t.* **2.** to assert.

con′tent¹ (kon′tent) *n.* **1.** Usu., **contents. a.** something contained. **b.** the subjects in a book, document, etc. **2.** meaning.

con·tent′² (kən tent′) *adj.* **1.** satisfied. —*v.t.* **2.** to make content. —*n.* **3.** Also, **con·tent′ment.** satisfaction.

con·ten′tion (-shən) *n.* **1.** conflict; dispute. **2.** something asserted in an argument. —**con·ten′tious,** *adj.*

con′test *n.* (kon′test) **1.** a competition. **2.** a struggle. —*v.t.* (kən test′) **3.** to compete for. **4.** to dispute. —**con·test′ant,** *n.*

con′text (kon′tekst) *n.* **1.** what comes before or follows a word or statement and influences its meaning. **2.** circumstances.

con·tig′u·ous (kən tig′yōō əs) *adj.* **1.** touching. **2.** near.

con′ti·nence (kon′tn əns) *n.* **1.** self-restraint. **2.** the ability to control bodily discharges.

con′ti·nent (kon′tn ənt) *n.* **1.** one of the seven main land masses of the earth. —*adj.* **2.** self-restrained. **3.** able to control bodily discharges.

con′ti·nen′tal (kon′ti nen′tl) *adj.* **1.** of a continent. **2. Continental,** European.

con·tin′gen·cy (kən tin′jən sē) *n., pl.,* **-cies. 1.** dependence on chance. **2.** a chance event.

con·tin′gent *adj.* **1.** dependent on something else. —*n.* **2.** a group that is part of a larger body.

con·tin′u·al (kən tin′yōō əl) *adj.* recurring regularly or frequently. —**con·tin′u·al·ly,** *adv.* —**Usage.** Use CONTINUAL for actions that occur over and over again (especially actions that are annoying): *The dog's continual barking was driving me crazy.* The word CONTINUOUS is used for actions that keep going and do not stop: *We had continuous electricity during the big storm.*

con·tin′ue *v.,* **-tinued, -tinuing.** —*v.i.* **1.** to go on without interruption. **2.** to resume. **3.** to last. **4.** to remain in a state or place. —*v.t.* **5.** to go on with. **6.** to extend.

con·ti·nu′i·ty (kon′tn ōō′i tē, -tn yōō′-) *n., pl.* **-ties. 1.** the state of being continuous. **2.** a continuous whole.

con·tin′u·ous (kən tin′yōō əs) *adj.* going on without interruption. —**con·tin′u·ous·ly,** *adv.* —**Usage.** See CONTINUAL.

con·tin′u·um (-yōō əm) *n., pl.* **-tinua.** a continuous extent, series, or whole.

con·tort′ (kən tôrt′) *v.t., v.i.* to twist or become twisted out of shape. —**con·tor′tion,** *n.*

con′tour (kon′tōōr) *n.* the outline of a figure or body.

contra- a prefix meaning against, opposite, or opposing.

con′tra·band′ (kon′trə band′) *n.* goods imported or exported illegally.

con′tra·cep′tion (-sep′shən) *n.* the deliberate prevention of conception. —**con′tra·cep′tive,** *adj., n.*

con·tract′ *n.* (kon′trakt) **1.** a formal agreement. —*v.t.* (kən trakt′) **2.** to make shorter or smaller. **3.** to catch, as an illness. **4.** to incur, as a debt —*v.i.* **5.** to shrink. **6.** to enter into a formal agreement.

con/trac·tor (kon/trak tər) *n.* a person who performs work or supplies goods by contract.

con/tra·dict/ (kon/trə dikt/) *v.t.* **1.** to assert the contrary of. **2.** to imply a denial of. —*v.i.* **3.** to utter a contrary statement. —**con/tra·dic/-tion,** *n.* —**con/tra·dic/to·ry,** *adj.*

con·tral/to (kən tral/tō) *n., pl.* **-tos. 1.** the lowest female voice. **2.** a singer with this voice.

con·trap/tion (kən trap/shən) *n.* a strange machine; gadget.

con/tra·ry (kon/trer ē) *adj., n., pl.* **-ries.** —*adj.* **1.** opposite. **2.** (*also* kən trâr/ē) stubbornly willful. —*n.* **3.** something opposite. —*Idiom.* **4. on the contrary,** in opposition to what has been stated. **5. to the contrary,** to the opposite effect.

con·trast/ *v.t.* (kən trast/) **1.** to compare in order to show differences. —*v.i.* **2.** to exhibit unlikeness when compared. —*n.* (kon/-trast) **3.** unlikeness shown by comparing. **4.** something unlike.

con/tra·vene/ (kon/trə vēn/) *v.t.,* **-vened, -vening.** to oppose.

con/tre·temps/ (kon/trə täN/) *n., pl.* **-temps.** an unfortunate happening.

con·trib/ute (kən trib/yōōt) *v.t., v.i.,* **-uted, -uting. 1.** to give (money, aid, etc.) together with others. —*Idiom.* **2. contribute to,** to be a factor in. —**con/tri·bu/tion** (kon/-trə byōō/shən) *n.* —**con·trib/u·tor,** *n.* —**con·trib/u·to/ry,** *adj.*

con·trite/ (kən trīt/) *adj.* penitent. —**con·tri/tion** (-trish/ən) *n.*

con·trive/ (kən trīv/) *v.t.,* **-trived, -triving.** to plan or scheme.

con·trol/ (kən trōl/) *v.,* **-trolled, -trolling,** *n.* —*v.t.* **1.** to have direction over. **2.** to restrain. —*n.* **3.** the act or power of controlling. **4.** a restraint. **5.** a regulating device.

con·trol/ler *n.* **1.** an officer who superintends finances. **2.** a regulator.

con/tro·ver/sy (kon/trə vûr/sē) *n., pl.* **-sies. 1.** a prolonged public dispute. **2.** an argument. —**con/tro·ver/sial** (-vûr/shəl) *adj.*

con/tro·vert/ (kon/trə vûrt/, kon/trə-vûrt/) *v.t.* to dispute; deny.

con/tu·ma/cious (kon/tōō mā/shəs, -tyōō-) *adj.* stubbornly disobedient.

con/tu·me·ly (kon/tōō mə lē, -tyōō-) *n., pl.* **-lies.** insulting or humiliating treatment or language.

con·tu/sion (kən tōō/zhən, -tyōō/-) *n.* a bruise.

co·nun/drum (kə nun/drəm) *n.* anything that puzzles.

con/ur·ba/tion (kon/ər bā/shən) *n.* a continuous group of towns or cities.

con/va·lesce/ (kon/və les/) *v.i.,* **-lesced, -lescing.** to recover from illness. —**con/va·les/cence,** *n.* —**con/va·les/cent,** *adj., n.*

con·vec/tion (kən vek/shən) *n.* the transfer of heat by the movement of the warm parts of a liquid or gas.

con·vene/ (kən vēn/) *v.i., v.t.,* **-vened, -vening.** to assemble.

con·ven/ient (-yənt) *adj.* **1.** suitable to the needs or purpose. **2.** at hand; accessible. —**con·ven/ience,** *n.*

con/vent (kon/vent, -vənt) *n.* a community of nuns or the building they occupy.

con·ven/tion (kən ven/shən) *n.* **1.** an assembly. **2.** an agreement. **3.** an accepted usage or custom.

con·ven/tion·al *adj.* **1.** conforming to accepted standards. **2.** ordinary.

con·verge/ (kən vûrj/) *v.i.,* **-verged, -verging.** to meet in a point.

con·ver/sant (-vûr/sənt) *adj.* familiar.

con/ver·sa/tion (kon/vər sā/shən) *n.* informal oral communication between people or an instance of this. —**con/ver·sa/tion·al,** *adj.*

con·verse/[1] (kən vûrs/) *v.i.,* **-versed, -versing.** to talk informally with someone.

con/verse[2] *adj.* (kən vûrs/) **1.** opposite or contrary. —*n.* (kon/vûrs) **2.** something opposite or contrary.

con·ver/sion *n.* **1.** the act or process of converting or the state of being converted. **2.** change in form or function. **3.** change from one belief, viewpoint, etc., to another.

con·vert/ *v.t.* (kən vûrt/) **1.** to change into a different form. **2.** to persuade to different beliefs. —*v.i.* **3.** to become converted. —*n.* (kon/vûrt) **4.** a converted person. —**con·vert/er,** *n.*

con·vert/i·ble *adj.* **1.** able to be converted. —*n.* **2.** a car with a folding top.

con·vex/ (kon veks/) *adj.* curved outward. —**con·vex/i·ty,** *n.*

con·vey/ (kən vā/) *v.t.* **1.** to transport; transmit. **2.** to communicate. —**con·vey/or, con·vey/er** *n.*

con·vey/ance *n.* **1.** the act of conveying. **2.** a vehicle.

con·vict/ *v.t.* (kən vikt/) **1.** to find guilty. —*n.* (kon/vikt) **2.** a convicted person in prison.

con·vic/tion *n.* **1.** convicting or being convicted. **2.** a firm belief.

con·vince/ (kən vins/) *v.t.,* **-vinced, -vincing.** to cause (a person) to believe something is true.

con·viv/i·al (kən viv/ē əl) *adj.* sociable and festive.

con·voke/ (kən vōk/) *v.t.,* **-voked,**

-voking. to call together. —con′-
vo•ca′tion (kon′vō kā′shən) n.

con′vo•lu′tion (kon′və loō′shən) n.
a coil. —con′vo•lut′ed, adj.

con′voy (kon′voi) v.t. **1.** to escort
for protection. —n. **2.** a group of
ships or vehicles traveling together.

con•vulse′ (kən vuls′) v.t., -vulsed,
-vulsing. to cause to shake violently with laughter, pain, etc.
—con•vul′sive, adj.

con•vul′sion n. **1.** a series of violent, involuntary muscular contractions. **2.** a violent disturbance.

co′ny (kō′nē, kun′ē) n., pl. -nies. a
rabbit.

coo (koō) v., cooed, cooing, n.
—v.i. **1.** to utter or imitate the soft
murmuring sound of a dove. —n.
2. such a sound.

cook (koŏk) v.t. **1.** to prepare (food)
by heating. —v.i. **2.** to prepare
food by heating. **3.** to undergo
cooking. —n. **4.** one who cooks.

cook′book′ n. a book with recipes
and instructions for cooking.

cook′er•y n. the art of cooking.

cook′ie n. a small sweet cake.

cool (koōl) adj. **1.** moderately cold.
2. calm. **3.** not enthusiastic. **4.**
Slang. great; excellent. —v.t., v.i. **5.**
to make or become cool.

cool′ant n. a substance used to reduce the temperature of a system.

cool′er n. a container for keeping
something cool.

coop (koōp, koŏp) n. **1.** a cage for
fowls. —v.t. **2.** to keep in or as if
in a coop.

coop′er n. a barrel maker.

co•op′er•ate′ (kō op′ə rāt′) v.i.,
-ated, -ating. to work or act together. —co•op′er•a′tion, n.

co•op′er•a•tive (-ər ə tiv) adj. **1.** cooperating or willing to cooperate.
—n. **2.** an enterprise owned and
operated by its members. **3.** Also,
co-op (kō′op′). an apartment house
jointly owned by its tenants.

co-opt′ (kō opt′) v.t. **1.** to choose
as a fellow member. **2.** to win over
into a larger group.

co•or′di•nate′ v., -nated, -nating,
adj., n. —v.t. (kō ôr′dn āt′) **1.** to
place in order. **2.** to combine in
harmonious relationship. —adj.
(-dn it) **3.** of equal order or degree.
—n. **4.** a coordinate person or
thing. —co•or′di•na′tion, n.

cop (kop) n. Informal. a police officer.

co′pay′ (kō′pā′) n. a fixed amount
paid by a patient to a health-care
provider. Also, co′pay′ment.

cope¹ (kōp) v.i., coped, coping. to
deal with problems or duties.

cope² (kōp) n. a long cloak worn
by the clergy.

cop′i•er (kop′ē ər) n. a machine for
making copies.

co′pi′lot (kō′pī′lət) n. an aircraft pilot who is second in command.

cop′ing (kō′ping) n. the top layer
of a wall.

co′pi•ous (kō′pē əs) adj. abundant.

cop′per (kop′ər) n. a soft reddish
metallic element.

cop′per•head′ n. a poisonous
snake with a copper-colored head.

copse (kops) n. a thicket of small
trees or bushes. Also, cop′pice.

cop′u•late′ (kop′yə lāt′) v.i., -lated,
-lating. to have sexual intercourse.
—cop′u•la′tion, n.

cop′y (kop′ē) n., pl. -ies, v., -ied,
-ying. —n. **1.** a reproduction or imitation. **2.** a specimen of a book,
magazine, etc. **3.** material to be
printed. —v.t., v.i. **4.** to make a
copy (of). **5.** to imitate.

cop′y•cat′ n. an imitator.

cop′y•right′ n. **1.** exclusive control
of a book, picture, etc. —v.t. **2.** to
secure the copyright on. —adj. **3.**
covered by copyright.

co•quette′ (kō ket′) n. a female
flirt. —co•quet′tish, adj.

cor′al (kôr′əl) n. **1.** a substance
formed of the skeletons of tiny
marine animals. **2.** a yellowish
pink.

cord (kôrd) n. **1.** a thin rope. **2.** a
small, flexible, insulated electrical
cable. **3.** 128 cu. ft. of firewood.

cor′dial (kôr′jəl) adj. **1.** hearty;
friendly. —n. **2.** a liqueur. —cor•
dial′i•ty (-jal′i tē, -jē al′-) n.

cord′less adj. (of an electrical appliance) having a self-contained
power supply.

cor′don (kôr′dn) n. a line of police,
soldiers, etc., guarding an area.

cor′do•van (kôr′də vən) n. a soft
leather.

cor′du•roy′ (kôr′də roi′) n. a ribbed
cotton fabric.

core (kôr) n., v., cored, coring. —n.
1. the central part. —v.t. **2.** to remove the core of.

co′ri•an′der (kôr′ē an′dər) n. an
herb with pungent leaves and
seeds.

cork (kôrk) n. **1.** the bark of a Mediterranean oak tree. **2.** a stopper of
cork, rubber, etc. —v.t. **3.** to close
with a cork.

cork′screw′ n. a spiral, pointed instrument for removing corks.

cor′mo•rant (kôr′mər ənt) n. a diving seabird.

corn¹ (kôrn) n. **1.** a cereal plant
bearing large ears with kernels. **2.**

Informal. something trite. —*v.t.* **3.** to preserve in brine.

corn² (kôrn) *n.* a horny growth, esp. on the toe.

corn′ bread′ *n.* a bread made with cornmeal.

corn′cob′ *n.* the core of an ear of corn that holds the grains.

cor′ne•a (kôr′nē ə) *n.* the transparent outer covering of the eye.

cor′ner (kôr′nər) *n.* **1.** the place or point where two lines or streets meet. **2.** a secluded place. **3.** a monopoly. —*v.t.* **4.** to drive into a corner. **5.** to gain exclusive control of (a stock or commodity). —*Idiom.* **6. cut corners,** to reduce cost, labor, etc.

cor′ner•stone′ *n.* **1.** a stone representing the starting place in the construction of a building. **2.** something essential.

cor•net′ (kôr net′) *n.* a wind instrument resembling the trumpet.

cor′nice (kôr′nis) *n.* a horizontal projection at the top of a wall.

corn′meal′ *n.* meal from corn.

corn′starch′ *n.* a starchy flour from corn.

cor′nu•co′pi•a (kôr′nə kō′pē ə, -nyə-) *n.* a horn of plenty.

corn′y *adj.,* **-ier, -iest.** trite, sentimental, or old-fashioned.

co•rol′la (kə rol′ə, -rō′lə) *n.* the petals of a flower.

cor′ol•lar′y (kôr′ə ler′ē) *n., pl.* **-laries.** a logical deduction.

co•ro′na (kə rō′nə) *n., pl.* **-nas, -nae** (-nē). a circle of light.

cor′o•nar′y (kôr′ə ner′ē) *adj., n., pl.* **-naries.** —*adj.* **1.** of the arteries supplying the heart with blood. —*n.* **2.** a heart attack.

cor′o•na′tion (kôr′ə nā′shən) *n.* the act of crowning.

cor′o•ner (kôr′ə nər) *n.* an official who investigates suspicious deaths.

cor′o•net′ (kôr′ə net′) *n.* a small crown.

corp. corporation.

cor′po•ral¹ (-pər əl) *adj.* physical.

cor′po•ral² (-pər əl) *n.* an officer ranking below a sergeant.

cor′po•ra′tion (-rā′shən) *n.* an association created by law and having the powers and liabilities of an individual. —**cor′po•rate** (-pər it, -prit) *adj.*

cor•po′re•al (-pôr′ē əl) *adj.* material; tangible.

corps (kôr) *n., pl.* **corps. 1.** a military unit. **2.** any group.

corpse (kôrps) *n.* a dead body.

cor′pu•lent (kôr′pyə lənt) *adj.* fat.

cor′pus (kôr′pəs) *n., pl.* **-pora** (-pər ə). **1.** a complete collection of writings. **2.** a body, esp. when dead.

cor′pus•cle (-pə səl) *n.* a blood cell.

cor•ral′ (kə ral′) *n., v.,* **-ralled, -ralling.** —*n.* **1.** a pen for livestock. —*v.t.* **2.** to keep in a corral. **3.** to corner or capture.

cor•rect′ (kə rekt′) *v.t.* **1.** to make right. **2.** to mark or remove errors. **3.** to rebuke or punish. —*adj.* **4.** right. —**cor•rec′tion,** *n.* —**cor•rec′tive,** *adj., n.*

cor′re•late′ (kôr′ə lāt′) *v.t.,* **-lated, -lating.** to establish in orderly connection. —**cor′re•la′tion,** *n.*

cor′re•spond′ (kôr′ə spond′) *v.i.* **1.** to match or be similar. **2.** to communicate by letters. —**cor′re•spond′ence,** *n.*

cor′re•spond′ent *n.* **1.** a letter writer. **2.** a person employed by a newspaper, television network, etc., to report news from a distant place. —*adj.* **3.** similar.

cor′ri•dor (kôr′i dər) *n.* **1.** a long hallway. **2.** a strip of land forming an outlet through foreign territory. **3.** a densely populated region with major transportation routes.

cor•rob′o•rate′ (kə rob′ə rāt′) *v.t.,* **-rated, -rating.** to confirm. —**cor•rob′o•ra′tion,** *n.* —**cor•rob′o•ra′tive** (-ə rā′tiv, -ər ə tiv) *adj.*

cor•rode′ (kə rōd′) *v.,* **-roded, -roding.** —*v.t.* **1.** to eat or wear away gradually. —*v.i.* **2.** to become corroded. —**cor•ro′sion** (-rō′zhən) *n.* —**cor•ro′sive,** *adj.*

cor′ru•gate′ (kôr′ə gāt′) *v.,* **-gated, -gating.** —*v.t.* **1.** to bend into grooves and ridges. —*v.i.* **2.** to become corrugated.

cor•rupt′ (kə rupt′) *adj.* **1.** dishonest. **2.** immoral. **3.** decayed. —*v.t., v.i.* **4.** to make or become corrupt. —**cor•rup′tion,** *n.*

cor•sage′ (kôr säzh′) *n.* a small bouquet to be worn.

cor′set (-sit) *n.* an undergarment for shaping the body.

cor•tege′ (-tezh′) *n.* a procession.

cor′tex (-teks) *n.* the outer covering of the brain or an organ.

cor′ti•sone′ (kôr′tə zōn′, -sōn′) *n.* a hormone used in treating autoimmune or inflammatory diseases.

cor•vette′ (kôr vet′) *n.* a small, fast sailing vessel.

cos•met′ic (koz met′ik) *n.* **1.** a beautifying product. —*adj.* **2.** of cosmetics. **3.** superficial.

cos′mic (koz′mik) *adj.* **1.** of the cosmos. **2.** vast.

cos•mol′o•gy (-mol′ə jē) *n.* the study of the origin and structure of the universe.

cos′mo•pol′i•tan (koz′mə pol′i tn) *adj.* worldly.

cos/mos (-məs, -mōs) *n.* the ordered universe.

cost (kôst) *n.* **1.** the price paid for something. **2.** a loss or penalty. —*v.t.* **3.** to require the payment of. **4.** to result in the loss of.

cost/-ef·fec/tive *adj.* producing optimum results for the expenditure.

cost/ of liv/ing *n.* the average amount paid for basic necessities.

cos/tume (kos/tōōm, -tyōōm) *n.* historical or theatrical dress.

co/sy (kō/zē) *adj.,* -sier, -siest, *n., pl.,* -sies. cozy.

cot (kot) *n.* a light, portable bed.

cote (kōt) *n.* a shelter for pigeons, sheep, etc.

co/te·rie (kō/tə rē) *n.* a group of social acquaintances.

co·til/lion (kə til/yən) *n.* a formal ball.

cot/tage (kot/ij) *n.* a small house.

cot/tage cheese/ *n.* a soft, mild cheese made from skim-milk curds.

cot/ton (kot/n) *n.* **1.** a soft white substance attached to the seeds of a tropical plant. **2.** cloth or thread made of this substance.

cot/ton·mouth/ (-mouth/) *n.* a poisonous snake of southeastern U.S. swamps. Also, **water moccasin.**

cot/ton·seed/ *n.* the seed of the cotton plant, yielding an oil **(cottonseed oil)** used in cooking and medicine.

couch (kouch) *n.* a long piece of furniture for sitting or lying.

cou/gar (kōō/gər) *n.* a large American wildcat.

cough (kôf) *v.i.* **1.** to expel air from the lungs suddenly and loudly. —*n.* **2.** the act or sound of coughing.

cough/ drop/ *n.* a lozenge for relieving a cough, sore throat, etc.

could (kŏŏd; *unstressed* kəd), *auxiliary v.* **1.** pt. of **can**[1]. **2.** (used to express politeness or doubt).

coun/cil (koun/səl) *n.* a deliberative or advisory body. —**coun/ci·lor, coun/cil·lor,** *n.*

coun/sel (-səl) *n., v.,* -seled, -seling. —*n.* **1.** advice. **2.** consultation. **3.** a lawyer. —*v.t.* **4.** to advise. —**coun/se·lor, coun/sel·lor,** *n.*

count[1] (kount) *v.t.* **1.** to find the total number of. **2.** to name the numbers up to. **3.** to consider. —*v.i.* **4.** to name the numbers in order. **5.** to be important. **6. count on,** to rely on. —*n.* **7.** the act of counting. **8.** the total. **9.** an item in an indictment.

count[2] (kount) *n.* a nobleman.

count/down/ *n.* a backward counting to zero, indicating the start of a scheduled event.

coun/te·nance (koun/tn əns) *n., v.,* -nanced, -nancing. —*n.* **1.** the face. **2.** facial expression. —*v.t.* **3.** to approve.

count/er[1] (-tər) *n.* **1.** a table on which goods can be shown, business transacted, etc. **2.** a small object used to keep account in games. —*Idiom.* **3. over the counter,** (of medicines) without requiring a prescription. **4. under the counter,** in a secretive manner.

count/er[2] (-tər) *adv.* **1.** in the opposite direction. —*adj.* **2.** opposite. —*n.* **3.** something opposite to something else. —*v.t., v.i.* **4.** to oppose.

counter- a prefix indicating: **1.** opposite. **2.** against. **3.** in response to.

coun/ter·act/ *v.t.* to act in opposition to.

coun/ter·at·tack/ *n.* **1.** an attack made in response to another attack. —*v.t., v.i.* **2.** to make a counterattack (against).

coun/ter·bal/ance *n., v.,* -anced, -ancing. —*n.* (koun/tər bal/əns) **1.** a weight or influence balancing another. —*v.t., v.i.* (koun/tər bal/əns) **2.** to act as a counterbalance (to).

coun/ter·clock/wise/ *adv., adj.* in a direction opposite to the movement of clock hands.

coun/ter·cul/ture *n.* those opposed to a prevailing culture.

coun/ter·feit (-fit) *adj.* **1.** fake. —*n.* **2.** a fraudulent imitation. —*v.t., v.i.* **3.** to make a counterfeit (of). **4.** to feign.

coun/ter·in·tel/li·gence *n.* activity thwarting espionage by an enemy power.

coun/ter·mand/ (-mand/) *v.t.* to cancel (an order).

coun/ter·part/ *n.* a person or thing corresponding to another.

coun/ter·point/ *n.* a method of combining melodies.

coun/ter·pro·duc/tive *adj.* giving results contrary to those intended.

coun/ter·sign/ *n.* **1.** a secret sign. —*v.t.* **2.** to sign (a document) to confirm the signature of another person.

count/ess (koun/tis) *n.* **1.** the wife of a count or earl. **2.** a woman equal in rank to a count or earl.

count/less *adj.* too many to count.

coun/try (kun/trē) *n., pl.* -tries. **1.** a nation or its land or people. **2.** areas with fields, farms, forests, etc., and few buildings or people.

coun/try·side/ *n.* a rural area.

coun/ty (koun/tē) *n., pl.* -ties. a political unit within a state.

coup (koo) *n., pl.* **coups.** a daring and successful act.

coup′ d′é.tat′ (koo′ dä tä′) *n., pl.* **coups d′état** (-dä täz′, -tä′). an overthrow of a government by force.

coupe (koop) *n.* a small, two-door car. Also, **cou•pé′** (koo pā′).

cou′ple (kup′əl) *n., v.,* **-pled, -pling.** —*n.* **1.** a combination of two of a kind. **2.** a grouping of two persons. —*v.t., v.i.* **3.** to join or unite. —**cou′pling,** *n.* —**Usage.** Do not confuse PAIR and COUPLE. Both words have the meaning "a group of two" but are used differently. PAIR is used when two things come as a set, with one not usually used without the other: *a pair of gloves* or when there is one item that has two parts, as in *a pair of scissors.* COUPLE is used for things of the same kind that happen to be two in number: *a couple of books.*

cou′plet (kup′lit) *n.* a pair of rhyming lines.

cou′pon (koo′pon, kyoo′-) *n.* a certificate entitling the holder to a gift or discount.

cour′age (kûr′ij, kur′-) *n.* bravery. —**cou•ra′geous** (kə rā′jəs) *adj.*

cour′i•er (kûr′ē ər) *n.* a messenger.

course (kôrs) *n., v.,* **coursed, coursing.** —*n.* **1.** a path, route, or channel. **2.** a direction taken. **3.** a manner of proceeding. **4.** a series of lessons. **5.** one part of a meal. —*v.i.* **6.** to run or move swiftly. —*Idiom.* **7. in due course,** in the proper order of events. **8. of course,** certainly.

court (kôrt) *n.* **1.** a place where justice is administered. **2.** an open space enclosed by buildings or walls. **3.** a sovereign's residence and retinue. **4.** an assembly held by a sovereign. **5.** homage or attention. **6.** a level area for certain games. —*v.t.* **7.** to seek to win the favor of. **8.** to woo. **9.** to act in a way that causes.

cour′te•ous (kûr′tē əs) *adj.* polite.

cour′te•san (kôr′tə zən) *n.* a prostitute with noble or wealthy clients.

cour′te•sy (kûr′tə sē) *n., pl.* **-sies. 1.** polite behavior. **2.** a courteous act.

cour′ti•er (kôr′tē ər) *n.* an attendant at a royal court.

court′ly *adj.* polite or elegant.

court′-mar′tial *n., pl.* **courts-martial,** *v.,* **-tialed, -tialing.** —*n.* **1.** a military court. —*v.t.* **2.** to try by court-martial.

cous′in (kuz′ən) *n.* the child of one's uncle or aunt.

cou•tu′ri•er (koo toor′ē ər, -ē ā′) *n.* a designer of fashionable clothes.

cove (kōv) *n.* a recess in a shoreline.

cov′en (kuv′ən, kō′vən) *n.* an assembly of witches.

cov′e•nant (kuv′ə nənt) *n.* a solemn agreement; oath or pact.

cov′er (kuv′ər) *v.t.* **1.** to place something over or upon. **2.** to hide from view. **3.** to deal with. **4.** to protect. **5.** to travel over. **6.** to meet or offset. —*v.i.* **7.** to substitute for someone. **8.** to provide an alibi. —*n.* **9.** something that covers. **10.** protection. **11.** an assumed identity. —*Idiom.* **12. take cover,** to seek shelter. **13. under cover,** secretly.

cov′er•age (-ij) *n.* **1.** protection by insurance. **2.** the reporting of news.

cov′er•let (-lit) *n.* a quilt.

cov′ert (kō′vərt) *adj.* **1.** secret. —*n.* **2.** a thicket giving shelter to animals. —**cov′ert•ly,** *adv.*

cov′er-up′ *n.* concealment of illegal activity, a blunder, etc.

cov′et (kuv′it) *v.t., v.i.* to desire (another's property) eagerly or wrongfully. —**cov′et•ous,** *adj.*

cov′ey (kuv′ē) *n., pl.* **-eys.** a small flock.

cow[1] (kou) *n.* the female of a bovine or other large animal, as the whale.

cow[2] (kou) *v.t.* to intimidate.

cow′ard (kou′ərd) *n.* one who lacks courage. —**cow′ard•ice** (-ər dis) *n.*

cow′boy′ or **cow′girl′** *n.* a cattle herder.

cow′er (kou′ər) *v.i.* to crouch in fear.

cowl (koul) *n.* a hooded garment or the hood itself.

cow′lick′ *n.* a tuft of hair growing in a different direction from the rest of the hair.

cow′slip′ *n.* a plant with fragrant yellow flowers.

cox′swain (kok′sən) *n.* a person who steers a boat or racing shell. Also, **cox.**

coy (koi) *adj.* pretending to be shy or embarrassed. —**coy′ness,** *n.*

coy•o•te (kī ō′tē) *n.* a wild animal related to the wolf.

coz′en (kuz′ən) *v.t., v.i.* to cheat or deceive.

co′zy (kō′zē) *adj.,* **-zier, -ziest,** *n.* —*adj.* **1.** snugly warm and comfortable. —*n.* **2.** a knitted or padded cover for keeping a teapot or coffeepot warm. —**co′zi•ness,** *n.*

CPA certified public accountant.

CPI consumer price index.

CPR cardiopulmonary resuscitation: a form of lifesaving.

CPU central processing unit: the

key component of a computer system.

crab (krab) *n.* a crustacean with a broad flat body and four pairs of legs.

crab′ ap′ple *n.* a small tart apple.

crab′by *adj.*, **-bier, -biest.** grouchy.

crack (krak) *v.i.* **1.** to make a sudden, sharp sound. **2.** to break without separating. **3.** (of the voice) to break abruptly. —*v.t.* **4.** to cause to make a sudden, sharp sound. **5.** to cause to break without separating. **6.** to strike forcefully. **7. crack down,** to take severe measures. —*n.* **8.** a sudden, sharp sound. **9.** a break without the separation of parts. **10.** a slight opening. **11.** a sharp blow. **12.** a witty remark. **13.** *Slang.* a potent, smokable form of cocaine. —*Idiom.* **14. get cracking,** to hurry up.

crack′down′ *n.* a stern enforcement of regulations.

crack′er *n.* **1.** a crisp, thin biscuit. **2.** a firecracker.

crack·le (krak′əl) *v.*, **-led, -ling,** *n.* —*v.i.* **1.** to make repeated, small sharp noises. —*n.* **2.** such a sound.

crack′pot′ *n.* a person with irrational ideas.

crack′up′ *n.* a mental breakdown.

cra′dle (krād′l) *n.*, *v.*, **-dled, -dling.** —*n.* **1.** a bed for a baby, usu. on rockers. —*v.t.* **2.** to place in a cradle. **3.** to hold protectively.

craft (kraft) *n.* **1.** a skill; skilled trade. **2.** cunning. **3.** vessels or aircraft.

craft′y *adj.*, **-ier, -iest.** cunning.

crag (krag) *n.* a steep, rugged rock.

cram (kram) *v.*, **crammed, cramming.** —*v.t.* **1.** to fill tightly; stuff. —*v.i.* **2.** to study hard for an examination.

cramp[1] (kramp) *n.* **1.** an involuntary muscular contraction. —*v.t.*, *v.i.* **2.** to affect or be affected with a cramp.

cramp[2] (kramp) *v.t.* to restrict or hinder.

cramped (krampt) *adj.* confined.

cran′ber′ry (kran′ber′ē) *n.*, *pl.* **-ries.** an edible sour red berry.

crane (krān) *n.*, *v.*, **craned, cran·ing.** —*n.* **1.** a tall wading bird. **2.** a device for lifting heavy weights. —*v.t.*, *v.i.* **3.** to stretch (the neck).

cra′ni·um (krā′nē əm) *n.*, *pl.* **-niums, -nia** (-nē ə). the skull.

crank (krangk) *n.* **1.** a right-angled lever used to operate a machine. **2.** *Informal.* an ill-tempered person. **3.** a person with strange ideas. —*v.t.* **4.** to start by turning a crank.

crank′y (krang′kē) *adj.*, **-ier, -iest.** ill-tempered. —**crank′i·ness,** *n.*

cran′ny (kran′ē) *n.*, *pl.* **-nies.** a narrow opening.

crap (krap) *n. Slang.* **1.** worthless material. **2.** false or meaningless statements.

crape (krāp) *n.* crepe (defs. 1, 2).

crap′pie (krap′ē) *n.* a type of large sunfish.

craps (kraps) *n.* a dice game.

crash (krash) *v.i.* **1.** to make a loud, clattering noise. **2.** to fall with damage. **3.** to strike, collide, or break noisily. **4.** to collapse suddenly. **5.** (of a computer) to fail suddenly. —*v.t.* **6.** to cause to break violently and noisily. **7.** to cause (a vehicle) to crash. **8.** to enter (a party) without invitation. —*n.* **9.** an act or instance of crashing. **10.** a sudden loud noise. **11.** a collapse.

crass (kras) *adj.* insensitive; crude.

crate (krāt) *n.*, *v.*, **crated, crating.** —*n.* **1.** a wooden box for packing. —*v.t.* **2.** to put in a crate.

cra′ter *n.* a cup-shaped hole, as in a volcano or on the moon.

cra·vat′ (krə vat′) *n.* a necktie.

crave (krāv) *v.t.*, **craved, craving.** to yearn or beg for.

cra′ven (krā′vən) *adj.* **1.** cowardly. —*n.* **2.** a coward.

crav′ing *n.* an intense yearning.

crawl (krôl) *v.i.* **1.** to move on hands and knees or with the belly close to the ground. **2.** to move slowly. —*n.* **3.** the act of crawling. **4.** a crawling pace. **5.** an overhand swimming stroke. —**crawl′er,** *n.*

cray′fish′ (krā′fish′) *n.* a crustacean resembling a lobster. Also, **craw′-fish′** (krô′-).

cray′on (krā′on) *n.* a stick of colored wax for drawing.

craze (krāz) *v.*, **crazed, crazing,** *n.* —*v.t.* **1.** to make or become insane. —*n.* **2.** a fad.

cra′zy (krā′zē) *adj.*, **-zier, -ziest. 1.** insane. **2.** impractical.

creak (krēk) *v.i.* **1.** to squeak sharply. —*n.* **2.** a creaking sound.

cream (krēm) *n.* **1.** the fatty part of milk. **2.** a thick, smooth substance to put on the skin. **3.** the best part of anything. —*v.t.* **4.** to make with cream. **5.** to mix until creamy.

cream′er·y *n.*, *pl.* **-ies.** a place where dairy goods are produced.

crease (krēs) *n.*, *v.*, **creased, creasing.** —*n.* **1.** a ridge produced by folding, striking, etc. **2.** a wrinkle. —*v.t.* **3.** to make creases in. —*v.i.* **4.** to become creased.

cre·ate′ (krē āt′) *v.t.*, **-ated, -ating.** to cause to exist. —**cre·a′tion,** *n.* —**cre·a′tive,** *adj.* —**cre·a′tor,** *n.*

crea/ture (krē/chər) *n.* an animal or human being.

cre/dence (krēd/ns) *n.* belief.

cre.den/tials (kri den/shəlz) *n. pl.* documents providing evidence of identity, qualifications, etc.

cre.den/za (kri den/zə) *n.* a sideboard, esp. one without legs.

cred/i.ble (kred/ə bəl) *adj.* believable. —**cred/i.bil/i.ty,** *n.*

cred/it (kred/it) *n.* **1.** the belief that something is true. **2.** commendation for an accomplishment. **3.** a source of honor. **4.** permission to pay for goods later. **5.** a balance in a person's favor. —*v.t.* **6.** to believe or trust. **7.** to give credit for or to. **cred/it.a.ble** *adj.* worthy.

cred/it card/ *n.* a card entitling the holder to make purchases and pay for them later.

cred/i.tor *n.* a person to whom money is owed.

cred/it un/ion *n.* a cooperative group that makes loans to its members at low interest rates.

cred/u.lous (krej/ə ləs) *adj.* willing to believe too readily. —**cre.du/li.ty** (krə dōō/li tē, -dyōō/-) *n.*

creed (krēd) *n.* a formal statement of beliefs.

creek (krēk, krik) *n.* a small stream.

creep (krēp) *v.,* **crept** (krept) or **creeped, creeping,** *n.* —*v.i.* **1.** to move slowly with the body close to the ground. **2.** to move slowly or stealthily. **3.** (of a plant) to grow along the ground, a wall, etc. —*n.* **4.** *Slang.* an obnoxious person. **5. the creeps,** a sensation of anxiety or disgust.

creep/y *adj.,* **-ier, -iest.** having or causing a sensation of horror.

cre/mate (krē/māt) *v.t.,* **-mated, -mating.** to burn (a dead body) to ashes. —**cre.ma/tion,** *n.* —**cre/ma.to/ry,** *n.*

cre/o.sote/ (krē/ə sōt/) *n.* an oily liquid from coal and wood tar, used as a wood preservative and an antiseptic.

crepe (krāp; *for 3 also* krep) *n.* **1.** a light crinkled fabric. **2.** Also, **crepe paper,** thin, wrinkled paper used for decorating. **3.** a thin, light pancake.

cre.scen/do (kri shen/dō) *n., pl.* **-dos.** a gradual increase in loudness.

cres/cent (kres/ənt) *n.* **1.** the shape of the moon in its first or last quarter. **2.** an object having this shape.

cress (kres) *n.* a plant with pungent leaves, eaten in salads.

crest (krest) *n.* **1.** the top of a hill. **2.** the highest point. **3.** a tuft on the head of a bird or animal. **4.** the foamy top of a wave. **5.** a heraldic device. —*v.i.* **6.** to form or rise to a crest.

crest/fal/len *adj.* discouraged or depressed.

cre/tin (krēt/n) *n.* a boorish person.

cre.vasse/ (krə vas/) *n.* a deep cleft, esp. in a glacier.

crev/ice (krev/is) *n.* a crack forming an opening.

crew (krōō) *n.* a group of persons working together, as on a ship.

crew/cut/ *n.* a haircut in which the hair is very closely cropped.

crib (krib) *n., v.,* **cribbed, cribbing.** —*n.* **1.** a child's bed with enclosed sides. **2.** a bin for storing grain. **3.** a manger. —*v.t.* **4.** to put in a crib.

crib/bage (krib/ij) *n.* a card game using a score-board with pegs.

crick (krik) *n.* a muscle spasm.

crick/et (krik/it) *n.* **1.** a leaping insect that makes a chirping sound. **2.** an outdoor ball game, popular in Britain, played by two teams with bats, balls, and wickets.

cri/er (krī/ər) *n.* one who makes announcements.

crime (krīm) *n.* an unlawful act.

crim/inal (krim/ə nl) *adj.* **1.** guilty of crime. **2.** dealing with crime or its punishment. —*n.* **3.** a person convicted of a crime.

crimp (krimp) *v.t.* **1.** to make wavy. —*n.* **2.** a crimped form. —*Idiom.* **3. put a crimp in,** to hinder.

crim/son (krim/zən) *n.* a deep red.

cringe (krinj) *v.i.,* **cringed, cringing.** to shrink in fear or embarrassment.

crin/kle (kring/kəl) *v.,* **-kled, -kling,** *n.* —*v.t., v.i.* **1.** to wrinkle. **2.** to rustle. —*n.* **3.** a wrinkle. **4.** a rustling sound. —**crin/kly,** *adj.*

crin/o.line (krin/l in) *n.* **1.** a stiff, coarse fabric. **2.** a petticoat.

crip/ple (krip/əl) *n., v.,* **-pled, -pling.** —*n.* **1.** *Sometimes Offensive.* a lame or disabled person or animal. —*v.t.* **2.** to disable.

cri/sis (krī/sis) *n., pl.* **-ses** (-sēz) a decisive stage or point.

crisp (krisp) *adj.* **1.** brittle. **2.** firm and fresh. **3.** brisk and decided. **4.** bracing. —*v.t., v.i.* **5.** to make or become crisp. —**crisp/ness,** *n.*

criss/cross/ (kris/krôs/) *adj.* **1.** marked with crossed lines. —*n.* **2.** a crisscross pattern. —*v.t.* **3.** to move back and forth over. **4.** to mark with crossed lines.

cri.te/ri.on (krī tēr/ē ən) *n., pl.* **-teria** (-tēr/ē ə) a standard for judgment.

crit/ic (krit/ik) *n.* **1.** a person who judges art or literature. **2.** a person who tends to make harsh judgments.

crit′i•cal *adj.* **1.** severe in judgment. **2.** involving criticism. **3.** crucial.

crit′i•cism *n.* **1.** faultfinding. **2.** the art of judging the merits of anything.

crit′i•cize′ (-sīz′) *v.i., v.t.,* **-cized, -cizing. 1.** to discuss as a critic. **2.** to find fault (with).

cri•tique′ (kri tēk′) *n., v.,* **-tiqued, -tiquing.** —*n.* **1.** an article evaluating a work. —*v.t.* **2.** to analyze critically.

crit′ter (krit′ər) *n. Dial.* a creature.

croak (krōk) *v.i.* **1.** to utter a hoarse cry, as that of a frog. —*n.* **2.** such a sound.

cro•chet′ (krō shā′) *v.i.* to form thread into designs with a hooked needle.

crock (krok) *n.* an earthen jar.

croc′o•dile′ (krok′ə dīl′) *n.* a large aquatic reptile with long, powerful jaws and tail.

cro′cus (krō′kəs) *n.* a small bulbous plant blooming in early spring.

crois•sant′ (*Fr.* krwä säN′; *Eng.* krə-sänt′) *n.* a crescent-shaped pastry.

crone (krōn) *n.* a witchlike old woman.

cro′ny (krō′nē) *n., pl.* **-nies.** a close friend.

crook (krŏŏk) *n.* **1.** a hooked stick. **2.** a bend. **3.** a dishonest person. —*v.t., v.i.* **4.** to bend; curve.

croon (krŏŏn) *v.i., v.t.* to sing softly.

crop (krop) *n., v.,* **cropped, cropping.** —*n.* **1.** the cultivated produce from the soil. **2.** a short whip. **3.** a pouch in the gullet of a bird. —*v.t.* **4.** to remove the ends of. **5.** to cut short. **6. crop up,** to appear.

cro•quet′ (krō kā′) *n.* a lawn game played with wooden balls and mallets.

cro′sier (krō′zhər) *n.* the staff of a bishop.

cross (krôs) *n.* **1.** a structure whose basic form has an upright with a transverse piece. **2.** the emblem of Christianity. **3.** a figure resembling a cross. **4.** a mixture of breeds. —*v.t.* **5.** to put, lie, or pass across. **6.** to oppose or frustrate. **7.** to mark (out). **8.** to mix (breeds). **9.** to make the sign of the cross over. —*v.i.* **10.** to intersect. **11.** to move or extend from one side to another. **12. cross off** *or* **out,** to cancel, as by drawing a line through. —*adj.* **13.** lying crosswise. **14.** angry. —*Idiom.* **15. cross one's mind,** to occur to one.

cross′bow′ (-bō′) *n.* a weapon consisting of a bow fixed on a stock like that of a rifle.

cross′breed′ *v.,* **crossbred, crossbreeding,** *n.* —*v.t., v.i.* **1.** to hybridize. —*n.* **2.** a hybrid.

cross′-coun′try *adj.* **1.** proceeding over fields, through woods, etc., rather than on a road or track. **2.** from one end of a country to the other. —*n.* **3.** the sport of cross-country racing.

cross′-ex•am′ine *v.t.,* **cross-examined, cross-examining.** to examine closely, as an opposing witness. —**cross′-ex•am′in•a′tion,** *n.*

cross′-eye′ *n.* a condition in which one or both eyes turn inward.

cross′ sec′tion *n.* **1.** a section made by cutting across something. **2.** a representative sample of a whole.

cross′walk′ *n.* a place where people can cross the street.

cross′word puz′zle *n.* a puzzle in which words determined from numbered clues are fitted into a pattern of squares.

crotch (kroch) *n.* a place where something divides, as the human body between the legs.

crotch′et (kroch′it) *n.* an odd fancy or whim.

crotch′et•y *adj.* grumpy.

crouch (krouch) *v.i.* **1.** to stoop low with the knees bent. —*n.* **2.** the act of crouching.

croup (krŏŏp) *n.* an inflammation of the throat causing coughing and difficult breathing.

crou′pi•er (krŏŏ′pē ər, -pē ā′) *n.* an attendant who handles bets and money at a gambling table.

crou′ton (krŏŏ′ton) *n.* a small cube of toasted bread.

crow¹ (krō) *n.* **1.** a large bird with black feathers. —*Idiom.* **2. as the crow flies,** in a straight line. **3. eat crow,** to admit a mistake.

crow² (krō) *v.i.* **1.** to utter the cry of a rooster. **2.** to boast. **3.** to utter a cry of pleasure. —*n.* **4.** the cry of a rooster. **5.** a cry of pleasure.

crow′bar′ *n.* an iron bar for prying something open.

crowd (kroud) *n.* **1.** a large group. —*v.i.* **2.** to press forward. —*v.t.* **3.** to cram. **4.** to push.

crown (kroun) *n.* **1.** an ornate ceremonial headgear worn by a monarch. **2.** the power of a sovereign. **3.** the top. —*v.t.* **4.** to place a crown on. **5.** to honor. **6.** to be at the top of.

CRT cathode-ray tube.

cru′cial (krŏŏ′shəl) *adj.* vitally important.

cru′ci•ble (krŏŏ′sə bəl) *n.* **1.** a vessel

for heating substances to high temperatures. **2.** a severe trial.

cru′ci•fix (krōō′sə fiks) *n.* a cross with a figure of Jesus crucified.

cru′ci•fy′ (-fī′) *v.t.*, **-fied, -fying. 1.** to put to death on a cross. **2.** to persecute. —**cru′ci•fix′ion,** *n.*

crude (krōōd) *adj.*, **cruder, crudest,** *n.* —*adj.* **1.** in a raw or unrefined state. **2.** unfinished; rough. **3.** vulgar. —*n.* **4.** unrefined petroleum.

cru′el (krōō′əl) *adj.* willfully causing pain. —**cru′el•ty,** *n.*

cru′et (krōō′it) *n.* a stoppered bottle for vinegar, oil, etc.

cruise (krōōz) *v.*, **cruised, cruising,** *n.* —*v.i.* **1.** to sail or fly at a moderate speed. **2.** to travel for pleasure. —*n.* **3.** a pleasure voyage on a ship.

cruis′er *n.* **1.** a kind of warship. **2.** a small pleasure boat.

crumb (krum) *n.* a small bit of bread, cookie, etc.

crum′ble (krum′bəl) *v.t., v.i.,* **-bled, -bling.** to break into small fragments.

crum′my (krum′ē) *adj.,* **-mier, -miest.** *Informal.* **1.** shabby. **2.** worthless. **3.** miserable.

crum′ple (krum′pəl) *v.,* **-pled, -pling.** —*v.t.* **1.** to crush into wrinkles. —*v.i.* **2.** to become crushed into wrinkles. **3.** to collapse.

crunch (krunch) *v.t.* **1.** to chew or crush noisily. —*n.* **2.** an act or sound of crunching. **3.** a critical situation.

cru•sade (krōō sād′) *n., v.,* **-saded, -sading.** —*n.* **1.** a medieval Christian expedition to recover the Holy Land from the Muslims. **2.** a campaign for a cause. —*v.i.* **3.** to engage in a crusade. —**cru•sad′er,** *n.*

crush (krush) *v.t.* **1.** to bruise or break by pressing. **2.** to pound into fragments. **3.** to suppress completely. —*v.i.* **4.** to become crushed. —*n.* **5.** a dense crowd. **6.** an infatuation.

crust (krust) *n.* **1.** a hard outer layer, as of bread. —*v.t., v.i.* **2.** to cover or become covered with a crust. —**crust′y,** *adj.*

crus•ta′cean (kru stā′shən) *n.* a sea animal having a hard shell, as the lobster, shrimp, etc.

crutch (kruch) *n.* **1.** a stick with a crosspiece under the armpit for support in walking. **2.** any aid or prop.

crux (kruks) *n., pl.* **cruxes, cruces** (krōō′sēz). the vital point.

cry (krī) *v.,* **cried, crying,** *n., pl.* **cries.** —*v.i.* **1.** to make sounds of grief or suffering. **2.** to weep. **3.** to shout. **4.** (of an animal) to make a characteristic sound. —*v.t.* **5.** to utter loudly. —*n.* **6.** a shout or scream. **7.** a fit of weeping. **8.** an animal's call. **9.** an appeal.

cry′o•gen′ics (krī′ə jen′iks) *n.* the study of extremely low temperatures. —**cry′o•gen′ic,** *adj.*

crypt (kript) *n.* an underground chamber, esp. for burial.

cryp′tic *adj.* mysterious.

crys′tal (kris′tl) *n.* **1.** a clear transparent mineral. **2.** a body with symmetrical plane faces. **3.** fine glass. —**crys′tal•line** (-in, -īn′) *adj.*

crys′tal•lize′ *v.i., v.t.,* **-lized, -lizing. 1.** to form or cause to form into crystals. **2.** to assume or cause to assume a definite form. —**crys′tal•li•za′tion,** *n.*

C′-sec′tion *n.* a Cesarean.

CST Central Standard Time.

CT Connecticut.

ct. 1. carat. **2.** cent. **3.** court.

cu. cubic.

cub (kub) *n.* a young fox, bear, etc.

cub′by•hole′ (kub′ē-) *n.* a small enclosed space.

cube (kyōōb) *n., v.,* **cubed, cubing.** —*n.* **1.** a solid bounded by six equal sides. **2.** *Math.* the third power of a quantity. —*v.t.* **3.** to cut into cubes. **4.** *Math.* to raise to the third power. —**cu′bic,** *adj.*

cu′bi•cle (kyōō′bi kəl) *n.* a small room.

cub′ism *n.* an artistic style marked by the reduction of natural forms to geometric shapes. —**cub′ist,** *adj., n.*

cuck′old (kuk′əld) *n.* the husband of an unfaithful wife.

cuck′oo (kōō′kōō, kŏŏk′ōō) *n.* a slim, stout-billed, long-tailed bird.

cu′cum•ber (kyōō′kum bər) *n.* a fleshy, green-skinned cylindrical fruit.

cud (kud) *n.* the food that a cow returns to its mouth from its stomach for further chewing.

cud′dle (kud′l) *v.,* **-dled, -dling.** —*v.t.* **1.** to hug tenderly. —*v.i.* **2.** to lie close. —*n.* **3.** a hug.

cudg′el (kuj′əl) *n., v.,* **-eled, -eling.** —*n.* **1.** a short thick stick. —*v.t.* **2.** to beat with a cudgel.

cue[1] (kyōō) *n.* (esp. on stage) something that signals speech or action.

cue[2] (kyōō) *n.* a rod used to strike the ball in billiards, pool, etc.

cuff[1] (kuf) *n.* **1.** a fold at the end of a sleeve or pants leg. —*Idiom.* **2. off the cuff,** impromptu.

cuff[2] (kuf) *v.t.* **1.** to slap. —*n.* **2.** a slap.

cui•sine′ (kwi zēn′) *n.* cookery.

cu′li•nar′y (kyōō′lə ner′ē, kul′ə-) *adj.* of cooking.

cull

cul′mi•nate′ (kul′mə nāt′) v.i., -nated, -nating. to reach the highest point. —cul′mi•na′tion, n.

cul′pa•ble (kul′pə bəl) adj. deserving blame. —cul′pa•bil′i•ty, n.

cul′prit (kul′prit) n. a person guilty of an offense.

cult (kult) n. 1. a religious sect or system. —adj. 2. popular with a particular group.

cul′ti•vate′ (kul′tə vāt′) v.t., -vated, -vating. 1. to prepare and care for (land). 2. to develop the possibilities of. —cul′ti•va′tion, n.

cul′ti•vat′ed adj. 1. prepared for raising crops. 2. cultured.

cul′ture (kul′chər) n. 1. artistic and intellectual pursuits. 2. development of the mind. 3. a state or form of civilization. 4. the growth of bacteria for study. 5. the raising of plants or animals.

cul′ture shock′ n. the distress of persons exposed to a new culture.

cul′vert (kul′vərt) n. a drain under a road, sidewalk, etc.

cum′ber•some (kum′bər səm) adj. clumsy or bulky.

cu′mu•la•tive (kyoo′myə lə tiv) adj. increasing by successive additions.

cu′mu•lus (kyoo′myə ləs) n., pl. -li. a puffy, rounded cloud.

cu•ne′i•form′ (kyoo nē′ə fôrm′) adj. composed of wedge-shaped elements, as some ancient writing.

cun′ning (kun′ing) adj. 1. clever. 2. sly. —n. 3. skill. 4. craftiness.

cup (kup) n., v., cupped, cupping. —n. 1. a small open drinking vessel, usu. with a handle. —v.t. 2. to form into a cup.

cup′board (kub′ərd) n. a closet with shelves for dishes, food, etc.

Cu′pid (kyoo′pid) n. the Roman god of carnal love.

cu•pid′i•ty (-pid′i tē) n. greed.

cu′po•la (kyoo′pə lə) n. a light, rounded structure on a roof.

cur (kûr) n. a mongrel dog.

cu′rate (kyoor′it) n. a member of the clergy assisting a rector or vicar.

cu•ra′tor (kyoo rā′tər, kyoor′ā-) n. a person in charge of a museum, art collection, etc.

curb (kûrb) n. 1. a strap for restraining a horse. 2. a restraint. 3. the edge of a sidewalk. —v.t. 4. to control.

curd (kûrd) n. a substance formed when milk coagulates, used in making cheese.

cur′dle (kûr′dl) v.t., v.i., -dled, -dling. to change into curds; congeal.

cure (kyoor) n., v., cured, curing.

—n. 1. a remedy. 2. restoration to health. —v.t. 3. to restore to health. 4. to preserve (meat, fish, etc.).

cur′few (kûr′fyoo) n. an order to be home or off the streets by a certain time.

cu′ri•o′ (kyoor′ē ō′) n., pl. -rios. an unusual valuable article.

cu′ri•os′i•ty (kyoor′ē os′i tē) n., pl. -ties. 1. the desire to know about anything. 2. a rare thing.

cu′ri•ous (-əs) adj. 1. eager to know. 2. prying. 3. strange.

curl (kûrl) v.t. 1. to form into ringlets. 2. to coil. —v.i. 3. to grow or form in ringlets. —n. 4. a ringlet. —curl′er, n. —curl′y, adj.

cur′lew (kûr′loo) n. a shorebird with a long curved bill.

cur•mudg′eon (kər muj′ən) n. a bad-tempered, difficult person.

cur′rant (kûr′ənt) n. 1. a small seedless raisin. 2. a small, edible sour berry.

cur′ren•cy (kûr′ən sē) n., pl. -cies. 1. the money in use in a country. 2. general acceptance.

cur′rent (kûr′ənt) adj. 1. present. 2. generally accepted. —n. 3. a flowing. 4. water, air, etc., moving in one direction. 5. the movement of electricity.

cur•ric′u•lum (kə rik′yə ləm) n., pl. -lums, -la (-lə) a course of study.

cur′ry¹ (kûr′ē, kur′ē) n., pl. -ries, v., -ried, -rying. —n. 1. an East Indian hot dish or powder (curry powder). —v.t. 2. to prepare with curry.

cur′ry² (kûr′ē, kur′ē) v.t., -ried, -rying. 1. to rub and comb (a horse). —Idiom. 2. curry favor, to seek to advance oneself through flattery.

curse (kûrs) n., v., cursed or curst, cursing. —n. 1. a wish that evil or misfortune befall someone or something. 2. a great evil or misfortune. 3. a profane or obscene word. —v.t. 4. to wish evil upon. 5. to swear at. 6. to afflict with evil. —v.i. 7. to swear profanely.

cur′sive (kûr′siv) adj. (of handwriting) in flowing strokes with letters joined together.

cur′sor (-sər) n. a movable symbol on a computer screen to indicate where data may be input.

cur′so•ry adj. hasty and superficial.

curt (kûrt) adj. rudely abrupt.

cur•tail′ (kər tāl′) v.t. to cut short or reduce. —cur•tail′ment, n.

cur′tain (kûr′tn) n. 1. a piece of fabric hung to adorn, conceal, etc. —v.t. 2. to cover with curtains.

curt′sy (kûrt′sē) n., pl. -sies, v., -sied, -sying. —n. 1. a respectful bow by women, made by bending the knees. —*v.i.* **2.** to make a curtsy.

cur'va·ture (kûr'və chər) *n.* **1.** a curved condition. **2.** the degree of curving.

curve (kûrv) *n., v.,* **curved, curving. —n. 1.** a continuously bending line. —*v.i., v.t.* **2.** to bend or move in a curve.

cush'ion (koosh'ən) *n.* **1.** a soft pad or pillow. **2.** something to absorb shocks. —*v.t.* **3.** to lessen the effects of. **4.** to provide with a cushion.

cush'y (koosh'ē) *adj.* **-ier, -iest.** *Informal.* easy and profitable.

cusp (kusp) *n.* a point.

cus'pid (kus'pid) *n.* one of the canine teeth in humans.

cus'tard (kus'tərd) *n.* a cooked dish of eggs and milk.

cus·to'di·an *n.* **1.** a person who has custody. **2.** the caretaker of a property.

cus'to·dy (-tə dē) *n., pl.* **-dies. 1.** guardianship and care. **2.** imprisonment. —**cus·to'di·al** (kə stō'dē-əl) *adj.*

cus'tom (kus'təm) *n.* **1.** a usual practice. **2.** habits or usages collectively. **3. customs, a.** duties on imports and exports. **b.** the agency collecting these. —*adj.* **4.** made for the individual.

cus'tom·ar'y *adj.* usual; habitual.

cus'tom·er *n.* a person who purchases something from another.

cus'tom·ize' *v.t.,* **-ized, -izing.** to make to individual specifications.

cut (kut) *v.,* **cut, cutting,** *n.* —*v.t.* **1.** to divide, sever, or penetrate with a sharp instrument. **2.** to harvest. **3.** to trim. **4.** to shorten or reduce. **5.** to dilute. **6.** to ignore. **7.** to absent oneself from. —*v.i.* **8.** to move or cross. **9. cut in, a.** to push oneself or a vehicle between others. **b.** to interrupt. —*n.* **10.** the act of cutting. **11.** the result of cutting. **12.** a straight passage. **13.** a share. **14.** a reduction. —*Idiom.* **15. a cut above,** superior to.

cut'-and-dried' *adj.* routine.

cu·ta'ne·ous (kyoo tā'nē əs) *adj.* of the skin.

cut'back' *n.* a reduction.

cute (kyoot) *adj.,* **cuter, cutest.** attractive or pretty in a dainty way.

cu'ti·cle (kyoo'ti kəl) *n.* the hardened skin around a fingernail or toenail.

cut'lass (kut'ləs) *n.* a short curved sword.

cut'ler·y (-lə rē) *n.* knives, forks, and spoons collectively.

cut'let (-lit) *n.* a slice of meat for frying or broiling.

cut'off' *n.* **1.** a point beyond which something is no longer effective or possible. **2.** a road that leaves another to make a shortcut.

cut'-rate' *adj.* offered at reduced prices.

cut'ter *n.* **1.** one that cuts. **2.** a single-masted sailing ship.

cut'throat' *n.* **1.** a murderer. —*adj.* **2.** ruthless.

cut'tle·fish' (kut'l fish') *n., pl.* **-fish, -fishes.** a marine mollusk with ten arms and a hard internal shell (**cut'tle·bone'**).

cy'a·nide' (sī'ə nīd') *n.* a highly poisonous compound of sodium or potassium.

cy'ber·net'ics (sī'bər net'iks) *n.* the study of control and communications systems in living beings and machines.

cy'ber·space' *n.* **1.** the realm of electronic communication. **2.** virtual reality.

cy'cle (sī'kəl) *n., v.,* **-cled, -cling. —n. 1.** a recurring series. **2.** a recurring period of time in which certain events repeat themselves in the same order. **3.** a bicycle, motorcycle, etc. —*v.i.* **4.** to ride a bicycle. **5.** to move in cycles.

cy'clone (sī'klōn) *n.* a violent weather system with circular wind motion. —**cy·clon'ic** (-klon'ik) *adj.*

cy'clo·tron' (-tron') *n.* a device used in splitting atoms.

cyg'net (sig'nit) *n.* a young swan.

cyl'in·der (sil'in dər) *n.* **1.** a round elongated solid with ends that are equal parallel circles. **2.** a machine part or opening in this form. —**cy·lin'dri·cal,** *adj.*

cym'bal (sim'bəl) *n.* a percussion instrument consisting of a concave brass plate that produces a sharp ringing sound when struck.

cyn'ic (sin'ik) *n.* a person who believes only selfishness motivates human action. —**cyn'i·cal,** *adj.* —**cyn'i·cism** (-ə siz'əm) *n.*

cy'no·sure' (sī'nə shoor') *n.* the center of attention.

cy'press (sī'prəs) *n.* an evergreen tree with dark green, scalelike leaves.

cyst (sist) *n.* an abnormal sac in or on the body, containing fluid or soft matter. —**cys'tic,** *adj.*

cys'tic fi·bro'sis (sis'tik fī brō'sis) *n.* a hereditary disease marked by breathing difficulties and the growth of excess fibrous tissue.

czar (zär) *n.* the former emperor of Russia. Also, **tsar.**

D

D, d (dē) *n.* the fourth letter of the English alphabet.

d. 1. date. **2.** deceased. **3.** degree. **4.** diameter. **5.** dose.

D.A. District Attorney.

dab (dab) *v.t., v.i.,* **dabbed, dabbing. 1.** to apply by light strokes. —*n.* **2.** a small quantity.

dab'ble (dab'əl) *v.i.,* **-bled, -bling. 1.** to play in water. **2.** to work at anything in a superficial manner.

dachs'hund' (däks'hŏŏnt', -hŏŏnd') *n.* a small dog with short legs and a long body.

dad (dad) *n. Informal.* father.

dad'dy (dad'ē) *n., pl.* **-dies.** *Informal.* father.

dad'dy-long'legs' or **dad'dy long'legs'** *n., pl.* **-longlegs.** a spiderlike arachnid with long, slender legs.

daf'fo·dil (daf'ə dil) *n.* a plant with trumpet-shaped yellow flowers.

daft (daft) *adj.* **1.** crazy. **2.** foolish.

dag'ger (dag'ər) *n.* a short, pointed two-edged weapon.

dahl'ia (dal'yə, däl'-) *n.* a showy cultivated flowering plant.

dai'ly (dā'lē) *adj.* of or occurring each day.

dain'ty (dān'tē) *adj.,* **-tier, -tiest,** *n., pl.* **-ties.** —*adj.* **1.** delicate. **2.** fastidious. —*n.* **3.** a delicacy.

dair'y (dâr'ē) *n., pl.* **-ies.** a place for making or selling milk, butter, etc.

da'is (dā'is) *n.* a raised platform.

dai'sy (dā'zē) *n., pl.* **-sies.** a flower with a yellow center and white petals.

dale (dāl) *n.* a valley.

dal'ly (dal'ē) *v.i.,* **-lied, -lying. 1.** to waste time. **2.** to flirt. —**dal'li·ance,** *n.*

Dal·ma'tian (dal mā'shən) *n.* a large white-and-black dog.

dam¹ (dam) *n., v.,* **dammed, damming.** —*n.* **1.** a barrier to obstruct the flow of water. —*v.t.* **2.** to stop up.

dam² (dam) *n.* a female parent of a four-footed domestic animal.

dam'age (dam'ij) *n., v.,* **-aged, -aging.** —*n.* **1.** injury or harm. **2. damages,** payment for loss or injury. —*v.t.* **3.** to cause damage to.

dam'ask (dam'əsk) *n.* a reversible fabric with a figured pattern.

dame (dām) *n.* **1. Dame,** in Britain, an official title of honor for a woman. **2.** *Slang: Sometimes Offensive.* a woman.

damn (dam) *v.t.* **1.** to declare to be bad. **2.** to condemn to hell. —**dam·na'tion,** *n.*

damp (damp) *adj.* **1.** moist. —*n.* **2.** moisture. —*v.t.* Also, **damp'en. 3.** to moisten. **4.** to discourage. **5.** to deaden. —**damp'ness,** *n.*

damp'er *n.* **1.** a control for air or smoke currents, as in a fireplace. **2.** a discouraging influence.

dam'sel (dam'zəl) *n.* a maiden.

dam'son (dam'zən, -sən) *n.* a small purple plum.

dance (dans) *v.,* **danced, dancing,** *n.* —*v.i.* **1.** to move the feet and body rhythmically to music. **2.** to leap or skip. —*n.* **3.** a pattern of motions performed to music. **4.** the art of dancing. **5.** a gathering for dancing. —**danc'er,** *n.*

dan'de·li·on (dan'dl ī'ən) *n.* a weedy plant with yellow flowers.

dan'der (-dər) *n.* **1.** loose skin scales shed from various animals. **2.** *Informal.* temper.

dan'dle (dan'dl) *v.t.,* **-dled, -dling.** to move (a child) lightly up and down.

dan'druff (-drəf) *n.* scales of dry skin on the scalp.

dan'dy (-dē) *n., pl.* **-dies,** *adj.,* **-dier, -diest.** —*n.* **1.** a man who is excessively concerned about his clothes. —*adj.* **2.** fine.

dan'ger (dān'jər) *n.* **1.** likelihood of harm. **2.** an instance of this. —**dan'ger·ous,** *adj.*

dan'gle (dang'gəl) *v.,* **-gled, -gling.** —*v.i.* **1.** to hang loosely. —*v.t.* **2.** to cause to hang loosely.

dank (dangk) *adj.* unpleasantly damp. —**dank'ness,** *n.*

dap'per (dap'ər) *adj.* neat and well-dressed.

dap'ple (dap'əl) *adj., v.,* **-pled, -pling,** *n.* —*adj.* **1.** marked with spots of dark and light. —*v.t.* **2.** to mark with spots of light and dark. —*n.* **3.** an animal with a dappled coat.

dare (dâr) *v.,* **dared, daring,** *n.* —*v.i.* **1.** to have the courage for something. —*v.t.* **2.** to have the boldness to try. **3.** to challenge (someone) to do something. —*n.* **4.** a challenge.

dare'dev'il *n.* **1.** a recklessly daring person. —*adj.* **2.** recklessly daring.

dar'ing *adj.* **1.** courageous. —*n.* **2.** adventurous courage.

dark (därk) *adj.* **1.** having little or no light. **2.** blackish. **3.** not pale or fair. **4.** gloomy. —*n.* **5.** the absence of light. **6.** night. —**dark'en,** *v.t., v.i.* —**dark'ly,** *adv.* —**dark'ness,** *n.*

Dark′ Ag′es *n.* the Middle Ages from A.D. 476 to about 1000.

dark′ horse′ *n.* an unexpected winner.

dark′room′ *n.* a darkened place for developing photographs.

dar′ling (där′ling) *n.* **1.** a loved one. **2.** a favorite. —*adj.* **3.** very dear. **4.** charming.

darn (därn) *v.t.* **1.** to mend by weaving stitches across a hole. —*n.* **2.** a darned place.

dart (därt) *n.* **1.** a slender pointed missile. **2. darts,** a game in which darts are thrown at a target. **3.** a tapered seam. —*v.i.* **4.** to move swiftly.

dash (dash) *v.t.* **1.** to strike or throw violently against something. **2.** to frustrate. **3. dash off, a.** to hurry away. **b.** to do something quickly. —*n.* **4.** a small quantity. **5.** a hasty movement. **6.** a punctuation mark (–) noting an abrupt break or pause. **7.** a short race.

dash′board′ *n.* the instrument panel on a motor vehicle.

dash′ing *adj.* **1.** lively. **2.** stylish.

das′tard (das′tərd) *n.* a coward.

da′ta (dā′tə, dat′ə) *n.pl., sing.* **da-tum** (dā′təm, dat′əm). facts or items of information.

da′ta·base′ *n.* a collection of data, esp. one accessible by computer.

da′ta proc′essing *n.* the high-speed handling of information by computer.

date¹ (dāt) *n., v.,* **dated, dating.** —*n.* **1.** a particular month, day, and year. **2.** an inscription on a writing, coin, etc., that shows the time of writing, casting, etc. **3.** a social engagement arranged before-hand. **4.** the period to which any event belongs. **5.** a person with whom one has a date. —*v.i.* **6.** to belong to a particular period. **7.** to go out on dates. —*v.t.* **8.** to mark with a date. **9.** to show the age of. **10.** to go out on a date with.

date² (dāt) *n.* the fleshy, edible fruit of the **date palm.**

dat′ed *adj.* **1.** having or showing a date. **2.** out-of-date.

da′tive (dā′tiv) *adj.* denoting a grammatical case that indicates the indirect object of a verb.

daub (dôb) *v.t., v.i.* **1.** to smear or paint clumsily. —*n.* **2.** something daubed on.

daugh′ter (dô′tər) *n.* a female child.

daugh′ter-in-law′ *n., pl.* **daugh-ters-in-law.** the wife of one's son.

daunt (dônt, dänt) *v.t.* to intimi-date or discourage.

daunt′less *adj.* bold; fearless.

dav′en·port′ (dav′ən pôrt′) *n.* a large sofa.

daw′dle (dôd′l) *v.,* **-dled, -dling.** —*v.i.* **1.** to waste time; idle. **2.** to walk slowly and aimlessly. —*v.t.* **3.** to waste (time) by trifling.

dawn (dôn) *n.* **1.** the break of day. **2.** the beginning of anything. —*v.i.* **3.** to begin to grow light. **4.** to become apparent.

day (dā) *n.* **1.** the period of light between two nights. **2.** a period of 24 hours. **3.** the part of a day given to work. **4.** a period of exist-ence or influence. —*Idiom.* **5. call it a day,** to stop working for the rest of the day.

day′break′ *n.* the first appearance of daylight; dawn.

day′ care′ *n.* supervised daytime care for young children or the eld-erly, usu. at a center outside the home. —**day′-care′,** *adj.*

day′dream′ *n.* **1.** pleasant idle thoughts indulged in while awake. —*v.i.* **2.** to have daydreams.

day′light′ *n.* **1.** the period of light during a day. **2.** public knowledge. **3.** dawn.

day′light-sav′ing time *n.* time one hour later than standard time, usu. used in the summer. Also, **day′-light-sav′ings time.**

day′time′ *n.* the time between sunrise and sunset.

day′-to-day′ *adj.* **1.** daily. **2.** rou-tine.

daze (dāz) *v.,* **dazed, dazing,** *n.* —*v.t.* **1.** to cause to feel stunned or overwhelmed. —*n.* **2.** a dazed state.

daz′zle (daz′əl) *v.t.,* **-zled, -zling. 1.** to overpower by intense light. **2.** to impress by splendor.

dba doing business as.

DC 1. direct current. **2.** District of Columbia.

D.D. Doctor of Divinity.

D.D.S. 1. Doctor of Dental Science. **2.** Doctor of Dental Surgery.

DDT a strong insecticide, now banned from use.

de- a prefix indicating: **1.** reverse. **2.** remove. **3.** down or lower.

dea′con (dē′kən) *n.* **1.** a cleric rank-ing below a priest. **2.** a lay church officer.

de·ac′ti·vate′ (dē ak′tə vāt′) *v.t.,* **-vated, -vating.** to make inactive.

dead (ded) *adj.* **1.** no longer alive or active. **2.** no longer in use or operation. **3.** exact. —*n.* **4.** the darkest, coldest time. **5. the dead,** dead persons. —*adv.* **6.** completely. **7.** directly. —**dead′en,** *v.t.*

dead′beat′ *n.* **1.** a person who avoids paying debts. **2.** a sponger.

dead′ end′ *n.* **1.** a street, corridor,

etc., with no exit. **2.** a position with no hope of progress. —**dead′-end′**, adj.

dead′ heat′ n. a race that finishes in a tie.

dead′line′ n. the time by which something must be finished.

dead′lock′ n. a state in which no progress can be made.

dead′ly adj., **-lier, -liest. 1.** causing death. **2.** very dreary. **3.** extremely accurate. —adv. **4.** extremely.

dead′pan′ adj. without expression.

dead′wood′ n. useless or extraneous persons or things.

deaf (def) adj. **1.** unable to hear. **2.** refusing to respond. —**deaf′en**, v.t.

deaf′-mute′ n. Often Offensive. a person who is unable to hear or speak.

deal (dēl) v., **dealt, dealing,** n. —v.i. **1.** to be concerned. **2.** to take action regarding someone or something. **3.** to do business. **4.** to distribute. —n. **5.** a business transaction. **6.** a bargain. **7.** a secret agreement. **8.** an undefined quantity.

deal′er n. **1.** a person who deals. **2.** a merchant or trader.

dean (dēn) n. **1.** an official in a university or college. **2.** the head of a cathedral.

dear (dēr) adj. **1.** much loved. **2.** expensive. —n. **3.** a beloved one. **4.** a kind or generous person.

dearth (dûrth) n. scarcity.

death (deth) n. **1.** the act of dying or the state of being dead. **2.** extinction; destruction. —**death′ly,** adj., adv.

death′bed′ n. **1.** the bed on which a person dies. **2.** the last hours before death.

death′less adj. not subject to death.

de•ba•cle (də bä′kəl, -bak′əl, dā-) n. **1.** a disaster. **2.** a general rout.

de•bar′ (di bär′) v.t., **-barred, -barring.** to shut out or exclude.

de•bark′ (di bärk′) v.i., v.t. to disembark. —**de′bar•ka′tion**, n.

de•base′ (di bās′) v.t., **-based, -basing.** to reduce in quality or value.

de•bate′ (di bāt′) n., v., **-bated, -bating.** —n. **1.** a discussion involving opposing viewpoints. —v.i., v.t. **2.** to discuss (a matter) by giving opposing viewpoints. —**de•bat′a•ble,** adj.

de•bauch′ (di bôch′) v.t. to corrupt; seduce. —**de•bauch′er•y,** n.

de•bil′i•tate′ (di bil′i tāt′) v.t., **-tated, -tating.** to make weak.

de•bil′i•ty n., pl. **-ties.** weakness.

deb′it (deb′it) n. **1.** a recorded item of debt. —v.t. **2.** to charge (a person or account) with a debt. **3.** to enter as a debt in an account.

deb′o•nair′ (deb′ə nâr′) adj. **1.** suave; worldly. **2.** carefree.

de•brief′ (dē brēf′) v.t. to question to gather information about a completed mission.

de•bris′ (də brē′, dā′brē) n. the remains of anything destroyed or broken; rubbish.

debt (det) n. **1.** something owed. **2.** a state of owing. —**debt′or,** n.

de•bunk′ (di bungk′) v.t. to expose as false.

de•but′ (dā byoō′, di-, dā′byoō) n. **1.** a first public appearance, as of a performer. **2.** a formal introduction of a young woman into society. —v.i. **3.** to make a debut. —v.t. **4.** to introduce to the public.

Dec. December.

dec′ade (dek′ād) n. a ten-year period.

dec′a•dence (dek′ə dəns, di kād′ns) n. **1.** moral deterioration. **2.** excessive self-indulgence. **3.** a falling into decay. —**dec′a•dent,** adj.

de•caf′fein•at′ed (dē kaf′ə nā′tad) adj. having the caffeine removed.

dec′a•he′dron (dek′ə hē′drən) n., pl. **-drons, -dra** (-drə). a solid figure with ten faces.

de′cal (dē′kal, di kal′) n. a design on specially prepared paper for transfer to wood, metal, etc.

Dec′a•logue′ (dek′ə lôg′) n. the Ten Commandments.

de•camp′ (di kamp′) v.i. to depart, esp. secretly.

de•cant′ (di kant′) v.t. to pour (liquid) into another container, leaving the sediment behind.

de•cant′er n. an ornamental bottle for wine, brandy, etc.

de•cap′i•tate′ (di kap′i tāt′) v.t., **-tated, -tating.** to behead.

de•cath′lon (di kath′lon) n. an athletic contest of ten track-and-field events.

de•cay′ (di kā′) v.i. **1.** to decline in quality, health, etc. **2.** to rot. —n. **3.** decomposition. **4.** a gradual decline.

de•cease′ (di sēs′) n., v., **-ceased, -ceasing.** —n. **1.** death. —v.i. **2.** to die. —**de•ceased′,** adj.

de•ceit′ (di sēt′) n. **1.** the act or process of deceiving. **2.** a trick.

de•ceit′ful adj. **1.** given to deceiving. **2.** misleading.

de•ceive′ (di sēv′) v.t., **-ceived, -ceiving.** to cause to believe something that is false; trick.

De•cem′ber (di sem′bər) n. the twelfth month of the year.

de′cen•cy (dē′sən sē) n., pl. **-cies. 1.**

the state or quality of being decent. **2.** courtesy; propriety.

de•cent *adj.* **1.** conforming to accepted standards of propriety. **2.** respectable. **3.** adequate. **4.** kind.

de•cen•tral•ize (dē sen'trə līz') *v.t.,* **-ized, -izing.** to end central control of.

de•cep•tion (di sep'shən) *n.* **1.** the act of deceiving. **2.** a trick. —**de• cep'tive,** *adj.*

dec•i•bel (des'ə bel', -bəl) *n.* a unit for expressing intensity of sound.

de•cide (di sīd') *v.,* **-cided, -ciding.** —*v.t.* **1.** to solve (a dispute). **2.** to make up one's mind about. —*v.i.* **3.** to come to a decision.

de•cid'ed *adj.* **1.** unquestionable; certain. **2.** determined.

de•cid'u•ous (di sij'ōō əs) *adj.* shedding the leaves annually.

dec'i•mal (des'ə məl) *adj.* **1.** of tenths or the number ten. **2.** proceeding by tens. —*n.* **3.** a fraction whose denominator is some power of 10, usu. indicated by a dot (**decimal point**) before the numerator.

dec'i•mate (-māt') *v.t.,* **-mated, -mating.** to destroy much of.

de•ci•pher (di sī'fər) *v.t.* to make out the meaning of. —**de•ci'pher• a•ble,** *adj.*

de•ci'sion (di sizh'ən) *n.* **1.** the act of deciding or of making up one's mind. **2.** something decided. **3.** a judgment. **4.** determination.

de•ci'sive (-sī'siv) *adj.* **1.** having the power to decide. **2.** displaying firmness. **3.** definite. —**de•ci'sive• ly,** *adv.* —**de•ci'sive•ness,** *n.*

deck (dek) *n.* **1.** a floor of a ship. **2.** a porch. **3.** a pack of playing cards. —*v.t.* **4.** to clothe in something festive.

de•claim' (di klām') *v.t., v.i.* to speak loudly and rhetorically.

dec•la•ma'tion (dek/lə mā'shən) *n.* oratorical speech.

de•clar'a•tive *adj.* serving to state or explain.

de•clare' (di klâr') *v.t.,* **-clared, -claring. 1.** to make known publicly. **2.** to state emphatically. **3.** to indicate. —**dec'la•ra'tion** (dek/lə- rā'shən) *n.*

de•clen'sion (di klen'shən) *n.* the inflection of nouns, pronouns, and adjectives.

de•cline' (di klīn') *v.,* **-clined, -clining,** *n.* —*v.t.* **1.** to refuse courteously. **2.** to cause to slope downward. **3.** to inflect (a noun, pronoun, or adjective). —*v.i.* **4.** to express courteous refusal. **5.** to lose strength. —*n.* **6.** a downward slope. **7.** a deterioration.

de•code' (dē kōd') *v.t.,* **-coded, -coding.** to translate from code.

de•com•mis'sion *v.t.* to retire (a vessel) from active service.

de•com•pose' (-kəm pōz') *v.t., v.i.,* **-posed, -posing. 1.** to separate into constituent parts. **2.** to rot. —**de'• com•po•si'tion,** *n.*

de•con•ges'tant (dē/kən jes'tənt) *adj.* **1.** relieving congestion of the upper respiratory tract. —*n.* **2.** a decongestant agent.

de•con•tam'i•nate (-nāt') *v.t.,* **-nated, -nating.** to make safe by removing or neutralizing harmful contaminants.

dé•cor' (dā kôr', di-) *n.* a style of decoration, as of a room. Also, **de• cor'.**

dec'o•rate (dek/ə rāt') *v.t.,* **-rated, -rating. 1.** to make attractive by adding something ornamental. **2.** to design the interior of, as a room. **3.** to confer an honor on. —**dec'o•ra'tion,** *n.* —**dec'o•ra•tive** (-ər ə tiv) *adj.* —**dec'o•ra'tor,** *n.*

dec'o•rous *adj.* proper; dignified.

de•co'rum (di kôr'əm) *n.* correctness of behavior.

de'coy *n.* (dē'koi, di koi') **1.** a person or animal who lures another into danger. **2.** anything used as a lure. —*v.t.* (di koi', dē'koi) **3.** to lure by a decoy.

de•crease' *v.,* **-creased, -creasing,** *n.* —*v.i., v.t.* (di krēs') **1.** to lessen, as in size or quantity. —*n.* (dē'krēs, di krēs') **2.** the act or process of decreasing. **3.** the amount by which something is decreased.

de•cree' (di krē') *n., v.,* **-creed, -creeing.** —*n.* **1.** a formal order. —*v.t., v.i.* **2.** to order by decree.

de•crep'it (di krep'it) *adj.* old and feeble. —**de•crep'i•tude',** *n.*

de•cre•scen'do (dē/kri shen'dō, dā/-) *adj., adv. Music.* gradually decreasing in loudness.

de•crim'i•nal•ize' (dē krim/ə nl īz') *v.t.,* **-ized, -izing.** to remove criminal penalties for. —**de•crim'i•nal•i• za'tion,** *n.*

de•cry' (di krī') *v.t.,* **-cried, -crying.** to denounce publicly.

ded'i•cate' (ded/i kāt') *v.t.,* **-cated, -cating. 1.** to set apart. **2.** to devote to some purpose, cause, or person. —**ded'i•ca'tion,** *n.*

de•duce' (di dōōs', -dyōōs') *v.t.,* **-duced, -ducing.** to arrive at (a conclusion) by reasoning; infer.

de•duct' (di dukt') *v.t.* to subtract.

de•duct'i•ble *adj.* **1.** able to be deducted. —*n.* **2.** the amount a person must pay on each claim made on an insurance policy.

de•duc'tion *n.* **1.** the act of deducting. **2.** something deducted. **3.** the act of deducing. **4.** something deduced. —**de•duc′tive,** *adj.*

deed (dēd) *n.* **1.** something done; an act. **2.** a document transferring property from one person to another. —*v.t.* **3.** to transfer by deed.

dee•jay′ (dē′jā′) *n.* a disc jockey.

deem (dēm) *v.t.* to think; estimate.

deep (dēp) *adj.* **1.** extending far down or in. **2.** difficult to understand. **3.** intense. **4.** involved. **5.** dark. **6.** obscure. **7.** low in pitch. —*n.* **8.** a deep part. —*adv.* **9.** at great depth. —**deep′en,** *v.t., v.i.*

deep′-freeze′ *v.,* **-froze, -frozen, -freezing,** *n.* —*v.t.* **1.** to freeze (food) quickly. —*n.* **2.** a refrigerator that deep-freezes.

deep′-fry′ *v.t.,* **-fried, -frying.** to cook in boiling fat deep enough to cover food. —**deep′-fry′er,** *n.*

deep′-seat′ed *adj.* firmly implanted.

deep′ space′ space beyond the solar system.

deer (dēr) *n.,* pl. **deer.** a hoofed, ruminant animal, the male of which usually has antlers.

de•face′ (di fās′) *v.t.,* **-faced, -facing.** to spoil the appearance of.

de fac′to (dē fak′tō, dā) *adv.* **1.** in fact. —*adj.* **2.** actually existing, esp. without legal authority.

de•fame′ (di fām′) *v.t.,* **-famed, -faming.** to attack the reputation of; slander or libel. —**def′a•ma′-tion** (def′ə mā′shən) *n.* —**de•fam′-a•to•ry** (-fam′ə tôr′ē) *adj.*

de•fault′ (di fôlt′) *n.* **1.** failure to act or to appear; neglect. —*v.i.* **2.** to fail to meet an obligation. —*v.t.* **3.** to lose by default.

de•feat′ (di fēt′) *v.t.* **1.** to overcome in a contest. **2.** to frustrate. —*n.* **3.** the act of defeating or the state of being defeated.

de•feat′ist *n.* one who accepts defeat too easily. —**de•feat′ism,** *n.*

def′e•cate′ (def′i kāt′) *v.i.,* **-cated, -cating.** to discharge feces from the bowels. —**def′e•ca′tion,** *n.*

de′fect *n.* (dē′fekt, di fekt′) **1.** a fault; imperfection. —*v.i.* (di fekt′) **2.** to desert a cause, country, etc. —**de•fec′tive,** *adj.*

de•fec′tion *n.* desertion of a cause, country, etc.

de•fend′ (di fend′) *v.t.* **1.** to protect against attack. **2.** to uphold by argument. **3.** to serve as attorney for (a defendant). —**de•fend′er,** *n.*

de•fend′ant *n.* a person accused of a crime or sued in court.

de•fense′ *n.* **1.** resistance to attack. **2.** something that defends. **3.** arguments defending against an accusation. —**de•fense′less,** *adj.*

defense′ mech′anism *n.* an unconscious process that protects a person from painful ideas.

de•fen′sive *adj.* **1.** intended for defense. **2.** sensitive to criticism. —*n.* **3.** an attitude of defense.

de•fer′¹ (-fûr′) *v.,* **-ferred, -ferring.** —*v.t.* **1.** to postpone. —*v.i.* **2.** to put off action. —**de•fer′ment,** *n.*

de•fer′² (-fûr′) *v.i.,* **-ferred, -ferring.** to yield respectfully to a person's wishes or opinion.

def′er•ence (def′ər əns) *n.* polite respect. —**def′er•en′tial** (-ə ren′-shəl) *adj.*

de•fi′ance (di fī′əns) *n.* **1.** bold resistance to authority. **2.** contempt. —**de•fi′ant,** *adj.*

de•fi′cien•cy (di fish′ən sē) *n.,* pl. **-cies. 1.** lack. **2.** the amount lacked. —**de•fi′cient,** *adj.*

def′i•cit (def′ə sit) *n.* the amount by which a total falls short of the required amount.

de•file′ (di fīl′) *v.t.,* **-filed, -filing.** to make foul or dirty.

de•fine′ (di fīn′) *v.t.,* **-fined, -fining. 1.** to state the meaning of (a word, phrase, etc.). **2.** to specify. **3.** to mark the limits of.

def′i•nite (def′ə nit) *adj.* **1.** clearly defined. **2.** having fixed limits. **3.** positive. —**def′i•nite•ly,** *adv.*

def′i•ni′tion *n.* **1.** the act of making definite or clear. **2.** the formal statement of the meaning of a word, phrase, etc. **3.** the condition of being definite.

de•fin′i•tive (di fin′i tiv) *adj.* **1.** most reliable. **2.** serving to define. **3.** conclusive.

de•flate′ (di flāt′) *v.t.,* **-flated, -flating. 1.** to release air or gas from. **2.** to reduce in importance or size. **3.** to reduce (currency, prices, etc.) from an inflated condition. —**de•fla′tion,** *n.*

de•flect′ (di flekt′) *v.t., v.i.* to turn from a course. —**de•flec′tion,** *n.*

de•fo′li•ate′ (dē fō′lē āt′) *v.t.,* **-ated, -ating. 1.** to strip of leaves. **2.** to clear of vegetation. —**de•fo′-li•a′tion,** *n.* —**de•fo′li•ant** (-ənt) *n.*

de•for′est (di fôr′ist) *v.t.* to clear of trees. —**de•for′es•ta′tion,** *n.*

de•form′ *v.t.* to mar the natural form, shape, or beauty of. —**de•form′i•ty,** *n.*

de•fraud′ *v.t.* to deprive by fraud. —**de•fraud′er,** *n.*

de•fray′ *v.t.* to pay all or part of.

de•frost′ *v.t.* **1.** to remove the frost or ice from. **2.** to thaw. —*v.i.* **3.** to become free of frost. **4.** to thaw.

deft (deft) *adj.* quick and skillful.

de·funct' (di fungkt') *adj.* no longer in existence.

de·fuse' (dē fyōōz') *v.t.*, **-fused, -fusing.** 1. to remove the detonating fuse from. 2. to make less dangerous or tense.

de·fy' (di fī') *v.t.*, **-fied, -fying.** 1. to resist boldly. 2. to challenge to do something.

de·gen'er·ate' *v.*, **-ated, -ating,** *adj., n.* —*v.t.* (di jen'ə rāt') 1. to decline physically, mentally, or morally. —*adj.* (-ər it) 2. having declined physically, mentally, or morally. —*n.* (-ər it) 3. a person who has declined, esp. morally.

de·grade' (di grād') *v.t.*, **-graded, -grading.** to lower in dignity, quality, or status. —**deg'ra·da'tion** (deg'ri dā'shən) *n.*

de·gree' (di grē') *n.* 1. any of a series of steps or stages in a process. 2. the 360th part of a circle. 3. a unit of measure for temperature. 4. an academic title conferred by a college or university on completion of a course of study.

de·hu'man·ize' (dē hyōō'mə nīz'; *often* -yōō'-) *v.t.*, **-ized, -izing.** to deprive of human qualities.

de'hu·mid'i·fi'er *n.* a device for removing moisture from the air. —**de'hu·mid'i·fy,** *v.t.*

de·hy'drate' *v.*, **-drated, -drating.** —*v.t.* 1. to remove water from. —*v.i.* 2. to lose fluids or water. —**de'hy·dra'tion,** *n.*

de'i·fy' (dē'ə fī') *v.t.*, **-fied, -fying.** to make a god of.

deign (dān) *v.t., v.i.* to condescend (to do or grant).

de'ism (dē'iz əm) *n.* belief in a god's existence based on reason rather than on divine revelation. —**de'ist,** *n.*

de'i·ty (dē'i tē) *n., pl.* **-ties.** a god or goddess.

dé'jà vu' (dā'zhä vōō') *n.* a feeling of having lived through the present moment before.

de·ject'ed (di jek'tid) *adj.* in low spirits. —**de·jec'tion,** *n.*

de ju're (di jōōr'ē, dā jōōr'ā) *adv., adj.* by right or according to law.

Del. Delaware.

de·lay' (di lā') *v.t.* 1. to postpone. 2. to hinder. —*v.i.* 3. to linger. —*n.* 4. the act of delaying. 5. an instance of being delayed.

de·lec'ta·ble (di lek'tə bəl) *adj.* delightful or delicious.

del'e·gate *n., v.*, **-gated, -gating.** —*n.* (del'i git, -gāt') 1. a person designated to represent another. —*v.t.* (-gāt') 2. to send or appoint as a delegate. 3. to give (powers) to another as agent.

del'e·ga'tion *n.* 1. a group of delegates. 2. a delegating or being delegated.

de·lete' (di lēt') *v.t.*, **-leted, -leting.** to strike out (something written). —**de·le'tion,** *n.*

del'e·te'ri·ous (del'i tēr'ē əs) *adj.* harmful.

del'i (del'ē) *n.* a delicatessen.

de·lib'er·ate *adj., v.*, **-ated, -ating.** —*adj.* (di lib'ər it) 1. intentional. 2. slow and careful. —*v.i.* (-ə rāt') 3. to think carefully. 4. to confer. —**de·lib'er·a'tion,** *n.*

del'i·ca·cy (del'i kə sē) *n., pl.* **-cies.** 1. the quality or state of being delicate. 2. something delightful, esp. a choice food.

del'i·cate (-kit) *adj.* 1. fine in texture, quality, etc. 2. fragile. 3. precise in action. 4. keenly sensitive. —**del'i·cate·ly,** *adv.*

del'i·ca·tes'sen (del'i kə tes'ən) *n.* a store that sells prepared foods.

de·li'cious (di lish'əs) *adj.* highly pleasing, esp. to taste.

de·light' (di līt') *n.* 1. a high degree of pleasure; joy. —*v.t.* 2. to give delight to. —*v.i.* 3. to have or take great pleasure. —**de·light'ed,** *adj.* —**de·light'ful,** *adj.*

de·lim'it (di lim'it) *v.t.* to fix the limits of. —**de·lim'i·ta'tion,** *n.*

de·lin'e·ate' (di lin'ē āt') *v.t.*, **-ated, -ating.** 1. to outline. 2. to describe.

de·lin'quent (di ling'kwənt) *adj.* 1. neglectful of an obligation. 2. guilty of an offense. —*n.* 3. a person who is delinquent. —**de·lin'quen·cy,** *n.*

de·lir'i·um (di lēr'ē əm) *n.* a temporary mental disorder marked by excitement, hallucinations, etc. —**de·lir'i·ous,** *adj.*

de·liv'er (di liv'ər) *v.t.* 1. to carry and turn over (letters, goods, etc.) to someone. 2. to hand over. 3. to utter. 4. to direct. 5. to set free. 6. to assist at the birth of. —*v.i.* 7. to give birth. 8. to do something.

de·liv'er·ance *n.* rescue.

de·liv'er·y *n.* 1. the delivering of something. 2. a giving up. 3. one's manner while speaking. 4. the act of striking or throwing. 5. childbirth. 6. something delivered.

dell (del) *n.* a small, wooded valley.

del·phin'i·um (del fin'ē əm) *n., pl.* **-iums, -ia** (-ē ə). a tall blue garden flower.

del'ta (del'tə) *n.* 1. the fourth letter of the Greek alphabet. 2. a triangular plain between the branches of the mouth of a river.

de·lude' (di lōōd') *v.t.*, **-luded, -luding.** to mislead or deceive.

del'uge (del'yōōj) *n.*, *v.*, **-uged, -ug-ing.** —*n.* **1.** a great flood. **2.** anything that overwhelms. —*v.t.* **3.** to flood. **4.** to overwhelm.

de·lu'sion (di lōō'zhən) *n.* a false opinion or conception.

de·luxe' (də luks') *adj.* of finest quality.

delve (delv) *v.i.*, **delved, delving.** to search carefully for information.

Dem. 1. Democrat. **2.** Democratic.

dem'a·gogue' (dem'ə gog') *n.* an orator or leader who gains power by arousing people's emotions and prejudices. —**dem'a·gogu'er·y,** *n.*

de·mand' (di mand') *v.t.* **1.** to claim as a right. **2.** to require. **3.** to ask for in an urgent or peremptory manner. —*v.i.* **4.** to ask. —*n.* **5.** a claim. **6.** an urgent requirement. **7.** consumers' desire for a product.

de·mar'cate (di mär'kāt, dē'mär-kāt') *v.t.*, **-cated, -cating.** to set the limits of. —**de'mar·ca'tion,** *n.*

de·mean' (di mēn') *v.t.* to lower in standing.

de·mean'or *n.* conduct; behavior.

de·ment'ed (di men'tid) *adj.* **1.** crazy. **2.** affected with dementia.

de·men'tia (-shə, -shē ə) *n.* severe mental impairment.

de·mer'it (di mer'it) *n.* a mark against a person for misconduct.

demi- a prefix indicating half.

dem'i·god' (dem'ē god') *n.* one partly divine and partly human.

de·mil'i·ta·rize' (dē mil'i tə rīz') *v.t.*, **-rized, -rizing.** to remove from military control. —**de·mil'i·ta·ri·za'tion,** *n.*

de·mise' (di mīz') *n.* death.

dem'i·tasse' (dem'i tas', -täs') *n.* a small coffee cup.

dem'o (dem'ō) *n.*, *pl.* **-os.** a product displayed or offered for trial.

de·mo'bi·lize' (dē mō'bə līz') *v.t.*, **-lized, -lizing.** to disband (troops).

de·moc'ra·cy (di mok'rə sē) *n.*, *pl.* **-cies. 1.** government in which the people hold supreme power, usu. through their elected representatives. **2.** a state having such government. **3.** social equality.

dem'o·crat' *n.* **1.** a supporter of democracy. **2.** **Democrat,** a member of the Democratic Party.

dem'o·crat'ic *adj.* **1.** of or advocating democracy. **2.** **Democratic,** of the **Democratic Party,** one of two major political parties in the U.S.

de·mol'ish (di mol'ish) *v.t.* to destroy. —**dem'o·li'tion** (dem'ə-lish'ən) *n.*

de'mon (dē'mən) *n.* **1.** an evil spirit. **2.** a cruel person.

de·mon'ic (di mon'ik) *adj.* **1.** in-spired as if by a demon. **2.** like a demon.

dem'on·strate' (dem'ən strāt') *v.*, **-strated, -strating.** —*v.t.* **1.** to describe or explain. **2.** to prove. **3.** to display. —*v.i.* **4.** to parade or picket in support or opposition. —**de·mon'stra·ble** (di mon'strə bəl) *adj.* —**dem'on·stra'tion,** *n.* —**dem'on·stra'tor,** *n.*

de·mon'stra·tive (də mon'strə tiv) *adj.* **1.** showing one's feelings openly. **2.** showing. **3.** proving.

de·mor'al·ize' (di môr'ə līz') *v.t.*, **-ized, -izing.** to destroy the confidence of.

de·mote' (di mōt') *v.t.*, **-moted, -moting.** to reduce the rank or position of. —**de·mo'tion,** *n.*

de·mur' (di mûr') *v.i.*, **-murred, -murring.** to raise objections. —**de·mur'ral,** *n.*

de·mure' (di myŏŏr') *adj.* shy and modest. —**de·mure'ly,** *adv.*

den (den) *n.* **1.** the lair of a wild animal. **2.** a room at home for re-laxing.

de·na'ture *v.t.*, **-tured, -turing. 1.** to change the natural character of. **2.** to make (alcohol) undrinkable.

de·ni'al (di nī'əl) *n.* **1.** a statement that something is not true. **2.** refusal to believe a doctrine. **3.** the refusal to grant a request.

den'i·grate' (den'i grāt') *v.t.*, **-grated, -grating.** to speak badly of.

den'im (den'əm) *n.* **1.** a heavy cotton fabric. **2.** **denims,** trousers of this.

den'i·zen (den'ə zən) *n.* an inhabitant.

de·nom'i·nate' (di nom'ə nāt') *v.t.*, **-nated, -nating.** to give a name to.

de·nom'i·na'tion *n.* **1.** a particular religious body. **2.** a grade in a series of values. **3.** a class or kind of persons or things.

de·nom'i·na'tor *n.* **1.** the lower term in a fraction. **2.** something held in common.

de·note' (di nōt') *v.t.*, **-noted, -noting. 1.** to indicate. **2.** to mean.

de'noue·ment' (dā'nōō mäN') *n.* the final resolution of a plot or story. Also, **dé'noue·ment'.**

de·nounce' (di nouns') *v.t.*, **-nounced, -nouncing. 1.** to speak against publicly. **2.** to inform against.

dense (dens) *adj.*, **denser, densest. 1.** having the parts crowded together; compact. **2.** stupid. **3.** opaque. —**dense'ly,** *adv.*

den'si·ty *n.* **1.** the state or quality of being dense. **2.** stupidity. **3.** the average number per unit of area.

dent (dent) *n.* **1.** a small depression in a surface. **2.** a slight effect. —*v.t., v.i.* **3.** to make a dent in or to become dented.

den'tal (den'tl) *adj.* of the teeth or dentistry.

den'tal floss' *n.* a thread used to clean between the teeth.

den'ti•frice (-tə fris) *n.* a substance for cleaning the teeth.

den'tin (-tn, -tin) *n.* the hard tissue forming the major part of a tooth.

den'tist (-tist) *n.* a person trained in the prevention and treatment of tooth and gum diseases. —**den'-tist•ry,** *n.*

den'ture (-chər, -choŏr) *n.* an artificial replacement for teeth.

de•nude' (di noōd', -nyoōd') *v.t.,* **-nuded, -nuding.** to strip bare.

de•nun'ci•a'tion (di nun'sē ā'shən) *n.* **1.** a condemnation. **2.** an accusation.

de•ny' (di nī') *v.t.,* **-nied, -nying. 1.** to declare that (a statement) is not true. **2.** to refuse to agree to or give. **3.** to disown.

de•o'dor•ant (dē ō'dər ənt) *n.* a substance for destroying odors.

de•o'dor•ize' *v.t.,* **-ized, -izing.** to get rid of odor.

de•part' (di pärt') *v.i.* to go away; leave. —**de•par'ture,** *n.*

de•part'ment *n.* a part or division of an organization. —**de'part•men'tal,** *adj.*

de•pend' (di pend') *v.i.* **1.** to rely. **2.** to be determined by something else. —**de•pend'ence,** *n.* —**de•pend'ent,** *adj., n.*

de•pend'a•ble *adj.* able to be depended on.

de•pict' (di pikt') *v.t.* to represent in a picture or in words. —**de•pic'tion,** *n.*

de•pil'a•to'ry (di pil'ə tôr'ē) *adj., n., pl.* **-ries.** —*adj.* **1.** capable of removing hair. —*n.* **2.** a depilatory agent.

de•plete' (di plēt') *v.t.,* **-pleted, -pleting.** to reduce by using up.

de•plore' *v.t.* (-plôr'-plōr'), **-plored, -ploring. 1.** to regret. **2.** to disapprove of. —**de•plor'a•ble,** *adj.*

de•ploy' (-ploi') *v.t.* to place strategically. —**de•ploy'ment,** *n.*

de•po•lit'i•cize' (dē'pə lit'ə sīz') *v.t.,* **-cized, -cizing.** to remove from the realm of politics.

de•pop'u•late' (dē pop'yə lāt') *v.t.,* **-lated, -lating.** to reduce the population of. —**de•pop'u•la'tion,** *n.*

de•port' (di pôrt') *v.t.* **1.** to expel from a country. **2.** to behave (oneself).

de•por•ta'tion (dē'pôr tā'shən) *n.* the lawful expulsion of a person from a country.

de•port'ment *n.* conduct.

de•pose' (di pōz') *v.t.,* **-posed, -posing. 1.** to remove from office. **2.** to testify under oath.

de•pos'it (di poz'it) *v.t.* **1.** to place in a bank account. **2.** to put down. **3.** to lay down by a natural process. **4.** to give as security. —*n.* **5.** money placed in a bank account. **6.** sediment. **7.** anything given as security.

dep'o•si'tion (dep'ə zish'ən) *n.* **1.** removal from an office. **2.** something deposited. **3.** written testimony under oath.

de•pos'i•to'ry (di poz'i tôr'ē) *n., pl.* **-ries.** a place where something is deposited for safekeeping.

de'pot (dē'pō; *Mil. or Brit.* dep'ō) *n.* **1.** a railroad or bus station. **2.** a storage place.

de•prave' (di prāv') *v.t.,* **-praved, -praving.** to corrupt morally. —**de•prav'i•ty** (-prav'i tē) *n.*

dep're•cate' (dep'ri kāt') *v.t.,* **-cated, -cating. 1.** to express disapproval of. **2.** to belittle. —**dep're•ca•to'ry,** *adj.*

de•pre'ci•ate' (di prē'shē āt') *v.,* **-ated, -ating.** —*v.t.* **1.** to lessen the value of. **2.** to belittle. —*v.i.* **3.** to decline in value.

dep're•da'tion (dep'ri dā'shən) *n.* plundering.

de•press' (di pres') *v.t.* **1.** to make sad. **2.** to press down. **3.** to lower in amount or value.

de•pres'sion *n.* **1.** a depressing or being depressed. **2.** an area lower than the surrounding one. **3.** sadness or gloom. **4.** a period of decline in business activity and employment. —**de•pres'sive,** *adj.*

de•prive' (-prīv') *v.t.,* **-prived, -priving.** to keep from possessing or enjoying something. —**dep'ri•va'tion** (dep'rə vā'shən) *n.*

dept. 1. department. **2.** deputy.

depth (depth) *n.* **1.** a measurement taken downward or inward through an object. **2.** deepness. **3.** intensity. **4.** Often, **depths.** a deep or inner part. —*Idiom.* **5.** in depth, thoroughly.

dep'u•ta'tion (dep'yə tā'shən) *n.* a group of people sent to represent others.

dep'u•ty (-tē) *n., pl.* **-ties.** a person authorized to act as a representative. —**dep'u•tize'** (-tīz') *v.t.*

de•rail' (dē rāl') *v.t.* **1.** to cause (a train) to run off the rails. **2.** to deflect from a purpose. —*v.i.* **3.** to become derailed.

de•range' (di rānj') *v.t.,* **-ranged,**

-ranging. **1.** to throw into disorder. **2.** to make insane.

der′by (dûr′bē; *Brit.* där′-) *n., pl.* **-bies. 1.** a stiff hat with a rounded crown. **2.** a race.

de·reg′u·late′ (dē reg′yə lāt′) *v.t.,* **-lated, -lating.** to free of regulation.

der′e·lict (der′ə likt) *adj.* **1.** abandoned. **2.** neglectful of duty. —*n.* **3.** anything abandoned. **4.** a person who lacks a home or means of support.

der′e·lic′tion *n.* **1.** deliberate neglect. **2.** an abandoning or being abandoned.

de·ride′ (di rīd′) *v.t.,* **-rided, -riding.** to ridicule. —**de·ri′sion** (-rizh′ən) *n.* —**de·ri′sive** (-rī′siv) *adj.*

de·riv′a·tive (di riv′ə tiv) *adj.* **1.** not original. —*n.* **2.** something derived.

de·rive′ (di rīv′) *v.,* **-rived, -riving.** —*v.t.* **1.** to obtain from a source. **2.** to obtain by reasoning. —*v.i.* **3.** to originate. —**der′i·va′tion** (der′ə-vā′shən) *n.*

der′ma·ti′tis (dûr′mə tī′tis) *n.* inflammation of the skin.

der′ma·tol′o·gy (-tol′ə jē) *n.* the branch of medicine dealing with treatment of the skin.

de·rog′a·to·ry (di rog′ə tôr′ē) *adj.* disparaging; belittling.

der′rick (der′ik) *n.* **1.** a boom for lifting heavy cargo. **2.** the towerlike framework over an oil well.

der′ri·ère (der′ē âr′) *n.* the buttocks.

de·scend′ (di send′) *v.i.* **1.** to go or move down. **2.** to slope downward. —**de·scent′,** *n.*

de·scend′ant *n.* a person descended from a specific ancestor; offspring.

de·scribe′ (di skrīb′) *v.t.,* **-scribed, -scribing. 1.** to tell in words what (a person or thing) is like. **2.** to draw the outline of. —**de·scrip′-tion,** *n.* —**de·scrip′tive,** *adj.*

de·scry′ (di skrī′) *v.t.,* **-scried, -scrying. 1.** to notice. **2.** to detect.

des′e·crate′ (des′i krāt′) *v.t.,* **-crated, -crating.** to treat (something sacred) with irreverence; profane. —**des′e·cra′tion,** *n.*

de·seg′re·gate′ *v.t., v.i.,* **-gated, -gating.** to eliminate racial segregation in (schools, housing, etc.).

de·sen′si·tize′ *v.t.,* **-tized, -tizing.** to make less sensitive.

des′ert¹ (dez′ərt) *n.* a very dry, often sandy, region.

de·sert² (di zûrt′) *v.t., v.i.* **1.** to leave or run away from (a person, duty, etc.). **2.** (of military personnel) to leave (service) without permission or intention to return. —**de·sert′er,** *n.* —**de·ser′tion,** *n.*

de·sert³ (di zûrt′) *n.* Often, **deserts.** due reward or punishment.

de·serve′ (di zûrv′) *v.t., v.i.,* **-served, -serving.** to be worthy of (reward, punishment, etc.); merit.

des′ic·cate′ (des′i kāt′) *v.t., v..i.,* **-cated, -cating.** to dry up.

de·sign′ (di zīn′) *v.t.* **1.** to prepare the preliminary plans for. **2.** to plan and fashion skillfully. **3.** to form in the mind. —*v.i.* **4.** to make sketches or plans. **5.** to plan an object, work of art, etc. —*n.* **6.** a sketch or plan. **7.** the organization of elements in an object. **8.** an ornamental pattern. **9.** purpose. —**de·sign′er,** *n.*

des′ig·nate′ (dez′ig nāt′) *v.,* **-nated, -nating,** *adj.* —*v.t.* **1.** to specify. **2.** to name. **3.** to select. —*adj.* (dez′ig nit) **4.** selected for an office but not yet installed. —**des′-ig·na′tion,** *n.*

des′ignated driv′er *n.* a person who does not drink alcohol at a gathering in order to drive companions home safely.

de·sign′ing *adj.* scheming.

de·sir′a·ble *adj.* **1.** pleasing. **2.** arousing desire. **3.** advisable.

de·sire′ (di zī°r′) *v.,* **-sired, -siring,** *n.* —*v.t.* **1.** to wish or long for. **2.** to ask for. —*n.* **3.** a longing. **4.** a request. **5.** something desired. **6.** sexual urge.

de·sist′ (di zist′, -sist′) *v.i.* to cease.

desk (desk) *n.* **1.** a table for writing. **2.** a section of an organization, as a newspaper office.

desk′top pub′lishing *n.* the design and production of publications using a microcomputer.

des′o·late (des′ə lit) *adj.* **1.** deserted; uninhabited. **2.** lonely. **3.** dismal. —**des′o·la′tion,** *n.*

de·spair′ (di spâr′) *n.* **1.** hopelessness or a cause of hopelessness. —*v.i.* **2.** to lose hope.

des′per·a·do (des′pə rä′dō, -rä′-) *n., pl.* **-does, -dos.** a reckless outlaw.

des′per·ate (des′pər it) *adj.* **1.** reckless from despair. **2.** having an urgent need or desire. **3.** extreme. —**des′per·a′tion,** *n.*

des′pi·ca·ble (des′pi kə bəl, di-spik′ə-) *adj.* contemptible.

de·spise′ (di spīz′) *v.t.,* **-spised, -spising.** to scorn or hate.

de·spite′ (di spīt′) *prep.* in spite of.

de·spoil′ (di spoil′) *v.t.* to rob or plunder.

de·spond′ent (di spon′dənt) *adj.* in low spirits; dejected. —**de·spond′-en·cy** *n.*

des′pot (des′pət, -pot) *n.* a tyrant. —**des•pot′ic,** *adj.*

des•sert′ (di zûrt′) *n.* a usu. sweet food served as the final course of a meal.

des′ti•na′tion (des′tə nā′shən) *n.* the place to which a person or thing travels or is sent.

des′tine (-tin) *v.t.,* **-tined, -tining. 1.** to set apart for a purpose. **2.** to determine beforehand.

des′ti•ny *n., pl.* **-nies. 1.** fate. **2.** the predetermined course of events.

des′ti•tute′ (-tōōt′, -tyōōt′) *adj.* **1.** very poor. **2.** deprived or lacking.

de•stroy′ (di stroi′) *v.t.* **1.** to demolish. **2.** to put an end to. **3.** to kill. **4.** to make useless.

de•stroy′er *n.* **1.** one that destroys. **2.** a fast warship.

de•struct′ (di strukt′) *v.i.* to be destroyed automatically.

de•struc′tion *n.* **1.** destroying or being destroyed. **2.** a cause or means of destroying. —**de•struc′tive,** *adj.*

des′ul•to′ry (des′əl tôr′ē) *adj.* **1.** lacking in consistency or order. **2.** random. —**des′ul•to′ri•ly,** *adv.*

de•tach′ (di tach′) *v.t.* to unfasten and separate. —**de•tach′a•ble,** *adj.*

de•tached′ (-tacht′) *adj.* **1.** not attached. **2.** impartial. **3.** not involved.

de•tach′ment *n.* **1.** a detaching or being detached. **2.** aloofness. **3.** impartiality.

de•tail′ (di tāl′, dē′tāl) *n.* **1.** an individual or minute part. **2.** such parts collectively. **3.** troops or a group selected for special duty. —*v.t.* **4.** to relate in detail. **5.** to assign for a particular duty.

de•tain′ (di tān′) *v.t.* **1.** to delay. **2.** to keep in custody.

de•tect′ (di tekt′) *v.t.* to discover or notice. —**de•tec′tion,** *n.* —**de•tec′tor,** *n.*

de•tec′tive *n.* one who investigates crimes, obtains evidence, etc.

dé•tente′ (dā tänt′) *n.* a relaxing of tensions, esp. between nations.

de•ten′tion (di ten′shən) *n.* **1.** the keeping of a person in custody. **2.** the keeping of a student after school hours as punishment.

de•ter′ (di tûr′) *v.t.,* **-terred, -terring. 1.** to discourage or restrain from acting. **2.** to prevent. —**de•ter′rence,** *n.* —**de•ter′rent,** *adj., n.*

de•ter′gent (di tûr′jənt) *n.* a cleansing agent.

de•te′ri•o•rate′ (-tēr′ē ə rāt′) *v.t., v.i.,* **-rated, -rating.** to make or become worse.

de•ter′mi•na′tion (-tûr′mə nā′shən)

n. **1.** the process of coming to a decision. **2.** firmness of purpose.

de•ter′mine (-tûr min) *v.,* **-mined, -mining.** —*v.t.* **1.** to settle or resolve (a dispute, question, etc.). **2.** to conclude, as after observation. **3.** to decide upon. —*v.i.* **4.** to decide.

de•ter′mined *adj.* **1.** full of determination. **2.** decided; settled.

de•test′ (di test′) *v.t.* to dislike intensely. —**de•test′a•ble,** *adj.*

de•throne′ (dē thrōn′) *v.t.,* **-throned, -throning.** to remove from a throne.

det′o•nate′ (det′n āt′) *v.i., v.t.,* **-nated, -nating.** to explode. —**det′o•na′tion,** *n.*

de′tour (dē′tŏŏr, di tŏŏr′) *n.* **1.** a roundabout course or route. —*v.i., v.t.* **2.** to make or cause to make a detour.

de′tox *n., v.,* **-toxed, -toxing.** *Informal.* —*n.* **1.** (dē′toks) detoxification. —*v.t.* **2.** (dē toks′) to detoxify.

de•tox′i•fy *v.t.,* **-fied, -fying.** to rid of the effects of alcohol or drug use. —**de•tox′i•fi•ca′tion,** *n.*

de•tract′ (di trakt′) *v.* **detract from,** to take away a part, as from quality or reputation.

det′ri•ment (de′trə mənt) *n.* **1.** damage or loss. **2.** a cause of damage or loss. —**det′ri•men′tal,** *adj.*

de•tri′tus (di trī′təs) *n.* **1.** rock particles worn away from a mass. **2.** debris.

deuce (dōōs, dyōōs) *n.* a card or die with two pips. **3.** the tie score.

dev′as•tate′ (dev′ə stāt′) *v.t.,* **-tated, -tating. 1.** to cause great destruction to. **2.** to overwhelm. —**dev′as•ta′tion,** *n.*

de•vel′op (di vel′əp) *v.t.* **1.** to make more advanced, effective, or usable. **2.** to cause to grow. **3.** to bring into being. **4.** to elaborate in detail. **5.** to treat (film) so as to make images visible. —*v.i.* **6.** to become more advanced, mature, etc. **7.** to come gradually into existence or operation. —**de•vel′op•ment,** *n.* —**de•vel′op•er,** *n.*

de′vi•ant (dē′vē ənt) *adj.* **1.** deviating from an accepted norm. —*n.* **2.** a deviant person or thing.

de′vi•ate′ (-āt′) *v.i.,* **-ated, -ating.** to turn aside from a course, standard, or topic. —**de′vi•a′tion,** *n.*

de•vice′ (di vīs′) *n.* **1.** a thing made or used for a specific purpose. **2.** a scheme. **3.** a slogan or emblem.

dev′il (dev′əl) *n.* **1. the Devil,** Satan. **2.** an evil spirit or person. **3.** a mischievous person. —**dev′il•ish,** *adj.* —**dev′il•try,** *n.*

de•vi•ous (dē′vē əs) *adj.* **1.** roundabout. **2.** not straightforward.

de•vise′ (di vīz′) *v.t.,* **-vised, -vising. 1.** to plan or contrive. **2.** to bequeath (property) by will.

de•void′ (di void′) *adj.* totally lacking.

de•volve′ (di volv′) *v.t., v.i.,* **-volved, -volving.** to pass or be passed on from one to another.

de•vote′ (di vōt′) *v.t.,* **-voted, -voting. 1.** to apply to a certain pursuit, cause, etc. **2.** to dedicate.

dev′o•tee′ (dev′ə tē′) *n.* a person who is greatly devoted to something.

de•vo′tion (di vō′shən) *n.* **1.** great love or loyalty. **2.** profound dedication. **3. devotions,** prayers.

de•vour′ (-vour′) *v.t.* **1.** to eat up hungrily. **2.** to take in eagerly with the senses or intellect.

de•vout′ (-vout′) *adj.* **1.** devoted to divine worship; pious. **2.** earnest.

dew (dōō, dyōō) *n.* atmospheric moisture condensed in droplets at night and deposited in small drops on a cool surface. —**dew′y,** *adj.*

dex•ter•i•ty (dek ster′i tē) *n.* skill. —**dex′ter•ous** (-əs, -strəs) *adj.*

dex′trose (-strōs) *n.* a type of sugar.

di•a•be•tes (dī′ə bē′tis, -tēz) *n.* a disease characterized by high levels of glucose in the blood. —**di′a•bet′ic** (-bet′ik) *adj., n.*

di•a•bol′ic (dī′ə bol′ik) *adj.* devilish. Also, **di′a•bol′i•cal.**

di•a•crit′ic (dī′ə krit′ik) *n.* Also called **di′a•crit′i•cal mark.** a mark added to a letter to give it a particular phonetic value.

di′a•dem′ (dī′ə dem′) *n.* a crown.

di′ag•nose′ (dī′əg nōs′, -nōz′) *v.t., v.i.,* **-nosed, -nosing.** to make a diagnosis (of).

di′ag•no′sis *n.* **1.** the process of identifying a disease or condition by medical examination. **2.** the decision reached. —**di′ag•nos′tic** (-nos′tik) *adj.*

di•ag′o•nal (-ag′ə nl) *adj.* **1.** extending from one corner to the opposite one. —*n.* **2.** a line extending from one corner to the opposite corner. —**di•ag′o•nal•ly,** *adv.*

di′a•gram′ (-gram′) *n., v.,* **-gramed, -graming.** —*n.* **1.** a drawing, chart, or plan that outlines and explains something. —*v.t.* **2.** to make a diagram of.

di′al (dī′əl, dīl) *n., v.,* **dialed, dialing.** —*n.* **1.** the numbered face on a watch or clock. **2.** a similar disk or plate with a movable pointer. **3.** a movable disk on a telephone.

—*v.t.* **4.** to select or contact by using a dial.

di•a•lect′ (dī′ə lekt′) *n.* pronunciation or words peculiar to an area.

di•a•lec′tic *adj.* **1.** Also **di′a•lec′ti•cal.** of the nature of logical argumentation. —*n.* **2.** Often **di′a•lec′tics.** the art or practice of debate or conversation by which the truth of a theory or opinion is arrived at logically.

di′a•logue′ (dī′ə lôg′) *n.* a conversation between two or more people. Also, **di′a•log′.**

di•al′y•sis (-al′ə sis) *n.* the removal of waste products from the blood of someone with kidney disease.

di•am′e•ter (dī am′i tər) *n.* a straight line through the center of a circle.

di′a•met′ri•cal (-ə me′tri kəl) *adj.* being in direct opposition. —**di′a•met′ri•cal•ly,** *adv.*

dia′mond (dī′mənd, dī′ə-) *n.* **1.** a very hard, brilliant, precious stone. **2.** a figure having four equal sides and two acute and two obtuse angles. **3. diamonds,** a suit of playing cards marked with such shapes. **4.** a baseball field.

dia′mond•back′ *n.* a rattlesnake with diamond-shaped markings.

di•a•per (dī′pər, dī′ə pər) *n.* **1.** a piece of absorbent material worn as underpants by a baby. —*v.t.* **2.** to put a diaper on.

di•aph′a•nous (dī af′ə nəs) *adj.* very sheer and light.

di′a•phragm′ (dī′ə fram′) *n.* **1.** the muscle between the chest and the abdomen. **2.** a vibrating disk, as in a telephone. **3.** a contraceptive device that fits over the cervix.

di•ar•rhe′a (dī′ə rē′ə) *n.* a disorder characterized by frequent and fluid bowel movements.

di′a•ry (dī′ə rē) *n., pl.* **-ries. 1.** a daily record of events. **2.** a book for recording these. —**di′a•rist,** *n.*

di′a•tribe′ (-trīb′) *n.* a bitter, abusive denunciation.

dib′ble (dib′əl) *n.* a pointed instrument for making holes in soil.

dice (dīs) *n.pl., sing.* **die,** *v.,* **diced, dicing.** —*n.* **1.** small cubes, marked on each side with one to six spots, used in games. **2.** a game played with these. —*v.t.* **3.** to cut into small cubes. —*v.i.* **4.** to play at dice.

dic′ey (dī′sē) *adj.,* **-ier, -iest.** risky.

di•chot′o•my (dī kot′ə mē) *n., pl.* **-mies.** division into two parts.

dick′er (dik′ər) *v.i.* to bargain.

di•cot′y•le′don (dī kot′l ēd′n, dī-kot l-) *n.* a plant having two embryonic seed leaves.

dic'tate (dik'tāt) *v.*, **-tated, -tating,** *n.* —*v.t., v.i.* **1.** to say or read aloud (something) to be written down or recorded. **2.** to command. —*n.* **3.** a command. —**dic·ta'tion,** *n.*

dic'ta·tor *n.* an absolute ruler. —**dic'ta·to'ri·al** (-tə tôr'ē əl) *adj.* —**dic·ta'tor·ship',** *n.*

dic'tion (dik'shən) *n.* style of speaking or writing.

dic'tion·ar'y (-shə ner'ē) *n., pl.* **-ar·ies.** a book that lists the words of a language with their meanings and other information.

dic'tum (-təm) *n., pl.* **-ta, -tums.** an authoritative declaration.

did (did) *v.* pt. of **do.**

di·dac'tic (dī dak'tik) *adj.* intended for instruction.

did'n't (did'nt) a contraction of **did not.**

die¹ (dī) *v.i.*, **died, dying. 1.** to cease to live. **2.** to cease to function. **3.** to lose force; fade.

die² (dī) *n., pl.* **dies** for 1; **dice** for 2. **1.** a device that cuts or shapes material. **2.** sing. of **dice.**

die'hard' *n.* a person who stubbornly resists change.

di·er'e·sis (dī er'ə sis) *n., pl.* **-ses.** a sign (¨) placed over the second of two vowels, indicating it is pronounced separately, as in Noël.

die'sel (dē'zəl, -səl) *n.* a vehicle powered by a diesel engine.

die'sel en'gine *n.* an internal-combustion engine in which fuel oil is ignited by the heat of compressed air.

di'et¹ (dī'it) *n.* **1.** the food one usually eats. **2.** a particular selection of food, as for health. —*v.i., v.t.* **3.** to go or put on a diet.

di'et² (dī'it) *n.* a legislative body.

di'e·tar'y (-i ter'ē) *adj.* of diet.

di'e·tet'ic (-tet'ik) *adj.* **1.** of diet. **2.** suitable for special diets. —*n.* **3.** **dietetics,** the science of nutrition and food preparation.

di'e·ti'tian (dī'i tish'ən) *n.* a person who is trained in nutrition and dietetics. Also, **di'e·ti'cian.**

dif'fer (dif'ər) *v.i.* **1.** to be unlike. **2.** to disagree.

dif'fer·ence (dif'ər əns, dif'rəns) *n.* **1.** the state or degree of being different. **2.** a disagreement. **3.** the amount separating two quantities.

dif'fer·ent *adj.* **1.** not alike. **2.** distinct. **3.** various. **4.** not ordinary. —**dif'fer·ent·ly,** *adv.* —**Usage.** DIFFERENT FROM is more common today in introducing a phrase, but DIFFERENT THAN is also used: *New York speech is different from/than that of Chicago.* DIFFERENT THAN is usually used when a clause follows, especially when the word "from" would create an awkward sentence: *The stream followed a different course than the map showed.*

dif·fer·en'ti·ate' (-en'shē āt') *v.*, **-ated, -ating.** —*v.t.* **1.** to distinguish. **2.** to perceive the difference in. —*v.i.* **3.** to become unlike. **4.** to make a distinction. —**dif·fer·en'ti·a'tion,** *n.*

dif'fi·cult' (dif'i kult', -kəlt) *adj.* **1.** requiring special effort or skill. **2.** hard to do or understand. **3.** hard to deal with.

dif'fi·cul'ty *n., pl.* **-ties. 1.** the condition of being difficult. **2.** a difficult situation. **3.** trouble. **4.** a disagreement.

dif'fi·dent (-dənt) *adj.* timid; shy.

dif·frac'tion (di frak'shən) *n.* a breaking up of light rays, producing a spectrum.

dif·fuse' *v.*, **-fused, -fusing,** *adj.* —*v.t., v.i.* (di fyōōz') **1.** to spread or scatter. —*adj.* (-fyōōs') **2.** wordy. **3.** spread or scattered.

dig (dig) *v.*, **dug** (dug) or **digged, digging,** *n.* —*v.i.* **1.** to break up and move earth. **2.** to make one's way by digging. —*v.t.* **3.** to break up, turn over, or loosen (earth). **4.** to uncover by removing earth. **5.** to form by removing material. —*n.* **6.** a thrust. **7.** a cutting remark. **8.** an excavation. —**dig'ger,** *n.*

dig'e·ra'ti (dij'ə rä'tē, -rä'-) *n.pl.* people skilled with or knowledgeable about computers.

di·gest' *v.t.* (di jest') **1.** to dissolve (food) in the stomach for absorption by the body. **2.** to absorb mentally. —*n.* (dī'jest) **3.** a collection or summary. —**di·ges'tion,** *n.* —**di·gest'ive,** *adj.*

dig'it (dij'it) *n.* **1.** a finger or toe. **2.** any Arabic numeral from 0 to 9.

dig'it·al (-i tl) *adj.* of, using, or expressing data in numerals.

dig'i·tal'is (-tal'is, -tā'lis) *n.* a medicine derived from foxglove leaves, used to stimulate the heart.

dig'i·tize' (-tīz') *v.t.*, **-tized, -tizing.** to convert (data) to digital form.

dig'ni·fied' (dig'nə fīd') *adj.* marked by dignity; stately.

dig'ni·fy' *v.t.*, **-fied, -fying.** to give honor or dignity to.

dig'ni·ta·ry (-ter'ē) *n., pl.* **-ries.** a high-ranking person.

dig'ni·ty *n., pl.* **-ties. 1.** formal or serious conduct or manner. **2.** worthiness. **3.** high rank, title, etc.

di·gress' (di gres', dī-) *v.i.* to wander from the main topic, argument, etc. —**di·gres'sion,** *n.*

dike (dīk) *n.* a long wall or bank built to prevent flooding.

di·lap′i·dat′ed (di lap′i dā′tid) *adj.* ruined or decayed.

di·late′ (dī lāt′) *v.t.*, *v.i.*, **-lated, -lating.** to make or become wider. —**di·la′tion,** *n.*

dil′a·to′ry (dil′ə tôr′ē) *adj.* delaying; tardy. —**dil′a·to′ri·ness,** *n.*

di·lem′ma (di lem′ə) *n.* a situation requiring a choice between equally unpleasant alternatives.

dil′et·tante′ (dil′i tänt′, dil′i tänt′) *n.* a person who dabbles in an activity or subject for amusement.

dil′i·gence (dil′i jəns) *n.* earnest effort. —**dil′i·gent,** *adj.*

dill (dil) *n.* an herb with aromatic seeds and leaves.

dil′ly-dal′ly (dil′ē dal′ē) *v.i.*, **-dallied, -dallying.** to waste time, esp. by indecision.

di·lute′ (di lōōt′, dī-) *v.t.*, **-luted, -luting. 1.** to make (a liquid) thinner or weaker, as by adding water. **2.** to reduce the strength of. —**di·lu′tion,** *n.*

dim (dim) *adj.*, **dimmer, dimmest,** *v.*, **dimmed, dimming.** —*adj.* **1.** not bright. **2.** indistinct. —*v.t.*, *v.i.* **3.** to make or become dim.

dime (dīm) *n.* a ten-cent coin.

di·men′sion (di men′shən, dī-) *n.* **1.** extension in a given direction. **2. dimensions,** measurement in length, width, and thickness. —**di·men′sion·al,** *adj.*

di·min′ish (di min′ish) *v.t.*, *v.i.* to make or become smaller, less, or less important.

di·min′u·en′do (di min′yŏŏ en′dō) *adj.*, *adv. Music.* gradually reducing in loudness.

di·min′u·tive (di min′yə tiv) *adj.* **1.** tiny. —*n.* **2.** a word denoting smallness, familiarity, or affection.

dim′ple (dim′pəl) *n.* a small natural hollow, esp. in the cheek.

dim′wit′ *n. Slang.* a stupid person. —**dim′wit′ted,** *adj.*

din (din) *n.*, *v.*, **dinned, dinning.** —*n.* **1.** a loud, confused noise. —*v.t.* **2.** to assail with a din.

dine (dīn) *v.i.*, **dined, dining.** to eat dinner.

din′er *n.* **1.** a person who dines. **2.** a railroad dining car. **3.** a restaurant resembling this.

di·nette′ (-net′) *n.* a small area or alcove for dining.

din′ghy (ding′gē) *n.*, *pl.* **-ghies.** a small boat.

din′gy (din′jē) *adj.*, **-gier, -giest.** of a dark, dull, or dirty color.

din′ner (din′ər) *n.* the main meal of the day.

di′no·saur′ (dī′nə sôr′) *n.* any of various extinct, prehistoric reptiles.

dint (dint) *n.* **1.** force. **2.** a dent.

di′o·cese′ (dī′ə sis, -sēz′, -sēs′) *n.* a district under a bishop. —**di·oc′e·san** (-os′ə sən) *adj.*, *n.*

di′o·ram′a (dī′ə ram′ə, -rä′mə) *n.* a miniature three-dimensional scene against a painted background.

di·ox′ide (dī ok′sīd, -sid) *n.* an oxide with two atoms of oxygen.

di·ox′in (-ok′sin) *n.* a toxic by-product of pesticide manufacture.

dip (dip) *v.*, **dipped, dipping,** *n.* —*v.t.* **1.** to plunge briefly into a liquid. **2.** to bail or scoop. —*v.i.* **3.** to go under water and emerge quickly. **4.** to drop suddenly. **5.** to slope down. —*n.* **6.** the act of dipping. **7.** a downward slope. **8.** a substance into which something is dipped. **9.** a brief swim.

diph·the′ri·a (dif thēr′ē ə, dip-) *n.* an infectious disease marked by high fever and breathing difficulty.

diph′thong (dif′thông, dip′-) *n.* a gliding speech sound containing two vowels.

di·plo′ma (di plō′mə) *n.* a document conferring a degree or certifying the successful completion of a course of study.

di·plo′ma·cy (-sē) *n.*, *pl.* **-cies. 1.** the conduct of international relations. **2.** skill in negotiation. —**dip′lo·mat′** (dip′lə mat′) *n.*

dip′lo·mat′ic *adj.* **1.** of diplomacy. **2.** tactful.

dip′so·ma′ni·a (dip′sə mā′nē ə, -sō-) *n.* an irresistible craving for alcohol. —**dip′so·ma′ni·ac,** *n.*

dire (dī⁰r) *adj.*, **direr, direst.** dreadful; ominous.

di·rect′ (di rekt′, dī-) *v.t.* **1.** to manage or guide. **2.** to command. **3.** to serve as director of. **4.** to show (a person) the way or how to do something. **5.** to address. —*adj.* **6.** proceeding in a straight line. **7.** without intermediary agents or conditions. **8.** straightforward. —**di·rect′ly,** *adv.* —**di·rect′ness,** *n.*

direct′ cur′rent *n.* an electric current flowing continuously in one direction.

di·rec′tion *n.* **1.** an act of directing. **2.** the line along which a thing faces or moves. **3.** supervision. —**di·rec′tion·al,** *adj.*

di·rec′tive *n.* an authoritative order or instruction.

di·rec′tor *n.* **1.** one that directs. **2.** one of the persons chosen to govern the affairs of a company. **3.** the person who guides the performers in a play or film.

di·rec′to·ry *n.*, *pl.* **-ries.** a list of names, locations, telephone numbers, etc.

dirge (dûrj) *n.* a song or poem commemorating the dead.

dir•i•gi•ble (dir′i jə bəl, di rij′ə-) *n.* a self-propelled, lighter-than-air aircraft; airship.

dirk (dûrk) *n.* a dagger.

dirt (dûrt) *n.* **1.** any foul or filthy substance. **2.** soil. **3.** obscene words. **4.** gossip.

dirt•y *adj.,* **-ier, -iest,** *v.,* **-ied, -ying.** —*adj.* **1.** soiled or soiling. **2.** vile. **3.** obscene. **4.** unpleasant. —*v.t., v.i.* **5.** to make or become dirty. —**dirt′i•ness,** *n.*

dis (dis) *v.,* **dissed, dissing,** *n. Slang.* —*v.t.* **1.** to show disrespect for. **2.** to disparage. —*n.* **3.** disparagement or criticism.

dis- a prefix indicating: **1.** reversal. **2.** negation or lack. **3.** removal.

dis•a•ble (-ā′bəl) *v.t.,* **-bled, -bling.** to make unable or unfit. —**dis′a•bil/i•ty,** *n.*

dis•a′bled *adj.* handicapped; incapacitated.

dis•a•buse′ (-byo͞oz′) *v.t.,* **-bused, -busing.** to free from deception.

dis•ad•van•tage *n.* an unfavorable condition; handicap.

dis•ad•van′taged *adj.* lacking economic and social opportunity.

dis•af•fect′ *v.t.* to make discontented.

dis•a•gree′ *v.i.,* **-greed, -greeing. 1.** to differ in opinion. **2.** to fail to agree. **3.** to quarrel. —**dis•a•gree′ment,** *n.*

dis•a•gree′a•ble *adj.* unpleasant; grouchy.

dis•al•low′ *v.t.* to refuse to allow.

dis•ap•pear′ *v.i.* **1.** to cease to be seen. **2.** to cease to exist. —**dis•ap•pear′ance,** *n.*

dis•ap•point′ *v.t.* to fail to fulfill the hopes of. —**dis•ap•point′ment,** *n.*

dis•ap•pro•ba′tion *n.* disapproval.

dis•ap•prove′ *v.,* **-proved, -proving.** —*v.t.* **1.** to think (something) wrong. **2.** to withhold approval from. —*v.i.* **3.** to have an unfavorable opinion. —**dis•ap•prov′al,** *n.*

dis•arm′ *v.t.* **1.** to deprive of weapons. **2.** to make less hostile.

dis•ar•range′ *v.t.,* **-ranged, -ranging.** to disturb the arrangement of.

dis•ar•ray′ *n.* lack of order.

dis•as•so•ci•ate′ (-āt′) *v.t., v.i.* **-ated, -ating.** to dissociate.

dis•as′ter (di zas′tər) *n.* an event that occurs suddenly and causes great damage. —**dis•as′trous,** *adj.*

dis•a•vow′ (dis′ə vou′) *v.t.* to deny knowledge of or responsibility for. —**dis•a•vow′al,** *n.*

dis•band′ *v.t.* to break up (an organization).

dis•bar′ *v.t.,* **-barred, -barring.** to expel from the legal profession.

dis•be•lieve′ *v.t., v.i.,* **-lieved, -lieving.** to refuse or be unable to believe. —**dis•be•lief′,** *n.*

dis•burse′ (dis bûrs′) *v.t.,* **-bursed, -bursing.** to pay out.

disc (disk) *n.* **1.** a disk. **2.** a phonograph record.

dis•card′ *v.t.* (di skärd′) **1.** to cast aside. —*n.* (dis′kärd) **2.** the act of discarding. **3.** something discarded.

dis•cern′ (di sûrn′, -zûrn′) *v.t., v.i.* to perceive by the sight or the mind. —**dis•cern′i•ble,** *adj.* —**dis•cern′ment,** *n.*

dis•cern′ing *adj.* showing good judgment and understanding.

dis•charge′ *v.,* **-charged, -charging,** *n.* —*v.t.* (dis chärj′) **1.** to remove the contents of. **2.** to send or pour forth. **3.** to shoot (a gun). **4.** to fulfill the requirements of (a duty). **5.** to dismiss from employment. **6.** to pay (a debt). —*v.i.* **7.** to get rid of a burden. **8.** to pour forth. **9.** to go off, as a gun. —*n.* (dis′chärj) **10.** the act of discharging. **11.** something discharged.

dis•ci′ple (di sī′pəl) *n.* a follower.

dis•ci•pline (dis′ə plin) *n., v.,* **-plined, -plining.** —*n.* **1.** training to act in accordance with rules. **2.** behavior in accord with rules of conduct. **3.** a branch of learning. **4.** punishment. —*v.t.* **5.** to train by instruction and exercise. **6.** to bring under control. **7.** to punish. —**dis′ci•pli•nar′y,** *adj.*

disc′ jockey′ *n.* a person who plays and comments on recorded music on a radio program.

dis•claim′ *v.t.* to disown.

dis•close′ *v.t.,* **-closed, -closing.** to reveal. —**dis•clo′sure,** *n.*

dis′co (dis′kō) *n., pl.* **-cos. 1.** a discotheque. **2.** a style of popular music having a heavy rhythmic beat.

dis•col′or *v.t., v.i.* to change color. —**dis•col′or•a′tion,** *n.*

dis′com•bob′u•late′ (dis′kəm bob′yə lāt′) *v.t.,* **-lated, -lating.** to confuse or disconcert.

dis•com′fit (dis kum′fit) *v.t.* **1.** to confuse; disconcert. **2.** to frustrate. —**dis•com′fi•ture,** *n.*

dis•com′fort *n.* **1.** lack of comfort. **2.** anything disturbing to comfort.

dis′com•mode′ (dis′kə mōd′) *v.t.,* **-moded, -moding.** to cause inconvenience to.

dis′com•pose′ *v.t.,* **-posed, -posing. 1.** to upset the order of. **2.** to disturb the composure of.

dis•con•cert′ (dis′kən sûrt′) *v.t.* to disturb the self-possession of; perturb.

dis•con•nect′ *v.t.* to break the connection of.

dis•con•so•late (-kon′sə lit) *adj.* sad; gloomy. —**dis•con′so•late•ly,** *adv.*

dis′con•tent′ (-kən tent′) *adj.* Also **dis′con•tent′ed. 1.** not contented. —*n.* **2.** lack of contentment.

dis′con•tin′ue *v.,* **-tinued, -tinuing.** —*v.t.* **1.** to put an end to; stop. —*v.i.* **2.** to come to an end.

dis′cord *n.* **1.** lack of harmony. **2.** difference of opinion. **3.** any harsh noise. —**dis•cord′ant,** *adj.*

dis′co•theque′ (dis′kə tek′, dis′kə tek′) *n.* a nightclub for dancing.

dis′count *v.t.* (dis′kount, dis kount′) **1.** to deduct an amount from. **2.** to sell at a reduced price. **3.** to disregard. —*n.* (dis′kount) **4.** an act of discounting. **5.** an amount deducted.

dis•cour′age *v.t.,* **-aged, -aging. 1.** to deprive of courage or confidence. **2.** to hinder.

dis′course *n., v.,* **-coursed, -coursing.** —*n.* (dis′kôrs) **1.** a conversation. **2.** a formal discussion of a subject. —*v.i.* (dis kôrs′) **3.** to talk. **4.** to treat a subject formally.

dis•cour′te•sy *n., pl.* **-sies. 1.** rudeness. **2.** an impolite act. —**dis•cour′te•ous,** *adj.*

dis•cov′er (di skuv′ər) *v.t.* to obtain sight or knowledge of. —**dis•cov′er•er,** *n.* —**dis•cov′er•y,** *n.*

dis•cred′it *v.t.* **1.** to injure the reputation of. **2.** to disbelieve. —*n.* **3.** loss or lack of belief. **4.** disgrace.

dis•creet′ (di skrēt′) *adj.* cautious in conduct or speech; prudent.

dis•crep′an•cy (di skrep′ən sē) *n., pl.* **-cies.** a difference; inconsistency.

dis•crete′ (di skrēt′) *adj.* separate.

dis•cre′tion (di skresh′ən) *n.* **1.** the freedom to decide something. **2.** the quality of being discreet.

dis•crim′i•nate′ (di skrim′ə nāt′) *v.i.,* **-nated, -nating. 1.** to show partiality. **2.** to note a difference. —**dis•crim′i•na′tion,** *n.*

dis•crim′i•nat′ing *adj.* having good taste or judgment.

dis•cur′sive (di skûr′siv) *adj.* rambling from one subject to another.

dis′cus (dis′kəs) *n.* a disk for throwing in athletic competition.

dis•cuss′ (di skus′) *v.t.* to consider or examine by argument, comment, etc. —**dis•cus′sion,** *n.*

dis•dain′ (dis dān′, di stān′) *v.t.* to scorn. —**dis•dain′ful,** *adj.*

dis•ease′ (di zēz′) *n.* an abnormal condition; an illness.

dis′em•bark′ (dis′em bärk′) *v.i.* to leave an airplane or ship. —**dis•em′bar•ka′tion,** *n.*

dis′en•chant′ *v.t.* to free from enchantment or illusion.

dis′en•gage′ *v.,* **-gaged, -gaging.** —*v.t.* **1.** to separate; disconnect. —*v.i.* **2.** to become disengaged.

dis•fa′vor *n.* displeasure; dislike.

dis•fig′ure *v.t.,* **-ured, -uring.** to spoil the appearance of. —**dis•fig′ure•ment′,** *n.*

dis•fran′chise or **dis′en•fran′chise** *v.t.,* **-chised, -chising.** to deprive of a right, esp. the right to vote.

dis•gorge′ (dis gôrj′) *v.t.,* **-gorged, -gorging.** to eject; throw up.

dis•grace′ *n., v.,* **-graced, -gracing.** —*n.* **1.** loss of respect or honor. **2.** a person or thing that causes loss of respect or honor. —*v.t.* **3.** to bring shame upon. —**dis•grace′ful,** *adj.*

dis•grun′tle (dis grun′tl) *v.t.,* **-tled, -tling.** to make discontented or resentful.

dis•guise′ (dis gīz′, di skīz′) *v.,* **-guised, -guising,** *n.* —*v.t.* **1.** to conceal the true identity or character of. —*n.* **2.** something that disguises.

dis•gust′ (dis gust′, di skust′) *v.t.* **1.** to cause loathing or nausea in. —*n.* **2.** a strong loathing. —**dis•gust′ed,** *adj.* —**dis•gust′ing,** *adj.*

dish (dish) *n.* **1.** an open, shallow container for holding food. **2.** a particular article of food.

dis′ha•bille′ (dis′ə bēl′, -bē′) *n.* the state of being partially dressed.

dis•heart′en *v.t.* to discourage.

dis•hon′est *adj.* not honest.

dis•hon′or *n.* **1.** lack or loss of honor; disgrace. —*v.t.* **2.** to disgrace. —**dis•hon′or•a•ble,** *adj.*

dish′wash′er *n.* a person or machine that washes dishes.

dis•il•lu′sion *v.t.* to free from pleasing but false beliefs.

dis′in•cline′ *v.t.,* **-clined, -clining.** to make unwilling or reluctant.

dis′in•fect′ *v.t.* to cleanse in order to destroy disease germs. —**dis′in•fect′ant,** *n., adj.*

dis•in′for•ma′tion *n.* deliberately misleading information.

dis′in•gen′u•ous *adj.* insincere.

dis′in•her′it *v.t.* to deprive of an inheritance.

dis•in′te•grate′ *v.i.,* **-grated, -grating.** to break into parts. —**dis•in′te•gra′tion,** *n.*

dis′in•ter′ *v.t.,* **-terred, -terring.** to unearth; dig up.

dis•in′ter•est′ed *adj.* not partial or biased. —**Usage.** Do not confuse DISINTERESTED and UNINTERESTED. DISINTERESTED means "able to act fairly; not partial or biased," while UNINTERESTED means "not taking an interest."

dis•joint′ed *adj.* disconnected; incoherent.

disk (disk) *n.* **1.** a thin, flat, circular plate. **2.** a plate for storing electronic data. **3.** a roundish, flat anatomical part, as in the spine. **4.** a phonograph record.

disk•ette′ *n.* a floppy disk.

dis•like′ *v.,* **-liked, -liking,** *n.* —*v.t.* **1.** to regard with displeasure. —*n.* **2.** a feeling of not liking.

dis′lo•cate′ (dis′lō kāt′, dis lō′kāt) *v.t.,* **-cated, -cating. 1.** to put out of place or order. **2.** to put out of joint, as a limb.

dis•lodge′ *v.t.,* **-lodged, -lodging.** to force out of place.

dis•loy′al *adj.* not loyal; faithless.

dis′mal (diz′məl) *adj.* **1.** gloomy. **2.** very bad. —**dis′mal•ly,** *adv.*

dis•man′tle *v.t.,* **-tled, -tling. 1.** to take away equipment from. **2.** to take apart.

dis•may′ (dis mā′) *v.t.* **1.** to surprise and discourage. —*n.* **2.** surprise and discouragement.

dis•mem′ber *v.t.* **1.** to remove the limbs of. **2.** to divide into parts.

dis•miss′ (dis mis′) *v.t.* **1.** to direct or allow to go. **2.** to discharge from service. **3.** to reject. —**dis•mis′sal,** *n.*

dis•mount′ *v.i.* to get down, as from a horse or a bicycle.

dis′o•be′di•ent *adj.* not obedient. —**dis′o•be′di•ence,** *n.*

dis′o•bey′ *v.t., v.i.* to neglect or refuse to obey.

dis•or′der *n.* **1.** lack of order; confusion. **2.** an illness. —*v.t.* **3.** to create disorder in. —**dis•or′der•ly,** *adj.*

dis•or′gan•ize′ *v.t.,* **-ized, -izing.** to destroy the orderly system or arrangement of. —**dis•or′gan•i•za′tion,** *n.*

dis•o′ri•ent′ *v.t.* **1.** to cause to lose one's way. **2.** to confuse mentally.

dis•own′ *v.t.* to refuse to acknowledge as belonging to oneself.

dis•par′age (di spar′ij) *v.t.,* **-aged, -aging.** to speak slightingly of.

dis′par•ate (dis′pər it, di spar′-) *adj.* different. —**dis′par•i•ty,** *n.*

dis•pas′sion•ate *adj.* impartial; calm. —**dis•pas′sion•ate•ly,** *adv.*

dis•patch′ *v.t.* **1.** to send off. **2.** to dispose of (a matter) quickly. **3.** to kill. —*n.* **4.** the act of sending off. **5.** execution. **6.** speedy action. **7.** a message or report sent quickly.

dis•pel′ (di spel′) *v.t.,* **-pelled, -pelling.** to drive off; scatter.

dis•pen′sa•ry (di spen′sə rē) *n., pl.* **-ries.** a place where medicine is dispensed.

dis′pen•sa′tion (dis′pən sā′shən, -pen-) *n.* **1.** an act of dispensing. **2.** the divine ordering of the world's affairs. **3.** an official exemption from a law or obligation.

dis•pense′ (di spens′) *v.t.,* **-pensed, -pensing. 1.** to distribute; administer. **2.** to make up and distribute (medicines). **3.** dispense with, to do without. —**dis•pens′er,** *n.*

dis•perse′ (di spûrs′) *v.,* **-persed, -persing.** *v.t.* **1.** to scatter. **2.** to dispel. —*v.i.* **3.** to become scattered. —**dis•per′sal,** *n.*

dis•pir′i•ted *adj.* downhearted.

dis•place′ *v.t.,* **-placed, -placing. 1.** to put out of the usual place. **2.** to take the place of. —**dis•place′ment,** *n.*

dis•play′ (di splā′) *v.t.* **1.** to show or exhibit. —*n.* **2.** an act or instance of displaying.

dis•please′ *v.t., v.i.,* **-pleased, -pleasing.** to annoy or offend. —**dis•pleas′ure** (-plezh′ər) *n.*

dis•pose′ *v.t.,* **-posed, -posing. 1.** to place or arrange. **2.** to make willing to do something. **3. dispose of, a.** to settle. **b.** to get rid of. —**dis•pos′a•ble,** *adj., n.* —**dis•pos′al,** *n.*

dis′po•si′tion (dis′pə zish′ən) *n.* **1.** one's mental outlook. **2.** tendency. **3.** arrangement. **4.** final settlement of a matter.

dis′pos•sess′ *v.t.* to put (a person) out of possession.

dis′pro•por′tion *n.* lack of proportion. —**dis′pro•por′tion•ate,** *adj.*

dis•prove′ *v.t.,* **-proved, -proving.** to prove to be false.

dis•pute′ (di spyo͞ot′) *v.,* **-puted, -puting,** *n.* —*v.i.* **1.** to engage in argument. **2.** to quarrel. —*v.t.* **3.** to argue about or against. **4.** to fight about. —*n.* **5.** an argument; quarrel. —**dis•put′a•ble,** *adj.* —**dis′pu•ta′tion,** *n.*

dis•qual′i•fy′ *v.t.,* **-fied, -fying.** to make ineligible. —**dis•qual′i•fi•ca′tion,** *n.*

dis•qui′et *n.* **1.** anxiety; uneasiness. —*v.t.* **2.** to cause disquiet to.

dis′re•gard′ *v.t.* **1.** to ignore. —*n.* **2.** neglect.

dis′re•pair′ *n.* the condition of needing repair.

dis′re•pute′ *n.* bad repute; disfavor. —**dis•rep′u•ta•ble,** *adj.*

dis′re•spect′ *n.* lack of respect. —**dis′re•spect′ful,** *adj.*

dis•robe′ *v.t., v.i.,* **-robed, -robing.** to undress.

dis•rupt′ (dis rupt′) *v.t.* **1.** to break

up. **2.** to disturb. —**dis·rup'tion,** *n.*
—**dis·rup'tive,** *adj.*

dis'sat·is·fac'tion *n.* **1.** lack of satisfaction. **2.** a cause or feeling of displeasure. —**dis·sat'is·fy',** *v.t.*

dis·sect' (di sekt', dī-) *v.t.* **1.** to cut apart for examination. **2.** to analyze in detail. —**dis·sec'tion,** *n.*

dis·sem'ble (di sem'bəl) *v.t., v.i.,* **-bled, -bling.** to conceal (motives or thoughts). —**dis·sem'bler,** *n.*

dis·sem'i·nate' (di sem'ə nāt') *v.t.,* **-nated, -nating.** to spread widely.

dis·sen'sion (di sen'shən) *n.* strong disagreement; discord.

dis·sent' (di sent') *v.i.* **1.** to differ in opinion or sentiment. —*n.* **2.** a difference of opinion.

dis·ser·ta'tion (dis'ər tā'shən) *n.* a formal essay or thesis.

dis·serv'ice *n.* harm or injury.

dis'si·dent (dis'i dənt) *n.* **1.** a person who dissents from established opinions. —*adj.* **2.** dissenting, as in opinion. —**dis'si·dence,** *n.*

dis·sim'i·lar *adj.* not similar. —**dis·sim'i·lar'i·ty** (-lar'i tē) *n.*

dis·sim'u·late' (di sim'yə lāt') *v.t., v.i.,* **-lated, -lating.** to dissemble.

dis'si·pate' (dis'ə pāt') *v.,* **-pated, -pating.** —*v.t.* **1.** to scatter. **2.** to use wastefully. —*v.i.* **3.** to become scattered. **4.** to indulge in dissolute behavior. —**dis'si·pa'tion,** *n.*

dis·so'ci·ate' (di sō'shē āt', -sē-) *v.t., v.i.,* **-ated, -ating.** to break the association of.

dis'so·lute' (dis'ə loōt') *adj.* lacking moral restraint.

dis·solve' (di zolv') *v.,* **-solved, -solving.** —*v.t.* **1.** to make a solution of. **2.** to melt. **3.** to break (a tie). **4.** to dismiss (an assembly). —*v.i.* **5.** to become dissolved. **6.** to disappear gradually. **7.** to break down emotionally. —**dis'so·lu'tion** (dis'ə loō'shən) *n.*

dis'so·nance (dis'ə nəns) *n.* inharmonious sound; discord.

dis·suade' (di swād') *v.t.,* **-suaded, -suading.** to persuade against.

dist. 1. distance. **2.** district.

dis'taff (dis'taf) *adj.* **1.** of women. —*n.* **2.** a staff for holding wool, flax, etc., in spinning.

dis'tance (dis'təns) *n.* **1.** the space between two things, points, etc. **2.** remoteness. **3.** a distant region. **4.** aloofness.

dis'tant *adj.* **1.** far off in space or time; remote. **2.** reserved or aloof. —**dis'tant·ly,** *adv.*

dis·taste' *n.* dislike; aversion. —**dis·taste'ful,** *adj.*

dis·tem'per (dis tem'pər) *n.* an infectious disease of dogs and cats.

dis·tend' (di stend') *v.t., v.i.* to swell. —**dis·ten'tion,** *n.*

dis·till' (di stil') *v.t., v.i.* **1.** to subject to or undergo distillation. **2.** to fall in drops. —**dis·till'er·y,** *n.*

dis·til·la'tion *n.* **1.** the process of heating, evaporating, and condensing a liquid. **2.** the purification of a substance by such a method.

dis·tinct' (di stingkt') *adj.* **1.** different in nature or quality. **2.** clear. **3.** separate. —**dis·tinct'ly,** *adv.*

dis·tinc'tion *n.* **1.** an act or instance of distinguishing. **2.** the recognizing of differences. **3.** a distinguishing quality. **4.** a special honor. —**dis·tinc'tive,** *adj.*

dis·tin'guish (di sting'gwish) *v.t.* **1.** to mark off as different. **2.** to recognize as distinct. **3.** to perceive clearly. **4.** to make prominent.

dis·tin'guished *adj.* **1.** characterized by distinction. **2.** dignified or elegant.

dis·tort' (di stôrt') *v.t.* **1.** to twist out of shape. **2.** to give a false meaning to.

dis·tract' (di strakt') *v.t.* to divert the attention of.

dis·trac'tion *n.* **1.** a distracting or being distracted. **2.** mental distress. **3.** a person or thing that prevents concentration. **4.** something that amuses.

dis·traught' (di strôt') *adj.* crazed with anxiety; deeply agitated.

dis·tress' (di stres') *n.* **1.** anxiety, pain, or sorrow. —*v.t.* **2.** to afflict with anxiety, pain, or sorrow.

dis·trib'ute (di strib'yoōt) *v.t.,* **-uted, -uting. 1.** to divide and give out in shares. **2.** to spread over a space. —**dis'tri·bu'tion,** *n.* —**dis·trib'u·tor,** *n.*

dis'trict (dis'trikt) *n.* **1.** a political division. **2.** a region.

dis'trict attor'ney *n.* an attorney for the government within a given district.

dis·trust' *v.t.* **1.** to have no trust in. —*n.* **2.** lack of trust; suspicion.

dis·turb' (di stûrb') *v.t.* **1.** to interrupt the rest or peace of. **2.** to put out of order. **3.** to trouble. —**dis·turb'ance,** *n.*

dis·use' (dis yoōs') *n.* the state of not being used.

ditch (dich) *n.* **1.** a long, narrow channel in the ground. —*v.t.* **2.** to crash-land on water and abandon (an aircraft). **3.** *Slang.* to get rid of.

dith'er (di*th*'ər) *n.* **1.** flustered excitement or fear. —*v.i.* **2.** to be indecisive.

dit'to (dit'ō) *n., pl.* **-tos,** *adv.* —*n.* **1.** the above or the same (used in accounts, lists, etc.). —*adv.* **2.** as stated before.

dit′to mark′ *n.* a mark (") used as a sign for ditto.

dit′ty (dit′ē) *n., pl.* **-ties.** a simple song.

di′u•ret′ic (dī′ə ret′ik) *adj.* **1.** causing more urine to be excreted. —*n.* **2.** a diuretic medicine.

di•ur′nal (dī ûr′nl) *adj.* **1.** occurring each day. **2.** of or active in the daytime.

div. 1. dividend. **2.** division. **3.** divorced.

di′va (dē′və, -vä) *n.* a principal female singer in an opera.

di•van′ (di van′) *n.* a sofa or couch.

dive (dīv) *v.*, **dived** or **dove** (dōv), **dived, diving.** —*v.t.* **1.** to plunge headfirst into water. **2.** to plunge, fall, or descend through the air. **3.** to rush. —*n.* **4.** an act of diving. **5.** a sudden decline. —**div′er**, *n.*

di•verge′ (di vûrj′, dī-) *v.i.*, **-verged, -verging. 1.** to move or extend in different directions from a point. **2.** to differ, as in opinion. **3.** to deviate, as from a path. —**di•ver′gence**, *n.* —**di•ver′gent**, *adj.*

di′vers (dī′vərz) *adj.* various.

di•verse′ (di vûrs′, dī-) *adj.* of different kinds.

di•ver′si•fy′ *v.*, **-fied, -fying.** —*v.t.* **1.** to vary. —*v.i.* **2.** to become diversified.

di•ver′sion *n.* **1.** the act of turning aside. **2.** a distraction.

di•ver′si•ty *n.* difference or variety.

di•vert′ (di vûrt′, dī-) *v.t.* **1.** to turn aside, as from a course. **2.** to distract. **3.** to amuse.

di•vest′ (di vest′, dī-) *v.t.* **1.** to strip of clothing, ornament, etc. **2.** to deprive, as of property rights.

di•vide′ (di vīd′) *v.*, **-vided, -viding**, *n.* —*v.t.* **1.** to separate into parts, sections, etc. **2.** to cut off. **3.** to separate into equal parts by mathematical division. —*v.i.* **4.** to become divided. **5.** to diverge. **6.** to perform mathematical division. —*n.* **7.** a ridge separating drainage basins. —**di•vid′er**, *n.*

div′i•dend′ (div′i dend′) *n.* **1.** a number to be divided. **2.** a sum paid to shareholders out of company earnings. **3.** a bonus.

di•vine′ (di vīn′) *adj., n., v.*, **-vined, -vining.** —*adj.* **1.** of, from, or like God or a god. **2.** devoted to God or a god. **3.** *Informal.* extremely good. —*n.* **4.** a theologian or cleric. —*v.t.* **5.** to prophesy. **6.** to perceive by intuition. —**di•vine′ly**, *adv.*

divin′ing rod′ *n.* a forked stick for finding underground water.

di•vin′i•ty (-vin′i tē) *n., pl.* **-ties. 1.** the quality of being divine. **2.** a divine being.

di•vi′sion (di vizh′ən) *n.* **1.** the act or result of dividing. **2.** the arithmetic operation of finding how many times one number is contained in another. **3.** something that divides. **4.** a section. **5.** disagreement. **6.** a major unit of the army or navy. —**di•vis′i•ble**, *adj.*

di•vi′sive (-vī′siv) *adj.* creating dissension.

di•vi′sor (-vī′zər) *n.* a number by which another number is divided.

di•vorce′ (di vôrs′) *n., v.*, **-vorced, -vorcing.** —*n.* **1.** legal dissolution of a marriage. **2.** total separation. —*v.t.* **3.** to separate by divorce. —*v.i.* **4.** to get a divorce.

di•vor′cee′ (-sē′) *n.* a divorced woman.

di•vulge′ (di vulj′, dī-) *v.t.*, **-vulged, -vulging.** to disclose or reveal.

Dix′ie•land′ *n.* a style of jazz marked by accented four-four rhythm and improvisation.

diz′zy (diz′ē) *adj.*, **-zier, -ziest. 1.** having a sensation of whirling and a tendency to fall. **2.** confused. **3.** *Informal.* foolish; silly.

D.J. (dē′jā′) disc jockey. Also, **DJ, deejay.**

DNA deoxyribonucleic acid, the substance that carries genes along its strands.

do¹ (dōō; *unstressed* dŏŏ, də) *v.*, **did, done, doing**, *n.* —*v.t.* **1.** to perform (an act). **2.** to execute (an amount of work). **3.** to accomplish. **4.** to be the cause of (good, harm, etc.). **5.** to deal with. **6.** to exert. **7.** to render. **8.** to suffice for. —*v.i.* **9.** to act. **10.** to proceed. **11.** to be enough. —*auxiliary v.* **12.** (used to ask questions, to make negative statements, to add emphasis, and to avoid repetition). **13. do away with,** to abolish. **14.** ~ **in, a.** to kill. **b.** to exhaust. **15.** ~ **out of,** *Informal.* to cheat. —*n.* **16.** *Informal.* a social gathering.

do² (dō) *n.* the musical syllable used for the first note of a scale.

DOA dead on arrival.

doc′ile (dos′əl) *adj.* readily trained; submissive.

dock¹ (dok) *n.* **1.** a wharf. **2.** a waterway between two piers for receiving a ship while in port. **3.** a platform for loading trucks, freight cars, etc. —*v.t.* **4.** to bring (a ship) into a dock. **5.** to join (a space vehicle) with another spacecraft. —*v.i.* **6.** to come into a dock. **7.** (of two space vehicles) to join together.

dock

dock² (dok) *v.t.* **1.** to cut off the end of. **2.** to deduct from (wages).

dock³ (dok) *n.* the place in a courtroom where a prisoner is placed during trial.

dock′et (dok′it) *n.* **1.** a list of court cases. **2.** a list of business to be transacted.

doc′tor (dok′tər) *n.* **1.** a person licensed to practice medicine. **2.** a person who has a doctor's degree. —*v.t.* **3.** to treat medically. **4.** to tamper with.

doc′tor·ate (-it) *n.* a doctor's degree.

doc′tor's degree′ *n.* the highest degree awarded by universities.

doc′tri·naire′ (-trə när′) *adj.* adhering stubbornly to a doctrine.

doc′trine (-trin) *n.* **1.** a particular principle of a religion or government. **2.** a body of teachings. —**doc′tri·nal,** *adj.*

doc′u·ment *n.* (-mənt) **1.** a paper giving information. **2.** a computer data file. —*v.t.* (-ment′) **3.** to support by documents.

doc′u·men′ta·ry (-men′tə rē) *adj., n., pl.* **-ries.** —*adj.* **1.** of or derived from documents. **2.** depicting an actual event, life story, etc. —*n.* **3.** a documentary film.

dod′der (dod′ər) *v.i.* to totter.

dodge (doj) *v.,* **dodged, dodging,** *n.* —*v.t.* **1.** to avoid by a quick movement or strategy. —*v.i.* **2.** to move suddenly. —*n.* **3.** a quick, evasive movement. **4.** a trick. —**dodg′er,** *n.*

do′do (dō′dō) *n., pl.* **-dos, -does.** a large, extinct flightless bird.

doe (dō) *n.* the female of the deer, rabbit, etc.

does (duz) *v.* third pers. sing. pres. indic. of **do.**

does′n't (duz′ənt) contraction of **does not.**

doff (dof) *v.t.* to remove, as one's hat.

dog (dôg) *n., v.,* **dogged, dogging.** —*n.* **1.** a domesticated carnivore. **2.** any animal belonging to the same family, as the wolf, fox, etc. —*v.t.* **3.** to follow closely.

dog′-ear′ *n.* a folded-down corner of a book page. —**dog′-eared′,** *adj.*

dog′ged (dô′gid) *adj.* persistent.

dog′house′ *n.* **1.** a shelter for a dog. —*Idiom.* **2. in the doghouse,** in disfavor.

dog′ma (-mə) *n.* a system of principles or beliefs, as of a church.

dog·mat′ic (-mat′ik) *adj.* **1.** of dogma. **2.** arrogantly asserting opinions. —**dog′ma·tism′** *n.*

dog′wood′ *n.* a tree with white or pink blossoms.

doi′ly (doi′lē) *n., pl.* **-lies.** a small ornamental mat.

dol′drums (dōl′drəmz, dol′-) *n.pl.* **1.** a belt of calms and light winds near the equator. **2.** a state of inactivity. **3.** a dull, depressed mood.

dole (dōl) *n., v.,* **doled, doling.** —*n.* **1.** an allotment of money or food given to the needy. —*v.t.* **2.** to distribute in charity. **3.** to give out in small quantities.

dole′ful *adj.* sorrowful; gloomy.

doll (dol) *n.* **1.** a toy representing a baby or other human being. **2.** an attractive or nice person.

dol′lar (dol′ər) *n.* the basic monetary unit in the U.S. and certain other countries.

dol′lop (dol′əp) *n.* a lump or blob of some soft substance.

dol′ly (dol′ē) *n., pl.* **-lies. 1.** a low cart for moving heavy loads. **2.** a movable platform for a movie or TV camera.

dol′or·ous (dō′lər əs, dol′ər-) *adj.* full of or causing pain or sorrow.

dol′phin (dol′fin) *n.* a marine mammal having a beaklike snout.

dolt (dōlt) *n.* a stupid person. —**dolt′ish,** *adj.*

-dom a suffix indicating: **1.** domain. **2.** rank or station. **3.** general condition,

do·main′ (dō mān′) *n.* **1.** a field of action, thought, influence, etc. **2.** the area governed by a single ruler or government.

dome (dōm) *n.* **1.** a rounded ceiling or roof. **2.** anything shaped like this.

do·mes′tic (də mes′tik) *adj.* **1.** of the home. **2.** of one's own country. —*n.* **3.** a servant. —**do′mes·tic′i·ty** (dō′me stis′i tē) *n.*

do·mes′ti·cate′ (-kāt′) *v.t.,* **-cated, -cating. 1.** to train (an animal) to live with humans. **2.** to accustom to household life.

domes′tic part′ner *n.* either member of an unmarried cohabiting couple.

dom′i·cile (dom′ə sīl′, -səl, dō′mə-) *n.* a house or home.

dom′i·nant *adj.* ruling or controlling. —**dom′i·nance,** *n.*

dom′i·nate′ (dom′ə nāt′) *v.,* **-nated, -nating.** —*v.t.* **1.** to rule over. **2.** to be the major influence in. **3.** to tower above. —*v.i.* **4.** to exercise power. **5.** to occupy a commanding position. —**dom′i·na′tion,** *adj.*

dom′i·neer′ (dom′ə nēr′) *v.i.* to act in a way that forces others to behave; bully.

do·min′ion (də min′yən) *n.* **1.** authority to govern. **2.** the territory governed.

dom′i·no′ (dom′ə nō′) *n., pl.* **-noes.** **1.** a small, flat block marked with dots. **2. dominoes,** a game played with dominoes.

don (don) *v.t.,* **donned, donning.** to put on.

do′nate (dō′nāt, dō nāt′) *v.t., v.i.,* **-nat·ed, -nat·ing.** to contribute or give. —**do·na′tion,** *n.*

don′key (dong′kē, dông′-, dung′-) *n.* a long-eared domesticated animal related to the horse.

do′nor (dō′nər) *n.* one who donates.

doo′dle (dōōd′l) *v.i., v.t.,* **-dled, -dling.** to draw or scribble idly.

doom (dōōm) *n.* **1.** adverse fate. **2.** ruin or death. **3.** an unfavorable judgment. —*v.t.* **4.** to destine to an adverse fate.

dooms′day′ *n.* the day of the Last Judgment.

door (dôr) *n.* **1.** a movable barrier for opening and closing an entrance, cabinet, etc. **2.** a doorway.

door′step′ *n.* a step in front of a door.

door′way′ *n.* the entrance to a building, room, etc.

dope (dōp) *n., v.,* **doped, doping.** —*n.* **1.** *Slang.* a narcotic. **2.** *Slang.* information. **3.** *Informal.* a stupid person. —*v.t.* **4.** *Slang.* to drug.

dop′ey *adj.,* **-ier, -iest.** *Informal.* **1.** stupid. **2.** sluggish or confused, as from drug use. Also, **dop′y.**

dor′mant (dôr′mənt) *adj.* **1.** temporarily inactive. **2.** undeveloped. —**dor′man·cy,** *n.*

dor′mer (dôr′mər) *n.* a vertical window in a projection built from a sloping roof.

dor′mi·to′ry (dôr′mi tôr′ē) *n., pl.* **-ries.** **1.** a building, as at a college, containing rooms for residents. **2.** communal sleeping quarters.

dor′mouse′ (dôr′mous′) *n., pl.* **-mice.** a small bushy-tailed rodent.

dor′sal (dôr′səl) *adj.* of or on the back.

do′ry (dôr′ē) *n., pl.* **-ries.** a flat-bottomed rowboat.

DOS (dôs) *n.* a disk operating system for microcomputers.

dose (dōs) *n., v.,* **dosed, dosing.** —*n.* **1.** the amount of medicine taken at one time. —*v.t.* **2.** to give a dose of medicine to.

dos′si·er′ (dos′ē ā′) *n.* a file of documents containing detailed information.

dot (dot) *n., v.,* **dotted, dotting.** —*n.* **1.** a small, roundish mark. **2.** the shorter signal in Morse code.

3. a period, esp. as used in an Internet address. —*v.t.* **4.** to mark with dots.

do′tage (dō′tij) *n.* a decline of mental faculties in old age.

dote (dōt) *v.,* **doted, doting. dote on,** to be excessively fond of.

dou′ble (dub′əl) *adj., n., v.,* **-bled, -bling.** —*adj.* **1.** twice as large, as many, etc. **2.** composed of two like parts. **3.** suitable for two. **4.** folded in two. —*n.* **5.** a double quantity. **6.** a duplicate. **7. doubles,** a game between two pairs of players. —*v.t.* **8.** to make double. **9.** to bend or fold with one part over the other. **10.** to repeat. —*v.i.* **11.** to become double. **12.** to turn back. **13.** to serve in two capacities.

dou′ble bass′ (bās) *n.* the lowest-pitched instrument of the violin family.

doub′le-cross′ *v.t.* to cheat.

dou′ble en·ten′dre (än tän′drə, -tänd′) *n., pl.* **dou′ble en·ten′dres** (än tän′drəz, -tändz′). a word or expression with two meanings, one of which is usually indecent.

dou′ble·head′er *n.* two games played on the same day in immediate succession.

dou′ble play′ *n.* a baseball play in which two players are put out.

dou′ble stand′ard *n.* any set of principles applied differently to one group than to another.

dou′ble take′ *n.* a delayed response, as to something not immediately recognized.

doub′le-talk′ *n.* speech that means something different from its apparent meaning.

doubt (dout) *v.t.* **1.** to be uncertain and undecided about. **2.** to distrust. —*v.i.* **3.** to be uncertain. —*n.* **4.** a feeling of uncertainty and indecision. **5.** distrust or suspicion.

doubt′ful *adj.* **1.** feeling doubt. **2.** causing doubt or suspicion.

douche (dōōsh) *n., v.,* **douched, douching.** —*n.* **1.** a jet of liquid applied to a body part or cavity. —*v.t., v.i.* **2.** to apply a douche (to).

dough (dō) *n.* a mixture of flour, liquid, etc., for baking into bread, pastry, etc.

dough′nut (dō′nət, -nut′) *n.* a ring-like cake of fried, sweet dough.

dour (dōōr, dou°r, dou′ər) *adj.* sullen; gloomy.

douse (dous) *v.t.,* **doused, dousing.** **1.** to throw water on. **2.** to extinguish. **3.** to plunge into water.

dove¹ (duv) *n.* a bird of the pigeon family.

dove² (dōv) *v.* a pt. of **dive.**

dovecote

dove′cote′ (-kōt′) *n.* a structure for housing tame pigeons.

dove′tail′ *n.* **1.** a wedge-shaped joint that interlocks two pieces of wood. —*v.t., v.i.* **2.** to join by means of a dovetail. **3.** to fit together harmoniously.

dow′a·ger (dou′ə jər) *n.* **1.** a titled or wealthy widow. **2.** a dignified elderly woman.

dow′dy (dou′dē) *adj.*, **-dier, -diest.** not stylish.

dow′el (dou′əl) *n.* a wooden or metal pin fitting into a hole to hold two pieces of wood or stone together.

dow′er (dou′ər) *n.* a widow's share of her husband's property.

down¹ (doun) *adv.* **1.** to, at, or in a lower place or state. **2.** to a lower value or rate. **3.** to a lesser pitch or volume. **4.** from an earlier to a later time. **5.** from a greater to a lesser strength, amount, etc. —*prep.* **6.** in a descending direction on or along. —*adj.* **7.** directed downward. **8.** being at a low position. **9.** depressed. —*v.t.* **10.** to knock, throw, or bring down. —*Idiom.* **11. down cold** or **pat,** learned perfectly. **12. down on,** hostile to.

down² (doun) *n.* the soft feathers of birds.

down′cast′ *adj.* dejected.

down′er *n. Informal.* **1.** a depressing experience. **2.** a sedative drug.

down′fall′ *n.* **1.** ruin. **2.** something causing ruin.

down′grade′ *v.*, **-graded, -grading,** *n.* —*v.t.* **1.** to reduce in rank, importance, etc. —*n.* **2.** a downward slope.

down′heart′ed *adj.* dejected.

down′hill′ (*adv.* -hil′; *adj.* -hil′) *adv.* **1.** down a slope. **2.** into a worse condition. —*adj.* **3.** going downward. **4.** free of obstacles.

down′play′ *v.t.* to minimize.

down′pour′ *n.* a heavy rain.

down′right′ *adj.* **1.** thorough. —*adv.* **2.** completely.

down′scale′ *adj.* of or for people at the lower end of the economic scale.

down′size′ *v.t.*, **-sized, -sizing.** to reduce in size or number.

down′stage′ *adv., adj.* at or toward the front of the stage.

down′stairs′ (*adv.* -stârz′; *adj.* -stârz′) *adv., adj.* to or on a lower floor.

Down′ syn′drome *n.* a genetic disorder characterized by mental retardation, a wide, flattened skull, and slanting eyes. Also, **Down's′ syn′drome.**

down′-to-earth′ *adj.* practical.

down′trod′den *adj.* oppressed.

down′turn′ *n.* a downward trend.

down′ward, *adv.* **1.** Also, **down′wards.** to a lower level or condition. —*adj.* **2.** moving down.

down′y *adj.*, **-ier, -iest.** like soft feathers.

dow′ry (dou′rē) *n., pl.* **-ries.** the property that a bride brings to her husband at marriage.

dowse (dous) *v.i.*, **dowsed, dowsing.** to search for underground water using a divining rod.

doz. dozen.

doze (dōz) *v.*, **dozed, dozing,** *n.* —*v.i.* **1.** to sleep lightly. —*n.* **2.** a light sleep.

doz′en (duz′ən) *n., pl.* **dozen, dozens.** a group of 12.

Dr. **1.** Doctor. **2.** Drive.

drab (drab) *adj.*, **-ber, -best.** dull; uninteresting.

draft (draft) *n.* **1.** a drawing or sketch. **2.** a rough preliminary form of any writing. **3.** a current of air. **4.** selection for military service, an athletic team, etc. **5.** a written order for payment. **6.** the act of pulling loads or the load pulled. **7.** beer drawn from a cask. **8.** a drink or dose. —*v.t.* **9.** to sketch. **10.** to compose. **11.** to select by draft.

draft·ee′ *n.* a person who has been drafted, as for military service.

drafts′man *n.* a person employed in making mechanical drawings.

draft′y *adj.*, **-ier, -iest.** letting in currents of air.

drag (drag) *v.*, **dragged, dragging,** *n.* —*v.t.* **1.** to pull slowly and with effort; haul. **2.** to search (the bottom of a body of water). —*v.i.* **3.** to be drawn along. **4.** to trail on the ground. **5.** to move slowly and with effort. —*n.* **6.** any device for searching the bottom of a body of water. **7.** a hindrance. **8.** *Slang.* a bore. **9.** a puff on a cigarette, pipe, etc. **10.** *Slang.* clothing characteristically worn by the opposite sex.

drag′net′ *n.* **1.** a fishing net drawn along the bottom of a stream. **2.** a system for catching a criminal.

drag′on (drag′ən) *n.* a mythical reptile able to breath out fire.

drag′on·fly′ *n., pl.* **-flies.** an insect with a long, narrow body and four gauzy wings.

dra·goon′ (drə gōōn′) *n.* **1.** a heavily armed mounted soldier. —*v.t.* **2.** to force; coerce.

drag′ race′ *n.* a race with cars accelerating from a standstill.

drift

drain (drān) *v.t.* **1.** to draw off (a liquid) gradually. **2.** to empty by drawing off liquid. **3.** to exhaust or use up gradually. —*v.i.* **4.** to flow off or empty gradually. —*n.* **5.** a channel or pipe for draining. **6.** a continuous outflow. —**drain′age,** *n.*

drake (drāk) *n.* a male duck.

dram (dram) *n.* an apothecaries' weight, equal to $\frac{1}{8}$ ounce.

dra′ma (drä′mə, dram′ə) *n.* **1.** a play for acting on the stage. **2.** a vivid series of events. **3.** dramatic quality.

dra·mat′ic (drə mat′ik) *adj.* **1.** of plays or the theater. **2.** highly vivid or compelling.

dra·mat′ics *n.* **1.** (*used with a sing. v.*) the performance of plays. **2.** (*used with a pl. v.*) exaggerated conduct or emotion.

dram′a·tist (dram′ə tist, drä′mə-) *n.* a writer of plays.

dram′a·tize′ *v.t.,* **-tized, -tizing. 1.** to put into a form suitable for acting. **2.** to express vividly.

drank (drangk) *v.* pt. and a pp. of **drink.**

drape (drāp) *v.,* **draped, draping,** *n.* —*v.t.* **1.** to cover or hang loosely with fabric. **2.** to arrange in folds. —*n.* **3.** a long, heavy curtain. —**dra′per·y,** *n.*

dras′tic (dras′tik) *adj.* having a violent or harsh effect.

draught (draft) *n. Brit.* a draft.

draw (drô) *v.,* **drew** (drōō), **drawn, drawing,** *n.* —*v.t.* **1.** to cause to move in a particular direction by pulling. **2.** to pull down, over, or out. **3.** to attract. **4.** to sketch. **5.** to take in, as a breath. **6.** to deduce. **7.** to stretch. **8.** to choose or have assigned to one at random. —*v.i.* **9.** to exert a pulling or attracting force. **10.** to move or pass. **11.** to take out a weapon. **12. draw on,** to make use of as a source. **13.** ~ **out, a.** to pull out. **b.** to prolong. **c.** to persuade to speak. —*n.* **14.** the act or result of drawing. **15.** something that attracts. **16.** something drawn. **17.** a contest that ends in a tie.

draw′back′ *n.* a disadvantage.

draw′bridge′ *n.* a bridge that can be raised.

draw′er (drôr *for 1, 2;* drô′ər *for 3*) *n.* **1.** a sliding, lidless box, as in a desk or bureau. **2. drawers,** underpants. **3.** a person who draws.

draw′ing *n.* **1.** a picture drawn with pencil or crayon. **2.** a lottery.

drawl (drôl) *v.t., v.i.* **1.** to speak slowly. —*n.* **2.** a drawled utterance.

drawn (drôn) *adj.* tense; haggard.

dray (drā) *n.* a low, strong cart without fixed sides.

dread (dred) *v.t.* **1.** to fear greatly. —*n.* **2.** great fear. —*adj.* **3.** feared.

dread′ful *adj.* **1.** causing dread. **2.** extremely bad.

dread′ful·ly *adv.* very.

dread′locks′ *n.* a hairstyle of many long, ropelike pieces.

dream (drēm) *n.* **1.** a series of images or thoughts passing through the mind during sleep. **2.** a daydream. **3.** a goal. **4.** something of unreal beauty. —*v.i.* **5.** to have a dream. —*v.t.* **6.** to see imagine in a dream. **7.** to imagine as possible.

dream′ team′ *n.* a group of highly skilled experts.

drear′y *adj.,* **-ier, -iest. 1.** gloomy; sad. **2.** boring. —**drear′i·ly,** *adv.*

dredge¹ (drej) *n., v.,* **dredged, dredging.** —*n.* **1.** a machine for scooping up mud. —*v.t.* **2.** to remove with a dredge.

dredge² (drej) *v.t.,* **dredged, dredging.** to coat (food) with flour.

dregs (dregz) *n.pl.* **1.** the matter that settles to the bottom of a liquid. **2.** the least valuable part of anything.

drench (drench) *v.t.* to soak.

dress (dres) *n.* **1.** a woman's garment consisting of bodice and skirt in one piece. **2.** clothing. —*v.t.* **3.** to clothe. **4.** to decorate. **5.** to prepare for cooking or for use. **6.** to treat (wounds). —*v.i.* **7.** to put on one's clothes. **8. dress down, a.** to scold. **b.** to dress informally. **9.** ~ **up, a.** to put on one's best clothing. **b.** to dress in costume.

dress′ cir′cle *n.* the first gallery of seats in a theater.

dress′er¹ *n.* a chest of drawers.

dress′er² *n.* a person employed to dress others.

dress′ing *n.* **1.** a sauce, as for a salad. **2.** a stuffing, as for a fowl. **3.** material to dress a wound.

dress′ rehears′al *n.* a final rehearsal with costumes.

dress′y *adj.,* **-ier, -iest.** fancy or formal.

drew (drōō) *v.* pt. of **draw.**

drib′ble (drib′əl) *v.,* **-bled, -bling,** *n.* —*v.i., v.t.* **1.** to fall or let fall in drops. **2.** to advance (a ball or puck) by bouncing it or pushing it. —*n.* **3.** a trickle or drop.

dri′er (drī′ər) *n.* a dryer.

drift (drift) *n.* **1.** an act or instance of being carried along by currents of water or air. **2.** a deviation from a set course. **3.** a tendency. **4.** something piled up by wind. —*v.i.* **5.** to be carried along by currents. **6.** to wander aimlessly. **7.** to be

driven into heaps, as snow. —*v.t.*
8. to cause to drift.
drift′er *n.* a person who moves frequently from one place or job to another.
drill¹ (dril) *n.* **1.** a shaftlike tool for making holes. **2.** any strict, methodical exercise. —*v.t., v.i.* **3.** to pierce with a drill. **4.** to perform or make perform training drills.
drill² (dril) *n.* **1.** a furrow for seeds. **2.** a machine for sowing seeds.
drink (dringk) *v.,* **drank** (drangk), **drunk** (drungk), **drinking,** *n.* —*v.t.* **1.** to swallow (a liquid). —*v.i.* **2.** to swallow a liquid. **3.** to consume alcoholic drinks, esp. to excess. —*n.* **4.** any liquid for drinking. **5.** alcoholic liquors.
drip (drip) *v.,* **dripped, dripping,** *n.* —*v.i., v.t.* **1.** to fall or let fall in drops. —*n.* **2.** the act or sound of dripping. **3.** liquid that drips.
drive (drīv) *v.,* **drove** (drōv), **driven, driving,** *n.* —*v.t.* **1.** to send or expel by force. **2.** to force in or down. **3.** to convey in a vehicle. **4.** to cause and guide the movement of. **5.** to urge. —*v.i.* **6.** to cause and guide the movement of a vehicle or animal. **7.** to travel in a vehicle. **8.** to strive toward a goal. **9. drive at,** to intend to convey. —*n.* **10.** a trip in a vehicle. **11.** an inner urge. **12.** a strong effort toward a goal. **13.** energy. **14.** a road for vehicles. **15.** a military offensive.
drive′-by′ *adj., n., pl.* **drive-bys.** —*adj.* **1.** occurring while driving past a person. **2.** casual; offhand. —*n.* **3.** a drive-by shooting.
drive′-in′ *n.* a facility or business that may be used without getting out of one's car.
driv′el (driv′əl) *n.* foolish talk.
drive′way′ *n.* a road on private property.
driz′zle (driz′əl) *v.,* **-zled, -zling,** *n.* —*v.i.* **1.** to rain in fine drops. —*n.* **2.** a very light rain.
droll (drōl) *adj.* amusing in an odd way.
drom′e·dar′y (drom′i der′ē) *n., pl.* **-daries.** a single-humped camel.
drone¹ (drōn) *n.* **1.** the male of the honeybee. **2.** a lazy person.
drone² (drōn) *v.,* **droned, droning,** *n.* —*v.i.* **1.** to make a deep humming sound. **2.** to speak in a dull, monotonous tone. —*n.* **3.** a deep humming sound.
drool (drōōl) *v.i.* **1.** to water at the mouth; salivate. —*n.* **2.** saliva dripping from the mouth.
droop (drōōp) *v.i.* **1.** to sink, bend, or hang down. **2.** to lose spirit or courage. —*n.* **3.** a drooping.

drop (drop) *n., v.,* **dropped, dropping.** —*n.* **1.** a small, rounded mass of liquid. **2.** a small quantity. **3. drops,** liquid medicine given in drops. **4.** an act of falling. **5.** the distance of a fall. **6.** a steep descent. **7.** a decline in amount, value, etc. —*v.i.* **8.** to fall in drops. **9.** to fall lower or backward. **10.** to sink. —*v.t.* **11.** to let fall in drops. **12.** to let or cause to fall. **13.** to reduce in value, quality, etc. **14.** to leave out; omit. **15.** to remove or dismiss.
drop′out′ *n.* a person who withdraws, esp. a student who leaves school before graduation.
drop′per *n.* a small tube with a squeezable bulb for drawing in a liquid and expelling it in drops.
dross (drôs) *n.* waste matter.
drought (drout) *n.* a long period of dry weather.
drove (drōv) *v.* **1.** pt. of **drive.** —*n.* **2.** a group of driven cattle. **3.** Usu., **droves.** a large crowd.
drown (droun) *v.i.* **1.** to die by suffocation in liquid. —*v.t.* **2.** to kill by suffocation in liquid. **3.** to flood. **4. drown out,** to overpower, as by a louder sound.
drow′sy (drou′zē) *adj.,* **-sier, -siest.** sleepy.
drub (drub) *v.t.,* **drubbed, drubbing. 1.** to beat. **2.** to defeat.
drudge (druj) *n., v.,* **drudged, drudging.** —*n.* **1.** a person who does dull or menial work. —*v.i.* **2.** to do such work. —**drudg′er·y,** *n.*
drug (drug) *n., v.,* **drugged, drugging.** —*n.* **1.** a chemical substance used in medicine. **2.** a narcotic. —*v.t.* **3.** to add or give a drug to.
drug′gist *n.* a person licensed to prepare and sell drugs and medicines; pharmacist.
drug′store′ *n.* a store that sells medicines, toiletries, etc.
drum (drum) *n., v.,* **drummed, drumming.** —*n.* **1.** a percussion instrument consisting of a round frame covered with a tightly stretched membrane that is struck to produce a sound. **2.** any cylindrical object. **3.** the eardrum. —*v.i.* **4.** to beat a drum. **5.** to tap one's fingers rhythmically. —*v.t.* **6.** to perform by beating a drum. **7. drum up,** to get by vigorous effort.
drum′ ma′jor *n.* the leader of a marching band.
drum′ majorette′ *n.* a majorette.
drum′stick′ *n.* **1.** a stick for beating a drum. **2.** the leg of a cooked fowl.
drunk (drungk) *adj.* **1.** having one's mental and physical powers im-

paired by alcoholic drink. —*n.* **2.** a
drunk person. —*v.* **3.** pp. of **drink.**

drunk′ard (drung′kərd) *n.* a person
who is habitually drunk.

drunk′en *adj.* **1.** intoxicated. **2.**
caused or marked by intoxication.

dry (drī) *adj.,* **drier, driest,** *v.,* **dried,
drying.** —*adj.* **1.** not wet. **2.** without rain. **3.** empty of or not yielding liquid. **4.** thirsty. **5.** dull; uninteresting. **6.** not expressing
emotion. **7.** not allowing the sale
of alcoholic beverages. **8.** (of wine)
not sweet. —*v.t., v.i.* **9.** to make or
become dry. —**dry′ly, dri′ly** *adv.*

dry′-clean′ *v.t.* to clean (clothing)
with solvents. —**dry′-clean′er,** *n.*

dry′er *n.* a machine for drying.

dry′ ice′ *n.* solid carbon dioxide,
used esp. as a refrigerant.

dry′ run′ *n.* a rehearsal or trial.

DST daylight-saving time.

du′al (dōō′əl, dyōō′-) *adj.* twofold.

dub¹ (dub) *v.t.,* **dubbed, dubbing.**
to name formally.

dub² (dub) *v.t.,* **dubbed, dubbing.**
to furnish (a film or tape) with a
new sound track.

du′bi·ous (dōō′bē əs) *adj.* doubtful.

du′cal (dōō′kəl, dyōō′-) *adj.* of
dukes.

duch′ess (duch′is) *n.* **1.** a duke's
wife. **2.** a woman equal in rank to
a duke.

duch′y (duch′ē) *n., pl.* **duchies.** the
territory of a duke or duchess.

duck¹ (duk) *n.* a web-footed swimming bird with a broad, flat bill.

duck² (duk) *v.i., v.t.* **1.** to lower or
bend (the head or body) suddenly.
2. to evade. **3.** to plunge under water.

duck³ (duk) *n.* a heavy cotton fabric.

duck′ling *n.* a young duck.

duct (dukt) *n.* any tube, canal,
pipe, etc., by which liquid or air is
conveyed. —**duct′less,** *adj.*

duc′tile (duk′tl, -til) *adj.* **1.** (of
metal) readily drawn out into wire.
2. capable of being shaped.

duct′ tape′ (duk, dukt) *n.* a
strongly adhesive cloth tape.

dud (dud) *n.* a failure.

dude (dōōd, dyōōd) *n.* **1.** a man excessively concerned with his
clothes. **2.** *Slang.* a fellow; guy.

dudg′eon (duj′ən) *n.* anger.

due (dōō, dyōō) *adj.* **1.** owing or
owed. **2.** proper. **3.** adequate. **4.**
expected. —*n.* **5.** something owed
or naturally belonging to someone.
6. dues, a regular fee for membership. —*adv.* **7.** directly or exactly.

du′el (dōō′əl, dyōō′-) *n., v.,* **-eled,
-eling.** —*n.* **1.** a planned combat
between two persons. —*v.t., v.i.* **2.**
to fight in a duel. —**du′el·ist,** *n.*

du·et′ (dōō et′, dyōō-) *n.* a musical
composition for two performers.

duf′fel bag′ (duf′əl) *n.* a large, cylindrical bag.

dug (dug) *v.* a pt. and pp. of **dig.**

dug′out′ *n.* **1.** a boat made by hol-
lowing out a log. **2.** a roofed structure where baseball players sit
when not on the field. **3.** a rough
shelter dug in the ground.

duke (dōōk, dyōōk) *n.* a nobleman
ranking immediately below a
prince. —**duke′dom,** *n.*

dul′ci·mer (dul′sə mər) *n.* a musical instrument with metal strings
that are struck with light hammers.

dull (dul) *adj.* **1.** not sharp. **2.** not
bright. **3.** boring; tedious. **4.** stupid. **5.** not lively. —*v.t., v.i.* **6.** to
make or become dull.

du′ly (dōō′lē, dyōō′-) *adv.* **1.** properly. **2.** punctually.

dumb (dum) *adj.* **1.** silly or stupid.
2. lacking the power of speech. **3.**
silent.

dumb′bell′ *n.* **1.** a bar with
weighted ends, used for exercising.
2. *Slang.* a stupid person.

dumb·found′ (dum found′, dum′-
found′) *v.t.* to astonish.

dumb′wait′er *n.* a small elevator
for moving food, garbage, etc.

dum′my *n., pl.* **-mies,** *adj.* —*n.* **1.**
an imitation or copy. **2.** a model
of the human figure, used for displaying clothes. **3.** *Informal.* a stupid person. —*adj.* **4.** counterfeit.

dump (dump) *v.t.* **1.** to drop in a
heap. **2.** to unload. **3.** to discard or
dismiss. —*n.* **4.** a place where garbage is deposited. **5.** *Informal.* a dilapidated, dirty place.

dump′ling (-ling) *n.* **1.** a mass of
boiled dough. **2.** a wrapping of
dough enclosing a filling.

dump′y *adj.,* **-ier, -iest.** short and
stout.

dun¹ (dun) *v.,* **dunned, dunning,** *n.*
—*v.t.* **1.** to make repeated demands
upon for the payment of a debt.
—*n.* **2.** a demand for payment.

dun² (dun) *adj.* a dull grayish
brown.

dunce (duns) *n.* a stupid person.

dune (dōōn, dyōōn) *n.* a sand hill
formed by the wind.

dung (dung) *n.* manure.

dun′ga·rees′ (dung′gə rēz′) *n.pl.*
overalls or trousers of blue denim.

dun′geon (dun′jən) *n.* a strong underground prison.

dunk (dungk) *v.t.* **1.** to dip in a
beverage before eating. **2.** to submerge briefly in liquid.

du′o (dōō′ō, dyōō′ō) *n.* **1.** a duet.
2. a couple or pair.

du′o·de′num (dōō′ə dē′nəm,

dyōō-; dōō od/n əm, dyōō-) n. the upper part of the small intestine.

dupe (dōōp, dyōōp) n., v., **duped, duping.** —n. **1.** a person who is easily fooled. —v.t. **2.** to deceive.

du/plex (dōō/pleks, dyōō/-) n. **1.** an apartment with two floors. **2.** a house for two families.

du/pli.cate adj., n., v., **-cated, -cat-ing.** —adj. (dōō/pli kit) **1.** exactly like something else. **2.** double. —n. (-kit) **3.** an exact copy. —v.t. (-kāt/) **4.** to make an exact copy of. **5.** to repeat.

du.plic/i.ty (dōō plis/i tē, dyōō-) n., pl. **-ties.** deceitfulness.

du/ra.ble (dōōr/ə bəl, dyōōr/-) adj. lasting. —**du/ra.bil/i.ty,** n.

du.ra/tion (dōō rā/shən, dyōō-) n. the length of time something con-tinues.

du.ress/ (dōō res/, dyōō-, dōōr/is, dyōōr/-) n. the use of force.

dur/ing (dōōr/ing, dyōōr/-) prep. **1.** throughout **2.** at some point in the course of.

du/rum (dōōr/əm, dyōōr/-) n. a wheat yielding flour used in pasta.

dusk (dusk) n. twilight.

dust (dust) n. **1.** fine particles of earth or other matter. —v.t. **2.** to wipe the dust from. **3.** to sprinkle with powder or dust. —v.i. **4.** to wipe dust from furniture, wood-work, etc. —**dust/y,** adj.

Dutch/ un/cle n. a mentor who criticizes very frankly.

du/te.ous (dōō/tē əs, dyōō/-) adj. dutiful; obedient.

du/ti.ful adj. performing the duties expected of one.

du/ty (dōō/tē, dyōō/-) n., pl. **-ties. 1.** moral or legal obligation. **2.** action required by one's position or occu-pation. **3.** a tax on imports and ex-ports.

DVD an optical disc that can store a very large amount of digital data, as text, music, or images.

dwarf (dwôrf) n. **1.** a person, ani-mal, or plant of abnormally small size. —adj. **2.** of small size. —v.t. **3.** to cause to seem small by compari-son. **4.** to stunt.

dweeb (dwēb) n. Slang. a nerd; wimp.

dwell (dwel) v.i., **dwelt** or **dwelled, dwelling. 1.** to live or stay as a res-ident. **2. dwell on,** to think, speak, or write about at length. —**dwell/-ing,** n.

dwin/dle (dwin/dl) v.i., v.t., **-dled, -dling.** to make or become less.

dye (dī) n., v., **dyed, dyeing.** —n. **1.** a substance used to color cloth, hair, etc. —v.t. **2.** to color with a dye.

dyed/-in-the-wool/ adj. complete.

dyke (dīk) n. **1.** a dike. **2.** Slang: Usu. Disparaging and Offensive. (a term used to refer to a female ho-mosexual.)

dy.nam/ic (dī nam/ik) adj. **1.** force-ful; energetic. **2.** of force or energy.

dy/na.mite/ (dī/nə mīt/) n., v., **-mited, -miting.** —n. **1.** a powerful explosive made of nitroglycerin. —v.t. **2.** to blow up with dynamite.

dy/na.mo/ (-mō/) n., pl. **-mos. 1.** a machine for generating electricity. **2.** an energetic, forceful person.

dy/nas.ty (dī/nə stē) n., pl. **-ties.** a line of rulers from the same family.

dys- a prefix meaning ill or bad.

dys/en.ter/y (dis/ən ter/ē) n. an in-fectious disease of the intestines.

dys.func/tion n. impairment of function or malfunctioning.

dys.lex/i.a (dis lek/sē ə) n. a learn-ing disorder causing abnormal dif-ficulty in reading and spelling. —**dys.lex/ic,** adj., n.

dys.pep/sia (dis pep/shə, -sē ə) n. indigestion.

dz. dozen.

E

E, e (ē) n. the fifth letter of the English alphabet.

E 1. east, eastern. **2.** English.

ea. each.

each (ēch) adj., pron. **1.** every one of two or more. —adv. **2.** to, from, or for each.

ea/ger (ē/gər) adj. full of desire or enthusiasm. —**ea/ger.ness,** n.

ea/gle (ē/gəl) n. a large bird of prey.

ea/gle-eyed/ adj. having unusually sharp eyesight.

ear¹ (ēr) n. **1.** the organ of hearing. **2.** the external part of this. **3.** the

sense of hearing. **4.** attention. **5.** an ear-shaped part. —**Idiom. 6. play it by ear,** to improvise.

ear² (ēr) n. the seed-bearing part of a cereal plant, as corn.

ear/drum/ n. a thin membrane in the ear that vibrates when struck by sound waves.

earl (ûrl) n. a nobleman ranking below a marquis. —**earl/dom,** n.

ear/lobe/ or **ear/ lobe/** n. the soft lower part of the external ear.

ear/ly (ûr/lē) adv., **-lier, -liest,** adj. **1.** in or during the first part of a period of time or series of events. **2.** before the expected time.

ear′mark′ (ēr′märk′) *v.t.* to set aside for a particular purpose.

ear′muffs′ *n.pl.* warm connected coverings for the ears.

earn (ûrn) *v.t.* **1.** to gain in return for labor or by one's merit. **2.** to produce as return or profit.

ear′nest (ûr′nist) *adj.* **1.** serious. **2.** showing sincerity of feeling.

earn′ings *n.pl.* wages or profits.

ear′phone′ (ēr′fōn′) *n.* a sound receiver that fits on the ear.

ear′ring′ (ēr′ring′, ēr′ing) *n.* an ornament worn on the earlobe.

ear′shot′ *n.* range of hearing.

ear′split′ting *adj.* extremely loud or shrill.

earth (ûrth) *n.* **1.** (*often cap.*) the planet third in order from the sun. **2.** the surface of the earth; ground. **3.** soil and dirt.

earth′en *adj.* made of clay or earth.

earth′en.ware *n.* pottery made of baked clay.

earth′ly *adj.*, **-lier, -liest. 1.** of the earth, as opposed to heaven. **2.** conceivable.

earth′quake′ *n.* a series of vibrations of the earth's surface.

earth′work′ *n.* a fortification formed of earth.

earth′worm′ *n.* a worm that burrows in the soil.

earth′y *adj.*, **-ier, -iest. 1.** of earth or soil. **2.** coarse; unrefined.

ease (ēz) *n., v.*, **eased, easing.** —*n.* **1.** freedom from pain, trouble, anxiety, effort, etc. —*v.t.* **2.** to free from care or pain. **3.** to make less difficult. —*v.i.* **4.** to become less difficult or painful.

ea′sel (ē′zəl) *n.* a support stand, as for a painting.

east (ēst) *n.* **1.** a cardinal point of the compass, the direction in which the sun rises. **2. the East,** a region in this direction. —*adj., adv.* **3.** toward, in, or from the east. —**east′ern,** *adj.* —**east′ern.er,** *n.* —**east′ward′,** *adv., adj.*

East′er (ē′stər) *n.* a festival celebrating Christ's resurrection.

east′er.ly *adj., adv.* toward or blowing from the east.

eas′y (ē′zē) *adj.*, **easier, easiest,** *adv.* **1.** not difficult. **2.** free from pain, worry, or care. **3.** not forced or hurried. —*adv.* **4.** in an easy manner. —**eas′i.ly,** *adv.*

eas′y-go.ing *adj.* casual; relaxed.

eat (ēt) *v.*, **ate** (āt), **eating, eaten.** —*v.t.* **1.** to take into the mouth and swallow. **2.** to wear away or dissolve. —*v.i.* **3.** to have a meal.

eat′ing disor′der *n.* a disorder characterized by severe disturbances in eating habits.

eaves (ēvz) *n.pl.* the overhanging lower edge of a roof.

eaves′drop′ *v.i.*, **-dropped, -dropping.** to listen secretly.

ebb (eb) *n.* **1.** the flowing back of the tide as the water returns to the sea. **2.** a decline. —*v.i.* **3.** to flow back. **4.** to decline.

eb′on.y (eb′ə nē) *n., pl.* **-ies. 1.** a hard black wood from trees of Africa and Asia. **2.** a deep black.

eBook (ē′book′) *n.* a portable electronic device used to download and read books or magazines that are in digital form. Also, **e-book.**

e.bul′lient (i bul′yənt, i bool′-) *adj.* full of enthusiasm and high spirits.

ec.cen′tric (ik sen′trik) *adj.* **1.** unconventional. **2.** not having the same center. **3.** not placed in the center. **4.** not circular, as an orbit. —*n.* **5.** an unconventional person. —**ec′cen.tric′i.ty** (-tris′i tē) *n.*

ec.cle′si.as′tic (i klē′zē as′tik) *n.* **1.** a member of the clergy. —*adj.* **2.** Also, **ec.cle′si.as′ti.cal.** of a church or the clergy.

ech′e.lon (esh′ə lon′) *n.* a level of command or rank.

ech′o (ek′ō) *n., pl.* **echoes,** *v.,* **echoed, echoing.** —*n.* **1.** a repetition of sound caused by the reflection of sound waves. **2.** an imitation. —*v.i.* **3.** to be repeated by an echo. —*v.t.* **4.** to repeat in imitation.

é.clair′ (ā klâr′) *n.* a cream- or custard-filled pastry.

é.clat′ (ā klä′) *n.* **1.** brilliance of success or reputation. **2.** acclaim.

ec.lec′tic (i klek′tik) *adj.* chosen from various sources.

e.clipse′ (i klips′) *n., v.*, **eclipsed, eclipsing.** —*n.* **1.** the blocking of the light of one heavenly body by another. **2.** loss of splendor or status. —*v.t.* **3.** to obscure.

e.clip′tic (i klip′tik) *n.* the apparent annual path of the sun.

e′co.cide′ (ek′ə sīd′, ē′kə-) *n.* the destruction of large areas of the natural environment.

e.col′o.gy (i kol′ə jē) *n.* the study of the relationship between organisms and the environment. —**e.col′o.gist,** *n.*

e′co.nom′i.cal (ek′ə nom′i kəl, ē′kə-) *adj.* avoiding waste; thrifty.

ec′o.nom′ics *n.* **1.** the science of the production, distribution, and use of goods and services. **2.** (*used with a pl. v.*) financial considerations. —**ec′o.nom′ic,** *adj.* —**e.con′o.mist** (i kon′ə mist) *n.*

e·con′o·mize (i kon′ə mīz′) *v.i.*, **-mized, -mizing.** to be thrifty.

e·con′o·my *n., pl.* **-mies. 1.** thrifty management. **2.** the management of the resources of an area. **3.** the prosperity or earnings of a place. **4.** the efficient use of something.

ec′o·sys′tem (ek′ō sis′təm, ē′kō-) *n.* a system formed by the interaction of a group of organisms with its environment.

ec′ru (ek′rōō) *n.* a light brown; beige. Also, **éc·ru** (ā′krōō).

ec′sta·sy (ek′stə sē) *n., pl.* **-sies. 1.** intense delight. **2.** an overpowering emotion. **—ec·stat′ic** (ek stat′ik) *adj.*

ec′u·men′i·cal (ek′yōō men′i kəl) *adj.* **1.** universal. **2.** pertaining to or fostering worldwide Christian unity.

ec′ze·ma (ek′sə mə, eg′zə-, ig zē′-) *n.* a skin disease causing itching and scaling.

ed′dy (ed′ē) *n., pl.* **-dies,** *v.,* **-died, -dying. —n. 1.** a current running counter to the main current. *—v.t., v.i.* **2.** to whirl in eddies.

e′del·weiss′ (ād′l vīs′, -wīs′) *n.* a small, flowering Alpine plant.

e·de′ma (i dē′mə) *n.* abnormal retention of fluid in body tissue.

E′den (ēd′n) *n.* the garden where Adam and Eve first lived; paradise.

edge (ej) *n., v.,* **edged, edging. —n. 1.** the line at which something ends. **2.** a verge. **3.** the thin, sharp side of a blade. **4.** sharpness. *—v.t.* **5.** to border. *—v.i.* **6.** to move gradually. **—edge′wise′,** *adv.*

edg′y *adj.,* **-ier, -iest.** nervous or tense.

ed′i·ble (ed′ə bəl) *adj.* fit to be eaten. **—ed′i·bil′i·ty,** *n.*

e′dict (ē′dikt) *n.* an official decree.

ed′i·fice (ed′ə fis) *n.* a large building.

ed′i·fy′ *v.t.,* **-fied, -fying.** to instruct and improve. **—ed′i·fi·ca′-tion,** *n.*

ed′it (ed′it) *v.t.* **1.** to prepare (a manuscript) for publication. **2.** to revise or correct. **3.** to prepare (film or tape) by arranging sections. **—ed′i·tor,** *n.*

e·di′tion (i dish′ən) *n.* **1.** the form in which a literary work is published. **2.** the number of copies printed at one time. **3.** a version of something.

ed′i·to′ri·al (ed′i tôr′ē əl) *n.* **1.** an article in a periodical presenting the opinion of the publishers or editors. *—adj.* **2.** of an editor or editing. **3.** of or resembling an editorial. **—ed′i·to′ri·al·ize′,** *v.i.*

ed′u·cate′ (ej′ōō kāt′) *v.t.,* **-cated,**

-cating. 1. to develop the mind and abilities of. **2.** to provide with training or information. **—ed′u·ca′tion,** *n.* **—ed′u·ca′tion·al,** *adj.*

EEG electroencephalogram.

eel (ēl) *n.* a snakelike fish.

e′er (âr) *adv. Poetic.* ever.

ee′rie (ēr′ē) *adj.,* **-rier, -riest.** strange and mysterious; unsettling. **—ee′ri·ly,** *adv.*

ef·face′ (i fās′) *v.t.,* **-faced, -facing. 1.** to wipe out. **2.** to make inconspicuous. **—ef·face′ment,** *n.*

ef·fect′ (i fekt′) *n.* **1.** a result; consequence. **2.** the power to produce results. **3.** operation. **4.** an impression. **5. effects,** personal property. *—v.t.* **6.** to accomplish or produce. **—Usage.** See AFFECT.

ef·fec′tive *adj.* **1.** producing the intended results. **2.** in operation. **3.** striking. **—ef·fec′tive·ness,** *n.*

ef·fec′tive·ly *adv.* **1.** in an effective way. **2.** for all practical purposes.

ef·fec′tu·al (-chōō əl) *adj.* producing an intended effect.

ef·fem′i·nate (i fem′ə nit) *adj.* (of a man) having traits usu. considered feminine.

ef′fer·vesce′ (ef′ər ves′) *v.i.,* **-vesced, -vescing. 1.** to give off bubbles of gas. **2.** to show liveliness. **—ef′fer·ves′cent,** *adj.*

ef·fete′ (i fēt′) *adj.* **1.** decadent. **2.** worn out.

ef′fi·ca′cious (ef′i kā′shəs) *adj.* producing the desired result. **—ef′fi·ca·cy** (-kə sē) *n.*

ef·fi′cient (i fish′ənt) *adj.* acting effectively without waste of time or effort. **—ef·fi′cien·cy,** *n.*

ef′fi·gy (ef′i jē) *n., pl.* **-gies.** an image of a person, esp. someone disliked.

ef′flu·ent (ef′lōō ənt) *adj.* **1.** flowing out. *—n.* **2.** something that flows out.

ef′fort (ef′ərt) *n.* **1.** exertion of energy. **2.** something achieved by exertion.

ef·fron′ter·y (i frun′tə rē) *n., pl.* **-teries.** impudence.

ef·fu′sion (i fyōō′zhən) *n.* **1.** the act or result of pouring forth. **2.** an unrestrained expression. **—ef·fu′sive,** *adj.*

e.g. for example.

e·gal′i·tar′i·an (i gal′i târ′ē ən) *adj.* asserting or resulting from belief in the equality of all people.

egg¹ (eg) *n.* **1.** the roundish reproductive body produced by the female of certain animals. **2.** a female reproductive cell; ovum.

egg² (eg) *v.* **egg on,** to urge on.

egg′nog′ *n.* a drink containing eggs, milk, sugar, and usu. rum.

egg′plant′ *n.* a dark-purple vegetable.

e′go (ē′gō) *n.* the self.

e′go·cen′tric (-sen′trik) *adj.* self-centered.

e′go·ism *n.* self-centeredness. —**e′go·ist,** *n.*

e′go·tism (ē′gə tiz′əm) *n.* **1.** conceit. **2.** selfishness. —**e′go·tist,** *n.* —**e′go·tis′tic, e′go·tis′ti·cal,** *adj.*

e·gre′gious (i grē′jəs) *adj.* extraordinarily bad; flagrant.

e′gress (ē′gres) *n.* an exit.

e′gret (ē′grit) *n.* a kind of heron.

eh (ā, e) *interj.* (an exclamation of surprise or doubt).

ei′der·down′ (ī′dər doun′) *n.* **1.** down from the female **eider duck,** a northern sea duck. **2.** a quilt filled with eiderdown.

eight (āt) *n., adj.* seven plus one. —**eighth,** *adj., n.*

eight′een′ (ā′tēn′) *n., adj.* ten plus eight. —**eight·eenth′,** *adj., n.*

eight′y *n., adj.* ten times eight. —**eight′i·eth,** *adj., n.*

ei′ther (ē′thər, ī′thər) *adj., pron.* **1.** one or the other of two. **2.** each of two. —*conj.* **3.** (used with *or* to indicate a choice.) —*adv.* **4.** as well.

—**Pronunciation.** The pronunciations (ē′thər) for the word EITHER and (nē′thər) for the word NEITHER, with the vowel of *see,* are the usual ones in American English. The pronunciations (ī′thər) and (nī′thər) with the vowel of *sigh,* occur occasionally in the U.S., chiefly in the speech of the educated and in standard broadcasting English. Since the 19th century, the (ī) has been the more common pronunciation in standard British speech.

e·jac′u·late′ (i jak′yə lāt′) *v.t., v.i.,* **-lated, -lating. 1.** to eject (semen). **2.** to exclaim. —**e·jac′u·la′tion,** *n.*

e·ject′ (i jekt′) *v.t.* to drive or force out.

eke (ēk) *v.,* **eked, eking. eke out, 1.** to supplement. **2.** to make (a living) with difficulty.

EKG 1. electrocardiogram. **2.** electrocardiograph.

e·lab′o·rate′ *adj., v.,* **-rated, -rating.** —*adj.* (i lab′ər it) **1.** worked out in great detail. **2.** ornate. —*v.t.* (-ə-rāt′) **3.** to work out in great detail. —*v.i.* **4.** to expand.

é·lan′ (ā län′, ā län′) *n.* dash or vivacity.

e·lapse′ (i laps′) *v.i.,* **elapsed, elapsing.** (of time) to slip by.

e·las′tic (i las′tik) *adj.* **1.** able to return to its original length or shape after being stretched. **2.** adaptable. **3.** springy. —*n.* **4.** elastic material.

e·late′ (i lāt′) *v.t.,* **elated, elating.** to make extremely happy. —**e·la′tion,** *n.*

el′bow (el′bō) *n.* **1.** the joint between the upper arm and the forearm. —*v.t.* **2.** to push aside with one's elbow.

el′bow grease′ *n.* hard work.

el′bow·room′ *n.* space to move or work freely.

eld′er¹ (el′dər) *adj.* **1.** older. —*n.* **2.** an older person.

eld′er² (el′dər) *n.* a small tree bearing clusters of red, black, or yellow **el′der·ber′ries.**

el′der·ly *adj.* approaching old age.

eld′est (el′dist) *adj.* oldest.

e·lect′ (i lekt′) *v.t.* **1.** to select by vote. **2.** to choose. —*adj.* **3.** chosen.

e·lec′tion *n.* **1.** the act of electing. **2.** the fact of being elected.

e·lec′tion·eer′ *v.i.* to work for a candidate in an election.

e·lec′tive *adj.* **1.** chosen by election. **2.** empowered to elect. **3.** optional. —*n.* **4.** an elective academic course.

e·lec′tor·al col′lege (-tər əl) *n.* a body of special voters (**electors**) chosen to elect the president and vice-president of U.S.

e·lec′tor·ate (-tər it) *n.* a body of voters.

e·lec′tric (i lek′trik) also **e·lec′tri· cal.** *adj.* **1.** pertaining to electricity. **2.** exciting. —**e·lec′tri·cal·ly,** *adv.*

e·lec·tri′cian (i lek trish′ən, ē′lek-) *n.* a person who installs or repairs electrical systems.

e·lec·tric′i·ty (-tris′i tē) *n.* **1.** a fundamental form of energy occurring in matter and having effects such as light, heat, etc. **2.** electric current.

e·lec′tri·fy (-trə fī′) *v.t.,* **-fied, -fying. 1.** to charge with electricity. **2.** to supply with or equip for use of electric power. **3.** to thrill. —**e·lec′tri·fi·ca′tion,** *n.*

e·lec′tro·car′di·o·gram′ (-trō kär′-dē ə gram′) *n.* a graphic record of heart action produced by an electrocardiograph.

e·lec′tro·car′di·o·graph′ *n.* an instrument that records heart movements.

e·lec′tro·cute′ (-trə kyōōt′) *v.t.,* **-cuted, -cuting.** to kill by electricity.

e·lec′trode (i lek′trōd) *n.* a conductor through which an electric current enters or exits a nonmetallic portion of a circuit.

e·lec′tro·en·ceph′a·lo·gram′ (-trō-en sef′ə lə gram′) *n.* the graphic record produced by an electroencephalograph.

e·lec′tro·en·ceph′a·lo·graph′ *n.* an instrument for measuring and recording the electric activity of the brain.

e·lec·trol′o·gist (-trol′ə jist) *n.* a person trained in electrolysis for removing unwanted hair.

e·lec·trol′y·sis (-ə sis) *n.* **1.** the passage of an electric current through an electrolyte. **2.** the destruction of hair roots by electric current.

e·lec′tro·lyte′ (-trə līt′) *n.* a substance that conducts electricity when melted or dissolved.

e·lec′tro·mag′net (i lek′trō-) *n.* a device with an iron or steel core that is magnetized by electric current in a surrounding coil. —**e·lec′tro·mag·net′ic,** *adj.*

e·lec′tron *n.* a particle containing a negative electric charge.

electron′ic mail′ *n.* e-mail.

e·lec·tron′ics *n.* the science dealing with the development of devices and systems involving the flow of electrons. —**e·lec·tron′ic,** *adj.* —**e·lec·tron′i·cal·ly,** *adv.*

el′e·gant (el′i gənt) *adj.* **1.** tastefully luxurious. **2.** dignified. **3.** of superior quality. —**el′e·gance,** *n.*

el′e·gy (el′i jē) *n., pl.* **-gies.** a mournful or melancholy poem. —**el′e·gi′ac** (-jī′ak) *adj.*

el′e·ment (el′ə mənt) *n.* **1.** a part of a whole. **2.** a substance that cannot be broken down chemically. **3.** a natural environment. **4. elements, a.** the basic principles. **b.** atmospheric forces. **c.** the bread and wine of the Eucharist.

el′e·men′ta·ry (-tə rē) *adj.* dealing with the simplest or basic aspects of something.

elemen′tary school′ *n.* a school giving instruction in basic subjects in six or eight grades.

el′e·phant (el′ə fənt) *n.* a very large mammal with a long trunk and large tusks.

el′e·phan′tine (-fan′tēn, -tīn) *adj.* **1.** huge. **2.** clumsy.

el′e·vate′ (el′ə vāt′) *v.t.,* **-vated, -vating.** to raise to a higher place or status.

el′e·va′tion *n.* **1.** an elevating or being elevated. **2.** the height to which something is elevated. **3.** altitude.

el′e·va′tor *n.* **1.** a moving platform or cage for lifting or lowering. **2.** a building for storing grain.

e·lev′en (i lev′ən) *n., adj.* ten plus one. —**e·lev′enth,** *adj.,* *n.*

elf (elf) *n., pl.* **elves.** a tiny, mischievous being in folklore.

e·lic′it (i lis′it) *v.t.* to draw forth.

e·lide′ (i līd′) *v.t.,* **-lided, -liding.** to omit (a vowel, consonant, etc.) in pronunciation.

el′i·gi·ble (el′i jə bəl) *adj.* **1.** being a worthy choice. **2.** qualified to be chosen. —**el′i·gi·bil′i·ty,** *n.*

e·lim′i·nate′ (i lim′ə nāt′) *v.t.,* **-nated, -nating. 1.** to get rid of. **2.** to leave out.

e·lite′ (i lēt′, ā lēt′) *n.* **1.** (*often used with a pl. v.*) the choice, best, or most powerful of a group, class, etc. —*adj.* **2.** of the best or most select.

e·lit′ism *n.* the practice of or belief in rule by an elite. —**e·lit′ist,** *adj.*

e·lix′ir (i lik′sər) *n.* **1.** a sweetened solution used as a flavoring in medicine. **2.** a preparation believed capable of prolonging life.

elk (elk) *n.* a large deer.

el·lipse′ (i lips′) *n.* a closed plane curve shaped like an oval.

el·lip′sis (i lip′sis) *n., pl.* **-ses.** the omission of a word or phrase.

elm (elm) *n.* a large shade tree.

el′o·cu′tion (el′ə kyoō′shən) *n.* the art of public speaking.

e·lon′gate (i lông′gāt) *v.i., v.t.,* **-gated, -gating.** to lengthen.

e·lope′ (i lōp′) *v.i.,* **eloped, eloping.** to run off secretly to be married. —**e·lope′ment,** *n.*

el′o·quent (el′ə kwənt) *adj.* skilled in fluent, forceful speaking. —**el′o·quence,** *n.*

else (els) *adj.* **1.** different. **2.** additional. —*adv.* **3.** otherwise.

else′where′ *adv.* in or to another place.

e·lu′ci·date′ (i loō′si dāt′) *v.t., v.i.,* **-dated, -dating.** to make clear by explaining. —**e·lu′ci·da′tion,** *n.*

e·lude′ (i loōd′) *v.t.,* **eluded, eluding. 1.** to skillfully escape detection or capture by. **2.** to escape the memory or understanding of. —**e·lu′sive,** *adj.* —**Usage.** See ESCAPE.

e·ma′ci·ate′ (i mā′shē āt′) *v.t.,* **-ated, -ating.** to make abnormally thin. —**e·ma′ci·a′tion,** *n.*

e′-mail′ or **e′mail′** or **E′-mail′** (ē′māl′) *n.* **1.** a system for sending messages between computers. **2.** a message sent by e-mail. —*v.t.* **3.** to send a message to by e-mail.

em′a·nate′ (em′ə nāt′) *v.i.,* **-nated, -nating.** to flow out or issue forth.

e·man′ci·pate′ (i man′sə pāt′) *v.t.,* **-pated, -pating.** to free from restraint; liberate. —**e·man′ci·pa′tion,** *n.*

e·mas′cu·late′ (i mas′kyə lāt′) *v.t.,* **-lated, -lating. 1.** to castrate. **2.** to weaken. —**e·mas′cu·la′tion,** *n.*

em·balm′ (em bäm′) *v.t.* to treat (a dead body) with chemicals to preserve it. —**em·balm′·er,** *n.*

em·bank′ment (em bank′mənt) *n.* a bank or mound to hold back water, carry a roadway, etc.

em·bar′go (em bär′gō) *n., pl.* **-goes.** a government order restricting movement of ships or goods.

em·bark′ (em bärk′) *v.i.* **1.** to board a ship or aircraft. **2.** to begin an enterprise. **—em′bar·ka′tion,** *n.*

em·bar′rass (em bar′əs) *v.t.* to make self-conscious or ashamed. **—em·bar′rass·ment,** *n.*

em′bas·sy (em′bə sē) *n., pl.* **-sies.** **1.** an ambassador's headquarters. **2.** an ambassador and staff.

em·bat′tled (em bat′ld) *adj.* prepared for or engaged in conflict.

em·bed′ (em bed′) *v.t., v.i.,* **-bedded, -bedding.** to fix or be fixed into a surrounding mass.

em·bel′lish (em bel′ish) *v.t.* **1.** to beautify with ornamentation. **2.** to enhance by adding detail. **—embel′lish·ment,** *n.*

em′ber (em′bər) *n.* a live coal.

em·bez′zle (em bez′əl) *v.t.,* **-zled, -zling.** to steal (money entrusted to one). **—em·bez′zle·ment,** *n.*

em·bit′ter *v.t.* to cause to feel bitterness.

em·bla′zon (em blā′zən) *v.t.* to decorate, as with heraldic devices.

em′blem (em′bləm) *n.* **1.** a symbol. **2.** a figure identifying something.

em·bod′y *v.t.,* **-ied, -ying.** to put in concrete form; exemplify. **—embod′i·ment,** *n.*

em′bo·lism (em′bə liz′əm) *n.* the closing off of a blood vessel.

em·boss′ (em bôs′) *v.t.* to decorate with a raised design.

em·brace′ (em brās′) *v.,* **-braced, -bracing,** *n.* **—v.t. 1.** to hug. **2.** to accept willingly. **3.** to include. **—n. 4.** a hug.

em·broi′der (em broi′dər) *v.t., v.i.* **1.** to decorate with needlework. **2.** to add fictitious details to (a story). **—em·broi′der·y,** *n.*

em·broil′ *v.t.* to involve in conflict.

em′bry·o (em′brē ō′) *n., pl.* **-bryos.** an organism in the first stages of development. **—em′bry·on′ic,** *adj.*

em′cee′ (em′sē′) *n., v.,* **-ceed, -ceeing. —n. 1.** a master of ceremonies. **—v.i., v.it. 2.** to serve or direct as master of ceremonies.

e·mend′ (i mend′) *v.t.* to change (a text) by correcting.

em′er·ald (em′ər əld) *n.* **1.** a precious green gem. **2.** a clear, deep green.

e·merge′ (i mûrj′) *v.i.,* **emerged, emerging. 1.** to come into existence. **2.** to come into view. **—e·mer′gence,** *n.*

e·mer′gen·cy (i mûr′jən sē) *n., pl.*
-cies. an urgent situation requiring immediate action.

em′er·y (em′ə rē) *n.* a mineral used for grinding and polishing.

e·met′ic (i met′ik) *n.* a medicine that causes vomiting.

em′i·grate (em′i grāt′) *v.i.,* **-grated, -grating.** to leave one country to settle in another. **—em′i·grant** (-grənt) *n., adj.* **—em′i·gra′tion,** *n.*

é′mi·gré′ (-i grā′) *n.* a person who emigrates, esp. one who flees for political reasons.

em′i·nence (em′ə nəns) *n.* high rank or place. **—em′i·nent,** *adj.*

em′is·sar′y (em′ə ser′ē) *n., pl.* **-saries.** an agent sent on a mission.

e·mit′ (i mit′) *v.t.,* **emitted, emitting.** to send forth. **—e·mis′sion,** *n.*

e·mol′lient (i mol′yənt) *adj.* **1.** softening; soothing. **—n. 2.** an emollient substance.

e·mol′u·ment (-yə mənt) *n.* a salary.

e·mote′ (i mōt′) *v.i.,* **emoted, emoting.** to show emotion in or as if in acting.

e·mo′tion (i mō′shən) *n.* a strong feeling. **—e·mo′tion·al,** *adj.*

em′pa·thy (em′pə thē) *n.* identification with the feelings of another. **—em′pa·thize′,** *v.i.*

em′per·or (em′pər ər) *n.* the male ruler of an empire.

em′pha·sis (em′fə sis) *n., pl.* **-ses.** special stress or importance. **—emphat′ic** (-fat′ik) *adj.* **—emphat′i·cal·ly,** *adv.* **—em′pha·size′,** *v.t.*

em′phy·se′ma (em′fə sē′mə) *n.* a chronic lung disease.

em′pire (em′pīər) *n.* **1.** a group of nations under one powerful ruler. **2.** a powerful enterprise controlled by one person or group.

em·pir′i·cal (-pir′i kəl) *adj.* drawing on experience or observation.

em·ploy′ (em ploi′) *v.t.* **1.** to engage the services of; hire. **2.** to make use of. **—n. 3.** employment; service. **—em·ploy′ee,** *n.* **—em·ploy′er,** *n.*

em·ploy′ment *n.* **1.** an employing or being employed. **2.** an occupation.

em·po′ri·um (em pôr′ē əm) *n.* a large store.

em·pow′er *v.t.* **1.** to give power or authority to. **2.** to enable. **—empow′er·ment,** *n.*

em′press *n.* **1.** the female ruler of an empire. **2.** the wife of an emperor.

emp′ty (emp′tē) *adj.,* **-tier, -tiest,** *v.,* **-tied, -tying. —adj. 1.** containing nothing. **2.** vacant. **3.** lacking force. **—v.t., v.i. 4.** to make or become empty. **5.** to discharge.

EMT emergency medical technician.

e′mu (ē′myo͞o) *n.* a large, flightless Australian bird.

em′u·late′ (em′yə lāt′) *v.t.,* **-lated, -lating.** to imitate in an effort to equal or surpass.

e·mul′si·fy′ (i mul′sə fī′) *v.t., v.i.,* **-fied, -fying.** to make into or form an emulsion.

e·mul′sion (-shən) *n.* **1.** a milklike mixture of liquids. **2.** a photosensitive coating on film.

en- a prefix meaning: **1.** to put into or on. **2.** to cover or surround with. **3.** to make or cause to be.

en·a′ble (en ā′bəl) *v.t.,* **-bled, -bling. 1.** to make able. **2.** to make possible.

en·act′ *v.t.* **1.** to make into law. **2.** to act the part of.

e·nam′el (i nam′əl) *n. v.,* **-eled, -eling.** —*n.* **1.** a glassy coating fused to metal, pottery, etc. **2.** a paint that dries to a glossy surface. **3.** the surface of the teeth. —*v.t.* **4.** to apply enamel to.

en·am′or (-ər) *v.t.* to fill with love.

en·camp′ *v.t., v.i.* to settle in a camp. —**en·camp′ment,** *n.*

en·cap′su·late′ (en kap′sə lāt′) *v.t.,* **-lated, -lating.** to summarize or condense.

en·case′ (en kās′) *v.t,* **-cased, -casing.** to enclose in or as if in a case.

en·ceph′a·li′tis (en sef′ə lī′tis) *n.* inflammation of the brain.

en·chant′ (en chant′) *v.t.* to bewitch; charm. —**en·chant′ment,** *n.*

en·cir′cle *v.t.,* **-cled, -cling.** to surround.

encl. 1. enclosed. **2.** enclosure.

en′clave (en′klāv, än′-) *n.* a small area surrounded by foreign territory.

en·close′ (en klōz′) *v.t.,* **-closed, -closing. 1.** to shut in on all sides. **2.** to surround, as with a fence. **3.** to put in an envelope along with something else. —**en·clo′sure,** *n.*

en·code′ *v.t.,* **-coded, -coding.** to convert into code.

en·co′mi·um (-kō′mē əm) *n., pl.* **-miums, -mia.** formal words of praise.

en·com′pass (-kum′pəs) *v.t.* **1.** to encircle; surround. **2.** to include.

en′core (äng′kôr, än′-) *n.* **1.** a demand by an audience for a repetition of a song, the performance of an additional piece, etc. **2.** a performance in response to an encore.

en·coun′ter (en koun′tər) *v.t.* **1.** to meet unexpectedly. —*n.* **2.** an unexpected meeting. **3.** a battle.

en·cour′age (en kûr′ij, -kur′-) *v.t.,* **-aged, -aging. 1.** to inspire with courage or confidence. **2.** to stimulate. —**en·cour′age·ment,** *n.*

en·croach′ (-krōch′) *v.i.* to trespass on the property or rights of another.

en·cum′ber (kum′bər) *v.t.* **1.** to hinder. **2.** to burden. —**en·cum′-brance,** *n.*

en·cyc′li·cal (-sik′li kəl) *n.* a letter from the pope to all bishops.

en·cy·clo·pe′di·a (-sī′klə pē′dē ə) *n.* a book with information on all branches of knowledge or on all aspects of one branch. —**en·cy′clo·pe′dic,** *adj.*

end (end) *n.* **1.** the last part. **2.** a point that indicates the limit of something. **3.** the farthest part or point of something. **4.** a purpose. **5.** an outcome. **6.** destruction. —*v.t., v.i.* **7.** to bring or come to an end. —**end′less,** *adj.*

en·dan′ger (en dān′jər) *v.t.* **1.** to expose to danger. **2.** to threaten with extinction.

en·dear′ (en dēr′) *v.t.* to make beloved.

en·deav′or (en dev′ər) *v.i.* **1.** to make an earnest effort. —*n.* **2.** an attempt.

en·dem′ic (en dem′ik) *adj.* belonging to a particular people or place.

end′ing *n.* a concluding part.

en′dive (en′dīv, än dēv′) *n.* **1.** a plant with curly leaves used in salad. **2.** Also called **Belgian endive.** a plant with a narrow head of whitish, edible leaves.

en′do·crine (en′də krin, -krīn′) *adj.* **1.** secreting internally into the blood or lymph. **2.** of glands that secrete hormones directly into the blood or lymph.

en·dorse′ (-dôrs′) *v.t.,* **-dorsed, -dorsing. 1.** to express approval or support of. **2.** to sign one′s name on the back of (a check).

en·dow′ (-dou′) *v.t.* **1.** to provide with a permanent source of income. **2.** to equip.

en·dure′ (-do͞or′, -dyo͞or′) *v.,* **-dured, -during.** —*v.t.* **1.** to hold up under (pain or hardship) without yielding. **2.** to tolerate. —*v.i.* **3.** to last. —**en·dur′ance,** *n.*

en′e·ma (en′ə mə) *n.* liquid injected into the rectum.

en′em·y (en′ə mē) *n., pl.* **-mies.** a person who is hostile to and wishes or tries to harm another.

en′er·gize′ (en′ər jīz′) *v.t.,* **-gized, -gizing.** to give energy to.

en′er·gy (-jē) *n., pl.* **-gies. 1.** the capacity for vigorous activity. **2.** the capacity to do work. **3.** a source of usable power, as oil. —**en·er·get′ic** (-jet′ik) *adj.*

en•er•vate (en'ər vāt') *v.t.*, **-vated, -vating.** to deprive of strength.

en•fee•ble (-fē'bəl) *v.t.*, **-bled, -bling.** to weaken.

en•fold *v.t.* **1.** to wrap up. **2.** to hug.

en•force *v.t.*, **-forced, -forcing. 1.** to compel obedience to. **2.** to obtain by force. **—en•force'ment,** *n.* **—en•forc'er,** *n.*

en•fran'chise *v.t.*, **-chised, -chising.** to grant voting rights to.

en•gage (-gāj') *v.*, **-gaged, -gaging. —v.t. 1.** to occupy the attention of. **2.** to employ. **3.** to attract and hold. **4.** to bind by a pledge, esp. a pledge to marry. **5.** to enter into conflict with. **6.** to cause (gears) to become interlocked. **—v.i. 7.** to be involved. **8.** to assume an obligation. **9.** to enter into conflict. **10.** to interlock. **—en•gaged',** *adj.*

en•gage'ment *n.* **1.** the act of engaging or the state of being engaged. **2.** an appointment. **3.** an agreement to marry. **4.** a battle.

en•gag'ing *adj.* attractive.

en•gen'der *v.t.* to cause.

en'gine (en'jən) *n.* **1.** a machine for converting energy into force and motion. **2.** a locomotive.

en•gi•neer (en'jə nēr') *n.* **1.** a person trained in engineering. **2.** an engine operator. **—v.t. 3.** to contrive; bring about.

en•gi•neer'ing *n.* the practical application of science and mathematics, as in the design of systems and structures.

en•gorge' *v.t.*, *v.i.*, **-gorged, -gorging. 1.** to swallow greedily. **2.** to fill or congest, esp. with blood. **—en•gorge'ment,** *n.*

en•grave' *v.t.*, **-graved, -graving. 1.** to cut (letters or a design) into a hard surface. **2.** to ornament by such cutting. **—en•grav'er,** *n.* **—en•grav'ing,** *n.*

en•gross' (en grōs') *v.t.* to occupy completely. **—en•gross'ing,** *adj.*

en•gulf' *v.t.* **1.** to swallow up. **2.** to overwhelm.

en•hance' (en hans') *v.t.*, **-hanced, -hancing. 1.** to intensify. **2.** to improve.

e•nig•ma (ə nig'mə) *n.* a puzzling person, event, or situation. **—en'ig•mat'ic,** *adj.*

en•join' *v.t.* to direct or order.

en•joy' *v.t.* **1.** to take pleasure in. **2.** to have the use of. **—en•joy'a•ble,** *adj.* **—en•joy'ment,** *n.*

en•large' *v.t.*, *v.i.*, **-larged, -larging.** to make or grow larger. **—en•large'ment,** *n.*

en•light•en (en līt'n) *v.t.* **1.** to give

understanding to. **2.** to free of ignorance. **—en•light'en•ment,** *n.*

en•list' *v.i.*, *v.t.* **1.** to enroll for military service. **2.** to secure for a cause. **—en•list'ment,** *n.*

en•liv'en (en lī'vən) *v.t.* to make active or lively.

en masse' (än mas', äɴ) *adv.* in a mass; all together.

en•mesh' *v.t.* to entangle.

en'mi•ty (en'mi tē) *n.*, *pl.* **-ties.** hatred.

en•nui' (än wē') *n.* boredom.

e•nor•mi•ty (i nôr'mi tē) *n.*, *pl.* **-ties. 1.** great wickedness. **2.** an outrageous crime; atrocity.

e•nor'mous (-məs) *adj.* huge.

e•nough' (i nuf') *adj.* **1.** sufficient for a purpose. *—n.* **2.** an adequate amount. *—adv.* **3.** sufficiently.

en•quire' (en kwī°r') *v.i.*, *v.t.*, **-quired, -quiring.** to inquire. **—en•quir'y,** *n.*

en•rage' *v.t.*, **-raged, -raging.** to make very angry.

en•rap'ture (en rap'chər) *v.t.*, **-tured, -turing.** to delight.

en•rich' *v.t.* **1.** to make rich. **2.** to improve. **—en•rich'ment,** *n.*

en•roll' *v.t.*, *v.i.* to accept as or become a member. **—en•roll'ment,** *n.*

en route' (än rōōt') *adv.* on the way.

en•sconce' (en skons') *v.t.*, **-sconced, -sconcing.** to settle securely or snugly.

en•sem'ble (än säm'bəl) *n.* **1.** all the parts of a thing taken together. **2.** a group performing together. **3.** an outfit.

en•shrine' *v.t.*, **-shrined, -shrining. 1.** to put in a shrine. **2.** to cherish as sacred.

en•shroud' *v.t.* to conceal.

en'sign (en'sin; *Mil.* -sən) *n.* **1.** a military flag. **2.** the lowest commissioned naval officer.

en•slave' *v.t.*, **-slaved, -slaving.** to make a slave of.

en•snare' *v.t.*, **-snared, -snaring.** to capture in a snare; entrap.

en•sue' (en sōō') *v.i.*, **-sued, -suing.** to follow in order or as a result.

en•sure' (en shŏŏr') *v.t.*, **-sured, -suring.** to make certain; secure.

en•tail' (en tāl') *v.t.* to cause or involve by necessity or as a consequence.

en•tan'gle *v.t.*, **-gled, -gling. 1.** to make tangled. **2.** to involve in difficulties or complications.

en•tente' (än tänt') *n.* an international agreement on a common policy.

en'ter (en'tər) *v.t.* **1.** to come or go in or into. **2.** to begin. **3.** to become involved in. **4.** to put on a list. —*v.i.* **5.** to come or go in.

en·ter·i·tis (en/tə rī/tis) *n.* inflammation of the intestines.

en·ter·prise/ (en/tər prīz/) *n.* **1.** a project, esp. one requiring boldness or originality. **2.** adventurous spirit. **3.** a business firm.

en·ter·pris/ing *adj.* showing imagination and initiative.

en·ter·tain/ (en/tər tān/) *v.t.* **1.** to amuse. **2.** to treat as a guest. **3.** to have in one's mind. —**en·ter·tain/er,** *n.* —**en·ter·tain/ment,** *n.*

en·thrall/ (en thrôl/) *v.t.* **1.** to captivate. **2.** to enslave.

en·throne/ *v.t.,* **-throned, -throning.** to place on or as if on a throne. —**en·throne/ment,** *n.*

en·thuse/ (en thōōz/) *v.,* **-thused, -thusing.** —*v.i.* **1.** to show enthusiasm. —*v.t.* **2.** to fill with enthusiasm.

en·thu/si·asm (-thōō/zē az/əm) *n.* lively, absorbing interest. —**en·thu/si·ast/,** *n.* —**en·thu/si·as/tic,** *adj.*

en·tice/ (en tīs/) *v.t.,* **-ticed, -tic·ing.** to lead on by exciting hope or desire; allure. —**en·tice/ment,** *n.*

en·tire/ (en tī°r/) *adj.* whole or complete. —**en·tire/ly,** *adv.* —**en·tire/ty,** *n.*

en·ti/tle *v.t.,* **-tled, -tling. 1.** to give a right to. **2.** to give a title to.

en/ti·ty (en/ti tē) *n., pl.* **-ties.** something that exists as a separate thing.

en·tomb/ *v.t.* to place in a tomb.

en·to·mol/o·gy (en/tə mol/ə jē) *n.* the study of insects. —**en/to·mol/o·gist,** *n.*

en/tou·rage/ (än/tōō räzh/) *n.* a group of attendants.

en/trails (en/trālz, -trəlz) *n.pl.* the inner organs, esp. the intestines.

en/trance¹ (-trəns) *n.* **1.** the act of entering. **2.** a place for entering. **3.** the right to enter.

en·trance/² (-trans/) *v.t.,* **-tranced, -trancing.** to fill with delight.

en/trant (en/trənt) *n.* a person who enters a competition or a contest.

en·trap/ *v.t.,* **-trapped, -trapping.** to catch in or as if in a trap.

en·treat/ (en trēt/) *v.t., v.i.* to ask earnestly. —**en·treat/y,** *n.*

en/tree (än/trā) *n.* **1.** the main course of a meal. **2.** access.

en·trench/ *v.t.* to establish firmly.

en/tre·pre·neur/ (än/trə prə nûr/) *n.* a person who organizes a business, esp. one involving risk. —**en/tre·pre·neur/i·al,** *adj.*

en/tro·py (en/trə pē) *n.* **1.** a measure of the energy in a system that is not available for conversion into

mechanical work. **2.** the tendency toward disorder in any system.

en·trust/ *v.t.* to give to as a trust.

en/try (en/trē) *n., pl.* **-tries. 1.** a place of entrance. **2.** permission or right to enter. **3.** the act of entering. **4.** an item entered in a list or contest.

en·twine/ *v.t.,* **-twined, -twining.** to twine around or together.

e·nu/mer·ate/ (i nōō/mə rāt/, i nyōō/-) *v.t.,* **-ated, -ating.** to name one by one; list. —**e·nu/mer·a/tion,** *n.*

e·nun/ci·ate/ (i nun/sē āt/) *v.t., v.i.,* **-ated, -ating. 1.** to pronounce. **2.** to state clearly.

en·vel/op (en vel/əp) *v.t.* **1.** to wrap up. **2.** to surround.

en/ve·lope/ (en/və lōp/, än/-) *n.* a flat paper container, as for a letter.

en·vi/ron·ment (en vī/rən mənt, -vī/ərn-) *n.* **1.** surroundings. **2.** the external factors, as air, water, etc., affecting an organism. —**en·vi/ron·men/tal** (-men/tl) *adj.* —**en·vi/ron·men/tal·ist,** *n.*

en·vi/rons *n.pl.* the surrounding districts, as of a city.

en·vis/age (en viz/ij) *v.t.,* **-aged, -aging.** to form a mental picture of. Also, **en·vi/sion.**

en/voy (en/voi, än/-) *n.* **1.** a diplomatic representative. **2.** a messenger.

en/vy (en/vē) *n., pl.* **-vies,** *v.,* **-vied, -vying.** —*n.* **1.** discontent at another's possessions or success. **2.** an object of envy. —*v.t.* **3.** to regard with envy. —**en/vi·ous,** *adj.*

en/zyme (en/zīm) *n.* a protein formed in living cells and capable of producing chemical changes in other substances.

e/on (ē/ən, ē/on) *n.* a long period of time.

EPA Environmental Protection Agency.

ep/au·let/ (ep/ə let/, -lit) *n.* an ornamental shoulder piece on a uniform. Also, **ep/au·lette/.**

e·phem/er·al (i fem/ər əl) *adj.* lasting a very short time.

ep/ic (ep/ik) *n.* **1.** a long poem or story describing heroic deeds. —*adj.* **2.** of or like an epic.

ep/i·cen/ter (ep/ə sen/tər) *n.* a point directly above the center of an earthquake.

ep/i·cure/ (ep/i kyŏŏr/) *n.* a person with refined taste in food and drink. —**ep/i·cu·re/an,** *adj.*

ep/i·dem/ic (ep/i dem/ik) *adj.* **1.** affecting many persons at once. —*n.* **2.** an epidemic disease.

ep/i·der/mis *n.* the outer layer of skin.

ep′i•glot′tis (-glot′is) *n.*, *pl.* **-glot-tises, -glottides** (-glot′i dēz′). a flap of cartilage that covers the wind-pipe during swallowing.

ep′i•gram′ (ep′i gram′) *n.* a short witty saying.

ep′i•lep′sy (ep′ə lep′sē) *n.* a nerv-ous disorder usu. marked by con-vulsions. —**ep′i•lep′tic,** *adj., n.*

ep′i•logue′ (ep′ə lôg′) *n.* a con-cluding part or speech.

e•piph′a•ny (i pif′ə nē) *n.* **1. Epiph-any,** a festival commemorating the Wise Men's visit to Christ, cele-brated on January 6. **2.** an appear-ance. **3.** a sudden realization.

e•pis′co•pal (i pis′kə pəl) *adj.* gov-erned by bishops.

ep′i•sode′ (ep′ə sōd′) *n.* an inci-dent in a series of events. —**ep′i•sod′ic** (-sod′ik) *adj.*

e•pis′tle (i pis′əl) *n.* a letter.

ep′i•taph′ (ep′i taf′) *n.* an inscrip-tion on a tomb.

ep′i•thet′ (ep′ə thet′) *n.* a descrip-tive term.

e•pit′o•me (i pit′ə mē) *n.* **1.** a per-fect example. **2.** a summary. —**e•pit′o•mize′,** *v.t.*

ep′och (ep′ək) *n.* a distinctive pe-riod of time. —**ep′och•al,** *adj.*

ep•ox′y (i pok′sē) *n.*, *pl.* **-ies.** a tough synthetic resin used in glue.

Ep′som salts′ (ep′səm) *n.pl.* salts used esp. as a cathartic.

eq′ua•ble (ek′wə bəl) *adj.* **1.** free from many changes. **2.** calm.

e′qual (ē′kwəl) *adj.*, *n.*, *v.*, **equaled, equaling.** —*adj.* **1.** alike in amount, rank, value, size, etc. **2.** the same in operation or effect. **3.** having adequate means or ability. —*n.* **4.** one that is equal. —*v.t.* **5.** to be or become equal to. **6.** to do something equal to. —**e•qual′i•ty,** *n.* —**e′qual•ize′,** *v.t.*

e′qual sign′ *n.* a symbol (=) indi-cating equality between the terms it separates. Also, **e′quals sign′.**

e′qua•nim′i•ty (ē′kwə nim′i tē) *n.* calmness.

e•quate′ (i kwāt′) *v.t.*, **equated, equating.** to make or consider as equivalent.

e•qua′tion (i kwā′zhən) *n.* **1.** an equating or being equated. **2.** an expression of the equality of two quantities.

e•qua′tor (-tər) *n.* an imaginary cir-cle around the earth midway be-tween the North Pole and the South Pole. —**e•qua•to′ri•al,** *adj.*

e•ques′tri•an (i kwes′trē ən) *adj.* **1.** of horseback riding or riders. —*n.* **2.** a person who rides horses.

e′qui•dis′tant (ē′kwi dis′tənt) *adj.* equally distant.

e′qui•lat′er•al *adj.* having all the sides equal.

e′qui•lib′ri•um (-lib′rē əm) *n.*, *pl.* **-riums, -ria.** a state of balance be-tween opposing forces, powers, or influences.

e′quine (ē′kwīn) *adj.* of horses.

e′qui•nox′ (ē′kwə noks′) *n.* one of the times when day and night are of equal length.

e•quip′ (i kwip′) *v.t.*, **equipped, equipping.** to provide with what is needed.

e•quip′ment *n.* **1.** an equipping or being equipped. **2.** the articles needed for a specific activity.

eq′ui•ta•ble (ek′wi tə bəl) *adj.* fair and impartial.

eq′ui•ty *n.*, *pl.* **-ties. 1.** fairness. **2.** the value of a property beyond any amounts owed on it.

e•quiv′a•lent (i kwiv′ə lənt) *adj.* **1.** equal in value, meaning, effect, etc. —*n.* **2.** something equivalent. —**e•quiv′a•lence,** *n.*

e•quiv′o•cal (-kəl) *adj.* **1.** ambigu-ous. **2.** questionable.

e•quiv′o•cate′ (-kāt′) *v.i.*, **-cated, -cating.** to express oneself ambigu-ously. —**e•quiv′o•ca′tion,** *n.*

e′ra (ēr′ə, er′ə) *n.* a period of his-tory.

ERA 1. Also, **era.** earned run aver-age. **2.** Equal Rights Amendment.

e•rad′i•cate′ (i rad′i kāt′) *v.t.*, **-cated, -cating.** to remove com-pletely.

e•rase′ (i rās′) *v.t.*, **erased, erasing. 1.** to rub out. **2.** to eliminate. —**e•ras′a•ble,** *adj.* —**e•ras′er,** *n.*

e•ra′sure *n.* **1.** an act of erasing. **2.** a place where something has been erased.

ere (âr) *prep., conj. Archaic.* before.

e•rect′ (i rekt′) *adj.* **1.** upright. —*v.t.* **2.** to build. **3.** to set up.

e•rec′tile (i rek′tl, -til, -tīl) *adj.* capa-ble of being distended with blood and becoming rigid.

e•rec′tion (-shən) *n.* **1.** something erected. **2.** a distended and rigid state of an organ, as the penis.

erg (ûrg) *n.* a unit of work or en-ergy.

er′go•nom′ics (ûr′gə nom′iks) *n.* an applied science that coordinates workplace design and equipment with workers' needs.

er′mine (ûr′min) *n.* **1.** a kind of weasel. **2.** its white winter fur.

e•rode′ (i rōd′) *v.*, **eroded, eroding.** —*v.t.* **1.** to wear away. —*v.i.* **2.** to become worn away. —**e•ro′sion,** *n.*

e•rog′e•nous (i roj′ə nəs) *adj.* sen-sitive to sexual stimulation.

e•rot′ic (i rot′ik) *adj.* **1.** of sexual

love. **2.** arousing sexual desire.
—e•rot′i•cism (-ə siz/əm) *n.*

err (ûr, er) *v.i.* **1.** to be mistaken. **2.** to sin.

er′rand (er′ənd) *n.* a short trip for a specific purpose.

er′rant (-ənt) *adj.* **1.** straying from the proper course. **2.** wandering.

er•rat′ic (i rat′ik) *adj.* irregular or unpredictable.

er•ra′tum (i rä′təm, i rat′əm) *n., pl.* **-ta.** an error in printing or writing.

er•ro′ne•ous (ə rō′nē əs, e rō′-) *adj.* incorrect.

er′ror (er′ər) *n.* **1.** a mistake. **2.** being wrong.

er•satz′ (er zäts′) *adj.* serving as a substitute; artificial.

erst′while′ *adj.* former.

ERT estrogen replacement therapy.

er′u•dite′ (er′yŏŏ dīt′) *adj.* learned.

e•rupt′ (i rupt′) *v.i.* **1.** to burst forth. **2.** (of a volcano, geyser, etc.) to eject matter. —**e•rup′tion,** *n.*

es•ca•late′ (es′kə lāt′) *v.i., v.t.,* **-lated, -lating.** to increase in intensity, amount, size, etc.

es•ca•la′tor *n.* a continuously moving stairway.

es•ca•pade′ (es′kə pād′) *n.* a reckless adventure.

es•cape′ (i skāp′) *v.,* **-caped, -caping,** *n.* —*v.i.* **1.** to get away. **2.** to avoid a danger. **3.** to get out of a container. —*v.t.* **4.** to get away from. **5.** to succeed in avoiding. **6.** to elude. —*n.* **7.** an act or means of escaping. **8.** avoidance of reality. **9.** leakage, as of gas. —**es•cap′ee,** *n.* ——**Usage.** ESCAPE, ELUDE, EVADE mean to keep away from something. To ESCAPE is to manage to keep away from danger, pursuit, observation, etc.: *to escape punishment.* To ELUDE is to slip through an apparently tight net, and implies using skill or cleverness: *The fox eluded the hounds.* To EVADE is to turn aside from or go out of reach of a person or thing, usually by moving or directing attention elsewhere: *We evaded the traffic jam by taking an alternate route.*

es•cape′ment (-mənt) *n.* the part of a clock that measures beats and controls the speed of the wheels.

es•cap′ism *n.* an attempt to forget reality through fantasy. —**es•cap′ist,** *n., adj.*

es′ca•role′ (es′kə rōl′) *n.* a broad-leaved endive.

es•carp′ment (i skärp′mənt) *n.* a long clifflike ridge.

es•chew′ (es chŏŏ′) *v.t.* to avoid.

es′cort *n.* (es′kôrt) **1.** someone accompanying another for protection or courtesy. **2.** a man accompanying a woman in public. —*v.t.* (i-skôrt′) **3.** to accompany as an escort.

es•cutch′eon (i skuch′ən) *n.* a shield with a coat of arms.

ESL English as a second language.

e•soph′a•gus (i sof′ə gəs) *n., pl.* **-gi** (-jī′). a tube connecting the throat and the stomach.

es′o•ter′ic (es′ə ter′ik) *adj.* understood only by a select few.

ESP extrasensory perception.

esp. especially.

es•pe′cial (i spesh′əl) *adj.* special. —**es•pe′cial•ly,** *adv.*

es′pi•o•nage′ (es′pē ə näzh′, -nij) *n.* the act or practice of spying.

es′pla•nade′ (es′plə näd′, -nād′) *n.* an open level space for public walks.

es•pouse′ (i spouz′, i spous′) *v.t.,* **-poused, -pousing. 1.** to adopt or support, as a cause. **2.** to marry. —**es•pous′al,** *n.*

es•prit′ de corps′ (ē sprē′ də kôr′) *n.* a sense of unity and common purpose.

es•py′ (i spī′) *v.t.,* **-pied, -pying.** to catch sight of.

es•quire′ (es′kwīᵊr) *n.* a title of respect, applied chiefly to lawyers. *Abbr.:* Esq.

es′say *n.* (es′ā) **1.** a short literary composition on a particular subject. **2.** an attempt. —*v.t.* (e sā′) **3.** to try.

es′say•ist *n.* a writer of essays.

es′sence (es′əns) *n.* **1.** the basic, real nature of a thing. **2.** a concentrated form of a substance. **3.** a perfume.

es•sen′tial (ə sen′shəl) *adj.* **1.** absolutely necessary. —*n.* **2.** something basic or necessary.

es•sen′tial•ly *adv.* basically.

EST Eastern Standard Time.

est. 1. established. **2.** estimate. **3.** estimated.

es•tab′lish (i stab′lish) *v.t.* **1.** to bring into being. **2.** to settle, as in a position. **3.** to cause to be accepted. **4.** to prove.

es•tab′lish•ment *n.* **1.** an establishing or being established. **2.** an institution or business. **3. the Establishment,** the group controlling government and social institutions.

es•tate′ (i stāt′) *n.* **1.** a piece of landed property. **2.** a person's possessions or property, esp. that of a deceased person.

es•teem′ (i stēm′) *v.t.* **1.** to regard with respect or admiration. —*n.* **2.** respect or admiration.

es′ter (es′tər) *n.* a chemical compound produced by the reaction between an acid and an alcohol.

es/thete *n.* an aesthete.

es/ti·ma·ble (es/tə mə bəl) *adj.* worthy of high regard.

es/ti·mate/ *v.,* **-mated, -mating,** *n.* —*v.t.* (es/tə māt/) **1.** to form an approximate judgment regarding the amount, worth, etc., of. —*v.i.* **2.** to make an estimate. —*n.* (-mit) **3.** an approximate judgment or calculation. **4.** a statement of the approximate cost. —**es/ti·ma/tion,** *n.*

es·trange/ (i strānj/) *v.t.,* **-tranged, -tranging.** to make unfriendly.

es/tro·gen (es/trə jən) *n.* any of several female sex hormones.

es/tu·ar/y (es/chōō er/ē) *n., pl.* **-aries.** the part of a river at which the current meets the sea tides.

ETA estimated time of arrival.

et al. (et al/, äl/, ôl/) and others.

et cet/er·a (et set/ər ə, se/trə) *adv.* and others, esp. of the same sort. *Abbr.:* etc.

etch (ech) *v.t.* to cut a design into (metal) with acid. —**etch/ing,** *n.*

e·ter/nal (i tûr/nl) *adj.* **1.** without beginning or end; existing always. **2.** not subject to change.

e·ter/ni·ty (-ni tē) *n.* **1.** infinite time. **2.** eternal existence.

eth/ane (eth/ān) *n.* a colorless, odorless, flammable gas used chiefly as a fuel.

e/ther (ē/thər) *n.* **1.** a colorless liquid used as a solvent and formerly as an anesthetic. **2.** the upper part of space.

e·the/re·al (i thēr/ē əl) *adj.* **1.** light or airy. **2.** heavenly.

eth/ics (eth/iks) *n.* **1.** a system of moral principles. **2.** the branch of philosophy dealing with right and wrong. —**eth/i·cal,** *adj.*

eth/nic (-nik) *adj.* **1.** of a group sharing a common culture. —*n.* **2.** a member of an ethnic group.

eth/nic cleans/ing *n.* the elimination of an ethnic group from a society, as by genocide or forced emigration.

eth·nic/i·ty (-nis/i tē) *n.* ethnic traits or association.

eth·nol/o·gy (-nol/ə jē) *n.* a branch of anthropology dealing with cultural comparisons. —**e·thol/o·gy** (ē thol/ə jē) *n.* the scientific study of animal behavior.

e/thos (ē/thos, eth/ōs) *n.* the distinguishing character or spirit of a person, group, or culture.

eth/yl (eth/əl) *n.* a fluid used in gasoline.

et/i·quette (et/i kit, -ket/) *n.* conventions of social behavior.

et seq. and the following.

é/tude (ā/tōōd, ā/tyōōd) *n.* a musical composition played to improve technique and for its artistic merit.

et/y·mol/o·gy (et/ə mol/ə jē) *n., pl.* **-gies.** the history of a word's origin and development.

eu- a prefix meaning good.

eu·ca·lyp/tus (yōō/kə lip/təs) *n., pl.* **-ti.** an evergreen tree with strong-smelling leaves.

Eu/cha·rist (yōō/kə rist) *n.* Holy Communion.

eu·gen/ics (yōō jen/iks) *n.* a science concerned with improving the genetic traits of the human race.

eu/lo·gy (-lə jē) *n., pl.* **-gies.** spoken or written praise of a person, esp. of someone who has died. —**eu/lo·gize/,** *v.t.*

eu/nuch (-nək) *n.* a castrated man.

eu/phe·mism (-fə miz/əm) *n.* the substitution of a mild expression for one thought to be offensive. —**eu/phe·mis/tic,** *adj.*

eu/pho·ny (-fə nē) *n., pl.* **-nies.** pleasantness of sound, esp. a pleasing combination of words. —**eu·pho/ni·ous** (-fō/nē əs) *adj.*

eu·pho/ri·a (-fôr/ē ə) *n.* a strong feeling of happiness or well-being. —**eu·phor/ic,** *adj.*

eu·re/ka (yōō rē/kə) *interj.* (an exclamation of triumph at a discovery.)

eu/ro (yōōr/ō, yûr/-) *n., pl.* **-ros.** the official common currency of most W European countries.

Eu·sta/chian tube (yōō stā/shən) *n.* (*often l.c.*) a canal between the middle ear and the pharynx.

eu/tha·na/sia (yōō/thə nā/zhə) *n.* painless killing of a person or animal suffering from an incurable disease.

e·vac/u·ate/ (i vak/yōō āt/) *v.t.,* **-ated, -ating. 1.** to make empty. **2.** to remove (persons or things) from (a place), esp. for safety. —**e·vac/u·a/tion,** *n.*

e·vade/ (i vād/) *v.t., v.i.,* **evaded, evading.** to avoid or escape, esp. by cleverness. —**e·va/sion,** *n.* —**e·va/sive,** *adj.* —**Usage.** See ESCAPE.

e·val/u·ate/ (i val/yōō āt/) *v.t.,* **-ated, -ating.** to determine the value, quality, or importance of. —**e·val/u·a/tion,** *n.*

ev/a·nes/cent (ev/ə nes/ənt) *adj.* fading away.

e/van·gel/i·cal (ē/van jel/i kəl, ev/-ən-) *adj.* **1.** of or in keeping with the Gospels. **2.** of those Christian churches that stress the authority of the Scriptures. **3.** marked by zeal.

e·van/ge·list (i van/jə list) *n.* **1.** a preacher of the Christian gospel. **2.**

Evangelist, one of the writers of the four Gospels. —**e·van′ge·lism,** *n.* —**e·van′ge·lize′,** *v.t., v.i.*

e·vap′o·rate′ (i vap′ə rāt′) *v.,* **-rated, -rating.** —*v.i.* **1.** to change into vapor. **2.** to disappear. —*v.t.* **3.** to convert into vapor.

eve (ēv) *n.* the evening or day before an event or holiday.

e′ven (ē′vən) *adj.* **1.** level. **2.** smooth. **3.** uniform. **4.** equal in quantity. **5.** divisible by two. **6.** calm. —*adv.* **7.** still; yet. **8.** (used to suggest an extreme case). **9.** indeed. —*v.t., v.i.* **10.** to make or become even.

e′ven·hand′ed *adj.* impartial; fair.

eve′ning (ēv′ning) *n.* the latter part of the day and early part of the night.

e·vent′ (i vent′) *n.* something that happens, esp. something important. —**e·vent′ful,** *adj.*

e·ven′tu·al (i ven′chōō əl) *adj.* happening at an indefinite future time. —**e·ven′tu·al·ly,** *adv.*

e·ven′tu·al′i·ty *n., pl.* **-ties.** a possible event or circumstance.

ev′er (ev′ər) *adv.* **1.** at any time. **2.** at all times. **3.** in any possible case.

ev′er·glade′ *n.* a tract of low, swampy land.

ev′er·green′ *adj.* **1.** having green leaves all year. —*n.* **2.** an evergreen plant.

ev′er·last′ing *adj.* lasting forever.

eve′ry (ev′rē) *adj.* **1.** each one in a group. **2.** all possible.

eve′ry·bod′y (-bod′ē, -bud′ē) *pron.* every person.

eve′ry·day′ *adj.* **1.** of or for ordinary days. **2.** ordinary.

eve′ry·one′ *pron.* everybody.

eve′ry·thing′ *pron.* all things.

eve′ry·where′ *adv.* in every place.

e·vict′ (i vikt′) *v.t.* to expel (a tenant) from property by legal means. —**e·vic′tion,** *n.*

e′vi·dence (ev′i dəns) *n., v.,* **-denced, -dencing.** —*n.* **1.** something establishing a fact as true. **2.** something presented in a law court to support a case. —*v.t.* **3.** to show clearly.

ev′i·dent *adj.* clear to the sight or mind. —**ev′i·dent·ly** (ev′i dənt lē, ev′i dent′lē) *adv.*

e′vil (ē′vəl) *adj.* **1.** wicked. **2.** harmful. **3.** unfortunate.

e′vil·do′er *n.* a person who does wrong.

e·vince′ (i vins′) *v.t., v.i.,* **evinced, evincing.** to make evident.

e·vis′cer·ate′ (i vis′ə rāt′) *v.t.,* **-ated, -ating. 1.** to remove the entrails of. **2.** to deprive of vital parts.

e·voke′ (i vōk′) *v.t.,* **evoked, evoking. 1.** to call up (memories, feelings, etc.). **2.** to draw forth. —**ev′o·ca′tion** (ev′ə kā′shən) *n.* —**e·voc′a·tive** (i vok′-) *adj.*

e·volve′ (i volv′) *v.t., v.i.,* **evolved, evolving.** to develop gradually.

ewe (yōō) *n.* a female sheep.

ew′er (yōō′ər) *n.* a wide-mouthed pitcher.

ex- a prefix meaning: **1.** out of or from, **2.** utterly or thoroughly. **3.** former.

ex. example.

ex·ac′er·bate′ (ig zas′ər bāt′, ek-sas′-) *v.t.,* **-bated, -bating.** to make more severe or violent.

ex·act′ (ig zakt′) *adj.* **1.** precise; accurate. —*v.t.* **2.** to demand; require.

ex·act′ing *adj.* **1.** severe in making demands. **2.** requiring close attention.

ex·ag′ger·ate′ (ig zaj′ə rāt′) *v.t.,* **-ated, -ating.** to make seem larger, better, etc., than is really true.

ex·alt′ (ig zôlt′) *v.t.* **1.** to raise in rank, power, etc. **2.** to praise. —**ex′al·ta′tion,** *n.*

ex·am′ (ig zam′) *n. Informal.* an examination.

ex·am′i·na′tion *n.* **1.** an examining or being examined. **2.** a test of knowledge or qualifications.

ex·am′ine (-in) *v.t.,* **-ined, -ining. 1.** to inspect carefully. **2.** to test the knowledge or qualifications of. —**ex·am′in·er,** *n.*

ex·am′ple (ig zam′pəl) *n.* **1.** one of a number of things that shows what others of the same kind are like. **2.** a person or thing worthy of being imitated. **3.** a fact illustrating a rule or method.

ex·as′per·ate′ (ig zas′pə rāt′) *v.t.,* **-ated, -ating.** to irritate or provoke greatly.

ex′ca·vate′ (eks′kə vāt′) *v.t.,* **-vated, -vating. 1.** to make a hole in. **2.** to dig out (earth, sand, etc.) **3.** to expose by digging. —**ex·ca·va′tion,** *n.* —**ex′ca·va′tor,** *n.*

ex·ceed′ (ik sēd′) *v.t.* **1.** to go beyond the limits of. **2.** to be superior to.

ex·ceed′ing·ly *adv.* extremely.

ex·cel′ (ik sel′) *v.i., v.t.,* **-celled, -celling.** to be superior (to); surpass (others).

ex′cel·lence (ek′sə ləns) *n.* the fact or state of excelling.

ex′cel·lent *adj.* remarkably good.

ex·cept′[1] (ik sept′) *prep.* **1.** not including; but. —*conj.* **2.** with the exception that; only. —Usage. See ACCEPT.

ex·cept/² (ik sept/) v.t. **1.** to leave out. —v.i. **2.** to object.

ex·cep/tion·a·ble adj. liable to exception.

ex·cep/tion·al adj. unusual, esp. superior.

ex/cerpt n. (ek/sûrpt) **1.** a passage or quotation, as from a book. —v.t. (ik sûrpt/, ek/sûrpt) **2.** to take (an excerpt) from a book, film, etc.

ex·cess/ n. (ik ses/) **1.** the amount by which one thing exceeds another. **2.** a surplus. —adj. (ek/ses) **3.** being more than necessary, usual, or desirable.

ex·ces/sive adj. too much.

ex·change/ (iks chānj/) v., -changed, -changing, n. —v.t. **1.** to give or receive in place of something else. —n. **2.** an act of exchanging. **3.** something exchanged. **4.** a place where commodities or securities are exchanged. **5.** a central office.

ex·cheq/uer (iks chek/ər) n. a treasury, as of a nation.

ex/cise¹ (ek/sīz) n. a tax on certain goods.

ex·cise/² (ik sīz/) v.t., -cised, -cising. to remove by cutting.

ex·cite/ (ik sīt/) v.t., -cited, -citing. **1.** to stir up the feelings of. **2.** to arouse (feelings). **3.** to stir to action. —**ex·cit/a·ble**, adj. —**ex·cite/ment**, n.

ex·claim/ (ik sklām/) v.i., v.t. to cry out. —**ex·cla·ma/tion** (ek/sklə mā/shən) n.

ex·clude/ (ik sklōōd/) v.t., -cluded, -cluding. **1.** to shut or keep out. **2.** to omit. —**ex·clu/sion**, n.

ex·clu/sive (ik sklōō/siv) adj. **1.** excluding others. **2.** single or sole. **3.** expensive or fashionable.

ex/com·mu/ni·cate/ (eks/kə myōō/-ni kāt/) v.t., -cated, -cating. to cut off from communion or membership of a church. —**ex/com·mu/ni·ca/tion**, n.

ex·co/ri·ate/ (ik skôr/ē āt/) v.t., -ated, -ating. to denounce.

ex/cre·ment (ek/skrə mənt) n. bodily waste.

ex·cres/cence (ik skres/əns) n. an abnormal outgrowth. —**ex·cres/cent**, adj.

ex·crete/ (ik skrēt/) v.t., -creted, -creting. to eliminate (waste) from the body. —**ex·cre/tion**, n.

ex·cru/ci·at/ing (ik skrōō/shē ā/-ting) adj. **1.** causing intense suffering. **2.** intense or extreme.

ex/cul·pate/ (ek/skul pāt/, ik skul/-pāt) v.t., -pated, -pating. to free of blame. —**ex/cul·pa/tion**, n.

ex·cur/sion (ik skûr/zhən) n. a short trip.

ex·cuse/ v., -cused, -cusing, n. —v.t. (ik skyōōz/) **1.** to pardon or forgive. **2.** to be a justification of. **3.** to release from an obligation. —n. (ik skyōōs/) **4.** a reason for excusing or being excused.

ex/e·crate/ (ek/si krāt/) v.t., -crated, -crating. **1.** to detest utterly. **2.** to denounce.

ex/e·cute/ (ek/si kyōōt/) v.t., -cuted, -cuting. **1.** to accomplish. **2.** to perform; do. **3.** to put to death according to law. —**ex/e·cu/tion**, n. —**ex/e·cu/tion·er**, n.

ex·ec/u·tive (ig zek/yə tiv) n. **1.** a person with administrative or managerial power in an organization. —adj. **2.** of or having such power.

ex·ec/u·tor (-tər) n. a person named to carry out a will.

ex·ec/u·trix/ (-triks) n. a woman named to carry out a will.

ex·em/plar (ig zem/plər, -plär) n. a model or pattern.

ex·em/pla·ry (-plə rē) adj. worthy of imitation.

ex·em/pli·fy/ (-plə fī/) v.t., -fied, -fying. to serve as an example of.

ex·empt/ (ig zempt/) v.t. **1.** to free from an obligation. —adj. **2.** not subject to an obligation. —**ex·emp/tion**, n.

ex/er·cise/ (ek/sər sīz/) n., v., -cised, -cising. —n. **1.** physical or mental exertion to increase skill or strength. **2.** a putting into action or use. **3.** exercises, a traditional ceremony. —v.t. **4.** to put through exercises. **5.** to put into action. —v.i. **6.** to take bodily exercise.

ex·ert/ (ig zûrt/) v.t. **1.** to put forth. **2.** to put in force. **3.** to put (oneself) into vigorous effort. —**ex·er/tion**, n.

ex·hale/ (eks hāl/) v.i., v.t., -haled, -haling. to breathe out.

ex·haust/ (ig zôst/) v.t. **1.** to use up completely. **2.** to tire out. —n. **3.** the steam or gases ejected from an engine. —**ex·haus/tion**, n.

ex·haus/tive adj. thorough.

ex·hib/it (ig zib/it) v.t. **1.** to show; display for public view. —n. **2.** an act of exhibiting. **3.** something exhibited. —**ex/hi·bi/tion** (ek/sə-bish/ən) n. —**ex·hib/i·tor**, n.

ex/hi·bi/tion·ism (-bish/ə niz/əm) n. a desire or tendency to display oneself. —**ex/hi·bi/tion·ist**, n.

ex·hil/a·rate/ (ig zil/ə rāt/) v.t., -rated, -rating. **1.** to make lively. **2.** to make joyful. —**ex·hil/a·ra/tion**, n.

ex·hort/ (ig zôrt/) v.t., v.i. to advise

or urge earnestly. —**ex′hor·ta′tion** (eg′zŏr tā′shən) *n.*

ex·hume′ (ig zōōm′, -zyōōm′) *v.t.,* **-humed, -huming.** to dig up (a dead body).

ex′i·gen·cy (ek′si jən sē) *n., pl.* **-cies.** 1. a state of urgency. 2. **exigencies,** things needed urgently. —**ex′i·gent,** *adj.*

ex′ile (eg′zīl, ek′sīl) *n., v.,* **-iled, -iling.** —*n.* 1. enforced absence from one's country. 2. an exiled person. —*v.t.* 3. to send into exile.

ex·ist′ (ig zist′) *v.i.* 1. to be. 2. to live. 3. to continue to be or live. —**ex·ist′ence,** *n.* —**ex·ist′ent,** *adj.*

ex·is·ten′tial (eg′zi sten′shəl, ek′si-) *adj.* of existence.

ex·is·ten′tial·ism *n.* a philosophy that stresses personal liberty and responsibility. —**ex·is·ten′tial·ist,** *n., adj.*

ex′it (eg′zit, ek′sit) *n.* 1. a way out. 2. a departure, as that of an actor from the stage. —*v.i., v.t.* 3. to leave.

exo- a prefix meaning outside.

ex′o·crine (ek′sə krin, -krīn′) *adj.* 1. secreting externally through a duct. 2. of glands that secrete externally through a duct.

ex′o·dus (ek′sə dəs) *n.* 1. a mass departure or emigration. 2. **Exodus,** the departure of the Israelites from Egypt under Moses.

ex′ of·fi′ci·o′ (eks′ ə fish′ē ō′) *adv., adj.* because of one's office.

ex·on′er·ate′ (ig zon′ə rāt′) *v.t.,* **-ated, -ating.** to clear of blame.

ex·or′bi·tant (ig zôr′bi tənt) *adj.* excessive, esp. in cost.

ex′or·cise′ (ek′sôr sīz′, -sər-) *v.t.,* **-cised, -cising.** 1. to expel (an evil spirit) by prayer. 2. to free (a person or place) of evil spirits. —**ex′or·cism,** *n.* —**ex′or·cist,** *n.*

ex′o·sphere′ (ek′sō sfēr′) *n.* the highest region of the atmosphere.

ex·ot′ic (ig zot′ik) *adj.* 1. foreign. 2. strikingly unusual.

ex·pand′ (ik spand′) *v.t., v.i.* to increase in size, scope, or extent; spread out. —**ex·pan′sion,** *n.*

ex·panse′ (ik spans′) *n.* a broad, unbroken space.

ex·pan′sive (ik span′siv) *adj.* 1. extensive; wide. 2. warm and cordial.

ex·pa′ti·ate′ (ik spā′shē āt′) *v.i.,* **-ated, -ating.** to talk or write at length.

ex·pa′tri·ate′ *v.,* **-ated, -ating,** *n., adj.* —*v.t., v.i.* (eks pā′trē āt′) 1. to banish; exile. 2. to withdraw (oneself) from residence in one's native country. —*n.* (-it) 3. an expatriated person. —*adj.* (-it) 4. dwelling in a foreign land.

ex·pect′ (ik spekt′) *v.t.* 1. to look for as likely to happen or arrive; look forward to. 2. to consider as due or proper. —**ex·pect′an·cy,** *n.* —**ex·pect′ant,** *adj.*

ex′pec·ta′tion *n.* 1. the act or state of expecting. 2. something expected.

ex·pec′to·rate′ (-rāt′) *v.i., v.t.,* **-rated, -rating.** to spit, esp. to cough and spit up mucus. —**ex·pec′to·rant,** *n.*

ex·pe′di·ent (ik spē′dē ənt) *adj.* 1. fit or suitable for a purpose. 2. marked by self-interest. —*n.* 3. a handy means to an end. —**ex·pe′di·en·cy,** *n.*

ex′pe·dite′ (ek′spi dīt′) *v.t.,* **-dited, -diting.** to speed up.

ex′pe·di′tion (-dish′ən) *n.* 1. a journey for a specific purpose. 2. a group on such a journey.

ex′pe·di′tious *adj.* prompt.

ex·pel′ (ik spel′) *v.t.,* **-pelled, -pelling.** to drive or force away.

ex·pend′ (-spend′) *v.t.* 1. to use up. 2. to spend. —**ex·pend′i·ture,** *n.*

ex·pend′a·ble *adj.* 1. available for spending. 2. capable of being sacrificed if necessary.

ex·pense′ (ik spens′) *n.* 1. cost. 2. a cause of spending. 3. **expenses,** charges incurred through business.

ex·pen′sive *adj.* costing much.

ex·pe′ri·ence (ik spēr′ē əns) *n., v.,* **-enced, -encing.** —*n.* 1. something lived through. 2. observation of events as they occur. 3. knowledge gained from such things. —*v.t.* 4. to have experience of.

ex·per′i·ment *n.* (ik sper′ə mənt) 1. an act or operation to discover something unknown or to test a supposition, principle, etc. —*v.i.* (-ment′) 2. to conduct an experiment. —**ex·per′i·men′tal** (-men′tl) *adj.* —**ex·per′i·men·ta′tion,** *n.*

ex′pert *n.* (eks′pûrt) 1. a person with special skill in a particular field. —*adj.* (ek′spûrt; *also* ik spûrt′) 2. skilled. —**ex·pert′ly,** *adv.*

ex′per·tise′ (ek′spər tēz′) *n.* expert skill or knowledge.

ex′pi·ate′ (ek′spē āt′) *v.t.,* **-ated, -ating.** to make amends for. —**ex′pi·a′tion,** *n.*

ex·pire′ (ik spī°r′) *v.i.,* **-pired, -piring.** 1. to come to an end. 2. to die. 3. to breathe out.

ex·plain′ (ik splān′) *v.t.* 1. to make clear. 2. to account for. —*v.i.* 3. to give an explanation. —**ex′pla·na′tion,** *n.* —**ex·plan′a·to·ry** (ik-splan′-) *adj.*

ex′ple·tive (ek′spli tiv) *n.* an often profane exclamation.

ex′pli.cate′ (-kāt′) v.t., -cated, -cat-
ing. to explain in detail.
ex.plic′it (ik splis′it) adj. fully and
clearly expressed.
ex.plode′ (ik splōd′) v., -ploded,
-ploding. —v.i. 1. to burst suddenly, noisily, and violently. 2. to
burst forth violently or emotionally. —v.t. 3. to cause to explode.
—ex.plo′sion, n. —ex.plo′sive,
adj., n.
ex′ploit¹ (eks′ploit) n. a notable
deed.
ex.ploit′² (ik sploit′) v.t. to use, esp.
selfishly or for profit. —ex′ploi.
ta′tion, n. —ex.ploit′a.tive, adj.
ex.plore′ (ik splôr′) v., -plored,
-ploring. —v.t. 1. to travel through
(an area) to learn about it. 2. to
examine. —v.i. 3. to engage in exploring. —ex′plo.ra′tion (ek′splə-
rā′shən) n. —ex.plor′a.to′ry, adj.
—ex.plor′er, n.
ex.po′nent (ik spō′nənt or, esp. for
2, ek′spō nənt) n. 1. a person who
promotes an idea, cause, etc. 2.
Math. a symbol placed to the upper right of another to indicate the
power to which the latter is to be
raised.
ex.port′ v.t. (ik spōrt′) 1. to send to
other countries. —n. (ek′spōrt) 2.
something exported.
ex.pose′ (ik spōz′) v.t., -posed,
-posing. 1. to lay open, as to danger. 2. to reveal. 3. to allow light
to reach (film).
ex′po.si′tion (ek′spə zish′ən) n. 1.
a large public exhibition. 2. the act
of explaining. 3. an explanation.
ex.pos′i.to′ry (ik spoz′i tôr′ē) adj.
serving to expound or explain.
ex′ post′ fac′to (eks′ pōst′ fak′tō)
adj. made or done after the fact;
retroactive.
ex.pos′tu.late′ (ik spos′chə lāt′)
v.i., -lated, -lating. to protest or re-
monstrate.
ex.po′sure (-spō′zhər) n. 1. an exposing or being exposed. 2. the action of exposing film to the light.
3. position with regard to weather
or direction.
ex.pound′ (ik spound′) v.t. to explain in detail.
ex.press′ (ik spres′) v.t. 1. to put
into words. 2. to make known, as
feelings or thoughts. 3. to squeeze
out. —adj. 4. clearly stated. 5.
moving fast, with few stops, as a
train. —n. 6. an express train.
ex.pres′sion n. 1. the act of expressing. 2. a word or phrase. 3. a
look or intonation that expresses
feeling.
ex.pres′sion.ism n. (often cap.) a
style in art, literature, etc., stressing

the subjective element in experience and the symbolic aspects of
objects. —ex.pres′sion.ist, n., adj.
—ex.pres′sion.is′tic, adj.
ex.pres′sive (ik spres′iv) adj. 1.
meaningful. 2. serving to express.
ex.press′way′ n. a road for high-
speed traffic.
ex.pro′pri.ate′ (eks prō′prē āt′) v.t.,
-ated, -ating. to take for public
use.
ex.pul′sion (ik spul′shən) n. the act
of driving out or the state of being
driven out.
ex.punge′ (ik spunj′) v.t., -punged,
-punging. to wipe out; obliterate.
ex′pur.gate′ (ek′spər gāt′) v.t.,
-gated, -gating. to remove objectionable parts from.
ex′qui.site (ik skwiz′it, ek′skwi zit)
adj. delicately beautiful.
ex′tant (ek′stənt, ik stant′) adj. still
existing.
ex.tem′po.ra′ne.ous (ik stem′pə-
rā′nē əs) adj. done, spoken, or performed without preparation. —ex.
tem′po.re (ik stem′pə rē) adv.
ex.tend′ (ik stend′) v.t. 1. to
stretch or draw out. 2. to make
longer or larger. 3. to offer. —ex.
ten′sion, n.
ex.ten′sive (-siv) adj. far-reaching.
ex.tent′ (-stent′) n. the space or
degree to which a thing extends;
scope.
ex.ten′u.ate′ (-sten′yŏŏ āt′) v.t.,
-ated, -ating. to make seem less serious.
ex.te′ri.or (-stēr′ē ər) adj. 1. being
on the outer side or the outside.
—n. 2. an exterior surface.
ex.ter′mi.nate′ (-stûr′mə nāt′) v.t.,
-nated, -nating. to get rid of by destroying. —ex.ter′mi.na′tion, n.
—ex.ter′mi.na′tor, n.
ex.ter′nal (-nl) adj. 1. outer. 2. acting from without. 3. superficial.
ex.tinct′ (ik stingkt′) adj. 1. no
longer existing. 2. no longer active. —ex.tinc′tion, n.
ex.tin′guish (-sting′gwish) v.t. 1. to
put out, as a fire. 2. to wipe out.
—ex.tin′guish.er, n.
ex′tir.pate′ (ek′stər pāt′) v.t.,
-pated, -pating. to destroy totally.
ex.tol′ (ik stōl′) v.t., -tolled, -toll-
ing. to praise highly.
ex.tort′ (ik stôrt′) v.t. to get
(money, information, etc.) by force
or threat. —ex.tor′tion, n.
ex.tor′tion.ate (ik stôr′shə nit) adj.
excessive.
ex′tra (ek′strə) adj. 1. more than is
usual, expected, or necessary; additional. —n. 2. an additional feature
or expense. —adv. 3. in excess of
what is usual.

extra- a prefix meaning outside or beyond.

ex·tract/ v.t. (ik strakt/) **1.** to pull or draw out with effort. **2.** to copy out, as from a book. **3.** to obtain by pressure, distillation, or use of chemicals. —n. (ek/strakt) **4.** something extracted. **5.** an excerpt. —**ex·trac/tion,** n.

ex/tra·cur·ric/u·lar (-kə rik/yə lər) adj. outside a regular curriculum.

ex/tra·dite/ (ek/strə dīt/) v.t., **-dited, -diting.** to deliver (a fugitive or criminal) to another state. —**ex/-tra·di/tion** (-dish/ən) n.

ex/tra·le/gal adj. beyond the authority of law.

ex/tra·mu/ral (-myŏŏr/əl) adj. involving members of more than one school.

ex·tra/ne·ous (ik·strā/nē əs) adj. not essential.

ex·traor/di·nar/y (ik strôr/dn er/ē) adj. unusual or remarkable. —**ex·traor/di·nar/i·ly,** adv.

ex·trap/o·late (ik strap/ə lāt/) v.t., v.i., **-lated, -lating.** to infer (an unknown) from something known. —**ex·trap/o·la/tion,** n.

ex/tra·sen/so·ry (ek/strə sen/sə rē) adj. beyond one's physical senses.

ex/tra·ter·res/tri·al adj. **1.** being or from outside the earth's limits. —n. **2.** an extraterrestrial being.

ex·trav/a·gant (ik strav/ə gənt) adj. **1.** spending more than is necessary or wise. **2.** excessive. —**ex·trav/a·gance,** n.

ex·trav/a·gan/za (-gan/zə) n. a lavish production.

ex·treme/ (ik strēm/) adj. **1.** going well beyond the moderate or ordinary. **2.** outermost. **3.** very great or intense. —n. **4.** one of two things that are complete opposites. **5.** an extreme degree, act, or condition.

ex·trem/ism n. a tendency to take extreme measures, esp. in politics.

ex·trem/i·ty (ik strem/i tē) n., pl. **-ties. 1.** the farthest part. **2.** an arm or leg. **3.** a condition of extreme need, danger, etc.

ex/tri·cate/ (ek/stri kāt/) v.t., **-cated, -cating.** to disentangle.

ex·trin/sic (ik strin/sik, -zik) adj. **1.** not inherent or essential. **2.** being or coming from without; external.

ex/tro·vert/ (ek/strə vûrt/) n. an outgoing person. —**ex/tro·ver/-sion,** n. —**ex/tro·vert/ed,** adj.

ex·trude/ (ik strōōd/) v.t., **-truded, -truding.** to force or press out.

ex·u/ber·ant (ig zōō/bər ənt) adj. **1.** uninhibitedly enthusiastic. **2.** abundant. —**ex·u/ber·ance,** n.

ex·ude/ (ig zōōd/, ik sōōd/) v.i., v.t., **-uded, -uding. 1.** to ooze or cause to ooze out. **2.** to radiate.

ex·ult/ (ig zult/) v.i. to rejoice triumphantly. —**ex·ult/ant,** adj. —**ex/ul·ta/tion,** n.

eye (ī) n., v., **eyed, eying** or **eye-ing.** —n. **1.** the organ of sight. **2.** sight; vision. **3.** an attentive look. **4.** something like an eye. —v.t. **5.** to look at.

eye/ball/ n. **1.** the globe of the eye. —v.t. **2.** Informal. to examine.

eye/brow/ n. the ridge and line of short hairs over the eye.

eye/ful/ (ī/fŏŏl) n., pl. **-fuls. 1.** a thorough view. **2.** Informal. an attractive person.

eye/glass/es n.pl. a pair of corrective lenses in a frame.

eye/lash/ n. one of the short hairs at the edge of the eyelid.

eye/let (ī/lit) n. a small hole, as for a lace.

eye/lid/ n. the movable skin covering the eye.

eye/o/pen·er n. something that causes sudden enlightenment.

eye/sight/ n. **1.** the power or act of seeing. **2.** one's range of vision.

eye/sore/ n. something unpleasant to look at.

eye/tooth/ n. a canine tooth in the upper jaw.

eye/wash/ n. **1.** a soothing solution for the eyes. **2.** nonsense.

eye/wit/ness n. a person who has seen an event and can give an account of it.

ey/rie (âr/ē, ēr/ē) n., pl. **-ries.** the lofty nest of a bird of prey; aerie.

F

F, f (ef) n. the sixth letter of the English alphabet.

F 1. Fahrenheit. **2.** female.

f. 1. feet. **2.** female. **3.** folio. **4.** foot. **5.** franc.

FAA Federal Aviation Administration.

fa/ble (fā/bəl) n. a short tale used to teach a moral.

fab/ric (fab/rik) n. **1.** a cloth made by weaving or knitting fibers. **2.** framework.

fab/ri·cate/ (-ri kāt/) v.t., **-cated, -cating. 1.** to construct. **2.** to invent; make up.

fab/u·lous (-yə ləs) adj. **1.** almost impossible to believe. **2.** marvelous.

fa·çade' (fə säd') *n.* **1.** the front of a building. **2.** outward appearance.

face (fās) *n.*, *v.*, **faced, facing.** —*n.* **1.** the front part of the head. **2.** an expression on the face. **3.** outward appearance. **4.** a grimace. **5.** the surface. **6.** the most important side; front. —*v.t.* **7.** to look toward. **8.** to confront directly or bravely. **9.** to put a facing on. —*v.i.* **10.** to turn or be turned. **11.** to have the face in a certain direction. **12. face up to, a.** to admit. **b.** to meet courageously. —*Idiom.* **13. face to face, a.** opposite one another. **b.** confronting one another. **14. to one's face,** in one's presence.

face'less *adj.* lacking identity.

face'-lift' *n.* **1.** surgery to eliminate facial sagging and wrinkles. **2.** renovation to improve the appearance of a building.

face'-sav'ing *adj.* saving one's prestige or dignity.

fac'et (fas'it) *n.* **1.** one of the surfaces of a cut gem. **2.** an aspect.

fa·ce'tious (fə sē'shəs) *adj.* not meant to be taken seriously.

face' val'ue (fās' val'yōō *for 1;* fās' val'yōō *for 2*) *n.* **1.** the value printed on the face of a stock, bond, etc. **2.** apparent value.

fa'cial (fā'shəl) *adj.* **1.** of or for the face. —*n.* **2.** a treatment to beautify the face.

fac'ile (fas'il) *adj.* **1.** easily done. **2.** superficial.

fa·cil'i·tate' (fə sil'i tāt') *v.t.*, **-tated, -tating.** to make easier. —**fa·cil'i·ta'tion,** *n.* —**fa·cil'i·ta'tor,** *n.*

fa·cil'i·ty (-i tē) *n.*, *pl.* **-ties. 1.** something designed or installed for a specific purpose. **2.** ease.

fac'ing (fā'sing) *n.* **1.** a decorative or protective outer layer. **2.** a lining applied along an edge of a garment.

fac·sim'i·le (fak sim'ə lē) *n.* **1.** an exact copy. **2.** a fax.

fact (fakt) *n.* **1.** something known to exist or to have happened. **2.** something known to be true. —**fac'tu·al,** *adj.*

fac'tion (fak'shən) *n.* **1.** a group within a larger group. **2.** dissension. —**fac'tion·al,** *adj.*

fac'tious (-shəs) *adj.* causing strife.

fac'tor (-tər) *n.* **1.** one of the elements contributing to a result. **2.** one of two numbers multiplied.

fac'to·ry (-tə rē) *n.*, *pl.* **-ries.** a place where goods are manufactured.

fac'ul·ty (-əl tē) *n.*, *pl.* **-ties. 1.** a special ability. **2.** one of the powers of the mind or body. **3.** the teaching staff of a school.

fad (fad) *n.* a temporary fashion.

fade (fād) *v.*, **faded, fading.** —*v.i.* **1.** to lose freshness, color, or vitality. **2.** to disappear gradually. —*v.t.* **3.** to cause to fade.

fag¹ (fag) *v.*, **fagged, fagging,** *n.* —*n.* **1.** *Slang.* a cigarette. **2.** a drudge. —*v.t.* **3.** to exhaust.

fag² (fag) *n. Slang: Usu. Disparaging and Offensive.* (a term used to refer to a male homosexual.)

fag'ot (fag'ət) *n.* a bundle of sticks bound together and used as fuel.

Fahr'en·heit' (far'ən hīt') *adj.* of a temperature scale in which water freezes at 32° and boils at 212°.

fail (fāl) *v.i.* **1.** to be unsuccessful. **2.** to weaken. **3.** to stop functioning. **4.** to die away. **5.** to become bankrupt. —*v.t.* **6.** to be unsuccessful in the performance of. **7.** to be of no help to. —**fail'ure,** *n.*

fail'ing *n.* **1.** a defect or fault. —*prep.* **2.** in the absence of.

fail'-safe' *adj.* ensured against failure of a mechanical system, nuclear reactor, etc.

faint (fānt) *adj.* **1.** lacking brightness or clarity. **2.** feeling weak or dizzy. —*v.i.* **3.** to lose consciousness briefly.

faint'heart'ed *adj.* lacking courage.

fair¹ (fâr) *adj.* **1.** free from bias or injustice. **2.** proper under the rules. **3.** moderately good or large. **4.** (of the weather) fine. **5.** having light-colored skin and hair. **6.** attractive. **7.** likely; promising. —**fair'ly,** *adv.* —**fair'ness,** *n.*

fair² (fâr) *n.* **1.** a usu. competitive exhibition, as of farm products. **2.** an exhibition and sale of goods.

fair'y (fâr'ē) *n.*, *pl.* **fairies. 1.** a tiny supernatural being. **2.** *Slang: Disparaging and Offensive.* (a contemptuous term used to refer to a male homosexual.)

fair'y·land' *n.* the imaginary realm of fairies.

fair'y tale' *n.* **1.** a story, usu. for children, about magical creatures. **2.** an improbable story.

faith (fāth) *n.* **1.** confidence or trust. **2.** religious belief. **3.** loyalty.

faith'ful *adj.* **1.** steady in allegiance or affection. **2.** reliable. **3.** true to fact or standard.

fake (fāk) *v.*, **faked, faking,** *n.*, *adj.* —*v.t.* **1.** to make an imitation of to mislead others. —*v.i.* **2.** to pretend. —*n.* **3.** an imitation intended to be passed off as genuine. **4.** one who fakes. **5.** not genuine.

fa·kir' (fə kēr') *n.* a Muslim or Hindu ascetic or mendicant considered to be a wonder-worker.

fal′con (fôl′kən, fal′-) *n.* a swift bird of prey.

fall (fôl) *v.,* **fell** (fel) **fallen, falling,** *n.* —*v.i.* **1.** to come down suddenly to a lower position; drop. **2.** to decline. **3.** to lose position. **4.** to be overthrown. **5.** to pass into a specified condition. **6.** to die in combat. —*n.* **7.** an act or instance of falling. **8.** autumn. **9.** surrender or capture, as of a city.

fal′la·cy (fal′ə sē) *n., pl.* **-cies. 1.** a false belief. **2.** an unsound argument. —**fal·la′cious** (fə lā′shəs) *adj.*

fall′ guy′ *n. Slang.* **1.** an easy victim. **2.** a scapegoat.

fal′li·ble (fal′ə bəl) *adj.* liable to be mistaken. —**fal′li·bil′i·ty,** *n.*

fall′ing-out′ *n., pl.* **fallings-out, falling-outs.** a quarrel.

fal·lo′pi·an tube′ or **Fal·lo′pi·an tube′** (fə lō′pē ən) *n.* either of a pair of long ducts in the female abdomen that transport ova from the ovary to the uterus.

fall′out′ *n.* **1.** radioactive particles carried by the air. **2.** an incidental outcome or product.

fal′low (fal′ō) *adj.* (of land) plowed and left unseeded for a season.

false (fôls) *adj.,* **falser, falsest. 1.** not true or correct. **2.** not loyal. **3.** deceptive. **4.** not genuine. —**false′hood,** *n.* —**fal′si·fy,** *v.t.*

fal·set′to (fôl set′ō) *n., pl.* **-tos.** an artificially high-pitched voice.

fal′ter (fôl′tər) *v.i.* **1.** to hesitate or waver. **2.** to speak hesitantly. **3.** to move unsteadily.

fame (fām) *n.* widespread reputation; renown. —**famed,** *adj.*

fa·mil′iar (fə mil′yər) *adj.* **1.** commonly known or seen. **2.** well-acquainted. **3.** intimate. **4.** too personal. —**fa·mil′i·ar′i·ty** (-ē ar′i tē, -yar′-) *n.* —**fa·mil′iar·ize′,** *v.t.*

fam′i·ly (fam′ə lē, fam′lē) *n., pl.* **-lies. 1.** parents and their children as a group. **2.** a group of persons descended from a common ancestor. **3.** a set of relatives. **4.** a group of related things or individuals. —**fa·mil′ial** (fə mil′yəl) *adj.*

fam′ily leave′ *n.* an unpaid leave of absence from work in order to take care of a baby or an ailing family member.

fam′ine (fam′in) *n.* extreme scarcity of food.

fam′ish (fam′ish) *v.t., v.i.* to suffer or cause to suffer extreme hunger.

fa′mous (fā′məs) *adj.* widely known; renowned.

fa′mous·ly *adv.* very well.

fan¹ (fan) *n., v.,* **fanned, fanning.** —*n.* **1.** a device, either waved in the hand or operated electrically, that produces a current of air. **2.** something resembling a fan. —*v.t.* **3.** to cause air to blow upon. **4.** to spread out from a central point.

fan² (fan) *n.* an enthusiastic devotee.

fa·nat′ic (fə nat′ik) *n.* **1.** a person who is excessively devoted to a cause. —*adj.* **2.** excessively devoted to a cause. —**fa·nat′i·cal,** *adj.* —**fa·nat′i·cism** (-ə siz′əm) *n.*

fan′ci·er (fan′sē ər) *n.* a person with a special interest in something, as in breeding animals.

fan′ci·ful *adj.* **1.** imaginary or unreal. **2.** imaginative or inventive.

fan′cy (fan′sē) *n., pl.* **-cies,** *adj.,* **-cier, -ciest,** *v.,* **-cied, -cying.** —*n.* **1.** imagination. **2.** the thing imagined. **3.** a whim. **4.** a liking. —*adj.* **5.** of high quality. **6.** decorative. —*v.t.* **7.** to imagine. **8.** to believe without being certain. **9.** to crave.

fan′cy-free′ *adj.* free from emotional ties, esp. from love.

fan′fare′ *n.* **1.** a flourish played on trumpets. **2.** a showy display.

fang (fang) *n.* a long, sharp tooth.

fan′ny *n., pl.* **-nies.** *Informal.* the buttocks.

fan·ta′sia (fan tā′zhə) *n.* a fanciful musical work.

fan′ta·size′ (-tə sīz′) *v.,* **-sized, -sizing.** —*v.i.* **1.** to have fanciful ideas. —*v.t.* **2.** to create in one's daydreams.

fan·tas′tic (-tas′tik) *adj.* **1.** wonderful and strange. **2.** excellent.

fan′ta·sy (-tə sē, -zē) *n., pl.* **-sies. 1.** imagination. **2.** a daydream or illusion. **3.** a fantasia.

FAQ (fak, ef′ā′kyōō′) *n., pl.* **FAQs, FAQ's.** *Computers.* frequently asked questions: a document that introduces newcomers to a topic.

far (fär) *adv., adj.,* **farther, farthest.** —*adv.* **1.** at or to a great distance or remote point. —*adj.* **2.** distant. —*Idiom.* **3. by far,** very much. **4. far and away,** without doubt. **5. far and wide,** everywhere. **6. so far,** up to a certain point.

far′a·way′ (fär′ə wā′) *adj.* **1.** distant. **2.** preoccupied; dreamy.

farce (färs) *n.* **1.** light comedy. **2.** a foolish or ridiculous display; pretense. —**far′ci·cal,** *adj.*

fare (fâr) *n., v.,* **fared, faring.** —*n.* **1.** the price charged a passenger for travel. **2.** a paying passenger. **3.** food. —*v.i.* **4.** to get along.

fare′well′ (fâr′wel′) *interj.* **1.** goodbye. —*n.* **2.** good wishes at parting. **3.** a departure. —*adj.* **4.** final.

far′-fetched′ *adj.* not reasonable or probable.

far′-flung′ *adj.* **1.** extending over a

great distance. **2.** widely distributed.

fa·ri′na (fə rē′nə) n. flour or grain cooked as a cereal.

farm (färm) n. **1.** a tract of land on which crops and livestock are raised. —v.t. **2.** to cultivate (land). —v.i. **3.** to operate a farm. **4. farm out,** to assign (work) to another. —**farm′er,** n. —**farm′ing,** n.

farm′yard′ n. an enclosed area surrounded by farm buildings.

far′-off′ adj. distant.

far′-reach′ing adj. extending far in influence or effect.

far′row (far′ō) n. **1.** a litter of pigs. —v.i. **2.** to give birth to young pigs.

far′-sight′ed (fär′sī′tid, -sī′-) adj. **1.** seeing distant objects best. **2.** planning for the future.

far′ther (fär′thər) adv., compar. of **far. 1.** at or to a greater distance or extent. —adj., compar. of **far. 2.** more distant. **3.** additional.
—**Usage.** FARTHER is used to indicate physical distance: Is it much farther to the hotel? FURTHER is used to refer to additional time, amount, or abstract ideas: I would rather not talk about this further. But both FARTHER and FURTHER are often used for distance of any kind: Here is the solution; look no farther/further. His study of the novel reaches farther/further than any earlier one.

far′thest (-thist) adv., superl. of **far. 1.** at or to the greatest distance. —adj., superl. of **far. 2.** most distant.

fas′ci·nate′ (fas′ə nāt′) v.t., -nated, -nating. **1.** to attract and hold, as by a unique power or a special quality. **2.** to arouse the interest of. —**fas′ci·na′tion,** n.

fas′cism (fash′iz əm) n. a dictatorship emphasizing aggressive nationalism, militarism, and racism. —**fas′cist,** n., adj. —**fa·scis′tic,** adj.

fash′ion (fash′ən) n. **1.** a prevailing style. **2.** manner. —v.t. **3.** to give shape to; make.

fash′ion·a·ble adj. in or using the latest style. —**fash′ion·a·bly,** adv.

fast¹ (fast) adj. **1.** acting or moving with speed. **2.** done in little time. **3.** (of a timepiece) ahead of the correct time. **4.** firmly fixed or held. —adv. **5.** quickly. **6.** firmly; tightly.

fast² (fast) v.i. **1.** to go without food or certain kinds of food. —n. **2.** the act of fasting. **3.** the period of fasting.

fas′ten (fas′ən) v.t. **1.** to fix or at-

tach firmly or securely. —v.i. **2.** to become fastened. —**fas′ten·er,** n.

fast′-food′ adj. specializing in food that is prepared and served quickly.

fas·tid′i·ous (fa stid′ē əs, fə-) adj. **1.** highly critical and demanding. **2.** marked by excessive care.

fast′ness n. a stronghold.

fat (fat) n., adj., **fatter, fattest.** —n. **1.** an oily substance found in animal tissue and many plant seeds. —adj. **2.** plump. **3.** containing fat. **4.** profitable. **5.** thick. —**fat′ten,** v.t., v.i. —**fat′ty,** adj.

fa′tal (fāt′l) adj. causing death or disaster. —**fa′tal·ly,** adv.

fa′tal·ism n. the belief that all events are determined by fate. —**fa′tal·ist,** n.

fa·tal′i·ty (fā tal′i tē, fə-) n., pl. -ties. a death caused by a disaster.

fate (fāt) n. **1.** the power believed to control events; destiny. **2.** something that happens unavoidably.

fat′ed adj. subject to fate; destined.

fate′ful adj. having important or disastrous consequences.

fa′ther (fä′thər) n. **1.** a male parent. **2.** a founder. **3.** a title for a priest. **4. Father,** God. —v.t. **5.** to beget. —**fa′ther·hood′,** n. —**fa′ther·ly,** adj.

fa′ther-in-law′ n., pl. **fathers-in-law.** the father of one's spouse.

fa′ther·land′ n. **1.** one's native country. **2.** the land of one's ancestors.

fath′om (fath′əm) n. **1.** a unit of nautical measure equal to 6 feet (1.8 m). —v.t. **2.** to understand.

fa·tigue′ (fə tēg′) n., v., -tigued, -tiguing. —n. **1.** weariness from exertion. **2.** the weakening of material from repeated stress. **3.** nonmilitary labor by military personnel. —v.t., v.i. **4.** to weary with exertion.

fat′ty ac′id n. an organic acid found in animal and vegetable fats.

fat′u·ous (fach′ōō əs) adj. foolish or silly.

fau′cet (fô′sit) n. a device for controlling the flow of liquid from a pipe; tap.

fault (fôlt) n. **1.** a defect or flaw. **2.** responsibility for something wrong. **3.** an error. **4.** a fracture in a body of rock. —**Idiom. 5. at fault,** blameworthy. —**faul′ty,** adj.

faun (fôn) n. an ancient Roman deity, part man and part goat.

fau′na (fô′nə) n., pl. -nas, -nae (-nē). the animals or animal life of a particular region or period.

faux pas′ (fō pä′) n. an embarrassing social error.

fa′vor (fā′vər) n. 1. a kind act. 2. approval. 3. preferential treatment. —v.t. 4. to regard with favor. 5. to prefer. 6. to show favor to. 7. to be favorable to. 8. to resemble. —**Idiom.** 9. **in favor of, a.** in support of. **b.** to the advantage of.

fa′vor·a·ble adj. 1. showing approval. 2. pleasing. 3. advantageous.

fa′vor·ite n. 1. a person or thing preferred. 2. the one most likely to win. —adj. 3. preferred.

fa′vor·it·ism (-ə tiz′əm) n. preference shown toward certain persons.

fawn[1] (fôn) n. a young deer.

fawn[2] (fôn) v.i. to try to win favor by being servile.

fax (faks) n. 1. a method or device for sending documents by telephone. 2. an item sent in this way. —v.t. 3. to send by fax.

faze (fāz) v.t., **fazed, fazing.** to cause to be disconcerted.

FBI Federal Bureau of Investigation.

FCC Federal Communications Commission.

FDA Food and Drug Administration.

FDIC Federal Deposit Insurance Corporation.

fear (fēr) n. 1. an unpleasant feeling aroused by the threat of danger, evil, or pain. 2. awe, esp. toward God. —v.t. 3. to be afraid of. 4. to hold in awe. —**fear′ful,** adj.

fea′si·ble (fē′zə bəl) adj. 1. capable of being done. 2. likely. —**fea′si·bil′i·ty,** n.

feast (fēst) n. 1. a large elaborate meal. 2. a religious celebration. —v.i., v.t. 3. to have or entertain with a feast.

feat (fēt) n. a remarkable achievement.

feath′er (feth′ər) n. 1. one of the structures consisting of a central shaft with fine interlocking barbs that form the principal covering of birds. —v.t. 2. to cover or provide with feathers. —**feath′er·y,** adj.

fea′ture (fē′chər) n., v., **-tured, -turing.** —n. 1. one of the parts of the face. 2. a noticeable characteristic. 3. a special attraction. 4. a full-length motion picture. 5. a prominent story, article, etc. —v.t. 6. to give prominence to. 7. to be a feature or mark of.

Feb. February.

Feb′ru·ar′y (feb′roo er′ē, feb′yoo-) n., pl. **-aries.** the second month of the year. —**Pronunciation.** The second pronunciation for FEBRUARY shown above, with the first (r) replaced by (y), occurs because neighboring sounds that are alike tend to become different. This word also conforms to the pattern (-yoo er′ē) by analogy with the pronunciation of the first month of the year, January. Although the pronunciation of FEBRUARY with (y) is often criticized, both pronunciations are used by educated speakers and are considered standard.

fe′ces (fē′sēz) n.pl. excrement.

feck′less (fek′lis) adj. 1. incompetent. 2. irresponsible and lazy.

fe′cund (fē′kund) adj. fertile.

fed. 1. federal. 2. federated. 3. federation.

fed′er·al (fed′ər əl) adj. of a system in which states unite under a central government distinct from the individual governments of the separate states.

fed′er·ate′ (fed′ə rāt′) v.t., v.i., **-ated, -ating.** to unite under a central authority.

fe·do′ra (fi dôr′ə) n. a soft felt hat with a curved brim.

fee (fē) n. a sum charged, as for professional service.

fee′ble (fē′bəl) adj., **-bler, -blest.** 1. weak. 2. ineffective.

feed (fēd) v., **fed** (fed) **feeding,** n. —v.t. 1. to give food to. 2. to provide as food. 3. to supply for growth or operation. —v.i. 4. (esp. of animals) to eat. —n. 5. food for livestock. —**feed′er,** n.

feed′back′ n. a reaction or response.

feel (fēl) v., **felt** (felt) **feeling,** n. —v.t. 1. to perceive or examine by touch. 2. to be conscious of. 3. to have a physical sensation of. —v.i. 4. to have perception by touch. 5. to have a sensation of being. —n. 6. a quality that is perceived by touching. 7. the sense of touch.

feel′er n. 1. a proposal or remark designed to elicit reaction. 2. an organ of touch, as an antenna.

feign (fān) v.t. to pretend.

feint (fānt) n. 1. a deceptive move. —v.i., v.t. 2. to make or deceive with a feint.

feist′y (fī′stē) adj., **-ier, -iest.** 1. lively. 2. ready to argue or fight.

fe·lic′i·tate′ (fə lis′i tāt′) v.t., **-tated, -tating.** to congratulate.

fe·lic′i·tous (-təs) adj. 1. well chosen for an occasion. 2. enjoyable.

fe·lic′i·ty n., pl. **-ties.** 1. happiness. 2. a capacity for skill or grace.

fe′line (fē′līn) adj. 1. of or like cats. —n. 2. an animal of the cat family.

fell (fel) v.t. to cut or strike down.

fel′low (fel′ō) n. 1. a man. 2. a companion. 3. an equal. 4. a graduate student who receives a stipend. **5.** a member of a learned or professional group.

fel′low•ship′ *n.* **1.** companionship. **2.** the position or stipend of an academic fellow.

fel′on (fel′ən) *n.* a person who has committed a felony.

fel′o•ny *n., pl.* **-nies.** a serious crime, as burglary or murder. —**fe• lo′ni•ous** (fə lō′nē əs) *adj.*

felt (felt) *v.* **1.** pt. and pp. of **feel.** —*n.* **2.** a fabric made by pressing fibers together. —*adj.* **3.** of felt.

fem. 1. female. **2.** feminine.

fe′male (fē′māl) *adj.* **1.** belonging to the sex that conceives and bears young. —*n.* **2.** a female person or animal.

fem′i•nine (fem′ə nin) *adj.* of, like, or suitable for women. —**fem′i• nin′i•ty,** *n.*

fem′i•nism (-i niz′əm) *n.* support of social, political, and economic rights for women equal to those of men. —**fem′i•nist,** *adj., n.*

fe′mur (fē′mər) *n.* the thighbone.

fen (fen) *n.* swampy ground.

fence (fens) *n., v.,* **fenced, fencing.** —*n.* **1.** a barrier around an open area, used to prevent entrance or mark a boundary. **2.** a person who receives and disposes of stolen goods. —*v.t.* **3.** to enclose or separate with a fence. **4.** to sell to a fence. —*v.i.* **5.** to practice the sport of fencing. **6.** to try to avoid giving direct answers.

fenc′ing *n.* **1.** the sport of fighting with foils. **2.** fences or material for fences.

fend (fend) *v.* **1. fend off,** to ward off. **2. fend for,** to try to manage.

fend′er *n.* a metal part mounted over the wheel of a vehicle.

fen′nel (fen′l) *n.* a plant with seeds used for flavoring.

fe′ral (fēr′əl, fer′-) *adj.* in a wild state; not tamed.

fer′ment *v.i., v.t.* (fər ment′) **1.** to undergo or cause to undergo fermentation. —*n.* (fûr′ment) **2.** a substance causing fermentation. **3.** agitation; excitement.

fer′men•ta′tion *n.* a chemical change caused by an organic substance, as yeast, mold, or bacteria, producing effervescence and heat.

fern (fûrn) *n.* a nonflowering plant with feathery leaves.

fe•ro′cious (fə rō′shəs) *adj.* savagely fierce or cruel. —**fe•roc′i•ty** (fə-ros′i tē) *n.*

fer′ret (fer′it) *n.* **1.** a kind of weasel. —*v.t.* **2.** to search out and bring to light.

Fer′ris wheel′ (fer′is) *n.* an amusement ride consisting of a large upright wheel with seats suspended from its rim.

fer′rous (fer′əs) *adj.* of or containing iron.

fer′ry (fer′ē) *n., pl.* **-ries,** *v.,* **-ried, -rying.** —*n.* **1.** a boat used for transporting persons or things across a river, bay, etc. **2.** a place where ferries operate. —*v.t.* **3.** to carry over a fixed route in a boat. —*v.i.* **4.** to go in a ferry.

fer′tile (fûr′tl) *adj.* **1.** producing abundantly. **2.** able to bear young. **3.** capable of developing.

fer′ti•lize′ *v.t.,* **-lized, -lizing. 1.** to render (an egg) capable of development through union with a sperm. **2.** to enrich, as soil. —**fer′ti•li•za′• tion,** *n.* —**fer′ti•liz′er,** *n.*

fer′vent (fûr′vənt) *adj.* having or showing intensity of feeling; ardent. —**fer′ven•cy** *n.*

fer′vid (-vid) *adj.* **1.** vehement; impassioned. **2.** very hot.

fes′ter (fes′tər) *v.i.* **1.** to form pus. **2.** to rankle, as bitterness.

fes′ti•val (fes′tə vəl) *n.* **1.** a time of celebration. **2.** a program of cultural events or entertainment.

fes′tive *adj.* **1.** of or suitable for a feast or festival. **2.** joyous.

fes•tiv′i•ty (-tiv′i tē) *n., pl.* **-ties.** a festive celebration.

fes•toon′ (fe stōon′) *n.* **1.** a chain of foliage hung between two points. —*v.t.* **2.** to decorate with or as if with festoons.

fetch (fech) *v.t.* **1.** to go and bring back. **2.** to cause to come. **3.** to sell for.

fetch′ing *adj.* charming.

fete (fāt, fet) *n., v.,* **feted, feting.** —*n.* **1.** a festive celebration or entertainment. **2.** a religious festival. —*v.t.* **3.** to honor with a fete.

fet′id (fet′id, fē′tid) *adj.* stinking.

fe′tish (fet′ish, fē′tish) *n.* **1.** an object believed to have magical power. **2.** something to which one is irrationally devoted. —**fet′ish• ism,** *n.*

fet′lock (fet′lok′) *n.* **1.** the part of a horse's leg behind the hoof. **2.** the tuft of hair on this part.

fet′ter (fet′ər) *n.* **1.** a chain or shackle put on the feet. **2. fetters,** anything that restrains. —*v.t.* **3.** to put fetters on. **4.** to restrain.

fet′tle (fet′l) *n.* condition.

fe′tus (fē′təs) *n.* the young of an animal in the womb or egg. —**fe′• tal,** *adj.*

feud (fyōod) *n.* **1.** lasting hostility. —*v.i.* **2.** to engage in a feud.

feu′dal•ism (fyōod′l iz′əm) *n.* a social and economic system in medieval Europe by which land was held by vassals in exchange for military and other service given to overlords. —**feu/dal,** adj.

fe/ver (fē/vər) n. an abnormally high body temperature. —**fe/ver.ish,** adj.

few (fyōō) adj. **1.** not many. —n. **2.** a small number. —pron. **3.** a small number of persons or things. —**Usage.** See LESS.

fey (fā) adj. **1.** strange; whimsical. **2.** supernatural; enchanted.

fez (fez) n., pl. **fezzes.** a flat-topped cone-shaped felt hat.

ff 1. folios. **2.** (and the) following (pages, verses, etc.).

fi/an.cé/ (fē/än sā/, fē än/sā) n. a man engaged to be married.

fi/an.cée/ n. a woman engaged to be married.

fi.as/co (fē as/kō) n., pl. **-cos, -coes.** a complete and humiliating failure.

fi/at (fē/ät, fī/ät) n. an authoritative order or decree.

fib (fib) n., v., **fibbed, fibbing.** —n. **1.** a mild lie. —v.i. **2.** to tell a fib.

fi/ber (fī/bər) n. **1.** a fine threadlike piece, as of cotton. **2.** matter or material formed of fibers. **3.** plant matter that is bulky and stimulates the action of the intestines. **4.** essential character, quality, or strength. —**fi/brous,** adj. —**fi/broid,** adj.

fi/ber.glass/ n. a material composed of fine glass fibers.

fi/ber op/tics n. the technology of sending light and images through glass or plastic fibers. —**fi/ber-op/tic,** adj.

fib/ril.la/tion (fib/rə lā/shən, fī/brə-) n. rapid and irregular contractions of the heart muscle.

fib/u.la (fib/yə lə) n., pl. **-lae** (-lē) **-las.** the outer and thinner of the two bones extending from the knee to the ankle.

FICA (fī/kə, fē/-) Federal Insurance Contributions Act.

fick/le (fik/əl) adj. not constant.

fic/tion (fik/shən) n. **1.** the class of literature consisting of works of imaginative narration in prose form. **2.** works of this class, as novels or short stories. **3.** something made up. —**fic/tion.al,** adj.

fic.ti/tious (-tish/əs) adj. **1.** false. **2.** of or consisting of fiction.

fid/dle (fid/l) n., v., **-dled, -dling.** —n. **1.** a violin. —v.i. **2.** to play the fiddle. **3.** to move the hands nervously.

fid/dle.sticks/ interj. (an exclamation of impatience, disbelief, etc.).

fi.del/i.ty (fi del/i tē, fī-) n., pl. **-ties. 1.** faithfulness. **2.** accuracy.

fidg/et (fij/it) v.i. **1.** to move about restlessly. —n. **2. fidgets,** restlessness.

field (fēld) n. **1.** a piece of open ground, as for cultivation. **2.** an area where sports are played. **3.** an area of activity or interest. **4.** an area rich in a natural resource. **5.** all the competitors in a contest.

field/ day/ 1. a day devoted to outdoor sports or contests. **2.** a chance for unrestricted enjoyment.

fiend (fēnd) n. **1.** an evil spirit. **2.** a cruel person. **3.** Informal. an addict. —**fiend/ish,** adj.

fierce (fērs) adj., **fiercer, fiercest. 1.** wild and savage. **2.** violent. **3.** eager or intense. —**fierce/ly,** adv.

fier/y (fī²r/ē, fī/ə rē) adj., **-ier, -iest. 1.** of or like fire. **2.** ardent or passionate.

fi.es/ta (fē es/tə) n. a festival.

fife (fīf) n. a small high-pitched flute.

fif/teen/ (fif/tēn/) n., adj. ten plus five. —**fif.teenth/,** adj., n.

fifth (fifth) adj. **1.** next after the fourth. —n. **2.** a fifth part or the fifth one of a series.

fifth/ col/umn n. a group of people who work for the enemy within a country at war.

fifth/ wheel/ n. one that is unnecessary or unwanted.

fif/ty (fif/tē) n., adj. ten times five. —**fif/ti.eth,** adj., n.

fig (fig) n. the pear-shaped fruit of a semitropical tree.

fig. (fig) **1.** figurative. **2.** figure.

fight (fīt) n., v., **fought, fighting.** —n. **1.** a battle. **2.** a struggle. **3.** an angry argument. —v.i. **4.** to engage in battle. **5.** to strive. —v.t. **6.** to contend with in battle. **7.** to carry on. —**fight/er,** n.

fig/ment (fig/mənt) n. something imagined.

fig/ur.a.tive (-yər ə tiv) adj. of the nature of or involving a figure of speech; metaphorical. —**fig/ur.a.tive.ly,** adv.

fig/ure n., v., **-ured, -uring.** —n. **1.** a written symbol of a number. **2.** an amount or value. **3.** a written symbol other than a letter. **4.** the form or shape of something. **5.** a pattern —v.t. **6.** to calculate. **7.** Informal. to conclude or think. —v.i. **8.** to work with numerical figures. **9.** to be or appear. **10. figure out,** to solve.

fig/ure.head/ n. **1.** a leader who has no real power. **2.** a carved figure on the bow of a ship.

fig/ure of speech/ n. an expression, as a metaphor, in which words are used in a nonliteral sense.

fig′ur•ine′ (-yə rēn′) *n.* a miniature statue.

fil′a•ment (fil′ə mənt) *n.* **1.** a very fine thread. **2.** a threadlike conductor in a light bulb.

filch (filch) *v.t.* to steal.

file¹ (fīl) *n., v.,* **filed, filing.** —*n.* **1.** a container in which papers are arranged in order. **2.** a collection of papers arranged in order. **3.** a collection of computer data stored by name. **4.** a line of persons or things. —*v.t.* **5.** to arrange or keep in a file. —*v.i.* **6.** to march in a line.

file² (fīl) *n., v.,* **filed, filing.** —*n.* **1.** a metal tool having rough surfaces for smoothing metal, wood, etc. —*v.t.* **2.** to smooth or reduce with a file.

fil′i•al (fil′ē əl) *adj.* of or befitting a son or daughter.

fil′i•bus′ter (fil′ə bus′tər) *n.* **1.** the use of long speeches to prevent or delay the adoption of legislation. —*v.i., v.t.* **2.** to impede (legislation) by making long speeches.

fil′i•gree′ (-i grē′) *n.* delicate ornamental work of fine wires.

fill (fil) *v.t.* **1.** to make full. **2.** to spread through completely. **3.** to occupy. **4.** to supply the requirements of. **5.** to stop up. —*v.i.* **6.** to become full. —*n.* **7.** a full supply. **8.** material for building up the level of an area.

fil•let′ (fi lā′) *n.* **1.** a narrow strip, esp. of meat or fish. —*v.t.* **2.** to cut (meat or fish) into a fillet.

fil′ly (fil′ē) *n., pl.* **-lies.** a young female horse.

film (film) *n.* **1.** a thin layer or coating. **2.** a thin sheet or strip with a photographically sensitive coating. **3.** a motion picture. —*v.t.* **4.** to cover with a film. **5.** to make a film of. —*v.i.* **6.** to become covered with a film. —**film′y,** *adj.*

film′strip′ *n.* a length of film containing still pictures for projecting on a screen.

fil′ter (fil′tər) *n.* **1.** a device or substance for straining the impurities out of liquid or gas. **2.** a screen that modifies light or sound waves. —*v.t., v.i.* **3.** to remove by or pass through a filter. —**fil•tra′tion,** *n.*

filth (filth) *n.* **1.** disgusting dirt. **2.** obscenity. —**filth′y,** *adj.*

fin (fin) *n.* a winglike or paddlelike organ on aquatic animals.

fi•na′gle (fi nā′gəl) *v.i., v.t.,* **-gled, -gling.** to practice or obtain by trickery.

fi′nal (fīn′l) *adj.* **1.** last. **2.** conclu-sive. —**fi•nal′i•ty** (fī nal′i tē) *n.* —**fi′nal•ize′,** *v.t.*

fi•na′le (fi nä′lē) *n.* the concluding part of something.

fi•nance′ (fi nans′, fī′nans) *n., v.,* **-nanced, -nancing.** —*n.* **1.** the management of funds. **2. finances,** monetary resources. —*v.t.* **3.** to supply with money. —**fi•nan′cial,** *adj.*

fin′an•cier′ (fin′ən sēr′, fī′nən-) *n.* a person who manages large financial operations.

finch (finch) *n.* a small songbird with a short bill.

find (fīnd) *v.,* **found** (found) **finding,** *n.* —*v.t.* **1.** to come upon. **2.** to locate or obtain. **3.** to learn. **4.** to recover (something lost). —*v.i.* **5.** (of a jury) to decide. —*n.* **6.** something found; a discovery.

fine¹ (fīn) *adj.,* **finer, finest,** *adv.* —*adj.* **1.** excellent. **2.** in small particles. **3.** delicate; very thin. **4.** highly skilled. **5.** refined. —*adv.* **6.** very well.

fine² (fīn) *n., v.,* **fined, fining.** —*n.* **1.** a sum of money exacted as a penalty. —*v.t.* **2.** to subject to a fine.

fine′ art′ *n.* painting, sculpture, music, etc.

fin′er•y *n.* fine or showy clothing.

fi•nesse′ (fi ness′) *n.* **1.** delicacy or subtlety of performance or skill. **2.** tact in handling a situation.

fin′ger (fing′gər) *n.* **1.** any of the five parts extending from the end of the hand. —*v.t.* **2.** to touch with the fingers. —**fin′ger•nail′,** *n.*

fin′ger•print′ *n.* **1.** an impression of the markings of the surface of the fingertip. —*v.t.* **2.** to take or record the fingerprints of.

fin′ger•tip *n.* the tip of a finger.

fin′ick•y (fin′i kē) *adj.* excessively particular.

fi′nis (fin′is, fē nē′, fī′nis) *n.* the end.

fin′ish (fin′ish) *v.t.* **1.** to bring to an end. **2.** to come to the end of. **3.** to use completely. **4.** to destroy. **5.** to complete in detail. **6.** to put a coating on. —*v.i.* **7.** to come to an end. —*n.* **8.** the final part. **9.** something that completes a thing. **10.** a surface coating or treatment.

fi′nite (fī′nīt) *adj.* having bounds or limits. —**fi′nite•ly,** *adv.*

fiord (fyôrd, fē ôrd′) *n.* a fjord.

fir (fûr) *n.* a cone-bearing evergreen tree of the pine family.

fire (fī°r) *n., v.,* **fired, firing.** —*n.* **1.** the light, heat, and flame given off by something burning. **2.** a burning mass. **3.** a destructive burning. **4.** brilliance. **5.** anger or excitement. —*v.t.* **6.** to set on fire. **7.** to fill with excitement. **8.** to shoot (a weapon). **9.** to bake in a kiln. **10.** to dismiss from a job. —*v.i.* **11.** to catch fire. **12.** to discharge a weapon.

fire′arm′ *n.* a gun.

fire′bomb′ *n.* **1.** an incendiary bomb. —*v.t.* **2.** to attack with firebombs.

fire′crack′er *n.* a small firework that makes a loud noise.

fire′fight′er *n.* a person who fights destructive fires.

fire′fly′ *n., pl.* **-flies.** a nocturnal beetle that produces light.

fire′place′ *n.* the part of a chimney that opens into a room and in which fuel is burned.

fire′plug′ *n.* a hydrant with water for fighting fires.

fire′proof′ *adj.* resistant to destruction by fire.

fire′trap′ *n.* a building likely to burn and difficult to escape from.

fire′works′ *n.pl.* devices ignited for a display of light or a loud noise.

firm¹ (fûrm) *adj.* **1.** not soft or yielding when pressed. **2.** securely fixed. **3.** resolute. —*v.t., v.i.* **4.** to make or become firm.

firm² (fûrm) *n.* a business organization.

fir′ma·ment (fûr′mə mənt) *n.* the sky.

first (fûrst) *adj.* **1.** being before all others. —*adv.* **2.** before all others. **3.** for the first time. —*n.* **4.** the person or thing that is first. **5.** the winning rank in a competition.

first′ aid′ *n.* emergency treatment.

first′ class′ *n.* **1.** the highest class or grade. **2.** the most expensive class in travel. **3.** the class of mail sealed against inspection. —**first′-class′,** *adj.*

first′hand′ or **first′-hand′** *adj., adv.* from the first or original source.

first′-rate′ *adj.* **1.** of the highest quality. —*adv.* **2.** very well.

fis′cal (fis′kəl) *adj.* of public revenues.

fish (fish) *n., pl.* **fish, fishes,** *v.* —*n.* **1.** a cold-blooded aquatic vertebrate having gills and fins. —*v.t.* **2.** to try to catch fish in. —*v.i.* **3.** to try to catch fish. **4.** to search carefully.

fisher·man′ *n.* a person who fishes.

fish′y *adj.,* **-ier, -iest. 1.** like a fish, esp. in taste or smell. **2.** of questionable character; dubious.

fis′sion (fish′ən) *n.* a splitting, esp. of the nucleus of an atom. —**fis′-sion·a·ble,** *adj.*

fis′sure (fish′ər) *n.* a narrow opening.

fist (fist) *n.* a closed hand.

fist′ful (-fŏol) *n., pl.* **-fuls.** a handful.

fit¹ (fit) *adj.,* **fitter, fittest,** *v.,* **fitted, fitting,** *n.* —*adj.* **1.** suitable. **2.** proper. **3.** healthy. —*v.t.* **4.** to be suitable or proper for. **5.** to be of the right size or shape for. **6.** to equip. —*v.i.* **7.** to be suitable or proper. **8.** to be of the right size or shape. —*n.* **9.** the manner in which a thing fits. —**fit′ness,** *n.*

fit² (fit) *n.* a sudden attack of illness or emotion.

fit′ful *adj.* irregular.

fit′ting *adj.* **1.** appropriate. —*n.* **2.** the process of trying on clothes that are being made or altered. **3.** anything provided as standard equipment.

five (fīv) *n., adj.* four plus one.

fix (fiks) *v.t.* **1.** to repair or mend. **2.** to make fast, steady, or definite. **3.** to direct or hold steadily. **4.** to establish.

fix·a′tion (fik sā′shən) *n.* an obsession.

fixed *adj.* not changing.

fix′ture (-chər) *n.* **1.** something securely fixed in place. **2.** a person or thing that is firmly established.

fizz (fiz) *v.i.* **1.** to make a hissing sound; effervesce. —*n.* **2.** a fizzing sound. **3.** an effervescent drink.

fiz′zle (fiz′əl) *v.,* **-zled, -zling,** *n.* —*v.i.* **1.** to hiss weakly. **2.** to fail. —*n.* **3.** a failure.

fjord (fyôrd, fē ôrd′) *n.* a narrow arm of the sea.

FL Florida.

fl. 1. (he or she) flourished. **2.** fluid.

Fla. Florida.

flab (flab) *n.* loose, excessive flesh.

flab′ber·gast′ (flab′ər gast′) *v.t.* to astound.

flab′by (flab′ē) *adj.,* **-bier, -biest.** not firm. —**flab′bi·ness,** *n.*

flac′cid (flak′sid, flas′id) *adj.* soft and limp.

flag¹ (flag) *n., v.,* **flagged, flagging.** —*n.* **1.** a piece of cloth with distinctive colors or design that is used as a symbol. **2.** something used to attract attention. —*v.t.* **3.** to place a flag on. **4.** to signal with a flag.

flag² (flag) *n.* a plant with long, sword-shaped leaves.

flag³ (flag) *v.i.,* **flagged, flagging.** to lose energy or interest.

flag′el·late′ (flaj′ə lāt′) *v.t.,* **-lated, -lating.** to whip; flog.

flag′on (flag′ən) *n.* a container for

liquids, esp. one with a handle, spout, and cover.

fla/grant (flā/grənt) *adj.* shockingly noticeable.

flag/ship/ *n.* **1.** a ship carrying the commander of a fleet. **2.** the most important one of a group.

flail (flāl) *n.* **1.** an instrument for threshing grain. —*v.t., v.i.* **2.** to strike or strike at, as with a flail.

flair (flâr) *n.* **1.** aptitude; talent. **2.** smartness of style or manner.

flak (flak) *n.* **1.** antiaircraft fire. **2.** critical or hostile reaction.

flake (flāk) *n., v.,* **flaked, flaking.** —*n.* **1.** a small, thin piece. —*v.i.* **2.** to peel off or form into flakes.

flak/y *adj.,* **-ier, -iest. 1.** of or like flakes. **2.** lying or coming off in flakes. **3.** *Slang.* eccentric; odd.

flam•boy/ant (flam boi/ənt) *adj.* showy; colorful.

flame (flām) *n., v.,* **flamed, flaming.** —*n.* **1.** tongue-shaped burning gas or vapor. —*v.i.* **2.** to burn with or glow like flames.

fla•min/go (flə ming/gō) *n., pl.* **-gos, -goes.** a tall wading bird with pink feathers and long legs.

flam/ma•ble (flam/ə bəl) *adj.* easily set on fire. —**flam/ma•bil/i•ty,** *n.*

flange (flanj) *n.* a projecting rim.

flank (flangk) *n.* **1.** a side, esp. the side of the body between the ribs and hip. —*v.t.* **2.** to stand or be placed at the side of.

flan/nel (flan/l) *n.* a soft wool or cotton fabric.

flap (flap) *v.,* **flapped, flapping,** *n.* —*v.i., v.t.* **1.** to swing or cause to swing loosely and noisily. **2.** to move up and down. —*n.* **3.** a flapping movement. **4.** something flat attached at one side and hanging loosely. **5.** *Informal.* a state of nervous excitement.

flare (flâr) *v.,* **flared, flaring,** *n.* —*v.i.* **1.** to blaze with a sudden unsteady flame. **2.** to burst out in sudden anger. **3.** to spread outward. —*n.* **4.** a signal fire. **5.** a sudden burst. **6.** an outward curve.

flare/up/ *n.* a sudden outburst or outbreak.

flash (flash) *n.* **1.** a sudden burst of light. **2.** a sudden, brief outburst. **3.** an instant. **4.** a brief news dispatch. —*v.i.* **5.** to break into sudden light. **6.** to appear suddenly. **7.** to move rapidly. —*v.t.* **8.** to cause to flash. **9.** to show briefly. **10.** to display ostentatiously.

flash/back/ *n.* an earlier event inserted out of order in a story.

flash/bulb/ *n.* a bulb giving a burst of light for photography.

flash/light/ *n.* a portable battery-powered light.

flash/y *adj.,* **-ier, -iest.** showy and tasteless.

flask (flask) *n.* a flat metal or glass bottle.

flat¹ (flat) *adj.,* **flatter, flattest,** *n.* —*adj.* **1.** level. **2.** horizontal. **3.** not thick. **4.** absolute. **5.** lacking flavor or effervescence. **6.** not shiny. **7.** *Music.* **a.** lowered a half tone in pitch. **b.** below an intended pitch. —*n.* **8.** something flat. **9.** a flat surface. **10.** *Music.* a sign indicating that a note is lowered a half tone. —**flat/ten,** *v.t., v.i.*

flat² (flat) *n.* an apartment.

flat/bed/ *n.* a truck with a trailer platform open on all sides.

flat/car/ *n.* a railroad car without sides or top.

flat/fish/ *n.* a fish with a broad, flat body, as a flounder.

flat/foot/ *n., pl.* **-feet** for 1b, **-foots** for 2. **1. a.** a condition in which the arch of the foot is flattened. **b.** Usu. **flatfeet.** feet with flattened arches. **2.** *Slang.* a police officer.

flat/-out/ *adj. Informal.* **1.** using full speed, resources, etc. **2.** downright.

flat/ter (flat/ər) *v.t.* **1.** to praise insincerely or excessively. **2.** to show favorably. —**flat/ter•y,** *n.*

flat/u•lent (flach/ə lənt) *adj.* **1.** having an accumulation of gas in the intestines. **2.** inflated and empty; pompous. —**flat/u•lence,** *n.*

flat/ware/ *n.* table utensils.

flaunt (flônt) *v.t.* to display boldly.

fla/vor (flā/vər) *n.* **1.** the distinctive taste of something. —*v.t.* **2.** to give flavor to. —**fla/vor•ing,** *n.*

flaw (flô) *n.* a defect or weakness. —**flawed,** *adj.* —**flaw/less,** *adj.*

flax (flaks) *n.* a plant with blue flowers that is cultivated for its edible, oil-producing seeds and for its fiber, used for making linen. —**flax/en,** *adj.*

flay (flā) *v.t.* **1.** to strip the skin from. **2.** to criticize severely.

flea (flē) *n.* a small, bloodsucking, leaping insect.

flea/ mar/ket *n.* a market, often outdoors, where used articles, antiques, etc., are sold.

fleck (flek) *n.* **1.** a small bit or spot. —*v.t.* **2.** to mark with flecks.

fledg/ling (flej/ling) *n.* a young bird that has just grown flight feathers.

flee (flē) *v.i., v.t.,* **fled** (fled) **fleeing.** to run away (from).

fleece (flēs) *n., v.,* **fleeced, fleecing.** —*n.* **1.** the woolly covering of a sheep. —*v.t.* **2.** to swindle. —**fleec/y,** *adj.*

fleet[1] (flēt) *n.* an organized group of ships, aircraft, or road vehicles.

fleet[2] (flēt) *adj.* swift.

fleet'ing *adj.* temporary.

flesh (flesh) *n.* **1.** the muscle and fat of an animal body. **2.** the body. **3.** the soft part of a fruit or vegetable. —**flesh'y,** *adj.*

flew (flōō) *v.* a pt. of **fly.**

flex (fleks) *v.t., v.i.* **1.** to bend. **2.** to tighten (a muscle) by contraction.

flex'i·ble *adj.* **1.** capable of bending. **2.** adaptable.

flick (flik) *n.* **1.** a quick light blow or stroke. —*v.t.* **2.** to strike, remove, or operate with a flick.

flick'er *v.i.* **1.** to burn unsteadily. —*n.* **2.** a flickering light or movement. **3.** a brief occurrence.

fli'er (flī'ər) *n.* **1.** a pilot. **2.** a small circular. Also, **fly'er.**

flight (flīt) *n.* **1.** the act or power of flying. **2.** a trip in an airplane. **3.** a hasty departure. **4.** a series of steps.

flight'less *adj.* incapable of flying.

flight'y *adj.,* **-ier, -iest.** frivolous and irresponsible.

flim'sy (flim'zē) *adj.,* **-sier, -siest.** weak or thin. —**flim'si·ness,** *n.*

flinch (flinch) *v.i.* to draw back; shrink; wince.

fling (fling) *v.,* **flung** (flung) **flinging,** *n.* —*v.t.* **1.** to throw with force, violence, or abandon. **2.** to involve (oneself) vigorously in an undertaking. —*v.i.* **3.** to move with haste or violence. —*n.* **4.** an act of flinging. **5.** a short period of indulgence in pleasure.

flint (flint) *n.* a hard stone that strikes sparks. —**flint'y,** *adj.*

flip (flip) *v.,* **flipped, flipping,** *n., adj.,* **flipper, flippest.** —*v.t.* **1.** to turn over by tossing. **2.** to move with a sudden stroke. —*n.* **3.** such a movement. —*adj.* **4.** flippant.

flip'-flop' *n.* **1.** a sudden reversal, as of opinion. **2.** a flat backless rubber shoe with a thong between the first two toes.

flip'pant (flip'ənt) *adj.* frivolously disrespectful or lacking in seriousness. —**flip'pan·cy,** *n.*

flip'per *n.* **1.** a broad flat limb, as of a seal, for swimming. **2.** a paddlelike rubber device worn on the foot as an aid in swimming.

flirt (flûrt) *v.i.* **1.** to act amorously without serious intentions. —*n.* **2.** a person who flirts. —**flir·ta'tion,** *n.* —**flir·ta'tious,** *adj.*

flit (flit) *v.i.,* **flitted, flitting.** to fly or move swiftly and lightly.

float (flōt) *v.i.* **1.** to rest or move gently on liquid, in the air, etc. —*v.t.* **2.** to cause to float. **3.** to issue (stocks, bonds, etc.) in order to raise money. —*n.* **4.** something that floats. **5.** a vehicle carrying a display in a parade. —**flo·ta'tion** (flō tā'shən) *n.*

flock (flok) *n.* **1.** a group of animals, as sheep or birds. **2.** a large group of people. **3.** a church congregation. —*v.i.* **4.** to gather or go in a flock.

floe (flō) *n.* a sheet of floating ice.

flog (flog) *v.t.,* **flogged, flogging.** to beat with a whip or stick.

flood (flud) *n.* **1.** a great overflow of water, esp. over land that is usually dry. **2.** a great outpouring. —*v.t.* **3.** to cover with a flood. —*v.i.* **4.** to become flooded.

flood'light' *n.* **1.** an artificial light that illuminates a large area. —*v.t.* **2.** to illuminate with a floodlight.

floor (flôr) *n.* **1.** the surface of a room on which one walks. **2.** a level in a building. **3.** the bottom surface, as of the ocean. **4.** the right to speak. —*v.t.* **5.** to furnish with a floor. **6.** to confound.

floor'ing *n.* floor covering.

flop (flop) *v.,* **flopped, flopping,** *n.* —*v.i.* **1.** to move or fall in a clumsy manner. **2.** to fail completely. —*n.* **3.** an act of flopping. **4.** a complete failure.

flop'py *adj.,* **-pier, -piest.** limp.

flop'py disk' *n.* a thin plastic disk for storing computer data.

flo'ra (flôr'ə) *n., pl.* **floras, florae** (flôr'ē). the plants or plant life of a particular region or period.

flo'ral *adj.* of flowers.

flor'id (flôr'id) *adj.* **1.** reddish in color. **2.** excessively ornate.

flo'rist *n.* a person who sells flowers and plants.

floss (flôs) *n.* **1.** the silky fiber from certain plants. **2.** embroidery thread. **3.** dental floss. —*v.i., v.t.* **4.** to use or clean with dental floss.

flo·til'la (flō til'ə) *n.* a group of small ships.

flot'sam (flot'səm) *n.* wreckage of a ship and its cargo found floating on the water.

flounce[1] (flouns) *v.,* **flounced, flouncing,** *n.* —*v.i.* **1.** to go with exaggerated or impatient movements. —*n.* **2.** a flouncing movement.

flounce[2] (flouns) *n.* a ruffle.

floun'der[1] (floun'dər) *v.i.* to struggle clumsily.

floun'der[2] (floun'dər) *n.* a flat edible fish.

flour (flou[ə]r, flou'ər) *n.* **1.** the finely ground meal of grain. —*v.t.* **2.** to cover with flour.

flour'ish (flûr'ish) *v.i.* **1.** to thrive

fob

or be successful. —*v.t.* **2.** to brandish. —*n.* **3.** a dramatic gesture. **4.** a decoration or embellishment. **5.** an elaborate musical passage.

flout (flout) *v.t., v.i.* to treat with or show scorn; scoff (at).

flow (flō) *v.i.* **1.** to move in a stream. **2.** to proceed smoothly. **3.** to hang loosely. —*n.* **4.** the act or rate of flowing. **5.** something that flows.

flow′ chart′ *n.* a chart showing the steps in a procedure or system.

flow′er (flou′ər) *n.* **1.** the blossom of a plant. **2.** the best part, product, or example. —*v.i.* **3.** to produce flowers. **4.** to develop fully. —**flow′er·y,** *adj.*

flow′er·pot′, *n.* a container in which to grow plants.

flown (flōn) *v.* a pp. of FLY¹.

flu (flōō) *n.* influenza.

fluc′tu·ate′ (fluk′chōō āt′) *v.i.,* **-ated, -ating.** to vary irregularly.

flue (flōō) *n.* a passage for smoke, air, or gas.

flu′ent (flōō′ənt) *adj.* spoken or able to speak with ease. —**flu′en·cy,** *n.*

fluff (fluf) *n.* **1.** light, downy particles. **2.** a soft, light mass. **3.** something light or frivolous. —*v.t.* **4.** to make or become fluffy. **5.** to make a mistake (in).

fluff′y *adj.,* **-ier, -iest. 1.** of, like, or covered with fluff. **2.** light and airy. **3.** frivolous.

flu′id (flōō′id) *n.* **1.** a substance that flows. —*adj.* **2.** flowing. **3.** not rigid.

fluke¹ (flōōk) *n.* **1.** the barbed part of an anchor or a spear. **2.** either half of a whale's tail.

fluke² (flōōk) *n.* a lucky chance.

fluke³ (flōōk) *n.* a flounder.

flume (flōōm) *n.* **1.** a deep, narrow gorge containing a stream. **2.** an artificial channel for water.

flung (flung) *v.* pt. and pp. of **fling.**

flunk (flungk) *v.i., v.t.* to fail, esp. in a course or examination.

flun′ky *n., pl.* **-kies.** a person who does menial work.

fluo·res′cence (flōō res′əns, flô-) *n.* the emission of visible light by a substance upon exposure to external radiation. —**fluo·res′cent,** *adj.*

fluores′cent lamp′ *n.* a tubular electric lamp in which light is produced by the fluorescence of phosphors coating the inside of the tube.

fluor′i·da′tion (flōōr′ə dā′shən, flôr′-) *n.* the addition of fluorides to drinking water to reduce tooth decay.

fluor′ide (-īd) *n.* a chemical compound containing fluorine.

fluor′ine (-ēn) *n.* a nonmetallic chemical element, a yellowish toxic gas.

flur′ry (flûr′ē) *n., pl.* **-ries. 1.** a light shower of snow. **2.** a sudden commotion or excitement.

flush¹ (flush) *n.* **1.** a rosy glow; blush. **2.** a rushing flow of water. **3.** a sudden rise of emotion. **4.** a sensation of heat. —*v.t.* **5.** to wash out with a rush of water. —*v.i.* **6.** to become red in the face.

flush² (flush) *adj.* **1.** even with an adjoining surface. **2.** well supplied. **3.** even with the right or left margin of a page of type.

flus′ter (flus′tər) *v.t.* to confuse and agitate.

flute (flōōt) *n.* **1.** a wind instrument with a high range, consisting of a tube with fingerholes or keys. **2.** a decorative groove. —**flut′ist,** *n.*

flut′ter (flut′ər) *v.i.* **1.** to wave or flap about. **2.** to beat rapidly and irregularly, as the heart. **3.** to be agitated. —*n.* **4.** a fluttering movement. **5.** a state of nervous excitement. —**flut′ter·y,** *adj.*

flux (fluks) *n.* **1.** a flowing. **2.** continuous change. **3.** a substance added to metal to aid in fusion.

fly¹ (flī) *v.,* **flew** (flōō) **flown** (flōn) **flying,** *n., pl.* **flies.** —*v.i.* **1.** to move or be carried through the air, using wings or in an aircraft. **2.** to move swiftly. —*v.t.* **3.** to cause to move through the air or transport by air. **4.** to operate (an aircraft). —*n.* **5.** a flap that conceals fasteners in a garment opening. **6. flies,** the space above a theater stage.

fly² (flī) *n., pl.,* **flies. 1.** a winged insect. **2.** a fishhook designed to resemble an insect.

fly′-blown′ *adj.* tainted; spoiled.

fly′er *n.* a flier.

fly′ing sau′cer *n.* a disk-shaped object reportedly seen flying at high speed and altitude.

fly′leaf′ *n., pl.* **-leaves.** a blank page in the front or back of a book.

fly′wheel′ *n.* a wheel that regulates the speed of machinery.

foal (fōl) *n.* **1.** a young horse or related mammal. —*v.i.* **2.** to give birth to a foal.

foam (fōm) *n.* **1.** a mass of tiny bubbles. **2.** a lightweight spongy material, as rubber or plastic. —*v.i.* **3.** to form foam.

foam′ rub′ber *n.* a spongy rubber used esp. in cushions.

fob¹ (fob) *n.* a watch chain or an ornament on such a chain.

fob² (fob) v., **fobbed, fobbing. fob off,** to dispose of (something inferior) by trickery; palm off.

fo′cus (fō′kəs) n., pl. **-cuses, -ci** (-sī) v., **-cused, -cusing.** —n. 1. a central point, as of attention. 2. a point at which rays meet. 3. the adjustment of an optical device to produce a clear image. —v.t. 4. to bring into focus. 5. to concentrate. —v.i. 6. to become focused. —**fo′cal,** adj.

fod′der (fod′ər) n. food for livestock.

foe (fō) n. an enemy.

fog (fog) n., v., **fogged, fogging.** —n. 1. thick mist. 2. mental confusion. —v.t., v.i. 3. to envelop or become enveloped with fog. —**fog′gy,** adj.

fo′gy (fō′gē) n., pl. **-gies.** an old-fashioned person.

foi′ble (foi′bəl) n. a minor weakness in a person's character.

foil¹ (foil) v.t. to frustrate or thwart.

foil² (foil) n. 1. metal in the form of very thin sheets. 2. a person or thing that makes another seem better by contrast.

foil³ (foil) n. a thin, flexible fencing sword with a blunt point.

foist (foist) v.t. to get a person to accept, buy, etc. (something inferior or undesirable).

fold¹ (fōld) v.t. 1. to bend (paper, cloth, etc.) over upon itself. 2. to bring together and intertwine or cross. 3. to enclose, wrap, or envelop. —v.i. 4. to be folded. 5. to fail, esp. to go out of business. —n. 6. a folded part. 7. a line or crease made by folding.

fold² (fōld) n. 1. an enclosure for sheep. 2. a group sharing common beliefs.

-fold a suffix meaning: 1. having so many parts. 2. times as many.

fold′er n. 1. a folded cover for holding loose papers. 2. a circular.

fo′li•age (fō′lē ij) n. leaves.

fo′lic ac′id (fō′lik, fol′ik) n. one of the B vitamins.

fo′li•o′ (fō′lē ō′) n., pl. **-ios.** 1. a sheet of paper folded once to make two leaves, or four pages, of a book. 2. a book having pages of the largest size. 3. a page number.

folk (fōk) n., pl. **folk** or **folks.** 1. people. 2. an ethnic group. 3. **folks,** Informal. one's relatives. —adj. 4. of the common people.

folk′lore′ n. the traditional customs and beliefs of a people.

folk′ song′ n. a song originating among the common people or a song of similar character written by a known composer.

folk′sy adj., **-sier, -siest.** friendly; informal.

fol′li•cle (fol′i kəl) n. Anatomy. a small cavity, sac, or gland.

fol′low (fol′ō) v.t. 1. to come or go after. 2. to pursue. 3. to conform to or obey. 4. to keep up with and understand. —v.i. 5. to come next after something else. 6. to result.

fol′low•er n. 1. a person who follows. 2. a disciple.

fol′low•ing n. a group of admirers or disciples.

fol′ly (fol′ē) n., pl. **-lies.** foolishness or a foolish action or idea.

fo•ment′ (fō ment′) v.t. to foster or instigate.

fond (fond) adj. 1. affectionate; loving. 2. doting. 3. cherished. 4. **fond of,** having a liking or affection for. —**fond′ly,** adv.

fon′dant (fon′dənt) n. a creamy sugar paste used in candies.

fon′dle (fon′dl) v.t., **-dled, -dling.** to caress.

font¹ (font) n. a basin for baptismal water in a church.

font² (font) n. Printing. a complete set of type of one style.

food (fōōd) n. a substance that is taken into the body to sustain life.

food′ proc′essor n. an appliance for chopping, shredding, or otherwise processing food.

fool (fōōl) n. 1. a silly or stupid person. 2. a court jester. —v.t. 3. to trick. —v.i. 4. to act like a fool. —**fool′ish,** adj.

fool′har′dy adj., **-dier, -diest.** recklessly bold.

fool′proof′ adj. 1. involving no risk or harm. 2. never-failing.

foot (fŏŏt) n., pl. **feet** (fēt) v. —n. 1. the part of the leg on which the body stands. 2. a part similar to a foot. 3. a unit of length equal to 12 inches. 4. the lowest part. 5. a metrical unit in verse. —v.t. 6. to pay. —Idiom. 7. **on foot,** by walking or running.

foot′ball′ n. 1. a game in which two opposing teams of 11 players defend goals at opposite ends of a field. 2. the ball used. 3. Chiefly Brit. rugby or soccer.

foot′hill′ n. a hill at the base of a mountain.

foot′hold′ n. 1. a support for the feet. 2. a firm basis for further progress.

foot′ing n. 1. a support for the foot. 2. a basis. 3. stability.

foot′less adj. having no basis.

foot′lights′ n.pl. the lights at the front of a stage floor.

foot′lock′er n. a small trunk.

foot′loose′ *adj.* free to go or travel about.

foot′man *n.* a male servant.

foot′note′ *n.* a note printed at the bottom of a page.

foot′print′ *n.* a mark left by the foot.

foot′step′ *n.* the setting down of a foot or the sound of this.

foot′stool′ *n.* a low stool for resting the feet.

for (fôr; *unstressed* fər) *prep.* **1.** with the purpose of. **2.** intended to benefit or be used by. **3.** as the price of. **4.** in favor of. **5.** appropriate to. **6.** on behalf of. **7.** during. —*conj.* **8.** because.

for′age (fôr′ij) *n., v.,* **-aged, -aging.** —*n.* **1.** food for horses or cattle. —*v.i.* **2.** to search about.

for′ay (fôr′ā) *n.* **1.** a quick raid. **2.** an attempt.

for·bear′ (fôr bâr′) *v.,* **-bore** (-bôr′) **-borne** (-bôrn′) **-bearing.** —*v.t.* **1.** to refrain from. —*v.i.* **2.** to be patient.

for·bid′ (fər bid′, fôr-) *v.t.,* **-bade** (-bad′, -bād′) or **-bad, -bidden** or **-bid, -bidding. 1.** to order (a person) not to do something. **2.** to prohibit (something). **3.** to prevent.

for·bid′ding *adj.* threatening or discouraging.

force (fôrs) *n., v.,* **forced, forcing.** —*n.* **1.** strength. **2.** violence. **3.** energy. **4.** power to influence or persuade. **5.** a body of military troops or police. —*v.t.* **6.** to compel to do something. **7.** to bring about or obtain by force. **8.** to break open. **9.** to cause (plants) to grow at an increased rate.

for′ceps (fôr′səps, -seps) *n.* a medical instrument for seizing and holding objects.

for′ci·ble (fôr′sə bəl) *adj.* done by force. —**for′ci·bly,** *adv.*

ford (fôrd) *n.* **1.** a place where a body of water may be crossed by wading or driving. —*v.t.* **2.** to cross at a ford. —**ford′a·ble,** *adj.*

fore (fôr) *adj.* **1.** situated in front. **2.** first in place, time, order, or rank. —*adv.* **3.** forward. —*n.* **4.** the front.

fore- a prefix meaning: **1.** before. **2.** front. **3.** preceding. **4.** chief.

fore′arm′ *n.* the part of the arm between the elbow and the wrist.

fore′bear′ *n.* an ancestor.

fore′cast′ *v., n.,* **-cast, -casting,** *n.* —*v.t.* **1.** to predict (a future condition or happening). —*n.* **2.** a prediction.

fore′cas·tle (fōk′səl, fôr′kas/əl) *n.* the forward part of a ship's upper deck.

fore·close′ (-klōz′) *v.,* **-closed, -closing.** —*v.t.* **1.** to take possession of property and keep (a mortgage) from being redeemed because the debt is not being repaid. —*v.i.* **2.** to foreclose a mortgage. —**fore·clo′sure,** *n.*

fore′fa′ther *n.* an ancestor.

fore′fin′ger *n.* the finger next to the thumb.

fore′front′ *n.* **1.** the foremost part. **2.** the leading position.

fore·go′ing *adj.* previous.

fore′ground′ *n.* the part of a scene nearest to the viewer.

fore′hand′ *n.* **1.** in sports, a stroke made with the palm of the hand facing the direction of movement. —*adj.* **2.** made with this stroke.

fore′head (fôr′id, fôr′hed′) *n.* the part of the face above the eyes.

for′eign (fôr′in) *adj.* **1.** of or from another country. **2.** not belonging to the place where found.

fore′man or **-wom′an** or **-per′son** *n., pl.* **-men** or **-women** or **-persons.** the person in charge of a work crew or jury.

fore′most′ *adj., adv.* first in place, rank, or importance.

fo·ren′sic (fə ren′sik) *adj.* of or used in courts of law or in public debate.

fore′play′ *n.* sexual stimulation leading to intercourse.

fore′run′ner *n.* a person or thing that precedes and foreshadows another.

fore·see′ *v.t.,* **-saw, -seen, -seeing.** to see or know in advance. —**fore′sight′,** *n.*

fore·shad′ow *v.t.* to show or indicate beforehand.

fore′skin′ *n.* the skin on the end of the penis.

for′est (fôr′ist) *n.* a large area of land covered with trees.

fore·stall′ *v.t.* to prevent or hinder by acting in advance.

for′est·a′tion (fôr′ə stā′shən) *n.* the planting of forests.

for′est·ry *n.* the science of planting and caring for forests.

fore·tell′ *v.t.,* **-told, -telling.** to tell of beforehand.

fore′thought′ *n.* careful thought and planning for the future.

for·ev′er (fôr ev′ər, fər-) *adv.* always.

fore·warn′ *v.t.* to warn in advance.

fore′word′ *n.* an introductory statement in a book.

for′feit (fôr′fit) *n.* **1.** something given up as a penalty. —*v.t.* **2.** to lose as a forfeit. —*adj.* **3.** forfeited.

for·gave' (fər gāv') v. pt. of **for·give.**

forge¹ (fôrj) v., **forged, forging,** n. —v.t. **1.** to shape (metal) by heating and hammering. **2.** to fashion by concerted effort. **3.** to imitate fraudulently. —n. **4.** a furnace in which metal is heated before shaping. —**for'ger·y,** n.

forge² (fôrj) v.i., **forged, forging.** to move ahead steadily.

for·get' (fər get') v., **-got** (-got') **-gotten, -getting.** —v.t. **1.** to be unable to remember. **2.** to stop thinking about. —v.i. **3.** to cease or fail to think of something. —**for·get'ta·ble,** adj.

for·get'ful adj. tending to forget.

for·get'-me-not' n. a small plant with blue flowers.

for·give' (fər giv') v., **-gave** (-gāv'), **-given, -giving.** —v.t. **1.** to grant pardon for to. **2.** to cancel (a debt). **3.** to cease to feel angry at or for. —v.i. **4.** to grant pardon.

for·go' (fôr gō') v.t., **-went** (-went') **-gone** (-gon'), **-going.** to do without.

fork (fôrk) n. **1.** a pronged instrument or tool. **2.** a point of division into branches or one of the branches. —v.t. **3.** to pierce, dig, or carry with a fork. —v.i. **4.** to divide into branches.

fork'lift' n. a vehicle with two power-operated prongs for lifting heavy weights.

for·lorn' (fôr lôrn') adj. **1.** miserable. **2.** forsaken.

form (fôrm) n. **1.** shape. **2.** a mold. **3.** the way in which something appears or exists. **4.** a kind, type, or variety. **5.** a customary method of doing something. **6.** a document with blank spaces to be filled in. —v.t. **7.** to shape. **8.** to make or produce. **9.** to develop. —v.i. **10.** to take form or a particular form.

for'mal (fôr'məl) adj. **1.** following accepted custom or standard practice. **2.** marked by form or ceremony. **3.** precisely stated. —**for'mal·ize',** v.t.

form·al'de·hyde' (fôr mal'də hīd', fər-) n. a toxic gas used as a disinfectant and preservative.

for·mal'i·ty (-mal'i tē) n., pl. **-ties. 1.** strict adherence to established rules. **2.** a formal act.

for'mat (fôr'mat) n., v., **-matted, -matting.** —n. **1.** the general style of a book, magazine, etc. **2.** the organization of something. **3.** the arrangement of data for computer input or output. —v.t. **4.** to provide a format for. **5.** to prepare (a computer disk) for use.

for·ma'tion (-mā'shən) n. **1.** the act of forming. **2.** the manner in which something is formed. **3.** something formed.

form'a·tive (-mə tiv) adj. **1.** giving form. **2.** relating to formation and development.

for'mer (-mər) adj. **1.** of an earlier time. **2.** being the first-mentioned. —**for'mer·ly,** adv.

for'mi·da·ble (-mi də bəl) adj. **1.** causing fear or awe. **2.** very difficult. —**for'mi·da·bly,** adv.

form' let'ter n. a standardized letter sent to many people.

for'mu·la (fôr'myə lə) n., pl. **-las, -lae** (-lē'). **1.** a scientific description or mathematical rule expressed in figures and symbols. **2.** a set form of words. **3.** a milk mixture for a baby.

for'mu·late' (fôr'myə lāt') v.t., **-lated, -lating. 1.** to state systematically. **2.** to devise.

for'ni·cate' (fôr'ni kāt') v.i., **-cated, -cating.** to have sexual intercourse with someone to whom one is not married. —**for'ni·ca'tion,** n.

for·sake' (fôr sāk') v.t., **-sook** (-sōōk') **-saken, -saking. 1.** to abandon. **2.** to give up.

for·swear' v., **-swore, -sworn, -swearing.** —v.t. **1.** to renounce under oath. **2.** to deny under oath. —v.i. **3.** to commit perjury.

for·syth'i·a (fôr sith'ē ə, fər-) n. a shrub bearing yellow flowers in early spring.

fort (fôrt) n. a fortified place.

forte¹ (fôrt, fôr'tā) n. a person's specialty.

for'te² (fôr'tā) adv. Music. loudly. —**Pronunciation.** In the noun sense (*She draws pretty well, but sculpture is really her forte*), the established pronunciation of FORTE is with one syllable: (fôrt). However, the two-syllable pronunciation (fôr'tā) which is correct for the adverb (a musical term borrowed from Italian), is increasingly heard for the noun as well.

forth (fôrth) adv. onward, outward, or forward.

forth'com'ing adj. **1.** about to appear. **2.** available.

forth'right' adj. direct in manner or speech.

forth'with' adv. at once.

for'ti·fy' (fôr'tə fī') v.t., **-fied, -fying.** to strengthen or make more effective. —**for'ti·fi·ca'tion,** n.

for·tis'si·mo' (fôr tis'ə mō') adv. Music. very loudly.

for'ti·tude' (fôr'ti tōōd', -tyōōd') n. strength and courage in facing danger or trouble.

fort'night' *n.* two weeks.

for'tress (fôr'tris) *n.* a fortified place.

for.tu'i.tous (fôr tōō'i təs, -tyōō'-) *adj.* **1.** happening by chance. **2.** lucky.

for'tu.nate (fôr'chə nit) *adj.* lucky.

for'tune *n.* **1.** wealth. **2.** chance; luck. **3.** fate; destiny.

for'tune-tell'er *n.* a person who claims to read the future.

for'ty (fôr'tē) *n., adj.* ten times four. —**for'ti.eth,** *adj., n.*

fo'rum (fôr'əm) *n.* a place or assembly for public discussion.

for'ward (fôr'wərd) *adv.* **1.** toward or to what is in front. **2.** into view. —*adj.* **3.** directed toward the front. **4.** advanced. **5.** bold. —*v.t.* **6.** to send on, as to a new address.

fos'sil (fos'əl) *n.* the preserved remains of an animal or plant. —**fos'sil.ize',** *v.t., v.i.*

fos'ter (fô'stər) *v.t.* **1.** to promote the growth of. **2.** to bring up (a child that is not own's one). —*adj.* **3.** giving or receiving parental care although not legally related.

foul (foul) *adj.* **1.** grossly offensive. **2.** filthy; dirty. **3.** clogged. **4.** entangled. **5.** stormy. **6.** contrary to the rules of a game. —*n.* **7.** a violation of the rules of a game. —*v.t.* **8.** to make foul. **9.** to clog or obstruct. **10.** to entangle. **11.** to disgrace. —*v.i.* **12.** to become foul. **13.** to commit a foul.

found¹ (found) *v.* pt. and pp. of **find.**

found² (found) *v.t.* **1.** to establish. **2.** to provide a firm basis for.

foun.da'tion *n.* **1.** basis. **2.** the base on which a building rests. **3.** an institution endowed for the public benefit. **4.** a founding or being founded.

foun'der (foun'dər) *v.i.* **1.** to fill with water and sink. **2.** to fail completely. —*n.* **3.** a person who founds an institution.

found'ling *n.* an abandoned child.

found'ry (foun'drē) *n., pl.* **-ries.** a place where molten metal is cast.

foun'tain (foun'tn) *n.* **1.** a spring of water. **2.** a source.

foun'tain.head' *n.* a source.

four (fôr) *n., adj.* three plus one. —**fourth,** *adj., n.*

401(k) (fôr'ō'wun'kā', fôr'-) *n.* a savings plan that allows employees to contribute a fixed amount of income to a retirement account.

four'-score' *adj.* eighty.

four'some (-səm) *n.* a group of four.

four'square' *adj.* **1.** firm; forthright. —*adv.* **2.** firmly; frankly.

four'teen' *n., adj.* ten plus four. —**four'teenth',** *adj., n.*

fowl (foul) *n.* a bird, esp. a domestic hen, rooster, turkey, etc.

fox (foks) *n.* **1.** a carnivorous animal of the dog family. **2.** a crafty person. —*v.t.* **3.** to trick.

fox'glove' *n.* a tall plant with bell-shaped purple flowers and leaves that yield digitalis.

fox'hole' *n.* a small pit used for cover in battle.

fox' trot' *n.* a ballroom dance for couples.

fox'y *adj.,* **-ier, -iest.** slyly clever.

foy'er (foi'ər, foi'ā) *n.* a lobby or entrance hall.

Fr. **1.** Father. **2.** French. **3.** Friar.

fra'cas (frā'kəs, frak'əs) *n.* a disorderly disturbance.

frac'tion (frak'shən) *n.* **1.** a number expressed in the form *a/b.* **2.** a part of a whole. —**frac'tion.al,** *adj.*

frac'tious (frak'shəs) *adj.* **1.** rebellious. **2.** irritable.

frac'ture (frak'chər) *n., v.,* **-tured, -turing.** —*n.* **1.** a break. —*v.t., v.i.* **2.** to break or crack.

frag'ile (fraj'əl) *adj.* easily damaged. —**fra.gil'i.ty** (frə jil'i tē) *n.*

frag'ment *n.* (frag'mənt) **1.** a part broken off. **2.** an unfinished part. —*v.i., v.t.* (frag'ment, frag ment') **3.** to break into fragments.

fra'grance (frā'grəns) *n.* a pleasant scent. —**fra'grant,** *adj.*

frail (frāl) *adj.* **1.** not physically strong. **2.** easily broken.

frame (frām) *n., v.,* **framed, framing.** —*n.* **1.** a decorative border. **2.** a rigid supporting structure. **3.** an enclosing case. **4.** a particular state. —*v.t.* **5.** to shape or devise. **6.** to put a frame around. **7.** to cause an innocent person to seem guilty.

frame'-up' *n.* a fraudulent incrimination of an innocent person.

frame'work' *n.* a skeletal supporting structure.

franc (frangk) *n.* the basic monetary unit of France, Belgium, Switzerland, and several other countries.

fran'chise (fran'chīz) *n.* **1.** the right to vote. **2.** the right to market a company's goods in a given area.

frank (frangk) *adj.* **1.** direct and honest in expression. —*n.* **2.** a mark indicating that a piece of mail may be sent postage free. —*v.t.* **3.** to mark (mail) with a frank.

frank'furt.er (frangk'fər tər) *n.* a cooked sausage.

frank'in.cense' (frang'kin sens') *n.* an aromatic resin used as incense.

fran'tic (fran'tik) *adj.* wild with emotion. —**fran'ti.cal.ly,** *adv.*

fraternal

fra·ter·nal (frə tûr′nl) *adj.* of or be-fitting a brother. —**fra·ter′nal·ly,** *adv.*

fra·ter·ni·ty *n., pl.* **-ties. 1.** brother-hood. **2.** a society of male students in a college or university.

frat′er·nize′ (frat′ər nīz′) *v.i.,* **-nized, -nizing. 1.** to associate in a friendly way. **2.** to associate cor-dially with members of a hostile or proscribed group.

frat′ri·cide′ (fra′tri sīd′, frā′-) *n.* **1.** the act of killing one's brother. **2.** a person who kills his or her brother.

fraud (frôd) *n.* **1.** deceit or trickery. **2.** a particular instance of deceit. **3.** a person who commits fraud. —**fraud′u·lent,** *adj.*

fraught (frôt) *adj.* filled.

fray¹ (frā) *n.* a noisy quarrel; fight.

fray² (frā) *v.t., v.i.* **1.** to make or be-come worn so that there are loose threads at the edge. **2.** to make or become strained or upset.

fraz′zle (fraz′əl) *v.,* **-zled, -zling,** *n.* —*v.t., v.i.* **1.** to make or become fa-tigued. **2.** to fray. —*n.* **3.** a state of fatigue.

freak (frēk) *n.* an abnormal phe-nomenon, person, or animal.

freck′le (frek′əl) *n.* a small brown-ish spot on the skin. —**freck′led,** *adj.*

free (frē) *adj.,* **freer, freest,** *adv., v.,* **freed, freeing.** —*adj.* **1.** having personal rights or liberty. **2.** inde-pendent. **3.** not attached. **4.** not occupied or in use. **5.** provided without charge. —*adv.* **6.** without charge. —*v.t.* **7.** to make free. **8.** to disentangle. —**free′dom,** *n.*

free′-for-all′ *n.* a fight or contest open to all.

free′lance′ (-lans′) *adj., n., v.,* **-lanced, -lancing.** **1.** Also, **free′-lanc′er.** a person who sells services without working on a regular basis for any employer. —*v.i.* **2.** to work as a freelance. —*adj.* **3.** of or being a freelance.

free′load′ *v.i. Informal.* to take ad-vantage of the generosity of others.

free′ rad′ical *n.* a molecule capa-ble of multiplying rapidly and harming the immune system.

free′way′ *n.* a major highway.

freeze (frēz) *v.,* **froze** (frōz) **frozen, freezing,** *n.* —*v.i.* **1.** to become hardened into ice. **2.** to become hardened or stiffened because of loss of heat. **3.** to be at the degree of cold at which water turns to ice. **4.** to suffer the effects of intense cold or fear. **5.** to become tempo-rarily inoperable. —*v.t.* **6.** to harden into ice. **7.** to harden or

stiffen by cold. **8.** to subject to freezing temperatures. **9.** to kill or damage by frost or cold. **10.** to fix (rents, prices, or wages) at a spe-cific level. **11.** to make unnegoti-able. —*n.* **12.** an act of freezing or the state of being frozen.

freight (frāt) *n.* **1.** transportation of goods or payment for such trans-portation. **2.** the goods trans-ported. —*v.t.* **3.** to load with freight. **4.** to transport by freight.

freight′er *n.* a ship or aircraft car-rying freight.

French′ fries′ *n.pl.* strips of potato that have been deep-fried.

French′ horn′ *n.* a coiled brass wind instrument.

fre·net′ic (frə net′ik) *adj.* frantic or frenzied.

fren′zy (fren′zē) *n., pl.* **-zies. 1.** a state of extreme agitation or wild excitement. **2.** mental derange-ment. —**fren′zied,** *adj.*

fre′quen·cy (frē′kwən sē) *n., pl.* **-cies. 1.** the state of being fre-quent. **2.** rate of recurrence. **3.** *Physics.* the number of cycles per unit of time of a wave or oscilla-tion.

fre′quent *adj.* (frē′kwənt) **1.** occur-ring often. —*v.t.* (fri kwent′) **2.** to visit often.

fres′co (fres′kō) *n., pl.* **-coes, -cos.** a painting on a damp plaster surface.

fresh (fresh) *adj.* **1.** new. **2.** not salty, as water. **3.** not stale or spoiled. **4.** not preserved by can-ning or pickling. **5.** refreshing, as air. **6.** inexperienced. **7.** *Informal.* impudent. —**fresh′en,** *v.t., v.i.*

fresh′et (fresh′it) *n.* a sudden flooding of a stream.

fresh′man *n., pl.* **-men. 1.** a first-year student. **2.** a beginner.

fresh′wa′ter *adj.* of or living in water that is not salty.

fret¹ (fret) *v., n.,* **fretted, fretting.** —*v.i., v.t.* **1.** to feel or cause to feel worry. —*n.* **2.** vexation. —**fret′ful,** *adj.*

fret² (fret) *n.* an angular design of intersecting bands.

fret³ (fret) *n.* a ridge across the strings of an instrument.

Fri. Friday.

fri·a·ble (frī′ə bəl) *adj.* crumbly.

fri′ar (frī′ər) *n.* a member of a mendicant religious order. —**fri′-ar·y,** *n.*

fric′tion (frik′shən) *n.* **1.** surface re-sistance to motion. **2.** the rubbing of one surface against another. **3.** conflict, as between persons.

Fri′day (frī′dā, -dē) *n.* the sixth day of the week.

friend (frend) *n.* a person attached

to another by affection or regard.
—**friend′ly**, *adj.* —**friend′ship**, *n.*

frieze (frēz) *n.* a decorative band around a room or building.

frig′ate (frig′it) *n.* a small fast warship.

fright (frīt) *n.* **1.** sudden and extreme fear. **2.** a shocking thing. —**fright′en**, *v.t., v.i.*

fright′ful *adj.* **1.** causing fright; horrible. **2.** *Informal.* ugly; tasteless. **3.** *Informal.* very great. **fright′ful•ly** *adv. Informal.* very.

frig′id (frij′id) *adj.* **1.** very cold. **2.** lacking warmth of feeling. **3.** (of a woman) sexually unresponsive. —**fri•gid′i•ty**, *n.*

frill (fril) *n.* **1.** a trimming, as lace, gathered at one edge. **2.** an unnecessary feature; luxury. —**frill′y**, *adj.*

fringe (frinj) *n., v.*, **fringed, fringing.** —*n.* **1.** a decorative border of hanging threads, cords, etc. **2.** an outer edge. **3.** something regarded as marginal or extreme. —*v.t.* **4.** to furnish with fringe.

frisk (frisk) *v.i.* **1.** to dance, leap, or skip playfully. —*v.t.* **2.** to search (a person) for a concealed weapon, drugs, etc.

frisk′y *adj.*, **-ier, -iest.** playful.

frit′ter¹ (frit′ər) *v.t.* to squander little by little.

frit′ter² (frit′ər) *n.* a small cake of fried batter, containing corn, apples, etc.

friv′o•lous (friv′ə ləs) *adj.* **1.** not serious or deserving serious notice. **2.** self-indulgent and carefree. —**fri•vol′i•ty** (fri vol′i tē) *n.*

frizz (friz) *v.i., v.t.* **1.** to form into small curls. —*n.* **2.** something frizzed, as hair. —**friz′zy**, *adj.*

fro (frō) *adv.* from; back.

frock (frok) *n.* a dress.

frog (frog) *n.* **1.** a small, tailless amphibian with long hind legs. **2.** a slight hoarseness.

frol′ic (frol′ik) *n., v.*, **-icked, -icking.** —*n.* **1.** fun; gaiety. —*v.i.* **2.** to play merrily. —**frol′ic•some**, *adj.*

from (frum, from; *unstressed* frəm) *prep.* **1.** having as a starting point. **2.** as removed, separated, or distinguished. **3.** having as a source, agent, or cause.

frond (frond) *n.* a large, finely divided leaf.

front (frunt) *n.* **1.** the part of something that faces forward. **2.** an area of activity. **3.** a pretense. **4.** a line of battle. **5.** land facing a road, river, etc. **6.** a person or thing serving as a cover or disguise. —*adj.* **7.** of or at the front. —*v.t., v.i.* **8.** to face. **9.** to serve as a front (for). —*Idiom.* **10. up front,** *Infor-*

mal. **a.** before anything else. **b.** open. —**fron′tal**, *adj.*

front′age (frun′tij) *n.* the front of a property.

fron•tier′ *n.* **1.** the border between countries. **2.** land that forms the outer edge of a country's settled regions. —**fron•tiers′man**, *n.*

fron′tis•piece′ (frun′tis pēs′, fron′-) *n.* a picture preceding a title page.

front′-run′ner *n.* a person who leads in a competition.

frost (frôst) *n.* **1.** a freezing condition. **2.** a cover of tiny ice particles. —*v.t.* **3.** to cover with frost or frosting.

frost′bite′ *n.* injury to a body part from prolonged exposure to cold.

frost′ing *n.* a sweet, creamy mixture for coating baked goods.

froth (frôth) *n.* **1.** foam. —*v.t., v.i.* **2.** to cover with or give out foam.

fro′ward (frō′wərd, frō′ərd) *adj.* willfully contrary.

frown (froun) *v.i.* **1.** to contract the brow, as in displeasure. **2. frown on,** to view with disapproval. —*n.* **3.** a frowning look.

frowz′y (frou′zē) *adj.*, **-ier, -iest.** dirty and untidy.

froze (frōz) *v.* pt. of **freeze.**

fro′zen *v.* **1.** pp. of **freeze.** —*adj.* **2.** turned into ice. **3.** very cold. **4.** preserved by freezing. **5.** fixed.

fruc′ti•fy′ (fruk′tə fī′, frōōk′-) *v.*, **-fied, -fying.** —*v.i.* **1.** to bear fruit. —*v.t.* **2.** to make productive. —**fruc′ti•fi•ca′tion**, *n.*

fruc′tose (-tōs) *n.* a very sweet sugar in honey and many fruits.

fru′gal (frōō′gəl) *adj.* thrifty.

fruit (frōōt) *n.* **1.** the edible part of a plant developed from a flower. **2.** a product or result.

fruit′ful *adj.* productive; successful.

fru•i′tion (frōō ish′ən) *n.* attainment of something hoped or worked for.

fruit′less *adj.* not producing results or success.

frump (frump) *n.* a dowdy, drab woman. —**frump′y**, *adj.*

frus′trate (frus′trāt) *v.t.*, **-trated, -trating. 1.** to defeat (plans, efforts, etc.). **2.** to cause disappointment. —**frus•tra′tion**, *n.*

fry¹ (frī) *v.*, **fried, frying,** *n., pl.* **fries.** —*v.t.* **1.** to cook in fat over direct heat. —*v.i.* **2.** to undergo frying. —*n.* **3.** something fried.

fry² (frī) *n., pl.* **fry.** the young of fish.

ft. 1. feet. **2.** foot. **3.** fort.

FTC Federal Trade Commission.

fuch′sia (fyōō′shə) *n.* **1.** a plant with pink to purplish drooping flowers. **2.** a purplish red color.

fudge

fudge (fuj) *n.* a kind of soft candy.

fuel (fyōō′əl) *n., v.,* **fueled, fueling.** —*n.* **1.** something, as coal, oil, etc., that can be burned to create heat or power. **2.** something that stimulates. —*v.t.* **3.** to supply with or take in fuel.

fu·gi·tive (fyōō′ji tiv) *n.* **1.** a person who flees. —*adj.* **2.** having run away. **3.** passing quickly.

-ful a suffix meaning: **1.** full of or characterized by. **2.** tending to or able to. **3.** as much as will fill.

ful′crum (fŏŏl′krəm, ful′-) *n., pl.* **-crums, -cra.** the support on which a lever turns.

ful·fill′ (fŏŏl fil′) *v.t.* **1.** to carry out (a prophecy or promise). **2.** to perform (a task or duty). **3.** to satisfy (requirements, obligations, etc.). —**ful·fill′ment,** *n.*

full (fŏŏl) *adj.* **1.** filled to the limit. **2.** complete. **3.** of maximum size, extent, degree, etc. **4.** well supplied. **5.** rounded in form. **6.** rich in sound. —*adv.* **7.** completely. **8.** exactly. —**ful′ly,** *adv.*

full′-bod′ied *adj.* of full strength, flavor, or richness.

full′-fledged′ *adj.* **1.** of full rank. **2.** fully developed.

full′-scale′ *adj.* **1.** having the exact size of an original. **2.** using all possible means.

ful′mi·nate′ (ful′mə nāt′) *v.i.,* **-nated, -nating. 1.** to explode loudly. **2.** to issue violent denunciations.

ful′some (fŏŏl′səm, ful′-) *adj.* sickeningly excessive, as praise.

fum′ble (fum′bəl) *v.,* **-bled, -bling,** *n.* —*v.i.* **1.** to grope about clumsily. —*v.t.* **2.** to handle clumsily. —*n.* **3.** an act of fumbling.

fume (fyōōm) *n., v.,* **fumed, fuming.** —*n.* **1.** smoke or vapor, esp. of an irritating nature. —*v.i.* **2.** to emit fumes. **3.** to show anger. —*v.t.* **4.** to subject to fumes.

fu′mi·gate′ (fyōō′mi gāt′) *v.t.,* **-gated, -gating.** to disinfect with fumes. —**fu′mi·ga′tion,** *n.*

fun (fun) *n.* **1.** enjoyment or amusement. **2.** something that provides amusement. —*Idiom.* **3. make fun of,** to ridicule.

func′tion (fungk′shən) *n.* **1.** the kind of activity or purpose proper to a person or thing. **2.** a ceremonious public occasion. —*v.i.* **3.** to work. **4.** to perform a function.

func′tion·ar′y (-shə ner′ē) *n., pl.* **-aries.** an official.

fund (fund) *n.* **1.** a sum of money for a specific purpose. **2.** a supply. —*v.t.* **3.** to provide money for.

fun′da·men′tal (fun′də men′tl) *adj.* **1.** of or being a foundation or basis. **2.** essential. —*n.* **3.** a basic principle.

fun′da·men′tal·ist *n.* a person who believes in the literal interpretation of a religious text.

fu′ner·al (fyōō′nər əl) *n.* the ceremony prior to burial or cremation.

fu′neral direc′tor *n.* a person who arranges funerals.

fu·ne′re·al (-nēr′ē əl) *adj.* **1.** gloomy. **2.** of funerals.

fun′gus (fung′gəs) *n., pl.* **fungi** (fun′jī). a plant of the group including mushrooms and molds.

funk (fungk) *n.* **1.** a state of fear. **2.** depression.

funk′y (fung′kē) *adj.,* **-ier, -iest. 1.** having an earthy, blues-based character, as jazz. **2.** *Slang.* offbeat.

fun′nel (fun′l) *n., v.,* **-neled, -neling.** —*n.* **1.** a tube with a cone-shaped top for pouring a substance through a small opening. **2.** a smokestack. —*v.t., v.i.* **3.** to pass through a funnel.

fun′ny (fun′ē) *adj.,* **-nier, -niest. 1.** causing laughter. **2.** strange; odd.

fun′ny bone′ *n.* the part of the elbow that tingles when hit.

fur (fûr) *n., v.,* **furred, furring.** —*n.* **1.** the soft, thick hairy coat of a mammal. **2.** a garment made of fur. **3.** a coating like fur. —*v.t., v.i.* **4.** to cover or become covered with fur. —**fur′ry,** *adj.*

fur′bish (fûr′bish) *v.t.* to restore to good condition.

fu·ri·ous (fyŏŏr′ē əs) *adj.* **1.** very angry. **2.** violent; intense.

furl (fûrl) *v.t.* to roll tightly.

fur′long (fûr′lông) *n.* ⅛ of a mile (0.2 km) or 220 yards (201 m).

fur′lough (fûr′lō) *n.* **1.** a leave of absence, esp. in the military. —*v.t.* **2.** to give a furlough to.

fur′nace (fûr′nis) *n.* a structure in which heat is generated.

fur′nish (fûr′nish) *v.t.* **1.** to provide. **2.** to fit out with furniture.

fur′nish·ings *n.pl.* **1.** articles of furniture for a room. **2.** articles of dress.

fur′ni·ture (-ni chər) *n.* movable articles as tables, chairs, beds, etc., for furnishing a room.

fu·ror (fyŏŏr′ôr, -ər) *n.* general excitement; uproar.

fur′ri·er (fûr′ē ər) *n.* a dealer in furs.

fur′row (fûr′ō) *n.* **1.** a narrow groove made by a plow. **2.** a wrinkle. —*v.t.* **3.** to make furrows in. —*v.i.* **4.** to become furrowed.

fur′ther (fûr′thər) *adv.* **1.** to or at a greater distance or extent. **2.** moreover. —*adj.* **3.** more distant or ex-

tended. **4.** more. —*v.t.* **5.** to promote. —**fur′ther•ance,** *n.*
—**Usage.** See FARTHER.

fur′ther•more′ *adv.* in addition; moreover; besides.

fur′ther•most′ *adj.* most distant.

fur′thest (-thist) *adj., adv.* farthest.

fur′tive (-tiv) *adj.* **1.** stealthy. **2.** sly; shifty.

fu′ry (fyoͦor′ē) *n., pl.* **-ries. 1.** violent passion, esp. anger. **2.** violence.

fuse¹ (fyoͦoz) *n.* a tube or cord of easily burnt material for igniting an explosive.

fuse² (fyoͦoz) *n., v.,* **fused, fusing.** —*n.* **1.** a safety device that breaks an electrical connection when excessive current runs through it. —*v.t., v.i.* **2.** to blend or unite by melting together. —**fu′si•ble,** *adj.*

fu′se•lage′ (fyoͦo′sə läzh′, -lij) *n.* the central structure of an airplane.

fu′sil•lade′ (fyoͦo′sə lād′, -läd′) *n.* **1.** a continuous discharge of guns. **2.** a general discharge of anything.

fuss (fus) *n.* **1.** needless or useless concern or activity. **2.** a complaint about something trivial. —*v.i.* **3.** to make a fuss. **4.** to complain about something trivial.

fus′ty (fus′tē) *adj.,* **-tier, -tiest. 1.** moldy; musty. **2.** old-fashioned.

fu′tile (fyoͦot′l, fyoͦo′tīl) *adj.* incapable of producing a useful result. —**fu•til′i•ty** (-til′i tē) *n.*

fu′ton (foͦo′ton) *n.* a cotton-covered quiltlike mattress placed on a low frame for sleeping or as seating.

fu′ture (fyoͦo′chər) *adj.* **1.** coming after the present time. **2.** of or being a verb tense that refers to events or states in time to come. —*n.* **3.** future time. **4.** an event or condition in the future. **5. futures,** commodities bought and sold speculatively for future delivery.

fu′tur•is′tic *adj.* of the future.

fuzz (fuz) *n.* loose, light, fluffy matter.

fuzz′y *adj.,* **-ier, -iest. 1.** covered with fuzz. **2.** blurred. —**fuzz′i•ly,** *adv.* —**fuzz′i•ness,** *n.*

FYI for your information.

G

G, g (jē) *n.* the seventh letter of the English alphabet.

g 1. gram. **2.** gravity.

GA 1. Gamblers Anonymous. **2.** general of the army. **3.** Georgia.

Ga. Georgia.

gab (gab) *n., v.,* **gabbed, gabbing.** *Informal.* —*n.* **1.** idle talk; chatter. —*v.i.* **2.** to chatter. —**gab′by,** *adj.*

gab′ar•dine′ (gab′ər dēn′) *n.* a twill fabric.

gab′ble (gab′əl) *n., v.,* **-bled, -bling.** —*n.* **1.** rapid, unintelligible talk. —*v.i.* **2.** to speak rapidly and unintelligibly.

ga′ble (gā′bəl) *n.* the triangular part of an outside wall, enclosed by the edges of a ridged roof.

gad (gad) *v.,* **gadded, gadding. gad about,** to move restlessly from one place to another in search of pleasure. —**gad′a•bout′,** *n.*

gad′fly′ *n., pl.* **-flies. 1.** a fly that bites livestock. **2.** a person who annoys or stirs up others.

gadg′et (gaj′it) *n.* a small mechanical device. —**gad′get•ry,** *n.*

gaff (gaf) *n.* a hook for landing fish.

gaffe (gaf) *n.* a social blunder.

gaf′fer *n.* **1.** the chief electrician on a film or TV show. **2.** *Informal.* an old man.

gag¹ (gag) *v.,* **gagged, gagging,** *n.* —*v.t.* **1.** to stop up the mouth of (a person) to prevent speech. **2.** to restrain from free speech. —*v.i.* **3.** to retch or choke. —*n.* **4.** something that gags. **5.** any suppression of free speech.

gag² (gag) *n., v.,* **gagged, gagging.** *Informal.* —*n.* **1.** a joke. —*v.i.* **2.** to tell jokes.

gage (gāj) *n., v.t.,* **gaged, gaging.** gauge.

gag′gle (gag′əl) *n.* a flock of geese.

gai′e•ty (gā′i tē) *n.* merriment.

gai′ly (gā′lē) *adv.* merrily.

gain (gān) *v.t.* **1.** to get as a result of one's efforts. **2.** to acquire as an addition. **3.** to obtain as a profit. **4.** (of a timepiece) to run fast. —*v.i.* **5.** to get nearer. **6.** to improve. —*n.* **7.** profit or advantage. **8.** an increase.

gain′say′ (gān′sā′, gān sā′) *v.t.,* **-said, -saying.** to deny; contradict.

gait (gāt) *n.* a manner of walking or running.

gal (gal) *n. Informal: Sometimes Offensive.* a girl.

gal. gallon.

ga′la (gā′lə, gal′ə; *esp. Brit.* gä′lə) *adj.* **1.** festive. —*n.* **2.** a festive occasion.

gal′ax•y (gal′ək sē) *n., pl.* **-axies. 1.** a very large system of stars. **2. the Galaxy,** the Milky Way. **3.** any large and brilliant group. —**ga•lac′tic** (gə lak′tik) *adj.*

gale (gāl) *n.* **1.** a strong wind. **2.** a noisy outburst, as of laughter.

gall

gall¹ (gôl) n. **1.** impudence. **2.** bile. **3.** bitterness of spirit.

gall² (gôl) v.t. **1.** to make sore by rubbing. **2.** to irritate. —n. **3.** a sore made by rubbing. **4.** something irritating.

gal′lant (gal′ənt; for 2 also gə lant′, -länt′) adj. **1.** brave. **2.** attentive to women.

gall′blad′der n. a sac attached to the liver in which bile is stored.

gal′le·on (gal′ē ən, gal′yən) n. a large sailing ship of the 15th to 17th centuries.

gal′ler·y (-ə rē) n., pl. **-eries. 1.** a balcony in a theater. **2.** a place for art exhibits. **3.** a corridor.

gal′ley (-ē) n. **1.** a ship propelled by many oars. **2.** a ship's kitchen.

gal′li·vant′ (-ə vant′) v.i. to travel about, seeking pleasure.

gal′lon (-ən) n. a unit of capacity equal to 4 quarts (3.7853 liters).

gal′lop (-əp) v.i. **1.** to run at full speed. —n. **2.** the fastest gait of a horse.

gal′lows (-ōz, -əz) n. a wooden frame for execution by hanging.

gall′stone′ n. a stony mass formed in the gallbladder.

ga·lore′ (gə lôr′) adv. in abundance.

ga·losh′es (-losh′iz) n.pl. overshoes.

gal′va·nize′ (gal′və nīz′) v.t., **-nized, -nizing. 1.** to stimulate by or as if by electric current. **2.** to coat with zinc.

gam′bit (gam′bit) n. a clever tactic used to gain an advantage.

gam′ble (-bəl) v., **-bled, -bling,** n. —v.i. **1.** to play a game of chance for money. —v.t. **2.** to wager or risk. —n. **3.** anything involving risk or chance. —**gam′bler,** n.

gam′bol (-bəl) v., **-boled, -boling,** n. —v.i. **1.** to skip about playfully. —n. **2.** a skipping about.

game¹ (gām) n. **1.** a pastime or amusement. **2.** a competitive activity involving skill and played according to rules. **3.** wild animals, hunted for sport. —adj. **4.** brave and willing. —**game′ly,** adv.

game² (gām) adj. lame.

game′ plan′ n. a carefully planned strategy or course of action.

gam′ete (gam′ēt) n. a mature reproductive cell that unites with another to form a new organism.

gam′ut (gam′ət) n. the full scale.

gam′y (gā′mē) adj., **-ier, -iest.** having the strong flavor of game.

gan′der (gan′dər) n. **1.** a male goose. **2.** Slang. a look.

gang (gaŋ) n. **1.** a group of people who associate or work together.

2. a band of criminals. —v. **3.** **gang up on,** to attack as a group.

gan′gling (gaŋ′gliŋ) adj. awkwardly tall and thin.

gan′gli·on (gaŋ′glē ən) n., pl. **-glia, -glions.** a mass of connected nerve cells.

gang′plank′ n. a movable structure used for boarding or leaving a ship.

gan′grene (gaŋ′grēn, gaŋ grēn′) n. death of soft body tissue. —**gan′gre·nous** (-grə nəs) adj.

gang′ster n. a member of a criminal gang.

gang′way′ n. (gaŋ′wā′) **1.** a gangplank. **2.** a narrow passage. —interj. (gaŋ′wā′) **3.** (make way!)

gan′try (gan′trē) n., pl. **-tries. 1.** a spanning framework, as on a crane. **2.** a multilevel scaffolding used to erect rockets.

gaol (jāl) n., v.t. Brit. jail.

gap (gap) n. **1.** an opening. **2.** a wide difference. **3.** a ravine.

gape (gāp, gap) v.i., **gaped, gaping. 1.** to stare with open mouth, as in wonder. **2.** to open wide.

ga·rage′ (gə räzh′, -räj′) n. a place where motor vehicles are kept or repaired.

garb (gärb) n. **1.** clothing. —v.t. **2.** to clothe.

gar′bage (gär′bij) n. trash; refuse.

gar′ble (-bəl) v.t., **-bled, -bling.** to distort or confuse.

gar′den (-dn) n. **1.** an area where flowers, vegetables, etc., are cultivated. —v.i. **2.** to tend a garden. —**gar′den·er,** n.

gar·de′nia (-dē′nyə, -nē ə) n. a shrub with shiny leaves and fragrant white flowers.

gar′den-vari′ety adj. common.

gar·gan′tu·an (gär gan′chōō ən) adj. gigantic; colossal.

gar′gle (-gəl) v., **-gled, -gling,** n. —v.t., v.i. **1.** to rinse (the throat) with liquid kept in motion by the breath. —n. **2.** liquid for gargling.

gar′goyle (-goil) n. a grotesquely carved figure on a building.

gar′ish (gâr′ish, gar′-) adj. tastelessly showy. —**gar′ish·ly,** adv.

gar′land (gär′lənd) n. **1.** a wreath of flowers, leaves, etc. —v.t. **2.** to deck with garlands.

gar′lic (-lik) n. a plant with a pungent bulb used in cooking. —**gar′lick·y,** adj.

gar′ment (-mənt) n. an article of clothing.

gar′ner (-nər) v.t. to gather; acquire.

gar′net (-nit) n. a deep-red gem.

gar′nish (-nish) v.t. **1.** to add something ornamental to. **2.** to deco-

gem

rate (a food). —*n.* **3.** a decoration for food.

gar′nish•ee′ (-ni shē′) *v.t.,* **-eed, -eeing.** to take (money or property of a debtor) by legal authority pending settlement in court.

gar′ret (gar′it) *n.* an attic.

gar′ri•son (gar′ə sən) *n.* **1.** a body of troops defending a fort. **2.** a military post. —*v.t.* **3.** to station (troops) in a fort.

gar•rote′ (gə rot′, -rōt′) *n., v.,* **-roted, -roting.** —*n.* **1.** a cord, wire, etc. used to strangle a person. —*v.t.* **2.** to strangle with a garrote.

gar′ru•lous (gar′ə ləs, gar′yə-) *adj.* very talkative. —**gar•ru′li•ty** (gə-rŏŏ′le tē) *n.*

gar′ter (gär′tər) *n.* a device for holding up a stocking.

gar′ter snake′ *n.* a common, harmless striped snake.

gas (gas) *n., pl.* **gases,** *v.,* **gassed, gassing.** —*n.* **1.** a fluid substance that can expand indefinitely. **2.** any such fluid used as a fuel, anesthetic, etc. **3.** gasoline. **4.** intestinal gas. —*v.t.* **5.** to overcome or poison with gas.

gash (gash) *n.* **1.** a long deep cut. —*v.t.* **2.** to make a gash in.

gas′ket (gas′kit) *n.* a rubber or metal ring used to make a joint watertight.

gas′o•line′ (gas′ə lēn′, gas′ə lēn′) *n.* a flammable liquid from petroleum, used as motor fuel.

gasp (gasp) *n.* **1.** a sudden short intake of breath. —*v.i.* **2.** to breathe with effort. —*v.t.* **3.** to utter with gasps.

gas′tric (gas′trik) *adj.* of the stomach.

gas′tro•nom′i•cal (gas′trə nom′i-kəl) *adj.* of good eating. Also, **gas′tro•nom′ic.** —**gas•tron′o•my** (ga-stron′ə mē) *n.*

gate (gāt) *n.* **1.** a movable hinged barrier in a fence, wall, etc. **2.** any means of entrance.

gat′ed (gā′tid) *adj.* being a residential neighborhood protected by gates, guards, etc.

gate′way′ *n.* a passage or entrance.

gath′er (gath′ər) *v.t.* **1.** to bring together into one group or place. **2.** to harvest. **3.** to conclude. **4.** to collect. **5.** to draw (cloth) into folds by stitching. —*v.i.* **6.** to come together. —*n.* **7. gathers,** a fold or pucker. —**gath′er•ing,** *n.*

gauche (gōsh) *adj.* lacking social grace.

gaud′y (gô′dē) *adj.,* **-ier, -iest.** tastelessly showy. —**gaud′i•ly,** *adv.*

gauge (gāj) *v.,* **gauged, gauging,** *n.*

—*v.t.* **1.** to estimate. **2.** to measure. —*n.* **3.** a standard of measure. **4.** a device for measuring.

gaunt (gônt) *adj.* extremely thin and bony; emaciated.

gaunt′let[1] (gônt′lit, gänt′-) *n.* **1.** a glove with a large cuff. —*Idiom.* **2. throw down the gauntlet,** to challenge someone.

gaunt′let[2] (gônt′lit, gänt′-) *n.* **1.** an ordeal. —*Idiom.* **2. run the gauntlet,** to suffer severe criticism or trouble.

gauze (gôz) *n.* a thin fabric.

gav′el (gav′əl) *n.* a small mallet used to signal for attention.

gawk (gôk) *v.i.* to stare stupidly.

gawk′y *adj.,* **-ier, -iest.** awkward.

gay (gā) *adj.,* **gayer, gayest,** *n.* —*adj.* **1.** merry. **2.** bright. **3.** homosexual. —*n.* **4.** a homosexual person. —**gay′ly,** *adv.*

gaze (gāz) *v.,* **gazed, gazing,** *n.* —*v.i.* **1.** to look steadily. —*n.* **2.** a steady look.

ga•ze′bo (gə zā′bō, -zē′-) *n., pl.* **-bos, -boes.** an open structure on a site with a pleasant view.

ga•zelle′ (-zel′) *n.* a small antelope of Africa and Asia.

ga•zette′ (-zet′) *n.* a newspaper.

gaz′et•teer′ (gaz′i tēr′) *n.* a geographical dictionary.

ga•zil′lion (gə zil′yən) *n. Informal.* an extremely large, indeterminate number.

gear (gēr) *n.* **1.** a toothed wheel that engages with another toothed wheel in machinery. **2.** equipment. —*v.t.* **3.** to provide with or connect by gears. **4.** to adjust.

gear′shift′ *n.* a gear-changing lever in an auto's transmission system.

geck′o (gek′ō) *n., pl.* **-os** or **-oes.** a small tropical lizard.

GED general equivalency diploma.

geek (gēk) *n. Slang.* **1.** a peculiar person, esp. one who is overly intellectual. **2.** a computer expert.

gee′zer (gē′zər) *n.* an odd or eccentric man, esp. an older one.

Gei′ger count′er (gī′gər) *n.* an instrument for measuring radioactivity.

gei′sha (gā′shə, gē′-) *n.* a Japanese woman trained to provide companionship for men.

gel (jel) *n., v.,* **gelled, gelling.** —*n.* **1.** a jellylike or gluelike substance. —*v.i.* **2.** to form a gel.

gel′a•tin (jel′ə tn) *n.* a substance made by boiling animal bones, used in jellies, glue, etc. —**ge•lat′i•nous** (jə lat′n əs) *adj.*

geld′ing (gel′ding) *n.* a castrated horse. —**geld,** *v.t.*

gem (jem) *n.* **1.** a precious stone.

2. something prized for its beauty or excellence.

Gen. General.

gen′der (jen′dər) *n.* **1.** the character of being male or female; sex. **2.** a set of grammatical categories applied to nouns, as masculine, feminine, or neuter.

gene (jēn) *n.* the biological unit that carries inherited traits.

ge′ne.al′o.gy (jē′nē ol′ə jē, -al′-, jen′ē-) *n., pl.* **-gies. 1.** an account of a person's ancestry. **2.** the study of family ancestries.

gen′er.al (jen′ər əl) *adj.* **1.** of, affecting, or including all in a group. **2.** not limited to one class, field, etc. **3.** not specific. —*n.* **4.** an army officer of any of the five highest ranks. —**gen′er.al.ly,** *adv.*

gen′er.al′i.ty (-al′i tē) *n., pl.* **-ties.** a general statement.

gen′er.al.ize′ *v.,* **-ized, -izing.** —*v.t.* **1.** to form a general conclusion from. —*v.i.* **2.** to form general principles, opinions, etc. **3.** to speak in general terms.

gen′eral practi′tioner *n.* a doctor whose practice is not limited to any specific branch of medicine.

gen′er.ate′ (jen′ə rāt′) *v.t.,* **-ated, -ating.** to bring into existence.

gen′er.a′tion *n.* **1.** all the people born at about the same time. **2.** the average period between the birth of parents and the birth of their offspring (about 30 years). **3.** a single step in natural descent. **4.** the act or process of generating.

gen′er.a′tor *n.* a machine that converts mechanical energy into electricity.

ge.ner′ic (jə ner′ik) *adj.* **1.** of or applying to all members of a group, class, genus, etc. **2.** (of a product) not having a brand name. —**ge.ner′i.cal.ly,** *adv.*

gen′er.ous (jen′ər əs) *adj.* **1.** giving freely. **2.** abundant. —**gen′er.os′i.ty** (-ə ros′i tē) *n.*

gen′e.sis (-ə sis) *n.* a beginning.

ge.net′ics (jə net′iks) *n.* the branch of biology that deals with heredity. —**ge.net′ic,** *adj.*

gen., genl. general.

gen′ial (jēn′yəl, jē′nē əl) *adj.* pleasantly cheerful or friendly.

ge′nie (jē′nē) *n.* a spirit, often appearing in human form.

gen′i.ta′li.a (jen′i tā′lē ə, -tāl′yə) *n.pl.* the genitals.

gen′i.tals (-tlz) *n.pl.* the sexual organs.

gen′i.tive (jen′i tiv) *n.* **1.** the grammatical case indicating possession or origin. —*adj.* **2.** of or relating to this case.

gen′i.to.u′ri.nar′y (jen′i tō-) *adj.* of the genital and urinary organs.

gen′ius (jēn′yəs) *n.* **1.** an exceptionally great natural ability. **2.** a person having such ability.

gen′o.cide′ (jen′ə sīd′) *n.* the planned extermination of a national or racial group.

gen′re (zhän′rə) *n.* a class or category of artistic work.

gen.teel′ (jen tēl′) *adj.* affectedly refined and polite.

gen′tian (jen′shən) *n.* a plant with blue flowers.

gen′tile (jen′tīl) *adj.* **1.** (*often cap.*) not Jewish. —*n.* **2.** a person who is not Jewish.

gen′tle (jen′tl) *adj.,* **-tler, -tlest. 1.** mild; kindly. **2.** not rough or severe; moderate.

gen′tle.man *n., pl.* **-men. 1.** a man who has good manners. **2.** a man of good family. **3.** (used as a polite term) any man.

gen′tri.fi.ca′tion (jen′trə fi kā′shən) *n.* the renovation of run-down urban neighborhoods by upper-income people, thus displacing lower-income families and small businesses. —**gen′tri.fy,** *v.t.*

gen′try *n.* wellborn people.

gen′u.flect′ (-yōō flekt′) *v.i.* to bend one knee in reverence.

gen′u.ine (-yōō in or, sometimes, -īn′) *adj.* real; authentic. —**gen′u.ine.ly,** *adv.*

ge′nus (jē′nəs) *n., pl.* **genera, ge.nuses. 1.** a biological group of similar animals or plants, usu. including several species. **2.** a kind.

geo- a prefix meaning earth.

ge′ode (jē′ōd) *n.* a hollow nodular stone often lined with crystals.

ge′o.des′ic dome′ (jē′ə des′ik, -dē′sik) *n.* a dome with a framework of straight members that form a grid of polygonal faces.

ge.og′ra.phy (jē og′rə fē) *n.* **1.** the study of the earth's surface, climate, population, etc. **2.** the features and arrangement of a region. —**ge.og′ra.pher,** *n.* —**ge′o.graph′i.cal** (-ə graf′i kəl) *adj.*

ge.ol′o.gy (jē ol′ə jē) *n.* the science that deals with the earth's physical history and changes. —**ge.ol′o.gist,** *n.*

ge′o.mag.net′ic (-′ō mag net′ik) *adj.* of the earth's magnetism.

ge′o.met′ric (-ə me′trik) *adj.* **1.** Also **ge′o.met′ri.cal.** of geometry or its principles. **2.** resembling the lines and figures used in geometry.

ge.om′e.try (-om′i trē) *n.* the branch of mathematics dealing with points, lines, angles, and solids.

ge′o•phys′ics n. the branch of geology that deals with the physics of the earth and its atmosphere.

ge′o•pol′i•tics n. the study of the influence of physical geography on the politics of a state.

ge′o•sta′tion•ar′y adj. of an orbiting satellite traveling at the same speed as the earth so as to remain in the same spot over the earth.

ge′o•ther′mal adj. of the earth's internal heat.

ge•ra′ni•um (ji rā′nē əm) n. a garden plant with showy red, white, or pink flowers.

ger′bil (jûr′bəl) n. a small burrowing rodent, popular as a pet.

ger′i•at′rics (jer′ē a′triks, jēr′-) n. the branch of medicine dealing with the aged. —**ger′i•at′ric,** adj.

germ (jûrm) n. **1.** a microscopic disease-producing organism. **2.** a seed or origin from which something may develop.

ger•mane′ (jər mān′) adj. relevant.

Ger′man mea′sles n. rubella.

Ger′man shep′herd n. a large dog with a thick, usu. gray or black-and-tan coat.

ger′mi•cide′ (jûr′mə sīd′) n. an agent that kills germs. —**ger′mi•cid′al,** adj.

ger′mi•nate′ v.i., v.t., **-nated, -nating.** to begin or cause to grow; sprout. —**ger′mi•na′tion,** n.

ger′on•tol′o•gy (jer′ən tol′ə jē, jēr′-) n. the study of aging and the problems and care of old people.

ger′ry•man′der (-i man′dər) v.t. to divide (a state, county, etc.) into voting districts so as to give one group or area an unequal advantage.

ger′und (jer′ənd) n. the *-ing* form of an English verb when functioning as a noun.

ges•ta′tion (je stā′shən) n. the period of carrying young in the womb.

ges•tic′u•late′ (je stik′yə lāt′) v.i., **-lated, -lating.** to make gestures.

ges′ture (jes′chər) n., v., **-tured, -turing.** —n. **1.** an expressive movement of the hand, body, head, etc. **2.** any act or communication demonstrating an attitude or emotion. —v.i. **3.** to make expressive movements.

get (get) v., **got** (got), **got** or **gotten, getting.** —v.t. **1.** to obtain or receive. **2.** to fetch. **3.** to cause or cause to become, move, etc. **4.** to capture. **5.** to prepare, as a meal. **6.** to understand. —v.i. **7.** to arrive at a place. **8.** to become. **9. get ahead,** to be successful. **10. ~ along,** to be on good terms. **11. ~**

over, to recover from. **12. ~ through, a.** to complete. **b.** to make oneself understood.

get′a•way n. **1.** an escape. **2.** a place for relaxing, a vacation, etc.

get′-up n. *Informal.* an outfit.

gey′ser (gī′zər, -sər) n. a hot spring that sends up water and steam.

ghast′ly (gast′lē) adj., **-lier, -liest. 1.** horrible. **2.** deathly pale.

gher′kin (gûr′kin) n. **1.** a small cucumber. **2.** a small pickle.

ghet′to (get′ō) n., pl. **-tos, -toes.** a section in which mostly poor minorities live. —**ghet′to•ize,** v.t.

ghost (gōst) n. the disembodied spirit of a dead person imagined as haunting the living.

ghost′writ′er n. a person who writes for another person who is presumed to be the author. —**ghost′write′,** v.t., v.i.

ghoul (gōōl) n. **1.** an evil spirit believed to rob graves, prey on corpses, etc. **2.** a person morbidly interested in misfortunes.

GI n., pl. **GIs** or **GI's.** an enlisted soldier.

gi′ant (jī′ənt) n. **1.** (in folklore) a being of superhuman size. **2.** a person of great size, achievement, etc. —adj. **3.** huge.

gib′ber (jib′ər) v.i. to speak unintelligibly. —**gib′ber•ish,** n.

gib′bet (jib′it) n. a gallows.

gib′bon (gib′ən) n. a small, long-armed ape.

gibe (jīb) v., **gibed, gibing,** n. —v.t. **1.** to mock; jeer. —n. **2.** a sarcastic remark.

gib′lets (jib′lits) n.pl. the heart, liver, and gizzard of a fowl.

gid′dy (gid′ē) adj., **-dier, -diest. 1.** dizzy. **2.** frivolous.

gift (gift) n. **1.** something given. **2.** the act of giving. **3.** a talent.

gift′ed adj. **1.** talented. **2.** highly intelligent.

gig¹ (gig) n. a single engagement, as of jazz musicians.

gig² (gig) n. a light carriage drawn by one horse.

giga- a prefix used in units of measure equal to one billion.

gig′a•byte′ (gig′ə bīt′, jig′-), n. *Computers.* **1.** 2^{30} (1,073,741,824) bytes; 1024 megabytes. **2.** 10^9, or one billion (1,000,000,000), bytes; 1000 megabytes.

gi•gan′tic (jī gan′tik, ji-) adj. very large. —**gi•gan′ti•cal•ly,** adv.

gig′gle (gig′əl) v., **-gled, -gling,** n. —v.i. **1.** to laugh lightly in a silly way. —n. **2.** a silly laugh.

gig′o•lo′ (jig′ə lō′) n., pl. **-los.** a man supported by his female lover.

Gi/la mon/ster (hē/lə) *n.* a large, venomous lizard.

gild (gild) *v.t.,* **gilded** or **gilt, gilding.** to coat with gold.

gill¹ (gil) *n.* the breathing organ of fish.

gill² (jil) *n.* a unit of liquid measure, ¼ pint (4 fluid ounces).

gilt (gilt) *n.* the gold used for gilding.

gilt/-edged/ or **gilt/-edge/** *adj.* of the highest quality.

gim/let (gim/lit) *n.* a small tool for boring holes.

gim/mick (-ik) *n.* a device or trick to attract attention.

gimp/y (-pē) *adj.,* **-ier, -iest.** *Slang.* limping or lame.

gin¹ (jin) *n.* **1.** an alcoholic liquor flavored with juniper berries. **2.** a card game.

gin² (jin) *n., v.,* **ginned, ginning.** —*n.* **1.** a machine for separating cotton from its seeds. **2.** a trap. —*v.t.* **3.** to put (cotton) through a gin.

gin/ger (jin/jər) *n.* a plant with a spicy root used in cooking.

gin/ger•bread/ *n.* a cake flavored with ginger and molasses.

gin/ger•ly *adj.* **1.** wary. —*adv.* **2.** warily.

gin/ger•snap/ *n.* a crisp cookie flavored with ginger.

ging/ham (ging/əm) *n.* a checked or striped cotton fabric.

gin/gi•vi/tis (jin/jə vī/tis) *n.* inflammation of the gums.

gink/go or **ging/ko** (ging/kō, jing/-) *n., pl.* **-goes** or **-koes.** a shade tree with fan-shaped leaves, native to China.

gin/seng (jin/seng) *n.* a plant with a root used medicinally.

gi•raffe/ (jə raf/) *n.* a tall, long-necked, spotted animal of Africa.

gird (gûrd) *v.t.,* **girt** or **girded, girding.** **1.** to encircle. **2.** to prepare for action

gird/er *n.* a horizontal metal beam supporting a structure.

gir/dle *n., v.,* **-dled, -dling.** —*n.* **1.** a light corset. **2.** anything that encircles. —*v.t.* **3.** to encircle.

girl (gûrl) *n.* a female child. —**girl/hood/,** *n.* —**girl/ish,** *adj.*

girl/friend/ *n.* a frequent or favorite female companion or friend.

girth (gûrth) *n.* **1.** the measure around a body or object. **2.** a band that passes underneath a horse to hold a saddle in place.

gist (jist) *n.* the essential point or meaning of a matter.

give (giv) *v.,* **gave** (gāv), **given, giving,** *n.* —*v.t.* **1.** to present. **2.** to hand to someone. **3.** to grant to

someone. **4.** to utter. **5.** to provide. **6.** to yield. —*v.i.* **7.** to make a gift. **8.** to yield under pressure. **9. give in,** to admit defeat. **10. ~ up, a.** to abandon hope or effort. **b.** to surrender. —*n.* **11.** elasticity.

giv/en *v.* **1.** pp. of **give.** —*adj.* **2.** specified. **3.** inclined. —*n.* **4.** an established fact or condition.

giz/zard (giz/ərd) *n.* the lower stomach of birds.

gla/cial (glā/shəl) *adj.* **1.** of glaciers or ice sheets. **2.** bitterly cold. **3.** moving very slowly.

gla/cier *n.* a great mass of ice moving very slowly.

glad (glad) *adj.,* **gladder, gladdest. 1.** pleased; happy; joyful. **2.** causing joy. —**glad/den,** *v.t.*

glade (glād) *n.* an open space in a forest.

glad/i•a/tor (glad/ē ā/tər) *n.* (in ancient Rome) a swordsman fighting to the death for public entertainment.

glad/i•o/lus (-ō/ləs) *n., pl.* **-lus, -li** (-lī) **-luses.** a plant bearing tall spikes of flowers.

glad/ly *adv.* **1.** with pleasure. **2.** willingly.

glam/or•ize/ (glam/ə rī/) *v.t.,* **-ized, -izing.** to make glamorous.

glam/our (glam/ər) *n.* alluring charm and attractiveness. —**glam/or•ous,** *adj.*

glance (glans) *v.,* **glanced, glancing,** *n.* —*v.i.* **1.** to look quickly or briefly. **2.** to strike a surface and bounce off. —*n.* **3.** a quick look.

gland (gland) *n.* any organ or group of cells that secretes some substance.

glans (glanz) *n.* the head of the penis or the clitoris.

glare (glâr) *n., v.,* **glared, glaring.** —*n.* **1.** a very harsh light. **2.** a fierce look. —*v.i.* **3.** to shine with a harsh light. **4.** to stare fiercely.

glar/ing *adj.* **1.** dazzlingly bright. **2.** very obvious.

glass (glas) *n.* **1.** a hard, brittle, transparent substance. **2. glasses,** eyeglasses. **3.** a drinking container made of glass. **4.** anything made of glass. —*adj.* **5.** of glass.

glass/ ceil/ing *n.* a not generally acknowledged upper limit to professional advancement, esp. for women or minorities.

glass/ware/ *n.* articles of glass.

glass/y *adj.,* **-ier, -iest. 1.** like glass. **2.** without expression; dull.

glau•co/ma (glô kō/mə, glou-) *n.* a condition of elevated fluid pressure within the eyeball, causing increasing loss of vision.

glaze (glāz) *v.,* **glazed, glazing,** *n.*

—*v.t.* **1.** to fit with glass. **2.** to put a smooth, glossy coating on. —*v.i.* **3.** to become glazed or glassy. —*n.* **4.** a smooth, glossy coating.

gla′zier (glā′zhər) *n.* a person who installs glass.

gleam (glēm) *n.* **1.** a beam of light or subdued or reflected light. **2.** a brief indication of a quality. —*v.i.* **3.** to send forth a gleam.

glean (glēn) *v.t., v.i.* **1.** to gather (grain) left by the reapers. **2.** to collect (information) little by little.

glee (glē) *n.* open delight or pleasure. —**glee′ful,** *adj.*

glee′ club′ *n.* a singing group.

glen (glen) *n.* a narrow valley.

glib (glib) *adj.* speaking very readily but insincerely.

glide (glīd) *v.,* **glided, gliding,** *n.* —*v.i.* **1.** to move smoothly. —*n.* **2.** a gliding movement.

glid′er *n.* a motorless aircraft.

glim′mer (glim′ər) *n.* **1.** a faint unsteady light. **2.** a small amount. —*v.i.* **3.** to shine or appear faintly. —**glim′mer·ing,** *n.*

glimpse (glimps) *n., v.,* **glimpsed, glimpsing.** —*n.* **1.** a brief look. —*v.t.* **2.** to catch a glimpse of. —*v.i.* **3.** to look briefly.

glint (glint) *n.* **1.** a tiny, quick flash of light. **2.** a trace. —*v.i.* **3.** to shine with a glint.

glis′ten (glis′ən) *v.i.* **1.** to sparkle. —*n.* **2.** a glistening; sparkle.

glitch (glich) *n. Informal.* a defect.

glit′ter (glit′ər) *v.i.* **1.** to reflect light with a brilliant sparkle. **2.** to make a brilliant show. —*n.* **3.** a sparkling light. **4.** showy brilliance. **5.** small glittering ornaments.

glitz′y (glit′sē) *adj.,* **-ier, -iest.** *Informal.* tastelessly showy.

gloam′ing (glō′ming) *n.* twilight.

gloat (glōt) *v.i.* to be maliciously triumphant.

glob (glob) *n.* a rounded lump or mass.

glo′bal warm′ing (glō′bəl) *n.* an increase in the average temperature of the earth's atmosphere that causes changes in climate.

globe (glōb) *n.* **1.** the planet Earth. **2.** a sphere with a map of the earth on it. **3.** anything shaped like a sphere. —**glob′al,** *adj.*

globe′trot′ter *n.* a person who travels regularly all over the world.

glob′ule (-yōol) *n.* a small spherical body. —**glob′u·lar,** *adj.*

gloom (glōōm) *n.* **1.** darkness. **2.** a feeling of depression. —**gloom′y,** *adj.*

glo′ri·fy′ (glôr′ə fī′) *v.t.,* **-fied, -fying. 1.** to praise highly. **2.** to treat

(something) as more splendid or excellent than it is.

glo′ry *n., pl.* **-ries,** *v.,* **-ried, -rying.** —*n.* **1.** very great praise or honor. **2.** magnificence. **3.** a state of absolute happiness. —*v.i.* **4.** to exult triumphantly. —**glor′i·ous,** *adj.*

gloss¹ (glos) *n.* **1.** a shine on a surface. —*v.t.* **2.** to put a gloss on. **3. gloss over,** to cover up, as a mistake. —**glos′sy,** *adj.*

gloss² (glos) *n.* **1.** an explanation of a word, usu. in the margin or between the lines of a text. —*v.t.* **2.** to insert glosses on.

glos′sa·ry (glos′ə rē) *n., pl.* **-ries.** a list of difficult or specialized words with definitions.

glot′tis (glot′is) *n.* the opening at the upper part of the windpipe. —**glot′tal,** *adj.*

glove (gluv) *n., v.,* **gloved, gloving.** —*n.* **1.** a covering for the hand with a separate piece for each finger. —*v.t.* **2.** to cover with a glove.

glow (glō) *n.* **1.** a light sent out by a heated substance. **2.** brightness or warmth. —*v.i.* **3.** to send out light and heat without flame. **4.** to show a bright, ruddy color. **5.** to show emotion or excitement.

glow′er (glou′ər) *v.i.* **1.** to stare with sullen dislike or anger. —*n.* **2.** a look of sullen dislike or anger.

glow′worm′ (glō′wûrm′) *n.* a beetle that emits a greenish light.

glu′cose (glōō′kōs) *n.* a sugar found in fruits and honey.

glue (glōō) *n., v.,* **glued, gluing.** —*n.* **1.** an adhesive substance obtained from gelatin. —*v.t.* **2.** to attach with glue.

glum (glum) *adj.,* **glummer, glummest.** silently gloomy.

glut (glut) *v.,* **glutted, glutting,** *n.* —*v.t.* **1.** to fill to excess. **2.** to flood (the market) with a particular item or service. —*n.* **3.** an excess.

glu′ten (glōōt′n) *n.* a sticky component of flour.

glu′tin·ous *adj.* sticky.

glut′ton (glut′n) *n.* **1.** a greedy person. **2.** a person who is eager for something. —**glut′ton·ous,** *adj.* —**glut′ton·y,** *n.*

glyc′er·in or **glyc′er·ine** (glis′ər in) *n.* a colorless liquid made from fats, used as a sweetener and in lotions.

gnarled (närld) *adj.* twisted and misshapen.

gnash (nash) *v.t., v.i.* to grind (the teeth) together, as in rage.

gnat (nat) *n.* a kind of small fly.

gnaw (nô) *v.t.* **1.** to bite on persistently. **2.** to wear away. —*v.i.* **3.** to

gnome

gnome (nōm) *n.* a dwarf in fairy tales.

GNP gross national product.

gnu (nōō, nyōō) *n., pl.* **gnus, gnu.** an African antelope.

go (gō) *v., n.,* **went** (went) **gone** (gôn) **going,** *pl.* **goes. —v.i. 1.** to move; proceed. **2.** to depart. **3.** to function. **4.** to extend. **5.** to become. **6.** to make a certain sound. **7.** (of time) to pass. **8.** (of colors) to harmonize. **9. go after,** to try to get. **10. ~ around, a.** to be enough for all. **b.** to circulate. **11. ~ for, a.** to try for. **b.** to attack. **c.** to like very much. **12. ~ over, a.** to review or examine. **b.** to succeed. **13. ~ through with,** to finish. **14. ~ under,** to fail or founder. **—n. 15.** energy. **16.** an attempt. **—Idiom. 17. on the go,** very busy. **18. to go,** (of food) to be taken away and eaten elsewhere.

goad (gōd) *n.* **1.** a pointed stick for driving animals. **2.** anything that urges on. **—v.t. 3.** to urge on.

goal (gōl) *n.* **1.** an aim. **2.** the end point or target in a race or game. **3.** a single score in various games.

goal′keep′er *n.* (in soccer, hockey, etc.) the player whose chief duty is to prevent the opposition from scoring a goal.

goat (gōt) *n.* a horned mammal related to the sheep.

goat•ee′ (gō tē′) *n.* a pointed beard.

gob (gob) *n.* **1.** a mass. **2. gobs,** *Informal.* a large quantity.

gob′ble¹ (gob′əl) *v.t., v.i.,* **-bled, -bling.** to eat greedily.

gob′ble² (gob′əl) *v.,* **-bled, -bling** *n.* **—v.i. 1.** to make the cry of a male turkey. **—n. 2.** this cry.

gob′ble•de•gook′ (-dē gōōk′) *n.* nonsense.

gob′bler *n.* a male turkey.

go′-be•tween′ *n.* an intermediary.

gob′let (gob′lit) *n.* a glass with a foot and stem.

gob′lin (gob′lin) *n.* an ugly, mischievous elf.

god (god) *n.* **1.** a superhuman being presiding over some part of human affairs. **2. God,** the creator and ruler of the universe in the Christian, Jewish, and Muslim religions. **3.** any person or object that is adored or admired.

god′child′ *n.* a child for whom a godparent serves as sponsor. **—god′daugh′ter,** *n.* **—god′son′,** *n.*

god′dess *n.* **1.** a female god. **2.** a woman admired for her beauty.

god′ly *adj.,* **-lier, -liest. 1.** devout. **2.** of God or gods.

god′par′ent *n.* a person who serves as sponsor of a child at baptism. **—god′fath′er,** *n.* **—god′-moth′er,**

god′send′ *n.* anything unexpected but welcome.

goes (gōz) *v.* third pers. sing. pres. indic. of **go.**

go′fer (gō′fər) *n. Slang.* an employee whose main duty is running errands.

gog′gle (gog′əl) *n., v.,* **-gled, -gling. —n. 1. goggles,** protective eyeglasses. **—v.i. 2.** to stare with wide-open eyes.

goi′ter (goi′tər) *n.* an enlargement of the thyroid gland.

gold (gōld) *n.* **1.** a precious yellow metal. **2.** riches. **3.** a bright yellow.

gold′en•rod′ *n.* a plant bearing clusters of small yellow flowers on long stalks.

gold′finch′ *n.* a yellow-feathered American finch.

gold′fish′ *n.* a small, gold-colored fish of the carp family.

golf (golf) *n.* a game in which clubs are used to hit a small ball into a series of holes. **—golf′er,** *n.*

go′nad (gō′nad, gon′ad) *n.* an ovary or testis. **—go•nad′al,** *adj.*

gon′do•la (gon′dl ə *or, esp. for 1,* gon dō′lə) *n.* **1.** a long, narrow boat used on the canals in Venice. **2.** a car suspended from a cable. **—gon′do•lier′** (-lēr′) *n.*

gon′er (gô′nər) *n. Informal.* one that is dead, lost, or past recovery.

gong (gông) *n.* a large bronze disk that gives a hollow sound when struck.

gon′or•rhe′a (gon′ə rē′ə) *n.* a venereal disease that causes a discharge from the genitals.

goo (gōō) *n., pl.* **goos.** *Informal.* **1.** a thick or sticky substance. **2.** sentimentality.

good (gōōd) *adj.* **1.** morally excellent. **2.** of high or adequate quality. **3.** well-behaved. **4.** kind. **5.** valid. **6.** favorable. **—n. 7.** profit or advantage. **8.** virtue. **9. goods,** possessions. **—Idiom. 10. for good,** permanently. **11. good for, a.** sure to repay. **b.** worth. **c.** useful for.

Good′ Fri′day *n.* the Friday before Easter, commemorating the Crucifixion of Christ.

good′ly *adj.,* **-lier, -liest.** numerous or abundant.

good′ Sa•mar′i•tan (sə mar′i tn) *n.* a person who helps those in need.

good′will′ *n.* friendly feelings or intentions.

good′y (gŏŏd′ē) n., pl. **-ies.** something pleasing to eat, as candy.

goof (gŏŏf) Informal. —n. **1.** a foolish or stupid person. **2.** a mistake. —v.i. **3.** to make a mistake. **4. goof off** or **around,** to waste time. —**goof′y,** adj.

goon (gŏŏn) n. Slang. **1.** a hired hoodlum. **2.** a stupid, foolish, or awkward person.

goose (gŏŏs) n., pl. **geese. 1.** a web-footed water bird, larger than a duck. **2.** the female of this bird.

goose′ber′ry n., pl. **-ries.** a sour, edible green berry.

goose′ flesh′ n. the bristling of hair on the skin, as from cold or fear. Also, **goose pimples, goose bumps.**

G.O.P. Grand Old Party (epithet of the Republican Party).

go′pher (gō′fər) n. a burrowing rodent.

gore¹ (gôr) n. **1.** clotted blood. **2.** bloodshed. —**gor′y,** adj.

gore² (gôr) v.t., **gored, goring.** to pierce with a horn.

gore³ (gôr) n. a triangular insert of cloth.

gorge (gôrj) n., v., **gorged, gorging.** —n. **1.** a narrow rocky ravine. —v.t., v.i. **2.** to stuff (oneself) with food.

gor′geous (gôr′jəs) adj. **1.** splendid. **2.** very beautiful.

go·ril′la (gə ril′ə) n. a large African ape.

gos′ling (goz′ling) n. a young goose.

gos′pel (gos′pəl) n. **1.** the teachings of Jesus and the apostles. **2. Gospel,** any of the first four New Testament books. **3.** absolute truth.

gos′sa·mer (-ə mər) n. **1.** a filmy cobweb. **2.** something very light and delicate. —adj. **3.** like gossamer.

gos′sip (gos′əp) n., v., **-siped, -siping.** —n. **1.** idle talk or rumor about others′ private affairs. **2.** a person who spreads gossip. —v.i. **3.** to spread gossip.

got (got) v. a pt. and pp. of **get.**

Goth′ic (goth′ik) adj. **1.** noting a style of medieval European architecture, marked by pointed arches. **2.** (often l.c.) noting a style of literature marked by gloomy settings and mysterious events.

got′ten v. a pp. of **get.**

gouge (gouj) n., v., **gouged, gouging.** —n. **1.** a chisel with a concave blade. **2.** a hole made by or as if by a gouge. —v.t. **3.** to dig out with a gouge. **4.** to swindle or overcharge.

gourd (gôrd, gŏŏrd) n. **1.** the hard-shelled fruit of a vine related to the squash. **2.** a dipper made from a dried gourd shell.

gour·mand′ (gŏŏr mänd′, gŏŏr′mənd) n. one who is fond of good eating, often to excess.

gour′met (gŏŏr mā′, gŏŏr′mā) n. a lover of fine food.

gout (gout) n. a painful disease of the joints. —**gout′y,** adj.

gov. 1. government. **2.** governor.

gov′ern (guv′ərn) v.t. **1.** to rule by authority. **2.** to influence. **3.** to control.

gov′ern·ess n. a woman employed to teach children in their home.

gov′ern·ment (-ərn mənt, -ər mənt) n. **1.** the system by which a state is governed. **2.** a governing body of persons. **3.** control; rule.

gov′er·nor (-ər nər, -ə nər) n. **1.** the head of a U.S. state. **2.** a person governing a colony, territory, etc. **3.** the head of an institution.

govt. government.

gown (goun) n. **1.** a woman′s formal dress. **2.** a loose robe worn by judges, the clergy, etc.

G.P. General Practitioner.

grab (grab) v., **grabbed, grabbing,** n. —v.t. **1.** to seize suddenly, eagerly, roughly, or forcibly. —n. **2.** the act of grabbing.

grace (grās) n., v., **graced, gracing.** —n. **1.** beauty of form, manner, etc. **2.** goodwill. **3.** mercy. **4.** God′s love or favor. **5.** a prayer of thanks said at mealtime. —v.t. **6.** to lend grace to. **7.** to favor or honor. —**grace′ful,** adj.

gra′cious (grā′shəs) adj. **1.** kind or courteous. **2.** marked by good taste or luxury.

grack′le (grak′əl) n. a blackbird with iridescent black plumage.

gra·da′tion (grā dā′shən) n. **1.** a change taking place in a series of stages. **2.** a stage in such a series.

grade (grād) n., v., **graded, grading.** —n. **1.** a degree in a scale, as of rank or quality. **2.** a category. **3.** a stage in a process. **4.** a division in a school. **5.** a mark showing the quality of a student′s work. —v.t. **6.** to arrange in grades. **7.** to make level. **8.** to assign a grade to (a student′s work).

grade′ cros′sing n. an intersection of a railroad track and a road.

grade′ school′ n. an elementary school.

grad′u·al (graj′ŏŏ əl) adj. changing, moving, etc., by degrees.

grad′u·ate n., adj., v., **-ated, -ating.** —n. (-it) **1.** a person who has received an academic degree or diploma. —*adj.* (-it) **2.** having an academic degree or diploma. **3.** of academic study beyond the baccalaureate level. —*v.i.* (-āt´) **4.** to receive a diploma or degree. —*v.t.* **5.** to grant an academic diploma or degree to. **6.** to divide into or mark with degrees or other divisions.

graf·fi´ti (grə fē´tē) *n.pl., sing.* **graf·fito** (-tō). markings scrawled or painted on public surfaces.

graft[1] (graft) *n.* **1.** a bud or shoot of a plant inserted into another plant to form a new plant. **2.** living tissue transplanted to another part of the body or from one person to another. —*v.t., v.i.* **3.** to insert (a graft). **4.** to transplant (living tissue) as a graft.

graft[2] (graft) *n.* **1.** obtaining money or advantage dishonestly, as by political influence. **2.** the advantage obtained.

gra´ham (grā´əm, gram) *adj.* made of whole-wheat flour.

Grail (grāl) *n.* (in medieval legend) the cup or chalice used at the Last Supper of Christ with the apostles.

grain (grān) *n.* **1.** a small, hard seed of a cereal plant. **2.** any small, hard particle. **3.** a tiny amount. **4.** the pattern of wood fibers. —**grain´y,** *adj.*

gram (gram) *n.* a metric unit of weight equal to ¹/₁₀₀₀ of a kilogram.

-gram a suffix meaning something written or drawn.

gram´mar (-ər) *n.* **1.** the features or constructions of a language as a whole. **2.** knowledge or usage of the preferred forms in speaking or writing. —**gram·mar´i·an** (grə-mar´ē ən) *n.* —**gram·mat´i·cal** (-mat´i kəl) *adj.*

gran´a·ry (grā´nə rē, gran´ə-) *n., pl.* **-ries.** a storehouse for grain.

grand (grand) *adj.* **1.** large or impressive. **2.** of great importance. **3.** splendid. —*n.* **4.** a grand piano. **5.** *Informal.* a thousand dollars.

grand´child´ (gran´chīld´) *n.* a child of one's son or daughter. —**grand´daugh´ter,** *n.* —**grand´son´,** *n.*

gran·dee´ (-dē´) *n.* a nobleman.

gran´deur (-jər, -jŏŏr) *n.* greatness; splendor.

gran·dil´o·quence (-dil´ə kwəns) *n.* lofty, often pompous speech. —**gran·dil´o·quent,** *adj.*

gran·di·ose´ (-dē ōs´) *adj.* grand or pompous.

grand´ ju´ry *n.* a jury designated to determine if a law has been violated and whether the evidence warrants prosecution.

grand´par´ent *n.* a parent of a parent. —**grand´fa´ther,** *n.* —**grand´moth´er,** *n.*

grand´ pian´o *n.* a piano with a horizontal case on three legs.

grand´stand´ (gran´-, grand´-) *n.* **1.** a main seating area, as of a stadium. —*v.i.* **2.** to conduct oneself to impress onlookers.

grange (grānj) *n.* a farmers' organization.

gran´ite (gran´it) *n.* a very hard, coarse-grained rock.

gra·no´la (grə nō´lə) *n.* a cereal of dried fruit, grains, nuts, etc.

grant (grant) *v.t.* **1.** to give; bestow. **2.** to admit to. —*n.* **3.** something granted, as a piece of land. —*Idiom.* **4.** take for granted, a. to accept as true. b. to fail to appreciate.

gran´u·late´ (gran´yə lāt´) *v.t., v.i.,* **-lated, -lating.** to form into granules or grains.

gran´ule (-yōōl) *n.* a small grain or particle.

grape (grāp) *n.* a smooth-skinned fruit that grows in clusters on a vine.

grape´fruit´ *n.* a large yellow citrus fruit.

grape´vine´ *n.* **1.** a vine on which grapes grow. **2.** a person-to-person route by which gossip spreads.

graph (graf) *n.* a diagram showing relations among things by dots, lines, etc.

-graph a suffix meaning: **1.** something written or drawn. **2.** an instrument that writes or records.

graph´ic *adj.* **1.** vivid. **2.** of writing, drawing, engraving, etc.

graph´ics *n.pl.* **1.** the arts of drawing, engraving, etc. **2.** drawings, charts, etc. **3.** a pictorial computer output.

graph´ite (-īt) *n.* a soft carbon.

graph·ol´o·gy (gra fol´ə jē) *n.* the study of handwriting.

-graphy a suffix meaning: **1.** the process or form of writing, printing, or describing. **2.** an art or science concerned with these.

grap´nel (grap´nl) *n.* a hooked device for grasping.

grap´ple (grap´əl) *n., v.,* **-pled, -pling.** —*n.* **1.** a hook for grasping; grapnel. **2.** a seizing. —*v.i.* **3.** to use a grapnel. **4.** to struggle. —*v.t.* **5.** to seize or hold.

grasp (grasp) *v.t.* **1.** to seize and hold. **2.** to understand. —*n.* **3.** the act of grasping. **4.** mastery.

grasp´ing *adj.* greedy.

grass (gras) *n.* **1.** a plant with jointed stems and bladelike leaves.

2. grass-covered ground. —**grass′y,** *adj.*

grass′hop′per *n.* a leaping insect.

grass′land′ *n.* open grass-covered land; prairie.

grass′ roots′ *n.* ordinary citizens, as contrasted with the leadership or elite. —**grass′-roots′,** *adj.*

grate[1] (grāt) *n.* **1.** a frame of metal bars for holding burning fuel. **2.** a framework of crossed bars used as a guard or cover.

grate[2] (grāt) *v.,* **grated, grating.** —*v.i.* **1.** to have an irritating effect. **2.** to make a rough scraping sound. —*v.t.* **3.** to reduce to small particles by rubbing against a rough surface. **4.** to rub together with a harsh sound. **5.** to irritate.

grate′ful *adj.* **1.** thankful. **2.** expressing gratitude. —**grate′ful•ly,** *adv.*

grat′i•fy′ (grat′ə fī′) *v.t.,* **-fied, -fying. 1.** to please. **2.** to satisfy. —**grat′i•fi•ca′tion,** *n.*

gra′tis (grat′is, grä′tis) *adv., adj.* free of charge.

grat′i•tude′ (-i tōōd′, -tyōōd′) *n.* the quality or feeling of being grateful.

gra•tu′i•tous (grə tōō′i təs, -tyōō′-) *adj.* **1.** free of charge. **2.** being without reasonable cause.

gra•tu′i•ty *n., pl.* **-ties.** a tip.

grave[1] (grāv) *n.* a place of or an excavation for burial of a dead body.

grave[2] (grāv) *adj.,* **graver, gravest. 1.** serious or solemn. **2.** important.

grav′el (grav′əl) *n.* small stones.

grav′el•ly *adj.* **1.** made up of or like gravel. **2.** harsh-sounding.

grave′yard′ *n.* a cemetery.

grav′i•ta′tion (grav′i tā′shən) *n.* the force of attraction between two bodies. —**grav′i•tate′,** *v.i.*

grav′i•ty *n., pl.* **-ties. 1.** the force attracting bodies to the earth's center. **2.** heaviness. **3.** seriousness.

gra′vy (grā′vē) *n., pl.* **-vies.** a sauce made from the juices of cooked meat.

gray (grā) *n.* **1.** a color between black and white. —*adj.* **2.** of this color. **3.** ambiguous. **4.** vaguely depressing.

gray′ mat′ter *n.* **1.** a reddish gray nerve tissue of the brain. **2.** *Informal.* brains.

graze[1] (grāz) *v.,* **grazed, grazing.** —*v.i.* **1.** to feed on grass. —*v.t.* **2.** to put (livestock) out to graze.

graze[2] (grāz) *v.t., v.i.,* **grazed, grazing.** to touch or rub (something) lightly in passing.

grease *n., v.,* **greased, greasing.** —*n.* (grēs) **1.** animal fat. **2.** any fatty or oily matter. —*v.t.* (grēs,

grēz) **3.** to put grease on or in. —**greas′y,** *adj.*

great (grāt) *adj.* **1.** very large in size, number, intensity, etc. **2.** excellent. **3.** famous. **4.** important. —**great′ly,** *adv.*

Great′ Dane′ *n.* a kind of very large and powerful dog.

grebe (grēb) *n.* a kind of diving bird.

greed (grēd) *n.* excessive desire, esp. for wealth. —**greed′i•ly,** *adv.* —**greed′y,** *adj.*

green (grēn) *adj.* **1.** of the color of growing foliage. **2.** unripe. **3.** inexperienced. —*n.* **4.** the color between blue and yellow. **5. greens,** the edible leaves of certain plants. **6.** grassy land.

green′back′ *n.* a U.S. legal-tender note.

green′belt′ *n.* an area of open land surrounding a community.

green′er•y *n.* plants.

green′horn′ *n.* an inexperienced person.

green′house′ *n.* a glass building where plants are grown.

green′house′ effect′ *n.* heating of the atmosphere resulting from the absorption by certain gases of solar radiation.

green′room′ *n.* a lounge in a theater for use by performers.

green′ thumb′ *n.* an exceptional skill in growing plants.

greet (grēt) *v.t.* **1.** to address on meeting. **2.** to receive. **3.** to show itself to. —**greet′ing,** *n.*

gre•gar′i•ous (gri gâr′ē əs) *adj.* fond of the company of others.

grem′lin (grem′lin) *n.* an imaginary mischievous being blamed for disruptions in any activity.

gre•nade′ (gri nād′) *n.* a small explosive thrown by hand.

gren′a•dier′ (gren′ə dēr′) *n.* a member of a British infantry regiment.

grew (grōō) *v.* pt. of **grow.**

grey (grā) *n., adj.* gray.

grey′hound′ *n.* a slender swift dog.

grid (grid) *n.* **1.** a grating of crossed bars. **2.** a network of crossed lines as on a map, chart, etc. **3.** a system of electrical distribution.

grid′dle (grid′l) *n.* a shallow frying pan.

grid′i•ron (grid′ī′ərn) *n.* **1.** a grill. **2.** a football field.

grid′lock′ *n.* a complete stoppage of movement in all directions due to traffic blocking intersections.

grief (grēf) *n.* deep sorrow.

griev′ance (grē′vəns) *n.* **1.** a wrong. **2.** a complaint against a wrong.

grieve (grēv) *v.i., v.t.,* **grieved,**

grieving. to feel or cause to feel sorrow.

griev′ous *adj.* **1.** causing grief. **2.** very serious.

grif′fin (grif′in) *n.* a fabled monster with the head and wings of an eagle and the body of a lion.

grill (gril) *n.* **1.** a utensil topped by a metal framework for cooking food over direct heat. —*v.t.* **2.** to broil on a grill. **3.** to question severely and persistently.

grille (gril) *n.* an ornamental metal barrier.

grim (grim) *adj.*, **grimmer, grimmest. 1.** stern. **2.** having a harsh or forbidding air. —**grim′ly,** *adv.*

grim′ace (grim′əs, gri mās′) *n., v.,* **-maced, -macing.** —*n.* **1.** a facial expression indicating pain, disapproval, etc. —*v.i.* **2.** to make grimaces.

grime (grīm) *n.* dirt adhering to a surface. —**grim′y,** *adj.*

grin (grin) *v.,* **grinned, grinning,** *n.* —*v.i.* **1.** to smile openly and broadly. —*n.* **2.** a broad smile.

grind (grīnd) *v.,* **ground** (ground) **grinding,** *n.* —*v.t.* **1.** to wear, crush, or sharpen by friction. **2.** to reduce to particles. **3.** to rub together harshly, as the teeth. **4.** to operate by turning a crank. —*n.* **5.** the act or sound of grinding. **6.** a grade of fineness. **7.** *Informal.* dreary, uninteresting work.

grind′stone *n.* a rotating stone wheel for sharpening, shaping, etc.

grip (grip) *n., v.,* **gripped, gripping.** —*n.* **1.** a firm grasp. **2.** control. **3.** a handclasp. **4.** a handle. **5.** mental hold. —*v.t.* **6.** to grasp. **7.** to hold the attention of. —*v.i.* **8.** to take firm hold. —*Idiom.* **9. come to grips with,** to face and cope with.

gripe (grīp) *v.,* **griped, griping,** *n.* —*v.i.* **1.** *Informal.* to complain. —*v.t.* **2.** to produce pain in the bowels of. **3.** to annoy. —*n.* **4.** *Informal.* a complaint. —**grip′er,** *n.*

gris′ly (griz′lē) *adj.,* **-lier, -liest.** gruesome.

grist (grist) *n.* grain to be ground.

gris′tle (gris′əl) *n.* cartilage in meat.

grit (grit) *n., v.,* **gritted, gritting.** —*n.* **1.** hard, abrasive particles. **2.** firmness of character. —*v.t.* **3.** to clamp (the teeth) together.

grits (grits) *n.pl.* ground hominy.

griz′zly (griz′lē) *adj.,* **-zlier, -zliest.** gray, as hair or fur.

griz′zly bear′ *n.* a large North American brown bear with coarse, gray-tipped fur.

groan (grōn) *n.* **1.** a low moan of pain, grief, disapproval, etc. —*v.i., v.t.* **2.** to utter (with) a groan.

gro′cer (grō′sər) *n.* the owner of a store that sells food and household articles.

gro′cer•y *n., pl.* **-ies. 1.** a store selling food and household articles. **2.** Usu., **groceries.** food bought at such a store.

grog (grog) *n.* **1.** a mixture of rum and water. **2.** any alcoholic drink.

grog′gy *adj.,* **-gier, -giest.** dazed and weakened.

groin (groin) *n.* the fold where the thigh joins the abdomen.

grom′met (grom′it, grum′-) *n.* a metal eyelet.

groom (grōōm, grŏŏm) *n.* **1.** a bridegroom. **2.** a person who takes care of horses. —*v.t.* **3.** to make neat. **4.** to clean and brush (an animal). **5.** to prepare for a position.

groove (grōōv) *n., v.,* **grooved, grooving.** —*n.* **1.** a long, narrow cut in a surface. —*v.t.* **2.** to cut a groove in.

grope (grōp) *v.,* **groped, groping.** —*v.i.* **1.** to feel about blindly or uncertainly. —*v.t.* **2.** to seek (one's way) by groping.

gros′beak′ (grōs′bēk′) *n.* a finch with a thick, conical bill.

gross (grōs) *adj.* **1.** without deductions. **2.** flagrant; extreme. **3.** disgusting. **4.** very fat or large. —*n.* **5.** the total amount before deductions. **6.** twelve dozen.

gross′ na′tional prod′uct *n.* the total monetary value of all goods and services produced in a country during one year.

gro•tesque′ (grō tesk′) *adj.* fantastically ugly or absurd.

grot′to (grot′ō) *n., pl.* **-tos, -toes.** a cave.

grouch (grouch) *n.* **1.** an ill-tempered person. —*v.i.* **2.** to be sulky. —**grouch′y,** *adj.*

ground (ground) *n.* **1.** the earth's solid surface. **2.** earth or soil. **3. grounds,** the land surrounding a building. **4.** Usu., **grounds,** the basis for a belief. **5. grounds,** coffee dregs. —*adj.* **6.** of or on ground. —*v.t.* **7.** to place on a foundation. **8.** to teach the basics to. **9.** to cause (a ship) to run aground. **10.** to restrict (an aircraft or pilot) to the ground. **11.** *Informal.* to restrict the social activities of. —*Idiom.* **12. gain (or lose) ground,** to advance (or fail to advance).

ground′hog′ *n.* a stocky North American burrowing rodent; woodchuck.

ground′less *adj.* without rational basis.

ground' rules' *n.pl.* the basic rules of conduct in a given situation.

ground'swell' *n.* a surge of feelings, esp. among the general public.

group (grōōp) *n.* **1.** a number of persons, animals, or things considered together. —*v.t., v.i.* **2.** to form into a group.

group'er (grōō'pər) *n., pl.* **-ers, -er.** a large warm-water sea bass.

grouse[1] (grous) *n.* a game bird with a short bill and feathered legs.

grouse[2] (grous) *v.i.,* **groused, grousing.** to complain.

grout (grout) *n.* a thin, coarse mortar used to fill crevices.

grove (grōv) *n.* a small wood or orchard.

grov'el (grov'əl, gruv'-) *v.i.,* **-eled, -eling.** to humble oneself.

grow (grō) *v.,* **grew** (grōō) **grown, growing.** —*v.i.* **1.** to increase in size; develop. **2.** to become. —*v.t.* **3.** to cause or allow to grow; cultivate. **4. grow on,** to become gradually more liked by. **5. ~ up,** to become mature. —**grow'er,** *n.*

growl (groul) *n.* **1.** a deep guttural sound, as of anger or hostility. —*v.i.* **2.** to utter a growl.

grown (grōn) *adj.* **1.** arrived at full growth. —*v.* **2.** pp. of **grow.**

grown'up' *n.* an adult. —**grown'-up',** *adj.*

growth (grōth) *n.* **1.** the act of growing. **2.** a size or stage of development. **3.** something that has grown. **4.** a tumor.

grub (grub) *n., v.,* **grubbed, grubbing.** —*n.* **1.** the thick-bodied larva of certain insects. **2.** *Slang.* food. —*v.t.* **3.** to uproot. —*v.i.* **4.** to search for by digging. **5.** to work hard.

grub'by *adj.,* **-bier, -biest.** dirty.

grudge (gruj) *n., v.,* **grudged, grudging.** —*n.* **1.** a feeling of ill will. —*v.t.* **2.** to give reluctantly. **3.** to resent the good fortune of. —**grudg'ing.ly,** *adv.*

gru'el (grōō'əl) *n.* a thin cooked cereal.

gru'el.ing (grōō'ə ling, grōō'ling) *adj.* exhausting; arduous.

grue'some (-səm) *adj.* causing horror and repugnance.

gruff (gruf) *adj.* **1.** low and hoarse. **2.** brusque or surly.

grum'ble (grum'bəl) *v.,* **-bled, -bling.** —*v.i.* **1.** to mutter in discontent. —*v.t.* **2.** to utter by grumbling. —*n.* **3.** a complaint.

grump'y (grum'pē) *adj.,* **-ier, -iest.** bad-tempered.

grunge (grunj) *n. Slang.* **1.** dirt; filth. **2.** a style or fashion marked by unkempt clothing, derived from a movement in rock music characterized by aggressive, nihilistic songs. —**grun'gy,** *adj.*

grunt (grunt) *v.i., v.t.* **1.** to utter (with) the deep, guttural sound of a hog. —*n.* **2.** such a sound.

gryph'on (grif'ən) *n.* a griffin.

gua'no (gwä'nō) *n.* a manure from the excrement of sea birds.

guar'an.tee' (gar'ən tē') *n., v.,* **-teed, -teeing.** —*n.* **1.** an assurance that something is of specified quality or content. **2.** something offered as security that an obligation will be fulfilled. **3.** something assuring a particular outcome. —*v.t.* **4.** to make or give a guarantee. **5.** to promise.

guar'an.tor' (-tôr') *n.* a person who guarantees.

guard (gärd) *v.t.* **1.** to watch over. **2.** to keep safe from harm. —*v.i.* **3.** to take precautions. —*n.* **4.** a person who guards. **5.** a close watch. **6.** a device that prevents injury, loss, etc.

guard'ed *adj.* **1.** cautious; prudent. **2.** protected or restrained.

guard'i.an *n.* **1.** a person who guards or protects. **2.** a person legally entrusted with the care of another.

gua'va (gwä'və) *n.* the large yellow fruit of a tropical tree.

gu'ber.na.to'ri.al (gōō'bər nə tôr'ē-əl, gyōō'-) *adj.* of a governor or the office of a governor.

guer.ril'la (gə ril'ə) *n.* a member of a band of soldiers that harasses the enemy.

guess (ges) *v.t., v.i.* **1.** to form an opinion about (something) without complete evidence. **2.** to be correct in such an opinion. —*n.* **3.** the act of guessing. **4.** an opinion reached by guessing.

guess'work' *n.* **1.** a guessing. **2.** conclusions drawn from guesses.

guest (gest) *n.* **1.** a person who spends time at another's home. **2.** a customer at a hotel, restaurant, etc.

guf.faw' (gu fô', gə-) *n.* **1.** a burst of loud laughter. —*v.i.* **2.** to laugh loudly.

guid'ance (gīd'ns) *n.* **1.** an act or instance of guiding. **2.** advice or counseling.

guide (gīd) *v.,* **guided, guiding,** *n.* —*v.t.* **1.** to show the way. **2.** to lead or direct in any action. —*n.* **3.** one that guides.

guide'book' *n.* a book of directions and information, as for tourists.

guid'ed mis'sile *n.* a radio-controlled aerial missile.

guide/line/ *n.* any guide or indication of a future course of action.

guild (gild) *n.* **1.** an organization of people having a common interest. **2.** a medieval association of merchants or artisans.

guile (gīl) *n.* deceitful cunning.

guil/lo·tine/ (gil/ə tēn/, gē/ə-) *n.* a machine for beheading people.

guilt (gilt) *n.* **1.** the fact of having committed an offense. **2.** a feeling of responsibility or regret for having done something wrong.

guin/ea fowl/ (gin/ē) *n.* a gray-speckled domesticated fowl.

guin/ea pig/ *n.* **1.** a tailless rodent raised as a pet and for use in laboratories. **2.** the subject of any experiment.

guise (gīz) *n.* outward appearance.

gui·tar/ (gi tär/) *n.* a musical instrument usu. having six strings that are plucked. —**gui·tar/ist,** *n.*

gulch (gulch) *n.* a deep, narrow ravine marking the course of a stream.

gulf (gulf) *n.* **1.** a large arm of the sea partly enclosed by land. **2.** an abyss. **3.** any wide gap.

gull[1] (gul) *n.* a long-winged sea bird, usu. white with gray or black wings and back.

gull[2] (gul) *v.t.* **1.** to trick or cheat. —*n.* **2.** a person who is easily deceived. —**gul/li·ble,** *adj.*

gul/let (gul/it) *n.* the esophagus or the throat.

gul/ly (gul/ē) *n., pl.* **-lies.** a deep channel cut by running water.

gulp (gulp) *v.t.* **1.** to swallow greedily. —*v.i.* **2.** to gasp, as if swallowing large amounts of a liquid. —*n.* **3.** the act of gulping.

gum[1] (gum) *n., v.,* **gummed, gumming.** —*n.* **1.** a sticky substance exuded from certain trees. **2.** chewing gum. —*v.t.* **3.** to smear, stick together, or clog with gum.

gum[2] (gum) *n.* Often, **gums.** the firm, fleshy tissue around the teeth.

gump/tion (gump/shən) *n.* **1.** initiative; resourcefulness. **2.** courage.

gum/shoe/ *n., pl.* **-shoes.** *Slang.* a detective. **2.** a rubber overshoe.

gun (gun) *n., v.,* **gunned, gunning.** —*n.* **1.** a weapon that shoots missiles from a metal tube by the force of an explosive. **2.** any device for shooting or ejecting something under pressure. —*v.t.* **3.** to shoot with a gun. **4.** to cause (an engine) to speed up quickly. —*Idiom.* **5. under the gun,** under pressure.

gun/fire/ *n.* the firing of guns.

gunk (gungk) *n. Slang.* any sticky or greasy matter.

gun/man *n., pl.* **-men.** an armed criminal.

gun/ny *n., pl.* **-nies.** a strong coarse material used for sacks.

gun/point/ *n.* —*Idiom.* **at gunpoint,** under threat of being shot.

gun/pow/der *n.* an explosive mixture used in guns and for blasting.

gun/shot/ *n.* a shot fired from a gun.

gun/smith/ *n.* a person who makes or repairs firearms.

gun/wale (gun/l) *n.* the upper edge of the side of a vessel.

gup/py (gup/ē) *n., pl.* **-pies.** a small fish often kept in aquariums.

gur/gle (gûr/gəl) *v.,* **-gled, -gling,** *n.* —*v.i.* **1.** to flow irregularly and noisily. —*n.* **2.** the sound of this.

gur/ney (gûr/nē) *n.* a wheeled table for transporting patients.

gu/ru (gŏŏr/ŏŏ, gŏŏ rŏŏ/) *n.* **1.** any person who teaches or advises. **2.** a Hindu spiritual teacher.

gush (gush) *v.i.* **1.** to flow out suddenly and forcibly. **2.** to talk effusively. —*n.* **3.** a sudden flow.

gush/er *n.* a flowing oil well.

gus/set (gus/it) *n.* a triangular piece of material inserted to improve fit or to reinforce.

gust (gust) *n.* **1.** a sudden blast of wind. **2.** an outburst of emotion. —**gust/y,** *adj.*

gus/ta·to/ry (gus/tə tôr/ē) *adj.* of taste.

gus/to (-tō) *n.* hearty enjoyment.

gut (gut) *n., v.,* **gutted, gutting.** —*n.* **1.** the intestine. **2. guts, a.** the bowels. **b.** courage. —*v.t.* **3.** to remove the guts of. **4.** to destroy the interior of, as a building. —*adj.* **5. a.** basic. **b.** based on instincts.

guts/y *adj.,* **-ier, -iest.** daring or courageous.

gut/ter (gut/ər) *n.* a channel for leading off rainwater.

gut/tur·al (- əl) *adj.* of or pronounced in the throat.

guy[1] (gī) *n.* **1.** a man or boy. **2. guys,** people.

guy[2] (gī) *n.* a rope or cable used to steady an object.

guz/zle (guz/əl) *v.i., v.t.,* **-zled, -zling.** to drink or eat greedily.

gym·na/si·um (jim nā/zē əm) *n., pl.* **-siums, -sia.** a room or building for physical exercise.

gym/nast (-nəst, -nast) *n.* a person trained in gymnastics.

gym·nas/tics (-nas/tiks) *n.pl.* physical exercises that demonstrate strength, balance, or agility.

gy/ne·col/o·gy (gī/ni kol/ə jē, jin/i-) *n.* the branch of medicine dealing with the health of women, esp. of the reproductive organs. —**gy′ne‧col′o‧gist,** *n.*

gyp (jip) *v.t., v.i.,* **gypped, gyp-ping.** *Informal.* to cheat.

gyp′sum (-səm) *n.* a chalk-like mineral.

Gyp′sy (-sē) *n., pl.* **-sies.** a member of a wandering people.

gy′rate (jī′rāt, jī rāt′) *v.i.,* **-rated, -rating.** to move in a circle or spiral —**gy‧ra′tion,** *n.*

gy′ro‧scope′ (jī′rə skōp′) *n.* a rotating wheel mounted so its axis can turn in all directions, used to maintain equilibrium and determine direction.

H

H, h (āch) *n.* the eighth letter of the English alphabet.

ha′be‧as cor′pus (hā′bē əs kôr′pəs) *n.* a writ requiring that an arrested person be brought before a court to determine whether he or she has been detained legally.

hab′er‧dash′er‧y (hab′ər dash′ə rē) *n., pl.* **-eries.** a shop selling men's shirts, ties, socks, etc. —**hab′er‧dash′er,** *n.*

hab′it (hab′it) *n.* **1.** a pattern of behavior. **2.** customary practice. **3.** a monk's or nun's garb. **4.** addiction.

hab′it‧a‧ble (hab′i tə bəl) *adj.* able to be lived in.

hab′i‧tat′ (-tat′) *n.* the natural environment of a plant or animal.

hab′i‧ta′tion *n.* a dwelling.

ha‧bit′u‧ate′ (hə bich′ŏŏ āt′) *v.t.,* **-ated, -ating.** to accustom.

ha‧bit′u‧é′ (-ŏŏ ā′) *n.* a regular visitor to a place.

hack¹ (hak) *v.t.* **1.** to cut roughly. —*v.i.* **2.** to cough dryly. —*n.* **3.** a cut or notch. **4.** a dry cough.

hack² *n.* **1.** a writer who does routine work. **2.** a horse or vehicle for hire. —*v.i.* **3.** to drive a taxi. **4.** to work as a hack. —*adj.* **5.** routine.

hack′er *n. Slang.* **1.** a skilled computer enthusiast. **2.** a computer user who tries to gain unauthorized access to systems.

hack′les (hak′əlz) *n.pl.* the hair that can bristle on the back of an animal's neck.

hack′neyed *adj.* trite.

hack′saw′ *n.* a saw for cutting metal.

had′dock (had′ək) *n.* a N Atlantic food fish of the cod family.

Ha′des (hā′dēz) *n.* **1.** the Greek god of the underworld. **2.** hell.

haft (haft) *n.* a handle.

hag (hag) *n.* an ugly old woman.

hag′gard (hag′ərd) *adj.* appearing gaunt, wasted, or exhausted.

hag′gle (hag′əl) *v.i.,* **-gled, -gling.** to argue about price.

hail¹ (hāl) *v.t.* **1.** to greet. **2.** to call out or signal to. —*n.* **3.** a call or greeting.

hail² (hāl) *n.* **1.** ice pellets falling in a shower. **2.** a shower of anything. —*v.i.* **3.** to fall like hail.

hair (hâr) *n.* **1.** a fine threadlike structure on the human head, the body of a mammal, etc. **2.** a mass of such structures. —**hair′less,** *adj.* —**hair′y,** *adj.*

hair′breadth′ or **hairs′breadth′** *n.* a very small space or distance.

hair′cut′ *n.* **1.** the act of cutting the hair. **2.** a hairstyle.

hair′do′ (-dŏŏ′) *n., pl.* **-dos.** a hairstyle.

hair′dress′er *n.* a person who cuts or arranges hair.

hair′piece′ *n.* a toupee or wig.

hair′pin *n.* **1.** a U-shaped pin for fastening up the hair. —*adj.* **2.** sharply curved back, as in a U shape.

hair′-rais′ing *adj.* terrifying.

hair′spray′ *n.* a liquid spray for holding the hair in place.

hair′style′ *n.* a way of arranging the hair. —**hair′styl′ist,** *n.*

hair′-trig′ger *adj.* easily set off.

hake (hāk) *n.* a codlike marine food fish.

hal′cy‧on (hal′sē ən) *adj.* peaceful; happy; carefree.

hale (hāl) *adj.* healthy.

half (haf) *n., pl.* **halves,** *adj., adv.* —*n.* **1.** one of two equal parts. —*adj.* **2.** being a half. **3.** incomplete. —*adv.* **4.** partly.

half′-baked′ *adj.* **1.** not sufficiently planned or prepared. **2.** foolish.

half′ broth′er *n.* a brother related through one parent only.

half′-cocked′ *adj.* ill-prepared.

half′-heart′ed *adj.* unenthusiastic.

half′ sis′ter *n.* a sister related through one parent only.

half′-truth′ *n.* a deceptive statement that is only partly true.

half′way′ (-wā′, -wā′) *adv.* **1.** to the midpoint. **2.** partially or almost. —*adj.* **3.** midway. **4.** partial or inadequate.

half′way house′ *n.* a residence for persons released from a hospital, prison, etc.

half′-wit′ *n.* a foolish person.

hal′i‧but (hal′ə bət, hol′-) *n.* a kind of large edible flounder.

hal′i•to′sis (-i tō′sis) *n.* bad breath.

hall (hôl) *n.* **1.** a corridor. **2.** the entrance room of a house or building. **3.** a large public room.

hal′le•lu′jah (hal′ə lōō′yə) *interj.* (Praise ye the Lord!)

hall′mark′ (hôl′-) *n.* **1.** any mark or indication of genuineness or quality. **2.** any distinguishing characteristic.

hal′low (hal′ō) *v.t.* to make or honor as holy.

Hal′low•een′ or **Hal′low•e′en′** (hal′ə wēn′, -ō ēn′, hol′-) *n.* the evening of October 31; the eve of All Saints' Day.

hal•lu•ci•na′tion (hə lōō′sə nā′shən) *n.* **1.** an experience of seeing or hearing something that does not exist outside the mind. **2.** an illusion. —**hal•lu′ci•nate′**, *v.i.*

hal•lu′ci•no•gen (-nə jən) *n.* a substance producing hallucinations.

hall′way′ *n.* a corridor.

ha′lo (hā′lō) *n., pl.* **-los, -loes.** a circle of light around the head of a holy personage in a picture.

halt¹ (hôlt) *v.i., v.t.* **1.** to stop or cause to stop. —*n.* **2.** a stop.

halt² *v.i.* **1.** to falter or hesitate. —*adj.* **2.** lame.

hal′ter (hôl′tər) *n.* **1.** a strap for leading or restraining a horse. **2.** a noose. **3.** a woman's top, tied behind the neck and back.

halve (hav) *v.t.,* **halved, halving. 1.** to divide into two equal parts. **2.** to reduce to half.

ham¹ (ham) *n.* **1.** a cut of meat from the rear thigh of a hog. **2.** the back of the human thigh.

ham² (ham) *n., v.,* **hammed, hamming.** —*n.* **1.** a performer who overacts. **2.** an amateur radio operator. —*v.i., v.t.* **3.** to overact.

ham′burg′er (-bûr′gər) *n.* a patty of ground beef or a sandwich of this.

ham′let (-lit) *n.* a small village.

ham′mer (-ər) *n.* **1.** a tool with a head set crosswise on a handle, used for driving nails, beating metal, etc. **2.** something resembling this. —*v.t., v.i.* **3.** to beat with a hammer. **4.** to strike repeatedly.

ham′mock (-ək) *n.* a hanging bed of canvas or cord.

ham′per¹ (-pər) *v.t.* to hold back; impede.

ham′per² (-pər) *n.* a large covered basket.

ham′ster (-stər) *n.* a short-tailed rodent often kept as a pet.

ham′string′ *n., v.,* **-strung, -stringing.** —*n.* **1.** a tendon behind the knee. —*v.t.* **2.** to disable by cutting the hamstring. **3.** to make powerless or ineffective.

hand (hand) *n.* **1.** the end part of the arm. **2.** anything resembling a hand in shape or function. **3.** a manual worker or crew member. **4.** means; agency. **5.** assistance. **6.** side or direction. **7.** a round of applause. **8.** a pledge of marriage. **9.** the cards held by a player. —*v.t.* **10.** to give or pass by hand. —*Idiom.* **11. at hand,** near. **12. hands down,** effortlessly. **13. on hand,** available.

hand′bag′ *n.* a woman's purse.

hand′ball′ *n.* a game in which players strike a ball against a wall with the hand.

hand′bill′ *n.* a small printed notice, usu. distributed by hand.

hand′book′ *n.* a guide or reference book; manual.

hand′cuff′ *n.* **1.** a metal ring, linked to another by a chain, that can be locked around a prisoner's wrist. —*v.t.* **2.** to put handcuffs on.

hand′ful (-fŏŏl) *n., pl.* **-fuls. 1.** the amount a hand can hold. **2.** *Informal.* a difficult person or thing.

hand′gun′ *n.* a firearm that can be held and fired with one hand.

hand′i•cap′ (han′dē kap′) *n., v.,* **-capped, -capping.** —*n.* **1.** a disadvantage. **2.** a physical or mental disability. —*v.t.* **3.** to place at a disadvantage.

hand′i•craft′ *n.* **1.** manual skill. **2.** products requiring such skill.

hand′i•work′ *n.* **1.** work done by hand. **2.** the work of a particular person.

hand′ker•chief (hang′kər chif, -chēf′) *n.* a small cloth for wiping the nose, face, etc.

han′dle (han′dl) *n., v.,* **-dled, -dling.** —*n.* **1.** a part by which a thing is grasped or held by the hand. —*v.t.* **2.** to touch or pick up with the hands. **3.** to manage or control. **4.** to deal in.

hand′made′ *adj.* made by hand.

hand′out′ *n.* **1.** something given to a needy person. **2.** printed material distributed to a group. **3.** anything given away for nothing.

hand′shake′ *n.* a gripping and shaking of each other's hand in greeting or agreement.

hands′-off′ *adj.* not intervening.

hand′some (han′səm) *adj.* **1.** good-looking. **2.** generous.

hands′-on′ *adj.* involving active personal participation.

hand′spring′ *n.* a complete flipping of the body, landing first on the hands, then on the feet.

hand′-to-mouth′ *adj.* providing barely enough to survive.

hand′writ′ing *n.* **1.** writing done by hand. **2.** a style of such writing. —**hand′writ′ten** (-rit′n) *adj.*

hand′y (han′dē) *adj.,* **-ier, -iest. 1.** within easy reach. **2.** easily used. **3.** skillful with the hands.

han′dy‧man′ *n., pl.* **-men.** a person hired to do small jobs, as repairs.

hang (hang) *v.,* **hung** (hung) or **hanged, hanging,** *n.* —*v.t.* **1.** to attach (a thing) so that it is supported from above with the lower part moving freely. **2.** to execute by suspending from a rope around the neck. **3.** to attach to a wall. **4.** to let (one's head) droop. —*v.i.* **5.** to be suspended so as to swing freely. **6.** to suffer death by hanging. **7.** to incline downward. **8.** to drape, as a garment. —*n.* **9.** the way a thing hangs.

hang′ar (hang′ər) *n.* a shelter for housing aircraft.

hang′dog′ *adj.* abject.

hang′man *n.* a person who hangs condemned criminals.

hang′nail′ *n.* a small piece of loose skin around a fingernail.

hang′o′ver *n.* a sick feeling from drinking too much alcohol.

hang′up′ *n. Slang.* a preoccupation or psychological block.

hank (hangk) *n.* a coil or loop of yarn, thread, hair, etc.

han′ker (hang′kər) *v.i.* to have a longing.

hank′y-pank′y *n. Informal.* **1.** mischief. **2.** illicit sexual relations.

han′som (han′səm) *n.* a two-wheeled covered cab.

Ha‧nuk‧kah (ᴋʜä′nə kə, hä′-) *n.* a Jewish festival commemorating the rededication of the Temple in Jerusalem.

hap′haz′ard (hap haz′ərd) *adj.* having no plan or order; random.

hap′less *adj.* unfortunate.

hap′pen (hap′ən) *v.i.* **1.** to take place; occur. **2.** to discover by chance. —**hap′pen‧ing,** *n.*

hap′pen‧stance′ (-stans′) *n.* a chance happening or event.

hap′py (hap′ē) *adj.,* **-pier, -piest. 1.** pleased or delighted. **2.** pleasing. **3.** bringing good luck; fortunate.

ha‧rangue′ (hə rang′) *n., v.,* **-rangued, -ranguing.** —*n.* **1.** a long, passionate speech. —*v.t.* **2.** to address in a harangue.

ha‧rass′ (hə ras′, har′əs) *v.t.* **1.** to disturb persistently. **2.** to attack repeatedly. —**har‧ass′ment,** *n.* —**Pronunciation.** ʜᴀʀᴀss has traditionally been pronounced (har′əs). A newer pronunciation, (hə ras′), which has developed in North American but not British English, is sometimes criticized. However, it is now the more common pronunciation among younger educated U.S. speakers.

har‧bin‧ger (här′bin jər) *n.* one that heralds the approach of something.

har′bor (här′bər) *n.* **1.** a sheltered part of a body of water where ships can anchor. **2.** a place of shelter. —*v.t.* **3.** to give shelter to.

hard (härd) *adj.* **1.** firm to the touch; not soft. **2.** difficult. **3.** harsh; severe. **4.** (of water) containing mineral salts that interfere with the action of soap. **5.** (of drugs) addictive. **6.** (of drinks) containing much alcohol. —*Idiom.* **7. hard up,** *Informal.* needing money. —**hard′en,** *v.t., v.i.* —**hard′ness,** *n.*

hard′-bit′ten *adj.* tough; stubborn.

hard′-boiled′ *adj.* **1.** (of an egg) boiled long enough for the yolk and white to solidify. **2.** not sentimental; tough.

hard′ ci′der *n.* fermented cider.

hard′-core′ *adj.* **1.** uncompromising. **2.** (of pornography) explicit. **3.** persistent or chronic.

hard′hat′ *n.* **1.** a protective helmet worn by construction workers. **2.** a construction worker.

hard′head′ed *adj.* **1.** practical; realistic; shrewd. **2.** obstinate; willful.

hard′heart′ed *adj.* unfeeling.

hard′-line′ or **hard′line′** *adj.* uncompromising, as in politics.

hard′ly *adv.* barely or scarcely.

hard′-nosed′ *adj. Informal.* practical and shrewd.

hard′ship *n.* suffering or need.

hard′tack′ *n.* a hard biscuit.

hard′ware′ *n.* **1.** metalware, as tools, locks, etc. **2.** the electronic devices of a computer system.

hard′wood′ *n.* the hard, compact wood of various trees.

har′dy (här′dē) *adj.,* **-dier, -diest.** sturdy; strong.

hare (hâr) *n.* a mammal related to but larger than the rabbit.

hare′brained′ *adj.* foolish.

hare′lip′ *n. Offensive.* a split upper lip; cleft lip.

har′em (hâr′əm, har′-) *n.* **1.** the women's section of a Muslim house. **2.** the women in a Muslim household.

hark (härk) *v.i.* **1.** to listen. **2. hark back,** to recollect a previous event or topic.

har′le‧quin (här′lə kwin, -kin) *n.* a character in comic theater, usu.

masked and dressed in multicolored, diamond-patterned tights.

har′lot (här′lət) *n.* a prostitute.

harm (härm) *n.* **1.** injury or damage. —*v.t.* **2.** to cause harm to. —**harm′ful,** *adj.* —**harm′less,** *adj.*

har·mon′i·ca (här mon′i kə) *n.* a wind instrument played by exhaling and inhaling through metal reeds.

har′mo·ny (-mə nē) *n., pl.* **-nies. 1.** agreement. **2.** a pleasing arrangement of parts. **3.** the combination of tones blended into pleasing chords. —**har′mo·nize′,** *v.t., v.i.* —**har·mon′i·ous** (-mō′nē əs) *adj.*

har′ness (-nis) *n.* **1.** the straps and bands by which a horse is controlled. —*v.t.* **2.** to put a harness on. **3.** to control and make use of.

harp (härp) *n.* **1.** a musical instrument with strings stretched on a triangular frame. —*v.i.* **2.** to play the harp. **3. harp on,** to repeat tediously. —**harp′ist,** *n.*

har·poon′ (här po͞on′) *n.* **1.** a spearlike missile attached to a rope, used in hunting whales. —*v.t.* **2.** to strike with a harpoon.

harp′si·chord′ (härp′si kôrd′) *n.* a keyboard instrument in which the strings are plucked by quill points connected with the keys. —**harp′-si·chord′ist,** *n.*

har′ri·dan (har′i dn) *n.* a scolding, vicious woman.

har′row (har′ō) *n.* **1.** an implement for leveling or breaking up plowed land. —*v.t.* **2.** to draw a harrow over. **3.** to disturb painfully.

har′row·ing *adj.* very distressing.

har′ry (har′ē) *v.t.,* **-ried, -rying.** to harass.

harsh (härsh) *adj.* **1.** rough or unpleasant to the senses. **2.** severe; cruel.

har′vest (här′vist) *n.* **1.** the gathering of crops. **2.** the season when crops are gathered. **3.** a yield of one season. **4.** the result of something. —*v.t., v.i.* **5.** to gather or reap. —**har′vest·er,** *n.*

has (haz; *unstressed* həz, əz) *v.* third pers. sing. pres. indic. of **have.**

has′-been′ *n.* a person or thing that is no longer effective, successful, etc.

hash[1] (hash) *n.* **1.** chopped meat and potatoes browned together. **2.** a mess. —*v.t.* **3.** to chop. **4.** to discuss thoroughly.

hash[2] (hash) *n. Slang.* hashish.

hash′ish (hash′ēsh, hä shēsh′) *n.* a narcotic made from Indian hemp.

hasn′t (haz′ənt) contraction of **has not.**

hasp (hasp) *n.* a clasp for a door or lid.

has′sle (has′əl) *n., v.,* **-sled, -sling.** *Informal.* —*n.* **1.** a disorderly dispute. **2.** a troublesome situation. —*v.i.* **3.** to quarrel. **4.** to be bothered or harassed. —*v.t.* **5.** to bother or harass.

has′sock (has′ək) *n.* a cushion used as a footstool.

haste (hāst) *n.* **1.** hurry. **2.** quick or rash action. —**hast′y,** *adj.* —**hast′-i·ness,** *n.*

has′ten (hā′sən) *v.i., v.t.* to hurry.

hat (hat) *n.* a shaped covering for the head.

hatch[1] (hach) *v.t.* **1.** to bring forth (young) from the egg. **2.** to plot. —*v.i.* **3.** to emerge from an egg. —**hatch′er·y,** *n.*

hatch[2] (hach) *n.* **1.** an opening in the floor, a ship's deck, etc. **2.** the cover for such an opening.

hatch′et (hach′it) *n.* a small ax.

hatch′et job′ *n.* a maliciously destructive critique.

hatch′way′ *n.* an opening in a ship's deck.

hate (hāt) *v.,* **hated, hating,** *n.* —*v.t.* **1.** to dislike intensely. —*v.i.* **2.** to feel hatred. —*n.* **3.** intense dislike. **4.** the object of hatred.

hate′ful *adj.* arousing or deserving hate. —**hate′ful·ly,** *adv.*

haugh′ty (hô′tē) *adj.,* **-tier, -tiest.** disdainfully proud; arrogant.

haul (hôl) *v.t., v.i.* **1.** to pull with force. **2.** to transport. —*n.* **3.** an act of hauling. **4.** the load hauled. **5.** the distance over which something is hauled.

haunch (hônch, hänch) *n.* **1.** the hip. **2.** the leg and loin of an animal.

haunt (hônt, hänt) *v.t.* **1.** to visit or appear to frequently as a ghost. **2.** to recur persistently in the mind of. **3.** to visit often. —*n.* **4.** a place frequently visited. —**haunt′ed,** *adj.*

haunt′ing *adj.* lingering in the mind.

haute′ cou·ture′ (ōt′ ko͞o to͞or′) *n.* high fashion.

haute′ cui·sine′ (ōt′ kwi zēn′) *n.* gourmet cooking.

have (hav; *unstressed* həv, əv;) *v.,* **had, having.** —*v.t.* **1.** to possess; hold. **2.** to get. **3.** to experience. **4.** to give birth to. **5.** to cause to or cause to be. **6.** to engage in. **7.** to permit. **8.** to outwit. —*auxiliary verb.* **9.** (used with a past participle to form perfect tenses). **10.** (used with an infinitive to express obligation). —*Idiom.* **11. have it in for,** to wish harm to. **12. have it out,** to reach an understanding

through discussion or fighting.
—**Usage.** See OF.

ha′ven (hā′vən) *n.* **1.** a harbor. **2.** a place of shelter.

have′-not′ *n.* Usu., **have-nots.** a poor individual or group.

haven't (hav′ənt) contraction of **have not.**

hav′er•sack′ (hav′ər sak′) *n.* a single-strapped shoulder bag for carrying supplies.

hav′oc (hav′ək) *n.* great destruction.

Haw. Hawaii.

hawk[1] (hôk) *n.* **1.** a bird of prey. **2.** a person who advocates war.

hawk[2] (hôk) *v.t.* to offer for sale by calling aloud in public. —**hawk′er,** *n.*

haw′thorn′ (hô′thôrn′) *n.* a small tree with thorns and red berries.

hay (hā) *n.* grass cut and dried for fodder.

hay′ fe′ver *n.* inflammation of the eyes and respiratory tract, caused by pollen.

hay′stack′ *n.* a stack of hay built up in the open air.

hay′wire′ *adj.* out of order.

haz′ard (haz′ərd) *n.* **1.** something causing danger. —*v.t.* **2.** to venture or risk. —**haz′ard•ous,** *adj.*

haze[1] (hāz) *n.* **1.** a fine mist. **2.** vagueness. —**ha′zy,** *adj.*

haze[2] (hāz) *v.t.,* **hazed, hazing.** to subject to humiliating tricks.

ha′zel (hā′zəl) *n.* **1.** a tree or shrub bearing small edible nuts. **2.** a light golden- or greenish-brown.

H′-bomb′ *n.* the hydrogen bomb.

HDTV high-definition television.

he (hē; *unstressed* ē) *pron.* **1.** the male last mentioned. —*n.* **2.** a male.

head (hed) *n.* **1.** the upper part of the body, containing the skull with mouth, eyes, nose, and brain. **2.** the mind. **3.** the top part of anything. **4.** a leader or chief. **5.** froth at the top of a liquid. **6.** the source of a river. —*adj.* **7.** leading or main. **8.** situated at the top or front. —*v.t.* **9.** to lead. **10.** to be the chief of. —*v.i.* **11.** to move in a certain direction. **12. head off,** to intercept. —*Idiom.* **13. come to a head,** to reach a crisis. **14. keep** (or **lose) one's head,** to keep (or lose) one's self-control. **15. over one's head,** beyond one's ability to understand.

head′ache′ *n.* **1.** a pain in the upper part of the head. **2.** an annoying person, situation, etc.

head′band′, *n.* a band worn around the head.

head′dress *n.* a covering or decoration for the head.

head′first′ *adv.* **1.** with the head in front. **2.** rashly.

head′ing *n.* **1.** something that serves as a head, top, or front. **2.** a title of a page, chapter, etc.

head′light′ *n.* a light with a reflector on the front of a vehicle.

head′line′ *n.* a heading in a newspaper.

head′long′ *adv.* **1.** headfirst. **2.** rashly. —*adj.* **3.** rash. **4.** done with the head foremost.

head′-on′ *adj., adv.* with the head or front foremost.

head′phone′ *n.* Usu., **headphones.** a device worn over the ears for listening to a radio, audiotape, etc.

head′quar′ters *n.* a center of command or operations.

head′stone′ *n.* a stone marker at the head of a grave.

head′strong′ *adj.* willful.

head′way′ *n.* progress.

head′y *adj.,* **-ier, -iest. 1.** giddy; dizzy. **2.** intoxicating; exciting.

heal (hēl) *v.t.* **1.** to restore to health. —*v.i.* **2.** to get well. —**heal′er,** *n.*

health (helth) *n.* **1.** the general condition of the body or mind. **2.** soundness of body or mind. —**health′ful,** *adj.* —**health′y,** *adj.*

heap (hēp) *n.* **1.** a group of things lying one on another; pile. —*v.t., v.i.* **2.** to pile or become piled.

hear (hēr) *v.,* **heard** (hûrd) **hearing.** —*v.t.* **1.** to perceive by the ear. **2.** to listen to. **3.** to receive a report of. —*v.i.* **4.** to be able to perceive sound. **5.** to receive information.

hear′say′ *n.* rumor.

hearse (hûrs) *n.* a vehicle used to carry a coffin.

heart (härt) *n.* **1.** the organ keeping the blood in circulation. **2.** the seat of life or emotion. **3.** compassion. **4.** the vital part. **5. hearts,** a suit of playing cards with heart-shaped figures. —*Idiom.* **6. at heart,** basically. **7. by heart,** from memory.

heart′ache′ *n.* grief.

heart′ attack′ *n.* any sudden insufficiency of oxygen supply to the heart that results in heart muscle damage.

heart′break′ *n.* great sorrow or anguish. —**heart′bro′ken,** *adj.*

heart′burn′ *n.* a burning sensation in the stomach and esophagus.

heart′en *v.t.* to encourage.

heart′felt′ *adj.* deeply felt.

hearth (härth) *n.* **1.** the floor of a fireplace. **2.** the fireside.

heart′less *adj.* lacking compassion.

heart'-rend/ing adj. causing or expressing intense grief.

heart/sick/ adj. extremely sad.

heart/-to-heart/ adj. sincere and intimate.

heart/y adj., **-ier, -iest. 1.** warmhearted. **2.** genuine. **3.** vigorous. **4.** substantial. —**heart/i•ly,** adv.

heat (hēt) n. **1.** the condition or quality of being hot. **2.** the sensation of hotness. **3.** energy that causes a rise in temperature, expansion, etc. **4.** intensity of feeling —v.t., v.i. **5.** to make or become hot. **6.** to make or become excited. —**heat/er,** n.

heat/ed adj. excited or angry. —**heat/ed•ly,** adv.

heath (hēth) n. **1.** an area of open, uncultivated land. **2.** any shrub common on such land.

hea/then (hē/thən) n. **1.** one who does not believe in an established religion; pagan. —adj. **2.** pagan.

heat/stroke/ n. headache, fever, etc., caused by too much heat.

heave (hēv) v., **heaved, heaving,** n. —v.t. **1.** to lift with effort. **2.** to lift and throw with effort. —v.i. **3.** to rise and fall rhythmically. **4.** to retch. —n. **5.** an act of heaving.

heav/en (hev/ən) n. **1.** the abode of God, the angels, and the spirits of the righteous dead. **2.** Usu., **heavens.** the sky. **3.** a place or state of bliss.

heav/y (hev/ē) adj., **-ier, -iest. 1.** of great weight, amount, size, force, or intensity. **2.** serious. **3.** intense. **4.** clumsy. —**heav/i•ly,** adv.

heav/y-du/ty adj. made for hard use.

heav/y-hand/ed adj. tactless.

heav/y-heart/ed adj. preoccupied with sorrow or worry.

heav/y-set/ adj. large in body.

heck/le (hek/əl) v.t., **-led, -ling.** to harass (a speaker) with comments or questions.

hec/tare (-târ) n. a unit of area equal to 10,000 square meters (2.47 acres).

hec/tic adj. marked by confusion, excitement, or hurried activity.

hec/tor (-tər) v.t. **1.** to harass by bullying. —v.i. **2.** to be a bully.

hedge (hej) n., v., **hedged, hedging.** —n. **1.** a dense row of bushes or small trees forming a boundary. **2.** an act or means of hedging. —v.t. **3.** to surround with a hedge. **4.** to offset a possible loss by counterbalancing (one's bets, investments, etc.). —v.i. **5.** to avoid a direct answer or commitment.

hedge/hog/ n. a small spiny mammal.

he/don•ist (hēd/n ist) n. a person who lives for pleasure. —**he/don•ism,** n.

heed (hēd) v.t., v.i. **1.** to give careful attention (to). —n. **2.** careful attention. —**heed/ful,** adj. —**heed/less,** adj.

heel¹ (hēl) n. **1.** the back part of the foot below the ankle. **2.** the part of a shoe, sock, etc., covering this. —v.t. **3.** to furnish (shoes) with heels. —v.i. **4.** (of a dog) to follow at one's heels on command. —*Idiom.* **5. down at heel,** dressed shabbily. **6. kick up one's heels,** to have a lively time. **7. on the heels of,** closely following.

heel² (hēl) v.i., v.t. to lean or cause to lean to one side.

heel³ (hēl) n. a dishonorable person.

heft (heft) n. **1.** heaviness. **2.** importance. —v.t. **3.** to test for weight by lifting.

hef/ty adj., **-tier, -tiest. 1.** heavy. **2.** large.

he•gem/o•ny (hi jem/ə nē, hej/ə-mō/-) n., pl. **-nies.** domination.

heif/er (hef/ər) n. a young cow that has not calved.

height (hīt) n. **1.** extent upward. **2.** the distance between the highest and lowest points. **3.** the highest point. —**height/en,** v.t., v.i.

Heim/lich maneu/ver (hīm/lik) n. a procedure to aid a choking person by applying sudden pressure to the upper abdomen.

hei/nous (hā/nəs) adj. evil.

heir (âr) n. a person who inherits or who has a right to inherit the property, title, etc., of another.

heir/ess n. a female heir.

heir/loom/ n. a family possession handed down from one generation to another.

heist (hīst) Slang. —n. **1.** a robbery. —v.t. **2.** to rob.

held (held) v. pt. and pp. of **held.**

hel/i•cop/ter (hel/i kop/tər, hē/li-) n. an aircraft lifted by blades that rotate on a horizontal axis.

he/li•um (hē/lē əm) n. a light, colorless gas.

he/lix (hē/liks) n., pl. **hel/i•ces** (hel/-ə sēz/), **helixes.** a spiral.

hell (hel) n. **1.** the place of punishment of the wicked after death. **2.** any place or state of misery. —**hell/ish,** adj.

hel•lo/ (he lō/, hə-, hel/ō) interj. an exclamation of greeting.

helm (helm) n. **1.** a device by which a ship is steered. **2.** the place of control.

hel/met (hel/mit) n. a protective, rigid head covering.

help (help) *v.t.* **1.** to provide what is necessary to accomplish something. **2.** to make easier. **3.** to be useful to. **4.** to serve (a customer). —*v.i.* **5.** to give aid. —*n.* **6.** aid; relief. **7.** a helping person or thing. —**help'er,** *n.* —**help'ful,** *adj.*

help'ing *n.* a portion of food served.

help'less *adj.* **1.** unable to help oneself. **2.** powerless.

help'mate' *n.* a companion and helper.

hel'ter-skel'ter (hel'tər skel'tər) *adv.* in disorderly haste.

hem (hem) *v.,* **hemmed, hemming,** *n.* —*v.t.* **1.** to fold back and sew down the edge of (cloth, a garment, etc.). **2. hem in,** to confine and restrict. —*n.* **3.** an edge made by hemming.

hem'i•sphere (-i sfēr') *n.* **1.** one of the halves of the earth. **2.** a half of a sphere.

hem'lock (-lok') *n.* **1.** a cone-bearing tree of the pine family. **2.** a poisonous plant of the parsley family.

he'mo•glo'bin (hē'mə glō'bin, hem'ə-) *n.* an oxygen-carrying compound in red blood cells.

he'mo•phil'i•a (hē'mə fil'ē ə) *n.* a genetic disorder marked by excessive bleeding. —**he'mo•phil'i•ac',** *n.*

hem'or•rhage (hem'ər ij) *n., v.,* **-rhaged, -rhaging.** —*n.* **1.** a discharge of blood. —*v.i.* **2.** to bleed profusely.

hem'or•rhoid' (hem'ə roid') *n.* Usu., **hemorrhoids.** a painful dilation of blood vessels in the anus.

hemp (hemp) *n.* **1.** a plant with tough fibers used for making rope. **2.** an intoxicating drug made from the hemp plant.

hen (hen) *n.* a female bird.

hence (hens) *adv.* **1.** therefore. **2.** from this time. **3.** from this place.

hence'forth' (hens'fôrth', hens'-fôrth') *adv.* from now on.

hench'man (hench'mən) *n., pl.,* **-men.** a trusted supporter.

hen'na (hen'ə) *n.* a reddish dye.

hep'a•ti'tis (hep'ə tī'tis) *n.* inflammation of the liver.

hep.tath'lon (hep tath'lən, -lon) *n.* an athletic contest comprising seven track-and-field events.

her (hûr; *unstressed* hər, ər) *pron.* **1.** the objective case of **she.** —*adj.* **2.** a form of the possessive case of **she.**

her'ald (her'əld) *n.* **1.** a messenger or forerunner. **2.** one that proclaims. —*v.t.* **3.** to proclaim. **4.** to usher in.

her'ald•ry *n.* the art of devising and describing coats of arms, tracing genealogies, etc. —**he•ral'dic** (he ral'dik, hə-) *adj.*

herb (ûrb; *esp. Brit.* hûrb) *n.* **1.** a flowering plant with a nonwoody stem. **2.** such a plant used in medicine or cooking. —**herb'al,** *adj.*

her•ba'ceous (hûr bā'shəs, ûr-) **1.** herblike. **2.** (of plants) not woody.

herb'i•cide' (hûr'bə sīd', ûr'-) *n.* a substance for killing plants, esp. weeds. —**her'bi•cid'al,** *adj.*

her•biv'o•rous (hûr biv'ər əs, ûr-) *adj.* feeding on plants. —**her'bi•vore'** (hûr'bə vôr', ûr'-) *n.*

her'cu•le'an (hûr'kyə lē'ən, hûr-kyōō'lē-) *adj.* requiring or showing extraordinary strength or effort.

herd (hûrd) *n.* **1.** a number of animals feeding or moving together. —*v.i., v.t.* **2.** to move or gather as a herd.

here (hēr) *adv.* **1.** in, at, or to this place. **2.** in the present. —*n.* **3.** this place or point.

here'a•bout' or **here'a•bouts'** *adv.* in this neighborhood.

here•af'ter 1. from now on. —*n.* **2.** a life after death. **3.** the future.

here•by' *adv.* by means of this.

he•red'i•tar'y (hə red'i ter'ē) *adj.* **1.** passing from parents to offspring; inherited. **2.** holding rights, a title, etc., by inheritance.

he•red'i•ty *n.* the passing on of traits from parents to offspring.

here•in' *adv.* in this place.

her'e•sy (her'ə sē) *n., pl.* **-sies. 1.** a religious opinion contrary to accepted doctrine. **2.** any belief contrary to established beliefs or customs. —**her'e•tic** (her'i tik) *n.*

here•to•fore' *adv.* before now.

here'with' *adv.* along with or by means of this.

her'it•a•ble (her'i tə bəl) *adj.* capable of being inherited.

her'it•age (her'i tij) *n.* **1.** something passed on by inheritance. **2.** traditions and history.

her•maph'ro•dite' (hûr maf'rə dīt') *n.* an animal or plant with reproductive organs of both sexes.

her•met'ic (-met'ik) *adj.* airtight. Also, **her•met'i•cal.**

her'mit (-mit) *n.* a person living apart from others.

her'mit•age (-mi tij) *n.* a hermit's dwelling.

her'ni•a (-nē ə) *n.* the protrusion of an organ or tissue through the surrounding wall.

he'ro (hēr'ō) *n., pl.* **-roes. 1.** a man admired for brave deeds, noble qualities, etc. **2.** the main male

character in a story, play, etc.
—**her′o·ism′** (her′ō iz′əm) *n.*

he·ro′ic (hi rō′ik) *adj.* **1.** brave, daring, or noble. **2.** dealing with the deeds of heroes.

her′o·in (her′ō in) *n.* a narcotic and addictive drug derived from morphine.

her′o·ine (her′ō in) *n.* **1.** a woman admired for brave deeds, noble qualities, etc. **2.** the main female character in a story, play, etc.

her′on (her′ən) *n.* a long-legged wading bird.

her′pes (hûr′pēz) *n.* a viral disease characterized by blisters on the skin or mucous membranes.

her′ring (her′ing) *n.* a food fish of the N Atlantic.

her′ring·bone′ *n.* **1.** a pattern of slanting lines in adjoining vertical rows. **2.** a fabric with this pattern.

hers (hûrz) *pron.* **1.** a possessive form of **she**, used as a predicate adjective. **2.** that or those belonging to her.

her·self′ *pron.* a reflexive or intensive form of **her**.

hertz (hûrts) *n., pl.* **hertz.** a unit of frequency equal to one cycle per second.

hes′i·tate′ (hez′i tāt′) *v.i.*, **-tated,** **-tating. 1.** to wait to act or speak because of fear, doubt, or reluctance. **2.** to pause. —**hes′i·tant** (-tənt) *adj.* —**hes′i·ta′tion, hes′i· tan·cy,** *n.*

het′er·o·dox′ (het′ər ə doks′) *adj.* not in accordance with established doctrine.

het′er·o·ge′ne·ous (-jē′nē əs) *adj.* composed of people or things of different kinds.

het′er·o·sex′u·al *adj.* **1.** sexually attracted to the opposite sex. —*n.* **2.** a heterosexual person. —**het′er· o·sex′u·al′i·ty,** *n.*

hew (hyōō; *often* yōō) *v.,* **hewed,** **hewed** or **hewn, hewing.** —*v.t.* **1.** to chop or cut with an ax, sword, etc. **2.** to make by cutting.

hex (heks) *v.t.* **1.** to cast a spell on. **2.** to bring bad luck to. —*n.* **3.** a spell or charm.

hex′a·gon′ (hek′sə gon′, -gən) *n.* a six-sided polygon. —**hex·ag′o·nal** (hek sag′ə nl) *adj.*

hex·am′e·ter (hek sam′i tər) *n.* a line of verse having six feet.

hey′day′ (hā′dā′) *n.* the time of greatest success, popularity, etc.

hgt. height.

hgwy. highway.

HI Hawaii.

hi·a′tus (hī ā′təs) *n., pl.* **-tuses, -tus.** a break or interruption.

hi·ba′chi (hi bä′chē) *n.* a small brazier covered with a grill.

hi′ber·nate′ (hī′bər nāt′) *v.i.,* **-nated, -nating.** to spend the winter in a dormant state. —**hi′ber· na′tion,** *n.*

hi·bis′cus (hī bis′kəs, hi-) *n.* a plant with large, showy flowers.

hic′cup or **hic′cough** (hik′up, -əp) *n.* **1.** a sudden involuntary drawing in of breath with a "hic" sound. —*v.i.* **2.** to make the sound of a hiccup.

hick (hik) *n.* a provincial, unsophisticated person.

hick′o·ry (-ə rē) *n., pl.* **-ries.** a N American tree of the walnut family, bearing an edible nut.

hide[1] (hīd) *v.,* **hid** (hid) **hidden** or **hid, hiding,** *n.* —*v.t.* **1.** to conceal from sight. **2.** to keep secret. —*v.i.* **3.** to conceal oneself.

hide[2] (hīd) *n.* an animal's skin.

hide′a·way′ *n.* a private retreat.

hide′bound′ *adj.* narrow and rigid in opinion.

hid′e·ous (hid′ē əs) *adj.* very ugly.

hide′-out′ *n.* a safe place to hide, esp. from the law.

hi′er·ar′chy (hī′ə rär′kē) *n., pl.* **-chies.** any system in which one person or thing is ranked one above another.

hi′er·o·glyph′ic (hī′ər ə glif′ik, hī′- rə-) *adj.* **1.** of picture writing, as among the ancient Egyptians. —*n.* **2.** a hieroglyphic symbol.

hi′-fi′ (hī′fī′) *n.* high fidelity.

high (hī) *adj.,* **-er, -est. 1.** lofty; tall. **2.** having a certain height. **3.** far above the ground. **4.** greater than normal. **5.** above others in rank. **6.** elevated in pitch. **7.** *Informal.* under the influence of alcohol or drugs. —*adv.* **8.** at or to a high place, rank, etc. —*n.* **9.** a high point or level. **10.** an atmospheric system of high pressure. **11.** a state of euphoria.

high′brow′ *n.* **1.** a cultured or intellectual person. —*adj.* **2.** typical of a highbrow.

high′ fidel′ity *n.* sound reproduction with little distortion of the original.

high′-flown′ *adj.* pretentious.

high′ fre′quency *n.* the range of radio frequencies between 3 and 30 megahertz.

high′-hand′ed *adj.* arrogant.

high′lands (-ləndz) *n.* a hilly area.

high′light′ *v.t.* **1.** to emphasize. **2.** to create highlights in. —*n.* **3.** an important event, scene, etc. **4.** an area of contrasting brightness.

high′ly *adv.* very; extremely.

high'-mind'ed *adj.* having or showing noble principles.

high'ness (-nis) *n.* **1.** the quality or state of being high. **2. Highness,** a title given to royalty.

high'-pres'sure *adj., v.,* **-sured, -suring.** —*adj.* **1.** having a pressure above the normal. **2.** stressful. **3.** aggressive. —*v.t.* **4.** to persuade aggressively.

high'rise' *adj.* **1.** (of a building) having many stories. —*n.* **2.** a tall building.

high'road' *n.* **1.** an honorable course. **2.** an easy course. **3.** *Chiefly Brit.* a highway.

high' school' *n.* a school consisting of grades 9 through 12.

high' seas' *n.* the open ocean.

high'-spir'it·ed *adj.* lively.

high'-strung' *adj.* highly sensitive or nervous.

high'-tech' *n.* **1.** technology using highly sophisticated and advanced equipment and techniques. —*adj.* **2.** using or suggesting high-tech.

high'-ten'sion *adj.* of relatively high voltage.

high'way' *n.* a main road.

high'way·man *n., pl.* **-men.** a highway robber.

hi'jack' (hī'jak') *v.t.* to seize (a plane, truck, etc.) by force.

hike (hīk) *v.,* **hiked, hiking,** *n.* —*v.i.* **1.** to walk a long distance, esp. through rural areas. —*n.* **2.** a long walk. —**hik'er,** *n.*

hi·lar'i·ous (hi lâr'ē əs, -lar'-) *adj.* **1.** very funny. **2.** noisily merry. —**hi·lar'i·ty,** *n.*

hill (hil) *n.* **1.** a raised part of the earth's surface, smaller than a mountain. **2.** a heap or mound. —**hill'y,** *adj.*

hill'ock (-ək) *n.* a small hill.

hilt (hilt) *n.* the handle of a sword or tool.

him (him) *pron.* the objective case of **he.**

him·self' (him self'; *medially often* im-) *pron.* the reflexive or emphatic form of **him.**

hind¹ (hīnd) *adj.* situated in the rear.

hind² (hīnd) *n.* the female red deer.

hin'der (hin'dər) *v.t.* to cause delay or difficulty in. —**hin'drance,** *n.*

hind'most' (hīnd'-) *adj.* nearest the rear.

hind'sight' *n.* keen understanding of an event after it has occurred.

Hin'du·ism (hin'do͞o iz'əm) *n.* the major religion of India. —**Hin'du,** *n., adj.*

hinge (hinj) *n., v.,* **hinged, hinging.** —*n.* **1.** a jointed device on which a door, lid, etc., moves. —*v.t., v.i.* **2.** to attach or be attached by a hinge. **3. hinge on,** to depend on.

hint (hint) *n.* **1.** an indirect suggestion. —*v.t., v.i.* **2.** to give a hint.

hin'ter·land' (hin'tər land') *n.* an area remote from cities.

hip¹ (hip) *n.* the projecting part on each side of the body below the waist.

hip² (hip) *adj.,* **-per, -pest.** *Slang.* familiar with the latest styles or ideas.

hip'-hop' *n. Slang.* the popular culture of usu. black urban youth as characterized by rap music.

hip'pie (hip'ē) *n.* a young person of the 1960s who rejected conventional social values.

hip'po (hip'ō) *n., pl.* **-pos.** a hippopotamus.

hip'po·drome' (hip'ə drōm') *n.* an arena, esp. for equestrian events.

hip'po·pot'a·mus (hip'ə pot'ə məs) *n., pl.* **-muses, -mi** (-mī'). a large African river mammal with short legs and a thick skin.

hire (hī°r) *v.,* **hired, hiring,** *n.* —*v.t.* **1.** to engage the services of (a person) or the use of (a thing) for a set price. —*n.* **2.** the act of hiring or the condition of being hired.

hire'ling (-ling) *n.* a person who works only for pay.

hir'sute (hûr'so͞ot, hûr so͞ot') *adj.* hairy. —**hir'sute·ness,** *n.*

his (hiz; *unstressed* iz) *pron.* **1.** the possessive form of **he. 2.** that or those belonging to him.

hiss (his) *v.i.* **1.** to make a prolonged *s* sound. **2.** to express disapproval in this way. —*n.* **3.** a hissing sound.

his·tor'ic (hi stôr'ik) *adj.* well-known in history.

his'to·ry (his'tə rē, -trē) *n., pl.* **-ries. 1.** the knowledge, study, or record of past events. **2.** a pattern of events determining the future. —**his·to'ri·an** (hi stôr'ē ən) *n.*

his'tri·on'ics (his'trē on'iks) *n.pl.* overly dramatic behavior or speech. —**his'tri·on'ic,** *adj.*

hit (hit) *v.,* **hit, hitting,** *n.* —*v.t.* **1.** to deal a blow to. **2.** to collide with. **3.** to reach with a missile, weapon, etc. **4.** to have a marked effect on. **5.** to come upon. —*v.i.* **6.** to strike. **7.** to come into collision. **8.** to come to light. —*n.* **9.** a collision. **10.** a blow. **11.** a success.

hitch (hich) *v.t.* **1.** to fasten by a hook, rope, etc. **2.** to raise jerkily. —*v.i.* **3.** to become fastened. **4.** to move jerkily. —*n.* **5.** a fastening or knot. **6.** an obstruction or problem. **7.** a jerk or pull.

hitch'hike' *v.i.,* **-hiked, -hiking.** to

travel by begging a ride from a stranger.

hith′er (hith′ər) *adv.* to this place.

hith′er•to′ *adv.* until now.

HIV human immunodeficiency virus, the cause of AIDS.

hive (hīv) *n.* **1.** a shelter for bees. **2.** the bees living in a hive.

hives (hīvz) *n.pl.* an eruption of itchy swellings on the skin.

HMO *pl.* **HMOs, HMO's.** health maintenance organization: a health-care plan that provides services to subscribers.

H.M.S. Her (or His) Majesty's Ship.

hoard (hôrd) *n.* **1.** a supply that is hidden for future use. —*v.t., v.i.* **2.** to accumulate a hoard (of). —**hoard′er,** *n.*

hoar′frost′ (hôr′frôst′) *n.* a cover of tiny ice particles.

hoarse (hôrs) *adj.* having a low and harsh voice.

hoary (hôr′ē) *adj.* **1.** white with age. **2.** old.

hoax (hōks) *n.* **1.** something intended to deceive. —*v.t.* **2.** to deceive; trick.

hob′ble (hob′əl) *v.,* **-bled, -bling.** —*v.i.* **1.** to limp. —*v.t.* **2.** to cause to limp. **3.** to fasten together the legs of (a horse, mule, etc.) to prevent free movement. **4.** to impede.

hob′by (hob′ē) *n., pl.* **-bies.** an activity pursued for pleasure rather than money.

hob′by•horse′ *n.* **1.** a stick with a horse's head, ridden by children. **2.** a favorite idea or project.

hob′gob′lin *n.* something causing superstitious fear.

hob′nob′ (-nob′) *v.i.,* **-nobbed, -nobbing.** to associate on friendly terms.

ho′bo (hō′bō) *n., pl.* **-bos, -boes.** a tramp; vagrant.

hock¹ (hok) *n.* the joint in the hind leg of a horse, cow, etc.

hock² (hok) *v.t.* **1.** to pawn. —*n.* **2.** the state of being held as security. **3.** the condition of owing.

hock′ey (hok′ē) *n.* a game played on a field or on ice with bent clubs (**hockey sticks**) and a ball or disk.

ho′cus-po′cus (hō′kəs pō′kəs) *n.* meaningless words used in magic tricks.

hod (hod) *n.* **1.** a trough for carrying mortar, bricks, etc. **2.** a coal scuttle.

hodge′podge′ (hoj′poj′) *n.* a mixture; jumble.

hoe (hō) *n., v.,* **hoed, hoeing.** —*n.* **1.** a tool for breaking the soil and weeding. —*v.t., v.i.* **2.** to dig or weed with a hoe.

hog (hôg) *n., v.,* **hogged, hogging.** —*n.* **1.** a domesticated swine. **2.** a greedy or filthy person. —*v.t.* **3.** to take more than one's share of. —**hog′gish,** *adj.*

hogs′head′ *n.* a large cask.

hog′wash′ *n.* nonsense; bunk.

hog′-wild′ *adj.* wildly enthusiastic.

hoi′ pol•loi′ (hoi′ pə loi′) *n.* the common people; the masses.

hoist (hoist) *v.t.* **1.** to lift, esp. by machine. —*n.* **2.** a hoisting apparatus. **3.** the act of lifting.

hok′ey (hō′kē) *adj.,* **-ier, -iest. 1.** overly sentimental. **2.** obviously contrived. —**hok′i•ness,** *n.*

hold (hōld) *v.,* **held** (held) **holding,** *n.* —*v.t.* **1.** to have in the hand. **2.** to support. **3.** to possess or occupy. **4.** to keep in a specified condition. **5.** to contain. **6.** to restrain or detain. **7.** to regard. **8.** to believe. —*v.i.* **9.** to remain in a specified condition. **10.** to remain valid. **11. hold forth,** to speak at length. **12. ~ out, a.** to offer. **b.** to last. **c.** to refuse to yield. —*n.* **13.** a grasp. **14.** a means of exerting influence. **15.** a cargo space below a ship's deck. —**hold′er,** *n.*

hold′ing *n.* **1.** a section of leased land, esp. for farming. **2. holdings,** legally owned property.

hold′out′ *n.* one who refuses to take part, give in, etc.

hold′up′ *n.* **1.** a delay. **2.** a robbery at gunpoint.

hole (hōl) *n., v.,* **holed, holing.** —*n.* **1.** an opening or gap. **2.** a hollow place. **3.** the burrow of an animal. **4.** an unpleasant situation.

hol′i•day′ (hol′i dā′) *n.* **1.** a day on which business is suspended to commemorate a person or event. **2.** a holy day. —*adj.* **3.** festive.

ho′li•ness (hō′lē nis) *n.* the quality or state of being holy.

ho•lis′tic (hō lis′tik) *adj.* of or using therapies that consider the body and the mind as an integrated whole.

hol′low (hol′ō) *adj.* **1.** empty. **2.** sunken. **3.** dull. **4.** meaningless; insincere. —*n.* **5.** a hole. **6.** a valley. —*v.t., v.i.* **7.** to make or become hollow.

hol′ly (hol′ē) *n., pl.* **-lies.** a shrub with glossy leaves and red berries.

hol′ly•hock′ (-hok′, -hôk′) *n.* a tall plant with showy, colored flowers.

hol′o•caust′ (hol′ə kôst′, hō′lə-) *n.* **1.** a great destruction, esp. by fire. **2. the Holocaust,** the slaughter of European Jews by the Nazis.

ho′lo•gram′ (hol′ə gram′, hō′lə-) *n.* a three-dimensional image made by a laser.

ho·log′ra·phy (hə log′rə fē) *n.* the technique of making holograms.

hol′ster (hōl′stər) *n.* a case for a pistol, worn on the body.

ho′ly (hō′lē) *adj.*, **-lier, -liest. 1.** recognized or revered as sacred. **2.** dedicated to God.

Ho′ly Spir′it, *n.* the third person of the Trinity. Also, **Holy Ghost.**

hom′age (hom′ij, om′-) *n.* reverence or respect.

home (hōm) *n., adj., adv., v.,* **homed, homing. —n. 1.** a place of residence. **2.** an institution for people needing special care. **3.** one's native place or country. *—adj.* **4.** of one's home. *—adv.* **5.** to or at home. *—v.i.* **6.** to go home or toward a specified point.

home′land′ *n.* one's native land.

home′less *adj.* lacking a home.

home′ly *adj.*, **-lier, -liest. 1.** plain; not beautiful. **2.** simple.

home′made′ *adj.* made at home or at the place where it is sold.

home′mak′er *n.* a person who manages a home.

home′ of′fice *n.* **1.** the main office of a company. **2.** work or office space set up in a person's home and used regularly and exclusively for business.

ho′me·op′a·thy (hō′mē op′ə thē) *n.* a method of treating disease with small doses of drugs that in a healthy person would cause symptoms like those of the disease. **—ho′me·o·path′ic** (-ə path′ik) *adj.*

home′ page′ *n.* the initial page of a Web site.

home′sick′ *adj.* longing for home.

home′spun′ *adj.* **1.** plain; simple. *—n.* **2.** cloth made at home.

home′stead (-sted, -stid) *n.* a dwelling with its land and buildings.

home′stretch′ *n.* the last part of a racetrack, endeavor, etc.

hom′ey *adj.*, **-ier, -iest.** cozy.

hom′i·cide′ (hom′ə sīd′, hō′mə-) *n.* the killing of one person by another. **—hom′i·cid′al,** *adj.*

hom′i·ly (hom′ə lē) *n., pl.* **-lies.** a sermon. **—hom′i·let′ic** (-let′ik) *adj.*

hom′i·ny (hom′ə nē) *n.* hulled corn from which the bran and germ have been removed.

homo- a prefix meaning same.

ho′mo·ge′ne·ous (hō′mə jē′nē əs) *adj.* **1.** composed of parts that are all of the same kind. **2.** of the same kind. **—ho′mo·ge·ne′i·ty** (-ji-nē′ə tē) *n.*

ho·mog′e·nize′ (hə moj′ə nīz′, hō-) *v.t.*, **-nized, -nizing. 1.** to make homogeneous. **2.** to treat (milk) so that the fat is evenly distributed.

ho′mo·graph′ (hom′ə graf′) *n.* a word spelled the same as another but having a different meaning.

hom′o·nym (-nim) *n.* a word that is like another in sound, but not in meaning.

ho′mo·pho′bi·a (hō′mə fō′bē ə) *n.* a hatred of homosexuals.

Ho′mo sa′pi·ens (hō′mō sā′pē ənz) *n.* the species to which human beings belong.

ho′mo·sex′u·al (hō′mə sek′shoo əl) *adj.* **1.** sexually attracted to persons of the same sex. **—***n.* **2.** a homosexual person. **—ho′mo·sex′u·al′i·ty** (-al′i tē) *n.*

Hon. 1. Honorable. **2.** Honorary.

hon′cho (hon′chō) *n., pl.* **-chos.** *Slang.* an important person.

hone (hōn) *v.t.*, **honed, honing.** to sharpen to a fine edge.

hon′est (on′ist) *adj.* **1.** honorable or trustworthy. **2.** gained fairly. **3.** sincere. **4.** truthful. **—hon′est·ly,** *adv.* **—hon′es·ty,** *n.*

hon′ey (hun′ē) *n.* a sweet fluid produced by bees from nectar.

hon′ey·comb′ *n.* **1.** a wax structure built by bees to store honey. **2.** anything resembling such a structure.

hon′ey·dew′ mel′on *n.* a melon with a pale greenish rind and light green flesh.

hon′ey·moon′ *n.* a vacation taken by a newly married couple.

hon′ey·suck′le *n.* a shrub bearing fragrant tubular flowers.

honk (hongk) *n.* **1.** the cry of a goose. **2.** any similar sound. **—***v.i.*, *v.t.* **3.** to make or cause to make such a sound.

hon′or (on′ər) *n.* **1.** honesty in one's beliefs and action. **2.** high respect or public esteem. **3.** a token of this. **—***v.t.* **4.** to hold in high respect. **5.** to show regard for. **6.** to confer an honor on. **7.** to accept as valid.

hon′or·a·ble *adj.* **1.** showing principles of honor. **2.** worthy of honor.

hon′or·ar′y (-rer′ē) *adj.* given for honor only.

hood[1] (hood) *n.* **1.** a flexible covering for the head and neck. **2.** something resembling this. **3.** the part of an automobile body that covers the engine. **—hood′ed,** *adj.*

hood[2] (hood) *n.* a hoodlum.

hood′lum (hood′ləm, hood′-) *n.* a young thug or ruffian.

hood′wink′ (hood′wingk′) *v.t.* to deceive.

hoof (hoof, hoof) *n., pl.* **hoofs, hooves** (hoovz, hoovz). the horny covering of an animal's foot. **—hoofed,** *adj.*

hook (hŏŏk) *n.* **1.** a curved piece of metal for catching, pulling, etc. **2.** something having a sharp curve. —*v.t.* **3.** to seize, fasten, or hold with a hook. —*v.i.* **4.** to curve or bend like a hook.

hook′er *n. Slang.* a prostitute.

hook′up′ *n.* a connection of parts or apparatus into a circuit, network, machine, or system.

hoo′li•gan (hōō′li gən) *n.* a hoodlum.

hoop (hōōp, hŏŏp) *n.* a rigid circular band of metal or wood.

hoop′la (hōōp′lä) *n. Informal.* excitement.

hoo•ray′ (hŏŏ rā′) *interj., n.* hurrah.

hoot (hōōt) *v.i.* **1.** to shout in scorn. **2.** to utter the cry of an owl. —*n.* **3.** an owl's cry. **4.** a scornful shout.

hop¹ (hop) *v.,* **hopped, hopping,** *n.* —*v.i.* **1.** to make a short, bouncing leap. **2.** to leap on one foot. **3.** to make a short, quick trip. —*v.t.* **4.** to jump over. **5.** to board (a vehicle). —*n.* **6.** a short leap, esp. on one foot. **7.** a short trip, esp. by air. **8.** *Informal.* a dance.

hop² (hop) *n.* **1.** a twining plant of the hemp family. **2. hops,** its dried ripe cones, used in brewing, medicine, etc.

hope (hōp) *n., v.,* **hoped, hoping.** —*n.* **1.** the feeling that something desired is possible. **2.** a person or thing giving cause for hope. **3.** something hoped for. —*v.t.* **4.** to look forward to with desire and confidence. —*v.i.* **5.** to have hope. —**hope′ful,** *adj.*

hop′per (hop′ər) *n.* a bin in which material is stored temporarily.

horde (hôrd) *n.* a crowd.

ho•ri′zon (hə rī′zən) *n.* the apparent line between earth and sky.

hor′i•zon′tal (hôr′ə zon′tl) *adj.* parallel to level ground.

hor′mone (hôr′mōn) *n.* a secretion of an endocrine gland that affects the functions of specific organs, tissues, etc.

horn (hôrn) *n.* **1.** a hard pointed growth on the heads of cattle, goats, etc. **2.** a hornlike part. **3.** a brass wind instrument. **4.** a device that sounds a warning.

hor′net (hôr′nit) *n.* a large wasp.

hor′o•scope′ (hôr′ə skōp′) *n.* a chart of the heavens used in astrology to predict events in a person's life.

hor•ren′dous (hə ren′dəs) *adj.* dreadful; horrible.

hor′ri•ble (hôr′ə bəl) *adj.* **1.** causing horror. **2.** very unpleasant.

hor′rid (-id) *adj.* extremely unpleasant.

hor′ror (hôr′ər) *n.* **1.** intense fear and loathing. **2.** anything causing such a feeling. **3.** a strong aversion. —**hor′ri•fy′,** *v.t.*

hors-d'oeuvre′ (ôr dûrv′) *n., pl.* **hors-d'oeuvres** (ôr dûrv′, -dûrvz′). a small portion of food served before a meal.

horse (hôrs) *n.* **1.** a large four-footed animal domesticated for pulling loads and riding. **2.** a frame with legs on which something is mounted.

horse′back′ *n.* **1.** the back of a horse. —*adv.* **2.** on horseback.

horse′man or **horse′wo′man** *n., pl.* **-men** or **-women.** a person skilled in riding a horse.

horse′play′ *n.* rough play.

horse′pow′er *n.* a unit of power equal to 550 foot-pounds per second.

horse′rad′ish *n.* a cultivated plant with a pungent root.

horse′ sense′ *n.* common sense.

horse′shoe′ *n.* **1.** a U-shaped iron plate nailed to a horse's hoof. **2.** something U-shaped.

hors′y *adj.,* **-ier, -iest. 1.** of or like a horse. **2.** dealing with or fond of horses.

hor′ti•cul′ture (hôr′ti kul′chər) *n.* the art of cultivating gardens.

ho•san′na (hō zan′ə) *interj.* an exclamation praising God.

hose (hōz) *n., v.,* **hosed, hosing.** —*n.* **1.** a flexible tube for conveying liquid. **2.** stockings. —*v.t.* **3.** to spray with a hose.

ho′sier•y (hō′zhə rē) *n.* stockings.

hos′pice (hos′pis) *n.* a facility for supportive care of the dying.

hos′pi•ta•ble (hos′pi tə bəl, hospit′ə-) *adj.* **1.** treating guests warmly and generously. **2.** favorably receptive.

hos′pi•tal (hos′pi tl) *n.* an institution for treatment of the sick and injured.

hos′pi•tal′i•ty (-tal′i tē) *n., pl.* **-ties.** the warm reception of guests or strangers.

hos′pi•tal•ize′ *v.t.,* **-ized, -izing.** to place in a hospital for care. —**hos′-pi•tal•i•za′tion,** *n.*

host¹ (hōst) *n.* **1.** a person who entertains guests. **2.** a moderator for a television or radio program. —*v.t., v.i.* **3.** to act as host (to).

host² (hōst) *n.* a great number.

Host (hōst) *n.* the bread consecrated in the celebration of the Eucharist.

hos′tage (hos′tij) *n.* a person given or held as security.

hos'tel (hos'tl) *n.* an inexpensive lodging for young travelers.

hos'tile (hos'tl; *esp. Brit.* -tīl) *adj.* **1.** opposed; unfriendly. **2.** of enemies. —**hos•til'i•ty** (ho stil'i tē) *n.*

hot (hot) *adj.,* **hotter, hottest. 1.** having a high temperature. **2.** feeling great heat. **3.** peppery. **4.** showing intense feeling. **5.** *Informal.* currently popular. **6.** *Slang.* recently stolen.

hot'bed' *n.* **1.** a glass-covered, heated bed of earth for growing plants. **2.** a place where something thrives and spreads.

hot'-blood'ed *adj.* **1.** excitable. **2.** passionate.

hot' cake' *n.* a pancake.

hot' dog' *n.* a frankfurter.

ho•tel' (hō tel') *n.* a building offering food and lodging to travelers.

hot' flash' *n.* a sudden, brief feeling of heat experienced by some menopausal women.

hot'head' *n.* an impetuous or short-tempered person.

hot'house' *n.* a greenhouse.

hot' line' *n.* a direct telephone line for immediate communications of major importance.

hot' plate' *n.* a portable electrical appliance for cooking.

hot' rod' *n. Slang.* a car with an engine built for increased speed. —**hot' rod'der,** *n.*

hot' tub' *n.* a large wooden tub of hot water big enough for several persons.

hot' wa'ter *n. Informal.* trouble.

hound (hound) *n.* **1.** any of several breeds of hunting dog. —*v.t.* **2.** to hunt or track. **3.** to harass.

hour (ouᵊr, ou'ər) *n.* **1.** a period of 60 minutes. **2.** any specific time of day. —**hour'ly,** *adj., adv.*

hour'glass' *n.* a device for measuring time by the draining of sand from the top part to the bottom part of a glass container.

house *n., v.,* **housed, housing.** —*n.* (hous) **1.** a building in which people live. **2.** a building for any special purpose. **3.** a legislative or deliberative body. **4.** a commercial firm. **5.** a family or dynasty. —*v.t.* (houz) **6.** to provide with shelter or space for work or storage.

house'break'er *n.* a person who breaks into another's house with the intent to steal.

house'bro'ken *adj.* (of an animal) trained to excrete outdoors or to behave appropriately indoors.

house'fly' *n., pl.* **-flies.** a medium-sized fly.

house'hold' *n.* **1.** the people of a house. **2.** a home and its related affairs. —*adj.* **3.** domestic.

house'hus'band *n.* a married man who stays at home to manage the household.

house'keep'er *n.* a person who manages a house. —**house'keep'ing,** *n.*

house'plant' *n.* an ornamental plant grown indoors.

house'warm'ing *n.* a party to celebrate a new home.

house'wife' *n., pl.* **-wives.** a married woman who stays at home to manage the household.

house'work' *n.* the work done in housekeeping.

hous'ing (hou'zing) *n.* **1.** any lodging or dwelling place. **2.** houses collectively. **3.** anything that protects.

hov'el (huv'əl, hov'-) *n.* a small, mean dwelling.

hov'er (huv'ər, hov'-) *v.i.* **1.** to hang suspended in air. **2.** to wait nearby.

how (hou) *adv.* **1.** in what way? **2.** to what extent or degree? **3.** in what state or condition? —*conj.* **4.** the way in which.

how•ev'er *conj.* **1.** nevertheless. —*adj.* **2.** to whatever extent. —*conj.* **3.** in whatever manner or state.

howl (houl) *v.t.* **1.** to utter the loud, long, mournful cry of a wolf, dog, etc. **2.** to utter a similar cry. —*n.* **3.** the cry of the wolf, dog, etc. **4.** any similar cry.

how'so•ev'er *adv.* however.

hoy'den (hoid'n) *n.* a tomboy.

HP horsepower.

HQ headquarters.

H.S. High School.

ht. height.

HTML HyperText Markup Language: a set of standards, a variety of SGML, used to tag the elements of a hypertext document on the World Wide Web.

hub (hub) *n.* **1.** the central part of a wheel. **2.** a center of activity.

hub'bub (hub'ub) *n.* an uproar.

hu'bris (hyōō'bris, hōō'-) *n.* excessive pride.

huck'le•ber'ry (huk'əl ber'ē) *n., pl.* **-ries.** the dark blue, edible berry of a shrub of the heath family.

huck'ster (huk'stər) *n.* **1.** a peddler. **2.** an aggressive seller or promoter.

HUD (hud) Department of Housing and Urban Development.

hud'dle (hud'l) *v.,* **-dled, -dling,** *n.* —*v.t., v.i.* **1.** to crowd together closely. —*n.* **2.** a closely gathered group or heap.

hue (hyōō) *n.* a color.

huff (huf) n. **1.** a fit of sulking anger. —v.i. **2.** to breathe heavily.

hug (hug) v., **hugged, hugging,** n. —v.t. **1.** to clasp in the arms affectionately. **2.** to stay close to. —n. **3.** a tight clasp with the arms.

huge (hyōōj; *often* yōōj) adj., **huger, hugest.** very large in size or extent.

hu′la (hōō′lə) n. a Hawaiian dance.

hulk (hulk) n. **1.** the body of an old ship. **2.** a bulky person or thing.

hulk′ing adj. heavy and clumsy.

hull¹ (hul) n. **1.** the outer covering of a seed or fruit. —v.t. **2.** to remove the hull of.

hull² (hul) n. the hollow lower part of a ship.

hul′la·ba·loo′ (hul′ə bə lōō′) n., pl. **-loos.** *Informal.* an uproar.

hum (hum) v., **hummed, humming,** n. —v.i. **1.** to make a low droning sound. **2.** to sing with closed lips. **3.** to be busy or active. —n. **4.** the act or sound of humming.

hu′man (hyōō′mən) adj. **1.** of or like people. —n. **2.** Also, **human being.** a person.

hu·mane′ (-mān′) adj. compassionate and sympathetic toward others.

hu′man·ism n. a system of thought focusing on human interests, values, and dignity. —**hu′man·ist,** n., adj.

hu·man·i·tar′i·an (-man′i târ′ē ən) adj. **1.** having concern for the welfare of people. —n. **2.** a person who promotes human welfare.

hu·man′i·ty n., pl. **-ties. 1.** the human race. **2.** the state or quality of being human. **3. the humanities,** literature, philosophy, art, etc., as distinguished from the sciences.

hu′man·ize′ (-mə nīz′) v.t., v.i., **-ized, -izing.** to make or become human or humane.

hu′man·kind′ n. the human race.

hu′man·ly adv. by human means.

hum′ble (hum′bəl) adj., **-bler, -blest,** v., **-bled, -bling.** —adj. **1.** not proud. **2.** low in rank, condition, etc. —v.t. **3.** to lower in status or condition. —**hum′ble·ness,** n. —**hum′bly,** adv.

hum′bug n. **1.** an impostor. **2.** something intended to deceive.

hum′drum′ adj. dull.

hu′mid (hyōō′mid) adj. moist. —**hu·mid′i·ty,** n.

hu·mid′i·fy′ v.t., **-fied, -fying.** to make humid. —**hu·mid′i·fi′er,** n.

hu·mil′i·ate′ (hyōō mil′ē āt′) v.t., **-ated, -ating.** to harm the pride or self-respect of. —**hu·mil′i·a′tion,** n.

hu·mil′i·ty n. the quality or state of being humble.

hum′ming·bird′ n. a tiny colorful bird with wings that beat rapidly.

hum′mock (hum′ək) n. a very small hill.

hu·mon′gous (hyōō mung′gəs, -mong′-) adj. *Slang.* huge.

hu′mor (hyōō′mər) n. **1.** the quality of being amusing or comical. **2.** the ability to perceive this. **3.** a mood. **4.** a whim. —v.t. **5.** to indulge. —**hu′mor·ist,** n. —**hu′mor·ous,** adj.

hump (hump) n. **1.** a rounded protruding part on the back. —v.t. **2.** to raise (the back) in a hump.

hump′back′ n. **1.** a back with a hump. **2.** a hunchback. **3.** a kind of whale.

hu′mus (hyōō′məs) n. the dark organic material in soils, produced by decomposing matter.

hunch (hunch) v.t. **1.** to push out or up in a hump. —n. **2.** an intuitive feeling.

hun′dred (hun′drid) n., adj. ten times ten. —**hun′dredth,** adj., n.

hung (hung) v. a pt. and pp. of **hang.**

hun′ger (hung′gər) n. **1.** a need or desire for food. **2.** a strong desire. —v.i. **3.** to be hungry. **4.** to have a strong desire.

hun′gry adj., **-grier, -griest. 1.** having a desire or need for food. **2.** desiring.

hunk (hungk) n. **1.** a large piece. **2.** *Slang.* a handsome, muscular man.

hun′ker (hung′kər) v.i. to squat on one's heels.

hunt (hunt) v.t. **1.** to chase to catch or kill. **2.** to search for. —v.i. **3.** to kill wild animals. —n. **4.** the act of hunting. **5.** a search. —**hunt′er,** n.

hur′dle (hûr′dl) n., v., **-dled, -dling.** —n. **1.** a barrier over which runners or horses leap in a race. **2.** an obstacle. —v.t. **3.** to leap over.

hurl (hûrl) v.t. to throw with great force.

hurl′y-burl′y (hûr′lē bûr′lē) n. noisy disorder and confusion.

hur·rah′ (hə rä′, -rô′) interj., n. an exclamation of joy, triumph, etc.

hur·ri·cane′ (hûr′i kān′, hur′-) n. a violent tropical storm.

hur′ry (hûr′ē, hur′ē) v., **-ried, -rying,** n., pl. **-ries.** —v.i. **1.** to move or act with haste. **2.** to cause to move or act with haste; rush. —n. **3.** a state of urgency. **4.** hurried movement. —**hur′ried·ly,** adv.

hurt (hûrt) v., **hurt, hurting,** n. —v.t. **1.** to cause injury, harm, or pain to. —v.i. **2.** to feel pain. **3.** to cause pain, damage, or distress. —n. **4.** injury or damage.

hur′tle (hûr′tl) *v.i., v.t.,* **-tled, -tling.** to move or fling violently.

hus′band (huz′bənd) *n.* **1.** a married man. —*v.t.* **2.** to manage prudently.

hus′band•ry *n.* the cultivation of crops and the raising of livestock.

hush (hush) *interj.* **1.** a command to be silent. —*v.t., v.i.* **2.** to make or become silent. —*n.* **3.** silence.

husk (husk) *n.* **1.** the dry covering of seeds. —*v.t.* **2.** to remove the husk from.

husk′y[1] *adj.,* **-ier, -iest. 1.** big and strong. **2.** (of the voice) hoarse.

husk′y[2] *n., pl.* **-ies.** (*sometimes cap.*) a sturdy sled dog of arctic regions.

hus′sy (hus′ē, huz′ē) *n., pl.* **-sies.** a disreputable woman.

hus′tle (hus′əl) *v.,* **-tled, -tling,** *n.* —*v.i.* **1.** to proceed or work energetically. **2.** to push. —*v.t.* **3.** to force or push roughly. **4.** to urge. —*n.* **5.** energetic activity. —**hus′tler,** *n.*

hut (hut) *n.* a small or humble dwelling.

hutch (huch) *n.* **1.** a pen for small animals. **2.** a chestlike cabinet with open shelves above.

hwy. highway.

hy′a•cinth (hī′ə sinth) *n.* a plant with a cylindrical cluster of fragrant flowers.

hy′brid (hī′brid) *n.* **1.** the offspring of two plants or animals of different breeds, species, etc. **2.** anything made by combining different elements.

hy′brid•ize *v.i., v.t.,* **-ized, -izing.** to produce or cause to produce hybrids.

hy•dran′gea (hī drān′jə) *n.* a shrub with large white, pink, or blue flower clusters.

hy′drant (-drənt) *n.* an upright pipe with an outlet for drawing water from a water main.

hy•drau′lic (-drô′lik) *adj.* **1.** of or operated by liquid under pressure. **2.** of hydraulics.

hy•drau′lics *n.* the science of moving liquids.

hydro- a prefix meaning: **1.** water. **2.** hydrogen.

hy′dro•car′bon (hī′drə kär′bən) *n.* a compound containing only hydrogen and carbon.

hy′dro•e•lec′tric (hī′drō-) *adj.* pertaining to electricity derived from the energy of falling water. —**hy′dro•e•lec•tric′i•ty,** *n.*

hy′dro•foil′ *n.* a boat with a structure that lifts the hull out of water when traveling at high speed.

hy′dro•gen (-jən) *n.* a colorless, odorless, flammable gas, the lightest of the elements.

hy′dro•gen•ate′ (hī′drə jə nāt′, hī-droj′ə-) *v.t.,* **-ated, -ating.** to combine with or treat with hydrogen.

hy′drogen bomb′ *n.* a powerful bomb that derives its explosive energy from the fusion of hydrogen isotopes.

hy′drogen perox′ide *n.* a liquid used as an antiseptic and a bleach.

hy′dro•pho′bi•a (-fō′bē ə) *n.* **1.** a fear of water. **2.** rabies.

hy′dro•plane′ *n.* **1.** an airplane that lands on water. **2.** a light, high-speed motorboat that planes along the surface of the water.

hy′dro•ther′a•py *n.* the use of water to treat disease or injury.

hy•e′na (hī ē′nə) *n.* a carnivorous mammal of Africa and Asia.

hy′giene (hī′jēn) *n.* a condition or practice conducive to health. —**hy′gi•en′ic** (-jē en′ik, -jen′-, -jē′-nik) *adj.* —**hy•gien′ist** (-jē′nist, -jen′ist) *n.*

hy•grom′e•ter (-grom′i tər) *n.* an instrument for measuring humidity.

hy′men (hī′mən) *n.* a fold of mucous membrane partly closing the vagina in a virgin.

hymn (him) *n.* a song of praise.

hym′nal (him′nl) *n.* a book of hymns. Also, **hym′nbook′.**

hype (hīp) *v.,* **hyped, hyping,** *n. Informal.* —*v.t.* **1.** to create interest in by flamboyant methods. —*n.* **2.** exaggerated promotion.

hyper- a prefix meaning over, above, or excessive.

hy′per•ac′tive (hī′pər-) *adj.* unusually active.

hy•per′bo•le (-pûr′bə lē) *n.* obvious exaggeration.

hy′per•crit′i•cal (hī′pər-) *adj.* excessively critical.

hy′per•gly•ce′mi•a (-glī sē′mē ə) *n.* an abnormally high level of glucose in the blood.

hy′per•ten′sion *n.* high blood pressure.

hy′per•text′ *n.* computerized data in which pieces of text, pictures, etc., are linked so that a user can move from one object or document to another.

hy′per•ven′ti•la′tion *n.* prolonged rapid or deep breathing. —**hy′per•ven′ti•late′,** *v.i.*

hy′phen (hī′fən) *n.* a short line (-) connecting parts or syllables of a word. —**hy′phen•ate′,** *v.t.*

hyp•no′sis (hip nō′sis) *n., pl.* **-ses** (-sēz). an artificially produced sleeplike state in which a person obeys suggestions. —**hyp•not′ic**

(-not′ik) *adj.* —**hyp′no•tism′** (-nə-tiz′əm) *n.* —**hyp′no•tist,** *n.* —**hyp′no•tize′,** *v.t.*

hy′po (hī′pō) *n., pl.* **-pos.** a hypodermic needle or injection.

hypo- a prefix meaning under.

hy′po•al′ler•gen′ic *adj.* designed to minimize the chance of an allergic reaction.

hy′po•chon′dri•a (hī′pə kon′drē ə) *n.* an excessive preoccupation with one's health. —**hy′po•chon′dri•ac′,** *n., adj.*

hy•poc′ri•sy (hi pok′rə sē) *n., pl.* **-sies.** the false professing of qualities such as virtue, piety, etc.

hyp′o•crite (hip′ə krit) *n.* a person given to hypocrisy. —**hyp′o•crit′i•cal,** *adj.*

hy′po•der′mic (hī′pə dûr′mik) *adj.* **1.** introduced under the skin, as a needle. —*n.* **2.** a syringe and needle for hypodermic injections.

hy′po•gly•ce′mi•a (hī′pō glī sē′-mē ə) *n.* an abnormally low level of glucose in the blood.

hy•pot′e•nuse (-pot′n ōōs′, -yōōs′) *n.* the side of a right triangle opposite the right angle.

hy′po•ther′mi•a (-pə thûr′mē ə) *n.* a body temperature that is below normal.

hy•poth′e•sis (-poth′ə sis, hi-) *n., pl.* **-ses** (-sēz′). a proposition set forth as an explanation of something, often as the basis for further investigation. —**hy′po•thet′i•cal** (-pə-thet′i kəl) *adj.*

hys′ter•ec′to•my (his′tə rek′tə mē) *n., pl.* **-mies.** surgical removal of the uterus.

hys•te′ri•a (hi ster′ē ə, -stēr′-) *n.* an uncontrollable emotional outburst. —**hys•ter′i•cal** (-ster′-) *adj.* —**hys•ter′i•cal•ly,** *adv.* —**hys•ter′ics,** *n.pl.*

Hz hertz.

I

I, i (ī) *n.* the ninth letter of the English alphabet.

I (ī) *pron.* the subject form of the singular pronoun used by a person speaking about himself or herself.

IA or **Ia.** Iowa.

i′bex (ī′beks) *n., pl.* **i′bex•es, ib′i•ces′** (ib′ə sēz′, ī′bə-), **ibex.** a wild goat with backward-curving horns.

ibid. (ib′id) ibidem.

i′bis (ī′bis) *n.* a large wading bird.

-ible a variant of *-able.*

i′bu•pro′fen (ī′byōō prō′fən) *n.* an anti-inflammatory drug.

-ic¹ an adjective suffix meaning: of or pertaining to; like or characteristic of; containing or made of.

-ic² a noun suffix meaning: person having; agent or drug; follower.

ICC Interstate Commerce Commission.

ice (īs) *n., v.,* **iced, icing.** —*n.* **1.** frozen water. **2.** a frozen dessert. —*v.t.* **3.** to freeze. **4.** to cool with ice. **5.** to cover with icing. —*v.i.* **6.** to change to or become coated with ice. —**iced,** *adj.*

ice′berg′ (-bûrg) *n.* a large mass of ice floating at sea.

ice′box′ *n.* an insulated food chest cooled by ice.

ice′ cream′ *n.* a frozen dessert made with cream and flavorings.

ice′ skate′ *n.* a shoe with a metal blade for skating on ice. —**ice-skate,** *v.i.*

ich′thy•ol′o•gy (ik′thē ol′ə jē) *n.* the study of fishes.

i′ci•cle (ī′si kəl) *n.* a hanging, tapering mass of ice.

ic′ing *n.* a sweet mixture for covering cakes, cookies, etc.

i′con (ī′kon) *n.* **1.** a sacred image. **2.** a symbol. **3.** a small graphic on a computer screen.

i•con′o•clast′ (-ə klast′) *n.* a person who attacks cherished beliefs. —**i•con′o•clas′tic,** *adj.*

ICU intensive care unit.

id (id) *n.* the unconscious, instinctive part of the psyche.

ID (ī′dē′) *n., pl.* **IDs, ID's.** a document, card, or other means of identification.

ID or **Id.** Idaho.

i•de′a (ī dē′ə, ī dēə′) *n.* **1.** a conception or plan formed in the mind. **2.** an opinion. **3.** a purpose.

i•de′al (ī dē′əl, ī dēl′) *n.* **1.** a conception or standard of perfection. **2.** a person or thing regarded as perfect. —*adj.* **3.** regarded as perfect. —**i•de′al•ize′,** *v.t.*

i•de′al•ism′ *n.* belief in or behavior according to one's ideals. —**i•de′al•ist,** *n.*

i•den′ti•cal (ī den′ti kəl, i den′-) *adj.* the same. —**i•den′ti•cal•ly,** *adv.*

i•den′ti•fy′ (-fī) *v.t.,* **-fied, -fying. 1.** to recognize as being a particular person or thing. **2.** to associate closely. —**i•den′ti•fi•ca′tion,** *n.*

i•den′ti•ty (-tē) *n., pl.* **-ties. 1.** the fact or state of remaining the same. **2.** the sense of self.

i′de•ol′o•gy (ī′dē ol′ə jē, id′ē-) *n., pl.* **-gies.** the beliefs that guide a person, institution, or group. —**i′de•o•log′i•cal,** *adj.*

id′i•om (id′ē əm) *n.* an expression

peculiar to a language. —id**/**i•o•mat**/**ic, *adj.*

id**/**i•o•syn**/**cra•sy (-sing**/**krə sē, -sin**/**-) *n., pl.* -sies. a habit or mannerism peculiar to an individual. —id**/**i•o•syn•crat**/**ic, *adj.*

id**/**i•ot (id**/**ē ət) *n.* a very stupid person. —id**/**i•ot**/**ic (-ot**/**ik) *adj.* —id**/**i•ot**/**i•cal•ly, *adv.* —id**/**i•o•cy, *n.*

i**/**dle (īd**/**l) *adj., v.,* idled, idling. —*adj.* 1. not active. 2. worthless. 3. lazy. —*v.i.* 4. to do nothing. 5. (of an engine) to operate at a low speed. —*v.t.* 6. to pass (time) doing nothing. —i**/**dler, *n.* —i**/**dly, *adv.*

i**/**dol (īd**/**l) *n.* 1. a person or thing that is worshiped. 2. an image representing a god. —i**/**dol•ize**/**, *v.t.*

i•dol**/**a•try (ī dol**/**ə trē) *n., pl.* -tries. 1. the worship of idols. 2. excessive admiration. —i•dol**/**a•ter, *n.*

i**/**dyll (īd**/**l) *n.* 1. a scene of charming peace and simplicity such a scene. 2. a literary work describing such a scene. Also, i**/**dyl. —i•dyl**/**lic (ī dil**/**ik) *adj.*

i.e. that is.

if (if) *conj.* 1. in case that. 2. even though. 3. whether.

if**/**fy *adj.,* -fier, -fiest. *Informal.* not resolved; indefinite.

ig**/**loo (ig**/**lōō) *n., pl.* -loos. a hut built of snow blocks.

ig**/**ne•ous (-nē əs) *adj.* 1. produced under intense heat. 2. of fire.

ig•nite**/** (-nīt**/**) *v.,* -nited, -niting. —*v.t., v.i.* to set on or catch fire. —ig•ni**/**tion (-nish**/**ən) *n.*

ig•no**/**ble (-nō**/**bəl) *adj.* not noble in character.

ig**/**no•min**/**i•ous (-nə min**/**ē əs) *adj.* 1. disgraceful. 2. contemptible.

ig**/**no•ra**/**mus (-rā**/**məs, -ram**/**əs) *n.* an ignorant person.

ig**/**no•rant (-nər ənt) *adj.* 1. lacking in knowledge or education. 2. unaware. —ig**/**no•rance, *n.*

ig•nore**/** (-nôr**/**) *v.t.,* -nored, -noring. to take no notice of.

i•gua**/**na (i gwä**/**nə) *n.* a large tropical lizard.

IL Illinois.

il- a prefix equivalent to *in-.*

ilk (ilk) *n.* family or kind.

ill (il) *adj.* 1. sick. 2. evil. 3. hostile; unkind. 4. unfavorable. —*n.* 5. trouble. 6. evil. 7. sickness. —*adv.* 8. badly or poorly. 9. with difficulty.

Ill. Illinois.

ill**/**-bred**/** *adj.* rude.

il•le**/**gal (i lē**/**gəl) *adj.* against the law.

il•leg**/**i•ble (-lej**/**ə bəl) *adj.* hard to read.

il•le•git**/**i•mate (il**/**i jit**/**ə mit) *adj.* 1. unlawful. 2. born to parents who are not married to each other. —il**/**le•git**/**i•ma•cy (-mə sē) *n.*

ill**/**-fat**/**ed *adj.* 1. destined to a bad fate. 2. bringing bad luck.

il•lib**/**er•al *adj.* 1. narrow-minded; bigoted. 2. not generous.

il•lic**/**it *adj.* unlawful; not allowed.

il•lim**/**it•a•ble (i lim**/**i tə bəl) *adj.* boundless.

il•lit**/**er•ate (i lit**/**ər it) *adj.* 1. unable to read and write. —*n.* 2. an illiterate person. —il•lit**/**er•a•cy, *n.*

ill**/**-man**/**nered *adj.* having bad manners.

ill**/**ness *n.* 1. the state of being ill. 2. a particular ailment; sickness.

il•log**/**i•cal (i loj**/**i kəl) *adj.* not logical. —il•log**/**i•cal•ly, *adv.*

ill**/**-starred**/** *adj.* unlucky; ill-fated.

ill**/**-treat**/** *v.t.* to treat badly or cruelly. —ill**/**-treat**/**ment, *n.*

il•lu**/**mi•nate**/** (i lōō**/**mə nāt**/**) *v.t.,* -nated, -nating. 1. to supply with light. 2. to make clear. —il•lu**/**mi•na**/**tion, *n.*

illus. 1. illustrated. 2. illustration.

ill**/**-use**/** *v.,* ill-used, ill-using, *n.* —*v.t.* (il**/**yōōz**/**) 1. to treat badly or unjustly. —*n.* (-yōōs**/**) 2. bad or unjust treatment.

il•lu**/**sion (i lōō**/**zhən) *n.* 1. a false belief. 2. something that creates a false impression of reality. —il•lu**/**so•ry (-sə rē, -zə-) *adj.*

il**/**lus•trate**/** (il**/**ə strāt**/**, i lus**/**trāt**/**) *v.t.,* -trated, -trating. 1. to furnish (a book or article) with pictures. 2. to make clear by examples. —il**/**lus•tra**/**tion, *n.* —il**/**lus•tra**/**tor, *n.*

il•lus**/**tri•ous (i lus**/**trē əs) *adj.* distinguished.

ill**/** will**/** *n.* hostile feeling.

im- a suffix equivalent to *in-.*

im**/**age (im**/**ij) *n.* 1. a likeness. 2. a picture in the mind. 3. an optical picture of a thing as produced by reflection in a mirror or through a lens. 4. a general or public perception; reputation.

im**/**age•ry *n., pl.* -ries. 1. mental images collectively. 2. the use of figures of speech.

im•ag**/**i•nar**/**y (i maj**/**ə ner**/**ē) *adj.* existing only in the imagination.

im•ag**/**i•na**/**tion (-nā**/**shən) *n.* 1. the act or faculty of imagining. 2. the ability to form mental images. 3. creativity. —im•ag**/**i•na•tive (-nə-tiv) *adj.*

im•ag**/**ine (-in) *v.t., v.i.,* -ined, -ining. 1. to form mental images (of). 2. to think. 3. to suppose or guess. —im•ag**/**i•na•ble, *adj.*

im•bal**/**ance (im bal**/**əns) *n.* lack of balance.

im**/**be•cile (im**/**bə sil) *n.* a stupid person.

im·bibe′ (im bīb′) v.t., -bibed, -bib-ing. **1.** to drink. **2.** to receive into the mind.

im·bro′glio (im brōl′yō) n., pl. -glios. a complicated situation.

im·bue′ (im byōō′) v.t., -bued, -bu-ing. **1.** to inspire. **2.** to saturate.

im′i·tate′ (im′i tāt′) v.t., -tated, -tating. **1.** to copy. **2.** to follow as a model or example. —**im′i·ta′-tive,** adj. —**im′i·ta′tion,** n.

im·mac′u·late (i mak′yə lit) adj. **1.** spotlessly clean. **2.** free from blem-ish or error.

im′ma·nent (im′ə nənt) adj. re-maining within; inherent. —**im′-ma·nence,** n.

im′ma·te′ri·al (im′ə tēr′ē əl) adj. **1.** unimportant. **2.** not physical.

im′ma·ture′ adj. not mature.

im·meas′ur·a·ble adj. limitless.

im·me′di·ate (i mē′dē it) adj. **1.** oc-curring without delay. **2.** nearest, with nothing in between. **3.** of the present time. —**im·me′di·a·cy** (-ə sē) n.

im′me·mo′ri·al adj. beyond mem-ory, record, or knowledge.

im·mense′ (i mens′) adj. vast. —**im·men′si·ty,** n.

im·merse′ (i mûrs′) v.t., -mersed, -mersing. **1.** to plunge into liquid. **2.** to involve deeply. —**im·mer′-sion,** n.

im′mi·grant (im′i grənt) n. a per-son who immigrates.

im′mi·grate′ (-grāt′) v.i., -grated, -grating. to come to a foreign country as a permanent resident. —**im′mi·gra′tion,** n.

im′mi·nent (im′ə nənt) adj. about to happen. —**im′mi·nence,** n.

im·mo′bile (i mō′bəl, -bēl) adj. **1.** incapable of moving or being moved. **2.** not moving. —**im′mo·bil′i·ty,** n. —**im·mo′bi·lize′,** v.t.

im·mod′er·ate (-it) adj. excessive.

im·mod′est adj. not modest.

im′mo·late′ (im′ə lāt′) v.t., -lated, -lating. **1.** to kill as a sacrifice. **2.** to destroy by fire. —**im′mo·la′-tion,** n.

im·mor′al adj. morally wrong. —**im′mo·ral′i·ty,** n.

im·mor′tal adj. **1.** living forever. **2.** remembered forever. —n. **3.** an im-mortal being. —**im′mor·tal′i·ty,** n. —**im·mor′tal·ize′,** v.t.

im·mov′a·ble (i mōō′və bəl) adj. **1.** fixed; stationary. **2.** unyielding.

im·mune′ (i myōōn′) adj. **1.** pro-tected from a disease or infection. **2.** exempt. —**im·mu′ni·ty,** n. —**im′mu·ni·za′tion,** n. —**im′mu·nize′,** v.t.

immune′ sys′tem n. the network of cells and tissues that protects the body from disease.

im′mu·nol′o·gy (-nol′ə jē) n. the branch of science dealing with the immune system.

im·mure′ (i myoor′) v.t., -mured, -muring. to enclose within walls.

im·mu′ta·ble adj. unchangeable.

imp (imp) n. **1.** a little demon. **2.** a mischievous child. —**imp′ish,** adj.

im′pact n. (im′pakt) **1.** a collision. **2.** effect. —v.t., v.i. (im pakt′) **3.** to make contact (with) forcefully. **4.** to have an effect (on).

im·pact′ed adj. (of a tooth) wedged too tightly in its socket to erupt properly.

im·pair′ (im pâr′) v.t. to damage; weaken. —**im·pair′ment,** n.

im·pale′ v.t., -paled, -paling. to pierce with something pointed.

im·pal′pa·ble adj. **1.** incapable of being felt by touch. **2.** difficult for the mind to grasp.

im·pan′el v.t., -eled, -eling. **1.** to enter on a list for jury duty. **2.** to select (a jury) from a panel.

im·part′ v.t. **1.** to make known. **2.** to give.

im·par′tial adj. not biased. —**im′-par·ti·al′i·ty** (-shē al′i tē) n.

im·pas′sa·ble adj. not able to be passed through.

im′passe (im′pas, im pas′) n. a po-sition from which there is no es-cape.

im·pas′sioned adj. filled with in-tense feeling.

im·pas′sive adj. showing or feeling no emotion. —**im·pas′sive·ly,** adv.

im·pa′tience n. lack of patience. —**im·pa′tient,** adj.

im·peach′ (im pēch′) v.t. to charge (a public official) with misconduct in office. —**im·peach′ment,** n.

im·pec′ca·ble (-pek′ə bəl) adj. faultless; flawless. —**im·pec′ca·bly,** adv.

im′pe·cu′ni·ous (-pi kyōō′nē əs) adj. having no money.

im·pede′ (-pēd′) v.t., -peded, -ped-ing. to hinder.

im·ped′i·ment (-ped′ə mənt) n. **1.** a hindrance. **2.** a speech defect.

im·pel′ v.t., -pelled, -pelling. to drive or urge forward.

im·pend′ v.i. to be about to hap-pen.

im·pen′e·tra·ble adj. **1.** not able to be penetrated or entered. **2.** not able to be understood. —**im·pen′e·tra·bil′i·ty,** n.

im·per′a·tive (-per′ə tiv) adj. **1.** ab-solutely necessary. **2.** expressing a command.

im′per·cep′ti·ble adj. very slight.

im·per′fect adj. **1.** having a defect.

2. not complete. **3.** designating a verb tense indicating a continuing or repeated action or a state in the past. —**im·per·fec′tion,** *n.* —**im·per′fect·ly,** *adv.*

im·pe′ri·al (im pēr′ē əl) *adj.* of an empire.

im·pe′ri·al·ism′ *n.* the policy of extending the rule of a nation over other peoples. —**im·pe′ri·al·ist,** *n., adj.*

im·per′il *v.t.,* -iled, -iling. to endanger.

im·pe′ri·ous (im pēr′ē əs) *adj.* domineering.

im·per′ish·a·ble *adj.* not subject to decay.

im·per′me·a·ble *adj.* not able to be penetrated by liquid. —**im·per′me·a·bil′i·ty,** *n.*

im·per′son·al *adj.* not referring to a particular person.

im·per′son·ate′ *v.t.,* -ated, -ating. to assume the character or appearance of. —**im·per′son·a′tion,** *n.* —**im·per′son·a′tor,** *n.*

im·per′ti·nent *adj.* **1.** disrespectful. **2.** not relevant. —**im·per′ti·nence,** *n.*

im′per·turb′a·ble *adj.* incapable of being upset or excited; calm.

im·per′vi·ous (im pûr′vē əs) *adj.* **1.** not allowing penetration. **2.** incapable of being affected.

im′pe·ti′go (im′pi tī′gō) *n.* a contagious skin infection.

im·pet′u·ous (im pech′ōō əs) *adj.* rash or hasty. —**im·pet′u·os′i·ty** (-os′i tē) *n.*

im′pe·tus (im′pi təs) *n.* a driving or moving force.

im·pi′e·ty *n., pl.* -ties. **1.** a lack of reverence. **2.** an impious act.

im·pinge′ (im pinj′) *v.i.,* -pinged, -pinging. **1.** to encroach or infringe. **2.** to strike.

im′pi·ous (im′pē əs, im pī′-) *adj.* **1.** not reverent; irreligious. **2.** disrespectful.

im·pla′ca·ble (im plak′ə bəl, -plā′kə-) *adj.* not to be appeased or pacified.

im·plant′ *v.t.* (im plant′) **1.** to establish or plant firmly. **2.** to insert (a tissue, organ, etc.) into the body. —*n.* (im′plant′) **3.** a device or material used to repair or replace a body part.

im·plau′si·ble *adj.* causing disbelief. —**im·plau′si·bil′i·ty,** *n.*

im′ple·ment *n.* (im′plə mənt) **1.** an instrument or tool. —*v.t.* (-ment′, -mənt) **2.** to put into effect. —**im′ple·men·ta′tion,** *n.*

im′pli·cate′ (-pli kāt′) *v.t.,* -cated, -cating. to show to be involved.

im′pli·ca′tion *n.* **1.** an implying or being implied. **2.** something implied. **3.** an implicating or being implicated.

im·plic′it (-plis′it) *adj.* **1.** implied; not explicit. **2.** unquestioning; absolute.

im·plode′ (-plōd′) *v.i., v.t.,* -ploded, -ploding. to burst inward. —**im·plo′sion,** *n.*

im·plore′ (-plôr′) *v.t.,* -plored, -ploring. to urge or beg.

im·ply′ (-plī′) *v.t.,* -plied, -plying. to indicate or suggest without stating directly.

im′po·lite′ *adj.* rude.

im·pol′i·tic *adj.* not wise or prudent.

im·pon′der·a·ble *adj.* incapable of being precisely measured or evaluated.

im·port′ *v.t.* (im pôrt′) **1.** to bring in from another country. **2.** to mean or signify. —*n.* (im′pôrt) **3.** anything imported. **4.** importance or significance. **5.** meaning. —**im′por·ta′tion,** *n.* —**im·port′er,** *n.*

im·por′tant (im pôr′tnt) *adj.* **1.** of much significance. **2.** having authority or distinction. —**im·por′tance,** *n.*

im′por·tune′ (im′pôr tōōn′, -tyōōn′, im pôr′chən) *v.t., v.i.,* -tuned, -tuning. to urge or beg persistently. —**im·por′tu·nate,** *adj.*

im·pose′ *v.t.,* -posed, -posing. **1.** to set as an obligation. **2.** to thrust upon others. **3. impose on,** to take unfair advantage of. —**im′po·si′tion** (-pə zish′shən) *n.*

im·pos′ing *adj.* impressive.

im·pos′si·ble *adj.* **1.** not capable of being or happening. **2.** not able to be done. —**im·pos′si·bil′i·ty,** *n.*

im′post (im′pōst) *n.* a tax or duty.

im·pos′tor or **im·pos′ter** (im pos′tər) *n.* a person who pretends to be someone else.

im′po·tent (im′pə tənt) *adj.* **1.** lacking power or force. **2.** (of a male) unable to attain or sustain an erection. —**im′po·tence,** *n.*

im·pound′ *v.t.* to seize and hold in legal custody.

im·pov′er·ish (im pov′ər ish, -pov′rish) *v.t.* **1.** to make poor. **2.** to exhaust the strength of.

im·prac′ti·ca·ble (-prak′ti kə bəl) *adj.* incapable of being put into practice or use.

im·prac′ti·cal *adj.* **1.** not practical or useful. **2.** not able to deal with practical matters.

im′pre·ca′tion (-pri kā′shən) *n.* a curse.

im′pre·cise′ *adj.* vague; not exact.

im·preg′na·ble (-preg′nə bəl) *adj.* strong enough to resist attack.

im·preg′nate (-nāt) *v.t.*, **-nated, -nating. 1.** to make pregnant. **2.** to permeate. —**im′preg·na′tion,** *n.*

im′pre·sa′ri·o (-prə sär′ē ō′, -sâr′-) *n., pl.* **-os.** a person who organizes or manages public entertainments, as operas.

im·press′ *v.t.* (im pres′) **1.** to affect strongly; influence. **2.** to fix in the mind. **3.** to produce (a mark) by pressure. —*n.* (im′pres) **4.** the act of impressing. **5.** a mark made by pressure.

im·pres′sion (-presh′ən) *n.* **1.** a strong effect on the mind or feelings. **2.** a vague awareness. **3.** a mark produced by pressure.

im·pres′sion·a·ble *adj.* easily influenced, esp. emotionally.

im·pres′sion·ism *n.* (*often cap.*) a style of 19th-century painting characterized by short brush strokes to represent the effect of light on objects. —**im·pres′sion·ist,** *n., adj.* —**im·pres′sion·is′tic, adj.**

im·pres′sive *adj.* causing admiration or respect.

im′pri·ma′tur (-pri mä′tər, -mā′-) *n.* sanction; approval.

im′print *n.* a mark made by pressure.

im·pris′on *v.t.* to put in prison. —**im·pris′on·ment,** *n.*

im·prob′a·ble *adj.* not likely to be true or to happen. —**im·prob′a·bil′i·ty,** *n.*

im·promp′tu (im promp′tōō, -tyōō) *adj., adv.* without preparation.

im·prop′er *adj.* not right, suitable, or proper. —**im′pro·pri′e·ty** (im′-prə prī′i tē) *n.* —**im·prop′er·ly, adv.**

im·prove′ *v.t., v.i.,* **-proved, -proving.** to make or become better. —**im·prove′ment,** *n.*

im·prov′i·dent *adj.* not providing for the future. —**im·prov′i·dence, n.** —**im·prov′i·dent·ly, adv.**

im′pro·vise′ (im′prə vīz′) *v.t., v.i.,* **-vised, -vising. 1.** to perform or deliver at short notice. **2.** to make from whatever is available. —**im·prov′i·sa′tion** (-prov′ə zā′shən) *n.*

im·pru′dent *adj.* not prudent; unwise.

im′pu·dent (im′pyə dənt) *adj.* impertinent; disrespectful. —**im′pu·dence, n.**

im·pugn′ (im pyōōn′) *v.t.* to cast doubt on.

im′pulse (im′puls) *n.* **1.** a sudden inclination to do something. **2.** a driving force. —**im·pul′sive, adj.**

im·pu′ni·ty (im pyōō′ni tē) *n.* exemption from punishment.

im·pure′ *adj.* not pure. —**im·pu′ri·ty, n.**

im·pute′ (im pyōōt′) *v.t.,* **-puted, -puting.** to attribute (esp. a fault) to someone.

in (in) *prep.* **1.** included within a place. **2.** during. **3.** into. —*adv.* **4.** in or into some place, position, etc. **5.** on the inside. —*adj.* **6.** fashionable. **7.** being in power. —*Idiom.* **8.** in that, because.

IN Indiana.

in- a prefix meaning not or lacking.

in. inch.

in ab·sen′tia (in ab sen′shə, -shē ə) *Latin.* in absence.

in·ac′ti·vate′ (in ak′tə vāt′) *v.t.,* **-vated, -vating.** to make inactive.

in′ad·vert′ent (in′əd vûr′tnt) *adj.* unintentional.

in·al′ien·a·ble *adj.* not to be taken away or transferred.

in·am′o·ra′ta (in am′ə rä′tə, in′am-) *n.* a female lover.

in·ane′ (i nān′) *adj.* silly; ridiculous. —**in·an′i·ty** (i nan′i tē) *n.*

in·ar·tic′u·late (-lit) *adj.* **1.** lacking the ability to express oneself clearly. **2.** not fully expressed.

in′as·much′ as′ *conj.* **1.** seeing that; since. **2.** to such a degree as.

in·au′gu·rate′ (in ô′gyə rāt′) *v.t.,* **-rated, -rating. 1.** to begin formally. **2.** to admit to office formally. —**in·au′gu·ral,** *adj., n.* —**in·au′gu·ra′tion, n.**

in′board′ *adj., adv.* located inside a hull or aircraft.

in′born′ *adj.* present at birth.

in′bound′ *adj.* inward bound.

in′breed′ *v.t.* to produce by breeding closely related individuals. —**in′breed′ing, n.** —**in′bred′, adj.**

inc. 1. incomplete. **2.** incorporated. **3.** increase.

in′can·des′cence (-kən des′əns) *n.* the glow caused by intense heat.

in′can·ta′tion (-kan tā′shən) *n.* the chanting of words as a magic spell.

in·ca·pac′i·tate′ (-kə pas′i tāt′) *v.t.,* **-tated, -tating.** to make unfit or unable. —**in·ca·pac′i·ty, n.**

in·car′cer·ate′ (-kär′sə rāt′) *v.t.,* **-ated, -ating.** to imprison.

in·car′nate (-kär′nit, -nāt) *adj.* **1.** given a bodily form. **2.** personified.

in·cen′di·ar′y (-sen′dē er′ē) *adj., n., pl.* **-aries.** *adj.* **1.** of or causing fires. **2.** arousing strife. —*n.* **3.** a person who maliciously sets fires.

in·cense[1] (in′sens) *n.* a substance giving a sweet odor when burned.

in·cense[2] (in sens′) *v.t.,* **-censed, -censing.** to make angry.

in·cen′tive (in sen′tiv) *n.* something that incites to action.

183

incursion

in·cep′tion (-sep′shən) *n.* beginning.

in·ces′sant (-ses′ənt) *adj.* not ceasing. —in·ces′sant·ly, *adv.*

in′cest (in′sest) *n.* sexual relations between close relatives. —in·ces′tu·ous (-ses′chōō əs) *adj.*

inch (inch) *n.* 1. a unit of length, $\frac{1}{12}$ foot. —*v.t., v.i.* 2. to move by small degrees.

in·cho′ate (in kō′it) *adj.* just begun; not fully developed.

inch′worm′ *n.* a moth larva that moves in a looping motion.

in′ci·dence (in′si dəns) *n.* the rate at which a thing occurs.

in′ci·dent *n.* 1. an occurrence or event. —*adj.* 2. likely to happen. —in′ci·den′tal (-den′tl) *adj., n.*

in·cin′er·ate′ (in sin′ə rāt′) *v.t., v.i.,* -ated, -ating. to burn to ashes. —in·cin′er·a′tor, *n.*

in·cip′i·ent (in sip′ē ənt) *adj.* beginning to exist.

in·cise′ (-sīz′) *v.t.,* -cised, -cising. to cut into; engrave. —in·ci′sion, *n.*

in·ci′sive (-sī′siv) *adj.* 1. cutting. 2. mentally sharp.

in·ci′sor (in sī′zər) *n.* a front tooth used for cutting.

in·cite′ (-sīt′) *v.t.,* -cited, -citing. to urge to action. —in·cite′ment, *n.*

incl. including.

in·cline′ *v.,* -clined, -clining, *n.* —*v.i.* (in klīn′) 1. to lean; bend. 2. to have a tendency or preference. —*n.* (in′klīn) 3. a slanted surface. —in′cli·na′tion, *n.*

in·clude′ (-klōōd′) *v.t.,* -cluded, -cluding. 1. to contain as part of a whole. 2. to put into a group. —in·clu′sion (-klōō′zhən) *n.* —in·clu′sive (-siv) *adj.*

in·cog′ni·to (in′kog nē′tō, in kog′ni-tō′) *adj., adv.* with one's identity hidden.

in′come (in′kum) *n.* money received as wages, interest, etc.

in′com·ing *adj.* coming in.

in′com·mu·ni·ca′do (in′kə myōō′ni-

kä′dō) *adv., adj.* without means of communicating.

in·com′pa·ra·ble *adj.* 1. beyond comparison. 2. unequaled.

in·con·sid′er·ate *adj.* thoughtless.

in·con′ti·nent *adj.* 1. unable to control discharges of urine or feces. 2. lacking in moderation. —in·con′ti·nence, *n.*

in·cor′po·rate′ (-pə rāt′) *v.,* -rated, -rating. —*v.t.* 1. to form into a corporation. 2. to include as a part. —*v.i.* 3. to form a corporation.

in·cor·po′re·al *adj.* not material.

in·cor′ri·gi·ble (in kôr′i jə bəl, -kor′-) *adj.* not able to be reformed.

in·crease′ *v.,* -creased, -creasing, *n.* —*v.t., v.i.* (in krēs′) 1. to make or become greater. —*n.* (in′krēs) 2. the act or process of increasing. 3. a growth or addition. —in·creas′ing·ly, *adv.*

in·cred′i·ble *adj.* unbelievable; amazing. —in·cred′i·bly, *adv.*

in·cred′u·lous *adj.* 1. unbelieving. 2. showing disbelief.

in′cre·ment (in′krə mənt, ing′-) *n.* an addition; increase. —in′cre·men′tal (-men′tl) *adj.*

in·crim′i·nate′ (in krim′ə nāt′) *v.t.,* -nated, -nating. to accuse of or indicate involvement in a crime. —in·crim′i·na′tion, *n.*

in′cu·bate′ (in′kyə bāt′, ing′-) *v.t., v.i.,* -bated, -bating. to hatch (eggs) by warmth. —in′cu·ba′tion, *n.*

in′cu·ba′tor *n.* 1. an apparatus for hatching eggs. 2. an apparatus for warming premature infants.

in·cul′cate (in kul′kāt, in′kul kāt′) *v.t.,* -cated, -cating. to implant (habits) by repeated urging.

in·cum′bent (in kum′bənt) *adj.* 1. currently holding an office. 2. obligatory. —*n.* 3. the holder of an office.

in·cur′ (in kûr′) *v.t.,* -curred, -curring. 1. to come into or acquire. 2. to bring upon oneself.

in·cur′sion (-zhən, -shən) *n.* a hostile invasion; raid.

in′a·bil′i·ty	in′at·ten′tive	in·com′pe·tent
in′ac·ces′si·ble	in′au·di·ble	in′com·plete′
in·ac′cu·ra·cy	in′aus·pi′cious	in′com·pre·hen′si·ble
in·ac′cu·rate	in·cal′cu·la·ble	in′con·ceiv′a·ble
in·ac′tive	in·ca′pa·ble	in′con·clu′sive
in′ad·e′qua·cy	in′ca·pac′i·ty	in·con′gru·ous
in′ad·e′quate	in·cau′tious	in′con·se·quen′tial
in′ad·mis′si·ble	in′ci·vil′i·ty	in′con·sist′en·cy
in′ad·vis′a·ble	in·clem′ent	in′con·sist′ent
in·an′i·mate	in′co·her′ence	in′con·sol′a·ble
in′ap·pro′pri·ate	in′co·her′ent	in′con·spic′u·ous
in·apt′	in·com·men′su·rate	in′con·stan·cy
in·apt′i·tude′	in′com·pat′i·bil′i·ty	in·con′stant
in′ar·tis′tic	in′com·pat′i·ble	in′con·test′a·ble
in′at·ten′tion	in·com·pe·tence	in′con·tro·vert′i·ble

Ind. Indiana.

in•debt'ed *adj.* **1.** owing money. **2.** obligated for favors received.

in'de•ci'pher•a•ble *adj.* not able to be read or deciphered.

in'de•ci'sion *n.* the inability to decide. —**in'de•ci'sive,** *adj.*

in•deed' (in dēd') *adv.* **1.** in fact; truly. —*interj.* **2.** an exclamation of surprise or skepticism.

in'de•fat'i•ga•ble (in'di fat'i gə bəl) *adj.* untiring.

in•del'i•ble (in del'ə bəl) *adj.* incapable of being removed or erased.

in•dem'ni•fy' (in dem'nə fī') *v.t.,* **-fied, -fying.** to compensate for or insure against damage or loss. —**in•dem'ni•ty,** *n.*

in•dent' (in dent') *v.t.* to set in from the margin.

in•den'ture (in den'chər) *n., v.,* **-tured, -turing.** —*n.* **1.** a contract binding a person to service. —*v.t.* **2.** to bind by indenture.

in'de•pend'ent *adj.* **1.** free. **2.** not controlled by or dependent on others. —**in'de•pend'ence,** *n.*

in'-depth' *adj.* intensive; thorough.

in'de•struct'i•ble *adj.* incapable of being destroyed.

in'dex (in'deks) *n., pl.* **-dexes, -dices** (-də sēz') *v.* —*n.* **1.** (in a book) an alphabetical list of names, topics, etc., with page references. **2.** an indication. **3.** a number expressing a property or ratio, as of economic growth. —*v.t.* **4.** to provide with or enter in an index.

In'dian sum'mer *n.* a period of mild, dry weather in late fall.

in'di•cate' (in'di kāt') *v.t.,* **-cated, -cating. 1.** to be a sign of. **2.** to point to. —**in'di•ca'tion,** *n.* —**in'•di•ca'tor,** *n.*

in•dic'a•tive (-dik'ə tive) *adj.* **1.** pointing out. **2.** of the grammatical mood used for ordinary statements and questions.

in•dict' (-dīt') *v.t.* to charge with a crime. —**in•dict'ment,** *n.*

in•dif'fer•ent *adj.* **1.** without inter-

est or concern. **2.** not very good. —**in•dif'fer•ence,** *n.*

in•dig'e•nous (-dij'ə nəs) *adj.* native.

in'di•gent (-di jənt) *adj.* needy; destitute. —**in'di•gence,** *n.*

in'di•ges'tion *n.* discomfort caused by difficulty in digesting food.

in'dig•na'tion (-dig nā'shən) *n.* anger aroused by something unjust or offensive. —**in•dig'nant,** *adj.*

in•dig'ni•ty *n., pl.* **-ties.** an injury to a person's dignity; humiliation.

in'di•go' (in'di gō') *n., pl.* **-gos, -goes.** a deep blue color or dye.

in•dis•crim'i•nate (in'di skrim'ə nit) *adj.* **1.** lacking in care, judgment, etc. **2.** thrown together.

in'dis•posed' *adj.* **1.** mildly ill. **2.** unwilling. —**in'dis•po•si'tion,** *n.*

in'dis•sol'u•ble (in'di sol'yə bəl) *adj.* unable to be dissolved, decomposed, undone, or destroyed.

in'di•vid'u•al (in'də vij'ōō əl) *adj.* **1.** single; particular. **2.** of, characteristic of, or for one person or thing only. —*n.* **3.** a single person, animal, or thing. —**in'di•vid'u•al'i•ty** (-al'i tē) *n.* —**in'di•vid'u•al•ly,** *adv.*

in'di•vid'u•al•ist *n.* a person who is very independent.

in•doc'tri•nate' (in dok'trə nāt') *v.t.,* **-nated, -nating.** to instruct in a doctrine or idea. —**in•doc'tri•na'tion,** *n.*

in'do•lent (in'dl ənt) *adj.* lazy. —**in'do•lence,** *n.*

in•dom'i•ta•ble (in dom'i tə bəl) *adj.* incapable of being dominated.

in'door' *adj.* located or used inside a building.

in•doors' *adv.* in or into a building.

in•du'bi•ta•ble (in dōō'bi tə bəl, -dyōō'-) *adj.* not to be doubted.

in•duce' (in dōōs', -dyōōs') *v.t.,* **-duced, -ducing. 1.** to persuade; influence. **2.** to cause; bring about. —**in•duce'ment,** *n.*

in•duct' (in dukt') *v.t.* to install in an office, military service, etc.

in•duc′tion *n.* **1.** reasoning from particular facts. **2.** an inducting or being inducted.

in•dulge′ (in dulj′) *v.t.,* **-dulged, -dulging. 1.** to yield to (desires, feelings, etc.). **2.** to yield to the wishes of (oneself or another). —**in•dul′gence,** *n.* —**in•dul′gent,** *adj.*

in•dus′tri•al *adj.* **1.** of, used in, or resulting from industry. **2.** having many industries.

in•dus′tri•al•ist *n.* the owner or manager of an industrial plant.

in•dus′tri•al•ize′ *v.t.,* **-ized, -izing.** —*v.t.* **1.** to introduce industry into. —*v.i.* **2.** to become industrial.

in•dus′tri•ous *adj.* hard-working.

in′dus•try (in′də strē) *n., pl.* **-tries. 1.** manufacture or production of goods. **2.** any general business activity. **3.** diligent work.

in•e′bri•ate′ *v.,* **-ated, -ating,** *n.* —*v.t.* (in ē′brī āt′) **1.** to make drunk. —*n.* (-it) **2.** a drunken person.

in•ef′fa•ble (in ef′ə bəl) *adj.* not able to be expressed in words.

in′ef•fec′tu•al *adj.* producing no effect.

in•ept′ (in ept′, i nept′) *adj.* **1.** incompetent. **2.** unsuitable. **3.** foolish. —**in•ept′i•tude′,** *n.*

in•eq′ui•ty *n., pl.* **-ties.** unfairness.

in•ert′ (in ûrt′, i nûrt′) *adj.* **1.** having no inherent power to move, resist, or act. **2.** slow-moving. **3.** having little or no ability to react chemically. —**in•er′tia,** *n.*

in•ev′i•ta•ble (in ev′i tə bəl) *adj.* not able to be avoided. —**in•ev′i•ta•bil′i•ty,** *n.* —**in•ev′i•ta•bly,** *adv.*

in•ex′o•ra•ble (in ek′sər ə bəl) *adj.* **1.** unyielding; relentless. **2.** not able to be persuaded.

in•ex′pert (in eks′pûrt, in′ik spûrt′) *adj.* unskilled.

in•ex′pli•ca•ble (in ek′spli kə bəl, in′ik splik′ə-) *adj.* incapable of being explained.

in•ex′tri•ca•ble (in ek′stri kə bəl, in′ik strik′ə-) *adj.* **1.** from which one cannot escape. **2.** incapable of being disentangled or loosed.

in•fal′li•ble (in fal′ə bəl) *adj.* never failing or making mistakes.

in′fa•mous (in′fə məs) *adj.* having or causing an evil reputation.

in′fa•my *n., pl.* **-mies. 1.** a very bad reputation as the result of an outrageous act. **2.** an infamous act.

in′fant (in′fənt) *n.* a child during the earliest period of its life. —**in′-fan•cy,** *n.* —**in′fan•tile′** (-fən tīl′) *adj.*

in′fan•try (in′fən trē) *n., pl.* **-tries.** the branch of an army composed of soldiers who fight on foot. —**in′fan•try•man,** *n.*

in′farct′ (in′ färkt′, in färkt′) *n.* an area of dead or dying tissue, as in the heart. Also, **in•farc′tion.**

in•fat′u•ate′ (in fach′oo āt′) *v.t.,* **-ated, -ating.** to inspire with a foolish love or admiration. —**in•fat′u•a′tion,** *n.*

in•fect′ (in fekt′) *v.t.* to affect or contaminate with disease or germs. —**in•fec′tion,** *n.*

in•fec′tious *adj.* causing or communicable by infection.

in•fer′ (in fûr′) *v.t.,* **-ferred, -ferring.** to conclude by reasoning or from facts; deduce. —**in′fer•ence,** *n.*

in•fe′ri•or (in fēr′ē ər) *adj.* **1.** lower in rank, importance, quality, value, or position. —*n.* **2.** a person inferior to others. —**in•fe′ri•or′i•ty** (-ôr′i tē) *n.*

in•fer′nal (in fûr′nl) *adj.* **1.** hellish; diabolical. **2.** of hell.

in•fer′no (-nō) *n., pl.* **-nos. 1.** a place of intense heat. **2.** hell.

in•fest′ (in fest′) *v.t.* to overrun in a troublesome manner. —**in′fes•ta′tion,** *n.*

in′fi•del (in′fi dl, -del′) *n.* a person who does not believe in a religion.

in′field′ *n.* the area of a baseball field inside the base lines.

in′fight′ing *n.* conflict within a group.

in•fil′trate (in fil′trāt, in′fil trāt′) *v.t., v.i.,* **-trated, -trating.** to move into

---

in•flex′i•ble	in•op′er•a•tive	in•suf′fer•a•ble
in•for′mal	in•op′por•tune′	in′suf•fi′cient
in′for•mal′i•ty	in′or•gan′ic	in′sup•press′i•ble
in•fre′quen•cy	in′se•cure′	in′sur•mount′a•ble
in•fre′quent	in•sen′si•tive	in′sus•cep′ti•ble
in•glo′ri•ous	in•sep′a•ra•ble	in•tan′gi•ble
in•grat′i•tude′	in′sig•nif′i•cance	in•tem′per•ance
in′har•mon′ic	in′sig•nif′i•cant	in•tem′per•ate
in′har•mo′ni•ous	in•sin•cere′	in•tol′er•a•ble
in•hos′pi•ta•ble	in′sin•cer′i•ty	in•tol′er•ance
in•hu•mane′	in•sol′u•ble	in•tol′er•ant
in′ju•di′cious *adj.*	in′sta•bil′i•ty	in•var′i•a•ble
in•jus′tice	in′sub•or′di•nate	in•vis′i•ble
in′of•fen′sive	in′sub•or′di•na′tion	in•vis′i•bly

(an organization, enemy area, etc.) gradually and without being noticed. —in′fil•tra′tion, *n.*

in′fi•nite (in′fə nit) *adj.* **1.** so great that it cannot be measured. **2.** endless. —*n.* **3.** something infinite. —in•fin′i•ty (in fin′i tē) *n.*

in′fin•i•tes′i•mal (in′fin i tes′ə məl) *adj.* exceedingly small.

in•fin′i•tive (in fin′i tiv) *n.* a verb form not indicating person, number, or tense, usu. preceded by *to* in English.

in•firm′ (-fûrm′) *adj.* feeble; weak. —in•fir′mi•ty, *n.*

in•fir′ma•ry (-fûr′mə rē) *n., pl.* -ries. a place for the care of the sick and injured.

in•flame′ *v.t., v.i.,* -flamed, -flaming. **1.** to kindle or excite (passions, desires, etc.). **2.** to affect or become affected with inflammation.

in•flam′ma•ble (-flam′ə bəl) *adj.* **1.** capable of being set on fire. **2.** easily aroused to passion or anger.

in′flam•ma′tion (-flə mā′shən) *n.* redness, swelling, and fever in an area of the body in response to an infection or injury.

in•flam′ma•to′ry (-tô′rē) *adj.* **1.** tending to arouse anger, passion, etc. **2.** of or caused by inflammation.

in•flate′ (in flāt′) *v.,* -flated, -flating. —*v.t.* **1.** to fill with air or gas so as to expand. **2.** to increase unduly, as prices. —*v.i.* **3.** to become inflated.

in•fla′tion (-shən) *n.* **1.** a steady rise in prices resulting in a loss of the value of money. **2.** an inflating or being inflated.

in•flect′ *v.t.* **1.** to change the pitch of (the voice). **2.** to change the form of (a word) by inflection.

in•flict′ *v.t.* to cause (anything unwelcome) to be suffered.

in′flu•ence (in′flōō əns) *n., v.,* -enced, -encing. —*n.* **1.** the power to affect another. **2.** something that does this. —*v.t.* **3.** to affect or alter. —in′flu•en′tial (-en′shəl) *adj.*

in′flu•en′za (-en′zə) *n.* a contagious viral disease with respiratory symptoms and fever.

in′flux′ *n.* a flowing or coming in.

in′fo•mer′cial (in′fō mûr′shəl) *n.* a program-length television commercial designed to appear to be standard programming.

in•form′ (in fôrm′) *v.t.* **1.** to supply with information. —*v.i.* **2.** to give incriminating evidence about someone. —in•form′ant, *n.* —in•form′er, *n.* —in•form′a•tive, *adj.*

in′for•ma′tion (-fər mā′shən) *n.*

knowledge given or received concerning particular facts. —in′for•ma′tion•al, *adj.*

in′forma′tion su′perhighway *n.* a large-scale communications network linking computers, television sets, etc.

in′fra (in′frə) *adv.* below, esp. in a text.

in•frac′tion (in frak′shən) *n.* a violation.

in′fra•red′ *adj.* of or using invisible radiation wavelengths that are just longer than red in the visible spectrum.

in′fra•struc′ture *n.* **1.** the basic framework of a system or organization. **2.** basic facilities, as transportation.

in•fringe′ (in frinj′) *v.,* -fringed, -fringing. —*v.t.* **1.** to violate. —*v.i.* **2.** to trespass or encroach on.

in•fu′ri•ate′ (in fyŏŏr′ē āt′) *v.t.,* -ated, -ating. to make very angry.

in•fuse′ (in fyōōz′) *v.t.,* -fused, -fusing. **1.** to put into as if by pouring. **2.** to fill with something. **3.** to soak (as tea or herbs) to extract the flavor. —in•fu′sion, *n.*

in•gen′ious (in jēn′yəs) *adj.* cleverly inventive. —in•ge•nu′i•ty (in′jə-nōō′i tē, -nyōō′-) *n.*

in′ge•nue′ (an′zhə nōō′) *n.* an artless, innocent young woman or such a role in a play.

in•gen′u•ous (in jen′yōō əs) *adj.* free from deceit; innocent.

in•gest′ (-jest′) *v.t.* to take into the body, as food or liquid.

in′got (ing′gət) *n.* a mass of metal cast in a form.

in•grained′ *adj.* fixed firmly in a surface or a person's character.

in′grate *n.* an ungrateful person.

in•gra′ti•ate′ (in grā′shē āt′) *v.t.,* -ated, -ating. to get (oneself) into someone's favor, esp. to gain an advantage.

in•gre′di•ent (in grē′dē ənt) *n.* an element or part of a mixture.

in′gress (in′gres) *n.* **1.** the act of entering. **2.** the right to enter.

in•hab′it (in hab′it) *v.t.* to live in. —in•hab′it•ant, *n.*

in′ha•la′tor (in′hə lā′tər) *n.* **1.** an apparatus to help one inhale anesthetics, medicine, etc. **2.** a respirator.

in•hale′ (in hāl′) *v.t., v.i.,* -haled, -haling. to breathe in. —in′ha•la′-tion, *n.*

in•hal′er *n.* **1.** an inhalator. **2.** a person who inhales.

in•here′ (in hēr′) *v.i.,* -hered, -hering. to be an inseparable part or element. —in•her′ent (-hēr′ənt, -her′-) *adj.*

in•her′it (in her′it) *v.t., v.i.* **1.** to receive (property, a title, etc.) by succession or will, esp. from someone who has died. **2.** to receive (a characteristic) from one's parents. —**in•her′it•ance,** *n.*

in•hib′it (in hib′it) *v.t.* to restrain or hinder. —**in′hi•bi′tion,** *n.*

in′house′ (*adj.* in′hous′; *adv.* -hous′) *adj., adv.* using an organization's own staff or resources.

in•hu′man *adj.* **1.** brutal; very cruel. **2.** not human. —**in′hu•man′i•ty,** *n.*

in•im′i•cal (i nim′i kəl) *adj.* hostile.

in•im′i•ta•ble (i nim′i tə bəl) *adj.* not able to be imitated.

in•iq′ui•ty (i nik′wi tē) *n., pl.* **-ties. 1.** great injustice. **2.** a wicked act.

in•i′tial (i nish′əl) *adj., n., v.,* **-tialed, -tialing.** —*adj.* **1.** of or occurring at the beginning. —*n.* **2.** the first letter of a word or a proper name. —*v.t.* **3.** to sign with initials. —**in•i′tial•ly,** *adv.*

in•i′ti•ate′ (i nish′ē āt′) *v.t.,* **-ated, -ating. 1.** to begin. **2.** to instruct in some subject. **3.** to admit into membership. —**in•i′ti•a′tion,** *n.*

in•i′ti•a•tive (i nish′ē ə tiv, i nish′ə-) *n.* **1.** an introductory step. **2.** readiness and ability to take action.

in•ject′ (in jekt′) *v.t.* **1.** to force (a fluid), as into tissue. **2.** to introduce (a remark), as into a conversation. —**in•jec′tion,** *n.*

in•junc′tion (in jungk′shən) *n.* a court order.

in′jure (in′jər) *v.t.,* **-jured, -juring. 1.** to cause harm to. **2.** to treat unjustly. —**in•ju′ri•ous** (-jŏŏr′ē əs) *adj.* —**in′ju•ry,** *n.*

ink (ingk) *n.* **1.** a colored writing fluid. —*v.t.* **2.** to mark with ink. —**ink′y,** *adj.*

ink′ling (ingk′ling) *n.* a slight suggestion.

in′land (*adj.* in′lənd; *adv.* -land′, -lənd) *adj.* **1.** of or in the interior of a region. —*adv.* **2.** of or toward an inland area.

in′-law′ (in lô′, in′lô′) *n.* a relative by marriage.

in•lay′ *v.,* **-laid, -laying,** *n.* —*v.t.* (in′lā′, in′lā′) **1.** to insert (pieces of wood, ivory, etc.) in a surface. —*n.* (in′lā′) **2.** an inlaid design.

in′let′ (-let, -lit) *n.* a narrow bay.

in′-line skate′ *n.* a roller skate with four wheels in a straight line.

in′mate′ *n.* a person confined in a prison, hospital, etc.

in me•mo′ri•am (in mə môr′ē əm) *prep.* in memory (of).

in′most′ *adj.* farthest within. Also, **in′ner•most′.**

inn (in) *n.* **1.** a hotel. **2.** a tavern.

in•nards (in′ərdz) *n.pl.* the internal parts.

in•nate′ (i nāt′, in′āt) *adj.* existing in one from birth.

in′ner (in′ər) *adj.* **1.** being farther within. **2.** internal.

in′ner cit′y *n.* a central part of a city.

in′ning (in′ing) *n. Baseball.* one round of play for both teams.

in′no•cence (in′ə səns) *n.* **1.** freedom from guilt or evil. **2.** lack of worldly knowledge. —**in′no•cent,** *adj., n.*

in•noc′u•ous (i nok′yŏŏ əs) *adj.* harmless.

in′no•vate′ (in′ə vāt′) *v.i., v.t.,* **-vated, -vating.** to bring in (something new). —**in′no•va′tion,** *n.* —**in′no•va′tor,** *n.* —**in′no•va′tive,** *adj.*

in′nu•en′do (in′yŏŏ en′dō) *n., pl.* **-dos, -does.** an indirect, usu. disparaging, remark.

in•nu′mer•a•ble *adj.* too numerous to be counted.

in•oc′u•late′ (i nok′yə lāt′) *v.t.,* **-lated, -lating.** to inject a vaccine into (a person or animal) to protect against a disease. —**in•oc′u•la′tion,** *n.*

in•or′di•nate (in ôr′dn it) *adj.* excessive. —**in•or′di•nate•ly,** *adv.*

in′pa′tient *n.* a patient who stays in a hospital while receiving treatment.

in′put′ *n., v.,* **-putted** or **-put, -putting.** —*n.* **1.** something that is put in. **2.** data put into a computer. —*v.t.* **3.** to enter (data) into a computer.

in′quest *n.* a judicial inquiry, esp. one into a death.

in•quire′ (in kwī²r′) *v.i.,* **-quired, -quiring.** to seek information by questioning; investigate. —**in•quir′y** (in kwī²r′ē, in′kwə rē) *n.*

in′qui•si′tion (in′kwə zish′ən, ing′-) *n.* **1.** an official investigation. **2.** harsh and prolonged questioning. —**in•quis′i•tor,** *n.*

in•quis′i•tive (-kwiz′i tiv) *adj.* very curious.

in′road′ *n.* **1.** an intrusion on someone's territory or rights. **2.** a hostile attack.

in•sane′ (in sān′) *adj.* **1.** mentally deranged. **2.** very foolish. —**in•san′i•ty** (-san′i tē) *n.*

in•sa′ti•a•ble (in sā′shə bəl, -shē ə-) *adj.* incapable of being satisfied.

in•scribe′ (in skrīb′) *v.t.,* **-scribed, -scribing.** to write or engrave. —**in•scrip′tion** (-skrip′shən) *n.*

in•scru′ta•ble (in skrŏŏ′tə bəl) *adj.* not easily understood; mysterious. —**in•scru′ta•bil′i•ty,** *n.*

in/sect (in/sekt) *n.* a small six-legged creature having a body divided into three parts.

in.sec/ti.cide/ (-sek/tə sīd/) *n.* a substance used for killing insects.

in.sem/i.nate/ (in sem/ə nāt/) *v.t.,* **-nated, -nating.** to insert semen into. —**in.sem/i.na/tion,** *n.*

in.sen/si.ble *adj.* **1.** incapable of feeling or perceiving. **2.** unaware; unconscious. —**in.sen/si.bil/i.ty,** *n.*

in.sert/ *v.t.* (in sûrt/) **1.** to put or place in. —*n.* (in/sûrt) **2.** something inserted. —**in.ser/tion,** *n.*

in/shore/ *adj.* **1.** on or close to the shore. —*adv.* **2.** toward the shore.

in/side/ (in/sīd/, in/sīd/) *n.* **1.** the inner part or side. —*adj.* **2.** inner. —*adv.* **3.** in or into the inner part. —*prep.* **4.** on or to the inside of.

in/sid/er *n.* a person who has influence, esp. one privy to confidential information.

in.sid/i.ous (in sid/ē əs) *adj.* proceeding harmfully without being noticed.

in/sight/ *n.* understanding of the true nature of something.

in.sig/ni.a (in sig/nē ə) *n., pl.* **-nia** or **-nias.** a badge or other symbol of rank, honor, etc.

in.sin/u.ate/ (in sin/yōō āt/) *v.t.,* **-ated, -ating. 1.** to hint slyly. **2.** to instill or insert subtly or artfully. —**in.sin/u.a/tion,** *n.*

in.sip/id (in sip/id) *adj.* lacking interest or color; dull.

in.sist/ (in sist/) *v.i.* **1.** to be firm or persistent. —*v.t.* **2.** to assert emphatically. —**in.sist/ence,** *n.* —**in.sist/ent,** *adj.*

in/so.far/ *adv.* to such an extent.

in/sole/ *n.* **1.** the inner sole of a shoe. **2.** a removable sole put into a shoe for comfort.

in/so.lent (in/sə lənt) *adj.* disrespectful. —**in/so.lence,** *n.*

in.sol/vent *adj.* unable to pay one's debts. —**in.sol/ven.cy,** *n.*

in.som/ni.a (in som/nē ə) *n.* sleeplessness. —**in.som/ni.ac/,** *n., adj.*

in/so.much/ *adv.* **1.** to such a degree (that). **2.** inasmuch (as).

in.sou/ci.ant (in sōō/sē ənt) *adj.* free from care.

in.spect/ (in spekt/) *v.t.* to look over carefully or officially. —**in.spec/tion,** *n.*

in.spec/tor *n.* **1.** a person who inspects. **2.** a police official.

in.spire/ (in spī^ər/) *v.t.,* **-spired, -spiring. 1.** to animate. **2.** to arouse (a feeling, thought, etc.). **3.** to prompt to action. —**in/spi.ra/tion** (in/spə rā/shən) *n.* —**in/spi.ra/tion.al,** *adj.*

Inst. 1. Institute. **2.** Institution.

in.stall/ (in stôl/) *v.t.* **1.** to put in position for use. **2.** to establish. **3.** to place (a person) in office formally. —**in/stal.la/tion,** *n.*

in.stall/ment *n.* a division, as of a payment or story.

in/stance (in/stəns) *n., v.,* **-stanced, -stancing.** —*n.* **1.** a particular case. **2.** an example. —*v.t.* **3.** to cite as an instance.

in/stant *n.* **1.** a moment. **2.** a particular moment. —*adj.* **3.** immediate. —**in/stant.ly,** *adv.*

in/stan.ta/ne.ous (-stən tā/nē əs) *adj.* occurring in an instant.

in.stead/ (in sted/) *adv.* as a substitute.

in/step/ *n.* the upper arch of the foot.

in/sti.gate/ (in/sti gāt/) *v.t.,* **-gated, -gating.** to incite or provoke to some action. —**in/sti.ga/tion,** *n.* —**in/sti.ga/tor,** *n.*

in.still/ *v.t.* to introduce slowly.

in/stinct (in/stingkt) *n.* **1.** a natural impulse. **2.** a natural tendency or talent. —**in.stinc/tive,** *adj.*

in/sti.tute/ (in/sti tōōt/, -tyōōt/) *v.,* **-tuted, -tuting,** *n.* —*v.t.* **1.** to establish. **2.** to start. —*n.* **3.** a society for promoting the arts, scientific research, etc.

in/sti.tu/tion *n.* **1.** an organization devoted to the promotion of a public cause. **2.** the building occupied by such an organization. **3.** an established tradition, rule, etc. **4.** a place for the care or confinement of people. —**in/sti.tu/tion.al,** *adj.* —**in/sti.tu/tion.al.ize/,** *v.t.*

in.struct/ (in strukt/) *v.t.* **1.** to teach. **2.** to direct; command. —**in.struc/tion,** *n.* —**in.struc/tive,** *adj.* —**in.struc/tor,** *n.*

in/stru.ment (in/strə mənt) *n.* **1.** a tool, esp. one for precision work. **2.** a device for producing music. **3.** a means; agent. **4.** a device for monitoring or controlling. **5.** a legal document. —**in/stru.men/tal** (-men/tl) *adj.*

in/su.lar (in/sə lər, ins/yə-) *adj.* **1.** of islands. **2.** narrow in viewpoint.

in/su.late/ (-lāt/) *v.t.,* **-lated, -lating. 1.** to cover with a material that prevents passage of heat, electricity, or sound. **2.** to place in an isolated situation. —**in/su.la/tion,** *n.* —**in/su.la/tor,** *n.*

in/su.lin (in/sə lin, ins/yə-) *n.* a hormone that regulates the body's absorption of sugar and other nutrients.

in.sult/ *v.t.* (in sult/) **1.** to treat with contemptuous rudeness. —*n.* (in/sult) **2.** a contemptuously rude remark or act.

in•su′per•a•ble (in soō′pər ə bəl) *adj.* unable to be overcome.

in•sure′ *v.t.,* **-sured, -suring. 1.** to guarantee compensation for loss, damage, etc. **2.** to make certain. —**in•sur′ance,** *n.* —**in•sur′er,** *n.*

in•sur′gent (in sûr′jənt) *n.* **1.** a rebel. —*adj.* **2.** rebellious.

in′sur•rec′tion (in′sə rek′shən) *n.* an armed rebellion.

in•tact′ (in takt′) *adj.* undamaged.

in′take′ *n.* **1.** the point at which something is taken in. **2.** the act of taking in. **3.** a quantity taken in.

in′te•ger (in′ti jər) *n.* a whole number.

in′te•gral (in′ti grəl, in teg′rəl) *adj.* necessary to form a whole.

in′te•grate′ (in′ti grāt′) *v.,* **-grated, -grating.** —*v.t.* **1.** to bring together into a unified whole. **2.** to make (a school, neighborhood, etc.) available to all racial or ethnic groups. —**in′te•gra′tion,** *n.*

in•teg′ri•ty (in teg′ri tē) *n.* **1.** honesty. **2.** the state of being whole.

in•teg′u•ment (in teg′yə mənt) *n.* a skin, rind, etc.

in′tel•lect′ (in′tl ekt′) *n.* the mind's power of reasoning and understanding.

in′tel•lec′tu•al *adj.* **1.** appealing to or relying on the intellect. **2.** having a strong intellect. —*n.* **3.** a person who pursues intellectual interests.

in•tel′li•gence (in tel′i jəns) *n.* **1.** ability to learn, reason, and understand. **2.** information, esp. secret information about an enemy. **3.** an organization that gathers secret information.

in•tel′li•gent *adj.* having a high mental capacity.

in•tel′li•gi•ble (-jə bəl) *adj.* understandable. —**in•tel′li•gi•bil′i•ty,** *n.*

in•tend′ (in tend′) *v.t.* to have in mind as something to be done.

in•tend′ed *n. Informal.* the person one plans to marry.

in•tense′ (in tens′) *adj.* **1.** existing in a high or extreme degree. **2.** having strong feeling. —**in•ten′si•fy′,** *v.t., v.i.* —**in•ten′si•ty,** *n.*

in•ten′sive *adj.* thorough.

in•tent′[1] (in tent′) *n.* **1.** something intended. **2.** the act of intending. —*Idiom.* **3. to** or **for all intents and purposes,** practically speaking.

in•tent′[2] (in tent′) *adj.* **1.** firmly fixed or directed. **2.** having the attention sharply focused. **3.** determined. —**in•tent′ly,** *adv.*

in•ten′tion *n.* **1.** purpose. **2.** meaning. —**in•ten′tion•al,** *adj.*

in•ter′ (in tûr′) *v.t.,* **-terred, -terring.** to bury (a body).

inter- a prefix meaning: **1.** between or among. **2.** reciprocally.

in′ter•act′ (in′tər akt′) *v.i.* to act upon one another. —**in′ter•ac′tion,** *n.* —**in′ter•ac′tive,** *adj.*

in′ter•breed′ *v.t., v.i.,* **-bred, -breeding.** to crossbreed (a plant or animal).

in′ter•cede′ (-sēd′) *v.i.,* **-ceded, -ceding.** to act or plead in behalf of one in trouble. —**in′ter•ces′sion,** *n.*

in′ter•cept′ (-sept′) *v.t.* to stop or interrupt the course or progress of.

in′ter•change′ *v.,* **-changed, -changing,** *n.* —*v.t.* (in′tər chānj′) **1.** to put each in the place of the other. **2.** to exchange. —*n.* (in′tər-chānj′) **3.** an act of interchanging. **4.** a highway intersection that allows vehicles to move without crossing the streams of traffic.

in′ter•con′ti•nen′tal *adj.* between or among continents.

in′ter•course′ *n.* **1.** dealings among individuals or nations. **2.** sexual relations; coitus.

in′ter•de•nom′i•na′tion•al *adj.* between or involving different religious denominations.

in′ter•de•pend′ent *adj.* mutually dependent.

in′ter•dict′ *n.* (in′tər dikt′) **1.** a decree that prohibits. —*v.t.* (in′tər-dikt′) **2.** to prohibit officially. —**in′ter•dic′tion,** *n.*

in′ter•est (in′tər ist, -trist) *n.* **1.** a feeling of attention, curiosity, etc. **2.** the object of one's attention, curiosity, etc. **3.** a business, cause, etc., in which a person has a share. **4.** advantage. **5. a.** a sum charged for borrowing money. **b.** the rate for such charge. —*v.t.* **6.** to excite or hold the attention of.

in′ter•est•ing (-tər ə sting, -trə-sting, -tə res′ting) *adj.* engaging the attention or curiosity.

in′ter•face′ *n., v.,* **-faced, -facing.** —*n.* (in′tər fās′) **1.** a common boundary. **2.** computer hardware or software that communicates information between entities. —*v.t., v.i.* (in′tər fās′, in′tər fās′) **3.** to interact or coordinate smoothly.

in′ter•fere′ (-fēr′) *v.i.,* **-fered, -fering. 1.** to hamper or obstruct action. **2.** to meddle. —**in′ter•fer′ence,** *n.*

in′ter•im (in′tər əm) *n.* **1.** an intervening time. —*adj.* **2.** temporary.

in•te′ri•or (in tēr′ē ər) *adj.* **1.** inner. —*n.* **2.** the inner part.

in′ter•ject′ (in′tər jekt′) *v.t.* to insert abruptly between other things.

in′ter•jec′tion (-jek′shən) *n.* **1.** the act of interjecting. **2.** something interjected. **3.** an exclamation that expresses emotion, as *indeed!*

in•ter•lace′ *v.i., v.t.,* **-laced, -lacing.** to unite by weaving together.

in•ter•lock′ *v.i., v.t.* to lock, join, or fit together closely.

in•ter•loc′u•tor (-lok′yə tər) *n.* a participant in a conversation.

in•ter•loc′u•to•ry (-tôr′ē) *adj. Law.* (of a decision or decree) not final.

in•ter•lop′er (-lō′pər) *n.* an intruder.

in•ter•lude′ (-lōōd′) *n.* **1.** an intervening episode, period, or space. **2.** something performed in this.

in•ter•mar′ry *v.i.,* **-ried, -rying. 1.** to become connected by marriage. **2.** to marry outside one's religion, ethnic group, etc. **—in′ter•mar′-riage,** *n.*

in•ter•me′di•ar′y (-mē′dē er′ē) *adj., n., pl.* **-aries.** *—adj.* **1.** being between; intermediate. *—n.* **2.** an intermediate agent; mediator.

in•ter•me′di•ate (-it) *adj.* being or acting between two points, stages, etc.

in•ter′ment (in tûr′mənt) *n.* burial.

in•ter′mi•na•ble (in tûr′mə nə bəl) *adj.* seeming to be without end; endless. **—in•ter′mi•na•bly,** *adv.*

in•ter•mis′sion (in′tər mish′ən) *n.* an interval between periods of action, as between the acts in a play.

in•ter•mit′tent (-mit′nt) *adj.* alternately ceasing and starting again.

in•tern′[1] (in tûrn′) *v.t.* to confine within limits, as prisoners of war. **—in•tern′ment,** *n.*

in•tern[2] (in′tûrn) *n.* **1.** a recent medical school graduate serving under supervision in a hospital. **2.** someone working as a trainee to gain experience. *—v.i.* **3.** to serve as an intern. **—in′tern•ship′,** *n.*

in•ter′nal (in tûr′nl) *adj.* **1.** inner. **2.** not foreign; domestic.

inter′nal med′icine *n.* the diagnosis and nonsurgical treatment of diseases.

in•ter•na′tion•al *adj.* **1.** among nations. **2.** of many nations. **—in′-ter•na′tion•al•ize,** *v.t., v.i.*

in•ter•ne′cine (-nē′sēn, -sīn, -nes′ēn, -īn) *adj.* involving conflict within a group.

In′ter•net′ *n.* a large computer network linking smaller networks worldwide.

in•tern•ist (in′tûr nist, in tûr′nist) *n.* a doctor specializing in internal medicine.

in•ter•per′son•al *adj.* between persons.

in′ter•plan′e•tar′y *adj.* between planets.

in′ter•play′ *n.* reciprocal relationship or action.

in•ter′po•late′ (in tûr′pə lāt′) *v.t.,* **-lated, -lating.** to insert to alter or clarify meaning.

in′ter•pose′ *v.t., v.i.,* **-posed, -posing. 1.** to place or come between (other things). **2.** to intervene.

in•ter′pret (in tûr′prit) *v.t.* **1.** to explain the meaning of. **2.** to translate. **—in•ter′pre•ta′tion,** *n.* **—in•ter′pret•er,** *n.*

in′ter•ra′cial *adj.* of, for, or between persons of different races.

in′ter•re•lat′ed *adj.* closely associated.

in•ter′ro•gate′ (in ter′ə gāt′) *v.t., v.i.,* **-gated, -gating.** to question, esp. formally. **—in•ter′ro•ga′tion,** *n.* **—in′ter•rog′a•tive** (in′tə rog′ə-tiv) *adj.* **—in•ter′ro•ga′tor,** *n.*

in′ter•rupt′ (in′tə rupt′) *v.t.* **1.** to break the continuity of. **2.** to stop (a person) in the midst of something. *—v.i.* **3.** to interfere with action or speech. **—in′ter•rup′tion,** *n.*

in′ter•scho•las′tic *adj.* existing or occurring between schools.

in′ter•sect′ (-sekt′) *v.t.* to divide by crossing; cross.

in′ter•sec′tion *n.* **1.** a place where roads meet. **2.** an intersecting.

in′ter•sperse′ (-spûrs′) *v.t.,* **-spersed, -spersing.** to scatter here and there.

in′ter•state′ *adj.* connecting or involving different states.

in′ter•stel′lar *adj.* situated or occurring between the stars.

in•ter′stice (in tûr′stis) *n.* a small space between things.

in′ter•twine′ *v.t., v.i.,* **-twined, -twining.** to unite by twining together.

in′ter•ur′ban *adj.* between cities.

in′ter•val (in′tər vəl) *n.* **1.** an intervening period of time. **2.** a space between things. **3.** the difference in musical pitch between two tones.

in′ter•vene′ (-vēn′) *v.i.,* **-vened, -vening. 1.** to come between disputing people. **2.** to occur between other events or periods. **—in′ter•ven′tion** (-ven′shən) *n.*

in′ter•view′ *n.* **1.** a formal meeting to assess someone or to get information from someone. *—v.t.* **2.** to have an interview with.

in•tes′tate (in tes′tāt, -tit) *adj.* not having made a will.

in•tes′tine (-tin) *n.* the lower part of the alimentary canal. **—in•tes′-ti•nal,** *adj.*

in′ti•mate′[1] *adj.* (in′tə mit) **1.** having a close personal relationship.

2. private or personal. —*n.* **3.** an intimate friend. —**in′ti•ma•cy** (-mə sē) *n.*

in′ti•mate′² (-māt′) *v.t.*, **-mated, -mating.** to make known indirectly; imply. —**in′ti•ma′tion,** *n.*

in•tim•i•date (in tim′i dāt′) *v.t.*, **-dat•ed, -dat•ing. 1.** to make fearful. **2.** to force into or deter from some action by causing fear. —**in•tim′i•da′tion,** *n.*

in′to (in′tōō; *unstressed* -tōō, -tə) *prep.* **1.** to the inside of. **2.** toward or in the direction of. **3.** to a particular action, circumstance, etc.

in•tone′ *v.t.*, **-toned, -toning. 1.** to use a particular spoken tone. **2.** to chant.

in•tox•i•cate (in tok′si kāt′) *v.t.*, **-cated, -cating. 1.** to make drunk. **2.** to make extremely happy.

in•trac′ta•ble *adj.* hard to manage or deal with.

in′tra•mu′ral (in′trə myōōr′əl) *adj.* within one school.

in′tra•net′ (in′trə net′) *n.* a computer network with restricted access, as within a corporation, that uses Internet technology.

in•tran•si•gent (in tran′si jənt) *adj.* refusing to compromise. —**in•tran′si•gence,** *n.*

in•tran•si•tive (-tiv) *adj.* (of a verb) not taking a direct object.

in′tra•ve′nous (in′trə vē′nəs) *adj.* within or into a vein.

in•trep′id (in trep′id) *adj.* fearless.

in′tri•cate (in′tri kit) *adj.* very complicated. —**in′tri•ca•cy** (-kə sē) *n.*

in•trigue′ *v.*, **-trigued, -triguing,** *n.* —*v.t.* (in trēg′) **1.** to arouse the curiosity of. —*v.i.* **2.** to plot craftily. —*n.* (in trēg′, in′trēg) **3.** a crafty design or plot.

in•trin′sic (in trin′sik, -zik) *adj.* belonging to a thing by its very nature. —**in•trin′si•cal•ly,** *adv.*

in′tro•duce′ (in′trə dōōs′, -dyōōs′) *v.t.*, **-duced, -ducing. 1.** to make (a person) known to another. **2.** to bring into notice or use. **3.** to begin. —**in′tro•duc′tion** (-duk′shən) *n.* —**in′tro•duc•to•ry** (-duk′tə rē) *adj.*

in′tro•spec′tion (-shən) *n.* examination of one's own thoughts and motives. —**in′tro•spec′tive,** *adj.*

in′tro•vert′ (-vûrt′) *n.* a shy person concerned chiefly with inner thoughts or feelings. —**in′tro•ver′sion** (-vûr′zhən) *n.*

in•trude′ (in trōōd′) *v.*, **-truded, -truding.** —*v.t.* **1.** to thrust in. —*v.i.* **2.** to come in without welcome. —**in•tru′sion** (-trōō′zhən) *n.* —**in•tru′sive** (-siv) *adj.*

in′tu•i′tion (in′tōō ish′ən, -tyōō-) *n.*

direct perception of truth, fact, etc., without reasoning. —**in•tu′i•tive** (-i tiv) *adj.*

in′un•date′ (in′ən dāt′, -un-) *v.t.*, **-dated, -dating. 1.** to flood. **2.** to overwhelm. —**in′un•da′tion,** *n.*

in•ure′ (in yōōr′, i nōōr′) *v.t.*, **-ured, -uring.** to toughen or accustom.

in•vade′ (in vād′) *v.t.*, **-vaded, -vading. 1.** to enter as an enemy. **2.** to enter and cause harm. —**in•va′sion** (-vā′zhən) *n.*

in′va•lid¹ (in′və lid) *n.* **1.** a sickly or infirm person. —*adj.* **2.** unable to care for oneself due to illness or disability. **3.** of or for invalids.

in•val′id² (in val′id) *adj.* without force or foundation; not valid. —**in•val′i•date′,** *v.t.*

in•val′u•a•ble *adj.* priceless.

in•vec′tive (in vek′tiv) *n.* vehement denunciation or abuse.

in•veigh′ (-vā′) *v.i.* to attack violently with words.

in•vei′gle (-vā′gəl, -vē′-) *v.t.*, **-gled, -gling.** to lure or entice.

in•vent′ *v.t.* **1.** to devise (something new). **2.** to make up. —**in•ven′tion,** *n.* —**in•ven′tive,** *adj.* —**in•ven′tor,** *n.*

in′ven•to′ry (in′vən tôr′ē) *n.*, *pl.* **-tories.** a list of stock or goods.

in•verse′ (-vûrs′, in′vûrs) *adj.* reversed in position or direction.

in•vert′ (-vûrt′) *v.t.* **1.** to turn upside down. **2.** to reverse in position, direction, or relationship. —**in•ver′sion,** *n.*

in•ver′te•brate *adj.* **1.** without a backbone. —*n.* **2.** an invertebrate animal.

in•vest′ *v.t.* **1.** to put (money) to use in hope of profit. **2.** to give or devote (time, effort, etc.). **3.** to give power or authority to. —**in•vest′ment,** *n.* —**in•ves′tor,** *n.*

in•ves′ti•gate′ (in ves′ti gāt′) *v.t.*, *v.i.*, **-gated, -gating.** to search or inquire (into) systematically. —**in•ves′ti•ga′tion,** *n.* —**in•ves′ti•ga′tive,** *adj.* —**in•ves′ti•ga′tor,** *n.*

in•vet′er•ate (-vet′ər it) *adj.* confirmed in habit, feeling, etc.

in•vid′i•ous (-vid′ē əs) *adj.* likely to cause ill will.

in•vig′or•ate′ (-vig′ə rāt′) *v.t.*, **-ated, -ating.** to fill with energy.

in•vin′ci•ble (in vin′sə bəl) *adj.* unable to be conquered. —**in•vin′ci•bil′i•ty,** *n.*

in•vi′o•la•ble (in vī′ə lə bəl) *adj.* incapable of being violated or destroyed.

in•vi′o•late (-lit, -lāt′) *adj.* free from violation, injury, or desecration.

in•vite′ (-vīt′) *v.t.*, **-vited, -viting. 1.** to request the presence of. **2.** to ask politely. **3.** to act so as to bring on. **4.** to attract. —**in'vi•ta'tion** (in/vi tā/shən) *n.*

in•vit'ing *adj.* attractive or tempting.

in vi'tro (in vē/trō) *adj.* (of a biological entity or process) developed or maintained in a controlled nonliving environment, as a laboratory vessel.

in•vo•ca'tion (in/və kā/shən) *n.* a prayer for aid, guidance, etc.

in'voice *n., v.,* **-voiced, -voicing.** —*n.* **1.** an itemized bill with the prices of goods sent or services provided to a buyer. —*v.t.* **2.** to present an invoice to or for.

in•voke' (in vōk/) *v.t.,* **-voked, -voking. 1.** to beg for. **2.** to call on in prayer. **3.** to cite as authoritative.

in•vol'un•tar'y *adj.* **1.** unintentional. **2.** without conscious control.

in•volve' (-volv/) *v.t.,* **-volved, -volving. 1.** to include as a necessary consequence. **2.** to include within itself. **3.** to bring into a troublesome matter. **4.** to preoccupy. —**in•volve'ment,** *n.*

in'ward (-wərd) *adv.* **1.** Also, **in'-wards.** toward the inside. —*adj.* **2.** situated on or directed toward the inside. **3.** mental or spiritual. —**in'ward•ly,** *adv.*

in'-your-face' *adj. Informal.* involving confrontation; defiant.

I/O input/output.

i'o•dine' (ī/ə dīn/, -din; *in Chem. also* -dēn/) *n.* a nonmetallic element used in medicine and dyes.

i'on (ī/ən, ī/on) *n.* an electrically charged particle.

i'on•ize' (ī/ə nīz/) *v.,* **-nized, -nizing.** —*v.t.* **1.** to separate or change into ions. **2.** to produce ions in. —*v.i.* **3.** to become ionized. —**i'on•i•za'tion,** *n.*

i•on'o•sphere (ī on/ə sfēr/) *n.* the outermost region of the earth's atmosphere, consisting of ionized layers.

i•o'ta (ī ō/tə) *n.* a very small quantity.

IOU *n., pl.* **IOUs, IOU's.** a written acknowledgment of a debt.

ip'so fac'to (ip/sō fak/tō) *adv.* by the fact itself.

IQ intelligence quotient.

IRA (*pronounced as initials or* ī/rə) individual retirement account.

i•ras'ci•ble (i ras/ə bəl) *adj.* easily angered.

ire (ī°r) *n.* anger. —**i•rate'** (ī rāt/, ī/rāt) *adj.*

ir/i•des'cence (ir/i des/əns) *n.* a display of lustrous colors like a rainbow. —**ir/i•des'cent,** *adj.*

i'ris (ī/ris) *n.* **1.** the colored part of the eye. **2.** a perennial plant with flowers having three upright petals.

irk (ûrk) *v.t.* to irritate or annoy. —**irk'some,** *adj.*

i'ron (ī/ərn) *n.* **1.** a hard gray metallic element, used for making tools, machinery, etc. **2.** something made of iron. **3.** an appliance with a flat metal bottom for pressing cloth. **4. irons,** shackles. —*adj.* **5.** of or like iron. —*v.t., v.i.* **6.** to press with a heated iron.

i'ron-clad' *adj.* **1.** iron-plated, as a ship. **2.** very rigid or exacting.

i'ron cur'tain *n.* (formerly) a barrier between the Soviet bloc and other countries after World War II.

i'ro•ny (ī/rə nē, ī/ər-) *n., pl.* **-nies. 1.** the use of words to convey a meaning that is the opposite of the literal meaning. **2.** an outcome contrary to expectations. —**i•ron'ic** (ī ron/ik) *adj.*

ir•ra'di•ate' (i rā/dē āt/) *v.t.,* **-ated, -ating. 1.** to shed rays of light upon. **2.** to expose to radiation.

ir•ra'tion•al (i rash/ə nl) *adj.* lacking reason or judgment.

ir•rec'on•cil'a•ble (i rek/ən sī/lə bəl) *adj.* unable to be brought into agreement.

ir/re•deem'a•ble (ir/i dē/mə bəl) *adj.* not able to be redeemed.

ir/re•duc'i•ble (ir/i dŏŏ/sə bəl, -dyŏŏ/-) *adj.* not able to be reduced.

ir/re•fut'a•ble (i ref/yə tə bəl) *adj.* impossible to refute.

ir•reg'u•lar (i reg/yə lər) *adj.* **1.** not symmetrical. **2.** not conforming to established rules.

ir•rel'e•vant (i rel/ə vənt) *adj.* not relevant or pertinent. —**ir•rel'e•vance,** *n.*

ir/re•li'gious (ir/i lij/əs) *adj.* **1.** not practicing a religion. **2.** hostile to religion.

ir•rep'a•ra•ble (i rep/ər ə bəl) *adj.* incapable of being made good or remedied.

ir/re•press'i•ble (ir/i pres/ə bəl) *adj.* incapable of being restrained.

ir/re•proach'a•ble (ir/i prō/chə bəl) *adj.* blameless.

ir/re•sist'i•ble (ir/i zis/tə bəl) *adj.* not able to be resisted.

ir/res'o•lute' (i rez/ə lŏŏt/) *adj.* undecided.

ir/re•spec'tive *adj.* without regard to.

ir/re•spon'si•ble (ir/i spon/sə bəl) *adj.* lacking a sense of responsibility. —**ir/re•spon'si•bly,** *adv.*

ir/re•triev'a•ble (ir/i trē/və bəl) *adj.* incapable of being recovered.

ir·rev′er·ent (i rev′ər ənt) *adj.* lacking reverence or respect.

ir·rev′o·ca·ble (i rev′ə kə bəl) *adj.* not to be revoked or recalled.

ir′ri·gate′ (ir′i gāt′) *v.t.,* **-gated, -gating.** to supply with water by artificial means. —**ir′ri·ga′tion,** *n.*

ir′ri·ta·ble (ir′i tə bəl) *adj.* easily annoyed or angered. —**ir′ri·ta·bil′i·ty,** *n.*

ir′ri·tate′ (-tāt′) *v.t.,* **-tated, -tating. 1.** to make annoyed or angry. **2.** to make sore. —**ir′ri·tant** (-tnt) *n.* —**ir′ri·ta′tion,** *n.*

IRS Internal Revenue Service.

is (iz) *v.* third pers. sing. pres. indic. of **be.**

Is·lam′ (is läm′, is′ləm, iz′-) *n.* the religion of the Muslims, as set forth in the Koran. —**Is·lam′ic,** *adj.*

is′land (ī′lənd) *n.* a body of land completely surrounded by water. —**is′land·er,** *n.*

isle (īl) *n.* an island, esp. a small one.

is′let (ī′lit) *n.* a tiny island.

ism (iz′əm) *n.* a distinctive doctrine, theory, or system.

-ism a suffix meaning: action or practice; condition; doctrine; distinctive feature or usage.

i′so·bar′ (ī′sə bär′) *n.* a line on a map connecting the points at which barometric pressure is the same.

i′so·late′ (ī′sə lāt′) *v.t.,* **-lated, -lating.** to place or keep alone. —**i′so·la′tion,** *n.*

i′so·la′tion·ist *n.* a person opposed to a country's participation in world affairs.

i′so·met′rics *n.pl.* exercises in which one body part is tensed against another. —**i′so·met′ric,** *adj.*

i·sos′ce·les′ (ī sos′ə lēz′) *adj.* (of a triangle) having two sides equal.

i′so·tope′ (ī′sə tōp′) *n.* one of two or more forms of a chemical element having the same atomic number but different atomic weights.

is′sue (ish′ōō) *v.,* **-sued, -suing,** *n.* —*v.t.* **1.** to send out; discharge. **2.**

to publish. —*v.i.* **3.** to go, pass, or flow out. **4.** to be published. —*n.* **5.** a sending out or putting forth. **6.** something issued. **7.** a point in question. **8.** offspring. **9.** a result. —*Idiom.* **10.** at issue, being disputed. **11.** take issue, to disagree. —**is′su·ance,** *n.*

isth′mus (is′məs) *n.* a strip of land surrounded by water and connecting two larger bodies.

it (it) *pron.* third pers. sing. neuter pronoun.

ital. italic.

i·tal′ic (i tal′ik, ī tal′-) *adj.* of a printing type that slopes to the right.

itch (ich) *v.i.* **1.** to feel a tingling irritation of the skin that causes a desire to scratch. —*n.* **2.** an itching sensation. **3.** a restless longing. —**itch′y,** *adj.*

i′tem (ī′təm) *n.* a separate article.

i′tem·ize′ *v.t.,* **-ized, -izing.** to state by items; list. —**i′tem·i·za′tion,** *n.*

i·tin′er·ant (ī tin′ər ənt, i tin′-) *adj.* **1.** traveling from place to place. —*n.* **2.** a person who goes from place to place.

i·tin′er·ar′y (-ə rer′ē) *n., pl.* **-aries.** a detailed plan for a journey; route.

its (its) *adj.* the possessive form of **it.**

it's (its) a contraction of **it is.**

it·self′ *pron.* a reflexive form of **it.**

IV (ī′vē′) *n., pl.,* **IVs, IV's.** an apparatus for intravenous delivery of medicines, nutrients, etc.

I've (īv) a contraction of **I have.**

i′vo·ry (ī′və rē, ī′vrē) *n., pl.* **-ries. 1.** a hard white substance composing the tusks of the elephant, walrus, etc. **2.** a yellowish white.

i′vory tow′er *n.* a place remote from worldly affairs.

i′vy (ī′vē) *n., pl.* **ivies.** a climbing vine with smooth, evergreen leaves. —**i′vied,** *adj.*

-ize a suffix meaning: **1.** to engage in. **2.** to treat in a certain way. **3.** to become or form into. **4.** to make or cause to be.

J

J, j (jā) *n.* the tenth letter of the English alphabet.

jab (jab) *v.,* **jabbed, jabbing,** *n.* —*v.t., v.i.* **1.** to poke or punch. —*n.* **2.** a sharp, quick thrust or punch.

jab′ber (jab′ər) *v.i., v.t.* **1.** to talk rapidly or indistinctly. —*n.* **2.** such talk.

jack (jak) *n.* **1.** a device for lifting heavy objects short heights. **2.** a playing card with a picture of a soldier or servant. **3.** an electrical connecting device. —*v.t.* **4.** to raise with a jack.

jack′al (jak′əl) *n.* a wild dog.

jack′ass′ *n.* **1.** a male donkey. **2.** a fool.

jack′et (jak′it) *n.* **1.** a short coat. **2.** an outer covering.

jack′ham′mer *n.* a compressed-air portable drill for rock, concrete, etc.

jack′-in-the-box′ *n., pl.* **jack-in--boxes.** a toy consisting of a box from which a figure springs up when the lid is opened.

jack′knife′ *n., pl.* **-knives,** *v.,* **-knifed, -knifing.** —*n.* **1.** a large folding pocketknife. —*v.i., v.t.* **2.** (of a trailer truck) to have or cause to have the cab and trailer swivel into a V.

jack′pot′ *n.* the cumulative prize in a contest, lottery, etc.

jack′ rab′bit *n.* a large rabbit of W North America.

Ja·cuz′zi (jə kōō′zē) *Trademark.* a brand name for a type of whirlpool bath.

jade¹ (jād) *n.* a hard green stone, used for carvings and jewelry.

jade² (jād) *n.* **1.** a broken-down horse. **2.** a disreputable woman.

jad′ed *adj.* weary and bored.

jag′ged *adj.* having ragged notches.

jag′uar (jag′wär) *n.* a large South American wildcat.

jai′ a·lai′ (hī′ lī′, hī′ ə lī′) *n.* a game played with basketlike rackets on a three-walled court.

jail (jāl) *n.* **1.** a prison. —*v.t.* **2.** to put in prison. —**jail′er,** *n.*

ja·la·pe′ño (hä′lə pān′yō) *n., pl.* **-ños.** a Mexican hot pepper.

ja·lop′y (jə lop′ē) *n., pl.* **-pies.** an old, decrepit automobile.

jam¹ (jam) *v.,* **jammed, jamming,** *n.* —*v.t.* **1.** to push into a space. **2.** to make unworkable. **3.** to interfere with (radio signals), making them unintelligible. —*v.i.* **4.** to become stuck or unworkable. —*n.* **5.** people or objects jammed together. **6.** *Informal.* a difficult situation.

jam² *n.* a preserve of crushed fruit with sugar.

jamb (jam) *n.* the side post of a door or window.

jam′bo·ree′ (jam′bə rē′) *n.* noisy merrymaking.

Jan. January.

jan′gle (jang′gəl) *v.,* **-gled, -gling,** *n.* —*v.i., v.t.* **1.** to make or cause a harsh metallic sound. —*n.* **2.** a harsh metallic sound.

jan′i·tor (jan′i tər) *n.* the caretaker of a building.

Jan′u·ar′y (jan′yōō er′ē) *n.* the first month of the year.

jar¹ (jär) *n.* a broad-mouthed bottle.

jar² (jär) *v.t., v.i.,* **jarred, jarring.** **1.** to jolt or shake. **2.** to have an unpleasant effect (on).

jar′gon (jär′gən, -gon) *n.* vocabulary meaningful only to a particular profession or group.

jas′mine (jaz′min, jas′-) *n.* a shrub with fragrant white or yellow flowers.

jas′per (jas′pər) *n.* a kind of quartz.

jaun′dice (jôn′dis, jän′-) *n.* a condition causing yellow discoloration of the skin, whites of the eyes, etc.

jaun′diced *adj.* **1.** affected with jaundice. **2.** envious and resentful.

jaunt (jônt, jänt) *n.* a short pleasure trip.

jaun′ty (jôn′tē, jän′-) *adj.,* **-tier, -tiest.** lively and cheerful.

ja′va (jä′və) *n.* **1.** *Slang.* coffee. **2. Java,** *Trademark.* a programming language used to create interactive Internet applications.

jave′lin (jav′lin, jav′ə-) *n.* a light spear.

jaw (jô) *n.* **1.** either of two bones forming the framework of the mouth. **2.** one of two or more parts that grip something. —*v.i.* **3.** *Slang.* to chat.

jaw′bone′ *n., v.,* **-boned, -boning.** —*n.* **1.** the bone of the jaw. —*v.t.* **2.** to influence by persuasion.

jay (jā) *n.* a noisy blue or gray songbird.

jay′walk′ *v.i.* to cross a street carelessly. —**jay′walk′er,** *n.*

jazz (jaz) *n.* **1.** popular music marked by strong rhythm and improvisation. **2.** *Slang.* insincere talk.

jazz′y *adj.,* **-ier, -iest. 1.** of or like jazz music. **2.** flashy.

J.D. Doctor of Jurisprudence; Doctor of Laws.

jeal′ous (jel′əs) *adj.* **1.** resentful and envious, as of another's success. **2.** watchful in guarding something. —**jeal′ous·y,** *n.*

jeans (jēnz) *n.pl.* trousers of twilled cotton.

Jeep (jēp) *Trademark.* a small rugged type of automobile.

jeer (jēr) *v.i., v.t.* **1.** to shout scornfully. —*n.* **2.** a scornful shout.

Je·ho′vah (ji hō′və) *n.* God.

je·june′ (ji jōōn′) *adj.* **1.** lacking interest or importance. **2.** lacking maturity; childish.

jell (jel) *v.i., v.t.* **1.** to become or cause to become jellylike in consistency. **2.** to become or cause to become clear.

jel′ly (jel′ē) *n., pl.* **-lies,** *v.,* **-lied, -lying.** —*n.* **1.** a sweet spread of fruit juice boiled down with sugar. **2.** any substance of such consist-

ency. —*v.i., v.t.* **3.** to become or
cause to become jellylike.

jel′ly·bean′ *n.* a small, bean-
shaped, chewy candy.

jel′ly·fish′ *n., pl.* **-fish, -fishes.** a
stinging marine animal with a soft,
jellylike body.

jel′ly roll′ *n.* a thin cake spread
with jelly and rolled up.

jeop′ard·ize′ (jep′ər dīz′) *v.t.,*
-ized, -izing. to expose to danger.
—**jeop′ard·y,** *n.*

jerk (jûrk) *n.* **1.** a quick, sharp pull.
2. *Slang.* a stupid person. —*v.t., v.i.*
3. to pull or move with a jerk.
—**jerk′y,** *adj.*

jer′kin (jûr′kin) *n.* a close-fitting,
usu. sleeveless jacket.

jerk′wa′ter *adj.* insignificant and
remote.

jer′ry-built′ (jer′ē-) *adj.* flimsily
made.

jer′sey (jûr′zē) *n.* **1.** a soft knitted
fabric. **2.** a shirt of this.

jest (jest) *n.* **1.** a joke. —*v.i.* **2.** to
joke or banter. —**jest′er,** *n.*

jet¹ (jet) *n., v.,* **jet·ted, jet·ting,** *adj.*
—*n.* **1.** a stream of gas or liquid
under pressure. **2.** Also, **jet plane.**
a plane operated by jet propulsion.
—*v.t., v.i.* **3.** to shoot (something)
forth in a stream.

jet² (jet) *n.* a hard black stone.

jet′ lag′ *n.* fatigue after a jet flight
to a different time zone.

jet′ propul′sion *n.* forward movement caused by a body's reaction
to the expulsion of jets of gas from
a rear vent. —**jet′-pro·pelled′,** *adj.*

jet′sam (jet′səm) *n.* goods thrown
overboard to lighten a ship.

jet′ti·son (jet′ə sən, -zən) *v.t.* to
cast (cargo) overboard.

jet′ty (jet′ē) *n., pl.* **-ties. 1.** a structure built into the water. **2.** a pier.

Jew (jōō) *n.* **1.** a member of a people who trace their descent from
the biblical Israelites. **2.** a follower
of Judaism. —**Jew′ish,** *adj.*

jew′el (jōō′əl) *n.* **1.** a precious
stone; gem. **2.** a treasured person
or thing.

jib (jib) *n.* a triangular sail set forward from a mast.

jibe¹ (jīb) *v.i.,* **jibed, jibing.** to be
in harmony or accord.

jibe² (jīb) *v.i., v.t.,* **jibed, jibing.** to
gibe.

jif′fy (jif′ē) *n., pl.* **-fies.** a short
time.

jig (jig) *n., v.,* **jigged, jigging.** —*n.*
1. a lively folk dance. —*v.i.* **2.** to
dance a jig.

jig′ger (jig′ər) *n.* a measure of 1½
oz. (45 ml) for liquors.

jig′gle *v.,* **-gled, -gling,** *n.* —*v.t.,*

v.i. **1.** to move with short, quick
jerks. —*n.* **2.** the act of jiggling.

jig′saw′ *n.* a saw with a narrow
vertical blade for cutting curves,
patterns, etc.

jig′saw puz′zle *n.* a set of irregularly cut flat pieces that form a picture when fitted together.

jilt (jilt) *v.t.* to reject (a previously
encouraged suitor).

Jim′ Crow′ (jim) *n. (sometimes l.c.)*
a policy of discrimination against
blacks. —**Jim′-Crow′,** *adj.*

jim′my (jim′ē) *n., pl.* **-mies,** *v.,*
-mied, -mying. —*n.* **1.** a short
crowbar. —*v.t.* **2.** to force open.

jim′son·weed′ (jim′sən wēd′) *n.* a
coarse weed with poisonous leaves.

jin′gle (jing′gəl) *v.,* **-gled, -gling,** *n.*
—*v.i., v.t.* **1.** to make or cause to
make repeated clinking sounds.
—*n.* **2.** a jingling sound. **3.** a very
simple verse.

jin′go·ism (jing′gō iz′əm) *n.* chauvinism marked by an aggressive
foreign policy. —**jin′go·is′tic,** *adj.*

jinx (jingks) *n.* **1.** a cause of bad
luck. —*v.t.* **2.** to cause bad luck.

jit′ters *n.pl. Informal.* nervousness.
—**jit′ter·y,** *adj.*

jive (jīv) *n., v.,* **jived, jiv·ing.** —*n.*
1. swing music or early jazz. **2.**
meaningless talk. —*v.t., v.i.* **3.**
Slang. to fool or kid (someone).

job (job) *n.* **1.** a piece of work. **2.**
employment. **3.** a task.

job′ ac′tion *n.* a work slowdown
by employees to win demands.

job′ber *n.* a dealer in odd lots of
merchandise.

job′ lot′ *n.* a large assortment of
goods sold as a single unit.

jock (jok) *n. Informal.* **1.** an athlete.
2. an enthusiast.

jock′ey (jok′ē) *n.* **1.** a person who
rides horses in races. —*v.i.* **2.** to
maneuver.

jo·cose′ (jō kōs′, jə-) *adj.* joking.
Also, **joc′und** (jok′ənd, jō′kənd).

joc′u·lar (jok′yə lər) *adj.* joking.
—**joc′u·lar′i·ty** (-lar′i tē) *n.*

jog (jog) *v.,* **jogged, jogging,** *n.*
—*v.t.* **1.** to push or shake. **2.** to stir
to activity. —*v.i.* **3.** to run at a
slow, steady pace, esp. for exercise.
—*n.* **4.** a nudge. **5.** a steady pace.
6. a bend or turn. —**jog′ger,** *n.*

joie de vi′vre (zhwAdə vē′vRə) *n.*
French. delight in being alive.

join (join) *v.t., v.i.* **1.** to put or
come together. **2.** to become a
member of (a group).

join′er *n.* an assembler of wood-
work. —**join′er·y,** *n.*

joint (joint) *n.* **1.** the place at
which two things join. **2.** the place
where two bones fit together. **3.**

Slang. a disreputable place. **4.** *Slang.* a marijuana cigarette. —*adj.* **5.** shared by, common to, or done by two or more. —*v.t.* **6.** to join or divide by a joint. —**joint′ly,** *adv.*

joist (joist) *n.* one of the parallel beams supporting a floor or ceiling.

joke (jōk) *n.*, *v.*, **joked, jok·ing.** —*n.* **1.** an amusing remark, story, etc. **2.** an object of ridicule. —*v.i.* **3.** to make or tell jokes. —**jok′ing·ly,** *adv.*

jol′ly (jol′ē) *adj.*, **-lier, -liest,** *v.*, **-lied, -lying,** *adv.* —*adj.* **1.** in good spirits; merry. —*v.t.* **2.** to try to keep (someone) in good humor. —*adv.* **3.** *Brit. Informal.* very. —**jol′li·ness, jol′li·ty,** *n.*

jolt (jōlt) *v.t.* **1.** to shake roughly. **2.** to shock. —*v.i.* **3.** to move jerkily. —*n.* **4.** a shock.

jon′quil (jong′kwil, jon′-) *n.* a fragrant yellow or white narcissus.

josh (josh) *v.t.*, *v.i.* **1.** to tease.

jos′tle (jos′əl) *v.t.*, *v.i.*, **-tled, -tling.** to push or shove rudely.

jot (jot) *v.*, **jot·ted, jot·ting,** *n.* —*v.t.* **1.** to write down quickly or briefly. —*n.* **2.** a little bit.

jounce (jouns) *v.*, **jounced, jounc·ing,** *n.* —*v.t.*, *v.i.* **1.** to move joltingly. —*n.* **2.** a jouncing movement.

jour′nal (jûr′nl) *n.* **1.** a daily record of events. **2.** a newspaper or periodical.

jour′nal·ism (-iz′əm) *n.* the occupation of writing, editing, and publishing or broadcasting news. —**jour′nal·ist,** *n.*

jour′ney (jûr′nē) *n.* **1.** the act or course of traveling. —*v.i.* **2.** to travel.

jour′ney·man *n.*, *pl.* **-men.** a skilled worker.

joust (joust) *n.* a combat between mounted knights.

jo′vi·al (jō′vē əl) *adj.* hearty and good-humored. —**jo′vi·al′i·ty** (-al′i-tē) *n.*

jowl (joul) *n.* **1.** the lower jaw. **2.** flesh hanging from the lower jaw.

joy (joi) *n.* **1.** happiness; delight. **2.** a source of delight. —**joy′ful, joy′ous,** *adj.*

joy′ride′ *n.* a pleasure ride, esp. in a recklessly driven vehicle.

joy′stick′ *n.* **1.** *Informal.* the control stick of an airplane. **2.** a lever for controlling the action in a computer game.

JP Justice of the Peace.

Jr. junior. Also, **jr.**

ju′bi·lant (jōō′bə lənt) *adj.* showing great joy. —**ju′bi·la′tion** (-lā′-shən) *n.*

ju′bi·lee′ (jōō′bə lē′) *n.* a celebration, esp. of an anniversary.

Ju′da·ism (-dē iz′əm, -də-) *n.* the religion of the Jewish people.

judge (juj) *n.*, *v.*, **judged, judging.** —*n.* **1.** a public officer who hears and decides cases in a court of law. **2.** a person who decides who has won a contest. **3.** a person able to pass critical judgment. —*v.t.* **4.** to pass legal judgment on. **5.** to form an opinion about. —*v.i.* **6.** to act as a judge.

judg′ment (-mənt) *n.* **1.** a decision, as in a court of law. **2.** good sense.

judg·men′tal (-men′tl) *adj.* making judgments, esp. on morality.

ju·di′cial (jōō dish′əl) *adj.* of justice, courts of law, or judges.

ju·di′ci·ar′y (-dish′ē er′ē, -dish′ə rē) *n.*, *pl.* **-ies,** *adj.* —*n.* **1.** the legal branch of a government. **2.** the system of courts in a country. —*adj.* **3.** of judges.

ju·di′cious *adj.* wise; prudent.

ju′do (jōō′dō) *n.* a martial art based on jujitsu.

jug (jug) *n.* **1.** a container for liquid, having a handle and a narrow neck. **2.** *Slang.* a jail; prison.

jug′ger·naut′ (jug′ər nôt′) *n.* any overpowering, irresistible force.

jug′gle (jug′əl) *v.*, **-gled, -gling.** —*v.t.* **1.** to do tricks by tossing and catching (several objects) at once. **2.** to manage the requirements of (several activities) at once. —*v.i.* **3.** to juggle objects. —**jug′gler,** *n.*

jug′u·lar (jug′yə lər) *adj.* **1.** of the neck. —*n.* **2.** a large vein in the neck.

juice (jōōs) *n.* **1.** the liquid part of plants, esp. fruits and vegetables. **2.** the natural fluid of an animal body. —**juic′y,** *adj.*

juic′er *n.* an appliance for extracting juice from fruits and vegetables.

ju·jit′su (jōō jit′sōō) *n.* a Japanese method of self-defense without weapons.

juke′box′ (jōōk′boks′) *n.* a coin-operated device for playing recorded music.

Jul. July.

ju′li·enne′ (jōō′lē en′) *adj.* (of vegetables) cut into thin strips.

Ju·ly′ (jōō lī′, jə-) *n.* the seventh month of the year.

jum′ble (jum′bəl) *n.*, *v.*, **-bled, -bling.** —*v.t.*, *v.i.* **1.** to mix or be mixed in a confused mass. —*n.* **2.** a disordered mass.

jum′bo (jum′bō) *adj.* very large.

jump (jump) *v.i.*, *v.t.* **1.** to spring or leap (over). **2.** to increase suddenly. —*n.* **3.** a spring; leap. **4.** a

sudden rise in amount, price, etc.
—**Idiom. 5. get** or **have the jump
on,** to have an advantage over.
jump′er¹ n. **1.** one that jumps. **2.**
one of a pair of electric cables for
starting a dead car battery.
jump′er² n. a sleeveless dress worn
over a shirt.
jump′-start′ n. **1.** the starting of a
car engine with jumpers. —v.t. **2.**
to give a jump-start to. **3.** to enliven or revive.
jump′suit′ n. a one-piece suit.
jump′y adj., **-ier, -iest.** nervous.
Jun. June.
junc′tion (jungk′shən) n. **1.** a joining or being joined. **2.** a place
where things meet.
junc′ture (-chər) n. **1.** a point of
time. **2.** a crisis. **3.** a point at
which two bodies are joined.
June (jōōn) n. the sixth month of
the year.
jun′gle (jung′gəl) n. wild land
overgrown with vegetation, esp. in
the tropics.
jun′ior (jōōn′yər) adj. **1.** younger.
2. of lower rank. —n. **3.** a third-
year high school or college student.
jun′ior col′lege n. a two-year college.
jun′ior high′ school′ n. a school
consisting of grades 7 through 9.
ju′ni·per (jōō′nə pər) n. an evergreen shrub or tree with berrylike
cones.
junk¹ (jungk) n. **1.** old or discarded
material. **2.** something worthless.
—v.t. **3.** to discard.
junk² (jungk) n. a flat-bottomed
Chinese ship.
jun′ket (jung′kit) n. **1.** a custardlike dessert. **2.** a pleasure trip, esp.
one made by a government official
at public expense.
junk′ food′ n. high-calorie food
having little nutritional value.
junk′ie n. Informal. **1.** a drug ad-

dict. **2.** a person who craves or is
enthusiastic about something.
junk′ mail′ n. unsolicited commercial material mailed in bulk.
jun′ta (hōōn′tə, jun′-, hun′-) n. a
small group ruling a country, esp.
after a seizure of power.
Ju′pi·ter (jōō′pi tər) n. the largest
planet in the solar system, fifth
from the sun.
ju′ris·dic′tion (jōōr′is dik′shən) n.
power; authority; control.
ju′ris·pru′dence (-prōōd′ns) n. the
science of law.
ju′rist n. an expert in law, as a
judge.
ju′ror (jōōr′ər, -ôr) n. a member of
a jury.
ju′ry (jōōr′ē) n., pl. **-ries.** a group
of persons selected to make a decision, esp. in a law court.
just (just) adj. **1.** fair; right. **2.** lawful. **3.** true. —adv. **4.** exactly. **5.**
simply. **6.** barely. **7.** only. **8.** very
recently.
jus′tice (jus′tis) n. **1.** fairness;
rightness. **2.** the administration of
punishment or reward. **3.** a judge.
jus′tice of the peace′ n. a local
public officer who performs marriages, tries minor cases, etc.
jus′ti·fy′ v.t., **-fied, -fying. 1.** to
show to be just, true, right, etc. **2.**
to defend. —**jus′ti·fi·ca′tion,** n.
jut (jut) v.i., **jutted, jutting.** to
project; protrude.
jute (jōōt) n. a strong fiber made
from certain East Indian plants.
ju′ve·nile (jōō′və nl, -nīl′) adj. **1.**
young. **2.** immature. **3.** for young
people. —n. **4.** a young person.
ju′venile delin′quency n. illegal or
antisocial behavior by a minor.
—**ju′venile delin′quent,** n.
jux′ta·pose′ (juk′stə pōz′, juk′stə-
pōz′) v.t., **-posed, -posing.** to place
close together, as for contrast.
—**jux′ta·po·si′tion** (-pə zish′ən) n.

K

K, k (kā) n. the eleventh letter of
the English alphabet.
K 1. karat. **2.** Kelvin. **3.** kilobyte. **4.**
kilometer. **5.** thousand.
k 1. karat. **2.** kilogram.
ka·bu′ki (kə bōō′kē, kä′bōō kē′) n. a
popular drama of Japan.
kai′ser (kī′zər) n. a German emperor.
kale (kāl) n. a cabbagelike plant
with wrinkled leaves.
ka·lei′do·scope′ (kə lī′də skōp′) n.
an optical device in which colored
bits change patterns continually.

kan·ga·roo′ (kang′gə rōō′) n., pl.
-roos, -roo. a leaping Australian
marsupial with long, powerful
hind legs.
kan′garoo court′ n. a self-appoint-
ed tribunal disregarding legal
principles or human rights.
Kans. Kansas.
ka′o·lin (kā′ə lin) n. a fine white
clay.
ka′pok (kā′pok) n. the silky down
from the seeds of certain trees.
ka·put′ (kä pōōt′, -pŏŏt′, kə-) adj.
Informal. ruined or broken.

kar′at (kar′ət) *n.* $\frac{1}{24}$ part: a unit for measuring the purity of gold.

ka•ra′te (kə rä′tē) *n.* a Japanese method of self-defense.

kar′ma (kär′mə) *n.* (in Hinduism and Buddhism) fate as the result of one's actions in successive incarnations.

ka′ty•did (kā′tē did) *n.* a large green grasshopper.

kay′ak (kī′ak) *n.* an Eskimo canoe or a small boat resembling this.

ka•zoo′ (kə zoō′) *n., pl.* **-zoos.** a tubular musical toy that buzzes when one hums into it.

KB kilobyte.

kc kilocycle.

ke•bab′ (kə bob′) *n.* cubes of marinated meat, vegetables, etc., broiled on a skewer.

keel (kēl) *n.* **1.** the central framing part in the bottom of a ship's hull. —*v.* **2. keel over, a.** to capsize. **b.** to fall or cause to fall over.

keen¹ (kēn) *adj.* **1.** sharp or piercing. **2.** intelligent. **3.** intense. **4.** eager. —**keen′ly,** *adv.*

keen² (kēn) *n.* **1.** a wailing lament. —*v.t., v.i.* **2.** to wail in lament (for the dead).

keep (kēp) *v.,* **kept** (kept) **keeping,** *n.* —*v.t.* **1.** to retain in one's possession. **2.** to cause to continue in a given position or state. **3.** to take care of. **4.** to prevent. **5.** to obey or fulfill. —*v.i.* **6.** to continue or go on. **7.** to stay in good condition. —*n.* **8.** board and lodging. —*Idiom.* **9. for keeps,** permanently. —**keep′er,** *n.*

keep′ing *n.* **1.** conformity. **2.** care.

keep′sake′ *n.* a souvenir.

keg (keg) *n.* a small barrel.

kelp (kelp) *n.* any large brown seaweed.

Kel′vin (kel′vin) *adj.* of or noting an absolute scale of temperature in which 0° equals −273.16° Celsius.

ken (ken) *n.* knowledge.

Ken. Kentucky.

ken′nel (ken′l) *n.* **1.** a shelter for a dog or cat. **2.** an establishment where dogs or cats are bred or boarded.

ken′te (ken′tā) *n.* a colorful Ghanaian fabric, often worn as a symbol of African-American pride.

kept (kept) *v.* pt. and pp. of **keep.**

ker′chief (kûr′chif, -chēf) *n.* a square scarf worn as a covering for the head or neck.

ker′nel (kûr′nl) *n.* the center part of a nut.

ker′o•sene′ (ker′ə sēn′) *n.* a type of oil used as fuel.

kes′trel (kes′trəl) *n.* a small falcon.

ketch′up (kech′əp, kach′-) *n.* a type of thick tomato sauce with spices.

ket′tle (ket′l) *n.* a metal container for boiling liquids.

ket′tle•drum′ *n.* a large drum with a round copper bottom.

key (kē) *n.* **1.** a metal piece for moving the bolt of a lock. **2.** something that explains or solves. **3.** a lever pressed by the finger on a computer, piano, etc. **4.** a system of related musical tones. —*adj.* **5.** chief; essential. —*v.t.* **6.** to regulate the pitch of. **7. key up,** to excite or make nervous.

key′board′ *n.* **1.** the row or set of keys on a piano, computer, etc. —*v.t., v.i.* **2.** to insert (data) into a computer. —**key′board′er,** *n.*

key′note′ *n.* **1.** the basic note of a scale. **2.** the basic idea or theme.

key′stone′ *n.* the stone forming the summit of an arch.

kg kilogram.

khak′i (kak′ē, kä′kē) *n.* a dull yellowish brown.

kHz kilohertz.

kib•butz′ (ki bootz′, -boots′) *n., pl.* **-butzim.** a collective farm in Israel.

kib′itz•er (kib′it sər) *n. Informal.* a person offering unwanted advice.

kick (kik) *v.t.* **1.** to strike with the foot. **2.** *Slang.* to give up (a habit). —*v.i.* **3.** to make a rapid thrust with the foot. **4.** (of a gun) to recoil. —*n.* **5.** the act of kicking. **6.** *Informal.* a thrill.

kick′back′ *n.* a part of an income given, usu. secretly, to someone who made the income possible.

kick′off′ *n.* **1.** the kick that begins play in football or soccer. **2.** the beginning of anything.

kick′stand′ *n.* the bar for holding a bicycle upright when not in use.

kid¹ (kid) *n.* **1.** *Informal.* a child. **2.** a young goat. **3.** leather made from the skin of a young goat.

kid² (kid) *v.t., v.i.,* **kidded, kidding.** *Informal.* to tease. —**kid′der,** *n.*

kid′nap (kid′nap) *v.t.,* **-napped** or **-naped, -napping** or **-naping.** to carry off by force, esp. for ransom. —**kid′nap•per, kid′nap•er,** *n.*

kid′ney (kid′nē) *n.* one of a pair of organs that filter waste from the blood and secrete urine.

kid′ney bean′ *n.* a red-skinned dried bean.

kid′ney stone′ *n.* an abnormal stony mass formed in the kidney.

kill (kil) *v.t.* **1.** to cause the death of. **2.** to spend (time) unprofitably. —*n.* **3.** a killing. **4.** an animal killed.

kil′ler whale′ *n.* a large, predatory, black-and-white dolphin.

kill′ing *n.* **1.** the act of one that kills. **2.** a quick, large profit. —*adj.* **3.** fatal. **4.** exhausting.

kill′-joy′ *n.* a person who spoils others' pleasure.

kiln (kil, kiln) *n.* a large furnace for making bricks, firing pottery, etc.

ki·lo (kē′lō, kil′ō) *n., pl.* **-los. 1.** a kilogram. **2.** a kilometer.

kilo- a prefix meaning thousand.

kil′o·byte′ (kil′ə bīt′) *n.* **1.** 1024 bytes. **2.** (loosely) 1000 bytes.

kil′o·gram′ *n.* 1000 grams. Also, **kilo.**

kil′o·hertz′ *n., pl.* **-hertz.** a unit of frequency equal to 1000 cycles per second.

kil′o·li·ter (-lē′-) *n.* 1000 liters.

ki·lom′e·ter (ki lom′i tər, kil′ə mē′-) *n.* 1000 meters.

kil′o·watt′ *n.* 1000 watts.

kilt (kilt) *n.* a pleated, knee-length tartan skirt worn by Scotsmen.

ki·mo′no (kə mō′nə, -nō) *n., pl.* **-nos.** a loose dressing gown.

kin (kin) *n.* relatives. Also, **kin′folk′.**

kind¹ (kīnd) *adj.* gentle; considerate. —**kind′ness,** *n.*

kind² (kīnd) *n.* **1.** a class or group of animals, objects, etc. **2.** variety; sort.

kin′der·gar′ten (kin′dər gär′tn, -dn) *n.* a class or school for young children.

kind′heart′ed (kīnd′-) *adj.* having or showing kindness.

kin′dle (kin′dl) *v.,* **-dled, -dling.** —*v.t.* **1.** to set fire to. **2.** to excite. —*v.i.* **3.** to begin to burn.

kin′dling *n.* material for starting a fire.

kind′ly (kīnd′lē) *adj.,* **-lier, -liest,** *adv.* —*adj.* **1.** kind. —*adv.* **2.** in a kind manner. **3.** favorably.

kin′dred (kin′drid) *adj.* **1.** related; similar. —*n.* **2.** relatives.

ki·net′ic (ki net′ik, kī-) *adj.* of motion.

king (king) *n.* **1.** a male sovereign or ruler. **2.** a man or thing supreme in its class. **3.** a playing card bearing a picture of a king. **4.** a chess piece. —**king′ly,** *adj., adv.*

king′dom (-dəm) *n.* **1.** a state ruled by a king or queen. **2.** one of the three divisions of natural objects.

king′fish′er *n.* a bright blue fish-eating bird.

king′-size′ *adj.* extra large.

kink (kingk) *n.* **1.** a twist or curl. —*v.i., v.t.* **2.** to curl or cause to curl. —**kink′y,** *adj.*

kin′ship *n.* **1.** family relationship. **2.** affinity; likeness.

ki′osk (kē′osk, kē osk′) *n.* a small open structure where newspapers, refreshments, etc., are sold.

kip′per (kip′ər) *n.* a salted, dried herring or salmon.

kiss (kis) *v.t., v.i.* **1.** to touch with the lips in affection, greeting, etc. —*n.* **2.** the act of kissing.

kit (kit) *n.* **1.** a set of supplies, tools, etc. **2.** a set of materials or parts for assembly.

kitch′en (kich′ən) *n.* a place for cooking.

kite (kīt) *n.* **1.** a light, paper-covered frame flown on a long string. **2.** a type of hawk.

kith′ and kin′ (kith) *n.* friends and relatives.

kitsch (kich) *n.* something pretentious and shallow showing a lack of good taste.

kit′ten (kit′n) *n.* a young cat.

kit′ten·ish *adj.* playfully coy or cute.

kit′ty-cor′nered *adj.* cater-cornered. Also, **kit′ty-cor′ner.**

ki′wi (kē′wē) *n.* **1.** a flightless bird of New Zealand. **2.** an egg-sized brown fruit with edible green pulp.

KKK Ku Klux Klan.

Klee′nex (klē′neks) *Trademark.* a soft paper tissue.

klep′to·ma′ni·a (klep′tə mā′nē ə) *n.* an irresistible compulsion to steal. —**klep′to·ma′ni·ac′,** *n.*

klutz (kluts) *n. Slang.* a clumsy person. —**klutz′y,** *adj.*

km kilometer.

knack (nak) *n.* a special skill.

knap′sack′ (nap′sak′) *n.* a supply bag carried on one's back.

knead (nēd) *v.t.* to work (dough) with the hands.

knee (nē) *n.* the joint in the middle part of the leg.

knee′cap′ *n.* the flat bone at the front of the knee.

knee′-jerk′ *adj. Informal.* reacting in an automatic, habitual way.

kneel (nēl) *v.i.,* **knelt** (nelt) or **kneeled, kneeling.** to go down or rest on one's knees.

knell (nel) *n.* the slow, deep sound of a bell.

knelt (nelt) *v.* a pt. and pp. of **kneel.**

knew (nōō, nyōō) *v.* pt. of **know.**

knick′ers (nik′ərz) *n.pl.* loose-fitting short trousers gathered at the knee.

knick′knack′ (nik′nak′) *n.* a trinket.

knife (nīf) *n., pl.* **knives** (nīvz), *v.,* **knifed, knif·ing.** —*n.* **1.** a cutting instrument having a sharp blade in a handle. —*v.t.* **2.** to stab with a knife.

knight (nīt) *n.* **1.** (in the Middle Ages) a chivalrous soldier. **2.** a man given a rank with the title

"Sir". **3.** a chess piece shaped like a horse's head. —*v.t.* **4.** to name a man a knight. —**knight′hood,** *n.*

knit (nit) *v.,* **knitted** or **knit, knitting,** *n.* —*v.t.* **1.** to make (a fabric or garment) by interlocking loops of yarn with needles. **2.** to join together firmly. —*n.* **3.** a knitted garment.

knob (nob) *n.* a rounded projecting part forming a handle.

knock (nok) *v.i.* **1.** to strike a sharp, sounding blow. **2.** to make a pounding noise. —*v.t.* **3.** to strike a sharp, sounding blow to. **4.** to make by striking. **5.** *Informal.* to criticize. **6. knock off,** to stop. **7.** ~ **out,** to make unconscious. —*n.* **8.** the act or sound of knocking. **9.** a blow or thump. **10.** *Informal.* criticism.

knock′-knee′ *n.* inward curvature of the legs at the knees.

knock′out′ *n.* **1.** a boxing blow that knocks the opponent to the canvas. **2.** *Informal.* one that is extremely attractive.

knoll (nōl) *n.* a small hill.

knot (not) *n., v.,* **knotted, knotting.** —*n.* **1.** an interlacing of a cord, rope, etc., drawn tight into a knob. **2.** a cluster of persons or things. **3.** a hard mass where a branch joins a tree trunk. **4.** one nautical mile per hour. —*v.t.* **5.** to form a knot in. —*v.i.* **6.** to become tied or tangled. —**knot′ty,** *adj.*

know (nō) *v.,* **knew** (nōō, nyōō) **known, knowing.** —*v.t.* **1.** to understand, remember, or experience. —*v.i.* **2.** to be aware. —**Idiom. 3. in the know,** having knowledge or information. —**know′a·ble,** *adj.*

know′ing *adj.* **1.** having or reveal-

ing knowledge. **2.** deliberate. —**know′ing·ly,** *adv.*

knowl′edge (nol′ij) *n.* **1.** the fact or state of knowing. **2.** understanding or information one has learned. **3.** all that is known.

know′ledge·a·ble (-i jə bəl) *adj.* well-informed.

knuck′le (nuk′əl) *n., v.,* **-led, -ling.** —*n.* **1.** a joint of a finger. —*v.* **2. knuckle down,** to apply oneself earnestly. **3.** ~ **under,** to submit.

knuck′le·head′ *n. Informal.* a stupid, inept person.

ko·al′a (kō ä′lə) *n.* a gray, tree-dwelling Australian marsupial.

kohl·ra′bi (kōl rä′bē, -rab′ē) *n., pl.* **-bies.** a variety of cabbage.

ko′la (kō′lə) *n.* a tropical African tree grown for its nuts, used to flavor soft drinks.

kook (kōōk) *n. Slang.* an eccentric person. —**kook′y,** *adj.*

Ko·ran′ (kə rän′, -ran′, kô-) *n.* the sacred scripture of Islam.

ko′sher (kō′shər) *adj.* permissible to eat according to Jewish law.

kow′tow′ (kou′tou′, -tou′, kō′-) *v.i.* to act in a servile manner.

kryp′ton (krip′ton) *n.* an inert gas.

KS Kansas.

ku′dos (kōō′dōz, -dōs, -dos, kyōō′-) *n.* honor; glory.

kum′quat (kum′kwot) *n.* a small, orange citrus fruit.

kung′ fu′ (kung′ fōō′, kōōng′) *n.* a Chinese technique of unarmed combat.

kvetch (kvech) *Slang.* —*v.i.* **1.** to complain chronically. —*n.* **2.** a person who kvetches.

KW kilowatt. Also, **kw.**

KY Kentucky. Also, **Ky.**

L

L, l (el) *n.* the twelfth letter of the English alphabet.

l. 1. left. **2.** length. **3.** line. **4.** liter.

LA Louisiana. Also, **La.**

lab (lab) *n.* a laboratory.

la′bel (lā′bəl) *n., v.,* **-beled, -beling.** —*n.* **1.** a piece of paper or cloth attached to an object and giving information about it. —*v.t.* **2.** to put a label on. **3.** to describe as.

la′bi·a (lā′bē ə) *n.pl., sing.* **-bium.** the liplike folds of the vulva.

la′bi·al (lā′bē əl) *adj.* of the lips or labia.

la′bor (lā′bər) *n.* **1.** bodily toil; work. **2.** childbirth. **3.** workers as a group. —*v.i.* **4.** to work hard. **5.** to move slowly and heavily. —*v.t.* **6.**

to emphasize excessively. Also, *Brit.,* **la′bour.** —**la′bor·er,** *n.*

lab′o·ra·to·ry (lab′rə tôr′ē, lab′ər-ə-) *n., pl.* **-ries.** a place for scientific research and experiment.

la′bored *adj.* done with difficulty.

la·bo′ri·ous (lə bôr′ē əs) *adj.* involving much effort.

la′bor un′ion *n.* an organization of workers for mutual benefit, esp. by collective bargaining.

la·bur′num (lə bûr′nəm) *n.* a poisonous shrub with yellow flowers.

lab′y·rinth (lab′ə rinth) *n.* a complicated network of passages; maze. —**lab′y·rin′thine,** *adj.*

lace (lās) *n., v.,* **laced, lacing.** —*n.* **1.** a delicate netlike fabric. **2.** a cord for tying; shoelace. —*v.t.* **3.** to fasten with a lace. —**lac′y,** *adj.*

lac′er·ate′ (las′ə rāt′) *v.t.*, **-ated, -ating.** to tear roughly; mangle. —**lac′er·a′tion,** *n.*

lach′ry·mal (lak′rə məl) *adj.* of or producing tears.

lach′ry·mose (-mōs′) *adj.* tearful.

lack (lak) *n.* **1.** the state or fact of being without something. —*v.t., v.i.* **2.** to be wanting or deficient (in).

lack′a·dai′si·cal (lak′ə dā′zi kəl) *adj.* listless; unenthusiastic.

lack′ey (lak′ē) *n.* a servile follower.

lack′lus′ter *adj.* dull.

la·con′ic (lə kon′ik) *adj.* using few words. —**la·con′i·cal·ly,** *adv.*

lac′quer (lak′ər) *n.* **1.** a kind of varnish. —*v.t.* **2.** to coat with lacquer.

la·crosse′ (lə krôs′) *n.* a game played with a ball that is carried in a net at the end of a stick.

lac′tate (lak′tāt) *v.i.*, **-tated, -tating.** to secrete milk. —**lac·ta′tion,** *n.*

lac′tose (-tōs) *n.* a sugar-like crystalline substance in milk.

la·cu′na (lə kyōō′nə) *n., pl.* **-nae** (nē) **-nas.** a gap.

lad (lad) *n.* a boy.

lad′der (lad′ər) *n.* uprights with steps between for climbing.

lad′en (lād′n) *adj.* loaded heavily.

lad′ing (lā′ding) *n.* cargo; freight.

la′dle (lād′l) *n., v.,* **-dled, -dling.** —*n.* **1.** a large deep-bowled spoon. —*v.t.* **2.** to serve with a ladle.

la′dy (lā′dē) *n., pl.* **-dies. 1.** a refined, polite woman. **2. Lady,** a British title for a noblewoman.

la′dy·bug′ *n.* a small, spotted, brightly colored beetle. Also, **la′dy·bird′.**

la′dy's-slip′per *n.* an orchid with a slipper-shaped flower lip.

lag (lag) *v.,* **lagged, lagging,** *n.* —*v.i.* **1.** to fall behind; move slowly or belatedly. —*n.* **2.** an instance of lagging. **3.** an interval.

la′ger (lä′gər, lô′-) *n.* a kind of light beer.

lag′gard (lag′ərd) *n.* **1.** a person who lags. —*adj.* **2.** moving slowly.

la·gniappe′ (lan yap′, lan′yap) *n.* a gratuity. Also, **la·gnappe′.**

la·goon′ (lə gōōn′) *n.* a saltwater lake or pond separated from the sea by sand dunes or bars.

laid′-back′ (lād′-) *adj. Informal.* relaxed; easygoing.

lair (lâr) *n.* a wild animal's den.

lais′sez faire′ (les′ā fâr′) *n.* a policy of non-interference in trade, others' affairs, etc. —**lais′sez-faire′,** *adj.*

la′i·ty (lā′i tē) *n.* laypersons.

lake (lāk) *n.* a large body of water enclosed by land.

lam (lam) *n., v.,* **lammed, lamming.** *Slang.* —*n.* **1.** a hasty escape. —*v.i.* **2.** to escape; flee.

la′ma (lä′mə) *n.* a Tibetan or Mongolian Buddhist monk.

La·maze′ meth′od (lə mäz′) *n.* a method by which an expectant mother is prepared for natural birth by physical conditioning and breathing exercises.

lamb (lam) *n.* **1.** a young sheep. **2.** its flesh as food.

lam·baste′ (lam bāst′, -bast′) *v.t.,* **-basted, -basting.** *Informal.* **1.** to beat severely. **2.** to reprimand harshly.

lam′bent (lam′bənt) *adj.* **1.** glowing lightly. **2.** (of wit) gently brilliant.

lame (lām) *adj., lamer, lamest, v.,* **lamed, laming.** —*adj.* **1.** crippled. **2.** stiff or sore. **3.** inadequate. —*v.t.* **4.** to make lame.

la·mé′ (la mā′, lä-) *n.* an ornamental fabric with metallic threads.

lame′ duck′ (lām) *n.* an elected official who is completing a term after the election of a successor.

la·ment′ (lə ment′) *v.t., v.i.* **1.** to mourn; express grief (for). —*n.* **2.** Also, **lam′en·ta′tion** (lam′ən tā′shən). an expression of grief. —**la·ment′a·ble,** *adj.*

lam′i·nate′ *v.t.,* **-nated, -nating,** *adj.* —*v.t.* (lam′ə nāt′) **1.** to form into thin plates or layers. **2.** to cover with layers. —*adj.* (-nāt′, -nit) **3.** Also, **lam′i·nat′ed.** made of layers. —**lam′i·na′tion,** *n.*

lamp (lamp) *n.* a device producing artificial light.

lam·poon′ (lam pōōn′) *n.* **1.** a broad, harsh satire. —*v.t.* **2.** to ridicule in a lampoon.

lam′prey (-prē) *n.* an eel-like fish.

lamp′shade *n.* a shade for screening the light of a lamp.

lance (lans) *n., v.,* **lanced, lanc·ing.** —*n.* **1.** a long spear. —*v.t.* **2.** to open with a lancet.

lan′cet (lan′sit) *n.* a sharp-pointed surgical tool.

land (land) *n.* **1.** the part of the earth's surface above water. **2.** ground or soil. **3.** country. —*v.t., v.i.* **4.** to bring or come to land. **5.** to fall to the earth or floor.

land′ed *adj.* **1.** owning land. **2.** consisting of land.

land′fall′ *n.* **1.** a sighting of land after a voyage or flight. **2.** the land sighted or reached.

land′fill′ *n.* **1.** an area of land built up from refuse material. **2.** material deposited on a landfill.

land′ing *n.* **1.** the act of one that

landlady

lands. **2.** a place for landing persons and goods. **3.** the level floor between flights of stairs.

land′la·dy *n., pl.* **-dies.** a woman who owns and leases property.

land′locked′ *adj.* **1.** shut in by land. **2.** having no access to the sea.

land′lord′ *n.* a person who owns and leases property.

land′lub·ber (-lub′ər) *n.* a person unused to the sea and ships.

land′mark′ *n.* **1.** a prominent object serving as a guide. **2.** a site of historical importance. **3.** an important event, achievement, etc.

land′mass′ *n.* a large area of land.

land′ mine′ *n.* an explosive charge hidden just under the surface of the ground and detonated by pressure.

land′scape′ (-skāp′) *n., v.,* **-scaped, -scaping.** —*n.* **1.** a broad view of natural scenery. **2.** a picture portraying such scenery. —*v.t.* **3.** to improve the appearance of (an area) by planting trees, shrubs, etc.

land′slide′ *n.* **1.** a fall of earth or rock. **2.** an overwhelming majority of votes in an election.

lane (lān) *n.* a narrow road.

lan′guage (lang′gwij) *n.* **1.** speech or writing. **2.** any means of communication.

lan′guid (lang′gwid) *adj.* moving slowly and weakly.

lan′guish (-gwish) *v.i.* **1.** to be or become weak. **2.** to long; pine. —**lan′guish·ing,** *adj.*

lan′guor (-gər) *n.* lack of energy or interest. —**lan′guor·ous,** *adj.*

lank (langk) *adj.* **1.** thin. Also, **lank′y. 2.** straight and limp.

lan′o·lin (lan′l in) *n.* a fat from wool, used in ointments and cosmetics.

lan′tern (lan′tərn) *n.* a lamp with a transparent or translucent protective case.

lan′yard (lan′yərd) *n.* a short rope.

lap¹ (lap) *n.* the top part of the thighs of a seated person.

lap² (lap) *n., v.,* **lapped, lapping.** —*n.* **1.** a circuit of a course in racing. **2.** a part of a journey. —*v.t.* **3.** to lay (something) partly over something underneath. **4.** to get a lap ahead of (a competitor). —*v.i.* **5.** to fold around something.

lap³ (lap) *v.t., v.i.,* **lapped, lapping. 1.** (of water) to wash (against something) lightly. **2.** to take in (liquid) with the tongue.

la·pel′ (lə pel′) *n.* the folded-back part on the front of a coat.

lap′i·dar·y (lap′i der′ē) *n., pl.* **-ries.** one who cuts or polishes gems.

lap′is laz′u·li (lap′is laz′o͞o lē, -lī′, laz′yo͞o-) **1.** a deep blue semiprecious gem. **2.** a sky-blue color.

lapse (laps) *n., v.,* **lapsed, lapsing.** —*n.* **1.** a slight error; slip of memory. **2.** an interval of time. —*v.i.* **3.** to fall from a previous standard. **4.** to come to an end. **5.** to fall, slip, or sink. **6.** to pass, as time.

lap′top′ *n.* a portable microcomputer.

lar′ce·ny (lär′sə nē) *n., pl.* **-nies.** theft. —**lar′ce·nist,** *n.*

larch (lärch) *n.* a deciduous tree of the pine family.

lard (lärd) *n.* **1.** pig fat used in cooking. —*v.t.* **2.** to put strips of fat in (lean meat) before cooking.

lard′er (lär′dər) *n.* a pantry.

large (lärj) *adj.,* **larger, largest. 1.** great in size or number. —**Idiom. 2. at large, a.** at liberty. **b.** in general. —**large′ness,** *n.*

large′ly *adv.* mostly.

large′-scale′ *adj.* extensive.

lar·gess′ (lär jes′, lär′jis) *n.* generosity. Also, **lar·gesse′.**

lar′go (lär′gō) *adj., adv. Music.* slowly and with dignity.

lar′i·at (lar′ē ət) *n.* a long, noosed rope used to tether an animal.

lark (lärk) *n.* **1.** a kind of songbird. **2.** a carefree adventure.

lark′spur′ (-spûr′) *n.* a plant with blue or pink flowers on tall stalks.

lar′va (lär′və) *n., pl.* **-vae** (-vē). an insect between the egg and pupal stages. —**lar′val,** *adj.*

lar′yn·gi′tis (lar′ən jī′tis) *n.* inflammation of the larynx, often with a loss of voice.

lar′ynx (lar′ingks) *n., pl.* **larynges** (lə rin′jēz), **larynxes.** the upper part of the windpipe containing the vocal cords. —**la·ryn′ge·al** (lə rin′jē-əl, lar′ən jē′əl) *adj.*

las·civ′i·ous (lə siv′ē əs) *adj.* lewd.

la′ser (lā′zər) *n.* a device for amplifying light and focusing it into an intense beam.

lash (lash) *n.* **1.** the flexible part of a whip. **2.** a blow with a whip. **3.** an eyelash. —*v.t.* **4.** to strike with or as if with a lash. **5.** to bind. **6. lash out,** to speak out angrily.

lass (las) *n.* a girl.

las′si·tude′ (las′i to͞od′, -tyo͞od′) *n.* weariness.

las′so (las′ō, la so͞o′) *n., pl.* **-sos, -soes,** *v.,* **-soed, -soing.** —*n.* **1.** a lariat for catching horses or cattle. —*v.t.* **2.** to catch with a lasso.

last (last) *adj.* **1.** latest. **2.** final. —*adv.* **3.** most recently. **4.** finally. —*n.* **5.** that which is last. **6.** a foot-shaped form on which shoes are made. —*v.i.* **7.** to endure. **8.** to

continue unexpended. —*Idiom.*
9. at (long) last, finally.
last′ing *adj.* permanent; enduring.
Last′ Sup′per *n.* the supper of Jesus and His disciples on the eve of His Crucifixion.
lat. latitude.
latch (lach) *n.* **1.** a device for fastening a door or gate. —*v.t.* **2.** to fasten with a latch. **3. latch onto,** to attach oneself to.
late (lāt) *adj., adv.,* **later, latest. 1.** after the usual or proper time. **2.** being or lasting well along in time. **3.** recent. **4.** deceased.
late′ly *adv.* recently.
la′tent (lāt′nt) *adj.* hidden; dormant; undeveloped.
lat′er·al (lat′ər əl) *adj.* on or from the side. —**lat′er·al·ly,** *adv.*
la′tex (lā′teks) *n.* **1.** a milky liquid from certain plants. **2.** a synthetic version of this.
lath (lath) *n.* **1.** a thin wood strip. **2.** a material for backing plaster. —*v.t.* **3.** to cover with laths.
lathe (lāth) *n.* a machine for shaping wood, metal, etc., by turning it against a cutting tool.
lath′er (lath′ər) *n.* **1.** foam made with soap and water. **2.** foam formed from sweating. —*v.i., v.t.* **3.** to form or cover with lather.
lat′i·tude (lat′i tōōd′, -tyōōd′) *n.* **1.** distance in degrees north or south of the equator. **2.** freedom to speak or act.
la·trine′ (lə trēn′) *n.* a communal toilet, esp. in a camp or barracks.
lat′ter (lat′ər) *adj.* **1.** being the second of two. **2.** near the end.
lat′tice (lat′is) *n.* a structure of criss-crossed strips.
laud (lôd) *v.t.* to praise. —**laud′a·ble,** *adj.* —**laud′a·to′ry,** *adj.*
laugh (laf) *v.i.* **1.** to express mirth audibly. **2. laugh at,** to ridicule. —*n.* **3.** an act or sound of laughing. —**laugh′ter,** *n.*
laugh′a·ble *adj.* ridiculous.
laugh′ing·stock′ *n.* an object of ridicule.
launch (lônch, länch) *v.t.* **1.** to set afloat or send off. **2.** to start. **3.** to throw. —*v.i.* **4.** to go into action. —*n.* **5.** a large open motorboat.
launch′ pad′ *n.* a platform for launching rockets.
laun·der (lôn′dər, län′-) *v.t., v.i.* to wash or wash and iron.
Laun′dro·mat′ (′-drə mat′) *Trademark.* a self-service laundry with coin-operated machines.
laun′dry *n., pl.* **-dries. 1.** clothes to be washed. **2.** a place where clothes are laundered.

lau′re·ate (lôr′ē it) *n.* a person who has been honored.
lau′rel (lôr′əl) *n.* **1.** a small glossy evergreen tree. **2. laurels,** honor won.
la′va (lä′və, lav′ə) *n.* molten rock from a volcano.
lav′a·to′ry (lav′ə tôr′ē) *n., pl.* **-ries. 1.** a toilet facility. **2.** a washbowl.
lav′en·der (lav′ən dər) *n.* **1.** a fragrant shrub with purple flowers. **2.** a pale purple.
lav′ish (lav′ish) *adj.* **1.** extravagant. —*v.t.* **2.** to expend or give in great amounts.
law (lô) *n.* **1.** the rules established by a government under which people live. **2.** a rule that must be obeyed. **3.** a statement of what always occurs under certain conditions. —**law′-abid′ing,** *adj.* —**law′break′er,** *n.*
law′ful *adj.* permitted by law.
law′less *adj.* **1.** without regard for the law. **2.** uncontrolled by law.
lawn¹ (lôn) *n.* grass-covered land that is kept mowed.
lawn² (lôn) *n.* a thin cotton or linen fabric.
law′suit′ *n.* a case brought before a court.
law′yer (lô′yər, loi′ər) *n.* a person trained and licensed to practice law.
lax (laks) *adj.* **1.** careless. **2.** slack.
lax′a·tive (lak′sə tiv) *adj.* **1.** helping to move the bowels. —*n.* **2.** a laxative agent.
lay¹ (lā) *v.,* **laid, laying,** *n.* —*v.t.* **1.** to place or put down, esp. on a flat surface. **2.** to place in proper position. **3.** to present for consideration. **4.** (of a hen) to produce (eggs). **5.** to attribute. **6.** pt. of **lie. 7. lay off, a.** to dismiss (an employee). **b.** *Informal.* to cease. —*n.* **8.** the position of something. —**Usage.** Many speakers confuse the verbs LAY and LIE because both include the meaning "in a flat position." LAY means "to put down" or "to place, especially in a flat position." A general rule to remember is that if the word "put" or "place" can be substituted in a sentence, then LAY is the verb to use: *Lay* (= put, place) *the books on the table. She laid* (= put, placed) *the baby in the cradle.* But the verb LIE means "to be in a flat position" or "to be situated": *Lie down and rest a moment. The baby is lying down.* For many speakers, the problem comes in the past tense for these two verbs, because the past tense of LIE is *lay,* which looks like, but is not, the present tense of LAY: *The dog will*

want to lie in the shade; yesterday it lay in the grass. Note that we can LAY an infant down in a crib; he or she will LIE there until picked up.

lay² (lā) *adj.* **1.** not ordained into the clergy. **2.** not a member of a profession.

lay'er *n.* **1.** one thickness of material. —*v.t.* **2.** to arrange in layers.

lay•ette' (-et') *n.* a complete outfit for a newborn baby.

lay'man or **lay'wom'an** or **lay'-per'son,** *n., pl.* **-men** or **-wom•en** or **-per•sons. 1.** a person who is not a member of the clergy. **2.** a person who is not a member of a given profession.

lay'off' *n.* the dismissal of employees.

lay'out' *n.* an arrangement.

la'zy (lā'zē) *adj.,* **-zier, -ziest. 1.** unwilling to work. **2.** slow-moving.

lb. *pl.* **lbs., lb.** pound.

l.c. lowercase.

leach (lēch) *v.i.* **1.** to soak through or in. —*v.t.* **2.** to dissolve by soaking.

lead¹ (lēd), *v.,* **led** (led) **leading,** *n.* —*v.t.* **1.** to guide by going before or with. **2.** to influence. **3.** to pass (one's life). **4.** to be or go at the head of. —*v.i.* **5.** to be a route to a place. **6.** to be or go first. **7.** to result in. —*n.* **8.** the position in advance of others. **9.** the extent of such advance. **10.** a clue. **11.** the main part in a play. —**lead'er,** *n.* —**lead'er•ship',** *n.*

lead² (led) *n.* **1.** a heavy gray metal. **2.** a plummet. **3.** graphite used in pencils. —**lead'en,** *adj.*

lead'ing ques'tion (lē'ding) *n.* a question worded to prompt the desired answer.

lead' time' (lēd) *n.* the time between the beginning of a process and the appearance of results.

leaf (lēf) *n., pl.* **leaves** (lēvz), *v.* —*n.* **1.** the flat green part on the stem of a plant. **2.** a thin sheet, as of paper or metal. —*v.* **3. leaf through,** to turn pages quickly. —**leaf'y,** *adj.*

leaf'let (-lit) *n.* **1.** a pamphlet. **2.** a small leaf.

league (lēg) *n., v.,* **leagued, leaguing.** —*n.* **1.** an alliance; pact. **2.** a group of sports teams organized for competition. **3.** a unit of distance, about three miles. —*v.t., v.i.* **4.** to unite in a league.

leak (lēk) *n.* **1.** an unintended hole or crack. **2.** a disclosure of secret information. —*v.i.* **3.** to pass in or out through a leak. —*v.t.* **4.** to let (fluid or light) enter or escape. **5.** to disclose. —**leak'age,** *n.*

lean¹ (lēn) *v.,* **leaned** or **leant, leaning.** —*v.i.* **1.** to bend from an upright position. **2.** to rest for support. **3.** to depend. **4.** to tend. —*v.t.* **5.** to cause to lean.

lean² (lēn) *adj.* **1.** not fat or rich. **2.** economical.

lean'-to' *n., pl.* **lean-tos.** a structure with a single-sloped roof abutting a wall.

leap (lēp) *v.,* **leaped** or **leapt** (lept, lēpt) **leaping,** *n.* —*v.i.* **1.** to spring through the air; jump. **2.** to act quickly. —*v.t.* **3.** to jump over. **4.** to cause to leap. —*n.* **5.** a jump.

leap'frog' *n., v.,* **-frogged, -frogging.** —*n.* **1.** a game in which players leap over each other's backs. —*v.t.* **2.** to jump over as in leapfrog.

leap' year' *n.* a year with February 29 as an extra day.

learn (lûrn) *v.t.* **1.** to acquire knowledge of or skill in. **2.** to commit to memory. **3.** to hear about. —*v.i.* **4.** to acquire knowledge or skill. —**learn'er,** *n.* —**learn'ing,** *n.*

learn'ed (lûr'nid) *adj.* scholarly.

learn'ing disabil'ity *n.* difficulty in reading, writing, etc., associated with impairment of the central nervous system.

lease (lēs) *n., v.,* **leased, leasing.** —*n.* **1.** a contract renting property for a certain time period. —*v.t.* **2.** to get by means of a lease.

leash (lēsh) *n.* **1.** a strap for controlling an animal. —*v.t.* **2.** to control by a leash.

least (lēst) *adj.* **1.** smallest in size, amount, etc. —*n.* **2.** the least amount, degree, etc. —*adv.* **3.** to the smallest extent, amount, etc. —*Idiom.* **4. at least, a.** at the lowest estimate. **b.** in any case. **5. not in the least,** not at all.

leath'er (leth'ər) *n.* material made from the skin of an animal, prepared by tanning. —**leath'er•y,** *adj.*

leath'er•neck' *n. Informal.* a U.S. marine.

leave¹ (lēv) *v.,* **left** (left) **leaving.** —*v.t.* **1.** to go away from or depart from permanently. **2.** to let remain. **3.** to abandon. **4.** to give for use after one's death. —*v.i.* **5.** to go away. **6. leave off,** to stop; discontinue. **7. ~ out,** to omit.

leave² (lēv) *n.* **1.** permission to do something. **2.** Also, **leave' of ab'-sence.** permission to be absent or the time this permission lasts.

leav'en (lev'ən) *n.* **1.** Also, **leav'en•ing.** a fermenting agent to raise dough. —*v.t.* **2.** to make dough rise with a leaven.

lech•er•ous (lech′ər əs) *adj.* lustful. —**lech′er,** *n.* —**lech′er•y,** *n.*

lec′tern (lek′tərn) *n.* a stand with a sloping top from which something is read.

lec′ture (-chər) *n., v.,* **-tured, -turing.** —*n.* **1.** an instructive speech. **2.** a lengthy reprimand. —*v.i.* **3.** to give a lecture. —*v.t.* **4.** to reprimand at length. —**lec′tur•er,** *n.*

ledge (lej) *n.* a narrow shelf.

ledg′er (lej′er) *n.* an account book.

lee (lē) *n.* **1.** the side away from the wind. **2.** shelter. —*adj.* **3.** of or on the lee. —**lee′ward,** *adj., n.*

leech (lēch) *n.* a bloodsucking worm.

leek (lēk) *n.* a vegetable related to the onion.

leer (lēr) *n.* **1.** a sly or lustful glance. —*v.i.* **2.** to look with a leer. **leer′y** (lēr′ē) *adj.,* **-ier, -iest.** wary.

lee′way′ *n.* **1.** extra time, space, etc. **2.** a degree of freedom of action.

left (left) *adj.* **1.** of or on the side that is toward the west when a person is facing north. —*n.* **2.** the left side. **3. the Left,** people favoring liberal reform or radical change. —**left′-hand′,** *adj.* —**left′-hand′ed,** *adj.*

left′ist *n.* (*sometimes cap.*) **1.** a member of the political Left. —*adj.* **2.** of the political Left.

leg (leg) *n.* **1.** one of the limbs supporting a body. **2.** any leglike part.

leg′a•cy (leg′ə sē) *n., pl.* **-cies.** anything bequeathed.

le′gal (lē′gəl) *adj.* of, permitted, or established by law. —**le•gal′i•ty** (-gal′i tē) *n.* —**le′gal•ize′,** *v.t.*

le•ga′tion (li gā′shən) *n.* **1.** a diplomatic minister and staff. **2.** the official headquarters of a diplomatic minister.

le•ga′to (lə gä′tō) *adj., adv. Music.* smooth and flowing; without breaks.

leg′end (lej′ənd) *n.* **1.** a story handed down by tradition. **2.** a person in such a story. **3.** a map key. —**leg′end•ar′y,** *adj.*

leg′er•de•main′ (lej′ər də mān′) *n.* sleight of hand.

leg′ging *n.* a covering for the leg.

leg′i•ble (lej′ə bəl) *adj.* easily read.

le′gion (lē′jən) *n.* **1.** a military unit. **2.** a great number. —**le′gion•naire′,** *n.*

leg′is•late′ (lej′is lāt′) *v.,* **-lated, -lating.** —*v.i.* **1.** to make laws. —*v.t.* **2.** to control by law. —**leg′is•la′tion,** *n.* —**leg′is•la′tive,** *adj.* —**leg′is•la′tor,** *n.*

leg′is•la•ture (-chər) *n.* a lawmaking body.

le•git′i•mate (li jit′ə mit) *adj.* **1.** lawful; valid. **2.** according to established rules. **3.** born of married parents. —**le•git′i•ma•cy** (-mə sē) *n.* —**le•git′i•mize′,** *v.t.*

leg′ume (leg′yoom, li gyoom′) *n.* **1.** any of a family of plants having pods that split open when dry, comprising beans, peas, etc. **2.** the pod or seed of such a plant.

lei (lā) *n.* a flower wreath for the neck.

lei′sure (lē′zhər, lezh′ər) *n.* **1.** time free from work or duty. —*adj.* **2.** unoccupied; having leisure.

lei′sure•ly *adj.* relaxed; unhurried.

leit′mo•tif′ (līt′mō tēf′) *n.* **1.** a recurring musical phrase in an opera. **2.** a dominant theme or underlying pattern in an artistic work.

lem′ming (lem′ing) *n.* a small arctic rodent noted for periodic mass migrations and mass drownings.

lem′on (lem′ən) *n.* **1.** the yellowish acid fruit of a citrus tree. **2.** *Informal.* a person or thing that is defective.

lem′on•ade′ (-ə nād′) *n.* a beverage of lemon juice, sugar, and water.

le′mur (lē′mər) *n.* a small treedwelling monkeylike animal.

lend (lend) *v.,* **lent, lending.** —*v.t.* **1.** to give temporary use of. **2.** to allow the use of (money) on payment of interest. **3.** to give or impart. —Usage. See BORROW.

length (lengkth, length, lenth) *n.* **1.** the size or extent from end to end. **2.** a piece (of cloth, string, etc.). **3.** a large extent of something. —*Idiom.* **4. at length, a.** finally. **b.** in detail. —**length′en,** *v.t., v.i.* —**length′wise′,** *adv., adj.* —**length′y,** *adj.*

le′ni•ent (lē′nē ənt, lēn′yənt) *adj.* not severe; gentle. —**le′ni•en•cy,** *n.*

lens (lenz) *n., pl.* **lenses. 1.** a glass for changing the convergence of light rays, used in eyeglasses, telescopes, etc. **2.** a similar part of the eye.

Lent (lent) *n.* the season of penitence and fasting before Easter. —**Lent′en,** *adj.*

len′til (len′til, -tl) *n.* the edible seed of a pealike plant.

le′o•nine′ (lē′ə nīn′) *adj.* of or like the lion.

leop′ard (lep′ərd) *n.* a large animal of the cat family, usu. tawny with black spots.

le′o•tard′ (lē′ə tärd′) *n.* a tight, flexible, one-piece garment worn by acrobats, dancers, etc.

lep′er (lep′ər) *n.* a person afflicted with leprosy.

lep•re•chaun′ (lep′rə kôn′) *n.* an elf in Irish folklore.

lep′ro•sy (lep′rə sē) *n.* a contagious disease marked by skin ulcerations.

les′bi•an (lez′bē ən) *n.* **1.** a female homosexual. —*adj.* **2.** pertaining to female homosexuals.

le′sion (lē′zhən) *n.* an area of diseased or injured tissue.

less (les) *adv.* **1.** to a smaller extent. —*adj.* **2.** smaller. **3.** lower in importance. —*n.* **4.** a smaller amount or quantity. **5.** minus. —**less•en,** *v.t., v.i.* —**Usage.** FEWER is the comparative form of FEW. It is properly used before plural nouns that refer to individuals or things that can be counted (*fewer words; no fewer than 31 states*). LESS is the comparative form of LITTLE. It should modify only singular mass nouns that refer to things that are abstract or cannot be counted (*less sugar; less doubt*). LESS may be used before plural nouns only when they involve measurements or mathematics (*less than $50; less than three miles.*)

les•see′ (le sē′) *n.* one granted a lease.

les′ser *adj.* a comparative of **little.**

les′son (les′ən) *n.* **1.** something to be learned. **2.** a chapter or exercise assigned to a student.

les′sor (les′ôr, le sôr′) *n.* a person who grants a lease.

lest (lest) *conj.* for fear that.

let (let) *v.t.,* **let, letting. 1.** to permit. **2.** to rent out. **3.** to cause to. **4. let down,** to disappoint; fail. **5.** ~ **off, a.** to release explosively. **b.** to release without punishment.

-let a suffix indicating: **1.** small. **2.** an article worn on.

let′down′ *n.* a disappointment.

le′thal (lē′thəl) *adj.* deadly.

leth′ar•gy (leth′ər jē) *n., pl.* **-gies.** lack of energy; drowsy dullness. —**le•thar′gic** (lə thar′jik) *adj.*

let′ter (let′ər) *n.* **1.** a written communication. **2.** a symbol that is part of an alphabet. **3.** literal meaning. **4. letters,** literature. —*v.t.* **5.** to mark with letters.

let′ter•head′ *n.* **1.** a printed heading on stationery. **2.** paper with a letterhead.

let′ter-per′fect *adj.* precise in every detail.

let′tuce (let′is) *n.* a plant with large crisp leaves used in salad.

let′up′ *n.* cessation; pause; relief.

leu•ke′mi•a (loo kē′mē ə) *n.* a cancerous disease of the bone marrow.

leu′ko•cyte (loo′kə sīt′) *n.* a white blood cell.

lev′ee (lev′ē) *n.* a river embankment to prevent floods.

lev′el (lev′əl) *adj., n., v.,* **-eled, -eling.** —*adj.* **1.** horizontal. **2.** equal. **3.** steady. **4.** sensible. —*n.* **5.** the horizontal line or plane in which something is located. **6.** height. **7.** a device for determining a horizontal plane. —*v.t.* **8.** to make level or equal. **9.** to knock down. —*v.i.* **10.** to become level.

lev′el•head′ed *adj.* sensible.

lev′el play′ing field′ *n.* a state of equality; an equal opportunity.

lev′er (lev′ər, lē′vər) *n.* a bar moving on a fixed support to exert force.

lev′er•age (-ij) *n.* the means of achieving a purpose.

le•vi′a•than (li vī′ə thən) *n.* something of immense size or power.

lev′i•tate′ (lev′i tāt′) *v.i., v.t.,* **-tated, -tating.** to rise or cause to rise into the air in apparent defiance of gravity. —**lev′i•ta′tion,** *n.*

lev′i•ty (-tē) *n.* lack of seriousness.

lev′y (lev′ē) *v.,* **levied, levying,** *n., pl.* **levies.** —*v.t.* **1.** to raise or collect a tax by authority. **2.** to make (war). —*n.* **3.** an act of levying. **4.** something levied.

lewd (lood) *adj.* obscene; indecent.

lex′i•cog′ra•phy (lek′si kog′rə fē) *n.* the process of writing dictionaries.

lex′i•con′ (-kon′, -kən) *n.* a dictionary.

lg. 1. large. **2.** long.

li′a•bil′i•ty (lī′ə bil′i tē) *n., pl.* **-ties. 1.** a debt. **2.** a disadvantage. **3.** the state of being liable.

li′a•ble *adj.* **1.** subject to legal obligation or penalty. **2.** likely.

li•ai′son (lē ā′zən, lē′ā zôn′) *n.* **1.** a contact or connection maintained to ensure cooperation. **2.** an illicit sexual relationship.

li′ar (lī′ər) *n.* one who tells lies.

li•ba′tion (lī bā′shən) *n.* **1.** the pouring out of wine or oil to honor a deity. **2.** the liquid poured. **3.** an alcoholic drink.

li′bel (lī′bəl) *n., v.,* **-beled, -beling.** —*n.* **1.** defamation falsely or unjustly in writing or print. —*v.t.* **2.** to publish libel against. —**li′bel•ous,** *adj.*

lib′er•al (lib′ər əl, lib′rəl) *adj.* **1.** favoring political reform and progressive government. **2.** tolerant. **3.** generous. **4.** not strict. —*n.* **5.** a person having liberal views. —**lib′er•al•ism,** *n.* —**lib′er•al′i•ty** (-ə ral′i tē) *n.* —**lib′er•al•ize′,** *v.t., v.i.*

lib′eral arts′ *n.pl.* college courses comprising the arts, humanities, and natural and social sciences.

lib′er•ate′ (-ə rāt′) *v.t.,* **-ated, -at-**

ing. to set free. —**lib′er·a′tion,** *n.*
—**lib′er·a′tor,** *n.*

lib′er·tar′i·an (lib′ər târ′ē ən) *n.* a person who advocates liberty in thought or conduct.

lib′er·tine′ (-tēn′, -tin) *n.* an unrestrained and immoral person.

lib′er·ty *n.,* *pl.* **-ties.** **1.** freedom; independence. **2. liberties,** impertinent freedom or familiarity.

li·bi′do (li bē′dō) *n.,* *pl.* **-dos.** sexual desire.

li′brar′y (lī′brer′ē, -brə rē, -brē) *n.,* *pl.* **-ries.** **1.** a place to house a collection of books, magazines, etc. **2.** a collection of books. —**li·brar′-i·an,** *n.* —**Pronunciation.** LI-BRARY, with two barely separated *r*-sounds, demonstrates the tendency for neighboring sounds that are alike to become different, or for one of them to disappear altogether. This can lead to forms like the pronunciation (lī′ber ē) which is likely to be heard from less educated or very young speakers and is often criticized. However, (lī′brē) the third pronunciation shown above, is considered perfectly standard, even though one of the *r*-sounds has been dropped.

li·bret′to (li bret′ō) *n.,* *pl.* **-brettos, -bretti** (-bret′ē). the text of an opera. —**li·bret′tist,** *n.*

li′cense (lī′səns) *n., v.,* **-censed, -censing.** —*n.* **1.** an official permit to own, use, or do something. **2.** deviation from rules, facts, etc. —*v.t.* **3.** to grant a license to.

li·cen′tious (-sen′shəs) *adj.* sexually immoral.

li′chen (lī′kən) *n.* a crustlike plant on rocks, trees, etc.

lic′it (lis′it) *adj.* lawful.

lick (lik) *v.t.* **1.** to pass the tongue over. **2.** (of waves or flames) to touch lightly. **3.** *Informal.* to beat or defeat. —*n.* **4.** an act of licking. **5.** a small amount.

lic′o·rice (lik′ər ish, -ə ris) *n.* a plant root used in candy.

lid (lid) *n.* **1.** a hinged or removable cover. **2.** an eyelid.

lie¹ (lī) *n., v.,* **lied, lying.** —*n.* **1.** a deliberately false statement. —*v.i.* **2.** to tell a lie.

lie² (lī) *v.,* **lay** (lā) **lain** (lān) **lying,** *n.* —*v.i.* **1.** to assume or have a reclining position. **2.** to be or remain. —*n.* **3.** a manner of lying. —**Usage.** See LAY.

lie′ detec′tor *n.* a device to detect lying in response to questions, by measuring changes in pulse, blood pressure, etc.; polygraph.

lien (lēn, lē′ən) *n.* the legal right to another's property until a debt is paid.

lieu (lōō) *n.* **in lieu of,** instead of.

lieu·ten′ant (lōō ten′ənt; *in Brit. use, except in the navy,* lef ten′ənt) *n.* **1.** a commissioned officer in the army or navy. **2.** an aide.

life (līf) *n., pl.* **lives** (līvz). **1.** the quality that distinguishes animals and plants from inanimate things. **2.** the period of being alive. **3.** living things. **4.** a manner of living. **5.** animation. —**life′like′,** *adj.*

life′blood′ *n.* **1.** the blood. **2.** a vital element.

life′boat′ *n.* a boat for rescuing passengers from a sinking ship.

life′-care′ *adj.* (of a facility or community) designed to provide for the basic needs of elderly residents.

life′guard′ *n.* a person employed to protect swimmers, as at a beach.

life′long′ *adj.* lasting all of one's life.

life′ part′ner *n.* one member of a monogamous relationship.

life′ preserv′er *n.* a buoyant device to keep a person afloat.

lif′er *n.* a person serving a term of imprisonment for life.

life′sav′er *n.* a person or thing that saves one from death or difficulty. —**life′sav′ing,** *adj., n.*

life′-size′ *adj.* of the actual size of a person, object, etc.

life′style′ *n.* a person's general pattern of living. Also, **life′-style′.**

life′-sup·port′ *adj.* of equipment or techniques that sustain or substitute for essential body functions.

life′time′ *n.* the duration of a person's life.

lift (lift) *v.t.* **1.** to move upward. **2.** to raise. **3.** to remove, as a restriction. —*v.i.* **4.** to go up. —*n.* **5.** the act of lifting. **6.** a ride given to a pedestrian. **7.** a feeling of exaltation. **8.** *Brit.* an elevator.

lift′-off′ *n.* the vertical ascent of a rocket.

lig′a·ment (lig′ə mənt) *n.* a band of tissue holding bones or organs together.

lig′a·ture (lig′ə chər, -chŏŏr′) *n.* **1.** a surgical thread or wire for tying blood vessels. **2.** two or more letters combined, as *fl.*

light¹ (līt) *n., adj., v.,* **lighted** or **lit** (līt), **lighting.** —*n.* **1.** something that makes things visible or gives illumination. **2.** daylight. **3.** aspect. **4.** enlightenment. **5.** a means of igniting. —*adj.* **6.** having light. **7.** pale. —*v.t.* **8.** to set burning. **9.** to brighten. —**Idiom.** **10. in light of,** considering.

light² (līt) *adj., adv.* **1.** not heavy.

2. not serious. **3.** (of food) easy to digest. **4.** (of sleep or a sleeper) easily disturbed.

light³ (līt) *v.i.,* **lighted** or **lit** (lit), **lighting. 1.** to land; alight. **2.** to happen upon.

light′en¹ *v.t., v.i.* to make or become less dark.

light′en² *v.t., v.i.* to make or become less heavy or burdensome.

light′er¹ *n.* something that lights.

light′er² *n.* a flat-bottomed barge.

light′-head′ed *adj.* dizzy and faint.

light′-heart′ed *adj.* cheerful.

light′house′ *n.* a tower displaying a beacon light to guide sailors.

light′ning (-ning) *n.* a flash of light in the sky caused by an electrical discharge.

light′ning bug′ *n.* a firefly.

light′ning rod′ *n.* a metal rod to divert lightning from a structure into the ground.

light′-year′ *n.* the distance that light travels in one year.

lig′ne·ous (lig′nē əs) *adj.* of the nature of or resembling wood.

lig′nite (lig′nīt) *n.* a kind of brown, wood-textured coal.

like¹ (līk) *adj.* **1.** of the same form, kind, appearance, etc. —*prep.* **2.** resembling. **3.** in the manner of. **4.** characteristic of. —*conj.* **5.** *Informal.* as; as if. —*n.* **6.** a similar person or thing; match. **7. the like,** something similar.

like² (līk) *v.,* **liked, liking,** *n.* —*v.t.* **1.** to find agreeable. **2.** to wish for. —*v.i.* **3.** to feel inclined. —*n.* **4. likes,** the things a person likes. —**lik′a·ble, like′a·ble,** *adj.*

like′ly *adj.,* **-lier, -liest,** *adv.* —*adj.* **1.** probable. **2.** suitable. —*adv.* **3.** probably. —**like′li·hood′,** *n.*

lik′en *v.t.* to point out the similarity of.

like′ness *n.* **1.** an image; picture. **2.** the fact of being similar.

like′wise′ *adv.* **1.** also. **2.** in like manner.

li′lac (lī′lək, -läk, -lak) *n.* a shrub with fragrant purple or white flowers.

Lil/li·pu′tian (lil′i pyoo′shən) *adj.* **1.** very small. **2.** trivial.

lilt (lilt) *n.* a rhythmic cadence.

lil′y (lil′ē) *n., pl.* **-ies.** a plant with erect stems and large funnel-shaped flowers.

lil′y-liv′ered (-liv′ərd) *adj.* cowardly.

lil′y of the val′ley *n., pl.* **lilies of the valley.** a plant with a spike of white bell-shaped flowers.

li′ma bean′ (lī′mə) *n.* a broad, flat, edible bean.

limb (lim) *n.* **1.** an arm, leg, or wing. **2.** a branch of a tree.

lim′ber (lim′bər) *adj.* **1.** flexible; supple. —*v.* **2. limber up,** to make or become limber.

lim′bo (lim′bō) *n., pl.* **-bos.** a place or state of oblivion.

lime¹ (līm) *n., v.,* **limed, liming.** —*n.* **1.** a white powder used in mortar, plaster, fertilizer, etc. —*v.t.* **2.** to treat with lime.

lime² (līm) *n.* the small, greenish, acid fruit of a tropical tree.

lime′light′ *n.* **1.** fame. **2.** a strong light formerly used on stage.

lim′er·ick (lim′ər ik) *n.* a humorous five-line rhymed verse.

lime′stone′ *n.* a rock consisting chiefly of powdered calcium.

lim′it (lim′it) *n.* **1.** the farthest extent; boundary. —*v.t.* **2.** to fix within limits. —**lim′i·ta′tion,** *n.*

lim′it·ed *adj.* restricted

lim′o (lim′ō) *n., pl.* **-os.** *Informal.* a limousine.

lim′ou·sine′ (lim′ə zēn′, lim′ə zēn′) *n.* a luxurious automobile for several passengers.

limp¹ (limp) *v.i.* **1.** to walk with a labored movement, as when lame. —*n.* **2.** a lame movement.

limp² (limp) *adj.* not stiff or firm. —**limp′ly,** *adv.*

lim′pet (lim′pit) *n.* a small shellfish that sticks to rocks.

lim′pid (-pid) *adj.* clear or transparent. —**lim·pid′i·ty, lim′pid·ness,** *n.*

linch′pin′ (linch′-) *n.* **1.** a pin inserted through the end of an axle to keep a wheel on. **2.** a key person or thing that holds an organization or structure together.

lin′den (lin′dən) *n.* a tree with heart-shaped leaves and fragrant flowers.

line¹ (līn) *n., v.,* **lined, lining.** —*n.* **1.** a long thin mark made on a surface. **2.** a row. **3.** a row of persons. **4.** a course of action, thought, etc. **5.** a boundary. **6.** a string, cord, etc. **7.** an occupation. —*v.i.* **8.** to form a line. —*v.t.* **9.** to mark with lines. —*Idiom.* **10. draw the line,** to impose a limit. **11. hold the line,** to maintain the status quo.

line² (līn) *v.t.,* **lined, lining.** to cover the inner side of.

lin′e·age (lin′ē ij) *n.* ancestry.

lin′e·al (-əl) *adj.* **1.** being in a direct line. **2.** linear.

lin′e·a·ment (-ə mənt) *n.* a feature, as of the face.

lin′e·ar (-ər) *adj.* **1.** of or using lines. **2.** involving measurement in one dimension only. **3.** long and narrow.

line′man *n., pl.* **-men.** a worker

who repairs telephone, telegraph, etc., wires.

lin/en (lin/ən) *n.* **1.** fabric made from flax. **2. linens**, bedding, tablecloths, etc., made of linen or cotton.

lin/er¹ (lī/nər) *n.* a ship or airplane on a regular route.

lin/er² (lī/nər) *n.* something serving as a lining.

line/-up/ *n.* **1.** people in a line for inspection. **2.** the arrangement of a sports team.

-ling a suffix meaning: **1.** a person connected with. **2.** little.

lin/ger (ling/gər) *v.i.* **1.** to remain in a place. **2.** to persist.

lin/ge•rie/ (län/zhə rā/, -jə-, lan/zhə-rē/) *n.* women's underwear.

lin/go (ling/gō) *n., pl.* **-goes.** *Informal.* jargon; unfamiliar language.

lin•gui/ni (-gwē/nē) *n.* a kind of slender, flat pasta.

lin/guist (-gwist) *n.* a person skilled in languages.

lin•guis/tics *n.* the science of language. **—lin•guis/tic,** *adj.*

lin/i•ment (lin/ə mənt) *n.* a liquid rubbed on the body to relieve muscular pain.

lin/ing (lī/ning) *n.* an inner covering, as in a coat.

link (lingk) *n.* **1.** a section of a chain. **2.** a bond. **—v.t., v.i. 3.** to unite. **—link/age,** *n.*

link/up/ *n.* **1.** a contact set up. **2.** a linking element or system.

lin/net (lin/it) *n.* a small finch.

li•no/le•um (li nō/lē əm) *n.* a hard, washable floor covering.

lin/seed/ (lin/sēd/) *n.* the seed of flax.

lint (lint) *n.* bits of thread.

lin/tel (lin/tl) *n.* a beam above a door or window.

li/on (lī/ən) *n.* a large tawny animal of the cat family, native to Africa and Asia.

li/on•ess *n.* a female lion.

li/on•heart/ed *adj.* brave.

li/on•ize/ *v.t.,* **-ized, -izing.** to treat as a celebrity.

lip (lip) *n.* **1.** either of the fleshy edges forming the margin of the mouth. **2.** a projecting edge. **3.** *Slang.* impudent talk.

lip/o•suc/tion (lip/ə suk/shən, lī/pə-) *n.* surgical withdrawal of excess fat from under the skin.

lip/read/ing *n.* a method of understanding spoken words by interpreting a speaker's lip movements. **—lip/read/,** *v.t., v.i.*

lip/ serv/ice *n.* insincere profession of admiration, support, etc.

lip/stick/ *n.* a cosmetic for coloring the lips.

liq/ue•fy/ (lik/wə fī/) *v.t., v.i.,* **-fied, -fying.** to make or become liquid. **—liq/ue•fac/tion** (-fak/shən) *n.*

li•queur/ (li kûr/, -kyŏor/) *n.* a strong sweet alcoholic drink.

liq/uid (lik/wid) *n.* **1.** a substance that flows, as water or oil. **—adj. 2.** of or being a liquid. **3.** (of assets) in or convertible to cash.

liq/ui•date/ (-wi dāt/) *v.t.,* **-dated, -dating. 1.** to settle, as debts. **2.** to convert (assets) into cash. **3.** to dissolve (a business or estate). **—liq/ui•da/tion,** *n.*

liq/uor (lik/ər) *n.* **1.** an alcoholic beverage. **2.** a liquid.

lisp (lisp) *n.* **1.** a speech defect in which *s* and *z* are pronounced like *th*. **—v.t., v.i. 2.** to speak with a lisp.

lis/some (lis/əm) *adj.* **1.** lithe; supple. **2.** agile. Also, **lis/som.**

list¹ (list) *n.* **1.** a written series of words, names, etc. **—v.t. 2.** to make a list of.

list² (list) *n.* **1.** a leaning to one side. **—v.i., v.t. 2.** to incline or cause to incline to one side.

lis/ten (lis/ən) *v.i.* to pay attention in order to hear. **—lis/ten•er,** *n.*

list/less (list/lis) *adj.* lacking energy.

list/ price/ *n.* the price at which something is sold to the public.

lit. 1. literally. **2.** literature.

lit/a•ny (lit/n ē) *n., pl.* **-nies. 1.** a form of prayer with responses. **2.** a prolonged account.

li/ter (lē/tər) *n.* a metric unit of liquid capacity, equal to 1.0567 U.S. quarts. Also, *Brit.,* **li/tre.**

lit/er•al (lit/ər əl) *adj.* in accordance with the strict meaning of a word or text.

lit/er•al-mind/ed *adj.* interpreting literally and without imagination.

lit/er•ar/y (-ə rer/ē) *adj.* of books and writings.

lit/er•ate (-ər it) *adj.* **1.** able to read and write. **2.** educated. **—lit/er•a•cy** (-ər ə sē) *n.*

lit/e•ra/ti (-ə rä/tē, -rä/-) *n.pl.* persons of literary attainments.

lit/er•a•ture (lit/ər ə chər, -chŏor/, li/trə-) *n.* **1.** writing in prose or verse that is regarded as having lasting worth because of its excellence. **2.** the writings dealing with a particular subject.

lithe (lī*th*) *adj.* limber; supple.

li•thog/ra•phy (li thog/rə fē) *n.* printing from a stone or metal plate treated with a combination of substances that either absorb or repel ink. **—lith/o•graph/,** *n.*

lit/i•gant (lit/i gənt) *n.* a person engaged in a lawsuit.

lit/i•gate/ (-gāt/) *v.,* **-gated, -gating.**

—*v.i.* **1.** to carry on a lawsuit. —*v.t.* **2.** to make the subject of a lawsuit. —**lit′i·ga′tion,** *n.*

lit′mus pa′per (-məs), *n.* paper that turns red in acid and blue in alkaline.

lit′mus test′ *n.* the use of a single factor as a basis for judgment.

Litt. D. Doctor of Letters; Doctor of Literature.

lit′ter (lit′ər) *n.* **1.** scattered objects, rubbish, etc. **2.** the young born to an animal at one birth. **3.** a stretcher for moving someone sick or injured. **4.** bedding for animals. **5.** material used to absorb animal waste. —*v.t.* **6.** to strew (a place) with litter. **7.** to scatter (objects) in disorder.

lit′ter·bug′ *n.* a person who litters public places with trash.

lit′tle (lit′l) *adj.,* **-tler, -tlest. 1.** small in size, amount, degree, etc. —*adv.* **2.** not at all. —*n.* **3.** a small amount.

lit′tor·al (lit′ər əl) *adj.* of the shore of a lake, sea, or ocean.

lit′ur·gy (lit′ər jē) *n., pl.* **-gies.** a form of public worship. —**li·tur′gi·cal** (li tûr′ji kəl) *adj.*

liv′a·ble (liv′ə bəl) *adj.* suitable for living.

live¹ (liv) *v.,* **lived, living.** —*v.i.* **1.** to be or remain alive. **2.** to continue in existence, memory, etc. **3.** to dwell. —*v.t.* **4.** to pass or spend.

live² (līv) *adj.* **1.** alive. **2.** burning. **3.** not exploded. **4.** connected to electric power.

live′li·hood′ (līv′lē hŏŏd′) *n.* a means of supporting oneself.

live′long′ (liv′-) *adj.* entire; whole.

live′ly (līv′lē) *adj.,* **-lier, -liest.** active; spirited.

liv′er (liv′ər) *n.* a large, vital abdominal organ that secretes bile.

liv′er·y (liv′ə rē, liv′rē) *n., pl.* **-eries. 1.** a uniform worn by male servants. **2.** the keeping of horses for hire.

live′stock′ (līv′stok′) *n.* domestic farm animals.

liv′id (liv′id) *adj.* **1.** furiously angry. **2.** dull bluish gray.

liv′ing (-ing) *adj.* **1.** being alive. **2.** sufficient for living. —*n.* **3.** the condition of one that lives. **4.** livelihood.

liv′ing room′ *n.* a room for leisure activities, entertaining, etc.

liv′ing will′ *n.* a document directing that no extraordinary measures be taken to prolong the signer's life during a terminal illness.

liz′ard (liz′ərd) *n.* a four-legged reptile with a long tail.

lla′ma (lä′mə, yä′-) *n.* a woolly South American animal related to the camel.

LL.B. Bachelor of Laws.

L.L.D. Doctor of Laws.

load (lōd) *n.* **1.** anything carried at one time. **2.** something that weighs down like a burden. —*v.t.* **3.** to put a load on. **4.** to oppress. **5.** to put ammunition into (a firearm). —**load′er,** *n.*

loaf (lōf) *n., pl.* **loaves** (lōvz), *v.* —*n.* **1.** a shaped mass of bread. —*v.i.* **2.** to spend time idly. —**loaf′er,** *n.*

loam (lōm) *n.* loose fertile soil.

loan (lōn) *n.* **1.** the act of lending. **2.** something lent. —*v.t., v.i.* **3.** to lend.

loan′ shark′ *n. Informal.* a person who lends money at exorbitant interest rates.

loan′word′ *n.* a word borrowed from another language.

loath (lōth, lōth) *adj.* reluctant.

loathe (lōth) *v.,* **loathed, loathing.** to feel intense dislike for. —**loath′some** (lōth′səm, lōth′-) *adj.*

lob (lob) *v.t.,* **lobbed, lobbing.** to strike or hurl in a high curve.

lob′by *n., pl.* **-bies,** *v.,* **-bied, -bying.** —*n.* **1.** an entrance hall. **2.** a group that tries to influence the votes of legislators. —*v.i.* **3.** to try to influence legislation. —*v.t.* **4.** to try to influence the votes of (legislators). —**lob′by·ist,** *n.*

lobe (lōb) *n.* a roundish projection.

lo·bot·o·my (lə bot′ə mē, lō-) *n., pl.* **-mies.** a surgical incision of the brain lobe to treat mental disorder.

lob′ster (lob′stər) *n.* an edible marine shellfish with large claws.

lo′cal (lō′kəl) *adj.* **1.** of or in a particular area. —*n.* **2.** a local branch of a trade union. **3.** a train that makes all stops. —**lo′cal·ly,** *adv.*

lo·cale′ (lō kal′, -käl′) *n.* a setting.

lo·cal′i·ty (-kal′i tē) *n., pl.* **-ties.** a place; area.

lo′cal·ize′ (-kə līz′) *v.t.,* **-ized, -izing.** to confine to a particular place.

lo′cate (lō′kāt, lō kāt′) *v.,* **-cated, -cating.** —*v.t.* **1.** to find or establish the place of. —*v.i.* **2.** to become settled.

lo·ca′tion *n.* **1.** an act or instance of locating. **2.** the place where something is.

loc. cit. (lok′ sit′) in the place cited.

lock¹ (lok) *n.* **1.** a device for fastening a door, lid, etc. **2.** a chamber in a canal for moving vessels from one water level to another. —*v.t.* **3.** to secure with a lock. **4.** to shut in or out. **5.** to join firmly.

lock² (lok) *n.* a curl of hair.

lock′er *n.* a chest, closet, etc., locked for safekeeping.

lock′et (-it) *n.* a small case for a keepsake, usu. worn on a necklace.

lock′jaw′ *n.* tetanus in which the jaws become tightly locked.

lock′out′ *n.* a business closure to force acceptance of an employer's terms of work.

lock′smith′ *n.* a person who makes or repairs locks.

lock′step′ *n.* **1.** a way of marching in close file. **2.** a rigidly inflexible pattern or process.

lock′up′ *n.* a jail.

lo′co (lō′kō) *adj. Slang.* crazy.

lo′co·mo′tion (lō′kə mō′shən) *n.* the act or power of moving about.

lo′co·mo′tive *n.* an engine that pulls railroad cars.

lo′co·weed′ (lō′kō-) *n.* a plant causing a disease in livestock.

lo′cust (lō′kəst) *n.* **1.** a grasshopper migrating in swarms that consume vegetation. **2.** a North American tree with white flowers.

lo·cu′tion (lō kyōō′shən) *n.* a word, phrase, or expression.

lode (lōd) *n.* a mineral deposit.

lode′star′ *n.* a guiding star.

lode′stone′ *n.* a magnetic stone.

lodge (loj) *n., v.,* **lodged, lodging.** —*n.* **1.** a temporary residence. **2.** the meeting place of a fraternal organization. —*v.i.* **3.** to live in a place temporarily. **4.** to be fixed in a place. —*v.t.* **5.** to furnish with temporary housing. —**lodg′er,** *n.*

lodg′ing *n.* **1.** temporary housing. **2. lodgings,** rooms.

loft (lôft) *n.* **1.** a space under a sloping roof; attic. **2.** an upper story of a warehouse.

loft′y *adj.,* **-ier, -iest. 1.** tall. **2.** exalted in rank or character. **3.** haughty. —**loft′i·ly,** *adv.*

log (lôg) *n., v.,* **logged, logging.** —*n.* **1.** a section of the trunk or limb of a felled tree. Also, **log′book′.** a record of events. —*v.t.* **3.** to cut (trees) into logs. **4.** to record in a log. —*v.i.* **5.** to fell trees and cut out logs for timber. **6. log in** or **on,** to gain access to a computer system. **7. ~ off** or **out,** to end a session on a computer system. —**log′ger,** *n.*

lo′gan·ber′ry (lō′gən ber′ē) *n., pl.* **-ries.** a dark red tart berry.

log′a·rithm (lô′gə riᵗʰ′əm) *n. Math.* the symbol of the number of times a number must be multiplied by itself to equal a given number.

loge (lōzh) *n.* the front section of the lowest balcony in a theater.

log′ger·head′ (lô′gər hed′, log′ər-)
n. —*Idiom.* **at loggerheads,** in conflict.

log′ic (loj′ik) *n.* a science or method of reasoning. —**lo·gi′cian** (lō jish′shən) *n.*

log′i·cal, *adj.* **1.** according to the principles of logic. **2.** reasonable. —**log′i·cal·ly,** *adv.*

lo·gis′tics (lō jis′tiks, lə-) *n.* the management of the details of an operation.

log′jam′ (lôg′-) *n.* **1.** a pileup of logs, as in a river. **2.** a blockage.

lo′go (lō′gō) *n.* a representation or symbol of a company name, trademark, etc. Also, **lo′go·type′.**

lo′gy (lō′gē) *adj.,* **-gier, -giest.** sluggish.

-logy a suffix meaning the study of.

loin (loin) *n.* the part of the body between the ribs and the hipbone.

loin′cloth′ *n.* a cloth worn around the loins or hips.

loi′ter (loi′tər) *v.i.* to linger aimlessly about a place.

loll (lol) *v.i.* **1.** to recline in a lazy manner. **2.** to hang loosely.

lol′li·pop′ (lol′ē pop′) *n.* hard candy on a stick.

lone (lōn) *adj.* solitary; sole.

lone′ly (lōn′lē) *adj.,* **-lier, -liest. 1.** solitary. **2.** having a depressing feeling of being alone. **3.** isolated. —**lone′li·ness,** *n.*

lon′er *n.* a person who spends much time alone.

lone′some (-səm) *adj.* **1.** depressed by being alone. **2.** remote.

long¹ (lông) *adj.* **1.** of great or specified length. —*adv.* **2.** for a long time.

long² (lông) *v.i.* to have a strong desire.

lon·gev′i·ty (lon jev′i tē) *n.* **1.** long life. **2.** length of life.

long′hand′ (lông′-) *n.* ordinary handwriting.

lon′gi·tude (lon′ji tōōd′, -tyōōd′) *n.* distance east or west of a point on the earth's surface.

lon′gi·tu′di·nal (-tōōd′n l, -tyōōd′-) *adj.* **1.** of longitude. **2.** lengthwise.

long′ jump′ *n.* a jump for distance from a running start.

long′-lived′ (-līvd′, -livd′) *adj.* having a long life or duration.

long′-range′ *adj.* spanning a long distance or time.

long′shore′man *n.* a person who loads and unloads ships.

long′ shot′ *n.* **1.** a racehorse, team, etc., with little chance of winning. **2.** an undertaking with little chance for success.

long′-term′ *adj.* involving a long time.

long′-wind′ed (-win′did) *adj.* continuing to speak for too long.

look (lŏok) *v.i.* **1.** to turn the eyes toward something in order to see. **2.** to seem. **3. look after,** to care for. **4. ~ down on,** to view with contempt. **5. ~ forward to,** to anticipate happily. **6. ~ up to,** to admire. —*n.* **7.** the act of looking. **8.** appearance.

look′ing glass′ *n.* a mirror.

look′out′ *n.* **1.** a watch. **2.** a person for keeping watch. **3.** a place for keeping watch.

loom¹ (lŏom) *n.* a device for weaving fabric.

loom² (lŏom) *v.i.* to come into view as large and indistinct.

loon (lŏon) *n.* a ducklike diving bird.

loon′y *adj.,* **-ier, -iest.** *Informal.* **1.** insane. **2.** extremely foolish.

loop (lŏop) *n.* **1.** a portion of a string, ribbon, etc., folded upon itself so as to leave an opening between the parts; anything shaped like this. —*v.i., v.t.* **2.** to form (into) a loop.

loop′hole′ *n.* **1.** a narrow opening in a wall. **2.** a means of evading a rule without breaking it.

loose (lŏos) *adj.,* **-er, -est,** *v.,* **loosed, loosing.** —*adj.* **1.** not firm or tight. **2.** not confined. **3.** not packed together. **4.** not exact. —*v.t.* **5.** to set free. **6.** to shoot (missiles). —**loos′en,** *v.t., v.i.*

loot (lŏot) *n.* **1.** plunder taken in war. **2.** anything taken by dishonesty, force, etc. **3.** *Slang.* money or gifts. —*v.t., v.i.* **4.** to take (as) loot. —**loot′er,** *n.*

lop (lop) *v.t.,* **lopped, lopping.** to cut off.

lope (lōp) *v.i.,* **loped, loping.** to move or run with a long, easy stride.

lop′sid′ed *adj.* uneven.

lo•qua′cious (lō kwā′shəs) *adj.* talkative. —**lo•quac′i•ty** (-kwas′ə tē) *n.*

lord (lôrd) *n.* **1.** a master. **2.** a British nobleman. **3. Lord,** God or Jesus Christ. —**lord′ly,** *adj.* —**lord′ship,** *n.*

lore (lôr) *n.* learning.

lor′ry (lôr′ē) *n., pl.* **-ries.** *Brit.* a truck.

lose (lŏoz) *v.,* **lost** (lôst) **losing.** —*v.t.* **1.** to fail to keep. **2.** to misplace. **3.** to be deprived of. **4.** to fail to win. —*v.i.* **5.** to suffer loss.

loss (lôs) *n.* **1.** the act of losing. **2.** disadvantage from losing. **3.** the thing, person, or amount lost. —**Idiom. 4. at a loss,** bewildered.

lost (lôst, lost) *adj.* **1.** no longer to be found. —*v.* **2.** pt. and pp. of **lose.**

lot (lot) *n.* **1.** an object drawn to decide a question by chance. **2.** allotted share; portion. **3.** a piece of land. **4.** Often, **lots.** *Informal.* a great number or amount. —**Usage.** See ALOT.

lo′tion (lō′shən) *n.* liquid to rub on the skin.

lot′ter•y (lot′ə rē) *n., pl.* **-ies.** a sale of tickets on prizes to be awarded by means of a drawing.

lot′to (lot′ō) *n.* a game of chance similar to bingo.

lo′tus (lō′təs) *n.* **1.** a water lily of Egypt and Asia. **2.** a mythical fruit that causes forgetfulness.

loud (loud) *adj.* **1.** easily heard. **2.** noisy. **3.** garish.

loud′speak′er *n.* a device for increasing the volume of sound.

lounge (lounj) *v.,* **lounged, lounging,** *n.* —*v.i.* **1.** to pass time idly. **2.** to loll. —*n.* **3.** a kind of sofa. **4.** a public room for socializing.

louse (lous) *n., pl.* **lice** (līs). **1.** a bloodsucking insect. **2.** a contemptible person.

lous′y (lou′zē) *adj.,* **-ier, -iest. 1.** *Informal.* bad. **2.** troubled with lice.

lout (lout) *n.* a clumsy ill-mannered person. —**lout′ish,** *adj.*

lou′ver (lŏo′vər) *n.* one of a set of slanting, overlapping slats to admit air and light but shut out rain.

lov′a•ble (luv′ə bəl) *adj.* attracting love. Also, **love′a•ble.**

love (luv) *n., v.,* **loved, loving.** —*n.* **1.** tender, passionate affection. **2.** strong personal liking. **3.** a person toward whom love is felt. —*v.t., v.i.* **4.** to have love (for). —**lov′er,** *n.* —**lov′ing,** *adj.*

love′lorn′ (-lôrn′) *adj.* deprived of love or a lover.

love′ly (luv′lē) *adj.,* **-lier, -liest.** charming. —**love′li•ness,** *n.*

lov′ing cup′ *n.* a large two-handled drinking cup.

low¹ (lō) *adj.* **1.** not high or tall. **2.** below the normal level. **3.** sad. **4.** humble or inferior. **5.** not loud. **6.** vulgar. —*adv.* **7.** in a low position. **8.** in a quiet tone. —*n.* **9.** a low point or level. **10.** an area of low atmospheric pressure. —**Idiom. 11. lay low,** to overpower. **12. lie low,** to hide oneself.

low² (lō) *v.i.* **1.** (of cattle) to make a deep mooing sound. —*n.* **2.** a deep mooing sound made by cattle.

low′brow′ *n.* **1.** an uncultured person. —*adj.* **2.** typical of a lowbrow.

low′down′ *n.* (lō′doun′) **1.** the real and unadorned facts. —*adj.* (-doun′) **2.** contemptible; mean.

low′er¹ (lō′ər) *adj.* **1.** comparative of **low¹.** —*v.t.* **2.** to reduce or diminish. **3.** to make lower. —*v.i.* **4.** to become lower. —*adj.*

low′er² (lou′ər) *v.i.* **1.** to be threatening. **2.** to frown.

low′er·case′ (lō′ər-) *adj.* **1.** (of a letter) of a form often different from and smaller than its corresponding capital letter. —*n.* **2.** a lowercase letter.

low′ fre′quency *n.* a radio frequency between 30 and 300 kilohertz.

low′-key′ *adj.* understated.

low′life′ *n., pl.* **-lifes.** a disreputable or degenerate person.

low′ly *adj.,* **-lier, -liest.** having a low rank; humble.

low′-mind′ed *adj.* coarse; vulgar.

low′ pro′file *n.* a deliberately inconspicuous manner.

lox (loks) *n.* smoked salmon.

loy′al (loi′əl) *adj.* faithful; steadfast. —**loy′al·ly,** *adv.* —**loy′al·ty,** *n.*

loz′enge (loz′inj) *n.* **1.** a flavored candy, often medicated. **2.** a diamond-shaped object.

LPN licensed practical nurse.

LSD lysergic acid diethylamide, a powerful psychedelic drug.

Lt. lieutenant.

Ltd. limited.

lu′bri·cant (loo′bri kənt) *n.* a lubricating substance.

lu′bri·cate′ (-kāt′) *v.t.,* **-cated, -cating.** to oil or grease, esp. to diminish friction.

lu′cid (loo′sid) *adj.* **1.** easily understood. **2.** clear. **3.** rational. —**lu·cid′i·ty,** *n.*

Lu′cite (loo′sīt) *Trademark.* a transparent plastic.

luck (luk) *n.* **1.** chance. **2.** good fortune. —**luck′less,** *adj.*

luck′y *adj.,* **-ier, -iest.** having or due to good luck. —**luck′i·ly,** *adv.*

lu′cra·tive (loo′krə tiv) *adj.* profitable.

lu′cre (loo′kər) *n.* gain or money.

lu′di·crous (loo′di krəs) *adj.* ridiculous. —**lu′di·crous·ly,** *adv.*

lug¹ (lug) *v.t., v.i.,* **lugged, lugging.** to pull or carry with effort.

lug² *n.* a projecting handle.

luge (loozh) *n., v.,* **luged, luging.** —*n.* **1.** a small racing sled. —*v.i.* **2.** to race on a luge.

lug′gage (lug′ij) *n.* suitcases, trunks, etc.; baggage.

lug′ nut′ *n.* a large nut, esp. for attaching a wheel to a vehicle.

lu·gu′bri·ous (loo goo′brē əs, -groo′-) *adj.* excessively mournful.

luke′warm′ (look′-) *adj.* slightly warm.

lull (lul) *v.t.* **1.** to soothe, esp. to

put to sleep. **2.** to give a false sense of security. —*n.* **3.** a brief stillness.

lull′a·by (-ə bī′) *n., pl.* **-bies.** a song used to lull a child to sleep.

lum·ba′go (lum bā′gō) *n.* pain in the lower back.

lum′bar (-bər, -bär) *adj.* of or close to the loins.

lum′ber¹ (-bər) *n.* **1.** timber made into boards, planks, etc. —*v.i.* **2.** to cut and prepare timber.

lum′ber² (-bər) *v.i.* to move heavily.

lum′ber·jack′ *n.* a person who fells trees.

lum′ber·yard′ *n.* a yard where lumber is stored for sale.

lu′mi·nar·y (loo′mə ner′ē) *n., pl.* **-ies. 1.** a celestial body. **2.** a person who inspires many.

lu·min·es′cent (-nes′ənt) *adj.* emitting light without heat. —**lu′min·es′cence,** *n.*

lu′mi·nous (-nəs) *adj.* **1.** reflecting light; shining. **2.** clear. —**lu′mi·nos′i·ty** (-nos′i tē) *n.*

lum′mox (lum′əks) *n. Informal.* a clumsy, stupid person.

lump (lump) *n.* **1.** an irregular mass. **2.** a swelling. —*adj.* **3.** including many. —*v.t.* **4.** to unite into one mass. —*v.i.* **5.** to form a lump.

lu′na·cy (loo′nə sē) *n.* insanity.

lu′nar (-nər) *adj.* **1.** of or according to the moon. **2.** crescent-shaped.

lu′na·tic (-tik) *n.* **1.** an insane person. —*adj.* **2.** for the insane. **3.** crazy.

lunch (lunch) *n.* **1.** Also, **lunch′eon** (lun′chən). a midday meal. —*v.i.* **2.** to eat lunch.

lung (lung) *n.* either of the two saclike respiratory organs.

lunge (lunj) *n., v.,* **lunged, lunging.** —*n.* **1.** a sudden forward movement. —*v.i.* **2.** to make a lunge.

lu′pine¹ (loo′pin) *n.* a plant with tall, dense clusters of blue, pink, or white flowers.

lu′pine² (loo′pin) *adj.* of or resembling the wolf.

lu′pus (loo′pəs) *n.* an autoimmune disease characterized by skin inflammation and joint pain.

lurch¹ (lûrch) *n.* **1.** a sudden lean to one side. —*v.i.* **2.** to stagger.

lurch² (lûrch) *n.* a difficult situation.

lure (loor) *n., v.,* **lured, luring.** —*n.* **1.** anything that entices or allures. —*v.t.* **2.** to attract; entice.

lu′rid (loor′id) *adj.* **1.** sensational; shocking. **2.** glaringly lighted.

lurk (lûrk) *v.i.* to lie hidden.

lus′cious (lush′əs) *adj.* delicious.

lush (lush) *adj.* **1.** tender and juicy. **2.** abundant.

lust (lust) *n.* **1.** strong sexual desire. **2.** any strong desire. —*v.i.* **3.** to have a strong desire. —**lust′ful,** *adj.*

lus′ter (lus′tər) *n.* gloss; radiance. Also, **lus′tre.** —**lus′trous,** *adj.*

lust′y *adj.,* **-ier, -iest.** vigorous.

lute (lōōt) *n.* a stringed instrument having a long neck and a hollow, pear-shaped body. —**lut′en•ist,** *n.*

lux•u′ri•ant (lug zhŏŏr′ē ənt, luk-shŏŏr′-) *adj.* richly abundant. —**lux•u′ri•ance,** *n.*

lux•u′ri•ate′ (-āt′) *v.i.,* **-ated, -ating.** to delight in something.

lux′u•ry (luk′shə rē, lug′zhə-) *n., pl.* **-ries. 1.** choice and costly comforts or pleasures. **2.** something enjoyable but not necessary. **3.** an unusual pleasure allowed oneself. —**lux•u′ri•ous** (lug zhŏŏr′ē əs, luk-shŏŏr′-) *adj.*

-ly a suffix meaning: in a specified manner; according to; to or from a specified direction; like or characteristic of; every.

ly•ce′um (lī sē′əm) *n.* a hall for public lectures, concerts, etc.

lye (lī) *n.* a white alkaline substance used for washing.

Lyme′ disease′ (līm) *n.* a tick-transmitted disease characterized esp. by joint pains and fatigue.

lymph (limf) *n.* a yellowish fluid containing lymphocytes and fats that surrounds body cells and carries away their wastes. —**lym•phat′ic** (lim fat′ik) *adj.*

lym′pho•cyte′ (lim′fə sīt′) *n.* a kind of white blood cell helping to produce antibodies.

lynch (linch) *v.t.* to put to death without legal authority.

lynx (lingks) *n., pl.* **lynxes, lynx.** a kind of wildcat having a short tail and tufted ears.

lyre (lī°r) *n.* an ancient harplike instrument.

lyr′ic (lir′ik) *adj.* Also, **lyr′i•cal. 1.** (of poetry) having the form of a song expressing the writer's feelings. **2.** of or writing such poetry. —*n.* **3.** a lyric poem. **4. lyrics,** the words for a song. —**lyr′i•cism** (-ə siz′m) *n.* —**lyr′i•cist,** *n.*

M

M, m (em) *n.* the thirteenth letter of the English alphabet.

ma (mä) *n. Informal.* mother.

MA Massachusetts.

M.A. Master of Arts.

ma′am (mam, mäm; *unstressed* məm) *n. Informal.* madam.

ma•ca′bre (mə kä′brə, -käb′) *adj.* gruesome.

mac•ad′am (mə kad′əm) *n.* a road-making material containing broken stones. —**mac•ad′am•ize′,** *v.t.*

mac′a•ro′ni (mak′ə rō′nē) *n.* tube-shaped pasta.

mac′a•roon′ (mak′ə rōōn′) *n.* an almond or coconut cookie.

ma•caw′ (mə kô′) *n.* a large, long-tailed parrot.

mace¹ (mās) *n.* **1.** a clublike armor-breaking weapon. **2.** a ceremonial staff.

mace² (mās) *n.* a spice made from the husk of the nutmeg.

Mace (mās) *n. Trademark.* a chemical spray for subduing attackers.

mac′er•ate′ (mas′ə rāt′) *v.t.,* **-ated, -ating.** to soften by steeping in liquid.

ma•che′te (mə shet′ē, -chet′ē) *n.* a heavy swordlike knife.

Mach′i•a•vel′li•an (mak′ē ə vel′ē-ən) *adj.* unscrupulously cunning.

mach′i•na′tion (mak′ə nā′shən) *n.* a cunning plan.

ma•chine′ (mə shēn′) *n.* **1.** a mechanical device. **2.** a group controlling a political party.

machine′ gun′ *n.* a firearm that shoots a continuous stream of bullets.

ma•chin′er•y *n.* machines or mechanical parts.

ma•chin′ist *n.* one who operates a powered tool, ship's engines, etc.

ma•chis′mo (mä chēz′mō) *n.* exaggerated masculinity.

Mach′ num′ber (mäk) *n.* the ratio of the speed of an object to the speed of sound.

ma′cho (mä′chō) *adj.* exaggeratedly virile.

mack′er•el (mak′ər əl) *n.* a N Atlantic food fish.

mack′i•naw (-ə nô′) *n.* a short, heavy, woolen coat.

mack′in•tosh (-in tosh′) *n.* a raincoat.

mac′ra•mé′ (mak′rə mā′) *n.* a decorative work of knotted cords.

macro- a prefix meaning large.

mac′ro•cosm (mak′rə koz′əm) *n.* the universe as a whole.

ma′cron (mā′kron, mak′ron) *n.* a horizontal line over a vowel to show it is long.

mac′u•la (mak′yə lə) *n., pl.* **-lae** (-lē′) **-las. 1.** a spot, esp. on the skin. **2.** the point of sharpest vision on the retina.

mac/ular degenera/tion *n.* deterioration of the macula in the center of the retina, resulting in a loss of central vision.

mad (mad) *adj.*, **madder, maddest. 1.** insane. **2.** angry. **3.** violent. —**mad/den,** *v.t.*

mad/am (mad/əm) *n.* **1.** a female term of address. **2.** a woman in charge of a brothel.

mad/ame (mad/əm, mə dam/, -däm/, mə-), *n., pl.* **mes•dames** (mā dam/, -däm/). (*often cap.*) a French title equivalent to Mrs.

mad/cap/ *adj.* impulsive; rash.

made *v.* pt. of **make.**

mad/e•moi•selle/ (mad/ə mə zel/, mad/mwə-, mam zel/) *n., pl.* **mademoiselles, mesdemoiselles** (mā/də-mə zel/, -zelz/, mād/mwä-). a French term of address for an unmarried woman.

Ma•don/na (mə don/ə) *n.* the Virgin Mary.

mad/ri•gal (mad/ri gəl) *n.* an unaccompanied song for several voices.

mael/strom (māl/strəm) *n.* **1.** a whirlpool. **2.** a state of confusion.

maes/tro (mī/strō) *n., pl.* **-tros.** a master, esp. of music.

Ma/fi•a (mä/fē ə, maf/ē ə) *n.* a secret society allegedly engaged in criminal activities.

ma/fi•o/so (mä/fē ō/sō) *n., pl.* **-si** (-sē) **-sos.** a member of the Mafia.

mag/a•zine/ (mag/ə zēn/) *n.* **1.** a periodical publication. **2.** a storehouse for ammunition. **3.** a cartridge chamber, as in a rifle.

ma•gen/ta (mə jen/tə) *n.* a reddish purple.

mag/got (mag/ət) *n.* the larva of a fly.

Ma/gi (mā/jī) *n.pl.* the three wise men who brought gifts to the infant Jesus.

mag/ic (maj/ik) *n.* **1.** the art of producing illusions or tricks. **2.** the use of techniques to exert control over the supernatural. —*adj.* Also, **mag/i•cal. 3.** used in or done by magic. **4.** enchanting. —**ma•gi/• cian** (mə jish/ən) *n.*

mag/is•te/ri•al (maj/ə stēr/ē əl) *adj.* masterlike; authoritative.

mag/is•trate/ (-strāt/, -strit) *n.* a civil public official.

mag/ma (mag/mə) *n.* molten rock.

mag•nan/i•mous (mag nan/ə məs) *adj.* generous; high-minded. —**mag/na•nim/i•ty** (-nə nim/i tē) *n.*

mag/nate (-nāt, -nit) *n.* a business leader.

mag•ne/sia (-nē/zhə) *n.* magnesium oxide, used in medicine.

mag•ne/si•um (-zē əm, -zhəm) *n.* a light, silvery, metallic element.

mag/net (-nit) *n.* **1.** a metal body that attracts iron or steel. **2.** something or someone that attracts.

mag•net/ic (-net/ik) *adj.* **1.** of a magnet or magnetism. **2.** attractive.

magnet/ic field/ *n.* a region near a magnet, electric current, or moving charged particle in which a magnetic force acts.

mag/net•ism (-ni tiz/əm) *n.* **1.** the characteristic properties of magnets. **2.** the science of magnets. **3.** great personal charm. —**mag/net• ize/,** *v.t.*

mag/net•ite/ (-ni tīt/) *n.* a common black mineral.

mag•ne/to (-nē/tō) *n., pl.* **-tos.** a small electric generator.

mag•nif/i•cent (-nif/ə sənt) *adj.* **1.** splendid. **2.** noble. —**mag•nif/i• cence,** *n.*

mag/ni•fy/ (-nə fī/) *v.t.,* **-fied, -fy-ing. 1.** to increase the apparent or actual size of. **2.** to exaggerate. —**mag/ni•fi/er,** *n.*

mag/ni•tude/ (-ni tōōd/, -tyōōd/) *n.* size or extent.

mag•no/li•a (mag nōl/yə, -nō/lē ə) *n.* a tree with large fragrant flowers.

mag/num o/pus *n.* the chief work of a great writer, musician, etc.

mag/pie/ (mag/pī/) *n.* a noisy black-and-white bird that steals.

ma•ha•ra/jah (mä/hə rä/jə, -zhə) *n.* (formerly) a ruling prince in India.

ma•ha•ra/nee (-nē) *n.* **1.** the wife of a maharajah. **2.** (formerly) an Indian princess.

ma•hat/ma (mə hät/mə, -hat/-) *n.* (in India) a person revered for wisdom and saintliness.

mah/-jongg/ (mä/jông/, -zhông/) *n.* a Chinese game played with tiles.

ma•hog/a•ny (mə hog/ə nē) *n., pl.* **-nies.** a tropical American tree or its hard red-brown wood.

maid (mād) *n.* **1.** a female servant. **2.** an unmarried woman.

maid/en *n.* **1.** a young unmarried woman. —*adj.* **2.** of maidens. **3.** unmarried. **4.** initial.

maid/en•hair/ *n.* a fern with finely divided fronds.

mail[1] (māl) *n.* **1.** letters, parcels, etc., delivered by a postal service. **2.** a system to deliver mail. —*v.t.* **3.** to send by mail. —**mail/box/,** *n.* —**mail/ car/rier,** *n.* —**mail/man/,** *n.*

mail[2] (māl) *n.* flexible armor.

maim (mām) *v.t.* to injure so as to lose the use of a body part.

main (mān) *adj.* **1.** chief. —*n.* **2.** a

chief pipe or duct. **3.** strength. **4.** the ocean. —**main′ly,** *adv.*

main′frame′ *n.* a large computer, often the hub of a system.

main′land′ (-land′, -lənd) *n.* continental land rather than an island.

main′stay′ *n.* a chief support.

main′stream′ *n.* the dominant course or trend.

main·tain′ (mān tān′) *v.t.* **1.** to support. **2.** to assert. **3.** to keep in order or condition. —**main′te·nance** (-tə nəns) *n.*

mai′tre d′hô·tel′ (mā′trə dō tel′) *n.* the head of a restaurant staff. Also, **mai′tre d′** (mā′tər dē′).

maize (māz) *n.* corn.

maj′es·ty (maj′ə stē) *n., pl.* **-ties. 1.** regal grandeur. **2.** a title of a sovereign. —**ma·jes′tic** (mə jes′tic) *adj.*

ma′jor (mā′jər) *n.* **1.** an army officer above a captain. **2.** a person of legal age. —*adj.* **3.** larger or more important.

ma′jor-do′mo (-dō′mō) *n.* a steward.

ma′jor·ette′ (-jə ret′) *n.* a young woman who leads a marching band.

ma′jor gen′eral *n.* a military officer above a brigadier.

ma·jor′i·ty (mə jôr′i tē) *n., pl.* **-ties. 1.** a number larger than half of a total. **2.** full legal age.

make (māk) *v.,* **made** (mād) **making,** *n.* —*v.t.* **1.** to create; form. **2.** to cause to be or exist. **3.** to prepare. **4.** to force. **7.** to appoint. **6.** to win or earn. **7.** to amount to. **8.** to reach. —*v.i.* **9.** to act or behave. **10.** to cause to be as specified. **11. make over,** to alter. **12.** ~ **up, a.** to invent. **b.** to compensate. **c.** to settle. **d.** to reconcile. —*n.* **13.** style. **14.** brand. —**Idiom. 15. make it,** to achieve success.

make′-be·lieve′ *n.* **1.** a pretending that a fanciful thing is true. —*adj.* **2.** imaginary.

make′shift′ *n.* **1.** a temporary substitute. —*adj.* **2.** substitute

make′up′ *n.* **1.** cosmetics. **2.** organization; composition.

mal- a prefix meaning bad or ill.

mal′a·chite′ (mal′ə kīt′) *n.* a green mineral, an ore of copper.

mal′ad·just′ed *adj.* badly adjusted, esp. to social conditions.

mal′a·droit′ (-ə droit′) *adj.* awkward.

mal′a·dy (-ə dē) *n., pl.* **-dies.** an illness.

ma·laise′ (ma lāz′, -lez′, mə-) *n.* **1.** weakness. **2.** a vague uneasiness.

mal′a·mute′ (mal′ə myōōt′) *n.* an Alaskan breed of large dogs.

mal′a·prop·ism (-ə prop iz′əm) *n.* a ludicrous misuse of similar words.

ma·lar′i·a (mə lâr′ē ə) *n.* a mosquito-borne disease. —**ma·lar′i·al,** *adj.*

ma·lar′key (mə lär′kē) *n. Slang.* nonsense.

mal′con·tent′ (mal′kən tent′) *n.* a dissatisfied person.

male (māl) *adj.* **1.** of the sex that produces sperm. —*n.* **2.** a male person or animal.

mal′e·dic′tion (mal′i dik′shən) *n.* a curse.

mal′e·fac′tor (-ə fak′tər) *n.* a criminal or evil person.

ma·lev′o·lent (mə lev′ə lənt) *adj.* wishing evil. —**ma·lev′o·lence,** *n.*

mal·fea′sance (mal fē′zəns) *n.* misconduct in office.

mal·formed′ *adj.* badly formed. —**mal′for·ma′tion,** *n.*

mal′ice (-is) *n.* evil intent. —**ma·li′cious** (mə lish′shəs) *adj.*

ma·lign′ (mə līn′) *v.t.* **1.** to speak ill of. —*adj.* **2.** evil.

ma·lig′nan·cy (mə lig′nən sē) *n., pl.* **-cies. 1.** a malignant state. **2.** a cancerous growth.

ma·lig′nant (-nənt) *adj.* **1.** causing harm or suffering. **2.** cancerous.

ma·lin′ger (mə ling′gər) *v.i.* to feign sickness to avoid work.

mall (môl) *n.* **1.** a covered shopping center. **2.** a shaded walk.

mal′lard (mal′ərd) *n.* a wild duck.

mal′le·a·ble (mal′ē ə bəl) *adj.* **1.** that may be hammered or rolled into shape. **2.** readily influenced.

mal′let (mal′it) *n.* a wooden-headed hammer.

mal′nu·tri′tion *n.* bad nutrition.

mal·o′dor·ous *adj.* smelling bad.

mal·prac′tice *n.* improper professional behavior.

malt (môlt) *n.* a germinated grain used in liquor-making.

mal·treat′ (mal trēt′) *v.t.* to abuse.

ma′ma (mä′mə, mə mä′) *n. Informal.* mother.

mam′mal (mam′əl) *n.* a vertebrate animal whose young are suckled.

mam′ma·ry (mam′ə rē) *adj.* of breasts.

mam′mo·gram′ (-gram′) *n.* an x-ray photograph of a breast, for detection of tumors.

mam′mon (mam′ən) *n.* material wealth.

mam′moth (mam′əth) *n.* **1.** a large extinct elephant. —*adj.* **2.** huge.

man (man) *n., pl.* **men** (men) *v.,* **manned, manning.** —*n.* **1.** an adult male person. **2.** a person. **3.** the human race. —*v.t.* **4.** to supply with a crew. **5.** to operate.

man′a·cle (man′ə kəl) *n., v.,* **-cled,**

-cling. —*n.* **1.** a handcuff. —*v.t.* **2.** to handcuff.

man′age (man′ij) *v.,* **-aged, -aging.** —*v.t.* **1.** to succeed in accomplishing. **2.** to supervise, direct, or control. —*v.i.* **3.** to cope. —**man′age•ment,** *n.* —**man′ag•er,** *n.*

man′a•tee′ (man′ə tē′) *n.* a plant-eating aquatic mammal.

man′da•rin (man′də rin) *n.* a public official in the Chinese Empire.

man′date (man′dāt) *n.* **1.** authority over territory granted to a nation. **2.** territory under such authority. **3.** an authorization to act granted by an electorate. **4.** a command.

man′da•to′ry (man′də tôr′ē) *adj.* officially required.

man′di•ble (man′də bəl) *n.* a bone comprising the lower jaw.

man′do•lin (man′dl in, man′dl in′) *n.* a stringed musical instrument.

man′drake (man′drāk, -drik) *n.* a narcotic plant whose root resembles a human form.

mane (mān) *n.* the long hair at the neck of horses or lions.

ma•neu′ver (mə nōō′vər) *n.* **1.** a planned movement or procedure, esp. in war. —*v.i., v.t.* **2.** to perform or cause to perform a maneuver. **3.** to position or manipulate skillfully. —**ma•neu′ver•a•ble,** *adj.*

man′ Fri′day *n., pl.* **men Friday.** a reliable male assistant.

man′ga•nese′ (mang′gə nēs′, -nēz′) *n.* a hard metallic element.

mange (mānj) *n.* a skin disease of animals. —**man′gy,** *adj.*

man′ger (mān′jər) *n.* a trough for feeding livestock.

man′gle (mang′gəl) *v.,* **-gled, -gling,** *n.* —*v.t.* **1.** to disfigure, esp. by crushing. **2.** to bungle. —*n.* **3.** a device with rollers for removing water in washing clothes.

man′go (mang′gō) *n., pl.* **-goes.** the fruit of a tropical tree.

man′grove (mang′grōv, man′-) *n.* a kind of tropical tree.

man′han′dle (man′han′dl) *v.t.,* **-dled, -dling.** to handle roughly.

man′hole′ *n.* an access hole to a sewer.

man′-hour′ *n.* the ideal amount of work done by a person in an hour.

man′hunt′ *n.* an intensive search for a fugitive.

ma′ni•a (mā′nē ə) *n.* **1.** great excitement. **2.** violent insanity.

ma′ni•ac′ *n.* a lunatic. —**ma•ni′a•cal** (mə nī′ə kəl) *adj.*

man′ic (man′ik) *adj.* irrationally excited or lively.

man′ic-depress′ive *adj.* suffering from a mental disorder in which

enthusiasm alternates with depression.

man′i•cure′ (man′i kyōōr′) *n., v.,* **-cured, -curing.** —*n.* **1.** a cosmetic treatment of the fingernails. —*v.t.* **2.** to give a manicure to.

man′i•fest′ (man′ə fest′) *adj.* **1.** evident. —*v.t.* **2.** to show plainly. —*n.* **3.** a list of cargo and passengers. —**man′i•fes•ta′tion,** *n.*

man′i•fes′to (-fes′tō) *n., pl.* **-toes.** a public declaration of intentions.

man′i•fold′ (man′ə fōld′) *adj.* **1.** of many kinds or parts. —*n.* **2.** a pipe with many outlets.

man′i•kin (man′i kin) *n.* a model of the human body.

Ma•nil′a pa′per (mə nil′ə) *n.* a strong, yellowish brown paper.

man′ in the street′ *n.* an ordinary person.

ma•nip′u•late′ (mə nip′yə lāt′) *v.t.,* **-lated, -lating.** to manage or handle with skill or cunning. —**ma•nip′u•la′tor,** *n.*

man′kind′ (man′kīnd′) *n.* the human race.

man′ly *adj.,* **-lier, -liest.** virile.

man′na (man′ə) *n.* divine food given to the Israelites.

man′ne•quin (man′i kin) *n.* a model for displaying clothes.

man′ner (man′ər) *n.* **1.** a way of doing or happening. **2.** **manners,** ways of behaving with reference to polite standards. **3.** sort.

man′ner•ism *n.* a peculiar way of doing something.

man′ner•ly *adj.* polite.

man′-of-war′ *n., pl.* **men-of-war.** a warship.

man′or (man′ər) *n.* a large estate.

man′pow′er *n.* power in terms of an available labor force.

man•qué′ (mäng kā′) *adj.* unfulfilled.

man′sard (man′särd) *n.* a roof with two slopes of different pitch on all sides.

manse (mans) *n.* a parson's house.

man′sion (man′shən) *n.* a large or stately house.

man′slaugh′ter *n.* the unlawful killing of a person without malice.

man′tel (man′tl) *n.* an ornamental structure around a fireplace.

man•til′la (man til′ə, -tē′ə) *n.* a lace head scarf for Spanish women.

man′tis (man′tis) *n.* a kind of carnivorous insect.

man′tle (man′tl) *n., v.,* **-tled, -tling.** —*n.* **1.** a loose cloak. **2.** something that covers. —*v.t.* **3.** to envelop.

man′tra (man′trə, män′-) *n.* a Hindu or Buddhist sacred incantation.

man′u•al (man′yōō əl) *adj.* **1.** of or

done with the hands or by human effort. —*n.* **2.** a small instruction book. —**man′u·al·ly,** *adv.*

man·u·fac′ture (man′yə fak′chər) *n., v.,* **-tured, -turing.** —*n.* **1.** the making of goods, esp. in great quantity. **2.** something made. —*v.t.* **3.** to make or fabricate.

man·u·mit′ (man′yə mit′) *v.t.,* **-mitted, -mitting.** to release from slavery. —**man′u·mis′sion,** *n.*

ma·nure′ (mə nŏŏr′, -nyŏŏr′) *n.* animal excrement used as fertilizer.

man′u·script′ (man′yə skript′) *n.* a handwritten or typed text.

man′y (men′ē) *adj.* **1.** comprising a large number; numerous. —*n.* **2.** a large number.

Mao′ism (mou′iz əm) *n.* the policies of the Chinese Communist leader Mao Zedong. —**Mao′ist,** *n., adj.*

map (map) *n., v.,* **mapped, mapping.** —*n.* **1.** a flat representation of all or part of the earth. —*v.t.* **2.** to show on a map. **3.** to plan.

ma′ple (mā′pəl) *n.* a broad-leaved tree grown for shade, ornament, sap, or timber.

mar (mär) *v.t.,* **marred, marring.** to damage or disfigure.

Mar. March.

ma·ra′ca (mə rä′kə, -rak′ə) *n.* a gourd-shaped rattle, used as a rhythm instrument.

mar′a·thon′ (mar′ə thon′, -thən) *n.* a long contest, esp. a foot race of 26 miles, 385 yards.

ma·raud′ (mə rôd′) *v.i., v.t.* to rove in quest of plunder. —**ma·raud′er,** *n.*

mar′ble (mär′bəl) *n.* **1.** a crystalline limestone used in sculpture and building. **2.** a small glass ball used in games. —*adj.* **3.** of marble.

mar′bling *n.* an intermixture of fat with lean in meat.

march (märch) *v.i.* **1.** to walk with measured tread. **2.** to advance. —*v.t.* **3.** to cause to march. —*n.* **4.** the act of marching. **5.** the distance covered in a march. **6.** music for marching.

March (märch) *n.* the third month of the year.

mar′chion·ess (mär′shə nis, -nes′) *n.* **1.** the wife of a marquess. **2.** a woman of a rank equal to a marquess.

Mar′di Gras (mär′dē grä′, grä′) *n.* the Tuesday before Lent, often celebrated as a carnival.

mare (mâr) *n.* a female horse.

mare′s′-nest′ *n.* a complicated situation.

mar′ga·rine (mär′jər in) *n.* a butter-like product made from vegetable oils and water or milk.

mar′gin (mär′jin) *n.* **1.** an edge. **2.** the space around text on a page. **3.** an amount beyond what is necessary.

mar′gin·al *adj.* **1.** of or at a margin. **2.** barely acceptable.

mar′gue·rite′ (mär′gə rēt′) *n.* a daisylike chrysanthemum.

mar′i·gold′ (mar′i gōld′) *n.* a common yellow- or orange-flowered plant.

ma·ri·jua′na (mar′ə wä′nə) *n.* a narcotic plant.

ma·rim′ba (mə rim′bə) *n.* a xylophone with chambers for resonance.

ma·ri′na (mə rē′nə) *n.* a docking area for small boats.

mar′i·nade′ (mar′ə nād′) *n.* a pungent liquid mixture for steeping food.

mar′i·nate′ *v.t.,* **-nated, -nating.** to season by steeping.

ma·rine′ (mə rēn′) *adj.* **1.** of the sea. —*n.* **2.** a member of the U.S. Marine Corps. **3.** a fleet of ships.

Marine′ Corps′ *n.* a military force trained for sea-launched assaults on land.

mar′i·ner (mar′ə nər) *n.* a sailor.

mar′i·o·nette′ (mar′ē ə net′) *n.* a puppet on strings.

mar′i·tal (mar′i tl) *adj.* of marriage.

mar′i·time′ (mar′i tīm′) *adj.* of the sea or shipping.

mar′jo·ram (mär′jər əm) *n.* an aromatic herb used as seasoning.

mark (märk) *n.* **1.** a visible sign. **2.** an object aimed at. **3.** a rating; grade. **4.** a lasting effect. —*v.t.* **5.** to be a feature of. **6.** to put a mark on, as a grade or price. **7.** to pay attention to. —**mark′er,** *n.*

mark′down′ *n.* a price reduction.

marked (märkt) *adj.* **1.** conspicuous; striking. **2.** singled out for revenge. —**mark′ed·ly,** *adv.*

mar′ket (mär′kit) *n.* **1.** a place for selling and buying. **2.** a food store. **3.** demand for a commodity. —*v.t.* **4.** to sell or buy. —**mar′ket·a·ble,** *adj.*

mar′ket·place′ *n.* **1.** an open area where a market is held. **2.** the world of business, trade, and economics.

marks′man *n., pl.* **-men.** a person who shoots well. —**marks′man·ship′,** *n.*

mark′up′ *n.* a price increase by a retailer.

mar′lin (mär′lin) *n.* a large game fish.

mar′ma·lade′ (mär′mə lād′) *n.* a citrus fruit preserve.

mar•mo•set (mär′mə zet′, -set′) n. a small tropical American monkey.

mar•mot (mär′mət) n. a bushy-tailed rodent.

ma•roon′[1] (mə rōōn′) n. a dark brownish red.

ma•roon′[2] (mə rōōn′) v.t. **1.** to put ashore and abandon on a deserted island. **2.** to isolate without aid.

mar•quee′ (mär kē′) n. **1.** a projecting structure over an entrance. **2.** a large tent.

mar′que•try (-ki trē) n. inlaid work forming a pattern.

mar′quis (-kwis, mär kē′) n. a European nobleman ranking below a duke.

mar•quise′ (-kēz′) n. **1.** the wife of a marquis. **2.** a woman of a rank equal to a marquis.

mar′riage (mar′ij) n. **1.** a legal union of a man and woman. **2.** a wedding. —**mar′riage•a•ble,** adj.

mar′row (mar′ō) n. the soft inner tissue of bone.

mar′ry (mar′ē) v., **-ried, -rying.** —v.t. **1.** to take as a husband or wife. **2.** to join in marriage. —v.i. **3.** to take a husband or wife.

Mars (märz) n. the planet fourth from the sun.

marsh (märsh) n. a tract of low, wet land. —**marsh′y,** adj.

mar′shal (mär′shəl) n., v., **-shaled, -shaling.** —n. **1.** a federal officer. —v.t. **2.** to rally; organize.

marsh′ gas′ n. a decomposition product of organic matter.

marsh′mal•low (-mel′ō, -mal′ō) n. a soft candy made from gelatin.

mar•su′pi•al (mär sōō′pē əl) n. an animal carrying its young in a pouch, as the kangaroo.

mart (märt) n. a market.

mar′ten (mär′tn) n. a small, American fur-bearing animal.

mar′tial (mär′shəl) adj. warlike.

mar′tial art′ n. any of various forms of East Asian self-defense or combat.

mar′tial law′ n. law imposed by military forces.

mar′tin (mär′tn) n. a bird of the swallow family.

mar′ti•net′ (mär′tn et′) n. a person who enforces strict discipline.

mar•ti′ni (mär tē′nē) n. a cocktail of gin and vermouth.

mar′tyr (mär′tər) n. **1.** a person who willingly dies for a belief. —v.t. **2.** to make a martyr of. —**mar′tyr•dom,** n.

mar′vel (mär′vəl) n., v., **-veled, -veling.** —n. **1.** a wonderful or astonishing thing. —v.i., v.t. **2.** to wonder (at or about).

mar′vel•ous adj. **1.** superbly fine.

2. arousing wonder or astonishment. —**mar′vel•ous•ly,** adv.

Marx′ism n. the system of thought developed by Karl Marx on which communism is based. —**Marx′ist,** n., adj.

mar′zi•pan′ (mär′zə pan′) n. a confection of almond paste and sugar.

mas•car′a (ma skar′ə) n. a cosmetic for eyelashes.

mas′cot (mas′kot, -kət) n. a person, animal, or thing bringing good luck.

mas′cu•line (mas′kyə lin) adj. of, like, or suitable for men. —**mas′-cu•lin′i•ty,** n.

ma′ser (mā′zər) n. a device for producing electromagnetic waves.

mash (mash) n. **1.** a soft pulpy mass. —v.t. **2.** to crush into a soft pulpy mass. —**mash′er,** n.

mask (mask) n. **1.** a disguise or protection for the face. —v.t. **2.** to disguise or cover.

mas′och•ism (mas′ə kiz′əm, maz′-) n. pleasure in suffering. —**masochist,** n. —**masochistic,** adj.

ma′son (mā′sən) n. a builder with stone, brick, etc. —**ma′son•ry,** n.

mas′quer•ade′ (mas′kə rād′) n., v., **-aded, -ading.** —n. **1.** a disguise. **2.** a party at which guests wear a disguise. —v.i. **3.** to be disguised.

mass[1] (mas) n. **1.** a body of coherent matter. **2.** a quantity or size. **3.** weight. **4.** the masses, the common people. —v.i., v.t. **5.** to form into a mass. —adj. **6.** of or affecting the masses. **7.** done on a large scale.

mass[2] (mas) n. (often cap.) the celebration of the Eucharist.

Mass. Massachusetts.

mas′sa•cre (mas′ə kər) n., v., **-cred, -cring.** —n. **1.** the killing of many people. —v.t. **2.** to slaughter.

mas•sage′ (mə säzh′, -säj′) v., **-saged, -saging,** n. —v.t. **1.** to manipulate the body by rubbing or kneading. —n. **2.** such treatment.

mas•seur′ (mə sûr′, -sōōr′) n. a man who provides massage.

mas•seuse′ (mə sōōs′, -sōōz′) n. a woman who provides massage.

mas′sive (mas′iv) adj. large; heavy.

mass′ me′dia n.pl. the means of communication that reach great numbers of people.

mass′ num′ber n. the number of nucleons in an atomic nucleus.

mass′-produce′ v.t., **-duced, -ducing.** to produce in large quantities. —**mass′ produc′tion,** n.

mast (mast) n. an upright pole on a ship.

mas•tec′to•my (ma stek′tə mē) n.,

pl. **-mies.** the surgical removal of a breast.

mas·ter (mas′tər) *n.* **1.** a person in control. **2.** a skilled person. —*adj.* **3.** chief. —*v.t.* **4.** to conquer. **5.** to become an expert in.

mas′ter·ful *adj.* asserting power.

mas′ter·ly *adj.* highly skilled.

mas′ter·mind′ *n.* **1.** one who originates or oversees a plan. —*v.t.* **2.** to plan as a mastermind.

mas′ter of cer′emonies *n.* a person who conducts events.

mas′ter·piece′ *n.* a work of highest skill.

mas′ter's degree′ *n.* a degree awarded to a student who has completed at least one year of graduate study.

mas′ter ser′geant *n.* a noncommissioned officer of the highest rank.

mas′ter·stroke′ *n.* an extremely skillful action.

mas′ter·y *n.* **1.** command; grasp. **2.** dominance. **3.** expert skill.

mas′ti·cate′ (mas′ti kāt′) *v.t.,* **-cated, -cating.** to chew.

mas′tiff (-tif) *n.* a powerful dog.

mas′to·don′ (mas′tə don′) *n.* a large extinct elephantlike mammal.

mas′toid (mas′toid) *n.* a protuberance of bone behind the ear.

mas′tur·bate′ (mas′tər bāt′) *v.i., v.t.,* **-bated, -bating.** to manually stimulate one's own genitals or the genitals of (another). —**mas′tur·ba′tion,** *n.*

mat (mat) *n., v.,* **matted, matting.** —*n.* **1.** a covering for a floor or other surface. **2.** material bordering a picture. **3.** a thick tangled mass. —*v.t., v.i.* **4.** to form into a mat.

mat′a·dor′ (-dôr′) *n.* a bullfighter.

match¹ (mach) *n.* **1.** a person or thing resembling or equaling another. **2.** a thing that goes well with another. **3.** a competition; contest. **4.** a marriage. —*v.t.* **5.** to equal. **6.** to fit together with. **7.** to arrange marriage for. —*v.i.* **8.** to go together well.

match² (mach) *n.* a stick chemically tipped to strike fire.

match′less *adj.* unequaled.

match′mak′er *n.* an arranger of marriages.

mate (māt) *n., v.,* **mated, mating.** —*n.* **1.** one of a pair. **2.** a husband or wife. **3.** an officer of a merchant ship. **4.** a companion. —*v.t., v.i.* **5.** to join; pair. **6.** to copulate.

ma·te′ri·al (mə tēr′ē əl) *n.* **1.** the substance of which a thing is made. **2.** fabric. —*adj.* **3.** physical. **4.** pertinent. —**ma·te′ri·al·ly,** *adv.*

ma·te′ri·al·ism *n.* **1.** devotion to material objects or wealth. **2.** the belief that all reality is material.

ma·te′ri·al·ize′ *v.i.,* **-ized, -izing. 1.** to be realized; appear. **2.** to assume material form.

ma·te′ri·el′ (mə tēr′ē el′) *n.* supplies, esp. military.

ma·ter′ni·ty (mə tûr′ni tē) *n.* **1.** the state of being a mother. —*adj.* **2.** for pregnant women or new mothers. —**ma·ter′nal,** *adj.*

math′e·mat′ics (math′ə mat′iks) *n.* the science of numbers. —**math′e·mat′i·cal,** *adj.* —**math′e·ma·ti′cian** (-mə tish′ən) *n.*

mat′i·née′ (mat′n ā′) *n.* an afternoon performance.

mat′ins (mat′nz) *n.* morning prayers.

ma′tri·arch′ (mā′trē ärk′) *n.* the female head of a family or tribe. —**ma′tri·ar′chy,** *n.*

mat′ri·cide′ (ma′tri sīd′, mā′-) *n.* **1.** the act of killing one's mother. **2.** a person who commits such an act. —**mat′ri·cid′al,** *adj.*

ma·tric·u·late (mə trik′yə lāt′) *v.t., v.i.,* **-lated, -lating.** to enroll as a student. —**ma·tric′u·la′tion,** *n.*

mat′ri·mo′ny (ma′trə mō′nē) *n.* marriage. —**mat′ri·mo′ni·al,** *adj.*

ma′trix (mā′triks, ma′-) *n., pl.* **-trices** (-tri sēz′), **-trixes. 1.** a place or point where something originates. **2.** a mold; model.

ma′tron (mā′trən) *n.* **1.** a dignified married woman. **2.** a female institutional officer. —**ma′tron·ly,** *adj.*

matte (mat) *adj.* **1.** having a dull surface, without luster. —*n.* **2.** a dull surface or finish.

mat′ter (mat′ər) *n.* **1.** the substance of which a physical object consists. **2.** trouble. **3.** pus. **4.** a subject of concern or discussion. —*v.i.* **5.** to be of importance.

mat′ter-of-fact′ *adj.* adhering to fact; straightforward.

mat′tock (-ək) *n.* a digging tool.

mat′tress (ma′tris) *n.* a thick filled case for sleeping on.

ma·ture′ (mə tŏŏr′, -tyŏŏr′, -chŏŏr′) *adj.,* **-turer, -turest,** *v.,* **-tured, -turing.** —*adj.* **1.** grown or developed. **2.** adult in manner or thought. **3.** payable. —*v.i., v.t.* **4.** to become or make mature. —**ma·tu′ri·ty,** *n.*

maud′lin (môd′lin) *adj.* weakly sentimental.

maul (môl) *v.t.* to injure by rough treatment.

maun′der (môn′dər) *v.i.* **1.** to talk in a rambling way. **2.** to wander.

mau·so·le·um (mô′sə lē′əm, -zə-) *n., pl.* **-leums, -lea** (-lē′ə). a tomb in the form of a building.

mauve (mōv, môv) *n.* a pale purple.

ma′ven (mā′vən) *n.* an expert.

mav′er•ick (mav′ər ik) *n.* **1.** a nonconformist. **2.** an unbranded animal.

maw (mô) *n.* the mouth, throat, or stomach of an animal.

mawk′ish (-kish) *adj.* sickeningly sentimental. —**mawk′ish•ly,** *adv.*

max′im (mak′sim) *n.* a proverb.

max′i•mum (mak′sə məm) *n.* **1.** the greatest degree or quantity. —*adj.* **2.** greatest possible.

may (mā) *aux. v., pres.* **may;** *past* **might** (mīt). (used to express possibility or permission.)

May (mā) *n.* the fifth month of the year.

may′be *adv.* it may be (that).

May′day′ *n.* an international radio distress call.

may′flow′er *n.* a plant that blossoms in May.

may′fly′ *n., pl.* **-flies.** an insect with large transparent forewings.

may′hem (mā′hem, -əm) *n.* **1.** the crime of willfully crippling or mutilating someone. **2.** random violence.

may′on•naise′ (mā′ə nāz′) *n.* a sauce made of egg yolks, oil, and vinegar. Also, *Informal.* **may′o.**

may′or (mā′ər) *n.* the chief officer of a city. —**may′or•al,** *adj.* —**may′or•al•ty,** *n.*

maze (māz) *n.* a confusing arrangement of paths.

MD Maryland. Also, **Md.**

M.D. Doctor of Medicine.

me (mē) *pron.* the objective case of I.

ME Maine.

mead (mēd) *n.* a liquor of fermented honey.

mead′ow (med′ō) *n.* a tract of level grassland.

mead′ow•lark′ *n.* a North American songbird.

mea′ger (mē′gər) *adj.* poor; scanty.

meal¹ (mēl) *n.* the food served and eaten at one time.

meal² (mēl) *n.* coarse powder ground from the seeds of a grain.

meal′y-mouthed′ *adj.* avoiding candid speech.

mean¹ (mēn) *v.,* **meant** (ment) **meaning.** —*v.t.* **1.** to intend (to do or signify). **2.** to signify. —*v.i.* **3.** to have specified intentions.

mean² (mēn) *adj.* **1.** unkind; malicious. **2.** poor; shabby. —**mean′ly,** *adv.* —**mean′ness,** *n.*

mean³ (mēn) *n.* **1. means,** a method for achieving a purpose. **2. means,** resources, esp. money. **3.** something midway between two extremes; average. —*adj.* **4.** middle.

—*Idiom.* **5. by all means,** certainly. **6. by no means,** not at all.

me•an′der (mē an′dər) *v.i.* to wander aimlessly.

mean′ing *n.* **1.** what is intended to be expressed. **2.** the aim or purpose. —**mean′ing•ful,** *adj.*

mean′time′ *n.* **1.** the time between. —*adv.* Also, **mean′while′.** **2.** in the time between.

mea′sles (mē′zəlz) *n.* an infectious disease marked by small red spots.

mea′sly (mē′zlē) *adj.,* **-slier, -sliest.** *Informal.* miserably small.

meas′ure (mezh′ər) *v.,* **-ured, -uring,** *n.* —*v.t.* **1.** to ascertain the size of. —*v.i.* **2.** to be of a specified size. **3. measure up,** to reach the necessary standard. —*n.* **4.** the process of measuring. **5.** the dimensions of something. **6.** an instrument or system used in measuring. **7.** Usu., **measures.** an action to achieve an end. —*Idiom.* **8. for good measure,** as an extra. —**meas′ure•ment,** *n.*

meas′ured *adj.* careful; deliberate.

meat (mēt) *n.* **1.** the flesh of animals used as food. **2.** the edible part of a fruit, nut, etc. **3.** the essential part; gist.

meat′y *adj.,* **-ier, -iest. 1.** like or full of meat. **2.** rich in content.

Mec′ca (mek′ə) *n.* **1.** the spiritual center of Islam. **2.** (*often l.c.*) a place that attracts many people.

me•chan′ic (mə kan′ik) *n.* a skilled worker with machinery.

me•chan′i•cal *adj.* of or operated by machinery.

me•chan′ics *n.* the science of motion and of the action of forces on bodies.

mech′an•ism (mek′ə niz′əm) *n.* **1.** the structure of a machine. **2.** a piece of machinery.

mech′a•nize′ *v.t.,* **-nized, -nizing. 1.** to make mechanical. **2.** to equip with machinery.

med′al (med′l) *n.* a badgelike metal object given for merit.

med′al•ist *n.* a medal winner.

me•dal′lion (mə dal′yən) *n.* a large medal or medallike ornament.

med′dle (med′l) *v.i.,* **-dled, -dling.** to interfere. —**med′dle•some,** *adj.*

me′di•a (mē′dē ə) *n.pl.* the means of mass communication.

me′di•an (mē′dē ən) *adj.* **1.** in the middle. —*n.* **2.** the middle number, point, etc.

me′di•ate′ (-āt′) *v.t., v.i.,* **-ated, -ating.** to settle or act as an intermediary. —**me′di•a′tor,** *n.*

med′ic (med′ik) *n. Informal.* a doctor or medical aide.

Med′i•caid′ (-i kād′) *n.* government-supported medical care for low-income persons.

med/i·cal *adj.* **1.** of medicine. **2.** curative. —**med/i·cal·ly,** *adv.*

me·dic/a·ment (mə dik/ə mənt, med/i kə-) *n.* a healing substance.

Med/i·care/ (med/i kâr/) *n.* government-supported medical insurance for those 65 and older.

med/i·cate/ *v.t.,* **-cated, -cating.** to treat with medicine. —**med/i·ca/- tion,** *n.*

me·dic/i·nal (mə dis/ə nl) *adj.* curative. —**me·dic/i·nal·ly,** *adv.*

med/i·cine (med/ə sin) *n.* **1.** a substance used in treating illness. **2.** the art of restoring physical health.

me/di·e/val (mē/dē ē/vəl, mid ē/-) *adj.* of the Middle Ages. Also, **me/- di·ae/val.** —**me/di·e/val·ist,** *n.*

me/di·o/cre (mē/dē ō/kər) *adj.* of ordinary or moderate quality. —**me/di·oc/ri·ty** (-ok/ri tē) *n.*

med/i·tate/ (med/i tāt/) *v.i.,* **-tated, -tating.** to think deeply. —**med/i· ta/tion,** *n.* —**med/i·ta/tive,** *adj.*

me/di·um (mē/dē əm) *n., pl.* **-dia** (-dē ə) except for 4, **-diums,** *adj.* —*n.* **1.** something intermediate or moderate. **2.** a means of doing or conveying something. **3.** a surrounding substance. **4.** a person believed able to communicate with the dead. **5.** a means of mass communication. —*adj.* **6.** intermediate.

med/ley (med/lē) *n.* a mixture.

meek (mēk) *adj.* submissive.

meer/schaum (mēr/shəm, -shôm) *n.* a claylike mineral, used for tobacco pipes.

meet (mēt) *v.,* **met** (met) **meeting,** *n., adj.* —*v.t.* **1.** to come upon. **2.** to come into contact with. **3.** to be introduced to. **4.** to pay or satisfy. —*v.i.* **5.** to come together. —*n.* **6.** a meeting of competitors for a sports contest. —*adj.* **7.** proper.

meet/ing *n.* **1.** a coming together. **2.** a gathering of persons.

mega- a prefix meaning: **1.** one million. **2.** large.

meg/a·hertz/ (meg/ə hûrts/) *n., pl.* **-hertz.** one million hertz.

meg/a·lo·ma/ni·a (-lō mā/nē ə) *n.* a delusion of greatness, riches, etc.

meg/a·phone/ (-fōn/) *n.* a cone-shaped device for magnifying sound.

meg/a·plex/ (-pleks/) *n.* a large building containing usu. more than a dozen movie theaters.

meg/a·ton/ *n.* an explosive force equal to that of one million tons of TNT.

mel/a·mine/ (mel/ə mēn/) *n.* a crystalline solid used in making resins.

mel/an·cho/li·a (mel/ən kō/lē ə) *n.* a severe form of depression.

mel/an·chol/y (-kol/ē) *n.* **1.** low spirits; depression. —*adj.* **2.** sad.

mé·lange/ (mā länzh/, -länj/) *n.* a mixture.

mel/a·nin (mel/ə nin) *n.* a pigment accounting for the dark color of skin, hair, etc.

mel/a·no/ma (-nō/mə) *n.* a darkly pigmented malignant skin tumor.

meld[1] (meld) *v.t., v.i.* to display (a combination of cards) for a score.

meld[2] (meld) *v.t., v.i.* **1.** to merge; blend. —*n.* **2.** a blend.

me/lee (mā/lā) *n.* a confused, general fight.

mel/io·rate/ (mēl/yə rāt/) *v.t., v.i.,* **-rated, -rating.** to ameliorate.

mel·lif/lu·ous (mə lif/lōō əs) *adj.* soft and sweet in speech.

mel/low (mel/ō) *adj.* **1.** soft and rich. **2.** genial. —*v.t., v.i.* **3.** to make or become mellow.

me·lo/di·ous *adj.* tuneful.

mel/o·dra/ma (mel/ə drä/mə, -dram/ə) *n.* a play emphasizing theatrical effects and strong emotions. —**mel/o·dra·mat/ic,** *adj.*

mel/o·dy (mel/ə dē) *n., pl.* **-dies.** an arrangement of musical sounds. —**me·lod/ic** (mə lod/ik) *adj.*

mel/on (mel/ən) *n.* an edible fruit of certain annual vines.

melt (melt) *v.t., v.i.* **1.** to make or become liquid, esp. by heat. **2.** to soften.

melt/down/ *n.* the melting of a nuclear reactor core.

melt/ing pot/ *n.* a locality in which a blending of peoples or cultures takes place.

mem/ber (mem/bər) *n.* **1.** a part of a structure. **2.** one belonging to an organization. —**mem/ber·ship/,** *n.*

mem/brane (-brān) *n.* a thin film of tissue in animals and plants.

me·men/to (mə men/tō) *n., pl.* **-tos, -toes.** something serving as a reminder.

mem/oir (mem/wär, -wôr) *n.* **1.** an autobiography. **2. memoirs,** a personal recollection.

mem/o·ra·bil/i·a (-ər ə bil/ē ə, -bil/yə) *n.pl.* souvenirs.

mem/o·ra·ble *adj.* worth remembering. —**mem/o·ra·bly,** *adv.*

mem/o·ran/dum (-ran/dəm) *n., pl.* **-dums, -da** (-də). a written statement or reminder. Also, **mem/o.**

me·mo/ri·al (mə môr/ē əl) *n.* **1.** something honoring the memory of a person or event. —*adj.* **2.** serving as a memorial.

mem/o·rize/ (mem/ə rīz/) *v.t., v.i.,* **-rized, -rizing.** to commit to memory.

mem•o•ry *n., pl.* **-ries. 1.** the faculty of remembering. **2.** something remembered. **3.** the length of time of recollection. **4.** the capacity of a computer to store data.

men′ace (men′is) *v.,* **-aced, -acing,** *n.* **—v.t., v.i. 1.** to threaten or be threatened. **—n. 2.** something that threatens.

me•nag′er•ie (mə naj′ə rē, -nazh′-) *n.* a collection of animals.

mend (mend) *v.t.* **1.** to repair. **2.** to improve. **—v.i. 3.** to heal. **—n. 4.** a mended place. **—Idiom. 5. on the mend,** improving.

men•da′cious (men dā′shəs) *adj.* untruthful. **—men•dac′i•ty** (-das′i-tē) *n.*

men′di•cant (men′di kənt) *n.* a beggar.

me′ni•al (mē′nē əl) *adj.* **1.** humble; servile. **—n. 2.** a servant.

me•nin′ges (mi nin′jēz) *n.pl., sing.* **me′ninx** (mē′ningks). the three membranes covering the brain and spinal cord.

men′in•gi′tis (men′in jī′tis) *n.* an inflammation of the meninges.

men′o•pause′ (men′ə pôz′) *n.* the period of cessation of menstruation.

me•nor′ah (mə nôr′ə) *n.* a symbolic candelabrum used during Hanukkah.

men′stru•a′tion (men′strōō ā′shən) *n.* the monthly discharge of blood from the uterus. **—men′stru•al,** *adj.* **—men′stru•ate′,** *v.i.*

men′sur•a•ble (-shər ə bəl, -sər ə-bəl) *adj.* capable of being measured.

-ment a suffix meaning: **1.** an action or resulting state. **2.** a product. **3.** a means.

men′tal (men′tl) *adj.* of or in the mind. **—men′tal•ly,** *adv.*

men•tal′i•ty (-tal′i tē) *n., pl.* **-ties. 1.** mental ability. **2.** a characteristic mental attitude.

men′thol (men′thôl, -thol) *n.* a colorless alcohol from peppermint oil. **—men′thol•at′ed** (-thə lā′tid) *adj.*

men′tion (men′shən) *v.t.* **1.** to speak or write about briefly. **—n. 2.** a brief reference.

men′tor (men′tôr, -tər) *n.* an adviser.

men′u (men′yōō, mā′nyōō) *n.* a list of dishes that can be served.

me•ow′ (mē ou′, myou) *n.* **1.** the sound a cat makes. **—v.i. 2.** to make such a sound.

mer′can•tile′ (mûr′kən tēl′, -tīl′, -til) *adj.* of or engaged in trade.

mer′ce•nar′y (mûr′sə ner′ē) *adj., n., pl.* **-naries. —adj. 1.** acting only for profit. **—n. 2.** a hired soldier.

mer′chan•dise′ *n., v.,* **-dised, -dising. —n.** (mûr′chən dīz′, -dīs′) **1.** goods; wares. **—v.t., v.i.** (-dīz′) **2.** to buy and sell.

mer′chant (-chənt) *n.* a person who buys and sells goods.

mer′chant marine′ *n.* the ships of a nation that are used for trade.

mer•cu′ri•al (mər kyŏŏr′ē əl) *adj.* **1.** of mercury. **2.** unpredictable.

mer′cu•ry (mûr′kyə rē) *n.* **1.** a heavy metallic element. **2. Mercury,** the smallest planet, nearest to the sun.

mer′cy (mûr′sē) *n., pl.* **-cies. 1.** pity; compassion. **2.** an act of compassion. **—mer′ci•ful,** *adj.*

mere (mēr) *adj.* being nothing more nor better than that specified. **—mere′ly,** *adv.*

merge (mûrj) *v.t., v.i.,* **merged, merging.** to combine. **—merg′er,** *n.*

me•rid′i•an (mə rid′ē ən) *n.* a circle on the earth's surface passing through the poles.

me•ringue′ (mə rang′) *n.* egg whites beaten with sugar and browned in an oven.

me•ri′no (mə rē′nō) *n., pl.* **-nos. 1.** a kind of sheep. **2.** soft wool.

mer′it (mer′it) *n.* **1.** worth. **2.** a commendable quality. **—v.t. 3.** to deserve. **—mer′i•to′ri•ous** (-i tôr′ē-əs) *adj.*

mer′maid′ (mûr′mād′) *n.* an imaginary sea creature, half woman and half fish.

mer′ry (mer′ē) *adj.,* **-rier, -riest.** joyous; cheerful. **—mer′ri•ly,** *adv.*

mer′ry-go-round′ *n.* a revolving amusement ride.

mer′ry•mak′ing *n.* festivity; revelry. **—mer′ry-ma′ker,** *n.*

me′sa (mā′sə) *n.* a high, steep-walled plateau.

mesh (mesh) *n.* **1.** a fabric of open texture. **2.** a network. **3.** the engagement of gear teeth. **—v.t., v.i. 4.** to engage or become engaged, as gear teeth. **5.** to match; coordinate.

mes′mer•ize′ (mez′mə rīz′) *v.t.,* **-ized, -izing.** to hypnotize. **—mes′mer•ism** (-mə riz′əm) *n.*

mes•quite′ (me skēt′, mes′kēt) *n.* a tree of the southwest U.S.

mess (mes) *n.* **1.** a dirty or disorderly condition. **2.** a group taking meals together regularly. **3.** meals so taken. **—v.t. 4.** to make dirty or untidy. **5.** to spoil; bungle. **—mess′y,** *adj.*

mes′sage (mes′ij) *n.* a communication.

mes′sen•ger (-ən jər) *n.* the bearer of a message.

Messiah

Mes•si′ah (mi sī′ə) *n.* **1.** the expected deliverer of the Jews. **2.** (in Christian theology) Jesus Christ.

mes•ti′zo (me stē′zō) *n., pl.* **-zos, -zoes.** a person who is part-Spanish, part-Indian.

meta- a prefix meaning: **1.** after or beyond. **2.** behind. **3.** change.

me•tab′o•lism (mə tab′ə liz′əm) *n.* the biological processes of converting food into energy. —**met′a•bol′ic** (met′ə bol′ik) *adj.*

met′al (met′l) *n.* an elementary substance such as gold or copper. —**me•tal′lic** (mə tal′ik) *adj.*

met′al•lur′gy (-ûr′jē) *n.* the science of working with metals.

met′a•mor′phose (met′ə môr′fōz, -fōs) *v.i., v.t.,* **-phosed, -phosing.** to transform.

met′a•mor′pho•sis (-fə sis) *n., pl.* **-ses** (-sēz′). a drastic change.

met′a•phor′ (-fôr′, -fər) *n.* a figure of speech in which a word or phrase is applied to an object or concept it does not literally denote in order to suggest comparison with its basic meaning. —**met′a•phor′i•cal,** *adj.*

met′a•phys′ics *n.* a branch of philosophy concerned with the ultimate nature of reality. —**met′a•phys′ical,** *adj.*

me•tas′ta•size′ (mə tas′tə sīz′) *v.i.,* **-sized, -sizing.** to spread from one to another part of the body. —**me•tas′ta•sis** (-sis) *n.*

mete (mēt) *v.t.,* **meted, meting.** to allot; distribute.

me′te•or (mē′tē ər, -ôr′) *n.* a small body of rock or metal passing through the earth's atmosphere.

me′te•or′ic (-ôr′ik) *adj.* **1.** of meteors. **2.** sudden and spectacular.

me′te•or•ite′ (-ə rīt′) *n.* a meteor reaching earth.

me′te•or•ol′o•gy (-ə rol′ə jē) *n.* the science of atmospheric phenomena, esp. weather. —**me′te•or•o•log′i•cal** (-ər ə loj′i kəl) *adj.* —**me′te•or•ol′o•gist,** *n.*

me′ter (mē′tər) *n.* **1.** a unit of length in the metric system, equal to 39.37 inches. **2.** the rhythmic element in music and poetry. **3.** a device for measuring flow. —*v.t.* **4.** to measure with a meter. Also, *Brit.,* **me′tre.**

meth′a•done′ (meth′ə dōn′) *n.* a synthetic narcotic used in treating heroin addiction.

meth′ane (-ān) *n.* a colorless, odorless, flammable gas.

meth′a•nol′ (-ə nôl′) *n.* a colorless liquid used as a solvent, fuel, etc.

meth′od (meth′əd) *n.* a system of doing something.

me•thod′i•cal (mə thod′i kəl) *adj.* **1.** done or acting in a systematic way. **2.** painstaking; deliberate. —**me•thod′i•cal•ly,** *adv.*

meth′od•ol′o•gy (-ə dol′ə jē) *n., pl.* **-gies.** a system of methods and principles.

meth′yl al′cohol *n.* methanol.

me•tic′u•lous (mə tik′yə ləs) *adj.* minutely careful.

mé′tier (mā′tyā) *n.* a field of activity in which one has special ability. Also, **me′tier.**

met′ric (me′trik) *adj.* of a decimal system of weights and measures, based on the meter and gram.

met′ro•nome′ (me′trə nōm′) *n.* a device for marking tempo.

me•trop′o•lis (mi trop′ə lis) *n.* a large, busy city.

met′ro•pol′i•tan (me′trə pol′i tn) *adj.* **1.** of or in a city. **2.** of cities and urban areas.

met′tle (met′l) *n.* **1.** spirit; fortitude. **2.** disposition.

met′tle•some (-səm) *adj.* spirited; courageous.

mew (myōō) *n.* **1.** the cry of a cat. —*v.i.* **2.** to emit a mew.

mews (myōōz) *n.* a street with dwellings converted from stables.

mez′za•nine′ (mez′ə nēn′, mez′ə nēn′) *n.* a low story between two main floors; balcony.

mez′zo-so•pran′o (met′sō-, med′zō-) *n.* a voice between soprano and contralto in range.

M.F.A. Master of Fine Arts.

MI Michigan.

mi•as′ma (mī az′mə, mē-) *n., pl.* **-mata** (-mə tə), **-mas.** a vapor from decaying organic matter.

mi′ca (mī′kə) *n.* a shiny mineral occurring in thin layers.

Mich. Michigan.

micro- a prefix meaning very small.

mi′crobe (mī′krōb) *n.* a microorganism, esp. one causing disease.

mi′cro•brew′er•y *n., pl.* **-ies.** a small brewery usu. producing exotic or high quality beer.

mi′cro•chip′ *n.* a chip (def. 5).

mi′cro•com•put′er *n.* a compact computer with less capability than a minicomputer.

mi′cro•cosm (mī′krə koz′əm) *n.* a world in miniature.

mi′cro•fi′ber *n.* a very fine polyester fiber.

mi′cro•fiche′ (-fēsh′) *n.* a small sheet of microfilm.

mi′cro•film′ *n.* **1.** a very small photograph of a page, document, etc. —*v.t.* **2.** to make a microfilm of.

mi′cro•man′age *v.t.,* **-aged, -aging.** to manage with excessive attention to minor details.

mi·crom/e·ter (-krom/i tər) n. a device for measuring tiny distances.

mi/cron (mī/kron) n. the millionth part of a meter.

mi/cro·or/gan·ism/ (mī/krō-) n. a microscopic organism.

mi/cro·phone/ (mī/krə fōn/) n. an instrument for changing sound waves into electric impulses.

mi/cro·proc/es·sor (mī/krō pros/es-ər, -ə sər; esp. Brit. -prō/ses ər, -sə-sər) n. a computer circuit that performs all the functions of a CPU.

mi/cro·scope/ (mī/krə skōp/) n. an instrument for inspecting minute objects.

mi/cro·scop/ic (-skop/ik) adj. 1. of microscopes. 2. extremely small.

mi/cro·sur/ger·y (mī/krō sûr/jə rē) n. surgery performed under magnification.

mi/cro·wave/ n., v. -waved, -waving. —n. 1. a short radio wave used in radar, cooking, etc. 2. an oven that uses microwaves to cook food. —v.t. 3. to cook in a microwave oven.

mid (mid) adj. 1. middle. —prep. 2. amid.

mid/day/ (-dā/, -dā/) n. noon.

mid/dle (mid/l) adj. 1. equally distant from given limits. 2. intermediate. —n. 3. a middle part.

Mid/dle Ag/es n. a period of European history, about A.D. 476 to 1500.

mid/dle class/ n. the class of people intermediate between the poor and the wealthy.

mid/dle·man/ n. a merchant who buys goods from the producer and resells them.

middle-of-the-road adj. moderate.

mid/dle school/ n. a school consisting of grades 5 or 6 through 8.

mid/dling adj. 1. medium. 2. mediocre.

midge (mij) n. a tiny fly.

midg/et (mij/it) n. a very small person or thing.

mid/land (-lənd) n. the interior of a country.

mid/night/ n. 12 o'clock at night.

mid/point/ n. a point at or near the middle.

mid/riff (-rif) n. a part of the body between the chest and abdomen.

mid/ship/man n., pl. -men. a student training to be an officer in the U.S. Navy or Marine Corps.

midst (midst) n. the middle.

mid/term n. 1. the halfway point of a school term. 2. an examination given at midterm.

mid/way/ adj., adv. (mid/wā/) 1. in the middle of the way or distance.

—n. (-wā/) 2. an area of games and sideshows at a carnival.

mid/wife/ n., pl. -wives. a woman who assists at childbirth.

mid/win/ter (-win/tər, -win/-) n. the middle of winter.

mien (mēn) n. demeanor; bearing.

miff (mif) n. a petty quarrel.

miffed (mift) adj. offended.

might¹ (mīt), aux. v., pres. sing. and pl. **might;** past **might.** 1. pt. of **may.** 2. (used to express possibility or obligation). 3. (used in polite requests for permission).

might² (mīt) n. strength or force.

might/y adj., -ier, -iest, adv. —adj. 1. powerful; huge. —adv. 2. Informal. very. —**might/i·ness, n.**

mi/graine (mī/grān) n. a severe headache, often with nausea.

mi/grate (-grāt) v.i., -grated, -grating. to go from one region to another. —**mi·gra/tion, n.** —**mi/gra·to/ry** (-grə tôr/ē) adj. —**mi/grant, adj., n.**

mi·ka/do (mi kä/dō) n., pl. -dos. a title of the emperor of Japan.

mike (mīk) n. Informal. a microphone.

mil (mil) n. one thousandth of an inch.

mild (mīld) adj. gentle; temperate.

mil/dew/ (mil/dōō/, -dyōō/) n. 1. a discoloration caused by fungus. —v.t., v.i. 2. to affect or become affected with mildew.

mile (mīl) n. a unit of distance, equal on land to 5280 ft.

mile/age (mī/lij) n. 1. the miles traveled. 2. an allowance for travel expenses.

mile/stone/ n. an important event.

mi·lieu/ (mil yōō/, mēl-; Fr. mē lyœ/) n., pl. -lieus, -lieux. surroundings; environment.

mil/i·tant (mil/i tənt) adj. aggressive.

mil/i·ta·rism (-tə riz/əm) n. military spirit. —**mil/i·ta·rist, n.**

mil/i·tar·ize/ v.t., -ized, -izing. to equip with military weapons.

mil/i·tar/y (-ter/ē) adj. 1. of armed forces, esp. on land. —n. 2. armed forces or soldiers collectively.

mil/i·tate/ (-tāt/) v.i., -tated, -tating. to act (for or against).

mi·li/tia (mi lish/ə) n. an organization for emergency military service. —**mi·li/tia·man, n.**

milk (milk) n. 1. a liquid secreted by female mammals to feed their young. —v.t. 2. to draw milk from. —**milk/y, adj.**

milk/weed/ n. a plant with milky juice.

Milk/y Way/ n. the galaxy containing our solar system.

mill (mil) n. 1. a place where manufacturing is done. **2.** a device for grinding. **3.** a place where grain is ground. **4.** one tenth of a cent. —*v.t.* **5.** to grind or treat with a mill. **6.** to groove the edges of (a coin). —*v.i.* **7.** to move about in confusion. —**mill′er,** *n.*

mil·len′ni·um (mi len′ē əm) *n., pl.* -niums, -nia (-nē ə). **1.** a period of a thousand years. **2.** a thousandth anniversary.

mil′let (-it) *n.* a cereal grass.

milli- a prefix meaning thousand or thousandth.

mil′liard (mil′yərd, -yärd) *n. Brit.* one billion.

mil′li·gram′ (mil′i gram′) *n.* one thousandth of a gram.

mil′li·li·ter *n.* one thousandth of a liter.

mil′li·me·ter *n.* one thousandth of a meter.

mil′li·ner (mil′ə nər) *n.* a person who makes or sells women's hats. —**mil′li·ner′y,** *n.*

mil′lion (mil′yən) *n.* 1000 times 1000. —**mil′lionth,** *adj., n.*

mil′lion·aire′ (-yə nâr′) *n.* a person having a million dollars or more.

mill′race′ *n.* a channel for the current of water driving a mill wheel.

mill′stone′ *n.* **1.** a stone for grinding grain. **2.** a heavy mental or emotional burden.

mill′stream′ *n.* the stream in a millrace.

mime (mīm, mēm) *n.* **1.** expression by mute gestures; pantomime. **2.** an actor skilled in mime.

mim′e·o·graph′ (mim′ē ə graf′) *n.* **1.** a stencil device for duplicating. —*v.t.* **2.** to copy with a mimeograph.

mim′ic (-ik) *v.,* -icked, -icking, *n.* —*v.t.* **1.** to imitate the speech or actions of. —*n.* **2.** a person who mimics. —**mim′ic·ry,** *n.*

mi·mo′sa (mi mō′sə, -zə) *n.* a semitropical tree or shrub.

min′a·ret′ (min′ə ret′) *n.* a tower for calling Muslims to prayer.

mince (mins) *v.,* minced, mincing. —*v.t.* **1.** to chop fine. **2.** to moderate (words). —*v.i.* **3.** to speak or behave with affected elegance.

mince′meat′ *n.* a cooked mixture of chopped meat, raisins, spices, etc., used in pies.

mind (mīnd) *n.* **1.** the thinking part of a human or animal. **2.** intellectual power. **3.** opinion. **4.** inclination. **5.** memory. —*v.t.* **6.** to obey. **7.** to attend to or care for. **8.** to object to. —*v.i.* **9.** to obey. **10.** to attend. **11.** to object.

mind′ful *adj.* careful.

mind′less *adj.* **1.** heedless. **2.** requiring no intelligence.

mine¹ (mīn) *pron.* **1.** a possessive form of I. **2.** that or those belonging to me.

mine² (mīn) *n., v.,* mined, mining. —*n.* **1.** an excavation in the earth for resources. **2.** a stationary explosive device. **3.** an abundant source. —*v.t.* **4.** to extract from a mine. **5.** to dig in to extract resources. **6.** to place explosive mines in. —*v.i.* **7.** to work in a mine. —**min′er,** *n.*

min′er·al (min′ər əl) *n.* **1.** a natural inorganic substance. **2.** a substance obtained by mining. —*adj.* **3.** of minerals.

min′er·al·o·gy (-ə rol′ə jē, -ral′ə-) *n.* the science of minerals.

min′eral wa′ter *n.* water containing dissolved mineral salts or gases.

mine′sweep′er *n.* a ship used to remove explosive mines.

min′gle (ming′gəl) *v.i., v.t.,* -gled, -gling. to mix or blend.

min′i (min′ē) *n.* a small version.

mini- a prefix meaning small.

min′i·a·ture (-ə chər, min′ə-) *n.* **1.** a very small version or representation of something. **2.** a tiny painting. —*adj.* **3.** on a small scale. —**min′i·a·tur·ize′,** *v.t.*

min′i·com·put′er *n.* a computer with capabilities between those of a microcomputer and mainframe.

min′im (min′əm) *n.* the smallest unit of liquid measure.

min′i·mal·ism (min′ə mə liz′əm) *n.* a spare and simple style.

min′i·mize′ (-miz′) *v.t.,* -mized, -mizing. **1.** to reduce to the minimum. **2.** to represent as being of minimum value or importance.

min′i·mum (-məm) *n.* **1.** the least possible quantity, degree, etc. —*adj.* **2.** Also, **min′i·mal** (-məl). lowest.

min′ion (-yən) *n.* a servile follower.

min′is·ter (-ə stər) *n.* **1.** a person authorized to conduct worship. **2.** a government representative abroad. **3.** the head of a governmental department. —*v.i.* **4.** to give care. —**min′is·te′ri·al** (-stēr′ē-əl) *adj.* —**min′is·tra′tion,** *n.*

min′is·try (-ə strē) *n., pl.* -tries. **1.** a religious calling. **2.** the clergy. **3.** the office of a department of government. **4.** a body of executive officials. **5.** the act of ministering.

mink (mingk) *n.* a semiaquatic mammal or its soft brown fur.

Minn. Minnesota.

min′now (min′ō) *n.* a tiny fish.

mi′nor (mī′nər) *adj.* **1.** lesser in size or importance. **2.** under legal age. —*n.* **3.** a person under legal age.

mishap

mi·nor′i·ty (mi nôr′i tē, mī-) *n., pl.* **-ties. 1.** a number or part forming less than half of a whole. **2.** a group differing from the majority, as in race. **3.** the state or time of being under legal age.

min′strel (min′strəl) *n.* **1.** a medieval musician or singer. **2.** a white performer in blackface singing black American songs in a variety show.

mint¹ (mint) *n.* **1.** a place where money is coined. **2.** a huge sum. —*v.t.* **3.** to make coins.

mint² (mint) *n.* an aromatic herb.

min′u·et′ (min′yōō et′) *n.* a stately dance.

mi′nus (mī′nəs) *prep.* **1.** less. **2.** lacking. —*adj.* **3.** less than. **4.** involving subtraction.

mi′nus·cule′ (min′ə skyōōl′, minus′kyōōl) *adj.* tiny.

min′ute¹ (min′it) *n.* **1.** sixty seconds. **2. minutes,** a record of proceedings.

mi′nute² (mī nōōt′, -nyōōt′) *adj.* extremely small. —**mi·nute′ly,** *adv.*

mi·nu′ti·ae′ (mi nōō′shē ē′) *n.pl.* trifling matters.

mir′a·cle (mir′ə kəl) *n.* a supernatural act or effect. —**mi·rac′u·lous** (mi rak′yə ləs) *adj.*

mi·rage′ (mi räzh′) *n.* an atmospheric illusion in which images of far-distant objects are seen.

mire (mīªr) *n., v.,* **mired, miring.** —*n.* **1.** a swamp. **2.** deep mud. —*v.i., v.t.* **3.** to sink or stick in or as if in mire.

mir′ror (mir′ər) *n.* **1.** a reflecting surface. —*v.t.* **2.** to reflect.

mirth (mûrth) *n.* gaiety and laughter. —**mirth′less,** *adj.*

mis- a prefix meaning: **1.** wrong. **2.** lack of.

mis′ad·ven′ture (mis′əd ven′chər) *n.* a misfortune; mishap.

mis′an·thrope′ (-ən thrōp′, miz′-) *n.* a hater of humanity. —**mis′an·throp′ic** (-throp′ik) *adj.*

mis′ap·ply′ *v.t.,* **-plied, -plying.** to use wrongly.

mis′ap·pre·hend′ *v.t.* to misunderstand. —**mis′ap·pre·hen′sion** (-hen′shən) *n.*

mis′ap·pro′pri·ate′ (-āt′) *v.t.,* **-ated, -ating.** to use wrongly as one's own.

mis′be·got′ten *adj.* ill-conceived.

mis′be·have′ *v.i.,* **-haved, -having.** to behave badly. —**mis′be·hav′ior,** *n.*

misc. miscellaneous.

mis·cal′cu·late′ *v.t.,* **-lated, -lating.** to judge badly.

mis·call′ *v.t.* to call by a wrong name.

mis·car′ry (mis kar′ē; *for 1 also* mis′kar′ē) *v.i.,* **-ried, -rying. 1.** to give birth to a fetus before it is viable. **2.** to be unsuccessful. —**mis·car′riage,** *n.*

mis·cast′ *v.t.* to cast in an unsuitable role.

mis·cel·la′ne·ous (mis′ə lā′nē əs) *adj.* unclassified; various.

mis·cel·la′ny (mis′ə lā′nē) *n., pl.* **-nies.** a collection of various items, esp. literary works.

mis·chance′ *n.* bad luck.

mis′chief (mis′chif) *n.* **1.** harm, trouble, or injury, caused willfully. **2.** annoying conduct or activity. —**mis′chie·vous** (mis′chə vəs) *adj.* —**Pronunciation.** The word MISCHIEVOUS is pronounced with three syllables. The pronunciation (mis chē′vē əs) with four syllables, is usually considered nonstandard. Note that although a spelling *mischievious,* which reflects this nonstandard pronunciation by including an extra *i* after the *v,* was occasionally seen between the 16th and 19th centuries, it is not considered a correct spelling today.

mis·con·ceive′ *v.t.,* **-ceived, -ceiving.** to misunderstand. —**mis′con·cep′tion,** *n.*

mis·con′duct *n.* improper or illegal conduct.

mis′con·strue′ (-kən strōō′) *v.t.,* **-strued, -struing.** to misinterpret.

mis′cre·ant (-krē ənt) *n.* a villain.

mis·deed′ *n.* an immoral deed.

mis′de·mean′or *n.* a minor offense.

mise-en-scène′ (mē zän sen′) *n., pl.* **mise-en-scènes** (-senz′). **1.** the placement of actors, scenery, and properties on stage. **2.** surroundings.

mi′ser (mī′zər) *n.* a hoarder of wealth. —**mi′ser·ly,** *adj.*

mis′er·a·ble (miz′ər ə bəl) *adj.* **1.** very unhappy. **2.** causing misery. **3.** contemptible; despicable.

mis′er·y *n., pl.* **-eries.** suffering or emotional distress.

mis·fire′ (-fiªr′) *v.t.,* **-fired, -firing.** to fail to fire.

mis·fit′ *n.* **1.** (mis fit′, mis′fit′) a poor fit. **2.** (mis′fit′) a maladjusted person.

mis·for′tune *n.* bad luck.

mis·giv′ing *n.* a doubt.

mis·guid′ed *adj.* mistaken; ill-informed.

mis·han′dle *v.t.,* **-dled, -dling. 1.** to handle roughly. **2.** to manage badly.

mis′hap (mis′hap, mis hap′) *n.* an unlucky accident.

mishmash

mish′mash′ (mish′mäsh′, -mash′) *n.* a jumble; hodgepodge.

mis′in·form′ *v.t.* to give false information to. —**mis′in·for·ma′tion,** *n.*

mis·in·ter·pret *v.t.* to interpret wrongly.

mis·judge′ *v.t.,* -judged, -judging. to judge wrongly.

mis·lay′ *v.t.,* -laid, -laying. **1.** to lay or place wrongly. **2.** to misplace.

mis·lead′ (-lēd′) *v.t.,* -led, -leading. **1.** to lead in the wrong direction. **2.** to lead into error, as in conduct.

mis·man′age *v.t.,* -aged, -aging. to manage badly.

mis·match′ *v.t.* **1.** (mis mach′) to match unsuitably. —*n.* (mis mach′, mis′mach′) **2.** an unsuitable match.

mis·no′mer (-nō′mər) *n.* a name applied wrongly.

mi·sog′a·my (mi sog′ə mē, mī-) *n.* hatred of marriage. —**mi·sog′a·mist,** *n.*

mi·sog′y·ny (mi soj′ə nē, mī-) *n.* hatred of women. —**mi·sog′y·nist,** *n.*

mis·place′ *v.t.,* -placed, -placing. **1.** to lose temporarily. **2.** to place unwisely.

mis′print′ (mis′print′, mis print′) *n.* an error in printing.

mis′pro·nounce′ *v.t.,* -nounced, -nouncing. to pronounce wrongly.

mis·quote′ *v.t.,* -quoted, -quoting. to quote incorrectly.

mis·read′ (-rēd′) *v.t.,* -read (red′) -reading. **1.** to read wrongly. **2.** to misinterpret.

mis′rep·re·sent′ *v.t.* to represent incorrectly or falsely.

mis·rule′ *n., v.,* -ruled, -ruling. —*n.* **1.** bad or unwise rule. —*v.t.* **2.** to rule badly.

miss¹ (mis) *v.t.* **1.** to fail to hit, do, meet, catch, etc. **2.** to regret the absence of. **3.** to escape or avoid. —*v.i.* **4.** to fail to hit something. **5.** to fail. —*n.* **6.** a failure, esp. a failure to hit something.

miss² (mis) *n.* **1. Miss,** a title of respect for an unmarried woman. **2.** a girl.

Miss. Mississippi.

mis′sal (-əl) *n.* a book of prayers and rites for celebrating Mass.

mis·shap′en *adj.* deformed.

mis′sile (-əl; *esp.* Brit. -īl) *n.* an object thrown or shot.

mis′sion (mish′ən) *n.* **1.** a group sent abroad for specific work. **2.** a duty. **3.** an air operation against an enemy. **4.** a missionary post.

mis′sion·ar′y (-ə ner′ē) *n., pl.* -aries, *adj.* —*n.* **1.** a person sent to propagate religious faith. —*adj.* **2.** of religious missions.

mis′sive (mis′iv) *n.* a letter.

mis·spell′ *v.t.* to spell wrongly.

mis·spend′ *v.t.,* -spent, -spending. to squander.

mis·state′ *v.t.,* -stated, -stating. to state wrongly.

mis·step′ *n.* an error.

mist (mist) *n.* a light, thin fog. —**mist′y,** *adj.*

mis·take′ (mi stāk′) *n., v.,* -took, -taken, -taking. —*n.* **1.** an error in judgment, action, or belief. —*v.t.* **2.** to identify, understand, interpret, or regard wrongly.

mis·tak′en *adj.* wrong; incorrect; in error. —**mis·tak′en·ly,** *adv.*

Mis′ter (-tər) *n.* a title of address for a man. *Abbr.:* **Mr.**

mis′tle·toe′ (-əl tō′) *n.* a parasitic plant with waxy white berries.

mis·treat′ *v.t.* to treat badly. —**mis·treat′ment,** *n.*

mis′tress (-tris) *n.* **1.** a female in control. **2.** a woman who has a sexual relationship with a married man.

mis·tri′al *n.* a trial ended without a verdict.

mis·trust′ *n.* **1.** a lack of trust. —*v.t.* **2.** to regard with mistrust.

mis′un·der·stand′ *v.t., v.i.,* -stood, -standing. to understand wrongly. —**mis′un·der·stand′ing,** *n.*

mis·use′ *n., v.,* -used, -using. —*n.* (-yōōs′) **1.** improper use. —*v.t.* (-yōōz′) **2.** to use badly or wrongly. **3.** to abuse.

mite (mīt) *n.* **1.** a tiny parasitic insect. **2.** a small thing or bit.

mi′ter (mī′tər) *n.* **1.** a headdress worn by a bishop. **2.** a joint formed by pieces of wood that fit together at an angle. —*v.t.* **3.** to join with a miter. Also, Brit., **mi′tre.**

mit′i·gate′ (mit′i gāt′) *v.t.,* -gated, -gating. to make less severe.

mi·to′sis (mī tō′sis) *n.* a method of cell division.

mitt (mit) *n.* a thick glove.

mit′ten (mit′n) *n.* a fingerless glove.

mix (miks) *v.t.* **1.** to put together; combine. —*v.i.* **2.** to associate. **3. mix up,** to confuse. —*n.* **4.** a mixture.

mixed′ num′ber *n.* a number consisting of a whole number and a fraction or decimal.

mix′ture (-chər) *n.* an act or product of mixing.

mix′-up′ *n.* a state of confusion.

ml milliliter.

mm millimeter.

MN Minnesota.

mne·mon′ic (ni mon′ik) *adj.* **1.** aiding memory. —*n.* **2.** a mnemonic device.

MO 1. Also, **Mo.** Missouri. **2.** modus operandi.

moan (mōn) *n.* **1.** a low groan. —*v.i.* **2.** to utter moans.

moat (mōt) *n.* a deep, water-filled ditch around a castle.

mob (mob) *n., v.,* **mobbed, mobbing.** —*n.* **1.** a crowd, esp. a disorderly one. —*v.t.* **2.** to crowd or crowd around.

mo'bile *adj.* (mō'bəl, -bēl) **1.** capable of moving or being moved. —*n.* (-bēl) **2.** a suspended artwork with parts that move in the breeze. —**mo·bil'i·ty,** *n.*

mo'bi·lize' (mō'bə līz') *v.t., v.i.* **-lized, -lizing.** to make or become ready, as for war.

mob'ster (mob'stər) *n.* a member of a criminal mob.

moc'ca·sin (mok'ə sin, -zən) *n.* **1.** a soft shoe. **2.** a poisonous snake.

mo'cha (mō'kə) *n.* **1.** a kind of coffee. **2.** a flavoring made from coffee and chocolate.

mock (mok) *v.t.* **1.** to mimic or ridicule. —*adj.* **2.** imitation. —**mock'er·y**

mock'ing·bird' *n.* a songbird that imitates other birds.

mock'-up' *n.* a model.

mode[1] (mōd) *n.* **1.** a method. **2.** a particular type or form.

mode[2] (mōd) *n.* fashion or style.

mod'el (mod'l) *n., adj., v.,* **-eled, -eling.** —*n.* **1.** a standard for imitation. **2.** a small-scale copy. **3.** a person paid to wear and display clothing. **4.** a person who poses for an artist. —*adj.* **5.** serving as a model. —*v.t.* **6.** to pattern after a model. **7.** to wear as a model. **8.** to form. —*v.i.* **9.** to work as a model.

mo'dem (mō'dəm, -dem) *n.* a device enabling transfer of data between computers via telephone lines.

mod'er·ate *adj., n., v.,* **-ated, -ating.** —*adj.* (mod'ər it) **1.** not extreme or excessive. —*n.* (-ər it) **2.** a person having moderate views. —*v.t., v.i.* **3.** to make or become moderate. **4.** to preside over or act as a moderator.

mod'er·a'tor *n.* the director of a group discussion.

mod'ern (-ərn) *adj.* of present and recent time. —**mo·der'ni·ty** (-dûr'ni tē) *n.* —**mod'ern·ize',** *v.t., v.i.*

mod'ern·ism *n.* **1.** modern character or tendencies. **2.** a modern usage.

mod'est (mod'ist) *adj.* **1.** humble in estimating oneself. **2.** simple; moderate. **3.** decent; moral. —**mod'est·ly,** *adv.* —**mod'es·ty,** *n.*

mod'i·cum (-i kəm) *n.* a small amount.

mod'i·fy (-ə fī') *v.t.,* **-fied, -fying.** to alter or moderate. —**mod'i·fi·ca'tion,** *n.* —**mod'i·fi'er,** *n.*

mod'ish (mō'dish) *adj.* fashionable.

mod'u·late' (moj'ə lāt') *v.t.,* **-lated, -lating. 1.** to adjust to a proper measure or proportion. **2.** to vary the amplitude, frequency, or intensity of. —**mod'u·la'tion,** *n.*

mod'ule (-ōol) *n.* **1.** a building unit. **2.** a self-contained segment of a spacecraft. —**mod'u·lar,** *adj.*

mo'dus op'e·ran'di (mō'dəs op'ə ran'dē, -dī) *n., pl.* **mo'di op'e·ran'di** (mō'dē, -dī). a method of operating.

mo'gul (mō'gəl) *n.* a powerful or influential person.

mo'hair' (mō'hâr') *n.* a fabric from the fleece of the Angora goat.

moi·ré' (mwä rā', mô-) *n., pl.* **-rés.** a fabric, as silk, with a watery appearance.

moist (moist) *adj.* damp. —**mois'ten** (moi'sən) *v.t., v.i.*

mois'ture (-chər) *n.* dampness; small beads of water.

mois'tur·ize' *v.t.,* **-ized, -izing.** to add moisture to. —**mois'tur·iz'er,** *n.*

mo'lar (mō'lər) *n.* a broad back tooth.

mo·las'ses (mə las'iz) *n.* a thick syrup produced in refining sugar.

mold[1] (mōld) *n.* **1.** a form for shaping molten or plastic material. **2.** something formed in a mold. **3.** distinctive character or type. —*v.t.* **4.** to form or shape.

mold[2] (mōld) *n.* **1.** a fungus growth on vegetable or animal matter. —*v.i.* **2.** to become covered with mold. —**mold'y,** *adj.*

mold'er *v.i.* to decay.

mold'ing *n.* a decorative strip of contoured material.

mole[1] (mōl) *n.* **1.** a burrowing mammal with fur. **2.** a spy who works from within an enemy intelligence agency.

mole[2] (mōl) *n.* a dark-colored spot on the skin.

mol'e·cule' (mol'ə kyōol') *n.* the smallest physical unit of a chemical element or compound. —**mo·lec'u·lar** (mə lek'yə lər) *adj.*

mole'hill' *n.* **1.** a small mound of earth raised by moles. **2.** something small and insignificant.

mole'skin' *n.* **1.** the fur of a mole. **2.** a heavy cotton fabric.

mo·lest' (mə lest') *v.t.* **1.** to annoy or bother. **2.** to make indecent sexual advances to. —**mo·lest'er,** *n.*

mol′li•fy′ (mol′ə fī′) *v.t.*, **-fied, -fy-ing.** to appease in temper.

mol′lusk (mol′əsk) *n.* a hard-shelled invertebrate animal.

mol′ly•cod′dle (mol′ē kod′l) *v.t.*, **-dled, -dling.** to pamper.

molt (mōlt) *v.i.* to shed skin or feathers.

mol′ten (mōl′tən) *adj.* melted.

mom (mom) *n. Informal.* mother.

mo′ment (mō′mənt) *n.* **1.** a very short space of time. **2.** importance.

mo′men•tar′y (-mən ter′ē) *adj.* very brief. **—mo′men•tar′i•ly,** *adv.*

mo•men′tous (-men′təs) *adj.* important.

mo•men′tum (-təm) *n., pl.* **-ta** (-tə) **-tums.** force or speed of movement.

mom′my (mom′ē) *n., pl.* **-mies.** *Informal.* mother.

Mon. Monday.

mon′arch (mon′ərk, -ärk) *n.* a hereditary sovereign.

mon′ar•chism *n.* advocacy of monarchy. **—mon′ar•chist,** *n., adj.*

mon′ar•chy *n., pl.* **-chies. 1.** government by a monarch. **2.** a country governed by a monarch.

mon′as•ter′y (mon′ə ster′ē) *n., pl.* **-teries.** a residence of monks.

mo•nas′tic (mə nas′tik) *adj.* of or characteristic of monks or nuns. **—mo•nas′ti•cism,** *n.*

Mon′day (mun′dā, -dē) *n.* the second day of the week.

mon′e•tar′y (mon′i ter′ē, mun′-) *adj.* of money.

mon′ey (mun′ē) *n., pl.* **moneys, monies. 1.** pieces of metal or certificates used to buy and sell. **2.** wealth.

mon′gol•ism (mong′gə liz′əm, mon′-) *n.* a former term for Down syndrome.

mon′goose (mong′gōōs′, mon′-) *n., pl.* **-gooses.** a carnivorous animal of Asia.

mon′grel (mung′grəl, mong′-) *n.* **1.** an animal or plant resulting from the crossing of different breeds. **—adj. 2.** of mixed breeds.

mon′i•tor (mon′i tər) *n.* **1.** a pupil who assists a teacher. **2.** a television or computer screen. **—v.t. 3.** to check or watch continuously.

monk (mungk) *n.* a male member of a religious order.

mon′key (mung′kē) *n.* **1.** a mammal strongly resembling a human being. **—v.i. 2.** to trifle idly; fool.

mon′key busi′ness *n.* mischievous behavior.

mon′key wrench′ *n.* a wrench with an adjustable jaw.

mono- a prefix meaning one.

mon′o•chrome (mon′ə krōm′) *adj.* of one color.

mon′o•cle (-kəl) *n.* an eyeglass for one eye.

mon′o•cot′y•le′don (-kot′l ēd′n) *n.* a plant having an embryo containing a single seed leaf.

mo•noc′u•lar (mə nok′yə lər) *adj.* **1.** having one eye. **2.** for the use of only one eye.

mo•nog′a•my (mə nog′ə mē) *n.* the practice of having one spouse at a time. **—mo•nog′a•mous,** *adj.* **—mo•nog′a•mist,** *n.*

mon′o•gram′ (mon′ə gram′) *n.* a design made of one's initials.

mon′o•graph′ (-graf′) *n.* a treatise on one subject.

mon′o•lith (-lith) *n.* a structure of a single block of stone. **—mon′o•lith′ic,** *adj.*

mon′o•logue′ (-lôg′) *n.* a talk by a single speaker. Also, **mon′o•log′.**

mon′o•ma′ni•a *n.* an obsessive zeal for or interest in a single thing. **—mon′o•ma′ni•ac,** *n.*

mon′o•nu′cle•o′sis (-nōō′klē ō′sis, -nyōō′-) *n.* a disease marked by fever, swelling of lymph nodes, etc.

mon′o•plane′ *n.* an airplane with one wing on each side.

mo•nop′o•ly (mə nop′ə lē) *n., pl.* **-lies. 1.** exclusive control. **2.** a company having exclusive control over a commodity or service. **3.** a commodity or service so controlled. **—mo•nop′o•lize′,** *v.t.*

mon′o•rail′ (mon′ə rāl′) *n.* **1.** a single rail serving as a track for wheeled vehicles. **2.** a car or train moving on such a rail.

mon′o•so′di•um glu′ta•mate′ (-sō′dē əm glōō′tə māt′) *n.* a white crystalline powder used to intensify the flavor of foods.

mon′o•syl′la•ble *n.* a word of one syllable. **—mon′o•syl•lab′ic,** *adj.*

mon′o•the•ism *n.* a doctrine or belief that there is only one God.

mon′o•tone′ *n.* a single tone of unvarying pitch.

mo•not′o•ny (mə not′n ē) *n.* wearisome uniformity. **—mo•not′o•nous,** *adj.*

mon•sieur′ (mə syœ′) *n., pl.* **mes•sieurs′** (me syœ′). a French term of address for a man.

mon•si′gnor (mon sē′nyər, mon′sē-nyôr′, môn′-) *n., pl.* **-gnors, -gnori** (môn′sē nyôr′ē). a title of certain Roman Catholic priests.

mon•soon′ (mon sōōn′) *n.* a seasonal wind of S Asia.

mon′ster (-stər) *n.* **1.** an animal or plant of abnormal form. **2.** a wicked creature. **3.** anything huge.

—mon•stros′i•ty (-stros′i tə), n.
—mon′strous, adj.

Mont. Montana.

mon•tage′ (mon täzh′; Fr. môN-
tAzh′) n. a blending of elements
from several pictures into one.

month (munth) n. any of twelve
parts of a calendar year.

month′ly adj., n., pl. **-lies,** adv.
—adj. **1.** occurring, appearing, etc.,
once a month. **2.** lasting for a
month. —n. **3.** a periodical published once a month. —adv. **4.**
once a month. **5.** by the month.

mon′u•ment (mon′yə mənt) n. a
memorial structure.

mon′u•men′tal (-men′tl) adj. **1.**
very great; significant. **2.** serving as
a monument.

moo (mōō) n. **1.** the sound a cow
makes. —v.t. **2.** to utter such a
sound.

mooch (mōōch) Slang. —v.i. **1.** to
borrow without intending to pay
back. —n. **2.** Also, **mooch′er.** a
person who mooches.

mood (mōōd) n. a frame of mind.

mood′y adj., **-ier, -iest.** given to
bad moods. —**mood′i•ly,** adv.

moon (mōōn) n. **1.** the earth's natural satellite. **2.** the natural satellite of any planet. —v.i. **3.** to behave dreamily.

moon′light′ n. **1.** light from the
moon. —v.i. **2.** to work at a second
job after the principal one.

moon′shine′ n. illegally made liquor. —**moon′shin′er,** n.

moon′stone′ n. a pearly gem.

moor[1] (mōōr) n. a tract of open
peaty wasteland.

moor[2] (mōōr) v.t., v.i. to secure or
be secured in place, as a ship.

moor′ing n. **1.** moorings, cables,
anchors, etc., by which a ship is
moored. **2.** a place where a ship is
moored.

moose (mōōs) n., pl. **moose.** a large
animal of the deer family.

moot (mōōt) adj. **1.** open to discussion or debate. **2.** of little practical
value.

mop (mop) n., v., **mopped, mop-
ping.** —n. **1.** a piece of cloth,
sponge, etc., fastened to a stick, for
washing or dusting. —v.t. **2.** to
clean with a mop.

mope (mōp) v.i., **moped, moping.**
to be in low spirits.

mo′ped′ (mō′ped′) n. a motorized
bicycle.

mop′pet (mop′it) n. a child.

mor′al (môr′əl) adj. **1.** of or concerned with right conduct. **2.** virtuous. —n. **3.** morals, principles of
conduct. **4.** a moral lesson.

—**mor′al•ist,** n. —**mor′al•is′tic,** adj.
—**mor′al•ly,** adv.

mo•rale′ (mə ral′) n. spirits; mood.

mo•ral′i•ty (-ral′i tē, mô-) n. **1.** conformity to rules of right conduct.
2. moral quality.

mor′al•ize′ (môr′ə līz′) v.i., **-ized,
-izing.** to think or pronounce on
moral questions.

mo•rass′ (mə ras′) n. a swamp.

mor′a•to′ri•um (môr′ə tôr′ē əm) n.,
pl. **-toria** (tôr′ē ə), **-toriums. 1.** legal permission to delay payment of
debts. **2.** any temporary cessation.

mo′ray (môr′ā, mô rā′) n. a tropical eel.

mor′bid (môr′bid) adj. **1.** unwhole-
somely gloomy. **2.** of disease.
—**mor•bid′i•ty,** n.

mor′dant (môr′dnt) adj. **1.** sarcastic; biting. **2.** burning; corrosive.

more (môr) adj. **1.** in greater
amount or degree. **2.** additional.
—n. **3.** an additional or greater
quantity or degree. —adv. **4.** in or
to a greater extent or degree. **5.** in
addition.

mo•rel′ (mə rel′) n. a kind of edible mushroom.

more•o•ver adv. in addition to
what has been said; besides.

mo′res (môr′āz, -ēz) n.pl. the social
and moral customs of a group.

morgue (môrg) n. a place where
corpses are taken for identification.

mor′i•bund′ (môr′ə bund′) adj. dying.

morn (môrn) n. morning.

morn′ing n. **1.** the first part of the
day. —adj. **2.** done or occurring in
the morning.

morn′ing-glo′ry n., pl. **morning-
glories.** a vine with funnel-shaped
flowers.

morn′ing sick′ness n. nausea occurring esp. in the morning during
the first months of pregnancy.

mo•roc′co (mə rok′ō) n. a fine
leather.

mo′ron (môr′on) n. a stupid person. —**mo•ron′ic** (mə ron′ik) adj.

mo•rose′ (mə rōs′) adj. gloomily
ill-humored. —**mo•rose′ly,** adv.

mor′pheme (-fēm) n. a minimal
grammatical unit.

mor′phine (-fēn) n. a narcotic
found in opium.

morph′ing (-fing) n. the smooth
transformation of one image into
another by computer.

mor•phol′o•gy (-fol′ə jē) n. **1.** the
study of the form and structure of
organisms. **2.** the study of word
formation.

Morse′ code′ (môrs) n. a telegraphic code of long and short signals.

morsel

mor′sel (môr′səl) *n.* a small amount.

mor′tal (-ytl) *adj.* **1.** liable to death. **2.** causing death. **3.** extreme. —*n.* **4.** a human being.

mor·tal′i·ty (-tal′i tē) *n., pl.* **-ties. 1.** mortal nature. **2.** the relative death rate.

mor′tar (-tər) *n.* **1.** a bowl in which drugs, foods, etc., are pulverized. **2.** a short cannon. **3.** material used to bind masonry.

mor′tar·board′ *n.* an academic cap with a square, flat top and tassel.

mort′gage (-gij) *n., v.,* **-gaged, -gaging.** —*n.* **1.** a conditional transfer of property as security for debt. —*v.t.* **2.** to put a mortgage on.

mor·ti′cian (-tish′ən) *n.* an undertaker.

mor′ti·fy′ (-tə fī′) *v.t.,* **-fied, -fying. 1.** to humiliate. **2.** to subdue (the body) by abstinence or pain.

mor′tise (-tis) *n.* a slot in wood for a tenon.

mor′tu·ar′y (-chōō er′ē) *n., pl.* **-aries.** a place where bodies are prepared for burial.

mo·sa′ic (mō zā′ik) *n.* a design made of small colored pieces of stone.

Mos′lem (moz′ləm, mos′-) *n., adj.* Muslim.

mosque (mosk) *n.* a Muslim place of prayer.

mos·qui′to (mə skē′tō) *n., pl.* **-toes, -tos.** a common biting insect.

moss (môs) *n.* a small, leafy-stemmed plant growing on rocks, moist ground, etc.

most (mōst) *adj.* **1.** the greatest, as in number. **2.** the majority of. —*n.* **3.** the greatest amount or degree. —*adv.* **4.** to the greatest extent or degree.

most′ly *adv.* **1.** in most cases. **2.** in greater part.

mote (mōt) *n.* a small particle.

mo·tel′ (mō tel′) *n.* a roadside hotel for automobile travelers.

moth (môth) *n.* an insect, some of whose larvae eat cloth.

moth′ball′ *n.* a ball of camphor, naphthalene, etc., for repelling moths.

moth′er (muth′ər) *n.* **1.** a female parent. **2.** the head of a group of nuns. **3.** a source. —*adj.* **4.** of, like, or being a mother. —*v.t.* **5.** to act as or like a mother to. —**moth′er·hood′,** *n.* —**moth′er·ly,** *adj.*

moth′er-in-law′ *n., pl.* **mothers-in-law.** the mother of one's spouse.

moth′er·land′ *n.* **1.** one's native land. **2.** the land of one's ancestors.

moth′er-of-pearl′ *n.* the inner layer of certain shells.

mo·tif′ (mō tēf′) *n.* a recurring subject or theme.

mo′tile (mōt′l, mō′til) *adj.* capable of moving spontaneously. —**mo·til′i·ty,** *n.*

mo′tion (mō′shən) *n.* **1.** the action or process of moving. **2.** a gesture. **3.** a formal proposal made in a meeting. —*v.t., v.i.* **4.** to direct by or make a motion.

mo′tion pic′ture *n.* **1.** a series of images projected so rapidly that things seem to move. **2.** a story in this form.

mo′ti·vate′ (mō′tə vāt′) *v.t.,* **-vated, -vating.** to give a motive to. —**mo′ti·va′tion,** *n.*

mo′tive (-tiv) *n.* a purpose; incentive.

mot′ley (mot′lē) *adj.* widely, often grotesquely, varied.

mo′tor (mō′tər) *n.* **1.** a small, powerful engine. —*adj.* **2.** of or causing motion. **3.** of or operated by a motor. **4.** of or for motor vehicles. —*v.i.* **5.** to travel by automobile. —**mo′tor·ist,** *n.*

mo′tor·boat′ *n.* a boat run by a motor.

mo′tor·cade′ (-kād′) *n.* a procession of automobiles.

mo′tor·cy′cle *n.* a heavy motor-driven bicycle. —**mo′tor·cy′clist,** *n.*

mo′tor·ize′ *v.t.,* **-ized, -izing.** to furnish with motors.

mot′tle (mot′l) *v.t.,* **-tled, -tling.** to mark with spots or blotches.

mot′to (mot′ō) *n., pl.* **-toes, -tos.** a phrase expressing one's guiding principle.

moue (mōō) *n., pl.* **moues** (mōō). a pouting grimace.

mould (mōld) *n., v.i.* Brit. mold.

mound (mound) *n.* a heap, as of earth; hill.

mount (mount) *v.t.* **1.** to go up; get up on. **2.** to organize and launch. **3.** to prepare for display. **4.** to fix in a setting. —*v.i.* **5.** to increase. **6.** to ascend or get up on something. —*n.* **7.** the act or manner of mounting. **8.** a horse for riding. **9.** a support, setting, etc. **10.** a mountain.

moun′tain (moun′tn) *n.* a lofty natural elevation on the earth's surface. —**moun′tain·ous,** *adj.*

moun′tain bike′ *n.* a sturdy bicycle designed for off-road use.

moun′tain·eer′ *n.* a mountain climber. —**moun′tain·eer′ing,** *n.*

moun′tain li′on *n.* a cougar.

moun′te·bank′ (moun′tə bangk′) *n.* a charlatan.

mourn (môrn) v.i., v.t. to grieve (for); feel or express sorrow (for). —**mourn′er,** n. —**mourn′ful,** adj.
mouse (mous) n., pl. **mice** (mīs) v., **moused, mousing.** —n. 1. a small rodent. 2. a palm-sized device used to select items on a computer screen. —v.i. 3. to hunt for mice.
mous•tache′ (mus′tash, mə stash′) n. a mustache.
mous′y (mou′sē, -zē) adj., -ier, -iest. 1. drab. 2. meek.
mouth n., pl. **mouths,** v. —n. (mouth) 1. an opening through which an animal eats. 2. any opening. —v.t. (mouth) 3. to utter pompously or dishonestly. 4. to form silently with the mouth. —**mouth′ful′,** n.
mouth′ or′gan n. a harmonica.
mouth′piece′ n. 1. a piece held in or to the mouth. 2. a spokesperson.
mouth′wash′ n. a solution for cleaning the mouth.
mouth′-wa′ter•ing adj. appetizing.
move (mōōv) v., **moved, moving,** n. —v.i. 1. to change place or position. 2. to change one's abode. 3. to advance. 4. to make a formal proposal in a meeting. —v.t. 5. to cause to change place or position. 6. to affect emotionally. —n. 7. the act of moving. 8. a purposeful action. —**Idiom.** 9. **on the move, a.** active. **b.** going from place to place. **c.** advancing.
move′ment n. 1. the act or process of moving. 2. a trend in thought. 3. the works of a mechanism. 4. a main division of a piece of music.
mov•ie (mōō′vē) n. 1. a motion picture. 2. **movies, a.** the motion-picture industry. **b.** the showing of a motion picture.
mow (mō) v.t., **mowed, mowed** or **mown, mowing.** to cut down (grass, grain, etc.). —**mow′er,** n.
moz′za•rel′la (mot′sə rel′ə, mōt′-) n. a mild, white, semisoft cheese.
MP 1. a member of Parliament. 2. Military Police.
mph miles per hour.
Mr. (mis′tər) pl. **Messrs.** (mes′ərz). Mister; a title of address for a man.
MRI magnetic resonance imaging: a process of producing images of the body using a magnetic field and radio waves.
Mrs. (mis′iz, miz′iz) pl. **Mmes.** (mā-däm′, -dam′). a title of address for a married woman.
MS 1. Also, **ms, ms.** manuscript. 2. Mississippi. 3. multiple sclerosis.
Ms. (miz) a title of address for a married or unmarried woman.
M.S. Master of Science.

MSG monosodium glutamate.
MT Montana.
much (much) adj. 1. great in quantity or degree. —n. 2. a great quantity. 3. a great or notable thing. —adv. 4. to a great extent or degree. 5. generally.
mu′ci•lage (myōō′sə lij) n. a gummy adhesive.
muck (muk) n. 1. dirt or mud. 2. moist barn refuse. —**muck′y,** adj.
muck′rake′ v.i., -raked, -raking. to expose scandal. —**muck′rak•er,** n.
mu′cous (myōō′kəs) adj. 1. secreting mucus. 2. of or like mucus.
mu′cous mem′brane n. a membrane lining all body passages open to the air.
mu′cus (-kəs) n. the sticky secretion of a mucous membrane.
mud (mud) n. 1. wet soft earth. 2. malicious statements. —**mud′dy,** adj., v.t.
mud′dle (mud′l) v., -dled, -dling, n. —v.t. 1. to mix up; confuse. 2. to act in a confused way. —n. 3. a state of confusion.
mud′dle•head′ed adj. confused in one's thinking.
mud′sling′ing n. efforts to discredit an opponent by malicious remarks.
mu•ez′zin (myōō ez′in, mōō-) n. a crier who summons Muslims to prayer.
muff (muf) n. 1. a tubular covering for the hands. —v.t., v.i. 2. to handle or act clumsily.
muf′fin (muf′in) n. a small round bread.
muf′fle (muf′əl) v.t., -fled, -fling. 1. to wrap in a scarf, cloak, etc. 2. to deaden (sound).
muf′fler n. 1. a heavy neck scarf. 2. a device for deadening sound.
muf′ti (muf′tē) n. civilian dress.
mug (mug) n., v., **mugged, mugging.** —n. 1. a cup with a handle. 2. Slang. the face. —v.t. 3. to assault, usually with intent to rob. —**mug′ger,** n.
mug′gy adj., -gier, -giest. hot and humid.
mug′ shot′ n. a photograph of the face of a criminal suspect.
mu•lat′to (mə lat′ō, -lä′tō) n., pl. -toes. a person with mixed black and white ancestry.
mul′ber′ry (mul′ber′ē, -bə rē) n., pl. -ries. a tree bearing a dark-purple, berrylike fruit.
mulch (mulch) n. 1. a loose covering of leaves, straw, etc., on plants. —v.t. 2. to surround with mulch.
mulct (mulkt) v.t. 1. to deprive of by trickery. 2. to fine.

mule (myōōl) *n.* the offspring of a donkey and a mare.

mul′ish (myōō′lish) *adj.* stubborn.

mull (mul) *v.t.* to think about carefully.

mul′let (mul′it) *n.* a common food fish.

mul′lion (mul′yən) *n.* a vertical member separating the lights of a window.

multi- a prefix meaning many.

mul′ti·cul′tur·al·ism (mul′tē kul′-chər ə liz′əm, mul′tī-) *n.* the recognition of different cultural identities within a unified society.

mul′ti·far′i·ous (mul′tə fâr′ē əs) *adj.* many and varied.

mul′ti·me′di·a (mul′tē-, mul′tī-) *n.* the combined use of several media or mass media.

mul′ti·na′tion·al *n.* **1.** a corporation with operations in many countries. —*adj.* **2.** of several nations or multinationals.

mul′ti·ple (mul′tə pəl) *adj.* **1.** consisting of or involving many. —*n.* **2.** a number evenly divisible by a stated other number.

mul′tiple sclero′sis *n.* a disease leading to neural and muscular impairments.

mul′ti·plic′i·ty (-plis′i tē) *n., pl.* **-ties.** a great number or variety.

mul′ti·ply′ (mul′tə plī′) *v.t., v.i.,* **-plied, -plying. 1.** to increase in number or quantity. **2.** to add (a number) to itself a stated number of times. —**mul′ti·pli′er,** *n.* —**mul′ti·pli·ca′tion,** *n.*

mul′ti·tude′ (mul′ti tōōd′, -tyōōd′) *n.* a great number.

mul′ti·tu′di·nous *adj.* **1.** numerous. **2.** having many parts.

mum (mum) *adj.* silent.

mum′ble (mum′bəl) *v.,* **-bled, -bling,** *n.* —*v.t., v.i.* **1.** to speak quietly and unintelligibly. —*n.* **2.** a mumbling sound.

mum′mer (mum′ər) *n.* **1.** a person in a festive disguise. **2.** an actor.

mum′my (mum′ē) *n., pl.* **-mies.** a dead body preserved by the ancient Egyptians.

mumps (mumps) *n.* a disease marked by swelling of the salivary glands.

munch (munch) *v.i., v.t.* to chew steadily or vigorously.

mun·dane′ (mun dān′, mun′dān) *adj.* commonplace.

mu·nic′i·pal (myōō nis′ə pəl) *adj.* of a city.

mu·nic′i·pal′i·ty (-pal′i tē) *n., pl.* **-ties.** a self-governing city.

mu·nif′i·cent (-nif′ə sənt) *adj.* extremely generous. —**mu·nif′i·cence,** *n.* —**mu·nif′i·cent·ly,** *adv.*

mu·ni′tions (-nish′ənz) *n.pl.* weapons and ammunition.

mu′ral (myōōr′əl) *n.* a picture painted on a wall.

mur′der (mûr′dər) *n.* **1.** an unlawful intentional killing. —*v.t.* **2.** to kill unlawfully and deliberately. —**mur′der·er,** *n.* —**mur′der·ous,** *adj.*

murk′y *adj.,* **-ier, -iest.** dark and gloomy. —**murk′i·ness,** *n.*

mur′mur (mûr′mər) *n.* **1.** a low, continuous, indistinct sound. **2.** a complaint. —*v.i., v.t.* **3.** to make or express in a murmur.

mus′cat (-kət, -kat) *n.* a sweet grape.

mus′cle (mus′əl) *n., v.,* **-cled, -cling.** —*n.* **1.** a bundle of fibers in the body that contract to produce motion. **2.** strength. —*v.i.* **3.** *Informal.* to force one's way. —**mus′cu·lar** (-kyə lər) *adj.*

mus′cle·bound′ *adj.* having enlarged and inelastic muscles.

mus′cular dys′tro·phy (dis′trə fē) *n.* a hereditary disease marked by gradual wasting of muscles.

muse (myōōz) *v.i.,* **mused, musing.** to reflect quietly.

Muse (myōōz) *n.* **1.** one of nine Greek goddesses of the arts. **2. muse,** the inspiration motivating a poet, artist, etc.

mu·se′um (myōō zē′əm) *n.* a place for permanent public exhibits.

mush¹ (mush *or, esp. for* 2, 3, mōōsh) *n.* **1.** meal, esp. cornmeal, boiled in water or milk. **2.** a thick, soft mass. **3.** maudlin sentiment. —**mush′y,** *adj.*

mush² (mush) *v.i.* to travel over snow with a dog team and sled.

mush′room (mush′rōōm, -rŏŏm) *n.* **1.** a fleshy fungus, usu. umbrella-shaped, sometimes edible. —*v.i.* **2.** to grow quickly.

mu′sic (myōō′zik) *n.* **1.** the art of arranging sounds for effect by rhythm, melody, etc. **2.** the score of a musical composition.

mus′i·cal *adj.* **1.** of music. **2.** pleasant-sounding. **3.** fond of or skilled in music. —*n.* **4.** Also, **mus′ical com′edy.** a play with music.

mu·si′cian (-zish′ən) *n.* a person who performs or composes music.

mu′si·col′o·gy (-zi kol′ə jē) *n.* the scholarly study of music. —**mu′si·col′o·gist,** *n.*

mu′sic vid′eo *n.* a videotape featuring a dramatized rendition of a pop song.

musk (musk) *n.* an animal secretion, used in perfume. —**musk′y,** *adj.*

mus′ket (mus′kit) *n.* an early rifle.

mus'ket·eer' *n.* a soldier armed with a musket.

musk'mel'on *n.* a sweet edible melon.

musk'ox' *n., pl.* **-oxen.** a large mammal of arctic regions.

musk'rat' *n.* a large aquatic American rodent.

Mus'lim (muz'lim, mooz'-, moos'-) *n.* **1.** a follower of Islam. —*adj.* **2.** of or pertaining to Islam.

mus'lin (muz'lin) *n.* a plain-weave cotton fabric.

muss (mus) —*v.t.* **1.** to make messy. —*n.* **2.** disorder.

mus'sel (mus'əl) *n.* a bivalve mollusk, sometimes edible.

must (must) *aux. v.* **1.** (used to express obligation or necessity). **2.** (used to express strong probability or inevitability). —*n.* **3.** something necessary or required.

mus'tache (mus'tash, mə stash') *n.* hair growing on the upper lip.

mus'tang (mus'tang) *n.* a small wild horse of the western U.S.

mus'tard (mus'tərd) *n.* a pungent yellow powder made from the seeds of the mustard plant.

mus'tard gas' *n.* an irritating and poisonous liquid used in warfare.

mus'ter (mus'tər) *v.t., v.i.* **1.** to assemble, as troops; gather. —*n.* **2.** an assembly. —*Idiom.* **3.** **pass muster,** to be found acceptable.

mus'ty (-tē) *adj.,* **-tier, -tiest. 1.** stale-smelling. **2.** outdated.

mu'ta·ble (myoo'tə bəl) *adj.* subject to change. —**mu'ta·bil'i·ty,** *n.*

mu'tant (myoot'nt) *n.* **1.** an organism resulting from mutation. —*adj.* **2.** resulting from mutation.

mu·ta'tion *n.* **1.** a sudden change in a genetic characteristic. **2.** an individual or species characterized by such a change. **3.** a change. —**mu'tate,** *v.i., v.t.*

mute (myoot) *adj.,* **muter, mutest,** *n., v.,* **muted, muting.** —*adj.* **1.** silent. **2.** incapable of speech. —*n.* **3.** a person unable to utter words. **4.** a device for muffling a musical instrument. —*v.t.* **5.** to deaden the sound of.

mu'ti·late' (-l āt') *v.t.,* **-lated, -lating.** to injure by depriving of or harming a part. —**mu'ti·la'tion,** *n.*

mu'ti·ny (myoot'n ē) *n., pl.* **-nies,** *v.,* **-nied, -nying.** —*n.* **1.** a military revolt against lawful authority. —*v.i.* **2.** to commit mutiny. —**mu'ti·neer',** *n.* —**mu'ti·nous,** *adj.*

mutt (mut) *n. Slang.* a mongrel dog.

mut'ter (mut'ər) *v.i., v.t.* **1.** to speak low and indistinctly; grumble. —*n.* **2.** the act or sound of muttering.

mut'ton (mut'n) *n.* the flesh of sheep, used as food.

mu'tu·al (myoo'choo əl) *adj.* **1.** done, experienced, etc., by two or more in relation to each other. **2.** common; shared.

mu'tual fund' *n.* an investment company that invests the pooled funds of its shareholders in a diversified list of securities.

muz'zle (muz'əl) *n., v.,* **-zled, -zling.** —*n.* **1.** an animal's jaws. **2.** a cagelike device for an animal's jaws. **3.** the mouth of a firearm. —*v.t.* **4.** to put a muzzle on. **5.** to silence.

my (mī) *pron.* the possessive form of I used before a noun.

my·col'o·gy (mī kol'ə jē) *n.* the study of fungi. —**my·col'o·gist,** *n.*

my'na (mī'nə) *n.* an Asiatic bird sometimes taught to talk.

my·o'pi·a (mī ō'pē ə) *n.* near-sightedness. —**my·op'ic** (-op'ik, -ō'pik) *adj.*

myr'i·ad (mir'ē əd) *n.* **1.** an indefinitely great number. —*adj.* **2.** consisting of a myriad.

myrrh (mûr) *n.* an aromatic substance from certain plants.

myr'tle (mûr'tl) *n.* **1.** an evergreen shrub. **2.** a periwinkle[2].

my·self' *pron., pl.* **ourselves. 1.** the reflexive form of **me. 2.** an intensive form of **I** or **me.**

mys'ter·y (mis'tə rē) *n., pl.* **-teries. 1.** anything secret, unknown, or unexplained. **2.** obscurity. **3.** a secret rite. —**mys·te'ri·ous** (mi stēr'ē-əs) *adj.* —**mys·te'ri·ous·ly,** *adv.*

mys'tic (mis'tik) *adj.* Also, **mys'ti·cal. 1.** of mysticism. **2.** occult. —*n.* **3.** a believer in mysticism.

mys'ti·cism (-tə siz'əm) *n.* a doctrine of direct spiritual intuition of God, truth, etc.

mys'ti·fy' *v.t.,* **-fied, -fying.** to bewilder purposely.

mys·tique' (mi stēk') *n.* an aura of mystery or power.

myth (mith) *n.* **1.** a legendary story, person, etc. **2.** a false popular belief. —**myth'i·cal,** *adj.*

my·thol'o·gy (mi thol'ə jē) *n., pl.* **-gies.** a body of myths. —**myth'o·log'i·cal** (mith'ə loj'i kəl) *adj.*

N

N, n (en) *n.* the fourteenth letter of the English alphabet.

N north, northern.

nab (nab) *v.t.*, **nabbed, nabbing.** *Informal.* to seize; arrest.

na′bob (nā′bob) *n.* a wealthy, influential, or powerful person.

na′cre (nā′kər) *n.* mother-of-pearl.

na′dir (nā′dər, -dēr) *n.* **1.** the lowest point. **2.** the point on a celestial sphere directly below a given point.

nag[1] (nag) *v.*, **nagged, nagging,** *n.* —*v.t.* **1.** to annoy or scold constantly. —*n.* **2.** a person who nags.

nag[2] (nag) *n.* an old horse.

nai′ad (nā′ad, -əd, nī′-) *n.* a water nymph.

nail (nāl) *n.* **1.** a slender piece of metal for holding pieces of wood together. **2.** a horny plate at the end of fingers and toes. —*v.t.* **3.** to fasten with nails. **4.** *Informal.* to secure or seize.

na·ive′ (nä ēv′) *adj.* **1.** simple. **2.** lacking experience. Also, **na·ïve′.**

na·ive·té′ (-tā′) *n.* artless simplicity. Also, **na·ïve·té′.**

na′ked (nā′kid) *adj.* **1.** without clothing or covering. **2.** (of the eye) unassisted in seeing. **3.** plain.

name (nām) *n.*, *v.*, **named, naming.** —*n.* **1.** the word or words by which a person, place, or thing is designated. **2.** a reputation. **3.** on the behalf or with the authority of. —*v.t.* **4.** to give a name to. **5.** to specify. **6.** to appoint.

name′less *adj.* **1.** having no name. **2.** not referred to by name.

name′ly *adv.* that is to say.

name′sake′ *n.* a person having the same name as another.

nan′ny (nan′ē) *n.*, *pl.* **-nies.** a person employed to take care of a child.

nan′ny goat′ *n.* a female goat.

nan′o·sec′ond (nan′ə sek′ənd, nā′-nə-) *n.* one billionth of a second.

nap[1] (nap) *n.*, *v.*, **napped, napping.** —*n.* **1.** a brief period of sleep. —*v.i.* **2.** to sleep for a short time.

nap[2] (nap) *n.* the short, fuzzy fibers on the surface of cloth.

na′palm (nā′päm) *n.* **1.** a highly incendiary jellylike substance used in bombs, flamethrowers, etc. —*v.t.* **2.** to attack with napalm.

nape (nāp, nap) *n.* the back of the neck.

naph′tha (naf′thə, nap′-) *n.* a petroleum derivative.

nap′kin (nap′kin) *n.* a piece of cloth or paper used while eating to wipe the lips or fingers.

nar′cis·sism (när′sə siz′em) *n.* an excessive admiration of oneself. —**nar′cis·sis′tic** (-sis′tik) *adj.*

nar·cis′sus (när sis′əs) *n.* a bulb plant that blooms in the spring.

nar·co′sis (när kō′sis) *n.* a state of drowsiness or stupor.

nar·cot′ic (-kot′ik) *adj.* **1.** sleep-inducing. —*n.* **2.** a substance that dulls pain, induces sleep, etc. **3.** an addictive drug, esp. an illegal one.

nar′rate (nar′āt, na rāt′) *v.t.*, **-rated, -rating.** to tell or relate (a story, event, etc.). —**nar·ra′tion,** *n.* —**nar′ra·tor,** *n.*

nar′ra·tive (-ə tiv) *n.* **1.** a story or account of events. —*adj.* **2.** that narrates. **3.** of narration.

nar′row (nar′ō) *adj.* **1.** not broad or wide. **2.** literal or strict in interpreting rules, laws, etc. **3.** minute. —*v.i.*, *v.t.* **4.** to make or become narrow. —*n.* **5.** a narrow place, thing, etc.

nar′row-mind′ed *adj.* unwilling to accept new ideas.

nar′whal (när′wəl) *n.* a small arctic whale.

NASA (nas′ə) *n.* National Aeronautics and Space Administration.

na′sal (nā′zəl) *adj.* **1.** of noses. **2.** spoken through the nose. —*n.* **3.** a nasal sound. —**na′sal·ly,** *adv.*

nas′cent (nas′ənt, nā′sənt) *adj.* beginning to exist or develop.

na·stur′tium (nə stûr′shəm, na-) *n.* a garden plant with yellow, orange, or red flowers.

nas′ty (nas′tē) *adj.*, **-tier, -tiest. 1.** spiteful or mean. **2.** objectionable. —**nas′ti·ly,** *adv.*

na′tal (nāt′l) *adj.* of a person's birth.

na′tion (nā′shən) *n.* **1.** a population living in one territory under the same government. **2.** people related by traditions or ancestry. —**na′tion·al** (nash′ə nl) *adj.*, *n.*

na′tion·al·ism (nash′ə nl iz′əm) *n.* devotion to one's nation. —**na′tion·al·ist,** *n.*, *adj.*

na′tion·al′i·ty (-nal′i tē) *n.*, *pl.* **-ties. 1.** the condition of being a member of a particular nation. **2.** a nation or people.

na′tion·al·ize′ *v.t.*, **-ized, -izing.** to bring under national control.

na′tion·wide′ (nā′shən-) *adj.*, *adv.* extending across an entire nation.

na′tive (nā′tiv) *adj.* **1.** belonging to by birth, nationality, or nature. **2.**

237 **need**

of natives. **3.** being the place of origin of a person or thing. —*n.* **4.** a person, animal, or plant native to a region.

na·tiv'i·ty (nə tiv'i tē) *n.*, *pl.* **-ties.** a birth.

NATO (nā'tō) *n.* North Atlantic Treaty Organization.

nat'u·ral (nach'ər əl) *adj.* **1.** of, existing in, or formed by nature. **2.** to be expected in circumstances. **3.** without affectation. **4.** *Music.* neither sharp nor flat. —**nat'u·ral·ly,** *adv.* —**nat'u·ral·ness,** *n.*

nat'ural child'birth *n.* childbirth without the use of any drugs.

nat'ural gas' *n.* a mixture of gaseous hydrocarbons that accumulates in porous sedimentary rocks.

nat'ural his'tory *n.* the study of natural objects.

nat'u·ral·ism (-ər ə liz'əm) *n.* the artistic or literary style that represents objects or events as they occur in nature or real life. —**nat'u·ral·is'tic,** *adj.*

nat'u·ral·ist *n.* **1.** a student of nature. **2.** an adherent of naturalism.

nat'u·ral·ize' *v.t.,* **-ized, -izing. 1.** to confer citizenship upon. **2.** to introduce to a region.

nat'ural re'source *n.* a source of wealth occurring in nature.

nat'ural selec'tion *n.* the process by which life forms having traits that enable them to adapt to the environment survive in greater numbers.

na'ture (nā'chər) *n.* **1.** the natural world as it exists without human beings. **2.** the universe. **3.** a person's character. **4.** a kind or sort.

naught (nôt) *n.* **1.** nothing. **2.** zero.

naugh'ty (nô'tē) *adj.,* **-tier, -tiest. 1.** disobedient; bad. **2.** improper.

nau'sea (nô'zē ə, -zhə, -sē ə, -shə) *n.* **1.** a feeling of impending vomiting. **2.** disgust. —**nau'se·ate'** (-zē āt', -zhē-, -sē-, -shē-) *v.t.*

nau'seous (-shəs, -zē əs) *adj.* **1.** affected with nausea. **2.** causing nausea.

nau'ti·cal (nô'ti kəl) *adj.* of ships, sailors, or navigation.

nau'tical mile' *n.* a unit of distance equal to 1.852 kilometers.

nau'ti·lus (nôt'l əs) *n.* a deep-sea mollusk having a pearly shell.

na'val (nā'vəl) *adj.* of or for ships or a navy.

nave (nāv) *n.* the main lengthwise part of a church.

na'vel (nā'vəl) *n.* the depression in the center surface of the belly where the umbilical cord was connected.

nav'i·gate' (nav'i gāt') *v.,* **-gated,** -gating. —*v.t.* **1.** to traverse (water or air). **2.** to direct (a ship or aircraft) on a course. —*v.i.* **3.** to walk or find one's way. —**nav'i·ga'tor,** *n.* —**nav'i·ga·ble,** *adj.*

na'vy (nā'vē) *n.,* *pl.* **-vies.** a nation's warships and crews.

na'vy blue' *n.* dark blue.

nay (nā) *adv.,* *n.* no.

NB nota bene.

NC North Carolina. Also, **N.C.**

ND North Dakota. Also, **N.D.**

N.Dak. North Dakota.

NE 1. Nebraska. **2.** northeast.

neap' tide' (nēp) *n.* the tide with the lowest high point, midway between spring tides.

near (nēr) *adv.* **1.** close by. —*adj.* **2.** close. **3.** intimate. —*v.t., v.i.* **4.** to approach. —**near'ness,** *n.*

near'by' *adj., adv.* close by.

near'ly *adv.* almost.

near'-sight'ed (-sī'tid, -sī'-) *adj.* seeing distinctly only at short distances. —**near'-sight'ed·ness,** *n.*

neat (nēt) *adj.* **1.** orderly. **2.** skillful. **3.** undiluted. —**neat'ly,** *adv.*

Neb. Nebraska.

neb'u·la (neb'yə lə) *n.,* *pl.* **-lae** (-lē') **-las.** a luminous mass of gas or stars. —**neb'u·lar,** *adj.*

neb'u·lous (-ləs) *adj.* **1.** hazy or vague. **2.** cloudlike.

nec'es·sar'y (nes'ə ser'ē) *adj., n., pl.* **-saries. 1.** essential. **2.** required by facts or reason. —*n.* **3.** something necessary.

ne·ces'si·tate' (nə ses'i tāt') *v.t.,* **-tated, -tating.** to make necessary or unavoidable.

ne·ces'si·ty *n.,* *pl.* **-ties. 1.** something necessary. **2.** the state or fact of being necessary. **3.** poverty.

neck (nek) *n.* **1.** the part of the body connecting the head and trunk. —*v.i.* **2.** *Slang.* to kiss and embrace amorously.

neck'lace (-lis) *n.* a piece of jewelry worn around the neck.

neck'tie' *n.* a decorative fabric strip worn under the collar and tied in front.

nec'ro·man'cy (nek'rə man'sē) *n.* magic. —**nec'ro·manc'er,** *n.*

ne·cro'sis (nə krō'sis) *n.* the death of a tissue or of an organ.

nec'tar (nek'tər) *n.* **1.** the sweet secretion of flowers. **2.** (in Greek myth) the drink of the gods.

nec'tar·ine' (-tə rēn') *n.* a variety of peach having a smooth skin.

nee (nā) *adj.* (of a woman) born; having as a maiden name. Also, **née.**

need (nēd) *n.* **1.** a requirement. **2.** a condition marked by necessity. —*v.t.* **3.** to have need of. —*v.i.* **4.**

to be in need. —*aux.v.* **5.** to be obliged.

nee′dle (nēd′l) *n., v.,* **-dled, -dling.** —*n.* **1.** a slender pointed implement for sewing, knitting, etc. **2.** anything similar, as for an indicator or gauge. **3.** a hypodermic syringe. —*v.t.* **4.** to prod or goad.

nee′dle·point′ *n.* embroidery on canvas.

need′less *adj.* not needed; unnecessary. —**need′less·ly,** *adv.*

nee′dle·work′ *n.* the art or product of working with a needle.

need′y *adj.,* **-ier, -iest.** very poor.

ne′er′-do-well′ (nâr′-) *n.* an idle, worthless person.

ne·far′i·ous (ni fâr′ē əs) *adj.* wicked.

ne·gate′ (ni gāt′, neg′āt) *v.t.,* **-gated, -gating.** to deny; nullify.

neg′a·tive (neg′ə tiv) *adj.* **1.** expressing denial or refusal. **2.** lacking positive attributes. **3.** *Math.* minus. **4.** *Photog.* having light and shade reversed. —*n.* **5.** a negative statement. **6.** *Photog.* a negative image.

ne·glect′ (ni glekt′) *v.t.* **1.** to disregard or fail to do. —*n.* **2.** disregard; negligence. —**ne·glect′ful,** *adj.*

neg′li·gee′ (neg′li zhā′, neg′li zhā′) *n.* a woman's sheer dressing gown.

neg′li·gent (neg′li jənt) *adj.* guilty of or characterized by neglect. —**neg′li·gence,** *n.*

neg′li·gi·ble (-jə bəl) *adj.* very small; unimportant.

ne·go′ti·a·ble (ni gō′shē ə bəl, -shə bəl) *adj.* **1.** capable of being negotiated. **2.** transferable, as securities. —**ne·go′ti·a·bil′i·ty,** *n.*

ne·go′ti·ate′ (-shē āt′) *v.,* **-ated, -ating.** —*v.i.* **1.** to deal or bargain with another. —*v.t.* **2.** to arrange for by discussion. —**ne·go′ti·a′-tion,** *n.* —**ne·go′ti·a′tor,** *n.*

neigh (nā) *n.* **1.** the cry of a horse. —*v.i.* **2.** to make such a sound.

neigh′bor (nā′bər) *n.* **1.** a person or thing near another. —*v.t., v.i.* **2.** to be near.

neigh′bor·hood *n.* **1.** a surrounding area. **2.** a district having a separate identity.

nei′ther (nē′thər, nī′-) *conj., adj.* not either. —**Pronunciation.** See EITHER.

nem′e·sis (nem′ə sis) *n., pl.* **-ses. 1.** a source of harm or failure. **2.** an unconquerable opponent.

neo- a prefix meaning new.

ne·ol′o·gism (nē ol′ə jiz′əm) *n.* a new word or phrase.

ne′on (nē′on) *n.* a gas used in some electrical signs.

ne′o·na′tal (nē′ō nāt′l) *adj.* referring to the care of newborn babies.

ne′o·nate′ (nē′ə nāt′) *n.* a newborn child.

ne′o·phyte′ (-fīt′) *n.* a beginner.

ne′o·plasm (-plaz′əm) *n.* a growth of abnormal tissue; a tumor.

neph′ew (nef′yōō) *n.* a son of one's brother or sister.

ne·phri′tis (nə frī′tis) *n.* inflammation of the kidneys.

ne′ plus′ ul′tra (nē′ plus′ ul′trə, nā′) *n.* the highest point.

nep′o·tism (nep′ə tiz′əm) *n.* favoritism based on family relationship.

Nep′tune (nep′tōōn, -tyōōn) *n.* the planet eighth from the sun.

nerd (nûrd) *n. Slang.* **1.** a dull or unattractive person. **2.** a person devoted to a nonsocial pursuit.

nerve (nûrv) *n., v.,* **nerved, nerving.** —*n.* **1.** a bundle of fiber that conveys impulses between the brain and other parts of the body. **2.** courage. **3.** *Informal.* presumption. **4. nerves,** anxiety; unease. —*v.t.* **5.** to give courage to.

nerve′ gas′ *n.* a poison gas that interferes with nerve functions.

nerv′ous *adj.* **1.** uneasy or anxious. **2.** having or caused by disordered nerves. **3.** of nerves.

nerv′y *adj.,* **-ier, -iest.** *Informal.* brashly bold; presumptuous.

-ness a suffix meaning quality or state.

nest (nest) *n.* **1.** a structure of grass, twigs, etc., prepared by a bird for its eggs. **2.** any place used by an animal for rearing its young. **3.** a group of things fitting tightly together. —*v.i.* **4.** to settle in a nest. —*v.t.* **5.** to fit one within another.

nest′ egg′ *n.* money saved for emergencies, retirement, etc.

nes′tle (nes′əl) *v.i.,* **-tled, -tling.** to lie close and snug.

net¹ (net) *n., v.,* **netted, netting.** —*n.* **1.** Also, **net′ting.** a lacelike fabric of uniform mesh. **2.** anything serving to catch or ensnare. **3.** a computer or telecommunications network. —*v.t.* **4.** to cover with a net. **5.** to ensnare.

net² (net) *adj., n., v.,* **netted, netting.** —*adj.* **1.** exclusive of loss or remaining after deductions. —*n.* **2.** the net income, profit, etc. —*v.t.* **3.** to gain as clear profit.

neth′er (neth′ər) *adj.* lower.

net′i·quette (net′i kit, -ket′) *n.* the etiquette of computer networks, esp. the Internet.

net′tle (net′l) *n., v.,* **-tled, -tling.** —*n.* **1.** a plant with stinging hairs. —*v.t.* **2.** to irritate; sting.

net′tle·some (-səm) *adj.* **1.** causing irritation. **2.** easily provoked.

net′work′ *n.* **1.** a netlike combination of intersecting elements. **2.** a group of associated radio or television stations. **3.** a computer or telecommunications system linked to permit information exchanges. —*v.i.* **4.** to engage in networking.

net′work compu′ter *n.* a computer with minimal processing power, designed primarily to provide access to networks.

net′work′ing *n.* the informal sharing of information among people who have common interests.

neu′ral (nŏŏr′əl, nyŏŏr′-) *adj.* of nerves or the nervous system.

neu·ral′gia (nŏŏ ral′jə, nyŏŏ-) *n.* a sharp pain along a nerve.

neu·ri′tis (-rī′tis, nyŏŏ-) *n.* inflammation of a nerve.

neu·rol′o·gy (-rol′ə jē) *n.* the branch of medicine dealing with the nervous system. —**neu·rol′o·gist,** *n.* —**neu′ro·log′i·cal** (nŏŏr′ə loj′i kəl) *adj.*

neu′ron (nŏŏr′on, nyŏŏr′-) *n.* a cell that is the basic unit of the nervous system.

neu·ro′sis (nŏŏ rō′sis, nyŏŏ-) *n., pl.* **-ses.** an emotional disorder characterized by anxiety, obsessional thoughts, compulsive acts, etc.

neu′ro·sur′ger·y (nŏŏr′ō sûr′jə rē, nyŏŏr′-) *n.* surgery of the brain or other nerve tissue.

neu·rot′ic (-rot′ik) *adj.* **1.** of or marked by neurosis. —*n.* **2.** a neurotic person.

neu′ro·trans′mit·ter *n.* a chemical substance that transmits nerve impulses across a synapse.

neu′ter (nŏŏ′tər, nyŏŏ′-) *adj.* **1.** neither male nor female. —*v.t.* **2.** to spay or castrate (a dog, cat, etc.).

neu′tral (-trəl, nyŏŏ′-) *adj.* **1.** taking no side in a controversy. **2.** not emphatic or positive. —*n.* **3.** a neutral person or state. —**neu·tral′i·ty** (-tral′i tē) *n.* —**neu′tral·ize′,** *v.t.,* —**neu′tral·ly,** *adv.*

neu′tron (-tron, nyŏŏ′-) *n.* an elementary particle having no charge, found in the nucleus of an atom.

Nev. Nevada.

nev′er (nev′ər) *adv.* not ever.

nev′er·the·less′ *adv.* in spite of that.

new (nŏŏ, nyŏŏ) *adj.* **1.** of recent origin or existence. **2.** unfamiliar. —*adv.* **3.** recently; freshly.

new′el (nŏŏ′əl, nyŏŏ′-) *n.* the post supporting the handrail at the head or foot of a flight of stairs.

new′fan′gled (-fang′gəld) *adj.* of a new kind or fashion.

new′ly *adv.* **1.** recently. **2.** anew.

new′ly·wed′ *n.* a person who has recently married.

news (nŏŏz, nyŏŏz) *n.* **1.** a report of a recent event. **2.** a report of recent events in a newspaper, on the radio, or on television.

news′cast′ *n.* a broadcast of the news on radio or television. —**news′cast′er,** *n.*

news′group′ *n.* an on-line discussion group on a specific topic.

news′let′ter *n.* a periodic informational report for a specialized group.

news′pa′per (nŏŏz′-, nyŏŏz′-) *n.* a periodical containing news, comment, features, advertising, etc.

news′print′ *n.* the paper on which newspapers are printed.

news′reel′ *n.* a short motion picture of recent news events.

news′stand′ *n.* a sales booth for newspapers, periodicals, etc.

news′wor′thy *adj.* interesting enough to warrant press coverage.

newt (nŏŏt, nyŏŏt) *n.* a salamander.

New′ Tes′tament *n.* the portion of the Christian Bible recording the life and teachings of Christ and His disciples.

new′ton (nŏŏt′n, nyŏŏt′n) *n.* a unit of force.

new′ wave′ *n.* a movement that breaks with traditional values, techniques, etc.

new′ year′ *n.* **1. New Year,** the first day of the year. **2.** the year approaching.

next (nekst) *adj.* **1.** immediately following in time, order, etc. —*adv.* **2.** in the nearest place after. **3.** at the first subsequent time.

next′-door′ *adj.* in the next house, apartment, etc.

nex′us (nek′səs) *n., pl.* **nexus.** a link or connection.

NH New Hampshire. Also, **N.H.**

ni′a·cin (nī′ə sin) *n.* nicotinic acid.

nib (nib) *n.* a pen point.

nib′ble *v.,* **-bled, -bling,** *n.* —*v.t., v.i.* **1.** to bite off in small bits. —*n.* **2.** a small morsel.

nice (nīs) *adj.,* **nicer, nicest. 1.** agreeable. **2.** precise. **3.** fastidious.

ni′ce·ty (nī′si tē) *n., pl.* **-ties. 1.** a subtle point. **2.** a refinement.

niche (nich) *n.* **1.** a recess in a wall. **2.** a suitable role or position.

nick (nik) *n.* **1.** a notch or hollow place in a surface. **2.** a precise or opportune moment. —*v.t.* **3.** to injure slightly. **4.** to make a nick in.

nick′el (nik′əl) *n.* **1.** a hard silver-white metal. **2.** a five-cent coin.

nick′name′ *n., v.,* **-named, -nam-**

ing. —*n.* 1. an informal name. —*v.t.* 2. to give a nickname to.

nic′o•tine′ (nik/ə tēn/) *n.* a toxic liquid alkaloid found in tobacco.

niece (nēs) *n.* a daughter of one's brother or sister.

nif′ty (nif/tē) *adj.*, -tier, -tiest. *Informal.* smart; fine.

nig′gard•ly (nig/ərd lē) *adj.* stingy.

nig′gling (-ling) *adj.* trivial.

nigh (nī) *adv.*, *adj.* near.

night (nīt) *n.* the period between sunset and sunrise.

night′cap′ *n.* 1. an alcoholic drink taken before bed. 2. a cap worn while sleeping.

night′club′ *n.* an establishment open at night, offering food, drink, and entertainment.

night′ crawl′er *n.* an earthworm.

night′fall′ *n.* the coming of night.

night′gown′ *n.* a gown for sleeping.

night′hawk′ *n.* a nocturnal American bird.

night′in•gale′ (nīt′n gāl/, nī/ting-) *n.* a small European thrush that sings at night.

night′ly *adj.*, *adv.* occurring every night.

night′mare′ (-mâr/) *n.* 1. a bad dream. 2. a harrowing event.

night′ owl′ *n.* a person who often stays up late at night.

night′shirt′ *n.* a loose shirtlike garment worn in bed.

night′ stick′ *n.* a club carried by police officers.

ni′hil•ism (nī/ə liz/əm, nē/-) *n.* 1. a belief that existence has no meaning. 2. total rejection of established laws and institutions. —ni′-hil•ist, *n.* —ni′hil•is′tic, *adj.*

nil (nil) *n.* nothing.

nim′ble (nim/bəl) *adj.*, -bler, -blest. agile; quick. —nim′bly, *adv.*

nim′bus (-bəs) *n.*, *pl.* -bi (-bī) -buses. 1. a halo. 2. a rain cloud.

nim′rod (-rod) *n.* a skilled hunter.

nin′com•poop′ (nin/kəm pōōp/, ning/-) *n.* a fool.

nine (nīn) *n.*, *adj.* eight plus one. —ninth, *adj.*, *n.*

nine′teen′ *n.*, *adj.* ten plus nine. —nine′teenth′, *n.*, *adj.*

nine′ty *n.*, *adj.* ten times nine. —nine′ti•eth, *adj.*, *n.*

nin′ny (nin/ē) *n.*, *pl.* -nies. a fool.

nip¹ (nip) *v.*, nipped, nipping, *n.* —*v.t.* 1. to pinch or bite. 2. to check the growth of. 3. to affect sharply. —*n.* 4. a pinch. 5. a biting quality.

nip² (nip) *v.*, nipped, nipping, *n.* —*v.i.* 1. to drink an alcoholic liquor in small sips. —*n.* 2. a small drink of alcoholic liquor.

nip′ple *n.* 1. a milk-discharging protuberance on the female breast. 2. a nipple-shaped object.

nip′py *adj.*, -pier, -piest. 1. chilly. 2. pungent.

nir•va′na (nir vä/nə, -van/ə, nər-) *n.* 1. (in Buddhism) freedom from all passion. 2. a state of bliss.

nit (nit) *n.* the egg of a louse.

ni′ter (nī/tər) *n.* the white salt used in gunpowder, fertilizer, etc. Also, ni′tre.

nit′-pick′ *v.i. Informal.* to argue or find fault pettily.

ni′trate (nī/trāt, -trit) *n.* the salt of nitric acid.

ni′tric ac′id (nī/trik) *n.* a caustic liquid used in the manufacture of explosives, fertilizers, etc.

ni′tro•gen (nī/trə jən) *n.* a colorless, odorless, tasteless gas.

ni′tro•glyc′er•in (-glis/ər in) *n.* a colorless, highly explosive oil.

ni′trous (nī/trəs) *adj.* 1. of niter. 2. Also, ni′tric. containing nitrogen.

nit′ty-grit′ty (nit/ē grit/ē) *n. Slang.* the crux of a matter.

nit′wit′ *n.* a foolish person.

nix (niks) *n.* 1. nothing. —*adv.* 2. no. —*v.t.* 3. to veto.

NJ New Jersey. Also, N.J.

NM New Mexico.

N. Mex. New Mexico.

no¹ (nō) *adv.*, *n.*, *pl.* noes, nos. —*adv.* 1. a word used to express dissent, denial, or refusal. —*n.* 2. a negative vote.

no² (nō) *adj.* not any.

no. 1. north. 2. number.

no•bil′i•ty (nō bil/i tē) *n.*, *pl.* -ties. 1. the noble class. 2. the state or quality of being noble.

no′ble (nō/bəl) *adj.*, -bler, -blest, *n.* —*adj.* 1. of high rank by birth. 2. admirable or magnificent. —*n.* 3. a person of noble rank.

no•blesse′ o•blige′ (nō bles/ ō-blēzh/) *n.* the moral obligation of the rich to show generosity to the less fortunate.

no′bod′y (nō/bod/ē, -bud/ē, -bə dē) *pron.*, *n.*, *pl.* -bodies. —*pron.* 1. no person. —*n.* 2. a person of no importance.

noc•tur′nal (nok tûr/nl) *adj.* 1. of the night. 2. occurring or active by night.

noc′turne (-tûrn) *n.* a dreamy or pensive musical composition.

nod (nod) *v.*, nodded, nodding, *n.* —*v.t.* 1. to incline (the head) briefly. —*v.i.* 2. to become sleepy. 3. to sway gently. —*n.* 4. a brief inclination of the head.

node (nōd) *n.* 1. a protuberance. 2. a joint in a plant stem.

nod′ule (noj′ool) *n.* a small knob or lump. —**nod′u•lar,** *adj.*

No•el′ (nō el′) *n.* Christmas.

no′-fault′ *adj.* (of auto accident insurance, divorces, etc.) effective without establishing fault.

nog′gin (nog′ən) *n.* **1.** a small mug. **2.** *Informal.* the head.

noise (noiz) *n., v.,* **noised, noising.** —*n.* **1.** a sound, esp. loud or harsh. —*v.t.* **2.** to spread, as rumors. —**nois′y,** *adj.* —**nois′i•ly,** *adv.*

noi′some (noi′səm) *adj.* **1.** offensive. **2.** harmful.

no′mad (nō′mad) *n.* a wanderer. —**no•mad′ic,** *adj.*

no′ man's′ land′ *n.* the area between warring armies.

nom de plume (nom′ də ploom′) *n.* the name used by a writer.

no′men•cla′ture (nō′mən klā′chər) *n.* a set or system of names.

nom′i•nal (nom′ə nl) *adj.* **1.** in name only; so-called. **2.** trifling.

nom′i•nate′ (-nāt′) *v.t.,* **-nated, -nating. 1.** to propose as a candidate. **2.** to appoint. —**nom′i•na′tion,** *n.*

nom′i•na•tive (-nə tiv) *adj.* **1.** denoting the grammatical case of a noun or pronoun used as the subject of a verb. —*n.* **2.** the nominative case.

nom′i•nee′ *n.* a person nominated.

non- a prefix meaning not.

non′age (non′ij, nō′nij) *n.* the period of legal minority.

non′a•ge•nar′i•an (non′ə jə när′ē-ən, nō′nə-) *n.* a person between 90 and 99 years old.

non′cha•lant′ (non′shə länt′) *adj.* coolly unconcerned. —**non′cha•lance′,** *n.* —**non′cha•lant′ly,** *adv.*

non′com•bat′ant (-kəm bat′nt, non kom′bə tnt) *n.* **1.** a member of a military force who is not a fighter. **2.** a civilian in wartime.

non′com•mit′tal *adj.* giving no particular view, feeling, etc.

non′ com′pos men′tis (non′ kom′-pəs men′tis) *adj. Law.* not of sound mind.

non′con•duc′tor *n.* a substance that does not readily conduct heat, electricity, etc.

non′con•form′ist *n.* a person who refuses to conform.

non′de•script′ (-di skript′) *adj.* of no particular kind.

none (nun) *pron. sing. and pl.* **1.** not one; not any. —*adv.* **2.** in no way.

non•en′ti•ty *n., pl.* **-ties.** an unimportant person or thing.

none′the•less′ *adv.* nevertheless.

non•met′al *n.* an element not hav-

ing the character of a metal, as carbon or nitrogen.

no′-no′ *n. Informal.* a forbidden thing.

non′pa•reil′ (-pə rel′) *adj.* **1.** having no equal. —*n.* **2.** a person or thing without equal.

non•par′ti•san *adj.* **1.** not taking sides. **2.** belonging to no party.

non•plus′ (non plus′, non′plus) *v.t.* **-plussed or -plused, -plussing or -plusing.** to confuse.

non•prof′it *adj.* not profit motivated.

non′rep•re•sen•ta′tion•al *adj.* not resembling any object in nature.

non′sec•tar′i•an *adj.* not affiliated with a religious denomination.

non′sense (non′sens, -səns) *n.* senseless or absurd words or actions. —**non•sen′si•cal,** *adj.*

non se′qui•tur (non sek′wi tər, -toor′) *n.* a statement unrelated to the preceding one.

non′stand′ard *adj.* not conforming to usage considered acceptable by educated native speakers.

non′stop′ *adj., adv.* without intermediate stops. Also, **non-stop.**

non′sup•port′ *n.* failure to provide financial support.

non•un′ion *adj.* **1.** not belonging to a labor union. **2.** not produced by union workers.

non•vi′o•lence *n.* the policy of refraining from using violence. —**non•vi′o•lent,** *adj.*

noo′dle (nood′l) *n.* a thin strip of dough, cooked in soup, casseroles, etc.

nook (nook) *n.* a corner of a room.

noon (noon) *n.* twelve o'clock in the daytime. —**noon′time′,** *n.*

no′ one′ *pron.* not anyone.

noose (noos) *n.* a loop with a running knot that pulls tight.

nor (nôr; *unstressed* nər) *conj.* or not: used with **neither.**

norm (nôrm) *n.* a standard or model.

nor′mal (nôr′məl) *adj.* **1.** of standard type; usual. —*n.* **2.** the standard or average. —**nor′mal•cy, nor•mal′i•ty** (-mal′i tē) *n.* —**nor′mal•ize′,** *v.t., v.i.*

nor′ma•tive (nôr′mə tiv) *adj.* establishing a norm.

north (nôrth) *n.* **1.** a cardinal point of the compass, lying to the left of a person facing the rising sun. **2. the North,** a region in this direction. —*adj., adv.* **3.** toward, in, or from the north. —**north′ern,** *adj.* —**north′ern•er,** *adj.* —**north′ward,** *adv., adj.*

north•east′ *n.* **1.** a point or direction midway between north and east. **2. the Northeast,** a region in this direction. —*adj., adv.* **3.** toward, in, or from the northeast. —**north′east′ern,** *adj.*

north′er•ly *adj., adv.* toward or blowing from the north.

North′ Star′ *n.* the bright star close to the North Pole; Polaris.

north′west′ *n.* **1.** a point or direction midway between north and west. **2. the Northwest,** a region in this direction. —*adj., adv.* **3.** toward, in, or from the northwest. —**north′west′ern,** *adj.*

nose (nōz) *n., v.,* **nosed, nosing.** —*n.* **1.** the part of the head containing the nostrils. **2.** the sense of smell. **3.** the projecting part of any object. —*v.t.* **4.** to perceive by smell. **5.** to push forward with the nose. —*v.i.* **6.** to pry. **7.** to head cautiously. —*Idiom.* **8. on the nose,** precisely.

nose′cone′ *n.* the forward section of a rocket.

nose′dive′ *n., v.,* **-dived** or **-dove, -dived, -diving.** —*n.* **1.** a downward plunge. —*v.i.* **2.** to go into a nosedive.

nose′gay′ *n.* a small bouquet.

nosh (nosh) *Informal.* —*v.i., v.t.* **1.** to snack (on). —*n.* **2.** a snack.

no′-show′ *n.* a person who neither uses nor cancels a reservation.

nos•tal•gia (no stal′jə) *n.* a sentimental yearning for the past.

nos′tril (nos′trəl) *n.* either of the two external openings of the nose for breathing.

nos′trum (nos′trəm) *n.* **1.** a quack remedy. **2.** a pet solution.

nos′y (nō′zē) *adj.,* **-ier, -iest.** *Informal.* unduly inquisitive.

not (not) *adv.* a word expressing negation, denial, or refusal.

no′ta be′ne (nō′tə ben′ē) *Latin.* note well.

no′ta•ble (nō′tə bəl) *adj.* **1.** worthy of note; important. —*n.* **2.** a prominent person. —**no′ta•bly,** *adv.*

no′ta•rize′ (nō′tə rīz′) *v.t.,* **-rized, -rizing.** to authenticate through a notary.

no′ta•ry (-rē) *n., pl.* **-ries.** an official authorized to verify documents. Also, **notary public.**

no•ta′tion (nō tā′shən) *n.* **1.** a short note. **2.** a special symbol.

notch (noch) *n.* **1.** an angular cut. —*v.t.* **2.** to make a notch in.

note (nōt) *n., v.,* **noted, noting.** —*n.* **1.** a brief record, comment, etc. **2.** a short letter. **3.** a distinction. **4.** an observation. **5.** a paper promising payment. **6.** a musical sound or written symbol. —*v.t.* **7.** to write down. **8.** to notice.

note′book′ *n.* **1.** a book with blank pages for writing notes. **2.** a lightweight laptop computer.

not′ed *adj.* famous.

note′wor′thy *adj.* worthy of attention.

noth′ing (nuth′ing) *n.* **1.** not anything. **2.** a trivial action, thing, etc. —*adv.* **3.** not at all. —**noth′-ing•ness,** *n.*

no′tice (nō′tis) *n., v.,* **-ticed, -ticing.** —*n.* **1.** information; warning. **2.** a note, sign, etc., that informs or warns. **3.** attention; heed. —*v.t.* **4.** to pay attention to or perceive. **5.** to mention.

no′tice•a•ble *adj.* attracting notice or attention. —**no′tice•a•bly,** *adv.*

no′ti•fy′ *v.t.,* **-fied, -fying.** to give notice to. —**no′ti•fi•ca′tion,** *n.*

no′tion (nō′shən) *n.* **1.** an idea. **2.** an opinion. **3.** a whim. **4. notions,** small items, as pins or trim.

no•to′ri•ous (nō tôr′ē əs, nə-) *adj.* widely known, esp. unfavorably. —**no′to•ri′e•ty** (-tə rī′i tē) *n.*

not′with•stand′ing *prep.* **1.** in spite of. —*adv.* **2.** nevertheless. —*conj.* **3.** although.

nou′gat (nōō′gət) *n.* a pastelike candy with nuts.

nought (nôt) *n.* naught.

noun (noun) *n.* a word denoting a person, place, or thing.

nour′ish (nûr′ish, nur′-) *v.t.* to sustain with food. —**nour′ish•ment,** *n.*

nou′veau riche′ (nōō′vō rēsh′) *n., pl.* **nou′veaux riches** (nōō′vō rēsh′). a newly rich person.

Nov. November.

no′va (nō′və) *n., pl.* **-vas, -vae** (-vē). a star that suddenly becomes much brighter, then gradually fades.

nov′el¹ (nov′əl) *n.* a long fictional narrative. —**nov′el•ist,** *n.*

nov′el² (nov′əl) *adj.* new or strange.

nov′el•ty *n., pl.* **-ties.** **1.** unfamiliarity. **2.** a new or amusing thing.

No•vem′ber (nō vem′bər) *n.* the eleventh month of the year.

nov′ice (nov′is) *n.* **1.** a beginner. **2.** a person just received into a religious order.

no•vi′ti•ate (nō vish′ē it, -āt′) *n.* the period of being a novice.

No′vo•caine′ (nō′və kān′) *Trademark.* a local anesthetic.

now (nou) *adv.* **1.** at the present time. **2.** immediately. —*conj.* **3.** since. —*n.* **4.** the present.

now′a•days′ (-ə dāz′) *adv.* in these times.

no′where′ *adv.* not anywhere.

nox′ious (nok′shəs) *adj.* harmful.

noz′zle (noz′əl) *n.* a projecting spout.

nth (enth) *adj.* utmost.

nu′ance (nōō′äns, nyōō′-) *n.* a shade of expression, color, or meaning.

nub (nub) *n.* **1.** the gist. **2.** a knob or lump.

nu′bile (nōō′bil, -bīl, nyōō′-) *adj.* **1.** (of a young woman) marriageable. **2.** (of a young woman) sexually attractive.

nu′cle·ar (nōō′klē ər, nyōō′-) *adj.* **1.** of or involving atomic weapons. **2.** powered by nuclear energy. **3.** of or forming a nucleus.

nu′clear en′ergy *n.* energy released by reactions within atomic nuclei, as in nuclear fission or fusion.

nu′clear fam′ily *n.* a social unit composed of a father, a mother, and children.

nu′clear phys′ics *n.* the branch of physics dealing with atoms.

nu′clear win′ter *n.* the devastation, darkness, and cold that could result from a nuclear war.

nu′cle·on (nōō′klē on′, nyōō′-) *n.* a proton or neutron.

nu′cle·us (-klē əs) *n., pl.* **-cle·i** (-klē ī) **-cleuses. 1.** a central part. **2.** the central body of a living cell. **3.** the core of an atom.

nude (nōōd, nyōōd) *adj.* **1.** naked. —*n.* **2.** a naked human figure.

nudge (nuj) *v.,* **nudged, nudging,** *n.* —*v.t.* **1.** to push slightly. —*n.* **2.** a slight push.

nud′ism (nōō′diz əm, nyōō′-) *n.* the practice of going nude. —**nud′ist,** *n.*

nug′get (nug′it) *n.* a lump (esp. of gold).

nui′sance (nōō′səns, nyōō′-) *n.* an annoying thing or person.

nuke (nōōk, nyōōk) *n., v.,* **nuked, nuking.** *Informal.* —*n.* **1.** a nuclear weapon or power plant. —*v.t.* **2.** to attack with nuclear weapons.

null (nul) *adj.* of no effect.

null′i·fy *v.t.,* **-fied, -fying. 1.** to make null. **2.** to make legally void.

numb (num) *adj.* **1.** deprived of feeling. —*v.t.* **2.** to make numb.

num′ber (num′bər) *n.* **1.** the sum of a group of units. **2.** a numeral. **3.** one of a series or group. **4.** a large quantity. —*v.t.* **5.** to mark with numbers. **6.** to count. —*v.i.* **7.** to amount to in numbers. —**Usage.** See AMOUNT.

num′ber·less *adj.* too many to count.

nu′mer·al (nōō′mər əl, nyōō′-) *n.* **1.** a word or sign representing a number. —*adj.* **2.** of numbers.

nu′mer·ate′ (-mə rāt′) *v.t.,* **-ated, -ating.** to count.

nu′mer·a′tor *n.* the part of a fraction written above the line.

nu·mer′i·cal (nōō mer′i kəl, nyōō′-) *adj.* of or denoting numbers.

nu′mer·ol′o·gy (-mə rol′ə jē, nyōō′-) *n.* the study of numbers to determine their supernatural meaning.

nu′mer·ous (-mər əs) *adj.* very many.

nu·mis·mat′ics (-miz mat′iks, -mis-, nyōō′-) *n.* the science of coins and medals.

num′skull′ (num′skul′) *n. Informal.* a stupid person. Also, **numb′skull′.**

nun (nun) *n.* a woman living with a religious group under vows.

nun′ci·o′ (nun′shē ō′,-sē ō′, nōōn′-) *n., pl.* **-cios.** a papal representative in a foreign capital.

nun′ner·y (nun′ə rē) *n., pl.* **-neries.** a convent.

nup′tial (nup′shəl, -chəl) *adj.* **1.** of marriage. —*n.* **2. nuptials,** the marriage ceremony.

nurse (nûrs) *n., v.,* **nursed, nursing.** —*n.* **1.** a person who cares for sick people or children. —*v.t.* **2.** to minister to in sickness. **3.** to look after carefully. **4.** to suckle.

nurs′er·y *n., pl.* **-eries. 1.** a room set apart for young children. **2.** a place where young plants are grown.

nurs′ery school′ *n.* a prekindergarten school for children.

nurs′ing home′ *n.* a residential institution caring for the aged or infirm.

nur′ture (nûr′chər) *v.,* **-tured, -turing,** *n.* —*v.t.* **1.** to feed and care for during growth. —*n.* **2.** upbringing. **3.** something that nourishes.

nut (nut) *n.* **1.** a dry fruit consisting of an edible kernel in a shell. **2.** the kernel. **3.** a perforated, threaded metal block used to screw on the end of a bolt. **4.** *Slang.* an insane or eccentric person. —**nut′-crack′er,** *n.* —**nut′shell′,** *n.*

nut′hatch′ *n.* a small songbird that seeks food along tree trunks.

nut′meg (-meg) *n.* the aromatic seed of an East Indian tree.

nu′tri·ent (nōō′trē ənt, nyōō′-) *adj.* **1.** nourishing. —*n.* **2.** a nutrient substance.

nu′tri·ment (-trə mənt) *n.* nourishment.

nu·tri′tion (-trish′ən) *n.* **1.** the process of nourishing or being nourished. **2.** the study of dietary requirements. —**nu·tri′tious, nu′-tri·tive,** *adj.* —**nu·tri′tion·ist,** *n.*

nuts (nuts) *adj. Slang.* crazy.

nut′ty *adj.,* **-tier, -tiest. 1.** tasting of or like nuts. **2.** *Slang.* insane; senseless. —**nut′ti·ness,** *n.*

nuz′zle (nuz′əl) *v.t, v.i.,* **-zled,**

-zling. 1. to touch or rub with the nose, snout, etc. **2.** to cuddle.

NV Nevada.

NW northwest. Also, **N.W.**

NY New York. Also, **N.Y.**

ny′lon (nī′lon) *n.* **1.** a tough, elastic synthetic substance used for yarn, bristles, etc. **2. nylons,** stockings of nylon.

nymph (nimf) *n.* **1.** a class of mythological goddess. **2.** a beautiful girl.

nym/pho•ma/ni•a (nim′fə mā′nē ə) *n.* uncontrollable sexual desire in women. —**nym′pho•ma/ni•ac′,** *n.*

O

O, o (ō) *n.* the fifteenth letter of the English alphabet.

O (ō) *interj.* (an expression of surprise, gladness, pain, etc.)

o′ (ə, ō) *prep.* a shortened form of **of.**

oaf (ōf) *n.* a clumsy, rude person. —**oaf′ish,** *adj.*

oak (ōk) *n.* a hardwood tree bearing acorns.

oar (ôr) *n.* a flat-bladed shaft for rowing a boat. —**oars′man,** *n.*

oar′lock′ *n.* a device providing a pivot for an oar.

o•a′sis (ō ā′sis) *n., pl.* **-ses.** a fertile place in the desert.

oat (ōt) *n.* a cereal grass grown for its edible grain.

oath (ōth) *n.* **1.** a solemn affirmation; vow. **2.** a curse.

oat′meal′ *n.* **1.** ground oats. **2.** a cooked breakfast food.

ob′du•rate (ob′dŏŏ rit, -dyŏŏ-) *adj.* stubborn. —**ob′du•ra•cy,** *n.*

o•be•di•ent (ō bē′dē ənt) *adj.* obeying or willing to obey. —**o•be′di•ence,** *n.*

o•bei′sance (ō bā′səns, ō bē′-) *n.* **1.** a bow or curtsy. **2.** homage.

ob′e•lisk (ob′ə lisk) *n.* a tapering, four-sided shaft of stone.

o•bese′ (ō bēs′) *adj.* very fat. —**o•bes′i•ty,** *n.*

o•bey′ (ō bā′) *v.t.* **1.** to do as ordered by. **2.** to comply with.

ob′fus•cate′ (ob′fə skāt′, ob fus′kāt) *v.t.,* **-cated, -cating.** to confuse. —**ob′fus•ca′tion,** *n.*

ob′i•ter dic′tum (ob′i tər dik′təm) *n., pl.* **obiter dicta** (-tə). an incidental remark.

o•bit′u•ar′y (ō bich′ŏŏ er′ē) *n., pl.* **-aries.** a notice of a person's death, as in a newspaper.

obj. 1. object. **2.** objective.

ob′ject *n.* (ob′jikt, -jekt) **1.** something solid. **2.** a thing or person to which attention is directed. **3.** an end; motive. **4.** a noun or pronoun that represents the goal of an action. —*v.i.* (əb jekt′) **5.** to say that one is opposed. —**ob•jec′tor,** *n.*

ob•jec′tion (əb jek′shən) *n.* **1.** an argument against. **2.** the act of objecting.

ob•jec′tion•a•ble (-shə nə bəl) *adj.* causing disapproval; offensive.

ob•jec′tive *n.* **1.** a purpose; goal. —*adj.* **2.** not influenced by personal feelings. **3.** of the grammatical case indicating the object of a verb or preposition. —**ob′jec•tiv′i•ty** (ob′jik tiv′i tē) *n.*

ob′ject les′son *n.* a practical illustration of a principle.

ob′jet d′art′ (ob′zhā där′) *n., pl.* **objets d′art** (ob′zhā där′). an object of artistic worth.

ob′late (ob′lāt, o blāt′) *adj.* flattened at the poles, as a spheroid.

ob•la′tion (o blā′shən) *n.* an offering; sacrifice.

ob′li•gate′ (ob′li gāt′) *v.t.,* **-gated, -gating.** to bind morally or legally. —**ob′li•ga′tion,** *n.*

ob•lig′a•to•ry (ə blig′ə tôr′ē) *adj.* compulsory; required.

o•blige′ (ə blīj′) *v.t.,* **obliged, obliging. 1.** to require. **2.** to do a favor for.

ob•lique′ (ə blēk′, ō blēk′) *adj.* **1.** slanting. **2.** indirect. —**ob•lique′ly,** *adv.*

ob•lit′er•ate′ (ə blit′ə rāt′) *v.t.,* **-ated, -ating.** to remove all traces of.

ob•liv′i•on (ə bliv′ē ən) *n.* **1.** the state of being forgotten. **2.** the state of forgetting.

ob′long (ob′lông′) *adj.* **1.** of a rectangular shape that is longer than it is broad. —*n.* **2.** an oblong figure.

ob′lo•quy (ob′lə kwē) *n., pl.* **-quies.** public disgrace.

ob•nox′ious (əb nok′shəs) *adj.* very offensive.

o′boe (ō′bō) *n.* a woodwind instrument with a double-reed mouthpiece. —**o′bo•ist,** *n.*

obs. obsolete.

ob•scene′ (əb sēn′) *adj.* **1.** offensive to decency or morality. **2.** disgusting. —**ob•scen′i•ty** (-sen′i tē, -sē′ni-) *n.*

ob•scure′ *adj., v.,* **-scured, -scuring.** —*adj.* **1.** not clear to the understanding. **2.** not easily noticed. **3.** not famous. —*v.t.* **4.** to make obscure. —**ob•scu′ri•ty,** *n.*

ob.se'qui.ous (əb sē'kwē əs) *adj.*
excessively deferential.

ob'se.quy (ob'si kwē) *n., pl.* **-quies.**
a funeral rite.

ob.serv'ance (əb zûr'vəns) *n.* **1.**
the act of observing a law, custom,
etc. **2.** the celebration of a holiday.

ob.serv'ant *adj.* **1.** quick to notice.
2. careful in the observing of a
law, ritual, etc.

ob.ser.va'tion (ob'zûr vā'shən) *n.*
1. an observing or being observed.
2. a remark.

ob.serv'a.to.ry (əb zûr'və tôr'ē) *n.,*
pl. **-ries.** a place equipped for observing astronomical phenomena.

ob.serve' *v.t.,* **-served, -serving. 1.**
to see; notice; watch. **2.** to remark.
3. to obey, as a law. **4.** to celebrate, as a holiday.

ob.sess' (əb ses') *v.t.* **1.** to preoccupy the thoughts of constantly.
—*v.i.* **2.** to think about something
constantly. —**ob.sess'ive,** *adj.*

ob.ses'sion (əb sesh'ən) *n.* **1.** the
domination of one's thoughts or
feelings by a persistent idea, desire,
etc. **2.** the idea or desire itself.

ob'so.les'cent (ob'sə les'ənt) *adj.*
becoming obsolete. —**ob'so.les'-
cence,** *n.*

ob'so.lete' (-lēt') *adj.* no longer in
use.

ob'sta.cle (ob'stə kəl) *n.* something
that is in the way.

ob.stet'rics (əb ste'triks) *n.* the
branch of medicine concerned
with pregnancy and childbirth.
—**ob'ste.tri'cian** (ob'sti trish'ən) *n.*

ob'sti.nate (ob'stə nit) *adj.* **1.** stubborn. **2.** not yielding to treatment.
—**ob'sti.na.cy** (-nə sē) *n.*

ob.strep'er.ous (əb strep'ər əs) *adj.*
unruly.

ob.struct' (əb strukt') *v.t.* **1.** to
block. **2.** to hinder the passage,
progress, etc., of. —**ob.struc'tion,**
n. —**ob.struc'tive,** *adj.*

ob.tain' (əb tān') *v.t.* **1.** to get or
acquire. —*v.i.* **2.** to be customary.

ob.trude' (əb trōōd') *v.,* **-truded,
-truding.** —*v.t.* **1.** to thrust forward. —*v.i.* **2.** to intrude. —**ob.
tru'sive** (-trōō'siv) *adj.*

ob.tuse' (əb tōōs', -tyōōs') *adj.* **1.**
not perceptive. **2.** not sharp. **3.** (of
an angle) between 90° and 180°.

ob'verse *n.* (ob'vûrs) **1.** the side, as
of a coin, bearing the principal design. **2.** a counterpart. —*adj.* (ob-
vûrs', ob'vûrs) **3.** facing the observer.

ob'vi.ate' (ob'vē āt') *v.t.,* **-ated,
-ating.** to make unnecessary.

ob'vi.ous (-əs) *adj.* easily seen or
understood. —**ob'vi.ous.ly,** *adv.*

oc.ca'sion (ə kā'zhən) *n.* **1.** a particular time. **2.** a special time or
event. **3.** an opportunity. **4.** the
immediate cause. —*v.t.* **5.** to cause.

oc.ca'sion.al *adj.* **1.** not occurring
frequently. **2.** of a special occasion.
—**oc.ca'sion.al.ly,** *adv.*

oc'ci.dent (ok'si dənt) *n.* the west.

oc.cult' (ə kult', ok'ult) *adj.* **1.** supernatural. **2.** secret. —*n.* **3.** occult
matters.

oc'cu.pa'tion (ok'yə pā'shən) *n.* **1.**
a person's work. **2.** an activity. **3.**
taking control of a place by force.
—**oc'cu.pa'tion.al,** *adj.*

occupa'tional ther'apy *n.* therapy
utilizing useful activities for psychological or physical rehabilitation.

oc'cu.py *v.t.,* **-pied, -pying. 1.** to
fill (time, space, etc.). **2.** to inhabit. **3.** to take possession of (an
area) by force. **4.** to keep busy.
—**oc'cu.pan.cy,** *n.* —**oc'cu.pant,** *n.*

oc.cur' (ə kûr') *v.i.,* **-curred, -curr-
ing. 1.** to happen. **2.** to appear. **3.**
to come to mind. —**oc.cur'rence,**
n.

o'cean (ō'shən) *n.* **1.** the large
body of salt water covering much
of the earth. **2.** any of its five
main parts. —**o'ce.an'ic** (ō'shē an'-
ik) *adj.*

o'cea.nog'ra.phy (ō'shə nog'rə fē,
ō'shē ə-) *n.* the study of oceans
and the life in them.

o'ce.lot' (os'ə lot', ō'sə-) *n.* a
small, spotted American wildcat.

o'cher (ō'kər) *n.* a yellow-to-red
earthy material used as a pigment.
Also, **o'chre.**

o'clock' (ə klok') *adv.* by the clock.

Oct. October.

oc'ta.gon' (ok'tə gon', -gən) *n.* a
plane figure with eight sides.

oc'tane (ok'tān) *n.* a colorless liquid hydrocarbon in petroleum.

oc'tave (ok'tiv, -tāv) *n.* **1.** a tone on
the eighth degree from a given
musical tone. **2.** the interval between such tones.

oc.tet' (ok tet') *n.* **1.** a group of
eight musicians. **2.** music composed for such a group.

Oc.to'ber (ok tō'bər) *n.* the tenth
month of the year.

oc'to.ge.nar'i.an (ok'tə jə nâr'ē ən)
n. a person between 80 and 89
years old.

oc'to.pus (-pəs) *n., pl.* **-puses, -pi**
(-pī). an eight-armed sea mollusk.

oc'u.lar (ok'yə lər) *adj.* of the eyes.

OD (ō'dē') *n., pl.* **ODs** or **OD's,** *v.,*
OD'd or **ODed, OD'ing.** *Slang.* —*n.*
1. an overdose of a drug, esp. a fatal one. —*v.i.* **2.** to take a drug
overdose.

odd (od) *adj.* **1.** unusual; eccentric.

2. not part of a set. **3.** (of a number) not exactly divisible by two.

odd/ball/ *n. Informal.* a peculiar person or thing.

odd/i•ty *n., pl.* **-ties. 1.** strangeness. **2.** a strange thing or person.

odds (odz) *n.* **1.** the probability that something is more or less likely to occur than something else. **2.** this probability expressed as a ratio. —*Idiom.* **3. at odds,** in disagreement.

odds/ and ends/ *n.pl.* **1.** miscellaneous items. **2.** scraps.

odds/-on/ *adj.* most likely.

ode (ōd) *n.* a poem of praise.

o/di•ous (ō/dē əs) *adj.* hateful.

o/di•um (-əm) *n.* intense disgust.

o/dor (ō/dər) *n.* a smell or scent. —**o/dor•ous,** *adj.*

o/dor•if/er•ous (ō/də rif/ər əs) *adj.* having an odor, esp. a bad one.

od/ys•sey (od/ə sē) *n.* a long, adventurous journey.

o/er (ôr) *prep., adv. Poetic.* over.

oeu/vre (Fr. Œ/VR͞ᵊ) *n., pl.* **oeu•vres** (Fr. Œ/VR͞ᵊ). all the works of a writer, painter, etc.

of (uv, ov; *unstressed* əv *or, esp. before consonants,* ə) *prep.* **1.** from. **2.** belonging to. **3.** by. **4.** containing. **5.** about. —*aux. v.* **6.** *Nonstandard.* have. —**Usage.** Because the preposition OF, when unstressed (*a piece of cake*), and the unstressed or contracted auxiliary verb HAVE (*could have gone; could've gone*) are both pronounced (əv) or (ə) in connected speech, inexperienced writers commonly confuse the two words, spelling HAVE as OF (*I would of handed in my book report, but the dog ate it*). Professional writers use this spelling deliberately, especially in fiction, to represent the speech of the uneducated: *If he could of went home, he would of.*

off (ôf) *adv.* **1.** away. **2.** no longer attached or covering. **3.** not operating or in effect. —*prep.* **4.** away from. —*adj.* **5.** not in effect. **6.** in error. **7.** free from duty. **8.** of less than the ordinary activity. **9.** unlikely. —*Idiom.* **10. off and on,** intermittently; at intervals.

of/fal (ô/fəl) *n.* **1.** the viscera and remains of a butchered animal. **2.** garbage.

off/beat/ *adj.* unconventional.

off/-col/or *adj.* of questionable taste.

of•fend/ (ə fend/) *v.t.* **1.** to irritate, annoy, or anger. **2.** to affect disagreeably. —*v.i.* **3.** to commit an offense. —**of•fend/er,** *n.*

of•fense/ *n.* **1.** (ə fens/) a breaking of a rule or law. **2.** (ə fens/) a feeling of resentment and displeasure. **3.** (ə fens/) an attack. **4.** (ô/fens) the attacking side. Also, **of•fence/.**

of•fen/sive *adj.* **1.** causing resentful displeasure. **2.** unpleasant; disagreeable. —*n.* **3.** an attack.

of/fer (ô/fər) *v.t.* **1.** to present for acceptance or refusal. **2.** to propose; suggest. **3.** to bid as a price. —*n.* **4.** a proposal; bid.

of/fer•ing *n.* **1.** something offered. **2.** the act of one who offers.

of/fer•to/ry (-tôr/ē) *n., pl.* **-ries. 1.** the offering to God of bread and wine in the Eucharistic service. **2.** the collection of money at a religious service. **3.** the music accompanying such an offering.

off/hand/ *adj.* **1.** done without previous thought. **2.** casual or curt. —*adv.* **3.** in an offhand way.

of/fice (ô/fis) *n.* **1.** a place of business. **2.** a position of authority or trust. **3.** a duty or function. **4.** a religious service.

of/fice•hold/er *n.* a public official.

of/fi•cer *n.* **1.** a person of authority in an organization. **2.** a person holding a commission in the armed services. **3.** a member of a police department.

of•fi/cial (ə fish/əl) *n.* **1.** a person who holds office. —*adj.* **2.** authorized. **3.** pertaining to public office.

of•fi/ci•ant (-ē ənt) *n.* a person who officiates at a religious service.

of•fi/ci•ate/ (-āt/) *v.i.,* **-ated, -ating.** to perform official duties.

of•fi/cious *adj.* too aggressive in offering unwanted help or advice.

off/ing (ô/fing) *n.* —*Idiom.* **in the offing,** in the near future.

off/-key/ *adj.* not in tune.

off/-lim/its *adj.* forbidden.

off/-put/ting *adj.* provoking uneasiness, annoyance, etc.

off/set/ *v.t.,* **-set, -setting.** to compensate for.

off/shoot/ *n.* a branch.

off/shore/ *adj., adv.* in the water and away from shore.

off/spring/ *n.* children.

off/stage/ *adv., adj.* out of sight of the audience.

off/-the-cuff/ *adj.* impromptu.

off/-the-rec/ord *adj.* not to be quoted.

off/-the-wall/ *adj. Informal.* bizarre.

off/ year/ *n.* **1.** a year without a major election. **2.** a year marked by reduced production.

oft (ôft) *adv. Poetic.* often.

of/ten (ô/fən, ôf/tən) *adv.* many times; frequently.

o/gle (ō/gəl) *v.,* **ogled, ogling,** *n.* —*v.t., v.i.* **1.** to look (at) amorously or flirtatiously. —*n.* **2.** an ogling glance.

o′gre (ō′gər) *n.* **1.** in fairy tales, a hideous giant who eats human flesh. **2.** a cruel person.

oh (ō) *interj.* (an exclamation of surprise, pain, sympathy, etc.)

OH Ohio.

ohm (ōm) *n.* a unit of electrical resistance.

-oid a suffix meaning like.

oil (oil) *n.* **1.** a greasy combustible liquid used for lubricating, heating, etc. —*v.t.* **2.** to smear or supply with oil. —*adj.* **3.** of oil.

oil′cloth′ *n.* a cotton fabric made waterproof with oil.

oil′skin′ *n.* **1.** a fabric made waterproof with oil. **2.** (*often pl.*) a garment made of this, as a raincoat.

oint′ment (oint′mənt) *n.* a soft, oily preparation, often medicated, for applying to the skin.

OK Oklahoma.

OK (ō′kā′) *adj., adv., v.,* **OK′d, OK′ing,** *n., pl.* **OK′s.** —*adj., adv.* **1.** all right. —*v.t.* **2.** to approve. —*n.* **3.** approval. Also, **O.K.,** **o′kay′.**

Okla. Oklahoma.

o′kra (ō′krə) *n.* a leafy vegetable with sticky, edible pods.

old (ōld) *adj.* **1.** having lived or existed for a long time. **2.** having lived or existed for a specified time. **3.** shabby through age or use. **4.** of long standing. **5.** Also, **old′en.** former; ancient. —*n.* **6.** time long past.

old′-fash′ioned *adj.* having the style, ideas, etc., of an earlier time.

Old′ Guard′ *n.* (*sometimes l.c.*) the conservative members of a group.

old′ hand′ *n.* a person with long experience.

old′ hat′ *adj.* old-fashioned; dated.

old′ school′ *n.* supporters of established custom.

old′ster *n. Informal.* an elderly person.

Old′ Tes′tament *n.* the complete Bible of the Jews, being the first division of the Christian Bible.

old′-tim′er *n. Informal.* an elderly person.

o′le·ag′i·nous (ō′lē aj′ə nəs) *adj.* **1.** oily. **2.** unctuous; fawning.

o′le·an′der (ō′lē an′dər) *n.* a poisonous evergreen shrub with pink, red, or white flowers.

o′le·o·mar′ga·rine (ō′lē ō′-) *n.* margarine. Also, **o′le·o′.**

ol·fac′to·ry (ol fak′tə rē, ōl-) *adj.* pertaining to the sense of smell.

ol′i·gar′chy (-i gär′kē) *n., pl.* **-chies.** government by a small group. —**ol′i·garch′,** *n.*

ol′ive (-iv) *n.* **1.** a small, oval fruit eaten as a relish and used as a source of oil. **2.** a yellowish green color.

om′buds·man′ (om′bədz mən, om-bōōdz′-) *n., pl.* **-men.** an official who investigates individuals' complaints against the government.

o·me′ga (ō mē′gə, ō meg′ə) *n.* the last letter of the Greek alphabet.

om′e·let (om′lit, om′ə-) *n.* a dish of beaten eggs cooked and folded. Also, **om′e·lette.**

o′men (ō′mən) *n.* an event believed to predict good or evil.

om′i·nous (om′ə nəs) *adj.* threatening evil. —**om′i·nous·ly,** *adv.*

o·mit′ (ō mit′) *v.t.,* **omitted, omitting.** **1.** to leave out. **2.** to fail (to do, make, use, etc.). —**o·mis′sion** (ō mish′ən) *n.*

omni- a prefix meaning all.

om′ni·bus′ (om′nə bus′, -bəs) *n., pl.* **-buses.** **1.** a bus. **2.** an anthology.

om·nip′o·tent (om nip′ə tənt) *adj.* having unlimited power. —**om·nip′o·tence,** *n.*

om′ni·pres′ent (om′nə prez′ənt) *adj.* present everywhere at once.

om·nis′cient (om nish′ənt) *adj.* knowing all things.

om·niv′o·rous (om niv′ər əs) *adj.* eating all kinds of foods.

on (on) *prep.* **1.** attached to, supported by, or suspended from. **2.** in contact with. **3.** near to. **4.** toward. **5.** at the time of. **6.** concerning. —*adv.* **7.** in, into, or onto a thing, place, or person. **8.** forward. **9.** into or in operation. —*adj.* **10.** in use. —*Idiom.* **11. on and off,** intermittently. **12. on and on,** at great length. —*Usage.* See ABOUT.

once (wuns) *adv.* **1.** formerly. **2.** a single time. **3.** at any time. —*conj.* **4.** as soon as. —*Idiom.* **5. at once, a.** at the same time. **b.** immediately. **6. once in a while,** occasionally.

once′-o′ver *n.* a quick look.

on·col′o·gy (ong kol′ə jē) *n.* the branch of medicine dealing with tumors and cancer. —**on·col′o·gist,** *n.*

on′com′ing *adj.* approaching.

one (wun) *adj.* **1.** single. **2.** individual. **3.** common to all. —*n.* **4.** the first and lowest whole number. **5.** a single person or thing. —*pron.* **6.** a person or thing. **7.** any person or thing.

one′ness *n.* unity.

on′er·ous (on′ər əs, ō′nər-) *adj.* burdensome.

one·self′ (wun self′, wunz-) *pron.* a person's self. Also, **one's self.**

one′-sid′ed *adj.* **1.** with all advantage on one side. **2.** biased.

one′-time′ *adj.* former.

one′-track′ *adj.* obsessed with one subject.

one′-way′ *adj.* moving or allowing movement in one direction only.

on′go′ing *adj.* continuing.

on′ion (un′yən) *n.* a common plant having an edible, pungent bulb.

on′-line′ *adj.* operating under the direct control of, or connected to, a main computer.

on′look′er *n.* a spectator; witness.

on′ly (ōn′lē) *adv.* **1.** alone; solely. **2.** merely. —*adj.* **3.** being the single one of the kind. —*conj.* **4.** but.

on′o·mat′o·poe′ia (on′ə mat′ə pē′-ə, -mä′tə-) *n.* the formation of a word by the imitation of a sound.

on′rush′ *n.* a rapid advance.

on′set′ *n.* **1.** a beginning. **2.** an attack.

on′slaught′ (on′slôt′) *n.* an attack.

on′to *prep.* upon; on.

on·tol′o·gy (on tol′ə jē) *n.* the branch of metaphysics studying existence or being.

o′nus (ō′nəs) *n.* **1.** an unfair burden. **2.** responsibility.

on′ward (-wərd) *adv.* **1.** forward. —*adj.* **2.** directed or moving forward.

on′yx (on′iks, ō′niks) *n.* a kind of varicolored quartz.

ooze (ōōz) *v.*, **oozed, oozing**, *n.* —*v.i.* **1.** to leak out slowly. —*n.* **2.** something that oozes. **3.** soft mud.

o·pac′i·ty (ō pas′i tē) *n.*, *pl.* **-ties.** the state of being opaque.

o′pal (ō′pəl) *n.* a precious iridescent stone.

o′pa·les′cent (ō′pə les′ənt) *adj.* with a play of colors like that of the opal.

o·paque′ (ō pāk′) *adj.* **1.** not allowing light to pass through. **2.** dark; dull. **3.** not clear.

op. cit. (op′ sit′) in the work cited.

OPEC (ō′pek) *n.* Organization of Petroleum Exporting Countries.

Op′-Ed′ (op′ed′) *n.* a newspaper section devoted to articles by commentators, essayists, etc.

o′pen (ō′pən) *adj.* **1.** not closed, locked, or covered. **2.** not restricted. **3.** available or accessible. **4.** frank. **5.** unfolded. **6.** undecided. —*v.t.*, *v.i.* **7.** to make or become open. **8.** to begin. **9.** to come apart. —*n.* **10.** any open space.

o′pen-and-shut′ *adj.* easily solved or decided; obvious.

o′pen-end′ed *adj.* **1.** unrestricted. **2.** having no fixed answer.

o′pen-hand′ed *adj.* generous.

o′pen·ing *n.* **1.** an unobstructed or unoccupied place. **2.** a gap or hole. **3.** a beginning. **4.** an opportunity.

o′pen-mind′ed *adj.* without prejudice.

op′er·a (op′ər ə, op′rə) *n.* a drama in which the words are sung to music. —**op′er·at′ic** (-ə rat′ik) *adj.*

op′er·a·ble (op′ər ə bəl) *adj.* **1.** able to be operated. **2.** curable by surgery.

op′era glass′es *n.pl.* small, low-power binoculars.

op′er·ate′ (-ə rāt′) *v.*, **-ated, -ating.** —*v.i.* **1.** to work or function. **2.** to exert force or influence. **3.** to perform surgery. —*v.t.* **4.** to manage or use (a machine). —**op′er·a′tor**, *n.*

op′erating sys′tem *n.* software that directs a computer's operations.

op′er·a′tion *n.* **1.** the act or manner of operating. **2.** a practical or mechanical process. **3.** a surgical procedure. —**op′er·a′tion·al**, *adj.*

op′er·a·tive (-ər ə tiv, -ə rā′tiv) *n.* **1.** a worker. **2.** a spy. —*adj.* **3.** in operation.

op′er·et′ta (op′ə ret′ə) *n.* a light opera.

oph′thal·mol′o·gy (of′thəl mol′ə jē, -thə-, -thal-, op′-) *n.* the branch of medicine dealing with the eye. —**oph′thal·mol′o·gist**, *n.*

o′pi·ate (ō′pē it, -āt′) *n.* a drug containing opium.

o·pine′ (ō pīn′) *v.t.*, *v.i.*, **-pined, -pining.** to express as an opinion.

o·pin′ion (ə pin′yən) *n.* a belief or judgment.

o·pin′ion·at′ed (-yə nā′tid) *adj.* stubborn regarding one's own opinions.

o′pi·um (ō′pē əm) *n.* a narcotic made from the juice of certain poppies.

o·pos′sum (ə pos′əm, pos′əm) *n.* a marsupial of the eastern U.S.

op·po′nent (ə pō′nənt) *n.* **1.** a person on the opposite side, as in a contest. **2.** a person opposed to something.

op′por·tune′ (op′ər tōōn′, -tyōōn′) *adj.* appropriate; timely. —**op′por·tune′ly**, *adv.*

op′por·tun′ism *n.* the grasping of opportunities without regard for consequences or ethical considerations. —**op′por·tun′ist**, *n.* —**op′por·tun·is′tic**, *adj.*

op′por·tu′ni·ty *n.*, *pl.* **-ties.** a favorable time or condition for doing something.

op·pose′ (ə pōz′) *v.t.*, **-posed, -posing.** **1.** to resist. **2.** to be hostile to. **3.** to set (something) opposite something else.

op•po•site (op′ə zit, -sit) *adj.* **1.** in the corresponding position on the other side. **2.** completely different. —*n.* **3.** one that is opposite.

op′po•si′tion (-zish′ən) *n.* **1.** the action of opposing. **2.** hostility. **3.** one that opposes, protests, etc.

op•press′ (ə pres′) *v.t.* **1.** to exercise harsh authority over. **2.** to lie heavily on. —**op•pres′sor,** *n.*

op•pro′bri•um (ə prō′brē əm) *n.* disgrace and reproach.

opt (opt) *v.i.* to make a choice.

op′tic (op′tik) *adj.* of the eye or sight.

op′ti•cal *adj.* **1.** made to assist sight. **2.** visual. **3.** of optics.

op′tical disc′ *n.* a disk on which digital data is stored and read by a laser.

op′tical scan′ner *n.* a device for scanning and digitizing printed material.

op•ti′cian (op tish′ən) *n.* a person who makes or sells eyeglasses.

op′tics *n.* the branch of science dealing with light and vision.

op′ti•mal *adj.* most favorable; best.

op′ti•mism (op′tə miz′əm) *n.* **1.** a tendency to have a favorable view of things. **2.** the belief that good will prevail. —**op′ti•mist,** *n.* —**op′ti•mis′tic,** *adj.*

op′ti•mum (-məm) *n.* **1.** the best (point, degree, amount, etc.). —*adj.* **2.** most favorable; best.

op′tion (op′shən) *n.* **1.** the power or right to choose. **2.** a choice. —**op′tion•al,** *adj.*

op•tom′e•try (op tom′i trē) *n.* the profession of examining the eyes for defects. —**op•tom′e•trist,** *n.*

op′u•lent (op′yə lənt) *adj.* **1.** wealthy. **2.** richly supplied. —**op′u•lence,** *n.*

o′pus (ō′pəs) *n., pl.* **op•er•a** (op′ər ə, op′rə). a musical or literary work.

or (ôr; *unstressed* ər) *conj.* (used to connect alternatives).

OR 1. operating room. **2.** Oregon.

-or¹ a suffix meaning condition or quality.

-or² a suffix meaning a person or thing that does something.

or′a•cle (ôr′ə kəl) *n.* **1.** (in the ancient world) one believed to give answers from the gods. **2.** a wise person. —**o•rac′u•lar,** *adj.*

o′ral (ôr′əl) *adj.* **1.** spoken. **2.** of the mouth.

or′ange (ôr′inj) *n.* **1.** a round, reddish-yellow citrus fruit. **2.** a reddish yellow.

o•rang′u•tan′ (ô rang′oo tan′, ə rang′-) *n.* a large, long-armed ape.

o•ra′tion (ô rā′shən) *n.* a speech.

or′a•tor (ôr′ə tər) *n.* an eloquent public speaker.

or′a•to′ri•o′ (-tôr′ē ō′) *n., pl.* **-rios.** a musical work for voices and orchestra, usu. on a religious theme.

or′a•to′ry *n.* **1.** eloquent public speaking. **2.** the art of public speaking. —**or′a•tor′i•cal** (ôr′ə tôr′-), *adj.*

orb (ôrb) *n.* a sphere or globe.

or′bit (ôr′bit) *n.* **1.** the curved path of a planet, satellite, etc., around a celestial body. **2.** a sphere of influence. —*v.t., v.i.* **3.** to travel in or send into an orbit. —**or′bit•al,** *adj.*

or′chard (ôr′chərd) *n.* a group of cultivated fruit trees.

or′ches•tra (ôr′kə strə, -kes trə) *n.* **1.** a large company of instrumental performers. **2.** the main floor of a theater. —**or•ches′tral,** *adj.*

or′ches•trate′ (-strāt′) *v.t.,* **-trated, -trating. 1.** to arrange (music) for an orchestra. **2.** to arrange the elements of to produce a certain effect. —**or′ches•tra′tion,** *n.*

or′chid (ôr′kid) *n.* a tropical plant with showy flowers having three petals.

or•dain′ (ôr dān′) *v.t.* **1.** to invest as a member of the clergy. **2.** to give orders for; decree.

or•deal′ (ôr dēl′, ôr′dēl) *n.* any severely difficult experience.

or•der (ôr′dər) *n.* **1.** an authoritative command. **2.** a methodical arrangement; sequence. **3.** obedience to authority. **4.** goods bought or sold. **5.** a group bound by common religious rules. —*v.t., v.i.* **6.** to give an order (to). **7.** to put in order. —*Idiom.* **8. in order, a.** appropriate. **b.** properly arranged. **c.** according to the rules. **9. in short order,** quickly. **10. out of order, a.** inappropriate. **b.** improperly arranged. **c.** not according to the rules. **d.** not operating.

or′der•ly *adj., adv., n., pl.* **-lies.** —*adj.* **1.** arranged in a tidy manner. **2.** well-behaved. —*adv.* **3.** methodically. **4.** according to established order. —*n.* **5.** a hospital attendant.

or′di•nal (-dn əl) *adj.* **1.** showing a position in a series, as *first* or *second.* —*n.* **2.** an ordinal number.

or′di•nance (-əns) *n.* a law.

or′di•nar′y (-dn er′ē) *adj.* **1.** commonplace. **2.** usual; normal. —**or′di•nar′i•ly,** *adv.*

or′di•na′tion (ôr′dn ā′shən) *n.* the act or ceremony of ordaining.

ord′nance (ôrd′nəns) *n.* military weapons of all kinds.

or′dure (ôr′jər, -dyŏor) *n.* dung.

ore (ôr) *n.* a rock or mineral containing metal.

Ore. Oregon.

o•reg′a•no (ə reg′ə nō′) *n.* an aromatic plant whose leaves are used as seasoning.

or′gan (ôr′gən) *n.* 1. a musical instrument having pipes activated by keyboard and foot pedals and sounded by compressed air. 2. a part of an animal or plant having a specific function. 3. a periodical. —**or′gan•ist,** *n.*

or′gan•dy (ôr′gən dē) *n., pl.* -dies. a thin stiff cotton fabric.

or•gan′ic (ôr gan′ik) *adj.* 1. of carbon compounds. 2. of living organisms. 3. grown without synthetic fertilizers, pesticides, etc.

or′gan•ism (-gə niz′əm) *n.* any individual life form.

or•gan•i•za•tion (ôr′gə nə zā′shən) *n.* 1. an organizing or being organized. 2. something organized. 3. a group organized for some purpose. —**or′gan•i•za′tion•al,** *adj.*

or′gan•ize′ (-gə nīz′) *v.,* -ized, -izing. —*v.t.* 1. to put in order. 2. to form into a whole. 3. to gather (people) into a group for a common purpose. —*v.i.* 4. to become organized.

or•gan′za (ôr gan′zə) *n.* a sheer fabric with a crisp finish.

or′gasm (ôr′gaz əm) *n.* a sexual climax.

or′gy (ôr′jē) *n., pl.* -gies. 1. any unrestrained indulgence. 2. a wild party.

o′ri•el (ôr′ē əl) *n.* a bay window.

o′ri•ent *n.* (ôr′ē ənt, -ē ent′) 1. the east. —*v.t.* (ôr′ē ent′) 2. to make familiar with new surroundings. 3. to place facing in a certain direction. —**o′ri•en•ta′tion,** *n.*

or′i•fice (ôr′ə fis) *n.* an opening.

o′ri•ga•mi (ôr′i gä′mē) *n.* the Japanese art of folding paper into decorative forms.

or′i•gin (ôr′i jin) *n.* 1. the source from which something arises. 2. the beginning of something. 3. a person's birth or ancestry.

o•rig′i•nal (ə rij′ə nl) *adj.* 1. first. 2. not copied from something else. 3. inventive; creative. —*n.* 4. a first type from which others are made. 5. an original work, document, etc. —**o•rig′i•nal′i•ty** (-nal′i tē) *n.* —**o•rig′i•nal•ly,** *adv.*

o•rig′i•nate′ *v.t., v.i.,* -nated, -nating. to bring or come into being.

o′ri•ole′ (ôr′ē ōl′) *n.* a bright-colored songbird.

or′i•son (ôr′i zən) *n.* a prayer.

or′mo•lu′ (ôr′mə loo′) *n., pl.* -lus. a copper-zinc alloy used to imitate gold.

or′na•ment *n.* (-nə mənt) 1. something added to beautify; decoration. —*v.t.* (-ment′, -mənt) 2. to decorate. —**or′na•men′tal,** *adj.*

or•nate′ (-nāt′) *adj.* elaborately decorated. —**or•nate′ly,** *adv.*

or′ner•y (-nə rē) *adj.* ill-tempered.

or′ni•thol′o•gy (ôr′nə thol′ə jē) *n.* the study of birds. —**or′ni•thol′o•gist,** *n.*

o′ro•tund′ (-tund′) *adj.* 1. (of the voice or speech) rich and clear. 2. (of speech or writing) pompous.

or′phan (ôr′fən) *n.* 1. a child whose parents are both dead. —*adj.* 2. of or for orphans. —*v.t.* 3. to cause to become an orphan.

or′phan•age (-fə nij) *n.* a home for orphans.

or′tho•don′tics (-thə don′tiks) *n.* the branch of dentistry dealing with the correction of irregular teeth. —**or′tho•don′tic,** *adj.* —**or′tho•don′tist,** *n.*

or′tho•dox′ (-thə doks′) *adj.* 1. conforming to the approved form of any doctrine, philosophy, etc. 2. conventional. 3. **Orthodox,** of the Eastern Christian Church. 4. **Orthodox,** of Orthodox Judaism.

or•thog′ra•phy (ôr thog′rə fē) *n., pl.* -phies. spelling. —**or′tho•graph′ic** (ôr′thə graf′ik) *adj.*

or′tho•pe′dics (ôr′thə pē′diks) *n.* the branch of medicine dealing with the skeletal system. —**or′tho•pe′dist,** *n.*

-ory a suffix meaning: 1. of, characterized by, or serving to. 2. a place or instrument for.

os′cil•late′ (os′ə lāt′) *v.i.,* -lated, -lating. to swing to and fro. —**os′cil•la′tion,** *n.*

os•cil′lo•scope′ (ə sil′ə skōp′) *n.* a device that uses a cathode-ray tube to show changes in electric quantity.

os′cu•late′ (os′kyə lāt′) *v.t., v.i.,* -lated, -lating. to kiss.

o′sier (ō′zhər) *n.* a tough, flexible willow twig used in wickerwork.

-osis a suffix meaning: 1. action or condition. 2. an abnormal state.

os•mo′sis (oz mō′sis, os-) *n.* the diffusion of a liquid through a membrane into another liquid.

os′prey (os′prē, -prā) *n.* a large bird of prey that feeds on fish.

os′se•ous (os′ē əs) *adj.* of, like, or containing bone.

os′si•fy′ (os′ə fī′) *v.t., v.i.,* -fied, -fying. to convert into bone.

os•ten′si•ble (o sten′sə bəl) *adj.* outwardly appearing as such. —**os•ten′si•bly,** *adv.*

os·ten·ta/tion (os/ten tā/shən, -tən-) *n.* pretentious display. —**os/ten·ta/tious,** *adj.*

os·te·o·ar·thri/tis (os/tē ō är thrī/-tis) *n.* arthritis marked by break-down of cartilage in the joints.

os·te·op/a·thy (-op/ə thē) *n.* the treatment of disease by manipulating the affected part. —**os/te·o·path/** (-ə path/) *n.* —**os/te·o·path/ic,** *adj.*

os·te·o·po·ro/sis (-ō pə rō/sis) *n.* a disorder in which the bones become increasingly brittle, porous, and prone to fracture.

os/tra·cize/ (os/trə sīz/) *v.t.,* **-cized, -cizing.** to exclude from society; banish. —**os/tra·cism** (-siz/əm) *n.*

os/trich (ô/strich) *n.* a large, swift-footed, flightless bird.

oth/er (uth/ər) *adj.* **1.** additional. **2.** different. **3.** remaining. **4.** not long past. —*pron.* **5.** Usu., **others.** other persons or things.

oth/er·wise/ *adv.* **1.** under other circumstances. **2.** in a different way. **3.** in other respects.

oth/er·world/ly *adj.* concerned with a spiritual or imaginary world.

ot/ter (ot/ər) *n.* a furbearing aquatic mammal.

ot/to·man (ot/ə mən) *n.* a low, cushioned seat.

ought (ôt) *aux. v.* **1.** (used to express obligation or advisability). **2.** (used to express probability).

ounce (ouns) *n.* a unit of weight equal to $\frac{1}{16}$ lb. avoirdupois or $\frac{1}{12}$ lb. troy.

our (ou°r, ou/ər; *unstressed* är) *pron.* the possessive form of **we,** used before a noun.

ours *pron.* the possessive form of **we,** used as a predicate adjective.

our·selves/ *pron.* **1.** a reflexive substitute for **us. 2.** an intensive with or substitute for **we** or **us.**

oust (oust) *v.t.* to expel or force out from a place or position.

oust/er *n.* expulsion.

out (out) *adv.* **1.** not in the usual place, position, etc. **2.** in or into the outdoors. **3.** so as to project or extend. **4.** known to the public. **5.** not in effective use or operation. **6.** to a state of nonexistence, exhaustion, etc. —*adj.* **7.** not at one's home or place of work. **8.** not operating. —*prep.* **9.** out from or through. **10.** out along or on. —*n.* **11.** a means of evasion. —*Idiom.* **12. on the outs,** quarreling.

out- a prefix meaning: **1.** outward. **2.** outside. **3.** to surpass.

out/age (ou/tij) *n.* an interruption or failure in a supply of power.

out/-and-out/ *adj.* complete; absolute.

out/back/ *n.* a remote area.

out/board/ *adj.* located on the exterior of a ship or boat.

out/break/ *n.* **1.** a sudden occurrence. **2.** a riot.

out/build/ing *n.* a detached building smaller than a main building.

out/burst/ *n.* a violent outpouring.

out/cast/ *n.* an exiled person.

out/class/ *v.t.* to outdo in style or excellence.

out/come/ *n.* a final result.

out/crop/ *n.* an underlying layer of rock that emerges on the earth's surface.

out/cry/ *n., pl.* **-cries.** an expression of distress or protest.

out·dat/ed *adj.* out-of-date.

out·dis/tance *v.t.,* **-tanced, -tancing.** to leave behind, as in racing.

out·do/ *v.t.,* **-did, -done, -doing.** to do better than.

out/door/ *adj.* done or occurring in the open air.

out/doors/ *adv.* **1.** in the open air. —*n.* **2.** the world away from buildings; open air.

out/er *adj.* **1.** situated farther out. **2.** situated on the outside.

out/er·most/ *adj.* situated farthest out.

out/er space/ *n.* **1.** space beyond the earth's atmosphere. **2.** space beyond the solar system.

out/field/ *n.* the area of a baseball field beyond the diamond.

out/fit/ *n., v.,* **-fitted, -fitting.** —*n.* **1.** a set of articles for any purpose. **2.** a set of clothes. **3.** an organized group of persons. —*v.t.* **4.** to equip.

out/go/ *n., pl.* **-goes.** money paid out.

out/go/ing *adj.* **1.** (-gō/ing) departing. **2.** (-gō/ing) retiring from a position or office. **3.** (-gō/ing, -gō/-) friendly; sociable.

out/grow/ *v.t.,* **-grew, -grown, -growing.** to grow too large or mature for.

out/growth/ *n.* an additional result.

out/house/ *n.* an outbuilding serving as a toilet.

out/ing *n.* a pleasure trip.

out·land/ish (-lan/dish) *adj.* strange or odd.

out/last/ *v.t.* to last longer than.

out/law/ *n.* **1.** a habitual criminal. —*v.t.* **2.** to declare illegal.

out/lay/ *n.* a sum of money spent.

out/let/ (-let, -lit) *n.* **1.** an opening or passage out. **2.** a market for goods. **3.** a means of expression.

out/line/ *n., v.,* **-lined, -lining.** —*n.*

1. the line by which an object is bounded. **2.** a drawing showing only an outer contour. **3.** a general description. —*v.t.* **4.** to draw or represent in outline.

out/live/ (-liv/) *v.t.,* **-lived, -living.** to live longer than.

out/look/ *n.* **1.** the view from a place. **2.** one's mental attitude. **3.** prospect for the future.

out/ly/ing *adj.* remote.

out/mod/ed (-mō/did) *adj.* **1.** no longer fashionable. **2.** obsolete.

out•num/ber *v.t.* to exceed in number.

out/-of-bod/y *adj.* characterized by the sensation that the mind has left the body.

out/-of-date/ *adj.* outmoded.

out/-of-doors/ *n.* outdoors.

out/-of-the-way/ *adj.* **1.** isolated; remote. **2.** unusual.

out/pa/tient *n.* a patient who receives treatment at a hospital without being admitted.

out/post/ *n.* an outlying military post.

out/put/ *n.* **1.** the quantity produced in a certain period. **2.** the power produced by an electrical device. **3.** information made available by computer.

out/rage *n., v.,* **-raged, -raging.** —*n.* **1.** an act of wanton violence. **2.** great anger. —*v.t.* **3.** to subject to outrage.

out•ra/geous (-rā/jəs) *adj.* **1.** grossly offensive. **2.** beyond reasonable limits.

ou•tré/ (ōō trā/) *adj.* bizarre.

out/reach/ *n.* **1.** an act of reaching out. —*adj.* **2.** concerned with extending community services.

out/right/ *adj.* (-rīt/) **1.** complete; thorough. —*adv.* (-rīt/, -rīt/) **2.** completely. **3.** openly.

out/run/ *v.t.,* **-ran, -run, -running. 1.** to run faster or farther than. **2.** to exceed.

out/sell/ *v.t.,* **-sold, -selling.** to sell more than.

out/set/ *n.* beginning.

out/shine/ *v.t.,* **-shone** or **-shined, -shining. 1.** to shine more brightly than. **2.** to surpass in excellence.

out/side/ *n.* (out/sīd/, -sīd/) **1.** the outer surface, appearance, etc. **2.** the space beyond an enclosure or boundary. —*adj.* (out/sīd/, out/-) **3.** of, being, done, etc., on the outside. **4.** remote. **5.** not belonging to a group. —*adv.* (out/sīd/) **6.** on or to the outside. —*prep.* (out/sīd/, out/sīd/) **7.** on the outside of.

out•sid/er *n.* a person who doesn't belong to a group.

out/skirts/ *n.pl.* the outlying district.

out•smart/ *v.t.* to outwit.

out/spo/ken *adj.* candid.

out/spread/ *adj.* extended.

out/stand/ing *adj.* **1.** excellent. **2.** prominent. **3.** not yet paid.

out/strip/ *v.t.,* **-stripped, -stripping. 1.** to exceed. **2.** to get ahead of.

out/take/ *n.* a segment of film edited out of the published version.

out/ward (-wərd) *adj.* **1.** on the outside. —*adv.* **2.** Also, **out/wards.** toward the outside. —**out/ward•ly,** *adv.*

out/weigh/ *v.t.* to exceed in importance.

out/wit/ *v.t.,* **-witted, -witting.** to get the better of by superior cleverness.

o/va (ō/və) *n.* pl. of **ovum.**

o/val (ō/vəl) *adj.* **1.** egg-shaped. —*n.* **2.** something oval in shape.

o/va•ry (ō/və rē) *n., pl.* **-ries.** the female reproductive gland. —**o•var/i•an** (ō vâr/ē ən) *adj.*

o/vate (ō/vāt) *adj.* egg-shaped.

o•va/tion (ō vā/shən) *n.* enthusiastic applause.

ov/en (uv/ən) *n.* a chamber for baking or drying.

o/ver (ō/vər) *prep.* **1.** above in position, authority, etc. **2.** on or to the other side of; across. **3.** so as to cover. **4.** in excess of. **5.** concerning. **6.** during. —*adv.* **7.** so as to affect the whole surface. **8.** from one side to another. **9.** from an upright position. **10.** once more. **11.** in addition. —*adj.* **12.** upper. **13.** surplus. **14.** too great. **15.** past.

o/ver•a•chieve/ *v.i.,* **-chieved, -chieving.** to perform better than expected, esp. in school.

o/ver•act/ *v.i.* to perform in an exaggerated manner.

o/ver•age¹ (ō/vər āj/) *adj.* beyond the acceptable or desirable age.

o/ver•age² (ō/vər ij) *n.* a surplus.

o/ver•all/ (ō/vər ôl/) *adv., adj.* **1.** from one end to the other. **2.** including everything. —*n.* **3. overalls,** loose, stout trousers.

o/ver•awe/ *v.t.,* **-awed, -awing.** to subdue by inspiring awe.

o/ver•bear/ing *adj.* domineering.

o/ver•blown/ *adj.* **1.** excessive. **2.** pretentious.

o/ver•board/ *adv.* over the side of a ship into the water.

o/ver•cast/ (-kast/, -kast/) *adj.* **1.** cloudy. **2.** gloomy.

o/ver•charge/ *v.,* **-charged, -charging.** —*v.t., v.i.* **1.** to charge too high a price. **2.** to overload. —*n.* (ō/vər chärj/) **3.** a charge exceeding a fair price. **4.** an excessive load.

o/ver·coat/ *n.* a coat worn over ordinary clothing.

o/ver·come/ *v.*, **-came, -come, -com·ing.** —*v.t.* **1.** to prevail over (opposition, temptations, etc.). **2.** to overpower. —*v.i.* **3.** to win.

o/ver·do/ *v.*, **-did, -done, -doing.** —*v.t.* **1.** to do to excess. —*v.i.* **2.** to do too much.

o/ver·dose/ *n.*, *v.*, **-dosed, -dosing.** —*n.* **1.** an excessive dose of a drug. —*v.i.* **2.** to take such a dose.

o/ver·draft/ *n.* **1.** the act of overdrawing a checking account. **2.** the amount overdrawn.

o/ver·draw/ *v.t.*, **-drew, -drawn, -drawing.** to draw upon (an account) in excess of the balance.

o/ver·drive/ *n.* a mechanism that reduces the power required to maintain speed by lowering the gear ratio.

o/ver·due/ *adj.* past due.

o/ver·flow/ *v.*, **-flowed, -flown, -flowing,** *n.* —*v.i.* (ō/vər flō/) **1.** to flow or run over; flood. —*n.* (ō/vər flō/) **2.** an instance of flooding. **3.** something that runs over.

o/ver·grow/ *v.t.*, **-grew, -grown, -growing.** to cover with growth.

o/ver·hand/ *adv.* with hand and arm raised above the shoulder.

o/ver·hang/ *v.*, **-hung, -hanging,** *n.* —*v.t.*, *v.i.* (ō/vər hang/) **1.** to project over (something). —*n.* (ō/vər-hang/) **2.** something that extends over.

o/ver·haul/ *v.t.* (ō/vər hôl/, ō/vər-hôl/) **1.** to investigate thoroughly, as for repair. **2.** to catch up with. —*n.* (ō/vər hôl/) **3.** a complete examination and repair.

o/ver·head/ *adv.* (ō/vər hed/) **1.** above one's head. —*n.* (ō/vər hed/) **2.** general business expenses, as rent and lighting.

o/ver·hear/ *v.t.*, **-heard, -hearing.** to hear (words or a speaker) without the speaker's knowledge.

o/ver·joyed/ (-joid/) *adj.* very happy.

o/ver·kill/ *n.* any greatly excessive amount.

o/ver·land/ (-land/, -lənd) *adv.*, *adj.* across open country.

o/ver·lap/ *v.*, **-lapped, -lapping,** *n.* —*v.t.*, *v.i.* (ō/vər lap/) **1.** to extend over and beyond. —*n.* (ō/vər lap/) **2.** an overlapping part.

o/ver·lay/ *v.t.*, **-laid, -laying. 1.** to lay or place (one thing) over another. **2.** to finish with a decorative layer.

o/ver·lie/ *v.i.*, **-lay, -lain, -lying.** to lie over or on.

o/ver·look/ *v.t.* **1.** to fail to notice.

2. to excuse. **3.** to give a view over.

o/ver·ly *adv.* excessively.

o/ver·night/ *adv.* (-nīt/) **1.** during the night. **2.** suddenly. —*adj.* (-nīt/) **3.** done, made, etc., during the night. **4.** staying for one night.

o/ver·pass/ *n.* a bridge crossing over traffic.

o/ver·play/ *v.t.* to exaggerate.

o/ver·pow/er *v.t.* **1.** to overwhelm in feeling. **2.** to subdue.

o/ver·rate/ *v.t.*, **-rated, -rating.** to rate too highly.

o/ver·reach/ *v.t.* **1.** to reach over or beyond. **2.** to defeat (oneself) by trying too hard.

o/ver·re·act/ *v.i.* to react too emotionally. —**o/ver·re·ac/tion,** *n.*

o/ver·ride/ *v.t.*, **-rode, -ridden, -riding.** to prevail over; overrule.

o/ver·rule/ *v.t.*, **-ruled, -ruling.** to rule against.

o/ver·run/ *v.t.*, **-ran, -run, -running.** to swarm over.

o/ver·seas/ *adv.* across the sea.

o/ver·see/ *v.t.*, **-saw, -seen, -seeing.** to supervise. —**o/ver·se/er,** *n.*

o/ver·shad/ow *v.t.* to be more important than.

o/ver·shoot/ *v.t.*, **-shot, -shooting.** to shoot or go beyond so as to miss.

o/ver·sight/ *n.* **1.** an error of neglect. **2.** supervision.

o/ver·sleep/ *v.i.*, **-slept, -sleeping.** to sleep beyond a desired time.

o/ver·state/ *v.t.*, **-stated, -stating.** to exaggerate in describing. —**o/ver·state/ment,** *n.*

o/ver·stay/ *v.i.* to stay too long.

o/ver·step/ *v.t.*, **-stepped, -stepping.** to go beyond.

o·vert/ (ō vûrt/, ō/vûrt) *adj.* not concealed.

o/ver·take/ *v.t.*, **-took, -taken, -taking.** to catch up with or pass.

o/ver-the-count/er *adj.* **1.** sold legally without a prescription. **2.** not listed on or traded through an organized securities exchange.

o/ver·throw/ *v.*, **-threw, -thrown, -throwing,** *n.* —*v.t.* (ō/vər thrō/) **1.** to defeat; depose. —*n.* (ō/vər thrō/) **2.** an act or instance of overthrowing or being overthrown.

o/ver·time/ *n.* time worked in addition to regular hours.

o/ver·tone/ *n.* an additional meaning or implication.

o/ver·ture (ō/vər chər, -chŏŏr/) *n.* **1.** an orchestral prelude, as to an opera. **2.** a first move in a relationship, negotiation, etc.

o/ver·turn/ *v.t.* **1.** to cause to turn over. **2.** to defeat. —*v.i.* **3.** to turn over.

o′ver•view′ n. a general perception or description.

o′ver•ween′ing (-wē′ning) adj. **1.** conceited. **2.** excessive.

o′ver•weight′ (ō′vər wāt′) adj. weighing more than is normal.

o′ver•whelm′ (-hwelm′, -welm′) v.t. **1.** to overpower emotionally. **2.** to overcome completely. **3.** to bury beneath a mass of something.

o′ver•work′ v.i., v.t. **-worked** or **-wrought, -working.** (ō′ver wûrk′) to work or cause to work too hard.

o′ver•wrought′ (ō′vər rôt′, ō′vər-) adj. extremely excited.

o′vi•duct′ (ō′vi dukt′) n. a tube through which ova are transported from the ovary to the uterus.

o′void (ō′void) adj. egg-shaped.

ov′u•late (ov′yə lāt′, ō′vyə-) v.i., **-lated, -lating.** to produce and discharge eggs from an ovary.

ov′ule (ov′yōol, ō′vyōol) n. **1.** the structure that develops into a seed after fertilization. **2.** a small egg.

o′vum (ō′vəm) n., pl. **ova** (ō və). a female reproductive cell.

owe (ō) v.t., **owed, owing. 1.** to be obligated to pay or give to another. **2.** to be indebted to or for.

owl (oul) n. a nocturnal bird of prey.

own (ōn) adj. **1.** of or belonging to. —v.t. **2.** to possess. **3.** to acknowledge. —**own′er,** n. —**own′er• ship′,** n.

ox (oks) n., pl. **oxen.** a bovine animal, esp. a castrated adult bull.

ox′ford (oks′fərd) n. a low shoe laced over the instep.

ox′i•dant (ok′si dənt) n. a chemical agent that oxidizes.

ox′ide (ok′sīd, -sid) n. a compound of oxygen and another element.

ox′i•dize′ (ok′si dīz′) v., **-dized, -dizing.** —v.t. **1.** to combine chemically with oxygen. —v.i. **2.** to become oxidized. —**ox′i•da′tion,** n.

ox′y•a•cet′y•lene′ (ok′sē ə set′l ēn′, -in) n. a mixture of oxygen and acetylene used for cutting and welding steel.

ox′y•gen (ok′si jən) n. a colorless, odorless gas necessary to life.

ox′y•gen•ate′ (-jə nāt′) v.t., **-ated, -ating.** to enrich with oxygen.

ox′y•mo′ron (ok′si môr′on) n., pl. **-mora.** a figure of speech that uses seeming contradictions.

oys′ter (oi′stər) n. an edible mollusk having an irregularly shaped shell.

oz. ounce.

o′zone (ō′zōn, ō zōn′) n. a form of oxygen in the upper atmosphere.

o′zone hole′ n. any part of the ozone layer depleted by atmospheric pollution.

o′zone lay′er n. the layer of the upper atmosphere where most ozone is concentrated.

P

P, p (pē) n. the sixteenth letter of the English alphabet.

PA **1.** Also, **Pa.** Pennsylvania. **2.** public-address system.

PAC (pak) n., pl. **PACs, PAC′s.** political action committee.

pace (pās) n., v., **paced, pacing.** —n. **1.** a rate of movement or progress. **2.** a single step. —v.t. **3.** to set the pace for. **4.** to measure by pacing. —v.i. **5.** to take slow, regular steps. —**pac′er,** n.

pace′mak′er n. an electronic device for controlling the heartbeat.

pace′set′ter n. a person who sets a pace for others to follow.

pach′y•derm′ (pak′i dûrm′) n. a large thick-skinned mammal, as the elephant.

pach′y•san′dra (pak′ə san′drə) n., pl. **-dras.** a low plant used as ground cover.

pa•cif′ic (pə sif′ik) adj. peaceful.

pac′i•fi′er (pas′ə fī′ər) n. **1.** a nipple-shaped device for a baby to suck on. **2.** one that pacifies.

pac′i•fism (-fiz′əm) n. opposition to war or violence. —**pac′i•fist,** n.

pac′i•fy′ v.t., **-fied, -fying. 1.** to calm. **2.** to appease.

pack (pak) n. **1.** a group of items wrapped together for easy handling or selling. **2.** a group of people or things. **3.** a group of wolves, dogs, etc. —v.t. **4.** to make into a pack. **5.** to fill with anything. **6.** to crowd together within. —v.i. **7.** to fill luggage with belongings for travel. **8.** to press together. —*Idiom.* **9.** pack it in, to abandon one's efforts. —**pack′er,** n.

pack′age (-ij) n., v., **-aged, -aging.** —n. **1.** a bundle; parcel. **2.** a container in which something is packed. **3.** a group of related things offered as a unit. —v.t. **4.** to put into a package.

pack′et n. a small package.

pack′ rat′ n. **1.** a rat that carries off shiny articles to its nest. **2.** *Informal.* a person who saves useless items.

pact (pakt) n. an agreement.

pad¹ (pad) *n.*, *v.*, **padded, padding.** —*n.* **1.** a cushionlike mass of soft material. **2.** a bound package of writing paper. **3.** a soft part under an animal's paw. —*v.t.* **4.** to furnish with soft material. **5.** to expand with false or useless matter.

pad² (pad) *n.*, *v.*, **padded, padding.** —*n.* **1.** a dull sound, as of footsteps. —*v.i.* **2.** to walk with a dull sound.

pad′dle¹ (pad′l) *n.*, *v.*, **-dled, -dling.** —*n.* **1.** a short oar for two hands. —*v.i.*, *v.t.* **2.** to propel (a canoe) with a paddle.

pad′dle² (pad′l) *v.i.*, **-dled, -dling.** to move the feet and hands in shallow water.

pad′dock (pad′ək) *n.* a fenced area for horses.

pad′dy (pad′ē) *n.*, *pl.* **-dies.** a rice field.

pad′dy wag′on *n.* a van for transporting prisoners.

pad′lock′ *n.* **1.** a detachable lock with a sliding U-shaped shackle. —*v.t.* **2.** to fasten with a padlock.

pa′dre (pä′drā) *n.*, *pl.* **-dres.** a clergyman.

pae′an (pē′ən) *n.* a song of praise.

pa′gan (pā′gən) *n.* **1.** a person who does not believe in an established religion; heathen. —*adj.* **2.** of pagans; heathen. —**pa′gan·ism**, *n.*

page¹ (pāj) *n.*, *v.*, **paged, paging.** —*n.* **1.** a written or printed surface, as in a book. —*v.* **2. page through,** to turn pages.

page² (pāj) *n.*, *v.*, **paged, paging.** —*n.* **1.** a boy servant. **2.** an employee who carries messages, runs errands, etc. —*v.t.* **3.** to summon (a person) in a public place by calling his or her name.

pag′eant (paj′ənt) *n.* an elaborate show or parade with people in costume. —**pag′eant·ry**, *n.*

pag′i·nate′ (-ə nāt′) *v.t.*, **-nated, -nating.** to number the pages of. —**pag′i·na′tion**, *n.*

pa·go′da (pə gō′də) *n.* a Far Eastern temple tower having a series of upward-curving roofs.

paid (pād) *v.* a pt. and pp. of **pay.**

pail (pāl) *n.* a bucket.

pain (pān) *n.* **1.** physical or mental suffering. **2. pains,** effort. —*v.t.* **3.** to hurt. —**pain′ful**, *adj.* —**pain′less**, *adj.*

pain′kil′ler *n.* something that relieves pain.

pains′tak′ing *adj.* careful.

paint (pānt) *n.* **1.** a liquid coloring matter used as a decorative or protective coating. —*v.t.* **2.** to represent in paint. **3.** to apply paint to.

—*v.i.* **4.** to engage in painting. —**paint′er**, *n.* —**paint′ing**, *n.*

pair (pâr) *n.*, *pl.* **pairs, pair**, *v.* —*n.* **1.** a combination of two things matched for use together. **2.** an object consisting of two joined parts. **3.** two associated persons or things. —*v.t.*, *v.i.* **4.** to form (into) a pair. —**Usage.** See COUPLE.

pais′ley (pāz′lē) *adj.* having a colorful, detailed pattern of curved figures.

pa·jam′as (pə jä′məz, -jam′əz) *n.pl.* a jacket and trousers for sleeping in.

pal (pal) *n. Informal.* a close friend.

pal′ace (pal′is) *n.* the official residence of a sovereign.

pal′an·quin′ (pal′ən kēn′) *n.* an enclosed chair or bed carried on men's shoulders.

pal′at·a·ble (pal′ə tə bəl) *adj.* acceptable to the taste.

pal′ate (-it) *n.* **1.** the roof of the mouth. **2.** the sense of taste.

pa·la′tial (pə lā′shəl) *adj.* splendidly built or furnished.

pa·lav′er (pə lav′ər) *n.* idle talk.

pale¹ (pāl) *adj.*, **paler, palest**, *v.*, **paled, paling.** —*adj.* **1.** without much color; near-white. —*v.t.*, *v.i.* **2.** to make or become pale.

pale² (pāl) *n.* **1.** a stake. **2.** limits.

pa′le·on·tol′o·gy (pā′lē ən tol′ə jē) *n.* the science of early life forms, as represented by their fossils.

pal′ette (pal′it) *n.* a thin board on which a painter lays and mixes colors.

pal′imp·sest′ (pal′imp sest′) *n.* a manuscript with text erased to make room for another text.

pal′in·drome′ (-in drōm′) *n.* a word or verse reading the same backward as forward.

pal′ing (pā′ling) *n.* a fence of stakes.

pal′i·sade′ (pal′ə sād′) *n.* **1.** a fence of stakes. **2. palisades,** a line of cliffs.

pall (pôl) *n.* **1.** a cloth spread on a coffin. **2.** something that covers with darkness. —*v.i.* **3.** to become wearisome or distasteful.

pall′bear′er *n.* one of the persons who carries the coffin at a funeral.

pal′let¹ (pal′it) *n.* **1.** a straw mattress. **2.** a small bed.

pal′let² (pal′it) *n.* a low platform on which goods are placed.

pal′li·ate′ (pal′ē āt′) *v.t.*, **-ated, -ating.** **1.** to relieve without curing. **2.** to try to reduce the seriousness of (an offense). —**pal′li·a·tive** (-ā′tiv, ə tiv), *n.*, *adj.*

pal′lid (pal′id) *adj.* pale.

pal′lor (-ər) *n.* paleness.

palm¹ (päm) *n.* **1.** the inner surface of the hand. —*v.t.* **2.** to conceal in the hand. **3. palm off,** to get someone to accept (something) by fraudulent means.

palm² (päm) *n.* a tall, unbranched tropical tree with a crown of large leaves.

pal·met'to (pal met'ō, päl-, pä-) *n., pl.* **-tos, -toes.** a species of palm.

palm'is·try (pä'mə strē) *n.* the art of telling fortunes from the lines on the palms of the hands. —**palm'ist,** *n.*

pal'o·mi'no (pal'ə mē'nō) *n., pl.* **-nos.** a light tan or golden horse.

pal'pa·ble (pal'pə bəl) *adj.* **1.** able to be touched. **2.** obvious. —**pal'pa·bly,** *adv.*

pal'pate (-pāt) *v.t.,* **-pated, -pating.** to examine by touch. —**pal·pa'tion,** *n.*

pal'pi·tate' (-pi tāt') *v.i.,* **-tated, -tating. 1.** to throb with unnatural rapidity. **2.** to quiver, as with excitement. —**pal'pi·ta'tion,** *n.*

pal'sy (pôl'zē) *n., pl.* **-sies.** paralysis and tremors.

pal'try (pôl'trē) *adj.,* **-trier, -triest.** worthless. —**pal'tri·ness,** *n.*

pam'pas (pam'pəz; *attributively* -pəs) *n.* the vast plains of South America.

pam'per (pam'pər) *v.t.* to treat with excessive indulgence.

pam'phlet (pam'flit) *n.* a thin booklet.

pan¹ (pan) *n., v.,* **panned, panning.** —*n.* **1.** a broad, shallow container for cooking, washing, etc. —*v.t.* **2.** *Informal.* to criticize. —*v.i.* **3.** to wash gravel, sand, etc., in a pan to search for gold. **4. pan out,** *Informal.* to have a successful outcome.

pan² (pan) *v.,* **panned, panning,** *n.* —*v.i., v.t.* **1.** to swivel (a camera) in filming. —*n.* **2.** the act of panning a camera.

pan- a prefix meaning all.

pan'a·ce'a (pan'ə sē'ə) *n.* a cure-all.

pa·nache' (pə nash', -näsh') *n.* a grand or flamboyant manner; flair.

pan'cake' *n.* a flat fried batter cake.

pan'cre·as (pan'krē əs, pang'-) *n.* a large gland near the stomach that secretes insulin into the blood. —**pan'cre·at'ic,** *adj.*

pan'da (pan'də) *n.* a black-and-white bearlike animal of China.

pan·dem'ic (pan dem'ik) *adj.* (of a disease) epidemic over a large area.

pan·de·mo'ni·um (-də mō'nē əm) *n.* wild disorder or uproar.

pan'der (-dər) *v.i.* to cater to the desires of others.

pane (pān) *n.* a glass section of a window or door.

pan'e·gyr'ic (pan'i jir'ik, -jī'rik) *n.* speech or writing in praise of a person or thing.

pan'el (pan'l) *n., v.,* **-eled, -eling.** —*n.* **1.** a bordered section of a wall, door, etc. **2.** a public discussion group. **3.** a list of persons called for jury duty. —*v.t.* **4.** to arrange in or ornament with panels.

pan'el·ist *n.* a member of a panel.

pang (pang) *n.* a sudden feeling of distress or pain.

pan'han'dle¹ *n.* a long, narrow strip of a larger territory.

pan'han'dle² *v.i.,* **-dled, -dling.** *Informal.* to beg from passersby.

pan'ic (pan'ik) *n., v.,* **-icked, -icking.** —*n.* **1.** sudden overwhelming fear. —*v.t., v.i.* **2.** to affect or be affected with panic. —**pan'ick·y,** *adj.* —**pan'ic-strick'en,** *adj.*

pan'nier (pan'yər, -ē ər) *n.* a large basket for carrying goods.

pan'o·ply (pan'ə plē) *n., pl.* **-plies.** an impressive display.

pan'o·ram'a (-ram'ə, -rä'mə) *n.* a view over a wide area or of changing events. —**pan'o·ram'ic,** *adj.*

pan'sy (pan'zē) *n., pl.* **-sies.** a kind of violet with bright, variously colored flowers.

pant (pant) *v.i.* **1.** to breathe hard and quickly. **2.** to long eagerly.

pan'ta·loons' (pan'tl ōōnz') *n.pl.* a man's close-fitting trousers.

pan'the·ism (pan'thē iz'əm) *n.* a religious belief or philosophical doctrine that identifies God with the universe. —**pan'the·is'tic,** *adj.*

pan'the·on (-on') *n.* **1.** a building with tombs or memorials of a nation's famous dead. **2.** the heroes of a nation, movement, etc., as a group.

pan'ther (pan'thər) *n.* a cougar or leopard, usu. black.

pan'ties (pan'tēz) *n.pl.* women's underpants. Also, **pan'ty.**

pan'to·mime' (pan'tə mīm') *n., v.,* **-mimed, -miming.** —*n.* **1.** gesture without speech. **2.** a play in which the performers express themselves by gesture only. —*v.t., v.i.* **3.** to express (oneself) in pantomime. —**pan'to·mim'ist,** *n.*

pan'try (pan'trē) *n., pl.* **-tries.** a room or closet in which food and kitchen supplies are kept.

pants (pants) *n.pl.* trousers.

pant'y·hose' *n.* (*used with a pl. v.*) one-piece stockings plus panties.

pan'zer (pan'zər) *adj.* **1.** armored. —*n.* **2.** a tank or armored vehicle.

pap (pap) *n.* soft food.

pa·pa (pä'pə, pə pä') *n.* father.

pa′pa•cy (pā′pə sē) *n., pl.* **-cies.** the office of the pope.

pa′pal (pā′pəl) *adj.* of the pope or the papacy.

pa•pa′ya (pə pä′yə) *n.* a yellow, melonlike tropical American fruit.

pa′per (pā′pər) *n.* **1.** a substance made in thin sheets from wood pulp, rags, etc., for writing on, wrapping, etc. **2.** a document. **3.** a newspaper. **4.** a scholarly essay, article, etc. **5.** wallpaper. —*v.t.* **6.** to cover with wallpaper. —*adj.* **7.** of paper. —**pa′per•y,** *adj.*

pa′per•back′ *n.* a book bound in a paper cover.

pa′per ti′ger *n.* a person or nation that seems strong but is actually weak.

pa′per•weight′ *n.* a small, heavy object placed on papers to keep them from scattering.

pa′pier-mâ•ché′ (pā′pər mə shā′) *n.* dampened paper pulp mixed with glue and molded to form objects.

pa•poose′ (pa po͞os′) *n.* a North American Indian baby.

pap•ri′ka (pa prē′kə) *n.* a red spice made from dried sweet peppers.

Pap′ test′ (pap) *n.* a test for cancer of the cervix.

pa•py′rus (pə pī′rəs) *n., pl.* **-ri. 1.** a tall aquatic plant made into a kind of paper by the ancient Egyptians. **2.** the paper made from this.

par (pär) *n.* **1.** an equality in value or standing. **2.** an average amount, degree, etc. **3.** in golf, a standard number of strokes for a hole or a course.

para- a prefix meaning: **1.** beside. **2.** beyond. **3.** auxiliary.

par′a•ble (par′ə bəl) *n.* a short allegory to teach a moral.

pa•rab′o•la (pə rab′ə lə) *n.* a U-shaped curve, surface, object, etc.

par′a•chute′ (par′ə sho͞ot′) *n., v.,* **-chuted, -chuting.** —*n.* **1.** a folding, umbrellalike apparatus used to descend slowly and safely through the air. —*v.t., v.i.* **2.** to drop by parachute. —**par′a•chut′ist,** *n.*

pa•rade′ (pə rād′) *n., v.,* **-raded, -rading.** —*n.* **1.** a public procession in honor of a holiday, person, etc. **2.** a military ceremony involving a formal assembly of troops. —*v.t.* **3.** to display ostentatiously. —*v.i.* **4.** to march in a procession. **5.** to assemble in military order.

par′a•digm′ (par′ə dīm′, -dim) *n.* an example or model.

par′a•dise′ (-dīs′, -dīz′) *n.* **1.** heaven. **2.** a place of perfect happiness. —**par′a•di•sa′i•cal,** *adj.*

par′a•dox′ (-doks′) *n.* a statement that seems self-contradictory. —**par′a•dox′i•cal,** *adj.*

par′af•fin (-fin) *n.* a waxy, solid substance.

par′a•gon′ (-gon′, -gən) *n.* a model of excellence.

par′a•graph′ (-graf′) *n.* **1.** a unit of written or printed matter, beginning on a new line that is usu. indented. —*v.t.* **2.** to divide into paragraphs.

par′a•keet′ (-kēt′) *n.* a small parrot with a long tail.

par′a•le′gal *n.* a lawyer's assistant.

par′al•lax′ (-ə laks′) *n.* the apparent displacement of an observed object due to the changed position of the viewer.

par′al•lel′ (-ə lel′, -ləl) *adj., n., v.,* **-leled, -leling.** —*adj.* **1.** (of lines or planes) going in the same direction and being the same distance apart at all points. **2.** having the same direction, nature, etc.; similar. —*n.* **3.** a parallel line or plane. **4.** anything parallel or similar to something else. —*v.t.* **5.** to be parallel to. —**par′al•lel•ism,** *n.*

par′al•lel′o•gram (-lel′ə gram′) *n.* a four-sided figure whose opposite sides are parallel.

pa•ral′y•sis (pə ral′ə sis) *n., pl.* **-ses.** a loss or impairment of the ability to move. —**par′a•lyt′ic** (par′ə lit′ik) *n., adj.* —**par′a•lyze′,** *v.t.*

par′a•med′ic *n.* a person trained to give emergency medical care.

pa•ram′e•ter (pə ram′i tər) *n.* **1.** a determining characteristic. **2.** parameters, limits or boundaries.

par′a•mil′i•ta•ry (par′ə mil′i ter′ē) *adj.* of organizations operating in place of or in addition to a regular military force.

par′a•mount′ (par′ə mount′) *adj.* greatest; utmost.

par′a•mour′ (-mo͞or′) *n.* a lover.

par′a•noi′a (par′ə noi′ə) *n.* a mental disorder marked by delusions of persecution. —**par′a•noid′,** *adj., n.*

par′a•pet (par′ə pit, -pet′) *n.* a wall at the edge of a roof or terrace.

par′a•pher•nal′ia (-fər nāl′yə, -fə-) *n.pl.* **1.** equipment for a particular activity. **2.** personal belongings.

par′a•phrase′ *v.,* **-phrased, -phrasing,** *n.* —*v.t., v.i.* **1.** to express in different words. —*n.* **2.** such a rephrasing.

par′a•ple′gi•a (-plē′jē ə, -jə) *n.* paralysis of both lower limbs. —**par′a•ple′gic,** *n., adj.*

par′a•pro•fes′sion•al *adj.* engaged in a profession in a partial or secondary capacity.

par′a•psy•chol′o•gy *n.* the branch of psychology that studies the power of perceiving things beyond the range of the senses.

par′a•site′ (par′ə sīt′) *n.* an animal or plant that lives on another organism. —**par′a•sit′ic** (-sit′ik) *adj.*

par′a•sol′ (-sôl′) *n.* a light umbrella used as a sunshade.

par′a•thy′roid gland′ *n.* one of the small glands near the thyroid.

par′boil′ (pär′boil′) *v.t.* to boil partially.

par′cel (pär′səl) *n., v.,* **-celed, -celing.** —*n.* **1.** a package. **2.** a part. —*v.* **3. parcel out,** to divide in portions.

parch (pärch) *v.t., v.i.* to make or become very dry by heat.

parch′ment (pärch′mənt) *n.* the skin of sheep, goats, etc., prepared for writing on.

par′don (pär′dn) *n.* **1.** a legal release from a penalty. **2.** forgiveness. —*v.t.* **3.** to excuse; forgive. —**par′don•a•ble,** *adj.*

pare (pâr) *v.t.,* **pared, paring.** to cut off the outer part of.

par′ent (pâr′ənt, par′-) *n.* **1.** a father or mother. **2.** a source or cause. —**pa•ren′tal** (pə ren′tl) *adj.*

par′ent•age (-ən tij) *n.* ancestry.

pa•ren′the•sis (pə ren′thə sis) *n., pl.* **-ses** (-sēz). **1.** one of the upright curves ( ) used to mark off an inserted word or phrase. **2.** material so inserted. —**par′en•thet′i•cal** (par′ən thet′i kəl) *adj.*

par ex′cel•lence′ (pär ek′sə läns′) *adj.* superior.

par•fait′ (pär fā′) *n.* a layered ice cream dessert.

pa•ri′ah (pə rī′ə) *n.* an outcast.

par′i-mu′tu•el (par′i myōō′chōō əl) *n.* a form of betting on races.

par′ish (par′ish) *n.* **1.** a district having its own church and clergy. **2.** a local church and its activities. —**pa•rish′ion•er,** *n.*

par′i•ty (par′i tē) *n.* equality.

park (pärk) *n.* **1.** a tract of land set apart for public use. —*v.t., v.i.* **2.** to put (a car) in a place temporarily.

par′ka (pär′kə) *n.* a warm hooded jacket.

Par′kin•son's disease′ (pär′kin-səns) *n.* a neurological disease characterized by tremors and a shuffling walk.

park′way′ *n.* a broad thoroughfare with a dividing strip or side strips planted with grass, trees, etc.

par′lance (pär′ləns) *n.* a way of speaking.

par′lay (pär′lā, -lē) *v.t.* to make use of (assets) for a large gain.

par′ley (pär′lē) *n.* **1.** a discussion. —*v.i.* **2.** to hold a parley.

par′lia•ment (pär′lə mənt) *n.* a national legislature.

par′lia•men•tar′ian (-men târ′ē ən, -mən-) *n.* an expert in parliamentary rules.

par′lia•men′ta•ry (-men′tə rē) *adj.* **1.** of, by, or having a parliament. **2.** in accordance with the rules of debate.

par′lor (pär′lər) *n.* a room for receiving guests.

Par′me•san′ (pär′mə zän′, -zən) *n.* a hard, dry Italian cheese.

pa•ro′chi•al (pə rō′kē əl) *adj.* **1.** of a parish. **2.** of very limited scope; provincial.

paro′chial school′ *n.* a school run by a religious organization.

par′o•dy (par′ə dē) *n., pl.* **-dies,** *v.,* **-died, -dying.** —*n.* **1.** a comic imitation of a literary or musical work. —*v.t.* **2.** to make a parody of.

pa•role′ (pə rōl′) *n., v.,* **-roled, -roling.** —*n.* **1.** a conditional release from prison. —*v.t.* **2.** to put on parole. —**pa•rol•ee′** (-rō lē′) *n.*

par′ox•ysm (par′ək siz′əm) *n.* a sudden, violent outburst.

par•quet′ (pär kā′) *n.* a floor made of wood pieces laid in a pattern.

par′ri•cide′ (par′ə sīd′) *n.* the crime of killing one's mother, father, or other close relative.

par′rot (par′ət) *n.* **1.** a hook-billed, bright-colored bird that can be taught to mimic speech. —*v.t.* **2.** to repeat without understanding.

par′ry (par′ē) *v.,* **-ried, -rying,** *n., pl.* **-ries.** —*v.t.* **1.** to ward off; evade. —*n.* **2.** an act of parrying.

parse (pärs) *v.,* **parsed, parsing.** —*v.t.* **1.** to analyze (a word or sentence) grammatically. —*v.i.* **2.** to admit of being parsed.

par′si•mo′ny (pär′sə mō′nē) *n.* stinginess. —**par′si•mo′ni•ous,** *adj.*

pars′ley (pär′slē) *n.* a garden herb with either curled leaf clusters or flat compound leaves.

pars′nip (-snip) *n.* a plant with a large, white edible root.

par′son (-sən) *n.* a member of the Protestant clergy.

par′son•age (-sə nij) *n.* the house provided for a parson.

part (pärt) *n.* **1.** a distinct portion of a whole. **2.** some but not all. **3.** a share. **4.** a role. —*v.t., v.i.* **5.** to separate; divide.

par•take′ (pär tāk′) *v.i.,* **-took, -taken, -taking. 1.** to participate. **2.** to take or have a portion.

par•terre′ (pär târ′) *n.* the rear section of theater seats under the balcony.

par′the•no•gen′e•sis (pär′thə nōjen**/**ə sis) *n.* the development of an egg without fertilization.

par/tial (pär**/**shəl) *adj.* **1.** being part; incomplete. **2.** favoring one group over another. —*Idiom.* **3. partial to,** especially fond of. —**par·tial/i·ty,** *n.*

par·tic/i·pate/ (-tis**/**ə pāt**/**) *v.i.,* **-pated, -pating.** to take part or have a share. —**par·tic/i·pant,** *n.* —**par·tic/i·pa/tion,** *n.*

par/ti·ci·ple (-tə sip**/**əl) *n.* a verbal form that can be used as an adjective or to form certain tenses with an auxiliary verb.

par/ti·cle (-ti kəl) *n.* a tiny piece.

par·tic/u·lar (pər tik**/**yə lər, pə-) *adj.* **1.** pertaining to a specific person, thing, etc. **2.** special; unusual. **3.** exacting; fussy. —*n.* **4.** a distinct part; detail.

par·tic/u·lar·ize/ *v.,* **-ized, -izing.** —*v.t.* **1.** to state in detail. —*v.i.* **2.** to give details.

par·tic/u·lar·ly *adv.* **1.** especially. **2.** specifically.

part/ing *n.* a departure or separation.

par/ti·san (pär**/**tə zən, -sən) *n.* **1.** a supporter of a person, cause, etc. **2.** a guerrilla.

par·ti/tion (-tish**/**ən) *n.* **1.** a division into parts. **2.** something that separates. —*v.t.* **3.** to divide into parts.

part/ly *adv.* not wholly.

part/ner (pärt**/**nər) *n.* **1.** a person who is associated with another; associate. **2.** a spouse or lover. —**part/ner·ship/,** *n.*

par/tridge (pär**/**trij) *n.* a game bird of the pheasant family.

part/-time/ *adj.* (-tīm**/**) **1.** involving or working less than the usual or full time. —*adv.* (-tīm**/**) **2.** on a part-time basis.

par/tu·ri/tion (pär**/**tŏŏ rish**/**ən, -tyŏŏ-) *n.* childbirth.

par/ty (pär**/**tē) *n., pl.* **-ties. 1.** a social gathering. **2.** a group working or traveling together. **3.** a group supporting a common cause or policy. **4.** a specific individual.

par/ty line/ (pär**/**tē lin**/** *for 1;* lin**/** *for 2*) *n.* **1.** the guiding policy of a political party. **2.** a telephone line connecting the telephones of several subscribers.

par/ve·nu/ (pär**/**və nōō**/**, -nyōō**/**) *n., pl.* **-nus.** a person who has new wealth but not social acceptance.

pass (pas) *v.,* **passed, passed** or **past, passing,** *n.* —*v.t.* **1.** to move past, by, across, or through. **2.** to undergo successfully. **3.** to go beyond. **4.** to approve. **5.** to transfer (a ball) to a teammate. —*v.i.* **6.** to go or move onward. **7.** to go by;

elapse. **8.** to be accepted, allowed, or approved. **9.** to get through successfully. **10.** to refuse one's turn. **11. pass away** *or* **on,** to die. **12. ~ out,** to faint. **13. ~ over,** to disregard. **14. ~ up,** to refuse to accept. —*n.* **15.** the act of passing. **16.** a route through the mountains. **17.** permission to come or go. **18.** a free ticket. **19.** a state of affairs.

pas/sa·ble *adj.* adequate.

pas/sage (-ij) *n.* **1.** passing from one place or condition to another. **2.** the right to pass. **3.** the route by which one passes. **4.** a corridor. **5.** a section of a written work or a musical composition. —**pas/sage·way/,** *n.*

pass/book/ *n.* a record of a depositor's bank balance.

pas·sé/ (pa sā**/**) *adj.* out-of-date.

pas/sen·ger (pas**/**ən jər) *n.* a traveler on a bus, train, ship, etc.

pass/er·by/ *n., pl.* **passersby.** a person who passes by.

pass/ing *adj.* brief; transitory.

pas/sion (pash**/**ən) *n.* **1.** any very strong emotion. **2.** sexual desire. **3.** enthusiasm. **4.** the object of one's passion. **5. Passion,** the sufferings of Christ. —**pas/sion·ate,** *adj.*

pas/sive (pas**/**iv) *adj.* **1.** acted upon by an external force. **2.** submitting without resistance. **3.** designating a voice, verb form, or construction indicating a subject acted upon by the verb. —**pas/sive·ly,** *adv.* —**pas·siv/i·ty,** *n.*

pas/sive resist/ance *n.* nonviolent opposition.

pas/sive smok/ing *n.* the inhaling of others' smoke.

pass/key/ *n.* a master key or skeleton key.

Pass/o·ver (pas**/**ō**/**vər) *n.* a Jewish festival commemorating the Israelites' Exodus from Egypt.

pass/port *n.* an official document proving a person's identity and used when traveling abroad.

pass/word/ *n.* a secret word used to gain access.

past (past) *adj.* **1.** gone by or elapsed in time. **2.** of an earlier time. **3.** designating a verb tense referring to times gone by. —*n.* **4.** past time or events. **5.** the history of a person, nation, etc. —*adv.* **6.** so as to pass by or beyond. —*prep.* **7.** after. **8.** beyond.

pas/ta (pä**/**stə) *n.* a dried flour-and-egg dough made into various shapes, as spaghetti.

paste (pāst) *n., v.,* **pasted, pasting.** —*n.* **1.** a soft, sticky mixture used as an adhesive. **2.** dough. **3.** heavy glass used for making artificial gems. —*v.t.* **4.** to fasten with paste.

paste′board′ *n.* a firm board made of layers of paper.

pas·tel′ (pa stel′) *n.* **1.** a soft, delicate color. **2.** a crayon made of ground pigment. **3.** a drawing made with such crayons.

pas′teur·ize′ (pas′chə rīz′) *v.t.*, **-ized**, **-izing**. to heat (a food) to a high temperature to destroy bacteria.

pas·tiche′ (pa stēsh′) *n.* an artistic work made up of selections from borrowed sources.

pas·tille′ (pa stēl′) *n.* a lozenge.

pas′time′ (pas′tīm′) *n.* something that makes time pass pleasantly.

past′ mas′ter *n.* an expert.

pas′tor (-tər) *n.* a minister or priest.

pas′to·ral *adj.* **1.** having rural charm. **2.** of shepherds. **3.** of pastors or spiritual guidance.

pas′to·rale′ (-rāl′) *n.* a dreamy musical composition.

pas·tra′mi (pə strä′mē) *n.* beef brisket cured and smoked before cooking.

pas′try (pā′strē) *n.*, *pl.* **-tries. 1.** dough, esp. when prepared with shortening. **2.** a sweet baked food with a crust of dough.

pas′ture *n.*, *v.*, **-tured, -turing.** —*n.* **1.** grassy land for the grazing of livestock. —*v.t.* **2.** to put out (livestock) to graze on pasture.

past′y (pā′stē) *adj.*, **-ier, -iest.** like paste in texture or color.

pat[1] (pat) *v.*, **patted, patting,** *n.* —*v.t.* **1.** to strike or tap gently. —*n.* **2.** a light stroke. **3.** a small mass of something soft, as butter.

pat[2] (pat) *adj.* **1.** exactly to the point —*Idiom.* **2. stand pat,** to cling firmly to one's decision.

patch (pach) *n.* **1.** a small piece of material used to mend a tear. **2.** a piece of material used to cover an injured part or to administer medication through the skin. **3.** a small area or a plot of land. —*v.t.* **4.** to mend or cover with a patch. **5. patch up, a.** to repair in a hasty way. **b.** to settle, as a quarrel.

patch′ test′ *n.* an allergy test in which a patch of material with an allergen is applied to the skin.

patch′y *adj.*, **-ier, -iest.** irregular in surface or quality.

pate (pāt) *n.* the top of the head.

pâ·té′ (pä tā′, pa-) *n.* a paste of puréed or chopped meat, liver, etc.

pa·tel′la (pə tel′ə) *n.*, *pl.* **-tellae** (tel′ē). the kneecap.

pat′ent (pat′nt) *n.* **1.** the exclusive right to be the only maker or seller of an invention for a specified number of years. **2.** an invention protected by this right. —*adj.* **3.** protected by a patent. **4.** obvious. —*v.t.* **5.** to obtain a patent on.

pat′ent leath′er *n.* a hard, glossy, smooth leather.

pat′ent med′icine *n.* a drug protected by a trademark.

pa·ter′nal (pə tûr′nl) *adj.* **1.** fatherly. **2.** related through or inherited from one's father.

pa·ter′nal·ism *n.* the practice of managing people in the way a father deals with his children. —**pa·ter′nal·is′tic,** *adj.*

pa·ter′ni·ty (-ni tē) *n.* fatherhood.

pa′ter·nos′ter (pā′tər nos′tər) *n.* the Lord's Prayer.

path (path) *n.* **1.** Also, **path′way′.** a way by which people or animals pass on foot. **2.** a route along which something moves. **3.** a course of action.

pa·thet′ic (pə thet′ik) *adj.* arousing pity. —**pa·thet′i·cal·ly,** *adv.*

path′o·gen (path′ə jən, -jen′) *n.* a disease-producing agent.

path′o·log′i·cal (-loj′i kəl) *adj.* **1.** of pathology. **2.** caused by disease; sick. **3.** characterized by an unhealthy compulsion.

pa·thol′o·gy (pə thol′ə jē) *n.* the study of the origin, nature, and cause of diseases. —**pa·thol′o·gist,** *n.*

pa′thos (pā′thos, -thōs) *n.* the quality or power of arousing pity.

-pathy a suffix meaning: **1.** feeling. **2.** method of treatment.

pa′tient (pā′shənt) *n.* **1.** a person under medical care. —*adj.* **2.** enduring delay, annoyance, etc., without complaint. —**pa′tience,** *n.*

pat′i·na (pat′n ə, pə tē′nə) *n.* a green film on old bronze.

pa′ti·o′ (pat′ē ō′) *n.*, *pl.* **-tios. 1.** an inner open courtyard. **2.** a paved recreational area adjoining a house.

pa′tri·arch′ (pā′trē ärk′) *n.* **1.** the male head of a family. **2.** a venerable old man. —**pa′tri·ar′chal,** *adj.* —**pa′tri·ar′chy,** *n.*

pa·tri′cian (pə trish′ən) *n.* **1.** a member of the aristocracy. —*adj.* **2.** aristocratic.

pat′ri·cide′ (pa′trə sīd′) *n.* **1.** the act of killing one's father. **2.** a person who commits such an act. —**pat′ri·cid′al,** *adj.*

pat′ri·mo′ny (-mō′nē) *n.*, *pl.* **-nies.** an inherited estate.

pa′tri·ot (pā′trē ət, -ot′) *n.* a person who supports his or her country. —**pa′tri·ot′ic,** *adj.* —**pa′tri·ot·ism** (-ə tiz′əm) *n.*

pa·trol′ (pə trōl′) *v.*, **-trolled, -troll-**

ing, n. —v.t., v.i. **1.** to pass regularly through or around (an area) in guarding. —n. **2.** a person or group assigned to patrol.

pa·trol/man n., pl. **-men.** a police officer who patrols a given route.

pa/tron (pā/trən) n. **1.** a person who supports an artist, charity, etc. **2.** a regular customer or client.

pa/tron·age (-trə nij, pā/-) n. **1.** business provided by customers, clients, etc. **2.** political control of appointments to office. **3.** a patron's support of an artist, charity, etc.

pa/tron·ize v.t., **-ized, -izing. 1.** to give a store, restaurant, etc., one's regular patronage. **2.** to treat condescendingly.

pa/tron saint/ n. a saint regarded as a special guardian.

pat/sy (pat/sē) n., pl. **-sies.** Slang. a person who is easily fooled or manipulated.

pat/ter¹ (pat/ər) v.i. **1.** to make a series of light tapping sounds. —n. **2.** a light tapping sound.

pat/ter² (pat/ər) n. **1.** rapid, glib talk. —v.i., v.t. **2.** to speak glibly or rapidly.

pat/tern (-ərn) n. **1.** a decorative design. **2.** a set of qualities, acts, etc., forming a characteristic arrangement. **3.** a model to be imitated. —v.t. **4.** to make after a pattern.

pat/ty (pat/ē) n., pl. **-ties.** a flat cake of ground or minced food.

pau/ci·ty (pô/si tē) n. smallness of quantity.

paunch (pônch) n. a large belly. —**paunch/y,** adj.

pau/per (pô/pər) n. a very poor person.

pause (pôz) n., v., **paused, pausing.** —n. **1.** a temporary stop or rest. —v.i. **2.** to make a pause.

pave (pāv) v.t., **paved, paving. 1.** to cover (a road, walk, etc.) with concrete, stones, or asphalt. —Idiom. **2. pave the way,** to prepare the way. —**pave/ment,** n.

pa·vil/ion (pə vil/yən) n. **1.** a light open building used for concerts, exhibits, etc. **2.** a large tent.

paw (pô) n. **1.** the foot of an animal. —v.t., v.i. **2.** to scrape or strike with the paws. **3.** to touch clumsily.

pawn¹ (pôn) v.t. **1.** to deposit as security for money borrowed. —n. **2.** the state of being pawned. **3.** something pawned. —**pawn/bro/ker,** n. —**pawn/shop/,** n.

pawn² (pôn) n. **1.** a chess piece of the lowest value. **2.** someone who is controlled by others.

paw/paw/ (pô/pô/, pə pô/) n. a tree bearing purple flowers and a fleshy edible fruit.

pay (pā) v., **paid, paying,** n. —v.t. **1.** to give (money) in exchange for goods or services. **2.** to settle (a debt). **3.** to transfer money to (a person) for goods or services. **4.** to be profitable to. **5.** to give (attention, a compliment, etc.) as due. **6.** to let out (rope). —v.i. **7.** to transfer money as in making a purchase or settling a debt. **8.** to be worthwhile. —n. **9.** wages, salary, etc. —**pay/a·ble,** adj. —**pay·ee/,** n. —**pay/er,** n. —**pay/ment,** n.

pay/ dirt/ n. **1.** profitable soil to mine. **2.** Informal. any source of wealth.

pay/load/ n. **1.** revenue-producing cargo. **2.** explosives, passengers, or cargo carried by an aircraft.

pay/mas/ter n. a person in charge of paying out wages.

pay/off/ n. **1.** the payment of a salary, debt, etc. **2.** the final result. **3.** Informal. a bribe.

pay·o/la (pā ō/lə) n. a bribe in return for the dishonest use of one's position.

pay/roll/ n. **1.** a list of employees to be paid, with the amount due to each. **2.** the total of these amounts.

PC 1. pl. **PCs** or **PC's.** personal computer. **2.** politically correct.

PCS Personal Communications Service: a system of digital wireless communications, used esp. for mobile phones.

PE physical education.

pea (pē) n. the round edible seed of a cultivated legume.

peace (pēs) n. **1.** freedom from war, trouble, or disturbance. **2.** a treaty ending a war. —**peace/ful,** adj. —**peace/mak/er,** n.

peach (pēch) n. a round, pinkish-yellow, fuzzy-skinned fruit.

pea/cock/ (pē/kok/) n. the male peafowl, having fanlike iridescent tail feathers.

pea/fowl/ n. a large Asiatic bird of the pheasant family.

pea/hen/ n. the female peafowl.

pea/ jack/et n. a short, heavy coat of navy-blue wool.

peak (pēk) n. **1.** the pointed top of something, esp. a mountain. **2.** the highest or most important point. —v.i. **3.** to reach a peak of activity, popularity, etc.

peaked (pē/kid) adj. sickly; haggard.

peal (pēl) n. **1.** a loud, prolonged sound, as of bells or thunder. **2.** a set of bells. —*v.t., v.i.* **3.** to sound or sound forth in a peal.

pea′nut′ *n.* the pod or edible seed of a plant of the legume family.

pear (pâr) *n.* an edible fruit with a rounded shape that grows smaller toward the stem.

pearl (pûrl) *n.* **1.** a hard, smooth, near-white gem formed within the shell of an oyster. **2.** something similar. —**pearl′y,** *adj.*

peas′ant (pez′ənt) *n.* a person who works on the land.

peat (pēt) *n.* decomposed vegetable matter found in bogs, cut and dried for fuel. —**peat′y,** *adj.*

peb′ble (peb′əl) *n.* a small, rounded stone. —**peb′bly,** *adj.*

pe·can′ (pi kän′, -kan′) *n.* the smooth-shelled edible nut of a tree of the hickory family, cultivated in the southern U.S. and Mexico.

pec′ca·dil′lo (pek′ə dil′ō) *n., pl.* **-loes, -los.** a trifling sin.

pec′ca·ry (pek′ə rē) *n., pl.* **-ries.** a small wild pig of Central and South America.

peck¹ (pek) *v.t.* **1.** to strike with the beak or with something pointed. —*v.i.* **2.** to make strokes with the beak or with something pointed. —*n.* **3.** a quick stroke. **4.** a quick kiss.

peck² (pek) *n.* a dry measure of 8 quarts.

peck′ing or′der *n.* a hierarchy within a group.

pec′tin (pek′tin) *n.* a substance in ripe fruit that causes jelly to set.

pec′to·ral (pek′tər əl) *adj.* of, in, or on the chest.

pe·cu′liar (pi kyōol′yər) *adj.* **1.** odd; strange. **2.** uncommon. **3.** belonging exclusively to some person, group, or thing. —**pe·cu′li·ar′i·ty** (-lē ar′i tē) *n.*

pe·cu′ni·ar′y (pi kyōō′nē er′ē) *adj.* of money.

ped′a·gogue′ (ped′ə gog′) *n.* a teacher. —**ped′a·go′gy** (-gō′jē, -goj′ē) *n.* —**ped′a·gog′ic, ped′a·gog′i·cal,** *adj.*

ped′al (ped′l) *n., v.,* **-aled, -aling,** *adj.* —*n.* **1.** a foot-operated lever. —*v.t., v.i.* **2.** to work the pedals (of).

ped′ant (ped′nt) *n.* **1.** a person who overemphasizes rules and details. **2.** a person who makes an excessive display of learning. —**pe·dan′tic,** *adj.* —**ped′ant·ry,** *n.*

ped′dle (ped′l) *v.t., v.i.,* **-dled, -dling.** to carry (small articles) about for sale. —**ped′dler,** *n.*

ped′es·tal (ped′ə stl) *n.* a base for a column, statue, etc.

pe·des′tri·an (pə des′trē ən) *n.* **1.** a person who is walking. —*adj.* **2.** walking. **3.** dull.

pe′di·at′rics (pē′dē a′triks) *n.* the branch of medicine dealing with the care and diseases of children. —**pe′di·a·tri′cian** (-ə trish′ən) *n.* —**pe′di·at′ric,** *adj.*

ped′i·cure (ped′i kyŏōr′) *n.* professional care of the feet.

ped′i·gree (-grē′) *n.* **1.** ancestry. **2.** a certificate of ancestry, esp. of a purebred animal.

ped′i·ment (ped′ə mənt) *n.* a low triangular gable above an end wall, colonnade, etc.

pe·dom′e·ter (pə dom′i tər) *n.* a device that measures the distance walked.

peek (pēk) *v.i.* **1.** to look quickly or furtively. —*n.* **2.** a quick, furtive look.

peel (pēl) *v.t.* **1.** to remove the skin or rind of. **2.** to strip away from something. —*v.i.* **3.** (of skin, paint, etc.) to come off in pieces. **4.** to lose the skin, paint, etc. —*n.* **5.** the skin or rind of a fruit or vegetable.

peep¹ (pēp) *v.i.* **1.** to look through a small opening or from a hidden location. **2.** to show slightly. —*n.* **3.** a quick look.

peep² (pēp) *n.* **1.** a short, shrill cry. —*v.i.* **2.** to utter a short, shrill cry.

peer¹ (pēr) *n.* **1.** a person who is the equal of another. **2.** a member of the British nobility. —**peer′age,** *n.*

peer² (pēr) *v.i.* to look searchingly or with difficulty.

peer′less *adj.* without equal.

peeve (pēv) *n., v.,* **peeved, peeving.** —*n.* **1.** a source of annoyance. —*v.t.* **2.** to make peevish; vex.

peev′ish (pē′vish) *adj.* cross.

peg (peg) *n., v.,* **pegged, pegging.** —*n.* **1.** a pin of wood, metal, etc. —*v.t.* **2.** to fasten with pegs.

peg′ leg′ *n.* a wooden leg.

peign·oir′ (pān wär′, pen-) *n.* a woman's loose dressing gown.

pe·jo′ra·tive (pi jôr′ə tiv) *adj.* disparaging; negative.

Pe′king·ese′ (pē′kə nēz′, -nēs′) *n., pl.* **Pekingese.** a small, long-haired Chinese dog with a flat muzzle.

pel′i·can (pel′i kən) *n.* a large fish-eating bird with a throat pouch.

pel·la′gra (pə lag′rə, -lā′grə, -lä′-) *n.* a disease caused by a lack of niacin in the diet.

pel′let (pel′it) *n.* a small, round mass, as of food.

pell′-mell′ (pel′mel′) *adv.* in disorderly haste.

pel·lu′cid (pə lōō′sid) *adj.* very clear.

pelt¹ (pelt) *v.t.* **1.** to attack with repeated blows. —*v.i.* **2.** (of rain) to come down hard and fast.

pelt[2] (pelt) *n.* the skin of an animal.

pel'vis (pel'vis) *n.* **1.** the cavity in the lower trunk of the body. **2.** the bones forming this. —**pel'vic,** *adj.*

pen[1] (pen) *n., v.,* **penned, penning.** —*n.* **1.** an instrument for writing or drawing with ink. —*v.t.* **2.** to write or draw with a pen.

pen[2] (pen) *n., v.,* **penned, penning.** —*n.* **1.** a small enclosure for animals. —*v.t.* **2.** to confine in a pen.

pe'nal (pēn'l) *adj.* of or prescribing punishment. —**pe'nal.ize',** *v.t.*

pen'al.ty (pen'l tē) *n., pl.* **-ties.** a punishment for violating a law.

pen'ance (-əns) *n.* a punishment as penitence for sin.

pen'chant (-chənt) *n.* a liking.

pen'cil (-səl) *n.* a slender stick of graphite or crayon enclosed in wood, metal, etc., used for writing or drawing.

pend'ant (-dənt) *n.* an ornament hanging from a chain around the neck.

pend'ent (-dənt) *adj.* hanging.

pend'ing *prep.* **1.** until. **2.** during. —*adj.* **3.** awaiting decision.

pen'du.lous (pen'jə ləs, pen'dyə-) *adj.* hanging loosely.

pen'du.lum (-ləm) *n.* a body suspended from a fixed point and swinging freely.

pen'e.trate' (pen'i trāt') *v.t., v.i.,* **-trated, -trating. 1.** to pierce or pass into or through (something). **2.** to understand; have insight. —**pen'e.tra'tion,** *n.*

pen'guin (peng'gwin, pen'-) *n.* a flightless aquatic bird of Antarctic regions.

pen'i.cil'lin (pen'ə sil'in) *n.* an antibiotic produced in certain molds.

pen.in'su.la (pə nin'sə lə) *n.* land almost completely surrounded by water. —**pen.in'su.lar,** *adj.*

pe'nis (pē'nis) *n.* the male organ of copulation and urination. —**pe'nile** (pēn'l) *adj.*

pen'i.tent (pen'i tənt) *adj.* **1.** sorry for a sin or fault. —*n.* **2.** a penitent person. —**pen'i.tence,** *n.*

pen'i.ten'tia.ry (-ten'shə rē) *n., pl.* **-ries.** a prison.

pen'knife' *n.* a small pocketknife.

pen'light' *n.* a flashlight shaped like a fountain pen.

Penn. Pennsylvania. Also, **Penna.**

pen' name' *n.* a writer's pseudonym.

pen'nant (pen'ənt) *n.* **1.** a long, tapering flag. **2.** a flag symbolizing a championship.

pen'ny (pen'ē) *n., pl.* **pennies,** *Brit.* **pence.** a small coin, equal to one cent in the U.S. and Canada, and to $\frac{1}{100}$ pound in the United Kingdom.

pen'ny pinch'er *n.* a stingy person.

pen'ny.weight' *n.* (in troy weight) 24 grains, or $\frac{1}{20}$ of an ounce.

pen' pal' *n.* a person with whom one exchanges letters regularly.

pen'sion (pen'shən) *n.* **1.** a fixed periodic payment for past service, injury sustained, etc. **2.** (pän sē-ōn') (in Europe) a boardinghouse or small hotel. —*v.t.* **3.** to give a pension to.

pen'sive (pen'siv) *adj.* gravely thoughtful. —**pen'sive.ly,** *adv.*

penta- a prefix meaning five.

pen'ta.gon' (pen'tə gon') *n.* a plane figure having five sides.

pen'ta.gram' (-gram') *n.* a five-pointed, star-shaped symbol.

pen.tam'e.ter (-tam'i tər) *n.* a verse or line of five feet.

pen.tath'lon (-tath'lən, -lon) *n.* an athletic contest consisting of five events.

Pen'te.cost' (pen'ti kôst') *n.* the seventh Sunday after Easter, commemorating the descent of the Holy Spirit upon the Apostles.

Pen'te.cos'tal *adj.* of Christian groups that emphasize the Holy Spirit.

pent'house' (pent'hous') *n.* a rooftop apartment.

pent'-up' *adj.* restrained; confined.

pe.nul'ti.mate (pi nul'tə mit) *adj.* being or occurring next to last.

pe.num'bra (pə num'brə) *n., pl.* **-brae** (-brē) **-bras.** the partial shadow outside the complete shadow of a celestial body in eclipse. —**pe.num'bral,** *adj.*

pe.nu'ri.ous (pə nŏŏr'ē əs, -nyŏŏr'-) *adj.* **1.** stingy. **2.** very poor.

pen'u.ry (pen'yə rē) *n.* poverty.

pe'on (pē'ən, -on) *n.* an unskilled worker.

pe'o.ny (pē'ə nē) *n., pl.* **-nies.** a plant with large, showy red, white, or pink flowers.

peo'ple (pē'pəl) *n., v.,* **-pled, -pling.** —*n.* **1.** persons in general. **2.** the body of persons constituting a nation or ethnic group. —*v.t.* **3.** to populate.

pep (pep) *n., v.,* **pepped, pepping.** —*n.* **1.** energy or liveliness. —*v.* **2. pep up,** to make or become vigorous. —**pep'py,** *adj.*

pep'per (pep'ər) *n.* **1.** a condiment made from the pungent dried berries of a tropical shrub. **2.** the usu. red or green edible fruit of certain plants, ranging from mild to hot in flavor. —*v.t.* **3.** to season with

pepper. **4.** to pelt with missiles.
—**pep/per•y,** adj.
pep/per•corn/ n. the dried berry of the pepper plant.
pep/per mill/ n. a device for grinding peppercorns.
pep/per•mint/ n. an aromatic herb of the mint family.
pep/sin (pep/sin) n. an enzyme, produced in the stomach, that digests proteins.
pep/tic (-tik) adj. of or aiding digestion.
per (pûr; unstressed pər) prep. for; by means of.
per•am/bu•late/ v., -lated, -lating. —v.t. **1.** to walk about or through. —v.i. **2.** to stroll.
per•am/bu•la/tor n. a baby carriage.
per an/num (pər an/əm) adv. yearly.
per•cale/ (pər kāl/) n. a smooth, closely woven cotton fabric.
per cap/i•ta (pər kap/i tə) adj., adv. by or for each person.
per•ceive/ (pər sēv/) v.t., -ceived, -ceiving. **1.** to become aware of by seeing, hearing, etc. **2.** to understand. —**per•ceiv/a•ble,** adj.
per•cent/ (-sent/) n. one one-hundredth part.
per•cent/age (-sen/tij) n. **1.** a rate or proportion per hundred. **2.** a proportion.
per•cen/tile (-tīl, -til) n. one of the values of a statistical variable that divides the distribution of the variable into 100 equal parts.
per•cep/ti•ble (-sep/tə bəl) adj. capable of being perceived.
per•cep/tion n. **1.** the act or faculty of perceiving. **2.** insight. **3.** the result of perceiving.
per•cep/tive adj. showing insight.
per•cep/tu•al (-chōō əl) adj. involving perception.
perch[1] (pûrch) n. **1.** a horizontal rod serving as a roosting place for birds. **2.** a high position, resting place, etc. —v.i., v.t. **3.** to rest or set on a perch.
perch[2] (pûrch) n. a small freshwater fish with a spiny fin.
per/co•late/ (pûr/kə lāt/) v., -lated, -lating. —v.t. **1.** to cause (a liquid) to filter through something porous. —v.i. **2.** to filter.
per/co•la/tor n. a coffee pot in which boiling water is forced up through a hollow stem and filters down through ground coffee.
per•cus/sion (pər kush/ən) n. the striking of one body against another.
percus/sion in/strument n. a musical instrument, as the drum or

cymbal, that is struck to produce a sound.
per di/em (pər dē/əm) adv. **1.** by the day. —n. **2.** a daily allowance for expenses.
per•di/tion (pər dish/ən) n. eternal damnation; hell.
per/e•gri•nate/ (per/i grə nāt/) v.i., v.t., -nated, -nating. to travel (over or through), esp. on foot. —**per/e•gri•na/tion,** n.
per/e•grine fal/con (-grin, -grēn/) n. a kind of falcon that feeds on birds taken in flight.
per•emp/to•ry (pə remp/tə rē) adj. permitting no denial or refusal. —**per•emp/to•ri•ly,** adv.
per•en/ni•al (pə ren/ē əl) adj. **1.** lasting indefinitely. **2.** (of plants) living more than two years. **3.** continuing. —n. **4.** a perennial plant. —**per•en/ni•al•ly,** adv.
per/fect (pûr/fikt) adj. **1.** without flaws. **2.** excellent. **3.** complete; thorough. **4.** designating a verb tense that indicates an action already completed. —v.t. (pər fekt/) **5.** to make faultless.
per•fec/tion n. **1.** a perfecting or being perfect. **2.** something perfect. **3.** the highest degree of excellence.
per•fec/tion•ism n. insistence on perfection. —**per•fec/tion•ist,** n.
per/fi•dy (pûr/fi dē) n., pl. -dies. treachery. —**per•fid/i•ous,** adj.
per/fo•rate/ (pûr/fə rāt/) v.t., -rated, -rating. to make holes through. —**per/fo•ra/tion,** n.
per•force/ (pər fôrs/) adv. of necessity.
per•form/ (-fôrm/) v.t. **1.** to carry out; do. **2.** to present (a play, musical work, etc.) before an audience. —v.i. **3.** to do something. **4.** to give a performance. —**per•form/er,** n.
per•for/mance (-fôr/məns) n. **1.** an entertainment presented before an audience. **2.** the act of performing. **3.** a specific action, deed, etc.
perform/ing arts/ arts requiring public performance.
per/fume n., v., -fumed, -fuming. —n. (pûr/fyōōm, pər fyōōm/) **1.** a sweet-smelling liquid for applying to the body. **2.** a pleasant fragrance. —v.t. (pər fyōōm/, pûr/fyōōm) **3.** to fill with a pleasant fragrance. —**per•fum/er•y,** n.
per•func/to•ry (pər fungk/tə rē) adj. done without care or attention. —**per•func/to•ri•ly,** adv.
per•haps/ (pər haps/) adv. maybe.
peri- a prefix meaning aroun, surrounding, or near.

per′i•car′di•um (per′i kär′dē əm) *n.* the sac enclosing the heart.

per′il (per′əl) *n.* **1.** danger. —*v.t.* **2.** to endanger. —**per′il•ous,** *adj.*

per•im′e•ter (pə rim′i tər) *n.* **1.** the outer boundary of a two-dimensional figure. **2.** the length of such a boundary.

per′i•ne′um (per′ə nē′əm) *n., pl.* **-nea.** the area between the genitals and the anus.

pe′ri•od (pēr′ē əd) *n.* **1.** a portion of time. **2.** the mark (.) indicating the end of a sentence. **3.** an occurrence of menstruation.

pe′ri•od′ic (-od′ik) *adj.* recurring regularly or intermittently. —**pe′ri•od′i•cal•ly,** *adv.*

pe′ri•od′i•cal *n.* **1.** a publication issued at regular intervals. —*adj.* **2.** of such publications. **3.** periodic.

pe′ri•od′ic ta′ble *n.* a table showing the chemical elements in related groups, arranged by atomic number.

per′i•pa•tet′ic (per′ə pə tet′ik) *adj.* walking or traveling about.

pe•riph′er•al (pə rif′ər əl), *adj.* **1.** located on the periphery. **2.** only partly relevant. —*n.* **3.** an external hardware device connected to a computer's CPU.

pe•riph′er•y *n., pl.* **-eries. 1.** the boundary of a surface or area. **2.** a surrounding region or area.

pe•riph′ra•sis (-rə sis) *n., pl.* **-ses** (-sēz′). the use of a roundabout form of expression.

per′i•scope′ (per′ə skōp′) *n.* an optical instrument consisting of a tube in which mirrors or prisms reflect to give a view from below or behind an obstacle.

per′ish (per′ish) *v.i.* **1.** to die. **2.** to decay.

per′ish•a•ble *adj.* **1.** subject to decay or destruction. —*n.* **2.** Usu., **perishables.** something perishable, esp. food.

per′i•stal′sis (per′ə stôl′sis, -stal′-) *n., pl.* **-ses** (-sēz). the muscle contractions and relaxations that move food along the alimentary canal.

per′i•to•ne′um (-i tn ē′əm, -tō′-) *n.* the lining of the abdominal cavity.

per′i•to•ni′tis (-tn ī′tis) *n.* inflammation of the peritoneum.

per′i•win′kle[1] (per′i wing′kəl) *n.* an edible marine snail.

per′i•win′kle[2] (per′i wing′kəl) *n.* a trailing evergreen plant with blue flowers.

per′jure (pûr′jər) *v.,* **-jured, -juring. perjure oneself,** to lie under oath. —**per′ju•ry,** *n.*

perk[1] (pûrk) *v.* **perk up,** to become or make lively or cheerful.

perk[2] (pûrk) *n.* a perquisite.

perk′y *adj.,* **-ier, -iest.** cheerful.

per′ma•frost′ (pûr′mə frôst′) *n.* permanently frozen subsoil.

per′ma•nent (-nənt) *adj.* **1.** lasting indefinitely. —*n.* **2.** a curl set in the hair by chemicals. —**per′ma•nence,** *n.* —**per′ma•nent•ly,** *adv.*

per′me•a•ble (pûr′mē ə bəl) *adj.* letting fluids through.

per′me•ate′ (-āt′) *v.t., v.i.,* **-ated, -ating.** to penetrate or spread through all parts (of).

per•mis′si•ble (pər mis′ə bəl) *adj.* allowable.

per•mis′sion (-mish′ən) *n.* authorization or consent to do something.

per•mis′sive (-mis′iv) *adj.* **1.** loose or lax in discipline. **2.** giving permission.

per•mit′ *v.,* **-mitted, -mitting,** *n.* —*v.t.* (pər mit′) **1.** to allow to do something. **2.** to allow to occur. —*v.i.* **3.** to afford opportunity. —*n.* (pûr′mit, pər mit′) **4.** a written order giving permission.

per′mu•ta′tion (pûr′myŏŏ tā′shən) *n.* alteration or transformation.

per•ni′cious (pər nish′əs) *adj.* causing serious harm.

per•ox′ide (pə rok′sīd) *n., v.,* **-ided, -iding.** —*n.* **1.** hydrogen peroxide. **2.** an oxide with two bonded oxygen atoms. —*v.t.* **3.** to bleach with peroxide.

per′pen•dic′u•lar (pûr′pən dik′yə lər) *adj.* **1.** vertical. **2.** meeting a given line at right angles. —*n.* **3.** a perpendicular line or position.

per′pe•trate′ (pûr′pi trāt′) *v.t.,* **-trated, -trating.** to carry out; commit. —**per′pe•tra′tion,** *n.* —**per′pe•tra′tor,** *n.*

per•pet′u•al (pər pech′ŏŏ əl) *adj.* **1.** continuing or lasting forever. **2.** not ceasing. —**per•pet′u•ate′,** *v.t.*

per′pe•tu′i•ty (pûr′pi tŏŏ′i tē, -tyŏŏ′-) *n.* **in perpetuity,** forever.

per•plex′ (pər pleks′) *v.t.* to cause to be confused. —**per•plex′i•ty,** *n.*

per′qui•site (pûr′kwə zit) *n.* a benefit beyond one's regular income.

per se′ (pûr sā′, sē′, pər) *adv.* by, of, for, or in itself; intrinsically.

per′se•cute′ (pûr′si kyŏŏt′) *v.t.,* **-cuted, -cuting.** to subject to cruel treatment, esp. because of religion or race. —**per′se•cu′tion,** *n.* —**per′se•cu′tor,** *n.*

per′se•vere′ (pûr′sə vēr′) *v.i.,* **-vered, -vering.** to continue steadfastly. —**per′se•ver′ance,** *n.*

per•sim′mon (pər sim′ən) *n.* a plumlike orange fruit.

per•sist′ (pər sist′, -zist′) *v.i.* **1.** to

continue firmly in spite of opposition. **2.** to endure. —**per·sist′ence,** *n.* —**per·sist′ent,** *adj.*

per·snick′et·y (pər snik′i tē) *adj. Informal.* fussy.

per′son (pûr′sən) *n.* **1.** a human being. **2.** the individual personality of a human being. **3.** the body of a living human being. **4.** a grammatical category applied to pronouns and verbs, used to distinguish the one speaking, the one spoken to, and the one or thing spoken about.

per′son·a·ble *adj.* attractive in appearance and manner.

per′son·age (-sə nij) *n.* a distinguished person.

per′son·al (-sə nl) *adj.* **1.** of, by, or relating to a certain person. **2.** done in person. **3.** of the body, clothing, or appearance. **4.** of grammatical person. **5.** *Law.* of property that is movable.

per′sonal comput′er *n.* a microcomputer for individual use.

per′sonal effects′ *n.pl.* belongings.

per·son·al′i·ty (-sə nal′ə tē) *n., pl.* -ties. **1.** distinctive personal character. **2.** a famous person.

per·son·al·ize′ *v.t.,* -ized, -izing. **1.** to have marked with one's name. **2.** to make personal.

per′son·al·ly *adv.* **1.** in person. **2.** as if directed at oneself. **3.** as regards oneself. **4.** as a person.

per·so′na non gra′ta (pər sō′nə non grä′tə) *n.* a person who is not welcome.

per·son′i·fy′ (pər son′ə fī′) *v.t.,* -fied, -fying. **1.** to embody; typify. **2.** to attribute a human character to. —**per·son′i·fi·ca′tion,** *n.*

per′son·nel′ (pûr′sə nel′) *n.* employees.

per·spec′tive (pər spek′tiv) *n.* **1.** a technique of depicting space relationships on a flat surface. **2.** the way objects appear from their relative distance and positions. **3.** a mental view or prospect.

per·spi·ca′cious (pûr′spi kā′shəs) *adj.* having keen insight. —**per′·spi·cac′i·ty** (-kas′i tē) *n.*

per·spire′ (pər spī°r′) *v.i.,* -spired, -spiring. to sweat. —**per′spi·ra′·tion** (pûr′spə rā′shən) *n.*

per·suade′ (pər swād′) *v.t.,* -suaded, -suading. **1.** to prevail upon (a person) to act as suggested. **2.** to convince. —**per·sua′·sive,** *adj.* —**per·sua′sive·ly,** *adv.*

per·sua′sion (-swā′zhən) *n.* **1.** the act or power of persuading. **2.** a belief. **3.** a religious system.

pert (pûrt) *adj.* **1.** impertinent; saucy. **2.** lively.

per·tain′ (pər tān′) *v.i.* **1.** to relate. **2.** to belong as a part.

per′ti·nent (-tn ənt) *adj.* relevant. —**per′ti·nence,** *n.*

per·turb′ (pər tûrb′) *v.t.* to disturb greatly. —**per′tur·ba′tion,** *n.*

pe·ruse′ (pə rōōz′) *v.t.,* -rused, -rusing. to read carefully. —**pe·ru′sal,** *n.*

per·vade′ (pər vād′) *v.t.,* -vaded, -vading. to become spread throughout all parts of. —**per·va′·sive,** *adj.*

per·verse′ (pər vûrs′) *adj.* stubbornly determined not to do what is expected. —**per·ver′si·ty,** *n.*

per·vert′ *v.t.* (-vûrt′) **1.** to corrupt. **2.** to turn to an improper use. **3.** to distort. —*n.* (pûr′vûrt) **4.** a perverted person. —**per·ver′sion,** *n.*

pes′ky (pes′kē) *adj.,* -kier, -kiest. annoying; troublesome.

pe′so (pā′sō) *n.* the basic monetary unit of many Latin American countries.

pes′si·mism (pes′ə miz′əm) *n.* the tendency to expect the worst. —**pes′si·mist,** *n.* —**pes′si·mis′tic,** *adj.* —**pes′si·mis′ti·cal·ly,** *adv.*

pest (pest) *n.* a troublesome person, animal, or thing.

pes′ter (pes′tər) *v.t.* to annoy continually, as with requests.

pes′ti·cide′ (pes′tə sīd′) *n.* a poison used to kill harmful insects or weeds.

pes·tif′er·ous (pe stif′ər əs) *adj.* **1.** bearing disease. **2.** dangerous **3.** troublesome.

pes′ti·lence (pes′tl əns) *n.* a deadly epidemic disease.

pes′tle (pes′əl, pes′tl) *n.* a tool for pounding or crushing.

pet (pet) *n., adj., v.,* **petted, petting.** —*n.* **1.** a tame animal that is cared for affectionately. **2.** a favorite. —*adj.* **3.** treated as a pet. **4.** favorite. —*v.t.* **5.** to caress. —*v.i.* **6.** to engage in amorous caressing.

pet′al (pet′l) *n.* one of the colored outer parts of a flower.

pe·tard′ (pi tärd′) *n.* an explosive device.

pe′ter (pē′tər) *v.* **peter out,** to diminish gradually.

pe·tite′ (pə tēt′) *adj.* small.

pe·ti′tion (pə tish′ən) *n.* **1.** a formal request signed by those submitting it and addressed to a person in authority. —*v.t.* **2.** to present a petition to.

pet′rel (pe′trəl) *n.* a small sea bird.

pet′ri·fy′ (pe′trə fī′) *v.t.,* -fied, -fying. **1.** to turn into stone. **2.** to paralyze with fear.

pet·ro·chem′i·cal (pe′trō kem′i kəl)

n. a chemical obtained from petroleum.

pet′rol (pe′trəl) *n. Brit.* gasoline.

pe·tro′le·um (-lē əm) *n.* an oily liquid found underground that yields gasoline, kerosene, etc.

pe·trol′o·gy (-trol′ə jē) *n.* the study of rocks.

pet′ti·coat′ (pet′ē kōt′) *n.* an underskirt.

pet′ti·fog′ (-fog′) *v.i.*, **-fogged, -fogging.** to quibble over trifles.

pet′tish (pet′ish) *adj.* petulant.

pet′ty (pet′ē) *adj.*, **-tier, -tiest. 1.** small or trivial. **2.** small-minded. —**pet′ti·ness,** *n.*

pet′ty cash′ *n.* a fund for paying minor expenses.

pet′ty ju′ry *n.* a jury impaneled in a civil or criminal trial.

pet′ty of′ficer *n.* a noncommissioned officer in the navy.

pet′u·lant (pech′ə lənt) *adj.* showing impatient irritation. —**pet′u·lance,** *n.*

pe·tu′ni·a (pi tōō′nyə, -tyōō′-) *n.* a garden plant with colorful funnel-shaped flowers.

pew (pyōō) *n.* one of the fixed benches with backs in a church.

pe′wee (pē′wē) *n.* any of several New World flycatchers.

pew′ter (pyōō′tər) *n.* an alloy of tin and another metal.

pg. page.

pH a symbol describing the acidity or alkalinity of a chemical solution.

pha′lanx (fā′langks, fal′angks) *n.*, *pl.* **-lanxes, -langes** (fə lan′jēz). **1.** a compact mass of persons, animals, or things. **2.** a bone of a finger or toe.

phal′lus (fal′əs) *n., pl.* **phalli** (fal′ī). **1.** the penis. **2.** an image of the penis as a symbol of male generative powers. —**phal′lic,** *adj.*

phan′tasm (fan′taz əm) *n.* an apparition; phantom.

phan·tas′ma·go′ri·a (-mə gôr′ē ə) *n.* a shifting series of phantasms or illusions, as in a dream.

phan′tom (-təm) *n.* **1.** a ghostlike image. —*adj.* **2.** unreal; illusory.

Phar′aoh (fâr′ō) *n.* a title of an ancient Egyptian king.

Phar′i·see′ (far′ə sē′) *n.* **1.** a member of an ancient Jewish sect. **2. pharisee,** a self-righteous person.

phar′ma·ceu′ti·cal (fär′mə sōō′ti-kəl) *adj.* pertaining to pharmacy.

phar′ma·col′o·gy (-kol′ə jē) *n.* the study of the uses and effects of drugs.

phar′ma·co·poe′ia (-kə pē′ə) *n.* a book that lists drugs, their formulas, etc.

phar′ma·cy (-sē) *n., pl.* **-cies. 1.** a drugstore. **2.** the art and science of preparing and dispensing drugs. —**phar′ma·cist,** *n.*

phar′ynx (far′ingks) *n., pl.* **pharynges** (fə rin′jēz), **pharynxes.** the tube connecting the mouth and nasal passages with the esophagus. —**pha·ryn′ge·al,** *adj.* —**phar′yn·gi′tis** (far′ən jī′tis) *n.*

phase (fāz) *n.* **1.** a stage in a process of change or development. —*v.* **2. phase in,** to put into use gradually. **3. ~ out,** to bring to an end gradually.

Ph.D. Doctor of Philosophy.

pheas′ant (fez′ənt) *n.* a large, long-tailed game bird.

phe′no·bar′bi·tal′ (fē′nō bär′bi-tôl′, -tal′) *n.* a white powder used as a sedative.

phe·nom′e·non′ (fi nom′ə non′, -nən) *n., pl.* **-ena** (-ə nə). **1.** a fact, occurrence, or circumstance that can be observed. **2.** an extraordinary thing or person. —**phe·nom′e·nal,** *adj.*

pher′o·mone′ (fer′ə mōn′) *n.* a chemical substance released by an animal that influences the behavior of other members of the species.

phi′al (fī′əl) *n.* a vial.

phil- a prefix meaning loving.

phi·lan′der·er (fi lan′dər ər) *n.* a man who has many love affairs. —**phi·lan′der,** *v.i.*

phi·lan′thro·py (-thrə pē) *n., pl.* **-pies. 1.** love of humanity, as shown in charitable acts. **2.** a benevolent act, work, or institution. —**phil′an·throp′ic** (fil′ən throp′ik) *adj.* —**phi·lan′thro·pist,** *n.*

phi·lat′e·ly (fi lat′l ē) *n.* the collection and study of postage stamps. —**phi·lat′e·list,** *n.*

phil′har·mon′ic (fil′här mon′ik) *adj.* **1.** music-loving. —*n.* **2.** a symphony orchestra.

phil′is·tine (-ə stēn′, -stīn′) *n.* a person who is indifferent to culture.

phil′o·den′dron (fil′ə den′drən) *n., pl.* **-drons, -dra.** a tropical climbing plant, grown as a houseplant.

phi·lol′o·gy (fi lol′ə jē) *n.* the study of languages. —**phi·lol′o·gist,** *n.*

phi·los′o·pher (fi los′ə fər) *n.* **1.** a person trained in philosophy. **2.** a person guided by reason.

phi·los′o·phy (-fē) *n., pl.* **-phies. 1.** the study of the truths and principles of being and knowledge. **2.** a system of philosophical belief. **3.** the principles of a particular field of knowledge or action.

—**phil′o•soph′i•cal** (fil′ə sof′i kəl) *adj.* —**phi•los′o•phize′**, *v.i.*

phle•bi′tis (flə bī′tis) *n.* inflammation of a vein.

phle•bot′o•my (-bot′ə mē) *n., pl.* **-mies.** the practice of opening a vein to let blood.

phlegm (flem) *n.* **1.** thick mucus in the respiratory passages. **2.** apathy.

phleg•mat′ic (fleg mat′ik) *adj.* unemotional or unenthusiastic.

phlo′em (flō′em) *n.* the tissue in a plant through which food passes.

phlox (floks) *n.* a garden plant with showy white or purple flowers.

pho′bi•a (fō′bē ə) *n.* a morbid fear.

-phobia a suffix meaning fear.

phoe′be (fē′bē) *n.* a small American flycatcher.

phoe′nix (fē′niks) *n.* a mythical bird that burns, then rises from its ashes.

phone (fōn) *n., v.t., v.i.,* **phoned, phoning.** *Informal.* telephone.

phone′ card′ *n.* a prepaid card used to make calls from any telephone.

pho′neme (fō′nēm) *n.* any minimal unit of speech sound that distinguishes one word from another.

pho•net′ics (fə net′iks) *n.* the study of speech sounds and their written representation. —**pho•net′ic,** *adj.*

phon′ics (fon′iks) *n.* a method of teaching reading and spelling based on phonetics.

phono- a prefix meaning sound.

pho′no•graph′ (fō′nə graf′) *n.* a sound-producing machine using records in the form of grooved disks. —**pho′no•graph′ic,** *adj.*

pho•nol′o•gy (fə nol′ə jē) *n., pl.* **-gies. 1.** the system of sounds in a language. **2.** the study of sounds in a language.

pho′ny (fō′nē) *adj.,* **-nier, -niest,** *n., pl.* **-nies.** —*adj.* **1.** false; fake. **2.** not sincere. —*n.* **3.** a phony person or thing. —**pho′ni•ness,** *n.*

phos′gene (fos′jēn) *n.* a poisonous, colorless liquid or gas.

phos′phate (-fāt) *n.* **1.** a salt of phosphoric acid. **2.** a fertilizer containing phosphorus.

phos′phor (-fər) *n.* a substance that is luminous when struck by certain kinds of light.

phos′pho•res′cent (-fə res′ənt) *adj.* luminous. —**phos′pho•res′cence,** *n.*

phos′pho•rus (-fər əs) *n.* a nonmetallic element used in matches and fertilizer.

pho′to (fō′tō) *n., pl.* **-tos.** *Informal.* a photograph.

photo- a prefix meaning light.

pho′to•cop′y *n., pl.* **-ies,** *v.,* **-ied,** **-ying.** —*n.* **1.** a photographic copy of a document. —*v.t.* **2.** to make a photocopy of.

pho′to•e•lec′tric *adj.* of or using electrical effects produced by light.

pho′to•en•grav′ing *n.* a photographic process of preparing printing plates for letterpress printing.

pho′to fin′ish *n.* a finish of a race so close as to require a photograph to determine the winner.

pho′to•gen′ic (fō′tə jen′ik) *adj.* looking attractive in photos.

pho′to•graph′ (-graf′) *n.* **1.** a picture produced by photography. —*v.t.* **2.** to take a photograph of.

pho•tog′ra•phy (fə tog′rə fē) *n.* the process of producing images on a sensitized surface by the action of light. —**pho•tog′ra•pher,** *n.* —**pho′to•graph′ic** (fō′tə graf′ik) *adj.*

pho′ton (fō′ton) *n.* a quantum of electromagnetic radiation.

pho′to•sen′si•tive *adj.* sensitive to light.

Pho′to•stat′ (fō′tə stat′) *n.* **1.** *Trademark.* a camera for photographing documents, drawings, etc. **2.** (*often l.c.*) the photograph so made. —*v.t.* **3.** **photostat,** to copy with this camera.

pho′to•syn′the•sis *n.* the conversion by plants of carbon dioxide and water into carbohydrates, aided by light and chlorophyll.

phrase (frāz) *n., v.,* **phrased, phrasing.** —*n.* **1.** a sequence of words forming a unit within a sentence or clause. **2.** a passage of four to eight measures of music. —*v.t.* **3.** to express in a particular way.

phra′se•ol′o•gy (frā′zē ol′ə jē) *n.* manner of verbal expression.

phy•log′e•ny (fī loj′ə nē) *n.* the development of a particular group of organisms.

phy′lum (fī′ləm) *n., pl.* **-la.** the primary classification of plants or animals.

phys′ic (fiz′ik) *n.* a medicine that purges.

phys′i•cal *adj.* **1.** of the body. **2.** of matter as opposed to spirit. **3.** of physics. —*n.* **4.** a full medical examination.

phys′ical anthropol′ogy *n.* the study of the evolutionary changes in human body structure.

phys′ical sci′ence *n.* a science that deals with inanimate matter or energy, as physics or chemistry.

phys′ical ther′apy *n.* the treatment of physical disability or pain by techniques such as exercise or massage.

phy·si/cian (fi zish/ən) *n.* a medical doctor.

phys/ics (fiz/iks) *n.* the science that deals with matter, motion, energy, and force. —**phys/i·cist,** *n.*

phys/i·og/no·my (fiz/ē og/nə mē, -on/ə-) *n., pl.* **-mies.** the face.

phys/i·og/ra·phy (-og/rə fē) *n.* the branch of geography concerned with features of the earth's surface.

phys/i·ol/o·gy (-ol/ə jē) *n.* the science dealing with the functions of living organisms. —**phys/i·o·log/i·cal** (-ə loj/i kəl) *adj.* —**phys/i·ol/o·gist,** *n.*

phys/i·o·ther/a·py (fiz/ē ō-) *n.* physical therapy.

phy·sique/ (fi zēk/) *n.* bodily structure.

pi (pī) *n., pl.* **pis.** the Greek letter π, used as the symbol for the ratio of the circumference of a circle to its diameter (3.14159+).

pi/a·nis/si·mo (pē/ə nis/ə mō/, pyä-) *adv. Music.* very softly.

pi·an/o (pē an/ō) *n., pl.* **-anos,** *adv.* —*n.* **1.** a musical instrument in which felt-covered hammers, operated from a keyboard, strike metal strings. —*adv.* (pē ä/nō) **2.** *Music.* softly. —**pi·an/ist** (pē an/ist, pē/ə-nist) *n.*

pi·az/za (pē az/ə) *n.* an open public square, esp. in Italy.

pi/ca (pī/kə) *n.* a unit of measure in printing.

pic/a·resque/ (pik/ə resk/) *adj.* of a form of fiction that describes the adventures of a roguish hero.

pic/a·yune/ (pik/ē yōōn/, pik/ə-) *adj.* insignificant; petty.

pic/co·lo/ (pik/ə lō/) *n., pl.* **-los.** a small flute.

pick¹ (pik) *v.t.* **1.** to choose. **2.** to pluck one by one. **3.** to dig or break into, esp. with a pointed instrument. **4. pick at,** to eat sparingly. **5. ~ on,** to criticize or tease. **6. ~ out,** to select. —*n.* **7.** the act of choosing. **8.** something chosen. **9.** the best part.

pick² (pik) *n.* **1.** Also, **pick/ax/, pick/axe/.** a sharp-pointed tool for breaking up soil, rock, etc. **2.** a pointed tool.

pick/er·el (-ər əl) *n.* a small pike.

pick/et (pik/it) *n.* **1.** a pointed stake driven into the ground. **2.** a person who demonstrates in front of a workplace. **3.** troops posted to warn of an enemy attack. —*v.t.* **4.** to enclose with pickets. **5.** to place pickets at (a building). —*v.i.* **6.** to demonstrate as a picket.

pick/et line/ *n.* a line of strikers or other pickets.

pick/le (pik/əl) *n., v.,* **-led, -ling.**

—*n.* **1.** a cucumber or other vegetable preserved in vinegar and spices. **2.** a predicament. —*v.t.* **3.** to preserve in vinegar or brine.

pick/pock/et *n.* a person who steals from others' pockets.

pick/up/ *n.* **1.** a small open-body truck. **2.** the ability to accelerate rapidly. **3.** an improvement.

pick/y *adj.,* **-ier, -iest.** extremely fussy or finicky.

pic/nic (pik/nik) *n., v.,* **-nicked, -nicking.** —*n.* **1.** an outing and outdoor meal. —*v.i.* **2.** to have a picnic. —**pic/nick·er,** *n.*

pic·to/ri·al (pik tôr/ē əl) *adj.* of, like, or expressed in pictures.

pic/ture (pik/chər) *n., v.,* **-tured, -turing.** —*n.* **1.** a representation of a person, object, or scene, as a painting or photograph **2.** a description. **3.** the embodiment of some quality. —*v.t.* **4.** to represent in a picture. **5.** to imagine.

pic/tur·esque/ (-chə resk/) *adj.* visually charming or quaint.

pid/dling *adj.* trivial; negligible.

pidg/in (pij/ən) *n.* a language developed to allow speakers of different languages to communicate.

pie (pī) *n.* a baked dish of fruit, meat, etc., in a pastry crust.

pie/bald/ (pī/bôld/) *adj.* having patches of different colors.

piece (pēs) *n., v.,* **pieced, piecing.** —*n.* **1.** one part or portion of a whole. **2.** a quantity of something forming a unit. **3.** an artistic work. **4.** an example of something. —*v.t.* **5.** to make by joining pieces.

pièce de ré·sis·tance/ (pyes də Rā-zē stäNs/) *n., pl.* **pièces de résistance** (pyes-). **1.** the principal dish of a meal. **2.** the principal item of a series.

piece/meal/ *adv.* gradually.

piece/work/ *n.* work done and paid for by the piece.

pie/ chart/ *n.* a graph in which sectors of a circle represent quantities.

pied (pīd) *adj.* many-colored.

pied/-à-terre/ (pyā/də târ/) *n., pl.* **pieds/-à-terre/** (pyā/-). an apartment for part-time use.

pier (pēr) *n.* **1.** a structure built out over the water, used as an entertainment area, a landing place for ships, etc. **2.** a vertical support for masonry, steel, etc.

pierce (pērs) *v.,* **pierced, piercing.** —*v.t.* **1.** to penetrate, as a pointed object does. **2.** to make a hole in. **3.** to force a way through. **4.** to sound sharply through. —*v.i.* **5.** to force a way through something.

pi/e·ty (pī/i tē) *n.* **1.** reverence for

God or devotion to religious duties. **2.** a pious act, belief, etc.

pif′fle (pif′əl) *n. Informal.* nonsense. **—pif′fling,** *adj.*

pig (pig) *n.* **1.** a swine. **2.** a gluttonous or sloppy person. **3.** a bar of metal. **—pig′gish,** *adj.*

pi′geon (pij′ən) *n.* a short-legged bird with a small head and compact body.

pi′geon•hole′ *n., v.,* **-holed, -holing.** **—n. 1.** a small compartment, as in a desk. **—v.t. 2.** to classify. **3.** to put aside indefinitely.

pi′geon-toed′ *adj.* having toes or feet turned inward.

pig′gy•back′ *adv.* **1.** on the back. **—adj. 2.** astride the back. **3.** attached to something else.

pig′head′ed *adj.* stubborn.

pig′ i′ron *n.* crude iron cast in pigs or blocks.

pig′let *n.* a baby pig.

pig′ment *n.* coloring matter.

pig′men•ta′tion *n.* coloration.

pig′pen′ *n.* **1.** a stall for pigs. **2.** a filthy or untidy place.

pig′tail′ *n.* a braid of hair.

pike¹ (pīk) *n.* a large, slender freshwater fish.

pike² (pīk) *n.* a long, heavy spear.

pike³ (pīk) *n.* a turnpike.

pik′er *n. Slang.* a stingy person.

pi•las′ter (pi las′tər) *n.* a shallow decorative feature projecting from a wall and imitating the form of a column.

pil′chard (pil′chərd) *n.* a marine fish, related to the herring.

pile¹ (pīl) *n., v.,* **piled, piling. —n. 1.** a group of things lying one upon the other. **2.** a large amount of anything. **—v.t. 3.** to lay or place in a pile. **4. pile up,** to accumulate.

pile² (pīl) *n.* Also, **pil′ing.** a long beam driven into the ground as part of a foundation or retaining wall.

pile³ (pīl) *n.* a soft surface on cloth or rugs, formed by upright threads.

piles (pīls) *n.pl.* hemorrhoids.

pil′fer (pil′fər) *v.i., v.t.* to steal, esp. in small amounts. **—pil′fer•age,** *n.*

pil′grim (pil′grim, -grəm) *n.* **1.** a traveler to a sacred place. **2. Pilgrim,** one of the early Puritan settlers in America. **—pil′grim•age,** *n.*

pill (pil) *n.* a small tablet or capsule of medicine.

pil′lage (pil′ij) *v.,* **-laged, -laging.** **—v.t., v.i. 1.** to loot and plunder. **—n. 2.** booty or spoils.

pil′lar (pil′ər) *n.* **1.** a slender vertical structure used as a support or ornament. **2.** a chief supporter of a community, organization, etc.

pill′box′ *n.* **1.** a box for pills. **2.** a small boxlike fortification for machine guns or antitank weapons.

pil′lo•ry (pil′ə rē) *n., pl.* **-ries,** *v.,* **-ried, -rying.** **—n. 1.** a wooden framework used to confine and expose offenders. **—v.t. 2.** to put in the pillory. **3.** to expose to public contempt.

pil′low (pil′ō) *n.* a cloth case filled with soft material, used to cushion the head. **—pil′low•case′,** *n.*

pi′lot (pī′lət) *n.* **1.** a person qualified to operate an aircraft. **2.** a person who steers a ship. **3.** a guide. **—v.t. 4.** to act as pilot of. **5.** to steer. **—adj. 6.** experimental.

pi′lot light′ *n.* a small flame used to relight the main burners.

pi•men′to (pi men′tō) *n., pl.* **-tos.** the red fruit of a sweet pepper.

pimp (pimp) *n.* **1.** a person who solicits customers for prostitutes. **—v.i. 2.** to act as a pimp.

pim′ple (pim′pəl) *n.* a small swelling of skin. **—pim′ply,** *adj.*

pin (pin) *n., v.,* **pinned, pinning. —n. 1.** a slender pointed piece of metal, wood, etc., for fastening or support. **—v.t. 2.** to fasten with a pin. **3.** to hold fast. **4. pin down,** to force (someone) to make a decision.

PIN (pin) *n.* a personal identification number.

pin′a•fore′ (pin′ə fôr′) *n.* a sleeveless, apronlike garment worn over a dress or blouse.

pin′ball′ *n.* a game in which a spring-driven ball rolls against pins on a sloping board.

pince′-nez′ (pans′nā′, pins′-) *n., pl.* **pince-nez.** eyeglasses held on by a spring that pinches the nose.

pin′cers (pin′sərz) *n.pl.* **1.** a gripping tool with a pair of pivoted jaws. **2.** a grasping organ, as the claws of a lobster.

pinch (pinch) *v.t.* **1.** to squeeze tightly between the finger and thumb. **2.** to constrict. **3.** *Slang.* to steal. **—v.i. 4.** to economize. **—n. 5.** a pinching. **6.** a tiny amount. **7.** an emergency. **—Idiom. 8. pinch pennies,** to be very frugal.

pinch′-hit′ *v.i.,* **-hit, -hitting.** to substitute for someone.

pine¹ (pīn) *n.* an evergreen tree with needle-shaped leaves and woody cones containing seeds.

pine² (pīn) *v.i.,* **pined, pining. 1.** to yearn painfully. **2.** to fail in health from grief, regret, etc.

pine′ap′ple (-ap′əl) *n.* a juicy tropical fruit with spiny-edged leaves.

pin′feath′er *n.* an undeveloped feather.

ping (ping) *v.i.* **1.** to produce a sharp sound like a bullet striking metal. —*n.* **2.** a pinging sound.

Ping′-Pong′ (ping′pong′) *Trademark.* table tennis.

pin′head′ *n.* **1.** the head of a pin. **2.** a stupid person.

pin′ion[1] (pin′yən) *n.* **1.** the wing of a bird. —*v.t.* **2.** to bind (a person's arms or hands) so they cannot be used.

pin′ion[2] (pin′yən) *n.* a small cogwheel.

pink (pingk) *n.* **1.** a pale red. **2.** a fragrant garden plant having pink, white, or red flowers. **3.** the highest degree.

pink′eye′ *n.* a contagious inflammation of the membrane that covers the eye and lines the eyelid.

pink′ing shears′ *n.* shears with notched blades.

pin′ mon′ey *n.* any small sum set aside.

pin′na•cle (pin′ə kəl) *n.* a lofty peak or position.

pin′nate (pin′āt, -it) *adj.* (of a leaf) having leaflets on each side of a common stalk.

pi′noch•le (pē′nuk əl, -nok-) *n.* a game using 48 cards.

pin′point′ *v.t.* to locate exactly.

pin′stripe′ *n.* a very thin stripe in fabrics. —**pin′striped′,** *adj.*

pint (pīnt) *n.* a liquid and dry measure equal to one-half of a quart.

pin′to (pin′tō, pēn′-) *adj., n., pl.* **-tos.** —*adj.* **1.** marked with spots of white and other colors. —*n.* **2.** a pinto horse.

pin′to bean′ *n.* a bean with pinkish mottled seeds.

pin′wheel′ *n.* a windmill-like toy that spins on a stick.

pi′o•neer′ (pī′ə nēr′) *n.* **1.** an early arrival in new territory. **2.** the first one in any effort. —*v.i.* **3.** to act as a pioneer.

pi′ous (pī′əs) *adj.* **1.** devout. **2.** hypocritically virtuous.

pip[1] (pip) *n.* a spot on a playing card, domino, etc.

pip[2] (pip) *n.* a small fruit seed.

pipe (pīp) *n., v.,* **piped, piping.** —*n.* **1.** a hollow cylinder for conveying fluid. **2.** a tube with a small bowl at one end for smoking tobacco. **3.** a tube used as a musical instrument. —*v.i.* **4.** to play on a pipe. —*v.t.* **5.** to convey by pipe. **6.** to play (music) on a pipe. **7.** to utter in a shrill tone.

pipe′ dream′ *n.* an unrealistic hope.

pipe′line′ *n.* **1.** linked pipes for transporting oil, water, etc. **2.** a route for supplies. **3.** a channel of information.

pip′ing *n.* **1.** pipes. **2.** the sound of pipes. **3.** a kind of trimming for clothing, upholstery, etc.

pip′pin (pip′in) *n.* a kind of apple.

pip′squeak′ (pip′skwēk′) *n. Informal.* an unimportant person.

pi′quant (pē′kənt, -känt) *adj.* **1.** agreeably sharp in taste. **2.** mentally stimulating. —**pi′quan•cy,** *n.*

pique (pēk) *v.,* **piqued, piquing,** *n.* —*v.t.* **1.** to arouse resentment in. **2.** to excite (interest, curiosity, etc.). —*n.* **3.** an irritated feeling.

pi•qué′ (pi kā′) *n.* a corded cotton fabric.

pi•ra•cy (pī′rə sē) *n., pl.* **-cies.** **1.** robbery at sea. **2.** the illegal use of copyrighted material.

pi•ra′nha (pi rän′yə, -ran′-, -rä′nə, -ran′ə) *n., pl.* **-nhas, -nha.** a small predatory South American fish.

pi•rate (pī′rət) *n., v.,* **-rated, -rating.** —*n.* **1.** a person who practices piracy. —*v.t.* **2.** to take by piracy. **3.** to reproduce (a book, invention, etc.) without authorization.

pir′ou•ette′ (pir′ŏŏ et′) *v.,* **-etted, -etting,** *n.* —*v.i.* **1.** to spin on the toes in dancing. —*n.* **2.** such spinning.

pis•ta′chi•o′ (pi stash′ē ō′) *n., pl.* **-chios.** a nut containing an edible, greenish kernel.

pis′til (pis′tl) *n.* the seed-bearing organ of a flower. —**pis′til•late** (-tl-it, -āt′) *adj.*

pis′tol (pis′tl) *n.* a short gun fired with one hand.

pis′tol-whip′ *v.t.,* **pistol-whipped, pistol-whipping.** to beat with a pistol.

pis′ton (pis′tən) *n.* a disk or cylinder sliding within a longer cylinder, as in an engine or pump.

pit[1] (pit) *n., v.,* **pitted, pitting.** —*n.* **1.** a hole in the ground. **2.** a hollow in a surface. **3. the pits,** *Slang.* an unpleasant place or situation. **4.** the space in the front of a theater in which the musicians sit. —*v.t.* **5.** to mark with pits. **6.** to set in opposition.

pit[2] (pit) *n., v.,* **pitted, pitting.** —*n.* **1.** the stone of a fruit. —*v.t.* **2.** to remove the pit from.

pi′ta (pē′tə) *n.* a round, flat bread with a pocket.

pitch[1] (pich) *v.t.* **1.** to throw. **2.** to set up, as a tent. **3.** to set at a certain point. —*v.i.* **4.** to fall forward. **5.** to plunge and rise, as a ship. **6. pitch in,** *Informal.* to contribute to a common cause. —*n.* **7.** a throw. **8.** relative point or degree. **9.** the degree of height or depth of a musical tone. **10.** the degree of slope. **11.** *Informal.* a sales talk.

pitch² (pich) *n.* a sticky dark substance from coal tar.

pitch′-black′ *adj.* extremely black.

pitch′blende′ (-blend′) *n.* a black mineral that is the principal ore of uranium and radium.

pitch′-dark′ *adj.* very dark.

pitch′er¹ (pich′ər) *n.* a container with a handle and spout, for pouring liquids.

pitch′er² (pich′ər) *n. Baseball.* the person who throws the ball to the batter.

pitch′fork′ *n.* a large, long-handled fork for lifting and pitching hay.

pitch′ pipe′ *n.* a small pipe producing pitches when blown into.

pit′e·ous (pit′ē əs) *adj.* pathetic.

pit′fall′ *n.* a trap; hazard.

pith (pith) *n.* **1.** the spongy central tissue in a plant stem. **2.** the important part.

pith′y *adj.*, **-ier, -iest.** brief and forceful in expression.

pit′i·a·ble (pit′ē ə bəl) *adj.* **1.** deserving pity. **2.** contemptible. —**pit′i·a·bly,** *adv.*

pit′i·ful (-i fəl) *adj.* **1.** deserving pity. **2.** arousing contempt. —**pit′i·ful·ly,** *adv.*

pit′tance (pit′ns) *n.* a very small amount, esp. of money.

pit′y (pit′ē) *n., pl.* **-ies,** *v.,* **-ied, -ying.** —*n.* **1.** sympathetic sorrow for another's suffering. **2.** cause for regret. —*v.t.* **3.** to feel pity for. —**pit′i·less,** *adj.*

piv′ot (piv′ət) *n.* **1.** a shaft on which something turns. —*v.i.* **2.** to turn on a pivot. —*v.t.* **3.** to place on a pivot. —**piv′ot·al,** *adj.*

pix′el (pik′səl, -sel) *n.* the smallest element of an image in a video display system.

pi·zazz′ (pə zaz′) *n. Informal.* **1.** energy. **2.** flair. Also, **piz·zazz′.**

piz′za (pēt′sə) *n.* a baked, open-faced pie topped with cheese, tomato sauce, etc.

piz′zi·ca′to (pit′si kä′tō) *adj. Music.* played by plucking the strings with the finger.

pkg. package.

pkwy. parkway.

pl. 1. place. **2.** plural.

plac′ard (plak′ärd, -ərd) *n.* a public sign or notice.

pla′cate (plā′kāt, plak′āt) *v.t.,* **-cated, -cating.** to appease.

place (plās) *n., v.,* **placed, placing.** —*n.* **1.** a particular portion of space. **2.** any part of a body or surface. **3.** position or situation. **4.** a region. **5.** a building, location, residence, etc. —*v.t.* **6.** to put in a par-

ticular position or situation. **7.** to identify. **8.** to make (a bet, phone call, etc.). —**place′ment,** *n.*

pla·ce′bo (-sē′bō) *n., pl.* **-bos, -boes.** a pill containing no medication, given to reassure a patient or as a control in testing a drug.

pla·cen′ta (plə sen′tə) *n.* the structure in the uterus which attaches to and nourishes the fetus.

plac′id (plas′id) *adj.* calm; serene. —**pla·cid′i·ty,** *n.* —**plac′id·ly,** *adv.*

plack′et (plak′it) *n.* a slit at the neck, waist, or wrist of a garment.

pla′gia·rize′ (plā′jə rīz′) *v.t., v.i.,* **-rized, -rizing.** to copy and claim as one's own work. —**pla′gia·rism,** *n.*

plague (plāg) *n., v.,* **plagued, plaguing.** —*n.* **1.** an often fatal epidemic disease. **2.** any affliction or vexation. —*v.t.* **3.** to trouble.

plaid (plad) *n.* a fabric woven in a cross-barred pattern of different colors.

plain (plān) *adj.* **1.** clear or distinct. **2.** easily understood. **3.** straightforward. **4.** ordinary. **5.** unadorned; simple. **6.** not beautiful. —*adv.* **7.** clearly and simply. —*n.* **8.** a level area of land. —**plain′ly,** *adv.*

plain′clothes′man *n., pl.* **-men.** a police officer who wears civilian clothes on duty.

plain′song′ *n.* the music of the early Christian Church, chanted in unison.

plaint (plānt) *n.* a complaint.

plain′tiff (plān′tif) *n.* one who brings a suit in a court.

plain′tive (-tiv) *adj.* mournful. —**plain′tive·ly,** *adv.*

plait (plāt, plat) *n.* **1.** a braid. **2.** a pleat. —*v.t.* **3.** to braid. **4.** to pleat.

plan (plan) *n., v.,* **planned, planning.** —*n.* **1.** a scheme or method of action or arrangement, developed in advance. **2.** an outline, diagram, or sketch. —*v.t., v.i.* **3.** to make a plan (for). —**plan′ner,** *n.*

plane¹ (plān) *n.* **1.** a flat or level surface. **2.** a level of character. **3.** an airplane. —*adj.* **4.** flat or level.

plane² (plān) *n., v.,* **planed, planing.** —*n.* **1.** a tool for smoothing wood or metal. —*v.t.* **2.** to smooth with a plane.

plan′et (plan′it) *n.* any of the nine heavenly bodies revolving around the sun. —**plan′e·tar′y,** *adj.*

plan′e·tar′i·um (-i târ′ē əm) *n., pl.* **-iums, -ia.** a building or room with an optical device that projects a representation of the stars and planets on a domed ceiling.

plane′ tree′ *n.* a large, spreading shade tree, esp. the North American sycamore.

plan′gent (plan′jənt) *adj.* resounding loudly.

plank (plangk) *n.* **1.** a long flat piece of timber. **2.** one of the principles in a political platform. —**plank′ing,** *n.*

plank′ton (plangk′tən) *n.* microscopic organisms floating in water.

plant (plant) *n.* **1.** a living organism that has no sense organs and cannot move about. **2.** the buildings, equipment, etc., necessary for an industrial business; factory. —*v.t.* **3.** to set in the ground for growth. **4.** to place firmly.

plan′tain (plan′tin) *n.* **1.** a tropical bananalike plant. **2.** a common flat-leaved weed.

plan.ta′tion (plan tā′shən) *n.* **1.** a large estate on which crops are cultivated. **2.** a group of planted trees.

plant′er *n.* **1.** a container for growing plants. **2.** a tool for planting seeds. **3.** a plantation owner.

plaque (plak) *n.* **1.** a metal plate or tablet attached to a wall as a memorial or an ornament. **2.** a sticky, whitish film formed on tooth surfaces.

plas′ma (plaz′mə) *n.* the clear liquid part of blood or lymph.

plas′ter (plas′tər) *n.* **1.** a pasty mixture of lime, sand, and water for covering walls. **2.** a medicinal preparation spread on cloth and applied to the body. —*v.t.* **3.** to cover or treat with plaster.

plas′ter.board′ *n.* a material for insulating or covering walls.

plas′ter of Par′is (par′is) *n.* a powdery form of gypsum used in making plasters and casts.

plas′tic (plas′tik) *n.* **1.** a synthetic or natural material that is hardened after shaping. **2.** a credit card. —*adj.* **3.** made of plastic. **4.** able to be molded. —**plas.tic.i.ty** (-tis′ə tē) *n.*

plas′tic sur′gery *n.* the branch of surgery dealing with the repair, replacement, or reshaping of parts of the body.

plate (plāt) *n.*, *v.*, **plated, plating.** —*n.* **1.** a shallow round dish for food. **2.** gold or silver ware. **3.** a thin sheet of metal, plastic, glass, etc. —*v.t.* **4.** to coat (metal) with a film of gold or silver. **5.** to cover with protective metal plates.

pla.teau′ (pla tō′) *n.*, *pl.* **-teaus, -teaux** (-tōz′). **1.** an area of high, level land. **2.** a period of little growth.

plate′ glass′ *n.* thick, smooth glass, as used for windows.

plat′en (plat′n) *n.* a plate in a printing press that presses the paper against an inked surface.

plat′form (plat′fôrm) *n.* **1.** a raised flooring or structure. **2.** a set of announced political principles.

plat′i.num (-n əm) *n.* a grayish white metallic element that is resistant to most chemicals.

plat′i.tude′ (-tōōd′, -tyōōd′) *n.* a trite remark.

pla.ton′ic (plə ton′ik) *adj.* spiritual, not sexual.

pla.toon′ (plə tōōn′) *n.* a small military unit.

plat′ter (plat′ər) *n.* a large, shallow serving dish.

plat′y.pus (plat′i pəs) *n.*, *pl.* **-puses, -pi** (-pī′). an aquatic, egg-laying Australian mammal having webbed feet and a ducklike bill.

plau′dits (plô′dits) *n.pl.* an expression of approval; applause.

plau′si.ble (plô′zə bəl) *adj.* credible; believable. —**plau′si.bil′i.ty,** *n.*

play (plā) *n.* **1.** a dramatic work or performance. **2.** recreation. **3.** fun or jest. **4.** freedom of movement. —*v.t.* **5.** to act the part of. **6.** to engage in (a game). **7.** to employ in a game. **8.** to perform on (a musical instrument). **9.** to perform (music). —*v.i.* **10.** to amuse oneself. **11.** to take part in a game. **12.** to perform on a musical instrument. **13.** to move about lightly. **14. play down,** to treat as unimportant. **15. ~ out,** to exhaust. **16. ~ up,** to emphasize. —**play′er,** *n.*

play′back′ *n.* **1.** a reproduction of a recording. **2.** the apparatus used in producing playbacks.

play′bill′ *n.* a program or announcement of a play.

play′boy′ *n.* a man who pursues a life of pleasure without responsibilities or attachments.

play′ful (-fəl) *adj.* **1.** full of fun. **2.** pleasantly humorous. —**play′ful.ly,** *adv.* —**play′ful.ness,** *n.*

play′ground′ *n.* an area used by children for outdoor recreation.

play′house′ *n.* **1.** a theater. **2.** a small house for children to play in.

play′mate′ *n.* a companion in play.

play′-off′ *n.* a series of games played to decide a championship.

play′ on words′ *n.* a pun.

play′pen′ *n.* a small enclosure in which a baby can play.

play′thing′ *n.* a toy.

play′wright′ (-rīt′) *n.* a writer of plays.

pla′za (plä′zə, plaz′ə) *n.* **1.** a public square. **2.** a shopping center.

plea (plē) *n.* **1.** an appeal or entreaty. **2.** a defendant's answer to a charge in a court of law.

plea′ bar′gain *n.* an agreement in which a criminal defendant pleads guilty to a lesser charge.

plead (plēd) *v.,* **pleaded** or **pled** (pled), **pleading.** —*v.i.* **1.** to entreat earnestly. **2.** to put forward a plea in a law court. —*v.t.* **3.** to offer as an excuse. **4.** to argue (a case) in a law court. **5.** to make a plea of. —**plead′er,** *n.*

pleas′ant (plez′ənt) *adj.* agreeable; pleasing. —**pleas′ant·ly,** *adv.*

pleas′ant·ry *n., pl.* **-ries.** a good-humored remark.

please (plēz) *adv., v.,* **pleased, pleasing.** —*adv.* **1.** (used in polite requests) be so kind as to. —*v.t., v.i.* **2.** to give pleasure or satisfaction (to).

pleas′ur·a·ble (plezh′ər ə bəl) *adj.* enjoyable.

pleas′ure *n.* **1.** enjoyment or a source of enjoyment. **2.** one's will or desire.

pleat (plēt) *n.* **1.** a double fold of cloth. —*v.t.* **2.** to fold in pleats.

ple·be′ian (pli bē′ən) *adj.* of the common people.

pleb′i·scite′ (pleb′ə sīt′) *n.* a direct vote by citizens on a question.

plec′trum (plek′trəm) *n., pl.* **-tra** (-trə) **-trums.** a small piece of metal or plastic for plucking the strings of a musical instrument.

pledge (plej) *n., v.,* **pledged, pledging.** —*n.* **1.** a solemn promise. **2.** something delivered as security on a loan. —*v.t.* **3.** to bind by pledge. **4.** to promise. **5.** to give as a pledge.

ple′na·ry (plē′nə rē, plen′ə-) *adj.* full; complete.

plen′i·po·ten′ti·ar′y (plen′ə pə ten′shē er′ē, -shə rē) *n., pl.* **-aries,** *adj.* —*n.* **1.** a diplomat with full authority. —*adj.* **2.** having full authority.

plen′i·tude′ (plen′i tōōd′, -tyōōd′) *n.* abundance.

plen′ty (-tē) *n.* **1.** an abundant supply. —*adv. Informal.* **2.** very.

pleth′o·ra (pleth′ər ə) *n.* an overabundance.

pleu·ra (plŏŏr′ə) *n., pl.* **pleur·ae** (plŏŏr′ē). one of a pair of membranes that cover the lungs and line the chest wall.

pleu·ri·sy (-sē) *n.* inflammation of the pleura.

Plex′i·glas′ (plek′si glas′) *Trademark.* a light, durable transparent plastic.

pli′a·ble (plī′ə bəl) *adj.* easily bent or influenced; flexible.

pli′ant (-ənt) *adj.* pliable.

pli′ers (plī′ərz) *n.pl.* small pincers for bending wire, holding objects, etc.

plight[1] (plīt) *n.* a distressing condition.

plight[2] (plīt) *v.t.* to pledge.

PLO Palestine Liberation Organization.

plod (plod) *v.i.,* **plodded, plodding. 1.** to walk heavily. **2.** to work slowly and steadily. —**plod′der,** *n.*

plop (plop) *v.,* **plopped, plopping,** *n.* —*v.t., v.i.* **1.** to drop with a sound like that of an object hitting water. **2.** to drop with direct impact. —*n.* **3.** a plopping sound or fall.

plot (plot) *n., v.,* **plotted, plotting.** —*n.* **1.** a secret plan. **2.** the main story of a novel, play, etc. **3.** a small piece of ground. —*v.t.* **4.** to plan secretly. **5.** to mark on a map. —*v.i.* **6.** to conspire. —**plot′ter,** *n.*

plov′er (pluv′ər, plō′vər) *n.* a kind of shore bird.

plow (plou) *n.* **1.** an implement for turning soil or removing snow. —*v.t.* **2.** to turn or remove with a plow. —*v.i.* **3.** to work with a plow. **4.** to make one's way laboriously. Also, **plough.**

plow′share′ *n.* the blade of a plow.

ploy (ploi) *n.* a clever maneuver.

pluck (pluk) *v.t.* **1.** to pull out (feathers, flowers, etc.) from a fixed position. **2.** to sound (the strings of a musical instrument). —*n.* **3.** a pull or tug. **4.** courage.

pluck′y *adj.,* **-ier, -iest.** courageous.

plug (plug) *n., v.,* **plugged, plugging.** —*n.* **1.** an object for stopping a hole. **2.** an attachment on an electrical cord that establishes contact in a socket. **3.** favorable mention. —*v.t.* **4.** to stop with a plug. **5.** to mention favorably. —*v.i.* **6.** to work steadily. **7. plug in,** to connect to a power source.

plum (plum) *n.* **1.** a juicy round fruit with a smooth skin. **2.** a deep purple. **3.** a desirable thing.

plum′age (plōō′mij) *n.* the feathers of a bird.

plumb (plum) *n.* **1.** a small weight suspended by a line (**plumb′ line′**) and used to measure depth or to ascertain a vertical line. —*adj.* **2.** perpendicular. —*adv.* **3.** vertically. **4.** exactly. **5.** completely. —*v.t.* **6.** to test by a plumb line. **7.** to examine closely.

plumb′er *n.* a person who installs and repairs plumbing.

plumb′ing *n.* the system of water pipes and drains in a building.

plume (plōōm) *n., v.,* **plumed,**

pluming. —*n.* **1.** a large feather. **2.** an ornamental tuft. —*v.t.* **3.** to preen. **4.** to adorn with plumes.

plum′met (plum′it) *n.* **1.** the weight on a plumb line. —*v.i.* **2.** to plunge.

plump¹ (plump) *adj.* having a full, rounded form. —**plump′ness,** *n.*

plump² (plump) *v.i., v.t.* **1.** to drop heavily. —*n.* **2.** a heavy fall. —*adv.* **3.** heavily. **4.** directly.

plun′der (plun′dər) *v.t.* **1.** to rob by force, as in war. —*n.* **2.** a plundering. **3.** something taken in plundering.

plunge (plunj) *v.,* **plunged, plunging,** *n.* —*v.t.* **1.** to thrust suddenly into something. —*v.i.* **2.** to fall or cast oneself into water from a height. **3.** to rush or dash. —*n.* **4.** an act or instance of plunging.

plung′er *n.* **1.** a pistonlike part moving within the cylinder of certain machines. **2.** a device with a handle and suction cup, used to unclog drains.

plu′ral (ploōr′əl) *adj.* **1.** of, being, or containing more than one. —*n.* **2.** a plural form. —**plur′al·ize′,** *v.t., v.i.*

plu′ral·ism *n.* a condition in which minority groups participate in society, yet maintain their distinctions.

plu·ral′i·ty (ploō ral′i tē) *n., pl.* **-ties. 1.** in an election with three or more candidates, the excess of votes received by the leading candidate over those received by the next candidate. **2.** a majority.

plus (plus) *prep.* **1.** increased by. —*adj.* **2.** involving addition. **3.** positive. —*n.* **4.** something additional.

plush (plush) *n.* **1.** a velvetlike fabric having a deep pile. —*adj.* **2.** luxurious.

Plu′to (ploō′tō) *n.* the planet ninth from the sun.

plu′to·crat′ (-tə krat′) *n.* **1.** a wealthy person. **2.** a member of a wealthy governing class. —**plu·toc′ra·cy** (-tok′rə sē) *n.*

plu·to′ni·um (-tō′nē əm) *n.* a radioactive metallic element.

plu′vi·al (ploō′vē əl) *adj.* of rain.

ply¹ (plī) *v.,* **plied, plying.** —*v.t.* **1.** to work with busily. **2.** to carry on, as a trade. **3.** to offer something pressingly to. **4.** to travel along regularly. —*v.i.* **5.** to travel regularly between certain places. **6.** to perform one's work busily.

ply² (plī) *n., pl.* **plies.** a thickness.

ply′wood′ *n.* a building material consisting of sheets of wood glued over each other.

p.m. after noon. Also, **P.M.**

PMS premenstrual syndrome.

pneu·mat′ic (noō mat′ik, nyoō-) *adj.* **1.** of gases. **2.** operated by air.

pneu·mo′nia (-mōn′yə, nyoō-) *n.* inflammation of the lungs.

P.O. post office.

poach¹ (pōch) *v.i., v.t.* to take (game or fish) illegally. —**poach′er,** *n.*

poach² (pōch) *v.t.* to cook (eggs, fish, etc.) in a small amount of simmering liquid.

pock′et (pok′it) *n.* **1.** a small pouch sewed on or into a garment. **2.** a pouchlike receptacle or cavity. **3.** an isolated group or area. —*adj.* **4.** small. —*v.t.* **5.** to put into one's pocket. **6.** to take as one's own, usu. dishonestly.

pock′et·book′ *n.* a purse.

pock′et·knife′ *n.* a small folding knife.

pock′mark (pok′märk′) *n.* a scar from acne, chickenpox, etc.

pod (pod) *n.* a long, narrow seed vessel.

po·di′a·try (pə dī′ə trē) *n.* the diagnosis and treatment of foot disorders. —**po·di′a·trist,** *n.*

po′di·um (pō′dē əm) *n., pl.* **-diums, -dia** (-dē ə). a small raised platform.

po′em (-əm) *n.* a composition in verse.

po′e·sy (-ə sē) *n.* poetry.

po′et (-it) *n.* one who writes poetry.

poet′ic jus′tice *n.* a fitting distribution of rewards and punishments.

poet′ic li′cense *n.* liberty taken by a writer in deviating from fact to produce a desired effect.

po′et·ry (-i trē) *n.* **1.** poems collectively. **2.** the art of writing poems. **3.** poetic qualities. —**po·et′ic** (pō-et′ik), **po·et′i·cal,** *adj.*

po·grom′ (pə grum′, -grom′) *n.* an organized massacre.

poign′ant (poin′yənt) *adj.* **1.** keenly distressing. **2.** affecting the emotions. —**poign′an·cy,** *n.*

poin·set′ti·a (poin set′ē ə, -set′ə) *n., pl.* **-as.** a tropical plant with scarlet, white, or pink flowers.

point (point) *n.* **1.** a sharp end. **2.** a projecting part. **3.** a dot. **4.** a definite position or time. **5.** a compass direction. **6.** a basic reason, purpose, etc. **7.** a detail. **8.** a unit in accounting, scoring, etc. —*v.t.* **9.** to indicate. **10.** to direct (the finger, a weapon, etc.). —*v.i.* **11.** to indicate position or direction. **12.** to be directed. —*Idiom.* **13.** beside the point, irrelevant. **14.** to the point, relevant.

point′-blank′ *adj.* **1.** direct; plain. —*adv.* **2.** directly.

point′ed *adj.* **1.** having a point. **2.**

sharp. **3.** aimed at a particular person. **4.** emphasized.

point′er *n.* **1.** one that points. **2.** a long stick for pointing. **3.** a breed of hunting dog.

poin′til•lism (pwan′tl iz′əm) *n.* the technique in painting of using dots of pure color that are optically mixed into the resulting hue by the viewer.

point′less *adj.* futile.

poise (poiz) *n., v.,* **poised, poising.** —*n.* **1.** balance. **2.** a dignified, self-confident manner. —*v.t., v.i.* **3.** to balance or be balanced.

poi′son (poi′zən) *n.* **1.** a substance that kills or harms seriously. —*v.t.* **2.** to kill or injure with poison. **3.** to put poison in or on. —**poi′son•er,** *n.* —**poi′son•ous,** *adj.*

poi′son i′vy *n.* **1.** a vine or shrub having shiny leaves with three leaflets. **2.** a rash caused by touching poison ivy.

poke (pōk) *v., n.,* **poked, poking.** —*v.t.* **1.** to prod with something pointed. **2.** to thrust. —*v.i.* **3.** to make a thrusting movement. **4.** to pry. —*n.* **5.** a thrust or push.

pok′er¹ (pō′kər) *n.* a rod for stirring a fire.

pok′er² (pō′kər) *n.* a gambling card game.

pok′er-faced′ *adj.* showing no emotion or intention.

pok′y (pō′kē) *adj.,* **pokier, pokiest.** slow; dull. Also, **poke′y.**

po′lar (pō′lər) *adj.* **1.** of the North or South Pole. **2.** of magnetic poles. —**po•lar′i•ty,** *n.*

po′lar bear′ *n.* a white arctic bear.

Po•lar′is (pō lâr′is, -lär′-, pə-) *n.* the bright star close to the north pole of the heavens.

po′lar•i•za′tion (-lər ə zā′shən) *n.* **1.** the division of a group into opposing factions. **2.** a state in which rays of light exhibit different properties in different directions. —**po′lar•ize′,** *v.t., v.i.*

pole¹ (pōl) *n., v.,* **poled, poling.** —*n.* **1.** a long slender rod. —*v.t.* **2.** to propel with a pole.

pole² (pōl) *n.* **1.** each end of the axis of a sphere, esp. the earth. **2.** one of two opposite principles.

pole′cat′ *n.* **1.** a European mammal that ejects a bad-smelling fluid. **2.** a skunk.

po•lem′ics (pə lem′iks) *n.* the art or practice of debate. —**po•lem′ic,** *n., adj.* —**po•lem′i•cist,** *n.*

pole′ vault′ *n.* an athletic event in which a vault over a horizontal bar is performed with a long pole.

po•lice′ (pə lēs′) *n., v.,* **-liced, -licing.** —*n.* **1.** an organized civil force

for keeping order and enforcing the law. —*v.t.* **2.** to keep in order.

pol′i•cy¹ (pol′ə sē) *n., pl.* **-cies.** a definite course of action.

pol′i•cy² (pol′ə sē) *n., pl.* **-cies.** an insurance contract.

po′li•o•my•e•li′tis (pō′lē ō mī′ə lī′tis) *n.* an infectious viral disease of the spinal cord, often resulting in paralysis. Also called **po′li•o′.**

pol′ish (pol′ish) *v.t.* **1.** to make glossy. **2.** to make refined. —*n.* **3.** a polishing substance. **4.** a gloss. **5.** refinement.

po•lite′ (pə līt′) *adj.* showing good manners. —**po•lite′ly,** *adv.*

pol′i•tic (pol′i tik) *adj.* **1.** prudent; expedient. **2.** political.

po•lit′i•cal (pə lit′i kəl) *adj.* of government or politics. —**po•lit′i•cal•ly,** *adv.*

polit′ically correct′ *adj.* marked by a progressive attitude on issues of race, gender, etc. —**polit′ical correct′ness,** *n.*

polit′ical sci′ence *n.* the social science dealing with political institutions and government.

pol•i•ti′cian (pol′i tish′ən) *n.* a person who is active in politics, esp. as a career.

po•lit′i•cize′ (pə lit′ə sīz′) *v.t.,* **-cized, -cizing.** to give a political character to.

pol′i•tick′ing (pol′i tik′ing) *n.* political campaigning.

pol′i•tics (-tiks) *n.* **1.** the science or conduct of government. **2.** political affairs, methods, or principles.

pol′ka (pōl′kə, pō′kə) *n.* a lively dance for couples.

pol′ka dot′ *n.* a pattern of dots.

poll (pōl) *n.* **1.** a sampling of public opinion. **2. polls,** the place where people vote. **3.** the act of voting or the votes cast in an election. **4.** a list of individuals, as for voting. —*v.t.* **5.** to take a sampling of the opinions of. **6.** to receive at the polls, as votes.

pol′len (pol′ən) *n.* the powdery fertilizing element of flowers.

pol′li•nate′ (-ə nāt′) *v.t.,* **-nated, -nating.** to convey pollen to the stigma of (a flower). —**pol′li•na′tion,** *n.*

pol′li•wog′ (-ē wog′) *n.* a tadpole.

poll′ster (pōl′stər) *n.* a person who takes public-opinion polls.

pol•lute′ (pə lōōt′) *v.t.,* **-luted, -luting.** to contaminate or make foul, as with chemicals or waste products. —**pol•lu′tion,** *n.* —**pol•lut′ant,** *n.*

po′lo (pō′lō) *n., pl.* **-los.** a game played on horseback by two teams who drive a ball with long-handled mallets.

pol′ter.geist′ (pōl′tər gīst′) *n.* a noisy spirit that throws things about.

pol.troon′ (pol trōon′) *n.* a coward.

poly- a prefix meaning many.

pol′y.es′ter (-es′tər) *n.* a polymer used to make plastics, textiles, etc.

pol′y.eth′yl.ene′ (-eth′ə lēn′) *n.* a plastic polymer used esp. for containers and packaging.

po.lyg′a.my (pə lig′ə mē) *n.* the practice of having more than one spouse, esp. a wife, at one time. —**po.lyg′a.mist,** *n.* —**po.lyg′a. mous,** *adj.*

pol′y.gon′ (-gon′) *n.* a figure having three or more straight sides.

pol′y.graph′ (pol′i graf′) *n.* a lie detector.

pol′y.he′dron (pol′ē hē′drən) *n., pl.* **-drons, -dra** (-drə). a solid figure having four or more sides.

pol′y.math′ (-math′) *n.* a person of great learning in several fields.

pol′y.mer (pol′ə mər) *n.* a compound formed by the combination of many smaller molecules. —**pol′. y.mer.i.za′tion,** *n.*

pol′yp (pol′ip) *n.* a projecting growth from a mucous surface.

po.lyph′o.ny (pə lif′ə nē) *n.* music in which two or more melodic lines are played or sung at the same time. —**pol′y.phon′ic** (pol′ē fon′ik) *adj.*

pol′y.sty′rene (pol′ē stī′rēn, -stēr′ēn) *n.* a polymer used in molded objects and as an insulator.

pol′y.tech′nic (-tek′nik) *adj.* offering instruction in many applied sciences, technical subjects, etc.

pol′y.the′ism *n.* belief in more than one god.

pol′y.un.sat′u.rat′ed *adj.* of a class of fats associated with low cholesterol content.

po.made′ (po mād′, -mäd′) *n.* a hair ointment.

pome′gran′ate (pom′gran′it, pom′i-) *n.* a round, red fruit with many seeds.

pom′mel (pom′əl, pom′-) *n., v.,* **-meled, -meling.** —*n.* **1.** a knob on the hilt of a sword or the front of a saddle. —*v.t.* **2.** to pummel.

pomp (pomp) *n.* stately display.

pom′pa.dour′ (pom′pə dôr′, -dōor′) *n.* an arrangement of hair in which it is brushed up high from the forehead.

pom′pom (pom′pom′) *n.* an ornamental tuft.

pomp′ous (pom′pəs) *adj.* full of ostentatious self-importance or dignity. —**pom.pos′i.ty** (-pos′i tē) *n.*

pon′cho (pon′chō) *n., pl.* **-chos.** a blanketlike cloak.

pond (pond) *n.* a small lake.

pon′der (pon′dər) *v.i., v.t.* to consider (something) thoughtfully.

pon′der.ous *adj.* not graceful.

pon′tiff (pon′tif) *n.* **1.** the pope. **2.** any chief priest; bishop. —**pon. tif′i.cal,** *adj.*

pon.tif′i.cate′ (-tif′i kāt′) *v.t., -cated, -cating.* to speak with an affected air of authority.

pon.toon′ (-tōon′) *n.* a floating support.

po′ny (pō′nē) *n., pl.* **-nies.** a small horse.

po′ny.tail′ *n.* hair gathered and fastened at the back of the head so as to hang freely.

poo′dle (pōod′l) *n.* a kind of dog with thick, curly hair.

pool[1] (pōol) *n.* **1.** a small pond. **2.** a collection of liquid on a surface. **3.** a large basin filled with water for swimming.

pool[2] (pōol) *n.* **1.** a game resembling billiards. **2.** a combination of resources, funds, etc., available for sharing. **3.** a shared facility or resource. —*v.t.* **4.** to put into a common fund or supply.

poop (pōop) *n.* the upper deck on the stern of a ship.

poor (pōor) *adj.* **1.** having little money. **2.** not very good. **3.** unfortunate.

pop[1] (pop) *v.,* **popped, popping,** *n.* —*v.i.* **1.** to make or burst with a quick, explosive sound. **2.** to come or go suddenly. —*v.t.* **3.** to thrust quickly. —*n.* **4.** a quick, explosive sound. **5.** a fizzy soft drink.

pop[2] (pop) *adj.* **1.** of popular songs or art. **2.** reflecting the tastes of the general public. —*n.* **3.** popular music.

pop′corn′ *n.* a kind of corn whose kernels burst in dry heat.

pope (pōp) *n.* (*often cap.*) the bishop of Rome as the head of the Roman Catholic Church.

pop′lar (pop′lər) *n.* any of several tall, slender, fast-growing trees.

pop′lin (pop′lin) *n.* a plain, usu. cotton fabric.

pop′py (pop′ē) *n., pl.* **-pies.** a plant with showy, usu. red flowers.

pop′py.cock′ *n.* nonsense.

pop′u.lace (pop′yə ləs) *n.* the general public.

pop′u.lar (-lər) *adj.* **1.** generally liked and approved. **2.** of the people. **3.** prevalent. —**pop′u.lar′i.ty** (-lar′i tē) *n.* —**pop′u.lar.ize′,** *v.t.*

populate

pop′u•late′ (-lāt′) v.t., **-lated, -lating.** to inhabit.

pop′u•la′tion n. the total number of persons inhabiting a given area.

pop′u•lism n. a political philosophy or movement promoting the interests of the common people. —**pop′u•list,** n., adj.

pop′u•lous adj. with many inhabitants.

por′ce•lain (pôr′sə lin, pôrs′lin) n. glassy ceramic ware; china.

porch (pôrch) n. **1.** an open or enclosed room attached to the outside of a house. **2.** a covered entrance to a building.

por′cu•pine′ (pôr′kyə pīn′) n. a large rodent with stiff, sharp quills.

pore¹ (pôr) v., **pored, poring. pore over,** to ponder or study intently.

pore² (pôr) n. a minute opening, as in the skin.

pork (pôrk) n. the flesh of hogs as food.

pork′ bar′rel n. government money for local improvements intended to ingratiate legislators with their constituents.

por•nog′ra•phy (pôr nog′rə fē) n. writings, photographs, etc., intended to cause sexual excitement. —**por′no•graph′ic** (-nə graf′ik) adj. —**por•nog′ra•pher,** n.

po′rous (pôr′əs) adj. permeable by water, air, etc. —**po′rous•ness,** n.

por′poise (-pəs) n. an aquatic mammal with a blunt, rounded snout.

por′ridge (pôr′ij, por′-) n. a thick cereal made of boiled oatmeal.

port¹ (pôrt) n. **1.** a place where ships load or unload. **2.** a harbor.

port² (pôrt) n. **1.** the left side of a vessel, facing forward. —adj. **2.** of or on the left side.

port³ (pôrt) n. a sweet, dark red wine.

port⁴ (pôrt) n. **1.** an opening in a ship's side. **2.** a data connection in a computer to which a peripheral device can be attached.

port′a•ble adj. readily carried.

por′tage (pôr′tij, pôr täzh′) n. **1.** an overland route between navigable streams. **2.** the carrying of boats, supplies, etc., over such a route.

por′tal (-tl) n. a door or gate, esp. a large one.

port•cul′lis (-kul′is) n. a heavy iron grating at the gateway of a castle.

por•tend′ (-tend′) v.t. to indicate in advance.

por′tent (-tent) n. **1.** an omen. **2.** threatening or disquieting significance. —**por•ten′tous,** adj.

por′ter (-tər) n. **1.** a railroad attendant. **2.** a baggage carrier. **3.** a person who cleans or maintains a building, store, etc.

por′ter•house′ n. a choice cut of beefsteak.

port•fo′li•o′ (pôrt fō′lē ō′) n., pl. **-lios. 1.** a flat, portable case for carrying loose sheets of paper. **2.** a collection of one's work, as drawings, photographs, etc. **3.** the investments held by one person.

port′hole′ n. a small, round window in a ship's side.

por′ti•co′ (pôr′ti kō′) n., pl. **-coes, -cos.** a structure with a roof supported by columns.

por′tion (pôr′shən) n. **1.** a part of a whole. **2.** a share. —v.t. **3.** to divide into shares.

port′ly (pôrt′lē) adj., **-lier, -liest.** rather heavy and dignified. —**port′li•ness,** n.

port•man′teau (pôrt man′tō) n., pl. **-teaus, -teaux** (-tōz, tō). a leather trunk opening into two halves.

por′trait (pôr′trit, -trāt) n. a picture, sculpture, etc., showing a specific person. —**por′trai•ture** (-tri chər) n.

por•tray′ (pôr trā′) v.t. **1.** to make a picture of. **2.** to depict in words. **3.** to represent on the stage. —**por•tray′al,** n.

Por′tuguese man′-of-war′ n. a poisonous marine animal.

pose (pōz) v., **posed, posing,** n. —v.i. **1.** to assume or hold a physical position, attitude, or character. **2.** to pretend to be what one is not. —v.t. **3.** to place in a specific position. **4.** to ask (a question). —n. **5.** a position or character assumed.

po′ser n. **1.** a person who poses, as for an artist. **2.** a difficult question.

po•seur′ (pō zûr′) n. an affected person.

posh (posh) adj. elegant; luxurious.

pos′it (poz′it) v.t. to lay down or assume as a fact or principle.

po•si′tion (pə zish′ən) n. **1.** the place occupied by a person or thing. **2.** an opinion on a question. **3.** situation. **4.** rank. **5.** a job. —v.t. **6.** to place.

pos′i•tive (poz′i tiv) adj. **1.** definite; certain. **2.** affirmative. **3.** confident. **4.** constructive. **5.** (of a quantity) greater than zero. **6.** deficient in electrons. **7.** revealing the presence of the thing tested for. **8.** denoting the first degree of comparison of an adjective or adverb. —n. **9.** something positive. **10.** a photographic image.

pos′i•tron′ (-tron′) n. a particle with the same mass as an electron but a positive charge.

pos′se (pos′ē) *n.* a body of persons assisting a sheriff.

pos·sess′ (pə zes′) *v.t.* **1.** to have under ownership or domination. **2.** to have as a quality. **3.** to control or dominate. —**pos·ses′sor,** *n.*

pos·sessed′ *adj.* controlled by a strong feeling or by the supernatural.

pos·ses′sion *n.* **1.** a possessing or being possessed. **2.** a thing possessed. **3. possessions,** property. **4.** a territory governed by a state.

pos·ses′sive *adj.* **1.** desiring to dominate another. **2.** of the grammatical case indicating ownership. —*n.* **3.** the possessive case.

pos′si·ble (pos′ə bəl) *adj.* that may be, happen, be done, etc. —**pos′si·bil′i·ty,** *n.* —**pos′si·bly,** *adv.*

pos′sum (pos′əm) *n.* an opossum.

post¹ (pōst) *n.* **1.** an upright support of timber or metal. **2.** a message sent to a newsgroup. —*v.t.* **3.** to attach (a notice) to a wall. **4.** to make publicly known, as by a poster. **5.** to send (a message) to a newsgroup.

post² (pōst) *n.* **1.** a position of duty, trust, etc. **2.** a station for soldiers or traders. —*v.t.* **3.** to station at a post. **4.** to provide, as bail.

post³ (pōst) *n.* **1.** *Chiefly Brit.* mail. —*v.t.* **2.** to inform. **3.** to enter in a ledger. **4.** *Chiefly Brit.* to mail.

post- a prefix meaning: after or behind.

post′age (pō′stij) *n.* the charge for mailing.

post′al (pōs′tl) *adj.* concerning mail.

post′card′ *n.* a small notecard usu. having a picture on one side and space for a stamp, address, and message on the other.

post·date′ (pōst dāt′, pōst′-) *v.t.,* **-dated, -dating. 1.** to mark with a date later than the actual date. **2.** to follow in time.

post′er (pō′stər) *n.* a large sign, notice, or picture announcing something.

pos·te′ri·or (po stēr′ē ər, pō-) *adj.* **1.** situated behind. **2.** coming after. —*n.* **3.** the buttocks.

pos·ter′i·ty (-ster′i tē) *n.* one's descendants.

post·grad′u·ate (pōst graj′ōo it, -āt′) *n.* **1.** a student taking advanced work after graduation. —*adj.* **2.** of postgraduates.

post′haste′ *adv.* speedily.

post′hu·mous (pos′chə məs, -chōo-) *adj.* occurring after a person's death.

post′mark′ *n.* **1.** an official mark on a piece of mail showing the place and time of mailing. —*v.t.* **2.** to stamp with a postmark.

post′mas′ter *n.* the official in charge of a post office.

post′mis′tress *n.* a woman in charge of a post office.

post·mor′tem (-môr′təm) *adj.* **1.** of or occurring in the time after death. —*n.* **2.** an examination of the body after death; autopsy.

post·na′tal (-nāt′l) *adj.* after childbirth.

post′ of′fice *n.* a place where mail is handled, stamps are sold, etc.

post′paid′ *adv., adj.* with the postage paid in advance.

post·par′tum (-pär′təm) *adj.* following childbirth.

post·pone′ (pōst pōn′, pōs-) *v.t.,* **-poned, -poning.** to put off to a later time. —**post·pone′ment,** *n.*

post′script′ *n.* a note added to a letter that has already been signed.

pos′tu·late *v., * **-lated, -lating,** *n.* —*v.t.* (pos′chə lāt′) **1.** to assume the truth of as a basis for reasoning. —*n.* (-lit) **2.** something postulated.

pos′ture (pos′chər) *n., v.,* **-tured, -turing.** —*n.* **1.** the position or carriage of the body. —*v.i.* **2.** to strike a pose.

post′war′ *adj.* after a war.

po′sy (pō′zē) *n., pl.* **-sies.** a flower or bouquet.

pot¹ (pot) *n., v.,* **potted, potting.** —*n.* **1.** a round deep container for cooking, serving, etc. **2.** a flowerpot. —*v.t.* **3.** to put into a pot. —*Idiom.* **4. go to pot,** to become ruined.

pot² (pot) *n. Slang.* marijuana.

po′ta·ble (pō′tə bəl) *adj.* drinkable.

pot′ash′ (pot′ash′) *n.* potassium carbonate, esp. from wood ashes.

po·tas′si·um (pə tas′ē əm) *n.* a silvery white metallic element.

po·ta′to (pə tā′tō, -tə) *n., pl.* **-toes.** the edible tuber of a cultivated plant.

pot′bel′ly *n., pl.* **-lies.** a belly that sticks out. —**pot′bel′lied,** *adj.*

pot′boil′er *n.* a mediocre work of literature or art produced merely for financial gain.

po′tent (pōt′nt) *adj.* **1.** powerful. **2.** (of a male) capable of sexual intercourse. —**po′ten·cy,** *n.*

po′ten·tate (-tāt′) *n.* a powerful person, as a monarch.

po·ten′tial (pə ten′shəl) *adj.* **1.** capable of being developed. —*n.* **2.** possibility. **3.** a latent ability that may or may not be developed. —**po·ten′tial·ly,** *adv.*

pot′hole′ *n.* a hole formed in pavement.

po′tion (pō′shən) *n.* a medicinal or magical drink.

pot′luck′ *n.* **1.** a meal to which people bring food to be shared. **2.** whatever is available.

pot′pour·ri′ (pō′pŏŏ rē′) *n.* **1.** a fragrant mixture of dried flowers and spices. **2.** any miscellaneous grouping.

pot′shot′ *n.* **1.** a casual or aimless shot. **2.** a random or incidental criticism.

pot′ter (pot′ər) *n.* a person who makes earthen pots.

pot′ter·y *n., pl.* **-teries. 1.** earthenware. **2.** a place where earthen vessels are made.

pouch (pouch) *n.* a small bag or sack or something shaped like this.

poul′tice (pōl′tis) *n.* a soft moist mass applied as medicine.

poul′try (pōl′trē) *n.* domestic fowl.

pounce (pouns) *v.*, **pounced, pouncing,** *n.* —*v.i.* **1.** to swoop down or spring suddenly. **2.** to seize eagerly. —*n.* **3.** a sudden swoop.

pound[1] (pound) *v.t.* **1.** to strike repeatedly and heavily. **2.** to crush by pounding. —*v.i.* **3.** to beat heavily, as the heart. **4.** to run heavily.

pound[2] (pound) *n., pl.* **pounds, pound. 1.** a unit of weight: in the U.S., **pound avoirdupois** (16 ounces) and **pound troy** (12 ounces). **2.** the British monetary unit.

pound[3] (pound) *n.* an enclosure for stray animals or for impounded vehicles.

pound′ cake′ *n.* a rich, sweet cake.

pour (pôr) *v.t.* **1.** to send (a liquid) flowing. **2.** to emit or utter continuously. —*v.i.* **3.** to flow along. **4.** to rain heavily.

pout (pout) *v.i.* **1.** to thrust out the lips in displeasure or sullenness. —*n.* **2.** a sullen look or mood.

pov′er·ty (pov′ər tē) *n.* **1.** the state of being poor. **2.** a lack.

POW *pl.* **POWs, POW′s.** prisoner of war.

pow′der (pou′dər) *n.* **1.** a solid substance crushed to fine loose particles. —*v.t.* **2.** to reduce to powder. **3.** to apply powder to. —**pow′der·y,** *adj.*

pow′der keg′ *n.* **1.** a container for gunpowder. **2.** an explosive situation.

pow′er (pou′ər) *n.* **1.** ability to act. **2.** strength. **3.** authority. **4.** a person, nation, etc., having great influence. **5.** mechanical energy. **6.** the product of repeated multiplications of a number by itself. **7.** the

magnifying capacity of an optical instrument. —*v.t.* **8.** to supply with power. —**pow′er·ful,** *adj.*

pow′er·house′ *n.* **1.** a building where electricity is generated. **2.** a dynamic person.

pow′er of attorn′ey *n.* a written legal authorization for another person to act in one's place.

pox (poks) *n.* a disease marked by skin eruptions.

pp. 1. pages. **2.** past participle.

ppd. 1. postpaid. **2.** prepaid.

P.P.S. an additional postscript.

PR public relations.

prac′ti·ca·ble (prak′ti kə bəl) *adj.* able to be put into practice.

prac′ti·cal *adj.* **1.** of or resulting from practice or action as opposed to theory. **2.** suitable for use. **3.** levelheaded. **4.** virtual. —**prac′ti·cal′i·ty,** *n.*

prac′ti·cal·ly *adv.* **1.** almost. **2.** in a practical way.

prac′tice (-tis) *n., v.,* **-ticed, -ticing.** —*n.* **1.** a habitual or customary way of doing something. **2.** the action of doing something. **3.** repeated performance to acquire skill. **4.** the exercise of a profession. —*v.t.* **5.** to do habitually or repeatedly or as a profession. —*v.i.* **6.** to do something repeatedly to acquire skill. Also, *Brit.*, **prac′tise** (for defs. 5–6).

prac·ti′tion·er (-tish′ə nər) *n.* a person engaged in a profession.

prag·mat′ic (prag mat′ik) *adj.* concerned with practical values and results. —**prag′ma·tism,** *n.* —**prag′ma·tist,** *n.*

prai′rie (prâr′ē) *n.* a broad, flat, treeless grassland.

prai′rie dog′ *n.* a burrowing squirrel of W North America.

praise (prāz) *n., v.,* **praised, praising.** —*n.* **1.** words of strong approval. **2.** worship of God. —*v.t.* **3.** to express approval of. **4.** to worship. —**praise′wor′thy,** *adj.*

pra′line (prā′lēn, prä′-) *n.* a confection of caramelized nuts and sugar.

pram (pram) *n. Chiefly Brit.* a baby carriage.

prance (prans) *v.,* **pranced, prancing,** *n.* —*v.i.* **1.** to step about gaily or proudly. —*n.* **2.** the act of prancing.

prank (prangk) *n.* a playful trick. —**prank′ster,** *n.*

prate (prāt) *v.i., v.t.,* **prated, prating.** to talk foolishly.

prat′fall′ (prat′fôl′) *n.* a fall on the buttocks.

prat′tle (prat′l) *v.,* **-tled, -tling,** *n.* —*v.i., v.t.* **1.** to talk in a foolish or childish way. —*n.* **2.** chatter.

prawn (prôn) *n.* a large shrimplike shellfish.

pray (prā) *v.i.* **1.** to say prayers. —*v.t.* **2.** to entreat earnestly.

prayer (prâr) *n.* **1.** a devout petition to or spiritual communication with God. **2.** a petition.

pre- a prefix meaning before or in front of.

preach (prēch) *v.t.* **1.** to deliver (a sermon). **2.** to advocate. —*v.i.* **3.** to preach a sermon. **4.** to advise in a tedious or moralizing way. —**preach′er,** *n.* —**preach′y,** *adj.*

pre•am′ble (prē′am′bəl, prē am′-) *n.* an introductory declaration.

pre•can′cer•ous *adj.* showing pathological changes that may be preliminary to malignancy.

pre•car′i•ous (pri kâr′ē əs) *adj.* uncertain; dangerous.

pre•cau′tion (pri kô′shən) *n.* a prudent advance measure. —**pre•cau′tion•ar′y,** *adj.*

pre•cede′ (pri sēd′) *v.t., v.i.,* -**ceded, -ceding.** to go or come before.

prec′e•dence (pres′i dens) *n.* the act, fact, or right of preceding.

prec′e•dent (pres′i dənt) *n.* a past case used as an example or guide.

pre′cept (prē′sept) *n.* a rule of conduct.

pre•cep′tor (pri sep′tər, prē′sep-) *n.* a teacher.

pre′cinct (prē′singkt) *n.* a bounded or defined area.

pre•ci•os′i•ty (presh′ē os′i tē) *n., pl.* -**ties.** fastidious refinement.

pre′cious (-əs) *adj.* **1.** valuable. **2.** beloved. **3.** affectedly refined.

prec′i•pice (pres′ə pis) *n.* a cliff.

pre•cip′i•tate′ *v.,* -**tated, -tating,** *adj., n.* —*v.t.* (pri sip′i tāt′) **1.** to hasten the occurrence of. **2.** to separate (a solid) from a solution. **3.** to fling down. —*v.i.* **4.** to condense from vapor and fall to the earth's surface as rain, snow, etc. **5.** to separate from a solution as a precipitate. —*adj.* (-tit) **6.** rash or impetuous; hasty. —*n.* (-tit) **7.** a substance precipitated from a solution. **8.** condensed moisture. —**pre•cip′i•tate•ly,** *adv.*

pre•cip′i•ta′tion *n.* **1.** rain, snow, etc., or the amount that has fallen at a place in a given period. **2.** the act or result of precipitating. **3.** sudden haste.

pre•cip′i•tous *adj.* **1.** extremely steep. **2.** precipitate.

pré•cis′ (prā sē′, prā′sē) *n.* a summary.

pre•cise′ (pri sīs′) *adj.* **1.** definitely stated, defined, or fixed. **2.** exact. —**pre•ci′sion** (-sizh′ən) *n.*

pre•clude′ (pri klōōd′) *v.t.,* -**cluded,** -**cluding.** to prevent or exclude the possibility of. —**pre•clu′sion** (-klōō′zhən) *n.* —**pre•clu′sive,** *adj.*

pre•co′cious (pri kō′shəs) *adj.* unusually advanced in mental development or talent. —**pre•coc′i•ty** (-kos′ə tē) *n.*

pre′cog•ni′tion (prē′kog nish′ən) *n.* knowledge of a future event through extrasensory means.

pre•con•ceive′ *v.t.,* -**ceived, -ceiving.** to form (an opinion) beforehand. —**pre′con•cep′tion,** *n.*

pre′con•di′tion *n.* something necessary for a subsequent result.

pre•cur′sor (pri kûr′sər, prē′kûr-) *n.* **1.** a predecessor. **2.** a harbinger.

pred′a•tor (pred′ə tər) *n.* one that preys on others. —**pred′a•tor′y,** *adj.*

pred′e•ces′sor (-ses′ər) *n.* one who precedes another.

pre•des′ti•na′tion (pri des′tə nā′shən) *n.* **1.** fate; destiny. **2.** the doctrine that everything has been determined in advance by God. —**pre•des′tine,** *v.t.*

pre′de•ter′mine (prē′di tûr′min) *v.t.,* -**mined, -mining.** to decide in advance. —**pre′de•ter′mi•na′tion,** *n.*

pre•dic′a•ment (pri dik′ə mənt) *n.* a difficult situation.

pred′i•cate *n., adj., v.,* -**cated, -cating.** —*n.* (pred′i kit) **1.** the part of a sentence that expresses the action performed by or the state of the subject. —*adj.* (-kit) **2.** belonging to the predicate of a sentence. —*v.t.* (-kāt′) **3.** to declare. **4.** to find a basis for.

pre•dict′ (pri dikt′) *v.t., v.i.* to tell (what will happen) in advance. —**pre•dict′a•ble,** *adj.* —**pre•dic′-tion,** *n.* —**pre•dic′tor,** *n.*

pre′di•lec′tion (pred′l ek′shən, prēd′-) *n.* a preference.

pre′dis•pose′ (prē′di spōz′) *v.t.,* -**posed, -posing.** **1.** to make susceptible. **2.** to incline. —**pre•dis′-po•si′tion,** *n.*

pre•dom′i•nate′ (pri dom′ə nāt′) *v.i.,* -**nated, -nating.** to be more powerful or common. —**pre•dom′-i•nance,** *n.* —**pre•dóm′i•nant,** *adj.*

pre•em′i•nent (prē em′ə nənt) *adj.* superior; outstanding. —**pre•em′i•nence,** *n.* —**pre•em′i•nent•ly,** *adv.*

pre•empt′ (prē empt′) *v.t.* **1.** to take the place of. **2.** to acquire before others can. **3.** to occupy (land) to establish a prior right to buy. —**pre•emp′tive,** *adj.*

preen (prēn) *v.t.* **1.** to trim or clean (feathers or fur) with the beak or tongue. **2.** to dress (oneself) carefully. **3.** to pride (oneself) on something.

pre·fab'ri·cate' *v.t.*, **-cated, -cating.** to build in parts for quick assembly. **—pre'fab·ri·ca'tion,** *n.*

pref'ace (pref'is) *n.*, *v.*, **-aced, -acing. —n. 1.** an introductory statement. **—v.t. 2.** to provide with or introduce by a preface. **—pref'a·to'ry** (-ə tôr'ē) *adj.*

pre'fect (prē'fekt) *n.* a chief magistrate. **—pre'fec·ture** (-fek shər) *n.*

pre·fer' (pri fûr') *v.t.*, **-ferred, -ferring. 1.** to like better. **—Idiom. 2. prefer charges,** to make an accusation of wrongdoing against another.

pref'er·a·ble (pref'ər ə bəl) *adj.* more desirable.

pref'er·ence (-əns) *n.* **1.** a preferring or being preferred. **2.** something preferred. **3.** an advantage given to one over others. **—pref'er·en'tial** (-ə ren'shəl) *adj.*

pre·fer'ment (pri fûr'mənt) *n.* advancement or promotion.

pre·fig'ure (prē fig'yər) *v.t.*, **-ured, -uring.** to foreshadow.

pre'fix *n.* (-fiks) **1.** a syllable or syllables put before a word to qualify its meaning. **—v.t.** (*also* prē fiks') **2.** to put before.

preg'nant (preg'nənt) *adj.* **1.** having a child developing in the body. **2.** full of meaning. **—preg'nan·cy,** *n.*

pre·hen'sile (pri hen'sil, -sīl) *adj.* adapted for grasping.

pre'his·tor'ic *adj.* of the time before recorded history.

pre·judge' *v.t.*, **-judged, -judging.** to judge prematurely.

prej'u·dice (prej'ə dis) *n.*, *v.*, **-diced, -dicing. —n. 1.** an opinion formed beforehand or without knowledge. **2.** unreasonable, hostile attitudes regarding a group. **—v.t. 3.** to affect with a prejudice. **—prej'u·di'cial** (-dish'əl) *adj.*

prel'ate (prel'it) *n.* a high church official.

pre·lim'i·nar'y (pri lim'ə ner'ē) *adj.*, *n.*, *pl.* **-naries. —adj. 1.** leading up to the main action or event. **—n. 2.** a preliminary action.

prel'ude (prel'yōōd, prā'lōōd) *n.* **1.** a preliminary to a major event. **2.** an introductory piece of music.

pre·mar'i·tal (prē mar'i tl) *adj.* before marriage.

pre'ma·ture' *adj.* born, coming, done, or occurring too soon. **—pre'ma·ture'ly,** *adv.*

pre·med'i·tate' *v.t.*, *v.i.*, **-tated, -tating.** to plan in advance.

pre·mier' (pri mēr', -myēr') *n.* **1.** a prime minister. **—adj. 2.** chief.

pre·miere' (-mēr', -myâr') *n.* the first public performance.

prem'ise (prem'is) *n.* **1.** a statement from which a conclusion is drawn. **2. premises,** a building with its grounds.

pre'mi·um (prē'mē əm) *n.* **1.** a periodic payment for an insurance policy. **2.** a bonus. **3.** an extra charge. **4.** great value.

pre'mo·ni'tion (prem'ə nish'ən, prē'mə-) *n.* a foreboding.

pre·na'tal (prē nāt'l) *adj.* before birth or before giving birth.

pre·oc'cu·py' *v.t.*, **-pied, -pying.** to engross completely.

pre'or·dain' *v.t.* to decree in advance.

prep (prep) *v.t.*, *v.i.*, **prepped, prepping.** to prepare.

prep'a·ra'tion (prep'ə rā'shən) *n.* **1.** a means by which one prepares for something. **2.** a preparing or being prepared. **3.** a substance prepared for use.

pre·par'a·to'ry (pri par'ə tôr'ē) *adj.* **1.** preparing. **2.** introductory.

prepar'atory school' *n.* a private secondary school preparing students for college. Also, **prep school.**

pre·pare' (pri pâr') *v.t.*, *v.i.*, **-pared, -paring.** to make or get ready.

pre·par'ed·ness (-pâr'id nis, -pârd'nis) *n.* the state of being prepared, esp. for war.

pre·pay' (prē pā') *v.t.*, **-paid, -paying.** to pay beforehand.

pre·pon'der·ant (pri pon'dər ənt) *adj.* superior in force or numbers.

prep'o·si'tion (prep'ə zish'ən) *n.* a word placed before a noun or pronoun to indicate space, time, means, etc.

pre'pos·sess'ing (prē'-) *adj.* impressing favorably.

pre·pos'ter·ous (pri pos'tər əs) *adj.* absurd.

pre'puce (prē'pyōōs) *n.* the skin covering the head of the penis.

pre·req'ui·site (pri rek'wə zit, prē-) *adj.* **1.** required in advance. **—n. 2.** something prerequisite.

pre·rog'a·tive (pri rog'ə tiv, pə rog'-) *n.* a special right or privilege.

pres. 1. present. **2.** president.

pres'age (pres'ij) *v.t.*, **-aged, -aging. 1.** to foreshadow. **2.** to predict.

pres'by·o'pi·a (prez'bē ō'pē ə, pres'-) *n.* farsightedness, usu. associated with aging.

pres'by·ter (-bi tər, pres'-) *n.* **1.** a priest. **2.** an elder.

pre'school' *adj.* (prē'skōōl') **1.** of or for children between infancy and kindergarten age. **—n.** (-skōōl') **2.** a school for preschool children.

pre•sci•ence (presh′ans, -ē ans) *n.* foresight. —**pre•sci•ent,** *adj.*

pre•scribe′ (pri skrīb′) *v.t.,* **-scribed, -scribing. 1.** to order for use, as medicine. **2.** to lay down as a rule to be followed. —**pre•scrip′tion** (-skrip′shan) *n.* —**pre•scrip′tive** (-skrip′tiv) *adj.*

pres′ence (prez′ans) *n.* **1.** the fact of being present. **2.** immediate vicinity. **3.** impressive personal appearance or bearing.

pres′ent¹ (prez′ant) *adj.* **1.** being or occurring now. **2.** being at a particular place. **3.** designating a verb tense referring to an action or state existing now. —*n.* **4.** the present time. **5.** the present tense.

pre′sent² *v.t.* (pri zent′) **1.** to give, bring, or offer. **2.** to bring before the public. —*n.* (prez′ant) **3.** a gift.

pre•sent′a•ble (pri zen′ta bal) *adj.* suitable in looks, dress, etc.

pres•en•ta•tion (prez′an tā′shan, prē′zen-) *n.* **1.** a presenting or being presented. **2.** a performance. **3.** a demonstration, lecture, etc.

pre•sen′ti•ment (-mant) *n.* a feeling of something impending.

pres′ent•ly (prez′ant lē) *adv.* **1.** soon. **2.** at the present time.

pres′er•va′tion•ist (prez′ar vā′sha-nist) *n.* one who advocates preservation, esp. of wildlife, historical places, etc.

pre•serv′a•tive (pri zûr′va tiv) *n.* **1.** a substance used to preserve foods from spoilage. —*adj.* **2.** tending to preserve.

pre•serve′ (-zûrv′) *v.,* **-served, -serving,** *n.* —*v.t.* **1.** to keep alive or safe. **2.** to maintain. **3.** to treat (food) to prevent spoilage. —*n.* **4. preserves,** preserved fruit. **5.** a place where animals are protected. —**pres′er•va′tion** (prez′ar vā′shan) *n.*

pre•side′ (pri zīd′) *v.i.,* **-sided, -siding.** to have charge of a meeting.

pres′i•dent (prez′i dant) *n.* **1.** the chief of state of a republic. **2.** the chief officer of a corporation, college, etc. —**pres′i•den•cy,** *n.*

press (pres) *v.t.* **1.** to act upon with steady weight or force. **2.** to squeeze. **3.** to make smooth by ironing. **4.** to urge to hurry or comply. —*v.i.* **5.** to exert force. **6.** to push forward. **7.** to crowd. —*n.* **8.** newspapers, magazines, etc., collectively. **9.** a device for printing. **10.** a device for stamping, crushing, etc. **11.** a crowd. **12.** urgency.

press′ a′gent *n.* a person employed to obtain favorable publicity for a client.

press′ con′ference *n.* an interview with reporters held by an official.

press′ing *adj.* urgent.

press′ release′ *n.* a statement distributed to the press.

pres′sure (presh′ar) *n., v.,* **-sured, -suring.** —*n.* **1.** the exertion of force by one body upon another. **2.** stress. **3.** urgency, as of business. —*v.t.* **4.** to put pressure on.

pres′sure cook′er *n.* a pot for cooking by steam under pressure.

pres′sure group′ *n.* a group that tries to influence legislation.

pres′sur•ize′ *v.t.,* **-ized, -izing.** to produce normal air pressure in (an airplane, spacesuit, etc.) at high altitudes. —**pres′sur•i•za′tion,** *n.*

pres′ti•dig′i•ta′tion (pres′ti dij′i tā′-shan) *n.* sleight of hand.

pres•tige′ (pre stēzh′, -stēj′) *n.* reputation as a result of success, rank, etc. —**pres•tig′ious** (-stij′as) *adj.*

pres′to (pres′tō) *adv.* very quickly.

pre•sume′ (pri zōōm′) *v.,* **-sumed, -suming.** —*v.t.* **1.** to take for granted or suppose to be true. —*v.i.* **2.** to act with unjustified boldness. —**pre•sum′a•bly,** *adv.*

pre•sump′tion (-zump′shan) *n.* **1.** something presumed; assumption. **2.** impertinent boldness.

pre•sump′tu•ous (-chōō as) *adj.* behaving with impertinent or unwarranted boldness.

pre′sup•pose′ (prē′sa pōz′) *v.t.,* **-posed, -posing. 1.** to assume beforehand. **2.** to assume the prior existence of. —**pre′sup•po•si′tion** (-sup azish′an) *n.*

pre•teen′ *n.* **1.** a child between 10 and 13 years old. —*adj.* **2.** of or for preteens.

pre•tend′ (pri tend′) *v.t.* **1.** to feign. **2.** to make believe. **3.** to claim falsely. —**pre•tend′er,** *n.*

pre•ten′sion (pri ten′shan) *n.* **1.** a claim to something. **2.** Often, **pretensions.** an unwarranted claim, as to importance.

pre•ten′tious *adj.* **1.** overly self-important. **2.** ostentatious. —**pre•ten′tious•ly,** *adv.*

pre′ter•nat′u•ral (prē′tar nach′ar al) *adj.* exceptional.

pre′text (prē′tekst) *n.* something put forward to conceal a true reason.

pret′ty (prit′ē) *adj.,* **-tier, -tiest,** *adv.* —*adj.* **1.** pleasingly attractive in a delicate way. —*adv.* **2.** moderately. **3.** very. —**pret′ti•fy′,** *v.t.* —**pret′ti•ly,** *adv.*

pret′zel (pret′sal) *n.* a crisp knotted or elongated biscuit, usu. salted.

pre•vail′ (pri vāl′) *v.i.* **1.** to be

widespread. **2.** to exercise persuasion. **3.** to gain victory.

pre•vail′ing *adj.* **1.** most common. **2.** having superior influence.

prev′a•lent (prev′ə lənt) *adj.* widespread; general. —**prev′a•lence,** *n.*

pre•var′i•cate′ (pri var′i kāt′) *v.i.,* **-cated, -cating.** to speak evasively; lie. —**pre•var′i•ca′tion,** *n.*

pre•vent′ (pri vent′) *v.t.* **1.** to keep from happening. **2.** to stop from doing something. —**pre•vent′a•ble,** *adj.* —**pre•ven′tion,** *n.*

pre•ven′tive (-tə tiv) *adj.* **1.** serving to prevent. —*n.* **2.** a preventive agent. Also, **pre•vent′a•tive.**

pre′view′ (prē′vyōō′) *n.* **1.** an earlier view or showing. —*v.t.* **2.** to view or show beforehand.

pre′vi•ous (-vē əs) *adj.* coming or occurring before something else. —**pre′vi•ous•ly,** *adv.*

prey (prā) *n.* **1.** an animal hunted as food by another animal. **2.** any victim. —*v.* **3.** **prey on, a.** to seize prey. **b.** to victimize another.

price (prīs) *n., v.,* **priced, pricing.** —*n.* **1.** the amount for which a thing is bought or sold. **2.** what must be given, done, etc., to obtain something. —*v.t.* **3.** to fix the price of. **4.** to ask the price of.

price′less *adj.* too valuable to set a price on.

prick (prik) *n.* **1.** a slight puncture by a pointed object. **2.** a sharp pain. —*v.t.* **3.** to pierce slightly with a sharp point. **4.** to cause sharp pain to. **5.** to point (the ears).

prick′le *n., v.,* **-led, -ling.** —*n.* **1.** a small, sharp point. **2.** a pricking feeling. —*v.t.* **3.** to cause a tingling sensation in. —*v.i.* **4.** to tingle.

prick′ly heat′ *n.* an itching rash caused by an inflammation of the sweat glands.

pride (prīd) *n., v.,* **prided, priding.** —*n.* **1.** self-respect. **2.** something causing one to be proud. **3.** conceit. **4.** a group of lions. —*v.* **5.** **pride oneself on,** to be proud of. —**pride′ful,** *adj.*

priest (prēst) *n.* **1.** a member of the clergy. **2.** a person authorized to perform religious rites. —**priest′-hood,** *n.*

priest′ess (prē′stis) *n.* a woman who officiates in sacred rites.

prig (prig) *n.* a self-righteous person. —**prig′gish,** *adj.*

prim (prim) *adj.* stiffly proper.

pri′ma•cy (prī′mə sē) *n., pl.* **-cies.** the state of being first in rank, importance, etc.

pri′ma don′na (prē′mə don′ə, prim′ə) *n.* **1.** a principal female

opera singer. **2.** a temperamental person.

pri′ma fa′ci•e (prī′mə fā′shē ē′, fā′-shē, prē′-) *adj.* sufficient to establish a fact unless rebutted.

pri′mal (prī′məl) *adj.* **1.** first; original. **2.** most important.

pri•ma′ri•ly (-mâr′ə lē, -mer′-) *adv.* **1.** chiefly. **2.** originally.

pri′ma•ry (-mer ē, -mə rē) *adj., n., pl.* **-ries.** —*adj.* **1.** first in importance, order, or time. —*n.* **2.** a preliminary election for choosing party candidates.

pri′mate (-māt *or, esp. for* 2, -mit) *n.* **1.** a mammal of the order including humans, apes, and monkeys. **2.** a high church official.

prime (prīm) *adj., n., v.,* **primed, priming.** —*adj.* **1.** first in importance or quality. **2.** basic. —*n.* **3.** the best stage or part. —*v.t.* **4.** to prepare for a special purpose or function.

prime′ merid′ian *n.* the meridian running through Greenwich, England, from which longitude east and west is reckoned.

prime′ min′ister *n.* the head of government and of the cabinet in a parliamentary system.

prim′er¹ (prim′ər; *esp. Brit.* prī′mər) *n.* an elementary book, esp. for reading.

prim′er² (prī′mər) *n.* a first coat of paint.

prime′ rate′ *n.* the minimum interest rate charged by banks to their best-rated customers.

prime′ time′ *n.* the hours having the largest television audience.

pri•me′val (prī mē′vəl) *adj.* of the first ages of the world.

prim′i•tive (prim′i tiv) *adj.* **1.** of early ages or an early state of development. **2.** simple or crude.

pri′mo•gen′i•ture (prī′mə jen′i-chər) *n.* the right of inheritance by the eldest son.

pri•mor′di•al (-môr′dē əl) *adj.* existing from the very beginning.

primp (primp) *v.t., v.i.* to dress (oneself) with care.

prim′rose′ (prim′rōz′) *n.* a plant with colorful, five-lobed flowers.

prince (prins) *n.* **1.** the son of a king or queen. **2.** a ruler.

prince′ly *adj.* **1.** lavish. **2.** of a prince.

prin′cess (prin′sis, -ses) *n.* **1.** the daughter of a king or queen. **2.** the consort of a prince.

prin′ci•pal (prin′sə pəl) *adj.* **1.** chief. —*n.* **2.** a chief, head, or leader. **3.** the head of a school. **4.** a person authorizing another to act for him or her. **5.** a capital sum, distinguished from interest.

prin′ci‧pal′i‧ty (-pal′i tē) *n., pl.* **-ties.** a state ruled by a prince.

prin′ci‧ple (-pəl) *n.* **1.** a rule of conduct or action. **2.** a fundamental truth or cause.

print (print) *v.t., v.i.* **1.** to reproduce from inked types, plates, etc. **2.** to write in letters like those of print. **3.** to produce (a photograph) from a negative. —*n.* **4.** printed lettering or material. **5.** a cloth having a design or pattern. **6.** a mark made by the pressure of one thing on another. **7.** a photograph.

print′out′ *n.* printed output of a computer.

pri′or¹ (prī′ər) *adj.* preceding in time, order, importance, etc.

pri′or² (prī′ər) *n.* an officer in a religious house. —**pri′o‧ry,** *n.*

pri′or‧ess (-is) *n.* a woman who is an officer in a religious house.

pri‧or′i‧tize′ (prī ôr′i tīz′) *v.t.,* **-tized, -tizing.** to arrange in order of priority.

pri‧or′i‧ty *n., pl.* **-ties. 1.** the right to take precedence over others. **2.** something given special or prior attention.

prism (priz′əm) *n.* a transparent body for dispersing light into a spectrum.

pris′on (-ən) *n.* a place where criminals are confined. —**pris′on‧er,** *n.*

pris′sy (pris′ē) *adj.,* **-sier, -siest.** excessively or affectedly proper.

pris′tine (-tēn, pri stēn′) *adj.* pure.

pri′vate (prī′vit) *adj.* **1.** of, belonging to, or confined to a particular person or group. **2.** not provided or maintained by public funds. **3.** personal; secret. —*n.* **4.** a soldier of one of the three lowest ranks. —**pri′va‧cy,** *n.* —**pri′vate‧ly,** *adv.*

pri′va‧teer′ (-və tēr′) *n.* a privately owned vessel commissioned to fight. —**pri′va‧teer′ing,** *n.*

pri′vate eye′ *n. Informal.* a private detective.

pri‧va′tion (-vā′shən) *n.* hardship.

priv′et (priv′it) *n.* an evergreen shrub often grown as a hedge.

priv′i‧lege (-ə lij, -lij) *n., v.,* **-leged, -leging.** —*n.* **1.** a special advantage enjoyed by a particular group. —*v.t.* **2.** to grant a privilege to.

priv′y (-ē) *adj., n., pl.* **privies.** —*adj.* **1.** having knowledge of something private. —*n.* **2.** an outdoor toilet.

priv′y coun′cil *n.* a board of personal advisors, as of a sovereign.

prize¹ (prīz) *n.* **1.** a reward for victory, superiority, etc. **2.** a thing worth striving for. —*adj.* **3.** worthy of a prize.

prize² (prīz) *v.t.,* **prized, prizing.** to esteem highly.

pro¹ (prō) *adv., n., pl.* **pros.** —*adv.* **1.** in favor of a plan, opinion, etc. —*n.* **2.** a vote in favor of something. **3.** a person upholding the affirmative in a debate.

pro² (prō) *adj., n., pl.* **pros.** professional.

pro- a prefix meaning: **1.** favoring. **2.** before or in front of.

prob′a‧ble (prob′ə bəl) *adj.* **1.** likely to occur or prove true. **2.** affording ground for belief. —**prob′-a‧bil′i‧ty,** *n.* —**prob′a‧bly,** *adv.*

pro′bate (prō′bāt) *n., adj., v.,* **-bated, -bating.** —*n.* **1.** the official authentication of a will. —*adj.* **2.** of probate. —*v.t.* **3.** to establish a will's validity.

pro‧ba′tion *n.* **1.** the testing of a person's conduct or character. **2.** the period of such testing. **3.** the conditional release of a prisoner.

probe (prōb) *v.,* **probed, probing,** *n.* —*v.t.* **1.** to examine thoroughly. —*n.* **2.** an investigation. **3.** an instrument for exploring a wound.

pro′bi‧ty (prō′bi tē, prob′i-) *n.* honesty.

prob′lem (prob′ləm) *n.* **1.** a matter involving uncertainty or difficulty. **2.** a question proposed for solution. —**prob′lem‧at′ic,** *adj.*

pro‧bos′cis (prō bos′is, -kis) *n., pl.* **-cises.** a flexible snout.

pro‧ced′ure (prə sē′jər) *n.* the act or manner of proceeding to accomplish something. —**pro‧ced′ur‧al,** *adj.*

pro‧ceed′ *v.i.* (-sēd′) **1.** to go forward. **2.** to carry on an action. **3.** to issue forth. —*n.* (prō′sēd) **4.** **proceeds,** the sum derived from a sale or other transaction.

pro‧ceed′ing *n.* **1.** an action or course of action. **2. proceedings, a.** a record of the business discussed at a meeting. **b.** legal action.

proc′ess (pros′es; *esp. Brit.* prō′ses) *n.* **1.** a series of actions directed to some end. **2.** a continuous action or series of changes. **3.** a legal summons. —*v.t.* **4.** to treat by a particular process. **5.** to handle according to a routine procedure.

pro‧ces′sion (prə sesh′ən) *n.* a line of persons, vehicles, etc., moving along in a ceremonious manner.

pro‧ces′sion‧al *n.* a piece of music for accompanying a procession.

pro‧choice′ (prō chois′) *adj.* supporting the right to legalized abortion.

pro‧claim′ (-klām′, prə-) *v.t.* to announce formally. —**proc′la•ma′-tion** (prok′lə mā′shən) *n.*

pro•cliv′i•ty (-kliv′i tē) *n.*, *pl.* **-ties.** a natural tendency.

pro•cras′ti•nate′ (-kras′tə nāt′, prə-) *v.i.*, *v.t.*, **-nated, -nating.** to delay (action). —**pro•cras′ti•na′tion,** *n.*

pro′cre•ate′ (-krē āt′) *v.t.*, *v.i.*, **-ated, -ating.** to produce (offspring). —**pro′cre•a′tion,** *n.*

proc′tor (prok′tər) *n.* **1.** a person who supervises students at examinations. —*v.t.*, *v.i.* **2.** to supervise or monitor.

pro•cure′ (prō kyŏŏr′, prə-) *v.t.*, **-cured, -curing. 1.** to obtain by effort. **2.** to obtain (a person) for prostitution. —**pro•cur′a•ble,** *adj.* —**pro•cure′ment,** *n.*

prod (prod) *v.*, **prodded, prodding,** *n.* —*v.t.* **1.** to jab or poke. **2.** to incite; goad. —*n.* **3.** a poke. **4.** a pointed instrument used to goad.

prod′i•gal (prod′i gəl) *adj.* **1.** wastefully extravagant. **2.** lavishly abundant. —*n.* **3.** a spendthrift. —**prod′i•gal′i•ty,** *n.*

pro•di′gious (prə dij′əs) *adj.* extraordinary in size, amount, etc. —**pro•di′gious•ly,** *adv.*

prod′i•gy (prod′i jē) *n.*, *pl.* **-gies.** a very gifted person, esp. a child.

pro•duce′ *v.*, **-duced, -ducing,** *n.* —*v.t.* (prə dōōs′, -dyōōs′) **1.** to bring into existence; create. **2.** to bear, as young, fruit, etc. **3.** to present; exhibit. —*v.i.* **4.** to yield products, offspring, etc. —*n.* (prod′ōōs, -yōōs, prō′dōōs, -dyōōs) **5.** agricultural products collectively.

prod′uct (prod′əkt) *n.* **1.** a thing produced by labor. **2.** a person or thing resulting from a process. **3.** the result obtained by multiplying.

pro•duc′tion (prə duk′shən) *n.* **1.** the act of producing. **2.** something produced. **3.** the amount produced. —**pro•duc′tive,** *adj.*

pro′duc•tiv′i•ty (prō′duk tiv′i tē, prod′ək) *n.* **1.** the quality of being productive. **2.** the rate at which things are produced.

pro•fane′ (prə fān′, prō-) *adj.*, *v.*, **-faned, -faning.** —*adj.* **1.** disrespectful toward sacred things. **2.** secular. —*v.t.* **3.** to defile. **4.** to treat (a sacred thing) with contempt. —**prof′a•na′tion** (prof′ə-nā′shən) *n.*

pro•fan′i•ty (-fan′i tē) *n.*, *pl.* **-ties. 1.** the quality of being profane. **2.** blasphemous or vulgar language.

pro•fess′ (prə fes′) *v.t.* **1.** to pretend to. **2.** to declare. **3.** to affirm one's faith in.

pro•fes′sion *n.* **1.** an occupation requiring advanced education. **2.** the persons engaged in such an occupation. **3.** a declaration.

pro•fes′sion•al *adj.* **1.** of or engaged in a profession. **2.** following an occupation for payment. —*n.* **3.** a professional person.

pro•fes′sor (prə fes′ər) *n.* a college teacher of the highest rank.

prof′fer (prof′ər) *v.t.* to offer.

pro•fi′cient (prə fish′ənt) *adj.* expert; skilled. —**pro•fi′cien•cy,** *n.*

pro′file (prō′fīl) *n.* **1.** a side view. **2.** a biographical sketch.

prof′it (prof′it) *n.* **1.** the monetary gain from a business transaction after expenses have been met. **2.** gain; benefit. —*v.i.*, *v.t.* **3.** to gain or cause to gain a profit. —**prof′it•a•ble,** *adj.*

prof′it•eer′ *n.* **1.** a person who makes an unfair profit. —*v.i.* **2.** to act as a profiteer.

prof′li•gate (-li git, -gāt′) *adj.* **1.** immoral. **2.** extravagant. —*n.* **3.** a profligate person. —**prof′li•ga•cy,** *n.*

pro for′ma (prō fôr′mə) *adj.* done as a matter of form or for the sake of form.

pro•found′ (prə found′) *adj.* **1.** showing deep thought or insight. **2.** intense. **3.** deep. —**pro•fun′di•ty** (-fun′di tē) *n.*

pro•fuse′ (-fyōōs′) *adj.* extravagant; abundant. —**pro•fuse′ly,** *adv.* —**pro•fu′sion** (-fyōō′zhən) *n.*

pro•gen′i•tor (prō jen′i tər) *n.* an ancestor.

prog′e•ny (proj′ə nē) *n.* offspring collectively.

pro•ges′ter•one (prō jes′tə rōn′) *n.* a female hormone that prepares the uterus for the fertilized egg.

prog•no′sis (prog nō′sis) *n.*, *pl.* **-noses** (-nō′sēz). a forecast, esp. of the course of a disease.

prog•nos′ti•cate′ (-nos′ti kāt′) *v.t.*, **-cated, -cating.** to predict.

pro′gram (prō′gram, -grəm) *n.*, *v.*, **-grammed, -gramming.** —*n.* **1.** a plan of things to do. **2.** a schedule of entertainments. **3.** a television or radio show. **4.** a series of instructions enabling a computer to perform a task. —*v.t.* **5.** to make a program for or including. —**pro′gram•ma•ble,** *adj.* —**pro′gram•mer,** *n.*

prog′ress *n.* (prog′res, -rəs; *esp. Brit.* prō′gres) **1.** advancement toward a goal. **2.** permanent improvement. **3.** forward movement. —*v.i.* (prə gres′) **4.** to go forward. **5.** to develop.

pro•gres′sion (prə gresh′ən) *n.* **1.** the act of progressing. **2.** a series.

pro·gres'sive *adj.* **1.** advocating reform. **2.** advancing step by step.

pro·hib'it (prō hib'it) *v.t.* to forbid; prevent.

pro'hi·bi'tion (-ə bish'ən) *n.* **1.** the act of prohibiting. **2. Prohibition**, the period, 1920–33, when the manufacture and sale of alcoholic drinks was forbidden in the U.S. —**pro'hi·bi'tion·ist**, *n.*

pro·hib'i·tive (-hib'ə tiv) *adj.* **1.** prohibiting. **2.** too expensive.

proj'ect *n.* (proj'ekt, -ikt; *esp. Brit.* prō'jekt) **1.** a plan. **2.** a large and important undertaking. —*v.t.* (prə jekt') **3.** to plan. **4.** to impel forward. **5.** to cast upon a surface, as a shadow. **6.** to cause to protrude. —**pro·jec'tion**, *n.*

pro·jec'tile (prə jek'til, -tīl) *n.* an object fired with explosive force.

pro·jec'tion·ist (-shə nist) *n.* an operator of a motion-picture projector.

pro·jec'tor *n.* an apparatus for casting an image onto a screen.

pro'le·tar'i·at (prō'li târ'ē ət) *n.* the working class. —**pro'le·tar'i·an**, *adj., n.*

pro-life' *adj.* opposed to legalized abortion.

pro·lif'er·ate' (prə lif'ə rāt') *v.i., v.t.*, **-ated, -ating.** to increase or spread rapidly.

pro·lif'ic (-ik) *adj.* highly productive.

pro·lix' (prō liks', prō'liks) *adj.* tediously long and wordy.

pro'logue (prō'lôg) *n.* the introductory part of a novel, play, etc.

pro·long' (prə lông') *v.t.* to extend the duration or length of. —**pro'lon·ga'tion** (prō'-) *n.*

prom (prom) *n.* a formal dance at a high school or college.

prom'e·nade' (prom'ə nād', -näd') *n., v.*, **-naded, -nading.** —*n.* **1.** a leisurely walk. **2.** a space for such a walk. —*v.t., v.i.* **3.** to stroll (through or about).

prom'i·nent (prom'ə nənt) *adj.* **1.** conspicuous. **2.** projecting. **3.** well-known. —**prom'i·nence**, *n.*

pro·mis'cu·ous (prə mis'kyŏŏ əs) *adj.* having numerous casual sexual partners. —**prom'is·cu'i·ty** (prom'i skyŏŏ'i tē) *n.*

prom'ise (prom'is) *n., v.*, **-ised, -ising.** —*n.* **1.** an assurance that one will act as specified. **2.** indication of future excellence. —*v.t., v.i.* **3.** to assure by a promise. **4.** to afford ground for expecting. —**prom'is·ing**, *adj.*

prom'is·so'ry (-ə sôr'ē) *adj.* containing a promise of payment.

prom'on·to'ry (-ən tôr'ē) *n., pl.* **-ries.** a high peak projecting into the sea or overlooking low land.

pro·mote' (prə mōt') *v.t.*, **-moted, -moting. 1.** to further the progress of. **2.** to advance. **3.** to encourage the sales or acceptance of. —**pro·mot'er**, *n.* —**pro·mo'tion**, *n.*

prompt (prompt) *adj.* **1.** done without delay. **2.** quick to act. —*v.t.* **3.** to induce to action; inspire. **4.** to give a cue to; remind. —**prompt'ness**, *n.*

prom'ul·gate (prom'əl gāt', prō·mul'gāt) *v.t.*, **-gated, -gating.** to proclaim formally.

prone (prōn) *adj.* **1.** likely; inclined. **2.** lying flat, esp. face downward.

prong (prông) *n.* a point.

pro'noun' (prō'noun') *n.* a word used as a substitute for a noun.

pro·nounce' (prə nouns') *v.t.*, **-nounced, -nouncing. 1.** to enunciate or articulate (sounds, words, etc.). **2.** to utter formally. —**pro·nounce'ment**, *n.*

pro·nounced' *adj.* **1.** strongly marked. **2.** decided.

pron'to (pron'tō) *adv.* quickly.

pro·nun'ci·a'tion (prə nun'sē ā'shən) *n.* the production of the sounds of speech.

proof (prŏŏf) *n.* **1.** evidence establishing a truth or fact. **2.** a copy of printed matter for correcting errors. —*adj.* **3.** invulnerable.

-proof a suffix meaning resistant.

proof'read' (-rēd') *v.t., v.i.*, **-read** (red') **-reading.** to read (printers' proofs, copy, etc.) to detect and mark errors. —**proof'read'er**, *n.*

prop (prop) *n., v.*, **propped, propping.** —*n.* **1.** a rigid support. **2.** a person serving as a support. —*v.t.* **3.** to support with a prop.

prop'a·gan'da (prop'ə gan'də) *n.* **1.** ideas or information spread to promote or injure a cause, nation, etc. **2.** the spreading of such ideas. —**prop'a·gan'dist**, *n.* —**prop'a·gan'dize**, *v.t., v.i.*

prop'a·gate' (-gāt') *v.*, **-gated, -gating.** —*v.t.* **1.** to cause (an organism) to reproduce. **2.** to spread or disseminate. —*v.i.* **3.** to multiply by natural reproduction. —**prop'a·ga'tion**, *n.*

pro'pane (prō'pān) *n.* a colorless flammable gas, used esp. as a fuel.

pro·pel' (prə pel') *v.t.*, **-pelled, -pelling.** to drive forward.

pro·pel'lant (-ənt) *n.* a propelling agent. Also, **pro·pel·lent.**

pro·pel'ler *n.* a screwlike device for propelling an airplane, ship, etc.

pro·pen'si·ty (prə pen'si tē) *n., pl.* **-ties.** an inclination or tendency.

prop'er (prop'ər) *adj.* **1.** suitable;

fitting. **2.** conforming to social conventions, manners, or good taste. **3.** correct. **4.** in the strict sense.

prop′er noun′ *n.* a noun that is the name of a particular person, place, or thing and is usu. capitalized.

prop′er•ty *n., pl.* **-ties. 1.** that which one owns. **2.** land or real estate. **3.** an attribute or quality.

proph′e•sy′ (-sī′) *v.t., v.i.,* **-sied, -sying.** to predict (future events). —**proph′e•cy** (-sē) *n.*

proph′et (-it) *n.* **1.** a person who speaks for God. **2.** an inspired leader. **3.** a person who predicts. —**pro•phet′ic** (prə fet′ik) *adj.*

pro′phy•lac′tic (prō′fə lak′tik) *adj.* **1.** preventing disease or infection. —*n.* **2.** a prophylactic medicine, measure, or device.

pro′phy•lax′is (prō′fə lak′sis) *n.* the prevention of disease, as by protective measures.

pro•pin′qui•ty (prō ping′kwi tē) *n.* nearness.

pro•pi′ti•ate′ (prə pish′ē āt′) *v.t.,* **-ated, -ating.** to make less angry.

pro•pi′tious (-əs) *adj.* favorable. —**pro•pi′tious•ly,** *adv.*

pro•po′nent (prə pō′nənt) *n.* an advocate; supporter.

pro•por′tion (-pôr′shən) *n.* **1.** comparative or proper relation of dimensions or quantities. **2.** symmetry. **3. proportions,** dimensions. —*v.t.* **4.** to adjust in proper relation.

pro•por′tion•ate (-shə nit) *adj.* being in due proportion.

pro•pose′ (-pōz′) *v.,* **-posed, -posing.** —*v.t.* **1.** to suggest. **2.** to plan; intend. —*v.i.* **3.** to make an offer of marriage. —**pro•pos′al,** *n.*

prop′o•si′tion (prop′ə zish′ən) *n.* **1.** the act of proposing or a plan proposed. **2.** a statement. **3.** a proposal of sexual relations. —*v.t.* **4.** to propose sexual relations to.

pro•pound′ (prə pound′) *v.t.* to offer for consideration.

pro•pri′e•tar′y (prə prī′i ter′ē) *adj.* **1.** made and sold only by the owner of the patent, trademark, etc. **2.** of a proprietor.

pro•pri′e•tor (prə prī′ə tər) *n.* the owner of a business, property, etc.

pro•pri′e•ty *n., pl.* **-ties.** conformity to established standards of behavior, manners, etc.

pro•pul′sion (prə pul′shən) *n.* a propelling force.

pro•rate′ (prō rāt′, prō′rāt′) *v.t., v.i.,* **-rated, -rating.** to divide or calculate proportionately.

pro•sa′ic (prō zā′ik) *adj.* commonplace. —**pro•sa′i•cal•ly,** *adv.*

pro•sce′ni•um (prō sē′nē əm, prə-) *n., pl.* **-niums, -nia** (-nē ə). the arch separating a stage from the auditorium. Also, **proscenium arch.**

pro•scribe′ (-skrīb′) *v.t.,* **-scribed, -scribing.** to prohibit.

prose (prōz) *n.* ordinary language as distinguished from verse.

pros′e•cute′ (pros′i kyōōt′) *v.t.,* **-cuted, -cuting. 1.** to begin legal proceedings against. **2.** to go on with (an undertaking) to the end. —**pros′e•cu′tion,** *n.* —**pros′e•cu′tor,** *n.*

pros′e•lyt•ize′ (pros′ə li tīz′) *v.t., v.i.,* **-ized, -izing.** to try to convert (someone) to another opinion, belief, etc. —**pros′e•lyte′** (-līt′), *n.*

pros′pect (-pekt) *n.* **1.** Usu., **prospects, a.** the likelihood of success. **b.** the outlook for the future. **2.** expectation. **3.** a potential customer. —*v.t., v.i.* **4.** to search (an area), as for gold. —**pros′pec•tor,** *n.*

pro•spec′tive (prə spek′tiv) *adj.* potential or likely.

pro•spec′tus (prə spek′təs) *n.* a description of a new investment or purchase.

pros′per (pros′pər) *v.i.* to be successful, esp. financially. —**pros•per′i•ty** (-per′ə tē) *n.* —**pros′per•ous,** *adj.*

pros′tate (-tāt) *n.* a gland surrounding the neck of the bladder in males.

pros•the′sis (-thē′sis) *n., pl.* **-ses** (-sēz). a device that substitutes for or supplements a missing or defective body part. —**pros•thet′ic** (-thet′ik) *adj.*

pros′ti•tute′ (-ti tōōt′, -tyōōt′) *n., v.,* **-tuted, -tuting.** —*n.* **1.** a person who engages in sexual intercourse for money. —*v.t.* **2.** to put to an unworthy use. —**pros′ti•tu′tion,** *n.*

pros′trate (-trāt) *v.,* **-trated, -trating,** *adj.* —*v.t.* **1.** to cast (oneself) facedown, as in humility. **2.** to overcome or exhaust. —*adj.* **3.** lying flat. **4.** helpless, weak, or exhausted.

pros′y (prō′zē) *adj.,* **-ier, -iest.** dull.

pro•tag′o•nist (prō tag′ə nist) *n.* the main character.

pro′te•an (-tē ən, -tē′-) *adj.* assuming different forms.

pro•tect′ (prə tekt′) *v.t.* to defend from injury, attack, etc. —**pro•tec′tion,** *n.* —**pro•tec′tive,** *adj.*

pro•tec′tion•ism (-shə niz′əm) *n.* the practice of protecting industries from foreign competition by imposing import duties.

pro·tec'tor·ate (-tər it) *n.* a weak state that is protected and partly controlled by a stronger one.

pro'té·gé' (prō'tə zhā') *n.* a person under the friendly patronage of someone interested in his or her welfare.

pro'tein (-tēn, -tē in) *n.* an organic compound forming a large portion of the mass of all life forms.

pro' tem'por·e' (prō' tem'pə rē', -rā') *adv.* 1. temporarily. —*adj.* 2. temporary.

pro'test *n.* (prō'test) 1. an objection. —*v.i.*, *v.t.* (prə test', prō'test) 2. to make a protest (against). —**prot'es·ta'tion,** *n.* —**pro·test'er,** *n.*

Prot'es·tant (prot'ə stənt) *n.* 1. a Christian who belongs to a church that began by breaking away from the Roman Catholic Church in the 16th century. —*adj.* 2. of Protestants or their religion. —**Prot'es·tant·ism',** *n.*

proto- a prefix meaning earliest.

pro'to·col' (prō'tə kôl') *n.* 1. the customs dealing with diplomatic precedence, etiquette, etc. 2. an original draft of a treaty. 3. a set of rules for exchanging messages between computers.

pro'ton (-ton) *n.* the part of an atom bearing a positive charge.

pro'to·plasm' (-tə plaz'əm) *n.* the substance of which cells are formed.

pro'to·type' *n.* the model on which something is based. —**pro'to·typ'i·cal,** *adj.*

pro'to·zo'an (-zō'ən) *n.*, *pl.* -zoans, -zoa (-zō'ə). a one-celled organism that obtains nourishment by ingesting food rather than by photosynthesis.

pro·tract' (prō trakt', prə-) *v.t.* to draw out, esp. in time.

pro·trac'tor *n.* an instrument for measuring angles.

pro·trude' (prō trōōd', prə-) *v.i.*, *v.t.*, -truded, -truding. to jut out or cause to jut out. —**pro·tru'sion** (-trōō'zhən) *n.*

pro·tu'ber·ant (-tōō'bər ənt) *adj.* bulging out. —**pro·tu'ber·ance,** *n.*

proud (proud) *adj.* 1. full of pride. 2. highly creditable. 3. arrogant. —**proud'ly,** *adv.*

prove (prōōv) *v.*, **proved, proving.** —*v.t.* 1. to establish the truth, validity, or worth of. —*v.i.* 2. to turn out. 3. to be found to be.

prov'e·nance (prov'ə nəns, -näns') *n.* a place or source of origin.

prov'en·der (prov'ən dər) *n.* food, esp. dry food for livestock.

prov'erb (prov'ərb) *n.* a popular saying expressing some commonplace truth. —**pro·ver'bi·al** (prə vûr'bē əl) *adj.*

pro·vide' (prə vīd') *v.*, -vided, -viding. —*v.t.* 1. to make available; supply. 2. to stipulate beforehand. —*v.i.* 3. to supply means of support. —**pro·vid'er,** *n.*

pro·vid'ed *conj.* on the condition that.

prov'i·dence (prov'i dəns) *n.* 1. God's care. 2. foresight.

prov'i·dent (-dənt) *adj.* showing foresight; prudent.

prov'i·den'tial (-den'shəl) *adj.* fortunate or lucky.

prov'ince (prov'ins) *n.* 1. an administrative unit of a country. 2. a sphere of activity.

pro·vin'cial (prə vin'shəl) *adj.* 1. of a particular province. 2. narrow-minded; unsophisticated.

pro·vi'sion (-vizh'ən) *n.* 1. something stated as necessary or binding. 2. the act of providing. 3. what is provided. 4. an arrangement made beforehand. 5. **provisions,** supplies of food.

pro·vi'sion·al *adj.* temporary.

pro·vi'so (-vī'zō) *n.*, *pl.* -sos, -soes. something required in an agreement; stipulation.

pro·voc'a·tive (-vok'ə tiv) *adj.* stimulating; exciting.

pro·voke' (-vōk') *v.t.*, -voked, -voking. 1. to anger or vex. 2. to arouse. —**prov'o·ca'tion** (prov'ə kā'shən) *n.*

pro'vost (prō'vōst) *n.* 1. a superintendent. 2. a high-ranking university administrator.

prow (prou) *n.* the front part of a ship.

prow'ess (-is) *n.* 1. exceptional ability. 2. bravery.

prowl (proul) *v.i.*, *v.t.* to roam or search stealthily. —**prowl'er,** *n.*

prox·im'i·ty (prok sim'i tē) *n.* nearness.

prox'y (prok'sē) *n.*, *pl.* **proxies.** a person authorized to act for another or the power to do so.

Pro'zac (prō'zak) *Trademark.* a drug used as an antidepressant.

prude (prōōd) *n.* a person who is excessively proper or modest, esp. in sexual matters. —**prud'er·y,** *n.* —**prud'ish,** *adj.*

pru'dence *n.* practical wisdom; caution. —**pru'dent,** *adj.*

prune¹ (prōōn) *n.* a dried plum

prune² (prōōn) *v.t.*, **pruned, pruning.** 1. to cut off undesirable twigs, branches, etc., from. 2. to remove (anything undesirable).

pru'ri·ent (prŏŏr'ē ənt) *adj.* having or causing lewd thoughts. —**pru'ri·ence,** *n.*

pry[1] (prī) *v.i.*, **pried, prying.** to inquire or look too closely.

pry[2] (prī) *v.t.*, **pried, prying.** 1. to move or open with a lever. 2. to obtain with difficulty.

P.S. 1. postscript. 2. Public School.

psalm (säm) *n.* a sacred song.

pseu·do (sōō′dō) *adj.* false.

pseu·do·nym (sōōd′n im) *n.* a false name used by a writer.

pso·ri·a·sis (sə rī′ə sis) *n.* a chronic, inflammatory skin disease.

psych (sīk) *v.t. Informal.* 1. to intimidate. 2. to prepare psychologically.

psy′che (sī′kē) *n.* the human soul or mind.

psy′che·del′ic (sī′ki del′ik) *adj.* of or causing a mental state of distorted sense perceptions and hallucinations.

psy·chi·a·try (si kī′ə trē, sī-) *n.* the branch of medicine concerned with mental diseases. —**psy′chi·at′ric** (sī′kē a′trik) *adj.* —**psy·chi·a·trist,** *n.*

psy′chic (sī′kik) *adj.* 1. of the psyche. 2. pertaining to an apparently nonphysical force or agency. —*n.* 3. a person sensitive to psychic influences.

psy′cho·a·nal′y·sis *n.* a professional technique for investigating conscious and unconscious psychological processes and treating mental illness. —**psy′cho·an′a·lyst,** *n.* —**psy′cho·an′a·lyze′,** *v.t.*

psy·chol′o·gy (sī kol′ə jē) *n.* the science of mental states and behavior. —**psy′cho·log′i·cal** (-kə loj′i·kəl) *adj.* —**psy·chol′o·gist,** *n.*

psy′cho·path′ (sī′kə path′) *n.* a person having a disorder marked by amoral or antisocial behavior. —**psy′cho·path′ic,** *adj.* —**psy·chop′a·thy** (-kop′ə thē), *n.*

psy·cho·sis (-kō′sis) *n., pl.* **-ses** (-sēz). a severe mental disorder marked by delusions. —**psy·chot′ic** (-kot′ik) *adj., n.*

psy′cho·so·mat′ic (-sə mat′ik) *adj.* (of a physical disorder) caused by one's emotional state.

psy′cho·ther′a·py *n., pl.* **-pies.** the treatment of mental disorders. —**psy′cho·ther′a·pist,** *n.*

pt. 1. part. 2. pint. 3. point.

pto′maine (tō′mān) *n.* a substance produced during the decay of plant and animal matter.

pub (pub) *n.* a tavern.

pu′ber·ty (pyōō′bər tē) *n.* the period of life when a person reaches sexual maturity. —**pu′ber·tal,** *adj.*

pu·bes′cent (-bes′ənt) *adj.* arriving at puberty. —**pu·bes′cence,** *n.*

pu′bic (-bik) *adj.* of or near the genitals.

pub′lic (pub′lik) *adj.* 1. of or for people generally. 2. open to the view or knowledge of all. —*n.* 3. people.

pub·li·ca′tion *n.* 1. the act of publishing a book, piece of music, etc. 2. something published.

pub′lic defend′er *n.* a lawyer who represents impoverished clients at public expense.

pub′lic domain′ *n.* the legal status of material no longer protected by copyright or patent.

pub·lic′i·ty (pu blis′i tē) *n.* 1. public attention directed to someone or something. 2. material promoting this.

pub′li·cize′ *v.t.*, **-cized, -cizing.** to bring to public notice.

pub′lic rela′tions *n.pl.* the actions of an organization in promoting goodwill with the public.

pub′lish (pub′lish) *v.t.* 1. to issue (printed matter) for general distribution. 2. to make publicly known. —*v.i.* 3. to issue newspapers, books, etc. —**pub′lish·er,** *n.*

puck (puk) *n.* a black rubber disk hit into the goal in hockey.

puck′er (puk′ər) *v.t., v.i.* 1. to draw or gather into wrinkles. —*n.* 2. a wrinkle.

puck′ish (puk′ish) *adj.* mischievous.

pud′ding (pōōd′ing) *n.* a soft, creamy dessert.

pud·dle (pud′l) *n.* a small pool of water.

pudg′y (puj′ē) *adj.*, **-ier, -iest.** short and fat. —**pudg′i·ness,** *n.*

pu′er·ile (pyōō′ər il, -ə rīl′) *adj.* childish. —**pu′er·il′i·ty,** *n.*

puff (puf) *n.* 1. a short, light blowing of air, smoke, etc. 2. a ball or pad of light, soft material. 3. an overenthusiastic review of a book, performance, etc. —*v.i.* 4. to blow with puffs. 5. to breathe hard and fast. —*v.t.* 6. to send forth in puffs. 7. to inflate. —**puff′i·ness,** *n.* —**puff′y,** *adj.*

puf′fin (puf′in) *n.* a sea bird with a short neck and a colorful bill.

pug (pug) *n.* a kind of small dog with a wrinkled face.

pu′gil·ism (pyōō′jə liz′əm) *n.* boxing. —**pu′gil·ist,** *n.*

pug·na′cious (pug nā′shəs) *adj.* always ready to fight. —**pug·nac′i·ty** (-nas′ə tē) *n.*

pul′chri·tude′ (pul′kri tōōd′, -tyōōd′) *n.* beauty.

pull (pōōl) *v.t.* 1. to draw; haul. 2. to move (something) toward oneself with force. 3. to strain (a muscle). 4. to tear. —*v.i.* 5. to exert a drawing or hauling force. **6.** to move or go. **7. pull for,** to support actively. **8. ~ off,** *Informal.* to perform successfully. **9. ~ through,** to come through safely. —*n.* **10.** the act of pulling. **11.** force. **12.** a handle. **13.** influence.

pul′let (pŏŏl′it) *n.* a young hen.

pul′ley (pŏŏl′ē) *n.* a wheel for guiding a rope.

Pull′man (pŏŏl′mən) *Trademark.* a railroad sleeping car.

pull′out′ *n.* **1.** a withdrawal. **2.** a section of a publication that can be pulled out.

pull′o′ver *adj.* **1.** put on by being drawn over the head. —*n.* **2.** a pullover garment.

pul′mo·nar′y (pul′mə ner′ē, pŏŏl′-) *adj.* of the lungs.

pulp (pulp) *n.* **1.** the soft fleshy part of fruit. **2.** the inner substance of the tooth. **3.** any soft, moist mass. —*v.t.* **4.** to reduce to pulp.

pul′pit (pŏŏl′pit, pul′-) *n.* a raised structure in a church from which a sermon is preached.

pul′sar (pul′sär) *n.* a celestial object that emits regular pulses of radiation.

pul′sate (-sāt) *v.i.,* **-sated, -sating.** to expand and contract rhythmically. —**pul·sa′tion,** *n.*

pulse (puls) *n., v.,* **pulsed, pulsing.** —*n.* **1.** the heartbeat. —*v.i.* **2.** to beat or throb.

pul′ver·ize′ (pul′və rīz′) *v.t., v.i.,* **-ized, -izing.** to reduce or be reduced to powder.

pu′ma (pyŏŏ′mə, pŏŏ′-) *n.* a cougar.

pum′ice (pum′is) *n.* a porous volcanic glass used as an abrasive.

pum′mel (pum′əl) *v.t.,* **-meled, -meling.** to strike or beat with the fists.

pump (pump) *n.* **1.** a device for raising or driving fluids. —*v.t.* **2.** to raise or drive with a pump. **3.** to move by an up and down action. **4.** to try to get information from.

pum′per·nick·el (pum′pər nik′əl) *n.* a coarse, dark rye bread.

pump′kin (pump′kin *or, commonly,* pung′kin) *n.* a large, edible orange fruit of a garden vine.

pun (pun) *n., v.,* **punned, punning.** —*n.* **1.** a humorous use of words alike in sound but different in meaning. —*v.i.* **2.** to make puns. —**pun′ster,** *n.*

punch¹ (punch) *n.* **1.** a thrusting blow with the fist. —*v.t.* **2.** to hit with the fist. **3.** to strike or hit in operating.

punch² (punch) *n.* **1.** a tool or machine for making holes, driving

nails, etc. —*v.t.* **2.** to make (a hole) with a punch.

punch³ (punch) *n.* a beverage of fruit juice, sugar, soda, and sometimes alcohol.

punch′ line′ *n.* the climactic phrase in a joke.

punch′y *adj.,* **-ier, -iest. 1.** befuddled; dazed. **2.** forceful.

punc·til′i·ous (pungk til′ē əs) *adj.* exact in the observance of the formalities of conduct.

punc′tu·al (-chŏŏ əl) *adj.* arriving on time; prompt. —**punc′tu·al′i·ty,** *n.*

punc′tu·ate′ (-āt′) *v.t.,* **-ated, -ating. 1.** to mark with punctuation. **2.** to interrupt periodically.

punc·tu·a′tion *n.* the use of commas, semicolons, etc.

punc′ture (-chər) *n., v.,* **-tured, -turing.** —*n.* **1.** the act of piercing with a pointed object. **2.** a hole so made. —*v.t., v.i.* **3.** to pierce with a pointed object.

pun′dit (pun′dit) *n.* an expert.

pun′gent (pun′jənt) *adj.* **1.** sharp in taste; biting. **2.** forceful and sharp. —**pun′gen·cy,** *n.*

pun′ish (pun′ish) *v.t.* to subject to pain, confinement, loss, etc., for an offense. —**pun′ish·ment,** *n.*

pu′ni·tive (pyŏŏ′ni tiv) *adj.* punishing.

punk (pungk) *n.* **1.** *Slang.* something or someone worthless or unimportant. **2.** *Slang.* a young hoodlum. **3.** Also, **punk rock.** rock music marked by aggressive lyrics. **4.** a style marked by bizarre clothing, hairstyles, etc., suggesting defiance of social norms. —*adj.* **5.** *Informal.* poor in quality. **6.** of punk rock or the punk style.

punt¹ (punt) *n.* **1.** a kick in football. —*v.t., v.i.* **2.** to kick (a dropped ball) before it touches the ground.

punt² (punt) *n.* **1.** a small, flat-bottomed boat. —*v.t., v.i.* **2.** to propel (a punt) with a pole.

pu′ny (pyŏŏ′nē) *adj.,* **-nier, -niest.** small and weak.

pup (pup) *n.* a young dog.

pu′pa (pyŏŏ′pə) *n., pl.* **-pae** (-pē) **-pas.** an insect in the stage between the larva and the winged adult. —**pu′pal,** *adj.*

pu′pil¹ (-pəl) *n.* a person being taught.

pu′pil² (-pəl) *n.* the opening in the iris of the eye.

pup′pet (pup′it) *n.* **1.** a doll or figure manipulated by the hand or by strings. **2.** a person, government, etc., whose actions are controlled

by another. —**pup′pet·eer′**, n.
—**pup′pet·ry**, n.
pup·py (pup′ē) n., pl. -pies. a
young dog.
pur′chase (pûr′chəs) v., -chased,
-chasing, n. —v.t. **1.** to buy. —n. **2.**
acquisition by payment. **3.** something bought. **4.** leverage.
pure (pyŏŏr) adj., purer, purest. **1.**
free of pollutants. **2.** being that
and nothing else. **3.** absolute. **4.**
theoretical, as science or mathematics. **5.** chaste. —**pure′ly**, adv.
pure′bred adj. (-bred′) **1.** having
ancestors over many generations
from a recognized breed. —n.
(pyŏŏr′bred′) **2.** a purebred animal.
pu·rée′ (pyŏŏ rā′, -rē′) n., v., -réed,
-réeing. —n. **1.** cooked food that
has been sieved or blended. —v.t.
2. to make a purée of.
pur′ga·to·ry (pûr′gə tôr′ē) n., pl.
-ries. **1.** (esp. in Roman Catholic
belief) a place or state in which
penitent souls are purified after
death. **2.** any condition or place of
temporary punishment.
purge (pûrj) v., purged, purging, n.
—v.t. **1.** to cleanse; purify. **2.** to
eliminate (undesirable members)
from an organization. **3.** to clear
(the stomach or intestines) by
causing evacuation. —n. **4.** the act
or means of purging. —**pur′ga·
tive** (-gə tiv) adj., n.
pu′ri·fy′ (pyŏŏr′ə fī′) v.t., v.i., -fied,
-fying. to make or become pure.
Pu′rim (pŏŏr′im) n. a Jewish festival
commemorating the saving of the
Jews in Persia from destruction.
pur′ism (pyŏŏr′iz əm) n. insistence
on purity in language, style, etc.
Pu′ri·tan (-i tn) n. **1.** a member of a
strict Protestant group originating
in 16th-century England. **2.** puritan, a person of strict moral views.
—**pu′ri·tan′i·cal**, adj.
pu′ri·ty (-i tē) n. the condition of
being pure.
purl (pûrl) v.t., v.i. to knit with an
inverted stitch.
pur′lieu (pûr′lŏŏ, pûrl′yŏŏ) n., pl.
-lieus. **1.** purlieus, neighborhood.
2. an outlying district.
pur·loin′ (pər loin′, pûr′loin) v.t.,
v.i. to steal.
pur′ple (pûr′pəl) n. a color blended
of red and blue.
pur·port′ v.t. (pər pôrt′) **1.** to
claim. **2.** to imply. —n. (pûr′pôrt)
3. meaning.
pur′pose (pûr′pəs) n., v., -posed,
-posing. —n. **1.** the reason for
which something is done, made,
etc. **2.** intention. —v.t., v.i. **3.** to
intend. —**Idiom. 4. on purpose,**
intentionally. —**pur′pose·ful**, adj.

purr (pûr) n. **1.** the low, continuous vibrating sound made by a cat.
—v.i. **2.** to make this sound.
purse (pûrs) n., v., pursed, pursing.
—n. **1.** a bag for money and small
things. **2.** a sum of money offered
as a prize or gift. —v.t. **3.** to
pucker, as the lips.
purs′er n. a financial officer on a
ship.
pur·su′ant (pər sŏŏ′ənt) adv. **pur-
suant to,** according to.
pur·sue′ v.t., -sued, -suing. **1.** to
follow in order to catch. **2.** to
carry on or engage in.
pur·suit′ (-sŏŏt′) n. **1.** the act of
pursuing. **2.** an occupation or pastime.
pur·vey′ (pər vā′) v.t. to provide;
supply. —**pur·vey′or**, n.
pus (pus) n. the liquid matter
found in sores, abscesses, etc.
push (pŏŏsh) v.t. **1.** to press against
with force to move forward. **2.** to
put demands on. **3.** to urge. **4.**
Slang. to peddle (illicit drugs).
—v.i. **5.** to exert a thrusting force
on something. **6.** to proceed by
strong effort. —n. **7.** the act of
pushing. **8.** a strong effort.
push′o·ver n. one easily victimized
or overcome.
push′y adj., -ier, -iest. obnoxiously
self-assertive. —**push′i·ness**, n.
pu·sil·lan·i·mous (pyŏŏ′sə lan′ə-
məs) adj. cowardly.
puss′y (pŏŏs′ē) n., pl. pussies. a
cat. Also, **puss.**
puss′y·foot′ v.i. **1.** to move
stealthily. **2.** to act irresolutely.
puss′y wil′low n. a small willow
with silky catkins.
pus′tule (pus′chŏŏl) n. a pimple
containing pus.
put (pŏŏt) v., put, putting, n. —v.t.
1. to cause to be in a specific place,
condition, relation, etc. **2.** to set to
a task. **3.** to express. **4.** to apply to
a purpose. **5.** to impose. **6.** to
throw. **7. put off, a.** to postpone.
b. to evade. **8. ~ up with,** to tolerate.
pu′ta·tive (pyŏŏ′tə tiv) adj. re-
puted; supposed.
put′-down′ n. Informal. a snubbing
remark.
pu′tre·fy′ (pyŏŏ′trə fī′) v.t., v.i.,
-fied, -fying. to rot. —**pu′tre·fac′-
tion** (-fak′shən) n.
pu·tres′cent (-tres′ənt) adj. becoming putrid. —**pu·tres′cence**, n.
pu′trid (-trid) adj. rotten.
putsch (pŏŏch) n. a sudden political revolt or uprising.
putt (put) v.t., v.i. **1.** to strike (a
golf ball) gently. —n. **2.** such a
strike.

put′ter[1] (-ər) *v.i.* to busy oneself in a leisurely manner.

put′ter[2] (-ər) *n.* a club for putting.

put′ty (put′ē) *n., v.,* **-tied, -tying.** —*n.* **1.** a compound of whiting and oil used to secure windowpanes, fill holes, etc. —*v.t.* **2.** to secure with putty.

puz′zle (puz′əl) *n., v.,* **-zled, -zling.** —*n.* **1.** a toy, game, or problem to be solved for amusement. **2.** a difficult question or matter. —*v.t.* **3.** to mystify. —*v.i.* **4.** to ponder a perplexing problem.

Pvt. Private.

PX post exchange.

pyg′my (pig′mē) *n., pl.* **-mies.** a dwarf.

py′lon (pī′lon) *n.* a tall thin metal structure used as a support.

pyr′a·mid (pir′ə mid) *n.* a solid with triangular sides meeting in a point at the top. —**py·ram′i·dal** (pə ram′ə dl) *adj.*

pyre (pī°r) *n.* a heap of wood, esp. for burning a corpse.

py′rite (pī′rīt) *n.* a common yellow mineral containing sulfur and iron.

py′ro·ma′ni·a (pī′rə mā′nē ə) *n.* a compulsion for setting fires. —**py′ro·ma′ni·ac′,** *n.*

py′ro·tech′nics (-tek′niks) *n.* a firework display. —**py′ro·tech′nic,** *adj.*

py′thon (pī′thon) *n.* a large snake that kills by crushing its prey.

Q

Q, q (kyōō) *n.* the seventeenth letter of the English alphabet.

Q.E.D. which was to be shown or demonstrated.

qt. *pl.* **qt., qts.** quart.

qty. quantity.

quack[1] (kwak) *n.* **1.** the harsh cry of a duck. —*v.i.* **2.** to utter a quack.

quack[2] (kwak) *n.* a fraudulent pretender to medical or other skill. —**quack′er·y,** *n.*

quad[1] (kwod) *n.* a quadrangle.

quad[2] (kwod) *n.* a quadruplet.

quad′ran·gle (-rang′gəl) *n.* **1.** a plane figure with four angles and four sides. **2.** a four-sided area surrounded by buildings.

quad′rant (-rənt) *n.* **1.** an arc of 90°. **2.** an instrument for measuring altitudes.

quad′ra·phon′ic (-rə fon′ik) *adj.* of sound reproduced through four recording tracks.

quad·ren′ni·al (-dren′ē əl) *adj.* **1.** occurring every four years. **2.** of or lasting for four years.

quad′ri·lat′er·al (-lat′ər əl) *adj.* **1.** four-sided. —*n.* **2.** a four-sided plane figure.

qua·drille′ (kwo dril′, kwə-) *n.* a square dance for four couples.

quad′ri·ple′gi·a (kwod′rə plē′jē ə, -jə) *n.* paralysis of the entire body below the neck. —**quad′ri·ple′gic,** *n., adj.*

quad′ru·ped′ (-rōō ped′) *n.* a four-footed animal.

quad·ru′ple (kwo drōō′pəl, -drup′əl) *adj., n., v.,* **-pled, -pling.** —*adj.* **1.** of four parts. **2.** four times as great. —*n.* **3.** a number or amount four times as great as another. —*v.t., v.i.* **4.** to make or become four times as great.

quad·ru′plet (-drup′lit, -drōō′plit) *n.*

one of four children born at one birth.

quad·ru′pli·cate (-drōō′pli kit) *n.* a group of four copies.

quaff (kwof, kwaf) *v.i., v.t.* **1.** to drink heartily. —*n.* **2.** a beverage quaffed.

quag′mire′ (kwag′mī°r′, kwog′-) *n.* boggy ground.

qua′hog (kwô′hog, kō′-) *n.* an edible American clam.

quail[1] (kwāl) *n., pl.* **quails, quail.** a game bird resembling domestic fowls.

quail[2] (kwāl) *v.i.* to shrink in fear.

quaint (kwānt) *adj.* pleasingly old-fashioned or odd. —**quaint′ly,** *adv.*

quake (kwāk) *v.i.,* **quaked, quaking.** to tremble.

qual′i·fy′ (kwol′ə fī′) *v.,* **-fied, -fy-ing.** —*v.t.* **1.** to make proper or fit, as for a job. **2.** to modify or limit. **3.** to moderate. —*v.i.* **4.** to show oneself fit, competent, or eligible. —**qual′i·fi·ca′tion,** *n.*

qual′i·ty (-i tē) *n., pl.* **-ties. 1.** a characteristic or property. **2.** relative merit. **3.** excellence.

qual′ity time′ *n.* time devoted exclusively to nurturing a cherished person or activity.

qualm (kwäm) *n.* a pang of conscience; misgiving.

quan′da·ry (kwon′də rē, -drē) *n., pl.* **-ries.** a dilemma.

quan′ti·fy′ (kwon′tə fī′) *v.t.,* **-fied, -fying.** to determine or express the quantity of.

quan′ti·ty (-ti tē) *n., pl.* **-ties. 1.** a definite or indefinite amount or measure. **2.** a large amount.

quan′tum (-təm) *n., pl.* **-ta,** *adj.* —*n.* **1.** quantity or amount. **2.** *Physics.* a very small, indivisible quantity of energy. —*adj.* **3.** sudden and significant.

quar•an•tine′ (kwôr′ən tēn′) *n., v.,* **-tined, -tining.** —*n.* **1.** strict isolation to prevent spread of disease. —*v.t.* **2.** to put in quarantine.

quark (kwôrk, kwärk) *n.* a subatomic particle thought to form the basis of all matter.

quar′rel (kwôr′əl) *n., v.,* **-reled, -reling.** —*n.* **1.** an angry dispute. —*v.i.* **2.** to disagree angrily. —**quar′rel•some,** *adj.*

quar′ry (-ē) *n., pl.* **-ries,** *v.,* **-ried, -rying.** —*n.* **1.** a pit from which stone is taken. **2.** an object of pursuit. —*v.t.* **3.** to get from a quarry.

quart (kwôrt) *n.* a measure of capacity: in liquid measure, $\frac{1}{4}$ gallon; in dry measure, $\frac{1}{8}$ peck.

quar′ter *n.* **1.** one of four equal parts. **2.** a coin worth 25 cents. **3. quarters,** lodgings; accommodations. **4.** mercy. —*v.t.* **5.** to divide into quarters. **6.** to lodge.

quar′ter•ly *adj., n., pl.* **-lies,** *adv.* —*adj.* **1.** occurring, done, etc., each quarter year. —*n.* **2.** a quarterly publication. —*adv.* **3.** once each quarter year.

quar′ter•mas′ter *n.* **1.** a military officer in charge of quarters, supplies, etc. **2.** a naval officer in charge of signals.

quar•tet′ (kwôr tet′) *n.* **1.** a group of four singers or players. **2.** a musical composition for four performers.

quar′to (-tō) *n., pl.* **-tos.** a book page of sheets folded twice.

quartz (kwôrts) *n.* a hard crystalline mineral.

qua′sar (kwā′zär, -zər) *n.* an astronomical source of powerful radio energy.

quash (kwosh) *v.t.* to subdue; suppress.

qua′si (kwā′zī, -sī, kwä′sē, -zē) *adj.* resembling; seeming to be.

quasi- a prefix meaning somewhat.

quat′rain (kwo′trān) *n.* a four-line stanza.

qua′ver (kwā′vər) *v.i.* **1.** to quiver. **2.** to speak in a trembling tone. —*n.* **3.** a quavering tone.

quay (kē) *n.* a landing place beside water; wharf.

quea′sy (kwē′zē) *adj.,* **-sier, -siest. 1.** nauseated. **2.** uneasy.

queen (kwēn) *n.* **1.** a female sovereign. **2.** the wife of a king. **3.** the fertile female of bees, ants, etc. —*v.t.* **4.** to crown as queen.

queer (kwēr) *adj.* **1.** strange; odd. —*n.* **2.** *Slang: Disparaging and Offensive.* (a contemptuous term used to refer to a homosexual.)

quell (kwel) *v.t.* to suppress.

quench (kwench) *v.t.* **1.** to satisfy or slake. **2.** to extinguish.

quer′u•lous (kwer′ə ləs, kwer′yə-) *adj.* complaining; whining.

que′ry (kwēr′ē) *n., pl.* **-ries,** *v.,* **-ried, -rying.** —*n.* **1.** a question. —*v.t.* **2.** to question.

quest (kwest) *n.* a search.

ques′tion (kwes′chən) *n.* **1.** a sentence in a form intended to elicit information. **2.** a matter for discussion or dispute. —*v.t.* **3.** to ask questions of. **4.** to doubt or dispute. —**ques′tion•er,** *n.*

ques′tion•a•ble *adj.* **1.** of doubtful honesty or morality. **2.** uncertain.

ques′tion mark′ *n.* a punctuation mark (?) indicating a question.

ques′tion•naire′ (-chə nâr′) *n.* a list of questions.

queue (kyoo) *n., v.,* **queued, queuing.** —*n.* **1.** a line of persons. **2.** a single braid of hair. —*v.i.* **3. queue up,** to form a line while waiting.

quib′ble (kwib′əl) *v.,* **-bled, -bling,** *n.* —*v.i.* **1.** to speak ambiguously in evasion. **2.** to make petty objections. —*n.* **3.** the act of quibbling.

quiche (kēsh) *n.* a pie of unsweetened custard and cheese, onion, etc.

quick (kwik) *adj.* **1.** prompt; done promptly. **2.** swift. **3.** alert. —*n.* **4.** living persons. **5.** sensitive flesh under the nails. —*adv.* **6.** in a quick manner. —**quick′ly,** *adv.*

quick′en *v.t.* **1.** to hasten. —*v.i.* **2.** to become livelier or more rapid.

quick′ie *n.* something done or enjoyed in only a short time.

quick′sand′ *n.* soft sand yielding easily to weight.

quick′sil′ver *n.* mercury.

quid pro quo (kwid′ prō kwō′) *n., pl.* **quid pro quos, quids pro quo.** something given or taken in return for something else.

qui•es′cent (kwē es′ənt, kwī-) *adj.* inactive. —**qui•es′cence,** *n.*

qui′et (kwī′it) *adj.* **1.** being at rest. **2.** peaceful. **3.** silent. **4.** restrained. —*v.t., v.i.* **5.** to make or become quiet. —*n.* **6.** tranquillity. **7.** silence. —**qui′et•ly,** *adv.*

quill (kwil) *n.* **1.** a large feather. **2.** a spine of a porcupine.

quilt (kwilt) *n.* a padded and lined bed covering. —**quilt′ed,** *adj.*

quince (kwins) *n.* a yellowish acid fruit.

qui′nine (kwī′nīn) *n.* a bitter substance used esp. to treat malaria.

quin•tes′sence (kwin tes′əns) *n.* the pure essence or most perfect example of something. —**quin′tes•sen′tial** (-tə sen′shəl) *adj.*

quin·tet′ (-tet′) *n.* **1.** a group of five singers or players. **2.** a musical composition for a quintet.

quin·tu′plet (-tup′lit, -tōō′plit, -tyōō′-) *n.* one of five children born at one birth.

quip (kwip) *n., v.,* **quipped, quipping.** —*n.* **1.** a witty or sarcastic remark. —*v.i.* **2.** to make a quip.

quirk (kwûrk) *n.* a peculiarity. —**quirk′y,** *adj.*

quit (kwit) *v.,* **quit** or **quitted, quitting.** —*v.t.* **1.** to stop. **2.** to give up or leave. —*v.i.* **3.** to give up a job or position.

quite (kwīt) *adv.* **1.** completely. **2.** really.

quits (kwits) *adj.* **1.** being on equal terms. —*Idiom.* **2. call it quits,** to end something.

quit′tance (kwit′ns) *n.* **1.** recompense. **2.** discharge from debt.

quiv′er¹ (kwiv′ər) *v.i.* **1.** to tremble. —*n.* **2.** the act of quivering.

quiv·er² (kwiv′ər) *n.* a case for arrows.

quix·ot′ic (kwik sot′ik) *adj.* extravagantly idealistic; impractical.

quiz (kwiz) *v.,* **quizzed, quizzing,** *n., pl.* **quizzes.** —*v.t.* **1.** to question. —*n.* **2.** a short test.

quiz′zi·cal *adj.* **1.** comical. **2.** puzzled. —**quiz′zi·cal·ly,** *adv.*

quoin (koin, kwoin) *n.* **1.** an external solid angle. **2.** a cornerstone.

quoit (kwoit, koit) *n.* a flat ring thrown to encircle a peg in the game of **quoits.**

quo′rum (kwôr′əm) *n.* the number of members needed to transact business legally.

quo′ta (kwō′tə) *n.* **1.** the proportional share due. **2.** the number or amount officially allowed.

quo·ta′tion (tā′shən) *n.* **1.** the act of quoting. **2.** the words quoted. **3.** a stated price.

quota′tion mark′ *n.* one of a pair of punctuation marks enclosing a quotation, shown as (″) at the beginning and (″) at the end.

quote (kwōt) *v.,* **quoted, quoting,** *n.* —*v.t.* **1.** to repeat verbatim. **2.** to cite. **3.** to state (a price). —*n.* **4.** *Informal.* a quotation.

quo·tid′i·an (kwō tid′ē ən) *adj.* **1.** daily; everyday. **2.** ordinary.

quo′tient (-shənt) *n.* the number of times one number is contained in another.

R

R, r (är) *n.* the eighteenth letter of the English alphabet.

rab′bi (rab′ī) *n.* a Jewish religious leader. —**rab·bin′ic** (rə bin′ik), **rab·bin′i·cal,** *adj.*

rab′bin·ate (rab′ə nit, -nāt′) *n.* **1.** the office of a rabbi. **2.** rabbis collectively.

rab′bit (rab′it) *n.* a long-eared hopping mammal.

rab′ble (rab′əl) *n.* **1.** a mob. **2.** the common people.

rab′ble-rous′er (-rou′zər) *n.* a person who stirs up the public.

rab′id (rab′id) *adj.* **1.** irrationally intense. **2.** having rabies.

ra′bies (rā′bēz) *n.* a fatal disease transmitted by the bite of an infected animal.

rac·coon′ (ra kōōn′) *n.* a small nocturnal carnivorous mammal.

race¹ (rās) *n., v.,* **raced, racing.** —*n.* **1.** a contest of speed. **2.** a competition. **3.** onward flow or course. —*v.i., v.t.* **4.** to run a race (against). **5.** to (cause to) run or go swiftly. —**rac′er,** *n.*

race² (rās) *n.* **1.** a group of people related by common descent, language, etc. **2.** a classification of humans based on physical characteristics. —**ra′cial** (rā′shəl) *adj.*

rac′ism (rā′siz əm) *n.* hatred of or prejudice against another race.

rack¹ (rak) *n.* **1.** a structure for storage. **2.** a toothed bar engaging with the teeth of a pinion. **3.** a torture device.

rack² (rak) *n.* **rack and ruin,** decline or destruction.

rack·et¹ (rak′it) *n.* **1.** loud noise. **2.** a dishonest or illegal activity.

rack·et² (rak′it) *n.* a bat with a netted frame, used in tennis, badminton, etc. Also, **rac′quet.**

rack′e·teer′ *n.* a criminal engaged in a racket.

rac′on·teur′ (rak′on tûr′, -tōōr′, -ən-) *n.* a skilled storyteller.

rac′quet·ball (rak′it-) *n.* a game like handball, played with rackets.

rac′y (rā′sē) *adj.,* **-ier, -iest. 1.** lively. **2.** risqué. —**rac′i·ly,** *adv.*

ra′dar (rā′där) *n.* an electronic device that locates unseen objects by measuring radio waves.

ra′di·al (-dē əl) *adj.* of rays or radii.

ra′di·ant (-ənt) *adj.* **1.** emitting rays of light. **2.** bright; exultant. **3.** emitted in rays. —**ra′di·ance,** *n.*

ra′di·ate′ (-āt′) *v.,* **-ated, -ating.** —*v.i.* **1.** to spread like rays from a center. **2.** to emit rays. —*v.t.* **3.** to emit in rays.

ra′di·a′tion *n.* **1.** the process in

which energy is emitted as particles or waves, transmitted, and absorbed. **2.** the process of radiating. **3.** something radiated.

ra·di·a·tor *n.* **1.** a heating device. **2.** an engine-cooling device.

rad·i·cal (rad′i kəl) *adj.* **1.** favoring drastic reforms. **2.** basic. —*n.* **3.** a person with radical ideas. **4.** an atom or group of atoms behaving as a unit. —**rad′i·cal·ism,** *n.*

ra·di·o (rā′dē ō′) *n., pl.* **-dios. 1.** a way of transmitting sound by electromagnetic waves, without wires. **2.** an apparatus for sending or receiving such waves.

ra·di·o·ac′tive *adj.* emitting radiation from the atomic nucleus. —**ra·di·o·ac·tiv′i·ty,** *n.*

ra·di·ol′o·gy (-ol′ə jē) *n.* the use of radiation, as x-rays, for medical diagnosis and treatment.

rad′ish (rad′ish) *n.* the crisp root of a garden plant, eaten raw.

ra′di·um (rā′dē əm) *n.* a radioactive metallic element.

ra′di·us (-əs) *n., pl.* **-dii** (-dē ī) **-di·uses. 1.** a straight line from the center of a circle to the circumference. **2.** a bone of the forearm.

ra′don (rā′don) *n.* an inert radioactive gaseous element produced by the decay of radium.

RAF Royal Air Force.

raf·fi·a (raf′ē ə) *n.* a fiber made from the leafstalks of a palm.

raff′ish (raf′ish) *adj.* **1.** jaunty; rakish. **2.** gaudily vulgar or cheap.

raf′fle (raf′əl) *n., v.,* **-fled, -fling.** —*n.* **1.** a lottery in which people buy chances to win a prize. —*v.t.* **2.** to dispose of by raffle.

raft (raft) *n.* a floating platform of logs or planks.

raft′er (raf′tər) *n.* a framing timber of a roof.

rag (rag) *n.* a torn or worn scrap of cloth.

rag′a·muf·fin (rag′ə muf′in) *n.* a ragged child.

rage (rāj) *n., v.,* **raged, raging.** —*n.* **1.** violent anger. **2.** an object of popular enthusiasm. —*v.i.* **3.** to be violently angry. **4.** to move or act violently.

rag′ged (rag′id) *adj.* **1.** clothed in torn garments. **2.** torn or tattered. **3.** rough or uneven.

rag′time′ *n.* syncopated jazz.

rag′weed′ *n.* a plant whose pollen causes hay fever.

raid (rād) *n.* **1.** a sudden assault or attack. —*v.t., v.i.* **2.** to attack suddenly.

rail¹ (rāl) *n.* **1.** a horizontal bar forming a support or barrier. **2.** one of a pair of steel bars forming a railroad track. **3.** the railroad.

rail² (rāl) *v.i.* to complain bitterly.

rail′ing *n.* a barrier of rails and posts.

rail′ler·y (rā′lə rē) *n.* good-humored kidding; banter.

rail′road′ *n.* **1.** a road with fixed rails on which trains run. **2.** a system of such roads and trains. —*v.t.* **3.** to push through hastily.

rail′way′ *n. Chiefly Brit.* a railroad.

rai′ment (rā′mənt) *n.* clothing.

rain (rān) *n.* **1.** water falling from the sky in drops. **2.** a heavy, continuous fall. —*v.i., v.t.* **3.** to fall or send down as rain. —**rain′y,** *adj.*

rain′bow′ (-bō′) *n.* an arc of colors sometimes seen in the sky opposite the sun during rain.

rain′ check′ *n.* **1.** a postponement of an invitation. **2.** a ticket for future admission to an event postponed by rain.

rain′coat′ *n.* a waterproof coat.

rain′fall′ *n.* the amount of rain falling in an area in a given time.

rain′for′est *n.* a tropical forest in an area of high annual rainfall.

raise (rāz) *v.,* **raised, raising,** *n.* —*v.t.* **1.** to lift up. **2.** to set upright. **3.** to cause to appear or arise. **4.** to grow. **5.** to increase, as in amount. **6.** to collect. **7.** to rear. —*n.* **8.** an increase in pay.

rai′sin (rā′zin) *n.* a dried grape.

rai·son d'ê·tre (rā′zōn de′trə) *n., pl.* **raisons d'être.** reason for existence.

ra′jah (rä′jə) *n.* (formerly) an Indian king or prince.

rake¹ (rāk) *n., v.,* **raked, raking.** —*n.* **1.** an agricultural tool with a handle and row of teeth. —*v.t.* **2.** to gather or smooth with a rake. **3.** to gather in abundance. **4.** to sweep with gunfire. —*v.i.* **5.** to use a rake.

rake² (rāk) *n.* a dissolute man.

rake′-off′ *n.* an amount received, esp. illicitly.

rak′ish (rā′kish) *adj.* jaunty.

ral′ly (ral′ē) *v.,* **-lied, -lying,** *n., pl.* **-lies.** —*v.t., v.i.* **1.** to bring or come into order. **2.** to call or come together. **3.** to (cause to) recover. —*n.* **4.** a sharp rise. **5.** a renewal of strength. **6.** a mass meeting.

ram (ram) *n., v.,* **rammed, ramming.** —*n.* **1.** a male sheep. **2.** a device for battering, forcing, etc. —*v.t.* **3.** to strike forcibly.

RAM (ram) *n.* random-access memory: computer memory for running programs and temporarily storing data.

ram′ble *v.,* **-bled, -bling,** *n.* —*v.i.* **1.**

to stroll idly. **2.** to talk vaguely.
—*n.* **3.** a stroll. —**ram′bler,** *n.*
ram•bunc′tious (-bungk′shəs) *adj.*
difficult to control or handle.
ram′i•fi•ca′tion (ram′ə fi kā′shən) *n.*
a consequence.
ram′i•fy′ (-ə fī′) *v.t., v.i.,* **-fied, -fy-
ing.** to divide into branches.
ramp (ramp) *n.* a sloping surface
between two levels.
ram′page (ram′pāj) *n., v.,* **-paged,
-paging.** —*n.* **1.** an eruption of violent behavior. —*v.i.* **2.** to move furiously about.
ramp′ant (-pənt) *adj.* vigorous; unrestrained.
ram′part (-pärt, -pərt) *n.* a mound
of earth raised for defense.
ram′rod′ *n.* a rod for cleaning or
loading a gun.
ram′shack′le *adj.* rickety.
ranch (ranch) *n.* a large farm, esp.
for raising livestock. —**ranch′er,** *n.*
ran′cid (ran′sid) *adj.* smelling or
tasting spoiled.
ran′cor (rang′kər) *n.* lasting resentment. —**ran′cor•ous,** *adj.*
ran′dom (ran′dəm) *adj.* occurring
or done without aim or pattern.
rand′y (ran′dē) *adj.,* **-ier, -iest.** sexually aroused; lustful.
rang (rang) *v.* pt. of **ring.**
range (rānj) *n., v.,* **ranged, ranging.**
—*n.* **1.** limits; extent. **2.** a row or
series. **3.** a mountain chain. **4.** a
grazing area. **5.** a cooking stove. **6.**
a place for target shooting. **7.** the
distance between gun and target.
—*v.t.* **8.** to arrange in a line. **9.** to
pass over (an area). —*v.i.* **10.** to
vary within limits.
rang′er (rān′jer) *n.* **1.** the warden
of a forest tract. **2.** a civil officer
who patrols a large area.
rang′y (rān′jē) *adj.,* **-ier, -iest.** slender and long-limbed.
rank[1] (rangk) *n.* **1.** a social or official position or standing. **2.** high
position. **3.** a row or series. **4.
ranks,** enlisted soldiers. —*v.t., v.i.*
5. to put or be in a particular rank.
rank[2] (rangk) *adj.* **1.** growing excessively. **2.** smelling bad. **3.** utter.
—**rank′ness,** *n.*
rank′ and file′ *n.* **1.** members apart
from leaders. **2.** enlisted soldiers.
rank′ing *adj.* **1.** senior. **2.** renowned.
ran•kle (rang′kəl) *v.i., v.t.,* **-kled,
-kling.** to cause resentment (in).
ran′sack (ran′sak) *v.t.* **1.** to search
thoroughly. **2.** to plunder; pillage.
ran′som (ran′səm) *n.* **1.** a sum demanded for the release of a captive. —*v.t.* **2.** to pay ransom for.
rant (rant) *v.i.* **1.** to speak wildly.
—*n.* **2.** violent speech. —**rant′er,** *n.*

rap (rap) *v.,* **rapped, rapping,** *n.*
—*v.t., v.i.* **1.** to hit quickly and
sharply. —*n.* **2.** a sharp blow. **3.**
popular music marked by rhythmical intoning of rhymed verses over
a repetitive beat. —**rap′per,** *n.*
ra•pa′cious (rə pā′shəs) *adj.* predatory; greedy.
rape (rāp) *n., v.,* **raped, rap•ing.**
—*n.* **1.** the act of forcing a person
to have sexual intercourse. **2.** an
act of plunder. —*v.i., v.t.* **3.** to
commit rape (on). —**rap′ist,** *n.*
rap′id (rap′id) *adj.* **1.** swift. —*n.* **2.
rapids,** the swift-moving part of a
river. —**ra•pid′i•ty,** *n.*
ra′pi•er (rā′pē ər) *n.* a slender
sword.
rap′ine (rap′in) *n.* plunder.
rap•port′ (ra pôr′) *n.* a sympathetic
relationship.
rap′proche•ment′ (rap′rōsh mäɴ′)
n. an establishment of harmonious
relations.
rapt (rapt) *adj.* engrossed.
rap′ture (rap′chər) *n.* ecstatic joy.
—**rap′tur•ous,** *adj.*
rare[1] (râr) *adj.,* **rarer, rarest. 1.** uncommon. **2.** not dense, as a gas.
—**rare′ness,** *n.* —**rar′i•ty,** *n.*
rare[2] (râr) *adj.,* **rarer, rarest.** (of
meat) cooked just slightly. —**rare′-
ness,** *n.*
rare′bit (-bit) *n.* a dish of melted
cheese.
rar′e•fy′ (-ə fī′) *v.t., v.i.,* **-fied, -fy-
ing.** to make or become thin, as
air.
rar′ing *adj.* very eager or anxious.
ras′cal (ras′kəl) *n.* a dishonest or
mischievous person.
rash[1] (rash) *adj.* recklessly hasty.
—**rash′ly,** *adv.* —**rash′ness,** *n.*
rash[2] (rash) *n.* a skin eruption.
rash′er *n.* a serving of bacon.
rasp (rasp) *v.t.* **1.** to scrape, as with
a file. **2.** to irritate. —*v.i.* **3.** to
speak gratingly. —*n.* **4.** a coarse
file. **5.** a rasping sound.
rasp′ber′ry (raz′ber′ē, -bə rē) *n., pl.*
-ries. a small juicy red or black
fruit.
rat (rat) *n.* a rodent larger than a
mouse.
ratch′et (rach′it) *n.* a wheel or bar
with teeth.
rate (rāt) *n., v.,* **rated, rating.** —*n.*
1. a charge in proportion to something that varies. **2.** degree of
speed or progress. —*v.t.* **3.** to estimate the value of. **4.** to consider;
judge.
rath′er (rath′ər) *adv.* **1.** somewhat.
2. in preference. **3.** on the contrary.
rat′i•fy′ (rat′ə fī′) *v.t.,* **-fied, -fying.**
to confirm formally.

ra′tio (rā′shō, -shē ō′) *n., pl.* **-tios.** relative number or extent; proportion.

ra′ti•oc′i•na′tion (rash′ē os′ə nā′shən) *n.* reasoning.

ra′tion (-ən, rā′shən) *n.* **1.** a fixed allowance. —*v.t.* **2.** to apportion. **3.** to put on a ration.

ra′tion•al (-ə nl) *adj.* **1.** sensible. **2.** sane. —**ra′tion•al′i•ty,** *n.*

ra′tion•ale′ (-nal′) *n.* a reasonable basis for action.

ra′tion•al•ism *n.* advocacy of precise reasoning as the source of truth. —**ra′tion•al•ist,** *n.*

ra′tion•al•ize′ *v.t., v.i.,* **-ized, -izing.** to find a plausible reason for (one's behavior or attitude).

rat′ race′ *n.* an exhausting, competitive routine activity.

rat•tan′ (ra tan′, rə-) *n.* the hollow stem of a climbing palm used for wickerwork.

rat′tle (rat′l) *v.,* **-tled, -tling,** *n.* —*v.i.* **1.** to make a series of short, sharp sounds. **2.** to chatter. —*v.t.* **3.** to cause to make a rattling noise. **4.** to disconcert; confuse. —*n.* **5.** a rattling sound. **6.** a baby's toy that rattles.

rat′tle•snake′ *n.* a venomous American snake.

rat′ty *adj.,* **-tier, -tiest.** shabby.

rau′cous (rô′kəs) *adj.* **1.** hoarse; harsh. **2.** rowdy; disorderly.

raun′chy (rôn′chē, rän′-) *adj.,* **-chier, -chiest. 1.** vulgar; smutty. **2.** lecherous. **3.** dirty; slovenly.

rav′age (rav′ij) *v.,* **-aged, -aging,** *n.* —*v.t., v.i.* **1.** to do ruinous damage (to). —*n.* **2.** ruinous damage. —**rav′ag•er,** *n.*

rave (rāv) *v.i.,* **raved, raving.** to talk wildly.

rav′el (rav′əl) *v.t.* **1.** to disentangle the threads of. **2.** to entangle. **3.** to make clear. —*v.i.* **4.** to fray.

ra′ven (rā′vən) *n.* a large shiny black bird.

rav′en•ing (rav′ə ning) *adj.* greedy for prey.

rav′en•ous (rav′ə nəs) *adj.* very hungry; greedy. —**rav′en•ous•ly,** *adv.*

ra•vine′ (rə vēn′) *n.* a deep, narrow valley.

rav′ish (rav′ish) *v.t.* **1.** to seize and carry off. **2.** to rape. **3.** to fill with strong emotion.

rav′ish•ing *adj.* extremely beautiful.

raw (rô) *adj.* **1.** in the natural state. **2.** uncooked. **3.** damp and chilly. **4.** untrained.

raw′boned′ *adj.* lean and bony.

raw′hide′ *n.* the untanned hide of cattle.

ray¹ (rā) *n.* **1.** a narrow beam of light. **2.** a trace. **3.** a line outward from the center.

ray² (rā) *n.* a flat-bodied deep-sea fish.

ray′on (rā′on) *n.* a silklike synthetic fabric.

raze (rāz) *v.t.,* **razed, razing.** to tear down; demolish.

ra′zor (rā′zər) *n.* a sharp-edged instrument for shaving.

R.C. Roman Catholic.

rd. road.

re¹ (rā) *n.* the musical syllable used for the second note of a scale.

re² (rē, rā) *prep.* with reference to.

re- 1. a prefix meaning: back or backward. **2.** again.

reach (rēch) *v.t.* **1.** to come to. **2.** to be able to touch. **3.** to stretch. **4.** to extend as far as. —*v.i.* **5.** to stretch with the hand. **6.** to extend. —*n.* **7.** the act of reaching. **8.** extent.

re•act′ (rē akt′) *v.i.* **1.** to act upon each other. **2.** to respond.

re•ac′tant (-ak′tənt) *n.* a substance that undergoes change in a chemical reaction.

re•ac′tion *n.* **1.** a responsive action. **2.** a reverse movement or tendency. **3.** a chemical change.

re•ac•tion•ar•y *adj., n., pl.* **-ar•ies.** —*adj.* **1.** extremely conservative politically. —*n.* **2.** a reactionary person.

re•ac′tor *n.* an apparatus for producing useful nuclear energy.

read (rēd) *v.,* **read** (red) **reading.** —*v.t.* **1.** to understand or utter aloud (something printed or written). **2.** to register. **3.** to access (computer data). —*v.i.* **4.** to read printed matter. —**read′er,** *n.*

read′ing (rē′ding) *n.* **1.** something read. **2.** an interpretation of a written or musical work. **3.** data indicated on an instrument.

read′-on′ly (rēd) *adj.* noting computer data that can be read but not changed.

read′y (red′ē) *adj.,* **-ier, -iest,** *v.,* **-ied, -ying,** *n.* —*adj.* **1.** fully prepared. **2.** willing. **3.** apt. —*v.t.* **4.** to make ready. —*n.* **5.** the state of being ready. —**read′i•ly,** *adv.* —**read′i•ness,** *n.*

read′y-made′ *adj.* ready for use when bought.

re•a′gent (rē ā′jənt) *n.* a chemical used in analysis and synthesis.

re′al (rē′əl, rēl) *adj.* **1.** actual. **2.** genuine. **3.** denoting immovable property. —**re′al•ness,** *n.*

re′al estate′ *n.* property in land and buildings. Also, **re′al•ty** (rē′əl tē, rēl′-).

re′al•ism *n.* **1.** a tendency to see

things as they really are. **2.** the representation of things as they really are. —**re′al·ist,** *n.* —**re′al·is′·tic,** *adj.* —**re′al·is′ti·cal·ly,** *adv.*

re·al′i·ty (rē al′i tē) *n., pl.* **-ties. 1.** the state or quality of being real. **2.** a real thing or fact.

re′al·ize′ *v.t.,* **-ized, -izing. 1.** to understand clearly. **2.** to make real. **3.** to get as profit. —**re′al·i·za′·tion,** *n.*

re′al·ly *adv.* **1.** actually. **2.** genuinely; truly. **3.** indeed.

realm (relm) *n.* **1.** a kingdom. **2.** a special field.

ream (rēm) *n.* a standard quantity of paper, usu. 500 sheets.

reap (rēp) *v.t.* to harvest. —**reap′er,** *n.*

rear (rēr) *n.* **1.** the back part. —*adj.* **2.** of or at the rear. —*v.t.* **3.** to care for to maturity. **4.** to raise; erect. —*v.i.* **5.** to rise on the hind legs.

rear′ ad′miral *n.* a naval officer above a captain.

rear′most′ *adj.* farthest back.

rear′ward (-wərd) *adv.* **1.** Also, **rear′wards,** toward the rear. —*adj.* **2.** located in the rear.

rea′son (rē′zən) *n.* **1.** a cause for a belief, act, etc. **2.** sound judgment. **3.** sanity. —*v.i.* **4.** to think or argue logically. —*v.t.* **5.** to infer. —**rea′son·ing,** *n.*

rea′son·a·ble (rē′zə nə bəl, rēz′nə-) *adj.* **1.** logical. **2.** moderate. **3.** not expensive. **4.** rational.

re′as·sure′ (rē′ə shŏŏr′, -shûr′) *v.t.,* **-sured, -suring.** to restore the confidence of. —**re′as·sur′ance,** *n.*

re′bate (rē′bāt) *n., v.,* **-bated, -bating.** —*n.* **1.** a return of part of the amount paid. —*v.t.* **2.** to return (part of a payment).

re·bel′ *v.,* **-belled, -belling,** *n.* —*v.i.* (ri bel′) **1.** to rise in arms against one's government. **2.** to resist any authority. —*n.* (reb′əl) **3.** one who rebels. —**re·bel′lion,** *n.* —**re·bel′lious,** *adj.* —**re·bel′lious·ly,** *adv.*

re·bound′ *v.i.* (ri bound′) **1.** to spring back after impact. —*n.* (rē′bound′) **2.** the act of rebounding.

re·buff′ (ri buf′) *n.* **1.** a blunt repulse or refusal. —*v.t.* **2.** to refuse or repel.

re·buke′ (- byōōk′) *v.,* **-buked, -buking,** *n.* —*v.t.* **1.** to scold sharply. —*n.* **2.** a sharp scolding.

re·but′ (ri but′) *v.t.,* **-butted, -butting.** to prove wrong; refute. —**re·but′tal,** *n.*

re·cal′ci·trant (ri kal′si trənt) *adj.* resisting control.

re·call′ *v.t.* (ri kôl′) **1.** to remember. **2.** to call back. **3.** to withdraw. —*n.* (rē′kôl) **4.** the act of recalling.

re·cant′ (ri kant′) *v.t.* to retract (a statement, opinion, etc.).

re′cap′ (rē′kap′) *v.,* **-capped, -capping,** *n.* —*v.t.* **1.** to recapitulate. **2.** to recondition (a tire) by adding a rubber strip. —*n.* **3.** a recapitulation. **4.** a recapped tire.

re′ca·pit′u·late (rē′kə pich′ə lāt′) *v.t., v.i.,* **-lated, -lating.** to summarize; sum up.

re·cap′ture *v.,* **-tured, -turing,** *n.* —*v.t.* **1.** to capture again. **2.** to experience again. —*n.* **3.** a recovery by capture.

recd. or **rec′d.** received.

re·cede′ (ri sēd′) *v.i.,* **-ceded, -ceding.** to move or appear to move back.

re·ceipt′ (ri sēt′) *n.* **1.** a written acknowledgment of receiving. **2. receipts,** an amount received. **3.** the act of receiving.

re·ceive′ *v.t.,* **-ceived, -ceiving. 1.** to take (something offered or delivered). **2.** to experience. **3.** to welcome (guests). **4.** to accept.

re·ceiv′er *n.* **1.** one that receives. **2.** a device that receives electrical signals and converts them. **3.** a person put in charge of property in litigation. —**re·ceiv′er·ship′,** *n.*

re′cent (rē′sənt) *adj.* happening, done, or made lately.

re·cep′ta·cle (ri sep′tə kəl) *n.* a container.

re·cep′tion (ri sep′shən) *n.* **1.** the act of receiving. **2.** the fact or manner of being received. **3.** a social function.

re·cep′tion·ist *n.* a person who receives callers in an office.

re·cep′tive (-tiv) *adj.* quick to understand and consider ideas.

re·cep′tor (-tər) *n.* a nerve ending that is sensitive to stimuli.

re·cess′ (ri ses′, rē′ses) *n.* **1.** a temporary cessation of work. **2.** an alcove. **3. recesses,** an inner part. —*v.i.* **4.** to take a recess. —*v.t.* **5.** to make a recess in.

re·ces′sion (-sesh′ən) *n.* **1.** an economic decline. **2.** a withdrawing procession.

re·ces′sive (-ses′iv) *adj.* receding.

re·cher·ché (rə shâr′shā, rə shâr·shā′) *adj.* **1.** very rare or choice. **2.** affectedly refined.

re·cid′i·vism (ri sid′ə viz′əm) *n.* repeated or habitual relapse, as into crime. —**re·cid′i·vist,** *n., adj.*

rec′i·pe (res′ə pē) *n.* instructions for preparing food or drink.

re·cip′i·ent (ri sip′ē ənt) *n.* **1.** one who receives. —*adj.* **2.** receiving.

re·cip′ro·cal (ri sip′rə kəl) *adj.* given and received in return; mutual. —**re·cip′ro·cal·ly,** *adv.*

re·cip·ro·cate' (-kāt') v.i., v.t., -cated, -cating. 1. to give, feel, etc., in return. 2. to move alternately backward and forward. —re·cip/ro·ca'tion, n.

rec/i·proc/i·ty (res'ə pros'i tē) n. mutual exchange.

re·cit/al (ri sīt'l) n. a musical or dance performance.

rec/i·ta·tive/ (res'i tə tēv') n. a style of vocal music intermediate between speaking and singing.

re·cite' (ri sīt') v.t., v.i., -cited, -citing. 1. to repeat (something) from memory. 2. to narrate (something) in detail.

reck/less (rek/lis) adj. heedless of danger or consequences; careless.

reck/on (rek'ən) v.t. 1. to calculate. 2. to regard as; esteem. 3. Informal. to suppose. 4. reckon with, to deal with.

reck/on·ing n. 1. a settling of accounts. 2. navigational calculation.

re·claim' (rē klām') v.t. to make usable, as land. —rec/la·ma'tion (rek/lə mā'shən) n.

re·cline' (ri klīn') v.i., v.t., -clined, -clining. to lean or cause to lean back.

re·clin/er n. a chair with an adjustable back and footrest.

rec/luse (rek/loōs, ri kloōs') n. a person living in seclusion.

re·cog·ni·zance (ri kog/nə zəns, -kon/ə-) n. a bond pledging one to do a particular act.

rec/og·nize/ (rek/əg nīz') v.t., -nized, -nizing. 1. to identify from previous knowledge. 2. to acknowledge formally. 3. to greet. —rec/og·ni/tion (-nish/ən) n.

re·coil' (rē koil') v.i. 1. to shrink back. 2. to spring back. —n. 3. the act of recoiling.

rec/ol·lect/ (rek/ə lekt') v.t., v.i. to remember. —rec/ol·lec/tion, n.

rec/om·mend/ (rek/ə mend') v.t. 1. to present as worthy. 2. to advise. —rec/om·men·da/tion, n.

rec/om·pense/ (rek/əm pens') v., -pensed, -pensing. —v.t. 1. to repay or reward for services, injury, etc. —n. 2. such compensation.

rec/on·cile/ (rek/ən sīl') v.t., -ciled, -ciling. 1. to bring into agreement. 2. to restore to friendliness. —rec/on·cil/i·a/tion (-sil/ē ā/shən) n.

rec/on·dite (rek/ən dīt') adj. 1. very profound or difficult; abstruse. 2. known by a few; esoteric.

re·con/nais·sance (ri kon/ə səns, -zəns) n. a survey of enemy territory.

re/con·noi·ter (rē/kə noi/tər, rek/ə-) v.t., v.i. to make a reconnaissance (of).

re·cord' v.t. (ri kôrd') 1. to set down in writing. 2. to register for mechanical reproduction. —n. (rek/ərd) 3. what is recorded. 4. a disk on which sound is recorded. 5. the best yet attained. —adj. (rek/ərd) 6. best. —Idiom. 7. off the record, not for publication. —re·cord/ing, n.

re·cord/er n. 1. a person who records. 2. a recording device. 3. a flute with eight finger holes.

re·count (rē kount') v.t. 1. to count again. —n. (rē/kount') 2. a second count. Also, **re-count**.

re·count' (ri kount') v.t. to narrate.

re·coup' (ri kōōp') v.t. to recover; make up.

re/course (rē/kôrs, ri kôrs') n. a source of help.

re·cov/er (ri kuv/ər) v.t. 1. to get back. 2. to reclaim. —v.i. 3. to regain health. —re·cov/er·a·ble, adj. —recov/er·y, n.

re/-cre·ate/ (rē/krē āt') v.t., re-created, re-creating. to create anew.

rec/re·a/tion (rek/rē ā/shən) n. 1. mental or physical refreshment after work. 2. a means of enjoyable relaxation. —rec/re·a/tion·al, adj.

re·crim/i·nate/ (ri krim/ə nāt') v.t., -nated, -nating. to accuse in return. —re·crim/i·na/tion, n.

re·cruit' (-krōōt') n. 1. a new member, esp. of the armed forces. —v.t. 2. to enlist. —re·cruit/ment, n.

rec/tan·gle (rek/tang/gəl) n. a parallelogram with four right angles. —rec·tan/gu·lar (-tang/gyə lər) adj.

rec/ti·fy/ (rek/tə fī') v.t., -fied, -fying. to correct. —rec/ti·fi/a·ble, adj. —rec/ti·fi·ca/tion, n.

rec/ti·lin/e·ar (rek/tl in/ē ər) adj. 1. forming a straight line. 2. formed by straight lines.

rec/ti·tude/ (rek/ti tōōd', -tyōōd') n. moral rightness.

rec/tor (rek/tər) n. 1. a member of the clergy in charge of a parish. 2. the head of some universities or schools.

rec/to·ry n., pl. -ries. a rector's house.

rec/tum (rek/təm) n. the lowest part of the intestine. —rec/tal, adj.

re·cum/bent (ri kum/bənt) adj. lying down. —re·cum/ben·cy, n.

re·cu/per·ate/ (ri kōō/pə rāt') v.i., -ated, -ating. to regain health. —re·cu/per·a/tion, n.

re·cur' (ri kûr') v.i., -curred, -curring. 1. to occur again. 2. to return in thought. —re·cur/rence, n. —re·cur/rent, adj.

re·cy/cle (rē sī/kəl) v.t., v.i., -cled, -cling. 1. to treat (refuse) to extract reusable material. **2.** to use again with minimal change.

red (red) *n., adj.,* **redder, reddest.** —*n.* **1.** the color of blood. **2.** (*often cap.*) a communist. —*adj.* **3.** of or like red. **4.** (*often cap.*) communist. —**red′den,** *v.t., v.i.* —**red′dish,** *adj.*

red′ blood′ cell′ *n.* a blood cell that contains hemoglobin and carries oxygen.

red′cap′ *n.* a baggage porter.

re•deem′ (ri dēm′) *v.t.* **1.** to pay off. **2.** to recover. **3.** to fulfill. **4.** to deliver from sin by sacrifice. —**re•deem′er,** *n.* —**re•demp′tion** (-demp′shən) *n.*

red′-hand′ed *adj., adv.* in the act of wrongdoing.

red′head′ *n.* a person with red hair. —**red′head′ed,** *adj.*

red′ her′ring *n.* something intended to distract attention from the real problem or issue.

red′-hot′ *adj.* **1.** red with heat. **2.** furious. **3.** very fresh or new.

re•di•al *v.t.* (rē dī′əl, -dīl′) **1.** to dial again. —*n.* (rē′dī′əl, -dīl′) **2.** a telephone function that automatically redials the last number called. **3.** a button that performs this function.

red′-let′ter *adj.* memorable.

red′lin′ing *n.* refusal by banks to grant mortgages in specified urban areas.

red′o•lent (red′l ənt) *adj.* **1.** odorous. **2.** suggestive.

re•doubt′ (ri dout′) *n.* a small isolated fort.

re•doubt′a•ble *adj.* evoking fear or respect.

re•dound′ (ri dound′) *v.i.* **1.** to have an effect. **2.** to result. **3.** to reflect upon a person.

re•dress′ *v.t.* (ri dress′) **1.** to set right (a wrong). —*n.* (rē′dres) **2.** the act of redressing.

red′ tape′ *n.* bureaucratic routine.

re•duce′ (ri dōōs′, -dyōōs′) *v.t.,* **-duced, -ducing. 1.** to make less in size, rank, etc. **2.** to put into a simpler form or state. —*v.i.* **3.** to lose weight. —**re•duc′i•ble,** *adj.* —**re•duc′tion** (-duk′shən) *n.*

re•dun′dant (ri dun′dənt) *adj.* **1.** excessive; superfluous. **2.** wordy. —**re•dun′dance, re•dun′dan•cy,** *n.*

red′wood′ (red′wŏŏd′) *n.* a huge evergreen tree of California.

reed (rēd) *n.* **1.** a tall marsh grass. **2.** a small piece of cane or metal at the mouth of a wind instrument.

reef (rēf) *n.* a narrow ridge near the surface of water.

reek (rēk) *v.i.* **1.** to smell strongly and unpleasantly. —*n.* **2.** such a smell.

reel¹ (rēl) *n.* **1.** a turning device for winding up cord or film. —*v.t.* **2.** to wind on a reel. **3.** **reel off,** to say fluently and quickly.

reel² (rēl) *v.i.* **1.** to sway or stagger. **2.** to whirl.

reel³ (rēl) *n.* a lively Scottish dance.

re•en′try (rē en′trē) *n., pl.* **-tries. 1.** a second entry. **2.** a return into the earth's atmosphere.

ref (ref) *n., v.t., v.i.,* **reffed, ref•fing** referee.

re•fec′to•ry (ri fek′tə rē) *n., pl.* **-ries.** a dining hall.

re•fer′ (ri fûr′) *v.,* **-ferred, -ferring.** —*v.t.* **1.** to direct for information or aid. —*v.i.* **2.** to direct attention. **3.** to have recourse, as for information. **4.** to make reference. —**re•fer′ral,** *n.*

ref′er•ee′ (ref′ə rē′) *n.* **-ees,** *v.* **-eed, -eeing.** —*n.* **1.** a judge. —*v.t., v.i.* **2.** to preside over or act as referee.

ref′er•ence (ref′ər əns) *n.* **1.** the act or fact of referring. **2.** something referred to. **3.** a person from whom one seeks a recommendation. **4.** a statement regarding a person's character or abilities.

ref′er•en′dum (ref′ə ren′dəm) *n., pl.* **-dums, -da.** the referring of a legislative measure to the vote of the electorate.

re•fill′ *v.t., v.i.* (rē fil′) **1.** to fill again. —*n.* (rē′fil′) **2.** a second filling.

re•fine′ (ri fīn′) *v.t.,* **-fined, -fining. 1.** to free from impurities or error. **2.** to teach good manners, taste, etc. —**re•fine′ment,** *n.*

re•fin′er•y *n., pl.* **-eries.** an establishment for refining.

re•flect′ (ri flekt′) *v.t.* **1.** to cast back. **2.** to show; mirror. **3.** to bring (credit or discredit) on one. —*v.i.* **4.** to think. —**re•flec′tion,** *n.* —**re•flec′tive,** *adj.* —**re•flec′tor,** *n.*

re′flex (rē′fleks) *adj.* **1.** denoting involuntary action. **2.** bent. —*n.* **3.** an involuntary movement.

re•flex′ive *adj.* **1.** (of a verb) having the same subject and object. **2.** (of a pronoun) showing identity with the subject.

re•form′ (rē fôrm′) *n.* **1.** the improvement of what is wrong. —*v.t., v.i.* **2.** to change for the better. —**re•form′er,** *n.* —**ref′or•ma′tion** (ref′ər mā′shən) *n.*

re•form′a•to•ry (ri fôr′mə tôr′ē) *n., pl.* **-ries.** a prison for young offenders.

re•frac′tion (ri frak′shən) *n.* the change of direction of light or heat rays in passing to another medium. —**re•fract′,** *v.t.* —**re•frac′tive,** *adj.*

re•frac′to•ry *adj.* stubborn.

re·frain'¹ (ri frān') *v.i.* to keep oneself from doing or saying something.

re·frain'² (ri frān') *n.* a recurring passage in a song or poem.

re·fresh' (ri fresh') *v.t.* **1.** to give new vigor and energy to. **2.** to stimulate. —**re·fresh'ing,** *adj.*

re·fresh'ment *n.* **1.** something that refreshes. **2.** refreshments, food and drink for a light meal. **3.** a refreshing or being refreshed.

re·frig'er·ate' (ri frij'ə rāt') *v.t.,* **-ated, -ating.** to make or keep cold. —**re·frig'er·ant** (-ə rənt) *adj., n.* —**re·frig'er·a'tion,** *n.*

re·frig'er·a'tor *n.* a cabinet for keeping food cold.

ref'uge (ref'yōōj) *n.* (a place giving) shelter from danger.

ref'u·gee' (ref'yōō jē') *n.* a person who flees for safety.

re·ful'gent (ri ful'jənt) *adj.* shining brightly. —**re·ful'gence,** *n.*

re·fund' (ri fund') *v.t.* **1.** to give back (money). —*n.* (rē'fund) **2.** the act of refunding. **3.** an amount refunded. —**re·fund'a·ble,** *adj.*

re·fur'bish (rē fûr'bish) *v.t.* to renovate.

re·fuse'¹ (ri fyōōz') *v.t., v.i.,* **-fused, -fus·ing.** to decline to accept, give, or do (something). —**re·fus'al,** *n.*

ref·use'² (ref'yōōs) *n.* rubbish.

re·fute' (ri fyōōt') *v.t.,* **-futed, -futing.** to prove wrong. —**ref'u·ta'tion,** *n.*

re·gain' (rē gān') *v.t.* to get again.

re'gal (rē'gəl) *adj.* royal.

re·gale' (ri gāl') *v.t.,* **-galed, -galing.** to entertain grandly.

re·ga'lia (-gāl'yə) *n.pl.* emblems of royalty, office, etc.

re·gard' (-gärd') *v.t.* **1.** to look upon in a particular way. **2.** to respect. **3.** to look at. **4.** to concern. —*n.* **5.** reference; relation. **6.** attention. **7.** respect and liking.

re·gard'ing *prep.* concerning.

re·gard'less *adv.* **1.** despite everything. —*adj.* **2.** unmindful.

re·gat'ta (ri gat'ə, -gä'tə) *n.* an organized series of boat races.

re·gen'er·ate' (ri jen'ə rāt') *v.,* **-ated, -ating.** —*v.t.* **1.** to give new life or spiritual vigor to. —*v.i.* **2.** to form anew. —**re·gen'er·a'tion,** *n.* —**re·gen'er·a'tive,** *adj.*

re'gent (rē'jənt) *n.* **1.** a person ruling in place of a monarch. **2.** a university governor. —**re'gen·cy,** *n.*

reg'i·cide' (rej'ə sīd') *n.* **1.** the act of killing a king. **2.** a person who kills a king.

re·gime' (rə zhēm', rā-) *n.* a system of rule.

reg'i·men (rej'ə mən) *n.* a regulated course of diet, exercise, etc., for health.

reg'i·ment *n.* (rej'ə mənt) **1.** an infantry unit. —*v.t.* (rej'ə ment') **2.** to subject to strict, uniform discipline. —**reg'i·men'tal,** *adj.*

re'gion (rē'jən) *n.* an area; district. —**re'gion·al,** *adj.*

re'gion·al·ism *n.* a feature peculiar to a geographical region.

reg'is·ter (rej'ə stər) *n.* **1.** a written list; record. **2.** the range of a voice or instrument. **3.** a device for controlling the passage of warm air. —*v.t.* **4.** to enter in a register. **5.** to show. —*v.i.* **6.** to enter oneself on a list of voters. —**reg'is·tra'tion** (-strā'shən) *n.*

reg'is·trar (-strär') *n.* an official recorder.

reg'is·try *n., pl.* **-tries. 1.** registration. **2.** a place where a register is kept. **3.** an official record.

re·gress' (ri gres') *v.i.* to return to a previous, inferior state. —**re·gres'sion,** *n.* —**re·gres'sive,** *adj.*

re·gret' (-gret') *v.,* **-gretted, -gretting,** *n.* —*v.t.* **1.** to feel sorry about. —*n.* **2.** a feeling of loss or sorrow. —**re·gret'ta·ble,** *adj.* —**re·gret'ful,** *adj.*

reg'u·lar (reg'yə lər) *adj.* **1.** usual. **2.** evenly or uniformly arranged. **3.** recurring at fixed times. **4.** orderly. **5.** (of verbs) having normal inflections. **6.** denoting a permanent army. —*n.* **7.** a regular soldier. **8.** a long-standing customer. —**reg'u·lar'i·ty,** *n.* —**reg'u·lar·ize',** *v.t.*

reg'u·late' (-lāt') *v.t.,* **-lated, -lating. 1.** to control by rule, method, etc. **2.** to adjust. —**reg'u·la·to'ry** (-lə tôr'ē) *adj.*

reg'u·la'tion *n.* **1.** the act of regulating. **2.** a rule.

re·gur'gi·tate' (ri gûr'ji tāt') *v.t.,* **-tated, -tating.** to bring up from the stomach.

re'ha·bil'i·tate' (rē'hə bil'i tāt', rē'ə-) *v.t.,* **-tated, -tating.** to restore to health or good condition. —**re'ha·bil'i·ta'tion,** *n.*

re·hash' *v.t.* (rē hash') **1.** to rework or reuse in a new form without significant change. —*n.* (rē'hash') **2.** the act of rehashing. **3.** something rehashed.

re·hearse' (ri hûrs') *v.t., v.i.,* **-hearsed, -hearsing.** to practice (a play, music, etc.) before performance. —**re·hears'al,** *n.*

reign (rān) *n.* **1.** (the period of) royal rule. —*v.i.* **2.** to have sovereign power or title.

re·im·burse' (rē'im bûrs') *v.t.,*

-bursed, -bursing. to repay, as for expenses. —re′im•burse′ment, n.

rein (rān) n. a narrow strap fastened to the bridle for controlling an animal.

re′in•car•na′tion (rē′in kär nā′shən) n. the continuation of the soul after death in a new body.

rein′deer′ (rān′dēr′) n. a large arctic deer.

re′in•force′ (rē′in fôrs′) v.t., -forced, -forcing. to strengthen with support, troops, etc. —re′in•force′ment, n.

re′in•state′ (rē′in stāt′) v.t., -stated, -stating. to put back into a former position or state.

re•it′er•ate′ (-it′ə rāt′) v.t., -ated, -ating. to repeat. —re•it′er•a′tion, n.

re•ject′ v.t. (ri jekt′) 1. to refuse or discard. —n. (rē′jekt) 2. something rejected. —re•jec′tion, n.

re•joice′ (ri jois′) v.i., -joiced, -joicing. to be glad.

re•join′ (-join′) v.t. 1. to answer. 2. to join again.

re•join′der (-dər) n. a response.

re•ju′ve•nate′ (ri jōō′və nāt′) v.t., -nated, -nating. to make young again.

re•lapse′ v., -lapsed, -lapsing, n. —v.i. (ri laps′) 1. to fall back into a former state or practice. 2. to fall back into illness after apparent recovery. —n. (ri laps′, rē′laps) 3. an act or instance of relapsing.

re•late′ (ri lāt′) v., -lated, -lating. —v.t. 1. to tell. 2. to connect in thought or meaning. —v.i. 3. to have relation. 4. to establish a sympathetic relationship.

re•lat′ed adj. 1. associated. 2. connected by blood or marriage.

re•la′tion n. 1. connection. 2. a relative. 3. the act of relating. —re•la′tion•ship′, n.

rel′a•tive (rel′ə tiv) n. 1. a person connected with another by blood or marriage. —adj. 2. comparative.

rel′a•tiv′i•ty n. the principle that time, mass, etc., are relative, not absolute, concepts.

re•lax′ (ri laks′) v.t., v.i. 1. to make or become less tense, firm, etc. 2. to rest from work. —re′lax•a′tion (rē′lak sā′shən) n.

re′lay (rē′lā) n. 1. a fresh supply of persons, animals, etc., to relieve others. —v.t. 2. to receive and carry forward.

re•lease′ (ri lēs′) v., -leased, -leasing, n. —v.t. 1. to let go. —n. 2. an act or instance of releasing.

rel′e•gate′ (rel′i gāt′) v.t., -gated, -gating. 1. to consign to an inferior position. 2. to turn over.

re•lent′ (ri lent′) v.i. to become more mild or forgiving. —re•lent′less, adj.

rel′e•vant (rel′ə vənt) adj. having to do with the matter in question.

re•li′a•ble (ri lī′ə bəl) adj. trustworthy. —re•li′a•bil′i•ty, n.

re•li′ance (-əns) n. 1. trust; dependence. 2. confidence. —re•li′ant, adj.

rel′ic (rel′ik) n. 1. an object surviving from the past. 2. a personal memorial of a sacred person.

re•lief′¹ (ri lēf′) n. 1. alleviation of pain or distress. 2. help given to poor people. 3. a pleasing change.

re•lief′² (ri lēf′) n. projection of a figure from its background, as in sculpture.

re•lieve′ (ri lēv′) v.t., -lieved, -lieving. 1. to ease. 2. to break the sameness of. 3. to discharge from duty.

re•li′gion (ri lij′ən) n. 1. belief in and worship of a God or other superhuman agency. 2. a particular system of these beliefs.

re•li′gious adj. 1. of religion. 2. pious; devout. 3. conscientious.

re•lin′quish (ri ling′kwish) v.t. to give up; surrender.

rel′i•quar′y (rel′i kwer′ē) n., pl. -ies. a receptacle for religious relics.

rel′ish (rel′ish) n. 1. enjoyment or liking. 2. something savory. —v.t. 3. to take enjoyment in.

re•live′ (rē liv′) v.t., -lived, -living. to experience again.

re•lo′cate v.t., v.i., -cated, -cating. to move. —re′lo•ca′tion, n.

re•luc′tant (ri luk′tənt) adj. unwilling. —re•luc′tance, n.

re•ly′ (ri lī′) v.i., -lied, -lying. to depend confidently.

REM (rem) n. quick, darting movement of the eyes during sleep.

re•main′ (ri mān′) v.i. 1. to continue to be. 2. to stay; be left. —n. remains, 3. that which remains. 4. a corpse.

re•main′der (-dər) n. that which is left over.

re•mand′ (ri mand′) v.t. to send back, as to a lower court of law.

re•mark′ (ri märk′) v.t. 1. to say casually. 2. to note; observe. —v.i. 3. to make a comment. —n. 4. notice or mention. 5. a casual comment.

re•mark′a•ble adj. extraordinary.

rem′e•dy (rem′i dē) v., -died, -dying, n., pl. -dies. —v.t. 1. to cure or alleviate. 2. to correct. —n. 3. something that remedies. —re•me′di•al, adj.

re•mem′ber (ri mem′bər) v.t. 1. to recall to or retain in memory. 2. to mention (a person) to another as sending greetings. —*v.i.* **3.** to recall something to memory. —**re•mem′•brance** (-brəns) *n.*

re•mind′ (ri mīnd′) *v.t.* to cause to remember. —**re•mind′er**, *n.*

rem′i•nisce′ (rem′ə nis′) *v.i.*, **-nisced, -niscing.** to recall past experiences. —**rem′i•nis′cence**, *n.* —**rem′i•nis′cent**, *adj.*

re•miss′ (ri mis′) *adj.* negligent.

re•mis′sion *n.* **1.** the act of forgiving. **2.** a period when symptoms of disease subside.

re•mit′ (-mit′) *v.t.*, **-mitted, -mitting. 1.** to send (money), usu. in payment. **2.** to pardon. **3.** to slacken; abate.

re•mit′tance *n.* money sent.

rem′nant (rem′nənt) *n.* **1.** a small remaining part. **2.** a trace.

re•mod′el (rē mod′l) *v.t.*, **-eled, -eling.** to alter in structure or form.

re•mon′strate (ri mon′strāt) *v.t.*, *v.i.*, **-strated, -strating.** to protest; plead in protest.

re•morse′ (ri môrs′) *n.* regret for wrongdoing. —**re•morse′ful**, *adj.* —**re•morse′less**, *adj.*

re•mote′ (ri mōt′) *adj.* **1.** far distant. **2.** faint. —*n.* **3.** a remote control (def. 2). —**re•mote′ly**, *adv.*

remote′ control′ *n.* **1.** control of an apparatus from a distance, as by radio signals. **2.** a device used for such control.

re•move′ (ri moov′) *v.*, **-moved, -moving,** *n.* —*v.t.* **1.** to take away or off. **2.** to move to another place. —*n.* **3.** a distance of separation. —**re•mov′al**, *n.* —**re•mov′a•ble**, *adj.*

re•mu′ner•ate′ (-myoo′nə rāt′) *v.t.*, **-ated, -ating.** to pay for work, services, etc. —**re•mu′ner•a′tion**, *n.*

ren′ais•sance′ (ren′ə säns′) *n.* **1.** a revival. **2. Renaissance,** a cultural period of the 14th-17th centuries marked by a great revival of interest in art, literature, and learning.

re′nal (rēn′l) *adj.* of the kidneys.

rend (rend) *v.t.* **1.** to tear apart. **2.** to disturb with noise. **3.** to distress.

ren′der *v.t.* **1.** to cause to be. **2.** to do, show, or furnish. **3.** to perform. **4.** to give back. **5.** to melt (fat).

ren′dez•vous′ (rän′də voo′, -dā-) *n.*, *pl.* **-vous.** an appointment or place to meet.

ren•di′tion (ren dish′ən) *n.* **1.** the act of rendering. **2.** a translation or interpretation, as of a role.

ren′e•gade′ (ren′i gād′) *n.* a deserter.

re•nege′ (ri nig′, -neg′) *v.i.*, **-neged, -neging.** to break a promise.

re•new′ (ri noo′, -nyoo′) *v.t.* **1.** to begin or do again. **2.** to make like new; replenish. **3.** to extend for an additional period. —**re•new′al**, *n.*

ren′net (ren′it) *n.* **1.** a membrane lining the stomach of a calf or other animal. **2.** a preparation of this used in making cheese.

re•nounce′ (ri nouns′) *v.t.*, **-nounced, -nouncing.** to give up voluntarily. —**re•nounce′ment**, *n.*

ren′o•vate′ (ren′ə vāt′) *v.t.*, **-vated, -vating.** to restore to good condition.

re•nown′ (ri noun′) *n.* fame. —**re•nowned′**, *adj.*

rent¹ (rent) *n.* **1.** a payment for the use of property. —*v.t.* **2.** to grant or have use of in return for rent. —*v.i.* **3.** to be leased for rent. —**rent′er**, *n.*

rent² (rent) *n.* a tear made by rending.

rent′al *n.* **1.** an amount given or received as rent. **2.** the act of renting. **3.** property rented.

re•nun′ci•a′tion (ri nun′sē ā′shən, -shē-) *n.* the act of renouncing.

Rep. 1. Representative. **2.** Republic. **3.** Republican.

re•pair′¹ (ri pâr′) *v.t.* **1.** to restore to sound condition. **2.** to remedy. —*n.* **3.** an act or instance of repairing. **4.** condition with respect to soundness.

re•pair′² (ri pâr′) *v.i.* to go.

rep′a•ra′tion (rep′ə rā′shən) *n.* amends for injury or damage.

rep′ar•tee′ (rep′ər tē′, -tā′, -är-) *n.* an exchange of wit; banter.

re•past′ (ri past′) *n.* a meal.

re•pa′tri•ate′ (rē pā′trē āt′) *v.t.*, **-ated, -ating.** to send back to one's native country.

re•pay′ (ri pā′) *v.t.*, **-paid, -paying.** to pay back. —**re•pay′ment**, *n.*

re•peal′ (ri pēl′) *v.t.* **1.** to revoke officially. —*n.* **2.** the act of repealing.

re•peat′ (ri pēt′) *v.t.* **1.** to say, tell, or do again. —*n.* **2.** the act of repeating. **3.** something repeated.

re•peat′ed *adj.* said or done again and again. —**re•peat′ed•ly**, *adv.*

re•pel′ (ri pel′) *v.t.*, **-pelled, -pelling. 1.** to drive back; thrust away. **2.** to arouse disgust or aversion in. —**re•pel′lent**, *adj.*, *n.*

re•pent′ (ri pent′) *v.i.*, *v.t.* to feel contrite or penitent (for). —**re•pent′ance**, *n.* —**re•pent′ant**, *adj.*

re′per•cus′sion (rē′pər kush′ən) *n.* **1.** an indirect result. **2.** an echo.

rep′er•toire′ (rep′ər twär′, -twôr′, rep′ə-) *n.* a group of works that a performer or company can perform. Also, **rep′er•to′ry.**

rep′e•ti′tion (rep′ə tish′ən) *n.* **1.** the act of repeating. **2.** something repeated. —**rep′e•ti′tious,** *adj.* —**re•pet′i•tive** (ri pet′ə tiv) *adj.*

repet′itive strain′ in′jury *n.* a debilitating disorder, esp. of the hand or arm, caused by the stress of repeated movements. Also, **repet′itive strain′ disor′der.**

re•pine′ (ri pīn′) *v.i.,* -**pined, -pining. 1.** to complain. **2.** to yearn.

re•place′ (ri plās′) *v.t.,* -**placed, -placing. 1.** to take the place of. **2.** to provide a substitute for. **3.** to put back.

re•play′ *v.t.* (rē plā′) **1.** to play again. —*n.* (rē′ plā) **2.** the act of replaying. **3.** something replayed.

re•plen′ish (ri plen′ish) *v.t.* to make full again.

re•plete′ (ri plēt′) *adj.* abundantly filled. —**re•ple′tion,** *n.*

rep′li•ca (rep′li kə) *n.* a copy.

rep′li•cate (-kāt′) *v.t.,* -**cated, -cating. 3.** to duplicate or reproduce.

re•ply′ (ri plī′) *v.,* -**plied, -plying,** *n., pl.* -**plies.** —*v.i., v.t.* **1.** to give or return as an answer. —*n.* **2.** an answer.

re•port′ (ri pôrt′) *n.* **1.** a statement of events or findings. **2.** rumor. **3.** a loud noise. —*v.t.* **4.** to tell of. **5.** to inform against. —*v.i.* **6.** to present oneself.

re•port′er *n.* **1.** one who reports. **2.** a person employed to gather and report news.

re•pose′ (ri pōz′) *n., v.,* -**posed, -posing.** —*n.* **1.** rest or sleep. **2.** tranquility. —*v.i.* **3.** to rest or sleep. —**re•pose′ful,** *adj.*

re•pos′i•tor′y (ri poz′i tôr′ē) *n., pl.* -**tories.** a place where things are stored.

re′pos•sess′ (rē′pə zes′) *v.t.* to take back.

rep′re•hen′si•ble (rep′rə hen′sə bəl) *adj.* blameworthy.

rep′re•sent′ (rep′ri zent′) *v.t.* **1.** to act or speak for. **2.** to portray. **3.** to express. —**rep′re•sen•ta′tion,** *n.*

rep′re•sent′a•tive (-zen′tə tiv) *n.* **1.** one that represents another. **2.** a member of a legislative body. —*adj.* **3.** representing. **4.** typical.

re•press′ (ri pres′) *v.t.* **1.** to inhibit. **2.** to suppress. —**re•pres′sive,** *adj.* —**re•pres′sion,** *n.*

re•prieve′ (ri prēv′) *v.,* -**prieved, -prieving,** *n.* —*v.t.* **1.** to delay the punishment of. —*n.* **2.** a delay in punishment. **3.** a respite.

rep′ri•mand′ (rep′rə mand′) *n.* **1.** severe criticism. —*v.t.* **2.** to scold or criticize severely.

re•pris′al (ri prī′zəl) *n.* infliction of injuries in retaliation.

re•proach′ (ri prōch′) *v.t.* **1.** to blame or censure. —*n.* **2.** blame; discredit. —**re•proach′ful,** *adj.*

rep′ro•bate′ (rep′rə bāt′) *n.* **1.** a hopelessly bad person. —*adj.* **2.** morally corrupt.

re′pro•duce′ (rē′prə dōōs′, -dyōōs′) *v.,* -**duced, -ducing.** —*v.t.* **1.** to copy or duplicate. **2.** to produce (new individuals). —*v.i.* **3.** to bear offspring. —**re′pro•duc′tion** (-duk′shən) *n.* —**re′pro•duc′tive,** *adj.*

re•proof′ (ri prōōf′) *n.* an act of reproving.

re•prove′ (-prōōv′) *v.t.,* -**proved, -proving.** to criticize or censure.

rep′tile (rep′til, -tīl) *n.* a scaly, air-breathing animal, as a snake.

re•pub′lic (ri pub′lik) *n.* a state governed by representatives elected by citizens.

re•pub′li•can *adj.* **1.** of or favoring a republic. **2. Republican,** of the **Republican Party,** one of two major political parties in the U.S. —*n.* **3. Republican,** a member of the Republican Party.

re•pu′di•ate′ (ri pyōō′dē āt′) *v.t.,* -**ated, -ating.** to reject as worthless, not binding, or false.

re•pug′nant (ri pug′nənt) *adj.* objectionable; offensive. —**re•pug′nance,** *n.*

re•pulse′ *v.,* -**pulsed, -pulsing,** *n.* —*v.t.* **1.** to drive back with force. —*n.* **2.** the act of repulsing. **3.** a rejection. —**re•pul′sion,** *n.*

re•pul′sive *adj.* disgusting.

rep′u•ta•ble (rep′yə tə bəl) *adj.* of good reputation.

rep′u•ta′tion (-tā′shən) *n.* **1.** a public estimation of character. **2.** good name.

re•pute′ (ri pyōōt′) *n., v.,* -**puted, -puting.** —*n.* **1.** reputation. —*v.t.* **2.** to consider; believe.

re•quest′ (ri kwest′) *v.t.* **1.** to ask for. —*n.* **2.** the act of requesting. **3.** what is requested.

req′ui•em (rek′wē əm) *n.* a mass for the dead or a musical setting of this.

re•quire′ (ri kwīᵊr′) *v.t.,* -**quired, -quiring. 1.** to need. **2.** to demand. —**re•quire′ment,** *n.*

req′ui•site (rek′wə zit) *adj.* **1.** necessary. —*n.* **2.** a necessary thing.

req′ui•si′tion (-zish′ən) *n.* **1.** a formal order or demand. —*v.t.* **2.** to take for official use.

re•quite′ (ri kwīt′) *v.t.,* -**quited, -quiting.** to give or do in return. —**re•quit′al** (-kwī′təl) *n.*

re′run′ (rē′run′) *n.* **1.** the showing of a motion picture or television program after its initial run. **2.** the program shown.

re•scind/ (ri sind/) *v.t.* to repeal.

res/cue (res/kyōō) *v.,* **-cued, -cuing,** *n.* —*v.t.* **1.** to free from danger, capture, etc. —*n.* **2.** the act of rescuing.

re•search/ (ri sûrch/, rē/sûrch) *n.* **1.** diligent investigation. —*v.i., v.t.* **2.** to investigate carefully.

re•sem/ble (ri zem/bəl) *v.t.,* **-bled, -bling.** to be similar to. —**re•sem/- blance,** *n.*

re•sent/ (ri zent/) *v.t.* to feel indignation or displeasure at. —**re• sent/ful,** *adj.* —**re•sent/ment,** *n.*

res/er•va/tion (rez/ər vā/shən) *n.* **1.** the act of withholding or setting apart. **2.** a particular doubt or misgiving. **3.** an advance assurance of accommodations. **4.** land for the use of an American Indian tribe.

re•serve/ (ri zûrv/) *v.,* **-served, -serving,** *n., adj.* —*v.t.* **1.** to keep back or set aside. —*n.* **2.** something reserved. **3.** part of a military force held in readiness to support active forces. **4.** reticence. —*adj.* **5.** kept in reserve.

re•served/ *adj.* **1.** held for future use. **2.** self-restrained.

re•serv/ist *n.* a member of the military reserves.

res/er•voir/ (rez/ər vwär/, -vwôr/, rez/ə-) *n.* **1.** a place where water is stored for use. **2.** a supply.

re•side/ (ri zīd/) *v.i.,* **-sided, -siding. 1.** to dwell. **2.** to be vested, as powers.

res/i•dence (rez/i dəns) *n.* **1.** a dwelling place. **2.** the act or fact of residing. —**res/i•dent,** *n.* —**res/i• den/tial** (-den/shəl) *adj.*

res/i•den•cy *n., pl.* **-cies. 1.** residence (def. 2). **2.** a period of advanced medical training.

res/i•due/ (-dōō/, -dyōō/) *n.* a part remaining. —**re•sid/u•al** (ri zij/ōō-əl) *adj.*

re•sign/ (ri zīn/) *v.t., v.i.* **1.** to give up (a job, right, etc.), esp. formally. **2.** to submit, as to fate or force.

re•signed/ *adj.* submissive or acquiescent.

re•sil/i•ent (-zil/yənt) *adj.* **1.** springing back. **2.** recovering readily from adversity. —**re•sil/i•ence,** *n.*

res/in (rez/in) *n.* a substance exuded from some plants, used in medicines, plastics, etc.

re•sist/ (ri zist/) *v.t., v.i.* to withstand; offer opposition (to). —**re• sist/ant,** *adj.*

re•sist/ance *n.* **1.** the act of resisting. **2.** the ability to resist disease. **3.** opposition to electric current.

re•sis/tor *n.* a device that introduces resistance into an electrical circuit.

res/o•lute/ (rez/ə lōōt/) *adj.* determined on an action or result.

res/o•lu/tion *n.* **1.** a formal expression of group opinion. **2.** determination. **3.** a solution of a problem.

re•solve/ (ri zolv/) *v.,* **-solved, -solving,** *n.* —*v.t.* **1.** to decide firmly. **2.** to state formally. **3.** to dispel. **4.** to solve. —*n.* **5.** resolution; determination.

res/o•nant (rez/ə nənt) *adj.* **1.** resounding. **2.** rich in sound.

res/o•nate (-nāt/) *v.i.,* **-nated, -nating.** to resound.

re•sort/ (ri zôrt/) *v.i.* **1.** to apply or turn (to) for use, help, etc. **2.** to go often. —*n.* **3.** a place much frequented, esp. for recreation. **4.** a source of help.

re•sound/ (-zound/) *v.i.* to ring with sound; sound loudly.

re•sound/ing *adj.* impressively complete. —**re•sound/ing•ly,** *adv.*

re/source (rē/sôrs, ri sôrs/) *n.* **1.** a source of aid or supply. **2. resources,** sources of wealth.

re•source/ful *adj.* able to deal with new situations or difficulties.

re•spect/ (ri spekt/) *n.* **1.** a detail; point. **2.** reference. **3.** esteem. —*v.t.* **4.** to hold in esteem.

re•spect/a•ble *adj.* **1.** worthy of respect. **2.** decent.

re•spect/ful *adj.* showing respect. —**re•spect/ful•ly,** *adv.*

re•spect/ing *prep.* concerning.

re•spec/tive *adj.* in the order previously named.

res/pi•ra/tion *n.* the act or process of breathing. —**res/pi•ra•to/ry** (-rə tôr/ē), *adj.*

res/pi•ra/tor (res/pə rā/tər) *n.* an apparatus to produce artificial breathing.

res/pite (res/pit) *n.* a temporary relief or delay.

re•splend/ent (-splen/dənt) *adj.* gleaming. —**re•splend/ence,** *n.*

re•spond/ (ri spond/) *v.i., v.t.* to answer or react.

re•spond/ent *n.* a defendant.

re•sponse/ (-spons/) *n.* a reply.

re•spon/si•bil/i•ty *n., pl.* **-ties. 1.** the state of being responsible. **2.** an obligation. **3.** initiative.

re•spon/si•ble *adj.* **1.** causing or allowing things to happen. **2.** capable of rational thought. **3.** reliable.

re•spon/sive *adj.* responding readily. —**re•spon/sive•ly,** *adv.*

rest¹ (rest) *n.* **1.** (a period of) quiet or sleep. **2.** inactivity after work or motion. **3.** *Music.* an interval of silence. **4.** a supporting device. —*v.i.* **5.** to refresh oneself. **6.** to cease from motion. **7.** to lie or lean. **8.** to be based or found. —*v.t.* **9.** to give rest to. **10.** to place for rest or support. —**rest′ful,** *adj.* —**rest′ful•ly,** *adv.*

rest[2] (rest) *n.* **1.** the remaining part. —*v.i.* **2.** to continue to be.

res′tau•rant (res′tər ənt, -tə ränt′) *n.* a public eating place.

res′tau•ra•teur′ (-tər ə tûr′) *n.* a restaurant owner.

res′ti•tu′tion (-ti tōō′shən, -tyōō′-) *n.* **1.** amends for damage. **2.** the return of rights, property, etc.

res′tive (-tiv) *adj.* restless.

rest′less *adj.* **1.** lacking rest. **2.** uneasy. **3.** always moving. —**rest′less•ly,** *adv.* —**rest′less•ness,** *n.*

re•store′ (ri stôr′) *v.t.,* **-stored, -storing. 1.** to bring back, as to use or good condition. **2.** to give back. —**res′to•ra′tion,** *n.* —**re•stor′a•tive,** *adj., n.*

re•strain′ (ri strān′) *v.t.* **1.** to hold back. **2.** to confine.

re•straint′ (-strānt′) *n.* **1.** a restraining influence. **2.** confinement. **3.** constraint.

re•strict′ (ri strikt′) *v.t.* to confine; limit. —**re•stric′tion,** *n.* —**re•stric′tive,** *adj.*

rest′ room′ *n.* a room in a public building with toilets and basins.

re•sult′ (ri zult′) *n.* **1.** an outcome; consequence. —*v.i.* **2.** to occur as a result. **3.** to end. —**re•sult′ant,** *adj., n.*

re•sume′ (ri zōōm′) *v.t., v.i.,* **-sumed, -suming.** to begin again after interruption. —**re•sump′tion** (-zump′shən) *n.*

ré′su•mé′ (rez′ōō mā′) *n.* a summary, esp. of a person's education and work.

re•sur′face (rē sûr′fis) *v.t.,* **-faced, -facing. 1.** to give a new surface to. **2.** to come to the surface again.

re•sur′gent (ri sûr′jənt) *adj.* rising again. —**re•sur′gence,** *n.*

res′ur•rect′ (rez′ə rekt′) *v.t.* to bring to life again. —**res′ur•rec′tion,** *n.*

re•sus′ci•tate′ (ri sus′i tāt′) *v.t.* to revive. —**re•sus′ci•ta′tion,** *n.*

re′tail (rē′tāl) *n.* **1.** the sale of goods to consumers. —*v.t., v.i.* **2.** to sell or be sold at a retail price. —**re′tail•er,** *n.*

re•tain′ (ri tān′) *v.t.* **1.** to keep or hold. **2.** to engage the services of.

re•tain′er *n.* **1.** a fee paid to secure services. **2.** an old servant.

re•take′ *v.,* **-took, -taken, -taking,** *n.* —*v.t.* **1.** to take again. **2.** to photograph again. —*n.* (rē′tāk) **3.** a picture photographed again.

re•tal′i•ate′ (ri tal′ē āt′) *v.i.,* **-ated, -ating.** to return like for like, esp. evil. —**re•tal′i•a′tion,** *n.* —**re•tal′i•a•to′ry** (-ə tôr′ē) *adj.*

re•tard′ (-tärd′) *v.t.* to delay.

re•tard′ed *adj.* slow or weak in mental development.

retch (rech) *v.i.* to try to vomit.

re•ten′tion (ri ten′shən) *n.* **1.** the act or power of retaining. **2.** memory. —**re•ten′tive,** *adj.*

ret′i•cent (ret′ə sənt) *adj.* saying little. —**ret′i•cence,** *n.*

ret′i•na (ret′n ə) *n.* a coating on the back part of the eyeball that receives images.

ret′i•nue′ (ret′n ōō′, -yōō′) *n.* a train of attendants.

re•tire′ (ri tī°r′) *v.,* **-tired, -tiring.** —*v.i.* **1.** to end one's working life. **2.** to withdraw. **3.** to go to bed. —*v.t.* **4.** to cause to retire. —**re•tire′ment,** *n.*

re•tired′ *adj.* withdrawn from office, occupation, etc.

re•tir•ee′ *n.* a person who has retired from work.

re•tir′ing *adj.* shy.

re•tort′[1] (ri tôrt′) *v.t.* **1.** to reply smartly. —*n.* **2.** a sharp or witty reply.

re•tort′[2] (ri tôrt′) *n.* a long-necked vessel used in distilling.

re•touch′ (rē tuch′) *v.t.* to touch up.

re•trace′ (rē trās′) *v.t.,* **-traced, -tracing.** to go back over.

re•tract′ (ri trakt′) *v.t.* to withdraw. —**re•trac′tion,** *n.* —**re•tract′a•ble,** *adj.*

re′tread′ (rē′tred′) *n.* a tire that has had new tread added.

re•treat′ (ri trēt′) *n.* **1.** a forced withdrawal. **2.** a private place. —*v.i.* **3.** to withdraw.

re•trench′ (ri trench′) *v.i.* to reduce expenses. —**re•trench′ment,** *n.*

ret′ri•bu′tion (re′trə byōō′shən) *n.* deserved punishment; retaliation.

re•trieve′ (ri trēv′) *v.t.,* **-trieved, -trieving. 1.** to regain or restore. **2.** to access in a computer.

ret′ro•ac′tive (re′trō ak′tiv) *adj.* applying also to the past.

ret′ro•fit′ *v.t.,* **-fitted, -fitting.** to furnish with newly developed equipment.

ret′ro•grade′ *adj.* moving backward.

ret′ro•gress′ (-gres′) *v.i.* to return to an earlier or more primitive condition. —**ret′ro•gres′sion,** *n.* —**ret′ro•gres′sive,** *adj.*

ret′ro•spect′ (re′trə spekt′) *n.* an occasion of looking back. —**ret′ro•spec′tive,** *adj., n.*

re•turn′ (ri tûrn′) *v.i.* **1.** to go or

come back. —*v.t.* **2.** to repay. **3.** to put, bring, or give back. —*n.* **4.** the act or fact of returning. **5.** a recurrence. **6.** a repayment or requital. **7.** Often, **returns.** profit. **8.** an official report. —**re•turn′ee,** *n.*

re′u•nite′ (rē′yə nīt′) *v.t., v.i.,* **-nited, -niting.** to unite after separation. —**re•un′ion,** *n.*

rev (rev) *n., v.,* **revved, revving.** —*n.* **1.** a revolution of a machine part. —*v.t.* **2.** to increase the speed of (a motor).

Rev. Reverend.

re•vamp′ (rē vamp′) *v.t.* to renovate or revise.

re•veal′ (ri vēl′) *v.t.* to disclose.

rev•eil•le (rev′ə lē) *n.* a signal to awaken military personnel.

rev•el (rev′əl) *v.i.,* **-eled, -eling. 1.** to enjoy greatly. **2.** to make merry. —*n.* **3.** revels, lively festivities; merrymaking. —**rev′el•ry,** *n.*

rev•e•la′tion *n.* an often surprising disclosure.

re•venge′ (ri venj′) *v.,* **-venged, -venging,** *n.* —*v.t.* **1.** to inflict harm in return for. —*n.* **2.** the act of revenging. **3.** vindictiveness. —**re•venge′ful,** *adj.*

rev′e•nue′ (rev′ən yōō′, -ə nōō′) *n.* income, esp. of a government or business.

re•ver′ber•ate′ (ri vûr′bə rāt′) *v.i.,* **-ated, -ating. 1.** to echo again and again. **2.** to reflect. —**re•ver′ber•a′tion,** *n.*

re•vere′ (ri vēr′) *v.t.,* **-vered, -vering.** to hold in deep respect.

rev′er•ence (rev′ər əns) *n., v.,* **-enced, -encing.** —*n.* **1.** deep respect and awe. —*v.t.* **2.** to regard with reverence. —**rev′er•ent, rev′er•en′tial** (-ə ren′shəl) *adj.*

Rev′er•end *adj.* a title used with the name of a member of the clergy.

rev′er•ie (rev′ə rē) *n.* a daydream.

re•verse′ (ri vûrs′) *adj., n., v.,* **-versed, -versing.** —*adj.* **1.** opposite in position, action, etc. **2.** of or for backward motion. —*n.* **3.** a reverse part, position, etc. **4.** a misfortune. —*v.t.* **5.** to turn in an opposite direction or position. —**re•ver′sal,** *n.* —**re•vers′i•ble,** *adj.*

re•vert′ (-vûrt′) *v.i.* to go back to an earlier state, topic, etc.

re•view′ *n.* **1.** a critical report, as on a book or film. **2.** a repeated viewing. **3.** a general survey. **4.** a formal inspection. —*v.t.* **5.** to go over or examine again. **6.** to inspect formally. **7.** to write a review of. —**re•view′er,** *n.*

re•vile′ (-vīl′) *v.t.,* **-viled, -viling.** to speak abusively to or about.

re•vise′ (ri vīz′) *v.t.,* **-vised, -vising.** to change or amend the content of. —**re•vi′sion** (-vizh′ən) *n.*

re•vi′sion•ism (-vizh′ə niz′əm) *n.* departure from an accepted doctrine. —**re•vi′sion•ist,** *n., adj.*

re•vi′tal•ize′ (rē vīt′l īz′) *v.t.,* **-ized, -izing.** to bring new vitality to.

re•viv′al (ri vī′vəl) *n.* **1.** restoration to life, use, etc. **2.** a religious awakening. —**re•viv′al•ist,** *n.*

re•vive′ *v.t., v.i.,* **-vived, -viving.** to bring or come back to life or use.

re•voke′ (ri vōk′) *v.t.,* **-voked, -voking.** to annul or repeal. —**rev′o•ca•ble** (rev′ə kə bəl) *adj.*

re•volt′ (ri vōlt′) *v.i.* **1.** to rebel. —*v.t.* **2.** to fill with disgust. —*n.* **3.** a rebellion. —**re•volt′ing,** *adj.*

rev′o•lu′tion (rev′ə lōō′shən) *n.* **1.** the overthrow of a government. **2.** a fundamental change. **3.** an act or instance of revolving. —**rev′o•lu′tion•ar′y,** *adj., n.*

rev′o•lu′tion•ize′ *v.t.,* **-ized, -izing.** to cause fundamental change in.

re•volve′ (ri volv′) *v.i.,* **-volved, -volving. 1.** to move in a circular course. **2.** to rotate.

re•volv′er *n.* a pistol with a revolving cylinder holding cartridges.

re•vue′ (-vyōō′) *n.* a theatrical show.

re•vul′sion (-vul′shən) *n.* a strong feeling of disgust.

re•ward′ (-wôrd′) *n.* **1.** recompense for merit, service, etc. —*v.t.* **2.** to give a reward (for).

re•ward′ing *adj.* giving satisfaction.

re•write′ *v.t.,* **-wrote, -written, -writing. 1.** to revise. **2.** to write again.

RFD rural free delivery.

rhap′so•dize′ (rap′sə dīz′) *v.i.,* **-dized, -dizing.** to talk with extravagant enthusiasm.

rhap′so•dy (-sə dē) *n., pl.* **-dies. 1.** an exaggerated expression of enthusiasm. **2.** a free-form musical composition.

rhe′o•stat′ (rē′ə stat′) *n.* a device for regulating electric current.

rhet′o•ric (ret′ər ik) *n.* **1.** the skillful use of language. **2.** exaggerated speech.

rhetor′ical ques′tion *n.* a question asked for effect, not an answer.

rheu′ma•tism (rōō′mə tiz′əm) *n.* a disease causing pain and stiffness in the joints or muscles. —**rheu•mat′ic** (rōō mat′ik) *adj., n.*

Rh factor *n.* an antigen in blood that may cause a severe reaction in an individual lacking it.

rhine′stone′ (rīn′stōn′) *n.* an artificial diamondlike gem.

rhi·noc′er·os (rī nos′ər əs) *n.* a
large thick-skinned mammal with a
horned snout.

rho′do·den′dron (rō′də den′drən)
n. a flowering evergreen shrub.

rhom′boid (rom′boid) *n.* an
oblique-angled parallelogram with
only the opposite sides equal.

rhom′bus (-bəs) *n.*, *pl.* **-buses, -bi**
(-bī). an oblique-angled parallelogram with all sides equal.

rhu′barb (rōō′bärb) *n.* a garden
plant with edible stalks.

rhyme (rīm) *n.*, *v.*, **rhymed, rhyming.** —*n.* **1.** agreement in the end
sounds of lines or words. **2.** a verse
with such correspondence. —*v.i.* **3.**
to make or form a rhyme.

rhythm (riᵺ′əm) *n.* **1.** movement
with a uniformly recurring element. **2.** a pattern of pulses in music resulting from strong and weak
beats. —**rhyth′mic, rhyth′mi·cal,**
adj.

RI Rhode Island. Also, **R.I.**

rib¹ (rib) *n.*, *v.*, **ribbed, ribbing.** —*n.*
1. one of the curved bones enclos-
ing the chest. **2.** a riblike part.
—*v.t.* **3.** to furnish with ribs.

rib² (rib) *v.t.*, **ribbed, ribbing.** to
tease.

rib′ald (rib′əld; *spelling pron.* rī′bəld)
adj. bawdy in speech. —**rib′ald·ry,**
n.

rib′bon (rib′ən) *n.* a strip of silk,
rayon, etc.

ri′bo·fla′vin (rī′bō flā′vin, -bə-) *n.*
an important vitamin in milk,
fresh meat, eggs, and leafy vegetables.

rice (rīs) *n.* an edible starchy grain.

rich (rich) *adj.* **1.** having abundant
and costly possessions. **2.** abounding. **3.** containing butter, eggs,
cream, etc. **4.** strong; vivid. **5.** mellow.

rich′es *n.pl.* abundant and valuable
possessions.

Rich′ter scale (rik′tər) *n.* a scale for
indicating the intensity of an
earthquake.

rick (rik) *n.* a stack of hay, straw,
etc.

rick′ets (-its) *n.* a childhood bone
disease caused by lack of vitamin D.

rick′et·y (-i tē) *adj.*, **-ier, -iest.**
likely to fall or collapse.

rick′shaw (-shô, -shä) *n.* a two-
wheeled passenger vehicle pulled
by a person.

ric′o·chet′ (rik′ə shā′) *v.*, **-cheted**
(-shād′) **-cheting** (-shā′ing) *n.* —*v.i.*
1. to rebound from a flat surface.
—*n.* **2.** such a movement.

ri·cot′ta (ri kot′ə, -kô′tə) *n.* a soft
Italian cheese.

rid (rid) *v.t.*, **rid** or **ridded, ridding.**
to clear or free of. —**rid′dance,** *n.*

rid′dle¹ (rid′l) *n.* **1.** a question requiring ingenuity to answer. **2.** a
puzzling thing or person.

rid′dle² (rid′l) *v.t.*, **-dled, -dling.** to
pierce with many holes.

ride (rīd) *v.*, **rode** (rōd) **ridden, riding,** *n.* —*v.i.* **1.** to be carried in
traveling. **2.** to rest on something.
—*v.t.* **3.** to sit on and manage (a
horse, bicycle, etc.). —*n.* **4.** a journey on a horse, camel, etc., or in a
vehicle. **5.** a vehicle in which people ride for amusement.

rid′er *n.* **1.** a person who rides. **2.**
a clause attached to a legislative
bill before passage.

ridge (rij) *n.*, *v.*, **ridged, ridging.**
—*n.* **1.** a long narrow elevation.
—*v.t.* **2.** to provide with ridges.

rid′i·cule′ (rid′i kyōōl′) *n.*, *v.*,
-culed, -culing. —*n.* **1.** speech or
action intended to make fun of
someone. —*v.t.* **2.** to make fun of;
mock.

ri·dic′u·lous (ri dik′yə ləs) *adj.* very
foolish; absurd.

rife (rīf) *adj.* **1.** widespread. **2.**
abounding.

riff (rif) *n.* a repeated phrase in jazz
or rock music.

riff′raff′ (rif′raf′) *n.* the lowest classes; rabble.

ri′fle¹ (rī′fəl) *n.* a shoulder firearm
with a spirally grooved barrel.

ri′fle² (rī′fəl) *v.t.*, **-fled, -fling.** to
ransack and rob.

rift (rift) *n.* **1.** a split or crack. **2.** a
disagreement.

rig (rig) *v.*, **rigged, rigging,** *n.* —*v.t.*
1. to fit with tackle and other
parts. **2.** to put together as makeshift. **3.** to manipulate fraudulently. —*n.* **4.** an arrangement of
masts, booms, tackle, etc. **5.** equipment.

rig′ging *n.* the ropes and chains
that support and work masts, sails,
etc.

right (rīt) *adj.* **1.** just or good. **2.**
correct. **3.** in good condition. **4.**
on the side that is toward the east
when one faces north. **5.** straight.
—*n.* **6.** that which is right. **7.** the
right side. **8.** something to which a
person is entitled. **9. the Right,**
people holding conservative political views. —*adv.* **10.** directly; completely. **11.** set correctly. **12.** in the
right position. **13.** correct.
—**right′ly,** *adv.* —**right′ist,** *adj.*, *n.*

right′ an′gle *n.* a 90-degree angle.

right′eous (rī′chəs) *adj.* acting in a
moral way.

right′ful *adj.* belonging by or having a just claim. **—right′ful•ly,** *adv.*

right′-hand′ed *adj.* **1.** using the right hand more easily. **2.** for the right hand.

right′ of way′ *n.* **1.** the right of one vehicle to proceed before another. **2.** a path that may lawfully be used.

right′-to-life′ *adj.* advocating laws making abortion illegal.

right′ wing′ *n.* the conservative element in an organization. **—right′-wing′,** *adj.*

rig′id (rij′id) *adj.* **1.** stiff; inflexible. **2.** strict; severe. **—ri•gid′i•ty,** *n.*

rig′ma•role′ (rig′mə rōl′) *n.* **1.** confused talk. **2.** a complicated procedure.

rig′or (rig′ər) *n.* **1.** strictness. **2.** hardship. **—rig′or•ous,** *adj.*

ri′gor mor′tis (rig′ər môr′tis) *n.* stiffening of the body after death.

rile (rīl) *v.t.,* **riled, riling.** to irritate.

rim (rim) *n., v.,* **rimmed, rimming.** **—n. 1.** an outer edge. **—v.t. 2.** to furnish with a rim.

rime¹ (rīm) *n.* rough white frost.

rime² (rīm) *n., v.i.,* **rimed, rim•ing.** rhyme.

rind (rīnd) *n.* a firm outer layer.

ring¹ (ring) *n.* **1.** a circular band worn on the finger. **2.** something shaped like a ring. **3.** a circular enclosed area. **4.** a group cooperating for unethical purposes. **—v.t. 5.** to surround with a ring.

ring² (ring) *v.,* **rang** (rang) **rung** (rung) **ringing,** *n.* **—v.i. 1.** to sound clearly and resonantly. **2.** to cause a bell to sound. **3.** to resound; reecho. **4.** to seem; appear. **—v.t. 5.** to cause to ring. **6.** to announce by a bell. **7.** to telephone. **—n. 8.** a ringing sound. **9.** a telephone call. **10.** a characteristic quality.

ring′er *n.* **1.** one that rings. **2.** a person or thing that closely resembles another. **3.** an athlete entered in competition in violation of eligibility rules.

ring′lead′er *n.* a leader in mischief.

ring′let (-lit) *n.* a curled lock of hair.

ring′mas′ter *n.* a person in charge of performances in a circus ring.

ring′worm′ *n.* a contagious skin disease.

rink (ringk) *n.* a floor or sheet of ice for skating on.

rinse (rins) *v.,* **rinsed, rinsing,** *n.* **—v.t. 1.** to wash in clean water. **2.** to remove soap, dirt, etc., by rinsing. **—n. 3.** the act of rinsing. **4.** liquid for rinsing.

ri′ot (rī′ət) *n.* **1.** a disturbance by a

mob. **2.** wild disorder. **—v.i. 3.** to take part in a riot. **—ri′ot•ous,** *adj.*

rip (rip) *v.,* **ripped, ripping,** *n.* **—v.t. 1.** to cut, tear apart, or tear off roughly. **—v.i. 2.** to become torn apart. **—n. 3.** a tear made by ripping. **—rip′per,** *n.*

R.I.P. may he, she, or they rest in peace.

rip′ cord′ *n.* a cord that opens a parachute.

ripe (rīp) *adj.,* **riper, ripest. 1.** fully developed; mature. **2.** ready. **—rip′en,** *v.t., v.i.* **—ripe′ness,** *n.*

rip′off′ *n. Slang.* a theft or exploitation.

ri•poste′ (ri pōst′) *n.* a quick, sharp reply or reaction.

rip′ple (rip′əl) *v.,* **-pled, -pling,** *n.* **—v.i. 1.** to form small waves. **—n. 2.** a pattern of small waves.

rip′ple effect′ *n.* a spreading effect.

rip′-roar′ing *adj.* boisterously exciting.

rip′tide′ *n.* a tide that opposes other tides.

rise (rīz) *v.,* **rose** (rōz) **risen** (riz′ən) **rising,** *n.* **—v.i. 1.** to get up. **2.** to revolt. **3.** to appear. **4.** to originate. **5.** to move upward. **6.** to increase. **7.** (of dough) to expand. **—n. 8.** an upward movement or slope. **9.** origin. **—ris′er,** *n.*

risk (risk) *n.* **1.** a chance of injury or loss. **—v.t. 2.** to expose to risk. **3.** to take the chance of. **—risk′y,** *adj.*

ris•qué′ (ri skā′) *adj.* bawdy; indecent.

rite (rīt) *n.* a ceremonial act.

rite′ of pas′sage *n.* an event marking a passage from one stage of life to another.

rit′u•al (rich′ŏŏ əl) *n.* a procedure for religious or other rites.

ri′val (rī′vəl) *n., adj., v.,* **-valed, -valing. —n. 1.** a competitor. **2.** an equal. **—adj. 3.** being a rival. **—v.t. 4.** to compete with. **5.** to match. **—ri′val•ry,** *n.*

riv′er (riv′ər) *n.* a large natural stream.

riv′et (-it) *n.* **1.** a metal bolt hammered after insertion. **—v.t. 2.** to fasten with or as if with rivets.

riv′u•let (-yə lit) *n.* a small stream.

RN registered nurse.

roach (rōch) *n.* a cockroach.

road (rōd) *n.* an open way for travel.

road′block′ *n.* an obstruction placed across a road to halt traffic.

road′kill′ *n.* the body of an animal killed on a road by a vehicle.

road′run′ner *n.* a terrestrial cuckoo of the western U.S.

roam (rōm) *v.i., v.t.* to wander; rove.

roan (rōn) *adj.* **1.** of a dark color with gray or white spots. —*n.* **2.** a roan horse.

roar (rôr) *v.i.* **1.** to make a loud, deep sound. —*v.t.* **2.** to express in a roar. —*n.* **3.** a loud, deep sound.

roast (rōst) *v.t.* **1.** to cook by dry heat. —*n.* **2.** roasted meat.

rob (rob) *v.t.,* **robbed, robbing.** to steal from. —**rob′ber,** *n.* —**rob′-ber•y,** *n.*

robe (rōb) *n.* a long loose garment.

rob′in (rob′in) *n.* a red-breasted songbird.

ro′bot (rō′bət, -bot) *n.* **1.** a human-like machine that performs tasks. **2.** a person who acts mechanically.

ro•bot′ics *n.* the technology of computer-controlled robots.

ro•bust′ (rō bust′, rō′bust) *adj.* healthy.

rock (rok) *n.* **1.** a mass of stone. **2.** Also, **rock-′n′-roll.** popular music with a steady, insistent rhythm. —*v.t., v.i.* **3.** to move back and forth. —**rock′y,** *adj.*

rock′ bot′tom *n.* the lowest level.

rock′er *n.* **1.** the curved support of a cradle or rocking chair. **2.** a rocking chair.

rock′et (rok′it) *n.* a tube propelled by discharge of gases from it.

rock′et•ry *n.* the science of rocket design.

rock′ing chair′ *n.* a chair mounted on rockers.

rock′ salt′ *n.* salt occurring in rocklike masses.

ro•co′co (rə kō′kō, rō′kə kō′) *adj., n.* (of or in) an elaborate decorative style of many curves.

rod (rod) *n.* **1.** a slender shaft. **2.** a linear measure of 5½ yards.

ro′dent (rōd′nt) *n.* a small gnawing or nibbling mammal.

ro′de•o′ (rō′dē ō′, rō dā′ō) *n., pl.* **-deos.** an exhibition of cowboy skills.

roe[1] (rō) *n.* fish eggs.

roe[2] (rō) *n., pl.* **roes, roe.** a small deer.

rog′er (roj′ər) *interj.* (message) received.

rogue (rōg) *n.* **1.** a dishonest person; scoundrel. **2.** a playfully mischievous person. —**ro′guer•y,** *n.* —**ro′guish,** *adj.*

roil (roil) *v.t.* **1.** to make muddy. **2.** to vex.

role (rōl) *n.* a part or function, as of a character in a play.

role′ mod′el *n.* a person imitated by others.

roll (rōl) *v.i.* **1.** to move by turning over and over. **2.** to move on wheels. **3.** to have a deep long sound. **4.** to rock from side to side. —*v.t.* **5.** to flatten, as with a rolling pin. **6.** to form into a roll or ball. —*n.* **7.** a list; register. **8.** anything cylindrical. **9.** a small cake of bread. **10.** a deep long sound. —**roll′er** *n.*

roll′back′ *n.* a return to a lower level.

roll′ call′ *n.* the calling of names for checking attendance.

Roll′er•blade′ *n., v.,* **-bladed, -blad-ing. 1.** *Trademark.* a brand of in-line skates. —*v.i.* **2.** (*often l.c.*) to skate on in-line skates.

roll′er coast′er *n.* an amusement-park railroad with a winding route and steep inclines.

roll′er skate′ *n.* a skate with four wheels. —**roll′er-skate′,** *v.i.*

rol′lick•ing (rol′i king) *adj.* jolly.

roll′o′ver *n.* a reinvestment of funds.

ro′ly-po′ly (rō′lē pō′lē, -pō′lē) *adj.* short and round.

ROM (rom) *n.* read-only memory: nonmodifiable computer memory containing instructions to the system.

ro•maine′ (rō mān′, rə-) *n.* a kind of lettuce with a cylindrical head.

ro′man (-mən) *n.* an upright style of printing type.

Ro′man Cath′olic Church′ *n.* the Christian church of which the pope is the supreme head.

ro•mance′ (-mans′) *n., v.,* **-manced, -mancing.** —*n.* **1.** a tale of heroic or marvelous exploits. **2.** a colorful, fanciful quality. **3.** a love affair. —*v.t.* **4.** to woo passionately.

Ro′man nu′merals *n.pl.* numbers using letters as symbols: I = 1, V = 5, X = 10, L = 50, C = 100, D = 500, M = 1,000.

ro•man′tic (-man′tik) *adj.* **1.** of romance. **2.** impractical or unrealistic. **3.** imbued with idealism. **4.** preoccupied with love. **5.** passionate; fervent. **6.** of a style of art stressing imagination and emotion. —*n.* **7.** a romantic person.

ro•man′ti•cism (-tə siz′əm) *n.* **1.** romantic spirit. **2.** (*often cap.*) an artistic style emphasizing imagination and emotion.

ro•man′ti•cize *v.t.,* **-cized, -cizing.** to invest with romantic character.

romp (romp) *v.i.* **1.** to play in a lively or boisterous manner. —*n.* **2.** a lively frolic.

romp′ers *n.pl.* a child's loose outer garment.

rood (rood) *n.* **1.** a crucifix. **2.** one-quarter of an acre.

roof (roof, roof) *n., pl.* **roofs. 1.** the

upper covering of a building. —v.t.
2. to provide with a roof.
—**roof'er,** n.
rook[1] (rŏŏk) n. **1.** a European crow.
—v.t. **2.** to cheat.
rook[2] (rŏŏk) n. a chess piece moving horizontally or vertically.
rook'ie n. a beginner.
room (rŏŏm, rŏŏm) n. **1.** a separate space within a building. **2.** space available for something. —v.i. **3.** to lodge. —**room'er,** n. —**room'-mate',** n. —**room'y,** adj.
roost (rŏŏst) n. **1.** a perch where fowls rest. —v.i. **2.** to sit on a roost.
roost'er n. a male chicken.
root[1] (rŏŏt, rŏŏt) n. **1.** a plant part that grows downward into the soil. **2.** the embedded portion of a hair, tooth, etc. **3.** a source. **4.** a quantity that when multiplied by itself a certain number of times produces a given quantity. —v.i. **5.** to become fixed. —v.t. **6.** to fix by or as if by roots. **7.** to dig up by the roots. **8. root out,** to remove completely.
root[2] (rŏŏt, rŏŏt) v.i. to turn up the soil with the snout.
root[3] (rŏŏt) v.i. to encourage a team by cheering enthusiastically.
root' beer' n. a soft drink flavored with extracts of roots, barks, and herbs.
root' canal' n. the root portion of the pulp cavity of a tooth.
rope (rōp) n., v., **roped, roping.**
—n. **1.** a strong twisted cord. —v.t. **2.** to fasten or catch with a rope.
Ror'schach test' (rôr'shäk) n. a diagnostic personality test based on interpretations of inkblot designs.
ro'sa.ry (rō'zə rē) n., pl. **-ries. 1.** a series of prayers recited by Roman Catholics. **2.** a string of beads counted in saying the rosary.
rose[1] (rōz) n. a thorny plant with showy, fragrant flowers.
rose[2] (rōz) v. pt. of **rise.**
ro.sé (rō zā') n. a pink wine.
rose'mar'y (rōz'mâr'ē, -mə rē) n. an aromatic shrub used for seasoning.
ro.sette' (rō zet') n. a rose-shaped ornament.
ros'ter (ros'tər) n. a list of persons, events, etc.
ros'trum (ros'trəm) n., pl. **-trums, -tra** (-trə). a speakers' platform.
ros'y (rō'zē) adj., **-ier, -iest. 1.** pink or pinkish-red. **2.** bright or promising. —**ros'i.ly,** adv.
rot (rot) v., **rotted, rotting,** n.
—v.i., v.t. **1.** to decay. —n. **2.** decay. **3.** a disease characterized by decay of tissue.

ro'tate (rō'tāt) v.i., v.t., **-tated, -tating. 1.** to turn on or as on an axis. **2.** to proceed or cause to proceed in a fixed succession. —**ro'ta.ry** (-tə rē) adj. —**ro.ta'tion,** n.
ROTC (är'ō tē sē', rot'sē) Reserve Officers Training Corps.
rote (rōt) n. **by rote,** from memory, in a mechanical way.
ro.tis'ser.ie (rō tis'ə rē) n. a machine with a revolving spit for roasting.
ro'tor (rō'tər) n. a rotating part.
rot'ten (rot'n) adj. **1.** decaying. **2.** corrupt. —**rot'ten.ness,** n.
ro.tund' (rō tund') adj. rounded; plump.
ro.tun'da (-tun'də) n. a round room.
rou.é' (rŏŏ ā') n. a dissolute man.
rouge (rŏŏzh) n., v., **rouged, rouging.** —n. **1.** a red cosmetic for cheeks. —v.t. **2.** to color with rouge.
rough (ruf) adj. **1.** not smooth. **2.** violent in action or motion. **3.** harsh. **4.** crude. **5.** approximate. —n. **6.** a rough thing or part.
rough'age (-ij) n. coarse or fibrous material in food.
rough'en v.t., v.i. to make or become rough.
rou.lette' (rŏŏ let') n. a gambling game based on a spinning disk.
round (round) adj. **1.** circular, curved, or spherical. **2.** complete. **3.** expressed as an approximate number. **4.** sonorous. —n. **5.** something round. **6.** a complete course, series, etc. **7.** a cut of beef between the rump and leg. **8.** a song in which voices enter at intervals. **9.** a stage of competition, as in a tournament. —adv. **10.** throughout. **11.** around. —prep. **12.** around. —v.t. **13.** to make round. **14.** to travel around. **15.** to express as a round number. —v.i. **16.** to become round. **16. round up,** to bring together. —**round'ness,** n.
round'a.bout' adj. indirect.
round'house' n. a building for servicing locomotives.
round'ly adv. unsparingly.
round' ta'ble n. a group gathered for a conference.
round' trip' n. a trip to a place and back.
round'up' n. **1.** a bringing together. **2.** a summary.
rouse (rouz) v.t., **roused, rousing.** to stir up; arouse.
roust'a.bout' (roust'ə bout') n. a laborer, as at a circus.
rout (rout) n. **1.** a defeat ending in disorderly flight. —v.t. **2.** to force to flee in disorder.

route (rōōt, rout) *n., v.,* **routed, routing.** —*n.* **1.** a course of travel. —*v.t.* **2.** to send by a particular route.

rou·tine′ (rōō tēn′) *n.* **1.** a regular order of action. —*adj.* **2.** like or by routine. **3.** ordinary.

rove (rōv) *v.i., v.t.,* **roved, roving.** to wander (over or through) aimlessly. —**rov′er,** *n.*

row¹ (rō) *n.* a number of persons or things in a line.

row² (rō) *v.t., v.i.* **1.** to propel (a boat) with oars. **2.** to convey in a rowboat. —**row′boat′,** *n.*

row³ (rou) *n.* a noisy dispute.

row·dy (rou′dē) *adj.,* **-dier, -diest,** *n., pl.* **-dies.** —*adj.* **1.** rough and disorderly. —*n.* **2.** a rowdy person.

roy·al (roi′əl) *adj.* of kings or queens. —**roy′al·ly,** *adv.*

roy′al·ist *n.* a person favoring rule by a king or queen.

roy·al·ty *n., pl.* **-ties. 1.** royal persons. **2.** royal power. **3.** an agreed share of proceeds paid to an author, inventor, etc.

rpm revolutions per minute.

RR 1. railroad. **2.** rural route.

RSVP please reply.

rub (rub) *v.,* **rubbed, rubbing,** *n.* —*v.t.* **1.** to apply pressure to in cleaning, smoothing, etc. **2.** to move or apply with pressure. **3.** to press against with friction. —*v.i.* **4.** to rub something. —*n.* **5.** the act of rubbing. **6.** a difficulty. —*Idiom.* **7. rub the wrong way,** to irritate.

rub′ber (rub′ər) *n.* **1.** elastic material from a tropical tree. **2. rubbers,** rubber overshoes. —**rub′ber·y,** *adj.*

rub′ber band′ *n.* a band of rubber used for holding things together.

rub′ber cement′ *n.* a liquid adhesive.

rub′ber·neck′ *Informal.* —*v.i.* **1.** to stare curiously. —*n.* **2.** a curious onlooker. **3.** a sightseer.

rub′ber stamp′ *n.* a stamp with a rubber printing surface.

rub′bish (rub′ish) *n.* **1.** waste or trash. **2.** nonsense.

rub′ble (rub′əl) *n.* broken stone.

rub′down′ *n.* a massage.

ru·bel·la (rōō bel′ə) *n.* a usu. mild viral infection. Also, **German measles.**

ru′ble (rōō′bəl) *n.* a monetary unit of Russia and of some former Soviet states.

ru′bric (rōō′brik) *n.* **1.** a title or heading. **2.** a class or category.

ru′by (rōō′bē) *n., pl.* **-bies.** a red gem.

ruck′sack′ (ruk′sak′, rōōk′-) *n.* a knapsack.

ruck′us (ruk′əs) *n.* a noisy commotion.

rud′der (rud′ər) *n.* a flat vertical piece for steering a ship, aircraft, etc.

rud′dy (rud′ē) *adj.,* **-dier, -diest.** having a healthy red color.

rude (rōōd) *adj.,* **ruder, rudest. 1.** not polite. **2.** rough or crude.

ru·di·ment (rōō′də mənt) *n.* a basic thing to learn. —**ru′di·men·ta·ry** (-men′tə rē) *adj.*

rue (rōō) *v.t.,* **rued, ruing.** to regret. —**rue′ful,** *adj.*

ruff (ruf) *n.* **1.** a gathered or pleated collar. **2.** a collar of hairs or feathers on an animal's neck.

ruf′fi·an (-ən) *n.* a rough or lawless person.

ruf′fle (-əl) *v.,* **-fled, -fling,** *n.* —*v.t.* **1.** to make uneven. **2.** to disturb. **3.** to gather in folds. —*n.* **4.** a break in evenness. **5.** a strip of fabric gathered on one edge.

rug (rug) *n.* a floor covering.

Rug′by (-bē) *n.* a British form of football.

rug′ged (-id) *adj.* **1.** roughly irregular. **2.** severe. **3.** strong.

ru·in (rōō′in) *n.* **1.** complete loss or destruction. **2. ruins,** the remains of fallen buildings, monuments, etc. —*v.t.* **3.** to bring or come to ruin or ruins. —**ru′in·a′tion,** *n.* —**ru′in·ous,** *adj.*

rule (rōōl) *n., v.,* **ruled, ruling.** —*n.* **1.** a principle; regulation. **2.** control or government. **3.** a ruler (def. 2). —*v.t., v.i.* **4.** to exercise control (over); govern. **5.** to decide in the manner of a judge. **6.** to mark with a ruler. —**rul′ing,** *n., adj.*

rul′er *n.* **1.** a person who rules. **2.** a straight-edged strip for measuring and drawing lines.

rum (rum) *n.* an alcoholic liquor made from sugarcane or molasses.

rum′ble (rum′bəl) *v.,* **-bled, -bling,** *n.* —*v.i.* **1.** to make a long, deep, heavy sound. —*n.* **2.** such a sound.

ru′mi·nant (rōō′mə nənt) *n.* **1.** a cud-chewing mammal, as a cow. —*adj.* **2.** cud-chewing.

ru′mi·nate′ (-nāt′) *v.i.,* **-nated, -nating. 1.** to chew cud. **2.** to meditate.

rum′mage (rum′ij) *v.i., v.t.,* **-maged, -maging.** to search thoroughly (through).

rum′my (rum′ē) *n.* a card game in which cards are matched in sets and sequences.

ru′mor (rōō′mər) *n.* **1.** an unconfirmed but widely repeated story. —*v.t.* **2.** to tell as a rumor.

rump (rump) *n.* **1.** the rear part of an animal's body. **2.** the buttocks.

rum′pus (rum′pəs) *n.* a noisy disturbance.

run (run) *v.*, **ran** (ran) **run, running,** *n.* —*v.i.* **1.** to go, move, or depart quickly. **2.** to take part in a race. **3.** to be a candidate. **4.** to flow. **5.** to extend or continue. **6.** to operate. **7.** to total. **8.** to recur persistently. —*v.t.* **9.** to manage. **10.** to operate. **11.** to compete in. **12. run out of,** to use up the supply of. —*n.* **13.** an act or period of running. **14.** a raveled line in knitting. **15.** freedom of action. **16.** a scoring unit in baseball. —*Idiom.* **17. in the long run,** over a long period.

run′a·round′ *n.* an evasive action or response.

run′a·way′ *n.* **1.** a fugitive. **2.** something that has broken away from control. —*adj.* **3.** escaped. **4.** uncontrolled.

run′-down′ *adj.* **1.** weary. **2.** fallen into disrepair. **3.** (of a clock or watch) not running because not wound.

run′down′ *n.* a short summary.

rung¹ (rung) *v.* pt. and pp. of **ring.**

rung² (rung) *n.* **1.** a ladder step. **2.** a bar between chair legs.

run′-in′ *n.* a confrontation.

run′ner *n.* **1.** one that runs. **2.** a messenger. **3.** a blade of a skate. **4.** a strip of fabric, carpet, etc.

run′ner-up′ *n.* a competitor finishing in second place.

run′off′ *n.* a final contest held to break a tie.

run′-of-the-mill′ *adj.* mediocre.

runt (runt) *n.* an undersized thing.

run′way′ *n.* a strip where airplanes take off and land.

rup′ture (rup′chər) *n.*, *v.*, **-tured, -turing.** —*n.* **1.** the act of breaking or state of being broken. **2.** a hernia. —*v.i.*, *v.t.* **3.** to suffer or cause to suffer a rupture.

ru′ral (rŏŏr′əl) *adj.* of or in the country.

ruse (rŏŏz) *n.* a deception or trick.

rush¹ (rush) *v.i.*, *v.t.* **1.** to move or cause to move with speed. —*n.* **2.** the act of rushing. **3.** hurried activity. **4.** a hurried state. —*adj.* **5.** requiring or done in haste.

rush² (rush) *n.* a grasslike marsh plant.

rusk (rusk) *n.* a sweet raised bread dried and baked again.

rus′set (rus′it) *n.* a reddish brown.

rust (rust) *n.* **1.** a red-orange coating that forms on iron and steel exposed to air and moisture. —*v.t.*, *v.i.* **2.** to form rust (on). —**rust′y,** *adj.*

rus′tic (rus′tik) *adj.* **1.** rural. **2.** simple. —*n.* **3.** a country person.

rus′tle (rus′əl) *v.i.*, *v.t.*, **-tled, -tling,** *n.* **1.** to make or cause to make small soft sounds. **2.** to steal (livestock). —*n.* **3.** a rustling sound.

rut¹ (rut) *n.* **1.** a groove worn in the ground. **2.** a fixed, dull way of proceeding.

rut² (rut) *n.* a period of sexual excitement in male deer, goats, etc.

ru′ta·ba·ga (rŏŏ′tə bā′gə) *n.* a yellow turnip.

ruth′less (rŏŏth′lis) *adj.* without pity or mercy. —**ruth′less·ness,** *n.*

RV recreational vehicle.

Rx prescription.

rye (rī) *n.* a cereal grass used for flour, feed, and whiskey.

S

S, s (es) *n.* the nineteenth letter of the English alphabet.

S south, southern.

Sab′bath (sab′əth) *n.* a day of religious observance and rest, observed on Saturday by Jews and on Sunday by most Christians.

sab·bat′i·cal (sə bat′i kəl) *n.* a paid leave of absence for study, writing, or travel, granted to teachers.

sa′ber (sā′bər) *n.* a one-edged sword. Also, **sa′bre.**

sa′ble (sā′bəl) *n.* a small mammal with dark-brown fur.

sab′o·tage′ (sab′ə täzh′) *n.*, *v.*, **-taged, -taging.** —*n.* **1.** deliberate injury to equipment or interference with production. —*v.t.* **2.** to injure or attack by sabotage.

sab′o·teur′ (-tûr′) *n.* a person who sabotages.

sac (sak) *n.* a baglike part.

sac′cha·rin (-ər in) *n.* a synthetic, noncaloric sugar substitute.

sac′cha·rine (-ər in, -ə rēn′) *adj.* overly sweet or sentimental.

sa·chet′ (sa shā′) *n.* a small bag of perfumed powder.

sack¹ (sak) *n.* **1.** a large stout bag. **2.** a bag. **3.** *Slang.* dismissal from a job. —*v.t.* **4.** *Slang.* to dismiss from a job.

sack² (sak) *v.t* **1.** to loot (a place) after capture; plunder. —*n.* **2.** the plundering of a captured place.

sack′cloth′ *n.* a coarse cloth worn for penance or mourning.

sac′ra·ment (sak′rə mənt) *n.* **1.** a

symbolic rite, as baptism, in the Christian church. **2. Sacrament,** the Eucharist.

sa′cred (sā′krid) *adj.* **1.** holy. **2.** connected with religion. **3.** dedicated to some person or purpose. **4.** regarded with reverence.

sac′ri•fice (sak′rə fīs′) *n., v.,* **-ficed, -ficing.** —*n.* **1.** the offering of something to a deity. **2.** something so offered. **3.** the giving up of something valued for the sake of something else. —*v.i.* **4.** to make a sacrifice (of). —**sac′ri•fi′cial** (-fish′əl) *adj.*

sac′ri•lege (-lij) *n.* violation or profanation of anything sacred. —**sac′ri•le′gious** (-lij′əs, -lē′jəs) *adj.*

sac′ris•ty (-ri stē) *n., pl.* **-ties.** a room in a church where sacred objects are kept.

sac′ro•il′i•ac′ (sak′rō il′ē ak′, sā′krō-) *n.* a joint in the lower back.

sac′ro•sanct′ (sak′rō sangkt′) *adj.* sacred.

sac′rum (sak′rəm, sā′krəm) *n., pl.* **sacra.** a bone forming the rear wall of the pelvis.

sad (sad) *adj.,* **sadder, saddest.** affected by, marked by, or causing sorrow. —**sad′den,** *v.t., v.i.*

sad′dle (sad′l) *n., v.,* **-dled, -dling.** —*n.* **1.** a seat for a rider on a horse. **2.** anything resembling a saddle. —*v.t.* **3.** to put a saddle on. **4.** to burden.

sad′dle•bag′ *n.* a pouch laid over the back of a horse or mounted over the rear wheel of a bicycle or motorcycle.

sad′ism (sā′diz əm, sad′iz-) *n.* pleasure in causing pain. —**sad′ist,** *n.* —**sa•dis′tic** (sə dis′tik) *adj.*

sa•fa′ri (sə fär′ē) *n.* **1.** a hunting expedition, esp. in E Africa. **2.** a long journey.

safe (sāf) *adj.,* **safer, safest,** *n.* —*adj.* **1.** offering security from danger. **2.** free from injury or risk. **3.** dependable. —*n.* **4.** a steel or iron box for valuables.

safe′-con′duct *n.* a document authorizing safe passage.

safe′-de•pos′it *adj.* providing safekeeping for valuables.

safe′guard′ *n.* **1.** something that ensures safety. —*v.t.* **2.** to protect.

safe′ sex′ *n.* sexual activity in which precautions are taken to avoid sexually transmitted diseases.

safe′ty *n.* **1.** the state of being safe. **2.** freedom from injury, danger, or loss. **3.** a device to prevent injury.

safe′ty pin′ *n.* a pin bent back on itself with a guard covering the point.

saf′flow•er (saf′lou′ər) *n.* a thistlelike plant whose seeds yield oil.

saf′fron (saf′rən) *n.* the orangecolored stigmas of a crocus, used to color and flavor foods.

sag (sag) *v.,* **sagged, sagging,** *n.* —*v.i.* **1.** to bend, esp. in the middle, from weight or pressure. **2.** to hang loosely. —*n.* **3.** a sagging place.

sa′ga (sä′gə) *n.* a heroic tale.

sa•ga′cious (sə gā′shəs) *adj.* shrewd. —**sa•gac′i•ty** (-gas′ə tē) *n.*

sage[1] (sāj) *n., adj.,* **sager, sagest.** —*n.* **1.** a wise person. —*adj.* **2.** wise.

sage[2] (sāj) *n.* a plant of the mint family, used in cooking.

sage′brush′ *n.* a bushy plant of the dry plains of the western U.S.

said (sed) *v.* pt. and pp. of **say.**

sail (sāl) *n.* **1.** a sheet of fabric spread to catch the wind to propel a vessel or a windmill. **2.** a trip on a sailing vessel. —*v.i.* **3.** to travel over water. **4.** to control a sailboat. **5.** to move smoothly and effortlessly. —*v.t.* **6.** to sail upon or over. **7.** to navigate (a ship). —**sail′or,** *n.*

sail′fish′ *n.* a large fish with an upright fin.

saint (sānt) *n.* **1.** a holy person, esp. one formally recognized by the Christian Church. **2.** an especially good or kind person. —**saint′hood,** *n.* —**saint′ly,** *adj.*

sake (sāk) *n.* **1.** benefit. **2.** purpose.

sa•la′cious (sə lā′shəs) *adj.* lewd; indecent.

sal′ad (sal′əd) *n.* a cold dish of raw vegetables or fruit.

sal′a•man′der (sal′ə man′dər) *n.* a small, tailed amphibian.

sa•la′mi (sə lä′mē) *n.* a spicy, garlic-flavored sausage.

sal′a•ry (sal′ə rē) *n., pl.* **-ries.** fixed payment for regular work.

sale (sāl) *n.* **1.** the act of selling. **2.** a special offering of goods at reduced prices. **3.** a transfer of property for money. —**sales′man,** *n.* —**sales′wom′an,** *n.fem.* —**sales′per′son,** *n.* —**sales′people,** *n.pl.*

sales′man•ship′ *n.* the skill of selling a product or idea.

sa′li•ent (sā′lē ənt) *adj.* **1.** prominent. **2.** pointing outward. —*n.* **3.** a projecting part. —**sa′li•ence,** *n.*

sa′line (sā′lēn, -līn) *adj.* salty.

sa•li′va (sə lī′və) *n.* a colorless fluid that forms in the mouth. —**sal′i•var′y** (sal′ə ver′ē) *adj.* —**sal′i•vate** (-vāt′) *v.i.* —**sal′i•va′tion,** *n.*

sal′low (sal′ō) *adj.* having a sickly complexion.

sal/ly (sal/ē) n., pl. **-lies. 1.** a sudden attack. **2.** a witty remark.

salm/on (sam/ən) n. a pink-fleshed food fish of northern waters.

sal/mo·nel/la (sal/mə nel/ə) n., pl. **-nellae** (-nel/ē) **-nellas.** a rod-shaped bacterium that causes food poisoning.

sa·lon/ (sə lon/; Fr. SA lôN/) n. **1.** an elegant drawing room. **2.** a gathering of leaders in the arts, politics, etc. **3.** a shop offering a special service to a fashionable clientele.

sa·loon/ (sə lōon/) n. a place where liquor is sold and drunk.

sal/sa (säl/sə, -sä) n. **1.** a hot sauce containing chilies. **2.** a type of Latin-American music with elements of jazz, rock, and soul.

salt (sôlt) n. **1.** sodium chloride, used for seasoning and preserving food. **2.** a chemical compound derived from an acid and a base. **3.** a sailor. —v.t. **4.** to season or preserve with salt. —*Idiom.* **5. take with a grain of salt,** to be skeptical about. —**salt/y,** adj.

salt/cel/lar n. a shaker or dish for salt.

sal·tine/ (sôl tēn/) n. a crisp, salted cracker.

salt/ lick/ n. a place where animals go to lick salt deposits.

salt/pe/ter (-pē/tər) n. potassium nitrate.

sa·lu/bri·ous (sə lōo/brē əs) adj. good for the health.

sal/u·tar/y (sal/yə ter/ē) adj. healthful; beneficial.

sal/u·ta/tion (sal/yə tā/shən) n. **1.** a greeting. **2.** the opening of a letter.

sa·lute/ (sə lōot/) v., **-luted, -luting,** n. —n. **1.** a gesture of greeting or respect. —v.t., v.i. **2.** to give a salute (to).

sal/vage (sal/vij) n., v., **-vaged, -vaging.** —v.t. **1.** to save from destruction. —n. **2.** the act of saving a ship or cargo at sea. **3.** the property saved.

sal·va/tion (-vā/shən) n. **1.** the act of saving or the means of being saved. **2.** deliverance from the consequences of sin.

salve (sav) n., v., **salved, salving.** —n. **1.** an ointment for sores. —v.t. **2.** to soothe with salve.

sal/ver (sal/vər) n. a tray.

sal/vo (sal/vō) n., pl. **-vos, -voes.** a simultaneous discharge of guns.

same (sām) adj. **1.** identical with what has just been mentioned. **2.** corresponding. **3.** unchanged. —pron. **4.** the same person or thing. —**same/ness,** n.

sam/ple (sam/pəl) n., adj., v., **-pled, -pling.** —n. **1.** a small part that shows the nature or quality of the whole. —adj. **2.** serving as a sample. —v.t. **3.** to take a sample of.

sam/pler n. a piece of needlework done to show a beginner's skill.

sam/u·rai/ (sam/ŏŏ rī/) n., pl. **-rai.** a member of a hereditary warrior class in feudal Japan.

san/a·to/ri·um (san/ə tôr/ē əm) n., pl. **-toriums, -toria** (-tôr/ē ə). **1.** a hospital for treating chronic diseases. **2.** a sanitarium.

sanc/ti·fy/ (sangk/tə fī/) v.t., **-fied, -fying.** to make holy. —**sanc/ti·fi·ca/tion,** n.

sanc/ti·mo/ni·ous (-mō/nē əs) adj. hypocritically devout.

sanc/tion (sangk/shən) n. **1.** permission or approval. **2.** action by one state against another to force compliance with an obligation. —v.t. **3.** to authorize; approve.

sanc/ti·ty (-ti tē) n. holiness; sacredness.

sanc/tu·ar/y (-chōo er/ē) n., pl. **-ies. 1.** a holy place, as the chancel of a church. **2.** a place of refuge.

sanc/tum (-təm) n., pl. **-tums, -ta.** a private place; retreat.

sand (sand) n. **1.** fine, loose grains of rock. **2. sands,** a sandy region. —v.t. **3.** to smooth or polish with sandpaper.

san/dal (san/dl) n. a shoe consisting of a sole fastened to the foot with straps.

san/dal·wood/ n. a fragrant wood.

sand/bag/ n. a sand-filled bag used as fortification, ballast, etc.

sand/bank/ n. a large mass of sand.

sand/ bar/ n. a bar of sand formed by tidal action in a river or sea.

sand/blast/ v.t. to clean with a blast of air laden with sand.

sand/box/ n. a receptacle holding sand for children to play in.

sand/ dol/lar n. a disklike sea animal.

sand/lot/ n. a vacant lot used by youngsters for games.

sand/man/ n. a figure in folklore who puts sand in children's eyes to make them sleepy.

sand/pa/per n. **1.** paper coated with sand for smoothing. —v.t. **2.** to smooth with sandpaper.

sand/pip/er (-pī/pər) n. a thin-billed shore bird.

sand/stone/ n. rock formed chiefly of sand.

sand/storm/ n. a windstorm with clouds of sand.

sand/wich (sand/wich, san/-) n. **1.** two slices of bread with a filling between them. —v.t. **2.** to insert between two other things.

sane (sān) *adj.*, **saner, sanest.** free from mental disorder; rational.

sang-froid′ (*Fr.* säN frwA′) *n.* coolness of mind; composure.

san′gui•nar′y (sang′gwə ner′ē) *adj.* **1.** bloody. **2.** bloodthirsty.

san′guine (-gwin) *adj.* optimistic.

san′i•tar′i•um (san′i târ′ē əm) *n., pl.* **-iums, -ia** (-ē ə). a place for the treatment of invalids and convalescents.

san′i•tar′y (-ter′ē) *adj.* **1.** of health. **2.** free from dirt and germs.

san′itary nap′kin *n.* a pad worn to absorb menstrual flow.

san′i•tize′ *v.t.*, **-tized, -tizing. 1.** to make free from dirt. **2.** to make less offensive by removing objectionable elements.

san′i•ty *n.* soundness of mind.

sap[1] (sap) *n.* **1.** the fluid that carries mineral salts and sugar through a woody plant. **2.** a fool.

sap[2] (sap) *v.t.*, **sapped, sapping.** to weaken or undermine gradually.

sa′pi•ent (sā′pē ənt) *adj.* wise.

sap′ling (sap′ling) *n.* a young tree.

sap′phire (saf′īᵊr) *n.* a deep-blue gem.

sar′casm (sär′kaz əm) *n.* scornful, ironic language. —**sar•cas′tic,** *adj.*

sar•co′ma (sär kō′mə) *n., pl.* **-mas, -mata** (-mə tə). a malignant tumor.

sar•coph′a•gus (sär kof′ə gəs) *n., pl.* **-gi** (-jī′, -gī′). a stone coffin.

sar•dine′ (sär dēn′) *n.* a small fish of the herring family.

sar•don′ic (sär don′ik) *adj.* scornfully mocking.

sa′ri (sär′ē) *n.* a long cloth wrapped around the body, worn as a woman's garment in India.

sa•rong′ (sə rông′) *n.* a skirtlike garment worn in Malaysia.

sar′sa•pa•ril′la (sas′pə ril′ə) *n.* **1.** a tropical American vine. **2.** a soft drink flavored with roots of this plant.

sar•to′ri•al (sär tôr′ē əl) *adj.* of tailors or tailoring.

SASE self-addressed stamped envelope.

sash[1] (sash) *n.* a band of cloth worn over the shoulder or around the waist.

sash[2] (sash) *n.* a framework in which the panes of a window are set.

sass (sas) *Informal.* —*n.* **1.** impudent back talk. —*v.t.* **2.** to answer back impudently. —**sas′sy,** *adj.*

sas′sa•fras′ (sas′ə fras′) *n.* an American tree with an aromatic root bark.

sat (sat) *v.* pt. and pp. of **sit.**

Sat. Saturday.

Sa′tan (sāt′n) *n.* the devil. —**sa•tan′ic** (sə tan′ik) *adj.*

satch′el (sach′əl) *n.* a small bag with a handle.

sate (sāt) *v.t.*, **sated, sating.** to satisfy fully.

sat′el•lite′ (sat′l īt′) *n.* **1.** a natural or artificial body that revolves around a planet. **2.** a country under the influence of another.

sat′ellite dish′ *n.* a dish-shaped reflector, used esp. for receiving satellite and microwave signals.

sa′ti•ate′ (sā′shē āt′) *v.t.*, **-ated, -ating.** to supply to excess.

sat′in (sat′n) *n.* a glossy silk or rayon fabric. —**sat′in•y,** *adj.*

sat′ire (sat′īᵊr) *n.* the use of irony or ridicule in exposing vice, folly, etc. —**sa•tir′i•cal** (sə tir′i kəl), **sa•tir′ic,** *adj.* —**sat′i•rist** (sat′ər ist) *n.* —**sat′i•rize′,** *v.t.*

sat′is•fac′tory (sat′is fak′tə rē) *adj.* serving to satisfy; adequate. —**sat′is•fac′to•ri•ly,** *adv.*

sat′is•fy′ (-fī′) *v.t.*, **-fied, -fying. 1.** to fulfill the desire, needs, or demands of. **2.** to fulfill the requirements of. **3.** to convince. —**sat′is•fac′tion** (-fak′shən) *n.*

sat′u•rate′ (sach′ə rāt′) *v.t.*, **-rated, -rating. 1.** to soak completely. **2.** to load or fill to the utmost.

Sat′ur•day (sat′ər dā′, -dē) *n.* the seventh day of the week.

Sat•urn (sat′ərn) *n.* the planet sixth from the sun.

sat′ur•nine′ (-ər nīn′) *adj.* gloomy.

sa′tyr (sā′tər, sat′ər) *n.* **1.** a deity of ancient Greece, part man and part goat. **2.** a lecherous man.

sauce (sôs) *n.* **1.** a liquid dressing for food. **2.** stewed fruit.

sauce′pan′ *n.* a cooking pot with a handle.

sau′cer *n.* a small shallow dish.

sau′cy *adj.*, **-cier, -ciest. 1.** impertinent. **2.** jaunty. —**sau′ci•ly,** *adv.*

sau′na (sô′nə) *n.* a bath heated by steam.

saun′ter (sôn′tər) *v.i.* **1.** to stroll. —*n.* **2.** a stroll.

sau′sage (sô′sij) *n.* minced seasoned meat, often in a casing.

sau•té′ (sō tā′, sô-) *v.t.*, **-téed, -tée- ing.** to fry in a small amount of fat.

sav′age (sav′ij) *adj.* **1.** wild; uncivilized. **2.** brutal; cruel. —*n.* **3.** an uncivilized person. **4.** a brutal or cruel person. —**sav′age•ly,** *adv.* —**sav′age•ry,** *n.*

sa•van′na (sə van′ə) *n.* a grassy plain with scattered trees. Also, **sa•van′nah.**

sa•vant′ (sa vänt′) *n.* a learned person.

save¹ (sāv) v., **saved, saving** —v.t.
1. to rescue from danger or harm.
2. to keep safe or unhurt. **3.** to set
aside in reserve. —v.i. **4.** to set
aside money.

save² (sāv) prep. **1.** with the exception of. —conj. **2.** except.

sav′ing n. **1.** a reduction in spending. **2. savings,** money put aside.

sav′ior (sāv′yər) n. **1.** one who res-
cues. **2. Savior,** Jesus Christ. Also,
sav′iour.

sa′voir-faire′ (sav′wär fâr′) n.
knowledge of how to behave in
any situation.

sa′vor (sā′vər) v.t. to taste, smell,
or experience with enjoyment.

sa′vor•y adj. **1.** pleasing in taste or
smell. —n. **2.** an aromatic herb of
the mint family.

sav′vy (sav′ē) n. **1.** practical understanding. —adj. **2.** shrewd and
well-informed.

saw¹ (sô) v. pt. of **see.**

saw² (sô) n., v., **sawed, sawed** or
sawn, sawing. —n. **1.** a cutting
tool with a toothed metal blade.
—v.t., v.i. **2.** to cut with a saw.

saw′dust′ n. fine particles of wood
produced in sawing.

saw′horse′ n. a frame for supporting wood while it is being sawed.

saw′mill′ n. a mill where timber is
sawed.

sax (saks) n. a saxophone.

sax′o•phone′ (sak′sə fōn′) n. a
wind instrument with a conical
tube and a reed mouthpiece.

say (sā) v., **said** (sed) **saying,** n.
—v.t. **1.** to speak; utter; recite. **2.** to
express in words; state. **3.** to state
as an opinion. —n. **4.** the right to
speak or choose.

say′ing n. a proverb.

say′-so′ n., pl. **say-sos.** one's personal assurance; word.

SC South Carolina. Also, **S.C.**

scab (skab) n., v., **scabbed, scab-
bing.** —n. **1.** a crust forming over a
sore. **2.** a worker who takes a striker's place on the job. —v.i. **3.** to
form a scab. **4.** to work as a scab.
—**scab′by,** adj.

scab′bard (skab′ərd) n. a sheath for
a sword, dagger, etc.

scad (skad) n. **scads,** a great quantity.

scaf′fold (skaf′əld, -ōld) n. **1.** Also,
scaf′fold•ing. a raised platform for
workers and materials, used in construction. **2.** a platform on which a
criminal is executed.

scald (skôld) v.t. **1.** to burn with
hot liquid or steam. **2.** to heat to
just below boiling. —n. **3.** a burn
caused by scalding.

scale¹ (skāl) n., v., **scaled, scaling.**

—n. **1.** one of the flat hard plates
covering fish, snakes, etc. **2.** a thin
flake or coating. —v.t. **3.** to remove
the scales from. —v.i. **4.** to come
off in scales. —**scal′y,** adj.

scale² (skāl) n. Often, **scales.** a device for weighing.

scale³ (skāl) n., v., **scaled, scaling.**
—n. **1.** an ordered series of steps or
degrees. **2.** a series of marks at regular intervals for measuring. **3.** relative size or extent. **4.** a succession
of musical tones. —v.t. **5.** to climb.
6. to make according to a scale.

scal′lion (skal′yən) n. a small green
onion.

scal′lop (skol′əp, skal′-) n. **1.** a bivalve mollusk with a fluted shell.
2. one of a series of curves on a
border. —v.t. **3.** to finish (an edge)
with scallops.

scalp (skalp) n. **1.** the skin and hair
of the top of the head. —v.t. **2.** to
cut the scalp from. **3.** to resell at
an inflated price.

scal′pel (skal′pəl) n. a small surgical knife.

scam (skam) n., v., **scammed, scam-
ming.** —n. **1.** a fraudulent scheme;
swindle. —v.t. **2.** to cheat.

scam′per v.i. **1.** to run quickly.
—n. **2.** a quick run.

scan (skan) v., **scanned, scanning.**
—v.t. **1.** to examine closely. **2.** to
glance at hastily. **3.** to read (data)
for use by a computer. —v.i. **4.** (of
verse) to conform to metrical rules.

scan′dal (skan′dl) n. **1.** a disgraceful act; disgrace. **2.** malicious gossip. —**scan′dal•ize,** v.t. —**scan′dal•
ous,** adj.

scan′dal•mon′ger n. a person who
spreads scandal.

scan′ner n. **1.** a person or thing
that scans. **2.** a device that moni-
tors selected radio frequencies and
reproduces any signal detected. **3.**
an optical scanner.

scant (skant) adj. barely adequate.
Also, **scant′y.** —**scant′i•ly,** adv.

scape′goat′ (skāp′gōt′) n. one who
is made to bear the blame for
others.

scap′u•la (skap′yə lə) n., pl. **-las,
-lae** (-lē′) either of two flat triangular bones forming the back part
of the shoulder; the shoulder
blade.

scar (skär) n., v., **scarred, scarring.**
—n. **1.** a mark left by a healed
wound. —v.t., v.i. **2.** to mark with
or form a scar.

scar′ab (skar′əb) n. **1.** a large beetle, sacred in ancient Egypt. **2.** a
representation of a scarab.

scarce (skârs) adj., **scarcer, scarcest.**

1. insufficient to fill a need. 2. rare. —**scar'ci•ty, scarce'ness,** n.
scarce'ly adv. 1. barely. 2. probably not.
scare (skâr) v., **scared, scaring,** n. —v.t., v.i. 1. to frighten or become frightened. —n. 2. a sudden fright.
scare'crow' n. an object, usu. a figure of a person, set up to frighten birds away from crops.
scarf (skärf) n., pl. **scarfs, scarves** (skärvz). a strip or square of cloth worn about the neck, shoulders, or head.
scar'i•fy' (skar'ə fī') v.t., **-fied, -fy-ing.** 1. to make scratches or slight cuts in. 2. to criticize harshly.
scar'let (skär'lit) n. a bright red.
scar'let fe'ver n. a contagious disease marked by a red rash.
scar'y (skâr'ē) adj., **-ier, -iest.** causing fear.
scat (skat) v.i., **scatted, scatting.** to run off.
scath'ing (skā'thing) adj. bitterly severe.
scat'o•log'i•cal (skat'l oj'i kəl) adj. concerned with obscenity.
scat'ter (skat'ər) v.t. 1. to throw loosely about. —v.i. 2. to separate and disperse.
scav'enge (skav'inj) v., **-enged, -enging.** —v.t. 1. to search for (usable objects) among discarded material. —v.i. 2. to act as a scavenger. —**scav'en•ger,** n.
sce•nar'i•o' (si nâr'ē ō', -när'-) n., pl. **-ios.** 1. a plot outline. 2. an imagined sequence of events.
scene (sēn) n. 1. the place where something occurs. 2. a view. 3. a division of a play, film, etc. 4. a public display of emotion. 5. a sphere of activity or interest. —**scen'er•y,** n. —**sce'nic,** adj.
scent (sent) n. 1. a distinctive odor, esp. an agreeable one. 2. a trail marked by this. 3. the sense of smell. —v.t. 4. to perceive by the sense of smell. 5. to perfume.
scep'ter (sep'tər) n. a rod carried as an emblem of royal power. Also, **scep'tre.**
scep'tic (skep'tik) n. a skeptic.
sched'ule (skej'ōōl, -ōōl; Brit. shed'-yōōl, shej'ōōl) n., v., **-uled, -uling.** —n. 1. a list of things to be done with the time allotted for each. 2. a timetable. —v.t. 3. to enter in a schedule. 4. to plan for a certain date.
scheme (skēm) n., v., **schemed, scheming.** —n. 1. a plan of action. 2. an intrigue; plot. —v.t., v.i. 3. to plan or plot. —**sche•mat'ic** (ski-mat'ik) adj.

scher'zo (skert'sō) n., pl. **-zos, -zi** (-sē). a playful musical movement.
schism (siz'əm, skiz'-) n. a division within a group, as a church.
schiz'o•phre'ni•a (skit'sə frē'nē ə) n. a severe mental disorder marked by delusions and hallucinations. —**schiz'o•phren'ic** (-fren'ik) adj., n.
schlep (shlep) v., **schlepped, schlepping,** n. Slang. —v.t., v.i. 1. to carry or move with great effort. —n. 2. a slow or awkward person. 3. a tedious journey.
schmaltz (shmälts, shmôlts) n. Informal. excessive sentimentalism, esp. in music. —**schmaltz'y,** adj.
schol'ar (skol'ər) n. 1. a learned person. 2. a student. —**schol'ar•ly,** adj.
schol'ar•ship' n. 1. the qualities or knowledge of scholars. 2. financial aid granted to a promising student.
scho•las'tic (skə las'tik) adj. of schools or scholars.
school[1] (skōōl) n. 1. an institution for teaching and learning. 2. the students and teachers at such an institution. 3. a group of persons following the same principles or beliefs. —v.t. 4. to educate; train.
school[2] (skōōl) n. a group of fish.
schoon'er (skōō'nər) n. a sailing ship with fore and aft sails.
schwa (shwä) n. the vowel sound in certain unstressed syllables, as a in sofa; usually represented by ə.
sci•at'i•ca (sī at'i kə) n. pain in the lower back and thigh. —**sci•at'ic,** adj.
sci'ence (sī'əns) n. systematic knowledge, esp. of the physical world, gained through observation and experimentation. —**sci'en•tif'ic** (-tif'ik) adj. —**sci'en•tif'i•cal•ly,** adv. —**sci'en•tist,** n.
sci'ence fic'tion n. fiction dealing with space travel, robots, etc.
sci-fi (sī'fī') n., adj. Informal. science fiction.
scim'i•tar (sim'i tər) n. a curved sword.
scin•til'la (sin til'ə) n. a tiny particle.
scin'til•late' (-tl āt') v.i., **-lated, -lating.** to sparkle.
sci'on (sī'ən) n. 1. a descendant. 2. a plant shoot cut for grafting.
scis'sors (siz'ərz) n.pl. a cutting instrument with two pivoted blades that work against each other.
scle•ro'sis (skli rō'sis) n. a hardening of a body tissue or part.
scoff (skôf) v.i. to express mockery or scorn.
scoff'law' n. a person who flouts the law, as by ignoring traffic tickets.

scold (skōld) *v.t., v.i.* **1.** to find fault (with) angrily. —*n.* **2.** a person who is constantly scolding.

sconce (skons) *n.* a wall bracket for candles or electric lights.

scoop (skōōp) *n.* **1.** a small deep shovel for food. **2.** the bucket of a steam shovel. **3.** the act of scooping. **4.** the quantity taken up. **5.** news published by one newspaper before its rivals. —*v.t.* **6.** to take up with a scoop. **7.** to publish news before (one's rivals).

scoot (skōōt) *v.i.* to go swiftly.

scoot'er *n.* **1.** a child's two-wheeled vehicle. **2.** a two-wheeled motor vehicle.

scope (skōp) *n.* extent or range.

scorch (skôrch) *v.t., v.i.* **1.** to burn or become burnt slightly. —*n.* **2.** a superficial burn.

score (skôr) *n., pl.* **scores,** (for 3) **score,** *v.,* **scored, scoring.** —*n.* **1.** a record of points made, as in a game. **2.** a notch, scratch, or mark. **3.** a group of twenty. **4.** the written or printed music for a movie, play, etc. —*v.t.* **5.** to earn in a game. **6.** to make notches, cuts, or marks in or on. **7.** to compose a score for. —*v.i.* **8.** to earn points, as in a game. **9.** to keep score, as of a game. **10.** to achieve success.

scorn (skôrn) *n.* **1.** contempt. **2.** mockery. —*v.t.* **3.** to treat, regard, or reject with scorn. —**scorn'ful,** *adj.*

scor'pi·on (skôr'pē ən) *n.* a small animal of the spider family with a poisonous stinger in the end of its long tail.

scotch (skoch) *v.t.* to put an end to.

Scotch *n.* a whiskey made in Scotland.

scoun'drel (skoun'drəl) *n.* a dishonorable person.

scour[1] (skou°r) *v.t., v.i.* **1.** to cleanse by rubbing. **2.** to clear out by the force of water.

scour[2] (skou°r) *v.t.* to search (a place) thoroughly.

scourge (skûrj) *n., v.,* **scourged, scourging.** —*n.* **1.** a whip. **2.** a cause of affliction. —*v.t.* **3.** to whip.

scout (skout) *n.* **1.** a person sent ahead to obtain information. **2.** a person employed to find new talent. —*v.t., v.i.* **3.** to search as a scout. **4.** to search (for).

scowl (skoul) *v.i.* **1.** to frown in a sullen or angry manner. —*n.* **2.** a scowling expression.

scrab'ble (skrab'əl) *v.i., v.t.,* **-bled, -bling. 1.** to scratch frantically with the hands or paws. **2.** to scribble.

scrag'gly *adj.,* **-glier, -gliest. 1.** uneven. **2.** shaggy.

scram (skram) *v.i.,* **scrammed, scramming.** *Informal.* to go away quickly.

scram'ble (-bəl) *v.,* **-bled, -bling,** *n.* —*v.i.* **1.** to move quickly, esp. on the hands and knees. —*v.t.* **2.** to mix together confusedly. **3.** to cook (eggs) while stirring. **4.** to make (a radio or television signal) unintelligible. —*n.* **5.** a quick climb. **6.** a disorderly struggle for possession.

scrap (skrap) *n., v.,* **scrapped, scrapping.** —*n.* **1.** a small piece. **2.** discarded material. —*v.t.* **3.** to discard as useless. —**scrap'py,** *adj.*

scrap'book' *n.* a blank book for mounting keepsakes.

scrape (skrāp) *v.,* **scraped, scraping,** *n.* —*v.t.* **1.** to draw something rough or sharp over (a surface) so as to smooth it. **2.** to remove by scraping. **3.** to injure by rubbing against something rough or sharp. **4.** to collect with difficulty. —*v.i.* **5.** to rub against something gratingly. **6.** to make a grating sound. **7.** to get by with difficulty; economize. —*n.* **8.** an act or sound of scraping. **9.** a scraped place. **10.** a distressing situation. —**scrap'er,** *n.*

scratch (skrach) *v.t.* **1.** to mark, tear, or rub with something sharp. **2.** to strike out or cancel. —*v.i.* **3.** to use nails or claws. —*n.* **4.** a mark or injury from scratching. **5.** the act or sound of scratching. —*adj.* **6.** gathered hastily and carelessly. —**Idiom.** **7.** from scratch, from the beginning or from nothing. **8.** up to scratch, satisfactory.

scrawl (skrôl) *v.t., v.i.* **1.** to write carelessly or awkwardly. —*n.* **2.** such handwriting.

scraw'ny (skrô'nē) *adj.,* **-nier, -niest.** excessively thin. —**scraw'ni·ness,** *n.*

scream (skrēm) *n.* **1.** a loud sharp cry. —*v.i., v.t.* **2.** to utter (with) a loud, sharp cry.

screech (skrēch) *n.* **1.** a harsh, shrill sound. —*v.t., v.i.* **2.** to utter with or make a harsh, shrill sound.

screen (skrēn) *n.* **1.** a movable or fixed device that protects or conceals. **2.** a frame holding a wire mesh, used in a window or doorway. **3.** a surface on which motion pictures can be shown. **4.** anything that shelters or conceals. **5.** a sieve. —*v.t.* **6.** to shelter, protect, or conceal with a screen. **7.** to sift, sort, or separate through a screen. **8.** to project on a screen.

screen′play′ *n.* the outline or full script of a motion picture.

screw (skrōō) *n.* **1.** a metal fastener with a spirally threaded shank, driven by twisting. **2.** something having a spiral form. **3.** a propeller. —*v.t.* **4.** to fasten with a screw. **5.** to attach, detach, or adjust by twisting. —*v.i.* **6.** to become attached, detached, or adjusted by being twisted.

screw′driv′er *n.* a tool for turning screws.

scrib′ble (skrib′əl) *v.,* **-bled, -bling,** *n.* —*v.t., v.i.* **1.** to write or draw hastily or carelessly. —*n.* **2.** hasty, careless writing or drawing.

scribe (skrīb) *n.* a person who writes or copies manuscripts.

scrim′mage (skrim′ij) *n., v.,* **-maged, -maging.** —*n.* **1.** in football, the action while the ball is in play. **2.** a practice game. —*v.i.* **3.** to engage in a scrimmage.

scrimp (skrimp) *v.i., v.t.* to be frugal (with).

scrip (skrip) *n.* **1.** paper money issued for temporary use. **2.** a certificate worth a fraction of a share of stock.

script (skript) *n.* **1.** the written text of a play, film, etc. **2.** handwriting.

scrip′ture (skrip′chər) *n.* **1.** sacred writing. **2. Scriptures,** the Bible. —**scrip′tur·al,** *adj.*

scrod (skrod) *n.* a young codfish or haddock.

scroll (skrōl) *n.* **1.** a roll of parchment, paper, etc., with writing on it. —*v.i.* **2.** to move a cursor smoothly, causing new data to appear on a computer screen.

scro′tum (skrō′təm) *n., pl.* **-ta** (-tə) **-tums.** the pouch of skin containing the testicles. —**scro′tal,** *adj.*

scrounge (skrounj) *v.,* **scrounged, scrounging.** —*v.t.* **1.** to beg or mooch. —*v.i.* **2.** to look around for what is needed. —**scroung′er,** *n.*

scrub¹ (skrub) *v.,* **scrubbed, scrubbing,** *n.* —*v.t.* **1.** to rub hard, esp. in washing. —*v.i.* **2.** to clean something by rubbing hard. —*n.* **3.** an act of rubbing.

scrub² (skrub) *n.* **1.** low trees or shrubs. **2.** anything small or poor. —**scrub′by,** *adj.*

scruff (skruf) *n.* the back of the neck; nape.

scruff′y (skruf′ē) *adj.,* **-ier, -iest.** untidy; shabby.

scrump′tious (skrump′shəs) *adj.* extremely pleasing; delicious.

scru′ple (skrōō′pəl) *n.* a moral or ethical consideration that affects one's actions.

scru′pu·lous (-pyə ləs) *adj.* **1.** having scruples. **2.** exact.

scru′ti·nize′ (skrōōt′n īz′) *v.t.,* **-nized, -nizing.** to examine closely. —**scru′ti·ny,** *n.*

scu′ba (skōō′bə) *n.* a portable breathing device for swimmers.

scud (skud) *v.i.,* **scudded, scudding.** to move quickly.

scuff (skuf) *v.t., v.i.* to mar or become marred by hard use.

scuf′fle *n., v.,* **-fled, -fling.** —*n.* **1.** a rough, confused struggle. —*v.i.* **2.** to engage in a scuffle.

scull (skul) *n.* **1.** a light racing boat. **2.** an oar mounted on the stern of a boat. —*v.t., v.i.* **3.** to propel (a boat) with sculls.

sculp′ture (skulp′chər) *n., v.,* **-tured, -turing. 1.** the art of carving or modeling wood, stone, etc., to make three-dimensional works of art. **2.** a work or works made in this way. —*v.t.* **3.** to carve or model (a piece of sculpture). —*v.i.* **4.** to work as a sculptor. —**sculp′tor** (-tər) *n.*

scum (skum) *n.* **1.** a film on top of a liquid. **2.** low, worthless persons.

scurf (skûrf) *n.* **1.** loose scales of skin. **2.** scaly matter on a surface.

scur′ril·ous (skûr′ə ləs) *adj.* coarsely or obscenely abusive.

scur′ry (skûr′ē, skur′ē) *v.i.,* **-ried, -rying.** to move with haste; hurry.

scur′vy (skûr′vē) *n., adj.,* **-vier, -viest.** —*n.* **1.** a disease caused by lack of vitamin C. —*adj.* **2.** contemptible.

scut′tle¹ (skut′l) *n.* a coal bucket.

scut′tle² (skut′l) *v.i.,* **-tled, -tling.** to run with short, quick steps.

scut′tle³ (skut′l) *v.t.,* **-tled, -tling.** to sink (a ship) by making holes in the bottom.

scut′tle·butt′ (-but′) *n. Informal.* rumor; gossip.

scythe (sīth) *n.* a tool with a long handle and a curved blade for cutting grass by hand.

SD South Dakota. Also, **S.D.**

S. Dak. South Dakota.

SE southeast.

sea (sē) *n.* **1.** the salt water covering much of the earth. **2.** an ocean. **3.** a large wave. **4.** a great quantity. —*Idiom.* **5. at sea,** uncertain. —**sea′coast′,** *n.* —**sea′port′,** *n.* —**sea′shore′,** *n.*

sea′ bass′ (bas) *n.* a marine food fish.

sea′bed′ *n.* the ocean floor.

sea′far′ing *adj.* traveling by or working at sea. —**sea′far′er,** *n.*

sea′food′ *n.* edible marine fish or shellfish.

sea′go′ing *adj.* fit for going to sea.

sea′ gull′ *n.* a gull.

sea′ horse′ *n.* a small fish with a head like that of a horse.

seal¹ (sēl) *n.* **1.** an emblem or symbol used to indicate that something is authentic. **2.** a means of closing something tightly. **3.** a stamplike label. —*v.t.* **4.** to affix a seal to. **5.** to fasten with a seal. **6.** to decide or settle. —**seal′ant,** *n.*

seal² (sēl) *n., pl.* **seals, seal.** a marine animal with large flippers.

sea′ lev′el *n.* the position of the sea's surface at mean level between low and high tide.

sea′ li′on *n.* a large seal.

seam (sēm) *n.* **1.** the line formed when two edges meet. **2.** a thin layer in the ground, as of coal. **3.** a wrinkle or scar. —*v.t.* **4.** to join together in a seam.

sea′man *n., pl.* **-men.** a sailor.

seam′stress (-stris) *n.* a woman whose occupation is sewing.

seam′y *adj.,* **-ier, -iest.** sordid.

sé′ance (sā′äns) *n.* a meeting to attempt communication with the spirits of the dead.

sea′plane′ *n.* an airplane equipped with floats.

sear (sēr) *v.t.* to burn the surface of.

search (sûrch) *v.t.* **1.** to look or feel through carefully in order to find something. —*n.* **2.** an act of searching. —**search′er,** *n.*

search′light′ *n.* a device for projecting a strong beam of light.

sea′shell′ *n.* the shell of a marine mollusk.

sea′sick′ness *n.* nausea from the motion of a ship. —**sea′sick′,** *adj.*

sea′son (sē′zən) *n.* **1.** any of four periods of the year. **2.** the usual time when something takes place or flourishes. —*v.t.* **3.** to flavor (food) with salt, spices, etc. **4.** to prepare for use. —**sea′son•al,** *adj.*

sea′son•a•ble *adj.* appropriate to the time of year.

sea′son•ing *n.* flavoring, as salt, spices, or herbs.

seat (sēt) *n.* **1.** something for sitting on. **2.** the part of something on which a person sits. **3.** a right to sit, as in Congress. **4.** a place in which something is established. —*v.t.* **5.** to place in or on a seat. **6.** to find seats for.

seat′ belt′ *n.* straps to keep a passenger secure in a vehicle.

sea′ ur′chin *n.* a small, round sea animal with a spiny shell.

sea′weed′ *n.* a plant growing in the sea.

sea′wor′thy *adj.,* **-thier, -thiest.** fit for sea travel.

se•ba′ceous (si bā′shəs) *adj.* of or secreting a fatty substance.

se•cede′ (si sēd′) *v.i.,* **-ceded, -ceding.** to withdraw from membership in a nation, alliance, etc. —**se•ces′-sion** (-sesh′ən) *n.*

se•clude′ (si klood′) *v.t.,* **-cluded, -cluding.** to remove from contact with others. —**se•clu′sion,** *n.*

sec′ond¹ (sek′ənd) *adj.* **1.** next after the first. **2.** other; another. —*n.* **3.** a second part or the second one of a series. **4.** a person who aids or supports another. **5. seconds, a.** an additional helping of food. **b.** imperfect goods. —*v.t.* **6.** to support. —*adv.* **7.** in the second place. —**sec′ond•ly,** *adv.*

sec′ond² (sek′ənd) *n.* the sixtieth part of a minute.

sec′ond•ar′y (-ən der′ē) *adj.* **1.** second in order, rank, or time. **2.** not primary. **3.** less important.

sec′ond-guess′ *v.t.* to use hindsight in criticizing or correcting.

sec′ond•hand′ *adj.* **1.** not new. **2.** not directly known or experienced.

sec′ond na′ture *n.* a deeply ingrained habit or tendency.

sec′ond-rate′ *adj.* inferior.

sec′ond string′ *n.* a squad of players available to replace those who start a game.

sec′ond wind′ *n.* (wind) energy for a renewed effort.

se′cret (sē′krit) *adj.* **1.** kept from the knowledge of others. —*n.* **2.** something secret. **3.** a mystery. —**se′cre•cy,** *n.*

sec′re•tar′i•at (sek′ri târ′ē ət) *n.* a group of administrative officials.

sec′re•tar′y (-ter′ē) *n., pl.* **-taries. 1.** an office assistant. **2.** the head of a governmental department. **3.** a tall writing desk. —**sec′re•tar′i•al,** *adj.*

se•crete′¹ (si krēt′) *v.t.,* **-creted, -creting.** to discharge or release by secretion.

se•crete′² (si krēt′) *v.t.,* **-creted, -creting.** to hide.

se•cre′tion (-krē′shən) *n.* **1.** the process of producing a substance within the body, as in a gland or cell. **2.** the product secreted.

se′cre•tive (sē′kri tiv, si krē′-) *adj.* tending to keep things secret.

sect (sekt) *n.* a group with a common religious faith.

sec•tar′i•an (sek târ′ē ən) *adj.* **1.** of a sect. **2.** limited in scope. —*n.* **3.** a sectarian person.

sec′tion (sek′shən) *n.* **1.** a separate or distinct part. —*v.t.* **2.** to cut or divide into sections.

sec′tor (sek′tər) *n.* **1.** a plane figure bounded by two radii and an arc. **2.** a distinct part.

sec•u•lar (sek/yə lər) *adj.* worldly; not religious. —**sec/u•lar•ism,** *n.*
—**sec/u•lar•ize/,** *v.t.*

se•cure/ (si kyŏŏr/) *adj., v.,* **-cured, -curing.** —*adj.* **1.** safe. **2.** firmly in place. **3.** certain. —*v.t.* **4.** to get hold of. **5.** to make secure.

se•cu/ri•ty (-kyŏŏr/i tē) *n., pl.* **-ties. 1.** safety. **2.** freedom from care. **3.** protection against crime, attack, etc. **4.** something given as a pledge. **5. securities,** stocks or bonds.

secu/rity blan/ket *n.* something that gives a feeling of safety.

se•dan/ (-dan/) *n.* an enclosed automobile for four or more.

se•date/ (-dāt/) *adj., v.* **-dated, -dating.** —*adj.* **1.** calm, dignified, and composed. —*v.t.* **2.** to give a sedative to. —**se•date/ly,** *adv.* —**se•da/tion,** *n.*

sed/a•tive (sed/ə tiv) *adj.* **1.** tending to soothe or relieve pain or agitation. —*n.* **2.** a sedative drug.

sed/en•tar/y (sed/n ter/ē) *adj.* characterized by or requiring sitting.

sedge (sej) *n.* a grassy marsh plant.

sed/i•ment (sed/ə mənt) *n.* matter settling to the bottom of a liquid. —**sed/i•men/ta•ry,** *adj.*

se•di/tion (si dish/ən) *n.* incitement to rebellion. —**se•di/tious,** *adj.*

se•duce/ (-dōōs/, -dyōōs/) *v.t.,* **-duced, -ducing. 1.** to lead astray. **2.** to induce to have sexual intercourse. —**se•duc/er,** *n.* —**se•duc/tion** (-duk/shən) *n.* —**se•duc/tive,** *adj.*

see¹ (sē) *v.,* **saw** (sô) **seen, seeing.** —*v.t.* **1.** to perceive with the eyes; look at. **2.** to understand. **3.** to visualize. **4.** to recognize. **5.** to find out. **6.** to make sure. **7.** to escort. **8.** to visit. —*v.i.* **9.** to have the power of sight. **10.** to understand.

see² (sē) *n.* a bishop's jurisdiction.

seed (sēd) *n.* **1.** a fertilized plant ovule from which a new plant will grow. **2.** sperm; semen. **3.** the source of something. **4.** offspring. —*v.t.* **5.** to sow with seed. **6.** to remove the seeds from. —*v.i.* **7.** to produce seed. —*Idiom.* **8. go to seed, a.** to stop growing as seed develops. **b.** to become shabby.

seed/ling *n.* a plant grown from seed.

seed/ mon/ey *n.* money for beginning an enterprise.

seed/y *adj.,* **-ier, -iest. 1.** shabby. **2.** having many seeds.

see/ing *conj.* inasmuch as.

seek (sēk) *v.t.,* **sought, seeking. 1.** to search for. **2.** to try; attempt.

seem (sēm) *v.i.* to appear to be.

seem/ing *adj.* apparent.

seem/ly *adj.,* **-lier, -liest.** proper.

seen (sēn) *v.* pp. of **see.**

seep (sēp) *v.i.* to pass, flow, or ooze gradually. —**seep/age,** *n.*

seer (sēr) *n.* a prophet.

seer/suck/er (sēr/suk/ər) *n.* a striped cotton fabric.

see/saw/ (sē/sô/) *n.* **1.** a balanced plank on which two children ride up and down while seated at opposite ends. **2.** going up and down or back and forth. —*v.i., v.t.* **3.** to move on or as if on a seesaw.

seethe (sēth) *v.i.,* **seethed, seething. 1.** to boil; foam. **2.** to be agitated or excited.

seg/ment (seg/mənt) *n.* **1.** a part; section. —*v.t., v.i.* **2.** to divide into segments. —**seg/men•ta/tion,** *n.*

seg/re•gate/ (seg/ri gāt/) *v.t.,* **-gated, -gating.** to separate from others. —**seg/re•ga/tion,** *n.*

se/gue (sā/gwā, seg/wā) *v.,* **segued, segueing,** *n.* —*v.i.* **1.** to continue at once with the next section. **2.** to make a smooth transition. —*n.* **3.** a smooth transition.

seine (sān) *n.* a fishing net.

seis/mic (sīz/mik, sīs/-) *adj.* of or caused by earthquakes.

seis/mo•graph/ (-mə graf/) *n.* an instrument for recording the intensity of earthquakes.

seis•mol/o•gy (-mol/ə jē) *n.* the science of earthquakes. —**seis/mo•log/i•cal,** *adj.* —**seis•mol/o•gist,** *n.*

seize (sēz) *v.t.,* **seized, seizing. 1.** to take hold of suddenly or forcibly. **2.** to take possession of.

seiz/ure (sē/zhər) *n.* **1.** an act of seizing. **2.** a sudden attack of illness.

sel/dom (sel/dəm) *adv.* not often.

se•lect/ (si lekt/) *v.t., v.i.* **1.** to choose. —*adj.* **2.** chosen carefully; choice. **3.** careful in choosing. —**se•lec/tion,** *n.* —**se•lec/tive,** *adj.*

self (self) *n., pl.* **selves** (selvz) **1.** a person referred to as an individual. **2.** a person's own nature. **3.** personal advantage or interests.

self/-ad•dressed/ *adj.* addressed for return to the sender.

self/-as•ser/tion *n.* an expression of one's own importance, opinions, etc. —**self/-as•ser/tive,** *adj.*

self/-as•sur/ance *n.* confidence in one's ability. —**self/-as•sured/,** *adj.*

self/-cen/tered *adj.* interested only in oneself.

self/-con/fi•dence *n.* faith in one's own judgment, ability, etc. —**self/-con/fi•dent,** *adj.*

self/-con/scious *adj.* embarrassed or uneasy.

self/-con•tained/ *adj.* **1.** containing

within itself all that is necessary. **2.** reserved in behavior.

self′-con·trol′ *n.* restraint of one's actions. —**self′-con·trolled′,** *adj.*

self′-de·fense′ *n.* **1.** the act of defending oneself or one's property. **2.** a plea that use of force was necessary in defending one's person.

self′-de·ni′al *n.* the sacrifice of one's desires.

self′-de·ter′mi·na′tion *n.* **1.** the freedom to act as one chooses. **2.** freedom of a nation to choose its own form of government.

self′-ef·fac′ing *adj.* keeping oneself in the background.

self′-ev′i·dent *adj.* obvious.

self′-im·por′tant *adj.* having or showing an exaggerated sense of one's own importance.

self′-in′ter·est *n.* one's personal benefit.

self′ish (sel′fish) *adj.* caring only for oneself. —**self′ish·ly,** *adv.*

self′less *adj.* having little concern for oneself; unselfish.

self′-made′ *adj.* owing one's success entirely to one's own efforts.

self′-pos·sessed′ *adj.* calm; poised.

self′-pres·er·va′tion *n.* the instinctive desire to guard one's safety.

self′-re·spect′ *n.* proper regard for oneself. —**self′-re·spect′ing,** *adj.*

self′-re·straint′ *n.* self-control.

self′-right′eous *adj.* smugly convinced that one is morally right.

self′same′ *adj.* identical.

self′-sat′is·fied′ *adj.* feeling or showing a smug satisfaction with oneself or one's achievements.

self′-seek′ing *n.* **1.** the selfish seeking of one's own interests or ends. —*adj.* **2.** given to or characterized by self-seeking.

self′-serv′ice *adj.* **1.** of a commercial establishment in which customers serve themselves. **2.** designed to be used without the aid of an attendant.

self′-serv′ing *adj.* serving to further one's own interests.

self′-styled′ *adj.* so called only by oneself.

self′-suf·fi′cient *adj.* able to supply one's own needs without external assistance.

sell (sel) *v.,* **sold** (sōld) **selling.** —*v.t.* **1.** to exchange (goods, property, or services) for money. **2.** to offer for sale. **3.** to promote the sale, acceptance, or approval of. —*v.i.* **4.** to engage in selling. **5.** to be offered for sale. **6. sell out, a.** to dispose of all of one's stock by selling. **b.** to betray. —**sell′er,** *n.*

sel′vage (sel′vij) *n.* a finished edge on fabric.

se·man′tics (si man′tiks) *n.* the study of meaning in language.

sem′a·phore′ (sem′ə fôr′) *n.* an apparatus for visual signaling.

sem′blance (sem′bləns) *n.* **1.** outward appearance. **2.** a likeness.

se′men (sē′mən) *n.* the male reproductive fluid.

se·mes′ter (si mes′tər) *n.* half of a school year.

semi- a prefix meaning half.

sem′i·cir′cle *n.* a half circle. —**sem′i·cir′cu·lar,** *adj.*

sem′i·co′lon *n.* a punctuation mark (;) between parts of a sentence.

sem′i·con·duc′tor *n.* a substance, as silicon, with electrical conductivity between that of an insulator and a conductor.

sem′i·fi′nal *adj.* **1.** of the next to last round in a tournament. —*n.* **2.** a semifinal round or bout.

sem′i·nal (sem′ə nl) *adj.* **1.** of or consisting of semen. **2.** influencing future development.

sem′i·nar′ (-när′) *n.* a class in which advanced students discuss their research.

sem′i·nar′y (-ner′ē) *n., pl.* **-ies.** a school that prepares students for the priesthood, ministry, or rabbinate.

sem′i·pre′cious (sem′ē-, sem′ī-) *adj.* having value as a gem, but not classified as precious.

sem′i·tone′ *n.* a musical pitch halfway between two whole tones.

sem′o·li′na (sem′ə lē′nə) *n.* ground durum wheat.

sen′ate (sen′it) *n.* a legislative body, esp. (*cap.*) the upper house of the legislatures of the United States, Canada, etc. —**sen′a·tor** (-i-tər) *n.*

send (send) *v.t.,* **sent, sending.** **1.** to cause or enable to go. **2.** to cause to be taken to a destination. **3.** to emit. —**send′er,** *n.*

se′nile (sē′nīl) *adj.* showing mental weakness because of old age. —**se·nil′i·ty** (si nil′ə tē) *n.*

sen′ior (sēn′yər) *adj.* **1.** older. **2.** of higher rank or longer service. **3.** denoting the final year in high school or college. —*n.* **4.** a senior person. **5.** a student in the final year of high school or college.

sen′ior cit′izen *n.* an older person.

sen·ior′i·ty (sēn yôr′i tē) *n.* the status conferred by length of service.

sen·sa′tion (sen sā′shən) *n.* **1.** perception through the senses. **2.** a feeling produced by stimulation of the senses or the mind. **3.** excited interest. **4.** the person or thing causing this.

sen·sa′tion·al *adj.* startling; shocking. —**sen·sa′tion·al·ism,** *n.*

sense (sens) *n., v.,* **sensed, sensing.** —*n.* **1.** one of the faculties, sight, hearing, smell, taste, or touch, by which humans and animals perceive the environment. **2.** a feeling based on one of the senses. **3.** a special ability for perception or appreciation. **4.** practical intelligence. **5.** meaning. —*v.t.* **6.** to perceive by the senses.

sen′si·bil′i·ty (sen′sə bil′i tē) *n., pl.* **-ties.** capacity for feeling.

sen′si·ble *adj.* **1.** having, using, or showing good sense. **2.** aware. **3.** capable of feeling or perceiving. —**sen′si·bly,** *adv.*

sen′si·tive *adj.* **1.** readily affected by outside stimuli. **2.** responsive to the feelings of others. **3.** easily offended. —**sen′si·tiv′i·ty,** *n.*

sen′si·tize′ (-tīz′) *v.t., v.i.,* **-tized, -tizing.** to make or become sensitive.

sen′sor (sen′sôr, -sər) *n.* a device sensitive to light, temperature, or radiation level that transmits a signal to another instrument.

sen′so·ry (-sə rē) *adj.* of sensation or the senses.

sen′su·al (sen′shoo əl) *adj.* **1.** pleasing the senses. **2.** indulging in physical pleasures. —**sen′su·al′i·ty** (-al′i tē) *n.* —**sen′su·al·ly,** *adv.*

sen′su·ous *adj.* of or affecting the senses.

sen′tence (sen′tns) *n., v.,* **-tenced, -tencing.** —*n.* **1.** a group of words expressing a complete thought. **2.** a punishment ordered by a court of law. —*v.t.* **3.** to pronounce sentence upon.

sen·ten′tious (-ten′shəs) *adj.* **1.** using maxims or pompous words. **2.** moralizing.

sen′tient (-shənt) *adj.* capable of perceiving through the senses.

sen′ti·ment (-tə mənt) *n.* **1.** an opinion or attitude. **2.** tender feelings. **3.** a thought influenced by emotion.

sen′ti·men′tal (-men′tl) *adj.* **1.** expressing or appealing to tender or romantic feelings. **2.** nostalgic.

sen′ti·nel (-tn l, -tə nl) *n.* one that stands watch.

sen′try (-trē) *n., pl.* **-tries.** a guard.

se′pal (sē′pəl) *n.* one of the leaflike parts of a flower calyx.

sep′a·rate′ *v.,* **-rated, -rating,** *adj.* —*v.t.* (sep′ə rāt′) **1.** to put or keep apart; divide. —*v.i.* **2.** to move or come apart. **3.** to stop living together as a married couple. —*adj.* (-rit) **4.** not connected. —**sep′a·ra′tion,** *n.* —**sep′a·ra·ble,** *adj.*

sep′a·ra·tist (-ər ə tist, -ə rā′-) *n.* an advocate of separation.

sep′a·ra′tor *n.* an apparatus for separating ingredients.

se′pi·a (sē′pē ə) *n.* **1.** a brown pigment. **2.** a dark brown.

sep′sis (sep′sis) *n.* invasion of the body by harmful microorganisms. —**sep′tic** (-tik) *adj.*

Sept. September.

Sep·tem′ber (sep tem′bər) *n.* the ninth month of the year.

sep·tet′ (-tet′) *n.* a group of seven.

sep′ti·ce′mi·a (-tə sē′mē ə) *n.* blood poisoning.

sep′tic tank′ *n.* a tank in which sewage is decomposed.

sep′tu·a·ge·nar′i·an (-chōō ə jə-nâr′ē ən) *n.* a person 70 to 79 years old.

sep′ul·cher (sep′əl kər) *n.* a burial place. Also, **sep′ul·chre.**

seq. **1.** sequel. **2.** the following.

se′quel (sē′kwəl) *n.* **1.** a literary work, film, etc., continuing the narrative of an earlier one. **2.** a subsequent development.

se′quence (-kwəns) *n.* **1.** the following of one thing after another. **2.** a continuous connected series.

se·ques′ter (si kwes′tər) *v.t.* **1.** to remove or withdraw into solitude. **2.** to set apart.

se′quin (sē′kwin) *n.* a small shiny disk used as ornamentation.

se·quoi′a (si kwoi′ə) *n.* a large coniferous tree of California.

ser′aph (ser′əf) *n., pl.* **-aphs, -aphim** (-ə fim). a member of the highest order of angels. —**se·raph′ic** (sə raf′ik) *adj.*

sere (sēr) *adj.* dry; withered.

ser′e·nade′ (ser′ə nād′) *n., v.,* **-naded, -nading.** —*n.* **1.** music performed in the open air at night, as by a lover to his lady. —*v.t., v.i.* **2.** to perform a serenade (for).

ser′en·dip′i·ty (ser′ən dip′i tē) *n.* luck in making desirable discoveries by accident. —**ser′en·dip′i·tous,** *adj.*

se·rene′ (sə rēn′) *adj.* **1.** peaceful; calm. **2.** clear; fair. —**se·ren′i·ty** (-ren′ə tē) *n.*

serf (sûrf) *n.* a person in feudal servitude. —**serf′dom,** *n.*

ser′geant (sär′jənt) *n.* **1.** a noncommissioned officer above a corporal. **2.** a police officer below a captain or lieutenant.

se′ri·al (sēr′ē əl) *n.* **1.** something appearing in installments at regular intervals. —*adj.* **2.** of a serial. **3.** of or in a series.

se′ries (sēr′ēz) *n.* a number of related things arranged or occurring in succession.

ser·if (ser′if) *n.* a smaller line used to finish off a main stroke of a printed letter.

se·ri·ous (sēr′ē əs) *adj.* **1.** of, requiring, or marked by deep thought. **2.** somber. **3.** important. **4.** critical or threatening.

ser′mon (sûr′mən) *n.* a religious speech delivered by a cleric.

ser′pent (sûr′pənt) *n.* a snake.

ser′pen·tine′ (-pən tēn′, -tīn′) *adj.* winding like a snake.

ser′rat·ed (ser′ā tid) *adj.* notched or toothed on the edge. Also, **ser′rate** (ser′it).

se·rum (sēr′əm) *n.*, *pl.* **serums, sera** (sēr′ə). **1.** the clear, pale yellow liquid that separates from the clot in blood. **2.** such liquid used as an inoculation against a certain disease. **3.** a watery animal fluid.

serv′ant (sûr′vənt) *n.* a person employed by another, esp. to do domestic work.

serve (sûrv) *v.*, **served, serving.** —*v.i.* **1.** to act as a servant. **2.** to present food or drink. **3.** to do one's official duty. **4.** to suffice. **5.** (in tennis, volleyball, etc.) to put the ball into play. —*v.t.* **6.** to offer food or drink to. **7.** to present (food or drink) to someone. **8.** to work for as a servant. **9.** to undergo (a term of imprisonment, service, etc.). **10.** (in tennis, volleyball, etc.) to put (the ball) into play. **11.** to render homage to. **12.** to make legal delivery of (a process or writ).

serv′ice (sûr′vis) *n.*, *v.*, **-iced, -icing.** —*n.* **1.** an act of helpful activity. **2.** the providing or a provider of maintenance or repair. **3.** the performance of duties or duties performed. **4.** an act of public worship. **5.** a set of dishes or utensils. **6.** domestic employment. **7.** (a branch of) the armed forces. **8.** (in tennis, volleyball, etc.) the act or manner of serving the ball. —*v.t.* **9.** to maintain, repair, or restore. **10.** to supply with services.

serv′ice·a·ble *adj.* usable.

ser′vile (-vil, -vīl) *adj.* slavishly submissive. —**ser·vil′i·ty** (-vil′ə tē) *n.*

ser′vi·tude′ (-tōōd′, -tyōōd′) *n.* bondage.

ses′a·me (ses′ə mē) *n.* the small edible seed of a tropical plant.

ses′sion (sesh′ən) *n.* a meeting, as of a court or class.

set (set) *v.*, **set, setting,** *n.*, *adj.* —*v.t.* **1.** to put or place. **2.** to fix definitely. **3.** to put (a broken bone) in position. **4.** to arrange (type) for printing. —*v.i.* **5.** to sink below the horizon. **6.** to become

firm. **7. set forth, a.** to state. **b.** to begin a trip. **8. ~ off, a.** to cause to explode. **b.** to begin. **9. ~ up, a.** to raise. **b.** to establish. —*n.* **10.** a group; complete collection. **11.** a radio or television receiver. **12.** a construction representing the setting of the action in a play. —*adj.* **13.** prearranged. **14.** resolved.

set′back′ *n.* a return to a worse condition.

set·tee′ (se tē′) *n.* a small sofa.

set′ter (set′ər) *n.* a long-haired hunting dog.

set′ting *n.* **1.** the position of something that has been set. **2.** surroundings. **3.** the locale and period of a story, play, etc. **4.** a mounting for a jewel. **5.** the music composed for certain words.

set′tle (set′l) *v.*, **-tled, -tling.** —*v.t.* **1.** to put in order. **2.** to pay. **3.** to colonize. **4.** to quiet or calm. **5.** to resolve. —*v.i.* **6.** to come to an agreement or decision. **7.** to take up residence. **8.** to come to rest. **9.** to sink gradually. —**set′tle·ment,** *n.* —**set′tler,** *n.*

sev′en (sev′ən) *n.*, *adj.* six plus one. —**sev′enth,** *adj.*, *n.*

sev′en·teen′ *n.*, *adj.* sixteen plus one. —**sev′en·teenth′,** *adj.*, *n.*

sev′enth heav′en *n.* bliss.

sev′en·ty *n.*, *adj.* ten times seven. —**sev′en·ti·eth,** *adj.*, *n.*

sev′er (-ər) *v.t.*, *v.i.* to separate; break off. —**sev′er·ance,** *n.*

sev′er·al (-əl) *adj.* **1.** some, but not many. **2.** respective; individual. **3.** various. —*n.* **4.** several persons or things.

se·vere′ (sə vēr′) *adj.*, **-verer, -verest.** **1.** harsh. **2.** serious or stern. **3.** austere. **4.** intense; violent. —**se·ver′i·ty** (-ver′i tē) *n.*

sew (sō) *v.*, **sewed, sewed** or **sewn, sewing.** —*v.t.* **1.** to make, repair, or attach by stitches. —*v.i.* **2.** to work with a needle and thread.

sew′age (sōō′ij) *n.* wastes that pass through sewers.

sew′er (sōō′ər) *n.* an underground passage for waste water, refuse, etc.

sex (seks) *n.* **1.** either the male or female division of a species. **2.** the differences by which the male and female are distinguished. **3.** the attraction drawing one individual sexually toward another. **4.** sexual intercourse. —**sex′u·al** (sek′shōō əl) *adj.* —**sex′u·al·i·ty,** *n.*

sex′a·ge·nar′i·an (sek′sə jə när′ē ən) *n.* a person 60 to 69 years old.

sex′ chro′mosome *n.* a chromosome that determines an individual's sex.

sex′ism *n.* discrimination because of sex, esp. against women. —**sex′ist,** *n., adj.*

sex′tant (sek′stənt) *n.* an instrument for finding one's position at sea.

sex•tet′ (seks tet′) *n.* a group of six musicians or a composition for such a group.

sex′ton (sek′stən) *n.* a church caretaker.

sex′ual harass′ment *n.* unwelcome sexual advances, esp. by a superior.

sex′ual in′tercourse *n.* genital contact between individuals, esp. penetration of the penis into the vagina.

sex′ually transmit′ted disease′ *n.* any disease transmitted by sexual contact.

sex′y *adj.,* **-ier, -iest.** sexually interesting or exciting; erotic.

SGML Standard Generalized Markup Language: a set of standards enabling a user to create a markup scheme for tagging the elements of an electronic document.

Sgt. Sergeant.

shab′by (shab′ē) *adj.,* **-bier, -biest.** **1.** worn out or run-down. **2.** mean. —**shab′bi•ness,** *n.*

shack (shak) *n.* a rough cabin.

shack′le (shak′əl) *n., v.,* **-led, -ling.** —*n.* **1.** an iron bond for the wrist, ankle, etc. —*v.t.* **2.** to put shackles on. **3.** to restrain; inhibit.

shad (shad) *n.* an edible marine fish that spawns in rivers upstream from the sea.

shade (shād) *n., v.,* **shaded, shading.** —*n.* **1.** a slightly dark, cool place. **2.** a place sheltered from the sun. **3.** something used to shut out light. **4.** the degree of darkness of a color. **5.** a slight amount. —*v.t.* **6.** to dim or darken. **7.** to protect from light or heat. —*v.i.* **8.** to change by degrees.

shad′ow (shad′ō) *n.* **1.** a dark image cast on a surface by a body intercepting light. **2.** comparative darkness. **3.** a trace. **4.** a cause of gloom. —*v.t.* **5.** to cast a shadow over. **6.** to follow secretly. —**shad′ow•y,** *adj.*

shad′y *adj.,* **-ier, -iest. 1.** giving or located in shade. **2.** dishonest.

shaft (shaft) *n.* **1.** a long slender rod. **2.** a ray or beam. **3.** a revolving bar in an engine. **4.** a vertical underground space, as in a mine. **5.** *Slang.* unfair treatment. —*v.t.* **6.** *Slang.* to treat unfairly.

shag (shag) *n.* **1.** matted wool, hair, etc. **2.** a long, thick pile or nap.

shah (shä) *n.* (formerly, in Iran) a king.

shake (shāk) *v.,* **shook** (shŏŏk), **shaken, shaking,** *n.* —*v.i., v.t.* **1.** to move up and down or back and forth with short, quick movements. **2.** to come or force off or out by quick movements. **3.** to tremble or cause to tremble. **4.** to clasp (a person's hand) in greeting. **5.** to disturb greatly. —*n.* **6.** an act of shaking. **7. shakes,** a spell of trembling.

shake′up′ *n.* a thorough organizational reform.

shak′y *adj.,* **-ier, -iest.** not firm.

shale (shāl) *n.* layered rock.

shall (shal; *unstressed* shəl) *auxiliary v., pres.* **shall;** *past* **should. 1.** plan to or intend to. **2.** will have to or is determined to. **3.** (in laws, directives, etc.) must. **4.** (used in questions). —**Usage.** Today, WILL is used in place of SHALL to indicate future time in all three persons and in all types of speech and writing. SHALL has some use, chiefly in formal contexts, to express determination: *I shall return. We shall overcome.* SHALL also occurs in the language of law and in directives: *All visitors shall observe posted regulations.*

shal′lot (shal′ət) *n.* an onionlike plant with a bulb used in cooking.

shal′low (shal′ō) *adj.* **1.** not deep. **2.** superficial. —*n.* **3. shallows,** a shallow part of a body of water.

sham (sham) *n., adj., v.,* **shammed, shamming.** —*n.* **1.** a pretense or imitation. —*adj.* **2.** pretended. —*v.t., v.i.* **3.** to pretend.

sham′ble *v.,* **-bled, -bling,** *n.* —*v.i.* **1.** to walk awkwardly. —*n.* **2.** a shambling gait. **3. shambles,** a scene of confusion.

shame (shām) *n., v.,* **shamed, shaming.** —*n.* **1.** distress and guilt over a wrong or foolish act. **2.** disgrace. —*v.t.* **3.** to cause to feel shame. **4.** to motivate by shame. —**shame′ful,** *adj.* —**shame′less,** *adj.*

sham•poo′ (sham pŏŏ′) *n.* **1.** a liquid soap for washing the hair. **2.** a cleansing agent for rugs, upholstery, etc. **3.** a cleansing with shampoo. —*v.t.* **4.** to wash or cleanse with shampoo.

sham′rock (sham′rok) *n.* a small clover with a three-part leaf.

shank (shangk) *n.* the part of the leg between the knee and the ankle.

shan′ty (shan′tē) *n., pl.* **-ties.** a crudely built hut or cabin.

shape (shāp) *n., v.,* **shaped, shap-**

ing. —*n.* **1.** the outline or form of something. **2.** condition. **3.** orderly arrangement. —*v.t.* **4.** to give shape to. **5.** to adjust to a certain condition. —**shape′less,** *adj.*

shape′ly *adj.,* **-lier, -liest.** having a pleasing shape. —**shape′li•ness,** *n.*

share (shâr) *n., v.,* **shared, sharing.** —*n.* **1.** a portion allotted to one person. **2.** one of the equal parts into which a company's stock is divided. —*v.t.* **3.** to divide and distribute in shares. **4.** to use, enjoy, etc., jointly. —*v.i.* **5.** to have a share.

share′crop′per *n.* a tenant farmer who pays part of the crop as rent.

share′hold′er *n.* one that owns shares of stock.

shark (shärk) *n.* **1.** a large marine fish, often ferocious. **2.** one who preys greedily on others.

sharp (shärp) *adj.* **1.** having a thin cutting edge or fine point. **2.** abrupt. **3.** clearly defined. **4.** (of taste) pungent. **5.** (of sound) piercing. **6.** felt acutely, as cold. **7.** mentally acute. **8.** shrewd. **9.** *Music.* above the true pitch. —*adv.* **10.** keenly or acutely. **11.** punctually. —*n.* **12.** a musical tone one half step above a given tone or the symbol indicating this. —**sharp′en,** *v.t., v.i.* —**sharp′en•er,** *n.* —**sharp′ness,** *n.*

sharp′shoot′er *n.* a skilled shooter.

shat′ter (shat′ər) *v.i., v.t.* to break or cause to break in pieces.

shat′ter•proof′ *adj.* made to resist shattering.

shave (shāv) *v.,* **shaved, shaved** or **shaven, shaving,** *n.* —*v.i.* **1.** to remove hair with a razor. —*v.t.* **2.** to remove hair from (face, legs, etc.) close to the skin. **3.** to cut thin slices from. —*n.* **4.** the act or result of shaving.

shav′ings *n.pl.* thin slices of wood.

shawl (shôl) *n.* a long covering for the head and shoulders.

she (shē) *pron.* **1.** the female last mentioned. —*n.* **2.** a female.

sheaf (shēf) *n., pl.* **sheaves.** a bundle.

shear (shēr) *v.t.,* **sheared, sheared** or **shorn, shearing.** **1.** to cut (something). **2.** to clip the hair, fleece, etc., from.

shears *n.pl.* large scissors.

sheath (shēth) *n.* **1.** a case for a blade. **2.** any similar covering.

sheathe (shē*th*) *v.t.,* **sheathed, sheathing.** to put into a sheath.

she•bang′ (shə bang′) *n. Informal.* a thing, contrivance, or affair.

shed¹ (shed) *n.* a simple shelter.

shed² (shed) *v.,* **shed, shedding.**

—*v.t.* **1.** to pour or give forth. **2.** to lose (leaves, skin, etc.) by a natural process. **3.** to throw off. —*v.i.* **4.** to cast off a natural covering.

sheen (shēn) *n.* brightness.

sheep (shēp) *n., pl.* **sheep.** a mammal bred for wool and meat.

sheep′ dog′ *n.* a dog trained to herd sheep.

sheep′fold′ *n.* an enclosure for sheep.

sheep′ish *adj.* embarrassed.

sheer¹ (shēr) *adj.* **1.** transparent and thin. **2.** complete; utter. **3.** very steep.

sheer² (shēr) *v.t., v.i.* to turn from a course.

sheet¹ (shēt) *n.* **1.** a large piece of cloth used as bedding. **2.** a broad thin layer or covering. **3.** a thin piece, as of glass, metal, etc.

sheet² (shēt) *n.* a rope or wire used to control a ship's sail.

sheik (shēk, shāk) *n.* (in Arab countries) a ruler.

shek′el (shek′əl) *n.* an ancient Hebrew and modern Israeli monetary unit.

shelf (shelf) *n., pl.* **shelves** (shelvz). **1.** a horizontal slab attached to a wall for holding objects. **2.** something resembling this, as a ledge.

shelf′ life′ *n.* the period during which a product is fit for use.

shell (shel) *n.* **1.** a hard outer covering of an animal or a seed, egg, nut, etc. **2.** a metal case filled with an explosive charge. **3.** a light racing boat. —*v.t.* **4.** to remove the shell of. **5.** to fire shells at.

shel•lac′ (shə lak′) *n., v.,* **-lacked, -lacking.** —*n.* **1.** a substance used in varnish. —*v.t.* **2.** to coat with shellac. **3.** *Slang.* to defeat.

shell′fish′ *n.* an aquatic animal having a shell.

shell′ shock′ *n.* combat fatigue.

shel′ter (shel′tər) *n.* **1.** a structure that offers protection against rain, cold, etc. **2.** the protection provided by a shelter. —*v.t., v.i.* **3.** to provide with or take shelter.

shelve (shelv) *v.t.,* **shelved, shelving.** **1.** to put on a shelf. **2.** to put off or aside. **3.** to remove from active use.

she•nan′i•gans (shə nan′i gənz) *n.pl. Informal.* mischief.

shep′herd (shep′ərd) *n.* **1.** a person who tends sheep. —*v.t.* **2.** to guide.

sher′bet (shûr′bit) *n.* a frozen, fruit-flavored dessert.

sher′iff (sher′if) *n.* a county law-enforcement officer.

sher′ry (sher′ē) *n., pl.* **-ries.** a fortified wine served as a cocktail.

shib'bo·leth (shib'ə lith) *n.* a common saying; slogan.

shield (shēld) *n.* **1.** a plate of armor carried on the arm. **2.** something or someone that protects. —*v.t.* **3.** to protect.

shift (shift) *v.t., v.i.* **1.** to move from one place or direction to another. —**2.** a change from one place or direction to another. **3.** a scheduled period of work.

shift'less *adj.* lacking ambition.

shift'y *adj.*, **-ier, -iest.** devious.

shill (shil) *n.* a person who poses as a customer to lure others.

shil'ling (shil'ing) *n.* a former British coin, the 20th part of a pound.

shim'mer (shim'ər) *v.i.* **1.** to glow faintly; flicker. —*n.* **2.** a faint glow.

shin (shin) *n.* the front of the leg from the knee to the ankle.

shin'dig' (shin'dig') *n. Informal.* an elaborate and usu. large party.

shine (shīn) *v., shone* (shōn) or (for 6) **shined, shining,** *n.* —*v.i.* **1.** to give forth or glow with light. **2.** to sparkle. **3.** to excel. —*v.t.* **4.** to cause to shine. **5.** to direct the light of. **6.** to polish. —*n.* **7.** brightness. **8.** a polish. —**shin'y,** *adj.*

shin'gle¹ (shing'gəl) *n., v.,* **-gled, -gling.** —*n.* **1.** a thin slab of wood, asbestos, etc., used in overlapping rows as covering for a roof or outside wall. **2.** a small signboard. —*v.t.* **3.** to cover with shingles.

shin'gle² (shing'gəl) *n.* **1.** smooth pebbles lying loose on a beach. **2.** an area of these.

shin'gles *n.* a viral disease marked by skin eruptions and pain in the involved nerves.

shin' splints' *n.pl.* a painful condition of the shins associated with strenuous activity.

Shin'to (shin'tō) *n.* a native religion of Japan.

ship (ship) *n., v.,* **shipped, shipping.** —*n.* **1.** a large vessel for navigating in water. —*v.t.* **2.** to transport by ship, rail, truck, etc. **3.** to put (as oars) in place for use on a ship or boat. **4.** to send away. —**ship'board',** *n.* —**ship'mate',** *n.*

-ship a suffix meaning: **1.** state or quality. **2.** position or rank. **3.** skill or art.

ship'ment *n.* **1.** the act of shipping. **2.** something that is shipped.

ship'shape' *adj., adv.* in good order.

ship'wreck' *n.* **1.** the destruction of a ship. —*v.i., v.t.* **2.** to suffer or cause to suffer shipwreck.

ship'wright' *n.* a carpenter who repairs or builds ships.

ship'yard' *n.* a place where ships are built or repaired.

shire (shī°r) *n.* a county in Great Britain.

shirk (shûrk) *v.t., v.i.* to evade (work or duty).

shirr (shûr) *v.t.* **1.** to gather (cloth) on parallel threads. **2.** to bake (eggs).

shirt (shûrt) *n.* a garment for the upper part of the body.

shirt'tail' *n.* the part of a shirt below the waistline.

shirt'waist' *n.* a tailored blouse.

shish' ke·bab' (shish' kə bob') *n.* cubes of meat broiled on a skewer.

shiv'er (shiv'ər) *v.i.* **1.** to tremble, as with cold. —*n.* **2.** a tremble or quiver. —**shiv'er·y,** *adj.*

shoal¹ (shōl) *n.* a shallow place in a body of water.

shoal² (shōl) *n.* a large number, esp. of fish.

shock (shok) *n.* **1.** a sudden, violent emotional upset. **2.** a sudden and violent blow, impact, etc. **3.** severely diminished blood circulation caused by trauma. **4.** the effect of an electric charge on the body. —*v.t.* **5.** to affect with horror, surprise, etc. **6.** to subject to electric shock.

shock' absorb'er *n.* a device for damping sudden, rapid motion.

shock' ther'apy *n.* a treatment for mental disorders using a drug or electricity.

shod'dy (shod'ē) *adj.*, **-dier, -diest.** of poor quality. —**shod'di·ly,** *adv.*

shoe (shoō) *n., v.,* **shod** (shod) **shoeing.** —*n.* **1.** an external covering for the foot. **2.** a horseshoe. **3.** the part of a brake that presses against a rotating wheel. —*v.t.* **4.** to provide with shoes.

shoe'horn' *n.* a curved device to assist in slipping on a shoe.

shoe'lace' *n.* a lace for fastening a shoe.

shoe'mak'er *n.* a person who makes or mends shoes.

shoe'string' *n.* **1.** a shoelace. **2.** a very small amount of money.

shoe'tree' *n.* a device placed inside a shoe to hold its shape.

sho'gun (shō'gən) *n.* one of the chief military commanders of Japan from the 8th to 12th centuries.

shoo (shoō) *interj., v.,* **shooed, shooing.** —*interj.* **1.** (used to drive away animals). —*v.t.* **2.** to drive away by shouting "shoo."

shoo'-in' *n.* one regarded as certain to win.

shook (shoōk) *v.* pt. of **shake.**

shoot (shoōt) *v.,* **shot, shooting,** *n.*

—*v.t.* **1.** to hit, wound, or kill with a missile. **2.** to discharge (a weapon). **3.** to send forth swiftly or suddenly. **4.** to photograph. —*v.i.* **5.** to move or pass swiftly or suddenly. **6.** to hunt with a gun. **7.** to put forth buds or shoots. —*n.* **8.** new growth from a plant. **9.** a shooting contest. —**shoot′er,** *n.*

shoot′ing star′ *n.* a meteor.

shop (shop) *n., v.,* **shopped, shopping.** —*n.* **1.** a store. **2.** a workshop. **3.** a factory, office, or business. —*v.i.* **4.** to look at or purchase goods.

shop′lift′er *n.* one who steals from shops while posing as a customer.

shop′talk′ *n.* conversation about one's work or occupation.

shore¹ (shôr) *n.* the land along the edge of a body of water.

shore² (shôr) *v.t.,* **shored, shoring.** to prop or support with a post or beam.

shorn (shôrn) *v.* a pp. of **shear.**

short (shôrt) *adj.* **1.** not long or tall. **2.** rudely brief. **3.** not sufficient. **4.** not reaching a target or standard. **5.** (of pastry) crisp and flaky. —*adv.* **6.** abruptly. —*n.* **7.** anything short. **8. shorts,** short trousers. **9.** a short circuit. —*v.i., v.t.* **10.** to form a short circuit (on). —**short′en,** *v.t., v.i.*

short′age (shôr′tij) *n.* scarcity.

short′bread′ *n.* a rich butter cookie.

short′cake′ *n.* a rich biscuit topped with fruit and cream.

short′change′ *v.t.,* **-changed, -changing. 1.** to give less than the correct change to. **2.** to cheat.

short′ cir′cuit *n.* an abnormal connection between two points in a circuit.

short′com′ing *n.* a deficiency.

short′cut′ *n.* a shorter way to get somewhere or to accomplish something.

short′en·ing (shôrt′ning) *n.* butter or another fat used to make pastry.

short′hand′ *n.* a system of rapid handwriting.

short′-hand′ed *adj.* not having enough workers.

short′-lived′ (-līvd, -livd) *adj.* lasting only a short time.

short′ly *adv.* **1.** in a short time. **2.** briefly.

short′ shrift′ *n.* little attention or consideration.

short′-sight′ed *adj.* lacking foresight.

short′-tem′pered *adj.* very irritable.

short′wave′ *n.* a radio wave of fre-

quencies over 1600 kilohertz, used for long-distance transmission.

shot¹ (shot) *v.* pt. and pp. of **shoot.**

shot² (shot) *n.* **1.** the discharge of a weapon. **2.** the sound of this. **3.** an act or instance of shooting. **4.** a person who shoots. **5.** a missile for discharge from a firearm. **6.** an attempt or try. **7.** a photograph. **8.** a stroke or throw in a game. **9.** an injection. **10.** a heavy metal ball used in the shot put.

shot′gun′ *n.* a smoothbore gun.

shot′ put′ *n.* a competition in which a heavy metal ball is thrown for distance. —**shot′-put′ter,** *n.*

should (shŏŏd) *v.* pt. of **shall.**

shoul′der (shōl′dər) *n.* **1.** the part of the body from the neck to the upper joint of the arm in humans or the foreleg in animals. **2.** a border along a highway. —*v.t.* **3.** to push with or as if with the shoulder. **4.** to take up, as a burden.

shoul′der blade′ *n.* the scapula.

shout (shout) *v.i., v.t.* **1.** to call or cry out loudly. —*n.* **2.** a loud call or cry.

shove (shuv) *v.,* **shoved, shoving,** *n.* —*v.t.* **1.** to push roughly. —*n.* **2.** a rough push.

shov′el *n., v.,* **-eled, -eling.** —*n.* **1.** a tool with a broad scoop and handle. —*v.t.* **2.** to dig or move with a shovel.

show (shō) *v.,* **showed, shown** or **showed, showing,** *n.* —*v.t.* **1.** to cause or allow to be seen. **2.** to point out. **3.** to explain. **4.** to guide. —*v.i.* **5.** to be visible. **6. show off, a.** to display proudly. **b.** to act in a way that attracts attention. —*n.* **7.** an exhibition. **8.** a performance. **9.** appearance.

show′case′ *n., v.,* **-cased, -casing.** —*n.* **1.** a setting for displaying something. —*v.t.* **2.** to exhibit to best advantage.

show′down′ *n.* a decisive confrontation.

show′er (shou′ər) *n.* **1.** a brief fall of rain, snow, etc. **2.** a bath in which water is sprayed on the body. **3.** a party at which gifts are given. —*v.t.* **4.** to give abundantly. —*v.i.* **5.** to bathe in a shower. **6.** to rain in a shower.

show′piece′ *n.* something worthy of being exhibited.

show′y *adj.,* **-ier, -iest.** making an impressive display; ostentatious.

shrank (shrangk) *v.* a pt. of **shrink.**

shrap′nel (shrap′nl) *n.* fragments from an exploding shell.

shred (shred) *n., v.,* **shredded** or **shred, shredding.** —*n.* **1.** a torn piece or strip. **2.** a bit. —*v.t.*, *v.i.* **3.** to reduce to shreds.

shrew (shrōō) *n.* **1.** a quarrelsome woman. **2.** a small mouselike mammal. —**shrew′ish**, *adj.*

shrewd (shrōōd) *adj.* clever.

shriek (shrēk) *n.* **1.** a loud shrill cry. —*v.i.*, *v.t.* **2.** to utter (with) a shriek.

shrill (shril) *adj.* **1.** high-pitched and piercing. —*v.t.*, *v.i.* **2.** to cry shrilly.

shrimp (shrimp) *n.* a small, long-tailed edible shellfish.

shrine (shrīn) *n.* a sacred place.

shrink (shringk) *v.*, **shrank** (shrangk) or **shrunk** (shrungk), **shrunk** or **shrunken, shrinking.** —*v.i.* **1.** to become smaller. **2.** to draw back. —*v.t.* **3.** to make smaller.

shrink′age (shring′kij) *n.* the process or amount of shrinking.

shrink′-wrap′ *v.*, **shrink-wrapped, shrink-wrapping,** *n.* —*v.t.* **1.** to seal in plastic film that when exposed to heat shrinks tightly around the object it covers. —*n.* **2.** the plastic used to shrink-wrap.

shriv′el (shriv′əl) *v.t.*, *v.i.*, **-eled, -eling.** to shrink and wrinkle, as from dryness.

shroud (shroud) *n.* **1.** a burial cloth. **2.** something that conceals. **3.** one of the ropes supporting the masts of a ship. —*v.t.* **4.** to hide from view.

shrub (shrub) *n.* a woody perennial plant smaller than a tree. —**shrub•ber•y,** *n.*

shrug (shrug) *v.*, **shrugged, shrugging,** *n.* —*v.t.*, *v.i.* **1.** to move (the shoulders) to show ignorance, indifference, etc. —*n.* **2.** this movement.

shrunk (shrungk) *v.* a pp. and pt. of **shrink.**

shuck (shuk) *n.* **1.** a husk, as of corn, or shell, as of an oyster. —*v.t.* **2.** to remove the shucks from. **3.** to remove.

shud′der (shud′ər) *v.i.* **1.** to tremble, as from horror. —*n.* **2.** this movement.

shuf′fle (shuf′əl) *v.*, **-fled, -fling,** *n.* —*v.i.* **1.** to drag the feet in walking. —*v.t.* **2.** to move (the feet) along the ground without lifting. **3.** to intermix (playing cards). —*n.* **4.** a shuffling gait. **5.** an act of shuffling cards.

shuf′fle•board′ *n.* a game in which disks are pushed with cues on a marked floor surface.

shun (shun) *v.t.*, **shunned, shunning.** to avoid.

shut (shut) *v.*, **shut, shutting,** *adj.* —*v.t.* **1.** to move into a closed position. **2.** to close by bringing together the parts of. **3.** to confine. —*v.i.* **4.** to become shut. **5.** **shut down,** to cease operations. **6.** ~ **out, a.** to exclude. **b.** to prevent (an opponent) from scoring. **7.** ~ **up,** to stop or cause to stop talking. —*adj.* **8.** closed.

shut′ter *n.* **1.** a solid or louvered movable cover for a window. **2.** a device for opening and closing a camera lens.

shut′tle (shut′l) *n.*, *v.*, **-tled, -tling.** —*n.* **1.** a bus, plane, etc., moving back and forth between two destinations. **2.** a device for moving thread back and forth in weaving. —*v.i.*, *v.t.* **3.** to move or cause to move quickly back and forth.

shut′tle•cock′ *n.* the feathered object hit in badminton.

shy (shī) *adj.*, **shyer** or **shier, shyest** or **shiest,** *v.*, **shied, shying.** —*adj.* **1.** bashful. **2.** easily frightened. **3.** lacking. —*v.i.* **4.** to start back or aside, as in fear.

Si′a•mese′ twins (sī′ə mēz′, -mēs′) *n.pl.* twins joined together by a body part.

sib′i•lant (sib′ə lənt) *adj.* **1.** hissing. —*n.* **2.** a hissing sound.

sib′ling (-ling) *n.* a brother or sister.

sib′yl (-əl) *n.* a female prophet.

sic (sik) *v.t.*, **sicked, sicking.** to urge to attack.

sic (sēk; Eng. sik) *adv. Latin.* so; thus: used in brackets to indicate that something has been used or spelled as quoted.

sick (sik) *adj.* **1.** not healthy; ill. **2.** nauseated. **3.** deeply distressed. **4.** gruesome. —**sick′en,** *v.t.*, *v.i.*

sick′le (sik′əl) *n.* a tool with a curved blade and a short handle, used for cutting grass, grain, etc.

sick′ly *adj.*, **-lier, -liest. 1.** not well. **2.** faint; weak.

side (sīd) *n.*, *adj.*, *v.*, **sided, siding.** —*n.* **1.** the surface of something, esp. a part other than the front, back, top, or bottom. **2.** the right or left half of the body. **3.** an aspect. **4.** region or position with reference to a central point. **5.** a contesting team or group. **6.** a faction. —*adj.* **7.** at, on, from, or toward one side. —*v.i.* **8.** **side with** (or **against**), to support (or oppose).

side′bar′ *n.* a short news feature highlighting a longer story.

side′board′ *n.* a piece of dining-room furniture for holding china.

side′burns′ *n.pl.* short whiskers in front of the ears.

side′ effect′ *n.* an often bad secondary effect, as of a drug.

side′kick′ *n.* **1.** a close friend. **2.** a confederate or assistant.

side′light′ *n.* an item of incidental information.

side′line′ *n., pl.* **-lines. 1.** a business or activity in addition to one's primary business. **2.** an additional line of goods. **3.** a line defining the side of an athletic field.

side′long′ *adj., adv.* to or toward the side.

side′sad′dle *n.* **1.** a saddle on which a person rides with both legs on one side of the horse. —*adv.* **2.** on a sidesaddle.

side′show′ *n.* a minor show connected with a principal one.

side′-step′ *v.i., v.t.,* **-stepped, -stepping.** to avoid, as by stepping aside.

side′swipe′ *v.t.,* **-swiped, -swiping.** to strike with a glancing blow along the side.

side′track′ *v.t., v.i.* to divert.

side′walk′ *n.* a paved walk along a street.

side′ways′ *adj., adv.* **1.** with one side forward. **2.** toward or from one side. Also, **side′wise′.**

sid′ing *n.* **1.** weatherproof facing for frame buildings. **2.** a short railroad track for halted cars.

si′dle (sīd′l) *v.i.,* **-dled, -dling.** to move sideways, esp. furtively.

SIDS (sidz) *n.* sudden infant death syndrome.

siege (sēj) *n.* **1.** the surrounding of a fortified place to force its surrender. **2.** a prolonged period of troubles.

si•en′na (sē en′ə) *n.* a yellowish- or reddish-brown pigment.

si•er′ra (-er′ə) *n.* a jagged chain of hills or mountains.

si•es′ta (-es′tə) *n.* a midday rest.

sieve (siv) *n.* a utensil with a meshed surface for straining.

sift (sift) *v.t.* **1.** to pass through a sieve. **2.** to separate by or as if by a sieve.

sigh (sī) *v.i.* **1.** to exhale audibly in grief, weariness, etc. **2.** to yearn. —*n.* **3.** the act or sound of sighing.

sight (sīt) *n.* **1.** the power of seeing. **2.** a glimpse. **3.** one's range of vision. **4.** a device, as on a firearm, for guiding one's aim. **5.** something worth seeing. —*v.t.* **6.** to see. **7.** to aim by a sight. —*Idiom.* **8. sight unseen,** without previous examination. —**sight′less,** *adj.*

sight′ed *adj.* not blind.

sight′read′ (-rēd) *v.t., v.i.,* **-read** (-red′) **-reading.** to perform without previous practice or study.

sight′see′ing *n.* visiting new places and things of interest.

sign (sīn) *n.* **1.** an indication. **2.** a conventional mark, figure, etc., used instead of a word. **3.** a board, placard, etc., bearing an advertisement, warning, or instruction. **4.** a gesture. **5.** a trace. **6.** an omen. —*v.t.* **7.** to put one's signature to. **8.** to engage by written agreement. **9.** to convey (a message) in sign language. —*v.i.* **10.** to write one's signature. **11.** to employ sign language.

sig′nal (sig′nl) *n., adj., v.,* **-naled, -naling.** —*n.* **1.** a sign or gesture that indicates, warns, or commands. —*adj.* **2.** serving as a signal. **3.** notable. —*v.t., v.i.* **4.** to communicate by symbols.

sig′nal•ly *adv.* notably.

sig′na•to′ry (-nə tôr′ē) *n., pl.* **-ries.** a signer.

sig′na•ture (-nə chər) *n.* **1.** a person's name in his or her own handwriting. **2.** *Music.* a sign indicating the key or meter of a piece.

sig′net (-nit) *n.* a small seal.

sig•nif′i•cance (-nif′i kəns) *n.* **1.** importance. **2.** meaning. —**sig•nif′i•cant,** *adj.*

sig′ni•fy′ *v.,* **-fied, -fying.** —*v.t.* **1.** to make known. **2.** to mean. —*v.i.* **3.** to be of importance.

sign′ lan′guage *n.* a visual-gestural language, used by deaf people.

si′lage (sī′lij) *n.* fodder preserved in a silo.

si′lence (-ləns) *n., v.,* **-lenced, -lencing.** —*n.* **1.** absence of sound or noise. —*v.t.* **2.** to make silent.

si′lenc•er *n.* a device for deadening the report of a firearm.

si′lent *adj.* **1.** making no sound. **2.** not speaking. **3.** unspoken. **4.** (of a letter) not pronounced.

sil′hou•ette′ (sil′ōō et′) *n., v.,* **-etted, -etting.** —*n.* **1.** a dark filled-in outline of an object against a light background. —*v.t.* **2.** to show in silhouette.

sil′i•ca (-i kə) *n.* silicon dioxide, appearing as quartz, sand, flint, etc.

sil′i•cate (-kit, -kāt′) *n.* a mineral, as quartz, consisting of silicon and oxygen with a metal.

sil′i•con (-kən, -kon′) *n.* a nonmetallic element that constitutes more than one fourth of the earth's crust in its combined forms.

sil′i•cone′ (-kōn′) *n.* a polymer with silicon and oxygen atoms, used in adhesives, lubricants, etc.

sil′i•co′sis (-kō′sis) *n.* a lung disease caused by inhaling silica particles.

silk (silk) *n.* **1.** the fine soft fiber from the cocoon of the silkworm.

2. thread or cloth made of it. —*adj.* **3.** Also, **silk′en, silk′y.** of silk.

silk′screen′ *n.* **1.** a printmaking technique in which color is forced through the pores of a mesh cloth. —*v.t.* **2.** to print by silkscreen.

silk′worm′ *n.* a moth caterpillar that spins silk to make its cocoon.

sill (sil) *n.* a horizontal piece beneath a window or door.

sil′ly (sil′ē) *adj.*, **-lier, -liest. 1.** foolish. **2.** ridiculous. —**sil′li•ness,** *n.*

si′lo (sī′lō) *n., pl.* **-los. 1.** a tower for storing fodder. **2.** an underground housing for a missile.

silt (silt) *n.* **1.** earth or sand carried and deposited by a stream. —*v.t., v.i.* **2.** to fill with silt.

sil′ver (sil′vər) *n.* **1.** a white metallic element used for making coins, jewelry, etc. **2.** coins, utensils, etc., of silver. **3.** a shiny grayish white. —*adj.* **4.** of or plated with silver.

sil′ver bul′let *n.* a quick solution to a difficult problem.

sil′ver•fish′ *n.* a wingless, silvery-gray insect that damages paper.

sil′ver lin′ing *n.* a prospect of hope or comfort.

sil′ver ni′trate *n.* a poisonous powder used in photography.

sil′ver•ware′ *n.* eating and serving utensils of silver or other metal.

sim′i•an (sim′ē ən) *n.* **1.** an ape or monkey. —*adj.* **2.** of or resembling apes or monkeys.

sim′i•lar (sim′ə lər) *adj.* having a general likeness or resemblance. —**sim′i•lar′i•ty** (-lar′i tē) *n.*

sim′i•le (-ə lē) *n.* a phrase comparing two things using "like" or "as."

si•mil′i•tude (si mil′i tood′, -tyood′) *n.* likeness; resemblance.

sim′mer (sim′ər) *v.i., v.t.* to remain or keep near the boiling point.

sim′per (-pər) *v.i.* **1.** to smile in a silly way. —*n.* **2.** such a smile.

sim′ple (-pəl) *adj.*, **-pler, -plest. 1.** not difficult; easy. **2.** not complicated; plain. **3.** mentally weak. —**sim•plic′i•ty** (-plis′i tē) *n.*

sim′ple in′terest *n.* interest payable only on the principal.

sim′ple-mind′ed *adj.* **1.** unsophisticated. **2.** mentally deficient.

sim′ple•ton (-tən) *n.* a fool.

sim′pli•fy′ (-plə fī′) *v.t.*, **-fied, -fying.** to make simpler.

sim•plis′tic (-plis′tik) *adj.* foolishly or naïvely simple.

sim′u•late′ (-yə lāt′) *v.t.*, **-lated, -lating.** to imitate the appearance or characteristics of.

si′mul•ta′ne•ous (-tā′nē əs) *adj.* occurring at the same time.

sin (sin) *n., v.*, **sinned, sinning.** —*n.*

1. an offense against a religious or moral law. —*v.i.* **2.** to commit a sin. —**sin′ner,** *n.* —**sin′ful,** *adj.*

since (sins) *prep.* **1.** continuously from. **2.** in the period after. —*conj.* **3.** from the time when. **4.** because. —*adv.* **5.** from then till now. **6.** subsequently.

sin•cere′ (sin sēr′) *adj.*, **-cerer, -cerest. 1.** honest. **2.** genuine. —**sin•cer′i•ty** (-ser′i tē) *n.* —**sin•cere′ly,** *adv.*

si′ne•cure′ (sī′ni kyŏŏr′) *n.* a well-paying job requiring little work.

si′ne qua non′ (sin′ā kwä nōn′) *n.* an indispensable condition.

sin′ew (sin′yōō) *n.* **1.** a tendon. **2.** strength. —**sin′ew•y,** *adj.*

sing (sing) *v.*, **sang** (sang) or **sung** (sung) **sung, singing.** —*v.i.* **1.** to use the voice to make musical sounds. **2.** to make a whistling or humming sound. —*v.t.* **3.** to perform (a song). **4.** to proclaim in song. —**sing′er,** *n.*

singe (sinj) *v.*, **singed, singeing,** *n.* —*v.t.* **1.** to burn superficially. —*n.* **2.** singeing.

sin′gle (sing′gəl) *adj., v.*, **-gled, -gling,** *n.* —*adj.* **1.** one only. **2.** intended for one person. **3.** unmarried. —*v.t.* **4.** to select (one) from others. —*n.* **5.** a single thing. **6.** an unmarried person.

sin′gle-hand′ed *adj.* **1.** by one's own effort; unaided. —*adv.* **2.** by one person alone.

sin′gle-mind′ed *adj.* having or showing a single aim or purpose.

sin′gly *adv.* **1.** separately. **2.** one at a time. **3.** single-handed.

sing′song′ *n.* a monotonous rhythmical rise and fall of the voice.

sin′gu•lar (sing′gyə lər) *adj.* **1.** extraordinary. **2.** strange. **3.** of the grammatical category denoting one person or thing. —*n.* **4.** the singular number or form.

sin′is•ter (sin′ə stər) *adj.* threatening evil.

sink (singk) *v.*, **sank** (sangk) or **sunk** (sungk), **sunk** or **sunken, sinking,** *n.* —*v.i.* **1.** to fall, drop, or descend to a lower level or state. **2.** to fail in health. **3.** to decrease in amount or intensity. —*v.t.* **4.** to cause to sink. **5.** to dig, as a shaft. —*n.* **6.** a basin connected with a water supply and a drain.

sink′hole′ *n.* a hole in rock through which surface water drains into an underground passage.

sin′u•ous (sin′yōō əs) *adj.* winding.

si′nus (sī′nəs) *n.* one of the cavities in the skull connecting with the nasal cavities.

sip (sip) *v.*, **sipped, sipping,** *n.*

—*v.t., v.i.* **1.** to drink a little at a time. —*n.* **2.** an act of sipping. **3.** the amount taken in a sip.

si′phon (sī′fən) *n.* **1.** a tube for drawing liquids by gravity and suction to another container. —*v.t., v.i.* **2.** to draw or pass through a siphon.

sir (sûr) *n.* **1.** a formal term of address for a man. **2.** **Sir,** the title of a knight or baronet.

sire (sī°r) *n., v.,* **sired, siring.** —*n.* **1.** a male parent. —*v.t.* **2.** to beget.

si′ren (sī′rən) *n.* **1.** a noise-making device used on emergency vehicles. **2.** a mythical creature whose seductive singing lured sailors to destruction. **3.** a seductively beautiful woman.

sir′loin (sûr′loin) *n.* a cut of beef from the loin.

si·roc′co (sə rok′ō) *n., pl.* **-cos.** a hot, dusty wind from N Africa.

si′sal (sī′səl, sis′əl) *n.* a fiber used in making ropes.

sis′sy (sis′ē) *n., pl.* **-sies.** a weak or timid person.

sis′ter (sis′tər) *n.* **1.** a female child of the same parents as another person. **2.** a woman connected, as by race, to another. **3.** a female member of a religious order. —*adj.* **4.** being in close relationship with another. —**sis′ter·ly,** *adj.*

sis′ter-in-law′ *n., pl.* **sisters-in-law. 1.** the sister of one's spouse. **2.** the wife of one's brother.

sit (sit) *v.,* **sat** (sat) **sitting.** —*v.i.* **1.** to rest with the body supported on the buttocks. **2.** to be located. **3.** to pose, as for an artist. **4.** to be in session. **5.** (of a bird) to cover eggs for hatching. —*v.t.* **6.** to cause to sit. **7.** **sit in on,** to be an observer at. **8.** **~ out,** to fail to take part in.

si·tar′ (si tär′) *n.* an Indian lute.

site (sīt) *n.* a position or location.

sit′-in′ *n.* a protest by demonstrators who occupy and refuse to leave a place.

sit′u·ate′ (sich′ōō āt′) *v.t.,* **-ated, -ating.** to locate.

sit′u·a′tion (-ā′shən) *n.* **1.** location. **2.** circumstances. **3.** a job.

six (siks) *n., adj.* five plus one. —**sixth,** *adj., n.*

six′teen′ *n., adj.* ten plus six. —**six·teenth′,** *adj., n.*

sixth′ sense′ *n.* intuition.

six′ty *n., adj.* ten times six. —**six′·ti·eth,** *adj., n.*

siz′a·ble (sī′zə bəl) *adj.* fairly large. Also, **size′a·ble.**

size¹ (sīz) *n., v.,* **sized, sizing.** —*n.* **1.** dimensions, magnitude, or extent. **2.** one of a series of standard measures for manufactured articles.

—*v.t.* **3.** to sort according to size. **4.** **size up,** to judge.

size² (sīz) *n., v.,* **sized, sizing.** —*n.* **1.** Also, **sizing.** a gluey coating for paper, cloth, etc. —*v.t.* **2.** to coat with size.

siz′zle (siz′əl) *v.,* **-zled, -zling,** *n.* —*v.i.* **1.** to make a hissing sound, as in frying. —*n.* **2.** a sizzling sound.

skate¹ (skāt) *n., pl.* **skates,** *v.,* **skated, skating.** —*n.* **1.** an ice skate. **2.** a roller skate. —*v.i.* **3.** to glide on skates. —**skat′er,** *n.*

skate² (skāt) *n., pl.* **skates, skate.** a flat-bodied marine fish; ray.

skate′board′ *n.* an oblong board on roller-skate wheels.

skein (skān) *n.* a coil of yarn.

skel·e·ton (skel′i tn) *n.* the bones that form the body's framework. —**skel′e·tal,** *adj.*

skel′eton key′ *n.* a key that opens various simple locks.

skep′tic (skep′tik) *n.* a person who doubts or questions. —**skep′ti·cal,** *adj.* —**skep′ti·cism** (-siz′əm) *n.*

sketch (skech) *n.* **1.** a simple hasty drawing. **2.** a rough plan. —*v.i., v.t.* **3.** to make a sketch (of).

sketch′y *adj.,* **-ier, -iest.** vague; approximate. —**sketch′i·ly,** *adv.*

skew (skyōō) *v.i., v.t.* to turn aside.

skew′er *n.* **1.** a pin for holding together pieces of meat while cooking. —*v.t.* **2.** to fasten with or as if with a skewer.

ski (skē) *n.* **1.** one of a pair of slender runners for gliding over snow. —*v.i., v.t.* **2.** to travel on skis (over).

skid (skid) *n., v.,* **skidded, skidding.** —*n.* **1.** an uncontrollable sideways slide on a surface. **2.** a surface on which to slide a heavy object. —*v.i.* **3.** to slip or slide sideways.

skid′ row′ (rō) *n.* a run-down urban area frequented by vagrants.

skiff (skif) *n.* a small boat.

skill (skil) *n.* **1.** the ability to do something well. **2.** a craft or trade. —**skilled,** *adj.* —**skill′ful,** *adj.*

skil′let (-it) *n.* a frying pan.

skim (skim) *v.,* **skimmed, skimming.** —*v.t.* **1.** to remove (floating matter) from the surface of a liquid. **2.** to move lightly over. **3.** to read superficially. —*v.i.* **4.** to move lightly over a surface. **5.** to read something superficially.

skim′ milk′ *n.* milk with the cream removed.

skimp (skimp) *v.i., v.t.* to scrimp.

skimp′y *adj.,* **-ier, -iest.** lacking in size or fullness.

skin (skin) *n., v.,* **skinned, skinning.** —*n.* **1.** the outer covering of an animal body. **2.** an outer layer, as the rind of fruit. —*v.t.* **3.** to remove the skin of.

skin′ div′ing *n.* underwater swimming with flippers and a face mask and sometimes with scuba gear.

skin′flint′ *n.* a stingy person.

skin′ny *adj.*, **-nier, -niest.** very thin.

skin′ny-dip′ *v.i.*, **skinny-dipped, skinny-dipping.** *Informal.* to swim in the nude.

skip (skip) *v.*, **skipped, skipping,** *n.* —*v.i.* **1.** to spring; leap. —*v.t.* **2.** to omit. —*n.* **3.** a light jump.

skip′per *n.* the master of a ship.

skir′mish (skûr′mish) *n.* **1.** a brief fight between small forces. —*v.i.* **2.** to engage in a skirmish.

skirt (skûrt) *n.* **1.** the part of a dress or coat below the waist. **2.** a woman's garment extending down from the waist. —*v.t.* **3.** to lie or pass along the edge of. **4.** to avoid.

skit (skit) *n.* a short, usu. amusing play.

skit′tish *adj.* **1.** easily frightened. **2.** frisky.

skul·dug′ger·y (skul dug′ə rē) *n.* dishonorable or deceitful behavior.

skulk (skulk) *v.i.* to sneak about.

skull (skul) *n.* the bony framework of the head.

skull′cap′ *n.* a small, brimless, close-fitting cap.

skunk (skungk) *n.* **1.** a small mammal with black-and-white fur that sprays a bad-smelling fluid as defense. **2.** a contemptible person.

sky (skī) *n.*, *pl.* **skies.** the upper atmosphere of the earth.

sky′jack′ *v.t.* to hijack (an airliner).

sky′light′ *n.* a window in a roof.

sky′line′ *n.* an outline of buildings against the sky.

sky′rock′et *n.* **1.** a firework that rises into the air before exploding. —*v.i.*, *v.t.* **2.** to rise or cause to rise rapidly.

sky′scrap′er *n.* a building with many stories.

sky′writ′ing *n.* writing in the sky by smoke released from an airplane.

slab (slab) *n.* a broad, flat, thick piece of material.

slack (slak) *adj.* **1.** loose. **2.** careless. **3.** slow or sluggish. **4.** inactive. —*n.* **5.** a slack condition. **6.** an inactive period. —*v.t.*, *v.i.* **7.** to slacken. —**slack′ly,** *adv.*

slack′en *v.t.*, *v.i.* to make or become slack.

slack′er *n.* one who evades work.

slacks *n.pl.* trousers for casual wear.

slag (slag) *n.* refuse matter separated during the smelting of a metal from its ore.

slake (slāk) *v.t.*, **slaked, slaking.** to quench (thirst, desire, etc.).

sla′lom (slä′ləm) *n.* a downhill ski race over a winding, zigzag course.

slam (slam) *v.*, **slammed, slamming,** *n.* —*v.t.*, *v.i.* **1.** to shut forcefully and noisily. —*n.* **2.** the act or sound of slamming.

slan′der (slan′dər) *n.* **1.** a false, malicious statement that damages a person's reputation. —*v.t.* **2.** to utter slander against.

slang (slang) *n.* very informal, colorful language. —**slang′y,** *adj.*

slant (slant) *v.i.* **1.** to slope. —*v.t.* **2.** to cause to slant. **3.** to present (news) with a particular point of view. —*n.* **4.** a slope. **5.** a particular point of view.

slap (slap) *v.*, **slapped, slapping,** *n.* —*v.t.* **1.** to strike sharply with the open hand. —*n.* **2.** such a blow.

slap′dash′ *adj.* hasty and careless.

slap′hap′py *adj.*, **-pier, -piest. 1.** befuddled. **2.** agreeably foolish.

slap′stick′ *n.* boisterous comedy with broad farce and horseplay.

slash (slash) *v.t.* **1.** to cut violently. **2.** to reduce sharply. —*n.* **3.** a violent sweeping stroke or cut. **4.** a stroke (/) used as a dividing line.

slat (slat) *n.* a thin narrow strip of wood or metal.

slate (slāt) *n.*, *v.*, **slated, slating.** —*n.* **1.** a kind of rock that splits horizontally. **2.** a thin piece of slate. **3.** a list of candidates. —*v.t.* **4.** to cover with slates.

slat′tern (slat′ərn) *n.* an untidy woman. —**slat′tern·ly,** *adj.*

slaugh′ter (slô′tər) *n.* **1.** the killing of animals, esp. for food. **2.** the brutal killing of people, esp. in great numbers. —*v.t.* **3.** to butcher for food. **4.** to massacre.

slave (slāv) *n.*, *v.*, **slaved, slaving.** —*n.* **1.** a person owned by another. **2.** a person under the domination of another. —*v.i.* **3.** to work like a slave. —**slav′er·y,** *n.* —**slav′ish,** *adj.*

slav′er (sla′vər) *v.i.* to drool.

slay (slā) *v.t.*, **slew** (slōō) **slain, slaying.** to kill. —**slay′er,** *n.*

slea′zy (slē′zē) *adj.*, **-zier, -ziest.** disreputable or squalid.

sled (sled) *n.*, *v.*, **sledded, sledding.** —*n.* **1.** a platform on runners for gliding over snow. —*v.i.*, *v.t.* **2.** to ride on or transport by sled.

sledge (slej) *n.* **1.** a heavy sledlike vehicle. **2.** Also, **sledge′ham′mer.** a large heavy hammer.

sleek (slēk) *adj.* **1.** smooth and

glossy. **2.** streamlined. —*v.t.* **3.** to make sleek. —**sleek′ly,** *adv.*

sleep (slēp) *v.,* **slept** (slept) **sleeping,** *n.* —*v.i.* **1.** to rest during the natural suspension of consciousness. —*n.* **2.** the state or period of sleeping. —**sleep′less,** *adj.* —**sleep′y,** *adj.*

sleep′er *n.* **1.** a person who sleeps. **2.** a railroad car equipped for sleeping. **3.** an unexpected success.

sleep′ing bag′ *n.* a warmly lined bag in which a person can sleep.

sleep′walk′ing *n.* the act of walking while asleep. —**sleep′walk′,** *v.i.* —**sleep′walk′er,** *n.*

sleet (slēt) *n.* **1.** rain that freezes as it falls. —*v.i.* **2.** to fall as sleet.

sleeve (slēv) *n.* **1.** the part of a garment covering the arm. **2.** a tubular piece fitting over another part. —**sleeve′less,** *adj.*

sleigh (slā) *n.* a horse-drawn vehicle on runners, used for traveling over snow.

sleight′ of hand′ (slīt) *n.* skill in conjuring or juggling.

slen·der (slen′dər) *adj.* **1.** thin. **2.** not adequate.

sleuth (slōōth) *n.* a detective.

slew (slōō) *v.* pt. of **slay.**

slice (slīs) *n., v.,* **sliced, slicing.** —*n.* **1.** a thin, flat piece cut from something. —*v.t.* **2.** to cut into slices. —**slic′er,** *n.*

slick (slik) *adj.* **1.** slippery. **2.** sly. **3.** clever. —*n.* **4.** an oil-covered area. **5.** a slippery place. —*v.t.* **6.** to make sleek or smooth.

slick′er *n.* a loose oilskin raincoat.

slide (slīd) *v.,* **slid, sliding,** *n.* —*v.i., v.t.* **1.** to move or cause to move easily. —*n.* **2.** an act of sliding. **3.** a smooth surface for sliding. **4.** a glass plate used to examine objects with a microscope. **5.** a transparent picture, mounted for projection on a screen.

slid′ing scale′ *n.* a scale, as of prices, that varies with such conditions as ability to pay.

slight (slīt) *adj.* **1.** trifling; small. **2.** slim. —*v.t.* **3.** to treat as unimportant. —*n.* **4.** such treatment; a snub. —**slight′ly,** *adv.*

slim (slim) *adj.,* **slimmer, slimmest. 1.** slender. **2.** scanty. —*v.t., v.i.* **3.** to make or become slim.

slime (slīm) *n.* **1.** thin sticky mud. **2.** a sticky secretion. —**slim′y,** *adj.*

sling (sling) *n., v.,* **slung** (slung) **slinging.** —*n.* **1.** a looped rope, bandage, etc., used to support or carry something. **2.** a straplike device for hurling stones. —*v.t.* **3.** to throw. **4.** to place in or move by a sling.

sling′shot′ *n.* a Y-shaped stick with an elastic strip between two prongs, for shooting small missiles.

slink (slingk) *v.i.,* **slunk** (slungk) **slinking.** to go furtively. —**slink′y,** *adj.*

slip (slip) *v.,* **slipped, slipping,** *n.* —*v.i.* **1.** to move easily. **2.** to slide suddenly and accidentally. **3.** to make a mistake. **4.** to decline in quality. —*v.t.* **5.** to cause to move smoothly. **6.** to put, pass, or insert quickly or stealthily. **7.** to escape (the memory). —*n.* **8.** a slipping. **9.** a mistake. **10.** a woman's garment worn under a dress. **11.** a space for a ship in a dock.

slip′cov′er *n.* an easily removable cloth cover for a piece of furniture.

slip′knot′ *n.* a knot that slips easily along a cord.

slipped′ disk′ *n.* an abnormal protrusion of a spinal disk between vertebrae.

slip′per *n.* a light shoe.

slip′per·y *adj.* **1.** causing slipping. **2.** tending to slip.

slip′shod′ (-shod′) *adj.* careless.

slip′-up′ *n.* a mistake.

slit (slit) *v.,* **slit, slitting,** *n.* —*v.t.* **1.** to make a long cut in. —*n.* **2.** a narrow cut or opening.

slith′er (slith′ər) *v.i.* to slide.

sliv·er (sliv′ər) *n.* **1.** a small, thin piece. —*v.t., v.i.* **2.** to cut into slivers.

slob (slob) *n.* a slovenly person.

slob′ber *v.i.* **1.** to let saliva dribble from the mouth. —*n.* **2.** saliva dribbling from the mouth.

sloe (slō) *n.* the small sour fruit of the blackthorn.

slog (slog) *v.i.,* **slogged, slogging. 1.** to plod heavily. **2.** to work hard.

slo′gan (slō′gən) *n.* a motto.

sloop (slōōp) *n.* a single-masted sailboat.

slop (slop) *v.,* **slopped, slopping,** *n.* —*v.t., v.i.* **1.** to spill or splash (liquid). —*n.* **2.** kitchen waste fed to swine. **3.** unappetizing food or drink.

slope (slōp) *v.,* **sloped, sloping,** *n.* —*v.i., v.t.* **1.** to incline or cause to incline; slant. —*n.* **2.** a sloping surface. **3.** the amount by which a thing slopes.

slop′py *adj.,* **-pier, -piest. 1.** untidy. **2.** careless. —**slop′pi·ly,** *adv.*

slosh (slosh) *v.i.* **1.** to splash through water, mud, etc. **2.** (of a liquid) to move noisily within a container.

slot (slot) *n.* **1.** a long, narrow opening. **2.** a place in a series.

sloth (slôth) *n.* **1.** laziness. **2.** a

slow-moving South American mammal. —**sloth′ful,** *adj.*

slouch (slouch) *v.i.* **1.** to sit, stand, or walk with a drooping posture. —*n.* **2.** a drooping posture or gait. —**slouch′y,** *adj.*

slough[1] (slou) *n.* **1.** a muddy area or swamp. **2.** a state of despair.

slough[2] (sluf) *v.t.* to shed.

slov′en (sluv′ən) *n.* an untidy or careless person.

slov′en.ly *adj.,* **-lier, -liest. 1.** untidy or unclean. **2.** slipshod; negligent. —**slov′en.li.ness,** *n.*

slow (slō) *adj.* **1.** not fast or quick. **2.** not intelligent or perceptive. **3.** running behind time. —*adv.* **4.** in a slow manner. —*v.t., v.i.* **5.** to make or become slow.

slow′down′ *n.* a slackening of pace or speed.

slow′ mo′tion *n.* the process of projecting a film or television sequence so that action appears to be slowed down.

slow′poke′ *n. Informal.* a person who moves, works, or acts very slowly.

slow′-wit′ted *adj.* slow to understand.

sludge (sluj) *n.* mud, mire, or ooze.

slue (slōō) *v.i., v.t.,* **slued, sluing.** to turn around.

slug[1] (slug) *n.* **1.** a slimy, crawling mollusk having no shell. **2.** a bullet. **3.** a metal disk used as a coin or token.

slug[2] (slug) *v.,* **slugged, slugging,** *n.* —*v.t.* **1.** to hit hard, esp. with the fist. —*n.* **2.** a hard blow, esp. with the fist. —**slug′ger,** *n.*

slug′gard (-ərd) *n.* a lazy person.

slug′gish *adj.* inactive; slow.

sluice (slōōs) *n., v.,* **sluiced, sluicing.** —*n.* **1.** a channel with a gate to control the flow of water. —*v.t.* **2.** to cleanse with flowing water.

slum (slum) *n.* a squalid, crowded residence or neighborhood.

slum′ber (slum′bər) *v.i.* **1.** to sleep. —*n.* **2.** a sleep.

slump (slump) *v.i.* **1.** to drop heavily or suddenly. —*n.* **2.** a slumping.

slur[1] (slûr) *v.,* **slurred, slurring,** *n.* —*v.t.* **1.** to pronounce indistinctly. **2.** to sing or play (two notes) without a break. —*n.* **3.** a slurred sound.

slur[2] (slûr) *n.* a disparaging remark.

slurp (slûrp) *v.t., v.i.* **1.** to eat or drink with loud sucking noises. —*n.* **2.** a slurping sound.

slush (slush) *n.* partly melted snow.

slut (slut) *n.* a slovenly or immoral woman.

sly (slī) *adj.,* **slyer, slyest** or **slier, sliest. 1.** cunning. **2.** stealthy.

smack[1] (smak) *v.t.* **1.** to open and close the lips) noisily. **2.** to strike or kiss loudly. —*n.* **3.** a loud slap or kiss. **4.** a smacking of the lips. —*adv.* **5.** directly.

smack[2] (smak) *n.* **1.** a slight flavor. **2.** a trace. —*v.i.* **3.** to have a slight flavor or trace.

smack[3] (smak) *n.* a small fishing boat.

small (smôl) *adj.* **1.** not big; little. **2.** not very important. **3.** meanspirited. —*adv.* **4.** in a small way. **5.** in small pieces. —*n.* **6.** a small or narrow part, as of the back.

small′ fry′ *n.pl.* **1.** young children. **2.** unimportant people.

small′-mind′ed *adj.* petty or selfish.

small′pox′ *n.* a contagious disease marked by fever and pustules.

small′-scale′ *adj.* **1.** of limited scope. **2.** being a small version of an original.

small′ talk′ *n.* light conversation.

smarm′y (smär′mē) *adj.,* **-ier, -iest.** excessively flattering or servile.

smart (smärt) *v.i.* **1.** to cause or feel a sharp stinging pain. —*adj.* **2.** clever; intelligent. **3.** sharp. **4.** stylish. —*n.* **5.** a sharp local pain.

smart′ bomb′ *n.* an air-to-surface missile guided by a laser beam.

smart′en *v.t., v.i.* to improve in appearance.

smash (smash) *v.t., v.i.* **1.** to break into pieces violently. **2.** to hit, collide, or strike with force. **3.** to destroy or be destroyed. —*n.* **4.** the act or sound of smashing. **5.** a collision or crash. **6.** ruin. **7.** *Informal.* a great success.

smat′ter.ing (smat′ər ing) *n.* slight knowledge.

smear (smēr) *v.t.* **1.** to spread or apply (an oily or dirty substance). **2.** to slander. —*n.* **3.** a stain or spot. **4.** a slanderous attack.

smell (smel) *v.,* **smelled** or **smelt, smelling,** *n.* —*v.t.* **1.** to perceive the odor of with the nose. —*v.i.* **2.** to have an odor. —*n.* **3.** the faculty of smelling. **4.** odor.

smelt[1] (smelt) *v.t.* **1.** to melt (ore) in order to separate the metal. **2.** to refine (metal) by smelting.

smelt[2] (smelt) *n., pl.* **smelts, smelt.** a small, silvery food fish.

smid′gen (smij′ən) *n.* a very small amount.

smile (smīl) *v.,* **smiled, smiling,** *n.* —*v.i.* **1.** to look pleased, amused, etc. —*n.* **2.** a smiling facial expression.

smirk (smûrk) *v.i.* **1.** to smile smugly, affectedly, or offensively. —*n.* **2.** such a smile.

smite 338

smite (smīt) v.t., smote (smōt), smit•ten (smit′n) or smote, smiting. 1. to strike hard. 2. to affect strongly.

smith (smith) n. a worker in metal.

smith′er•eens′ (smith′ə rēnz′) n.pl. small pieces.

smith′y (smith′ē, smith′ē) n., pl. -ies. a blacksmith's shop.

smit′ten (smit′n) adj. infatuated.

smock (smok) n. a long, loose garment worn to protect the clothing while working.

smog (smog) n. smoke and fog.

smoke (smōk) n., v., smoked, smoking. —n. 1. the visible vapor and gases from a burning substance. —v.i. 2. to give off smoke. 3. to inhale and puff out tobacco smoke. —v.t. 4. to inhale and puff out the smoke of. 5. to cure (meat, fish, etc.) by exposure to smoke. —smoke′less, adj. —smok′y, adj.

smoke′ detec′tor n. an alarm activated by the presence of smoke.

smoke′house′ n. a building in which meat or fish is cured with smoke.

smoke′ screen′ n. 1. a mass of dense smoke for concealment. 2. something intended to deceive.

smoke′stack′ n. a pipe for the escape of smoke, gases, etc.

smol′der (smōl′dər) v.i. 1. to burn without flame. 2. to exist in a suppressed state. Also, smoul′der.

smooch (smōōch) Informal. —v.i. 1. to kiss. —n. 2. a kiss.

smooth (smōōth) adj. 1. having an even surface; not rough. 2. not lumpy. 3. moving or flowing freely. 4. tranquil. —v.t. 5. to make smooth.

smor′gas•bord′ (smôr′gəs bôrd′; often shmôr′-) n. a buffet meal of assorted foods.

smoth′er (smuth′ər) v.t. 1. to suffocate or stifle. 2. to cover closely. 3. to suppress.

smudge (smuj) n., v., smudged, smudging. —n. 1. a dirty mark or smear. —v.t., v.i. 2. to make or become dirty.

smug (smug) adj. self-satisfied; complacent.

smug′gle v.t., -gled, -gling. 1. to import or export secretly and illegally. 2. to bring or take secretly.

smut (smut) n. 1. soot. 2. a dirty mark. 3. obscenity. 4. a fungous disease of plants. —smut′ty, adj.

snack (snak) n. 1. a light meal. —v.i. 2. to eat a snack.

snag (snag) n., v., snagged, snagging. —n. 1. a sharp projection. 2. an obstacle. 3. a tear or pull in a fabric. —v.t. 4. to catch on a snag.

snail (snāl) n. a slow-moving, spiral-shelled mollusk.

snail′ mail′ n. physical delivery of mail, as contrasted with e-mail.

snake (snāk) n., v., snaked, snaking. —n. 1. a long, limbless, scaly reptile. —v.i. 2. to wind like a snake.

snap (snap) v., snapped, snapping, n., adj. —v.i., v.t. 1. to make or cause to make a sudden sharp sound. 2. to break abruptly. 3. to grasp with a quick bite. 4. to say or speak quickly and sharply. 5. to take a snapshot (of). —n. 6. a snapping sound. 7. a kind of fastener. 8. Informal. an easy task. —adj. 9. made or done suddenly.

snap′drag′on n. a plant with spikes of two-lipped flowers.

snap′pish adj. cross or irritable.

snap′py adj., -pier, -piest. Informal. 1. quick. 2. smart; stylish.

snap′shot′ n. an unposed photograph.

snare (snâr) n., v., snared, snaring. —n. 1. a trap with a noose. —v.t. 2. to trap with a snare.

snarl¹ (snärl) v.i. 1. to growl. —n. 2. an act or sound of snarling.

snarl² (snärl) n. 1. a tangle, as of thread. —v.i., v.t. 2. to become or cause to become tangled.

snatch (snach) v.t. 1. to grab suddenly. —n. 2. a grabbing motion. 3. a bit or fragment.

sneak (snēk) v.i., v.t. 1. to go, act, or take furtively. —n. 2. a person who sneaks.

sneak′er n. a rubber-soled shoe.

sneak′ pre′view′ n. a preview of a motion picture, often shown in addition to an announced film.

sneer (snēr) v.i. 1. to smile or laugh contemptuously. —n. 2. a contemptuous look.

sneeze (snēz) v., sneezed, sneezing, n. —v.i. 1. to expel the breath suddenly and audibly through the nose. —n. 2. an act of sneezing.

snick′er (snik′ər) v.i. 1. to laugh in a half-suppressed or disrespectful manner. —n. 2. a snickering laugh.

snide (snīd) adj., snider, snidest. derogatory in a nasty, insinuating way.

sniff (snif) v.i., v.t. 1. to inhale quickly and audibly. 2. to draw in by sniffing. —n. 3. the act or sound of sniffing.

snif′ter (-tər) n. a pear-shaped glass for brandy.

snip (snip) v., snipped, snipping, n. —v.t., v.i. 1. to cut with small, quick strokes. —n. 2. a small piece cut off. 3. the act of snipping.

snipe (snīp) n., v., sniped, sniping.

—*n.* **1.** a long-billed sandpiper. —*v.i.* **2.** to shoot from a hidden position. **3.** to make snide remarks. —**snip′er,** *n.*

snip′pet (snip′it) *n.* a small bit, scrap, or fragment.

snip′py *adj.,* **-pier, -piest.** sharp or curt, esp. in a haughty way.

snit (snit) *n.* an agitated state.

snitch¹ (snich) *v.t. Informal.* to steal; pilfer.

snitch² (snich) *Informal.* —*v.i.* **1.** to turn informer; tattle. —*n.* **2.** an informer.

sniv′el (sniv′əl) *v.i.* **1.** to weep weakly. **2.** to have a runny nose.

snob (snob) *n.* a person overconcerned with position, wealth, etc. —**snob′bish,** *adj.* —**snob′ber·y,** *n.*

snoop (sno̅o̅p) *Informal.* —*v.i.* **1.** to prowl or pry. —*n.* **2.** Also, **snoop′er.** a person who snoops.

snoot′y (sno̅o̅′tē) *adj.,* **-ier, -iest.** *Informal.* snobbish; condescending.

snooze (sno̅o̅z) *v.,* **snoozed, snoozing,** *n.* —*v.i.* **1.** to sleep for a short time. —*n.* **2.** a short sleep.

snore (snôr) *v.,* **snored, snoring,** *n.* —*v.i.* **1.** to breathe with hoarse or harsh sounds in sleep. —*n.* **2.** an act or sound of snoring.

snor′kel (snôr′kəl) *n.* **1.** a tube through which a swimmer can breathe while underwater. —*v.i.* **2.** to swim while using a snorkel.

snort (snôrt) *v.i.* **1.** to exhale loudly and harshly. **2.** to express contempt by snorting. —*n.* **3.** an act or sound of snorting.

snot (snot) *n.* **1.** *Vulgar.* nasal mucus. **2.** *Informal.* an impudently disagreeable young person. —**snot′ty,** *adj.*

snout (snout) *n.* the projecting nose and jaw of an animal.

snow (snō) *n.* **1.** white crystalline ice flakes that fall to earth. —*v.i., v.t.* **2.** to fall or let fall as or like snow. —**snow′y,** *adj.* —**snow′fall,** *n.* —**snow′storm,** *n.*

snow′ball′ *n.* **1.** a ball of snow. —*v.i., v.t.* **2.** to increase or cause to increase rapidly.

snow′board′ *n.* a board for gliding on snow, resembling a wide ski ridden in a standing position.

snow′drift′ *n.* a mound or bank of snow driven together by the wind.

snow′drop′ *n.* an early-blooming plant with white flowers.

snow′flake′ *n.* a small crystal or flake of snow.

snow′man′ *n.* a figure of a person made of packed snow.

snow′mo·bile′ (-mə bēl′) *n.* a motor vehicle for travel on snow.

snow′shoe′ *n.* a racketlike shoe for walking on snow.

snow′suit′ *n.* a child's warmly insulated outer garment.

snow′ tire′ *n.* a tire with a deep tread for increased traction on snow.

snub (snub) *v.,* **snubbed, snubbing,** *n.* —*v.t.* **1.** to treat with scorn. —*n.* **2.** an affront or slight.

snuff¹ (snuf) *v.t., v.i.* **1.** to inhale noisily. **2.** to smell. —*n.* **3.** powdered tobacco that is inhaled.

snuff² (snuf) *v.t.* to extinguish (a candle).

snuf′fle *v.,* **-fled, -fling,** *n.* —*v.i.* **1.** to sniff or snuff. —*n.* **2.** an act or sound of snuffling.

snug (snug) *adj.,* **snugger, snuggest. 1.** cozy. **2.** trim; neat.

snug′gle *v.i., v.t.,* **-gled, -gling.** to nestle or cuddle.

so (sō) *adv.* **1.** in this or that way. **2.** to such a degree. **3.** as stated. —*conj.* **4.** with the result that. **5.** in order that.

soak (sōk) *v.i.* **1.** to lie in a liquid and become thoroughly wet. —*v.t.* **2.** to wet thoroughly. **3.** to absorb.

so′-and-so′ *n., pl.* **so-and-sos.** a person or thing not definitely named.

soap (sōp) *n.* **1.** a substance used for washing. —*v.t.* **2.** to rub with soap.

soap′box′ *n.* an improvised platform on which a speaker stands.

soap′stone′ *n.* a variety of talc.

soar (sôr) *v.i.* to fly upward.

sob (sob) *v.,* **sobbed, sobbing,** *n.* —*v.i., v.t.* **1.** to weep with uneven catching of the breath. —*n.* **2.** an act or sound of sobbing.

so′ber (sō′bər) *adj.* **1.** not drunk. **2.** serious. **3.** restrained. —*v.t., v.i.* **4.** to make or become sober. —**so·bri′e·ty,** *n.*

so′bri·quet′ (sō′bri kā′, -ket′) *n.* a nickname.

so′-called′ *adj.* called thus.

soc′cer (sok′ər) *n.* a form of football played by kicking a large, round ball.

so′cia·ble (sō′shə bəl) *adj.* friendly. —**so′cia·bil′i·ty,** *n.*

so′cial (sō′shəl) *adj.* **1.** of or marked by friendly relations. **2.** living with others in a community. **3.** of or based on status in a society. —**so′cial·ly,** *adv.*

so′cial·ism (-shə liz′əm) *n.* a theory or system of social organization based on government or community ownership of the means of production and distribution of goods. —**so′cial·ist,** *n.*

so′cial•ite′ (-shə līt′) n. a socially prominent person.

so′cial•ize′ v., **-ized, -izing. —v.t. 1.** to make fit for life in society. **2.** to establish according to the theories of socialism. **—v.i. 3.** to mingle with others in a friendly way.

so′cial secu′rity n. (often caps.) a federal program of old age, unemployment, health, disability, and survivors' insurance.

so′cial work′ n. services or activities designed to improve social conditions among poor, sick, or troubled persons.

so•ci•e′ty (sə sī′i tē) n., pl. **-ties. 1.** an organized group of people living together. **2.** a group of persons united by common interests. **3.** companionship; company. **4.** the class of fashionable people.

so′ci•o•ec•o•nom′ic (sō′sē ō-, sō′-shē ō-) adj. pertaining to a combination of social and economic factors.

so′ci•ol′o•gy (sō′sē ol′ə jē, sō′shē-) n. the study of human social relations and institutions. —**so′ci•ol′o•gist,** n.

sock¹ (sok) n. a short stocking.

sock² (sok) v.t. to hit hard.

sock′et (sok′it) n. a hollow part for holding another part.

sod (sod) n. grass with its roots.

so′da (sō′də) n. **1.** a carbonated, flavored sweet soft drink. **2.** a drink made with soda water, flavored syrup, and ice cream. **3.** a preparation containing sodium.

so′da crack′er n. a crisp cracker.

so′da foun′tain n. a counter at which ice cream, sodas, etc., are served.

so′da wa′ter n. water charged with carbon dioxide.

sod′den (sod′n) adj. soaked.

so′di•um (sō′dē əm) n. a soft, silver-white metallic element.

so′dium bicar′bonate n. baking soda.

so′dium chlo′ride n. salt.

sod′o•my (sod′ə mē) n. anal or oral copulation.

so′fa (sō′fə) n. a couch with a back and arms.

soft (sôft) adj. **1.** yielding readily to touch or pressure. **2.** not rough or harsh. **3.** gentle; pleasant. **4.** not hard. **5.** (of water) free from mineral salts. —**sof′ten,** v.t., v.i.

soft′ball′ n. **1.** a form of baseball played with a larger, softer ball. **2.** the ball used.

soft′-boiled′ adj. (of an egg) boiled only until the yolk is partially set.

soft′ drink′ n. a nonalcoholic drink.

soft′-heart′ed adj. very sympathetic.

soft′ mon′ey n. money contributed to a political candidate or party that is not subject to federal regulations.

soft′-ped′al v.t., **soft-pedaled, soft-pedaling.** to make less obvious; play down.

soft′ sell′ n. a quietly persuasive method of selling.

soft′ware′ n. programs for use with a computer.

sog′gy (sog′ē) adj., **-gier, -giest. 1.** soaked. **2.** damp and heavy.

soi•gné′ (swän yā′; Fr. swa nyā′) adj. elegant. Also, **soi•gnée′.**

soil¹ (soil) n. **1.** the loose surface layer of the earth. **2.** ground. **3.** dirt. **4.** a land.

soil² (soil) v.t., v.i. to make or become dirty.

soi•rée′ (swä rā′) n. an evening party.

so′journ v.i. (sō′jûrn, sō jûrn′) **1.** to dwell briefly. —n. (sō′jûrn) **2.** a short stay.

sol′ace (sol′is) n., v., **-aced, -acing.** —n. **1.** comfort in sorrow. —v.t. **2.** to comfort.

so′lar (sō′lər) adj. of the sun.

so′lar cell′ n. a cell that converts sunlight into electricity.

so•lar′i•um (sə lâr′ē əm, sō-) n., pl. **-iums, -ia** (-ē ə). a glass-enclosed room for enjoying sunlight.

so′lar plex′us n. a point on the stomach wall just below the sternum.

so′lar sys′tem n. the sun and all the celestial bodies revolving around it.

sol′der (sod′ər) n. **1.** an alloy that can be fused for joining metal. —v.t., v.i. **2.** to join with solder.

sol′dier (sōl′jər) n. **1.** a person in military service. —v.i. **2.** to serve as a soldier.

sole¹ (sōl) adj. being the only one. —**sole′ly,** adv.

sole² (sōl) n., v., **soled, soling.** —n. **1.** the bottom of a foot or shoe. —v.t. **2.** to put a sole on (a shoe).

sole³ (sōl) n. an edible marine flatfish.

sol′emn (sol′əm) adj. **1.** grave; serious. **2.** formal or ceremonious. —**so•lem′ni•ty** (sə lem′ni tē) n.

sol′em•nize′ (-nīz′) v.t., **-nized, -nizing. 1.** to observe with formality. **2.** to perform the ceremony of (marriage).

so•lic′it (sə lis′it) v.t. **1.** to try to obtain by asking for. —v.i. **2.** to solicit something desired. —**so•lic′i•ta′tion,** n.

so·lic/i·tor (-i tər) *n.* **1.** a person who solicits. **2.** *Brit.* a lawyer.

so·lic/it·ous *adj.* anxious; concerned. —**so·lic/i·tude/,** *n.*

sol·id (sol/id) *adj.* **1.** having length, breadth, and thickness. **2.** not hollow. **3.** not liquid or gaseous. **4.** substantial. **5.** consisting entirely of one material. —*n.* **6.** a solid body or substance. —**so·lid/i·fy/,** *v.t., v.i.* —**so·lid/i·ty,** *n.*

sol/i·dar/i·ty (-i dar/i tē) *n.* unity of attitude or purpose.

sol/id·ly *adv.* **1.** firmly. **2.** wholeheartedly; fully.

so·lil/o·quy (sə lil/ə kwē) *n., pl.* **-quies. 1.** a speech in a play in which a character speaks as if alone. **2.** the act of talking to oneself. —**so·lil/o·quize/,** *v.i., v.t.*

sol/i·taire/ (sol/i târ/) *n.* **1.** a card game for one person. **2.** a gem set by itself.

sol/i·tar/y (-ter/ē) *adj.* **1.** alone. **2.** single. **3.** remote. —**sol/i·tude/,** *n.*

so/lo (sō/lō) *n., pl.* **-los,** *adj., adv.* —*n.* **1.** a performance by one person. —*adj., adv.* **2.** (performed) alone. —**so/lo·ist,** *n.*

sol/stice (sol/stis, sōl/-) *n.* the time in summer (June 21) or winter (Dec. 21) when the sun is at its greatest distance from the celestial equator.

sol·u·ble (sol/yə bəl) *adj.* able to be dissolved. —**sol/u·bil/i·ty,** *n.*

so·lu/tion (sə lōō/shən) *n.* **1.** the process of solving a problem. **2.** an explanation or answer. **3.** the process of dissolving one substance in another. **4.** the resulting liquid.

solve (solv) *v.t.,* **solved, solving.** to find the answer for.

sol/vent (sol/vənt) *adj.* **1.** able to pay one's debts. **2.** causing dissolving. —*n.* **3.** an agent that dissolves.

som/ber (som/bər) *adj.* **1.** gloomy; dark. **2.** very serious.

som·bre·ro (som brâr/ō) *n., pl.* **-ros.** a tall, wide-brimmed hat.

some (sum; *unstressed* səm) *adj.* **1.** being an unknown or unnamed one. **2.** unspecified in number, amount, etc. —*pron.* **3.** an unspecified number or amount. —*adv.* **4.** approximately. —**Usage.** SOME is used in sentences that are affirmative: *I'd like some milk.* ANY is used instead of SOME with negative phrases or in questions: *I don't want any milk. I never see any of my friends these days. Do you have any milk?* But SOME can be used in questions when the answer is expected to be "yes": *Can I have some milk, please?*

some/bod/y (sum/bod/ē, -bud/ē, -bə dē) *pron.* some person. Also, **some/one/.**

some/day/ *adv.* at some distant time.

some/how/ *adv.* in some way.

som/er·sault (sum/ər sôlt/) *n.* **1.** a heels-over-head roll of the body. —*v.i.* **2.** to perform a somersault.

some/thing/ *n.* an unspecified thing.

some/time/ *adv.* **1.** at an indefinite time. —*adj.* **2.** former.

some/times/ *adv.* now and then.

some/what/ *adv.* to some extent.

some/where/ *adv.* in, at, or to an unspecified place.

som·nam/bu·lism (som nam/byə liz/əm, səm-) *n.* sleepwalking.

som/no·lent (-nə lənt) *adj.* sleepy. —**som/no·lence,** *n.*

son (sun) *n.* a male offspring.

so/nar (sō/när) *n.* a method or apparatus for detecting objects in water by means of sound waves.

so·na/ta (sə nä/tə) *n.* an instrumental composition, usu. in several movements.

song (sông) *n.* **1.** music for singing. **2.** the art or act of singing.

song/bird/ *n.* a bird that sings.

son/ic (son/ik) *adj.* of sound.

son/ic boom/ *n.* a loud noise caused by an aircraft moving at supersonic speed.

son/-in-law/ *n., pl.* **sons-in-law.** the husband of one's daughter.

son/net (son/it) *n.* a poem of 14 lines.

son/o·gram (son/ə gram/, sō/nə-) *n.* the visual image made by reflected sound waves in an ultrasound examination.

so·no/rous (sə nôr/əs, son/ər əs) *adj.* resonant, with a rich, full sound. —**so·nor/i·ty,** *n.*

soon (sōōn) *adv.* in a short time.

soot (sŏōt, sōōt) *n.* a black powdery substance in smoke. —**soot/y,** *adj.*

soothe (sōōth) *v.t.,* **soothed, soothing. 1.** to calm. **2.** to ease or allay.

sooth/say/er (sōōth/sā/ər) *n.* a person who predicts events.

sop (sop) *n., v.,* **sopped, sopping.** —*n.* **1.** something given to pacify. —*v.t.* **2.** to soak or dip in liquid. **3.** to absorb (liquid).

so·phis/ti·cat/ed (sə fis/ti kā/tid) *adj.* **1.** worldly; not naive. **2.** complex; intricate. —**so·phis/ti·cate** (-kit) *n.* —**so·phis/ti·ca/tion,** *n.*

soph/ist·ry (sof/ə strē) *n., pl.* **-ries.** clever but unsound reasoning.

soph/o·more/ (sof/ə môr/) *n.* a second-year high school or college student.

soph/o·mor/ic (-môr/ik) *adj.* intellectually immature.

so•po•rif•ic (sop/ə rif/ik) *adj.* **1.** causing sleep. —*n.* **2.** a soporific agent.

so•pran•o (sə pran/ō) *n., pl.* **-pranos. 1.** the highest singing voice in women and boys. **2.** a singer with such a voice. —*adj.* **3.** of the highest pitch in music.

sor•bet/ (sôr bā/, sôr/bit) *n.* a fruit or vegetable ice.

sor/cer•y (-sə rē), *n., pl.* **-cer•ies.** the exercise of supernatural powers granted by evil spirits. —**sor/-cer•er,** *n.*

sor/did (-did) *adj.* **1.** morally base. **2.** filthy.

sore (sôr) *adj.,* **sorer, sorest,** *n.* —*adj.* **1.** painful or tender. **2.** causing or suffering pain or distress. **3.** annoyed. —*n.* **4.** a sore spot.

sor/ghum (sôr/gəm) *n.* a cereal grass used in making syrup.

so•ror•i•ty (sə rôr/i tē) *n., pl.* **-ties.** a club of women or girls.

sor/rel¹ (sôr/əl) *n.* **1.** a reddish brown. **2.** a horse of this color.

sor/rel² (sôr/əl) *n.* a salad plant with acid leaves.

sor/row (sor/ō) *n.* **1.** grief or the cause or expression of grief. —*v.i.* **2.** to feel or express sorrow. —**sor/-row•ful,** *adj.*

sor/ry (sor/ē) *adj.* **-rier, -riest. 1.** feeling regret or pity. **2.** wretched.

sort (sôrt) *n.* **1.** a particular kind or class. **2.** character or quality. —*v.t.* **3.** to arrange by kind. —*Idiom.* **4. out of sorts,** irritable.

sor/tie (sôr/tē) *n.* **1.** an attack by defending troops. **2.** a combat mission.

SOS (es/ō/es/) *n.* a call for help.

so/-so/ *adj.* **1.** neither good nor bad. —*adv.* **2.** tolerably.

sot/to vo/ce (sot/ō vō/chē) *adv.* in a low voice; softly.

souf•fle/ (sōō flā/) *n.* a light, puffy baked dish made with egg whites.

sough (sou, suf) *v.i.* **1.** to rustle or murmur, as wind. —*n.* **2.** a soughing sound.

sought (sôt) *v.* pt. and pp. of **seek.**

soul (sōl) *n.* **1.** the spiritual part of a human being. **2.** an essential part. **3.** a person. **4.** shared ethnic awareness and pride among black Americans. —*adj.* **5.** of black American customs and culture.

sound¹ (sound) *n.* **1.** the sensation affecting the organs of hearing. **2.** vibrations that can be perceived by the ear. **3.** something heard. —*v.i.* **4.** to make a sound. **5.** to give a certain impression. —*v.t.* **6.** to cause to sound. **7.** to pronounce.

sound² (sound) *adj.* **1.** healthy; strong. **2.** secure; reliable. **3.** valid. —**sound/ly,** *adv.*

sound³ (sound) *v.t.* **1.** to measure the depth of (water). **2.** to try to find out the views of.

sound⁴ (sound) *n.* a strait or inlet of the sea.

sound/ bar/rier *n.* an abrupt increase in drag experienced by an aircraft approaching the speed of sound.

sound/ bite/ *n.* a brief statement excerpted for broadcast news.

sound/ing board/ *n.* **1.** a thin board placed in a musical instrument to enhance resonance. **2.** a person whose reactions reveal the acceptability of an idea.

sound/proof/ *adj.* **1.** not able to be penetrated by sound. —*v.t.* **2.** to make soundproof.

sound/track/ *n.* the band on a strip of motion-picture film on which sound is recorded.

soup (sōōp) *n.* a liquid food of vegetables, seasonings, meat, etc.

soup/y *adj.,* **-ier, -iest. 1.** resembling soup in consistency. **2.** very thick. **3.** overly sentimental.

sour (sou°r) *adj.* **1.** acid in taste; tart. **2.** spoiled. **3.** disagreeable. —*v.t., v.i.* **4.** to make or become sour. —**sour/ly,** *adv.*

source (sôrs) *n.* **1.** any thing or place from which something comes. **2.** the place where a river begins. **3.** something or someone that supplies information.

sour/ grapes/ *n.* pretended scorn for something one cannot have.

south (south) *n.* **1.** a cardinal point of the compass lying directly opposite north. **2. the South,** a region in this direction. —*adj., adv.* **3.** toward, in, or from the south. —**south/ern,** *adj.* —**south/ern•er,** *n.* —**south/ward,** *adv., adj.*

south/east/ *n.* **1.** the point or direction midway between south and east. **2. the Southeast,** a region in this direction. —*adj., adv.* **3.** toward, in, or from the southeast. —**south/east/ern,** *adj.*

south/er•ly (suth/ər lē) *adj., adv.* toward or blowing from the south.

south/paw/ *n. Informal.* a left-handed person.

south/west/ *n.* **1.** the point or direction midway between south and west. **2. the Southwest,** a region in this direction. —*adj., adv.* **3.** toward, in, or from the southwest. —**south/west/ern,** *adj.*

sou•ve•nir/ (sōō/və nēr/) *n.* a memento.

sov/er•eign (sov/rin, -ər in) *n.* **1.** a supreme ruler. —*adj.* **2.** supreme in power. **3.** independent. —**sov′er‐eign‐ty,** *n.*

sow¹ (sō) *v.t.* **1.** to scatter (seed) for growth. **2.** to scatter seed over. **3.** to implant or introduce. —*v.i.* **4.** to sow seed. —**sow′er,** *n.*

sow² (sou) *n.* an adult female swine.

soy′bean′ (soi′-) *n.* the seed of a plant of the legume family.

soy′ sauce′ *n.* a salty sauce made from fermented soybeans.

spa (spä) *n.* a resort with a mineral spring.

space (spās) *n.*, *v.*, **spaced, spacing.** —*n.* **1.** the unlimited expanse in which all objects are located. **2.** a particular part of this. **3.** space beyond the earth's atmosphere. **4.** an empty area. **5.** an interval of time. —*v.t.* **6.** to separate by spaces.

space′craft′ *n.*, *pl.* **-craft.** a vehicle for traveling in outer space.

space′ship′ *n.* a spacecraft.

space′ shut′tle *n.* a reusable space-craft.

space′ sta′tion *n.* a manned space-craft orbiting the earth and serving as a base for research.

spa′cious (spā′shəs) *adj.* roomy.

spade¹ (spād) *n.*, *v.*, **spaded, spad-ing.** —*n.* **1.** a tool with a flat blade for digging. —*v.t.* **2.** to dig with a spade.

spade² (spād) *n.* a playing card with a black figure shaped like an inverted heart with a short stem.

spa‐ghet′ti (spə get′ē) *n.* pasta in the form of long strings.

spam (spam) *n.*, *v.*, **spammed, spamming.** —*n.* **1.** a disruptive message posted on a computer net-work. —*v.i.* **2.** to send spam.

span¹ (span) *n.*, *v.*, **spanned, span-ning.** —*n.* **1.** the full extent of something. **2.** the space between two supports. **3.** a short period of time. —*v.t.* **4.** to extend across.

span² (span) *n.* a pair of animals driven together.

span′gle (spang′gəl) *n.*, *v.*, **-gled, -gling.** —*n.* **1.** a small, thin piece of glittering metal, used to deco-rate a garment. —*v.t.* **2.** to decorate with spangles.

span′iel (span′yəl) *n.* a kind of dog having droopy ears and a silky coat.

spank (spangk) *v.t.* **1.** to slap on the buttocks. —*n.* **2.** such a blow.

spank′ing *n.* **1.** a series of spanks on the buttocks, esp. in punish-ment. —*adj.* **2.** brisk; vigorous.

spar¹ (spär) *n.* a stout pole, as a mast, for supporting sails.

spar² (spär) *v.i.*, **sparred, sparring.** **1.** to box with light blows. **2.** to engage in a dispute.

spare (spâr) *v.*, **spared, sparing,** *adj.*, **sparer, sparest.** —*v.t.* **1.** to re-frain from harming or punishing. **2.** to do without. —*adj.* **3.** kept in reserve. **4.** extra. **5.** thin.

spare′rib′ *n.* a cut of meat from the ribs, esp. of pork.

spark (spärk) *n.* **1.** a burning parti-cle. **2.** a flash of electricity. **3.** something that stimulates. **4.** a small amount.

spar′kle *v.*, **-kled, -kling,** *n.* —*v.i.* **1.** to shine with flashes of light; glit-ter. **2.** to be vivacious. **3.** to pro-duce little bubbles. —*n.* **4.** a spar-kling light.

spark′ plug′ *n.* a device in an in-ternal-combustion engine that ig-nites the fuel.

spar′row (spar′ō) *n.* a small, com-mon, gray-brown songbird.

sparse *adj.*, **sparser, sparsest.** thinly distributed.

spar′tan *adj.* austere.

spasm (spaz′əm) *n.* **1.** a sudden in-voluntary muscular contraction. **2.** a sudden burst of activity.

spas‐mod′ic (spaz mod′ik) *adj.* **1.** of or marked by spasms. **2.** inter-mittent.

spas′tic (spas′tik) *adj.* of or marked by spasms.

spat (spat) *n.* a petty quarrel.

spate (spāt) *n.* a sudden outpour-ing.

spa′tial (spā′shəl) *adj.* of or in space.

spat′ter (spat′ər) *v.t.*, *v.i.* **1.** to sprinkle in many fine drops. —*n.* **2.** an act or sound of spattering.

spat′u‐la (spach′ə lə) *n.* an imple-ment with a broad flexible blade.

spawn (spôn) *n.* **1.** the eggs of fish, frogs, etc. —*v.i.*, *v.t.* **2.** to deposit (spawn). **3.** to bring forth.

spay (spā) *v.t.* to remove the ova-ries of (a female dog, cat, etc.).

speak (spēk) *v.*, **spoke** (spōk) **spo-ken, speaking.** —*v.i.* **1.** to utter words; talk. **2.** to deliver a speech. —*v.t.* **3.** to utter or express with the voice. —**speak′er,** *n.*

speak′eas′y *n.*, *pl.* **-easies.** a place selling alcoholic beverages illegally.

spear (spēr) *n.* **1.** a long staff with a sharp-pointed head. —*v.t.* **2.** to pierce with a spear.

spear′head′ *n.* **1.** the head of a spear. **2.** a leader. —*v.t.* **3.** to lead.

spear′mint′ *n.* an aromatic herb.

spe′cial (spesh′əl) *adj.* **1.** particular in nature or purpose. **2.** unusual or unique. **3.** exceptional. —*n.* **4.** a special thing or person.

spe′cial‐ize *v.i.*, **-ized, -izing.** to

study or work in a special field.
—**spe′cial•ist**, *n.* —**spe′cial•i•za′-
tion**, *n.*

spe′cial•ty *n., pl.* **-ties. 1.** a person's field of special interest or competence. **2.** a special article, service, feature, etc.

spe′cie (spē′shē, -sē) *n.* coined money.

spe′cies (spē′shēz, -sēz) *n.* a group of related animals or plants that can breed among themselves.

spe•cif′ic (spi sif′ik) *adj.* **1.** precise or explicit. **2.** peculiar or limited to someone or something. —**spe•cif′i•cal•ly**, *adv.*

spec′i•fi•ca′tion (spes′ə fi kā′shən) *n.* **1.** something specified. **2.** a detailed statement of requirements.

specif′ic grav′ity *n.* the ratio of the density of a substance to the density of a standard substance, water being the standard.

spec′i•fy′ *v.t.,* **-fied, -fying.** to mention or require explicitly.

spec′i•men (spes′ə mən) *n.* a part or an individual taken as an example or a sample to be tested.

spe′cious (spē′shəs) *adj.* apparently true or good but lacking real merit.

speck (spek) *n.* a small spot or bit.

speck′le *n., v.,* **-led, -ling.** —*n.* **1.** a small speck. —*v.t.* **2.** to mark with speckles.

spec′ta•cle (spek′tə kəl) *n.* **1.** anything presented to view. **2.** a public display. **3. spectacles**, eyeglasses.

spec•tac′u•lar (-tak′yə lər) *adj.* dramatic; thrilling.

spec′ta•tor (-tā tər) *n.* an observer.

spec′ter (-tər) *n.* a ghost. Also, **spec′tre.**

spec′tral (-trəl) *adj.* of a specter or a spectrum.

spec′trum (-trəm) *n., pl.* **-tra** (-trə), **-trums. 1.** a band of colors formed when a light ray is dispersed. **2.** a broad range.

spec′u•late′ (-yə lāt′) *v.i.,* **-lated, -lating. 1.** to think; conjecture. **2.** to invest at some risk in the hope of making a large profit. —**spec′u•la′tion**, *n.* —**spec′u•la′tive** (-lā′tiv, -lə tiv) *adj.* —**spec′u•la′tor**, *n.*

speech (spēch) *n.* **1.** the power of speaking. **2.** the act or manner of speaking. **3.** something spoken. **4.** a talk before an audience. —**speech′less**, *adj.*

speed (spēd) *n., v.,* **sped** (sped) or **speeded, speeding.** —*n.* **1.** swiftness. **2.** relative rate of motion —*v.t.* **3.** to increase the rate of speed of. —*v.i.* **4.** to go fast. **5.** to drive at an illegal rate of speed. —**speed′y**, *adj.* —**speed′i•ly**, *adv.*

speed•om′e•ter (spē dom′i tər, spi-) *n.* an instrument for indicating speed.

spe′le•ol′o•gy (spē′lē ol′ə jē) *n.* the exploration and study of caves.

spell[1] (spel) *v.,* **spelled** or **spelt**, **spelling.** —*v.t.* **1.** to give the letters of in order. **2.** (of letters) to form (a word). **3.** to mean. —*v.i.* **4.** to spell words.

spell[2] (spel) *n.* **1.** words believed to have magic power. **2.** a fascination.

spell[3] (spel) *n.* **1.** a period of activity, time, or weather. —*v.t.* **2.** to take the place of for a time.

spell′bound′ *adj.* fascinated.

spe•lunk′er (spi lung′kər) *n.* a person who explores caves.

spend (spend) *v.,* **spent, spending.** —*v.t.* **1.** to pay out (money). **2.** to pass (time). **3.** to use up.

spend′thrift′ *n.* a person who spends extravagantly.

spent (spent) *v.* pt. and pp. of **spend.**

sperm (spûrm) *n.* **1.** a male reproductive cell. **2.** semen. —**sper•mat′ic** (-mat′ik) *adj.*

sper•mat′o•zo′on (spûr mat′ə-zō′ən, -on) *n., pl.* **-zoa** (-zō′ə) a mature male reproductive cell.

sper′mi•cide′ (-mə sīd′) *n.* a sperm-killing agent.

spew (spyōō) *v.i., v.t.* **1.** to gush or pour out. **2.** to vomit.

sphere (sfēr) *n.* **1.** a round solid geometric figure. **2.** a field of activity. —**spher′i•cal**, *adj.*

sphe′roid (-oid) *n.* a solid figure similar to a sphere in shape.

sphinc′ter (sfingk′tər) *n.* a circular band of muscle that closes a body opening.

sphinx (sfingks) *n.* an ancient Egyptian figure with a human head and a lion's body.

spice (spīs) *n., v.,* **spiced, spicing.** —*n.* **1.** an aromatic plant substance used to season food. —*v.t.* **2.** something that gives zest. **3.** to season with spice. **4.** to give zest to. —**spic′y**, *adj.*

spick′-and-span′ (spik′ən span′) *adj.* spotlessly clean.

spi′der (spī′dər) *n.* a web-spinning insectlike animal with eight legs.

spiel (spēl, shpēl) *n. Slang.* a glib speech intended to persuade.

spig′ot (spig′ət) *n.* a faucet.

spike[1] (spīk) *n., v.,* **spiked, spiking.** —*n.* **1.** a long thick nail. **2.** a stiff, pointed part. —*v.t.* **3.** to fasten with spikes. **4.** to suppress or stop. —**spik′y**, *adj.*

spike[2] (spīk) *n.* **1.** an ear of grain. **2.** a stalk of flowers.

spill (spil) v., **spilled** or **spilt, spilling.** —v.t. **1.** to cause to run or flow from a container, esp. accidentally. **2.** to shed (blood). —v.i. **3.** to run or flow from a container. —**spil′lage,** n.

spill′way′ n. a passage through which excess water escapes.

spin (spin) v., **spun** (spun) **spinning,** n. —v.t. **1.** to make (yarn) by drawing out and twisting fibers. **2.** to form (fibers) into yarn. **3.** to cause to rotate rapidly. —v.i. **4.** to rotate rapidly. **5.** to spin yarn or thread. —n. **6.** a spinning motion. **7.** a short ride. **8.** *Slang.* a viewpoint or bias.

spin′ach (-ich) n. a plant with edible, dark green leaves.

spi′nal (spīn′l) adj. of the spine or spinal cord.

spi′nal col′umn n. the series of vertebrae forming the axis of the skeleton.

spi′nal cord′ n. the cord of nerve tissue extending through the spinal column.

spin′ control′ n. *Slang.* an attempt to give a bias to news coverage.

spin′dle (spin′dl) n. **1.** a tapered rod on which thread is wound in spinning. **2.** any shaft or axis.

spin′dly, adj., **-dli·er, -dli·est.** tall and thin.

spine (spīn) n. **1.** the backbone. **2.** the back of a book binding. **3.** a stiff bristle or thorn. —**spin′y,** adj.

spine′less adj. weak in character.

spin′et (spin′it) n. a small piano.

spin′ning wheel′ n. a device for spinning yarn or thread.

spin′-off′ n. a by-product or secondary development.

spin′ster (-stər) n. *Usu. Disparaging.* an unmarried woman, esp. elderly.

spi′ral (spī′rəl) n., adj., v., **-raled, -raling.** —n. **1.** a curve made by circling a fixed point while approaching or receding from it. —adj. **2.** of or like a spiral. —v.i., v.t. **3.** to move or cause to move on a spiral course.

spire (spī^ər) n. a tall, sharply pointed roof forming the top of a tower or steeple.

spi·re′a (spī rē′ə) n. a garden shrub with white or pink flowers.

spir′it (spir′it) n. **1.** the vital force in humans; mind or soul. **2.** a ghost. **3. spirits,** mood or feelings. **4.** vigor. **5.** general meaning. **6. spirits,** alcoholic liquor. —v.t. **7.** to carry off mysteriously.

spir′it·u·al (-chōō əl) adj. **1.** of the spirit or the soul. **2.** religious. —n. **3.** a religious song originating among blacks in the southern U.S.

—**spir′it·u·al·ly,** adv. —**spir′it·u·al′i·ty** (-al′i tē) n.

spir′it·u·al·ism n. the belief that spirits of the dead communicate with the living. —**spir′it·u·al·ist,** n., adj.

spit¹ (spit) v., **spat** (spat) or **spit, spitting,** n. —v.i., v.t. **1.** to eject (saliva) from the mouth. —n. **2.** saliva. **3.** the act of spitting.

spit² (spit) n., v., **spitted, spitting.** —n. **1.** a pointed rod for roasting meat. **2.** a narrow point of land. —v.t. **3.** to pierce with a spit.

spite (spīt) n., v., **spited, spiting.** —n. **1.** a malicious desire to harm or annoy someone. —v.t. **2.** to treat with spite. —*Idiom.* **3. in spite of,** not being hindered by. —**spite′ful,** adj.

spit′fire′ n. a person with a fiery temper.

spit′tle n. saliva.

spit·toon′ (spi tōōn′) n. a large bowl serving as a receptacle for spit, esp. from chewing tobacco.

splash (splash) v.t. **1.** to dash (water, mud, etc.) about in drops. **2.** to wet or soil with such drops. —v.i. **3.** to fall or move with a splash. —n. **4.** an act or sound of splashing. **5.** a spot. **6.** a striking impression. —**splash′y,** adj.

splash′down′ n. the landing of a space vehicle in the ocean.

splat (splat) n. a sound made by splattering or slapping.

splat′ter v.t., v.i. to splash widely.

splay (splā) v.t., v.i. **1.** to spread out. **2.** to slant.

spleen (splēn) n. **1.** an abdominal organ that helps maintain the proper condition of the blood. **2.** ill humor.

splen′did (splen′did) adj. gorgeous; superb; fine. —**splen′dor,** n.

splice (splīs) v., **spliced, splicing,** n. —v.t. **1.** to join by interweaving or overlapping, as ropes, film, etc. —n. **2.** a union made by splicing.

splint (splint) n. **1.** a piece of rigid material for immobilizing a broken part of the body while it heals. —v.t. **2.** to brace with a splint.

splin′ter n. **1.** a thin sharp fragment, as of wood or glass. —v.t., v.i. **2.** to break into splinters.

split (split) v., **split, splitting,** n., adj. —v.t., v.i. **1.** to separate or divide, esp. lengthwise. **2.** to burst. —n. **3.** the act of splitting. **4.** a breach. —adj. **5.** cleft; divided.

split′-lev′el adj. **1.** (of a house) having rooms on levels a half story apart. —n. **2.** a split-level house.

split′ pea′ n. a dried green pea.

split′ personal′ity n. a mental disorder in which a person acquires several personalities.

splotch (sploch) *n.* **1.** a large spot. —*v.t.* **2.** to mark with splotches.

splurge (splûrj) *n., v.,* **splurged, splurging.** —*n.* **1.** a big expenditure. —*v.i.* **2.** to be extravagant.

splut′ter (splut′ər) *v.i.* **1.** to talk rapidly and confusedly. —*n.* **2.** spluttering talk.

spoil (spoil) *v.,* **spoiled** or **spoilt, spoiling,** *n.* —*v.t.* **1.** to damage. **2.** to harm the character of (esp. a child) by excessive indulgence. —*v.i.* **3.** to become unfit for use. —*n.* **4. spoils,** plunder. —**spoil′-age,** *n.*

spoil′sport′ *n.* a person who spoils the pleasure of others.

spoils′ sys′tem *n.* the practice of filling nonelective public offices with supporters of the victor.

spoke[1] (spōk) *v.* a pt. of **speak.**

spoke[2] (spōk) *n.* a bar between the hub and the rim of a wheel.

spokes′man or **spokes′wom′an** or **spokes′per′son** *n., pl.* **-men** or **-wom•en** or **-per•sons.** a person who speaks for another or for a group.

sponge (spunj) *n., v.,* **sponged, sponging.** —*n.* **1.** a marine animal with a porous skeleton. **2.** its absorbent skeleton or an imitation, used for cleaning. —*v.t.* **3.** to clean with a sponge. **4.** to get by imposing on another. —*v.i.* **5.** to impose or live on another. —**spong′er,** *n.*

sponge′ cake′ *n.* a light cake without shortening.

spon′sor (spon′sər) *n.* **1.** one who recommends or supports. **2.** an advertiser on radio or television. **3.** a godparent. —*v.t.* **4.** to act as sponsor for. —**spon′sor•ship′,** *n.*

spon•ta•ne•ous (spon tā′nē əs) *adj.* **1.** occurring naturally or without planning. **2.** impulsive. —**spon′ta•ne′i•ty** (-tə nē′i tē, -nā′-) *n.*

sponta′neous combus′tion *n.* the ignition of a substance without heat from an external source.

spoof (spoof) *n.* **1.** a parody. —*v.t., v.i.* **2.** to make fun (of) lightly.

spook (spook) *n.* **1.** a ghost. —*v.t., v.i.* **2.** to frighten or become frightened. —**spook′y,** *adj.*

spool (spool) *n.* a cylinder on which something is wound.

spoon (spoon) *n.* **1.** a utensil for stirring or taking up food. —*v.t.* **2.** to eat with or lift in a spoon. —**spoon′ful,** *n.*

spoon′-feed′ *v.t.* **1.** to feed with a spoon. **2.** to provide with information in a simplified way.

spoor (spoor) *n.* a track or scent of a wild animal.

spo•rad′ic (spə rad′ik) *adj.* occasional; scattered.

spore (spôr) *n.* the asexual reproductive cell of a fungus, fern, etc.

sport (spôrt) *n.* **1.** a competitive athletic activity. **2.** recreation. **3.** a sportsmanlike person. **4.** mockery. —*adj.* **5.** of or for sport. —*v.i.* **6.** to amuse oneself. —*v.t.* **7.** to wear or display.

spor′tive *adj.* playful.

sports′ car′ *n.* a small, high-powered car.

sports′man *n., pl.* **-men. 1.** a person who engages in sports, esp. hunting and fishing. **2.** a person who shows fairness and grace in winning and defeat. —**sports′man•like′,** *adj.* —**sports′man•ship′,** *n.*

sport′-util′ity ve′hicle *n.* a rugged vehicle with a trucklike chassis, designed for occasional off-road use.

sport′y *adj.,* **-ier, -iest.** flashy.

spot *n., v.,* **spotted, spotting,** *adj.* —*n.* **1.** a discolored mark; stain. **2.** a small part. **3.** a place. —*v.t.* **4.** to stain with spots. **5.** to notice. —*v.i.* **6.** to make a spot. —*adj.* **7.** made, done, etc., at once. —**spot′-less,** *adj.* —**spot′ty,** *adj.*

spot′ check′ *n.* a random sampling or investigation. —**spot′-check′,** *v.t., v.i.*

spot′light′ *n.* **1.** an intense light focused on a person or thing. **2.** intense public attention.

spouse (spous) *n.* a husband or wife.

spout (spout) *v.t., v.i.* **1.** to discharge or issue with force. **2.** to say or speak insincerely. —*n.* **3.** a pipe or lip on a container.

sprain (sprān) *v.t.* **1.** to injure by wrenching. —*n.* **2.** such an injury.

sprang (sprang) *v.* a pt. of **spring.**

sprat (sprat) *n.* a herringlike fish.

sprawl (sprôl) *v.i.* **1.** to stretch out ungracefully. —*n.* **2.** a sprawling position.

spray[1] (sprā) *n.* **1.** liquid falling through the air in fine droplets. **2.** a device for producing a spray. —*v.t., v.i.* **3.** to scatter as spray. **4.** to apply in a spray. —**spray′er,** *n.*

spray[2] (sprā) *n.* an arrangement of flowers, leaves, etc.

spread (spred) *v.,* **spread, spreading,** *n.* —*v.t., v.i.* **1.** to stretch or open out. **2.** to force or move apart. **3.** to distribute over an area. **4.** to apply in a layer. **5.** to become or make widely known. —*n.* **6.** the act of spreading. **7.** expanse; range. **8.** a cloth cover for a bed. **9.** a food for spreading.

spread/-ea/gle *adj., v.,* **-gled, -gl-ing.** —*adj.* **1.** suggestive of an eagle with outstretched wings. —*v.t.* **2.** to stretch out in this way.

spread/sheet/ *n.* **1.** an outsize ledger sheet. **2.** such a sheet simulated by computer software.

spree (sprē) *n.* a spell or bout of indulgence.

sprig (sprig) *n.* a twig or shoot.

spright/ly (sprīt/lē) *adj.,* **-lier, -liest.** lively. —**spright/li•ness,** *n.*

spring (spring) *v.,* **sprang** (sprang) or **sprung** (sprung) **sprung, spring-ing,** *n.* —*v.i.* **1.** to rise or leap suddenly. **2.** to come into being; arise. —*v.t.* **3.** to cause to spring. **4.** to cause to operate suddenly. **5.** to develop. —*n.* **6.** the season after winter. **7.** a jump. **8.** a place where water issues from the ground. **9.** an elastic device that recovers its shape after being bent, stretched, etc. —**spring/time/,** *n.*

spring/board/ *n.* **1.** a flexible board used in diving and gymnastics. **2.** a starting point.

spring/ tide/ *n.* the large rise and fall of the tide at the time of the new or the full moon.

sprin/kle (spring/kəl) *v.,* **-kled, -kl-ing,** *n.* —*v.t., v.i.* **1.** to scatter in drops. **2.** to rain slightly in scattered drops. —*n.* **3.** an instance of sprinkling. **4.** something sprinkled.

sprint (sprint) *v.i.* **1.** to run fast for a short distance. —*n.* **2.** a short fast run. —**sprint/er,** *n.*

sprite (sprīt) *n.* an elf; fairy.

sprock/et (sprok/it) *n.* a tooth on a wheel engaging with a chain.

sprout (sprout) *v.i.* **1.** to begin to grow; bud. —*n.* **2.** a plant shoot.

spruce[1] (sprōōs) *n.* a cone-bearing evergreen tree.

spruce[2] (sprōōs) *adj.,* **sprucer, sprucest,** *v.,* **spruced, sprucing.** —*adj.* **1.** trim; neat. —*v.t., v.i.* **2.** to make or become spruce.

sprung (sprung) *v.* a pt. and pp. of **spring.**

spry (sprī) *adj.,* **spryer** or **sprier, spryest** or **spriest.** nimbly energetic.

spume (spyōōm) *n.* foam.

spunk (spungk) *n. Informal.* courage; spirit. —**spunk/y,** *adj.*

spur (spûr) *n., v.,* **spurred, spurring.** —*n.* **1.** a sharp device worn on a boot heel to goad a horse. **2.** a spurlike part. —*v.t.* **3.** to urge on. —*Idiom.* **4. on the spur of the moment,** suddenly.

spu/ri•ous (spyŏŏr/ē əs) *adj.* not genuine. —**spu/ri•ous•ly,** *adv.*

spurn (spûrn) *v.t.* to scorn; reject.

spurt (spûrt) *n.* **1.** a sudden, force-ful gush. **2.** a brief increase of effort. —*v.i., v.t.* **3.** to gush, expel in, or make a spurt.

sput/ter (sput/ər) *v.i.* **1.** to make rapid popping sounds. **2.** to talk incoherently. —*n.* **3.** an act or sound of sputtering.

spu/tum (spyōō/təm) *n.* spittle.

spy (spī) *n., pl.* **spies,** *v.,* **spied, spy-ing.** —*n.* **1.** a person employed by a government to gather information about another country. **2.** a person who keeps secret watch on others. —*v.i.* **3.** to act as a spy. —*v.t.* **4.** to catch sight of.

spy/ glass/ *n.* a small telescope.

squab (skwob) *n.* a young pigeon.

squab/ble (-əl) *n., v.,* **-bled, -bling.** —*n.* **1.** a petty quarrel. —*v.i.* **2.** to engage in a petty quarrel.

squad (skwod) *n.* a small group, esp. of soldiers or police officers.

squad/ car/ *n.* a police car.

squad/ron (-rən) *n.* a unit in the Navy, Air Force, etc.

squal/id (skwol/id) *adj.* filthy and repulsive. —**squal/or,** *n.*

squall[1] (skwôl) *n.* a sudden, strong gust of wind, often with rain or snow.

squall[2] (skwôl) *v.i.* **1.** to cry out loudly. —*n.* **2.** a loud cry.

squan/der (skwon/dər) *v.t.* to use or spend wastefully.

square (skwâr) *n., v.,* **squared, squaring,** *adj.,* **squarer, squarest,** *adv.* —*n.* **1.** a rectangle with four equal sides and four right angles. **2.** anything shaped like a square. **3.** an open area formed by intersecting streets. **4.** the product of a number multiplied by itself. **5.** *Slang.* a conventional, unimaginative person. —*v.t.* **6.** to make square in form. **7.** to multiply (a number) by itself. **8.** to make even. **9.** to adjust. —*v.i.* **10.** to agree. —*adj.* **11.** forming a right angle. **12.** of square shape. **13.** having all accounts settled. **14.** honest. **15.** *Slang.* conventional. —*adv.* **16.** honestly. —**square/ly,** *adv.*

square/ dance/ *n.* a dance by four couples arranged in a square.

square/ root/ *n.* the quantity of which a given quantity is the square.

squash[1] (skwosh) *v.t.* **1.** to crush into a pulplike mass. **2.** to suppress. —*n.* **3.** a squashed mass. **4.** a game resembling tennis.

squash[2] (skwosh) *n.* the edible fruit of plants of the gourd family.

squat (skwot) *v.,* **squatted** or **squat, squatting,** *adj., n.* —*v.i.* **1.** to sit on the haunches or heels. **2.** to occupy another's property illegally.

—*adj.* **3.** stocky. —*n.* **4.** a squatting position.

squawk (skwôk) *n.* **1.** a loud harsh cry. —*v.i.* **2.** to utter squawks. **3.** to complain.

squeak (skwēk) *n.* **1.** a small shrill sound. —*v.i., v.t.* **2.** to utter (with) a squeak. —**squeak′y,** *adj.*

squeal (skwēl) *n.* **1.** a long shrill cry. —*v.t., v.i.* **2.** to utter (with) a squeal.

squeam′ish (skwē′mish) *adj.* easily nauseated or disgusted.

squee′gee (skwē′jē) *n.* an implement for cleaning glass surfaces.

squeeze (skwēz) *v.,* **squeezed, squeezing,** *n.* —*v.t.* **1.** to press forcibly together. **2.** to extract by pressing. —*v.i.* **3.** to exert pressure. **4.** to force one's way. —*n.* **5.** an act of squeezing. **6.** a hug.

squelch (skwelch) *v.t.* **1.** to silence, as with a crushing retort. —*n.* **2.** a crushing retort.

squib (skwib) *n.* **1.** a short witty item. **2.** a hissing firecracker.

squid (skwid) *n.* a 10-armed marine animal with a long, slender body.

squig′gle (skwig′əl) *n.* a short, irregular twist. —**squig′gly,** *adj.*

squint (skwint) *v.i.* **1.** to look with the eyes partly closed. **2.** to be cross-eyed. —*n.* **3.** a squinting look. **4.** a cross-eyed condition.

squire (skwi⁹r) *n., v.,* **squired, squiring.** —*n.* **1.** an English country gentleman. **2.** an escort. —*v.t.* **3.** to escort.

squirm (skwûrm) *v.i.* to wriggle or writhe.

squir′rel (skwûr′əl) *n.* a bushytailed, tree-living rodent.

squirt (skwûrt) *v.i.* **1.** to eject liquid in a thin stream. —*v.t.* **2.** to cause to squirt. **3.** to wet in this way. —*n.* **4.** a jet of liquid.

squish (skwish) *v.t.* **1.** to squash. —*v.i.* **2.** to make a gushing sound when walked in. —*n.* **3.** a squishing sound.

Sr. 1. Senior. **2.** Sister.

SRO 1. single-room occupancy. **2.** standing room only.

SS social security.

SST supersonic transport.

St. 1. Saint. **2.** Street.

stab (stab) *v.,* **stabbed, stabbing,** *n.* —*v.t., v.i.* **1.** to pierce with a pointed weapon. —*n.* **2.** a thrust with a pointed weapon.

sta′bi•lize′ (stā′bə līz′) *v.t., v.i.,* **-lized, -lizing.** to make, keep, or become stable.

sta′ble¹ (stā′bəl) *n., v.,* **-bled, -bling,** *adj.* —*n.* **1.** a building for horses. —*v.t., v.i.* **2.** to put or stay in a stable.

sta′ble² (stā′bəl) *adj.* steady. —**sta•bil′i•ty,** *n.*

stac•ca′to (stə kä′tō) *adj. Music.* shortened and detached when played or sung.

stack (stak) *n.* **1.** an orderly pile or heap. **2. stacks,** a book storage area. **3.** a great quantity. —*v.t.* **4.** to pile in a stack.

sta′di•um (stā′dē əm) *n., pl.* **-diums, -dia.** an open structure for games, surrounded by rows of tiered seats.

staff (staf) *n., pl.* **staves** (stāvz) or **staffs** (for 1, 3); **staffs** (for 2); *v.* —*n.* **1.** a stick carried as a support, weapon, etc. **2.** a body of administrators or assistants. **3.** a set of five lines on which music is written. —*v.t.* **4.** to provide with a staff.

stag (stag) *n.* **1.** an adult male deer. —*adj.* **2.** for men only. —*adv.* **3.** without a date.

stage (stāj) *n., v.,* **staged, staging.** —*n.* **1.** a single step in a process or series. **2.** a raised platform, esp. one on which actors perform. **3. the stage,** the theater as a profession. —*v.t.* **4.** to present on stage.

stage′coach′ *n.* a horse-drawn public coach that traveled over a fixed route.

stage′hand′ *n.* a theater worker who deals with props and scenery.

stage′struck′ *adj.* obsessed with the theater.

stag′ger (stag′ər) *v.i.* **1.** to move unsteadily. —*v.t.* **2.** to astonish. **3.** to arrange in an alternating pattern. —*n.* **4.** a staggering movement.

stag′ger•ing *adj.* amazing.

stag′nant (stag′nənt) *adj.* **1.** not flowing; foul; stale. **2.** inactive. —**stag′nate** (-nāt) *v.i.*

staid (stād) *adj.* sedate or solemn.

stain (stān) *n.* **1.** a discolored patch; blemish. **2.** a kind of dye. —*v.t.* **3.** to discolor. **4.** to color with a stain. —*v.i.* **5.** to become stained.

stain′less steel′ *n.* steel allied with chromium to resist rust.

stair (stâr) *n.* **1.** one of a series of steps between levels. **2. stairs,** a flight of steps. —**stair′case′, stair′way′,** *n.*

stair′well′ *n.* a vertical shaft containing stairs.

stake¹ (stāk) *n., v.,* **staked, staking.** —*n.* **1.** a pointed stick. —*v.t.* **2.** to mark off with stakes. **3.** to support with a stake.

stake² (stāk) *n., v.,* **staked, staking.** —*n.* **1.** something wagered. **2.** a share. **3. stakes,** a prize. —*v.t.* **4.** to risk. **5.** to provide money for. —*Idiom.* **6. at stake,** at risk.

stake′out′ *n.* surveillance by the police.

sta·lac′tite (stə lak′tīt) *n.* an icicle-shaped formation hanging from a cave roof.

sta·lag′mite (-lag′mīt) *n.* a cone-shaped deposit on a cave floor.

stale (stāl) *adj.,* **staler, stalest.** not fresh.

stale′mate′ (-māt′) *n.* a deadlocked position.

stalk[1] (stôk) *n.* a plant stem.

stalk[2] (stôk) *v.i.* **1.** to walk stiffly. —*v.t.* **2.** to pursue (a person or animal) stealthily. —**stalk′er,** *n.*

stall[1] (stôl) *n.* **1.** a compartment in a stable for one animal. **2.** a sales booth. **3.** a condition in which an engine stops. —*v.t., v.i.* **4.** to put or keep in a stall. **5.** to stop, esp. unintentionally.

stall[2] (stôl) *v.i., v.t.* **1.** to delay. —*n.* **2.** a pretext for delay.

stal′lion (stal′yən) *n.* a male horse.

stal′wart (stôl′wərt) *adj.* **1.** robust. **2.** brave. **3.** steadfast. —*n.* **4.** a stalwart person.

sta′men (stā′mən) *n.* the pollen-bearing organ of a flower.

stam·i•na (stam′ə nə) *n.* endurance.

stam′mer *v.i., v.t.* **1.** to speak or say with involuntary breaks or repetitions. —*n.* **2.** such speech.

stamp (stamp) *v.t.* **1.** to bring (the foot) down forcibly. **2.** to pound with the foot. **3.** to impress (something) with a mark. **4.** to impress (a mark) on something. —*v.i.* **5.** to bring the foot down forcibly. —*n.* **6.** a gummed printed label showing that postage has been paid. **7.** a marking device. **8.** an official mark.

stam•pede′ (stam pēd′) *n., v.,* **-peded, -peding.** —*n.* **1.** a panicky rush or flight. —*v.i., v.t.* **2.** to flee or cause to flee in a stampede.

stamp′ing ground′ *n.* a favorite haunt.

stance (stans) *n.* a way of standing.

stanch (stônch, stanch) *v.t.* **1.** to stop the flow of, esp. blood. —*v.i.* **2.** to stop flowing.

stan′chion (stan′shən) *n.* an upright post.

stand (stand) *v.,* **stood** (sto̅o̅d) **standing,** *n.* —*v.i.* **1.** to rise to, be in, or remain in an upright position. **2.** to remain firm. **3.** to be located. **4.** to remain unchanged. —*v.t.* **5.** to set upright. **6.** to endure. **7. stand by, a.** to abide by. **b.** to be loyal to. **c.** to be ready to act. **8. ~ for, a.** to represent. **b.** to tolerate. **9. ~ out,** to be prominent. **10. ~ up, a.** to be convinc-

ing. **b.** to be lasting. **c.** to fail to keep an appointment. —*n.* **11.** a position or attitude. **12.** the place occupied by a witness giving testimony in court. **13.** a raised platform. **14. stands,** a section of seats for spectators. **15.** a support for small articles. **16.** an outdoor salesplace. **17.** an area of trees.

stand′ard (stan′dərd) *n.* **1.** something serving as a basis for comparison or judgment. **2.** a flag. **3.** an upright support. —*adj.* **4.** being a model or basis for comparison.

stan′dard-bear′er *n.* the leader of a cause.

stand′ard•ize′ *v.t.,* **-ized, -izing.** to make conform with a standard.

stand′ard time′ *n.* the civil time officially adopted for a region.

stand′by′ *n., pl.* **-bys.** **1.** a person or thing that can be depended on. **2.** one ready to be a substitute.

stand′-in′ *n.* a substitute.

stand′ing *n.* **1.** status or reputation. **2.** duration. —*adj.* **3.** upright. **4.** not flowing. **5.** lasting; fixed.

stand′off′ *n.* a tie or draw.

stand′off′ish *adj.* aloof.

stand′pipe′ *n.* a vertical pipe into which water is pumped to obtain a required pressure.

stand′point′ *n.* a viewpoint.

stand′still′ *n.* a complete halt.

stan′za (stan′zə) *n.* a division of a poem.

sta′ple[1] (stā′pəl) *n., v.,* **-pled, -pling.** —*n.* **1.** a thin, bracket-shaped wire fastener. —*v.t.* **2.** to fasten with a staple. —**sta′pler,** *n.*

sta•ple[2] (stā′pəl) *n.* **1.** a basic item, as of food. —*adj.* **2.** basic or chief.

star (stär) *n., adj., v.,* **starred, starring.** —*n.* **1.** a heavenly body that appears as a fixed point of light at night. **2.** a figure with five or six points. **3.** a principal or famous performer. **4.** an asterisk. —*adj.* **5.** principal. —*v.i.* **6.** to be outstanding. **7.** to perform as a star. —**star′ry,** *adj.*

star′board′ (-bərd, -bôrd′) *n.* **1.** the right side of a ship, facing forward. —*adj.* **2.** of or on the right side.

starch (stärch) *n.* **1.** a white tasteless substance found in rice, corn, wheat, potatoes, etc. **2.** a preparation of starch used to stiffen fabrics. —*v.t.* **3.** to stiffen with starch.

stare (stâr) *v.,* **stared, staring,** *n.* —*v.i.* **1.** to gaze fixedly. —*n.* **2.** a fixed look.

star′fish′ *n.* a star-shaped sea animal.

star′gaze′ *v.i.,* **-gazed, -gazing.** **1.** to gaze at the stars. **2.** to daydream.

stark (stärk) *adj.* **1.** complete; utter. **2.** bleak. —*adv.* **3.** completely.

star'light' *n.* light emanating from the stars. —**star'lit'**, *adj.*

star'ling (-ling) *n.* a songbird with speckled black plumage.

star'ry-eyed' *adj.* overly romantic or idealistic.

start (stärt) *v.i.* **1.** to begin to move, go, or act. **2.** to give a sudden jerk, as from shock. —*v.t.* **3.** to set moving or acting. **4.** to establish. —*n.* **5.** a beginning. **6.** a startled movement. **7.** a lead.

star'tle *v.*, **-tled, -tling.** —*v.t.*, *v.i.* to surprise or be surprised.

starve (stärv) *v.*, **starved, starving.** —*v.i.* **1.** to die or suffer from hunger. —*v.t.* **2.** to kill or weaken by hunger. —**star•va'tion,** *n.*

stash (stash) *v.t.* **1.** to hide away. —*n.* **2.** something hidden away. **3.** a hiding place.

stat (stat) *n.* a statistic.

state (stāt) *n.*, *adj.*, *v.*, **stated, stating.** —*n.* **1.** the condition of a person or thing. **2.** a nation. **3.** a political unit of a federal union. **4.** formality. —*adj.* **5.** of a state or government. **6.** ceremonial. —*v.t.* **7.** to declare. —**state'hood,** *n.*

state'house' *n.* the building in which a state legislature sits.

state'less *adj.* lacking nationality.

state'ly *adj.*, **-lier, -liest.** dignified.

state'ment *n.* **1.** a declaration. **2.** a report on a business account.

state' of the art' *n.* the most advanced stage of a science, art, etc.

state'room' *n.* a private room on a ship.

states'man *n.* a highly respected and influential political leader who is devoted to public service. —**states'man•ship',** *n.*

stat'ic (stat'ik) *adj.* **1.** fixed; at rest; showing no change. —*n.* **2.** atmospheric electricity. **3.** interference caused by such electricity.

sta'tion (stā'shən) *n.* **1.** a regular stopping place for trains or buses. **2.** a place from which broadcasts are sent. **3.** an assigned place or office. **4.** status. —*v.t.* **5.** to assign a place to.

sta'tion•ar'y (-shə ner'ē) *adj.* not moving; not movable; fixed.

sta'tion•er'y (-shə ner'ē) *n.* writing materials.

sta•tis'tics (stə tis'tiks) *n.* the science of collecting, classifying, and using numerical data. —**stat'is•ti'cian** (stat'ə stish'ən) *n.*

stat'u•ar'y (stach'ōō er'ē) *n.* statues.

stat'ue (stach'ōō) *n.* a carved, molded, or cast figure.

stat'u•esque' (-esk') *adj.* tall and dignified.

stat'ure (-ər) *n.* **1.** height. **2.** status from achievement.

sta'tus (stā'təs, stat'əs) *n.* **1.** present condition. **2.** social standing.

sta'tus quo' (kwō) *n.* the existing state.

stat'ute (stach'ōōt) *n.* a law.

stat'ute of limita'tions *n.* a law defining the period within which legal action may be taken.

staunch (stônch) *adj.* firm; steadfast; strong.

stave (stāv) *n.*, *v.*, **staved** or (for 3) **stove** (stōv), **staving.** —*n.* **1.** a narrow strip of wood. **2.** a stick or rod. —*v.t.* **3.** to break a hole in. **4. stave off,** to prevent.

stay (stā) *v.i.* **1.** to remain in a place or condition; continue. **2.** to dwell. —*v.t.* **3.** to stop or restrain. —*n.* **4.** a period of time spent at one place. **5.** a stop; pause.

stay'ing pow'er *n.* endurance.

STD sexually transmitted disease.

stead (sted) *n.* **1.** the place of a person taken by another. —*Idiom.* **2. stand in good stead,** to prove useful to.

stead'fast' *adj.* **1.** fixed in place. **2.** firm in purpose or loyalty.

stead'y *adj.*, **-ier, -iest,** *v.*, **-ied, -ying.** —*adj.* **1.** firmly fixed. **2.** regular. **3.** calm; not excitable. **4.** unwavering. —*v.t.*, *v.i.* **5.** to make or become steady. —**stead'i•ly,** *adv.*

steak (stāk) *n.* a slice of meat or fish.

steal (stēl) *v.*, **stole** (stōl) **stolen, stealing.** —*v.t.* **1.** to take wrongfully. —*v.i.* **2.** to commit theft. **3.** to move very quietly.

stealth (stelth) *n.* secret action.

steam (stēm) *n.* **1.** water in the form of gas or vapor. **2.** power or energy. —*v.i.* **3.** to pass off as or give off steam. —*v.t.* **4.** to treat with steam, as in cooking. —*adj.* **5.** operated by steam. **6.** conducting steam. —**steam'boat',** **steam'ship',** *n.*

steam'er *n.* **1.** a vessel moved by steam. **2.** a device for cooking, treating, etc., with steam.

steam'roll'er *n.* **1.** a heavy vehicle with a roller used for paving roads. —*v.t.* **2.** to crush, flatten, or overwhelm as if with a steamroller.

steed (stēd) *n.* a horse.

steel (stēl) *n.* **1.** an alloy of iron with carbon. —*adj.* **2.** of or like steel. —*v.t.* **3.** to make resolute.

steel' wool' *n.* a mass of steel shavings, used for scouring and smoothing.

stiff-necked

steep[1] (stēp) *adj.* **1.** sloping sharply. **2.** exorbitant. —**steep′ly,** *adv.*

steep[2] (stēp) *v.t.* **1.** to soak in a liquid. **2.** to saturate. —*v.i.* **3.** to lie soaking in a liquid.

stee′ple (stē′pəl) *n.* a structure topped with a spire, as on a church.

stee′ple•chase′ *n.* a horse race with artificial obstacles.

steer[1] (stēr) *v.t.* **1.** to guide the course of. **2.** to direct; guide. —*v.i.* **3.** to steer a vessel or vehicle.

steer[2] (stēr) *n.* a castrated ox.

steer′age (-ij) *n.* the part of a ship for passengers paying the least.

stein (stīn) *n.* a mug, esp. for beer.

stel′lar (stel′ər) *adj.* **1.** of stars. **2.** outstanding.

stem[1] (stem) *n., v.,* **stemmed, stemming.** —*n.* **1.** the supporting stalk of a plant. **2.** something resembling this. **3.** a family's line of descent. **4.** the part of a word that does not change. —*v.t.* **5.** to remove the stem of. —*v.i.* **6.** to originate.

stem[2] (stem) *v.t.,* **stemmed, stemming.** to stop or check.

stem[3] (stem) *n., v.,* **stemmed, stemming.** —*n.* **1.** the front of a ship. —*v.t.* **2.** to advance against.

stench (stench) *n.* a bad odor.

sten′cil (sten′səl) *n., v.,* **-ciled, -ciling.** —*n.* **1.** a sheet with a cut-out design to color over and reproduce on an underlying surface. —*v.t.* **2.** to make with a stencil.

ste•nog′ra•phy (-rə fē) *n.* shorthand writing. —**ste•nog′ra•pher,** *n.*

sten•to′ri•an (-tôr′ē ən) *adj.* very loud.

step (step) *n., v.,* **stepped, stepping.** —*n.* **1.** the movement of the foot in walking. **2.** the distance of such movement. **3.** a pace. **4.** a footprint. **5.** a stage in a process. **6.** a level on a stair. —*v.i.* **7.** to move in steps. **8.** to walk a short way. **9.** to press with the foot.

step- a prefix showing a relation created by the remarriage of a parent. —**step′broth′er,** *n.* —**step′child,** *n.* —**step′daugh′ter,** *n.* —**step′fath′er,** *n.* —**step′moth′er,** *n.* —**step′par′ent,** *n.* —**step′sis′ter,** *n.* —**step′son′,** *n.*

step′lad′der *n.* a ladder with a hinged supporting frame.

steppe (step) *n.* a vast plain.

-ster a suffix meaning one who is; one who is associated with; or one who makes or does.

ster′e•o (ster′ē ō′, stēr′-) *n., pl.* **-eos.** stereophonic sound or equipment.

ster′e•o•phon′ic (-ē ə fon′ik, stēr′-) *adj.* (of recorded sound) played through two or more speakers.

ster′e•o•type′ *n., v.,* **-typed, -typing.** —*n.* **1.** a simplified image of a person, group, etc. **2.** an idea, expression, etc., without originality. —*v.t.* **3.** to regard as a stereotype.

ster′ile (ster′il; *esp. Brit.* -īl) *adj.* **1.** free from living germs. **2.** unable to produce offspring; barren. —**ste•ril′i•ty** (stə ril′i tē) *n.*

ster′i•lize′ *v.t.,* **-lized, -lizing.** to make sterile. —**ster′i•li•za′tion,** *n.* —**ster′i•liz′er,** *n.*

ster′ling (stûr′ling) *adj.* **1.** containing 92.5% silver. **2.** of British money. **3.** excellent.

stern[1] (stûrn) *adj.* strict; grim.

stern[2] (stûrn) *n.* the rear part of a ship or boat.

ster′num (stûr′nəm) *n., pl.* **-na, -nums.** the bony plate to which the ribs are attached.

ste′roid (stēr′oid, ster′-) *n.* a fat-soluble organic compound.

stet (stet) *v.,* **stetted, stetting.** —*v.i.* **1.** let it stand (a direction to retain printed material previously deleted). —*v.t.* **2.** to mark with the word "stet."

steth′o•scope′ (steth′ə skōp′) *n.* a medical instrument for listening to sounds in the body.

ste′ve•dore′ (stē′vi dôr′) *n.* a person who loads and unloads ships.

stew (stoo, styoo) *v.t.* **1.** to cook by simmering. —*v.i.* **2.** to worry. —*n.* **3.** a stewed dish of vegetables, meat, etc. **4.** a state of worry.

stew′ard (stoo′ərd, styoo′-) *n.* **1.** a person who manages another's affairs, property, etc. **2.** a person in charge of food, supplies, etc., for a ship, club, etc. **3.** a domestic employee on a ship or airplane. —**stew′ard•ship′,** *n.*

stick[1] (stik) *n.* **1.** a cut or broken branch. **2.** a long, slender piece.

stick[2] (stik) *v.,* **stuck** (stuk) **sticking,** *n.* —*v.t.* **1.** to pierce; stab. **2.** to thrust (into or through). **3.** to fasten or attach. —*v.i.* **4.** to be fastened or attached. **5.** to become jammed. **6.** to protrude. **7. stick up for,** to defend.

stick′er *n.* an adhesive label.

stick′ler *n.* someone who insists on something difficult.

stick′ shift′ *n.* a manual transmission.

stick′y *adj.,* **-ier, -iest,** *n.* —*adj.* **1.** adhesive. **2.** humid. —**stick′i•ness,** *n.*

stiff (stif) *adj.* **1.** rigid. **2.** not moving easily. **3.** very formal in manner. —**stiff′en,** *v.t., v.i.*

stiff′-necked′ *adj.* stubborn.

stifle

sti′fle (stī′fəl) v., **-fled, -fling.** —v.t. **1.** to smother. **2.** to repress. —v.i. **3.** to suffocate.

stig′ma (stig′mə) n., pl. **stig·ma·ta** (stig mä′tə, -mə-) **-mas. 1.** a mark of disgrace. **2.** the pollen-receiving part of a pistil. **3. stigmata,** marks resembling the wounds of Christ.

stig′ma·tize′ (-tīz′) v.t., **-tized, -tiz· ing.** to set a mark of disgrace or discredit upon.

stile (stīl) n. a set of steps over a fence, wall, etc.

sti·let′to (sti let′ō) n., pl. **-tos, -toes.** a thin-bladed dagger.

still[1] (stil) adj. **1.** motionless. **2.** silent. **3.** tranquil. —adv. **4.** until now. **5.** yet. **6.** even then. —conj. **7.** and yet. —v.t., v.i. **8.** to make or become still. —n. **9.** silence. —**still′ness,** n.

still[2] n. a distilling apparatus.

still′born′ adj. born dead.

still′ life′ n. a picture of inanimate objects, as flowers, fruit, etc.

stilt (stilt) n. one of two poles with foot supports enabling the user to walk above the ground.

stilt′ed adj. stiffly dignified.

stim′u·lant (stim′yə lənt) n. a drug or drink that temporarily stimulates the body or mind.

stim′u·late′ (-lāt′) v.t., **-lated, -lating. 1.** to rouse to action. **2.** to excite. —**stim′u·la′tion,** n.

stim′u·lus (-ləs) n., pl. **-li.** something that stimulates.

sting (sting) v., **stung** (stung), **stinging,** n. —v.t. **1.** to wound with a sharp-pointed organ, as bees do. **2.** to cause to feel a sharp pain. —v.i. **3.** to feel a sharp pain. —n. **4.** a wound or pain caused by stinging. —**sting′er,** n.

stin′gy (stin′jē) adj., **-gier, -giest. 1.** not wanting to give or spend. **2.** scanty.

stink (stingk) v., **stank** (stangk) or **stunk** (stungk), **stunk, stinking,** n. —v.i. **1.** to emit a bad odor. —n. **2.** a bad odor.

stint (stint) v.i. **1.** to be frugal. —v.t. **2.** to limit unduly. —n. **3.** a period of time spent on a task. **4.** a limitation.

sti′pend (stī′pend) n. a periodic fixed payment.

stip′u·late′ (stip′yə lāt′) v.t., **-lated, -lating.** to require as a condition.

stir (stûr) v., **stirred, stirring,** n. —v.t., v.i. **1.** to mix or agitate (a substance) by moving a spoon around in it. **2.** to move. **3.** to affect or be moved strongly. **4.** to incite, rouse, or be roused. —n. **5.** movement. **6.** excitement.

stir′-fry′ v.t., **stir-fried, stir-frying.** to fry quickly while stirring constantly over high heat.

stir′rup (stûr′əp, stir′-) n. a looplike support for the foot, suspended from a saddle.

stitch (stich) n. **1.** one complete movement of a needle in sewing, knitting, etc. **2.** a sudden pain, esp. in the side. —v.t. **3.** to join with stitches. —v.i. **4.** to sew.

stock (stok) n. **1.** a supply of goods on hand. **2.** the shares of a company. **3.** livestock. **4.** a line of descent. **5.** meat broth. **6. stocks,** a framework in which prisoners were publicly confined. —adj. **7.** standard; common. **8.** kept on hand. —v.t. **9.** to supply. **10.** to store for future use. —v.i. **11.** to lay in a stock of something. —**Idiom. 12. take stock, a.** to make an inventory of stock. **b.** to appraise prospects.

stock·ade′ (sto kād′) n. an enclosure built of upright posts driven into the ground.

stock′brok′er n. a broker who buys and sells securities for customers.

stock′ com′pany n. a theatrical company acting a repertoire of plays.

stock′ exchange′ n. a place where securities are bought and sold. Also, **stock market.**

stock′hold′er n. an owner of stock in a corporation.

stock′ing n. a close-fitting covering for the foot and leg.

stock′pile′ n., v., **-piled, -piling.** —n. **1.** a supply of something kept in reserve. —v.t., v.i. **2.** to accumulate for eventual use.

stock′-still′ adj. motionless.

stock′y adj., **-ier, -iest.** sturdy and short.

stock′yard′ n. an enclosure for livestock about to be slaughtered.

stodg′y (stoj′ē) adj., **-ier, -iest. 1.** dull; boring. **2.** old-fashioned.

sto′ic (stō′ik) adj. **1.** Also, **sto′i·cal.** not reacting to pain or stress. —n. **2.** a person who represses emotion.

stoke (stōk) v.t., v.i., **stoked, stoking.** to stir up and feed (a fire).

stole[1] (stōl) v. pt. of **steal.**

stole[2] (stōl) n. a long scarf or narrow strip worn over the shoulders.

sto′len (stō′lən) v. pp. of **steal.**

stol′id (stol′id) adj. unemotional; not easily moved. —**sto·lid′i·ty,** n.

stom′ach (stum′ək) n. **1.** the organ in which food is stored and partly digested. **2.** appetite; desire. —v.t. **3.** to endure; tolerate.

stomp (stomp) v.t., v.i. to tread (on) heavily.

stone (stōn) n., pl. **stones** or (for 4)

stone, *adj., v.,* **stoned, stoning.** —*n.* **1.** a hard, mineral substance. **2.** a small rock. **3.** a gem. **4.** *Brit.* a unit of weight equal to 14 pounds. **5.** a stonelike seed. **6.** a hard substance formed in the body, as in the kidney. —*adj.* **7.** of stone. —*v.t.* **8.** to throw stones at. **9.** to remove stones from. —**ston'y,** *adj.*

stone'wall' *v.i.* to be evasive or uncooperative.

stood (stŏŏd) *v.* pt. and pp. of **stand.**

stooge (stŏŏj) *n.* **1.** a person who feeds lines to a comedian. **2.** an underling or assistant.

stool (stŏŏl) *n.* **1.** a seat without arms or back. **2.** fecal matter.

stoop[1] (stŏŏp) *v.i.* **1.** to bend the body forward and downward. **2.** to condescend. —*n.* **3.** a stooping posture.

stoop[2] (stŏŏp) *n.* a small doorway or porch.

stop (stop) *v.,* **stopped, stopping,** *n.* —*v.t.* **1.** to put an end to the progress, movement, or operation of. **2.** to prevent. **3.** to block (an opening). —*v.i.* **4.** to cease moving, acting, or operating. **5.** to halt for a stay or visit. —*n.* **6.** an act, instance, or place of stopping. **7.** a hindrance. **8.** a set of organ pipes producing tones of the same quality or the knobs controlling these.

stop'gap' *n.* a temporary substitute.

stop'o'ver *n.* a temporary stop on a journey.

stop'per *n.* a plug.

stop'watch' *n.* a watch that can be stopped or started at any instant, used for timing.

stor'age (stôr'ij) *n.* **1.** a storing or being stored. **2.** capacity for storing.

store (stôr) *n., v.,* **stored, storing.** —*n.* **1.** a place where merchandise is sold. **2.** a supply or quantity. —*v.t.* **3.** to put away for future use. —*Idiom.* **4. set store by,** to value. —**store'keep'er,** *n.*

store'front' *n.* **1.** a small street-level store. —*adj.* **2.** located in a storefront.

store'house' *n.* a building for storage.

store'room' *n.* a room in which supplies or goods are stored.

stork (stôrk) *n.* a wading bird with long legs and a long neck and bill.

storm (stôrm) *n.* **1.** heavy rain, snow, etc., with wind. **2.** a violent assault. —*v.i.* **3.** to blow, rain, etc., strongly. **4.** to rage. —*v.t.* **5.** to attack. —**storm'y,** *adj.*

sto'ry[1] (stôr'ē) *n., pl.* **-ries. 1.** a written or spoken account of something. **2.** a fictitious tale. **3.** a news report. **4.** a lie.

story[2] (stôr'ē) *n., pl.* **-ries.** a horizontal section of a building.

stout (stout) *adj.* **1.** solidly built. **2.** strong; sturdy. **3.** firm. —*n.* **4.** a dark ale.

stout'-heart'ed *adj.* brave and resolute.

stove (stōv) *n.* an apparatus for giving heat for warmth or cooking.

stow (stō) *v.t.* **1.** to put away, as cargo. **2. stow away,** to hide on a ship or airplane to get free passage. —**stow'age,** *n.* —**stow'a·way',** *n.*

strad'dle (strad'l) *v.,* **-dled, -dling,** *n.* —*v.i., v.t.* **1.** to have one leg on either side (of). —*n.* **2.** an act of straddling.

strafe (strāf, sträf) *v.t.,* **strafed, strafing.** to shoot from airplanes.

strag'gle (strag'əl) *v.i.,* **-gled, -gling.** to stray from the course; ramble. —**strag'gler,** *n.*

straight (strāt) *adj.* **1.** without a bend or curve. **2.** direct. **3.** honest. **4.** right. **5.** in order. **6.** undiluted. **7.** *Informal.* heterosexual. —*adv.* **8.** directly. **9.** in a straight line. **10.** honestly. —*n.* **11.** a straight part. **12.** a five-card sequence in poker. —**straight'en,** *v.t., v.i.*

straight'-arm' *v.t.* to deflect (an opponent) by pushing away with the arm held straight.

straight' ar'row *n.* an often righteously conventional person.

straight'a·way' *adv.* **1.** at once. —*n.* **2.** a straight stretch.

straight' face' *n.* an expression that conceals one's feelings.

straight'for'ward *adj.* direct; frank.

straight' man' *n.* an entertainer who acts as a foil for a comedian.

strain[1] (strān) *v.t.* **1.** to exert to the utmost. **2.** to draw tight. **3.** to injure by stretching. **4.** to filter. —*v.i.* **5.** to make a great effort. —*n.* **6.** great effort. **7.** an injury from overexertion. **8.** severe pressure.

strain[2] (strān) *n.* **1.** the descendants of a common ancestor. **2.** ancestry. **3.** hereditary trait. **4.** a trace.

strain[3] (strān) *n.* a melody.

strained *adj.* not natural.

strait (strāt) *n.* **1.** a narrow waterway connecting two large bodies of water. **2. straits,** distress.

strait'en *v.t.* **1.** to put into financial difficulties. **2.** to restrict.

strait'jack/et *n.* **1.** a garment of strong material designed to restrain a violent person. **2.** anything that severely confines or hinders.

strait'-laced' *adj.* excessively strict in conduct or morality.

strand¹ (strand) *v.t.* **1.** to run aground. **2.** to leave helpless —*n.* **3.** a shore.

strand² *n.* **1.** one of the fibers twisted to form a rope, cable, etc. **2.** a lock of hair. **3.** a string, as of beads.

strange (strānj) *adj.,* **stranger, strangest. 1.** unusual; odd. **2.** unfamiliar. —**strange'ly,** *adv.*

stran'ger (strān'jər) *n.* **1.** a person who is not known. **2.** a newcomer.

stran'gle (strang'gəl) *v.,* **-gled, -gling.** —*v.t.* **1.** to kill by choking. **2.** to stifle. —*v.i.* **3.** to become strangled. —**stran'gu·la'tion** (-gyə lā'shən) *n.*

stran'gle·hold' *n.* a restrictive force.

stran'gu·late' (-gyə lāt') *v.t.,* **-lated, -lating.** to constrict.

strap (strap) *n., v.,* **strapped, strapping.** —*n.* **1.** a narrow strip or band of leather for fastening or holding things together. —*v.t.* **2.** to fasten with a strap.

strapped *adj.* needing money.

strat'a·gem (strat'ə jəm) *n.* a plan; trick.

strat'e·gy (-i jē) *n., pl.* **-gies. 1.** a plan for achieving a goal. **2.** the planning and direction of military operations. —**stra·te'gic** (strə tē'jik) *adj.* —**strat'e·gist,** *n.*

strat'i·fy' (-ə fī') *v.t., v.i.,* **-fied, -fying.** to form into or become arranged in layers. —**strat'i·fi·ca'tion,** *n.*

strat'o·sphere' (-ə sfēr') *n.* the upper region of the atmosphere.

stra'tum (strā'təm, strat'əm) *n., pl.* **-ta** (-tə), **-tums.** a layer of material.

straw (strô) *n.* **1.** a stalk of cereal grass. **2.** a mass of dried stalks. **3.** a tube for sucking up a liquid.

straw'ber'ry (-ber'ē, -bə rē) *n., pl.* **-ries.** a red, juicy fruit having seeds on the surface.

straw' boss' *n.* an assistant foreman.

straw' vote' *n.* an unofficial vote taken to determine the general trend of opinion.

stray (strā) *v.i.* **1.** to go from one's course or rightful place. —*adj.* **2.** straying or having strayed. **3.** isolated. —*n.* **4.** a lost or homeless creature.

streak (strēk) *n.* **1.** a long, narrow mark or smear. **2.** a vein; stratum. **3.** a series. —*v.t.* **4.** to mark with streaks. —*v.i.* **5.** to flash rapidly.

stream (strēm) *n.* **1.** a flowing body of water. **2.** a steady flow. —*v.i.* **3.** to flow in or as if in a stream.

stream'er *n.* a long narrow flag.

stream'lined' *adj.* **1.** shaped to offer the least resistance to a current. **2.** designed for greatest efficiency. —**stream'line',** *v.t.*

street (strēt) *n.* a paved public road in a town or city.

street'car' *n.* a public conveyance running on rails along city streets.

street' smarts' *n.pl.* shrewd awareness of how to survive in an urban environment. —**street'-smart',** *adj.*

strength (strengkth, strength) *n.* **1.** the quality or state of being strong. **2.** intensity. **3.** force in numbers. **4.** a strong or valuable quality. —**strengthen,** *v.t., v.i.*

stren'u·ous (stren'yōō əs) *adj.* vigorous; active.

strep' throat' (strep) *n.* an acute sore throat caused by streptococci.

strep'to·coc'cus (strep'tə kok'əs) *n., pl.* **-ci** (-sī, -sē). one of a group of bacteria causing serious diseases.

stress (stres) *v.t.* **1.** to emphasize. **2.** to subject to strain. —*n.* **3.** physical, mental, or emotional strain or tension. **4.** emphasis.

stretch (strech) *v.t.* **1.** to spread out. **2.** to extend. **3.** to draw tight. —*v.i.* **4.** to extend one's limbs or body. **5.** to extend over a time or distance. —*n.* **6.** a stretching or being stretched. **7.** an extension; expansion. **8.** a continuous length.

stretch'er *n.* **1.** a canvas-covered frame for carrying the sick and injured. **2.** a device for stretching.

strew (strōō) *v.t.,* **strewed, strewed** or **strewn, strewing.** to scatter.

stri'at·ed (strī'ā tid) *adj.* furrowed; streaked. —**stri·a'tion** (-ā'shən) *n.*

strick'en (strik'ən) *adj.* afflicted, as by disease or sorrow.

strict (strikt) *adj.* **1.** narrowly limited; exact; precise. **2.** severe; exacting. —**strict'ly,** *adv.*

stric'ture (strik'chər) *n.* **1.** an abnormal contraction of a body passage. **2.** an adverse criticism.

stride (strīd) *v.,* **strode** (strōd) **stridden** (strid'n) **striding,** *n.* —*v.i., v.t.* **1.** to walk (over or along) with long steps. —*n.* **2.** a long step. **3.** a step forward, as in development.

stri'dent (strīd'nt) *adj.* harsh in sound. —**stri'den·cy,** *n.*

strife (strīf) *n.* bitter conflict.

strike (strīk) *v.,* **struck** (struk), **struck** or **strick·en** (strik'ən), **striking,** *n.* —*v.t.* **1.** to hit forcibly. **2.** to ignite (a match). **3.** to impress. **4.** to cancel. **5.** to afflict or affect. **6.** to find, as gold or oil. **7.** to mark by chimes, as the hour. —*v.i.* **8.** to deal a blow. **9.** to make an attack. **10.** to stop work to compel an employer's agreement to workers' demands. **11.** to sound by percussion. **12. strike out,** *Baseball.* to put or be put out on three strikes. —*n.* **13.** an act of striking. **14.** a group work stoppage to compel agreement to workers' demands. **15.** *Baseball.* the failure of a batter to hit a pitched ball. **16.** *Bowling.* the knocking-down of all the pins at once.

strik′ing *adj.* conspicuously attractive or impressive.

string (string) *n., v.,* **strung** (strung) **stringing.** —*n.* **1.** a thin cord or thread for tying. **2.** a series or set. **3.** a tightly stretched cord or wire on a musical instrument. **4.** a plant fiber. **5. strings,** conditions. —*v.t.* **6.** to supply with strings. **7.** to arrange in a row. **8.** to thread on a string. —**string′y,** *adj.*

string′ bean′ *n.* a bean with an edible pod.

stringed *adj.* fitted with strings.

strin′gent (strin′jənt) *adj.* very strict. —**strin′gen•cy,** *n.*

strip[1] (strip) *v.,* **stripped, stripping.** —*v.t.* **1.** to remove covering or clothing from. **2.** to take away. **3.** to clear out; empty. —*v.i.* **4.** to remove one's clothes.

strip[2] (strip) *n.* a long narrow piece.

stripe (strīp) *n., v.,* **striped, striping.** —*n.* **1.** a band differing in color, material, or texture from the background. **2.** a strip of braid or fabric worn on a sleeve to indicate military rank. —*v.t.* **3.** to mark with stripes.

strip′ling (strip′ling) *n.* a youth.

strip′ mall′ *n.* stores or restaurants in adjacent spaces in one long building.

strip′ mine′ *n.* a mine in an open pit. —**strip′-mine′,** *v.t., v.i.*

strive (strīv) *v.i.,* **strove** (strōv), **striven** (striv′ən), **striving.** to try hard; struggle.

strobe (strōb) *n.* an electronic flash producing rapid bursts of light.

stroke[1] (strōk) *n.* **1.** an act of striking. **2.** a blockage or hemorrhage of a blood vessel leading to the brain. **3.** a single complete movement, as in swimming. **4.** a single mark made by a pen, brush, etc. **5.** a sudden happening.

stroke[2] (strōk) *v.,* **stroked, stroking,** *n.* —*v.t.* **1.** to rub gently; caress. —*n.* **2.** an act or instance of stroking.

stroll (strōl) *v.i., v.t.* **1.** to walk idly (along or through). —*n.* **2.** a walk.

stroll′er *n.* a chairlike carriage in which young children are pushed.

strong (strông) *adj.* **1.** powerful;

vigorous. **2.** not weak; intense. **3.** able to resist strain or force.

strong′-arm′ *adj.* **1.** involving force. —*v.t.* **2.** to use force on.

strong′box′ *n.* a strongly made box for money.

strong′hold′ *n.* a fortress.

strop (strop) *n., v.,* **stropped, stropping.** —*n.* **1.** a flexible strap for sharpening razors. —*v.t.* **2.** to sharpen on a strop.

struck (struk) *v.* pt. and a pp. of **strike.**

struc′ture (struk′chər) *n.* **1.** the manner in which something is built or arranged. **2.** something constructed. —**struc′tur•al,** *adj.*

strug′gle (strug′əl) *v.,* **-gled, -gling,** *n.* —*v.i.* **1.** to contend; strive. —*n.* **2.** a strong effort. **3.** a conflict.

strum (strum) *v.t., v.i.,* **strummed, strumming.** to play lightly on (a stringed instrument).

strut[1] (strut) *v.,* **strutted, strutting,** *n.* —*v.i.* **1.** to walk in a vain, pompous manner. —*n.* **2.** a strutting walk.

strut[2] (strut) *n.* a prop; truss.

strych′nine (strik′nin, -nēn, -nīn) *n.* a colorless poison that affects the central nervous system.

stub (stub) *n., v.,* **stubbed, stubbing.** —*n.* **1.** a short remaining piece. —*v.t.* **2.** to strike (one's toe) against something. —**stub′by,** *adj.*

stub′ble (-əl) *n.* **1.** short stumps, as of grain stalks. **2.** a short growth of beard. —**stub′bly,** *adj.*

stub′born (stub′ərn) *adj.* **1.** unreasonably obstinate. **2.** persistent.

stuc′co (stuk′ō) *n., pl.* **-coes, -cos,** *v.,* **-coed, -coing.** —*n.* **1.** a plaster finish for exterior walls. —*v.t.* **2.** to cover with stucco.

stuck′-up′ *adj. Informal.* snobbishly conceited.

stud[1] (stud) *n., v.,* **studded, studding.** —*n.* **1.** a projecting knob, pin, etc. **2.** one of the upright posts forming the frame of a wall. **3.** a detachable button. —*v.t.* **4.** to set with studs. **5.** to be scattered over the surface of.

stud[2] (stud) *n.* a male animal kept for breeding.

stu′dent (stōōd′nt, styōōd′-) *n.* a person who studies.

stud′ied (stud′ēd) *adj.* deliberate.

stu′di•o′ (stōō′dē ō′, styōō′-) *n., pl.* **-dios. 1.** an artist's workroom. **2.** a place equipped for radio or television broadcasting.

stud′y (stud′ē) *n., pl.* **-ies,** *v.,* **-ied, -ying.** —*n.* **1.** applying the mind in an effort to learn. **2.** the object of study. **3.** a detailed analysis. **4.** deep thought. **5.** a room for studying, writing, etc. —*v.i.* **6.** to apply the mind to acquiring knowledge. —*v.t.* **7.** to make a study of.

stuff (stuf) *n.* **1.** material used to make something. **2.** personal belongings. **3.** unspecified matter or objects. **4.** worthless ideas or talk. —*v.t.* **5.** to cram full; pack.

stuff′ing *n.* **1.** material stuffed in something. **2.** a filling for poultry, vegetables, etc.

stuff′y *adj.,* **-ier, -iest. 1.** lacking fresh air. **2.** pompous; pedantic.

stul′ti·fy′ (stul′tə fī′) *v.t.,* **-fied, -fy-ing. 1.** to cause to look foolish **2.** to make futile or ineffectual.

stum′ble (stum′bəl) *v.,* **-bled, -bling,** *n.* —*v.i.* **1.** to lose one's balance. **2. stumble upon,** to discover by chance. —*n.* **3.** a stumbling.

stum′bling block′ *n.* an obstacle.

stump (stump) *n.* **1.** the lower end of a tree after the top is gone. **2.** any short remaining part. —*v.t.* **3.** to baffle. —*v.i.* **4.** to campaign politically. **5.** to walk heavily.

stun (stun) *v.t.,* **stunned, stunning. 1.** to render unconscious. **2.** to amaze.

stun′ning *adj.* strikingly attractive.

stunt[1] (stunt) *v.t.* to stop or slow the growth of.

stunt[2] (stunt) *n.* a feat showing skill or daring.

stu·pe·fy′ (stōō′pə fī′, styōō′-) *v.t.,* **-fied, -fying. 1.** to put into a stupor. **2.** to astonish.

stu·pen′dous (-pen′dəs, styōō-) *adj.* **1.** amazing. **2.** immense.

stu′pid (stōō′pid, styōō′-) *adj.* lacking intelligence. —**stu·pid′i·ty,** *n.*

stu′por (-pər) *n.* a dazed or insensible state.

stur′dy (stûr′dē) *adj.,* **-dier, -diest. 1.** strongly built. **2.** firm.

stur′geon (stûr′jən) *n.* a large fish of fresh and salt water, valued as a source of caviar.

stut′ter (stut′ər) *v.i., v.t.* **1.** to speak or say with repetitions, prolongations, etc. —*n.* **2.** stuttering or a speech defect marked by stuttering.

sty[1] (stī) *n., pl.* **sties.** a pigpen.

sty[2] (stī) *n., pl.* **sties.** an inflamed swelling on the eyelid.

style (stīl) *n., v.,* **styled, styling.** —*n.* **1.** a distinct way of acting, speaking, or writing. **2.** the current fashion. **3.** elegance. —*v.t.* **4.** to design in accordance with a particular style. **5.** to name.

styl′ish *adj.* fashionable.

styl′ist *n.* a person who cultivates a distinctive style. —**sty·lis′tic,** *adj.*

styl′ize *v.t.,* **-ized, -izing.** to cause to conform to a conventionalized style.

sty′lus (stī′ləs) *n.* a pointed tool used in artwork.

sty′mie (stī′mē) *v.t.,* **-mied, -mying.** to hinder or obstruct.

styp′tic (stip′tik) *adj.* checking bleeding.

Sty′ro·foam′ (stī′rə fōm′) *Trademark.* a lightweight plastic.

suave (swäv) *adj.* smoothly polite and agreeable. —**suav′i·ty,** *n.*

sub- a prefix meaning under, below, or beneath; secondary.

sub·a·tom′ic *adj.* of particles within an atom.

sub·con′scious *adj.* **1.** existing beneath one's consciousness. —*n.* **2.** ideas, feelings, etc., of which one is unaware. —**sub·con′scious·ly,** *adv.*

sub·con′ti·nent (sub kon′tn ənt, sub′kon′-) *n.* a large subdivision of a continent.

sub′cul′ture *n.* a group with social, economic, or other traits distinguishing it from others within the larger society.

sub′cu·ta′ne·ous *adj.* beneath the skin.

sub′di·vide′ (sub′di vīd′, sub′di-vīd′) *v.t., v.i.,* **-vided, -viding.** to divide into smaller parts. —**sub′di·vi′sion,** *n.*

sub·due′ (səb dōō′, -dyōō′) *v.t.,* **-dued, -duing. 1.** to overcome. **2.** to bring down the force or intensity of. **3.** to bring under control.

sub·fam′i·ly (sub fam′ə lē, sub′-fam′ə lē) *n., pl.* **-lies. 1.** a category of related organisms within a family. **2.** a group of related languages within a family.

sub′head′ *n.* **1.** a heading of a subdivision. **2.** a subordinate division of a title.

sub′ject *n.* (sub′jikt) **1.** a matter of thought, concern, etc. **2.** a person under the rule of a government. **3.** a noun or pronoun that performs the action or is in the state of the predicate. **4.** something or someone represented in a work of art. —*adj.* (sub′jikt) **5.** being a subject. **6.** liable; exposed. —*v.t.* (səb jekt′) **7.** to cause to experience. **8.** to make liable. —**sub·jec′tion,** *n.*

sub·jec′tive *adj.* dependent on personal views. —**sub′jec·tiv′i·ty,** *n.*

sub′ju·gate′ (sub′jə gāt′) *v.t.,* **-gated, -gating.** to subdue; conquer. —**sub′ju·ga′tion,** *n.*

sub·junc′tive (səb jungk′tiv) *adj.* **1.** designating a verb mood used for doubtful or hypothetical statements or questions. —*n.* **2.** the subjunctive mood or a verb in this mood.

sub′lease′ *n., v.,* **-leased, -leasing.** —*n.* (sub′lēs′) **1.** a lease granted to another by the tenant of a property. —*v.t., v.i.* (sub lēs′) **2.** to rent by sublease (of).

sub•let′ (sub let′, sub′let′) *v.t., v.i.,* **-let, -letting.** to sublease.

sub′li•mate′ (sub′lə māt′) *v.t.,* **-mated, -mating.** to divert (biological impulses) to other channels.

sub•lime′ (sə blīm′) *adj.* **1.** lofty; noble. —*n.* **2.** that which is sublime. —**sub•lim′i•ty** (-blim′i tē) *n.*

sub•lim′i•nal (sub lim′ə nl) *adj.* below the threshold of consciousness.

sub′ma•rine′ *n.* (sub′mə rēn′, sub′mə rēn′) **1.** a vessel that can navigate under water. —*adj.* (sub′mə-rēn′) **2.** of submarines. **3.** being under the sea.

sub•merge′ (səb mûrj′) *v.t., v.i.,* **-merged, -merging.** to put or sink under water. —**sub•mer′gence,** *n.*

sub•merse′ (-mûrs′) *v.t.,* **-mersed, -mersing.** to submerge. —**sub•mer′sion,** *n.* —**sub•mers′i•ble,** *adj.*

sub•mis′sive *adj.* yielding or obeying readily. —**sub•mis′sive•ly,** *adv.*

sub•mit′ (səb mit′) *v.,* **-mitted, -mitting.** —*v.t.* **1.** to yield; surrender. **2.** to offer for consideration. —*v.i.* **3.** to yield oneself to another's authority. —**sub•mis′sion** (-mish′ən) *n.*

sub•nor′mal (sub nôr′məl) *adj.* of less than normal intelligence.

sub•or′di•nate *adj., n., v.,* **-nated, -nating.** —*adj.* (sə bôr′dn it) **1.** of lower rank or importance. —*n.* (sə-bôr′dn it) **2.** a subordinate person or thing. —*v.t.* (-dn āt′) **3.** to make or treat as subordinate. —**sub•or′-di•na′tion,** *n.*

sub•orn′ (sə bôrn′) *v.t.* to bribe or incite to crime, esp. to perjury.

sub′plot′ (sub′plot′) *n.* a secondary plot.

sub•poe′na (sə pē′nə, səb-) *n., v.,* **-naed, -naing.** —*n.* **1.** a summons to appear in court. —*v.t.* **2.** to serve with a subpoena.

sub ro′sa (sub rō′zə) *adv.* secretly.

sub•scribe′ (səb skrīb′) *v.t., v.i.,* **-scribed, -scribing. 1.** to pay or pledge (money) as a contribution. **2.** to obtain a subscription, as to a publication. **3.** to give one's consent (to).

sub′script (sub′skript) *n.* a letter, number, etc., written low on a line of text.

sub•scrip′tion *n.* the right to receive a publication or to attend a series of performances for a sum paid.

sub•se•quent (sub′si kwənt) *adj.* later; following.

sub•ser′vi•ent (səb sûr′vē ənt) *adj.*

1. servile; submissive. **2.** subordinate. —**sub•ser′vi•ence,** *n.*

sub•side′ *v.i.,* **-sided, -siding. 1.** to sink; settle. **2.** to become less active or violent.

sub•sid′i•ar′y (-sid′ē er′ē) *adj., n., pl.* **-aries.** —*adj.* **1.** auxiliary. **2.** subordinate. —*n.* **3.** anything subsidiary.

sub′si•dy (-si dē) *n., pl.* **-dies.** direct financial aid, esp. by a government. —**sub′si•dize′,** *v.t.*

sub•sist′ (səb sist′) *v.i.* to continue to exist.

sub′soil′ *n.* the layer of earth immediately under the surface soil.

sub′stance (sub′stəns) *n.* **1.** physical matter or material. **2.** solid quality. **3.** the essential part. **4.** wealth.

sub•stand′ard *adj.* below standard.

sub•stan′tial (səb stan′shəl) *adj.* **1.** of real worth or effect. **2.** fairly large. **3.** strong. **4.** real. **5.** wealthy.

sub•stan′ti•ate′ (-shē āt′) *v.t.,* **-ated, -ating.** to support with evidence.

sub•stan•tive (sub′stən tiv) *adj.* **1.** essential. **2.** real. —*n.* **3.** a noun, pronoun, or word used as a noun.

sub′sti•tute′ (sub′sti tōōt′, -tyōōt′) *v., n.,* **-tuted, -tuting.** —*n.* **1.** a person or thing serving in place of another. —*v.t.* **2.** to put in place of another. —*v.i.* **3.** to serve as a substitute.

sub′struc′ture *n.* a structure forming a foundation.

sub•sume′ (səb sōōm′) *v.t.,* **-sumed, -suming.** to consider or include as part of something larger.

sub′ter•fuge′ (sub′tər fyōōj′) *n.* a means used to evade or conceal.

sub′ter•ra′ne•an (-tə rā′nē ən) *adj.* underground.

sub′text *n.* an underlying or implicit meaning.

sub′ti′tle *n., v.,* **-tled, -tling.** —*n.* **1.** a secondary or subordinate title, as of a book. **2.** a translation of dialogue, appearing at the bottom of a motion-picture screen. —*v.t.* **3.** to give subtitles to.

sub′tle (sut′l) *adj.,* **-tler, -tlest. 1.** difficult to perceive; delicate or fine. **2.** discerning. **3.** clever. —**sub′tle•ty,** *n.*

sub′to′tal (sub′tōt′l, sub tōt′-) *n., v.,* **-totaled, -totaling.** —*n.* **1.** the total of a part of a group of figures. —*v.t., v.i.* **2.** to determine a subtotal (for).

sub•tract′ *v.t., v.i.* to take (one number) from another. —**sub•trac′tion,** *n.*

sub•trop′i•cal *adj.* bordering on the tropics.

sub′urb (sub′ûrb′) n. a residential district just outside a city. —**sub•ur′ban,** adj. —**sub•ur′ban•ite′** n.

sub•ur′bi•a (-bē ə) n. 1. suburbs or suburbanites collectively. 2. life in the suburbs.

sub•vert′ (-vûrt′) v.t. to overthrow. —**sub•ver′sion,** n. —**sub•ver′sive,** adj., n.

sub′way′ n. an underground electric railway.

sub•ze′ro adj. indicating lower than zero on some scale.

suc•ceed′ (sək sēd′) v.i. 1. to turn out successfully. 2. to come next. —v.t. 3. to come after.

suc•cess′ (-ses′) n. 1. a favorable outcome. 2. good fortune. 3. a successful thing or person. —**suc•cess′ful,** adj.

suc•ces′sion (-sesh′ən) n. 1. the act of following in sequence. 2. a sequence of persons or things. 3. the right or process of succeeding another. —**suc•ces′sive,** adj.

suc•ces′sor n. one that succeeds another.

suc•cinct′ (sək singkt′) adj. without useless words; concise.

suc′cor (suk′ər) n. 1. help; aid. —v.t. 2. to help.

suc′cu•lent (suk′yə lənt) adj. juicy.

suc•cumb′ (sə kum′) v.i. 1. to yield. 2. to die.

such (such) adj. 1. of that kind, extent, etc. —n. 2. such a person or thing.

suck (suk) v.t. 1. to draw into the mouth by using the lips and tongue. 2. to draw (liquid) from. 3. to draw upon in the mouth. —v.i. 4. to draw something in by sucking. —n. 5. the act of sucking.

suck′er n. 1. one that sucks. 2. Informal. a gullible person. 3. a lollipop. 4. a shoot from an underground stem or root.

suck′le v.t., v.i., **-led, -ling.** to nurse at the breast.

suck′ling (-ling) n. 1. an infant. 2. an unweaned animal.

su′crose (soo′krōs) n. sugar.

suc′tion (suk′shən) n. 1. sucking. 2. the force that draws a substance into a vacuum.

sud′den (sud′n) adj. abrupt; quick; unexpected. —**sud′den•ly,** adv.

suds (sudz) n.pl. 1. soapy water. 2. foam; lather. —**suds′y,** adj.

sue (soo) v.t., v.i., **sued, suing.** to bring a civil action (against).

suede (swād) n. soft, napped leather.

su′et (soo′it) n. the hard fat around the kidneys of cattle and sheep.

suf′fer (suf′ər) v.i., v.t. 1. to undergo (pain, loss, etc.) 2. to tolerate.

suf′fer•ance (-əns) n. 1. tolerance. 2. endurance.

suf•fice′ (sə fīs′) v.i., v.t., **-ficed, -ficing.** to be enough (for).

suf•fi′cient (-fish′ənt) adj. enough. —**suf•fi′cien•cy,** n.

suf′fix (suf′iks) n. an element added to the end of a word to form another word.

suf′fo•cate (-ə kāt′) v., **-cated, -cating.** —v.t. 1. to kill or choke by cutting off air to the lungs. —v.i. 2. to become suffocated. —**suf′fo•ca′tion,** n.

suf′frage (-rij) n. the right to vote.

suf•fuse′ (sə fyooz′) v.t. to overspread; pervade.

sug′ar (shoog′ər) n. 1. a sweet substance obtained from sugar cane or sugar beet. —v.t. 2. to sweeten with sugar. —**sug′ar•less,** adj. —**sug′ar•y,** adj.

sug′ar beet′ n. a beet with a white root having a high sugar content.

sug′ar cane′ n. a tall grass that is the chief source of sugar.

sug′ar•coat′ v.t. to make more pleasant or acceptable.

sug′ar ma′ple n. a maple with a sweet sap.

sug′ar•plum′ n. a candy.

sug•gest′ (səg jest′, sə-) v.t. 1. to mention or propose for consideration or action. 2. to call to mind.

sug•gest′i•ble adj. easily led or influenced. —**sug•gest′i•bil′i•ty,** n.

sug•ges′tion n. 1. the act of suggesting. 2. something suggested. 3. a slight trace.

sug•ges′tive adj. suggesting.

su′i•cide′ (soo′ə sīd′) n. 1. the intentional killing of oneself. 2. a person who commits suicide. —**su′i•cid′al,** adj.

su′i ge′ne•ris (soo′ē jen′ər is, soo′ī) adj. being one of a kind.

suit (soot) n. 1. a set of clothes. 2. a legal action. 3. a class of playing cards. —v.t. 4. to be becoming to. 5. to please. —v.i. 6. to be appropriate.

suit′a•ble adj. appropriate; fitting.

suit′case′ n. a rectangular piece of luggage.

suite (swēt) n. 1. a series or set, as of rooms or furniture. 2. a retinue.

suit′or (soo′tər) n. a man who courts a woman.

sul′fa drug′ (sul′fə), n. a group of drugs used in the treatment of wounds, burns, and infections.

sul′fate (-fāt) n. a salt of sulfuric acid.

sul′fide (-fīd, -fid) n. a sulfur compound.

supercilious

sul'fur (-fər) *n.* a yellow nonmetallic element. —**sul·fur'ic, sul'fur'ous,** *adj.*

sulfu'ric ac'id *n.* a corrosive liquid used in chemicals and explosives.

sulk (sulk) *v.i.* **1.** to be sullen and aloof. —*n.* **2.** a fit of sulking.

sulk'y *adj.,* **-ier, -iest,** *n., pl.* **-ies.** —*adj.* **1.** sullen; ill-humored. —*n.* **2.** a two-wheeled racing carriage for one person. —**sulk'i·ly,** *adv.*

sul'len (sul'ən) *adj.* **1.** silently ill-humored. **2.** gloomy.

sul'ly (sul'ē) *v.t.,* **-lied, -lying.** to soil; defile.

sul'phur (-fər) *n.* sulfur.

sul'tan (sul'tn) *n.* a ruler of an Islamic country. —**sul'tan·ate',** *n.*

sul·tan'a (-tan'ə) *n.* a small raisin.

sul'try (-trē) *adj.,* **-trier, -triest. 1.** hot and humid. **2.** (of a woman) passionate. —**sul'tri·ness,** *n.*

sum (sum) *n., v.,* **summed, summing.** —*n.* **1.** the result obtained by adding two or more numbers. **2.** an amount. —*v.t.* **3.** to total. **4. sum up,** to summarize.

su'mac (soo'mak, shoo'-) *n.* a small tree with long pinnate leaves.

sum'ma·rize' (sum'ə rīz') *v.t.,* **-rized, -rizing.** to make or be a summary of.

sum'ma·ry (-rē) *n., pl.* **-ries,** *adj.* —*n.* **1.** a brief presentation of the main points. —*adj.* **2.** concise. **3.** prompt.

sum·ma'tion (sə mā'shən) *n.* the act or result of summing up.

sum'mer (sum'ər) *n.* **1.** the season between spring and fall. —*adj.* **2.** of, like, or for summer. —*v.i.* **3.** to spend or pass the summer. —**sum'mer·y,** *adj.*

sum'mit (sum'it) *n.* the highest point, part, or degree.

sum'mon (-ən) *v.t.* **1.** to order to appear. **2.** to gather together.

sum'mons *n.* **1.** an order to appear before a court. **2.** a command ordering someone to appear somewhere.

su'mo (soo'mō) *n.* a Japanese form of wrestling featuring extremely heavy contestants.

sump (sump) *n.* a pit, basin, or reservoir into which liquid drains.

sump'tu·ous (sump'choo əs) *adj.* revealing great expense; luxurious.

sun (sun) *n., v.,* **sunned, sunning.** —*n.* **1.** the star that is the heat- and light-giving body of the solar system. **2.** sunshine. —*v.t.* **3.** to expose to sunshine.

Sun. Sunday.

sun'bathe' *v.i.,* **-bathed, -bathing.** to expose the body to sunlight.

sun'block' *n.* a substance that protects against sunburn and prevents most tanning.

sun'burn' *n., v.,* **-burned** or **-burnt, -burning.** —*n.* **1.** a superficial burn from the sun's rays. —*v.i., v.t.* **2.** to suffer or cause to suffer from sunburn.

sun'dae (-dā, -dē) *n.* ice cream topped with syrup, nuts, fruit, etc.

Sun'day (-dā, -dē) *n.* the first day of the week.

sun'der (-dər) *v.t., v.i.* to separate.

sun'di'al *n.* an outdoor instrument for telling time by the shadow of a pointer cast by the sun on a dial.

sun·dries (-drēz) *n.pl.* small, miscellaneous items.

sun'dry (-drē) *adj.* various.

sun'fish' *n.* a freshwater fish.

sun'flow'er *n.* a tall plant with yellow flowers and edible seeds.

sung (sung) *v.* a pt. and pp. of **sing.**

sun'glass'es *n.pl.* eyeglasses with tinted lenses to protect the eyes from the sun.

sun'light' *n.* the light of the sun.

sun'lit' *adj.* lighted by the sun.

sun'ny *adj.,* **-nier, -niest. 1.** full of sunshine. **2.** cheerful; jolly.

sun'rise' *n.* the rise of the sun above the horizon. Also, **sun'up'.**

sun'roof' *n.* a section of an automobile roof that can be opened.

sun'screen' *n.* a substance that protects skin from ultraviolet light.

sun'set' *n.* the setting of the sun below the horizon. Also, **sun'down'.**

sun'shine' *n.* the direct light of the sun.

sun'spot' *n.* a dark spot on the sun.

sun'stroke' *n.* illness from overexposure to the sun's rays.

sun'tan' *n.* a darkening of the skin caused by exposure to the sun.

sup (sup) *v.i.,* **supped, supping.** to eat supper.

su'per (soo'pər) *n.* **1.** a superintendent, esp. of an apartment building. —*adj.* **2.** first-rate.

super- a prefix meaning above or over; exceeding; larger or more.

su'per·a·bun'dant *adj.* exceedingly abundant.

su'per·an'nu·at'ed (-an'yoo ā'tid) *adj.* too old for use or work.

su·perb' (soo pûrb', sə-) *adj.* very fine. —**su·perb'ly,** *adv.*

su'per·charge' (soo'pər charj') *v.t.,* **-charged, -charging. 1.** to charge with abundant energy. **2.** to supply air to (an engine) at high pressure.

su'per·cil'i·ous (sil'ē əs) *adj.* haughtily disdainful.

su′per•con•duc•tiv′i•ty *n.* the disappearance of electrical resistance in certain metals at extremely low temperatures. —**su′per•con′•duct′or,** *n.*

su′per•e′go *n.* the part of the personality representing the conscience.

su′per•fi′cial (-fish′əl) *adj.* **1.** of, on, or near the surface. **2.** shallow, obvious, or insignificant. —**su′per•fi′•ci•al′i•ty** (-fish′ē al′i tē) *n.*

su•per•flu•ous (soo pûr′floo əs) *adj.* being more than is necessary. —**su′per•flu′i•ty** (-floo′i tē) *n.*

su′per•high′way (soo′pər hi′wā, soo′pər hi′wā′) *n.* a highway for travel at high speeds.

su′per•hu′man *adj.* **1.** beyond what is human. **2.** exceeding human strength.

su′per•im•pose′ *v.t.,* **-posed, -posing.** to place over something else.

su′per•in•tend′ (soo′pər in tend′, soo′prin-) *v.t.* to oversee and direct.

su′per•in•tend′ent (soo′pər in ten′dənt, soo′prin-) *n.* **1.** a person who oversees a department, district, etc. **2.** a custodian in an apartment building.

su•pe′ri•or (sə pēr′ē ər, soo-) *adj.* **1.** higher in rank, degree, grade, or quality. **2.** above average; better. **3.** arrogant. —*n.* **4.** a superior person. **5.** the head of a convent or monastery. —**su•pe′ri•or′i•ty,** *n.*

su•per′la•tive (sə pûr′lə tiv, soo-) *adj.* **1.** of the highest kind; best. **2.** designating the highest degree of comparison of adjectives and adverbs. —*n.* **3.** anything superlative.

su′per•man′ (soo′pər-) *n., pl.* **-men.** a person of extraordinary powers.

su′per•mar′ket *n.* a large self-service store that sells food and household goods.

su′per•nat′u•ral *adj.* **1.** being beyond what can be explained by the laws of nature; ghostly. —*n.* **2.** the realm of supernatural beings or things.

su′per•no′va *n., pl.* **-vas, -vae** (-vē). a nova millions of times brighter than the sun.

su′per•nu′mer•ar′y (-noo′mə rer′ē, -nyoo′-) *adj., n., pl.* **-aries.** —*adj.* **1.** extra. —*n.* **2.** an extra person or thing. **3.** a performer with no speaking lines.

su′per•pow′er *n.* a large, powerful nation greatly influencing world affairs.

su′per•script′ *n.* a number, symbol, etc., written high on a line of text.

su′per•sede′ (-sēd′) *v.t.,* **-seded, -seding.** to take the place of.

su′per•son′ic *adj.* faster than the speed of sound.

su′per•star′ *n.* an entertainer or sports figure of world renown.

su′per•sti′tion (-stish′ən) *n.* an irrational belief in the ominous significance of a particular thing, event, etc. —**su′per•sti′tious,** *adj.*

su′per•store′ *n.* a very large store that stocks a wide variety of merchandise.

su′per•struc′ture *n.* the upper part of a building or vessel.

su′per•vene′ (-vēn′) *v.i.,* **-vened, -vening.** to occur as something extraneous. —**su′per•ven′tion** (-ven′shən) *n.*

su′per•vise′ (-vīz′) *v.t.,* **-vised, -vising.** to watch over and direct. —**su′per•vi′sion** (-vizh′ən) *n.* —**su′•per•vi′sor,** *n.*

su′per•wom′an *n., pl.* **-women. 1.** a woman of extraordinary powers. **2.** a woman who copes successfully with the demands of career, marriage, and motherhood.

su•pine′ (soo pīn′) *adj.* **1.** lying on the back. **2.** passive.

sup′per (sup′ər) *n.* the evening meal.

sup•plant′ (sə plant′) *v.t.* to take the place of, esp. by force.

sup•ple (sup′əl) *adj.,* **-pler, -plest.** flexible; limber.

sup′ple•ment *n.* (sup′lə mənt) **1.** something added to complete or improve a thing. —*v.t.* (-ment′) **2.** to add to or complete. —**sup′ple•men′tal** (-men′tl), **sup′ple•men′ta•ry,** *adj.*

sup′pli•cate′ (sup′li kāt′) *v.t., v.i.,* **-cated, -cating.** to beg (for) humbly. —**sup′pli•ant** (sup′lē ənt), **sup′pli•cant,** *n., adj.*

sup•ply′ (sə plī′) *v.,* **-plied, -plying,** *n., pl.* **-plies.** —*v.t.* **1.** to furnish; provide. **2.** to fill (a need). —*n.* **3.** the act of supplying. **4.** something supplied. **5.** a stock of items. —**sup•pli′er,** *n.*

supply′-side′ *adj.* of the economic theory that reduced taxes will stimulate economic growth.

sup•port′ (sə pôrt′) *v.t.* **1.** to hold up; bear. **2.** to provide a living for. **3.** to uphold or advocate (a cause). **4.** to corroborate (a statement). —*n.* **5.** a supporting or being supported. **6.** a thing or person that supports. —**sup•port′a•ble,** *adj.* —**sup•port′ive,** *adj.*

support′ group′ *n.* a group of people who meet regularly to discuss shared problems.

sup•pose′ (sə pōz′) *v.,* **-posed, -posing.** —*v.t.* **1.** to assume to be true. **2.** to think. —*v.i.* **3.** to as-

sume something. **4. to be supposed to,** to be expected to.
—**sup•pos′ed•ly** (-pō′zid lē), *adv.*
—**sup′po•si′tion** (sup′ə zish′ən) *n.*
sup•pos′i•to•ry (sə poz′i tôr′ē) *n.,*
pl. **-ries.** a solid mass of medication that melts on insertion into the rectum or vagina.
sup•press′ (sə pres′) *v.t.* **1.** to put an end to by force. **2.** to restrain. **3.** to withhold from circulation.
—**sup•pres′sion** (-presh′ən) *n.*
sup′pu•rate′ (sup′yə rāt′) *v.i.,*
-rated, -rating. to form or discharge pus. —**sup′pu•ra′tion,** *n.*
su′pra (sōō′prə) *adv.* above, esp. in a text.
su••prem′a•cist (sə prem′ə sist, sōō-) *n.* a person who advocates the supremacy of a particular group.
su•preme′ (sə prēm′, sōō-) *adj.* highest in rank, authority, quality, or importance. —**su•prem′a•cy** (-prem′ə sē) *n.* —**su•preme′ly,** *adv.*
sur′charge′ *n., v.,* **-charged, -charging.** —*n.* (sûr′chärj′) **1.** an extra charge. —*v.t.* (sûr chärj′, sûr′chärj′) **2.** to put a surcharge on.
sure (shōōr, shûr) *adj.,* **surer, surest. 1.** certain; positive. **2.** reliable. —*adv.* **3.** certainly. —**sure′ly,** *adv.*
sure′foot′ed *adj.* not likely to stumble.
sure′ty (shōōr′i tē, shōōr′tē, shûr′-) *n., pl.* **-ties. 1.** security against loss or damage. **2.** a person who accepts responsibility for another.
surf (sûrf) *n.* **1.** waves breaking on a shore. —*v.i.* **2.** to ride on the crest of a wave while standing or lying on a **surfboard. 3.** to search randomly, as for information on the Internet or a program on TV. —*v.t.* **4.** to search through (a computer network or TV channels). —**surf′er,** *n.*
sur′face (sûr′fis) *n., adj., v.,* **-faced, -facing.** —*n.* **1.** the outermost layer of something; outside. **2.** outward appearance. —*adj.* **3.** of or on a surface. —*v.t.* **4.** to finish the surface of. —*v.i.* **5.** to come to the surface.
sur′feit (sûr′fit) *n.* **1.** an excess, esp. of food or drink. —*v.t.* **2.** to supply or feed to excess.
surf′ing *n.* the sport of riding the surf, usu. on a **surf′board′.**
surge (sûrj) *n., v.,* **surged, surging.** —*n.* **1.** a wavelike forward movement. **2.** a sudden strong rush. —*v.i.* **3.** to move in a surge.
sur′geon (sûr′jən) *n.* a physician who specializes in surgery.
surge′ protec′tor *n.* a device to protect a computer, telephone,

etc., from damage by high-voltage electrical surges.
sur′ger•y (-jə rē) *n., pl.* **-geries. 1.** the treatment of disease, injuries, etc., by operating on the body with instruments. **2.** treatment by a surgeon. —**sur′gi•cal** (-ji kəl) *adj.*
sur′ly (sûr′lē) *adj.,* **-lier, -liest.** rude and sullen. —**sur′li•ness,** *n.*
sur•mise′ (sər mīz′) *v.,* **-mised, -mising,** *n.* —*v.t., v.i.* **1.** to guess. —*n.* (sər mīz′, sûr′mīz) **2.** a guess or conjecture.
sur•mount′ (sər mount′) *v.t.* **1.** to get over or on top of. **2.** to overcome.
sur′name′ (sûr′nām′) *n.* a family name.
sur•pass′ (sər pas′) *v.t.* **1.** to exceed. **2.** to excel. **3.** to transcend.
sur′plice (sûr′plis) *n.* a loose white robe worn over a cassock.
sur′plus (sûr′plus, -pləs) *n.* **1.** an amount beyond that needed; excess. —*adj.* **2.** being a surplus.
sur•prise′ (sər prīz′, sə-) *v.,* **-prised, -prising,** *n.* —*v.t.* **1.** to strike with astonishment. **2.** to come upon unexpectedly. —*n.* **3.** something that surprises. **4.** the feeling of being surprised. **5.** the act of surprising.
sur•re′al•ism (sə rē′ə liz′əm) *n.* a 20th-century style of art and literature that attempts to express the subconscious meaning of images. —**sur•re′al•ist,** *n., adj.*
sur•ren′der (sə ren′dər) *v.t.* **1.** to yield to the power or control of another. **2.** to abandon. —*v.i.* **3.** to give oneself up. —*n.* **4.** a surrendering.
sur′rep•ti′tious (sûr′əp tish′əs) *adj.* stealthy; secret.
sur′ro•gate′ (sûr′ə gāt′, -git, sur′-) *n.* **1.** a substitute. **2.** a judge concerned with wills, estates, etc.
sur′rogate moth′er *n.* a woman who bears a child for another.
sur•round′ (sə round′) *v.t.* to encircle; enclose.
sur•round′ings *n.pl.* environment.
sur′tax′ (sûr′taks′) *n.* an additional tax, esp. on high incomes.
sur•veil′lance (sər vā′ləns) *n.* a close watch kept over someone or something.
sur•vey′ *v.t.* (sər vā′) **1.** to view or study. **2.** to measure or determine the dimensions or nature of. —*n.* (sûr′vā) **3.** a comprehensive view. **4.** the act of surveying land or a description that results.
sur•vey′ing *n.* the science of making land surveys. —**sur•vey′or,** *n.*
sur•vive′ (sər vīv′) *v.,* **-vived, -viving.** —*v.i.* **1.** to remain alive. —*v.t.*

2. to outlive. **3.** to live through.
—**sur·viv'al,** n. —**sur·vi'vor,** n.

sus·cep'ti·ble (sə sep'tə bəl) adj.
likely to be affected or influenced.
—**sus·cep'ti·bil'i·ty,** n.

sus·pect' v.t. (sə spekt') **1.** to believe to be guilty, false, etc. **2.** to
mistrust. **3.** to think likely. —n.
(sus'pekt) **4.** one suspected of a
crime. —adj. (sus'pekt) **5.** liable to
doubt.

sus·pend' (-spend') v.t. **1.** to hang.
2. to keep from falling by hanging.
3. to make temporarily inactive. **4.**
to postpone.

sus·pend'ers n.pl. straps for holding up trousers.

sus·pense' (-spens') n. uncertainty;
anxiety.

sus·pen'sion n. **1.** a suspending or
being suspended. **2.** temporary inactivity. **3.** a state in which undis-
solved particles are dispersed in a
fluid.

suspen'sion bridge' n. a bridge
with a deck suspended from cables.

sus·pi'cion (sə spish'ən) n. **1.** a sus-
pecting or being suspected. **2.** a
trace.

sus·pi'cious adj. **1.** having suspi-
cions. **2.** causing suspicion.

sus·tain' (sə stān') v.t. **1.** to support. **2.** to keep going; maintain.
3. to uphold as valid.

sus'te·nance (sus'tə nəns) n. food;
nourishment.

su'ture (sōō'chər) n., v., **-tured,**
-turing. —n. **1.** the joining of the
edges of a wound. **2.** a stitch used
to close a wound. —v.t. **3.** to join
by suture.

SUV pl. **SUVs.** a sport-utility vehicle.

su'ze·rain (sōō'zə rin, -rān') n. **1.** a
state having control over a dependent state. **2.** a feudal overlord.
—**su'ze·rain·ty,** n.

svelte (svelt, sfelt) adj. gracefully
slender.

SW southwest.

swab (swob) n., v., **swabbed,**
swabbing. —n. **1.** a bit of cloth,
cotton, etc., esp. on a stick, used
for cleaning or applying medicine.
—v.t. **2.** to clean with a swab.

swad'dle (swod'l) v.t., **-dled, -dl-**
ing. to bind (a newborn infant)
with strips of cloth.

swag'ger v.i. **1.** to walk with an
insolent air. —n. **2.** such a gait.

swal'low¹ (swol'ō) v.t. **1.** to take
into the stomach through the
throat. **2.** to take in and envelop.
3. to accept without question.
—v.i. **4.** to perform the act of swallowing. —n. **5.** the act of swallowing. **6.** an amount swallowed.

swal'low² (swol'ō) n. a graceful
songbird with long wings and a
forked tail.

swal'low·tail' n. **1.** a deeply forked
tail like that of a swallow. **2.** a butterfly with long hind wings.

swam (swam) v. pt. of **swim.**

swa'mi (swä'mē) n. a Hindu religious teacher.

swamp (swomp) n. **1.** an area of
wet, spongy ground. —v.t. **2.** to
flood with water. **3.** to overwhelm.
—**swamp'y,** adj.

swan (swon) n. a large, usu. white
long-necked swimming bird.

swank (swangk) adj. **1.** stylish or elegant. **2.** pretentiously stylish. Also,
swank'y.

swan' song' n. a final act or farewell appearance.

swap (swop) v., **swapped, swap-**
ping, n. —v.t., v.i. **1.** to trade. —n.
2. a trade or exchange.

swarm (swôrm) n. **1.** a group of
honeybees. **2.** a large moving mass
of people, insects, etc. —v.i. **3.** to
move in a swarm.

swarth'y (swôr'thē, -thē) adj., **-ier,**
-iest. dark in skin color.

swash'buck·ler (swosh'buk'lər) n. a
swaggering fellow. —**swash'buck'-**
ling, adj., n.

swas'ti·ka (swos'ti kə) n. a figure
of a cross with the arms bent at
right angles: the emblem of the
Nazi Party.

swat (swot) v., **swatted, swatting,**
n. —v.t. **1.** to hit sharply. —n. **2.** a
sharp blow. —**swat'ter,** n.

swatch (swoch) n. a sample, as of
cloth.

swath (swoth) n. a long cut made
by a scythe or mowing machine.

swathe (swoth, swāth) v., **swathed,**
swathing, n. —v.t. **1.** to wrap or
bind closely. —n. **2.** a bandage.

sway (swā) v.i. **1.** to swing or move
to and fro. —v.t. **2.** to influence.
—n. **3.** a swaying movement. **4.**
controlling influence.

sway'back' n. an excessive downward curvature of the back, esp. of
horses. —**sway'backed',** adj.

swear (swâr) v., **swore** (swôr),
sworn, swearing. —v.i. **1.** to make
a solemn declaration by something
sacred. **2.** to bind oneself by an
oath; vow. **3.** to use profane language. —v.t. **4.** to state on oath. **5.**
swear in, to office by ad-
ministering an oath to.

sweat (swet) v., **sweat** or **sweated,**
sweating, n. —v.i. **1.** to excrete
moisture through the pores; perspire. **2.** to gather moisture from
the surrounding air. **3.** *Informal.* to
work hard. —v.t. **4.** to excrete

(moisture) through the pores. —*n.*
5. moisture given off by the body through the pores; perspiration. **6.** *Informal.* a state of anxiety. —**sweat′y,** *adj.*

sweat′er *n.* a knitted jacket.

sweat′ gland′ *n.* a tubular gland in the skin that secretes sweat.

sweat′pants′ *n.* loose pants of absorbent fabric.

sweat′shirt′ *n.* a loose pullover of absorbent fabric.

sweat′shop′ *n.* a shop employing workers at low wages, for long hours.

sweep (swēp) *v.*, **swept** (swept), **sweeping,** *n.* —*v.t.* **1.** to move or clear with a broom or brush. **2.** to pass or draw over a surface with a smooth, rapid movement. —*v.i.* **3.** to sweep a floor or room with a broom. **4.** to move swiftly and smoothly. —*n.* **5.** the act of sweeping. **6.** extent.

sweep′ing *adj.* of wide scope.

sweep′stakes′ *n.* **1.** a contest in which the prize consists of stakes put up by the competitors. **2.** a lottery.

sweet (swēt) *adj.* **1.** having the taste of sugar. **2.** fragrant. **3.** fresh. **4.** pleasant in sound. **5.** amiable. —*n.* **6.** anything sweet. —**sweet′en,** *v.t., v.i.*

sweet′bread′ *n.* the thymus or pancreas, esp. of a calf or lamb, used for food.

sweet′bri′er *n.* a wild rose.

sweet′en•er *n.* a substance, esp. a substitute for sugar, used to sweeten food or drink.

sweet′heart′ *n.* a beloved person.

sweet′ pea′ *n.* an annual vine with fragrant blooms.

sweet′ pep′per *n.* a mild-flavored bell-shaped pepper.

sweet′ pota′to *n.* a plant with a sweet edible root.

sweet′-talk′ *v.t., v.i.* to cajole.

sweet′ tooth′ *n.* a liking or craving for sweets.

sweet′ wil′liam (wil′yəm) *n.* a low plant with dense clusters of pink, red, and white flowers.

swell (swel) *v.*, **swelled, swelled** or **swollen, swelling,** *n., adj.* —*v.i., v.t.* **1.** to grow or cause to grow in size, degree, force, etc. —*n.* **2.** an act or state of swelling. **3.** a long, unbroken wave. **4.** an increase in amount, intensity, etc. —*adj.* **5.** *Informal.* excellent.

swel′ter (swel′tər) *v.i.* to suffer from oppressive heat.

swel′ter•ing *adj.* very hot.

swept (swept) *v.* pt. and pp. of **sweep.**

swerve (swûrv) *v.*, **swerved, swerving,** *n.* —*v.i., v.t.* **1.** to turn or cause to turn aside. —*n.* **2.** the act of swerving.

swift (swift) *adj.* **1.** moving with great speed. **2.** prompt or quick. —*n.* **3.** a swallowlike bird known for its swift flight. —**swift′ly,** *adv.*

swig (swig) *n., v.*, **swigged, swigging.** *Informal.* —*n.* **1.** a swallow of liquid. —*v.t., v.i.* **2.** to drink heartily.

swill (swil) *n.* **1.** moist garbage fed to hogs. —*v.i., v.t.* **2.** to guzzle.

swim (swim) *v.*, **swam** (swam), **swum,** (swum), **swimming,** *n.* —*v.i.* **1.** to move in water by the action of the limbs, fins, etc. **2.** to be immersed. **3.** to be dizzy. —*v.t.* **4.** to move in or across by swimming. —*n.* **5.** an act or period of swimming.

swim′suit′ *n.* a bathing suit.

swin′dle (swin′dl) *v.*, **-dled, -dling,** *n.* —*v.t., v.i.* **1.** to cheat; defraud. —*n.* **2.** an act of swindling; fraud.

swine (swīn) *n., pl.* **swine.** **1.** an animal with short legs, a disklike snout, and cloven hooves; pig or hog. **2.** a contemptible person.

swing (swing) *v.*, **swung** (swung) **swinging,** *n., adj.* —*v.i., v.t.* **1.** to move or cause to move to and fro. **2.** to move or cause to move on a fixed axis. **3.** to hang or cause to hang freely. —*n.* **4.** the act, way, or extent of swinging. **5.** a suspended seat for swinging. **6.** a style of jazz marked by a smooth beat and flowing phrasing. —*adj.* **7.** capable of determining an outcome.

swipe (swīp) *n., v.*, **swiped, swiping.** —*n.* **1.** a strong, sweeping blow. —*v.t.* **2.** to strike with a swipe. **3.** to slide (a magnetic card) quickly through an electronic device. **4.** *Informal.* to steal.

swirl (swûrl) *v.i., v.t.* **1.** to move or cause to move with a whirling motion. —*n.* **2.** a swirling movement.

swish (swish) *v.i., v.t.* **1.** to rustle. —*n.* **2.** a swishing sound.

Swiss′ cheese′ (swis) *n.* a firm, pale yellow cheese with holes.

switch (swich) *n.* **1.** a device for turning electric current on or off. **2.** a change. **3.** a flexible rod. —*v.t.* **4.** to whip with a switch. **5.** to change or exchange. **6.** to turn (electric current) on or off. —*v.i.* **7.** to change or shift. **8.** to make an exchange. **9.** to lash.

switch′back′ *n.* a zigzag highway or railroad track arrangement for climbing a steep grade.

switch′blade′ *n.* a pocketknife with a blade released by a spring.

switch′board′ *n.* a panel for controlling electric circuits.

swiv′el (swiv′əl) *v.,* **-eled, -eling,** *n.* —*v.t., v.i.* **1.** to rotate. —*n.* **2.** a device permitting the rotation of the thing mounted on it.

swol′len (swō′lən) *v.* pp. of **swell.**

swoon (swoon) *v.i.* **1.** to faint. —*n.* **2.** a faint.

swoop (swoop) *v.i.* **1.** to sweep down through the air. —*n.* **2.** a sweeping descent.

sword (sôrd) *n.* a weapon with a blade fixed in a hilt or handle.

sword′fish′ *n.* a marine fish with a swordlike upper jaw.

swore (swôr) *v.* pt. of **swear.**

sworn (swôrn) *v.* **1.** pp. of **swear.** —*adj.* **2.** bound by an oath.

swum (swum) *v.* pp. of **swim.**

syb′a·rite′ (sib′ə rīt′) *n.* a person devoted to pleasure.

syc′a·more′ (sik′ə môr′) *n.* a plane tree with lobed leaves.

syc′o·phant (sik′ə fənt, -fant′, sī′kə-) *n.* a servile flatterer.

syl·lab′i·cate′ (si lab′i kāt′) *v.t.,* **-cated, -cating.** to divide into syllables. Also, **syl·lab′i·fy′** (-fī′).

syl′la·ble (sil′ə bəl) *n.* a single unit of speech or the letters representing this.

syl′la·bus (-bəs) *n., pl.* **-buses, -bi** (-bī′). an outline of a course of study.

syl′lo·gism (-jiz′əm) *n.* a form of logical reasoning that contains two statements which lead to a conclusion.

sylph (silf) *n.* **1.** a graceful woman. **2.** an imaginary being supposed to inhabit the air.

syl′van (sil′vən) *adj.* of forests.

sym′bi·o′sis (sim′bē ō′sis, -bī-) *n., pl.* **-ses** (-sēz). the living together of two dissimilar organisms. —**sym′bi·ot′ic** (-ot′ik) *adj.*

sym′bol (sim′bəl) *n.* **1.** an emblem; token; sign. **2.** a thing that represents something else. —**sym·bol′ic** (-bol′ik), *adj.* —**sym′bol·ize′,** *v.t.*

sym′bol·ism *n.* **1.** representing things by symbols. **2.** symbolic meaning.

sym′me·try (-i trē) *n.* pleasing balance or proportion. —**sym·met′ri·cal** (si me′tri kəl) *adj.*

sym′pa·thize′ (-pə thīz′) *v.i.,* **-thized, -thizing. 1.** to share in a feeling. **2.** to feel or express sympathy.

sym′pa·thy (-thē) *n., pl.* **-thies. 1.** sharing or the ability to share the feelings of another. **2.** a feeling or expression of compassion. —**sym′pa·thet′ic** (-thet′ik) *adj.*

sym′pho·ny (-fə nē) *n., pl.* **-nies. 1.** a long composition for a large orchestra. **2.** harmony of sounds. —**sym·phon′ic** (-fon′ik) *adj.*

sym·po′si·um (sim pō′zē əm) *n., pl.* **-siums, -sia** (-zē ə). a meeting for discussion of one topic.

symp′tom (simp′təm) *n.* a sign or indication, esp. of disease. —**symp′to·mat′ic** (-mat′ik) *adj.*

syn′a·gogue′ (sin′ə gog′) *n.* **1.** a Jewish house of worship. **2.** a congregation of Jews.

sync (singk) *n., v.,* **synced, syncing.** —*n.* **1.** synchronization. **2.** harmonious relationship. —*v.t., v.i.* **3.** to synchronize.

syn′chro·nize′ (sing′krə nīz′) *v.,* **-nized, -nizing.** —*v.t.* **1.** to cause to show the same time. **2.** to cause to move or work exactly together. —*v.i.* **3.** to occur at the same time. —**syn′chro·ni·za′tion,** *n.* —**syn′chro·nous,** *adj.*

syn′co·pate′ (sing′kə pāt′, sin′-) *v.t.,* **-pated, -pating.** to shift (a musical accent) to a beat that is normally unaccented. —**syn′co·pa′tion,** *n.*

syn′di·cate *n., v.,* **-cated, -cating.** —*n.* (sin′də kit) **1.** a combination of persons or companies for a large joint enterprise. **2.** an agency selling news stories to a number of publications at the same time. —*v.t.* (sin′di kāt′) **3.** to combine into a syndicate. **4.** to publish through a syndicate. —*v.i.* **5.** to combine to form a syndicate.

syn′drome (sin′drōm) *n.* a group of symptoms characteristic of a disease.

syn′er·gism (sin′ər jiz′əm) *n.* the joint action of agents so that their combined effect is greater than the sum of their individual effects. Also, **synergy.**

syn′od (-əd) *n.* an assembly of church delegates.

syn′o·nym (-ə nim) *n.* a word meaning the same as another. —**syn·on′y·mous** (si non′ə məs) *adj.*

syn·op′sis (si nop′sis) *n., pl.* **-ses** (-sēz). a brief summary.

syn′tax (sin′taks) *n.* the arrangement of words into sentences and phrases.

syn′the·sis (sin′thə sis) *n., pl.* **-ses** (-sēz). the combining of parts into a whole.

syn′the·size′ *v.,* **-sized, -sizing.** —*v.t.* **1.** to form by combining parts or elements. —*v.i.* **2.** to make or form a synthesis.

syn′the·siz′er *n.* an electronic, usu. computerized device for creating or modifying musical sounds.

syn·thet′ic (-thet′ik) *adj.* **1.** produced artificially rather than by nature. **2.** of synthesis.

synthet′ic fu′el *n.* fuel made esp. from coal or shale.

syph′i·lis (sif′ə lis) *n.* an infectious venereal disease.

syr·inge′ (sə rinj′, sir′inj) *n.* a tube with a piston or rubber bulb for drawing in and ejecting fluids.

syr′up (sir′əp, sûr′-) *n.* a sweet thick liquid. —**syr′up·y,** *adj.*

sys′tem (sis′təm) *n.* **1.** an orderly assemblage of facts, parts, etc., forming a whole. **2.** a method. **3.** a group of bodily organs concerned with the same function. **4.** the body as a whole functioning unit. —**sys′tem·at′ic** (-tə mat′ik) *adj.* —**sys′tem·a·tize′,** *v.t.*

sys·tem′ic (si stem′ik) *adj.* affecting the entire body.

sys′to·le′ (sis′tə lē′) *n.* the normal rhythmic contraction of the heart. —**sys·tol′ic** (si stol′ik) *adj.*

T

T, t (tē) *n.* the twentieth letter of the English alphabet.

tab (tab) *n.* **1.** a small projecting flap. —*Idiom.* **2. keep tabs on,** keep watch over.

tab′by (tab′ē) *n., pl.* **-bies.** a striped or brindled cat.

tab′er·nac·le (tab′ər nak′əl) *n.* **1.** a large church. **2.** (*often cap.*) a portable place of worship used by the Israelites in the wilderness. **3.** a receptacle for the reserved Eucharist.

ta′ble (tā′bəl) *n., v.,* **-bled, -bling.** —*n.* **1.** a piece of furniture consisting of a flat part resting on legs. **2.** the food served at a table. **3.** a compact arrangement of information in parallel columns. —*v.t.* **4.** to postpone discussion of.

tab·leau′ (ta blō′, tab′lō) *n., pl.* **-leaux** (ta blōz′). a representation of a scene by silent, posed, costumed people.

ta′ble d'hôte′ (tä′bəl dōt′, tab′əl) *n.* a restaurant meal of fixed courses and price.

ta′ble·land′ *n.* an elevated level land area; plateau.

ta′ble·spoon′ *n.* **1.** a large spoon. **2.** a measuring spoon holding ½ fluid ounce. —**ta′ble·spoon·ful′,** *n.*

tab′let (tab′lit) *n.* **1.** a pad of writing paper. **2.** a small slab of stone. **3.** a pill.

ta′ble ten′nis *n.* a game resembling tennis, played on a table with paddles and a small hollow ball.

ta′ble·ware′ *n.* the dishes, utensils, etc., used at the table.

tab′loid (tab′loid) *n.* a newspaper with small pages, usu. concentrating on sensational news.

ta·boo′ (tə bōō′, ta-) *adj., n., pl.* **-boos.** —*adj.* **1.** forbidden by religion or custom. —*n.* **2.** a social prohibition.

tab′u·late′ (tab′yə lāt′) *v.t.,* **-lated, -lating.** to arrange in a table. —**tab′u·lar,** *adj.* —**tab′u·la′tion,** *n.*

ta·chom′e·ter (ta kom′i tər, tə-) *n.* an instrument measuring the speed of rotation of a vehicle's engine.

tach′y·car′di·a (tak′i kär′dē ə) *n.* excessively rapid heartbeat.

tac′it (tas′it) *adj.* understood or implied without being expressed in words. —**tac′it·ly,** *adv.*

tac′i·turn′ (tas′i tûrn′) *adj.* silent. —**tac′i·tur′ni·ty,** *n.*

tack (tak) *n.* **1.** a short nail with a flat head. **2.** a ship's direction relative to the direction of the wind. **3.** a long temporary stitch. —*v.t.* **4.** to fasten with a tack. **5.** to add on. —*v.i.* **6.** to change course.

tack′le *v.,* **-led, -ling,** *n.* —*v.t.* **1.** to undertake to handle or solve. —*n.* **2.** fishing equipment. **3.** hoisting apparatus.

tack′y¹ *adj.,* **-ier, -iest.** slightly sticky. —**tack′i·ness,** *n.*

tack′y² *adj.,* **-ier, -iest.** in poor taste. —**tack′i·ness,** *n.*

ta′co (tä′kō) *n.* a fried tortilla folded and filled with chopped meat, cheese, lettuce, etc.

tact (takt) *n.* skill in handling delicate situations. —**tact′ful,** *adj.*

tac·ti′cian (tak tish′ən) *n.* a person skilled in tactics.

tac′tics (-tiks) *n.* **1.** the maneuvering of armed forces. **2.** (*used with a pl. v.*) methods for attaining success. —**tac′ti·cal,** *adj.*

tac′tile (-til, -tīl) *adj.* of the sense of touch.

tad (tad) *n. Informal.* **1.** a small amount or degree. **2.** a small child.

tad′pole (tad′pōl) *n.* the larval form of frogs and toads.

taf′fe·ta (taf′i tə) *n.* a lustrous silk or rayon fabric.

taf′fy (taf′ē) *n., pl.* **-fies.** a chewy candy made from boiled sugar or molasses.

tag¹ (tag) *n., v.,* **tagged, tagging.** —*n.* **1.** a small piece of paper, plastic, etc., attached as a marker or label. —*v.t.* **2.** to furnish with a tag. **3. tag along,** to follow closely.

tag² (tag) *n.*, *v.*, **tagged, tagging.**
1. a children's game in which one player chases the others. —*v.t.* **2.** to touch in a game of tag.

t'ai chi ch'uan (tī′ jē′ chwän′, chē′) *n.* a Chinese system of meditative exercises. Also, **tai′ chi′.**

tail (tāl) *n.* **1.** the rear part of an animal, esp. that forming an appendage. **2.** something resembling this. **3.** the reverse of a coin. **4.** the bottom or end part. —*v.t.* **5.** to follow closely.

tail′gate′ *n.*, *v.*, **-gated, -gating.** —*n.* **1.** the hinged board or gate at the back of a vehicle. —*v.i.*, *v.t.* **2.** to drive too closely behind (another vehicle).

tail′light′ *n.* a red light at the rear of a vehicle.

tai′lor (tā′lər) *n.* **1.** a person who makes, mends, or alters clothes. —*v.t.* **2.** to fashion to a particular style or purpose.

tail′pipe′ *n.* an exhaust pipe at the rear of a motor vehicle.

tail′spin′ *n.* the descent of an airplane in a steep spiral dive.

tail′wind′ (-wind′) *n.* a wind coming from directly behind.

taint (tānt) *v.t.* **1.** to affect with something bad; contaminate. —*n.* **2.** a trace of something bad.

take (tāk) *v.*, **took** (tŏok) **taken, taking,** *n.* —*v.t.* **1.** to get possession of; seize. **2.** to receive. **3.** to choose. **4.** to react to. **5.** to remove. **6.** to absorb. **7.** to travel by. **8.** to occupy. **9.** to endure. **10.** to require. **11. take after,** to resemble. **12. ~ over,** to assume possession of. —*n.* **13.** something taken.

take′off′ *n.* **1.** the leaving of the ground in leaping or flying. **2.** a humorous imitation.

take′out′ *adj.* **1.** intended to be taken from a restaurant and eaten elsewhere. —*n.* **2.** food taken out from a restaurant.

take′o′ver *n.* **1.** a seizing of authority or control. **2.** the acquisition of a corporation through the purchase of stock.

talc (talk) *n.* a soft green-to-gray mineral. Also, **tal′cum.**

tal′cum pow′der (tal′kəm) *n.* a powder for the skin made of purified talc.

tale (tāl) *n.* **1.** a story. **2.** a lie.

tal′ent (tal′ənt) *n.* a special natural ability.

tal′is·man (tal′is mən, -iz-) *n.* an object worn or carried to bring good luck.

talk (tôk) *v.i.* **1.** to exchange ideas by speaking. —*v.t.* **2.** to express in words. **3.** to discuss. —*n.* **4.** the act of talking. **5.** an informal speech. **6.** a conference. **7.** gossip. —**talk′·a·tive,** *adj.*

talk′ing-to′ *n.*, *pl.* **talking-tos.** a scolding.

tall (tôl) *adj.* **1.** of great height. **2.** of a specified height.

tal′low (tal′ō) *n.* the hard fat of sheep and cattle, used to make candles and soap.

tal′ly (tal′ē) *n.*, *pl.* **-lies,** *v.*, **-lied, -lying.** —*n.* **1.** a record of amounts. —*v.t.* **2.** to record or count. —*v.i.* **3.** to match.

Tal′mud (täl′mŏod) *n.* a collection of Jewish law and tradition.

tal′on (tal′ən) *n.* a claw.

ta·ma′le (tə mä′lē) *n.* a Mexican dish of cornmeal and meat wrapped in corn husks.

tam′a·rack (tam′ə rak′) *n.* a N American larch.

tam′a·rind (-ə rind) *n.* a tropical fruit containing seeds in a juicy acid pulp.

tam′bou·rine′ (-bə rēn′) *n.* a small drum with metal jingles in a frame.

tame (tām) *adj.*, **tamer, tamest,** *v.*, **tamed, taming.** —*adj.* **1.** not wild; domesticated. **2.** dull. —*v.t.* **3.** to make tame. —**tame′ly,** *adv.*

tamp (tamp) *v.t.* to pack in tightly.

tam′per *v.* **tamper with,** to meddle or interfere with.

tam′pon (tam′pon) *n.* a plug of cotton or the like inserted into a wound or body cavity to absorb blood.

tan (tan) *v.*, **tanned, tanning,** *n.* —*v.t.* **1.** to make or become brown by exposure to sun. **2.** to convert (a hide) into leather. —*n.* **3.** the light brown color of skin that has been exposed to the sun. **4.** a yellowish brown. —**tan′ner·y,** *n.*

tan′dem (tan′dəm) *adv.* **1.** one behind the other. —*n.* **2.** a bicycle for two persons.

tang (tang) *n.* a strong flavor or odor.

tan′ge·lo′ (tan′jə lō′) *n.*, *pl.* **-los.** a fruit that is a cross between a grapefruit and a tangerine.

tan′gent (tan′jənt) *adj.* **1.** touching. —*n.* **2.** a tangent line, plane, etc. —*Idiom.* **3. off on a tangent,** changing suddenly from one course or thought to another.

tan·gen′tial (-jen′shəl) *adj.* **1.** touching. **2.** not relevant.

tan′ge·rine′ (-jə rēn′) *n.* a loose-skinned fruit similar to an orange.

tan′gi·ble (tan′jə bəl) *adj.* **1.** able to be touched. **2.** real. —**tan′gi·bil′i·ty,** *n.*

tan′gle (tang′gəl) *v.*, **-gled, -gling,**

n. —*v.t.* **1.** to bring together into a confused mass. **2.** to catch in a snare. —*v.i.* **3.** to become tangled. **4.** to come into conflict. —*n.* **5.** a tangled state or mass.

tan′go (tang′gō) *n., pl.* **-gos,** *v.,* **-goed, -going.** —*n.* **1.** a Latin-American ballroom dance. —*v.i.* **2.** to dance the tango.

tank (tangk) *n.* **1.** a large receptacle for liquid or gas. **2.** an armored combat vehicle.

tank′ard (tang′kərd) *n.* a large cup with a handle.

tank′er *n.* a ship, truck, or airplane for transporting liquid bulk cargo.

tan′nin (tan′in) *n.* an astringent compound used in tanning.

tan′ta•lize′ (tan′tl īz′) *v.t.,* **-lized, -lizing.** to torment with something desired but out of reach.

tan′ta•mount′ (-tə mount′) *adj.* equivalent.

tan′trum (-trəm) *n.* a noisy outburst of bad temper.

tap¹ (tap) *n., v.,* **tapped, tapping.** —*v.t., v.i.* **1.** to strike lightly. —*n.* **2.** a light blow or the sound of this.

tap² (tap) *n., v.,* **tapped, tapping.** —*n.* **1.** a plug or faucet through which liquid is drawn. **2.** a connection on an electrical circuit. **3.** an act of wiretapping. —*v.t.* **4.** to draw liquid from. **5.** to draw upon. **6.** to furnish with a tap. **7.** to wiretap.

tap′ dance′ *n.* a dance in which the rhythm is audibly tapped out by the foot. —**tap′-dance,** *v.i.*

tape (tāp) *n., v.,* **taped, taping.** —*n.* **1.** a narrow strip of fabric, paper, etc., sometimes with an adhesive surface. **2.** a magnetic tape. —*v.t.* **3.** to tie, bind, or attach with tape. **4.** to record on tape.

tape′ deck′ *n.* an audio system component for playing tapes.

tape′ meas′ure *n.* a tape marked for measuring.

ta′per (tā′pər) *v.t., v.i.* **1.** to make or become narrower toward one end. **2. taper off,** to decrease gradually. —*n.* **3.** a gradual decrease. **4.** a slender candle.

tape′ record′er *n.* an electrical device for recording or playing back sound recorded on magnetic tape.

tap′es•try (tap′ə strē) *n., pl.* **-tries.** a heavy, decorative, woven fabric used esp. for wall hangings.

tape′worm′ *n.* a long, flat parasitic worm found in the digestive tract.

tap′i•o•ca (tap′ē ō′kə) *n.* a starchy preparation from the cassava, used as a thickener.

ta′pir (tā′pər, tə pēr′) *n.* a tropical piglike animal.

tap′root′ *n.* a main, central root pointing downward and giving off small lateral roots.

tar (tär) *n., v.,* **tarred, tarring.** —*n.* **1.** a dark, sticky product from coal, wood, etc. **2.** smoke components. —*v.t.* **3.** to cover with tar.

tar′an•tel′la (tar′ən tel′ə) *n.* a rapid, whirling southern Italian dance.

ta•ran′tu•la (tə ran′chə lə) *n.* a large, hairy spider.

tar′dy (tär′dē) *adj.,* **-dier, -diest.** late. —**tar′di•ness,** *n.*

tare¹ (târ) *n.* a kind of vetch.

tare² (târ) *n.* the weight of a wrapping or receptacle.

tar′get (tär′git) *n.* **1.** an object aimed at, as in shooting. **2.** a goal. **3.** an object of abuse. —*v.t.* **4.** to make a target of.

tar′iff (tar′if) *n.* **1.** a list of export or import duties. **2.** one such duty.

tar′nish (tär′nish) *v.t.* **1.** to dull the luster of. **2.** to disgrace. —*v.i.* **3.** to become tarnished. —*n.* **4.** a tarnished coating or state.

ta′ro (tär′ō, târ′ō, tar′ō) *n.* a tropical plant with an edible tuber.

ta′rot (tar′ō, ta rō′) *n.* any of a set of 22 playing cards used for fortune-telling.

tar•pau′lin (tär pô′lin, tär′pə lin) *n.* a waterproofed covering.

tar′ra•gon′ (tar′ə gon′, -gən) *n.* a plant with aromatic leaves used as seasoning.

tar′ry (tar′ē) *v.i.,* **-ried, -rying. 1.** to stay. **2.** to delay.

tart¹ (tärt) *adj.* **1.** sour; acid. **2.** sharp in manner or expression.

tart² (tärt) *n.* a pastry shell filled with fruit or custard.

tar′tan (tär′tn) *n.* a woolen cloth with a crisscross pattern, originally worn in Scotland.

tar′tar (tär′tər) *n.* a hard deposit on the teeth. —**tar•tar′ic** (-tar′ik, -tär′-) *adj.*

task (task) *n.* **1.** a piece of work, esp. one that is difficult. —*v.t.* **2.** to put a strain on. —*Idiom.* **3. take to task,** to reprimand.

task′ force′ *n.* a group for carrying out a specific task.

task′mas′ter *n.* a person who assigns burdensome tasks.

tas′sel (tas′əl) *n.* a fringed ornament hanging from a roundish knob.

taste (tāst) *v.,* **tasted, tasting,** *n.* —*v.t.* **1.** to test the flavor of by taking some in the mouth. **2.** to eat or drink a little of. **3.** to perceive the flavor of. —*v.i.* **4.** to have a particular flavor. —*n.* **5.** the sense by which flavor is perceived. **6.** the act of tasting. **7.** flavor. **8.** a sense of what is harmonious or beautiful. —**taste′ful**, *adj.* —**taste′less**, *adj.*

taste′ bud′ *n.* one of numerous small bodies that are organs for the sense of taste.

tast′y *adj.*, **-ier, -iest.** good-tasting; savory. —**tast′i•ness**, *n.*

tat′tle (tat′l) *v.*, **-tled, -tling**, *n.* —*v.i.* **1.** to tell something secret about another person. —*n.* **2.** gossip. —**tat′tler, tat′tle•tale′,** *n.*

tat•too′ (ta tōō′) *n.* **1.** an indelible marking on the skin made by puncturing and dyeing. —*v.t.* **2.** to mark by tattoo. **3.** to put (tattoos) on the skin.

taunt (tônt, tänt) *v.t.* **1.** to reproach scornfully. —*n.* **2.** a scornful remark.

taupe (tōp) *n.* a brownish gray.

taut (tôt) *adj.* tight; tense.

tau•tol′o•gy (tô tol′ə jē) *n.* needless repetition of an idea in different words. —**tau′to•log′i•cal** (-tl oj′i•kəl) *adj.*

tav′ern (tav′ərn) *n.* a saloon.

taw′dry (tô′drē) *adj.*, **-drier, -driest.** gaudy; cheap.

taw′ny (tô′nē) *adj.* yellow-brown.

tax (taks) *n.* **1.** a sum of money paid to a government. **2.** a burdensome duty. —*v.t.* **3.** to impose a tax. **4.** to burden. **5.** to accuse. —**tax′a•ble,** *adj.* —**tax•a′tion,** *n.*

tax′i (tak′sē) *n.*, *v.*, **taxied, taxiing.** —*n.* **1.** a taxicab. —*v.i.* **2.** to ride in a taxicab. **3.** (of an airplane) to move on the ground under its own power.

tax′i•cab′ *n.* an automobile carrying paying passengers.

tax′i•der′my (tak′si dûr′mē) *n.* the art of preserving, stuffing, and mounting the skins of animals. —**tax′i•der′•mist,** *n.*

tax′pay′er *n.* a person who pays a tax.

tax′ shel′ter *n.* a financial arrangement that reduces or eliminates the taxes due.

TB tuberculosis. Also, **T.B.**

tbs. tablespoon. Also, **tbsp.**

T cell *n.* a cell involved in regulating the immune system's response to infected or malignant cells.

tea (tē) *n.* **1.** the dried aromatic leaves of an Asian shrub. **2.** a beverage made by the infusion of these leaves in hot water. **3.** a similar beverage made by steeping the leaves or flowers of other plants. **4.** a light afternoon meal.

teach (tēch) *v.*, **taught, teaching.**

—*v.t.*, *v.i.* to give instruction (to or about). —**teach′er,** *n.*

tea′cup′ *n.* a cup in which tea is served.

teak (tēk) *n.* an East Indian tree with hard wood.

tea′ket•tle *n.* a kettle with a cover, spout, and handle, used for boiling water.

teal (tēl) *n.* **1.** any of several small freshwater ducks. **2.** a greenish blue.

team (tēm) *n.* **1.** the persons forming a side in a contest. **2.** persons or animals working together. —*v.i.* **3.** to join in a team. —**team′-mate′,** *n.* —**team′work′,** *n.*

team′ster (-stər) *n.* a person who drives a team or a truck.

tea′pot′ *n.* a container with a spout, in which tea is made.

tear[1] (târ) *v.*, **tore** (tôr), **torn, tearing,** *n.* —*v.t.* **1.** to pull apart by force. **2.** to divide. **3.** to produce by tearing. **4.** to injure by tearing. —*v.i.* **5.** to become torn. **6.** to move hastily. —*n.* **7.** the act of tearing. **8.** a rip or hole.

tear[2] (tēr) *n.* **1.** a drop of the saline fluid that lubricates and flows from the eye. —*v.i.* **2.** (of the eyes) to fill with tears. —**tear′ful** (tēr′-) *adj.*

tear′ gas′ (tēr) *n.* a gas that makes the eyes smart and water.

tear′jerk′er (tēr′jûr′kər) *n. Informal.* a sentimental story, play, etc.

tease (tēz) *v.*, **teased, teasing,** *n.* —*v.t.* **1.** to annoy with taunts, mockery, etc. —*v.i.* **2.** to tease a person or animal. —*n.* **3.** a person who teases. —**teas′er,** *n.*

tea′spoon′ *n.* **1.** a small spoon. **2.** a measuring spoon holding $\frac{1}{6}$ fluid ounce. —**tea′spoon•ful′,** *n.*

teat (tēt, tit) *n.* a nipple.

tech′ni•cal (tek′ni kəl) *adj.* **1.** of the mechanical or industrial arts and applied sciences. **2.** of an art, science, or trade. **3.** considered in a strict sense.

tech′ni•cal′i•ty (-kal′i tē) *n.*, *pl.* **-ties. 1.** a technical point or detail. **2.** technical character.

Tech′ni•col′or *Trademark.* the system of making color motion pictures.

tech•nique′ (-nēk′) *n.* a method used to accomplish something.

tech•noc′ra•cy (-nok′rə sē) *n.*, *pl.* **-cies.** government by technological experts.

tech•nol′o•gy (-nol′ə jē) *n.*, *pl.* **-gies. 1.** the study of the applied sciences, engineering, etc. **2.** the practical application of knowledge. —**tech•no•log′i•cal** (-nə loj′i kəl) *adj.* —**tech•nol′o•gist,** *n.*

tec·ton·ics (-ton′iks) *n.* the branch of geology that studies the forces that cause the earth's crust to be deformed.

ted′dy bear′ (ted′ē) *n.* a stuffed toy bear.

Te De′um (tā dā′əm) *n.* a hymn of praise and thanksgiving.

te·di·ous (tē′dē əs, tē′jəs) *adj.* long and tiresome. —**te′di·um,** *n.*

tee (tē) *n., v.,* **teed, teeing. 1.** a mound of earth or a peg from which a golf ball is driven. —*v.t.* **2.** to place (a ball) on a tee. **3. tee off,** to strike a ball from a tee.

teem (tēm) *v.i.* to abound; swarm.

teens (tēnz) *n.pl.* **1.** the numbers 13 through 19. **2.** the ages 13 through 19. —**teen′ag′er,** *n.*

tee′ter (tē′tər) *v.i.* **1.** to move unsteadily. **2.** to waver.

teethe (tēth) *v.i.,* **teethed, teething.** to grow or cut teeth.

tee·to′tal·er (tē tōt′l ər, tē′tōt′-) *n.* a person who does not drink alcoholic beverages.

Tef′lon (tef′lon) *Trademark.* **1.** a polymer with nonsticking properties, used to coat cookware. —*adj.* **2.** impervious to blame or criticisms.

tel. 1. telegram. **2.** telegraph. **3.** telephone.

tel′e·cast′ (tel′i kast′) *v.,* **-cast** or **-casted, -casting,** *n.* —*v.t., v.i.* **1.** to broadcast by television. —*n.* **2.** a television broadcast.

tel′e·com·mu·ni·ca′tions *n.* the science and technology of transmitting information in the form of electromagnetic signals.

tel′e·gen′ic (-jen′ik) *adj.* having qualities that televise well.

tel′e·graph′ (-graf′) *n.* **1.** an electrical apparatus or process for sending a message (**tel′e·gram′**). —*v.t.* **2.** to send by telegraph. —**tel′e·graph′ic,** *adj.* —**te·leg′ra·phy** (tə leg′rə fē) *n.*

tel′e·mar·ket·ing *n.* selling or advertising by telephone.

te·lep′a·thy (tə lep′ə thē) *n.* communication between minds without sensory means. —**tel′e·path′ic** (tel′ə path′ik) *adj.*

tel′e·phone′ (tel′ə fōn′) *n., v.,* **-phoned, -phoning.** —*n.* **1.** an electrical apparatus or process for transmitting speech. —*v.t., v.i.* **2.** to send (a message) to (a person) by telephone.

tel′ephone tag′ *n.* repeated unsuccessful attempts by two persons to reach each other by telephone.

tel′e·pho′to *adj.* of a lens producing a large image of a small or distant object.

tel′e·scope′ *n., v.,* **-scoped, -scoping.** —*n.* **1.** an optical instrument for enlarging an image of distant objects. —*v.t., v.i.* **2.** to force or slide (one section) into another. **3.** to condense or become condensed. —**tel′e·scop′ic** (-skop′ik) *adj.*

tel′e·thon′ (-thon′) *n.* a television broadcast to raise money for charity.

tel′e·van′ge·list (-i van′jə list) *n.* an evangelist who conducts religious services on television. —**tel′e·van′ge·lism** (-liz′əm) *n.*

tel′e·vi′sion *n.* **1.** the broadcasting of images via radio waves to receivers that project them on screens. **2.** a set for receiving such broadcasts. —**tel′e·vise,** *v.t., v.i.*

tell (tel) *v.,* **told** (tōld) **telling.** —*v.t.* **1.** to narrate. **2.** to communicate in words. **3.** to reveal. **4.** to recognize. **5.** to inform. **6.** to order. —*v.i.* **7.** to give an account. **8.** to produce a marked effect.

tell′-all′ *adj.* thoroughly revealing.

tell′er *n.* a bank cashier.

tell′tale′ *adj.* revealing.

te·mer′i·ty (tə mer′i tē) *n.* rash boldness.

temp (temp) *n.* a temporary worker.

tem′per *n.* **1.** a state of mind or feelings. **2.** heat of mind or passion. **3.** calmness when provoked. —*v.t.* **4.** to moderate. **5.** to heat and cool (metal) to obtain the proper hardness and strength.

tem′per·a (tem′pər ə) *n.* a technique of painting using a medium containing egg and water or oil.

tem′per·a·ment (tem′pər ə mənt, -prə mənt) *n.* mental disposition.

tem′per·a·men′tal (-men′tl) *adj.* moody or sensitive.

tem′per·ance (tem′pər əns) *n.* **1.** moderation. **2.** total abstinence from alcohol.

tem′per·ate (-pər it) *adj.* moderate.

Tem′perate Zone′ *n.* the part of the earth's surface lying between either tropic and the nearest polar circle.

tem′per·a·ture (-pər ə chər, -prə-) *n.* the degree of warmth or coldness.

tem′pest (-pist) *n.* a violent storm or disturbance. —**tem·pes′tu·ous** (-pes′chōō əs) *adj.*

tem′plate (-plit) *n.* a pattern, mold, etc., serving as a gauge or guide in mechanical work.

tem′ple¹ (-əl) *n.* a building dedicated to worship.

tem′ple² (-əl) *n.* the flat area at the side of the forehead.

tem′po (-pō) *n., pl.* **-pos, -pi** (-pē).

the rate of speed of a musical passage.

tem′po•ral (-pər əl) *adj.* **1.** of time. **2.** worldly.

tem′po•rar′y (-pə rer′ē) *adj.* not permanent. —**tem′po•rar′i•ly,** *adv.*

tem′po•rize′ (-rīz′) *v.i.,* **-rized, -rizing.** to delay by evasion.

tempt (tempt) *v.t.* **1.** to entice to do something wrong. **2.** to appeal strongly to. —**temp•ta′tion,** *n.*

tem•pur′a (tem pŏŏr′ə) *n.* a Japanese deep-fried dish of vegetables or seafood.

ten (ten) *n., adj.* nine plus one. —**tenth,** *n., adj.*

ten′a•ble (ten′ə bəl) *adj.* able to be held, maintained, or defended. —**ten′a•bil′i•ty,** *n.*

te•na′cious (tə nā′shəs) *adj.* **1.** holding fast. **2.** highly retentive. —**te•nac′i•ty** (-nas′i tē) *n.*

ten′an•cy (ten′ən sē) *n., pl.* **-cies.** occupancy of land, a house, a position, etc.; tenure.

ten′ant (-ənt) *n.* **1.** one renting from a landlord. **2.** an occupant.

Ten′ Command′ments *n.pl.* the laws given to Moses by God on Mount Sinai.

tend¹ (tend) *v.i.* **1.** to be inclined to do something. **2.** to lead in a certain direction.

tend² (tend) *v.t.* to take care of.

tend′en•cy (ten′dən sē) *n., pl.* **-cies.** a disposition to behave or act in a certain way.

ten•den′tious (-den′shəs) *adj.* having or showing bias.

ten′der¹ *adj.* **1.** soft; delicate; weak. **2.** young. **3.** soft-hearted. **4.** affectionate. **5.** very sensitive. —**ten′der•ness,** *n.* —**ten′der•ize′,** *v.t.*

ten′der² *v.t.* **1.** to present or offer formally. —*n.* **2.** something offered.

ten′der³ *n.* **1.** a person who tends. **2.** a ship carrying provisions to other ships. **3.** a car carrying fuel and water for a locomotive.

ten′der•foot′ *n., pl.* **-foots, -feet.** *Informal.* an inexperienced person.

ten′der-heart′ed *adj.* soft-hearted.

ten′der•loin′ *n.* **1.** tender meat on a loin of beef, pork, etc. **2.** the brothel district of a city.

ten•di•ni′tis (ten′də nī′tis) *n.* inflammation of a tendon.

ten′don (-dən) *n.* a band of dense tissue connecting a muscle to a bone or part.

ten′dril (-dril) *n.* a clinging thread-like organ of a climbing plant.

ten′e•ment (-ə mənt) *n.* a run-down apartment house.

ten′et (-it) *n.* a principle, doctrine, dogma, etc.

Tenn. Tennessee.

ten′nis (-is) *n.* a game played with a ball and rackets (**tennis rackets**) on a rectangular court (**tennis court**).

ten′on (-ən) *n.* a projection inserted into a cavity (**mortise**) to form a joint.

ten′or (-ər) *n.* **1.** the highest ordinary adult male singing voice. **2.** a singer with this voice. **3.** general sense. **4.** continuous course or progress. —*adj.* **5.** of the pitch between alto and bass.

ten′pins′ *n.* a bowling game played with ten wooden pins.

tense¹ (tens), *adj.,* **tenser, tensest,** *v.,* **tensed, tensing.** —*adj.* **1.** taut; rigid. **2.** emotionally strained. —*v.t., v.i.* **3.** to make or become tense. —**tense′ly,** *adv.*

tense² (tens) *n.* the inflected form of a verb indicating time of an action or state.

ten′sile (ten′səl, -sil, -sīl) *adj.* **1.** of tension. **2.** able to be stretched.

ten′sion (-shən) *n.* **1.** a stretching or being stretched. **2.** mental or emotional strain.

tent (tent) *n.* a portable shelter, usu. of fabric supported by poles.

ten′ta•cle (ten′tə kəl) *n.* a long, flexible part of certain animals, used for touching, grasping, etc.

ten′ta•tive (-tə tiv) *adj.* **1.** experimental. **2.** unsure.

ten′ter•hook′ (-tər hŏŏk′) *n.* —*Idiom.* **on tenterhooks,** in suspense.

ten′u•ous (ten′yŏŏ əs) *adj.* **1.** lacking a sound basis. **2.** thin or slender. **3.** rare. —**ten′u•ous•ly,** *adv.*

ten′ure (-yər) *n.* the holding of property or a position.

te′pee (tē′pē) *n.* a cone-shaped tent used by the Plains Indians.

tep′id (tep′id) *adj.* lukewarm.

te•qui′la (tə kē′lə) *n.* a strong Mexican liquor.

ter′cen•ten′ni•al (tûr′-) *n.* a 300th anniversary or its celebration. Also, **ter′cen•ten′a•ry.**

term (tûrm) *n.* **1.** a name for something. **2.** the time through which something lasts. **3.** an appointed time. **4. terms,** the conditions of an agreement or bargain. —*v.t.* **5.** to name; designate.

ter′mi•nal (tû′mə nl) *adj.* **1.** situated at the end; concluding. **2.** leading to death. —*n.* **3.** an end or extremity. **4.** the terminating point for trains, buses, etc. **5.** a point of electrical connection. **6.** a device for entering information into or receiving information from a computer. —**ter′mi•nal•ly,** *adv.*

ter′mi·nate′ (-nāt′) v., **-nated, -nat-ing.** —v.i., v.t. to come or bring to an end. —**ter′mi·na′tion,** n.

ter′mi·nol′o·gy (-nol′ə jē) n., pl. **-gies.** the terms of a specialized subject.

ter′mi·nus (-nəs) n. **1.** the end of anything. **2.** the end of the line for buses, trains, etc.

ter′mite (tûr′mīt) n. a destructive wood-eating insect.

tern (tûrn) n. a gull-like aquatic bird.

ter′race (ter′əs) n., v., **-raced, -rac-ing.** —n. **1.** a raised level of earth with vertical or sloping sides. **2.** an open area connected with a house. **3.** a porch or balcony. —v.t. **4.** to make into a terrace.

ter′ra cot′ta (ter′ə kot′ə) n. a hard, brownish-red clay used for making pottery.

ter′ra fir′ma (fûr′mə) n. solid land.

ter·rain′ (tə rān′) n. an area of land of a specified nature.

ter′ra·pin (ter′ə pin) n. an edible North American turtle.

ter·rar′i·um (tə râr′ē əm) n., pl. **-iums, -ia** (-ē ə). a glass tank for raising plants or land animals.

ter·raz′zo (tə rä′tsō, -raz′ō) n. mosaic flooring composed of stone chips and cement.

ter·res′tri·al (tə res′trē əl) adj. **1.** of or living on earth. **2.** of land as distinct from water.

ter′ri·ble (ter′ə bəl) adj. dreadful; horrible. —**ter′ri·bly,** adv.

ter′ri·er (ter′ē ər) n. a small lively dog.

ter·rif′ic (tə rif′ik) adj. **1.** extremely great or intense. **2.** excellent. —**ter·rif′i·cal·ly,** adv.

ter′ri·fy′ (ter′ə fī′) v.t., **-fied, -fy-ing.** to fill with terror.

ter′ri·to·ry (ter′i tôr′ē) n., pl. **-ries. 1.** any large area of land. **2.** the land and waters under a state's control. **3.** a field of action, thought, etc. —**ter′ri·to′ri·al,** adj.

ter′ror (ter′ər) n. intense fear.

ter′ror·ism n. the use of violence and threats to obtain political demands. —**ter′ror·ist,** n., adj.

ter′ror·ize′ v.t., **-ized, -izing.** to fill with terror. —**ter′ror·i·za′tion,** n.

ter′ry (ter′ē) n., pl. **-ries.** a pile fabric with uncut loops, used for towels. Also, **terry cloth.**

terse (tûrs) adj. **1.** concise. **2.** curt; brusque. —**terse′ly,** adv.

ter′ti·ar′y (tûr′shē er′ē) adj. of the third rank or stage.

tes′sel·late′ (tes′ə lāt′) v.t., **-lated, -lating.** to form in a mosaic pattern of small squares.

test (test) n. **1.** the means used to determine the quality, content, etc., of something. **2.** an examination to evaluate a student or class. —v.t. **3.** to subject to a test.

tes′ta·ment (tes′tə mənt) n. **1.** either of two sections of the Bible. **2.** a legal will. —**tes′ta·men′ta·ry** (-men′tə rē) adj.

tes′tate (-tāt) adj. having left a valid will. —**tes′ta·tor,** n.

tes′ti·cle (-ti kəl) n. either of two male sex glands located in the scrotum. Also, **tes′tis** (tes′tis).

tes′ti·fy′ (-tə fī′) v.i., **-fied, -fying. 1.** to serve as evidence. **2.** to give testimony.

tes′ti·mo′ni·al (-mō′nē əl) n. **1.** a recommendation of a person or thing. **2.** a tribute.

tes′ti·mo′ny n., pl. **-nies. 1.** the statement of a witness under oath. **2.** proof.

tes·tos′ter·one (-tos′tə rōn′) n. a male sex hormone.

test′ tube′ n. a slender glass tube used in laboratories.

tes′ty (tes′tē) adj., **-tier, -tiest.** irritable. —**tes′ti·ly,** adv.

tet′a·nus (tet′n əs) n. a bacterial disease marked by muscular rigidity.

tête′-à-tête′ (tāt′ə tāt′, tet′ə tet′) n. a private conversation.

teth′er (teth′ər) n. **1.** a rope, chain, etc., for fastening an animal to a stake. —v.t. **2.** to fasten with a tether. —**Idiom. 3. at the end of one's tether,** having reached the end of one's ability or resources.

tet′ra (te′trə) n., pl. **-ras.** a small, brightly colored fish of tropical American waters.

tetra- a prefix meaning four.

tet′ra·he′dron (-hē′drən) n., pl. **-drons, -dra.** a solid contained by four plane faces.

Tex. Texas.

text (tekst) n. **1.** the main body of matter in a book or manuscript. **2.** the actual words spoken or written. **3.** a quotation from Scripture. —**tex′tu·al** (-chōō əl) adj.

text′book′ n. a book used by students in a course.

tex′tile (teks′tīl, -til) n. **1.** any woven material. —adj. **2.** of textiles or weaving.

tex′ture (-chər) n. the physical structure or composition of a material, object, etc. —**tex′tur·al,** adj.

thal′a·mus (thal′ə məs) n. the part of the brain that transmits and integrates sensory impulses.

tha·lid′o·mide′ (thə lid′ə mīd′) n. a drug formerly used as a sedative, found to cause fetal abnormalities when taken during pregnancy.

thal′li·um (thal′ē əm) *n.* a rare metallic element.

than (*t͟han*, *t͟hen; unstressed t͟hən, ən*) *conj.* **1.** (used to introduce the second member of a comparison). **2.** (used to indicate a difference in kind, place, etc.).

thank (thangk) *v.t.* **1.** to express gratitude to. —*n.* **2. thanks,** an expression of gratitude. —**thank′ful,** *adj.*

thank′less *adj.* not likely to be appreciated.

thanks′giv′ing *n.* **1.** an expression of thanks, esp. to God. **2. Thanksgiving,** a U.S. holiday observed on the fourth Thursday of November.

that (*t͟hat; unstressed t͟hət*) *pron., pl.* **those** (*t͟hōz*), *adj., adv., conj.* —*pron., adj.* **1.** a demonstrative word indicating **a.** the person, thing, etc., more remote. **b.** one of two persons, things, etc., pointed out or mentioned before (opposed to **this**). **2.** a relative pronoun used as: **a.** the subject or object of a relative clause. **b.** the object of a preposition. —*adv.* **3.** to that extent. —*conj.* **4.** a word used to introduce a dependent clause or one expressing reason, result, etc.

thatch (thach) *n.* **1.** rushes, straw, etc., woven together for covering roofs. —*v.t.* **2.** to cover with thatch.

thaw (thô) *v.i.* **1.** to melt. —*v.t.* **2.** to remove ice or frost from. —*n.* **3.** an act or instance of thawing.

the (*stressed t͟hē; unstressed before a consonant t͟hə, unstressed before a vowel t͟hē*) *def. article.* **1.** (used to indicate a particular person or thing). **2.** (used to mark a noun indicating the best, most important, etc.). **3.** (used to mark a noun standing for one or all of a kind). **4.** (used before adjectives that are used as nouns).

the′a·ter (thē′ə tər, thēᵊ′-) *n.* **1.** a building for the presentation of plays, movies, etc. **2. the theater,** dramatic art. **3.** a place of action. Also, **the′a·tre.** —**the·at′ri·cal** (-a′tri kəl) *adj.*

thee (*t͟hē*) *pron. Archaic.* the objective case of **thou.**

theft (theft) *n.* an act or instance of stealing.

their (*t͟hâr; unstressed t͟hər*) *pron.* **1.** the possessive form of **they** used before a noun. **2. theirs,** that which belongs to them.

the′ism (thē′iz əm) *n.* belief in the existence of a god or gods.

them (*t͟hem; unstressed t͟həm, əm*) *pron.* the objective case of **they.**

theme (thēm) *n.* **1.** the central subject of a work of art. **2.** a subject of discussion. **3.** a short essay. **4.** a principal melody in a musical composition. —**the·mat′ic** (-mat′ik) *adj.*

them·selves′ (*t͟həm selvz′, t͟hem′-*) *pron.* an emphatic or reflexive form of **them.**

then (*t͟hen*) *adv.* **1.** at that time. **2.** soon afterward. **3.** at another time. **4.** besides. **5.** in that case. —*adj.* **6.** being such at that time.

thence (*t͟hens*) *adv.* **1.** from that place or time. **2.** therefore.

thence′forth′ (*t͟hens′fôrth′, t͟hens′-fôrth′*) *adv.* from that place or time on.

the·ol′o·gy (-ol′ə jē) *n.* **1.** the study of religious truth. **2.** a particular form, system, or branch of this study. —**the′o·lo′gian** (-ə lō′jən, -jē ən) *n.* —**the′o·log′i·cal** (-loj′i kəl) *adj.*

the′o·rem (thē′ər əm, thēr′əm) *n. Math.* a proposition or formula containing something to be proved.

the′o·ret′i·cal (thē′ə ret′i kəl) *adj.* of, consisting in, or existing only in theory.

the′o·ry (thē′ə rē, thēr′ē) *n., pl.* **-ries. 1.** a group of propositions used as principles to explain a class of phenomena. **2.** a proposed explanation. **3.** the branch of a field of knowledge that deals with its principles rather than its practice. —**the′o·rist,** *n.* —**the′o·rize′,** *v.i.*

ther′a·py (ther′ə pē) *n., pl.* **-pies.** the treatment of disease or disorders. —**ther′a·pist** (-pist) *n.* —**ther′a·peu′tic** (-pyōō′tik) *adj.* —**ther′a·peu′tics,** *n.*

there (*t͟hâr; unstressed t͟hər*) *adv.* **1.** in, at, or to that place. **2.** at that point; in that matter. —*n.* **3.** that place or point. —*interj.* **4.** an exclamation of relief or satisfaction.

there′a·bout′ or **there′a·bouts′** *adv.* near that place, time, number, amount, etc.

there′af′ter *adv.* after that.

there′by′ (*t͟hâr′bī′*) *adv.* by means of that.

there′fore′ *adv.* as a result.

there′in′ *adv.* in that place.

there·of′ *adv.* of or from that.

there·on′ *adv.* **1.** on that. **2.** immediately after that.

there′up·on′ *adv.* **1.** immediately after that. **2.** because of that. **3.** upon that.

there·with′ *adv.* with or in addition to that.

ther′mal (thûr′məl) *adj.* of or retaining heat.

ther′mo·dy·nam′ics (thûr′mō dīnam′iks) n. the science concerned with the relations between heat and mechanical energy or work.

ther•mom′e•ter (thər mom′i tər) n. an instrument for measuring temperature.

ther′mo•nu′cle•ar (thûr′mō-) adj. of nuclear-fusion reactions at extremely high temperatures.

Ther′mos (thûr′məs) Trademark. a container with a vacuum between double walls for heat insulation.

ther′mo•sphere′ n. the region of the upper atmosphere in which temperature increases continually with altitude.

ther′mo•stat′ (-mə stat′) n. a device that automatically sets and maintains a desired temperature. —ther′mo•stat′ic, adj.

the•sau′rus (thi sôr′əs) n., pl. -sauruses, -sauri (-sôr′ī). a dictionary of synonyms and antonyms.

these (thēz) pron. pl. of this.

the′sis (thē′sis) n., pl. -ses (-sēz). 1. a proposition to be proved. 2. a lengthy essay presented for a university degree.

thes′pi•an (thes′pē ən) adj. 1. of dramatic art. —n. 2. an actor or actress.

they (thā) pron.pl. nominative plural of he, she, and it.

thi′a•mine (thī′ə min, -mēn′) n. vitamin B₁. Also, thi′a•min.

thick (thik) adj. 1. not thin. 2. measured between opposite surfaces. 3. dense. 4. heavy. —n. 5. the thickest part. —thick′en, v.t., v.i. —thick′en•er, n.

thick′et n. a thick growth of shrubs, bushes, etc.

thick′set′ adj. 1. set closely; dense. 2. heavily or solidly built.

thick′-skinned′ adj. not sensitive to criticism or contempt.

thief (thēf) n., pl. thieves (thēvz). a person who steals. —thieve, v.t., v.i. —thiev′er•y (thē′və rē) n.

thigh (thī) n. the part of the leg between the hip and the knee.

thim′ble (thim′bəl) n. a cap to protect the finger while sewing.

thin (thin) adj., thinner, thinnest, v., thinned, thinning. —adj. 1. having little extent between opposite sides; slender. 2. lean. 3. widely separated. 4. rarefied; diluted. 5. flimsy. 6. weak. —v.t., v.i. 7. to make or become thin.

thing (thing) n. 1. an inanimate object. 2. a matter. 3. an action. 4. an event. 5. a thought or idea. 6. things, personal possessions.

think (thingk) v., thought (thôt), thinking. —v.i. 1. to use one's mind rationally. 2. to have something as the subject of one's thoughts. 3. to form an idea. 4. to have a belief or opinion. —v.t. 5. to have in the mind. 6. to believe. —think′er, n.

think′ tank′ n. a research organization employed to analyze problems and plan future developments.

thin′ner n. a liquid used to dilute paint.

thin′-skinned′ adj. sensitive to criticism or contempt.

third (thûrd) adj. 1. next after the second. 2. being one of three equal parts. —n. 3. a third part or the third one of a series.

third′-class′ adj. of the lowest class or quality.

third′ degree′ n. the use of brutal measures by police (or others) in obtaining information.

third′ dimen′sion n. 1. thickness or depth. 2. an aspect that heightens reality.

third′ par′ty n. 1. any party to a case or quarrel who is incidentally involved. 2. in a two-party political system, a usu. temporary party composed of independents.

third′-rate′ adj. of poor quality.

thirst (thûrst) n. 1. the sensation caused by the need of drink. —v.i. 2. to be thirsty. —thirst′y, adj. —thirst′i•ly, adv.

thir′teen′ (thûr′tēn′) n., adj. ten plus three. —thir•teenth′, adj., n.

thir′ty (thûr′tē) n., adj. ten times three. —thir′ti•eth, adj., n.

this (this) pron., pl. these (thēz), adj., adv. —pron., adj. 1. a demonstrative word indicating something as just mentioned, present, near, etc. —adv. 2. to the indicated extent.

this′tle (this′əl) n. a prickly plant.

thith′er (thith′ər, thith′-) adv. to that place, point, etc.

tho (thō) conj., adv. a simplified spelling of though.

thong (thông) n. 1. a strip of leather. 2. a sandal with a strip of leather, plastic, etc., passing between the first two toes.

tho′rax (thôr′aks) n., pl. thoraxes, thoraces (thôr′ə sēz′). the part of the body between the neck and the abdomen. —tho•rac′ic (thō-ras′ik) adj.

thorn (thôrn) n. a sharp spine on a plant. —thorn′y, adj.

thor′ough (thûr′ō, thur′ō) adj. 1. complete. 2. having or done with great attention to detail.

thor′ough•bred′ (-ō bred′, -ə bred′) adj. 1. of pure breed or stock. —n. 2. a thoroughbred animal, esp. a horse.

thor′ough.fare′ n. a road, street, etc., that is open at both ends.

thor′ough.go.ing adj. extremely thorough.

those (t͡hōz) pron., adj. pl. of **that**.

thou (t͡hou) pron. Archaic (except in elevated prose or in addressing God). you (the second person singular in the nominative case).

though (t͡hō) conj. **1.** in spite of the fact that. **2.** even if. —adv. **3.** however.

thought[1] (thôt) n. **1.** the result of mental activity. **2.** an idea. **3.** the act, process, or capacity of thinking. **4.** an opinion.

thought[2] (thôt) v. pt. and pp. of **think**.

thought′ful adj. **1.** occupied with thought. **2.** careful. **3.** considerate. **—thought′ful.ly,** adv.

thought′less adj. **1.** showing lack of thought. **2.** careless; inconsiderate. **—thought′less.ly,** adv.

thou′sand (thou′zənd) n., adj. ten times one hundred. **—thou′-sandth,** adj., n.

thrall (thrôl) n. **1.** slavery; bondage. **2.** a person in bondage; slave.

thrash (thrash) v.t. **1.** to beat thoroughly. —v.i. **2.** to toss about wildly.

thread (thred) n. **1.** a fine spun cord of flax, cotton, etc., used for sewing. **2.** the ridge of a screw. —v.t. **3.** to pass thread through. **4.** to make (one's way) through obstacles.

thread′bare′ adj. shabby.

threat (thret) n. **1.** an expression of intent to harm. **2.** an indication of possible trouble. **—threat′en,** v.t., v.i.

three (thrē) n., adj. two plus one.

three′-di.men′sion.al adj. having or seeming to have depth as well as width and height.

three′fold′ adj. **1.** having three parts. **2.** three times as great.

three′score′ adj. sixty.

thresh (thresh) v.t., v.i. to separate (grain or seeds) from (a plant).

thresh′old (thresh′ōld, -hōld) n. **1.** a doorway sill. **2.** an entrance or beginning.

thrice (thrīs) adv. three times.

thrift (thrift) n. economical management. **—thrift′y,** adj.

thrill (thril) v.t. **1.** to affect with sudden emotion or excitement. —v.i. **2.** to vibrate. —n. **3.** a sudden wave of emotion or excitement.

thrill′er n. a suspenseful story.

thrive (thrīv) v.i., **thrived, thriving.** to prosper or flourish.

throat (thrōt) n. the passage from the mouth to the lungs or esophagus.

throat′y adj., **-ier, -iest.** (of a sound) husky; hoarse.

throb (throb) v., **throbbed, throbbing,** n. —v.i. **1.** to beat violently or rapidly. **2.** to vibrate. —n. **3.** an act of throbbing.

throe (thrō) n. **1.** a violent spasm. **—Idiom. 2. in the throes of,** in a violent struggle with.

throm.bo′sis (throm bō′sis) n. clotting of blood in the blood vessels or heart.

throne (thrōn) n. the official chair of a sovereign, bishop, etc.

throng (thrông) n. **1.** a crowd. —v.i. **2.** to gather in large numbers.

throt′tle (throt′l) n., v., **-tled, -tling.** —n. **1.** a device controlling the flow of fuel. —v.t. **2.** to choke. **3.** to silence or check.

through (thro͞o) prep. **1.** in one side and out the other side of. **2.** past; beyond. **3.** between or among. **4.** done with. **5.** by the means or reason of. —adv. **6.** in at one side and out at the other. **7.** all the way. **8.** to the end. —adj. **9.** finished. **10.** extending from one side to the other.

through.out′ prep. **1.** in every part of. —adv. **2.** in or during every part.

throw (thrō) v., **threw** (thro͞o), **thrown, throwing,** n. —v.t. **1.** to propel or cast forth. **2.** to cause to fall. **3.** to move (a lever or switch). **4.** to confuse. —n. **5.** an act of throwing. **6.** the distance something is thrown. **7.** a light blanket.

throw′a.way′ adj. **1.** to be discarded after use. —n. **2.** a notice distributed free.

throw′back′ n. a reversion to an earlier type.

thru (thro͞o) prep., adv., adj. an informal spelling of **through.**

thrush (thrush) n. **1.** a migratory songbird with dull feathers. **2.** a fungal infection.

thrust (thrust) v., **thrust, thrusting,** n. —v.t. **1.** to push. —v.i. **2.** to make a lunge or stab. **3.** to force one's way. —n. **4.** a thrusting movement. **5.** a force propelling a missile, ship, etc. **6.** the main point.

thru′way′ (thro͞o′wā′) n. an expressway providing a direct route between distant areas.

thud (thud) n., v., **thudded, thudding.** —n. **1.** a dull striking sound. —v.i. **2.** to make a thudding sound.

thug (thug) n. a violent criminal.

thumb (thum) n. **1.** the short, thick

finger next to the forefinger. —*v.t.*
2. to manipulate with the thumb.

thumb/nail/ *n.* **1.** the nail of the thumb. —*adj.* **2.** brief and concise.

thumb/screw/ *n.* a screw turned by the thumb and forefinger.

thumb/tack/ *n.* **1.** a tack with a large, flat head. —*v.t.* **2.** to secure with a thumbtack.

thump (thump) *n.* **1.** a heavy blow. —*v.t., v.i.* **2.** to strike heavily.

thump/ing *adj.* **1.** exceptional. **2.** of or like a thump.

thun/der (thun/dər) *n.* **1.** the loud noise accompanying lightning. **2.** any loud noise. —*v.i.* **3.** to give forth thunder. **4.** to make a noise like thunder. **5.** to speak loudly. —**thun/der·ous,** *adj.*

thun/der·bolt/ *n.* a flash of lightning with thunder.

thun/der·clap/ *n.* a crash of thunder.

thun/der·cloud/ *n.* an electrically charged cloud producing lightning and thunder.

thun/der·head/ *n.* a mass of clouds warning of thunderstorms.

thun/der·struck/ *adj.* astonished.

Thurs. Thursday.

Thurs/day (thûrz/dā, -dē) *n.* the fifth day of the week.

thus (*th*us) *adv.* **1.** in this way. **2.** as a result. **3.** to this extent.

thwack (thwak) *v.t.* **1.** to strike hard with something flat. —*n.* **2.** a sharp blow with something flat.

thwart (thwôrt) *v.t.* to oppose or frustrate.

thy (*th*ī) *pron. Archaic.* the possessive case of **thou.**

thyme (tīm; *spelling pron.* thīm) *n.* an aromatic plant of the mint family used as seasoning.

thy/mus (thī/məs) *n.* a gland at the base of the neck that helps produce T cells.

thy/roid (thī/roid) *n.* **1.** a ductless gland near the windpipe, involved in controlling metabolism and growth. —*adj.* **2.** of this gland.

thy·self/ (*th*ī self/) *pron.* a reflexive and intensive form of **thou** or **thee.**

ti·ar/a (tē ar/ə, -är/ə, -âr/ə) *n.* a woman's ornamental coronet.

tib/i·a (tib/ē ə) *n., pl.* **-iae** (-ē ē/) **-ias.** the bone from the knee to the ankle.

tic (tik) *n.* a sudden twitch.

tick¹ (tik) *n.* **1.** a slight, sharp, recurring click. —*v.i.* **2.** to make a ticking sound.

tick² (tik) *n.* a bloodsucking mite.

tick/er *n.* **1.** one that ticks. **2.** a telegraphic instrument that prints stock prices, market reports, etc.,

on tape (**ticker tape**). **3.** *Slang.* the heart.

tick/et (-it) *n.* **1.** a printed slip indicating the right to admission, transportation, etc. **2.** a tag. **3.** a summons for a traffic or parking violation. —*v.t.* **4.** to attach a ticket to.

tick/ing *n.* a cotton fabric used to cover mattresses and pillows.

tick/le *v.*, **-led, -ling,** *n.* —*v.t.* **1.** to touch lightly so as to make tingle or itch. **2.** to gratify. —*v.i.* **3.** to have or produce a tingling sensation. —*n.* **4.** a tickling sensation. —**tick/lish,** *adj.*

tick/-tack-toe/ (tik/tak tō/) *n.* a game for two players, each trying to complete a row of three X's or three O's on a nine-square grid.

tid/al wave/ *n.* a large, destructive ocean wave.

tid/bit/ (tid/bit/) *n.* a choice bit, as of food.

tid/dly·winks/ (-lē wingks/) *n.* a game in which small disks are snapped with larger disks into a cup.

tide (tīd) *n., v.,* **tided, tiding.** —*n.* **1.** the periodic rise and fall of the ocean. **2.** a tendency. —*v.* **3. tide over,** to help to get through a difficult period. —**tid/al,** *adj.*

ti/dings (tī/dingz) *n.pl.* news.

ti/dy (tī/dē) *adj.,* **-dier, -diest,** *v.,* **-died, -dying.** —*adj.* **1.** neat and orderly. **2.** fairly large. —*v.t.* **3.** to make tidy. —**ti/di·ly,** *adv.*

tie (tī) *v.,* **tied, tying,** *n.* —*v.t.* **1.** to fasten with a cord, string, etc. **2.** to make into a bow. **3.** to bind. **4.** to make the same score as. —*v.i.* **5.** to make the same score. —*n.* **6.** something used to tie or join. **7.** a necktie. **8.** equality in scores, votes, etc. **9.** a contest in which this occurs. **10.** a bond of kinship, affection, etc.

tie/-dye/ing *n.* a method of dyeing with sections of garment bound so as not to receive dye.

tie/-in/ *n.* a link or association.

tier (tēr) *n.* a row or rank.

tie/-up/ *n.* a temporary stoppage of business, traffic, etc.

tiff (tif) *n.* a petty quarrel.

ti/ger (tī/gər) *n.* a large striped Asian cat.

ti/ger lil/y *n.* a lily with flowers of a dull-orange color spotted with black.

tight (tīt) *adj.* **1.** firmly fixed in place. **2.** stretched so as to be tense. **3.** fitting closely. **4.** firm; rigid. **5.** scarce. **6.** stingy. —**tight/-en,** *v.t., v.i.* —**tight/ness,** *n.*

tight/-fist/ed *adj.* stingy.

tight´-lipped´ *adj.* reluctant to speak.

tight´rope´ *n.* a taut wire or cable on which acrobats perform.

tights *n.pl.* a skintight garment covering the hips, legs, and feet.

tight´wad´ *n.* a stingy person.

til´de (til´də) *n.* a diacritical mark (˜) placed over a letter.

tile (tīl) *n.*, *v.*, **tiled, tiling.** —*n.* **1.** a thin piece of baked clay or linoleum, used for covering roofs, floors, etc. —*v.t.* **2.** to cover with tiles.

till¹ (til) *prep.*, *conj.* until. —**Usage.** TILL and UNTIL are used interchangeably in speech and writing: *It rained till/until nearly midnight.* TILL is not a shortened form of UNTIL and is not spelled ´till. ´TIL is usually considered a spelling error, though commonly used in business and advertising: *open ´til ten.*

till² (til) *v.t.*, *v.i.* to prepare (land) for raising crops. —**till´age,** *n.*

till³ (til) *n.* a drawer in which money is kept in a shop.

till´er *n.* a handle for turning the rudder in steering.

tilt (tilt) *v.t.* **1.** to cause to slope. —*v.i.* **2.** to slope. **3.** to charge with a lance. —*n.* **4.** a slope. **5.** a tournament.

tim´ber (tim´bər) *n.* **1.** wood suitable for building. **2.** trees. **3.** a wooden beam.

tim´ber·line´ *n.* the altitude above sea level at which timber ceases to grow.

tim´ber wolf´ *n.* a large brindled wolf of northern North America.

tim´bre (tam´bər, tim´-) *n.* the characteristic quality of a sound.

time (tīm) *n.*, *v.*, **timed, timing.** —*n.* **1.** the length of all existence, past, present, and future. **2.** a limited or particular period of time. **3.** a definite point in time. **4.** an occasion. **5.** an appointed or proper time. **6.** a system of measuring time. **7.** **times,** an era. **8.** rhythm in music. —*v.t.* **9.** to determine, record, or schedule the time of. —*Idiom.* **10. ahead of time,** early. **11. at the same time,** nevertheless. **12. for the time being,** temporarily. —**tim´er,** *n.*

time´ clock´ *n.* a clock with an attachment that records the times of arrival and departure of employees.

time´-hon´ored *adj.* long valued or used; traditional.

time´keep´er *n.* an official who times, regulates, and records the length of a contest.

time´less *adj.* restricted to no particular time.

time´ line´ *n.* **1.** a linear representation of events in the order in which they occurred. **2.** a schedule.

time´ly *adj.*, **-lier, -liest.** occurring at a suitable time.

time´-out´ *n.* a brief suspension of activity, as in a sports contest.

time´piece´ *n.* a clock or watch.

times *prep.* multiplied by.

time´-shar´ing *n.* **1.** a plan in which several people share the cost of a vacation home. **2.** a system in which users at different terminals simultaneously use a single computer.

time´ta´ble *n.* a schedule of times of arrivals, departures, etc.

time´worn´ *adj.* **1.** showing the effects of long use. **2.** trite.

time´ zone´ *n.* one of 24 divisions of the globe coinciding with meridians at successive hours from the observatory at Greenwich, England.

tim´id (tim´id) *adj.* easily alarmed; shy. —**ti·mid´i·ty,** *n.*

tim´ing (tī´ming) *n.* the control of the time or speed of an action, event, etc., so that it occurs at the proper moment.

tim´or·ous (tim´ər əs) *adj.* fearful or timid. —**tim´or·ous·ly,** *adv.*

tim´pa·ni (tim´pə nē) *n.pl.* a set of kettledrums. —**tim´pa·nist,** *n.*

tin (tin) *n.*, *v.*, **tinned, tinning.** —*n.* **1.** a malleable metallic element. —*v.t.* **2.** to cover with tin.

tinc´ture (tingk´chər) *n.* a medicinal solution in alcohol.

tin´der (tin´dər) *n.* any dry substance that ignites easily.

tin´der·box´ *n.* **1.** a box for tinder. **2.** a potential source of violence.

tine (tīn) *n.* a prong of a fork.

tin´foil´ *n.* tin or a tin and lead alloy in a thin sheet.

tinge (tinj) *v.*, **tinged, tingeing** or **tinging,** *n.* —*v.t.* **1.** to impart a trace of color, taste, etc., to. —*n.* **2.** a slight trace.

tin´gle (ting´gəl) *v.*, **-gled, -gling,** *n.* —*v.i.*, *v.t.* **1.** to feel or cause slight stings. —*n.* **2.** a tingling sensation.

tink´er (ting´kər) *n.* **1.** a mender of pots, kettles, pans, etc. —*v.i.* **2.** to putter. **3.** to work clumsily.

tin´kle (ting´kəl) *v.*, **-kled, -kling,** *n.* —*v.i.*, *v.t.* **1.** to make or cause light ringing sounds. —*n.* **2.** a tinkling sound.

tin´ plate´ *n.* a thin iron or steel sheet coated with tin.

tin´sel (tin´səl) *n.* **1.** thin strips of glittering metal, paper, etc. **2.** anything showy and worthless.

tint (tint) *n.* **1.** a shade of a color.

2. a delicate color. —*v.t.* **3.** to give a tint to.

tin′tin•nab′u•la′tion (-ti nab′yə lā′shən) *n.* the ringing or sound of bells.

ti′ny (tī′nē) *adj.*, **-nier, -niest.** very small.

-tion a suffix meaning action or process; result of action; or state or condition.

tip¹ (tip) *n.*, *v.*, **tipped, tipping.** —*n.* **1.** a slender or pointed end of something. **2.** a small piece covering the end of something. —*v.t.* **3.** to furnish with a tip. **4.** to form or adorn the tip of.

tip² (tip) *v.*, **tipped, tipping,** *n.* —*v.t.*, *v.i.* **1.** to tilt. **2.** to overturn. —*n.* **3.** a tipping or being tipped.

tip³ (tip) *n.*, *v.*, **tipped, tipping.** —*n.* **1.** a gift of money for service provided; gratuity. **2.** a piece of confidential information. **3.** a useful hint. —*v.t.*, *v.i.* **4.** to give a tip (to).

tip′-off′ *n.* a hint or warning.

tip′sy *adj.*, **-sier, -siest.** slightly drunk.

tip′toe′ *n.*, *v.*, **-toed, -toeing.** —*n.* **1.** the tip of the toe. —*v.i.* **2.** to move on tiptoes.

tip′top′ (-top′, -top′) *n.* **1.** the extreme top. —*adj.* **2.** situated at the very top. **3.** of the highest quality.

ti′rade (tī′rād, tī rād′) *n.* a long, angry outburst.

tire¹ (tī°r) *v.t.*, *v.i.*, **tired, tiring.** to make or become exhausted or bored. —**tire′less,** *adj.*

tire² (tī°r) *n.* a ring of rubber, metal, etc., around a wheel.

tired (tī°rd) *adj.* **1.** exhausted; fatigued. **2.** weary. —**tired′ly,** *adv.*

tire′some *adj.* causing annoyance or boredom.

tis′sue (tish′ōō) *n.* **1.** a substance forming the body of an animal or plant. **2.** a soft, absorbent paper. **3.** a light, gauzy fabric.

tis′sue pa′per *n.* very thin paper used for wrapping.

ti′tan (tīt′n) *n.* a person or thing of great size or power. —**ti•tan′ic** (tī-tan′ik) *adj.*

tithe (tīth) *n.*, *v.*, **tithed, tithing.** —*n.* **1.** a tenth part of goods or income, paid to support a church. —*v.t.*, *v.i.* **2.** to give or pay a tithe (of).

ti′tian (tish′ən) *n.* a bright golden brown.

tit′il•late′ (tit′l āt′) *v.t.*, **-lated, -lating.** to excite agreeably.

tit′i•vate′ (-ə vāt′) *v.t.*, *v.i.*, **-vated, -vating.** to make (oneself) smart or spruce.

ti′tle (tīt′l) *n.*, *v.*, **-tled, -tling.** —*n.* **1.** the name of a book, picture, etc.

2. a caption. **3.** a word indicating rank or office. **4.** a championship. **5.** the right to something. **6.** a document showing this. —*v.t.* **7.** to furnish with a title.

tit′mouse′ (tit′mous′) *n.*, *pl.* **-mice.** a small bird with a crest and a conical bill.

tit′ter (tit′ər) *n.* **1.** a giggle. —*v.i.* **2.** to giggle.

tit′tle (tit′l) *n.* a very small thing.

tit′u•lar (tich′ə lər, tit′yə-) *adj.* **1.** being such in title only. **2.** of or having a title.

tiz′zy (tiz′ē) *n.*, *pl.* **-zies.** *Slang.* a nervous, distracted state.

TN Tennessee.

TNT trinitrotoluene.

to (tōō; *unstressed* tŏŏ, tə) *prep.* **1.** as far as. **2.** in the direction of; toward. **3.** to the limit of. **4.** before; until. **5.** as compared with. —*adv.* **6.** toward a closed position. **7.** toward action or work. —*Idiom.* **8. to and fro,** back and forth.

toad (tōd) *n.* a froglike animal living mostly on land.

toad′stool′ *n.* a fungus with an umbrellalike cap.

toad′y *n.*, *pl.* **-ies,** *v.*, **-ied, -ying.** —*n.* **1.** a person who flatters to gain favors. —*v.i.* **2.** to behave in this way.

toast¹ (tōst) *n.* **1.** sliced bread browned by dry heat. —*v.t.* **2.** to brown (bread, cheese, etc.) by heat. —*v.i.* **3.** to become toasted.

toast² (tōst) *n.* **1.** words of welcome or congratulations said before drinking to a person or event. —*v.t.*, *v.i.* **2.** to propose or drink a toast (to).

toast′er *n.* an appliance for toasting bread.

toast′mas′ter *n.* a person who introduces after-dinner speakers or proposes toasts.

to•bac′co (tə bak′ō) *n.*, *pl.* **-cos, -coes. 1.** a plant with leaves prepared for smoking or chewing. **2.** a product made from such leaves.

to•bog′gan (tə bog′ən) *n.* **1.** a long, narrow, flat-bottomed sled. —*v.i.* **2.** to coast on a toboggan.

to•day′ (tə dā′) *n.* **1.** this day, time, or period. —*adv.* **2.** on this day. **3.** at the present time.

tod′dle (tod′l) *v.i.*, **-dled, -dling.** to move with short, unsteady steps, like a young child. —**tod′dler,** *n.*

tod′dy (tod′ē) *n.*, *pl.* **-dies.** a drink made of liquor, hot water, and sugar.

to-do′ *n.*, *pl.* **to-dos.** a fuss.

toe (tō) *n.* **1.** one of the five parts on the front of the foot. **2.** the part of a shoe or sock covering the toes. —**toe′nail′**, n.

toe′hold′ n. **1.** a small niche that supports the toes. **2.** any slight advantage.

tof′fee (tô′fē) n. a candy made of brown sugar, butter, and vinegar.

to′fu (tō′fōō) n. a soft cheeselike food made from soybean milk.

to′ga (tō′gə) n. (in ancient Rome) a man's formal outer garment.

to·geth′er (tə geth′ər) adv. **1.** into or in one gathering, association, or single mass. **2.** at the same time. **3.** in cooperation.

to·geth′er·ness n. warm fellowship.

togs n.pl. Informal. clothes.

toil (toil) n. **1.** hard, exhausting work. —v.i. **2.** to work hard.

toi′let (toi′lit) n. **1.** a bathroom fixture for urination and defecation. **2.** a bathroom; lavatory. **3.** Also, **toi·lette′.** the act or process of dressing or grooming oneself.

toi′let·ry n., pl. **-ries.** an article or preparation used in grooming.

toi′let wa′ter n. a scented liquid used as a light perfume.

to′ken (tō′kən) n. **1.** something expressing or representing a feeling, fact, etc.; sign or symbol. **2.** a metal disk used in place of money. —adj. **3.** being merely a token.

to′ken·ism n. making a minimal effort to conform to a law or social pressure.

tol′er·a·ble (tol′ər ə bəl) adj. **1.** capable of being tolerated. **2.** fairly good.

tol′er·ance (-əns) n. **1.** fairness toward those whose race, religion, etc., differ from one's own. **2.** the capacity to endure something. —**tol′er·ant,** adj.

tol′er·ate′ (-ə rāt′) v.t., **-ated, -ating. 1.** to allow; permit. **2.** to put up with. —**tol′er·a′tion,** n.

toll¹ (tōl) n. **1.** a payment, as for driving on a highway or crossing a bridge. **2.** a payment for a long-distance telephone call.

toll² (tōl) v.t. **1.** to ring (a bell) with slow, repeated strokes. —v.i. **2.** (of a bell) to ring slowly.

toll′booth′ n. a booth where a toll is collected.

tom (tom) n. the male of various animals.

tom′a·hawk′ (tom′ə hôk′) n. a light ax used by North American Indians.

to·ma′to (tə mā′tō) n., pl. **-toes.** a pulpy, juicy red fruit used as a vegetable.

tomb (tōōm) n. a burial chamber for a dead body; grave.

tom′boy′ (tom′-) n. an energetic, boisterous girl whose behavior is considered boyish.

tomb′stone′ n. a stone marker on a grave.

tom′cat′ n. a male cat.

tome (tōm) n. a large, heavy book.

tom′fool′er·y (tom′fōō′lə rē) n. foolish or silly behavior.

to·mor′row (tə môr′ō) n. **1.** the day after today. —adv. **2.** on the day after today.

tom′-tom′ n. a primitive drum played with the hands.

ton (tun) n. a unit of weight, equal to 2000 pounds (**short ton**) in the U.S. and 2240 pounds (**long ton**) in Great Britain.

to·nal′i·ty (tō nal′i tē) n., pl. **-ties.** the sum of relations between the tones of a musical scale.

tone (tōn) n., v., **toned, toning.** —n. **1.** any sound with reference to its quality, pitch, etc. **2.** quality of sound. **3.** a vocal sound. **4.** a particular style or manner. **5.** firmness. **6.** elegance. —v.t. **7.** to give a certain tone to. —**ton′al,** adj.

tone′-deaf′ adj. unable to distinguish differences in musical pitch.

tongs (tôngz) n.pl. a two-armed implement for picking up an object.

tongue (tung) n. **1.** an organ in the mouth, used for tasting, eating, and speaking. **2.** a language. **3.** anything resembling a tongue.

tongue′-lash′ing n. a severe scolding.

tongue′-tied′ adj. unable to speak, as from shyness.

tongue′ twist′er n. a sequence of words that is difficult to pronounce rapidly.

ton′ic (ton′ik) n. **1.** an invigorating medicine. —adj. **2.** invigorating.

to·night′ (tə nīt′) n. **1.** this night. —adv. **2.** on this night.

ton′nage (tun′ij) n. **1.** the carrying capacity or total volume of a ship. **2.** ships collectively.

ton′sil (ton′səl) n. an oval mass of lymphoid tissue in the throat.

ton′sil·lec′to·my (-sə lek′tə mē) n., pl. **-mies.** the surgical removal of the tonsils.

ton′sil·li′tis (-lī′tis) n. inflammation of the tonsils.

ton·so′ri·al (-sôr′ē əl) adj. of barbers.

ton′sure (-shər) n. the shaved part of the head of a monk.

too (tōō) adv. **1.** in addition. **2.** excessively; extremely.

tool (tōōl) n. **1.** a hand implement, as a hammer or saw. **2.** the working part of a machine. **3.** anything used for accomplishing a purpose.

4. a person exploited by another; dupe. —*v.t.* **5.** to shape, work, or decorate with a tool.

toot (tōōt) *v.i., v.t.* to sound (a horn or whistle) in quick blasts.

tooth (tōōth) *n., pl.* **teeth** (tēth). **1.** one of the hard white structures attached to the jaw, used for biting and chewing. **2.** a toothlike projection, as on a comb or saw. —**tooth′ache′** *n.*

tooth′ and nail′ *adv.* with all one's resources and energy.

tooth′paste′ *n.* a paste for cleaning the teeth.

tooth′pick′ *n.* a small pointed stick for removing bits of food from between the teeth.

tooth′some (-səm) *adj.* tasty.

tooth′y (tōō′thē, -thē) *adj.,* **-ier, -iest.** having or displaying conspicuous teeth.

top[1] (top) *n., v.,* **topped, topping.** —*n.* **1.** the highest or uppermost point, surface, rank, etc. **2.** a lid. **3.** a garment for the upper part of the body. —*adj.* **4.** highest. —*v.t.* **5.** to put a top on. **6.** to reach or be at the top of. **7.** to outdo.

top[2] (top) *n.* a child's spinning toy.

to′paz (tō′paz) *n.* a yellowish or brownish crystalline gem.

top′ brass′ *n.* high-ranking officials.

top′coat′ *n.* a light overcoat.

top′flight′ (top′-) *adj.* excellent.

top′ hat′ *n.* a man's tall silk hat.

top′-heav′y *adj.* heavier at the top than at the bottom.

top′ic (top′ik) *n.* a subject of discussion or writing.

top′i·cal *adj.* of or dealing with matters of current interest.

top′mast′ *n.* the mast next above a lower mast on a sailing ship.

top′most *adj.* highest.

top′-notch′ *adj.* first-rate.

to·pog′ra·phy (tə pog′rə fē) *n.* **1.** the surface features of an area. **2.** the detailed mapping of such features.

top′ping *n.* a sauce or garnish placed on food.

top′ple *v.i., v.t.,* **-pled, -pling.** to fall or cause to fall over.

top′-se′cret *adj.* extremely secret.

top′soil′ *n.* fertile upper soil.

top′sy-tur′vy (top′sē tûr′vē) *adv., adj.* **1.** upside down. **2.** in confusion.

tor (tôr) *n.* a hill.

To′rah (tôr′ə, tôr′ə) *n. (sometimes l.c.)* **1.** the five books of Moses. **2.** the whole Jewish scripture, law, and teaching.

torch (tôrch) *n.* a burning stick used for light.

torch′bear′er *n.* **1.** a person who carries a torch. **2.** a leader in a movement.

tor′e·a·dor′ (tôr′ē ə dôr′) *n.* a bullfighter.

tor·ment′ *v.t.* (tôr ment′) **1.** to cause great suffering to. —*n.* (tôr′-ment) **2.** great suffering or its cause. —**tor·men′tor,** *n.*

tor·na′do (tôr nā′dō) *n., pl.* **-does, -dos.** a violent windstorm with a funnel-shaped cloud.

tor·pe′do (tôr pē′dō) *n., pl.* **-does,** *v.,* **-doed, -doing.** —*n.* **1.** a selfpropelled missile launched in water and exploding on impact. —*v.t.* **2.** to strike with a torpedo.

tor′pid (tôr′pid) *adj.* **1.** inactive. **2.** dull or lethargic.

tor′por (-pər) *n.* **1.** inactivity. **2.** indifference; apathy.

torque (tôrk) *n.* a force producing rotation.

tor′rent (tôr′ənt) *n.* a rapid, violent stream. —**tor·ren′tial** (tô ren′shəl, tə-) *adj.*

tor′rid (-id) *adj.* **1.** very hot. **2.** passionate.

tor′sion (shən) *n.* **1.** a twisting or being twisted. **2.** the twisting of an object by two equal opposing torques.

tor′so (tôr′sō) *n., pl.* **-sos, -si.** the trunk of the body.

tort (tôrt) *n. Law.* a civil wrong (other than breach of contract or trust) for which the law requires that damages be paid.

torte (tôrt) *n., pl.* **tortes.** a rich cake.

tor′tel·li·ni (tôr′tl ē′nē) *n. (used with a sing. or pl. v.)* small ring-shaped pieces of pasta filled with meat, cheese, or vegetables.

tor·til′la (tôr tē′ə) *n.* a flat, round Mexican bread, made from cornmeal or wheat flour.

tor′toise (tôr′təs) *n.* a turtle, esp. one living on land.

tor′toise·shell′ *n.* **1.** the horny brown and yellow shell of certain turtles, used for combs and ornaments. **2.** synthetic tortoiseshell.

tor′tu·ous (tôr′chōō əs) *adj.* **1.** twisting. **2.** indirect; devious.

tor′ture (tôr′chər) *n., v.,* **-tured, -turing.** —*n.* **1.** extreme pain. **2.** the infliction of great pain, esp. for punishment or coercion. —*v.t.* **3.** to subject to torture.

tor′tur·ous *adj.* involving or causing torture or suffering.

toss (tôs) *v.t.* **1.** to throw lightly. **2.** to fling about. **3.** to jerk upward. —*v.i.* **4.** to move irregularly or restlessly. —*n.* **5.** a throw or pitch.

toss′up′ *n.* **1.** the tossing of a coin

to decide something. **2.** an even chance.

tot (tot) *n.* a small child.

to'tal (tōt'l) *adj., n., v.,* **-taled, -tal-ing.** —*adj.* **1.** entire. **2.** complete. —*n.* **3.** the total amount. —*v.t.* **4.** to add together. **5.** to add up to. **6.** to damage beyond repair. —*v.i.* **7.** to amount. —**to•tal'i•ty** (-tal'i-tē) *n.* —**to'tal•ly,** *adv.*

to•tal'i•tar'i•an (tō tal'i târ'ē ən) *adj.* of a government in which one party has dictatorial control. —**to•tal'i•tar'i•an•ism,** *n.*

tote (tōt) *v.,* **toted, toting,** *n.* —*v.t.* **1.** to carry. —*n.* **2.** an open hand-bag or shopping bag; tote bag.

tote' bag' *n.* a large open hand-bag.

to'tem (tō'təm) *n.* an object in nature assumed as the emblem of a clan, family, or related group.

to'tem pole' *n.* a pole with carved and painted figures, erected by Indians of the NW coast of North America.

tot'ter (tot'ər) *v.i.* **1.** to walk unsteadily. **2.** to sway as if about to fall.

tou'can (tōo'kan, -kän) *n.* a brightly colored tropical American bird with a large bill.

touch (tuch) *v.t.* **1.** to put the hand, finger, etc., into contact with. **2.** to bring or come into contact with. **3.** to reach. **4.** to affect with tenderness or sympathy. —*v.i.* **5.** to touch someone or something. **6.** to come into or be in contact. —*n.* **7.** a touching or being touched. **8.** the sense by which a thing is perceived by physical contact. **9.** ability. **10.** a slight trace.

touch' and go' *n.* an uncertain state of affairs.

touch'down' *n.* **1.** the act of scoring in football by touching the ball to the ground behind the opponent's goal line. **2.** the act of landing, as of an airplane.

tou•ché' (tōo shā') *interj.* (used to acknowledge a touch in fencing or a telling remark or rejoinder).

touch'stone' *n.* a test for the qualities of a thing.

touch'y *adj.,* **-ier, -iest.** easily offended. —**touch'i•ness,** *n.*

tough (tuf) *adj.* **1.** not easily broken, cut, or chewed. **2.** sturdy. **3.** unyielding. **4.** difficult. **5.** unruly or rough. —*n.* **6.** a brutal, lawless person. —**tough'en,** *v.t., v.i.*

tou•pee' (tōo pā') *n.* a patch of false hair worn to cover a bald spot.

tour (tōor) *n.* **1.** a long journey, visiting places of interest or giving performances. **2.** a period of duty in one place. —*v.i., v.t.* **3.** to go on a tour (through).

tour'de force' (tōor' də fôrs') *n., pl.* **tours de force.** an exceptional achievement.

tour'ism *n.* **1.** the occupation of providing various services to tourists. **2.** the promotion of tourist travel.

tour'ist *n.* a person who makes a tour, as for sightseeing.

tour'na•ment (tōor'nə mənt, tûr'-) *n.* **1.** a contest involving a series of matches between competitors. **2.** a medieval contest between knights on horseback.

tour'ni•quet (tûr'ni kit, tōor'-) *n.* a bandlike device for stopping bleeding.

tou'sle (tou'zəl, -səl) *v.t.,* **-sled, -sling.** to disorder or dishevel, as hair.

tout (tout) *Informal.* —*v.i.* **1.** to solicit business, votes, etc., in a persistent and annoying way. —*v.t.* **2.** to solicit in a persistent and annoying way. **3.** to praise highly.

tow (tō) *v.t.* **1.** to pull or haul (a car, barge, etc.) by rope or chain. —*n.* **2.** an act of towing. **3.** something towed.

to•ward' (tôrd, twôrd) *prep.* Also, **to•wards'.** **1.** in the direction of. **2.** with respect to. **3.** shortly before.

tow'el (tou'əl, toul) *n.* an absorbent cloth or paper for wiping.

tow'er (tou'ər) *n.* **1.** a tall structure, either standing alone or forming part of another building. —*v.i.* **2.** to stand high.

tow'er•ing *adj.* **1.** very high or tall. **2.** extreme or intense.

tow'head' (tō'hed') *n.* a person with very light-colored hair.

town (toun) *n.* **1.** a small city. **2.** the central business area of a city. **3.** the people who live in a town. —**towns'man,** *n.* —**towns'wom'an,** *n.fem.* —**towns'peo'ple, towns'folk',** *n.pl.*

town' house' *n.* one of a group of similar houses joined by common side walls.

town' meet'ing *n.* a meeting of the voters of a town.

town'ship *n.* a division of a county.

tow'path' (tō'path') *n.* a path along the bank of a canal or river, for use in towing boats.

tox•e•mi•a (tok sē'mē ə) *n.* blood poisoning resulting from the presence of toxins in the blood. —**tox•e'mic,** *adj.*

tox′ic (tok′sik) *adj.* **1.** of or caused by a toxin. **2.** poisonous. —**tox·ic′·i·ty,** *n.*

tox′i·col′o·gy (-si kol′ə jē) *n.* the study of poisons.

tox′ic shock′ syn′drome *n.* a rapidly developing toxemia.

tox′in (tok′sin) *n.* a poison produced by an animal, plant, or bacterium.

toy (toi) *n.* **1.** a thing to play with. —*v.* **2. toy with,** to play or trifle with.

trace (trās) *n., v.,* **traced, tracing.** —*n.* **1.** a mark or sign left by something. **2.** a very small amount. —*v.t.* **3.** to follow the course of. **4.** to find out by investigating. **5.** to copy (a drawing) by following its lines on a transparent sheet placed over it.

trac′er·y *n., pl.* **-eries.** an ornamental pattern of interlacing lines.

tra′che·a (trā′kē ə) *n., pl.* **-cheae** (-kē ē′). the windpipe.

tra′che·ot′o·my (-ot′ə mē) *n., pl.* **-mies.** the operation of cutting into the trachea to help a person breathe.

track (trak) *n.* **1.** a pair of parallel rails on which a train runs. **2.** marks left by an animal, person, or vehicle. **3.** a path. **4.** a course for running. **5.** a band of recorded sound, as on a compact disc. —*v.t.* **6.** to follow; pursue.

track′ball′ *n.* a computer input device for controlling the pointer on a screen by rotating a ball set inside a case.

track′ rec′ord *n.* a record of achievements or performance.

tract[1] (trakt) *n.* **1.** an area of land. **2.** a specific area of the body.

tract[2] (trakt) *n.* a brief pamphlet, esp. on religion or politics.

trac′ta·ble (trak′tə bəl) *adj.* easily managed or controlled.

trac′tion (-shən) *n.* **1.** the adhesive friction of a body on a surface. **2.** a pulling or being pulled.

trac′tor (-tər) *n.* a powerful vehicle for pulling farm machinery.

trade (trād) *n., v.,* **traded, trading.** —*n.* **1.** the buying, selling, or exchange of goods; commerce. **2.** an exchange. **3.** an occupation. —*v.t.* **4.** to buy and sell. **5.** to exchange. —*v.i.* **6.** to carry on trade. **7.** to make an exchange. —**trad′er,** *n.* —**trades′man,** *n.*

trade′-in′ *n.* goods given in whole or part payment for a purchase.

trade′mark′ *n.* any registered name, symbol, etc., used by a manufacturer to identify its goods.

trade′ name′ *n.* a word or phrase by which a particular class of goods is designated.

trade′-off′ *n.* the exchange of one thing for another.

trade′ un′ion *n.* a labor union.

trade′ wind′ (wind) *n.* any sea wind blowing from the northeast in the Northern Hemisphere and from the southeast in the Southern Hemisphere.

tra·di′tion (trə dish′ən) *n.* **1.** the handing down of beliefs, customs, etc., through generations. **2.** something so handed down. —**tra·di′tion·al,** *adj.* —**tra·di′tion·al·ist,** *n.*

tra·duce′ (trə dōōs′, -dyōōs′) *v.t.,* **-duced, -ducing.** to slander.

traf′fic (traf′ik) *n., v.,* **-ficked, -ficking.** —*n.* **1.** vehicles, persons, etc., moving over a route. **2.** trade. —*v.i.* **3.** to trade.

traf′fic cir′cle *n.* a circular roadway at a multiple intersection.

traf′fic light′ *n.* a set of signal lights at an intersection.

tra·ge′di·an (trə jē′dē ən) *n.* an actor in or writer of tragedy.

trag′e·dy (traj′i dē) *n., pl.* **-dies. 1.** a serious drama with an unhappy ending. **2.** a sad event. —**trag′ic,** *adj.*

trail (trāl) *n.* **1.** a path, as in a forest. **2.** the track, scent, etc., left by an animal or person. —*v.t.* **3.** to draw or drag along behind. **4.** to follow the track of. **5.** to follow behind, as in a race. —*v.i.* **6.** to drag, esp. along the ground. **7.** to lag behind. **8. trail off,** to gradually become weaker.

trail′blaz′er *n.* a pioneer.

trail′er *n.* **1.** a vehicle drawn by a truck for hauling freight. **2.** a vehicle with accommodations for living, attached to a car.

train *n.* **1.** connected railroad cars pulled by a locomotive. **2.** a moving line of persons, vehicles, etc. **3.** part of a long skirt that trails behind. **4.** a series of events, ideas, etc. —*v.t.* **5.** to form the behavior of by discipline and instruction. **6.** to make fit. **7.** to aim, as a gun. —*v.i.* **8.** to become trained. —**train·ee′,** *n.* —**train′er,** *n.*

traipse (trāps) *v.i.,* **traipsed, traipsing.** to walk aimlessly.

trait (trāt) *n.* a characteristic.

trai′tor (trā′tər) *n.* a person who betrays another or any trust. —**trai′tor·ous,** *adj.*

tra·jec′to·ry (trə jek′tə rē) *n., pl.* **-ries.** the curve described by a projectile in flight.

tram (tram) *n. Brit.* a streetcar.

tram′mel (tram′əl) *n., v.,* **-meled, -meling.** —*n.* **1.** something that

tramp

382

hinders action; restraint. —*v.t.* **2.** to hinder or restrain.

tramp (tramp) *v.i.* **1.** to walk with a firm, heavy step. **2.** to hike. —*n.* **3.** a vagrant; vagabond. **4.** a firm, heavy tread or the sound of this. **5.** a hike.

tram′ple *v.t., v.i.,* **-pled, -pling.** to step roughly (on).

tram′po•line′ (tram′pə lēn′, -lin) *n.* a canvas sheet attached by springs to a frame, used for tumbling.

trance (trans) *n.* a half-conscious or hypnotic state.

tran′quil (trang′kwil) *adj.* peaceful; calm. —**tran•quil′li•ty,** *n.* —**tran′quil•ize′,** *v.t., v.i.*

tran′quil•iz′er (-kwi lī′zər) *n.* a drug that has a calming effect.

trans- a prefix meaning across, through, or on the other side; changing thoroughly; beyond or surpassing.

trans•act′ (tran sakt′, -zakt′) *v.t.* to carry on (business, negotiations, etc.). —**trans•ac′tion,** *n.*

trans′at•lan′tic (trans′ət lan′tik, tranz′-) *adj.* **1.** crossing the Atlantic. **2.** on the other side of the Atlantic.

trans•ceiv′er (tran sē′vər) *n.* a radio transmitter and receiver combined.

tran•scend′ (tran send′) *v.t.* **1.** to go beyond the ordinary limits of. **2.** to surpass; exceed. —**tran•scend′ent** *adj.*

tran′scen•den′tal (tran′sen den′tl, -sən-) *adj.* beyond ordinary human experience.

trans′con•ti•nen′tal (trans′kon tn-en′tl) *adj.* **1.** extending across a continent. **2.** on the other side of a continent.

tran•scribe′ (tran skrīb′) *v.t.,* **-scribed, -scribing. 1.** to make a written or typed copy of (spoken material). **2.** to arrange (music) for a different instrument. —**tran′script,** *n.* —**tran•scrip′tion** (-skrip′shən) *n.*

trans•duc′er (trans dōō′sər, -dyōō′-, tranz-) *n.* a device, as a microphone, that converts a signal from one form of energy to another.

tran′sept (tran′sept) *n.* the part of a church crossing the nave at right angles.

trans•fer′ *v.,* **-ferred, -ferring,** *n.* —*v.t.* (trans fûr′, trans′fər) **1.** to convey or hand over. —*v.i.* **2.** to transfer oneself or be transferred. **3.** to change from one bus, train, etc., to another. —*n.* (trans′fər) **4.** the means or act of transferring. —**trans•fer′a•ble,** *adj.* —**trans•fer′al,** *n.* —**trans•fer′ence,** *n.*

trans•fig′ure *v.t.,* **-ured, -uring. 1.** to transform. **2.** to change in appearance to something more beautiful or glorious. —**trans′fig•u•ra′tion,** *n.*

trans•fix′ *v.t.* **1.** to make motionless, as with awe. **2.** to pierce.

trans•form′ *v.t.* to change in form, appearance, condition, nature, etc. —**trans•for•ma′tion,** *n.*

trans•form′er *n.* a device for converting electrical currents.

trans•fuse′ (-fyōōz′) *v.t.,* **-fused, -fusing. 1.** to transfer (blood) by injecting into a blood vessel. **2.** to diffuse into or through. —**trans•fu′sion,** *n.*

trans•gen′dered (trans jen′dərd, tranz-) *adj.* **1.** appearing or attempting to be a member of the opposite sex, as a transsexual. **2.** pertaining to transgendered people.

trans•gress′ (trans gres′, tranz-) *v.i.* **1.** to violate a law, moral code, etc. —*v.t.* **2.** to go beyond (a limit). —**trans•gres′sion** (-gresh′ən) *n.* —**trans•gres′sor,** *n.*

tran′sient (tran′shənt, -zhənt, -zē-ənt) *adj.* lasting or staying only a short time.

tran•sis′tor (-zis′tər) *n.* a small electronic device that controls the flow of an electric current.

trans′it (-sit, -zit) *n.* the act or fact of passing across, over, or through.

tran•si′tion (-zish′ən, -sish′-) *n.* passage from one position, condition, etc., to another. —**tran•si′tion•al,** *adj.*

tran′si•tive (-si tiv, -zi-) *adj.* (of a verb) taking a direct object.

tran′si•to′ry (-si tôr′ē, -zi-) *adj.* lasting only a short time.

trans•late′ (trans lāt′, tranz-, trans′-lāt, tranz′-) *v.t.,* **-lated, -lating. 1.** to turn from one language into another. **2.** to change the form or condition of. —**trans•la′tion,** *n.* —**trans•lat′a•ble,** *adj.* —**trans•lat′or,** *n.*

trans•lit′er•ate′ (-lit′ə rāt′) *v.t.,* **-ated, -ating.** to change (letters or words) into the corresponding characters of another alphabet.

trans•lu′cent (-lōō′sənt) *adj.* not transparent but allowing light to pass through.

trans•mi•gra′tion *n.* the passage of a soul into another body.

trans•mis′sion (-mish′ən) *n.* **1.** the act or process of transmitting. **2.** something transmitted. **3.** a set of gears to transfer force between mechanisms, as in an automobile. **4.** a broadcast.

trans•mit′ (-mit′) *v.t.,* **-mitted, -mitting. 1.** to send from one person or place to another. **2.** to pass on by heredity. **3.** to cause (light, heat, etc.,) to pass through a medium. **4.** to emit (radio or television signals). —**trans•mit′ter,** *n.*

trans•mog′ri•fy′ (-mog′rə fī′) *v.t.,* -**fied, -fying.** to change in appearance or form; transform.

trans•mute′ (-myōōt′) *v.t., v.i.,* -**muted, -muting.** to change from one nature or form into another. —**trans•mut′a•ble,** *adj.* —**trans•mu•ta′tion,** *n.*

tran′som (tran′səm) *n.* **1.** a crosspiece separating a door or window from a window above it. **2.** a window above such a crosspiece.

trans′pa•cif′ic (trans′-) *adj.* **1.** crossing the Pacific. **2.** on the other side of the Pacific.

trans•par′ent (-pâr′ənt) *adj.* **1.** able to be seen clearly through. **2.** easily understood; obvious. —**trans•par′en•cy,** *n.*

tran•spire′ (tran spī°r′) *v.i.,* -**spired, -spiring. 1.** to occur. **2.** to give off waste matter, watery vapor, etc., through the surface.

trans•plant′ *v.t.* (trans plant′) **1.** to remove and put or plant in another place. —*n.* (trans′plant′) **2.** the act of transplanting. **3.** something transplanted. —**trans′plan•ta′tion,** *n.*

trans•port′ *v.t.* (trans pôrt′) **1.** to convey from one place to another. **2.** to carry away by strong emotion. —*n.* (trans′pōrt) **3.** the act of transporting. **4.** something that transports. —**trans•port′er,** *n.*

trans•pose′ (-pōz′) *v.t.,* -**posed, -posing. 1.** to reverse the position or order of. **2.** to put (a musical composition) into a different key. —**trans′po•si′tion,** *n.*

trans•sex′u•al *n.* **1.** a person feeling an identity with the opposite sex. **2.** a person whose sex has been surgically altered.

trans′sub•stan′ti•a′tion *n.* (in the Eucharist) the conversion of the whole substance of bread and wine into the body and blood of Christ.

trans•verse′ (trans vûrs′, tranz-; trans′vûrs, tranz′-) *adj.* **1.** lying or reaching across. —*n.* **2.** something transverse. —**trans•verse′ly,** *adv.*

trans•ves′tite (trans ves′tīt, tranz-) *n.* a person who dresses in clothing of the opposite sex.

trap (trap) *n., v.,* **trapped, trapping.** —*n.* **1.** a device for catching animals. **2.** a scheme for catching a person unawares. **3.** a U-shaped section in a pipe to prevent the escape of air or gases. —*v.t.* **4.** to catch in a trap. —*v.i.* **5.** to trap animals for their fur.

tra•peze′ (tra pēz′, trə-) *n.* a suspended bar used in acrobatics.

trap′e•zoid′ (trap′ə zoid′) *n.* a four-sided figure with two parallel sides.

trap′pings *n.pl.* **1.** ornamental articles of equipment or dress. **2.** conventional outward forms.

trash (trash) *n.* **1.** anything worthless. —*v.t.* **2.** to vandalize.

trau′ma (trou′mə, trô′-) *n., pl.* -**mata, -mas. 1.** a bodily injury. **2.** an experience causing lasting psychological harm. —**trau•mat′ic** (trə -mat′ik) *adj.*

tra•vail′ (trə vāl′, trav′āl) *n.* painfully difficult work.

trav′el (trav′əl) *v.,* -**eled, -eling,** *n.* —*v.i.* **1.** to go from one place to another. **2.** to pass or be transmitted. —*n.* **3.** the act of traveling, esp. to faraway places. —**trav′el•er,** *n.*

trav′erse *v.,* -**ersed, -ersing,** *n.* —*v.t.* (trə vûrs′, trav′ərs) **1.** to pass over, through, or along. —*n.* (trav′ərs, trə vûrs′) **2.** something that crosses.

trav′es•ty (trav′ə stē) *n., pl.* -**ties,** *v.,* -**tied, -tying.** —*n.* **1.** a grotesque imitation. —*v.t.* **2.** to make a travesty of.

trawl (trôl) *n.* **1.** a fishing net dragged along the sea bottom. —*v.i., v.t.* **2.** to fish with a trawl. —**trawl′er,** *n.*

tray (trā) *n.* a flat, shallow receptacle with raised edges.

treach′er•y (trech′ə rē) *n.* betrayal of trust. —**treach′er•ous,** *adj.*

tread (tred) *v.,* **trod** (trod), **trodden** or **trod, treading,** *n.* —*v.i.* **1.** to step or walk. **2.** to walk on, in, or along. —*v.t.* **2.** to trample underfoot. —*n.* **4.** the act, sound, or manner of walking. **5.** something on which one walks or stands. **6.** the raised pattern on a rubber tire.

trea′dle (tred′l) *n.* a lever worked by the foot to drive a machine.

tread′mill′ *n.* a device worked by treading on moving steps or an endless moving belt.

trea′son (trē′zən) *n.* a violation of allegiance to one's sovereign or state.

treas′ure (trezh′ər) *n., v.,* -**ured, -uring.** —*n.* **1.** accumulated wealth. **2.** anything greatly valued. —*v.t.* **3.** to prize. **4.** to put away for future use.

treas′ure-trove′ (-trōv′) *n.* **1.** anything valuable that one finds. **2.** treasure of unknown ownership, found hidden.

treas′ur•y *n., pl.* -**uries. 1.** a place for keeping public or private funds. **2.** funds. **3. Treasury,** the government department that handles funds. —**treas′ur•er,** *n.*

treat (trēt) *v.t.* **1.** to act, behave toward, or regard in a certain way. **2.** to buy food, gifts, etc., for. **3.** to give medical care to. **4.** to subject to some agent or action. **5.** to deal with in speech, writing, etc. —*n.* **6.** entertainment, food, etc., paid for by someone else. **7.** something special and enjoyable.

trea′tise (trē′tis) *n.* formal writing on a particular subject.

trea′ty (trē′tē) *n., pl.* **-ties.** a formal agreement between nations.

tre′ble (treb′əl) *adj., n., v.,* **-bled, -bling.** —*adj.* **1.** triple. **2.** of the highest musical pitch or range. —*n.* **3.** the treble part, voice, or instrument. —*v.t., v.i.* **4.** to triple.

tree (trē) *n., v.,* **treed, treeing.** —*n.* **1.** a large plant with a woody trunk and branches. **2.** something shaped like this. —*v.t.* **3.** to drive up a tree, as one pursued.

tre′foil (trē′foil, tref′oil) *n.* **1.** a plant having leaves with three leaflets. **2.** something shaped like this.

trek (trek) *n., v.,* **trekked, trekking.** —*n.* **1.** a slow and difficult journey. —*v.i.* **2.** to make a trek.

trel′lis (trel′is) *n.* a lattice supporting vines.

trem′ble (trem′bəl) *v.,* **-bled, -bling,** *n.* —*v.i.* **1.** to quiver; shake. **2.** to be afraid. —*n.* **3.** the act or state of trembling.

tre•men′dous (tri men′dəs) *adj.* extraordinarily great.

trem′o•lo (trem′ə lō′) *n., pl.* **-los.** a vibrating effect produced on an instrument or in the voice.

trem′or (trem′ər, trē′mər) *n.* **1.** involuntary shaking. **2.** any vibration.

trem′u•lous (trem′yə ləs) *adj.* **1.** trembling. **2.** fearful.

trench (trench) *n.* **1.** a long, narrow ditch dug by soldiers for defense. **2.** a deep furrow or ditch.

trench′ant (tren′chənt) *adj.* **1.** incisive; keen. **2.** vigorous.

trench′ coat′ *n.* a belted, double-breasted raincoat with epaulets.

trench′ foot′ *n.* a disease of the feet caused by prolonged exposure to cold and wet.

trench′ mouth′ *n.* an ulcerating infection of the gums and teeth.

trend (trend) *n.* **1.** the general tendency. **2.** style.

trend′y *adj.,* **-ier, -iest.** following the latest fad.

trep′i•da′tion (trep′i dā′shən) *n.* fearful anxiety.

tres′pass (tres′pəs, -pas) *v.i.* **1.** to enter property or land unlawfully.

2. to commit an offense. —*n.* **3.** the act of trespassing.

tress (tres) *n.* Usu., **tresses.** long locks of hair.

tres′tle (tres′əl) *n.* a supporting frame composed of a bar on two pairs of spreading legs.

tri- a prefix meaning three.

tri′ad (trī′ad, -əd) *n.* a group of three.

tri•age′ (trē äzh′) *n.* the process of sorting victims to determine priority of medical treatment.

tri′al (trī′əl) *n.* **1.** the hearing and deciding of a case in a court of law. **2.** a test. **3.** an attempt. **4.** something annoying. **5.** a source of suffering.

tri′an′gle (trī′ang′gəl) *n.* a figure with three straight sides and three angles. —**tri•an′gu•lar,** *adj.*

tribe (trīb) *n.* a group of people united by common descent and sharing common customs. —**trib′al,** *adj.* —**tribes′man,** *n.*

trib′u•la′tion (trib′yə lā′shən) *n.* severe trial or suffering or an instance of this.

tri•bu′nal (trī byōōn′l, tri-) *n.* **1.** a court of justice. **2.** a place of judgment.

trib′une (trib′yōōn, tri byōōn′) *n.* a person who defends the rights of the people.

trib′u•tar′y (-yə ter′ē) *n., pl.* **-taries,** *adj.* —*n.* **1.** a stream flowing into a larger body of water. —*adj.* **2.** flowing into a larger body of water.

trib′ute (-yōot) *n.* **1.** a speech or gift expressing gratitude or respect. **2.** (formerly) a tax paid by one state to acknowledge subjugation to another.

trice (trīs) *n.* an instant.

tri′cen•ten′ni•al (trī′sen ten′ē əl) *n.* a tercentennial.

tri′ceps (trī′seps) *n.* the muscle at the back of the upper arm.

trick (trik) *n.* **1.** something intended to deceive or cheat. **2.** a practical joke. **3.** a knack. **4.** the set of cards played and won in one round. —*v.t.* **5.** to deceive or cheat. —**trick′er•y,** *n.* —**trick′ster,** *n.* —**trick′y,** *adj.*

trick′le (trik′əl) *v.,* **-led, -ling,** *n.* —*v.i.* **1.** to flow in a small, gentle stream. **2.** to move slowly. —*n.* **3.** a trickling flow.

tri′col′or (trī′kul′ər) *adj.* **1.** of three colors. —*n.* **2.** a three-colored flag, esp. that of France.

tri•cus′pid *adj.* having three cusps or points, as a tooth.

tri′cy•cle (trī′si kəl, -sik′əl) *n.* a child's vehicle with one large front wheel and two smaller rear wheels.

tri•dent (trīd′nt) *n.* a three-pronged spear.

tried (trīd) *adj.* tested; proved.

tri•en•ni•al (trī en′ē əl) *adj.* **1.** lasting three years. **2.** occurring every three years. —*n.* **3.** a period of three years. **4.** a third anniversary.

tri′fle (trī′fəl) *n., v.,* **-fled, -fling.** —*n.* **1.** an article of small value. **2.** a trivial matter or amount. —*v.* **3. trifle with,** to deal lightly with; play or toy with. —**tri′fling,** *adj.*

trig′ger (trig′ər) *n.* **1.** a projecting tongue pressed to fire a gun. **2.** a device pressed to release a spring. —*v.t.* **3.** to cause (a reaction, process, etc.).

tri′go•nom′e•try (trig′ə nom′i trē) *n.* the mathematical study of the relations between the sides and angles of triangles.

trill (tril) *n.* **1.** a rapid alternation of two nearby musical tones. **2.** a similar sound, as that made by a bird. —*v.t., v.i.* **3.** to sing or play with a trill.

tril′lion (tril′yən) *n., adj.* a number represented by 1 followed by 12 zeroes.

tril′o•gy (tril′ə jē) *n., pl.* **-gies.** a group of three works on a related theme.

trim (trim) *v.,* **trimmed, trimming,** *n., adj.,* **trimmer, trimmest.** —*v.t.* **1.** to make neat or to reduce by cutting, clipping, etc. **2.** to decorate with ornaments. **3.** to adjust (a ship's sails) to the direction of the wind. —*n.* **4.** ornamentation. **5.** a trimming by cutting, as of hair. —*adj.* **6.** neat. **7.** in good condition. —**trim′mer,** *n.*

tri•mes′ter (trī mes′tər, trī′mes-) *n.* **1.** a period of three months. **2.** one of three terms of the academic year.

trim′ming (trim′ing) *n.* **1.** something used to decorate. **2. trimmings,** something accompanying a main dish. **3.** pieces cut off in trimming.

tri•ni′tro•tol′u•ene′ (trī nī′trō tol′-yōō ēn′) *n.* a high explosive, known as TNT.

Trin′i•ty (trin′i tē) *n.* the union of Father, Son, and Holy Spirit.

trin′ket (tring′kit) *n.* a small ornament of little value.

tri′o (trē′ō) *n., pl.* **trios. 1.** a group of three. **2.** music for three voices or instruments.

trip (trip) *n., v.,* **tripped, tripping.** —*n.* **1.** a journey. **2.** a stumble. **3.** *Slang.* a drug-induced event. —*v.i., v.t.* **4.** to stumble or cause to stumble. **5.** to make or cause to make a mistake. **6.** to release suddenly, as a switch. **7.** to move lightly and quickly. —**trip′per,** *n.*

tri•par′tite (trī pär′tīt) *adj.* **1.** consisting of three parts. **2.** involving three parties.

tripe (trīp) *n.* **1.** the stomach of a ruminant, as an ox, used as food. **2.** *Slang.* worthless statements or writing.

tri′ple (trip′əl) *adj., n., v.,* **-pled, -pling.** —*adj.* **1.** consisting of three parts. **2.** three times as great. —*n.* **3.** *Baseball.* a hit allowing a batter to reach third base. —*v.t., v.i.* **4.** to make or become triple.

tri′plet (trip′lit) *n.* one of three children born at a single birth.

trip′li•cate (-li kit, -kāt′) *adj.* **1.** consisting of three identical parts. —*n.* **2.** one of a set of three copies.

tri′pod (trī′pod) *n.* a three-legged stand or support.

trip′tych (trip′tik) *n.* a set of three panels side by side, with pictures or carvings.

trite (trīt) *adj.,* **triter, tritest.** commonplace; hackneyed.

tri′umph (trī′əmf, -umf) *n.* **1.** victory; success. **2.** joy over victory or success. —*v.i.* **3.** to be victorious or successful. **4.** to rejoice over victory or success. —**tri•um′phal,** *adj.* —**tri•um′phant,** *adj.*

tri•um′vi•rate (-vər it, -və rāt′) *n.* a group of three officials governing jointly, as in ancient Rome.

triv′et (triv′it) *n.* a device protecting a table top from hot objects.

triv′i•a (triv′ē ə) *n.* (*used with a sing. or pl. v.*) things that are very unimportant.

triv′i•al *adj.* of very little importance. —**triv′i•al′i•ty,** *n.*

trog′lo•dyte′ (trog′lə dīt′) *n.* **1.** a prehistoric cave dweller. **2.** a hermit.

troi′ka (troi′kə) *n.* **1.** a Russian vehicle drawn by three horses. **2.** a ruling group of three.

troll (trōl) *n.* in folklore, a supernatural being living underground or in caves.

trol′ley (trol′ē) *n.* **1.** Also **trolley car,** an electric streetcar receiving current from an overhead wire. **2.** a small cart or table on wheels. **3.** a carriage or truck traveling on an overhead track.

trol′lop (trol′əp) *n.* **1.** an untidy or slovenly woman. **2.** a prostitute.

trom•bone′ (trom bōn′, trom′bōn) *n.* a brass wind instrument with a U-shaped metal tube and a slide. —**trom•bon′ist,** *n.*

troop (trōōp) *n.* **1.** an assemblage of persons or things. **2.** a cavalry unit. —*v.i.* **3.** to gather or move in great numbers. **4.** to walk, as if in a march.

tro/phy (trō/fē) n., pl. **-phies. 1.** anything taken in competition, war, etc., and preserved as a memento. **2.** something given as a prize.

trop/ic (trop/ik) n. **1.** either of two lines of latitude, one **(trop/ic of Can/cer)** 23 ½° N, and the other **(trop/ic of Cap/ricorn)** 23 ½° S of the equator. **2. the tropics,** the regions lying between these latitudes, having a hot climate.

trop/o.sphere/ (trop/ə sfēr/, trō/pə-) n. the lowest layer of the atmosphere.

trot (trot) v., **trotted, trotting,** n. —v.i., v.t. **1.** (of a horse) to go or cause to go at a gait in which the legs move in diagonal pairs. **2.** to hurry. —n. **3.** a trotting gait. —**trot/ter,** n.

troth (trôth, trōth) n. Archaic. **1.** faithfulness. **2.** one's promise.

trou/ba.dour/ (trōō/bə dôr/) n. a medieval lyric poet of S France.

trou/ble (trub/əl) v., **-bled, -bling,** n. —v.t. **1.** to distress. **2.** to inconvenience. **3.** to cause pain or discomfort to. —n. **4.** difficulty, annoyance, or disturbance. **5.** physical or mental distress. **6.** inconvenience. —**trou/ble.some,** adj.

trou/bled adj. **1.** emotionally or mentally distressed. **2.** economically or socially distressed.

trou/ble.mak/er n. a person who causes trouble.

troub/le.shoot/er n. an expert in eliminating causes of trouble.

trough (trôf) n. **1.** a long, narrow open container out of which animals eat or drink. **2.** a long depression, as between two waves. **3.** an area of low atmospheric pressure.

trounce (trouns) v.t., **trounced, trouncing.** to defeat decisively.

troupe (trōōp) n. a company of performers. —**troup/er,** n.

trou/sers (trou/zərz) n.pl. a two-legged outer garment covering the lower part of the body.

trous/seau (trōō/sō, trōō sō/) n., pl. **-seaux, -seaus** (-sōz). an outfit of clothing, linen, etc., for a bride.

trout (trout) n. a freshwater game fish of the salmon family.

trow/el (trou/əl) n. **1.** a flat-bladed tool for spreading or smoothing. **2.** a small digging tool.

troy/ weight/ (troi), n. a system of weights for precious metals and gems.

tru/ant (trōō/ənt) n. **1.** a student absent from school without permission. —adj. **2.** absent from

school without permission. —**tru/-an.cy,** n.

truce (trōōs) n. a temporary suspension of military hostilities.

truck[1] (truk) n. **1.** a large motor vehicle for carrying goods. **2.** a wheeled cart for moving heavy objects. —v.t. **3.** to transport by truck. —**truck/er,** n.

truck[2] (truk) n. **1.** vegetables raised for the market. **2.** dealings.

truck/le v.i., **-led, -ling.** to submit humbly.

truc/u.lent (truk/yə lənt, trōō/kyə-) adj. aggressively hostile. —**truc/u.lence,** n.

trudge (truj) v., **trudged, trudging,** n. —v.i. **1.** to walk, esp. wearily. —n. **2.** a tiring walk.

true (trōō) adj., **truer, truest. 1.** conforming to reality or fact. **2.** real. **3.** loyal. **4.** legitimate. **5.** correct. —**tru/ly,** adv.

true/-blue/ adj. totally loyal.

truf/fle (truf/əl) n. **1.** a kind of edible fungus that grows under the ground. **2.** a chocolate confection resembling a truffle in shape.

tru/ism (trōō/iz əm) n. an obvious truth.

trump (trump) n. **1.** any playing card of a suit outranking other suits. **2.** the suit itself. —v.t., v.i. **3.** to take (a trick) with a trump. **4. trump up,** to invent deceitfully.

trump/er.y n., pl. **-eries. 1.** something without use or value. **2.** nonsense.

trum/pet (trum/pit) n. **1.** a brass wind instrument with a curved tube and a flaring bell. **2.** something shaped like a trumpet. —v.i. **3.** to make a loud, trumpetlike sound. —v.t. **4.** to proclaim loudly. —**trum/pet.er,** n.

trun/cate (trung/kāt) v.t., **-cated, -cating.** to shorten by cutting off a part.

trun/cheon (trun/chən) n. a short club carried as a weapon.

trun/dle (trun/dl) v.i., v.t., **-dled, -dling.** to roll along.

trun/dle bed/ n. a low bed on casters.

trunk (trungk) n. **1.** the main stem of a tree. **2.** a large, heavy box for carrying or storing clothes, personal items, etc. **3.** a large storage compartment in a car. **4.** the body of a person or animal excluding the head and limbs. **5.** an elephant's long, flexible nasal appendage. **6. trunks,** shorts worn for athletics.

trunk/ line/ n. **1.** a major long-distance transportation line. **2.** a

tumor

telephone line between two switching devices.

truss (trus) *v.t.* **1.** to bind or tie. **2.** to fasten the legs and wings of (a fowl) before cooking. **3.** to support with a truss. —*n.* **4.** a rigid supporting framework. **5.** a device worn for supporting a hernia.

trust (trust) *n.* **1.** firm reliance on the integrity, ability, etc., of a person or thing. **2.** confident expectation. **3.** responsibility; care. **4.** something entrusted to one's care. **5.** the holding of legal title for another's benefit. —*v.t.* **6.** to have confidence in. **7.** to hope. —*v.i.* **8.** to have confidence. —**trust′wor′thy,** *adj.* —**trust′y,** *adj.*

trus•tee′ *n.* **1.** a person appointed to administer the affairs of a company, institution, etc. **2.** a person who holds title to property for another's benefit.

trus•tee′ship *n.* **1.** the office of a trustee. **2.** the control of a territory granted by the United Nations. **3.** the territory.

trust′ fund′ *n.* money, stocks, etc., held in trust.

truth (trooth) *n.* **1.** something true. **2.** the quality of being true. —**truth′ful,** *adj.*

try (trī) *v.,* **tried, trying.** —*v.t.* **1.** to make an effort to do. **2.** to test or sample. **3.** to examine and determine judicially. **4.** to strain the endurance, patience, etc., of. —*v.i.* **5.** to make an effort. **6. try out, a.** to experiment with. **b.** to take part in a test for a job, role, etc.

try′ing *adj.* annoying; irksome.

try′out′ *n.* a trial or test of fitness, ability, etc.

tryst (trist, trīst) *n.* **1.** an appointment, as of lovers, to meet. **2.** the meeting or place of meeting.

tsar (zär, tsär) *n.* a czar.

tset′se fly (tset′sē, tsē/tsē) an African fly that can transmit sleeping sickness.

T′-shirt′ *n.* a short-sleeved pullover shirt.

tsp. teaspoon.

T square *n.* a T-shaped ruler used in mechanical drawing.

tub (tub) *n.* **1.** a bathtub. **2.** a deep, round, open container.

tu′ba (too′bə, tyoo′-) *n.* a low-pitched brass wind instrument.

tub′by (tub′ē) *adj.,* **-bier, -biest.** short and fat.

tube (toob, tyoob) *n.* **1.** a hollow pipe for conveying fluids. **2.** a compressible container from which paste may be squeezed. **3.** a railroad or vehicular tunnel. **4. the tube,** *Informal.* television. **5.** *Brit.*

the subway. —**tu′bu•lar** (-byə lər) *adj.* —**tub′ing,** *n.*

tu′ber (too′bər, tyoo′-) *n.* a fleshy thickening of an underground stem or shoot. —**tu′ber•ous,** *adj.*

tu′ber•cle (-kəl) *n.* a small roundish projection, nodule, or swelling.

tu•ber′cu•lo′sis (-lō′sis) *n.* an infectious disease marked by the formation of tubercles, esp. in the lungs. —**tu•ber′cu•lar,** *adj.*

tu′bule (-byool) *n.* a small tube.

tuck (tuk) *v.t.* **1.** to put into a small or concealing space. **2.** to push in the edge of (a sheet, shirt, etc.) so as to hold in place. **3.** to draw up in folds. **4.** to cover snugly. —*n.* **5.** a flat fold sewn into cloth.

tuck′er *v.* **tucker out,** *Informal.* to tire; exhaust.

Tues. Tuesday. Also, **Tue.**

Tues′day (tooz′dā, -dē, tyooz′-) *n.* the third day of the week.

tuft (tuft) *n.* **1.** a bunch of feathers, hairs, grass, etc., growing or fastened together. **2.** a cluster of threads tied together at the base. —*v.t.* **3.** to furnish or decorate with tufts. —**tuft′ed,** *adj.*

tug (tug) *v.,* **tugged, tugging,** *n.* —*v.t., v.i.* **1.** to pull (at) with force or effort. —*n.* **2.** an act of tugging. **3.** a tugboat.

tug′boat′ *n.* a small, powerful boat used for towing.

tug′ of war′ *n.* **1.** a contest between teams pulling on the opposite ends of a rope. **2.** a struggle for supremacy.

tu•i′tion (too ish′ən, tyoo-) *n.* the fee for instruction, as at a college.

tu′lip (too′lip, tyoo′-) *n.* a plant bearing cup-shaped flowers of various colors.

tulle (tool) *n.* a thin silk or rayon net.

tum′ble (tum′bəl) *v.,* **-bled, -bling,** *n.* —*v.i.* **1.** to fall over or down. **2.** to perform gymnastic feats. **3.** to roll about; toss. —*n.* **4.** the act of tumbling.

tum′ble-down′ *adj.* dilapidated.

tum′bler *n.* **1.** a drinking glass. **2.** a part of a lock that engages a bolt. **3.** a performer of tumbling feats.

tum′ble•weed′ *n.* a plant whose upper part becomes detached and is driven about by the wind.

tum′brel (tum′brəl) *n.* a farmer's cart that can be tilted to discharge its load. Also, **tum′bril.**

tu′mid (too′mid, tyoo-) *adj.* **1.** swollen. **2.** pompous.

tum′my (tum′ē) *n., pl.* **-mies.** *Informal.* the stomach or abdomen.

tu′mor (too′mər, tyoo′-) *n.* an uncontrolled, abnormal growth of cells in a part of the body.

tu′mult (tōo′mult, -məlt, tyōo′-) *n.* violent disturbance, commotion, or uproar. —**tu·mul′tu·ous** (-mul′-chōo əs) *adj.*

tun (tun) *n.* a large cask.

tu′na (tōo′nə, tyōo′-) *n.* a large marine fish, used as food.

tun′dra (tun′drə, tōon′-) *n.* a vast, treeless, arctic plain.

tune (tōon, tyōon) *n., v.,* **tuned, tuning.** —*n.* **1.** a melody. **2.** the state of proper pitch, frequency, or condition. **3.** agreement. —*v.t.* **4.** to adjust (a musical instrument) to the correct pitch. **5.** to adjust (a radio or television) to receive a broadcast. **6.** to adjust (a motor) to run smoothly. —**tune′ful,** *adj.* —**tune′less,** *adj.* —**tun′er,** *n.*

tune′-up′ *n.* an adjustment, as of a motor, to improve working condition.

tung′sten (tung′stən) *n.* a metallic element used for electric-lamp filaments.

tu′nic (tōo′nik, tyōo′-) *n.* **1.** a gownlike garment worn by the ancient Greeks and Romans. **2.** a woman's straight upper garment. **3.** the coat of a uniform.

tun′ing fork′ *n.* a two-pronged steel instrument producing a tone of constant pitch when struck.

tun′nel (tun′l) *n., v.,* **-neled, -neling.** —*n.* **1.** an underground passage. —*v.t., v.i.* **2.** to make a tunnel (through or under).

tur′ban (tûr′bən) *n.* a head covering made of a long cloth wound around the head.

tur′bid (tûr′bid) *adj.* **1.** (of liquids) muddy or unclear. **2.** confused.

tur′bine (-bin, -bīn) *n.* a motor driven by a wheel turned by the pressure of a moving fluid or gas.

tur′bo·jet′ (tûr′bō-) *n.* **1.** a jet engine that compresses air for combustion by a turbine-driven compressor. **2.** an airplane with such engines.

tur′bo·prop′ *n.* **1.** a turbojet engine with a turbine-driven propeller. **2.** an airplane with such engines.

tur′bot (-bət) *n.* a kind of flatfish.

tur′bu·lent (-byə lənt) *adj.* **1.** being in a state of agitation. **2.** marked by disturbance or disorder.

tu·reen′ (tōo rēn′, tyōo-) *n.* a large covered dish for soup, stew, etc.

turf (tûrf) *n.* **1.** a layer of matted earth formed by grass and roots. **2.** a familiar area, as of residence or expertise. **3. the turf,** horse racing.

tur′gid (tûr′jid) *adj.* **1.** swollen. **2.** pompous. —**tur·gid′i·ty,** *n.*

tur′key (tûr′kē) *n.* a large, edible N American bird with brown feathers.

tur′key vul′ture *n.* a blackish brown New World vulture.

tur′mer·ic (tûr′mər ik) *n.* an aromatic spice from an Asian plant.

tur′moil (tûr′moil) *n.* great excitement or disturbance.

turn (tûrn) *v.t.* **1.** to rotate. **2.** to move around. **3.** to reverse. **4.** to change the course or position of. **5.** to change or alter. **6.** to put to some use. **7.** to reach or pass (a certain age, amount, etc.). **8.** to shape on a lathe. —*v.i.* **9.** to rotate. **10.** to move around. **11.** to change position or course. **12.** to change in form or appearance. **13.** to become spoiled. **14.** to become. **15. turn down,** to reject. **16. ~ off, a.** to stop the flow of. **b.** to extinguish. **c.** *Slang.* to alienate. **17. ~ on, a.** to cause to flow. **b.** to switch on. **c.** *Slang.* to arouse the interest of. **d.** to become hostile to. —*n.* **18.** a rotation. **19.** a change or point of change. **20.** one's due time or opportunity. **21.** a trend. **22.** a short walk, ride, etc. **23.** an inclination or aptitude. **24.** a service or disservice.

turn′a·bout′ *n.* a change of opinion, loyalty, etc.

turn′coat′ *n.* a person who changes to the opposite faction.

turn′ing point′ *n.* the point at which a decisive change takes place.

tur′nip (tûr′nip) *n.* the fleshy, edible root of either of two plants of the mustard family.

turn′off′ *n.* a small road that branches off from a larger one.

turn′out′ *n.* the attendance at a meeting, show, etc.

turn′o′ver *n.* **1.** the rate at which workers are replaced. **2.** the amount of business done in a given time. **3.** a small folded pastry with a filling.

turn′pike′ (-pīk′) *n.* an express highway on which tolls are charged.

turn′stile′ *n.* a gate with revolving arms to allow people through one by one.

turn′ta′ble *n.* a rotating platform.

tur′pen·tine′ (tûr′pən tīn′) *n.* a strong-smelling oil derived from coniferous trees, used as a paint thinner and solvent.

tur′pi·tude′ (-pi tōod′, -tyōod′) *n.* vile character; depravity.

tur′quoise (-ykoiz, -kwoiz) *n.* **1.** a

greenish-blue mineral used as a gem. **2.** a greenish blue.

tur′ret (tûr′it, tur′-) *n.* **1.** a small tower. **2.** a revolving structure for mounting a gun on a tank or ship.

tur′tle (tûr′tl) *n.* a water- or land-dwelling reptile with a shell-encased body.

tur′tle•dove′ (-duv′) *n.* a small dove noted for its soft cooing.

tur′tle•neck′ *n.* **1.** a high, close-fitting collar. **2.** a garment with a turtleneck.

tusk (tusk) *n.* a very long tooth, as of an elephant or walrus.

tus′sle (tus′əl) *v.*, **-sled, -sling,** *n.* —*v.i.* **1.** to struggle or fight. —*n.* **2.** a vigorous struggle.

tus′sock (tus′ək) *n.* a tuft of growing grass.

tu′te•lage (tōōt′l ij, tyōōt′-) *n.* **1.** guardianship. **2.** instruction.

tu′tor (tōō′tər, tyōō′-) *n.* **1.** a private instructor. —*v.t., v.i.* **2.** to act as a tutor (to). —**tu•to′ri•al** (-tôr′ē-əl) *adj.*

tu′tu′ (tōō′tōō′) *n.* a short, full skirt worn by a ballerina.

tux (tuks) *n. Informal.* a tuxedo.

tux•e′do (tuk sē′dō) *n., pl.* **-dos.** a man's semiformal suit.

TV television.

twad′dle (twod′l) *n.* nonsense.

twain (twān) *adj., n.* two.

twang (twang) *v.i., v.t.* **1.** to make or cause a sharp, vibrating sound. **2.** to speak or utter with a nasal tone. —*n.* **3.** a twanging sound.

tweak (twēk) *v.t.* **1.** to seize and pull or twist. **2.** to make a minor adjustment to. —*n.* **3.** a sharp pull and twist.

tweed (twēd) *n.* a thick, coarse woolen cloth.

tweet (twēt) *n.* **1.** a chirping sound. —*v.i.* **2.** to chirp.

tweez′ers (twē′zərz) *n.pl.* small pincers.

twelve (twelv) *n., adj.* ten plus two. —**twelfth,** *adj., n.*

Twelve′ Step′ *adj.* of or based on a program for recovery from addiction that provides 12 progressive levels toward attainment.

twen′ty (twen′tē) *n., adj.* ten times two. —**twen′ti•eth,** *adj., n.*

24-7 (twen′tē fôr′ sev′ən) *adv. Slang.* continually; constantly (alluding to twenty-four hours a day, seven days a week).

twerp (twûrp) *n. Slang.* an insignificant or despicable person.

twice (twīs) *adv.* **1.** two times. **2.** doubly.

twig (twig) *n.* a small offshoot of a branch or tree.

twi′light′ (twī′līt′) *n.* **1.** light from the sky after sunset. **2.** the period of this light.

twill (twil) *n.* a fabric woven in parallel diagonal lines.

twin (twin) *n.* either of two children born at a single birth.

twine (twīn) *n., v.,* **twined, twining.** —*n.* **1.** a strong thread or string of twisted strands. —*v.t.* **2.** to twist together. **3.** to wind or coil. —*v.i.* **4.** to wind around something.

twinge (twinj) *n., v.,* **twinged, twinging.** —*n.* **1.** a sudden, sharp pain. —*v.t., v.i.* **2.** to affect with or have a twinge.

twin′kle (twing′kəl) *v.,* **-kled, -kling,** *n.* —*v.i.* **1.** to shine with a flickering gleam. —*n.* **2.** a flickering gleam.

twin′kling *n.* an instant.

twirl (twûrl) *v.i., v.t.* **1.** to spin; whirl. —*n.* **2.** a twirling.

twist (twist) *v.t.* **1.** to turn by rotating. **2.** to combine (strands) by winding together. **3.** to form into a coil by winding, rolling, etc. **4.** to distort. **5.** to wrench. —*v.i.* **6.** to become twisted. **7.** to writhe or squirm. **8.** to turn to face another direction. —*n.* **9.** a curve or turn. **10.** a spin. **11.** distortion, as of meaning. **12.** a wrench. **13.** a sudden, unexpected change.

twist′er *n. Informal.* a tornado.

twit (twit) *v.,* **twitted, twitting,** *n.* —*v.t.* **1.** to taunt; tease. —*n.* **2.** Informal. a fool.

twitch (twich) *v.t., v.i.* **1.** to pull (at) or move with a jerk. —*n.* **2.** a quick jerky movement.

twit′ter (twit′ər) *v.i.* **1.** to utter small, tremulous sounds, as a bird. **2.** to tremble with excitement. —*n.* **3.** a twittering sound. **4.** a state of excitement.

two (tōō) *n., adj.* one plus one.

two′-bit′ *adj. Informal.* inferior or unimportant.

two′ bits′ *n. Informal.* 25 cents.

two′-faced′ *adj.* hypocritical.

two′-fist′ed *adj.* strong and vigorous.

two′fold′ *adj.* (-fōld′) **1.** having two parts. **2.** twice as great. —*adv.* (fōld′) **3.** in two-fold measure.

two′-ply′ *adj.* consisting of two layers, strands, etc.

two′some (-səm) *n.* a pair.

two′-time′ *v.t.,* **-timed, -timing.** *Informal.* to be unfaithful to.

two′-way′ *adj.* **1.** allowing movement in two directions. **2.** involving two participants.

twp. township.

TX Texas.

-ty a suffix meaning state or condition.

ty·coon′ (tī koon′) n. a businessperson having great wealth and power.

tyke (tīk) n. a small child.

tym·pan′ic mem′brane (tim pan′ik) n. a membrane separating the middle from the external ear.

tym′pa·num (tim′pə nəm) n. 1. the middle ear. 2. the tympanic membrane.

type (tīp) n., v., **typed, typing.** —n. 1. a kind or class. 2. a thing or person that is typical of a class or group. 3. a set of characters used in printing. —v.t. 4. to write on a typewriter, computer keyboard, etc. —v.i. 5. to write using a typewriter, computer keyboard, etc.

type′cast′ v.t., **-cast, -casting.** to cast (an actor) exclusively in the same kind of role.

type′script′ n. typewritten matter.

type′set′ter n. 1. a person who sets type. 2. a machine for setting type. —**type′set′,** v.t.

type′writ′er n. a machine for writing mechanically.

ty′phoid (tī′foid) n. an infectious disease marked by fever and intestinal inflammation. Also, **ty′phoid fe′ver.**

ty·phoon′ (tī foon′) n. a tropical hurricane in the W Pacific.

ty′phus (tī′fəs) n. an infectious disease transmitted by lice and fleas and characterized by reddish spots on the skin.

typ′i·cal (tip′i kəl) adj. having the essential characteristics of a particular type or group.

typ′i·fy′ v.t., **-fied, -fying.** to serve as a typical example or symbol of.

ty′po (tī′pō) n., pl. **-pos.** an error in typography or typing.

ty·pog′ra·phy (tī pog′rə fē) n. the art, process, or style of printing.

tyr′an·ny (tir′ə nē) n., pl. **-nies.** 1. arbitrary or unrestrained exercise of power. 2. the government of a tyrant. —**ty·ran′ni·cal** (ti ran′i kəl, tī-) adj. —**tyr′an·nize′,** v.t., v.i.

ty′rant (tī′rənt) n. an oppressive, unjust, or absolute ruler.

ty′ro (tī′rō) n., pl. **-ros.** a beginner.

tzar (zär, tsär) n. czar.

U

U, u (yoo) n. the twenty-first letter of the English alphabet.

u·biq′ui·tous (yoo bik′wi təs) adj. present everywhere at the same time.

ud′der (ud′ər) n. a baggy mammary gland, esp. of a cow.

UFO (yoo′ef′ō′; sometimes yoo′fō) n., pl. **UFOs, UFO′s.** an unidentified flying object.

ug′ly (ug′lē) adj., **-lier, -liest.** 1. very unattractive; repulsive. 2. threatening; dangerous. 3. quarrelsome.

u′ku·le′le (yoo′kə lā′lē) n. a small guitar.

ul′cer (ul′sər) n. an open sore, as on the stomach lining. —**ul′cer·ous,** adj. —**ul′cer·ate′,** v.i., v.t.

ul′na (ul′nə) n. the larger bone of the forearm. —**ul′nar,** adj.

ul·te′ri·or (ul tēr′ē ər) adj. not acknowledged; concealed.

ul′ti·mate (-mit) adj. 1. farthest. 2. basic. 3. final. —**ul′ti·mate·ly,** adv.

ul′ti·ma′tum (-mā′təm, -mä′-) n., pl. **-tums, -ta** (-tə). a final demand.

ultra- a prefix meaning beyond; extremely.

ul′tra·high′ fre′quency (ul′trə hī′) n. a radio frequency between 300 and 3000 megahertz.

ul′tra·ma·rine′ n. a deep blue.

ul′tra·sound′ n. the application of

sound above human hearing to medical diagnosis and therapy.

ul′tra·vi′o·let adj. of or producing invisible rays beyond violet in the spectrum.

um′ber (um′bər) n. a reddish brown.

umbil′ical cord′ (um bil′i kəl) n. a cordlike structure connecting the fetus with the placenta, conveying nourishment and removing wastes.

um·bil′i·cus (-kəs) n., pl. **-ci** (-sī). the navel. —**um·bil′i·cal,** adj.

um′brage (um′brij) n. offense.

um·brel′la (um brel′ə) n. a cloth-covered folding metal framework on a carrying stick, used for protection from rain or sun.

ump (ump) n., v.t., v.i. umpire.

um′pire (um′pīʳr) n., v., **-pired, -piring.** —n. 1. a rules official in certain sports. —v.t., v.i. 2. to decide or act as umpire.

UN United Nations.

un- a prefix indicating negative or opposite sense.

un·a′ble (un ā′bəl) adj. lacking the necessary power, skill, or resources.

un′ac·count′a·ble adj. 1. impossible to account for. 2. not responsible.

un′af·fect′ed adj. 1. without affectation. 2. not concerned.

u·nan′i·mous (yoo nan′ə məs) adj.

being in complete agreement.
—**u′na·nim′i·ty** (-nə nim′i tē) n.

un·as·sum′ing (un′-) adj. modest; without vanity.

un·at·tached′ adj. **1.** not attached. **2.** not engaged or married.

un′a·vail′ing adj. futile.

un·a·wares′ adv. not knowingly.

un·bal′anced adj. **1.** out of balance. **2.** irrational; deranged.

un·bear′a·ble adj. intolerable.

un′be·com′ing adj. unattractive or unseemly.

un·bend v.t., v.i., -**bent, -bending. 1.** to straighten. **2.** to relax.

un·bend′ing adj. rigidly formal or unyielding.

un·bid′den adj. **1.** not commanded. **2.** not asked.

un·blush′ing adj. showing no remorse; shameless.

un·bos′om v.t. to disclose (a confidence, secret, etc.).

un·bowed′ (-boud′) adj. **1.** not bent. **2.** not subjugated.

un·brid′led adj. unrestrained.

un·bro′ken adj. **1.** not broken. **2.** undisturbed. **3.** not tamed.

un·bur′den v.t. **1.** to free from a burden. **2.** to relieve (one's mind, conscience, etc.) by confessing.

un·called′-for′ adj. not warranted.

un·can′ny adj. strange; mysterious.

un·cer′e·mo′ni·ous adj. **1.** informal. **2.** rudely abrupt.

un·chart′ed adj. unexplored.

un·clad′ adj. naked.

un·cle (ung′kəl) n. **1.** the brother of one's father or mother. **2.** the husband of one's aunt.

un·com′pro·mis′ing adj. rigid.

un′con·cern′ n. indifference.

un′con·di′tion·al adj. absolute; without conditions or reservations.

un·con′scion·a·ble (-shən-) adj. not restrained by conscience; unscrupulous.

un·con′scious adj. **1.** lacking awareness, sensation, or cognition. **2.** not perceived at the level of awareness. **3.** done without intent. —n. **4. the unconscious,** the part of

the mind rarely accessible to awareness but influencing behavior.

un·couth′ (un kōōth′) adj. rude; boorish.

unc′tion (ungk′shən) n. **1.** anointment with oil. **2.** excessive earnestness of manner.

unc′tu·ous (-chōō əs) adj. **1.** overly suave or smug. **2.** oily.

un·cut′ (un-) adj. **1.** not shortened; unabridged. **2.** not yet given shape, as a gemstone.

un·daunt′ed adj. not discouraged.

un′de·mon′stra·tive adj. not expressing emotion; reserved.

un′der (un′dər) prep. **1.** beneath; below. **2.** less than. **3.** below in rank. **4.** subject to the authority of. **5.** within the category of. —adv. **6.** below or beneath something. **7.** in or into a lower degree, amount, position, or condition. —adj. **8.** lower.

under- a prefix meaning: **1.** below. **2.** lower in grade. **3.** of lesser degree or amount.

un′der·a·chieve′ v.i., -**achieved, -achieving.** to perform below one's potential.

un′der·age′ adj. being below the legal or required age.

un′der·bel′ly n., pl. -**ies. 1.** the lower abdomen. **2.** a vulnerable area.

un′der·brush′ n. low shrubs, vines, etc., in a forest.

un′der·car′riage n. the supporting framework underneath a vehicle.

un′der·cov′er adj. secret.

un′der·cur′rent n. a hidden tendency or feeling.

un′der·cut′ v.t., -**cut, -cutting.** to sell at a lower price than.

un′der·de·vel′oped adj. insufficiently developed.

un′der·dog′ n. **1.** a person expected to lose a contest or conflict. **2.** a victim of injustice.

un′der·done′ adj. not cooked enough.

un′der·es′ti·mate′ (-māt′) v.t.,

un′ac·cept′a·ble	un·com′mon	un·e′ven
un′ack·now′ledged	un′con·trol′la·ble	un′ex·pect′ed
un′a·void′a·ble	un·cork′	un·fail′ing
un·a′ware′	un·cov′er	un·fair′
un′be·liev′a·ble	un′de·cid′ed	un·faith′ful
un·born′	un′de·clared′	un′fa·mil′iar
un·bound′ed	un′de·feat′ed	un·fas′ten
un·but′ton	un′de·ni′a·ble	un·fit′
un·cer′tain	un·doubt′ed	un·fold′
un·civ′il	un·dress′	un′for·get′ta·ble
un·clean′	un·due′	un′for·giv′a·ble
un·cloak′	un·du′ly	un′for·tu·nate
un·clothe′	un·e′qual	un·friend′ly
un·com′fort·a·ble	un·err′ing	un·god′ly

-mated, -mating. to estimate too low.

un′der·ex·pose′ v.t., -posed, -posing. to expose (film) to insufficient light or for too short a period.

un′der·gar′ment n. an item of underwear.

un′der·go′ v.t., -went, -gone, -going. to experience; endure.

un′der·grad′u·ate (-it) n. a college student who has not received a first degree.

un′der·ground′ (un′dər ground′) adv. 1. under the ground. 2. in secrecy. —adj. (-ground′) 3. existing underground. 4. secret. 5. reflecting nonconformist views. —n. (-ground′) 6. a secret resistance army.

un′der·growth′ n. underbrush.

un′der·hand′ adj. sly; secret.

un′der·line′ v.t., -lined, -lining. 1. to draw a line under. 2. to stress.

un′der·ling′ (-ling) n. a subordinate.

un′der·mine′ (un′dər mīn′, un′dər-mīn′) v.t., -mined, -mining. to weaken or destroy, esp. secretly.

un′der·neath′ (-nēth′, -nēth′) prep. 1. beneath; under. —adv. 2. below.

un′der·pass′ n. a passage running underneath.

un′der·pin′ning n. 1. a system of supports. 2. underpinnings, a foundation; basis.

un′der·priv′i·leged adj. denied the normal privileges of a society.

un′der·score′ v.t., -scored, -scoring. to underline; stress.

un′der-signed′ n. the undersigned, the person or persons signing a document.

un′der-staffed′ adj. not having enough workers.

un′der·stand′ v., -stood, -standing. —v.t. 1. to see the meaning of. 2. to have a thorough knowledge of. 3. to regard as settled. 4. to infer. —v.i. 5. to perceive what is meant. 6. to accept sympathetically.

un′der·stand′ing n. 1. comprehension. 2. personal interpretation. 3. intellectual ability; intelligence. 4. a mutual agreement. —adj. 5. marked by tolerance or sympathy.

un′der·state′ v.t., -stated, -stating. 1. to state less strongly than the facts warrant. 2. to set forth in restrained terms. —un′der·state′-ment, n.

un′der·stud′y n., pl. -studies, v., -ied, -ying. —n. 1. an actor who learns another's part in order to serve as a substitute if necessary. —v.t., v.i. 2. to learn (a role) as an understudy (for).

un′der·take′ v.t., -took, -taken, -taking. 1. to take upon oneself, as a task. 2. to promise.

un′der·tak′er n. a funeral director; mortician.

un′der·tak′ing (un′dər tā′king, un′-dər tā′-) n. 1. something undertaken. 2. a promise.

un′der-the-coun′ter adj. illegal; unauthorized.

un′der·tone′ n. 1. a low tone. 2. an underlying quality. 3. a subdued color.

un′der·tow′ (-tō′) n. a strong current under the surface that is moving in a direction opposite that of the surface current.

un′der·wear′ n. garments worn under outer clothing.

un′der·world′ n. 1. the criminal element of a society. 2. the realm of the spirits of the dead.

un′der·write′ (un′dər rīt′, un′dər-rīt′) v.t., -wrote, -written, -writing. 1. to agree to finance. 2. to guarantee the security of.

un·do′ (un dōō′) v.t., -did, -done, -doing. 1. to reverse or annul. 2. to unfasten. 3. to destroy.

un·do′ing n. 1. a reversing. 2. ruin. 3. a cause of ruin.

un′du·late′ (un′jə lāt′, -dyə-) v.i., v.t., -lated, -lating. to move or cause to move with a wavy motion. —un′du·la′tion, n.

un·dy′ing adj. eternal; unending.

un·earned′ adj. 1. not earned by service. 2. not deserved. 3. (of income) derived from investments.

un·gra′cious	un·lock′	un·tan′gle
un·guard′ed	un·mask′	un·true′
un·hap′py	un′mis·tak′a·ble	un·truth′
un·heard′-of′	un·mor′al	un·twist′
un·ho′ly	un·nat′u·ral	un·typ′i·cal
un′in·tel′lig·i·ble	un·nec′es·sar′y	un·used′
un′in·ter·rupt′ed	un·pack′	un·u′su·al
un·kind′	un·pop′u·lar	un·veil′
un′known′	un·rea′son·a·ble	un·wind′
un·lace′	un·roll′	un·wise′
un·law′ful	un·screw′	un·worn′
un·like′	un·shack′le	un·wor′thy
un·like′ly	un·sight′ly	un·wrap′
un·load′	un·skilled′	un·yoke′

un·earth′ *v.t.* to discover.

un·earth′ly *adj.* **1.** supernatural; weird. **2.** unreasonable; absurd.

un·eas′y *adj.,* **-ier, -iest.** anxious.

un′e·quiv′o·cal *adj.* definite.

un′e·vent′ful *adj.* routine.

un′ex·cep′tion·al *adj.* ordinary.

un·feel′ing *adj.* lacking sympathy.

un·fledged′ (-flejd′) *adj.* **1.** lacking sufficient feathers for flight. **2.** immature.

un·found′ed *adj.* not supported by evidence.

un·frock′ *v.t.* to deprive of ecclesiastical rank, authority, etc.

un·gain′ly (-gān′lē) *adj.* clumsy.

un′guent (ung′gwənt) *n.* an ointment.

un·hand′ *v.t.* to release.

un·hinge′ *v.t.,* **-hinged, -hinging. 1.** to remove from hinges. **2.** to make mentally unstable.

uni- a prefix meaning one.

u′ni·corn′ (yōō′ni kôrn′) *n.* a mythical horselike animal with one horn.

u′ni·form′ (yōō′nə fôrm′) *adj.* **1.** exactly like others. **2.** constant. —*n.* **3.** the distinctive clothing of a specific group. —*v.t.* **4.** to clothe in a uniform. —**u′ni·form′i·ty,** *n.*

u′ni·fy′ (-fī′) *v.t., v.i.,* **-fied, -fying.** to make or become a single unit. —**u′ni·fi·ca′tion,** *n.*

u′ni·lat′er·al *adj.* one-sided.

un′im·peach′a·ble (un′im pē′chə bəl) *adj.* above reproach.

un′in·hib′it·ed *adj.* unrestrained by convention.

un·in′ter·est·ed *adj.* not interested; indifferent. —**Usage.** See DISINTERESTED.

un′ion (yōōn′yən) *n.* **1.** a uniting or being united. **2.** a combination. **3.** a group joined for a common purpose. **4.** a labor union.

un′ion·ize′ *v.t., v.i.,* **-ized, -iz·ing.** to organize into a labor union.

u·nique′ (yōō nēk′) *adj.* **1.** only. **2.** most unusual or rare. —**Usage.** UNIQUE is an adjective representing an absolute state that cannot exist in degrees. Therefore, it cannot be sensibly used with a limiting or comparative adverb such as "very," "most," or "extremely": *She has a unique* (not "*very unique*" or "*most unique*") *style of singing.*

u′ni·sex′ (yōō′nə seks′) *adj.* suitable for both sexes.

u′ni·son (-sən, -zən) *n.* **1.** perfect agreement. **2.** *Music.* identity in pitch.

u′nit (yōō′nit) *n.* **1.** a single entity. **2.** one of a number of identical or similar parts within a whole.

u·nite′ (yōō nīt′) *v.t., v.i.,* **united,** uniting. **1.** to bring or come together in a single unit. **2.** to join in a common goal.

u′ni·ty (yōō′ni tē) *n., pl.* **-ties. 1.** the state of being united; oneness. **2.** agreement.

u′ni·ver′sal (yōō′nə vûr′səl) *adj.* **1.** of, affecting, or understood by all. **2.** applicable or existing everywhere. —**u′ni·ver·sal′i·ty** (-sal′i tē) *n.*

U′niver′sal Prod′uct Code′ *n.* a standardized bar code used in ringing up purchases in a store.

u′ni·verse′ (-vûrs′) *n.* all things that exist, including heavenly bodies.

u′ni·ver′si·ty (-vûr′si tē) *n., pl.* **-ties.** an institution of higher learning composed of various specialized colleges and at least one graduate school.

un·kempt′ (un kempt′) *adj.* untidy.

un·lead′ed (-led′id) *adj.* (of gasoline) free of pollution-causing lead.

un·less′ (un les′, ən-) *conj.* except when.

un·let′tered *adj.* illiterate.

un·mit′i·gat′ed *adj.* **1.** not lessened. **2.** absolute.

un·nerve′ *v.t.,* **-nerved, -nerving.** to deprive of courage, strength, or determination.

un·par′al·leled′ *adj.* without equal.

un·plumbed′ *adj.* not explored in depth.

un·prin′ci·pled *adj.* without principles or ethics.

un·print′a·ble *adj.* unfit for print, esp. because obscene.

un·rav′el *v.,* **-eled, -eling.** —*v.t.* **1.** to separate the threads of. **2.** to solve. —*v.i.* **3.** to become unraveled.

un′re·con·struct′ed *adj.* stubbornly maintaining beliefs considered out of date.

un′re·mit′ting *adj.* not ceasing.

un·rest′ *n.* disturbance or turmoil.

un·ruf′fled *adj.* calm.

un·ru′ly (un rōō′lē) *adj.,* **-lier, -liest.** difficult to control.

un·sa′vo·ry *adj.* **1.** unpleasant in taste or smell. **2.** morally objectionable.

un·scru′pu·lous *adj.* not scrupulous; unprincipled.

un·sea′son·a·ble *adj.* **1.** being out of season. **2.** not timely.

un·seat′ *v.t.* **1.** to dislodge from a seat. **2.** to remove from political office.

un·seem′ly *adj.,* **-lier, -liest.** improper.

un·set′tle *v.t.,* **-tled, -tling. 1.** to cause to be unstable; disturb. **2.** to agitate the mind or emotions of.

un·sound′ *adj.* **1.** unhealthy. **2.** not solid or secure. **3.** not valid.

un·spar′ing *adj.* **1.** profuse. **2.** unmerciful.

un·speak′a·ble *adj.* **1.** exceeding the power of speech. **2.** inexpressibly bad or objectionable.

un·sta′ble *adj.* **1.** unsteady. **2.** emotionally unbalanced.

un·strung′ *adj.* nervously upset; unnerved.

un·sung′ *adj.* unappreciated.

un·ten′a·ble *adj.* indefensible.

un·think′a·ble *adj.* not to be imagined; impossible.

un·ti′dy *adj.*, **-dier, -diest.** not tidy or neat. **—un·tid′i·ly,** *adv.*

un·tie′ *v.*, **-tied, -tying.** **—***v.t.* **1.** to loosen or open (something tied). **—***v.i.* **2.** to become untied.

un·til′ (un til′) *conj.* **1.** up to the time when. **2.** before. **—***prep.* **3.** onward to the time of. **4.** before. **—Usage.** See TILL.

un′to (un′tōō; *unstressed* -tə) *prep.* **1.** to. **2.** until.

un·told′ *adj.* countless.

un·touch′a·ble *adj.* **1.** not allowed to be touched. **2.** beyond control or criticism.

un·to·ward′ *adj.* **1.** unfortunate. **2.** not proper.

un·well′ *adj.* ill or ailing.

un·wield′y *adj.*, **-ier, -iest.** awkward to handle.

un·wit′ting *adj.* not aware.

un·wont′ed (un wôn′tid, -wōn′-, -wun′-) *adj.* not habitual or usual.

up (up) *adv.*, *prep.*, *adj.*, *v.*, **upped, upping.** **—***adv.* **1.** to, toward, in, or on a higher place or level. **2.** to or in an erect position. **3.** out of bed. **4.** to or at an equal point. **5.** into existence or view. **—***prep.* **6.** to, toward, or at a higher place or farther point on or in. **—***adj.* **7.** moving or facing upward. **—***v.t.* **8.** to increase or raise. **—Idiom.** **9. ups and downs,** alternating good and bad fortune.

up′-and-com′ing *adj.* likely to succeed; promising.

up′beat′ *adj.* optimistic; happy.

up·braid′ (up brād′) *v.t.* to reproach severely.

up′bring′ing *n.* the care and training of children.

UPC Universal Product Code.

up′com′ing *adj.* about to take place or appear.

up′coun′try *adj.*, *adv.* of, toward, or in the interior of a region.

up′date′ (up′dāt′, up′dāt′) *v.*, **-dated, -dating.** **—***v.t.* **1.** to bring up to date. **—***n.* **2.** new information. **3.** an updated version.

up·end′ *v.t.*, *v.i.* to set on end.

up′-front′ *adj.* **1.** invested or paid in advance. **2.** honest; candid.

up′grade′ *n.*, *v.*, **-graded, -grading.** **—***n.* (up′grād′) **1.** an improved or enhanced version. **2.** an increase, rise, or improvement. **3.** an upward incline. **—***v.t.* (up grād′, up′-grād′) **4.** to raise in rank, quality, value, etc.

up·heav′al (up hē′vəl) *n.* a sudden and great movement or change.

up′hill′ *adv.* up a slope or incline.

up·hold′ *v.t.*, **-held, -holding.** to defend or support.

up·hol′ster (up hōl′stər, ə pōl′-) *v.t.* to provide (furniture) with coverings, stuffing, etc. **—up·hol′ster·er,** *n.* **—up·hol′ster·y,** *n.*

up′keep′ *n.* **1.** maintaining something in good condition. **2.** the cost of upkeep.

up′land (up′lənd, -land′) *n.* an elevated region.

up·lift′ *v.t.* (up lift′) **1.** to lift up. **2.** to improve. **—***n.* (up′lift′) **3.** a lifting up. **4.** improvement.

up·on′ (ə pon′, ə pôn′) *prep.* on.

up′per *adj.* higher.

up′per·case′ *adj.* **1.** (of a letter) capital. **—***n.* **2.** a capital letter.

up′per hand′ *n.* the controlling position; advantage.

up′pi·ty (up′i tē) *adj. Informal.* haughty, snobbish, or arrogant.

up′right′ (up′rīt′, up rīt′) *adj.* **1.** in a vertical position; erect. **2.** righteous or honest. **—***n.* **3.** something standing upright.

up′ris′ing (up′rī′zing, up rī′-) *n.* a revolt.

up′roar′ *n.* tumult; noise; din.

up·roar′i·ous (-ē əs) *adj.* **1.** characterized by uproar. **2.** very funny.

up·root′ *v.t.* **1.** to tear up by the roots. **2.** to remove to a new place.

up′scale′ *adj.* for people at the upper end of the economic scale.

up·set′ *v.*, **-set, -setting,** *n.*, *adj.* **—***v.t.* (up set′) **1.** to knock over. **2.** to distress emotionally or physically. **3.** to defeat. **—***n.* (up′set′) **4.** upsetting or being upset. **5.** a defeat. **—***adj.* (up set′) **6.** overturned. **7.** disturbed.

up′shot′ *n.* the final result.

up′side down′ *adv.* **1.** with the upper part undermost. **2.** in or into complete disorder. **—up′side-down′,** *adj.*

up′stage′ *adv.*, *adj.*, *v.*, **-staged, -staging.** **—***adv.* **1.** at or toward the back of a stage. **—***adj.* **2.** of the back of a stage. **—***v.t.* **3.** to draw attention away from, as by moving upstage. **4.** to outdo professionally or socially.

up′stairs′ *adv., adj.* on or to an upper floor.

up′start′ *n.* a person newly risen to wealth or importance.

up′-to-date′ *adj.* modern.

up′ward (up′wərd) *adv.* **1.** toward a higher place. —*adj.* **2.** moving upward. Also, **up′wards.**

u.ra′ni.um (yoō rā′nē əm) *n.* a white, radioactive metallic element, important in the development of atomic energy.

U′ra.nus (yoōr′ə nəs, yoō rā′-) *n.* the planet seventh from the sun.

ur′ban (ûr′bən) *adj.* of a city.

ur.bane′ (ûr bān′) *adj.* suave and sophisticated. —**ur.ban′i.ty** (-ban′i-tē) *n.*

ur′chin (ûr′chin) *n.* a ragged child.

u.re′a (yoō rē′ə, yoōr′ē ə) *n.* a compound occurring in body fluids, esp. urine.

u.re′ter (yoō rē′tər) *n.* a duct that conveys urine from a kidney to the bladder.

u.re′thra (yoō rē′thrə) *n., pl.* **-thrae** (-thrē) **-thras.** a duct that conveys urine and, in males, semen.

urge (ûrj) *v.,* **urged, urging,** *n.* —*v.t.* **1.** to push along, encourage, or incite. **2.** to insist on. —*n.* **3.** a desire; impulse.

ur′gent (ûr′jənt) *adj.* requiring immediate attention. —**ur′gen.cy,** *n.*

u′ri.nal (yoōr′ə nl) *n.* **1.** a wall fixture used by men for urinating. **2.** a receptacle for urine.

u′ri.nar′y (-ner′ē) *adj.* **1.** of urine. **2.** of the organs that secrete and discharge urine.

u′ri.nate′ (-nāt′) *v.i.,* **-nated, -nating.** to pass urine. —**u′ri.na′tion,** *n.*

u′rine (yoōr′in) *n.* the yellowish liquid secreted by the kidneys. —**u′ric** (yoōr′ik) *adj.*

urn (ûrn) *n.* **1.** a container with a faucet for serving coffee or tea. **2.** a vase with a pedestal.

u.rol′o.gy (yoō rol′ə jē) *n.* the branch of medicine dealing with the urinary or genitourinary tract. —**u.rol′o.gist,** *n.*

us (us) *pron.* the objective case of **we.**

us′age (yoō′sij, -zij) *n.* **1.** a custom or practice. **2.** the way in which something is used.

use *v.,* **used, using,** *n.* —*v.t.* (yoōz or, for *pt.* form of 5, yoōst) **1.** to put into service. **2.** to consume. **3.** to treat. **4.** to take unfair advantage of. —*v.i.* **5.** to be accustomed. —*n.* (yoōs) **6.** a using or being used. **7.** the purpose for which something is used. **8.** the power of using something. —**use′ful,** *adj.* —**use′less,** *adj.* —**us′er,** *n.*

ush′er (ush′ər) *n.* **1.** a person who escorts people to their seats. —*v.t.* **2.** to act as an usher to.

u′su.al (yoō′zhoō əl) *adj.* customary; common. —**u′su.al.ly,** *adv.*

u.surp′ (yoō sûrp′, -zûrp′) *v.t.* to seize (a position, power, etc.) by force or without legal right. —**u.surp′er,** *n.*

u′su.ry (yoō′zhə rē) *n.* lending money at exorbitant rates of interest. —**u′sur.er,** *n.*

UT Utah. Also, **Ut.**

u.ten′sil (yoō ten′səl) *n.* a tool or instrument, esp. for the kitchen.

u′ter.us (-tər əs) *n., pl.* **-teri** (-tə rī′). a hollow organ in female mammals in which the fertilized egg develops. —**u′ter.ine** (-in) *adj.*

u.til′i.tar′i.an (-til/i târ′ē ən) *adj.* of practical use.

u.til′i.ty *n., pl.* **-ties. 1.** usefulness. **2.** a public service, as the providing of electricity.

u′ti.lize′ (yoōt′l īz′) *v.t.,* **-lized, -lizing.** to put to practical use. —**u′ti.li.za′tion,** *n.*

ut′most′ (ut′mōst′) *adj.* **1.** greatest. **2.** furthest.

U.to′pi.an (yoō tō′pē ən) *adj.* impossibly perfect.

ut′ter[1] (ut′ər) *v.t.* to speak; say.

ut′ter[2] (ut′ər) *adj.* complete; total.

u′vu.la (yoō′vyə lə) *n., pl.* **-las, -lae.** the small, fleshy part on the soft palate.

V

V, v (vē) *n.* the twenty-second letter of the English alphabet.

VA Virginia. Also, **Va.**

va′cant (-kənt) *adj.* **1.** empty. **2.** unoccupied. —**va′can.cy,** *n.*

va′cate (vā′kāt) *v.t.,* **-cated, -cating.** to cause to be vacant.

va.ca′tion (vā kā′shən, və-) *n.* **1.** a period of rest or freedom from duty, business, etc. —*v.i.* **2.** to take a vacation.

vac′ci.nate′ (vak′sə nāt′) *v.t.,* **-nated, -nating.** to inoculate against disease. —**vac′ci.na′tion,** *n.*

vac.cine′ (vak sēn′) *n.* a substance injected into the bloodstream to give immunity from infection.

vac′il.late′ (vas′ə lāt′) *v.i.,* **-lated, -lating. 1.** to be indecisive. **2.** to waver. —**vac′il.la′tion,** *n.*

vac′u.ous (vak′yoō əs) *adj.* **1.**

empty. **2.** showing a lack of intelligence. —**va·cu'i·ty,** *n.*

vac'u·um (vak'yōōm, -yōō əm, -yəm) *n.* **1.** a space from which all matter has been removed. —*v.t., v.i.* **2.** to clean with a vacuum cleaner.

vac'uum bot'tle *n.* a bottle with a double wall enclosing a vacuum, used to keep liquids hot or cold.

vac'uum clean'er *n.* an electrical appliance for cleaning by suction.

vac'uum-packed' *adj.* packed with as much air as possible evacuated before sealing.

vag'a·bond' (vag'ə bond') *adj.* **1.** wandering. —*n.* **2.** a wanderer. **3.** a vagrant.

va·gar'y (və gâr'ē, vā'gə rē) *n., pl.* **-garies.** a capricious act or idea.

va·gi'na (və jī'nə) *n., pl.* **-nas, -nae.** the passage from the uterus to the vulva. —**vag'i·nal** (vaj'ə nl) *adj.*

va'grant (vā'grənt) *n.* **1.** a person who has no home. —*adj.* **2.** wandering. —**va'gran·cy,** *n.*

vague (vāg) *adj.,* **vaguer, vaguest. 1.** not clearly expressed. **2.** indistinct.

vain (vān) *adj.* **1.** conceited. **2.** futile. —**Idiom. 3. in vain,** without effect. —**vain'ly,** *adv.*

vain'glo'ry *n.* excessive vanity. —**vain·glo'ri·ous,** *adj.*

val'ance (val'əns, vā'ləns) *n.* a drapery across the top of a window.

vale (vāl) *n.* a valley.

val'e·dic·to'ri·an (val'i dik tôr'ē ən) *n.* a graduating student who delivers the valedictory.

val'e·dic'to·ry (-tə rē) *n., pl.* **-ries.** a farewell address, esp. one delivered at commencement.

va'lence (vā'ləns) *n.* the relative combining capacity of an atom compared with that of the hydrogen atom.

val'en·tine' (val'ən tīn') *n.* **1.** an affectionate card or gift sent on February 14 (**St. Valentine's Day**). **2.** a sweetheart greeted on that day.

val'et (va lā', val'it, val'ā) *n.* a personal manservant.

val'iant (val'yənt) *adj.* brave.

val'id (val'id) *adj.* **1.** sound; logical. **2.** legally binding. —**val'i·date',** *v.t.* —**val'i·da'tion,** *n.* —**va·lid'i·ty** (və lid'i tē) *n.*

va·lise' (və lēs') *n.* a traveling bag.

val'ley (val'ē) *n.* a long depression between uplands or mountains.

val'or (val'ər) *n.* bravery.

val'u·a·ble (-yōō ə bəl, -yə bəl) *adj.* **1.** of great worth, importance, etc. —*n.* **2. valuables,** articles of great value.

val·u·a'tion (-yōō ā'shən) *n.* an estimate of a thing's value.

val'ue *n., v.,* **-ued, -uing.** —*n.* **1.** worth or importance. **2.** equivalent worth in money, goods, etc. **3. values,** the abstract concepts of what is right or good. —*v.t.* **4.** to estimate the worth of. **5.** to regard highly. —**val'ue·less,** *adj.*

valve (valv) *n.* **1.** a device for controlling the flow of a liquid or gas. **2.** a structure allowing a body fluid to flow in one direction only.

vam'pire (vam'pī³r) *n.* (in folklore) a corpse that is said to be reanimated and to suck the blood of living persons.

van (van) *n.* **1.** a covered truck for moving furniture, animals, etc. **2.** a small closed trucklike vehicle.

van'dal (van'dl) *n.* a person who willfully damages or destroys another's property. —**van'dal·ism,** *n.* —**van'dal·ize,** *v.t.*

vane (vān) *n.* **1.** a weathervane. **2.** one of a set of blades set on a rotor to be moved by fluid or air.

van'guard' (van'-) *n.* the foremost part of an advancing army, a movement, etc.

va·nil'la (və nil'ə; *often* -nel'ə) *n.* **1.** a tropical orchid, whose fruit (**vanilla bean**) yields a flavoring extract. **2.** this flavoring.

van'ish (van'ish) *v.i.* to disappear.

van'i·ty (van'i tē) *n., pl.* **-ties. 1.** excessive pride in oneself, esp. in one's appearance. **2.** futility.

van'quish (vang'kwish, van'-) *v.t.* to conquer; defeat.

van'tage (van'tij) *n.* **1.** a place or condition offering some advantage. **2.** an advantage.

vap'id (vap'id) *adj.* insipid; dull.

va'por (vā'pər) *n.* **1.** visible matter, as mist, suspended in air. **2.** a gas.

va'por·ize' *v.t., v.i.,* **-ized, -izing.** to change into vapor. —**va'por·i·za'tion,** *n.* —**va'por·iz'er,** *n.*

var'i·a·ble (vâr'ē ə bəl) *adj.* **1.** changeable. **2.** inconstant. —*n.* **3.** something variable. —**var'i·a·bil'i·ty,** *n.*

var'i·ance (-əns) *n.* **1.** the state of being variable. **2.** disagreement.

var'i·ant *adj.* **1.** varying. **2.** differing. —*n.* **3.** a variant form, spelling, etc.

var'i·a'tion (-ā'shən) *n.* **1.** a change. **2.** amount of change. **3.** a different form of something. **4.** the transformation of a melody with changes in harmony, rhythm, etc.

var'i·col'ored (vâr'i kul'ərd) *adj.* having various colors.

var'i·cose' (var'i kōs') *adj.* abnormally swollen, as veins.

var′i•e•gate′ (vâr′ē i gāt′, vâr′i-)
v.t., **-gated, -gating. 1.** to make
varied in appearance. **2.** to give variety to.

va•ri′e•ty (və rī′i tē) *n.*, *pl.* **-ties. 1.**
diversity. **2.** a number of different
things. **3.** a kind or sort.

var′i•ous (vâr′ē əs) *adj.* **1.** of different kinds. **2.** several.

var′mint (vär′mənt) *n.* an undesirable, usu. verminous animal.

var′nish (vär′nish) *n.* **1.** a resinous
solution that dries to form a hard,
glossy coat. **2.** a gloss. —*v.t.* **3.** to
coat with varnish.

var′y (vâr′ē) *v.t.*, **varied, varying.
1.** to change. **2.** to cause to be different. —*v.i.* **3.** to differ.

vas′cu•lar (vas′kyə lər) *adj.* of vessels that convey fluids, as blood.

vase (vās, vāz, väz) *n.* a tall container, esp. for flowers.

vas•ec′to•my (va sek′tə mē, və-) *n.*,
pl. **-mies.** surgical removal of part
of the sperm-carrying duct of the
testis, resulting in sterility.

vas′sal (vas′əl) *n.* **1.** a feudal holder
of land who renders service to a
lord. **2.** a subject, servant, etc.

vast (vast) *adj.* immense; huge.

vat (vat) *n.* a large container, as a
tank, for liquids.

vaude′ville (vôd′vil, vōd′-, vô′də-)
n. a form of popular entertainment
made up of separate acts.

vault¹ (vôlt) *n.* **1.** an arched ceiling
or roof. **2.** an arched space, chamber, etc. **3.** a room for the safekeeping of valuables. —*v.t.*, *v.i.* **4.**
to build or cover with a vault.
—**vault′ed,** *adj.*

vault² (vôlt) *v.i.*, *v.t.* to leap (over).
vault′ing *adj.* **1.** leaping. **2.** excessive.

vaunt (vônt, vänt) *v.t.*, *v.i.* **1.** to
boast (of). —*n.* **2.** a boast.

VCR videocassette recorder.

VD venereal disease.

V′-Day′ *n.* a day of military victory.

VDT video display terminal.

veal (vēl) *n.* the flesh of a calf as
used for food.

vec′tor (vek′tər) *n.* a quantity possessing both magnitude and direction.

veer (vēr) *v.i.* to change direction.

veg′e•ta•ble (vej′tə bəl, vej′i tə-) *n.*
1. a plant grown for food. —*adj.* **2.**
of vegetables.

veg′e•tar′i•an (vej′i târ′ē ən) *n.* **1.** a
person who does not eat meat,
fish, or fowl. —*adj.* **2.** of vegetari-
ans. **3.** consisting solely of vegetables. —**veg′e•tar′i•an•ism,** *n.*

veg′e•tate′ (-tāt′) *v.i.*, **-tated, -tat-
ing. 1.** to grow as plants do. **2.** to

live a dull, inactive life. —**veg′e•
ta′tive,** *adj.*

veg′e•ta′tion *n.* plants collectively.

ve′he•ment (vē′ə mənt) *adj.* showing strong feeling. —**ve′he•mence,
ve′he•men′cy,** *n.*

ve′hi•cle (vē′i kəl) *n.* **1.** a conveyance for passengers or goods, as a
car, truck, etc. **2.** a means by
which something is transmitted.
—**ve•hic′u•lar** (-hik′yə lər) *adj.*

veil (vāl) *n.* **1.** a piece of material
concealing the face. **2.** a part of a
headdress, as of a nun or a bride.
3. a cover; screen. **4.** a pretense.
—*v.t.* **5.** to cover with a veil.

vein (vān) *n.* **1.** one of the vessels
conveying blood to the heart. **2.** a
tubular riblike thickening, as in a
leaf or insect wing. **3.** a layer of
ore, coal, etc., in rock. **4.** a quality.
—*v.t.* **5.** to furnish or mark with
veins.

Vel′cro (vel′krō) *Trademark.* a fastening tape with opposing pieces
of nylon that interlock.

veld (velt, felt) *n.* the open grassy
country in South Africa. Also,
veldt.

vel′lum (vel′əm) *n.* parchment.

ve•loc′i•ty (və los′i tē) *n.*, *pl.* **-ties.**
speed.

ve′lo•drome′ (vē′lə drōm′) *n.* an
indoor arena with a banked track
for cycling.

ve•lour′ (və lŏŏr′) *n.* a velvetlike
fabric used for clothing and upholstery.

vel′vet (vel′vit) *n.* a woven fabric
with a thick, soft pile.

vel′vet•een′ (-vi tēn′) *n.* a cotton
fabric resembling velvet.

ve′nal (vēn′l) *adj.* corrupt.

vend (vend) *v.t.*, *v.i.* to sell.

ven•det′ta (ven det′ə) *n.* a long,
bitter feud.

vend′ing machine′ *n.* a coin-
operated machine for selling small
articles.

ven′dor *n.* one that sells. Also,
vend′er.

ve•neer′ (və nēr′) *n.* **1.** a thin layer
of material for covering wood. **2.** a
superficial appearance. —*v.t.* **3.** to
cover with a veneer.

ven′er•a•ble (ven′ər ə bəl) *adj.*
worthy of reverence.

ven′er•ate′ (-ə rāt′) *v.t.*, **-ated, -at-
ing.** to revere. —**ven′er•a′tion,** *n.*

ve•ne′re•al (və nēr′ē əl) *adj.* of or
transmitted by sexual intercourse.

ve•ne′tian blind′ (-nē′shən) *n.* a
window blind with horizontal
slats.

venge′ance (ven′jəns) *n.* **1.** infliction of harm in retaliation for a

wrong. —*Idiom.* **2. with a vengeance,** to an extreme degree.

venge′ful *adj.* seeking vengeance.

ve′ni•al (vē′nē əl, vēn′yəl) *n.* (of a sin) pardonable.

ven′i•son (ven′ə sən, -zən) *n.* the flesh of a deer used for food.

ven′om (ven′əm) *n.* **1.** a poisonous fluid secreted by some snakes, spiders, etc. **2.** spite; malice. —**ven′om•ous,** *adj.*

ve′nous (vē′nəs) *adj.* **1.** of or having veins. **2.** of or being the blood carried back to the heart by veins.

vent (vent) *n.* **1.** an opening serving as an outlet, as for fluid or fumes. **2.** expression; utterance. —*v.t.* **3.** to express freely. **4.** to release or discharge through a vent.

ven′ti•late′ (ven′tl āt′) *v.t.,* **-lated, -lating.** to provide with fresh air. —**ven′ti•la′tion,** *n.* —**ven′ti•la′tor,** *n.*

ven′tral (ven′trəl) *adj.* of or near the belly; abdominal.

ven′tri•cle (ven′tri kəl) *n.* either of two lower chambers of the heart.

ven•tril′o•quism′ (ven tril′ə kwiz′əm) *n.* the art of speaking so that the voice seems to come from another source. —**ven•tril′o•quist,** *n.*

ven′ture (ven′chər) *n., v.,* **-tured, -turing.** —*n.* **1.** an undertaking involving risk. —*v.t.* **2.** to risk; dare. —*v.i.* **3.** to undertake a venture. —**ven′ture•some** (-səm), *adj.*

ven′ue (ven′yōō) *n.* the scene or locale of an action or event.

Ve′nus (vē′nəs) *n.* the second planet from the sun.

Ven′us's-fly′trap *n.* a plant with hinged leaves that trap insects.

ve•rac′i•ty (və ras′ə tē) *n.* truthfulness or accuracy. —**ve•ra′cious** (-rā′shəs) *adj.*

ve•ran′da (-ran′də) *n.* an open porch. Also, **ve•ran′dah.**

verb (vûrb) *n.* a part of speech expressing action, state, or occurrence.

ver′bal (vûr′bəl) *adj.* **1.** of or in the form of words. **2.** oral. —**ver′bal•ly,** *adv.*

ver′bal•ize′ *v.,* **-ized, -izing.** —*v.t.* **1.** to express in words. —*v.i.* **2.** to express something verbally.

ver•ba′tim (vər bā′tim) *adv.* word for word.

ver′bi•age (vûr′bē ij) *n.* an overabundance of words.

ver•bose′ (vər bōs′) *adj.* excessively wordy. —**ver•bos′i•ty** (-bos′i tē) *n.*

ver′dant (vûr′dnt) *adj.* green with vegetation. —**ver′dan•cy,** *n.*

ver′dict (vûr′dikt) *n.* a judgment or decision.

ver′dure (vûr′jər) *n.* **1.** greenness. **2.** green vegetation.

verge (vûrj) *n., v.,* **verged, verging.** —*n.* **1.** an edge or margin. —*v.i.* **2.** to border.

ver′i•fy′ (ver′ə fī′) *v.t.,* **-fied, -fying. 1.** to prove to be true. **2.** to ascertain the correctness of. —**ver′i•fi′a•ble,** *adj.* —**ver′i•fi•ca′tion,** *n.*

ver′i•ly (-lē) *adv. Archaic.* truly.

ver′i•si•mil′i•tude′ (-si mil′i tōōd′, -tyōōd′) *n.* the appearance of truth.

ver′i•ta•ble (-tə bəl) *adj.* genuine.

ver′i•ty (-tē) *n.* truth.

ver•mil′ion (vər mil′yən) *n.* a bright red.

ver′min (vûr′min) *n.pl.* small, objectionable animals or insects. —**ver′min•ous,** *adj.*

ver•mouth′ (vər mōōth′) *n.* a white wine flavored with herbs.

ver•nac′u•lar (vər nak′yə lər, və nak′-) *n.* **1.** the native speech of an area. **2.** the language of a particular group. —*adj.* **3.** (of language) used locally or in everyday speech.

ver′nal (vûr′nl) *adj.* of spring.

ver′sa•tile (vûr′sə tl; *esp. Brit.* -tīl′) *adj.* capable of doing a variety of things well. —**ver′sa•til′i•ty,** *n.*

verse (vûrs) *n.* **1.** a line of a poem. **2.** a type of metrical composition. **3.** a poem. **4.** poetry. **5.** a division of a Biblical chapter.

versed *adj.* expert; skilled.

ver′si•fy′ (vûr′sə fī′) *v.,* **-fied, -fying.** —*v.t.* **1.** to treat in or turn into verse. —*v.i.* **2.** to compose verses. —**ver′si•fi•ca′tion,** *n.*

ver′sion (vûr′zhən, -shən) *n.* **1.** a particular account of something. **2.** a special form. **3.** a translation.

ver′so (vûr′sō) *n., pl.* **-sos.** the left-hand page of a book.

ver′sus (-səs, -səz) *prep.* in opposition or contrast to.

ver′te•bra (-tə brə) *n., pl.* **-brae, -bras.** one of the bones of the spinal column. —**ver′te•bral,** *adj.*

ver′te•brate′ (-brit, -brāt′) *adj.* **1.** having vertebrae. —*n.* **2.** a vertebrate animal.

ver′tex (vûr′teks) *n., pl.* **-texes, -tices** (-tə sēz′). the highest point.

ver′ti•cal (vûr′ti kəl) *adj.* **1.** perpendicular to level ground; upright. —*n.* **2.** something vertical.

ver•tig′i•nous (vər tij′ə nəs) *adj.* **1.** whirling. **2.** affected with or liable to cause vertigo.

ver′ti•go′ (vûr′ti gō′) *n., pl.* **-goes.** dizziness.

verve (vûrv) *n.* vivaciousness.

ver′y (ver′ē) *adv., adj.,* **-ier, -iest.** —*adv.* **1.** extremely. **2.** absolutely. —*adj.* **3.** precise. **4.** mere **5.** sheer; utter. **6.** actual.

ves′i•cle (ves′i kəl) *n.* a small sac in the body.

ves′pers (-pərz) *n.* an evening religious service.

ves′sel (-əl) *n.* **1.** a ship or boat. **2.** a container, esp. one for liquids. **3.** a tube or duct that conveys a bodily fluid.

vest (vest) *n.* **1.** a waist-length sleeveless garment. —*v.t.* **2.** to clothe. **3.** to endow with powers, rights, etc.

vest′ed *adj.* held completely and permanently.

vest′ed in′terest *n.* a special interest in a system, arrangement, or institution for personal reasons.

ves′ti•bule′ (ves′tə byool′) *n.* a small room between the outer door and the interior of a building.

ves′tige (-tij) *n.* **1.** a trace of something extinct. **2.** a very small amount of something. —**ves•tig′i•al** (ve stij′ē əl, -stij′əl) *adj.*

vest′ing *n.* the granting to an employee of the right to pension benefits despite early retirement.

vest′ment *n.* a ceremonial garment, esp. that worn by clergy during a religious service.

vest′-pock′et *adj.* very small.

ves′try (ves′trē) *n., pl.* **-tries. 1.** a room in a church for vestments or for meetings. **2.** a committee managing temporal affairs in the Episcopal church.

vet (vet) *n. Informal.* **1.** a veterinarian. **2.** a veteran.

vet′er•an (vet′ər ən) *n.* **1.** a person who has served in the armed forces. **2.** an experienced person. —*adj.* **3.** experienced.

vet•er•i•nar′i•an (-ə när′ē ən) *n.* a doctor qualified to treat the diseases and injuries of animals.

vet′er•i•nar′y (-ner′ē) *n., pl.* **-naries,** *adj.* —*n.* **1.** a veterinarian. —*adj.* **2.** of or for the medical and surgical treatment of animals.

ve′to (vē′tō) *n., pl.* **-toes,** *v.,* **-toed, -toing.** —*n.* **1.** the power of the executive branch of government to reject an action of the legislative branch. **2.** a strong prohibition. —*v.t.* **3.** to reject (a bill) by veto.

vex (veks) *v.t.* **1.** to irritate. **2.** to worry. —**vex•a′tion,** *n.* —**vex•a′tious,** *adj.* —**vexed,** *adj.*

vi′a (vī′ə, vē′ə) *prep.* by way of.

vi′a•ble (vī′ə bəl) *adj.* **1.** capable of living. **2.** practicable; workable.

vi′a•duct′ *n.* a bridge carrying a road or railroad.

Vi•ag•ra (-ag′rə) *Trademark.* a drug used to treat impotence.

vi′al (vī′əl, vīl) *n.* a small glass container.

vi′and (vī′ənd) *n.* an article of food.

vi′brant (vī′brənt) *adj.* **1.** vibrating. **2.** energetic; vital. —**vi′bran•cy,** *n.*

vi′brate (vī′brāt) *v.i.,* **-brated, -brating. 1.** to move to and fro very rapidly and continuously. **2.** to resonate. —**vi•bra′tion,** *n.* —**vi′bra•tor,** *n.*

vi•bra′to (vi brä′tō) *n., pl.* **-tos.** a pulsating effect produced by rapid but slight alterations in pitch.

vic′ar (vik′ər) *n.* **1.** a parish priest in the Anglican church. **2.** a representative of a bishop in the Roman Catholic church. —**vic′ar•age,** *n.*

vi•car′i•ous (vī kâr′ē əs, vi-) *adj.* **1.** done or suffered in place of another. **2.** felt through imagined participation in the experience of another. —**vi•car′i•ous•ly,** *adv.*

vice (vīs) *n.* **1.** an evil habit or practice. **2.** immoral conduct. **3.** a personal fault.

vice- a prefix meaning deputy.

vice′-ad′mi•ral (vīs′) *n.* a commissioned officer ranking above a rear admiral.

vice′ pres′i•dent *n.* an officer next in rank to a president. —**vice′ pres′i•den•cy,** *n.*

vice′roy (vīs′roi) *n.* a person who rules an area as the deputy of the sovereign.

vi′ce ver′sa (vī′sə vûr′sə, vīs′, vī′sē) *adv.* in reverse order.

vi•cin′i•ty (vi sin′i tē) *n., pl.* **-ties.** the neighborhood; nearby area.

vi′cious (vish′əs) *adj.* **1.** evil. **2.** malicious. **3.** savage.

vi•cis′si•tude′ (vi sis′i tood′, -tyood′) *n.* change or variation.

vic′tim (vik′təm) *n.* **1.** a person who suffers from an injurious action or event. **2.** a person who is cheated. **3.** a creature sacrificed in a religious rite. —**vic′tim•ize′,** *v.t.*

vic′tor (-tər) *n.* a winner. —**vic•to′ri•ous** (-tôr′ē əs) *adj.*

vic′to•ry (-tə rē) *n., pl.* **-ries.** success in winning a contest, battle, etc.

vict′uals (vit′lz) *n.pl.* food.

vid′e•o′ (vid′ē ō′) *n., pl.* **-eos,** *adj.* —*n.* **1.** the visual elements of a telecast. **2.** a videotape or videocassette. —*adj.* **3.** of television.

vid′e•o′cas•sette′ *n.* a cassette containing videotape.

vid′eocassette′ record′er *n.* an electronic device for recording and playing videocassettes.

vid′e•o•disc′ *n.* a disc on which pictures and sound are recorded for playback on a TV set.

vid′eo game′ *n.* an electronic game played on a screen.

vid′e•o•tape′ *n., v.,* **-taped, -tap-**

ing. —*n.* **1.** magnetic tape on which a TV program, motion picture, etc., can be recorded. —*v.t.* **2.** to record on videotape.

vie (vī) *v.i.,* **vied, vying.** to contend for superiority.

view (vyōō) *n.* **1.** seeing or beholding. **2.** a range of vision. **3.** a sight, as of a landscape. **4.** a picture of a scene. **5.** a manner of looking at something. **6.** a personal opinion. —*v.t.* **7.** to see; look at. **8.** to consider. —**view′er,** *n.*

view′point′ *n.* **1.** a point of view. **2.** a place from which there is a good view.

vig′il (vij′əl) *n.* a period of staying awake to watch or pray.

vig′i.lant (-lənt) *adj.* **1.** watchful. **2.** wary. —**vig′i.lance,** *n.*

vig′i.lan′te (-lan′tē) *n.* a person who takes the law into his or her own hands.

vi.gnette′ (vin yet′) *n.* a literary sketch.

vig′or (vig′ər) *n.* **1.** active strength. **2.** vitality. —**vig′or.ous,** *adj.*

vile (vīl) *adj.,* **viler, vilest. 1.** very bad. **2.** highly offensive. **3.** evil.

vil′i.fy′ (vil′ə fī′) *v.t.,* **-fied, -fying.** to speak ill of. —**vil′i.fi.ca′tion,** *n.*

vil′la (vil′ə) *n.* a country residence.

vil′lage (vil′ij) *n.* a small town. —**vil′lag.er,** *n.*

vil′lain (vil′ən) *n.* a wicked person. —**vil′lain.ous,** *adj.* —**vil′lain.y,** *n.*

vim (vim) *n.* vitality.

vin′ai.grette′ (vin′ə gret′) *n.* a dressing, esp. for salad, of oil and vinegar usu. with herbs.

vin′di.cate′ (vin′di kāt′) *v.t.,* **-cated, -cating. 1.** to clear, as from a suspicion. **2.** to uphold or justify. —**vin′di.ca′tion,** *n.*

vin.dic′tive (-dik′tiv) *adj.* holding a grudge; vengeful.

vine (vīn) *n.* a creeping or climbing plant with a slender stem.

vin′e.gar (vin′i gər) *n.* a sour liquid obtained by fermentation of wine or cider. —**vin′e.gar.y,** *adj.*

vine′yard (-yərd) *n.* a plantation of grapevines.

vin′tage (vin′tij) *n.* **1.** the wine or grapes from one harvest. **2.** the output of a particular time. —*adj.* **3.** of a specified vintage. **4.** being the best of a kind. **5.** of a style of the past.

vint′ner (vint′nər) *n.* a person who makes wine.

vi′nyl (vīn′l) *n.* a type of plastic.

vi.o′la (vē ō′lə) *n.* a stringed instrument resembling the violin but slightly larger and deeper in tone.

vi′o.late′ (vī′ō lāt′) *v.t.,* **-lated, -lating. 1.** to break or transgress. **2.** to break through or into. **3.** to desecrate. **4.** to rape. —**vi′o.la′tion,** *n.* —**vi′o.la′tor,** *n.*

vi′o.lent *adj.* **1.** uncontrolled, strong, or rough. **2.** caused by destructive force. **3.** intense; severe. —**vi′o.lence,** *n.* —**vi′o.lent.ly,** *adv.*

vi′o.let (vī′ə lit) *n.* **1.** a low plant bearing bluish purple flowers. **2.** a bluish purple.

vi′o.lin′ (vī′ə lin′) *n.* a stringed instrument of treble pitch, played with a bow. —**vi′o.lin′ist,** *n.*

VIP (vē′ī′pē′) *Informal.* very important person.

vi′per (vī′pər) *n.* **1.** a kind of venomous snake. **2.** a treacherous person. —**vi′per.ous,** *adj.*

vi.ra′go (vi rä′gō, -rā′-) *n., pl.* **-goes, -gos.** a shrewish woman.

vi′ral (vī′rəl) *adj.* of or caused by a virus.

vir′gin (vûr′jin) *n.* **1.** a person who has not had sexual intercourse. **2. the Virgin,** Mary, the mother of Jesus. —*adj.* **3.** of or like a virgin. **4.** untouched; unused. —**vir′gin.al,** *adj.* —**vir′gin.i.ty,** *n.*

vir′gule (vûr′gyōōl) *n.* an oblique stroke (/) used as a dividing line.

vir′ile (vir′əl) *adj.* **1.** manly. **2.** vigorous. **3.** capable of procreating. —**vi.ril′i.ty,** *n.*

vir′tu.al (vûr′chōō əl) *adj.* **1.** being such in effect, though not actually. **2.** simulated by a computer.

vir′tual real′ity *n.* realistic simulation of an environment by a computer program.

vir′tue (vûr′chōō) *n.* **1.** moral excellence. **2.** chastity. **3.** an admirable quality.

vir.tu.o′so (-ō′sō) *n., pl.* **-sos, -si.** a person of special skill, esp. in music. —**vir′tu.os′i.ty** (-os′i tē) *n.*

vir′tu.ous (-əs) *adj.* **1.** conforming to moral principles. **2.** chaste. —**vir′tu.ous.ly,** *adv.*

vir′u.lent (vir′yə lənt, vir′ə-) *adj.* **1.** very poisonous or infectious. **2.** violently hostile. —**vir′u.lence,** *n.*

vi′rus (vī′rəs) *n.* **1.** a tiny infectious agent that causes disease. **2.** a self-replicating code planted illegally in a computer program.

vi′sa (vē′zə) *n.* a passport endorsement permitting the bearer to enter a foreign country.

vis′age (viz′ij) *n.* **1.** the face. **2.** aspect.

vis′-à-vis′ (vē′zə vē′) *prep.* **1.** in relation to. **2.** opposite. —*adv., adj.* **3.** face to face.

vis′cer.a (vis′ər ə) *n.pl.* the internal organs of the body.

vis′cer.al *adj.* **1.** proceeding from

instinct rather than intellect. **2.** of the viscera. —**vis′cer•al•ly,** *adv.*

vis′count (vī′kount′) *n.* a nobleman ranking below an earl or count. —**vis′count•ess,** *n.fem.*

vis′cous (vis′kəs) *adj.* sticky; gluey. Also, **vis′cid** (vis′id).

vise (vīs) *n.* a device, usu. with two jaws, for holding an object firmly.

vis′i•bil′i•ty (viz′ə bil′i tē) *n.* the range of vision under given conditions.

vis′i•ble (-bəl) *adj.* **1.** capable of being seen. **2.** perceptible.

vi′sion (vizh′ən) *n.* **1.** the power or sense of sight. **2.** imagination or unusually keen perception. **3.** a mental image of something imaginary.

vi′sion•ar′y (vizh′ə ner′ē) *adj., n., pl.* **-ies.** —*adj.* **1.** given to or marked by fanciful or impractical ideas. **2.** seen in a vision. —*n.* **3.** a person of unusual foresight. **4.** a seer of visions. **5.** a dreamer.

vis′it (viz′it) *v.t.* **1.** to go or come to see. **2.** to stay temporarily at. **3.** to afflict. **4.** to access (a Web site). —*v.i.* **5.** to make a visit. —*n.* **6.** an act of visiting. **7.** a stay as a guest. —**vis′i•tor, vis′i•tant,** *n.*

vis′it•a′tion (-i tā′shən) *n.* **1.** a formal visit. **2.** a punishment, as from God.

vi′sor (vī′zər) *n.* the projecting front part of a cap, helmet, etc.

vis′ta (vis′tə) *n.* an extended view in one direction.

vis′u•al (vizh′o͞o əl) *adj.* **1.** of or used in seeing. **2.** visible.

vis′u•al•ize′ *v.i., v.t.,* **-ized, -izing.** to form a mental image (of).

vi′tal (vīt′l) *adj.* **1.** of or necessary to life. **2.** essential. **3.** energetic.

vi•tal′i•ty (-tal′i tē) *n., pl.* **-ties. 1.** physical or mental vigor. **2.** power to live or grow.

vi′tal signs′ *n.pl.* essential body functions, comprising pulse rate, body temperature, and respiration.

vi′tal statis′tics *n.pl.* statistics concerning deaths, births, and marriages.

vi′ta•min (vī′tə min) *n.* an organic substance found in food and essential to maintain life.

vi′ti•ate′ (vish′ē āt′) *v.t.,* **-ated, -ating. 1.** to impair the quality or effectiveness of. **2.** to make legally invalid.

vit′re•ous (vi′trē əs) *adj.* of or like glass.

vit′reous hu′mor *n.* the transparent gelatinous substance that fills the eyeball.

vit′ri•fy′ *v.t., v.i.,* **-fied, -fying.** to change into glass.

vit′ri•ol (vi′trē əl) *n.* **1.** a glassy metallic compound. **2.** sulfuric acid. **3.** savagely caustic criticism. —**vit′-ri•ol′ic** (-ol′ik) *adj.*

vi•tu′per•ate′ (vī to͞o′pə rāt′, -tyo͞o′-, vi-) *v.t.,* **-ated, -ating.** to criticize harshly. —**vi•tu′per•a′tive,** *adj.*

vi•va′cious (vi vā′shəs, vī-) *adj.* lively. —**vi•vac′i•ty** (-vas′i tē) *n.*

viv′id (viv′id) *adj.* **1.** strikingly bright or intense, as color or an image. **2.** clearly perceptible. **3.** full of life. —**viv′id•ly,** *adv.*

viv′i•sec′tion (viv′ə sek′shən) *n.* the dissection of a live animal.

vix′en (vik′sən) *n.* **1.** a female fox. **2.** an ill-tempered woman.

vi•zier′ (vi zēr′, viz′yər) *n.* a high official in some Muslim countries.

vo•cab′u•lar′y (vō kab′yə ler′ē) *n., pl.* **-laries. 1.** all the words used by a person or group. **2.** an alphabetical list of defined words.

vo′cal (vō′kəl) *adj.* **1.** of the voice. **2.** of or for singing. **3.** outspoken.

vo′cal cords′ *n.pl.* membranes in the larynx that vibrate to produce sound.

vo′cal•ist (-kə list) *n.* a singer.

vo′cal•ize′ *v.,* **-ized, -iz•ing.** —*v.t.* **1.** to articulate. —*v.i.* **2.** to utter sounds with the vocal cords.

vo•ca′tion (vō kā′shən) *n.* an occupation, business, or profession. —**vo•ca′tion•al,** *adj.*

voc′a•tive (vok′ə tiv) *adj.* of or being a grammatical case used to indicate the one being addressed.

vo•cif′er•ous, *adj.* making a loud or vehement outcry.

vod′ka (vod′kə) *n.* a colorless distilled liquor made from rye or wheat.

vogue (vōg) *n.* **1.** the current fashion. **2.** popularity.

voice (vois) *n., v.,* **voiced, voicing.** —*n.* **1.** sound uttered through the mouth. **2.** an expressed will or desire. **3.** the right to express an opinion. **4.** a verb form indicating whether the subject is acting or acted upon. —*v.t.* **5.** to express or declare. —**voice′less,** *adj.*

voice′ mail′ *n.* an electronic system that routes voice messages to appropriate recipients.

void (void) *adj.* **1.** without legal force. **2.** useless. **3.** empty. —*n.* **4.** emptiness. —*v.t.* **5.** to invalidate. **6.** to empty. —**void′a•ble,** *adj.*

voile (voil) *n.* a lightweight, semisheer fabric.

vol. volume.

vol′a•tile (vol′ə tl) *adj.* **1.** evaporating rapidly. **2.** explosive. **3.** unstable.

vol•ca′no (vol kā′nō) *n., pl.* **-noes,**

-nos. 1. a vent in the earth's crust from which lava, steam, and ashes are expelled. **2.** a mountain formed from this lava and ash. —**vol•can′ic** (-kan′ik) *adj.*

vole (vōl) *n.* a short-tailed, stocky rodent.

vo•li′tion (vō lish′ən, və-) *n.* will.

vol′ley (vol′ē) *n.* **1.** a discharge of many missiles together. **2.** a burst of many things at once. **3.** the return of a ball before it hits the ground, as in tennis. —*v.t., v.i.* **4.** to discharge or be discharged in a volley. **5.** to return (a ball) before it hits the ground.

vol′ley•ball′ *n.* **1.** a game in which a large ball is volleyed back and forth over a net. **2.** the ball used in this game.

volt (vōlt) *n.* a unit of electromotive force.

volt′age (vōl′tij) *n.* electromotive force expressed in volts.

volt′me′ter *n.* an instrument for measuring the voltage between two points.

vol′u•ble (vol′yə bəl) *adj.* fluent; talkative. —**vol′u•bil′i•ty,** *n.*

vol′ume (vol′yōōm, -yəm) *n.* **1.** a book. **2.** the amount of space occupied by or contained in an object. **3.** a quantity; mass. **4.** loudness of sound.

vo•lu′mi•nous (və lōō′mə nəs) *adj.* **1.** filling volumes. **2.** of great size.

vol′un•tar′y (vol′ən ter′ē) *adj.* **1.** done, made, given, etc., by free choice and without expecting compensation. **2.** depending on voluntary action. **3.** done by or consisting of volunteers. **4.** controlled by the will. —**vol′un•tar′i•ly,** *adv.*

vol′un•teer′ *n.* **1.** a person who offers to serve or work without expecting payment. —*v.i.* **2.** to offer oneself as a volunteer. —*v.t.* **3.** to offer or perform voluntarily.

vo•lup′tu•ous (və lup′chōō əs) *adj.* **1.** luxurious; sensuous. **2.** full and shapely. —**vo•lup′tu•ous•ly,** *adv.*

vo•lute′ (və lōōt′) *n.* a spiral object.

vom′it (vom′it) *v.i., v.t.* **1.** to eject (the contents of the stomach) through the mouth. **2.** to eject or be ejected with force. —*n.* **3.** vomited matter.

voo′doo (vōō′dōō) *n.* a polytheistic religion deriving chiefly from African cult worship.

vo•ra′cious (vô rā′shəs) *adj.* greedy; ravenous. —**vo•rac′i•ty** (-ras′i tē) *n.*

vor′tex (vôr′teks) *n., pl.* **-texes, -tices** (-tə sēz′). a whirling mass or movement.

vo′ta•ry (vō′tə rē) *n., pl.* **-ries.** a worshiper; devotee.

vote (vōt) *n., v.,* **voted, voting.** —*n.* **1.** a formal expression of opinion or choice, as in an election. **2.** the right to this; suffrage. **3.** the number of votes cast. —*v.i.* **4.** to cast one's vote. —*v.t.* **5.** to establish or determine by vote. —**vot′er,** *n.*

vouch (vouch) *v.* **vouch for,** to give a guarantee of the dependability or accuracy of.

vouch′er *n.* a document, receipt, etc., proving an expenditure.

vouch•safe′ *v.t.,* **-safed, -safing.** to grant or give.

vow (vou) *n.* **1.** a solemn promise or pledge. —*v.t.* **2.** to promise solemnly. —*v.i.* **3.** to make a vow.

vow′el (vou′əl) *n.* **1.** a speech sound made without obstructing the flow of air. **2.** a letter representing a vowel.

voy′age (voi′ij) *n., v.,* **-aged, -aging.** —*n.* **1.** a journey. —*v.i.* **2.** to make a voyage.

vo•yeur′ (vwä yûr′, voi ûr′) *n.* a person who obtains sexual gratification by looking at sexual objects or acts. —**vo•yeur′ism,** *n.*

V.P. Vice President. Also, **VP.**

vs. versus.

VT Vermont. Also, **Vt.**

vul′can•ize′ (vul′kə nīz′) *v.t.,* **-ized, -izing.** to treat (rubber) with sulfur and heat to strengthen it. —**vul′can•i•za′tion,** *n.*

vul′gar (-gər) *adj.* **1.** lacking good breeding or taste. **2.** obscene. **3.** of the ordinary people in a society. **4.** expressed in their language. —**vul•gar′i•ty** (-gar′i tē) *n.*

vul′ner•a•ble (-nər ə bəl) *adj.* **1.** liable to physical or emotional hurt. **2.** open to attack.

vul′ture (vul′chər) *n.* a large, carrion-eating bird.

vul′va (vul′və) *n., pl.* **-vae, -vas.** the external female genitalia.

vy′ing (vī′ing) *n.* pres. part. of **vie.**

W

W, w (dub'əl yōō', -yōō) *n.* the twenty-third letter of the English alphabet.

W west, western.

WA Washington.

wack'y (wak'ē) *adj.*, **-ier, -iest.** *Slang.* odd or irrational.

wad (wod) *n., v.*, **wadded, wadding.** —*n.* **1.** a small soft mass. **2.** a large quantity. —*v.t.* **3.** to form into a wad. **4.** to stuff with a wad.

wad'dle (wod'l) *v.*, **-dled, -dling,** *n.* —*v.i.* **1.** to sway in walking, as a duck. —*n.* **2.** a waddling gait.

wade (wād) *v.i.*, **waded, wading. 1.** to walk through water, mud, snow, etc. **2.** to walk laboriously.

wa'fer (wā'fər) *n.* **1.** a thin crisp biscuit. **2.** a small disk of unleavened bread used in the Eucharist.

waf'fle¹ (wof'əl) *n.* a batter cake baked in a double griddle (**waffle iron**).

waf'fle² (wof'əl) *v.i.*, **-fled, -fling.** to speak or write equivocally.

waft (wäft, waft) *v.t., v.i.* **1.** to float lightly and smoothly through the air. —*n.* **2.** the sound, odor, etc., wafted.

wag (wag) *v.*, **wagged, wagging,** *n.* —*v.t., v.i.* **1.** to move rapidly back and forth. —*n.* **2.** the act of wagging. **3.** a witty person.

wage (wāj) *n., v.*, **waged, waging.** —*n.* **1.** Often, **wages.** money for work done. **2.** **wages,** recompense. —*v.t.* **3.** to carry on (an argument, war, etc.).

wa'ger (wā'jər) *n.* **1.** a bet. —*v.t., v.i.* **2.** to bet.

wag'on (wag'ən) *n.* a four-wheeled vehicle for moving heavy loads.

wag'on train' *n.* a train of wagons and horses.

waif (wāf) *n.* a homeless child.

wail (wāl) *n.* **1.** a long mournful cry. **2.** a sound like this. —*v.i.* **3.** to express sorrow with a long mournful cry.

wain'scot (wān'skət, -skot, -skōt) *n.* wood paneling lining an interior wall.

waist (wāst) *n.* **1.** the narrow part of the body between the ribs and the hips. **2.** the part of a garment covering the waist.

waist'band' *n.* a band, as on a skirt, encircling the waist.

waist'coat' (wes'kət, wāst'kōt') *n. Brit.* a vest.

waist'line' (wāst'līn') *n.* the circumference of the body at the waist.

wait (wāt) *v.i.* **1.** to remain inactive until a specified time or until an event occurs. **2.** to be ready. —*v.t.* **3.** to await. **4.** to postpone. **5. wait on,** to serve. —*n.* **6.** an act or period of waiting. —*Idiom.* **7. lie in wait,** to lie in ambush.

wait'er *n.* a man who waits on tables. —**wait'ress,** *n.fem.*

wait'ing list' *n.* a list of persons waiting, as for reservations.

waive (wāv) *v.t.*, **waived, waiving.** to refrain from claiming (a right).

waiv'er *n.* a statement relinquishing a right.

wake¹ (wāk) *v.*, **waked** or **woke** (wōk), **waked, waking,** *n.* —*v.i.* **1.** to become roused from sleep. **2.** to become aware of something. —*v.t.* **3.** to rouse from sleep. —*n.* **4.** a vigil beside a corpse awaiting burial.

wake² (wāk) *n.* the track of waves left by a vessel.

wake'ful *adj.* awake; alert.

wak'en *v.t., v.i.* to awake; awaken.

wale (wāl) *n., v.*, **waled, waling.** —*n.* **1.** a mark left on the skin by a rod or whip. **2.** a vertical cord in fabric. —*v.t.* **3.** to mark with wales.

walk (wôk) *v.i.* **1.** to move on foot at a moderate pace. —*v.t.* **2.** to go along, through, or over on foot. **3.** to cause or help to walk. —*n.* **4.** an act, course, or manner of walking. **5.** a distance walked. **6.** a sidewalk or path. **7.** a line of work or position in society.

walk'ie-talk'ie (wô'kē tô'kē) *n.* a portable radio transmitter and receiver.

walk'ing stick' *n.* a stick used for support in walking.

walk'out' *n.* a strike in which workers leave their place of work.

wall (wôl) *n.* **1.** an upright structure that divides, encloses, etc. **2.** a barrier or obstruction. —*v.t.* **3.** to enclose, divide, etc., with a wall.

wal'let (wol'it) *n.* a small flat case for paper money, cards, etc.

wall'eye' (wôl'ī-) *n.* **1.** a N American freshwater food fish. **2.** a condition in which the eye or eyes are turned outward.

wall'flow'er *n.* **1.** a shy person who remains at the side at a party. **2.** a plant with fragrant yellow or orange flowers.

wal'lop (wol'əp) *Informal.* —*v.t.* **1.** to thrash or defeat. —*n.* **2.** a hard blow.

wal'low (wol'ō) *v.i.* **1.** to roll around, as in mud. **2.** to indulge oneself.

wall′pa′per *n.* decorative paper for covering walls and ceilings.

wal′nut′ (wôl′nut′, -nət) *n.* a meaty edible nut with a wrinkled shell.

wal•rus (wôl′rəs) *n.* a large tusked mammal of Arctic seas.

waltz (wôlts) *n.* **1.** a ballroom dance in triple rhythm. —*v.i., v.t.* **2.** to dance a waltz (with).

wan (won) *adj.,* **wanner, wannest.** pale; worn-looking. —**wan′ly,** *adv.*

wand (wond) *n.* a slender rod, as one used by a magician.

wan′der (won′dər) *v.i.* **1.** to roam from one place to another without a definite purpose. **2.** to go astray. —*v.t.* **3.** to travel about, on, or through. —**wan′der•er,** *n.*

wan′der•lust′ *n.* a strong desire to travel.

wane (wān) *v.,* **waned, waning,** *n.* —*v.i.* **1.** to decline or decrease. —*n.* **2.** a decline or decrease.

wan′gle (wang′gəl) *v.t.,* **-gled, -gling.** to bring out or obtain by scheming or underhand methods.

want (wont) *v.t.* **1.** to feel a need or desire for. **2.** to lack; be deficient in. —*v.i.* **3.** to have a need. —*n.* **4.** lack. **5.** poverty.

want′ing *adj., prep.* lacking.

wan′ton (won′tn) *adj.* **1.** malicious or unjustifiable. **2.** unrestrained. —*n.* **3.** a wanton person.

war (wôr) *n., v.,* **warred, warring.** —*n.* **1.** armed conflict. —*v.t.* **2.** to make or carry on war.

war′ble (wôr′bəl) *v.,* **-bled, -bling,** *n.* —*v.i., v.t.* **1.** to sing with trills, as birds. —*n.* **2.** a warbled song.

war′bler *n.* a small songbird, often brightly colored.

ward (wôrd) *n.* **1.** a division of a city. **2.** a division of a hospital. **3.** a person under the legal care of a guardian or court. **4.** custody. —*v.* **5. ward off,** to repel or avert.

ward′en (wôr′dn) *n.* **1.** a keeper. **2.** the head of a prison.

ward′er *n.* a guard.

ward′robe′ *n.* **1.** a collection of clothes. **2.** a clothes closet.

ware (wâr) *n.* **1. wares,** goods for sale. **2.** a particular kind of merchandise.

ware′house′ *n., v.,* **-housed, -housing.** —*n.* (wâr′hous′) **1.** a storehouse for goods or merchandise. —*v.t.* (-houz′, -hous′) **2.** to place or store in a warehouse.

war′fare′ *n.* the waging of war.

war′head′ *n.* the section of a missile containing the explosive.

war′-horse′ *n. Informal.* a veteran of many conflicts.

war′lock′ *n.* a male witch.

warm (wôrm) *adj.* **1.** having, giving, or feeling moderate heat. **2.** friendly; affectionate. **3.** heated or angry. —*v.t., v.i.* **4.** to make or become warm. —**warmth,** *n.*

warm′-blood′ed *adj.* (of an animal) having a relatively constant body temperature that is independent of the environment.

warmed′-o′ver *adj.* **1.** reheated. **2.** stale; not new.

warm′heart′ed *adj.* having emotional warmth.

war′mon′ger (wôr′mung′ər, -mong′-) *n.* a person who advocates war.

warn (wôrn) *v.t.* **1.** to give advance notice of danger, evil, etc. **2.** to advise to be careful. —**warn′ing,** *n., adj.*

warp (wôrp) *v.t.* **1.** to bend out of shape; distort. —*v.i.* **2.** to become warped. —*n.* **3.** a bend or twist. **4.** the lengthwise threads in a loom.

war′rant (wôr′ənt) *n.* **1.** justification or authorization. **2.** a guarantee. **3.** a document authorizing something. —*v.t.* **4.** to authorize or justify. **5.** to guarantee.

war′rant of′ficer *n.* a military officer ranking below a commissioned officer.

war′ran•ty *n., pl.* **-ties.** a written guarantee.

war′ren (wôr′ən) *n.* a place where rabbits live.

war′ri•or (wôr′ē ər) *n.* a soldier.

war′ship′ *n.* a ship armed for combat.

wart (wôrt) *n.* a small hard growth on the skin. —**wart′y,** *adj.*

war′y (wâr′ē) *adj.,* **-ier, -iest. 1.** watchful. **2.** careful. —**war′i•ly,** *adv.*

was (wuz, woz; *unstressed* wəz) *v.* the first and third pers. sing., past indicative of **be.**

wash (wosh) *v.t.* **1.** to cleanse with liquid, esp. water. **2.** to flow through or over. **3.** to carry in flowing. **4.** to overlay with a thin coating, as of paint. —*v.i.* **5.** to wash oneself, clothes, etc. **6.** to be carried by water. —*n.* **7.** the act of washing. **8.** Also, **wash′ing.** items to be washed. **9.** a liquid covering. **10.** rough water or air behind a moving ship or plane. —**wash′a•ble,** *adj.*

Wash. Washington.

wash′board′ *n.* a board to scrub clothes on.

wash′bowl′ *n.* a large bowl for washing the hands and face. Also, **wash′ba′sin.**

wash′cloth′ *n.* a cloth for washing the face or body.

washed/-out/ *adj.* **1.** faded. **2.** *Informal.* weary or tired-looking.

washed/-up/ *adj.* *Informal.* done for; having failed.

wash/er *n.* **1.** a machine for washing. **2.** a flat ring of rubber, metal, etc., used under a bolt to give tightness.

wash/out/ *n.* **1.** a washing out of earth by water. **2.** *Slang.* a failure.

wash/room/ *n.* a room with washbowls and toilets.

wasn't (wuz/ənt, woz/-) a contraction of **was not.**

wasp (wosp) *n.* a slender winged stinging insect.

wasp/ish *adj.* irritable; snappish.

was/sail (wos/əl, wo sāl/) *n.* **1.** a toast to a person's health. **2.** a festivity with much drinking.

waste (wāst) *v.,* **wasted, wasting,** *n., adj.* —*v.t.* **1.** to spend or consume uselessly or carelessly. **2.** to fail to use. **3.** to make weak. —*v.i.* **4.** to be consumed or spent uselessly or carelessly. **5.** to become gradually used up. **6.** to become weak. —*n.* **7.** useless expenditure. **8.** neglect. **9.** gradual decay. **10.** devastation or a devastated area. **11.** anything left over. —*adj.* **12.** not used. **13.** left over or worthless. **14.** desolate. —**waste/ful,** *adj.*

waste/land/ *n.* barren land.

wast/rel (wā/strəl) *n.* **1.** a spendthrift. **2.** an idler.

watch (woch) *v.i.* **1.** to look attentively. **2.** to be careful. **3.** to remain vigilant. —*v.t.* **4.** to view attentively. **5.** to guard. **6. watch out,** to be on one's guard. —*n.* **7.** close, constant observation. **8.** a guard. **9.** a period of watching. **10.** a small timepiece. —**watch/ful,** *adj.*

watch/band/ *n.* a band for holding a wristwatch on the wrist.

watch/dog/ *n.* **1.** a dog that guards property. **2.** a guardian, as against illegal conduct.

watch/man *n.* a person who keeps watch.

watch/tow/er *n.* a tower for a guard.

watch/word/ *n.* **1.** a password. **2.** a slogan.

wa/ter (wô/tər) *n.* **1.** an odorless, tasteless liquid composed of hydrogen and oxygen that forms rivers, seas, lakes, rain, etc. **2.** a body of water. **3. waters,** the sea that borders and is controlled by a country. **4.** a liquid organic secretion. —*v.t.* **5.** to sprinkle or supply with water. **6.** to dilute. —*v.i.* **7.** to fill with or secrete water. —*adj.* **8.** of, for, or powered by water.

wa/ter buf/falo *n.* a domesticated Asian buffalo with curved horns.

wa/ter•col/or *n.* **1.** a pigment mixed with water. **2.** a painting using such pigments.

wa/ter•course/ *n.* **1.** a stream of water. **2.** the bed of a stream.

wa/ter•cress/ *n.* a plant that grows in streams and bears pungent leaves used in salad.

wa/ter•fall/ *n.* a steep fall of water from a height.

wa/ter•fowl/ *n., pl.* **-fowl, -fowls.** an aquatic bird.

wa/ter•front/ *n.* a part of a city on the edge of a body of water.

wa/ter lil/y *n.* an aquatic plant with showy flowers.

wa/ter•logged/ *adj.* filled or soaked with water.

wa/ter•mark/ *n.* **1.** a design impressed on paper that is visible when light shines through it. **2.** a mark showing the height to which water has risen. —*v.t.* **3.** to put a watermark in (paper).

wa/ter•mel/on *n.* a large melon with sweet red pulp.

wa/ter moc/casin *n.* the cottonmouth.

wa/ter•proof/ *adj.* **1.** impervious to water. —*v.t.* **2.** to make waterproof.

wa/ter-repel/lent *adj.* repelling water but not entirely waterproof.

wa/ter•shed/ *n.* **1.** an area drained by a river or stream. **2.** a ridge dividing such areas. **3.** an important point of division or transition.

wa/ter ski/ *n.* a short, broad ski for gliding over water while being towed by a boat. —**wa/ter-ski/,** *v.i.*

wa/ter•spout/ *n.* a tornadolike storm over a lake or ocean.

wa/ter ta/ble *n.* the underground level beneath which soil and rock are saturated with water.

wa/ter•tight/ *adj.* **1.** constructed or fitted to be impervious to water. **2.** allowing no doubt.

wa/ter•way/ *n.* a body of water as a route of travel.

wa/ter wheel/ *n.* a wheel turned by water to provide power for machinery.

wa/ter•works/ *n.pl.* a system by which water is collected, stored, purified, and pumped for a city.

wa/ter•y *adj.* of, like, or full of water.

watt (wot) *n.* a unit of electric power.

wat/tle[1] (wot/l) *n.* flesh hanging from the throat or chin of certain birds, as the turkey.

wat/tle[2] (wot/l) *n.* interwoven rods and twigs, used for making walls and fences.

wave (wāv) n., v., **waved, waving.**
—n. **1.** a moving ridge on the surface of water. **2.** a surge; rush. **3.** an outward curve. **4.** a wavelike vibration, as in the transmission of sound or light. **5.** a sign with a moving hand, flag, etc. —v.i. **6.** to move back and forth or up and down. **7.** to curve. **8.** to signal by moving the hand. —v.t. **9.** to cause to wave. **10.** to express by a waving movement. —Idiom. **11.** **make waves,** Informal. to disturb the status quo. —**wav′y,** adj.

wave′length′ n. the distance between two successive points in a wave, as of light or sound.

wa′ver (wā′vər) v.i. **1.** to be unsteady. **2.** to flicker or quiver. **3.** to feel or show indecision.

wax¹ (waks) n. **1.** a solid, yellowish substance secreted by bees. **2.** any similar substance. —v.t. **3.** to rub or polish with wax. —**wax′en,** adj. —**wax′y,** adj.

wax² (waks) v.i. **1.** to increase. **2.** to become.

wax′ pa′per n. paper made moisture-resistant by a paraffin coating.

wax′wing′ n. a small crested songbird with red-tipped wing feathers.

way (wā) n. **1.** a method or means. **2.** manner. **3.** a direction. **4.** a road or route. **5.** space for passing. **6.** condition. —Idiom. **7.** **by the way,** incidentally. **8.** **by way of,** by the route of; through. **9.** **give way, a.** to yield. **b.** to collapse.

way′far′er n. a traveler.

way′lay′ (wā′lā′, wā lā′) v.t., -**laid,** -**laying.** to lie in wait for.

ways′ and means′ n.pl. methods of raising revenue.

way′side′ n. land next to a road.

way′ward (-wərd) adj. stubbornly willful.

we (wē) pron. the nominative plural of I.

weak (wēk) adj. **1.** not strong; frail. **2.** lacking in strength, force, intensity, etc. **3.** deficient. —**weak′en,** v.t., v.i. —**weak′ly,** adv. —**weak′-ness,** n.

weak′-kneed′ adj. yielding readily to opposition or intimidation.

weak′ling (-ling) n. a weak creature.

weal (wēl) n. well-being.

wealth (welth) n. **1.** abundance of possessions or riches. **2.** plentiful amount. —**wealth′y,** adj.

wean (wēn) v.t. **1.** to accustom (a child or young animal) to food other than the mother's milk. **2.** to rid of an undesirable object or habit.

weap′on (wep′ən) n. **1.** a device
for attack or defense. **2.** something used against an adversary.

weap′on·ry n. weapons collectively.

wear (wâr) v., **wore** (wôr), **worn, wearing,** n. —v.t. **1.** to have on the body for covering or ornament. **2.** to cause to deteriorate gradually through use. **3.** to fatigue. —v.i. **4.** to deteriorate from use. **5.** to withstand continued use. **6.** **wear down,** to overcome by persistence. **7.** ~ **off,** to diminish gradually. —n. **8.** a wearing or being worn. **9.** clothing of a specific kind. **10.** gradual deterioration. **11.** durability. —**wear′a·ble,** adj.

wea′ri·some (wēr′ē səm) adj. tiring or tedious.

wea′ry adj., -**rier, -riest,** v., -**ried, -rying.** —adj. **1.** tired. **2.** dissatisfied. —v.t., v.i. **3.** to make or become tired. —**wea′ri·ly,** adv.

wea′sel (wē′zəl) n. a small flesh-eating animal with a long, slender body.

weath′er (weth′ər) n. **1.** the state of the atmosphere with respect to moisture, temperature, etc. —v.t. **2.** to expose to weather. **3.** to withstand. —v.i. **4.** to endure exposure to the weather.

weath′er-beat′en adj. worn or marked by weather.

weath′er·ing n. the action of wind and water on exposed rock.

weath′er·ize′ v.t., -**ized, -izing.** to make secure against cold weather.

weath′er·proof′ adj. **1.** able to withstand all kinds of weather. —v.t. **2.** to make weatherproof.

weath′er·vane′ n. a device to show the direction of the wind.

weave (wēv) v., **wove** (wōv), **woven** or **wove, weaving,** n. —v.t. **1.** to interlace (threads, strands, etc.) so as to form cloth. **2.** to form by weaving. **3.** to combine into a connected whole. —v.i. **4.** to make something by weaving. **5.** to move in a winding course. —n. **6.** a pattern or method of weaving. —**weav′er,** n.

web (web) n., v., **webbed, web-bing.** —n. **1.** something woven. **2.** a cobweb. **3.** something that entangles. **4.** a membrane between the toes of ducks, geese, etc. **5.** **the Web,** the World Wide Web. —v.t. **6.** to cover with a web.

web′foot′ n. a foot with webbed toes. —**web′foot′ed,** adj.

Web′mas·ter (web′mas′tər, -mä′-stər) n. a person who designs or maintains a Web site.

Web′ site′ n. a group of pages on the World Wide Web devoted to one topic or several related topics. Also, **website.**

Web'ster (web'stər) *n.* a dictionary of the English language. Also, **Web'ster's.**

wed (wed) *v.t., v.i.,* **wedded, wedded** or **wed, wedding. 1.** to marry. **2.** to unite.

Wed. Wednesday.

wed'ding *n.* a marriage ceremony.

wedge (wej) *n., v.,* **wedged, wedging.** —*n.* **1.** a tapered triangular piece of hard material. **2.** something that splits or divides. —*v.t.* **3.** to split with a wedge. **4.** to pack tightly into a space. —*v.i.* **5.** to force a way like a wedge.

wed'lock *n.* the state of being married.

Wednes'day (wenz'dā, -dē) *n.* the fourth day of the week.

weed (wēd) *n.* **1.** an undesirable plant growing in cultivated ground. —*v.t.* **2.** to free from weeds. **3.** to remove as undesirable. —*v.i.* **4.** to remove weeds. —**weed'y,** *adj.*

weeds (wēdz) *n.pl.* black clothes for mourning.

week (wēk) *n.* **1.** a period of seven successive days. **2.** the working part of a week.

week'day' *n.* any day except Sunday, or, often, Saturday and Sunday.

week'end' (-end', -end') *n.* the period between Friday evening and Monday morning.

week'ly *adj., adv., n., pl.* **-lies.** —*adj.* **1.** happening, appearing, etc., once a week. **2.** lasting a week. —*adv.* **3.** once a week. —*n.* **4.** a weekly periodical.

weep (wēp) *v.i.,* **wept** (wept), **weeping.** to shed tears.

wee'vil (wē'vəl) *n.* a beetle destructive to grain, fruit, etc.

weft (weft) *n.* (in weaving) the woof.

weigh (wā) *v.t.* **1.** to measure the heaviness of. **2.** to consider. —*v.i.* **3.** to have weight or importance. **4.** to bear down as a burden.

weight (wāt) *n.* **1.** amount of heaviness. **2.** a system of units for expressing weight. **3.** a unit of heaviness or mass. **4.** a solid mass. **5.** a burden. **6.** importance. —*v.t.* **7.** to add weight to. —**weight'y,** *adj.* —**weight'less,** *adj.*

weir (wēr) *n.* **1.** a dam in a stream. **2.** a fence set in a stream to catch fish.

weird (wērd) *adj.* **1.** supernatural. **2.** strange; peculiar.

weird'o (wēr'dō) *n., pl.* **-os.** *Slang.* an odd or eccentric person.

wel'come (wel'kəm) *n., v.,* **-comed, -coming,** *adj.* —*n.* **1.** a friendly reception. —*v.t.* **2.** to receive or greet with pleasure. —*adj.* **3.** gladly received. **4.** given permission or consent.

weld (weld) *v.t.* **1.** to unite, esp. by heating and pressing. —*n.* **2.** a welded joint. —**weld'er,** *n.*

wel'fare' (wel'fâr') *n.* **1.** well-being. **2.** assistance given, esp. by the government, to those in need.

well[1] (wel) *adv., compar.* **better,** *superl.* **best,** *adj.* —*adv.* **1.** in a good or satisfactory manner. **2.** excellently; properly. **3.** thoroughly. **4.** with approval. **5.** with good reason. —*adj.* **6.** in good health. **7.** satisfactory or good.

well[2] (wel) *n.* **1.** a hole drilled in the earth to reach water, oil, etc. **2.** a natural or abundant source. **3.** a vertical shaft for air, stairs, or an elevator. —*v.i.* **4.** to rise or gush.

well'-ad·vised' *adj.* prudent.

well'-ap·point'ed *adj.* attractively furnished.

well'-be'ing *n.* a good or prosperous condition.

well'-bred' *adj.* showing good manners.

well'-dis·posed' *adj.* feeling favorable, sympathetic, or kind.

well'-done' *adj.* **1.** done accurately and skillfully. **2.** thoroughly cooked.

well'-found'ed *adj.* based on good reasons, sound information, etc.

well'-ground'ed *adj.* having good basic knowledge of a subject.

well'-heeled' *adj.* prosperous.

well'-in·formed' *adj.* having extensive knowledge.

well'man'nered *adj.* polite.

well'-mean'ing *adj.* having good intentions. —**well'-meant',** *adj.*

well'-nigh' *adv.* very nearly.

well'-off' *adj.* **1.** prosperous. **2.** in a good or favorable condition.

well'spring' *n.* a source.

well'-to-do' *adj.* wealthy.

well'-worn' *adj.* **1.** showing the effects of extensive use. **2.** trite.

welt (welt) *n.* **1.** a ridge on the skin, as from a blow. **2.** a strip around the edge of a shoe. **3.** a strip or cord sewn along a seam.

wel'ter (wel'tər) *v.i.* **1.** to toss or roll, as waves. **2.** to wallow. —*n.* **3.** a confused mass.

wen (wen) *n.* a small cyst.

wench (wench) *n.* a girl or young woman.

wend (wend) *v.* **wend one's way,** to go.

went (went) *v.* pt. of **go.**

were (wûr; *unstressed* wər) *v.* past plural and pres. subjunctive of **be.**

weren't (wûrnt, wûr′ənt) a contraction of **were not.**

were′wolf′ (wâr′wŏŏlf′, wēr′-,) *n., pl.* **-wolves.** (in folklore) a human turned into a wolf.

west (west) *n.* **1.** a cardinal point of the compass, the direction in which the sun sets. **2. the West,** a region in this direction. —*adj., adv.* **3.** toward, in, or from the west.

west′ern·ize′ (wes′tər nīz′) *v.t.,* **-ized, -izing.** to influence with western ideas and customs.

west′ward (-wərd) *adv.* **1.** toward the west. —*adj.* **2.** moving or facing toward the west.

wet (wet) *adj.,* **wetter, wettest,** *n., v.,* **wet** or **wetted, wetting.** —*adj.* **1.** covered or soaked with water. **2.** rainy. —*n.* **3.** moisture. **4.** wet weather. —*v.t., v.i.* **5.** to make or become wet.

wet′ blan′ket *n.* one that dampens enthusiasm.

wet′ nurse′ *n.* a woman hired to suckle another's infant.

wet′ suit′ *n.* a close-fitting rubber suit worn for body warmth, as by scuba divers.

whack (hwak, wak) *Informal.* —*v.t., v.i.* **1.** to strike sharply. —*n.* **2.** a smart blow.

whale (hwāl, wāl) *n., pl.* **whales** or **whale,** *v.,* **whaled, whaling.** —*n.* **1.** a large marine mammal with a fishlike body. —*v.i.* **2.** to hunt and kill whales.

whale′bone′ *n.* an elastic horny substance in the upper jaw of some whales.

wharf (hwôrf, wôrf) *n., pl.* **wharves.** a structure where ships moor to load and unload.

what (hwut, hwot, wut, wot; *unstressed* hwət, wət) *pron.* **1.** (used as a request for information). **2.** (used to ask about the character, identity, or worth of a person or thing). **3.** how much? **4.** that which. **5.** as much or as many. —*adj.* **6.** (used interrogatively before nouns). **7.** whatever or whichever. —*adv.* **8.** to what extent or degree?

what·ev′er *pron.* **1.** anything that. **2.** no matter what. —*adj.* **3.** no matter what. —*interj.* **4.** (used to indicate indifference).

what′not′ *n.* a small open cupboard for knickknacks.

what′so·ev′er *pron., adj.* whatever.

wheat (hwēt, wēt) *n.* the grain of a common cereal grass, used esp. for flour.

whee′dle (hwēd′l, wēd′l) *v.t., v.i.,* **-dled, -dling.** to influence (a person) by flattery.

wheel (hwēl, wēl) *n.* **1.** a circular frame or disk turning on an axis. —*v.t., v.i.* **2.** to turn, rotate, or revolve. **3.** to move on wheels.

wheel′bar′row *n.* a one-wheeled cart for conveying small loads.

wheel′base′ *n.* the distance between the front and rear axles.

wheel′chair′ *n.* a chair mounted on wheels for use by persons who cannot walk.

wheeze (hwēz, wēz) *v.,* **wheezed, wheezing,** *n.* —*v.i.* **1.** to breathe with difficulty and with a whistling sound. —*n.* **2.** a wheezing breath.

whelp (hwelp, welp) *n.* **1.** the young of a dog, wolf, bear, etc. —*v.t., v.i.* **2.** to give birth to (whelps).

when (hwen, wen; *unstressed* hwən, wən) *adv.* **1.** at what time? —*conj.* **2.** at what time. **3.** at the time that. —*pron.* **4.** what or which time.

whence (hwens, wens) *adv., conj.* from what place, source, or cause?

when·ev′er *adv.* at whatever time.

where (hwâr, wâr) *adv.* **1.** in, at, or to what place? **2.** in what respect? —*conj.* **3.** in, at, or to what place or situation. —*pron.* **4.** what place? **5.** the place in or point at which.

where′a·bouts′ *adv.* **1.** about where? —*n.* **2.** the place where someone or something is.

where·as′ *conj.* **1.** while on the contrary. **2.** considering that.

where·by′ *conj.* by what or which; under the terms of which.

where′fore′ *adv., conj.* **1.** for that cause or reason. **2.** *Archaic.* why? —*n.* **3.** a reason.

where·in′ *conj.* **1.** in what or in which. —*adv.* **2.** in what way or respect?

where·of′ *adv., conj.* of what.

where′up·on′ *conj.* **1.** upon which. **2.** at or after which.

wher·ev′er *conj.* in, at, or to whatever place or circumstance.

where′with·al′ (-with ôl′, -with-) *n.* means with which to do something.

whet (hwet, wet) *v.t.,* **whetted, whetting. 1.** to sharpen. **2.** to stimulate (appetite, interest, etc.).

wheth′er (hweth′ər, weth′-) *conj.* (used to introduce an alternative.)

whet′stone′ *n.* a stone for sharpening blades by friction.

whey (hwā, wā) *n.* the watery part of curdled milk.

which (hwich, wich) *pron.* **1.** what

one or ones? **2.** the one that. —*adj.* **3.** what one or ones of (those mentioned).

which·ev′er *pron.* any that.

whiff (hwif, wif) *n.* a slight puff or trace.

while (hwīl, wīl) *n., conj., v.,* **whiled, whiling.** —*n.* **1.** an interval of time. —*conj.* **2.** during the time that. **3.** even though. —*v.* **4. while away,** to cause (time) to pass pleasantly.

whim (hwim, wim) *n.* an irrational or fanciful decision or idea.

whim′per (hwim′pər, wim′-) *v.i., v.t.* **1.** to cry softly and plaintively. —*n.* **2.** a whimpering cry.

whim′sy (hwim′zē, wim′-) *n., pl.* **-sies.** a fanciful idea; whim. —**whim′si·cal,** *adj.*

whine (hwīn, wīn) *v.,* **whined, whining,** *n.* —*v.i., v.t.* **1.** to utter (with) a low, nasal complaining sound. —*n.* **2.** a whining sound or complaint.

whin′ny (hwin′ē, win′ē) *n., pl.* **-nies,** *v.,* **-nied, -nying.** —*n.* **1.** a gentle neigh. —*v.i.* **2.** to utter a whinny.

whip (hwip, wip) *v.,* **whipped, whipping,** *n.* —*v.t.* **1.** to strike repeatedly or flog as punishment. **2.** to move, pull, or seize suddenly. **3.** to defeat. **4.** to beat to a froth. —*v.i.* **5.** to move quickly and suddenly; lash about. —*n.* **6.** an instrument with a lash and a handle for striking a person or animal. **7.** a party manager in a legislature.

whip′lash′ *n.* **1.** the lash of a whip. **2.** a neck injury caused by a sudden jerking of the head.

whip′pet (whip′it, wip′-) *n.* a type of slender swift dog.

whip′poor·will′ (hwip′ər wil′, wip′-) *n.* a nocturnal American bird.

whir (hwûr, wûr) *v.,* **whirred, whirring,** *n.* —*v.i., v.t.* **1.** to move quickly with a humming sound. —*n.* **2.** such a sound.

whirl (hwûrl, wûrl) *v.i.* **1.** to spin or turn rapidly. **2.** to move quickly. —*v.t.* **3.** to cause to whirl. —*n.* **4.** a whirling movement. **5.** a rapid round of events. **6.** an attempt.

whirl′pool′ *n.* water in a swift circular downward motion.

whirl′wind′ (-wind′) *n.* a whirling mass of air.

whisk (hwisk, wisk) *v.t.* **1.** to move with a rapid sweeping stroke. **2.** to move or carry lightly. **3.** to whip or blend with a whisk. —*n.* **4.** the act of whisking. **5.** a wire implement for beating food.

whisk′er *n.* **1.** one of the long bris-

tly hairs growing near the mouth of some animals, as the cat. **2. whiskers,** the hair on a man's face.

whis′key (hwis′kē, wis′-) *n.* a distilled alcoholic liquor made from grain or corn. Also, **whis′ky.**

whis′per (hwis′pər, wis′pər) *v.i., v.t.* **1.** to speak or utter very softly. —*n.* **2.** the sound of whispering. **3.** something whispered.

whist (hwist, wist) *n.* a card game that is an early form of bridge.

whis′tle (hwis′əl, wis′-) *v.,* **-tled, -tling,** *n.* —*v.i.* **1.** to make a high clear sound with breath, air, or steam. —*n.* **2.** a device for making such sounds. **3.** the sound of whistling.

whis′tle-blow′er *n.* a person who publicly discloses wrongdoing.

whis′tle stop′ *n.* a small town.

whit (hwit, wit) *n.* a particle; bit.

white (hwīt, wīt) *adj.* **1.** of the color of pure snow. **2.** having light skin. **3.** pale. —*n.* **4.** a color without hue that is the opposite of black. **5.** a light-skinned person. **6.** a white or light material or part. —**whit′en,** *v.t., v.i.*

white′ blood′ cell′ *n.* a nearly colorless blood cell of the immune system.

white′-bread′ *adj.* bland; conventional.

white′-col′lar *adj.* of professional or office workers whose jobs usu. do not involve manual labor.

white′ el′ephant *n.* a possession of no use to the owner but of use to another.

white′fish′ *n.* a small freshwater food fish.

white′ goods′ *n.pl.* household linens.

white′ lie′ *n.* a small, harmless lie.

white′wash′ *n.* **1.** a substance for whitening walls, woodwork, etc. —*v.t.* **2.** to cover with whitewash. **3.** to cover the faults or errors of.

white′ wa′ter *n.* frothy water, as in rapids.

whith′er (hwith′ər, with′-) *adv., conj.* **1.** to what place, point, end, or action? —*conj.* **2.** to which or whatever place.

whit′ing[1] (hwī′ting, wī′-) *n.* a small Atlantic food fish.

whit′ing[2] (hwī′ting, wī′-) *n.* purewhite chalk powder.

Whit′sun·day (hwit′sun′dā, -dē, -sən dā′, wit′-) *n.* Pentecost.

whit′tle (hwit′l, wit′l) *v.,* **-tled, -tling.** —*v.t.* **1.** to cut, trim, or shape (wood) bit by bit with a knife. **2.** to reduce. —*v.i.* **3.** to whittle wood. —**whit′tler,** *n.*

whiz (hwiz, wiz) *v.,* **whizzed, whiz-**

who

who   410

zing, *n.* —*v.i.* **1.** to move with a humming, buzzing, or hissing sound. —*n.* **2.** a whizzing sound. **3.** *Informal.* a person who is very good at something. Also, **whizz.**

who (hoō) *pron.* **1.** what person? **2.** the person that.

whoa (hwō, wō) *interj.* (a command to stop).

who·dun′it (-dun′it) *n.* a detective story.

who·ev′er *pron.* anyone that.

whole (hōl) *adj.* **1.** entire; total; complete; undivided. **2.** not damaged or injured. **3.** *Math.* not fractional. —*n.* **4.** the entire amount or extent. **5.** a complete thing. —**whol′ly,** *adv.* —**whole′ness,** *n.*

whole′-heart′ed *adj.* sincere.

whole′sale′ *n., adj., v.,* **-saled, -saling.** —*n.* **1.** the sale of goods in quantity, as to retailers. —*adj.* **2.** of or engaged in sale by wholesale. —*v.t., v.i.* **3.** to sell by wholesale. —**whole′sal′er,** *n.*

whole′some (-səm) *adj.* healthful.

whole′-wheat′ *adj.* prepared with the complete wheat kernel.

whom (hoōm) *pron.* the objective case of **who.**

whom·ev′er *pron.* the objective case of **whoever.**

whoop (hwoōp, hwo͝op, woōp, wo͝op; *esp. for 2* hoōp, ho͝op) *n.* **1.** a loud shout or cry. **2.** a gasping sound characteristic of whooping cough. —*v.i., v.t.* **3.** to utter (with) a loud cry.

whoop′ing cough′ (hoō′ping, ho͝op′ing) *n.* an infectious disease characterized by short, convulsive coughs followed by whoops.

whop′per (hwop′ər, wop′-) *n. Informal.* **1.** something very large. **2.** a big lie.

whop′ping *adj. Informal.* very large.

whore (hôr; *often* ho͝or) *n.* a prostitute.

whorl (hwûrl, hwôrl, wûrl, wôrl) *n.* a circular arrangement; spiral.

whose (hoōz) *pron.* the possessive case of **who.**

who′so·ev′er *pron.* whoever.

why (hwī, wī) *adv., conj., n., pl.* **whys.** —*adv.* **1.** for what reason or purpose? —*conj.* **2.** for what cause. **3.** the reason for which. —*n.* **4.** the cause or reason.

WI Wisconsin.

wick (wik) *n.* a twist of soft threads that absorb fuel and burn in a candle, lamp, etc.

wick′ed (wik′id) *adj.* **1.** morally bad; evil; sinful. **2.** harmful. **3.** very unpleasant. —**wick′ed·ly,** *adv.*

wick′er *n.* **1.** a slender, pliant twig. **2.** things made of wicker. —*adj.* **3.** made of wicker.

wick′et (wik′it) *n.* **1.** a small gate or opening. **2.** a hoop in croquet. **3.** a framework in cricket.

wide (wīd) *adj.,* **wider, widest,** *adv.* —*adj.* **1.** of great size from side to side; broad. **2.** having a specified width. **3.** of great range. **4.** far from an objective. —*adv.* **5.** to the utmost. **6.** away from an objective. **7.** over a large area. —**wid′en,** *v.t., v.i.*

wide′-awake′ *adj.* **1.** fully awake. **2.** alert or observant.

wide′spread′ *adj.* occurring or distributed over a wide area.

wid·ow (wid′ō) *n.* **1.** a woman whose husband has died. —*v.t.* **2.** to make a widow of. —**wid′ow·er,** *n.masc.* —**wid′ow·hood,** *n.*

width (width, witth) *n.* **1.** extent from side to side; breadth. **2.** something of a specific width.

wield (wēld) *v.t.* **1.** to exercise (power, influence, etc.). **2.** to handle.

wife (wīf) *n., pl.* **wives** (wīvz). a married woman. —**wife′ly,** *adj.*

wig (wig) *n.* a covering of natural or artificial hair for the head.

wig′gle (wig′əl) *v.,* **-gled, -gling,** *n.* —*v.i., v.t.* **1.** to move with quick, irregular side-to-side movements. —*n.* **2.** a wiggling movement. —**wig′gly,** *adj.* —**wig′gler,** *n.*

wig′wam (-wom) *n.* an American Indian dwelling of rounded shape.

wild (wīld) *adj.* **1.** not cultivated. **2.** not civilized. **3.** violent. **4.** not inhabited or developed. **5.** disorderly. —*adv.* **6.** in a wild manner. —*n.* **7.** a wilderness. —**wild′ly,** *adv.*

wild′cat′ *n., v.,* **-catted, -catting.** —*n.* **1.** a medium-sized cat, as the bobcat. —*v.i., v.t.* **2.** to search (an unknown area) for oil, gas, or ore. —*adj.* **3.** not sanctioned by a labor union.

wil′der·ness (wil′dər nis) *n.* a wild or desolate region.

wild′-eyed′ *adj.* **1.** having a wild expression in the eyes. **2.** extreme or radical.

wild′fire′ *n.* an outdoor fire that spreads rapidly and is hard to extinguish.

wild′flow′er *n.* the flower of a plant that grows wild.

wild′-goose′ chase′ *n.* a senseless search for something unobtainable.

wild′life′ *n.* animals living in the wild.

wile (wīl) *n.* a trick to fool, trap, or entice.

will¹ (wil) *auxiliary v.* and *v., pres.* will; *past* would. —*auxiliary verb.*

1. (used to express a future tense). **2.** (used to express willingness or determination). **3.** (used to express capability). —*v.t., v.i.* **4.** to wish; like. —**Usage.** See SHALL.

will² (wil) *n.* **1.** the power of conscious action or choice. **2.** wish; pleasure. **3.** attitude toward another. **4.** a legal document declaring one's wishes for the disposition of one's property after death. —*v.t.* **5.** to decide upon or bring about by an act of the will. **6.** to give by will; bequeath. **7.** to influence by the power of the will.

will′ful *adj.* **1.** intentional. **2.** headstrong; stubborn. Also, **wil′ful.**

wil′lies (wil′ēz) *n.pl. Slang.* nervousness.

will′ing *adj.* **1.** inclined. **2.** cheerfully done, given, etc. —**will′ing•ly,** *adv.* —**will′ing•ness,** *n.*

will′-o′-the-wisp′ (wil′ə *th*ə wisp′) *n.* **1.** a flitting, elusive light. **2.** something that fascinates and deludes.

wil′low (wil′ō) *n.* a slender tree or shrub with tough, pliant branches.

wil′low•y *adj.,* **-ier, -iest.** tall and slender.

wil′ly-nil′ly (wil′ē nil′ē) *adv.* whether one wishes or not.

wilt (wilt) *v.i.* **1.** to wither or droop. —*v.t.* **2.** to cause to wilt.

wil′y (wī′lē) *adj.,* **-ier, -iest.** crafty; cunning.

wimp (wimp) *n. Informal.* a weak, ineffectual person. —**wimp′y,** *adj.*

win (win) *v.,* **won** (wun), **winning,** *n.* —*v.i.* **1.** to finish first in a competition. **2.** to succeed by effort. —*v.t.* **3.** to succeed in reaching. **4.** to get by effort. **5.** to be victorious in. —*n.* **6.** a victory.

wince (wins) *v.,* **winced, wincing,** *n.* —*v.i.* **1.** to shrink back, as from pain or a blow. —*n.* **2.** a wincing movement.

winch (winch) *n.* **1.** the crank or handle of a machine. **2.** a windlass for hoisting.

wind¹ (wind) *n.* **1.** air in motion. **2.** breath or breathing. **3. winds,** the wind instruments in an orchestra. **4.** a hint or intimation. **5.** gas in the stomach or intestines. —*v.t.* **6.** to make short of breath. **7.** to follow by scent. —*Idiom.* **8. in the wind,** about to occur. —**wind′y** (win′dē) *adj.*

wind² (wīnd) *v.,* **wound** (wound) **winding,** *n.* —*v.i.* **1.** to have or take a curving or spiral course. —*v.t.* **2.** to wrap around. **3.** to roll (thread, yarn, etc.) into a ball or on a spool. **4.** to tighten the spring of (a clock, toy, etc.). **5. wind up,**

a. to bring or come to an end. **b.** to excite. —*n.* **6.** a turn.

wind′break′ (wind′-) *n.* something that shelters from the wind.

wind′chill fac′tor (wind′chil′) *n.* the apparent temperature felt on exposed skin owing to the combination of temperature and wind speed.

wind′ed (win′did) *adj.* breathless.

wind′fall′ (wind′-) *n.* **1.** an unexpected piece of good fortune. **2.** something, as fruit, blown down.

wind′ing sheet′ (wīn′ding) *n.* a shroud.

wind′ in′strument (wind) *n.* a musical instrument sounded by an air current, esp. the breath.

wind′lass (wind′ləs) *n.* a device for hoisting, consisting of a horizontal drum around which a rope is wound.

wind′mill′ (wind′-) *n.* a mill that is driven by the wind acting on vanes or sails.

win′dow (win′dō) *n.* **1.** an opening in a building, vehicle, etc., for air and light, usu. fitted with glass in a frame. **2.** the glass in a window frame. **3.** a period of time for doing something. **4.** a portion of a computer screen, surrounded by borders, on which data is displayed.

win′dow dress′ing *n.* **1.** the art, act, or technique of decorating store display windows. **2.** something done solely to create a favorable impression.

win′dow•pane′ *n.* a pane of glass for a window.

win′dow-shop′ *v.i.,* **-shopped, -shopping.** to look at articles in store windows without making purchases.

wind′pipe′ (wind′-) *n.* the trachea.

wind′shield′ (wind′-, win′-) *n.* a glass shield above the dashboard of an automobile.

wind′sock′ (wind′-) *n.* a mounted cloth cone that catches the wind to indicate wind direction.

wind′storm′ (wind′-) *n.* a storm with heavy wind but little or no precipitation.

wind′surf′ing (wind′-) *n.* the sport of riding on a surfboard mounted with a sail. —**wind′surf′,** *v.i.*

wind′-swept′ (wind′-) *adj.* exposed to or blown by the wind.

wind′up′ (wīnd′-) *n.* the conclusion of an action or activity.

wind′ward (wind′wərd) *adv.* **1.** toward the wind. —*adj.* **2.** of, in, or toward the direction from which the wind blows. —*n.* **3.** the direction from which the wind blows.

wine (wīn) *n.*, *v.*, **wined, wining.**
—*n.* **1.** the fermented juice of grapes. **2.** a dark purplish red. —*v.t.*, *v.i.* **3.** to supply with or drink wine.

win'er·y *n.*, *pl.* **-eries.** a place where wine is made.

wing (wing) *n.* **1.** either of two forelimbs or appendages by which birds, insects, and bats are able to fly. **2.** any winglike or projecting structure. **3.** flight. **4.** one of the winglike structures on an airplane. **5. wings,** the space at the side of a stage. **6.** an extreme faction within an organization. —*v.i.* **7.** to travel on wings. —*v.t.* **8.** to transport on wings. **9.** to wound in the wing or arm. **10. wing it,** to improvise. —*Idiom.* **11. under one's wing,** under one's protection.

wink (wingk) *v.i.* **1.** to close and open an eye quickly. **2.** to signal by winking. **3.** to twinkle. —*v.t.* **4.** to make (an eye) wink. **5. wink at,** to ignore (wrongdoing). —*n.* **6.** the act of winking.

win'ner (win'ər) *n.* one that wins.

win'ning *n.* **1. winnings,** that which is won. —*adj.* **2.** charming.

win'now (win'ō) *v.t.* **1.** to free (grain) of chaff by a forced current of air. **2.** to separate.

win'some (win'səm) *adj.* sweetly or innocently charming.

win'ter (win'tər) *n.* **1.** the cold season between autumn and spring. —*adj.* **2.** of, like, or for winter. —*v.i.* **3.** to spend the winter. —**win'try,** *adj.*

win'ter·green' *n.* a creeping aromatic evergreen shrub bearing white flowers and red berries.

win-win *adj.* advantageous to both sides, as in a negotiation.

wipe (wīp) *v.*, **wiped, wiping,** *n.* —*v.t.* **1.** to clean or dry by rubbing lightly. **2.** to rub (something) over a surface. —*n.* **3.** the act of wiping. —**wip'er,** *n.*

wire (wīᵊr) *n.*, *adj.*, *v.*, **wired, wiring.** —*n.* **1.** a slender, flexible piece of metal. **2.** a length of wire used as a conductor of current. **3.** a telegram or telegraph. —*adj.* **4.** made of wire. —*v.t.* **5.** to equip, furnish, or connect with wire. **6.** to send by telegraph.

wire'less *adj.* **1.** activated by electromagnetic waves rather than wires. —*n.* **2.** *Brit.* a radio.

wire' serv'ice *n.* an agency that sends syndicated news by wire to its subscribers.

wire'tap' *n.*, *v.*, **-tapped, -tapping.** —*n.* **1.** an act or instance of connecting secretly into a telephone.

—*v.t.* **2.** to listen in on by means of a wiretap. —*v.i.* **3.** to tap a telephone wire.

wir'ing *n.* a system of electric wires.

wir'y *adj.*, **-ier, -iest.** like wire; lean and strong. —**wir'i·ness,** *n.*

Wis. Wisconsin.

wis'dom (wiz'dəm) *n.* **1.** the quality of being wise. **2.** wise sayings.

wis'dom tooth' *n.* the third molar on each side of the upper and lower jaws.

wise¹ (wīz) *adj.* **1.** having good judgment and understanding. **2.** having scholarly knowledge. **3.** informed. —**wise'ly,** *adv.*

wise² (wīz) *n.* way; manner.

wise'a'cre (-ā'kər) *n.* a conceited, often insolent person.

wise'crack' *n.* **1.** a smart or facetious remark. —*v.i.*, *v.t.* **2.** to make or say as a wisecrack.

wish (wish) *v.t.* **1.** to want; desire. **2.** to express a hope or desire for. —*v.i.* **3.** to yearn. **4.** to make a wish. —*n.* **5.** a desire or an expression of a desire. **6.** the thing desired. —**wish'ful,** *adj.*

wish'bone' *n.* a forked bone in front of the breastbone in most birds.

wish'y-wash'y (wish'ē wosh'ē) *adj.* weak.

wisp (wisp) *n.* **1.** a thin tuft, lock, or mass. **2.** a thin puff or streak. —**wisp'y,** *adj.*

wis·te'ri·a (wi stēr'ē ə) *n.* a climbing shrub with long clusters of pale purple flowers.

wist'ful (wist'fəl) *adj.* marked by pensive longing. —**wist'ful·ly,** *adv.*

wit¹ (wit) *n.* **1.** the power of combining perception with clever expression. **2.** a person having this. **3. wits,** mental faculties.

wit² (wit) —*Idiom.* **to wit,** namely.

witch (wich) *n.* a woman thought to practice magic.

witch'craft' *n.* the practices of witches; sorcery.

witch' doc'tor *n.* a person in some cultures who uses magic esp. to cure illness.

witch'er·y *n.* **1.** witchcraft; magic. **2.** charm.

witch ha'zel (hā'zəl) *n.* **1.** a shrub bearing small yellow flowers. **2.** an astringent lotion made from its leaves and bark.

with (with, wiŧh) *prep.* **1.** accompanied by. **2.** by means of. **3.** having. **4.** owing to. **5.** at the same time as. **6.** in a manner showing.

with·draw' (wiŧh drô', with-) *v.*, **-drew, -drawn, -drawing.** —*v.t.* **1.**

to draw back, away, or aside. **2.** to retract. —*v.i.* **3.** to remove oneself from a place or activity.

with·draw′al *n.* **1.** a withdrawing or being withdrawn. **2.** ceasing to use an addictive drug.

with′er (wi*th*′ər) *v.i.*, *v.t.* to (cause to) shrivel or fade.

with′ers *n.pl.* the high part of a horse's back at the base of the neck.

with·hold′ (with hōld′, with-) *v.t.*, -held, -holding. to hold or keep back.

withhold′ing tax′ *n.* that part of an employee's tax liability withheld by an employer from wages.

with·in′ (wi*th* in′, with-) *adv.* **1.** inside; inwardly. —*prep.* **2.** in or into the interior or compass of. **3.** in the scope of.

with·out′ *prep.* **1.** not having. **2.** not accompanied by. **3.** at or to the outside of. —*adv.* **4.** outside. **5.** lacking something.

with·stand′ (with stand′, with-) *v.t.*, -stood, -standing. to resist.

wit′less *adj.* stupid.

wit′ness (wit′nis) *v.t.* **1.** to see, hear, or know by personal experience. **2.** to testify. **3.** to attest by one's signature. —*n.* **4.** a person who has witnessed something. **5.** one who gives testimony. **6.** testimony.

wit′ti·cism′ (wit′ə siz′əm) *n.* a witty remark.

wit′ting *adj.* knowing; aware.

wit′ty *adj.*, -tier, -tiest. having or showing wit. —**wit′ti·ly**, *adv.*

wiz′ard (wiz′ərd) *n.* a magician or sorcerer. —**wiz′ard·ry**, *n.*

wiz′ened (wiz′ənd, wē′zənd) *adj.* shriveled.

wk. week.

w/o without.

wob·ble (wob′əl) *v.i.*, -bled, -bling. to move unsteadily from side to side. —**wob′bly**, *adj.*

woe (wō) *n.* grief, trouble, or affliction. —**woe′ful**, *adj.*

woe′be·gone′ (-bi gôn′) *adj.* showing woe; forlorn.

wok (wok) *n.* a bowl-shaped Chinese cooking pan.

wolf (woolf) *n.*, *pl.* **wolves** (woolvz). —*n.* **1.** a wild carnivorous animal of the dog family. **2.** a cruelly greedy person. **3.** a man who makes amorous advances to women. —*v.t.* **4.** to eat ravenously.

wol′ver·ine′ (wool′və rēn′) *n.* a North American mammal of the weasel family.

wom′an (woom′ən) *n.*, *pl.* **women** (wim′in). an adult female person.

womb (woom) *n.* the uterus.

wom′bat (wom′bat) *n.* a burrowing, herbivorous Australian marsupial.

won′der (wun′dər) *v.i.* **1.** to think or speculate curiously. **2.** to marvel. —*n.* **3.** a cause of amazement, admiration, etc. **4.** Also, **won′der·ment.** a feeling of amazement, puzzlement, etc.

won′der·ful *adj.* **1.** excellent. **2.** exciting wonder.

won′drous *adj.* remarkable.

wont (wônt, wōnt, wunt) *adj.* **1.** accustomed. —*n.* **2.** habit. —**wont′ed,** *adj.*

won′t (wōnt) a contraction of **will not.**

woo (woo) *v.t.* to seek to win, esp. in marriage. —**woo′er,** *n.*

wood (wood) *n.* **1.** the hard, fibrous substance under the bark of trees. **2.** timber or firewood. **3. woods,** forest. —*adj.* **4.** made of wood. **5.** living in the woods. —*v.t.* **6.** to plant with trees. —**wood′craft′,** *n.* —**wood′y,** *adj.*

wood′bine′ (-bīn′) *n.* any of various vines, as the honeysuckle.

wood′chuck′ *n.* a bushy-tailed burrowing rodent. Also called **ground′hog′.**

wood′cut′ *n.* a print made from a carved block of wood.

wood′ed *adj.* covered with trees.

wood′en *adj.* **1.** made of wood. **2.** without feeling or expression.

wood′land′ (-land′, -lənd) *n.* land covered with trees.

wood′peck′er *n.* a bird with a hard bill for boring into wood in search of insects.

wood′ruff (-rəf, -ruf′) *n.* a fragrant plant with small white flowers.

wood′wind′ (-wind′) *n.* a musical instrument of the group including the flute, clarinet, oboe, and bassoon.

wood′work′ *n.* the wooden fittings inside a building.

woof (woof, woof) *n.* the threads running from side to side in a loom.

woof′er (woof′ər) *n.* a loudspeaker to reproduce low-frequency sounds.

wool (wool) *n.* **1.** the soft curly hair of sheep, goats, etc. **2.** a garment, yarn, or fabric of wool. **3.** a substance resembling the wool of sheep. —**wool′en** or (*esp. Brit.*) **wool′len,** *adj.*, *n.*

wool′gath′er·ing *n.* daydreaming.

wool′ly *adj.* **1.** of or resembling wool. **2.** confused or disorganized.

wool′ly bear′ *n.* a caterpillar with woolly hairs.

word (wûrd) *n.* **1.** one or more

spoken sounds carrying meaning and forming a basic unit of speech. **2.** the written representation of this. **3. words, a.** the text of a song. **b.** a quarrel. **4.** something said. **5.** a promise. **6.** a command. —*v.t.* **7.** to express in words. —**word′less,** *adj.*

word′ing *n.* the way of expressing something.

word′ of mouth′ *n.* oral communication.

word′play′ *n.* witty repartee.

word′ proc′essing *n.* the production and storage of documents using computers. —**word′ proc′essor,** *n.*

word′y *adj.,* **-ier, -iest.** using too many words; verbose. —**word′i•ness,** *n.*

work (wûrk) *n.* **1.** exertion; labor. **2.** a task. **3.** employment. **4.** a place of employment. **5.** the materials on which one works. **6.** the result of exertion, labor, etc. **7. works,** an industrial plant. —*adj.* **8.** of or for work. —*v.i.* **9.** to do work. **10.** to function. **11.** to prove effective. —*v.t.* **12.** to use or operate. **13.** to bring about. **14.** to cause to work. **15.** to solve (a puzzle, problem, etc.). **16.** to cause a strong emotion in. —*Idiom.* **17. in the works,** in preparation. —**work′a•ble,** *adj.* —**work′er,** *n.*

work′a•hol′ic (-hô′lik) *n.* a person who works compulsively.

work′horse′ *n.* a person who works tirelessly.

work′house′ *n.* a penal institution for minor offenders.

work′load′ *n.* the amount of work that a machine or employee is expected to perform.

work′man *n., pl.* **-men.** a man skilled in manual, mechanical, or industrial work.

work′man•like′ *adj.* skillful.

work′man•ship′ *n.* **1.** the skill of a workman. **2.** the quality of work done.

work′out′ *n.* **1.** practice or a test to maintain or determine physical ability or endurance. **2.** a structured regimen of physical exercise.

work′shop′ *n.* **1.** a place where work is done. **2.** a seminar to develop a skill or technique.

work′sta′tion *n.* a work area for one person, as in an office, usu. with electronic equipment.

world (wûrld) *n.* **1.** the earth. **2.** a particular part of the earth. **3.** a realm or domain. **4.** humanity. **5.** the universe. **6.** Often, **worlds.** a great quantity.

world′-class′ *adj.* of the highest caliber.

world′ly *adj.,* **-lier, -liest. 1.** of this world. **2.** sophisticated; experienced. —**world′li•ness,** *n.*

world′ly-wise′ *adj.* wise as to the affairs of this world.

world′-wea′ry *adj.* blasé.

World′ Wide′ Web′ *n.* a system of extensively interlinked hypertext documents: a branch of the Internet.

worm (wûrm) *n.* **1.** a long, soft-bodied creeping animal. **2.** something resembling a worm. **3. worms,** an intestinal disorder caused by parasites. —*v.i.* **4.** to creep or crawl slowly and stealthily. —*v.t.* **5.** to extract (a secret) craftily. **6.** to insinuate. **7.** to free from intestinal worms.

worm′wood′ *n.* a bitter aromatic herb.

worn (wôrn) *v.* **1.** pp. of **wear.** —*adj.* **2.** exhausted; spent.

worn′-out′ *adj.* **1.** exhausted. **2.** destroyed by wear.

wor′ry (wûr′ē, wur′ē) *v.,* **-ried, -rying,** *n., pl.* **-ries.** —*v.i.* **1.** to feel anxious. —*v.t.* **2.** to make anxious. **3.** to seize with the teeth and shake. —*n.* **4.** anxiety. **5.** a cause of anxiety. —**wor′ri•some,** *adj.*

worse (wûrs) *adj.* **1.** less good; less favorable. —*n.* **2.** that which is worse. —*adv.* **3.** in a worse way. —**wors′en,** *v.t., v.i.*

wor′ship (wûr′ship) *n., v.,* **-shiped, -shiping** or **-shipped, -shipping.** —*n.* **1.** reverence for a god. **2.** adoring reverence. **3.** a formal expression of reverence. —*v.t.* **4.** to render religious reverence to. **5.** to feel adoring regard for. —*v.i.* **6.** to engage in religious worship. —**wor′ship•er,** *n.*

worst (wûrst) *adj.* **1.** least satisfactory; least well. **2.** in the poorest condition. —*n.* **3.** that which is worst. —*adv.* **4.** in the worst way. —*v.t.* **5.** to defeat.

wor′sted (woos′tid, wûr′stid) *n.* **1.** firmly twisted wool yarn or thread. **2.** fabric made of it.

worth (wûrth) *adj.* **1.** good enough to justify. **2.** having a value of. —*n.* **3.** excellence; importance. **4.** wealth. **5.** a quantity of something of a specified value. —**worth′less,** *adj.*

worth′while′ *adj.* repaying time and effort spent.

wor′thy (wûr′thē) *adj.,* **-thier, -thiest 1.** having merit or value. **2.** deserving. —**wor′thi•ly,** *adv.*

would (wood; *unstressed* wəd) *v.* pt. of **will**[1].

would'-be' adj. wishing, pretending, or intended to be.

wound (wōōnd) n. **1.** an injury from external violence. —v.t. **2.** to inflict a wound upon. **3.** to grieve with an insult or reproach.

wrack (rak) n. damage or destruction.

wraith (rāth) n. a ghost.

wran'gle (rang'gəl) v., **-gled, -gl-ing,** n. —v.i. **1.** to argue noisily. —v.t. **2.** to round up (livestock). —n. **3.** a noisy argument.

wrap (rap) v., **wrapped** or **wrapt, wrapping,** n. —v.t. **1.** to enclose or envelop. **2.** to wind or fold about. —v.i. **3.** to become wrapped. **4. wrap up,** to conclude. —n. **5.** a shawl.

wrap'per n. **1.** one that wraps. **2.** Also, **wrapping.** an outer cover. **3.** a long loose garment.

wrath (rath) n. fierce anger.

wreak (rēk) v.t. to inflict (punishment, vengeance, etc.).

wreath (rēth) n. a circular band of leaves, flowers, etc.

wreathe (rēth) v.t., **wreathed, wreathing. 1.** to encircle with a wreath. **2.** to envelop.

wreck (rek) n. **1.** anything reduced to ruins. **2.** destruction. **3.** a person in ruined health. —v.t. **4.** to damage or destroy.

wreck'age n. **1.** wrecking or being wrecked. **2.** the remains of something wrecked.

wreck'er n. **1.** a vehicle for towing wrecked automobiles. **2.** one that demolishes buildings.

wren (ren) n. a small brown-gray songbird.

wrench (rench) v.t. **1.** to twist or pull forcibly. **2.** to injure by wrenching. —n. **3.** a wrenching movement. **4.** a tool for turning bolts, nuts, etc.

wrest (rest) v.t. **1.** to take away by force. **2.** to get by effort. —n. **3.** a twist or wrench.

wres'tle (res'əl) v., **-tled, -tling,** n. —v.t. **1.** to contend with by trying to force another person down. —v.i. **2.** to engage in wrestling. **3.** to struggle. —n. **4.** a struggle.

wretch (rech) n. a pitiable person.

wretch'ed adj. **1.** miserable or pitiable. **2.** contemptible. **3.** worthless.

wrig'gle (rig'əl) v., **-gled, -gling,** n. —v.i. **1.** to twist to and fro; squirm. —v.t. **2.** to cause to wriggle. —n. **3.** the act of wriggling.

wring (ring) v., **wrung** (rung) **wringing,** n. —v.t. **1.** to twist or compress forcibly. **2.** to clasp tightly. —n. **3.** a twist or squeeze. —**wring'er,** n.

wrin'kle (ring'kəl) n., v., **-kled, -kl-ing.** —n. **1.** a small crease in the skin, in fabric, etc. **2.** a problem. —v.t., v.i. **3.** to form wrinkles (in). —**wrin'kly,** adj.

wrist (rist) n. the joint between the hand and the arm.

writ (rit) n. a court order directing a person to do or not to do something.

write (rīt) v., **wrote** (rōt) **written** (rit'n) **writing.** —v.t. **1.** to form (letters, words, etc.) by hand on paper. **2.** to express in writing. **3.** to be the author or composer of. —v.i. **4.** to express ideas in writing. **5.** to write a letter.

write'-in' n. a candidate or vote for a candidate not listed on a ballot but written in by the voter.

write'-off' n. something cancelled, as a debt.

writ'er n. a person engaged in writing, esp. as an occupation.

writhe (rīth) v., **writhed, writhing,** n. —v.i. **1.** to twist and turn, as in pain. —n. **2.** a writhing movement.

wrong (rông) adj. **1.** not morally good. **2.** deviating from truth or fact; incorrect. **3.** not proper or suitable. —n. **4.** evil; injury; error. —adv. **5.** in a wrong manner. —v.t. **6.** to do wrong to. **7.** to misjudge. —**wrong'ly,** adv.

wrong'do'er n. a person who does wrong, esp. a sinner or transgressor. —**wrong'do'ing,** n.

wrong'ful adj. not fair or legal. —**wrong'ful·ly,** adv.

wrong'head'ed adj. misguided and stubborn.

wrought (rôt) adj. **1.** worked. **2.** shaped by beating.

wrought'-up' adj. excited or disturbed.

wry (rī) adj., **wrier, wriest. 1.** contorted; twisted. **2.** ironic. —**wry'ly,** adv. —**wry'ness,** n.

wuss (wōōs) n. Slang. a weakling; wimp.

WV West Virginia. Also, **W. Va.**

WWW World Wide Web.

WY Wyoming. Also, **Wyo.**

WYSIWYG (wiz'ē wig') adj. of or being a computer display screen that shows text exactly as it will appear when printed.

X Y Z

X, x (eks) *n.* the twenty-fourth letter of the English alphabet.

X′ chro′mosome *n.* a sex chromosome that determines femaleness when paired with another X chromosome and that occurs singly in males.

xen′o·pho′bi·a (zen′ə fō′bē ə, zē′nə-) *n.* an unreasonable fear or hatred of foreigners. —**xen′o·pho′bic,** *adj.*

xe·rog′ra·phy (zi rog′rə fē) *n.* a copying process in which resins are fused to paper electrically.

Xe′rox (zēr′oks) *n.* **1.** *Trademark.* a brand name for a copying machine using xerography. **2.** (*sometimes l.c.*) a copy made on a Xerox. —*v.t., v.i.* **3.** (*sometimes l.c.*) to print or reproduce by Xerox.

Xmas (kris′məs; *often* eks′məs) *n.* Christmas.

X-rat·ed (eks′rā′tid) *adj.* sexually explicit; obscene.

x′-ray′ *n.* **1.** a highly penetrating type of electromagnetic ray, used esp. in medicine. **2.** a photograph made by x-rays. —*v.t.* **3.** to photograph or examine with x-rays.

xy′lo·phone′ (zī′lə fōn′) *n.* a musical instrument of wooden bars struck with small wooden hammers. —**xy′lo·phon′ist,** *n.*

Y, y (wī) *n.* the twenty-fifth letter of the English alphabet.

-y a suffix meaning: **1.** full of or like. **2.** inclined to. **3.** dear or little. **4.** action of. **5.** quality or state.

yacht (yot) *n.* **1.** a boat or ship used for private cruising or racing. —*v.i.* **2.** to sail in a yacht. —**yacht′ing,** *n.* —**yachts′man,** *n.*

ya′da-ya′da-ya′da (yä′də yä′də-yä′də) *adv. Slang.* and so on; and so forth. Also, **yad′da-yad′da-yad′da.**

ya′hoo (yä′hōō) *n.* an uncultivated or boorish person.

yak¹ (yak) *n.* a long-haired Tibetan ox.

yak² (yak) *v.,* **yakked, yakking,** *n. Slang.* —*v.i.* **1.** to gab; chatter. —*n.* **2.** incessant idle or gossipy talk.

yam (yam) *n.* the edible potatolike root of an African climbing vine.

yank (yangk) *v.i., v.t.* **1.** to pull sharply; jerk. —*n.* **2.** a sudden, sharp pull; jerk.

yap (yap) *v.,* **yapped, yapping,** *n.* —*v.i.* **1.** to bark sharply; yelp. **2.** *Slang.* to talk noisily or foolishly. —*n.* **3.** a sharp bark. **4.** *Slang.* noisy, foolish talk.

yard¹ (yärd) *n.* **1.** a linear unit equal to 3 feet or 36 inches. **2.** a long spar supporting the head of a sail.

yard² (yärd) *n.* **1.** the ground adjoining or surrounding a building. **2.** an enclosed outdoor area for a specific purpose.

yard′age (yär′dij) *n.* an amount in yards.

yard′arm′ *n.* either of the yards of a square sail.

yard′stick′ *n.* **1.** a measuring stick one yard long. **2.** a criterion.

yar′mul·ke (yär′məl kə, -mə-, yä′-) *n.* a skullcap worn by Jewish males.

yarn (yärn) *n.* **1.** a strand or thread used for knitting or weaving. **2.** a tale.

yar′row (yar′ō) *n.* a plant with flat-topped clusters of white-to-yellow flowers.

yaw (yô) *v.i.* **1.** to deviate from a straight course, as a ship. —*n.* **2.** the movement of yawing.

yawl (yôl) *n.* a small sailboat.

yawn (yôn) *v.i.* **1.** to open the mouth wide involuntarily, as from sleepiness or boredom. —*n.* **2.** the act of yawning.

Y′ chro′mosome *n.* a sex chromosome present only in males and paired with an X chromosome.

ye (yē) *pron. Archaic.* you.

yea (yā) *adv.* **1.** yes. —*n.* **2.** an affirmative vote.

year (yēr) *n.* **1.** a period of 365 or 366 days. **2. years, a.** age. **b.** a long time. —**year′ly,** *adv., adj.*

year′book′ *n.* **1.** a book published annually with information on the past year. **2.** a commemorative book published by a graduating class.

year′ling (-ling) *n.* an animal in its second year.

yearn (yûrn) *v.i.* to have a strong desire; long.

year′-round′ *adj.* **1.** continuing, available, or used throughout the year. —*adv.* **2.** throughout the year.

yeast (yēst) *n.* a fungus causing fermentation, used in brewing alcoholic beverages and as a leaven in baking bread.

yell (yel) *v.i., v.t.* **1.** to shout loudly. —*n.* **2.** such a shout.

yel′low (yel′ō) *n.* **1.** the color of butter, lemons, etc. —*adj.* **2.** of or like yellow. **3.** cowardly. —*v.t., v.i.* **4.** to make or become yellow.

yel′low fe′ver *n.* an infectious

tropical disease transmitted by mosquitoes.

yelp (yelp) *v.i., v.t.* **1.** to give a sharp, shrill cry. —*n.* **2.** such a cry.

yen (yen) *n.* a desire or craving.

yeo'man (yō'mən) *n.* **1.** a petty officer in the navy. **2.** an independent farmer.

yes (yes) *adv.* **1.** (used to express affirmation or agreement). —*n.* **2.** an affirmative reply.

ye•shi'va (yə shē'və) *n.* an Orthodox Jewish school.

yes'-man' *n., pl.* **yes-men.** a person who always agrees with superiors.

yes'ter•day (yes'tər dā', -dē) *adv., n.* **1.** (on) the day before today. **2.** (in) the recent past.

yet (yet) *adv.* **1.** up to this (or that) time; still. **2.** besides; in addition. **3.** even. **4.** nevertheless. —*conj.* **5.** still; nevertheless.

yew (yōō) *n.* an evergreen tree with needlelike foliage.

yield (yēld) *v.t.* **1.** to produce; give forth. **2.** to surrender or relinquish. **3.** to give as required. —*v.i.* **4.** to give way. **5.** to give a return. —*n.* **6.** a quantity yielded or produced.

yip (yip) *v., pl.* **yipped, yipping,** *n.* —*v.i.* **1.** to bark sharply. —*n.* **2.** a sharp bark.

yo'del (yōd'l) *v.,* **-deled, -deling.** —*v.t., v.i.* **1.** to sing with quick changes to and from falsetto. —*n.* **2.** a yodeled song.

yo'ga (yō'gə) *n.* a series of postures and breathing exercises practiced to attain physical and mental control and tranquillity.

yo'gurt (yō'gərt) *n.* a custardlike food made from milk curdled by bacterial action. Also, **yo'ghurt.**

yoke (yōk) *n., v.,* **yoked, yoking.** —*n.* **1.** a wooden piece put across the necks of oxen pulling a cart, plow, etc. **2.** a frame resting on a person's shoulders to carry two loads. **3.** the fitted upper part of a garment. **4.** oppression or servitude. —*v.t.* **5.** to put a yoke on. **6.** to join or unite.

yo'kel (yō'kəl) *n.* a country bumpkin.

yolk (yōk) *n.* the yellow part of an egg.

Yom Kip•pur (yom kip'ər; *Heb.* yōm' kē pŏŏr') *n.* the holiest Jewish holiday, observed by fasting and prayers of repentance.

yon'der (yon'dər) *adj., adv.* over there. Also, **yon.**

yore (yôr) *n.* time past.

you (yōō; *unstressed* yŏŏ, yə) *pron.* the person or persons addressed.

young (yung) *adj.* **1.** in the early stages of life, operation, etc. **2.** of

youth. —*n.* **3.** young persons. **4.** young offspring. —**young'ish,** *adj.*

young'ster (-stər) *n.* a child.

your (yōōr, yôr; *unstressed* yər) *pron., adj.* a possessive form of **you;** (without noun following) **yours.** —**Usage.** Do not confuse YOUR and YOU'RE. YOUR is the possessive form of "you": *Your book is overdue at the library.* YOU'RE is the contraction of "you are": *You're just the person we need for this job.*

you're (yōōr; *unstressed* yər) a contraction of **you are.** —**Usage.** See YOUR.

your•self' *pron.* an emphatic or reflexive form of **you.**

youth (yōōth) *n.* **1.** the state or time of being young. **2.** young persons. **3.** a young person, esp. a young man. —**youth'ful,** *adj.*

yowl (youl) *v.i.* **1.** to howl. —*n.* **2.** a yowling cry.

yo'-yo (yō'yō) *n., pl.* **yo-yos,** *v.,* **yo-yoed, yo-yoing.** —*n.* **1.** a spoollike toy that is spun out and reeled in by a string looped on the player's finger. —*v.i.* **2.** to move up and down or back and forth.

yr. year.

yuc'ca (yuk'ə) *n.* an American plant with sword-shaped leaves and white flowers.

yule (yōōl) *n.* Christmas.

yule'tide' (-tīd') *n.* the Christmas season.

yum'my (yum'ē) *adj.,* **-mier, -miest.** very pleasing, esp. to the taste.

yup'pie (yup'ē) *n.* a young, ambitious, and affluent professional who lives in or near a city.

Z, z (zē; *esp. Brit.* zed) *n.* the twenty-sixth letter of the English alphabet.

za'ny (zā'nē) *adj.,* **-nier, -niest.** crazily funny. —**za'ni•ness,** *n.*

zap (zap) *v.t.,* **zapped, zapping.** *Informal.* to kill or defeat.

zeal (zēl) *n.* intense ardor or eagerness. —**zeal'ous** (zel'əs) *adj.*

zeal'ot (zel'ət) *n.* an excessively zealous person; fanatic. —**zeal'ot•ry,** *n.*

ze'bra (zē'brə) *n.* a wild, striped horselike animal.

Zen (zen) *n.* a Buddhist movement emphasizing enlightenment by meditation and direct, intuitive insight. Also, **Zen Buddhism.**

ze'nith (zē'nith) *n.* the highest point.

zeph'yr (zef'ər) *n.* a mild breeze.

zep'pe•lin (zep'ə lin) *n.* a large dirigible of the early 20th century.

ze'ro (zēr'ō) *n., pl.* **-ros, -roes. 1.** the figure or numerical symbol 0. **2.** nothing. **3.** the lowest point or degree.

ze′ro hour′ *n.* the starting time for an event or action.

zest (zest) *n.* something adding flavor, interest, etc. —**zest′ful,** *adj.*

zig′zag′ (zig′zag′) *n., adj., adv., v.,* **-zagged, -zagging.** —*n.* **1.** a line going sharply from side to side. —*adj.* **2.** having sharp turns back and forth. —*adv.* **3.** in a zigzag manner. —*v.t., v.i.* **4.** to make into or go in a zigzag.

zilch (zilch) *n. Slang.* zero; nothing.

zil′lion (zil′yən) *n. Informal.* an extremely large, indeterminate number.

zinc (zingk) *n.* a bluish white metallic element.

zinc′ ox′ide *n.* a white powder used in pigments and ointments.

zin′ni•a (zin′ē ə) *n.* a plant with dense, colorful flowers.

zip[1] (zip) *v.,* **zipped, zipping,** *n.* —*v.i.* **1.** to act or go with great energy. —*n.* **2.** energy.

zip[2] (zip) *v.t., v.i.,* **zipped, zipping.** to fasten (with) a zipper.

ZIP (zip) *n.* a way of compressing electronic files for storage and transfer.

ZIP′ code′ *Trademark.* a system to expedite mail delivery by assigning a numerical code to every postal area in the U.S.

zip′per *n.* a fastener with tracks of teeth that can be interlocked by pulling a sliding piece.

zip′py *adj.,* **-pier, -piest.** lively; smart.

zir′con (zûr′kon) *n.* a mineral that is used as a gem when transparent.

zit (zit) *n. Slang.* a pimple.

zith′er (zith′ər, zith′-) *n.* a stringed musical instrument that is played with a plectrum and the fingertips.

zo′di•ac′ (zō′dē ak′) *n.* an imaginary belt in the heavens containing paths of the sun, moon, and the major planets, divided into 12 signs, each named after a constellation.

zom′bie (zom′bē) *n.* **1.** (in voodoo) a reanimated corpse. **2.** a person whose behavior is listless or mechanical.

zone (zōn) *n., v.,* **zoned, zoning.** —*n.* **1.** a special area. **2.** one of five divisions of the earth's surface based on climate and latitude. —*v.t.* **3.** to divide into or mark with zones. —**zon′al,** *adj.*

zoo (zōō) *n.* a parklike area where live animals are exhibited.

zo•ol′o•gy (zō ol′ə jē) *n.* the scientific study of animals. —**zo′o•log′i•cal** (-ə loj′i kəl) *adj.* —**zo•ol′o•gist,** *n.*

zoom (zōōm) *v.i.* **1.** to move with a loud hum or buzz. **2.** to move suddenly and sharply.

zo′o•pho′bi•a (zō′ə-) *n.* fear of animals.

zo′o•phyte′ (-fīt′) *n.* an invertebrate animal resembling a plant, as a coral.

zuc•chi′ni (zōō kē′nē) *n.* a cucumber-shaped summer squash.

zwie′back′ (zwī′bak′, -bäk′, swē′-) *n.* a biscuit of dried, twice-baked bread.

Rules of Punctuation

1. **Period (.):** Ends a sentence which makes a statement or expresses a request, order, or command. It is also used after most abbreviations.
2. **Question Mark (?):** Ends a sentence which asks a question.
3. **Exclamation Point (!):** Ends a sentence which expresses strong emotion or feeling.
4. **Colon (:):** Used (a) to introduce a formal or long direct quotation; (b) to introduce a long series of items or illustrations; (c) in the salutation of a formal letter.
5. **Semicolon (;):** Used (a) to separate long clauses of a compound sentence; (b) to separate independent clauses if the conjunction is omitted; (c) to separate long items in a series.
6. **Comma (,):** Used (a) to separate independent clauses connected by conjunctions *and, but, or, nor, for, yet, so*; (b) to separate a non-restrictive clause from the rest of the sentence; (c) to separate three or more words, phrases, or clauses in a series; (d) to set off appositives and nouns in direct address; (e) to set off mild interjections; (f) to separate words in dates and addresses; (g) to introduce a direct quotation.
7. **Dash (—):** Used (a) to show a definite interruption or change of thought; (b) to indicate the omission of words, letters, or numbers.
8. **Apostrophe ('):** Used (a) in the possessive forms of nouns and indefinite pronouns; (b) to indicate the omission of one or more letters in contractions; (c) to form plurals of numbers or letters.
9. **Hyphen (-):** Used (a) to mark the break in an unfinished word at the end of a line; (b) between a prefix and a proper name or when the emphasis is on the prefix; (c) in fractions and in compound numerals from twenty-one to ninety-nine; (d) between the parts of certain compound words.
10. **Parentheses ( ):** Used to set off words, phrases, or clauses which are not basic to the main point of the sentence.
11. **Brackets ([ ]):** Used to indicate editorial explanation.
12. **Quotation Marks (" "):** Used (a) to enclose direct quotations; (b) to set off titles.

Rules of Spelling

No spelling rule should be followed blindly, for every rule has exceptions, and words analogous in some forms may differ in others.

1. **Silent *e* dropped.** Silent *e* at the end of a word is usually dropped before a suffix beginning with a vowel: *abide, abiding; recite, recital.* **Exceptions:** Words ending in *ce* or *ge* retain the *e* before a suffix beginning with *a* or *o* to keep the soft sound of the consonant: *notice, noticeable; courage, courageous.*

2. **Silent _e_ kept.** A silent _e_ following a consonant (or another _e_) is usually retained before a suffix beginning with a consonant: _late, lateness; spite, spiteful._ **Exceptions:** _fledgling, acknowledgment, judgment, wholly,_ and a few similar words.

3. **Final consonant doubled.** A final consonant following a single vowel in one-syllable words or in a syllable that will take the main accent when combined with a suffix is doubled before a suffix beginning with a vowel: _begin, beginning; occur, occurred._ **Exceptions:** _h_ and _x (ks)_ in final position; _transferable, gaseous,_ and a few others.

4. **Final consonant single.** A final consonant following another consonant or a double vowel or diphthong or not in a stressed syllable is not doubled before a suffix beginning with a vowel: _part, parting; remark, remarkable._ **Exceptions:** An unaccented syllable does not prevent doubling of the final consonant, especially in British usage: _traveller_ beside _traveler,_ etc.

5. **Double consonants remain.** Double consonants are usually retained before a suffix except when a final _l_ is to be followed by _ly_ or _less._ To avoid a triple _lll,_ one _l_ is usually dropped: _full, fully._ **Exceptions:** Usage is divided, with _skilful_ beside _skillful, instalment_ beside _installment,_ etc.

6. **Final _y._** If the _y_ follows a consonant, change _y_ to _i_ before all endings except _ing._ Do not change it before _ing_ or if it follows a vowel: _bury, buried, burying; try, tries;_ but _attorney, attorneys._ **Exceptions:** _day, daily; gay, gaily; lay, laid; say, said._

7. **Final _ie_ to _y._** Words ending in _ie_ change to _y_ before _ing: die, dying; lie, lying._

8. **Double and triple _e_ reduced.** Words ending in double _e_ drop one _e_ before an ending beginning in _e,_ to avoid a triple _e._ Words ending in silent _e_ usually drop the _e_ before endings beginning in _e_ to avoid forming a syllable. Other words ending in a vowel sound commonly retain the letters indicating the sound. _Free-ed = freed._

9. **_ei_ or _ie._** Words having the sound of $\bar{e}$ are commonly spelled _ie_ following all letters but _c;_ with a preceding _c,_ the common spelling is _ei._ Examples: _believe, achieve, besiege_ but _conceit, ceiling, receive, conceive._ When the sound is $\bar{a}$, the common spelling is _ei_ regardless of the preceding letter. Examples: _eight, weight, deign._ **Exceptions:** _either, neither, seize, financier;_ some words in which _e_ and _i_ are pronounced separately, such as _notoriety._

10. **Words ending in _c._** Before an ending beginning with _e, i,_ or _y,_ words ending in _c_ commonly add _k_ to keep the _c_ hard: _panic, panicky._

11. **Compounds.** Some compounds written as a unit bring together unusual combinations of letters. They are seldom changed on this account. _Bookkeeper, roommate._ **Exceptions:** A few words are regularly clipped when compounded, such as _full_ in _awful, cupful,_ etc.

Facts About the United States

State	Capital	Population	Area (sq. mi.)
Alabama	Montgomery	4,447,100	51,609
Alaska	Juneau	626,932	586,400
Arizona	Phoenix	5,130,632	113,909
Arkansas	Little Rock	2,673,400	53,103
California	Sacramento	33,871,648	158,693
Colorado	Denver	4,301,261	104,247
Connecticut	Hartford	3,405,565	5009
Delaware	Dover	783,600	2057
Florida	Tallahassee	15,982,378	58,560
Georgia	Atlanta	8,186,453	38,876
Hawaii	Honolulu	1,211,537	6424
Idaho	Boise	1,293,953	83,557
Illinois	Springfield	12,419,293	36,400
Indiana	Indianapolis	6,080,485	36,291
Iowa	Des Moines	2,926,324	56,290
Kansas	Topeka	2,688,418	82,276
Kentucky	Frankfort	4,041,769	40,395
Louisiana	Baton Rouge	4,468,976	48,522
Maine	Augusta	1,274,923	33,215
Maryland	Annapolis	5,296,486	10,577
Massachusetts	Boston	6,349,097	8257
Michigan	Lansing	9,938,444	58,216
Minnesota	St. Paul	4,919,479	84,068
Mississippi	Jackson	2,844,658	47,716
Missouri	Jefferson City	5,595,211	69,674
Montana	Helena	902,195	147,138
Nebraska	Lincoln	1,711,263	77,237
Nevada	Carson City	1,998,257	110,540
New Hampshire	Concord	1,235,786	9304
New Jersey	Trenton	8,414,350	7836
New Mexico	Santa Fe	1,819,046	121,666
New York	Albany	18,976,457	49,576
North Carolina	Raleigh	8,049,313	52,586
North Dakota	Bismarck	642,200	70,665
Ohio	Columbus	11,353,140	41,222
Oklahoma	Oklahoma City	3,450,654	69,919
Oregon	Salem	3,421,399	96,981
Pennsylvania	Harrisburg	12,281,054	45,333
Rhode Island	Providence	1,048,319	1214
South Carolina	Columbia	4,012,012	31,055

Facts About the United States *(Continued)*

State	Capital	Population	Area (sq. mi.)
South Dakota	Pierre	754,844	77,047
Tennessee	Nashville	5,689,283	42,246
Texas	Austin	20,851,820	267,339
Utah	Salt Lake City	2,233,169	84,916
Vermont	Montpelier	608,827	9609
Virginia	Richmond	7,078,515	40,815
Washington	Olympia	5,894,121	68,192
West Virginia	Charleston	1,808,344	24,181
Wisconsin	Madison	5,363,675	56,154
Wyoming	Cheyenne	493,782	97,914
Washington, D.C.	—	572,059	63
Total U.S.		**281,421,906**	**3,615,122**

Chief American Holidays

New Year's Day	January 1
Martin Luther King Day	January 15[1]
Inauguration Day	January 20
Lincoln's Birthday	February 12[2]
Washington's Birthday	February 22[2]
Good Friday	Friday before Easter
Memorial Day	May 30[3]
Independence Day	July 4
Labor Day	First Monday in September
Columbus Day	October 12[4]
Veterans Day	November 11
Election Day	Tuesday after first Monday in November
Thanksgiving Day	Fourth Thursday in November
Christmas Day	December 25

[1] officially observed on 3rd Monday in January
[2] officially observed as Presidents' Day on 3rd Monday in February
[3] officially observed on last Monday in May
[4] officially observed on 2nd Monday in October

Presidents of the United States

Name (and party)	Birth State	Born	Term	Died
George Washington (F)	Va.	1732	1789–1797	1799
John Adams (F)	Mass.	1735	1797–1801	1826
Thomas Jefferson (D-R)	Va.	1743	1801–1809	1826
James Madison (D-R)	Va.	1751	1809–1817	1836
James Monroe (D-R)	Va.	1758	1817–1825	1831
John Quincy Adams (D-R)	Mass.	1767	1825–1829	1848
Andrew Jackson (D)	S.C.	1767	1829–1837	1845
Martin Van Buren (D)	N.Y.	1782	1837–1841	1862
William Henry Harrison (W)	Va.	1773	1841–1841	1841
John Tyler (W)	Va.	1790	1841–1845	1862
James Knox Polk (D)	N.C.	1795	1845–1849	1849
Zachary Taylor (W)	Va.	1784	1849–1850	1850
Millard Fillmore (W)	N.Y.	1800	1850–1853	1874
Franklin Pierce (D)	N.H.	1804	1853–1857	1869
James Buchanan (D)	Pa.	1791	1857–1861	1868
Abraham Lincoln (R)	Ky.	1809	1861–1865	1865
Andrew Johnson (R)	N.C.	1808	1865–1869	1875
Ulysses Simpson Grant (R)	Ohio	1822	1869–1877	1885
Rutherford Birchard Hayes (R)	Ohio	1822	1877–1881	1893
James Abram Garfield (R)	Ohio	1831	1881–1881	1881
Chester Alan Arthur (R)	Vt.	1830	1881–1885	1886
Grover Cleveland (D)	N.J.	1837	1885–1889	1908
Benjamin Harrison (R)	Ohio	1833	1889–1893	1901
Grover Cleveland (D)	N.J.	1837	1893–1897	1908
William McKinley (R)	Ohio	1843	1897–1901	1901
Theodore Roosevelt (R)	N.Y.	1858	1901–1909	1919
William Howard Taft (R)	Ohio	1857	1909–1913	1930
Woodrow Wilson (D)	Va.	1856	1913–1921	1924
Warren Gamaliel Harding (R)	Ohio	1865	1921–1923	1923
Calvin Coolidge (R)	Vt.	1872	1923–1929	1933
Herbert Clark Hoover (R)	Iowa	1874	1929–1933	1964
Franklin Delano Roosevelt (D)	N.Y.	1882	1933–1945	1945
Harry S. Truman (D)	Mo.	1884	1945–1953	1972
Dwight D. Eisenhower (R)	Tex.	1890	1953–1961	1969

Presidents of the United States *(Continued)*

Name (and party)	Birth State	Born	Term	Died
John Fitzgerald Kennedy (D)	Mass.	1917	1961–1963	1963
Lyndon Baines Johnson (D)	Tex.	1908	1963–1969	1973
Richard Milhous Nixon (R)	Cal.	1913	1969–1974	1994
Gerald R. Ford (R)	Neb.	1913	1974–1977	
James Earl Carter, Jr. (D)	Ga.	1924	1977–1981	
Ronald Wilson Reagan (R)	Ill.	1911	1981–1989	
George H. W. Bush (R)	Mass.	1924	1989–1993	
William J. Clinton (D)	Ark.	1946	1993–2001	
George W. Bush (R)	Conn.	1946	2001–	

F–Federalist; D–Democrat; R–Republican; W–Whig.

Distances Between U.S. Cities

	Atlanta	Chicago	Dallas	Denver	Los Angeles	New York	St. Louis	Seattle
Atlanta	—	592	738	1421	1981	762	516	2354
Boston	946	879	1565	1786	2739	184	1118	2831
Chicago	592	—	857	909	1860	724	251	1748
Cincinnati	377	255	870	1102	1910	613	550	2003
Cleveland	587	307	1080	1216	2054	458	558	2259
Dallas	738	857	—	683	1243	1391	547	2199
Denver	1421	909	683	—	838	1633	781	1074
Detroit	619	247	1045	1156	2052	486	463	1947
Kansas City	745	405	452	552	1360	1117	229	1626
Los Angeles	1981	1860	1243	838	—	2624	1589	956
Miami	614	1199	1405	1911	2611	1106	1123	2947
Minneapolis	942	350	860	840	1768	1020	492	1398
New Orleans	427	860	437	1120	1680	1186	609	2608
New York	762	724	1381	1633	2624	—	888	2418
Philadelphia	667	671	1303	1578	2467	95	841	2647
Pittsburgh	536	461	1318	1349	2157	320	568	2168
St. Louis	516	251	547	781	1589	888	—	1890
San Francisco	2308	1856	1570	956	327	2580	1916	687
Seattle	2354	1748	2199	1074	956	2418	1890	—
Washington, D.C.	547	600	1183	1519	2426	215	719	2562

Weights and Measures

Troy Weight

24 grains	=	1 pennyweight
20 pennyweights	=	1 ounce
12 ounces	=	1 pound

Avoirdupois Weight

$27\,^{11}/_{32}$ grains	=	1 dram
16 drams	=	1 ounce
16 ounces	=	1 pound
100 pounds	=	1 short hundredweight
20 short hundredweight	=	1 short ton

Apothecaries' Weight

20 grains	=	1 scruple
3 scruples	=	1 dram
8 drams	=	1 ounce
12 ounces	=	1 pound

Linear Measure

12 inches	=	1 foot
3 feet	=	1 yard
$5\,^1/_2$ yards	=	1 rod
40 rods	=	1 furlong
8 furlongs (5280 feet)	=	1 statute mile

Mariners' Measure

6 feet	=	1 fathom
1000 fathoms (approx.)	=	1 nautical mile
3 nautical miles	=	1 league

Apothecaries' Fluid Measure

60 minims	=	1 fluid dram
8 fluid drams	=	1 fluid ounce
16 fluid ounces	=	1 pint
2 pints	=	1 quart
4 quarts	=	1 gallon

Square Measure

144 square inches	=	1 square foot
9 square feet	=	1 square yard
$30\,^1/_4$ square yards	=	1 square rod
160 square rods	=	1 acre
640 acres	=	1 square mile

Cubic Measure

1728 cubic inches	=	1 cubic foot
27 cubic feet	=	1 cubic yard

Weights and Measures *(Continued)*

Surveyors' Measure
7.92 inches	=	1 link
100 links	=	1 chain

Liquid Measure
4 gills	=	1 pint
2 pints	=	1 quart
4 quarts	=	1 gallon
31 $\frac{1}{2}$ gallons	=	1 barrel
2 barrels	=	1 hogshead

Dry Measure
2 pints	=	1 quart
8 quarts	=	1 peck
4 pecks	=	1 bushel

Wood Measure
16 cubic feet	=	1 cord foot
8 cord feet	=	1 cord

Angular and Circular Measure
60 seconds	=	1 minute
60 minutes	=	1 degree
90 degrees	=	1 right angle
180 degrees	=	1 straight angle
360 degrees	=	1 circle

10 dekaliters	=	1 hectoliter
10 hectoliters	=	1 kiloliter

Weights
10 milligrams	=	1 centigram
10 centigrams	=	1 decigram
10 decigrams	=	1 gram
10 grams	=	1 dekagram
10 dekagrams	=	hectogram
10 hectograms	=	1 kilogram
100 kilograms	=	1 quintal
10 quintals	=	1 ton

Webster's
Spanish–English
Dictionary

Pronunciation Key for Spanish

IPA Symbols	Key Words	Approximate Equivalents
a	alba, banco, cera	father, depart
e	esto, del, parte, mesa	bet; like rain when e ends syllable and is not followed by r, rr, or t
i	ir, fino, adiós, muy	like beet, but shorter
o	oler, flor, grano	like vote, but shorter
u	un, luna, cuento, vergüenza, guarda	fool, group
b	bajo, ambiguo, vaca	by, abet
β	hablar, escribir, lavar	like vehicle, but with lips almost touching
d	dar, desde, andamio, dueña	deal, adept
ð	pedir, edredón, verdad	that, gather
f	fecha, afectar, golf	fan, after
g	gato, grave, gusto, largo, guerra	garden, ugly
h	gemelo, giro, junta, bajo	horse
k	cacao, claro, cura, cuenta, que, quinto	kind, actor
l	lado, lente, habla, papel	lot, altar
ʎ	(in Spain) llama, calle, olla	like million, but with tongue behind teeth
m	mal, amor	more, commit

IPA Symbols	Key Words	Approximate Equivalents
n	nada, nuevo, mano, bien	not, enter
ɲ	ñapa, año	canyon, companion
ŋ	angosto, aunque	ring, anchor
p	peso, guapo	pill, applaud
r	real, faro, deber	like rice, but with single flap of tongue on roof of mouth
rr	perro, sierra	like rice, but with trill, or vibration of tongue, against upper teeth
s	sala, espejo, mas; (in Latin America) cena, hacer, vez	say, clasp
θ	(in Spain) cena, hacer, cierto, cine, zarzuela, lazo, vez	thin, myth
t	tocar, estado, cenit	table, attract
y	ya, ayer; (in Latin America) llama, calle	you, voyage
tʃ	chica, mucho	chill, batch

Diphthongs

ai	baile, hay	high, rye
au	audacia, laudable	out, round
ei	veinte, seis, rey	ray
ie	miel, tambien	fiesta
oi	estoico, hoy	coin, loyal
ua	cuanto	quantity
ue	buena, suerte	sway, quaint

Spanish Stress

In a number of words, spoken stress is marked by an accent (´): *nación, país, médico, día.*

Words which are not so marked are, generally speaking, stressed on the next-to-the-last syllable if they end in a vowel, *n,* or *s;* and on the last syllable if they end in a consonant other than *n* or *s.*

Note: An accent is placed over some words to distinguish them from others having the same spelling and pronunciation but differing in meaning.

Spanish Alphabetization

In Spanish, *ch* and *ll* are no longer considered to be separate letters of the alphabet. They are now alphabetized as they would be in English. However, words with *ñ* are alphabetized after *n.*

Guía de Pronunciación del inglés

Símbolos del AFI	Ejemplos
/æ/	*ingl.* hat; como la **a** de *esp.* paro, pero más cerrada
/ei/	*ingl.* stay; *esp.* reina
/ɛə/ [followed by /r/]	*ingl.* hair; *esp.* ver
/ɑ/	*ingl.* father; similar a las **as** de *esp.* casa, pero más larga
/ɛ/	*ingl.* bet; *esp.* entre
/i/	*ingl.* bee; como la **i** de *esp.* vida, pero más larga
/ɪə/ [followed by /r/]	*ingl.* hear; como la **i** de *esp.* venir, pero menos cerrada
/ɪ/	*ingl.* sit; como la **i** de *esp.* Chile, pero menos cerrada
/ai/	*ingl.* try; *esp.* hay
/ɒ/	*ingl.* hot; *esp.* poner
/ou/	*ingl.* boat; similar a la **o** de *esp.* saco, pero más cerrada
/ɔ/	*ingl.* saw; similar a la **o** de *esp.* corte, pero más cerrada
/ɔi/	*ingl.* toy; *esp.* hoy
/ʊ/	*ingl.* book; como la **u** de *esp.* insulto, pero menos cerrada
/u/	*ingl.* too; como la **u** de *esp.* luna, pero más larga
/au/	*ingl.* cow; *esp.* pausa
/ʌ/	*ingl.* up; entre la **o** de *esp.* borde y la **a** de *esp.* barro
/ɜ/ [followed by /r/]	*ingl.* burn; *fr.* fleur
/ə/	*ingl.* alone; *fr.* demain
/ᵊ/	*ingl.* fire (fiᵊr); *fr.* bastille
/b/	*ingl.* boy; como la **b** de *esp.* boca, pero más aspirada
/tʃ/	*ingl.* child; *esp.* mucho
/d/	*ingl.* dad; *esp.* dar
/f/	*ingl.* for; *esp.* fecha
/g/	*ingl.* give; *esp.* gato

Símbolos del AFI	Ejemplos
/h/	*ingl.* happy; como la j de *esp.* jabón, pero más aspirada y menos aspera
/dʒ/	*ingl.* just; *it.* giorno
/k/	*ingl.* kick; similar a la k de *esp.* kilogramo, pero más aspirada
/l/	*ingl.* love; *esp.* libro
/m/	*ingl.* mother; *esp.* limbo
/n/	*ingl.* now; *esp.* noche
/ŋ/	*ingl.* sing; *esp.* blanco
/p/	*ingl.* pot; como las ps de *esp.* papa, pero más aspirada
/r/	*ingl.* read; como la r de *esp.* para, pero con la lengua elevada hacia el paladar, sin tocarlo
/s/	*ingl.* see; *esp.* hasta
/ʃ/	*ingl.* shop; *fr.* chercher
/t/	*ingl.* ten; similar a la t de *esp.* tomar, pero más aspirada
/θ/	*ingl.* thing; *esp.* (en España) cerdo, zapato
/ð/	*ingl.* father; *esp.* codo
/v/	*ingl.* victory; como la b de *esp.* haba, pero es labiodental en vez de bilabial
/w/	*ingl.* witch; como la u de *esp.* puesto, pero con labios más cerrados
/y/	*ingl.* yes; *esp.* yacer
/z/	*ingl.* zipper; fr. zéro
/ʒ/	*ingl.* pleasure; *fr.* jeune

Las consonantes /ḷ/, /m̩/, y /n̩/ son similar a las l, m, y n del español, pero alargada y resonante.

English Abbreviations/ Abreviaturas inglesas

a.	adjective	*Govt.*	government
abbr.	abbreviation	*Gram.*	grammar
adv.	adverb	*interj.*	interjection
Aero.	aeronautics	*interrog.*	interrogative
Agr.	agriculture	*Leg.*	legal
Anat.	anatomy	*m.*	masculine
art.	article	*Mech.*	mechanics
Auto.	automotive	*Mex.*	Mexico
Biol.	biology	*Mil.*	military
Bot.	botany	*Mus.*	music
Carib.	Caribbean	*n.*	noun
Chem.	chemistry	*Naut.*	nautical
Colloq.	colloquial	*Phot.*	photography
Com.	commerce	*pl.*	plural
conj.	conjunction	*Pol.*	politics
dem.	demonstrative	*prep.*	preposition
Econ.	economics	*pron.*	pronoun
Elec.	electrical	*Punct.*	punctuation
esp.	especially	*rel.*	relative
f.	feminine	*Relig.*	religion
Fig.	figurative	*S.A.*	Spanish America
Fin.	finance	*Theat.*	theater
Geog.	geography	*v.*	verb

Note: If a main entry term is repeated in a boldface subentry in exactly the same form, it is abbreviated. Example: **comedor** *n.m.* dining room. **coche c.,** dining car.

SPANISH-ENGLISH

A

a /a/ *prep.* to; at.
abacería /aβaθe'ria; aβase'ria/ *n. f.* grocery store.
abacero /aβa'θero; aβa'sero/ *n. m.* grocer.
ábaco /'aβako/ *n. m.* abacus.
abad /a'βaδ/ *n. m.* abbot.
abadía /aβa'δia/ *n. f.* abbey.
abajar /aβa'har/ *v.* lower; go down.
abajo /a'βaho/ *adv.* down; downstairs.
abandonar /aβando'nar/ *v.* abandon.
abandono /aβan'dono/ *n. m.* abandonment.
abanico /aβa'niko/ *n. m.* fan. **—abanicar,** *v.*
abaratar /aβara'tar/ *v.* cheapen.
abarcar /aβar'kar/ *v.* comprise; clasp.
abastecer /aβaste'θer; aβaste'ser/ *v.* supply, provide.
abatido /aβa'tiδo/ *a.* dejected, despondent.
abatir /aβa'tir/ *v.* knock down; dismantle; depress, dishearten.
abdicación /aβδika'θion; aβδika'sion/ *n. f.* abdication.
abdicar /aβδi'kar/ *v.* abdicate.
abdomen /aβ'δomen/ *n. m.* abdomen.
abdominal /aβδomi'nal/ *a.* **1.** abdominal. **—***n.* **2.** *m.* sit-up.
abecé /aβe'θe; aβe'se/ *n. m.* ABCs, rudiments.
abecedario /aβeθe'δario; aβese'δario/ *n. m.* alphabet; reading book.
abeja /a'βeha/ *n. f.* bee.
abejarrón /aβeha'rron/ *n. m.* bumblebee.
aberración /aβerra'θion; aβerra'sion/ *n. f.* aberration.
abertura /aβer'tura/ *n. f.* opening, aperture, slit.
abeto /a'βeto/ *n. m.* fir.
abierto /a'βierto/ *a.* open; overt.
abismal /aβis'mal/ *a.* abysmal.
abismo /a'βismo/ *n. m.* abyss, chasm.
ablandar /aβlan'dar/ *v.* soften.
abnegación /aβnega'θion; aβnega'sion/ *n. f.* abnegation.
abochornar /aβotʃor'nar/ *v.* overheat; embarrass.

abogado /aβo'gaδo/ **-da** *n.* lawyer, attorney.
abolengo /aβo'lengo/ *n. m.* ancestry.
abolición /aβoli'θion; aβoli'sion/ *n. f.* abolition.
abolladura /aβoʎa'δura; aβoya'δura/ *n. f.* dent. **—abollar,** *v.*
abominable /aβomi'naβle/ *a.* abominable.
abominar /aβomi'nar/ *v.* abhor.
abonado /aβo'naδo/ **-da** *n. m. & f.* subscriber.
abonar /aβo'nar/ *v.* pay; fertilize.
abonarse /aβo'narse/ *v.* subscribe.
abono /a'βono/ *n. m.* fertilizer; subscription; season ticket.
aborigen /aβor'ihen/ *a. & n.* aboriginal.
aborrecer /aβorre'θer; aβorre'ser/ *v.* hate, loathe, abhor.
abortar /aβor'tar/ *v.* abort, miscarry.
aborto /a'βorto/ *n. m.* abortion.
abovedar /aβoβe'δar/ *v.* vault.
abrasar /aβra'sar/ *v.* burn.
abrazar /aβra'θar; aβra'sar/ *v.* embrace; clasp.
abrazo /a'βraθo; a'βraso/ *n. m.* embrace.
abrelatas /aβre'latas/ *n. m.* can opener.
abreviar /aβre'βiar/ *v.* abbreviate, abridge, shorten.
abreviatura /aβreβia'tura/ *n. f.* abbreviation.
abrigar /aβri'gar/ *v.* harbor, shelter.
abrigarse /aβri'garse/ *v.* bundle up.
abrigo /a'βrigo/ *n. m.* overcoat; shelter; (*pl.*) wraps.
abril /a'βril/ *n. m.* April.
abrir /a'βrir/ *v.* open; *Med.* lance.
abrochar /aβro'tʃar/ *v.* clasp.
abrogación /aβroga'θion; aβroga'sion/ *n. f.* abrogation, repeal.
abrogar /aβro'gar/ *v.* abrogate.
abrojo /a'βroho/ *n. m.* thorn.
abrumar /aβru'mar/ *v.* overwhelm, crush, swamp.
absceso /aβs'θeso; aβ'sseso/ *n. m.* abscess.
absolución /aβsolu'θion; aβsolu'sion/ *n. f.* absolution; acquittal.

absoluto /aβso'luto/ *a.* absolute; downright.

absolver /aβsol'βer/ *v.* absolve, pardon.

absorbente /aβsor'βente/ *a.* absorbent.

absorber /aβsor'βer/ *v.* absorb.

absorción /aβsor'θion; aβsor'sion/ *n. f.* absorption.

abstemio /aβs'temio/ *a.* abstemious.

abstenerse /aβste'nerse/ *v.* abstain; refrain.

abstinencia /aβsti'nenθia; aβsti'nensia/ *n. f.* abstinence.

abstracción /aβstrak'θion; aβstrak'sion/ *n. f.* abstraction.

abstracto /aβ'strakto/ *a.* abstract.

abstraer /aβstra'er/ *v.* abstract.

absurdo /aβ'surðo/ *a.* **1.** absurd. —*n.* **2.** *m.* absurdity.

abuchear /aβutʃe'ar/ *v.* boo.

abuela /a'βuela/ *n. f.* grandmother.

abuelo /a'βuelo/ *n. m.* grandfather; *(pl.)* grandparents.

abultado /aβul'taðo/ *a.* bulky.

abultamiento /aβulta'miento/ *n. m.* bulge. —**abultar,** *v.*

abundancia /aβun'danθia; aβun'dansia/ *n. f.* abundance, plenty.

abundante /aβun'dante/ *a.* abundant, plentiful.

abundar /aβun'dar/ *v.* abound.

aburrido /aβu'rriðo/ *a.* boring, tedious.

aburrimiento /aβurri'miento/ *n. m.* boredom.

aburrir /aβu'rrir/ *v.* bore.

abusar /aβu'sar/ *v.* abuse, misuse.

abusivo /aβu'siβo/ *a.* abusive.

abuso /a'βuso/ *n. m.* abuse.

abyecto /aβ'yekto/ *a.* abject, low.

a.C., *abbr.* **(antes de Cristo)** BC.

acá /a'ka/ *adv.* here.

acabar /aka'βar/ *v.* finish. **a. de...,** to have just....

acacia /a'kaθia; a'kasia/ *n. f.* acacia.

academia /aka'ðemia/ *n. f.* academy.

académico /aka'ðemiko/ *a.* academic.

acaecer /akae'θer; akae'ser/ *v.* happen.

acanalar /akana'lar/ *v.* groove.

acaparar /akapa'rar/ *v.* hoard; monopolize.

acariciar /akari'θiar; akari'siar/ *v.* caress, stroke.

acarrear /akarre'ar/ *v.* cart, transport; occasion, entail.

acaso /a'kaso/ *n. m.* chance. **por si a.,** just in case.

acceder /akθe'ðer; akse'ðer/ *v.* accede.

accesible /akθe'siβle; akse'siβle/ *a.* accessible.

acceso /ak'θeso; ak'seso/ *n. m.* access, approach.

accesorio /akθe'sorio; akse'sorio/ *a.* accessory.

accidentado /akθiðen'taðo; aksiðen'taðo/ *a.* hilly.

accidental /akθiðen'tal; aksiðen'tal/ *a.* accidental.

accidente /akθi'ðente; aksi'ðente/ *n. m.* accident, wreck.

acción /ak'θion; ak'sion/ *n. f.* action, act; *Com.* share of stock.

accionista /akθio'nista; aksio'nista/ *n. m. & f.* shareholder.

acechar /aθe'tʃar; ase'tʃar/ *v.* ambush, spy on.

acedia /a'θeðia; a'seðia/ *n. f.* heartburn.

aceite /a'θeite; a'seite/ *n. m.* oil.

aceite de hígado de bacalao /a'θeite de i'gaðo de baka'lao; a'seite/ cod-liver oil.

aceitoso /aθei'toso; asei'toso/ *a.* oily.

aceituna /aθei'tuna; asei'tuna/ *n. f.* olive.

aceleración /aθelera'θion; aselera'sion/ *n. f.* acceleration.

acelerar /aθele'rar; asele'rar/ *v.* accelerate, speed up.

acento /a'θento; a'sento/ *n. m.* accent.

acentuar /aθen'tuar; asen'tuar/ *v.* accent, accentuate, stress.

acepillar /aθepi'ʎar; asepi'yar/ *v.* brush; plane (wood).

aceptable /aθep'taβle; asep'taβle/ *a.* acceptable.

aceptación /aθepta'θion; asepta'sion/ *n. f.* acceptance.

aceptar /aθep'tar; asep'tar/ *v.* accept.

acequía /aθe'kia; ase'kia/ *n. f.* ditch.

acera /a'θera; a'sera/ *n. f.* sidewalk.

acerca de /a'θerka de; a'serka de/ *prep.* about, concerning.

acercar /aθer'kar; aser'kar/ *v.* bring near.

acercarse /aθer'karse; aser'karse/ v. approach, come near, go near.

acero /a'θero; a'sero/ n. m. steel.

acero inoxidable /a'θero inoksi-'ðaβle; a'sero inoksi'ðaβle/ stainless steel.

acertar /aθer'tar; aser'tar/ v. guess right. **a. en,** hit (a mark).

acertijo /aθer'tiho; aser'tiho/ n. m. puzzle, riddle.

achicar /atʃi'kar/ v. diminish, dwarf; humble.

acidez /aθi'ðeθ; asi'ðes/ n. f. acidity.

ácido /'aθiðo; 'asiðo/ a. **1.** sour. —n. **2.** m. acid.

aclamación /aklama'θion; aklama'sion/ n. f. acclamation.

aclamar /akla'mar/ v. acclaim.

aclarar /akla'rar/ v. brighten; clarify, clear up.

acoger /ako'her/ v. welcome, receive.

acogida /ako'hiða/ n. f. welcome, reception.

acometer /akome'ter/ v. attack.

acomodador /akomoða'ðor/ n. m. usher.

acomodar /akomo'ðar/ v. accommodate, fix up.

acompañamiento /akompaɲa'miento/ n. m. accompaniment; following.

acompañar /akompa'ɲar/ v. accompany.

acondicionar /akondiθio'nar; akondisio'nar/ v. condition.

aconsejable /akonse'haβle/ a. advisable.

aconsejar /akonse'har/ v. advise.

acontecer /akonte'θer; akonte'ser/ v. happen.

acontecimiento /akonteθi'miento; akontesi'miento/ n. m. event, happening.

acorazado /akora'θaðo; akora'saðo/ n. **1.** m. battleship. —a. **2.** armor-plated, ironclad.

acordarse /akor'ðarse/ v. remember, recollect.

acordeón /akorðe'on/ n. m. accordion.

acordonar /akorðo'nar/ v. cordon off.

acortar /akor'tar/ v. shorten.

acosar /ako'sar/ v. beset, harry.

acostar /ako'star/ v. lay down; put to bed.

acostarse /akos'tarse/ v. lie down; go to bed.

acostumbrado /akostum'braðo/ a. accustomed; customary.

acostumbrar /akostum'brar/ v. accustom.

acrecentar /akreθen'tar; akresen'tar/ v. increase.

acreditar /akreði'tar/ v. accredit.

acreedor /akree'ðor/ -ra n. creditor.

acróbata /a'kroβata/ n. m. & f. acrobat.

acrobático /akro'βatiko/ a. acrobatic.

actitud /akti'tuð/ n. f. attitude.

actividad /aktiβi'ðað/ n. f. activity.

activista /akti'βista/ a. & n. activist.

activo /ak'tiβo/ a. active.

acto /'akto/ n. m. act.

actor /ak'tor/ n. m. actor.

actriz /ak'triθ; ak'tris/ n. f. actress.

actual /ak'tual/ a. present; present day.

actualidades /aktuali'ðaðes/ n. f.pl. current events.

actualmente /aktual'mente/ adv. at present; nowadays.

actuar /ak'tuar/ v. act.

acuarela /akua'rela/ n. f. watercolor.

acuario /a'kuario/ n. m. aquarium.

acuático /a'kuatiko/ a. aquatic.

acuchillar /akutʃi'ʎar; akutʃi'yar/ v. slash, knife.

acudir /aku'ðir/ v. rally; hasten; be present.

acuerdo /a'kuerðo/ n. m. accord, agreement; settlement. **de a.,** in agreement, agreed.

acumulación /akumula'θion; akumula'sion/ n. f. accumulation.

acumular /akumu'lar/ v. accumulate.

acuñar /aku'ɲar/ v. coin, mint.

acupuntura /akupun'tura/ n. f. acupuncture.

acusación /akusa'θion; akusa'sion/ n. f. accusation, charge.

acusado /aku'saðo/ -da a. & n. accused; defendant.

acusador /akusa'ðor/ -ra n. accuser.

acusar /aku'sar/ v. accuse; acknowledge.

acústica /a'kustika/ n. f. acoustics.

adaptación /aðapta'θion; aðapta'sion/ *n. f.* adaptation.
adaptador /aðapta'ðor/ *n. m.* adapter.
adaptar /aðap'tar/ *v.* adapt.
adecuado /aðe'kuaðo/ *a.* adequate.
adelantado /aðelan'taðo/ *a.* advanced; fast (clock).
adelantamiento /aðelanta'miento/ *n. m.* advancement, promotion.
adelantar /aðelan'tar/ *v.* advance.
adelante /aðe'lante/ *adv.* ahead, forward, onward, on.
adelanto /aðe'lanto/ *n. m.* advancement, progress, improvement.
adelgazar /aðelga'θar; aðelga'sar/ *v.* make thin.
ademán /aðe'man/ *n. m.* attitude; gesture.
además /aðe'mas/ *adv.* in addition, besides, also.
adentro /a'ðentro/ *adv.* in, inside.
adepto /a'ðepto/ *a.* adept.
aderezar /aðere'θar; aðere'sar/ *v.* prepare; trim.
adherirse /aðe'rirse/ *v.* adhere, stick.
adhesivo /aðe'siβo/ *a.* adhesive.
adicción /aðik'θion; aðik'sion/ *n. f.* adiction.
adición /aði'θion; aði'sion/ *n. f.* addition.
adicional /aðiθio'nal; aðisio'nal/ *a.* additional, extra.
adicto /a'ðikto/ **-ta** *a.* & *n.* addicted; addict.
adinerado /aðine'raðo/ **-a** *a.* wealthy.
adiós /aðios/ *n. m.* & *interj.* goodbye, farewell.
adivinar /aðiβi'nar/ *v.* guess.
adjetivo /aðhe'tiβo/ *n. m.* adjective.
adjunto /að'hunto/ *a.* enclosed.
administración /aðministra'θion; aðministra'sion/ *n. f.* administration.
administrador /aðministra'ðor/ **-ra** *n.* administrator.
administrar /aðminis'trar/ *v.* administer; manage.
administrativo /aðministra'tiβo/ *a.* administrative.
admirable /aðmi'raβle/ *a.* admirable.
admiración. /aðmira'θion; að-mira'sion/ *n. f.* admiration; wonder.
admirar /aðmi'rar/ *v.* admire.
admisión /aðmi'sion/ *n. f.* admission.
admitir /aðmi'tir/ *v.* admit, acknowledge.
ADN, *abbr.* (**ácido deoxirribonucleico**) DNA (deoxyribonucleic acid).
adobar /ado'βar/ *v.* marinate.
adolescencia /aðoles'θenθia; aðoles'sensia/ *n. f.* adolescence, youth.
adolescente /aðoles'θente; aðoles'sente/ *a.* & *n.* adolescent.
adónde /a'ðonde/ *adv.* where.
adondequiera /a,ðonde'kiera/ *conj.* wherever.
adopción /aðop'θion; aðop'sion/ *n. f.* adoption.
adoptar /aðop'tar/ *v.* adopt.
adoración /aðora'θion; aðora'sion/ *n. f.* worship, love, adoration. —**adorar,** *v.*
adormecer /aðorme'θer; aðorme'ser/ *v.* drowse.
adornar /aðor'nar/ *v.* adorn; decorate.
adorno /a'ðorno/ *n. m.* adornment, trimming.
adquirir /aðki'rir/ *v.* acquire, obtain.
adquisición /aðkisi'θion; aðkisi'sion/ *n. f.* acquisition, attainment.
aduana /a'ðuana/ *n. f.* custom house, customs.
adujada /aðu'haða/ *n. f. Naut.* coil of rope.
adulación /aðula'θion; aðula'sion/ *n. f.* flattery.
adular /aðu'lar/ *v.* flatter.
adulterar /aðulte'rar/ *v.* adulterate.
adulterio /aðul'terio/ *n. m.* adultery.
adulto /a'ðulto/ **-ta** *a.* & *n.* adult.
adusto /a'ðusto/ *a.* gloomy; austere.
adverbio /að'βerβio/ *n. m.* adverb.
adversario /aðβer'sario/ *n. m.* adversary.
adversidad /aðβersi'ðað/ *n. f.* adversity.
adverso /að'βerso/ *a.* adverse.
advertencia /aðβer'tenθia; aðβer'tensia/ *n. f.* warning.

advertir /aðβer'tir/ *v.* warn; notice.

adyacente /aðya'θente; aðya'sente/ *a.* adjacent.

aéreo /'aereo/ *a.* aerial; air.

aerodeslizador /aeroðesliθa'ðor; aeroðeslisa'ðor/ *n. m.* hovercraft.

aeromoza /aero'moθa; aero'mosa/ *n. f.* stewardess, flight attendant.

aeroplano /aero'plano/ *n. m.* light plane.

aeropuerto /aero'puerto/ *n. m.* airport.

aerosol /aero'sol/ *n. m.* aerosol, spray.

afable /a'faβle/ *a.* affable, pleasant.

afanarse /afa'narse/ *v.* toil.

afear /afe'ar/ *v.* deface, mar, deform.

afectación /afekta'θion; afekta'sion/ *n. f.* affectation.

afectar /afek'tar/ *v.* affect.

afecto /a'fekto/ *n. m.* affection, attachment.

afeitada /afei'taða/ *n. f.* shave. —**afeitarse**, *v.*

afeminado /afemi'naðo/ *a.* effeminate.

afición /afi'θion; afi'sion/ *n. f.* fondness, liking; hobby.

aficionado /afiθio'naðo; afisio'naðo/ *a.* fond.

aficionado -da *n.* fan, devotee; amateur.

aficionarse a /afiθio'narse a; afisio'narse a/ *v.* become fond of.

afilado /afi'laðo/ *a.* sharp.

afilar /afi'lar/ *v.* sharpen.

afiliación /afilia'θion; afilia'sion/ *n. f.* affiliation.

afiliado /afi'liaðo/ **-da** *n.* affiliate. —**afiliar**, *v.*

afinar /afi'nar/ *v.* polish; tune up.

afinidad /afini'ðað/ *n. f.* relationship, affinity.

afirmación /afirma'θion; afirma'sion/ *n. f.* affirmation, statement.

afirmar /afir'mar/ *v.* affirm, assert.

afirmativa /afirma'tiβa/ *n. f.* affirmative. —**afirmativo**, *a.*

aflicción /aflik'θion; aflik'sion/ *n. f.* affliction; sorrow, grief.

afligido /afli'hiðo/ *a.* sorrowful, grieved.

afligir /afli'hir/ *v.* grieve, distress.

aflojar /aflo'har/ *v.* loosen.

afluencia /a'fluenθia; a'fluensia/ *n. f.* influx.

afortunado /afortu'naðo/ *a.* fortunate, successful, lucky.

afrenta /a'frenta/ *n. f.* insult, outrage, affront. —**afrentar**, *v.*

afrentoso /afren'toso/ *a.* shameful.

africano /afri'kano/ **-na** *a. & n.* African.

afuera /a'fuera/ *adv.* out, outside.

afueras /a'fueras/ *n. f.pl.* suburbs.

agacharse /aga'tʃarse/ *v.* squat, crouch; cower.

agarrar /aga'rrar/ *v.* seize, grasp, clutch.

agarro /a'garro/ *n. m.* clutch, grasp.

agencia /a'henθia; a'hensia/ *n. f.* agency.

agencia de colocaciones /a'henθia de koloka'θiones; a'hensia de koloka'siones/ employment agency.

agencia de viajes /a'henθia de 'biahes; a'hensia de 'biahes/ travel agency.

agente /a'hente/ *n. m. & f.* agent, representative.

agente de aduana /a'hente de a'ðuana/ *mf.* customs officer.

agente inmobiliario /a'hente imoβi'liario/ **-ria** *n.* real-estate agent.

ágil /'ahil/ *a.* agile, spry.

agitación /ahita'θion; ahita'sion/ *n. f.* agitation, ferment.

agitado /ahi'taðo/ *a.* agitated; excited.

agitador /ahita'ðor/ *n. m.* agitator.

agitar /ahi'tar/ *v.* shake, agitate, excite.

agobiar /ago'βiar/ *v.* oppress, burden.

agosto /a'gosto/ *n. m.* August.

agotamiento /a,gota'miento/ *n. m.* exhaustion.

agotar /ago'tar/ *v.* exhaust, use up, sap.

agradable /agra'ðaβle/ *a.* agreeable, pleasant.

agradar /agra'ðar/ *v.* please.

agradecer /agraðe'θer; agraðe'ser/ *v.* thank; appreciate, be grateful for.

agradecido /agraðe'θiðo; agraðe'siðo/ *a.* grateful, thankful.

agradecimiento /agraðeθi'miento; agraðesi'miento/ *n. m.* gratitude, thanks.

agravar /agra'ßar/ v. aggravate, make worse.

agravio /a'graßio/ n. m. wrong. —**agraviar,** v.

agregado /agre'gaðo/ a. & n. aggregate; Pol. attaché.

agregar /agre'gar/ v. add; gather.

agresión /agre'sion/ n. f. aggression; Leg. battery.

agresivo /agre'sißo/ a. aggressive.

agresor /agre'sor/ -ra n. aggressor.

agrícola /a'grikola/ a. agricultural.

agricultor /agrikul'tor/ n. m. farmer.

agricultura /agrikul'tura/ n. f. agriculture, farming.

agrio /'agrio/ a. sour.

agrupar /agru'par/ v. group.

agua /'agua/ n. f. water. —**aguar,** v.

aguacate /agua'kate/ n. m. avocado, alligator pear.

aguafuerte /ˌagua'fuerte/ n. f. etching.

agua mineral /'agua mine'ral/ mineral water.

aguantar /aguan'tar/ v. endure, stand, put up with.

aguardar /aguar'ðar/ v. await; expect.

aguardiente /aguar'ðiente/ n. m. brandy.

aguas abajo /'aguas a'ßaho/ adv. downriver, downstream.

aguas arriba /'aguas a'rrißa/ adv. upriver, upstream.

agudo /a'guðo/ a. sharp, keen, shrill, acute.

agüero /a'guero/ n. m. omen.

águila /'agila/ n. f. eagle.

aguja /a'guha/ n. f. needle.

agujero /agu'hero/ n. m. hole.

aguzar /agu'θar; agu'sar/ v. sharpen.

ahí /a'i/ adv. there.

ahogar /ao'gar/ v. drown; choke; suffocate.

ahondar /aon'dar/ v. deepen.

ahora /a'ora/ adv. now.

ahorcar /aor'kar/ v. hang (execute).

ahorrar /ao'rrar/ v. save, save up; spare.

ahorros /a'orros/ n. m.pl. savings.

ahumar /au'mar/ v. smoke.

airado /ai'raðo/ a. angry, indignant.

aire /'aire/ n. m. air. —**airear,** v.

aire acondicionado /'aire akondi-θio'naðo; 'aire akondisio'naðo/ air conditioning.

aislamiento /aisla'miento/ n. m. isolation.

aislar /ais'lar/ v. isolate.

ajedrez /ahe'ðreθ; ahe'ðres/ n. m. chess.

ajeno /a'heno/ a. alien; someone else's.

ajetreo /ahe'treo/ n. m. hustle and bustle.

ají /'ahi/ n. m. chili.

ajo /'aho/ n. m. garlic.

ajustado /ahus'taðo/ a. adjusted; trim; exact.

ajustar /ahus'tar/ v. adjust.

ajuste /a'huste/ n. m. adjustment, settlement.

al /al/ contr. of **a + el**.

ala /'ala/ n. f. wing; brim (of hat).

alabanza /ala'ßanθa; ala'ßansa/ n. f. praise. —**alabar,** v.

alabear /alaße'ar/ v. warp.

ala delta /'ala 'delta/ hang glider.

alambique /alam'bike/ n. m. still.

alambre /a'lambre/ n. m. wire. **a. de púas,** barbed wire.

alarde /a'larðe/ n. m. boasting, ostentation.

alargar /alar'gar/ v. lengthen; stretch out.

alarma /a'larma/ n. f. alarm. —**alarmar,** v.

alba /'alßa/ n. f. daybreak, dawn.

albanega /alßa'nega/ n. f. hair net.

albañil /alßa'ɲil/ n. m. bricklayer; mason.

albaricoque /alßari'koke/ n. m. apricot.

alberca /al'ßerka/ n. f. swimming pool.

albergue /al'ßerge/ n. m. shelter. —**albergar,** v.

alborotar /alßoro'tar/ v. disturb, make noise, brawl, riot.

alboroto /alßo'roto/ n. m. brawl, disturbance, din, tumult.

álbum /'alßum/ n. m. album.

álbum de recortes /'alßum de rre'kortes/ scrapbook.

alcachofa /alka'tʃofa/ n. f. artichoke.

alcalde /al'kalde/ n. m. mayor.

alcance /al'kanθe; al'kanse/ n. m. reach; range, scope.

alcanfor /alkan'for/ n. m. camphor.

alcanzar /alkan'θar; alkan'sar/ v. reach, overtake, catch.

alcayata /alka'yata/ n. f. spike.

alce /'alθe; 'alse/ n. m. elk.

alcoba /al'koβa/ n. f. bedroom; alcove.

alcoba de huéspedes /al'koβa de 'uespeðes/ guest room.

alcoba de respeto /al'koβa de rres'peto/ guest room.

alcohol /al'kool/ n. m. alcohol.

alcohólico /alko'oliko/ **-ca** a. & n. alcoholic.

aldaba /al'daβa/ n. f. latch.

aldea /al'dea/ n. f. village.

alegación /alega'θion; alega'sion/ n. f. allegation.

alegar /ale'gar/ v. allege.

alegrar /ale'grar/ v. make happy, brighten.

alegrarse /ale'grarse/ v. be glad.

alegre /a'legre/ a. glad, cheerful, merry.

alegría /ale'gria/ n. f. gaiety, cheer.

alejarse /ale'harse/ v. move away, off.

alemán /ale'man/ **-ana** a. & n. German.

Alemania /ale'mania/ n. f. Germany.

alentar /alen'tar/ v. cheer up, encourage.

alergia /aler'hia/ n. f. allergy.

alerta /a'lerta/ adv. on the alert.

aleve /a'leβe/ **alevoso** a. treacherous.

alfabeto /alfa'βeto/ n. m. alphabet.

alfalfa /al'falfa/ n. f. alfalfa.

alfarería /alfare'ria/ n. f. pottery.

alférez /al'fereθ; al'feres/ n. m. (naval) ensign.

alfil /al'fil/ n. m. (chess) bishop.

alfiler /alfi'ler/ n. m. pin.

alfombra /al'fombra/ n. f. carpet, rug.

alforja /al'forha/ n. f. knapsack; saddlebag.

alga /'alga/ n. f. seaweed.

alga marina /'alga ma'rina/ seaweed.

algarabía /algara'βia/ n. f. jargon; din.

álgebra /'alheβra/ n. f. algebra.

algo /'algo/ pron. & adv. something, somewhat; anything.

algodón /algo'ðon/ n. m. cotton.

algodón hidrófilo /algo'ðon i'ðrofilo/ absorbent cotton.

alguien /'algien/ pron. somebody, someone; anybody, anyone.

algún /al'gun/ **-no -na** a. & pron. some; any.

alhaja /al'aha/ n. f. jewel.

aliado /a'liaðo/ **-da** a. & n. allied; ally. —**aliar,** v.

alianza /a'lianθa; a'liansa/ n. f. alliance.

alicates /ali'kates/ n. m.pl. pliers.

aliento /a'liento/ n. m. breath. **dar a.,** encourage.

aligerar /alihe'rar/ v. lighten.

alimentar /alimen'tar/ v. feed, nourish.

alimento /ali'mento/ n. m. nourishment, food.

alinear /aline'ar/ v. line up; Pol. align.

aliñar /ali'ɲar/ v. dress (a salad).

aliño /a'liɲo/ n. m. salad dressing.

alisar /ali'sar/ v. smooth.

alistamiento /alista'miento/ n. m. enlistment.

alistar /alis'tar/ v. make ready, prime.

alistarse /alis'tarse/ v. get ready; Mil. enlist.

aliviar /ali'βiar/ v. alleviate, relieve, ease.

alivio /a'liβio/ n. m. relief.

allá /a'ʎa; a'ya/ adv. there. **más a.,** beyond, farther on.

allanar /aʎa'nar; aya'nar/ v. flatten, smooth, plane.

allí /a'ʎi; a'yi/ adv. there. **por a.,** that way.

alma /'alma/ n. f. soul.

almacén /alma'θen; alma'sen/ n. m. department store; storehouse, warehouse.

almacenaje /almaθe'nahe; almase'nahe/ n. m. storage.

almacenar /almaθe'nar; almase'nar/ v. store.

almanaque /alma'nake/ n. m. almanac.

almeja /al'meha/ n. f. clam.

almendra /al'mendra/ n. f. almond.

almíbar /al'miβar/ n. m. syrup.

almidón /almi'ðon/ n. m. starch. —**almidonar,** v.

almirante /almi'rante/ n. m. admiral.

almohada /almo'aða/ n. f. pillow.

almuerzo /al'muerθo; al'muerso/ n. m. lunch. —**almorzar,** v.

alojamiento /aloha'miento/ n. m. lodging, accommodations.

alojar /alo'har/ v. lodge, house.

alojarse /alo'harse/ v. stay, room.

alquiler /alki'ler/ *n. m.* rent.
—alquilar, *v.*
alrededor /alreðe'ðor/ *adv.* around.
alrededores /alreðe'ðores/ *n. m.pl.* environs.
altanero /alta'nero/ *a.* haughty.
altar /al'tar/ *n. m.* altar.
altavoz /ˌalta'βoθ; ˌalta'βos/ *n. m.* loudspeaker.
alteración /altera'θion; altera-'sion/ *n. f.* alteration.
alterar /alte'rar/ *v.* alter.
alternativa /alterna'tiβa/ *n. f.* alternative. **—alternativo,** *a.*
alterno /al'terno/ *a.* alternate. **—alternar,** *v.*
alteza /al'teθa; al'tesa/ *n. f.* highness.
altivo /al'tiβo/ *a.* proud, haughty; lofty.
alto /'alto/ *a.* **1.** high, tall; loud. **—n. 2.** *m.* height, story (house).
altura /al'tura/ *n. f.* height, altitude.
alud /a'luð/ *n. m.* avalanche.
aludir /alu'ðir/ *v.* allude.
alumbrado /alum'braðo/ *n. m.* lighting.
alumbrar /alum'brar/ *v.* light.
aluminio /alu'minio/ *n. m.* aluminum.
alumno /a'lumno/ **-na** *n.* student, pupil.
alusión /alu'sion/ *n. f.* allusion.
alza /'alθa; 'alsa/ *n. f.* rise; boost.
alzar /al'θar; al'sar/ *v.* raise, lift.
ama /'ama/ *n. f.* housewife, mistress (of house). **a. de llaves,** housekeeper.
amable /a'maβle/ *a.* kind; pleasant, sweet.
amalgamar /amalga'mar/ *v.* amalgamate.
amamantar /amaman'tar/ *v.* suckle, nurse.
amanecer /amane'θer; amane'ser/ *n.* **1.** *m.* dawn, daybreak. **—v. 2.** dawn; awaken.
amante /a'mante/ *n. m. & f.* lover.
amapola /ama'pola/ *n. f.* poppy.
amar /a'mar/ *v.* love.
amargo /a'margo/ *a.* bitter.
amargón /amar'gon/ *n. m.* dandelion.
amargura /amar'gura/ *n. f.* bitterness.
amarillo /ama'riʎo; ama'riyo/ *a.* yellow.

amarradero /amarra'ðero/ *n. m.* mooring.
amarrar /ama'rrar/ *v.* hitch, moor, tie up.
amartillar /amarti'ʎar; amarti'yar/ *v.* hammer; cock (a gun).
amasar /ama'sar/ *v.* knead, mold.
ámbar /'ambar/ *n. m.* amber.
ambarino /amba'rino/ *a.* amber.
ambición /ambi'θion; ambi'sion/ *n. f.* ambition.
ambicionar /ambiθio'nar; ambisio'nar/ *v.* aspire to.
ambicioso /ambi'θioso; ambi-'sioso/ *a.* ambitious.
ambientalista /ambienta'lista/ *n. m. & f.* environmentalist.
ambiente /am'biente/ *n. m.* environment, atmosphere.
ambigüedad /ambigue'ðað/ *n. f.* ambiguity.
ambiguo /am'biguo/ *a.* ambiguous.
ambos /'ambos/ *a. & pron.* both.
ambulancia /ambu'lanθia; ambu'lansia/ *n. f.* ambulance.
amenaza /ame'naθa; ame'nasa/ *n. f.* threat, menace.
amenazar /amena'θar; amena'sar/ *v.* threaten, menace.
ameno /a'meno/ *a.* pleasant.
americana /ameri'kana/ *n. f.* suit coat.
americano /ameri'kano/ **-na** *a. & n.* American.
ametralladora /ametraʎa'ðora; ametraya'ðora/ *n. f.* machine gun.
amigable /ami'gaβle/ *a.* amicable, friendly.
amígdala /a'migðala/ *n. f.* tonsil.
amigo /a'migo/ **-ga** *n.* friend.
aminorar /amino'rar/ *v.* lessen, reduce.
amistad /amis'tað/ *n. f.* friendship.
amistoso /amis'toso/ *a.* friendly.
amniocéntesis /amnioθen'tesis; amniosen'tesis/ *n. m.* amniocentesis.
amo /'amo/ *n. m.* master.
amonestaciones /amonesta-'θiones; amonesta'siones/ *n. f.pl.* banns.
amonestar /amones'tar/ *v.* admonish.
amoníaco /amo'niako/ *n. m.* ammonia.
amontonar /amonto'nar/ *v.* amass, pile up.

amor /a'mor/ *n. m.* love. **a. propio,** self-esteem.

amorío /amo'rio/ *n. m.* romance, love affair.

amoroso /amo'roso/ *a.* amorous; loving.

amortecer /amorte'θer; amorte-'ser/ *v.* deaden.

amparar /ampa'rar/ *v.* aid, befriend; protect, shield.

amparo /am'paro/ *n. m.* protection.

ampliar /amp'liar/ *v.* enlarge; elaborate.

amplificar /amplifi'kar/ *v.* amplify.

amplio /'amplio/ *a.* ample, roomy.

ampolla /am'poʎa; am'poya/ *n. f.* bubble; bulb; blister.

amputar /ampu'tar/ *v.* amputate.

amueblar /amue'βlar/ *v.* furnish.

analfabeto /analfa'βeto/ **-ta** *a.* & *n.* illiterate.

analgésico /anal'hesiko/ *n. m.* pain killer.

análisis /a'nalisis/ *n. m.* analysis.

analizar /anali'θar; anali'sar/ *v.* analyze.

analogía /analo'hia/ *n. f.* analogy.

análogo /a'nalogo/ *a.* similar, analogous.

anarquía /anar'kia/ *n. f.* anarchy.

anatomía /anato'mia/ *n. f.* anatomy.

ancho /'antʃo/ *a.* wide, broad.

anchoa /an'tʃoa/ *n. f.* anchovy.

anchura /an'tʃura/ *n. f.* width, breadth.

anciano /an'θiano; an'siano/ **-na** *a.* & *n.* old, aged (person).

ancla /'ankla/ *n. f.* anchor. **—anclar,** *v.*

anclaje /an'klahe/ *n. m.* anchorage.

andamio /an'damio/ *n. m.* scaffold.

andar /an'dar/ *v.* walk; move, go.

andén /an'den/ *n. m.* (railroad) platform.

andrajoso /andra'hoso/ *a.* ragged, uneven.

anécdota /a'nekδota/ *n. f.* anecdote.

anegar /ane'gar/ *v.* flood, drown.

anestesia /anes'tesia/ *n. f.* anesthetic.

anexar /anek'sar/ *v.* annex.

anexión /anek'sion/ *n. f.* annexation.

anfitrión /anfitri'on/ **-na** *n.* host.

ángel /'anhel/ *n. m.* angel.

angosto /aŋ'gosto/ *a.* narrow.

anguila /aŋ'gila/ *n. f.* eel.

angular /aŋgu'lar/ *a.* angular.

ángulo /'aŋgulo/ *n. m.* angle.

angustia /aŋ'gustia/ *n. f.* anguish, agony.

angustiar /aŋgus'tiar/ *v.* distress.

anhelar /ane'lar/ *v.* long for.

anidar /ani'δar/ *v.* nest, nestle.

anillo /a'niʎo; a'niyo/ *n. m.* ring; circle.

animación /anima'θion; anima-'sion/ *n. f.* animation; bustle.

animado /ani'maδo/ *a.* animated, lively; animate.

animal /ani'mal/ *a.* & *n.* animal.

ánimo /'animo/ *n. m.* state of mind, spirits; courage.

aniquilar /aniki'lar/ *v.* annihilate, destroy.

aniversario /aniβer'sario/ *n. m.* anniversary.

anoche /a'notʃe/ *adv.* last night.

anochecer /anotʃe'θer; anotʃe'ser/ *n.* **1.** *m.* twilight, nightfall. —*v.* **2.** get dark.

anónimo /a'nonimo/ *a.* anonymous.

anorexia /ano'reksia/ *n. f.* anorexia.

anormal /anor'mal/ *a.* abnormal.

anotación /anota'θion; anota'sion/ *n. f.* annotation.

anotar /ano'tar/ *v.* annotate.

ansia /'ansia/ **ansiedad** *n. f.* anxiety.

ansioso /an'sioso/ *a.* anxious.

antagonismo /antago'nismo/ *n. m.* antagonism.

antagonista /antago'nista/ *n. m.* & *f.* antagonist, opponent.

anteayer /antea'yer/ *adv.* day before yesterday.

antebrazo /ante'βraθo; ante-'βraso/ *n. m.* forearm.

antecedente /anteθe'δente; antese'δente/ *a.* & *m.* antecedent.

anteceder /anteθe'δer; antese'δer/ *v.* precede.

antecesor /anteθe'sor; antese'sor/ *n. m.* ancestor.

antemano /ante'mano/ *de a.,* in advance.

antena /an'tena/ *n. f.* antenna.

antena parabólica /an'tena para'βolika/ satellite dish.

anteojos /ante'ohos/ *n. m.pl.* eyeglasses.

antepasado /antepa'saðo/ *n. m.*
ancestor.

antepenúltimo /antepe'nultimo/
a. antepenultimate.

anterior /ante'rior/ *a.* previous,
former.

antes /'antes/ *adv.* before; formerly.

antibala /anti'bala/ *a.* bulletproof.

anticipación /antiθipa'θion; antisi-
pa'sion/ *n. f.* anticipation.

anticipar /antiθi'par; antisi'par/ *v.*
anticipate; advance.

anticonceptivo /antikonθep'tiβo;
antikonsep'tiβo/ *a. & n.* contraceptive.

anticongelante /antikoŋge'lante/
n. m. antifreeze.

anticuado /anti'kuaðo/ *a.* antiquated, obsolete.

antídoto /an'tiðoto/ *n. m.* antidote.

antigüedad /antigue'ðað/ *n. f.*
antiquity; antique.

antiguo /an'tiguo/ *a.* former; old;
antique.

antihistamínico /antiista'miniko/
n. m. antihistamine.

antílope /an'tilope/ *n. m.* antelope.

antinuclear /antinukle'ar/ *a.* antinuclear.

antipatía /antipa'tia/ *n. f.* antipathy.

antipático /anti'patiko/ *a.* disagreeable, nasty.

antiséptico /anti'septiko/ *a. & m.*
antiseptic.

antojarse /anto'harse/ *v.* **se me
antoja...** etc., I desire..., take a
fancy to..., etc.

antojo /an'toho/ *n. m.* whim,
fancy.

antorcha /an'tortʃa/ *n. f.* torch.

antracita /antra'θita; antra'sita/ *n.
f.* anthracite.

anual /a'nual/ *a.* annual, yearly.

anudar /anu'ðar/ *v.* knot; tie.

anular /anu'lar/ *v.* annul, void.

anunciar /anun'θiar; anun'siar/ *v.*
announce; proclaim, advertise.

anuncio /a'nunθio; a'nunsio/ *n.
m.* announcement; advertisement.

añadir /aɲa'ðir/ *v.* add.

añil /a'ɲil/ *n. m.* bluing; indigo.

año /'aɲo/ *n. m.* year.

apacible /apa'θiβle; apa'siβle/ *a.*
peaceful, peaceable.

apaciguamiento /a,paθigua-
'miento; a,pasigua'miento/ *n. m.*
appeasement.

apaciguar /apaθi'guar; apasi'guar/
v. appease; placate.

apagado /apa'gaðo/ *a.* dull.

apagar /apa'gar/ *v.* extinguish,
quench, put out.

apagón /apa'gn/ *n. m.* blackout.

aparador /apara'ðor/ *n. m.* buffet,
cupboard.

aparato /apa'rato/ *n. m.* apparatus; machine; appliance, set.

aparcamiento /aparka'miento/ *n.
m.* parking lot; parking space.

aparecer /apare'θer; apare'ser/ *v.*
appear, show up.

aparejo /apa'reho/ *n. m.* rig.
—**aparejar,** *v.*

aparentar /aparen'tar/ *v.* pretend;
profess.

aparente /apa'rente/ *a.* apparent.

apariencia /apa'rienθia; apa'rien-
sia/ **aparición** *n. f.* appearance.

apartado /apar'taðo/ *a.* **1.** aloof;
separate. —*n.* **2.** *m.* post-office
box.

apartamento /aparta'mento/ *n.
m.* apartment. **a. en propiedad,**
condominium.

apartar /apar'tar/ *v.* separate; remove.

aparte /a'parte/ *adv.* apart; aside.

apartheid /apar'teið/ *n. m.* apartheid.

apasionado /apasio'naðo/ *a.* passionate.

apatía /apa'tia/ *n. f.* apathy.

apearse /ape'arse/ *v.* get off,
alight.

apedrear /apeðre'ar/ *v.* stone.

apelación /apela'θion; apela'sion/
n. f. appeal. —**apelar,** *v.*

apellido /ape'ʎiðo; ape'yiðo/ *n.
m.* family name.

apellido materno /ape'ʎiðo
ma'terno; ape'yiðo ma'terno/
mother's family name.

apellido paterno /ape'ʎiðo
pa'terno; ape'yiðo pa'terno/ father's family name.

apenas /a'penas/ *adv.* scarcely,
hardly.

apéndice /a'pendiθe; a'pendise/ *n.
m.* appendix.

apercibir /aperθi'βir; apersi'βir/ *v.*
prepare, warn.

aperitivo /aperi'tiβo/ *n. m.* appetizer.

aperos /a'peros/ *n. m.pl.* imple-
ments.

apestar /apes'tar/ v. infect; stink.
apetecer /apete'θer; apete'ser/ v. desire, have appetite for.
apetito /ape'tito/ n. m. appetite.
ápice /'apiθe; 'apise/ n. m. apex.
apilar /api'lar/ v. stack.
apio /'apio/ n. m. celery.
aplacar /apla'kar/ v. appease; placate.
aplastar /aplas'tar/ v. crush, flatten.
aplaudir /aplau'ðir/ v. applaud, cheer.
aplauso /a'plauso/ n. m. applause.
aplazar /apla'θar; apla'sar/ v. postpone, put off.
aplicable /apli'kaβle/ a. applicable.
aplicado /apli'kaðo/ a. industrious, diligent.
aplicar /apli'kar/ v. apply.
aplomo /a'plomo/ n. m. aplomb, poise.
apoderado /apoðe'raðo/ **-da** n. attorney.
apoderarse de /apoðe'rarse de/ v. get hold of, seize.
apodo /a'poðo/ n. m. nickname. —**apodar,** v.
apologético /apolo'hetiko/ a. apologetic.
apoplejía /apople'hia/ n. f. apoplexy.
aposento /apo'sento/ n. m. room, flat.
apostar /apos'tar/ v. bet, wager.
apóstol /a'postol/ n. m. apostle.
apoyar /apo'yar/ v. support, prop; lean.
apoyo /a'poyo/ n. m. support; prop; aid; approval.
apreciable /apreθia'βle; apresia'βle/ a. appreciable.
apreciar /apre'θiar; apre'siar/ v. appreciate, prize.
aprecio /a'preθio; a'presio/ n. m. appreciation, regard.
apremio /a'premio/ n. m. pressure, compulsion.
aprender /apren'der/ v. learn.
aprendiz /apren'diθ; apren'dis/ n. m. apprentice.
aprendizaje /aprendi'θahe; aprendi'sahe/ n. m. apprenticeship.
aprensión /apren'sion/ n. f. apprehension.
aprensivo /apren'siβo/ a. apprehensive.

apresurado /apresu'raðo/ a. hasty, fast.
apresurar /apresu'rar/ v. hurry, speed up.
apretado /apre'taðo/ a. tight.
apretar /apre'tar/ v. squeeze, press; tighten.
apretón /apre'ton/ n. m. squeeze.
aprieto /a'prieto/ n. m. plight, predicament.
aprobación /aproβa'θion; aproβa'sion/ n. f. approbation, approval.
aprobar /apro'βar/ v. approve.
apropiación /apropia'θion; apropia'sion/ n. f. appropriation.
apropiado /apro'piaðo/ a. appropriate. —**apropiar,** v.
aprovechar /aproβe'tʃar/ v. profit by.
aprovecharse /aproβe'tʃarse/ v. take advantage.
aproximado /aproksi'maðo/ a. approximate.
aproximarse a /aproksi'marse a/ v. approach.
aptitud /apti'tuð/ n. f. aptitude.
apto /'apto/ a. apt.
apuesta /a'puesta/ n. f. bet, wager, stake.
apuntar /apun'tar/ v. point, aim; prompt; write down.
apunte /a'punte/ n. m. annotation, note; promptings, cue.
apuñalar /apuɲa'lar/ v. stab.
apurar /apu'rar/ v. hurry; worry.
apuro /a'puro/ n. m. predicament, scrape, trouble.
aquel /a'kel/ **aquella** dem. a. that.
aquél /a'kel/ **aquélla** dem. pron. that (one); the former.
aquello /a'keʎo; a'keyo/ dem. pron. that.
aquí /a'ki/ adv. here. **por a.,** this way.
aquietar /akie'tar/ v. allay; lull, pacify.
ara /'ara/ n. f. altar.
árabe /'araβe/ a. & n. Arab, Arabic.
arado /a'raðo/ n. m. plow. —**arar,** v.
arándano /a'randano/ n. m. cranberry.
araña /a'raɲa/ n. f. spider. **a. de luces,** chandelier.
arbitración /arβitra'θion; arβitra'sion/ n. f. arbitration.

arbitrador /arβitra'ðor/ **-ra** *n.* arbitrator.

arbitraje /arβi'trahe/ *n. m.* arbitration.

arbitrar /arβi'trar/ *v.* arbitrate.

arbitrario /arβi'trario/ *a.* arbitrary.

árbitro /'arβitro/ *n. m.* arbiter, umpire, referee.

árbol /'arβol/ *n. m.* tree; mast.

árbol genealógico /'arβol henea'lohiko/ family tree.

arbusto /ar'βusto/ *n. m.* bush, shrub.

arca /'arka/ *n. f.* chest; ark.

arcada /ar'kaða/ *n. f.* arcade.

arcaico /ar'kaiko/ *a.* archaic.

arce /'arθe; 'arse/ *n. m.* maple.

archipiélago /artʃi'pielago/ *n. m.* archipelago.

archivador /artʃiβa'ðor/ *n. m.* file cabinet.

archivo /ar'tʃiβo/ *n. m.* archive; file. —**archivar,** *v.*

arcilla /ar'θiʎa; ar'siya/ *n. f.* clay.

arco /'arko/ *n. m.* arc; arch; (archer's) bow. **a. iris,** rainbow.

arder /ar'ðer/ *v.* burn.

ardid /ar'ðið/ *n. m.* stratagem, cunning.

ardiente /ar'ðiente/ *a.* ardent, burning, fiery.

ardilla /ar'ðiʎa; ar'ðiya/ *n. f.* squirrel.

ardor /ar'ðor/ *n. m.* ardor, fervor.

ardor de estómago /ar'ðor de es'tomago/ heartburn.

arduo /'arðuo/ *a.* arduous.

área /'area/ *n. f.* area.

arena /a'rena/ *n. f.* sand; arena.

arenoso /are'noso/ *a.* sandy.

arenque /a'renke/ *n. m.* herring.

arete /a'rete/ *n.* earring.

argentino /arhen'tino/ **-na** *a. & n.* Argentine.

argüir /ar'guir/ *v.* dispute, argue.

árido /'ariðo/ *a.* arid.

aristocracia /aristo'kraθia; aristo'krasia/ *n. f.* aristocracy.

aristócrata /aris'tokrata/ *n. f.* aristocrat.

aristocrático /aristo'kratiko/ *a.* aristocratic.

aritmética /arit'metika/ *n. f.* arithmetic.

arma /'arma/ *n. f.* weapon, arm.

armadura /arma'ðura/ *n. f.* armor; reinforcement; framework.

armamento /arma'mento/ *n. m.* armament.

armar /ar'mar/ *v.* arm.

armario /ar'mario/ *n. m.* cabinet, bureau, wardrobe.

armazón /arma'θon; arma'son/ *n. m.* framework, frame.

armería /arme'ria/ *n. f.* armory.

armisticio /armis'tiθio; armis'tisio/ *n. m.* armistice.

armonía /armo'nia/ *n. f.* harmony.

armonioso /armo'nioso/ *a.* harmonious.

armonizar /armoni'θar; armoni'sar/ *v.* harmonize.

arnés /ar'nes/ *n. m.* harness.

aroma /a'roma/ *n. f.* aroma, fragrance.

aromático /aro'matiko/ *a.* aromatic.

arpa /'arpa/ *n. f.* harp.

arquear /arke'ar/ *v.* arch.

arquitecto /arki'tekto/ *n. m.* architect.

arquitectura /arkitek'tura/ *n. f.* architecture.

arquitectural /arkitektu'ral/ *a.* architectural.

arrabal /arra'βal/ *n. m.* suburb.

arraigar /arrai'gar/ *v.* take root, settle.

arrancar /arran'kar/ *v.* pull out, tear out; start up.

arranque /a'rranke/ *n. m.* dash, sudden start; fit of anger.

arrastrar /arras'trar/ *v.* drag.

arrebatar /arreβa'tar/ *v.* snatch, grab.

arrebato /arre'βato/ *n. m.* sudden attack, fit of anger.

arrecife /arre'θife; arre'sife/ *n. m.* reef.

arreglar /arre'glar/ *v.* arrange; repair, fix; adjust, settle.

arreglárselas /arre'glarselas/ *v.* manage, shift for oneself.

arreglo /a'rreglo/ *n. m.* arrangement, settlement.

arremangarse /arremaŋ'garse/ *v.* roll up one's sleeves; roll up one's pants.

arremeter /arreme'ter/ *v.* attack.

arrendar /arren'dar/ *v.* rent.

arrepentimiento /arrepenti'miento/ *n. m.* repentance.

arrepentirse /arrepen'tirse/ *v.* repent.

arrestar /arres'tar/ *v.* arrest.

arriba /a'rriβa/ *adv.* up; upstairs.

arriendo /a'rriendo/ *n. m.* lease.

arriero /a'rriero/ *n. m.* muleteer.

arriesgar /arries'gar/ *v.* risk.

arrimarse /arri'marse/ *v.* lean.

arrodillarse /arroði'ʎarse; arroði-'yarse/ *v.* kneel.

arrogancia /arro'ganθia; arro-'gansia/ *n. f.* arrogance.

arrogante /arro'gante/ *a.* arrogant.

arrojar /arro'har/ *v.* throw, hurl; shed.

arrollar /arro'ʎar; arro'yar/ *v.* roll, coil.

arroyo /a'rroyo/ *n. m.* brook; gully; gutter.

arroz /a'rroθ; a'rros/ *n. m.* rice.

arruga /a'rruga/ *n. f.* ridge; wrinkle.

arrugar /arru'gar/ *v.* wrinkle, crumple.

arruinar /arrui'nar/ *v.* ruin, destroy, wreck.

arsenal /arse'nal/ *n. m.* arsenal; armory.

arsénico /ar'seniko/ *n. m.* arsenic.

arte /'arte/ *n. m.* (*f.* in *pl.*) art, craft; wiliness.

arteria /ar'teria/ *n. f.* artery.

artesa /ar'tesa/ *n. f.* trough.

artesano /arte'sano/ **-na** *n.* artisan, craftsman.

ártico /'artiko/ *a.* arctic.

articulación /artikula'θion; artikula'sion/ *n. f.* articulation; joint.

articular /artiku'lar/ *v.* articulate.

artículo /ar'tikulo/ *n. m.* article.

artífice /ar'tifiθe; ar'tifise/ *n. m. & f.* artisan.

artificial /artifi'θial; artifi'sial/ *a.* artificial.

artificio /arti'fiθio; arti'fisio/ *n. m.* artifice, device.

artificioso /artifi'θioso; artifi-'sioso/ *a.* affected.

artillería /artiʎe'ria; artiye'ria/ *n. f.* artillery.

artista /ar'tista/ *n. m. & f.* artist.

artístico /ar'tistiko/ *a.* artistic.

artritis /ar'tritis/ *n. f.* arthritis.

arzobispo /arθo'βispo; arso'βispo/ *n. m.* archbishop.

as /as/ *n. m.* ace.

asado /a'saðo/ *a. & n.* roast.

asaltador /asalta'ðor/ **-ra** *n.* assailant.

asaltante /asal'tante/ *n. m. & f.* mugger.

asaltar /asal'tar/ *v.* assail, attack.

asalto /a'salto/ *n. m.* assault. —**asaltar,** *v.*

asamblea /asam'βlea/ *n. f.* assembly.

asar /a'sar/ *v.* roast; broil, cook (meat).

asaz /a'saθ; a'sas/ *adv.* enough; quite.

ascender /asθen'der; assen'der/ *v.* ascend, go up; amount.

ascenso /as'θenso; as'senso/ *n. m.* ascent.

ascensor /asθen'sor; assen'sor/ *n. m.* elevator.

ascensorista /asθenso'rista; assenso'rista/ *n. m. & f.* (elevator) operator.

asco /'asko/ *n. m.* nausea; disgusting thing. **qué a.,** how disgusting.

aseado /ase'aðo/ *a.* tidy. —**asear,** *v.*

asediar /ase'ðiar/ *v.* besiege.

asedio /a'seðio/ *n. m.* siege.

asegurar /asegu'rar/ *v.* assure; secure.

asegurarse /asegu'rarse/ *v.* make sure.

asemejarse a /aseme'harse a/ *v.* resemble.

asentar /asen'tar/ *v.* settle; seat.

asentimiento /asenti'miento/ *n. m.* assent. —**asentir,** *v.*

aseo /a'seo/ *n. m.* neatness, tidiness.

aseos /a'seos/ *n. m.pl.* restroom.

asequible /ase'kiβle/ *a.* attainable; affordable.

aserción /aser'θion; aser'sion/ *n. f.* assertion.

aserrar /ase'rrar/ *v.* saw.

asesinar /asesi'nar/ *v.* assassinate; murder, slay.

asesinato /asesi'nato/ *n. m.* assassination, murder.

asesino /ase'sino/ **-na** *n.* murderer, assassin.

aseveración /aseβera'θion; aseβera'sion/ *n. f.* assertion.

aseverar /aseβe'rar/ *v.* assert.

asfalto /as'falto/ *n. m.* asphalt.

así /a'si/ *adv.* so, thus, this way, that way. **a. como,** as well as. **a. que,** as soon as.

asiático /a'siatiko/ **-ca** *a. & n.* Asiatic.

asiduo /a'siðuo/ *a.* assiduous.

asiento /a'siento/ *n. m.* seat; chair; site.

asiento delantero /a'siento delan'tero/ front seat.

asiento trasero /a'siento tra'sero/ back seat.

asignar /asig'nar/ *v.* assign; allot.

asilo /a'silo/ n. m. asylum, sanctuary.

asimilar /asimi'lar/ v. assimilate.

asir /a'sir/ v. grasp.

asistencia /asis'tenθia; asistensia/ n. f. attendance, presence.

asistir /asis'tir/ v. be present, attend.

asno /'asno/ n. m. donkey.

asociación /asoθia'θion; asosia-'sion/ n. f. association.

asociado /aso'θiaðo; aso'siaðo/ n. m. associate, partner.

asociar /aso'θiar; aso'siar/ v. associate.

asolar /aso'lar/ v. desolate; burn, parch.

asoleado /asole'aðo/ a. sunny.

asomar /aso'mar/ v. appear, loom up, show up.

asombrar /asom'βrar/ v. astonish, amaze.

asombro /a'sombro/ n. m. amazement, astonishment.

aspa /'aspa/ n. f. reel. —**aspar**, v.

aspecto /as'pekto/ n. m. aspect.

aspereza /aspe'reθa; aspe'resa/ n. f. harshness.

áspero /'aspero/ a. rough, harsh.

aspiración /aspira'θion; aspira-'sion/ n. f. aspiration.

aspirador /aspira'ðor/ n. m. vacuum cleaner.

aspirar /aspi'rar/ v. aspire.

aspirina /aspi'rina/ n. f. aspirin.

asqueroso /aske'roso/ a. dirty, nasty, filthy.

asta /'asta/ n. f. shaft.

asterisco /aste'risko/ n. m. asterisk.

astilla /as'tiʎa; as'tiya/ n. f. splinter, chip. —**astillar**, v.

astillero /asti'ʎero; asti'yero/ n. m. dry dock.

astro /'astro/ n. m. star.

astronauta /astro'nauta/ n. m. & f. astronaut.

astronave /astro'naβe/ n. f. spaceship.

astronomía /astrono'mia/ n. f. astronomy.

astucia /as'tuθia; as'tusia/ n. f. cunning.

astuto /as'tuto/ a. astute, sly, shrewd.

asumir /asu'mir/ v. assume.

asunto /a'sunto/ n. m. matter, affair, business; subject.

asustar /asus'tar/ v. frighten, scare, startle.

atacar /ata'kar/ v. attack, charge.

atajo /a'taho/ n. m. shortcut.

ataque /a'take/ n. m. attack, charge; spell, stroke.

ataque cardíaco /a'take kar'ðiako/ heart attack.

atar /a'tar/ v. tie, bind, fasten.

atareado /atare'aðo/ a. busy.

atascar /atas'kar/ v. stall, stop, obstruct.

atasco /a'tasko/ n. m. traffic jam.

ataúd /ata'uð/ n. m. casket, coffin.

atavío /ata'βio/ n. m. dress; gear, equipment.

atemorizar /atemori'θar; atemori'sar/ v. frighten.

atención /aten'θion; aten'sion/ n. f. attention.

atender /aten'der/ v. heed; attend to, wait on.

atenerse a /ate'nerse a/ v. count on, depend on.

atentado /aten'taðo/ n. m. crime, offense.

atento /a'tento/ a. attentive, courteous.

ateo /a'teo/ n. m. atheist.

aterrizaje /aterri'θahe; aterri'sahe/ n. m. landing (of aircraft).

aterrizaje forzoso /aterri'θahe for'θoso; aterri'sahe for'soso/ emergency landing, forced landing.

aterrizar /aterri'θar; aterri'sar/ v. land.

atesorar /ateso'rar/ v. hoard.

atestar /ates'tar/ v. witness.

atestiguar /atesti'guar/ v. attest, testify.

atinar /ati'nar/ v. hit upon.

atisbar /atis'βar/ v. scrutinize, pry.

Atlántico /at'lantiko/ n. m. Atlantic.

atlántico a. Atlantic.

atlas /'atlas/ n. m. atlas.

atleta /at'leta/ n. m. & f. athlete.

atlético /at'letiko/ a. athletic.

atletismo /atle'tismo/ n. m. athletics.

atmósfera /at'mosfera/ n. f. atmosphere.

atmosférico /atmos'feriko/ a. atmospheric.

atolladero /atoʎa'ðero; atoya'ðero/ n. m. dead end, impasse.

atómico /a'tomiko/ a. atomic.

átomo /'atomo/ n. m. atom.

atormentar /atormen'tar/ v. torment, plague.

atornillar /atorni'ʎar; atorni'yar/ v. screw.

atracción /atrak'θion; atrak'sion/ n. f. attraction.

atractivo /atrak'tiβo/ a. **1.** attractive. —n. **2.** m. attraction.

atraer /atra'er/ v. attract; lure.

atrapar /atra'par/ v. trap, catch.

atrás /a'tras/ adv. back; behind.

atrasado /atra'saðo/ a. belated; backward; slow (clock).

atrasar /atra'sar/ v. delay, retard; be slow.

atraso /a'traso/ n. m. delay; backwardness; (pl.) arrears.

atravesar /atraβe'sar/ v. cross.

atreverse /atre'βerse/ v. dare.

atrevido /atre'βiðo/ a. daring, bold.

atrevimiento /atreβi'miento/ n. m. boldness.

atribuir /atri'βuir/ v. attribute, ascribe.

atributo /atri'βuto/ n. m. attribute.

atrincherar /atrintʃe'rar/ v. entrench.

atrocidad /atroθi'ðað; atrosi'ðað/ n. f. atrocity, outrage.

atronar /atro'nar/ v. deafen.

atropellar /atrope'ʎar; atrope'yar/ v. trample; fell.

atroz /a'troθ; a'ntros/ a. atrocious.

atún /a'tun/ n. m. tuna.

aturdir /atur'ðir/ v. daze, stun, bewilder.

audacia /au'ðaθia; au'ðasia/ n. f. audacity.

audaz /au'ðaθ; au'ðas/ a. audacious, bold.

audible /au'ðiβle/ a. audible.

audífono /au'ðifono/ n. m. hearing aid.

audiovisual /auðioβi'sual/ a. audiovisual.

auditorio /auði'torio/ n. m. audience.

aula /'aula/ n. f. classroom, hall.

aullar /au'ʎar; au'yar/ v. howl, bay.

aullido /au'ʎiðo; au'yiðo/ n. m. howl.

aumentar /aumen'tar/ v. augment; increase, swell.

aun /a'un/ **aún** adv. still; even. **a. cuando,** even though, even if.

aunque /'aunke/ conj. although, though.

áureo /'aureo/ a. golden.

aureola /aure'ola/ n. f. halo.

auriculares /auriku'lares/ n. m.pl. headphones.

aurora /au'rora/ n. f. dawn.

ausencia /au'senθia; au'sensia/ n. f. absence.

ausentarse /ausen'tarse/ v. stay away.

ausente /au'sente/ a. absent.

auspicio /aus'piθio; aus'pisio/ n. m. auspice.

austeridad /austeri'ðað/ n. f. austerity.

austero /aus'tero/ a. austere.

austriaco /aus'triako/ **-ca** a. & n. Austrian.

auténtico /au'tentiko/ a. authentic.

auto /'auto/ **automóvil** n. m. auto, automobile.

autobús /auto'βus/ n. m. bus.

autocine /auto'θine; auto'sine/ **autocinema** n. m. drive-in (movie theater).

automático /auto'matiko/ a. automatic.

autonomía /autono'mia/ n. f. autonomy.

autopista /auto'pista/ n. f. expressway.

autor /au'tor/ n. m. author.

autoridad /autori'ðað/ n. f. authority.

autoritario /autori'tario/ a. authoritarian; authoritative.

autorizar /autori'θar; autori'sar/ v. authorize.

autostop /auto'stop/ n. m. hitchhiking. **hacer a.,** to hitchhike.

auxiliar /auksi'liar/ a. **1.** auxiliary. —v. **2.** assist, aid.

auxilio /auk'silio/ n. m. aid, assistance.

avaluar /aβa'luar/ v. evaluate, appraise.

avance /a'βanθe; a'βanse/ n. m. advance. —**avanzar,** v.

avaricia /aβa'riθia; aβa'risia/ n. f. avarice.

avariento /aβa'riento/ a. miserly, greedy.

avaro /a'βaro/ **-ra** a. & m. miser; miserly.

ave /'aβe/ n. f. bird.

avellana /aβe'ʎana; aβe'yana/ n. f. hazelnut.

Ave María /aβema'ria/ *n. m.* Hail Mary.

avena /a'βena/ *n. f.* oat.

avenida /aβe'niða/ *n. f.* avenue; flood.

avenirse /aβe'nirse/ *v.* compromise; agree.

aventajar /aβenta'har/ *v.* surpass, get ahead of.

aventar /aβen'tar/ *v.* fan; scatter.

aventura /aβen'tura/ *n. f.* adventure.

aventurar /aβentu'rar/ *v.* venture, risk, gamble.

aventurero /aβentu'rero/ **-ra** *a.* & *n.* adventurous; adventurer.

avergonzado /aβergon'θaðo; aβergon'saðo/ *a.* ashamed, abashed.

avergonzar /aβergon'θar; aβergon'sar/ *v.* shame, abash.

avería /aβe'ria/ *n. f.* damage. —**averiar,** *v.*

averiguar /aβeri'guar/ *v.* ascertain, find out.

aversión /aβer'sion/ *n. f.* aversion.

avestruz /aβes'truθ; aβes'trus/ *n. m.* ostrich.

aviación /aβia'θion; aβia'sion/ *n. f.* aviation.

aviador /aβia'ðor/ **-ra** *n.* aviator.

ávido /'aβiðo/ *a.* avid; eager.

avión /a'βion/ *n. m.* airplane.

avisar /aβi'sar/ *v.* notify, let know; warn, advise.

aviso /a'βiso/ *n. m.* notice, announcement; advertisement; warning.

avispa /a'βispa/ *n. f.* wasp.

avivar /aβi'βar/ *v.* enliven, revive.

axila /ak'sila/ *n. f.* armpit.

aya /'aya/ *n. f.* governess.

ayatolá /aya'tola/ *n. m.* ayatollah.

ayer /a'yer/ *adv.* yesterday.

ayuda /a'yuða/ *n. f.* help, aid. —**ayudar,** *v.*

ayudante /ayu'ðante/ *a.* assistant, helper; adjutant.

ayuno /a'yuno/ *n. m.* fast. —**ayunar,** *v.*

ayuntamiento /ayunta'miento/ *n. m.* city hall.

azada /a'θaða; a'saða/ *n. f.*, **azadón,** *m.* hoe.

azafata /aθa'fata; asa'fata/ *n. f.* stewardess, flight attendant.

azar /a'θar; a'sar/ *n. m.* hazard, chance. **al a.,** at random.

azotar /aθo'tar; aso'tar/ *v.* whip, flog; belabor.

azote /a'θote; a'sote/ *n. m.* scourge, lash.

azúcar /a'θukar; a'sukar/ *n. m.* sugar.

azucarero /aθuka'rero; asuka'rero/ *n. m.* sugar bowl.

azúcar moreno /a'θukar mo'reno; a'sukar mo'reno/ brown sugar.

azul /a'θul; a'sul/ *a.* blue.

azulado /aθu'laðo; asu'laðo/ *a.* blue, bluish.

azulejo /aθu'leho; asu'leho/ *n. m.* tile; bluebird.

azul marino /a'θul ma'rino; a'sul ma'rino/ navy blue.

B

baba /'baβa/ *n. f.* drivel. —**babear,** *v.*

babador /baβa'ðor, ba'βero/ *n. m.* bib.

babucha /ba'βutʃa/ *n. f.* slipper.

bacalao /baka'lao/ *n. m.* codfish.

bachiller /batʃi'ʎer; batʃi'yer/ **-ra** *n.* bachelor (degree).

bacía /ba'θia; ba'sia/ *n. f.* washbasin.

bacterias /bak'terias/ *n. f.pl.* bacteria.

bacteriología /bakteriolo'hia/ *n. f.* bacteriology.

bahía /ba'ia/ *n. f.* bay.

bailador /baila'ðor/ **-ra** *n.* dancer.

bailar /bai'lar/ *v.* dance.

bailarín /baila'rin/ **-ina** *n.* dancer.

baile /'baile/ *n. m.* dance.

baja /'baha/ *n. f.* fall (in price); *Mil.* casualty.

bajar /ba'har/ *v.* lower; descend.

bajeza /ba'heθa; ba'hesa/ *n. f.* baseness.

bajo /'baho/ *prep.* **1.** under, below. —*a.* **2.** low; short; base.

bala /'bala/ *n. f.* bullet; ball; bale.

balada /ba'laða/ *n. f.* ballad.

balancear /balanθe'ar; balanse'ar/ *v.* balance; roll, swing, sway.

balanza /ba'lanθa; ba'lansa/ *n. f.* balance; scales.

balbuceo /balβu'θeo; balβu'seo/ *n. m.* stammer; babble. —**balbucear,** *v.*

Balcanes /bal'kanes/ *n. m.pl.* Balkans.

balcón /bal'kon/ *n. m.* balcony.

balde /'balde/ *n. m.* bucket, pail. **de b.,** gratis. **en b.,** in vain.

balística /ba'listika/ *n. f.* ballistics.

ballena /ba'ʎena; ba'yena/ *n. f.* whale.

balneario /balne'ario/ *n. m.* bathing resort; spa.

balompié /balom'pie/ *n. m.* football.

balón /ba'lon/ *n. m.* football; *Auto.* balloon tire.

baloncesto /balon'θesto; balon-'sesto/ *n. m.* basketball.

balota /ba'lota/ *n. f.* ballot, vote. —**balotar,** *v.*

balsa /'balsa/ *n. f.* raft.

bálsamo /'balsamo/ *n. m.* balm.

baluarte /ba'luarte/ *n. m.* bulwark.

bambolearse /bambole'arse/ *v.* sway.

bambú /bam'βu/ *n.* bamboo.

banal /ba'nal/ *a.* banal, trite.

banana /ba'nana/ *n. f.* banana.

banano /ba'nano/ *n. m.* banana tree.

bancarrota /banka'rrota/ *n. f.* bankruptcy.

banco /'banko/ *n. m.* bank; bench; school of fish.

banco cooperativo /'banko koopera'tiβo/ credit union.

banda /'banda/ *n. f.* band.

bandada /ban'daða/ *n. f.* covey; flock.

banda sonora /'banda so'nora/ *n. f.* soundtrack.

bandeja /ban'deha/ *n. f.* tray.

bandera /ban'dera/ *n. f.* flag; banner; ensign.

bandido /ban'diðo/ **-da** *n.* bandit.

bando /'bando/ *n. m.* faction.

bandolero /bando'lero/ **-ra** *n.* bandit, robber.

banquero /ban'kero/ **-ra** *n.* banker.

banqueta /ban'keta/ *n. f.* stool; (Mex.) sidewalk.

banquete /ban'kete/ *n. m.* feast, banquet.

banquillo /ban'kiʎo; ban'kiyo/ *n. m.* stool.

bañar /ba'ɲar/ *v.* bathe.

bañera /ba'ɲera/ *n. f.* bathtub.

baño /'baɲo/ *n. m.* bath; bathroom.

bar /bar/ *n. m.* bar, pub.

baraja /ba'raha/ *n. f.* pack of cards; game of cards.

baranda /ba'randa/ *n. f.* railing, banister.

barato /ba'rato/ *a.* cheap.

barba /'barβa/ *n. f.* beard; chin.

barbacoa /barβa'koa/ *n. f.* barbecue; stretcher.

barbaridad /barβari'ðað/ *n. f.* barbarity; *Colloq.* excess (in anything).

bárbaro /'barβaro/ *a.* barbarous; crude.

barbería /barβe'ria/ *n. f.* barbershop.

barbero /bar'βero/ *n. m.* barber.

barca /'barka/ *n. f.* (small) boat.

barcaza /bar'kaθa; bar'kasa/ *n. f.* barge.

barco /'barko/ *n. m.* ship, boat.

barniz /bar'niθ; bar'nis/ *n. m.* varnish. —**barnizar,** *v.*

barómetro /ba'rometro/ *n. m.* barometer.

barón /ba'ron/ *n. m.* baron.

barquilla /bar'kiʎa; bar'kiya/ *n. f.* *Naut.* log.

barra /'barra/ *n. f.* bar.

barraca /ba'rraka/ *n. f.* hut, shed.

barrear /barre'ar/ *v.* bar, barricade.

barreno /ba'rreno/ *n. m.* blast, blasting. —**barrenar,** *v.*

barrer /ba'rrer/ *v.* sweep.

barrera /ba'rrera/ *n. f.* barrier.

barricada /barri'kaða/ *n. f.* barricade.

barriga /ba'rriga/ *n. f.* belly.

barril /ba'rril/ *n. m.* barrel; cask.

barrio /'barrio/ *n. m.* district, ward, quarter.

barro /'barro/ *n. m.* clay, mud.

base /'base/ *n. f.* base; basis. —**basar,** *v.*

base de datos /'base de 'datos/ database.

bastante /bas'tante/ *a.* **1.** enough, plenty of. —*adv.* **2.** enough; rather, quite.

bastar /bas'tar/ *v.* suffice, be enough.

bastardo /bas'tarðo/ **-a** *a. & n.* bastard.

bastear /baste'ar/ *v.* baste.

bastidor /basti'ðor/ *n. m.* wing (in theater).

bastón /bas'ton/ *n. m.* (walking) cane.

bastos /'bastos/ *n. m.pl.* clubs (cards).

basura /ba'sura/ *n. f.* refuse, dirt; garbage; junk.

basurero /basu'rero/ **-ra** *n.* scavenger.

batalla /ba'taʎa; ba'taya/ *n. f.* battle. —**batallar,** *v.*

batallón /bata'ʎon; bata'yon/ *n. m.* batallion.

batata /ba'tata/ *n. f.* sweet potato.

bate /'bate/ *n. m.* bat. —**batear,** *v.*

batería /bate'ria/ *n. f.* battery.

batido /ba'tiðo/ *n. m.* (cooking) batter; milkshake.

batidora /bati'ðora/ *n. f.* mixer (for food).

batir /ba'tir/ *v.* beat; demolish; conquer.

baúl /ba'ul/ *n. m.* trunk.

bautismo /bau'tismo/ *n. m.* baptism.

bautista /bau'tista/ *n. m. & f.* Baptist.

bautizar /bauti'θar; bauti'sar/ *v.* christen, baptize.

bautizo /bau'tiθo; bau'tiso/ *n. m.* baptism.

baya /'baia/ *n. f.* berry.

bayoneta /bayo'neta/ *n. f.* bayonet.

beato /be'ato/ *a.* blessed.

bebé /be'βe/ *n. m.* baby.

beber /be'βer/ *v.* drink.

bebible /be'βiβle/ *a.* drinkable.

bebida /be'βiða/ *n. f.* drink, beverage.

beca /'beka/ *n. f.* grant, scholarship.

becado /be'kaðo/ **-da** *n.* scholar.

becerro /be'θerro; be'serro/ *n. m.* calf; calfskin.

beldad /bel'dað/ *n. f.* beauty.

belga /'belga/ *a. & n.* Belgian.

Bélgica /'belhika/ *n. f.* Belgium.

belicoso /beli'koso/ *a.* warlike.

beligerante /belihe'rante/ *a. & n.* belligerent.

bellaco /be'ʎako; be'yako/ *a.* **1.** sly, roguish. —*n.* **2.** *m.* rogue.

bellas artes /'beʎas 'artes; 'beyas 'artes/ *n. f.pl.* fine arts.

belleza /be'ʎeθa; be'yesa/ *n. f.* beauty.

bello /'beʎo; 'beyo/ *a.* beautiful.

bellota /be'ʎota; be'yota/ *n. f.* acorn.

bendecir /bende'θir; bende'sir/ *v.* bless.

bendición /bendi'θion; bendi'sion/ *n. f.* blessing, benediction.

bendito /ben'dito/ *a.* blessed.

beneficio /bene'fiθio; bene'fisio/ *n. m.* benefit. —**beneficiar,** *v.*

beneficioso /benefi'θioso; benefi'sioso/ *a.* beneficial.

benevolencia /beneβo'lenθia; beneβo'lensia/ *n. f.* benevolence.

benévolo /be'neβolo/ *a.* benevolent.

benigno /be'nigno/ *a.* benign.

beodo /be'oðo/ **-da** *a. & n.* drunk.

berenjena /beren'hena/ *n. f.* eggplant.

beso /'beso/ *n. m.* kiss. —**besar,** *v.*

bestia /'bestia/ *n. f.* beast, brute.

betabel /beta'βel/ *n. m.* beet.

Biblia /'biβlia/ *n. f.* Bible.

bíblico /'biβliko/ *a.* Biblical.

biblioteca /biβlio'teka/ *n. f.* library.

bicarbonato /bikarβo'nato/ *n. m.* bicarbonate.

bicicleta /biθi'kleta; bisi'kleta/ *n. f.* bicycle.

bien /bien/ *adv.* **1.** well. —*n.* **2.** good; (*pl.*) possessions.

bienes inmuebles /'bienes i'mueβles/ *n. m.pl.* real estate.

bienestar /bienes'tar/ *n. m.* well-being, welfare.

bienhechor /biene'tʃor/ **-ra** *n.* benefactor.

bienvenida /biembe'niða/ *n. f.* welcome.

bienvenido /biembe'niðo/ *a.* welcome.

biftec /bif'tek/ *n. m.* steak.

bifurcación /bifurka'θion; bifurka'sion/ *n. f.* fork. —**bifurcar,** *v.*

bigamia /bi'gamia/ *n. f.* bigamy.

bígamo /'bigamo/ **-a** *n.* bigamist.

bigotes /bi'gotes/ *n. m.pl.* mustache.

bikini /bi'kini/ *n. m.* bikini.

bilingüe /bi'lingue/ *a.* bilingual.

bilingüismo /bilin'guismo/ *n. m.* bilingualism.

bilis /'bilis/ *n. f.* bile.

billar /bi'ʎar; bi'yar/ *n. m.* billiards.

billete /bi'ʎete; bi'yete/ *n. m.* ticket; bank note, bill.

billete de banco /bi'ʎete de 'banko; bi'yete de 'banko/ bank note.

billón /bi'ʎon; bi'yon/ *n. m.* billion.

bingo /'biŋgo/ *n. m.* bingo.

biodegradable /bioðegra'ðaβle/ *a.* biodegradable.

biografía /biogra'fia/ *n. f.* biography.

biología /biolo'hia/ *n. f.* biology.

biombo /'biombo/ *n. m.* folding screen.

bisabuela /bisa'βuela/ *n. f.* great-grandmother.

bisabuelo /bisa'βuelo/ *n. m.* great-grandfather.

bisel /bi'sel/ *n. m.* bevel. —**biselar,** *v.*

bisonte /bi'sonte/ *n. m.* bison.

bisté /bis'te/ **bistec** *n. m.* steak.

bisutería /bisute'ria/ *n. f.* costume jewelry.

bizarro /bi'θarro; bi'sarro/ *a.* brave; generous; smart.

bizco /'biθko/ **-ca** *n.* **1.** cross-eyed person. —*a.* **2.** cross-eyed, squinting.

bizcocho /biθ'kotʃo; bis'kotʃo/ *n. m.* biscuit, cake.

blanco /'blanko/ *a.* **1.** white; blank. —*n.* **2.** *m.* white; target.

blandir /blan'dir/ *v.* brandish, flourish.

blando /'blando/ *a.* soft.

blanquear /blanke'ar/ *v.* whiten; bleach.

blasfemar /blasfe'mar/ *v.* blaspheme, curse.

blasfemia /blas'femia/ *n. f.* blasphemy.

blindado /blin'daðo/ *a.* armored.

blindaje /blin'dahe/ *n. m.* armor.

bloque /'bloke/ *n. m.* block. —**bloquear,** *v.*

bloqueo /blo'keo/ *n. m.* blockade. —**bloquear,** *v.*

blusa /'blusa/ *n. f.* blouse.

bobada /bo'βaða/ *n. f.* stupid, silly thing.

bobo /'boβo/ **-ba** *a. & n.* fool; foolish.

boca /'boka/ *n. f.* mouth.

bocado /bo'kaðo/ *n. m.* bit; bite, mouthful.

bocanada /boka'naða/ *n. f.* puff (of smoke); mouthful (of liquor).

bocazas /bo'kaθas/ *n. m. & f. Colloq.* bigmouth.

bochorno /bo'tʃorno/ *n. m.* sultry weather; embarrassment.

bocina /bo'θina; bo'sina/ *n. f.* horn.

boda /'boða/ *n. f.* wedding.

bodega /bo'ðega/ *n. f.* wine cellar; *Naut.* hold; (Carib.) grocery store.

bofetada /bofe'taða/ *n. f.* **bofetón,** *m.* slap.

boga /'boga/ *n. f.* vogue; fad.

bogar /bo'gar/ *v.* row (a boat).

bohemio /bo'emio/ **-a** *a. & n.* Bohemian.

boicoteo /boiko'teo/ *n. m.* boycott. —**boicotear,** *v.*

boina /'boina/ *n. f.* beret.

bola /'bola/ *n. f.* ball.

bola de nieve /'bola de 'nieβe/ snowball.

bolas de billar /'bolas de bi'ʎar; 'bolas de bi'yar/ billiard balls.

bolera /bo'lera/ *n. f.* bowling alley.

boletín /bole'tin/ *n. m.* bulletin.

boletín informativo /bole'tin informa'tiβo/ news bulletin.

boleto /bo'leto/ *n. m.* ticket. **b. de embarque,** boarding pass.

boliche /bo'litʃe/ *n. m.* bowling alley.

bolígrafo /bo'ligrafo/ *n. m.* ballpoint pen.

boliviano /boli'βiano/ **-a** *a. & n.* Bolivian.

bollo /'boʎo; 'boyo/ *n. m.* bun, loaf.

bolos /'bolos/ *n. m.pl.* bowling.

bolsa /'bolsa/ *n. f.* purse; stock exchange.

bolsa de agua caliente /'bolsa de 'agua ka'liente/ hot-water bottle.

bolsillo /bol'siʎo; bol'siyo/ *n. m.* pocket.

bomba /'bomba/ *n. f.* pump; bomb; gas station.

bombardear /bombarðe'ar/ *v.* bomb; bombard, shell.

bombear /bombe'ar/ *v.* pump.

bombero /bom'βero/ *n. m.* fireman.

bombilla /bom'βiʎa; bom'βiya/ *n. f.* (light) bulb.

bonanza /bo'nanθa; bo'nansa/ *n. f.* prosperity; fair weather.

bondad /bon'dað/ *n. f.* kindness; goodness.

bondadoso /bonda'ðoso/ *a.* kind, kindly.

bongó /boŋ'go/ *n. m.* bongo drum.

bonito /bo'nito/ *a.* pretty.

bono /'bono/ *n. m.* bonus; *Fin.* bond.

boqueada /boke'aða/ n. f. gasp; gape. —**boquear,** v.
boquilla /bo'kiʎa; bo'kiya/ n. f. cigarette holder.
bordado /bor'ðaðo/ n. m., **bordadura,** f. embroidery.
bordar /bor'ðar/ v. embroider.
borde /'borðe/ n. m. border, rim, edge, brink, ledge.
borde de la carretera /'borðe de la karre'tera/ roadside.
borla /'borla/ n. f. tassel.
borracho /bo'rratʃo/ -a a. & n. drunk.
borrachón /borra'tʃon/ -na n. drunkard.
borrador /borra'ðor/ n. m. eraser.
borradura /borra'ðura/ n. f. erasure.
borrar /bo'rrar/ v. erase, rub out.
borrasca /bo'rraska/ n. f. squall, storm.
borrico /bo'rriko/ n. m. donkey.
bosque /'boske/ n. m. forest, wood.
bosquejo /bos'keho/ n. m. sketch, draft. —**bosquejar,** v.
bostezo /bos'teθo; bos'teso/ n. m. yawn. —**bostezar,** v.
bota /'bota/ n. f. boot.
botalón /bota'lon/ n. m. Naut. boom.
botánica /bo'tanika/ n. f. botany.
botar /bo'tar/ v. throw out, throw away.
bote /'bote/ n. m. boat; can, box.
bote salvavidas /'bote salβa-'βiðas/ lifeboat.
botica /bo'tika/ n. f. pharmacy, drugstore.
boticario /boti'kario/ n. m. pharmacist, druggist.
botín /bo'tin/ n. m. booty, plunder, spoils.
botiquín /boti'kin/ n. m. medicine chest.
boto /'boto/ a. dull, stupid.
botón /bo'ton/ n. m. button.
botones /bo'tones/ n. m. bellboy (in a hotel).
bóveda /b'oβeða/ n. f. vault.
boxeador /boksea'ðor/ n. m. boxer.
boxeo /bok'seo/ n. m. boxing. —**boxear,** v.
boya /'boya/ n. f. buoy.
boyante /bo'yante/ a. buoyant.
bozal /bo'θal; bo'sal/ n. m. muzzle.
bragas /'bragas/ n. f.pl. panties.

bramido /bra'miðo/ n. m. roar, bellow. —**bramar,** v.
brasa /'brasa/ n. f. embers, grill. —**brasear,** v.
brasileño /brasi'leɲo/ -ña a. & n. Brazilian.
bravata /bra'βata/ n. f. bravado.
bravear /braβe'ar/ v. bully.
braza /'braθa; 'brasa/ n. f. fathom.
brazada /bra'θaða; bra'saða/ n. f. (swimming) stroke.
brazalete /braθa'lete; brasa'lete/ n. m. bracelet.
brazo /'braθo; 'braso/ n. m. arm.
brea /'brea/ n. f. tar, pitch.
brecha /'bretʃa/ n. f. gap, breach.
brécol /'brekol/ n. m. broccoli.
bregar /bre'gar/ v. scramble.
breña /'breɲa/ n. f. rough country with brambly shrubs.
Bretaña /bre'taɲa/ n. f. Britain.
breve /'breβe/ a. brief, short. **en b.,** shortly, soon.
brevedad /breβe'ðað/ n. f. brevity.
bribón /bri'βon/ -na n. rogue, rascal.
brida /'briða/ n. f. bridle.
brigada /bri'gaða/ n. f. brigade.
brillante /bri'ʎante; bri'yante/ a. 1. brilliant, shiny. —n. 2. m. diamond.
brillo /'briʎo; 'briyo/ n. m. shine, glitter. —**brillar,** v.
brinco /'brinko/ n. m. jump; bounce, skip. —**brincar,** v.
brindis /'brindis/ n. m. toast. —**brindar,** v.
brío /'brio/ n. m. vigor.
brioso /'brioso/ a. vigorous, spirited.
brisa /'brisa/ n. f. breeze.
brisa marina /'brisa ma'rina/ sea breeze.
británico /bri'taniko/ a. British.
brocado /bro'kaðo/ -da a. & n. brocade.
brocha /'brotʃa/ n. f. brush.
broche /'brotʃe/ n. m. brooch, clasp, pin.
broma /'broma/ n. f. joke. —**bromear,** v.
bronca /'bronka/ n. f. Colloq. quarrel, row, fight.
bronce /'bronθe; 'bronse/ n. m. bronze; brass.
bronceador /bronθea'ðor; bronsea'ðor/ n. m. suntan lotion, suntan oil.

bronquitis /bron'kitis/ *n. f.* bronchitis.

brotar /bro'tar/ *v.* gush; sprout; bud.

brote /'brote/ *n. m.* bud, shoot.

bruja /'bruha/ *n. f.* witch.

brújula /'bruhula/ *n. f.* compass.

bruma /'bruma/ *n. f.* mist.

brumoso /bru'moso/ *a.* misty.

brusco /'brusko/ *a.* brusque; abrupt, curt.

brutal /bru'tal/ *a.* savage, brutal.

brutalidad /brutali'ðað/ *n. f.* brutality.

bruto /'bruto/ **-ta** *a.* **1.** brutish; ignorant. —*n.* **2.** blockhead.

bucear /buθe'ar/ buse'ar/ *v.* dive.

bueno /'bueno/ *a.* good, fair; well (in health).

buey /buei/ *n. m.* ox, steer.

búfalo /'bufalo/ *n. m.* buffalo.

bufanda /bu'fanda/ *n. f.* scarf.

bufón /bu'fon/ **-ona** *a. & n.* fool, buffoon, clown.

búho /'buo/ *n. m.* owl.

buhonero /buo'nero/ *n. m.* peddler, vendor.

bujía /bu'hia/ *n. f.* spark plug.

bulevar /bule'βar/ *n. m.* boulevard.

bulimia /bu'limia/ *n. f.* bulimia.

bullicio /bu'ʎiθio; bu'yisio/ *n. m.* bustle, noise.

bullicioso /buʎi'θioso; buyi'sioso/ *a.* boisterous, noisy.

bulto /'bulto/ *n. m.* bundle; lump.

buñuelo /bu'ɲuelo/ *n. m.* bun.

buque /'buke/ *n. m.* ship.

buque de guerra /'buke de 'gerra/ warship.

buque de pasajeros /'buke de pasa'heros/ passenger ship.

burdo /'burðo/ *a.* coarse.

burgués /bur'ges/ **-esa** *a. & n.* bourgeois.

burla /'burla/ *n. f.* mockery; fun.

burlador /burla'ðor/ **-ra** *n.* trickster, jokester.

burlar /bur'lar/ *v.* mock, deride.

burlarse de /bur'larse de/ *v.* scoff at; make fun of.

burro /'burro/ *n. m.* donkey.

busca /'buska/ *n. f.* search, pursuit, quest.

buscar /bus'kar/ *v.* seek, look for; look up.

busto /'busto/ *n. m.* bust.

butaca /bu'taka/ *n. f.* armchair; *Theat.* orchestra seat.

buzo /'buθo; 'buso/ *n. m.* diver.

buzón /bu'θon; bu'son/ *n. m.* mailbox.

C

cabal /ka'βal/ *a.* exact; thorough.

cabalgar /kaβal'gar/ *v.* ride horseback.

caballeresco /kaβaʎe'resko; kaβaye'resko/ *a.* gentlemanly, chivalrous.

caballería /kaβaʎe'ria; kaβaye'ria/ *n. f.* cavalry; chivalry.

caballeriza /kaβaʎe'riθa; kaβaye-'risa/ *n. f.* stable.

caballero /kaβa'ʎero; kaβa'yero/ *n. m.* gentleman; knight.

caballete /kaβa'ʎete; kaβa'yete/ *n. m.* sawhorse; easel; ridge (of roof).

caballo /ka'βaʎo; ka'βayo/ *n. m.* horse.

cabaña /ka'βaɲa/ *n. f.* cabin; booth.

cabaré /kaβa're/ *n. m.* nightclub.

cabaretero /kaβare'tero/ **-a** *n. m. & f.* nightclub owner.

cabecear /kaβeθe'ar; kaβese'ar/ *v.* pitch (as a ship).

cabecera /kaβe'θera; kaβe'sera/ *n. f.* head (of bed, table).

cabello /ka'βeʎo; ka'βeyo/ *n. m.* hair.

caber /ka'βer/ *v.* fit into, be contained in. **no cabe duda,** there is no doubt.

cabeza /ka'βeθa; ka'βesa/ *n. f.* head; warhead.

cabildo /ka'βildo/ *n. m.* city hall.

cabildo abierto /ka'βildo a'βierto/ town meeting.

cabizbajo /kaβiθ'βaho; kaβis-'βaho/ *a.* downcast.

cablegrama /kaβle'grama/ *n. m.* cablegram.

cabo /'kaβo/ *n. m.* end; *Geog.* cape; *Mil.* corporal. **llevar a c.,** carry out, accomplish.

cabra /'kaβra/ *n. f.* goat.

cacahuete /kaka'uete/ *n. m.* peanut.

cacao /ka'kao/ *n. m.* cocoa; chocolate.

cacerola /kaθe'rola; kase'rola/ *n. f.* pan, casserole.

cachondeo /katʃon'deo/ *n. m.* fun, hilarity.

cachondo /ka'tʃondo/ *a.* funny; *Colloq.* horny.

cachorro /ka'tʃorro/ *n. m.* cub; puppy.

cada /'kaða/ *a.* each, every.

cadáver /ka'ðaβer/ *n. m.* corpse.

cadena /ka'ðena/ *n. f.* chain.

cadera /ka'ðera/ *n. f.* hip.

cadete /ka'ðete/ *n. m.* cadet.

caer /ka'er/ *v.* fall.

café /ka'fe/ *n. m.* coffee; café.

café exprés /ka'fe eks'pres/ espresso.

café soluble /ka'fe so'luβle/ instant coffee.

cafetal /kafe'tal/ *n. m.* coffee plantation.

cafetera /kafe'tera/ *n. f.* coffee pot.

caída /ka'iða/ *n. f.* fall, drop; collapse.

caimán /kai'man/ *n. m.* alligator.

caja /'kaha/ *n. f.* box, case; checkout counter.

caja de ahorros /'kaha de a'orros/ savings bank.

caja de cerillos /'kaha de θe-'riʎos; 'kaha de se'riyos/ matchbox.

caja de fósforos /'kaha de 'fosforos/ matchbox.

caja torácica /'kaha to'raθika; 'kaha to'rasika/ rib cage.

cajero /ka'hero/ **-ra** *n.* cashier.

cajón /ka'hon/ *n. m.* drawer.

cal /kal/ *n. f.* lime.

calabaza /kala'βaθa; kala'βasa/ *n. f.* calabash, pumpkin.

calabozo /kala'βoθo; kala'βoso/ *n. m.* jail, cell.

calambre /ka'lambre/ *n. m.* cramp.

calamidad /kalami'ðað/ *n. f.* calamity, disaster.

calcetín /kalθe'tin; kalse'tin/ *n. m.* sock.

calcio /'kalθio; 'kalsio/ *n. m.* calcium.

calcular /kalku'lar/ *v.* calculate, figure.

cálculo /'kalkulo/ *n. m.* calculation, estimate.

caldera /kal'dera/ *n. f.* kettle, caldron; boiler.

caldo /'kaldo/ *n. m.* broth.

calefacción /kalefak'θion; kalefak'sion/ *n. f.* heat, heating.

calendario /kalen'dario/ *n. m.* calendar.

calentar /kalen'tar/ *v.* heat, warm.

calidad /kali'ðað/ *n. f.* quality, grade.

caliente /ka'liente/ *a.* hot, warm.

calificar /kalifi'kar/ *v.* qualify.

callado /ka'ʎaðo; ka'yaðo/ *a.* silent, quiet.

callarse /ka'ʎarse; ka'yarse/ *v.* quiet down; keep still; stop talking.

calle /'kaʎe; 'kaye/ *n. f.* street.

callejón /kaʎe'hon; kaye'hon/ *n. m.* alley.

calle sin salida /'kaʎe sin sa'liða; 'kaye sin sa'liða/ dead end.

callo /'kaʎo; 'kayo/ *n. m.* callus, corn.

calma /'kalma/ *n. f.* calm, quiet.

calmado /kal'maðo/ *a.* calm.

calmante /kal'mante/ *a.* soothing, calming.

calmar /kal'mar/ *v.* calm, quiet, lull, soothe.

calor /ka'lor/ *n.* heat, warmth. **tener c.,** to be hot, warm; feel hot, warm. **hacer c.,** to be hot, warm (weather).

calorífero /kalo'rifero/ *a.* **1.** heat-producing. —*n.* **2.** *m.* radiator.

calumnia /ka'lumnia/ *n. f.* slander. —**calumniar,** *v.*

caluroso /kalu'roso/ *a.* warm, hot.

calvario /kal'βario/ *n. m.* Calvary.

calvo /'kalβo/ *a.* bald.

calzado /kal'θaðo; kal'saðo/ *n. m.* footwear.

calzar /kal'θar; kal'sar/ *v.* wear (as shoes).

calzoncillos /kalθon'θiʎos; kalson'siyos/ *n. m.pl.* shorts.

calzones /kal'θones; kal'sones/ *n. m.pl.* trousers.

cama /'kama/ *n. f.* bed.

cámara /'kamara/ *n. f.* chamber; camera.

camarada /kama'raða/ *n. m. & f.* comrade.

camarera /kama'rera/ *n. f.* chambermaid; waitress.

camarero /kama'rero/ *n. m.* steward; waiter.

camarón /kama'ron/ *n. m.* shrimp.

camarote /kama'rote/ *n. m.* stateroom, berth.

cambiar /kam'βiar/ v. exchange, change, trade; cash.

cambio /'kambio/ n. m. change, exchange. **en c.,** on the other hand.

cambista /kam'βista/ n. m. & f. money changer; banker, broker.

cambur /kam'βur/ n. m. banana.

camello /ka'meʎo; ka'meyo/ n. m. camel.

camilla /ka'miʎa; ka'miya/ n. f. stretcher.

caminar /kami'nar/ v. walk.

caminata /kami'nata/ n. f. tramp, hike.

camino /ka'mino/ n. m. road; way.

camión /ka'mion/ n. m. truck.

camisa /ka'misa/ n. f. shirt.

camisería /kamise'ria/ n. f. haberdashery.

camiseta /kami'seta/ n. f. undershirt; T-shirt.

campamento /kampa'mento/ n. m. camp.

campana /kam'pana/ n. f. bell.

campanario /kampa'nario/ n. m. bell tower, steeple.

campaneo /kampa'neo/ n. m. chime.

campaña /kam'paɲa/ n. f. campaign.

campeón /kampe'on/ **-na** n. champion.

campeonato /kampeo'nato/ n. m. championship.

campesino /kampe'sino/ **-na** n. peasant.

campestre /kam'pestre/ a. country, rural.

campo /'kampo/ n. m. field; (the) country.

campo de concentración /'kampo de konθentra'θion; 'kampo de konsentra'sion/ concentration camp.

campo de golf /'kampo de 'golf/ golf course.

Canadá /kana'ða/ n. m. Canada.

canadiense /kana'ðiense/ a. & n. Canadian.

canal /ka'nal/ n. m. canal; channel.

Canal de la Mancha /ka'nal de la 'mantʃa/ n. m. English Channel.

canalla /ka'naʎa; ka'naya/ n. f. rabble.

canario /ka'nario/ n. m. canary.

canasta /ka'nasta/ n. f. basket.

cáncer /'kanθer; 'kanser/ n. m. cancer.

cancha de tenis /'kantʃa de 'tenis/ n. f. tennis court.

canciller /kanθi'ʎer; kansi'yer/ n. m. chancellor.

canción /kan'θion; kan'sion/ n. f. song.

candado /kan'daðo/ n. m. padlock.

candela /kan'dela/ n. f. fire; light; candle.

candelero /kande'lero/ n. m. candlestick.

candidato /kandi'ðato/ **-ta** n. candidate; applicant.

candidatura /kandiða'tura/ n. f. candidacy.

canela /ka'nela/ n. f. cinnamon.

cangrejo /kaŋ'greho/ n. m. crab.

caníbal /ka'niβal/ n. m. cannibal.

caniche /ka'nitʃe/ n. m. poodle.

canje /'kanhe/ n. m. exchange, trade. —**canjear,** v.

cano /'kano/ a. gray.

canoa /ka'noa/ n. f. canoe.

cansado /kan'saðo/ a. tired, weary.

cansancio /kan'sanθio; kan'sansio/ n. m. fatigue.

cansar /kan'sar/ v. tire, fatigue, wear out.

cantante /kan'tante/ n. m. & f. singer.

cantar /kan'tar/ n. **1.** m. song. —v. **2.** sing.

cántaro /'kantaro/ n. m. pitcher.

cantera /kan'tera/ n. f. (stone) quarry.

cantidad /kanti'ðað/ n. f. quantity, amount.

cantina /kan'tina/ n. f. bar, tavern; restaurant.

canto /'kanto/ n. m. chant, song, singing; edge.

caña /'kaɲa/ n. f. cane, reed; sugar cane; small glass of beer.

cañón /ka'ɲon/ n. m. canyon; cannon; gun barrel.

caoba /ka'oβa/ n. f. mahogany.

caos /'kaos/ n. m. chaos.

caótico /ka'otiko/ a. chaotic.

capa /'kapa/ n. f. cape, cloak; coat (of paint).

capacidad /kapaθi'ðað; kapasi-'ðað/ n. f. capacity; capability.

capacitar /kapaθi'tar; kapasi'tar/ v. enable.

capataz /kapa'taθ; kapa'tas/ n. m. foreman.

capaz /ka'paθ; ka'pas/ *a.* capable, able.

capellán /kape'ʎan; kape'yan/ *n. m.* chaplain.

caperuza /kape'ruθa; kape'rusa/ *n. f.* hood.

capilla /ka'piʎa; ka'piya/ *n. f.* chapel.

capital /kapi'tal/ *n.* **1.** *m.* capital. **2.** *f.* capital (city).

capitalista /kapita'lista/ *a. & n.* capitalist.

capitán /kapi'tan/ *n. m.* captain.

capitular /kapitu'lar/ *v.* yield.

capítulo /ka'pitulo/ *n. m.* chapter.

capota /ka'pota/ *n. f.* hood.

capricho /ka'pritʃo/ *n. m.* caprice; fancy, whim.

caprichoso /kapri'tʃoso/ *a.* capricious.

cápsula /'kapsula/ *n. f.* capsule.

capturar /kaptu'rar/ *v.* capture.

capucha /ka'putʃa/ *n. f.* hood.

capullo /ka'puʎo; ka'puyo/ *n. m.* cocoon.

cara /'kara/ *n. f.* face.

caracol /kara'kol/ *n. m.* snail.

carácter /ka'rakter/ *n. m.* character.

característica /karakte'ristika/ *n. f.* characteristic.

característico /karakte'ristiko/ *a.* characteristic.

caramba /ka'ramba/ mild exclamation.

caramelo /kara'melo/ *n. m.* caramel; candy.

carátula /ka'ratula/ *n. f.* dial.

caravana /kara'βana/ *n. f.* caravan.

carbón /kar'βon/ *n. m.* carbon; coal.

carbonizar /karβoni'θar; karβoni'sar/ *v.* char.

carburador /karβura'ðor/ *n. m.* carburetor.

carcajada /karka'haða/ *n. f.* burst of laughter.

cárcel /'karθel; 'karsel/ *n. f.* prison, jail.

carcelero /karθe'lero; karse'lero/ *n. m.* jailer.

carcinogénico /karθino'heniko; karsino'heniko/ *a.* carcinogenic.

cardenal /karðe'nal/ *n. m.* cardinal.

cardiólogo /kar'ðiologo/ **-a** *m & f.* cardiologist.

carecer /kare'θer; kare'ser/ *v.* lack.

carestía /kares'tia/ *n. f.* scarcity; famine.

carga /'karga/ *n. f.* cargo; load, burden; freight.

cargar /kar'gar/ *v.* carry; load; charge.

cargo /'kargo/ *n. m.* load; charge, office.

caricatura /karika'tura/ *n. f.* caricature; cartoon.

caricaturista /karikatu'rista/ *n. m. & f.* caricaturist; cartoonist.

caricia /ka'riθia; ka'risia/ *n. f.* caress.

caridad /kari'ðað/ *n. f.* charity.

cariño /ka'riɲo/ *n. m.* affection, fondness.

cariñoso /kari'ɲoso/ *a.* affectionate, fond.

carisma /ka'risma/ *n. m.* charisma.

caritativo /karita'tiβo/ *a.* charitable.

carmesí /karme'si/ *a. & m.* crimson.

carnaval /karna'βal/ *n. m.* carnival.

carne /'karne/ *n. f.* meat, flesh; pulp.

carne acecinada /'karne aθe-θi'naða; 'karne asesi'naða/ *n. f.* corned beef.

carnero /kar'nero/ *n. m.* ram; mutton.

carnicería /karniθe'ria; karnise'ria/ *n. f.* meat market; massacre.

carnicero /karni'θero; karni'sero/ **-ra** *n.* butcher.

carnívoro /kar'niβoro/ *a.* carnivorous.

caro /'karo/ *a.* dear, costly, expensive.

carpa /'karpa/ *n. f.* tent.

carpeta /kar'peta/ *n. f.* folder; briefcase.

carpintero /karpin'tero/ *n. m.* carpenter.

carrera /ka'rrera/ *n. f.* race; career.

carrera de caballos /ka'rrera de ka'βaʎos; ka'rrera de ka'βayos/ horse race.

carreta /ka'rreta/ *n. f.* wagon, cart.

carrete /ka'rrete/ *n. m.* reel, spool.

carretera /karre'tera/ *n. f.* road, highway.

carril /ka'rril/ *n. m.* rail.

carrillo /ka'rriʎo; ka'rriyo/ *n. m.* cart (for baggage or shopping).

carro /'karro/ *n. m.* car, automobile; cart.

carroza /ka'rroθa; ka'rrosa/ *n. f.* chariot.

carruaje /ka'rruahe/ *n. m.* carriage.

carta /'karta/ *n. f.* letter; (*pl.*) cards.

cartel /kar'tel/ *n. m.* placard, poster; cartel.

cartelera /karte'lera/ *n. f.* billboard.

cartera /kar'tera/ *n. f.* pocketbook, handbag, wallet; portfolio.

cartero /kar'tero/ **(-ra)** *n.* mail carrier.

cartón /kar'ton/ *n. m.* cardboard.

cartón piedra /kar'ton 'pieðra/ *n. m.* papier-mâché.

cartucho /kar'tutʃo/ *n. m.* cartridge; cassette.

casa /'kasa/ *n. f.* house, dwelling; home.

casaca /ka'saka/ *n. f.* dress coat.

casa de pisos /'kasa de 'pisos/ apartment house.

casado /ka'saðo/ *a.* married.

casamiento /kasa'miento/ *n. m.* marriage.

casar /ka'sar/ *v.* marry, marry off.

casarse /ka'sarse/ *v.* get married. **c. con,** marry.

cascabel /kaska'βel/ *n. m.* jingle bell.

cascada /kas'kaða/ *n. f.* waterfall, cascade.

cascajo /kas'kaho/ *n. m.* gravel.

cascanueces /kaska'nueθes; kaska'nueses/ *n. m.* nutcracker.

cascar /kas'kar/ *v.* crack, break, burst.

cáscara /'kaskara/ *n. f.* shell, rind, husk.

casco /'kasko/ *n. m.* helmet; hull.

casera /ka'sera/ *n. f.* landlady; housekeeper.

caserío /kase'rio/ *n. m.* settlement.

casero /ka'sero/ *a.* **1.** homemade. —*n.* **2.** *m.* landlord, superintendent.

caseta /ka'seta/ *n. f.* cottage, hut.

casi /'kasi/ *adv.* almost, nearly.

casilla /ka'siʎa; ka'siya/ *n. f.* booth; ticket office; pigeonhole.

casimir /kasi'mir/ *n. m.* cashmere.

casino /ka'sino/ *n. m.* club; clubhouse.

caso /'kaso/ *n. m.* case. **hacer c. a,** pay attention to.

casorio /ka'sorio/ *n. m.* informal wedding.

caspa /'kaspa/ *n. f.* dandruff.

casta /'kasta/ *n. f.* caste.

castaña /kas'taɲa/ *n. f.* chestnut.

castaño /kas'taɲo/ *a.* **1.** brown. —*n.* **2.** *m.* chestnut tree.

castañuela /kasta'ɲuela/ *n. f.* castanet.

castellano /kaste'ʎano; kaste-'yano/ **-na** *a. & n.* Castilian.

castidad /kasti'ðað/ *n. f.* chastity.

castigar /kasti'gar/ *v.* punish, castigate.

castigo /kas'tigo/ *n. m.* punishment.

castillo /kas'tiʎo; kas'tiyo/ *n. m.* castle.

castizo /kas'tiθo; kas'tiso/ *a.* pure, genuine; noble.

casto /'kasto/ *a.* chaste.

castor /kas'tor/ *n. m.* beaver.

casual /ka'sual/ *adj.* accidental, coincidental.

casualidad /kasuali'ðað/ *n. f.* coincidence. **por c.,** by chance.

casuca /ka'suka/ *n. f.* hut, shanty, hovel.

cataclismo /kata'klismo/ *n. m.* cataclysm.

catacumba /kata'kumba/ *n. f.* catacomb.

catadura /kata'ðura/ *n. f.* act of tasting; appearance.

catalán /kata'lan/ **-na** *a. & n.* Catalonian.

catálogo /ka'talogo/ *n. m.* catalogue. —**catalogar,** *v.*

catapulta /kata'putta/ *n. f.* catapult.

catar /ka'tar/ *v.* taste; examine, try; bear in mind.

catarata /kata'rata/ *n. f.* cataract, waterfall.

catarro /ka'tarro/ *n. m.* head cold, catarrh.

catástrofe /ka'tastrofe/ *n. f.* catastrophe.

catecismo /kate'θismo; kate-'sismo/ *n. m.* catechism.

cátedra /'kateðra/ *n. f.* professorship.

catedral /kate'ðral/ *n. f.* cathedral.

catedrático /kate'ðratiko/ **-ca** *n.* professor.

categoría /katego'ria/ *n. f.* category.

categórico /kate'goriko/ *a.* categorical.

catequismo /kate'kismo/ *n. m.* catechism.

catequizar /kateki'θar; kateki'sar/ *v.* catechize.

cátodo /'katoðo/ *n. m.* cathode.

catolicismo /katoli'θismo; katoli'sismo/ *n. m.* Catholicism.

católico /ka'toliko/ **-ca** *a. & n.* Catholic.

catorce /ka'torθe; ka'torse/ *a. & pron.* fourteen.

catre /'katre/ *n. m.* cot.

cauce /'kauθe; 'kause/ *n. m.* river-bed; ditch.

cauchal /kau'tʃal/ *n. m.* rubber plantation.

caucho /'kautʃo/ *n. m.* rubber.

caución /kau'θion; kau'sion/ *n. f.* precaution; security, guarantee.

caudal /kau'ðal/ *n. m.* means, fortune; (*pl.*) holdings.

caudaloso /kauða'loso/ *a.* prosperous, rich.

caudillaje /kauði'ʎahe; kauði-'yahe/ *n. m.* leadership; tyranny.

caudillo /kau'ðiʎo; kau'ðiyo/ *n. m.* leader, chief.

causa /'kausa/ *n. f.* cause.
—causar, *v.*

cautela /kau'tela/ *n. f.* caution.

cauteloso /kaute'loso/ *n. m.* cautious.

cautivar /kauti'βar/ *v.* captivate.

cautiverio /kauti'βerio/ *n. m.* captivity.

cautividad /kautiβi'ðað/ *n. f.* captivity.

cautivo /kau'tiβo/ **-va** *a. & n.* captive.

cauto /'kauto/ *a.* cautious.

cavar /ka'βar/ *v.* dig.

caverna /ka'βerna/ *n. f.* cavern, cave.

cavernoso /kaβer'noso/ *a.* cavernous.

cavidad /kaβi'ðað/ *n. f.* cavity, hollow.

cavilar /kaβi'lar/ *v.* criticize, cavil.

cayado /ka'yaðo/ *n. m.* shepherd's staff.

cayo /'kayo/ *n. m.* small rocky islet, key.

caza /'kaθa; 'kasa/ *n. f.* hunting, pursuit, game.

cazador /kaθa'ðor; kasa'ðor/ *n. m.* hunter.

cazar /ka'θar; ka'sar/ *v.* hunt.

cazatorpedero /kaθatorpe'ðero;

kasatorpe'ðero/ *n. m.* torpedo-boat, destroyer.

cazo /'kaθo; 'kaso/ *n. m.* ladle, dipper; pot.

cazuela /ka'θuela; ka'suela/ *n. f.* crock.

cebada /θe'βaða; se'βaða/ *n. f.* barley.

cebiche /θe'bitʃe/ *n. m.* dish of marinated raw fish.

cebo /'θeβo; 'seβo/ *n. m.* bait.
—cebar, *v.*

cebolla /θe'βoʎa; se'βoya/ *n. f.* onion.

cebolleta /θeβo'ʎeta; seβo'yeta/ *n. f.* spring onion.

ceceo /θe'θeo; se'seo/ *n. m.* lisp.
—cecear, *v.*

cecina /θe'θina; se'sina/ *n. f.* dried beef.

cedazo /θe'ðaθo; se'ðaso/ *n. m.* sieve, sifter.

ceder /θe'ðer; se'ðer/ *v.* cede; transfer; yield.

cedro /'θeðro; 'seðro/ *n. m.* cedar.

cédula /'θeðula; 'seðula/ *n. f.* decree. **c. personal,** identification card.

céfiro /'θefiro; 'sefiro/ *n. m.* zephyr.

cegar /θe'gar; se'gar/ *v.* blind.

ceguedad /θege'ðað, θe'gera; sege'ðað, se'gera/ **ceguera** *n. f.* blindness.

ceja /'θeha; 'seha/ *n. f.* eyebrow.

cejar /θe'har; se'har/ *v.* go backwards; yield, retreat.

celada /θe'laða; se'laða/ *n. f.* trap; ambush.

celaje /θe'lahe; se'lahe/ *n. m.* appearance of the sky.

celar /θe'lar; se'lar/ *v.* watch carefully, guard.

celda /'θelda; 'selda/ *n. f.* cell.

celebración /θeleβra'θion; seleβra'sion/ *n. f.* celebration.

celebrante /θele'βrante; sele'βrante/ *n. m.* officiating priest.

celebrar /θele'βrar; sele'βrar/ *v.* celebrate, observe.

célebre /'θeleβre; 'seleβre/ *a.* celebrated, noted, famous.

celebridad /θeleβri'ðað; seleβri-'ðað/ *n. f.* fame; celebrity; pageant.

celeridad /θeleri'ðað; seleri'ðað/ *n. f.* speed, rapidity.

celeste /θe'leste; se'leste/ *a.* celestial.

celestial /θeles'tial; seles'tial/ *a.* heavenly.

celibato /θeli'βato; seli'βato/ *n. m.* celibacy.

célibe /'θeliβe; 'seliβe/ *a.* **1.** unmarried. —*n.* **2.** *m. & f.* unmarried person.

celista /θe'lista; se'lista/ *n. m. & f.* cellist.

cellisca /θe'ʎiska; se'yiska/ *n. f.* sleet. —**cellisquear,** *v.*

celo /'θelo; 'selo/ *n. m.* zeal; (*pl.*) jealousy.

celofán /θelo'fan; selo'fan/ *n. m.* cellophane.

celosía /θelo'sia; selo'sia/ *n. f.* Venetian blind.

celoso /θe'loso; se'loso/ *a.* jealous; zealous.

céltico /'θeltiko; 'seltiko/ *a.* Celtic.

célula /'θelula; 'selula/ *n. f. Biol.* cell.

celuloide /θelu'loiðe; selu'loiðe/ *n. m.* celluloid.

cementar /θemen'tar; semen'tar/ *v.* cement.

cementerio /θemen'terio; semen'terio/ *n. m.* cemetery.

cemento /θe'mento; se'mento/ *n. m.* cement.

cena /'θena; 'sena/ *n. f.* supper.

cenagal /θena'gal; sena'gal/ *n. m.* swamp, marsh.

cenagoso /θena'goso; sena'goso/ *a.* swampy, marshy, muddy.

cenar /θe'nar; se'nar/ *v.* dine, eat.

cencerro /θen'θerro; sen'serro/ *n. m.* cowbell.

cendal /θen'dal; sen'dal/ *n. m.* thin, light cloth; gauze.

cenicero /θeni'θero; seni'sero/ *n. m.* ashtray.

ceniciento /θeni'θiento; seni-'siento/ *a.* ashen.

cenit /'θenit; 'senit/ *n. m.* zenith.

ceniza /θe'niθa; se'nisa/ *n. f.* ash, ashes.

censo /'θenso; 'senso/ *n. m.* census.

censor /θen'sor; sen'sor/ *n. m.* censor.

censura /θen'sura; sen'sura/ *n. f.* reproof, censure; censorship.

censurable /θensu'raβle; sensu'raβle/ *a.* objectionable.

censurar /θensu'rar; sensu'rar/ *v.* censure, criticize.

centavo /θen'taβo; sen'taβo/ *n. m.* cent.

centella /θen'teʎa; sen'teya/ *n. f.* thunderbolt, lightning.

centellear /θenteʎe'ar; senteye'ar/ *v.* twinkle, sparkle.

centelleo /θente'ʎeo; sente'yeo/ *n. m.* sparkle.

centenar /θente'nar; sente'nar/ *n. m.* (a) hundred.

centenario /θente'nario; sente-'nario/ *n. m.* centennial, centenary.

centeno /θen'teno; sen'teno/ *m.* rye.

centígrado /θen'tigraðo; sen'tigraðo/ *a.* centigrade.

centímetro /θenti'metro; senti'metro/ *n. m.* centimeter.

céntimo /'θentimo; 'sentimo/ *n. m.* cent.

centinela /θenti'nela; senti'nela/ *n. m.* sentry, guard.

central /θen'tral; sen'tral/ *a.* central.

centralita /θentra'lita; sentra'lita/ *n. f.* switchboard.

centralizar /θentrali'θar; sentrali'sar/ *v.* centralize.

centrar /θen'trar; sen'trar/ *v.* center.

céntrico /'θentriko; 'sentriko/ *a.* central.

centro /'θentro; 'sentro/ *n. m.* center.

centroamericano /θentroameri'kano; sentroameri'kano/ -**na** *a. & n.* Central American.

centro de mesa /'θentro de 'mesa; 'sentro de 'mesa/ centerpiece.

ceñidor /θeɲi'ðor; seɲi'ðor/ *n. m.* belt, sash; girdle.

ceñir /θe'ɲir; se'ɲir/ *v.* gird.

ceño /'θeɲo; 'seɲo/ *n. m.* frown.

ceñudo /θe'ɲuðo; se'ɲuðo/ *a.* frowning, grim.

cepa /'θepa; 'sepa/ *n. f.* stump.

cepillo /θe'piʎo; se'piyo/ *n. m.* brush; plane. —**cepillar,** *v.*

cera /'θera; 'sera/ *n. f.* wax.

cerámica /θe'ramika; se'ramika/ *n. m.* ceramics.

cerámico /θe'ramiko; se'ramiko/ *a.* ceramic.

cerca /'θerka; 'serka/ *adv.* **1.** near. —*n.* **2.** *f.* fence, hedge.

cercado /θer'kaðo; ser'kaðo/ *n. m.* enclosure; garden.

cercamiento /θerka'miento; serka'miento/ *n. m.* enclosure.

cercanía /θerka'nia; serka'nia/ *n. f.* proximity.

cercano /θer'kano; ser'kano/ *a.* near, nearby.

cercar /θer'kar; ser'kar/ *v.* surround.

cercenar /θerθe'nar; serse'nar/ *v.* clip; lessen, reduce.

cerciorar /θerθio'rar; sersio'rar/ *v.* make sure; affirm.

cerco /'θerko; 'serko/ *n. m.* hoop; siege.

cerda /'θerða; 'serða/ *n. f.* bristle.

cerdo /'θerðo; 'serðo/ **-da** *n.* hog.

cerdoso /θer'ðoso; ser'ðoso/ *a.* bristly.

cereal /θere'al; sere'al/ *a. & m.* cereal.

cerebro /θe're βro; se're βro/ *n. m.* brain.

ceremonia /θere'monia; sere'monia/ *n. f.* ceremony.

ceremonial /θeremo'nial; seremo'nial/ *a. & m.* ceremonial, ritual.

ceremonioso /θeremo'nioso; seremo'nioso/ *a.* ceremonious.

cereza /θe're θa; se'resa/ *n. f.* cherry.

cerilla /θe'riʎa; se'riya/ *n. f.*, **cerillo,** *m.* match.

cerner /θer'ner; ser'ner/ *v.* sift.

cero /'θero; 'sero/ *n. m.* zero.

cerrado /θe'rraðo; se'rraðo/ *a.* closed; cloudy; obscure; taciturn.

cerradura /θerra'ðura; serra'ðura/ *n. f.* lock.

cerrajero /θerra'hero; serra'hero/ *n. m.* locksmith.

cerrar /θe'rrar; se'rrar/ *v.* close, shut.

cerro /'θerro; 'serro/ *n. m.* hill.

cerrojo /θe'rroho; se'rroho/ *n. m.* latch, bolt.

certamen /θer'tamen; ser'tamen/ *n. m.* contest; competition.

certero /θer'tero; ser'tero/ *a.* accurate, exact; certain, sure.

certeza /θer'teθa; ser'tesa/ *n. f.* certainty.

certidumbre /θerti'ðumbre; serti'ðumbre/ *n. f.* certainty.

certificado /θertifi'kaðo; sertifi'kaðo/ *n. m.* certificate.

certificado de compra /θertifi'kaðo de 'kompra; sertifi'kaðo de 'kompra/ proof of purchase.

certificar /θertifi'kar; sertifi'kar/ *v.* certify; register (a letter).

cerúleo /θe'ruleo; se'ruleo/ *a.* cerulean, sky-blue.

cervecería /θerβeθe'ria; serβese'ria/ *n. f.* brewery; beer saloon.

cervecero /θerβe'θero; serβe'sero/ *n. m.* brewer.

cerveza /θer'βeθa; ser'βesa/ *n. f.* beer.

cesante /θe'sante; se'sante/ *a.* unemployed.

cesar /θe'sar; se'sar/ *v.* cease.

césped /'θespeð; 'sespeð/ *n. m.* sod, lawn.

cesta /'θesta; 'sesta/ *n. f.*, **cesto,** *m.* basket.

cetrino /θe'trino; se'trino/ *a.* yellow, lemon-colored.

cetro /'θetro; 'setro/ *n. m.* scepter.

chabacano /tʃaβa'kano/ *a.* vulgar.

chacal /tʃa'kal/ *n. m.* jackal.

chacó /'tʃako/ *n. m.* shako.

chacona /tʃa'kona/ *n. f.* chaconne.

chacota /tʃa'kota/ *n. f.* fun, mirth.

chacotear /tʃakote'ar/ *v.* joke.

chacra /'tʃakra/ *n. f.* small farm.

chafallar /tʃafa'ʎar; tʃafa'yar/ *v.* mend badly.

chagra /'tʃagra/ *n.* rustic; rural person.

chal /tʃal/ *n. m.* shawl.

chalán /tʃa'lan/ *n. m.* horse trader.

chaleco /tʃa'leko/ *n. m.* vest.

chaleco salvavidas /tʃa'leko salβa'βiðas/ life jacket.

chalet /tʃa'le; tʃa'let/ *n. m.* chalet.

challí /tʃa'ʎi; tʃa'yi/ *n. m.* challis.

chamada /tʃa'maða/ *n. f.* brushwood.

chamarillero /tʃamari'ʎero; tʃamari'yero/ *n. m.* gambler.

chamarra /tʃa'marra/ *n. f.* coarse linen jacket.

chambelán /tʃambe'lan/ *n. m.* chamberlain.

champaña /tʃam'paɲa/ *n. m.* champagne.

champú /tʃam'pu/ *n. m.* shampoo.

chamuscar /tʃamus'kar/ *v.* scorch.

chancaco /tʃan'kako/ *a.* brown.

chance /'tʃanθe/ *n. m. & f.* opportunity, break.

chancear /tʃanθe'ar; tʃanse'ar/ *v.* jest, joke.

chanciller /tʃanθi'ʎer; tʃansi'yer/ *n. m.* chancellor.

chancillería /tʃanθiʎe'ria; tʃansi-ye'ria/ *n. f.* chancery.

chancla /'tʃankla/ *n. f.* old shoe.

chancleta /tʃan'kleta/ *n. f.* slipper.

chanclos /'tʃanklos/ *n. m.pl.* galoshes.

chancro /'tʃankro/ *n. m.* chancre.

changador /tʃaŋga'ðor/ *n. m.* porter; handyman.

chantaje /tʃan'tahe/ *n. m.* blackmail.

chantajista /tʃanta'hista/ *n. m. & f.* blackmailer.

chantejear /tʃantehe'ar/ *v.* blackmail.

chanto /'tʃanto/ *n. m.* flagstone.

chantre /'tʃantre/ *n. m.* precentor.

chanza /'tʃanθa; 'tʃansa/ *n. f.* joke, jest. —**chancear,** *v.*

chanzoneta /tʃanθo'neta; tʃanso'neta/ *n. f.* chansonette.

chapa /'tʃapa/ *n. f.* (metal) sheet, plate; lock.

chapado en oro /tʃa'paðo en 'oro/ *a.* gold-plated.

chapado en plata /tʃa'paðo en 'plata/ *a.* silver-plated.

chaparrada /tʃapa'rraða/ *n. f.* downpour.

chaparral /tʃapa'rral/ *n. m.* chaparral.

chaparreras /tʃapa'rreras/ *n. f.pl.* chaps.

chaparrón /tʃapa'rron/ *n. m.* downpour.

chapear /tʃape'ar/ *v.* veneer.

chapeo /tʃa'peo/ *n. m.* hat.

chapero /tʃa'pero/ *n. m. Colloq.* male homosexual prostitute.

chapitel /tʃapi'tel/ *n. m.* spire, steeple; (architecture) capital.

chapodar /tʃapo'ðar/ *v.* lop.

chapón /tʃa'pon/ *n. m.* inkblot.

chapotear /tʃapote'ar/ *v.* paddle or splash in the water.

chapoteo /tʃapo'teo/ *n. m.* splash.

chapucear /tʃapuθe'ar; tʃapuse'ar/ *v.* fumble, bungle.

chapucero /tʃapu'θero; tʃapu'sero/ *a.* sloppy, bungling.

chapurrear /tʃapurre'ar/ *v.* speak (a language) brokenly.

chapuz /tʃa'puθ; tʃa'pus/ *n. m.* dive; ducking.

chapuzar /tʃapu'θar; tʃapu'sar/ *v.* dive; duck.

chaqueta /tʃa'keta/ *n. f.* jacket, coat.

chaqueta deportiva /tʃa'keta depor'tiβa/ *n. f.* sport jacket.

charada /tʃa'raða/ *n. f.* charade.

charamusca /tʃara'muska/ *n. f.* twisted candy stick.

charanga /tʃa'raŋga/ *n. f.* military band.

charanguero /tʃaraŋ'guero/ *n. m.* peddler.

charca /'tʃarka/ *n. f.* pool, pond.

charco /'tʃarko/ *n. m.* pool, puddle.

charla /'tʃarla/ *n. f.* chat; chatter, prattle. —**charlar,** *v.*

charladuría /tʃarlaðu'ria/ *n. f.* chatter.

charlatán /tʃarla'tan/ **-ana** *n.* charlatan.

charlatanismo /tʃarlata'nismo/ *n. m.* charlatanism.

charol /tʃa'rol/ *n. m.* varnish.

charolar /tʃaro'lar/ *v.* varnish; polish.

charquear /tʃarke'ar/ *v.* jerk (beef).

charquí /tʃar'ki/ *n. m.* jerked beef.

charrán /tʃa'rran/ *a.* roguish.

chascarillo /tʃaska'riʎo; tʃaska'riyo/ *n. m.* risqué story.

chasco /'tʃasko/ *n. m.* disappointment, blow; practical joke.

chasis /'tʃasis/ *n. m.* chassis.

chasquear /tʃaske'ar/ *v.* fool, trick; disappoint; crack (a whip).

chasquido /tʃas'kiðo/ *n. m.* crack (sound).

chata /'tʃata/ *n. f.* bedpan.

chatear /tʃate'ar/ *v.* chat (on the Internet).

chato /'tʃato/ *a.* flat-nosed, pugnosed.

chauvinismo /tʃauβi'nismo/ *n. m.* chauvinism.

chauvinista /tʃauβi'nista/ *n. & a.* chauvinist.

chelín /tʃe'lin/ *n. m.* shilling.

cheque /'tʃeke/ *n. m.* (bank) check.

chica /'tʃika/ *n. f.* girl.

chicana /tʃi'kana/ *n. f.* chicanery.

chicha /'tʃitʃa/ *n. f.* an alcoholic drink.

chícharo /'tʃitʃaro/ *n. f.* pea.

chicharra /tʃi'tʃarra/ *n. f.* cicada; talkative person.

chicharrón /tʃitʃa'rron/ *n. m.* crisp fried scrap of meat.

chichear /tʃitʃe'ar/ v. hiss in disapproval.

chichón /tʃi'tʃon/ n. m. bump, bruise, lump.

chicle /'tʃikle/ n. m. chewing gum.

chico /'tʃiko/ a. 1. little. —n. 2. m. boy.

chicote /tʃi'kote/ n. m. cigar; cigar butt.

chicotear /tʃikote'ar/ v. whip, flog.

chifladura /tʃifla'ðura/ n. f. mania; whim; jest.

chiflar /tʃi'flar/ v. whistle; become insane.

chiflido /tʃi'fliðo/ n. m. shrill whistle.

chile /'tʃile/ n. m. chili.

chileno /tʃi'leno/ **-na** a. & n. Chilean.

chillido /tʃi'ʎiðo; tʃi'yiðo/ n. m. shriek, scream, screech. —**chillar,** v.

chillón /tʃi'ʎon; tʃi'yon/ a. shrill.

chimenea /tʃime'nea/ n. f. chimney, smokestack; fireplace.

china /'tʃina/ n. f. pebble; maid; Chinese woman.

chinarro /tʃi'narro/ n. m. large pebble, stone.

chinche /'tʃintʃe/ n. f. bedbug; thumbtack.

chincheta /tʃin'tʃeta/ n. f. thumbtack.

chinchilla /tʃin'tʃiʎa; tʃin'tʃiya/ n. f. chinchilla.

chinchorro /tʃin'tʃorro/ n. m. fishing net.

chinela /tʃi'nela/ n. f. slipper.

chinero /tʃi'nero/ n. m. china closet.

chino /'tʃino/ **-na** a. & n. Chinese.

chipirón /tʃipi'ron/ n. m. baby squid.

chiquero /tʃi'kero/ n. m. pen for pigs, goats, etc.

chiquito /tʃi'kito/ **-ta** a. 1. small, tiny. —n. 2. m. & f. small child.

chiribitil /tʃiriβi'til/ n. m. small room, den.

chirimía /tʃiri'mia/ n. f. flageolet.

chiripa /tʃi'ripa/ n. f. stroke of good luck.

chirla /'tʃirla/ n. f. mussel.

chirle /'tʃirle/ a. insipid.

chirona /tʃi'rona/ n. f. prison, jail.

chirrido /tʃi'rriðo/ n. m. squeak, chirp. —**chirriar,** v.

chis /tʃis/ interj. hush!

chisgarabís /tʃisgara'βis/ n. meddler; unimportant person.

chisguete /tʃis'gete/ n. m. squirt, splash.

chisme /'tʃisme/ n. m. gossip. —**chismear,** v.

chismero /tʃis'mero/ **-ra** n. gossiper.

chismoso /tʃis'moso/ adj. gossiping.

chispa /'tʃispa/ n. f. spark.

chispeante /tʃispe'ante/ a. sparkling.

chispear /tʃispe'ar/ v. sparkle.

chisporrotear /tʃisporrote'ar/ v. emit sparks.

chistar /tʃis'tar/ v. speak.

chiste /'tʃiste/ n. m. joke, gag; witty saying.

chistera /tʃis'tera/ n. f. fish basket; top hat.

chistoso /tʃis'toso/ a. funny, comic, amusing.

chito /'tʃito/ interj. hush!

chiva /'tʃiβa/ n. f. female goat.

chivato /tʃi'βato/ n. m. kid, young goat.

chivo /'tʃiβo/ n. m. male goat.

chocante /tʃo'kante/ a. striking; shocking; unpleasant.

chocar /tʃo'kar/ v. collide, clash, crash; shock.

chocarrear /tʃokarre'ar/ v. joke, jest.

chochear /tʃotʃe'ar/ v. be in one's dotage.

chochera /tʃo'tʃera/ n. f. dotage, senility.

choclo /'tʃoklo/ n. m. clog; overshoe; ear of corn.

chocolate /tʃoko'late/ n. m. chocolate.

chocolate con leche /tʃoko'late kon 'letʃe/ milk chocolate.

chocolatería /tʃokolate'ria/ n. f. chocolate shop.

chofer /'tʃofer/ **chófer** n. m. chauffeur, driver.

chofeta /tʃo'feta/ n. f. chafing dish.

cholo /'tʃolo/ n. m. half-breed.

chopo /'tʃopo/ n. m. black poplar.

choque /'tʃoke/ n. m. collision, clash, crash; shock.

chorizo /tʃo'riθo; tʃo'riso/ n. m. sausage.

chorrear /tʃorre'ar/ v. spout; drip.

chorro /'tʃorro/ n. m. spout; spurt, jet. **llover a chorros,** to pour (rain).

choto /'tʃoto/ *n. m.* calf, kid.

choza /'tʃoθa; 'tʃosa/ *n. f.* hut, cabin.

chozno /'tʃoθno; 'tʃosno/ **-na** *n.* great-great-great-grandchild.

chubasco /tʃu'βasko/ *n. m.* shower, squall.

chubascoso /tʃuβas'koso/ *a.* squally.

chuchería /tʃutʃe'ria/ *n. f.* trinket, knickknack.

chucho /'tʃutʃo/ *n. m. Colloq.* mutt.

chulería /tʃule'ria/ *n. f.* pleasant manner.

chuleta /tʃu'leta/ *n. f.* chop, cutlet.

chulo /'tʃulo/ *n. m.* rascal, rogue; joker.

chupa /'tʃupa/ *n. f.* jacket.

chupada /tʃu'paða/ *n. f.* suck, sip.

chupado /tʃu'paðo/ *a.* very thin.

chupaflor /tʃupa'flor/ *n. m.* hummingbird.

chupar /tʃu'par/ *v.* suck.

churrasco /tʃu'rrasko/ *n. m.* roasted meat.

churros /'tʃuros/ *n. m.pl.* long, slender fritters.

chuscada /tʃus'kaða/ *n. f.* joke, jest.

chusco /'tʃusko/ *a.* funny, humorous.

chusma /'tʃusma/ *n. f.* mob, rabble.

chuzo /'tʃuθo; 'tʃuso/ *n. m.* pike.

CI, *abbr.* **(coeficiente intelectual)** IQ (intelligence quotient).

ciberespacio /θiβeres'paθio/ *n. m.* cyberspace.

cibernauta /θiβer'nauta/ *n. m. & f.* cybernaut.

cicatero /θika'tero; sika'tero/ *a.* stingy.

cicatriz /θika'triθ; sika'tris/ *n. f.* scar.

cicatrizar /θikatri'θar; sikatri'sar/ *v.* heal.

ciclamato /θi'klamato; si'klamato/ *n. m.* cyclamate.

ciclista /θi'klista; si'klista/ *m & f.* cyclist.

ciclo /'θiklo; 'siklo/ *n. m.* cycle.

ciclón /θi'klon; si'klon/ *n. m.* cyclone.

ciego /'θiego; 'siego/ **-ga** *n.* **1.** blind. —*n.* **2.** blind person.

cielo /'θielo; 'sielo/ *n. m.* heaven; sky, heavens; ceiling.

ciempiés /θiem'pies; siem'pies/ *n. m.* centipede.

cien /θien; sien/ **ciento** *a. & pron.* hundred. **por c.,** per cent.

ciénaga /'θienaga; 'sienaga/ *n. f.* swamp, marsh.

ciencia /'θienθia; 'siensia/ *n. f.* science.

cieno /'θieno; 'sieno/ *n. m.* mud.

científico /θien'tifiko; sien'tifiko/ **-ca** *a.* **1.** scientific. —*n.* **2.** scientist.

cierre /'θierre; 'sierre/ *n. m.* fastener, snap, clasp.

cierto /'θierto; 'sierto/ *a.* certain, sure, true.

ciervo /'θierβo; 'sierβo/ *n. m.* deer.

cierzo /'θierθo; 'sierso/ *n. m.* northerly wind.

cifra /'θifra; 'sifra/ *n. f.* cipher, number. —**cifrar,** *v.*

cigarra /θi'garra; si'garra/ *n. f.* locust.

cigarrera /θiga'rrera; siga'rrera/ **cigarrillera** *f.* cigarette case.

cigarrillo /θiga'rriʎo; siga'rriyo/ *n. m.* cigarette.

cigarro /θi'garro; si'garro/ *n. m.* cigar; cigarette.

cigüeña /θi'gueɲa; si'gueɲa/ *n. f.* stork.

cilíndrico /θi'lindriko; si'lindriko/ *a.* cylindrical.

cilindro /θi'lindro; si'lindro/ *n. m.* cylinder.

cima /'θima; 'sima/ *n. f.* summit, peak.

cimarrón /θima'rron; sima'rron/ *a.* **1.** wild, untamed. —*n.* **2.** *m.* runaway slave.

címbalo /'θimbalo; 'simbalo/ *n. m.* cymbal.

cimbrar /θim'βrar, θimbre'ar; sim'βrar, simbre'ar/ *v.* shake, brandish.

cimientos /θi'mientos; si'mientos/ *n. m.pl.* foundation.

cinc /θink; sink/ *n. m.* zinc.

cincel /θin'θel; sin'sel/ *n. m.* chisel. —**cincelar,** *v.*

cincha /'θintʃa; 'sintʃa/ *n. f.* (harness) cinch. —**cinchar,** *v.*

cinco /'θinko; 'sinko/ *a. & pron.* five.

cincuenta /θin'kuenta; sin'kuenta/ *a. & pron.* fifty.

cine /'θine; 'sine/ *n. m.* movies; movie theater.

cíngulo /'θiŋgulo; 'siŋgulo/ *n. m.* cingulum.

cínico /'θiniko; 'siniko/ -ca *a.* & *n.* cynical; cynic.

cinismo /θi'nismo; si'nismo/ *n. m.* cynicism.

cinta /'θinta; 'sinta/ *n. f.* ribbon, tape; (movie) film.

cintilar /θinti'lar; sinti'lar/ *v.* glitter, sparkle.

cinto /'θinto; 'sinto/ *n. m.* belt; girdle.

cintura /θin'tura; sin'tura/ *n. f.* waist.

cinturón /θintu'ron; sintu'ron/ *n. m.* belt.

cinturón de seguridad /θintu'ron de seguri'ðað; sintu'ron de seguri'ðað/ safety belt.

ciprés /θi'pres; si'pres/ *n. m.* cypress.

circo /'θirko; 'sirko/ *n. m.* circus.

circuito /θir'kuito; sir'kuito/ *n. m.* circuit.

circulación /θirkula'θion; sirkula-'sion/ *n. f.* circulation.

circular /θirku'lar; sirku'lar/ *a.* & *m.* **1.** circular. —*v.* **2.** circulate.

círculo /'θirkulo; 'sirkulo/ *n. m.* circle, club.

circundante /θirkun'dante; sirkun'dante/ *a.* surrounding.

circundar /θirkun'dar; sirkun'dar/ *v.* encircle, surround.

circunferencia /θirkunfe'renθia; sirkunfe'rensia/ *n. f.* circumference.

circunlocución /θirkunloku'θion; sirkunloku'sion/ *n.* circumlocution.

circunscribir /θirkunskri'βir; sirkunskri'βir/ *v.* circumscribe.

circunspección /θirkunspek'θion; sirkunspek'sion/ *n.* decorum, propriety.

circunspecto /θirkuns'pekto; sirkuns'pekto/ *a.* circumspect.

circunstancia /θirkuns'tanθia; sirkuns'tansia/ *n. f.* circumstance.

circunstante /θirkuns'tante; sirkuns'tante/ *n. m.* bystander.

circunvecino /θirkumbe'θino; sirkumbe'sino/ *a.* neighboring, adjacent.

cirio /'θirio; 'sirio/ *n. m.* candle.

cirrosis /θi'rrosis; si'rrosis/ *n. f.* cirrhosis.

ciruela /θi'ruela; si'ruela/ *n. f.* plum; prune.

cirugía /θiru'hia; siru'hia/ *n. f.* surgery.

cirujano /θiru'hano; siru'hano/ *n. m.* surgeon.

cisne /'θisne; 'sisne/ *n. m.* swan.

cisterna /θis'terna; sis'terna/ *n. f.* cistern.

cita /'θita; 'sita/ *n. f.* citation; appointment, date.

citación /θita'θion; sita'sion/ *n. f.* citation; (legal) summons.

citar /θi'tar; si'tar/ *v.* cite, quote; summon; make an appointment with.

cítrico /'θitriko; 'sitriko/ *a.* citric.

ciudad /θiu'ðað; siu'ðað/ *n. f.* city.

ciudadanía /θiuðaða'nia; siuða-ða'nia/ *n. f.* citizenship.

ciudadano /θiuða'ðano; siu-ða'ðano/ -na *n.* citizen.

ciudadela /θiuða'ðela; siuða'ðela/ *n. f.* fortress, citadel.

cívico /'θiβiko; 'siβiko/ *a.* civic.

civil /θi'βil; si'βil/ *a.* & *n.* civil; civilian.

civilidad /θiβili'ðað; siβili'ðað/ *n. f.* politeness, civility.

civilización /θiβiliθa'θion; siβilisa'sion/ *n. f.* civilization.

civilizador /θiβiliθa'ðor; siβilisa-'ðor/ *a.* civilizing.

civilizar /θiβili'θar; siβili'sar/ *v.* civilize.

cizallas /θi'θaʎas; si'sayas/ *n. f.pl.* shears. —**cizallar**, *v.*

cizaña /θi'θaɲa; si'saɲa/ *n. f.* weed; vice.

clamar /kla'mar/ *v.* clamor.

clamor /kla'mor/ *n. m.* clamor.

clamoreo /klamo'reo/ *n. m.* persistent clamor.

clamoroso /klamo'roso/ *a.* clamorous.

clandestino /klandes'tino/ *a.* secret, clandestine.

clara /'klara/ *n. f.* white (of egg).

claraboya /klara'βoya/ *n. m.* skylight; bull's-eye.

clara de huevo /'klara de 'ueβo/ egg white.

clarear /klare'ar/ *v.* clarify; become light, dawn.

clarete /kla'rete/ *n. m.* claret.

claridad /klari'ðað/ *n. f.* clarity.

clarificar /klarifi'kar/ *v.* clarify.

clarín /kla'rin/ *n. m.* bugle, trumpet.

clarinete /klari'nete/ *n. m.* clarinet.

clarividencia /klariβi'ðenθia; klariβi'ðensia/ *n. f.* clairvoyance.

clarividente /klariβi'ðente/ *a.* clairvoyant.

claro /'klaro/ *a.* clear; bright; light (in color); of course.

clase /'klase/ *n. f.* class; classroom; kind, sort.

clase nocturna /'klase nok'turna/ evening class.

clásico /'klasiko/ *a.* classic, classical.

clasificar /klasifi'kar/ *v.* classify, rank.

claustro /'klaustro/ *n. m.* cloister.

claustrofobia /klaustro'foβia/ *n. f.* claustrophobia.

cláusula /'klausula/ *n. f.* clause.

clausura /klau'sura/ *n. f.* cloister; inner sanctum; closing.

clavado /kla'βaðo/ *a.* **1.** nailed. —*n.* **2.** *m.* & *f.* dive.

clavar /kla'βar/ *v.* nail, peg, pin.

clave /'klaβe/ *n. f.* code; *Mus.* key.

clavel /kla'βel/ *n. m.* carnation.

clavetear /klaβete'ar/ *v.* nail.

clavícula /kla'βikula/ *n. f.* collarbone.

clavija /kla'βiha/ *n. f.* pin, peg.

clavo /'klaβo/ *n. m.* nail, spike; clove.

clemencia /kle'menθia; kle'mensia/ *n. f.* clemency.

clemente /kle'mente/ *a.* merciful.

clementina /klemen'tina/ *n. f.* tangerine.

clerecía /klere'θia; klere'sia/ *n. f.* clergy.

clerical /kleri'kal/ *a.* clerical.

clérigo /'klerigo/ *n. m.* clergyman.

clero /'klero/ *n. m.* clergy.

cliente /'kliente/ *n. m.* & *f.* customer, client.

clientela /klien'tela/ *n. f.* clientele, practice.

clima /'klima/ *n. m.* climate.

clímax /'klimaks/ *n. m.* climax.

clínca de reposo /'klinka de rre'poso/ convalescent home.

clínica /'klinika/ *n. f.* clinic.

clínico /'kliniko/ *a.* clinical.

clíper /'kliper/ *n. m.* clipper ship.

cloaca /klo'aka/ *n. f.* sewer.

cloquear /kloke'ar/ *v.* cluck, cackle.

cloqueo /klo'keo/ *n. m.* cluck.

cloro /'kloro/ *n. m.* chlorine.

club /kluβ/ *n. m.* club, association.

club juvenil /kluβ huβe'nil/ youth club.

clueca /'klueka/ *n. f.* brooding hen.

coacción /koak'θion; koak'sion/ *n.* compulsion.

coagular /koagu'lar/ *v.* coagulate, clot.

coágulo /ko'agulo/ *n. m.* clot.

coalición /koali'θion; koali'sion/ *n. f.* coalition.

coartada /koar'taða/ *n. f.* alibi.

coartar /koar'tar/ *v.* limit.

cobarde /ko'βarðe/ *a. & n.* cowardly; coward.

cobardía /koβar'ðia/ *n. f.* cowardice.

cobayo /ko'βayo/ *n. m.* guinea pig.

cobertizo /koβer'tiθo; koβer'tiso/ *n. m.* shed.

cobertor /koβer'tor/ *n. m.*, **cobija**, *f.* blanket.

cobertura /koβer'tura/ *n. f.* cover, wrapping.

cobijar /koβi'har/ *v.* cover; protect.

cobrador /koβra'ðor/ *n. m.* collector.

cobranza /ko'βranθa; ko'βransa/ *n. f.* collection or recovery of money.

cobrar /ko'βrar/ *v.* collect; charge; cash.

cobre /'koβre/ *n. m.* copper.

cobrizo /ko'βriθo; ko'βriso/ *a.* coppery.

cobro /'koβro/ *n. m.* collection or recovery of money.

coca /'koka/ *n. f.* coca leaves.

cocaína /koka'ina/ *n. f.* cocaine.

cocal /ko'kal/ *n. m.* coconut plantation.

cocear /koθe'ar; kose'ar/ *v.* kick; resist.

cocer /ko'θer; ko'ser/ *v.* cook, boil, bake.

coche /'kotʃe/ *n. m.* coach; car, automobile.

cochecito de niño /kotʃe'θito de 'niɲo; kotʃe'sito de 'niɲo/ baby carriage.

coche de choque /'kotʃe de 'tʃoke/ dodgem.

cochera /ko'tʃera/ *n. f.* garage.

cochero /ko'tʃero/ *n. m.* coachman; cab driver.

cochinada /kotʃi'naða/ *n. f.* filth; herd of swine.

cochino /ko'tʃino/ *n. m.* pig, swine.

cocido /ko'θiðo; ko'siðo/ *n. m.* stew.

cociente /ko'θiente; ko'siente/ *n. m.* quotient.

cocimiento /koθi'miento; kosi'miento/ *n. m.* cooking.

cocina /ko'θina; ko'sina/ *n. f.* kitchen.

cocinar /koθi'nar; kosi'nar/ *v.* cook.

cocinero /koθi'nero; kosi'nero/ **-ra** *n.* cook.

coco /'koko/ *n. m.* coconut; coconut tree.

cocodrilo /koko'ðrilo/ *n. m.* crocodile.

cóctel /kok'tel/ *n. m.* cocktail.

codazo /ko'ðaθo; ko'ðaso/ *n. m.* nudge with the elbow.

codicia /ko'ðiθia; ko'ðisia/ *n. f.* avarice, greed; lust.

codiciar /koðiθi'ar; koðisi'ar/ *v.* covet.

codicioso /koðiθi'oso; koðisi'oso/ *a.* covetous; greedy.

código /'koðigo/ *n. m.* (law) code.

codo /'koðo/ *n. m.* elbow.

codorniz /koðor'niθ; koðor'nis/ *n. f.* quail.

coeficiente /koefi'θiente; koefi'siente/ *n. m.* quotient.

coeficiente intelectual /koefi'θiente intelek'tual; koefi'siente intelek'tual/ intelligence quotient.

coetáneo /koe'taneo/ *a.* contemporary.

coexistir /koeksis'tir/ *v.* coexist.

cofrade /ko'fraðe/ *n. m.* fellow member of a club, etc.

cofre /'kofre/ *n. m.* coffer; chest; trunk.

coger /ko'her/ *v.* catch; pick; take.

cogote /ko'gote/ *n. m.* nape.

cohecho /ko'etʃo/ *n. m.* bribe. —**cohechar,** *v.*

coheredero /koere'ðero/ **-ra** *n.* coheir.

coherente /koe'rente/ *a.* coherent.

cohesión /koe'sion/ *n. f.* cohesion.

cohete /ko'ete/ *n. m.* firecracker; rocket.

cohibición /koiβi'θion; koiβi'sion/ *n.* restraint; repression.

cohibir /koi'βir/ *v.* restrain; repress.

coincidencia /koinθi'ðenθia; koinsi'ðensia/ *n. f.* coincidence.

coincidir /koinθi'ðir; koinsi'ðir/ *v.* coincide.

cojear /kohe'ar/ *v.* limp.

cojera /ko'hera/ *n. m.* limp.

cojín /ko'hin/ *n. m.* cushion.

cojinete /kohi'nete/ *n. m.* small cushion, pad.

cojo /'koho/ **-a** *a.* **1.** lame. —*n.* **2.** lame person.

col /kol/ *n. f.* cabbage.

cola /'kola/ *n. f.* tail; glue; line, queue. **hacer c.,** stand in line.

colaboración /kolaβora'θion; kolaβora'sion/ *n. f.* collaboration.

colaborar /kolaβo'rar/ *v.* collaborate.

cola de caballo /'kola de ka'βaʎo; 'kola de ka'βayo/ ponytail.

coladera /kola'ðera/ *n. f.* strainer.

colador /kola'ðor/ *n. m.* colander, strainer.

colapso /ko'lapso/ *n. m.* collapse, prostration.

colar /ko'lar/ *v.* strain; drain.

colateral /kolate'ral/ *a.* collateral.

colcha /'koltʃa/ *n. f.* bedspread, quilt.

colchón /kol'tʃon/ *n. m.* mattress.

colear /kole'ar/ *v.* wag the tail.

colección /kolek'θion; kolek'sion/ *n. f.* collection, set.

coleccionar /kolekθio'nar; koleksio'nar/ *v.* collect.

colecta /ko'lekta/ *n. f.* collection; collect (a prayer).

colectivo /kolek'tiβo/ *a.* collective.

colector /kolek'tor/ *n. m.* collector.

colega /ko'lega/ *n. m. & f.* colleague.

colegial /kole'hial/ *n. m.* college student.

colegiatura /kolehia'tura/ *n. f.* scholarship; tuition.

colegio /ko'lehio/ *n. m.* (private) school, college.

colegir /kole'hir/ *v.* infer, deduce.

cólera /'kolera/ *n.* **1.** *f.* rage, wrath. **2.** *m.* cholera.

colérico /ko'leriko/ *adj.* angry, irritated.

colesterol /koleste'rol/ *n. m.* cholesterol.

coleta /ko'leta/ *n. f.* pigtail; postscript.

coleto /ko'leto/ *n. m.* leather jacket.

colgado /kol'gaðo/ **-da** *n.* **1.** crazy person. —*a.* **2.** hanging, pending.
colgador /kolga'ðor/ *n. m.* rack, hanger.
colgaduras /kolga'ðuras/ *n. f.pl.* drapery.
colgante /kol'gante/ *a.* hanging.
colgar /kol'gar/ *v.* hang up, suspend.
colibrí /koli'βri/ *n. m.* hummingbird.
coliflor /koli'flor/ *n. f.* cauliflower.
coligarse /koli'garse/ *v.* band together, unite.
colilla /ko'liʎa; ko'liya/ *n. f.* butt of a cigar or cigarette.
colina /ko'lina/ *n. f.* hill, hillock.
colinabo /koli'naβo/ *n. m.* turnip.
colindante /kolin'dante/ *a.* neighboring, adjacent.
colindar /kolin'dar/ *v.* neighbor, abut.
coliseo /koli'seo/ *n. m.* theater; coliseum.
colisión /koli'sion/ *n. f.* collision.
collado /ko'ʎaðo; ko'yaðo/ *n. m.* hillock.
collar /ko'ʎar; ko'yar/ *n. m.* necklace; collar.
colmar /kol'mar/ *v.* heap up, fill liberally.
colmena /kol'mena/ *n. f.* hive.
colmillo /kol'miʎo; kol'miyo/ *n. m.* eyetooth; tusk; fang.
colmo /'kolmo/ *n. m.* height, peak, extreme.
colocación /koloka'θion; koloka'sion/ *n. f.* place, position; employment, job; arrangement.
colocar /kolo'kar/ *v.* place, locate, put, set.
colombiano /kolom'biano/ **-na** *a.* & *n.* Colombian.
colon /'kolon/ *n. m.* colon (of intestines).
colonia /ko'lonia/ *n. f.* colony; eau de Cologne.
Colonia *n. f.* Cologne.
colonial /kolo'nial/ *a.* colonial.
colonización /koloniθa'θion; kolonisa'sion/ *n. f.* colonization.
colonizador /koloniθa'ðor; kolonisa'ðor/ **-ra** *n.* colonizer.
colonizar /koloni'θar; koloni'sar/ *v.* colonize.
colono /ko'lono/ *n. m.* colonist; tenant farmer.
coloquio /ko'lokio/ *n. m.* conversation, talk.

color /ko'lor/ *n. m.* color. —**colorar,** *v.*
coloración /kolora'θion; kolora'sion/ *n. f.* coloring.
colorado /kolo'raðo/ *a.* red, ruddy.
colorar /kolo'rar/ *v.* color, paint; dye.
colorete /kolo'rete/ *n. m.* rouge.
colorformo /kolor'formo/ *n. m.* chloroform.
colorido /kolo'riðo/ *n. m.* color, coloring. —**colorir,** *v.*
colosal /kolo'sal/ *a.* colossal.
columbrar /kolum'brar/ *v.* discern.
columna /ko'lumna/ *n. f.* column, pillar, shaft.
columpiar /kolum'piar/ *v.* swing.
columpio /ko'lumpio/ *n. m.* swing.
coma /'koma/ *n. f.* coma; comma.
comadre /ko'maðre/ *n. f.* midwife; gossip; close friend.
comadreja /koma'ðreha/ *n. f.* weasel.
comadrona /koma'ðrona/ *n. f.* midwife.
comandancia /koman'danθia; koman'dansia/ *n. m.* command; command post.
comandante /koman'dante/ *n. m.* commandant; commander; major.
comandar /koman'dar/ *v.* command.
comandita /koman'dita/ *n. f.* silent partnership.
comanditario /komandi'tario/ **-ra** *n.* silent partner.
comando /ko'mando/ *n. m.* command.
comarca /ko'marka/ *n. f.* region; border, boundary.
comba /'komba/ *n. f.* bulge.
combar /kom'bar/ *v.* bend; bulge.
combate /kom'bate/ *n. m.* combat. —**combatir,** *v.*
combatiente /komba'tiente/ *a.* & *m.* combatant.
combinación /kombina'θion; kombina'sion/ *n. f.* combination; slip (garment).
combinar /kombi'nar/ *v.* combine.
combustible /kombus'tiβle/ *a.* **1.** combustible. —*n.* **2.** *m.* fuel.
combustión /kombus'tion/ *n. f.* combustion.
comedero /kome'ðero/ *n. m.* trough.

comedia /ko'meðia/ *n. f.* comedy; play.

comediante /kome'ðiante/ *n. m.* actor; comedian.

comedido /kome'ðiðo/ *a.* polite, courteous; obliging.

comedirse /kome'ðirse/ *v.* to be polite or obliging.

comedor /kome'ðor/ *n. m.* dining room. **coche c.,** dining car.

comendador /komenda'ðor/ *n. m.* commander.

comensal /komen'sal/ *n. m.* table companion.

comentador /komenta'ðor/ -ra *n.* commentator.

comentario /komen'tario/ *n. m.* commentary.

comento /ko'mento/ *n. m.* comment. —**comentar,** *v.*

comenzar /komen'θar; komen'sar/ *v.* begin, start, commence.

comer /ko'mer/ *v.* eat, dine.

comercial /komer'θial; komer'sial/ *a.* commercial.

comercializar /komerθiali'θar; komersiali'sar/ *v.* market.

comerciante /komer'θiante; komer'siante/ -ta *n.* merchant, trader, businessperson.

comerciar /komer'θiar; komer'siar/ *v.* trade, deal, do business.

comercio /ko'merθio; ko'mersio/ *n. m.* commerce, trade, business; store.

comestible /komes'tiβle/ *a.* **1.** edible. —*n.* **2.** *m. (pl.)* groceries, provisions.

cometa /ko'meta/ *n.* **1.** *m.* comet. **2.** *f.* kite.

cometer /kome'ter/ *v.* commit.

cometido /kome'tiðo/ *n. m.* commission; duty; task.

comezón /kome'θon; kome'son/ *n. f.* itch.

comicios /ko'miθios; ko'misios/ *n. m.pl.* primary elections.

cómico /'komiko/ -ca *a. & n.* comic, comical; comedian.

comida /ko'miða/ *n. f.* food; dinner; meal.

comidilla /komi'ðiʎa; komi'ðiya/ *n. f.* light meal; gossip.

comienzo /ko'mienθo; ko'mienso/ *n. m.* beginning.

comilitona /komili'tona/ *n. f.* spread, feast.

comillas /ko'miʎas; ko'miyas/ *n. f.pl.* quotation marks.

comilón /komi'lon/ -na *n.* glutton; heavy eater.

comisario /komi'sario/ *n. m.* commissary.

comisión /komi'sion/ *n. f.* commission. —**comisionar,** *v.*

comisionado /komisio'naðo/ -da *n.* agent, commissioner.

comisionar /komisio'nar/ *v.* commission.

comiso /ko'miso/ *n. m.* (law) confiscation of illegal goods.

comistrajo /komis'traho/ *n. m.* mess, hodgepodge.

comité /komi'te/ *n. m.* committee.

comitiva /komi'tiβa/ *n. f.* retinue.

como /'komo/ *conj. & adv.* like, as.

cómo *adv.* how.

cómoda /'komoða/ *n. f.* bureau, chest (of drawers).

cómodamente /komoða'mente/ *adv.* conveniently.

comodidad /komoði'ðað/ *n. f.* convenience, comfort; commodity.

comodín /komo'ðin/ *n. m.* joker (playing card).

cómodo /'komoðo/ *a.* comfortable; convenient.

comodoro /komo'ðoro/ *n. m.* commodore.

compacto /kom'pakto/ *a.* compact.

compadecer /kompaðe'θer; kompaðe'ser/ *v.* be sorry for, pity.

compadraje /kompa'ðrahe/ *n. m.* clique.

compadre /kom'paðre/ *n. m.* close friend.

compaginar /kompahi'nar/ *v.* put in order; arrange.

compañerismo /kompaɲe'rismo/ *n. m.* companionship.

compañero /kompa'ɲero/ -ra *n.* companion, partner.

compañía /kompa'ɲia/ *n. f.* company.

comparable /kompa'raβle/ *a.* comparable.

comparación /kompara'θion; kompara'sion/ *n. f.* comparison.

comparar /kompa'rar/ *v.* compare.

comparativamente /komparatiβa'mente/ *adv.* comparatively.

comparativo /kompara'tiβo/ *a.* comparative.

comparecer /kompare'θer; kompare'ser/ *v.* appear.

comparendo /kompa'rendo/ n. m. summons.

comparsa /kom'parsa/ n. f. carnival masquerade; retinue.

compartimiento /komparti'miento/ n. m. compartment.

compartir /kompar'tir/ v. share.

compás /kom'pas/ n. m. compass; beat, rhythm.

compasar /kompa'sar/ v. measure exactly.

compasión /kompa'sion/ n. f. compassion.

compasivo /kompa'siβo/ a. compassionate.

compatibilidad /kompatiβili'ðað/ n. f. compatibility.

compatible /kompa'tiβle/ a. compatible.

compatriota /kompa'triota/ n. m. & f. compatriot.

compeler /kompe'ler/ v. compel.

compendiar /kompen'diar/ v. summarize; abridge.

compendiariamente /kompendiaria'mente/ adv. briefly.

compendio /kom'pendio/ n. m. summary; abridgment.

compendiosamente /kompendiosa'mente/ adv. briefly.

compensación /kompensa'θion; kompensa'sion/ n. f. compensation.

compensar /kompen'sar/ v. compensate.

competencia /kompe'tenθia; kompe'tensia/ n. f. competence; competition.

competente /kompe'tente/ a. competent.

competentemente /kompetente'mente/ adv. competently.

competición /kompeti'θion; kompeti'sion/ n. f. competition.

competidor /kompeti'ðor/ **-ra** a. & n. competitive; competitor.

competir /kompe'tir/ v. compete.

compilación /kompila'θion; kompila'sion/ n. f. compilation.

compilar /kompi'lar/ v. compile.

compinche /kom'pintʃe/ n. m. pal.

complacencia /kompla'θenθia; kompla'sensia/ n. f. complacency.

complacer /kompla'θer; kompla'ser/ v. please, oblige, humor.

complaciente /kompla'θiente; kompla'siente/ a. pleasing, obliging.

complejidad /komplehi'ðað/ n. f. complexity.

complejo /kom'pleho/ **-ja** a. & n. complex.

complemento /komple'mento/ n. m. complement; Gram. object.

completamente /kompleta'mente/ adv. completely.

completamiento /kompleta'miento/ n. m. completion, finish.

completar /komple'tar/ v. complete.

completo /kom'pleto/ a. complete, full, perfect.

complexión /komplek'sion/ n. f. nature, temperament.

complicación /komplika'θion; komplika'sion/ n. f. complication.

complicado /kompli'kaðo/ a. complicated.

complicar /kompli'kar/ v. complicate.

cómplice /'kompliθe; 'komplise/ n. m. & f. accomplice, accessory.

complicidad /kompliθi'ðað; komplisi'ðað/ n. f. complicity.

complot /kom'plot/ n. m. conspiracy.

componedor /kompone'ðor/ **-ra** n. typesetter.

componenda /kompo'nenda/ n. f. compromise; settlement.

componente /kompo'nente/ a. & m. component.

componer /kompo'ner/ v. compose; fix, repair.

componible /kompo'niβle/ a. reparable.

comportable /kompor'taβle/ a. endurable.

comportamiento /komporta'miento/ n. m. behavior.

comportarse /kompor'tarse/ v. behave.

comporte /kom'porte/ n. m. behavior.

composición /komposi'θion; komposi'sion/ n. f. composition.

compositivo /komposi'tiβo/ a. synthetic; composite.

compositor /komposi'tor/ **-ra** n. composer.

compost /kom'post/ n. m. compost.

compostura /kompos'tura/ n. f. composure; repair; neatness.

compota /kom'pota/ n. f. (fruit) sauce.

compra /'kompra/ n. f. purchase.
 ir de compras, to go shopping.

comprador /kompra'ðor/ -ra *n.*
buyer, purchaser.

comprar /kom'prar/ *v.* buy, purchase.

comprender /kompren'der/ *v.*
comprehend, understand; include,
comprise.

comprensibilidad /komprensiβili'ðað/ *n. f.* comprehensibility.

comprensible /kompren'siβle/ *a.*
understandable.

comprensión /kompren'sion/ *n. f.*
comprehension, understanding.

comprensivo /kompren'siβo/ *n.*
m. comprehensive.

compresa /kom'presa/ *n. f.* medical compress.

compresión /kompre'sion/ *n. f.*
compression.

comprimir /kompri'mir/ *v.* compress; restrain, control.

comprobación /komproβa'θion;
komproβa'sion/ *n. f.* proof.

comprobante /kompro'βante/ *a.*
1. proving. —*n.* **2.** *m.* proof.

comprobar /kompro'βar/ *v.* prove;
verify, check.

comprometer /komprome'ter/ *v.*
compromise.

comprometerse /komprome-
'terse/ *v.* become engaged.

compromiso /kompro'miso/ *n. m.*
compromise; engagement.

compuerta /kom'puerta/ *n. f.*
floodgate.

compuesto /kom'puesto/ *n. m.*
composition; compound.

compulsión /kompul'sion/ *n. f.*
compulsion.

compulsivo /kompul'siβo/ *a.* compulsive.

compunción /kompun'θion; kompun'sion/ *n. f.* compunction.

compungirse /kompuŋ'girse/ *v.*
regret, feel remorse.

computación /komputa'θion;
komputa'sion/ *n. f.* computation.

computador /komputa'ðor/ *n. m.*
computer.

computadora de sobremesa
/komputa'ðora de soβre'mesa/ *n.*
f. desktop computer.

computadora doméstica /komputa'ðora do'mestika/ *n. f.* home
computer.

computar /kompu'tar/ *v.* compute.

cómputo /'komputo/ *n. m.* computation.

comulgar /komul'gar/ *v.* take
communion.

comulgatorio /komulga'torio/ *n.*
m. communion altar.

común /ko'mun/ *a.* common,
usual.

comunal /komu'nal/ *a.* communal.

comunero /komu'nero/ *n. m.*
commoner.

comunicable /komuni'kaβle/ *a.*
communicable.

comunicación /komunika'θion;
komunika'sion/ *n. f.* communication.

comunicante /komuni'kante/ *n.*
m. & f. communicant.

comunicar /komuni'kar/ *v.* communicate; convey.

comunicativo /komunika'tiβo/ *a.*
communicative.

comunidad /komuni'ðað/ *n. f.*
community.

comunión /komu'nion/ *n. f.* communion.

comunismo /komu'nismo/ *n. m.*
communism.

comunista /komu'nista/ *a. & n.*
communistic; communist.

comúnmente /komu'mente/ *adv.*
commonly; usually; often.

con /kon/ *prep.* with.

concavidad /konkaβi'ðað/ *n. f.*
concavity.

cóncavo /'konkaβo/ *a.* **1.** concave.
—*n.* **2.** *m.* concavity.

concebible /konθe'βiβle; konse-
'βiβle/ *a.* conceivable.

concebir /konθe'βir; konse'βir/ *v.*
conceive.

conceder /konθe'ðer; konse'ðer/
v. concede.

concejal /konθe'hal; konse'hal/ *n.*
m. councilman.

concejo /kon'θeho; kon'seho/ *n.*
m. city council.

concento /kon'θento; kon'sento/
n. m. harmony (of singing
voices).

concentración /konθentra'θion;
konsentra'sion/ *n. f.* concentration.

concentrar /konθen'trar; konsen'trar/ *v.* concentrate.

concepción /konθep'θion; konsep'sion/ *n. f.* conception.

conceptible /konθep'tiβle; konsep'tiβle/ *a.* conceivable.

concepto /kon'θepto; kon'septo/
n. m. concept; opinion.

concerniente /konθer'niente; konser'niente/ *a.* concerning.

concernir /konθer'nir; konser'nir/ *v.* concern.

concertar /konθer'tar; konser'tar/ *v.* arrange.

concertina /konθer'tina; konser'tina/ *n. f.* concertina.

concesión /konθe'sion; konse'sion/ *n. f.* concession.

concha /'kontʃa/ *n. f. S.A.* shell.

conciencia /kon'θienθia; kon'siensia/ *n. f.* conscience; consciousness; conscientiousness.

concienzudo /konθien'θuðo; konsien'suðo/ *a.* conscientious.

concierto /kon'θierto; kon'sierto/ *n. m.* concert.

conciliación /konθilia'θion; konsilia'sion/ *n. f.* conciliation.

conciliador /konθilia'ðor; konsilia'ðor/ **-ra** *n.* conciliator.

conciliar /konθi'liar; konsi'liar/ *v.* conciliate.

concilio /kon'θilio; kon'silio/ *n. m.* council.

concisión /konθi'sion; konsi'sion/ *n. f.* conciseness.

conciso /kon'θiso; kon'siso/ *a.* concise.

concitar /konθi'tar; konsi'tar/ *v.* instigate, stir up.

conciudadano /konθiuða'ðano; konsiuða'ðano/ **-na** *n.* fellow citizen.

concluir /kon'kluir/ *v.* conclude.

conclusión /konklu'sion/ *n. f.* conclusion.

conclusivo /konklu'siβo/ *a.* conclusive.

concluso /kon'kluso/ *a.* concluded; closed.

concluyentemente /konkluyente'mente/ *adv.* conclusively.

concomitante /konkomi'tante/ *a.* concomitant, attendant.

concordador /konkorða'ðor/ **-ra** *n.* moderator; conciliator.

concordancia /konkor'ðanθia; konkor'ðansia/ *n. f.* agreement, concord.

concordar /konkor'ðar/ *v.* agree; put or be in accord.

concordia /kon'korðia/ *n. f.* concord, agreement.

concretamente /konkreta'mente/ *adv.* concretely.

concretar /konkre'tar/ *v.* summarize; make concrete.

concretarse /konkre'tarse/ *v.* limit oneself to.

concreto /kon'kreto/ *a. & m.* concrete.

concubina /konku'βina/ *n. f.* concubine, mistress.

concupiscente /konkupis'θente; konkupis'sente/ *a.* lustful.

concurrencia /konku'rrenθia; konku'rrensia/ *n. f.* assembly; attendance; competition.

concurrente /konku'rrente/ *a.* concurrent.

concurrido /konku'rriðo/ *a.* heavily attended or patronized.

concurrir /konku'rrir/ *v.* concur; attend.

concurso /kon'kurso/ *n. m.* contest, competition; meeting.

conde /'konde/ *n. m.* (title) count.

condecente /konde'θente; konde'sente/ *a.* appropriate, proper.

condecoración /kondekora'θion; kondekora'sion/ *n. f.* decoration; medal; badge.

condecorar /kondeko'rar/ *v.* decorate with a medal.

condena /kon'dena/ *n. f.* prison sentence.

condenación /kondena'θion; kondena'sion/ *n. f.* condemnation.

condenar /konde'nar/ *v.* condemn; sentence.

condensación /kondensa'θion; kondensa'sion/ *n. f.* condensation.

condensar /konden'sar/ *v.* condense.

condesa /kon'desa/ *n. f.* countess.

condescendencia /kondesθen'denθia; kondessen'densia/ *n. f.* condescension.

condescender /kondesθen'der; kondessen'der/ *v.* condescend, deign.

condescendiente /kondesθen'diente; kondessen'diente/ *a.* condescending.

condición /kondi'θion; kondi'sion/ *n. f.* condition.

condicional /kondiθio'nal; kondisio'nal/ *a.* conditional.

condicionalmente /kondiθional'mente; kondisional'mente/ *adv.* conditionally.

condimentar /kondimen'tar/ *v.* season, flavor.

condimento /kondi'mento/ *n. m.* condiment, seasoning, dressing.

condiscípulo /kondis'θipulo; kondis'sipulo/ **-la** n. schoolmate.

condolencia /kondo'lenθia; kondo'lensia/ n. f. condolence, sympathy.

condolerse de /kondo'lerse de/ v. sympathize with.

condominio /kondo'minio/ n. m. condominium.

condómino /kon'domino/ n. m. co-owner.

condonar /kondo'nar/ v. condone.

cóndor /'kondor/ n. m. condor (bird).

conducción /konduk'θion; konduk'sion/ n. f. conveyance.

conducente /kondu'θente; kondu'sente/ a. conducive.

conducir /kondu'θir; kondu'sir/ v. conduct, escort, lead; drive.

conducta /kon'dukta/ n. f. conduct, behavior.

conducto /kon'dukto/ n. m. pipe, conduit; sewer.

conductor /konduk'tor/ **-ra** n. driver; conductor.

conectar /konek'tar/ v. connect.

conejera /kone'hera/ n. f. rabbit warren; place of ill repute.

conejillo de Indias /kone'hiʎo de 'indias; kone'hiyo de 'indias/ guinea pig.

conejo /ko'neho/ **-ja** n. rabbit.

conexión /konek'sion/ n. f. connection; coupling.

conexivo /konek'siβo/ a. connective.

conexo /ko'nekso/ a. connected, united.

confalón /konfa'lon/ n. m. ensign, standard.

confección /konfek'θion; konfek'sion/ n. f. workmanship; ready-made article; concoction.

confeccionar /konfekθio'nar; konfeksio'nar/ v. concoct.

confederación /konfeðera'θion; konfeðera'sion/ n. f. confederation.

confederado /konfeðe'raðo/ **-da** a. & n. confederate.

confederar /konfeðe'rar/ v. confederate, unite, ally.

conferencia /konfe'renθia; konfe'rensia/ n. f. lecture; conference. **c. interurbana,** long-distance call.

conferenciante /konferen'θiante; konferen'siante/ n. m. & f. lecturer, speaker.

conferenciar /konferen'θiar; konferen'siar/ v. confer.

conferencista /konferen'θista; konferen'sista/ n. m. & f. lecturer, speaker.

conferir /konfe'rir/ v. confer.

confesar /konfe'sar/ v. confess.

confesión /konfe'sion/ n. f. confession.

confesionario /konfesio'nario, konfeso'nario/ n. m. confessional.

confesor /konfe'sor/ **-ra** n. confessor.

confeti /kon'feti/ n. m.pl. confetti.

confiable /kon'fiaβle/ a. dependable.

confiado /kon'fiaðo/ a. confident; trusting.

confianza /kon'fianθa; kon'fiansa/ n. f. confidence, trust, faith.

confiar /kon'fiar/ v. entrust; trust, rely.

confidencia /konfi'ðenθia; konfi'ðensia/ n. f. confidence, secret.

confidencial /konfiðen'θial; konfiðen'sial/ a. confidential.

confidente /konfi'ðente/ n. m. & f. confidant.

confidentemente /konfiðente'mente/ adv. confidently.

confín /kon'fin/ n. m. confine.

confinamiento /konfina'miento/ n. m. confinement.

confinar /konfi'nar/ v. confine, imprison; border on.

confirmación /konfirma'θion; konfirma'sion/ n. f. confirmation.

confirmar /konfir'mar/ v. confirm.

confiscación /konfiska'θion; konfiska'sion/ n. f. confiscation.

confiscar /konfis'kar/ v. confiscate.

confitar /konfi'tar/ v. sweeten; make into candy or jam.

confite /kon'fite/ n. m. candy.

confitería /konfite'ria/ n. f. confectionery; candy store.

confitura /konfi'tura/ n. f. confection.

conflagración /konflagra'θion; konflagra'sion/ n. f. conflagration.

conflicto /kon'flikto/ n. m. conflict.

confluencia /kon'fluenθia; kon'fluensia/ n. f. confluence, junction.

confluir /kon'fluir/ v. flow into each other.

conformación /konforma'θion;

konforma'sion/ n. f. conformation.

conformar /konfor'mar/ v. conform.

conforme /kon'forme/ a. **1.** acceptable, right, as agreed; in accordance, in agreement. —*conj.* **2.** according, as.

conformidad /konformi'ðað/ n. f. conformity; agreement.

conformismo /konfor'mismo/ n. m. conformism.

conformista /konfor'mista/ n. m. & f. conformist.

confortar /konfor'tar/ v. comfort.

confraternidad /konfraterni'ðað/ n. f. brotherhood, fraternity.

confricar /konfri'kar/ v. rub vigorously.

confrontación /konfronta'θion; konfronta'sion/ n. f. confrontation.

confrontar /konfron'tar/ v. confront.

confucianismo /konfuθia'nismo; konfusia'nismo/ n. m. Confucianism.

confundir /konfun'dir/ v. confuse; puzzle, mix up.

confusamente /konfusa'mente/ adv. confusedly.

confusión /konfu'sion/ n. f. confusion, mix-up; clutter.

confuso /kon'fuso/ a. confused; confusing.

confutación /konfuta'θion; konfuta'sion/ n. f. disproof.

confutar /konfu'tar/ v. refute, disprove.

congelable /konge'laβle/ a. congealable.

congelación /konhela'θion; konhela'sion/ n. f. congealment; deep freeze.

congelado /konge'laðo/ a. frozen, congealed.

congelar /konhe'lar/ v. congeal, freeze.

congenial /konge'nial/ a. congenial; analogous.

congeniar /konhe'niar/ v. be congenial.

congestión /konhes'tion/ n. f. congestion.

conglomeración /konglomera'θion; konglomera'sion/ n. f. conglomeration.

congoja /kon'goha/ n. f. grief, anguish.

congraciamiento /kongraθia'miento; kongrasia'miento/ n. m. flattery; ingratiation.

congraciar /kongra'θiar; kongra'siar/ v. flatter; ingratiate oneself.

congratulación /kongratula'θion; kongratula'sion/ n. f. congratulation.

congratular /kongratu'lar/ v. congratulate.

congregación /kongrega'θion; kongrega'sion/ n. f. congregation.

congregar /kongre'gar/ v. congregate.

congresista /kongre'sista/ n. m. & f. congressional representative.

congreso /kon'greso/ n. m. congress; conference.

conjetura /konhe'tura/ n. f. conjecture. —**conjeturar,** v.

conjetural /konhetu'ral/ a. conjectural.

conjugación /konhuga'θion; konhuga'sion/ n. f. conjugation.

conjugar /konhu'gar/ v. conjugate.

conjunción /konhun'θion; konhun'sion/ n. f. union; conjunction.

conjuntamente /konhunta'mente/ adv. together, jointly.

conjunto /kon'hunto/ a. **1.** joint, unified. —*n.* **2.** m. whole.

conjuración /konhura'θion; konhura'sion/ n. f. conspiracy, plot.

conjurado /konhu'raðo/ **-da** n. conspirator, plotter.

conjurar /konhu'rar/ v. conjure.

conjuro /kon'huro/ n. m. exorcism; spell; plea.

conllevador /konʎeβa'ðor; konyeβa'ðor/ n. m. helper, aide.

conmemoración /komemora'θion; komemora'sion/ n. f. commemoration; remembrance.

conmemorar /komemo'rar/ v. commemorate.

conmemorativo /komemora'tiβo/ a. commemorative, memorial.

conmensal /komen'sal/ n. m. messmate.

conmigo /ko'migo/ adv. with me.

conmilitón /komili'ton/ n. m. fellow soldier.

conminación /komina'θion; komina'sion/ n. f. threat, warning.

conminar /komi'nar/ v. threaten.

conminatorio /komina'torio/ a. threatening, warning.

conmiseración /komisera'θion; komisera'sion/ *n. f.* sympathy.

conmoción /komo'θion; komo'sion/ *n. f.* commotion, stir.

conmovedor /komoβe'ðor/ *a.* moving, touching.

conmover /komo'βer/ *v.* move, affect, touch.

conmutación /komuta'θion; komuta'sion/ *n. f.* commutation.

conmutador /komuta'ðor/ *n. m.* electric switch.

conmutar /komu'tar/ *v.* exchange.

connatural /konnatu'ral/ *a.* innate, inherent.

connotación /konnota'θion; konnota'sion/ *n. f.* connotation.

connotar /konno'tar/ *v.* connote.

connubial /konnu'βial/ *a.* connubial.

connubio /ko'nnuβio/ *n. m.* matrimony.

cono /'kono/ *n. m.* cone.

conocedor /konoθe'ðor; konose'ðor/ **-ra** *n.* expert, connoisseur.

conocer /kono'θer; kono'ser/ *v.* know, be acquainted with; meet, make the acquaintance of.

conocible /kono'θiβle; kono'siβle/ *a.* knowable.

conocido /kono'θiðo; kono'siðo/ **-da** *a.* **1.** familiar, well-known. —*n.* **2.** acquaintance, person known.

conocimiento /konoθi'miento; konosi'miento/ *n. m.* knowledge, acquaintance; consciousness.

conque /'konke/ *conj.* so then; and so.

conquista /kon'kista/ *n. f.* conquest.

conquistador /konkista'ðor/ **-ra** *n.* conqueror.

conquistar /konkis'tar/ *v.* conquer.

consabido /konsa'βiðo/ *a.* aforesaid.

consagración /konsagra'θion; konsagra'sion/ *n. f.* consecration.

consagrado /konsa'graðo/ *a.* consecrated.

consagrar /konsa'grar/ *v.* consecrate, dedicate, devote.

consanguinidad /konsaŋguini'ðað/ *n. f.* consanguinity.

consciente /kons'θiente; kons'siente/ *a.* conscious, aware.

conscientemente /konsθiente'mente; konssiente'mente/ *adv.* consciously.

conscripción /konskrip'θion; konskrip'sion/ *n. f.* conscription for military service.

consecución /konseku'θion; konseku'sion/ *n. f.* attainment.

consecuencia /konse'kuenθia; konse'kuensia/ *n. f.* consequence.

consecuente /konse'kuente/ *a.* consequent; consistent.

consecuentemente /konsekuente'mente/ *adv.* consequently.

consecutivamente /konsekutiβa'mente/ *adv.* consecutively.

consecutivo /konseku'tiβo/ *a.* consecutive.

conseguir /konse'gir/ *v.* obtain, get, secure; succeed in, manage to.

conseja /kon'seha/ *n. f.* fable.

consejero /konse'hero/ **-ra** *n.* adviser, counselor.

consejo /kon'seho/ *n. m.* council; counsel; (piece of) advice. **c. de redacción,** editorial board.

consenso /kon'senso/ *n. m.* consensus.

consentido /konsen'tiðo/ *a.* spoiled, bratty.

consentimiento /konsenti'miento/ *n. m.* consent.

consentir /konsen'tir/ *v.* allow, permit.

conserje /kon'serhe/ *n. m.* superintendent, keeper.

conserva /kon'serβa/ *n. f.* conserve, preserve.

conservación /konserβa'θion; konserβa'sion/ *n. f.* conservation.

conservador /konserβa'ðor/ **-ra** *a. & n.* conservative.

conservar /konser'βar/ *v.* conserve.

conservativo /konserβa'tiβo/ *a.* conservative, preservative.

conservatorio /konserβa'torio/ *n. m.* conservatory.

considerable /konsiðe'raβle/ *a.* considerable, substantial.

considerablemente /konsiðeraβle'mente/ *adv.* considerably.

consideración /konsiðera'θion; konsiðera'sion/ *n. f.* consideration.

consideradamente /konsiðeraða'mente/ *adv.* considerably.

considerado /konsiðe'raðo/ *a.* considerate; considered.

considerando /konsiðe'rando/ *conj.* whereas.

considerar /konsiðe'rar/ *v.* consider.

consigna /kon'signa/ *n. f.* watchword.

consignación /konsigna'θion; konsigna'sion/ *n. f.* consignment.

consignar /konsig'nar/ *v.* consign.

consignatorio /konsigna'torio/ **-ria** *n.* consignee; trustee.

consigo /kon'sigo/ *adv.* with herself, with himself, with oneself, with themselves, with yourself, with yourselves.

consiguiente /konsi'giente/ *a.* **1.** consequent. —*n.* **2.** *m.* consequence.

consiguientemente /konsigiente'mente/ *adv.* consequently.

consistencia /konsis'tenθia; konsis'tensia/ *n. f.* consistency.

consistente /konsis'tente/ *a.* consistent.

consistir /konsis'tir/ *v.* consist.

consistorio /konsis'torio/ *n. m.* consistory.

consocio /kon'soθio; kon'sosio/ *n. m.* associate; partner; comrade.

consola /kon'sola/ *n. f.* console.

consolación /konsola'θion; konsola'sion/ *n. f.* consolation.

consolar /konso'lar/ *v.* console.

consolativo /konsola'tiβo/ *a.* consolatory.

consolidación /konsoliða'θion; konsoliða'sion/ *n.* consolidation.

consolidado /konsoli'ðaðo/ *a.* consolidated.

consolidar /konsoli'ðar/ *v.* consolidate.

consonancia /konso'nanθianb; konso'nansia/ *n. f.* agreement, accord, harmony.

consonante /konso'nante/ *a. & f.* consonant.

consonar /konso'nar/ *v.* rhyme.

consorte /kon'sorte/ *n. m. & f.* consort, mate.

conspicuo /kons'pikuo/ *a.* conspicuous.

conspiración /konspira'θion; konspira'sion/ *n. f.* conspiracy, plot.

conspirador /konspira'ðor/ **-ra** *n.* conspirator.

conspirar /konspi'rar/ *v.* conspire, plot.

constancia /kons'tanθia; kons'tansia/ *n. f.* perseverance; record.

constante /kons'tante/ *a.* constant.

constantemente /konstante'mente/ *adv.* constantly.

constar /kons'tar/ *v.* consist; be clear, be on record.

constelación /konstela'θion; konstela'sion/ *n. f.* constellation.

consternación /konsterna'θion; konsterna'sion/ *n. f.* consternation.

consternar /konster'nar/ *v.* dismay.

constipación /konstipa'θion; konstipa'sion/ *n. f.* head cold.

constipado /konsti'paðo/ *a.* **1.** having a head cold. —*n.* **2.** *m.* head cold.

constitución /konstitu'θion; konstitu'sion/ *n. f.* constitution.

constitucional /konstituθio'nal; konstitusio'nal/ *a.* constitutional.

constitucionalidad /konstituθionali'ðað; konstitusionali'ðað/ *n. f.* constitutionality.

constituir /konsti'tuir/ *v.* constitute.

constitutivo /konstitu'tiβo/ *n. m.* constituent.

constituyente /konstitu'yente, konstitu'tiβo/ *a.* constituent.

constreñidamente /konstreɲiða'mente/ *adv.* compulsively; with constraint.

constreñimiento /konstreɲi'miento/ *n. m.* compulsion; constraint.

constreñir /konstre'ɲir/ *v.* constrain.

constricción /konstrik'θion; konstrik'sion/ *n. f.* constriction.

construcción /konstruk'θion; konstruk'sion/ *n. f.* construction.

constructivo /konstruk'tiβo/ *a.* constructive.

constructor /konstruk'tor/ **-ra** *n.* builder.

construir /kons'truir/ *v.* construct, build.

consuelo /kon'suelo/ *n. m.* consolation.

cónsul /'konsul/ *n. m.* consul.

consulado /konsu'laðo/ *n. m.* consulate.

consular /konsu'lar/ *a.* consular.

consulta /kon'sulta/ *n. f.* consultation.

consultación /konsulta'θion; konsulta'sion/ *n. f.* consultation.

consultante 44

consultante /konsul'tante/ *n. m. & f.* consultant.
consultar /konsul'tar/ *v.* consult.
consultivo /konsul'tiβo/ *a.* consultative.
consultor /konsul'tor/ **-ra** *n.* adviser.
consumación /konsuma'θion; konsuma'sion/ *n. f.* consummation; end.
consumado /konsu'maðo/ *a.* consummate, downright.
consumar /konsu'mar/ *v.* consummate.
consumidor /konsumi'ðor/ **-ra** *n.* consumer.
consumir /konsu'mir/ *v.* consume.
consumo /kon'sumo/ *n. m.* consumption.
consunción /konsun'θion; konsun'sion/ *n. m.* consumption, tuberculosis.
contabilidad /kontaβili'ðað/ *n. f.* accounting, bookkeeping.
contabilista /kontaβi'lista/ **contable** *n. m. & f.* accountant.
contacto /kon'takto/ *n. m.* contact.
contado /kon'taðo/ *n. m.* **al c.,** (for) cash.
contador /konta'ðor/ **-ra** *n.* accountant, bookkeeper; meter.
contagiar /konta'hiar/ *v.* infect.
contagio /kon'tahio/ *n. m.* contagion.
contagioso /konta'hioso/ *a.* contagious.
contaminación /kontamina'θion; kontamina'sion/ *n. f.* contamination, pollution. **c. del aire, c. atmosférica,** air pollution.
contaminar /kontami'nar/ *v.* contaminate, pollute.
contar /kon'tar/ *v.* count; relate, recount, tell. **c. con,** count on.
contemperar /kontempe'rar/ *v.* moderate.
contemplación /kontempla'θion; kontempla'sion/ *n. f.* contemplation.
contemplador /kontempla'ðor/ **-ra** *n.* thinker.
contemplar /kontem'plar/ *v.* contemplate.
contemplativamente /kontemplatiβa'mente/ *adv.* thoughtfully.
contemplativo /kontempla'tiβo/ *a.* contemplative.
contemporáneo /kontempo'raneo/ **-nea** *a. & n.* contemporary.
contención /konten'θion; konten'sion/ *n. f.* contention.
contencioso /konten'θioso; konten'sioso/ *a.* quarrelsome; argumentative.
contender /konten'der/ *v.* cope, contend; conflict.
contendiente /konten'diente/ *n. m. & f.* contender.
contenedor /kontene'ðor/ *n. m.* container.
contener /konte'ner/ *v.* contain; curb, control.
contenido /konte'niðo/ *n. m.* contents.
contenta /kon'tenta/ *n. f.* endorsement.
contentamiento /kontenta'miento/ *n. m.* contentment.
contentar /konten'tar/ *v.* content, satisfy.
contentible /konten'tiβle/ *a.* contemptible.
contento /kon'tento/ *a.* **1.** contented, happy. —*n.* **2.** *m.* contentment, satisfaction, pleasure.
contérmino /kon'termino/ *a.* adjacent, abutting.
contestable /kontes'taβle/ *a.* disputable.
contestación /kontesta'θion; kontesta'sion/ *n. f.* answer. —**contestar,** *v.*
contestador automático /kontesta'ðor auto'matiko/ *n. m.* answering machine.
contextura /konteks'tura/ *n. f.* texture.
contienda /kon'tienda/ *n. f.* combat; match; strife.
contigo /kon'tigo/ *adv.* with you.
contiguamente /kontigua'mente/ *adv.* contiguously.
contiguo /kon'tiguo/ *a.* adjoining, next.
continencia /konti'nenθia; konti'nensia/ *n. f.* continence, moderation.
continental /konti'nental/ *a.* continental.
continente /konti'nente/ *n. m.* continent; mainland.
continentemente /kontinente'mente/ *adv.* in moderation.
contingencia /kontin'henθia; kontin'hensia/ *n. f.* contingency.
contingente /kontin'hente/ *a.* contingent; incidental.

continuación /kontinua'θion; kontinua'sion/ *n. f.* continuation. **a c.,** thereupon, hereupon.

continuamente /kontinua'mente/ *adv.* continuously.

continuar /konti'nuar/ *v.* continue, keep on.

continuidad /kontinui'ðað/ *n. f.* continuity.

continuo /kon'tinuo/ *a.* continual; continuous.

contorcerse /kontor'θerse; kontor'serse/ *v.* writhe, twist.

contorción /kontor'θion; kontor'sion/ *n. f.* contortion.

contorno /kon'torno/ *n. m.* contour; profile, outline; neighborhood.

contra /'kontra/ *prep.* against.

contraalmirante /kontraalmi'rante/ *n. m.* rear admiral.

contraataque /kontraa'take/ *n. m.* counterattack.

contrabajo /kontra'βaho/ *n. m.* double bass.

contrabalancear /kontraβalanθe'ar; kontraβalanse'ar/ *v.* counterbalance.

contrabandear /kontraβande'ar/ *v.* smuggle.

contrabandista /kontraβan'dista/ *n. m. & f.* smuggler.

contrabando /kontra'βando/ *n. m.* contraband, smuggling.

contracción /kontrak'θion; kontrak'sion/ *n. f.* contraction.

contracepción /kontraθep'θion; kontrasep'sion/ *n. f.* contraception, birth control.

contractual /kontrak'tual/ *a.* contractual.

contradecir /kontraðe'θir; kontraðe'sir/ *v.* contradict.

contradicción /kontraðik'θion; kontraðik'sion/ *n. f.* contradiction.

contradictorio /kontraðik'torio/ *adj.* contradictory.

contraer /kontra'er/ *v.* contract; shrink.

contrahacedor /kontraaθe'ðor; kontraase'ðor/ **-ra** *n.* imitator.

contrahacer /kontraa'θer; kontraa'ser/ *v.* forge.

contralor /kontra'lor/ *n. m.* comptroller.

contramandar /kontraman'dar/ *v.* countermand.

contraorden /kontra'orðen/ *n. f.* countermand.

contraparte /kontra'parte/ *n. f.* counterpart.

contrapesar /kontrape'sar/ *v.* counterbalance; offset.

contrapeso /kontra'peso/ *n. m.* counterweight.

contraproducente /kontraproðu'θente; kontraproðu'sente/ *a.* counterproductive.

contrapunto /kontra'punto/ *n. m.* counterpoint.

contrariamente /kontraria'mente/ *adv.* contrarily.

contrariar /kontra'riar/ *v.* contradict; vex; antagonize; counteract.

contrariedad /kontrarie'ðað/ *n. f.* contrariness; opposition; contradiction; disappointment; trouble.

contrario /kon'trario/ *a. & m.* contrary, opposite.

contrarrestar /kontrarres'tar/ *v.* resist; counteract.

contrasol /kontra'sol/ *n. m.* sunshade.

contraste /kon'traste/ *n. m.* contrast. **—contrastar,** *v.*

contratar /kontra'tar/ *v.* engage, contract.

contratiempo /kontra'tiempo/ *n. m.* accident; misfortune.

contratista /kontra'tista/ *n. m. & f.* contractor.

contrato /kon'trato/ *n. m.* contract.

contribución /kontriβu'θion; kontriβu'sion/ *n. f.* contribution; tax.

contribuir /kontri'βuir/ *v.* contribute.

contribuyente /kontriβu'yente/ *n. m. & f.* contributor; taxpayer.

contrición /kontri'θion; kontri'sion/ *n. f.* contrition.

contristar /kontris'tar/ *v.* afflict.

contrito /kon'trito/ *a.* contrite, remorseful.

control /kon'trol/ *n. m.* control. **—controlar,** *v.*

controlador aéreo /kontrola'ðor a'ereo/ *n. m.* air traffic controller.

controversia /kontro'βersia/ *n. f.* controversy.

controversista /kontroβer'sista/ *n. m. & f.* controversialist.

controvertir /kontroβer'tir/ *v.* dispute.

contumacia /kontu'maθia; kontu'masia/ *n. f.* stubbornness.

contumaz /kontu'maθ; kontu'mas/ *adj.* stubborn.

contumelia /kontu'melia/ n. f. contumely; abuse.

conturbar /kontur'βar/ v. trouble, disturb.

contusión /kontu'sion/ n. f. contusion; bruise.

convalecencia /kombale'θenθia; kombale'sensia/ n. f. convalescence.

convalecer /kombale'θer; kombale'ser/ v. convalesce.

convaleciente /kombale'θiente; kombale'siente/ a. convalescent.

convecino /kombe'θino; kombe'sino/ **-na** a. **1.** near, close. —n. **2.** neighbor.

convencedor /kombenθe'ðor; kombense'ðor/ adj. convincing.

convencer /komben'θer; komben'ser/ v. convince.

convencimiento /kombenθi-'miento; kombensi'miento/ n. m. conviction, firm belief.

convención /komben'θion; komben'sion/ n. f. convention.

convencional /kombenθio'nal; kombensio'nal/ a. conventional.

conveniencia /kombe'nienθia; kombe'niensia/ n. f. suitability; advantage, interest.

conveniente /kombe'niente/ a. suitable; advantageous, opportune.

convenio /kom'benio/ n. m. pact, treaty; agreement.

convenir /kombe'nir/ v. assent, agree, concur; be suitable, fitting, convenient.

convento /kom'bento/ n. m. convent.

convergencia /komber'henθia; komber'hensia/ n. f. convergence.

convergir /komber'hir/ v. converge.

conversación /kombersa'θion; kombersa'sion/ n. f. conversation.

conversar /komber'sar/ v. converse.

conversión /komber'sion/ n. f. conversion.

convertible /komber'tiβle/ a. convertible.

convertir /komber'tir/ v. convert.

convexidad /kombeksi'ðað/ n. f. convexity.

convexo /kom'bekso/ a. convex.

convicción /kombik'θion; kombik'sion/ n. f. conviction.

convicto /kom'bikto/ a. found guilty.

convidado /kombi'ðaðo/ **-da** n. guest.

convidar /kombi'ðar/ v. invite.

convincente /kombin'θente; kombin'sente/ a. convincing.

convite /kom'bite/ n. m. invitation, treat.

convocación /komboka'θion; komboka'sion/ n. f. convocation.

convocar /kombo'kar/ v. convoke, assemble.

convoy /kom'boi/ n. m. convoy, escort.

convoyar /kombo'yar/ v. convey; escort.

convulsión /kombul'sion/ n. f. convulsion.

convulsivo /kombul'siβo/ a. convulsive.

conyugal /konyu'gal/ a. conjugal.

cónyuge /'konyuhe/ n. m. & f. spouse, mate.

coñac /ko'ɲak/ n. m. cognac, brandy.

cooperación /koopera'θion; koopera'sion/ n. f. cooperation.

cooperador /koopera'ðor/ a. cooperative.

cooperar /koope'rar/ v. cooperate.

cooperativa /koopera'tiβa/ n. f. (food, etc.) cooperative, co-op.

cooperativo /koopera'tiβo/ a. cooperative.

coordinación /koorðina'θion; koorðina'sion/ n. f. coordination.

coordinar /koorði'nar/ v. coordinate.

copa /'kopa/ n. f. goblet.

copartícipe /kopar'tiθipe; kopar'tisipe/ m & f. partner.

copete /ko'pete/ n. m. tuft; toupee.

copia /'kopia/ n. f. copy. —**copiar**, v.

copiadora /kopia'ðora/ n. f. copier.

copioso /ko'pioso/ a. copious.

copista /ko'pista/ n. m. & f. copyist.

copla /'kopla/ n. f. popular song.

coplero /kop'lero/ n. m. poetaster.

cópula /'kopula/ n. f. connection.

coqueta /ko'keta/ n. f. flirt. —**coquetear**, v.

coraje /ko'rahe/ n. m. courage, bravery; anger.

coral /ko'ral/ a. **1.** choral. —n. **2.** m. coral.

coralino /kora'lino/ a. coral.

Corán /ko'ran/ n. m. Koran.

corazón /kora'θon; kora'son/ *n. m.* heart.

corazonada /koraθo'naða; koraso'naða/ *n. f.* foreboding.

corbata /kor'βata/ *n. f.* necktie.

corbeta /kor'βeta/ *n. f.* corvette.

corcho /'kortʃo/ *n. m.* cork.

corcova /kor'koβa/ *n. f.* hump, hunchback.

corcovado /korko'βaðo/ **-da** *a. & n.* hunchback.

cordaje /kor'ðahe/ *n. m.* rigging.

cordel /kor'ðel/ *n. m.* string, cord.

cordero /kor'ðero/ *n. m.* lamb.

cordial /kor'ðial/ *a.* cordial; hearty.

cordialidad /korðiali'ðað/ *n. f.* cordiality.

cordillera /korði'ʎera; korði'yera/ *n. f.* mountain range.

cordón /kor'ðon/ *n. m.* cord; (shoe) lace.

cordura /kor'ðura/ *n. f.* sanity.

Corea /ko'rea/ *n. f.* Korea.

coreano /kore'ano/ **-a** *a. & n.* Korean.

coreografía /koreogra'fia/ *n. f.* choreography.

corista /ko'rista/ *n. f.* chorus girl.

corneja /kor'neha/ *n. f.* crow.

córneo /'korneo/ *a.* horny.

corneta /kor'neta/ *n. f.* bugle, horn, cornet.

corniforme /korni'forme/ *a.* horn-shaped.

cornisa /kor'nisa/ *n. f.* cornice.

cornucopia /kornu'kopia/ *n. f.* cornucopia.

coro /'koro/ *n. m.* chorus; choir.

corola /ko'rola/ *n. f.* corolla.

corolario /koro'lario/ *n. m.* corollary.

corona /ko'rona/ *n. f.* crown; halo; wreath.

coronación /korona'θion; korona'sion/ *n. f.* coronation.

coronamiento /korona'miento/ *n. m.* completion of a task.

coronar /koro'nar/ *v.* crown.

coronel /koro'nel/ *n. m.* colonel.

coronilla /koro'niʎa; koro'niya/ *n. f.* crown, top of the head.

corporación /korpora'θion; korpora'sion/ *n. f.* corporation.

corporal /korpo'ral/ *adj.* corporeal, bodily.

corpóreo /kor'poreo/ *a.* corporeal.

corpulencia /korpu'lenθia; korpu'lensia/ *n. f.* corpulence.

corpulento /korpu'lento/ *a.* corpulent, stout.

corpuscular /korpusku'lar/ *a.* corpuscular.

corpúsculo /kor'puskulo/ *n. m.* corpuscle.

corral /ko'rral/ *n. m.* corral, pen, yard.

correa /ko'rrea/ *n. f.* belt, strap.

correa transportadora /korrea transporta'ðora/ conveyor belt.

corrección /korrek'θion; korrek'sion/ *n. f.* correction.

correcto /ko'rrekto/ *a.* correct, proper, right.

corrector /korrek'tor/ **-ra** *n.* corrector, proofreader.

corredera /korre'ðera/ *n. f.* race course.

corredizo /korre'ðiθo; korre'ðiso/ *a.* easily untied.

corredor /korre'ðor/ *n. m.* corridor; runner.

corregible /korre'hiβle/ *a.* corrigible.

corregidor /korrehi'ðor/ *n. m.* corrector; magistrate, mayor.

corregir /korre'hir/ *v.* correct.

correlación /korrela'θion; korrela'sion/ *n. f.* correlation.

correlacionar /korrelaθio'nar; korrelasio'nar/ *v.* correlate.

correlativo /korrela'tiβo/ *a.* correlative.

correo /ko'rreo/ *n. m.* mail.

correoso /korre'oso/ *a.* leathery.

correr /ko'rrer/ *v.* run.

correría /korre'ria/ *n. f.* raid; escapade.

correspondencia /korrespon'denθia; korrespon'densia/ *n. f.* correspondence.

corresponder /korrespon'der/ *v.* correspond.

correspondiente /korrespon'diente/ *a. & m.* corresponding; correspondent.

corresponsal /korrespon'sal/ *n. m.* correspondent.

corretaje /korre'tahe/ *n. m.* brokerage.

correvedile /korreβe'ðile/ *n. m.* tale bearer; gossip.

corrida /ko'rriða/ *n. f.* race. **c. (de toros),** bullfight.

corrido /ko'rriðo/ *a.* abashed; expert.

corriente /ko'rriente/ *a.* **1.** current, standard. —*n.* **2.** *f.* current, stream. **3.** *m.* **al c.,** informed, up to date. **contra la c.,** against the current; upriver, upstream.

corroboración /korroβora'θion; korroβora'sion/ *n. f.* corroboration.

corroborar /korroβo'rar/ *v.* corroborate.

corroer /korro'er/ *v.* corrode.

corromper /korrom'per/ *v.* corrupt.

corrompido /korrom'piðo/ *a.* corrupt.

corrupción /korrup'θion; korrup'sion/ *n. f.* corruption.

corruptela /korrup'tela/ *n. f.* corruption; vice.

corruptibilidad /korruptiβili'ðað/ *n. f.* corruptibility.

corruptor /korrup'tor/ **-ra** *n.* corrupter.

corsario /kor'sario/ *n. m.* corsair.

corsé /kor'se/ *n. m.* corset.

corso /'korso/ *n. m.* piracy.

cortacésped /korta'θespeð; korta'sespeð/ *n. m.* lawnmower.

cortadillo /korta'ðiʎo; korta'ðiyo/ *n. m.* small glass.

cortado /kor'taðo/ *a.* cut.

cortadura /korta'ðura/ *n. f.* cut.

cortante /kor'tante/ *a.* cutting, sharp, keen.

cortapisa /korta'pisa/ *n. f.* obstacle.

cortaplumas /korta'plumas/ *n. m.* penknife.

cortar /kor'tar/ *v.* cut, cut off, cut out.

corte /'korte/ *n. f.* court, *m.* cut.

cortedad /korte'ðað/ *n. f.* smallness; shyness.

cortejar /korte'har/ *v.* pay court to, woo.

cortejo /kor'teho/ *n. m.* court; courtship; sweetheart.

cortés /kor'tes/ *a.* civil, courteous, polite.

cortesana /korte'sana/ *n. f.* courtesan.

cortesano. 1. /korte'sano/ *a.* **1.** courtly, courteous. —*n.* **2.** *m.* courtier.

cortesía /korte'sia/ *n. f.* courtesy.

corteza /kor'teθa; kor'tesa/ *n. f.* bark; rind; crust.

cortijo /kor'tiho/ *n. m.* farmhouse.

cortina /kor'tina/ *n. f.* curtain.

corto /'korto/ *a.* short.

corva /'korβa/ *n. f.* back of the knee.

cosa /'kosa/ *n. f.* thing. **c. de,** a matter of, roughly.

cosecha /ko'setʃa/ *n. f.* crop, harvest. —**cosechar,** *v.*

coser /ko'ser/ *v.* sew, stitch.

cosmético /kos'metiko/ *a. & m.* cosmetic.

cósmico /'kosmiko/ *a.* cosmic.

cosmonauta /kosmo'nauta/ *n. m. & f.* cosmonaut.

cosmopolita /kosmopo'lita/ *a. & n.* cosmopolitan.

cosmos /'kosmos/ *n. m.* cosmos.

coso /'koso/ *n. m.* arena for bull fights.

cosquilla /kos'kiʎa; kos'kiya/ *n. f.* tickle. —**cosquillar,** *v.*

cosquilloso /koski'ʎoso; koski'yoso/ *a.* ticklish.

costa /'kosta/ *n. f.* coast; cost, expense.

costado /kos'taðo/ *n. m.* side.

costal /kos'tal/ *n. m.* sack, bag.

costanero /kosta'nero/ *a.* coastal.

costar /kos'tar/ *v.* cost.

costarricense /kostarri'θense; kostarri'sense/ *a. & n.* Costa Rican.

coste /'koste/ *n. m.* cost, price.

costear /koste'ar/ *v.* defray, sponsor; sail along the coast of.

costilla /kos'tiʎa; kos'tiya/ *n. f.* rib; chop.

costo /'kosto/ *n. m.* cost, price.

costoso /kos'toso/ *a.* costly.

costra /'kostra/ *n. f.* crust.

costumbre /kos'tumbre/ *n. f.* custom, practice, habit.

costura /kos'tura/ *n. f.* sewing; seam.

costurera /kostu'rera/ *n. f.* seamstress, dressmaker.

costurero /kostu'rero/ *n. m.* sewing basket.

cota de malla /'kota de 'maʎa; 'kota de 'maya/ coat of mail.

cotejar /kote'har/ *v.* compare.

cotidiano /koti'ðiano/ *a.* daily; everyday.

cotillón /koti'ʎon; koti'yon/ *n. m.* cotillion.

cotización /kotiθa'θion; kotisa'sion/ *n. f.* quotation.

cotizar /koti'θar; koti'sar/ *v.* quote (a price).

coto /'koto/ *n. m.* enclosure; boundary.

cotón /ko'ton/ *n. m.* printed cotton cloth.

cotufa /ko'tufa/ *n. f.* Jerusalem artichoke.

coturno /ko'turno/ *n. m.* buskin.
covacha /ko'βatʃa/ *n. f.* small cave.
coxal /kok'sal/ *a.* of the hip.
coy /koi/ *n. m.* hammock.
coyote /ko'yote/ *n. m.* coyote.
coyuntura /koyun'tura/ *n. f.* joint; juncture.
coz /koθ; kos/ *n. f.* kick.
crac /krak/ *n. m.* failure.
cráneo /'kraneo/ *n. m.* skull.
craniano /kra'niano/ *a.* cranial.
crapuloso /krapu'loso/ *a.* drunken.
crasiento /kra'siento/ *a.* greasy, oily.
craso /'kraso/ *a.* fat; gross.
cráter /'krater/ *n. m.* crater.
craza /'kraθa; 'krasa/ *n. f.* crucible.
creación /krea'θion; krea'sion/ *n. f.* creation.
creador /krea'ðor/ **-ra** *a. & n.* creative; creator.
crear /kre'ar/ *v.* create.
creativo /krea'tiβo/ *a.* creative.
crébol /'kreβol/ *n. m.* holly tree.
crecer /kre'θer; kre'ser/ *v.* grow, grow up; increase.
creces /'kreθes; 'kreses/ *n. f.pl.* increase, addition.
crecidamente /kreθiða'mente; kresiða'mente/ *adv.* abundantly.
crecido /kre'θiðo; kre'siðo/ *a.* increased, enlarged; swollen.
creciente /kre'θiente; kre'siente/ *a.* **1.** growing. —*n.* **2.** *m.* crescent.
crecimiento /kreθi'miento; kresi'miento/ *n. m.* growth.
credenciales /kreðen'θiales; kreðen'siales/ *f.pl.* credentials.
credibilidad /kreðiβili'ðað/ *n. f.* credibility.
crédito /'kreðito/ *n. m.* credit.
credo /'kreðo/ *n. m.* creed, belief.
crédulamente /kreðula'mente/ *adv.* credulously, gullibly.
credulidad /kreðuli'ðað/ *n. f.* credulity.
crédulo /'kreðulo/ *a.* credulous.
creedero /kree'ðero/ *a.* credible.
creedor /kree'ðor/ *a.* credulous, believing.
creencia /kre'enθia; kre'ensia/ *n. f.* belief.
creer /kre'er/ *v.* believe; think.
creíble /kre'iβle/ *a.* credible, believable.
crema /'krema/ *n. f.* cream.

cremación /krema'θion; krema'sion/ *n. f.* cremation.
crema dentífrica /'krema den'tifrika/ toothpaste.
cremallera /krema'ʎera; krema'yera/ *n. f.* zipper.
crémor tártaro /'kremor 'tartaro/ *n. m.* cream of tartar.
cremoso /kre'moso/ *a.* creamy.
creosota /kreo'sota/ *n. f.* creosote.
crepitar /krepi'tar/ *v.* crackle.
crepuscular /krepusku'lar/ *a.* of or like the dawn or dusk; crepuscular.
crépusculo /kre'puskulo/ *n. m.* dusk, twilight.
crescendo /kres'θendo; kres'sendo/ *n. m.* crescendo.
crespo /'krespo/ *a.* curly.
crespón /kres'pon/ *n. m.* crepe.
cresta /'kresta/ *n. f.* crest; heraldic crest.
crestado /kres'taðo/ *a.* crested.
creta /'kreta/ *n. f.* chalk.
cretáceo /kre'taθeo; kre'taseo/ *a.* chalky.
cretinismo /kreti'nismo/ *n. m.* cretinism.
cretino /kre'tino/ **-na** *n. & a.* cretin.
cretona /kre'tona/ *n. f.* cretonne.
creyente /kre'yente/ *a.* **1.** believing. —*n.* **2.** believer.
creyón /kre'yon/ *n. m.* crayon.
cría /'kria/ *n. f.* (stock) breeding; young (of an animal), litter.
criada /kri'aða/ *n. f.* maid.
criadero /kria'ðero/ *n. m. Agr.* nursery.
criado /kri'aðo/ **-da** *n.* servant.
criador /kria'ðor/ *a.* fruitful, prolific.
crianza /kri'anθa; kri'ansa/ *n. f.* breeding; upbringing.
criar /kri'ar/ *v.* raise, rear; breed.
criatura /kria'tura/ *n. f.* creature; infant.
criba /'kriβa/ *n. f.* sieve.
cribado /kri'βaðo/ *a.* sifted.
cribar /kri'βar/ *v.* sift.
crimen /'krimen/ *n. m.* crime.
criminal /krimi'nal/ *a. & n.* criminal.
criminalidad /kriminali'ðað/ *n. f.* criminality.
criminalmente /kriminal'mente/ *adv.* criminally.
criminología /kriminolo'hia/ *n. f.* criminology.

criminoso /krimi'noso/ *a.* criminal.

crines /'krines/ *n. f.pl.* mane of a horse.

crinolina /krino'lina/ *n. f.* crinoline.

criocirugía /krioθiru'hia; kriosiru'hia/ *n. f.* cryosurgery.

criollo /'krioʎo; 'krioyo/ **-lla** *a.* & *n.* native; Creole.

cripta /'kripta/ *n. f.* crypt.

criptografía /kriptogra'fia/ *n. f.* cryptography.

crisantemo /krisan'temo/ *n. m.* chrysanthemum.

crisis /'krisis/ *n. f.* crisis.

crisis nerviosa /'krisis ner'βiosa/ nervous breakdown.

crisma /'krisma/ *n. m.* chrism.

crisol /kri'sol/ *n. m.* crucible.

crispamiento /krispa'miento/ *n. m.* twitch, contraction.

crispar /kris'par/ *v.* contract (the muscles); twitch.

cristal /kri'stal/ *n. m.* glass; crystal; lens.

cristalería /kristale'ria/ *n. f.* glassware.

cristalino /krista'lino/ *a.* crystalline.

cristalización /kristaliθa'θion; kristalisa'sion/ *n. f.* crystallization.

cristalizar /kristali'θar; kristali'sar/ *v.* crystallize.

cristianar /kristia'nar/ *v.* baptize.

cristiandad /kristian'dað/ *n. f.* Christendom.

cristianismo /kristia'nismo/ *n. m.* Christianity.

cristiano /kris'tiano/ **-na** *a.* & *n.* Christian.

Cristo /'kristo/ *n. m.* Christ.

criterio /kri'terio/ *n. m.* criterion; judgment.

crítica /'kritika/ *n. f.* criticism; critique.

criticable /kriti'kaβle/ *a.* blameworthy.

criticador /kritika'ðor/ *a.* critical.

criticar /kriti'kar/ *v.* criticize.

crítico /'kritiko/ **-ca** *a.* & *n.* critical; critic.

croar /kro'ar/ *v.* croak.

crocante /kro'kante/ *n. m.* almond brittle.

crocitar /kroθi'tar; krosi'tar/ *v.* crow.

cromático /kro'matiko/ *a.* chromatic.

cromo /'kromo/ *n. m.* chromium.

cromosoma /kromo'soma/ *n. m.* chromosome.

cromotipia /kromo'tipia/ *n. f.* color printing.

crónica /'kronika/ *n. f.* chronicle.

crónico /'kroniko/ *a.* chronic.

cronicón /kroni'kon/ *n. m.* concise chronicle.

cronista /kro'nista/ *n. m.* & *f.* chronicler.

cronología /kronolo'hia/ *n. f.* chronology.

cronológicamente /kronolohika'mente/ *adv.* chronologically.

cronológico /krono'lohiko/ *a.* chronologic.

cronometrar /kronome'trar/ *v.* time.

cronómetro /kro'nometro/ *n. m.* stopwatch; chronometer.

croqueta /kro'keta/ *n. f.* croquette.

croquis /'krokis/ *n. m.* sketch; rough outline.

crótalo /'krotalo/ *n. m.* rattlesnake; castanet.

cruce /'kruθe; 'kruse/ *n. m.* crossing, crossroads, junction.

crucero /kru'θero; kru'sero/ *n. m.* cruiser.

crucífero /kru'θifero; kru'sifero/ *a.* cross-shaped.

crucificado /kruθifi'kaðo; krusifi'kaðo/ *a.* crucified.

crucificar /kruθifi'kar; krusifi'kar/ *v.* crucify.

crucifijo /kruθi'fiho; krusi'fiho/ *n. m.* crucifix.

crucifixión /kruθifik'sion; krusifik'sion/ *n. f.* crucifixion.

crucigrama /kruθi'grama; krusi'grama/ *n. m.* crossword puzzle.

crudamente /kruða'mente/ *adv.* crudely.

crudeza /kru'ðeθa; kru'ðesa/ *n. f.* crudeness.

crudo /'kruðo/ *a.* crude, raw.

cruel /kruel/ *a.* cruel.

crueldad /kruel'dað/ *n. f.* cruelty.

cruelmente /kruel'mente/ *adv.* cruelly.

cruentamente /kruenta'mente/ *adv.* bloodily.

cruento /'kruento/ *a.* bloody.

crujía /kru'hia/ *n. f.* corridor.

crujido /kru'hiðo/ *n. m.* creak.

crujir /kru'hir/ *v.* crackle; creak; rustle.

cruórico /'kruoriko/ *a.* bloody.

crup /krup/ *n. m.* croup.

crupié /kru'pie/ *n. m. & f.* croupier.

crustáceo /krus'taθeo; krus'taseo/ *n. & a.* crustacean.

cruz /kruθ; krus/ *n. f.* cross.

cruzada /kru'θaða; kru'saða/ *n. f.* crusade.

cruzado /kru'θaðo; kru'saðo/ **-da** *n.* crusader.

cruzamiento /kruθa'miento; krusa'miento/ *n. m.* crossing.

cruzar /kru'θar; kru'sar/ *v.* cross.

cruzarse con /kru'θarse kon; kru'sarse kon/ *v.* to (meet and) pass.

cuaderno /kua'ðerno/ *n. m.* notebook.

cuadra /'kuaðra/ *n. f.* block; (hospital) ward.

cuadradamente /kuaðraða'mente/ *adv.* exactly, precisely; completely, in full.

cuadradillo /kuaðra'ðiʎo; kuaðra'ðiyo/ *n. m.* lump of sugar.

cuadrado /kua'ðraðo/ **-da** *a. & n.* square.

cuadrafónico /kuaðra'foniko/ *a.* quadraphonic.

Cuadragésima /kuaðra'hesima/ *n. f.* Lent.

cuadragesimal /kuaðrahesi'mal/ *a.* Lenten.

cuadrángulo /kua'ðraŋgulo/ *n. m.* quadrangle.

cuadrante /kua'ðrante/ *n. m.* quadrant; dial.

cuadrar /kua'ðrar/ *v.* square; suit.

cuadricular /kuaðriku'lar/ *a.* in squares.

cuadrilátero /kuaðri'latero/ *a.* quadrilateral.

cuadrilla /kua'ðriʎa; kua'ðriya/ *n. f.* band, troop, gang.

cuadro /'kuaðro/ *n. m.* picture; painting; frame. **a cuadros,** checked, plaid.

cuadro de servicio /'kuaðro de ser'βiθio; 'kuaðro de ser'βisio/ timetable.

cuadrupedal /kuaðrupe'ðal/ *a.* quadruped.

cuádruplo /'kuaðruplo/ *a.* fourfold.

cuajada /kua'haða/ *n. f.* curd.

cuajamiento /kuaha'miento/ *n. m.* coagulation.

cuajar /kua'har/ *v.* coagulate; overdecorate.

cuajo /'kuaho/ *n. m.* rennet; coagulation.

cual /kual/ *rel. pron.* which.

cuál *a. & pron.* what, which.

cualidad /kuali'ðað/ *n. f.* quality.

cualitativo /kualita'tiβo/ *a.* qualitative.

cualquiera /kual'kiera/ *a. & pron.* whatever, any; anyone.

cuando /'kuando/ *conj.* when.

cuando *adv.* when. **de cuando en cuando,** from time to time.

cuantía /kuan'tia/ *n. f.* quantity; amount.

cuantiar /kuan'tiar/ *v.* estimate.

cuantiosamente /kuantiosa'mente/ *adv.* abundantly.

cuantioso /kuan'tioso/ *a.* abundant.

cuantitativo /kuantita'tiβo/ *a.* quantitative.

cuanto /'kuanto/ *a., adv. & pron.* as much as, as many as; all that which. **en c.,** as soon as. **en c. a,** as for. **c. antes,** as soon as possible. **c. más... tanto más,** the more... the more. **unos cuantos,** a few.

cuánto *a. & adv.* how much, how many.

cuaquerismo /kuake'rismo/ *n. m.* Quakerism.

cuáquero /'kuakero/ **-ra** *n. & a.* Quaker.

cuarenta /kua'renta/ *a. & pron.* forty.

cuarentena /kuaren'tena/ *n. f.* quarantine.

cuaresma /kua'resma/ *n. f.* Lent.

cuaresmal /kuares'mal/ *a.* Lenten.

cuarta /'kuarta/ *n. f.* quarter; quadrant; quart.

cuartear /kuarte'ar/ *v.* divide into quarters.

cuartel /kuar'tel/ *n. m. Mil.* quarters; barracks; *Naut.* hatch. **c. general,** headquarters. **sin c.,** giving no quarter.

cuartelada /kuarte'laða/ *n. f.* military uprising.

cuarterón /kuarte'ron/ *n. & a.* quadroon.

cuarteto /kuar'teto/ *n. m.* quartet.

cuartillo /kuar'tiʎo; kuar'tiyo/ *n. m.* pint.

cuarto /'kuarto/ *a.* **1.** fourth. —*n.* **2.** *m.* quarter; room.

cuarto de baño /'kuarto de 'baɲo/ bathroom.

cuarto de dormir /'kuarto de dor'mir/ bedroom.

cuarto para invitados /'kuarto para imbi'taðos/ guest room.

cuarzo /'kuarθo; 'kuarso/ *n. m.* quartz.

cuasi /'kuasi/ *adv.* almost, nearly.

cuate /'kuate/ *a. & n.* twin.

cuatrero /kua'trero/ *n. m.* cattle rustler.

cuatrillón /kuatri'ʎon; kuatri'yon/ *n. m.* quadrillion.

cuatro /'kuatro/ *a. & pron.* four.

cuatrocientos /kuatro'θientos; kuatro'sientos/ *a. & pron.* four hundred.

cuba /'kuβa/ *n. f.* cask, tub, vat.

cubano /ku'βano/ **-na** *a. & n.* Cuban.

cubero /ku'βero/ *n. m.* cooper.

cubeta /ku'βeta/ *n. f.* small barrel, keg.

cúbico /'kuβiko/ *a.* cubic.

cubículo /ku'βikulo/ *n. m.* cubicle.

cubierta /ku'βierta/ *n. f.* cover; envelope; wrapping; tread (of a tire); deck.

cubiertamente /kuβierta'mente/ *adv.* secretly, stealthily.

cubierto /ku'βierto/ *n. m.* place (at table).

cubil /ku'βil/ *n. m.* lair.

cubismo /ku'βismo/ *n. m.* cubism.

cubito de hielo /ku'βito de 'ielo/ *n. m.* ice cube.

cubo /'kuβo/ *n. m.* cube; bucket.

cubo de la basura /'kuβo de la ba'sura/ trash can.

cubrecama /kuβre'kama/ *n. f.* bedspread.

cubrir /ku'βrir/ *v.* cover.

cubrirse /ku'βrirse/ *v.* put on one's hat.

cucaracha /kuka'ratʃa/ *n. f.* cockroach.

cuchara /ku'tʃara/ *n. f.* spoon, tablespoon.

cucharada /kutʃa'raða/ *n. f.* spoonful.

cucharita /kutʃa'rita/ **cucharilla** *n. f.* teaspoon.

cucharón /kutʃa'ron/ *n. m.* dipper, ladle.

cuchicheo /kutʃi'tʃeo/ *n. m.* whisper. —**cuchichear**, *v.*

cuchilla /ku'tʃiʎa; ku'tʃiya/ *n. f.* cleaver.

cuchillada /kutʃi'ʎaða; kutʃi'yaða/ *n. f.* slash.

cuchillería /kutʃiʎe'ria; kutʃiye'ria/ *n. f.* cutlery.

cuchillo /ku'tʃiʎo; ku'tʃiyo/ *n. m.* knife.

cucho /'kutʃo/ *n. m.* fertilizer.

cuchufleta /kutʃu'fleta/ *n. f.* jest.

cuclillo /ku'kliʎo; ku'kliyo/ *n. m.* cuckoo.

cuco /'kuko/ *a.* sly.

cuculla /ku'kuʎa; ku'kuya/ *n. f.* hood, cowl.

cuelga /'kuelga/ *n. f.* cluster, bunch.

cuelgacapas /kuelga'kapas/ *n. m.* coat rack.

cuello /'kueʎo; 'kueyo/ *n. m.* neck; collar.

cuenca /'kuenka/ *n. f.* socket; (river) basin; wooden bowl.

cuenco /'kuenko/ *n. m.* earthen bowl.

cuenta /'kuenta/ *n. f.* account; bill. **darse c.,** to realize. **tener en c.,** to keep in mind.

cuenta bancaria /'kuenta ban'karia/ bank account.

cuenta de ahorros /'kuenta de a'orros/ savings account.

cuentagotas /kuenta'gotas/ *n. m.* dropper (for medicine).

cuentista /kuen'tista/ *n. m. & f.* storyteller; informer.

cuento /'kuento/ *n. m.* story, tale.

cuerda /'kuerða/ *n. f.* cord; chord; rope; string; spring (of clock). **dar c. a,** to wind (clock).

cuerdamente /kuerða'mente/ *adv.* sanely; prudently.

cuerdo /'kuerðo/ *a.* sane; prudent.

cuerno /'kuerno/ *n. m.* horn.

cuero /'kuero/ *n. m.* leather; hide.

cuerpo /'kuerpo/ *n. m.* body; corps.

cuervo /'kuerβo/ *n. m.* crow, raven.

cuesco /'kuesko/ *n. m.* pit, stone (of fruit).

cuesta /'kuesta/ *n. f.* hill, slope. **llevar a cuestas,** to carry on one's back.

cuestación /kuesta'θion; kuesta'sion/ *n. f.* solicitation for charity.

cuestión /kues'tion/ *n. f.* question; affair; argument.

cuestionable /kuestio'naβle/ *a.* questionable.

cuestionar /kuestio'nar/ *v.* question; discuss; argue.

cuestionario /kuestio'nario/ *n. m.* questionnaire.

cuete /'kuete/ *n. m.* firecracker.
cueva /'kueβa/ *n. f.* cave; cellar.
cuguar /ku'guar/ *n. m.* cougar.
cugujada /kugu'haða/ *n. f.* lark.
cuidado /kui'ðaðo/ *n. m.* care, caution, worry. **tener c.,** to be careful.
cuidadosamente /kuiðaðosa-'mente/ *adv.* carefully.
cuidadoso /kuiða'ðoso/ *a.* careful, painstaking.
cuidante /kui'ðante/ *n.* caretaker, custodian.
cuidar /kui'ðar/ *v.* take care of.
cuita /'kuita/ *n. f.* trouble, care; grief.
cuitado /kui'taðo/ *a.* unfortunate; shy, timid.
cuitamiento /kuita'miento/ *n. m.* timidity.
culata /ku'lata/ *n. f.* haunch, buttock; butt of a gun.
culatada /kula'taða/ *n. f.* recoil.
culatazo /kula'taθo; kula'taso/ *n. m.* blow with the butt of a gun; recoil.
culebra /ku'leβra/ *n. f.* snake.
culero /ku'lero/ *a.* lazy, indolent.
culinario /kuli'nario/ *a.* culinary.
culminación /kulmina'θion; kulmina'sion/ *n. f.* culmination.
culminar /kulmi'nar/ *v.* culminate.
culpa /'kulpa/ *n. f.* fault, guilt, blame. **tener la c.,** to be at fault. **echar la culpa a,** to blame.
culpabilidad /kulpaβili'ðað/ *n. f.* guilt, fault, blame.
culpable /kul'paβle/ *a.* at fault, guilty, to blame, culpable.
culpar /kul'par/ *v.* blame, accuse.
cultamente /kulta'mente/ *adv.* politely, elegantly.
cultivable /kulti'βaβle/ *a.* arable.
cultivación /kultiβa'θion; kultiβa-'sion/ *n. f.* cultivation.
cultivador /kultiβa'ðor/ **-ra** *n.* cultivator.
cultivar /kulti'βar/ *v.* cultivate.
cultivo /kul'tiβo/ *n. m.* cultivation; (growing) crop.
culto /'kulto/ *a.* **1.** cultured, cultivated. —*n.* **2.** *m.* cult; worship.
cultura /kul'tura/ *n. f.* culture; refinement.
cultural /kultu'ral/ *a.* cultural.
culturar /kultu'rar/ *v.* cultivate.
culturismo /kultu'rismo/ *n. m.* body building.
culturista /kultu'rista/ *n. m. & f.* body builder.

cumbre /'kumbre/ *n. m.* summit, peak.
cumpleaños /kumple'aɲos/ *n. m.pl.* birthday.
cumplidamente /kumpliða'mente/ *adv.* courteously, correctly.
cumplido /kum'pliðo/ *a.* polite, polished.
cumplimentar /kumplimen'tar/ *v.* compliment.
cumplimiento /kumpli'miento/ *n. m.* fulfillment; compliment.
cumplir /kum'plir/ *v.* comply; carry out, fulfill; reach (years of age).
cumulativo /kumula'tiβo/ *a.* cumulative.
cúmulo /'kumulo/ *n. m.* heap, pile.
cuna /'kuna/ *n. f.* cradle.
cundir /kun'dir/ *v.* spread; expand; propagate.
cuneiforme /kunei'forme/ *a.* cuneiform, wedge-shaped.
cuneo /ku'neo/ *n. m.* rocking.
cuña /'kuɲa/ *n. f.* wedge.
cuñada /ku'ɲaða/ *n. f.* sister-in-law.
cuñado /ku'ɲaðo/ *n. m.* brother-in-law.
cuñete /ku'ɲete/ *n. m.* keg.
cuota /'kuota/ *n. f.* quota; dues.
cuotidiano /kuoti'ðiano/ *a.* daily.
cupé /ku'pe/ *n. m.* coupé.
Cupido /ku'piðo/ *n. m.* Cupid.
cupo /'kupo/ *n. m.* share; assigned quota.
cupón /ku'pon/ *n. m.* coupon.
cúpula /'kupula/ *n. f.* dome.
cura /'kura/ *n. m.* priest; *f.* treatment, (medical) care. **c. de urgencia,** first aid.
curable /ku'raβle/ *a.* curable.
curación /kura'θion; kura'sion/ *n. f.* healing; cure; (surgical) dressing.
curado /ku'raðo/ *a.* cured, healed.
curador /kura'ðor/ **-ra** *n.* healer.
curandero /kuran'dero/ **-ra** *n.* healer, medicine man.
curar /ku'rar/ *v.* cure, heal, treat.
curativo /kura'tiβo/ *a.* curative, healing.
curia /'kuria/ *n. f.* ecclesiastical court.
curiosear /kuriose'ar/ *v.* snoop, pry, meddle.
curiosidad /kuriosi'ðað/ *n. f.* curiosity.
curioso /ku'rioso/ *a.* curious.

curro /'kurro/ *a.* showy, loud, flashy.

cursante /kur'sante/ *n.* student.

cursar /kur'sar/ *v.* frequent; attend.

cursi /'kursi/ *a.* vulgar, shoddy, in bad taste.

curso /'kurso/ *n. m.* course.

curso por correspondencia /'kurso por korrespon'denθia; 'kurso por korrespon'densia/ *n. m.* correspondence course.

cursor /kur'sor/ *n. m.* cursor.

curtidor /kurti'ðor/ *n. m.* tanner.

curtir /kur'tir/ *v.* tan.

curva /'kurβa/ *n. f.* curve; bend.

curvatura /kurβa'tura, kurβi'ðað/ *n. f.* curvature.

cúspide /'kuspiðe/ *n. f.* top, peak.

custodia /kus'toðia/ *n. f.* custody.

custodiar /kusto'ðiar/ *v.* guard, watch.

custodio /kus'toðio/ *n. m.* custodian.

cutáneo /ku'taneo/ *a.* cutaneous.

cutícula /ku'tikula/ *n. f.* cuticle.

cutis /'kutis/ *n. m. or f.* skin, complexion.

cutre /'kutre/ *a.* shoddy.

cuyo /'kuyo/ *a.* whose.

D

dable /'daβle/ *a.* possible.

dactilógrafo /dakti'lografo/ **-fa** *n.* typist.

dádiva /'daðiβa/ *n. f.* gift.

dadivosamente /daðiβosa'mente/ *adv.* generously.

dadivoso /daði'βoso/ *a.* generous, bountiful.

dado /'daðo/ *n. m.* die.

dador /da'ðor/ **-ra** *n.* giver.

dados /'daðos/ *n. m.pl.* dice.

daga /'daga/ *n. f.* dagger.

dalia /'dalia/ *n. f.* dahlia.

dallador /daʎa'ðor; daya'ðor/ *n. m.* lawn mower.

dallar /da'ʎar; da'yar/ *v.* mow.

daltonismo /dalto'nismo/ *n. m.* color blindness.

dama /'dama/ *n. f.* lady.

damasco /da'masko/ *n. m.* apricot; damask.

damisela /dami'sela/ *n. f.* young lady, girl.

danés /da'nes/ **-esa** *a. & n.* Danish, Dane.

danza /'danθa; 'dansa/ *n. f.* (the) dance. **—danzar,** *v.*

danzante /dan'θante; dan'sante/ **-ta** *n.* dancer.

dañable /da'ɲaβle/ *a.* condemnable.

dañar /da'ɲar/ *v.* hurt, harm; damage.

dañino /da'ɲino/ *a.* harmful.

daño /'daɲo/ *n. m.* damage; harm.

dañoso /da'ɲoso/ *a.* harmful.

dar /dar/ *v.* give; strike (clock). **d. a,** face, open on. **d. con,** find, locate. **¡Dalo por hecho!** Consider it done!

dardo /'darðo/ *n. m.* dart.

dársena /'darsena/ *n. f.* dock.

datar /'datar/ *v.* date.

dátil /'datil/ *n. m.* date (fruit).

dativo /da'tiβo/ *n. m. & a.* dative.

datos /'datos/ *n. m.pl.* data.

de /de/ *prep.* of; from; than.

debajo /de'βaho/ *adv.* underneath. **d. de,** under.

debate /de'βate/ *n. m.* debate.

debatir /deβa'tir/ *v.* debate, argue.

debe /'deβe/ *n. m.* debit.

debelación /deβela'θion; deβela'sion/ *n. f.* conquest.

debelar /deβe'lar/ *v.* conquer.

deber /de'βer/ *v.* **1.** owe; must; be to, be supposed to. **—***n.* **2.** *m.* obligation.

deberes /de'βeres/ *n. m.pl.* homework.

debido /de'βiðo/ *a.* due.

débil /'deβil/ *a.* weak, faint.

debilidad /deβili'ðað/ *n. f.* weakness.

debilitación /deβilita'θion; deβilitasion/ *n. f.* weakness.

debilitar /deβili'tar/ *v.* weaken.

débito /'deβito/ *n. m.* debit.

debutar /deβu'tar/ *v.* make a debut.

década /'dekaða/ *n. f.* decade.

decadencia /deka'ðenθia; dekaðensia/ *n. f.* decadence, decline, decay.

decadente /deka'ðente/ *a.* decadent, declining, decaying.

decaer /deka'er/ *v.* decay, decline.

decalitro /deka'litro/ *n. m.* decaliter.

decálogo /de'kalogo/ *n. m.* m. decalogue.

decámetro /de'kametro/ *n. m.* decameter.

decano /de'kano/ *n. m.* dean.

decantado /dekan'taðo/ *a.* much discussed; overexalted.

decapitación /dekapita'θion; dekapitasion/ *n. f.* beheading.

decapitar /dekapi'tar/ *v.* behead.

decencia /de'θenθia; de'sensia/ *n. f.* decency.

decenio /de'θenio; de'senio/ *n. m.* decade.

decente /de'θente; de'sente/ *a.* decent.

decentemente /deθente'mente; desente'mente/ *adv.* decently.

decepción /deθep'θion; desep'sion/ *n. f.* disappointment, letdown; delusion.

decepcionar /deθepθio'nar; desepsio'nar/ *v.* disappoint, disillusion.

dechado /de'tʃaðo/ *n. m.* model; sample; pattern; example.

decibelio /deθi'βelio; desi'βelio/ *n. m.* decibel.

decididamente /deθiðiða'mente; desiðiða'mente/ *adv.* decidedly.

decidir /deθi'ðir; desi'ðir/ *v.* decide.

decigramo /deθi'gramo; desi'gramo/ *n. m.* decigram.

decilitro /deθi'litro; desi'litro/ *n. m.* deciliter.

décima /'deθima; 'desima/ *n. f.* ten-line stanza.

decimal /deθi'mal; desi'mal/ *a.* decimal.

décimo /'deθimo; 'desimo/ *a.* tenth.

decir /de'θir; de'sir/ *v.* tell, say. **es d.,** that is (to say).

decisión /deθi'sion; desi'sion/ *n. f.* decision.

decisivamente /deθisiβa'mente; desisiβa'mente/ *adv.* decisively.

decisivo /deθi'siβo; desi'siβo/ *a.* decisive.

declamación /deklama'θion; deklama'sion/ *n. f.* declamation, speech.

declamar /dekla'mar/ *v.* declaim.

declaración /deklara'θion; deklara'sion/ *n. f.* declaration; statement; plea.

declaración de la renta /deklara'θion de la 'rrenta; deklara'sion de la 'rrenta/ tax return.

declarar /dekla'rar/ *v.* declare, state.

declarativo /deklara'tiβo, deklara'torio/ *a.* declarative.

declinación /deklina'θion; deklina'sion/ *n. f.* descent; decay; decline; declension.

declinar /dekli'nar/ *v.* decline.

declive /de'kliβe,/ *n. m.* declivity, slope.

decocción /dekok'θion; dekok'sion/ *n. f.* decoction.

decomiso /deko'miso/ *n. m.* seizure, confiscation.

decoración /dekora'θion; dekora'sion/ *n. f.* decoration, trimming.

decorado /deko'raðo/ *n. m. Theat.* scenery, set.

decorar /deko'rar/ *v.* decorate, trim.

decorativo /dekora'tiβo/ *a.* decorative, ornamental.

decoro /de'koro/ *n. m.* decorum; decency.

decoroso /deko'roso/ *a.* decorous.

decrecer /dekre'θer; dekre'ser/ *v.* decrease.

decrépito /de'krepito/ *a.* decrepit.

decreto /de'kreto/ *n. m.* decree. —**decretar,** *v.*

dedal /de'ðal/ *n. m.* thimble.

dédalo /'deðalo/ *n. m.* labyrinth.

dedicación /deðika'θion; deðika'sion/ *n. f.* dedication.

dedicar /deði'kar/ *v.* devote; dedicate.

dedicatoria /deðika'toria/ *n. f.* dedication, inscription.

dedo /'deðo/ *n. m.* finger, toe.

dedo anular /'deðo anu'lar/ ring finger.

dedo corazón /'deðo kora'θon; 'deðo kora'son/ middle finger.

dedo índice /'deðo 'indiθe; 'deðo 'indise/ index finger.

dedo meñique /'deðo me'ɲike/ little finger, pinky.

dedo pulgar /'deðo pul'gar/ thumb.

deducción /deðuk'θion; deðuk'sion/ *n. f.* deduction.

deducir /deðu'θir; deðu'sir/ *v.* deduce; subtract.

defectivo /defek'tiβo/ *a.* defective.

defecto /de'fekto/ *n. m.* defect, flaw.

defectuoso /defek'tuoso/ *a.* defective, faulty.

defender /defen'der/ *v.* defend.

defensa /de'fensa/ *n. f.* defense.

defensivo /defen'siβo/ *a.* defensive.

defensor /defen'sor/ **-ra** *n.* defender.

deferencia /defe'renθia; deferensia/ *n. f.* deference.

deferir /defe'rir/ *v.* defer.

deficiente /defi'θiente; defi'siente/ *a.* deficient.

déficit /'defiθit; 'defisit/ *n. m.* deficit.

definición /defini'θion; defini'sion/ *n. f.* definition.

definido /defi'niðo/ *a.* definite.

definir /defi'nir/ *v.* define; establish.

definitivamente /definitiβa-'mente/ *adv.* definitely.

definitivo /defini'tiβo/ *a.* definitive.

deformación /deforma'θion; deforma'sion/ *n. f.* deformation.

deformar /defor'mar/ *v.* deform.

deforme /de'forme/ *a.* deformed; ugly.

deformidad /deformi'ðað/ *n. f.* deformity.

defraudar /defrau'ðar/ *v.* defraud.

defunción /defun'θion; defun'sion/ *n. f.* death.

degeneración /dehenera'θion; dehenera'sion/ *n. f.* degeneration.

degenerado /dehene'raðo/ *a.* degenerate. —**degenerar,** *v.*

deglutir /deglu'tir/ *v.* swallow.

degollar /dego'ʎar; dego'yar/ *v.* behead.

degradación /degraða'θion; degraða'sion/ *n. f.* degradation.

degradar /degra'ðar/ *v.* degrade, debase.

deidad /dei'ðað/ *n. f.* deity.

deificación /deifika'θion; deifika'sion/ *n. f.* deification.

deificar /deifi'kar/ *v.* deify.

deífico /de'ifiko/ *a.* divine, deific.

deísmo /de'ismo/ *n. m.* deism.

dejadez /deha'ðeθ; deha'ðes/ *n. f.* neglect, untidiness; laziness.

dejado /de'haðo/ *a.* untidy; lazy.

dejar /de'har/ *v.* let, allow; leave. **d. de,** stop, leave off. **no d. de,** not fail to.

dejo /'deho/ *n. m.* abandonment; negligence; aftertaste; accent.

del /del/ *contr. of* de + el.

delantal /delan'tal/ *n. m.* apron; pinafore. **delantal de niña,** pinafore.

delante /de'lante/ *adv.* ahead, forward; in front.

delantero /delan'tero/ *a.* forward, front, first.

delator /dela'tor/ *n. m.* informer; accuser.

delegación /delega'θion; delega'sion/ *n. f.* delegation.

delegado /dele'gaðo/ **-da** *n.* delegate. —**delegar,** *v.*

deleite /de'leite/ *n. m.* delight. —**deleitar,** *v.*

deleitoso /delei'toso/ *a.* delightful.

deletrear /deletre'ar/ *v.* spell; decipher.

delfín /del'fin/ *n. m.* dolphin; dauphin.

delgadez /delga'ðeθ; delga'ðes/ *n. f.* thinness, slenderness.

delgado /del'gaðo/ *a.* thin, slender, slim, slight.

deliberación /deliβera'θion; deliβera'sion/ *n. f.* deliberation.

deliberadamente /deliβeraða-'mente/ *adv.* deliberately.

deliberar /deliβe'rar/ *v.* deliberate.

deliberativo /deliβera'tiβo/ *a.* deliberative.

delicadamente /delikaða'mente/ *adv.* delicately.

delicadeza /delika'ðeθa; delika-'ðesa/ *n. f.* delicacy.

delicado /deli'kaðo/ *a.* delicate, dainty.

delicia /deli'θia; deli'sia/ *n. f.* delight; deliciousness.

delicioso /deli'θioso; deli'sioso/ *a.* delicious.

delincuencia /delin'kuenθia; delin'kuensia/ *n. f.* delinquency.

delincuencia de menores /delin'kuenθia de me'nores; delin'kuensia de me'nores/ **delincuencia juvenil** juvenile delinquency.

delincuente /delin'kuente/ *a. & n.* delinquent; culprit, offender.

delineación /delinea'θion; delinea'sion/ *n. f.* delineation, sketch.

delinear /deline'ar/ *v.* delineate, sketch.

delirante /deli'rante/ *a.* delirious.

delirar /deli'rar/ *v.* rave, be delirious.

delirio /de'lirio/ *n. m.* delirium; rapture, bliss.

delito /de'lito/ *n. m.* crime, offense.

delta /'delta/ *n. m.* delta (of river); hang glider.

demacrado /dema'kraðo/ *a.* emaciated.

demagogia /dema'gohia/ *n. f.* demagogy.

demagogo /dema'gogo/ *n. m.* demagogue.

demanda /de'manda/ *n. f.* demand, claim.

demandador /demanda'ðor/ **-ra** *n.* plaintiff.

demandar /deman'dar/ *v.* sue; demand.

demarcación /demarka'θion; demarka'sion/ *n. f.* demarcation.

demarcar /demar'kar/ *v.* demarcate, limit.

demás /de'mas/ *a. & n.* other; (the) rest (of). **por d.,** too much.

demasía /dema'sia/ *n. f.* excess; audacity; iniquity.

demasiado /dema'siaðo/ *a. & adv.* too; too much; too many.

demencia /de'menθia; de'mensia/ *n. f.* dementia; insanity.

demente /de'mente/ *a.* demented.

democracia /demo'kraθia; demo'krasia/ *n. f.* democracy.

demócrata /de'mokrata/ *n. m. & f.* democrat.

democrático /demo'kratiko/ *a.* democratic.

demoler /demo'ler/ *v.* demolish, tear down.

demolición /demoli'θion; demoli'sion/ *n. f.* demolition.

demonio /de'monio/ *n. m.* demon, devil.

demontre /de'montre/ *n. m.* devil.

demora /de'mora/ *n. f.* delay, —**demorar,** *v.*

demostración /demostra'θion; demostra'sion/ *n. f.* demonstration.

demostrador /demostra'ðor/ **-ra** *n.* demonstrator.

demostrar /demos'trar/ *v.* demonstrate, show.

demostrativo /demostra'tiβo/ *a.* demonstrative.

demudar /demu'ðar/ *v.* change; disguise, conceal.

denegación /denega'θion; denega'sion/ *n. f.* denial; refusal.

denegar /dene'gar/ *v.* deny; refuse.

dengue /'deŋgue/ *n. m.* prudishness; dengue.

denigración /denigra'θion; deni-gra'sion/ *n. f.* defamation, disgrace.

denigrar /deni'grar/ *v.* defame, disgrace.

denodado /deno'ðaðo/ *a.* brave, dauntless.

denominación /denomina'θion; denomina'sion/ *n. f.* denomination.

denominar /denomi'nar/ *v.* name, call.

denotación /denota'θion; denota-'sion/ *n. f.* denotation.

denotar /deno'tar/ *v.* denote, betoken, express.

densidad /densi'ðað/ *n. f.* density.

denso /'denso/ *a.* dense.

dentado /den'taðo/ *a.* toothed; serrated; cogged.

dentadura /denta'ðura/ *n. f.* set of teeth.

dentadura postiza /denta'ðura pos'tiθa; denta'ðura pos'tisa/ false teeth, dentures.

dental /den'tal/ *a.* dental.

dentífrico /den'tifriko/ *n. m.* dentifrice, toothpaste.

dentista /den'tista/ *n. m. & f.* dentist.

dentistería /dentiste'ria/ *n. f.* dentistry.

dentro /'dentro/ *adv.* within, inside. **d. de poco,** in a short while.

dentudo /den'tuðo/ *a.* toothy (person).

denuedo /de'nueðo/ *n. m.* bravery, courage.

denuesto /de'nuesto/ *n. m.* insult, offense.

denuncia /de'nunθia; de'nunsia/ *n. f.* denunciation; declaration; complaint.

denunciación /denunθia'θion; denunsia'sion/ *n. f.* denunciation.

denunciar /denun'θiar; denun'siar/ *v.* denounce.

deparar /depa'rar/ *v.* offer; grant.

departamento /departa'mento/ *n. m.* department, section.

departir /depar'tir/ *v.* talk, chat.

dependencia /depen'denθia; depen'densia/ *n. f.* dependence; branch office.

depender /depen'der/ *v.* depend.

dependiente /depen'diente/ *a. & m.* dependent; clerk.

depilar /depi'lar/ *v.* depilate, pluck.

depilatorio /depila'torio/ a. & n. depilatory.

depistar v. mislead, put off the track.

deplorable /deplo'raßle/ a. deplorable, wretched.

deplorablemente /deploraßle-'mente/ adv. deplorably.

deplorar /deplo'rar/ v. deplore.

deponer /depo'ner/ v. depose.

deportación /deporta'θion; deporta'sion/ n. f. deportation; exile.

deportar /depor'tar/ v. deport.

deporte /de'porte/ n. m. sport. —**deportivo,** a.

deposición /deposi'θion; deposi'sion/ n. f. assertion, deposition; removal; movement.

depositante /deposi'tante/ n. m. & f. depositor.

depósito /de'posito/ n. m. deposit. —**depositar,** v.

depravación /depraßa'θion; depraßa'sion/ n. f. depravation; depravity.

depravado /depra'ßaðo/ a. depraved, wicked.

depravar /depra'ßar/ v. deprave, corrupt, pervert.

depreciación /depreθia'θion; depresia'sion/ n. f. depreciation.

depreciar /depre'θiar; depre'siar/ v. depreciate.

depredación /depreða'θion; depreða'sion/ n. f. depredation.

depredar /depre'ðar/ v. pillage, depredate.

depresión /depre'sion/ n. f. depression.

depresivo /depre'sißo/ a. depressive.

deprimir /depri'mir/ v. depress.

depurar /depu'rar/ v. purify.

derecha /de'retʃa/ n. f. right (hand, side).

derechera /dere'tʃera/ n. f. shortcut.

derecho /de'retʃo/ a. **1.** right; straight. —n. **2.** m. right; (the) law. **derechos,** Com. duty.

derechos civiles /de'retʃos θi'ßiles; de'retʃos si'ßiles/ n. m.pl. civil rights.

derechos de aduana /de'retʃos de a'ðuana/ n. m.pl. customs duty.

derechura /dere'tʃura/ n. f. straightness.

derelicto /dere'likto/ a. abandoned, derelict.

deriva /de'rißa/ n. f. Naut. drift.

derivación /derißa'θion; derißa'sion/ n. f. derivation.

derivar /deri'ßar/ v. derive.

dermatólogo /derma'tologo/ -a n. dermatologist, skin doctor.

derogar /dero'gar/ v. derogate; repeal, abrogate.

derramamiento /derrama'miento/ n. m. overflow.

derramar /derra'mar/ v. spill, pour, scatter.

derrame /de'rrame/ n. m. overflow; discharge.

derretir /derre'tir/ v. melt, dissolve.

derribar /derri'ßar/ v. demolish, knock down; bowl over, floor, fell.

derrocamiento /derroka'miento/ n. m. overthrow.

derrocar /derro'kar/ v. overthrow; oust; demolish.

derrochar /derro'tʃar/ v. waste.

derroche /de'rrotʃe/ n. m. waste.

derrota /de'rrota/ n. f. rout, defeat. —**derrotar,** v.

derrotismo /derro'tismo/ n. m. defeatism.

derrumbamiento /derrumba-'miento/ **derrumbe** m. collapse; landslide.

derrumbarse /derrum'ßarse/ v. collapse, tumble.

derviche /der'ßitʃe/ n. m. dervish.

desabotonar /desaßoto'nar/ v. unbutton.

desabrido /desa'ßriðo/ a. insipid, tasteless.

desabrigar /desaßri'gar/ v. uncover.

desabrochar /desaßro'tʃar/ v. unbutton, unclasp.

desacato /desa'kato/ n. m. disrespect, lack of respect.

desacierto /desa'θierto; desa-'sierto/ n. m. error.

desacobardar /desakoßar'ðar/ v. remove fear; embolden.

desacomodadamente /desakomoðaða'mente/ adv. inconveniently.

desacomodado /desakomo'ðaðo/ a. unemployed.

desacomodar /desakomo'ðar/ v. molest; inconvenience; dismiss.

desacomodo /desako'moðo/ n. m. loss of employment.

desaconsejar /desakonse'har/ v. dissuade (someone); advise against (something).

desacordadamente /desakorða-ða'mente/ adv. unadvisedly.

desacordar /desakor'ðar/ v. differ, disagree; be forgetful.

desacorde /desa'korðe/ a. discordant.

desacostumbradamente /de-sakostumbraða'mente/ adv. unusually.

desacostumbrado /desakostum-'braðo/ a. unusual, unaccustomed.

desacostumbrar /desakostum-'brar/ v. give up a habit or custom.

desacreditar /desakreði'tar/ v. discredit.

desacuerdo /desa'kuerðo/ n. m. disagreement.

desadeudar /desaðeu'ðar/ v. pay one's debts.

desadormecer /desaðorme'θer; desaðorme'ser/ v. waken, rouse.

desadornar /desaðor'nar/ v. divest of ornament.

desadvertidamente /desaðβerti-ða'mente/ adv. inadvertently.

desadvertido /desaðβer'tiðo/ a. imprudent.

desadvertimiento /desaðβerti-'miento/ n. m. imprudence, rashness.

desadvertir /desaðβer'tir/ v. act imprudently.

desafección /desafek'θion; desafek'sion/ n. f. disaffection.

desafecto /desa'fekto/ a. disaffected.

desafiar /desa'fiar/ v. defy; challenge.

desafinar /desafi'nar/ v. be out of tune.

desafío /desa'fio/ n. m. defiance; challenge.

desaforar /desafo'rar/ v. infringe one's rights; be outrageous.

desafortunado /desafortu'naðo/ a. unfortunate.

desafuero /desa'fuero/ n. m. violation of the law; outrage.

desagraciado /desagra'θiaðo; desagra'siaðo/ a. graceless.

desagradable /desagra'ðaβle/ a. disagreeable, unpleasant.

desagradablemente /desagra-ðaβle'mente/ adv. disagreeably.

desagradecido /desagraðe'θiðo; desagraðe'siðo/ a. ungrateful.

desagradecimiento /desagraðe-θi'miento; desagraðesimiento/ n. m. ingratitude.

desagrado /desa'graðo/ n. m. displeasure.

desagraviar /desagra'βiar/ v. make amends.

desagregar /desagre'gar/ v. separate, disintegrate.

desagriar /desa'griar/ v. mollify, appease.

desaguadero /desagua'ðero/ n. m. drain, outlet; cesspool; sink.

desaguador /desagua'ðor/ n. m. water pipe.

desaguar /desa'guar/ v. drain.

desaguisado /desagi'saðo/ n. m. offense; injury.

desahogadamente /desaogaða-'mente/ adv. impudently; brazenly.

desahogado /desao'gaðo/ a. impudent, brazen; cheeky.

desahogar /desao'gar/ v. relieve.

desahogo /desa'ogo/ n. m. relief; nerve, cheek.

desahuciar /desau'θiar; desau'siar/ v. give up hope for; despair of.

desairado /desai'raðo/ a. graceless.

desaire /des'aire/ n. m. slight; scorn. —**desairar,** v.

desajustar /desahus'tar/ v. mismatch, misfit; make unfit.

desalar /desa'lar/ v. hurry, hasten.

desalentar /desalen'tar/ v. make out of breath; discourage.

desaliento /desa'liento/ n. m. discouragement.

desaliñar /desali'ɲar/ v. disarrange; make untidy.

desaliño /desa'liɲo/ n. m. slovenliness, untidiness.

desalivar /desali'βar/ v. remove saliva from.

desalmadamente /desalmaða-'mente/ adv. mercilessly.

desalmado /desal'maðo/ a. merciless.

desalojamiento /desaloha'miento/ n. m. displacement; dislodging.

desalojar /desalo'har/ v. dislodge.

desalquilado /desalki'laðo/ a. vacant, unrented.

desamar /desa'mar/ v. cease loving.

desamasado /desama'saðo/ *a.* dissolved, disunited, undone.

desamistarse /desamis'tarse/ *v.* quarrel, disagree.

desamor /desa'mor/ *n. m.* disaffection, dislike; hatred.

desamorado /desamo'raðo/ *a.* cruel; harsh; rude.

desamparador /desampara'ðor/ *n. m.* deserter.

desamparar /desampa'rar/ *v.* desert, abandon.

desamparo /desam'paro/ *n. m.* desertion, abandonment.

desamueblado /desamue'βlaðo/ *a.* unfurnished.

desamueblar /desamue'βlar/ *v.* remove furniture from.

desandrajado /desandra'haðo/ *a.* shabby, ragged.

desanimadamente /desanimaða'mente/ *adv.* in a discouraged manner; spiritlessly.

desanimar /desani'mar/ *v.* dishearten, discourage.

desánimo /des'animo/ *n. m.* discouragement.

desanudar /desanu'ðar/ *v.* untie; loosen; disentangle.

desapacible /desapa'θiβle; desapa'siβle/ *a.* rough, harsh; unpleasant.

desaparecer /desapare'θer; desapare'ser/ *v.* disappear.

desaparición /desapari'θion; desapari'sion/ *n. f.* disappearance.

desapasionadamente /desapasionaða'mente/ *adv.* dispassionately.

desapasionado /desapasio'naðo/ *a.* dispassionate.

desapego /desa'pego/ *n. m.* impartiality.

desapercibido /desaperθi'βiðo; desapersi'βiðo/ *a.* unnoticed; unprepared.

desapiadado /desapia'ðaðo/ *a.* merciless, cruel.

desaplicación /desaplika'θion; desaplika'sion/ *n. f.* indolence, laziness; negligence.

desaplicado /desapli'kaðo/ *a.* indolent, lazy; negligent.

desaposesionar /desaposesio'nar/ *v.* dispossess.

desapreciar /desapre'θiar; desapre'siar/ *v.* depreciate.

desapretador /desapreta'ðor/ *n. m.* screwdriver.

desapretar /desapre'tar/ *v.* loosen; relieve, ease.

desaprisionar /desaprisio'nar/ *v.* set free, release.

desaprobación /desaproβa'θion; desaproβa'sion/ *n. f.* disapproval.

desaprobar /desapro'βar/ *v.* disapprove.

desaprovechado /desaproβe'tʃaðo/ *a.* useless, profitless; backward.

desaprovechar /desaproβe'tʃar/ *v.* waste; be backward.

desarbolar /desarβo'lar/ *v.* unmast.

desarmado /desar'maðo/ *a.* disarmed, defenseless.

desarmar /desar'mar/ *v.* disarm.

desarme /de'sarme/ *n. m.* disarmament.

desarraigado /desarrai'gaðo/ *a.* rootless.

desarraigar /desarrai'gar/ *v.* uproot; eradicate; expel.

desarreglar /desarre'glar/ *v.* disarrange, mess up.

desarrollar /desarro'ʎar; desarro'yar/ *v.* develop.

desarrollo /desa'rroʎo; des'arroyo/ *n. m.* development.

desarropar /desarro'par/ *v.* undress; uncover.

desarrugar /desarru'gar/ *v.* remove wrinkles from.

desaseado /desase'aðo/ *a.* dirty; disorderly.

desasear /desase'ar/ *v.* make dirty or disorderly.

desaseo /desa'seo/ *n. m.* dirtiness; disorder.

desasir /desa'sir/ *v.* loosen; disengage.

desasociable /desaso'θiaβle; desaso'siaβle/ *a.* unsociable.

desasosegar /desasose'gar/ *v.* disturb.

desasosiego /desaso'siego/ *n. m.* uneasiness.

desastrado /desas'traðo/ *a.* ragged, wretched.

desastre /de'sastre/ *n. m.* disaster.

desastroso /desas'troso/ *a.* disastrous.

desatar /desa'tar/ *v.* untie, undo.

desatención /desaten'θion; desaten'sion/ *n. f.* inattention; disrespect; rudeness.

desatender /desaten'der/ *v.* ignore; disregard.

desatentado /desaten'taðo/ *a.* inconsiderate; imprudent.

desatinado /desati'naðo/ *a.* foolish; insane, wild.

desatino /desa'tino/ *n. m.* blunder. **—desatinar,** *v.*

desatornillar /desatorni'ʎar; desatorni'yar/ *v.* unscrew.

desautorizado /desautori'θaðo; desautori'saðo/ *a.* unauthorized.

desautorizar /desautori'θar; desautori'sar/ *v.* deprive of authority.

desavenencia /desaβe'nenθia; desaβe'nensia/ *n. f.* disagreement, discord.

desaventajado /desaβenta'haðo/ *a.* disadvantageous.

desayuno /desa'yuno/ *n. m.* breakfast. **—desayunar,** *v.*

desazón /desa'θon; desa'son/ *n. f.* insipidity; uneasiness.

desazonado /desaθo'naðo; desaso'naðo/ *a.* insipid; uneasy.

desbandada /desβan'daða/ *n. f.* disbanding.

desbandarse /desβan'darse/ *v.* disband.

desbarajuste /desβara'huste/ *n. m.* disorder, confusion.

desbaratar /desβara'tar/ *v.* destroy.

desbastar /desβas'tar/ *v.* plane, smoothen.

desbocado /desβo'kaðo/ *a.* foulspoken, indecent.

desbocarse /desβo'karse/ *v.* use obscene language.

desbordamiento /desβorða'miento/ *n. m.* overflow; flood.

desbordar /desβor'ðar/ *v.* overflow.

desbrozar /desβro'θar; desβro'sar/ *v.* clear away rubbish.

descabal /deska'βal/ *a.* incomplete.

descabalar /deskaβa'lar/ *v.* render incomplete; impair.

descabellado /deskaβe'ʎaðo; deskaβe'yaðo/ *a.* absurd, preposterous.

descabezar /deskaβe'θar; deskaβe'sar/ *v.* behead.

descaecimiento /deskaeθi'miento; deskaesi'miento/ *n. m.* weakness; dejection.

descafeinado /deskafei'naðo/ *a.* decaffeinated.

descalabrar /deskala'βrar/ *v.* injure, wound (esp. the head).

descalabro /deska'laβro/ *n. m.* accident, misfortune.

descalzarse /deskal'θarse; deskal'sarse/ *v.* take off one's shoes.

descalzo /des'kalθo; des'kalso/ *a.* shoeless; barefoot.

descaminado /deskami'naðo/ *a.* wrong, misguided.

descaminar /deskami'nar/ *v.* mislead; lead into error.

descamisado /deskami'saðo/ *a.* shirtless; shabby.

descansillo /deskan'siʎo; deskan'siyo/ *n. m.* landing (of stairs).

descanso /des'kanso/ *n. m.* rest. **—descansar,** *v.*

descarado /deska'raðo/ *a.* saucy, fresh.

descarga /des'karga/ *n. f.* discharge.

descargar /deskar'gar/ *v.* discharge, unload, dump.

descargo /des'kargo/ *n. m.* unloading; acquittal.

descarnar /deskar'nar/ *v.* skin.

descaro /des'karo/ *n. m.* gall, effrontery.

descarriar /deska'rriar/ *v.* lead or go astray.

descarrilamiento /deskarrila'miento/ *n. m.* derailment.

descarrilar /deskarri'lar/ *v.* derail.

descartar /deskar'tar/ *v.* discard.

descascarar /deskaska'rar/ *v.* peel; boast, brag.

descendencia /desθen'denθia; dessen'densia/ *n. f.* descent, origin; progeny.

descender /desθen'der; dessen'der/ *v.* descend.

descendiente /desθen'diente; dessen'diente/ *n. m. & f.* descendant.

descendimiento /desθendi'miento; dessendi'miento/ *n. m.* descent.

descenso /des'θenso; des'senso/ *n. m.* descent.

descentralización /desθentraliθa'θion; dessentralisa'sion/ *n. f.* decentralization.

descifrar /desθi'frar; dessi'frar/ *v.* decipher, puzzle out.

descoco /des'koko/ *n. m.* boldness, brazenness.

descolgar /deskol'gar/ *v.* take down.

descollar /desko'ʎar; desko'yar/ *v.* stand out; excel.

descolorar 62

descolorar /deskolo'rar/ v. discolor.

descolorido /deskolo'riðo/ a. pale, faded.

descomedido /deskome'ðiðo/ a. disproportionate; rude.

descomedirse /deskome'ðirse/ v. be rude.

descomponer /deskompo'ner/ v. decompose; break down, get out of order.

descomposición /deskomposi'θion; deskomposi'sion/ n. f. discomposure; disorder, confusion.

descompuesto /deskom'puesto/ a. impudent, rude.

descomulgar /deskomul'gar/ v. excommunicate.

descomunal /deskomu'nal/ a. extraordinary, huge.

desconcertar /deskonθer'tar; deskonser'tar/ v. disconcert, baffle.

desconcierto /deskon'θierto; deskon'sierto/ n. m. confusion, disarray.

desconectar /deskonek'tar/ v. disconnect.

desconfiado /deskon'fiaðo/ a. distrustful.

desconfianza /deskon'fianθa; deskon'fiansa/ n. f. distrust.

desconfiar /deskon'fiar/ v. distrust, mistrust; suspect.

descongelar /deskoŋge'lar/ v. defrost.

descongestionante /deskoŋgestio'nante/ n. m. decongestant.

desconocer /deskono'θer; deskono'ser/ v. ignore, fail to recognize.

desconocido /deskono'θiðo; deskonos'iðo/ **-da** n. stranger.

desconocimiento /deskonoθi'miento; deskonosi'miento/ n. m. ingratitude; ignorance.

desconsejado /deskonse'haðo/ a. imprudent, ill advised, rash.

desconsolado /deskonso'laðo/ a. disconsolate, wretched.

desconsuelo /deskon'suelo/ n. m. grief.

descontar /deskon'tar/ v. discount, subtract.

descontentar /deskonten'tar/ v. dissatisfy.

descontento /deskon'tento/ n. m. discontent.

descontinuar /deskonti'nuar/ v. discontinue.

desconvenir /deskombe'nir/ v. disagree.

descorazonar /deskoraθo'nar; deskoraso'nar/ v. dishearten.

descorchar /deskor'tʃar/ v. uncork.

descortés /deskor'tes/ a. discourteous, impolite, rude.

descortesía /deskorte'sia/ n. f. discourtesy, rudeness.

descortezar /deskorte'θar; deskorte'sar/ v. peel.

descoyuntar /deskoyun'tar/ v. dislocate.

descrédito /des'kreðito/ n. m. discredit.

describir /deskri'βir/ v. describe.

descripción /deskrip'θion; deskrip'sion/ n. f. description.

descriptivo /deskrip'tiβo/ a. descriptive.

descuartizar /deskuarti'θar; deskuarti'sar/ v. dismember, disjoint.

descubridor /deskuβri'ðor/ **-ra** n. discoverer.

descubrimiento /deskuβri'miento/ n. m. discovery.

descubrir /desku'βrir/ v. discover; uncover; disclose.

descubrirse /desku'βrirse/ v. take off one's hat.

descuento /des'kuento/ n. m. discount.

descuidado /deskui'ðaðo/ a. reckless, careless; slack.

descuido /des'kuiðo/ n. m. neglect. —**descuidar,** v.

desde /'desðe/ prep. since; from. **d. luego,** of course.

desdén /des'ðen/ n. m. disdain. —**desdeñar,** v.

desdeñoso /desðe'ɲoso/ a. contemptuous, disdainful, scornful.

desdicha /des'ðitʃa/ n. f. misfortune.

deseable /dese'aβle/ a. desirable.

desear /dese'ar/ v. desire, wish.

desecar /dese'kar/ v. dry, desiccate.

desechable /dese'tʃaβle/ a. disposable.

desechar /dese'tʃar/ v. scrap, reject.

desecho /de'setʃo/ n. m. remainder, residue; (pl.) waste.

desembalar /desemba'lar/ v. unpack.

desembarazado /desembara'θaðo; desembara'saðo/ a. free; unrestrained.

desembarazar /desembara'θar; desembara'sar/ *v.* free; extricate; unburden.

desembarcar /desembar'kar/ *v.* disembark, go ashore.

desembocar /desembo'kar/ *v.* flow into.

desembolsar /desembol'sar/ *v.* disburse; expend.

desembolso /desem'bolso/ *n. m.* disbursement.

desemejante /deseme'hante/ *a.* unlike, dissimilar.

desempacar /desempa'kar/ *v.* unpack.

desempeñar /desempe'ɲar/ *v.* carry out; redeem.

desempeño /desempe'ɲo/ *n. m.* fulfillment.

desencajar /desenka'har/ *v.* disjoint; disturb.

desencantar /desenkan'tar/ *v.* disillusion.

desencanto /desen'kanto/ *n. m.* disillusion.

desencarcelar /desenkarθe'lar; desenkarse'lar/ *v.* set free; release.

desenchufar /desentʃu'far/ *v.* unplug.

desenfadado /desenfa'ðaðo/ *a.* free; unembarrassed; spacious.

desenfado /desen'faðo/ *n. m.* freedom; ease; calmness.

desenfocado /desenfo'kaðo/ *a.* out of focus.

desengaño /deseŋ'gaɲo/ *m.* disillusion. **—desengañar** *v.*

desenlace /desen'laθe; desen'lase/ *n. m.* outcome, conclusion.

desenredar /desenre'ðar/ *v.* disentangle.

desensartar /desensar'tar/ *v.* unthread (pearls).

desentenderse /desenten'derse/ *v.* overlook; avoid noticing.

desenterrar /desente'rrar/ *v.* disinter, exhume.

desenvainar /desembai'nar/ *v.* unsheath.

desenvoltura /desembol'tura/ *n. f.* confidence; impudence, boldness.

desenvolver /desembol'βer/ *v.* evolve, unfold.

deseo /de'seo/ *n. m.* wish, desire, urge.

deseoso /dese'oso/ *a.* desirous.

deserción /deser'θion; deser'sion/ *n. f.* desertion.

desertar /deser'tar/ *v.* desert.

desertor /deser'tor/ **-ra** *n.* deserter.

desesperación /desespera'θion; desespera'sion/ *n. f.* despair, desperation.

desesperado /desespe'raðo/ *a.* desperate; hopeless.

desesperar /desespe'rar/ *v.* despair.

desfachatez /desfatʃa'teθ; desfatʃa'tes/ *n. f.* cheek (gall).

desfalcar /desfal'kar/ *v.* embezzle.

desfase horario /des'fase o'rario/ *n. m.* jet lag.

desfavorable /desfaβo'raβle/ *a.* unfavorable.

desfigurar /desfigu'rar/ *v.* disfigure, mar.

desfiladero /desfila'ðero/ *n. m.* defile.

desfile /des'file/ *n. m.* parade. **—desfilar,** *v.*

desfile de modas /des'file de 'moðas/ fashion show.

desgaire /des'gaire/ *n. m.* slovenliness.

desgana /des'gana/ *n. f.* lack of appetite; unwillingness; repugnance.

desgarrar /desga'rrar/ *v.* tear, lacerate.

desgastar /desgas'tar/ *v.* wear away; waste; erode.

desgaste /des'gaste/ *n. m.* wear; erosion.

desgracia /des'graθia; des'grasia/ *n. f.* misfortune.

desgraciado /desgra'θiaðo; desgra'siaðo/ *a.* unfortunate.

desgranar /desgra'nar/ *v.* shell.

desgreñar /desgre'ɲar/ *v.* dishevel.

deshacer /desa'θer; desa'ser/ *v.* undo, take apart, destroy.

deshacerse de /desa'θerse de; desa'serse de/ *v.* get rid of, dispose of.

deshecho /des'etʃo/ *a.* undone; wasted.

deshelar /dese'lar/ *v.* thaw; melt.

desheredamiento /desereða'miento/ *n. m.* disinheriting.

desheredar /desere'ðar/ *v.* disinherit.

deshielo /des'ielo/ *n. m.* thaw, melting.

deshinchar /desin'tʃar/ *v.* reduce a swelling.

deshojarse /deso'harse/ *v.* shed (leaves).

deshonestidad /desonesti'ðað/ *n. f.* dishonesty.

deshonesto /deso'nesto/ *a.* dishonest.

deshonra /de'sonra/ *n. f.* dishonor.

deshonrar /deson'rar/ *v.* disgrace; dishonor.

deshonroso /deson'roso/ *a.* dishonorable.

desierto /de'sierto/ *n. m.* desert, wilderness.

designar /desig'nar/ *v.* appoint, name.

designio /de'signio/ *n. m.* purpose, intent.

desigual /desi'gual/ *a.* uneven, unequal.

desigualdad /desigual'dað/ *n. f.* inequality.

desilusión /desilu'sion/ *n. f.* disappointment.

desinfección /desinfek'θion; desinfek'sion/ *n. f.* disinfection.

desinfectar /desinfek'tar/ *v.* disinfect.

desintegrar /desinte'grar/ *v.* disintegrate, zap.

desinterés /desinte'res/ *n. m.* indifference.

desinteresado /desintere'saðo/ *a.* disinterested, unselfish.

desistir /desis'tir/ *v.* desist, stop.

desleal /desle'al/ *a.* disloyal.

deslealtad /desleal'tað/ *n. f.* disloyalty.

desleir /desle'ir/ *v.* dilute, dissolve.

desligar /desli'gar/ *v.* untie, loosen; free, release.

deslindar /deslin'dar/ *v.* make the boundaries of.

deslinde /des'linde/ *n. m.* demarcation.

desliz /des'liθ; des'lis/ *n. m.* slip; false step; weakness.

deslizarse /desli'θarse; desli'sarse/ *v.* slide; slip; glide; coast.

deslumbramiento /deslumbra-'miento/ *n. m.* dazzling glare; confusion.

deslumbrar /deslumb'rar/ *v.* dazzle; glare.

deslustre /des'lustre/ *n. m.* tarnish. —**deslustrar,** *v.*

desmán /des'man/ *n. m.* mishap; misbehavior; excess.

desmantelar /desmante'lar/ *v.* dismantle.

desmañado /desma'ɲaðo/ *a.* awkward, clumsy.

desmaquillarse /desmaki'ʎarse; desmaki'yarse/ *v.* remove one's makeup.

desmayar /desma'yar/ *v.* depress, dishearten.

desmayo /des'mayo/ *n. m.* faint. —**desmayarse,** *v.*

desmejorar /desmeho'rar/ *v.* make worse; decline.

desmembrar /desmem'brar/ *v.* dismember.

desmemoria /desme'moria/ *n. f.* forgetfulness.

desmemoriado /desmemo'riaðo/ *a.* forgetful.

desmentir /desmen'tir/ *v.* contradict, disprove.

desmenuzable /desmenu'θaβle; desmenu'saβle/ *a.* crisp, crumbly.

desmenuzar /desmenu'θar; desmenu'sar/ *v.* crumble, break into bits.

desmesurado /desmesu'raðo/ *a.* excessive.

desmobilizar /desmoβili'θar; desmoβili'sar/ *v.* demobilize.

desmonetización /desmonetiθa-'θion; desmonetisa'sion/ *n. f.* demonetization.

desmonetizar /desmoneti'θar; desmoneti'sar/ *v.* demonetize.

desmontado /desmon'taðo/ *a.* dismounted.

desmontar /desmon'tar/ *v.* dismantle.

desmontarse /desmon'tarse/ *v.* dismount.

desmoralización /desmoraliθa-'θion; desmoralisa'sion/ *n. f.* demoralization.

desmoralizar /desmorali'θar; desmorali'sar/ *v.* demoralize.

desmoronar /desmoro'nar/ *v.* crumble, decay.

desmovilizar /desmoβili'θar; desmoβili'sar/ *v.* demobilize.

desnatar /desna'tar/ *v.* skim.

desnaturalización /desnaturaliθa-'θion; desnaturalisa'sion/ *n. f.* denaturalization.

desnaturalizar /desnaturali'θar; desnaturali'sar/ *v.* denaturalize.

desnegamiento /desnega'miento/ *n. m.* denial, contradiction.

desnervar /desner'βar/ *v.* enervate.

desnivel /desni'βel/ *n. m.* unevenness or difference in elevation.

desnudamente /desnuða'mente/ *adv.* nakedly.

desnudar /desnu'ðar/ *v.* undress.

desnudez /desnu'ðeθ; desnu'ðes/ *n. f.* bareness, nudity.

desnudo /des'nuðo/ *a.* bare, naked.

desnutrición /desnutri'θion; desnutri'sion/ *n. f.* malnutrition.

desobedecer /desoβeðe'θer; desoβeðe'ser/ *v.* disobey.

desobediencia /desoβeðien'θia; desoβeðien'sia/ *n. f.* disobedience.

desobediente /desoβe'ðiente/ *a.* disobedient.

desobedientemente /desoβeðiente'mente/ *adv.* disobediently.

desobligar /desoβli'gar/ *v.* release from obligation; offend.

desocupado /desoku'paðo/ *a.* idle, not busy; vacant.

desocupar /desoku'par/ *v.* vacate.

desolación /desola'θion; desola-'sion/ *n. f.* desolation; ruin.

desolado /deso'laðo/ *a.* desolate. —**desolar**, *v.*

desollar /deso'ʎar; deso'yar/ *v.* skin.

desorden /de'sorðen/ *n. m.* disorder.

desordenar /desorðe'nar/ *v.* disarrange.

desorganización /desorganiθa-'θion; desorganisa'sion/ *n. f.* disorganization.

desorganizar /desorgani'θar; desorgani'sar/ *v.* disorganize.

despabilado /despaβi'laðo/ *a.* vigilant, watchful; lively.

despachar /despa't ʃar/ *v.* dispatch, ship, send.

despacho /despa't ʃo/ *n. m.* shipment; dispatch, promptness; office.

despacio /des'paθio; des'pasio/ *adv.* slowly.

desparpajo /despar'paho/ *n. m.* glibness; fluency of speech.

desparramar /desparra'mar/ *v.* scatter.

despavorido /despaβo'riðo/ *a.* terrified.

despecho /des'pet ʃo/ *n. m.* spite.

despedazar /despeða'θar; despeða'sar/ *v.* tear up.

despedida /despe'ðiða/ *n. f.* farewell; leave-taking; discharge.

despedir /despe'ðir/ *v.* dismiss, discharge; see off.

despedirse de /despe'ðirse de/ *v.* say good-bye to, take leave of.

despegar /despe'gar/ *v.* unglue; separate; *Aero.* take off.

despego /des'pego/ *n. m.* indifference; disinterest.

despejar /despe'har/ *v.* clear, clear up.

despejo /des'peho/ *n. m.* sprightliness; clarity; without obstruction.

despensa /des'pensa/ *n. f.* pantry.

despensero /despen'sero/ *n. m.* butler.

despeñar /despe'ɲar/ *v.* throw down.

desperdicio /desper'ðiθio; desper'ðisio/ *n. m.* waste. —**desperdiciar**, *v.*

despertador /desperta'ðor/ *n. m.* alarm clock.

despertar /desper'tar/ *v.* wake, wake up.

despesar /despe'sar/ *n. m.* dislike.

despicar /despi'kar/ *v.* satisfy.

despidida /despi'ðiða/ *n. f.* gutter.

despierto /des'pierto/ *a.* awake; alert, wide-awake.

despilfarrado /despilfa'rraðo/ *a.* wasteful, extravagant.

despilfarrar /despilfa'rrar/ *v.* waste, squander.

despilfarro /despil'farro/ *n. m.* waste, extravagance.

despique /des'pike/ *n. m.* revenge.

despistar /despis'tar/ *v.* mislead, put off the track.

desplazamiento /desplaθa-'miento; desplasa'miento/ *n. m.* displacement.

desplegar /desple'gar/ *v.* display; unfold.

desplome /des'plome/ *n. m.* collapse. —**desplomarse**, *v.*

desplumar /desplu'mar/ *v.* defeather, pluck.

despoblar /despo'βlar/ *v.* depopulate.

despojar /despo'har/ *v.* strip; despoil, plunder.

despojo /des'poho/ *n. m.* plunder, spoils; (*pl.*) remains, debris.

desposado /despo'saðo/ *a.* newly married.

desposar /despo'sar/ *v.* marry.

desposeer /despose'er/ *v.* dispossess.

déspota /'despota/ *n. m. & f.* despot.

despótico /des'potiko/ a. despotic.

despotismo /despo'tismo/ n. m. despotism, tyranny.

despreciable /despre'θiaβle; despre'siaβle/ a. contemptible.

despreciar /despre'θiar; despre'siar/ v. spurn, despise, scorn.

desprecio /des'preθio; des'presio/ n. m. scorn, contempt.

desprender /despren'der/ v. detach, unfasten.

desprenderse /despren'derse/ v. loosen, come apart. **d. de,** part with.

desprendido /despren'diðo/ a. disinterested.

despreocupado /despreoku'paðo/ a. unconcerned; unprejudiced.

desprevenido /despreβe'niðo/ a. unprepared, unready.

desproporción /despropor'θion; despropor'sion/ n. f. disproportion.

despropósito /despro'posito/ n. m. nonsense.

desprovisto /despro'βisto/ a. devoid.

después /des'pues/ adv. afterwards, later; then, next. **d. de, d. que,** after.

despuntar /despun'tar/ v. blunt; remove the point of.

desquiciar /deski'θiar; deski'siar/ v. unhinge; disturb, unsettle.

desquitar /deski'tar/ v. get revenge, retaliate.

desquite /des'kite/ n. m. revenge, retaliation.

desrazonable /desraθo'naβle; desraso'naβle/ a. unreasonable.

destacamento /destaka'mento/ n. m. Mil. detachment.

destacarse /desta'karse/ v. stand out, be prominent.

destajero /desta'hero/ **-a** n. **destajista,** m. & f. pieceworker.

destapar /desta'par/ v. uncover.

destello /des'teʎo; deste'yo/ n. m. sparkle, gleam.

destemplar /destem'plar/ v. Mus. untune; disturb, upset.

desteñir /deste'ɲir/ v. fade, discolor.

desterrado /deste'rraðo/ **-da** n. exile.

desterrar /deste'rrar/ v. banish, exile.

destetar /deste'tar/ v. wean.

destierro /des'tierro/ n. m. banishment, exile.

destilación /destila'θion; destila'sion/ n. f. distillation.

destilar /desti'lar/ v. distill.

destilería /destile'ria/ n. f. distillery.

destilería de petróleo /destile'ria de pe'troleo/ oil refinery.

destinación /destina'θion; destina'sion/ n. f. destination.

destinar /desti'nar/ v. destine, intend.

destinatario /destina'tario/ **-ria** n. addressee (mail); payee (money).

destino /des'tino/ n. m. destiny, fate; destination.

destitución /destitu'θion; destitu'sion/ n. f. dismissal; abandonment.

destituido /desti'tuiðo/ a. destitute.

destorcer /destor'θer; destor'ser/ v. undo, straighten out.

destornillado /destorni'ʎaðo; destorni'yaðo/ a. reckless, careless.

destornillador /destorni'ʎaðor; destorni'yaðor/ n. m. screwdriver.

destraillar /destrai'ʎar; destrai'yar/ v. unleash; set loose.

destral /des'tral/ n. m. hatchet.

destreza /des'treθa; des'tresa/ n. f. cleverness; dexterity, skill.

destripar /destri'par/ v. eviscerate, disembowel.

destrísimo /des'trisimo/ a. extremely dexterous.

destronamiento /destrona'miento/ n. m. dethronement.

destronar /destro'nar/ v. dethrone.

destrozador /destroθa'ðor; destrosa'ðor/ n. m. destroyer, wrecker.

destrozar /destro'θar; destro'sar/ v. destroy, wreck.

destrozo /des'troθo; des'troso/ n. m. destruction, ruin.

destrucción /destruk'θion; destruk'sion/ n. f. destruction.

destructibilidad /destruktiβili'ðað/ n. f. destructibility.

destructible /destruk'tiβle/ a. destructible.

destructivamente /destruktiβa'mente/ adv. destructively.

destructivo /destruk'tiβo/ a. destructive.

destruir /destruir/ *v.* destroy; wipe out.

desuello /desue'ʎo; desue'yo/ *n. m.* impudence.

desunión /desu'nion/ *n. f.* disunion; discord; separation.

desunir /desu'nir/ *v.* disconnect, sever.

desusadamente /desusaða'mente/ *adv.* unusually.

desusado /desu'saðo/ *a.* archaic; obsolete.

desuso /de'suso/ *n. m.* disuse.

desvalido /des'βaliðo/ *a.* helpless; destitute.

desvalijador /desβaliha'ðor/ *n. m.* highwayman.

desván /des'βan/ *n. m.* attic.

desvanecerse /desβane'θerse; desβane'serse/ *v.* vanish; faint.

desvariado /desβa'riaðo/ *a.* delirious; disorderly.

desvarío /desβa'rio/ *n. m.* raving. —**desvariar,** *v.*

desvedado /desβe'ðaðo/ *a.* free; unrestrained.

desveladamente /desβelaða-'mente/ *adv.* watchfully, alertly.

desvelado /desβe'laðo/ *a.* watchful; alert.

desvelar /desβe'lar/ *v.* be watchful; keep awake.

desvelo /des'βelo/ *n. m.* vigilance; uneasiness; insomnia.

desventaja /desβen'taha/ *n. f.* disadvantage.

desventar /desβen'tar/ *v.* let air out of.

desventura /desβen'tura/ *n. f.* misfortune.

desventurado /desβentu'raðo/ *a.* unhappy; unlucky.

desvergonzado /desβergon'θaðo; desβergonsaðo/ *a.* shameless, brazen.

desvergüenza /desβer'guenθa; desβer'guensa/ *n. f.* shamelessness.

desvestir /desβes'tir/ *v.* undress.

desviación /desβia'θion; desβia-'sion/ *n. f.* deviation.

desviado /des'βiaðo/ *a.* deviant; remote.

desviar /des'βiar/ *v.* divert; deviate, detour.

desvío /des'βio/ *n. m.* detour; side track; indifference.

desvirtuar /desβir'tuar/ *v.* decrease the value of.

deszumar /desθu'mar; dessu'mar/ *v.* remove the juice from.

detalle /de'taʎe; de'taye/ *n. m.* detail. —**detallar,** *v.*

detective /de'tektiβe/ *n. m.* & *f.* detective.

detención /deten'θion; deten'sion/ *n. f.* detention, arrest.

detenedor /detene'ðor/ **-ra** *n.* stopper; catch.

detener /dete'ner/ *v.* detain, stop; arrest.

detenidamente /deteniða'mente/ *adv.* carefully, slowly.

detenido /dete'niðo/ *adv.* stingy; thorough.

detergente /deter'hente/ *a.* detergent.

deterioración /deteriora'θion; deteriora'sion/ *n. f.* deterioration.

deteriorar /deterio'rar/ *v.* deteriorate.

determinable /determi'naβle/ *a.* determinable.

determinación /determina'θion; determina'sion/ *n. f.* determination.

determinar /determi'nar/ *v.* determine, settle, decide.

determinismo /determi'nismo/ *n. m.* determinism.

determinista /determi'nista/ *n.* & *a.* determinist.

detestable /detes'taβle/ *a.* detestable, hateful.

detestablemente /detestaβle-'mente/ *adv.* detestably, hatefully, abhorrently.

detestación /detesta'θion; detesta'sion/ *n. f.* detestation, hatefulness.

detestar /detes'tar/ *v.* detest.

detonación /detona'θion; detona'sion/ *n. f.* detonation.

detonar /deto'nar/ *v.* detonate, explode.

detracción /detrak'θion; detrak-'sion/ *n. f.* detraction, defamation.

detractar /detrak'tar/ *v.* detract, defame, vilify.

detraer /detra'er/ *v.* detract.

detrás /de'tras/ *adv.* behind; in back.

detrimento /detri'mento/ *n. m.* detriment, damage.

deuda /'deuða/ *n. f.* debt.

deudo /'deuðo/ **-da** *n.* relative, kin.

deudor /deu'ðor/ **-ra** *n.* debtor.

Deuteronomio /deutero'nomio/ *n. m.* Deuteronomy.

devalar /deβa'lar/ *v.* drift off course.

devanar /deβa'nar/ *v.* to wind, as on a spool.

devanear /deβane'ar/ *v.* talk deliriously, rave.

devaneo /deβa'neo/ *n. m.* frivolity; idle pursuit; delirium.

devastación /deβasta'θion; deβasta'sion/ *n. f.* devastation, ruin, havoc.

devastador /deβasta'ðor/ *a.* devastating.

devastar /deβas'tar/ *v.* devastate.

devenir /deβe'nir/ *v.* happen, occur; become.

devoción /deβo'θion; deβo'sion/ *n. f.* devotion.

devocionario /deβoθio'nario; deβosio'nario/ *n. m.* prayer book.

devocionero /deβoθio'nero; deβosio'nero/ *a.* devotional.

devolver /deβol'βer/ *v.* return, give back.

devorar /deβo'rar/ *v.* devour.

devotamente /deβota'mente/ *adv.* devotedly, devoutly, piously.

devoto /de'βoto/ *a.* devout; devoted.

deyección /deiek'θion; deiek'sion/ *n. f.* depression, dejection.

día /dia/ *n. m.* day. **buenos días,** good morning.

diabetes /dia'βetes/ *n. f.* diabetes.

diabético /dia'βetiko/ *a.* diabetic.

diablear /diaβle'ar/ *v.* play pranks.

diablo /'diaβlo/ *n. m.* devil.

diablura /dia'βlura/ *n. f.* mischief.

diabólicamente /diaβolika'mente/ *adv.* diabolically.

diabólico /dia'βoliko/ *a.* diabolic, devilish.

diaconato /diako'nato/ *n. m.* deaconship.

diaconía /diako'nia/ *n. f.* deaconry.

diácono /'diakono/ *n. m.* deacon.

diacrítico /dia'kritiko/ *a.* diacritic.

diadema /dia'ðema/ *n. f.* diadem; crown.

diáfano /'diafano/ *a.* transparent.

diafragma /dia'fragma/ *n. m.* diaphragm.

diagnosticar /diagnosti'kar/ *v.* diagnose.

diagonal /diago'nal/ *n. f.* diagonal.

diagonalmente /diagonal'mente/ *adv.* diagonally.

diagrama /dia'grama/ *n. m.* diagram.

dialectal /dialek'tal/ *a.* dialectal.

dialéctico /dia'lektiko/ *a.* dialectic.

dialecto /dia'lekto/ *n. m.* dialect.

diálogo /'dialogo/ *n. m.* dialogue.

diamante /dia'mante/ *n. m.* diamond.

diamantista /diaman'tista/ *n. m. & f.* diamond cutter; jeweler.

diametral /diame'tral/ *a.* diametric.

diametralmente /diametral'mente/ *adv.* diametrically.

diámetro /'diametro/ *n. m.* diameter.

diana /'diana/ *n. f.* reveille; dartboard.

diapasón /diapa'son/ *n. m.* standard pitch; tuning fork.

diaplejía /diaple'hia/ *n. f.* paralysis.

diariamente /diaria'mente/ *adv.* daily.

diario /'diario/ *a. & m.* daily; daily paper; diary; journal.

diarrea /dia'rrea/ *n. f.* diarrhea.

diatriba /dia'triβa/ *n. f.* diatribe, harangue.

dibujo /di'βuho/ *n. m.* drawing, sketch. **—dibujar,** *v.*

dicción /dik'θion; dik'sion/ *n. f.* diction.

diccionario /dikθio'nario; diksio'nario/ *n. m.* dictionary.

diccionarista /dikθiona'rista; diksiona'rista/ *n. m. & f.* lexicographer.

dicha /'ditʃa/ *n. f.* happiness.

dicho /'ditʃo/ *n. m.* saying.

dichoso /di'tʃoso/ *a.* happy; fortunate.

diciembre /di'θiembre; di'siembre/ *n. m.* December.

dicotomía /dikoto'mia/ *n. f.* dichotomy.

dictado /dik'taðo/ *n. m.* dictation.

dictador /dikta'ðor/ **-ra** *n.* dictator.

dictadura /dikta'ðura/ *n. f.* dictatorship.

dictamen /dik'tamen/ *n. m.* dictate.

dictar /dik'tar/ *v.* dictate; direct.

dictatorial /diktato'rial/ **dictatorio** *a.* dictatorial.

didáctico /di'ðaktiko/ *a.* didactic.

diecinueve /dieθi'nueβe; diesi-'nueβe/ *a. & pron.* nineteen.

dieciocho /die'θiotʃo; die'siotʃo/ *a. & pron.* eighteen.

dieciseis /dieθi'seis; diesi'seis/ *a. & pron.* sixteen.

diecisiete /dieθi'siete; diesi'siete/ *a. & pron.* seventeen.

diente /diente/ *n. m.* tooth.

diestramente /diestra'mente/ *adv.* skillfully, ably; ingeniously.

diestro /'diestro/ *a.* dexterous, skillful; clever.

dieta /'dieta/ *n. f.* diet; allowance.

dietética /die'tetika/ *n. f.* dietetics.

dietético /die'tetiko/ *a.* **1.** dietetic; dietary. —*n.* **2. -ca.** dietician.

diez /dieθ; dies/ *a. & pron.* ten.

diezmal /dieθ'mal; dies'mal/ *a.* decimal.

diezmar /dieθ'mar; dies'mar/ *v.* decimate.

difamación /difama'θion; difama'sion/ *n. f.* defamation, smear.

difamar /difa'mar/ *v.* defame, smear, libel.

difamatorio /difama'torio/ *a.* defamatory.

diferencia /dife'renθia; dife'rensia/ *n. f.* difference.

diferencial /diferen'θial; diferen-'sial/ *a. & f.* differential.

diferenciar /diferen'θiar; diferen-'siar/ *v.* differentiate, distinguish.

diferente /dife'rente/ *a.* different.

diferentemente /diferente'mente/ *adv.* differently.

diferir /dife'rir/ *v.* differ; defer, put off.

difícil /di'fiθil; di'fisil/ *a.* difficult, hard.

difícilmente /difiθil'mente; difisil-'mente/ *adv.* with difficulty or hardship.

dificultad /difikul'taδ/ *n. f.* difficulty.

dificultar /difikul'tar/ *v.* make difficult.

dificultoso /difikul'toso/ *a.* difficult, hard.

difidencia /difi'δenθia; difi'δensia/ *n. f.* diffidence.

difidente /difi'δente/ *a.* diffident.

difteria /dif'teria/ *n. f.* diphtheria.

difundir /difun'dir/ *v.* diffuse, spread.

difunto /di'funto/ *a.* **1.** deceased, dead, late. —*n.* **2. -ta,** deceased person.

difusamente /difusa'mente/ *adv.* diffusely.

difusión /difu'sion/ *n. f.* diffusion, spread.

digerible /dihe'riβle/ *a.* digestible.

digerir /dihe'rir/ *v.* digest.

digestible /dihes'tiβle/ *a.* digestible.

digestión /dihes'tion/ *n. f.* digestion.

digestivo /dihes'tiβo/ *a.* digestive.

digesto /di'hesto/ *n. m.* digest or code of laws.

digitado /dihi'taδo/ *a.* digitate.

digital /dihi'tal/ *a.* **1.** digital. —*n.* **2.** *f.* foxglove, digitalis.

dignación /digna'θion; digna'sion/ *f.* condescension; deigning.

dignamente /digna'mente/ *adv.* with dignity.

dignarse /dig'narse/ *v.* condescend, deign.

dignatario /digna'tario/ **-ra** *n.* dignitary.

dignidad /digni'δaδ/ *n. f.* dignity.

dignificar /dignifi'kar/ *v.* dignify.

digno /'digno/ *a.* worthy; dignified.

digresión /digre'sion/ *n. f.* digression.

digresivo /digre'siβo/ *a.* digressive.

dij, dije /dih; 'dihe/ *n. m.* trinket, piece of jewelry.

dilación /dila'θion; dila'sion/ *n. f.* delay.

dilapidación /dilapiδa'θion; dilapi-'δasion/ *n. f.* dilapidation.

dilapidado /dilapi'δaδo/ *a.* dilapidated.

dilatación /dilata'θion; dilata'sion/ *n. f.* dilatation, enlargement.

dilatar /dila'tar/ *v.* dilate; delay; expand.

dilatoria /dila'toria/ *n. f.* delay.

dilatorio /dila'torio/ *a.* dilatory.

dilecto /di'lekto/ *a.* loved.

dilema /di'lema/ *n. m.* dilemma.

diligencia /dili'henθia; dili'hensia/ *n. f.* diligence, industriousness.

diligente /dili'hente/ *a.* diligent, industrious.

diligentemente /dilihente'mente/ *adv.* diligently.

dilogía /dilo'hia/ *n. f.* ambiguous meaning.

dilución /dilu'θion; dilu'sion/ *n. f.* dilution.

diluir /di'luir/ *v.* dilute.

diluvial /dilu'βial/ *a.* diluvial.

diluvio /di'luβio/ *n. m.* flood, deluge.

dimensión /dimen'sion/ *n. f.* dimension; measurement.

diminución /diminu'θion; diminu-'sion/ *n. f.* diminution.

diminuto /dimi'nuto/ **diminutivo** *a.* diminutive, little.

dimisión /dimi'sion/ *n. f.* resignation.

dimitir /dimi'tir/ *v.* resign.

Dinamarca /dina'marka/ *n. f.* Denmark.

dinamarqués /dinamar'kes/ **-esa** *a. & n.* Danish, Dane.

dinámico /di'namiko/ *a.* dynamic.

dinamita /dina'mita/ *n. f.* dynamite.

dinamitero /dinami'tero/ **-ra** *n.* dynamiter.

dínamo /'dinamo/ *n. m.* dynamo.

dinasta /di'nasta/ *n. m.* dynast, king, monarch.

dinastía /dinas'tia/ *n. f.* dynasty.

dinástico /di'nastiko/ *a.* dynastic.

dinero /di'nero/ *n. m.* money, currency.

dinosauro /dino'sauro/ *n. m.* dinosaur.

diócesis /'dioθesis; 'diosesis/ *n. f.* diocese.

Dios /dios/ *n. m.* God.

dios -sa *n.* god, goddess.

diploma /di'ploma/ *n. m.* diploma.

diplomacia /diplo'maθia; diplo-'masia/ *n. f.* diplomacy.

diplomado /diplo'maðo/ **-da** *n.* graduate.

diplomarse /diplo'marse/ *v.* graduate (from a school).

diplomática /diplo'matika/ *n. f.* diplomacy.

diplomático /diplo'matiko/ **-ca** *a. & n.* diplomat; diplomatic.

dipsomanía /dipsoma'nia/ *n. f.* dipsomania.

diptongo /dip'toŋgo/ *n. m.* diphthong.

diputación /diputa'θion; diputa'sion/ *n. f.* deputation, delegation.

diputado /dipu'taðo/ **-da** *n.* deputy; delegate.

diputar /dipu'tar/ *v.* depute, delegate; empower.

dique /'dike/ *n. m.* dike; dam.

dirección /direk'θion; direk'sion/ *n. f.* direction; address; guidance; *Com.* management.

directamente /direkta'mente/ *adv.* directly.

directo /di'rekto/ *a.* direct.

director /direk'tor/ **-ra** *n.* director; manager.

directorio /direk'torio/ *n. m.* directory.

dirigente /diri'hente/ *a.* directing, controlling, managing.

dirigible /diri'hiβle/ *n. m.* dirigible.

dirigir /diri'hir/ *v.* direct; lead; manage.

dirigirse a /diri'hirse a/ *v.* address; approach, turn to; head for.

dirruir /di'rruir/ *v.* destroy, devastate.

disanto /di'santo/ *n. m.* holy day.

discantar /diskan'tar/ *v.* sing (esp. in counterpoint); discuss.

disceptación /disθepta'θion; dissepta'sion/ *n. f.* argument, quarrel.

disceptar /disθep'tar; dissep'tar/ *v.* argue, quarrel.

discernimiento /disθerni'miento; disserni'miento/ *n. m.* discernment.

discernir /disθer'nir; disser'nir/ *v.* discern.

disciplina /disθi'plina; dissi'plina/ *n. f.* discipline.

disciplinable /disθipli'naβle; dissipli'naβle/ *a.* disciplinable.

disciplinar /disθipli'nar; dissipli'nar/ *v.* discipline, train, teach.

discípulo /dis'θipulo; dis'sipulo/ **-la** *n.* disciple, follower; pupil.

disco /'disko/ *n. m.* disk; (phonograph) record.

disco compacto /'disko kom'pakto/ compact disk.

disco duro /'disko 'duro/ hard disk.

disco flexible /'disko flek'siβle/ floppy disk.

discontinuación /diskontinua-'θion; diskontinua'sion/ *n. f.* discontinuation.

discontinuar /diskonti'nuar/ *v.* discontinue, break off, cease.

discordancia /diskor'ðanθia; diskor'ðansia/ *n. f.* discordance.

discordar /diskor'ðar/ *v.* disagree, conflict.

discordia /dis'korðia/ *n. f.* discord.

discoteca /disko'teka/ *n. f.* disco, discotheque.

disonancia

discreción /diskre'θion; diskre-'sion/ n. f. discretion.
discrecional /diskreθio'nal; diskre-sio'nal/ a. optional.
discrecionalmente /diskreθional-'mente; diskresional'mente/ adv. optionally.
discrepancia /diskre'panθia; diskre'pansia/ n. f. discrepancy.
discretamente /diskreta'mente/ adv. discreetly.
discreto /dis'kreto/ a. discreet.
discrimen /dis'krimen/ n. m. risk, hazard.
discriminación /diskrimina'θion; diskrimina'sion/ n. f. discrimination.
discriminar /diskrimi'nar/ v. discriminate.
disculpa /dis'kulpa/ n. f. excuse; apology.
disculpar /diskul'par/ v. excuse; exonerate.
disculparse /diskul'parse/ v. apologize.
discurrir /disku'rrir/ v. roam; flow; think; plan.
discursante /diskur'sante/ n. lecturer, speaker.
discursivo /diskur'siβo/ a. discursive.
discurso /dis'kurso/ n. m. speech, talk.
discusión /disku'sion/ n. f. discussion.
discutible /disku'tiβle/ a. debatable.
discutir /disku'tir/ v. discuss; debate; contest.
disecación /diseka'θion; diseka-'sion/ n. f. dissection.
disecar /dise'kar/ v. dissect.
disección /disek'θion; disek'sion/ n. f. dissection.
diseminación /disemina'θion; disemina'sion/ n. f. dissemination.
diseminar /disemi'nar/ v. disseminate, spread.
disensión /disen'sion/ n. f. dissension; dissent.
disenso /di'senso/ n. m. dissent.
disentería /disente'ria/ n. f. dysentery.
disentir /disen'tir/ v. disagree, dissent.
diseñador /diseɲa'ðor/ -ra n. designer.
diseño /di'seɲo/ n. m. design.
—**diseñar,** v.

disertación /diserta'θion; diserta-'sion/ n. f. dissertation.
disforme /dis'forme/ a. deformed, monstrous, ugly.
disformidad /disformi'ðað/ n. f. deformity.
disfraz /dis'fraθ; dis'fras/ n. m. disguise. —**disfrazar,** v.
disfrutar /disfru'tar/ v. enjoy.
disfrute /dis'frute/ n. m. enjoyment.
disgustar /disgus'tar/ v. displease; disappoint.
disgusto /dis'gusto/ n. m. displeasure; disappointment.
disidencia /disi'ðenθia; disi-'ðensia/ n. f. dissidence.
disidente /disi'ðente/ a. & n. dissident.
disímil /di'simil/ a. unlike.
disimilitud /disimili'tuð/ n. f. dissimilarity.
disimulación /disimula'θion; disimula'sion/ n. f. dissimulation.
disimulado /disimu'laðo/ a. dissembling, feigning; sly.
disimular /disimu'lar/ v. hide; dissemble.
disimulo /di'simulo/ n. m. pretense.
disipación /disipa'θion; disipa'sion/ n. f. dissipation.
disipado /disi'paðo/ a. dissipated; wasted; scattered.
disipar /disi'par/ v. waste; scatter.
dislexia /dis'leksia/ n. f. dyslexia.
disléxico /dis'leksiko/ a. dyslexic.
dislocación /disloka'θion; disloka'sion/ n. f. dislocation.
dislocar /dislo'kar/ v. dislocate; displace.
disminuir /dismi'nuir/ v. diminish, lessen, reduce.
disociación /disoθia'θion; disosia'sion/ n. f. dissociation.
disociar /diso'θiar; diso'siar/ v. dissociate.
disolubilidad /disoluβili'ðað/ n. f. dissolubility.
disoluble /diso'luβle/ a. dissoluble.
disolución /disolu'θion; disolu-'sion/ n. f. dissolution.
disolutamente /disoluta'mente/ adv. dissolutely.
disoluto /diso'luto/ a. dissolute.
disolver /disol'βer/ v. dissolve.
disonancia /diso'nanθia; diso-'nansia/ n. f. dissonance; discord.

disonante /diso'nante/ *a.* dissonant; discordant.
disonar /diso'nar/ *v.* be discordant; clash in sound.
dísono /di'sono/ *a.* dissonant.
dispar /dis'par/ *a.* unlike.
disparadamente /disparaða-
'mente/ *adv.* hastily, hurriedly.
disparar /dispa'rar/ *v.* shoot, fire
(a weapon).
disparatado /dispara'taðo/ *a.*
nonsensical.
disparatar /dispara'tar/ *v.* talk
nonsense.
disparate /dispa'rate/ *n. m.* nonsense, tall tale.
disparejo /dispa'reho/ *a.* uneven,
unequal.
disparidad /dispari'ðað/ *n. f.* dis-
parity.
disparo /dis'paro/ *n. m.* shot.
dispendio /dis'pendio/ *n. m.* extravagance.
dispendioso /dispen'dioso/ *a.* expensive; extravagant.
dispensa /dis'pensa/ **dispensación** *n. f.* dispensation.
dispensable /dispen'saβle/ *a.* dispensable; excusable.
dispensar /dispen'sar/ *v.* dispense,
excuse; grant.
dispensario /dispen'sario/ *n. m.*
dispensary.
dispepsia /dis'pepsia/ *n. f.*
dyspepsia.
dispéptico /dis'peptiko/ *a.*
dyspeptic.
dispersar /disper'sar/ *v.* scatter;
dispel; disband.
dispersión /disper'sion/ *n. f.* dis-
persion, dispersal.
disperso /dis'perso/ *a.* dispersed.
displicente /displi'θente; displi-
'sente/ *a.* unpleasant.
disponer /dispo'ner/ *v.* dispose. **d.
de,** have at one's disposal.
disponible /dispo'niβle/ *a.* available.
disposición /disposi'θion; disposi-
'sion/ *n. f.* disposition; disposal.
dispuesto /dis'puesto/ *a.* disposed, inclined; attractive.
disputa /dis'puta/ *n. f.* dispute,
argument.
disputable /dispu'taβle/ *a.* disputable.
disputador /disputa'ðor/ **-ra** *n.*
disputant.
disputar /dispu'tar/ *v.* argue; dispute.

disquete /dis'kete/ *n. m.* diskette.
disquetera /diske'tera/ *n. f.* disk
drive.
disquisición /diskisi'θion; diskisi-
'sion/ *n. f.* disquisition.
distancia /dis'tanθia; dis'tansia/ *n.
f.* distance.
distante /dis'tante/ *a.* distant.
distantemente /distante'mente/
adv. distantly.
distar /dis'tar/ *v.* be distant, be
far.
distender /disten'der/ *v.* distend,
swell, enlarge.
distensión /disten'sion/ *n. f.* dis-
tension, swelling.
dístico /'distiko/ *n. m.* couplet.
distinción /distin'θion; distin'sion/
n. f. distinction, difference.
distingo /dis'tiŋgo/ *n. m.* restriction.
distinguible /distiŋ'guiβle/ *a.* dis-
tinguishable.
distinguido /distiŋ'guiðo/ *a.* distinguished, prominent.
distinguir /distiŋ'guir/ *v.* distinguish; make out, spot.
distintamente /distinta'mente/
adv. distinctly, clearly; differently.
distintivo /distin'tiβo/ *a.* distinctive.
distintivo del país /distin'tiβo del
pa'is/ country code.
distinto /dis'tinto/ *a.* distinct; different.
distracción /distrak'θion; distrak-
'sion/ *n. f.* distraction, pastime;
absent-mindedness.
distraer /distra'er/ *v.* distract.
distraídamente /distraiða'mente/
adv. absent-mindedly, distract-
edly.
distraído /distra'iðo/ *a.* absent-
minded; distracted.
distribución /distriβu'θion; dis-
triβu'sion/ *n. f.* distribution.
distribuidor /distriβui'ðor/ **-ra** *n.*
distributor.
distribuir /distri'βuir/ *v.* distribute.
distributivo /distriβu'tiβo/ *a.* dis-
tributive.
distributor /distriβu'tor/ *n. m.*
distributor.
distrito /dis'trito/ *n. m.* district.
disturbar /distur'βar/ *v.* disturb,
trouble.
disturbio /dis'turβio/ *n. m.*
disturbance, outbreak; turmoil.
disuadir /disua'ðir/ *v.* dissuade.

disuasión /disua'sion/ n. f. dissuasion; deterrence.

disuasivo /disua'siβo/ a. dissuasive.

disyunción /disyun'θion; disyun'sion/ n. f. disjunction.

ditirambo /diti'rambo/ n. m. dithyramb.

diurno /'diurno/ a. diurnal.

diva /'diβa/ n. f. diva, prima donna.

divagación /diβaga'θion; diβaga'sion/ n. f. digression.

divagar /diβa'gar/ v. digress, ramble.

diván /di'βan/ n. m. couch.

divergencia /diβer'henθia; diβer'hensia/ n. f. divergence.

divergente /diβer'hente/ a. divergent, differing.

divergir /diβer'hir/ v. diverge.

diversamente /diβersa'mente/ adv. diversely.

diversidad /diβersi'ðað/ n. f. diversity.

diversificar /diβersifi'kar/ v. diversify, vary.

diversión /diβer'sion/ n. f. diversion, pastime.

diverso /di'βerso/ a. diverse, different; (pl.) various, several.

divertido /diβer'tiðo/ a. humorous, amusing.

divertimiento /diβerti'miento/ n. m. diversion; amusement.

divertir /diβer'tir/ v. entertain, amuse.

divertirse /diβer'tirse/ v. enjoy oneself, have a good time.

dividendo /diβi'ðendo/ n. m. dividend.

divididero /diβiði'ðero/ a. to be divided.

dividido /diβi'ðiðo/ a. divided.

dividir /diβi'ðir/ v. divide; separate.

divieso /di'βieso/ n. m. Med. boil.

divinamente /diβina'mente/ adv. divinely.

divinidad /diβini'ðað/ n. f. divinity.

divinizar /diβini'θar; diβini'sar/ v. deify.

divino /di'βino/ a. divine; heavenly.

divisa /di'βisa/ n. f. badge, emblem.

divisar /diβi'sar/ v. sight, make out.

divisibilidad /diβisiβili'ðað/ n. f. divisibility.

divisible /diβi'siβle/ a. divisible.

división /diβi'sion/ n. f. division.

divisivo /diβi'siβo/ a. divisive.

divo /'diβo/ n. m. movie star.

divorcio /di'βorθio; di'βorsio/ n. m. divorce. —**divorciar,** v.

divulgable /diβul'gaβle/ a. divulgable.

divulgación /diβulga'θion; diβulga'sion/ n. f. divulgation.

divulgar /diβul'gar/ v. divulge, reveal.

dobladamente /doβlaða'mente/ adv. doubly.

dobladillo /doβla'ðiʎo; doβla'ðiyo/ n. m. hem of a skirt or dress.

dobladura /doβla'ðura/ n. f. fold; bend.

doblar /do'βlar/ v. fold; bend.

doble /'doβle/ a. double.

doblegable /doβle'gaβle/ a. flexible, foldable.

doblegar /doβle'gar/ v. fold, bend; yield.

doblez /do'βleθ; doβles/ n. m. fold; duplicity.

doblón /do'βlon/ n. m. doubloon.

doce /'doθe; 'dose/ a. & pron. twelve.

docena /do'θena; do'sena/ n. f. dozen.

docente /do'θente; do'sente/ a. educational.

dócil /'doθil; 'dosil/ a. docile.

docilidad /doθili'ðað; dosili'ðað/ n. f. docility, tractableness.

dócilmente /doθil'mente; dosil'mente/ adv. docilely, meekly.

doctamente /dokta'mente/ adv. learnedly, profoundly.

docto /'dokto/ a. learned, expert.

doctor /dok'tor/ -ra n. doctor.

doctorado /dokto'raðo/ n. m. doctorate.

doctoral /dokto'ral/ a. doctoral.

doctrina /dok'trina/ n. f. doctrine.

doctrinador /doktrina'ðor/ -ra n. teacher.

doctrinal /doktri'nal/ n. m. doctrinal.

doctrinar /doktri'nar/ v. teach.

documentación /dokumenta'θion; dokumenta'sion/ n. f. documentation.

documental /dokumen'tal/ a. documentary.

documento /doku'mento/ *n. m.* document.

dogal /do'gal/ *n. m.* noose.

dogma /'dogma/ *n. m.* dogma.

dogmáticamente /dog'matikamente/ *adv.* dogmatically.

dogmático /dog'matiko/ *n. m.* dogmatic.

dogmatismo /dogma'tismo/ *n. m.* dogmatism.

dogmatista /dogma'tista/ *n. m. & f.* dogmatist.

dogo /'dogo/ *n. m.* bulldog.

dolar /'dolar/ *v.* cut, chop, hew.

dólar *n. m.* dollar.

dolencia /do'lenθia; do'lensia/ *n. f.* pain; disease.

doler /do'ler/ *v.* ache, hurt, be sore.

doliente /do'liente/ *a.* ill; aching.

dolor /do'lor/ *n. m.* pain; grief, sorrow, woe.

dolor de cabeza /do'lor de ka'βeθa; do'lor de ka'βesa/ headache.

dolor de espalda /do'lor de es'palda/ backache.

dolor de estómago /do'lor de es'tomago/ stomachache.

dolorido /dolo'riðo/ *a.* painful, sorrowful.

dolorosamente /dolorosa'mente/ *adv.* painfully, sorrowfully.

doloroso /dolo'roso/ *a.* painful, sorrowful.

dolosamente /dolosa'mente/ *adv.* deceitfully.

doloso /do'loso/ *a.* deceitful.

domable /do'maβle/ *a.* that can be tamed or managed.

domar /do'mar/ *v.* tame; subdue.

dombo /'dombo/ *n. m.* dome.

domesticable /domesti'kaβle/ *a.* that can be domesticated.

domesticación /domestika'θion; domestika'sion/ *n. f.* domestication.

domésticamente /domestika'mente/ *adv.* domestically.

domesticar /domesti'kar/ *v.* tame, domesticate.

domesticidad /domestiθi'ðað; domestisi'ðað/ *n. f.* domesticity.

doméstico /do'mestiko/ *a.* domestic.

domicilio /domi'θilio; domi'silio/ *n. m.* dwelling, home, residence, domicile.

dominación /domina'θion; domina'sion/ *n. f.* domination.

dominador /domina'ðor/ *a.* dominating.

dominante /domi'nante/ *a.* dominant.

dominar /domi'nar/ *v.* rule, dominate; master.

dómine /'domine/ *n. m.* teacher.

domingo /do'miŋgo/ *n. m.* Sunday.

dominio /'dominio/ *n. m.* domain; rule; power.

dominó /domi'no/ *n. m.* domino.

domo /'domo/ *n. m.* dome.

Don /don/ *title used before a man's first name.*

don *n. m.* gift.

donación /dona'θion; dona'sion/ *n. f.* donation.

donador /dona'ðor/ **-ra** *n.* giver, donor.

donaire /do'naire/ *n. m.* grace.

donairosamente /donairosa'mente/ *adv.* gracefully.

donairoso /donai'roso/ *a.* graceful.

donante /do'nante/ *n.* giver, donor.

donar /do'nar/ *v.* donate.

donativo /dona'tiβo/ *n. m.* donation, contribution; gift.

doncella /don'θeʎa; don'seya/ *n. f.* lass; maid.

donde /'donde/ **dónde** *conj. & adv.* where.

dondequiera /donde'kiera/ *adv.* wherever, anywhere.

donosamente /donosa'mente/ *adv.* gracefully; wittily.

donoso /do'noso/ *a.* graceful; witty.

donosura /dono'sura/ *n. f.* gracefulness; wittiness.

Doña /'doɲa/ *title used before a lady's first name.*

dopar /do'par/ *v.* drug, dope.

dorado /do'raðo/ *a.* gilded.

dorador /dora'ðor/ **-ra** *n.* gilder.

dorar /do'rar/ *v.* gild.

dórico /'doriko/ *a.* Doric.

dormidero /dormi'ðero/ *a.* sleep-inducing; soporific.

dormido /dor'miðo/ *a.* asleep.

dormir /dor'mir/ *v.* sleep.

dormirse /dor'mirse/ *v.* fall asleep, go to sleep.

dormitar /dormi'tar/ *v.* doze.

dormitorio /dormi'torio/ *n. m.* dormitory; bedroom.

dorsal /dor'sal/ *a.* dorsal.

dorso /'dorso/ *n. m.* spine.

dos /dos/ *a.* & *pron.* two. **los d.,** both.
dosañal /dosa'ɲal/ *a.* biennial.
doscientos /dos'θientos; dos-'sientos/ *a.* & *pron.* two hundred.
dosel /do'sel/ *n. m.* canopy; platform, dais.
dosificación /dosifika'θion; dosifika'sion/ *n. f.* dosage.
dosis /'dosis/ *n. f.* dose.
dotación /dota'θion; dota'sion/ *n. f.* endowment; *Naut.* crew.
dotador /dota'ðor/ **-ra** *n.* donor.
dotar /do'tar/ *v.* endow; give a dowry to.
dote /'dote/ *n. f.* dowry; (*pl.*) talents.
dragaminas /draga'minas/ *n. m.* mine sweeper.
dragar /dra'gar/ *v.* dredge; sweep.
dragón /dra'gon/ *n. m.* dragon; dragoon.
dragonear /dragone'ar/ *v.* pretend to be.
drama /'drama/ *n. m.* drama; play.
dramática /dra'matika/ *n. f.* drama, dramatic art.
dramáticamente /dramatika-'mente/ *adv.* dramatically.
dramático /dra'matiko/ *a.* dramatic.
dramatizar /dramati'θar; dramati-'sar/ *v.* dramatize.
dramaturgo /drama'turgo/ **-ga** *n.* playwright, dramatist.
drástico /'drastiko/ *a.* drastic.
drenaje /dre'nahe/ *n. m.* drainage.
dríada /'driaða/ *n. f.* dryad.
dril /dril/ *n. m.* denim.
driza /'driθa; 'drisa/ *n. f.* halyard.
droga /'droga/ *n. f.* drug.
drogadicto /droga'ðikto/ **-ta** *n.* drug addict.
droguería /droge'ria/ *n. f.* drugstore.
droguero /dro'gero/ *n. m.* druggist.
dromedario /drome'ðario/ *n. m.* dromedary.
druida /'druiða/ *n. m.* & *f.* Druid.
dualidad /duali'ðað/ *n. f.* duality.
dubitable /duβi'taβle/ *a.* doubtful.
dubitación /duβita'θion; duβita-'sion/ *n. f.* doubt.
ducado /du'kaðo/ *n. m.* duchy.
ducal /du'kal/ *a.* ducal.
ducha /'dutʃa/ *n. f.* shower (bath).

ducharse /du'tʃarse/ *v.* take a shower.
dúctil /'duktil/ *a.* ductile.
ductilidad /duktili'ðað/ *n. f.* ductility.
duda /'duða/ *n. f.* doubt.
dudable /du'ðaβle/ *a.* doubtful.
dudar /du'ðar/ *v.* doubt; hesitate; question.
dudosamente /duðosa'mente/ *adv.* doubtfully.
dudoso /du'ðoso/ *a.* dubious; doubtful.
duela /'duela/ *n. f.* stave.
duelista /due'lista/ *n. m.* & *f.* duelist.
duelo /'duelo/ *n. m.* duel; grief; mourning.
duende /'duende/ *n. m.* elf, hobgoblin.
dueño /'dueɲo/ **-ña** *n.* owner; landlord -lady; master, mistress.
dulce /'dulθe; dulse/ *a.* **1.** sweet. **agua d.,** fresh water. —*n.* **2.** *m.* piece of candy; (*pl.*) candy.
dulcedumbre /dulθe'ðumbre; dulse'ðumbre/ *n. f.* sweetness.
dulcemente /dulθe'mente; dulse-'mente/ *adv.* sweetly.
dulcería /dulθe'ria; dulse'ria/ *n. f.* confectionery; candy shop.
dulcificar /dulθifi'kar; dulsifi'kar/ *v.* sweeten.
dulzura /dul'θura; dul'sura/ *n. f.* sweetness; mildness.
duna /'duna/ *n. f.* dune.
dúo /'duo/ *n. m.* duo, duet.
duodenal /duoðe'nal/ *a.* duodenal.
duplicación /duplika'θion; duplika'sion/ *n. f.* duplication; doubling.
duplicadamente /duplikaða-'mente/ *adv.* doubly.
duplicado /dupli'kaðo/ *a.* & *m.* duplicate.
duplicar /dupli'kar/ *v.* double, duplicate, repeat.
duplicidad /dupliθi'ðað; duplisi-'ðað/ *n. f.* duplicity.
duplo /'duplo/ *a.* double.
duque /'duke/ *n. m.* duke.
duquesa /du'kesa/ *n. f.* duchess.
durabilidad /duraβili'ðað/ *n. f.* durability.
durable /du'raβle/ *a.* durable.
duración /dura'θion; dura'sion/ *n. f.* duration.
duradero /dura'ðero/ *a.* lasting, durable.

duramente /dura'mente/ *adv.* harshly, roughly.

durante /du'rante/ *prep.* during.

durar /du'rar/ *v.* last.

durazno /du'raθno; du'rasno/ *n. m.* peach; peach tree.

dureza /du'reθa; du'resa/ *n. f.* hardness.

durmiente /dur'miente/ *a.* sleeping.

duro /'duro/ *a.* hard; stiff; stern; stale.

dux /duks/ *n. m.* doge.

E

e /e/ *conj.* and.

ebanista /eβa'nista/ *n. m. & f.* cabinetmaker.

ebanizar /eβani'θar; eβani'sar/ *v.* give an ebony finish to.

ébano /'eβano/ *n. m.* ebony.

ebonita /eβo'nita/ *n. f.* ebonite.

ebrio /'eβrio/ *a.* drunken, inebriated.

ebullición /eβuʎi'θion; eβuyi'sion/ *n. f.* boiling.

echada /e'tʃaða/ *n. f.* throw.

echadillo /etʃa'ðiʎo; etʃa'ðiyo/ *m.* foundling; orphan.

echar /e'tʃar/ *v.* throw, toss; pour. **e. a,** start to. **e. a perder,** spoil, ruin. **e. de menos,** miss.

echarse /e'tʃarse/ *v.* lie down.

eclecticismo /eklekti'θismo; eklekti'sismo/ *n. m.* eclecticism.

ecléctico /e'klektiko/ *n. & a.* eclectic.

eclesiástico /ekle'siastiko/ *a. & m.* ecclesiastic.

eclipse /e'klipse/ *n. m.* eclipse. **—eclipsar,** *v.*

écloga /'ekloga/ *n. f.* eclogue.

eco /'eko/ *n. m.* echo.

ecología /ekolo'hia/ *n. f.* ecology.

ecológico /eko'lohiko/ *n. f.* ecological.

ecologista /ekolo'hista/ *n. m. & f.* ecologist.

economía /ekono'mia/ *n. f.* economy; thrift; economics. **e. política,** political economy.

económicamente /ekonomika'mente/ *adv.* economically.

económico /eko'nomiko/ *a.* economic; economical, thrifty; inexpensive.

economista /ekono'mista/ *n. m. & f.* economist.

economizar /ekonomi'θar; ekonomi'sar/ *v.* save, economize.

ecuación /ekua'θion; ekua'sion/ *n. f.* equation.

ecuador /ekua'ðor/ *n. m.* equator.

ecuanimidad /ekuanimi'ðað/ *n. f.* equanimity.

ecuatorial /ekuato'rial/ *a.* equatorial.

ecuatoriano /ekuato'riano/ **-na** *a. & n.* Ecuadorian.

ecuestre /e'kuestre/ *a.* equestrian.

ecuménico. /eku'meniko/ *a.* ecumenical.

edad /e'ðað/ *n. f.* age.

edecán /eðe'kan/ *n. m.* aide-de-camp.

Edén /e'ðen/ *n. m.* Eden.

edición /eði'θion; eði'sion/ *n. f.* edition; issue.

edicto /e'ðikto/ *n. m.* edict, decree.

edificación /eðifika'θion; eðifika'sion/ *n. f.* construction; edification.

edificador /eðifika'ðor/ *n.* constructor; builder.

edificar /eðifi'kar/ *v.* build.

edificio /eði'fiθio; eði'fisio/ *n. m.* edifice, building.

editar /eði'tar/ *v.* publish, issue; edit.

editor /eði'tor/ *n. m.* publisher; editor.

editorial /eðito'rial/ *n. m.* editorial; publishing house.

edredón /eðre'ðon/ *n. m.* quilt.

educación /eðuka'θion; eðuka'sion/ *n. f.* upbringing, breeding; education.

educado /eðu'kaðo/ *a.* well-mannered; educated.

educador /eðuka'ðor/ **-ra** *n.* educator.

educar /eðu'kar/ *v.* educate; bring up; train.

educativo /eðuka'tiβo/ *a.* educational.

educción /eðuk'θion; eðuk'sion/ *n. f.* deduction.

educir /eðu'θir; eðu'sir/ *v.* educe.

efectivamente /efektiβa'mente/ *adv.* actually, really.

efectivo /efek'tiβo/ *a.* effective; actual, real. **en e.,** *Com.* in cash.

efecto /e'fekto/ *n. m.* effect.

efecto invernáculo /e'fekto imber'nakulo/ greenhouse effect.

efectuar /efek'tuar/ v. effect; cash.

eferente /efe'rente/ a. efferent.

efervescencia /eferβes'θenθia; eferβes'sensia/ n. f. effervescence; zeal.

eficacia /efi'kaθia; efi'kasia/ n. f. efficacy.

eficaz /efi'kaθ; efi'kas/ a. efficient, effective.

eficazmente /efikaθ'mente; efikas'mente/ adv. efficaciously.

eficiencia /efi'θienθia; efi'siensia/ n. f. efficiency.

eficiente /efi'θiente; efi'siente/ a. efficient.

efigie /e'fihie/ n. f. effigy.

efímera /efi'mera/ n. f. mayfly.

efímero /e'fimero/ a. ephemeral, passing.

efluvio /e'fluβio/ n. m. effluvium.

efundir /efun'dir/ v. effuse; pour out.

efusión /efu'sion/ n. f. effusion.

egipcio /e'hipθio; e'hipsio/ -cia a. & n. Egyptian.

Egipto /e'hipto/ n. m. Egypt.

egoísmo /ego'ismo/ n. m. egoism, egotism, selfishness.

egoísta /ego'ista/ a. & n. selfish, egoistic; egoist.

egotismo /ego'tismo/ n. m. egotism.

egotista /ego'tista/ n. m. & f. egotist.

egreso /e'greso/ n. m. expense, outlay.

eje /'ehe/ n. m. axis; axle.

ejecución /eheku'θion; eheku'sion/ n. f. execution; performance; enforcement.

ejecutar /eheku'tar/ v. execute; enforce; carry out.

ejecutivo /eheku''tiβo/ -va a. & n. executive.

ejecutor /eheku'tor/ -ra n. executor.

ejemplar /ehem'plar/ a. 1. exemplary. —n. 2. m. copy.

ejemplificación /ehemplifika'θion; ehemplifika'sion/ n. f. exemplification.

ejemplificar /ehemplifi'kar/ v. illustrate.

ejemplo /e'hemplo/ n. m. example.

ejercer /eher'θer; eher'ser/ v. exert; practice.

ejercicio /eher'θiθio; eher'sisio/ n. m. exercise, drill. —**ejercitar,** v.

ejercitación /eherθita'θion; ehersita'sion/ n. f. exercise, training, drill.

ejercitar /eherθi'tar; ehersi'tar/ v. exercise, train, drill.

ejército /e'herθito; e'hersito/ n. m. army.

ejotes /e'hotes/ n. m.pl. string beans.

el /el/ art. & pron. the; the one.

él pron. he, him; it.

elaboración /elaβora'θion; elaβora'sion/ n. f. elaboration; working up.

elaborado /elaβo'raðo/ a. elaborate.

elaborador /elaβora'ðor/ n. m. manufacturer, maker.

elaborar /elaβo'rar/ v. elaborate; manufacture; brew.

elación /ela'θion; ela'sion/ n. f. elation; magnanimity; turgid style.

elasticidad /elasti'θi'ðað; elastisi'ðað/ n. f. elasticity.

elástico /e'lastiko/ n. m. elastic.

elección /elek'θion; elek'sion/ n. f. election; option, choice.

electivo /elek'tiβo/ a. elective.

electo /e'lekto/ a. elected, chosen, appointed.

electorado /elekto'raðo/ n. m. electorate.

electoral /elekto'ral/ a. electoral.

electricidad /elektri'θi'ðað; elektrisi'ðað/ n. f. electricity.

electricista /elektri'θista; elektri'sista/ n. m. & f. electrician.

eléctrico /e'lektriko/ a. electric.

electrización /elektriθa'θion; elektrisa'sion/ n. f. electrification.

electrocardiograma /e,lektrokarðio'grama/ n. m. electrocardiogram.

electrocución /elektroku'θion; elektroku'sion/ n. f. electrocution.

electrocutar /elektroku'tar/ v. electrocute.

electrodo /elek'troðo/ n. m. electrode.

electrodoméstico /e,lektroðo-r'ɑprim;mestiko/ n. m. electrical appliance, home appliance.

electroimán /elektroi'man/ n. m. electromagnet.

electrólisis /elek'trolisis/ n. f. electrolysis.

electrólito /elek'trolito/ n. m. electrolyte.

electrón /elek'tron/ *n. m.* electron.

electrónico /elek'troniko/ *a.* electronic.

elefante /ele'fante/ *n. m.* elephant.

elegancia /ele'ganθia; ele'gansia/ *n. f.* elegance.

elegante /ele'gante/ *a.* elegant, smart, stylish, fine.

elegantemente /elegante'mente/ *adv.* elegantly.

elegía /ele'hia/ *n. f.* elegy.

elegibilidad /elehiβili'ðað/ *n. f.* eligibility.

elegible /ele'hiβle/ *a.* eligible.

elegir /ele'hir/ *v.* select, choose; elect.

elemental /elemen'tal/ *a.* elementary.

elementalmente /elemental'mente/ *adv.* elementally; fundamentally.

elemento /ele'mento/ *n. m.* element.

elepé /ele'pe/ *n. m.* long-playing (record), LP.

elevación /eleβa'θion; eleβa'sion/ *n. f.* elevation; height.

elevador /eleβa'ðor/ *n. m.* elevator.

elevamiento /eleβa'miento/ *n. m.* elevation.

elevar /ele'βar/ *v.* elevate; erect, raise.

elidir /eli'ðir/ *v.* elide.

eliminación /elimina'θion; elimina'sion/ *n. f.* elimination.

eliminar /elimi'nar/ *v.* eliminate.

elipse /e'lipse/ *n. f.* ellipse.

elipsis /e'lipsis/ *n. f.* ellipsis.

elíptico /e'liptiko/ *a.* elliptic.

ella /'eʎa; 'eya/ *pron.* she, her; it.

ello /'eʎo; 'eyo/ *pron.* it.

ellos /'eʎos; 'eyos/ **-as** *pron. pl.* they, them.

elocuencia /elo'kuenθia; elo'kuensia/ *n. f.* eloquence.

elocuente /elo'kuente/ *a.* eloquent.

elocuentemente /elokuente'mente/ *adv.* eloquently.

elogio /e'lohio/ *n. m.* praise, compliment. **—elogiar,** *v.*

elucidación /eluθiða'θion; elusiða'sion/ *n. f.* elucidation.

elucidar /eluθi'ðar; elusi'ðar/ *v.* elucidate.

eludir /elu'ðir/ *v.* elude.

emanar /ema'nar/ *v.* emanate, stem.

emancipación /emanθipa'θion; emansipa'sion/ *n. f.* emancipation; freeing.

emancipador /emanθipa'ðor; emansipa'ðor/ **-ra** *n.* emancipator.

emancipar /emanθi'par; emansi'par/ *v.* emancipate; free.

embajada /emba'haða/ *n. f.* embassy; legation; *Colloq.* errand.

embajador /embaha'ðor/ **-ra** *n.* ambassador.

embalar /emba'lar/ *v.* pack, bale.

embaldosado /embaldo'saðo/ *n. m.* tile floor.

embalsamador /embalsama'ðor/ *n. m.* embalmer.

embalsamar /embalsa'mar/ *v.* embalm.

embarazada /embara'θaða; embara'saða/ *a.* pregnant.

embarazadamente /embaraθaða'mente; embarasaða'mente/ *adv.* embarrassedly.

embarazar /embara'θar; embara'sar/ *v.* make pregnant; embarrass.

embarazo /emba'raθo; emba'raso/ *n. m.* embarrassment; pregnancy.

embarbascado /embarβas'kaðo/ *a.* difficult; complicated.

embarcación /embarka'θion; embarka'sion/ *n. f.* boat, ship; embarkation.

embarcadero /embarka'ðero/ *n. m.* wharf, pier, dock.

embarcador /embarka'ðor/ *n. m.* shipper, loader, stevedore.

embarcar /embar'kar/ *v.* embark, board ship.

embarcarse /embar'karse/ *v.* embark; sail.

embargador /embarga'ðor/ *n. m.* one who impedes; one who orders an embargo.

embargante /embar'gante/ *a.* impeding, hindering.

embargar /embar'gar/ *v.* impede, restrain; *Leg.* seize, embargo.

embargo /em'bargo/ *n. m.* seizure, embargo. **sin e.,** however, nevertheless.

embarnizar /embarni'θar; embarni'sar/ *v.* varnish.

embarque /em'barke/ *n. m.* shipment.

embarrador /embarra'ðor/ **-ra** *n.* plasterer.

embarrancar /embarran'kar/ *v.*

get stuck in mud; *Naut.* run aground.

embarrar /emba'rrar/ *v.* plaster; besmear with mud.

embasamiento /embasa'miento/ *n. m.* foundation of a building.

embastecer /embaste'θer; embaste'ser/ *v.* get fat.

embaucador /embauka'ðor/ **-ra** *n.* impostor.

embaucar /embau'kar/ *v.* deceive, trick, hoax.

embaular /embau'lar/ *v.* pack in a trunk.

embausamiento /embausa'miento/ *n. m.* amazement.

embebecer /embeβe'θer; embeβe'ser/ *v.* amaze, astonish; entertain.

embeber /embe'βer/ *v.* absorb; incorporate; saturate.

embelecador /embeleka'ðor/ **-ra** *n.* impostor.

embeleco /embe'leko/ *n. m.* fraud, perpetration.

embeleñar /embele'ɲar/ *v.* fascinate, charm.

embelesamiento /embelesa'miento/ *n. m.* rapture.

embelesar /embele'sar/ *v.* fascinate, charm.

embeleso /embe'leso/ *n. m.* rapture, bliss.

embellecer /embeʎe'θer; embeye'ser/ *v.* beautify, embellish.

embestida /embes'tiða/ *n. f.* violent assault; attack.

emblandecer /emblande'θer; emblande'ser/ *v.* soften; moisten; move to pity.

emblema /em'blema/ *n. m.* emblem.

emblemático /emble'matiko/ *a.* emblematic.

embocadura /emboka'ðura/ *n. f.* narrow entrance; mouth of a river.

embocar /embo'kar/ *v.* eat hastily; gorge.

embolia /em'bolia/ *n. f.* embolism.

émbolo /'embolo/ *n. m.* piston.

embolsar /embol'sar/ *v.* pocket.

embonar /embo'nar/ *v.* improve, fix, repair.

emborrachador /emborratʃa'ðor/ *a.* intoxicating.

emborrachar /emborra'tʃar/ *v.* get drunk.

emboscada /embos'kaða/ *n. f.* ambush.

emboscar /embos'kar/ *v.* put or lie in ambush.

embotado /embo'taðo/ *a.* blunt, dull (edged). —**embotar,** *v.*

embotadura /embota'ðura/ *n. f.* bluntness; dullness.

embotellamiento /emboteʎa'miento; emboteya'miento/ *n. m.* bottling (liquids); traffic jam.

embotellar /embote'ʎar; embote'yar/ *v.* put in bottles.

embozado /embo'θaðo; embo'saðo/ *v.* muzzled; muffled.

embozar /embo'θar; embo'sar/ *v.* muzzle; muffle.

embozo /em'boθo; em'boso/ *n. m.* muffler.

embrague /em'brage/ *n. m. Auto.* clutch.

embravecer /embraβe'θer; embraβe'ser/ *v.* be or make angry.

embriagado /embria'gaðo/ *a.* drunken, intoxicated.

embriagar /embria'gar/ *v.* intoxicate.

embriaguez /embria'geθ; embria'ges/ *n. f.* drunkenness.

embrión /em'brion/ *n. m.* embryo.

embrionario /embrio'nario/ *a.* embryonic.

embrochado /embro'tʃaðo/ *a.* embroidered.

embrollo /em'broʎo; em'broyo/ *n. m.* muddle. —**embrollar,** *v.*

embromar /embro'mar/ *v.* tease; joke.

embuchado /embu'tʃaðo/ *n. m.* pork sausage.

embudo /em'buðo/ *n. m.* funnel.

embuste /em'buste/ *n. m.* lie, fib.

embustear /embuste'ar/ *v.* lie, fib.

embustero /embus'tero/ **-ra** *n.* liar.

embutir /embu'tir/ *v.* stuff, cram.

emergencia /emer'henθia; emer'hensia/ *n. f.* emergency.

emérito /e'merito/ *a.* emeritus.

emético /e'metiko/ *n. m. & a.* emetic.

emigración /emigra'θion; emigra'sion/ *n. f.* emigration.

emigrante /emi'grante/ *a. & n.* emigrant.

emigrar /emi'grar/ *v.* emigrate.

eminencia /emi'nenθia; emi'nensia/ *n. f.* eminence, height.

eminente /emi'nente/ *a.* eminent.

emisario /emi'sario/ **-ria** *n.* emissary, spy; outlet.

emisión /emi'sion/ *n. f.* issue; emission.

emisor /emi'sor/ *n. m.* radio transmitter.

emitir /emi'tir/ *v.* emit.

emoción /emo'θion; emo'sion/ *n. f.* feeling, emotion, thrill.

emocional /emo'θional; emo'sional/ *a.* emotional.

emocionante /emoθio'nante; emosio'nante/ *a.* exciting.

emocionar /emoθio'nar; emosio'nar/ *v.* touch, move, excite.

emolumento /emolu'mento/ *n. m.* emolument; perquisite.

empacar /empa'kar/ *v.* pack.

empacho /em'patʃo/ *n. m.* shyness, timidity; embarrassment.

empadronamiento /empaðrona'miento/ *n. m.* census; list of taxpayers.

empalizada /empali'θaða; empali'saða/ *n. f.* palisade, stockade.

empanada /empa'naða/ *n. f.* meat pie.

empañar /empa'ɲar/ *v.* blur; soil, sully.

empapar /empa'par/ *v.* soak.

empapelado /empape'laðo/ *n. m.* wallpaper.

empapelar /empape'lar/ *v.* wallpaper.

empaque /em'pake/ *n. m.* packing; appearance, mien.

empaquetar /empake'tar/ *v.* pack, package.

emparedado /empare'ðaðo/ *n. m.* sandwich.

emparejarse /empare'harse/ *v.* match, pair off; level, even off.

emparentado /emparen'taðo/ *a.* related by marriage.

emparrado /empa'rraðo/ *n. m.* arbor.

empastadura /empasta'ðura/ *n. f.* (dental) filling.

empastar /empas'tar/ *v.* fill (a tooth); paste.

empate /em'pate/ *n. m.* tie, draw. —**empatarse**, *v.*

empecer /empe'θer; empe'ser/ *v.* hurt, harm, injure; prevent.

empedernir /empeðer'nir/ *v.* harden.

empeine /em'peine/ *n. m.* groin; instep; hoof.

empellar /empe'ʎar; empe'yar/ *v.* shove, jostle.

empellón /empe'ʎon; empe'yon/ *n. m.* hard push, shove.

empeñar /empe'ɲar/ *v.* pledge; pawn.

empeñarse en /empe'ɲarse en/ *v.* persist in, be bent on.

empeño /em'peɲo/ *n. m.* persistence; pledge; pawning.

empeoramiento /empeora'miento/ *n. m.* deterioration.

empeorar /empeo'rar/ *v.* get worse.

emperador /empera'ðor/ *n. m.* emperor.

emperatriz /empera'triθ; empera'tris/ *n. f.* empress.

empernar /emper'nar/ *v.* bolt.

empero /em'pero/ *conj.* however; but.

emperramiento /emperra'miento/ *n. m.* stubbornness.

empezar /empe'θar; empe'sar/ *v.* begin, start.

empinado /empi'naðo/ *a.* steep.

empinar /empi'nar/ *v.* raise; exalt.

empíreo /em'pireo/ *a.* celestial, heavenly; divine.

empíricamente /empirika'mente/ *adv.* empirically.

empírico /em'piriko/ *a.* empirical.

empirismo /empi'rismo/ *n. m.* empiricism.

emplastarse /emplas'tarse/ *v.* get smeared.

emplasto /em'plasto/ *n. m.* salve.

emplazamiento /emplaθa'miento; emplasa'miento/ *n. m.* court summons.

emplazar /empla'θar; empla'sar/ *v.* summon to court.

empleado /emple'aðo/ **-da** *n.* employee.

emplear /em'plear/ *v.* employ; use.

empleo /em'pleo/ *n. m.* employment, job; use.

empobrecer /empoβre'θer; empoβre'ser/ *v.* impoverish.

empobrecimiento /empoβreθi'miento; empoβresi'miento/ *n. m.* impoverishment.

empollador /empoʎa'ðor; empoya'ðor/ *n. m.* incubator.

empollar /empo'ʎar; empo'yar/ *v.* hatch.

empolvado /empol'βaðo/ *a.* dusty.

empolvar /empol'βar/ *v.* powder.

emporcar /empor'kar/ *v.* soil, make dirty.

emporio /em'porio/ *n. m.* emporium.

emprendedor /emprende'ðor/ *a.* enterprising.

emprender /empren'der/ *v.* undertake.

empreñar /empre'ɲar/ *v.* make pregnant; beget.

empresa /em'presa/ *n. f.* enterprise, undertaking; company.

empresario /empre'sario/ **-ria** *n.* businessperson; impresario.

empréstito /em'prestito/ *n. m.* loan.

empujón /empu'hon/ *n. m.* push; shove. —**empujar,** *v.*

empuñar /empu'ɲar/ *v.* grasp, seize; wield.

emulación /emula'θion; emula'sion/ *n. f.* emulation; envy; rivalry.

emulador /emula'ðor/ *n. m.* emulator; rival.

émulo /'emulo/ *a.* rival. —**emular,** *v.*

emulsión /emul'sion/ *n. f.* emulsion.

emulsionar /emulsio'nar/ *v.* emulsify.

en /en/ *prep.* in, on, at.

enaguas /e'naguas/ *n. f.pl.* petticoat; skirt.

enajenable /enahe'naβle/ *a.* alienable.

enajenación /enahena'θion; enahena'sion/ *n. f.* alienation; derangement, insanity.

enajenar /enahe'nar/ *v.* alienate.

enamoradamente /enamoraða'mente/ *adv.* lovingly.

enamorado /enamo'raðo/ *a.* in love.

enamorador /enamora'ðor/ *n. m.* wooer; suitor; lover.

enamorarse /enamo'rarse/ *v.* fall in love.

enano /e'nano/ **-na** *n.* midget; dwarf.

enardecer /enarðe'θer; enarðe'ser/ *v.* inflame.

enastado /enas'taðo/ *a.* horned.

encabestrar /enkaβe'strar/ *v.* halter.

encabezado /enkaβe'θaðo; enkaβe'saðo/ *n. m.* headline.

encabezamiento /enkaβeθa'miento; enkaβesa'miento/ *n. m.* title; census; tax roll.

encabezar /enkaβe'θar; enkaβe'sar/ *v.* head.

encachar /enka't∫ar/ *v.* hide.

encadenamiento /enkaðena'miento/ *n. m.* connection, linkage.

encadenar /enkaðe'nar/ *v.* chain; link, connect.

encajar /enka'har/ *v.* fit in, insert.

encaje /en'kahe/ *n. m.* lace.

encalar /enka'lar/ *v.* whitewash.

encallarse /enka'ʎarse; enka'yarse/ *v.* be stranded.

encallecido /enkaʎe'θiðo; enkaye'siðo/ *a.* hardened; calloused.

encalvecer /enkalβe'θer; enkalβe'ser/ *v.* lose one's hair.

encaminar /enkami'nar/ *v.* guide; direct; be on the way to.

encandilar /enkandi'lar/ *v.* dazzle; daze.

encantación /enkanta'θion; enkanta'sion/ *n. f.* incantation.

encantado /enkan'taðo/ *a.* charmed, fascinated, enchanted.

encantador /enkanta'ðor/ *a.* charming, delightful.

encante /en'kante/ *n. m.* public auction.

encanto /en'kanto/ *n. m.* charm, delight. —**encantar,** *v.*

encapillado /enkapi'ʎaðo; enkapi'yaðo/ *n. m.* clothes one is wearing.

encapotar /enkapo'tar/ *v.* cover, cloak; muffle.

encaprichamiento /enkaprit∫a'miento/ *n. m.* infatuation.

encaramarse /enkara'marse/ *v.* perch; climb.

encararse con /enka'rarse kon/ *v.* face.

encarcelación /enkarθela'θion; enkarsela'sion/ *n. f.* imprisonment.

encarcelar /enkarθe'lar; enkarse'lar/ *v.* jail, imprison.

encarecer /enkare'θer; enkare'ser/ *v.* recommend; extol.

encarecidamente /enkareθiða'mente; enkaresiða'mente/ *adv.* extremely; ardently.

encargado /enkar'gaðo/ **-da** *n.* agent; attorney; representative.

encargar /enkar'gar/ *v.* entrust; order.

encargarse /enkar'garse/ *v.* take charge, be in charge.

encargo /en'kargo/ *n. m.* errand; assignment; *Com.* order.

encarnación /enkarna'θion; enkarna'sion/ n. f. incarnation.

encarnado /enkar'naðo/ a. red.

encarnar /enkar'nar/ v. embody.

encarnecer /enkarne'θer; enkarne-'ser/ v. grow fat or heavy.

encarnizado /enkarni'θaðo; enkarni'saðo/ a. bloody, fierce.

encarrilar /enkarri'lar/ v. set right; put on the track.

encartar /enkar'tar/ v. ban, outlaw; summon.

encastar /enkas'tar/ v. improve by crossbreeding.

encastillar /enkasti'ʎar; enkasti'yar/ v. be obstinate or unyielding.

encatarrado /enkata'rraðo/ a. suffering from a cold.

encausar /enkau'sar/ v. prosecute; take legal action against.

encauzar /enkau'θar; enkau'sar/ v. channel; direct.

encefalitis /enθefa'litis; ensefa-'litis/ n. f. encephalitis.

encelamiento /enθela'miento; ensela'miento/ n. m. envy, jealousy.

encelar /enθe'lar; ense'lar/ v. make jealous.

encenagar /enθena'gar; ensena-'gar/ v. wallow in mud.

encendedor /enθende'ðor; ensende'ðor/ n. m. lighter.

encender /enθen'der; ensen'der/ v. light; set fire to, kindle; turn on.

encendido /enθen'diðo; ensen-'diðo/ n. m. ignition.

encerado /enθe'raðo; ense'raðo/ n. m. oilcloth; tarpaulin.

encerar /enθe'rar; ense'rar/ v. wax.

encerrar /enθe'rrar; ense'rrar/ v. enclose; confine, shut in.

enchapado /entʃa'paðo/ n. m. veneer.

enchufe /en'tʃufe/ n. m. Elec. plug, socket.

encía /en'θia; en'sia/ n. f. gum.

encíclico /en'θikliko; en'sikliko/ a. 1. encyclic. —n. 2. f. encyclical.

enciclopedia /enθiklo'peðia; ensiklo'peðia/ n. f. encyclopedia.

enciclopédico /enθiklo'peðiko; ensiklo'peðiko/ a. encyclopedic.

encierro /en'θierro; en'sierro/ n. m. confinement; enclosure.

encima /en'θima; en'sima/ adv. on top. **e. de,** on. **por e. de,** above.

encina /en'θina; en'sina/ n. f. oak.

encinta /en'θinta; en'sinta/ a. pregnant.

enclavar /enkla'βar/ v. nail.

enclenque /en'klenke/ a. frail, weak, sickly.

encogerse /enko'herse/ v. shrink. **e. de hombros,** shrug the shoulders.

encogido /enko'hiðo/ a. shy, bashful, timid.

encojar /enko'har/ v. make or become lame; cripple.

encolar /enko'lar/ v. glue, paste, stick.

encolerizar /enkoleri'θar; enkoleri'sar/ v. make or become angry.

encomendar /enkomen'dar/ v. commend; recommend.

encomiar /enko'miar/ v. praise, laud, extol.

encomienda /enko'mienda/ n. f. commission, charge; (postal) package.

encomio /en'komio/ n. m. encomium, eulogy.

enconar /enko'nar/ v. irritate, annoy, anger.

encono /en'kono/ n. m. rancor, resentment.

enconoso /enko'noso/ a. rancorous, resentful.

encontrado /enkon'traðo/ a. opposite.

encontrar /enkon'trar/ v. find; meet.

encorajar /enkora'har/ v. encourage; incite.

encornar /enkor'nar/ v. gore.

encorralar /enkorra'lar/ v. corral.

encorvadura /enkorβa'ðura/ n. f. bend, curvature.

encorvar /enkor'βar/ v. arch, bend.

encorvarse /enkor'βarse/ v. stoop.

encrucijada /enkruθi'haða; enkrusi'haða/ n. f. crossroads.

encuadrar /enkuað'rar/ v. frame.

encubierta /enku'βierta/ a. 1. secret, fraudulent. —n. 2. f. fraud.

encubrir /enkuβ'rir/ v. hide, conceal.

encuentro /en'kuentro/ n. m. encounter; match, bout.

encurtido /enkur'tiðo/ n. m. pickle.

endeble /en'deβle/ a. rail, weak, sickly.

enderezar /endere'θar; endere-'sar/ v. straighten; redress.

endeudarse /endeu'ðarse/ *v.* get into debt.

endiablado /endia'βlaðo/ *a.* devilish.

endibia /en'diβia/ *n. f.* endive.

endiosar /endio'sar/ *v.* deify.

endorso /en'dorso/ **endoso** *n. m.* endorsement.

endosador /endosa'ðor/ **-ra** *n.* endorser.

endosar /endo'sar/ *v.* endorse.

endosatario /endosa'tario/ **-ria** *n.* endorsee.

endulzar /endul'θar; endul'sar/ *v.* sweeten; soothe.

endurar /endu'rar/ *v.* harden.

endurecer /endure'θer; endure-'ser/ *v.* harden.

enemigo /ene'migo/ **-ga** *n.* foe, enemy.

enemistad /enemis'taδ/ *n. f.* enmity.

éneo /'eneo/ *a.* brass.

energía /ener'hia/ *n. f.* energy.

energía nuclear /ener'hia nukle-'ar/ atomic energy, nuclear energy.

energía vital /ener'hia bi'tal/ élan vital, vitality.

enérgicamente /e'nerhikamente/ *adv.* energetically.

enérgico /e'nerhiko/ *a.* forceful; energetic.

enero /e'nero/ *n. m.* January.

enervación /enerβa'θion; enerβa-'sion/ *n. f.* enervation.

enfadado /enfa'ðaðo/ *a.* angry.

enfadar /enfa'ðar/ *v.* anger, vex.

enfado /en'faðo/ *n. m.* anger, vexation.

énfasis /'enfasis/ *n. m. or f.* emphasis, stress.

enfáticamente /en'fatikamente/ *adv.* emphatically.

enfático /en'fatiko/ *a.* emphatic.

enfermar /enfer'mar/ *v.* make ill; fall ill.

enfermedad /enferme'ðaδ/ *n. f.* illness, sickness, disease.

enfermera /enfer'mera/ *n. f.* nurse.

enfermería /enferme'ria/ *n. f.* sanatorium.

enfermo /en'fermo/ **-ma** *a. & n.* ill, sick; sickly; patient.

enfilar /enfi'lar/ *v.* line up; put in a row.

enflaquecer /enflake'θer; enflake-'ser/ *v.* make thin; grow thin.

enfoque /en'foke/ *n. m.* focus. —**enfocar,** *v.*

enfrascamiento /enfraska'miento/ *n. m.* entanglement.

enfrascar /enfras'kar/ *v.* bottle; entangle oneself.

enfrenar /enfre'nar/ *v.* bridle, curb; restrain.

enfrentamiento /enfrenta'miento/ *n. m.* clash, confrontation.

enfrente /en'frente/ *adv.* across, opposite; in front.

enfriadera /enfria'ðera/ *n. f.* icebox; cooler.

enfriar /enf'riar/ *v.* chill, cool.

enfurecer /enfure'θer; enfure'ser/ *v.* infuriate, enrage.

engalanar /eŋgala'nar/ *v.* adorn, trim.

enganchar /eŋgan'tʃar/ *v.* hook, hitch, attach.

engañar /eŋga'ɲar/ *v.* deceive, cheat.

engaño /eŋ'gaɲo/ *n. m.* deceit; delusion.

engañoso /eŋga'ɲoso/ *a.* deceitful.

engarce /eŋ'garθe; eŋgarse/ *n. m.* connection, link.

engastar /eŋgas'tar/ *v.* to put (gems) in a setting.

engaste /eŋ'gaste/ *n. m.* setting.

engatusar /eŋgatu'sar/ *v.* deceive, trick.

engendrar /enhen'drar/ *v.* engender, beget, produce.

engendro /en'hendro/ *n. m.* fetus, embryo.

englobar /eŋglo'βar/ *v.* include.

engolfar /eŋgol'far/ *v.* be deeply absorbed.

engolosinar /eŋgolosi'nar/ *v.* allure, charm, entice.

engomar /eŋgo'mar/ *v.* gum.

engordador /eŋgor'ðaðor/ *a.* fattening.

engordar /eŋgor'ðar/ *v.* fatten; grow fat.

engranaje /eŋgra'nahe/ *n. m. Mech.* gear.

engranar /eŋgra'nar/ *v.* gear; mesh together.

engrandecer /eŋgrande'θer; eŋgrande'ser/ *v.* increase, enlarge; exalt; exaggerate.

engrasación /eŋgrasa'θion; eŋgrasa'sion/ *n. f.* lubrication.

engrasar /eŋgra'sar/ *v.* grease, lubricate.

engreído /eŋgre'iðo/ *a.* conceited.

engreimiento

84

engreimiento /eŋgrei'miento/ *n. m.* conceit.

engullidor /eŋgu'ʎi'ðor; eŋguyi-'ðor/ **-ra** *n.* devourer.

engullir /eŋgu'ʎir; eŋgu'yir/ *v.* devour.

enhebrar /ene'βrar/ *v.* thread.

enhestadura /enesta'ðura/ *n. f.* raising.

enhestar /enes'tar/ *v.* raise, erect, set up.

enhiesto /en'iesto/ *a.* erect, upright.

enhorabuena /enora'βuena/ *n. f.* congratulations.

enigma /e'nigma/ *n. m.* enigma, puzzle.

enigmáticamente /enigmatika'mente/ *adv.* enigmatically.

enigmático /enig'matiko/ *a.* enigmatic.

enjabonar /enhaβo'nar/ *v.* soap, lather.

enjalbegar /enhalβe'gar/ *v.* whitewash.

enjambradera /enhambra'ðera/ *n. f.* queen bee.

enjambre /en'hambre/ *n. m.* swarm. —**enjambrar**, *v.*

enjaular /enhau'lar/ *v.* cage, coop up.

enjebe /en'heβe/ *n. m.* lye.

enjuagar /enhua'gar/ *v.* rinse.

enjuague bucal /en'huage bu'kal/ *n. m.* mouthwash.

enjugar /enhu'gar/ *v.* wipe, dry off.

enjutez /enhu'teθ; enhu'tes/ *n. f.* dryness.

enjuto /en'huto/ *a.* dried; lean, thin.

enlace /en'laθe; en'lase/ *n. m.* attachment; involvement; connection.

enladrillador /enlaðriʎa'ðor; enlaðriya'ðor/ **-ra** *n.* bricklayer.

enlardar /enlar'ðar/ *v.* baste.

enlatado /enla'taðo/ **-da** *a.* canned (food).

enlatar /enla'tar/ *v.* can (food).

enlazar /enla'θar; enla'sar/ *v.* lace; join, connect; wed.

enlodar /enlo'ðar/ *v.* cover with mud.

enloquecer /enloke'θer; enloke-'ser/ *v.* go insane; drive crazy.

enloquecimiento /enlokeθi-'miento; enlokesi'miento/ *n. m.* insanity.

enlustrecer /enlustre'θer; enlustre'ser/ *v.* polish, brighten.

enmarañar /emara'ɲar/ *v.* entangle.

enmendación /enmenda'θion; enmenda'sion/ *n. f.* emendation.

enmendador /enmenda'ðor/ **-ra** *n.* emender, reviser.

enmendar /enmen'dar/ *v.* amend, correct.

enmienda /en'mienda/ *n. f.* amendment; correction.

enmohecer /enmoe'θer; enmoe'ser/ *v.* rust; mold.

enmohecido /enmoe'θiðo; enmoe-'siðo/ *a.* rusty; moldy.

enmudecer /enmuðe'θer; enmuðe-'ser/ *v.* silence; become silent.

ennegrecer /ennegre'θer; ennegre'ser/ *v.* blacken.

ennoblecer /ennoβle'θer; ennoβle'ser/ *v.* ennoble.

enodio /e'noðio/ *n. m.* young deer.

enojado /eno'haðo/ *a.* angry, cross.

enojarse /eno'harse/ *v.* get angry.

enojo /e'noho/ *n. m.* anger. —**enojar**, *v.*

enojosamente /enohosa'mente/ *adv.* angrily.

enorme /e'norme/ *a.* enormous, huge.

enormemente /enorme'mente/ *adv.* enormously; hugely.

enormidad /enormi'ðað/ *n. f.* enormity; hugeness.

enraizar /enrai'θar; enrai'sar/ *v.* take root, sprout.

enramada /enra'maða/ *n. f.* bower.

enredadera /enreða'ðera/ *n. f.* climbing plant.

enredado /enre'ðaðo/ *a.* entangled, snarled.

enredar /enre'ðar/ *v.* entangle, snarl; mess up.

enredo /en'reðo/ *n. m.* tangle, entanglement.

enriquecer /enrike'θer; enrike'ser/ *v.* enrich.

enrojecerse /enrohe'θerse; enrohe'serse/ *v.* color; blush.

enrollar /enro'ʎar; enro'yar/ *v.* wind, coil, roll up.

enromar /enro'mar/ *v.* make dull, blunt.

enronquecimiento /enronkeθi-'miento; enronkesi'miento/ *n. m.* hoarseness.

enroscar /enros'kar/ *v.* twist, curl, wind.

ensacar /ensa'kar/ *v.* put in a bag.

ensalada /ensa'laða/ *n. f.* salad.

ensaladera /ensala'ðera/ *n. f.* salad bowl.

ensalmo /en'salmo/ *n. m.* charm, enchantment.

ensalzamiento /ensalθa'miento; ensalsa'miento/ *n. m.* praise.

ensalzar /ensal'θar; ensal'sar/ *v.* praise, laud, extol.

ensamblar /ensam'blar/ *v.* join; unite; connect.

ensanchamiento /ensantʃa-'miento/ *n. m.* widening, expansion, extension.

ensanchar /ensan'tʃar/ *v.* widen, expand, extend.

ensangrentado /ensaŋgren'taðo/ *a.* bloody; bloodshot.

ensañar /ensa'ɲar/ *v.* enrage, infuriate; rage.

ensayar /ensa'yar/ *v.* try out; rehearse.

ensayista /ensa'yista/ *n. m. & f.* essayist.

ensayo /ensa'yo/ *n. m.* attempt; trial; rehearsal.

ensenada /ense'naða/ *n. f.* cove.

enseña /en'seɲa/ *n. f.* ensign, standard.

enseñador /enseɲa'ðor/ **-ra** *n.* teacher.

enseñanza /ense'ɲanθa; enseɲan-sa/ *n. f.* education; teaching.

enseñar /ense'ɲar/ *v.* teach, train; show.

enseres /en'seres/ *n. m.pl.* household goods.

ensilaje /ensi'lahe/ *n. m.* ensilage.

ensillar /ensi'ʎar; ensi'yar/ *v.* saddle.

ensordecedor /ensorðeθe'ðor; ensorðese'ðor/ *a.* deafening.

ensordecer /ensorðe'θer; ensorðe'ser/ *v.* deafen.

ensordecimiento /ensorðeθi-'miento; ensorðesi'miento/ *n. m.* deafness.

ensuciar /ensu'θiar; ensu'siar/ *v.* dirty, muddy, soil.

ensueño /en'sueɲo/ *n. m.* illusion, dream.

entablar /enta'βlar/ *v.* board up; initiate, begin.

entallador /entaʎa'ðor; entaya'ðor/ *n. m.* sculptor, carver.

entapizar /entapi'θar; entapi'sar/ *v.* upholster.

ente /'ente/ *n. m.* being.

entenada /ente'naða/ *n. f.* stepdaughter.

entenado /ente'naðo/ *n. m.* stepson.

entender /enten'der/ *v.* understand.

entendimiento /entendi'miento/ *n. m.* understanding.

entenebrecer /entene βre'θer; eneneβre'ser/ *v.* darken.

enterado /ente'raðo/ *a.* aware, informed.

enteramente /entera'mente/ *adv.* entirely, completely.

enterar /ente'rar/ *v.* inform.

enterarse /ente'rarse/ *v.* find out.

entereza /ente'reθa; ente'resa/ *n. f.* entirety; integrity; firmness.

entero /en'tero/ *a.* entire, whole, total.

enterramiento /enterra'miento/ *n. m.* burial, interment.

enterrar /ente'rrar/ *v.* bury.

entestado /entes'taðo/ *a.* stubborn, willful.

entibiar /enti'βiar/ *v.* to cool; moderate.

entidad /enti'ðað/ *n. f.* entity.

entierro /en'tierro/ *n. m.* interment, burial.

entonación /entona'θion; entona-'sion/ *n. f.* intonation.

entonamiento /entona'miento/ *n. m.* intonation.

entonar /ento'nar/ *v.* chant; harmonize.

entonces /en'tonθes; entonses/ *adv.* then.

entono /en'tono/ *n. m.* intonation; arrogance; affectation.

entortadura /entorta'ðura/ *n. f.* crookedness.

entortar /entor'tar/ *v.* make crooked; bend.

entrada /en'traða/ *n. f.* entrance; admission, admittance.

entrambos /en'trambos/ *a. & pron.* both.

entrante /en'trante/ *a.* coming, next.

entrañable /entra'ɲaβle/ *a.* affectionate.

entrañas /en'traɲas/ *n. f.pl.* entrails, bowels; womb.

entrar /en'trar/ *v.* enter, go in, come in.

entre /'entre/ *prep.* among; between.

entreabierto /entrea'βierto/ *a.* ajar, half-open.

entreabrir /entrea'βrir/ *v.* set ajar.

entreacto /entre'akto/ *n. m.* intermission.

entrecejo /entre'θeho; entre'seho/ *n. m.* frown; space between the eyebrows.

entrecuesto /entre'kuesto/ *n. m.* spine, backbone.

entredicho /entre'ðitʃo/ *n. m.* prohibition.

entrega /en'trega/ *n. f.* delivery.

entregar /entre'gar/ *v.* deliver, hand; hand over.

entrelazar /entrela'θar; entrela'sar/ *v.* intertwine, entwine.

entremedias /entre'meðias/ *adv.* meanwhile; halfway.

entremés /entre'mes/ *n. m.* side dish.

entremeterse /entreme'terse/ *v.* meddle, intrude.

entremetido /entreme'tiðo/ **-da** *n.* meddler.

entrenador /entrena'ðor/ **-ra** *n.* coach. —**entrenar,** *v.*

entrenarse /entre'narse/ *v.* train.

entrepalado /entrepa'laðo/ *a.* variegated; spotted.

entrerenglonar /entrerengloʼnar/ *v.* interline.

entresacar /entresa'kar/ *v.* select, choose; sift.

entresuelo /entre'suelo/ *n. m.* mezzanine.

entretanto /entre'tanto/ *adv.* meanwhile.

entretenedor /entretene'ðor/ **-ra** *n.* entertainer.

entretener /entrete'ner/ *v.* entertain, amuse; delay.

entretenimiento /entreteni'miento/ *n. m.* entertainment, amusement.

entrevista /entre'βista/ *n. f.* interview. —**entrevistar,** *v.*

entrevistador /entreβista'ðor/ **-ra** *n.* interviewer.

entristecedor /entristeθe'ðor; entristese'ðor/ *a.* sad.

entristecer /entriste'θer; entriste'ser/ *v.* sadden.

entronar /entro'nar/ *v.* enthrone.

entroncar /entron'kar/ *v.* be related or connected.

entronización /entroniθa'θion; entronisa'sion/ *n. f.* enthronement.

entronque /entron'ke/ *n. m.* relationship; connection.

entumecer /entume'θer; entume'ser/ *v.* become or be numb; swell.

entusiasmado /entusias'maðo/ *a.* enthusiastic.

entusiasmo /entu'siasmo/ *n. m.* enthusiasm.

entusiasta /entu'siasta/ *n. m. & f.* enthusiast.

entusiástico /entu'siastiko/ *a.* enthusiastic.

enumeración /enumera'θion; enumera'sion/ *n. f.* enumeration.

enumerar /enume'rar/ *v.* enumerate.

enunciación /enunθia'θion; enunsia'sion/ *n. f.* enunciation; statement.

enunciar /enun'θiar; enun'siar/ *v.* enunciate.

envainar /embai'nar/ *v.* sheathe.

envalentonar /embalento'nar/ *v.* encourage, embolden.

envanecimiento /embaneθi'miento; embanesi'miento/ *n. m.* conceit, vanity.

envasar /emba'sar/ *v.* put in a container; bottle.

envase /em'base/ *n. m.* container.

envejecer /embehe'θer; embehe'ser/ *v.* age, grow old.

envejecimiento /embeheθi'miento; embehesi'miento/ *n. m.* oldness, aging.

envenenar /embene'nar/ *v.* poison.

envés /em'bes/ *n. m.* wrong side; back.

envestir /embes'tir/ *v.* put in office; invest.

enviada /em'biaða/ *n. f.* shipment.

enviado /em'biaðo/ **-da** *n.* envoy.

enviar /em'biar/ *v.* send; ship.

envidia /em'biðia/ *n. f.* envy. —**envidiar,** *v.*

envidiable /embi'ðiaβle/ *a.* enviable.

envidioso /embi'ðioso/ *a.* envious.

envilecer /embile'θer; embile'ser/ *v.* vilify, debase, disgrace.

envío /em'bio/ *n. m.* shipment.

envión /em'bion/ *n. m.* shove.

envoltura /embol'tura/ *n. f.* wrapping.

envolver /embol'βer/ *v.* wrap, wrap up.

enyesar /enye'sar/ *v.* plaster.

enyugar /enyu'gar/ *v.* yoke.

eperlano /eper'lano/ *n. m.* smelt (fish).

épica /'epika/ *n. f.* epic.

épico /'epiko/ *a.* epic.

epicureísmo /epikure'ismo/ *n. m.* epicureanism.

epicúreo /epi'kureo/ *n.* & *a.* epicurean.

epidemia /epi'ðemia/ *n. f.* epidemic.

epidémico /epi'ðemiko/ *a.* epidemic.

epidermis /epi'ðermis/ *n. f.* epidermis.

epigrama /epi'grama/ *n. m.* epigram.

epigramático /epigra'matiko/ **-ca** *a.* epigrammatic.

epilepsia /epi'lepsia/ *n. f.* epilepsy.

epiléptico /epi'leptiko/ **-ca** *n.* & *a.* epileptic.

epílogo /e'pilogo/ *n. m.* epilogue.

episcopado /episko'paðo/ *n. m.* bishopric; episcopate.

episcopal /episko'pal/ *a.* episcopal.

episódico /epi'soðiko/ *a.* episodic.

episodio /epi'soðio/ *n. m.* episode.

epístola /e'pistola/ *n. f.* epistle, letter.

epitafio /epi'tafio/ *n. m.* epitaph.

epitomadamente /epitomaða-'mente/ *adv.* concisely.

epitomar /epito'mar/ *v.* epitomize, summarize.

época /'epoka/ *n. f.* epoch, age.

epopeya /epo'peya/ *n. f.* epic.

epsomita /epso'mita/ *n. f.* Epsom salts.

equidad /eki'ðað/ *n. f.* equity.

equilibrado /ekili'βraðo/ *a.* stable.

equilibrio /eki'liβrio/ *n. m.* equilibrium, balance.

equinoccio /eki'nokθio; ekinoksio/ *n. m.* equinox.

equipaje /eki'pahe/ *n. m.* luggage, baggage. **e. de mano,** luggage.

equipar /eki'par/ *v.* equip.

equiparar /ekipa'rar/ *v.* compare.

equipo /e'kipo/ *n. m.* equipment; team.

equitación /ekita'θion; ekita'sion/ *f.* horsemanship; horseback riding, riding.

equitativo /ekita'tiβo/ *a.* fair, equitable.

equivalencia /ekiβa'lenθia; ekiβa'lensia/ *n. f.* equivalence.

equivalente /ekiβa'lente/ *a.* equivalent.

equivaler /ekiβa'ler/ *v.* equal, be equivalent.

equivocación /ekiβoka'θion; ekiβoka'sion/ *n. f.* mistake.

equivocado /ekiβo'kaðo/ *a.* wrong, mistaken.

equivocarse /ekiβo'karse/ *v.* make a mistake, be wrong.

equívoco /e'kiβoko/ *a.* equivocal, ambiguous.

era /'era/ *n. f.* era, age.

erario /e'rario/ *n. m.* exchequer.

erección /erek'θion; erek'sion/ *n. f.* erection; elevation.

eremita /ere'mita/ *n. m.* hermit.

erguir /er'gir/ *v.* erect; straighten up.

erigir /eri'hir/ *v.* erect, build.

erisipela /erisi'pela/ *n. f.* erysipelas.

erizado /eri'θaðo; eri'saðo/ *a.* bristly.

erizarse /eri'θarse; eri'sarse/ *v.* bristle.

erizo /e'riθo; e'riso/ *n. m.* hedgehog; sea urchin.

ermita /er'mita/ *n. f.* hermitage.

ermitaño /ermi'taɲo/ *n. m.* hermit.

erogación /eroga'θion; eroga'sion/ *n. f.* expenditure. —**erogar,** *v.*

erosión /ero'sion/ *n. f.* erosion.

erótico /e'rotiko/ *a.* erotic.

erradicación /erraðika'θion; erraðika'sion/ *n. f.* eradication.

erradicar /erraði'kar/ *v.* eradicate.

errado /e'rraðo/ *a.* mistaken, erroneous.

errante /e'rrante/ *a.* wandering, roving.

errar /e'rrar/ *v.* be mistaken.

errata /e'rrata/ *n. f.* erratum.

errático /e'rratiko/ *a.* erratic.

erróneamente /erronea'mente/ *adv.* erroneously.

erróneo /e'rroneo/ *a.* erroneous.

error /e'rror/ *n. m.* error, mistake.

eructo /e'rukto/ *n. m.* belch. —**eructar,** *v.*

erudición /eruði'θion; eruði'sion/ *n. f.* scholarship, learning.

eruditamente /eruðita'mente/ *adv.* learnedly.

erudito /eru'ðito/ **-ta** *n.* **1.** scholar. —*a.* **2.** scholarly.

erupción /erup'θion; erup'sion/ *n. f.* eruption; rash.

eruptivo /erup'tiβo/ *a.* eruptive.

esbozo /es'βoθo; es'βoso/ *n. m.* outline, sketch. —**esbozar,** *v.*

escabechar /eskaβe't∫ar/ *v.* pickle; preserve.

escabeche /eska'βet∫e/ *n. m.* brine.

escabel /eska'βel/ *n. m.* small stool or bench.

escabroso /eska'βroso/ *a.* rough, irregular; craggy; rude.

escabullirse /eskaβu'ʎirse; eskaβu'yirse/ *v.* steal away, sneak away.

escala /es'kala/ *n. f.* scale; ladder. **hacer e.,** to make a stop.

escalada /eska'laða/ *n. f.* escalation.

escalador /eskala'ðor/ **-ra** *n.* climber.

escalar /eska'lar/ *v.* climb; scale.

escaldar /eskal'dar/ *v.* scald.

escalera /eska'lera/ *n. f.* stairs, staircase; ladder.

escalfado /eskal'faðo/ *a.* poached.

escalofriado /eskalo'friaðo/ *a.* chilled.

escalofrío /eskalo'frio/ *n. m.* chill.

escalón /eska'lon/ *n. m.* step.

escalonar /eskalo'nar/ *v.* space out, stagger.

escaloña /eska'loɲa/ *n. f.* scallion.

escalpar /eskal'par/ *v.* scalp.

escalpelo /eskal'pelo/ *n. m.* scalpel.

escama /es'kama/ *n. f.* (fish) scale. —**escamar,** *v.*

escamondar /eskamon'dar/ *v.* trim, cut; prune.

escampada /eskam'paða/ *n. f.* break in the rain, clear spell.

escandalizar /eskandali'θar; eskandali'sar/ *v.* shock, scandalize.

escandalizativo /eskandaliθa'tiβo; eskandalisa'tiβo/ *a.* scandalous.

escándalo /es'kandalo/ *n. m.* scandal.

escandaloso /eskanda'loso/ *a.* scandalous; disgraceful.

escandinavo /eskandi'naβo/ **-va** *n. & a.* Scandinavian.

escandir /eskan'dir/ *v.* scan.

escanear /eskane'ar/ *v.* scan (on a computer).

escáner /es'kaner/ *n. m.* scanner (of a computer).

escanilla /eska'niʎa; eska'niya/ *n. f.* cradle.

escañuelo /eska'ɲuelo/ *n. m.* small footstool.

escapada /eska'paða/ *n. f.* escapade.

escapar /eska'par/ *v.* escape.

escaparate /eskapa'rate/ *n. m.* shop window, store window.

escape /es'kape/ *n. m.* escape; *Auto.* exhaust.

escápula /es'kapula/ *n. f.* scapula.

escarabajo /eskara'βaho/ *n. m.* black beetle; scarab.

escaramucear /eskaramuθe'ar; eskaramuse'ar/ *v.* skirmish; dispute.

escarbadientes /eskarβa'ðientes/ *n. m.* toothpick.

escarbar /eskar'βar/ *v.* scratch; poke.

escarcha /es'kart∫a/ *n. f.* frost.

escardar /eskar'ðar/ *v.* weed.

escarlata /eskar'lata/ *n. f.* scarlet.

escarlatina /eskarla'tina/ *n. f.* scarlet fever.

escarmentar /eskarmen'tar/ *v.* correct severely.

escarnecedor /eskarneθe'ðor; eskarneseðor/ **-ra** *n.* scoffer; mocker.

escarnecer /eskarne'θer; eskarne'ser/ *v.* mock, make fun of.

escarola /eska'rola/ *n. f.* endive.

escarpa /es'karpa/ *n. m.* escarpment.

escarpado /eskar'paðo/ *a.* **1.** steep. —*n.* **2.** *m.* bluff.

escasamente /eskasa'mente/ *adv.* scarcely; sparingly; barely.

escasear /eskase'ar/ *v.* be scarce.

escasez /eska'seθ; eska'ses/ *n. f.* shortage, scarcity.

escaso /es'kaso/ *a.* scant; scarce.

escatimar /eskati'mar/ *v.* be stingy, skimp; save.

escatimoso /eskati'moso/ *a.* malicious; sly, cunning.

escena /es'θena; es'sena/ *n. f.* scene; stage.

escenario /esθe'nario; esse'nario/ *n. m.* stage (of theater); scenario.

escénico /es'θeniko; es'seniko/ *a.* scenic.

escépticamente /esθeptika'mente; esseptika'mente/ *adv.* skeptically.

escepticismo /esθepti'θismo; essepti'sismo/ *n. m.* skepticism.

escéptico /es'θeptiko; es'septiko/ **-ca** *a. & n.* skeptic; skeptical.

esclarecer /esklare'θer; esklare'ser/ *v.* clear up.

esclavitud /esklaβi'tuð/ *n. f.* slavery; bondage.

esclavizar /esklaβi'θar; esklaβi-'sar/ v. enslave.

esclavo /es'klaβo/ -va n. slave.

escoba /es'koβa/ n. f. broom.

escocés /esko'θes; esko'ses/ -esa a. & n. Scotch, Scottish; Scot.

Escocia /es'koθia; eskosia/ n. f. Scotland.

escofinar /eskofi'nar/ v. rasp.

escoger /esko'her/ v. choose, select.

escogido /esko'hiðo/ a. chosen, selected.

escogimiento /eskohi'miento/ n. m. choice.

escolar /esko'lar/ a. 1. scholastic, (of) school. —n. 2. m.& f. student.

escolasticismo /eskolasti'θismo; eskolasti'sismo/ n. m. scholasticism.

escollo /es'koʎo; es'koyo/ n. m. reef.

escolta /es'kolta/ n. f. escort. —escoltar, v.

escombro /es'kombro/ n. m. mackerel.

escombros /es'kombros/ n. m.pl. debris, rubbish.

esconce /es'konθe; es'konse/ n. m. corner.

escondedero /eskonde'ðero/ n. m. hiding place.

esconder /eskon'der/ v. hide, conceal.

escondidamente /eskondiða-'mente/ adv. secretly.

escondimiento /eskondi'miento/ n. m. concealment.

escondrijo /eskon'driho/ n. m. hiding place.

escopeta /esko'peta/ n. f. shotgun.

escopetazo /eskope'taθo; eskope-'taso/ n. m. gunshot.

escoplo /es'koplo/ n. m. chisel.

escorbuto /eskor'βuto/ n. m. scurvy.

escorpena /eskor'pena/ n. f. grouper.

escorpión /eskor'pion/ n. m. scorpion.

escorzón /eskor'θon; eskor'son/ n. m. toad.

escotado /eskota'ðo/ a. low-cut, with a low neckline.

escote /es'kote/ n. m. low neckline.

escribiente /eskri'βiente/ n. m. & f. clerk.

escribir /eskri'βir/ v. write.

escritor /eskri'tor/ -ra n. writer, author.

escritorio /eskri'torio/ n. m. desk.

escritura /eskri'tura/ n. f. writing, handwriting.

escrófula /es'krofula/ n. f. scrofula.

escroto /es'kroto/ n. m. scrotum.

escrúpulo /es'krupulo/ n. m. scruple.

escrupuloso /eskrupu'loso/ a. scrupulous.

escrutinio /eskru'tinio/ n. m. scrutiny; examination.

escuadra /es'kuaðra/ n. f. squad; fleet.

escuadrón /eskuað'ron/ n. m. squadron.

escualidez /eskuali'ðeθ; eskuali-'ðes/ n. f. squalor; poverty; emaciation.

escuálido /es'kualiðo/ a. squalid.

escualo /es'kualo/ n. m. shark.

escuchar /esku'tʃar/ v. listen; listen to.

escudero /esku'ðero/ n. m. squire.

escudo /es'kuðo/ n. m. shield; protection; coin of certain countries.

escuela /es'kuela/ n. f. school.

escuela nocturna /es'kuela nok-'turna/ night school.

escuela por correspondencia /es'kuela por korrespon'denθia; es'kuela por korrespon'densia/ correspondence school.

escuerzo /es'kuerθo; es'kuerso/ n. m. toad.

esculpir /eskul'pir/ v. carve, sculpture.

escultor /eskul'tor/ -ra n. sculptor.

escultura /eskul'tura/ n. f. sculpture.

escupidera /eskupi'ðera/ n. f. cuspidor.

escupir /esku'pir/ v. spit.

escurridero /eskurri'ðero/ n. m. drain board.

escurridor /eskurri'ðor/ n. m. colander, strainer.

escurrir /esku'rrir/ v. drain off; wring out.

escurrirse /esku'rrirse/ v. slip; sneak away.

ese /'ese/ esa dem. a. that.

ése, ésa dem. pron. that (one).

esencia /e'senθia; e'sensia/ *n. f.* essence; perfume.

esencial /esen'θial; esen'sial/ *a.* essential.

esencialmente /esenθial'mente; esensial'mente/ *adv.* essentially.

esfera /es'fera/ *n. f.* sphere.

esfinge /es'finhe/ *n. f.* sphinx.

esforzar /esfor'θar; esfor'sar/ *v.* strengthen.

esforzarse /esfor'θarse; esfor'sarse/ *v.* strive, exert oneself.

esfuerzo /es'fuerθo; es'fuerso/ *n. m.* effort, attempt; vigor.

esgrima /es'grima/ *n. f.* fencing.

esguince /es'ginθe; es'ginse/ *n. m.* sprain.

eslabón /esla'βon/ *n. m.* link (of a chain).

eslabonar /eslaβo'nar/ *v.* link, join, connect.

eslavo /es'laβo/ **-va** *a. & n.* Slavic; Slav.

esmalte /es'malte/ *n. m.* enamel, polish. —**esmaltar,** *v.*

esmerado /esme'raðo/ *a.* careful, thorough.

esmeralda /esme'ralda/ *n. f.* emerald.

esmerarse /esme'rarse/ *v.* take pains, do one's best.

esmeril /es'meril/ *n. m.* emery.

eso /'eso/ *dem. pron.* that.

esófago /e'sofago/ *n. m.* esophagus.

esotérico /eso'teriko/ *a.* esoteric.

espacial /espa'θial; espa'sial/ *a.* spatial.

espacio /es'paθio; es'pasio/ *n. m.* space. —**espaciar,** *v.*

espaciosidad /espaθiosi'ðað; espasiosi'ðað/ *n. f.* spaciousness.

espacioso /espa'θioso; espa'sioso/ *a.* spacious.

espada /es'paða/ *n. f.* sword; spade (in cards).

espadarte /espa'ðarte/ *n. m.* swordfish.

espaguetis /espa'getis/ *n. m.pl.* spaghetti.

espalda /es'palda/ *n. f.* back.

espaldera /espal'dera/ *n. f.* espalier.

espantar /espan'tar/ *v.* frighten, scare; scare away.

espanto /es'panto/ *n. m.* fright.

espantoso /espan'toso/ *a.* frightening, frightful.

España /es'paɲa/ *n. f.* Spain.

español /espa'ɲol/ **-ola** *a. & n.* Spanish; Spaniard.

esparcir /espar'θir; espar'sir/ *v.* scatter, disperse.

espárrago /es'parrago/ *n. m.* asparagus.

espartano /espar'tano/ **-na** *n. & a.* Spartan.

espasmo /es'pasmo/ *n. m.* spasm.

espasmódico /espas'moðiko/ *a.* spasmodic.

espata /es'pata/ *n. f.* spathe.

espato /es'pato/ *n. m.* spar (mineral).

espátula /es'patula/ *n. f.* spatula.

especia /es'peθia; es'pesia/ *n. f.* spice. —**especiar,** *v.*

especial /espe'θial; espe'sial/ *a.* special, especial.

especialidad /espeθiali'ðað; espesiali'ðað/ *n. f.* specialty.

especialista /espeθia'lista; espesia'lista/ *n. m. & f.* specialist.

especialización /espeθialiθa'θion; espesialisa'sion/ *n. f.* specialization.

especialmente /espeθial'mente; espesial'mente/ *adv.* especially.

especie /es'peθie; es'pesie/ *n. f.* species; sort.

especiería /espeθie'ria; espesie'ria/ *n. f.* grocery store; spice store.

especiero /espe'θiero; espe'siero/ **-ra** *n.* spice dealer; spice box.

especificar /espeθifi'kar; espesifi'kar/ *v.* specify.

específico /espe'θifiko; espe'sifiko/ *a.* specific.

espécimen /es'peθimen; es'pesimen/ *n. m.* specimen.

especioso /espe'θioso; espe'sioso/ *a.* neat; polished; specious.

espectacular /espektaku'lar/ *a.* spectacular.

espectáculo /espek'takulo/ *n. m.* spectacle, show.

espectador /espekta'ðor/ **-ra** *n.* spectator.

espectro /es'pektro/ *n. m.* specter, ghost.

especulación /espekula'θion; espekula'sion/ *n. f.* speculation.

especulador /espekula'ðor/ **-ra** *n.* speculator.

especular /espeku'lar/ *v.* speculate.

especulativo /espekula'tiβo/ *a.* speculative.

espejo /es'peho/ *n. m.* mirror.

espelunca /espe'lunka/ *n. f.* dark cave, cavern.

espera /es'pera/ *n. f.* wait.

esperanza /espe'ranθa; espe'ransa/ *n. f.* hope, expectation.

esperar /espe'rar/ *v.* hope; expect; wait, wait for, watch for.

espesar /espe'sar/ *v.* thicken.

espeso /es'peso/ *a.* thick, dense, bushy.

espesor /espe'sor/ *n. m.* thickness, density.

espía /es'pia/ *n. m. & f.* spy.
—**espiar**, *v.*

espigón /espi'gon/ *n. m.* bee sting.

espina /es'pina/ *n. f.* thorn.

espinaca /espi'naka/ *n. f.* spinach.

espina dorsal /es'pina dor'sal/ spine.

espinal /espi'nal/ *a.* spinal.

espinazo /espi'naθo; espi'naso/ *n. m.* backbone.

espineta /espi'neta/ *n. f.* spinet.

espino /es'pino/ *n. m.* briar.

espinoso /espi'noso/ *a.* spiny, thorny.

espión /es'pion/ *n. m.* spy.

espionaje /espio'nahe/ *n. m.* espionage.

espiral /espi'ral/ *a. & m.* spiral.

espirar /espi'rar/ *v.* expire; breathe, exhale.

espíritu /es'piritu/ *n. m.* spirit.

espiritual /espiri'tual/ *a.* spiritual.

espiritualidad /espirituali'ðað/ *n. f.* spirituality.

espiritualmente /espiritual-'mente/ *adv.* spiritually.

espita /es'pita/ *n. f.* faucet, spigot.

espléndido /es'plendiðo/ *a.* splendid.

esplendor /esplen'dor/ *n. m.* splendor.

espolear /espole'ar/ *v.* incite, urge on.

espoleta /espo'leta/ *n. f.* wishbone.

esponja /es'ponha/ *n. f.* sponge.

esponjoso /espon'hoso/ *a.* spongy.

esponsales /espon'sales/ *n. m.pl.* engagement, betrothal.

esponsalicio /esponsa'liθio; esponsa'lisio/ *a.* nuptial.

espontáneamente /espontanea-'mente/ *adv.* spontaneously.

espontaneidad /espontanei'ðað/ *n. f.* spontaneity.

espontáneo /espon'taneo/ *a.* spontaneous.

espora /es'pora/ *n. f.* spore.

esporádico /espo'raðiko/ *a.* sporadic.

esposa /es'posa/ *n. f.* wife.

esposar /espo'sar/ *v.* shackle; handcuff.

esposo /es'poso/ *n. m.* husband.

espuela /es'puela/ *n. f.* spur.
—**espolear**, *v.*

espuma /es'puma/ *n. f.* foam.
—**espumar,** *v.*

espumadera /espuma'ðera/ *n. f.* whisk; skimmer.

espumajear /espumahe'ar/ *v.* foam at the mouth.

espumajo /espu'maho/ *n. m.* foam.

espumar /espu'mar/ *v.* foam, froth; skim.

espumoso /espu'moso/ *a.* foamy; sparkling (wine).

espurio /es'purio/ *a.* spurious.

esputar /espu'tar/ *v.* spit, expectorate.

esputo /es'puto/ *n. m.* spit, saliva.

esquela /es'kela/ *n. f.* note.

esqueleto /eske'leto/ *n. m.* skeleton.

esquema /es'kema/ *n. m.* scheme; diagram.

esquero /es'kero/ *n. m.* leather sack, leather pouch.

esquiar /es'kiar/ *v.* ski.

esquiciar /eski'θiar; eski'siar/ *v.* outline, sketch.

esquicio /es'kiθio; es'kisio/ *n. m.* rough sketch, rough outline.

esquife /es'kife/ *n. m.* skiff.

esquilar /eski'lar/ *v.* fleece, shear.

esquilmo /es'kilmo/ *n. m.* harvest.

esquimal /eski'mal/ *n. & a.* Eskimo.

esquina /es'kina/ *n. f.* corner.

esquivar /eski'βar/ *v.* evade, shun.

estabilidad /estaβili'ðað/ *n. f.* stability.

estable /es'taβle/ *a.* stable.

establecedor /estaβleθe'ðor; estaβlese'ðor/ *n. m.* founder, originator.

establecer /estaβle'θer; estaβle-'ser/ *v.* establish, set up.

establecimiento /estaβleθi-'miento; estaβlesi'miento/ *n. m.* establishment.

establero /estaβ'lero/ *n. m.* groom.

establo /es'taβlo/ *n. m.* stable.

estaca /es'taka/ *n. f.* stake.

estación /esta'θion; esta'sion/ *n. f.* station; season.

estacionamiento /estaθiona'miento; estasiona'miento/ *n. m.* parking; parking lot; parking space.

estacionar /estaθio'nar; estasio'nar/ *v.* station; park (a vehicle).

estacionario /estaθio'nario; estasio'nario/ *a.* stationary.

estación de servicio /esta'θion de ser'βiθio; esta'sion de ser'βisio/ service station.

estación de trabajo /esta'θion de tra'βaho; esta'sion de tra'βaho/ work station.

estadista /esta'ðista/ *n. m. & f.* statesman.

estadística /esta'ðistika/ *n. f.* statistics.

estadístico /esta'ðistiko/ *a.* statistical.

estado /es'taðo/ *n. m.* state; condition; status.

Estados Unidos /es'taðos u'niðos/ *n. m.pl.* United States.

estafa /es'tafa/ *n. f.* swindle, fake. **—estafar,** *v.*

estafeta /esta'feta/ *n. f.* post office.

estagnación /estagna'θion; estagna'sion/ *n. f.* stagnation.

estallar /esta'ʎar; esta'yar/ *v.* explode; burst; break out.

estallido /esta'ʎiðo; esta'yiðo/ *n. m.* crash; crack; explosion.

estampa /es'tampa/ *n. f.* stamp. **—estampar,** *v.*

estampado /estam'paðo/ *n. m.* printed cotton cloth.

estampida /estam'piða/ *n. f.* stampede.

estampilla /estam'piʎa; estam'piya/ *n. f.* (postage) stamp.

estancado /estan'kaðo/ *a.* stagnant.

estancar /estan'kar/ *v.* stanch, stop, check.

estancia /es'tanθia; es'tansia/ *n. f.* stay; (S.A.) small farm.

estanciero /estan'θiero; estan'siero/ **-ra** *n.* small farmer.

estandarte /estan'darte/ *n. m.* banner.

estanque /es'tanke/ *n. m.* pool; pond.

estante /es'tante/ *n. m.* shelf.

estaño /es'taɲo/ *n. m.* tin. **—estañar,** *v.*

estar /es'tar/ *v.* be; stand; look.

estática /es'tatika/ *n. f.* static.

estático /es'tatiko/ *a.* static.

estatua /es'tatua/ *n. f.* statue.

estatura /esta'tura/ *n. f.* stature.

estatuto /esta'tuto/ *n. m.* statute, law.

este /'este/ *n. m.* east.

este, esta *dem. a.* this.

éste, ésta *dem. pron.* this (one); the latter.

estelar /este'lar/ *a.* stellar.

estenografía /estenogra'fia/ *n. f.* stenography.

estenógrafo /este'nografo/ **-fa** *n.* stenographer.

estera /es'tera/ *n. f.* mat, matting.

estereofónico /estereo'foniko/ *a.* stereophonic.

estéril /es'teril/ *a.* barren; sterile.

esterilidad /esterili'ðað/ *n. f.* sterility, fruitlessness.

esterilizar /esterili'θar; esterili'sar/ *v.* sterilize.

esternón /ester'non/ *n. m.* breastbone.

estética /es'tetika/ *n. f.* esthetics.

estético /es'tetiko/ *a.* esthetic.

estetoscopio /esteto'skopio/ *n. m.* stethoscope.

estibador /estiβa'ðor/ *n. m.* stevedore.

estiércol /es'tierkol/ *n. m.* dung, manure.

estigma /es'tigma/ *n. m.* stigma; disgrace.

estilarse /esti'larse/ *v.* be in fashion, be in vogue.

estilo /es'tilo/ *n. m.* style; sort.

estilográfica /estilo'grafika/ *n. f.* (fountain) pen.

estima /es'tima/ *n. f.* esteem.

estimable /esti'maβle/ *a.* estimable, worthy.

estimación /estima'θion; estima'sion/ *n. f.* estimation.

estimar /esti'mar/ *v.* esteem; value; estimate; gauge.

estimular /estimu'lar/ *v.* stimulate.

estímulo /es'timulo/ *n. m.* stimulus.

estío /es'tio/ *n. m.* summer.

estipulación /estipula'θion; estipula'sion/ *n. f.* stipulation.

estipular /estipu'lar/ *v.* stipulate.

estirar /esti'rar/ *v.* stretch.

estirpe /es'tirpe/ *n. m.* stock, lineage.

esto /'esto/ *dem. pron.* this.

estocada /esto'kaða/ *n. f.* stab, thrust.

estofado /esto'faðo/ *n. m.* stew. —**estofar,** *v.*

estoicismo /estoi'θismo; estoi'sismo/ *n. m.* stoicism.

estoico /es'toiko/ *n. & a.* stoic.

estómago /es'tomago/ *n. m.* stomach.

estorbar /estor'βar/ *v.* bother, hinder, interfere with.

estorbo /es'torβo/ *n. m.* hindrance.

estornudo /estor'nuðo/ *n. m.* sneeze. —**estornudar,** *v.*

estrabismo /estra'βismo/ *n. m.* strabismus.

estrago /es'trago/ *n. m.* devastation, havoc.

estrangulación /estraŋgula'θion; estraŋgula'sion/ *n. f.* strangulation.

estrangular /estraŋgu'lar/ *v.* strangle.

estraperlista /estraper'lista/ *n. m. & f.* black marketeer.

estraperlo /estra'perlo/ *n. m.* black market.

estratagema /estrata'hema/ *n. f.* stratagem.

estrategia /estra'tehia/ *n. f.* strategy.

estratégico /estra'tehiko/ *a.* strategic.

estrato /es'trato/ *n. m.* stratum.

estrechar /estre'tʃar/ *v.* tighten; narrow.

estrechez /estre'tʃeθ; estre'tʃes/ *n. f.* narrowness; tightness.

estrecho /es'tretʃo/ *a.* **1.** narrow, tight. —*n.* **2.** *m.* strait.

estregar /estre'gar/ *v.* scour, scrub.

estrella /es'treʎa; es'treya/ *n. f.* star.

estrellamar /estreʎa'mar; estreya'mar/ *n. f.* starfish.

estrellar /estre'ʎar; estre'yar/ *v.* shatter, smash.

estremecimiento /estremeθi'miento; estremesi'miento/ *n. m.* shudder. —**estremecerse,** *v.*

estrenar /estre'nar/ *v.* wear for the first time; open (a play).

estreno /es'treno/ *n. m.* debut, first performance.

estrenuo /es'trenuo/ *a.* strenuous.

estreñido /estre'ɲiðo/ -**da** *a.* constipated.

estreñimiento /estreɲi'miento/ *n. m.* constipation.

estreñir /estre'ɲir/ *v.* constipate.

estrépito /es'trepito/ *n. m.* din.

estreptococo /estrepto'koko/ *n. m.* streptococcus.

estría /es'tria/ *n. f.* groove.

estribillo /estri'βiʎo; estri'βiyo/ *n. m.* refrain.

estribo /es'triβo/ *n. m.* stirrup.

estribor /estri'βor/ *n. m.* starboard.

estrictamente /estrikta'mente/ *adv.* strictly.

estrictez /estrik'teθ; estrik'tes/ *f.* strictness.

estricto /es'trikto/ *a.* strict.

estrofa /es'trofa/ *n. f.* stanza.

estropajo /estro'paho/ *n. m.* mop.

estropear /estrope'ar/ *v.* cripple, damage, spoil.

estructura /estruk'tura/ *n. f.* structure.

estructural /estruktu'ral/ *a.* structural.

estruendo /es'truendo/ *n. m.* din, clatter.

estuario /es'tuario/ *n. m.* estuary.

estuco /es'tuko/ *n. m.* stucco.

estudiante /estu'ðiante/ -**ta** *n.* student.

estudiar /estu'ðiar/ *v.* study.

estudio /es'tuðio/ *n. m.* study; studio.

estudioso /estu'ðioso/ *a.* studious.

estufa /es'tufa/ *n. f.* stove.

estufa de aire /es'tufa de 'aire/ fan heater.

estulto /es'tulto/ *a.* foolish.

estupendo /estu'pendo/ *a.* wonderful, grand, fine.

estupidez /estupi'ðeθ; estupi'ðes/ *n. f.* stupidity.

estúpido /es'tupiðo/ *a.* stupid.

estupor /estu'por/ *n. m.* stupor.

estuque /es'tuke/ *n. m.* stucco.

esturión /estu'rion/ *n. m.* sturgeon.

etapa /e'tapa/ *n. f.* stage.

éter /'eter/ *n. m.* ether.

etéreo /e'tereo/ *a.* ethereal.

eternal /eter'nal/ *a.* eternal.

eternidad /eterni'ðað/ *n. f.* eternity.

eterno /e'terno/ *a.* eternal.

ética /'etika/ *n. f.* ethics.

ético /'etiko/ *a.* ethical.

etimología /etimolo'hia/ *n. f.* etymology.

etiqueta /eti'keta/ *n. f.* etiquette; tag, label.

étnico /'etniko/ *a.* ethnic.

etrusco /e'trusko/ **-ca** *n.* & *a.* Etruscan.

eucaristía /eukaris'tia/ *n. f.* Eucharist.

eufemismo /eufe'mismo/ *n. m.* euphemism.

eufonía /eufo'nia/ *n. f.* euphony.

Europa /eu'ropa/ *n. f.* Europe.

europeo /euro'peo/ **-pea** *a.* & *n.* European.

eutanasia /euta'nasia/ *n. f.* euthanasia.

evacuación /eβakua'θion; eβakua-'sion/ *n. f.* evacuation.

evacuar /eβa'kuar/ *v.* evacuate.

evadir /eβa'ðir/ *v.* evade.

evangélico /eβan'heliko/ *a.* evangelical.

evangelio /eβan'helio/ *n. m.* gospel.

evangelista /eβanhe'lista/ *n. m.* evangelist.

evaporación /eβapora'θion; eβapora'sion/ *n. f.* evaporation.

evaporarse /eβapo'rarse/ *v.* evaporate.

evasión /eβa'sion, eβa'siβa/ *n. f.* evasion.

evasivamente /eβasiβa'mente/ *adv.* evasively.

evasivo /eβa'siβo/ *a.* evasive.

evento /e'βento/ *n. m.* event, occurrence.

eventual /eβen'tual/ *a.* eventual.

eventualidad /eβentuali'ðað/ *n. f.* eventuality.

evicción /eβik'θion; eβik'sion/ *n. f.* eviction.

evidencia /eβi'ðenθia; eβiðensia/ *n. f.* evidence.

evidenciar /eβiðen'θiar; eβiðen-'siar/ *v.* prove, show.

evidente /eβi'ðente/ *a.* evident.

evitación /eβita'θion; eβita'sion/ *n. f.* avoidance.

evitar /eβi'tar/ *v.* avoid, shun.

evocación /eβoka'θion; eβoka-'sion/ *n. f.* evocation.

evocar /eβo'kar/ *v.* evoke.

evolución /eβolu'θion; eβolu'sion/ *n. f.* evolution.

exacerbar /eksaθer'βar; eksaser-'βar/ *v.* irritate deeply; exacerbate.

exactamente /eksakta'mente/ *adv.* exactly.

exactitud /eksakti'tuð/ *n. f.* precision, accuracy.

exacto /ek'sakto/ *a.* exact, accurate.

exageración /eksahera'θion; eksahera'sion/ *n. f.* exaggeration.

exagerar /eksahe'rar/ *v.* exaggerate.

exaltación /eksalta'θion; eksalta-'sion/ *n. f.* exaltation.

exaltamiento /eksalta'miento/ *n. m.* exaltation.

exaltar /eksal'tar/ *v.* exalt.

examen /ek'samen/ *n. m.* test, examination.

examen de ingreso /ek'samen de iŋ'greso/ entrance examination.

examinar /eksami'nar/ *v.* test, examine.

exánime /eksa'nime/ *a.* spiritless, weak.

exasperación /eksaspera'θion; eksaspera'sion/ *n. f.* exasperation.

exasperar /eksaspe'rar/ *v.* exasperate.

excavación /ekskaβa'θion; ekskaβa'sion/ *n. f.* excavation.

excavar /ekska'βar/ *v.* excavate.

exceder /eksθe'ðer; eksse'ðer/ *v.* exceed, surpass; outrun.

excelencia /eksθe'lenθia; eksse-'lensia/ *n. f.* excellence.

excelente /eksθe'lente; eksse-'lente/ *a.* excellent.

excéntrico /eks'θentriko; eks-'sentriko/ *a.* eccentric.

excepción /eksθep'θion; ekssep-'sion/ *n. f.* exception.

excepcional /eksθepθio'nal; ekssepsio'nal/ *a.* exceptional.

excepto /eks'θepto; eks'septo/ *prep.* except, except for.

exceptuar /eksθep'tuar; ekssep-'tuar/ *v.* except.

excesivamente /eksθesiβa'mente; ekssesiβa'mente/ *adv.* excessively.

excesivo /eksθe'siβo; eksse'siβo/ *a.* excessive.

exceso /eks'θeso; eks'seso/ *n. m.* excess.

excitabilidad /eksθitaβili'ðað; ekssitaβili'ðað/ *n. f.* excitability.

excitación /eksθita'θion; ekssita-'sion/ *n. f.* excitement.

excitar /eksθi'tar; ekssi'tar/ *v.* excite.

exclamación /eksklama'θion; eksklama'sion/ *n. f.* exclamation.

exclamar /ekskla'mar/ *v.* exclaim.

excluir /eksk'luir/ *v.* exclude, bar, shut out.

exclusión /eksklu'sion/ *n. f.* exclusion.

exclusivamente /eksklusiβa-'mente/ *adv.* exclusively.

exclusivo /eksklu'siβo/ *a.* exclusive.

excomulgar /ekskomul'gar/ *v.* excommunicate.

excomunión /ekskomu'nion/ *n. f.* excommunication.

excreción /ekskre'θion; ekskre-'sion/ *n. f.* excretion.

excremento /ekskre'mento/ *n. m.* excrement.

excretar /ekskre'tar/ *v.* excrete.

exculpar /ekskul'par/ *v.* exonerate.

excursión /ekskur'sion/ *n. f.* excursion.

excursionista /ekskursio'nista/ *n. m. & f.* excursionist; tourist.

excusa /eks'kusa/ *n. f.* excuse. —**excusar,** *v.*

excusado /eksku'saðo/ *n. m.* toilet.

excusarse /eksku'sarse/ *v.* apologize.

exención /eksen'θion; eksen'sion/ *n. f.* exemption.

exento /ek'sento/ *a.* exempt. —**exentar,** *v.*

exhalación /eksala'θion; eksala-'sion/ *n. f.* exhalation.

exhalar /eksa'lar/ *v.* exhale, breathe out.

exhausto /ek'sausto/ *a.* exhausted.

exhibición /eksiβi'θion; eksiβi-'sion/ *n. f.* exhibit, exhibition.

exhibir /eksi'βir/ *v.* exhibit, display.

exhortación /eksorta'θion; eksorta'sion/ *n. f.* exhortation.

exhortar /eksor'tar/ *v.* exhort, admonish.

exhumación /eksuma'θion; eksuma'sion/ *n. f.* exhumation.

exhumar /eksu'mar/ *v.* exhume.

exigencia /eksi'henθia; eksi'hensia/ *n. f.* requirement, demand.

exigente /eksi'hente/ *a.* exacting, demanding.

exigir /eksi'hir/ *v.* require, exact, demand.

eximir /eksi'mir/ *v.* exempt.

existencia /eksis'tenθia; eksis-'tensia/ *n. f.* existence; *Econ.* supply.

existente /eksis'tente/ *a.* existent.

existir /eksis'tir/ *v.* exist.

éxito /'eksito/ *n. m.* success.

éxodo /'eksoðo/ *n. m.* exodus.

exoneración /eksonera'θion; eksonera'sion/ *n. f.* exoneration.

exonerar /eksone'rar/ *v.* exonerate, acquit.

exorar /ekso'rar/ *v.* beg, implore.

exorbitancia /eksorβi'tanθia; eksorβi'tansia/ *n. f.* exorbitance.

exorbitante /eksorβi'tante/ *a.* exorbitant.

exorcismo /eksor'θismo; eksor-'sismo/ *n. m.* exorcism.

exornar /eksor'nar/ *v.* adorn, decorate.

exótico /ek'sotiko/ *a.* exotic.

expansibilidad /ekspansiβili'ðað/ *n. f.* expansibility.

expansión /ekspan'sion/ *n. f.* expansion.

expansivo /ekspan'siβo/ *a.* expansive; effusive.

expatriación /ekspatria'θion; ekspatria'sion/ *n. f.* expatriation.

expatriar /ekspa'triar/ *v.* expatriate.

expectación /ekspekta'θion; ekspekta'sion/ *n. f.* expectation.

expectorar /ekspekto'rar/ *v.* expectorate.

expedición /ekspeði'θion; ekspeði'sion/ *n. f.* expedition.

expediente /ekspe'ðiente/ *n. m.* expedient; means.

expedir /ekspe'ðir/ *v.* send off, ship; expedite.

expeditivo /ekspeði'tiβo/ *a.* speedy, prompt.

expedito /ekspe'ðito/ *a.* speedy, prompt.

expeler /ekspe'ler/ *v.* expel, eject.

expendedor /ekspende'ðor/ **-ra** *n.* dealer.

expender /ekspen'der/ *v.* expend.

expensas /eks'pensas/ *n. f.pl.* expenses, costs.

experiencia /ekspe'rienθia; ekspe'riensia/ *n. f.* experience.

experimentado /eksperimen'taðo/ *a.* experienced.

experimental /eksperimen'tal/ *a.* experimental.

experimentar /eksperimen'tar/ *v.* experience.

experimento /eksperi'mento/ *n. m.* experiment.

expertamente /eksperta'mente/ *adv.* expertly.

experto /ek'sperto/ **-ta** *a. & n.* expert.

expiación /ekspia'θion; ekspia-'sion/ *n. f.* atonement.

expiar /eks'piar/ *v.* atone for.

expiración /ekspira'θion; ekspira-'sion/ *n. f.* expiration.

expirar /ekspi'rar/ *v.* expire.

explanación /eksplana'θion; eksplana'sion/ *n. f.* explanation.

explanar /ekspla'nar/ *v.* make level.

expletivo /eksple'tiβo/ *n. & a.* expletive.

explicable /ekspli'kaβle/ *a.* explicable.

explicación /eksplika'θion; eksplika'sion/ *n. f.* explanation.

explicar /ekspli'kar/ *v.* explain.

explicativo /eksplika'tiβo/ *a.* explanatory.

explícitamente /ekspliθita'mente; eksplisita'mente/ *adv.* explicitly.

explícito /eks'pliθito; eksplisito/ *adj.* explicit.

exploración /eksplora'θion; eksplorasion/ *n. f.* exploration.

explorador /eksplora'ðor/ **-ra** *n.* explorer; scout.

explorar /eksplo'rar/ *v.* explore; scout.

exploratorio /eksplora'torio/ *a.* exploratory.

explosión /eksplo'sion/ *n. f.* explosion; outburst.

explosivo /eksplo'siβo/ *a. & m.* explosive.

explotación /eksplota'θion; eksplota'sion/ *n. f.* exploitation.

explotar /eksplo'tar/ *v.* exploit.

exponer /ekspo'ner/ *v.* expose; set forth.

exportación /eksporta'θion; eksporta'sion/ *n. f.* exportation; export.

exportador /eksporta'ðor/ **-ra** *n.* exporter.

exportar /ekspor'tar/ *v.* export.

exposición /eksposi'θion; eksposi'sion/ *n. f.* exhibit; exposition; exposure.

expósito /eks'posito/ **-ta** *n.* foundling; orphan.

expresado /ekspre'saðo/ *a.* aforesaid.

expresamente /ekspresa'mente/ *adv.* clearly, explicitly.

expresar /ekspre'sar/ *v.* express.

expresión /ekspre'sion/ *n. f.* expression.

expresivo /ekspre'siβo/ *a.* expressive; affectionate.

expreso /eks'preso/ *a. & m.* express.

exprimidera de naranjas /eksprimi'ðera de na'ranhas/ *n. f.* orange squeezer.

exprimir /ekspri'mir/ *v.* squeeze.

expropiación /ekspropia'θion; ekspropia'sion/ *n. f.* expropriation.

expropiar /ekspro'piar/ *v.* expropriate.

expulsar /ekspul'sar/ *v.* expel, eject; evict.

expulsión /ekspul'sion/ *n. f.* expulsion.

expurgación /ekspurga'θion; ekspurga'sion/ *n. f.* expurgation.

expurgar /ekspur'gar/ *v.* expurgate.

exquisitamente /ekskisita'mente/ *adv.* exquisitely.

exquisito /eks'kisito/ *a.* exquisite.

éxtasis /'ekstasis/ *n. m.* ecstasy.

extemporáneo /ekstempo'raneo/ *a.* extemporaneous, impromptu.

extender /eksten'der/ *v.* extend; spread; widen; stretch.

extensamente /ekstensa'mente/ *adv.* extensively.

extensión /eksten'sion/ *n. f.* extension, spread, expanse.

extenso /eks'tenso/ *a.* extensive, widespread.

extenuación /ekstenua'θion; ekstenua'sion/ *n. f.* weakening; emaciation.

extenuar /ekste'nuar/ *v.* extenuate.

exterior /ekste'rior/ *a. & m.* exterior; foreign.

exterminar /ekstermi'nar/ *v.* exterminate.

exterminio /ekster'minio/ *n. m.* extermination, ruin.

extinción /ekstin'θion; ekstin-'sion/ *n. f.* extinction.

extinguir /ekstiŋ'guir/ *v.* extinguish.

extinto /eks'tinto/ *a.* extinct.

extintor /ekstin'tor/ *n. m.* fire extinguisher.

extirpar /ekstir'par/ *v.* eradicate.

extorsión /ekstor'sion/ n. f. extortion.

extra /'ekstra/ n. extra.

extracción /ekstrak'θion; ekstrak-'sion/ n. f. extraction.

extractar /ekstrak'tar/ v. summarize.

extracto /eks'trakto/ n. m. extract; summary.

extradición /ekstraði'θion; ekstra-ði'sion/ n. f. extradition.

extraer /ekstra'er/ v. extract.

extranjero /ekstran'hero/ **-ra** a. **1.** foreign. —n. **2.** foreigner; stranger.

extrañar /ekstra'ɲar/ v. surprise; miss.

extraño /eks'traɲo/ a. strange, queer.

extraordinariamente /ˌekstraor-ðinaria'mente/ adv. extraordinarily.

extraordinario /ekstraorði'nario/ a. extraordinary.

extravagancia /ekstraβa'ganθia; ekstraβa'gansia/ n. f. extravagance.

extravagante /ekstraβa'gante/ a. extravagant.

extraviado /ekstra'βiaðo/ a. lost, misplaced.

extraviarse /ekstra'βiarse/ v. stray, get lost.

extravío /ekstra'βio/ n. m. misplacement; aberration, deviation.

extremadamente /ekstrema-ða'mente/ adv. extremely.

extremado /ekstre'maðo/ a. extreme.

extremaunción /ekstremaun'θion; ekstremaun'sion/ n. f. extreme unction.

extremidad /ekstremi'ðað/ n. f. extremity.

extremista /ekstre'mista/ n. & a. extremist.

extremo /eks'tremo/ a. & m. extreme, end.

extrínseco /ekstrin'seko/ a. extrinsic.

exuberancia /eksuβe'ranθia; eksu-βeransia/ n. f. exuberance.

exuberante /eksuβe'rante/ a. exuberant.

exudación /eksuða'θion; eksuða-'sion/ n. f. exudation.

exudar /eksu'ðar/ v. exude, ooze.

exultación /eksulta'θion; eksulta-'sion/ n. f. exultation.

eyaculación /eyakula'θion; eyaku-la'sion/ n. f. ejaculation.

eyacular /eyaku'lar/ v. ejaculate.

eyección /eyek'θion; eyek'sion/ n. f. ejection.

eyectar /eyek'tar/ v. eject.

F

fábrica /'faβrika/ n. f. factory.

fabricación /faβrika'θion; faβrika'sion/ n. f. manufacture, manufacturing.

fabricante /faβri'kante/ n. m. & f. manufacturer, maker.

fabricar /faβri'kar/ v. manufacture, make.

fabril /fa'βril/ a. manufacturing, industrial.

fábula /'faβula/ n. f. fable, myth.

fabuloso /faβu'loso/ a. fabulous.

facción /fak'θion; fak'sion/ n. f. faction, party; (pl.) features.

faccioso /fak'θioso; fak'sioso/ a. factious.

fachada /fa'tʃaða/ n. f. façade, front.

fácil /'faθil; 'fasil/ a. easy.

facilidad /faθili'ðað; fasili'ðað/ n. f. facility, ease.

facilitar /faθili'tar; fasili'tar/ v. facilitate, make easy.

fácilmente /ˌfaθil'mente; ˌfasil-'mente/ adv. easily.

facsímile /fak'simile/ n. m. facsimile.

factible /fak'tiβle/ a. feasible.

factor /fak'tor/ n. m. factor.

factótum /fak'totum/ n. m. factotum; jack of all trades.

factura /fak'tura/ n. f. invoice, bill.

facturar /faktu'rar/ v. bill; check (baggage).

facultad /fakulta'ð/ /fakul'tað/ n. f. faculty; ability.

facultativo /fakulta'tiβo/ a. optional.

faena /fa'ena/ n. f. task; work.

faisán /fai'san/ n. m. pheasant.

faja /'faha/ n. f. band; sash; zone.

falacia /fa'laθia; fa'lasia/ n. f. fallacy; deceitfulness.

falda /'falda/ n. f. skirt; lap.

falibilidad /faliβili'ðað/ *n. f.* fallibility.

falla /'faʎa; faya/ /'faʎa; 'faya/ *n. f.* failure; fault.

fallar /fa'ʎar; fa'yar/ *v.* fail.

fallecer /faʎe'θer; faye'ser/ *v.* pass away, die.

fallo /'faʎo; 'fayo/ *n. m.* verdict; shortcoming.

falsear /false'ar/ *v.* falsify, counterfeit; forge.

falsedad /false'ðað/ *n. f.* falsehood; lie; falseness.

falsificación /falsifika'θion; falsifika'sion/ *n. f.* falsification; forgery.

falsificar /falsifi'kar/ *v.* falsify, counterfeit, forge.

falso /'falso/ *a.* false; wrong.

falta /'falta/ *n. f.* error, mistake; fault; lack. **hacer f.,** to be lacking, to be necessary. **sin f.,** without fail.

faltar /fal'tar/ *v.* be lacking, be missing; be absent.

faltriquera /faltri'kera/ *n. f.* pocket.

fama /'fama/ *n. f.* fame; reputation; glory.

familia /fa'milia/ *n. f.* family; household.

familiar /fami'liar/ *a.* familiar; domestic; (of) family.

familiaridad /familiari'ðað/ *n. f.* familiarity, intimacy.

familiarizar /familiari'θar; familiari'sar/ *v.* familiarize, acquaint.

famoso /fa'moso/ *a.* famous.

fanal /fa'nal/ *n. m.* lighthouse; lantern, lamp.

fanático /fa'natiko/ **-ca** *a. & n.* fanatic.

fanatismo /fana'tismo/ *n. m.* fanaticism.

fanfarria /fan'farria/ *n. f.* bluster. **—fanfarrear,** *v.*

fango /'faŋgo/ *n. m.* mud.

fantasía /fanta'sia/ *n. f.* fantasy; fancy, whim.

fantasma /fan'tasma/ *n. m.* phantom; ghost.

fantástico /fan'tastiko/ *a.* fantastic.

faquín /fa'kin/ *n. m.* porter.

faquir /fa'kir/ *n. m.* fakir.

farallón /fara'ʎon; fara'yon/ *n. m.* cliff.

Faraón /fara'on/ *n. m.* Pharaoh.

fardel /far'ðel/ *n. m.* bag; package.

fardo /far'ðo/ /'farðo/ *n. m.* bundle.

farináceo /fari'naθeo; fari'naseo/ *a.* farinaceous.

faringe /fa'rinhe/ *n. f.* pharynx.

fariseo /fari'seo/ *n. m.* pharisee, hypocrite.

farmacéutico /farma'θeutiko; farma'seutiko/ **-ca** *a.* **1.** pharmaceutical. **—n. 2.** pharmacist.

farmacia /far'maθia; far'masia/ *n. f.* pharmacy.

faro /'faro/ *n. m.* beacon; lighthouse; headlight.

farol /fa'rol/ *n. m.* lantern; (street) light, street lamp.

farra /'farra/ *n. f.* spree.

fárrago /'farrago/ *n. m.* medley; hodgepodge.

farsa /'farsa/ *n. f.* farce.

fascinación /fasθina'θion; fassina'sion/ *n. f.* fascination.

fascinar /fasθi'nar; fassi'nar/ *v.* fascinate, bewitch.

fase /'fase/ *n. f.* phase.

fastidiar /fasti'ðiar/ *v.* disgust; irk, annoy.

fastidio /fasti'ðio/ *n. m.* disgust; annoyance.

fastidioso /fasti'ðioso/ *a.* annoying; tedious.

fasto /'fasto/ *a.* happy, fortunate.

fatal /fa'tal/ *a.* fatal.

fatalidad /fatali'ðað/ *n. f.* fate; calamity, bad luck.

fatalismo /fata'lismo/ *n. m.* fatalism.

fatalista /fata'lista/ *n. & a.* fatalist.

fatiga /fa'tiga/ *n. f.* fatigue. **—fatigar,** *v.*

fauna /'fauna/ *n. f.* fauna.

fauno /'fauno/ *n. m.* faun.

favor /fa'βor/ *n. m.* favor; behalf. **por f.,** please.

¡Favor! Puh-lease!

favorable /faβo'raβle/ *a.* favorable.

favorablemente /faβoraβle-'mente/ *adv.* favorably.

favorecer /faβore'θer; faβore'ser/ *v.* favor; flatter.

favoritismo /faβori'tismo/ *n. m.* favoritism.

favorito /faβo'rito/ **-ta** *a. & n.* favorite.

fax /faks/ *n. m.* fax.

faz /faθ; fas/ *n. f.* face.

fe /fe/ *n. f.* faith.

fealdad /feal'dað/ *n. f.* ugliness, homeliness.

febrero /fe'βrero/ *n. m.* February.

febril /fe'βril/ *a.* feverish.

fecha /'fetʃa/ *n. f.* date. **—fechar,** *v.*

fecha de caducidad /'fetʃa de kaðuθi'ðað; 'fetʃa de kaðusi'ðað/ expiration date.

fécula /'fekula/ *n. f.* starch.

fecundar /fekun'dar/ *v.* fertilize.

fecundidad /fekundi'ðað/ *n. f.* fecundity, fertility.

fecundo /fe'kundo/ *a.* fecund, fertile.

federación /feðera'θion; feðera-'sion/ *n. f.* federation.

federal /feðe'ral/ *a.* federal.

felicidad /feliθi'ðað; felisi'ðað/ *n. f.* happiness; bliss.

felicitación /feliθita'θion; felisita-'sion/ *n. f.* congratulation.

felicitar /feliθi'tar; felisi'tar/ *v.* congratulate.

feligrés /feli'gres/ **-esa** *n.* parishioner.

feliz /fe'liθ; fe'lis/ *a.* happy; fortunate.

felón /fe'lon/ *n. m.* felon.

felonía /felo'nia/ *n. f.* felony.

felpa /'felpa/ *n. f.* plush.

felpudo /fel'puðo/ *n. m.* doormat.

femenino /feme'nino/ *a.* feminine.

feminismo /femi'nismo/ *n. m.* feminism.

feminista /femi'nista/ *n. m. & f.* feminist.

fenecer /fene'θer; fene'ser/ *v.* conclude; die.

fénix /'feniks/ *n. m.* phoenix; model.

fenomenal /fenome'nal/ *a.* phenomenal.

fenómeno /fe'nomeno/ *n. m.* phenomenon.

feo /'feo/ *a.* ugly, homely.

feracidad /feraθi'ðað; ferasi'ðað/ *n. f.* feracity, fertility.

feraz /'feraθ; 'feras/ *a.* fertile, fruitful; copious.

feria /'feria/ *n. f.* fair; market.

feriado /fe'riaðo/ *a.* **día f.,** holiday.

fermentación /fermenta'θion; fermenta'sion/ *n. f.* fermentation.

fermento /fer'mento/ *n. m.* ferment. **—fermentar,** *v.*

ferocidad /feroθi'ðað; ferosi'ðað/ *n. f.* ferocity, fierceness.

feroz /fe'roθ; fe'ros/ *a.* ferocious, fierce.

férreo /'ferreo/ *a.* of iron.

ferrería /ferre'ria/ *n. f.* ironworks.

ferretería /ferrete'ria/ *n. f.* hardware; hardware store.

ferrocarril /ferroka'rril/ *n. m.* railroad.

fértil /'fertil/ *a.* fertile.

fertilidad /fertili'ðað/ *n. f.* fertility.

fertilizar /fertili'θar; fertili'sar/ *v.* fertilize.

férvido /'ferβiðo/ *a.* fervid, ardent.

ferviente /fer'βiente/ *a.* fervent.

fervor /fer'βor/ *n. m.* fervor, zeal.

fervoroso /ferβo'roso/ *a.* zealous, eager.

festejar /feste'har/ *v.* entertain, fete.

festejo /feste'ho/ *n. m.* feast.

festín /fes'tin/ *n. m.* feast.

festividad /festiβi'ðað/ *n. f.* festivity.

festivo /fes'tiβo/ *a.* festive.

fétido /'fetiðo/ *adj.* fetid.

feudal /feu'ðal/ *a.* feudal.

feudo /'feuðo/ *n. m.* fief; manor.

fiado /'fiaðo, al/ *adj.* on trust, on credit.

fiambrera /fiam'brera/ *n. f.* lunch box.

fianza /'fianθa; 'fiansa/ *n. f.* bail.

fiar /fi'ar/ *v.* trust, sell on credit; give credit.

fiarse de /'fiarse de/ *v.* trust (in), rely on.

fiasco /'fiasko/ *n. m.* fiasco.

fibra /'fiβra/ *n. f.* fiber; vigor.

fibroso /fi'βroso/ *a.* fibrous.

ficción /fik'θion; fik'sion/ *n. f.* fiction.

ficha /'fitʃa/ *n. f.* slip, index card; chip.

fichero /fi'tʃero/ *n. m.* computer file, filing cabinet, card catalog.

ficticio /fik'tiθio; fik'tisio/ *a.* fictitious.

fidedigno /fiðe'ðigno/ *a.* trustworthy.

fideicomisario /fiðeikomi'sario/ **-ria** *n.* trustee.

fideicomiso /fiðeiko'miso/ *n. m.* trust.

fidelidad /fiðeli'ðað/ *n. f.* fidelity.

fideo /fi'ðeo/ *n. m.* noodle.

fiebre /'fieβre/ *n. f.* fever.

fiebre del heno /'fieβre del 'eno/ hayfever.

fiel /fiel/ *a.* faithful.

fieltro /'fieltro/ *n. m.* felt.
fiera /'fiera/ *n. f.* wild animal.
fiereza /fie'reθa; fie'resa/ *n. f.* fierceness, wildness.
fiero /'fiero/ *a.* fierce; wild.
fiesta /'fiesta/ *n. f.* festival, feast; party.
figura /fi'gura/ *n. f.* figure. —**figurar,** *v.*
figurarse /figu'rarse/ *v.* imagine.
figurón /figu'ron/ *n. m.* dummy.
fijar /fi'har/ *v.* fix; set, establish; post.
fijarse en /fi'harse en/ *v.* notice.
fijeza /fi'heθa; fi'hesa/ *n. f.* firmness.
fijo /'fiho/ *a.* fixed, stationary, permanent, set.
fila /'fila/ *n. f.* row, rank, file, line.
filantropía /filantro'pia/ *n. f.* philanthropy.
filatelia /fila'telia/ *n. f.* philately, stamp collecting.
filete /fi'lete/ *n. m.* fillet; steak.
film /film/ *n. m.* film. —**filmar,** *v.*
filo /'filo/ *n. m.* (cutting) edge.
filón /fi'lon/ *n. m.* vein (of ore).
filosofía /filoso'fia/ *n. f.* philosophy.
filosófico /filo'sofiko/ *a.* philosophical.
filósofo /fi'losofo/ **-fa** *n.* philosopher.
filtro /'filtro/ *n. m.* filter. —**filtrar,** *v.*
fin /fin/ *n. m.* end, purpose, goal. **a f. de que,** in order that. **en f.,** in short. **por f.,** finally, at last.
final /fi'nal/ *a.* 1. final. —*n.* 2. *m.* end.
finalidad /finali'ðað/ *n. f.* finality.
finalmente /final'mente/ *adv.* at last.
financiero /finan'θiero; finan'siero/ **-ra** *a.* 1. financial. —*n.* 2. financier.
finca /'finka/ *n. f.* real estate; estate; farm.
finés /fi'nes/ **-esa** *a. & n.* Finnish; Finn.
fineza /fi'neθa; fi'nesa/ *n. f.* courtesy, politeness; fineness.
fingimiento /finhi'miento/ *n. m.* pretense.
fingir /fin'hir/ *v.* feign, pretend.
fino /'fino/ *a.* fine; polite, courteous.
firma /'firma/ *n. f.* signature; *Com.* firm.

firmamento /firma'mento/ *n. m.* firmament, heavens.
firmar /fir'mar/ *v.* sign.
firme /'firme/ *a.* firm, fast, steady, sound.
firmemente /firme'mente/ *adv.* firmly.
firmeza /fir'meθa; fir'mesa/ *n. f.* firmness.
fisco /'fisko/ *n. m.* exchequer, treasury.
física /'fisika/ *n. f.* physics.
físico /'fisiko/ **-ca** *a. & n.* physical; physicist.
fisiología /fisiolo'hia/ *n. f.* physiology.
fláccido /'flakθiðo; 'flaksiðo/ *a.* flaccid, soft.
flaco /'flako/ *a.* thin, gaunt.
flagelación /flahela'θion; flahela'sion/ *n. f.* flagellation.
flagelar /flahe'lar/ *v.* flagellate, whip.
flagrancia /fla'granθia; fla'gransia/ *n. f.* flagrancy.
flagrante /fla'grante/ *a.* flagrant.
flama /'flama/ *n. f.* flame; ardor, zeal.
flamante /fla'mante/ *a.* flaming.
flamenco /fla'menko/ *n. m.* flamingo.
flan /flan/ *n. m.* custard.
flanco /'flanko/ *n. m.* side; *Mil.* flank.
flanquear /flanke'ar/ *v.* flank.
flaqueza /fla'keθa; fla'kesa/ *n. f.* thinness; weakness.
flauta /'flauta/ *n. f.* flute.
flautín /flau'tin/ *n. m.* piccolo.
flautista /flau'tista/ *n. m. & f.* flutist, piper.
flecha /'fletʃa/ *n. f.* arrow.
flechazo /fle'tʃaθo; fle'tʃaso/ *n. m.* love at first sight.
flechero /fle'tʃero/ **-ra** *n.* archer.
fleco /'fleko/ *n. m.* fringe; flounce.
flema /'flema/ *n. f.* phlegm.
flemático /fle'matiko/ *a.* phlegmatic.
flequillo /fle'kiʎo; fle'kiyo/ *n. m.* fringe; bangs (of hair).
flete /'flete/ *n. m.* freight. —**fletar,** *v.*
flexibilidad /fleksiβili'ðað/ *n. f.* flexibility.
flexible /fle'ksiβle/ *a.* flexible, pliable.
flirtear /flirte'ar/ *v.* flirt.

flojo /'floho/ *a.* limp; loose, flabby, slack.

flor /flor/ *n. f.* flower; compliment.

flora /'flora/ *n. f.* flora.

floral /flo'ral/ *a.* floral.

florecer /flore'θer; flore'ser/ *v.* flower, bloom; flourish.

floreo /flo'reo/ *n. m.* flourish.

florero /flo'rero/ *n. m.* flower pot; vase.

floresta /flo'resta/ *n. f.* forest.

florido /flo'riðo/ *a.* flowery; flowering.

florista /flo'rista/ *n. m. & f.* florist.

flota /'flota/ *n. f.* fleet.

flotante /flo'tante/ *a.* floating.

flotar /flo'tar/ *v.* float.

flotilla /flo'tiʎa; flo'tiya/ *n. f.* flotilla, fleet.

fluctuación /fluktua'θion; fluktua'sion/ *n. f.* fluctuation.

fluctuar /fluktu'ar/ *v.* fluctuate.

fluente /'fluente/ *a.* fluent; flowing.

fluidez /flui'ðeθ; flui'ðes/ *n. f.* fluency.

flúido /'fluiðo/ *a. & m.* fluid, liquid.

fluir /flu'ir/ *v.* flow.

flujo /'fluho/ *n. m.* flow, flux.

fluor /fluor/ *n. m.* fluorine.

fluorescencia /fluores'θenθia; fluores'sensia/ *n. f.* fluorescence.

fluorescente /fluores'θente; fluores'sente/ *a.* fluorescent.

fobia /'foβia/ *n. f.* phobia.

foca /'foka/ *n. f.* seal.

foco /'foko/ *n. m.* focus, center; floodlight.

fogata /fo'gata/ *n. f.* bonfire.

fogón /fo'gon/ *n. m.* hearth, fireplace.

fogosidad /fogosi'ðað/ *n. f.* vehemence, ardor.

fogoso /fo'goso/ *a.* vehement, ardent.

folclore /fol'klore/ *n. m.* folklore.

follaje /fo'ʎahe; fo'yahe/ *n. m.* foliage.

folleto /fo'ʎeto; fo'yeto/ *n. m.* pamphlet, booklet.

follón /fo'ʎon; fo'yon/ *n. m.* mess, chaos.

fomentar /fomen'tar/ *v.* develop, promote, further, foster.

fomento /fo'mento/ *n. m.* fomentation.

fonda /'fonda/ *n. f.* eating house, inn.

fondo /'fondo/ *n. m.* bottom; back (part); background; (*pl.*) funds; finances. **a f.,** thoroughly.

fonética /fo'netika/ *n. f.* phonetics.

fonético /fo'netiko/ *a.* phonetic.

fonógrafo /fo'nografo/ *n. m.* phonograph.

fontanero /fonta'nero/ **-era** *n.* plumber.

forastero /foras'tero/ **-ra** *a.* **1.** foreign, exotic. —*n.* **2.** stranger.

forjar /for'har/ *v.* forge.

forma /'forma/ *n. f.* form, shape. —**formar,** *v.*

formación /forma'θion; forma'sion/ *n. f.* formation.

formal /for'mal/ *a.* formal.

formaldehido /formalde'iðo/ *n. m.* formaldehyde.

formalidad /formali'ðað/ *n. f.* formality.

formalizar /formali'θar; formali'sar/ *v.* finalize; formulate.

formidable /formi'ðaβle/ *a.* formidable.

formidablemente /formiðaβle'mente/ *adv.* formidably.

formón /for'mon/ *n. m.* chisel.

fórmula /'formula/ *n. f.* formula.

formular /formu'lar/ *v.* formulate, draw up.

formulario /formu'lario/ *n. m.* form.

foro /'foro/ *n. m.* forum.

forrado /fo'rraðo/ *a.* stuffed; *Colloq.* filthy rich.

forraje /fo'rrahe/ *n. m.* forage, fodder.

forrar /fo'rrar/ *v.* line.

forro /'forro/ *n. m.* lining; condom.

fortalecer /fortale'θer; fortale'ser/ *v.* fortify.

fortaleza /forta'leθa; forta'lesa/ *n. f.* fort, fortress; fortitude.

fortificación /fortifika'θion; fortifika'sion/ *n. f.* fortification.

fortitud /forti'tuð/ *n. f.* fortitude.

fortuitamente /fortuita'mente/ *adv.* fortuitously.

fortuito /for'tuito/ *a.* fortuitous.

fortuna /for'tuna/ *n. f.* fortune; luck.

forúnculo /fo'runkulo/ *n. m.* boil.

forzar /for'θar; for'sar/ *v.* force, compel, coerce.

forzosamente /forθosa'mente;

forsosa'mente/ *adv.* compulsorily; forcibly.

forzoso /for'θoso; for'soso/ *a.* compulsory; necessary. **paro f.,** unemployment.

forzudo /for'θuðo; for'suðo/ *a.* powerful, vigorous.

fosa /'fosa/ *n. f.* grave; pit.

fósforo /'fosforo/ *n. m.* match; phosphorus.

fósil /'fosil/ *n. m.* fossil.

foso /'foso/ *n. m.* ditch, trench; moat.

fotocopia /foto'kopia/ *n. f.* photocopy.

fotocopiadora /fotokopia'ðora/ *n. f.* photocopier.

fotografía /fotogra'fia/ *n. f.* photograph; photography.
—**fotografiar,** *v.*

frac /frak/ *n. m.* dress coat.

fracasar /fraka'sar/ *v.* fail.

fracaso /fra'kaso/ *n. m.* failure.

fracción /frak'θion; frak'sion/ *n. f.* fraction.

fractura /frak'tura/ *n. f.* fracture, break.

fragancia /fra'ganθia; fra'gansia/ *n. f.* fragrance; perfume; aroma.

fragante /fra'gante/ *a.* fragrant.

frágil /'frahil/ *a.* fragile, breakable.

fragilidad /frahili'ðað/ *n. f.* fragility.

fragmentario /fragmen'tario/ *a.* fragmentary.

fragmento /frag'mento/ *n. m.* fragment, bit.

fragor /fra'gor/ *n. m.* noise, clamor.

fragoso /fra'goso/ *a.* noisy.

fragua /'fragua/ *n. f.* forge.
—**fraguar,** *v.*

fraile /'fraile/ *n. m.* monk.

frambuesa /fram'buesa/ *n. f.* raspberry.

francamente /franka'mente/ *adv.* frankly, candidly.

francés /fran'θes; fran'ses/ **-esa** *a.* & *n.* French; Frenchman, Frenchwoman.

Francia /'franθia; 'fransia/ *n. f.* France.

franco /'franko/ *a.* frank.

franela /fra'nela/ *n. f.* flannel.

frangible /fraŋ'giβle/ *a.* breakable.

franqueo /fran'keo/ *n. m.* postage.

franqueza /fran'keθa; fran'kesa/ *n. f.* frankness.

franquicia /fran'kiθia; fran'kisia/ *n. f.* franchise.

frasco /'frasko/ *n. m.* flask, bottle.

frase /'frase/ *n. f.* phrase; sentence.

fraseología /fraseolo'hia/ *n. f.* phraseology; style.

fraternal /frater'nal/ *a.* fraternal, brotherly.

fraternidad /fraterni'ðað/ *n. f.* fraternity, brotherhood.

fraude /'frauðe/ *n. m.* fraud.

fraudulento /frauðu'lento/ *a.* fraudulent.

frazada /fra'θaða; fra'saða/ *n. f.* blanket.

frecuencia /fre'kuenθia; fre'kuensia/ *n. f.* frequency.

frecuente /fre'kuente/ *a.* frequent.

frecuentemente /frekuente'mente/ *adv.* frequently, often.

fregadero /frega'ðero/ *n. m.* sink.

fregadura /frega'ðura/ *n. f.* scouring, scrubbing.

fregar /fre'gar/ *v.* scour, scrub, mop.

fregona /fre'gona/ *n. f.* mop.

freír /fre'ir/ *v.* fry.

fréjol /'frehol/ *n. m.* kidney bean.

frenazo /fre'naθo; fre'naso/ *n. m.* sudden braking, slamming on the brakes.

frenesí /frene'si/ *n. m.* frenzy.

frenéticamente /fre'netikamente/ *adv.* frantically.

frenético /fre'netiko/ *a.* frantic, frenzied.

freno /'freno/ *n. m.* brake.
—**frenar,** *v.*

freno de auxilio /'freno de auk'silio/ emergency brake.

freno de mano /'freno de 'mano/ hand brake.

frente /'frente/ *n.* **1.** *f.* forehead. **2.** *m.* front. **en f., al f.,** opposite, across. **f. a,** in front of.

fresa /'fresa/ *n. f.* strawberry.

fresca /'freska/ *n. f.* fresh, cool air.

fresco /'fresko/ *a.* fresh; cool; crisp.

frescura /fres'kura/ *n. f.* coolness, freshness.

fresno /'fresno/ *n. m.* ash tree.

fresquería /freske'ria/ *n. f.* soda fountain.

friabilidad /friaβili'ðað/ *n. f.* brittleness.

friable /'friaβle/ *a.* brittle.

frialdad /frial'dað/ *n. f.* coldness.

fríamente /fria'mente/ *adv.* coldly; coolly.

frícandó /'frikando/ *n. m.* fricandeau.

fricar /fri'kar/ *v.* rub together.

fricción /frik'θion; frik'sion/ *n. f.* friction.

friccionar /frikθio'nar; friksio'nar/ *v.* rub.

friega /'friega/ *n. f.* friction; massage.

frigidez /frihi'ðeθ; frihi'ðes/ *n. f.* frigidity.

frígido /'frihiðo/ *a.* frigid.

frijol /fri'hol/ *n. m.* bean.

frío /'frio/ *a. & n.* cold. **tener f.,** to be cold, feel cold. **hacer f.,** to be cold (weather).

friolento /frio'lento/ **friolero** *a.* chilly; sensitive to cold.

friolera /frio'lera/ *n. f.* trifle, trinket.

friso /'friso/ *n. m.* frieze.

fritillas /fri'tiʎas; fri'tiyas/ *n. f.pl.* fritters.

frito /'frito/ *a.* fried.

fritura /fri'tura/ *n. f.* fritter.

frívolamente /'friβolamente/ *adv.* frivolously.

frivolidad /friβoli'ðað/ *n. f.* frivolity.

frívolo /'friβolo/ *a.* frivolous.

frondoso /fron'doso/ *a.* leafy.

frontera /fron'tera/ *n. f.* frontier; border.

frotar /fro'tar/ *v.* rub.

fructífero /fruk'tifero/ *a.* fruitful.

fructificar /fruktifi'kar/ *v.* bear fruit.

fructuosamente /fruktuosa-'mente/ *adv.* fruitfully.

fructuoso /fruk'tuoso/ *a.* fruitful.

frugal /fru'gal/ *a.* frugal; thrifty.

frugalidad /frugali'ðað/ *n. f.* frugality; thrift.

frugalmente /frugal'mente/ *adv.* frugally, thriftily.

fruncir /frun'θir; frun'sir/ *v.* gather, contract. **f. el entrecejo,** frown.

fruslería /frusle'ria/ *n. f.* trinket.

frustrar /frus'trar/ *v.* frustrate, thwart.

fruta /'fruta/ *n. f.* fruit.

frutería /frute'ria/ *n. f.* fruit store.

fruto /'fruto/ *n. m.* fruit; product; profit.

fucsia /'fuksia/ *n. f.* fuchsia.

fuego /'fuego/ *n. m.* fire.

fuelle /'fueʎe; 'fueye/ *n. m.* bellows.

fuente /'fuente/ *n. f.* fountain; source; platter.

fuera /'fuera/ *adv.* without, outside.

fuero /'fuero/ *n. m.* statute.

fuerte /'fuerte/ *a.* **1.** strong; loud. —*n.* **2.** *m.* fort.

fuertemente /fuerte'mente/ *adv.* strongly; loudly.

fuerza /'fuerθa; 'fuersa/ *n. f.* force, strength.

fuga /'fuga/ *n. f.* flight, escape.

fugarse /fu'garse/ *v.* flee, escape.

fugaz /fu'gaθ; fu'gas/ *a.* fugitive, passing.

fugitivo /fuhi'tiβo/ **-va** *a. & n.* fugitive.

fulano /fu'lano/ **-na** *n.* Mr., Mrs. so-and-so.

fulcro /'fulkro/ *n. m.* fulcrum.

fulgor /ful'gor/ *n. m.* gleam, glow. —**fulgurar,** *v.*

fulminante /fulmi'nante/ *a.* explosive.

fumador /fuma'ðor/ **-ra** *n.* smoker.

fumar /fu'mar/ *v.* smoke.

fumigación /fumiga'θion; fumiga'sion/ *n. f.* fumigation.

fumigador /fumiga'ðor/ **-ra** *n.* fumigator.

fumigar /fumi'gar/ *v.* fumigate.

fumoso /fu'moso/ *a.* smoky.

función /fun'θion; fun'sion/ *n. f.* function; performance, show.

funcionar /funθio'nar; funsio'nar/ *v.* function; work, run.

funcionario /funθio'nario; funsio-'nario/ **-ria** *n.* official, functionary.

funda /'funda/ *n. f.* case, sheath, slipcover.

fundación /funda'θion; funda-'sion/ *n. f.* foundation.

fundador /funda'ðor/ **-ra** *n.* founder.

fundamental /funda'mental/ *a.* fundamental, basic.

fundamentalmente /fundamen-tal'mente/ *adv.* fundamentally.

fundamento /funda'mento/ *n. m.* base, basis, foundation.

fundar /fun'dar/ *v.* found, establish.

fundición /fundi'θion; fundi'sion/ *n. f.* foundry; melting; meltdown.

fundir /fun'dir/ *v.* fuse; smelt.

fúnebre /'funeβre/ *a.* dismal.

funeral /fune'ral/ *n. m.* funeral.

funeraria /fune'raria/ *n. f.* funeral home, funeral parlor.

funestamente /funesta'mente/ *adv.* sadly.

fungo /'fuŋgo/ *n. m.* fungus.

furente /fu'rente/ *a.* furious, enraged.

furgoneta /furgo'neta/ *n. f.* van.

furia /'furia/ *n. f.* fury.

furiosamente /furiosa'mente/ *adv.* furiously.

furioso /fu'rioso/ *a.* furious.

furor /fu'ror/ *n. m.* furor; fury.

furtivamente /furtiβa'mente/ *adv.* furtively.

furtivo /fur'tiβo/ *a.* furtive, sly.

furúnculo /fu'runkulo/ *n. m.* boil.

fusibilidad /fusiβili'ðað/ *n. f.* fusibility.

fusible /fu'siβle/ *n. m.* fuse.

fusil /fu'sil/ *n. m.* rifle, gun.

fusilar /fusi'lar/ *v.* shoot, execute.

fusión /fu'sion/ *n. f.* fusion; merger.

fusionar /fusio'nar/ *v.* unite, fuse, merge.

fútbol /'futβol/ *n. m.* football, soccer.

fútil /'futil/ *a.* trivial.

futilidad /futili'ðað/ *n. f.* triviality.

futuro /fu'turo/ *a. & m.* future.

futurología /futurolo'hia/ *n. f.* futurology.

G

gabán /ga'βan/ *n. m.* overcoat.

gabardina /gaβar'ðina/ *n. f.* raincoat.

gabinete /gaβi'nete/ *n. m.* closet; cabinet; study.

gacela /ga'θela; ga'sela/ *n. f.* gazelle.

gaceta /ga'θeta; ga'seta/ *n. f.* gazette, newspaper.

gacetilla /gaθe'tiʎa; gase'tiya/ *n. f.* personal news section of a newspaper.

gaélico /ga'eliko/ *a.* Gaelic.

gafas /'gafas/ *n. f.pl.* eyeglasses.

gaguear /gage'ar/ *v.* stutter, stammer.

gaita /'gaita/ *n. f.* bagpipes.

gaje /'gahe/ *n. m.* salary; fee.

gala /'gala/ *n. f.* gala, ceremony; (*pl.*) regalia. **tener a g.,** be proud of.

galán /ga'lan/ *n. m.* gallant.

galano /ga'lano/ *a.* stylishly dressed; elegant.

galante /ga'lante/ *a.* gallant.

galantería /galante'ria/ *n. f.* gallantry, compliment.

galápago /ga'lapago/ *n. m.* freshwater turtle.

galardón /galar'ðon/ *n. m.* prize; reward.

gáleo /'galeo/ *n. m.* swordfish.

galera /ga'lera/ *n. f.* wagon; shed; galley.

galería /gale'ria/ *n. f.* gallery, *Theat.* balcony.

galés /'gales/ **-esa** *a. & n.* Welsh; Welshman, Welshwoman.

galgo /'galgo/ *n. m.* greyhound.

galillo /ga'liʎo; ga'liyo/ *n. m.* uvula.

galimatías /galima'tias/ *n. m.* gibberish.

gallardete /gaʎar'ðete; gayar'ðete/ *n. m.* pennant.

galleta /ga'ʎeta; ga'yeta/ *n. f.* cracker.

gallina /ga'ʎina; ga'yina/ *n. f.* hen.

gallinero /gaʎi'nero; gayi'nero/ *n. m.* chicken coop.

gallo /ga'ʎo; ga'yo/ *n. m.* rooster.

galocha /ga'lotʃa/ *n. f.* galosh.

galón /ga'lon/ *n. m.* gallon; *Mil.* stripe.

galope /ga'lope/ *n. m.* gallop. **—galopar,** *v.*

galopín /galo'pin/ *n. m.* ragamuffin, urchin (child).

gamba /'gamba/ *n. f.* prawn.

gamberro /gam'βerro/ **-ra** *n.* hooligan.

gambito /gam'bito/ *n. m.* gambit.

gamuza /ga'muθa; ga'musa/ *n. f.* chamois.

gana /'gana/ *n. f.* desire, wish, mind (to). **de buena g.,** willingly. **tener ganas de,** to feel like.

ganado /ga'naðo/ *n. m.* cattle.

ganador /gana'ðor/ **-ra** *n.* winner.

ganancia /ga'nanθia; ga'nansia/ *n. f.* gain, profit; (*pl.*) earnings.

ganapán /gana'pan/ n. m. drudge.
ganar /ga'nar/ v. earn; win; beat.
ganchillo /gan'tʃiʎo; gan'tʃiyo/ n. m. crochet work.
gancho /'gantʃo/ n. m. hook, hanger, clip, hairpin.
gandul /gan'dul/ -la n. idler, tramp, hobo.
ganga /'gaŋga/ n. f. bargain.
gangrena /gaŋ'grena/ n. f. gangrene.
gansarón /gansa'ron/ n. m. gosling.
ganso /'ganso/ n. m. goose.
garabato /gara'βato/ n. m. hook; scrawl, scribble.
garaje /ga'rahe/ n. m. garage.
garantía /garan'tia/ n. f. guarantee; collateral, security.
garantizar /garanti'θar; garanti-'sar/ v. guarantee, secure, pledge.
garbanzo /gar'βanθo; gar'βanso/ n. m. chickpea.
garbo /'garβo/ n. m. grace.
garboso /gar'βoso/ a. graceful, sprightly.
gardenia /gar'ðenia/ n. f. gardenia.
garfa /'garfa/ n. f. claw, talon.
garganta /gar'ganta/ n. f. throat.
gárgara /'gargara/ n. f. gargle. —**gargarizar,** v.
garita /ga'rita/ n. f. sentry box.
garito /ga'rito/ n. m. gambling house.
garlopa /gar'lopa/ n. f. carpenter's plane.
garra /'garra/ n. f. claw.
garrafa /ga'rrafa/ n. f. decanter, carafe.
garrideza /garri'ðeθa; garri'ðesa/ n. f. elegance, handsomeness.
garrido /ga'rriðo/ a. elegant, handsome.
garrote /ga'rrote/ n. m. club, cudgel.
garrotillo /garro'tiʎo; garro'tiyo/ n. m. croup.
garrudo /ga'rruðo/ a. powerful, brawny.
garza /'garθa; 'garsa/ n. f. heron.
gas /gas/ n. m. gas.
gasa /'gasa/ n. f. gauze.
gaseosa /gase'osa/ n. f. carbonated water.
gaseoso /gase'oso/ a. gaseous.
gasolina /gaso'lina/ n. f. gasoline.
gasolinera /gasoli'nera/ n. f. gas station.

gastar /gas'tar/ v. spend; use up, wear out; waste.
gastritis /gas'tritis/ n. f. gastritis.
gastrómano /gas'tromano/ n. m. glutton.
gastrónomo /gas'tronomo/ -ma n. gourmet, epicure, gastronome.
gatear /gate'ar/ v. creep.
gatillo /ga'tiʎo; ga'tiyo/ n. m. trigger.
gato /'gato/ -ta n. cat.
gaucho /'gautʃo/ n. m. Argentine cowboy.
gaveta /ga'βeta/ n. f. drawer.
gavilla /ga'βiʎa; ga'βiya/ n. f. sheaf.
gaviota /ga'βiota/ n. f. seagull.
gayo /ga'yo/ a. merry, gay.
gayola /ga'yola/ n. m. cage; Colloq. prison.
gazapera /gaθa'pera; gasa'pera/ n. f. rabbit warren.
gazapo /ga'θapo; ga'sapo/ n. m. rabbit.
gazmoñada /gaθmo'ɲaða; gasmo-'ɲaða/ n. f. prudishness.
gazmoño /gaθ'moɲo; gas'moɲo/ n. m. prude.
gaznate /gaθ'nate; gas'nate/ n. m. windpipe.
gazpacho /gaθ'patʃo; gas'patʃo/ n. m. cold tomato soup; gazpacho.
gelatina /hela'tina/ n. f. gelatine.
gemelo /he'melo/ -la n. twin.
gemelos /he'melos/ n. m.pl. cuff links; opera glasses; -as, twins.
gemido /he'miðo/ n. m. moan, groan, wail. —**gemir,** v.
genciana /hen'θiana; hen'siana/ n. f. gentian.
genealogía /heneloo'hia/ n. f. genealogy, pedigree.
generación /henera'θion; henera-'sion/ n. f. generation.
generador /henera'ðor/ n. m. generator.
general /hene'ral/ a. & m. general.
generalidad /henerali'ðað/ n. f. generality.
generalización /heneraliθa'θion; heneralisa'sion/ n. f. generalization.
generalizar /henerali'θar; henerali'sar/ v. generalize.
generalmente /heneral'mente/ adv. generally.
género /'henero/ n. 1. m. gender; kind. 2. (pl.) goods, material.

generosidad /henerosi'ðað/ *n. f.*
generosity.

generoso /hene'roso/ *a.* generous.

génesis /'henesis/ *n. m.* genesis.

genético /he'netiko/ *a.* genetic.

genial /he'nial/ *a.* genial; brilliant.

genio /'henio/ *n. m.* genius; temper; disposition.

genitivo /heni'tiβo/ *n. m.* genitive.

genocidio /heno'θiðio; heno'siðio/ *n. m.* genocide.

gente /'hente/ *n. f.* people, folk.

gentil /hen'til/ *a.* gracious; graceful.

gentileza /henti'leθa; henti'lesa/ *n. f.* grace, graciousness.

gentío /hen'tio/ *n. m.* mob, crowd.

genuino /he'nuino/ *a.* genuine.

geografía /heogra'fia/ *n. f.* geography.

geográfico /heo'grafiko/ *a.* geographical.

geométrico /heo'metriko/ *a.* geometric.

geranio /he'ranio/ *n. m.* geranium.

gerencia /he'renθia; he'rensia/ *n. f.* management.

gerente /he'rente/ *n. m. & f.* manager, director.

germen /'hermen/ *n. m.* germ.

germinar /hermi'nar/ *v.* germinate.

gerundio /he'rundio/ *n. m.* gerund.

gesticulación /hestikula'θion; hestikula'sion/ *n. f.* gesticulation.

gesticular /hestiku'lar/ *v.* gesticulate, gesture.

gestión /hes'tion/ *n. f.* conduct; effort; action.

gesto /'hesto/ *n. m.* gesture, facial expression.

gigante /hi'gante/ *a. & n.* gigantic, giant.

gigantesco /higan'tesko/ *a.* gigantic, huge.

gilipollas /gili'poʎas; gili'poyas/ *n. m. & f. Colloq.* fool, idiot.

gimnasio /him'nasio/ *n. m.* gymnasium.

gimnástica /him'nastika/ *n. f.* gymnastics.

gimotear /himote'ar/ *v.* whine.

ginebra /hi'neβra/ *n. f.* gin.

ginecólogo /hine'kologo/ **-ga** *n.* gynecologist.

gira /'hira/ *n. f.* tour, trip.

girado /hi'raðo/ **-da** *n. Com.* drawee.

girador /hira'ðor/ **-ra** *n. Com.* drawer.

girar /hi'rar/ *v.* revolve, turn, spin, whirl.

giratorio /hira'torio/ *a.* rotary, revolving.

giro /'hiro/ *n. m.* whirl, turn, spin; *Com.* draft. **g. postal,** money order.

gitano /hi'tano/ **-na** *a. & n.* Gypsy.

glacial /gla'θial; gla'sial/ *a.* glacial, icy.

glaciar /gla'θiar; gla'siar/ *n. m.* glacier.

gladiador /glaðia'ðor/ *n. m.* gladiator.

glándula /'glandula/ *n. f.* gland.

glándula endocrina /'glandula endo'krina/ endocrine gland.

glándula pituitaria /'glandula pi-tui'taria/ pituitary gland.

glándula prostática /'glandula pros'tatika/ prostate gland.

glasé /gla'se/ *n. m.* glacé.

glicerina /gliθe'rina; glise'rina/ *n. f.* glycerine.

globo /'gloβo/ *n. m.* globe; balloon.

gloria /'gloria/ *n. f.* glory.

glorieta /glo'rieta/ *n. f.* bower.

glorificación /glorifika'θion; glorifika'sion/ *n. f.* glorification.

glorificar /glorifi'kar/ *v.* glorify.

glorioso /glo'rioso/ *a.* glorious.

glosa /'glosa/ *n. f.* gloss.
—glosar, *v.*

glosario /glo'sario/ *n. m.* glossary.

glotón /glo'ton/ **-ona** *a. & n.* gluttonous; glutton.

glucosa /glu'kosa/ *n. f.* glucose.

gluten /'gluten/ *n. m.* gluten; glue.

gobernación /goβerna'θion; goβerna'sion/ *n. f.* government.

gobernador /goβerna'ðor/ **-ra** *n.* governor.

gobernalle /goβer'naʎe; goβer'naye/ *n. m.* rudder, tiller, helm.

gobernante /goβer'nante/ *n. m. & f.* ruler.

gobernar /goβer'nar/ *v.* govern.

gobierno /go'βierno/ *n. m.* government.

goce /'goθe; 'gose/ *n. m.* enjoyment.

gola /'gola/ *n. f.* throat.

golf /golf/ *n. m.* golf.

golfista /gol'fista/ *n. m. & f.* golfer.

golfo /'golfo/ *n. m.* gulf.

gollete /go'ʎete; go'yete/ *n. m.* upper portion of one's throat.

golondrina /golon'drina/ *n. f.* swallow.

golosina /golo'sina/ *n. f.* delicacy.

goloso /go'loso/ *a.* sweet-toothed.

golpe /'golpe/ *n. m.* blow, stroke. **de g.**, suddenly.

golpear /golpe'ar/ *v.* strike, beat, pound.

goma /'goma/ *n. f.* rubber; gum; glue; eraser.

góndola /'gondola/ *n. f.* gondola.

gordo /'gorðo/ *a.* fat.

gordura /gor'ðura/ *n. f.* fatness.

gorila /go'rila/ *n. m.* gorilla.

gorja /'gorha/ *n. f.* gorge.

gorjeo /gor'heo/ *n. m.* warble, chirp. —**gorjear,** *v.*

gorrión /go'rrion/ *n. m.* sparrow.

gorro /'gorro/ *n. m.* cap.

gota /'gota/ *n. f.* drop (of liquid).

gotear /gote'ar/ *v.* drip, leak.

goteo /go'teo/ *n. m.* leak.

gotera /go'tera/ *n. f.* leak; gutter.

gótico /'gotiko/ *a.* Gothic.

gozar /go'θar; go'sar/ *v.* enjoy.

gozne /'goθne; 'gosne/ *n. m.* hinge.

gozo /'goθo; 'goso/ *n. m.* enjoyment, delight, joy.

gozoso /go'θoso; go'soso/ *a.* joyful, joyous.

grabado /gra'βaðo/ *n.* **1.** *m.* engraving, cut, print. —*a.* **2.** recorded.

grabador /graβa'ðor/ *n. m.* engraver.

grabadora /graβa'ðora/ *n. f.* tape recorder.

grabar /gra'βar/ *v.* engrave; record.

gracia /'graθia; 'grasia/ *n. f.* grace; wit, charm. **hacer g.**, to amuse, strike as funny. **tener g.**, to be funny, to be witty.

gracias /'graθias; 'grasias/ *n. f.pl.* thanks, thank you.

gracioso /gra'θioso; gra'sioso/ *a.* witty, funny.

grada /'graða/ *n. f.* step.

gradación /graða'θion; graða'sion/ *n. f.* gradation.

grado /'graðo/ *n. m.* grade; rank; degree.

graduado /gra'ðuaðo/ **-da** *n.* graduate.

gradual /gra'ðual/ *a.* gradual.

graduar /gra'ðuar/ *v.* grade; graduate.

gráfico /'grafiko/ *a.* graphic, vivid.

grafito /gra'fito/ *n. m.* graphite.

grajo /'graho/ *n. m.* jackdaw.

gramática /gra'matika/ *n. f.* grammar.

gramo /'gramo/ *n. m.* gram.

gran /gran/ **grande** *a.* big, large; great.

granada /gra'naða/ *n. f.* grenade; pomegranate.

granar /gra'nar/ *v.* seed.

grandes almacenes /'grandes alma'θenes; 'grandes alma'senes/ *n. m.pl.* department store.

grandeza /gran'deθa; gran'desa/ *n. f.* greatness.

grandiosidad /grandiosi'ðað/ *n. f.* grandeur.

grandioso /gran'dioso/ *a.* grand, magnificent.

grandor /gran'dor/ *n. m.* size.

granero /gra'nero/ *n. m.* barn; granary.

granito /gra'nito/ *n. m.* granite.

granizada /grani'θaða; grani'saða/ *n. f.* hailstorm.

granizo /gra'niθo; gra'niso/ *n. m.* hail. —**granizar,** *v.*

granja /'granha/ *n. f.* grange; farm; farmhouse.

granjear /granhe'ar/ *v.* earn, gain; get.

granjero /gran'hero/ **-era** *n.* farmer.

grano /'grano/ *n. m.* grain; kernel.

granuja /gra'nuha/ *n. m.* waif, urchin.

grapa /'grapa/ *n. f.* clamp, clip.

grapadora /grapa'ðora/ *n. f.* stapler.

grasa /'grasa/ *n. f.* grease, fat.

grasiento /gra'siento/ *a.* greasy.

gratificación /gratifika'θion; gratifika'sion/ *n. f.* gratification; reward; tip.

gratificar /gratifi'kar/ *v.* gratify; reward; tip.

gratis /'gratis/ *adv.* gratis, free.

gratitud /grati'tuð/ *n. f.* gratitude.

grato /'grato/ *a.* grateful; pleasant.

gratuito /gra'tuito/ *a.* gratuitous; free.

gravamen /gra'βamen/ *n. m.* tax; burden; obligation.

grave /'graβe/ *a.* grave, serious, severe.

gravedad /graβe'ðað/ *n. f.* gravity, seriousness.

gravitación /graβita'θion; graβita-'sion/ *n. f.* gravitation.

gravitar /graβi'tar/ *v.* gravitate.

gravoso /gra'βoso/ *a.* burdensome.

graznido /graθ'niðo; gras'niðo/ *n. m.* croak. —**graznar**, *v.*

Grecia /'greθia; 'gresia/ *n. f.* Greece.

greco /'greko/ **-ca** *a.* & *n.* Greek.

greda /'greða/ *n. f.* clay.

gresca /'greska/ *n. f.* revelry; quarrel.

griego /'griego/ **-ga** *a.* & *n.* Greek.

grieta /'grieta/ *n. f.* opening; crevice, crack.

grifo /'grifo/ *n. m.* faucet.

grillo /'griʎo; 'griyo/ *n. m.* cricket.

grima /'grima/ *n. f.* fright.

gringo /'gringo/ **-ga** *n.* foreigner (usually North American).

gripa /'gripa/ **gripe** *n. f.* grippe.

gris /gris/ *a.* gray.

grito /'grito/ *n. m.* shout, scream, cry. —**gritar**, *v.*

grosella /gro'seʎa; gro'seya/ *n. f.* currant.

grosería /grose'ria/ *n. f.* grossness; coarseness.

grosero /gro'sero/ *a.* coarse, vulgar, discourteous.

grotesco /gro'tesko/ *a.* grotesque.

grúa /'grua/ *n. f.* crane; tow truck.

gruesa /'gruesa/ *n. f.* gross.

grueso /'grueso/ *a.* **1.** bulky; stout; coarse, thick. —*n.* **2.** *m.* bulk.

grulla /'gruʎa; 'gruya/ *n. f.* crane.

gruñido /gru'ɲiðo/ *n. m.* growl, snarl, mutter. —**gruñir**, *v.*

grupo /'grupo/ *n. m.* group, party.

gruta /'gruta/ *n. f.* cavern.

guacamol /guaka'mol/ **guaca-mole** *n. m.* avocado sauce; guacamole.

guadaña /gua'ðaɲa/ *n. f.* scythe. —**guadañar**, *v.*

guagua /'guagua/ *n. f.* (S.A.) baby; (Carib.) bus.

gualdo /'gualdo/ *n. m.* yellow, golden.

guano /'guano/ *n. m.* guano (fertilizer).

guante /'guante/ *n. m.* glove.

guantera /guan'tera/ *n. f.* glove compartment.

guapo /'guapo/ *a.* handsome.

guarda /'guarða/ *n. m. or f.* guard.

guardabarros /guarða'βarros/ *n. m.* fender.

guardacostas /guarða'kostas/ *n. m.* revenue ship.

guardaespaldas /,guarðaes-'paldas/ *n. m.* & *f.* bodyguard.

guardameta /guarða'meta/ *n. m.* & *f.* goalkeeper.

guardar /guar'ðar/ *v.* keep, store, put away; guard.

guardarropa /guarða'rropa/ *n. f.* coat room.

guardarse de /guar'ðarse de/ *v.* beware of, avoid.

guardia /'guarðia/ *n.* **1.** *f.* guard; watch. —*n.* **2.** *m.* policeman.

guardián /guar'ðian/ **-na** *n.* guardian, keeper, watchman.

guardilla /guar'ðiʎa; guar'ðiya/ *n. f.* attic.

guarida /gua'riða/ *n. f.* den.

guarismo /gua'rismo/ *n. m.* number, figure.

guarnecer /guarne'θer; guarne-'ser/ *v.* adorn.

guarnición /guarni'θion; guarni-'sion/ *n. f.* garrison; trimming.

guasa /'guasa/ *n. f.* joke, jest.

guayaba /gua'yaβa/ *n. f.* guava.

gubernativo /guβerna'tiβo/ *a.* governmental.

guerra /'gerra/ *n. f.* war.

guerrero /ge'rrero/ **-ra** *n.* warrior.

guía /'gia/ *n.* **1.** *m.* & *f.* guide. **2.** *f.* guidebook, directory.

guiar /giar/ *v.* guide; steer, drive.

guija /'giha/ *n. f.* pebble.

guillotina /giʎo'tina; giyo'tina/ *n. f.* guillotine.

guindar /gin'dar/ *v.* hang.

guinga /'ginga/ *n. f.* gingham.

guiñada /gi'ɲaða/ *n. f.*, **guiño**, *m.* wink. —**guiñar**, *v.*

guión /gi'on/ *n. m.* dash, hyphen; script.

guirnalda /gir'nalda/ *n. f.* garland, wreath.

guisa /'gisa/ *n. f.* guise, manner.

guisado /gi'saðo/ *n. m.* stew.

guisante /gi'sante/ *n. f.* pea.

guisar /gi'sar/ *v.* cook.

guiso /'giso/ *n. m.* stew.

guita /'gita/ *n. f.* twine.

guitarra /gi'tarra/ *n. f.* guitar.

guitarrista /gita'rrista/ *n. m. & f.*
guitarist.
gula /'gula/ *n. f.* gluttony.
gurú /gu'ru/ *n. m.* guru.
gusano /gu'sano/ *n. m.* worm,
caterpillar.
gustar /gus'tar/ *v.* please; taste.

gustillo /gus'tiʎo; gus'tiyo/ *n. m.*
aftertaste, slight pleasure.
gusto /'gusto/ *n. m.* pleasure;
taste; liking.
gustoso /gus'toso/ *a.* pleasant;
tasteful.
gutural /gutu'ral/ *a.* guttural.

H

haba /'aβa/ *n. f.* bean.
habanera /aβa'nera/ *n. f.* Cuban
dance melody.
haber /a'βer/ *v.* have. **h. de,** be
to, be supposed to.
haberes /a'βeres/ *n. m.pl.* property; worldly goods.
habichuela /aβi'tʃuela/ *n. f.* bean.
hábil /'aβil/ *a.* skillful; capable;
clever.
habilidad /aβili'ðað/ *n. f.* ability;
skill; talent.
habilidoso /aβili'ðoso/ *a.* able,
skillful, talented.
habilitado /aβili'taðo/ **-da** *n.* pay-
master.
habilitar /aβili'tar/ *v.* qualify; supply, equip.
hábilmente /'aβilmente/ *adv.* ably.
habitación /aβita'θion; aβita'sion/
n. f. dwelling; room. **h. individual,** single room.
habitante /aβi'tante/ *n. m. & f.*
inhabitant.
habitar /aβi'tar/ *v.* inhabit; dwell.
hábito /'aβito/ *n. m.* habit; custom.
habitual /aβi'tual/ *a.* habitual.
habituar /aβi'tuar/ *v.* accustom,
habituate.
habla /'aβla/ *n. f.* speech.
hablador /aβla'ðor/ *a.* talkative.
hablar /a'βlar/ *v.* talk, speak.
haca /'aka/ *n. f.* pony.
hacedor /aθe'ðor; ase'ðor/ *n. m.*
maker.
hacendado /aθen'daðo;
asen'daðo/ **-da** *n.* hacienda
owner; farmer.
hacendoso /aθen'doso; asen'doso/
a. industrious.
hacer /a'θer; a'ser/ *v.* do; make.
hace dos años, etc., two years
ago, etc.
hacerse /a'θerse; a'serse/ *v.* become, get to be.
hacha /'atʃa/ *n. f.* ax, hatchet.
hacia /'aθia; 'asia/ *prep.* toward.
hacienda /a'θienda; a'sienda/ *n. f.*
property; estate; ranch; farm;
Govt. treasury.
hada /'aða/ *n. f.* fairy.
hado /'aðo/ *n. m.* fate.
halagar /ala'gar/ *v.* flatter.
halar /a'lar/ *v.* haul, pull.
halcón /al'kon/ *n. m.* hawk, falcon.
haleche /a'letʃe/ *n. m.* anchovy.
hallado /a'ʎaðo; a'yaðo/ *a.* found.
bien h., welcome. **mal h.,** uneasy.
hallar /a'ʎar; a'yar/ *v.* find, locate.
hallarse /a'ʎarse; a'yarse/ *v.* be
located; happen to be.
hallazgo /a'ʎaθgo; a'yasgo/ *n. m.*
find, thing found.
hamaca /a'maka/ *n. f.* hammock.
hambre /'ambre/ *n. f.* hunger.
tener h., estar con h., to be
hungry.
hambrear /ambre'ar/ *v.* hunger;
starve.
hambriento /am'briento/ *a.* starving, hungry.
hamburguesa /ambur'gesa/ *n. f.*
beefburger, hamburger.
haragán /ara'gan/ **-na** *n.* idler,
lazy person.
haraganear /aragane'ar/ *v.* loiter.
harapo /a'rapo/ *n. m.* rag, tatter.
haraposo /ara'poso/ *a.* ragged,
shabby.
harén /a'ren/ *n. m.* harem.
harina /a'rina/ *n. f.* flour, meal.
harnero /ar'nero/ *n. m.* sieve.
hartar /ar'tar/ *v.* satiate.
harto /'arto/ *a.* stuffed; fed up.
hartura /ar'tura/ *n. f.* superabun-
dance, glut.
hasta /'asta/ *prep.* **1.** until, till; as
far as, up to. **h. luego,** good-bye,
so long. —*adv.* **2.** even.
hastío /as'tio/ *n. m.* distaste,
loathing.
hato /'ato/ *n. m.* herd.
hay /ai/ *v.* there is, there are. **h.
que,** it is necessary to. **no h. de**

qué, you're welcome, don't mention it.

haya /'aya/ *n. f.* beech tree.

haz /aθ; as/ *n. f.* bundle, sheaf; face.

hazaña /a'θaɲa; a'saɲa/ *n. f.* deed; exploit, feat.

hebdomadario /eβðoma'ðario/ *a.* weekly.

hebilla /e'βiʎa; e'βiya/ *n. f.* buckle.

hebra /'eβra/ *n. f.* thread, string.

hebreo /e'βreo/ **-rea** *a. & n.* Hebrew.

hechicero /etʃi'θero; etʃi'sero/ **-ra** *n.* wizard, witch.

hechizar /etʃi'θar; etʃi'sar/ *v.* bewitch.

hechizo /e'tʃiθo; e'tʃiso/ *n. m.* spell.

hecho /'etʃo/ *n. m.* fact; act; deed.

hechura /e'tʃura/ *n. f.* workmanship, make.

hediondez /eðion'deθ; eðion'des/ *n. f.* stench.

hégira /'ehira/ *n. f.* hegira.

helada /e'laða/ *n. f.* frost.

heladería /elaðe'ria/ *n. f.* ice-cream parlor.

helado /e'laðo/ *n. m.* ice cream.

helar /e'lar/ *v.* freeze.

helecho /e'letʃo/ *n. m.* fern.

hélice /'eliθe; 'elise/ *n. f.* propeller; helix.

helicóptero /eli'koptero/ *n. m.* helicopter.

helio /'elio/ *n. m.* helium.

hembra /'embra/ *n. f.* female.

hemisferio /emis'ferio/ *n. m.* hemisphere.

hemoglobina /emoglo'βina/ *n. f.* hemoglobin.

hemorragia /emo'rrahia/ *n. f.* hemorrhage.

hemorragia nasal /emo'rrahia na'sal/ nosebleed.

henchir /en'tʃir/ *v.* stuff.

hendedura /ende'ðura/ *n. f.* crevice, crack.

hendido /en'diðo/ *a.* cloven, cleft (lip).

heno /'eno/ *n. m.* hay.

hepática /e'patika/ *n. f.* liverwort.

hepatitis /epa'titis/ *n. f.* hepatitis.

heraldo /e'raldo/ *n. m.* herald.

herbáceo /er'βaθeo; er'βaseo/ *a.* herbaceous.

herbívoro /er'βiβoro/ *a.* herbivorous.

heredar /ere'ðar/ *v.* inherit.

heredero /ere'ðero/ **-ra** *n.* heir; successor.

hereditario /ereði'tario/ *a.* hereditary.

hereje /e'rehe/ *n. m. & f.* heretic.

herejía /ere'hia/ *n. f.* heresy.

herencia /e'renθia; e'rensia/ *n. f.* inheritance; heritage.

herético /e'retiko/ *a.* heretical.

herida /e'riða/ *n. f.* wound, injury.

herir /e'rir/ *v.* wound, injure.

hermafrodita /ermafro'ðita/ *a. & n.* hermaphrodite.

hermana /er'mana/ *n. f.* sister.

hermano /er'mano/ *n. m.* brother.

hermético /er'metiko/ *a.* airtight.

hermoso /er'moso/ *a.* beautiful, handsome.

hermosura /ermo'sura/ *n. f.* beauty.

hernia /'ernia/ *n. f.* hernia, rupture.

héroe /'eroe/ *n. m.* hero.

heroico /e'roiko/ *a.* heroic.

heroína /ero'ina/ *n. f.* heroine.

heroísmo /ero'ismo/ *n. m.* heroism.

herradura /erra'ðura/ *n. f.* horseshoe.

herramienta /erra'mienta/ *n. f.* tool; implement.

herrería /erre'ria/ *n. f.* blacksmith's shop.

herrero /e'rrero/ *n. m.* blacksmith.

herrumbre /e'rrumbre/ *n. f.* rust.

hertzio /'ertθio; 'ertsio/ *n. m.* hertz.

hervir /er'βir/ *v.* boil.

hesitación /esita'θion; esita'sion/ *n. f.* hesitation.

heterogéneo /etero'heneo/ *a.* heterogeneous.

heterosexual /eterosek'sual/ *a.* heterosexual.

hexagonal /eksago'nal/ *a.* hexagonal.

hexágono /e'ksagono/ *n. m.* hexagon.

hez /eθ; es/ *n. f.* dregs, sediment.

híbrido /'iβriðo/ **-da** *n. & a.* hybrid.

hidalgo /i'ðalgo/ **-ga** *a. & n.* noble.

hidalguía /iðal'gia/ *n. f.* nobility; generosity.

hidráulico /i'ðrauliko/ *a.* hydraulic.

hidroavión /iðroa'βion/ n. m. seaplane, hydroplane.
hidrofobia /iðro'foβia/ n. f. rabies.
hidrógeno /i'ðroheno/ n. m. hydrogen.
hidropesía /iðrope'sia/ n. f. dropsy.
hiedra /'ieðra/ n. f. ivy.
hiel /iel/ n. f. gall.
hielo /'ielo/ n. m. ice.
hiena /'iena/ n. f. hyena.
hierba /'ierβa/ n. f. grass; herb; marijuana.
hierbabuena /ierβa'βuena/ n. f. mint.
hierro /'ierro/ n. m. iron.
hígado /'igaðo/ n. m. liver.
higiene /i'hiene/ n. f. hygiene.
higiénico /i'hieniko/ a. sanitary, hygienic.
higo /'igo/ n. m. fig.
higuera /i'gera/ n. f. fig tree.
hija /'iha/ n. f. daughter.
hija adoptiva /'iha aðop'tiβa/ adopted daughter.
hijastro /i'hastro/ **-tra** n. stepchild.
hijo /'iho/ n. m. son.
hijo adoptivo /'iho aðop'tiβo/ n. m. adopted child, adopted son.
hila /'ila/ n. f. line.
hilandero /ilan'dero/ **-ra** n. spinner.
hilar /i'lar/ v. spin.
hilera /i'lera/ n. f. row, line, tier.
hilo /'ilo/ n. m. thread; string; wire; linen.
himno /'imno/ n. m. hymn.
hincar /in'kar/ v. drive, thrust; sink into.
hincarse /in'karse/ v. kneel.
hinchar /in'tʃar/ v. swell.
hindú /in'du/ n. & a. Hindu.
hinojo /i'noho/ n. m. knee.
hiperenlace /iperen'laθe, iperen'lase/ n. m. hyperlink.
hipermercado /ipermer'kaðo/ n. m. hypermarket.
hipertexto /iper'teksto/ n. m. hypertext.
hipnótico /ip'notiko/ a. hypnotic.
hipnotismo /ipno'tismo/ n. m. hypnotism.
hipnotista /ipno'tista/ n. m. & f. hypnotist.
hipnotizar /ipnoti'θar; ipnoti'sar/ v. hypnotize.
hipo /'ipo/ n. m. hiccough.

hipocresía /ipokre'sia/ n. f. hypocrisy.
hipócrita /i'pokrita/ a. & n. hypocritical; hypocrite.
hipódromo /i'poðromo/ n. m. race track.
hipoteca /ipo'teka/ n. f. mortgage. —**hipotecar,** v.
hipótesis /i'potesis/ n. f. hypothesis.
hirsuto /ir'suto/ a. hairy, hirsute.
hispano /is'pano/ a. Hispanic, Spanish American.
Hispanoamérica /ispanoa'merika/ f. Spanish America.
hispanoamericano /ispanoameri'kano/ **-na** a. & n. Spanish American.
histerectomía /isterekto'mia/ n. f. hysterectomy.
histeria /is'teria/ n. f. hysteria.
histérico /is'teriko/ a. hysterical.
historia /is'toria/ n. f. history; story.
historiador /istoria'ðor/ **-ra** n. historian.
histórico /is'toriko/ a. historic, historical.
histrión /is'trion/ n. m. actor.
hocico /o'θiko; o'siko/ n. m. snout, muzzle.
hogar /o'gar/ n. m. hearth; home.
hoguera /o'gera/ n. f. bonfire, blaze.
hoja /'oha/ n. f. leaf; sheet (of paper); pane; blade.
hoja de cálculo /'oha de 'kalkulo/ spreadsheet.
hoja de inscripción /'oha de inskrip'θion; 'oha de inskrip'sion/ entry blank.
hoja de pedidos /'oha de pe'ðiðos/ order blank.
hoja informativa /'oha informa'tiβa/ newsletter.
hojalata /oha'lata/ n. f. tin.
hojalatero /ohala'tero/ **-ra** n. tinsmith.
hojear /ohe'ar/ v. scan, skim through.
hola /'ola/ interj. hello.
Holanda /o'landa/ n. f. Holland, Netherlands.
holandés /olan'des/ **-esa** a. & n. Dutch; Hollander.
holganza /ol'ganθa; ol'gansa/ n. f. leisure; diversion.
holgazán /olga'θan; olga'san/ **-ana** a. **1.** idle, lazy. —n. **2.** m. idler, loiterer, tramp.

holgazanear /olgaθane'ar; olga-sane'ar/ v. idle, loiter.
hollín /o'ʎin; o'yin/ n. m. soot.
holografía /ologra'fia/ n. f. holography.
holograma /olo'grama/ n. m. hologram.
hombre /'ombre/ n. m. man.
hombría /om'βria/ n. f. manliness.
hombro /'ombro/ n. m. shoulder.
hombruno /om'bruno/ a. mannish, masculine (woman).
homenaje /ome'nahe/ n. m. homage.
homeópata /ome'opata/ n. m. homeopath.
homicidio /omi'θiðio; omi'siðio/ n. m. homicide.
homilía /omi'lia/ n. f. homily.
homosexual /omose'ksual/ a. homosexual, gay.
honda /'onda/ n. f. sling.
hondo /'ondo/ a. deep.
hondonada /ondo'naða/ n. f. ravine.
hondura /on'dura/ n. f. depth.
honestidad /onesti'ðað/ n. f. modesty, unpretentiousness.
honesto /o'nesto/ a. honest; pure; just.
hongo /'oŋgo/ n. m. fungus; mushroom.
honor /o'nor/ n. m. honor.
honorable /ono'raβle/ a. honorable.
honorario /ono'rario/ a. **1.** honorary. —n. **2.** m. honorarium, fee.
honorífico /ono'rifiko/ a. honorary.
honra /'onra/ n. f. honor. —**honrar,** v.
honradez /onra'ðeθ; onra'ðes/ n. f. honesty.
honrado /on'raðo/ a. honest, honorable.
hora /'ora/ n. f. hour; time (of day).
horadar /ora'ðar/ v. perforate.
hora punta /'ora 'punta/ rush hour.
horario /o'rario/ n. m. timetable, schedule.
horca /'orka/ n. f. gallows; pitchfork.
horda /'orða/ n. f. horde.
horizontal /oriθon'tal; orison'tal/ a. horizontal.
horizonte /ori'θonte; ori'sonte/ n. m. horizon.

hormiga /or'miga/ n. f. ant.
hormiguear /ormige'ar/ v. itch.
hormiguero /ormi'gero/ n. m. ant hill.
hornero /or'nero/ **-ra** n. baker.
hornillo /or'niʎo; or'niyo/ n. m. stove.
horno /'orno/ n. m. oven; kiln.
horóscopo /o'roskopo/ n. m. horoscope.
horrendo /o'rrendo/ a. dreadful, horrendous.
horrible /o'rriβle/ a. horrible, hideous, awful.
hórrido /'orriðo/ a. horrid.
horror /o'rror/ n. m. horror.
horrorizar /orrori'θar; orrori'sar/ v. horrify.
horroroso /orro'roso/ a. horrible, frightful.
hortelano /orte'lano/ n. m. horticulturist.
hospedaje /ospe'ðahe/ n. m. lodging.
hospedar /ospe'ðar/ v. give or take lodgings.
hospital /ospi'tal/ n. m. hospital.
hospitalario /ospita'lario/ a. hospitable.
hospitalidad /ospitali'ðað/ n. f. hospitality.
hospitalmente /ospital'mente/ adv. hospitably.
hostia /'ostia/ n. f. host; Colloq. hit, blow.
hostil /'ostil/ a. hostile.
hostilidad /ostili'ðað/ n. f. hostility.
hotel /'otel/ n. m. hotel.
hoy /oi/ adv. today. **h. día, h. en día,** nowadays.
hoya /'oya/ n. f. dale, valley.
hoyo /'oyo/ n. m. pit, hole.
hoyuelo /o'yuelo/ n. m. dimple.
hoz /oθ; os/ n. f. sickle.
hucha /'utʃa/ n. f. chest, money box; savings.
hueco /'ueko/ a. **1.** hollow, empty. —n. **2.** m. hole, hollow.
huelga /'uelga/ n. f. strike.
huelgista /uel'hista/ n. m. & f. striker.
huella /'ueʎa; 'ueya/ n. f. track, trace; footprint.
huérfano /'uerfano/ **-na** a. & n. orphan.
huero /'uero/ a. empty.
huerta /'uerta/ n. f. (vegetable) garden.
huerto /'uerto/ n. m. orchard.

hueso /'ueso/ *n. m.* bone; fruit pit.

huésped /'uespeð/ *n. m. & f.* guest.

huesudo /ue'suðo/ *a.* bony.

huevo /'ueβo/ *n. m.* egg.

huída /'uiða/ *n. f.* flight, escape.

huir /uir/ *v.* flee.

hule /'ule/ *n. m.* oilcloth.

humanidad /umani'ðað/ *n. f.* humanity, mankind; humaneness.

humanista /uma'nista/ *n. m. & f.* humanist.

humanitario /umani'tario/ *a.* humane.

humano /u'mano/ *a.* human; humane.

humareda /uma'reða/ *n. f.* dense cloud of smoke.

humear /ume'ar/ *v.* emit smoke or steam.

humedad /ume'ðað/ *n. f.* humidity, moisture, dampness.

humedecer /umeðe'θer; umeðe-'ser/ *v.* moisten, dampen.

húmedo /'umeðo/ *a.* humid, moist, damp.

humildad /umil'dað/ *n. f.* humility, meekness.

humilde /u'milde/ *a.* humble, meek.

humillación /umiʎa'θion; umiya-'sion/ *n. f.* humiliation.

humillar /umi'ʎar; umi'yar/ *v.* humiliate.

humo /'umo/ *n. m.* smoke; (*pl.*) airs, affectation.

humor /u'mor/ *n. m.* humor, mood.

humorista /umo'rista/ *n. m. & f.* humorist.

hundimiento /undi'miento/ *n. m.* collapse.

hundir /un'dir/ *v.* sink; collapse.

húngaro /'uŋgaro/ **-ra** *a. & n.* Hungarian.

Hungría /uŋ'gria/ *n. f.* Hungary.

huracán /ura'kan/ *n. m.* hurricane.

huraño /u'raɲo/ *a.* shy, bashful.

hurgar /ur'gar/ *v.* stir.

hurón /u'ron/ *n. m.* ferret.

hurtadillas /urta'ðiʎas; urta'ðiyas/ *n. f.pl.* **a h.,** on the sly.

hurtador /urta'ðor/ **-ra** *n.* thief.

hurtar /ur'tar/ *v.* steal, rob of; hide.

hurtarse /ur'tarse/ *v.* hide; withdraw.

husmear /usme'ar/ *v.* scent, smell.

huso /'uso/ *n. m.* spindle; bobbin.

huso horario /'uso o'rario/ time zone.

I

ibérico /i'βeriko/ *a.* Iberian.

iberoamericano /iβeroameri'kano/ **-na** *a. & n.* Latin American.

ida /'iða/ *n. f.* departure; trip out. **i. y vuelta,** round trip.

idea /i'ðea/ *n. f.* idea.

ideal /i'ðeal/ *a. & m.* ideal.

idealismo /iðea'lismo/ *n. m.* idealism.

idealista /iðea'lista/ *n. m. & f.* idealist.

idear /iðe'ar/ *v.* plan, conceive.

idéntico /i'ðentiko/ *a.* identical.

identidad /iðenti'ðað/ *n. f.* identity; identification.

identificar /iðentifi'kar/ *v.* identify.

idilio /i'ðilio/ *n. m.* idyll.

idioma /i'ðioma/ *n. m.* language.

idiota /i'ðiota/ *a. & n.* idiotic; idiot.

idiotismo /iðio'tismo/ *n. m.* idiom; idiocy.

idolatrar /iðola'trar/ *v.* idolize, adore.

ídolo /'iðolo/ *n. m.* idol.

idóneo /i'ðoneo/ *a.* suitable, fit, apt.

iglesia /i'glesia/ *n. f.* church.

ignición /igni'θion; igni'sion/ *n. f.* ignition.

ignominia /igno'minia/ *n. f.* ignominy, shame.

ignominioso /ignomi'nioso/ *a.* ignominious, shameful.

ignorancia /igno'ranθia; igno-'ransia/ *n. f.* ignorance.

ignorante /igno'rante/ *a.* ignorant.

ignorar /igno'rar/ *v.* be ignorant of, not know.

ignoto /ig'noto/ *a.* unknown.

igual /i'gual/ *a.* equal; the same; (*pl.*) alike. *m.* equal.

igualar /igua'lar/ *v.* equal; equalize; match.

igualdad /igual'dað/ *n. f.* equality; sameness.

ijada /i'haða/ *n. f.* flank (of an animal).

ilegal /ile'gal/ *a.* illegal.
ilegítimo /ile'hitimo/ *a.* illegitimate.
ileso /i'leso/ *a.* unharmed.
ilícito /i'liθito; i'lisito/ *a.* illicit, unlawful.
iluminación /ilumina'θion; iluminina'sion/ *n. f.* illumination.
iluminar /ilumi'nar/ *v.* illuminate.
ilusión /ilu'sion/ *n. f.* illusion.
ilusión de óptica /ilu'sion de 'optika/ optical illusion.
ilusorio /ilu'sorio/ *a.* illusive.
ilustración /ilustra'θion; ilustra'sion/ *n. f.* illustration; learning.
ilustrador /ilustra'ðor/ **-ra** *n.* illustrator.
ilustrar /ilus'trar/ *v.* illustrate.
ilustre /i'lustre/ *a.* illustrious, honorable, distinguished.
imagen /i'mahen/ *n. f.* image.
imaginación /imahina'θion; imahina'sion/ *n. f.* imagination.
imaginar /imahi'nar/ *v.* imagine.
imaginario /imahi'nario/ *a.* imaginary.
imaginativo /imahina'tiβo/ *a.* imaginative.
imán /i'man/ *n. m.* magnet; imam.
imbécil /im'beθil; im'besil/ *a. & n.* imbecile; stupid, foolish; fool.
imbuir /im'buir/ *v.* imbue, instil.
imitación /imita'θion; imita'sion/ *n. f.* imitation.
imitador /imita'ðor/ **-ra** *n.* imitator.
imitar /imi'tar/ *v.* imitate.
impaciencia /impa'θienθia; impa'siensia/ *n. f.* impatience.
impaciente /impa'θiente; impa'siente/ *a.* impatient.
impar /im'par/ *a.* unequal, uneven, odd.
imparcial /impar'θial; impar'sial/ *a.* impartial.
impasible /impa'siβle/ *a.* impassive, unmoved.
impávido /im'paβiðo/ *adj.* fearless, intrepid.
impedimento /impeði'mento/ *n. m.* impediment, obstacle.
impedir /impe'ðir/ *v.* impede, hinder, stop, obstruct.
impeler /impe'ler/ *v.* impel; incite.
impensado /impen'saðo/ *a.* unexpected.
imperar /impe'rar/ *v.* reign; prevail.
imperativo /impera'tiβo/ *a.* imperative.

imperceptible /imperθep'tiβle; impersep'tiβle/ *a.* imperceptible.
imperdible /imper'ðiβle/ *n. m.* safety pin.
imperecedero /impereθe'ðero; imperese'ðero/ *a.* imperishable.
imperfecto /imper'fekto/ *a.* imperfect, faulty.
imperial /impe'rial/ *a.* imperial.
imperialismo /imperia'lismo/ *n. m.* imperialism.
impericia /impe'riθia; impe'risia/ *n. f.* inexperience.
imperio /im'perio/ *n. m.* empire.
imperioso /impe'rioso/ *a.* imperious, domineering.
impermeable /imperme'aβle/ *a.* waterproof. *m.* raincoat.
impersonal /imperso'nal/ *a.* impersonal.
impertinencia /impertinen'θia; impertinen'sia/ *n. f.* impertinence.
ímpetu /'impetu/ *n. m.* impulse; impetus.
impetuoso /impe'tuoso/ *a.* impetuous.
impiedad /impie'ðað/ *n. f.* impiety.
impío /im'pio/ *a.* impious.
implacable /impla'kaβle/ *a.* implacable, unrelenting.
implicar /impli'kar/ *v.* implicate, involve.
implorar /implo'rar/ *v.* implore.
imponente /impo'nente/ *a.* impressive.
imponer /impo'ner/ *v.* impose.
impopular /impopu'lar/ *a.* unpopular.
importación /importa'θion; importa'sion/ *n. f.* importation, importing.
importador /importa'ðor/ **-ra** *n.* importer.
importancia /impor'tanθia; impor'tansia/ *n. f.* importance.
importante /impor'tante/ *a.* important.
importar /impor'tar/ *v.* be important, matter; import.
importe /im'porte/ *n. m.* value; amount.
importunar /importu'nar/ *v.* beg, importune.
imposibilidad /imposiβili'ðað/ *n. f.* impossibility.
imposibilitado /imposiβili'taðo/ *a.* helpless.
imposible /impo'siβle/ *a.* impossible.

imposición /imposi'θion; imposi-'sion/ *n. f.* imposition.

impostor /impos'tor/ **-ra** *n.* imposter, faker.

impotencia /impo'tenθia; impo-'tensia/ *n. f.* impotence.

impotente /impo'tente/ *a.* impotent.

imprecar /impre'kar/ *v.* curse.

impreciso /impre'θiso; impre'siso/ *adj.* inexact.

impregnar /impreg'nar/ *v.* impregnate.

imprenta /im'prenta/ *n. f.* press; printing house.

imprescindible /impresθin'diβle; impressin'diβle/ *a.* essential.

impresión /impre'sion/ *n. f.* impression.

impresionable /impresio'naβle/ *a.* impressionable.

impresionar /impresio'nar/ *v.* impress.

impresor /impre'sor/ *n. m.* printer.

imprevisión /impreβi'sion/ *n. f.* oversight; thoughtlessness.

imprevisto /impre'βisto/ *a.* unexpected, unforeseen.

imprimir /impri'mir/ *v.* print; imprint.

improbable /impro'βaβle/ *a.* improbable.

improbo /im'proβo/ *a.* dishonest.

improductivo /improðuk'tiβo/ *a.* unproductive.

improperio /impro'perio/ *n. m.* insult.

impropio /im'propio/ *a.* improper.

improvisación /improβisa'θion; improβisa'sion/ *n. f.* improvisation.

improvisar /improβi'sar/ *v.* improvise.

improviso /impro'βiso, impro-'βisto/ *a.* unforeseen.

imprudencia /impru'ðenθia; impru'ðensia/ *n. f.* imprudence.

imprudente /impru'ðente/ *a.* imprudent, reckless.

impuesto /im'puesto/ *n. m.* tax.

impuesto sobre la renta /im'puesto soβre la 'rrenta/ income tax.

impulsar /impul'sar/ *v.* prompt, impel.

impulsivo /impul'siβo/ *a.* impulsive.

impulso /im'pulso/ *n. m.* impulse.

impureza /impu're θa; impu'resa/ *n. f.* impurity.

impuro /im'puro/ *a.* impure.

imputación /imputa'θion; imputa'sion/ *n. f.* imputation.

imputar /impu'tar/ *v.* impute, attribute.

inaccesible /inakθe'siβle; inakse-'siβle/ *a.* inaccessible.

inacción /inak'θion; inak'sion/ *n. f.* inaction; inactivity.

inaceptable /inaθep'taβle; inasep'taβle/ *a.* unacceptable.

inactivo /inak'tiβo/ *a.* inactive; sluggish.

inadecuado /inaðe'kuaðo/ *a.* inadequate.

inadvertencia /inaðβer'tenθia; inaðβer'tensia/ *n. f.* oversight.

inadvertido /inaðβer'tiðo/ *a.* inadvertent, careless; unnoticed.

inagotable /inago'taβle/ *a.* inexhaustible.

inalterado /inalte'raðo/ *a.* unchanged.

inanición /inani'θion; inani'sion/ *n. f.* starvation.

inanimado /inani'maðo/ *adj.* inanimate.

inapetencia /inape'tenθia; inape-'tensia/ *n. f.* lack of appetite.

inaplicable /inapli'kaβle/ *a.* inapplicable; unfit.

inaudito /inau'ðito/ *a.* unheard of.

inauguración /inaugura'θion; inaugura'sion/ *n. f.* inauguration.

inaugurar /inaugu'rar/ *v.* inaugurate, open.

incandescente /inkandes'θente; inkandes'sente/ *a.* incandescent.

incansable /inkan'saβle/ *a.* tireless.

incapacidad /inkapaθi'ðað; inkapasi'ðað/ *n. f.* incapacity.

incapacitar /inkapaθi'tar; inkapasi'tar/ *v.* incapacitate.

incapaz /inka'paθ; inka'pas/ *a.* incapable.

incauto /in'kauto/ *a.* unwary.

incendiar /inθen'diar; insen'diar/ *v.* set on fire.

incendio /in'θendio; in'sendio/ *n. m.* fire; conflagration.

incertidumbre /inθerti'ðumbre; inserti'ðumbre/ *n. f.* uncertainty, suspense.

incesante /inθe'sante; inse'sante/ *a.* continual, incessant.

incidente /inθi'ðente; insi'ðente/ *n. m.* incident, event.

incienso /in'θienso; in'sienso/ *n.*
m. incense.

incierto /in'θierto; in'sierto/ *a.*
uncertain, doubtful.

incinerar /inθine'rar; insine'rar/ *v.*
incinerate; cremate.

incisión /inθi'sion; insi'sion/ *n. f.*
incision, cut.

incitamiento /inθita'miento;
insita'miento/ *n. m.* incitement,
motivation.

incitar /inθi'tar; insi'tar/ *v.* incite,
instigate.

incivil /inθi'βil; insi'βil/ *a.* impolite, rude.

inclemencia /inkle'menθia; inkle-
'mensia/ *n. f.* inclemency.

inclemente /inkle'mente/ *a.* in-
clement, merciless.

inclinación /inklina'θion; inklina-
'sion/ *n. f.* inclination, bent;
slope.

inclinar /inkli'nar/ *v.* incline; influence.

inclinarse /inkli'narse/ *v.* slope;
lean, bend over; bow.

incluir /in'kluir/ *v.* include; enclose.

inclusivo /inklu'siβo/ *a.* inclusive.

incluso /in'kluso/ *prep.* including.

incógnito /in'kognito/ *a.* unknown.

incoherente /inkoe'rente/ *a.* incoherent.

incombustible /inkombus'tiβle/ *a.*
fireproof.

incomible /inko'miβle/ *a.* inedible.

incomodar /inkomo'ðar/ *v.* disturb, bother, inconvenience.

incomodidad /inkomoði'ðað/ *n. f.*
inconvenience.

incómodo /in'komoðo/ *n. m.* uncomfortable; cumbersome; inconvenient.

incomparable /inkompa'raβle/ *a.*
incomparable.

incompatible /inkompa'tiβle/ *a.*
incompatible.

incompetencia /inkompe'tenθia;
inkompe'tensia/ *n. f.* incompe-
tence.

incompetente /inkompe'tente/ *a.*
incompetent.

incompleto /inkom'pleto/ *a.* incomplete.

incondicional /inkondiθio'nal; in-
kondisio'nal/ *a.* unconditional.

inconexo /inkone'kso/ *a.* incoherent; unconnected.

incongruente /inkoŋgru'ente/ *a.*
incongruous.

inconsciencia /inkon'sθienθia; in-
konssiensia/ *n. f.* unconsciousness.

inconsciente /inkon'sθiente; in-
kons'siente/ *a.* unconscious.

inconsecuencia /inkonse'kuenθia;
inkonse'kuensia/ *n. f.* inconsistency.

inconsecuente /inkonse'kuente/
a. inconsistent.

inconsiderado /inkonsiðe'raðo/ *a.*
inconsiderate.

inconstancia /inkons'tanθia; in-
kons'tansia/ *n. f.* changeableness.

inconstante /inkons'tante/ *a.*
changeable.

inconveniencia /inkombe'nienθia;
inkombe'niensia/ *n. f.* inconvenience; unsuitability.

inconveniente /inkombe'niente/
a. unsuitable. *m.* disadvantage;
objection.

incorporar /inkorpo'rar/ *v.* incorporate, embody.

incorporarse /inkorpo'rarse/ *v.* sit
up.

incorrecto /inko'rrekto/ *a.* incorrect, wrong.

incredulidad /inkreðuli'ðað/ *n. f.*
incredulity.

incrédulo /in'kreðulo/ *a.* incredulous.

increíble /inkre'iβle/ *a.* incredible.

incremento /inkre'mento/ *n. m.*
increase.

incubadora /inkuβa'ðora/ *n. f.* incubator.

incubar /inku'βar/ *v.* hatch.

inculto /in'kulto/ *a.* uncultivated.

incumplimento de contrato /in-
kumpli'mento de kon'trato/ *n. m.*
breach of contract.

incurable /inku'raβle/ *a.* incurable.

incurrir /inku'rrir/ *v.* incur.

indagación /indaga'θion; indaga-
'sion/ *n. f.* investigation, inquiry.

indagador /indaga'ðor/ **-ra** *n.* investigator.

indagar /inda'gar/ *v.* investigate,
inquire into.

indebido /inde'βiðo/ *a.* undue.

indecencia /inde'θenθia; inde-
'sensia/ *n. f.* indecency.

indecente /inde'θente; inde'sente/
a. indecent.

indeciso /inde'θiso; inde'siso/ *a.*
undecided.

indefenso /inde'fenso/ *a.* defenseless.

indefinido /indefi'niðo/ *a.* indefinite; undefined.

indeleble /inde'leβle/ *a.* indelible.

indemnización de despido /indemniθa'θion de des'piðo; indemnisa'sion de des'piðo/ *n. f.* severance pay.

indemnizar /indemni'θar; indemni'sar/ *v.* indemnify.

independencia /indepen'denθia; indepen'densia/ *n. f.* independence.

independiente /indepen'diente/ *a.* independent.

indesmallable /indesma'ʎaβle; indesma'yaβle/ *a.* runproof.

India /'india/ *n. f.* India.

indicación /indika'θion; indika'sion/ *n. f.* indication.

indicar /indi'kar/ *v.* indicate, point out.

indicativo /indika'tiβo/ *a. & m.* indicative.

índice /'indiθe; 'indise/ *n. m.* index; forefinger.

índice de materias /'indiθe de ma'terias; 'indise de ma'terias/ table of contents.

indicio /in'diθio; in'disio/ *n. m.* hint, clue.

indiferencia /indife'renθia; indife'rensia/ *n. f.* indifference.

indiferente /indife'rente/ *a.* indifferent.

indígena /in'dihena/ *a. & n.* native.

indigente /indi'hente/ *a.* indigent, poor.

indignación /indigna'θion; indigna'sion/ *n. f.* indignation.

indignado /indig'naðo/ *a.* indignant, incensed.

indignar /indig'nar/ *v.* incense.

indigno /in'digno/ *a.* unworthy.

indio /'indio/ **-dia** *a. & n.* Indian.

indirecto /indi'rekto/ *a.* indirect.

indiscreción /indiskre'θion; indiskre'sion/ *n. f.* indiscretion.

indiscreto /indis'kreto/ *a.* indiscreet.

indiscutible /indisku'tiβle/ *a.* unquestionable.

indispensable /indispen'saβle/ *a.* indispensable.

indisposición /indisposi'θion; indisposi'sion/ *n. f.* indisposition, ailment; reluctance.

indistinto /indis'tinto/ *a.* indistinct, unclear.

individual /indiβi'ðual/ *a.* individual.

individualidad /indiβiðuali'ðað/ *n. f.* individuality.

individuo /indi'βiðuo/ *a. & m.* individual.

indócil /in'doθil; in'dosil/ *a.* headstrong, unruly.

índole /'indole/ *n. f.* nature, character, disposition.

indolencia /indo'lenθia; indo'lensia/ *n. f.* indolence.

indolente /indo'lente/ *a.* indolent.

indómito /in'domito/ *a.* untamed, wild; unruly.

inducir /indu'θir; indu'sir/ *v.* induce, persuade.

indudable /indu'ðaβle/ *a.* certain, indubitable.

indulgencia /indul'henθia; indul'hensia/ *n. f.* indulgence.

indulgente /indul'hente/ *a.* indulgent.

indultar /indul'tar/ *v.* free; pardon.

industria /in'dustria/ *n. f.* industry.

industrial /indus'trial/ *a.* industrial.

industrioso /indus'trioso/ *a.* industrious.

inédito /i'neðito/ *a.* unpublished.

ineficaz /inefi'kaθ; inefi'kas/ *a.* inefficient.

inepto /i'nepto/ *a.* incompetent.

inequívoco /ine'kiβoko/ *a.* unmistakable.

inercia /i'nerθia; i'nersia/ *n. f.* inertia.

inerte /i'nerte/ *a.* inert.

inesperado /inespe'raðo/ *a.* unexpected.

inestable /ines'taβle/ *a.* unstable.

inevitable /ineβi'taβle/ *a.* inevitable.

inexacto /ine'ksakto/ *a.* inexact.

inexperto /ineks'perto/ *a.* unskilled.

inexplicable /inekspli'kaβle/ *a.* inexplicable, unexplainable.

infalible /infa'liβle/ *a.* infallible.

infame /in'fame/ *a.* infamous, bad.

infamia /in'famia/ *n. f.* infamy.

infancia /in'fanθia; in'fansia/ *n. f.* infancy; childhood.

infante /in'fante/ **-ta** *n.* infant.

infantería /infante'ria/ n. f. infantry.

infantil /infan'til/ a. infantile, childish.

infarto (de miocardio) /in'farto de mio'karðio/ n. m. heart attack.

infatigable /infati'gaβle/ a. untiring.

infausto /in'fausto/ a. unlucky.

infección /infek'θion; infek'sion/ n. f. infection.

infeccioso /infek'θioso; infek'sioso/ a. infectious.

infectar /infek'tar/ v. infect.

infeliz /infe'liθ; infe'lis/ a. unhappy, miserable.

inferior /infe'rior/ a. inferior; lower.

inferir /infe'rir/ v. infer; inflict.

infernal /infer'nal/ a. infernal.

infestar /infes'tar/ v. infest.

infiel /in'fiel/ a. unfaithful.

infierno /in'fierno/ n. m. hell.

infiltrar /infil'trar/ v. infiltrate.

infinidad /infini'ðað/ n. f. infinity.

infinito /infi'nito/ a. infinite.

inflación /infla'θion; infla'sion/ n. f. inflation.

inflamable /infla'maβle/ a. flammable.

inflamación /inflama'θion; inflama'sion/ n. f. inflammation.

inflamar /infla'mar/ v. inflame, set on fire.

inflar /in'flar/ v. inflate, pump up, puff up.

inflexible /infle'ksiβle/ a. inflexible, rigid.

inflexión /infle'ksion/ n. f. inflection.

infligir /infli'hir/ v. inflict.

influencia /influ'enθia; influ'ensia/ n. f. influence.

influenza /in'fluenθa; in'fluensa/ n. f. influenza, flu.

influir /in'fluir/ v. influence, sway.

influyente /influ'yente/ a. influential.

información /informa'θion; informa'sion/ n. f. information.

informal /infor'mal/ a. informal.

informar /infor'mar/ v. inform; report.

informática /infor'matika/ n. f. computer science; information technology.

informe /in'forme/ n. m. report; (pl.) information, data.

infortunio /infor'tunio/ n. m. misfortune.

infracción /infrak'θion; infrak'sion/ n. f. violation.

infracetructura /infraθetruk'tura; infrasetruk'tura/ n. f. infrastructure.

infrascrito /infras'krito/ **-ta** n. signer, undersigned.

infringir /infrin'hir/ v. infringe, violate.

infructuoso /infruk'tuoso/ a. fruitless.

infundir /infun'dir/ v. instil, inspire with.

ingeniería /inhenie'ria/ n. f. engineering.

ingeniero /inhe'niero/ **-ra** n. engineer.

ingenio /in'henio/ n. m. wit; talent.

ingeniosidad /inheniosi'ðað/ n. f. ingenuity.

ingenioso /inhe'nioso/ a. witty; ingenious.

ingenuidad /inhenui'ðað/ n. f. candor; naïveté.

ingenuo /in'henuo/ a. ingenuous, naïve, candid.

Inglaterra /ingla'terra/ n. f. England.

ingle /'ingle/ n. f. groin.

inglés /in'gles/ **-esa** a. & n. English; Englishman; Englishwoman.

ingratitud /ingrati'tuð/ n. f. ingratitude.

ingrato /in'grato/ a. ungrateful.

ingravidez /ingraβi'ðeθ; ingraβi'ðes/ n. f. weightlessness.

ingrávido /in'graβiðo/ a. weightless.

ingrediente /ingre'ðiente/ n. m. ingredient.

ingresar en /ingre'sar en/ v. enter; join.

ingreso /in'greso/ n. m. entrance; (pl.) earnings, income.

inhábil /in'aβil/ a. unskilled; incapable.

inhabilitar /inaβili'tar/ v. disqualify.

inherente /ine'rente/ a. inherent.

inhibir /ini'βir/ v. inhibit.

inhumano /inu'mano/ a. cruel, inhuman.

iniciador /iniθia'ðor; inisia'ðor/ **-ra** n. initiator.

inicial /ini'θial; ini'sial/ a. initial.

iniciar /ini'θiar; ini'siar/ v. initiate, begin.

iniciativa /iniθia'tiβa; inisia'tiβa/ n. f. initiative.

inicuo /ini'kuo/ *a.* wicked.

iniquidad /iniki'ðað/ *n. f.* iniquity; sin.

injuria /in'huria/ *n. f.* insult.

—**injuriar,** *v.*

injusticia /inhus'tiθia; inhus'tisia/ *n. f.* injustice.

injusto /in'husto/ *a.* unjust, unfair.

inmaculado /imaku'laðo/ *a.* immaculate; pure.

inmediato /ime'ðiato/ *a.* immediate.

inmensidad /imensi'ðað/ *n. f.* immensity.

inmenso /i'menso/ *a.* immense.

inmersión /imer'sion/ *n. f.* immersion.

inmigración /imigra'θion; imigra-'sion/ *n. f.* immigration.

inmigrante /imi'grante/ *a. & n.* immigrant.

inmigrar /imi'grar/ *v.* immigrate.

inminente /imi'nente/ *a.* imminent.

inmoderado /imoðe'raðo/ *a.* immoderate.

inmodesto /imo'ðesto/ *a.* immodest.

inmoral /imo'ral/ *a.* immoral.

inmoralidad /imorali'ðað/ *n. f.* immorality.

inmortal /imor'tal/ *a.* immortal.

inmortalidad /imortali'ðað/ *n. f.* immortality.

inmóvil /i'moβil/ *a.* immobile, motionless.

inmundicia /imun'diθia; imun-'disia/ *n. f.* dirt, filth.

inmune /i'mune/ *a.* immune; exempt.

inmunidad /imuni'ðað/ *n. f.* immunity.

innato /in'nato/ *a.* innate, inborn.

innecesario /inneθe'sario; innese-'sario/ *a.* unnecessary, needless.

innegable /inne'gaβle/ *a.* undeniable.

innoble /in'noβle/ *a.* ignoble.

innocuo /inno'kuo/ *a.* innocuous.

innovación /innoβa'θion; inno-βa'sion/ *n. f.* innovation.

innumerable /innume'raβle/ *a.* innumerable, countless.

inocencia /ino'θenθia; ino'sensia/ *n. f.* innocence.

inocentada /inoθen'taða; inosen-'taða/ *n. f.* practical joke.

inocente /ino'θente; ino'sente/ *a.* innocent.

inocular /inoku'lar/ *v.* inoculate.

inodoro /ino'ðoro/ *n. m.* toilet.

inofensivo /inofen'siβo/ *a.* inoffensive, harmless.

inolvidable /inolβi'ðaβle/ *a.* unforgettable.

inoportuno /inopor'tuno/ *a.* inopportune.

inoxidable /inoksi'ðaβle/ *a.* stainless.

inquietante /inkie'tante/ *a.* disturbing, worrisome, worrying, upsetting.

inquietar /inkie'tar/ *v.* disturb, worry, trouble.

inquieto /in'kieto/ *a.* anxious, uneasy, worried; restless.

inquietud /inkie'tuð/ *n. f.* concern, anxiety, worry; restlessness.

inquilino /inki'lino/ **-na** *n.* occupant, tenant.

inquirir /inki'rir/ *v.* inquire into, investigate.

inquisición /inkisi'θion; inkisi-'sion/ *n. f.* inquisition, investigation.

insaciable /insa'θiaβle; insa'siaβle/ *a.* insatiable.

insalubre /insa'luβre/ *a.* unhealthy.

insano /in'sano/ *a.* insane.

inscribir /inskri'βir/ *v.* inscribe; record.

inscribirse /inskri'βirse/ *v.* register, enroll.

inscripción /inskrip'θion; inskrip-'sion/ *n. f.* inscription; registration.

insecticida /insekti'θiða; insekti-'siða/ *n. m.* insecticide.

insecto /in'sekto/ *n. m.* insect.

inseguro /inse'guro/ *a.* unsure, uncertain; insecure, unsafe.

insensato /insen'sato/ *a.* stupid, senseless.

insensible /insen'siβle/ *a.* unfeeling, heartless.

inseparable /insepa'raβle/ *a.* inseparable.

inserción /inser'θion; inser'sion/ *n. f.* insertion.

insertar /inser'tar/ *v.* insert.

inservible /inser'βiβle/ *a.* useless.

insidioso /insi'ðioso/ *a.* insidious, crafty.

insigne /in'signe/ *a.* famous, noted.

insignia /in'signia/ *n. f.* insignia, badge.

insignificante /insignifi'kante/ *a.* insignificant, negligible.

insincero /insin'θero; insin'sero/ *a.* insincere.

insinuación /insinua'θion; insinua'sion/ *n. f.* insinuation; hint.

insinuar /insi'nuar/ *v.* insinuate, suggest, hint.

insipidez /insipi'ðeθ; insipi'ðes/ *n. f.* insipidity.

insípido /in'sipiðo/ *a.* insipid.

insistencia /insis'tenθia; insis'tensia/ *n. f.* insistence.

insistente /insis'tente/ *a.* insistent.

insistir /insis'tir/ *v.* insist.

insolación /insola'θion; insola'sion/ *n. f.* sunstroke.

insolencia /inso'lenθia; inso'lensia/ *n. f.* insolence.

insolente /inso'lente/ *a.* insolent.

insólito /in'solito/ *a.* unusual.

insolvente /insol'βente/ *a.* insolvent.

insomnio /in'somnio/ *n. m.* insomnia.

insonorizado /insonori'θaðo; insonori'saðo/ *a.* soundproof.

insonorizar /insonori'θar; insonori'sar/ *v.* soundproof.

insoportable /insopor'taβle/ *a.* unbearable.

inspección /inspek'θion; inspek'sion/ *n. f.* inspection.

inspeccionar /inspekθio'nar; inspeksio'nar/ *v.* inspect, examine.

inspector /inspek'tor/ **-ra** *n.* inspector.

inspiración /inspira'θion; inspira'sion/ *n. f.* inspiration.

inspirar /inspi'rar/ *v.* inspire.

instalación /instala'θion; instala'sion/ *n. f.* installation, fixture.

instalar /insta'lar/ *v.* install, set up.

instantánea /instan'tanea/ *n. f.* snapshot.

instantáneo /instan'taneo/ *a.* instantaneous.

instante /ins'tante/ *a. & m.* instant. **al i.,** at once.

instar /ins'tar/ *v.* coax, urge.

instigar /insti'gar/ *v.* instigate, urge.

instintivo /instin'tiβo/ *a.* instinctive.

instinto /ins'tinto/ *n. m.* instinct. **por i.,** by instinct, instinctively.

institución /institu'θion; institu'sion/ *n. f.* institution.

instituto /insti'tuto/ *n. m.* institute. **—instituir,** *v.*

institutriz /institu'triθ; institu'tris/ *n. f.* governess.

instrucción /instruk'θion; instruk'sion/ *n. f.* instruction; education.

instructivo /instruk'tiβo/ *a.* instructive.

instructor /instruk'tor/ **-ra** *n.* instructor.

instruir /ins'truir/ *v.* instruct, teach.

instrumento /instru'mento/ *n. m.* instrument.

insuficiente /insufi'θiente; insufi'siente/ *a.* insufficient.

insufrible /insu'friβle/ *a.* intolerable.

insular /insu'lar/ *a.* island, insular.

insulto /in'sulto/ *n. m.* insult. **—insultar,** *v.*

insuperable /insupe'raβle/ *a.* insuperable.

insurgente /insur'hente/ *n. & a.* insurgent, rebel.

insurrección /insurrek'θion; insurrek'sion/ *n. f.* insurrection, revolt.

insurrecto /insu'rrekto/ **-ta** *a. & n.* insurgent.

intacto /in'takto/ *a.* intact.

integral /inte'gral/ *a.* integral.

integridad /integri'ðað/ *n. f.* integrity; entirety.

íntegro /'integro/ *a.* entire; upright.

intelecto /inte'lekto/ *n. m.* intellect.

intelectual /intelek'tual/ *a. & n.* intellectual.

inteligencia /inteli'henθia; inteli'hensia/ *n. f.* intelligence.

inteligente /inteli'hente/ *a.* intelligent.

inteligible /inteli'hiβle/ *a.* intelligible.

intemperie /intem'perie/ *n. f.* bad weather.

intención /inten'θion; inten'sion/ *n. f.* intention.

intendente /inten'dente/ *n. m.* manager.

intensidad /intensi'ðað/ *n. f.* intensity.

intensificar /intensifi'kar/ *v.* intensify.

intensivo /inten'siβo/ *a.* intensive.

intenso /in'tenso/ *a.* intense.

intentar /inten'tar/ *v.* attempt, try.

intento /in'tento/ *n. m.* intent; attempt.

intercambiable /interkam'biaβle/ *a.* interchangeable.

intercambiar /interkam'βiar/ *v.* exchange, interchange.

interceptar /interθep'tar; intersep'tar/ *v.* intercept.

intercesión /interθe'sion; interse-'sion/ *n. f.* intercession.

interés /inte'res/ *n. m.* interest; concern; appeal.

interesante /intere'sante/ *a.* interesting.

interesar /intere'sar/ *v.* interest, appeal to.

interfaz /inter'faθ; inter'fas/ *n. f.* interface.

interferencia /interfe'renθia; interfe'rensia/ *n. f.* interference.

interino /inte'rino/ *a.* temporary.

interior /inte'rior/ *a.* **1.** interior, inner. —*n.* **2.** *m.* interior.

interjección /interhek'θion; interhek'sion/ *n. f.* interjection.

intermedio /inter'meðio/ *a.* **1.** intermediate. —*n.* **2.** *m.* intermediary; intermission.

interminable /intermi'naβle/ *a.* interminable, endless.

intermisión /intermi'sion/ *n. f.* intermission.

intermitente /intermi'tente/ *a.* intermittent.

internacional /internaθio'nal; internasio'nal/ *a.* international.

internarse en /inter'narse en/ *v.* enter into, go into.

Internet, el /inter'net/ *n. m.* the Internet.

interno /in'terno/ *a.* internal.

interpelar /interpe'lar/ *v.* ask questions; implore.

interponer /interpo'ner/ *v.* interpose.

interpretación /interpreta'θion; interpreta'sion/ *n. f.* interpretation.

interpretar /interpre'tar/ *v.* interpret; construe.

intérprete /in'terprete/ *n. m. & f.* interpreter; performer.

interrogación /interroga'θion; interroga'sion/ *n. f.* interrogation.

interrogar /interro'gar/ *v.* question, interrogate.

interrogativo /interroga'tiβo/ *a.* interrogative.

interrumpir /interrum'pir/ *v.* interrupt.

interrupción /interrup'θion; interrup'sion/ *n. f.* interruption.

intersección /intersek'θion; intersek'sion/ *n. f.* intersection.

intervalo /inter'βalo/ *n. m.* interval.

intervención /interβen'θion; interβen'sion/ *n. f.* intervention.

intervenir /interβe'nir/ *v.* intervene, interfere.

intestino /intes'tino/ *n. m.* intestine.

intimación /intima'θion; intima'sion/ *n. f.* intimation, hint.

intimar /inti'mar/ *v.* suggest, hint.

intimidad /intimi'ðað/ *n. f.* intimacy.

intimidar /intimi'ðar/ *v.* intimidate.

íntimo /'intimo/ **-ma** *a. & n.* intimate.

intolerable /intole'raβle/ *a.* intolerable.

intolerancia /intole'ranθia; intole-'ransia/ *n. f.* intolerance, bigotry.

intolerante /intole'rante/ *a.* intolerant.

intoxicación alimenticia /intoksika'θion alimen'tiθia; intoksika'sion alimen'tisia/ *n. f.* food poisoning.

intranquilo /intran'kilo/ *a.* uneasy.

intravenoso /intraβe'noso/ *a.* intravenous.

intrepidez /intrepi'ðeθ; intrepi'ðes/ *n. f.* daring.

intrépido /in'trepiðo/ *a.* intrepid.

intriga /in'triga/ *n. f.* intrigue, plot, scheme. —**intrigar,** *v.*

intrincado /intrin'kaðo/ *a.* intricate, involved; impenetrable.

introducción /introðuk'θion; introðuk'sion/ *n. f.* introduction.

introducir /introðu'θir; introðu'sir/ *v.* introduce.

intruso /in'truso/ **-sa** *n.* intruder.

intuición /intui'θion; intui'sion/ *n. f.* intuition.

inundación /inunda'θion; inunda'sion/ *n. f.* flood. —**inundar,** *v.*

inútil /i'nutil/ *a.* useless.

invadir /imba'ðir/ *v.* invade.

inválido /im'baliðo/ **-da** *a. & n.* invalid.

invariable /imba'riaβle/ *a.* constant.

invasión /imba'sion/ *n. f.* invasion.

invasor /imba'sor/ **-ra** *n.* invader.

invencible /imben'θiβle; imben-'siβle/ a. invincible.

invención /imben'θion; imben-'sion/ n. f. invention.

inventar /imben'tar/ v. invent; devise.

inventario /imben'tario/ n. m. inventory.

inventivo /imben'tiβo/ a. inventive.

invento /im'bento/ n. m. invention.

inventor /imben'tor/ -ra n. inventor.

invernáculo /imber'nakulo/ n. m. greenhouse.

invernal /imber'nal/ a. wintry.

inverosímil /imbero'simil/ a. improbable, unlikely.

inversión /imber'sion/ n. f. inversion; Com. investment.

inverso /im'berso/ a. inverse, reverse.

inversor /imber'sor/ -ra n. investor.

invertir /imber'tir/ v. invert; reverse; Com. invest.

investigación /imbestiga'θion; imbestiga'sion/ n. f. investigation.

investigador /imbestiga'ðor/ -ra n. investigator; researcher.

investigar /imbesti'gar/ v. investigate.

invierno /im'bierno/ n. m. winter.

invisible /imbi'siβle/ a. invisible.

invitación /imbita'θion; imbita-'sion/ n. f. invitation.

invitar /imbi'tar/ v. invite.

invocar /imbo'kar/ v. invoke.

involuntario /imbolun'tario/ a. involuntary.

inyección /inyek'θion; inyek'sion/ n. f. injection.

inyectar /inyek'tar/ v. inject.

ir /ir/ v. go. **irse,** go away, leave.

ira /'ira/ n. f. anger, ire.

iracundo /ira'kundo/ a. wrathful, irate.

iris /'iris/ n. m. iris. **arco i.,** rainbow.

Irlanda /ir'landa/ n. f. Ireland.

irlandés /irlan'des/ **-esa** a. & n. Irish; Irishman, Irishwoman.

ironía /iro'nia/ n. f. irony.

irónico /i'roniko/ a. ironical.

irracional /irraθio'nal; irrasio'nal/ a. irrational; insane.

irradiación /irraðia'θion; irraðia-'sion/ n. f. irradiation.

irradiar /irra'ðiar/ v. radiate.

irrazonable /irraθo'naβle; irraso-'naβle/ a. unreasonable.

irregular /irregu'lar/ a. irregular.

irreligioso /irreli'hioso/ a. irreligious.

irremediable /irreme'ðiaβle/ a. irremediable, hopeless.

irresistible /irresis'tiβle/ a. irresistible.

irresoluto /irreso'luto/ a. irresolute, wavering.

irrespetuoso /irrespe'tuoso/ a. disrespectful.

irreverencia /irreβe'renθia; irre-βe'rensia/ n. f. irreverence.

irreverente /irreβe'rente/ adj. irreverent.

irrigación /irriga'θion; irriga'sion/ n. f. irrigation.

irrigar /irri'gar/ v. irrigate.

irritación /irrita'θion; irrita'sion/ n. f. irritation.

irritar /irri'tar/ v. irritate.

irrupción /irrup'θion; irrup'sion/ n. f. raid, attack.

isla /'isla/ n. f. island.

isleño /is'leɲo/ **-ña** n. islander.

israelita /israe'lita/ n. & a. Israelite.

Italia /i'talia/ n. f. Italy.

italiano /ita'liano/ **-na** a. & n. Italian.

itinerario /itine'rario/ n. m. itinerary; timetable.

IVA, abbrev. (**impuesto sobre el valor añadido**) VAT (value-added tax).

izar /i'θar; i'sar/ v. hoist.

izquierda /iθ'kierða; is'kierða/ n. f. left (hand, side).

izquierdista /iθ'kierðista; is'kier-ðista/ n. & a. leftist.

izquierdo /iθ'kierðo; is'kierðo/ a. left.

jabalí /haβa'li/ *n. m.* wild boar.
jabón /ha'βon/ *n. m.* soap. **j. en polvo,** soap powder.
jabonar /haβo'nar/ *v.* soap.
jaca /'haka/ *n. f.* nag.
jacinto /ha'θinto; ha'sinto/ *n. m.* hyacinth.
jactancia /hak'tanθia; hak'tansia/ *n. f.* boast. —**jactarse,** *v.*
jactancioso /haktan'θioso; haktan'sioso/ *a.* boastful.
jadear /haðe'ar/ *v.* pant, puff.
jaez /ha'eθ; ha'es/ *n. m.* harness; kind.
jalar /ha'lar/ *v.* haul, pull.
jalea /ha'lea/ *n. f.* jelly.
jaleo /ha'leo/ *n. m.* row, uproar; hassle.
jamás /ha'mas/ *adv.* never, ever.
jamón /ha'mon/ *n. m.* ham.
Japón /ha'pon/ *n. m.* Japan.
japonés /hapo'nes/ **-esa** *a. & n.* Japanese.
jaqueca /ha'keka/ *n. f.* headache.
jarabe /ha'raβe/ *n. m.* syrup.
jaranear /harane'ar/ *v.* jest; carouse.
jardín /har'ðin/ *n. m.* garden.
jardín de infancia /har'ðin de in'fanθia; har'ðin de in'fansia/ nursery school.
jardinero /harði'nero/ **-ra** *n.* gardener.
jarra /'harra/ *n. f.* jar; pitcher.
jarro /'harro/ *n. m.* jug, pitcher.
jaspe /'haspe/ *n. m.* jasper.
jaula /'haula/ *n. f.* cage; coop.
jauría /hau'ria/ *n. f.* pack of hounds.
jazmín /haθ'min; has'min/ *n. m.* jasmine.
jefatura /hefa'tura/ *n. f.* headquarters.
jefe /'hefe/ **-fa** *n.* chief, boss.
jefe de comedor /'hefe de kome-'ðor/ headwaiter.
jefe de sala /'hefe de 'sala/ maître d'.
jefe de taller /'hefe de ta'ʎer; 'hefe de ta'yer/ foreman.
Jehová /heo'βa/ *n. m.* Jehovah.
jengibre /hen'hiβre/ *n. m.* ginger.
jerez /he're θ; he'res/ *n. m.* sherry.
jerga /'herga/ *n. f.* slang.
jergón /her'gon/ *n. m.* straw mattress.

jerigonza /heri'gonθa; heri'gonsa/ *n. f.* jargon.
jeringa /he'riŋga/ *n. f.* syringe.
jeringar /heriŋ'gar/ *v.* inject; annoy.
jeroglífico /hero'glifiko/ *n. m.* hieroglyph.
jersey /her'sei/ *n. m.* pullover; **j. de cuello alto,** turtleneck sweater.
Jerusalén /herusa'len/ *n. m.* Jerusalem.
jesuita /he'suita/ *n. m.* Jesuit.
Jesús /he'sus/ *n. m.* Jesus.
jeta /'heta/ *n. f.* snout.
jícara /'hikara/ *n. f.* cup.
jinete /hi'nete/ **-ta** *n.* horseman.
jingoísmo /hiŋgo'ismo/ *n. m.* jingoism.
jingoísta /hiŋgo'ista/ *n. & a.* jingoist.
jira /'hira/ *n. f.* picnic; outing.
jirafa /hi'rafa/ *n. f.* giraffe.
jiu-jitsu /hiu'hitsu/ *n. m.* jujitsu.
jocundo /ho'kundo/ *a.* jovial.
jornada /hor'naða/ *n. f.* journey; day's work.
jornal /hor'nal/ *n. m.* day's wage.
jornalero /horna'lero/ *n. m.* day laborer, workman.
joroba /ho'roβa/ *n. f.* hump.
jorobado /horo'βaðo/ *a.* humpbacked.
joven /'hoβen/ *a.* **1.** young. —*n.* **2.** *m. & f.* young person.
jovial /ho'βial/ *a.* jovial, jolly.
jovialidad /hoβiali'ðað/ *n. f.* joviality.
joya /'hoia/ *n. f.* jewel, gem.
joyas de fantasía /'hoias de fanta'sia/ *n. f.pl.* costume jewelry.
joyelero /hoie'lero/ *n. m.* jewel box.
joyería /hoie'ria/ *n. f.* jewelry; jewelry store.
joyero /ho'iero/ *n. m.* jeweler; jewel case.
juanete /hua'nete/ *n. m.* bunion.
jubilación /huβila'θion; huβila'-sion/ *n. f.* retirement; pension.
jubilar /huβi'lar/ *v.* retire, pension.
jubileo /huβi'leo/ *n. m.* jubilee, public festivity.
júbilo /'huβilo/ *n. m.* glee, rejoicing.
jubiloso /huβi'loso/ *a.* joyful, gay.
judaico /hu'ðaiko/ *a.* Jewish.

judaísmo /huða'ismo/ *n. m.* Judaism.

judía /hu'ðia/ *n. f.* bean, string bean.

judicial /huði'θial; huði'sial/ *a.* judicial.

judío /hu'ðio/ **-día** *a. & n.* Jewish; Jew.

juego /'huego/ *n. m.* game; play; gambling; set. **j. de damas,** checkers. **j. limpio,** fair play.

Juegos Olímpicos /huegos o'limpikos/ *n. m.pl.* Olympic Games.

juerga /'huerga/ *n. f.* spree.

jueves /'hueβes/ *n. m.* Thursday.

juez /hueθ; hues/ *n. m.* judge.

jugador /huga'ðor/ **-ra** *n.* player.

jugar /hu'gar/ *v.* play; gamble.

juglar /hug'lar/ *n. m.* minstrel.

jugo /'hugo/ *n. m.* juice. **j. de naranja,** orange juice.

jugoso /hu'goso/ *a.* juicy.

juguete /hu'gete/ *n. m.* toy, plaything.

juguetear /hugete'ar/ *v.* trifle.

juguetón /huge'ton/ *a.* playful.

juicio /'huiθio; 'huisio/ *n. m.* sense, wisdom, judgment; sanity; trial.

juicioso /hui'θioso; hui'sioso/ *a.* wise, judicious.

julio /'hulio/ *n. m.* July.

jumento /hu'mento/ *n. m.* donkey.

junco /'hunko/ *n. m.* reed, rush.

jungla /'huŋgla/ *n. f.* jungle.

junio /'hunio/ *n. m.* June.

junípero /hu'nipero/ *n. m.* juniper.

junquillo /hun'kiʎo; hun'kiyo/ *n. m.* jonquil.

junta /'hunta/ *n. f.* board, council; joint, coupling.

juntamente /hunta'mente/ *adv.* jointly.

juntar /hun'tar/ *v.* join; connect; assemble.

junto /'hunto/ *a.* together. **j. a,** next to.

juntura /hun'tura/ *n. f.* joint, juncture.

jurado /hu'raðo/ *n. m.* jury.

juramento /hura'mento/ *n. m.* oath.

jurar /hu'rar/ *v.* swear.

jurisconsulto /huriskon'sulto/ *n. m.* jurist.

jurisdicción /hurisðik'θion; hurisðik'sion/ *n. f.* jurisdiction; territory.

jurisprudencia /hurispru'ðenθia; hurispru'ðensia/ *n. f.* jurisprudence.

justa /'husta/ *n. f.* joust. —**justar,** *v.*

justicia /hus'tiθia; hus'tisia/ *n. f.* justice, equity.

justiciero /husti'θiero; husti'siero/ *a.* just.

justificación /hustifika'θion; hustifika'sion/ *n. f.* justification.

justificadamente /hustifikaða'mente/ *adv.* justifiably.

justificar /hustifi'kar/ *v.* justify, warrant.

justo /'husto/ *a.* right; exact; just; righteous.

juvenil /huβe'nil/ *a.* youthful.

juventud /huβen'tuð/ *n. f.* youth.

juzgado /huθ'gaðo; hus'gaðo/ *n. m.* court.

juzgar /huθ'gar; hus'gar/ *v.* judge, estimate.

K L

káiser /'kaiser/ *n. m.* kaiser.

karate /ka'rate/ *n. m.* karate.

kepis /'kepis/ *n. m.* military cap.

kerosena /kero'sena/ *n. f.* kerosene.

kilo /'kilo/ **kilogramo** *n. m.* kilogram.

kilohercio /kilo'erθio; kilo'ersio/ *n. m.* kilohertz.

kilolitro /kilo'litro/ *n. m.* kiloliter.

kilometraje /kilome'trahe/ *n. m.* mileage.

kilómetro /ki'lometro/ *n. m.* kilometer.

kiosco /'kiosko/ *n. m.* newsstand; pavilion.

la /la/ *art. & pron.* **1.** the; the one. —*pron.* **2.** her, it, you; (*pl.*) them, you.

laberinto /laβe'rinto/ *n. m.* labyrinth, maze.

labia /'laβia/ *n. f.* eloquence, fluency.

labio /'laβio/ *n. m.* lip.

labor /la'βor/ *n. f.* labor, work.

laborar /laβo'rar/ *v.* work; till.

laboratorio /laβora'torio/ *n. m.* laboratory.

laborioso /laβo'rioso/ *a.* industrious.

labrador /laβra'ðor/ *n. m.* farmer.

labranza /la'βranθa; la'βransa/ *n. f.* farming; farmland.

labrar /la'βrar/ *v.* work, till.

labriego /la'βriego/ **-ga** *n.* peasant.

laca /'laka/ *n. f.* shellac.

lacio /'laθio; 'lasio/ *a.* withered; limp; straight.

lactar /lak'tar/ *v.* nurse, suckle.

lácteo /'lakteo/ *a.* milky.

ladear /laðe'ar/ *v.* tilt, tip; sway.

ladera /la'ðera/ *n. f.* slope.

ladino /la'ðino/ *a.* cunning, crafty.

lado /'laðo/ *n. m.* side. **al l. de,** beside. **de l.,** sideways.

ladra /'laðra/ *n. f.* barking. **—ladrar,** *v.*

ladrillo /la'ðriʎo; la'ðriyo/ *n. m.* brick.

ladrón /la'ðron/ **-ona** *n.* thief, robber.

lagarto /la'garto/ *n. m.* lizard; (Mex.) alligator.

lago /'lago/ *n. m.* lake.

lágrima /'lagrima/ *n. f.* tear.

lagrimear /lagrime'ar/ *v.* weep, cry.

laguna /la'guna/ *n. f.* lagoon; gap.

laico /'laiko/ *a.* lay.

laja /'laha/ *n. f.* stone slab.

lamentable /lamen'taβle/ *a.* lamentable.

lamentación /lamenta'θion; lamenta'sion/ *n. f.* lamentation.

lamentar /lamen'tar/ *v.* lament; wail; regret, be sorry.

lamento /la'mento/ *n. m.* lament, wail.

lamer /la'mer/ *v.* lick; lap.

lámina /'lamina/ *n. f.* print, illustration.

lámpara /'lampara/ *n. f.* lamp.

lampiño /lam'piɲo/ *a.* beardless.

lana /'lana/ *n. f.* wool.

lanar /la'nar/ *a.* woolen.

lance /'lanθe; 'lanse/ *n. m.* throw; episode; quarrel.

lancha /'lantʃa/ *n. f.* launch; small boat.

lanchón /lan'tʃon/ *n. m.* barge.

langosta /laŋ'gosta/ *n. f.* lobster; locust.

langostino /laŋgos'tino/ *n. m.* king prawn.

languidecer /laŋguiðe'θer; laŋguiðe'ser/ *v.* languish, pine.

languidez /laŋgui'ðeθ; laŋgui'ðes/ *n. f.* languidness.

lánguido /'laŋguiðo/ *a.* languid.

lanza /'lanθa; 'lansa/ *n. f.* lance, spear.

lanzada /lan'θaða; lan'saða/ *n. f.* thrust, throw.

lanzar /lan'θar; lan'sar/ *v.* throw, hurl; launch.

lañar /la'ɲar/ *v.* cramp; clamp.

lapicero /lapi'θero; lapi'sero/ *n. m.* mechanical pencil.

lápida /'lapiða/ *n. f.* stone; tombstone.

lápiz /'lapiθ; 'lapis/ *n. m.* pencil; crayon.

lápiz de ojos /'lapiθ de 'ohos; 'lapis de 'ohos/ *n. m.* eyeliner.

lapso /'lapso/ *n. m.* lapse.

lardo /'larðo/ *n. m.* lard.

largar /lar'gar/ *v.* loosen; free.

largo /'largo/ *a.* **1.** long. **a lo l. de,** along. **—n. 2.** *m.* length.

largometraje /largome'trahe/ *n. m.* feature film.

largor /lar'gor/ *n. m.* length.

largueza /lar'geθa; lar'gesa/ *n. f.* generosity; length.

largura /lar'gura/ *n. f.* length.

laringe /la'rinhe/ *n. f.* larynx.

larva /'larβa/ *n. f.* larva.

lascivia /las'θiβia; las'siβia/ *n. f.* lasciviousness.

lascivo /las'θiβo; las'siβo/ *a.* lascivious.

láser /'laser/ *n. m.* laser.

laso /'laso/ *a.* weary.

lástima /'lastima/ *n. f.* pity. **ser l.,** to be a pity, to be too bad.

lastimar /lasti'mar/ *v.* hurt, injure.

lastimoso /lasti'moso/ *a.* pitiful.

lastre /'lastre/ *n. m.* ballast. **—lastrar,** *v.*

lata /'lata/ *n. f.* tin can; tin (plate); *Colloq.* annoyance, bore.

latente /la'tente/ *a.* latent.

lateral /late'ral/ *a.* lateral, side.

latigazo /lati'gaθo; lati'gaso/ *n. m.* lash, whipping.

látigo /'latigo/ *n. m.* whip.

latín /la'tin/ *n. m.* Latin (language).

latino /la'tino/ *a.* Latin.

latir /la'tir/ *v.* beat, pulsate.

latitud /lati'tuð/ *n. f.* latitude.

latón /la'ton/ *n. m.* brass.

laúd /la'uð/ *n. m.* lute.

laudable /lau'ðaβle/ *a.* laudable.

láudano /'lauðano/ *n. m.* laudanum.

laurel /lau'rel/ *n. m.* laurel.

lava /'laβa/ *n. f.* lava.

lavabo /la'βaβo/ **lavamanos** *n. m.* washroom, lavatory.

lavadora /laβa'ðora/ *n. f.* washing machine.

lavandera /laβan'dera/ *n. f.* washerwoman, laundress.

lavandería /laβande'ria/ *f.* laundry; laundromat.

lavaplatos /laβa'platos/ *n.* **1.** *m.* dishwasher (machine). —*n.* **2.** *m. & f.* dishwasher (person).

lavar /la'βar/ *v.* wash.

lavatorio /laβa'torio/ *n. m.* lavatory.

laya /'laia/ *n. f.* spade. —**layar,** *v.*

lazar /la'θar; la'sar/ *v.* lasso.

lazareto /laθa'reto; lasa'reto/ *n. m.* isolation hospital; quarantine station.

lazo /'laθo; 'laso/ *n. m.* tie, knot; bow; loop.

le /le/ *pron.* him, her, you; (*pl.*) them, you.

leal /le'al/ *a.* loyal.

lealtad /leal'taŏ/ *n. f.* loyalty, allegiance.

lebrel /le'βrel/ *n. m.* greyhound.

lección /lek'θion; lek'sion/ *n. f.* lesson.

leche /'letʃe/ *n. f.* milk.

lechería /letʃe'ria/ *n. f.* dairy.

lechero /le'tʃero/ *n. m.* milkman.

lecho /'letʃo/ *n. m.* bed; couch.

lechón /le'tʃon/ *n. m.* pig.

lechoso /le'tʃoso/ *a.* milky.

lechuga /le'tʃuga/ *n. f.* lettuce.

lechuza /le'tʃuθa; le'tʃusa/ *n. f.* owl.

lecito /le'θito; le'sito/ *n. m.* yolk.

lector /lek'tor/ **-ra** *n.* reader.

lectura /lek'tura/ *n. f.* reading.

leer /le'er/ *v.* read.

legación /lega'θion; lega'sion/ *n. f.* legation.

legado /le'gaðo/ *n. m.* bequest.

legal /le'gal/ *a.* legal, lawful.

legalizar /legali'θar; legali'sar/ *v.* legalize.

legar /le'gar/ *v.* bequeath, leave, will.

legible /le'hiβle/ *a.* legible.

legión /le'hion/ *n. f.* legion.

legislación /lehisla'θion; lehisla'sion/ *n. f.* legislation.

legislador /lehisla'ðor/ **-ra** *n.* legislator.

legislar /lehis'lar/ *v.* legislate.

legislativo /lehisla'tiβo/ *a.* legislative.

legislatura /lehisla'tura/ *n. f.* legislature.

legítimo /le'hitimo/ *a.* legitimate.

lego /'lego/ *n. m.* layman.

legua /'legua/ *n. f.* league (measure).

legumbre /le'gumbre/ *n. f.* vegetable.

lejano /le'hano/ *a.* distant, far-off.

lejía /le'hia/ *n. f.* lye.

lejos /'lehos/ *adv.* far. **a lo l.,** in the distance.

lelo /'lelo/ *a.* stupid, foolish.

lema /'lema/ *n. m.* theme; slogan.

lengua /'leŋgua/ *n. f.* tongue; language.

lenguado /leŋ'guaðo/ *n. m.* sole, flounder.

lenguaje /leŋ'guahe/ *n. m.* speech; language.

lenguaraz /leŋgua'raθ; leŋgua'ras/ *a.* talkative.

lente /'lente/ *n.* **1.** *m. or f.* lens. **2.** *m.pl.* eyeglasses.

lenteja /len'teha/ *n. f.* lentil.

lentilla /len'tiʎa; len'tiya/ *n. f.* contact lens.

lentitud /lenti'tuð/ *n. f.* slowness.

lento /'lento/ *a.* slow.

leña /'leɲa/ *n. f.* wood, firewood.

león /le'on/ *n. m.* lion.

leopardo /leo'parðo/ *n. m.* leopard.

lerdo /'lerðo/ *a.* dull-witted.

lesbiana /les'βiana/ *n. f.* lesbian.

lesión /le'sion/ *n. f.* wound; damage.

letanía /leta'nia/ *n. f.* litany.

letárgico /le'tarhiko/ *a.* lethargic.

letargo /le'targo/ *n. m.* lethargy.

letra /'letra/ *n. f.* letter (of alphabet); print; words (of a song).

letrado /le'traðo/ *a.* **1.** learned. —*n.* **2.** *m.* lawyer.

letrero /le'trero/ *n. m.* sign, poster.

leva /'leβa/ *n. f. Mil.* draft.

levadura /leβa'ðura/ *n. f.* yeast, leavening, baking powder.

levantador /leβanta'ðor/ *n. m.* lifter; rebel, mutineer.

levantar /leβan'tar/ *v.* raise, lift.

levantarse /leβan'tarse/ *v.* rise, get up; stand up.

levar /le'βar/ *v.* weigh (anchor).

leve /'leβe/ *a.* slight, light.

levita /le'βita/ *n. f.* frock coat.

léxico /'leksiko/ *n. m.* lexicon, dictionary.
ley /lei/ *n. f.* law, statute.
leyenda /le'ienda/ *n. f.* legend.
lezna /'leθna; 'lesna/ *n. f.* awl.
libación /liβa'θion; liβa'sion/ *n. f.* libation.
libelo /li'βelo/ *n. m.* libel.
libélula /li'βelula/ *n. f.* dragonfly.
liberación /liβera'θion; liβera'sion/ *n. f.* liberation, release.
liberal /liβe'ral/ *a.* liberal.
libertad /liβer'taδ/ *n. f.* liberty, freedom.
libertador /liβerta'δor/ **-ra** *n.* liberator.
libertar /liβer'tar/ *v.* free, liberate.
libertinaje /liβerti'nahe/ *n. m.* licentiousness.
libertino /liβer'tino/ **-na** *n.* libertine.
libídine /li'βiδine/ *n. f.* licentiousness; lust.
libidinoso /liβiδi'noso/ *a.* libidinous; lustful.
libra /'liβra/ *n. f.* pound.
libranza /li'βranθa; li'βransa/ *n. f.* draft, bill of exchange.
librar /li'βrar/ *v.* free, rid.
libre /'liβre/ *a.* free, unoccupied.
librería /liβre'ria/ *n. f.* bookstore.
librero /li'βrero/ **-ra** *n.* bookseller.
libreta /li'βreta/ *n. f.* notebook; booklet.
libreto /li'βreto/ *n. m.* libretto.
libro /'liβro/ *n. m.* book.
libro de texto /'liβro de 'teksto/ textbook.
licencia /li'θenθia; li'sensia/ *n. f.* permission, license, leave; furlough. **l. de armas,** gun permit.
licenciado /liθen'θiaδo; lisen'siaδo/ **-da** *n.* graduate.
licencioso /liθen'θioso; lisen'sioso/ *a.* licentious.
lícito /'liθito; 'lisito/ *a.* lawful.
licor /li'kor/ *n. m.* liquor.
licuadora /likua'δora/ *n. f.* blender (for food).
lid /liδ/ *n. f.* fight. —**lidiar,** *v.*
líder /'liδer/ *n. m. & f.* leader.
liebre /'lieβre/ *n. f.* hare.
lienzo /'lienθo; 'lienso/ *n. m.* linen.
liga /'liga/ *n. f.* league, confederacy; garter.
ligadura /liga'δura/ *n. f.* ligature.
ligar /li'gar/ *v.* tie, bind, join.
ligero /li'hero/ *a.* light; fast, nimble.

ligustro /li'gustro/ *n. m.* privet.
lija /'liha/ *n. f.* sandpaper.
lijar /li'har/ *v.* sandpaper.
lima /'lima/ *n. f.* file; lime.
limbo /'limbo/ *n. m.* limbo.
limitación /limita'θion; limita'sion/ *n. f.* limitation.
límite /'limite/ *n. m.* limit. —**limitar,** *v.*
limo /'limo/ *n. m.* slime.
limón /li'mon/ *n. m.* lemon.
limonada /limo'naδa/ *n. f.* lemonade.
limonero /limo'nero/ *n. m.* lemon tree.
limosna /li'mosna/ *n. f.* alms.
limosnero /limos'nero/ **-ra** *n.* beggar.
limpiabotas /limpia'βotas/ *n. m.* bootblack.
limpiadientes /limpia'δientes/ *n. m.* toothpick.
limpiar /lim'piar/ *v.* clean, wash, wipe.
límpido /'limpiδo/ *a.* limpid, clear.
limpieza /lim'pieθa; lim'piesa/ *n. f.* cleanliness.
limpio /'limpio/ *n. m.* clean.
limusina /limu'sina/ *n. f.* limousine.
linaje /li'nahe/ *n. m.* lineage, ancestry.
linaza /li'naθa; li'nasa/ *n. f.* linseed.
lince /'linθe; 'linse/ *a.* sharpsighted, observing.
linchamiento /lintʃa'miento/ *n. m.* lynching.
linchar /lin'tʃar/ *v.* lynch.
lindar /lin'dar/ *v.* border, bound.
linde /'linde/ *n. m.* boundary; landmark.
lindero /lin'dero/ *n. m.* boundary.
lindo /'lindo/ *a.* pretty, lovely, nice.
línea /'linea/ *n. f.* line.
línea de puntos /'linea de 'puntos/ dotted line.
lineal /line'al/ *a.* lineal.
linfa /'linfa/ *n. f.* lymph.
lingüista /liŋ'guista/ *n. m. & f.* linguist.
lingüístico /liŋ'guistiko/ *a.* linguistic.
linimento /lini'mento/ *n. m.* liniment.
lino /'lino/ *n. m.* linen; flax.
linóleo /li'noleo/ *n. m.* linoleum.
linterna /lin'terna/ *n. f.* lantern; flashlight.

lío /'lio/ *n. m.* pack, bundle; mess; scrape; hassle.

liquidación /likiða'θion; likiða-'sion/ *n. f.* liquidation.

liquidar /liki'ðar/ *v.* liquidate; settle up.

líquido /'likiðo/ *a. & m.* liquid.

lira /'lira/ *n. f.* lyre.

lírico /'liriko/ *a.* lyric.

lirio /'lirio/ *n. m.* lily.

lirismo /li'rismo/ *n. m.* lyricism.

lis /lis/ *n. f.* lily.

lisiar /li'siar/ *v.* cripple, lame.

liso /'liso/ *a.* smooth, even.

lisonja /li'sonha/ *n. f.* flattery.

lisonjear /lisonhe'ar/ *v.* flatter.

lisonjero /lison'hero/ **-ra** *n.* flatterer.

lista /'lista/ *n. f.* list; stripe; menu.

lista negra /'lista 'negra/ blacklist.

listar /lis'tar/ *v.* list; put on a list.

listo /'listo/ *a.* ready; smart, clever.

listón /lis'ton/ *n. m.* ribbon.

litera /li'tera/ *n. f.* litter, bunk, berth.

literal /lite'ral/ *a.* literal.

literario /lite'rario/ *a.* literary.

literato /lite'rato/ *n. m.* literary person, writer.

literatura /litera'tura/ *n. f.* literature.

litigación /litiga'θion; litiga'sion/ *n. f.* litigation.

litigio /li'tihio/ *n. m.* litigation; lawsuit.

litoral /lito'ral/ *n. m.* coast.

litro /'litro/ *n. m.* liter.

liturgia /li'turhia/ *n. f.* liturgy.

liviano /li'βiano/ *a.* light (in weight).

lívido /'liβiðo/ *a.* livid.

llaga /'ʎaga; 'yaga/ *n. f.* sore.

llama /'ʎama; 'yama/ *n. f.* flame; llama.

llamada /ʎa'maða; ya'maða/ *n. f.* call; knock. —**llamar,** *v.*

llamarse /ʎa'marse; ya'marse/ *v.* be called, be named. **se llama...** etc., his name is... etc.

llamativo /ʎama'tiβo; yama'tiβo/ *a.* gaudy, showy.

llamear /ʎame'ar; yame'ar/ *v.* blaze.

llaneza /ʎa'neθa; ya'nesa/ *n. f.* simplicity.

llano /'ʎano; 'yano/ *a.* **1.** flat, level; plain. —*n.* **2.** *m.* plain.

llanta /'ʎanta; 'yanta/ *n. f.* tire.

llanto /'ʎanto; 'yanto/ *n. m.* crying, weeping.

llanura /ʎa'nura; ya'nura/ *n. f.* prairie, plain.

llave /'ʎaβe; 'yaβe/ *n. f.* key; wrench; faucet; *Elec.* switch. **ll. inglesa,** monkey wrench.

llegada /ʎe'gaða; ye'gaða/ *n. f.* arrival.

llegar /ʎe'gar; ye'gar/ *v.* arrive; reach. **ll. a ser,** become, come to be.

llenar /ʎe'nar; ye'nar/ *v.* fill.

lleno /'ʎeno; 'yeno/ *a.* full.

llenura /ʎe'nura; ye'nura/ *n. f.* abundance.

llevadero /ʎeβa'ðero; yeβa'ðero/ *a.* tolerable.

llevar /ʎe'βar; ye'βar/ *v.* take, carry, bear; wear (clothes). **ll. a cabo,** carry out.

llevarse /ʎe'βarse; ye'βarse/ *v.* take away, run away with. **ll. bien,** get along well.

llorar /ʎo'rar; yo'rar/ *v.* cry, weep.

lloroso /ʎo'roso; yo'roso/ *a.* sorrowful, tearful.

llover /ʎo'βer; yo'βer/ *v.* rain.

llovido /ʎo'βiðo; yo'βiðo/ *n. m.* stowaway.

llovizna /ʎo'βiθna; yo'βisna/ *n. f.* drizzle, sprinkle. —**lloviznar,** *v.*

lluvia /'ʎuβia; 'yuβia/ *n. f.* rain.

lluvia ácida /'ʎuβia 'aθiða; 'yuβia 'asiða/ acid rain.

lluvioso /ʎu'βioso; yu'βioso/ *a.* rainy.

lo /lo/ *pron.* the; him, it, you; (*pl.*) them, you.

loar /lo'ar/ *v.* praise, laud.

lobina /lo'βina/ *n. f.* striped bass.

lobo /'loβo/ *n. m.* wolf.

lóbrego /'loβrego/ *a.* murky; dismal.

local /lo'kal/ *a.* **1.** local. —*n.* **2.** *m.* site.

localidad /lokali'ðað/ *n. f.* locality, location; seat (in theater).

localizar /lokali'θar; lokali'sar/ *v.* localize.

loción /lo'θion; lo'sion/ *n. f.* lotion.

loco /'loko/ **-ca** *a.* **1.** crazy, insane, mad. —*n.* **2.** lunatic.

locomotora /lokomo'tora/ *n. f.* locomotive.

locuaz /lo'kuaθ; lo'kuas/ *a.* loquacious.

locución /loku'θion; loku'sion/ *n. f.* locution, expression.

locura /lo'kura/ *n. f.* folly; madness, insanity.

lodo /'loðo/ *n. m.* mud.

lodoso /lo'ðoso/ *a.* muddy.

lógica /'lohika/ *n. f.* logic.

lógico /'lohiko/ *a.* logical.

lograr /lo'grar/ *v.* achieve; succeed in.

logro /'logro/ *n. m.* accomplishment.

lombriz /lom'βriθ; lom'βris/ *n. f.* earthworm.

lomo /'lomo/ *n. m.* loin; back (of an animal).

lona /'lona/ *n. f.* canvas, tarpaulin.

longevidad /lonheβi'ðað/ *n. f.* longevity.

longitud /lonhi'tuð/ *n. f.* longitude; length.

lonja /'lonha/ *n. f.* shop; market.

lontananza /lonta'nanθa; lonta-'nansa/ *n. f.* distance.

loro /'loro/ *n. m.* parrot.

losa /'losa/ *n. f.* slab.

lote /'lote/ *n. m.* lot, share.

lotería /lote'ria/ *n. f.* lottery.

loza /'loθa; 'losa/ *n. f.* china, crockery.

lozanía /loθa'nia; losa'nia/ *n. f.* freshness, vigor.

lozano /lo'θano; lo'sano/ *a.* fresh, spirited.

lubricación /luβrika'θion; luβrika-'sion/ *n. f.* lubrication.

lubricar /luβri'kar/ *v.* lubricate.

lucero /lu'θero; lu'sero/ *n. m.* (bright) star.

lucha /'lutʃa/ *n. f.* fight, struggle; wrestling. **—luchar,** *v.*

luchador /lutʃa'ðor/ **-ra** *n.* fighter, wrestler.

lúcido /lu'θiðo; lu'siðo/ *a.* lucid, clear.

luciente /lu'θiente; lu'siente/ *a.* shining, bright.

luciérnaga /lu'θiernaga; lu'siernaga/ *n. f.* firefly.

lucimiento /luθi'miento; lusi-'miento/ *n. m.* success; splendor.

lucir /lu'θir; lu'sir/ *v.* shine, sparkle; show off.

lucrativo /lukra'tiβo/ *a.* lucrative, profitable.

luego /'luego/ *adv.* right away; afterwards, next. **l. que,** as soon as. **desde l.,** of course. **hasta l.,** good-bye, so long.

lugar /lu'gar/ *n. m.* place, spot; space, room.

lúgubre /'luguβre/ *a.* gloomy; dismal.

lujo /'luho/ *n. m.* luxury. **de l.,** deluxe.

lujoso /lu'hoso/ *a.* luxurious.

lumbre /'lumbre/ *n. f.* fire; light.

luminoso /lumi'noso/ *a.* luminous.

luna /'luna/ *n. f.* moon.

lunar /lu'nar/ *n. m.* beauty mark, mole; polka dot.

lunático /lu'natiko/ **-ca** *a. & n.* lunatic.

lunes /'lunes/ *n. m.* Monday.

luneta /lu'neta/ *n. f. Theat.* orchestra seat.

lupa /'lupa/ *n. f.* magnifying glass.

lustre /'lustre/ *n. m.* polish, shine. **—lustrar,** *v.*

lustroso /lus'troso/ *a.* shiny.

luto /'luto/ *n. m.* mourning.

luz /luθ; lus/ *n. f.* light. **dar a l.,** give birth to.

M

maca /'maka/ *n. f.* blemish, flaw.

macaco /ma'kako/ *a.* ugly, horrid.

macareno /maka'reno/ *a.* boasting.

macarrones /maka'rrones/ *n. m.pl.* macaroni.

macear /maθe'ar; mase'ar/ *v.* molest, push around.

macedonia de frutas /maθe'ðonia de 'frutas; mase'ðonia de 'frutas/ *n. f.* fruit salad.

maceta /ma'θeta; ma'seta/ *n. f.* vase; mallet.

machacar /matʃa'kar/ *v.* pound; crush.

machina /ma't ʃina/ *n. f.* derrick.

machista /ma'tʃista/ *a.* macho.

macho /'matʃo/ *n. m.* male.

machucho /ma'tʃutʃo/ *a.* mature, wise.

macizo /ma'θiθo; ma'siso/ *a.* **1.** solid. **—n. 2.** *m.* bulk; flower bed.

macular /maku'lar/ *v.* stain.

madera /ma'ðera/ *n. f.* lumber; wood.

madero /ma'ðero/ *n. m.* beam, timber.

madrastra /ma'ðrastra/ *n. f.* stepmother.

madre /'maðre/ n. f. mother. **m. política,** mother-in-law.

madreperla /maðre'perla/ n. f. mother-of-pearl.

madriguera /maðri'gera/ n. f. burrow; lair, den.

madrina /ma'ðrina/ n. f. god-mother.

madroncillo /maðron'θiʎo; maðron'siyo/ n. m. strawberry.

madrugada /maðru'gaða/ n. f. daybreak.

madrugar /maðru'gar/ v. get up early.

madurar /maðu'rar/ v. ripen.

madurez /maðu'reθ; maðu'res/ n. f. maturity.

maduro /ma'ðuro/ a. ripe; mature.

maestría /maes'tria/ n. f. mastery; master's degree.

maestro /ma'estro/ n. m. master; teacher.

mafia /'mafia/ n. f. mafia.

maganto /ma'ganto/ a. lethargic, dull.

magia /'mahia/ n. f. magic.

mágico /'mahiko/ a. & m. magic; magician.

magistrado /mahis'traðo/ n. m. magistrate.

magnánimo /mag'nanimo/ a. magnanimous.

magnético /mag'netiko/ a. magnetic.

magnetismo /magne'tismo/ n. m. magnetism.

magnetófono /magne'tofono/ n. m. tape recorder.

magnificar /magnifi'kar/ v. magnify.

magnificencia /magnifi'θenθia; magnifi'sensia/ n. f. magnificence.

magnífico /mag'nifiko/ a. magnificent.

magnitud /magni'tuð/ n. f. magnitude.

magno /'magno/ a. great, grand.

magnolia /mag'nolia/ n. f. magnolia.

mago /'mago/ n. m. magician; wizard.

magosto /ma'gosto/ n. m. chestnut roast; picnic fire for roasting chestnuts.

magro /'magro/ a. meager; thin.

magullar /magu'ʎar; magu'yar/ v. bruise.

mahometano /maome'tano/ n. & a. Mohammedan.

mahometismo /maome'tismo/ n. m. Mohammedanism.

maíz /ma'iθ; ma'is/ n. m. corn.

majadero /maha'ðero/ -ra a. & n. foolish; fool.

majar /ma'har/ v. mash.

majestad /mahes'tað/ n. f. majesty.

majestuoso /mahes'tuoso/ a. majestic.

mal /mal/ adv. **1.** badly; wrong. —n. **2.** m. evil, ill; illness.

mala /'mala/ n. f. mail.

malacate /mala'kate/ n. m. hoist.

malandanza /malan'danθa; malan'dansa/ n. f. misfortune.

malaventura /malaβen'tura/ n. f. misfortune.

malcomido /malko'miðo/ a. underfed; malnourished.

malcontento /malkon'tento/ a. disssatisfied.

maldad /mal'dað/ n. f. badness; wickedness.

maldecir /malde'θir; malde'sir/ v. curse, damn.

maldición /maldi'θion; maldi'sion/ n. f. curse.

maldito /mal'dito/ a. accursed, damned.

malecón /male'kon/ n. m. embankment.

maledicencia /maleði'θenθia; maleði'sensia/ n. f. slander.

maleficio /male'fiθio; male'fisio/ n. m. spell, charm.

malestar /males'tar/ n. m. indisposition.

maleta /ma'leta/ n. f. suitcase, valise.

malévolo /ma'leβolo/ a. malevolent.

maleza /ma'leθa; ma'lesa/ n. f. weeds; underbrush.

malgastar /malgas'tar/ v. squander.

malhechor /male't∫or/ -ra n. malefactor, evildoer.

malhumorado /malumo'raðo/ a. morose, ill-humored.

malicia /ma'liθia; ma'lisia/ n. f. malice.

maliciar /mali'θiar; mali'siar/ v. suspect.

malicioso /mali'θioso; mali'sioso/ a. malicious.

maligno /ma'ligno/ a. malignant, evil.

malla /'maʎa; 'maya/ *n. f.* mesh, net.

mallas /'maʎas; 'mayas/ *n. f.pl.* leotard.

mallete /ma'ʎete; ma'yete/ *n. m.* mallet.

malo /'malo/ *a.* bad; evil, wicked; naughty; ill.

malograr /malo'grar/ *v.* miss, lose.

malparto /mal'parto/ *n. m.* abortion, miscarriage.

malquerencia /malke'renθia; malke'rensia/ *n. f.* hatred.

malquerer /malke'rer/ *v.* dislike; bear ill will.

malsano /mal'sano/ *a.* unhealthy; unwholesome.

malsín /mal'sin/ *n. m.* malicious gossip.

malta /'malta/ *n. f.* malt.

maltratar /maltra'tar/ *v.* mistreat.

malvado /mal'βaðo/ **-da** *a.* **1.** wicked. —*n.* **2.** villain.

malversar /malβer'sar/ *v.* embezzle.

malvís /mal'βis/ *n. m.* redwing.

mamá /'mama/ *n. f.* mama, mother.

mamar /ma'mar/ *v.* suckle; suck.

mamífero /ma'mifero/ *n. m.* mammal.

mampara /mam'para/ *n. f.* screen.

mampostería /mamposte'ria/ *n. f.* masonry.

mamut /ma'mut/ *n. m.* mammoth.

manada /ma'naða/ *n. f.* flock, herd, drove.

manantial /manan'tial/ *n. m.* spring (of water).

manar /ma'nar/ *v.* gush, flow out.

mancebo /man'θeβo; man'seβo/ *n. m.* young man.

mancha /'mantʃa/ *n. f.* stain, smear, blemish, spot. —**manchar,** *v.*

mancilla /man'θiʎa; man'siya/ *n. f.* stain; blemish.

manco /'manko/ *a.* armless; one-armed.

mandadero /manda'ðero/ *n. m.* messenger.

mandado /man'daðo/ *n. m.* order, command.

mandamiento /manda'miento/ *n. m.* commandment; command.

mandar /man'dar/ *v.* send; order, command.

mandatario /manda'tario/ *n. m.* attorney; representative.

mandato /man'dato/ *n. m.* mandate, command.

mandíbula /man'diβula/ *n. f.* jaw; jawbone.

mando /'mando/ *n. m.* command, order; leadership.

mando a distancia /'mando a dis'tanθia; 'mando a dis'tansia/ remote control.

mandón /man'don/ *a.* domineering.

mandril /man'dril/ *n. m.* baboon.

manejar /mane'har/ *v.* handle, manage; drive (a car).

manejo /ma'neho/ *n. m.* management; horsemanship.

manera /ma'nera/ *n. f.* way, manner, means. **de m. que,** so, as a result.

manga /'maŋga/ *n. f.* sleeve.

mangana /maŋ'gana/ *n. f.* lariat, lasso.

manganeso /maŋga'neso/ *n. m.* manganese.

mango /'maŋgo/ *n. m.* handle; mango (fruit).

mangosta /maŋ'gosta/ *n. f.* mongoose.

manguera /maŋ'guera/ *n. f.* hose.

manguito /maŋ'guito/ *n. m.* muff.

maní /ma'ni/ *n. m.* peanut.

manía /ma'nia/ *n. f.* mania, madness; hobby.

maníaco /ma'niako/ **-ca, maniático -ca** *a. & n.* maniac.

manicomio /mani'komio/ *n. m.* insane asylum.

manicura /mani'kura/ *n. f.* manicure.

manifactura /manifak'tura/ *n. f.* manufacture.

manifestación /manifesta'θion; manifesta'sion/ *n. f.* manifestation.

manifestar /manifes'tar/ *v.* manifest, show.

manifiesto /mani'fiesto/ *a. & m.* manifest.

manija /ma'niha/ *n. f.* handle; crank.

maniobra /ma'nioβra/ *n. f.* maneuver. —**maniobrar,** *v.*

manipulación /manipula'θion; manipula'sion/ *n. f.* manipulation.

manipular /manipu'lar/ *v.* manipulate.

maniquí /mani'ki/ *n. m.* mannequin.

manivela /mani'βela/ *n. f. Mech.* crank.

manjar /man'har/ *n. m.* food, dish.

manlieve /man'lieβe/ *n. m.* swindle.

mano /'mano/ *n. f.* hand.

manojo /ma'noho/ *n. m.* handful; bunch.

manómetro /ma'nometro/ *n. m.* gauge.

manopla /ma'nopla/ *n. f.* gauntlet.

manosear /manose'ar/ *v.* handle, feel, touch.

manotada /mano'taða/ *n. f.* slap, smack. —**manotear,** *v.*

mansedumbre /manse'ðumbre/ *n. f.* meekness, tameness.

mansión /man'sion/ *n. f.* mansion; abode.

manso /'manso/ *a.* tame, gentle.

manta /'manta/ *n. f.* blanket.

manteca /man'teka/ *n. f.* fat, lard; butter.

mantecado /mante'kaðo/ *n. m.* ice cream.

mantecoso /mante'koso/ *a.* buttery.

mantel /man'tel/ *n. m.* tablecloth.

mantener /mante'ner/ *v.* maintain, keep; sustain; support.

mantenimiento /manteni'miento/ *n. m.* maintenance.

mantequera /mante'kera/ *n. f.* butter dish; churn.

mantequilla /mante'kiʎa; mante'kiya/ *n. f.* butter.

mantilla /man'tiʎa; man'tiya/ *n. f.* mantilla; baby clothes.

mantillo /man'tiʎo; man'tiyo/ *n. m.* humus; manure.

manto /'manto/ *n. m.* mantle, cloak.

manual /ma'nual/ *a. & m.* manual.

manubrio /ma'nuβrio/ *n. m.* handle; crank.

manufacturar /manufaktu'rar/ *v.* manufacture; make.

manuscrito /manus'krito/ *n. m.* manuscript.

manzana /man'θana; man'sana/ *n. f.* apple; block (of street).

manzanilla /manθa'niʎa; mansa'niya/ *n. f.* dry sherry.

manzano /man'θano; man'sano/ *n. m.* apple tree.

maña /'maɲa/ *n. f.* skill; cunning; trick.

mañana /ma'ɲana/ *adv.* **1.** tomorrow. —*n.* **2.** *f.* morning.

mañanear /maɲane'ar/ *v.* rise early in the morning.

mañero /ma'ɲero/ *a.* clever; skillful; lazy.

mapa /'mapa/ *n. m.* map, chart.

mapache /ma'patʃe/ *n. m.* raccoon.

mapurito /mapu'rito/ *n. m.* skunk.

máquina /'makina/ *n. f.* machine. **m. de coser,** sewing machine. **m. de lavar,** washing machine.

maquinación /makina'θion; makina'sion/ *n. f.* machination; plot.

maquinador /makina'ðor/ **-ra** *n.* plotter, schemer.

maquinal /maki'nal/ *a.* mechanical.

maquinar /maki'nar/ *v.* scheme, plot.

maquinaria /maki'naria/ *n. f.* machinery.

maquinista /maki'nista/ *n. m.* machinist; engineer.

mar /mar/ *n. m. or f.* sea.

marabú /mara'βu/ *n. m.* marabou.

maraña /ma'raɲa/ *n. f.* tangle; maze; snarl; plot.

maravilla /mara'βiʎa; mara'βiya/ *n. f.* marvel, wonder. —**maravillarse,** *v.*

maravilloso /maraβi'ʎoso; maraβi'yoso/ *a.* marvelous, wonderful.

marbete /mar'βete/ *n. m.* tag, label; check.

marca /'marka/ *n. f.* mark, sign; brand, make.

marcador /marka'ðor/ *n. m.* highlighter.

marcapáginas /marka'pahinas/ *n. m.* bookmark.

marcar /mar'kar/ *v.* mark; observe, note.

marcha /'martʃa/ *n. f.* march; progress. —**marchar,** *v.*

marchante /mar'tʃante/ *n. m.* merchant; customer.

marcharse /mar'tʃarse/ *v.* go away, depart.

marchitable /martʃi'taβle/ *a.* perishable.

marchitar /martʃi'tar/ *v.* fade, wilt, wither.

marchito /mar'tʃito/ *a.* faded, withered.

marcial /mar'θial; mar'sial/ *a.* martial.

marco /'marko/ *n. m.* frame.

marea /ma'rea/ *n. f.* tide.

mareado /mare'aðo/ *a.* seasick.

marearse /mare'arse/ v. get dizzy; be seasick.

mareo /ma'reo/ n. m. dizziness; seasickness.

marfil /mar'fil/ n. m. ivory.

margarita /marga'rita/ n. f. pearl; daisy.

margen /'marhen/ n. m. or f. margin, edge, rim.

marido /ma'riðo/ n. m. husband.

marijuana /mari'huana/ n. f. marijuana.

marimacha /mari'matʃa/ n. f. lesbian.

marimacho /mari'matʃo/ n. m. mannish woman.

marimba /ma'rimba/ n. f. marimba.

marina /ma'rina/ n. f. navy; seascape.

marinero /mari'nero/ n. m. sailor, seaman.

marino /ma'rino/ a. & m. marine, (of) sea; mariner, seaman.

marión /ma'rion/ n. m. sturgeon.

mariposa /mari'posa/ n. f. butterfly.

mariquita /mari'kita/ n. f. ladybird.

mariscal /maris'kal/ n. m. marshal.

marisco /ma'risko/ n. m. shellfish; mollusk.

marital /mari'tal/ a. marital.

marítimo /ma'ritimo/ a. maritime.

marmita /mar'mita/ n. f. pot, kettle.

mármol /'marmol/ n. m. marble.

marmóreo /mar'moreo/ a. marble.

maroma /ma'roma/ n. f. rope.

marqués /mar'kes/ n. m. marquis.

marquesa /mar'kesa/ n. f. marquise.

Marruecos /ma'rruekos/ n. m. Morocco.

Marte /'marte/ n. m. Mars.

martes /'martes/ n. m. Tuesday.

martillo /mar'tiʎo; mar'tiyo/ n. m. hammer. **—martillar,** v.

mártir /'martir/ n. m. & f. martyr.

martirio /mar'tirio/ n. m. martyrdom.

martirizar /martiri'θar; martiri'sar/ v. martyrize.

marzo /'marθo; 'marso/ n. m. March.

mas /mas/ conj. but.

más a. & adv. more, most; plus. **no m.,** only; no more.

masa /'masa/ n. f. mass; dough.

masaje /ma'sahe/ n. m. massage.

mascar /mas'kar/ v. chew.

máscara /'maskara/ n. f. mask.

mascarada /maska'raða/ n. f. masquerade.

mascota /mas'kota/ n. f. mascot; good-luck charm.

masculino /masku'lino/ a. masculine.

mascullar /masku'ʎar; masku'yar/ v. mumble.

masón /ma'son/ n. m. Freemason.

masticar /masti'kar/ v. chew.

mástil /'mastil/ n. m. mast; post.

mastín /mas'tin/ n. m. mastiff.

mastín danés /mas'tin da'nes/ Great Dane.

mastuerzo /mas'tuerθo; mas'tuerso/ n. m. fool, ninny.

mata /'mata/ n. f. plant; bush.

matadero /mata'ðero/ n. m. slaughterhouse.

matador /mata'ðor/ **-ra** n. matador.

matafuego /mata'fuego/ n. m. fire extinguisher.

matanza /ma'tanθa; ma'tansa/ n. f. killing, bloodshed, slaughter.

matar /ma'tar/ v. kill, slay; slaughter.

matasanos /mata'sanos/ n. m. quack.

mate /'mate/ n. m. checkmate; Paraguayan tea.

matemáticas /mate'matikas/ n. f.pl. mathematics.

matemático /mate'matiko/ a. mathematical.

materia /ma'teria/ n. f. material; subject (matter).

material /mate'rial/ a. & m. material.

materialismo /materia'lismo/ n. m. materialism.

materializar /materiali'θar; materiali'sar/ v. materialize.

maternal /mater'nal/ **materno** a. maternal.

maternidad /materni'ðað/ n. f. maternity; maternity hospital.

matiné /mati'ne/ n. f. matinee.

matiz /ma'tiθ; ma'tis/ n. m. hue, shade.

matizar /mati'θar; mati'sar/ v. blend; tint.

matón /ma'ton/ n. m. bully.

matorral /mato'rral/ n. m. thicket.

matoso /ma'toso/ a. weedy.

matraca /ma'traka/ *n. f.* rattle.
—**matraquear,** *v.*

matrícula /ma'trikula/ *n. f.* registration; tuition.

matricularse /matriku'larse/ *v.* enroll, register.

matrimonio /matri'monio/ *n. m.* matrimony, marriage; married couple.

matriz /ma'triθ; ma'tris/ *n. f.* womb; *Mech.* die, mold.

matrona /ma'trona/ *n. f.* matron.

maullar /mau'ʎar; mau'yar/ *v.* mew.

máxima /'maksima/ *n. f.* maxim.

máxime /'maksime/ *a.* principally.

máximo /'maksimo/ *a. & m.* maximum.

maya /'maya/ *n. f.* daisy.

mayo /'mayo/ *n. m.* May.

mayonesa /mayo'nesa/ *n. f.* mayonnaise.

mayor /ma'yor/ *a.* larger, largest; greater, greatest; elder, eldest, senior. **m. de edad,** major, of age. **al por m.,** at wholesale. *m.* major.

mayoral /mayo'ral/ *n. m.* head shepherd; boss; foreman.

mayordomo /mayor'ðomo/ *n. m.* manager; butler, steward.

mayoría /mayo'ria/ *n. f.* majority, bulk.

mayorista /mayo'rista/ *n. m. & f.* wholesaler.

mayúscula /ma'yuskula/ *n. f.* capital letter, upper-case letter.

mazmorra /maθ'morra; mas'morra/ *n. f.* dungeon.

mazorca /ma'θorka; ma'sorka/ *n. f.* ear of corn.

me /me/ *pron.* me; myself.

mecánico /me'kaniko/ **-ca** *a. & n.* mechanical; mechanic.

mecanismo /meka'nismo/ *n. m.* mechanism.

mecanizar /mekani'θar; mekani-'sar/ *v.* mechanize.

mecanografía /mekanogra'fia/ *n. f.* typewriting.

mecanógrafo /meka'nografo/ **-fa** *n.* typist.

mecedor /meθe'ðor; mese'ðor/ *n. m.* swing.

mecedora /meθe'ðora; mese'ðora/ *n. f.* rocking chair.

mecer /me'θer; me'ser/ *v.* rock; swing, sway.

mecha /'metʃa/ *n. f.* wick; fuse.

mechón /me'tʃon/ *n. m.* lock (of hair).

medalla /me'ðaʎa; me'ðaya/ *n. f.* medal.

médano /'meðano/ *n. m.* sand dune.

media /'meðia/ *n. f.* stocking.

mediación /meðia'θion; meðia-'sion/ *n. f.* mediation.

mediador /meðia'ðor/ **-ra** *n.* mediator.

mediados /me'ðiaðos/ *n. m.pl.* **a m. de,** about the middle of (a period of time).

medianero /meðia'nero/ *n. m.* mediator.

medianía /meðia'nia/ *n. f.* mediocrity.

mediano /me'ðiano/ *a.* medium; moderate; mediocre.

medianoche /meðia'notʃe/ *n. f.* midnight.

mediante /me'ðiante/ *prep.* by means of.

mediar /me'ðiar/ *v.* mediate.

medicamento /meðika'mento/ *n. m.* medicine, drug.

medicastro /meði'kastro/ *n. m.* quack.

medicina /meði'θina; meði'sina/ *n. f.* medicine.

medicinar /meðiθi'nar; meðisi'nar/ *v.* treat (as a doctor).

médico /'meðiko/ *a.* **1.** medical. —*n.* **2.** *m. & f.* doctor, physician.

medida /me'ðiða/ *n. f.* measure, step.

medidor /meði'ðor/ *n. m.* meter.

medieval /meðie'βal/ *a.* medieval.

medio /'meðio/ *a.* **1.** half; mid, middle of. —*n.* **2.** *m.* middle; means.

mediocre /me'ðiokre/ *a.* mediocre.

mediocridad /meðiokri'ðað/ *n. f.* mediocrity.

mediodía /meðio'ðia/ *n. m.* midday, noon.

medir /me'ðir/ *v.* measure, gauge.

meditación /meðita'θion; meðita'sion/ *n. f.* meditation.

meditar /meði'tar/ *v.* meditate.

mediterráneo /meðite'rraneo/ *a.* Mediterranean.

medrar /me'ðrar/ *v.* thrive; grow.

medroso /me'ðroso/ *a.* fearful, cowardly.

megáfono /me'gafono/ *n. m.* megaphone.

megahercio /mega'erθio; mega-'ersio/ *n. f.* megahertz.

mejicano /mehi'kano/ **-na** *a. & n.* Mexican.

mejilla /me'hiʎa; me'hiya/ *n. f.* cheek.

mejillón /mehi'ʎon; mehi'yon/ *n. m.* mussel.

mejor /me'hor/ *a. & adv.* better; best. **a lo m.,** perhaps.

mejora /me'hora/ *n. f.,* **mejoramiento,** *m.* improvement.

mejorar /meho'rar/ *v.* improve, better.

mejoría /meho'ria/ *n. f.* improvement; superiority.

melancolía /melanko'lia/ *n. f.* melancholy.

melancólico /melan'koliko/ *a.* melancholy.

melaza /me'laθa; me'lasa/ *n. f.* molasses.

melena /me'lena/ *n. f.* mane; long or loose hair.

melenudo /mele'nuðo/ **-da** *a.* long-haired.

melindroso /melin'droso/ *a.* fussy.

mella /'meʎa; 'meya/ *n. f.* notch; dent. **—mellar,** *v.*

mellizo /me'ʎiθo; me'yiso/ **-za** *n. & a.* twin.

melocotón /meloko'ton/ *n. m.* peach.

melodía /melo'ðia/ *n. f.* melody.

melodioso /melo'ðioso/ *a.* melodious.

melón /me'lon/ *n. m.* melon.

meloso /me'loso/ *a.* like honey.

membrana /mem'brana/ *n. f.* membrane.

membrete /mem'brete/ *n. m.* memorandum; letterhead.

membrillo /mem'briʎo; mem-'briyo/ *n. m.* quince.

membrudo /mem'bruðo/ *a.* strong, muscular.

memorable /memo'raβle/ *a.* memorable.

memorándum /memo'randum/ *m.* memorandum; notebook.

memoria /me'moria/ *n. f.* memory; memoir; memorandum.

mención /men'θion; men'sion/ *f.* mention. **—mencionar,** *v.*

mendigar /mendi'gar/ *v.* beg (for alms).

mendigo /men'digo/ **-a** *n.* beggar.

mendrugo /men'drugo/ *n. m.* (hard) crust, chunk.

menear /mene'ar/ *v.* shake, wag; stir.

menester /menes'ter/ *n. m.* need, want; duty, task. **ser m.,** to be necessary.

menesteroso /meneste'roso/ *a.* needy.

mengua /'mengua/ *n. f.* decrease; lack; poverty.

menguar /meŋ'guar/ *v.* abate, decrease.

meningitis /meniŋ'gitis/ *n. f.* meningitis.

menopausia /meno'pausia/ *n. f.* menopause.

menor /me'nor/ *a.* smaller, smallest; lesser, least; younger, youngest, junior. **m. de edad,** minor, under age. **al por m.,** at retail.

menos /'menos/ *a. & adv.* less, least; minus. **a m. que,** unless. **echar de m.,** to miss.

menospreciar /menospre'θiar; menospre'siar/ *v.* cheapen; despise; slight.

mensaje /men'sahe/ *n. m.* message.

mensajero /mensa'hero/ **-ra** *n.* messenger.

menstruar /menstru'ar/ *v.* menstruate.

mensual /men'sual/ *a.* monthly.

mensualidad /mensuali'ðað/ *n. f.* monthly income or allowance; monthly payment.

menta /'menta/ *n. f.* mint, peppermint.

mentado /men'taðo/ *a.* famous.

mental /men'tal/ *a.* mental.

mentalidad /mentali'ðað/ *n. f.* mentality.

menta romana /'menta rro'mana/ spearmint.

mente /'mente/ *n. f.* mind.

mentecato /mente'kato/ *a.* foolish, stupid.

mentir /men'tir/ *v.* lie, tell a lie.

mentira /men'tira/ *n. f.* lie, falsehood. **parece m.,** it seems impossible.

mentiroso /menti'roso/ *a.* lying, untruthful.

mentol /'mentol/ *n. m.* menthol.

menú /me'nu/ *n. m.* menu.

menudeo /menu'ðeo/ *n. m.* retail.

menudo /menu'ðo/ *a.* small, minute. **a m.,** often.

meñique /me'ɲike/ *a.* tiny.

meple /'meple/ *n. m.* maple.

merca /'merka/ *n. f.* purchase.

mercader /merka'ðer/ n. m. merchant.

mercaderías /merkaðe'rias/ n. f.pl. merchandise, commodities.

mercado /mer'kaðo/ n. m. market.

Mercado Común /mer'kaðo ko'mun/ Common Market.

mercado negro /mer'kaðo 'negro/ black market.

mercancía /merkan'θia; merkan'sia/ n. f. merchandise; (pl.) wares.

mercante /mer'kante/ a. merchant.

mercantil /merkan'til/ a. mercantile.

merced /mer'θeð; mer'seð/ n. f. mercy, grace.

mercenario /merθe'nario; merse'nario/ **-ria** a. & n. mercenary.

mercurio /mer'kurio/ n. m. mercury.

merecedor /mereθe'ðor; merese'ðor/ a. worthy.

merecer /mere'θer; mere'ser/ v. merit, deserve.

merecimiento /mereθi'miento; meresi'miento/ n. m. merit.

merendar /meren'dar/ v. eat lunch; snack.

merendero /meren'dero/ n. m. lunchroom.

meridional /meriðio'nal/ a. southern.

merienda /me'rienda/ n. f. midday meal, lunch; afternoon snack.

mérito /'merito/ n. m. merit, worth.

meritorio /meri'torio/ a. meritorious.

merla /'merla/ n. f. blackbird.

merluza /mer'luθa; mer'lusa/ n. f. haddock.

mermelada /merme'laða/ n. f. marmalade.

mero /'mero/ a. mere.

merodeador /meroðea'ðor/ **-ra** n. prowler.

mes /'mes/ n. m. month.

mesa /'mesa/ n. f. table.

meseta /me'seta/ n. f. plateau.

mesón /me'son/ n. m. inn.

mesonero /meso'nero/ **-ra** n. innkeeper.

mestizo /mes'tiθo; mes'tiso/ **-za** a. & n. half-caste.

meta /'meta/ n. f. goal, objective.

metabolismo /metaβo'lismo/ n. m. metabolism.

metafísica /meta'fisika/ n. f. metaphysics.

metáfora /me'tafora/ n. f. metaphor.

metal /me'tal/ n. m. metal.

metálico /me'taliko/ a. metallic.

metalurgia /metalur'hia/ n. f. metallurgy.

meteoro /mete'oro/ n. m. meteor.

meteorología /meteorolo'hia/ n. f. meteorology.

meter /me'ter/ v. put (in).

meterse /me'terse/ v. interfere, meddle; go into.

metódico /me'toðiko/ a. methodic.

método /'metoðo/ n. m. method, approach.

metralla /me'traʎa; me'traya/ n. f. shrapnel.

métrico /'metriko/ a. metric.

metro /'metro/ n. m. meter (measure); subway.

metrópoli /me'tropoli/ n. f. metropolis.

mexicano /meksi'kano/ **-na** a. & n. Mexican.

mezcla /'meθkla; 'meskla/ n. f. mixture; blend.

mezclar /meθ'klar; mes'klar/ v. mix; blend.

mezcolanza /meθko'lanθa; mesko'lansa/ n. f. mixture; hodgepodge.

mezquino /meθ'kino; mes'kino/ a. stingy; petty.

mezquita /meθ'kita; mes'kita/ n. f. mosque.

mi /'mi/ a. my.

mí /'mi/ pron. me; myself.

microbio /mi'kroβio/ n. m. microbe, germ.

microbús /mikro'βus/ n. m. minibus.

microchip /mikro'tʃip/ n. m. microchip.

microficha /mikro'fitʃa/ n. f. microfiche.

micrófono /mi'krofono/ n. m. microphone.

microforma /mikro'forma/ n. f. microform.

microscópico /mikros'kopiko/ a. microscopic.

microscopio /mikros'kopio/ n. m. microscope.

microtaxi /mikro'taksi/ n. m. minicab.

miedo /'mieðo/ n. m. fear. **tener m.,** fear, be afraid.

miedoso /mie'ðoso/ *a.* fearful.

miel /miel/ *n. f.* honey.

miembro /mi'embro/ *n. m. & f.* member; limb.

mientras /'mientras/ *conj.* while. **m. tanto,** meanwhile. **m. más... más,** the more... the more.

miércoles /'mierkoles/ *n. m.* Wednesday.

miércoles de ceniza /'mierkoles de θe'niθa; 'mierkoles de se'nisa/ Ash Wednesday.

miga /'miga/ **migaja** *n. f.* scrap; crumb.

migración /migra'θion; migra-'sion/ *n. f.* migration.

migratorio /migra'torio/ *a.* migratory.

mil /mil/ *a. & pron.* thousand.

milagro /mi'lagro/ *n. m.* miracle.

milagroso /mila'groso/ *a.* miraculous.

milicia /mi'liθia; mi'lisia/ *n. f.* militia.

militante /mili'tante/ *a.* militant.

militar /mili'tar/ *a.* **1.** military. —*n.* **2.** *m.* military man.

militarismo /milita'rismo/ *n. m.* militarism.

milla /'miʎa; 'miya/ *n. f.* mile.

millar /mi'ʎar; mi'yar/ *n. m.* (a) thousand.

millón /mi'ʎon; mi'yon/ *n. m.* million.

millonario /miʎo'nario; miyo'nario/ **-ria** *n.* millionaire.

mimar /mi'mar/ *v.* pamper, spoil (a child).

mimbre /'mimbre/ *n. m.* willow; wicker.

mímico /'mimiko/ *a.* mimic.

mimo /'mimo/ *n. m.* mime, mimic.

mina /'mina/ *n. f.* mine. —**minar,** *v.*

mineral /mine'ral/ *a. & m.* mineral.

minero /mi'nero/ **-ra** *n.* miner.

miniatura /minia'tura/ *n. f.* miniature.

miniaturizar /miniaturi'θar; miniaturi'sar/ *v.* miniaturize.

mínimo /'minimo/ *a. & m.* minimum.

ministerio /minis'terio/ *n. m.* ministry; cabinet.

ministro /mi'nistro/ **-a** *n. Govt.* minister, secretary.

minoría /mino'ria/ *n. f.* minority.

minoridad /minori'ðað/ *n. f.* minority (of age).

minucioso /minu'θioso; minu-'sioso/ *a.* minute; thorough.

minué /mi'nue/ *n. m.* minuet.

minúscula /mi'nuskula/ *n. f.* lower-case letter, small letter.

minuta /mi'nuta/ *n. f.* draft.

mío /'mio/ *a.* mine.

miopía /mio'pia/ *n. f.* myopia.

mira /'mira/ *n. f.* gunsight.

mirada /mi'raða/ *n. f.* look; gaze, glance.

miramiento /mira'miento/ *n. m.* consideration; respect.

mirar /mi'rar/ *v.* look, look at; watch. **m. a,** face.

miríada /mi'riaða/ *n. f.* myriad.

mirlo /'mirlo/ *n. m.* blackbird.

mirón /mi'ron/ **-ona** *n.* bystander, observer.

mirra /'mirra/ *n. f.* myrrh.

mirto /'mirto/ *n. m.* myrtle.

misa /'misa/ *n. f.* mass, church service.

misceláneo /misθe'laneo; misse-'laneo/ *a.* miscellaneous.

miserable /mise'raβle/ *a.* miserable, wretched.

miseria /mi'seria/ *n. f.* misery.

misericordia /miseri'korðia/ *n. f.* mercy.

misericordioso /miserikor'ðioso/ *a.* merciful.

misión /mi'sion/ *n. f.* assignment; mission.

misionario /misio'nario/ **-ria, misionero -ra** *n.* missionary.

mismo /'mismo/ *a. & pron.* **1.** same; -self, -selves. —*adv.* **2.** right, exactly.

misterio /mis'terio/ *n. m.* mystery.

misterioso /miste'rioso/ *a.* mysterious, weird.

místico /'mistiko/ **-ca** *a. & n.* mystical, mystic.

mitad /mi'tað/ *n. f.* half.

mítico /'mitiko/ *a.* mythical.

mitigar /miti'gar/ *v.* mitigate.

mitin /'mitin/ *n. m.* meeting; rally.

mito /'mito/ *n. m.* myth.

mitón /mi'ton/ *n. m.* mitten.

mitra /'mitra/ *n. f.* miter (bishop's).

mixto /'miksto/ *a.* mixed.

mixtura /miks'tura/ *n. f.* mixture.

mobiliario /moβi'liario/ *n. m.* household goods.

mocasín /moka'sin/ *n. m.* moccasin.

mocedad /moθe'ðað; mose'ðað/ *n. f.* youthfulness.

mochila /mo'tʃila/ *n. f.* knapsack, backpack.

mocho /'motʃo/ *a.* cropped, trimmed, shorn.

moción /mo'θion; mo'sion/ *n. f.* motion.

mocoso /mo'koso/ **-sa** *n.* brat.

moda /'moða/ *n. f.* mode, fashion, style.

modales /mo'ðales/ *n. m.pl.* manners.

modelo /mo'ðelo/ *n. m.* model, pattern.

módem /'moðem/ *n. m.* modem.

moderación /moðera'θion; moðerasion/ *n. f.* moderation.

moderado /moðe'raðo/ *a.* moderate. —**moderar,** *v.*

modernizar /moðerni'θar; moðerni'sar/ *v.* modernize.

moderno /mo'ðerno/ *a.* modern.

modestia /mo'ðestia/ *n. f.* modesty.

modesto /mo'ðesto/ *a.* modest.

módico /'moðiko/ *a.* reasonable, moderate.

modificación /moðifi'kaθion; moðifika'sion/ *n. f.* modification.

modificar /moðifi'kar/ *v.* modify.

modismo /mo'ðismo/ *n. m. Gram.* idiom.

modista /mo'ðista/ *n. f.* dressmaker; milliner.

modo /'moðo/ *n. m.* way, means.

modular /moðu'lar/ *v.* modulate.

mofarse /mo'farse/ *v.* scoff, sneer.

mofletudo /mofle'tuðo/ *a.* fatcheeked.

mohín /mo'in/ *n. m.* grimace.

moho /'moo/ *n. m.* mold, mildew.

mohoso /mo'oso/ *a.* moldy.

mojar /mo'har/ *v.* wet.

mojón /mo'hon/ *n. m.* landmark; heap.

molde /'molde/ *n. m.* mold, form.

molécula /mo'lekula/ *n. f.* molecule.

moler /mo'ler/ *v.* grind, mill.

molestar /moles'tar/ *v.* molest, bother, disturb, annoy, trouble.

molestia /mo'lestia/ *n. f.* bother, annoyance, trouble; hassle.

molesto /mo'lesto/ *a.* bothersome; annoyed; uncomfortable.

molicie /mo'liθie; mo'lisie/ *n. f.* softness.

molinero /moli'nero/ *n. m.* miller.

molino /mo'lino/ *n. m.* mill. **m. de viento,** windmill.

mollera /mo'ʎera; mo'yera/ *n. f.* top of the head.

molusco /mo'lusko/ *n. m.* mollusk.

momentáneo /momen'taneo/ *a.* momentary.

momento /mo'mento/ *n. m.* moment.

mona /'mona/ *n. f.* female monkey.

monarca /mo'narka/ *n. m. & f.* monarch.

monarquía /monar'kia/ *n. f.* monarchy.

monarquista /monar'kista/ *n. & a.* monarchist.

monasterio /mona'sterio/ *n. m.* monastery.

mondadientes /monda'ðientes/ *n. m.* toothpick.

moneda /mo'neða/ *n. f.* coin; money.

monetario /mone'tario/ *a.* monetary.

monición /moni'θion; moni'sion/ *n. m.* warning.

monigote /moni'gote/ *n. m.* puppet.

monja /'monha/ *n. f.* nun.

monje /'monhe/ *n. m.* monk.

mono /'mono/ **-na** *a.* **1.** *Colloq.* cute. —*n.* **2.** *m. & f.* monkey.

monólogo /mo'nologo/ *n. m.* monologue.

monopatín /monopa'tin/ *n. m.* skateboard.

monopolio /mono'polio/ *n. m.* monopoly.

monopolizar /monopoli'θar; monopoli'sar/ *v.* monopolize.

monosílabo /mono'silaβo/ *n. m.* monosyllable.

monotonía /monoto'nia/ *n. f.* monotony.

monótono /mo'notono/ *a.* monotonous, dreary.

monstruo /'monstruo/ *n. m.* monster.

monstruosidad /monstruosi'ðað/ *n. f.* monstrosity.

monstruoso /mon'struoso/ *a.* monstrous.

monta /'monta/ *n. f.* amount; price.

montaña /mon'taɲa/ *n. f.* mountain.

montañoso /monta'ɲoso/ *a.* mountainous.

montar /mon'tar/ *v.* mount, climb; amount; *Mech.* assemble. **m. a caballo,** ride horseback.

montaraz /monta'raθ; monta'ras/ *a.* wild, barbaric.

monte /'monte/ *n. m.* mountain; forest.

montón /mon'ton/ *n. m.* heap, pile.

montuoso /mon'tuoso/ *a.* mountainous.

montura /mon'tura/ *n. f.* mount; saddle.

monumental /monumen'tal/ *a.* monumental.

monumento /monu'mento/ *n. m.* monument.

mora /'mora/ *n. f.* blackberry.

morada /mo'raða/ *n. f.* residence, dwelling.

morado /mo'raðo/ *a.* purple.

moral /mo'ral/ *a.* **1.** moral. —*n.* **2.** *f.* morale.

moraleja /mora'leha/ *n. f.* moral.

moralidad /morali'ðað/ *n. f.* morality, morals.

moralista /mora'lista/ *n. m. & f.* moralist.

morar /mo'rar/ *v.* dwell, live, reside.

mórbido /'morβiðo/ *a.* morbid.

mordaz /mor'ðaθ; mor'ðas/ *a.* caustic; sarcastic.

mordedura /morðe'ðura/ *n. f.* bite.

morder /mor'ðer/ *v.* bite.

moreno /mo'reno/ **-na** *a. & n.* brown; dark-skinned; dark-haired, brunette.

morfina /mor'fina/ *n. f.* morphine.

moribundo /mori'βundo/ *a.* dying.

morir /mo'rir/ *v.* die.

morisco /mo'risko/ **-ca, moro -ra** *a. & n.* Moorish; Moor.

morriña /mo'rriɲa/ *n. f.* sadness.

morro /'morro/ *n. m.* bluff; snout.

mortaja /mor'taha/ *n. f.* shroud.

mortal /mor'tal/ *a. & n.* mortal.

mortalidad /mortali'ðað/ *n. f.* mortality.

mortero /mor'tero/ *n. m.* mortar.

mortífero /mor'tifero/ *a.* fatal, deadly.

mortificar /mortifi'kar/ *v.* mortify.

mortuorio /mor'tuorio/ *a.* funereal.

mosaico /mo'saiko/ *a. & m.* mosaic.

mosca /'moska/ *n. f.* fly.

mosquito /mos'kito/ *n. m.* mosquito.

mostacho /mos'tatʃo/ *n. m.* mustache.

mostaza /mos'taθa; mos'tasa/ *n. f.* mustard.

mostrador /mostra'ðor/ *n. m.* counter; showcase.

mostrar /mos'trar/ *v.* show, display.

mote /'mote/ *n. m.* nickname; alias.

motel /mo'tel/ *n. m.* motel.

motín /mo'tin/ *n. m.* mutiny; riot.

motivo /mo'tiβo/ *n. m.* motive, reason.

motocicleta /motoθi'kleta; motosi'kleta/ *n. f.* motorcycle.

motociclista /motoθi'klista; motosi'klista/ *n. m. & f.* motorcyclist.

motor /mo'tor/ *n. m.* motor.

motorista /moto'rista/ *n. m. & f.* motorist.

movedizo /moβe'ðiθo; moβe'ðiso/ *a.* movable; shaky.

mover /mo'βer/ *v.* move; stir.

movible /mo'βiβle/ *a.* movable.

móvil /'moβil/ *a.* mobile.

movilización /moβiliθa'θion; moβilisa'sion/ *n. f.* mobilization.

movilizar /moβili'θar; moβili'sar/ *v.* mobilize.

movimiento /moβi'miento/ *n. m.* movement, motion.

mozo /'moθo; 'moso/ *n. m.* boy; servant, waiter, porter.

muaré /mua're/ *n. m.* moiré.

muchacha /mu'tʃatʃa/ *n. f.* girl, youngster; maid (servant).

muchachez /mutʃa'tʃeθ; mutʃa'tʃes/ *n. m.* boyhood, girlhood.

muchacho /mu'tʃatʃo/ *n. m.* boy; youngster.

muchedumbre /mutʃe'ðumbre/ *n. f.* crowd, mob.

mucho /'mutʃo/ *a.* **1.** much, many. —*adv.* **2.** much.

mucoso /mu'koso/ *a.* mucous.

muda /'muða/ *n. f.* change.

mudanza /mu'ðanθa; mu'ðansa/ *n. f.* change; change of residence.

mudar /mu'ðar/ *v.* change, shift.

mudarse /mu'ðarse/ *v.* change residence, move.

mudo /'muðo/ **-da** *a. & n.* mute.

mueble /'mueβle/ *n. m.* piece of furniture; (*pl.*) furniture.

mueca /'mueka/ *n. f.* grimace.

muela /'muela/ *n. f.* (back) tooth.

muelle /'mueʎe; 'mueye/ *n. m.* pier, wharf; *Mech.* spring.

muerte /'muerte/ *n. f.* death.

muerto /'muerto/ **-ta** *a.* **1.** dead. —*n.* **2.** dead person.

muesca /'mueska/ *n. f.* notch; groove.

muestra /'muestra/ *n. f.* sample, specimen; sign.

mugido /mu'hiðo/ *n. m.* lowing; mooing.

mugir /mu'hir/ *v.* low, moo.

mugre /'mugre/ *n. f.* filth, dirt.

mugriento /mu'griento/ *a.* dirty.

mujer /mu'her/ *f.* woman; wife. **m. de la limpieza,** cleaning lady, charwoman.

mujeril /muhe'ril/ *a.* womanly, feminine.

mula /'mula/ *n. f.* mule.

mulato /mu'lato/ **-ta** *a. & n.* mulatto.

muleta /mu'leta/ *n. f.* crutch; prop.

mulo /'mulo/ **-la** *n.* mule.

multa /'multa/ *n. f.* fine, penalty.

multicolor /multiko'lor/ *a.* many-colored.

multinacional /multinaθio'nal; multinasio'nal/ *a.* multinational.

múltiple /'multiple/ *a.* multiple.

multiplicación /multiplika'θion; multiplika'sion/ *n. f.* multiplication.

multiplicar /multipli'kar/ *v.* multiply.

multiplicidad /multipliθi'ðað; multiplisi'ðað/ *n. f.* multiplicity.

multitud /multi'tuð/ *n. f.* multitude, crowd.

mundanal /munda'nal/ *a.* worldly.

mundano /mun'dano/ *a.* worldly, mundane.

mundial /mun'dial/ *a.* worldwide; (of the) world.

mundo /'mundo/ *n. m.* world.

munición /muni'θion; muni'sion/ *n. f.* ammunition.

municipal /muniθi'pal; munisi'pal/ *a.* municipal.

municipio /muni'θipio; muni'sipio/ *n. m.* city hall.

muñeca /mu'ɲeka/ *n. f.* doll; wrist.

muñeco /mu'ɲeko/ *n. m.* doll; puppet.

mural /mu'ral/ *a. & m.* mural.

muralla /mu'raʎa; mu'raya/ *n. f.* wall.

murciélago /mur'θielago; mur'sielago/ *n. m.* bat.

murga /'murga/ *n. f.* musical band.

murmullo /mur'muʎo; mur'muyo/ *n. m.* murmur; rustle.

murmurar /murmu'rar/ *v.* murmur; rustle; grumble.

musa /'musa/ *n. f.* muse.

muscular /musku'lar/ *a.* muscular.

músculo /'muskulo/ *n. m.* muscle.

muselina /muse'lina/ *n. f.* muslin.

museo /mu'seo/ *n. m.* museum.

música /'musika/ *n. f.* music.

musical /musi'kal/ *a.* musical.

músico /'musiko/ **-ca** *a. & n.* musical; musician.

muslo /'muslo/ *n. m.* thigh.

mustio /'mustio/ *a.* sad.

musulmano /musul'mano/ **-na** *a. & n.* Muslim.

muta /'muta/ *n. f.* pack of hounds.

mutabilidad /mutaβili'ðað/ *n. f.* mutability.

mutación /muta'θion; muta'sion/ *n. f.* mutation.

mutilación /mutila'θion; mutila-'sion/ *n. f.* mutilation.

mutilar /muti'lar/ *v.* mutilate; mangle.

mutuo /'mutuo/ *a.* mutual.

muy /'mui/ *adv.* very.

N Ñ

nabo /'naβo/ *n. m.* turnip.

nácar /'nakar/ *n. m.* mother-of-pearl.

nacarado /naka'raðo, na'kareo/ *a.* pearly.

nacer /na'θer; na'ser/ *v.* be born.

naciente /na'θiente; na'siente/ *a.* rising; nascent.

nacimiento /naθi'miento; nasi-'miento/ *n. m.* birth.

nación /na'θion; na'sion/ *n. f.* nation.

nacional /naθio'nal; nasio'nal/ *a.* national.

nacionalidad /naθionali'ðað; nasionali'ðað/ *n. f.* nationality.

nacionalismo /naθiona'lismo; nasiona'lismo/ *n. m.* nationalism.

nacionalista /naθiona'lista; nasiona'lista/ *n. & a.* nationalist.

nacionalización /naθionaliθa'θion; nasionalisa'sion/ *n. f.* nationalization.

nacionalizar /naθionali'θar; nasionali'sar/ *v.* nationalize.

Naciones Unidas /na'θiones u'niðas; na'siones u'niðas/ *n. f.pl.* United Nations.

nada /'naða/ *pron.* **1.** nothing; anything. **de n.,** you're welcome. —*adv.* **2.** at all.

nadador /naða'ðor/ **-ra** *n.* swimmer.

nadar /na'ðar/ *v.* swim.

nadie /'naðie/ *pron.* no one, nobody; anyone, anybody.

nafta /'nafta/ *n. f.* naphtha.

naipe /'naipe/ *n. m.* (playing) card.

naranja /na'ranha/ *n. f.* orange.

naranjada /naran'haða/ *n. f.* orangeade.

naranjo /na'ranho/ *n. m.* orange tree.

narciso /nar'θiso; nar'siso/ *n. m.* daffodil; narcissus.

narcótico /nar'kotiko/ *a. & m.* narcotic.

nardo /'narðo/ *n. m.* spikenard.

nariz /na'riθ; na'ris/ *n. f.* nose; (*pl.*) nostrils.

narración /narra'θion; narra'sion/ *n. f.* account.

narrador /narra'ðor/ **-ra** *n.* narrator.

narrar /na'rrar/ *v.* narrate.

narrativa /narra'tiβa/ *n. f.* narrative.

nata /'nata/ *n. f.* cream.

nata batida /'nata ba'tiða/ whipped cream.

natación /nata'θion; nata'sion/ *n. f.* swimming.

natal /na'tal/ *a.* native; natal.

natalicio /nata'liθio; nata'lisio/ *n. m.* birthday.

natalidad /natali'ðað/ *n. f.* birth rate.

natillas /na'tiʎas; na'tiyas/ *n. f.pl.* custard.

nativo /na'tiβo/ *a.* native; innate.

natural /natu'ral/ *a.* **1.** natural. —*n.* **2.** *m. & f.* native. **3.** *m.* nature, disposition.

naturaleza /natura'leθa; natura'lesa/ *n. f.* nature.

naturalidad /naturali'ðað/ *n. f.* naturalness; nationality.

naturalista /natura'lista/ *a. & n.* naturalistic; naturalist.

naturalización /naturaliθa'θion; naturalisa'sion/ *n. f.* naturalization.

naturalizar /naturali'θar; naturali'sar/ *v.* naturalize.

naufragar /naufra'gar/ *v.* be shipwrecked; fail.

naufragio /nau'frahio/ *n. m.* shipwreck; disaster.

náufrago /'naufrago/ **-ga** *a. & n.* shipwrecked (person).

náusea /'nausea/ *n. f.* nausea.

nausear /nause'ar/ *v.* feel nauseous.

náutico /'nautiko/ *a.* nautical.

navaja /na'βaha/ *n. f.* razor; pen knife.

naval /na'βal/ *a.* naval.

navasca /na'βaska/ *n. f.* blizzard, snowstorm.

nave /'naβe/ *n. f.* ship.

nave espacial /'naβe espa'θial; 'naβe es'pasial/ spaceship.

navegable /naβe'gaβle/ *a.* navigable.

navegación /naβega'θion; naβega'sion/ *n. f.* navigation.

navegador /naβega'ðor/ **-ra** *n.* navigator.

navegante /naβe'gante/ *n. m. & f.* navigator.

navegar /naβe'gar/ *v.* sail; navigate.

Navidad /naβi'ðað/ *n. f.* Christmas.

navío /na'βio/ *n. m.* ship.

neblina /ne'βlina/ *n. f.* mist, fog.

nebuloso /neβu'loso/ *a.* misty; nebulous.

necedad /neθe'ðað; nese'ðað/ *n. f.* stupidity; nonsense.

necesario /neθe'sario; nese'sario/ *a.* necessary.

necesidad /neθesi'ðað; nesesi'ðað/ *n. f.* necessity, need, want.

necesitado /neθesi'taðo; nesesi'taðo/ *a.* needy, poor.

necesitar /neθesi'tar; nesesi'tar/ *v.* need.

necio /'neθio; 'nesio/ **-cia** *a.* **1.** stupid, silly. —*n.* **2.** fool.

néctar /'nektar/ *n. m.* nectar.

nectarina /nekta'rina/ *n. f.* nectarine.

nefando /ne'fando/ *a.* nefarious.

nefasto /ne'fasto/ *a.* unlucky, ill-fated.

negable /ne'gaβle/ *a.* deniable.

negación /nega'θion; nega'sion/ *n. f.* denial, negation.

negar /ne'gar/ v. deny.

negarse /ne'garse/ v. refuse, decline.

negativa /nega'tiβa/ n. f. negative, refusal.

negativamente /negatiβa'mente/ adv. negatively.

negativo /nega'tiβo/ a. negative.

negligencia /negli'henθia; negli'hensia/ n. f. negligence, neglect.

negligente /negli'hente/ a. negligent.

negociación /negoθia'θion; negosia'sion/ n. f. negotiation, deal.

negociador /negoθia'ðor; negosia'ðor/ -ra n. negotiator.

negociante /nego'θiante; nego'siante/ -ta n. businessperson.

negociar /nego'θiar; nego'siar/ v. negotiate, trade.

negocio /ne'goθio; ne'gosio/ n. m. trade; business.

negro /'negro/ -gra a. 1. black. —n. 2. m. Black.

nene /'nene/ -na n. baby.

neo /'neo/ **neón** n. m. neon.

nervio /'nerβio/ n. m. nerve.

nerviosamente /nerβiosa'mente/ adv. nervously.

nervioso /ner'βioso/ a. nervous.

nesciencia /nesθien'θia; nessien'sia/ n. f. ignorance.

nesciente /nes'θiente; nes'siente/ a. ignorant.

neto /'neto/ a. net.

neumático /neu'matiko/ a. 1. pneumatic. —n. 2. m. (pneumatic) tire.

neumático de recambio /neu'matiko de rre'kambio/ spare tire.

neumonía /neumo'nia/ n. f. pneumonia.

neurótico /neu'rotiko/ a. neurotic.

neutral /neu'tral/ a. neutral.

neutralidad /neutrali'ðað/ n. f. neutrality.

neutro /'neutro/ a. neuter; neutral.

neutrón /neu'tron/ n. m. neutron.

nevada /ne'βaða/ n. f. snowfall.

nevado /ne'βaðo/ a. snow-white; snow-capped.

nevar /ne'βar/ v. snow.

nevera /ne'βera/ n. f. icebox.

nevoso /ne'βoso/ a. snowy.

ni /ni/ conj. 1. nor. **ni... ni,** neither... nor. —adv. 2. not even.

nicho /'nitʃo/ n. m. recess; niche.

nido /'niðo/ n. m. nest.

niebla /'nieβla/ n. f. fog; mist.

nieto /'nieto/ -ta n. grandchild.

nieve /'nieβe/ n. f. snow.

nilón /ni'lon/ n. m. nylon.

nimio /'nimio/ adj. stingy.

ninfa /'ninfa/ n. f. nymph.

ningún /niŋ'gun/ **-no -na** a. & pron. no, none, neither (one); any, either (one).

niñera /ni'ɲera/ n. f. nursemaid, nanny.

niñez /ni'ɲeθ; ni'ɲes/ n. f. childhood.

niño /'niɲo/ **-ña 1.** a. 1. young; childish; childlike. —n. 2. child.

níquel /'nikel/ n. m. nickel.

niquelado /nike'laðo/ a. nickel-plated.

nítido /'nitiðo/ a. neat, clean, bright.

nitrato /ni'trato/ n. m. nitrate.

nitro /'nitro/ n. m. niter.

nitrógeno /ni'troheno/ n. m. nitrogen.

nivel /ni'βel/ n. m. level; grade. —**nivelar,** v.

no /no/ adv. 1. not. **no más,** only. —interj. 2. no.

noble /'noβle/ a. & m. noble; nobleman.

nobleza /no'βleθa; no'βlesa/ n. f. nobility; nobleness.

noche /'notʃe/ n. f. night; evening.

Nochebuena /notʃe'βuena/ n. f. Christmas Eve.

noción /no'θion; no'sion/ n. f. notion, idea.

nocivo /no'θiβo; no'siβo/ a. harmful.

noctiluca /nokti'luka/ n. f. glowworm.

nocturno /nok'turno/ a. nocturnal.

nodriza /no'ðriθa; no'ðrisa/ n. f. wet nurse.

no fumador /no fuma'ðor/ **-ra** n. m. & f. nonsmoker.

nogal /no'gal/ n. m. walnut.

nombradía /nom'βraðia/ n. f. fame.

nombramiento /nombra'miento/ n. m. appointment, nomination.

nombrar /nom'βrar/ v. name, appoint, nominate; mention.

nombre /'nombre/ n. m. name; noun.

nombre y apellidos /'nombre i ape'ʎiðos; 'nombre i ape'yiðos/ (person's) full name.

nómina /'nomina/ *n. f.* list; payroll.

nominación /nomina'θion; nomina'sion/ *n. f.* nomination.

nominal /nomi'nal/ *a.* nominal.

nominar /nomi'nar/ *v.* nominate.

non /non/ *a.* uneven, odd.

nonada /no'naða/ *n. f.* trifle.

nordeste /nor'ðeste/ *n. m.* northeast.

nórdico /'norðiko/ *a.* Nordic; northerly.

norma /'norma/ *n. f.* norm, standard.

normal /nor'mal/ *a.* normal, standard.

normalidad /normali'ðað/ *n. f.* normality.

normalizar /normali'θar; normali'sar/ *v.* normalize; standardize.

noroeste /noro'este/ *n. m.* northwest.

norte /'norte/ *n. m.* north.

norteamericano /norteameri'kano/ **-na** *a. & n.* North American.

Noruega /no'ruega/ *n. f.* Norway.

noruego /no'ruego/ **-ga** *a. & n.* Norwegian.

nos /nos/ *pron.* us; ourselves.

nosotros /no'sotros, no'sotras/ **-as** *pron.* we, us; ourselves.

nostalgia /nos'talhia/ *n. f.* nostalgia, homesickness.

nostálgico /nos'talhiko/ *a.* nostalgic.

nota /'nota/ *n. f.* note; grade, mark.

notable /no'taβle/ *a.* notable, remarkable.

notación /nota'θion; nota'sion/ *n. f.* notation; note.

notar /no'tar/ *v.* note, notice.

notario /no'tario/ **-ria** *n.* notary.

noticia /no'tiθia; no'tisia/ *n. f.* notice; piece of news; (*pl.*) news.

noticia de última hora /no'tiθia de 'ultima 'ora; no'tisia de 'ultima 'ora/ news flash.

notificación /notifika'θion; notifika'sion/ *n. f.* notification.

notificación de reclutamiento /notifika'θion de rrekluta'miento; notifika'sion de rrekluta'miento/ draft notice.

notificar /notifi'kar/ *v.* notify.

notorio /no'torio/ *a.* well-known.

novato /no'βato/ **-ta** *n.* novice.

novecientos /noβe'θientos; noβe'sientos/ *a. & pron.* nine hundred.

novedad /noβe'ðað/ *n. f.* novelty; piece of news.

novel /no'βel/ *a.* new; inexperienced.

novela /no'βela/ *n. f.* novel.

novelista /noβe'lista/ *n. m. & f.* novelist.

novena /no'βena/ *n. f.* novena.

noveno /no'βeno/ *a.* ninth.

noventa /no'βenta/ *a. & pron.* ninety.

novia /'noβia/ *n. f.* bride; sweetheart; fiancée.

noviazgo /no'βiaθgo; no'βiasgo/ *n. m.* engagement.

novicio /no'βiθio; no'βisio/ **-cia** *n.* novice, beginner.

noviembre /no'βiembre/ *n. m.* November.

novilla /no'βiʎa; no'βiya/ *n. f.* heifer.

novio /'noβio/ *n. m.* bridegroom; sweetheart; fiancé.

nube /'nuβe/ *n. f.* cloud.

núbil /'nuβil/ *a.* marriageable.

nublado /nu'βlaðo/ *a.* cloudy.

nuclear /nukle'ar/ *a.* nuclear.

núcleo /'nukleo/ *n. m.* nucleus.

nudo /'nuðo/ *n. m.* knot.

nuera /'nuera/ *n. f.* daughter-in-law.

nuestro /'nuestro/ *a.* our, ours.

nueva /'nueβa/ *n. f.* news.

nueve /'nueβe/ *a. & pron.* nine.

nuevo /'nueβo/ *a.* new. **de n.,** again, anew.

nuez /nueθ; nues/ *n. f.* nut; walnut.

nulidad /nuli'ðað/ *n. f.* nonentity; nullity.

nulo /'nulo/ *a.* null, void.

numeración /numera'θion; numera'sion/ *n. f.* numeration.

numerar /nume'rar/ *v.* number.

numérico /nu'meriko/ *a.* numerical.

número /'numero/ *n. m.* number; size (of shoe, etc.). **n. impar,** odd number. **n. par,** even number.

numeroso /nume'roso/ *a.* numerous.

numismática /numis'matika/ *n. f.* numismatics.

nunca /'nunka/ *adv.* never; ever.

nupcial /nup'θial; nup'sial/ *a.* nuptial.

nupcias /'nupθias; 'nupsias/ *n. f.pl.* nuptials, wedding.

nutrición /nutri'θion; nutri'sion/ *n. f.* nutrition.

nutrimento /nutri'mento/ *n. m.* nourishment.

nutrir /nu'trir/ *v.* nourish.

nutritivo /nutri'tiβo/ *a.* nutritious.

nylon /'nilon/ *n. m.* nylon.

ñame /'ɲame/ *n. m.* yam.

ñapa /'ɲapa/ *n. f.* something extra.

ñoñeria /ɲoɲe'ria/ *n. f.* dotage.

ñoño /'ɲoɲo/ *a.* feeble-minded, senile.

O

o /o/ *conj.* or. **o... o,** either... or.

oasis /o'asis/ *n. m.* oasis.

obedecer /oβeðe'θer; oβeðe'ser/ *v.* obey, mind.

obediencia /oβe'ðienθia; oβe-'ðiensia/ *n. f.* obedience.

obediente /oβe'ðiente/ *a.* obedient.

obelisco /oβe'lisko/ *n. m.* obelisk.

obertura /oβer'tura/ *n. f.* overture.

obeso /o'βeso/ *a.* obese.

obispo /o'βispo/ *n. m.* bishop.

obituario /oβi'tuario/ *n. m.* obituary.

objeción /oβhe'θion; oβhe'sion/ *n. f.* objection.

objetivo /oβhe'tiβo/ *a. & m.* objective.

objeto /oβ'heto/ *n. m.* object. **—objetar,** *v.*

objetor de conciencia /oβhe'tor de kon'θienθia; oβhe'tor de kon'siensia/ *n. m.* conscientious objector.

oblicuo /o'βlikuo/ *a.* oblique.

obligación /oβliga'θion; oβliga-'sion/ *n. f.* obligation, duty.

obligar /oβli'gar/ *v.* oblige, require, compel; obligate.

obligatorio /oβliga'torio/ *a.* obligatory, compulsory.

oblongo /o'βloŋgo/ *a.* oblong.

oboe /o'βoe/ *n. m.* oboe.

obra /'oβra/ *n. f.* work. **—obrar,** *v.*

obrero /o'βrero/ **-ra** *n.* worker, laborer.

obscenidad /oβsθeni'ðað; oβsseni'ðað/ *n. f.* obscenity.

obsceno /oβs'θeno; oβs'seno/ *a.* obscene.

obscurecer /oβskure'θer; oβskure-ɾ'aprim;ser/ *v.* obscure; darken.

obscuridad /oβskuri'ðað/ *n. f.* obscurity; darkness.

obscuro /oβs'kuro/ *a.* obscure; dark.

obsequiar /oβse'kiar/ *v.* court; make presents to, fete.

obsequio /oβ'sekio/ *n. m.* obsequiousness; gift; attention.

observación /oβserβa'θion; oβserβa'sion/ *n. f.* observation.

observador /oβserβa'ðor/ **-ra** *n.* observer.

observancia /oβser'βanθia; oβser-'βansia/ *n. f.* observance.

observar /oβser'βar/ *v.* observe, watch.

observatorio /oβserβa'torio/ *n. m.* observatory.

obsesión /oβse'sion/ *n. f.* obsession.

obstáculo /oβs'takulo/ *n. m.* obstacle.

obstante /oβs'tante/ *adv.* **no o.,** however, yet, nevertheless.

obstar /oβs'tar/ *v.* hinder, obstruct.

obstetricia /oβste'triθia; oβste'trisia/ *n. f.* obstetrics.

obstinación /oβstina'θion; oβstina'sion/ *n. f.* obstinacy.

obstinado /oβsti'naðo/ *a.* obstinate, stubborn.

obstinarse /oβsti'narse/ *v.* persist, insist.

obstrucción /oβstruk'θion; oβstruk'sion/ *n. f.* obstruction.

obstruir /oβs'truir/ *v.* obstruct, clog, block.

obtener /oβte'ner/ *v.* obtain, get, secure.

obtuso /oβ'tuso/ *a.* obtuse.

obvio /'oββio/ *a.* obvious.

ocasión /oka'sion/ *n. f.* occasion; opportunity, chance. **de o.,** secondhand.

ocasional /okasio'nal/ *a.* occasional.

ocasionalmente /okasional-'mente/ *adv.* occasionally.

ocasionar /okasio'nar/ *v.* cause, occasion.

occidental /okθiðen'tal; oksiðen-'tal/ *a.* western.

occidente /okθi'ðente; oksi'ðente/ *n. m.* west.

océano /o'θeano; o'seano/ *n. m.* ocean.

Océano Atlántico /o'θeano a'tlantiko; o'seano a'tlantiko/ Atlantic Ocean.

Océano Pacífico /o'θeano pa'θifiko; o'seano pa'sifiko/ Pacific Ocean.

ocelote /oθe'lote; ose'lote/ *n. m.* ocelot.

ochenta /o'tʃenta/ *a. & pron.* eighty.

ocho /'otʃo/ *a. & pron.* eight.

ochocientos /otʃo'θientos; otʃo'sientos/ *a. & pron.* eight hundred.

ocio /'oθio; 'osio/ *n. m.* idleness, leisure.

ociosidad /oθiosi'ðað; osiosi'ðað/ *n. f.* idleness, laziness.

ocioso /o'θioso; o'sioso/ *a.* idle, lazy.

ocre /'okre/ *n. m.* ochre.

octagonal /oktago'nal/ *a.* octagonal.

octava /ok'taβa/ *n. f.* octave.

octavo /ok'taβo/ *a.* eighth.

octubre /ok'tuβre/ *n. m.* October.

oculista /oku'lista/ *n. m. & f.* oculist.

ocultación /okulta'θion; okulta'sion/ *n. f.* concealment.

ocultar /okul'tar/ *v.* hide, conceal.

oculto /o'kulto/ *a.* hidden.

ocupación /okupa'θion; okupa'sion/ *n. f.* occupation.

ocupado /oku'paðo/ *a.* occupied; busy.

ocupante /oku'pante/ *n. m. & f.* occupant.

ocupar /oku'par/ *v.* occupy.

ocuparse de /oku'parse de/ *v.* take care of, take charge of.

ocurrencia /oku'rrenθia; oku'rrensia/

ocurrente /oku'rrente/ *a.* witty.

ocurrir /oku'rrir/ *v.* occur, happen.

oda /'oða/ *n. f.* ode.

odio /'oðio/ *n. m.* hate. —**odiar,** *v.*

odiosidad /oðiosi'ðað/ *n. f.* odiousness; hatred.

odioso /o'ðioso/ *a.* obnoxious, odious.

odisea /oði'sea/ *n. f.* odyssey.

OEA, *abbr.* (**Organización de los Estados Americanos**). OAS (**Organization of American States**).

oeste /o'este/ *n. m.* west.

ofender /ofen'der/ *v.* offend, wrong.

ofenderse /ofen'derse/ *v.* be offended, take offense.

ofensa /o'fensa/ *n. f.* offense.

ofensiva /ofen'siβa/ *n. f.* offensive.

ofensivo /ofen'siβo/ *a.* offensive.

ofensor /ofen'sor/ **-ra** *n.* offender.

oferta /o'ferta/ *n. f.* offer, proposal.

ofertorio /ofer'torio/ *n. m.* offertory.

oficial /ofi'θial; ofi'sial/ *a. & m.* official; officer.

oficialmente /ofiθial'mente; ofisial'mente/ *adv.* officially.

oficiar /ofi'θiar; ofi'siar/ *v.* officiate.

oficina /ofi'θina; ofi'sina/ *n. f.* office.

oficio /o'fiθio; o'fisio/ *n. m.* office; trade; church service.

oficioso /ofi'θioso; ofi'sioso/ *a.* officious.

ofrecer /ofre'θer; ofre'ser/ *v.* offer.

ofrecimiento /ofreθi'miento; ofresi'miento/ *n. m.* offer, offering. **o. de presentación,** introductory offer.

ofrenda /o'frenda/ *n. f.* offering.

oftalmía /oftal'mia/ *n. f.* ophthalmia.

ofuscamiento /ofuska'miento/ *n. m.* obfuscation; bewilderment.

ofuscar /ofus'kar/ *v.* obfuscate; bewilder.

ogro /'ogro/ *n. m.* ogre.

oído /o'iðo/ *n. m.* ear; hearing.

oír /o'ir/ *v.* hear; listen.

ojal /o'hal/ *n. m.* buttonhole.

ojalá /oha'la/ *interj.* expressing wish or hope. **o. que...** would that...

ojeada /ohe'aða/ *n. f.* glance; peep; look.

ojear /ohe'ar/ *v.* eye, look at, glance at, stare at.

ojeriza /ohe'riθa; ohe'risa/ *n. f.* spite; grudge.

ojiva /o'hiβa/ *n. f.* pointed arch, ogive.

ojo /'oho/ *n. m.* eye. **¡Ojo!** Look out!

ola /'ola/ *n. f.* wave.

olaje /o'lahe/ *n. m.* surge of waves.

oleada /ole'aða/ *n. f.* swell.

oleo /'oleo/ *n. m.* oil; holy oil; extreme unction.

oleoducto /oleo'ðukto/ *n. m.* pipeline.

oleomargarina /oleomarga'rina/ *n. f.* oleomargarine.

oleoso /ole'oso/ *a.* oily.

oler /o'ler/ *v.* smell.

olfatear /olfate'ar/ *v.* smell.

olfato /ol'fato/ *n. m.* scent, smell.

oliva /o'liβa/ *n. f.* olive.

olivar /oli'βar/ *n. m.* olive grove.

olivo /o'liβo/ *n. m.* olive tree.

olla /'oʎa; 'oya/ *n. f.* pot, kettle.
o. podrida, stew.

olmo /'olmo/ *n. m.* elm.

olor /o'lor/ *n. m.* odor, smell, scent.

oloroso /olo'roso/ *a.* fragrant, scented.

olvidadizo /olβiða'ðiθo; olβiða-'ðiso/ *a.* forgetful.

olvidar /olβi'ðar/ *v.* forget.

olvido /ol'βiðo/ *n. m.* omission; forgetfulness.

ombligo /om'βligo/ *n. m.* navel.

ominar /omi'nar/ *v.* foretell.

ominoso /omi'noso/ *a.* ominous.

omisión /omi'sion/ *n. f.* omission.

omitir /omi'tir/ *v.* omit, leave out.

ómnibus /'omniβus/ *n. m.* bus.

omnipotencia /omnipo'tenθia; omnipo'tensia/ *n. f.* omnipotence.

omnipotente /omnipo'tente/ *a.* almighty.

omnipresencia /omnipre'senθia; omnipre'sensia/ *n. f.* omnipresence.

omnisciencia /omnis'θienθia; omnis'siensia/ *n. f.* omniscience.

omnívoro /om'niβoro/ *a.* omnivorous.

omóplato /omo'plato/ *n. m.* shoulder blade.

once /'onθe; 'onse/ *a. & pron.* eleven.

onda /'onda/ *n. f.* wave, ripple.

ondear /onde'ar/ *v.* ripple.

ondulación /ondula'θion; ondula-'sion/ *n. f.* wave, undulation.

ondular /ondu'lar/ *v.* undulate, ripple.

onza /'onθa; 'onsa/ *n. f.* ounce.

opaco /o'pako/ *a.* opaque.

ópalo /'opalo/ *n. m.* opal.

opción /op'θion; op'sion/ *n. f.* option.

ópera /'opera/ *n. f.* opera.

operación /opera'θion; opera'sion/ *n. f.* operation.

operar /ope'rar/ *v.* operate; operate on.

operario /ope'rario/ **-ria** *n.* operator; (skilled) worker.

operarse /ope'rarse/ *v.* have an operation.

operativo /opera'tiβo/ *a.* operative.

opereta /ope'reta/ *n. f.* operetta.

opiato /o'piato/ *n. m.* opiate.

opinar /opi'nar/ *v.* opine.

opinión /opi'nion/ *n. f.* opinion, view.

opio /'opio/ *n. m.* opium.

oponer /opo'ner/ *v.* oppose.

Oporto /o'porto/ *n. m.* port (wine).

oportunidad /oportuni'ðað/ *n. f.* opportunity.

oportunismo /oportu'nismo/ *n. m.* opportunism.

oportunista /oportu'nista/ *n. & a.* opportunist.

oportuno /opor'tuno/ *a.* opportune, expedient.

oposición /oposi'θion; oposi'sion/ *n. f.* opposition.

opresión /opre'sion/ *n. f.* oppression.

opresivo /opre'siβo/ *a.* oppressive.

oprimir /opri'mir/ *v.* oppress.

oprobio /o'proβio/ *n. m.* infamy.

optar /op'tar/ *v.* select, choose.

óptica /'optika/ *n. f.* optics.

óptico /'optiko/ *a.* optic.

optimismo /opti'mismo/ *n. m.* optimism.

optimista /opti'mista/ *a. & n.* optimistic; optimist.

óptimo /'optimo/ *a.* best.

opuesto /o'puesto/ *a.* opposite; opposed.

opugnar /opug'nar/ *v.* attack.

opulencia /opu'lenθia; opu'lensia/ *n. f.* opulence, wealth.

opulento /opu'lento/ *a.* opulent, wealthy.

oración /ora'θion; ora'sion/ *n. f.* sentence; prayer; oration.

oráculo /o'rakulo/ *n. m.* oracle.

orador /ora'ðor/ **-ra** *n.* orator, speaker.

oral /o'ral/ *a.* oral.

orangután /oraŋgu'tan/ *n. m.* orangutan.

orar /o'rar/ *v.* pray.

oratoria /ora'toria/ *n. f.* oratory.

oratorio /ora'torio/ *a.* oratorical.

orbe /'orβe/ *n. m.* orb; globe.

órbita /'orβita/ *n. f.* orbit.

orden /'orðen/ *n. m. or f.* order.

ordenador /orðena'ðor/ *n. m.* computer; regulator.

ordenador de sobremesa /orðena'ðor de soβre'mesa/ desktop computer.

ordenador doméstico /orðena-'ðor do'mestiko/ home computer.

ordenanza /orðe'nanθa; orðe-'nansa/ *n. f.* ordinance.

ordenar /orðe'nar/ *v.* order; put in order; ordain.

ordeñar /orðe'ɲar/ *v.* milk.

ordinal /orði'nal/ *a. & m.* ordinal.

ordinario /orði'nario/ *a.* ordinary; common, usual.

oreja /o'reha/ *n. f.* ear.

orejera /ore'hera/ *n. f.* earmuff.

orfanato /orfa'nato/ *n. m.* orphanage.

organdí /organ'di/ *n. m.* organdy.

orgánico /or'ganiko/ *a.* organic.

organigrama /organi'grama/ *n. m.* flow chart.

organismo /orga'nismo/ *n. m.* organism.

organista /orga'nista/ *n. m. & f.* organist.

organización /organiθa'θion; organisa'sion/ *n. f.* organization.

organizar /organi'θar; organi'sar/ *v.* organize.

órgano /'organo/ *n. m.* organ.

orgía /or'hia/ *n. f.* orgy, revel.

orgullo /or'guʎo; or'guyo/ *n. m.* pride.

orgulloso /orgu'ʎoso; orgu'yoso/ *a.* proud.

orientación /orienta'θion; orienta'sion/ *n. f.* orientation.

oriental /orien'tal/ *a.* Oriental; eastern.

orientar /orien'tar/ *v.* orient.

oriente /o'riente/ *n. m.* orient, east.

orificación /orifika'θion; orifika'sion/ *n. f.* gold filling (for tooth).

origen /o'rihen/ *n. m.* origin; parentage, descent.

original /orihi'nal/ *a.* original.

originalidad /orihinali'ðað/ *n. f.* originality.

originalmente /orihinal'mente/ *adv.* originally.

originar /orihi'nar/ *v.* originate.

orilla /o'riʎa; o'riya/ *n. f.* shore; bank; edge.

orín /o'rin/ *n. m.* rust.

orina /o'rina/ *n. f.* urine.

orinar /ori'nar/ *v.* urinate.

orines /o'rines/ *n. m.pl.* urine.

oriol /o'riol/ *n. m.* oriole.

orla /'orla/ *n. f.* border; edging.

ornado /or'naðo/ *a.* ornate.

ornamentación /ornamenta'θion; ornamenta'sion/ *n. f.* ornamentation.

ornamento /orna'mento/ *n. m.* ornament. —**ornamentar,** *v.*

ornar /or'nar/ *v.* ornament, adorn.

oro /'oro/ *n. m.* gold.

oropel /oro'pel/ *n. m.* tinsel.

orquesta /or'kesta/ *n. f.* orchestra.

ortiga /or'tiga/ *n. f.* nettle.

ortodoxo /orto'ðokso/ *a.* orthodox.

ortografía /ortogra'fia/ *n. f.* orthography, spelling.

ortóptero /or'toptero/ *a.* orthopterous.

oruga /o'ruga/ *n. f.* caterpillar.

orzuelo /or'θuelo; or'suelo/ *n. m.* sty.

os /os/ *pron.* you (*pl.*); yourselves.

osadía /osa'ðia/ *n. f.* daring.

osar /o'sar/ *v.* dare.

oscilación /osθila'θion; ossila'sion/ *n. f.* oscillation.

oscilar /osθi'lar; ossi'lar/ *v.* oscillate, rock.

ósculo /'oskulo/ *n. m.* kiss.

oscurecer /oskure'θer; oskure'ser/ *v.* obscure. **oscuridad,** *n.* obscurity; darkness. **oscuro,** *adj.* obscure; dark.

oso /'oso/ **osa** *n.* bear.

oso de felpa /'oso de 'felpa/ teddy bear.

ostentación /ostenta'θion; ostenta'sion/ *n. f.* ostentation, showiness.

ostentar /osten'tar/ *v.* show off.

ostentoso /osten'toso/ *a.* ostentatious, flashy.

ostra /'ostra/ *n. f.* oyster.

ostracismo /ostra'θismo; ostra-'sismo/ *n. m.* ostracism.

otalgia /o'talhia/ *n. f.* earache.

otero /o'tero/ *n. m.* hill, knoll.

otoño /o'toɲo/ *n. m.* autumn, fall.

otorgar /otor'gar/ *v.* grant, award.

otro /'otro/ *a. & pron.* other, another. **o. vez,** again. **el uno al o.,** one another, each other.

ovación /oβa'θion; oβa'sion/ *n. f.* ovation.

oval /o'βal/ **ovalado** *a.* oval.

óvalo /'oβalo/ *n. m.* oval.

ovario /o'βario/ *n. m.* ovary.

oveja /o'βeha/ *n. f.* sheep.

ovejero /oβe'hero/ *n. m.* sheep dog.

ovillo /o'βiʎo; o'βiyo/ *n. m.* ball of yarn.

OVNI /'oβni/ *abbr.* (objeto volador no identificado) UFO (unidentified flying object).

oxidación /oksiða'θion; oksiða-'sion/ *n. f.* oxidation.

oxidar /oksi'ðar/ *v.* oxidize; rust.

óxido /'oksiðo/ *n. m.* oxide.

oxígeno /ok'siheno/ *n. m.* oxygen.

oyente /o'iente/ *n. m. & f.* hearer; (*pl.*) audience.

ozono /o'θono; o'sono/ *n. m.* ozone.

P

pabellón /paβe'ʎon; paβe'yon/ *n. m.* pavilion. **p. de deportes,** sports center.

pabilo /pa'βilo/ *n. m.* wick.

paciencia /pa'θienθia; pa'siensia/ *n. f.* patience.

paciente /pa'θiente; pa'siente/ *a. & n.* patient.

pacificar /paθifi'kar; pasifi'kar/ *v.* pacify.

pacífico /pa'θifiko; pa'sifiko/ *a.* pacific.

pacifismo /paθi'fismo; pasi'fismo/ *n. m.* pacifism.

pacifista /paθi'fista; pasi'fista/ *n. & a.* pacifist.

pacto /'pakto/ *n. m.* pact, treaty.

padecer /paðe'θer; paðe'ser/ *v.* suffer. **p. del corazón,** have heart trouble.

padrastro /pa'ðrastro/ *n. m.* stepfather.

padre /'paðre/ *n. m.* father; priest; (*pl.*) parents.

padrenuestro /paðre'nuestro/ *n. m.* paternoster, Lord's Prayer.

padrino /pa'ðrino/ *n. m.* godfather; sponsor.

paella /pa'eʎa; pa'eya/ *n. f.* dish of rice with meat or chicken.

paga /'paga/ *n. f.* pay, wages. **p. extra,** bonus.

pagadero /paga'ðero/ *a.* payable.

pagador /paga'ðor/ **-ra** *n.* payer.

paganismo /paga'nismo/ *n. m.* paganism.

pagano /pa'gano/ **-na** *a. & n.* heathen, pagan.

pagar /pa'gar/ *v.* pay, pay for. **p. en metálico,** pay cash.

página /'pahina/ *n. f.* page.

pago /'pago/ *n. m.* pay, payment.

país /pa'is/ *n. m.* country, nation.

paisaje /pai'sahe/ *n. m.* landscape, scenery, countryside.

paisano /pai'sano/ **-na** *n.* countryman; compatriot; civilian.

paja /'paha/ *n. f.* straw.

pajar /pa'har/ *n. m.* barn.

pajarita /paha'rita/ *n. f.* bow tie.

pájaro /'paharo/ *n. m.* bird.

paje /'pahe/ *n. m.* page (person).

pala /'pala/ *n. f.* shovel, spade.

palabra /pa'laβra/ *n. f.* word.

palabrero /pala'βrero/ *a.* talkative; wordy.

palabrista /pala'βrista/ *n. m. & f.* talkative person.

palacio /pa'laθio; pa'lasio/ *n. m.* palace.

paladar /pala'ðar/ *n. m.* palate.

paladear /palaðe'ar/ *v.* taste; relish.

palanca /pa'lanka/ *n. f.* lever. **p. de cambio,** gearshift.

palangana /palaŋ'gana/ *n. f.* washbasin.

palco /'palko/ *n. m.* theater box.

palenque /pa'lenke/ *n. m.* palisade.

paleta /pa'leta/ *n. f.* mat, pallet.

paletilla /pale'tiʎa; pale'tiya/ *n. f.* shoulder blade.

palidecer /paliðe'θer; paliðe'ser/ *v.* turn pale.

palidez /pali'ðeθ; pali'ðes/ *n. f.* paleness.

pálido /'paliðo/ *a.* pale.

paliza /pa'liθa; pa'lisa/ *n. f.* beating.

palizada /pali'θaða; pali'saða/ *n. m.* palisade.

palma /'palma/ **palmera** *n. f.* palm (tree).

palmada /pal'maða/ *n. f.* slap, clap.

palmear /palme'ar/ *v.* applaud.

palo /'palo/ *n. m.* pole, stick; suit (in cards); *Naut.* mast.

paloma /pa'loma/ *n. f.* dove, pigeon.

palpar /pal'par/ *v.* touch, feel.

palpitación /palpita'θion; palpita-'sion/ *n. f.* palpitation.

palpitar /palpi'tar/ *v.* palpitate.

paludismo /palu'ðismo/ *n. m.* malaria.

pampa /'pampa/ *n. f.* (*S.A.*) prairie, plain.

pan /pan/ *n. m.* bread; loaf. **p. de centeno**, rye bread.

pana /'pana/ *n. f.* corduroy.

panacea /pana'θea; pana'sea/ *n. f.* panacea.

panadería /panaðe'ria/ *n. f.* bakery.

panadero /pana'ðero/ **-ra** *n.* baker.

panameño /pana'meɲo/ **-ña** *a. & n.* Panamanian, of Panama.

panamericano /panameri'kano/ *a.* Pan-American.

páncreas /'pankreas/ *n. m.* páncreas.

pandeo /pan'deo/ *n. m.* bulge.

pandilla /pan'diʎa; pan'diya/ *n. f.* band, gang.

panecillo /pane'θiʎo; pane'siyo/ *n. m.* roll, muffin.

panegírico /pane'hiriko/ *n. m.* panegyric.

pánico /'paniko/ *n. m.* panic.

panocha /pa'notʃa/ *n. f.* ear of corn.

panorama /pano'rama/ *n. m.* panorama.

panorámico /pano'ramiko/ *a.* panoramic.

pantalla /pan'taʎa; pan'taya/ *n. f.* (movie) screen; lamp shade.

pantalones /panta'lones/ *n. m.pl.* trousers, pants.

pantano /pan'tano/ *n. m.* bog, marsh, swamp.

pantanoso /panta'noso/ *a.* swampy, marshy.

pantera /pan'tera/ *n. f.* panther.

pantomima /panto'mima/ *n. f.* pantomime.

pantorrilla /panto'rriʎa; panto-'rriya/ *n. f.* calf (of body).

panza /'panθa; 'pansa/ *n. f.* belly, paunch.

pañal /pa'ɲal/ *n. m.* diaper.

paño /'paɲo/ *n. m.* piece of cloth.

pañuelo /pa'ɲuelo/ *n. m.* handkerchief.

Papa /'papa/ *n. m.* Pope.

papa *n. f.* potato.

papá *n. m.* papa, father.

papado /pa'paðo/ *n. m.* papacy.

papagayo /papa'gaio/ *n. m.* parrot.

papal /pa'pal/ *a.* papal.

Papá Noel /pa'pa no'el/ *n. m.* Santa Claus.

papel /pa'pel/ *n. m.* paper; role, part.

papel crespón /pa'pel kres'pon/ crepe paper.

papel de aluminio /pa'pel de alu'minio/ aluminum foil.

papel de escribir /pa'pel de es-kri'βir/ writing paper.

papel de estaño /pa'pel de es'taɲo/ tin foil.

papel de lija /pa'pel de 'liha/ sandpaper.

papelera /pape'lera/ *n. f.* file cabinet; wastepaper basket.

papelería /papele'ria/ *n. f.* stationery store.

papel moneda /pa'pel mo'neða/ paper money.

paperas /pa'peras/ *n. f.pl.* mumps.

paquete /pa'kete/ *n. m.* package.

par /par/ *a.* **1.** even, equal. —*n.* **2.** *m.* pair; equal, peer. **abierto de p. en p.,** wide open.

para /'para/ *prep.* for; in order to. **p. que,** in order that. **estar p.,** to be about to.

parabién /para'βien/ *n. m.* congratulation.

parabrisa /para'βrisa/ *n. m.* windshield.

paracaídas /paraka'iðas/ *n. m.* parachute.

parachoques /para'tʃokes/ *n. m. Auto.* bumper.

parada /pa'raða/ *n. f.* stop, halt; stopover; parade.

paradero /para'ðero/ *n. m.* whereabouts; stopping place.

paradigma /para'ðigma/ *n. m.* paradigm.

paradoja /para'ðoha/ *n. f.* paradox.

parafina /para'fina/ *n. f.* paraffin.

parafrasear /parafrase'ar/ *v.* paraphrase.

paraguas /pa'raguas/ *n. m.* umbrella.

paraguayano /paragua'yano/ **-na** *n. & a.* Paraguayan.

paraíso /para'iso/ *n. m.* paradise.

paralelo /para'lelo/ *a. & m.* parallel.

parálisis /pa'ralisis/ *n. f.* paralysis.

paralizar /parali'θar; parali'sar/ *v.* paralyze.

paramédico /para'meðiko/ *n. m.* paramedic.

parámetro /pa'rametro/ *n. m.* parameter.

parapeto /para'peto/ *n. m.* parapet.

parar /pa'rar/ *v.* stop, stem, ward off; stay.

pararse /pa'rarse/ *v.* stop; stand up.

parasítico /para'sitiko/ *a.* parasitic.

parásito /pa'rasito/ *n. m.* parasite.

parcela /par'θela; par'sela/ *n. f.* plot of ground.

parcial /par'θial; par'sial/ *a.* partial.

parcialidad /parθiali'ðað; parsiali-'ðað/ *n. f.* partiality; bias.

parcialmente /parθial'mente; parsial'mente/ *adv.* partially.

pardo /'parðo/ *a.* brown.

parear /pare'ar/ *v.* pair; match; mate.

parecer /pare'θer; pare'ser/ *n.* **1.** *m.* opinion. —*v.* **2.** seem, appear, look.

parecerse /pare'θerse; pare'serse/ *v.* look alike. **p. a,** look like.

parecido /pare'θiðo; pare'siðo/ *a.* similar.

pared /pa'reð/ *n. f.* wall.

pareja /pa'reha/ *n. f.* pair, couple; (dancing) partner.

parentela /paren'tela/ *n. f.* kinfolk.

parentesco /paren'tesko/ *n. m.* parentage, lineage; kin.

paréntesis /pa'rentesis/ *n. m.* parenthesis.

paria /'paria/ *n. m.* outcast, pariah.

paricipante /pariθi'pante; parisi'pante/ *n. m. & f.* participant.

paridad /pari'ðað/ *n. f.* parity.

pariente /pa'riente/ *n. m. & f.* relative.

parir /pa'rir/ *v.* give birth.

parisiense /pari'siense/ *n. & a.* Parisian.

parlamentario /parlamen'tario/ *a.* parliamentary.

parlamento /parla'mento/ *n. m.* parliament.

paro /'paro/ *n. m.* stoppage; strike. **p. forzoso,** unemployment.

parodia /pa'roðia/ *n. f.* parody.

parodista /paro'ðista/ *n. m. & f.* parodist.

paroxismo /parok'sismo/ *n. m.* paroxysm.

párpado /'parpaðo/ *n. m.* eyelid.

parque /'parke/ *n. m.* park.

parquímetro /par'kimetro/ *n. m.* parking meter.

parra /'parra/ *n. f.* grapevine.

párrafo /'parrafo/ *n. m.* paragraph.

parranda /pa'rranda/ *n. f.* spree.

parrandear /parrande'ar/ *v.* carouse.

parrilla /pa'rriʎa; pa'rriya/ *n. f.* grill; grillroom.

párroco /'parroko/ *n. m.* parish priest.

parroquía /pa'rrokia/ *n. f.* parish.

parroquial /parro'kial/ *a.* parochial.

parsimonia /parsi'monia/ *n. f.* economy, thrift.

parsimonioso /parsimo'nioso/ *a.* economical, thrifty.

parte /'parte/ *n. f.* part. **de p. de,** on behalf of. **alguna p.,** somewhere. **por otra p.,** on the other hand. **dar p. a,** to notify.

partera /par'tera/ *n. f.* midwife.

partición /parti'θion; parti'sion/ *n. f.* distribution.

participación /partiθipa'θion; partisipa'sion/ *n. f.* participation.

participar /partiθi'par; partisi'par/ *v.* participate; announce.

participio /parti'θipio; parti'sipio/ *n. m.* participle.

partícula /par'tikula/ *n. f.* particle.

particular /partiku'lar/ *a.* **1.** particular; private. —*n.* **2.** *m.* particular; detail; individual.

particularmente /partikular-'mente/ *adv.* particularly.

partida /par'tiða/ *n. f.* departure; *Mil.* party; (sport) game.

partida de defunción /par'tiða de defun'θion; par'tiða de defun'sion/ death certificate.

partida de matrimonio /par'tiða de matri'monio/ marriage certificate.

partida de nacimiento /par'tiða de naθi'miento; par'tiða de nasi'miento/ birth certificate.

partidario /parti'ðario/ **-ria** *n.* partisan.

partido /par'tiðo/ *n. m.* side, party, faction; game, match.

partir /par'tir/ *v.* leave, depart; part, cleave, split.

parto /'parto/ *n. m.* delivery, childbirth.

pasa /'pasa/ *n. f.* raisin.

pasado /pa'saðo/ *a.* **1.** past; last. —*n.* **2.** *m.* past.

pasaje /pa'sahe/ *n. m.* passage, fare.

pasajero /pasa'hero/ **-ra** *a.* **1.** passing, transient. —*n.* **2.** passenger.

pasamano /pasa'mano/ *n. m.* banister.

pasaporte /pasa'porte/ *n. m.* passport.

pasar /pa'sar/ *v.* pass; happen; spend (time). **p. por alto,** overlook. **p. lista,** call the roll. **p. sin,** do without.

pasatiempo /pasa'tiempo/ *n. m.* pastime; hobby.

pascua /'paskua/ *n. f.* religious holiday; (*pl.*) Christmas (season). **P. Florida,** Easter.

pase de modelos /'pase de mo'ðelos/ *n. m.* fashion show.

paseo /pa'seo/ *n. m.* walk, stroll; drive. —**pasear,** *v.*

pasillo /pa'siʎo; pa'siyo/ *n. m.* aisle; hallway.

pasión /pa'sion/ *n. f.* passion.

pasivo /pa'siβo/ *a.* passive.

pasmar /pas'mar/ *v.* astonish, astound, stun.

pasmo /'pasmo/ *n. m.* spasm; wonder.

paso /'paso/ *a.* **1.** dried (fruit). —*n.* **2.** *m.* pace, step; (mountain) pass.

paso cebra /'paso 'θeβra; 'paso 'seβra/ crosswalk.

paso de ganso /'paso de 'ganso/ goose step.

paso de peatones /'paso de pea'tones/ pedestrian crossing.

pasta /'pasta/ *n. f.* paste; batter; plastic.

pasta dentífrica /'pasta den'tifrika/ toothpaste.

pastar /pas'tar/ *v.* graze.

pastel /pas'tel/ *n. m.* pastry; pie.

pastelería /pastele'ria/ *n. f.* pastry; pastry shop.

pasteurización /pasteuriθa'θion; pasteurisa'sion/ *n. f.* pasteurization.

pasteurizar /pasteuri'θar; pasteuri'sar/ *v.* pasteurize.

pastilla /pas'tiʎa; pas'tiya/ *n. f.* tablet, lozenge, coughdrop.

pasto /'pasto/ *n. m.* pasture; grass.

pastor /pas'tor/ *n. m.* pastor; shepherd.

pastorear /pastore'ar/ *v.* pasture, tend (a flock).

pastrón /pas'tron/ *n. m.* pastrami.

pastura /pas'tura/ *n. f.* pasture.

pata /'pata/ *n. f.* foot (of animal).

patada /pa'taða/ *n. f.* kick.

patán /pa'tan/ *n. m.* boor.

patanada /pata'naða/ *n. f.* rudeness.

patata /pa'tata/ *n. f.* potato. **p. asada,** baked potato.

patear /pate'ar/ *v.* stamp, tramp, kick.

patente /pa'tente/ *a. & m.* patent. —**patentar,** *v.*

paternal /pater'nal/ **paterno** *a.* paternal.

paternidad /paterni'ðað/ *n. f.* paternity, fatherhood.

patético /pa'tetiko/ *a.* pathetic.

patíbulo /pa'tiβulo/ *n. m.* scaffold; gallows.

patín /pa'tin/ *n. m.* skate. —**patinar,** *v.*

patín de ruedas /pa'tin de 'rrueðas/ roller skate.

patio /'patio/ *n. m.* yard, court, patio.

pato /'pato/ *n. m.* duck.

patria /'patria/ *n. f.* native land.

patriarca /pa'triarka/ *n. m. & f.* patriarch.

patrimonio /patri'monio/ *n. m.* inheritance.

patriota /pa'triota/ *n. m. & f.* patriot.

patriótico /pa'triotiko/ *a.* patriotic.

patriotismo /patrio'tismo/ *n. m.* patriotism.

patrocinar /patroθi'nar; patrosi'nar/ *v.* patronize, sponsor.

patrón /pa'tron/ **-ona** *n.* patron; boss; (dress) pattern.

patrulla /pa'truʎa; pa'truya/ *n. f.* patrol. —**patrullar,** *v.*

paulatino /paula'tino/ *a.* gradual.

pausa /'pausa/ *n. f.* pause. —**pausar,** *v.*

pausa para el café /'pausa 'para el ka'fe/ coffee break.

pauta /'pauta/ *n. f.* guideline.

pavesa /pa'βesa/ *n. f.* spark, cinder.

pavimentar /paβimen'tar/ *v.* pave.

pavimento /paβi'mento/ *n. m.* pavement.

pavo /'paβo/ *n. m.* turkey. **p. real,** peacock.

pavor /pa'βor/ *n. m.* terror.
payaso /pa'iaso/ **-sa** *n.* clown.
paz /paθ; pas/ *n. f.* peace.
peatón /pea'ton/ **-na** *n.* pedestrian.
peca /'peka/ *n. f.* freckle.
pecado /pe'kaðo/ *n. m.* sin.
—**pecar,** *v.*
pecador /peka'ðor/ **-ra** *a. & n.* sinful; sinner.
pecera /pe'θera; pe'sera/ *n. f.* aquarium, fishbowl.
pechera /pe'tʃera/ *n. f.* shirt front.
pecho /'petʃo/ *n. m.* chest; breast; bosom.
pechuga /pe'tʃuga/ *n. f.* breast (of fowl).
pecoso /pe'koso/ *a.* freckled, freckly.
peculiar /peku'liar/ *a.* peculiar.
peculiaridad /pekuliari'ðað/ *n. f.* peculiarity.
pedagogía /peðago'hia/ *n. f.* pedagogy.
pedagogo /peða'gogo/ **-ga** *n.* pedagogue, teacher.
pedal /pe'ðal/ *n. m.* pedal.
pedantesco /peðan'tesko/ *a.* pedantic.
pedazo /pe'ðaθo; pe'ðaso/ *n. m.* piece.
pedernal /peðer'nal/ *n. m.* flint.
pedestal /peðes'tal/ *n. m.* pedestal.
pediatra /pe'ðiatra/ *n. m. & f.* pediatrician.
pediatría /peðia'tria/ *n. f.* pediatrics.
pedicuro /peði'kuro/ *n. m.* chiropodist.
pedir /pe'ðir/ *v.* ask, ask for, request; apply for; order.
pedo /'pedo/ *n. m.* fart; intoxication.
pedregoso /peðre'goso/ *a.* rocky.
pegajoso /pega'hoso/ *a.* sticky.
pegamento /pega'mento/ *n. m.* glue.
pegar /pe'gar/ *v.* beat, strike; adhere, fasten, stick.
peinado /pei'naðo/ *n. m.* coiffure, hairdo.
peine /'peine/ *n. m.* comb.
—**peinar,** *v.*
peineta /pei'neta/ *n. f.* (ornamental) comb.
pelagra /pe'lagra/ *n. f.* pellagra.
pelar /pe'lar/ *v.* skin, pare, peel.

pelea /pe'lea/ *n. f.* fight, row.
—**pelearse,** *v.*
pelícano /pe'likano/ *n. m.* pelican.
película /pe'likula/ *n. f.* movie, motion picture, film. **p. de terror** horror film.
peligrar /peli'grar/ *v.* be in danger.
peligro /pe'ligro/ *n. m.* peril, danger.
peligroso /peli'groso/ *a.* perilous, dangerous.
pelirrojo /peli'rroho/ **-ja** *a. & n.* redhead.
pellejo /pe'ʎeho; pe'yeho/ *n. m.* skin; peel (of fruit).
pellizco /pe'ʎiθko; pe'yisko/ *n. m.* pinch. —**pellizcar,** *v.*
pelo /'pelo/ *n. m.* hair.
pelota /pe'lota/ *n. f.* ball.
peltre /'peltre/ *n. m.* pewter.
peluca /pe'luka/ *n. f.* wig.
peludo /pe'luðo/ *a.* hairy.
peluquería /peluke'ria/ *n. f.* hairdresser's shop, beauty parlor.
peluquero /pelu'kero/ **-ra** *n.* hairdresser.
pena /'pena/ *n. f.* pain, grief, trouble, woe; penalty. **valer la p.,** to be worthwhile.
penacho /pe'natʃo/ *n. m.* plume.
penalidad /penali'ðað/ *n. f.* trouble; penalty.
pender /pen'der/ *v.* hang, dangle; be pending.
pendiente /pen'diente/ *a.* **1.** hanging; pending. —*n.* **2.** *m.* incline, slope; earring, pendant.
pendón /pen'don/ *n. m.* pennant, flag.
penetración /penetra'θion; penetra'sion/ *n. f.* penetration.
penetrar /pene'trar/ *v.* penetrate, pierce.
penicilina /peniθi'lina; penisi'lina/ *n. f.* penicillin.
península /pe'ninsula/ *n. f.* peninsula.
penitencia /peni'tenθia; peni'tensia/ *n. f.* penitence, penance.
penitenciaría /penitenθia'ria; penitensia'ria/ *n. f.* penitentiary.
penoso /pe'noso/ *a.* painful, troublesome, grievous, distressing.
pensador /pensa'ðor/ **-ra** *n.* thinker.
pensamiento /pensa'miento/ *n. m.* thought.
pensar /pen'sar/ *v.* think; intend, plan.

pensativo /pensa'tiβo/ *a.* pensive, thoughtful.

pensión /pen'sion/ *n. f.* pension; boardinghouse.

pensionista /pensio'nista/ *n. m. & f.* boarder.

pentagonal /pentago'nal/ *a.* pentagonal.

penúltimo /pe'nultimo/ *a.* next-to-the-last, last but one, penultimate.

penuria /pe'nuria/ *n. f.* penury, poverty.

peña /'peɲa/ *n. f.* rock.

peñascoso /peɲas'koso/ *a.* rocky.

peñón /pe'ɲon/ *n. m.* rock, crag.

Peñón de Gibraltar /pe'ɲon de hiβral'tar/ Rock of Gibraltar.

peón /pe'on/ *n. m.* unskilled laborer; infantryman.

peonada /peo'naða/ *n. f.* group of laborers.

peonía /peo'nia/ *n. f.* peony.

peor /pe'or/ *a.* worse, worst.

pepino /pe'pino/ *n. m.* cucumber.

pepita /pe'pita/ *n. f.* seed (in fruit).

pequeñez /peke'ɲeθ; peke'ɲes/ *n. f.* smallness; trifle.

pequeño /pe'keɲo/ **-ña** *a.* **1.** small, little, short, slight. —*n.* **2.** child.

pera /'pera/ *n. f.* pear.

peral /pe'ral/ *n. m.* pear tree.

perca /'perka/ *n. f.* perch (fish).

percal /per'kal/ *n. m.* calico, percale.

percance /per'kanθe; per'kanse/ *n. m.* mishap, snag, hitch.

percepción /perθep'θion; persep'sion/ *n. f.* perception.

perceptivo /perθep'tiβo; persep'tiβo/ *a.* perceptive.

percha /'pertʃa/ *n. f.* perch; clothes hanger, rack.

percibir /perθi'βir; persi'βir/ *v.* perceive, sense; collect.

perder /per'ðer/ *v.* lose; miss; waste. **echar a p.,** spoil. **p. el conocimiento,** lose consciousness.

perdición /perði'θion; perði'sion/ *n. f.* perdition, downfall.

pérdida /'perðiða/ *n. f.* loss.

perdiz /per'ðiθ; per'ðis/ *n. f.* partridge.

perdón /per'ðon/ *n. m.* pardon, forgiveness.

perdonar /perðo'nar/ *v.* forgive, pardon; spare.

perdurable /perðu'raβle/ *a.* enduring, everlasting.

perdurar /perðu'rar/ *v.* endure, last.

perecedero /pereθe'ðero; perese'ðero/ *a.* perishable.

perecer /pere'θer; pere'ser/ *v.* perish.

peregrinación /peregrina'θion; peregrina'sion/ *n. f.* peregrination; pilgrimage.

peregrino /pere'grino/ **-na** *n.* pilgrim.

perejil /pere'hil/ *n. m.* parsley.

perenne /pe'renne/ *a.* perennial.

pereza /pe'reθa; pe'resa/ *n. f.* laziness.

perezoso /pere'θoso; pere'soso/ *a.* lazy, sluggish.

perfección /perfek'θion; perfek'sion/ *n. f.* perfection.

perfeccionar /perfekθio'nar; perfeksio'nar/ *v.* perfect.

perfeccionista /perfekθio'nista; perfeksio'nista/ *a. & n.* perfectionist.

perfectamente /perfekta'mente/ *adv.* perfectly.

perfecto /per'fekto/ *a.* perfect.

perfidia /per'fiðia/ *n. f.* falseness, perfidy.

pérfido /'perfiðo/ *a.* perfidious.

perfil /per'fil/ *n. m.* profile.

perforación /perfora'θion; perfora'sion/ *n. f.* perforation.

perforar /perfo'rar/ *v.* pierce, perforate.

perfume /per'fume/ *n. m.* perfume, scent. —**perfumar,** *v.*

pergamino /perga'mino/ *n. m.* parchment.

pericia /pe'riθia; pe'risia/ *n. f.* skill, expertness.

perico /pe'riko/ *n. m.* parakeet.

perímetro /pe'rimetro/ *n. m.* perimeter.

periódico /pe'rioðiko/ *a.* **1.** periodic. —*n.* **2.** *m.* newspaper.

periodista /perio'ðista/ *n. m. & f.* journalist.

período /pe'rioðo/ *n. m.* period.

periscopio /peris'kopio/ *n. m.* periscope.

perito /pe'rito/ **-ta** *a. & n.* experienced; expert, connoisseur.

perjudicar /perhuði'kar/ *v.* damage, hurt; impair.

perjudicial /perhuði'θial; perhuði'sial/ *a.* harmful, injurious.

perjuicio /per'huiθio; per'huisio/ *n. m.* injury, damage.

perjurar /perhu'rar/ *v.* commit perjury.

perjurio /per'hurio/ *n. m.* perjury.

perla /'perla/ *n. f.* pearl.

permanecer /permane'θer; permane'ser/ *v.* remain, stay.

permanencia /perma'nenθia; perma'nensia/ *n. f.* permanence; stay.

permanente /perma'nente/ *a.* permanent.

permiso /per'miso/ *n. m.* permission; permit; furlough.

permitir /permi'tir/ *v.* permit, enable, let, allow.

permuta /per'muta/ *n. f.* exchange, barter.

pernicioso /perni'θioso; perni'sioso/ *a.* pernicious.

perno /'perno/ *n. m.* bolt.

pero /'pero/ *conj.* but.

peróxido /pe'roksiðo/ *n. m.* peroxide.

perpendicular /perpendiku'lar/ *n. m. & a.* perpendicular.

perpetración /perpetra'θion; perpetra'sion/ *n. f.* perpetration.

perpetrar /perpe'trar/ *v.* perpetrate.

perpetuar /perpe'tuar/ *v.* perpetuate.

perpetuidad /perpetui'ðað/ *n. f.* perpetuity.

perpetuo /per'petuo/ *a.* perpetual.

perplejo /per'pleho/ *a.* perplexed, puzzled.

perrito caliente /pe'rrito ka'liente/ *n. m.* hot dog.

perro /'perro/ **-rra** *n.* dog.

persecución /perseku'θion; perseku'sion/ *n. f.* persecution.

perseguir /perse'gir/ *v.* pursue; persecute.

perseverancia /perseβe'ranθia; perseβe'ransia/ *n. f.* perseverance.

perseverar /perseβe'rar/ *v.* persevere.

persiana /per'siana/ *n. f.* shutter, Venetian blind.

persistente /persis'tente/ *a.* persistent.

persistir /persis'tir/ *v.* persist.

persona /per'sona/ *n. f.* person.

personaje /perso'nahe/ *n. m.* personage; *Theat.* character.

personal /perso'nal/ *a.* **1.** personal. —*n.* **2.** *m.* personnel, staff.

personalidad /personali'ðað/ *n. f.* personality.

personalmente /personal'mente/ *adv.* personally.

perspectiva /perspek'tiβa/ *n. f.* perspective; prospect.

perspicaz /perspi'kaθ; perspi'kas/ *a.* perspicacious, acute.

persuadir /persua'ðir/ *v.* persuade.

persuasión /persua'sion/ *n. f.* persuasion.

persuasivo /persua'siβo/ *a.* persuasive.

pertenecer /pertene'θer; pertene'ser/ *v.* pertain; belong.

pertinencia /perti'nenθia; perti'nensia/ *n. f.* pertinence.

pertinente /perti'nente/ *a.* pertinent; relevant.

perturbar /pertur'βar/ *v.* perturb, disturb.

peruano /pe'ruano/ **-na** *a. & n.* Peruvian.

perversidad /perβersi'ðað/ *n. f.* perversity.

perverso /per'βerso/ *a.* perverse.

pesadez /pesa'ðeθ; pesa'ðes/ *n. f.* dullness.

pesadilla /pesa'ðiʎa; pesa'ðiya/ *n. f.* nightmare.

pesado /pe'saðo/ *a.* heavy; dull, dreary, boring.

pésame /'pesame/ *n. m.* condolence.

pesar /pe'sar/ *n. m.* sorrow; regret. **a p. de,** in spite of. *v.* weigh.

pesca /'peska/ *n. f.* fishing; catch (of fish).

pescadería /peskaðe'ria/ *n. f.* fish store.

pescado /pes'kaðo/ *n. m.* fish. —**pescar,** *v.*

pescador /peska'ðor/ *n. m.* fisherman.

pesebre /pe'seβre/ *n. m.* stall, manger; crib.

peseta /pe'seta/ *n. f.* peseta (monetary unit).

pesimismo /pesi'mismo/ *n. m.* pessimism.

pesimista /pesi'mista/ *a. & n.* pessimistic; pessimist.

pésimo /'pesimo/ *a.* awful, terrible, very bad.

peso /'peso/ *n. m.* weight; load; peso (monetary unit).

pesquera /pes'kera/ *n. f.* fishery.

pesquisa /pesˈkisa/ *n. f.* investigation.

pestaña /pesˈtaɲa/ *n. f.* eyelash.

pestañeo /pestaˈɲeo/ *n. m.* wink, blink. **—pestañear,** *v.*

peste /ˈpeste/ *n. f.* plague.

pesticida /pestiˈθiða; pestiˈsiða/ *n. m.* pesticide.

pestilencia /pestiˈlenθia; pestiˈlensia/ *n. f.* pestilence.

pétalo /ˈpetalo/ *n. m.* petal.

petardo /peˈtarðo/ *n. m.* firecracker.

petición /petiˈθion; petiˈsion/ *n. f.* petition.

petirrojo /petiˈrroho/ *n. m.* robin.

petrel /peˈtrel/ *n. m.* petrel.

pétreo /ˈpetreo/ *a.* rocky.

petrificar /petrifiˈkar/ *v.* petrify.

petróleo /peˈtroleo/ *n. m.* petroleum.

petrolero /petroˈlero/ *n. m.* oil tanker.

petunia /peˈtunia/ *n. f.* petunia.

pez /peθ; pes/ *n.* **1.** *m.* fish (in the water). **—***n.* **2.** *f.* pitch, tar.

pezuña /peˈθuɲa; peˈsuɲa/ *n. f.* hoof.

piadoso /piaˈðoso/ *a.* pious; merciful.

pianista /piaˈnista/ *n. m. & f.* pianist.

piano /ˈpiano/ *n. m.* piano.

picadero /pikaˈðero/ *n. m.* riding school.

picadura /pikaˈðura/ *n. f.* sting, bite, prick.

picamaderos /pikamaˈðeros/ *n. m.* woodpecker.

picante /piˈkante/ *a.* hot, spicy.

picaporte /pikaˈporte/ *n. m.* latch.

picar /piˈkar/ *v.* sting, bite, prick; itch; chop up, grind up.

pícaro /ˈpikaro/ **-ra** *a.* **1.** knavish, mischievous. **—***n.* **2.** rogue, rascal.

picarse /piˈkarse/ *v.* be offended, piqued.

picazón /pikaˈθon; pikaˈson/ *n. f.* itch.

pícea /ˈpiθea; ˈpisea/ *n. f.* spruce.

pichón /piˈtʃon/ *n. m.* pigeon, squab.

pico /ˈpiko/ *n. m.* peak; pick; beak; spout; small amount.

picotazo /pikoˈtaθo; pikoˈtaso/ *n. m.* peck. **—picotear,** *v.*

pictórico /pikˈtoriko/ *a.* pictorial.

pie /pie/ *n. m.* foot. **al p. de la letra,** literally; thoroughly.

piedad /pieˈðað/ *n. f.* piety; pity, mercy.

piedra /ˈpieðra/ *n. f.* stone.

piel /piel/ *n. f.* skin, hide; fur.

pienso /ˈpienso/ *n. m.* fodder.

pierna /ˈpierna/ *n. f.* leg.

pieza /ˈpieθa; ˈpiesa/ *n. f.* piece; room; *Theat.* play.

pijama /piˈhama/ *n. m. or m.pl.* pajamas.

pila /ˈpila/ *n. f.* pile, stack; battery; sink.

pilar /piˈlar/ *n. m.* pillar, column.

píldora /ˈpildora/ *n. f.* pill.

pillo /ˈpiʎo; ˈpiyo/ **-a** *n.* thief; rascal.

piloto /piˈloto/ *n. m. & f.* pilot.

pimentón /pimenˈton/ *n. m.* paprika.

pimienta /piˈmienta/ *n. f.* pepper (spice).

pimiento /piˈmiento/ *n. m.* pepper (vegetable).

pináculo /piˈnakulo/ *n. m.* pinnacle.

pincel /pinˈθel; pinˈsel/ *n. m.* (artist's) brush.

pinchadiscos /pintʃaˈðiskos/ *m. & f.* disk jockey.

pinchazo /pinˈtʃaθo; pinˈtʃaso/ *n. m.* puncture; prick. **—pinchar,** *v.*

pingajo /pinˈgaho/ *n. m.* rag, tatter.

pino /ˈpino/ *n. m.* pine.

pinta /ˈpinta/ *n. f.* pint.

pintar /pinˈtar/ *v.* paint; portray, depict.

pintor /pinˈtor/ **-ra** *n.* painter.

pintoresco /pintoˈresko/ *a.* picturesque.

pintura /pinˈtura/ *n. f.* paint; painting.

pinzas /ˈpinθas; ˈpinsas/ *n. f.pl.* pincers, tweezers; claws.

piña /ˈpiɲa/ *n. f.* pineapple.

pío /ˈpio/ *a.* pious; merciful.

piojo /ˈpioho/ *n. m.* louse.

pionero /pioˈnero/ **-ra** *n.* pioneer.

pipa /ˈpipa/ *n. f.* tobacco pipe.

pique /ˈpike/ *n. m.* resentment, pique. **echar a p.,** sink (ship).

pira /ˈpira/ *n. f.* pyre.

piragua /piˈragua/ *n. f.* canoe.

piragüismo /piraˈguismo/ *n. m.* canoeing.

piragüista /piraˈguista/ *n. m. & f.* canoeist.

pirámide /piˈramiðe/ *n. f.* pyramid.

pirata /pi'rata/ *n. m. & f.* pirate.
p. de aviones, hijacker.
pisada /pi'saða/ *n. f.* tread, step.
—**pisar,** *v.*
pisapapeles /pisapa'peles/ *n. m.*
paperweight.
piscina /pis'θina; pis'sina/ *n. f.*
fishpond; swimming pool.
piso /'piso/ *n. m.* floor.
pista /'pista/ *n. f.* trace, clue,
track; racetrack.
pista de tenis /'pista de 'tenis/
tennis court.
pistola /pis'tola/ *n. f.* pistol.
pistón /pis'ton/ *n. m.* piston.
pitillo /pi'tiʎo; pi'tiyo/ *n. m.* cigarette.
pito /'pito/ *n. m.* whistle. —**pitar,**
v.
pizarra /pi'θarra; pi'sarra/ *n. f.*
slate; blackboard.
pizca /'piθka; 'piska/ *n. f.* bit,
speck; pinch.
pizza /'piθθa; 'pissa/ *n. f.* pizza.
placentero /plaθen'tero; plasen-
'tero/ *a.* pleasant.
placer /pla'θer; pla'ser/ *n.* **1.** *m.*
pleasure. —*v.* **2.** please.
plácido /'plaθiðo; 'plasiðo/ *a.*
placid.
plaga /'plaga/ *n. f.* plague,
scourge.
plagio /'plahio/ *n. m.* plagiarism;
(*S.A.*) kidnapping.
plan /plan/ *n. m.* plan. —**planear,**
v.
plancha /'plantʃa/ *n. f.* plate;
slab, flatiron.
planchar /plan'tʃar/ *v.* iron, press.
planeta /pla'neta/ *n. m.* planet.
planificación /planifika'θion;
planifika'sion/ *n. f.* planning.
planificar /planifi'kar/ *v.* plan.
plano /'plano/ *a.* **1.** level, flat.
—*n.* **2.** *m.* plan; plane.
planta /'planta/ *n. f.* plant; sole
(of foot).
planta baja /'planta 'baha/ *n. f.*
ground floor.
plantación /planta'θion; planta-
'sion/ *n. f.* plantation.
plantar /plan'tar/ *v.* plant.
plantear /plante'ar/ *v.* pose, present.
plantel /plan'tel/ *n. m.* educational institution; *Agr.* nursery.
plasma /'plasma/ *n. m.* plasma.
plástico /'plastiko/ *a. & m.* plastic.

plata /'plata/ *n. f.* silver; *Colloq.*
money.
plataforma /plata'forma/ *n. f.*
platform.
plátano /'platano/ *n. m.* plantain;
banana.
platel /pla'tel/ *n. m.* platter.
plática /'platika/ *n. f.* chat, talk.
—**platicar,** *v.*
platillo /pla'tiʎo; pla'tiyo/ *n. m.*
saucer.
platillo volante /pla'tiʎo bo'lante;
pla'tiyo bo'lante/ flying saucer.
plato /'plato/ *n. m.* plate, dish.
playa /'plaia/ *n. f.* beach, shore.
plaza /'plaθa; 'plasa/ *n. f.* square.
p. de toros, bullring.
plazo /'plaθo; 'plaso/ *n. m.* term,
deadline; installment.
plebe /'pleβe/ *n. f.* common people; masses.
plebiscito /pleβis'θito; pleβis'sito/
n. m. plebiscite.
plegable /ple'gaβle/ *a.* foldable,
folding.
plegadura /plega'ðura/ *n. f.* fold,
pleat. —**plegar,** *v.*
pleito /'pleito/ *n. m.* lawsuit; dispute.
plenitud /pleni'tuð/ *n. f.* fullness;
abundance.
pleno /'pleno/ *a.* full. **en pleno...**
in the middle of...
pliego /'pliego/ *n. m.* sheet of paper.
pliegue /'pliege/ *n. m.* fold, pleat,
crease.
plomería /plome'ria/ *n. f.* plumbing.
plomero /plo'mero/ *n. m.*
plumber.
plomizo /plo'miθo; plo'miso/ *a.*
leaden.
plomo /'plomo/ *n. m.* lead; fuse.
pluma /'pluma/ *n. f.* feather;
(writing) pen.
pluma estilográfica /'pluma es-
tiglo'grafika/ fountain pen.
plumafuente /pluma'fuente/ *n. f.*
fountain pen.
plumaje /plu'mahe/ *n. m.* plumage.
plumero /plu'mero/ *n. m.* feather
duster; plume.
plumoso /plu'moso/ *a.* feathery.
plural /plu'ral/ *a. & m.* plural.
pluriempleo /pluriem'pleo/ *n. m.*
moonlighting.
PNB, *abbr.* (producto nacional

bruto), GNP (gross national product).

población /poβla'θion; poβla'sion/ *n. f.* population; town.

poblador /poβla'ðor/ **-ra** *n.* settler.

poblar /po'βlar/ *v.* populate; settle.

pobre /'poβre/ *a. & n.* poor; poor person.

pobreza /po'βreθa; po'βresa/ *n. f.* poverty, need.

pocilga /po'θilga; po'silga/ *n. f.* pigpen.

poción /po'θion; po'sion/ *n. f.* drink; potion.

poco /'poko/ *a. & adv.* **1.** little, not much, (*pl.*) few. **por p.,** almost, nearly. —*n.* **2.** *m.* **un p. (de),** a little, a bit (of).

poder /po'ðer/ *n.* **1.** *m.* power. —*v.* **2.** be able to, can; be possible, may, might. **no p. menos de,** not be able to help.

poder adquisitivo /po'ðer aðki-si'tiβo/ purchasing power.

poderío /poðe'rio/ *n. m.* power, might.

poderoso /poðe'roso/ *a.* powerful, mighty, potent.

podrido /po'ðriðo/ *a.* rotten.

poema /po'ema/ *n. m.* poem.

poesía /poe'sia/ *n. f.* poetry; poem.

poeta /po'eta/ *n. m. & f.* poet.

poético /po'etiko/ *a.* poetic.

polaco /po'lako/ **-ca** *a. & n.* Polish; Pole.

polar /po'lar/ *a.* polar.

polaridad /polari'ðað/ *n. f.* polarity.

polea /po'lea/ *n. f.* pulley.

polen /'polen/ *n. m.* pollen.

policía /poli'θia; poli'sia/ *n.* **1.** *f.* police. —*n.* **2.** *m.* policeman.

polideportivo /poliðepor'tiβo/ *n. m.* sports center.

poliéster /poli'ester/ *n. m.* polyester.

poligamia /poli'gamia/ *n. f.* polygamy.

poligloto /poli'gloto/ **-ta** *n.* polyglot.

polígono industrial /po'ligono in-dus'trial/ *n. m.* industrial park.

polilla /po'liʎa; po'liya/ *n. f.* moth.

política /po'litika/ *n. f.* politics; policy.

político /po'litiko/ **-ca** *a. & n.* politic; political; politician.

póliza /'poliθa; 'polisa/ *n. f.* (insurance) policy; permit, ticket.

polizonte /poli'θonte; poli'sonte/ *n. m.* policeman.

pollada /po'ʎaða; po'yaða/ *n. f.* brood.

pollería /poʎe'ria; poye'ria/ *n. f.* poultry shop.

pollino /po'ʎino; po'yino/ *n. m.* donkey.

pollo /'poʎo; 'poyo/ *n. m.* chicken.

polo /'polo/ *n. m.* pole; polo; popsicle.

polonés /polo'nes/ *a.* Polish.

Polonia /po'lonia/ *n. f.* Poland.

polvera /pol'βera/ *n. f.* powder box; powder puff.

polvo /'polβo/ *n. m.* powder; dust.

polvora /'polβora/ *n. f.* gunpowder.

pompa /'pompa/ *n. f.* pomp.

pomposo /pom'poso/ *a.* pompous.

pómulo /'pomulo/ *n. m.* cheekbone.

ponche /'pontʃe/ *n. m.* punch (beverage).

ponchera /pon'tʃera/ *n. f.* punch bowl.

ponderar /ponde'rar/ *v.* ponder.

ponderoso /ponde'roso/ *a.* ponderous.

poner /po'ner/ *v.* put, set, lay, place.

ponerse /po'nerse/ *v.* put on; become, get; set (sun). **p. a,** start to.

poniente /po'niente/ *n. m.* west.

pontífice /pon'tifiθe; pon'tifise/ *n. m.* pontiff.

popa /'popa/ *n. f.* stern.

popular /popu'lar/ *a.* popular.

popularidad /populari'ðað/ *n. f.* popularity.

populazo /popu'laθo; popu'laso/ *n. m.* populace; masses.

por /por/ *prep.* by, through, because of; via; for. **p. qué,** why?

porcelana /porθe'lana; porse'lana/ *n. f.* porcelain, chinaware.

porcentaje /porθen'tahe; porsen-'tahe/ *n. m.* percentage.

porche /'portʃe/ *n. m.* porch; portico.

porción /por'θion; por'sion/ *n. f.* portion, lot.

porfiar /por'fiar/ *v.* persist; argue.
pormenor /porme'nor/ *n. m.* detail.
pornografía /pornogra'fia/ *n. f.* pornography.
poro /'poro/ *n. m.* pore.
poroso /po'roso/ *a.* porous.
porque /'porke/ *conj.* because.
porqué *n. m.* reason, motive.
porra /'porra/ *n. f.* stick, club.
porrazo /po'rraθo; po'rraso/ *n. m.* blow.
porro /'porro/ *n. m. Colloq.* joint (marijuana).
portaaviones /portaa'βiones/ *n. m.* aircraft carrier.
portador /porta'ðor/ **-ra** *n.* bearer.
portal /por'tal/ *n. m.* portal.
portar /por'tar/ *v.* carry.
portarse /por'tarse/ *v.* behave, act.
portátil /por'tatil/ *a.* portable.
portavoz /porta'βoθ; porta'βos/ *n.* **1.** *m.* megaphone. **2.** *m. & f.* spokesperson.
porte /'porte/ *n. m.* bearing; behavior; postage.
portero /por'tero/ *n. m.* porter; janitor.
pórtico /'portiko/ *n. m.* porch.
portorriqueño /portorri'keɲo/ **-ña** *n. & a.* Puerto Rican.
portugués /portu'ges/ **-esa** *a. & n.* Portuguese.
posada /po'saða/ *n. f.* lodge, inn.
posar /po'sar/ *v.* pose.
posdata /pos'ðata/ *n. f.* postscript.
poseer /pose'er/ *v.* possess, own.
posesión /pose'sion/ *n. f.* possession.
posibilidad /posiβili'ðað/ *n. f.* possibility.
posible /po'siβle/ *a.* possible.
posiblemente /posiβle'mente/ *adv.* possibly.
posición /posi'θion; posi'sion/ *n. f.* position, stand.
positivo /posi'tiβo/ *a.* positive.
posponer /pospo'ner/ *v.* postpone.
postal /pos'tal/ *a.* postal; postcard.
poste /'poste/ *n. m.* post, pillar.
posteridad /posteri'ðað/ *n. f.* posterity.
posterior /poste'rior/ *a.* posterior, rear.

postizo /pos'tiθo; pos'tiso/ *a.* false, artificial.
postrado /pos'traðo/ *a.* prostrate. **—postrar,** *v.*
postre /'postre/ *n. m.* dessert.
póstumo /'postumo/ *a.* posthumous.
postura /pos'tura/ *n. f.* posture, pose; bet.
potable /po'taβle/ *a.* drinkable.
potaje /po'tahe/ *n. m.* porridge; pot stew.
potasa /po'tasa/ *n. f.* potash.
potasio /po'tasio/ *n. m.* potassium.
pote /'pote/ *n. m.* pot, jar.
potencia /po'tenθia; po'tensia/ *n. f.* potency, power.
potencial /poten'θial; poten'sial/ *a. & m.* potential.
potentado /poten'taðo/ *n. m.* potentate.
potente /po'tente/ *a.* potent, powerful.
potestad /potes'tað/ *n. f.* power.
potro /'potro/ *n. m.* colt.
pozo /'poθo; 'poso/ *n. m.* well.
práctica /'praktika/ *n. f.* practice. **—practicar,** *v.*
práctico /'praktiko/ *a.* practical.
pradera /pra'ðera/ *n. f.* prairie, meadow.
prado /'praðo/ *n. m.* meadow; lawn.
pragmatismo /pragma'tismo/ *n. m.* pragmatism.
preámbulo /pre'ambulo/ *n. m.* preamble.
precario /pre'kario/ *a.* precarious.
precaución /prekau'θion; prekau'sion/ *n. f.* precaution.
precaverse /preka'βerse/ *v.* beware.
precavido /preka'βiðo/ *a.* cautious, guarded, wary.
precedencia /preθe'ðenθia; prese'ðensia/ *n. f.* precedence, priority.
precedente /preθe'ðente; prese'ðente/ *a. & m.* preceding; precedent.
preceder /preθe'ðer; prese'ðer/ *v.* precede.
precepto /pre'θepto; pre'septo/ *n. m.* precept.
preciar /pre'θiar; pre'siar/ *v.* value, prize.
preciarse de /pre'θiarse de; pre'siarse de/ *v.* take pride in.
precio /'preθio; 'presio/ *n. m.* price. **p. del billete de avión** air

fare. **p. del cubierto** cover charge.

precioso /pre'θioso; pre'sioso/ *a.* precious; beautiful, gorgeous.

precipicio /preθi'piθio; presi'pisio/ *n. m.* precipice, cliff.

precipitación /preθipita'θion; presipita'sion/ *n. f.* precipitation.

precipitar /preθipi'tar; presipi'tar/ *v.* precipitate, rush; throw headlong.

precipitoso /preθipi'toso; presipi'toso/ *a.* precipitous; rash.

precisar /preθi'sar; presi'sar/ *v.* fix, specify; be necessary.

precisión /preθi'sion; presi'sion/ *n. f.* precision; necessity.

preciso /pre'θiso; pre'siso/ *a.* precise; necessary.

precocidad /prekoθi'ðað; prekosi'ðað/ *n. f.* precocity.

precocinado /prekoθi'naðo; prekosi'naðo/ *a.* precooked, readycooked.

precoz /pre'koθ; pre'kos/ *a.* precocious.

precursor /prekur'sor/ **-ra** *a.* **1.** preceding. —*n.* **2.** precursor, forerunner.

predecesor /preðeθe'sor; preðese'sor/ **-ra** *a. & n.* predecessor.

predecir /preðe'θir; preðe'sir/ *v.* predict, foretell.

predicación /preðika'θion; preðika'sion/ *n. f.* sermon.

predicador /preðika'ðor/ **-ra** *n.* preacher.

predicar /preði'kar/ *v.* preach.

predicción /preðik'θion; preðik'sion/ *n. f.* prediction.

predilecto /preði'lekto/ *a.* favorite, preferred.

predisponer /preðispo'ner/ *v.* predispose.

predisposición /preðisposi'θion; preðisposi'sion/ *n. f.* predisposition; bias.

predominante /preðomi'nante/ *a.* prevailing, prevalent, predominant.

predominar /preðomi'nar/ *v.* prevail, predominate.

predominio /preðo'minio/ *n. m.* predominance, sway.

prefacio /pre'faθio; pre'fasio/ *n. m.* preface.

preferencia /prefe'renθia; prefe'rensia/ *n. f.* preference.

preferentemente /preferente'mente/ *adv.* preferably.

preferible /prefe'riβle/ *a.* preferable.

preferir /prefe'rir/ *v.* prefer.

prefijo /pre'fiho/ *n. m.* prefix; area code, dialing code. —**prefijar,** *v.*

pregón /pre'gon/ *n. m.* proclamation; street cry.

pregonar /prego'nar/ *v.* proclaim; cry out.

pregunta /pre'gunta/ *n. f.* question, inquiry. **hacer una p.,** to ask a question.

preguntar /pregun'tar/ *v.* ask, inquire.

preguntarse /pregun'tarse/ *v.* wonder.

prehistórico /preis'toriko/ *a.* prehistoric.

prejuicio /pre'huiθio; pre'huisio/ *n. m.* prejudice.

prelacía /prela'θia; prela'sia/ *n. f.* prelacy.

preliminar /prelimi'nar/ *a. & m.* preliminary.

preludio /pre'luðio/ *n. m.* prelude.

prematuro /prema'turo/ *a.* premature.

premeditación /premeðita'θion; premeðita'sion/ *n. f.* premeditation.

premeditar /premeði'tar/ *v.* premeditate.

premiar /pre'miar/ *v.* reward; award a prize to.

premio /'premio/ *n. m.* prize, award; reward. **p. de consuelo,** consolation prize.

premisa /pre'misa/ *n. f.* premise.

premura /pre'mura/ *n. f.* pressure; urgency.

prenda /'prenda/ *n. f.* jewel; (personal) quality. **p. de vestir,** garment.

prender /pren'der/ *v.* seize, arrest, catch; pin, clip. **p. fuego a,** set fire to.

prensa /'prensa/ *n. f.* printing press; (the) press.

prensar /pren'sar/ *v.* press, compress.

preñado /pre'ɲaðo/ *a.* pregnant.

preocupación /preokupa'θion; preokupa'sion/ *n. f.* worry, preoccupation.

preocupar /preoku'par/ *v.* worry, preoccupy.

preparación /prepara'θion; prepara'sion/ *n. f.* preparation.

preparar /prepa'rar/ *v.* prepare.
preparativo /prepara'tiβo/ *n. m.* preparation.
preparatorio /prepara'torio/ *n. m.* preparatory.
preponderante /preponde'rante/ *a.* preponderant.
preposición /preposi'θion; preposi'sion/ *n. f.* preposition.
prerrogativa /prerroga'tiβa/ *n. f.* prerogative, privilege.
presa /'presa/ *n. f.* capture; (water) dam.
presagiar /presa'hiar/ *v.* presage, forebode.
presbiteriano /presβite'riano/ **-na** *n. & a.* Presbyterian.
presbítero /pres'βitero/ *n. m.* priest.
prescindir de /presθin'dir de; pressin'dir de/ *v.* dispense with; omit.
prescribir /preskri'βir/ *v.* prescribe.
prescripción /preskrip'θion; preskrip'sion/ *n. f.* prescription.
presencia /pre'senθia; pre'sensia/ *n. f.* presence.
presenciar /presen'θiar; presen'siar/ *v.* witness, be present at.
presentable /presen'taβle/ *a.* presentable.
presentación /presenta'θion; presenta'sion/ *n. f.* presentation; introduction.
presentar /presen'tar/ *v.* present; introduce.
presente /pre'sente/ *a. & m.* present.
presentimiento /presenti'miento/ *n. m.* premonition.
preservación /preserβa'θion; preserβa'sion/ *n. f.* preservation.
preservar /preser'βar/ *v.* preserve, keep.
preservativo /preserβa'tiβo/ *a. & m.* preservative; condom.
presidencia /presi'ðenθia; presi'ðensia/ *n. f.* presidency.
presidencial /presiðen'θial; presiðen'sial/ *a.* presidential.
presidente /presi'ðente/ **-ta** *n.* president.
presidiario /presi'ðiario/ **-ria** *n. m. & f.* prisoner.
presidio /pre'siðio/ *n. m.* prison; garrison.
presidir /presi'ðir/ *v.* preside.
presión /pre'sion/ *n. f.* pressure.

presión arterial /pre'sion arte'rial/ blood pressure.
preso /'preso/ **-sa** *n.* prisoner.
presta /'presta/ *n. f.* mint (plant).
prestador /presta'ðor/ **-ra** *n.* lender.
prestamista /presta'mista/ *n. m. & f.* money lender.
préstamo /'prestamo/ *n. m.* loan.
prestar /pres'tar/ *v.* lend.
presteza /pres'teθa; pres'tesa/ *n. f.* haste, promptness.
prestidigitación /prestiðihita'θion; prestiðihita'sion/ *n. f.* sleight of hand.
prestigio /pres'tihio/ *n. m.* prestige.
presto /'presto/ *a.* **1.** quick, prompt; ready. —*adv.* **2.** quickly; at once.
presumido /presu'miðo/ *a.* conceited, presumptuous.
presumir /presu'mir/ *v.* presume; boast; claim; be conceited.
presunción /presun'θion; presun'sion/ *n. f.* presumption; conceit.
presunto /pre'sunto/ *a.* presumed; prospective.
presuntuoso /presun'tuoso/ *a.* presumptuous.
presupuesto /presu'puesto/ *n. m.* premise; budget.
pretender /preten'der/ *v.* pretend; intend; aspire.
pretendiente /preten'diente/ *n. m.* suitor; pretender (to throne).
pretensión /preten'sion/ *n. f.* pretension; claim.
pretérito /pre'terito/ *a. & m.* preterit, past (tense).
pretexto /pre'teksto/ *n. m.* pretext.
prevalecer /preβale'θer; preβale'ser/ *v.* prevail.
prevención /preβen'θion; preβen'sion/ *n. f.* prevention.
prevenir /preβe'nir/ *v.* prevent; forewarn; prearrange.
preventivo /preβen'tiβo/ *a.* preventive.
prever /pre'βer/ *v.* foresee.
previamente /preβia'mente/ *adv.* previously.
previo /'preβio/ *a.* previous.
previsible /preβi'siβle/ *a.* predictable.
previsión /preβi'sion/ *n. f.* foresight. **p. social,** social security.
prieto /'prieto/ *a.* blackish, very dark.

primacía /prima'θia; prima'sia/ *n. f.* primacy.

primario /pri'mario/ *a.* primary.

primavera /prima'ßera/ *n. f.* spring (season).

primero /pri'mero/ *a. & adv.* first.

primitivo /primi'tiβo/ *a.* primitive.

primo /'primo/ **-ma** *n.* cousin.

primor /pri'mor/ *n. m.* beauty; excellence; lovely thing.

primoroso /primo'roso/ *a.* exquisite, elegant; graceful.

princesa /prin'θesa; prin'sesa/ *n. f.* princess.

principal /prinθi'pal; prinsi'pal/ *a.* **1.** principal, main. —*n.* **2.** *m.* chief, head, principal.

principalmente /prinθipal'mente; prinsipal'mente/ *adv.* principally.

príncipe /'prinθipe; 'prinsipe/ *n. m.* prince.

Príncipe Azul /'prinθipe a'θul; 'prinsipe a'sul/ Prince Charming.

principiar /prinθi'piar; prinsi'piar/ *v.* begin, initiate.

principio /prin'θipio; prin'sipio/ *n. m.* beginning, start; principle.

pringado /priŋ'gaðo/ *n. m.* low-life, loser.

prioridad /priori'ðað/ *n. f.* priority.

prisa /'prisa/ *n. f.* hurry, haste. **darse p.,** hurry, hasten. **tener p.,** be in a hurry.

prisión /pri'sion/ *n. f.* prison; imprisonment.

prisionero /prisio'nero/ **-ra** *n.* captive, prisoner.

prisma /'prisma/ *n. m.* prism.

prismático /pris'matiko/ *a.* prismatic.

privación /priβa'θion; priβa'sion/ *n. f.* privation, want.

privado /pri'βaðo/ *a.* private, secret; deprived.

privar /pri'βar/ *v.* deprive.

privilegio /priβi'lehio/ *n. m.* privilege.

pro /pro/ *n. m. or f.* benefit, advantage. **en p. de,** in behalf of. **en p. y en contra,** pro and con.

proa /'proa/ *n. f.* prow, bow.

probabilidad /proβaβili'ðað/ *n. f.* probability.

probable /pro'βaβle/ *a.* probable, likely.

probablemente /proβaβle'mente/ *adv.* probably.

probador /proβa'ðor/ *n. m.* fitting room.

probar /pro'βar/ *v.* try, sample; taste; test; prove.

probarse /pro'βarse/ *v.* try on.

probidad /proβi'ðað/ *n. f.* honesty, integrity.

problema /pro'βlema/ *n. m.* problem.

probo /'proβo/ *a.* honest.

procaz /pro'kaθ; pro'kas/ *a.* impudent, saucy.

proceder /proθe'ðer; prose'ðer/ *v.* proceed.

procedimiento /proθeði'miento; proseði'miento/ *n. m.* procedure.

procesar /proθe'sar; prose'sar/ *v.* prosecute; sue; process.

procesión /proθe'sion; prose'sion/ *n. f.* procession.

proceso /pro'θeso; pro'seso/ *n. m.* process; (court) trial.

proclama /pro'klama/ **proclamación** *n. f.* proclamation.

proclamar /prokla'mar/ *v.* proclaim.

procreación /prokrea'θion; prokrea'sion/ *n. f.* procreation.

procrear /prokre'ar/ *v.* procreate.

procurar /proku'rar/ *v.* try; see to it; get, procure.

prodigalidad /proðigali'ðað/ *n. f.* prodigality.

prodigar /proði'gar/ *v.* lavish; squander, waste.

prodigio /pro'ðihio/ *n. m.* prodigy.

pródigo /'proðigo/ *a.* prodigal; profuse; lavish.

producción /proðuk'θion; proðuk'sion/ *n. f.* production.

producir /proðu'θir; proðu'sir/ *v.* produce.

productivo /proðuk'tiβo/ *a.* productive.

producto /pro'ðukto/ *n. m.* product.

producto nacional bruto /pro'ðukto naθio'nal 'bruto; pro'ðukto nasio'nal 'bruto/ gross national product.

proeza /pro'eθa; pro'esa/ *n. f.* prowess.

profanación /profana'θion; profana'sion/ *n. f.* profanation.

profanar /profa'nar/ *v.* defile, desecrate.

profanidad /profani'ðað/ *n. f.* profanity.

profano /pro'fano/ *a.* profane.

profecía /profe'θia; profe'sia/ *n. f.* prophecy.

proferir /profe'rir/ *v.* utter, express.

profesar /profe'sar/ *v.* profess.

profesión /profe'sion/ *n. f.* profession.

profesional /profesio'nal/ *a.* professional.

profesor /profe'sor/ **-ra** *n.* professor, teacher.

profeta /pro'feta/ *n. m.* prophet.

profético /pro'fetiko/ *a.* prophetic.

profetizar /profeti'θar; profeti-'sar/ *v.* prophesy.

proficiente /profi'θiente; profi-'siente/ *a.* proficient.

profundamente /profunda'mente/ *adv.* profoundly, deeply.

profundidad /profundi'ðað/ *n. f.* profundity, depth.

profundizar /profundi'θar; profundi'sar/ *v.* deepen.

profundo /pro'fundo/ *a.* profound, deep.

profuso /pro'fuso/ *a.* profuse.

progenie /pro'henie/ *n. f.* progeny, offspring.

programa /pro'grama/ *n. m.* program; schedule.

programador /programa'ðor/ **-ra** *n.* (computer) programmer.

progresar /progre'sar/ *v.* progress, advance.

progresión /progre'sion/ *n. f.* progression.

progresista /progre'sista/ **progresivo** *a.* progressive.

progreso /pro'greso/ *n. m.* progress.

prohibición /proiβi'θion; proiβi'sion/ *n. f.* prohibition.

prohibir /proi'βir/ *v.* prohibit, forbid.

prohibitivo /proiβi'tiβo, proiβi-'torio/ *a.* prohibitive.

prole /'prole/ *n. f.* progeny.

proletariado /proleta'riaðo/ *n. m.* proletariat.

proliferación /prolifera'θion; prolifera'sion/ *n. f.* proliferation.

prolijo /pro'liho/ *a.* prolix, tedious; long-winded.

prólogo /'prologo/ *n. m.* prologue; preface.

prolongar /proloŋ'gar/ *v.* prolong.

promedio /pro'meðio/ *n. m.* average.

promesa /pro'mesa/ *n. f.* promise.

prometer /prome'ter/ *v.* promise.

prometido /prome'tiðo/ *a.* promised; engaged (to marry).

prominencia /promi'nenθia; promi'nensia/ *n. f.* prominence.

promiscuamente /promiskua-'mente/ *adv.* promiscuously.

promiscuo /pro'miskuo/ *a.* promiscuous.

promisorio /promi'sorio/ *a.* promissory.

promoción /promo'θion; promo-'sion/ *n. f.* promotion.

promocionar /promoθio'nar; promosio'nar/ *v.* advertise, promote.

promover /promo'βer/ *v.* promote, further.

promulgación /promulga'θion; promulga'sion/ *n. f.* promulgation.

promulgar /promul'gar/ *v.* promulgate.

pronombre /pro'nombre/ *n. m.* pronoun.

pronosticación /pronostika'θion; pronostika'sion/ *n. f.* prediction, forecast.

pronosticar /pronosti'kar/ *v.* predict, forecast.

pronóstico /pro'nostiko/ *n. m.* prediction.

prontamente /pronta'mente/ *adv.* promptly.

prontitud /pronti'tuð/ *n. f.* promptness.

pronto /'pronto/ *a.* **1.** prompt; ready. —*adv.* **2.** soon; quickly. **de p.,** abruptly.

pronunciación /pronunθia'θion; pronunsia'sion/ *n. f.* pronunciation.

pronunciar /pronun'θiar; pronun'siar/ *v.* pronounce.

propagación /propaga'θion; propaga'sion/ *n. f.* propagation.

propaganda /propa'ganda/ *n. f.* propaganda.

propagandista /propagan'dista/ *n. m. & f.* propagandist.

propagar /propa'gar/ *v.* propagate.

propicio /pro'piθio; pro'pisio/ *a.* propitious, auspicious, favorable.

propiedad /propie'ðað/ *n. f.* property.

propietario /propie'tario/ **-ria** *n.* proprietor; owner; landlord, landlady.

propina /pro'pina/ *n. f.* gratuity, tip.

propio /'propio/ *a.* proper, suitable; typical; (one's) own; -self.

proponer /propo'ner/ *v.* propose.

proporción /propor'θion; propor'sion/ *n. f.* proportion.

proporcionado /proporθio'naðo; proporsio'naðo/ *a.* proportionate.

proporcionar /proporθio'nar; proporsio'nar/ *v.* provide with, supply, afford.

proposición /proposi'θion; proposi'sion/ *n. f.* proposition, offer; proposal.

propósito /pro'posito/ *n. m.* purpose; plan; **a p.,** by the way, apropos; on purpose.

propuesta /pro'puesta/ *n. f.* proposal, motion.

prorrata /pro'rrata/ *n. f.* quota.

prórroga /'prorroga/ *n. f.* renewal, extension.

prorrogar /prorro'gar/ *v.* renew, extend.

prosa /'prosa/ *n. f.* prose.

prosaico /pro'saiko/ *a.* prosaic.

proscribir /proskri'βir/ *v.* prohibit, proscribe, ban.

prosecución /proseku'θion; proseku'sion/ *n. f.* prosecution.

proseguir /prose'gir/ *v.* pursue; proceed, go on.

prosélito /pro'selito/ **-ta** *n.* proselyte.

prospecto /pros'pekto/ *n. m.* prospectus.

prosperar /prospe'rar/ *v.* prosper, thrive, flourish.

prosperidad /prosperi'ðað/ *n. f.* prosperity.

próspero /'prospero/ *a.* prosperous, successful.

prosternado /proster'naðo/ *a.* prostrate.

prostitución /prostitu'θion; prostitu'sion/ *n. f.* prostitution.

prostituir /prosti'tuir/ *v.* prostitute; debase.

prostituta /prosti'tuta/ *n. f.* prostitute.

protagonista /protago'nista/ *n. m. & f.* protagonist, hero, heroine.

protección /protek'θion; protek'sion/ *n. f.* protection.

protector /protek'tor/ **-ra** *a. & n.* protective; protector.

proteger /prote'her/ *v.* protect, safeguard. **p. contra escritura,** write-protect (diskette).

protegido /prote'hiðo/ **-da** *n.* **1.**

protégé. —*a.* **2.** protected. **p. contra escritura,** write-protected.

proteína /prote'ina/ *n. f.* protein.

protesta /pro'testa/ *n. f.* protest. **—protestar,** *v.*

protestante /protes'tante/ *a. & n.* Protestant.

protocolo /proto'kolo/ *n. m.* protocol.

protuberancia /protuβe'ranθia; protuβe'ransia/ *n. f.* protuberance, lump.

protuberante /protuβe'rante/ *a.* bulging.

provecho /pro'βetʃo/ *n. m.* profit, gain, benefit. **¡Buen provecho!** May you enjoy your meal!

provechoso /proβe'tʃoso/ *a.* beneficial, advantageous, profitable.

proveer /proβe'er/ *v.* provide, furnish.

provenir de /proβe'nir de/ *v.* originate in, be due to, come from.

proverbial /proβer'βial/ *a.* proverbial.

proverbio /pro'βerβio/ *n. m.* proverb.

providencia /proβi'ðenθia; proβi'ðensia/ *n. f.* providence.

providente /proβi'ðente/ *a.* provident.

provincia /pro'βinθia; pro'βinsia/ *n. f.* province.

provincial /proβin'θial; proβin'sial/ *a.* provincial.

provinciano /proβin'θiano; proβin'siano/ **-na** *a. & n.* provincial.

provisión /proβi'sion/ *n. f.* provision, supply, stock.

provisional /proβisio'nal/ *a.* provisional.

provocación /proβoka'θion; proβoka'sion/ *n. f.* provocation.

provocador /proβoka'ðor/ **-ra** *n.* provoker.

provocar /proβo'kar/ *v.* provoke, excite.

provocativo /proβoka'tiβo/ *a.* provocative.

proximidad /proksimi'ðað/ *n. f.* proximity, vicinity.

próximo /'proksimo/ *a.* next; near.

proyección /proiek'θion; proiek'sion/ *n. f.* projection.

proyectar /proiek'tar/ *v.* plan, project.

proyectil /proyek'til/ *n. m.* projectile, missile, shell.

proyecto /pro'iekto/ *n. m.* plan, project, scheme.
proyector /proiek'tor/ *n. m.* projector.
prudencia /pru'ðenθia; pru'ðensia/ *n. f.* prudence.
prudente /pru'ðente/ *a.* prudent.
prueba /'prueβa/ *n. f.* proof; trial; test.
psicoanálisis /psikoa'nalisis/ *n. m.* psychoanalysis.
psicoanalista /psikoana'lista/ *n. m. & f.* psychoanalyst.
psicodélico /psiko'ðeliko/ *a.* psychedelic.
psicología /psikolo'hia/ *n. f.* psychology.
psicológico /psiko'lohiko/ *a.* psychological.
psicólogo /psi'kologo/ **-ga** *n.* psychologist.
psiquiatra /psi'kiatra/ *n. m. & f.* psychiatrist.
psiquiatría /psikia'tria/ *n. f.* psychiatry.
publicación /puβlika'θion; puβlika'sion/ *n. f.* publication.
publicar /puβli'kar/ *v.* publish.
publicidad /puβliði'ðað; puβlisi-'ðað/ *n. f.* publicity.
publicista /puβli'θista; puβli'sista/ *n. m. & f.* publicity agent.
público /'puβliko/ *a. & m.* public.
puchero /pu'tʃero/ *n. m.* pot.
pudiente /pu'ðiente/ *a.* powerful; wealthy.
pudín /pu'ðin/ *n. m.* pudding.
pudor /pu'ðor/ *n. m.* modesty.
pudoroso /puðo'roso/ *a.* modest.
pudrirse /pu'ðrirse/ *v.* rot.
pueblo /'pueβlo/ *n. m.* town, village; (the) people.
puente /'puente/ *n. m.* bridge.
puente para peatones /'puente para pea'tones/ *n. m.* footbridge.
puerco /'puerko/ **-ca** *n.* pig.
puericultura /puerikul'tura/ *n. f.* pediatrics
pueril /pue'ril/ *a.* childish.
puerilidad /puerili'ðað/ *n. f.* puerility.
puerta /'puerta/ *n. f.* door; gate.
puerta giratoria /'puerta hira-'toria/ revolving door.
puerta principal /'puerta prinθi'pal; 'puerta prinsi'pal/ front door.
puerto /'puerto/ *n. m.* port, harbor.

puertorriqueño /puertorri'keɲo/ **-ña** *a. & n.* Puerto Rican.
pues /pues/ *adv.* 1. well... —*conj.* 2. as, since, for.
puesto /'puesto/ *n. m.* appointment, post, job; place; stand. **p. que,** since.
pugilato /puhi'lato/ *n. m.* boxing.
pugna /'pugna/ *n. f.* conflict.
pugnacidad /pugnaθi'ðað; pugnasi'ðað/ *n. f.* pugnacity.
pugnar /pug'nar/ *v.* fight; oppose.
pulcritud /pulkri'tuð/ *n. f.* neatness; exquisitness.
pulga /'pulga/ *n. f.* flea.
pulgada /pul'gaða/ *n. f.* inch.
pulgar /pul'gar/ *n. m.* thumb.
pulir /pu'lir/ *v.* polish; beautify.
pulmón /pul'mon/ *n. m.* lung.
pulmonía /pulmo'nia/ *n. f.* pneumonia.
pulpa /'pulpa/ *n. f.* pulp.
púlpito /'pulpito/ *n. m.* pulpit.
pulque /'pulke/ *n. m.* pulque (fermented maguey juice).
pulsación /pulsa'θion; pulsa'sion/ *n. f.* pulsation, beat.
pulsar /pul'sar/ *v.* pulsate, beat.
pulsera /pul'sera/ *n. f.* wristband; bracelet.
pulso /'pulso/ *n. m.* pulse.
pulverizar /pulβeri'θar; pulβeri-'sar/ *v.* pulverize.
puma /'puma/ *n. m.* puma.
pundonor /pundo'nor/ *n. m.* point of honor.
punta /'punta/ *n. f.* point, tip, end.
puntada /pun'taða/ *n. f.* stitch.
puntapié /punta'pie/ *n. m.* kick.
puntería /punte'ria/ *n. f.* (marksman's) aim.
puntiagudo /puntia'guðo/ *a.* sharp-pointed.
puntillas /pun'tiʎas; pun'tiyas/ *n. f.pl.* **de p., en p.,** on tiptoe.
punto /'punto/ *n. m.* point; period; spot, dot. **dos puntos,** *Punct.* colon. **a p. de,** about to. **al p.,** instantly.
punto de admiración /'punto de aðmira'θion; 'punto de aðmira'sion/ exclamation mark.
punto de congelación /'punto de koŋgela'θion; 'punto de koŋgela'sion/ freezing point.
punto de ebullición /'punto de eβuʎi'θion; 'punto de eβuyi'sion/ boiling point.

punto de vista /'punto de 'bista/ point of view, viewpoint.

puntuación /puntua'θion; puntua-'sion/ *n. f.* punctuation.

puntual /pun'tual/ *a.* punctual, prompt.

puntuar /pun'tuar/ *v.* punctuate.

puñada /pu'ɲaða/ *n. f.* punch.

puñado /pu'ɲaðo/ *n. m.* handful.

puñal /pu'ɲal/ *n. m.* dagger.

puñalada /puɲa'laða/ *n. f.* stab.

puñetazo /puɲe'taθo; puɲe'taso/ *n. m.* punch, fist blow.

puño /'puɲo/ *n. m.* fist; cuff; handle.

pupila /pu'pila/ *n. f.* pupil (of eye).

pupitre /pu'pitre/ *n. m.* writing desk, school desk.

pureza /pu'reθa; pu'resa/ *n. f.* purity; chastity.

purgante /pur'gante/ *n. m.* laxative.

purgar /pur'gar/ *v.* purge, cleanse.

purgatorio /purga'torio/ *n. m.* purgatory.

puridad /puri'ðað/ *n. f.* secrecy.

purificación /purifika'θion; puri-fika'sion/ *n. f.* purification.

purificar /purifi'kar/ *v.* purify.

purismo /pu'rismo/ *n. m.* purism.

purista /pu'rista/ *n. m. & f.* purist.

puritanismo /purita'nismo/ *n. m.* puritanism.

puro /'puro/ *a.* 1. pure. —*n.* 2. *m.* cigar.

púrpura /'purpura/ *n. f.* purple.

purpúreo /pur'pureo/ *a.* purple.

purulencia /puru'lenθia; puru-'lensia/ *n. f.* purulence.

purulento /puru'lento/ *a.* purulent.

pus /pus/ *n. m.* pus.

pusilánime /pusi'lanime/ *a.* pusillanimous.

puta /'puta/ **-to** *n.* prostitute.

putrefacción /putrefak'θion; putrefak'sion/ *n. f.* putrefaction, rot.

putrefacto /putre'fakto/ *a.* putrid, rotten.

pútrido /'putriðo/ *a.* putrid.

puya /'puya/ *n. f.* goad.

——— Q R ———

que /ke/ *rel. pron.* 1. who, whom; that, which. —*conj.* 2. than.

qué *a. & pron.* what. **por q., para q.,** why? *adv.* how.

quebrada /ke'βraða/ *n. f.* ravine, gully, gulch; stream.

quebradizo /keβra'ðiθo; keβra-'ðiso/ *a.* fragile, brittle.

quebraley /keβra'lei/ *n. m. & f.* lawbreaker, outlaw.

quebrar /ke'βrar/ *v.* break.

queda /'keða/ *n. f.* curfew.

quedar /ke'ðar/ *v.* remain, be located; be left. **q. bien a,** be becoming to.

quedarse /ke'ðarse/ *v.* stay, remain. **q. con,** keep, hold on to; remain with.

quedo /'keðo/ *a.* quiet; gentle.

quehacer /kea'θer; kea'ser/ *n. m.* task; chore.

queja /'keha/ *n. f.* complaint.

quejarse /ke'harse/ *v.* complain, grumble.

quejido /ke'hiðo/ *n. m.* moan.

quejoso /ke'hoso/ *a.* complaining.

quema /'kema/ *n. f.* burning.

quemadura /kema'ðura/ *n. f.* burn.

quemar /ke'mar/ *v.* burn.

querella /ke'reʎa; ke'reya/ *n. f.* quarrel; complaint.

querencia /ke'renθia; ke'rensia/ *n. f.* affection, liking.

querer /ke'rer/ *v.* want, wish; will; love (a person). **q. decir,** mean. **sin q.,** without meaning to; unwillingly.

querido /ke'riðo/ *a.* dear, loved, beloved.

quesería /kese'ria/ *n. f.* dairy.

queso /'keso/ *n. m.* cheese.

queso crema /'keso 'krema/ cream cheese.

quetzal /ket'θal; ket'sal/ *n. m.* quetzal.

quiche /'kitʃe/ *n. f.* quiche.

quiebra /'kieβra/ *n. f.* break, fracture; damage; bankruptcy.

quien /kien/ *rel. pron.* who, whom.

quién *interrog. pron.* who, whom.

quienquiera /kien'kiera/ *pron.* whoever, whomever.

quietamente /kieta'mente/ *adv.* quietly.

quieto /'kieto/ *a.* quiet, still.

quietud /kie'tuð/ *n. f.* quiet, quietude.

quijada /ki'haða/ *n. f.* jaw.
quijotesco /kiho'tesko/ *a.* quixotic.
quilate /ki'late/ *n. m.* carat.
quilla /'kiʎa; 'kiya/ *n. f.* keel.
quimera /ki'mera/ *n. f.* chimera; vision; quarrel.
química /'kimika/ *n. f.* chemistry.
químico /'kimiko/ **-ca** *a. & n.* chemical; chemist.
quimoterapia /kimote'rapia/ *n. f.* chemotherapy.
quincalla /kin'kaʎa; kin'kaya/ *n. f.* (computer) hardware.
quincallería /kinkaʎe'ria; kinkaye-'ria/ *n. f.* hardware store.
quince /'kinθe; 'kinse/ *a. & pron.* fifteen.
quinientos /ki'nientos/ *a. & pron.* five hundred.
quinina /ki'nina/ *n. f.* quinine.
quintana /kin'tana/ *n. f.* country home.
quinto /'kinto/ *a.* fifth.
quirúrgico /ki'rurhiko/ *a.* surgical.
quiste /'kiste/ *n. m.* cyst.
quitamanchas /kita'mantʃas/ *n. m.* stain remover.
quitanieves /kita'nieβes/ *n. m.* snowplow.
quitar /ki'tar/ *v.* take away, remove.
quitarse /ki'tarse/ *v.* take off; get rid of.
quitasol /kita'sol/ *n. m.* parasol, umbrella.
quitasueño /kita'sueɲo/ *n. m. Colloq.* nightmare; worry.
quizá /ki'θa; ki'sa/ **quizás** *adv.* perhaps, maybe.
quórum /'korum/ *n. m.* quorum.
rábano /'rraβano/ *n. m.* radish.
rabí /rra'βi/ **rabino** *n. m.* rabbi.
rabia /'rraβia/ *n. f.* rage; grudge; rabies.
rabiar /rra'βiar/ *v.* rage, be furious.
rabieta /rra'βieta/ *n. f.* tantrum.
rabioso /rra'βioso/ *a.* furious; rabid.
rabo /'rraβo/ *n. m.* tail.
racha /'rratʃa/ *n. f.* streak.
racimo /rra'θimo; rra'simo/ *n. m.* bunch, cluster.
ración /rra'θion; rra'sion/ *n. f.* ration. —**racionar,** *v.*
racionabilidad /rraθionaβili'ðað; rrasionaβili'ðað/ *n. f.* rationality.
racional /rraθio'nal; rrasio'nal/ *a.* rational.

racionalismo /rraθiona'lismo; rrasiona'lismo/ *n. m.* rationalism.
racionalmente /rraθional'mente; rrasional'mente/ *adv.* rationally.
radar /rra'ðar/ *n. m.* radar.
radiación /rraðia'θion; rraðia'sion/ *n. f.* radiation.
radiador /rraðia'ðor/ *n. m.* radiator.
radiante /rra'ðiante/ *a.* radiant.
radical /rraði'kal/ *a. & n.* radical.
radicalismo /rraðika'lismo/ *n. m.* radicalism.
radicoso /rraði'koso/ *a.* radical.
radio /'rraðio/ *n. m. or f.* radio.
radioactividad /rraðioaktiβi'ðað/ *n. f.* radioactivity.
radioactivo /rraðioak'tiβo/ *a.* radioactive.
radiocasete /rraðioka'sete/ *n. m.* radio cassette.
radiodifundir /rraðioðifun'dir/ *v.* broadcast.
radiodifusión /rraðioðifu'sion/ *n. f.* (radio) broadcasting.
radiografía /rraðiogra'fia/ *n. f.* X-ray.
radiografiar /rraðiogra'fiar/ *v.* X-ray.
ráfaga /'rrafaga/ *n. f.* gust (of wind).
raíz /rra'iθ; rra'is/ *n. f.* root.
raja /'rraha/ *n. f.* rip; split, crack. —**rajar,** *v.*
ralea /rra'lea/ *n. f.* stock, breed.
ralo /'rralo/ *a.* thin, scattered.
rama /'rrama/ *n. f.* branch, bough.
ramillete /rrami'ʎete; rrami'yete/ *n. m.* bouquet.
ramo /'rramo/ *n. m.* branch, bough; bouquet.
ramonear /rramone'ar/ *v.* browse.
rampa /'rrampa/ *n. f.* ramp.
rana /'rrana/ *n. f.* frog.
ranchero /rran'tʃero/ **-ra** *n.* small farmer.
rancho /'rrantʃo/ *n. m.* ranch.
rancidez /rranθi'ðeθ; rransi'ðes/ *n. f.* rancidity.
rancio /'rranθio; 'rransio/ *a.* rancid, rank, stale, sour.
rango /'rrango/ *n. m.* rank.
ranúnculo /rra'nunkulo/ *n. m.* ranunculus; buttercup.
ranura /rra'nura/ *n. f.* slot.
ranura de expansión /rra'nura de ekspan'sion/ expansion slot.
rapacidad /rrapaθi'ðað; rrapasi'ðað/ *n. f.* rapacity.

rapaz /rra'paθ; rra'pas/ *a.* **1.** rapacious. —*n.* **2.** *m.* young boy.
rapé /'rrape/ *n. m.* snuff.
rápidamente /rrapiða'mente/ *adv.* rapidly.
rapidez /rrapi'ðeθ; rrapi'ðes/ *n. f.* rapidity, speed.
rápido /'rrapiðo/ *a.* **1.** rapid, fast, speedy. —*n.* **2.** *m.* express (train).
rapiña /rra'piɲa/ *n. f.* robbery, plundering.
rapsodia /rrap'soðia/ *n. f.* rhapsody.
rapto /'rrapto/ *n. m.* kidnapping.
raquero /rra'kero/ **-ra** *n.* beachcomber.
raqueta /rra'keta/ *n. f.* (tennis) racket.
rareza /rra'reθa; rra'resa/ *n. f.* rarity; freak.
raridad /rrari'ðað/ *n. f.* rarity.
raro /'rraro/ *a.* rare, strange, unusual, odd, queer.
rasar /rra'sar/ *v.* skim.
rascacielos /rraska'θielos; rraska'sielos/ *n. m.* skyscraper.
rascar /rras'kar/ *v.* scrape; scratch.
rasgadura /rrasga'ðura/ *n. f.* tear, rip. —**rasgar,** *v.*
rasgo /'rrasgo/ *n. m.* trait.
rasgón /rras'gon/ *n. m.* tear.
rasguño /rras'guɲo/ *n. m.* scratch. —**rasguñar,** *v.*
raso /'rraso/ *a.* **1.** plain. **soldado r.,** *Mil.* private. —*n.* **2.** *m.* satin.
raspar /rras'par/ *v.* scrape; erase.
rastra /'rrastra/ *n. f.* trail, track. —**rastrear,** *v.*
rastrillar /rrastri'ʎar; rrastri'yar/ *v.* rake.
rastro /'rrastro/ *n. m.* track, trail, trace; rake; flea market.
rata /'rrata/ *n. f.* rat.
ratificación /rratifika'θion; rratifika'sion/ *n. f.* ratification.
ratificar /rratifi'kar/ *v.* ratify.
rato /'rrato/ *n. m.* while, spell, short time.
ratón /rra'ton/ *n. m.* mouse.
ratonera /rrato'nera/ *n. f.* mousetrap.
raya /'rraya/ *n. f.* dash, line, streak, stripe.
rayar /rra'yar/ *v.* rule, stripe; scratch; cross out.
rayo /'rrayo/ *n. m.* lightning bolt; ray; flash.
rayón /rra'yon/ *n. m.* rayon.
raza /'rraθa; 'rrasa/ *n. f.* race; breed, stock.

razón /rra'θon; rra'son/ *n. f.* reason; ratio. **a r. de,** at the rate of. **tener r.,** to be right.
razonable /rraθo'naβle; rraso'naβle/ *a.* reasonable, sensible.
razonamiento /rraθona'miento; rrasona'miento/ *n. m.* argument.
razonar /rraθo'nar; rraso'nar/ *v.* reason.
reacción /rreak'θion; rreak'sion/ *n. f.* reaction.
reaccionar /rreakθio'nar; rreaksio'nar/ *v.* react.
reaccionario /rreakθio'nario; rreaksio'nario/ **-ria** *a. & n.* reactionary.
reacondicionar /rreakondiθio'nar; rreakondisio'nar/ *v.* recondition.
reactivo /rreak'tiβo/ *a. & m.* reactive; *Chem.* reagent.
reactor /rreak'tor/ *n. m.* reactor.
real /rre'al/ *a.* royal, regal; real, actual.
realdad /rreal'dað/ *n. f.* royal authority.
realeza /rrea'leθa; rrea'lesa/ *n. f.* royalty.
realidad /rreali'ðað/ *n. f.* reality.
realidad virtual /rreali'ðað βir'tual/ virtual reality.
realista /rrea'lista/ *a. & n.* realistic; realist.
realización /rrealiθa'θion; rrealisa'sion/ *n. f.* achievement, accomplishment.
realizar /rreali'θar; rreali'sar/ *v.* accomplish; fulfill; effect; *Com.* realize.
realmente /rreal'mente/ *adv.* in reality, really.
realzar /rreal'θar; rreal'sar/ *v.* enhance.
reata /rre'ata/ *n. f.* rope; lasso, lariat.
rebaja /rre'βaha/ *n. f.* reduction.
rebajar /rreβa'har/ *v.* cheapen; reduce (in price); lower.
rebanada /rreβa'naða/ *n. f.* slice. —**rebanar,** *v.*
rebaño /rre'βaɲo/ *n. m.* flock, herd.
rebato /rre'βato/ *n. m.* alarm; sudden attack.
rebelarse /rreβe'larse/ *v.* rebel, revolt.
rebelde /rre'βelde/ *a. & n.* rebellious; rebel.
rebelión /rreβe'lion/ *n. f.* rebellion, revolt.
reborde /rre'βorðe/ *n. m.* border.

rebotar /rreβo'tar/ v. rebound.
rebozo /rre'βoθo; rre'βoso/ n. m. shawl.
rebuscar /rreβus'kar/ v. search thoroughly.
rebuznar /rreβuθ'nar; rreβus'nar/ v. bray.
recado /rre'kaðo/ n. m. message; errand.
recaída /rreka'iða/ n. f. relapse. —**recaer,** v.
recalcar /rrekal'kar/ v. stress, emphasize.
recalentar /rrekalen'tar/ v. reheat.
recámara /rre'kamara/ n. f. (Mex.) bedroom.
recapitulación /rrekapitula'θion; rrekapitula'sion/ n. f. recapitulation.
recapitular /rrekapitu'lar/ v. recapitulate.
recatado /rreka'taðo/ n. m. coy; prudent.
recaudador /rrekauða'ðor/ **-ra** n. tax collector.
recelar /rreθe'lar; rrese'lar/ v. fear, distrust.
receloso /rreθe'loso; rrese'loso/ a. distrustful.
recepción /rreθep'θion; rresep'sion/ n. f. reception.
recepcionista /rreθepθio'nista; rresepsio'nista/ n. m. & f. desk clerk.
receptáculo /rreθep'takulo; rresep'takulo/ n. m. receptacle.
receptividad /rreθeptiβi'ðað; rreseptiβi'ðað/ n. f. receptivity.
receptivo /rreθep'tiβo; rresep'tiβo/ a. receptive.
receptor /rreθep'tor; rresep'tor/ n. m. receiver.
receta /rre'θeta; rre'seta/ n. f. recipe; prescription.
recetar /rreθe'tar; rrese'tar/ v. prescribe.
rechazar /rretʃa'θar; rretʃa'sar/ v. reject, spurn, discard.
rechinar /rretʃi'nar/ v. chatter.
recibimiento /rreθiβi'miento; rresiβi'miento/ n. m. reception; welcome; anteroom.
recibir /rreθi'βir; rresi'βir/ v. receive.
recibo /rre'θiβo; rre'siβo/ n. m. receipt.
reciclaje /reθi'klahe; resi'klahe/ n. m. recycling.
reciclar /rreθi'klar; rresi'klar/ v. recycle.

recidiva /rreθi'ðiβa; rresi'ðiβa/ n. f. relapse.
recién /rre'θien; rre'sien/ adv. recently, newly, just.
reciente /rre'θiente; rre'siente/ a. recent.
recinto /rre'θinto; rre'sinto/ n. m. enclosure.
recipiente /rreθi'piente; rresi'piente/ n. m. recipient.
reciprocación /rreθiproka'θion; rresiproka'sion/ n. f. reciprocation.
recíprocamente /rreθiproka'mente; rresiproka'mente/ adv. reciprocally.
reciprocar /rreθipro'kar; rresipro'kar/ v. reciprocate.
reciprocidad /rreθiproθi'ðað; rresiprosi'ðað/ n. f. reciprocity.
recitación /rreθita'θion; rresita'sion/ n. f. recitation.
recitar /rreθi'tar; rresi'tar/ v. recite.
reclamación /rreklama'θion; rreklama'sion/ n. f. claim; complaint.
reclamar /rrekla'mar/ v. claim; complain.
reclamo /rre'klamo/ n. m. claim; advertisement, advertising; decoy.
reclinar /rrekli'nar/ v. recline, repose, lean.
recluta /rre'kluta/ n. m. & f. recruit.
reclutar /rreklu'tar/ v. recruit, draft.
recobrar /rreko'βrar/ v. recover, salvage, regain.
recobro /rre'koβro/ n. m. recovery.
recoger /rreko'her/ v. gather; collect; pick up. **r. el conocimiento,** regain consciousness.
recogerse /rreko'herse/ v. retire (for night).
recolectar /rrekolek'tar/ v. gather, assemble; harvest.
recomendación /rrekomenda-'θion; rrekomenda'sion/ n. f. recommendation; commendation.
recomendar /rrekomen'dar/ v. recommend; commend.
recompensa /rrekom'pensa/ n. f. recompense; compensation.
recompensar /rrekompen'sar/ v. reward; compensate.
reconciliación /rrekonθilia'θion; rrekonsilia'sion/ n. f. reconciliation.

reconciliar /rrekonθi'liar; rrekon-si'liar/ *v.* reconcile.

reconocer /rrekono'θer; rrekono-'ser/ *v.* recognize; acknowledge; inspect, examine; *Mil.* reconnoiter.

reconocimiento /rrekonoθi-'miento; rrekonosi'miento/ *n. m.* recognition; appreciation, gratitude.

reconstituir /rrekonsti'tuir/ *v.* reconstitute.

reconstruir /rrekons'truir/ *v.* reconstruct, rebuild.

record /'rrekorð/ *n. m.* (sports) record.

recordar /rrekor'ðar/ *v.* recall, recollect; remind.

recorrer /rreko'rrer/ *v.* go over; read over; cover (distance).

recorte /rre'korte/ *n. m.* clipping, cutting.

recostarse /rrekos'tarse/ *v.* recline, lean back, rest.

recreación /rrekrea'θion; rrekrea-'sion/ *n. f.* recreation.

recreo /rre'kreo/ *n. m.* recreation.

recriminación /rrekrimina'θion; rrekrimina'sion/ *n. f.* recrimination.

rectangular /rrektaŋgu'lar/ *a.* rectangular.

rectángulo /rrek'taŋgulo/ *n. m.* rectangle.

rectificación /rrektifika'θion; rrektifika'sion/ *n. f.* rectification.

rectificar /rrektifi'kar/ *v.* rectify.

recto /'rrekto/ *a.* straight; just, fair. **ángulo r.,** right angle.

recuento /rre'kuento/ *n. m.* recount.

recuerdo /rre'kuerðo/ *n. m.* memory; souvenir; remembrance; (*pl.*) regards.

reculada /rreku'laða/ *n. f.* recoil. —**recular,** *v.*

recuperación /rrekupera'θion; rrekupera'sion/ *n. f.* recuperation.

recuperar /rrekupe'rar/ *v.* recuperate.

recurrir /rreku'rrir/ *v.* revert; resort, have recourse.

recurso /rre'kurso/ *n. m.* resource; recourse.

red /rreð/ *n. f.* net; trap. **r. local** local area network.

redacción /rreðak'θion; rreðak-'sion/ *n. f.* (editorial) staff; composition (of written material).

redactar /rreðak'tar/ *v.* draft, draw up; edit.

redactor /rreðak'tor/ **-ra** *n.* editor.

redada /rre'ðaða/ *n. f.* netful, catch, haul.

redargución /rreðargu'θion; rreðargu'sion/ *n. f.* retort. —**redargüir,** *v.*

redención /rreðen'θion; rreðen-'sion/ *n. f.* redemption, salvation.

redentor /rreðen'tor/ *n. m.* redeemer.

redimir /rreði'mir/ *v.* redeem.

redoblante /rreðo'βlante/ *n. m.* snare drum; snare dummer.

redonda /rre'ðonda/ *n. f.* neighborhood, vicinity.

redondo /rre'ðondo/ *a.* round, circular.

reducción /rreðuk'θion; rreðuk-'sion/ *n. f.* reduction.

reducir /rreðu'θir; rreðu'sir/ *v.* reduce.

reembolso /rreem'βolso/ *n. m.* refund. —**reembolsar,** *v.*

reemplazar /rreempla'θar; rreempla'sar/ *v.* replace, supersede.

reencarnación /rreenkarna'θion; rreenkarna'sion/ *n. f.* reincarnation.

reexaminar /rreeksami'nar/ *v.* reexamine.

reexpedir /rreekspe'ðir/ *v.* forward (mail).

referencia /rrefe'renθia; rrefe-'rensia/ *n. f.* reference.

referéndum /rrefe'rendum/ *n. m.* referendum.

referir /rrefe'rir/ *v.* relate, report on.

referirse /rrefe'rirse/ *v.* refer.

refinamiento /rrefina'miento/ *n. m.* refinement.

refinar /rrefi'nar/ *v.* refine.

refinería /rrefine'ria/ *n. f.* refinery.

reflejar /rrefle'har/ *v.* reflect; think, ponder.

reflejo /rre'fleho/ *n. m.* reflection; glare.

reflexión /rreflek'sion/ *n. f.* reflection, thought.

reflexionar /rrefleksio'nar/ *v.* reflect, think.

reflujo /rre'fluho/ *n. m.* ebb; ebb tide.

reforma /rre'forma/ *n. f.* reform. —**reformar,** *v.*

reformación /rreforma'θion; rreforma'sion/ *n. f.* reformation.

reformador /rreforma'ðor/ **-ra** *n.* reformer.

reforma tributaria /rre'forma triβu'taria/ tax reform.

reforzar /rrefor'θar; rrefor'sar/ v. reinforce, strengthen; encourage.

refractario /rrefrak'tario/ a. refractory.

refrán /rre'fran/ n. m. proverb, saying.

refrenar /rrefre'nar/ v. curb, rein; restrain.

refrescar /rrefres'kar/ v. refresh, freshen, cool.

refresco /rre'fresko/ n. m. refreshment; cold drink.

refrigeración /rrefrihera'θion; rrefrihera'sion/ n. f. refrigeration.

refrigerador /rrefrihera'ðor/ n. m. refrigerator.

refrigerar /rrefrihe'rar/ v. refrigerate.

refuerzo /rre'fuerθo; rre'fuerso/ n. m. reinforcement.

refugiado /rrefu'hiaðo/ **-da** refugee.

refugiarse /rrefu'hiarse/ v. take refuge.

refugio /rre'fuhio/ n. m. refuge, asylum, shelter.

refulgencia /rreful'henθia; rreful'hensia/ n. f. refulgence.

refulgente /rreful'hente/ a. refulgent.

refulgir /rreful'hir/ v. shine.

refunfuñar /rrefunfu'ɲar/ v. mutter, grumble, growl.

refutación /rrefuta'θion; rrefuta'sion/ n. f. refutation; rebuttal.

refutar /rrefu'tar/ v. refute.

regadera /rrega'ðera/ n. f. watering can.

regadizo /rrega'ðiθo; rrega'ðiso/ a. irrigable.

regadura /rrega'ðura/ n. f. irrigation.

regalar /rrega'lar/ v. give (a gift), give away.

regaliz /rrega'liθ; rrega'lis/ n. m. licorice.

regalo /rre'galo/ n. m. gift, present, **con r.,** in luxury.

regañar /rrega'ɲar/ v. reprove; scold.

regaño /rre'gaɲo/ n. m. reprimand; scolding.

regar /rre'gar/ v. water, irrigate.

regatear /rregate'ar/ v. haggle.

regateo /rrega'teo/ n. m. bargaining, haggling.

regazo /rre'gaθo; rre'gaso/ n. m. lap.

regencia /rre'henθia; rre'hensia/ n. f. regency.

regeneración /rrehenera'θion; rrehenera'sion/ n. f. regeneration.

regenerar /rrehene'rar/ v. regenerate.

regente /rre'hente/ **-ta** a. & n. regent.

régimen /'rrehimen/ n. m. regime; diet.

regimentar /rrehimen'tar/ v. regiment.

regimiento /rrehi'miento/ n. m. regiment.

región /rre'hion/ n. f. region.

regional /rrehio'nal/ a. regional, sectional.

regir /rre'hir/ v. rule; be in effect.

registrar /rrehis'trar/ v. register; record; search.

registro /rre'histro/ n. m. register; record; search.

regla /'rregla/ n. f. rule, regulation. **en r.,** in order.

reglamento /rregla'mento/ n. m. code of regulations.

regocijarse /rregoθi'harse; rregosi'harse/ v. rejoice, exult.

regocijo /rrego'θiho; rrego'siho/ n. f. rejoicing; merriment, joy.

regordete /rregor'ðete/ a. chubby, plump.

regresar /rregre'sar/ v. go back, return.

regresión /rregre'sion/ n. f. regression.

regresivo /rregre'siβo/ a. regressive.

regreso /rre'greso/ n. m. return.

regulación /rregula'θion; rregula'sion/ n. f. regulation.

regular /rregu'lar/ a. **1.** regular; fair, middling. —v. **2.** regulate.

regularidad /rregulari'ðað/ n. f. regularity.

regularmente /rregular'mente/ adv. regularly.

rehabilitación /rreaβilita'θion; rreaβilita'sion/ n. f. rehabilitation.

rehabilitar /rreaβili'tar/ v. rehabilitate.

rehén /rre'en/ n. m. hostage.

rehogar /rreo'gar/ v. brown.

rehusar /rreu'sar/ v. refuse; decline.

reina /'rreina/ n. f. queen.

reinado /rrei'naðo/ n. m. reign. —**reinar,** v.

reino /'rreino/ n. m. kingdom; realm; reign.

reír /rre'ir/ *v.* laugh.

reiteración /rreitera'θion; rreitera'sion/ *n. f.* reiteration.

reiterar /rreite'rar/ *v.* reiterate.

reja /'rreha/ *n. f.* grating, grill-work.

relación /rrela'θion; rrela'sion/ *n. f.* relation; account, report.

relacionar /rrelaθio'nar; rrelasio'nar/ *v.* relate, connect.

relajamiento /rrelaha'miento/ *n. m.* laxity, laxness.

relajar /rrela'har/ *v.* relax, slacken.

relámpago /rre'lampago/ *n. m.* lightning; flash (of lightning).

relatador /rrelata'ðor/ **-ra** *n.* teller.

relatar /rrela'tar/ *v.* relate, recount.

relativamente /rrelatiβa'mente/ *adv.* relatively.

relatividad /rrelatiβi'ðað/ *n. f.* relativity.

relativo /rrela'tiβo/ *a.* relative.

relato /rre'lato/ *n. m.* account, story.

relegación /rrelega'θion; rrelega'sion/ *n. f.* relegation.

relegar /rrele'gar/ *v.* relegate.

relevar /rrele'βar/ *v.* relieve.

relicario /rreli'kario/ *n. m.* reliquary; locket.

relieve /rre'lieβe/ *n. m.* (sculpture) relief.

religión /rreli'hion/ *n. f.* religion.

religiosidad /rrelihiosi'ðað/ *n. f.* religiosity.

religioso /rreli'hioso/ **-sa** *a.* **1.** religious. —*n.* **2.** *m.* member of a religious order.

reliquia /rre'likia/ *n. f.* relic.

rellenar /rreʎe'nar; rreye'nar/ *v.* refill; fill up, stuff.

relleno /rre'ʎeno; rre'yeno/ *n. m.* filling; stuffing.

reloj /rre'loh/ *n. m.* clock; watch.

reloj de pulsera /rre'loh de pul'sera/ *n.* wrist watch.

relojería /rrelohe'ria/ *n. f.* watchmaker's shop.

relojero /rrelo'hero/ **-ra** *n.* watchmaker.

relucir /rrelu'θir; rrelu'sir/ *v.* glow, shine; excel.

relumbrar /rrelum'βrar/ *v.* glitter, sparkle.

remache /rre'matʃe/ *n. m.* rivet. —**remachar,** *v.*

remar /rre'mar/ *v.* row (a boat).

rematado /rrema'taðo/ *a.* finished; sold.

remate /rre'mate/ *n. m.* end, finish; auction. **de r.,** utterly.

remedador /rremeða'ðor/ **-ra** *n.* imitator.

remedar /rreme'ðar/ *v.* imitate.

remedio /rre'meðio/ *n. m.* remedy. —**remediar,** *v.*

remendar /rremen'dar/ *v.* mend, patch.

remesa /rre'mesa/ *n. f.* shipment; remittance.

remiendo /rre'miendo/ *n. m.* patch.

remilgado /rremil'gaðo/ *a.* prudish; affected.

reminiscencia /rreminis'θenθia; rreminis'sensia/ *n. f.* reminiscence.

remitir /rremi'tir/ *v.* remit.

remo /'rremo/ *n. m.* oar.

remolacha /rremo'latʃa/ *n. f.* beet.

remolcador /rremolka'ðor/ *n. m.* tug (boat); tow truck.

remolino /rremo'lino/ *n. m.* whirl; whirlpool; whirlwind.

remolque /rre'molke/ *n. m.* tow. —**remolcar,** *v.*

remontar /rremon'tar/ *v.* ascend, go up.

remontarse /rremon'tarse/ *v.* get excited; soar. **r. a,** date from; go back to (in time).

remordimiento /rremorði'miento/ *n. m.* remorse.

remotamente /rremota'mente/ *adv.* remotely.

remoto /rre'moto/ *a.* remote.

remover /rremo'βer/ *v.* remove; stir; shake; loosen.

rempujar /rrempu'har/ *v.* jostle.

remuneración /rremunera'θion; rremunera'sion/ *n. f.* remuneration.

remunerar /rremune'rar/ *v.* remunerate.

renacido /rrena'θiðo; rrena'siðo/ *a.* reborn, born-again.

renacimiento /rrenaθi'miento; rrenasi'miento/ *n. m.* rebirth; renaissance.

rencor /rren'kor/ *n. m.* rancor, bitterness, animosity; grudge.

rencoroso /rrenko'roso/ *a.* rancorous, bitter.

rendición /rrendi'θion; rrendi'sion/ *n. f.* surrender.

rendido /rren'diðo/ *a.* weary, worn out.

rendir /rren'dir/ *v.* yield; surrender, give up; win over.

renegado /rrene'gaðo/ **-da** *n.* renegade.

renglón /rreŋ'glon/ *n. m.* line; *Com.* item.

reno /'rreno/ *n. m.* reindeer.

renombre /rre'nombre/ *n. m.* renown.

renovación /rrenoβa'θion; rrenoβa'sion/ *f.* renovation, renewal.

renovar /rreno'βar/ *v.* renew; renovate.

renta /'rrenta/ *n. f.* income; rent.

rentar /rren'tar/ *v.* yield; rent.

renuencia /rre'nuenθia; rre'nuensia/ *n. f.* reluctance.

renuente /rre'nuente/ *a.* reluctant.

renuncia /rre'nunθia; rre'nunsia/ *n. f.* resignation; renunciation.

renunciar /rrenun'θiar; rrenun'siar/ *v.* resign; renounce, give up.

reñir /rre'ɲir/ *v.* scold, berate; quarrel, wrangle.

reo /'rreo/ *a. & n.* criminal; convict.

reorganizar /rreorgani'θar; rreorgani'sar/ *v.* reorganize.

reparación /rrepara'θion; rrepara'sion/ *n. f.* reparation, atonement; repair.

reparar /rrepa'rar/ *v.* repair; mend; stop, stay over. **r. en,** notice; consider.

reparo /rre'paro/ *n. m.* repair; remark; difficulty; objection.

repartición /rreparti'θion; rreparti'sion/ *n. f.,* **repartimiento, reparto,** *m.* division, distribution.

repartir /rrepar'tir/ *v.* divide, apportion, distribute; *Theat.* cast.

repaso /rre'paso/ *n. m.* review. —**repasar,** *v.*

repatriación /rrepatria'θion; rrepatria'sion/ *n. f.* repatriation.

repatriar /rrepa'triar/ *v.* repatriate.

repeler /rrepe'ler/ *v.* repel.

repente /rre'pente/ *n. m.* **de r.,** suddenly; unexpectedly.

repentinamente /rrepentina'mente/ *adv.* suddenly.

repentino /rrepen'tino/ *a.* sudden.

repercusión /rreperku'sion/ *n. f.* repercussion.

repertorio /rreper'torio/ *n. m.* repertoire.

repetición /rrepeti'θion; rrepeti'sion/ *n. f.* repetition; action replay.

repetidamente /rrepetiða'mente/ *adv.* repeatedly.

repetir /rrepe'tir/ *v.* repeat.

repisa /rre'pisa/ *n. f.* shelf.

réplica /'rreplika/ *n. f.* reply; objection; replica.

replicar /rrepli'kar/ *v.* reply; answer back.

repollo /rre'poʎo; rre'poyo/ *n. m.* cabbage.

reponer /rrepo'ner/ *v.* replace; repair.

reponerse /rrepo'nerse/ *v.* recover, get well.

reporte /rre'porte/ *n. m.* report; news.

repórter /rre'porter/ **reportero -ra** *n.* reporter.

reposado /rrepo'saðo/ *a.* tranquil, peaceful, quiet.

reposo /rre'poso/ *n. m.* repose, rest. —**reposar,** *v.*

reposte /rre'poste/ *n. f.* pantry.

represalia /rrepre'salia/ *n. f.* reprisal.

representación /rrepresenta'θion; rrepresenta'sion/ *n. f.* representation; *Theat.* performance.

representante /rrepresen'tante/ *n. m. & f.* representative, agent.

representar /rrepresen'tar/ *v.* represent; depict; *Theat.* perform.

representativo /rrepresenta'tiβo/ *a.* representative.

represión /rrepre'sion/ *n. f.* repression.

represivo /rrepre'siβo/ *a.* repressive.

reprimenda /rrepri'menda/ *n. f.* reprimand.

reprimir /rrepri'mir/ *v.* repress, quell.

reproche /rre'protʃe/ *n. m.* reproach. —**reprochar,** *v.*

reproducción /rreproðuk'θion; rreproðuk'sion/ *n. f.* reproduction.

reproducir /rreproðu'θir; rreproðu'sir/ *v.* reproduce.

reptil /rrep'til/ *n. m.* reptile.

república /rre'puβlika/ *n. f.* republic.

republicano /rrepuβli'kano/ **-na** *a. & n.* republican.

repudiación /rrepuðia'θion; rrepuðia'sion/ *n. f.* repudiation.

repudiar /rrepu'ðiar/ *v.* repudiate; disown.

repuesto /rre'puesto/ *n. m.* spare part. **de r.,** spare.

repugnancia /rrepug'nanθia; rrepug'nansia/ *n. f.* repugnance.

repugnante /rrepug'nante/ *a.* disgusting, repugnant, repulsive, revolting.

repugnar /rrepug'nar/ *v.* disgust.

repulsa /rre'pulsa/ *n. f.* refusal; repulse.

repulsivo /rrepul'siβo/ *a.* repulsive.

reputación /rreputa'θion; rreputa'sion/ *n. f.* reputation.

reputar /rrepu'tar/ *v.* repute; appreciate.

requerir /rreke'rir/ *v.* require.

requesón /rreke'son/ *n. m.* cottage cheese.

requisición /rrekisi'θion; rrekisi'sion/ *n. f.* requisition.

requisito /rreki'sito/ *n. m.* requisite, requirement.

res /rres/ *n. f.* head of cattle.

resaca /rre'saka/ *n. f.* hangover.

resbalar /rresβa'lar/ *v.* slide; slip.

resbaloso /rresβa'loso/ *a.* slippery.

rescate /rres'kate/ *n. m.* rescue; ransom. **—rescatar,** *v.*

rescindir /rresθin'dir; rressin'dir/ *v.* rescind.

resentimiento /rresenti'miento/ *n. m.* resentment.

resentirse /rresen'tirse/ *v.* resent.

reserva /rre'serβa/ *n. f.* reserve. **—reservar,** *v.*

reservación /rreserβa'θion; rreserβa'sion/ *n. f.* reservation.

resfriado /rres'friaðo/ *n. m. Med.* cold.

resfriarse /rres'friarse/ *v.* catch cold.

resguardar /rresguar'ðar/ *v.* guard, protect.

residencia /rresi'ðenθia; rresi'ðensia/ *n. f.* residence; seat, headquarters.

residente /rresi'ðente/ *a. & n.* resident.

residir /rresi'ðir/ *v.* reside.

residuo /rre'siðuo/ *n. m.* remainder.

resignación /rresigna'θion; rresigna'sion/ *n. f.* resignation.

resignar /rresig'nar/ *v.* resign.

resina /rre'sina/ *n. f.* resin; rosin.

resistencia /rresis'tenθia; rresis'tensia/ *n. f.* resistance.

resistir /rresis'tir/ *v.* resist; endure.

resolución /rresolu'θion; rresolu'sion/ *n. f.* resolution.

resolutivamente /rresolutiβa'mente/ *adv.* resolutely.

resolver /rresol'βer/ *v.* resolve; solve.

resonante /rreso'nante/ *a.* resonant.

resonar /rreso'nar/ *v.* resound.

resorte /rre'sorte/ *n. m. Mech.* spring.

respaldar /rrespal'dar/ *v.* endorse; back.

respaldo /rres'paldo/ *n. m.* back (of a seat).

respectivo /rrespek'tiβo/ *a.* respective.

respecto /rres'pekto/ *n. m.* relation, proportion; **r. a,** concerning, regarding.

respetabilidad /rrespetaβili'ðað/ *n. f.* respectability.

respetable /rrespe'taβle/ *a.* respectable.

respeto /rres'peto/ *n. m.* respect. **—respetar,** *v.*

respetuosamente /rrespetuosa'mente/ *adv.* respectfully.

respetuoso /rrespe'tuoso/ *a.* respectful.

respiración /rrespira'θion; rrespira'sion/ *n. f.* respiration, breath.

respirar /rrespi'rar/ *v.* breathe.

resplandeciente /rresplande'θiente; rresplande'siente/ *a.* resplendent.

resplandor /rresplan'dor/ *n. m.* brightness, glitter.

responder /rrespon'der/ *v.* respond, answer.

responsabilidad /rresponsaβili'ðað/ *n. f.* responsibility.

responsable /rrespon'saβle/ *a.* responsible.

respuesta /rres'puesta/ *n. f.* answer, response, reply.

resquicio /rres'kiθio; rres'kisio/ *n. m.* crack, slit.

resta /'rresta/ *n. f.* subtraction; remainder.

restablecer /rrestaβle'θer; rrestaβle'ser/ *v.* restore; reestablish.

restablecerse /rrestaβle'θerse; rrestaβle'serse/ *v.* recover, get well.

restar /rres'tar/ *v.* remain; subtract.

restauración /rrestaura'θion; rrestaura'sion/ *n. f.* restoration.

restaurante /rrestau'rante/ *n. m.* restaurant.

restaurar /rrestau'rar/ *v.* restore.

restitución /rrestitu'θion; rrestitu'sion/ *n. f.* restitution.

restituir /rresti'tuir/ *v.* restore, give back.

resto /'rresto/ *n. m.* remainder, rest; (*pl.*) remains.

restorán /rresto'ran/ *n. m.* restaurant.

restregar /rrestre'gar/ *v.* rub hard; scrub.

restricción /rrestrik'θion; rrestrik-'sion/ *n. f.* restriction.

restrictivo /rrestrik'tiβo/ *a.* restrictive.

restringir /rrestriŋ'gir/ *v.* restrict, curtail.

resucitar /rresuθi'tar; rresusi'tar/ *v.* revive, resuscitate.

resuelto /rre'suelto/ *a.* resolute.

resultado /rresul'taðo/ *n. m.* result.

resultar /rresul'tar/ *v.* result; turn out; ensue.

resumen /rre'sumen/ *n. m.* résumé, summary, **en r.,** in brief.

resumir /rresu'mir/ *v.* sum up.

resurgir /rresur'hir/ *v.* resurge, reappear.

resurrección /rresurrek'θion; rresurrek'sion/ *n. f.* resurrection.

retaguardia /rreta'guarðia/ *n. f.* rear guard.

retal /rre'tal/ *n. m.* remnant.

retardar /rretar'ðar/ *v.* retard, slow.

retardo /rre'tarðo/ *n. m.* delay.

retención /rreten'θion; rreten-'sion/ *n. f.* retention.

retener /rrete'ner/ *v.* retain, keep; withhold.

reticencia /rreti'θenθia; rreti'sensia/ *n. f.* reticence.

reticente /rreti'θente; rreti'sente/ *a.* reticent.

retirada /rreti'raða/ *n. f.* retreat, retirement.

retirar /rreti'rar/ *v.* retire, retreat, withdraw.

retiro /rre'tiro/ *n. m.* retirement.

retorcer /rretor'θer; rretor'ser/ *v.* wring.

retórica /rre'torika/ *n. f.* rhetoric.

retórico /rre'toriko/ *a.* rhetorical.

retorno /rre'torno/ *n. m.* return.

retozo /rre'toθo; rre'toso/ *n. m.* frolic, romp. —**retozar,** *v.*

retozón /rreto'θon; rreto'son/ *a.* frisky.

retracción /rretrak'θion; rretrak-'sion/ *n. f.* retraction.

retractar /rretrak'tar/ *v.* retract.

retrasar /rretra'sar/ *v.* delay, set back.

retrasarse /rretra'sarse/ *v.* be slow.

retraso /rre'traso/ *n. m.* delay, lag, slowness.

retratar /rretra'tar/ *v.* portray; photograph.

retrato /rre'trato/ *n. m.* portrait; picture, photograph.

retreta /rre'treta/ *n. f. Mil.* retreat.

retrete /rre'trete/ *n. m.* toilet.

retribución /rretriβu'θion; rretriβu'sion/ *n. f.* retribution.

retroactivo /rretroak'tiβo/ *a.* retroactive.

retroalimentación /rretroalimenta'θion; rretroalimenta'sion/ *n. f.* feedback.

retroceder /rretroθe'ðer; rretrose-'ðer/ *v.* recede, go back, draw back, back up.

retumbar /rretum'βar/ *v.* resound, rumble.

reumático /rreu'matiko/ *a.* rheumatic.

reumatismo /rreuma'tismo/ *n. m.* rheumatism.

reunión /rreu'nion/ *n. f.* gathering, meeting, party; reunion.

reunir /rreu'nir/ *v.* gather, collect, bring together.

reunirse /rreu'nirse/ *v.* meet, assemble, get together.

reutilizar /rreutili'zar/ *v.* reuse.

revelación /rreβela'θion; rreβela-'sion/ *n. f.* revelation.

revelar /rreβe'lar/ *v.* reveal; betray; *Phot.* develop.

reventa /rre'βenta/ *n. f.* resale.

reventar /rreβen'tar/ *v.* burst; split apart.

reventón /rreβen'ton/ *n. m.* blowout (of tire).

reverencia /rreβeren'θia; rreβeren'sia/ *n. f.* reverence.

reverendo /rreβe'rendo/ *a.* reverend.

reverente /rreβe'rente/ *a.* reverent.

revertir /rreβer'tir/ *v.* revert.

revés /rre'βes/ *n. m.* reverse; back, wrong side. **al r.,** just the opposite; inside out.

revisar /rreβi'sar/ *v.* revise; review.

revisión /rreβi'sion/ *n. f.* revision.

revista /rre'βista/ *n. f.* magazine, periodical; review.

revivir /rreβi'βir/ *v.* revive.

revocación /rreβoka'θion; rreβoka'sion/ *n. f.* revocation.

revocar /rreβo'kar/ *v.* revoke, reverse.

revolotear /rreβolote'ar/ *v.* hover.

revolución /rreβolu'θion; rreβolu'sion/ *n. f.* revolution.

revolucionario /rreβoluθio'nario; rreβolusio'nario/ **-ria** *a. & n.* revolutionary.

revolver /rreβol'βer/ *v.* revolve; stir, agitate.

revólver *n. m.* revolver, pistol.

revuelta /rre'βuelta/ *n. f.* revolt; turn.

rey /rrei/ *n. m.* king.

reyerta /rre'yerta/ *n. f.* quarrel, wrangle.

rezar /rre'θar; rre'sar/ *v.* pray.

rezongar /rreθoŋ'gar; rresoŋ'gar/ *v.* grumble; mutter.

ría /'rria/ *n. f.* estuary.

riachuelo /rria'tʃuelo/ *n. m.* creek.

riba /'rriβa/ *n. f.* embankment.

rico /'rriko/ *a.* rich, wealthy; delicious.

ridículamente /rri'ðikulamente/ *adv.* ridiculously.

ridiculizar /rriðikuli'θar; rriðikuli'sar/ *v.* ridicule.

ridículo /rri'ðikulo/ *a. & m.* ridiculous; ridicule.

riego /'rriego/ *n. m.* irrigation.

rienda /'rrienda/ *n. f.* rein.

riesgo /'rriesgo/ *n. m.* risk, gamble.

rifa /'rrifa/ *n. f.* raffle; lottery; scuffle.

rifle /'rrifle/ *n. m.* rifle.

rígidamente /'rrihiðamente/ *adv.* rigidly.

rigidez /rrihi'ðeθ; rrihi'ðes/ *n. f.* rigidity.

rígido /'rrihiðo/ *a.* rigid, stiff.

rigor /rri'gor/ *n. m.* rigor.

riguroso /rrigu'roso/ *a.* rigorous, strict.

rima /'rrima/ *n. f.* rhyme. **—rimar,** *v.*

rimel /rri'mel/ *n. f.* mascara.

rincón /rrin'kon/ *n. m.* corner, nook.

rinoceronte /rrinoθe'ronte; rrinose'ronte/ *n. m.* rhinoceros.

riña /'rriɲa/ *n. f.* quarrel, feud.

riñón /rri'ɲon/ *n. m.* kidney.

río /'rrio/ *n. m.* river. **r. abajo** downstream, downriver. **r. arriba,** upstream, upriver.

ripio /'rripio/ *n. m.* debris.

riqueza /rri'keθa; rri'kesa/ *n. f.* wealth.

risa /'rrisa/ *n. f.* laugh; laughter.

risco /'rrisko/ *n. m.* cliff.

risibilidad /rrisiβili'ðað/ *n. f.* risibility.

risotada /rriso'taða/ *n. f.* peal of laughter.

risueño /rri'sueɲo/ *a.* cheerful, smiling.

rítmico /'rritmiko/ *a.* rhythmical.

ritmo /'rritmo/ *n. m.* rhythm.

rito /'rrito/ *n. m.* rite.

ritual /rri'tual/ *a. & m.* ritual.

rivalidad /rriβali'ðað/ *n. f.* rivalry.

rivera /rri'βera/ *n. f.* brook.

rizado /rri'θaðo; rri'saðo/ *a.* curly.

rizo /'rriθo; 'rriso/ *n. m.* curl. **—rizar,** *v.*

robar /rro'βar/ *v.* rob, steal.

roble /'rroβle/ *n. m.* oak.

roblón /rro'βlon/ *n. m.* rivet. **—roblar,** *v.*

robo /'rroβo/ *n. m.* robbery, theft.

robustamente /rroβusta'mente/ *adv.* robustly.

robusto /rro'βusto/ *a.* robust.

roca /'rroka/ *n. f.* rock; cliff.

rociada /rro'θiaða; rro'siaða/ *n. f.* spray, sprinkle. **—rociar,** *v.*

rocío /'rroθio; 'rrosio/ *n. m.* dew.

rocoso /rro'koso/ *a.* rocky.

rodar /rro'ðar/ *v.* roll; roam.

rodear /rroðe'ar/ *v.* surround, encircle.

rodeo /rro'ðeo/ *n. m.* turn, winding; roundup.

rodilla /rro'ðiʎa; rro'ðiya/ *n. f.* knee.

rodillo /rro'ðiʎo; rro'ðiyo/ *n. m.* roller.

rodio /'rroðio/ *n. m.* rhodium.

rododendro /rroðo'ðendro/ *n. m.* rhododendron.

roedor /rroe'ðor/ *n. m.* rodent.

roer /rro'er/ *v.* gnaw.

rogación /rroga'θion; rroga'sion/ *n. f.* request, entreaty.

rogar /rro'gar/ *v.* beg, plead with, supplicate.

rojizo /rro'hiθo; rro'hiso/ *a.* reddish.

rojo /'rroho/ *a.* red.

rollizo /rro'ʎiθo; rro'yiso/ *a.* chubby.

rollo /'rroʎo; 'rroyo/ *n. m.* roll; coil.

romadizo /rroma'ðiθo; rroma-'ðiso/ *n. m.* head cold.

romance /rro'manθe; rro'manse/ *n. m.* romance; ballad.

románico /rro'maniko/ *a.* Romance.

romano /rro'mano/ **-na** *a. & n.* Roman.

romántico /rro'mantiko/ *a.* romantic.

romería /rrome'ria/ *n. f.* pilgrimage; picnic.

romero /rro'mero/ **-ra** *n.* pilgrim.

rompecabezas /rrompeka'βeθas; rrompeka'βesas/ *n. m.* puzzle (pastime).

romper /rrom'per/ *v.* break, smash, shatter; sever; tear.

rompible /rrom'piβle/ *a.* breakable.

ron /rron/ *n. m.* rum.

roncar /rron'kar/ *v.* snore.

ronco /'rronko/ *a.* hoarse.

ronda /'rronda/ *n. f.* round.

rondar /rron'dar/ *v.* prowl.

ronquido /rron'kiðo/ *n. m.* snore.

ronronear /rronrone'ar/ *v.* purr.

ronzal /rron'θal; rron'sal/ *n. m.* halter.

roña /'rroɲa/ *n. f.* scab; filth.

ropa /'rropa/ *n. f.* clothes, clothing. **r. blanca,** linen. **r. interior,** underwear.

ropa de marca /'rropa de 'marka/ designer clothing.

ropero /rro'pero/ *n. m.* closet.

rosa /'rrosa/ *n. f.* rose. **r. náutica,** compass.

rosado /rro'saðo/ *a.* pink, rosy.

rosal /rro'sal/ *n. m.* rose bush.

rosario /rro'sario/ *n. m.* rosary.

rosbif /rros'βif/ *n. m.* roast beef.

rosca /'rroska/ *n. f.* thread (of screw).

róseo /'rroseo/ *a.* rosy.

rostro /'rrostro/ *n. m.* face, countenance.

rota /'rrota/ *n. f.* defeat; *Naut.* course.

rotación /rrota'θion; rrota'sion/ *n. f.* rotation.

rotatorio /rrota'torio/ *a.* rotary.

rótula /'rrotula/ *n. f.* kneecap.

rotulador /rrotula'ðor/ *n. m.* felt-tipped pen.

rótulo /'rrotulo/ *n. m.* label. —**rotular,** *v.*

rotundo /rro'tundo/ *a.* round; sonorous.

rotura /rro'tura/ *n. f.* break, fracture, rupture.

rozar /rro'θar; rro'sar/ *v.* rub against, chafe; graze.

rubí /rru'βi/ *n. m.* ruby.

rubio /'rruβio/ **-bia** *a. & n.* blond.

rubor /rru'βor/ *n. m.* blush; bashfulness.

rúbrica /'rruβrika/ *n. f.* caption; scroll.

rucho /'rrutʃo/ *n. m.* donkey.

rudeza /rru'ðeθa; rru'ðesa/ *n. f.* rudeness; roughness.

rudimentario /rruðimen'tario/ *a.* rudimentary.

rudimento /rruði'mento/ *n. m.* rudiment.

rudo /'rruðo/ *a.* rude, rough.

rueda /'rrueða/ *n. f.* wheel.

rueda de feria /'rrueða de 'feria/ Ferris wheel.

ruego /'rruego/ *n. m.* plea; entreaty.

rufián /rru'fian/ *n. m.* ruffian.

rufo /'rrufo/ *a.* sandy haired.

rugir /rru'hir/ *v.* bellow, roar.

rugoso /rru'goso/ *a.* wrinkled.

ruibarbo /rrui'βarβo/ *n. m.* rhubarb.

ruido /'rruiðo/ *n. m.* noise.

ruidoso /rrui'ðoso/ *a.* noisy.

ruina /'rruina/ *n. f.* ruin, wreck.

ruinar /rrui'nar/ *v.* ruin, destroy.

ruinoso /rrui'noso/ *a.* ruinous.

ruiseñor /rruise'ɲor/ *n. m.* nightingale.

ruleta /rru'leta/ *n. f.* roulette.

rumba /'rrumba/ *n. f.* rumba (dance or music).

rumbo /'rrumbo/ *n. m.* course, direction.

rumor /rru'mor/ *n. m.* rumor; murmur.

runrún /rrun'run/ *n. m.* rumor.

ruptura /rrup'tura/ *n. f.* rupture, break.

rural /rru'ral/ *a.* rural.

Rusia /'rrusia/ *n. f.* Russia.

ruso /'rruso/ **-sa** *a. & n.* Russian.

rústico /'rrustiko/ **-ca** *a. & n.* rustic. **en r.,** paperback *f.*

ruta /'rruta/ *n. f.* route.

rutina /rru'tina/ *n. f.* routine.

rutinario /rruti'nario/ *a.* routine.

S

sábado /'saβaðo/ *n. m.* Saturday.

sábalo /'saβalo/ *n. m.* shad.

sábana /sa'βana/ *n. f.* sheet.

sabañon /saβa'ɲon/ *n. m.* chilblain.

saber /sa'βer/ *n.* **1.** *m.* knowledge. —*v.* **2.** know; learn, find out; know how to; taste. **a s.,** namely, to wit.

sabiduría /saβiðu'ria/ *n. f.* wisdom; learning.

sabio /'saβio/ **-a** *a.* **1.** wise; scholarly. —*n.* **2.** sage; scholar.

sable /'saβle/ *n. m.* saber.

sabor /sa'βor/ *n. m.* flavor, taste, savor.

saborear /saβore'ar/ *v.* savor, relish.

sabotaje /saβo'tahe/ *n. m.* sabotage.

sabroso /sa'βroso/ *a.* savory, tasty.

sabueso /sa'βueso/ *n. m.* hound.

sacacorchos /saka'kortʃos/ *n. m.* corkscrew.

sacapuntas /saka'puntas/ *n. f.* pencil sharpener.

sacar /sa'kar/ *v.* draw out; take out; take.

sacerdocio /saθer'ðoθio; saser-'ðosio/ *n. m.* priesthood.

sacerdote /saθer'ðote; saser'ðote/ *n. m.* priest.

saciar /sa'θiar; sa'siar/ *v.* satiate.

saco /'sako/ *n. m.* sack, bag, pouch; suit coat, jacket.

sacramento /sakra'mento/ *n. m.* sacrament.

sacrificio /sakri'fiθio; sakri'fisio/ *n. m.* sacrifice. —**sacrificar,** *v.*

sacrilegio /sakri'lehio/ *n. m.* sacrilege.

sacristán /sakris'tan/ *n. m.* sexton.

sacro /'sakro/ *a.* sacred, holy.

sacrosanto /sakro'santo/ *a.* sacrosanct.

sacudir /saku'ðir/ *v.* shake, jerk, jolt.

sádico /'saðiko/ *a.* sadistic.

sadismo /sa'ðismo/ *n. m.* sadism.

sagacidad /sagaθi'ðað; sagasi'ðað/ *n. f.* sagacity.

sagaz /sa'gaθ; sa'gas/ *a.* sagacious, sage.

sagrado /sa'graðo/ *a.* sacred, holy.

sal /sal/ *n. f.* salt; *Colloq.* wit.

sala /'sala/ *n. f.* room; living room, parlor; hall, auditorium.

salado /sa'laðo/ *a.* salted, salty; *Colloq.* witty.

salar /sa'lar/ *v.* salt; steep in brine.

salario /sa'lario/ *n. m.* salary, wages.

salchicha /sal'tʃitʃa/ *n. f.* sausage.

sal de la Higuera /sal de la i'gera/ Epsom salts.

saldo /'saldo/ *n. m.* remainder, balance; (bargain) sale.

saldo acreedor /'saldo akree'ðor/ credit balance.

saldo deudor /'saldo deu'ðor/ debit balance.

salero /sa'lero/ *n. m.* salt shaker.

salida /sa'liða/ *n. f.* exit, outlet; departure.

salida de urgencia /sa'liða de ur'henθia; sa'liða de ur'hensia/ emergency exit, fire exit.

salir /sa'lir/ *v.* go out, come out; set out, leave, start; turn out, result.

salirse de /sa'lirse de/ *v.* get out of. **s. con la suya,** have one's own way.

salitre /sa'litre/ *n. m.* saltpeter.

saliva /sa'liβa/ *n. f.* saliva.

salmo /'salmo/ *n. m.* psalm.

salmón /sal'mon/ *n. m.* salmon.

salmonete /salmo'nete/ *n. m.* red mullet.

salmuera /sal'muera/ *n. f.* pickle; brine.

salobre /sa'loβre/ *a.* salty.

salón /sa'lon/ *n. m.* parlor, living room; hall. **s. de baile,** dance hall. **s. de belleza** beauty parlor.

salpicar /salpi'kar/ *v.* spatter, splash.

salpullido /salpu'ʎiðo; salpu'yiðo/ *n. m.* rash.

salsa /'salsa/ *n. f.* sauce; gravy.

saltamontes /salta'montes/ *n. m.* grasshopper.

salteador /saltea'ðor/ *n. m.* highwayman.

saltear /salte'ar/ *v.* hold up, rob; sauté.

salto /'salto/ *n. m.* jump, leap, spring. —**saltar,** *v.*

saltón /sal'ton/ *n. m.* grasshopper.

salubre /sa'luβre/ *a.* salubrious, healthful.

salubridad /saluβri'ðað/ *n. f.* health.

salud /sa'luð/ *n. f.* health.

saludable /salu'ðaβle/ *a.* healthful, wholesome.

saludar /salu'ðar/ *v.* greet; salute.

saludo /sa'luðo/ *n. m.* greeting; salutation; salute.

salutación /saluta'θion; saluta-'sion/ *n. f.* salutation.

salva /'salβa/ *n. f.* salvo.

salvación /salβa'θion; salβa'sion/ *n. f.* salvation; deliverance.

salvador /salβa'ðor/ **-ra** *n.* savior; rescuer.

salvaguardia /salβa'guarðia/ *n. m.* safeguard.

salvaje /sal'βahe/ *a. & n.* savage, wild (person).

salvamento /salβa'mento/ *n. m.* salvation; rescue.

salvar /sal'βar/ *v.* save; salvage; rescue; jump over.

salvavidas /salβa'βiðas/ *n. m.* life preserver.

salvia /'salβia/ *n. f.* sage (plant).

salvo /'salβo/ *a.* **1.** safe. —*prep.* **2.** except, save (for). **s. que,** unless.

San /san/ *title.* Saint.

sanar /sa'nar/ *v.* heal, cure.

sanatorio /sana'torio/ *n. m.* sanatorium.

sanción /san'θion; san'sion/ *n. f.* sanction. —**sancionar,** *v.*

sancochar /sanko'tʃar/ *v.* parboil.

sandalia /san'dalia/ *n. f.* sandal.

sandez /san'deθ; san'des/ *n. f.* stupidity.

sandía /san'dia/ *n. f.* watermelon.

saneamiento /sanea'miento/ *n. m.* sanitation.

sangrar /saŋ'grar/ *v.* bleed.

sangre /'saŋgre/ *n. f.* blood.

sangriento /saŋ'griento/ *a.* bloody.

sanguinario /saŋgi'nario/ *a.* bloodthirsty.

sanidad /sani'ðað/ *n. f.* health.

sanitario /sani'tario/ *a.* sanitary.

sano /'sano/ *a.* healthy, sound, sane; healthful, wholesome.

santidad /santi'ðað/ *n. f.* sanctity, holiness.

santificar /santifi'kar/ *v.* sanctify.

santo /'santo/ **-ta** *a.* **1.** holy, saintly. —*n.* **2.** *m.* saint.

Santo -ta *title.* Saint.

santuario /san'tuario/ *n. m.* sanctuary, shrine.

saña /'saɲa/ *n. f.* rage, anger.

sapiente /sa'piente/ *a.* wise.

sapo /'sapo/ *n. m.* toad.

saquear /sake'ar/ *v.* sack; ransack; plunder.

sarampión /saram'pion/ *n. m.* measles.

sarape /sa'rape/ *n. m.* (Mex.) woven blanket; shawl.

sarcasmo /sar'kasmo/ *n. m.* sarcasm.

sarcástico /sar'kastiko/ *a.* sarcastic.

sardina /sar'ðina/ *n. f.* sardine.

sargento /sar'hento/ *n. m.* sergeant.

sarna /'sarna/ *n. f.* itch.

sartén /sar'ten/ *n. m.* frying pan.

sastre /'sastre/ *n. m.* tailor.

satánico /sa'taniko/ *a.* satanic.

satélite /sa'telite/ *n. m.* satellite.

sátira /'satira/ *n. f.* satire.

satírico /sa'tiriko/ *a. & m.* satirical; satirist.

satirizar /satiri'θar; satiri'sar/ *v.* satirize.

sátiro /'satiro/ *n. m.* satyr.

satisfacción /satisfak'θion; satisfak'sion/ *n. f.* satisfaction.

satisfacer /satisfa'θer; satisfa'ser/ *v.* satisfy.

satisfactorio /satisfak'torio/ *a.* satisfactory.

saturación /satura'θion; satura-'sion/ *n. f.* saturation.

saturar /satu'rar/ *v.* saturate.

sauce /'sauθe; 'sause/ *n. m.* willow.

sauna /'sauna/ *n. f.* sauna.

savia /'saβia/ *n. f.* sap.

saxofón /sakso'fon/ **saxófono** *n. m.* saxophone.

saya /'saya/ *n. f.* skirt.

sazón /sa'θon; sa'son/ *n. f.* season; seasoning. **a la s.,** at that time.

sazonar /saθo'nar; saso'nar/ *v.* flavor, season.

se /se/ *pron.* -self, -selves.

seca /'seka/ *n. f.* drought.

secador /seka'ðor/ **secador de pelo** *n. m.* hair dryer.

secante /se'kante/ *a.* **papel s.,** blotting paper.

secar /se'kar/ *v.* dry.

sección /sek'θion; sek'sion/ *n. f.* section.

seco /'seko/ *a.* dry; curt.

secreción /sekre'θion; sekre'sion/ n. f. secretion.

secretar /sekre'tar/ v. secrete.

secretaría /sekreta'ria/ n. f. secretary's office; secretariat.

secretario /sekre'tario/ -ra n. secretary.

secreto /se'kreto/ a. & m. secret.

secta /'sekta/ n. f. denomination; sect.

secuela /se'kuela/ n. f. result; sequel.

secuestrar /sekues'trar/ v. abduct, kidnap; hijack.

secuestro /se'kuestro/ n. m. abduction, kidnapping.

secular /seku'lar/ a. secular.

secundario /sekun'dario/ a. secondary.

sed /seð/ n. f. thirst. **tener s., estar con s.,** to be thirsty.

seda /'seða/ n. f. silk.

sedar /se'ðar/ v. quiet, allay.

sedativo /seða'tiβo/ a. & m. sedative.

sede /'seðe/ n. f. seat, headquarters.

sedentario /seðen'tario/ a. sedentary.

sedición /seði'θion; seði'sion/ n. f. sedition.

sedicioso /seði'θioso; seði'sioso/ a. seditious.

sediento /se'ðiento/ a. thirsty.

sedimento /seði'mento/ n. m. sediment.

sedoso /se'ðoso/ a. silky.

seducir /seðu'θir; seðu'sir/ v. seduce.

seductivo /seðuk'tiβo/ a. seductive, alluring.

segar /se'gar/ v. reap, harvest; mow.

seglar /seg'lar/ n. m. & f. layman, laywoman.

segmento /seg'mento/ n. m. segment.

segregar /segre'gar/ v. segregate.

seguida /se'giða/ n. f. succession. **en s.,** right away, at once.

seguido /se'giðo/ a. consecutive.

seguir /se'gir/ v. follow; continue, keep on, go on.

según /se'gun/ prep. **1.** according to. —conj. **2.** as.

segundo /se'gundo/ a. & m. second. —**segundar,** v.

seguridad /seguri'ðað/ n. f. safety, security; assurance.

seguro /se'guro/ a. **1.** safe, secure; sure, certain. —n. **2.** m. insurance.

seis /seis/ a. & pron. six.

seiscientos /seis'θientos; seis'sientos/ a. & pron. six hundred.

selección /selek'θion; selek'sion/ n. f. selection, choice.

seleccionar /selekθio'nar; seleksio'nar/ v. select, choose.

selecto /se'lekto/ a. select, choice, elite.

sello /'seʎo; 'seyo/ n. m. seal; stamp. —**sellar,** v.

selva /'selβa/ n. f. forest; jungle.

selvoso /sel'βoso/ a. sylvan.

semáforo /se'maforo/ n. m. semaphore; traffic light.

semana /se'mana/ n. f. week.

semana inglesa /se'mana iŋ'glesa/ five-day work week.

semanal /sema'nal/ a. weekly.

semana laboral /se'mana laβo'ral/ work week.

semántica /se'mantika/ n. f. semantics.

semblante /sem'βlante/ n. m. look, expression.

sembrado /sem'βraðo/ n. m. sown field.

sembrar /sem'βrar/ v. sow, seed.

semejante /seme'hante/ a. **1.** like, similar; such (a). —n. **2.** m. fellow man.

semejanza /seme'hanθa; seme'hansa/ n. f. similarity, likeness.

semejar /seme'har/ v. resemble.

semilla /se'miʎa; se'miya/ n. f. seed.

seminario /semi'nario/ n. m. seminary.

sémola /'semola/ n. f. semolina.

senado /se'naðo/ n. m. senate.

senador /sena'ðor/ -ra n. senator.

sencillez /senθi'ʎeθ; sensi'yes/ n. f. simplicity; naturalness.

sencillo /sen'θiʎo; sen'siyo/ a. simple, natural; single.

senda /'senda/ n. f. **sendero,** m. path, footpath.

senectud /senek'tuð/ n. f. old age.

senil /se'nil/ a. senile.

seno /'seno/ n. m. breast, bosom.

sensación /sensa'θion; sensa'sion/ n. f. sensation.

sensacional /sensaθio'nal; sensasio'nal/ a. sensational.

sensato /sen'sato/ a. sensible, wise.

sensibilidad /sensiβili'ðað/ *n. f.* sensibility; sensitiveness.

sensible /sen'siβle/ *a.* sensitive; emotional.

sensitivo /sensi'tiβo/ *a.* sensitive.

sensual /sen'sual/ *a.* sensual.

sensualidad /sensuali'ðað/ *n. f.* sensuality.

sentar /sen'tar/ *v.* seat. **s. bien,** fit well, be becoming.

sentarse /sen'tarse/ *v.* sit, sit down.

sentencia /sen'tenθia; sen'tensia/ *n. f.* (court) sentence.

sentidamente /sentiða'mente/ *adv.* feelingly.

sentido /sen'tiðo/ *n. m.* meaning, sense; consciousness.

sentido común /sen'tiðo ko'mun/ common sense.

sentimental /sentimen'tal/ *a.* sentimental.

sentimiento /senti'miento/ *n. m.* sentiment, feeling.

sentir /sen'tir/ *v.* feel, sense; hear; regret, be sorry.

seña /'seɲa/ *n. f.* sign, indication; (*pl.*) address.

señal /se'ɲal/ *n. f.* sign, signal; mark.

señalar /seɲa'lar/ *v.* designate, point out; mark.

señal de marcar /se'ɲal de mar'kar/ dial tone.

señor /se'ɲor/ *n. m.* gentleman; lord; (title) Mr., Sir.

señora /se'ɲora/ *n. f.* lady; wife; (title) Mrs., Madam.

señora de la limpieza /se'ɲora de la lim'pieθa; se'ɲora de la lim'piesa/ cleaning woman.

señorita /seɲo'rita/ *n. f.* young lady; (title) Miss.

sépalo /'sepalo/ *n. m.* sepal.

separación /separa'θion; separa'sion/ *n. f.* separation, parting.

separadamente /separaða'mente/ *adv.* separately.

separado /sepa'raðo/ *a.* separate; separated. —**separar,** *v.*

septentrional /septentrio'nal/ *a.* northern.

septiembre /sep'tiembre/ *n. m.* September.

séptimo /'septimo/ *a.* seventh.

sepulcro /se'pulkro/ *n. m.* sepulcher.

sepultar /sepul'tar/ *v.* bury, entomb.

sepultura /sepul'tura/ *n. f.* grave.

sequedad /seke'ðað/ *n. f.* dryness.

sequía /se'kia/ *n. f.* drought.

ser /ser/ *v.* be.

serenata /sere'nata/ *n. f.* serenade.

serenidad /sereni'ðað/ *n. f.* serenity.

sereno /se'reno/ *a.* **1.** serene, calm. —*n.* **2.** *m.* dew; watchman.

ser humano /ser u'mano/ *n.* human being.

serie /'serie/ *n. f.* series, sequence.

seriedad /serie'ðað/ *n. f.* seriousness.

serio /'serio/ *a.* serious. **en s.,** seriously.

sermón /ser'mon/ *n. m.* sermon.

seroso /se'roso/ *a.* watery.

serpiente /ser'piente/ *n. f.* serpent, snake.

serpiente de cascabel /ser'piente de kaska'βel/ rattlesnake.

serrano /se'rrano/ **-na** *n.* mountaineer.

serrar /se'rrar/ *v.* saw.

serrín /se'rrin/ *n. m.* sawdust.

servicial /serβi'θial; serβi'sial/ *a.* helpful, of service.

servicio /ser'βiθio; ser'βisio/ *n. m.* service; toilet.

servidor /serβi'ðor/ **-ra** *n.* servant.

servidumbre /serβi'ðumbre/ *n. f.* bondage; staff of servants.

servil /ser'βil/ *a.* servile, menial.

servilleta /serβi'ʎeta; serβi'yeta/ *n. f.* napkin.

servir /ser'βir/ *v.* serve. **s. para,** be good for.

servirse /ser'βirse/ *v.* help oneself.

sesenta /se'senta/ *a. & pron.* sixty.

sesgo /'sesgo/ *n. m.* slant. —**sesgar,** *v.*

sesión /se'sion/ *n. f.* session; sitting.

seso /'seso/ *n. m.* brain.

seta /'seta/ *n. f.* mushroom.

setecientos /sete'θientos; sete'sientos/ *a. & pron.* seven hundred.

setenta /se'tenta/ *a. & pron.* seventy.

seto /'seto/ *n. m.* hedge.

severamente /seβera'mente/ *adv.* severely.

severidad /seβeri'ðað/ *n. f.* severity.

severo /se'βero/ *a.* severe, strict, stern.

sexismo /sek'sismo/ *n. m.* sexism.

sexista /sek'sista/ *a. & n.* sexist.

sexo /'sekso/ *n. m.* sex.

sexto /'seksto/ *a.* sixth.

sexual /sek'sual/ *a.* sexual.

si /si/ *conj.* if; whether.

sí *pron.* **1.** -self, -selves. —*interj.* **2.** yes.

sico-. See **psicoanálisis, psicología,** etc.

sicómoro /siko'moro/ *n. m.* sycamore.

SIDA /'siða/ *n. m.* AIDS.

sidra /'siðra/ *n. f.* cider.

siempre /'siempre/ *adv.* always. **para s.,** forever. **s. que,** whenever; provided that.

sierra /'sierra/ *n. f.* saw; mountain range.

siervo /'sierβo/ **-va** *n.* slave; serf.

siesta /'siesta/ *n. f.* (afternoon) nap.

siete /'siete/ *a. & pron.* seven.

sifón /si'fon/ *n. m.* siphon; siphon bottle.

siglo /'siglo/ *n. m.* century.

signatura /signa'tura/ *n. f. Mus.* signature.

significación /signifika'θion; signifika'sion/ *n. f.* significance.

significado /signifi'kaðo/ *n. m.* meaning.

significante /signifi'kante/ *a.* significant.

significar /signifi'kar/ *v.* signify, mean.

significativo /signifika'tiβo/ *a.* significant.

signo /'signo/ *n. m.* sign, symbol; mark.

siguiente /si'giente/ *a.* following, next.

sílaba /'silaβa/ *n. f.* syllable.

silbar /sil'βar/ *v.* whistle; hiss, boo.

silbato /sil'βato/ **silbido** *n. m.* whistle.

silencio /si'lenθio; si'lensio/ *n. m.* silence, stillness.

silenciosamente /silenθiosa'mente; silensiosa'mente/ *a.* silently.

silencioso /silen'θioso; silen'sioso/ *a.* silent, still.

silicato /sili'kato/ *n. m.* silicate.

silicio /si'liθio; si'lisio/ *n. m.* silicon.

silla /'siʎa; 'siya/ *n. f.* chair; saddle.

sillón /si'ʎon; si'yon/ *n. m.* armchair.

silueta /si'lueta/ *n. f.* silhouette.

silvestre /sil'βestre/ *a.* wild, uncultivated. **fauna s.,** wildlife.

sima /'sima/ *n. f.* chasm; cavern.

simbólico /sim'boliko/ *a.* symbolic.

símbolo /'simbolo/ *n. m.* symbol.

simetría /sime'tria/ *n. f.* symmetry.

simétrico /si'metriko/ *a.* symmetrical.

símil /'simil/ **similar** *a.* similar, alike.

similitud /simili'tuð/ *n. f.* similarity.

simpatía /simpa'tia/ *n. f.* congeniality; friendly feeling.

simpático /sim'patiko/ *a.* likeable, nice, congenial.

simple /'simple/ *a.* simple.

simpleza /sim'pleθa; sim'plesa/ *n. f.* silliness; trifle.

simplicidad /simpliθi'ðað; simplisi'ðað/ *n. f.* simplicity.

simplificación /simplifika'θion; simplifika'sion/ *n. f.* simplification.

simplificar /simplifi'kar/ *v.* simplify.

simular /simu'lar/ *v.* simulate.

simultáneo /simul'taneo/ *a.* simultaneous.

sin /sin/ *prep.* without. **s. sentido,** meaningless.

sinagoga /sina'goga/ *n. f.* synagogue.

sinceridad /sinθeri'ðað; sinseri'ðað/ *n. f.* sincerity.

sincero /sin'θero; sin'sero/ *a.* sincere.

sincronizar /sinkroni'θar; sinkroni'sar/ *v.* synchronize.

sindicato /sindi'kato/ *n. m.* syndicate; labor union.

síndrome /'sindrome/ *n. m.* syndrome.

sinfonía /sinfo'nia/ *n. f.* symphony.

sinfónico /sin'foniko/ *a.* symphonic.

singular /siŋgu'lar/ *a. & m.* singular.

siniestro /si'niestro/ *a.* sinister, ominous.

sino /'sino/ *conj.* but.

sinónimo /si'nonimo/ *n. m.* synonym.

sinrazón /sinra'θon; sinra'son/ *n. f.* wrong, injustice.

sinsabor /sinsa'βor/ *n. m.* displeasure, distaste; trouble.

sintaxis /sin'taksis/ *n. f.* syntax.

síntesis /'sintesis/ *n. f.* synthesis.

sintético /sin'tetiko/ *a.* synthetic.

síntoma /'sintoma/ *n. m.* symptom.

siquiera /si'kiera/ *adv.* **ni s.,** not even.

sirena /si'rena/ *n. f.* siren.

sirviente /sir'βiente/ **-ta** *n.* servant.

sistema /sis'tema/ *n. m.* system.

sistemático /siste'matiko/ *a.* systematic.

sistematizar /sistemati'θar; sistemati'sar/ *v.* systematize.

sitiar /si'tiar/ *v.* besiege.

sitio /'sitio/ *n. m.* site, location, place, spot.

situación /situa'θion; situa'sion/ *n. f.* situation; location.

situar /si'tuar/ *v.* situate; locate.

smoking /'smokiŋ/ *n. m.* tuxedo, dinner jacket.

so /so/ *prep.* under.

soba /'soβa/ *n. f.* massage. —**sobar,** *v.*

sobaco /so'βako/ *n. m.* armpit.

sobaquero /soβa'kero/ *n. f.* armhole.

soberano /soβe'rano/ **-na** *a. & n.* sovereign.

soberbia /so'βerβia/ *n. f.* arrogance.

soberbio /so'βerβio/ *a.* superb; arrogant.

soborno /so'βorno/ *n. m.* bribe. —**sobornar,** *v.*

sobra /'soβra/ *n. f.* excess, surplus. **de sobra,** to spare.

sobrado /so'βraðo/ *n. m.* attic.

sobrante /so'βrante/ *a. & m.* surplus.

sobras /'soβras/ *n. f.pl.* leftovers.

sobre /'soβre/ *prep.* **1.** about; above, over. —*n.* **2.** *m.* envelope.

sobrecama /soβre'kama/ *n. f.* bedspread.

sobrecargo /soβre'kargo/ *n. m.* supercargo.

sobredicho /soβre'ðitʃo/ *a.* aforesaid.

sobredosis /soβre'ðosis/ *n. f.* overdose.

sobrehumano /soβreu'mano/ *a.* superhuman.

sobrenatural /soβrenatu'ral/ *a.* supernatural, weird.

sobrepasar /soβrepa'sar/ *v.* surpass.

sobresalir /soβresa'lir/ *v.* excel.

sobretodo /soβre'toðo/ *n. m.* overcoat.

sobrevivir /soβreβi'βir/ *v.* survive, outlive.

sobriedad /soβrie'ðað/ *n. f.* sobriety; moderation.

sobrina /so'βrina/ *n. f.* niece.

sobrino /so'βrino/ *n. m.* nephew.

sobrio /'soβrio/ *a.* sober, temperate.

socarrén /soka'rren/ *n. m.* eaves.

sociable /so'θiaβle; so'siaβle/ *a.* sociable.

social /so'θial; so'sial/ *a.* social.

socialismo /soθia'lismo; sosia'lismo/ *n. m.* socialism.

socialista /soθia'lista; sosia'lista/ *a. & n.* socialist.

sociedad /soθie'ðað; sosie'ðað/ *n. f.* society; association.

sociedad de consumo /soθie'ðað de kon'sumo; sosie'ðað de kon'sumo/ consumer society.

socio /'soθio; 'sosio/ **-cia** *n.* associate, partner; member.

sociología /soθiolo'hia; sosiolo'hia/ *n. f.* sociology.

sociológico /soθio'lohiko; sosio'lohiko/ *a.* sociological.

sociólogo /so'θiologo; so'siologo/ **-ga** *n.* sociologist.

socorrista /soko'rrista/ *n. m. & f.* lifeguard.

socorro /so'korro/ *n. m.* help, aid. —**socorrer,** *v.*

soda /'soða/ *n. f.* soda.

sodio /'soðio/ *n. m.* sodium.

soez /so'eθ; so'es/ *a.* vulgar.

sofá /so'fa/ *n. m.* sofa, couch.

sofisma /so'fisma/ *n. m.* sophism.

sofista /so'fista/ *n. m. & f.* sophist.

sofocación /sofoka'θion; sofoka'sion/ *n. f.* suffocation.

sofocar /sofo'kar/ *v.* smother, suffocate, stifle, choke.

sofrito /so'frito/ *n. m.* sauce of sautéed tomatoes, peppers, onions, and garlic.

software /'sofθwer/ *n. m.* software.

soga /'soga/ *n. f.* rope.

soja /'soha/ *n. f.* soya.

sol /sol/ *n. m.* sun.

solada /so'laða/ *n. f.* dregs.

solanera /sola'nera/ *n. f.* sunburn.

solapa /so'lapa/ *n. f.* lapel.

solar /so'lar/ *a.* **1.** solar. —*n.* **2.** *m.* building lot.

solaz /so'laθ; so'las/ *n. m.* solace, comfort. —**solazar,** *v.*

soldado /sol'daðo/ *n. m.* soldier.

soldar /sol'dar/ *v.* solder, weld.

soledad /sole'ðað/ *n. f.* solitude, privacy.

solemne /so'lemne/ *a.* solemn.

solemnemente /solemne'mente/ *adv.* solemnly.

solemnidad /solemni'ðað/ *n. f.* solemnity.

soler /so'ler/ *v.* be in the habit of.

solicitador /soliθita'ðor; solisita-'ðor/ **-ra** *n.* applicant, petitioner.

solicitar /soliθi'tar; solisi'tar/ *v.* solicit; apply for.

solícito /so'liθito; so'lisito/ *a.* solicitous.

solicitud /soliθi'tuð; solisi'tuð/ *n. f.* solicitude; application.

sólidamente /soliða'mente/ *adv.* solidly.

solidaridad /soliðari'ðað/ *n. f.* solidarity.

solidez /soli'ðeθ; soli'ðes/ *n. f.* solidity.

solidificar /soliðifi'kar/ *v.* solidify.

sólido /'soliðo/ *a. & m.* solid.

soliloquio /soli'lokio/ *n. m.* soliloquy.

solitario /soli'tario/ *a.* solitary, lone.

sollozo /so'ʎoθo; so'yoso/ *n. m.* sob. —**sollozar,** *v.*

solo /'solo/ *a.* **1.** only; single; alone; lonely. **a solas,** alone. —*n.* **2.** *m. Mus.* solo.

sólo *adv.* only, just.

solomillo /solo'miʎo; solo'miyo/ *n. m.* sirloin.

soltar /sol'tar/ *v.* release; loosen.

soltero /sol'tero/ **-ra** *a. & n.* single, unmarried (person).

soltura /sol'tura/ *n. f.* poise, ease, facility.

solubilidad /soluβili'ðað/ *n. f.* solubility.

solución /solu'θion; solu'sion/ *n. f.* solution.

solucionar /soluθio'nar; solusio-'nar/ *v.* solve, settle.

solvente /sol'βente/ *a.* solvent.

sombra /'sombra/ *n. f.* shade; shadow. —**sombrear,** *v.*

sombra de ojos /'sombra de 'ohos/ eye shadow.

sombrerera /sombre'rera/ *n. f.* hatbox.

sombrero /som'βrero/ *n. m.* hat.

sombrilla /som'βriʎa; som'βriya/ *n. f.* parasol.

sombrío /som'βrio/ *a.* somber, bleak, gloomy.

sombroso /som'βroso/ *a.* very shady.

someter /some'ter/ *v.* subject; submit.

somnífero /som'nifero/ *n. m.* sleeping pill.

somnolencia /somno'lenθia; somno'lensia/ *n. f.* drowsiness.

son /son/ *n. m.* sound. —**sonar,** *v.*

sonata /so'nata/ *n. f.* sonata.

sondar /son'dar/ *v.* sound, fathom.

sonido /so'niðo/ *n. m.* sound.

sonoridad /sonori'ðað/ *n. f.* sonority.

sonoro /so'noro/ *a.* sonorous.

sonrisa /son'risa/ *n. f.* smile. —**sonreír,** *v.*

sonrojo /son'roho/ *n. m.* flush, blush. —**sonrojarse,** *v.*

soñador /soɲa'ðor/ **-ra** *a. & n.* dreamy; dreamer.

soñar /so'ɲar/ *v.* dream.

soñoliento /soɲo'liento/ *a.* sleepy.

sopa /'sopa/ *n. f.* soup.

soplar /so'plar/ *v.* blow.

soplete /so'plete/ *n. m.* blowtorch.

soplo /'soplo/ *n. m.* breath; puff, gust.

soportar /sopor'tar/ *v.* abide, bear, stand.

soprano /so'prano/ *n. m. & f.* soprano.

sorbete /sor'βete/ *n. m.* sherbet.

sorbo /'sorβo/ *n. m.* sip. —**sorber,** *v.*

sordera /sor'ðera/ *n. f.* deafness.

sórdidamente /sorðiða'mente/ *adv.* sordidly.

sordidez /sorði'ðeθ; sorði'ðes/ *n. f.* sordidness.

sórdido /'sorðiðo/ *a.* sordid.

sordo /'sorðo/ *a.* deaf; muffled, dull.

sordomudo /sorðo'muðo/ **-da** *a. & n.* deaf-mute.

sorpresa /sor'presa/ *n. f.* surprise. —**sorprender,** *v.*

sorteo /sor'teo/ *n. m.* drawing lots; raffle.

sortija /sor'tiha/ *n. f.* ring.

sosa /'sosa/ *n. f. Chem.* soda.

soso /'soso/ *a.* dull, insipid, tasteless.

sospecha /sos'petʃa/ *n. f.* suspicion.

sospechar /sospe'tʃar/ *v.* suspect.

sospechoso /sospe'tʃoso/ *a.* suspicious.

sostén /sos'ten/ *n. m.* bra, brassiere; support.

sostener /soste'ner/ *v.* hold, support; maintain.

sostenimiento /sosteni'miento/ *n. m.* sustenance.

sota /'sota/ *n. f.* jack (in cards).

sótano /'sotano/ *n. m.* basement, cellar.

soto /'soto/ *n. m.* grove.

soviet /so'βiet/ *n. m.* soviet.

soya /'soya/ *n. f.* soybean.

su /su/ *a.* his, her, its, their, your.

suave /'suaβe/ *a.* smooth; gentle, soft, mild.

suavidad /suaβi'ðað/ *n. f.* smoothness; gentleness, softness, mildness.

suavizar /suaβi'θar; suaβi'sar/ *v.* soften.

subalterno /suβal'terno/ **-na** *a. & n.* subordinate.

subasta /su'βasta/ *n. f.* auction.

subcampeón /suβkampe'on/ **-na** *n.* runner-up.

subconsciencia /suβkons'θienθia; suβkons'siensia/ *n. f.* subconscious.

súbdito /'suβðito/ **-ta** *n.* subject.

subestimar /suβesti'mar/ *v.* underestimate.

subida /su'βiða/ *n. f.* ascent, rise.

subilla /su'βiʎa; su'βiya/ *n. f.* awl.

subir /su'βir/ *v.* rise, climb, ascend, mount. **s. a,** amount to.

súbito /'suβito/ *a.* sudden.

subjetivo /suβhe'tiβo/ *a.* subjective.

subjuntivo /suβhun'tiβo/ *a. & m.* subjunctive.

sublimación /suβlima'θion; suβlima'sion/ *n. f.* sublimation.

sublimar /suβli'mar/ *v.* elevate; sublimate.

sublime /su'βlime/ *a.* sublime.

submarinismo /suβmari'nismo/ *n. m.* scuba diving.

submarino /suβma'rino/ *a. & m.* submarine.

subordinación /suβorðina'θion; suβorðina'sion/ *n. f.* subordination.

subordinado /suβorði'naðo/ **-da** *a. & n.* subordinate.
—**subordinar,** *v.*

subrayar /suβra'yar/ *v.* underline.

subscribirse /suβskri'βirse/ *v.* subscribe; sign one's name.

subscripción /suβskrip'θion; suβskrip'sion/ *n. f.* subscription.

subsecuente /suβse'kuente/ *a.* subsequent.

subsidiario /suβsi'ðiario/ *a.* subsidiary.

subsiguiente /suβsi'giente/ *a.* subsequent.

substancia /suβs'tanθia; suβs'tansia/ *n. f.* substance.

substancial /suβs'tanθial; suβs'tansial/ *a.* substantial.

substantivo /suβstan'tiβo/ *n. m.* substantive, noun.

substitución /suβstitu'θion; suβstitu'sion/ *n. f.* substitution.

substituir /suβsti'tuir/ *v.* replace; substitute.

substitutivo /suβstitu'tiβo/ *a.* substitute.

substituto /suβsti'tuto/ **-ta** *n.* substitute.

substraer /suβstra'er/ *v.* subtract.

subsuelo /suβ'suelo/ *n. m.* subsoil.

subterfugio /suβter'fuhio/ *n. m.* subterfuge.

subterráneo /suβte'rraneo/ *a.* **1.** subterranean, underground. —*n.* **2.** *m.* place underground; subway.

subtítulo /suβ'titulo/ *n. m.* subtitle.

suburbio /su'βurβio/ *n. m.* suburb.

subvención /suββen'θion; suββen'sion/ *n. f.* subsidy, grant.

subversión /suββer'sion/ *n. f.* subversion.

subversivo /suββer'siβo/ *a.* subversive.

subvertir /suββer'tir/ *v.* subvert.

subyugación /suβyuga'θion; suβyuga'sion/ *n. f.* subjugation.

subyugar /suβyu'gar/ *v.* subjugate, quell.

succión /suk'θion; suk'sion/ *n. f.* suction.

suceder /suθe'ðer; suse'ðer/ *v.* happen, occur, befall. **s. a,** succeed, follow.

sucesión /suθe'sion; suse'sion/ *n. f.* succession.

sucesivo /suθe'siβo; suse'siβo/ *a.* successive. **en lo s.,** in the future.

suceso /su'θeso; su'seso/ *n. m.* event.

sucesor /suθe'sor; suse'sor/ **-ra** *n.* successor.

suciedad /suθie'ðaθ; susie'ðaθ/ *n. f.* filth, dirt.

sucio /'suθio; 'susio/ *a.* filthy, dirty.

suculento /suku'lento/ *a.* succulent.

sucumbir /sukum'βir/ *v.* succumb.

sud /suθ/ *n. m.* south.

sudadera /suða'ðera/ *n. f.* sweatshirt.

Sudáfrica /su'ðafrika/ *n. f.* South Africa.

sudafricano /suðafri'kano/ **-na** *a.* & *n.* South African..

sudamericano /suðameri'kano/ **-na** *a.* & *n.* South American.

sudar /su'ðar/ *v.* perspire, sweat.

sudeste /su'ðeste/ *n. m.* southeast.

sudoeste /suðo'este/ *n. m.* southwest.

sudor /su'ðor/ *n. m.* perspiration, sweat.

Suecia /'sueθia; 'suesia/ *n. f.* Sweden.

sueco /'sueko/ **-ca** *a.* & *n.* Swedish; Swede.

suegra /'suegra/ *n. f.* mother-in-law.

suegro /'suegro/ *n. m.* father-in-law.

suela /'suela/ *n. f.* sole.

sueldo /'sueldo/ *n. m.* salary, wages.

suelo /'suelo/ *n. m.* soil; floor; ground.

suelto /'suelto/ *a.* **1.** loose; free; odd, separate. —*n.* **2.** loose change.

sueño /'sueɲo/ *n. m.* sleep; sleepiness; dream. **tener s.,** to be sleepy.

suero /'suero/ *n. m.* serum.

suerte /'suerte/ *n. f.* luck; chance; lot.

suéter /'sueter/ *n. m.* sweater.

suficiente /sufi'θiente; sufi'siente/ *a.* sufficient.

sufragio /su'frahio/ *n. m.* suffrage.

sufrimiento /sufri'miento/ *n. m.* suffering, agony.

sufrir /su'frir/ *v.* suffer; undergo; endure.

sugerencia /suhe'renθia; suhe'rensia/ *n. f.* suggestion.

sugerir /suhe'rir/ *v.* suggest.

sugestión /suhes'tion/ *n. f.* suggestion.

sugestionar /suhestio'nar/ *v.* influence; hypnotize.

suicida /sui'θiða; sui'siða/ *n. m.* & *f.* suicide (person).

suicidarse /suiθi'ðarse; suisi'ðarse/ *v.* commit suicide.

suicidio /sui'θiðio; sui'siðio/ *n. m.* (act of) suicide.

Suiza /'suiθa; 'suisa/ *n. f.* Switzerland.

suizo /'suiθo; 'suiso/ **-za** *a.* & *n.* Swiss.

sujeción /suhe'θion; suhe'sion/ *n. f.* subjection.

sujetador /suheta'ðor/ *n. m.* bra, brassiere.

sujetapapeles /su'hetapa'peles/ *n. m.* paper clip.

sujetar /suhe'tar/ *v.* hold, fasten, clip.

sujeto /su'heto/ *a.* **1.** subject, liable. —*n.* **2.** *m. Gram.* subject.

sulfato /sul'fato/ *n. m.* sulfate.

sulfuro /sul'furo/ *n. m.* sulfide.

sultán /sul'tan/ *n. m.* sultan.

suma /'suma/ *n. f.* sum, amount. **en s.,** in short. **s. global,** lump sum.

sumar /su'mar/ *v.* add up.

sumaria /su'maria/ *n. f.* indictment.

sumario /su'mario/ *a.* & *m.* summary.

sumergir /sumer'hir/ *v.* submerge.

sumersión /sumer'sion/ *n. f.* submersion.

sumisión /sumi'sion/ *n. f.* submission.

sumiso /su'miso/ *a.* submissive.

sumo /'sumo/ *a.* great, high, utmost.

suntuoso /sun'tuoso/ *a.* sumptuous.

superar /supe'rar/ *v.* overcome, surpass.

superficial /superfi'θial; superfi'sial/ *a.* superficial, shallow.

superficie /super'fiθie; super'fisie/ *n. f.* surface.

supérfluo /su'perfluo/ *a.* superfluous.

superhombre /super'ombre/ *n. m.* superman.

superintendente /superinten-'dente/ *n. m.* & *f.* superintendent.

superior /supe'rior/ *a.* **1.** superior; upper, higher. —*n.* **2.** *m.* superior.

superioridad /superiori'ðað/ *n. f.* superiority.

superlativo /superla'tiβo/ *n. m.* & *a.* superlative.

superstición /supersti'θion; supersti'sion/ *n. f.* superstition.

supersticioso /supersti'θioso; supersti'sioso/ *a.* superstitious.

supervisar /superβi'sar/ *v.* supervise.

supervivencia /superβi'βenθia; superβi'βensia/ *n. f.* survival.

suplantar /suplan'tar/ *v.* supplant.

suplementario /suplemen'tario/ *a.* supplementary.

suplemento /suple'mento/ *n. m.* supplement. —**suplementar,** *v.*

suplente /su'plente/ *a.* & *n.* substitute.

súplica /'suplika/ *n. f.* request, entreaty, plea.

suplicación /suplika'θion; suplika'sion/ *n. f.* supplication; request, entreaty.

suplicar /supli'kar/ *v.* request, entreat; implore.

suplicio /su'pliθio; su'plisio/ *n. m.* torture, ordeal.

suplir /su'plir/ *v.* supply.

suponer /supo'ner/ *v.* suppose, pressume, assume.

suposición /suposi'θion; suposi'sion/ *n. f.* supposition, assumption.

supositorio /suposi'torio/ *n. m.* suppository.

supremacía /suprema'θia; suprema'sia/ *n. f.* supremacy.

supremo /su'premo/ *a.* supreme.

supresión /supre'sion/ *n. f.* suppression.

suprimir /supri'mir/ *v.* suppress; abolish.

supuesto /su'puesto/ *a.* supposed. **por s.,** of course.

sur /sur/ *n. m.* south.

surco /'surko/ *n. m.* furrow. —**surcar,** *v.*

surgir /sur'hir/ *v.* arise; appear suddenly.

surtido /sur'tiðo/ *n. m.* assortment; supply, stock.

surtir /sur'tir/ *v.* furnish, supply.

susceptibilidad /susθeptiβili'ðað; sussepтιβili'ðað/ *n. f.* susceptibility.

susceptible /susθep'tiβle; sussep'tiβle/ *a.* susceptible.

suscitar /susθi'tar; sussi'tar/ *v.* stir up.

suscri- = subscri-

suspender /suspen'der/ *v.* withhold; suspend; fail (in a course).

suspensión /suspen'sion/ *n. f.* suspension.

suspenso /sus'penso/ *n. m.* failing grade. **en s.,** in suspense.

suspicacia /suspi'kaθia; suspi'kasia/ *n. f.* suspicion, distrust.

suspicaz /suspi'kaθ; suspi'kas/ *a.* suspicious.

suspicazmente /suspikaθ'mente; suspikas'mente/ *adv.* suspiciously.

suspiro /sus'piro/ *n. m.* sigh. —**suspirar,** *v.*

sustan- = substan-

sustentar /susten'tar/ *v.* sustain, support.

sustento /sus'tento/ *n. m.* sustenance, support, living.

susti- = substi-

susto /'susto/ *n. m.* fright, scare.

sustraer /sustra'er/ = substraer.

susurro /su'surro/ *n. m.* rustle; whisper. —**susurrar,** *v.*

sutil /'sutil/ *a.* subtle.

sutileza /suti'leθa, sutili'ðað; suti'lesa, sutili'ðað/ **sutilidad** *n. f.* subtlety.

sutura /su'tura/ *n. f.* suture.

suyo /'suyo/ *a.* his, hers, theirs, yours.

T

tabaco /ta'βako/ *n. m.* tobacco.

tábano /'taβano/ *n. m.* horsefly.

tabaquería /taβake'ria/ *n. f.* tobacco shop.

taberna /ta'βerna/ *n. f.* tavern, bar.

tabernáculo /taβer'nakulo/ *n. m.* tabernacle.

tabique /ta'βike/ *n. m.* dividing wall, partition.

tabla /'taβla/ *n. f.* board, plank; table, list. **t. de planchar,** ironing board.

tablado /ta'βlaðo/ *n. m.* stage, platform.

tablero /ta'βlero/ *n. m.* panel.

tableta /ta'βleta/ *n. f.* tablet.

tablilla /ta'βliʎa; ta'βliya/ *n. f.* bulletin board.

tabú /ta'βu/ *n. m.* taboo.

tabular /taβu'lar/ *a.* tabular.

tacaño /ta'kaɲo/ *a.* stingy.

tacha /'tatʃa/ *n. f.* fault, defect.

tachar /ta'tʃar/ *v.* find fault with; cross out.

tachuela /ta'tʃuela/ *n. f.* tack.

tácitamente /'taθitamente; 'tasitamente/ *adv.* tacitly.

tácito /'taθito; 'tasito/ *a.* tacit.

taciturno /taθi'turno; tasi'turno/ *a.* taciturn.

taco /'tako/ *n. m.* heel (of shoe); billiard cue.

tacón /ta'kon/ *n. m.* heel (of shoe).

táctico /'taktiko/ *a.* tactical.

tacto /'takto/ *n. m.* (sense of) touch; tact.

tafetán /tafe'tan/ *n. m.* taffeta.

taimado /tai'maðo/ *a.* sly.

tajada /ta'haða/ *n. f.* cut, slice. **—tajar,** *v.*

tajea /ta'hea/ *n. f.* channel.

tal /tal/ *a.* such. **con t. que.,** provided that. **t. vez,** perhaps.

taladrar /tala'ðrar/ *v.* drill.

taladro /ta'laðro/ *n. m. Mech.* drill.

talante /ta'lante/ *n. m.* humor, disposition.

talco /'talko/ *n. m.* talc.

talega /ta'lega/ *n. f.* bag, sack.

talento /ta'lento/ *n. m.* talent.

talla /'taʎa; 'taya/ *n. f.* engraving; stature; size (of suit).

tallador /taʎa'ðor; taya'ðor/ **-ra** *n.* engraver; dealer (at cards).

talle /'taʎe; 'taye/ *n. m.* figure; waist; fit.

taller /ta'ʎer; ta'yer/ *n. m.* workshop, factory.

tallo /'taʎo; 'tayo/ *n. m.* stem, stalk.

talón /ta'lon/ *n. m.* heel (of foot); (baggage) check, stub.

tamal /ta'mal/ *n. m.* tamale.

tamaño /ta'maɲo/ *n. m.* size.

tambalear /tambale'ar/ *v.* stagger, totter.

también /tam'bien/ *adv.* also, too.

tambor /tam'bor/ *n. m.* drum.

tamiz /ta'miθ; ta'mis/ *n. m.* sieve, sifter.

tampoco /tam'poko/ *adv.* neither, either.

tan /tan/ *adv.* so.

tanda /'tanda/ *n. f.* turn, relay.

tándem /'tandem/ *n. m.* tandem; pair.

tangencia /taŋ'genθia; taŋ'gensia/ *n. f.* tangency.

tangible /taŋ'giβle/ *a.* tangible.

tango /'taŋgo/ *n. m.* tango (dance or music).

tanque /'tanke/ *n. m.* tank.

tanteo /tan'teo/ *n. m.* estimate. **—tantear,** *v.*

tanto /'tanto/ *a. & pron.* **1.** so much, so many; as much, as many. **entre t., mientras t.,** meanwhile. **por lo t.,** therefore. **un t.,** somewhat, a bit. **—n. 2.** *m.* point (in games) **3.** (*pl.*) score. **estar al t.,** to be up to date.

tañer /ta'ɲer/ *v.* play (an instrument); ring (bells).

tapa /'tapa/ *n. f.* cap, cover; snack served in a bar. **—tapar,** *v.*

tapadero /tapa'ðero/ *n. m.* stopper, lid.

tápara /'tapara/ *n. f.* caper.

tapete /ta'pete/ *n. m.* small rug, mat, cover.

tapia /'tapia/ *n. f.* wall.

tapicería /tapiθe'ria; tapise'ria/ *n. f.* tapestry.

tapioca /ta'pioka/ *n. f.* tapioca.

tapiz /ta'piθ; ta'pis/ *n. m.* tapestry; carpet.

tapizado (de pared) /tapi'θaðo de pa'reð; tapi'saðo de pa'reð/ *n. m.* (wall) covering.

tapón /ta'pon/ *n. m.* plug; cork.

taquigrafía /takigra'fia/ n. f. shorthand.

taquilla /ta'kiʎa; ta'kiya/ n. f. ticket office; box office; ticket window.

tara /'tara/ n. f. hang-up.

tarántula /ta'rantula/ n. f. tarantula.

tararear /tarare'ar/ v. hum.

tardanza /tar'ðanθa; tar'ðansa/ n. f. delay; lateness.

tardar /tar'ðar/ v. delay; be late; take (of time). **a más t.**, at the latest.

tarde /'tarðe/ adv. **1.** late. —n. **2.** f. afternoon.

tardío /tar'ðio/ a. late, belated.

tarea /ta'rea/ n. f. task, assignment.

tarifa /ta'rifa/ n. f. rate; tariff; price list.

tarjeta /tar'heta/ n. f. card.

tarjeta bancaria /tar'heta ban-'karia/ bank card.

tarjeta de crédito /tar'heta de 'kreðito/ credit card.

tarjeta de embarque /tar'heta de em'ßarke/ boarding pass.

tarta /'tarta/ n. f. tart.

tartamudear /tartamuðe'ar/ v. stammer, falter.

tasa /'tasa/ n. f. rate.

tasación /tasa'θion; tasa'sion/ n. f. valuation.

tasar /ta'sar/ v. assess, appraise.

tasca /'taska/ n. f. bar, pub.

tasugo /ta'sugo/ n. m. badger.

tatuar /tatu'ar/ v. tattoo.

tautología /tautolo'hia/ n. f. tautology.

taxi /'taksi/ **taxímetro** n. m. taxi.

taxista /tak'sista/ n. m. & f. taxi driver.

taxonomía /taksono'mia/ n. f. taxonomy.

taza /'taθa; 'tasa/ n. f. cup.

te /te/ pron. you; yourself.

té n. m. tea.

team /tim/ n. m. team.

teátrico /te'atriko/ a. theatrical.

teatro /te'atro/ n. m. theater.

tebeo /te'ßeo/ n. m. comic book.

techo /'tetʃo/ n. m. roof. —**techar**, v.

tecla /'tekla/ n. f. key (of a piano, etc.).

teclado /te'klaðo/ n. m. keyboard.

teclado numérico /te'klaðo nu'meriko/ numeric keypad.

técnica /'teknika/ n. f. technique.

técnicamente /'teknikamente/ adv. technically.

técnico /'tekniko/ a. **1.** technical; —m. **2.** repairman, technician.

tecnología /teknolo'hia/ n. f. technology.

tedio /'teðio/ n. m. tedium, boredom.

tedioso /te'ðioso/ a. tedious.

teísmo /te'ismo/ n. m. theism.

teja /'teha/ n. f. tile.

tejado /te'haðo/ n. m. roof.

tejano /te'hano/ **-na** a. & n. Texan.

tejanos /te'hanos/ n. m.pl. jeans.

tejer /te'her/ v. weave; knit.

tejido /te'hiðo/ n. m. fabric; weaving.

tejón /te'hon/ n. m. badger.

tela /'tela/ n. f. cloth, fabric, web. **t. metálica,** screen; screening. **t. vaquera,** denim.

telar /te'lar/ n. m. loom.

telaraña /tela'raɲa/ n. f. cobweb, spiderweb.

telefonista /telefo'nista/ n. m. & f. (telephone) operator.

teléfono /te'lefono/ n. m. telephone. —**telefonear,** v.

teléfono gratuito /te'lefono gra'tuito/ toll-free number.

teléfono público /te'lefono 'pußliko/ pay phone, public telephone.

teléfono rojo /te'lefono 'rroho/ hotline.

telégrafo /te'legrafo/ n. m. telegraph. —**telegrafear,** v.

telegrama /tele'grama/ n. m. telegram.

telescopio /teles'kopio/ n. m. telescope.

televisión /teleßi'sion/ n. f. television.

telón /te'lon/ n. m. Theat. curtain.

telurio /te'lurio/ n. m. tellurium.

tema /'tema/ n. m. theme, subject.

temblar /tem'blar/ v. tremble, quake; shake, shiver.

temblor /tem'blor/ n. m. tremor; shiver.

temer /te'mer/ v. fear, be afraid of, dread.

temerario /teme'rario/ a. rash.

temeridad /temeri'ðað/ n. f. temerity.

temerosamente /temerosa'mente/ adv. timorously.

temeroso /teme'roso/ a. fearful.

temor /te'mor/ *n. m.* fear.
témpano /'tempano/ *n. m.* kettle-drum; iceberg.
temperamento /tempera'mento/ *n. m.* temperament.
temperancia /tempe'ranθia; tempe'ransia/ *n. f.* temperance.
temperatura /tempera'tura/ *n. f.* temperature.
tempestad /tempes'taδ/ *n. f.* tempest, storm.
tempestuoso /tempes'tuoso/ *a.* tempestuous, stormy.
templado /tem'plaδo/ *a.* temperate, mild, moderate.
templanza /tem'planθa; tem'plansa/ *n. f.* temperance; mildness.
templar /tem'plar/ *v.* temper; tune (an instrument).
templo /'templo/ *n. m.* temple.
temporada /tempo'raδa/ *n. f.* season, time, spell.
temporal /tempo'ral/ **temporáneo** *a.* temporary.
temprano /tem'prano/ *a. & adv.* early.
tenacidad /tenaθi'δaδ; tenasi'δaδ/ *n. f.* tenacity.
tenaz /te'naθ; te'nas/ *a.* tenacious, stubborn.
tenazmente /tenaθ'mente; tenas'mente/ *adv.* tenaciously.
tendencia /ten'denθia; tendensia/ *n. f.* tendency, trend.
tender /ten'der/ *v.* stretch, stretch out.
tendero /ten'dero/ **-ra** *n.* shopkeeper, storekeeper.
tendón /ten'don/ *n. m.* tendon, sinew.
tenebrosidad /teneβrosi'δaδ/ *n. f.* gloom.
tenebroso /tene'βroso/ *a.* dark, gloomy.
tenedor /tene'δor/ *n.* **1.** *m. & f.* keeper; holder. **2.** *m.* fork.
tener /te'ner/ *v.* have; own; hold. **t. que**, have to, must.
teniente /te'niente/ *n. m.* lieutenant.
tenis /'tenis/ *n. m.* tennis; (*pl.*) sneakers.
tenor /te'nor/ *n. m.* tenor.
tensión /ten'sion/ *n. f.* tension, stress, strain.
tenso /'tenso/ *a.* tense.
tentación /tenta'θion; tenta'sion/ *n. f.* temptation.

tentáculo /ten'takulo/ *n. m.* tentacle.
tentador /tenta'δor/ *a.* alluring, tempting.
tentar /ten'tar/ *v.* tempt, lure; grope, probe.
tentativa /tenta'tiβa/ *n. f.* attempt.
tentativo /tenta'tiβo/ *a.* tentative.
teñir /te'ɲir/ *v.* tint, dye.
teología /teolo'hia/ *n. f.* theology.
teológico /teo'lohiko/ *a.* theological.
teoría /teo'ria/ *n. f.* theory.
teórico /te'oriko/ *a.* theoretical.
terapéutico /tera'peutiko/ *a.* therapeutic.
tercero /ter'θero; ter'sero/ *a.* third.
tercio /'terθio; 'tersio/ *n. m.* third.
terciopelo /terθio'pelo; tersio'pelo/ *n. m.* velvet.
terco /'terko/ *a.* obstinate, stubborn.
termal /ter'mal/ *a.* thermal.
terminación /termina'θion; termina'sion/ *n. f.* termination; completion.
terminal aérea /termi'nal 'airea/ *n. f.* air terminal.
terminar /termi'nar/ *v.* terminate, finish.
término /'termino/ *n. m.* term; end.
terminología /terminolo'hia/ *n. f.* terminology.
termómetro /ter'mometro/ *n. m.* thermometer.
termos /'termos/ *n. m.* thermos.
termostato /ter'mostato/ *n. m.* thermostat.
ternero /ter'nero/ **-ra** *n.* calf.
ternura /ter'nura/ *n. f.* tenderness.
terquedad /terke'δaδ/ *n. f.* stubbornness.
terraza /te'rraθa; te'rrasa/ *n. f.* terrace.
terremoto /terre'moto/ *n. m.* earthquake.
terreno /te'rreno/ *a.* **1.** earthly, terrestrial. —*n.* **2.** *m.* ground, terrain; lot, plot.
terrible /te'rriβle/ *a.* terrible, awful.
terrífico /te'rrifiko/ *a.* terrifying.
territorio /terri'torio/ *n. m.* territory.
terrón /te'rron/ *n. m.* clod, lump; mound.

terror /te'rror/ n. m. terror.

terso /'terso/ a. smooth, glossy; terse.

tertulia /ter'tulia/ n. f. social gathering, party.

tesis /'tesis/ n. f. thesis.

tesorería /tesore'ria/ n. f. treasury.

tesorero /teso'rero/ **-ra** n. treasurer.

tesoro /te'soro/ n. m. treasure.

testamento /testa'mento/ n. m. will, testament.

testarudo /testa'ruðo/ a. stubborn.

testificar /testifi'kar/ v. testify.

testigo /tes'tigo/ n. m. & f. witness.

testimonial /testimo'nial/ a. testimonial.

testimonio /testi'monio/ n. m. testimony.

teta /'teta/ n. f. teat.

tetera /te'tera/ n. f. teapot.

tétrico /'tetriko/ a. sad; gloomy.

texto /'teksto/ n. m. text.

textura /teks'tura/ n. f. texture.

tez /teθ; tes/ n. f. complexion.

ti /ti/ pron. you; yourself.

tía /'tia/ n. f. aunt.

tibio /'tiβio/ a. lukewarm.

tiburón /tiβu'ron/ n. m. shark.

tiemblo /'tiemblo/ n. m. aspen.

tiempo /'tiempo/ n. m. time; weather; Gram. tense.

tienda /'tienda/ n. f. shop, store; tent.

tientas /'tientas/ n. f.pl. **andar a t.,** to grope (in the dark).

tierno /'tierno/ a. tender.

tierra /'tierra/ n. f. land; ground; earth, dirt, soil.

tieso /'tieso/ a. taut, stiff, hard, strong.

tiesto /'tiesto/ n. m. flower pot.

tiesura /tie'sura/ n. f. stiffness; harshness.

tifo /'tifo/ n. m. typhus.

tifoideo /tifoi'ðeo/ n. m. typhoid fever.

tigre /'tigre/ n. m. tiger.

tijeras /ti'heras/ n. f.pl. scissors.

tila /'tila/ n. f. linden.

timbre /'timbre/ n. m. seal, stamp; tone; (electric) bell.

tímidamente /'timiðamente/ adv. timidly.

timidez /timi'ðeθ; timi'ðes/ n. f. timidity.

tímido /'timiðo/ a. timid, shy.

timón /ti'mon/ n. m. rudder, helm.

tímpano /'timpano/ n. m. kettledrum; eardrum.

tina /'tina/ n. f. tub, vat.

tinaja /ti'naha/ n. f. jar.

tinta /'tinta/ n. f. ink.

tinte /'tinte/ n. m. tint, shade.

tintero /tin'tero/ n. m. inkwell.

tinto /'tinto/ a. wine-colored; red (of wine).

tintorería /tintore'ria/ n. f. dry cleaning shop.

tintorero /tinto'rero/ **-ra** n. dyer; dry cleaner.

tintura /tin'tura/ n. f. tincture; dye.

tiñoso /ti'ɲoso/ a. scabby; stingy.

tío /'tio/ n. m. uncle.

tiovivo /tio'βiβo/ n. m. merry-go-round.

típico /'tipiko/ a. typical.

tipo /'tipo/ n. m. type, sort; (interest) rate; Colloq. guy, fellow.

tipo de cambio /'tipo de 'kambio/ exchange rate.

tipo de interés /'tipo de inte'res/ interest rate.

tira /'tira/ n. f. strip.

tirabuzón /tiraβu'θon; tiraβu'son/ n. m. corkscrew.

tirada /ti'raða/ n. f. edition.

tirado /ti'raðo/ **-da** a. dirt-cheap.

tiranía /tira'nia/ n. f. tyranny.

tiránico /ti'raniko/ n. m. tyrannical.

tirano /ti'rano/ **-na** n. tyrant.

tirante /ti'rante/ a. **1.** tight, taut; tense. —n. **2.** m.pl. suspenders.

tirar /ti'rar/ v. throw; draw; pull; fire (a weapon).

tiritar /tiri'tar/ v. shiver.

tiro /'tiro/ n. m. throw; shot.

tirón /ti'ron/ n. m. pull. **de un t.,** at a stretch, at one stroke.

tísico /'tisiko/ n. & a. consumptive.

tisis /'tisis/ n. f. consumption, tuberculosis.

titanio /ti'tanio/ n. m. titanium.

títere /'titere/ n. m. puppet.

titilación /titila'θion; titila'sion/ n. f. twinkle.

titubear /tituβe'ar/ v. stagger; totter; waver.

titulado /titu'laðo/ a. entitled; so-called.

titular /titu'lar/ a. **1.** titular. —v. **2.** entitle.

título /'titulo/ n. m. title, headline.

tiza /'tiθa; 'tisa/ n. f. chalk.

tiznar /tiθ'nar; tis'nar/ *v.* smudge; stain.

toalla /to'aʎa; to'aya/ *n. f.* towel.

t. sanitaria, sanitary napkin.

toalleta /toa'ʎeta; toa'yeta/ *n. f.* small towel.

tobillo /to'βiʎo; to'βiyo/ *n. m.* ankle.

tobogán /toβo'gan/ *n. m.* toboggan.

tocadiscos /toka'ðiskos/ *n. m.* record player.

tocadiscos compacto /toka'ðiskos kom'pakto/ **tocadiscos digital** /diɣi'tal/ CD player.

tocado /to'kaðo/ *n. m.* hairdo.

tocador /toka'ðor/ *n. m.* boudoir; dressing table.

tocante /to'kante/ *a.* touching. **t. a,** concerning, relative to.

tocar /to'kar/ *v.* touch; play (an instrument). **t. a uno,** be one's turn; be up to one.

tocayo /to'kayo/ **-ya** *n.* namesake.

tocino /to'θino; to'sino/ *n. m.* bacon.

tocólogo /to'kologo/ **-ga** *n.* obstetrician.

todavía /toða'βia/ *adv.* yet, still.

todo /'toðo/ *a.* **1.** all, whole. **todos los,** every. —*pron.* **2.** all, everything. **con t.,** still, however. **del t.,** wholly; at all.

todopoderoso /toðopoðe'roso/ *a.* almighty.

toldo /'toldo/ *n. m.* awning.

tolerancia /tole'ranθia; tole'ransia/ *n. f.* tolerance.

tolerante /tole'rante/ *a.* tolerant.

tolerar /tole'rar/ *v.* tolerate.

toma /'toma/ *n. f.* taking, capture, seizure.

tomaína /to'maina/ *n. f.* ptomaine.

tomar /to'mar/ *v.* take; drink. **t. el sol,** sunbathe.

tomate /to'mate/ *n. m.* tomato.

tomillo /to'miʎo; to'miyo/ *n. m.* thyme.

tomo /'tomo/ *n. m.* volume.

tonada /to'naða/ *n. f.* tune.

tonel /to'nel/ *n. m.* barrel, cask.

tonelada /tone'laða/ *n. f.* ton.

tonelaje /tone'lahe/ *n. m.* tonnage.

tónico /'toniko/ *a. & m.* tonic.

tono /'tono/ *n. m.* tone, pitch, shade. **darse t.,** to put on airs.

tonsila /ton'sila/ *n. f.* tonsil.

tonsilitis /tonsi'litis/ *n. f.* tonsilitis.

tontería /tonte'ria/ *n. f.* nonsense, foolishness.

tontifútbol /tonti'futβol/ *n. m.* excessively defensive strategy (in soccer).

tonto /'tonto/ **-ta** *a. & n.* foolish, silly; fool.

topacio /to'paθio; to'pasio/ *n. m.* topaz.

topar /to'par/ *v.* run into. **t. con,** come upon.

tópico /'topiko/ *a.* **1.** topical. —*n.* **2.** *m.* cliché.

topo /'topo/ *n. m.* mole (animal).

toque /'toke/ *n. m.* touch.

tórax /'toraks/ *n. m.* thorax.

torbellino /torβe'ʎino; torβe'yino/ *n. m.* whirlwind.

torcer /tor'θer; tor'ser/ *v.* twist; wind; distort.

toreador /torea'ðor/ **-a** *n.* toreador.

torero /to'rero/ **-ra** *n.* bullfighter.

torio /'torio/ *n. m.* thorium.

tormenta /tor'menta/ *n. f.* storm.

tormento /tor'mento/ *n. m.* torment.

tornado /tor'naðo/ *n. m.* tornado.

tornar /tor'nar/ *v.* return; turn.

tornarse en /tor'narse en/ *v.* turn into, become.

torneo /tor'neo/ *n. m.* tournament.

tornillo /tor'niʎo; tor'niyo/ *n. m.* screw.

toro /'toro/ *n. m.* bull.

toronja /to'ronha/ *n. f.* grapefruit.

torpe /'torpe/ *a.* awkward, clumsy; sluggish.

torpedero /torpe'ðero/ *n. m.* torpedo boat.

torpedo /tor'peðo/ *n. m.* torpedo.

torre /'torre/ *n. f.* tower.

torre de mando /'torre de 'mando/ control tower.

torrente /tor'rente/ *n. m.* torrent.

tórrido /'torriðo/ *a.* torrid.

torta /'torta/ *n. f.* cake; loaf.

tortilla /tor'tiʎa; tor'tiya/ *n. f.* omelet; (Mex.) tortilla, pancake.

tórtola /'tortola/ *n. f.* dove.

tortuga /tor'tuga/ *n. f.* turtle.

tortuoso /tor'tuoso/ *a.* tortuous.

tortura /tor'tura/ *n. f.* torture. —**torturar,** *v.*

tos /tos/ *n. m.* cough. —**toser,** *v.*

tosco /'tosko/ *a.* coarse, rough, uncouth.

tosquedad /toske'ðað/ *n. f.* coarseness, roughness.

tostador /tosta'ðor/ *n. m.* toaster.

tostar /'tostar/ *v.* toast; tan.

total /to'tal/ *a. & m.* total.

totalidad /totali'ðað/ *n. f.* totality, entirety, whole.

totalitario /totali'tario/ *a.* totalitarian.

totalmente /total'mente/ *adv.* totally; entirely.

tótem /'totem/ *n. m.* totem.

tóxico /'toksiko/ *a.* toxic.

toxicómano /toksi'komano/ **-na** *n. m. & f.* drug addict.

trabajador /traβaha'ðor/ **-ra** *a.* **1.** hardworking. —*n.* **2.** worker.

trabajo /tra'βaho/ *n. m.* work; labor. —**trabajar,** *v.*

trabar /tra'βar/ *v.* fasten, shackle; grasp; strike up.

tracción /trak'θion; trak'sion/ *n. f.* traction.

tracto /'trakto/ *n. m.* tract.

tractor /trak'tor/ *n. m.* tractor.

tradición /traði'θion; traði'sion/ *n. f.* tradition.

tradicional /traðiθio'nal; traðisio'nal/ *a.* traditional.

traducción /traðuk'θion; traðuk'sion/ *n. f.* translation.

traducir /traðu'θir; traðu'sir/ *v.* translate.

traductor /traðuk'tor/ **-ra** *n.* translator.

traer /tra'er/ *v.* bring; carry; wear.

tráfico /'trafiko/ *n. m.* traffic. —**traficar,** *v.*

tragaperras /traga'perras/ *n. f.* slot machine, one-armed bandit.

tragar /tra'gar/ *v.* swallow.

tragedia /tra'heðia/ *n. f.* tragedy.

trágicamente /'trahikamente/ *adv.* tragically.

trágico /'trahiko/ **-ca** *a.* **1.** tragic. —*n.* **2.** tragedian.

trago /'trago/ *n. m.* swallow; drink.

traición /trai'θion; trai'sion/ *n. f.* treason, betrayal.

traicionar /traiθio'nar; traisio'nar/ *v.* betray.

traidor /trai'ðor/ **-ra** *a. & n.* traitorous; traitor.

traje /'trahe/ *n. m.* suit; dress; garb, apparel.

traje de baño /'trahe de 'baɲo/ bathing suit.

trama /'trama/ *v.* plot (of a story).

tramador /trama'ðor/ **-ra** *n.* weaver; plotter.

tramar /tra'mar/ *v.* weave; plot, scheme.

trámite /'tramite/ *n. m.* (business) deal, transaction.

tramo /'tramo/ *n. m.* span, stretch, section.

trampa /'trampa/ *n. f.* trap, snare.

trampista /tram'pista/ *n. m. & f.* cheater; swindler.

trance /'tranθe; 'transe/ *n. m.* critical moment or stage. **a todo t.,** at any cost.

tranco /'tranko/ *n. m.* stride.

tranquilidad /trankili'ðað/ *n. f.* tranquility, calm, quiet.

tranquilizante /trankili'θante; trankili'sante/ *n. m.* tranquilizer.

tranquilizar /trankili'θar; trankili'sar/ *v.* quiet, calm down.

tranquilo /tran'kilo/ *a.* tranquil, calm.

transacción /transak'θion; transak'sion/ *n. f.* transaction.

transbordador /transβorða'ðor/ *n. m.* ferry.

transbordador espacial /transβorða'ðor espa'θial; transβorða'ðor espa'sial/ space shuttle.

transcribir /transkri'βir/ *v.* transcribe.

transcripción /transkrip'θion; transkrip'sion/ *n. f.* transcription.

transcurrir /transku'rrir/ *v.* elapse.

transeúnte /tran'seunte/ *a. & n.* transient; passerby.

transexual /transek'sual/ *a.* transsexual.

transferencia /transfe'renθia; transfe'rensia/ *n. f.* transference.

transferir /transfe'rir/ *v.* transfer.

transformación /transforma'θion; transforma'sion/ *n. f.* transformation.

transformar /transfor'mar/ *v.* transform.

transfusión /transfu'sion/ *n. f.* transfusion.

transgresión /transgre'sion/ *n. f.* transgression.

transgresor /transgre'sor/ **-ra** *n.* transgressor.

transición /transi'θion; transi'sion/ *n. f.* transition.

transigir /transi'hir/ *v.* compromise, settle; agree.

transistor /transis'tor/ *n. m.* transistor.

transitivo /transi'tiβo/ *a.* transitive.

tránsito /'transito/ *n. m.* transit, passage.

transitorio /transi'torio/ *a.* transitory.

transmisión /transmi'sion/ *n. f.* transmission; broadcast.

transmisora /transmi'sora/ *n. f.* broadcasting station.

transmitir /transmi'tir/ *v.* transmit; broadcast.

transparencia /transpa'renθia; transpa'rensia/ *n. f.* transparency.

transparente /transpa'rente/ *a.* **1.** transparent. —*n.* **2.** *m.* (window) shade.

transportación /transporta'θion; transporta'sion/ *n. f.* transportation.

transportar /transpor'tar/ *v.* transport, convey.

transporte /trans'porte/ *n. m.* transportation; transport.

tranvía /tram'bia/ *n. m.* streetcar, trolley.

trapacero /trapa'θero; trapa'sero/ **-ra** *n.* cheat; swindler.

trapo /'trapo/ *n. m.* rag.

tráquea /'trakea/ *n. f.* trachea.

tras /tras/ *prep.* after; behind.

trasegar /trase'gar/ *v.* upset, overturn.

trasero /tra'sero/ *a.* rear, back.

traslado /tras'laðo/ *n. m.* transfer. —**trasladar,** *v.*

traslapo /tras'lapo/ *n. m.* overlap. —**traslapar,** *v.*

trasnochar /trasno'tʃar/ *v.* stay up all night.

traspalar /traspa'lar/ *v.* shovel.

traspasar /traspa'sar/ *v.* go beyond; cross; violate; pierce.

trasquilar /traski'lar/ *v.* shear; clip.

trastornar /trastor'nar/ *v.* overturn, overthrow, upset.

trastorno /tras'torno/ *m.* overthrow; upheaval.

trastorno mental /tras'torno men'tal/ mental disorder.

trasvasar /trasβa'sar/ *v.* download; download.

tratado /tra'taðo/ *n. m.* treaty; treatise.

tratamiento /trata'miento/ *n. m.* treatment.

tratar /tra'tar/ *v.* treat, handle. **t. de,** deal with; try to; call (a name).

tratarse de /tra'tarse de/ *v.* be a question of.

trato /'trato/ *n. m.* treatment; manners; *Com.* deal.

través /tra'βes/ *adv.* **a t. de,** through, across. **de t.,** sideways.

travesía /traβe'sia/ *n. f.* crossing; voyage.

travesti /tra'βesti/ *n. m.* transvestite.

travestido /traβes'tiðo/ *a.* disguised.

travesura /traβe'sura/ *n. f.* prank; mischief.

travieso /tra'βieso/ *a.* naughty, mischievous.

trayectoria /trayek'toria/ *n. f.* trajectory.

trazar /tra'θar; tra'sar/ *v.* plan, devise; trace; draw.

trazo /'traθo; 'traso/ *n.* plan, outline; line, stroke.

trébol /'treβol/ *n. m.* clover.

trece /'treθe; 'trese/ *a. & pron.* thirteen.

trecho /'tretʃo/ *n. m.* space, distance, stretch.

tregua /'tregua/ *n. f.* truce; respite, lull.

treinta /'treinta/ *a. & pron.* thirty.

tremendo /tre'mendo/ *a.* tremendous.

tremer /tre'mer/ *v.* tremble.

tren /tren/ *n. m.* train.

trenza /'trenθa; 'trensa/ *n. f.* braid. —**trenzar,** *v.*

trepar /tre'par/ *v.* climb, mount.

trepidación /trepiða'θion; trepiða'sion/ *n. f.* trepidation.

tres /tres/ *a. & pron.* three.

trescientos /tres'θientos; tres'sientos/ *a. & pron.* three hundred.

triángulo /tri'aŋgulo/ *n. m.* triangle.

triar /triar/ *v.* sort, separate.

tribu /'triβu/ *n. f.* tribe.

tribulación /triβula'θion; triβula'sion/ *n. f.* tribulation.

tribuna /tri'βuna/ *n. f.* rostrum, stand; (*pl.*) grandstand.

tribunal /triβu'nal/ *n. m.* court, tribunal.

tributario /triβu'tario/ *a. & m.* tributary.

tributo /tri'βuto/ *n. m.* tribute.

triciclo /tri'θiklo; tri'siklo/ *n. m.* tricycle.

trigo /'trigo/ *n. m.* wheat.

trigonometría /trigonome'tria/ *n. f.* trigonometry.

trigueño /tri'geɲo/ *a.* swarthy, dark.

trilogía /trilo'hia/ *n. f.* trilogy.

trimestral /trimes'tral/ *a.* quarterly.

trinchar /trin'tʃar/ *v.* carve (meat).

trinchera /trin'tʃera/ *n. f.* trench, ditch.

trineo /tri'neo/ *n. m.* sled; sleigh.

trinidad /trini'ðað/ *n. f.* trinity.

tripa /'tripa/ *n. f.* tripe, entrails.

triple /'triple/ *a.* triple. —**triplicar,** *v.*

trípode /'tripoðe/ *n. m.* tripod.

tripulación /tripula'θion; tripula'sion/ *n. f.* crew.

tripulante /tripu'lante/ *m & f.* crew member.

tripular /tripu'lar/ *v.* man.

triste /'triste/ *a.* sad, sorrowful; dreary.

tristemente /triste'mente/ *adv.* sadly.

tristeza /tris'teθa; tris'tesa/ *n. f.* sadness; gloom.

triunfal /triun'fal/ *a.* triumphal.

triunfante /triun'fante/ *a.* triumphant.

triunfo /'triunfo/ *n. m.* triumph; trump. —**triunfar,** *v.*

trivial /tri'βial/ *a.* trivial, commonplace.

trivialidad /triβiali'ðað/ *n. f.* triviality.

trocar /tro'kar/ *v.* exchange, switch; barter.

trofeo /tro'feo/ *n. m.* trophy.

trombón /trom'bon/ *n. m.* trombone.

trompa /'trompa/ **trompeta** *n. f.* trumpet, horn.

tronada /tro'naða/ *n. f.* thunderstorm.

tronar /tro'nar/ *v.* thunder.

tronco /'tronko/ *n. m.* trunk, stump.

trono /'trono/ *n. m.* throne.

tropa /'tropa/ *n. f.* troop.

tropel /tro'pel/ *n. m.* crowd, throng.

tropezar /trope'θar; trope'sar/ *v.* trip, stumble. **t. con,** come upon, run into.

trópico /'tropiko/ *a. & m.* tropical; tropics.

tropiezo /tro'pieθo; tro'pieso/ *n. m.* stumble; obstacle; slip, error.

trote /'trote/ *n. m.* trot. —**trotar,** *v.*

trovador /troβa'ðor/ *n. m.* troubadour.

trozo /'troθo; 'troso/ *n. m.* piece, portion, fragment; selection, passage.

trucha /'trutʃa/ *n. f.* trout.

trueco /'trueko/ **trueque** *n. m.* exchange, barter.

trueno /'trueno/ *n. m.* thunder.

trufa /'trufa/ *n. f.* truffle.

tu /tu/ *a.* your.

tú *pron.* you.

tuberculosis /tuβerku'losis/ *n. f.* tuberculosis.

tubo /'tuβo/ *n. m.* tube, pipe.

tubo de ensayo /'tuβo de en'sayo/ test tube.

tubo de escape /'tuβo de es'kape/ exhaust pipe.

tuerca /'tuerka/ *n. f. Mech.* nut.

tulipán /tuli'pan/ *n. m.* tulip.

tumba /'tumba/ *n. f.* tomb, grave.

tumbar /tum'bar/ *v.* knock down.

tumbarse /tum'βarse/ *v.* lie down.

tumbo /'tumbo/ *n. m.* tumble; somersault.

tumbona /tum'βona/ *n. f.* deck chair.

tumor /tu'mor/ *n. m.* tumor; growth.

tumulto /tu'multo/ *n. m.* tumult, commotion.

tumultuoso /tumul'tuoso/ *a.* tumultuous, boisterous.

tunante /tu'nante/ *n. m.* rogue.

tunda /'tunda/ *n. f.* spanking, whipping.

túnel /'tunel/ *n. m.* tunnel.

túnel de Canal de la Mancha /'tunel de ka'nal de la 'mantʃa/ Channel Tunnel, Chunnel.

tungsteno /tuŋgs'teno/ *n. m.* tungsten.

túnica /'tunika/ *n. f.* tunic, robe.

tupir /tu'pir/ *v.* pack tight, stuff; stop up.

turbación /turβa'θion; turβa'sion/ *n. f.* confusion, turmoil.

turbamulta /turβa'multa/ *n. f.* mob, disorderly crowd.

turbar /tur'βar/ *v.* disturb, upset; embarrass.

turbina /tur'βina/ *n. f.* turbine.

turbio /'turβio/ *a.* turbid; muddy.

turco /'turko/ **-ca** *a. & n.* Turkish; Turk.

turismo /tu'rismo/ *n. m.* touring, (foreign) travel, tourism.

turista /tu'rista/ *n. m. & f.* tourist.
turno /'turno/ *n. m.* turn; (work) shift.
turquesa /tur'kesa/ *n. f.* turquoise.
Turquía /tur'kia/ *n. f.* Turkey.
turrón /tu'rron/ *n. m.* nougat.
tusa /'tusa/ *n. f.* corncob; corn.

tutear /tute'ar/ *v.* address as **tú,** etc.
tutela /tu'tela/ *n. f.* guardianship; aegis.
tutor /tu'tor/ **-ra** *n.* tutor; guardian.
tuyo /'tuyo/ *a.* your, yours.

——— U V Y Z ———

u /u/ *conj.* or.
ubre /'uβre/ *n. f.* udder.
Ucrania /u'krania/ *n. f.* Ukraine.
ucranio /u'kranio/ **-ia** *a. & n.* Ukrainian.
ufano /u'fano/ *a.* proud, haughty.
úlcera /'ulθera; 'ulsera/ *n. f.* ulcer.
ulterior /ulte'rior/ *a.* ulterior.
último /'ultimo/ *a.* last, final; ultimate; latest. **por ú.,** finally. **ú. minuto,** last minute, eleventh hour.
ultraje /ul'trahe/ *n. m.* outrage. **—ultrajar,** *v.*
ultrasónico /ultra'soniko/ *a.* ultrasonic.
umbral /um'bral/ *n. m.* threshold.
umbroso /um'broso/ *a.* shady.
un /un/ **una** *art. & a.* a, an; one; (*pl.*) some.
unánime /u'nanime/ *a.* unanimous.
unanimidad /unanimi'ðað/ *n. f.* unanimity.
unción /un'θion; un'sion/ *n. f.* unction.
ungüento /uŋ'guento/ *n. m.* ointment, salve.
único /'uniko/ *a.* only, sole; unique.
unicornio /uni'kornio/ *n. m.* unicorn.
unidad /uni'ðað/ *n. f.* unit; unity.
unidad de cuidados intensivos /uni'ðað de kui'ðaðos inten'siβos/ **unidad de vigilancia intensiva** intensive-care unit.
unidad de disco /uni'ðað de 'disko/ disk drive.
unificar /unifi'kar/ *v.* unify.
uniforme /uni'forme/ *a. & m.* uniform.
uniformidad /uniformi'ðað/ *n. f.* uniformity.
unión /u'nion/ *n. f.* union; joining.
unir /u'nir/ *v.* unite, join.
universal /uniβer'sal/ *a.* universal.
universalidad /uniβersali'ðað/ *n. f.* universality.

universidad /uniβersi'ðað/ *n. f.* university; college.
universo /uni'βerso/ *n. m.* universe.
uno /'uno/ **una** *pron.* one; (*pl.*) some.
untar /un'tar/ *v.* spread; grease; anoint.
uña /'uɲa/ *n. f.* fingernail.
urbanidad /urβani'ðað/ *n. f.* urbanity; good breeding.
urbanismo /urβa'nismo/ *n. m.* city planning.
urbano /ur'βano/ *a.* urban; urbane; well-bred.
urbe /'urβe/ *n. f.* large city.
urgencia /ur'henθia; ur'hensia/ *n. f.* urgency.
urgente /ur'hente/ *a.* urgent, pressing. **entrega u.,** special delivery.
urgir /ur'hir/ *v.* be urgent.
urna /'urna/ *n. f.* urn; ballot box; (*pl.*) polls.
urraca /u'rraka/ *n. f.* magpie.
usanza /u'sanθa; usansa/ *n. f.* usage, custom.
usar /u'sar/ *v.* use; wear.
uso /'uso/ *n. m.* use; usage; wear.
usted /us'teð/ *pron.* you.
usual /u'sual/ *a.* usual.
usualmente /usual'mente/ *adv.* usually.
usura /u'sura/ *n. f.* usury.
usurero /usu'rero/ **-ra** *n.* usurer.
usurpación /usurpa'θion; usurpa'sion/ *n. f.* usurpation.
usurpar /usur'par/ *v.* usurp.
utensilio /uten'silio/ *n. m.* utensil.
útero /'utero/ *n. m.* uterus.
útil /'util/ *a.* useful, handy.
utilidad /utili'ðað/ *n. f.* usefulness.
utilizar /utili'θar; utili'sar/ *v.* use, utilize.
útilmente /util'mente/ *adv.* usefully.
utópico /u'topiko/ *a.* utopian.
uva /'uβa/ *n. f.* grape.
vaca /'baka/ *n. f.* cow; beef.
vacaciones /baka'θiones; baka-

'siones/ *n. f.pl.* vacation, holidays.

vacancia /ba'kanθia; ba'kansia/ *n. f.* vacancy.

vacante /ba'kante/ *a.* **1.** vacant. —*n.* **2.** *f.* vacancy.

vaciar /ba'θiar; ba'siar/ *v.* empty; pour out.

vacilación /baθila'θion; basila-'sion/ *n. f.* vacillation.

vacilante /baθi'lante; basi'lante/ *a.* vacillating.

vacilar /baθi'lar; basi'lar/ *v.* falter, hesitate; waver; stagger.

vacío /ba'θio; ba'sio/ *a.* **1.** empty. —*n.* **2.** *m.* void, empty space.

vacuna /ba'kuna/ *n. f.* vaccine.

vacunación /bakuna'θion; bakuna-'sion/ *n. f.* vaccination.

vacunar /baku'nar/ *v.* vaccinate.

vacuo /'bakuo/ *a.* **1.** empty, vacant. —*n.* **2.** *m.* vacuum.

vadear /baðe'ar/ *v.* ford.

vado /'baðo/ *n. m.* ford.

vagabundo /baga'βundo/ **-da** *a.* & *n.* vagabond.

vagar /ba'gar/ *v.* wander; loiter.

vago /'bago/ **-ga** *a.* **1.** vague, hazy; wandering, vagrant. —*n.* **2.** vagrant, tramp.

vagón /ba'gon/ *n. m.* railroad car.

vahído /ba'iðo/ *n. m.* dizziness.

vaina /'baina/ *n. f.* sheath; pod.

vainilla /bai'niʎa; bai'niya/ *n. f.* vanilla.

vaivén /bai'βen/ *n. m.* vibration, sway.

vajilla /ba'hiʎa; ba'hiya/ *n. f.* (dinner) dishes.

valentía /balen'tia/ *n. f.* valor, courage.

valer /ba'ler/ *n.* **1.** *m.* worth. —*v.* **2.** be worth.

valerse de /ba'lerse de/ *v.* make use of, avail oneself of.

valía /ba'lia/ *n. f.* value.

validez /bali'ðeθ; bali'ðes/ *n. f.* validity.

válido /ba'liðo/ *a.* valid.

valiente /ba'liente/ *a.* valiant.

valija /ba'liha/ *n. f.* valise.

valioso /ba'lioso/ *a.* valuable.

valla /'baʎa; 'baya/ *n. f.* fence, barrier.

valle /'baʎe; 'baye/ *n. m.* valley.

valor /ba'lor/ *n. m.* value, worth; bravery, valor; (*pl., Com.*) securities.

valoración /balora'θion; balora-'sion/ *n. f.* appraisal.

valorar /balo'rar/ *v.* value, appraise.

vals /bals/ *n. m.* waltz.

valsar /bal'sar/ *v.* waltz.

valuación /balua'θion; balua'sion/ *n. f.* valuation.

valuar /balu'ar/ *v.* value; rate.

válvula /'balβula/ *n. f.* valve.

válvula de seguridad /'balβula de seguri'ðað/ safety valve.

vandalismo /banda'lismo/ *n. m.* vandalism.

vándalo /'bandalo/ **-la** *n.* vandal.

vanidad /bani'ðað/ *n. f.* vanity.

vanidoso /bani'ðoso/ *a.* vain, conceited.

vano /'bano/ *a.* vain; inane.

vapor /ba'por/ *n. m.* vapor; steam; steamer, steamship.

vaquero /ba'kero/ **-ra** *n.* cowboy.

vara /'bara/ *n. f.* wand, stick, switch.

varadero /bara'ðero/ *n. m.* shipyard.

varar /ba'rar/ *v.* launch; be stranded; run aground.

variable /ba'riaβle/ *a.* variable.

variación /baria'θion; baria'sion/ *n. f.* variation.

variar /ba'riar/ *v.* vary.

varicela /bari'θela; bari'sela/ *n. f.* chicken pox.

variedad /barie'ðað/ *n. f.* variety.

varios /'barios/ *a.* & *pron. pl.* various; several.

variz /ba'riθ; ba'ris/ *n. f.* varicose vein.

varón /ba'ron/ *n. m.* man; male.

varonil /baro'nil/ *a.* manly, virile.

vasallo /ba'saʎo; ba'sayo/ *n. m.* vassal.

vasectomía /basekto'mia/ *n. f.* vasectomy.

vasija /ba'siha/ *n. f.* bowl, container (for liquids).

vaso /'baso/ *n. m.* water glass; vase. **v. de papel,** paper cup.

vástago /'bastago/ *n. m.* bud, shoot; twig; offspring.

vasto /'basto/ *a.* vast.

vecindad /beθin'dað; besin'dað/ *n. f.* **vecindario,** *m.* neighborhood, vicinity.

vecino /be'θino; be'sino/ **-na** *a.* & *n.* neighboring; neighbor.

vedar /be'ðar/ *v.* forbid; impede.

vega /'bega/ *n. f.* meadow.

vegetación /beheta'θion; beheta-'sion/ *n. f.* vegetation.

vegetal /behe'tal/ *n. m.* vegetable.

vehemente /bee'mente/ *a.* vehement.

vehículo /be'ikulo/ *n. m.* vehicle; conveyance.

veinte /'beinte/ *a. & pron.* twenty.

vejez /be'heθ; be'hes/ *n. f.* old age.

vejiga /be'higa/ *n. f.* bladder.

vela /'bela/ *n. f.* vigil, watch; candle; sail.

velar /be'lar/ *v.* stay up, sit up; watch over.

vellón /be'ʎon; be'yon/ *n. m.* fleece.

velloso /be'ʎoso; be'yoso/ *a.* hairy; fuzzy.

velludo /be'ʎuðo; be'yuðo/ *a.* downy.

velo /'belo/ *n. m.* veil.

velocidad /beloθi'ðað; belosi'ðað/ *n. f.* velocity, speed; rate. **v. máxima,** speed limit.

velomotor /belomo'tor/ *n. m.* motorbike, moped.

veloz /be'loθ; be'los/ *a.* speedy, fast, swift.

vena /'bena/ *n. f.* vein.

venado /be'naðo/ *n. m.* deer.

vencedor /benθe'ðor; bense'ðor/ **-ra** *n.* victor.

vencer /ben'θer; ben'ser/ *v.* defeat, overcome, conquer; *Com.* become due, expire.

vencimiento /benθi'miento; bensi'miento/ *n. m.* defeat; expiration.

venda /'benda/ *n. f.* **vendaje,** *m.* bandage. —**vendar,** *v.*

vendedor /bende'ðor/ **-ra** *n.* seller, trader; sales clerk.

vender /ben'der/ *v.* sell.

vendimia /ben'dimia/ *n. f.* vintage; grape harvest.

Venecia /be'neθia; be'nesia/ *n. f.* Venice.

veneciano /bene'θiano; bene'siano/ **-na** *a. & n.* Venetian.

veneno /be'neno/ *n. m.* poison.

venenoso /bene'noso/ *a.* poisonous.

veneración /benera'θion; benera'sion/ *n. f.* veneration.

venerar /bene'rar/ *v.* venerate, revere.

venero /be'nero/ *n. m.* spring; origin.

véneto /'beneto/ *a.* Venetian.

venezolano /beneθo'lano; beneso'lano/ **-na** *a. & n.* Venezuelan.

vengador /benga'ðor/ **-ra** *n.* avenger.

venganza /beŋ'ganθa; beŋ'gansa/ *n. f.* vengeance, revenge.

vengar /beŋ'gar/ *v.* avenge.

venida /be'niða/ *n. f.* arrival, advent, coming.

venidero /beni'ðero/ *a.* future; coming.

venir /be'nir/ *v.* come.

venta /'benta/ *n. f.* sale; sales.

ventaja /ben'taha/ *n. f.* advantage; profit.

ventajoso /benta'hoso/ *a.* advantageous; profitable.

ventana /ben'tana/ *n. f.* window.

ventero /ben'tero/ **-ra** *n.* innkeeper.

ventilación /bentila'θion; bentila'sion/ *n. m.* ventilation.

ventilador /bentila'ðor/ *n. m.* ventilator, fan.

ventilar /benti'lar/ *v.* ventilate, air.

ventisquero /bentis'kero/ *n. m.* snowdrift; glacier.

ventoso /ben'toso/ *a.* windy.

ventura /ben'tura/ *n. f.* venture; happiness; luck.

ver /ber/ *v.* see. **tener que v. con,** have to do with.

vera /'bera/ *n. f.* edge.

veracidad /beraθi'ðað; berasi'ðað/ *n. f.* truthfulness, veracity.

verano /be'rano/ *n. m.* summer. —**veranear,** *v.*

veras /'beras/ *n. f.pl.* **de v.,** really, truly.

veraz /be'raθ; be'ras/ *a.* truthful.

verbigracia /berβi'graθia; berβi'grasia/ *adv.* for example.

verbo /'berβo/ *n. m.* verb.

verboso /ber'βoso/ *a.* verbose.

verdad /ber'ðað/ *n. f.* truth. **ser v.,** to be true.

verdadero /berða'ðero/ *a.* true, real.

verde /'berðe/ *a.* green; risqué, off-color.

verdor /ber'ðor/ *n. m.* greenness, verdure.

verdugo /ber'ðugo/ *n. m.* hangman.

verdura /ber'ðura/ *n. f.* verdure, vegetation; (*pl.*) vegetables.

vereda /be'reða/ *n. f.* path.

veredicto /bere'ðikto/ *n. m.* verdict.

vergonzoso /bergon'θoso; bergon'soso/ *a.* shameful, embarrassing; shy, bashful.

vergüenza /ber'guenθa; ber-

'guensa/ *n. f.* shame; disgrace; embarrassment.

verificar /berifi'kar/ *v.* verify, check.

verja /'berha/ *n. f.* grating, railing.

verosímil /bero'simil/ *a.* likely, plausible.

verraco /be'rrako/ *n. m.* boar.

verruga /be'rruga/ *n. f.* wart.

versátil /ber'satil/ *a.* versatile.

verse /'berse/ *v.* look, appear.

versión /ber'sion/ *n. f.* version.

verso /'berso/ *n. m.* verse, stanza; line (of poetry).

verter /ber'ter/ *v.* pour, spill; shed; empty.

vertical /berti'kal/ *a.* vertical.

vertiente /ber'tiente/ *n. f.* slope; watershed.

vertiginoso /bertihi'noso/ *a.* dizzy.

vértigo /'bertigo/ *n. m.* vertigo, dizziness.

vestíbulo /bes'tiβulo/ *n. m.* vestibule, lobby.

vestido /bes'tiðo/ *n. m.* dress; clothing.

vestigio /bes'tihio/ *n. m.* vestige, trace.

vestir /bes'tir/ *v.* dress, clothe.

veterano /bete'rano/ **-na** *a. & n.* veteran.

veterinario /beteri'nario/ **-ria** *a.* **1.** veterinary. —*n.* **2.** veterinarian.

veto /'beto/ *n. m.* veto.

vetusto /be'tusto/ *a.* ancient, very old.

vez /beθ; bes/ *n. f.* time; turn. **tal v.,** perhaps. **a la v.,** at the same time. **en v. de,** instead of. **una v.,** once. **otra v.,** again.

vía /'bia/ *n. f.* track; route, way.

viaducto /bia'ðukto/ *n. m.* viaduct.

viajante /bia'hante/ *a. & n.* traveling; traveler.

viajar /bia'har/ *v.* travel; journey; tour.

viaje /'biahe/ *n. m.* trip, journey, voyage; (*pl.*) travels.

viaje de estudios /'biahe de es'tuðios/ field trip.

viajero /bia'hero/ **-ra** *n.* traveler; passenger.

viaje todo incluido /'biahe 'toðo in'kluiðo/ package tour.

viandas /'biandas/ *n. f.pl.* victuals, food.

víbora /'biβora/ *n. f.* viper.

vibración /biβra'θion; biβra'sion/ *n. f.* vibration.

vibrar /bi'βrar/ *v.* vibrate.

vicepresidente /biθepresi'ðente; bisepresi'ðente/ **-ta** *n.* vice president.

vicio /'biθio; 'bisio/ *n. m.* vice.

vicioso /bi'θioso; bi'sioso/ *a.* vicious; licentious.

víctima /'biktima/ *n. f.* victim.

victoria /bik'toria/ *n. f.* victory.

victorioso /bikto'rioso/ *a.* victorious.

vid /bið/ *n. f.* grapevine.

vida /'biða/ *n. f.* life; living.

vídeo /bi'ðeo/ *n. m.* videotape.

videocámara /biðeo'kamara/ *n. f.* video camera.

videodisco /biðeo'ðisko/ *n. m.* videodisc.

videojuego /biðeo'huego/ *n. m.* video game.

vidrio /'biðrio/ *n. m.* glass.

viejo /'bieho/ **-ja** *a. & n.* old; old person.

viento /'biento/ *n. m.* wind. **hacer v.,** to be windy.

vientre /'bientre/ *n. m.* belly.

viernes /'biernes/ *n. m.* Friday.

viga /'biga/ *n. f.* beam, rafter.

vigente /bi'hente/ *a.* in effect (prices, etc.).

vigilante /bihi'lante/ *a. & m.* vigilant, watchful; watchman.

vigilante nocturno /bihi'lante nok'turno/ night watchman.

vigilar /bihi'lar/ *v.* guard, watch over.

vigilia /bi'hilia/ *n. f.* vigil, watchfulness; *Relig.* fast.

vigor /bi'gor/ *n. m.* vigor. **en v.,** in effect, in force.

vil /bil/ *a.* vile, low, contemptible.

vileza /bi'leθa; bi'lesa/ *n. f.* baseness; vileness.

villa /'biʎa; 'biya/ *n. f.* town; country house.

villancico /biʎan'θiko; biyan'siko/ *n. m.* Christmas carol.

villanía /biʎa'nia; biya'nia/ *n. f.* villainy.

villano /bi'ʎano; bi'yano/ *n. m.* boor.

vinagre /bi'nagre/ *n. m.* vinegar.

vinagrera /bina'grera/ *n. f.* cruet.

vínculo /'binkulo/ *n. m.* link. —**vincular,** *v.*

vindicar /bindi'kar/ *v.* vindicate.

vino /'bino/ *n. m.* wine.

viña /'biɲa/ *n. f.* vineyard.

violación /biola'θion; biola'sion/ *n. f.* violation; rape.

violador /biola'ðor/ **-ra** *n. m. & f.* rapist.

violar /bio'lar/ *v.* violate; rape.

violencia /bio'lenθia; bio'lensia/ *n. f.* violence.

violento /bio'lento/ *a.* violent; impulsive.

violeta /bio'leta/ *n. f.* violet.

violín /bio'lin/ *n. m.* violin.

violón /bio'lon/ *n. m.* bass viol.

virar /bi'rar/ *v.* veer, change course.

virgen /bir'hen/ *n. f.* virgin.

viril /bi'ril/ *a.* virile, manly.

virilidad /birili'ðað/ *n. f.* virility, manhood.

virtual /bir'tual/ *a.* virtual.

virtud /bir'tuð/ *n. f.* virtue; efficacy, power.

virtuoso /bir'tuoso/ *a.* virtuous.

viruela /bi'ruela/ *n. f.* smallpox.

viruelas locas /bi'ruelas 'lokas/ *n. f.pl.* chicken pox.

virus /'birus/ *n. m.* virus.

visa /'bisa/ *n. f.* visa.

visaje /bi'sahe/ *n. m.* grimace.

visera /bi'sera/ *n. f.* visor.

visible /bi'siβle/ *a.* visible.

visión /bi'sion/ *n. f.* vision.

visionario /bisio'nario/ **-ria** *a. & n.* visionary.

visita /bi'sita/ *n. f.* visit; *m. & f.* visitor, caller. **v. con guía, v. explicada, v. programada,** guided tour.

visitación /bisita'θion; bisita'sion/ *n. f.* visitation.

visitante /bisi'tante/ *a. & n.* visiting; visitor.

visitar /bisi'tar/ *v.* visit; inspect, examine.

vislumbrar /bislum'βrar/ *v.* glimpse.

vislumbre /bis'lumbre/ *n. f.* glimpse.

viso /'biso/ *n. m.* looks; outlook.

víspera /'bispera/ *n. f.* eve, day before.

vista /'bista/ *n. f.* view; scene; sight.

vista de pájaro /'bista de 'paharo/ bird's-eye view.

vistazo /bis'taθo; bis'taso/ *n. m.* glance, glimpse.

vistoso /bis'toso/ *a.* beautiful; showy.

visual /bi'sual/ *a.* visual.

vital /bi'tal/ *a.* vital.

vitalidad /bitali'ðað/ *n. f.* vitality.

vitamina /bita'mina/ *n. f.* vitamin.

vitando /bi'tando/ *a.* hateful.

vituperar /bitupe'rar/ *v.* vituperate; revile.

viuda /'biuða/ *n. f.* widow.

viudo /'biuðo/ *n. m.* widower.

vivaz /bi'βaθ; bi'βas/ *a.* vivacious, buoyant; clever.

víveres /'biβeres/ *n. m.pl.* provisions.

viveza /bi'βeθa; bi'βesa/ *n. f.* animation, liveliness.

vívido /bi'βiðo/ *a.* vivid, bright.

vivienda /bi'βienda/ *n. f.* (living) quarters, dwelling.

vivificar /biβifi'kar/ *v.* vivify, enliven.

vivir /bi'βir/ *v.* live.

vivo /'biβo/ *a.* live, alive, living; vivid; animated, brisk.

vocablo /bo'kaβlo/ *n. m.* word.

vocabulario /bokaβu'lario/ *n. m.* vocabulary.

vocación /boka'θion; boka'sion/ *n. f.* vocation, calling.

vocal /bo'kal/ *a.* **1.** vocal. —*n.* **2.** *f.* vowel.

vocear /boθe'ar; bose'ar/ *v.* vociferate.

vodca /'boðka/ *n. m.* vodka.

vodevil /boðe'βil/ *n. m.* vaudeville.

volante /bo'lante/ *a.* **1.** flying. —*n.* **2.** *m.* memorandum; (steering) wheel.

volar /bo'lar/ *v.* fly; explode.

volcán /bol'kan/ *n. m.* volcano.

volcar /bol'kar/ *v.* upset, capsize.

voltaje /bol'tahe/ *n. m.* voltage.

voltear /bolte'ar/ *v.* turn, whirl; overturn.

voltio /'boltio/ *n. m.* volt.

volumen /bo'lumen/ *n. m.* volume.

voluminoso /bolumi'noso/ *a.* voluminous.

voluntad /bolun'tað/ *n. f.* will. **buena v.** goodwill.

voluntario /bolun'tario/ **-ria** *a. & n.* voluntary; volunteer.

voluntarioso /bolunta'rioso/ *a.* willful.

volver /bol'βer/ *v.* turn; return, go back, come back. **v. a hacer** (etc.), do (etc.) again.

volverse /bol'βerse/ *v.* turn around; turn, become.

vómito /'bomito/ *n. m.* vomit. —**vomitar,** *v.*

voracidad /boraθi'ðað; borasi'ðað/ *n. f.* voracity; greed.

voraz /bo'raθ; bo'ras/ *a.* greedy, ravenous.

vórtice /'bortiθe; 'bortise/ *n. m.* whirlpool.

vosotros /bo'sotros, bo'sotras/ **-as** *pron.pl.* you; yourselves.

votación /bota'θion; bota'sion/ *n. f.* voting; vote.

voto /'boto/ *n. m.* vote; vow. **—votar,** *v.*

voz /boθ; bos/ *n. f.* voice; word. **a voces,** by shouting. **en v. alta,** aloud.

vuelco /'buelko/ *n. m.* upset.

vuelo /'buelo/ *n. m.* flight. **v. libre,** hang gliding.

vuelo chárter /'buelo 'tʃarter/ charter flight.

vuelo regular /'buelo rregu'lar/ scheduled flight.

vuelta /'buelta/ *n. f.* turn, bend; return. **a la v. de,** around. **dar una v.,** to take a walk.

vuestro /'buestro/ *a.* your, yours.

vulgar /bul'gar/ *a.* vulgar, common.

vulgaridad /bulgari'ðað/ *n. f.* vulgarity.

vulgo /'bulgo/ *n. m.* (the) masses, (the) common people.

vulnerable /bulne'raβle/ *a.* vulnerable.

y /i/ *conj.* and.

ya /ya/ *adv.* already; now; at once. **y. no,** no longer, any more. **y. que,** since.

yacer /ya'θer; ya'ser/ *v.* lie.

yacimiento /yaθi'miento; yasi-'miento/ *n. m.* deposit.

yanqui /'yanki/ *a. & n.* North American.

yate /'yate/ *n. m.* yacht.

yegua /'yegua/ *n. f.* mare.

yelmo /'yelmo/ *n. m.* helmet.

yema /'yema/ *n. f.* yolk (of an egg).

yerba /'yerβa/ *n. f.* grass; herb.

yerno /'yerno/ *n. m.* son-in-law.

yerro /'yerro/ *n. m.* error, mistake.

yeso /'yeso/ *n. m.* plaster.

yídish /'yiðis/ *n. m.* Yiddish.

yo /yo/ *pron.* I.

yodo /'yoðo/ *n. m.* iodine.

yoduro /jo'ðuro/ *n. m.* iodide.

yonqui /'yonki/ *m. &amp. f. Colloq.* drug addict, junkie.

yugo /'yugo/ *n. m.* yoke.

yunque /'yunke/ *n. m.* anvil.

yunta /'yunta/ *n. f.* team (of animals).

zafarse /θa'farse; sa'farse/ *v.* run away, escape. **z. de,** get rid of.

zafio /'θafio; 'safio/ *a.* coarse, uncivil.

zafiro /θa'firo; sa'firo/ *n. m.* sapphire.

zaguán /θa'guan; sa'guan/ *n. m.* vestibule, hall.

zalamero /θala'mero; sala'mero/ **-ra** *n.* flatterer, wheedler.

zambullir /θambu'ʎir; sambu'yir/ *v.* plunge, dive.

zampar /θam'par; sam'par/ *v. Colloq.* gobble down, wolf down.

zanahoria /θana'oria; sana'oria/ *n. f.* carrot.

zanja /'θanha; 'sanha/ *n. f.* ditch, trench.

zapatería /θapate'ria; sapate'ria/ *n. f.* shoe store; shoemaker's shop.

zapatero /θapa'tero; sapa'tero/ *n. m.* shoemaker.

zapato /θa'pato; sa'pato/ *n. m.* shoe.

zar /θar; sar/ *n. m.* czar.

zaraza /θa'raθa; sa'rasa/ *n. f.* calico; chintz.

zarza /'θarθa; 'sarsa/ *n. f.* bramble.

zarzuela /θar'θuela; sar'suela/ *n. f.* musical comedy.

zodíaco /θo'ðiako; so'ðiako/ *n. m.* zodiac.

zona /'θona; 'sona/ *n. f.* zone.

zoología /θoolo'hia; soolo'hia/ *n. f.* zoology.

zoológico /θoo'lohiko; soo'lohiko/ *a.* zoological.

zorro /'θorro; 'sorro/ **-rra** *n.* fox.

zozobra /θo'θoβra; so'soβra/ *n. f.* worry, anxiety; capsizing.

zozobrar /θoθo'βrar; soso'βrar/ *v.* capsize; worry.

zumba /'θumba; 'sumba/ *n. f.* spanking.

zumbido /θum'βiðo; sum'βiðo/ *n. m.* buzz, hum. **—zumbar,** *v.*

zumo /'θumo; 'sumo/ *n. m.* juice. **z. de naranja,** orange juice.

zurcir /θur'θir; sur'sir/ *v.* darn, mend.

zurdo /'θurðo; 'surðo/ *a.* left-handed.

zurrar /θu'rrar; su'rrar/ *v.* flog, drub.

A

a /ə, *when stressed* ā/ *art.* un, una.

abacus /'æbəkəs/ *n.* ábaco *m.*

abandon /ə'bændən/ *n.* **1.** desenfreno, abandono *m.* —*v.* **2.** abandonar, desamparar.

abandoned /ə'bændənd/ *a.* abandonado.

abandonment /ə'bændənmənt/ *n.* abandono, desamparo *m.*

abase /ə'beis/ *v.* degradar, humillar.

abasement /ə'beismənt/ *n.* degradación, humillación *f.*

abash /ə'bæʃ/ *v.* avergonzar.

abate /ə'beit/ *v.* menguar, moderarse.

abatement /ə'beitmənt/ *n.* disminución *f.*

abbess /'æbis/ *n.* abadesa *f.*

abbey /'æbi/ *n.* abadía *f.*

abbot /'æbət/ *n.* abad *m.*

abbreviate /ə'brivi,eit/ *v.* abreviar.

abbreviation /ə,brivi'eiʃən/ *n.* abreviatura *f.*

abdicate /'æbdɪ,keit/ *v.* abdicar.

abdication /,æbdɪ'keiʃən/ *n.* abdicación *f.*

abdomen /'æbdəmən/ *n.* abdomen *m.*

abdominal /æb'dɒmənļ/ *a.* abdominal.

abduct /æb'dʌkt/ *v.* secuestrar.

abduction /æb'dʌkʃən/ *n.* secuestración *f.*

abductor /æb'dʌktər/ *n.* secuestrador -ra.

aberrant /ə'bɛrənt, 'æbər-/ *a.* aberrante.

aberration /,æbə'reiʃən/ *n.* aberración *f.*

abet /ə'bɛt/ *v.* apoyar, favorecer.

abetment /ə'bɛtmənt/ *n.* apoyo *m.*

abettor /ə'bɛtər/ *n.* cómplice *m. & f.*

abeyance /ə'beiəns/ *n.* suspensión *f.*

abhor /æb'hɔr/ *v.* abominar, odiar.

abhorrence /æb'hɔrəns/ *n.* detestación *f.;* aborrecimiento *m.*

abhorrent /æb'hɔrənt/ *a.* detestable, aborrecible.

abide /ə'baid/ *v.* soportar. **to a. by,** cumplir con.

abiding /ə'baidɪŋ/ *a.* perdurable.

ability /ə'bɪlɪti/ *n.* habilidad *f.*

abject /'æbdʒɛkt/ *a.* abyecto; desanimado.

abjuration /,æbdʒə'reiʃən/ *n.* renuncia *f.*

abjure /æb'dʒʊr/ *v.* renunciar.

ablative /'æblətɪv/ *a. & n. Gram.* ablativo *m.*

ablaze /ə'bleiz/ *a.* en llamas.

able /'eibəl/ *a.* capaz; competente. **to be a.,** poder.

able-bodied /'eibəl 'bɒdid/ *a.* robusto.

ablution /ə'bluʃən/ *n.* ablución *f.*

ably /'eibli/ *adv.* hábilmente.

abnegate /'æbnɪ,geit/ *v.* repudiar; negar.

abnegation /,æbnɪ'geiʃən/ *n.* abnegación; repudiación *f.*

abnormal /æb'nɔrməl/ *a.* anormal.

abnormality /,æbnɔr'mælɪti/ *n.* anormalidad, deformidad *f.*

abnormally /æb'nɔrməli/ *adv.* anormalmente.

aboard /ə'bɔrd/ *adv.* a bordo.

abode /ə'boud/ *n.* residencia *f.*

abolish /ə'bɒlɪʃ/ *v.* suprimir.

abolishment /ə'bɒlɪʃmənt/ *n.* abolición *f.*

abolition /,æbə'lɪʃən/ *n.* abolición *f.*

abominable /ə'bɒmənəbəl/ *a.* abominable.

abominate /ə'bɒmə,neit/ *v.* abominar, detestar.

abomination /ə,bɒmə'neiʃən/ *n.* abominación *f.*

aboriginal /,æbə'rɪdʒənļ/ *a. & n.* aborigen *f.*

abortion /ə'bɔrʃən/ *n.* aborto *m.*

abortive /ə'bɔrtɪv/ *a.* abortivo.

abound /ə'baund/ *v.* abundar.

about /ə'baut/ *adv.* **1.** como. **about to,** para; a punto de. —*prep.* **2.** de, sobre, acerca de.

about-face /ə'baut,feis, ə'baut-'feis/ *n. Mil.* media vuelta.

above /ə'bʌv/ *adv.* **1.** arriba. —*prep.* **2.** sobre; por encima de.

aboveboard /ə'bʌv,bɔrd/ *a. & adv.* sincero, franco.

abrasion /ə'breiʒən/ *n.* raspadura *f.; Med.* abrasión *f.*

abrasive /ə'breisɪv/ *a.* raspante. *n.* abrasivo *m.*

abreast /ə'brɛst/ *adv.* de frente.

abridge /ə'brɪdʒ/ v. abreviar.

abridgment /ə'brɪdʒmənt/ n. abreviación f.; compendio m.

abroad /ə'brɔd/ adv. en el extranjero, al extranjero.

abrogate /'æbrə,geit/ v. abrogar, revocar.

abrogation /,æbrə'geiʃən/ n. abrogación, revocación f.

abrupt /ə'brʌpt/ a. repentino; brusco.

abruptly /ə'brʌptli/ adv. bruscamente, precipitadamente.

abruptness /ə'brʌptnɪs/ n. precipitación; brusquedad f.

abscess /'æbsɛs/ n. absceso m.

abscond /æb'skɒnd/ v. fugarse.

absence /'æbsəns/ n. ausencia, falta f.

absent /'æbsənt/ a. ausente.

absentee /,æbsən'ti/ a. & n. ausente m. & f.

absent-minded /'æbsənt 'maindɪd/ a. distraído.

absinthe /'æbsɪnθ/ n. absenta f.

absolute /'æbsə,lut/ a. absoluto.

absolutely /,æbsə'lutli/ adv. absolutamente.

absoluteness /,æbsə'lutnɪs/ n. absolutismo m.

absolution /,æbsə'luʃən/ n. absolución f.

absolutism /'æbsəlu,tɪzəm/ n. absolutismo, despotismo m.

absolve /æb'zɒlv/ v. absolver.

absorb /æb'sɔrb/ v. absorber; preocupar.

absorbed /æb'sɔrbd/ a. absorbido; absorto.

absorbent /æb'sɔrbənt/ a. absorbente.

absorbent cotton algodón hidrófilo m.

absorbing /æb'sɔrbɪŋ/ a. interesante.

absorption /æb'sɔrpʃən/ n. absorción; preocupación f.

abstain /æb'stein/ v. abstenerse.

abstemious /æb'stimiəs/ a. abstemio, sobrio.

abstinence /'æbstənəns/ n. abstinencia f.

abstract /a, v æb'strækt, 'æbstrækt; n 'æbstrækt/ a. 1. abstracto. —n. 2. resumen m. —v. 3. abstraer.

abstracted /æb'stræktɪd/ a. distraído.

abstraction /æb'strækʃən/ n. abstracción f.

abstruse /æb'strus/ a. abstruso.

absurd /æb'sɜrd/ a. absurdo, ridículo.

absurdity /æb'sɜrdɪti/ n. absurdo m.

absurdly /æb'sɜrdli/ adv. absurdamente.

abundance /ə'bʌndəns/ n. abundancia f.

abundant /ə'bʌndənt/ a. abundante.

abundantly /ə'bʌndəntli/ adv. abundantemente.

abuse /n ə'byus; v ə'byuz/ n. 1. abuso m. —v. 2. abusar de; maltratar.

abusive /ə'byusɪv/ a. abusivo.

abusively /ə'byusɪvli/ adv. abusivamente, ofensivamente.

abutment /ə'bʌtmənt/ n. (building) estribo, contrafuerte m.

abut (on) /ə'bʌt/ v. terminar (en); lindar (con).

abyss /ə'bɪs/ n. abismo m.

Abyssinian /,æbə'sɪniən/ a. & n. abisinio -nia.

acacia /ə'keiʃə/ n. acacia f.

academic /,ækə'dɛmɪk/ a. académico.

academy /ə'kædəmi/ n. academia f.

acanthus /ə'kænθəs/ n. Bot. acanto m.

accede /æk'sid/ v. acceder; consentir.

accelerate /æk'sɛlə,reit/ v. acelerar.

acceleration /æk,sɛlə'reiʃən/ n. aceleración f.

accelerator /æk'sɛlə,reitər/ n. Auto. acelerador m.

accent /'æksɛnt/ n. 1. acento m. —v. 2. acentuar.

accentuate /æk'sɛntʃu,eit/ v. acentuar.

accept /æk'sɛpt/ v. aceptar.

acceptability /æk,sɛptə'bɪlɪti/ n. aceptabilidad f.

acceptable /æk'sɛptəbəl/ a. aceptable.

acceptably /æk'sɛptəbli/ adv. aceptablemente.

acceptance /æk'sɛptəns/ n. aceptación f.

access /'æksɛs/ n. acceso m., entrada f.

accessible /æk'sɛsəbəl/ a. accesible.

accessory /æk'sɛsəri/ a. 1. accesorio. —n. 2. cómplice m. & f.

accident /'æksɪdənt/ n. accidente m. **by a.,** por casualidad.
accidental /,æksɪ'dɛntḷ/ a. accidental.
accidentally /,æksɪ'dɛntḷi/ adv. accidentalmente, casualmente.
acclaim /ə'kleim/ v. aclamar.
acclamation /,æklə'meiʃən/ n. aclamación f.
acclimate /'æklə,meit/ v. aclimatar.
acclivity /ə'klɪvɪti/ n. subida f.
accolade /'ækə,leid/ n. acolada f.
accommodate /ə'kɒmə,deit/ v. acomodar.
accommodating /ə'kɒmə,deitɪŋ/ a. bondadoso, complaciente.
accommodation /ə,kɒmə'deiʃən/ n. servicio m.; (pl.) alojamiento m.
accompaniment /ə'kʌmpənimənt/ n. acompañamiento m.
accompanist /ə'kʌmpənɪst/ n. acompañante m. & f.
accompany /ə'kʌmpəni/ v. acompañar.
accomplice /ə'kɒmplɪs/ n. cómplice m. & f.
accomplish /ə'kɒmplɪʃ/ v. llevar a cabo; realizar.
accomplished /ə'kɒmplɪʃt/ a. acabado, cumplido; culto.
accomplishment /ə'kɒmplɪʃmənt/ n. realización f.; logro m.
accord /ə'kɔrd/ n. **1.** acuerdo m. —v. **2.** otorgar.
accordance /ə'kɔrdṇs/ n.: **in a. with,** de acuerdo con.
accordingly /ə'kɔrdɪŋli/ adv. en conformidad.
according to /ə'kɔrdɪŋ/ prep. según.
accordion /ə'kɔrdiən/ n. acordeón m.
accost /ə'kɔst/ v. dirigirse a.
account /ə'kaunt/ n. **1.** relato m.; Com. cuenta f. **on a. of,** a causa de. **on no a.,** de ninguna manera. —v. **2. a. for,** explicar.
accountable /ə'kauntəbəl/ a. responsable.
accountant /ə'kauntṇt/ n. contador -ra.
accounting /ə'kauntɪŋ/ n. contabilidad f.
accouter /ə'kutər/ v. equipar, ataviar.
accouterments /ə'kutərmənts/ n. equipo, atavío m.
accredit /ə'krɛdɪt/ v. acreditar.

accretion /ə'kriʃən/ n. aumento m.
accrual /ə'kruəl/ n. aumento, incremento m.
accrue /ə'kru/ v. provenir; acumularse.
accumulate /ə'kyumyə,leit/ v. acumular.
accumulation /ə,kyumyə'leiʃən/ n. acumulación f.
accumulative /ə'kyumyə,leitɪv/ a. acumulativo.
accumulator /ə'kyumyə,leitər/ n. acumulador m.
accuracy /'ækyərəsi/ n. exactitud, precisión f.
accurate /'ækyərɪt/ a. exacto.
accursed /ə'kɜrsɪd, ə'kɜrst/ a. maldito.
accusation /,ækyu'zeiʃən/ n. acusación f., cargo m.
accusative /ə'kyuzətɪv/ a. & n. acusativo m.
accuse /ə'kyuz/ v. acusar.
accused /ə'kyuzd/ a. & n. acusado -da, procesado -da.
accuser /ə'kyuzər/ n. acusador -ra.
accustom /ə'kʌstəm/ v. acostumbrar.
accustomed /ə'kʌstəmd/ a. acostumbrado.
ace /eis/ a. **1.** sobresaliente. —n. **2.** as m.
acerbity /ə'sɜrbɪti/ n. acerbidad, amargura f.
acetate /'æsɪ,teit/ n. Chem. acetato m.
acetic /ə'sitɪk/ a. acético.
acetylene /ə'sɛtḷ,in/ a. **1.** acetilénico. —n. **2.** Chem. acetileno m.
ache /eik/ n. **1.** dolor m. —v. **2.** doler.
achieve /ə'tʃiv/ v. lograr, llevar a cabo.
achievement /ə'tʃivmənt/ n. realización f.; hecho notable m.
acid /'æsɪd/ a. & n. ácido m.
acidify /ə'sɪdə,fai/ v. acidificar.
acidity /ə'sɪdɪti/ n. acidez f.
acidosis /,æsɪ'dousɪs/ n. Med. acidismo m.
acid rain lluvia ácida f.
acid test prueba decisiva.
acidulous /ə'sɪdʒələs/ a. agrio, acídulo.
acknowledge /æk'nɒlɪdʒ/ v. admitir; (receipt) acusar.

acme /'ækmi/ *n.* apogeo, colmo *m.*

acne /'ækni/ *n. Med.* acné *m. & f.*

acolyte /'ækə,lait/ *n.* acólito *m.*

acorn /'eikɔrn/ *n.* bellota *f.*

acoustics /ə'kustiks/ *n.* acústica *f.*

acquaint /ə'kweint/ *v.* familiarizar. **to be acquainted with,** conocer.

acquaintance /ə'kweintṇs/ *n.* conocimiento *m.;* (person known) conocido -da. **to make the a. of,** conocer.

acquiesce /,ækwi'ɛs/ *v.* consentir.

acquiescence /,ækwi'ɛsəns/ *n.* consentimiento *m.*

acquire /ə'kwaiᵊr/ *v.* adquirir.

acquirement /ə'kwaiᵊrmənt/ *n.* adquisición *f.;* (pl.) conocimientos *m.pl.*

acquisition /,ækwə'ziʃən/ *n.* adquisición *f.*

acquisitive /ə'kwizitiv/ *a.* adquisitivo.

acquit /ə'kwit/ *v.* exonerar, absolver.

acquittal /ə'kwitḷ/ *n.* absolución *f.*

acre /'eikər/ *n.* acre *m.*

acreage /'eikəridʒ/ *número de* acres.

acrid /'ækrid/ *a.* acre, punzante.

acrimonious /,ækrə'mouniəs/ *a.* acrimonioso, mordaz.

acrimony /'ækrə,mouni/ *n.* acrimonia, aspereza *f.*

acrobat /'ækrə,bæt/ *n.* acróbata *m. & f.*

acrobatic /,ækrə'bætik/ *a.* acrobático.

across /ə'krɔs/ *adv.* **1.** a través, al otro lado. —*prep.* **2.** al otro lado de, a través de.

acrostic /ə'krɔstik/ *n.* acróstico *m.*

act /ækt/ *n.* **1.** acción *f.;* acto *m.* —*v.* **2.** actuar, portarse. **act as,** hacer de. **act on,** decidir sobre.

acting /'æktiŋ/ *a.* **1.** interino. —*n.* **2.** acción *f.; Theat.* representación *f.*

actinism /'æktə,nizəm/ *n.* actinismo *m.*

actinium /æk'tiniəm/ *n. Chem.* actinio *m.*

action /'ækʃən/ *n.* acción *f.* **take a.,** tomar medidas.

action replay /'ri,plei/ repetición *f.*

activate /'æktə,veit/ *v.* activar.

activation /,æktə'veiʃən/ *n.* activación *f.*

activator /'æktə,veitər/ *n. Chem.* activador *m.*

active /'æktiv/ *a.* activo.

activity /æk'tiviti/ *n.* actividad *f.*

actor /'æktər/ *n.* actor *m.*

actress /'æktris/ *n.* actriz *f.*

actual /'æktʃuəl/ *a.* real, efectivo.

actuality /,æktʃu'æliti/ *n.* realidad, actualidad *f.*

actually /'æktʃuəli/ *adv.* en realidad.

actuary /'æktʃu,ɛri/ *n.* actuario *m.*

actuate /'æktʃu,eit/ *v.* impulsar, mover.

acumen /ə'kyumən/ *n.* cacumen *m.,* perspicacia *f.*

acupuncture /'ækyu,pʌŋktʃər/ *n.* acupuntura *f.*

acute /ə'kyut/ *a.* agudo; perspicaz.

acutely /ə'kyutli/ *adv.* agudamente.

acuteness /ə'kyutnis/ *n.* agudeza *f.*

adage /'ædidʒ/ *n.* refrán, proverbio *m.*

adamant /'ædəmənt/ *a.* firme.

Adam's apple /'ædəmz/ nuez de la garganta.

adapt /ə'dæpt/ *v.* adaptar.

adaptability /ə,dæptə'biliti/ *n.* adaptabilidad *f.*

adaptable /ə'dæptəbəl/ *a.* adaptable.

adaptation /,ædəp'teiʃən/ *n.* adaptación *f.*

adapter /ə'dæptər/ *n. Elec.* adaptador *m.; Mech.* ajustador *m.*

adaptive /ə'dæptiv/ *a.* adaptable, acomodable.

add /æd/ *v.* agregar, añadir. **a. up,** sumar.

adder /'ædər/ *n.* víbora; serpiente *f.*

addict /'ædikt/ *n.* adicto -ta; (fan) aficionado -da.

addition /ə'diʃən/ *n.* adición *f.* **in a. to,** además de.

additional /ə'diʃənḷ/ *a.* adicional.

addle /'ædḷ/ *v.* confundir.

address /*n* ə'drɛs, 'ædrɛs; *v* ə'drɛs/ *n.* **1.** dirección *f.;* señas *f.pl.;* (speech) discurso. —*v.* **2.** dirigirse a.

addressee /,ædrɛ'si/ *n.* destinatario -ia.

adduce /ə'dus/ *v.* aducir.

adenoid /'ædṇ,ɔid/ *a.* adenoidea.

adept /ə'dɛpt/ *a.* adepto.

adeptly /ə'dɛptli/ *adv.* diestramente.

adeptness /ə'dɛptnɪs/ *n.* destreza *f.*

adequacy /'ædɪkwəsi/ *n.* suficiencia *f.*

adequate /'ædɪkwɪt/ *a.* adecuado.

adequately /'ædɪkwɪtli/ *adv.* adecuadamente.

adhere /æd'hɪər/ *v.* adherirse, pegarse.

adherence /æd'hɪərəns/ *n.* adhesión *f.;* apego *m.*

adherent /æd'hɪərənt/ *n.* adherente *m.*, partidario -ria.

adhesion /æd'hiʒən/ *n.* adhesión *f.*

adhesive /æd'hisɪv/ *a.* adhesivo. **a. tape,** esparadrapo *m.*

adhesiveness /æd'hisɪvnɪs/ *n.* adhesividad *f.*

adieu /ə'du/ *interj.* **1.** adiós. —*n.* **2.** despedida *f.*

adjacent /ə'dʒeisənt/ *a.* adyacente.

adjective /'ædʒɪktɪv/ *n.* adjetivo *m.*

adjoin /ə'dʒɔin/ *v.* lindar (con).

adjoining /ə'dʒɔinɪŋ/ *a.* contiguo.

adjourn /ə'dʒɜrn/ *v.* suspender, levantar.

adjournment /ə'dʒɜrnmənt/ *n.* suspensión *f.;* Leg. espera *f.*

adjunct /'ædʒʌŋkt/ *n.* adjunto *m.;* Gram. atributo *m.*

adjust /ə'dʒʌst/ *v.* ajustar, acomodar; arreglar.

adjuster /ə'dʒʌstər/ *n.* ajustador -ra.

adjustment /ə'dʒʌstmənt/ *n.* ajuste; arreglo *m.*

adjutant /'ædʒətənt/ *n.* Mil. ayudante *m.*

administer /æd'mɪnəstər/ *v.* administrar.

administration /æd,mɪnə'streiʃən/ *n.* administración *f.;* gobierno *m.*

administrative /æd'mɪnə,streitɪv/ *a.* administrativo.

administrator /æd'mɪnə,streitər/ *n.* administrador -ra.

admirable /'ædmərəbəl/ *a.* admirable.

admirably /'ædmərəbli/ *adv.* admirablemente.

admiral /'ædmərəl/ *n.* almirante *m.*

admiralty /'ædmərəlti/ *n.* Ministerio de Marina.

admiration /,ædmə'reiʃən/ *n.* admiración *f.*

admire /æd'maiᵊr/ *v.* admirar.

admirer /æd'maiᵊrər/ *n.* admirador -ra; enamorado -da.

admiringly /æd'maiᵊrɪŋli/ *adv.* admirativamente.

admissible /æd'mɪsəbəl/ *a.* admisible, aceptable.

admission /æd'mɪʃən/ *n.* admisión; entrada *f.*

admit /æd'mɪt/ *v.* admitir.

admittance /æd'mɪtn̩s/ *n.* entrada *f.*

admittedly /æd'mɪtɪdli/ *adv.* reconocidamente.

admixture /æd'mɪkstʃər/ *n.* mezcla *f.*

admonish /æd'mɒnɪʃ/ *v.* amonestar.

admonition /,ædmə'nɪʃən/ *n.* admonición *f.*

adolescence /,ædl̩'ɛsəns/ *n.* adolescencia *f.*

adolescent /,ædl̩'ɛsənt/ *n. & a.* adolescente.

adopt /ə'dɒpt/ *v.* adoptar.

adopted child /ə'dɒptɪd/ hija adoptiva *f.*, hijo adoptivo *m.*

adoption /ə'dɒpʃən/ *n.* adopción *f.*

adorable /ə'dɔrəbəl/ *a.* adorable.

adoration /,ædə'reiʃən/ *n.* adoración *f.*

adore /ə'dɔr/ *v.* adorar.

adorn /ə'dɔrn/ *v.* adornar.

adornment /ə'dɔrnmənt/ *n.* adorno *m.*

adrenalin /ə'drɛnl̩ɪn/ *n.* adrenalina *f.*

adrift /ə'drɪft/ *adv.* a la ventura.

adroit /ə'drɔit/ *a.* diestro.

adulate /'ædʒə,leit/ *v.* adular.

adulation /,ædʒə'leiʃən/ *n.* adulación *f.*

adult /ə'dʌlt/ *a. & n.* adulto -a.

adulterant /ə'dʌltərənt/ *a. & n.* adulterante *m.*

adulterate /ə'dʌltə,reit/ *v.* adulterar.

adulterer /ə'dʌltərər/ *n.* adúltero -ra.

adulteress /ə'dʌltərɪs/ *n.* adúltera *f.*

adultery /ə'dʌltəri/ *n.* adulterio *m.*

advance /æd'væns/ *n.* **1.** avance; adelanto *m.* **in a.,** de antemano, antes. —*v.* **2.** avanzar, adelantar.

advanced /æd'vænst/ a. avanzado, adelantado.

advancement /æd'vænsmənt/ n. adelantamiento m.; promoción f.

advantage /æd'væntɪdʒ/ n. ventaja f. **take a. of,** aprovecharse de.

advantageous /ˌædvən'teidʒəs/ a. provechoso, ventajoso.

advantageously /ˌædvən'teidʒəsli/ adv. ventajosamente.

advent /'ædvɛnt/ n. venida, llegada f.

adventitious /ˌædvən'tɪʃəs/ a. adventicio, espontáneo.

adventure /æd'vɛntʃər/ n. aventura f.

adventurer /æd'vɛntʃərər/ n. aventurero -ra.

adventurous /æd'vɛntʃərəs/ a. aventurero, intrépido.

adventurously /æd'vɛntʃərəsli/ adv. arriesgadamente.

adverb /'ædvɜrb/ n. adverbio m.

adverbial /æd'vɜrbiəl/ a. adverbial.

adversary /'ædvərˌsɛri/ n. adversario -a.

adverse /æd'vɜrs/ a. adverso.

adversely /æd'vɜrsli/ adv. adversamente.

adversity /æd'vɜrsɪti/ n. adversidad f.

advert /æd'vɜrt/ v. hacer referencia a.

advertise /'ædvərˌtaiz/ v. avisar, anunciar; (promote) promocionar.

advertisement /ˌædvər'taizmənt, æd'vɜrtɪsmənt/ n. aviso, anuncio m.

advertiser /'ædvərˌtaizər/ n. anunciante m. & f., avisador -ra.

advertising /'ædvərˌtaizɪŋ/ n. publicidad f.

advice /æd'vais/ n. consejos m.pl.

advisability /ædˌvaizə'bɪlɪti/ n. prudencia, propiedad f.

advisable /æd'vaizəbəl/ a. aconsejable, prudente.

advisably /æd'vaizəbli/ adv. prudentemente.

advise /æd'vaiz/ v. aconsejar. **a. against,** desaconsejar.

advisedly /æd'vaizɪdli/ adv. avisadamente, prudentemente.

advisement /æd'vaizmənt/ n. consideración f.; **take under a.,** someter a estudio.

adviser /æd'vaizər/ n. consejero -ra.

advocacy /'ædvəkəsi/ n. abogacía; defensa f.

advocate /n 'ædvəkɪt; v -ˌkeit/ n. **1.** abogado -da. —v. **2.** apoyar.

aegis /'idʒɪs/ n. amparo m.

aerate /'ɛəreit/ v. airear, ventilar.

aeration /ˌɛə'reiʃən/ n. aeración, ventilación f.

aerial /'ɛəriəl/ a. aéreo.

aerie /'ɛəri/ n. nido de águila.

aeronautics /ˌɛərə'nɔtɪks/ n. aeronáutica f.

aerosol bomb /'ɛərəˌsɔl/ bomba insecticida.

afar /ə'fɑr/ adv. lejos. **from a.,** de lejos, desde lejos.

affability /ˌæfə'bɪlɪti/ n. afabilidad, amabilidad f.

affable /'æfəbəl/ a. afable.

affably /'æfəbli/ adv. afablemente.

affair /ə'fɛər/ n. asunto m. **love a.,** aventura amorosa.

affect /ə'fɛkt/ v. afectar; (emotionally) conmover.

affectation /ˌæfɛk'teiʃən/ n. afectación f.

affected /ə'fɛktɪd/ a. artificioso.

affecting /ə'fɛktɪŋ/ a. conmovedor.

affection /ə'fɛkʃən/ n. cariño m.

affectionate /ə'fɛkʃənɪt/ a. afectuoso, cariñoso.

affectionately /ə'fɛkʃənɪtli/ adv. afectuosamente, con cariño.

affiance /ə'faiəns/ v. dar palabra de casamiento; **become affianced,** comprometerse.

affidavit /ˌæfɪ'deivɪt/ n. Leg. declaración, deposición f.

affiliate /n ə'fɪliˌit; v ə'fɪliˌeit/ n. **1.** afiliado -da. —v. **2.** afiliar.

affiliation /əˌfɪli'eiʃən/ n. afiliación f.

affinity /ə'fɪnɪti/ n. afinidad f.

affirm /ə'fɜrm/ v. afirmar.

affirmation /ˌæfər'meiʃən/ n. afirmación, aserción f.

affirmative /ə'fɜrmətɪv/ n. **1.** afirmativa f. —a. **2.** afirmativo.

affirmatively /ə'fɜrmətɪvli/ adv. afirmativamente, aseveradamente.

affix /n 'æfɪks; v ə'fɪks/ n. **1.** Gram. afijo m. —v. **2.** fijar, pegar, poner.

afflict /ə'flɪkt/ v. afligir.

affliction /ə'flɪkʃən/ n. aflicción f.; mal m.

affluence /'æfluəns/ n. abundancia, opulencia f.

affluent /'æfluənt/ *a.* opulento, afluente.

afford /ə'fɔrd/ *v.* proporcionar. **be able to a.**, tener con que comprar.

affordable /ə'fɔrdəbəl/ *a.* asequible.

affront /ə'frʌnt/ *n.* **1.** afrenta *f.* —*v.* **2.** afrentar, insultar.

afield /ə'fild/ *adv.* lejos de casa; lejos del camino; lejos del asunto.

afire /ə'faiᵊr/ *adv.* ardiendo.

afloat /ə'flout/ *adv. Naut.* a flote.

aforementioned /ə'fɔr,mɛnʃənd/ *a.* dicho, susodicho.

afraid /ə'freid/ *a.* **to be a.**, tener miedo, temer.

African /'æfrɪkən/ *n. & a.* africano -na.

aft /æft/ *adv. Naut.* a popa, en popa.

after /'æftər/ *prep.* **1.** después de. —*conj.* **2.** después que.

aftermath /'æftər,mæθ/ *n.* resultados *m.pl.*, consecuencias *f.pl.*

afternoon /,æftər'nun/ *n.* tarde *f.* **good a.**, buenas tardes.

aftertaste /'æftər,teist/ *n.* gustillo *m.*

afterthought /'æftər,θɔt/ *n.* idea tardía.

afterward(s) /'æftərwərdz/ *adv.* después.

again /ə'gɛn/ *adv.* otra vez, de nuevo. **to do a.**, volver a hacer.

against /ə'gɛnst/ *prep.* contra; en contra de.

agape /ə'geip/ *adv.* con la boca abierta.

agate /'ægɪt/ *n.* ágata *f.*

age /eidʒ/ *n.* **1.** edad *f.* **of a.**, mayor de edad. **old a.**, vejez *f.* —*v.* **2.** envejecer.

aged /eidʒd; 'eidʒɪd/ *a.* viejo, anciano, añejo.

ageism /'eidʒɪzəm/ *n.* discriminación contra las personas de edad.

ageless /'eidʒlɪs/ *a.* sempiterno.

agency /'eidʒənsi/ *n.* agencia *f.*

agenda /ə'dʒɛndə/ *n.* agenda *f.*, orden *m.*

agent /'eidʒənt/ *n.* agente; representante *m. & f.*

agglutinate /ə'glutn,eit/ *v.* aglutinar.

agglutination /ə,glutn'eiʃən/ *n.* aglutinación *f.*

aggrandize /ə'grændaiz/ *v.* agrandar; elevar.

aggrandizement /ə'grændɪzmənt/ *n.* engrandecimiento *m.*

aggravate /'ægrə,veit/ *v.* agravar; irritar.

aggravation /,ægrə'veiʃən/ *n.* agravamiento; empeoramiento *m.*

aggregate /'ægrɪgɪt, -,geit/ *a. & n.* agregado *m.*

aggregation /,ægrɪ'geiʃən/ *n.* agregación *f.*

aggression /ə'grɛʃən/ *n.* agresión *f.*

aggressive /ə'grɛsɪv/ *a.* agresivo.

aggressively /ə'grɛsɪvli/ *adv.* agresivamente.

aggressiveness /ə'grɛsɪvnɪs/ *n.* agresividad *f.*

aggressor /ə'grɛsər/ *n.* agresor -ra.

aghast /ə'gæst/ *a.* horrorizado.

agile /'ædʒəl/ *a.* ágil.

agility /æ'dʒɪlɪti/ *n.* agilidad, ligereza, prontitud *f.*

agitate /'ædʒɪ,teit/ *v.* agitar.

agitation /,ædʒɪ'teiʃən/ *n.* agitación *f.*

agitator /'ædʒɪ,teitər/ *n.* agitador -ra.

agnostic /æg'nɒstɪk/ *a. & n.* agnóstico -ca.

ago /ə'gou/ *adv.* hace. **two days a.**, hace dos días.

agonized /'ægə,naizd/ *a.* angustioso.

agony /'ægəni/ *n.* sufrimiento *m.*; angustia *f.*

agrarian /ə'grɛəriən/ *a.* agrario.

agree /ə'gri/ *v.* estar de acuerdo; convenir. **a. with one**, sentar bien.

agreeable /ə'griəbəl/ *a.* agradable.

agreeably /ə'griəbli/ *adv.* agradablemente.

agreement /ə'grimənt/ *n.* acuerdo *m.*

agriculture /'ægrɪ,kʌltʃər/ *n.* agricultura *f.*

ahead /ə'hɛd/ *adv.* adelante.

aid /eid/ *n.* **1.** ayuda *f.* —*v.* **2.** ayudar.

aide /eid/ *n.* ayudante -ta.

AIDS /eidz/ *n.* SIDA *m.*

ailing /'eilɪŋ/ *adj.* enfermo.

ailment /'eilmənt/ *n.* enfermedad *f.*

aim /eim/ *n.* **1.** puntería *f.*; (purpose) propósito *m.* —*v.* **2.** apuntar.

aimless /'eimlɪs/ *a.* sin objeto.

air /ɛər/ *n.* **1.** aire *m.* **by a.** por avión. —*v.* **2.** ventilar, airear.

airbag /'ɛər,bæg/ *n.* (in automobiles) saco de aire *m.*

air-conditioned /'ɛər kən,dɪʃənd/ *a.* con aire acondicionado.

air-conditioning /ɛər kən,dɪʃənɪŋ/ acondicionamiento del aire.

aircraft /'ɛər,kræft/ *n.* avión *m.*

aircraft carrier portaaviones *m.*

airfare /'ɛər,fɛər/ *n.* precio del billete de avión *m.*

airing /'ɛərɪŋ/ *n.* ventilación *f.*

airline /'ɛər,laɪn/ *n.* línea aérea *f.*

airliner /'ɛər,laɪnər/ *n.* avión de pasajeros.

airmail /'ɛər,meɪl/ *n.* correo aéreo.

airplane /'ɛər,pleɪn/ *n.* avión, aeroplano *m.*

air pollution contaminación atmosférica, contaminación del aire.

airport /'ɛər,pɔrt/ *n.* aeropuerto *m.*

air pressure presión atmosférica.

air raid ataque aéreo.

airsick /'ɛər,sɪk/ *a.* mareado.

air terminal terminal aérea *f.*

airtight /'ɛər,taɪt/ *a.* hermético.

air traffic controller controlador aéreo *m.*

aisle /aɪl/ *n.* pasillo *m.*

ajar /ə'dʒɑr/ *a.* entreabierto.

akin /ə'kɪn/ *a.* emparentado, semejante.

alacrity /ə'lækrɪti/ *n.* alacridad, presteza *f.*

alarm /ə'lɑrm/ *n.* **1.** alarma *f.* —*v.* **2.** alarmar.

alarmist /ə'lɑrmɪst/ *n.* alarmista *m. & f.*

albino /æl'baɪnou/ *n.* albino -na.

album /'ælbəm/ *n.* álbum *m.*

alcohol /'ælkə,hɔl/ *n.* alcohol *m.*

alcoholic /,ælkə'hɔlɪk/ *a.* alcohólico.

alcove /'ælkouv/ *n.* alcoba *f.*

ale /eɪl/ *n.* cerveza inglesa.

alert /ə'lɜrt/ *n.* **1.** alarma *f.* **on the a.,** alerta, sobre aviso. —*a.* **2.** listo, vivo. —*v.* **3.** poner sobre aviso.

alfalfa /æl'fælfə/ *n.* alfalfa *f.*

algebra /'ældʒəbrə/ *n.* álgebra *f.*

alias /'eɪliəs/ *n.* alias *m.*

alibi /'ælə,baɪ/ *n.* excusa *f.*; *Leg.* coartada *f.*

alien /'eɪliən/ *a.* **1.** ajeno, extranjero. —*n.* **2.** extranjero -ra.

alienate /'eɪliə,neɪt/ *v.* enajenar.

alight /ə'laɪt/ *v.* bajar, apearse.

align /ə'laɪn/ *v.* alinear.

alike /ə'laɪk/ *a.* **1.** semejante, igual. —*adv.* **2.** del mismo modo, igualmente.

alimentary canal /,ælə'mɛntəri/ *n.* tubo digestivo *m.*

alive /ə'laɪv/ *a.* vivo; animado.

alkali /'ælkə,laɪ/ *n. Chem.* álcali, cali *m.*

alkaline /'ælkə,laɪn/ *a.* alcalino.

all /ɔl/ *a. & pron.* todo. **not at a.,** de ninguna manera, nada.

allay /ə'leɪ/ *v.* aquietar.

allegation /,ælɪ'geɪʃən/ *n.* alegación *f.*

allege /ə'lɛdʒ/ *v.* alegar; pretender.

allegiance /ə'lidʒəns/ *n.* lealtad *f.*; (to country) homenaje *m.*

allegory /'ælə,gɔri/ *n.* alegoría *f.*

allergy /'ælərdʒi/ *n.* alergia *f.*

alleviate /ə'livi,eɪt/ *v.* aliviar.

alley /'æli/ *n.* callejón *m.* **bowling a.,** bolera *f.*, boliche *m.*

alliance /ə'laɪəns/ *n.* alianza *f.*

allied /'ælaɪd/ *a.* aliado.

alligator /'ælɪ,geɪtər/ *n.* caimán *m.*; (Mex.) lagarto *m.* **a. pear,** aguacate *m.*

allocate /'ælə,keɪt/ *v.* colocar, asignar.

allot /ə'lɒt/ *v.* asignar.

allotment /ə'lɒtmənt/ *n.* lote, porción *f.*

allow /ə'laʊ/ *v.* permitir, dejar.

allowance /ə'laʊəns/ *n.* abono *m.*; dieta *f.* **make a. for,** tener en cuenta.

alloy /'ælɔɪ/ *n.* mezcla *f.*; (metal) aleación *f.*

all right está bien.

allude /ə'lud/ *v.* aludir.

allure /ə'lʊr/ *n.* **1.** atracción *f.* —*v.* **2.** atraer, tentar.

alluring /ə'lʊrɪŋ/ *a.* tentador, seductivo.

allusion /ə'luʒən/ *n.* alusión *f.*

ally /*n* 'ælaɪ, *v* ə'laɪ/ *n.* **1.** aliado -da. —*v.* **2.** aliar.

almanac /'ɔlmə,næk/ *n.* almanaque *m.*

almighty /ɔl'maɪti/ *a.* todopoderoso.

almond /'ɑmənd/ *n.* almendra *f.*

almost /'ɔlmoust/ *adv.* casi.

alms /ɑmz/ *n.* limosna *f.*

aloft /ə'lɔft/ *adv.* arriba, en alto.

alone /ə'loun/ *adv.* solo, a solas. **to leave a.,** dejar en paz.

amputate

along /ə'lɔŋ/ *prep.* por; a lo largo de. **a. with,** junto con.

alongside /ə'lɔŋ'said/ *adv.* **1.** al lado. —*prep.* **2.** junto a.

aloof /ə'luf/ *a.* apartado.

aloud /ə'laud/ *adv.* en voz alta.

alpaca /æl'pækə/ *n.* alpaca *f.*

alphabet /'ælfə,bɛt/ *n.* alfabeto *m.*

alphabetical /,ælfə'bɛtɪkəl/ *a.* alfabético.

alphabetize /'ælfəbɪ,taiz/ *v.* alfabetizar.

already /ɔl'rɛdi/ *adv.* ya.

also /'ɔlsou/ *adv.* también.

altar /'ɔltər/ *n.* altar *m.*

alter /'ɔltər/ *v.* alterar.

alteration /,ɔltə'reiʃən/ *n.* alteración *f.*

alternate /a, *n* 'ɔltərnɪt; *v* -,neit/ *a.* **1.** alterno. —*n.* **2.** substituto -ta. —*v.* **3.** alternar.

alternative /ɔl'tɜrnətɪv/ *a.* **1.** alternativo. —*n.* **2.** alternativa *f.*

although /ɔl'ðou/ *conj.* aunque.

altitude /'æltɪ,tud/ *n.* altura *f.*

alto /'æltou/ *n.* contralto *m.*

altogether /,ɔltə'gɛðər/ *adv.* en junto; enteramente.

altruism /'æltru,ɪzəm/ *n.* altruismo *m.*

alum /'æləm/ *n.* alumbre *m.*

aluminum /ə'lumənəm/ *n.* aluminio *m.*

aluminum foil papel de aluminio *m.*

always /'ɔlweiz/ *adv.* siempre.

amalgam /ə'mælgəm/ *n.* amalgama *f.*

amalgamate /ə'mælgə,meit/ *v.* amalgamar.

amass /ə'mæs/ *v.* amontonar.

amateur /'æmə,tʃʊr/ *n.* aficionado -da.

amaze /ə'meiz/ *v.* asombrar; sorprender.

amazement /ə'meizmənt/ *n.* asombro *m.*

amazing /ə'meizɪŋ/ *a.* asombroso, pasmoso.

ambassador /æm'bæsədər/ *n.* embajador -ra.

amber /'æmbər/ *a.* **1.** ambarino. —*n.* **2.** ámbar *m.*

ambidextrous /,æmbɪ'dɛkstrəs/ *a.* ambidextro.

ambiguity /,æmbɪ'gyuɪti/ *n.* ambigüedad *f.*

ambiguous /æm'bɪgyuəs/ *a.* ambiguo.

ambition /æm'bɪʃən/ *n.* ambición *f.*

ambitious /æm'bɪʃəs/ *a.* ambicioso.

ambulance /'æmbyələns/ *n.* ambulancia *f.*

ambush /'æmbuʃ/ *n.* **1.** emboscada *f.* —*v.* **2.** acechar.

ameliorate /ə'milyə,reit/ *v.* mejorar.

amenable /ə'minəbəl/ *a.* tratable, dócil.

amend /ə'mɛnd/ *v.* enmendar.

amendment /ə'mɛndmənt/ *n.* enmienda *f.*

amenity /ə'mɛnɪti/ *n.* amenidad *f.*

American /ə'mɛrɪkən/ *a. & n.* americano -na, norteamericano -na.

amethyst /'æməθɪst/ *n.* amatista *f.*

amiable /'eimiəbəl/ *a.* amable.

amicable /'æmɪkəbəl/ *a.* amigable.

amid /ə'mɪd/ *prep.* entre, en medio de.

amidships /ə'mɪd,ʃɪps/ *adv. Naut.* en medio del navío.

amiss /ə'mɪs/ *adv.* mal. **to take a.,** llevar a mal.

amity /'æmɪti/ *n.* amistad, armonía *f.*

ammonia /ə'mounyə/ *n.* amoníaco *m.*

ammunition /,æmyə'nɪʃən/ *n.* municiones *f.pl.*

amnesia /æm'niʒə/ *n.* amnesia *f.*

amnesty /'æmnəsti/ *n.* amnistía *f.,* indulto *m.*

amniocentesis /,æmniousɛn'tisɪs/ *n.* amniocéntesis *f.*

amoeba /ə'mibə/ *n.* amiba *f.*

among /ə'mʌŋ/ *prep.* entre.

amoral /ei'mɔrəl/ *a.* amoral.

amorous /'æmərəs/ *a.* amoroso.

amorphous /ə'mɔrfəs/ *a.* amorfo.

amortize /'æmər,taiz/ *v. Com.* amortizar.

amount /ə'maunt/ *n.* **1.** cantidad, suma *f.* —*v.* **2. a. to,** subir a.

ampere /'æmpɪər/ *n. Elec.* amperio *m.*

amphibian /æm'fɪbiən/ *a. & n.* anfibio *m.*

amphitheater /'æmfə,θiətər/ *n.* anfiteatro, circo *m.*

ample /'æmpəl/ *a.* amplio; suficiente.

amplify /'æmplə,fai/ *v.* amplificar.

amputate /'æmpyu,teit/ *v.* amputar.

amuse /ə'myuz/ v. entretener, divertir.

amusement /ə'myuzmənt/ n. diversión f.

an /ən, when stressed an/ art. un, una.

anachronism /ə'nækrə,nızəm/ n. anacronismo, m.

analogous /ə'næləgəs/ a. análogo, parecido.

analogy /ə'nælədʒi/ n. analogía f.

analysis /ə'næləsıs/ n. análisis m.

analyst /'ænƖıst/ n. analista m. & f.

analytic /,ænƖ'ıtık/ a. analítico.

analyze /'ænƖ,aiz/ v. analizar.

anarchy /'ænərki/ n. anarquía f.

anatomy /ə'nætəmi/ n. anatomía f.

ancestor /'ænsɛstər/ n. antepasado m.

ancestral /æn'sɛstrəl/ a. de los antepasados, hereditario.

ancestry /'ænsɛstri/ n. linaje, abolengo m.

anchor /'æŋkər/ n. 1. ancla f. **weigh a.,** levar el ancla. —v. 2. anclar.

anchorage /'æŋkərıdʒ/ n. Naut. ancladero, anclaje m.

anchovy /'æntʃouvi/ n. anchoa f.

ancient /'einʃənt/ a. & n. antiguo -ua.

and /ænd, ənd/ conj. y, (before i-, hi-) e.

anecdote /'ænık,dout/ n. anécdota f.

anemia /ə'nimiə/ n. Med. anemia f.

anesthetic /,ænəs'θɛtık/ n. anestesia f.

anew /ə'nu/ adv. de nuevo.

angel /'eindʒəl/ n. ángel m.

anger /'æŋgər/ n. 1. ira f., enojo m. —v. 2. enfadar, enojar.

angle /'æŋgəl/ n. ángulo m.

angry /'æŋgri/ a. enojado, enfadado.

anguish /'æŋgwıʃ/ n. angustia f.

angular /'æŋgyələr/ a. angular.

aniline /'ænƖın/ n. Chem. anilina f.

animal /'ænəməl/ a. & n. animal m.

animate /v 'ænə,meit; a -mɪt/ v. 1. animar. —a. 2. animado.

animated /'ænə,meitɪd/ a. vivo, animado.

animation /,ænə'meiʃən/ n. animación, viveza f.

animosity /,ænə'mɒsıti/ n. rencor m.

anise /'ænıs/ n. anís m.

ankle /'æŋkəl/ n. tobillo m.

annals /'ænƖz/ n.pl. anales m.pl.

annex /n 'ænɛks; v ə'nɛks, 'ænɛks/ n. 1. anexo m., adición f. —v. 2. anexar.

annexation /,ænık'seiʃən/ n. anexión, adición f.

annihilate /ə'naiə,leit/ v. aniquilar, destruir.

anniversary /,ænə'vɜrsəri/ n. aniversario m.

annotate /'ænə,teit/ v. anotar.

annotation /,ænə'teiʃən/ n. anotación f., apunte m.

announce /ə'nauns/ v. anunciar.

announcement /ə'naunsmənt/ n. anuncio, aviso m.

announcer /ə'naunsər/ n. anunciador -ra; (radio) locutor -ra.

annoy /ə'nɔi/ v. molestar.

annoyance /ə'nɔiəns/ n. molestia, incomodidad f.

annual /'ænyuəl/ a. anual.

annuity /ə'nuıti/ n. anualidad, pensión f.

annul /ə'nʌl/ v. anular, invalidar.

anode /'ænoud/ n. Elec. ánodo m.

anoint /ə'nɔint/ v. untar; Relig. ungir.

anomalous /ə'nɒmələs/ a. anómalo, irregular.

anonymous /ə'nɒnəməs/ a. anónimo.

anorexia /,ænə'rɛksiə/ n. anorexia f.

another /ə'nʌðər/ a. & pron. otro.

answer /'ænsər, 'an-/ n. 1. contestación, respuesta f. —v. 2. contestar, responder. **a. for,** ser responsable de.

answerable /'ænsərəbəl/ a. discutible, refutable.

answering machine /'ænsərıŋ/ contestador automático m.

ant /ænt/ n. hormiga f.

antacid /ænt'æsıd/ a. & n. antiácido m.

antagonism /æn'tægə,nızəm/ n. antagonismo m.

antagonist /æn'tægənıst/ n. antagonista m. & f.

antagonistic /æn,tægə'nıstık/ a. antagónico, hostil.

antagonize /æn'tægə,naiz/ v. contrariar.

antarctic /ænt'arktık/ a. & n. antártico m.

antecedent /ˌæntəˈsidn̩t/ *a. & n.* antecedente *m.*

antedate /ˈæntɪˌdeit/ *v.* antedatar.

antelope /ˈæntl̩ˌoup/ *n.* antílope *m.*, gacela *f.*

antenna /ænˈtɛnə/ *n.* antena *f.*

antepenultimate /ˌæntipɪˈnʌltəmɪt/ *a.* antepenúltimo.

anterior /ænˈtɪəriər/ *a.* anterior.

anteroom /ˈæntiˌrum/ *n.* antecámara *f.*

anthem /ˈænθəm/ *n.* himno *m.*; (religious) antífona *f.*

anthology /ænˈθɒlədʒi/ *n.* antología *f.*

anthracite /ˈænθrəˌsait/ *n.* antracita *f.*

anthrax /ˈænθræks/ *n. Med.* ántrax *m.*

anthropology /ˌænθrəˈpɒlədʒi/ *n.* antropología *f.*

antiaircraft /ˌæntiˈɛərˌkræft, ˌæntai-/ *a.* antiaéreo.

antibody /ˈæntɪˌbɒdi/ *n.* anticuerpo *m.*

anticipate /ænˈtɪsəˌpeit/ *v.* esperar, anticipar.

anticipation /ænˌtɪsəˈpeiʃən/ *n.* anticipación *f.*

anticlerical /ˌæntiˈklɛrɪkəl, ˌæntai-/ *a.* anticlerical.

anticlimax /ˌæntiˈklaimæks, ˌæntai-/ *n.* anticlímax *m.*

antidote /ˈæntɪˌdout/ *n.* antídoto *m.*

antifreeze /ˈæntɪˌfriz/ *n.* anticongelante *m.*

antihistamine /ˌæntiˈhɪstəˌmin, -mɪn, ˌæntai-/ *n.* antihistamínico *m.*

antimony /ˈæntəˌmouni/ *n.* antimonio *m.*

antinuclear /ˌæntiˈnukliər, æntai-/ *a.* antinuclear.

antipathy /ænˈtɪpəθi/ *n.* antipatía *f.*

antiquated /ˈæntɪˌkweitɪd/ *a.* anticuado.

antique /ænˈtik/ *a.* **1.** antiguo. —*n.* **2.** antigüedad *f.*

antiquity /ænˈtɪkwɪti/ *n.* antigüedad *f.*

antiseptic /ˌæntəˈsɛptɪk/ *a. & n.* antiséptico *m.*

antisocial /ˌæntiˈsouʃəl, ˌæntai-/ *a.* antisocial.

antitoxin /ˌæntɪˈtɒksɪn/ *n. Med.* antitoxina *f.*

antler /ˈæntlər/ *n.* asta *f.*

anvil /ˈænvɪl/ *n.* yunque *m.*

anxiety /æŋˈzaiɪti/ *n.* ansia, ansiedad *f.*

anxious /ˈæŋkʃəs, ˈæŋʃəs/ *a.* inquieto, ansioso.

any /ˈɛni/ *a.* alguno; (at all) cualquiera; (after *not*) ninguno.

anybody /ˈɛniˌbɒdi/ *pron.* alguien; (at all) cualquiera; (after *not*) nadie.

anyhow /ˈɛniˌhau/ *adv.* de todos modos; en todo caso.

anyone /ˈɛniˌwʌn/ *pron.* = anybody.

anything /ˈɛniˌθɪŋ/ *pron.* algo; (at all) cualquier cosa; (after *not*) nada.

anyway /ˈɛniˌwei/ *adv.* = anyhow.

anywhere /ˈɛniˌwɛər/ *adv.* en alguna parte; (at all) dondequiera; (after *not*) en ninguna parte.

apart /əˈpɑrt/ *adv.* aparte. **to take a.,** deshacer.

apartheid /əˈpɑrtheit, -hait/ *n.* apartheid *m.*

apartment /əˈpɑrtmənt/ *n.* apartamento, piso *m.*

apartment house casa de pisos *f.*

apathetic /ˌæpəˈθɛtɪk/ *a.* apático.

apathy /ˈæpəθi/ *n.* apatía *f.*

ape /eip/ *n.* **1.** mono -na. —*v.* **2.** imitar.

aperture /ˈæpərtʃər/ *n.* abertura *f.*

apex /ˈeipɛks/ *n.* ápice *m.*

aphorism /ˈæfəˌrɪzəm/ *n.* aforismo *m.*

apiary /ˈeipiˌɛri/ *n.* colmenario, abejar *m.*

apiece /əˈpis/ *adv.* por persona; cada uno.

apologetic /əˌpɒləˈdʒɛtɪk/ *a.* apologético.

apologist /əˈpɒlədʒɪst/ *n.* apologista *m. & f.*

apologize /əˈpɒləˌdʒaiz/ *v.* excusarse, disculparse.

apology /əˈpɒlədʒi/ *n.* excusa; apología *f.*

apoplectic /ˌæpəˈplɛktɪk/ *a.* apopléctico.

apoplexy /ˈæpəˌplɛksi/ *n.* apoplejía *f.*

apostate /əˈpɒsteit/ *n.* apóstata *m. & f.*

apostle /əˈpɒsəl/ *n.* apóstol *m.*

apostolic /ˌæpəˈstɒlɪk/ *a.* apostólico.

appall /əˈpɔl/ *v.* horrorizar; consternar.

apparatus /ˌæpəˈrætəs/ *n.* aparato *m.*

apparel /əˈpærəl/ *n.* ropa *f.*

apparent /əˈpærənt/ *a.* aparente; claro.

apparition /ˌæpəˈrɪʃən/ *n.* aparición *f.;* fantasma *m.*

appeal /əˈpil/ *n.* **1.** súplica *f.;* interés *m.; Leg.* apelación *f.* —*v.* **2.** apelar, suplicar; interesar.

appear /əˈpɪər/ *v.* aparecer, asomar; (seem) parecer; *Leg.* comparecer.

appearance /əˈpɪərəns/ *n.* apariencia *f.,* aspecto *m.;* aparición *f.*

appease /əˈpiz/ *v.* aplacar, apaciguar.

appeasement /əˈpizmənt/ *n.* apaciguamiento *m.*

appeaser /əˈpizər/ *n.* apaciguador -ra, pacificador -ra.

appellant /əˈpɛlənt/ *n.* apelante, demandante *m.* & *f.*

appellate /əˈpɛlɪt/ *a. Leg.* de apelación.

appendage /əˈpɛndɪdʒ/ *n.* añadidura *f.*

appendectomy /ˌæpənˈdɛktəmi/ *n.* apendectomía *f.*

appendicitis /əˌpɛndəˈsaɪtɪs/ *n.* apendicitis *f.*

appendix /əˈpɛndɪks/ *n.* apéndice *m.*

appetite /ˈæpɪˌtaɪt/ *n.* apetito *m.*

appetizer /ˈæpɪˌtaɪzər/ *n.* aperitivo *m.*

appetizing /ˈæpɪˌtaɪzɪŋ/ *a.* apetitoso.

applaud /əˈplɒd/ *v.* aplaudir.

applause /əˈplɒz/ *n.* aplauso *m.*

apple /ˈæpəl/ *n.* manzana *f.* **a. tree,** manzano *m.*

applesauce /ˈæpəlˌsɒs/ *n.* compota de manzana.

appliance /əˈplaɪəns/ *n.* aparato *m.*

applicable /ˈæplɪkəbəl/ *a.* aplicable.

applicant /ˈæplɪkənt/ *n.* suplicante *m.* & *f.;* candidato -ta.

application /ˌæplɪˈkeɪʃən/ *n.* solicitud *f.,* (computer) programa *m.*

applied /əˈplaɪd/ *a.* aplicado. **a. for,** pedido.

appliqué /ˌæplɪˈkeɪ/ *n.* (sewing) aplicación *f.*

apply /əˈplaɪ/ *v.* aplicar. **a. for,** solicitar, pedir.

appoint /əˈpɔɪnt/ *v.* nombrar.

appointment /əˈpɔɪntmənt/ *n.* nombramiento *m.;* puesto *m.*

apportion /əˈpɔrʃən/ *v.* repartir.

apposition /ˌæpəˈzɪʃən/ *n. Gram.* aposición *f.*

appraisal /əˈpreɪzəl/ *n.* valoración *f.*

appraise /əˈpreɪz/ *v.* evaluar; tasar; estimar.

appreciable /əˈpriʃiəbəl/ *a.* apreciable; notable.

appreciate /əˈpriʃiˌeɪt/ *v.* apreciar, estimar.

appreciation /əˌpriʃiˈeɪʃən/ *n.* aprecio; reconocimiento *m.*

apprehend /ˌæprɪˈhɛnd/ *v.* prender, capturar.

apprehension /ˌæprɪˈhɛnʃən/ *n.* aprensión *f.;* detención *f.*

apprehensive /ˌæprɪˈhɛnsɪv/ *a.* aprensivo.

apprentice /əˈprɛntɪs/ *n.* aprendiz -iza.

apprenticeship /əˈprɛntɪsˌʃɪp/ *n.* aprendizaje *m.*

apprise /əˈpraɪz/ *v.* informar.

approach /əˈproʊtʃ/ *n.* **1.** acceso; método *m.* —*v.* **2.** acercarse.

approachable /əˈproʊtʃəbəl/ *a.* accesible.

approbation /ˌæprəˈbeɪʃən/ *n.* aprobación *f.*

appropriate /a əˈproʊpriɪt; v -ˌeɪt/ *a.* **1.** apropiado. —*v.* **2.** apropiar.

appropriation /əˌproʊpriˈeɪʃən/ *n.* apropiación *f.*

approval /əˈpruvəl/ *n.* aprobación *f.*

approve /əˈpruv/ *v.* aprobar.

approximate /a əˈprɒksəmɪt; v -ˌmeɪt/ *a.* **1.** aproximado. —*v.* **2.** aproximar.

approximately /əˈprɒksəmɪtli/ *adv.* aproximadamente.

approximation /əˌprɒksəˈmeɪʃən/ *n.* aproximación *f.*

appurtenance /əˈpɜrtnəns/ *n.* dependencia *f.*

apricot /ˈæprɪˌkɒt/ *n.* albaricoque, damasco *m.*

April /ˈeɪprəl/ *n.* abril *m.*

apron /ˈeɪprən/ *n.* delantal *m.*

apropos /ˌæprəˈpoʊ/ *adv.* a propósito.

apt /æpt/ *a.* apto; capaz.

aptitude /ˈæptɪˌtud/ *n.* aptitud; facilidad *f.*

aquarium /əˈkwɛəriəm/ *n.* acuario *m.,* pecera *f.*

aquatic /əˈkwætɪk/ *a.* acuático.

aqueduct /'ækwɪ,dʌkt/ n. acueducto m.

aqueous /'ækwiəs/ a. ácueo, acuoso, aguoso.

aquiline /'ækwə,lain/ a. aquilino, aguileño.

Arab /'ærəb/ a. & n. árabe m. & f.

arable /'ærəbəl/ a. cultivable.

arbitrary /'ɑrbɪ,trɛri/ a. arbitrario.

arbitrate /'ɑrbɪ,treit/ v. arbitrar.

arbitration /,ɑrbɪ'treiʃən/ n. arbitraje m., arbitración f.

arbitrator /'ɑrbɪ,treitər/ n. arbitrador -ra.

arbor /'ɑrbər/ n. emparrado m.

arboreal /ɑr'bɔriəl/ a. arbóreo.

arc /ɑrk/ n. arco m.

arch /ɑrtʃ/ n. **1.** arco m. —v. **2.** arquear, encorvar.

archaeology /,ɑrki'ɒlədʒi/ n. arqueología f.

archaic /ɑr'keiɪk/ a. arcaico.

archbishop /'ɑrtʃ'biʃəp/ n. arzobispo m.

archdiocese /,ɑrtʃ'daiə,sis, -sɪs/ n. archidiócesis f.

archduke /'ɑrtʃ'duk/ n. archiduque m.

archer /'ɑrtʃər/ n. arquero m.

archery /'ɑrtʃəri/ n. ballestería f.

archipelago /,ɑrkə'pɛlə,gou/ n. archipiélago m.

architect /'ɑrkɪ,tɛkt/ n. arquitecto -ta.

architectural /,ɑrkɪ'tɛktʃərəl/ a. arquitectural.

architecture /'ɑrkɪ,tɛktʃər/ n. arquitectura f.

archive /'ɑrkaiv/ n. archivo m.

archway /'ɑrtʃ,wei/ n. arcada f.

arctic /'ɑrktɪk, 'ɑrtɪk/ a. ártico.

ardent /'ɑrdn̩t/ a. ardiente.

ardor /'ɑrdər/ n. ardor m., pasión f.

arduous /'ɑrdʒuəs/ a. arduo, difícil.

area /'ɛəriə/ n. área; extensión f.

area code prefijo m.

arena /ə'rinə/ n. arena f.

Argentine /'ɑrdʒəntin, -,tain/ a. & n. argentino -na.

argue /'ɑrgyu/ v. disputar; sostener.

argument /'ɑrgyəmənt/ n. disputa f.; razonamiento m.

argumentative /,ɑrgyə'mɛntətɪv/ a. argumentoso.

aria /'ɑriə/ n. aria f.

arid /'ærɪd/ a. árido, seco.

arise /ə'raiz/ v. surgir; alzarse.

aristocracy /,ærə'stɒkrəsi/ n. aristocracia f.

aristocrat /ə'rɪstə,kræt/ n. aristócrata m.

aristocratic /ə,rɪstə'krætɪk/ a. aristocrático.

arithmetic /ə'rɪθmətɪk/ n. aritmética f.

ark /ɑrk/ n. arca f.

arm /ɑrm/ n. **1.** brazo m.; (weapon) arma f. —v. **2.** armar.

armament /'ɑrməmənt/ n. armamento m.

armchair /'ɑrm,tʃɛər/ n. sillón m., butaca f.

armed forces /'ɑrmd 'fɔrsɪz/ fuerzas militares.

armful /'ɑrm,fʊl/ n. brazada f.

armhole /'ɑrm,houl/ n. (sew.) sobaquera f.

armistice /'ɑrməstɪs/ n. armisticio m.

armor /'ɑrmər/ n. armadura f., blindaje m.

armored /'ɑrmərd/ a. blindado.

armory /'ɑrməri/ n. armería f., arsenal m.

armpit /'ɑrm,pɪt/ n. axila f., sobaco m.

army /'ɑrmi/ n. ejército m.

arnica /'ɑrnɪkə/ n. árnica f.

aroma /ə'roumə/ n. fragancia f.

aromatic /,ærə'mætɪk/ a. aromático.

around /ə'raund/ prep. alrededor de, a la vuelta de; cerca de. **a. here,** por aquí.

arouse /ə'rauz/ v. despertar; excitar.

arraign /ə'rein/ v. Leg. procesar criminalmente.

arrange /ə'reindʒ/ v. arreglar; concertar; Mus. adaptar.

arrangement /ə'reindʒmənt/ n. arreglo; orden m.

array /ə'rei/ n. **1.** orden; adorno m. —v. **2.** adornar.

arrears /ə'rɪərz/ n. atrasos m.pl.

arrest /ə'rɛst/ n. **1.** detención f. —v. **2.** detener, arrestar.

arrival /ə'raivəl/ n. llegada f.

arrive /ə'raiv/ v. llegar.

arrogance /'ærəgəns/ n. arrogancia f.

arrogant /'ærəgənt/ a. arrogante.

arrogate /'ærə,geit/ v. arrogarse, usurpar.

arrow /'ærou/ n. flecha f.

arrowhead /'ærou,hɛd/ n. punta de flecha f.

arsenal /'ɑrsənḷ/ n. arsenal m.

arsenic /'ɑrsənɪk/ n. arsénico m.

arson /'ɑrsən/ n. incendio premeditado.

art /ɑrt/ arte m. (f. in pl.); (skill) maña f.

arterial /ɑr'tɪəriəl/ a. arterial.

arteriosclerosis /ɑr,tɪəriousklə'rousɪs/ n. arteriosclerosis f.

artery /'ɑrtəri/ n. arteria f.

artesian well /ɑr'tiʒən/ pozo artesiano.

artful /'ɑrtfəl/ a. astuto.

arthritis /ɑr'θraitɪs/ n. artritis f.

artichoke /'ɑrtɪ,tʃouk/ n. alcachofa f.

article /'ɑrtɪkəl/ n. artículo m.

articulate /ɑr'tɪkyə,leit/ v. articular.

articulation /ɑr,tɪkyə'leiʃən/ n. articulación f.

artifice /'ɑrtəfɪs/ n. artificio m.

artificial /,ɑrtə'fɪʃəl/ a. artificial.

artificially /,ɑrtə'fɪʃəli/ adv. artificialmente.

artillery /ɑr'tɪləri/ n. artillería f.

artisan /'ɑrtəzən/ n. artesano -na.

artist /'ɑrtɪst/ n. artista m. & f.

artistic /ɑr'tɪstɪk/ a. artístico.

artistry /'ɑrtɪstri/ n. arte m. & f.

artless /'ɑrtlɪs/ a. natural, cándido.

as /æz/ adv. & conj. como; **as... as** tan... como.

asbestos /æs'bɛstəs/ n. asbesto m.

ascend /ə'sɛnd/ v. ascender.

ascendancy /ə'sɛndənsi/ n. ascendiente m.

ascendant /ə'sɛndənt/ a. ascendente.

ascent /ə'sɛnt/ n. subida f., ascenso m.

ascertain /,æsər'tein/ v. averiguar.

ascetic /ə'sɛtɪk/ a. **1.** ascético. —n. **2.** asceta m. & f.

ascribe /ə'skraib/ v. atribuir.

ash /æʃ/ n. ceniza f.

ashamed /ə'ʃeimd/ a. avergonzado.

ashen /'æʃən/ a. pálido.

ashore /ə'ʃɔr/ adv. a tierra. **go a.,** desembarcar.

ashtray /'æʃ,trei/ n. cenicero m.

Ash Wednesday miércoles de ceniza m.

Asiatic /,eiʒi'ætɪk/ a. & n. asiático -ca.

aside /ə'said/ adv. al lado. **a. from.** aparte de.

ask /æsk/ v. preguntar; invitar; (request) pedir. **a. for,** pedir. **a. a question,** hacer una pregunta.

askance /ə'skæns/ adv. de soslayo; con recelo.

asleep /ə'slip/ a. dormido. **to fall a.,** dormirse.

asparagus /ə'spærəgəs/ n. espárrago m.

aspect /'æspɛkt/ n. aspecto m., apariencia f.

asperity /ə'spɛriti/ n. aspereza f.

aspersion /ə'spɜrʒən/ n. calumnia f.

asphalt /'æsfɔlt/ n. asfalto m.

asphyxia /æs'fɪksiə/ n. asfixia f.

asphyxiate /æs'fɪksi,eit/ v. asfixiar, sofocar.

aspirant /'æspərənt/ a. & n. aspirante m. & f.

aspirate /'æspə,reit/ v. aspirar.

aspiration /,æspə'reiʃən/ n. aspiración f.

aspirator /'æspə,reitər/ n. aspirador m.

aspire /ə'spaiᵊr/ v. aspirar. **a. to,** ambicionar.

aspirin /'æspərɪn/ n. aspirina f.

ass /æs/ n. asno, burro m.

assail /ə'seil/ v. asaltar, acometer.

assailant /ə'seilənt/ n. asaltador -ra.

assassin /ə'sæsɪn/ n. asesino -na.

assassinate /ə'sæsə,neit/ v. asesinar.

assassination /ə,sæsə'neiʃən/ n. asesinato m.

assault /ə'sɔlt/ n. **1.** asalto m. —v. **2.** asaltar, atacar.

assay /'æsei/ v. examinar; ensayar.

assemblage /ə'sɛmblɪdʒ/ n. asamblea f.

assemble /ə'sɛmbəl/ v. juntar, convocar; (mechanism) montar.

assembly /ə'sɛmbli/ n. asamblea, concurrencia f.

assent /ə'sɛnt/ n. **1.** asentimiento m. —v. **2.** asentir, convenir.

assert /ə'sɜrt/ v. afirmar, aseverar. **a. oneself,** hacerse sentir.

assertion /ə'sɜrʃən/ n. aserción f., aseveración f.

assertive /ə'sɜrtɪv/ a. asertivo.

assess /ə'sɛs/ v. tasar, evaluar.

assessor /ə'sɛsər/ n. asesor -ra.

asset /'æsɛt/ n. ventaja f. **assets,** Com. capital m.

asseverate /ə'sɛvə,reit/ v. aseverar, afirmar.

asseveration /ə,sɛvə'reiʃən/ n. aseveracinewlin f.

assiduous /ə'sɪdʒuəs/ a. asiduo.

assiduously /ə'sɪdʒuəsli/ adv. asiduamente.

assign /ə'sain/ v. asignar; destinar.

assignable /ə'sainəbəl/ a. asignable, transferible.

assignation /,æsɪg'neiʃən/ n. asignación f.

assignment /ə'sainmənt/ n. misión; tarea f.

assimilate /ə'sɪmə,leit/ v. asimilar.

assimilation /ə,sɪmə'leiʃən/ n. asimilación f.

assimilative /ə'sɪmələtɪv/ a. asimilativo.

assist /ə'sɪst/ v. ayudar, auxiliar.

assistance /ə'sɪstəns/ n. ayuda f., auxilio m.

assistant /ə'sɪstənt/ n. ayudante -ta, asistente -ta.

associate /n ə'sousiit; v -si,eit/ n. **1.** socio -cia. —v. **2.** asociar.

association /ə,sousi'eiʃən/ n. asociación; sociedad f.

assonance /'æsənəns/ n. asonancia f.

assort /ə'sɔrt/ v. surtir con variedad.

assorted /ə'sɔrtɪd/ a. variado, surtido.

assortment /ə'sɔrtmənt/ n. surtido m.

assuage /ə'sweidʒ/ v. mitigar, aliviar.

assume /ə'sum/ v. suponer; asumir.

assuming /ə'sumɪŋ/ a. presuntuoso. **a. that,** dado que.

assumption /ə'sʌmpʃən/ n. suposición; *Relig.* asunción f.

assurance /ə'ʃurəns/ n. seguridad; confianza f.; garantía f.

assure /ə'ʃur/ v. asegurar; dar confianza.

assured /ə'ʃurd/ a. **1.** seguro. —a. & n. **2.** *Com.* asegurado -da.

assuredly /ə'ʃurɪdli/ adv. ciertamente.

aster /'æstər/ n. aster f.

asterisk /'æstərɪsk/ n. asterisco m.

astern /ə'stɜrn/ adv. *Naut.* a popa.

asteroid /'æstə,rɔid/ n. asteroide m.

asthma /'æzmə/ n. *Med.* asma f.

astigmatism /ə'stɪgmə,tɪzəm/ n. astigmatismo m.

astir /ə'stɜr/ adv. en movimiento.

astonish /ə'stɒnɪʃ/ v. asombrar, pasmar.

astonishment /ə'stɒnɪʃmənt/ n. asombro m., sorpresa f.

astound /ə'staund/ v. pasmar, sorprender.

astral /'æstrəl/ a. astral, estelar.

astray /ə'strei/ a. desviado.

astride /ə'straid/ adv. a horcajadas.

astringent /ə'strɪndʒənt/ a. & n. astringente m.

astrology /ə'strɒlədʒi/ n. astrología f.

astronaut /'æstrə,nɔt/ n. astronauta m. & f.

astronomy /ə'strɒnəmi/ n. astronomía f.

astute /ə'stut/ a. astuto; agudo.

asunder /ə'sʌndər/ adv. en dos.

asylum /ə'sailəm/ n. asilo, refugio m.

asymmetry /ei'sɪmɪtri/ n. asimetría f.

at /æt/ prep. a, en; cerca de.

ataxia /ə'tæksiə/ n. *Med.* ataxia f.

atheist /'eiθiɪst/ n. ateo -tea.

athlete /'æθlit/ n. atleta m. & f.

athletic /æθ'lɛtɪk/ a. atlético.

athletics /æθ'lɛtɪks/ n. atletismo m., deportes m.pl.

athwart /ə'θwɔrt/ prep. a través de.

Atlantic /æt'læntɪk/ a. **1.** atlántico. —n. **2.** Atlántico m.

Atlantic Ocean Océano Atlántico m.

atlas /'ætləs/ n. atlas m.

atmosphere /'ætməs,fɪər/ n. atmósfera f.; *Fig.* ambiente m.

atmospheric /,ætməs'fɛrɪk/ a. atmosférico.

atoll /'ætɒl/ n. atolón m.

atom /'ætəm/ n. átomo m.

atomic /ə'tɒmɪk/ a. atómico.

atomic bomb bomba atómica f.

atomic energy energía atómica, energía nuclear f.

atomic theory teoría atómica. f.

atomic weight peso atómico m.

atonal /ei'tounl/ a. *Mus.* atonal.

atone /ə'toun/ v. expiar, compensar.

atonement /ə'tounmənt/ n. expiación; reparación f.

atrocious /ə'trouʃəs/ a. atroz.

atrocity /ə'trɒsɪti/ n. atrocidad f.

atrophy /'ætrəfi/ n. **1.** *Med.* atrofia f. —v. **2.** atrofiar.

atropine /'ætrə,pin, -pɪn/ *n.* atropina *f.*

attach /ə'tætʃ/ *v.* juntar; prender; (hook) enganchar; *Fig.* atribuir.

attaché /ætæ'ʃei/ *n.* agregado -da.

attachment /ə'tætʃmənt/ enlace *m.;* accesorio *m.;* (emotional) afecto, cariño *m.*

attack /ə'tæk/ *n.* **1.** ataque *m.* —*v.* **2.** atacar.

attacker /ə'tækər/ *n.* asaltador -ra.

attain /ə'tein/ *v.* lograr, alcanzar.

attainable /ə'teinəbəl/ *a.* accesible, realizable.

attainment /ə'teinmənt/ *n.* logro; *(pl.)* dotes *f.pl.*

attempt /ə'tɛmpt/ *n.* **1.** ensayo; esfuerzo *m.;* tentativa *f.* —*v.* **2.** ensayar, intentar.

attend /ə'tɛnd/ *v.* atender; (a meeting) asistir a.

attendance /ə'tɛndəns/ *n.* asistencia; presencia *f.*

attendant /ə'tɛndənt/ *a.* **1.** concomitante. —*n.* **2.** servidor -ra.

attention /ə'tɛnʃən/ *n.* atención *f.;* obsequio *m.* **to pay a. to,** hacer caso a.

attentive /ə'tɛntɪv/ *a.* atento.

attentively /ə'tɛntɪvli/ *adv.* atentamente.

attenuate /ə'tɛnyu,eit/ *v.* atenuar, adelgazar.

attest /ə'tɛst/ *v.* confirmar, atestiguar.

attic /'ætɪk/ *n.* desván *m.,* guardilla *f.*

attire /ə'taiᵊr/ *n.* **1.** traje *m.* —*v.* **2.** vestir.

attitude /'ætɪ,tud/ *n.* actitud *f.,* ademán *m.*

attorney /ə'tɜrni/ *n.* abogado -da, apoderado -da.

attract /ə'trækt/ *v.* atraer. **a. attention,** llamar la atención.

attraction /ə'trækʃən/ *n.* atracción *f.,* atractivo *m.*

attractive /ə'træktɪv/ *a.* atractivo; simpático.

attributable /ə'trɪbyutəbəl/ *a.* atribuible, imputable.

attribute /*n* 'ætrə,byut; *v* ə'trɪbyut/ *n.* **1.** atributo *m.* —*v.* **2.** atribuir.

attrition /ə'trɪʃən/ *n.* roce, desgaste *m.;* atrición *f.*

attune /ə'tun/ *v.* armonizar.

auction /'ɔkʃən/ *n.* subasta *f.,* S.A. venduta *f.*

auctioneer /,ɔkʃə'nɪər/ *n.* subastador -ra, S.A. martillero -ra.

audacious /ɔ'deiʃəs/ *a.* audaz.

audacity /ɔ'dæsɪti/ *n.* audacia *f.*

audible /'ɔdəbəl/ *a.* audible.

audience /'ɔdiəns/ *n.* auditorio, público *m.;* entrevista *f.*

audiovisual /,ɔdiou'vɪʒuəl/ *a.* audiovisual.

audit /'ɔdɪt/ *n.* **1.** revisión de cuentas *f.* —*v.* **2.** revisar cuentas.

audition /ɔ'dɪʃən/ *n.* audición *f.*

auditor /'ɔdɪtər/ *n.* interventor -ora, revisor -ora.

auditorium /,ɔdɪ'tɔriəm/ *n.* sala *f.;* teatro *m.*

auditory /'ɔdɪ,tɔri/ *a. & n.* auditorio *m.*

augment /ɔg'mɛnt/ *v.* aumentar.

augur /'ɔgər/ *v.* augurar, pronosticar.

August /'ɔgəst/ *n.* agosto *m.*

aunt /ænt, ɑnt/ *n.* tía *f.*

auspice /'ɔspɪs/ *n.* auspicio *m.*

auspicious /ɔ'spɪʃəs/ *a.* favorable; propicio.

austere /ɔ'stɪər/ *a.* austero.

austerity /ɔ'stɛrɪti/ *n.* austeridad, severidad *f.*

Austrian /'ɔstriən/ *a. & n.* austríaco -ca.

authentic /ɔ'θɛntɪk/ *a.* auténtico.

authenticate /ɔ'θɛntɪ,keit/ *v.* autenticar.

authenticity /,ɔθɛn'tɪsɪti/ *n.* autenticidad *f.*

author /'ɔθər/ *n.* autor -ra, escritor -ra.

authoritarian /ə,θɔrɪ'tɛəriən/ *a. & n.* autoritario -ria.

authoritative /ə'θɔrɪ,teitɪv/ *a.* autoritativo; autorizado.

authoritatively /ə'θɔrɪ,teitɪvli/ *adv.* autoritativamente.

authority /ə'θɔrɪti/ *n.* autoridad *f.*

authorization /,ɔθərə'zeiʃən/ *n.* autorización *f.*

authorize /'ɔθə,raiz/ *v.* autorizar.

auto /'ɔtou/ *n.* auto, automóvil *m.*

autobiography /,ɔtəbai'ɒgrəfi/ *n.* autobiografía *f.*

autocracy /ɔ'tɒkrəsi/ *n.* autocracia *f.*

autocrat /'ɔtə,kræt/ *n.* autócrata *m. & f.*

autograph /'ɔtə,græf/ *n.* autógrafo *m.*

automatic /,ɔtə'mætɪk/ *a.* automático.

automatically /ˌɔtəˈmætɪkəli/ *adv.* automáticamente.

automobile /ˌɔtəməˈbil/ *n.* automóvil, coche *m.*

automotive /ˌɔtəˈmoutɪv/ *a.* automotriz.

autonomy /ɔˈtɒnəmi/ *n.* autonomía *f.*

autopsy /ˈɔtɒpsi/ *n.* autopsia *f.*

autumn /ˈɔtəm/ *n.* otoño *m.*

auxiliary /ɔɡˈzɪlyəri/ *a.* auxiliar.

avail /əˈveil/ *n.* **1. of no a.,** en vano. —*v.* **2. a. oneself of,** aprovecharse.

available /əˈveiləbəl/ *a.* disponible.

avalanche /ˈævəˌlæntʃ/ *n.* alud *m.*

avarice /ˈævərɪs/ *n.* avaricia, codicia *f.*

avariciously /ˌævəˈrɪʃəsli/ *adv.* avaramente.

avenge /əˈvɛndʒ/ *v.* vengar.

avenger /əˈvɛndʒər/ *n.* vengador -ra.

avenue /ˈævəˌnu/ *n.* avenida *f.*

average /ˈævərɪdʒ/ *a.* **1.** medio; común. —*n.* **2.** promedio, término medio *m.* —*v.* **3.** calcular el promedio.

averse /əˈvɜrs/ *a.* **to be a. to,** tener antipatía a, opuesto a.

aversion /əˈvɜrʒən/ *n.* aversión *f.*

avert /əˈvɜrt/ *v.* desviar; impedir.

aviary /ˈeivi.ɛri/ *n.* pajarera, avería *f.*

aviation /ˌeiviˈeiʃən/ *n.* aviación *f.*

aviator /ˈeivi.eitər/ *n.* aviador -ra.

aviatrix /ˌeiviˈeitrɪks/ *n.* aviatriz *f.*

avid /ˈævɪd/ *a.* ávido.

avocado /ˌævəˈkɑdou, ˌɑvə-/ *n.* aguacate *m.*

avocation /ˌævəˈkeiʃən/ *n.* pasatiempo *f.*

avoid /əˈvɔid/ *v.* evitar.

avoidable /əˈvɔidəbəl/ *a.* evitable.

avoidance /əˈvɔidn̩s/ *n.* evitación *f.; Leg.* anulación *f.*

avow /əˈvau/ *v.* declarar; admitir.

avowal /əˈvauəl/ *n.* admisión *f.*

avowed /əˈvaud/ *a.* reconocido; admitido.

avowedly /əˈvauɪdli/ *adv.* reconocidamente; confesadamente.

await /əˈweit/ *v.* esperar, aguardar.

awake /əˈweik/ *a.* despierto.

awaken /əˈweikən/ *v.* despertar.

award /əˈwɔrd/ *n.* **1.** premio *m.* —*v.* **2.** otorgar.

aware /əˈwɛər/ *a.* enterado, consciente.

awash /əˈwɒʃ/ *a. & adv. Naut.* a flor de agua.

away /əˈwei/ *adv.* (see under verb: **go away, put away, take away,** etc.)

awe /ɔ/ *n.* pavor *m.*

awesome /ˈɔsəm/ *a.* pavoroso; aterrador.

awful /ˈɔfəl/ *a.* horrible, terrible, muy malo, pésimo.

awhile /əˈwail/ *adv.* por un rato.

awkward /ˈɔkwərd/ *a.* torpe, desmañado; *Fig.* delicado, embarazoso.

awning /ˈɔnɪŋ/ *n.* toldo *m.*

awry /əˈrai/ *a.* oblicuo, torcido.

ax /æks/ *n.* hacha *f.*

axiom /ˈæksiəm/ *n.* axioma *m.*

axis /ˈæksɪs/ *n.* eje *m.*

axle /ˈæksəl/ *n.* eje *m.*

ayatollah /ˌayəˈtoulə/ *n.* ayatolá *m.*

azure /ˈæʒər/ *a.* azul.

B

---

babble /ˈbæbəl/ *n.* **1.** balbuceo, murmullo *m.* —*v.* **2.** balbucear.

babbler /ˈbæblər/ *n.* hablador -ra, charlador -ra.

baboon /bæˈbun/ *n.* mandril *m.*

baby /ˈbeibi/ *n.* nene, bebé *m.*

baby carriage cochecito de niño *m.*

babyish /ˈbeibiɪʃ/ *a.* infantil.

baby squid /skwɪd/ chipirón *m.*

bachelor /ˈbætʃələr/ *n.* soltero *m.*

bacillus /bəˈsɪləs/ *n.* bacilo, microbio *m.*

back /bæk/ *adv.* **1.** atrás. **to be**

b., estar de vuelta. **b. of,** detrás de. —*n.* **2.** espalda *f.;* (of animal) lomo *m.*

backache /ˈbæk.eik/ *n.* dolor de espalda *m.*

backbone /ˈbæk.boun/ *n.* espinazo *m.; Fig.* firmeza *f.*

backer /ˈbækər/ *n.* sostenedor -ra.

background /ˈbæk.graund/ *n.* fondo *m.* antecedentes *m.pl.*

backing /ˈbækɪŋ/ *n.* apoyo *m.,* garantía *f.*

backlash /ˈbæk.læʃ/ *n.* repercusión negativa.

backlog /'bæk,lɔg/ n. atrasos m.pl.

backpack /'bæk,pæk/ n. mochila f.

back seat asiento trasero m.

backstage /'bæk'steidʒ/ n. entre bastidores m.

backup /'bæk,ʌp/ n. copia de seguridad f.

backward /'bækwərd/ a. **1.** atrasado. —adv. **2.** hacia atrás.

backwardness /'bækwərdnis/ n. atraso m.

backwater /'bæk,wɔtər/ n. parte de río estancada f.

backwoods /'bæk'wudz/ n. región del monte apartada f.

bacon /'beikən/ n. tocino m.

bacteria /bæk'tɪəriə/ n. bacterias f.pl.

bacteriologist /,bæktɪəri'ɒlədʒɪst/ n. bacteriólogo -a.

bacteriology /,bæktɪəri'ɒlədʒi/ n. bacteriología f.

bad /bæd/ a. malo.

badge /bædʒ/ n. insignia, divisa f.

badger /'bædʒər/ n. **1.** tejón m. —v. **2.** atormentar.

badly /'bædli/ adv. mal.

badness /'bædnis/ n. maldad f.

bad-tempered /'bæd'tɛmpərd/ a. de mal humor.

baffle /'bæfəl/ v. desconcertar.

bafflement /'bæfəlmənt/ n. contrariedad; confusión f.

bag /bæg/ n. **1.** saco m.; bolsa f. —v. **2.** ensacar, cazar.

baggage /'bægɪdʒ/ n. equipaje m. **b. check,** talón m.

baggage cart (airport) carrillo para llevar equipaje.

baggy /'bægi/ a. abotagado; bolsudo; hinchado.

bagpipe /'bæg,paip/ n. gaita f.

bail /beil/ n. **1.** fianza f. —v. **2.** desaguar.

bailiff /'beilif/ n. alguacil m.

bait /beit/ n. **1.** cebo m. —v. **2.** cebar.

bake /beik/ v. cocer en horno.

baked potato /beikt/ patata asada f.

baker /'beikər/ n. panadero -ra, hornero -ra.

bakery /'beikəri, 'beikri/ n. panadería f.

baking /'beikɪŋ/ n. hornada f. **b. powder,** levadura f.

balance /'bæləns/ n. balanza f.; equilibrio m.; Com. saldo m.

balcony /'bælkəni/ n. balcón m.; Theat. galería f.

bald /bɔld/ a. calvo.

baldness /'bɔldnis/ n. calvicie f.

bale /beil/ n. **1.** bala f. —v. **2.** embalar.

balk /bɔk/ v. frustrar; rebelarse.

Balkans /'bɔlkənz/ n.pl. Balcanes m.pl.

balky /'bɔki/ a. rebelón.

ball /bɔl/ n. bola, pelota f.; (dance) baile m.

ballad /'bæləd/ n. romance, m.; balada f.

ballast /'bæləst/ n. **1.** lastre m. —v. **2.** lastrar.

ball bearing cojinete de bolas m.

ballerina /,bælə'rinə/ n. bailarina f.

ballet /bæ'lei/ n. danza f.; ballet m.

ballistics /bə'lɪstɪks/ n. balística f.

balloon /bə'lun/ n. globo m. **b. tire,** neumático de balón.

ballot /'bælət/ n. **1.** balota f., voto m. —v. **2.** balotar, votar.

ballpoint pen /'bɔl,pɔint/ bolígrafo m.

ballroom /'bɔl,rum/ n. salón de baile m.

balm /bam/ n. bálsamo; ungüento m.

balmy /'bami/ a. fragante; reparador; calmante.

balsa /'bɔlsə/ n. balsa f.

balsam /'bɔlsəm/ n. bálsamo m.

balustrade /'bælə,streid/ n. barandilla f.

bamboo /bæm'bu/ n. bambú m., caña f.

ban /bæn/ n. **1.** prohibición f. —v. **2.** prohibir; proscribir.

banal /bə'næl/ a. trivial; vulgar.

banana /bə'nænə/ n. banana f., cambur m. **b. tree,** banano, plátano m.

band /bænd/ n. **1.** banda f.; (of men) banda, cuadrilla, partida f. —v. **2.** asociarse.

bandage /'bændɪdʒ/ n. **1.** vendaje m. —v. **2.** vendar.

bandanna /bæn'dænə/ n. pañuelo (grande) m.; bandana f.

bandbox /'bænd,bɒks/ n. caja de cartón.

bandit /'bændɪt/ n. bandido -da.

bandmaster /'bænd,mæstər/ n. director de una banda musical m.

bandstand /'bænd,stænd/ n. kiosco de música.

bang /bæŋ/ *interj.* **1.** ¡pum! —*n.*
2. ruido de un golpe. —*v.* **3.** golpear ruidosamente.
banish /'bænɪʃ/ *v.* desterrar.
banishment /'bænɪʃmənt/ *n.* destierro *m.*
banister /'bænəstər/ *n.* pasa-
manos *m.pl.*
bank /bæŋk/ *n.* **1.** banco *m.;* (of a
river) margen *f.* —*v.* **2.** depositar.
bank account cuenta bancaria *f.*
bankbook /'bæŋk,bʊk/ *n.* libreta
de depósitos *f.*
bank card tarjeta bancaria *f.*
banker /'bæŋkər/ *n.* banquero -ra.
banking /'bæŋkɪŋ/ *a.* bancaria. *n.*
banca *f.*
bank note billete de banco *m.*
bankrupt /'bæŋkrʌpt/ *a.* insolvente.
bankruptcy /'bæŋkrʌptsi/ *n.* bancarrota *f.*
banner /'bænər/ *n.* bandera *f.;* estandarte *m.*
banquet /'bæŋkwɪt/ *n.* banquete
m.
banter /'bæntər/ *n.* **1.** choteo *m.;*
zumba; burla *f.* —*v.* **2.** chotear;
zumbar; burlarse.
baptism /'bæptɪzəm/ *n.* bautismo,
bautizo *m.*
baptismal /bæp'tɪzməl/ *a.* bautis-
mal.
Baptist /'bæptɪst/ *n.* bautista *m.* &
f.
baptize /bæp'taiz, 'bæptaiz/ *v.*
bautizar.
bar /bɑr/ *n.* **1.** barra *f.;* obstáculo
m.; (tavern) taberna *f.,* bar *m.*
—*v.* **2.** barrear; prohibir, excluir.
barbarian /bɑr'bɛəriən/ *a.* bárbaro. *n.* bárbaro -ra.
barbarism /'bɑrbə,rɪzəm/ *n.* bar-
barismo *m.,* barbarie *f.*
barbarous /'bɑrbərəs/ *a.* bárbaro,
cruel.
barbecue /'bɑrbɪ,kyu/ *n.* animal
asado entero; (Mex.) barbacoa *f.*
barber /'bɑrbər/ *n.* barbero *m.* **b.
shop,** barbería *f.*
barbiturate /bɑr'bɪtʃərɪt/ *n.* bar-
bitúrico *m.*
bar code código de barras *m.*
bare /bɛər/ *a.* **1.** desnudo; descubierto. —*v.* **2.** desnudar; descubrir.
bareback /'bɛər,bæk/ *adv.* sin
silla.
barefoot(ed) /'bɛər,fʊtɪd/ *a.* descalzo.

barely /'bɛərli/ *adv.* escasamente,
apenas.
bareness /'bɛərnɪs/ *n.* desnudez
f.; pobreza *f.*
bargain /'bɑrgən/ *n.* **1.** ganga *f.,*
compra ventajosa *f.;* contrato *m.*
—*v.* **2.** regatear; negociar.
barge /bɑrdʒ/ *n.* lanchón *m.,* barcaza *f.*
baritone /'bærɪ,toun/ *n.* barítono
m.
barium /'bɛəriəm/ *n.* bario *m.*
bark /bɑrk/ *n.* **1.** corteza *f.;* (of
dog) ladrido *f.* —*v.* **2.** ladrar.
barley /'bɑrli/ *n.* cebada *f.*
barn /bɑrn/ *n.* granero *m.*
barnacle /'bɑrnəkəl/ *n.* lapa *f.*
barnyard /'bɑrn,yɑrd/ *n.* corral *m.*
barometer /bə'rɒmɪtər/ *n.* barómetro *m.*
barometric /,bærə'mɛtrɪk/ *a.*
barométrico.
baron /'bærən/ *n.* barón *m.*
baroness /'bærənɪs/ *n.* baronesa *f.*
baronial /bə'rouniəl/ *a.* baronial.
baroque /bə'rouk/ *a.* barroco.
barracks /'bærəks/ *n.* cuartel *m.*
barrage /bə'rɑʒ/ *n.* cortina de
fuego *f.*
barred /bɑrd/ *a.* excluído; prohi-
bido.
barrel /'bærəl/ *n.* barril *m.;* (of
gun) cañón *m.*
barren /'bærən/ *a.* estéril.
barrenness /'bærən,nɪs/ *n.* esterilidad *f.*
barricade /'bærɪ,keid/ *n.* barricada, barrera *f.*
barrier /'bæriər/ *n.* barrera *f.;*
obstáculo *m.*
barroom /'bɑr,rum, -,rʊm/ *n.* cantina *f.*
bartender /'bɑr,tɛndər/ *n.* taber-
nero; cantinero *m.*
barter /'bɑrtər/ *n.* **1.** cambio,
trueque *m.* —*v.* **2.** cambiar, trocar.
base /beis/ *a.* **1.** bajo, vil. —*n.* **2.**
base *f.* —*v.* **3.** basar.
baseball /'beis,bɔl/ *n.* béisbol *m.*
baseboard /'beis,bɔrd/ *n.* tabla de
resguardo.
basement /'beismənt/ *n.* sótano
m.
baseness /'beisnɪs/ *n.* bajeza,
vileza *f.*
bashful /'bæʃfəl/ *a.* vergonzoso,
tímido.
bashfully /'bæʃfəli/ *adv.* tímidamente; vergonzosamente.

bashfulness /'bæʃfəlnɪs/ *n.* vergüenza; timidez *f.*

basic /'beisɪk/ *a.* fundamental, básico.

basin /'beisən/ *n.* bacía *f.;* (of river) cuenca *f.*

basis /'beisɪs/ *n.* base *f.*

bask /bæsk/ *v.* tomar el sol.

basket /'bæskɪt/ *n.* cesta, canasta *f.*

bass /bæs; beis/ *n.* (fish) lobina *f.; Mus.* bajo profundo *m.* **b. viol.** violón *m.*

bassinet /ˌbæsə'nɛt/ *n.* bacinete *m.*

bassoon /bæ'sun/ *n.* bajón *m.*

bastard /'bæstərd/ *a. & n.* bastardo -da; hijo -a natural.

baste /beist/ *v.* (sew) bastear; (cooking) pringar.

bat /bæt/ *n.* **1.** (animal) murciélago *m.;* (baseball) bate *m.* —*v.* **2.** batear.

batch /bætʃ/ *n.* cantidad de cosas.

bath /bæθ/ *n.* baño *m.*

bathe /beið/ *v.* bañar, bañarse.

bather /'beiðər/ *n.* bañista *m. & f.*

bathing resort /'beiðɪŋ/ balneario *m.*

bathing suit /'beiðɪŋ/ traje de baño.

bathrobe /'bæθˌroub/ *n.* bata de baño *f.*

bathroom /'bæθˌrum, -ˌrʊm/ *n.* cuarto de baño.

bathtub /'bæθˌtʌb/ *n.* bañera *f.*

baton /bə'tɒn/ *n.* bastón *m.; Mus.* batuta *f.*

battalion /bə'tælyən/ *n.* batallón *m.*

batter /'bætər/ *n.* **1.** (cooking) batido *m.;* (baseball) voleador *m.* —*v.* **2.** batir; derribar.

battery /'bætəri/ *n.* batería; *Elec.* pila *f.*

batting /'bætɪŋ/ *n.* agramaje, moldeaje *m.*

battle /'bætḷ/ *n.* **1.** batalla *f.;* combate *m.* —*v.* **2.** batallar.

battlefield /'bætḷˌfild/ *n.* campo de batalla.

battleship /'bætḷˌʃɪp/ *n.* acorazado *m.*

bauxite /'bɔksait, 'bouzait/ *n.* bauxita *f.*

bawl /bɔl/ *v.* gritar; vocear.

bay /bei/ *n.* bahía *f. v.* aullar.

bayonet /'beiənɛt/ *n.* bayoneta *f.*

bazaar /bə'zɑr/ *n.* bazar *m.,* feria *f.*

BC *abbr.* (**before Christ**) a.C. (antes de Cristo).

be /bi/ *v.* ser; estar. (See **hacer; hay; tener** in Sp.-Eng. section.)

beach /bitʃ/ *n.* playa *f.*

beachcomber /'bitʃˌkoumər/ *n.* raquero -ra *m. & f.*

beacon /'bikən/ *n.* faro *m.*

bead /bid/ *n.* cuenta *f.; pl. Relig.* rosario *m.*

beading /'bidɪŋ/ *n.* abalorio *m.*

beady /'bidi/ *a.* globuloso; burbujoso.

beak /bik/ *n.* pico *m.*

beaker /'bikər/ *n.* vaso con pico *m.*

beam /bim/ *n.* viga *f.;* (of wood) madero *m.;* (of light) rayo *m.*

beaming /'bimɪŋ/ *a.* radiante.

bean /bin/ *n.* haba, habichuela *f.,* frijol *m.*

bear /bɛər/ *n.* **1.** oso -sa. —*v.* **2.** llevar; (endure) aguantar.

bearable /'bɛərəbəl/ *a.* sufrible; soportable.

beard /bɪərd/ *n.* barba *f.*

bearded /'bɪərdɪd/ *a.* barbado; barbudo.

beardless /'bɪərdlɪs/ *a.* lampiño; imberbe.

bearer /'bɛərər/ *n.* portador -ra.

bearing /'bɛərɪŋ/ *n.* porte, aguante *m.*

bearskin /'bɛərˌskɪn/ *n.* piel de oso *f.*

beast /bist/ *n.* bestia *f.;* bruto -ta.

beat /bit/ *v.* golpear; batir; pulsar; (in games) ganar, vencer.

beaten /'bitṇ/ *a.* vencido; batido.

beatify /bi'ætəˌfai/ *v.* beatificar.

beating /'bitɪŋ/ *n.* paliza *f.*

beau /bou/ *n.* novio *m.*

beautiful /'byutəfəl/ *a.* hermoso, bello.

beautifully /'byutəfəli/ *adv.* bellamente.

beautify /'byutəˌfai/ *v.* embellecer.

beauty /'byuti/ *n.* hermosura, belleza *f.* **b. parlor,** salón de belleza.

beaver /'bivər/ *n.* castor *m.*

becalm /bɪ'kɑm/ *v.* calmar; sosegar; encalmarse.

because /bɪ'kɔz/ *conj.* porque. **b. of,** a causa de.

beckon /'bɛkən/ *v.* hacer señas.

become /bɪ'kʌm/ *v.* hacerse; ponerse.

becoming /bɪ'kʌmɪŋ/ *a.* propio,

correcto; **be b.,** quedar bien, sentar bien.

bed /bɛd/ n. cama f.; lecho m.; (of river) cauce m.

bedbug /'bɛd,bʌg/ n. chinche m.

bedclothes /'bɛd,klouz, -,klouðz/ n. ropa de cama f.

bedding /'bɛdɪŋ/ n. colchones m.pl.

bedfellow /'bɛd,fɛlou/ n. compañero -ra de cama.

bedizen /bɪ'daizən, -'dɪzən/ v. adornar; aderezar.

bedridden /'bɛd,rɪdn̩/ a. postrado (en cama).

bedrock /'bɛd,rɒk/ n. (mining) lecho de roca m.; Fig. fundamento m.

bedroom /'bɛd,rum/ n. alcoba f.; (Mex.) recámara f.

bedside /'bɛd,said/ n. al lado de una cama m.

bedspread /'bɛd,sprɛd/ n. cubrecama, sobrecama f.

bedstead /'bɛd,stɛd/ n. armadura de cama f.

bedtime /'bɛd,taim/ n. hora de acostarse.

bee /bi/ n. abeja f.

beef /bif/ n. carne de vaca.

beefburger /'bif,bɜrgər/ n. hamburguesa f.

beefsteak /'bif,steik/ n. bistec, bisté m.

beehive /'bi,haiv/ n. colmena f.

beer /bɪər/ n. cerveza f.

beeswax /'biz,wæks/ n. cera de abejas.

beet /bit/ n. remolacha f.; (Mex.) betabel m.

beetle /'bitl̩/ n. escarabajo m.

befall /bɪ'fɔl/ v. suceder, sobrevenir.

befitting /bɪ'fɪtɪŋ/ a. conveniente; propio; digno.

before /bɪ'fɔr/ adv. antes. prep. antes de; (in front of) delante de. conj. antes que.

beforehand /bɪ'fɔr,hænd/ adv. de antemano.

befriend /bɪ'frɛnd/ v. amparar.

befuddle /bɪ'fʌdl̩/ v. confundir; aturdir.

beg /bɛg/ v. rogar, suplicar; (for alms) mendigar.

beget /bɪ'gɛt/ v. engendrar; producir.

beggar /'bɛgər/ n. mendigo -ga; S.A. limosnero -ra.

beggarly /'bɛgərli/ a. pobre, miserable.

begin /bɪ'gɪn/ v. empezar, comenzar, principiar.

beginner /bɪ'gɪnər/ n. principiante -ta.

beginning /bɪ'gɪnɪŋ/ n. principio, comienzo m.

begrudge /bɪ'grʌdʒ/ v. envidiar.

behalf /bɪ'hæf/ n.: **in, on b. of,** a favor de, en pro de.

behave /bɪ'heiv/ v. portarse, comportarse.

behavior /bɪ'heivyər/ n. conducta f.; comportamiento m.

behead /bɪ'hɛd/ v. decapitar.

behind /bɪ'haind/ adv. atrás, detrás. prep. detrás de.

behold /bɪ'hould/ v. contemplar.

beige /beiʒ/ a. beige.

being /'biɪŋ/ n. existencia f.; (person) ser m.

bejewel /bɪ'dʒuəl/ v. adornar con joyas.

belated /bɪ'leitɪd/ a. atrasado, tardío.

belch /bɛltʃ/ n. **1.** eructo m. —v. **2.** vomitar; eructar.

belfry /'bɛlfri/ n. campanario m.

Belgian /'bɛldʒən/ a. & n. belga m. & f.

Belgium /'bɛldʒəm/ n. Bélgica f.

belie /bɪ'lai/ v. desmentir.

belief /bɪ'lif/ n. creencia f.; parecer m.

believable /bɪ'livəbəl/ a. creíble.

believe /bɪ'liv/ v. creer.

believer /bɪ'livər/ n. creyente m. & f.

belittle /bɪ'lɪtl̩/ v. dar poca importancia a.

bell /bɛl/ n. campana f.; (of house) campanilla f.; (electric) timbre m.

bellboy /'bɛl,bɔi/ n. mozo, botones m.

bellicose /'bɛli,kous/ a. guerrero.

belligerence /bə'lɪdʒərəns/ n. beligerancia f.

belligerent /bə'lɪdʒərənt/ a. & n. beligerante m. & f.

belligerently /bə'lɪdʒərəntli/ adv. belicosamente.

bellow /'bɛlou/ v. bramar, rugir.

bellows /'bɛlouz/ n. fuelle m.

belly /'bɛli/ n. vientre m.; panza, barriga f.

belong /bɪ'lɔŋ/ v. pertenecer.

belongings /bɪ'lɔŋɪŋz/ n. propiedad f.

beloved /bɪˈlʌvɪd/ a. querido, amado.

below /bɪˈlou/ adv. **1.** debajo, abajo. —prep. **2.** debajo de.

belt /bɛlt/ n. cinturón m.

bench /bɛntʃ/ n. banco m.

bend /bɛnd/ n. vuelta; curva f. v. encorvar, doblar.

beneath /bɪˈniθ/ adv. **1.** debajo, abajo. —prep. **2.** debajo de.

benediction /ˌbɛnɪˈdɪkʃən/ n. bendición f.

benefactor /ˈbɛnəˌfæktər/ n. bienhechor -ra.

benefactress /ˈbɛnəˌfæktrɪs/ n. bienhechora f.

beneficial /ˌbɛnəˈfɪʃəl/ a. provechoso, beneficioso.

beneficiary /ˌbɛnəˈfɪʃiˌɛri/ n. beneficiario -ria, beneficiado -da.

benefit /ˈbɛnəfɪt/ n. **1.** provecho, beneficio m. —v. **2.** beneficiar.

benevolence /bəˈnɛvələns/ n. benevolencia f.

benevolent /bəˈnɛvələnt/ a. benévolo.

benevolently /bəˈnɛvələntli/ adv. benignamente.

benign /bɪˈnain; bɪˈnɪgnənt/ a. benigno.

benignity /bɪˈnɪgnɪti/ n. benignidad; bondad f.

bent /bɛnt/ a. **1.** encorvado. **b. on,** resuelto a. —n. **2.** inclinación f.

benzene /ˈbɛnzin, bɛnˈzin/ n. benceno m.

bequeath /bɪˈkwið/ v. legar.

bequest /bɪˈkwɛst/ n. legado m.

berate /bɪˈreit/ v. reñir, regañar.

bereave /bɪˈriv/ v. despojar; desolar.

bereavement /bɪˈrivmənt/ n. privación f.; despojo m.; (mourning) luto m.

berry /ˈbɛri/ n. baya f.

berth /bɔrθ/ n. camarote m.; Naut. litera f.; (for vessel) amarradero m.

beseech /bɪˈsitʃ/ v. suplicar; implorar.

beseechingly /bɪˈsitʃɪŋli/ adv. suplicantemente.

beset /bɪˈsɛt/ v. acosar; rodear.

beside /bɪˈsaid/ prep. al lado de.

besides /bɪˈsaidz/ adv. además, por otra parte.

besiege /bɪˈsidʒ/ v. sitiar; asediar.

besieged /bɪˈsidʒd/ a. sitiado.

besieger /bɪˈsidʒər/ n. sitiador -ra.

besmirch /bɪˈsmɔrtʃ/ v. manchar; deshonrar.

best /bɛst/ a. & adv. mejor. **at b.,** a lo más.

bestial /ˈbɛstʃəl/ a. bestial; brutal.

bestir /bɪˈstɔr/ v. incitar; intrigar.

best man n. padrino de boda.

bestow /bɪˈstou/ v. conferir.

bestowal /bɪˈstouəl/ n. dádiva; presentación f.

bet /bɛt/ n. **1.** apuesta f. —v. **2.** apostar.

betoken /bɪˈtoukən/ v. presagiar, anunciar.

betray /bɪˈtrei/ v. traicionar; revelar.

betrayal /bɪˈtreiəl/ n. traición f.

betroth /bɪˈtrouð/ v. contraer esponsales; prometerse.

betrothal /bɪˈtrouðəl/ n. esponsales m.pl.

better /ˈbɛtər/ a. & adv. **1.** mejor. —v. **2.** mejorar.

between /bɪˈtwin/ prep. entre, en medio de.

bevel /ˈbɛvəl/ n. **1.** cartabón m. —v. **2.** cortar al sesgo.

beverage /ˈbɛvərɪdʒ/ n. bebida f.; (cold) refresco m.

bewail /bɪˈweil/ v. llorar; lamentar.

beware /bɪˈwɛər/ v. guardarse, precaverse.

bewilder /bɪˈwɪldər/ v. aturdir.

bewildered /bɪˈwɪldərd/ a. descarriado.

bewildering /bɪˈwɪldərɪŋ/ a. aturdente.

bewilderment /bɪˈwɪldərmənt/ n. aturdimiento m.; perplejidad f.

bewitch /bɪˈwɪtʃ/ v. hechizar; embrujar.

beyond /bɪˈɒnd/ prep. más allá de.

biannual /baiˈænyuəl/ a. semianual; semestral.

bias /ˈbaiəs/ n. **1.** parcialidad f.; prejuicio m. **on the b.,** al sesgo. —v. **2.** predisponer, influir.

bib /bɪb/ n. babador m.

Bible /ˈbaibəl/ n. Biblia f.

Biblical /ˈbɪblɪkəl/ a. bíblico.

bibliography /ˌbɪbliˈɒɡrəfi/ n. bibliografía f.

bicarbonate /baiˈkɑrbənɪt/ n. bicarbonato m.

bicentennial /ˌbaisɛnˈtɛniəl/ a. & n. bicentenario m.

biceps /ˈbaisɛps/ n. bíceps m.

bicker /ˈbɪkər/ v. altercar.

bicycle /'baɪsɪkəl/ n. bicicleta f.
bicyclist /'baɪsɪklɪst/ n. biciclista m. & f.
bid /bɪd/ n. **1.** proposición, oferta f. —v. **2.** mandar; ofrecer.
bidder /'bɪdər/ n. postor -ra.
bide /baɪd/ v. aguardar; esperar.
bier /bɪər/ n. ataúd m.
bifocal /baɪ'foukəl/ a. bifocal.
big /bɪg/ a. grande.
bigamist /'bɪgəmɪst/ n. bígamo -ma.
bigamy /'bɪgəmi/ n. bigamia f.
bigot /'bɪgət/ n. persona intolerante.
bigotry /'bɪgətri/ n. intolerancia f.
bikini /bɪ'kini/ n. bikini m.
bilateral /baɪ'lætərəl/ a. bilateral.
bile /baɪl/ n. bilis f.
bilingual /baɪ'lɪŋgwəl/ a. bilingüe.
bilingualism /baɪ'lɪŋgwə,lɪzəm/ n. bilingüismo m.
bilious /'bɪlyəs/ a. bilioso.
bill /bɪl/ **1.** n. cuenta, factura f.; (money) billete m.; (of bird) pico m. —v. **2.** facturar.
billboard /'bɪl,bɔrd/ n. cartelera f.
billet /'bɪlɪt/ n. **1.** billete m.; Mil. boleta f. —v. **2.** aposentar.
billfold /'bɪl,fould/ n. cartera f.
billiard balls /'bɪlyərd bɔlz/ bolas de billar.
billiards /'bɪlyərdz/ n. billar m.
billion /'bɪlyən/ n. billón m.
bill of health n. certificado de sanidad.
bill of lading /'leɪdɪŋ/ n. conocimiento de embarque.
bill of sale n. escritura de venta.
billow /'bɪlou/ n. ola; oleada f.
bimetallic /,baɪmə'tælɪk/ a. bimetálico.
bimonthly /baɪ'mʌnθli/ a. & adv. bimestral.
bin /bɪn/ n. hucha f.; depósito m.
bind /baɪnd/ v. atar; obligar; (book) encuadernar.
bindery /'baɪndəri/ n. taller de encuadernación m.
binding /'baɪndɪŋ/ n. encuadernación f.
bingo /'bɪŋgou/ n. bingo m.
binocular /bə'nɒkyələr/ a. binocular. n.pl. gemelos m.pl.
biochemistry /,baɪou'kɛməstri/ n. bioquímica f.
biodegradable /,baɪoudɪ'greɪdəbəl/ a. biodegradable.
biofeedback /,baɪou'fid,bæk/ n. biofeedback.

biographer /baɪ'ɒgrəfər/ n. biógrafo -fa.
biographical /,baɪə'græfɪkəl/ a. biográfico.
biography /baɪ'ɒgrəfi/ n. biografía f.
biological /,baɪə'lɒdʒɪkəl/ a. biológico.
biologically /,baɪə'lɒdʒɪkəli/ adv. biológicamente.
biology /baɪ'ɒlədʒi/ n. biología f.
bipartisan /baɪ'pɑrtəzən/ a. bipartito.
biped /'baɪpɛd/ n. bípedo m.
bird /bɜrd/ n. pájaro m.; ave f.
birdie /'bɜrdi/ n. (golf) uno bajo par m.
bird of prey n. ave de rapiña f.
bird's-eye view /'bɜrdz,aɪ/ n. vista de pájaro f.
birth /bɜrθ/ n. nacimiento m. **give b. to,** dar a luz.
birth certificate partida de nacimiento f.
birth control n. contracepción f.
birthday /'bɜrθ,deɪ/ n. cumpleaños m.
birthmark /'bɜrθ,mɑrk/ n. marca de nacimiento f.
birthplace /'bɜrθ,pleɪs/ n. natalicio m.
birth rate n. natalidad f.
birthright /'bɜrθ,raɪt/ n. primogenitura f.
biscuit /'bɪskɪt/ n. bizcocho m.
bisect /baɪ'sɛkt/ v. bisecar.
bishop /'bɪʃəp/ n. obispo m.; (chess) alfil m.
bishopric /'bɪʃəprɪk/ n. obispado m.
bismuth /'bɪzməθ/ n. bismuto m.
bison /'baɪsən/ n. bisonte m.
bit /bɪt/ n. pedacito m.; Mech. taladro m.; (for horse) bocado m.; (computer) bit m.
bitch /bɪtʃ/ n. perra f.
bite /baɪt/ n. **1.** bocado m.; picada f. —v. **2.** morder; picar.
biting /'baɪtɪŋ/ a. penetrante; mordaz.
bitter /'bɪtər/ a. amargo.
bitterly /'bɪtərli/ adv. amargamente; agriamente.
bitterness /'bɪtərnɪs/ n. amargura f.; rencor m.
bivouac /'bɪvu,æk/ n. **1.** vivaque m. —v. **2.** vivaquear.
biweekly /baɪ'wikli/ a. quincenal.
black /blæk/ a. negro.

Black /blæk/ n. (person) negro -gra; persona de color.

blackberry /'blæk,bɛri/ n. mora f.

blackbird /'blæk,bərd/ n. mirlo m.

blackboard /'blæk,bɔrd/ n. pizarra f.

blacken /'blækən/ v. ennegrecer.

black eye n. ojo amoratado.

blackguard /'blægard/ n. tunante; pillo m.

blacklist /'blæk,lɪst/ n. lista negra f.

blackmail /'blæk,meil/ n. **1.** chantaje m. —v. **2.** amenazar con chantaje, chantajear.

black market mercado negro, estraperlo m.

black marketeer /,markɪ'tir/ estraperlista mf.

blackout /'blæk,aut/ n. oscurecimiento, apagamiento m.

blacksmith /'blæk,smɪθ/ n. herrero -ra.

bladder /'blædər/ n. vejiga f.

blade /bleid/ n. (sword) hoja f.; (oar) pala f.; (grass) brizna f.

blame /bleim/ v. culpar, echar la culpa a.

blameless /'bleimlɪs/ a. inculpable.

blanch /blæntʃ/ v. blanquear; escaldar.

bland /blænd/ a. blando.

blank /blæŋk/ a. & n. en blanco.

blanket /'blæŋkɪt/ n. manta f.; cobertor m.

blare /blɛər/ n. sonido de trompeta. v. sonar como trompeta.

blaspheme /blæs'fim/ v. blasfemar.

blasphemer /blæs'fimər/ n. blasfemo -ma, blasfemador -ra.

blasphemous /'blæsfəməs/ a. blasfemo, impío.

blasphemy /'blæsfəmi/ n. blasfemia f.

blast /blæst/ n. **1.** barreno m.; (wind) ráfaga f. —v. **2.** barrenar.

blatant /'bleitnt/ a. bramante; descarado.

blaze /bleiz/ n. **1.** llama, hoguera f. —v. **2.** encenderse en llama.

blazing /'bleizɪŋ/ a. flameante.

bleach /blitʃ/ n. **1.** lejía, blanqueador. —v. **2.** blanquear.

bleachers /'blitʃərz/ n. asientos al aire libre.

bleak /blik/ a. frío y sombrío.

bleakness /'bliknɪs/ n. desolación f.

bleed /blid/ v. sangrar.

blemish /'blɛmɪʃ/ n. **1.** mancha f.; lunar m. —v. **2.** manchar.

blend /blɛnd/ n. **1.** mezcla f. —v. **2.** mezclar, combinar.

blended /'blɛndɪd/ a. mezclado.

blender /'blɛndər/ n. (for food) licuadora f.

bless /blɛs/ v. bendecir.

blessed /'blɛsɪd/ a. bendito.

blessing /'blɛsɪŋ/ a. bendición f.

blight /blait/ n. **1.** plaga f.; tizón m. —v. **2.** atizonar.

blind /blaind/ a. ciego.

blindfold /'blaind,fould/ v. vendar los ojos.

blinding /'blaindɪŋ/ a. deslumbrante; ofuscante.

blindly /'blaindli/ adv. ciegamente.

blindness /'blaindnɪs/ n. ceguedad, ceguera f.

blink /blɪŋk/ n. **1.** guiñada f. —v. **2.** guiñar.

bliss /blɪs/ n. felicidad f.

blissful /'blɪsfəl/ a. dichoso; bienaventurado.

blissfully /'blɪsfəli/ adv. felizmente.

blister /'blɪstər/ n. ampolla f.

blithe /blaið/ a. alegre; jovial; gozoso.

blizzard /'blɪzərd/ n. nevasca f.

bloat /blout/ v. hinchar.

bloc /blɒk/ n. grupo (político); bloc.

block /blɒk/ n. **1.** bloque m.; (street) manzana, cuadra f. —v. **2.** bloquear.

blockade /blɒ'keid/ n. **1.** bloqueo m. —v. **2.** bloquear.

blond /blɒnd/ a. & n. rubio -ia.

blood /blʌd/ n. sangre f.; parentesco, linaje m.

bloodhound /'blʌd,haund/ n. sabueso m.

bloodless /'blʌdlɪs/ a. exangüe; desangrado.

blood poisoning /'pɔizənɪŋ/ envenenamiento de sangre.

blood pressure presión arterial.

bloodshed /'blʌd,ʃɛd/ n. matanza f.

bloodthirsty /'blʌd,θərsti/ a. cruel, sanguinario.

bloody /'blʌdi/ a. ensangrentado, sangriento.

bloom /blum/ n. **1.** flor f. —v. **2.** florecer.

blooming /'blumɪŋ/ a. lozano; fresco; floreciente.

blossom /'blɒsəm/ n. **1.** flor f.
—v. **2.** florecer.

blot /blɒt/ n. **1.** mancha f. —v. **2.**
manchar.

blotch /blɒtʃ/ n. **1.** mancha,
roncha f. —v. **2.** manchar.

blotter /'blɒtər/ n. papel secante.

blouse /blaus/ n. blusa f.

blow /blou/ n. **1.** golpe m.; Fig.
chasco m. —v. **2.** soplar.

blowout /'blou,aut/ n. reventón
de neumático m.

blubber /'blʌbər/ n. grasa de ballena.

bludgeon /'blʌdʒən/ n. porra f. v.
apalear.

blue /blu/ a. azul; triste, melancólico.

bluebird /'blu,bɜrd/ n. azulejo m.

blue jeans jeans; vaqueros m.pl.

blueprint /'blu,prɪnt/ n. heliogra-
fía f.

bluff /blʌf/ n. risco m. v. alarde-
ar; baladronar.

bluing /'bluɪŋ/ n. añil m.

blunder /'blʌndər/ n. **1.** desatino
m. —v. **2.** desatinar.

blunderer /'blʌndərər/ n. desatinado -da.

blunt /blʌnt/ a. embotado; descortés. v. embotar.

bluntly /'blʌntli/ a. bruscamente.

bluntness /'blʌntnɪs/ n. grosería
f.; brusquedad.

blur /blɜr/ n. **1.** trazo confuso.
—v. **2.** hacer indistinto.

blush /blʌʃ/ n. **1.** rubor, sonrojo
m. —v. **2.** sonrojarse.

bluster /'blʌstər/ n. **1.** fanfarria f.
—v. **2.** fanfarrear.

boar /bɔr/ n. verraco m. **wild b.,**
jabalí.

board /bɔrd/ n. **1.** tabla; Govt.
consejo m.; junta f. **b. and room,**
cuarto y comida, casa y comida.
—v. **2.** (ship) abordar.

boarder /'bɔrdər/ n. pensionista
m. & f.

boardinghouse /'bɔrdɪŋ/ n. pensión f., casa de huéspedes.

boarding pass /'bɔrdɪŋ/ boleto de
embarque m., tarjeta de embarque f.

boast /boust/ n. **1.** jactancia f.
—v. **2.** jactarse.

boaster /'boustər/ n. fanfarrón
-na.

boastful /'boustfəl/ a. jactancioso.

boastfulness /'boustfəlnɪs/ n. jactancia f.

boat /bout/ n. barco, buque, bote
m.

boathouse /'bout,haus/ n. casilla
de botes f.

boatswain /'bousən/ n. contrama-
estre m.

bob /bɒb/ v. menear.

bobbin /'bɒbɪn/ n. bobina f.

bobby pin /'bɒbi/ n. gancho m.,
horquilla.

bodice /'bɒdɪs/ n. corpiño m.

bodily /'bɒdli/ a. corporal.

body /'bɒdi/ n. cuerpo m.

body builder culturista mf.

body building culturismo m.

bodyguard /'bɒdi,gɑrd/ n. guardaespaldas.

bog /bɒg/ n. pantano m.

bogey /'bougi/ n. (golf) uno sobre
par m.

Bohemian /bou'himiən/ a. & n.
bohemio -mia.

boil /bɔil/ n. **1.** hervor m.; Med.
divieso m. —v. **2.** hervir.

boiler /'bɔilər/ n. marmita; caldera
f.

boiling point /'bɔilɪŋ/ punto de
ebullición m.

boisterous /'bɔistərəs/ a. tumultuoso.

boisterously /'bɔistərəsli/ adv. tu-
multuosamente.

bold /bould/ a. atrevido, audaz.

boldface /'bould,feis/ n. (type)
letra negra.

boldly /'bouldli/ adv. audazmente;
descaradamente.

boldness /'bouldnɪs/ n. atrevimiento m.; osadía f.

Bolivian /bou'lɪviən/ a. & n. boliviano -na.

bologna /bə'louni/ n. salchicha f.,
mortadela.

bolster /'boulstər/ n. **1.** travesero,
cojín m. —v. **2.** apoyar, sostener.

bolt /boult/ n. perno m.; (of door)
cerrojo m.; (lightning) rayo m. v.
acerrojar.

bomb /bɒm/ n. **1.** bomba f. —v.
2. bombardear.

bombard /bɒm'bɑrd/ v. bombardear.

bombardier /,bɒmbər'diər/ n.
bombardero -ra.

bombardment /bɒm'bɑrdmənt/ n.
bombardeo m.

bomber /'bɒmər/ n. avión de
bombardeo.

bombproof /'bɒm,pruf/ a. a
prueba de granadas.

bombshell /'bɒm,ʃɛl/ *n.* bomba *f.*
bonbon /'bɒn,bɒn/ *n.* dulce, bombón *m.*
bond /bɒnd/ *n.* lazo *m.; Com.* bono *m.*
bondage /'bɒndɪdʒ/ *n.* esclavitud, servidumbre *f.*
bonded /'bɒndɪd/ *a.* garantizado.
bone /boun/ *n.* hueso *m.*
boneless /'bounlɪs/ *a.* sin huesos.
bonfire /'bɒn,faiᵊr/ *n.* hoguera, fogata *f.*
bonnet /'bɒnɪt/ *n.* gorra *f.*
bonus /'bounəs/ *n.* sobrepaga *f.*
bony /'bouni/ *a.* huesudo.
boo /bu/ *v.* abuchear.
book /bʊk/ *n.* libro *m.*
bookbinder /'bʊk,baindər/ *n.* encuadernador -ora.
bookcase /'bʊk,keis/ *n.* armario para libros.
bookkeeper /'bʊk,kipər/ *n.* tenedor -ra de libros.
bookkeeping /'bʊk,kipɪŋ/ *n.* contabilidad *f.*
booklet /'bʊklɪt/ *n.* folleto *m.*, libreta *f.*
bookmark /'bʊk,mɑrk/ *n.* marca-páginas *m.*
bookseller /'bʊk,sɛlər/ *n.* librero -ra.
bookstore /'bʊk,stɔr/ *n.* librería *f.*
boom /bum/ *n. Naut.* botalón *m.;* prosperidad repentina.
boon /bun/ *n.* dádiva *f.*
boor /bʊr/ *n.* patán, rústico *m.*
boorish /'bʊrɪʃ/ *a.* villano.
boost /bust/ *n.* **1.** alza; ayuda *f.* —*v.* **2.** levantar, alzar; fomentar.
booster /'bustər/ *n.* fomentador *m.*
boot /but/ *n.* bota *f.*
bootblack /'but,blæk/ *n.* limpia-botas *m.*
booth /buθ/ *n.* cabaña; casilla *f.*
booty /'buti/ *n.* botín *m.*
border /'bɔrdər/ *n.* **1.** borde *m.;* frontera *f.* —*v.* **2. b. on,** lindar con.
borderline /'bɔrdər,lain/ *a.* marginal. *n.* margen *m.*
bore /bɔr/ *n.* lata *f.;* persona pesada. *v.* aburrir, fastidiar; *Mech.* taladrar.
boredom /'bɔrdəm/ *n.* aburrimiento *m.*
boric acid /'bɔrɪk/ *n.* ácido bórico *m.*
boring /'bɔrɪŋ/ *a.* aburrido, pesado.

born /bɔrn/ *a.* nacido. **be born,** nacer.
born-again /'bɔrn ə'gɛn/ *a.* renacido.
borrow /'bɒrou/ *v.* pedir prestado.
bosom /'bʊzəm/ *v.* seno, pecho *m.*
boss /bɒs/ *n.* jefe, patrón *m.*
botany /'bɒtṇi/ *n.* botánica *f.*
both /bouθ/ *pron. & a.* ambos, los dos.
bother /'bɒðər/ *n.* molestia *f. v.* molestar, incomodar.
bothersome /'bɒðərsəm/ *a.* molesto.
bottle /'bɒtḷ/ *n.* **1.** botella *f.* —*v.* **2.** embotellar.
bottling /'bɒtḷɪŋ/ *n.* embotellamiento *m.*
bottom /'bɒtəm/ *n.* fondo *m.*
boudoir /'budwɑr/ *n.* tocador *m.*
bough /bau/ *n.* rama *f.*
boulder /'bouldər/ *n.* canto rodado.
boulevard /'bulə,vard/ *n.* bulevar *m.*
bounce /bauns/ *n.* **1.** brinco *m.* —*v.* **2.** brincar; hacer saltar.
bound /baund/ *n.* **1.** salto *m.* —*v.* **2.** limitar.
boundary /'baundəri/ *n.* límite, lindero *m.*
bouquet /bou'kei, bu-/ *n.* ramillete de flores.
bourgeois /bʊr'ʒwɑ/ *a. & n.* burgués -esa.
bout /baut/ *n.* encuentro; combate *m.*
bow /n bau, bou; v bau/ *n.* **1.** saludo *m.;* (of ship) proa *f.;* (archery) arco *m.;* (ribbon) lazo *m.* —*v.* **2.** saludar, inclinar.
bowels /'bauəlz/ *n.* intestinos *m.pl.;* entrañas *f.pl.*
bowl /boul/ *n.* **1.** vasija *f.;* platón *m.* —*v.* **2.** jugar a los bolos. **b. over,** derribar.
bowlegged /'bou,lɛgɪd/ *a.* pernia-bierto.
bowling /'boulɪŋ/ *n.* bolos *m.pl.*
bow tie /bou/ pajarita *f.*
box /bɒks/ *n.* **1.** caja *f.; Theat.* palco *m.* —*v.* **2.** (sports) boxear.
boxcar /'bɒks,kɑr/ *n.* vagón *m.*
boxer /'bɒksər/ *n.* boxeador -ra, pugilista *m. & f.*
boxing /'bɒksɪŋ/ *n.* boxeo *m.*
box office *n.* taquilla *f.*
boy /bɔi/ *n.* muchacho, chico, niño *m.*

boycott /'bɔikɒt/ n. **1.** boicoteo m. —v. **2.** boicotear.

boyhood /'bɔihʊd/ n. muchachez f.

boyish /'bɔiiʃ/ a. pueril.

boyishly /'bɔiiʃli/ adv. puerilmente.

bra /brɑ/ n. sujetador, sostén m.

brace /breis/ n. **1.** grapón m.; pl. tirantes m.pl. —v. **2.** reforzar.

bracelet /'breislɪt/ n. brazalete m., pulsera f.

bracket /'brækɪt/ n. ménsula f.

brag /bræg/ v. jactarse.

braggart /'brægərt/ a. **1.** jactancioso. —n. **2.** jaque m.

braid /breid/ n. **1.** trenza f. —v. **2.** trenzar.

brain /brein/ n. cerebro, seso m.

brainy /'breini/ a. sesudo, inteligente.

brake /breik/ n. **1.** freno m. —v. **2.** frenar.

bran /bræn/ n. salvado m.

branch /bræntʃ, brɑntʃ/ n. ramo m.; (of tree) rama f.

brand /brænd/ n. marca f.

brandish /'brændɪʃ/ v. blandir.

brand-new /'bræn'nu/ a. enteramente nuevo.

brandy /'brændi/ n. aguardiente, coñac m.

brash /bræʃ/ a. impetuoso.

brass /bræs/ n. bronce, latón m.

brassiere /brə'zɪər/ n. corpiño, sujetador, sostén m.

brat /bræt/ n. mocoso m.

bravado /brə'vɑdou/ n. bravata f.

brave /breiv/ a. valiente.

bravery /'breivəri/ n. valor m.

brawl /brɔl/ n. alboroto m. v. alborotar.

brawn /brɔn/ n. músculo m.

bray /brei/ v. rebuznar.

brazen /'breizən/ a. desvergonzado.

Brazil /brə'zɪl/ n. Brasil m.

Brazilian /brə'zɪlyən/ a. & n. brasileño -ña.

breach /britʃ/ n. rotura; infracción f.

breach of contract incumplimiento de contrato m.

bread /brɛd/ n. pan m.

breadth /brɛdθ/ n. anchura f.

break /breik/ n. **1.** rotura; pausa f. —v. **2.** quebrar, romper.

breakable /'breikəbəl/ a. rompible, frágil.

breakage /'breikɪdʒ/ n. rotura f., destrozo m.

breakfast /'brɛkfəst/ n. **1.** desayuno, almuerzo m. —v. **2.** desayunar, almorzar.

breakneck /'breik,nɛk/ a. rápido, precipitado, atropellado.

breast /brɛst/ n. (of human) pecho, seno m.; (of fowl) pechuga f.

breastbone /'brɛst,boun/ n. esternón m.

breath /brɛθ/ n. aliento; soplo m.

breathe /brið/ v. respirar.

breathless /'brɛθlɪs/ a. desalentado.

breathlessly /'brɛθlɪsli/ adv. jadeantemente, intensamente.

bred /brɛd/ a. criado; educado.

breeches /'brɪtʃɪz/ n.pl. calzones; pantalones, m.pl.

breed /brid/ n. **1.** raza f. —v. **2.** engendrar; criar.

breeder /'bridər/ n. criador -ra.

breeding /'bridɪŋ/ n. cría f.

breeze /briz/ n. brisa f.

breezy /'brizi/ a.: **it is b.**, hace brisa.

brevity /'brɛvɪti/ n. brevedad f.

brew /bru/ v. fraguar; elaborar.

brewer /'bruər/ n. cervecero -ra.

brewery /'bruəri/ n. cervecería f.

bribe /braib/ n. **1.** soborno, cohecho m. —v. **2.** sobornar, cohechar.

briber /'braibər/ n. sobornador -ra.

bribery /'braibəri/ n. soborno, cohecho m.

brick /brɪk/ n. ladrillo m.

bricklayer /'brɪk,leiər/ n. albañil m.

bridal /'braidl/ a. nupcial.

bride /braid/ n. novia f.

bridegroom /'braid,grum/ n. novio m.

bridesmaid /'braidz,meid/ n. madrina de boda.

bridge /brɪdʒ/ n. puente m.

bridged /brɪdʒd/ a. conectado.

bridgehead /'brɪdʒ,hɛd/ n. Mil. cabeza de puente.

bridle /'braidl/ n. brida f.

brief /brif/ a. breve.

briefcase /'brif,keis/ n. maletín m.

briefly /'brifli/ adv. brevemente.

briefness /'brifnɪs/ n. brevedad f.

brier /'braiər/ n. zarza f.

brig /brɪg/ n. bergantín m.

brigade /brɪ'geid/ n. brigada f.

bright /brait/ *a.* claro, brillante.

brighten /'braitṇ/ *v.* abrillantar; alegrar.

brightness /'braitnis/ *n.* resplandor *m.*

brilliance /'brilyəns/ *n.* brillantez *f.*

brilliant /'brilyənt/ *a.* brillante.

brim /brim/ *n.* borde *m.; (of hat)* ala *f.*

brine /brain/ *n.* escabeche, *m.* salmuera *f.*

bring /briŋ/ *v.* traer. **b. about,** efectuar, llevar a cabo.

brink /briŋk/ *n.* borde *m.*

briny /'braini/ *a.* salado.

brisk /brisk/ *a.* vivo; enérgico.

briskly /'briskli/ *adv.* vivamente.

briskness /'brisknis/ *n.* viveza *f.*

bristle /'brisəl/ *n.* cerda *f.*

bristly /'brisli/ *a.* hirsuto.

Britain /'britṇ/ *n.* **Great B.,** Gran Bretaña *f.*

British /'britiʃ/ *a.* británico.

British Empire imperio británico *m.*

British Isles /ailz/ islas británicas *f.*

Briton /'britṇ/ *n.* inglés *m.*

brittle /'britḷ/ *a.* quebradizo, frágil.

broad /brɔd/ *a.* ancho.

broadcast /'brɔd,kæst/ *n.* **1.** radiodifusión *f.* —*v.* **2.** radiodifundir.

broadcaster /'brɔd,kæstər/ *n.* locutor -ra.

broadcloth /'brɔd,klɔθ/ *n.* paño fino.

broaden /'brɔdṇ/ *v.* ensanchar.

broadly /'brɔdli/ *adv.* ampliamente.

broadminded /'brɔd'maindid/ *a.* tolerante, liberal.

brocade /brou'keid/ *n.* brocado *m.*

brocaded /brou'keidid/ *a.* espolinado.

broccoli /'brɒkəli/ *n.* brécol *m.*

broil /brɔil/ *v.* asar.

broiler /'brɔilər/ *n.* parrilla *f.*

broken /'broukən/ *a.* roto, quebrado.

broken-hearted /'broukən'hartid/ *a.* angustiado.

broker /'broukər/ *n.* corredor -ra, bolsista *m.* & *f.*

brokerage /'broukəridʒ/ *n.* corretaje *m.*

bronchial /'brɒŋkiəl/ *a.* bronquial.

bronchitis /brɒŋ'kaitis/ *n.* bronquitis *f.*

bronze /brɒnz/ *n.* bronce *m.*

brooch /broutʃ/ *n.* broche *m.*

brood /brud/ *n.* **1.** cría, progenie *f.* —*v.* **2.** empollar; cobijar.

brook /bruk/ *n.* arroyo *m.*, quebrada *f.*

broom /brum/ *n.* escoba *f.*

broomstick /'brum,stik/ *n.* palo de escoba.

broth /brɔθ/ *n.* caldo *m.*

brothel /'brɒθəl/ *n.* burdel *m.*

brother /'brʌðər/ *n.* hermano *m.*

brotherhood /'brʌðər,hud/ *n.* fraternidad *f.*

brother-in-law /'brʌðər in ,lɔ/ *n.* cuñado *m.*

brotherly /'brʌðərli/ *a.* fraternal.

brow /brau/ *n.* ceja; frente *f.*

brown /braun/ *a.* pardo, moreno; marrón. *v.* rehogar.

brown sugar azúcar moreno *m.*

browse /brauz/ *v.* curiosear; ramonear.

browser /'brauzər/ *n.* (Internet) nagegador *m.*, visualizador *m.*, visor *m.*

bruise /bruz/ *n.* **1.** contusión *f.* —*v.* **2.** magullar.

brunette /bru'nɛt/ *a.* & *n.* moreno -na, trigueño -ña.

brush /brʌʃ/ *n.* **1.** cepillo *m.*; brocha *f.* —*v.* **2.** cepillar.

brushwood /'brʌʃ,wud/ *n.* matorral *m.*

brusque /brʌsk/ *a.* brusco.

brusquely /'brʌskli/ *adv.* bruscamente.

brutal /'brutḷ/ *a.* brutal.

brutality /bru'tæliti/ *n.* brutalidad *f.*

brutalize /'brutḷ,aiz/ *v.* embrutecer.

brute /brut/ *n.* bruto -ta, bestia *f.*

bubble /'bʌbəl/ *n.* ampolla *f.*

bucket /'bʌkit/ *n.* cubo *m.*

buckle /'bʌkəl/ *n.* hebilla *f.*

buckram /'bʌkrəm/ *n.* bucarán *m.*

bucksaw /'bʌk'sɔ/ *n.* sierra de bastidor.

buckshot /'bʌk,ʃɒt/ *n.* posta *f.*

buckwheat /'bʌk,wit/ *n.* trigo sarraceno *m.*

bud /bʌd/ *n.* **1.** brote *m.* —*v.* **2.** brotar.

budding /'bʌdiŋ/ *a.* en capullo.

budge /bʌdʒ/ *v.* moverse.

budget /'bʌdʒit/ *n.* presupuesto *m.*

buffalo /'bʌfə,lou/ n. búfalo m.
buffer /'bʌfər/ n. parachoques m.
buffet /bə'fei/ n. bufet m.; (furniture) aparador m.
buffoon /bə'fun/ n. bufón m.
bug /bʌg/ n. insecto m.; (computer) error m.
bugle /'byugəl/ n. clarín m.; corneta f.
build /bɪld/ v. construir.
builder /'bɪldər/ n. constructor -ra.
building /'bɪldɪŋ/ n. edificio m.
bulb /bʌlb/ n. bulbo m.; (of lamp) bombilla, ampolla f.
bulge /bʌldʒ/ n. abultamiento m. v. abultar.
bulging /'bʌldʒɪŋ/ a. protuberante.
bulimia /bu'limiə/ n. bulimia f.
bulk /bʌlk/ n. masa f.; grueso m.; mayoría f.
bulkhead /'bʌlk,hed/ n. frontón m.
bulky /'bʌlki/ a. grueso, abultado.
bull /bʊl/ n. toro m.
bulldog /'bʊl,dɔg/ n. perro de presa.
bullet /'bʊlɪt/ n. bala f.
bulletin /'bʊlɪtɪn/ n. boletín m.
bulletproof /'bʊlɪt,pruf/ a. a prueba de bala.
bullfight /'bʊl,fait/ n. corrida de toros.
bullfighter /'bʊl,faitər/ n. torero -ra.
bullfinch /'bʊl,fɪntʃ/ n. pinzón real m.
bully /'bʊli/ n. **1.** rufián m. —v. **2.** bravear.
bulwark /'bʊlwərk/ n. baluarte m.
bum /bʌm/ n. holgazán m.
bump /bʌmp/ n. **1.** golpe, choque m. —v. **2. b. into,** chocar contra.
bumper /'bʌmpər/ n. parachoques m.
bun /bʌn/ n. bollo m.
bunch /bʌntʃ/ n. racimo; montón m.
bundle /'bʌndl/ n. **1.** bulto m. —v. **2. b. up,** abrigar.
bungalow /'bʌŋgə,lou/ n. casa de un solo piso.
bungle /'bʌŋgəl/ v. estropear.
bunion /'bʌnyən/ n. juanete m.
bunk /bʌŋk/ n. litera f.
bunny /'bʌni/ n. conejito -ta.
bunting /'bʌntɪŋ/ n. lanilla; banderas f.
buoy /'bui/ n. boya f.

buoyant /'bɔiənt/ a. boyante; vivaz.
burden /'bɔrdn/ n. **1.** carga f. —v. **2.** cargar.
burdensome /'bɔrdnsəm/ a. gravoso.
bureau /'byʊrou/ n. (furniture) cómoda f.; departamento m.
burglar /'bɔrglər/ n. ladrón -ona.
burglarize /'bɔrglə,raiz/ v. robar.
burglary /'bɔrgləri/ n. robo m.
burial /'beriəl/ n. entierro m.
burlap /'bɔrlæp/ n. arpillera f.
burly /'bɔrli/ a. corpulento.
burn /bɔrn/ v. quemar; arder.
burner /'bɔrnər/ n. mechero m.
burning /'bɔrnɪŋ/ a. ardiente.
burnish /'bɔrnɪʃ/ v. pulir; acicalar.
burrow /'bɔrou/ v. minar; horadar.
burst /bɔrst/ v. reventar.
bury /'beri/ v. enterrar.
bus /bʌs/ n. autobús m.
bush /bʊʃ/ n. arbusto m.
bushy /'bʊʃi/ a. matoso; peludo.
business /'bɪznɪs/ n. negocios m.pl.; comercio m.
businesslike /'bɪznɪs,laik/ a. directo, práctico.
businessman /'bɪznɪs,mæn/ n. hombre de negocios, comerciante m.
businesswoman /'bɪznɪs,wʊmən/ n. mujer de negocios.
bust /bʌst/ n. busto; pecho m.
bustle /'bʌsəl/ n. bullicio m.; animación f.
busy /'bɪzi/ a. ocupado, atareado.
busybody /'bɪzi,bɒdi/ n. entremetido -da.
but /bʌt/ conj. pero; sino.
butcher /'bʊtʃər/ n. carnicero -ra.
butchery /'bʊtʃəri/ n. carnicería; matanza f.
butler /'bʌtlər/ n. mayordomo m.
butt /bʌt/ n. punta f.; cabo extremo m.
butter /'bʌtər/ n. manteca, mantequilla f.
buttercup /'bʌtər,kʌp/ n. ranúnculo m.
butterfat /'bʌtər,fæt/ n. mantequilla f.
butterfly /'bʌtər,flai/ n. mariposa f.
buttermilk /'bʌtər,mɪlk/ n. suero (de leche) m.
button /'bʌtn/ n. botón m.
buttonhole /'bʌtn,houl/ n. ojal m.

buttress /'bʌtrɪs/ n. sostén; refuerzo m.

buxom /'bʌksəm/ a. regordete.

buy /bai/ v. comprar.

buyer /'baiər/ n. comprador -ra.

buzz /bʌz/ n. **1.** zumbido m. —v. **2.** zumbar.

buzzard /'bʌzərd/ n. gallinazo m.

buzzer /'bʌzər/ n. zumbador m.; timbre m.

buzz saw n. sierra circular f.

by /bai/ prep. por; (near) cerca de, al lado de; (time) para.

by-and-by /,baiən'bai/ adv. pronto; luego.

bygone /'bai,gɔn/ a. pasado.

bylaw /'bai,lɔ/ n. estatuto, reglamento m.

bypass /'bai,pæs/ n. desvío m.

byproduct /'bai,prɒdəkt/ n. subproducto m.

bystander /'bai,stændər/ n. espectador -ra; mirón -na.

byte /bait/ n. en teoría de la información: ocho bits, byte m.

byway /'bai,wei/ n. camino desviado m.

C

cab /kæb/ n. taxi, coche de alquiler m.

cabaret /,kæbə'rei/ n. cabaret m.

cabbage /'kæbɪdʒ/ n. repollo m.

cabin /'kæbɪn/ n. cabaña f.

cabinet /'kæbənɪt/ n. gabinete; ministerio m.

cabinetmaker /'kæbənɪt,meikər/ n. ebanista m.

cable /'keibəl/ n. cable m.

cablegram /'keibəl,græm/ n. cablegrama m.

cache /kæʃ/ n. escondite m.

cackle /'kækəl/ n. charla f.; cacareo m. v. cacarear.

cacophony /kə'kɒfəni/ n. cacofonía f.

cactus /'kæktəs/ n. cacto m.

cad /kæd/ n. persona vil.

cadaver /kə'dævər/ n. cadáver m.

cadaverous /kə'dævərəs/ a. cadavérico.

caddie /'kædi/ n. (golf) ayudante m. & f.

cadence /'keidns/ n. cadencia f.

cadet /kə'dɛt/ n. cadete m.

cadmium /'kædmiəm/ n. cadmio m.

cadre /'kædri, 'kɑdrei/ n. núcleo; Mil. cuadro m.

café /kæ'fei/ n. café m., cantina f.

cafeteria /,kæfɪ'tɪəriə/ n. cafetería f.

caffeine /kæ'fin/ n. cafeína f.

cage /keidʒ/ n. jaula f. v. enjaular.

caged /keidʒd/ a. enjaulado.

caisson /'keisɒn, -sən/ n. arcón m.; Mil. furgón m.

cajole /kə'dʒoul/ v. lisonjear; adular.

cake /keik/ n. torta f.; bizcocho m.

calamitous /kə'læmɪtəs/ a. calamitoso.

calamity /kə'læmɪti/ n. calamidad f.

calcify /'kælsə,fai/ v. calcificar.

calcium /'kælsiəm/ n. calcio m.

calculable /'kælkyələbəl/ a. calculable.

calculate /'kælkyə,leit/ v. calcular.

calculating /'kælkyə,leitɪŋ/ a. interesado.

calculation /,kælkyə'leiʃən/ n. calculación f.; cálculo m.

calculus /'kælkyələs/ n. cálculo m.

caldron /'kɔldrən/ n. caldera f.

calendar /'kæləndər/ n. calendario m.

calf /kæf/ n. ternero m. (animal); pantorrilla f. (of the body).

calfskin /'kæf,skɪn/ n. piel de becerro.

caliber /'kælɪbər/ n. calibre m.

calico /'kælɪ,kou/ n. calicó m.

caliper /'kæləpər/ n. calibrador m.

calisthenics /,kæləs'θɛnɪks/ n. calistenia, gimnasia f.

calk /kɔk/ v. calafatear; rellenar.

calker /'kɔkər/ n. calafate -ta.

call /kɔl/ n. **1.** llamada f. —v. **2.** llamar.

calligraphy /kə'lɪgrəfi/ n. caligrafía f.

calling /'kɔlɪŋ/ n. vocación f.

calling card tarjeta (de visita) f.

callously /'kæləsli/ adv. insensiblemente.

callow /'kælou/ a. sin experiencia.

callus /'kæləs/ n. callo m.

calm /kɑm/ a. **1.** tranquilo, calmado. —n. **2.** calma f. —v. **3.** calmar.

calmly /'kɑmli/ adv. serenamente.

calmness /'kɑmnɪs/ n. calma f.

caloric /kəˈlɔrɪk/ a. calórico.
calorie /ˈkæləri/ n. caloría f.
calorimeter /ˌkæləˈrɪmɪtər/ n. calorímetro m.
calumniate /kəˈlʌmniˌeit/ v. calumniar.
calumny /ˈkæləmni/ n. calumnia f.
Calvary /ˈkælvəri/ n. Calvario m.
calve /kæv/ v. parir (la vaca).
calyx /ˈkeilɪks/ n. cáliz m.
camaraderie /ˌkɑməˈrɑdəri/ n. compañerismo m., compadrería f.
cambric /ˈkeimbrɪk/ n. batista f.
camcorder /ˈkæmˌkɔrdər/ n. videocámara f.
camel /ˈkæməl/ n. camello -lla.
camellia /kəˈmilyə/ n. camelia f.
camel's hair /ˈkæməlz/ pelo de camello.
cameo /ˈkæmiˌou/ n. camafeo m.
camera /ˈkæmərə/ n. cámara f.
camouflage /ˈkæməˌflɑʒ/ n. camuflaje m.
camouflaging /ˈkæməˌflɑʒɪŋ/ n. simulacro, disfraz m.
camp /kæmp/ n. **1.** campamento m. —v. **2.** acampar.
campaign /kæmˈpein/ n. campaña f.
camper /ˈkæmpər/ n. acampado m.
campfire /ˈkæmpˌfaiᵊr/ n. fogata de campamento.
camphor /ˈkæmfər/ n. alcanfor m.
camphor ball bola de alcanfor.
campus /ˈkæmpəs/ n. campo de colegio (o universidad), campus m.
can /kæn/ v. (be able) poder.
can /kæn/ n. **1.** lata f. —v. **2.** conservar en latas, enlatar.
Canada /ˈkænədə/ n. Canadá m.
Canadian /kəˈneidiən/ a. & n. canadiense.
canal /kəˈnæl/ n. canal m.
canalize /ˈkænlˌaiz/ v. canalizar.
canard /kəˈnɑrd/ n. embuste m.
canary /kəˈneəri/ n. canario -ria.
cancel /ˈkænsəl/ v. cancelar.
cancellation /ˌkænsəˈleiʃən/ n. cancelación f.
cancer /ˈkænsər/ n. cáncer m.
candelabrum /ˌkændlˈɑbrəm/ n. candelabro m.
candid /ˈkændɪd/ a. cándido, sincero.
candidacy /ˈkændɪdəsi/ n. candidatura f.
candidate /ˈkændɪˌdeit/ n. candidato -ta.

candidly /ˈkændɪdli/ adv. cándidamente.
candidness /ˈkændɪdnɪs/ n. candidez; sinceridad f.
candied /ˈkændid/ a. garapiñado.
candle /ˈkændl/ n. vela f.
candlestick /ˈkændlˌstɪk/ n. candelero m.
candor /ˈkændər/ n. candor m.; sinceridad f.
candy /ˈkændi/ n. dulces m.pl.
cane /kein/ n. caña f.; (for walking) bastón m.
canine /ˈkeinain/ a. canino.
canister /ˈkænəstər/ n. frasco m.; lata f.
canker /ˈkæŋkər/ n. llaga; úlcera f.
cankerworm /ˈkæŋkərˌwɜrm/ n. oruga f.
canned /kænd/ a. envasado, enlatado.
canner /ˈkænər/ n. envasador m.
cannery /ˈkænəri/ n. fábrica de conservas alimenticias f.
cannibal /ˈkænəbəl/ n. caníbal m. & f.
cannon /ˈkænən/ n. cañón m.
cannonade /ˌkænəˈneid/ n. cañoneo m.
cannoneer /ˌkænəˈnɪər/ n. cañonero -ra.
canny /ˈkæni/ a. sagaz; prudente.
canoe /kəˈnu/ n. canoa, piragua f.
canoeing /kəˈnuɪŋ/ n. piragüismo m.
canoeist /kəˈnuɪst/ n. piragüista m. & f.
canon /ˈkænən/ n. canon m.; Relig. canónigo m.
canonical /kəˈnɒnɪkəl/ a. canónico.
canonize /ˈkænəˌnaiz/ v. canonizar.
can opener /ˈoupənər/ abrelatas m.
canopy /ˈkænəpi/ n. dosel m.
cant /kænt/ n. hipocresía f.
cantaloupe /ˈkæntlˌoup/ n. melón m.
canteen /kænˈtin/ n. cantina f.
canter /ˈkæntər/ n. **1.** medio galope m. —v. **2.** galopar.
cantonment /kænˈtɒnmənt/ n. Mil. acuartelamiento m.
canvas /ˈkænvəs/ n. lona f.
canyon /ˈkænyən/ n. cañón, desfiladero m.
cap /kæp/ n. **1.** tapa f.; (headwear) gorro m. —v. **2.** tapar.

capability /ˌkeipə'bɪlɪti/ n. capacidad f.

capable /'keipəbəl/ a. capaz.

capably /'keipəbli/ adv. hábilmente.

capacious /kə'peiʃəs/ a. espacioso.

capacity /kə'pæsɪti/ n. capacidad f.

cape /keip/ n. capa f., Geog. cabo m.

caper /'keipər/ n. zapateta f.; Bot. alcaparra f.

capillary /'kæpə,lɛri/ a. capilar.

capital /'kæpɪtl̩/ n. capital m.; Govt. capital f.

capitalism /'kæpɪtl̩,ɪzəm/ n. capitalismo m.

capitalist /'kæpɪtl̩ɪst/ n. capitalista m. & f.

capitalistic /ˌkæpɪtl̩'ɪstɪk/ a. capitalista.

capitalization /ˌkæpɪtl̩ə'zeiʃən/ n. capitalización f.

capitalize /'kæpɪtl̩,aiz/ v. capitalizar.

capital letter n. mayúscula f.

capitulate /kə'pɪtʃə,leit/ v. capitular.

capon /'keipɒn/ n. capón m.

caprice /kə'pris/ n. capricho m.

capricious /kə'prɪʃəs/ a. caprichoso.

capriciously /kə'prɪʃəsli/ adv. caprichosamente.

capriciousness /kə'prɪʃəsnɪs/ n. capricho m.

capsize /'kæpsaiz/ v. zozobrar, volcar.

capsule /'kæpsəl/ n. cápsula f.

captain /'kæptən/ n. capitán -tana.

caption /'kæpʃən/ n. título m.; (motion pictures) subtítulo m.

captious /'kæpʃəs/ a. capcioso.

captivate /'kæptə,veit/ v. cautivar.

captivating /'kæptə,veitɪŋ/ a. encantador.

captive /'kæptɪv/ n. cautivo -va, prisionero -ra.

captivity /kæp'tɪvɪti/ n. cautividad f.

captor /'kæptər/ n. apresador -ra.

capture /'kæptʃər/ n. **1.** captura f. —v. **2.** capturar.

car /kar/ n. coche, carro m.; (of train) vagón, coche m. **baggage c.,** vagón de equipajes. **parlor c.,** coche salón.

carafe /kə'ræf/ n. garrafa f.

caramel /'kærəməl/ n. caramelo m.

carat /'kærət/ n. quilate m.

caravan /'kærə,væn/ n. caravana f.

caraway /'kærə,wei/ n. alcaravea f.

carbide /'karbaid/ n. carburo m.

carbine /'karbin/ n. carabina f.

carbohydrate /ˌkarbou'haidreit/ n. hidrato de carbono.

carbon /'karbən/ n. carbón m.

carbon dioxide /dai'ɒksaid/ anhídrido carbónico.

carbon monoxide /mɒn'ɒksaid/ monóxido de carbono.

carbon paper papel carbón m.

carbuncle /'karbʌŋkəl/ n. carbúnculo m.

carburetor /'karbə,reitər/ n. carburador m.

carcinogenic /ˌkarsənə'dʒɛnɪk/ a. carcinogénico.

card /kard/ n. tarjeta f. **playing c.,** naipe m.

cardboard /'kard,bord/ n. cartón m.

cardiac /'kardi,æk/ a. cardíaco.

cardigan /'kardɪgən/ n. chaqueta de punto.

cardinal /'kardn̩l/ a. **1.** cardinal. —n. **2.** cardenal m.

cardiologist /ˌkardi'ɒlədʒɪst/ n. cardiólogo, -ga m. & f.

care /kɛər/ n. **1.** cuidado. —v. **2.** **c. for,** cuidar.

careen /kə'rin/ v. carenar; echarse de costado.

career /kə'rɪər/ n. carrera f.

carefree /'kɛər,fri/ a. descuidado.

careful /'kɛərfəl/ a. cuidadoso. **be. c.,** tener cuidado.

carefully /'kɛərfəli/ adv. cuidadosamente.

carefulness /'kɛərfəlnɪs/ n. esmero; cuidado m.; cautela f.

careless /'kɛərlɪs/ a. descuidado.

carelessly /'kɛərlɪsli/ adv. descuidadamente; negligentemente.

carelessness /'kɛərlɪsnɪs/ n. descuido m.

caress /kə'rɛs/ n. **1.** caricia f. —v. **2.** acariciar.

caretaker /'kɛər,teikər/ n. guardián -ana.

cargo /'kargou/ n. carga f.

caricature /'kærɪkətʃər/ n. caricatura f.

caricaturist /'kærɪkə,tʃʊrɪst/ *n.* caricaturista *m. & f.*

caries /'kɛəriz/ *n.* caries *f.*

carjacking /'kɑr,dʒækɪŋ/ *n.* robo de coche *m.*

carload /'kɑr,loud/ *a.* furgonada, vagonada.

carnal /'kɑrnļ/ *a.* carnal.

carnation /kɑr'neiʃən/ *n.* clavel *m.*

carnival /'kɑrnəvəl/ *n.* carnaval *m.*

carnivorous /kɑr'nɪvərəs/ *a.* carnívoro.

carol /'kærəl/ *n.* villancico *m.*

carouse /kə'rauz/ *v.* parrandear.

carpenter /'kɑrpəntər/ *n.* carpintero -ra.

carpet /'kɑrpɪt/ *n.* alfombra *f.*

carpeting /'kɑrpɪtɪŋ/ *n.* alfombrado *m.*

car pool /'kɑr,pul/ uso habitual, por varias personas, de un automóvil perteneciente a una de ellas.

carriage /'kærɪdʒ/ *n.* carruaje; (bearing) porte *m.*

carrier /'kæriər/ *n.* portador -ra.

carrier pigeon paloma mensajera.

carrot /'kærət/ *n.* zanahoria *f.*

carrousel /,kærə'sɛl/ *n.* volantín, carrusel *m.*

carry /'kæri/ *v.* llevar, cargar. **c. out,** cumplir, llevar a cabo.

cart /kɑrt/ *n.* carreta *f.*

cartage /'kɑrtɪdʒ/ *n.* acarreo, carretaje *m.*

cartel /kɑr'tɛl/ *n.* cartel *m.*

cartilage /'kɑrtļɪdʒ/ *n.* cartílago *m.*

carton /'kɑrtņ/ *n.* caja de cartón.

cartoon /kɑr'tun/ *n.* caricatura *f.*

cartoonist /kɑr'tunɪst/ *n.* caricaturista *m. & f.*

cartridge /'kɑrtrɪdʒ/ *n.* cartucho *m.*

carve /kɑrv/ *v.* esculpir; (meat) trinchar.

carver /'kɑrvər/ *n.* tallador -ra; grabador -ra.

carving /'kɑrvɪŋ/ *n.* entalladura *f.*; arte de trinchar. **c. knife,** trinchante *m.*

cascade /kæs'keid/ *n.* cascada *f.*

case /keis/ *n.* caso *m.*; (box) caja *f.* **in any c.,** sea como sea.

cash /kæʃ/ *n.* **1.** dinero contante. —*v.* **2.** efectuar, cambiar.

cashier /kæ'ʃɪər/ *n.* cajero -ra.

cashmere /'kæʒmɪər/ *n.* casimir *m.*

casino /kə'sinou/ *n.* casino *m.*

cask /kæsk/ *n.* barril *m.*

casket /'kæskɪt/ *n.* ataúd *m.*

casserole /'kæsə,roul/ *n.* cacerola *f.*

cassette /kə'sɛt/ *n.* cassette *m.*, cartucho *m.*

cast /kæst/ *n.* **1.** *Theat.* reparto de papeles. —*v.* **2.** echar; *Theat.* repartir.

castanet /,kæstə'nɛt/ *n.* castañuela *f.*

castaway /'kæstə,wei/ *n.* náufrago -ga.

caste /kæst/ *n.* casta *f.*

caster /'kæstər/ *n.* tirador *m.*

castigate /'kæstɪ,geit/ *v.* castigar.

Castilian /kæ'stɪlyən/ *a.* castellano.

cast iron *n.* hierro colado *m.*

castle /'kæsəl/ *n.* castillo *m.*

castoff /'kæst,ɔf/ *a.* descartado.

casual /'kæʒuəl/ *a.* casual.

casually /'kæʒuəli/ *adv.* casualmente.

casualness /'kæʒuəlnɪs/ *n.* casualidad *f.*

casualty /'kæʒuəlti/ *n.* víctima *f.; Mil.* baja *f.*

cat /kæt/ *n.* gato -ta.

cataclysm /'kætə,klɪzəm/ *n.* cataclismo *m.*

catacomb /'kætə,koum/ *n.* catacumba *f.*

catalogue /'kætļ,ɔg/ *n.* catálogo *m.*

catapult /'kætə,pʌlt/ *n.* catapulta *f.*

cataract /'kætə,rækt/ *n.* catarata *f.*

catarrh /kə'tɑr/ *n.* catarro *m.*

catastrophe /kə'tæstrəfi/ *n.* catástrofe *f.*

catch /kætʃ/ *v.* alcanzar, atrapar, coger.

catchy /'kætʃi/ *a.* contagioso.

catechism /'kætɪ,kɪzəm/ *n.* catequismo *m.*

catechize /'kætɪ,kaiz/ *v.* catequizar.

categorical /,kætɪ'gɔrɪkəl/ *a.* categórico.

category /'kætɪ,gɔri/ *n.* categoría *f.*

cater /'keitər/ *v.* abastecer; proveer. **c. to,** complacer.

caterpillar /'kætə,pɪlər/ *n.* gusano *m.*

catgut /'kæt,gʌt/ *n.* cuerda (de tripa).

catharsis /kə'θɑrsɪs/ *n.* catarsis, purga *f.*

cathartic /kə'θɑrtɪk/ *a.* **1.** catártico; purgante. —*n.* **2.** purgante *m.*

cathedral /kə'θidrəl/ *n.* catedral *f.*

cathode /'kæθoud/ *n.* cátodo *m.*

Catholic /'kæθəlɪk/ *a.* católico & *n.* católico -ca.

Catholicism /kə'θɒlə,sɪzəm/ *n.* catolicismo *m.*

catnap /'kæt,næp/ *n.* siesta corta.

catsup /'kætsəp, 'ketʃəp/ *n.* salsa de tomate.

cattle /'kætl/ *n.* ganado *m.*

cattleman /'kætl̩mən,ˈ-,mæn/ *n.* ganadero *m.*

cauliflower /'kɔlə,flauər/ *n.* coliflor *m.*

causation /kɔ'zeiʃən/ *n.* causalidad *f.*

cause /kɔz/ *n.* causa *f.*

causeway /'kɔz,wei/ *n.* calzada elevada *f.;* terraplén *m.*

caustic /'kɔstɪk/ *a.* cáustico.

cauterize /'kɔtə,raiz/ *v.* cauterizar.

cautery /'kɔtəri/ *n.* cauterio *m.*

caution /'kɔʃən/ *n.* cautela *f.*

cautious /'kɔʃəs/ *a.* cauteloso.

cavalcade /,kævəl'keid/ *n.* cabalgata *f.*

cavalier /,kævə'lɪər/ *n.* caballero *m.*

cavalry /'kævəlri/ *n.* caballería *f.*

cave /keiv/ **cavern** *n.* caverna, gruta *f.*

cave-in /'keiv ,ɪn/ *n.* hundimiento *m.*

caviar /'kævi,ɑr/ *n.* caviar *m.*

cavity /'kævɪti/ *n.* hueco *m.*

cayman /'keimən/ *n.* caimán *m.*

CD player tocadiscos compacto, tocadiscos digital *m.*

cease /sis/ *v.* cesar.

ceaseless /'sislɪs/ *a.* incesante.

cedar /'sidər/ *n.* cedro *m.*

cede /sid/ *v.* ceder.

ceiling /'silɪŋ/ *n.* techo; cielo *m.*

celebrant /'sɛləbrənt/ *n.* celebrante -ta.

celebrate /'sɛlə,breit/ *v.* celebrar.

celebration /,sɛlə'breiʃən/ *n.* celebración *f.*

celebrity /sə'lɛbrɪti/ *n.* celebridad.

celerity /sə'lɛrɪti/ *n.* celeridad; prontitud *f.*

celery /'sɛləri/ *n.* apio *m.*

celestial /sə'lɛstʃəl/ *a.* celeste.

celibacy /'sɛləbəsi/ *n.* celibato -ta.

celibate /'sɛləbɪt/ *a.* & *n.* célibe *m.* & *f.*

cell /sɛl/ *n.* celda *f.; Biol.* célula *f.*

cellar /'sɛlər/ *n.* sótano *m.*

cellist /'tʃɛlɪst/ *a.* celista *m.* & *f.*

cello /'tʃɛlou/ *n.* violonchelo *m.*

cellophane /'sɛlə,fein/ *n.* celofán *m.*

cellular /'sɛlyələr/ *a.* celular.

cellular phone /foun/ teléfono móvil *m.*

celluloid /'sɛlyə,lɔid/ *n.* celuloide *m.*

cellulose /'sɛlyə,lous/ *a.* **1.** celuloso. —*n.* **2.** celulosa *f.*

Celtic /'kɛltɪk, 'sɛl-/ *a.* céltico.

cement /sɪ'mɛnt/ *n.* cemento *m.*

cemetery /'sɛmɪ,tɛri/ *n.* cementerio *m.;* campo santo *m.*

censor /'sɛnsər/ *n.* censor -ra.

censorious /sɛn'sɔriəs/ *a.* severo; crítico.

censorship /'sɛnsər,ʃɪp/ *n.* censura *f.*

censure /'sɛnʃər/ *n.* **1.** censura *f.* —*v.* **2.** censurar.

census /'sɛnsəs/ *n.* censo *m.*

cent /sɛnt/ *n.* centavo, céntimo *m.*

centenary /sɛn'tɛnɛri/ *a.* & *n.* centenario *m.*

centennial /sɛn'tɛniəl/ *a.* & *n.* centenario *m.*

center /'sɛntər/ *n.* centro *m.*

centerfold /'sɛntər,fould/ *n.* página central desplegable en una revista.

centerpiece /'sɛntər,pis/ *n.* centro de mesa.

centigrade /'sɛntɪ,greid/ *a.* centígrado.

centigrade thermometer termómetro centígrado.

central /'sɛntrəl/ *a.* central.

Central American *a.* & *n.* centroamericano -na.

centralize /'sɛntrə,laiz/ *v.* centralizar.

century /'sɛntʃəri/ *n.* siglo *m.*

century plant maguey *m.*

ceramic /sə'ræmɪk/ *a.* cerámico.

ceramics /sə'ræmɪks/ *n.* cerámica *f.*

cereal /'sɪəriəl/ *n.* cereal *m.*

cerebral /sə'ribrəl/ *a.* cerebral.

ceremonial /,sɛrə'mouniəl/ *a.* ceremonial.

ceremonious /,sɛrə'mouniəs/ *a.* ceremonioso.

ceremony /'sɛrə,mouni/ *n.* ceremonia *f.*

certain /'sɜrtn/ *a.* cierto, seguro.

certainly /'sɜrtnli/ *adv.* sin duda, seguramente.

certainty /'sɜrtnti/ *n.* certeza *f.*

certificate /sər'tɪfɪkɪt/ *n.* certificado *m.*

certification /ˌsɜrtəfɪ'keiʃən, sər,tɪfə-/ *n.* certificación *f.*

certified /'sɜrtə,faid/ *a.* certificado.

certify /'sɜrtə,fai/ *v.* certificar.

certitude /'sɜrtɪ,tyud/ *n.* certeza *f.*

cessation /sɛ'seiʃən/ *n.* cesación, descontinuación *f.*

cession /'sɛʃən/ *n.* cesión *f.*

chafe /tʃeif/ *v.* irritar.

chafing dish /'tʃeifɪŋ/ *n.* escalfador *m.*

chagrin /ʃə'grɪn/ *n.* disgusto *m.*

chain /tʃein/ *n.* **1.** cadena *f.* —*v.* **2.** encadenar.

chair /tʃɛər/ *n.* silla *f.*

chairman /'tʃɛərmən/ *n.* presidente -ta.

chairperson /'tʃɛər,pɜrsən/ *n.* presidente -ta; persona que preside.

chalk /tʃɔk/ *n.* tiza *f.*

challenge /'tʃælɪndʒ/ *n.* **1.** desafío *m.* —*v.* **2.** desafiar.

challenger /'tʃælɪndʒər/ *n.* desafiador -ra.

chamber /'tʃeimbər/ *n.* cámara *f.*

chamberlain /'tʃeimbərlɪn/ *n.* camarero *m.*

chambermaid /'tʃeimbər,meid/ *n.* camarera *f.*

chameleon /kə'miliən/ *n.* camaleón *m.*

chamois /'ʃæmi/ *n.* gamuza *f.*

champagne /ʃæm'pein/ *n.* champán *m.*, champaña *f.*

champion /'tʃæmpiən/ *n.* **1.** campeón -na —*v.* **2.** defender.

championship /'tʃæmpiən,ʃip/ *n.* campeonato *m.*

chance /tʃæns/ *n.* oportunidad, ocasión *f.* **by c.,** por casualidad, por acaso. **take a c.,** aventurarse.

chancel /'tʃænsəl/ *n.* antealtar *m.*

chancellery /'tʃænsələri/ *n.* cancillería *f.*

chancellor /'tʃænsələr/ *n.* canciller *m.*

chandelier /ˌʃændl'iər/ *n.* araña de luces.

change /tʃeindʒ/ *n.* **1.** cambio; (from a bill) moneda *f.* —*v.* **2.** cambiar.

changeability /ˌtʃeindʒə'bɪliti/ *n.* mutabilidad *f.*

changeable /'tʃeindʒəbəl/ *a.* variable, inconstante.

changer /'tʃeindʒər/ *n.* cambiador -ra.

channel /'tʃænl/ *n.* **1.** canal *m.* —*v.* **2.** encauzar.

Channel Tunnel túnel del Canal de la Mancha *m.*

chant /tʃænt/ *n.* **1.** canto llano *m.* —*v.* **2.** cantar.

chaos /'keiɒs/ *n.* caos *m.*

chaotic /kei'ɒtɪk/ *a.* caótico.

chap /tʃæp/ *n.* **1.** *Colloq.* tipo *m.* —*v.* **2.** rajar.

chapel /'tʃæpəl/ *n.* capilla *f.*

chaperon /'ʃæpə,roun/ *n.* acompañante -ta de señorita.

chaplain /'tʃæplɪn/ *n.* capellán *m.*

chapter /'tʃæptər/ *n.* capítulo *m.*

char /tʃɑr/ *v.* carbonizar.

character /'kærɪktər/ *n.* carácter *m.*

characteristic /ˌkærɪktə'rɪstɪk/ *a.* **1.** característico. —*n.* **2.** característica *f.*

characterization /ˌkærɪktərə'zeiʃən/ *n.* caracterización *f.*

characterize /'kærɪktə,raiz/ *v.* caracterizar.

charcoal /'tʃɑr,koul/ *n.* carbón leña.

charge /tʃɑrdʒ/ *n.* **1.** acusación *f.;* ataque *m.* —*v.* **2.** cargar; acusar; atacar.

chariot /'tʃæriət/ *n.* carroza *f.*

charisma /kə'rɪzmə/ *n.* carisma *m.*

charitable /'tʃærɪtəbəl/ *a.* caritativo.

charitableness /'tʃærɪtəbəlnɪs/ *n.* caridad *f.*

charitably /'tʃærɪtəbli/ *adv.* caritativamente.

charity /'tʃærɪti/ *n.* caridad *f.;* (alms) limosna *f.*

charlatan /'ʃɑrlətn/ *n.* charlatán -na.

charlatanism /'ʃɑrlətn,ɪzəm/ *n.* charlatanería *f.*

charm /tʃɑrm/ *n.* **1.** encanto *m.;* (witchcraft) hechizo *m.* —*v.* **2.** encantar; hechizar.

charming /'tʃɑrmɪŋ/ *a.* encantador.

charred /tʃɑrd/ *a.* carbonizado.

chart /tʃɑrt/ *n.* tabla, esquema *f.*

charter /'tʃɑrtər/ *n.* **1.** carta *f.* —*v.* **2.** alquilar.

charter flight vuelo chárter *m.*

charwoman /'tʃɑr,wʊmən/ n. mujer de la limpieza f.

chase /tʃeis/ n. **1.** caza f. —v. **2.** cazar; perseguir.

chaser /'tʃeisər/ n. perseguidor -ra.

chasm /'kæzəm/ n. abismo m.

chassis /'tʃæsi/ n. chasis m.

chaste /tʃeist/ a. casto.

chasten /'tʃeisən/ v. corregir, castigar.

chastise /tʃæs'taiz/ v. castigar.

chastisement /tʃæs'taizmənt/ n. castigo m.

chastity /'tʃæstɪti/ n. castidad, pureza f.

chat /tʃæt/ n. **1.** plática, charla f. —v. **2.** platicar, charlar.

chateau /ʃæ'tou/ n. castillo m.

chattels /'tʃætəlz/ n.pl. bienes m.

chatter /'tʃætər/ v. **1.** cotorrear; (teeth) rechinar. —n. **2.** cotorreo m.

chatterbox /'tʃæt,ər bɒks/ n. charlador -ra.

chauffeur /'ʃoufər/ n. chofer m.

cheap /tʃip/ a. barato.

cheapen /'tʃipən/ v. rebajar, menospreciar.

cheaply /'tʃipli/ adv. barato.

cheapness /'tʃipnɪs/ n. baratura f.

cheat /tʃit/ v. engañar.

cheater /'tʃitər/ n. engañador -ra.

check /tʃɛk/ n. **1.** verificación f.; (bank) cheque m.; (restaurant) cuenta f.; (chess) jaque m. —v. **2.** verificar.

checkers /'tʃɛkərz/ n. juego de damas.

checkmate /'tʃɛk,meit/ v. dar mate.

checkout counter /'tʃɛk,aut/ caja f.

cheek /tʃik/ n. mejilla f. (of face), desfachatez f. (gall).

cheekbone /'tʃik,boun/ n. pómulo m.

cheeky /'tʃiki/ a. fresco, descarado, chulo.

cheer /tʃɪər/ n. **1.** alegría f.; aplauso m. —v. **2.** alegrar; aplaudir.

cheerful /'tʃɪərfəl/ a. alegre.

cheerfully /'tʃɪərfəli/ adv. alegremente.

cheerfulness /'tʃɪərfəlnɪs/ n. alegría f.

cheerless /'tʃɪərlɪs/ a. triste.

cheery /'tʃɪəri/ a. alegre.

cheese /tʃiz/ n. queso m. **cottage c.,** requesón m.

chef /ʃɛf/ n. cocinero en jefe.

chemical /'kɛmɪkəl/ a. **1.** químico. —n. **2.** reactivo m.

chemically /'kɛmɪkli/ adv. químicamente.

chemist /'kɛmɪst/ n. químico -ca.

chemistry /'kɛməstri/ n. química f.

chemotherapy /,kimou'θɛrəpi/ n. quimioterapia f.

chenille /ʃə'nil/ n. felpilla f.

cherish /'tʃɛrɪʃ/ v. apreciar.

cherry /'tʃɛri/ n. cereza f.

cherub /'tʃɛrəb/ n. querubín m.

chess /tʃɛs/ n. ajedrez m.

chest /tʃɛst/ n. arca f.; (physiology) pecho m.

chestnut /'tʃɛs,nʌt/ n. castaña f.

chevron /'ʃɛvrən/ n. sardineta f.

chew /tʃu/ v. mascar, masticar.

chewer /'tʃuər/ n. mascador -ra.

chic /ʃik/ a. elegante, paquete.

chicanery /ʃɪ'keinəri/ n. trampería f.

chick /tʃɪk/ n. pollito -ta.

chicken /'tʃɪkən/ n. pollo m., gallina f.

chicken-hearted /'tʃɪkən 'hɑrtɪd/ a. cobarde.

chicken pox /pɒks/ viruelas locas, varicela f.

chicle /'tʃɪkəl/ n. chicle m.

chicory /'tʃɪkəri/ n. achicoria f.

chide /tʃaid/ v. regañar, reprender.

chief /tʃif/ a. **1.** principal. —n. **2.** jefe -fa.

chiefly /'tʃifli/ adv. principalmente, mayormente.

chieftain /'tʃiftən/ n. caudillo m.; (Indian c.) cacique m.

chiffon /ʃɪ'fɒn/ n. chifón m., gasa f.

chilblain /'tʃɪlblein/ n. sabañón m.

child /tʃaild/ n. niño -ña; hijo -ja.

childbirth /'tʃaild,bɜrθ/ n. parto m.

childhood /'tʃaildhʊd/ n. niñez f.

childish /'tʃaildɪʃ/ a. pueril.

childishness /'tʃaildɪʃnɪs/ n. puerilidad f.

childless /'tʃaildlɪs/ a. sin hijos.

childlike /'tʃaild,laik/ a. infantil.

Chilean /'tʃɪliən/ a. & n. chileno -na.

chili /'tʃɪli/ n. chile, ají m.

chill /tʃɪl/ n. **1.** frío; escalofrío m.
—v. **2.** enfriar.
chilliness /'tʃɪlɪnɪs/ n. frialdad f.
chilly /'tʃɪli/ a. frío; friolento.
chimes /tʃaɪmz/ n. juego de campanas.
chimney /'tʃɪmni/ n. chimenea f.
chimpanzee /,tʃɪmpæn'zi, tʃɪm-
'pænzi/ n. chimpancé m.
chin /tʃɪn/ n. barba f.
china /'tʃaɪnə/ n. loza f.
chinchilla /tʃɪn'tʃɪlə/ n. chinchilla
f.
Chinese /tʃaɪ'niz/ a. & n. chino
-na.
chink /tʃɪŋk/ n. grieta f.
chintz /tʃɪnts/ n. zaraza f.
chip /tʃɪp/ n. **1.** astilla f. —v. **2.**
astillar.
chiropodist /kɪ'rɒpədɪst/ n. pedicuro -ra.
chiropractor /'kaɪrə,præktər/ n.
quiropráctico -ca.
chirp /tʃɜrp/ n. **1.** chirrido m. —v.
2. chirriar, piar.
chisel /'tʃɪzəl/ n. **1.** cincel m. —v.
2. cincelar, talar.
chivalrous /'ʃɪvəlrəs/ a. caballeroso.
chivalry /'ʃɪvəlri/ n. caballería f.
chive /tʃaɪv/ n. cebollino m.
chloride /'klɔraɪd/ n. cloruro m.
chlorine /'klɔrin/ n. cloro m.
chloroform /'klɔrə,fɔrm/ n. cloroformo m.
chlorophyll /'klɔrəfɪl/ n. clorofila
f.
chock-full /'tʃɒk'fʊl/ a. repleto,
colmado.
chocolate /'tʃɔkəlɪt/ n. chocolate
m.
choice /tʃɔɪs/ a. **1.** selecto, escogido. —n. **2.** selección f.; escogimiento m.
choir /kwaɪər/ n. coro m.
choke /tʃoʊk/ v. sofocar, ahogar.
cholera /'kɒlərə/ n. cólera f.
choleric /'kɒlərɪk/ a. colérico, irascible.
cholesterol /kə'lɛstə,roʊl/ n. colesterol m.
choose /tʃuz/ v. elegir, escoger.
chop /tʃɒp/ n. **1.** chuleta, costilla
f. —v. **2.** tajar; cortar.
chopper /'tʃɒpər/ n. tajador -ra.
choppy /'tʃɒpi/ a. agitado.
choral /'kɔrəl/ a. coral.
chord /kɔrd/ n. cuerda f.; acorde
m.

chore /tʃɔr/ n. tarea f., quehacer
m.
choreography /,kɔri'ɒgrəfi,
,koʊr-/ n. coreografía f.
chorister /'kɔrəstər/ n. corista m.
chorus /'kɔrəs/ n. coro m.
christen /'krɪsən/ v. bautizar.
Christendom /'krɪsəndəm/ n. cristiandad f.
Christian /'krɪsʃən/ a. & n. cristiano -na.
Christianity /,krɪsʃi'ænɪti/ n. cristianismo m.
Christmas /'krɪsməs/ n. Navidad,
Pascua f. **Merry C.,** felices
Pascuas. **C. Eve,** Nochebuena f.
chromatic /krou'mætɪk/ a. cromático.
chromium /'kroumiəm/ n. cromo
m.
chromosome /'kroumə,soum/ n.
cromosoma m.
chronic /'krɒnɪk/ a. crónico.
chronicle /'krɒnɪkəl/ n. crónica f.
chronological /,krɒnl'ɒdʒɪkəl/ a.
cronológico.
chronology /krə'nɒlədʒi/ n.
cronología f.
chrysalis /'krɪsəlɪs/ n. crisálida f.
chrysanthemum /krɪ'sænθəməm/
n. crisantemo m.
chubby /'tʃʌbi/ a. regordete, rollizo.
chuck /tʃʌk/ v. (cluck) cloquear;
(throw) echar, tirar.
chuckle /'tʃʌkəl/ v. reír entre
dientes.
chum /tʃʌm/ n. amigo -ga; compinche m.
chummy /'tʃʌmi/ a. íntimo.
chunk /tʃʌŋk/ n. trozo m.
chunky /'tʃʌŋki/ a. fornido, trabado.
Chunnel /'tʃʌnl/ n. túnel del Canal de la Mancha m.
church /tʃɜrtʃ/ n. iglesia f.
churchman /'tʃɜrtʃmən/ n. eclesiástico m.
churchyard /'tʃɜrtʃ,yɑrd/ n. cementerio m.
churn /tʃɜrn/ n. **1.** mantequera f.
—v. **2.** agitar, revolver.
chute /ʃut/ n. conducto; canal m.
cicada /sɪ'keɪdə/ n. cigarra, chicharra f.
cider /'saɪdər/ n. sidra f.
cigar /sɪ'gɑr/ n. cigarro, puro m.
cigarette /,sɪgə'rɛt/ n. cigarrillo,
cigarro, pitillo m. **c. case,** cigarrillera f. **c. lighter,** encendedor m.

cinchona /sɪŋ'kounə/ n. cinchona f.

cinder /'sɪndər/ n. ceniza f.

cinema /'sɪnəmə/ n. cine m.

cinnamon /'sɪnəmən/ n. canela f.

cipher /'saifər/ n. cifra f.

circle /'sɜrkəl/ n. círculo m.

circuit /'sɜrkɪt/ n. circuito m.

circuitous /sər'kyuɪtəs/ a. tortuoso.

circuitously /sər'kyuɪtəsli/ adv. tortuosamente.

circular /'sɜrkyələr/ a. circular, redondo.

circularize /'sɜrkyələ,raiz/ v. hacer circular.

circulate /'sɜrkyə,leit/ v. circular.

circulation /,sɜrkyə'leiʃən/ n. circulación f.

circulator /'sɜrkyə,leitər/ n. diseminador -ra.

circulatory /'sɜrkyələ,tori/ a. circulatorio.

circumcise /'sɜrkəm,saiz/ v. circuncidar.

circumcision /,sɜrkəm'sɪʒən/ n. circuncisión f.

circumference /sər'kʌmfərəns/ n. circunferencia f.

circumlocution /,sɜrkəmlou'kyuʃən/ n. circunlocución f.

circumscribe /'sɜrkəm,skraib/ v. circunscribir; limitar.

circumspect /'sɜrkəm,spɛkt/ a. discreto.

circumstance /'sɜrkəm,stæns/ n. circunstancia f.

circumstantial /,sɜrkəm'stænʃəl/ a. circunstancial, indirecto.

circumstantially /,sɜrkəm'stænʃəli/ adv. minuciosamente.

circumvent /,sɜrkəm'vɛnt/ v. evadir, evitar.

circumvention /,sɜrkəm'vɛnʃən/ n. trampa f.

circus /'sɜrkəs/ n. circo m.

cirrhosis /sɪ'rousɪs/ n. cirrosis f.

cistern /'sɪstərn/ n. cisterna f.

citadel /'sɪtədl/ n. ciudadela f.

citation /sai'teiʃən/ n. citación f.

cite /sait/ v. citar.

citizen /'sɪtəzən/ n. ciudadano -na.

citizenship /'sɪtəzən,ʃɪp/ n. ciudadanía f.

citric /'sɪtrɪk/ a. cítrico.

city /'sɪti/ n. ciudad f.

city hall ayuntamiento, municipio m.

city planning urbanismo m.

civic /'sɪvɪk/ a. cívico.

civics /'sɪvɪks/ n. ciencia del gobierno civil.

civil /'sɪvəl/ a. civil; cortés.

civilian /sɪ'vɪlyən/ a. & n. civil m. & f.

civility /sɪ'vɪlɪti/ n. cortesía f.

civilization /,sɪvələ'zeiʃən/ n. civilización f.

civilize /'sɪvə,laiz/ v. civilizar.

civil rights /raits/ derechos civiles m. pl.

civil service n. servicio civil oficial m.

civil war n. guerra civil f.

clabber /'klæbər/ n. 1. cuajo m. —v. 2. cuajarse.

clad /klæd/ a. vestido.

claim /kleim/ n. 1. demanda; pretensión f. —v. 2. demandar, reclamar.

claimant /'kleimənt/ n. reclamante -ta.

clairvoyance /klɛər'vɔiəns/ n. clarividencia f.

clairvoyant /klɛər'vɔiənt/ a. clarividente.

clam /klæm/ n. almeja f.

clamber /'klæmbər/ v. trepar.

clamor /'klæmər/ n. 1. clamor m. —v. 2. clamar.

clamorous /'klæmərəs/ a. clamoroso.

clamp /klæmp/ n. 1. prensa de sujeción f. —v. 2. asegurar, sujetar.

clan /klæn/ n. tribu f., clan m.

clandestine /klæn'dɛstɪn/ a. clandestino.

clandestinely /klæn'dɛstɪnli/ adv. clandestinamente.

clangor /'klæŋər, 'klæŋgər/ n. estruendo m., estrépito m.

clannish /'klænɪʃ/ a. unido; exclusivista.

clap /klæp/ v. aplaudir.

clapboard /'klæbərd, 'klæp,bɔrd/ n. chilla f.

claque /klæk/ n. claque f.

claret /'klærɪt/ n. clarete m.

clarification /,klærəfə'keiʃən/ n. clarificación f.

clarify /'klærə,fai/ v. clarificar.

clarinet /,klærə'nɛt/ n. clarinete m.

clarinetist /,klærə'nɛtɪst/ n. clarinetista m. & f.

clarity /'klærɪti/ n. claridad f.

clash /klæʃ/ n. 1. choque, enfrentamiento m. —v. 2. chocar.

clasp /klæsp/ *n.* **1.** broche *m.* —*v.* **2.** abrochar.
class /klæs/ *n.* clase *f.*
classic, /'klæsɪk/ **classical** *a.* clásico.
classicism /'klæsə,sɪzəm/ *n.* clasicismo *m.*
classifiable /'klæsə,faiəbəl/ *a.* clasificable, calificable.
classification /,klæsəfɪ'keiʃən/ *n.* clasificación *f.*
classify /'klæsə,fai/ *v.* clasificar.
classmate /'klæs,meit/ *n.* compañero -ra de clase.
classroom /'klæs,rum, -,rʊm/ *n.* sala de clase.
clatter /'klætər/ *n.* **1.** alboroto *m.* —*v.* **2.** alborotar.
clause /klɔz/ *n.* cláusula *f.*
claustrophobia /,klɔstrə'foubiə/ *n.* claustrofobia *f.*
claw /klɔ/ *n.* garra *f.*
clay /klei/ *n.* arcilla *f.;* barro *m.*
clean /klin/ *a.* **1.** limpio. —*v.* **2.** limpiar.
cleaner /'klinər/ *n.* limpiador -ra.
cleaning lady, cleaning woman /'klinɪŋ/ señora de la limpieza, mujer de la limpieza *f.*
cleanliness /'klɛnlinɪs/ *n.* limpieza *f.*
cleanse /klɛnz/ *v.* limpiar, purificar.
cleanser /'klɛnzər/ *n.* limpiador *m.,* purificador *m.*
clear /klɪər/ *a.* claro.
clearance /'klɪərəns/ *n.* espacio libre. **c. sale,** venta de liquidación.
clearing /'klɪərɪŋ/ *n.* despejo *m.;* desmonte *m.*
clearly /'klɪərli/ *adv.* claramente, evidentemente.
clearness /'klɪərnɪs/ *n.* claridad *f.*
cleavage /'klivɪdʒ/ *n.* resquebradura *f.*
cleaver /'klivər/ *n.* partidor *m.,* hacha *f.*
clef /klɛf/ *n.* clave, llave *f.*
clemency /'klɛmənsi/ *n.* clemencia *f.*
clench /klɛntʃ/ *v.* agarrar.
clergy /'klɜrdʒi/ *n.* clero *m.*
clergyman /'klɜrdʒimən/ *n.* clérigo *m.*
clerical /'klɛrɪkəl/ *a.* clerical. **c. work,** trabajo de oficina.
clericalism /'klɛrɪkə,lɪzəm/ *n.* clericalismo *m.*
clerk /klɜrk/ *n.* dependiente, escribiente *m.*

clerkship /'klɜrkʃɪp/ *n.* escribanía *f.,* secretaría *f.*
clever /'klɛvər/ *a.* diestro, hábil.
cleverly /'klɛvərli/ *adv.* diestramente, hábilmente.
cleverness /'klɛvərnɪs/ *n.* destreza *f.*
cliché /kli'ʃei/ *n.* tópico *m.*
client /'klaiənt/ *n.* cliente -ta.
clientele /,klaiən'tɛl/ *n.* clientela *f.*
cliff /klɪf/ *n.* precipicio, risco *m.*
climate /'klaimɪt/ *n.* clima *m.*
climatic /klai'mætɪk/ *a.* climático.
climax /'klaimæks/ *n.* colmo *m.,* culminación *f.*
climb /klaim/ *v.* escalar; subir.
climber /'klaimər/ *n.* trepador -ra, escalador -ra; *Bot.* enredadera *f.*
climbing plant /'klaimɪŋ/ enredadera *f.*
clinch /klɪntʃ/ *v.* afirmar.
cling /klɪŋ/ *v.* pegarse.
clinic /'klɪnɪk/ *n.* clínica *f.*
clinical /'klɪnɪkəl/ *a.* clínico.
clinically /'klɪnɪkəli/ *adv.* clínicamente.
clip /klɪp/ *n.* **1.** grapa *f.* **paper c.,** gancho *m.* —*v.* **2.** prender; (shear) trasquilar.
clipper /'klɪpər/ *n.* recortador *m.;* *Aero.* clíper *m.*
clipping /'klɪpɪŋ/ *n.* recorte *m.*
clique /klik/ *n.* camarilla *f.,* compadraje *m.*
cloak /klouk/ *n.* capa *f.,* manto *m.*
clock /klɒk/ *n.* reloj *m.* **alarm c.,** despertador *m.*
clod /klɒd/ *n.* terrón *m.;* césped *m.*
clog /klɒg/ *v.* obstruir.
cloister /'klɔistər/ *n.* claustro *m.*
clone /kloun/ *n.* clon *m.* & *f.* *v.* clonar.
close /a, adv. klous; v klouz/ *a.* **1.** cercano. —*adv.* **2.** cerca. **c. to,** cerca de. —*v.* **3.** cerrar; tapar.
closely /'klousli/ *adv.* (near) de cerca; (tight) estrechamente; (care) cuidadosamente.
closeness /'klousnɪs/ *n.* contigüidad *f.,* apretamiento *m.;* (airless) falta de ventilación *f.*
closet /'klɒzɪt/ *n.* gabinete *m.* **clothes c.,** ropero *m.*
clot /klɒt/ *n.* **1.** coágulo *f.* —*v.* **2.** coagularse.
cloth /klɔθ/ *n.* paño *m.;* tela *f.*
clothe /klouð/ *v.* vestir.
clothes /klouz/ *n.* ropa *f.*

clothing /'klouðɪŋ/ n. vestidos m., ropa f.

cloud /klaud/ n. nube f.

cloudburst /'klaud,bɜrst/ n. chaparrón m.

cloudiness /'klaudinɪs/ n. nebulosidad f.; obscuridad f.

cloudless /'klaudlɪs/ a. despejado, sin nubes.

cloudy /'klaudi/ a. nublado.

clove /klouv/ n. clavo m.

clover /'klouvər/ n. trébol m.

clown /klaun/ n. bufón -na, payaso -sa.

clownish /'klaunɪʃ/ a. grosero; bufonesco.

cloy /klɔi/ v. saciar, empalagar.

club /klʌb/ n. **1.** porra f.; (social) círculo, club m.; (cards) basto m. —v. **2.** golpear con una porra.

clubfoot /'klʌb,fut/ n. pateta m., pie zambo m.

clue /klu/ n. seña, pista f.

clump /klʌmp/ n. grupo m., masa f.

clumsiness /'klʌmzinɪs/ n. tosquedad f.; desmaña f.

clumsy /'klʌmzi/ a. torpe, desmañado.

cluster /'klʌstər/ n. **1.** grupo m.; (fruit) racimo m. —v. **2.** agrupar.

clutch /klʌtʃ/ n. **1.** Auto. embrague m. —v. **2.** agarrar.

clutter /'klʌtər/ n. **1.** confusión f. —v. **2.** poner en desorden.

coach /koutʃ/ n. **1.** coche, vagón m.; coche ordinario; (sports) entrenador m. —v. **2.** entrenar.

coachman /'koutʃmən/ n. cochero -ra.

coagulate /kou'ægyə,leit/ v. coagular.

coagulation /kou,ægyə'leiʃən/ n. coagulación f.

coal /koul/ n. carbón m.

coalesce /,kouə'les/ v. unirse, soldarse.

coalition /,kouə'lɪʃən/ n. coalición f.

coal oil n. petróleo m.

coal tar n. alquitrán m.

coarse /kɔrs/ a. grosero, burdo; (material) tosco, grueso.

coarsen /'kɔrsən/ v. vulgarizar.

coarseness /'kɔrsnɪs/ n. grosería; tosquedad f.

coast /koust/ n. **1.** costa f., litoral m. —v. **2.** deslizarse.

coastal /'koustḷ/ a. costanero.

coast guard guardacostas m. & f.

coat /kout/ n. **1.** saco m., chaqueta f.; (paint) capa f. —v. **2.** cubrir.

coat of arms /armz/ n. escudo m.

coax /kouks/ v. instar.

cobalt /'koubɔlt/ n. cobalto m.

cobbler /'kɒblər/ n. zapatero -ra.

cobblestone /'kɒbəl,stoun/ n. guijarro m.

cobra /'koubrə/ n. cobra f.

cobweb /'kɒb,web/ n. telaraña f.

cocaine /kou'kein/ n. cocaína f.

cock /kɒk/ n. (rooster) gallo m.; (water, etc.) llave f.; (gun) martillo m.

cockfight /'kɒk,fait/ n. riña de gallos f.

cockpit /'kɒk,pɪt/ n. gallera f.; reñidero de gallos m.; Aero. cabina f.

cockroach /'kɒk,routʃ/ n. cucaracha f.

cocktail /'kɒk,teil/ n. cóctel m.

cocky /'kɒki/ a. confiado, atrevido.

cocoa /'koukou/ n. cacao m.

coconut /'koukə,nʌt/ n. coco m.

cocoon /kə'kun/ n. capullo m.

cod /kɒd/ n. bacalao m.

code /koud/ n. código m.; clave f.

codeine /'koudin/ n. codeína f.

codfish /'kɒd,fɪʃ/ n. bacalao m.

codify /'kɒdə,fai/ v. compilar.

cod-liver oil /'kɒd 'lɪvər/ aceite de hígado de bacalo m.

coeducation /,kouɛdʒu'keiʃən/ n. coeducación f.

coequal /kou'ikwəl/ a. mutuamente igual.

coerce /kou'ɜrs/ v. forzar.

coercion /kou'ɜrʃən/ n. coerción f.

coercive /kou'ɜrsɪv/ a. coercitivo.

coexist /,kouɪg'zɪst/ v. coexistir.

coffee /'kɔfi/ n. café m. **c. plantation,** cafetal m. **c. shop,** café m.

coffee break pausa para el café f.

coffer /'kɔfər/ n. cofre m.

coffin /'kɔfɪn/ n. ataúd m.

cog /kɒg/ n. diente de rueda m.

cogent /'koudʒənt/ a. convincente.

cogitate /'kɒdʒɪ,teit/ v. pensar, reflexionar.

cognizance /'kɒgnəzəns/ n. conocimiento m., comprensión f.

cognizant /'kɒgnəzənt/ a. conocedor, informado.

cogwheel /'kɒg,wil/ n. rueda dentada f.

cohere /kou'hɪər/ v. pegarse.
coherent /kou'hɪərənt/ a. coherente.
cohesion /kou'hiʒən/ n. cohesión f.
cohesive /kou'hisɪv/ a. cohesivo.
cohort /'kouhɔrt/ n. cohorte f.
coiffure /kwɑ'fyur/ n. peinado, tocado m.
coil /kɔil/ n. **1.** rollo m.; *Naut.* adujada f. —v. **2.** enrollar.
coin /kɔin/ n. moneda f.
coinage /'kɔinɪdʒ/ n. sistema monetario m.
coincide /ˌkouɪn'said/ v. coincidir.
coincidence /kou'ɪnsɪdəns/ n. coincidencia; casualidad f.
coincident /kou'ɪnsɪdənt/ a. coincidente.
coincidental /kouˌɪnsɪ'dɛntl̩/ a. coincidental.
coincidentally /kouˌɪnsɪ'dɛntl̩i/ adv. coincidentalmente, al mismo tiempo.
colander /'kɒləndər/ n. colador m.
cold /kould/ a. & n. frío -a; *Med.* resfriado m. **to be c.,** tener frío; (weather) hacer frío.
coldly /'kouldli/ adv. fríamente.
coldness /'kouldnɪs/ n. frialdad f.
collaborate /kə'læbəˌreit/ v. colaborar.
collaboration /kəˌlæbə'reiʃən/ n. colaboración f.
collaborator /kə'læbəˌreitər/ n. colaborador -ra.
collapse /kə'læps/ n. **1.** desplome m.; *Med.* colapso m. —v. **2.** desplomarse.
collar /'kɒlər/ n. cuello m.
collarbone /'kɒlərˌboun/ n. clavícula f.
collate /kou'leit/ v. comparar.
collateral /kə'lætərəl/ a. **1.** colateral. —n. **2.** garantía f.
collation /kə'leiʃən/ n. comparación f.; (food) colación f., merienda f.
colleague /'kɒlig/ n. colega m. & f.
collect /'kɒlɛkt/ v. cobrar; recoger; coleccionar.
collection /kə'lɛkʃən/ n. colección f.
collective /kə'lɛktɪv/ a. colectivo.
collectively /kə'lɛktɪvli/ adv. colectivamente, en masa.
collector /kə'lɛktər/ n. colector -ra; coleccionista m. & f.

college /'kɒlɪdʒ/ n. colegio m.; universidad f.
collegiate /kə'lidʒɪt/ n. colegiado m.
collide /kə'laid/ v. chocar.
collision /kə'lɪʒən/ n. choque m.
colloquial /kə'loukwiəl/ a. familiar.
colloquially /kə'loukwiəli/ adv. familiarmente.
colloquy /'kɒləkwi/ n. conversación f., coloquio m.
collusion /kə'luʒən/ n. colusión f., connivencia f.
Cologne /kə'loun/ n. Colonia f.
Colombian /kə'lʌmbiən/ a. & n. colombiano -na.
colon /'koulən/ n. colon m.; *Punct.* dos puntos.
colonel /'kɜrnl̩/ n. coronel m.
colonial /kə'louniəl/ a. colonial.
colonist /'kɒlənɪst/ n. colono -na.
colonization /ˌkɒlənə'zeiʃən/ n. colonización f.
colonize /'kɒləˌnaiz/ v. colonizar.
colony /'kɒləni/ n. colonia f.
color /'kʌlər/ n. **1.** color; colorido m. —v. **2.** colorar; colorir.
coloration /ˌkʌlə'reiʃən/ n. colorido m.
colored /'kʌlərd/ a. de color.
colorful /'kʌlərfəl/ a. vívido.
colorless /'kʌlərlɪs/ a. descolorido, sin color.
colossal /kə'lɒsəl/ a. colosal.
colt /koult/ n. potro m.
column /'kɒləm/ n. columna f.
coma /'koumə/ n. coma m.
comb /koum/ n. **1.** peine m. —v. **2.** peinar.
combat /n 'kɒmbæt; v kəm'bæt/ n. **1.** combate m. —v. **2.** combatir.
combatant /kəm'bætnt/ n. combatiente -ta.
combative /kəm'bætɪv/ a. combativo.
combination /ˌkɒmbə'neiʃən/ n. combinación f.
combine /kəm'bain/ v. combinar.
combustible /kəm'bʌstəbəl/ a. & n. combustible m.
combustion /kəm'bʌstʃən/ n. combustión f.
come /kʌm/ v. venir. **c. back,** volver. **c. in,** entrar. **c. out,** salir. **c. up,** subir. **c. upon,** encontrarse con.
comedian /kə'midiən/ n. cómico -ca.

comedienne /kə,midi'ɛn/ *n.* cómica *f.*, actriz *f.*

comedy /'kɒmɪdi/ *n.* comedia *f.*

comet /'kɒmɪt/ *n.* cometa *m.*

comfort /'kʌmfərt/ *n.* **1.** confort *m.*; solaz *m.* —*v.* **2.** confortar; solazar.

comfortable /'kʌmftəbəl/ *a.* cómodo.

comfortably /'kʌmftəbli/ *adv.* cómodamente.

comforter /'kʌmfərtər/ *n.* colcha *f.*

comfortingly /'kʌmfərtɪŋli/ *adv.* confortantemente.

comfortless /'kɒmfərtlɪs/ *a.* sin consuelo; sin comodidades.

comic /'kɒmɪk/ **comical** *a.* cómico.

comic book *n.* tebeo *m.*

coming /'kʌmɪŋ/ *n.* **1.** venida *f.*, llegada *f.* —*a.* **2.** próximo, que viene, entrante.

comma /'kɒmə/ *n.* coma *f.*

command /kə'mænd/ *n.* **1.** mando *m.* —*v.* **2.** mandar.

commandeer /,kɒmən'dɪər/ *v.* reclutir forzosamente, expropiar.

commander /kə'mændər/ *n.* comandante -ta.

commander in chief *n.* generalísimo, jefe supremo.

commandment /kə'mændmənt/ *n.* mandato; mandamiento *m.*

commemorate /kə'mɛmə,reit/ *v.* conmemorar.

commemoration /kə,mɛmə-'reiʃən/ *n.* conmemoración *f.*

commemorative /kə'mɛmə,reitɪv/ *a.* conmemorativo.

commence /kə'mɛns/ *v.* comenzar, principiar.

commencement /kə'mɛnsmənt/ *n.* comienzo *m.*; graduación *f.*

commend /kə'mɛnd/ *v.* encomendar; elogiar.

commendable /kə'mɛndəbəl/ *a.* recomendable.

commendably /kə'mɛndəbli/ *adv.* loablemente.

commendation /,kɒmən'deiʃən/ *n.* recomendación *f.*; elogio *m.*

commensurate /kə'mɛnsərɪt/ *a.* proporcionado.

comment /'kɒmɛnt/ *n.* **1.** comentario *m.* —*v.* **2.** comentar.

commentary /'kɒmən,tɛri/ *n.* comentario *m.*

commentator /'kɒmən,teitər/ *n.* comentador -ra.

commerce /'kɒmərs/ *n.* comercio *m.*

commercial /kə'mɜrʃəl/ *a.* comercial.

commercialism /kə'mɜrʃə,lɪzəm/ *n.* comercialismo *m.*

commercialize /kə'mɜrʃə,laiz/ *v.* mercantilizar, explotar.

commercially /kə'mɜrʃəli/ *a. & adv.* comercialmente.

commiserate /kə'mɪzə,reit/ *v.* compadecerse.

commissary /'kɒmə,sɛri/ *n.* comisario *m.*

commission /kə'mɪʃən/ *n.* **1.** comisión *f.* —*v.* **2.** comisionar.

commissioner /kə'mɪʃənər/ *n.* comisario -ria.

commit /kə'mɪt/ *v.* cometer.

commitment /kə'mɪtmənt/ *n.* compromiso *m.*

committee /kə'mɪti/ *n.* comité *m.*

commodious /kə'moudiəs/ *a.* cómodo.

commodity /kə'mɒdɪti/ *n.* mercadería *f.*

common /'kɒmən/ *a.* común; ordinario.

commonly /'kɒmənli/ *adv.* comúnmente, vulgarmente.

Common Market Mercado Común *m.*

commonplace /'kɒmən,pleis/ *a.* trivial, banal.

common sense sentido común *m.*

commonwealth /'kɒmən,wɛlθ/ *n.* estado *m.*; nación *f.*

commotion /kə'mouʃən/ *n.* tumulto *m.*

communal /kə'myunḷ/ *a.* comunal, público.

commune /'kɒmyun/ *n.* **1.** distrito municipal *m.*; comuna *f.* —*v.* **2.** conversar.

communicable /kə'myunɪkəbəl/ *a.* comunicable; *Med.* transmisible.

communicate /kə'myunɪ,keit/ *v.* comunicar.

communication /kə,myunɪ'keiʃən/ *n.* comunicación *f.*

communicative /kə'myunɪ,keitɪv/ *a.* comunicativo.

communion /kə'myunyən/ *n.* comunión *f.* **take c.,** comulgar.

communiqué /kə,myunɪ'kei/ *n.* comunicación *f.*

communism /'kɒmyə,nɪzəm/ *n.* comunismo *m.*

communist /'kɒmyənɪst/ *n.* comunista *m. & f.*

communistic /ˌkɒmyəˈnɪstɪk/ *a.* comunístico.

community /kəˈmyunɪti/ *n.* comunidad *f.*

commutation /ˌkɒmyəˈteiʃən/ *n.* conmutación *f.*

commuter /kəˈmyutər/ *n.* empleado que viaja diariamente desde su domicilio hasta la ciudad donde trabaja.

compact /*a* kəmˈpækt; *n* ˈkɒmpækt/ *a.* **1.** compacto. —*n.* **2.** pacto *m.;* (lady's) polvera *f.*

compact disk disco compacto *m.*

companion /kəmˈpænyən/ *n.* compañero -ra.

companionable /kəmˈpænyənəbəl/ *a.* sociable.

companionship /kəmˈpænyənˌʃɪp/ *n.* compañerismo *m.*

company /ˈkʌmpəni/ *n.* compañía *f.*

comparable /ˈkɒmpərəbəl/ *a.* comparable.

comparative /kəmˈpærətɪv/ *a.* comparativo.

comparatively /kəmˈpærətɪvli/ *a.* relativamente.

compare /kəmˈpɛər/ *v.* comparar.

comparison /kəmˈpærəsən/ *n.* comparación *f.*

compartment /kəmˈpɑrtmənt/ *n.* compartimiento *m.*

compass /ˈkʌmpəs/ *n.* compás *m.; Naut.* brújula *f.*

compassion /kəmˈpæʃən/ *n.* compasión *f.*

compassionate /kəmˈpæʃənɪt/ *a.* compasivo.

compassionately /kəmˈpæʃənɪtli/ *adv.* compasivamente.

compatible /kəmˈpætəbəl/ *a.* compatible.

compatriot /kəmˈpeitriət/ *n.* compatriota *m.* & *f.*

compel /kəmˈpɛl/ *v.* obligar.

compensate /ˈkɒmpənˌseit/ *v.* compensar.

compensation /ˌkɒmpənˈseiʃən/ *n.* compensación *f.*

compensatory /kəmˈpɛnsəˌtɔri/ *a.* compensatorio.

compete /kəmˈpit/ *v.* competir.

competence /ˈkɒmpɪtəns/ *n.* competencia *f.*

competent /ˈkɒmpɪtənt/ *a.* competente, capaz.

competently /ˈkɒmpɪtəntli/ *adv.* competentemente.

competition /ˌkɒmpɪˈtɪʃən/ *n.* concurrencia *f.;* concurso *m.*

competitive /kəmˈpɛtɪtɪv/ *a.* competidor.

competitor /kəmˈpɛtɪtər/ *n.* competidor -ra.

compile /kəmˈpail/ *v.* compilar.

complacency /kəmˈpleisənsi/ *n.* complacencia *f.*

complacent /kəmˈpleisənt/ *a.* complaciente.

complacently /kəmˈpleisəntli/ *adv.* complacientemente.

complain /kəmˈplein/ *v.* quejarse.

complaint /kəmˈpleint/ *n.* queja *f.*

complement /ˈkɒmpləmənt/ *n.* complemento *m.*

complete /kəmˈplit/ *a.* **1.** completo —*v.* **2.** completar.

completely /kəmˈplitli/ *adv.* completamente, enteramente.

completeness /kəmˈplitnɪs/ *n.* integridad *f.*

completion /kəmˈpliʃən/ *n.* terminación *f.*

complex /kəmˈplɛks/ *a.* complejo.

complexion /kəmˈplɛkʃən/ *n.* tez *f.*

complexity /kəmˈplɛksɪti/ *n.* complejidad *f.*

compliance /kəmˈplaiəns/ *n.* consentimiento *m.* **in c. with,** de - acuerdo con.

compliant /kəmˈplaiənt/ *a.* dócil; complaciente.

complicate /ˈkɒmplɪˌkeit/ *v.* complicar.

complicated /ˈkɒmplɪˌkeitɪd/ *a.* complicado.

complication /ˌkɒmplɪˈkeiʃən/ *n.* complicación *f.*

complicity /kəmˈplɪsɪti/ *n.* complicidad *f.*

compliment /*n* ˈkɒmpləmənt; *v* -ˌmɛnt/ *n.* **1.** elogio *m. Fig.* —*v.* **2.** felicitar; echar flores.

complimentary /ˌkɒmpləˈmɛntəri/ *a.* galante, obsequioso, regaloso.

comply /kəmˈplai/ *v.* cumplir.

component /kəmˈpounənt/ *a.* & *n.* componente *m.*

comport /kəmˈpɔrt/ *v.* portarse.

compose /kəmˈpouz/ *v.* componer.

composed /kəmˈpouzd/ *a.* tranquilo; (made up) compuesto.

composer /kəmˈpouzər/ *n.* compositor -ra.

composite /kəmˈpɒzɪt/ *a.* compuesto.

composition /ˌkɒmpə'zɪʃən/ *n.* composición *f.*

composure /kəm'pouʒər/ *n.* serenidad *f.;* calma *f.*

compote /'kɒmpout/ *n.* compota *f.*

compound /'kɒmpaund/ *a. & n.* compuesto *m.*

comprehend /ˌkɒmprɪ'hɛnd/ *v.* comprender.

comprehensible /ˌkɒmprɪ'hɛnsəbəl/ *a.* comprensible.

comprehension /ˌkɒmprɪ'hɛnʃən/ *n.* comprensión *f.*

comprehensive /ˌkɒmprɪ'hɛnsɪv/ *a.* comprensivo.

compress /n 'kɒmprɛs; v kəm'prɛs/ *n.* **1.** cabezal *m.* —*v.* **2.** comprimir.

compressed /kəm'prɛst/ *a.* comprimido.

compression /kəm'prɛʃən/ *n.* compresión *f.*

compressor /kəm'prɛsər/ *n.* compresor *m.*

comprise /kəm'praiz/ *v.* comprender; abarcar.

compromise /'kɒmprə,maiz/ *n.* **1.** compromiso *m.* —*v.* **2.** comprometer.

compromiser /'kɒmprə,maizər/ *n.* compromisario *m.*

compulsion /kəm'pʌlʃən/ *n.* compulsión *f.*

compulsive /kəm'pʌlsɪv/ *a.* compulsivo.

compulsory /kəm'pʌlsəri/ *a.* obligatorio.

compunction /kəm'pʌŋkʃən/ *n.* compunción *f.;* escrúpulo *m.*

computation /ˌkɒmpyu'teiʃən/ *n.* computación *f.*

compute /kəm'pyut/ *v.* computar, calcular.

computer /kəm'pyutər/ *n.* computadora *f.,* ordenador *m.*

computerize /kəm'pyutə,raiz/ *v.* procesar en computadora, computerizar.

computer programmer /'prougræmər/ programador -ra de ordenadores.

computer science informática *f.*

comrade /'kɒmræd/ *n.* camarada *m. & f.;* compañero -ra.

comradeship /'kɒmræd,ʃɪp/ *n.* camaradería *f.*

concave /kɒn'keiv/ *a.* cóncavo.

conceal /kən'sil/ *v.* ocultar, esconder.

concealment /kən'silmənt/ *n.* ocultación *f.*

concede /kən'sid/ *v.* conceder.

conceit /kən'sit/ *n.* amor propio; engreimiento *m.*

conceited /kən'sitɪd/ *a.* engreído.

conceivable /kən'sivəbəl/ *a.* concebible.

conceive /kən'siv/ *v.* concebir.

concentrate /'kɒnsən,treit/ *v.* concentrar.

concentration /ˌkɒnsən'treiʃən/ *n.* concentración *f.*

concentration camp campo de concentración *m.*

concept /'kɒnsɛpt/ *n.* concepto *m.*

conception /kən'sɛpʃən/ *n.* concepción *f.;* concepto *m.*

concern /kən'sɜrn/ *n.* **1.** interés *m.;* inquietud *f.;* Com. negocio *m.* —*v.* **2.** concernir.

concerning /kən'sɜrnɪŋ/ *prep.* respecto a.

concert /'kɒnsɜrt/ *n.* concierto *m.*

concerted /kən'sɜrtɪd/ *a.* convenido.

concession /kən'sɛʃən/ *n.* concesión *f.*

conciliate /kən'sɪli,eit/ *v.* conciliar.

conciliation /kən,sɪli'eiʃən/ *n.* conciliación *f.*

conciliator /kən'sɪli,eitər/ *n.* conciliador -ra.

conciliatory /kən'sɪliə,tɔri/ *a.* conciliatorio.

concise /kən'sais/ *a.* conciso.

concisely /kən'saisli/ *adv.* concisamente.

conciseness /kən'saisnɪs/ *n.* concisión *f.*

conclave /'kɒnkleiv/ *n.* conclave *m.*

conclude /kən'klud/ *v.* concluir.

conclusion /kən'kluʒən/ *n.* conclusión *f.*

conclusive /kən'klusɪv/ *a.* conclusivo, decisivo.

conclusively /kən'klusɪvli/ *adv.* concluyentemente.

concoct /kɒn'kɒkt/ *v.* confeccionar.

concomitant /kɒn'kɒmɪtənt/ *n. & a.* concomitante *m.*

concord /'kɒnkɔrd/ *n.* concordia *f.*

concordat /kɒn'kɔrdæt/ *n.* concordato *m.*

concourse /'kɒnkɔrs/ *n.* concurso *m.;* confluencia *f.*

concrete /'kɒnkrit/ *a.* concreto.

concretely /kɒnˈkritli/ *adv.* concretamente.

concubine /ˈkɒŋkyəˌbain/ *n.* concubina, amiga *f.*

concur /kənˈkɜr/ *v.* concurrir.

concurrence /kənˈkɜrəns/ *n.* concurrencia *f.;* casualidad *f.*

concurrent /kənˈkɜrənt/ *a.* concurrente.

concussion /kənˈkʌʃən/ *n.* concusión *f.;* (c. of the brain) conmoción cerebral *f.*

condemn /kənˈdɛm/ *v.* condenar.

condemnable /kənˈdɛmnəbəl/ *a.* culpable, condenable.

condemnation /ˌkɒndɛmˈneiʃən/ *n.* condenación *f.*

condensation /ˌkɒndɛnˈseiʃən/ *n.* condensación *f.*

condense /kənˈdɛns/ *v.* condensar.

condenser /kənˈdɛnsər/ *n.* condensador *m.*

condescend /ˌkɒndəˈsɛnd/ *v.* condescender.

condescension /ˌkɒndəˈsɛnʃən/ *n.* condescendencia *f.*

condiment /ˈkɒndəmənt/ *n.* condimento *m.*

condition /kənˈdɪʃən/ *n.* **1.** condición *f.;* estado *m.* —*v.* **2.** acondicionar.

conditional /kənˈdɪʃənl/ *a.* condicional.

conditionally /kənˈdɪʃənli/ *adv.* condicionalmente.

condole /kənˈdoul/ *v.* condolerse.

condolence /kənˈdoulɒns/ *n.* pésame *m.*

condom /ˈkɒndəm/ *n.* forro, preservativo *m.*

condominium /ˌkɒndəˈmɪniəm/ *n.* condominio *m.*

condone /kənˈdoun/ *v.* condonar.

conducive /kənˈdusɪv, -ˈdyu-/ *a.* conducente.

conduct /*n* ˈkɒndʌkt; *v* kənˈdʌkt/ *n.* **1.** conducta *f.* —*v.* **2.** conducir.

conductivity /ˌkɒndʌkˈtɪvɪti/ *n.* conductividad *f.*

conductor /kənˈdʌktər/ *n.* conductor *m.*

conduit /ˈkɒnduit/ *n.* caño *m.*, canal *f.;* conducto *m.*

cone /koun/ *n.* cono *m.* **ice-cream c.,** barquillo de helado.

confection /kənˈfɛkʃən/ *n.* confitura *f.*

confectioner /kənˈfɛkʃənər/ *n.* confitero -ra.

confectionery /kənˈfɛkʃəˌnɛri/ *n.* dulcería *f.*

confederacy /kənˈfɛdərəsi/ *n.* federación *f.*

confederate / kənˈfɛdərɪt/ *a.* & *n.* confederado *m.*

confederation /kənˌfɛdəˈreiʃən/ *n.* confederación *f.*

confer /kənˈfɜr/ *v.* conferenciar; conferir.

conference /ˈkɒnfərəns/ *n.* conferencia *f.;* congreso *m.*

confess /kənˈfɛs/ *v.* confesar.

confession /kənˈfɛʃən/ *n.* confesión *f.*

confessional /kənˈfɛʃənl/ *n.* **1.** confesionario *m.* —*a.* **2.** confesional.

confessor /kənˈfɛsər/ *n.* confesor *m.*

confetti /kənˈfɛti/ *n.* confetti *m.*

confidant /ˈkɒnfɪˌdænt/ **confidante** *n.* confidente *m.* & *f.*

confide /kənˈfaid/ *v.* confiar.

confidence /ˈkɒnfɪdəns/ *n.* confianza *f.*

confident /ˈkɒnfɪdənt/ *a.* confiado; cierto.

confidential /ˌkɒnfɪˈdɛnʃəl/ *a.* confidencial.

confidentially /ˌkɒnfɪˈdɛnʃəli/ *adv.* confidencialmente, en secreto.

confidently /ˈkɒnfɪdəntli/ *adv.* confiadamente.

confine /kənˈfain/ *n.* **1.** confín *m.* —*v.* **2.** confinar; encerrar.

confirm /kənˈfɜrm/ *v.* confirmar.

confirmation /ˌkɒnfərˈmeiʃən/ *n.* confirmación *f.*

confiscate /ˈkɒnfəˌskeit/ *v.* confiscar.

confiscation /ˌkɒnfəˈskeiʃən/ *n.* confiscación *f.*

conflagration /ˌkɒnfləˈgreiʃən/ *n.* incendio *m.*

conflict /*n* ˈkɒnflɪkt; *v* kənˈflɪkt/ *n.* **1.** conflicto *m.* —*v.* **2.** oponerse; estar en conflicto.

conform /kənˈfɔrm/ *v.* conformar.

conformation /ˌkɒnfərˈmeiʃən/ *n.* conformación *f.*

conformer /kənˈfɔrmər/ *n.* conformista *m.* & *f.*

conformist /kənˈfɔrmɪst/ *n.* conformista *m.* & *f.*

conformity /kənˈfɔrmɪti/ *n.* conformidad *f.*

confound /kɒnˈfaund/ *v.* confundir.

confront /kənˈfrʌnt/ v. confrontar.

confrontation /ˌkɒnfrənˈteiʃən/ n. enfrentamiento m.

confuse /kənˈfyuz/ v. confundir.

confusion /kənˈfyuʒən/ n. confusión f.

congeal /kənˈdʒil/ v. congelar, helar.

congealment /kənˈdʒilmənt/ n. congelación f.

congenial /kənˈdʒinyəl/ a. congenial.

congenital /kənˈdʒenɪtl̩/ a. congénito.

congenitally /kənˈdʒenɪtli/ adv. congenitalmente.

congestion /kənˈdʒestʃən/ n. congestión f.

conglomerate /v kənˈglɒmə,reit; a, n kənˈglɒmərɪt/ v. **1.** conglomerar. —a. & n. **2.** conglomerado.

conglomeration /kən,glɒmə-ˈreiʃən/ n. conglomeración f.

congratulate /kənˈgrætʃə,leit/ v. felicitar.

congratulation /kən,grætʃə-ˈleiʃən/ n. felicitación f.

congratulatory /kənˈgrætʃələ,tɔri/ a. congratulatorio.

congregate /ˈkɒŋgrɪ,geit/ v. congregar.

congregation /ˌkɒŋgrɪˈgeiʃən/ n. congregación f.

congress /ˈkɒŋgrɪs/ n. congreso m.

conic /ˈkɒnɪk/ n. **1.** cónica f. —a. **2.** cónico.

conjecture /kənˈdʒektʃər/ n. **1.** conjetura f. —v. **2.** conjeturar.

conjugal /ˈkɒndʒəgəl/ a. conyugal, matrimonial.

conjugate /ˈkɒndʒə,geit/ v. conjugar.

conjugation /ˌkɒndʒəˈgeiʃən/ n. conjugación f.

conjunction /kənˈdʒʌŋkʃən/ n. conjunción f.

conjunctive /kənˈdʒʌŋktɪv/ n. **1.** Gram. conjunción f. —a. **2.** conjuntivo.

conjunctivitis /kən,dʒʌŋktəˈvaitɪs/ n. conjuntivitis f.

conjure /ˈkɒndʒər/ v. conjurar.

connect /kəˈnekt/ v. juntar; relacionar.

connection /kəˈnekʃən/ n. conexión f.

connivance /kəˈnaivəns/ n. consentimiento m.

connive /kəˈnaiv/ v. disimular.

connoisseur /ˌkɒnəˈsɜr/ n. perito -ta.

connotation /ˌkɒnəˈteiʃən/ n. connotación f.

connote /kəˈnout/ v. connotar.

connubial /kəˈnubiəl/ a. conyugal.

conquer /ˈkɒŋkər/ v. conquistar.

conquerable /ˈkɒŋkərəbəl/ a. conquistable, vencible.

conqueror /ˈkɒŋkərər/ n. conquistador -ra.

conquest /ˈkɒŋkwest/ n. conquista f.

conscience /ˈkɒnʃəns/ n. conciencia f.

conscientious /ˌkɒnʃiˈɛnʃəs/ a. concienzudo.

conscientiously /ˌkɒnʃiˈɛnʃəsli/ adv. escrupulosamente.

conscientious objector /ɒbˈdʒektər/ objetor de conciencia m.

conscious /ˈkɒnʃəs/ a. consciente.

consciously /ˈkɒnʃəsli/ adv. con conocimiento.

consciousness /ˈkɒnʃəsnɪs/ n. consciencia f.

conscript /n ˈkɒnskrɪpt; v kənˈskrɪpt/ n. **1.** conscripto m., recluta m. —v. **2.** reclutar, alistar.

conscription /kənˈskrɪpʃən/ n. conscripción f., alistamiento m.

consecrate /ˈkɒnsɪ,kreit/ v. consagrar.

consecration /ˌkɒnsɪˈkreiʃən/ n. consagración f.

consecutive /kənˈsekyətɪv/ a. consecutivo, seguido.

consecutively /kənˈsekyətɪvli/ adv. consecutivamente, de seguida.

consensus /kənˈsensəs/ n. consenso m., acuerdo general m.

consent /kənˈsent/ n. **1.** consentimiento m. —v. **2.** consentir.

consequence /ˈkɒnsɪ,kwens/ n. consecuencia f.

consequent /ˈkɒnsɪ,kwent/ a. consiguiente.

consequential /ˌkɒnsɪˈkwenʃəl/ a. importante.

consequently /ˈkɒnsɪ,kwentli/ adv. por lo tanto, por consiguiente.

conservation /ˌkɒnsərˈveiʃən/ n. conservación f.

conservatism /kənˈsɜrvə,tɪzəm/ n. conservatismo m.

conservative /kənˈsɜrvətɪv/ a. conservador, conservativo.

contact

conservatory /kən'sɜrvə,tɔri/ *n.* (plants) invernáculo *m.;* (school) conservatorio *m.*

conserve /kən'sɜrv/ *v.* conservar.

consider /kən'sɪdər/ *v.* considerar.
C. it done! ¡Dalo por hecho!

considerable /kən'sɪdərəbəl/ *a.* considerable.

considerably /kən'sɪdərəbli/ *adv.* considerablemente.

considerate /kən'sɪdərɪt/ *a.* considerado.

considerately /kən'sɪdərɪtli/ *adv.* consideradamente.

consideration /kən,sɪdə'reɪʃən/ *n.* consideración *f.*

considering /kən'sɪdərɪŋ/ *prep.* visto que, en vista de.

consign /kən'saɪn/ *v.* consignar.

consignment /kən'saɪnmənt/ *n.* consignación *f.,* envío *m.*

consist /kən'sɪst/ *v.* consistir.

consistency /kən'sɪstənsi/ *n.* consistencia *f.*

consistent /kən'sɪstənt/ *a.* consistente.

consolation /,kɒnsə'leɪʃən/ *n.* consolación *f.*

consolation prize premio de consuelo *m.*

console /kən'soul/ *v.* consolar.

consolidate /kən'sɒlɪ,deɪt/ *v.* consolidar.

consommé /,kɒnsə'meɪ/ *n.* caldo *m.*

consonant /'kɒnsənənt/ *n.* consonante *f.*

consort /*n* 'kɒnsɔrt, *v* kən'sɔrt/ *n.* **1.** cónyuge *m. & f.;* socio. —*v.* **2.** asociarse.

conspicuous /kən'spɪkyuəs/ *a.* conspicuo.

conspicuously /kən'spɪkyuəsli/ *adv.* visiblemente, llamativamente.

conspicuousness /kən'spɪkyuəsnɪs/ *n.* visibilidad *f.;* evidencia *f.;* fama *f.*

conspiracy /kən'spɪrəsi/ *n.* conspiración *f.;* complot *m.*

conspirator /kən'spɪrətər/ *n.* conspirador -ra.

conspire /kən'spaɪ³r/ *v.* conspirar.

conspirer /kən'spaɪ³rər/ *n.* conspirante *m. & f.*

constancy /'kɒnstənsi/ *n.* constancia *f.,* lealtad *f.*

constant /'kɒnstənt/ *a.* constante.

constantly /'kɒnstəntli/ *adv.* constantemente, de continuo.

constellation /,kɒnstə'leɪʃən/ *n.* constelación *f.*

consternation /,kɒnstər'neɪʃən/ *n.* consternación *f.*

constipate /'kɒnstə,peɪt/ *v.* estreñir.

constipated /'kɒnstə,peɪtɪd/ *a.* estreñido, *m.*

constipation /,kɒnstə'peɪʃən/ *n.* estreñimiento, *m.*

constituency /kən'stɪtʃuənsi/ *n.* distrito electoral *m.*

constituent /kən'stɪtʃuənt/ *a.* **1.** constituyente. —*n.* **2.** elector *m.*

constitute /'kɒnstɪ,tut/ *v.* constituir.

constitution /,kɒnstɪ'tuʃən/ *n.* constitución *f.*

constitutional /,kɒnstɪ'tuʃənļ/ *a.* constitucional.

constrain /kən'streɪn/ *v.* constreñir.

constraint /kən'streɪnt/ *n.* constreñimiento *m.,* compulsión *f.*

constrict /kən'strɪkt/ *v.* apretar, estrechar.

construct /kən'strʌkt/ *v.* construir.

construction /kən'strʌkʃən/ *n.* construcción *f.*

constructive /kən'strʌktɪv/ *a.* constructivo.

constructively /kən'strʌktɪvli/ *adv.* constructivamente; por deducción.

constructor /kən'strʌktər/ *n.* constructor *m.*

construe /kən'stru/ *v.* interpretar.

consul /'kɒnsəl/ *n.* cónsul *m.*

consular /'kɒnsələr/ *a.* consular.

consulate /'kɒnsəlɪt/ *n.* consulado *m.*

consult /kən'sʌlt/ *v.* consultar.

consultant /kən'sʌltənt/ *n.* consultor -ora.

consultation /,kɒnsəl'teɪʃən/ *n.* consulta *f.*

consume /kən'sum/ *v.* consumir.

consumer /kən'sumər/ *n.* consumidor -ra.

consumer society sociedad de consumo *f.*

consummation /,kɒnsə'meɪʃən/ *n.* consumación *f.*

consumption /kən'sʌmpʃən/ *n.* consumo *m.; Med.* tisis.

consumptive /kən'sʌmptɪv/ *n.* **1.** tísico *m.* —*a.* **2.** consuntivo.

contact /'kɒntækt/ *n.* **1.** contacto

m. —*v.* **2.** ponerse en contacto con.

contact lens lentilla *f.*

contagion /kən'teidʒən/ *n.* contagio *m.*

contagious /kən'teidʒəs/ *a.* contagioso.

contain /kən'tein/ *v.* contener.

container /kən'teinər/ *n.* envase *m.*

contaminate /kən'tæmə,neit/ *v.* contaminar.

contemplate /'kɒntəm,pleit/ *v.* contemplar.

contemplation /,kɒntəm'pleiʃən/ *n.* contemplación *f.*

contemplative /kən'templətɪv/ *a.* contemplativo.

contemporary /kən'tempə,reri/ *n.* & *a.* contemporáneo -nea.

contempt /kən'tempt/ *n.* desprecio *m.*

contemptible /kən'temptəbəl/ *a.* vil, despreciable.

contemptuous /kən'temptʃuəs/ *a.* desdeñoso.

contemptuously /kən'temptʃuəsli/ *adv.* desdeñosamente.

contend /kən'tend/ *v.* contender; competir.

contender /kən'tendər/ *n.* competidor -ra.

content /*a, v* kən'tent; *n* 'kɒntent/ *a.* **1.** contento. —*n.* **2.** contenido *m.* —*v.* **3.** contentar.

contented /kən'tentɪd/ *a.* contento.

contention /kən'tenʃən/ *n.* contención *f.*

contentment /kən'tentmənt/ *n.* contentamiento *m.*

contest /*n* 'kɒntest; *v* kən'test/ *n.* **1.** concurso *m.* —*v.* **2.** disputar.

contestable /kən'testəbəl/ *a.* contestable.

context /'kɒntekst/ *n.* contexto *m.*

contiguous /kən'tɪgyuəs/ *a.* contiguo.

continence /'kɒntn̩əns/ *n.* continencia *f.*, castidad *f.*

continent /'kɒntn̩ənt/ *n.* continente *m.*

continental /,kɒntn̩'entl/ *a.* continental.

contingency /kən'tɪndʒənsi/ *n.* eventualidad *f.*, casualidad *f.*

contingent /kən'tɪndʒənt/ *a.* contingente.

continual /kən'tɪnyuəl/ *a.* continuo.

continuation /kən,tɪnyu'eiʃən/ *n.* continuación *f.*

continue /kən'tɪnyu/ *v.* continuar.

continuity /,kɒntn̩'uiti/ *n.* continuidad *f.*

continuous /kən'tɪnyuəs/ *a.* continuo.

continuously /kən'tɪnyuəsli/ *adv.* continuamente.

contour /'kɒntur/ *n.* contorno *m.*

contraband /'kɒntrə,bænd/ *n.* contrabando *m.*

contraception /,kɒntrə'sepʃən/ *n.* contracepción *f.*

contraceptive /,kɒntrə'septɪv/ *n.* & *a.* anticeptivo *m.*

contract /*n* 'kɒntrækt; *v* kən'trækt/ *n.* **1.** contrato *m.* —*v.* **2.** contraer.

contraction /kən'trækʃən/ *n.* contracción *f.*

contractor /'kɒntræktər/ *n.* contratista *m.* & *f.*

contradict /,kɒntrə'dɪkt/ *v.* contradecir.

contradiction /,kɒntrə'dɪkʃən/ *n.* contradicción *f.*

contradictory /,kɒntrə'dɪktəri/ *a.* contradictorio.

contralto /kən'træltou/ *n.* contralto *m.*

contrary /'kɒntreri/ *a.* & *n.* contrario -ria.

contrast /*n* 'kɒntræst; *v* kən'træst/ *n.* **1.** contraste *m.* —*v.* **2.** contrastar.

contribute /kən'trɪbyut/ *v.* contribuir.

contribution /,kɒntrə'byuʃən/ *n.* contribución *f.*

contributor /kən'trɪbyətər/ *n.* contribuidor -ra.

contributory /kən'trɪbyə,tɔri/ *a.* contribuyente.

contrite /kən'trait/ *a.* contrito.

contrition /kən'trɪʃən/ *n.* contrición *f.*

contrivance /kən'traivəns/ *n.* aparato *m.*; estratagema *f.*

contrive /kən'traiv/ *v.* inventar, tramar; darse maña.

control /kən'troul/ *n.* **1.** control *m.* —*v.* **2.** controlar.

controllable /kən'troulabəl/ *a.* controlable, dominable.

controller /kən'troulər/ *n.* interventor -ra; contralor -ra.

control tower torre de mando *f.*

controversial /ˌkɒntrəˈvɜrʃəl/ a. contencioso.

controversy /ˈkɒntrəˌvɜrsi/ n. controversia f.

contusion /kənˈtuʒən/ n. contusión f.

convalesce /ˌkɒnvəˈlɛs/ v. convalecer.

convalescence /ˌkɒnvəˈlɛsəns/ n. convalecencia f.

convalescent /ˌkɒnvəˈlɛsənt/ n. convaleciente m. & f.

convalescent home clínica de reposo f.

convene /kənˈvin/ v. juntarse; convocar.

convenience /kənˈvinyəns/ n. comodidad f.

convenient /kənˈvinyənt/ a. cómodo; oportuno.

conveniently /kənˈvinyəntli/ adv. cómodamente.

convent /ˈkɒnvɛnt/ n. convento m.

convention /kənˈvɛnʃən/ n. convención f.

conventional /kənˈvɛnʃənl/ a. convencional.

conventionally /kənˈvɛnʃənli/ adv. convencionalmente.

converge /kənˈvɜrdʒ/ v. convergir.

convergence /kənˈvɜrdʒəns/ n. convergencia f.

convergent /kənˈvɜrdʒənt/ a. convergente.

conversant /kənˈvɜrsənt/ a. versado; entendido (de).

conversation /ˌkɒnvərˈseiʃən/ n. conversación, plática f.

conversational /ˌkɒnvərˈseiʃənl/ a. de conversación.

conversationalist /ˌkɒnvərˈseiʃənlɪst/ n. conversador -ra.

converse /kənˈvɜrs/ v. conversar.

conversely /kənˈvɜrsli/ adv. a la inversa.

convert /n ˈkɒnvɜrt; v kənˈvɜrt/ n. **1.** convertido da-. —v. **2.** convertir.

converter /kənˈvɜrtər/ n. convertidor m.

convertible /kənˈvɜrtəbəl/ a. convertible.

convex /kɒnˈvɛks/ a. convexo.

convey /kənˈvei/ v. transportar; comunicar.

conveyance /kənˈveiəns/ n. transporte; vehículo m.

conveyor /kənˈveiər/ n. conductor m.; Mech. transportador m.

conveyor belt correa transportadora f.

convict /n ˈkɒnvɪkt; v kənˈvɪkt/ n. **1.** reo m. —v. **2.** declarar culpable.

conviction /kənˈvɪkʃən/ n. convicción f.

convince /kənˈvɪns/ v. convencer.

convincing /kənˈvɪnsɪŋ/ a. convincente.

convivial /kənˈvɪviəl/ a. convival.

convocation /ˌkɒnvəˈkeiʃən/ n. convocación; asamblea f.

convoke /kənˈvouk/ v. convocar, citar.

convoy /ˈkɒnvɔi/ n. convoy m.; escolta f.

convulse /kənˈvʌls/ v. convulsionar; agitar violentamente.

convulsion /kənˈvʌlʃən/ n. convulsión f.

convulsive /kənˈvʌlsɪv/ a. convulsivo.

cook /kʊk/ n. **1.** cocinero -ra. —v. **2.** cocinar, cocer.

cookbook /ˈkʊkˌbʊk/ n. libro de cocina m.

cookie /ˈkʊki/ n. galleta dulce f.

cool /kul/ a. **1.** fresco. —v. **2.** refrescar.

cooler /ˈkulər/ n. enfriadera f.

coolness /ˈkulnɪs/ n. frescura f.

coop /kup/ n. **1.** jaula f. **chicken c.**, gallinero m. —v. **2.** enjaular.

cooperate /kouˈɒpəˌreit/ v. cooperar.

cooperation /kouˌɒpəˈreiʃən/ n. cooperación f.

cooperative /kouˈɒpərətɪv/ a. cooperativo.

cooperatively /kouˈɒpərətɪvli/ adv. cooperativamente.

coordinate /kouˈɔrdɪˌeit/ v. coordinar.

coordination /kouˌɔrdn̩ˈeiʃən/ n. coordinación f.

coordinator /kouˈɔrdn̩ˌeitər/ n. coordinador -ra.

cope /koup/ v. contender. **c. with,** superar, hacer frente a.

copier /ˈkɒpiər/ n. copiadora f.

copious /ˈkoupiəs/ a. copioso, abundante.

copiously /ˈkoupiəsli/ adv. copiosamente.

copiousness /ˈkoupiəsnɪs/ n. abundancia f.

copper /ˈkɒpər/ n. cobre m.

copy /'kɒpi/ n. **1.** copia f.; ejemplar m. —v. **2.** copiar.

copyist /'kɒpiɪst/ n. copista m. & f.

copyright /'kɒpi,rait/ n. derechos de propiedad literaria m.pl.

coquetry /'koukɪtri/ n. coquetería f.

coquette /kou'kɛt/ n. coqueta f.

coral /'kɔrəl/ n. coral m.

cord /kɔrd/ n. cuerda f.

cordial /'kɔrdʒəl/ a. cordial.

cordiality /kɔr'dʒæliti/ n. cordialidad f.

cordially /'kɔrdʒəli/ adv. cordialmente.

cordon off /'kɔrdn̩/ v. acordonar.

cordovan /'kɔrdəvən/ n. cordobán m.

corduroy /'kɔrdə,rɔi/ n. pana f.

core /kɔr/ n. corazón; centro m.

cork /kɔrk/ n. corcho m.

corkscrew /'kɔrk,skru/ n. tirabuzón m.

corn /kɔrn/ n. maíz m.

cornea /'kɔrniə/ n. córnea f.

corned beef /kɔrnd/ carne acecinada f.

corner /'kɔrnər/ n. rincón m.; (of street) esquina f.

cornet /kɔr'nɛt/ n. corneta f.

cornetist /kɔr'nɛtɪst/ n. cornetín m.

cornice /'kɔrnɪs/ n. cornisa f.

cornstarch /'kɔrn,stɑrtʃ/ n. maicena f.

corollary /'kɔrə,lɛri/ n. corolario m.

coronary /'kɔrə,nɛri/ a. coronario.

coronation /,kɔrə'neiʃən/ n. coronación f.

corporal /'kɔrpərəl/ a. **1.** corpóreo. —n. **2.** cabo m.

corporate /'kɔrpərɪt/ a. corporativo.

corporation /,kɔrpə'reiʃən/ n. corporación f.

corps /kɔr/ n. cuerpo m.

corpse /kɔrps/ n. cadáver m.

corpulent /'kɔrpyələnt/ a. corpulento.

corpuscle /'kɔrpəsəl/ n. corpúsculo m.

corral /kə'ræl/ n. **1.** corral m. —v. **2.** acorralar.

correct /kə'rɛkt/ a. **1.** correcto. —v. **2.** corregir.

correction /kə'rɛkʃən/ n. corrección; enmienda f.

corrective /kə'rɛktɪv/ n. & a. correctivo.

correctly /kə'rɛktli/ adv. correctamente.

correctness /kə'rɛktnɪs/ n. exactitud f.

correlate /'kɔrə,leit/ v. correlacionar.

correlation /,kɔrə'leiʃən/ n. correlación f.

correspond /,kɔrə'spɒnd/ v. corresponder.

correspondence /,kɔrə'spɒndəns/ n. correspondencia f.

correspondence course curso por correspondencia m.

correspondence school escuela por correspondencia f.

correspondent /,kɔrə'spɒndənt/ a. & n. correspondiente m. & f.

corresponding /,kɔrə'spɒndɪŋ/ a. correspondiente.

corridor /'kɔrɪdər/ n. corredor, pasillo m.

corroborate /kə'rɒbə,reit/ v. corroborar.

corroboration /kə,rɒbə'reiʃən/ n. corroboración f.

corroborative /kə'rɒbə,reitɪv/ a. corroborante.

corrode /kə'roud/ v. corroer.

corrosion /kə'rouʒən/ n. corrosión f.

corrugate /'kɔrə,geit/ v. arrugar; ondular.

corrupt /kə'rʌpt/ a. **1.** corrompido. —v. **2.** corromper.

corruptible /kə'rʌptəbəl/ a. corruptible.

corruption /kə'rʌpʃən/ n. corrupción f.

corruptive /kə'rʌptɪv/ a. corruptivo.

corset /'kɔrsɪt/ n. corsé m., (girdle) faja f.

cortege /kɔr'tɛʒ/ n. comitiva f., séquito m.

corvette /kɔr'vɛt/ n. corbeta f.

cosmetic /kɒz'mɛtɪk/ a. & n. cosmético m.

cosmic /'kɒzmɪk/ a. cósmico.

cosmonaut /'kɒzmə,nɒt/ n. cosmonauta m. & f.

cosmopolitan /,kɒzmə'pɒlitn̩/ a. & n. cosmopolita m. & f.

cosmos /'kɒzməs/ n. cosmos m.

cost /kɒst/ n. **1.** coste m.; costa f. —v. **2.** costar.

Costa Rican /'kɒstə'rikən/ a. & n. costarricense m. & f.

costly /'kɒstli/ a. costoso, caro.

costume /'kɒstum/ n. traje; disfraz m.

costume jewelry bisutería f., joyas de fantasía f.pl.

cot /kɒt/ n. catre m.

coterie /'koutəri/ n. camarilla f.

cotillion /kə'tɪlyən/ n. cotillón m.

cottage /'kɒtɪdʒ/ n. casita f.

cottage cheese requesón m.

cotton /'kɒtn̩/ n. algodón m.

cottonseed /'kɒtn̩,sid/ n. semilla del algodón f.

couch /kautʃ/ n. sofá m.

cougar /'kugər/ n. puma m.

cough /kɔf/ n. **1.** tos f. —v. **2.** toser.

council /'kaunsəl/ n. consejo, concilio m.

counsel /'kaunsəl/ n. **1.** consejo; (law) abogado -da. —v. **2.** aconsejar. **to keep one's c.,** no decir nada.

counselor /'kaunsələr/ n. consejero -ra; (law) abogado -da.

count /kaunt/ n. **1.** cuenta f.; (title) conde m. —v. **2.** contar.

countenance /'kauntn̩əns/ n. **1.** aspecto m.; cara f. —v. **2.** aprobar.

counter /'kauntər/ adv. **1. c. to,** contra, en contra de. —n. **2.** mostrador m.

counteract /,kauntər'ækt/ v. contrarrestar.

counteraction /,kauntər'ækʃən/ n. neutralización f.

counterbalance /'kauntər,bæləns/ n. **1.** contrapeso m. —v. **2.** contrapesar.

counterfeit /'kauntər,fɪt/ a. **1.** falsificado. —v. **2.** falsear.

countermand /,kauntər'mænd/ v. contramandar.

counteroffensive /,kauntərə-'fɛnsɪv/ n. contraofensiva f.

counterpart /'kauntər,pɑrt/ n. contraparte f.

counterproductive /,kauntərprə'dʌktɪv/ a. contraproducente.

countess /'kauntɪs/ n. condesa f.

countless /'kauntlɪs/ a. innumerable.

country /'kʌntri/ n. campo m.; Pol. país m.; (homeland) patria f.

country code distintivo del país m.

countryman /'kʌntrimən/ n. paisano m. **fellow c.,** compatriota m.

countryside /'kʌntri,said/ n. campo, paisaje m.

county /'kaunti/ n. condado m.

coupé /kup/ n. cupé m.

couple /'kʌpəl/ n. **1.** par m. —v. **2.** unir.

coupon /'kupɒn/ n. cupón, talón m.

courage /'kɜrɪdʒ/ n. valor m.

courageous /kə'reidʒəs/ a. valiente.

course /kɔrs/ n. curso m. **of c.,** por supuesto, desde luego.

court /kɔrt/ n. **1.** corte f.; cortejo m.; (of law) tribunal m. —v. **2.** cortejar.

courteous /'kɜrtiəs/ a. cortés.

courtesy /'kɜrtəsi/ n. cortesía f.

courthouse /'kɔrt,haus/ n. palacio de justicia m., tribunal m.

courtier /'kɔrtiər/ n. cortesano m.

courtly /'kɔrtli/ a. cortés, galante.

courtroom /'kɔrt,rum, -,rʊm/ n. sala de justicia f.

courtship /'kɔrtʃɪp/ n. cortejo m.

courtyard /'kɔrt,yard/ n. patio m.

cousin /'kʌzən/ n. primo -ma.

covenant /'kʌvənənt/ n. contrato, convenio m.

cover /'kʌvər/ n. **1.** cubierta, tapa f. —v. **2.** cubrir, tapar.

cover charge precio del cubierto m.

covet /'kʌvɪt/ v. ambicionar, suspirar por.

covetous /'kʌvɪtəs/ a. codicioso.

cow /kau/ n. vaca f.

coward /'kauərd/ n. cobarde m. & f.

cowardice /'kauərdɪs/ n. cobardía f.

cowardly /'kauərdli/ a. cobarde.

cowboy /'kau,bɔi/ n. vaquero, gaucho m.

cower /'kauər/ v. agacharse (de miedo).

cowhide /'kau,haid/ n. cuero m.

coy /kɔi/ a. recatado, modesto.

coyote /kai'outi/ n. coyote m.

cozy /'kouzi/ a. cómodo y agradable.

crab /kræb/ n. cangrejo m.

crab apple n. manzana silvestre f.

crack /kræk/ n. **1.** hendedura f.; (noise) crujido m. —v. **2.** hender; crujir.

cracker /'krækər/ n. galleta f.

cradle /'kreidl̩/ n. cuna f.

craft /kræft/ n. arte m.

craftsman /'kræftsmən/ n. artesano -na.

craftsmanship /'kræftsmən,ʃɪp/ n. artesanía f.

crafty /'kræfti/ a. ladino.

crag /kræg/ n. despeñadero m.; peña f.

cram /kræm/ v. rellenar, hartar.

cramp /kræmp/ n. calambre m.

cranberry /'kræn,bɛri/ n. arándano m.

crane /krein/ n. (bird) grulla f.; Mech. grúa f.

cranium /'kreiniəm/ n. cráneo m.

crank /kræŋk/ n. Mech. manivela f.

cranky /'kræŋki/ a. chiflado, caprichoso.

crash /kræʃ/ n. **1.** choque; estallido m. —v. **2.** estallar.

crate /kreit/ n. canasto m.

crater /'kreitər/ n. cráter m.

crave /kreiv/ v. desear; anhelar.

craven /'kreivən/ a. cobarde.

craving /'kreivɪŋ/ n. sed m., anhelo m.

crawl /krɔl/ v. andar a gatas, arrastrarse.

crayon /'kreiɒn/ n. creyón; lápiz m.

crazy /'kreizi/ a. loco.

creak /krik/ v. crujir.

creaky /'kriki/ a. crujiente.

cream /krim/ n. crema f.

cream cheese queso crema m.

creamery /'krimɒri/ n. lechería f.

creamy /'krimi/ a. cremoso.

crease /kris/ n. **1.** pliegue m. —v. **2.** plegar.

create /kri'eit/ v. crear.

creation /kri'eiʃən/ n. creación f.

creative /kri'eitɪv/ a. creativo, creador.

creator /kri'eitər/ n. creador -ra.

creature /'kritʃər/ n. criatura f.

credence /'kridns/ n. creencia f.

credentials /krɪ'dɛnʃəlz/ n. credenciales f.pl.

credibility /,krɛdə'bɪlɪti/ n. credibilidad f.

credible /'krɛdəbəl/ a. creíble.

credit /'krɛdɪt/ n. **1.** crédito m. **on c.,** al fiado. —v. **2.** Com. abonar.

creditable /'krɛdɪtəbəl/ a. fidedigno.

credit balance saldo acreedor.

credit card n. tarjeta de crédito f.

creditor /'krɛdɪtər/ n. acreedor -ra.

credit union banco cooperativo m.

credo /'kridou/ n. credo m.

credulity /krə'dulɪti/ n. credulidad f.

credulous /'krɛdʒələs/ a. crédulo.

creed /krid/ n. credo m.

creek /krik/ n. riachuelo m.

creep /krip/ v. gatear.

cremate /'krimeit/ v. incinerar.

crematory /'krimə,tɔri/ n. crematorio m.

creosote /'kriə,sout/ n. creosota f.

crepe /kreip/ n. crespón m.

crepe paper papel crespón m.

crescent /'krɛsənt/ a. & n. creciente f.

crest /krɛst/ n. cresta; cima f.; (heraldry) timbre m.

cretonne /krɪ'tɒn/ n. cretona f.

crevice /'krɛvɪs/ n. grieta f.

crew /kru/ n. tripulación f.

crew member tripulante m. & f.

crib /krɪb/ n. pesebre m.; cuna.

cricket /'krɪkɪt/ n. grillo m.

crime /kraim/ n. crimen m.

criminal /'krɪmənl/ a. & n. criminal m. & f.

criminologist /,krɪmə'nɒlədʒɪst/ n. criminólogo -ga, criminalista m. & f.

criminology /,krɪmə'nɒlədʒi/ n. criminología f.

crimson /'krɪmzən, -sən/ a. & n. carmesí m.

cringe /krɪndʒ/ v. encogerse, temblar.

cripple /'krɪpəl/ n. **1.** lisiado -da. —v. **2.** estropear, lisiar.

crisis /'kraisɪs/ n. crisis f.

crisp /krɪsp/ a. crespo, fresco.

crispness /'krɪspnɪs/ n. encrespadura f.

crisscross /'krɪs,krɔs/ a. entrelazado.

criterion /krai'tɪəriən/ n. criterio m.

critic /'krɪtɪk/ n. crítico -ca.

critical /'krɪtɪkəl/ a. crítico.

criticism /'krɪtə,sɪzəm/ n. crítica; censura f.

criticize /'krɪtə,saiz/ v. criticar; censurar.

critique /krɪ'tik/ n. crítica f.

croak /krouk/ n. **1.** graznido m. —v. **2.** graznar.

crochet /krou'ʃei/ n. **1.** crochet m. —v. **2.** hacer crochet.

crochet work ganchillo m.

crock /krɒk/ n. cazuela f.; olla de barro.

crockery /'krɒkəri/ n. loza f.

crocodile /'krɒkə,dail/ n. cocodrilo m.

crony /'krouni/ n. compinche m.

crooked /'krʊkɪd/ a. encorvado; deshonesto.

croon /krun/ v. canturrear.

crop /krɒp/ n. cosecha f.

croquet /krou'kei/ n. juego de croquet m.

croquette /krou'kɛt/ n. croqueta f.

cross /krɔs/ a. **1.** enojado, mal humorado. —n. **2.** cruz f. —v. **3.** cruzar, atravesar.

crossbreed /'krɔs,brid/ n. **1.** mestizo m. —v. **2.** cruzar (animales o plantas).

cross-examine /'krɔs ɪg,zæmɪn/ v. interrogar.

cross-eyed /'krɔs ,aid/ a. bizco.

cross-fertilization /'krɔs ,fɜrtlə-'zeiʃən/ n. alogamia f.

crossing /'krɔsɪŋ/ **crossroads** n. cruce m.

cross section corte transversal m.

crosswalk /'krɔs,wɔk/ n. paso cebra m.

crossword puzzle /'krɔs ,wɜrd/ crucigrama m.

crotch /krɒtʃ/ n. bifurcación f.; Anat. bragadura f.

crouch /krautʃ/ v. agacharse.

croup /krup/ n. Med. crup m.

croupier /'krupiər/ n. crupié m. & f.

crow /krou/ n. cuervo m.

crowd /kraud/ n. **1.** muchedumbre f.; tropel m. —v. **2.** apretar.

crowded /'kraudɪd/ a. lleno de gente.

crown /kraun/ n. **1.** corona f. —v. **2.** coronar.

crown prince príncipe heredero m.

crucial /'kruʃəl/ a. crucial.

crucible /'krusəbəl/ n. crisol m.

crucifix /'krusəfɪks/ n. crucifijo m.

crucifixion /,krusə'fɪkʃən/ n. crucifixión f.

crucify /'krusə,fai/ v. crucificar.

crude /krud/ a. crudo; (oil) bruto.

crudeness /'krudnɪs/ a. crudeza f.

cruel /'kruəl/ a. cruel.

cruelty /'kruəlti/ n. crueldad f.

cruet /'kruɪt/ n. vinagrera f.

cruise /kruz/ n. **1.** viaje por mar. —v. **2.** navegar.

cruiser /'kruzər/ n. crucero m.

crumb /krʌm/ n. miga; migaja f.

crumble /'krʌmbəl/ v. desmigajar; desmoronar.

crumple /'krʌmpəl/ v. arrugar; encogerse.

crusade /kru'seid/ n. cruzada f.

crusader /kru'seidər/ n. cruzado m.

crush /krʌʃ/ v. aplastar.

crust /krʌst/ n. costra; corteza f.

crustacean /krʌ'steiʃən/ n. crustáceo m.

crutch /krʌtʃ/ n. muleta f.

cry /krai/ n. **1.** grito m. —v. **2.** gritar; (weep) llorar.

cryosurgery /,kraiou'sɜrdʒəri/ n. criocirugía f.

crypt /krɪpt/ n. gruta f., cripta f.

cryptic /'krɪptɪk/ a. secreto.

cryptography /krɪp'tɒgrəfi/ n. criptografía f.

crystal /'krɪstl/ n. cristal m.

crystalline /'krɪstlɪn/ a. cristalino, transparente.

crystallize /'krɪstl,aiz/ v. cristalizar.

cub /kʌb/ n. cachorro m.

Cuban /'kyubən/ n. & a. cubano -na.

cube /kyub/ n. cubo m.

cubic /'kyubɪk/ a. cúbico.

cubicle /'kyubɪkəl/ n. cubículo m.

cubic measure medida de capacidad f.

cubism /'kyubɪzəm/ n. cubismo m.

cuckoo /'kuku/ n. cuco m.

cucumber /'kyukʌmbər/ n. pepino m.

cuddle /'kʌdl/ v. abrazar.

cudgel /'kʌdʒəl/ n. palo m.

cue /kyu/ n. apunte m.; (billiards) taco m.

cuff /kʌf/ n. puño de camisa. **c. links,** gemelos.

cuisine /kwɪ'zin/ n. arte culinario m.

culinary /'kyulə,nɛri/ a. culinario.

culminate /'kʌlmə,neit/ v. culminar.

culmination /,kʌlmə'neiʃən/ n. culminación f.

culpable /'kʌlpəbəl/ a. culpable.

culprit /'kʌlprɪt/ n. criminal; delincuente m. & f.

cult /kʌlt/ n. culto m.

cultivate /'kʌltə,veit/ v. cultivar.

cultivated /'kʌltə,veitɪd/ a. cultivado.

cultivation /,kʌltə'veiʃən/ n. cultivo m.; cultivación f.

cultivator /'kʌltə,veitər/ n. cultivador -ra.

cultural /'kʌltʃərəl/ a. cultural.

culture /'kʌltʃər/ n. cultura f.

cultured /'kʌltʃərd/ a. culto.

cumbersome /'kʌmbərsəm/ a. pesado, incómodo.

cumulative /'kyumyələtɪv/ a. acumulativo.

cunning /'kʌnɪŋ/ a. **1.** astuto. —n. **2.** astucia f.

cup /kʌp/ n. taza, jícara f.

cupboard /'kʌbərd/ n. armario, aparador m.

cupidity /kyu'pɪdɪti/ n. avaricia f.

curable /'kyurəbəl/ a. curable.

curator /kyu'reitər/ n. guardián -ana.

curb /kɜrb/ n. **1.** freno m. —v. **2.** refrenar.

curd /kɜrd/ n. cuajada f.

curdle /'kɜrdl/ v. cuajarse, coagularse.

cure /kyur/ n. **1.** remedio m. —v. **2.** curar, sanar.

curfew /'kɜrfyu/ n. toque de queda m.

curio /'kyuri,ou/ n. objeto curioso.

curiosity /,kyuri'ɒsɪti/ n. curiosidad f.

curious /'kyuriəs/ a. curioso.

curl /kɜrl/ n. **1.** rizo m. —v. **2.** rizar.

curly /'kɜrli/ a. rizado.

currant /'kɜrənt/ n. grosella f.

currency /'kɜrənsi/ n. circulación f.; dinero m.

current /'kɜrənt/ a. & n. corriente f.

current events /ɪ'vɛnts/ actualidades f.pl.

currently /'kɜrəntli/ adv. corrientemente.

curriculum /kə'rɪkyələm/ n. plan de estudio m.

curse /kɜrs/ n. **1.** maldición f. —v. **2.** maldecir.

cursor /'kɜrsər/ n. cursor m.

cursory /'kɜrsəri/ a. sumario.

curt /kɜrt/ a. brusco.

curtail /kər'teil/ v. reducir; restringir.

curtain /'kɜrtn/ n. cortina f.; Theat. telón m.

curtsy /'kɜrtsi/ n. **1.** reverencia f. —v. **2.** hacer una reverencia.

curvature /'kɜrvətʃər/ n. curvatura f.

curve /kɜrv/ n. **1.** curva f. —v. **2.** encorvar.

cushion /'kuʃən/ n. cojín m.; almohada f.

cuspidor /'kʌspɪ,dɔr/ n. escupidera f.

custard /'kʌstərd/ n. flan m.; natillas f.pl.

custodian /kʌ'stoudiən/ n. custodio m.

custody /'kʌstədi/ n. custodia f.

custom /'kʌstəm/ n. costumbre f.

customary /'kʌstə,mɛri/ a. acostumbrado, usual.

customer /'kʌstəmər/ n. cliente m. & f.

customhouse /'kʌstəm,haus/ **customs** n. aduana f.

customs duty /'kʌstəmz/ derechos de aduana m.pl.

customs officer /'kʌstəmz/ agente de aduana m. & f.

cut /kʌt/ n. **1.** corte m.; cortada f.; tajada f.; (printing) grabado m. —v. **2.** cortar; tajar.

cute /kyut/ a. mono, lindo.

cut glass cristal tallado m.

cuticle /'kyutɪkəl/ n. cutícula f.

cutlery /'kʌtləri/ n. cuchillería f.

cutlet /'kʌtlɪt/ n. chuleta f.

cutter /'kʌtər/ n. cortador -ra; Naut. cúter m.

cutthroat /'kʌt,θrout/ n. asesino -na.

cyberpunk /'saibər,pʌŋk/ n. ciberpunk m. & f.

cyberspace /'saibər,speis/ n. ciberespacio m.

cyclamate /'saiklə,meit, 'sɪklə-/ n. ciclamato m.

cycle /'saikəl/ n. ciclo m.

cyclist /'saiklɪst/ n. ciclista m. & f.

cyclone /'saikloun/ n. ciclón, huracán m.

cyclotron /'saiklə,trɒn, 'sɪklə-/ n. ciclotrón m.

cylinder /'sɪlɪndər/ n. cilindro m.

cylindrical /sɪ'lɪndrɪkəl/ a. cilíndrico.

cymbal /'sɪmbəl/ n. címbalo m.

cynic /'sɪnɪk/ n. cínico -ca.

cynical /'sɪnɪkəl/ a. cínico.

cynicism /'sɪnə,sɪzəm/ n. cinismo m.

cypress /'saiprəs/ n. ciprés m. **c. nut,** piñuela f.

cyst /sɪst/ n. quiste m.

D

dad /dæd/ *n.* papá *m.*, papito *m.*
daffodil /'dæfədɪl/ *n.* narciso *m.*
dagger /'dægər/ *n.* puñal *m.*
dahlia /'dælyə/ *n.* dalia *f.*
daily /'deili/ *a.* diario, cotidiano.
daintiness /'deintɪnɪs/ *n.* delicadeza *f.*
dainty /'deinti/ *a.* delicado.
dairy /'dɛəri/ *n.* lechería, quesería *f.*
dais /'deiɪs/ *n.* tablado *m.*
daisy /'deizi/ *n.* margarita *f.*
dale /deil/ *n.* valle *m.*
dally /'dæli/ *v.* holgar; perder el tiempo.
dam /dæm/ *n.* presa *f.*; dique *m.*
damage /'dæmɪdʒ/ *n.* **1.** daño *m.* —*v.* **2.** dañar.
damask /'dæməsk/ *n.* damasco *m.*
damn /dæm/ *v.* condenar.
damnation /dæm'neiʃən/ *n.* condenación *f.*
damp /dæmp/ *a.* húmedo.
dampen /'dæmpən/ *v.* humedecer.
dampness /'dæmpnɪs/ *n.* humedad *f.*
damsel /'dæmzəl/ *n.* doncella *f.*
dance /dæns/ *n.* **1.** baile *m.*; danza *f.* —*v.* **2.** bailar.
dance hall salón de baile *m.*
dancer /'dænsər/ *n.* bailador -ra; (professional) bailarín -na.
dancing /'dænsɪŋ/ *n.* baile *m.*
dandelion /'dændḷ,aiən/ *n.* amargón *m.*
dandruff /'dændrəf/ *n.* caspa *f.*
dandy /'dændi/ *n.* petimetre *m.*
danger /'deindʒər/ *n.* peligro *m.*
dangerous /'deindʒərəs/ *a.* peligroso.
dangle /'dæŋgəl/ *v.* colgar.
Danish /'deinɪʃ/ *a.* & *n.* danés -sa; dinamarqués -sa.
dapper /'dæpər/ *a.* gallardo.
dare /dɛər/ *v.* atreverse, osar.
daredevil /'dɛər,dɛvəl/ *n.* atrevido *m.*, -da *f.*
daring /'dɛərɪŋ/ *a.* **1.** atrevido. —*n.* **2.** osadía *f.*
dark /dɑrk/ *a.* **1.** obscuro; moreno. —*n.* **2.** obscuridad *f.*
darken /'dɑrkən/ *v.* obscurecer.
darkness /'dɑrknɪs/ *n.* obscuridad *f.*
darkroom /'dɑrk,rum, -,rʊm/ *n.* cámara obscura *f.*

darling /'dɑrlɪŋ/ *a.* & *n.* querido -da, amado -da.
darn /dɑrn/ *v.* zurcir.
darning needle /'dɑrnɪŋ/ aguja de zurcir *m.*
dart /dɑrt/ *n.* dardo *m.*
dartboard /'dɑrt,bɔrd/ *n.* diana *f.*
dash /dæʃ/ *n.* arranque *m.*; *Punct.* guión *m.*
data /'deitə/ *n.* datos *m.*
database /'deitəbeis/ *n.* base de datos *m.*
data processing /'prɒsɛsɪŋ/ proceso de datos *m.*
date /deit/ *n.* fecha *f.*; (engagement) cita *f.*; (fruit) dátil *m.*
daughter /'dɔtər/ *n.* hija *f.*
daughter-in-law /'dɔ,tər ɪn lɔ/ *n.* nuera *f.*
daunt /dɔnt, dɑnt/ *v.* intimidar.
dauntless /'dɔntlɪs/ *a.* intrépido.
davenport /'dævən,pɔrt/ *n.* sofá *m.*
dawn /dɔn/ *n.* **1.** alba, madrugada *f.* —*v.* **2.** amanecer.
day /dei/ *n.* día *m.* **good d.,** buenos días.
daybreak /'dei,breik/ *n.* alba, madrugada *f.*
daydream /'dei,drim/ *n.* fantasía *f.*
daylight /'dei,lait/ *n.* luz del día.
daze /deiz/ *v.* aturdir.
dazzle /'dæzəl/ *v.* deslumbrar.
deacon /'dikən/ *n.* diácono *m.*
dead /dɛd/ *a.* muerto.
deaden /'dɛdṇ/ *v.* amortecer.
dead end atolladero *m.* (impasse); callejón sin salida *m.* (street).
deadline /'dɛd,lain/ *n.* fecha límite *f.*
deadlock /'dɛd,lɒk/ *n.* paro *m.*
deadly /'dɛdli/ *a.* mortal.
deaf /dɛf/ *a.* sordo.
deafen /'dɛfən/ *v.* ensordecer.
deafening /'dɛfənɪŋ/ *a.* ensordecedor.
deaf-mute /'dɛf 'myut/ *n.* sordomudo -da.
deafness /'dɛfnɪs/ *n.* sordera *f.*
deal /dil/ *n.* **1.** trato *m.*; negociación *f.* **a great d., a good d.,** mucho. —*v.* **2.** tratar; negociar.
dealer /'dilər/ *n.* comerciante *m.*, (at cards) tallador -ra.
dean /din/ *n.* decano -na.

dear /dɪər/ a. querido; caro.

dearth /dɜrθ/ n. escasez f.

death /dɛθ/ n. muerte f.

death certificate partida de defunción f.

deathless /'dɛθlɪs/ a. inmortal.

debacle /də'bɑkəl/ n. desastre m.

debase /dɪ'beis/ v. degradar.

debatable /dɪ'beitəbəl/ a. discutible.

debate /dɪ'beit/ n. **1.** debate m. —v. **2.** disputar, deliberar.

debauch /dɪ'bɔtʃ/ v. corromper.

debilitate /dɪ'bɪlɪˌteit/ v. debilitar.

debit /'dɛbɪt/ n. débito m.

debit balance saldo deudor m.

debonair /ˌdɛbə'nɛər/ a. cortés; alegre, vivo.

debris /dei'bri/ n. escombros m.pl.

debt /dɛt/ n. deuda f. **get into d.** endeudarse.

debtor /'dɛtər/ n. deudor -ra.

debug /di'bʌg/ v. depurar, limpiar.

debunk /dɪ'bʌŋk/ v. desacreditar; desenmascarar.

debut /dei'byu/ n. debut, estreno m.

debutante /'dɛbyuˌtɑnt/ n. debutante f.

decade /'dɛkeid/ n. década f.

decadence /'dɛkədəns/ n. decadencia f.

decadent /'dɛkədənt/ a. decadente.

decaffeinated /di'kæfɪˌneitɪd/ a. descafeinado.

decalcomania /dɪˌkælkə'meiniə/ n. calcomanía f.

decanter /dɪ'kæntər/ n. garrafa f.

decapitate /dɪ'kæpɪˌteit/ v. descabezar.

decay /dɪ'kei/ n. **1.** descaecimiento m.; (dental) caries f. —v. **2.** decaer; (dental) cariarse.

deceased /dɪ'sist/ a. muerto, difunto.

deceit /dɪ'sit/ n. engaño m.

deceitful /dɪ'sitfəl/ a. engañoso.

deceive /dɪ'siv/ v. engañar.

December /dɪ'sɛmbər/ n. diciembre m.

decency /'disənsi/ n. decencia f.; decoro m.

decent /'disənt/ a. decente.

decentralize /di'sɛntrəˌlaiz/ v. descentralizar.

deception /dɪ'sɛpʃən/ n. decepción f.

deceptive /dɪ'sɛptɪv/ a. deceptivo.

decibel /'dɛsəˌbɛl/ n. decibelio m.

decide /dɪ'said/ v. decidir.

decimal /'dɛsəməl/ a. decimal.

decipher /dɪ'saifər/ v. descifrar.

decision /dɪ'sɪʒən/ n. decisión f.

decisive /dɪ'saisɪv/ a. decisivo.

deck /dɛk/ n. cubierta f.

deck chair tumbona f.

declamation /ˌdɛklə'meiʃən/ n. declamación f.

declaration /ˌdɛklə'reiʃən/ n. declaración f.

declarative /dɪ'klærətɪv/ a. declarativo.

declare /dɪ'klɛər/ v. declarar.

declension /dɪ'klɛnʃən/ n. declinación f.

decline /dɪ'klain/ n. **1.** decadencia f. —v. **2.** decaer; negarse; *Gram.* declinar.

decompose /ˌdikəm'pouz/ v. descomponer.

decongestant /ˌdikən'dʒɛstənt/ n. descongestionante m.

decorate /'dɛkəˌreit/ v. decorar, adornar.

decoration /ˌdɛkə'reiʃən/ n. decoración f.

decorative /'dɛkərətɪv/ a. decorativo.

decorator /'dɛkəˌreitər/ n. decorador -ra.

decorous /'dɛkərəs/ a. correcto.

decorum /dɪ'kɔrəm/ n. decoro m.

decrease /dɪ'kris/ v. disminuir.

decree /dɪ'kri/ n. decreto m.

decrepit /dɪ'krɛpɪt/ a. decrépito.

decry /dɪ'krai/ v. desacreditar.

dedicate /'dɛdɪˌkeit/ v. dedicar; consagrar.

dedication /ˌdɛdɪ'keiʃən/ n. dedicación; dedicatoria f.

deduce /dɪ'dus/ v. deducir.

deduction /dɪ'dʌkʃən/ n. rebaja; deducción f.

deductive /dɪ'dʌktɪv/ a. deductivo.

deed /did/ n. acción; hazaña f.

deem /dim/ v. estimar.

deep /dip/ a. hondo, profundo.

deepen /'dipən/ v. profundizar, ahondar.

deep freeze congelación f.

deeply /'dipli/ adv. profundamente.

deer /dɪər/ n. venado, ciervo m.

deface /dɪ'feis/ v. mutilar.

defamation /ˌdɛfə'meiʃən/ n. calumnia f.

defame /dɪ'feim/ v. difamar.

default /dɪ'fɔlt/ *n.* **1.** defecto *m.* —*v.* **2.** faltar.

defeat /dɪ'fit/ *n.* **1.** derrota *f.* —*v.* **2.** derrotar.

defeatism /dɪ'fitɪzəm/ *n.* derrotismo *m.*

defect /'difɛkt, dɪ'fɛkt/ *n.* defecto *m.*

defective /dɪ'fɛktɪv/ *a.* defectivo.

defend /dɪ'fɛnd/ *v.* defender.

defendant /dɪ'fɛndənt/ *n.* acusado -da.

defender /dɪ'fɛndər/ *n.* defensor -ra.

defense /dɪ'fɛns/ *n.* defensa *f.*

defensive /dɪ'fɛnsɪv/ *a.* defensivo.

defer /dɪ'fɜr/ *v.* aplazar; deferir.

deference /'dɛfərəns/ *n.* deferencia *f.*

defiance /dɪ'faɪəns/ *n.* desafío *m.*

defiant /dɪ'faɪənt/ *a.* desafiador.

deficiency /dɪ'fɪʃənsi/ *n.* defecto *m.*

deficient /dɪ'fɪʃənt/ *a.* deficiente.

deficit /'dɛfəsɪt/ *n.* déficit, descubierto *m.*

defile /dɪ'faɪl/ *n.* **1.** desfiladero *m.* —*v.* **2.** profanar.

define /dɪ'faɪn/ *v.* definir.

definite /'dɛfənɪt/ *a.* exacto; definitivo.

definitely /'dɛfənɪtli/ *adv.* definitivamente.

definition /ˌdɛfə'nɪʃən/ *n.* definición *f.*

definitive /dɪ'fɪnɪtɪv/ *a.* definitivo.

deflation /dɪ'fleɪʃən/ *n.* desinflación *f.*

deflect /dɪ'flɛkt/ *v.* desviar.

deform /dɪ'fɔrm/ *v.* deformar.

deformity /dɪ'fɔrmɪti/ *n.* deformidad *f.*

defraud /dɪ'frɔd/ *v.* defraudar.

defray /dɪ'freɪ/ *v.* costear.

defrost /dɪ'frɔst/ *v.* descongelar.

deft /dɛft/ *a.* diestro.

defy /dɪ'faɪ/ *v.* desafiar.

degenerate /a dɪ'dʒɛnərɪt; v -ˌreɪt/ *a.* **1.** degenerado. —*v.* **2.** degenerar.

degeneration /dɪˌdʒɛnə'reɪʃən/ *n.* degeneración *f.*

degradation /ˌdɛgrɪ'deɪʃən/ *n.* degradación *f.*

degrade /dɪ'greɪd/ *v.* degradar.

degree /dɪ'gri/ *n.* grado *m.*

deign /deɪn/ *v.* condescender.

deity /'diɪti/ *n.* deidad *f.*

dejected /dɪ'dʒɛktɪd/ *a.* abatido.

dejection /dɪ'dʒɛkʃən/ *n.* tristeza *f.*

delay /dɪ'leɪ/ *n.* **1.** retardo *m.*, demora *f.* —*v.* **2.** tardar, demorar.

delegate /*n* 'dɛlɪgɪt; *v* -ˌgeɪt/ *n.* **1.** delegado -da. —*v.* **2.** delegar.

delegation /ˌdɛlɪ'geɪʃən/ *n.* delegación *f.*

delete /dɪ'lit/ *v.* suprimir, tachar.

deliberate /a dɪ'lɪbərɪt; v -əˌreɪt/ *a.* **1.** premeditado. —*v.* **2.** deliberar.

deliberately /dɪ'lɪbərɪtli/ *adv.* deliberadamente.

deliberation /dɪˌlɪbə'reɪʃən/ *n.* deliberación *f.*

deliberative /dɪ'lɪbərətɪv/ *a.* deliberativo.

delicacy /'dɛlɪkəsi/ *n.* delicadeza *f.*

delicate /'dɛlɪkɪt/ *a.* delicado.

delicious /dɪ'lɪʃəs/ *a.* delicioso.

delight /dɪ'laɪt/ *n.* deleite *m.*

delightful /dɪ'laɪtfəl/ *a.* deleitoso.

delinquency /dɪ'lɪŋkwənsi/ *a.* delincuencia *f.*

delinquent /dɪ'lɪŋkwənt/ *a. & n.* delincuente. *m. & f.*

delirious /dɪ'lɪəriəs/ *a.* delirante.

deliver /dɪ'lɪvər/ *v.* entregar.

deliverance /dɪ'lɪvərəns/ *n.* liberación; salvación *f.*

delivery /dɪ'lɪvəri/ *n.* entrega *f.*; *Med.* parto *m.*

delude /dɪ'lud/ *v.* engañar.

deluge /'dɛlyudʒ/ *n.* inundación *f.*

delusion /dɪ'luʒən/ *n.* decepción *f.*; engaño *m.*

delve /dɛlv/ *v.* cavar, sondear.

demagogue /'dɛməˌgɒg/ *n.* demagogo -ga.

demand /dɪ'mænd/ *n.* **1.** demanda *f.* —*v.* **2.** demandar; exigir.

demarcation /ˌdimɑr'keɪʃən/ *n.* demarcación *f.*

demeanor /dɪ'minər/ *n.* conducta *f.*

demented /dɪ'mɛntɪd/ *a.* demente, loco.

demilitarize /di'mɪlɪtəˌraɪz/ *v.* desmilitarizar.

demobilize /di'moubəˌlaɪz/ *v.* desmovilizar.

democracy /dɪ'mɒkrəsi/ *n.* democracia *f.*

democrat /'dɛməˌkræt/ *n.* demócrata *m. & f.*

democratic /ˌdɛmə'krætɪk/ *a.* democrático.

demolish /dɪ'mɒlɪʃ/ *v.* demoler.

demon /'dimən/ *n.* demonio *m.*

demonstrate /'dɛmən,streit/ *v.* demostrar.

demonstration /,dɛmən'streiʃən/ *n.* demostración *f.*

demonstrative /də'mɒnstrətɪv/ *a.* demostrativo.

demoralize /dɪ'mɔrə,laiz, -'mɒr-/ *v.* desmoralizar.

demure /dɪ'myʊr/ *a.* modesto, serio.

den /dɛn/ *n.* madriguera, caverna *f.*

denature /di'neitʃər/ *v.* alterar.

denial /dɪ'naiəl/ *n.* negación *f.*

denim /'dɛnəm/ *n.* dril, tela vaquera.

Denmark /'dɛnmɑrk/ *n.* Dinamarca *f.*

denomination /dɪ,nɒmə'neiʃən/ *n.* denominación; secta *f.*

denote /dɪ'nout/ *v.* denotar.

denounce /dɪ'nauns/ *v.* denunciar.

dense /dɛns/ *a.* denso, espeso; estúpido.

density /'dɛnsɪti/ *n.* densidad *f.*

dent /dɛnt/ *n.* **1.** abolladura *f.* —*v.* **2.** abollar.

dental /'dɛntl̩/ *a.* dental.

dentist /'dɛntɪst/ *n.* dentista *m.* & *f.*

dentistry /'dɛntəstri/ *n.* odontología *f.*

denture /'dɛntʃər/ *n.* dentadura *f.*

denunciation /dɪ,nʌnsi'eiʃən/ *n.* denunciación *f.*

deny /dɪ'nai/ *v.* negar, rehusar.

deodorant /di'oudərənt/ *n.* desodorante *m.*

depart /dɪ'pɑrt/ *v.* partir; irse, marcharse.

department /dɪ'pɑrtmənt/ *n.* departamento *m.*

departmental /dɪ,pɑrt'mɛntl̩/ *a.* departamental.

department store grandes almacenes *m.pl.*

departure /dɪ'pɑrtʃər/ *n.* salida; desviación *f.*

depend /dɪ'pɛnd/ *v.* depender.

dependability /dɪ,pɛndə'bɪlɪti/ *n.* confiabilidad *f.*

dependable /dɪ'pɛndəbəl/ *a.* confiable.

dependence /dɪ'pɛndəns/ *n.* dependencia *f.*

dependent /dɪ'pɛndənt/ *a.* & *n.* dependiente *m.* & *f.*

depict /dɪ'pɪkt/ *v.* pintar; representar.

deplete /dɪ'plit/ *v.* agotar.

deplorable /dɪ'plɔrəbəl/ *a.* deplorable.

deplore /dɪ'plɔr/ *v.* deplorar.

deport /dɪ'pɔrt/ *v.* deportar.

deportation /,dipɔr'teiʃən/ *n.* deportación *f.*

deportment /dɪ'pɔrtmənt/ *n.* conducta *f.*

depose /dɪ'pouz/ *v.* deponer.

deposit /dɪ'pɒzɪt/ *n.* **1.** depósito *m.* (of money); yacimiento (of ore, etc.) *m.* —*v.* **2.** depositar.

depositor /dɪ'pɒzɪtər/ *n.* depositante *m.* & *f.*

depot /'dipou/ *n.* depósito *m.;* (railway) estación *f.*

depravity /dɪ'prævɪti/ *n.* depravación *f.*

deprecate /'dɛprɪ,keit/ *v.* deprecar.

depreciate /dɪ'priʃi,eit/ *v.* depreciar.

depreciation /dɪ,priʃi'eiʃən/ *n.* depreciación *f.*

depredation /,dɛprə'deiʃən/ *n.* depredación *f.*

depress /dɪ'prɛs/ *v.* deprimir; desanimar.

depression /dɪ'prɛʃən/ *n.* depresión *f.*

deprive /dɪ'praiv/ *v.* privar.

depth /dɛpθ/ *n.* profundidad, hondura *f.*

depth charge carga de profundidad *f.*

deputy /'dɛpyəti/ *n.* diputado -da.

deride /dɪ'raid/ *v.* burlar.

derision /dɪ'rɪʒən/ *n.* burla *f.*

derivation /,dɛrə'veiʃən/ *n.* derivación *f.*

derivative /dɪ'rɪvətɪv/ *a.* derivativo.

derive /dɪ'raiv/ *v.* derivar.

dermatologist /,dɜrmə'tɒlədʒɪst/ *n.* dermatólogo -ga.

derogatory /dɪ'rɒgə,tɔri/ *a.* derogatorio.

derrick /'dɛrɪk/ *n.* grúa *f.*

descend /dɪ'sɛnd/ *v.* descender, bajar.

descendant /dɪ'sɛndənt/ *n.* descendiente *m.* & *f.*

descent /dɪ'sɛnt/ *n.* descenso *m.;* origen *m.*

describe /dɪ'skraib/ *v.* describir.

description /dɪ'skrɪpʃən/ *n.* descripción *f.*

descriptive /dɪ'skrɪptɪv/ *a.* descriptivo.

desecrate /'dɛsɪ,kreit/ v. profanar.
desert /n 'dɛzərt; v dɪ'zɜrt/ n. **1.** desierto m. —v. **2.** abandonar.
deserter /dɪ'zɜrtər/ n. desertor -ra.
desertion /dɪ'zɜrʃən/ n. deserción f.
deserve /dɪ'zɜrv/ v. merecer.
design /dɪ'zain/ n. **1.** diseño m. —v. **2.** diseñar.
designate /'dɛzɪg,neit/ v. señalar, apuntar; designar.
designation /,dɛzɪg'neiʃən/ n. designación f.
designer /dɪ'zainər/ n. diseñador -ra; (technical) proyectista m. & f.
designer clothes, designer clothing ropa de marca f.
desirability /dɪ,zaiᵊrə'bɪlɪti/ n. conveniencia f.
desirable /dɪ'zaiᵊrəbəl/ a. deseable.
desire /dɪ'zaiᵊr/ n. **1.** deseo m. —v. **2.** desear.
desirous /dɪ'zaiᵊrəs/ a. deseoso.
desist /dɪ'sɪst/ v. desistir.
desk /dɛsk/ n. escritorio m.
desk clerk recepcionista m. & f.
desktop computer /'dɛsk,tɒp/ computadora de sobremesa f., ordenador de sobremesa f.
desolate /a 'dɛsəlɪt; v -,leit/ a. **1.** desolado. —v. **2.** desolar.
desolation /,dɛsə'leiʃən/ n. desolación, ruina f.
despair /dɪ'spɛər/ n. **1.** desesperación f. —v. **2.** desesperar.
despatch /dɪ'spætʃ/ **dispatch** n. **1.** despacho m.; prontitud f. —v. **2.** despachar.
desperado /,dɛspə'radou/ n. bandido m.
desperate /'dɛspərɪt/ a. desesperado.
desperation /,dɛspə'reiʃən/ n. desesperación f.
despicable /'dɛspɪkəbəl/ a. vil.
despise /dɪ'spaiz/ v. despreciar.
despite /dɪ'spait/ prep. a pesar de.
despondent /dɪ'spɒndənt/ a. abatido; desanimado.
despot /'dɛspət/ n. déspota m. & f.
despotic /dɛs'pɒtɪk/ a. despótico.
dessert /dɪ'zɜrt/ n. postre m.
destination /,dɛstə'neiʃən/ n. destinación f.
destine /'dɛstɪn/ v. destinar.
destiny /'dɛstəni/ n. destino m.

destitute /'dɛstɪ,tut/ a. destituído, indigente.
destitution /,dɛstɪ'tuʃən/ n. destitución f.
destroy /dɪ'strɔi/ v. destrozar, destruir.
destroyer /dɪ'strɔiər/ n. destruidor -ra; (naval) destructor m.
destruction /dɪ'strʌkʃən/ n. destrucción f.
destructive /dɪ'strʌktɪv/ a. destructivo.
desultory /'dɛsəl,tɔri/ a. inconexo; casual.
detach /dɪ'tætʃ/ v. separar, desprender.
detachment /dɪ'tætʃmənt/ n. Mil. destacamento; desprendimiento m.
detail /dɪ'teil/ n. **1.** detalle m. —v. **2.** detallar.
detain /dɪ'tein/ v. detener.
detect /dɪ'tɛkt/ v. descubrir.
detection /dɪ'tɛkʃən/ n. detección f.
detective /dɪ'tɛktɪv/ n. detective m. & f.
déténte /dei'tɑnt/ n. distensión f.; Pol. deténte.
detention /dɪ'tɛnʃən/ n. detención; cautividad f.
deter /dɪ'tɜr/ v. disuadir.
detergent /dɪ'tɜrdʒənt/ n. & a. detergente m.
deteriorate /dɪ'tɪəriə,reit/ v. deteriorar.
deterioration /dɪ,tɪəriə'reiʃən/ n. deterioración f.
determination /dɪ,tɜrmə'neiʃən/ n. determinación f.
determine /dɪ'tɜrmɪn/ v. determinar.
deterrence /dɪ'tɜrəns/ n. disuasión f.
detest /dɪ'tɛst/ v. detestar.
detonate /'dɛtn,eit/ v. detonar.
detour /'ditur/ n. desvío m. v. desviar.
detract /dɪ'trækt/ v. disminuir.
detriment /'dɛtrəmənt/ n. detrimento m., daño m.
detrimental /,dɛtrə'mɛntl/ a. dañoso.
devaluate /di'vælyu,eit/ v. depreciar.
devastate /'dɛvə,steit/ v. devastar.
develop /dɪ'vɛləp/ v. desarrollar; Phot. revelar.

developing nation /dɪ'vɛləpɪŋ/ nación en desarrollo.

development /dɪ'vɛləpmənt/ n. desarrollo m.

deviate /'divi,eit/ v. desviar.

deviation /,divi'eiʃən/ n. desviación f.

device /dɪ'vais/ n. aparato; artificio m.

devil /'dɛvəl/ n. diablo, demonio m.

devious /'diviəs/ a. desviado.

devise /dɪ'vaiz/ v. inventar.

devoid /dɪ'vɔid/ a. desprovisto.

devote /dɪ'vout/ v. dedicar, consagrar.

devoted /dɪ'voutɪd/ a. devoto.

devotee /,dɛvə'ti/ n. aficionado -da.

devotion /dɪ'vouʃən/ n. devoción f.

devour /dɪ'vaur/ v. devorar.

devout /dɪ'vaut/ a. devoto.

dew /du/ n. rocío, sereno m.

dexterity /dɛk'stɛrɪti/ n. destreza f.

dexterous /'dɛkstrəs/ a. diestro.

diabetes /,daiə'bitɪs/ n. diabetes f.

diabolic /,daiə'bɒlɪk/ a. diabólico.

diadem /'daiə,dɛm/ n. diadema f.

diagnose /'daiəg,nous/ v. diagnosticar.

diagnosis /,daiəg'nousɪs/ n. diagnóstico m.

diagonal /dai'ægənl/ n. diagonal f.

diagram /'daiə,græm/ n. diagrama m.

dial /'daiəl/ n. **1.** cuadrante m., carátula f. —v. **2. dial up** marcar.

dialect /'daiə,lɛkt/ n. dialecto m.

dialing code /'daiəlɪŋ/ prefijo m.

dialogue /'daiə,lɔg/ n. diálogo m.

dial tone señal de marcar f.

diameter /dai'æmɪtər/ n. diámetro m.

diamond /'daimənd/ n. diamante, brillante m.

diaper /'daipər/ n. pañal m.

diarrhea /,daiə'riə/ n. diarrea f.

diary /'daiəri/ n. diario m.

diathermy /'daiə,θɜrmi/ n. diatermia f.

dice /dais/ n. dados m.pl.

dictate /'dɪkteit/ n. **1.** mandato m. —v. **2.** dictar.

dictation /dɪk'teiʃən/ n. dictado m.

dictator /'dɪkteitər/ n. dictador -ra.

dictatorship /dɪk'teitər,ʃɪp/ n. dictadura f.

diction /'dɪkʃən/ n. dicción f.

dictionary /'dɪkʃə,nɛri/ n. diccionario m.

die /dai/ n. **1.** matriz f.; (game) dado m. —v. **2.** morir.

diet /'daiɪt/ n. dieta f.

dietary /'daiɪ,tɛri/ a. dietético.

dietitian /,daiɪ'tɪʃən/ n. & a. dietético -ca.

differ /'dɪfər/ v. diferir.

difference /'dɪfərəns/ n. diferencia f. **to make no d.,** no importar.

different /'dɪfərənt/ a. diferente, distinto.

differential /,dɪfə'rɛnʃəl/ n. diferencial f.

differentiate /,dɪfə'rɛnʃi,eit/ v. diferenciar.

difficult /'dɪfɪ,kʌlt/ a. difícil.

difficulty /'dɪfɪ,kʌlti/ n. dificultad f.

diffident /'dɪfɪdənt/ a. tímido.

diffuse /dɪ'fyuz/ v. difundir.

diffusion /dɪ'fyuʒən/ n. difusión f.

dig /dɪg/ v. cavar.

digest /n 'daidʒest; v dɪ'dʒɛst, dai-/ n. **1.** extracto m. —v. **2.** digerir.

digestible /dɪ'dʒɛstəbəl, dai-/ a. digerible.

digestion /dɪ'dʒɛstʃən, dai-/ n. digestión f.

digestive /dɪ'dʒɛstɪv, dai-/ a. digestivo.

digital /'dɪdʒɪtl/ a. digital.

digitalis /,dɪdʒɪ'tælɪs/ n. digital f.

dignified /'dɪgnə,faid/ a. digno.

dignify /'dɪgnə,fai/ v. dignificar.

dignitary /'dɪgnɪ,tɛri/ n. dignatario -ria.

dignity /'dɪgnɪti/ n. dignidad f.

digress /dɪ'grɛs, dai-/ v. divagar.

digression /dɪ'grɛʃən, dai-/ n. digresión f.

dike /daik/ n. dique m.

dilapidated /dɪ'læpɪ,deitɪd/ a. dilapidado.

dilapidation /dɪ,læpə'deiʃən/ n. dilapidación f.

dilate /dai'leit/ v. dilatar.

dilatory /'dɪlə,tɔri/ a. dilatorio.

dilemma /dɪ'lɛmə/ n. dilema m.

dilettante /'dɪlɪ,tɑnt/ n. diletante m. & f.

diligence /'dɪlɪdʒəns/ n. diligencia f.

diligent /'dɪlɪdʒənt/ *a.* diligente, aplicado.

dilute /dɪ'lut, dai-/ *v.* diluir.

dim /dɪm/ *a.* **1.** oscuro. —*v.* **2.** oscurecer.

dimension /dɪ'mɛnʃən/ *n.* dimensión *f.*

diminish /dɪ'mɪnɪʃ/ *v.* disminuir.

diminution /ˌdɪmə'nuʃən/ *n.* disminución *f.*

diminutive /dɪ'mɪnyətɪv/ *a.* diminutivo.

dimness /'dɪmnɪs/ *n.* oscuridad *f.*

dimple /'dɪmpəl/ *n.* hoyuelo *m.*

din /dɪn/ *n.* alboroto, estrépito *m.*

dine /dain/ *v.* comer, cenar.

diner /'dainər/ *n.* coche comedor *m.*

dingy /'dɪndʒi/ *a.* deslucido, deslustrado.

dining room /'dainɪŋ/ comedor *m.*

dinner /'dɪnər/ *n.* comida, cena *f.*

dinosaur /'dainə,sɔr/ *n.* dinosauro *m.*

diocese /'daiəsɪs/ *n.* diócesis *f.*

dip /dɪp/ *v.* sumergir, hundir.

diphtheria /dɪf'θɪəriə/ *n.* difteria *f.*

diploma /dɪ'ploumə/ *n.* diploma *m.*

diplomacy /dɪ'plouməsi/ *n.* diplomacia *f.*

diplomat /'dɪplə,mæt/ *n.* diplomático -ca.

diplomatic /ˌdɪplə'mætɪk/ *a.* diplomático.

dipper /'dɪpər/ *n.* cucharón *m.*

dire /daiᵊr/ *a.* horrendo.

direct /dɪ'rɛkt, dai-/ *a.* **1.** directo. —*v.* **2.** dirigir.

direction /dɪ'rɛkʃən, 'dai-/ *n.* dirección *f.*

directive /dɪ'rɛktɪv, dai-/ *n.* directiva *f.*

directly /dɪ'rɛktli, dai-/ *adv.* directamente.

director /dɪ'rɛktər, dai-/ *n.* director -ra.

directory /dɪ'rɛktəri, dai-/ *n.* directorio *m.*, guía *f.*

dirigible /'dɪrɪdʒəbəl/ *n.* dirigible *m.*

dirt /dɜrt/ *n.* basura *f.*; (earth) tierra *f.*

dirt-cheap /'dɜrt 'tʃip/ *a.* tirado.

dirty /'dɜrti/ *a.* sucio.

dis /dɪs/ *v. Colloq.* ofender, faltar al respeto.

disability /ˌdɪsə'bɪlɪti/ *n.* inhabilidad *f.*

disable /dɪs'eibəl/ *v.* incapacitar.

disabuse /ˌdɪsə'byuz/ *v.* desengañar.

disadvantage /ˌdɪsəd'væntɪdʒ/ *n.* desventaja *f.*

disagree /ˌdɪsə'gri/ *v.* desconvenir; disentir.

disagreeable /ˌdɪsə'griəbəl/ *a.* desagradable.

disagreement /ˌdɪsə'grimənt/ *n.* desacuerdo *m.*

disappear /ˌdɪsə'pɪər/ *v.* desaparecer.

disappearance /ˌdɪsə'pɪərəns/ *n.* desaparición *f.*

disappoint /ˌdɪsə'pɔint/ *v.* disgustar, desilusionar.

disappointment /ˌdɪsə'pɔintmənt/ *n.* disgusto *m.*, desilusión *f.*

disapproval /ˌdɪsə'pruvəl/ *n.* desaprobación *f.*

disapprove /ˌdɪsə'pruv/ *v.* desaprobar.

disarm /dɪs'ɑrm/ *v.* desarmar.

disarmament /dɪs'ɑrməmənt/ *n.* desarme *m.*

disarrange /ˌdɪsə'reindʒ/ *v.* desordenar; desarreglar.

disaster /dɪ'zæstər/ *n.* desastre *m.*

disastrous /dɪ'zæstrəs/ *a.* desastroso.

disavow /ˌdɪsə'vau/ *v.* repudiar.

disavowal /ˌdɪsə'vauəl/ *n.* repudiación *f.*

disband /dɪs'bænd/ *v.* dispersarse.

disbelieve /ˌdɪsbɪ'liv/ *v.* descreer.

disburse /dɪs'bɜrs/ *v.* desembolsar, pagar.

discard /dɪ'skɑrd/ *v.* descartar.

discern /dɪ'sɜrn/ *v.* discernir.

discerning /dɪ'sɜrnɪŋ/ *a.* discernidor, perspicaz.

discernment /dɪ'sɜrnmənt/ *n.* discernimiento *m.*

discharge /dɪs'tʃɑrdʒ/ *v.* descargar; despedir.

disciple /dɪ'saipəl/ *n.* discípulo -la.

disciplinary /'dɪsəplə,nɛri/ *a.* disciplinario.

discipline /'dɪsəplɪn/ *n.* disciplina *f.*

disclaim /dɪs'kleim/ *v.* repudiar.

disclaimer /dɪs'kleimər/ *n.* negación *f.*

disclose /dɪ'sklouz/ *v.* revelar.

disclosure /dɪ'sklouʒər/ *n.* revelación *f.*

disco /'dɪskou/ *n.* discoteca *f.*

discolor /dɪs'kʌlər/ v. descolorar.
discomfort /dɪs'kʌmfərt/ n. incomodidad f.
disconcert /ˌdɪskən'sɜrt/ v. desconcertar.
disconnect /ˌdɪskə'nɛkt/ v. desunir; desconectar.
disconnected /ˌdɪskə'nɛktɪd/ a. desunido.
disconsolate /dɪs'kɒnsəlɪt/ a. desconsolado.
discontent /ˌdɪskən'tɛnt/ n. descontento m.
discontented /ˌdɪskən'tɛntɪd/ a. descontento.
discontinue /ˌdɪskən'tɪnyu/ v. descontinuar.
discord /'dɪskɔrd/ n. discordia f.
discordant /dɪs'kɔrdənt/ a. disonante.
discotheque /'dɪskə,tɛk/ n. discoteca f.
discount /'dɪskaunt/ n. descuento m.
discourage /dɪ'skɜrɪdʒ/ v. desalentar, desanimar.
discouragement /dɪ'skɜrɪdʒmənt/ n. desaliento, desánimo m.
discourse /'dɪskɔrs/ n. discurso m.
discourteous /dɪs'kɜrtiəs/ a. descortés.
discourtesy /dɪs'kɜrtəsi/ n. descortesía f.
discover /dɪ'skʌvər/ v. descubrir.
discoverer /dɪ'skʌvərər/ n. descubridor -ra.
discovery /dɪ'skʌvəri/ n. descubrimiento m.
discreet /dɪ'skrit/ a. discreto.
discrepancy /dɪ'skrɛpənsi/ n. discrepancia f.
discretion /dɪ'skrɛʃən/ n. discreción f.
discriminate /dɪ'skrɪm,əneit/ v. distinguir. **d. against** discriminar contra.
discrimination /dɪ,skrɪmə'neiʃən/ n. discernimiento m.; discriminación f.
discuss /dɪ'skʌs/ v. discutir.
discussion /dɪ'skʌʃən/ n. discusión f.
disdain /dɪs'dein/ n. **1.** desdén m. —v. **2.** desdeñar.
disdainful /dɪs'deinfəl/ a. desdeñoso.
disease /dɪ'ziz/ n. enfermedad f., mal m.

disembark /ˌdɪsɛm'bark/ v. desembarcar.
disentangle /ˌdɪsɛn'tæŋgəl/ v. desenredar.
disfigure /dɪs'fɪgyər/ v. desfigurar.
disgrace /dɪs'greis/ n. **1.** vergüenza; deshonra f. —v. **2.** deshonrar.
disgraceful /dɪs'greisfəl/ a. vergonzoso.
disguise /dɪs'gaiz/ n. **1.** disfraz m. —v. **2.** disfrazar.
disgust /dɪs'gʌst/ n. **1.** repugnancia —v. **2.** fastidiar; repugnar.
dish /dɪʃ/ n. plato m.
dishearten /dɪs'hartn̩/ v. desanimar; descorazonar.
dishonest /dɪs'ɒnɪst/ a. deshonesto.
dishonesty /dɪs'ɒnəsti/ n. deshonestidad f.
dishonor /dɪs'ɒnər/ n. **1.** deshonra f. —v. **2.** deshonrar.
dishonorable /dɪs'ɒnərəbəl/ a. deshonroso.
dishwasher /'dɪʃ,wɒʃər/ n. lavaplatos m.
disillusion /ˌdɪsɪ'luʒən/ n. **1.** desengaño m. —v. **2.** desengañar.
disinfect /ˌdɪsɪn'fɛkt/ v. desinfectar.
disinfectant /ˌdɪsɪn'fɛktənt/ n. desinfectante m.
disinherit /ˌdɪsɪn'hɛrɪt/ v. desheredar.
disintegrate /dɪs'ɪntə,greit/ v. desintegrar.
disinterested /dɪs'ɪntə,rɛstɪd, -trɪstɪd/ a. desinteresado.
disk /dɪsk/ n. disco m.
disk drive disquetera f.
diskette /dɪ'skɛt/ n. disquete m.
disk jockey pinchadiscos m. & f.
dislike /dɪs'laik/ n. **1.** antipatía f. —v. **2.** no gustar de.
dislocate /'dɪslou,keit/ v. dislocar.
dislodge /dɪs'lɒdʒ/ v. desalojar; desprender.
disloyal /dɪs'lɔiəl/ a. desleal; infiel.
disloyalty /dɪs'lɔiəlti/ n. deslealtad f.
dismal /'dɪzməl/ a. lúgubre.
dismantle /dɪs'mæntl̩/ v. desmantelar, desmontar.
dismay /dɪs'mei/ n. **1.** consternación f. —v. **2.** consternar.
dismiss /dɪs'mɪs/ v. despedir.

dismissal /dɪs'mɪsəl/ n. despedida f.

dismount /dɪs'maunt/ v. apearse, desmontarse.

disobedience /ˌdɪsə'bidiəns/ n. desobediencia f.

disobedient /ˌdɪsə'bidiənt/ a. desobediente.

disobey /ˌdɪsə'bei/ v. desobedecer.

disorder /dɪs'ɔrdər/ n. desorden m.

disorderly /dɪs'ɔrdərli/ a. desarreglado, desordenado.

disown /dɪs'oun/ v. repudiar.

dispassionate /dɪs'pæʃənɪt/ a. desapasionado; templado.

dispatch /dɪ'spætʃ/ n. **1.** despacho m. —v. **2.** despachar.

dispel /dɪ'spɛl/ v. dispersar.

dispensary /dɪ'spɛnsəri/ n. dispensario m.

dispensation /ˌdɪspən'seiʃən/ n. dispensación f.

dispense /dɪ'spɛns/ v. dispensar.

dispersal /dɪ'spɜrsəl/ n. dispersión f.

disperse /dɪ'spɜrs/ v. dispersar.

displace /dɪs'pleis/ v. dislocar.

display /dɪ'splei/ n. **1.** despliegue m., exhibición f. —v. **2.** desplegar, exhibir.

displease /dɪs'pliz/ v. disgustar; ofender.

displeasure /dɪs'plɛʒər/ n. disgusto, sinsabor m.

disposable /dɪ'spouzəbəl/ a. disponible; desechable.

disposal /dɪ'spouzəl/ n. disposición f.

dispose /dɪ'spouz/ v. disponer.

disposition /ˌdɪspə'zɪʃən/ n. disposición f.; índole f., genio m.

dispossess /ˌdɪspə'zɛs/ v. desposeer.

disproportionate /ˌdɪsprə'pɔrʃənɪt/ a. desproporcionado.

disprove /dɪs'pruv/ v. confutar.

dispute /dɪ'spyut/ n. **1.** disputa f. —v. **2.** disputar.

disqualify /dɪs'kwɒlə,fai/ v. inhabilitar.

disregard /ˌdɪsrɪ'gɑrd/ n. **1.** desatención f. —v. **2.** desatender.

disrepair /ˌdɪsrɪ'pɛər/ n. descompostura f.

disreputable /dɪs'rɛpyətəbəl/ a. desacreditado.

disrespect /ˌdɪsrɪ'spɛkt/ n. falta de respeto, f., desacato m.

disrespectful /ˌdɪsrɪ'spɛktfəl/ a. irrespetuoso.

disrobe /dɪs'roub/ v. desvestir.

disrupt /dɪs'rʌpt/ v. romper; desbaratar.

dissatisfaction /ˌdɪssætɪs'fækʃən/ n. descontento m.

dissatisfy /dɪs'sætɪs,fai/ v. descontentar.

dissect /dɪ'sɛkt/ v. disecar.

dissemble /dɪ'sɛmbəl/ v. disimular.

disseminate /dɪ'sɛmə,neit/ v. diseminar.

dissension /dɪ'sɛnʃən/ n. disensión f.

dissent /dɪ'sɛnt/ n. **1.** disensión f. —v. **2.** disentir.

dissertation /ˌdɪsər'teiʃən/ n. disertación f.

dissimilar /dɪ'sɪmələr/ a. desemejante.

dissipate /'dɪsə,peit/ v. disipar.

dissipation /ˌdɪsə'peiʃən/ n. disipación f.; libertinaje m.

dissolute /'dɪsə,lut/ a. disoluto.

dissolution /ˌdɪsə'luʃən/ n. disolución f.

dissolve /dɪ'zɒlv/ v. disolver; derretirse.

dissonant /'dɪsənənt/ a. disonante.

dissuade /dɪ'sweid/ v. disuadir.

distance /'dɪstəns/ n. distancia f. **at a d., in the d.,** a lo lejos.

distant /'dɪstənt/ a. distante, lejano.

distaste /dɪs'teist/ n. disgusto, sinsabor m.

distasteful /dɪs'teistfəl/ a. desagradable.

distill /dɪ'stɪl/ v. destilar.

distillation /ˌdɪstl̩'eiʃən/ n. destilación f.

distillery /dɪ'stɪləri/ n. destilería f.

distinct /dɪ'stɪŋkt/ a. distinto.

distinction /dɪ'stɪŋkʃən/ n. distinción f.

distinctive /dɪ'stɪŋktɪv/ a. distintivo; característico.

distinctly /dɪ'stɪŋktli/ adv. distintamente.

distinguish /dɪ'stɪŋgwɪʃ/ v. distinguir.

distinguished /dɪ'stɪŋgwɪʃt/ a. distinguido.

distort /dɪ'stɔrt/ v. falsear; torcer.

distract /dɪ'strækt/ v. distraer.

distraction /dɪ'strækʃən/ n. distracción f.

distraught /dɪ'strɔt/ a. aturrullado; demente.

distress /dɪ'strɛs/ n. **1.** dolor m. —v. **2.** afligir.

distressing /dɪ'strɛsɪŋ/ a. penoso.

distribute /dɪ'strɪbyut/ v. distribuir.

distribution /ˌdɪstrə'byuʃən/ n. distribución f.; reparto m.

distributor /dɪ'strɪbyətər/ n. distribuidor -ra.

district /'dɪstrɪkt/ n. distrito m.

distrust /dɪs'trʌst/ n. **1.** desconfianza f. —v. **2.** desconfiar.

distrustful /dɪs'trʌstfəl/ a. desconfiado; sospechoso.

disturb /dɪ'stɜrb/ v. incomodar; inquietar.

disturbance /dɪ'stɜrbəns/ n. disturbio m.

disturbing /dɪ'stɜrbɪŋ/ a. inquietante.

ditch /dɪtʃ/ n. zanja f.; foso m.

divan /dɪ'væn/ n. diván m.

dive /daiv/ n. **1.** clavado m.; Colloq. leonera f. —v. **2.** echar un clavado; bucear.

diver /'daivər/ n. buzo m.

diverge /dɪ'vɜrdʒ/ v. divergir.

divergence /dɪ'vɜrdʒəns/ n. divergencia f.

divergent /dɪ'vɜrdʒənt/ a. divergente.

diverse /dɪ'vɜrs/ a. diverso.

diversion /dɪ'vɜrʒən/ n. diversión f.; pasatiempo m.

diversity /dɪ'vɜrsɪti/ n. diversidad f.

divert /dɪ'vɜrt/ v. desviar; divertir.

divest /dɪ'vɛst/ v. desnudar, despojar.

divide /dɪ'vaid/ v. dividir.

dividend /'dɪvɪˌdɛnd/ n. dividendo m.

divine /dɪ'vain/ a. divino.

divinity /dɪ'vɪnɪti/ n. divinidad f.

division /dɪ'vɪʒən/ n. división f.

divorce /dɪ'vɔrs/ n. **1.** divorcio m. —v. **2.** divorciar.

divorcee /dɪvɔr'sei/ n. divorciado -da.

divulge /dɪ'vʌldʒ/ v. divulgar, revelar.

dizziness /'dɪzɪnɪs/ n. vértigo, mareo m.

dizzy /'dɪzi/ a. mareado.

DNA abbr. (deoxyribonucleic acid) ADN (ácido deoxirríbonucleico) m.

do /du/ v. hacer.

docile /'dɒsəl/ a. dócil.

dock /dɒk/ n. **1.** muelle m. **dry d.,** astillero m. —v. **2.** entrar en muelle.

doctor /'dɒktər/ n. médico m.; doctor -ra.

doctorate /'dɒktərɪt/ n. doctorado m.

doctrine /'dɒktrɪn/ n. doctrina f.

document /'dɒkyəmənt/ n. documento m.

documentary /ˌdɒkyə'mɛntəri/ a. documental.

documentation /ˌdɒkyəmɛn'teiʃən/ n. documentación f.

dodge /dɒdʒ/ n. **1.** evasión f. —v. **2.** evadir.

dodgem /'dɒdʒɪm/ n. coche de choque m.

doe /dou/ n. gama f.

dog /dɔg/ n. perro -a.

dogma /'dɔgmə/ n. dogma m.

dogmatic /dɔg'mætɪk/ a. dogmático.

dogmatism /'dɔgməˌtɪzəm/ n. dogmatismo m.

doily /'dɔili/ n. servilletita f.

doleful /'doulfəl/ a. triste.

doll /dɒl/ n. muñeca -co.

dollar /'dɒlər/ n. dólar m.

dolorous /'doulərəs/ a. lastimoso.

dolphin /'dɒlfɪn/ n. delfín m.

domain /dou'mein/ n. dominio m.

dome /doum/ n. domo m.

domestic /də'mɛstɪk/ a. doméstico.

domesticate /də'mɛstɪˌkeit/ v. domesticar.

domicile /'dɒməˌsail/ n. domicilio m.

dominance /'dɒmənəns/ n. dominación f.

dominant /'dɒmənənt/ a. dominante.

dominate /'dɒməˌneit/ v. dominar.

domination /ˌdɒmə'neiʃən/ n. dominación f.

domineer /ˌdɒmə'nɪər/ v. dominar.

domineering /ˌdɒmə'nɪərɪŋ/ a. tiránico, mandón.

dominion /də'mɪnyən/ n. dominio; territorio m.

domino /'dɒməˌnou/ n. dominó m.

donate /'douneit/ v. donar; contribuir.

donation /dou'neiʃən/ n. donación f.

donkey /'dɒŋki/ *n.* asno, burro *m.*

doom /dum/ *n.* **1.** perdición, ruina *f.* —*v.* **2.** perder, ruinar.

door /dɔr/ *n.* puerta *f.*

doorman /'dɔr,mæn, -mən/ *n.* portero *m.*

doormat /'dɔr,mæt/ *n.* felpudo *m.*

doorway /'dɔr,wei/ *n.* entrada *f.*

dope /doup/ *n. Colloq.* narcótico *m.; idiota m.*

dormant /'dɔrmənt/ *a.* durmiente; inactivo.

dormitory /'dɔrmɪ,tɔri/ *n.* dormitorio *m.*

dosage /'dousɪdʒ/ *n.* dosificación *f.*

dose /dous/ *n.* dosis *f.*

dot /dɒt/ *n.* punto *m.*

dotted line /'dɒtɪd/ línea de puntos *f.*

double /'dʌbəl/ *a.* **1.** doble. —*v.* **2.** duplicar.

double bass /beis/ contrabajo *m.*

double-breasted /'dʌbəl 'brɛstɪd/ *a.* cruzado.

double-cross /'dʌbəl 'krɔs/ *v.* traicionar.

doubly /'dʌbli/ *adv.* doblemente.

doubt /daut/ *n.* **1.** duda *f.* —*v.* **2.** dudar.

doubtful /'dautfəl/ *a.* dudoso, incierto.

doubtless /'dautlɪs/ *a.* **1.** indudable. —*adv.* **2.** sin duda.

dough /dou/ *n.* pasta, masa *f.*

doughnut /'dounət, -,nʌt/ *n.* buñuelo *m.*

dove /duv/ *n.* paloma *f.*

dowager /'dauədʒər/ *n.* viuda (con título) *f.*

down /daun/ *adv.* **1.** abajo. —*prep.* **2. d. the street,** *etc.* calle abajo, *etc.*

downcast /'daun,kæst/ *a.* cabizbajo.

downfall /'daun,fɔl/ *n.* ruina, perdición *f.*

downhearted /'daun'hartɪd/ *a.* descorazonado.

download /'daun,loud/ *v.* bajar, descargar.

downpour /'daun,pɔr/ *n.* chaparrón *m.*

downright /'daun,rait/ *a.* absoluto, completo.

downriver /'daun'rɪvər/ *adv.* aguas abajo, río abajo.

downstairs /'daun'stɛərz/ *adv.* **1.** abajo. —*n.* **2.** primer piso.

downstream /'daun'strim/ *adv.* aguas abajo, río abajo.

downtown /'daun'taun/ *adv.* al centro, en el centro.

downward /'daunwərd/ *a.* **1.** descendente. —*adv.* **2.** hacia abajo.

dowry /'dauri/ *n.* dote *f.*

doze /douz/ *v.* dormitar.

dozen /'dʌzən/ *n.* docena *f.*

draft /dræft/ *n.* **1.** dibujo *m.; Com.* giro *m.; Mil.* conscripción *f.* —*v.* **2.** dibujar; *Mil.* reclutar.

draftee /dræf'ti/ *n.* conscripto *m.*

draft notice notificación de reclutamiento *f.*

drag /dræg/ *v.* arrastrar.

dragon /'drægən/ *n.* dragón *m.*

drain /drein/ *n.* **1.** desaguadero *m.* —*v.* **2.** desaguar.

drainage /'dreinɪdʒ/ *n.* drenaje *m.*

drain board escurridero *m.*

drama /'drɑmə, 'dræmə/ *n.* drama *m.*

dramatic /drə'mætɪk/ *a.* dramático.

dramatics /drə'mætɪks/ *n.* dramática *f.*

dramatist /'dræmətɪst, 'drɑmə-/ *n.* dramaturgo -ga.

dramatize /'dræmə,taiz, 'drɑmə-/ *v.* dramatizar.

drape /dreip/ *n.* cortinas *f.pl. v.* vestir; adornar.

drapery /'dreipəri/ *n.* colgaduras *f.pl.; ropaje m.*

drastic /'dræstɪk/ *a.* drástico.

draw /drɔ/ *v.* dibujar; atraer. **d. up,** formular.

drawback /'drɔ,bæk/ *n.* desventaja *f.*

drawer /drɔr/ *n.* cajón *m.*

drawing /'drɔɪŋ/ *n.* dibujo *m.; rifa f.*

dread /drɛd/ *n.* **1.** terror *m.* —*v.* **2.** temer.

dreadful /'drɛdfəl/ *a.* terrible.

dreadfully /'drɛdfəli/ *adv.* horrendamente.

dream /drim/ *n.* **1.** sueño, ensueño *m.* —*v.* **2.** soñar.

dreamer /'drimər/ *n.* soñador -ra; visionario -ia.

dreamy /'drimi/ *a.* soñador, contemplativo.

dreary /'drɪəri/ *a.* monótono y pesado.

dredge /drɛdʒ/ *n.* **1.** rastra *f.* —*v.* **2.** rastrear.

dregs /drɛgz/ *n.* sedimento *m.*

drench /drɛntʃ/ *v.* mojar.

dress /drɛs/ *n.* **1.** vestido; traje *m.* —*v.* **2.** vestir.

dresser /'drɛsər/ *n.* (furniture) tocador.

dressing /'drɛsɪŋ/ *n. Med.* curación *f.;* (cookery) relleno *m.,* salsa *f.*

dressing gown bata *f.*

dressing table tocador *m.*

dressmaker /'drɛs,meikər/ *n.* modista *m.* & *f.*

drift /drɪft/ *n.* **1.** tendencia *f.; Naut.* deriva *f.* —*v.* **2.** *Naut.* derivar; (snow) amontonarse.

drill /drɪl/ *n.* **1.** ejercicio *m.; Mech.* taladro *m.* —*v.* **2.** *Mech.* taladrar.

drink /drɪŋk/ *n.* **1.** bebida *f.* —*v.* **2.** beber, tomar.

drinkable /'drɪŋkəbəl/ *a.* potable, bebible.

drip /drɪp/ *v.* gotear.

drive /draiv/ *n.* **1.** paseo *m.* —*v.* **2.** impeler; *Auto.* guiar, conducir.

drive-in (movie theater) /'draiv ˌɪn/ *n.* autocine, autocinema *m.*

driver /'draivər/ *n.* conductor -ra; chofer *m.* **d.'s license,** permiso de conducir.

driveway /'draiv,wei/ *n.* entrada para coches.

drizzle /'drɪzəl/ *n.* **1.** llovizna *f.* —*v.* **2.** lloviznar.

dromedary /'drɒmɪ,dɛri/ *n.* dromedario *m.*

droop /drup/ *v.* inclinarse.

drop /drɒp/ *n.* **1.** gota *f.* —*v.* **2.** soltar; dejar caer.

dropout /'drɒp,aut/ *n.* joven que abandona sus estudios.

dropper /'drɒpər/ *n.* cuentagotas *f.*

dropsy /'drɒpsi/ *n.* hidropesía *f.*

drought /draut/ *n.* sequía *f.*

drove /drouv/ *n.* manada *f.*

drown /draun/ *v.* ahogar.

drowse /drauz/ *v.* adormecer.

drowsiness /'drauzɪnɪs/ *n.* somnolencia *f.*

drowsy /'drauzi/ *a.* soñoliento.

drudge /drʌdʒ/ *n.* ganapán *m.*

drudgery /'drʌdʒəri/ *n.* trabajo penoso.

drug /drʌg/ *n.* **1.** droga *f.* —*v.* **2.** narcotizar.

drug addict drogadicto -ta, toxicómano -na *m.* & *f.*

druggist /'drʌgɪst/ *n.* farmacéutico -ca, boticario -ria.

drugstore /'drʌg,stɔr/ *n.* farmacia, botica, droguería *f.*

drum /drʌm/ *n.* tambor *m.*

drummer /'drʌmər/ *n.* tambor *m.*

drumstick /'drʌm,stɪk/ *n.* palillo *m.; Leg.* pierna *f.*

drunk /drʌŋk/ *a.* & *n.* borracho, -a.

drunkard /'drʌŋkərd/ *n.* borrachón *m.*

drunken /'drʌŋkən/ *a.* borracho; ebrio.

drunkenness /'drʌŋkənnɪs/ *n.* embriaguez *f.*

dry /drai/ *a.* **1.** seco, árido. —*v.* **2.** secar.

dry cell *n.* pila seca *f.*

dry cleaner tintorero -ra.

dryness /'drainɪs/ *n.* sequedad *f.*

dual /'duəl/ *a.* doble.

dubious /'dubiəs/ *a.* dudoso.

duchess /'dʌtʃɪs/ *n.* duquesa *f.*

duck /dʌk/ *n.* **1.** pato *m.* —*v.* **2.** zambullir; (avoid) esquivar.

duct /dʌkt/ *n.* canal *m.*

due /du/ *a.* **1.** debido; *Com.* vencido. —*n.* **2. dues** cuota *f.*

duel /'duəl/ *n.* duelo *m.*

duelist /'duəlɪst/ *n.* duelista *m.*

duet /du'ɛt/ *n.* dúo *m.*

duke /duk/ *n.* duque *m.*

dull /dʌl/ *a.* apagado, desteñido; sin punta; *Fig.* pesado, soso.

dullness /'dʌlnɪs/ *n.* estupidez *f.;* pesadez *f.;* deslustre *m.*

duly /'duli/ *adv.* debidamente.

dumb /dʌm/ *a.* mudo; *Colloq.* estúpido.

dumbwaiter /'dʌm,weitər/ *n.* montaplatos *m.*

dumfound /dʌm'faund/ *v.* confundir.

dummy /'dʌmi/ *n.* maniquí *m.*

dump /dʌmp/ *n.* **1.** depósito *m.* —*v.* **2.** descargar.

dune /dun/ *n.* duna *f.*

dungeon /'dʌndʒən/ *n.* calabozo *m.*

dunk /dʌŋk/ *v.* mojar.

dupe /dup/ *v.* engañar.

duplicate /*a, n* 'duplɪkɪt; *v* -ˌkeit/ *a.* & *n.* **1.** duplicado *m.* —*v.* **2.** duplicar.

duplication /ˌduplɪ'keiʃən/ *n.* duplicación *f.*

duplicity /du'plɪsɪti/ *n.* duplicidad *f.*

durability /ˌdurə'bɪlɪti/ *n.* durabilidad *f.*

durable /'durəbəl/ *a.* durable, duradero.

duration /du'reiʃən/ *n.* duración *f.*

duress /dʊ'rɛs/ *n.* compulsión *f.;* encierro *m.*

during /'dʊrɪŋ/ *prep.* durante.

dusk /dʌsk/ *n.* crepúsculo *m.*

dusky /'dʌski/ *a.* oscuro; moreno.

dust /dʌst/ *n.* **1.** polvo *m.* —*v.* **2.** polvorear; despolvorear.

dusty /'dʌsti/ *a.* empolvado.

Dutch /dʌtʃ/ *a.* holandés -sa.

dutiful /'dutəfəl/ *a.* respetuoso.

dutifully /'dutəfəli/ *adv.* respetuosamente, obedientemente.

duty /'duti/ *n.* deber *m.;* Com. derechos *m.pl.*

duty-free /'duti 'fri/ *a.* libre de derechos.

dwarf /dwɔrf/ *n.* **1.** enano -na. —*v.* **2.** achicar.

dwell /dwɛl/ *v.* habitar, residir. **d. on,** espaciarse en.

dwelling /'dwɛlɪŋ/ *n.* morada, casa *f.*

dwindle /'dwɪndļ/ *v.* disminuirse.

dye /dai/ *n.* **1.** tintura *f.* —*v.* **2.** teñir.

dyer /'daiər/ *n.* tintorero -ra.

dynamic /dai'næmɪk/ *a.* dinámico.

dynamite /'dainə,mait/ *n.* dinamita *f.*

dynamo /'dainə,mou/ *n.* dínamo *m.*

dynasty /'dainəsti/ *n.* dinastía *f.*

dysentery /'dɪsən,tɛri/ *n.* disentería *f.*

dyslexia /dɪs'lɛksiə/ *n.* dislexia *f.*

dyslexic /dɪs'lɛksɪk/ *a.* disléxico.

dyspepsia /dɪs'pɛpʃə/ *n.* dispepsia *f.*

E

each /itʃ/ *a.* **1.** cada. —*pron.* **2.** cada uno -na. **e. other,** el uno al otro.

eager /'igər/ *a.* ansioso.

eagerly /'igərli/ *adv.* ansiosamente.

eagerness /'igərnɪs/ *n.* ansia *f.*

eagle /'igəl/ *n.* águila *f.*

ear /iər/ *n.* oído *m.;* (outer) oreja *f.;* (of corn) mazorca *f.*

earache /'iər,eik/ *n.* dolor de oído *m.*

earl /ɜrl/ *n.* conde *m.*

early /'ɜrli/ *a. & adv.* temprano.

earn /ɜrn/ *v.* ganar.

earnest /'ɜrnɪst/ *a.* serio.

earnestly /'ɜrnɪstli/ *adv.* seriamente.

earnings /'ɜrnɪŋz/ *n.* ganancias *f.pl.;* Com. ingresos *m.pl.*

earphone /'iər,foun/ *n.* auricular *m.*

earring /'iər,rɪŋ/ *n.* pendiente, arete *m.*

earth /ɜrθ/ *n.* tierra *f.*

earthquake /'ɜrθ,kweik/ *n.* terremoto *m.*

ease /iz/ *n.* **1.** reposo *m.;* facilidad *f.* —*v.* **2.** aliviar.

easel /'izəl/ *n.* caballete *m.*

easily /'izəli/ *adv.* fácilmente.

east /ist/ *n.* oriente, este *m.*

Easter /'istər/ *n.* Pascua Florida.

eastern /'istərn/ *a.* oriental.

eastward /'istwərd/ *adv.* hacia el este.

easy /'izi/ *a.* fácil.

eat /it/ *v.* comer.

eau de Cologne /'ou də kə'loun/ colonia *f.*

eaves /ivz/ *n.* socarrén *m.*

ebb /ɛb/ *n.* **1.** menguante *f.* —*v.* **2.** menguar.

ebony /'ɛbəni/ *n.* ébano *m.*

eccentric /ɪk'sɛntrɪk/ *a.* excéntrico.

eccentricity /,ɛksən'trɪsiti/ *n.* excentricidad *f.*

ecclesiastic /ɪ,klizi'æstɪk/ *a. & n.* eclesiástico *m.*

echelon /'ɛʃə,lɒn/ *n.* escalón *m.*

echo /'ɛkou/ *n.* eco *m.*

eclipse /ɪ'klɪps/ *n.* **1.** eclipse *m.* —*v.* **2.** eclipsar.

ecological /,ɛkə'lɒdʒɪkəl/ *a.* ecológico.

ecology /ɪ'kɒlədʒi/ *n.* ecología *f.*

economic /,ɛkə'nɒmɪk, ,ikə-/ *a.* económico.

economical /,ɛkə'nɒmɪkəl, ,ikə-/ *a.* económico.

economics /,ɛkə'nɒmɪks, ,ikə-/ *n.* economía política.

economist /ɪ'kɒnəmɪst/ *n.* economista *m. & f.*

economize /ɪ'kɒnə,maiz/ *v.* economizar.

economy /ɪ'kɒnəmi/ *n.* economía *f.*

ecstasy /'ɛkstəsi/ *n.* éxtasis *m.*

Ecuadorian /,ɛkwə'dɔriən/ *a. & n.* ecuatoriano -na.

ecumenical /'ɛkyu'mɛnɪkəl/ *a.* ecuménico.

eczema /'ɛksəmə/ n. eczema f.
eddy /'ɛdi/ n. **1.** remolino m. —v. **2.** remolinar.
edge /ɛdʒ/ n. **1.** filo; borde m. —v. **2. e. one's way,** abrirse paso.
edible /'ɛdəbəl/ a. comestible.
edict /'idɪkt/ n. edicto m.
edifice /'ɛdəfɪs/ n. edificio m.
edify /'ɛdə,fai/ v. edificar.
edition /ɪ'dɪʃən/ n. edición f.
editor /'ɛdɪtər/ n. redactor -ra.
editorial /,ɛdɪ'tɔriəl/ n. editorial m. **e. board,** consejo de redacción m. **e. staff,** redacción f.
educate /'ɛdʒʊ,keit/ v. educar.
education /,ɛdʒʊ'keiʃən/ n. instrucción; enseñanza f.
educational /,ɛdʒʊ'keiʃənl/ a. educativo.
educator /'ɛdʒʊ,keitər/ n. educador -ra, pedagogo -ga.
eel /il/ n. anguila f.
efface /ɪ'feis/ v. tachar.
effect /ɪ'fɛkt/ n. **1.** efecto m. **in e.,** en vigor. —v. **2.** efectuar, realizar.
effective /ɪ'fɛktɪv/ a. eficaz; efectivo; en vigor.
effectively /ɪ'fɛktɪvli/ adv. eficazmente.
effectiveness /ɪ'fɛktɪvnɪs/ n. efectividad f.
effectual /ɪ'fɛktʃuəl/ a. eficaz.
effeminate /ɪ'fɛmənɪt/ a. afeminado.
efficacy /'ɛfɪkəsi/ n. eficacia f.
efficiency /ɪ'fɪʃənsi/ n. eficiencia f.
efficient /ɪ'fɪʃənt/ a. eficaz.
efficiently /ɪ'fɪʃəntli/ adv. eficazmente.
effigy /'ɛfɪdʒi/ n. efigie f.
effort /'ɛfərt/ n. esfuerzo m.
effrontery /ɪ'frʌntəri/ n. impudencia f.
effusive /ɪ'fyusɪv/ a. efusivo.
egg /ɛg/ n. huevo m. **fried e.,** huevo frito. **soft-boiled e.,** h. pasado por agua. **scrambled eggs,** huevos revueltos.
eggplant /'ɛg,plænt/ n. berenjena f.
egg white clara de huevo f.
egoism /'igou,ɪzəm/ **egotism** n. egoísmo m.
egoist /'igouɪst/ **egotist** n. egoísta m. & f.
egotism /'igə,tɪzəm/ n. egotismo m.

egotist /'igətɪst/ n. egotista m. & f.
Egypt /'idʒɪpt/ n. Egipto m.
Egyptian /ɪ'dʒɪpʃən/ a. & n. egipcio -ia.
eight /eit/ a. & pron. ocho.
eighteen /'ei'tin/ a. & pron. dieciocho.
eighth /eitθ, eiθ/ a. octavo.
eightieth /'eitiɪθ/ n. octogésimo m.
eighty /'eiti/ a. & pron. ochenta.
either /'iðər/ a. & pron. **1.** cualquiera de los dos. —adv. **2.** tampoco. —conj. **3. either... or,** o... o.
ejaculate /ɪ'dʒækyə,leit/ v. exclamar; eyacular.
ejaculation /ɪ,dʒækyə'leiʃən/ n. eyaculación f.
eject /ɪ'dʒɛkt/ v. expeler; eyectar.
ejection /ɪ'dʒɛkʃən/ n. expulsión f.; eyección f.
elaborate /a ɪ'læbərɪt; v -ə,reit/ a. **1.** elaborado. —v. **2.** elaborar; ampliar.
elapse /ɪ'læps/ v. transcurrir; pasar.
elastic /ɪ'læstɪk/ a. & n. elástico m.
elasticity /ɪlæ'stɪsɪti/ n. elasticidad f.
elate /ɪ'leit/ v. exaltar.
elation /ɪ'leiʃən/ n. exaltación f.
elbow /'ɛlbou/ n. codo m.
elder /'ɛldər/ a. **1.** mayor. —n. **2.** anciano -na.
elderly /'ɛldərli/ a. de edad.
eldest /'ɛldɪst/ a. mayor.
elect /ɪ'lɛkt/ v. elegir.
election /ɪ'lɛkʃən/ n. elección f.
elective /ɪ'lɛktɪv/ a. electivo.
electorate /ɪ'lɛktərɪt/ n. electorado m.
electric /ɪ'lɛktrɪk/ **electrical** a. eléctrico.
electrician /ɪlɛk'trɪʃən/ n. electricista m. & f.
electricity /ɪlɛk'trɪsɪti/ n. electricidad f.
electrocardiogram /ɪ,lɛktrou'kɑrdiə,græm/ n. electrocardiograma m.
electrocute /ɪ'lɛktrə,kyut/ v. electrocutar.
electrode /ɪ'lɛktroud/ n. electrodo m.
electrolysis /ɪlɛk'trɒləsɪs/ n. electrólisis f.
electron /ɪ'lɛktrɒn/ n. electrón m.

electronic /ɪlɛk'trɒnɪk/ *a.* electrónico.

electronics /ɪlɪk'trɒnɪks/ *n.* electrónica *f.*

elegance /'ɛlɪgəns/ *n.* elegancia *f.*

elegant /'ɛlɪgənt/ *a.* elegante.

elegy /'ɛlɪdʒi/ *n.* elegía *f.*

element /'ɛləmənt/ *n.* elemento *m.*

elemental /ˌɛlə'mɛntl̩/ *a.* elemental.

elementary /ˌɛlə'mɛntəri/ *a.* elemental.

elephant /'ɛləfənt/ *n.* elefante -ta.

elevate /'ɛlə,veit/ *v.* elevar.

elevation /ˌɛlə'veiʃən/ *n.* elevación *f.*

elevator /'ɛlə,veitər/ *n.* ascensor *m.*

eleven /ɪ'lɛvən/ *a. & pron.* once.

eleventh /ɪ'lɛvənθ/ *a.* undécimo.

eleventh hour último minuto *m.*

elf /ɛlf/ *n.* duende *m.*

elicit /ɪ'lɪsɪt/ *v.* sacar; despertar.

eligibility /ˌɛlɪdʒə'bɪlɪti/ *n.* elegibilidad *f.*

eligible /'ɛlɪdʒəbəl/ *a.* elegible.

eliminate /ɪ'lɪmə,neit/ *v.* eliminar.

elimination /ɪ,lɪmə'neiʃən/ *n.* eliminación *f.*

elixir /ɪ'lɪksər/ *n.* elixir *m.*

elk /ɛlk/ *n.* alce *m.*, anta *m.*

elm /ɛlm/ *n.* olmo *m.*

elocution /ˌɛlə'kyuʃən/ *n.* elocución *f.*

elongate /ɪ'lɒŋgeit/ *v.* alargar.

elope /ɪ'loup/ *v.* fugarse.

eloquence /'ɛləkwəns/ *n.* elocuencia *f.*

eloquent /'ɛləkwənt/ *a.* elocuente.

eloquently /'ɛləkwəntli/ *adv.* elocuentemente.

else /ɛls/ *adv.* más. **someone e.,** otra persona. **something e.,** otra cosa. **or e.,** de otro modo.

elsewhere /'ɛls,wɛər/ *adv.* en otra parte.

elucidate /ɪ'lusɪ,deit/ *v.* elucidar.

elude /ɪ'lud/ *v.* eludir.

elusive /ɪ'lusɪv/ *a.* evasivo.

emaciated /ɪ'meiʃi,eitɪd/ *a.* demacrado, enflaquecido.

e-mail /'i,meil/ *n.* correo electrónico *m.*

emanate /'ɛmə,neit/ *v.* emanar.

emancipate /ɪ'mænsə,peit/ *v.* emancipar.

emancipation /ɪ,mænsə'peiʃən/ *n.* emancipación *f.*

emancipator /ɪ'mænsə,peitər/ *n.* libertador -ra.

embalm /ɛm'bam/ *v.* embalsamar.

embankment /ɛm'bæŋkmənt/ *n.* malecón, dique *m.*

embargo /ɛm'bargou/ *n.* embargo *m.*

embark /ɛm'bark/ *v.* embarcar.

embarrass /ɛm'bærəs/ *v.* avergonzar; turbar.

embarrassing /ɛm'bærəsɪŋ/ *a.* penoso, vergonzoso.

embarrassment /ɛm'bærəsmənt/ *n.* turbación; vergüenza *f.*

embassy /'ɛmbəsi/ *n.* embajada *f.*

embellish /ɛm'bɛlɪʃ/ *v.* hermosear, embellecer.

embellishment /ɛm'bɛlɪʃmənt/ *n.* embellecimiento *m.*

embezzle /ɛm'bɛzəl/ *v.* desfalcar, malversar.

emblem /'ɛmbləm/ *n.* emblema *m.*

embody /ɛm'bɒdi/ *v.* incorporar; personificar.

embrace /ɛm'breis/ *n.* **1.** abrazo *m.* —*v.* **2.** abrazar.

embroider /ɛm'brɔidər/ *v.* bordar.

embroidery /ɛm'brɔidəri, -dri/ *n.* bordado *m.*

embryo /'ɛmbri,ou/ *n.* embrión *m.*

embryonic /ˌɛmbri'ɒnɪk/ *a.* embrionario.

emerald /'ɛmərəld/ *n.* esmeralda *f.*

emerge /ɪ'mɔrdʒ/ *v.* salir.

emergency /ɪ'mɔrdʒənsi/ *n.* emergencia *f.*

emergency brake freno de auxilio *m.*

emergency exit salida de urgencia *f.*

emergency landing aterrizaje forzoso *m.*

emergent /ɪ'mɔrdʒənt/ *a.* emergente.

emery /'ɛməri/ *n.* esmeril *m.*

emetic /ɪ'mɛtɪk/ *n.* emético *m.*

emigrant /'ɛmɪgrənt/ *a. & n.* emigrante *m. & f.*

emigrate /'ɛmɪ,greit/ *v.* emigrar.

emigration /ˌɛmə'greiʃən/ *n.* emigración *f.*

eminence /'ɛmənəns/ *n.* altura; eminencia *f.*

eminent /'ɛmənənt/ *a.* eminente.

emissary /'ɛmə,sɛri/ *n.* emisario *m.*

emission /ɪ'mɪʃən/ *n.* emisión *f.*

emit /ɪˈmɪt/ v. emitir.

emolument /ɪˈmɒlyəmənt/ n. emolumento m.

emotion /ɪˈmouʃən/ n. emoción f.

emotional /ɪˈmouʃənl̩/ a. emocional; sentimental.

emperor /ˈɛmpərər/ n. emperador m.

emphasis /ˈɛmfəsɪs/ n. énfasis m. or f.

emphasize /ˈɛmfəˌsaiz/ v. acentuar, recalcar.

emphatic /ɛmˈfætɪk/ a. enfático.

empire /ˈɛmpaiˀr/ n. imperio m.

empirical /ɛmˈpɪrɪkəl/ a. empírico.

employ /ɛmˈplɔi/ v. emplear.

employee /ɛmˈplɔii/ n. empleado -da.

employer /ɛmˈplɔiər/ n. patrón -ona.

employment /ɛmˈplɔimənt/ n. empleo m.

employment agency agencia de colocaciones f.

empower /ɛmˈpauər/ v. autorizar.

emptiness /ˈɛmptinɪs/ n. vaciedad; futilidad f.

empty /ˈɛmpti/ a. **1.** vacío. —v. **2.** vaciar.

emulate /ˈɛmyəˌleit/ v. emular.

emulsion /ɪˈmʌlʃən/ n. emulsión f.

enable /ɛnˈeibəl/ v. capacitar; permitir.

enact /ɛnˈækt/ v. promulgar, decretar.

enactment /ɛnˈæktmənt/ n. ley f., estatuto m.

enamel /ɪˈnæməl/ n. **1.** esmalte m. —v. **2.** esmaltar.

enamored /ɪˈnæmərd/ a. enamorado.

enchant /ɛnˈtʃænt/ v. encantar.

enchantment /ɛnˈtʃæntmənt/ n. encanto m.

encircle /ɛnˈsɜrkəl/ v. circundar.

enclose /ɛnˈklouz/ v. encerrar. **enclosed,** (in letter) adjunto.

enclosure /ɛnˈklouʒər/ n. recinto m.; (in letter) incluso m.

encompass /ɛnˈkʌmpəs/ v. circundar.

encounter /ɛnˈkauntər/ n. **1.** encuentro m. —v. **2.** encontrar.

encourage /ɛnˈkɜrɪdʒ/ v. animar.

encouragement /ɛnˈkɜrɪdʒmənt/ n. estímulo m.

encroach /ɛnˈkroutʃ/ v. usurpar; meterse.

encryption /ɛnˈkrɪpʃən/ n. encriptación f., cifrado m.

encyclical /ɛnˈsɪklɪkəl/ n. encíclica f.

encyclopedia /ɛnˌsaiklɪˈpidiə/ n. enciclopedia f.

end /ɛnd/ n. **1.** fin, término, cabo; extremo; (aim) propósito m. —v. **2.** acabar; terminar.

endanger /ɛnˈdeindʒər/ v. poner en peligro.

endear /ɛnˈdiər/ v. hacer querer.

endeavor /ɛnˈdɛvər/ n. **1.** esfuerzo m. —v. **2.** esforzarse.

ending /ˈɛndɪŋ/ n. conclusión f.

endless /ˈɛndlɪs/ a. sin fin.

endocrine gland /ˈɛndəkrɪn/ glándula endocrina f.

endorse /ɛnˈdɔrs/ v. endosar; apoyar.

endorsement /ɛnˈdɔrsmənt/ n. endoso m.

endow /ɛnˈdau/ v. dotar, fundar.

endowment /ɛnˈdaumənt/ n. dotación f., fundación f.

endurance /ɛnˈdurəns/ n. resistencia f.

endure /ɛnˈdur/ v. soportar, resistir, aguantar.

enema /ˈɛnəmə/ n. enema; lavativa f.

enemy /ˈɛnəmi/ n. enemigo -ga.

energetic /ˌɛnərˈdʒɛtɪk/ a. enérgico.

energy /ˈɛnərdʒi/ n. energía f.

enervate /ˈɛnərˌveit/ v. enervar.

enervation /ˌɛnərˈveiʃən/ n. enervación f.

enfold /ɛnˈfould/ v. envolver.

enforce /ɛnˈfɔrs/ v. ejecutar.

enforcement /ɛnˈfɔrsmənt/ n. ejecución f.

engage /ɛnˈgeidʒ/ v. emplear; ocupar.

engaged /ɛnˈgeidʒd/ a. (to marry) prometido.

engagement /ɛnˈgeidʒmənt/ n. combate; compromiso; contrato m.; cita f.

engine /ˈɛndʒən/ n. máquina f. (railroad) locomotora f.

engineer /ˌɛndʒəˈniər/ n. ingeniero -ra; maquinista m.

engineering /ˌɛndʒəˈniərɪŋ/ n. ingeniería f.

England /ˈɪŋglənd/ n. Inglaterra f.

English /ˈɪŋglɪʃ/ a. & n. inglés -esa.

English Channel Canal de la Mancha m.

Englishman /'ɪŋglɪʃmən/ *n.* inglés *m.*

Englishwoman /'ɪŋglɪʃ,wumən/ *n.* inglesa *f.*

engrave /ɛn'greiv/ *v.* grabar.

engraver /ɛn'greivər/ *n.* grabador *m.*

engraving /ɛn'greivɪŋ/ *n.* grabado *m.*

engross /ɛn'grous/ *v.* absorber.

enhance /ɛn'hæns/ *v.* aumentar en valor; realzar.

enigma /ə'nɪɡmə/ *n.* enigma *m.*

enigmatic /,ɛnɪɡ'mætɪk/ *a.* enigmático.

enjoy /ɛn'dʒɔi/ *v.* gozar de; disfrutar de. **e. oneself,** divertirse.

enjoyable /ɛn'dʒɔiəbəl/ *a.* agradable.

enjoyment /ɛn'dʒɔimənt/ *n.* goce *m.*

enlarge /ɛn'lɑrdʒ/ *v.* agrandar; ampliar.

enlargement /ɛn'lɑrdʒmənt/ *n.* ensanchamiento *m.*, ampliación *f.*

enlarger /ɛn'lɑrdʒər/ *n.* amplificador *m.*

enlighten /ɛn'laitn̩/ *v.* informar.

enlightenment /ɛn'laitn̩mənt/ *n.* esclarecimiento *m.*; cultura *f.*

enlist /ɛn'lɪst/ *v.* reclutar; alistarse.

enlistment /ɛn'lɪstmənt/ *n.* alistamiento *m.*

enliven /ɛn'laivən/ *v.* avivar.

enmesh /ɛn'mɛʃ/ *v.* entrampar.

enmity /'ɛnmɪti/ *n.* enemistad *f.*

enormity /ɪ'nɔrmɪti/ *v.* enormidad *f.*

enormous /ɪ'nɔrməs/ *a.* enorme.

enough /ɪ'nʌf/ *a. & adv.* bastante. **to be e.,** bastar.

enrage /ɛn'reidʒ/ *v.* enfurecer.

enrich /ɛn'rɪtʃ/ *v.* enriquecer.

enroll /ɛn'roul/ *v.* registrar; matricularse.

enrollment /ɛn'roulmənt/ *n.* matriculación *f.*

ensign /'ɛnsən/ *n.* bandera *f.*; (naval) subteniente *m.*

enslave /ɛn'sleiv/ *v.* esclavizar.

ensue /ɛn'su/ *v.* seguir, resultar.

entail /ɛn'teil/ *v.* acarrear, ocasionar.

entangle /ɛn'tæŋgəl/ *v.* enredar.

enter /'ɛntər/ *v.* entrar.

enterprise /'ɛntər,praiz/ *n.* empresa *f.*

enterprising /'ɛntər,praizɪŋ/ *a.* emprendedor.

entertain /,ɛntər'tein/ *v.* entretener; divertir.

entertainment /,ɛntər'teinmənt/ *n.* entretenimiento *m.*; diversión *f.*

enthrall /ɛn'θrɔl/ *v.* esclavizar; cautivar.

enthusiasm /ɛn'θuzi,æzəm/ *n.* entusiasmo *m.*

enthusiast /ɛn'θuzi,æst, -ɪst/ *n.* entusiasta *m. & f.*

enthusiastic /ɛn,θuzi'æstɪk/ *a.* entusiasmado.

entice /ɛn'tais/ *v.* inducir.

entire /ɛn'taiᵊr/ *a.* entero.

entirely /ɛn'taiᵊrli/ *adv.* enteramente.

entirety /ɛn'taiᵊrti/ *n.* totalidad *f.*

entitle /ɛn'taitl̩/ *v.* autorizar; (book) titular.

entity /'ɛntɪti/ *n.* entidad *f.*

entrails /'ɛntreilz/ *n.* entrañas *f.pl.*

entrance /'ɛntrəns/ *n.* entrada *f.*

entrance examination examen de ingreso *m.*

entrant /'ɛntrənt/ *n.* competidor -ra.

entreat /ɛn'trit/ *v.* rogar, suplicar.

entreaty /ɛn'triti/ *n.* ruego *m.*, súplica *f.*

entrench /ɛn'trɛntʃ/ *v.* atrincherar.

entrust /ɛn'trʌst/ *v.* confiar.

entry /'ɛntri/ *n.* entrada *f.*; Com. partida *f.*

entry blank hoja de inscripción *f.*

enumerate /ɪ'numə,reit/ *v.* enumerar.

enumeration /ɪ,numə'reiʃən/ *n.* enumeración *f.*

enunciate /ɪ'nʌnsi,eit/ *v.* enunciar.

enunciation /ɪ,nʌnsi'eiʃən/ *n.* enunciación *f.*

envelop /ɛn'vɛləp/ *v.* envolver.

envelope /'ɛnvə,loup/ *n.* sobre *m.*; cubierta *f.*

enviable /'ɛnviəbəl/ *a.* envidiable.

envious /'ɛnviəs/ *a.* envidioso.

environment /ɛn'vairənmənt/ *n.* ambiente *m.*

environmentalist /ɛn,vairən'mɛntl̩ɪst/ *n.* ambientalista, ecologista *m. & f.*

environmental protection /ɛn,vairən'mɛntəl/ protección del ambiente.

environs /ɛn'vairənz/ *n.* alrededores *m.*

envoy /'ɛnvɔɪ/ *n.* enviado *m.*
envy /'ɛnvi/ *n.* **1.** envidia *f.* —*v.*
2. envidiar.
eon /'iən/ *n.* eón *m.*
ephemeral /ɪ'fɛmərəl/ *a.* efímero.
epic /'ɛpɪk/ *a.* **1.** épico. —*n.* **2.**
epopeya *f.*
epicure /'ɛpɪ,kyur/ *n.* epicúreo *m.*
epidemic /,ɛpɪ'dɛmɪk/ *a.* **1.**
epidémico. —*n.* **2.** epidemia *f.*
epidermis /,ɛpɪ'dɜrmɪs/ *n.* epidermis *f.*
epigram /'ɛpɪ,græm/ *n.* epigrama *m.*
epilepsy /'ɛpə,lɛpsi/ *n.* epilepsia *f.*
epilogue /'ɛpə,lɔg/ *n.* epílogo *m.*
episode /'ɛpə,soud/ *n.* episodio *m.*
epistle /ɪ'pɪsəl/ *n.* epístola *f.*
epitaph /'ɛpɪ,tæf/ *n.* epitafio *m.*
epithet /'ɛpə,θɛt/ *n.* epíteto *m.*
epitome /ɪ'pɪtəmi/ *n.* epítome *m.*
epoch /'ɛpək/ *n.* época, era *f.*
Epsom salts /'ɛpsəm/ *n.pl.* sal de
la Higuera *f.*
equal /'ikwəl/ *a. & n.* **1.** igual *m.*
—*v.* **2.** igualar; equivaler.
equality /ɪ'kwɒlɪti/ *n.* igualdad *f.*
equalize /'ikwə,laiz/ *v.* igualar.
equanimity /,ikwə'nɪmɪti/ *n.*
ecuanimidad *f.*
equate /ɪ'kweit/ *v.* igualar.
equation /ɪ'kweiʒən/ *n.* ecuación *f.*
equator /ɪ'kweitər/ *n.* ecuador *m.*
equatorial /,ikwə'tɔriəl/ *a.* ecuatorial
equestrian /ɪ'kwɛstriən/ *n.* **1.** jinete *m.* —*a.* **2.** ecuestre.
equilibrium /,ikwə'lɪbriəm/ *n.*
equilibrio *m.*
equinox /'ikwə,nɒks/ *n.* equinoccio *m.*
equip /ɪ'kwɪp/ *v.* equipar.
equipment /ɪ'kwɪpmənt/ *n.*
equipo *m.*
equitable /'ɛkwɪtəbəl/ *a.* equitativo.
equity /'ɛkwɪti/ *n.* equidad, justicia *f.*
equivalent /ɪ'kwɪvələnt/ *a. & n.*
equivalente *m.*
equivocal /ɪ'kwɪvəkəl/ *a.* equívoco, ambiguo.
era /'ɪərə, 'ɛrə/ *n.* era, época,
edad *f.*
eradicate /ɪ'rædɪ,keit/ *v.* extirpar.
erase /ɪ'reis/ *v.* borrar.
eraser /ɪ'reisər/ *n.* borrador *m.*
erasure /ɪ'reiʃər/ *n.* borradura *f.*

erect /ɪ'rɛkt/ *a.* **1.** derecho, erguido. —*v.* **2.** erigir.
erection /ɪ'rɛkʃən/ **erectness** *n.*
erección *f.*
ermine /'ɜrmɪn/ *n.* armiño *m.*
erode /ɪ'roud/ *v.* corroer.
erosion /ɪ'rouʒən/ *n.* erosión *f.*
erotic /ɪ'rɒtɪk/ *a.* erótico.
err /ɜr, ɛr/ *v.* equivocarse.
errand /'ɛrənd/ *n.* encargo, recado *m.*
errant /'ɛrənt/ *a.* errante.
erratic /ɪ'rætɪk/ *a.* errático.
erroneous /ə'rouniəs/ *a.* erróneo.
error /'ɛrər/ *n.* error *m.*
erudite /'ɛryu,dait/ *a.* erudito.
erudition /,ɛryu'dɪʃən/ *n.* erudición *f.*
eruption /ɪ'rʌpʃən/ *n.* erupción,
irrupción *f.*
erysipelas /,ɛrə'sɪpələs/ *n.* erisipela *f.*
escalate /'ɛskə,leit/ *v.* escalar; intensificarse.
escalator /'ɛskə,leitər/ *n.* escalera
mecánica *f.*
escapade /'ɛskə,peid/ *n.* escapada; correría *f.*
escape /ɪ'skeip/ *n.* **1.** fuga, huída
f. **fire e.,** escalera de salvamento.
—*v.* **2.** escapar; fugarse.
eschew /ɛs'tʃu/ *v.* evadir.
escort /*n.* 'ɛskɔrt; *v.* ɪ'skɔrt/ *n.* **1.**
escolta *f.* —*v.* **2.** escoltar.
escrow /'ɛskrou/ *n.* plica *f.*
escutcheon /ɪ'skʌtʃən/ *n.* escudo
de armas *m.*
esophagus /ɪ'sɒfəgəs/ *n.* esófago *m.*
esoteric /,ɛsə'tɛrɪk/ *a.* esotérico.
especially /ɪ'spɛʃəli/ *adv.* especialmente.
espionage /'ɛspiə,nɑʒ/ *n.* espionaje *m.*
espresso /ɛ'sprɛsou/ *n.* café exprés, *m.*
essay /'ɛsei/ *n.* ensayo *m.*
essayist /'ɛseiɪst/ *n.* ensayista *m.*
& f.
essence /'ɛsəns/ *n.* esencia *f.*; perfume *m.*
essential /ə'sɛntʃəl/ *a.* esencial.
essentially /ə'sɛntʃəli/ *adv.* esencialmente.
establish /ɪ'stæblɪʃ/ *v.* establecer.
establishment /ɪ'stæblɪʃmənt/ *n.*
establecimiento *m.*
estate /ɪ'steit/ *n.* estado *m.*; hacienda *f.*; bienes *m.pl.*

esteem /ɪ'stim/ n. **1.** estima f. —v. **2.** estimar.

estimable /'ɛstəməbəl/ a. estimable.

estimate /n 'ɛstəmɪt; v -,meit/ n. **1.** cálculo; presupuesto m. —v. **2.** estimar.

estimation /,ɛstə'meifən/ n. estimación f.; cálculo m.

estrange /ɪ'streindʒ/ v. extrañar; enajenar.

estuary /'ɛstʃu,ɛri/ n. estuario m.

etch /ɛtʃ/ v. grabar al agua fuerte.

etching /'ɛtʃɪŋ/ n. aguafuerte.

eternal /ɪ'tɜrnḷ/ a. eterno.

eternity /ɪ'tɜrnɪti/ n. eternidad f.

ether /'iθər/ n. éter m.

ethereal /ɪ'θɪəriəl/ a. etéreo.

ethical /'ɛθɪkəl/ a. ético.

ethics /'ɛθɪks/ n. ética f.

ethnic /'ɛθnɪk/ a. étnico.

etiquette /'ɛtɪkɪt/ n. etiqueta f.

etymology /,ɛtə'mɒlədʒi/ n. etimología f.

eucalyptus /,yukə'lɪptəs/ n. eucalipto m.

eugenic /yu'dʒɛnɪk/ a. eugenésico.

eugenics /yu'dʒɛnɪks/ n. eugenesia f.

eulogize /'yulə,dʒaiz/ v. elogiar.

eulogy /'yulədʒi/ n. elogio m.

eunuch /'yunək/ n. eunuco m.

euphonious /yu'founiəs/ a. eufónico.

Europe /'yʊrəp/ n. Europa f.

European /,yʊrə'piən/ a. & n. europeo -pea.

euthanasia /,yuθə'neiʒə, -ʒiə, -ziə/ n. eutanasia f.

evacuate /ɪ'vækyu,eit/ v. evacuar.

evade /ɪ'veid/ v. evadir.

evaluate /ɪ'vælyu,eit/ v. evaluar.

evaluation /ɪ,vælyu'eifən/ n. valoración f.

evangelist /ɪ'vændʒəlɪst/ n. evangelista m. & f.

evaporate /ɪ'væpə,reit/ v. evaporarse.

evaporation /ɪ,væpə'reifən/ n. evaporación f.

evasion /ɪ'veiʒən/ n. evasión f.

evasive /ɪ'veisɪv/ a. evasivo.

eve /iv/ n. víspera f.

even /'ivən/ a. **1.** llano; igual. —adv. **2.** aun; hasta. **not e.,** ni siquiera.

evening /'ivnɪŋ/ n. noche, tarde f. **good e.!** ¡buenas tardes! ¡buenas noches!

evening class clase nocturna f.

evenness /'ivənnɪs/ n. uniformidad f.

even number número par m.

event /ɪ'vɛnt/ n. acontecimiento, suceso m.

eventful /ɪ'vɛntfəl/ a. memorable.

eventual /ɪ'vɛntʃuəl/ a. eventual.

ever /'ɛvər/ adv. alguna vez; (after not) nunca. **e. since,** desde que.

everlasting /,ɛvər'læstɪŋ/ a. eterno.

every /'ɛvri/ a. cada, todos los.

everybody /'ɛvri,bɒdi, -,bʌdi/ pron. todo el mundo; cada uno.

everyday /'ɛvri,dei/ a. ordinario, de cada día.

everyone /'ɛvri,wʌn/ pron. todo el mundo; cada uno; cada cual.

everything /'ɛvri,θɪŋ/ pron. todo m.

everywhere /'ɛvri,wɛər/ adv. por todas partes, en todas partes.

evict /ɪ'vɪkt/ v. expulsar.

eviction /ɪ'vɪkʃən/ n. evicción f.

evidence /'ɛvɪdəns/ n. evidencia f.

evident /'ɛvɪdənt/ a. evidente.

evidently /'ɛvɪdəntli/ adv. evidentemente.

evil /'ivəl/ a. **1.** malo; maligno. —n. **2.** mal m.

evince /ɪ'vɪns/ v. revelar.

evoke /ɪ'vouk/ v. evocar.

evolution /,ɛvə'luʃən/ n. evolución f.

evolve /ɪ'vɒlv/ v. desenvolver; desarrollar.

ewe /yu/ v. oveja f.

exact /ɪg'zækt/ a. **1.** exacto. —v. **2.** exigir.

exacting /ɪg'zæktɪŋ/ a. exigente.

exactly /ɪg'zæktli/ adv. exactamente.

exaggerate /ɪg'zædʒə,reit/ v. exagerar.

exaggeration /ɪg,zædʒə'reifən/ n. exageración f.

exalt /ɪg'zɔlt/ v. exaltar.

exaltation /,ɛgzɔl'teifən/ n. exaltación f.

examination /ɪg,zæmə'neifən/ n. examen m.; (legal) interrogatorio m.

examine /ɪg'zæmɪn/ v. examinar.

example /ɪg'zæmpəl/ n. ejemplo m.

exasperate /ɪg'zæspə,reit/ v. exasperar.

exasperation /ɪg,zæspə'reiʃən/ n. exasperación f.

excavate /'ɛkskə,veit/ v. excavar, cavar.

exceed /ɪk'sid/ v. exceder.

exceedingly /ɪk'sidɪŋli/ adv. sumamente, extremadamente.

excel /ɪk'sɛl/ v. sobresalir.

excellence /'ɛksələns/ n. excelencia f.

Excellency /'ɛksələnsi/ n. (title) Excelencia f.

excellent /'ɛksələnt/ a. excelente.

except /ɪk'sɛpt/ prep. **1.** salvo, excepto. —v. **2.** exceptuar.

exception /ɪk'sɛpʃən/ n. excepción f.

exceptional /ɪk'sɛpʃənl/ a. excepcional.

excerpt /'ɛksɜrpt/ n. extracto.

excess /ɪk'sɛs, 'ɛksɛs/ n. exceso m.

excessive /ɪk'sɛsɪv/ a. excesivo.

exchange /ɪks'tʃeindʒ/ n. **1.** cambio; canje m. **stock e.,** bolsa f. **telephone e.,** central telefónica. —v. **2.** cambiar, canjear, intercambiar.

exchangeable /ɪks'tʃeindʒəbəl/ a. cambiable.

exchange rate tipo de cambio m.

excise /n 'ɛksaiz; v ɪk'saiz/ n. **1.** sisa f. —v. **2.** extirpar.

excite /ɪk'sait/ v. agitar; provocar; emocionar.

excitement /ɪk'saitmənt/ n. agitación, conmoción f.

exciting /ɪk'saitɪŋ/ a. emocionante.

exclaim /ɪk'skleim/ v. exclamar.

exclamation /,ɛksklə'meiʃən/ n. exclamación f.

exclamation mark punto de admiración m.

exclude /ɪk'sklud/ v. excluir.

exclusion /ɪk'skluʒən/ n. exclusión f.

exclusive /ɪk'sklusɪv/ a. exclusivo.

excommunicate /,ɛkskə'myunɪ,keit/ v. excomulgar, descomulgar.

excommunication /,ɛkskə,myunɪ'keiʃən/ n. excomunión f.

excrement /'ɛkskrəmənt/ n. excremento m.

excruciating /ɪk'skruʃi,eitɪŋ/ a. penosísimo.

exculpate /'ɛkskʌl,peit/ v. exculpar.

excursion /ɪk'skɜrʒən/ n. excursión, jira f.

excuse /n ɪk'skyus; v ɪk'skyuz/ n. **1.** excusa f. —v. **2.** excusar, perdonar, disculpar; dispensar.

execrable /'ɛksɪkrəbəl/ a. execrable.

execute /'ɛksɪ,kyut/ v. ejecutar.

execution /,ɛksɪ'kyuʃən/ n. ejecución f.

executioner /,ɛksɪ'kyuʃənər/ n. verdugo m.

executive /ɪg'zɛkyətɪv/ a. & n. ejecutivo -va.

executor /ɪg'zɛkyətər/ n. testamentario m.

exemplary /ɪg'zɛmpləri/ a. ejemplar.

exemplify /ɪg'zɛmplə,fai/ v. ejemplificar.

exempt /ɪg'zɛmpt/ a. **1.** exento. —v. **2.** exentar.

exercise /'ɛksər,saiz/ n. **1.** ejercicio m. —v. **2.** ejercitar.

exert /ɪg'zɜrt/ v. esforzar.

exertion /ɪg'zɜrʃən/ n. esfuerzo m.

exhale /ɛks'heil/ v. exhalar.

exhaust /ɪg'zɔst/ n. **1.** Auto. escape m. —v. **2.** agotar.

exhaustion /ɪg'zɔstʃən/ n. agotamiento m.

exhaustive /ɪg'zɔstɪv/ a. exhaustivo.

exhaust pipe tubo de escape m.

exhibit /ɪg'zɪbɪt/ n. **1.** exhibición, exposición f. —v. **2.** exhibir.

exhibition /,ɛksə'bɪʃən/ n. exhibición f.

exhilarate /ɪg'zɪlə,reit/ v. alegrar; estimular.

exhort /ɪg'zɔrt/ v. exhortar.

exhortation /,ɛgzɔr'teiʃən/ n. exhortación f.

exhume /ɪg'zum/ v. exhumar.

exigency /'ɛksɪdʒənsi/ n. exigencia f., urgencia f.

exile /'ɛgzail/ n. **1.** destierro m., (person) desterrado m. —v. **2.** desterrar.

exist /ɪg'zɪst/ v. existir.

existence /ɪg'zɪstəns/ n. existencia f.

existent /ɪg'zɪstənt/ a. existente.

exit /'ɛgzɪt, 'ɛksɪt/ n. salida f.

exodus /'ɛksədəs/ n. éxodo m.

exonerate /ɪg'zɒnə,reit/ v. exonerar.

exorbitant /ɪg'zɔrbɪtənt/ a. exorbitante.

exorcise /'ɛksɔr͵saiz/ v. exorcizar.

exotic /ɪg'zɒtɪk/ a. exótico.

expand /ɪk'spænd/ v. dilatar; ensanchar.

expanse /ɪk'spæns/ n. espacio m.; extensión f.

expansion /ɪk'spænʃən/ n. expansión f.

expansion slot ranura de expansión f.

expansive /ɪk'spænsɪv/ a. expansivo.

expatiate /ɪk'speiʃi͵eit/ v. espaciarse.

expatriate /n, a ɛks'peitriɪt; v ɛks'peitri͵eit/ n. & a. **1.** expatriado m. —v. **2.** expatriar.

expect /ɪk'spɛkt/ v. esperar; contar con.

expectancy /ɪk'spɛktənsi/ n. esperanza f.

expectation /͵ɛkspɛk'teiʃən/ n. esperanza f.

expectorate /ɪk'spɛktə͵reit/ v. expectorar.

expediency /ɪk'spidiənsi/ n. conveniencia f.

expedient /ɪk'spidiənt/ a. **1.** oportuno. —n. **2.** expediente m.

expedite /'ɛkspɪ͵dait/ v. acelerar, despachar.

expedition /͵ɛkspɪ'dɪʃən/ n. expedición f.

expel /ɪk'spɛl/ v. expeler; expulsar.

expend /ɪk'spɛnd/ v. desembolsar, expender.

expenditure /ɪk'spɛndɪtʃər/ n. desembolso; gasto m.

expense /ɪk'spɛns/ n. gasto m.; costa f.

expensive /ɪk'spɛnsɪv/ a. caro, costoso.

expensively /ɪk'spɛnsɪvli/ adv. costosamente.

experience /ɪk'spɪəriəns/ n. **1.** experiencia f. —v. **2.** experimentar.

experienced /ɪk'spɪəriənst/ a. experimentado, perito.

experiment /n ɪk'spɛrəmənt; v -͵mɛnt/ n. **1.** experimento m. —v. **2.** experimentar.

experimental /ɪk͵spɛrə'mɛntl̩/ a. experimental.

expert /'ɛkspɜrt/ a. & n. experto -ta.

expertise /͵ɛkspər'tiz/ n. pericia f.

expiate /'ɛkspi͵eit/ v. expiar.

expiration /͵ɛkspə'reiʃən/ n. expiración f.

expiration date fecha de caducidad f.

expire /ɪk'spaiᵊr/ v. expirar; Com. vencerse.

explain /ɪk'splein/ v. explicar.

explanation /͵ɛksplə'neiʃən/ n. explicación f.

explanatory /ɪk'splænə͵tɔri/ a. explicativo.

expletive /'ɛksplɪtɪv/ n. **1.** interjección f. —a. **2.** expletivo.

explicit /ɪk'splɪsɪt/ a. explícito, claro.

explode /ɪk'sploud/ v. estallar, volar; refutar.

exploit /ɪk'splɔit/ n. **1.** hazaña f. —v. **2.** explotar.

exploitation /͵ɛksplɔi'teiʃən/ n. explotación f.

exploration /͵ɛksplə'reiʃən/ n. exploración f.

exploratory /ɪk'splɔrə͵tɔri/ a. exploratorio.

explore /ɪk'splɔr/ v. explorar.

explorer /ɪk'splɔrər/ n. explorador -ra.

explosion /ɪk'splouʒən/ n. explosión f.

explosive /ɪk'splousɪv/ a. explosivo.

export /n 'ɛkspɔrt; v ɪk'spɔrt/ n. **1.** exportación f. —v. **2.** exportar.

exportation /͵ɛkspɔr'teiʃən/ n. exportación f.

expose /ɪk'spouz/ v. exponer; descubrir.

exposition /͵ɛkspə'zɪʃən/ n. exposición f.

expository /ɪk'spɒzɪ͵tɔri/ a. expositivo.

expostulate /ɪk'spɒstʃə͵leit/ v. altercar.

exposure /ɪk'spouʒər/ n. exposición f.

expound /ɪk'spaund/ v. exponer, explicar.

express /ɪk'sprɛs/ a. & n. **1.** expreso m. **e. company,** compañía de porteo. —v. **2.** expresar.

expression /ɪk'sprɛʃən/ n. expresión f.

expressive /ɪk'sprɛsɪv/ a. expresivo.

expressly /ɪk'sprɛsli/ adv. expresamente.

expressman /ɪk'sprɛsmən, -͵mæn/ n. empresario de expresos m.

expressway /ɪk'sprɛs͵wei/ n. autopista f.

expropriate /ɛks'proupri,eit/ v. expropriar.

expulsion /ɪk'spʌlʃən/ n. expulsión f.

expunge /ɪk'spʌndʒ/ v. borrar, expurgar.

expurgate /'ɛkspər,geit/ v. expurgar.

exquisite /ɪk'skwɪzɪt/ a. exquisito.

extant /'ɛkstənt/ a. existente.

extemporaneous /ɪk,stɛmpə-'reiniəs/ a. improvisado.

extend /ɪk'stɛnd/ v. extender.

extension /ɪk'stɛnʃən/ n. extensión f.

extensive /ɪk'stɛnsɪv/ a. extenso.

extensively /ɪk'stɛnsɪvli/ adv. extensamente.

extent /ɪk'stɛnt/ n. extensión f.; grado m. **to a certain e.,** hasta cierto punto.

extenuate /ɪk'stɛnyu,eit/ v. extenuar.

exterior /ɪk'stɪəriər/ a. & n. exterior m.

exterminate /ɪk'stɜrmə,neit/ v. exterminar.

extermination /ɪk,stɜrmə'neiʃən/ n. exterminio m.

external /ɪk'stɜrnl̩/ a. externo, exterior.

extinct /ɪk'stɪŋkt/ a. extinto.

extinction /ɪk'stɪŋkʃən/ n. extinción f.

extinguish /ɪk'stɪŋgwɪʃ/ v. extinguir, apagar.

extol /ɪk'stoul/ v. alabar.

extort /ɪk'stɔrt/ v. exigir dinero sin derecho.

extortion /ɪk'stɔrʃən/ n. extorsión f.

extra /'ɛkstrə/ a. **1.** extraordinario; adicional. —n. **2.** (newspaper) extra m.

extract /n 'ɛkstrækt; v ɪk'strækt/ n. **1.** extracto m. —v. **2.** extraer.

extraction /ɪk'strækʃən/ n. extracción f.

extraneous /ɪk'streiniəs/ a. extraño; ajeno.

extraordinary /ɪk'strɔrdn̩,ɛri/ a. extraordinario.

extravagance /ɪk'strævəgəns/ n. extravagancia f.

extravagant /ɪk'strævəgənt/ a. extravagante.

extreme /ɪk'strim/ a. & n. extremo m.

extremity /ɪk'strɛmɪti/ n. extremidad f.

extricate /'ɛkstrɪ,keit/ v. desenredar.

exuberant /ɪg'zubərənt/ a. exuberante.

exude /ɪg'zud/ v. exudar.

exult /ɪg'zʌlt/ v. regocijarse.

exultant /ɪg'zʌltn̩t/ a. triunfante.

eye /ai/ n. **1.** ojo m. —v. **2.** ojear.

eyeball /'ai,bɔl/ n. globo del ojo.

eyebrow /'ai,brau/ n. ceja f.

eyeglasses /'ai,glæsɪz/ n. lentes m.pl.

eyelash /'ai,læʃ/ n. pestaña f.

eyelid /'ai,lɪd/ n. párpado m.

eyeliner /'ai,lainər/ n. lápiz de ojos m.

eye shadow n. sombra de ojos f.

eyesight /'ai,sait/ n. vista f.

F

fable /'feibəl/ n. fábula; ficción f.

fabric /'fæbrɪk/ n. tejido m., tela f.

fabricate /'fæbrɪ,keit/ v. fabricar.

fabulous /'fæbyələs/ a. fabuloso.

façade /fə'sɑd/ n. fachada f.

face /feis/ n. **1.** cara f. **make faces,** hacer muecas. —v. **2.** encararse con. **f. the street,** dar a la calle.

facet /'fæsɪt/ n. faceta f.

facetious /fə'siʃəs/ a. chistoso.

facial /'feiʃəl/ n. **1.** masaje facial m. —a. **2.** facial.

facile /'fæsɪl/ a. fácil.

facilitate /fə'sɪlɪ,teit/ v. facilitar.

facility /fə'sɪlɪti/ n. facilidad f.

facsimile /fæk'sɪməli/ n. facsímile m.

fact /fækt/ n. hecho m. **in f.,** en realidad.

faction /'fækʃən/ n. facción f.

factor /'fæktər/ n. factor m.

factory /'fæktəri/ n. fábrica f.

factual /'fæktʃuəl/ a. verdadero.

faculty /'fækəlti/ n. facultad f.

fad /fæd/ n. boga; novedad f.

fade /feid/ v. desteñirse; (flowers) marchitarse.

fail /feil/ n. **1. without f.,** sin falla. —v. **2.** fallar; fracasar. **not to f. to,** no dejar de.

failure /'feilyər/ n. fracaso m.

faint /feint/ a. **1.** débil; vago;

pálido. —*n.* **2.** desmayo *m.* —*v.*
3. desmayarse.

faintly /'feintli/ *adv.* débilmente;
indistintamente.

fair /fɛər/ *a.* **1.** razonable, justo;
(hair) rubio; (weather) bueno.
—*n.* **2.** feria *f.*

fairly /'fɛərli/ *adv.* imparcial-
mente; regularmente; claramente;
bellamente.

fairness /'fɛərnɪs/ *n.* justicia *f.*

fair play juego limpio *m.*

fairway /'fɛər,wei/ *n.* (golf) calle
f.

fairy /'fɛəri/ *n.* hada *f.*, duende *m.*

faith /feiθ/ *n.* fe; confianza *f.*

faithful /'feiθfəl/ *a.* fiel.

fake /feik/ *a.* **1.** falso; postizo.
—*n.* **2.** imitación; estafa *f.* —*v.* **3.**
imitar; fingir.

faker /'feikəer/ *n.* imitador *m.;*
farsante *m.*

falcon /'fɔlkən/ *n.* halcón *m.*

fall /fɔl/ *n.* **1.** caída; catarata *f.;*
(season) otoño *m.;* (in price) baja
f. —*v.* **2.** caer; bajar. **f. asleep,**
dormirse; **f. in love,** enamorarse.

fallacious /fə'leiʃəs/ *a.* falaz.

fallacy /'fæləsi/ *n.* falacia *f.*

fallible /'fæləbəl/ *a.* falible.

fallout /'fɔl,aut/ *n.* lluvia radiac-
tiva, polvillo radiactivo.

fallow /'fælou/ *a.* sin cultivar;
barbecho.

false /fɔls/ *a.* falso; postizo.

falsehood /'fɔlshʊd/ *n.* falsedad;
mentira *f.*

falseness /'fɔlsnɪs/ *n.* falsedad,
perfidia *f.*

false teeth /tiθ/ dentadura postiza
f.

falsetto /fɔl'sɛtou/ *n.* falsete *m.*

falsification /,fɔlsəfɪ'keiʃən/ *n.*
falsificación *f.*

falsify /'fɔlsəfai/ *v.* falsificar.

falter /'fɔltər/ *v.* vacilar; (in
speech) tartamudear.

fame /feim/ *n.* fama *f.*

familiar /fə'mɪlyər/ *a.* familiar;
conocido. **be f. with,** estar fami-
liarizado con.

familiarity /fə,mɪli'ærɪti/ *n.* familiaridad *f.*

familiarize /fə'mɪlyə,raiz/ *v.*
familiarizar.

family /'fæməli/ *n.* familia; especie *f.*

family name apellido *m.*

family tree árbol genealógico *m.*

famine /'fæmɪn/ *n.* hambre; carestía *f.*

famished /'fæmɪʃt/ *a.* hambriento.

famous /'feiməs/ *a.* famoso, célebre.

fan /fæn/ *n.* abanico; ventilador
m. (sports) aficionado -da.

fanatic /fə'nætɪk/ *a. & n.* fanático
-ca.

fanatical /fə'nætɪkəl/ *a.* fanático.

fanaticism /fə'nætə,sɪzəm/ *n.*
fanatismo *m.*

fanciful /'fænsɪfəl/ *a.* caprichoso;
fantástico.

fancy /'fænsi/ *a.* **1.** fino, elegante.
f. foods, novedades *f.pl.* —*n.* **2.**
fantasía *f.;* capricho *m.* —*v.* **3.**
imaginar.

fanfare /'fænfɛər/ *n.* fanfarria *f.*

fang /fæŋ/ *n.* colmillo *m.*

fan heater estufa de aire *f.*

fantastic /fæn'tæstɪk/ *a.* fantástico.

fantasy /'fæntəsi/ *n.* fantasía *f.*

FAQ /fæk/ *n.* (Frequently Asked
Questions) preguntas más fre-
cuentes *f.pl.*

far /fɑr/ *a.* **1.** lejano, distante.
—*adv.* **2.** lejos. **how f.,** a qué distancia. **as f. as,** hasta. **so f., thus
f.,** hasta aquí.

farce /fɑrs/ *n.* farsa *f.*

fare /fɛər/ *n.* pasaje *m.*

farewell /,fɛər'wɛl/ *n.* **1.** despedida *f.* **to say f.** despedirse.
—*interj.* **2.** ¡adiós!

farfetched /'fɑr'fɛtʃt/ *a.* forzado,
inverosímil.

farm /fɑrm/ *n.* **1.** granja; hacienda
f. —*v.* **2.** cultivar, labrar la tierra.

farmer /'fɑrmər/ *n.* labrador,
agricultor *m.*

farmhouse /'fɑrm,haus/ *n.* hacienda, alquería *f.*

farming /'fɑrmɪŋ/ *n.* agricultura
f.; cultivo *m.*

fart /fɑrt/ *n.* *Colloq.* pedo *m.*

fascinate /'fæsə,neit/ *v.* fascinar,
embelesar.

fascination /,fæsə'neiʃən/ *n.* fascinación *f.*

fascism /'fæʃ,ɪzəm/ *n.* fascismo
m.

fashion /'fæʃən/ *n.* **1.** moda; costumbre; guisa *f.* **be in f.,** estilarse. —*v.* **2.** formar.

fashionable /'fæʃənəbəl/ *a.* de
moda, en boga.

fashion show desfile de modas, pase de modelos *m.*

fast /fæst/ *a.* **1.** rápido, veloz; (watch) adelantado; (color) firme. —*adv.* **2.** ligero, de prisa. —*n.* **3.** ayuno *m.* —*v.* **4.** ayunar.

fasten /'fæsən/ *v.* afirmar; atar; fijar.

fastener /'fæsənər/ *n.* asegurador *m.*

fastidious /fæ'stɪdiəs/ *a.* melindroso.

fat /fæt/ *a.* **1.** gordo. —*n.* **2.** grasa, manteca *f.*

fatal /'feitl/ *a.* fatal.

fatality /fei'tælɪti/ *n.* fatalidad *f.*

fatally /'feitli/ *adv.* fatalmente.

fate /feit/ *n.* destino *m.*; suerte *f.*

fateful /'feitfəl/ *a.* fatal; ominoso.

father /'faðər/ *n.* padre *m.*

fatherhood /'faðər,hʊd/ *n.* paternidad *f.*

father-in-law /'fɑ,ðər ɪn lɔ/ *n.* suegro *m.*

fatherland /'faðər,lænd/ *n.* patria *f.*

fatherly /'faðərli/ *a.* **1.** paternal. —*adv.* **2.** paternalmente.

fathom /'fæðəm/ *n.* **1.** braza *f.* —*v.* **2.** sondar; *Fig.* penetrar en.

fatigue /fə'tig/ *n.* **1.** fatiga *f.*, cansancio *m.* —*v.* **2.** fatigar, cansar.

fatten /'fætn/ *v.* engordar, cebar.

faucet /'fɔsɪt/ *n.* grifo *m.*, llave *f.*

fault /fɔlt/ *n.* culpa *f.*; defecto *m.* **at f.,** culpable.

faultless /'fɔltlɪs/ *a.* sin tacha, perfecto.

faultlessly /'fɔltlɪsli/ *adv.* perfectamente.

faulty /'fɔlti/ *a.* defectuoso, imperfecto.

fauna /'fɔnə/ *n.* fauna *f.*

favor /'feivər/ *n.* **1.** favor *m.* —*v.* **2.** favorecer.

favorable /'feivərəbəl/ *a.* favorable.

favorite /'feivərɪt/ *a.* & *n.* favorito -ta.

favoritism /'feivərɪ,tɪzəm/ *n.* favoritismo *m.*

fawn /fɔn/ *n.* **1.** cervato *m.* —*v.* **2.** halagar, adular.

fax /fæks/ *n.* **1.** fax *m.* —*v.* **2.** mandar un fax.

faze /feiz/ *v.* desconcertar.

fear /fɪər/ *n.* **1.** miedo, temor *m.* —*v.* **2.** temer.

fearful /'fɪərfəl/ *a.* temeroso, medroso.

fearless /'fɪərlɪs/ *a.* intrépido; sin temor.

fearlessness /'fɪərlɪsnɪs/ *n.* intrepidez *f.*

feasible /'fizəbəl/ *a.* factible.

feast /fist/ *n.* banquete *m.*; fiesta *f.*

feat /fit/ *n.* hazaña *f.*; hecho *m.*

feather /'fɛðər/ *n.* pluma *f.*

feature /'fitʃər/ *n.* **1.** facción *f.*; rasgo *m.*; (movies) película principal *f.*, largometraje *m.* —*v.* **2.** presentar como atracción especial.

February /'fɛbru,ɛri, 'fɛbyu-/ *n.* febrero *m.*

federal /'fɛdərəl/ *a.* federal.

federation /,fɛdə'reiʃən/ *n.* confederación, federación *f.*

fee /fi/ *n.* honorarios *m.pl.*

feeble /'fibəl/ *a.* débil.

feeble-minded /'fibəl 'maindɪd/ *a.* imbécil.

feebleness /'fibəlnɪs/ *a.* debilidad *f.*

feed /fid/ *n.* **1.** pasto *m.* —*v.* **2.** alimentar; dar de comer. **fed up with,** harto de.

feedback /'fid,bæk/ *n.* feedback *m.*, retroalimentación *f.*

feel /fil/ *n.* **1.** sensación *f.* —*v.* **2.** sentir; palpar. **f. like,** tener ganas de.

feeling /'filɪŋ/ *n.* sensación; sentimiento.

feign /fein/ *v.* fingir.

felicitate /fɪ'lɪsɪ,teit/ *v.* felicitar.

felicitous /fɪ'lɪsɪtəs/ *a.* feliz.

felicity /fɪ'lɪsɪti/ *n.* felicidad *f.*, dicha *f.*

feline /'filain/ *a.* felino.

fellow /'fɛlou/ *n.* compañero; socio *m.*; *Colloq.* tipo *m.*

fellowship /'fɛlou,ʃɪp/ *n.* compañerismo; (for study) beca *f.*

felon /'fɛlən/ *n.* reo *m.* & *f.*, felón -ona.

felony /'fɛləni/ *n.* felonía *f.*

felt /fɛlt/ *n.* fieltro *m.*

felt-tipped pen /'fɛlt ,tɪpt/ rotulador *m.*

female /'fimeil/ *a.* & *n.* hembra *f.*

feminine /'fɛmənɪn/ *a.* femenino.

feminist /'fɛmənɪst/ *a.* & *n.* feminista *m.* & *f.*

fence /fɛns/ *n.* **1.** cerca *f.* —*v.* **2.** cercar.

fender /'fɛndər/ *n.* guardabarros *m.pl.*

ferment /*n* 'fɜrmɛnt; *v* fər'mɛnt/

n. **1.** fermento *m.*; *Fig.* agitación *f.* —*v.* **2.** fermentar.

fermentation /ˌfɔrmɛn'teiʃən/ *n.* fermentación *f.*

fern /fɔrn/ *n.* helecho *m.*

ferocious /fə'rouʃəs/ *a.* feroz, fiero.

ferociously /fə'rouʃəsli/ *adv.* ferozmente.

ferocity /fə'rɒsiti/ *n.* ferocidad, fiereza *f.*

Ferris wheel /'fɛris/ rueda de feria *f.*

ferry /'fɛri/ *n.* transbordador *m.*, barca de transporte.

fertile /'fɔrtl/ *a.* fecundo; (land) fértil.

fertility /fər'tiliti/ *n.* fertilidad *f.*

fertilization /ˌfɔrtlə'zeiʃən/ *n.* fertilización *f.*

fertilize /'fɔrtlˌaiz/ *v.* fertilizar, abonar.

fertilizer /'fɔrtlˌaizər/ *n.* abono *m.*

fervency /'fɔrvənsi/ *n.* ardor *m.*

fervent /'fɔrvənt/ *a.* fervoroso.

fervently /'fɔrvəntli/ *adv.* fervorosamente.

fervid /'fɔrvid/ *a.* férvido.

fervor /'fɔrvər/ *n.* fervor *m.*

fester /'fɛstər/ *v.* ulcerarse.

festival /'fɛstəvəl/ *n.* fiesta *f.*

festive /'fɛstiv/ *a.* festivo.

festivity /fɛ'stiviti/ *n.* festividad *f.*

festoon /fɛ'stun/ *n.* **1.** festón *m.* —*v.* **2.** festonear.

fetch /fɛtʃ/ *v.* ir por; traer.

fete /feit/ *n.* **1.** fiesta *f.* —*v.* **2.** festejar.

fetid /'fɛtid/ *a.* fétido.

fetish /'fɛtiʃ/ *n.* fetiche *m.*

fetter /'fɛtər/ *n.* **1.** grillete *m.* —*v.* **2.** engrillar.

fetus /'fitəs/ *n.* feto *m.*

feud /fyud/ *n.* riña *f.*

feudal /'fyudl/ *a.* feudal.

feudalism /'fyudlˌizəm/ *n.* feudalismo *m.*

fever /'fivər/ *n.* fiebre *f.*

feverish /'fivəriʃ/ *a.* febril.

feverishly /'fivəriʃli/ *adv.* febrilmente.

few /fyu/ *a.* pocos. **a. f.,** algunos, unos cuantos.

fiancé, fiancée /ˌfian'sei/ *n.* novio -via.

fiasco /fi'æskou/ *n.* fiasco *m.*

fiat /'fiat/ *n.* fiat *m.*, orden *f.*

fib /fib/ *n.* **1.** mentira *f.* —*v.* **2.** mentir.

fiber /'faibər/ *n.* fibra *f.*

fibrous /'faibrəs/ *a.* fibroso.

fickle /'fikəl/ *a.* caprichoso.

fickleness /'fikəlnis/ *n.* inconstancia *f.*

fiction /'fikʃən/ *n.* ficción *f.*; (literature) novelas *f.pl.*

fictitious /fik'tiʃəs/ *a.* ficticio.

fidelity /fi'dɛliti/ *n.* fidelidad *f.*

fidget /'fidʒit/ *v.* inquietar.

field /fild/ *n.* campo *m.*

field trip viaje.de estudios *m.*

fiend /find/ *n.* demonio *m.*

fiendish /'findiʃ/ *a.* diabólico, malvado.

fierce /fiərs/ *a.* fiero, feroz.

fiery /'faiəri/ *a.* ardiente.

fiesta /fi'ɛstə/ *n.* fiesta *f.*

fife /faif/ *n.* pífano *m.*

fifteen /'fif'tin/ *a. & pron.* quince.

fifteenth /'fif'tinθ/ *n. & a.* décimoquinto.

fifth /fifθ/ *a.* quinto.

fifty /'fifti/ *a. & pron.* cincuenta.

fig /fig/ *n.* higo *m.* **f. tree,** higuera *f.*

fight /fait/ *n.* **1.** lucha, pelea *f.* —*v.* **2.** luchar, pelear.

fighter /'faitər/ *n.* peleador -ra, luchador -ra.

figment /'figmənt/ *n.* invención *f.*

figurative /'figyərətiv/ *a.* metafórico.

figuratively /'figyərətivli/ *adv.* figuradamente.

figure /'figyər/ *n.* **1.** figura; cifra *f.* —*v.* **2.** figurar; calcular.

filament /'filəmənt/ *n.* filamento *m.*

file /fail/ *n.* **1.** archivo *m.*; (instrument) lima *f.*; (row) fila *f.* —*v.* **2.** archivar; limar.

file cabinet archivador *m.*

filial /'filiəl/ *a.* filial.

filigree /'filəˌgri/ *n.* filigrana *f.*

fill /fil/ *v.* llenar.

fillet /'filit/ *n.* filete *m.*

filling /'filiŋ/ *n.* relleno *m.*; (dental) empastadura *f.* **f. station,** gasolinera *f.*

film /film/ *n.* **1.** película *f.*, film *m.* —*v.* **2.** filmar.

filter /'filtər/ *n.* **1.** filtro *m.* —*v.* **2.** filtrar.

filth /filθ/ *n.* suciedad, mugre *f.*

filthy /'filθi/ *a.* sucio.

fin /fin/ *n.* aleta *f.*

final /'fainl/ *a.* **1.** final, último. —*n.* **2.** examen final. **finals** (sports) final *f.*

finalist /'fainļist/ n. finalista m. & f.

finally /'fainļi/ adv. finalmente.

finances /'fainænsəz/ n. recursos, fondos m.pl.

financial /fɪ'nænʃəl/ a. financiero.

financier /,fɪnən'sɪər, ,fainən-/ n. financiero -ra.

find /faind/ n. **1.** hallazgo m. —v. **2.** hallar; encontrar. **f. out,** averiguar, enterarse, saber.

fine /fain/ a. **1.** fino; bueno. —adv. **2.** muy bien. —n. **3.** multa f. —v. **4.** multar.

fine arts /arts/ bellas artes f.pl.

finery /'fainəri/ n. gala f., adorno m.

finesse /fɪ'nɛs/ n. **1.** artificio m. —v. **2.** valerse de artificio.

finger /'fɪŋgər/ n. dedo m.

finger bowl n. enjuagatorio m.

fingernail /'fɪŋgər,neil/ n. uña f.

fingerprint /'fɪŋgər,prɪnt/ n. **1.** impresión digital f. —v. **2.** tomar las impresiones digitales.

finicky /'fɪnɪki/ a. melindroso.

finish /'fɪnɪʃ/ n. **1.** conclusión f. —v. **2.** acabar, terminar.

finished /'fɪnɪʃt/ a. acabado.

finite /'fainait/ a. finito.

fir /fɜr/ n. abeto m.

fire /faiər/ n. **1.** fuego; incendio m. —v. **2.** disparar, tirar; Colloq. despedir.

fire alarm n. alarma de incendio f.

firearm /'faiər,arm/ n. arma de fuego.

firecracker /'faiər,krækər/ n. triquitraque m., buscapiés m., petardo m.

fire engine bomba de incendios f.

fire escape escalera de incendios f.

fire exit salida de urgencia f.

fire extinguisher /ɪk'stɪŋgwɪʃər/ matafuego m.

firefly /'faiər,flai/ n. luciérnaga f.

fireman /'faiərmən/ n. bombero m.; (railway) fogonero m.

fireplace /'faiər,pleis/ n. hogar, fogón m.

fireproof /'faiər,pruf/ a. incombustible.

fireside /'faiər,said/ n. hogar, fogón m.

fireworks /'faiər,wɜrks/ n. fuegos artificiales.

firm /fɜrm/ a. **1.** firme. —n. **2.** firma, empresa f.

firmness /'fɜrmnɪs/ n. firmeza f.

first /fɜrst/ a. & adv. primero. **at f.,** al principio.

first aid primeros auxilios.

first-class /'fɜrst 'klæs/ a. de primera clase.

fiscal /'fɪskəl/ a. fiscal.

fish /fɪʃ/ n. **1.** (food) pescado m.; (alive) pez m. —v. **2.** pescar.

fisherman /'fɪʃərmən/ n. pescador m.

fishhook /'fɪʃ,hʊk/ n. anzuelo m.

fishing /'fɪʃɪŋ/ n. pesca f. **go f.,** ir de pesca.

fishmonger /'fɪʃ,mʌŋgər/ n. pescadero m.

fish store pescadería f.

fission /'fɪʃən/ n. fisión f.

fissure /'fɪʃər/ n. grieta f., quebradura f.; fisura.

fist /fɪst/ n. puño m.

fit /fɪt/ a. **1.** capaz; justo. —n. **2.** corte, talle m.; Med. convulsión f. —v. **3.** caber; quedar bien, sentar bien.

fitful /'fɪtfəl/ a. espasmódico; caprichoso.

fitness /'fɪtnɪs/ n. aptitud; conveniencia f.

fitting /'fɪtɪŋ/ a. **1.** conveniente. **be f.,** convenir. —n. **2.** ajuste m.

fitting room probador m.

five /faiv/ a. & pron. cinco.

five-day work week /'faiv 'dei/ semana inglesa f.

fix /fɪks/ n. **1.** apuro m. —v. **2.** fijar; arreglar; componer, reparar.

fixation /fɪk'seiʃən/ n. fijación f.; fijeza f.

fixed /fɪkst/ a. fijo.

fixture /'fɪkstʃər/ n. instalación; guarnición f.

flabby /'flæbi/ a. flojo.

flaccid /'flæksɪd, 'flæsɪd/ a. flojo; flácido.

flag /flæg/ n. bandera f.

flagellant /'flædʒələnt/ n. & a. flagelante m.

flagon /'flægən/ n. frasco m.

flagrant /'fleigrənt/ a. flagrante.

flagrantly /'fleigrəntli/ adv. notoriamente.

flair /flɛər/ n. aptitud especial f.

flake /fleik/ n. **1.** escama f.; copo de nieve. —v. **2.** romperse en láminas.

flamboyant /flæm'bɔiənt/ a. flamante, llamativo.

flame /fleim/ n. **1.** llama f. —v. **2.** llamear.

flaming /'fleimiŋ/ a. llameante, flamante.

flamingo /flə'miŋgou/ n. flamenco m.

flammable /'flæməbəl/ a. inflamable.

flank /flæŋk/ n. **1.** ijada f.; Mil. flanco m. —v. **2.** flanquear.

flannel /'flænḷ/ n. franela f.

flap /flæp/ n. **1.** cartera f. —v. **2.** aletear; sacudirse.

flare /fleər/ n. **1.** llamarada f. —v. **2.** brillar; Fig. enojarse.

flash /flæʃ/ n. **1.** resplandor m.; (lightning) rayo, relámpago m.; Fig. instante m. —v. **2.** brillar.

flashcube /'flæʃ,kyub/ n. cubo de flash m.

flashlight /'flæʃ,lait/ n. linterna (eléctrica).

flashy /'flæʃi/ a. ostentoso.

flask /flæsk/ n. frasco m.

flat /flæt/ a. **1.** llano; (tire) desinflado. —n. **2.** llanura f.; apartamento m.

flatness /'flætnis/ n. llanura f.

flatten /'flætṇ/ v. aplastar, allanar; abatir.

flatter /'flætər/ v. adular, lisonjear.

flatterer /'flætərər/ n. lisonjero -ra; zalamero -ra.

flattery /'flætəri/ n. adulación, lisonja f.

flaunt /flɔnt/ v. ostentar.

flavor /'fleivər/ n. **1.** sabor m. —v. **2.** sazonar.

flavoring /'fleivəriŋ/ n. condimento m.

flaw /flɔ/ n. defecto m.

flax /flæks/ n. lino m.

flay /flei/ v. despellejar; excoriar.

flea /fli/ n. pulga f.

flea market rastro m.

fleck /flek/ n. **1.** mancha f. —v. **2.** varetear.

flee /fli/ v. huir.

fleece /flis/ n. **1.** vellón m. —v. **2.** esquilar.

fleet /flit/ a. **1.** veloz. —n. **2.** flota f.

fleeting /'flitiŋ/ a. fugaz, pasajero.

flesh /fleʃ/ n. carne f.

fleshy /'fleʃi/ a. gordo; carnoso.

flex /fleks/ n. **1.** doblez m. —v. **2.** doblar.

flexibility /,fleksə'biliti/ n. flexibilidad f.

flexible /'fleksəbəl/ a. flexible.

flier /'flaiər/ n. aviador -ra.

flight /flait/ n. vuelo m.; fuga f.

flight attendant n. azafata f.; ayudante de vuelo m.

flimsy /'flimzi/ a. débil.

flinch /flintʃ/ v. acobardarse.

fling /fliŋ/ v. lanzar.

flint /flint/ n. pedernal m.

flip /flip/ v. lanzar.

flippant /'flipənt/ a. impertinente.

flippantly /'flipəntli/ adv. impertinentemente.

flirt /flɜrt/ n. **1.** coqueta f. —v. **2.** coquetear, flirtear.

flirtation /flɜr'teiʃən/ n. coqueteo m.

float /flout/ v. flotar.

flock /flɒk/ n. **1.** rebaño m. —v. **2.** congregarse.

flog /flɒg/ v. azotar.

flood /flʌd/ n. **1.** inundación f. —v. **2.** inundar.

floor /flɔr/ n. **1.** suelo, piso m. —v. **2.** derribar.

floppy disk /'flɒpi/ floppy, m., disquete, m.

floral /'flɔrəl/ a. floral.

florid /'flɔrid/ a. florido.

florist /'flɔrist/ n. florista m. & f.

flounce /flauns/ n. **1.** (sewing) volante m. —v. **2.** pernear.

flounder /'flaundər/ n. rodaballo m.

flour /flauᵊr/ n. harina f.

flourish /'flɔriʃ/ n. **1.** Mus. floreo m. —v. **2.** florecer; prosperar; blandir.

flow /flou/ n. **1.** flujo m. —v. **2.** fluir.

flow chart organigrama m.

flower /'flauər/ n. **1.** flor f. —v. **2.** florecer.

flowerpot /'flauər,pɒt/ n. maceta f.

flowery /'flauəri/ a. florido.

fluctuate /'flʌktʃu,eit/ v. fluctuar.

fluctuation /,flʌktʃu'eiʃən/ n. fluctuación f.

flue /flu/ n. humero m.

fluency /'fluənsi/ n. fluidez f.

fluent /'fluənt/ a. fluido; competente.

fluffy /'flʌfi/ a. velloso.

fluid /'fluid/ a. & n. fluido m.

fluidity /flu'iditi/ n. fluidez f.

fluoroscope /'flurə,skoup/ n. fluoroscopio m.

flurry /'flɜri/ n. agitación f.

flush /flʌʃ/ a. **1.** bien provisto. —n. **2.** sonrojo m. —v. **3.** limpiar con un chorro de agua; sonrojarse.

flute /flut/ *n.* flauta *f.*

flutter /'flʌtər/ *n.* **1.** agitación *f.* —*v.* **2.** agitarse.

flux /flʌks/ *n.* flujo *m.*

fly /flai/ *n.* **1.** mosca *f.* —*v.* **2.** volar.

flying saucer /'flaiiŋ/ platillo volante *m.*

foam /foum/ *n.* **1.** espuma *f.* —*v.* **2.** espumar.

focal /'foukəl/ *a.* focal.

focus /'foukəs/ *n.* **1.** enfoque *m.* —*v.* **2.** enfocar.

fodder /'fɒdər/ *n.* forraje *m.*, pienso *m.*

foe /fou/ *n.* adversario -ria, enemigo -ga.

fog /fɒg/ *n.* niebla *f.*

foggy /'fɒgi/ *a.* brumoso.

foil /fɔil/ *v.* frustrar.

foist /fɔist/ *v.* imponer.

fold /fould/ *n.* **1.** pliegue *m.* —*v.* **2.** doblar, plegar.

foldable /'fouldəbəl/ *a.* plegable.

folder /'fouldər/ *n.* circular *m.*; (for filing) carpeta *f.*

folding /'fouldiŋ/ *a.* plegable.

foliage /'fouliidʒ/ *n.* follaje *m.*

folio /'fouli,ou/ *n.* infolio; folio *m.*

folklore /'fouk,lɔr/ *n.* folklore *m.*

folks /fouks/ *n.* gente; familia *f.*

follicle /'fɒlikəl/ *n.* folículo *m.*

follow /'fɒlou/ *v.* seguir.

follower /'fɒlouər/ *n.* partidario -ria

folly /'fɒli/ *n.* locura *f.*

foment /fou'mɛnt/ *v.* fomentar.

fond /fɒnd/ *a.* cariñoso, tierno. **be f. of,** ser aficionado a.

fondle /'fɒndl/ *v.* acariciar.

fondly /'fɒndli/ *adv.* tiernamente.

fondness /'fɒndnis/ *n.* afición *f.*; cariño *m.*

food /fud/ *n.* alimento *m.*; comida *f.*

foodie /'fudi/ *n. Colloq.* gastrónomo -ma, gourmet *m. & f.*

food poisoning /'pɔizəniŋ/ intoxicación alimenticia *f.*

foodstuffs /'fud,stʌfs/ *n.pl.* comestibles, víveres *m.pl.*

fool /ful/ **1.** tonto -ta; bobo -ba; bufón -ona. —*v.* **2.** engañar.

foolhardy /'ful,hɑrdi/ *a.* temerario.

foolish /'fuliʃ/ *a.* bobo, tonto, majadero.

foolproof /'ful,pruf/ *a.* seguro.

foot /fut/ *n.* pie *m.*

footage /'futidʒ/ *n.* longitud en pies.

football /'fut,bɔl/ *n.* fútbol, balompié *m.*

footbridge /'fut,bridʒ/ *n.* puente para peatones *m.*

foothold /'fut,hould/ *n.* posición establecida.

footing /'futiŋ/ *n.* base *f.*, fundamento *m.*

footlights /'fut,laits/ *n.pl.* luces del proscenio.

footnote /'fut,nout/ *n.* nota al pie de una página.

footpath /'fut,pæθ/ *n.* sendero *m.*

footprint /'fut,print/ *n.* huella *f.*

footstep /'fut,stɛp/ *n.* paso *m.*

footstool /'fut,stul/ *n.* escañuelo *m.*, banqueta *f.*

fop /fɒp/ *n.* petimetre *m.*

for /fɔr; *unstressed* fər/ *prep.* **1.** para; por. **as f.,** en cuanto a. **what f.,** ¿para qué? —*conj.* **2.** porque, pues.

forage /'fɔridʒ/ *n.* **1.** forraje *m.* —*v.* **2.** forrajear.

foray /'fɔrei/ *n.* correría *f.*

forbear /fɔr,bɛər/ *v.* cesar; abstenerse.

forbearance /fɔr'bɛərəns/ *n.* paciencia *f.*

forbid /fər'bid/ *v.* prohibir.

forbidding /fər'bidiŋ/ *a.* repugnante.

force /fɔrs/ *n.* **1.** fuerza *f.* —*v.* **2.** forzar.

forced landing /fɔrst/ aterrizaje forzoso *m.*

forceful /'fɔrsfəl/ *a.* fuerte; enérgico.

forcible /'fɔrsəbəl/ *a.* a la fuerza; enérgico.

ford /fɔrd/ *n.* **1.** vado *m.* —*v.* **2.** vadear.

fore /fɔr/ *a.* **1.** delantero. —*n.* **2.** delantera *f.*

fore and aft de popa a proa.

forearm /fɔr'ɑrm/ *n.* antebrazo *m.*

forebears /'fɔr,bɛərz/ *n.pl.* antepasados *m.pl.*

forebode /fɔr'boud/ *v.* presagiar.

foreboding /fɔr'boudiŋ/ *n.* presentimiento *m.*

forecast /'fɔr,kæst/ *n.* **1.** pronóstico *m.*; profecía *f.* —*v.* **2.** pronosticar.

forecastle /'fouksəl/ *n. Naut.* castillo de proa.

forefathers /'fɔr,faðərz/ *n.* antepasados *m.pl.*

forefinger /'fɔr,fɪŋgər/ *n.* índice *m.*

forego /fɔr'gou/ *v.* renunciar.

foregone /fɔr'gɔn/ *a.* predeterminado.

foreground /'fɔr,graund/ *n.* primer plano.

forehead /'fɔrɪd/ *n.* frente *f.*

foreign /'fɔrɪn/ *a.* extranjero.

foreign aid *n.* ayuda exterior *f.*

foreigner /'fɔrənər/ *n.* extranjero -ra; forastero -ra.

foreleg /'fɔr,lɛg/ *n.* pierna delantera.

foreman /'fɔrmən/ *n.* capataz, jefe de taller *m.*

foremost /'fɔr,moust/ *a.* **1.** primero. —*adv.* **2.** en primer lugar.

forenoon /'fɔr,nun/ *n.* mañana *f.*

forensic /fə'rɛnsɪk/ *a.* forense.

forerunner /'fɔr,rʌnər/ *n.* precursor -ra.

foresee /fɔr'si/ *v.* prever.

foreshadow /fɔr'ʃædou/ *v.* prefigurar, anunciar.

foresight /'fɔr,sait/ *n.* previsión *f.*

forest /'fɔrɪst/ *n.* bosque *m.;* selva *f.*

forestall /fɔr'stɔl/ *v.* anticipar; prevenir.

forester /'fɔrəstər/ *n.* silvicultor -ra; guardamontes *m.pl. & f.pl.*

forestry /'fɔrəstri/ *n.* silvicultura *f.*

foretell /fɔr'tɛl/ *v.* predecir.

forever /fɔr'ɛvər/ *adv.* por siempre, para siempre.

forevermore /fɔr,ɛvər'mɔr/ *adv.* siempre.

forewarn /fɔr'wɔrn/ *v.* advertir, avisar.

foreword /'fɔr,wɜrd/ *n.* prefacio *m.*

forfeit /'fɔrfɪt/ *n.* **1.** prenda; multa *f.* —*v.* **2.** perder.

forfeiture /'fɔrfɪtʃər/ *n.* decomiso *m.*, multa *f.;* pérdida.

forgather /fɔr'gæðər/ *v.* reunirse.

forge /fɔrdʒ/ *n.* **1.** fragua *f.* —*v.* **2.** forjar; falsear.

forger /'fɔrdʒər/ *n.* forjador -ra; falsificador -ra.

forgery /'fɔrdʒəri/ *n.* falsificación *f.*

forget /fər'gɛt/ *v.* olvidar.

forgetful /fər'gɛtfəl/ *a.* olvidadizo.

forgive /fər'gɪv/ *v.* perdonar.

forgiveness /fər'gɪvnɪs/ *n.* perdón *m.*

fork /fɔrk/ *n.* **1.** tenedor *m.;* bifurcación *f.* —*v.* **2.** bifurcarse.

forlorn /fɔr'lɔrn/ *a.* triste.

form /fɔrm/ *n.* **1.** forma *f.;* (document) formulario *m.* —*v.* **2.** formar.

formal /'fɔrməl/ *a.* formal; ceremonioso. **f. dance,** baile de etiqueta. **f. dress,** traje de etiqueta.

formality /fɔr'mælɪti/ *n.* formalidad *f.*

formally /'fɔrməli/ *adv.* formalmente.

format /'fɔrmæt/ *n.* formato *m.*

formation /fɔr'meiʃən/ *n.* formación *f.*

formative /'fɔrmətɪv/ *a.* formativo.

formatting /'fɔrmætɪŋ/ *n.* formateo *m.*

former /'fɔrmər/ *a.* anterior; antiguo. **the f.,** aquél.

formerly /'fɔrmərli/ *adv.* antiguamente.

formidable /'fɔrmɪdəbəl/ *a.* formidable.

formless /'fɔrmlɪs/ *a.* sin forma.

formula /'fɔrmyələ/ *n.* fórmula *f.*

formulate /'fɔrmyə,leit/ *v.* formular.

formulation /,fɔrmy'leiʃən/ *n.* formulación *f.;* expresión *f.*

forsake /fɔr'seik/ *v.* abandonar.

fort /fɔrt/ *n.* fortaleza *f.;* fuerte *m.*

forte /'fɔrtei/ *a. & adv. Mus.* forte; fuerte.

forth /fɔrθ/ *adv.* adelante. **back and f.,** de aquí allá. **and so f.,** etcétera.

forthcoming /'fɔrθ'kʌmɪŋ/ *a.* futuro, próximo.

forthright /'fɔrθ,rait/ *a.* franco.

forthwith /,fɔrθ'wɪθ/ *adv.* inmediatamente.

fortification /,fɔrtəfɪ'keiʃən/ *n.* fortificación *f.*

fortify /'fɔrtə,fai/ *v.* fortificar.

fortissimo /fɔr'tɪsə,mou/ *a. & adv. Mus.* fortísimo.

fortitude /'fɔrtɪ,tud/ *n.* fortaleza; fortitud *f.*

fortnight /'fɔrt,nait/ *n.* quincena *f.*

fortress /'fɔrtrɪs/ *n.* fuerte *m.*, fortaleza *f.*

fortuitous /fɔr'tuɪtəs/ *a.* fortuito.

fortunate /'fɔrtʃənɪt/ *a.* afortunado.

fortune /'fɔrtʃən/ n. fortuna; suerte f.

fortune-teller /'fɔrtʃən ,tɛlər/ n. sortílego -ga, adivino -na.

forty /'fɔrti/ a. & pron. cuarenta.

forum /'fɔrəm/ n. foro m.

forward /'fɔrwərd/ a. **1.** delantero; atrevido. —adv. **2.** adelante. —v. **3.** trasmitir, reexpedir.

foster /'fɔstər/ n. **1. f. child,** hijo adoptivo. —v. **2.** fomentar; criar.

foul /faul/ a. sucio; impuro.

found /faund/ v. fundar.

foundation /faun'deiʃən/ n. fundación f.; (of building) cimientos m.pl.

founder /'faundər/ n. **1.** fundador -ra. —v. **2.** irse a pique.

foundry /'faundri/ n. fundición f.

fountain /'fauntn̩/ n. fuente f.

fountain pen pluma estilográfica, plumafuente f.

four /fɔr/ a. & pron. cuatro.

fourteen /'fɔr'tin/ a. & pron. catorce.

fourth /fɔrθ/ a. & n. cuarto m.

fowl /faul/ n. ave f.

fox /fɔks/ n. zorro -rra.

fox-trot /'fɔks,trɔt/ n. foxtrot m.

foxy /'fɔksi/ a. astuto.

foyer /'fɔiər/ n. salón de entrada.

fracas /'freikəs, 'frækəs/ n. riña f.

fraction /'frækʃən/ n. fracción f.

fracture /'fræktʃər/ n. **1.** fractura, rotura f. —v. **2.** fracturar, romper.

fragile /'frædʒəl/ a. frágil.

fragment /'frægmənt/ n. fragmento, trozo m.

fragmentary /'frægmən,tɛri/ a. fragmentario.

fragrance /'freigrəns/ n. fragancia f.

fragrant /'freigrənt/ a. fragante.

frail /freil/ a. débil, frágil.

frailty /'freilti/ n. debilidad, fragilidad f.

frame /freim/ n. **1.** marco; armazón; cuadro; cuerpo m. —v. **2.** fabricar; formar; encuadrar.

frame-up /'freim ,ʌp/ n. Colloq. conspiración f.

framework /'freim,wɜrk/ n. armazón m.

France /fræns/ n. Francia f.

franchise /'fræntʃaiz/ n. franquicia f.

frank /fræŋk/ a. **1.** franco. —n. **2.** carta franca. —v. **3.** franquear.

frankfurter /'fræŋkfərtər/ n. salchicha f.

frankly /'fræŋkli/ adv. francamente.

frankness /'fræŋknɪs/ n. franqueza f.

frantic /'fræntɪk/ a. frenético.

fraternal /frə'tɜrnl̩/ a. fraternal.

fraternity /frə'tɜrniti/ n. fraternidad f.

fraternization /,frætərnə'zeiʃən/ n. fraternización f.

fraternize /'frætər,naiz/ v. confraternizar.

fratricide /'frætri,said/ n. fratricida m. & f.; fratricidio m.

fraud /frɔd/ n. fraude m.

fraudulent /'frɔdʒələnt/ a. fraudulento.

fraudulently /'frɔdʒələntli/ adv. fraudulentamente.

fraught /frɔt/ a. cargado.

freak /frik/ n. rareza f.; monstruosidad.

freckle /'frɛkəl/ n. peca f.

freckled /'frɛkəld/ a. pecoso.

free /fri/ a. **1.** libre; gratis. —v. **2.** libertar, librar.

freedom /'fridəm/ n. libertad f.

freeze /friz/ v. helar, congelar.

freezer /'frizər/ n. heladora f.

freezing point /'frizɪŋ/ punto de congelación m.

freight /freit/ n. **1.** carga f.; flete m. —v. **2.** cargar; fletar.

freighter /'freitər/ n. Naut. fletador m.

French /frɛntʃ/ a. & n. francés -esa.

Frenchman /'frɛntʃmən/ n. francés m.

Frenchwoman /'frɛntʃ,wumən/ n. francesa f.

frenzied /'frɛnzid/ a. frenético.

frenzy /'frɛnzi/ n. frenesí m.

frequency /'frikwənsi/ n. frecuencia f.

frequency modulation /,mɒdʒə'leiʃən/ modulación de frequencia.

frequent /'frikwənt/ a. frecuente.

frequently /'frikwəntli/ adv. frecuentemente.

fresco /'frɛskou/ n. fresco.

fresh /frɛʃ/ a. fresco. **f. water,** agua dulce.

freshen /'frɛʃən/ v. refrescar.

freshness /'frɛʃnɪs/ n. frescura f.

fret /frɛt/ v. quejarse, irritarse; Mus. traste m.

fretful /'frɛtfəl/ a. irritable.

fretfully /'frɛtfəli/ adv. de mala gana.

fretfulness /'frɛtfəlnɪs/ n. mal humor.

friar /'fraiər/ n. fraile m.

fricassee /ˌfrɪkə'si/ n. fricasé m.

friction /'frɪkʃən/ n. fricción f.

Friday /'fraidei/ n. viernes m.

Good F., Viernes Santo m.

fried /fraid/ a. frito.

friend /frɛnd/ n. amigo -ga.

friendless /'frɛndlɪs/ a. sin amigos.

friendliness /'frɛndlinɪs/ n. amistad f.

friendly /'frɛndli/ a. amistoso.

friendship /'frɛndʃɪp/ n. amistad f.

fright /frait/ n. susto m.

frighten /'fraitn/ v. asustar, espantar.

frightful /'fraitfəl/ a. espantoso.

frigid /'frɪdʒɪd/ a. frígido; frío.

frill /frɪl/ n. (sewing) lechuga f.

fringe /frɪndʒ/ n. fleco; borde m.

frisky /'frɪski/ a. retozón.

fritter /'frɪtər/ n. fritura f.

frivolity /frɪ'vɒliti/ n. frivolidad f.

frivolous /'frɪvələs/ a. frívolo.

frivolousness /'frɪvələsnɪs/ n. frivolidad f.

frock /frɒk/ n. vestido de mujer.

f. coat, levita f.

frog /frɒg/ n. rana f.

frolic /'frɒlɪk/ n. **1.** retozo m. —v. **2.** retozar.

from /frʌm, unstressed frəm/ prep. de; desde.

front /frʌnt/ n. frente; (of building) fachada f. **in f. of,** delante de.

frontal /'frʌntl/ a. frontal.

front door puerta principal f.

frontier /frʌn'tɪər/ n. frontera f.

front seat asiento delantero m.

frost /frɒst/ n. helada, escarcha f.

frosty /'frɒsti/ a. helado.

froth /frɔθ/ n. espuma f.

frown /fraun/ n. **1.** ceño m. —v. **2.** fruncir el entrecejo.

frowzy /'frauzi/ a. desaliñado.

frozen /'frouzən/ a. helado; congelado.

fructify /'frʌktəˌfai/ v. fructificar.

frugal /'frugəl/ a. frugal.

frugality /fru'gæliti/ n. frugalidad f.

fruit /frut/ n. fruta f.; (benefits) frutos m.pl. **f. tree,** árbol frutal.

fruitful /'frutfəl/ a. productivo.

fruition /fru'ɪʃən/ n. fruición f.

fruitless /'frutlɪs/ a. inútil, en vano.

fruit salad macedonia de frutas f.

fruit store frutería f.

frustrate /'frʌstreit/ v. frustrar.

frustration /frʌ'streiʃən/ n. frustración f.

fry /frai/ v. freír.

fuel /'fyuəl/ n. combustible m.

fugitive /'fyudʒɪtɪv/ a. & n. fugitivo -va.

fugue /fyug/ n. fuga f.

fulcrum /'fulkrəm/ n. fulcro m.

fulfill /fʊl'fɪl/ v. cumplir.

fulfillment /fʊl'fɪlmənt/ n. cumplimiento m.; realización f.

full /fʊl/ a. lleno; completo; pleno.

full name nombre y apellidos.

fullness /'fʊlnɪs/ n. plenitud f.

fulminate /'fʌlməˌneit/ v. volar; fulminar.

fulmination /ˌfʌlmə'neiʃən/ n. fulminación; detonación f.

fumble /'fʌmbəl/ v. chapucear.

fume /fyum/ n. **1.** humo m. —v. **2.** humear.

fumigate /'fyumɪˌgeit/ v. fumigar.

fumigator /'fyumɪˌgeitər/ n. fumigador m.

fun /fʌn/ n. diversión f. **to make f. of,** burlarse de. **to have f.,** divertirse.

function /'fʌŋkʃən/ n. **1.** función f. —v. **2.** funcionar.

functional /'fʌŋkʃənl/ a. funcional.

fund /fʌnd/ n. fondo m.

fundamental /ˌfʌndə'mɛntl/ a. fundamental.

funeral /'fyunərəl/ n. funeral m.

funeral home, funeral parlor funeraria f.

fungus /'fʌŋgəs/ n. hongo m.

funnel /'fʌnl/ n. embudo m.; (of ship) chimenea f.

funny /'fʌni/ a. divertido, gracioso. **to be f.,** tener gracia.

fur /fɜr/ n. piel f.

furious /'fyuriəs/ a. furioso.

furlough /'fɜrlou/ n. permiso m.

furnace /'fɜrnɪs/ n. horno m.

furnish /'fɜrnɪʃ/ v. surtir, proveer; (a house) amueblar.

furniture /'fɜrnɪtʃər/ n. muebles m.pl.

furrow /'fɜrou/ n. **1.** surco m. —v. **2.** surcar.

further /'fɜrðər/ a. & adv. **1.** más. —v. **2.** adelantar, fomentar.

furthermore /'fɜrðər,mɔr/ *adv.* además.

fury /'fyʊri/ *n.* furor *m.*; furia *f.*

fuse /fyuz/ *n.* **1.** fusible *m.* —*v.* **2.** fundir.

fuss /fʌs/ *n.* **1.** alboroto *m.* —*v.* **2.** preocuparse por pequeñeces.

fussy /'fʌsi/ *a.* melindroso.

futile /'fyutl/ *a.* fútil.

future /'fyutʃər/ *a.* **1.** futuro. —*n.* **2.** porvenir *m.*

futurology /,fyutʃə'rɒlədʒi/ *n.* futurología *f.*

fuzzy logic /'fʌzi/ lógica matizada *f.*

FYI *abbr.* (For Your Information) para su información.

G

gag /gæg/ *n.* chiste *m.*; mordaza *f.*

gaiety /'geiɪti/ *n.* alegría *f.*

gain /gein/ **1.** ganancia *f.* —*v.* **2.** ganar.

gait /geit/ *n.* paso *m.*

gale /geil/ *n.* ventarrón *m.*

gall /gɔl/ *n.* hiel *f.*; *Fig.* amargura *f.*; descaro *m.*

gallant /'gælənt, gə'lænt, -'lɑnt/ *a.* **1.** galante. —*n.* **2.** galán *m.*

gallery /'gæləri/ *n.* galería *f.*; *Theat.* paraíso *m.*

gallon /'gælən/ *n.* galón *m.*

gallop /'gæləp/ *n.* **1.** galope *m.* —*v.* **2.** galopar.

gallows /'gælouz/ *n.* horca *f.*

gamble /'gæmbəl/ *n.* **1.** riesgo *m.* —*v.* **2.** jugar, aventurar.

game /geim/ *n.* juego *m.*; (match) partida *f.*; (hunting) caza *f.*

gang /gæŋ/ *n.* cuadrilla; pandilla *f.*

gangster /'gæŋstər/ *n.* rufián *m.*

gap /gæp/ *n.* raja *f.*

gape /geip/ *v.* boquear.

garage /gə'rɑʒ/ *n.* garaje *m.*

garbage /'gɑrbɪdʒ/ *n.* basura *f.*

garden /'gɑrdn/ *n.* jardín *m.*; (vegetable) huerta *f.*

gardener /'gɑrdnər/ *n.* jardinero -ra.

gargle /'gɑrgəl/ *n.* **1.** gárgara *f.* —*v.* **2.** gargarizar.

garland /'gɑrlənd/ *n.* guirnalda *f.*

garlic /'gɑrlɪk/ *n.* ajo *m.*

garment /'gɑrmənt/ *n.* prenda de vestir.

garrison /'gærəsən/ *n.* guarnición *f.*

garter /'gɑrtər/ *n.* liga *f.*; ataderas *f.pl.*

gas /gæs/ *n.* gas *m.*

gasohol /'gæsə,hɔl, -,hɒl/ *n.* gasohol *m.*

gasoline /,gæsə'lin/ *n.* gasolina *f.*

gasp /gæsp/ *n.* **1.** boqueada *f.* —*v.* **2.** boquear.

gas station gasolinera *f.*

gate /geit/ *n.* puerta; entrada; verja *f.*

gather /'gæðər/ *v.* recoger; inferir; reunir.

gaudy /'gɔdi/ *a.* brillante; llamativo.

gauge /geidʒ/ *n.* **1.** manómetro, indicador *m.* —*v.* **2.** medir; estimar.

gaunt /gɔnt/ *a.* flaco.

gauze /gɔz/ *n.* gasa *f.*

gay /gei/ *a.* **1.** alegre; homosexual. —*n.* **2.** homosexual.

gaze /geiz/ *n.* **1.** mirada *f.* —*v.* **2.** mirar con fijeza.

gear /gɪər/ *n.* engranaje *m.* **in g.,** en juego.

gearshift /'gɪər,ʃɪft/ *n.* palanca de cambio *f.*

gem /dʒem/ *n.* joya *f.*

gender /'dʒendər/ *n.* género *m.*

general /'dʒenərəl/ *a.* & *n.* general *m.*

generality /,dʒenə'ræliti/ *n.* generalidad *f.*

generalize /'dʒenərə,laiz/ *v.* generalizar.

generation /,dʒenə'reiʃən/ *n.* generación *f.*

generator /'dʒenə,reitər/ *n.* generador *m.*

generosity /,dʒenə'rɒsiti/ *n.* generosidad *f.*

generous /'dʒenərəs/ *a.* generoso.

genetic /dʒə'netɪk/ *a.* genético.

genial /'dʒinyəl/ *a.* genial.

genius /'dʒinyəs/ *n.* genio *m.*

genocide /'dʒenə,said/ *n.* genocidio *m.*

gentle /'dʒentl/ *a.* suave; manso; benigno.

gentleman /'dʒentlmən/ *n.* señor; caballero *m.*

gentleness /'dʒentlnɪs/ *n.* suavidad *f.*

genuine /'dʒenyuɪn/ *a.* genuino.

genuineness /'dʒɛnyuɪnnɪs/ n. pureza f.

geographical /,dʒiə'græfɪkəl/ a. geográfico.

geography /dʒi'ɒɡrəfi/ n. geografía f.

geometric /,dʒiə'mɛtrɪk/ a. geométrico.

geranium /dʒə'reiniəm/ n. geranio m.

germ /dʒɜrm/ n. germen; microbio m.

German /'dʒɜrmən/ a. & n. alemán -mana.

Germany /'dʒɜrməni/ n. Alemania f.

gesticulate /dʒɛ'stɪkyə,leit/ v. gesticular.

gesture /'dʒɛstʃər/ n. 1. gesto m. —v. 2. gesticular, hacer gestos.

get /ɡɛt/ v. obtener; conseguir; (become) ponerse. **go and g.,** ir a buscar; **g. away,** irse; escaparse; **g. together,** reunirse; **g. on,** subirse; **g. off,** bajarse; **g. up,** levantarse; **g. there,** llegar.

ghastly /'ɡæstli/ a. pálido; espantoso.

ghost /ɡoust/ n. espectro, fantasma m.

giant /'dʒaiənt/ n. gigante m.

gibberish /'dʒɪbərɪʃ/ n. galimatías, m.

gift /ɡɪft/ n. regalo, don; talento m.

gigabyte /'ɡɪɡə,bait, 'dʒɪɡ-/ n. giga m.

gild /ɡɪld/ v. dorar.

gin /dʒɪn/ n. ginebra f.

ginger /'dʒɪndʒər/ n. jengibre m.

gingerbread /'dʒɪndʒər,brɛd/ n. pan de jengibre.

gingham /'ɡɪŋəm/ n. guinga f.

gird /ɡɜrd/ v. ceñir.

girdle /'ɡɜrdl/ n. faja f.

girl /ɡɜrl/ n. muchacha, niña, chica f.

give /ɡɪv/ v. dar; regalar. **g. back,** devolver. **g. up,** rendirse; renunciar.

giver /'ɡɪvər/ n. dador -ra; donador -ra.

glacier /'ɡleiʃər/ n. glaciar; ventisquero m.

glad /ɡlæd/ a. alegre, contento. **be g.,** alegrarse.

gladly /'ɡlædli/ adj. con mucho gusto.

gladness /'ɡlædnɪs/ n. alegría f.; placer m.

glamor /'ɡlæmər/ n. encanto m.; elegancia f.

glamorous /'ɡlæmərəs/ a. encantador; elegante.

glamour /'ɡlæmər/ n. encanto m.; elegancia f.

glance /ɡlæns/ n. 1. vistazo m., ojeada f. —v. 2. ojear.

gland /ɡlænd/ n. glándula f.

glare /ɡlɛər/ n. 1. reflejo; brillo m. —v. 2. deslumbrar; echar miradas indignadas.

glass /ɡlæs/ n. vidrio; vaso m.; **(eyeglasses),** lentes, anteojos m.pl.

gleam /ɡlim/ n. 1. fulgor m. —v. 2. fulgurar.

glee /ɡli/ n. alegría f.; júbilo m.

glide /ɡlaid/ v. deslizarse.

glimpse /ɡlɪmps/ n. 1. vislumbre, vistazo m. —v. 2. vislumbrar, ojear.

glisten /'ɡlɪsən/ n. 1. brillo m. —v. 2. brillar.

glitter /'ɡlɪtər/ n. 1. resplandor m. —v. 2. brillar.

globe /ɡloub/ n. globo; orbe m.

gloom /ɡlum/ n. oscuridad; tristeza f.

gloomy /'ɡlumi/ a. oscuro; sombrío, triste.

glorify /'ɡlɔrə,fai/ v. glorificar.

glorious /'ɡlɔriəs/ a. glorioso.

glory /'ɡlɔri/ n. gloria, fama f.

glossary /'ɡlɒsəri/ n. glosario m.

glove /ɡlʌv/ n. guante m.

glove compartment guantera f.

glow /ɡlou/ n. 1. fulgor m. —v. 2. relucir; arder.

glucose /'ɡlukous/ f. glucosa.

glue /ɡlu/ n. 1. cola f., pegamento m. —v. 2. encolar, pegar.

glum /ɡlʌm/ a. de mal humor.

glutton /'ɡlʌtn/ n. glotón -ona.

gnaw /nɔ/ v. roer.

GNP (abbr. **gross national product**), **PNB** (producto nacional bruto).

go /ɡou/ v. ir, irse. **g. away,** irse, marcharse. **g. back,** volver, regresar. **g. down,** bajar. **g. in,** entrar. **g. on,** seguir. **g. out,** salir. **g. up,** subir.

goal /ɡoul/ n. meta f.; objeto m.

goalkeeper /'ɡoul,kipər/ n. guardameta m.

goat /ɡout/ n. cabra f.

goblet /'ɡɒblɪt/ n. copa f.

God /ɡɒd/ n. Dios m.

gold /ɡould/ n. oro m.

golden /'gouldən/ a. áureo.
gold-plated /'gould ˌpleitɪd/ a. chapado en oro.
golf /gɒlf/ n. golf m.
golf course campo de golf m.
golfer /'gɒlfər/ n. golfista m. & f.
good /gud/ a. **1.** bueno. —n. **2.** bienes m.pl.; Com. géneros m.pl.
good-bye /ˌgud'bai/ n. **1.** adiós m. —interj. **2.** ¡adiós!, ¡hasta la vista!, ¡hasta luego! **say g. to,** despedirse de.
goodness /'gudnɪs/ n. bondad f.
goodwill /'gud'wɪl/ n. buena voluntad. f.
goose /gus/ n. ganso m.
gooseberry /'gus,bɛri/ n. uva crespa f.
gooseneck /'gus,nɛk/ n. **1.** cuello de cisne m. —a. **2.** curvo.
goose step /'gus,stɛp/ paso de ganso m.
gore /gɔr/ n. **1.** sangre f. —v. **2.** acornear.
gorge /gɔrdʒ/ n. **1.** gorja f. —v. **2.** engullir.
gorgeous /'gɔrdʒəs/ a. magnífico; precioso.
gorilla /gə'rɪlə/ n. gorila m.
gory /'gɔri/ a. sangriento.
gosling /'gɒzlɪŋ/ n. gansarón m.
gospel /'gɒspəl/ n. evangelio m.
gossamer /'gɒsəmər/ n. **1.** telaraña f. —a. **2.** delgado.
gossip /'gɒsəp/ n. **1.** chisme m. —v. **2.** chismear.
Gothic /'gɒθɪk/ a. gótico.
gouge /gaudʒ/ n. **1.** gubia f. —v. **2.** escoplear.
gourd /gɔrd/ n. calabaza f.
gourmand /gur'mɑnd/ n. glotón m.
gourmet /gur'mei/ a. gastrónomo -ma.
govern /'gʌvərn/ v. gobernar.
governess /'gʌvərnɪs/ n. aya, institutriz f.
government /'gʌvərnmənt, -ərmənt/ n. gobierno m.
governmental /ˌgʌvərn'mɛntḷ, ˌgʌvər-/ a. gubernamental.
governor /'gʌvərnər/ n. gobernador -ra.
governorship /'gʌvərnər,ʃɪp/ n. gobernatura f.
gown /gaun/ n. vestido m. **dressing g.,** bata f.
grab /græb/ v. agarrar, arrebatar.
grace /greis/ n. gracia; gentileza; merced f.

graceful /'greisfəl/ a. agraciado.
graceless /'greislɪs/ a. réprobo; torpe.
gracious /'greiʃəs/ a. gentil, cortés.
grackle /'grækəl/ n. grajo m.
grade /greid/ n. **1.** grado; nivel m.; pendiente; nota; calidad f. —v. **2.** graduar.
grade crossing n. paso a nivel m.
gradual /'grædʒuəl/ a. gradual, paulatino.
gradually /'grædʒuəli/ adv. gradualmente.
graduate /n 'grædʒuit; v -,eit/ n. **1.** graduado -da, diplomado -da. —v. **2.** graduar; diplomarse.
graft /græft/ n. **1.** injerto m.; soborno público. —v. **2.** injertar.
graham /'greiəm/ a. centeno; acemita.
grail /greil/ n. grial m.
grain /grein/ n. grano; cereal m.
grain alcohol n. alcohol de madera m.
gram /græm/ n. gramo m.
grammar /'græmər/ n. gramática f.
grammarian /grə'mɛəriən/ n. gramático -ca.
grammar school n. escuela elemental f.
grammatical /grə'mætɪkəl/ a. gramatical.
gramophone /'græmə,foun/ n. gramófono m.
granary /'greinəri/ n. granero m.
grand /grænd/ a. grande, ilustre; estupendo.
grandchild /'græn,tʃaild/ n. nieto -ta.
granddaughter /'græn,dɔtər/ n. nieta f.
grandee /græn'di/ n. noble m.
grandeur /'grændʒər/ n. grandeza f.
grandfather /'græn,faðər/ n. abuelo m.
grandiloquent /græn'dɪləkwənt/ a. grandílocuo.
grandiose /'grændi,ous/ a. grandioso.
grand jury jurado de acusación, jurado de juicio m.
grandly /'grændli/ adv. grandiosamente.
grandmother /'græn,mʌðər/ n. abuela f.
grand opera ópera grande f.

grandparents /'grænd,pɛərənts/ n. abuelos m.pl.

grandson /'græn,sʌn/ n. nieto m.

grandstand /'græn,stænd/ n. andanada f., tribuna f.

grange /greindʒ/ n. granja f.

granger /'greindʒər/ n. labriego m.

granite /'grænɪt/ n. granito m.

granny /'græni/ n. abuelita f.

grant /grænt/ n. **1.** concesión; subvención f. —v. **2.** otorgar; conceder; conferir. **take for granted,** tomar por cierto.

granular /'grænyələr/ a. granular.

granulate /'grænyə,leit/ v. granular.

granulation /,grænyə'leiʃən/ n. granulación f.

granule /'grænyul/ n. gránulo m.

grape /greip/ n. uva f.

grapefruit /'greip,frut/ n. toronja f.

grape harvest vendimia f.

grapeshot /'greip,ʃɒt/ n. metralla f.

grapevine /'greip,vain/ n. vid; parra f.

graph /græf/ n. gráfica f.

graphic /'græfɪk/ a. gráfico.

graphite /'græfait/ n. grafito m.

graphology /græ'fɒlədʒi/ n. grafología f.

grapple /'græpəl/ v. agarrar.

grasp /græsp/ n. **1.** puño; poder; conocimiento m. —v. **2.** empuñar, agarrar; comprender.

grasping /'græspɪŋ/ a. codicioso.

grass /græs/ n. hierba f.; (marijuana) marijuana f.

grasshopper /'græs,hɒpər/ n. saltamontes m.

grassy /'græsi/ a. herboso.

grate /greit/ n. reja f.

grateful /'greitfəl/ a. agradecido.

gratify /'grætə,fai/ v. satisfacer.

grating /'greitɪŋ/ n. **1.** enrejado m. —a. **2.** discordante.

gratis /'grætɪs/ adv. & a. gratis.

gratitude /'grætɪ,tud/ n. agradecimiento m.

gratuitous /grə'tuɪtəs/ adj. gratuito.

gratuity /grə'tuɪti/ n. propina f.

grave /greiv/ a. **1.** grave. —n. **2.** sepultura; tumba f.

gravel /'grævəl/ n. cascajo m.

gravely /'greivli/ adv. gravemente.

gravestone /'greiv,stoun/ n. lápida sepulcral f.

graveyard /'greiv,yard/ n. cementerio m.

gravitate /'grævɪ,teit/ v. gravitar.

gravitation /,grævɪ'teiʃən/ n. gravitación f.

gravity /'grævɪti/ n. gravedad; seriedad f.

gravure /grə'vyʊr/ n. fotograbado m.

gravy /'greivi/ n. salsa f.

gray /grei/ a. gris; (hair) cano.

grayish /'greiɪʃ/ a. pardusco.

gray matter substancia gris f.

graze /greiz/ v. rozar; (cattle) pastar.

grazing /'greizɪŋ/ a. pastando.

grease /gris/ n. **1.** grasa f. —v. **2.** engrasar.

greasy /'grisi/ a. grasiento.

great /greit/ a. grande, ilustre; estupendo.

Great Dane /dein/ mastín danés m.

great-grandfather /,greit 'græn,fɑðər/ n. bisabuelo.

great-grandmother /,greit 'græn,mʌðər/ f. bisabuela.

greatness /'greitnɪs/ n. grandeza f.

Greece /gris/ n. Grecia f.

greed /grid/ **greediness** n. codicia, voracidad f.

greedy /'gridi/ a. voraz.

Greek /grik/ a. & n. griego -ga.

green /grin/ a. & n. verde m.

greens, n. verduras f.pl.

greenery /'grinəri/ n. verdor m.

greenhouse /'grin,haus/ n. invernáculo m.

greenhouse effect n. efecto invernáculo m.

greet /grit/ v. saludar.

greeting /'gritɪŋ/ n. saludo m.

gregarious /grɪ'gɛəriəs/ a. gregario; sociable.

grenade /grɪ'neid/ n. granada; bomba f.

greyhound /'grei,haund/ n. galgo m.

grid /grid/ n. parrilla f.

griddle /'gridl/ n. tortera f.

griddlecake /'gridl,keik/ n. tortita de harina f.

gridiron /'grid,aiərn/ n. parrilla f.; campo de fútbol m.

grief /grif/ n. dolor m.; pena f.

grievance /'grivəns/ n. pesar; agravio m.

grieve /griv/ v. afligir.

grievous /'grivəs/ a. penoso.

grill /grɪl/ n. **1.** parrilla f. —v. **2.** asar a la parrilla.

grillroom /'grɪl,rum, -,rʊm/ n. parrilla f.

grim /grɪm/ a. ceñudo.

grimace /'grɪməs/ n. **1.** mueca f. —v. **2.** hacer muecas.

grime /graim/ n. mugre f.

grimy /'graimi/ a. sucio; mugroso.

grin /grɪn/ n. **1.** sonrisa f. —v. **2.** sonreír.

grind /graind/ v. moler; afilar.

grindstone /'graind,stoun/ n. amoladera f.

gringo /'grɪŋgou/ n. gringo; yanqui m.

grip /grɪp/ n. **1.** maleta f. —v. **2.** agarrar.

gripe /graip/ v. **1.** agarrar. —n. **2.** asimiento m., opresión f.

grippe /grɪp/ n. gripe f.

grisly /'grɪzli/ a. espantoso.

grist /grɪst/ n. molienda f.

gristle /'grɪsəl/ n. cartílago m.

grit /grɪt/ n. arena f.; entereza f.

grizzled /'grɪzəld/ a. tordillo.

groan /groun/ n. **1.** gemido m. —v. **2.** gemir.

grocer /'grousər/ n. abacero m.

grocery /'grousəri/ n. tienda de comestibles, abacería; (Carib.) bodega f.

grog /grɒg/ n. brebaje m.

groggy /'grɒgi/ a. medio borracho; vacilante.

groin /grɔin/ n. ingle f.

groom /grum/ n. (of horses) establero; (at wedding) novio m.

groove /gruv/ n. **1.** estría f. —v. **2.** acanalar.

grope /group/ v. tentar; andar a tientas.

gross /grous/ a. **1.** grueso; grosero. —n. **2.** gruesa f.

grossly /'grousli/ adv. groseramente.

gross national product producto nacional bruto m.

grossness /'grousnɪs/ n. grosería f.

grotesque /grou'tɛsk/ a. grotesco.

grotto /'grɒtou/ n. gruta f.

grouch /grautʃ/ n. gruñón; descontento m.

ground /graund/ n. tierra f.; terreno; suelo; campo; fundamento m.

ground floor planta baja f.

groundhog /'graund,hɒg/ n. marmota f.

groundless /'graundlɪs/ a. infundado.

groundwork /'graund,wɜrk/ n. base f., fundamento m.

group /grup/ n. **1.** grupo m. —v. **2.** agrupar.

groupie /'grupi/ n. persona aficionada que acompaña a un grupo de música moderna.

grouse /graus/ v. quejarse

grove /grouv/ n. arboleda f.

grovel /'grɒvəl/ v. rebajarse; envilecerse.

grow /grou/ v. crecer; cultivar.

growl /graul/ n. **1.** gruñido m. —v. **2.** gruñir.

grown /groun/ a. crecido; desarrollado.

grownup /'groun,ʌp/ n. adulto -ta.

growth /grouθ/ n. crecimiento m.; vegetación f.; Med. tumor m.

grub /grʌb/ n. gorgojo m., larva f.

grubby /'grʌbi/ a. gorgojoso, mugriento.

grudge /grʌdʒ/ n. rencor m. **bear a g.,** guardar rencor.

gruel /'gruəl/ n. **1.** atole m. —v. **2.** agotar.

gruesome /'grusəm/ a. horripilante.

gruff /grʌf/ a. ceñudo.

grumble /'grʌmbəl/ v. quejarse.

grumpy /'grʌmpi/ a. gruñón; quejoso.

grunt /grʌnt/ v. gruñir.

guarantee /,gærən'ti/ n. **1.** garantía f. —v. **2.** garantizar.

guarantor /'gærən,tɔr/ n. fiador -ra.

guaranty /'gærən,ti/ n. garantía f.

guard /gard/ n. **1.** guardia m. & f. —v. **2.** vigilar.

guarded /'gardɪd/ a. cauteloso.

guardhouse /'gard,haus/ n. prisión militar f.

guardian /'gardiən/ n. guardián -ana.

guardianship /'gardiən,ʃɪp/ n. tutela f.

guardsman /'gardzmən/ n. centinela m.

guava /'gwavə/ n. guayaba f.

gubernatorial /,gubərnə'tɔriəl/ a. gubernativo.

guerrilla /gə'rɪlə/ n. guerrilla f.; guerrillero -ra.

guess /gɛs/ n. **1.** conjetura f. —v. **2.** adivinar; Colloq. creer.

guesswork /'gɛs,wɔrk/ n. conjetura f.

guest /gɛst/ n. huésped m. & f.

guest room alcoba de huéspedes f., alcoba de respeto f., cuarto para invitados m.

guffaw /gʌ'fɔ/ n. risotada f.

guidance /'gaidn̩s/ n. dirección f.

guide /gaid/ n. **1.** guía m. & f. —v. **2.** guiar.

guidebook /'gaid,bʊk/ n. guía f.

guided tour /'gaidɪd/ visita explicada, visita programada, visita con guía f.

guideline /'gaid,lain/ n. pauta f.

guidepost /'gaid,poust/ n. poste indicador m.

guild /gɪld/ n. gremio m.

guile /gail/ n. engaño m.

guillotine /'gɪlə,tin/ n. **1.** guillotina f. —v. **2.** guillotinar.

guilt /gɪlt/ n. culpa f.

guiltily /'gɪltəli/ adv. culpablemente.

guiltless /'gɪltlɪs/ a. inocente.

guilty /'gɪlti/ a. culpable.

guinea fowl /'gɪni/ gallina de Guinea f.

guinea pig /'gɪni/ cobayo m., conejillo de Indias m.

guise /gaiz/ n. modo m.

guitar /gɪ'tɑr/ n. guitarra f.

guitarist /gɪ'tɑrɪst/ n. guitarrista m. & f.

gulch /gʌltʃ/ n. quebrada f.

gulf /gʌlf/ n. golfo m.

gull /gʌl/ n. gaviota f.

gullet /'gʌlɪt/ n. esófago m.; zanja f.

gullible /'gʌləbəl/ a. crédulo.

gully /'gʌli/ n. barranca f.

gulp /gʌlp/ n. **1.** trago m. —v. **2.** tragar.

gum /gʌm/ n. **1.** goma f.; Anat. encía f. **chewing g.,** chicle m. —v. **2.** engomar.

gumbo /'gʌmbou/ n. quimbombó m.

gummy /'gʌmi/ a. gomoso.

gun /gʌn/ n. fusil, revólver m.

gunboat /'gʌn,bout/ n. cañonero m.

gunman /'gʌnmən/ n. bandido m.

gunner /'gʌnər/ n. artillero m.

gun permit licencia de armas f.

gunpowder /'gʌn,paudər/ n. pólvora f.

gunshot /'gʌn,ʃɒt/ n. escopetazo m.

gunwale /'gʌnl̩/ n. borda f.

gurgle /'gɔrgəl/ n. **1.** gorgoteo m. —v. **2.** gorgotear.

guru /'gʊru, gʊ'ru/ n. gurú m.

gush /gʌʃ/ n. **1.** chorro m. —v. **2.** brotar, chorrear.

gusher /'gʌʃər/ n. pozo de petróleo m.

gust /gʌst/ n. soplo m.; ráfaga f.

gustatory /'gʌstə,tɔri/ a. gustativo.

gusto /'gʌstou/ n. gusto; placer m.

gusty /'gʌsti/ a. borrascoso.

gut /gʌt/ n. intestino m.; tripa f.

gutter /'gʌtər/ n. canal; zanja f.

guttural /'gʌtərəl/ a. gutural.

guy /gai/ n. tipo m.

guzzle /'gʌzəl/ v. engullir; tragar.

gym /dʒɪm/ n. gimnasio m.

gymnasium /gɪm'naziəm/ n. gimnasio m.

gymnast /'dʒɪmnæst/ n. gimnasta m. & f.

gymnastic /dʒɪm'næstɪk/ a. gimnástico.

gymnastics /dʒɪm'næstɪks/ n. gimnasia f.

gynecologist /,gaini'kɒlədʒɪst/ n. ginecólogo, -ga m. & f.

gynecology /,gaini'kɒlədʒi/ n. ginecología f.

gypsum /'dʒɪpsəm/ n. yeso m.

Gypsy /'dʒɪpsi/ a. & n. gitano -na.

gyrate /'dʒaireit/ v. girar.

gyroscope /'dʒairə,skoup/ n. giroscopio m.

H

habeas corpus /'heibiəs 'kɔrpəs/ habeas corpus m.

haberdasher /'hæbər,dæʃər/ n. camisero m.

haberdashery /'hæbər,dæʃəri/ n. camisería f.

habiliment /hə'bɪləmənt/ n. vestuario m.

habit /'hæbɪt/ n. costumbre f., hábito m. **be in the h. of,** estar acostumbrado a; soler.

habitable /'hæbɪtəbəl/ a. habitable.

habitat /'hæbɪ,tæt/ n. habitación f., ambiente m.

habitation /ˌhæbɪ'teiʃən/ n. habitación f.
habitual /hə'bɪtʃuəl/ a. habitual.
habituate /hə'bɪtʃu,eit/ v. habituar.
habitué /hə'bɪtʃu,ei/ n. parroquiano m.
hack /hæk/ n. **1.** coche de alquiler. —v. **2.** tajar.
hacker /'hækər/ n. pirata m. & f.
hackneyed /'hæknid/ a. trillado.
hacksaw /'hæk,sɔ/ n. sierra para cortar metal f.
haddock /'hædək/ n. merluza f.
haft /hæft/ n. mango m.
hag /hæg, hɑg/ n. bruja f.
haggard /'hægərd/ a. trasnochado.
haggle /'hægəl/ v. regatear.
hail /heil/ n. **1.** granizo; (greeting) saludo m. —v. **2.** granizar; saludar.
Hail Mary /'mɛəri/ Ave María m.
hailstone /'heil,stoun/ n. piedra de granizo f.
hailstorm /'heil,stɔrm/ n. granizada f.
hair /hɛər/ n. pelo; cabello m.
haircut /'hɛər,kʌt/ n. corte de pelo.
hairdo /'hɛər,du/ n. peinado m.
hairdresser /'hɛər,drɛsər/ n. peluquero m.
hair dryer /'draiər/ secador de pelo, secador m.
hairpin /'hɛər,pɪn/ n. horquilla f.; gancho m.
hair's-breadth /'hɛərz,brɛdθ/ n. ancho de un pelo m.
hairspray /'hɛərsprei/ n. aerosol para cabello.
hairy /'hɛəri/ a. peludo.
halcyon /'hælsiən/ n. **1.** alcedón m. —a. **2.** tranquilo.
hale /heil/ a. sano.
half /hæf/ a. **1.** medio. —n. **2.** mitad f.
half-and-half /'hæf ən 'hæf/ a. mitad y mitad.
half-baked /'hæf 'beikt/ a. medio crudo.
half-breed /'hæf ,brid/ n. mestizo m.
half brother n. medio hermano m.
half-hearted /'hæf'hɑrtɪd/ a. sin entusiasmo.
half-mast /'hæf 'mæst/ a. & n. media asta m.

halfpenny /'heipəni/ n. medio penique m.
halfway /'hæf'wei/ adv. a medio camino.
half-wit /'hæf ,wɪt/ n. bobo m.
halibut /'hæləbət/ n. hipogloso m.
hall /hɔl/ n. corredor m.; (for assembling) sala f. **city h.,** ayuntamiento m.
hallmark /'hɔl,mɑrk/ n. marca del contraste f.
hallow /'hælou/ v. consagrar.
Halloween /ˌhælə'win/ n. víspera de Todos los Santos f.
hallucination /hə,lusə'neiʃən/ n. alucinación f.
hallway /'hɔl,wei/ n. pasadizo m.
halo /'heilou/ n. halo m.; corona f.
halt /hɔlt/ a. **1.** cojo. —n. **2.** parada f. —v. **3.** parar. —interj. **4.** ¡alto!
halter /'hɔltər/ n. cabestro m.
halve /hæv/ v. dividir en dos partes.
halyard /'hælyərd/ n. driza f.
ham /hæm/ n. jamón m.
hamburger /'hæm,bɜrgər/ n. albóndiga f.
hamlet /'hæmlɪt/ n. aldea f.
hammer /'hæmər/ n. **1.** martillo m. —v. **2.** martillar.
hammock /'hæmək/ n. hamaca f.
hamper /'hæmpər/ n. canasta f., cesto m.
hamstring /'hæm,strɪŋ/ n. **1.** tendón de la corva m. —v. **2.** desjarretar.
hand /hænd/ n. **1.** mano f. **on the other h.,** en cambio. —v. **2.** pasar. **h. over,** entregar.
handbag /'hænd,bæg/ n. cartera f.
handball /'hænd,bɔl/ n. pelota f.
handbook /'hænd,bʊk/ n. manual m.
handbrake /'hændbreik/ n. freno de mano m.
handcuff /'hænd,kʌf/ n. esposa v. esposar.
handful /'hændfʊl/ n. puñado m.
handicap /'hændi,kæp/ n. desventaja f.
handicraft /'hændi,kræft/ n. artífice m.; destreza manual.
handiwork /'hændi,wɜrk/ n. artefacto m.
handkerchief /'hæŋkərtʃif/ n. pañuelo m.
handle /'hændl/ n. **1.** mango m. —v. **2.** manejar.

hand luggage equipaje de mano *m.*

handmade /'hænd'meid/ *a.* hecho a mano.

handmaid /'hænd,meid/ *n.* criada de mano, sirvienta *f.*

hand organ organillo *m.*

handsome /'hænsəm/ *a.* guapo; hermoso.

hand-to-hand /'hænd tə 'hænd/ *adv.* de mano a mano.

handwriting /'hænd,raitɪŋ/ *n.* escritura *f.*

handy /'hændi/ *a.* diestro; útil; a la mano.

hang /hæŋ/ *v.* colgar; ahorcar.

hangar /'hæŋər/ *n.* hangar *m.*

hangdog /'hæŋ,dɔg/ *a.* & *n.* camastrón *m.*

hanger /'hæŋər/ *n.* colgador, gancho *m.*

hanger-on /'hæŋər 'ɒn/ *n.* dependiente; mogollón *m.*

hang glider /'glaidər/ aparato para vuelo libre, delta, ala delta.

hanging /'hæŋɪŋ/ *n.* **1.** ahorcadura *f.* —*a.* **2.** colgante.

hangman /'hæŋmən/ *n.* verdugo *m.*

hangnail /'hæŋ,neil/ *n.* padrastro *m.*

hang out *v.* enarbolar.

hangover /'hæŋ,ouvər/ *n.* resaca *f.*

hangup /'hæŋʌp/ *n.* tara (psicológica) *f.*

hank /hæŋk/ *n.* madeja *f.*

hanker /'hæŋkər/ *v.* ansiar; apetecer.

haphazard. /,hæp'hæzərd/ *a.* casual.

happen /'hæpən/ *v.* acontecer, suceder, pasar.

happening /'hæpənɪŋ/ *n.* acontecimiento *m.*

happiness /'hæpinɪs/ *n.* felicidad; dicha *f.*

happy /'hæpi/ *a.* feliz; contento; dichoso.

happy-go-lucky /'hæpi gou 'lʌki/ *a.* & *n.* descuidado *m.*

harakiri /'hɑrə'kɪəri/ *n.* harakiri (suicidio japonés) *m.*

harangue /hə'ræŋ/ *n.* **1.** arenga *f.* —*v.* **2.** arengar.

harass /hə'ræs/ *v.* acosar; atormentar.

harbinger /'hɑrbɪndʒər/ *n.* presagio *m.*

harbor /'hɑrbər/ *n.* **1.** puerto; albergue *m.* —*v.* **2.** abrigar.

hard /hɑrd/ *a.* **1.** duro; difícil. —*adv.* **2.** mucho.

hard coal antracita *m.*

hard disk disco duro *m.*

harden /'hɑrdṇ/ *v.* endurecer.

hard-headed /'hɑrd 'hɛdɪd/ *a.* terco.

hard-hearted /'hɑrd'hɑrtɪd/ *a.* empedernido.

hardiness /'hɑrdinɪs/ *n.* vigor *m.*

hardly /'hɑrdli/ *adv.* apenas.

hardness /'hɑrdnɪs/ *n.* dureza; dificultad *f.*

hardship /'hɑrdʃɪp/ *n.* penalidad *f.;* trabajo *m.*

hardware /'hɑrd,wɛər/ *n.* hardware *m.;* (computer) quincalla *f.*

hardwood /'hɑrd,wʊd/ *n.* madera dura *f.*

hardy /'hɑrdi/ *a.* fuerte, robusto.

hare /hɛər/ *n.* liebre *f.*

harebrained /'hɛər,breind/ *a.* tolondro.

harelip /'hɛər,lɪp/ *n.* **1.** labio leporino *m.* —*a.* **2.** labihendido.

harem /'hɛərəm/ *n.* harén *m.*

hark /hɑrk/ *v.* escuchar; atender.

Harlequin /'hɑrləkwɪn/ *n.* arlequín *m.*

harlot /'hɑrlət/ *n.* ramera *f.*

harm /hɑrm/ *n.* **1.** mal, daño; perjuicio *m.* —*v.* **2.** dañar.

harmful /'hɑrmfəl/ *a.* dañoso.

harmless /'hɑrmlɪs/ *a.* inocente.

harmonic /hɑr'mɒnɪk/ *n.* armónico *m.*

harmonica /hɑr'mɒnɪkə/ *n.* armónica *f.*

harmonious /hɑr'mouniəs/ *a.* armonioso.

harmonize /'hɑrmə,naiz/ *v.* armonizar.

harmony /'hɑrməni/ *n.* armonía *f.*

harness /'hɑrnɪs/ *n.* arnés *m.*

harp /hɑrp/ *n.* arpa *f.*

harpoon /hɑr'pun/ *n.* arpón *m.*

harridan /'hɑrɪdṇ/ *n.* vieja regañona *f.*

harrow /'hærou/ *n.* **1.** rastro *m.;* grada *f.* —*v.* **2.** gradar.

harry /'hæri/ *v.* acosar.

harsh /hɑrʃ/ *a.* áspero.

harshness /'hɑrʃnɪs/ *n.* aspereza *f.*

harvest /'hɑrvɪst/ *n.* **1.** cosecha *f.* —*v.* **2.** cosechar.

hash /hæʃ/ *n.* picadillo *m.*

hashish /'hæʃiʃ/ *n.* haxis *m.*

hasn't /'hæzənt/ v. no tiene (neg. + tener).

hassle /'hæsəl/ n. lío m., molestia f.; controversia f.

hassock /'hæsək/ n. cojín m.

haste /heist/ n. prisa f.

hasten /'heisən/ v. apresurarse, darse prisa.

hasty /'heisti/ a. apresurado.

hat /hæt/ n. sombrero m.

hat box /'hæt,bɒks/ sombrerera f.

hatch /hætʃ/ n. **1.** Naut. cuartel m. —v. **2.** incubar; Fig. tramar.

hatchery /'hætʃəri/ n. criadero m.

hatchet /'hætʃɪt/ n. hacha pequeña.

hate /heit/ n. **1.** odio m. —v. **2.** odiar, detestar.

hateful /'heitfəl/ a. detestable.

hatred /'heitrɪd/ n. odio m.

haughtiness /'hɔtinɪs/ n. arrogancia f.

haughty /'hɔti/ a. altivo.

haul /hɔl/ n. **1.** (fishery) redada f. —v. **2.** tirar, halar.

haunch /hɔntʃ/ n. anca f.

haunt /hɔnt/ n. **1.** lugar frecuentado. —v. **2.** frecuentar, andar por.

have /hæv; unstressed həv, əv/ v. tener; haber.

haven /'heivən/ n. puerto; asilo m.

haven't /'hævənt/ v. no tiene (neg. + tener).

havoc /'hævək/ n. ruina f.

hawk /hɔk/ n. halcón m.

hawker /'hɔkər/ n. buhonero m.

hawser /'hɔzər/ n. cable m.

hawthorn /'hɔ,θɔrn/ n. espino m.

hay /hei/ n. heno m.

hay fever n. fiebre del heno f.

hayfield /'heifild/ n. henar m.

hayloft /'hei,lɔft/ n. henil m.

haystack /'hei,stæk/ n. hacina de heno f.

hazard /'hæzərd/ n. **1.** azar m. —v. **2.** aventurar.

hazardous /'hæzərdəs/ a. peligroso.

haze /heiz/ n. niebla f.

hazel /'heizəl/ n. avellano m.

hazelnut /'heizəl,nʌt/ avellana f.

hazy /'heizi/ a. brumoso.

he /hei/ pron. él m.

head /hɛd/ n. **1.** cabeza f.; jefe m. —v. **2.** dirigir; encabezar.

headache /'hɛd,eik/ n. dolor de cabeza m.

headband /'hɛd,bænd/ n. venda para cabeza f.

headfirst /'hɛd'fɜrst/ adv. de cabeza.

headgear /'hɛd,gɪər/ n. tocado m.

headlight /'hɛd,lait/ n. linterna delantera f., farol de tope m.

headline /'hɛd,lain/ n. encabezado m.

headlong /'hɛd,lɔŋ/ a. precipitoso.

head-on /'hɛd 'ɒn/ adv. de frente.

headphones /'hɛd,founz/ n.pl. auriculares m.pl.

headquarters /'hɛd,kwɔrtərz/ n. jefatura f.; Mil. cuartel general.

headstone /'hɛd,stoun/ n. lápida mortuoria f.

headstrong /'hɛd,strɔŋ/ a. terco.

headwaiter /'hɛd'weitər/ jefe de comedor m. & f.

headwaters /'hɛd,wɔtərz/ n. cabeceras f.pl.

headway /'hɛd,wei/ n. avance m., progreso m.

headwork /'hɛd,wɜrk/ n. trabajo mental m.

heady /'hɛdi/ a. impetuoso.

heal /hil/ v. curar, sanar.

health /hɛlθ/ n. salud f.

healthful /'hɛlθfəl/ a. saludable.

healthy /'hɛlθi/ a. sano; salubre.

heap /hip/ n. montón m.

hear /hɪər/ v. oír. **h. from,** tener noticias de. **h. about, h. of,** oír hablar de.

hearing /'hɪərɪŋ/ n. oído m.

hearing aid audífono m.

hearsay /'hɪər,sei/ n. rumor m.

hearse /hɜrs/ n. ataúd m.

heart /hɑrt/ n. corazón m. **by h.,** de memoria. **have h. trouble** padecer del corazón.

heartache /'hɑrt,eik/ n. angustia f.

heart attack ataque cardíaco, infarto, infarto de miocardio m.

heartbreak /'hɑrt,breik/ n. angustia f.; pesar m.

heartbroken /'hɑrt,broukən/ a. acongojado.

heartburn /'hɑrt,bɜrn/ n. acedía f., ardor de estómago m.

heartfelt /'hɑrt,fɛlt/ a. sentido.

hearth /hɑrθ/ n. hogar m., chimenea f.

heartless /'hɑrtlɪs/ a. empedernido.

heartsick /'hɑrt,sɪk/ a. desconsolado.

heart-stricken /'hɑrt 'strɪkən/ a. afligido.

heart-to-heart /'hɑrt tə 'hɑrt/ adv. franco; sincero.

hearty /'hɑrti/ a. cordial; vigoroso.

heat /hit/ n. **1.** calor; ardor m.; calefacción f. —v. **2.** calentar.

heated /'hitɪd/ a. acalorado.

heater /'hitər/ n. calentador m.

heath /hiθ/ n. matorral m.

heathen /'hiðən/ a. & n. pagano -na.

heather /'hɛðər/ n. brezo m.

heating /'hitɪŋ/ n. calefacción f.

heatstroke /'hit,strouk/ n. insolación f.

heat wave onda de calor f.

heave /hiv/ v. tirar.

heaven /'hɛvən/ n. cielo m.

heavenly /'hɛvənli/ a. divino.

heavy /'hɛvi/ a. pesado; oneroso.

Hebrew /'hibru/ a. & n. hebreo -ea.

hectic /'hɛktɪk/ a. turbulento.

hedge /hɛdʒ/ n. seto m.

hedgehog /'hɛdʒ,hɒg/ n. erizo m.

hedonism /'hidṇ,ɪzəm/ n. hedonismo m.

heed /hid/ n. **1.** cuidado m. —v. **2.** atender.

heedless /'hidlɪs/ a. desatento; incauto.

heel /hil/ n. talón m.; (of shoe) tacón m.

heifer /'hɛfər/ n. novilla f.

height /hait/ n. altura f.

heighten /'haitṇ/ n. elevar; exaltar.

heinous /'heinəs/ a. nefando.

heir /ɛər/ **heiress** n. heredero -ra.

helicopter /'hɛlɪ,kɒptər/ n. helicóptero m.

heliotrope /'hiliə,troup/ n. heliotropo m.

helium /'hiliəm/ n. helio m.

hell /hɛl/ n. infierno m.

Hellenism /'hɛlə,nɪzəm/ n. helenismo m.

hellish /'hɛlɪʃ/ a. infernal.

hello /hɛ'lou/ interj. ¡hola!; (on telephone) aló; bueno.

helm /hɛlm/ n. timón m.

helmet /'hɛlmɪt/ n. yelmo, casco m.

helmsman /'hɛlmzmən/ n. limonero m.

help /hɛlp/ n. **1.** ayuda f. **help!** ¡socorro! —v. **2.** ayudar. **h. one-**self, servirse. **can't help (but),** no poder menos de.

helper /'hɛlpər/ n. ayudante m.

helpful /'hɛlpfəl/ a. útil; servicial.

helpfulness /'hɛlpfəlnɪs/ n. utilidad f.

helpless /'hɛlplɪs/ a. imposibilitado.

hem /hɛm/ n. **1.** ribete m. —v. **2.** ribetear.

hemisphere /'hɛmɪ,sfɪər/ n. hemisferio m.

hemlock /'hɛm,lɒk/ n. abeto m.

hemoglobin /'himə,gloubɪn/ n. hemoglobina f.

hemophilia /,himə'fɪliə/ n. hemofilia f.

hemorrhage /'hɛmərɪdʒ/ n. hemorragia f.

hemorrhoids /'hɛmə,rɔidz/ n. hemorroides f.pl.

hemp /hɛmp/ n. cáñamo m.

hemstitch /'hɛm,stɪtʃ/ n. **1.** vainica f. —v. **2.** hacer una vainica.

hen /hɛn/ n. gallina f.

hence /hɛns/ adv. por lo tanto.

henceforth /,hɛns'fɔrθ/ adv. de aquí en adelante.

henchman /'hɛntʃmən/ n. paniaguado m.

henna /'hɛnə/ n. alheña f.

hepatitis /,hɛpə'taitɪs/ n. hepatitis f.

her /hɜr; unstressed hər, ər/ a. **1.** su. —pron. **2.** ella; la; le.

herald /'hɛrəld/ n. heraldo m.

heraldic /hɛ'rældɪk/ a. heráldico.

heraldry /'hɛrəldri/ n. heráldica f.

herb /ɜrb; esp. Brit. hɜrb/ n. yerba, hierba f.

herbaceous /hɜr'beiʃəs, ɜr-/ a. herbáceo.

herbarium /hɜr'bɛəriəm, ɜr-/ n. herbario m.

herd /hɜrd/ n. **1.** hato, rebaño m. —v. **2.** reunir en hatos.

here /hɪər/ adv. aquí; acá.

hereafter /hɪər'æftər/ adv. en lo futuro.

hereby /hɪər'bai/ adv. por éstas, por la presente.

hereditary /hə'rɛdɪ,tɛri/ a. hereditario.

heredity /hə'rɛdɪti/ n. herencia f.

herein /hɪər'ɪn/ adv. aquí dentro; incluso.

heresy /'hɛrəsi/ n. herejía f.

heretic /'hɛrɪtɪk/ a. **1.** herético. —n. **2.** hereje m. & f.

heretical /hə'rɛtɪkəl/ a. herético.
heretofore /ˌhɪərtə'fɔr/ adv. hasta ahora.
herewith /hɪər'wɪθ/ adv. con esto, adjunto.
heritage /'hɛrɪtɪdʒ/ n. herencia f.
hermetic /hɜr'mɛtɪk/ a. hermético.
hermit /'hɜrmɪt/ n. ermitaño m.
hernia /'hɜrniə/ n. hernia f.
hero /'hɪərou/ n. héroe m.
heroic /hɪ'rouɪk/ a. heroico.
heroically /hɪ'rouɪkəli/ adv. heroicamente.
heroin /'hɛrouɪn/ n. heroína f.
heroine /'hɛrouɪn/ n. heroína f.
heroism /'hɛrou,ɪzəm/ n. heroísmo m.
heron /'hɛrən/ n. garza f.
herring /'hɛrɪŋ/ n. arenque m.
hers /hɜrz/ pron. suyo, de ella.
herself /hər'sɛlf/ pron. sí, sí misma, se. **she h.,** ella misma. **with h.,** consigo.
hertz /hɜrts/ n. hertzio m.
hesitancy /'hɛzɪtənsi/ n. hesitación f.
hesitant /'hɛzɪtənt/ a. indeciso.
hesitate /'hɛzɪ,teɪt/ v. vacilar.
hesitation /ˌhɛzɪ'teɪʃən/ n. duda; vacilación f.
heterogeneous /ˌhɛtərə'dʒiniəs/ a. heterogéneo.
heterosexual /ˌhɛtərə'sɛkʃuəl/ a. heterosexual.
hexagon /'hɛksə,gɒn/ n. hexágono m.
hibernate /'haɪbər,neɪt/ v. invernar.
hibernation /ˌhaɪbər'neɪʃən/ n. invernada f.
hibiscus /haɪ'bɪskəs/ n. hibisco m.
hiccup /'hɪkʌp/ n. **1.** hipo m. —v. **2.** tener hipo.
hickory /'hɪkəri/ n. nogal americano m.
hidden /'hɪdn̩/ a. oculto; escondido.
hide /haɪd/ n. **1.** cuero m.; piel f. —v. **2.** esconder; ocultar.
hideous /'hɪdiəs/ a. horrible.
hide-out /'haɪd ,aut/ n. escondite m.
hiding place /'haɪdɪŋ/ escondrijo m.
hierarchy /'haɪə,rɑrki/ n. jerarquía f.
high /haɪ/ a. alto, elevado; (in price) caro.

highbrow /'haɪ,brau/ n. erudito m.
highfalutin /ˌhaɪfə'lutn̩/ a. pomposo, presumido.
high fidelity de alta fidelidad.
highlighter /'haɪ,laɪtər/ n. marcador m.
highly /'haɪli/ adv. altamente; sumamente.
high school escuela secundaria f.
highway /'haɪ,weɪ/ n. carretera f.; camino real m.
hijacker /'haɪ,dʒækər/ n. secuestrador, pirata de aviones m.
hike /haɪk/ n. caminata f.
hilarious /hɪ'lɛəriəs/ a. alegre, bullicioso.
hilarity /hɪ'lærɪti/ n. hilaridad f.
hill /hɪl/ n. colina f.; cerro m.; **down h.,** cuesta abajo. **up h.,** cuesta arriba.
hilly /'hɪli/ a. accidentado.
hilt /hɪlt/ n. puño m. **up to the h.,** a fondo.
him /hɪm/ pron. él; lo; le.
himself /hɪm'sɛlf/ pron. sí, sí mismo; se. **he h.,** él mismo. **with h.,** consigo.
hinder /'hɪndər/ v. impedir.
hindmost /'haɪnd,moust/ a. último.
hindquarter /'haɪnd,kwɔrtər/ n. cuarto trasero m.
hindrance /'hɪndrəns/ n. obstáculo m.
hinge /hɪndʒ/ n. **1.** gozne m. —v. **2.** engoznar. **h. on,** depender de.
hint /hɪnt/ n. **1.** insinuación f.; indicio m. —v. **2.** insinuar.
hip /hɪp/ n. cadera f.
hippopotamus /ˌhɪpə'pɒtəməs/ n. hipopótamo m.
hire /haɪər/ v. alquilar.
his /hɪz; unstressed ɪz/ a. **1.** su. —pron. **2.** suyo, de él.
Hispanic /hɪ'spænɪk/ a. hispano.
hiss /hɪs/ v. silbar, sisear.
historian /hɪ'stɔriən/ n. historiador m.
historic /hɪ'stɔrɪk/ **historical** a. histórico.
history /'hɪstəri/ n. historia f.
histrionic /ˌhɪstri'ɒnɪk/ a. histriónico.
hit /hɪt/ n. **1.** golpe m.; Colloq. éxito m.; (Internet) hit m. —v. **2.** golpear.
hitch /hɪtʃ/ v. amarrar; enganchar.
hitchhike /'hɪtʃ,haɪk/ v. hacer autostop.

hitchhiker /'hɪtʃ,haikər/ n. autostopista f.

hitchhiking /'hɪtʃ,haikɪŋ/ n. autostop m.

hither /'hɪðər/ adv. acá, hacia acá.

hitherto /'hɪðər,tu/ adv. hasta ahora.

hive /haiv/ n. colmena f.

hives /haivz/ n. urticaria f.

hoard /hɔrd/ n. **1.** acumulación f. —v. **2.** acaparar; atesorar.

hoarse /hɔrs/ a. ronco.

hoax /houks/ n. **1.** engaño m. —v. **2.** engañar.

hobby /'hɒbi/ n. afición f., pasatiempo m.

hobgoblin /'hɒb,gɒblɪn/ n. trasgo m.

hobnob /'hɒb,nɒb/ v. tener intimidad.

hobo /'houbou/ n. vagabundo m.

hockey /'hɒki/ n. hockey m. **ice-h.**, hockey sobre hielo.

hod /hɒd/ n. esparavel m.

hodgepodge /'hɒdʒ,pɒdʒ/ n. baturrillo m.; mezcolanza f.

hoe /hou/ n. **1.** azada f. —v. **2.** cultivar con azada.

hog /hɒg/ n. cerdo, puerco m.

hoist /hɔist/ n. **1.** grúa f., elevador m. —v. **2.** elevar, enarbolar.

hold /hould/ n. **1.** presa f.; agarro m.; Naut. bodega f. **to get h. of,** conseguir, apoderarse de. —v. **2.** tener; detener; sujetar; celebrar.

holder /'houldər/ n. tenedor m. **cigarette h.**, boquilla f.

holdup /'hould,ʌp/ n. salteamiento m.

hole /houl/ n. agujero; hoyo; hueco m.

holiday /'hɒlɪ,dei/ n. día de fiesta.

holiness /'houlɪnɪs/ n. santidad f.

Holland /'hɒlənd/ n. Holanda f.

hollow /'hɒlou/ a. **1.** hueco. —n. **2.** cavidad f. —v. **3.** ahuecar; excavar.

holly /'hɒli/ n. acebo m.

hollyhock /'hɒli,hɒk/ n. malva real f.

holocaust /'hɒlə,kɔst/ n. holocausto m.

hologram /'hɒlə,græm/ n. holograma m.

holography /hə'lɒgrəfi/ n. holografía f.

holster /'houlstər/ n. pistolera f.

holy /'houli/ a. santo.

holy day disanto m.

Holy See Santa Sede f.

Holy Spirit Espíritu Santo m.

Holy Week Semana Santa f.

homage /'hɒmɪdʒ/ n. homenaje m.

home /houm/ n. casa, morada f; hogar m. **at h.**, en casa. **to go h.**, ir a casa.

home appliance electrodoméstica m.

home computer ordenador doméstico m., computadora doméstica f.

homeland /'houm,lænd/ n. patria f.

homely /'houmli/ a. feo; casero.

home rule n. autonomía f.

homesick /'houm,sɪk/ a. nostálgico.

homespun /'houm,spʌn/ a. casero; tocho.

homeward /'houmwərd/ adv. hacia casa.

homework /'houm,wɜrk/ n. deberes m.pl.

homicide /'hɒmə,said/ n. homicida m. & f.

homily /'hɒməli/ n. homilía f.

homogeneous /,houmə'dʒiniəs/ a. homogéneo.

homogenize /hə'mɒdʒə,naiz/ v. homogenezar.

homosexual /,houmə'sɛkʃuəl/ n. & a. homosexual m.

Honduras /hɒn'durəs/ n. Honduras f.

hone /houn/ n. **1.** piedra de afilar f. —v. **2.** afilar.

honest /'ɒnɪst/ a. honrado, honesto; sincero.

honestly /'ɒnɪstli/ adv. honradamente; de veras.

honesty /'ɒnəsti/ n. honradez, honestidad f.

honey /'hʌni/ n. miel f.

honeybee /'hʌni,bi/ n. abeja obrera f.

honeymoon /'hʌni,mun/ n. luna de miel.

honeysuckle /'hʌni,sʌkəl/ n. madreselva f.

honor /'ɒnər/ n. **1.** honra f.; honor m. —v. **2.** honrar.

honorable /'ɒnərəbəl/ a. honorable; ilustre.

honorary /'ɒnə,rɛri/ a. honorario.

hood /hʊd/ n. capota; capucha f.; Auto. cubierta del motor.

hoodlum /'hudləm/ n. pillo m., rufián m.

hoodwink /'hud,wɪŋk/ v. engañar.

hoof /hʊf/ n. pezuña f.
hook /hʊk/ n. **1.** gancho m. —v.
2. enganchar.
hooligan /'hulɪgən/ n. gamberro
-rra.
hoop /hup/ n. cerco m.
hop /hɒp/ n. **1.** salto m. —v. **2.**
saltar.
hope /houp/ n. **1.** esperanza f.
—v. **2.** esperar.
hopeful /'houpfəl/ a. lleno de es-
peranzas.
hopeless /'houplɪs/ a. desesperado; sin remedio.
horde /hɔrd/ n. horda f.
horehound /'hɔr,haund/ n. marru-
bio m.
horizon /hə'raizən/ n. horizonte
m.
horizontal /,hɔrə'zɒntl̩/ a. horizontal.
hormone /'hɔrmoun/ n. hormón
m.
horn /hɔrn/ n. cuerno m.; (music)
trompa f.; Auto. bocina f.
hornet /'hɔrnɪt/ n. avispón m.
horny /'hɔrni/ a. córneo; calloso.
horoscope /'hɔrə,skoup/ n. horóscopo m.
horrendous /hə'rɛndəs/ a. horrendo.
horrible /'hɔrəbəl/ a. horrible.
horrid /'hɔrɪd/ a. horrible.
horrify /'hɔrə,fai/ v. horrorizar.
horror /'hɔrər/ n. horror m.
horror film película de terror f.
hors d'oeuvre /ɔr 'dɜrv/ n. entremés m.
horse /hɔrs/ n. caballo m. **to ride
a h.,** cabalgar.
horseback /'hɔrs,bæk/ n. **on h.,** a
caballo. **to ride h.,** montar a caballo.
horseback riding equitación f.
horsefly /'hɔrs,flai/ n. tábano m.
horsehair /'hɔrs,hɛər/ n. pelo de
caballo m.; tela de crin f.
horseman /'hɔrsmən/ n. jinete m.
horsemanship /'hɔrsmən,ʃɪp/ n.
manejo m., equitación f.
horsepower /'hɔrs,pauər/ n. caballo de fuerza m.
horse race carrera de caballos f.
horseradish /'hɔrs,rædɪʃ/ n. rábano picante m.
horseshoe /'hɔrs,ʃu/ n. herradura
f.
hortatory /'hɔrtə,tɔri/ a. exhorta-
torio.

horticulture /'hɔrtɪ,kʌltʃər/ n.
horticultura f.
hose /houz/ n. medias f.pl; (garden) manguera f.
hosiery /'houʒəri/ n. calcetería f.
hospitable /'hɒspɪtəbəl/ a.
hospitalario.
hospital /'hɒspɪtl̩/ n. hospital m.
hospitality /,hɒspɪ'tælɪti/ n.
hospitalidad f.
hospitalization /,hɒspɪtl̩ɪ'zeiʃən/
n. hospitalización f.
hospitalize /'hɒspɪtl̩,aiz/ v. hospi-
talizar.
host /houst/ n. anfitrión m.,
dueño de la casa; Relig. hostia f.
hostage /'hɒstɪdʒ/ n. rehén m.
hostel /'hɒstl̩/ n. hostería f.
hostelry /'hɒstl̩ri/ n. fonda f., pa-
rador m.
hostess /'houstɪs/ n. anfitriona f.,
dueña de la casa.
hostile /'hɒstl̩/ a. hostil.
hostility /hɒ'stɪlɪti/ n. hostilidad f.
hot /hɒt/ a. caliente; (sauce) picante. **to be h.,** tener calor;
(weather) hacer calor.
hotbed /'hɒt,bɛd/ n. estercolero
m. Fig. foco m.
hot dog perrito caliente m.
hotel /hou'tɛl/ n. hotel m.
hotelier /,outəl'yei, ,houtl̩'ɪər/ n.
hotelero -ra.
hot-headed /'hɒt 'hɛdɪd/ a. turbulento, alborotadizo.
hothouse /'hɒt,haus/ n. invernáculo m.
hot-water bottle /'hɒt 'wɔtər/
bolsa de agua caliente f.
hound /haund/ n. **1.** sabueso m.
—v. **2.** perseguir; seguir la pista.
hour /auᵊr/ n. hora f.
hourglass /'auᵊr,glæs/ n. reloj de
arena m.
hourly /'auᵊrli/ a. **1.** por horas.
—adv. **2.** a cada hora.
house /n haus; v hauz/ n. **1.** casa
f.; Theat. público m. —v. **2.** alojar, albergar.
housefly /'haus,flai/ n. mosca
ordinaria f.
household /'haus,hould/ n.
familia; casa f.
housekeeper /'haus,kipər/ n. ama
de llaves.
housemaid /'haus,meid/ n. criada
f., sirvienta f.
housewife /'haus,waif/ n. ama de
casa.

housework /'haus,wɜrk/ *n.* tareas domésticas.

hovel /'hʌvəl/ *n.* choza *f.*

hover /'hʌvər/ *v.* revolotear.

hovercraft /'hʌvər,kræft/ *n.* aerodeslizador *m.*

how /hau/ *adv.* cómo. **h. much,** cuánto. **h. many,** cuántos. **h. far,** a qué distancia.

however /hau'ɛvər/ *adv.* como quiera; sin embargo.

howl /haul/ *n.* **1.** aullido *m.* —*v.* **2.** aullar.

HTML *abbr.* (HyperText Markup Language) Lenguaje de Marcado de Hipertexto *m.*

hub /hʌb/ *n.* centro *m.*; eje *m.* **h. of a wheel,** cubo de la rueda *m.*

hubbub /'hʌbʌb/ *n.* alboroto *m.*, bulla *f.*

hue /hyu/ *n.* matiz; color *m.*

hug /hʌg/ *n.* **1.** abrazo *m.* —*v.* **2.** abrazar.

huge /hyudʒ/ *a.* enorme.

hulk /hʌlk/ *n.* casco de buque *m.*

hull /hʌl/ *n.* **1.** cáscara *f.*; (naval) casco *m.* —*v.* **2.** decascarar.

hum /hʌm/ *n.* **1.** zumbido *m.* —*v.* **2.** tararear; zumbar.

human /'hyumən/ *a.* & *n.* humano -na.

human being ser humano *m.*

humane /hyu'mein/ *a.* humano, humanitario.

humanism /'hyumə,nɪzəm/ *n.* humanidad *f.*; benevolencia *f.*

humanitarian /hyu,mænɪ'tɛəriən/ *a.* humanitario.

humanity /hyu'mænɪti/ *n.* humanidad *f.*

humanly /'hyumənli/ *a.* humanamente.

humble /'hʌmbəl/ *a.* humilde.

humbug /'hʌm,bʌg/ *n.* farsa *f.*, embaucador *m.*

humdrum /'hʌm,drʌm/ *a.* monótono.

humid /'hyumɪd/ *a.* húmedo.

humidity /hyu'mɪdɪti/ *n.* humedad *f.*

humiliate /hyu'mɪli,eit/ *v.* humillar.

humiliation /hyu,mɪli'eiʃən/ *n.* mortificación *f.*; bochorno *m.*

humility /hyu'mɪlɪti/ *n.* humildad *f.*

humor /'hyumər/ *n.* **1.** humor; capricho *m.* —*v.* **2.** complacer.

humorist /'hyumərɪst/ *n.* humorista *m.*

humorous /'hyumərəs/ *a.* divertido.

hump /hʌmp/ *n.* joroba *f.*

humpback /'hʌmp,bæk/ *n.* jorobado *m.*

humus /'hyuməs/ *n.* humus *m.*

hunch /hʌntʃ/ *n.* giba *f.*; (idea) corazonada *f.*

hunchback /'hʌntʃ,bæk/ *n.* jorobado *m.*

hundred /'hʌndrɪd/ *a.* & *pron.* **1.** cien, ciento. **200,** doscientos. **300,** trescientos. **400,** cuatrocientos. **500,** quinientos. **600,** seiscientos. **700,** setecientos. **800,** ochocientos. **900,** novecientos. —*n.* **2.** centenar *m.*

hundredth /'hʌndrɪdθ/ *n.* & *a.* centésimo *m.*

Hungarian /hʌŋ'gɛəriən/ *a.* & *n.* húngaro -ra.

Hungary /'hʌŋgəri/ Hungría *f.*

hunger /'hʌŋgər/ *n.* hambre *f.*

hunger strike huelga de hambre *f.*

hungry /'hʌŋgri/ *a.* hambriento. **to be h.,** tener hambre.

hunt /hʌnt/ *n.* **1.** caza *f.* —*v.* **2.** cazar. **h. up,** buscar.

hunter /'hʌntər/ *n.* cazador *m.*

hunting /'hʌntɪŋ/ *n.* caza *f.* **to go h.,** ir de caza.

hurdle /'hɜrdl/ *n.* zarzo *m.*, valla *f.*; dificultad *f.*

hurl /hɜrl/ *v.* arrojar.

hurricane /'hɜrɪ,kein/ *n.* huracán *m.*

hurry /'hɜri/ *n.* **1.** prisa *f.* **to be in a h.,** tener prisa. —*v.* **2.** apresurar; darse prisa.

hurt /hɜrt/ *n.* **1.** daño, perjuicio *m.* —*v.* **2.** dañar; lastimar; doler; ofender.

hurtful /'hɜrtfəl/ *a.* perjudicial, dañino.

hurtle /'hɜrtl/ *v.* lanzar.

husband /'hʌzbənd/ *n.* marido, esposo *m.*

husk /hʌsk/ *n.* **1.** cáscara *f.* —*v.* **2.** descascarar.

husky /'hʌski/ *a.* fornido.

hustle /'hʌsəl/ *v.* empujar.

hustle and bustle ajetreo *m.*

hut /hʌt/ *n.* choza *f.*

hyacinth /'haiəsɪnθ/ *n.* jacinto *m.*

hybrid /'haibrɪd/ *a.* híbrido.

hydrangea /hai'dreindʒə/ *n.* hortensia *f.*

hydraulic /hai'drɔlɪk/ *a.* hidráulico.

hydroelectric

00

hydroelectric /,haidrouɪ'lɛktrɪk/ *a.*
hidroeléctrico.
hydrogen /'haidrədʒən/ *n.* hidrógeno *m.*
hydrophobia /,haidrə'foubiə/ *n.*
hidrofobia. *f.*
hydroplane /'haidrə,plein/ *n.* hidroavión *m.*
hydrotherapy /,haidrə'θɛrəpi/ *n.*
hidroterapia *f.*
hyena /hai'inə/ *n.* hiena *f.*
hygiene /'haidʒin/ *n.* higiene *f.*
hygienic /,haidʒi'ɛnɪk/ *a.* higiénico.
hymn /hɪm/ *n.* himno *m.*
hymnal /'hɪmnl/ *n.* himnario *m.*
hype /haip/ *n. Colloq.* **1.** bomba
publicitario *f.* —*v.* **2.** promocionar
a bombo y platillo.
hypercritical /,haipər'krɪtɪkəl/ *a.*
hipercrítico.
hyperlink /'haipər,lɪŋk/ *n.* (Internet) hiperenlace *m.*
hypermarket /'haipər,mɑrkɪt/ *n.*
hipermercado *m.*
hypertension /,haipər'tɛnʃən/ *n.*
hipertensión *f.*
hypertext /'haipər,tɛkst/ *n.* (Internet) hipertexto *m.*
hyphen /'haifən/ *n.* guión *m.*
hyphenate /'haifə,neit/ *v.* separar
con guión.

hypnosis /hɪp'nousɪs/ *n.* hipnosis
f.
hypnotic /hɪp'nɒtɪk/ *a.* hipnótico.
hypnotism /'hɪpnə,tɪzəm/ *n.* hipnotismo *m.*
hypnotize /'hɪpnə,taiz/ *v.* hipnotizar.
hypochondria /,haipə'kɒndriə/ *n.*
hipocondría *f.*
hypochondriac /,haipə'kɒndri,æk/
n. & a. hipocondríaco *m.*
hypocrisy /hɪ'pɒkrəsi/ *n.* hipocresía *f.*
hypocrite /'hɪpəkrɪt/ *n.* hipócrita
m. & f.
hypocritical /,hɪpə'krɪtɪkəl/ *a.*
hipócrita.
hypodermic /,haipə'dɜrmɪk/ *a.* hi-
podérmico.
hypotenuse /hai'pɒtṇ,us/ *n.* hipo-
tenusa *f.*
hypothesis /hai'pɒθəsɪs/ *n.* hipótesis *f.*
hypothetical /,haipə'θɛtɪkəl/ *a.*
hipotético.
hysterectomy /,hɪstə'rɛktəmi/ *n.*
histerectomía *f.*
hysteria /hɪ'stɛriə/ **hysterics** *n.*
histeria *f.*
hysterical /hɪ'stɛrɪkəl/ *a.*
histérico.

I

I /ai/ *pron.* yo.
iambic /ai'æmbɪk/ *a.* yámbico.
ice /ais/ *n.* hielo *m.*
iceberg /'aisbɜrg/ *n.* iceberg *m.*
icebox /'ais,bɒks/ *n.* refrigerador
m.
ice cream helado, mantecado *m.*;
i.-c. cone, barquillo de helado;
i.-c. parlor heladería *f.*
ice cube cubito de hielo *m.*
ice skate patín de cuchilla *m.*
icon /'aikɒn/ *n.* ícon *m.*
icy /'aisi/ *a.* helado; indiferente.
idea /ai'diə/ *n.* idea *f.*
ideal /ai'diəl/ *a.* ideal.
idealism /ai'diə,lɪzəm/ *n.*
idealismo *m.*
idealist /ai'diəlɪst/ *n.* idealista *m.*
& *f.*
idealistic /ai,diə'lɪstɪk/ *a.* idealista.
idealize /ai'diə,laiz/ *v.* idealizar.
ideally /ai'diəli/ *adv.* idealmente.
identical /ai'dɛntɪkəl/ *a.* idéntico.

identifiable /ai,dɛntɪ'faiəbəl/ *a.*
identificable.
identification /ai,dɛntəfɪ'keiʃən/
n. identificación *f.* **i. papers,** cédula de identidad *f.*
identify /ai'dɛntə,fai/ *v.* identificar.
identity /ai'dɛntɪti/ *n.* identidad *f.*
ideology /,aidi'ɒlədʒi/ *n.* ideología
f.
idiocy /'ɪdiəsi/ *n.* idiotez *f.*
idiom /'ɪdiəm/ *n.* modismo *m.*;
idioma *m.*
idiot /'ɪdiət/ *n.* idiota *m. & f.*
idiotic /,ɪdi'ɒtɪk/ *a.* idiota, tonto.
idle /'aidl/ *a.* desocupado; perezoso.
idleness /'aidlnɪs/ *n.* ociosidad,
pereza *f.*
idol /'aidl/ *n.* ídolo *m.*
idolatry /ai'dɒlətri/ *n.* idolatría *f.*
idolize /'aidl,aiz/ *v.* idolatrar.
idyl /'aidl/ *n.* idilio *m.*
idyllic /ai'dɪlɪk/ *a.* idílico.

if /ɪf/ *conj.* si. **even if,** aunque.
ignite /ɪg'naɪt/ *v.* encender.
ignition /ɪg'nɪʃən/ *n.* ignición *f.*
ignoble /ɪg'noubəl/ *a.* innoble, indigno.
ignominious /ˌɪgnə'mɪniəs/ *a.* ignominioso.
ignoramus /ˌɪgnə'reɪməs/ *n.* ignorante *m.*
ignorance /'ɪgnərəns/ *n.* ignorancia *f.*
ignorant /'ɪgnərənt/ *a.* ignorante. **to be i. of,** ignorar.
ignore /ɪg'nɔr/ *v.* desconocer, pasar por alto.
ill /ɪl/ *a.* enfermo, malo.
illegal /ɪ'ligəl/ *a.* ilegal.
illegible /ɪ'lɛdʒəbəl/ *a.* ilegible.
illegibly /ɪ'lɛdʒəbli/ *a.* ilegiblemente.
illegitimacy /ˌɪlɪ'dʒɪtəməsi/ *n.* ilegitimidad *f.*
illegitimate /ˌɪlɪ'dʒɪtəmɪt/ *a.* ilegítimo; desautorizado.
illicit /ɪ'lɪsɪt/ *a.* ilícito.
illiteracy /ɪ'lɪtərəsi/ *n.* analfabetismo *m.*
illiterate /ɪ'lɪtərɪt/ *a. & n.* analfabeto -ta.
illness /'ɪlnɪs/ *n.* enfermedad, maldad *f.*
illogical /ɪ'lɒdʒɪkəl/ *a.* ilógico.
illuminate /ɪ'lumə,neɪt/ *v.* iluminar.
illumination /ɪ,lumə'neɪʃən/ *n.* iluminación *f.*
illusion /ɪ'luʒən/ *n.* ilusión *f.*; ensueño *m.*
illusive /ɪ'lusɪv/ *a.* ilusivo.
illustrate /'ɪlə,streɪt/ *v.* ilustrar; ejemplificar.
illustration /ˌɪlə'streɪʃən/ *n.* ilustración *f.*; ejemplo; grabado *m.*
illustrative /ɪ'lʌstrətɪv/ *a.* ilustrativo.
illustrious /ɪ'lʌstriəs/ *a.* ilustre.
ill will *n.* malevolencia *f.*
image /'ɪmɪdʒ/ *n.* imagen, estatua *f.*
imagery /'ɪmɪdʒri/ *n.* imaginación *f.*
imaginable /ɪ'mædʒənəbəl/ *a.* imaginable.
imaginary /ɪ'mædʒə,nɛri/ *a.* imaginario.
imagination /ɪ,mædʒə'neɪʃən/ *n.* imaginación *f.*
imaginative /ɪ'mædʒənətɪv/ *a.* imaginativo.

imagine /ɪ'mædʒɪn/ *v.* imaginarse, figurarse.
imam /ɪ'mɑm/ *n.* imán *m.*
imbecile /'ɪmbəsɪl/ *n. & a.* imbécil *m.*
imitate /'ɪmɪ,teɪt/ *v.* imitar.
imitation /ˌɪmɪ'teɪʃən/ *n.* imitación *f.*
imitative /'ɪmɪ,teɪtɪv/ *a.* imitativo.
immaculate /ɪ'mækyəlɪt/ *a.* inmaculado.
immanent /'ɪmənənt/ *a.* inmanente.
immaterial /ˌɪmə'tɪəriəl/ *a.* inmaterial; sin importancia.
immature /'ɪmə'tʃʊr/ *a.* inmaturo.
immediate /ɪ'midiɪt/ *a.* inmediato.
immediately /ɪ'midiɪtli/ *adv.* inmediatamente.
immense /ɪ'mɛns/ *a.* inmenso.
immerse /ɪ'mɜrs/ *v.* sumergir.
immigrant /'ɪmɪgrənt/ *n. & a.* inmigrante *m. & f.*
immigrate /'ɪmɪ,greɪt/ *v.* inmigrar.
imminent /'ɪmənənt/ *a.* inminente.
immobile /ɪ'moubəl/ *a.* inmóvil.
immoderate /ɪ'mɒdərɪt/ *a.* inmoderado.
immodest /ɪ'mɒdɪst/ *a.* inmodesto; atrevido.
immoral /ɪ'mɔrəl/ *a.* inmoral.
immorality /ˌɪmə'rælɪti/ *n.* inmoralidad *f.*
immorally /ɪ'mɔrəli/ *adv.* licenciosamente.
immortal /ɪ'mɔrtl/ *a.* inmortal.
immortality /ˌɪmɔr'tælɪti/ *n.* inmortalidad *f.*
immortalize /ɪ'mɔrtl,aɪz/ *v.* inmortalizar.
immune /ɪ'myun/ *a.* inmune.
immunity /ɪ'myunɪti/ *n.* inmunidad *f.*
immunize /'ɪmyə,naɪz/ *v.* inmunizar.
impact /'ɪmpækt/ *n.* impacto *m.*
impair /ɪm'pɛər/ *v.* empeorar, perjudicar.
impale /ɪm'peɪl/ *v.* empalar.
impart /ɪm'pɑrt/ *v.* impartir, comunicar.
impartial /ɪm'pɑrʃəl/ *a.* imparcial.
impatience /ɪm'peɪʃəns/ *n.* impaciencia *f.*
impatient /ɪm'peɪʃənt/ *a.* impaciente.
impede /ɪm'pid/ *v.* impedir, estorbar.

impediment /ɪm'pɛdəmənt/ n. impedimento m.

impel /ɪm'pɛl/ v. impeler.

impenetrable /ɪm'pɛnɪtrəbəl/ a. impenetrable.

impenitent /ɪm'pɛnɪtənt/ n. & a. impenitente m.

imperative /ɪm'pɛrətɪv/ a. imperativo.

imperceptible /ˌɪmpər'sɛptəbəl/ a. imperceptible.

imperfect /ɪm'pɜrfɪkt/ a. imperfecto.

imperfection /ˌɪmpər'fɛkʃən/ n. imperfección f.

imperial /ɪm'pɪəriəl/ a. imperial.

imperialism /ɪm'pɪəriəˌlɪzəm/ n. imperialismo m.

imperious /ɪm'pɪəriəs/ a. imperioso.

impersonal /ɪm'pɜrsənḷ/ a. impersonal.

impersonate /ɪm'pɜrsəˌneit/ v. personificar; imitar.

impersonation /ɪmˌpɜrsə'neiʃən/ n. personificación f.; imitación f.

impertinence /ɪm'pɜrtṇəns/ n. impertinencia f.

impervious /ɪm'pɜrviəs/ a. impermeable.

impetuous /ɪm'pɛtʃuəs/ a. impetuoso.

impetus /'ɪmpɪtəs/ n. ímpetu m., impulso m.

impinge /ɪm'pɪndʒ/ v. tropezar; infringir.

implacable /ɪm'plækəbəl/ a. implacable.

implant /ɪm'plænt/ v. implantar; inculcar.

implement /'ɪmpləmənt/ n. herramienta f.

implicate /'ɪmplɪˌkeit/ v. implicar; embrollar.

implication /ˌɪmplɪ'keiʃən/ n. inferencia f.; complicidad f.

implicit /ɪm'plɪsɪt/ a. implícito.

implied /ɪm'plaid/ a. implícito.

implore /ɪm'plor/ v. implorar.

imply /ɪm'plai/ v. significar; dar a entender.

impolite /ˌɪmpə'lait/ a. descortés.

import /n 'ɪmpɔrt; v ɪm'pɔrt/ n. 1. importación f. —v. 2. importar.

importance /ɪm'pɔrtns/ n. importancia f.

important /ɪm'pɔrtṇt/ a. importante.

importation /ˌɪmpɔr'teiʃən/ n. importación f.

importune /ˌɪmpɔr'tun/ v. importunar.

impose /ɪm'pouz/ v. imponer.

imposition /ˌɪmpə'zɪʃən/ n. imposición f.

impossibility /ɪmˌpɒsə'bɪlɪti/ n. imposibilidad f.

impossible /ɪm'pɒsəbəl/ a. imposible.

impotence /'ɪmpətəns/ n. impotencia f.

impotent /'ɪmpətənt/ a. impotente.

impregnable /ɪm'prɛgnəbəl/ a. impregnable.

impregnate /ɪm'prɛgneit/ v. impregnar; fecundizar.

impresario /ˌɪmprə'sɑriˌou/ n. empresario m.

impress /ɪm'prɛs/ v. impresionar.

impression /ɪm'prɛʃən/ n. impresión f.

impressive /ɪm'prɛsɪv/ a. imponente.

imprison /ɪm'prɪzən/ v. encarcelar.

imprisonment /ɪm'prɪzənmənt/ n. prisión, encarcelación f.

improbable /ɪm'prɒbəbəl/ a. improbable.

impromptu /ɪm'prɒmptu/ a. extemporáneo.

improper /ɪm'prɒpər/ a. impropio.

improve /ɪm'pruv/ v. mejorar; progresar.

improvement /ɪm'pruvmənt/ n. mejoramiento; progreso m.

improvise /'ɪmprəˌvaiz/ v. improvisar.

impudent /'ɪmpyədənt/ a. descarado.

impugn /ɪm'pyun/ v. impugnar.

impulse /'ɪmpʌls/ n. impulso m.

impulsive /ɪm'pʌlsɪv/ a. impulsivo.

impunity /ɪm'pyunɪti/ n. impunidad f.

impure /ɪm'pyʊr/ a. impuro.

impurity /ɪm'pyʊrɪti/ n. impureza f.; deshonestidad f.

impute /ɪm'pyut/ v. imputar.

in /ɪn/ prep. 1. en; dentro de. —adv. 2. adentro.

inadvertent /ˌɪnəd'vɜrtṇt/ a. inadvertido.

inalienable /ɪn'eilyənəbəl/ a. inalienable.

inane /ɪ'nein/ a. mentecato.

inaugural /ɪn'ɔgyərəl/ a. inaugural.

inaugurate /ɪn'ɔgyə,reit/ v. inaugurar.

inauguration /ɪn,ɔgyə'reiʃən/ n. inauguración f.

Inca /'ɪŋkə/ n. inca m.

incandescent /,ɪnkən'dɛsənt/ a. incandescente.

incantation /,ɪnkæn'teiʃən/ n. encantación f., conjuro m.

incapacitate /,ɪnkə'pæsɪ,teit/ v. incapacitar.

incarcerate /ɪn'karsə,reit/ v. encarcelar.

incarnate /ɪn'karnɪt/ a. encarnado; personificado.

incarnation /,ɪnkar'neiʃən/ n. encarnación f.

incendiary /ɪn'sɛndi,ɛri/ a. incendario.

incense /ɪn'sɛns/ n. **1.** incienso m. —v. **2.** indignar.

incentive /ɪn'sɛntɪv/ n. incentivo m.

inception /ɪn'sɛpʃən/ n. comienzo m.

incessant /ɪn'sɛsənt/ a. incesante.

incest /'ɪnsɛst/ n. incesto m.

inch /ɪntʃ/ n. pulgada f.

incidence /'ɪnsɪdəns/ n. incidencia f.

incident /'ɪnsɪdənt/ n. incidente m.

incidental /,ɪnsɪ'dɛntl̩/ a. incidental.

incidentally /,ɪnsɪ'dɛntl̩i/ adv. incidentalmente; entre paréntesis.

incinerate /ɪn'sɪnə,reit/ v. incinerar.

incinerator /ɪn'sɪnə,reitər/ n. incinerador m.

incipient /ɪn'sɪpiənt/ a. incipiente.

incision /ɪn'sɪʒən/ n. incisión f.; cortadura f.

incisive /ɪn'saisɪv/ a. incisivo; mordaz.

incisor /ɪn'saizər/ n. incisivo m.

incite /ɪn'sait/ v. incitar, instigar.

inclination /,ɪnklə'neiʃən/ n. inclinación f.; declive m.

incline /n 'ɪnklain; v ɪn'klain/ n. **1.** pendiente m. —v. **2.** inclinar.

inclose /ɪn'klouz/ v. incluir.

include /ɪn'klud/ v. incluir, englobar.

including /ɪn'kludɪŋ/ prep. incluso.

inclusive /ɪn'klusɪv/ a. inclusivo.

incognito /,ɪnkɒg'nitou/ n. & adv. incógnito m.

income /'ɪnkʌm/ n. renta f.; ingresos m.pl.

income tax impuesto sobre la renta m.

incomparable /ɪn'kɒmpərəbəl/ a. incomparable.

inconvenience /,ɪnkən'vinyəns/ n. **1.** incomodidad f. —v. **2.** incomodar.

inconvenient /,ɪnkən'vinyənt/ a. incómodo.

incorporate /ɪn'kɔrpə,reit/ v. incorporar; dar cuerpo.

incorrigible /ɪn'kɔrɪdʒəbəl/ a. incorregible.

increase /ɪn'kris/ v. crecer; aumentar.

incredible /ɪn'krɛdəbəl/ a. increíble.

incredulity /,ɪnkrɪ'dulɪti/ n. incredulidad f.

incredulous /ɪn'krɛdʒələs/ a. incrédulo.

increment /'ɪnkrəmənt/ n. incremento m., aumento m.

incriminate /ɪn'krɪmə,neit/ v. incriminar.

incrimination /ɪn,krɪmə'neiʃən/ n. incriminación f.

incrust /ɪn'krʌst/ v. incrustar.

incubator /'ɪnkyə,beitər/ n. incubadora f.

inculcate /ɪn'kʌlkeit/ v. inculcar.

incumbency /ɪn'kʌmbənsi/ n. incumbencia f.

incumbent /ɪn'kʌmbənt/ a. obligatorio; colocado sobre.

incur /ɪn'kɜr/ v. incurrir.

incurable /ɪn'kyʊrəbəl/ a. incurable.

indebted /ɪn'dɛtɪd/ a. obligado; adeudado.

indeed /ɪn'did/ adv. verdaderamente, de veras. **no i.,** de ninguna manera.

indefatigable /,ɪndɪ'fætɪgəbəl/ a. incansable.

indefinite /ɪn'dɛfənɪt/ a. indefinido.

indefinitely /ɪn'dɛfənɪtli/ adv. indefinidamente.

indelible /ɪn'dɛləbəl/ a. indeleble.

indemnify /ɪn'dɛmnə,fai/ v. indemnizar.

indemnity /ɪn'dɛmnɪti/ n. indemnificación f.

indent /ɪn'dɛnt/ n. **1.** diente f., mella f. —v. **2.** indentar, mellar.

indentation /,ɪndɛn'teiʃən/ n. indentación f.

independence /ˌɪndɪˈpɛndəns/ n. independencia f.

independent /ˌɪndɪˈpɛndənt/ a. independiente.

in-depth /ˈɪn ˈdɛpθ/ adj. en profundidad.

index /ˈɪndɛks/ n. índice m.; (of book) tabla f.

index card ficha f.

index finger dedo índice m.

India /ˈɪndiə/ n. India f.

Indian /ˈɪndiən/ a. & n. indio -dia.

indicate /ˈɪndɪˌkeɪt/ v. indicar.

indication /ˌɪndɪˈkeɪʃən/ n. indicación f.

indicative /ɪnˈdɪkətɪv/ a. & n. indicativo m.

indict /ɪnˈdaɪt/ v. encausar.

indictment /ɪnˈdaɪtmənt/ n. (law) sumaria; denuncia f.

indifference /ɪnˈdɪfərəns/ n. indiferencia f.

indifferent /ɪnˈdɪfərənt/ a. indiferente.

indigenous /ɪnˈdɪdʒənəs/ a. indígena.

indigent /ˈɪndɪdʒənt/ a. indigente, pobre.

indigestion /ˌɪndɪˈdʒɛstʃən/ n. indigestión f.

indignant /ɪnˈdɪgnənt/ a. indignado.

indignation /ˌɪndɪgˈneɪʃən/ n. indignación f.

indignity /ɪnˈdɪgnɪti/ n. indignidad f.

indirect /ˌɪndəˈrɛkt/ a. indirecto.

indiscreet /ˌɪndɪˈskrit/ a. indiscreto.

indiscretion /ˌɪndɪˈskrɛʃən/ n. indiscreción f.

indiscriminate /ˌɪndɪˈskrɪmənɪt/ a. promiscuo.

indispensable /ˌɪndɪˈspɛnsəbəl/ a. indispensable.

indisposed /ˌɪndɪˈspouzd/ a. indispuesto.

individual /ˌɪndəˈvɪdʒuəl/ a. & n. individuo m.

individuality /ˌɪndə,vɪdʒuˈælɪti/ n. individualidad f.

individually /ˌɪndəˈvɪdʒuəli/ adv. individualmente.

indivisible /ˌɪndəˈvɪzəbəl/ a. indivisible.

indoctrinate /ɪnˈdɒktrəˌneɪt/ v. doctrinar, enseñar.

indolent /ˈɪndlənt/ a. indolente.

indoor /ˈɪn,dɔr/ a. 1. interior. **in-**

doors —adv. 2. en casa; bajo techo.

indorse /ɪnˈdɔrs/ v. endosar.

induce /ɪnˈdus/ v. inducir, persuadir.

induct /ɪnˈdʌkt/ v. instalar, iniciar.

induction /ɪnˈdʌkʃən/ n. introducción f.; instalación f.

inductive /ɪnˈdʌktɪv/ a. inductivo; introductor.

indulge /ɪnˈdʌldʒ/ v. favorecer. **i. in,** entregarse a.

indulgence /ɪnˈdʌldʒəns/ n. indulgencia f.

indulgent /ɪnˈdʌldʒənt/ a. indulgente.

industrial /ɪnˈdʌstriəl/ a. industrial.

industrialist /ɪnˈdʌstriəlɪst/ n. industrial m.

industrial park polígono industrial m.

industrious /ɪnˈdʌstriəs/ a. industrioso, trabajador.

industry /ˈɪndəstri/ n. industria f.

inedible /ɪnˈɛdəbəl/ a. incomible.

ineligible /ɪnˈɛlɪdʒəbəl/ a. inelegible.

inept /ɪnˈɛpt/ a. inepto.

inert /ɪnˈɜrt/ a. inerte.

inertia /ɪnˈɜrʃə/ n. inercia f.

inevitable /ɪnˈɛvɪtəbəl/ a. inevitable.

inexpensive /ˌɪnɪkˈspɛnsɪv/ a. económico.

inexplicable /ɪnˈɛksplɪkəbəl/ a. inexplicable.

infallible /ɪnˈfæləbəl/ a. infalible.

infamous /ˈɪnfəməs/ a. infame.

infamy /ˈɪnfəmi/ n. infamia f.

infancy /ˈɪnfənsi/ n. infancia f.

infant /ˈɪnfənt/ n. nene m.; criatura f.

infantile /ˈɪnfənˌtaɪl/ a. infantil.

infantry /ˈɪnfəntri/ n. infantería f.

infatuated /ɪnˈfætʃuˌeɪtɪd/ a. infatuado.

infatuation /ɪn,fætʃuˈeɪʃən/ a. encaprichamiento m.

infect /ɪnˈfɛkt/ v. infectar.

infection /ɪnˈfɛkʃən/ n. infección f.

infectious /ɪnˈfɛkʃəs/ a. infeccioso.

infer /ɪnˈfɜr/ v. inferir.

inference /ˈɪnfərəns/ n. inferencia f.

inferior /ɪnˈfɪəriər/ a. inferior.

infernal /ɪnˈfɜrnl/ a. infernal.

inferno /ɪnˈfɜrnou/ n. infierno m.

infest /ɪn'fɛst/ *v.* infestar.

infidel /'ɪnfɪdl/ *n.* **1.** infiel *m.* & *f.*; pagano -na. —*a.* **2.** infiel.

infidelity /ˌɪnfɪ'dɛlɪti/ *n.* infidelidad *f.*

infiltrate /ɪn'fɪltreit/ *v.* infiltrar.

infinite /'ɪnfənɪt/ *a.* infinito.

infinitesimal /ˌɪnfɪnɪ'tɛsəməl/ *a.* infinitesimal.

infinitive /ɪn'fɪnɪtɪv/ *n.* & *a.* infinitivo *m.*

infinity /ɪn'fɪnɪti/ *n.* infinidad *f.*

infirm /ɪn'fɜrm/ *a.* enfermizo.

infirmary /ɪn'fɜrməri/ *n.* hospital *m.*, enfermería *f.*

infirmity /ɪn'fɜrmɪti/ *n.* enfermedad *f.*

inflame /ɪn'fleim/ *v.* inflamar.

inflammable /ɪn'flæməbəl/ *a.* inflamable.

inflammation /ˌɪnflə'meiʃən/ *n.* inflamación *f.*

inflammatory /ɪn'flæməˌtɔri/ *a.* inflamante; *Med.* inflamatorio.

inflate /ɪn'fleit/ *v.* inflar.

inflation /ɪn'fleiʃən/ *n.* inflación *f.*

inflection /ɪn'flɛkʃən/ *n.* inflexión *f.*; (of the voice) modulación de la voz *f.*

inflict /ɪn'flɪkt/ *v.* infligir.

infliction /ɪn'flɪkʃən/ *n.* imposición *f.*

influence /'ɪnfluəns/ *n.* **1.** influencia *f.* —*v.* **2.** influir en.

influential /ˌɪnflu'ɛnʃəl/ *a.* influyente.

influenza /ˌɪnflu'ɛnzə/ *n.* gripe *f.*

influx /'ɪnˌflʌks/ *n.* afluencia *f.*

inform /ɪn'fɔrm/ *v.* informar. **i. oneself,** enterarse.

informal /ɪn'fɔrməl/ *a.* informal.

information /ˌɪnfər'meiʃən/ *n.* informaciones *f.pl.*

information technology *n.* informática *f.*

infrastructure /'ɪnfrəˌstrʌktʃər/ *n.* infraestructura *f.*

infringe /ɪn'frɪndʒ/ *v.* infringir.

infuriate /ɪn'fyuriˌeit/ *v.* enfurecer.

ingenious /ɪn'dʒinyəs/ *a.* ingenioso.

ingenuity /ˌɪndʒə'nuɪti/ *n.* ingeniosidad; destreza *f.*

ingredient /ɪn'gridiənt/ *n.* ingrediente *m.*

inhabit /ɪn'hæbɪt/ *v.* habitar.

inhabitant /ɪn'hæbɪtənt/ *n.* habitante *m.* & *f.*

inhale /ɪn'heil/ *v.* inhalar.

inherent /ɪn'hɪərənt/ *a.* inherente.

inherit /ɪn'hɛrɪt/ *v.* heredar.

inheritance /ɪn'hɛrɪtəns/ *n.* herencia *f.*

inhibit /ɪn'hɪbɪt/ *v.* inhibir.

inhibition /ˌɪnɪ'bɪʃən/ *n.* inhibición *f.*

inhuman /ɪn'hyumən/ *a.* inhumano.

inimical /ɪ'nɪmɪkəl/ *a.* hostil.

inimitable /ɪ'nɪmɪtəbəl/ *a.* inimitable.

iniquity /ɪ'nɪkwɪti/ *n.* iniquidad *f.*

initial /ɪ'nɪʃəl/ *a.* & *n.* inicial *f.*

initiate /ɪ'nɪʃiˌeit/ *v.* iniciar.

initiation /ɪˌnɪʃi'eiʃən/ *n.* iniciación *f.*

initiative /ɪ'nɪʃiətɪv/ *n.* iniciativa *f.*

inject /ɪn'dʒɛkt/ *v.* inyectar.

injection /ɪn'dʒɛkʃən/ *n.* inyección *f.*

injunction /ɪn'dʒʌŋkʃən/ *n.* mandato *m.*; (law) embargo *m.*

injure /'ɪndʒər/ *v.* herir; lastimar; ofender.

injurious /ɪn'dʒuriəs/ *a.* perjudicial.

injury /'ɪndʒəri/ *n.* herida; afrenta *f.*; perjuicio *m.*

injustice /ɪn'dʒʌstɪs/ *n.* injusticia *f.*

ink /ɪŋk/ *n.* tinta *f.*

inland /'ɪnlænd/ *a.* **1.** interior. —*adv.* **2.** tierra adentro.

inlet /'ɪnlɛt/ *n.* entrada *f.*; ensenada *f.*; estuario *m.*

inmate /'ɪnˌmeit/ *n.* residente *m.* & *f.*; (of a prison) preso -sa.

inn /ɪn/ *n.* posada *f.*; mesón *m.*

inner /'ɪnər/ *a.* interior. **i. tube,** cámara de aire.

innocence /'ɪnəsəns/ *n.* inocencia *f.*

innocent /'ɪnəsənt/ *a.* inocente.

innocuous /ɪ'nɒkyuəs/ *a.* innocuo.

innovation /ˌɪnə'veiʃən/ *n.* innovación *f.*

innuendo /ˌɪnyu'ɛndou/ *n.* insinuación *f.*

innumerable /ɪ'numərəbəl/ *a.* innumerable.

inoculate /ɪ'nɒkyəˌleit/ *v.* inocular.

inoculation /ɪˌnɒkyə'leiʃən/ *n.* inoculación *f.*

input /'ɪnˌpʊt/ *n.* aducto *m.*, ingreso *m.*, entrada *f.*

inquest /'ɪnkwɛst/ *n.* indagación *f.*

inquire /ın'kwaiᵊr/ v. preguntar; inquirir.

inquiry /ın'kwaiᵊri/ n. pregunta; investigación f.

inquisition /ˌınkwə'zıʃən/ n. escudriñamiento m.; (church) Inquisición f.

insane /ın'sein/ a. loco. **to go i.**, perder la razón; volverse loco.

insanity /ın'sæniti/ n. locura f., demencia f.

inscribe /ın'skraib/ v. inscribir.

inscription /ın'skrıpʃən/ n. inscripción; dedicatoria f.

insect /'ınsɛkt/ n. insecto m.

insecticide /ın'sɛktə,said/ n. & a. insecticida m.

inseparable /ın'sɛpərəbəl/ a. inseparable.

insert /ın'sɜrt/ v. insertar, meter.

insertion /ın'sɜrʃən/ n. inserción f.

inside /ˌın'said/ a. & n. **1.** interior m. —adv. **2.** adentro, por dentro. **i. out**, al revés. —prep. **3.** dentro de.

insidious /ın'sıdiəs/ a. insidioso.

insight /'ın,sait/ n. perspicacia f.; comprensión f.

insignia /ın'sıgniə/ n. insignias f.pl.

insignificance /ˌınsıg'nıfıkəns/ n. insignificancia f.

insignificant /ˌınsıg'nıfıkənt/ a. insignificante.

insinuate /ın'sınyu,eit/ v. insinuar.

insinuation /ın,sınyu'eiʃən/ n. insinuación f.

insipid /ın'sıpıd/ a. insípido.

insist /ın'sıst/ v. insistir.

insistence /ın'sıstəns/ n. insistencia f.

insistent /ın'sıstənt/ a. insistente.

insolence /'ınsələns/ n. insolencia f.

insolent /'ınsələnt/ a. insolente.

insomnia /ın'sɒmniə/ n. insomnio m.

inspect /ın'spɛkt/ v. inspeccionar, examinar.

inspection /ın'spɛkʃən/ n. inspección f.

inspector /ın'spɛktər/ n. inspector -ora.

inspiration /ˌınspə'reiʃən/ n. inspiración f.

inspire /ın'spaiᵊr/ v. inspirar.

install /ın'stɔl/ v. instalar.

installation /ˌınstə'leiʃən/ n. instalación f.

installment /ın'stɔlmənt/ n. plazo m.

instance /'ınstəns/ n. ocasión f. **for i.**, por ejemplo.

instant /'ınstənt/ a. & n. instante m.

instantaneous /ˌınstən'teiniəs/ a. instantáneo.

instant coffee café soluble m.

instantly /'ınstəntli/ adv. al instante.

instead /ın'stɛd/ adv. en lugar de eso. **i. of**, en vez de, en lugar de.

instigate /'ınstı,geit/ v. instigar.

instill /ın'stıl/ v. instilar.

instinct /ın'stıŋkt/ n. instinto m. **by i.** por instinto.

instinctive /ın'stıŋktıv/ a. instintivo.

instinctively /ın'stıŋktıvli/ adv. por instinto.

institute /'ınstı,tut/ n. **1.** instituto m. —v. **2.** instituir.

institution /ˌınstı'tuʃən/ n. institución f.

instruct /ın'strʌkt/ v. instruir.

instruction /ın'strʌkʃən/ n. instrucción f.

instructive /ın'strʌktıv/ a. instructivo.

instructor /ın'strʌktər/ n. instructor -ora.

instrument /'ınstrəmənt/ n. instrumento m.

instrumental /ˌınstrə'mɛntl̩/ a. instrumental.

insufficient /ˌınsə'fıʃənt/ a. insuficiente.

insular /'ınsələr/ a. insular; estrecho de miras.

insulate /'ınsə,leit/ v. aislar.

insulation /ˌınsə'leiʃən/ n. aislamiento m.

insulator /'ınsə,leitər/ n. aislador m.

insulin /'ınsəlın/ n. insulina f.

insult /n. 'ınsʌlt; v. ın'sʌlt/ n. **1.** insulto m. —v. **2.** insultar.

insuperable /ın'supərəbəl/ a. insuperable.

insurance /ın'ʃurəns/ n. seguro m.

insure /ın'ʃur, -'ʃɜr/ v. asegurar.

insurgent /ın'sɜrdʒənt/ a. & n. insurgente m. & a.

insurrection /ˌınsə'rɛkʃən/ n. insurrección f.

intact /ın'tækt/ a. intacto.

intangible /ɪn'tændʒəbəl/ *a.* intangible, impalpable.

integral /'ɪntɪgrəl/ *a.* íntegro.

integrate /'ɪntɪ,greit/ *v.* integrar.

integrity /ɪn'tɛgrɪti/ *n.* integridad *f.*

intellect /'ɪntḷ,ɛkt/ *n.* intelecto *m.*

intellectual /,ɪntḷ'ɛktʃuəl/ *a.* & *n.* intelectual *m.* & *f.*

intelligence /ɪn'tɛlɪdʒəns/ *n.* inteligencia *f.*

intelligence quotient /'kwouʃənt/ coeficiente intelectual *m.*

intelligent /ɪn'tɛlɪdʒənt/ *a.* inteligente.

intelligible /ɪn'tɛlɪdʒəbəl/ *a.* inteligible.

intend /ɪn'tɛnd/ *v.* pensar; intentar; destinar.

intense /ɪn'tɛns/ *a.* intenso.

intensify /ɪn'tɛnsə,fai/ *v.* intensificar.

intensity /ɪn'tɛnsɪti/ *n.* intensidad *f.*

intensive /ɪn'tɛnsɪv/ *a.* intensivo.

intensive-care unit /ɪn'tɛnsɪv'kɛər/ unidad de cuidados intensivos, unidad de vigilancia intensiva *f.*

intent /ɪn'tɛnt/ *n.* intento *m.*

intention /ɪn'tɛnʃən/ *n.* intención *f.*

intentional /ɪn'tɛnʃənḷ/ *a.* intencional.

intercede /,ɪntər'sid/ *v.* interceder.

intercept /,ɪntər'sɛpt/ *v.* interceptar; detener.

interchange /,ɪntər'tʃɛndʒ/ *v.* intercambiar.

interchangeable /,ɪntər'tʃɛindʒəbəl/ *a.* intercambiable.

intercourse /'ɪntər,kɔrs/ *n.* tráfico *m.*; comunicación *f.*; coito *m.*

interest /'ɪntərɪst/ *n.* **1.** interés *m.* —*v.* **2.** interesar.

interesting /'ɪntərəstɪŋ/ *a.* interesante.

interest rate *n.* tipo de interés *m.*

interface /'ɪntər,feis/ *n.* interfaz.

interfere /,ɪntər'fɪər/ *v.* entrometerse, intervenir. **i. with,** estorbar.

interference /,ɪntər'fɪərəns/ *n.* intervención *f.*; obstáculo *m.*

interior /ɪn'tɪəriər/ *a.* interior.

interject /,ɪntər'dʒɛkt/ *v.* interponer; intervenir.

interjection /,ɪntər'dʒɛkʃən/ *n.* interjección *f.*; interposición *f.*

interlude /'ɪntər,lud/ *n.* intervalo *m.*; *Theat.* intermedio *m.*; (music) interludio *m.*

intermediary /,ɪntər'midi,ɛri/ *n.* intermediario -ria.

intermediate /,ɪntər'midi,eit/ *a.* intermedio.

interment /ɪn'tɜrmənt/ *n.* entierro.

intermission /,ɪntər'mɪʃən/ *n.* intermisión *f.*; *Theat.* entreacto *m.*

intermittent /,ɪntər'mɪtṇt/ *a.* intermitente.

intern /ɪn'tɜrn/ *n.* **1.** interno -na, internado -da. —*v.* **2.** internar.

internal /ɪn'tɜrnḷ/ *a.* interno.

international /,ɪntər'næʃənḷ/ *a.* internacional.

internationalism /,ɪntər'næʃənḷ,ɪzəm/ *n.* internacionalismo *m.*

Internet, the /'ɪntər,nɛt/ *n.* el Internet *m.*

interpose /,ɪntər'pouz/ *v.* interponer.

interpret /ɪn'tɜrprɪt/ *v.* interpretar.

interpretation /ɪn,tɜrprɪ'teiʃən/ *n.* interpretación *f.*

interpreter /ɪn'tɜrprɪtər/ *n.* intérprete *m.* & *f.*

interrogate /ɪn'tɛrə,geit/ *v.* interrogar.

interrogation /ɪn,tɛrə'geiʃən/ *n.* interrogación; pregunta *f.*

interrogative /,ɪntə'rɒgətɪv/ *a.* interrogativo.

interrupt /,ɪntə'rʌpt/ *v.* interrumpir.

interruption /,ɪntə'rʌpʃən/ *n.* interrupción *f.*

intersect /,ɪntər'sɛkt/ *v.* cortar.

intersection /,ɪntər'sɛkʃən/ *n.* intersección *f.*; (street) bocacalle *f.*

intersperse /,ɪntər'spɜrs/ *v.* entremezclar.

interval /'ɪntərvəl/ *n.* intervalo *m.*

intervene /,ɪntər'vin/ *v.* intervenir.

intervention /,ɪntər'vɛnʃən/ *n.* intervención *f.*

interview /'ɪntər,vyu/ *n.* **1.** entrevista *f.* —*v.* **2.** entrevistar.

interviewer /'ɪntər,vyuər/ *n.* entrevistador -ora *m.* & *f.*

intestine /ɪn'tɛstɪn/ *n.* intestino *m.*

intimacy /'ɪntəməsi/ *n.* intimidad; familiaridad *f.*

intimate /'ɪntəmɪt/ *a.* **1.** íntimo, familiar. —*n.* **2.** amigo -ga íntimo -ma. —*v.* **3.** insinuar.

intimidate /ɪn'tɪmɪ,deit/ *v.* intimidar.

intimidation /ɪn,tɪmɪ'deiʃən/ *n.* intimidación *f.*

into /'ɪntu; *unstressed* -tʊ, -tə/ *prep.* en, dentro de.

intonation /,ɪntou'neiʃən/ *n.* entonación *f.*

intone /ɪn'toun/ *v.* entonar.

intoxicate /ɪn'tɒksɪ,keit/ *v.* embriagar.

intoxication /ɪn,tɒksɪ'keiʃən/ *n.* embriaguez *f.*

intravenous /,ɪntrə'vinəs/ *a.* intravenoso.

intrepid /ɪn'trepɪd/ *a.* intrépido.

intricacy /'ɪntrɪkəsi/ *n.* complejidad *f.;* enredo *m.*

intricate /'ɪntrɪkɪt/ *a.* intrincado; complejo.

intrigue /ɪn'trig; *n. also* 'ɪntrig/ *n.* **1.** intriga *f.* —*v.* **2.** intrigar.

intrinsic /ɪn'trɪnsɪk/ *a.* intrínseco.

introduce /,ɪntrə'dus/ *v.* introducir; (a person) presentar.

introduction /,ɪntrə'dʌkʃən/ *n.* presentación; introducción *f.*

introductory /,ɪntrə'dʌktəri/ *a.* introductor; preliminar. **i. offer,** ofrecimiento de presentación *m.*

introvert /'ɪntrə,vɜrt/ *n. & a.* introvertido -da.

intrude /ɪn'trud/ *v.* entremeterse.

intruder /ɪn'trudər/ *n.* intruso -sa.

intuition /,ɪntu'ɪʃən/ *n.* intuición *f.*

intuitive /ɪn'tuɪtɪv/ *a.* intuitivo.

inundate /'ɪnən,deit/ *v.* inundar.

invade /ɪn'veid/ *v.* invadir.

invader /ɪn'veidər/ *n.* invasor -ra.

invalid /ɪn'vælɪd/ *a. & n.* inválido -da.

invariable /ɪn'veəriəbəl/ *a.* invariable.

invasion /ɪn'veiʒən/ *n.* invasión *f.*

invective /ɪn'vektɪv/ *n.* **1.** invectiva *f.* —*a.* **2.** ultrajante.

inveigle /ɪn'veigəl/ *v.* seducir.

invent /ɪn'vent/ *v.* inventar.

invention /ɪn'venʃən/ *n.* invención *f.*

inventive /ɪn'ventɪv/ *a.* inventivo.

inventor /ɪn'ventər/ *n.* inventor -ra.

inventory /'ɪnvən,tɔri/ *n.* inventario *m.*

invertebrate /ɪn'vɜrtəbrɪt/ *n. & a.* invertebrado *m.*

invest /ɪn'vest/ *v.* investir; Com. invertir.

investigate /ɪn'vestɪ,geit/ *v.* investigar.

investigation /ɪn,vestɪ'geiʃən/ *n.* investigación *f.*

investment /ɪn'vestmənt/ *n.* inversión *f.*

investor /ɪn'vestər/ *n.* inversor, -ra.

inveterate /ɪn'vetərɪt/ *a.* inveterado.

invidious /ɪn'vɪdiəs/ *a.* abominable, odioso, injusto.

invigorate /ɪn'vɪgə,reit/ *v.* vigorizar, fortificar.

invincible /ɪn'vɪnsəbəl/ *a.* invencible.

invisible /ɪn'vɪzəbəl/ *a.* invisible.

invitation /,ɪnvɪ'teiʃən/ *n.* invitación *f.*

invite /ɪn'vait/ *v.* invitar, convidar.

invocation /,ɪnvə'keiʃən/ *n.* invocación *f.*

invoice /'ɪnvɔis/ *n.* factura *f.*

invoke /ɪn'vouk/ *v.* invocar.

involuntary /ɪn'vɒlən,teri/ *a.* involuntario.

involve /ɪn'vɒlv/ *v.* envolver; implicar.

involved /ɪn'vɒlvd/ *a.* complicado.

invulnerable /ɪn'vʌlnərəbəl/ *a.* invulnerable.

inward /'ɪnwərd/ *adv.* hacia adentro.

inwardly /'ɪnwərdli/ *adv.* interiormente.

iodine /'aiə,dain/ *n.* iodo *m.*

IQ *abbr.* CI (coeficiente intelectual) *m.*

irate /ai'reit/ *a.* encolerizado.

Ireland /'aiᵊrlənd/ *n.* Irlanda *f.*

iris /'airɪs/ *n.* Anat. iris *m.;* (botany) flor de lis *f.*

Irish /'airɪʃ/ *a.* irlandés.

irk /ɜrk/ *v.* fastidiar.

iron /'aiərn/ *n.* **1.** hierro *m.;* (appliance) plancha *f.* —*v.* **2.** planchar.

ironical /ai'rɒnɪkəl/ *a.* irónico.

ironing board /'aiərnɪŋ/ tabla de planchar *f.*

irony /'airəni/ *n.* ironía *f.*

irrational /ɪ'ræʃənļ/ *a.* irracional; ilógico.

irregular /ɪ'regyələr/ *a.* irregular.

irregularity /ɪ,regyə'lærɪti/ *n.* irregularidad *f.*

irrelevant /ɪ'reləvənt/ *a.* ajeno.

irresistible /,ɪrɪ'zɪstəbəl/ *a.* irresistible.

irresponsible /ˌɪrɪ'spɒnsəbəl/ *a.* irresponsable.

irreverent /ɪ'rɛvərənt/ *a.* irreverente.

irrevocable /ɪ'rɛvəkəbəl/ *a.* irrevocable.

irrigate /'ɪrɪˌgeit/ *v.* regar; *Med.* irrigar.

irrigation /ˌɪrɪ'geifən/ *n.* riego *m.*

irritability /ˌɪrɪtə'bɪlɪti/ *n.* irritabilidad *f.*

irritable /'ɪrɪtəbəl/ *a.* irritable.

irritant /'ɪrɪtn̩t/ *n. & a.* irritante *m.*

irritate /'ɪrɪˌteit/ *v.* irritar.

irritation /ˌɪrɪ'teifən/ *n.* irritación *f.*

island /'ailənd/ *n.* isla *f.*

isolate /'aisəˌleit/ *v.* aislar.

isolation /ˌaisə'leifən/ *n.* aislamiento *m.*

isosceles /ai'sɒsəˌliz/ *a.* isósceles.

issuance /'ɪʃuəns/ *n.* emisión *f.;* publicación *f.*

issue /'ɪʃu/ *n.* **1.** emisión; edición; progenie *f.;* número *m.;* punto en disputa. —*v.* **2.** emitir; publicar.

isthmus /'ɪsməs/ *n.* istmo *m.*

it /ɪt/ *pron.* ello; él, ella; lo, la.

Italian /ɪ'tælyən/ *a. & n.* italiano -na.

Italy /'ɪtļi/ *n.* Italia *f.*

itch /ɪtʃ/ *n.* **1.** picazón *f.* —*v.* **2.** picar.

item /'aitəm/ *n.* artículo; detalle *m.;* inserción *f.; Com.* renglón *m.*

itemize /'aitəˌmaiz/ *v.* detallar.

itinerant /ai'tɪnərənt/ *n.* **1.** viandante *m.* —*a.* **2.** ambulante.

itinerary /ai'tɪnə'rɛri/ *n.* itinerario *m.*

its /ɪts/ *a.* su.

itself /ɪt'sɛlf/ *pron.* sí; se.

ivory /'aivəri/ *n.* marfil *m.*

ivy /'aivi/ *n.* hiedra *f.*

J

jab /dʒæb/ *n.* **1.** pinchazo *m.* —*v.* **2.** pinchar.

jack /dʒæk/ *n.* (for lifting) gato *m.;* (cards) sota *f.*

jackal /'dʒækəl/ *n.* chacal *m.*

jackass /'dʒækˌæs/ *n.* asno *m.*

jacket /'dʒækɪt/ *n.* chaqueta *f.;* saco *m.*

jack-of-all-trades /'dʒæk əv 'ɔl 'treidz/ *n.* estuche *m.*

jade /dʒeid/ *n.* (horse) rocín *m.;* (woman) picarona *f.;* (mineral) jade *m.*

jaded /'dʒeidɪd/ *a.* rendido.

jagged /'dʒægɪd/ *a.* mellado.

jaguar /'dʒægwər/ *n.* jaguar *m.*

jail /dʒeil/ *n.* cárcel *f.*

jailer /'dʒeilər/ *n.* carcelero *m.*

jam /dʒæm/ *n.* **1.** conserva *f.;* aprieto, apretón *m.* —*v.* **2.** apiñar, apretar; trabar.

janitor /'dʒænɪtər/ *n.* portero *m.*

January /'dʒænyuˌɛri/ *n.* enero *m.*

Japan /dʒə'pæn/ *n.* Japón *m.*

Japanese /ˌdʒæpə'niz/ *a. & n.* japonés -esa.

jar /dʒɑr/ *n.* **1.** jarro *m.* —*v.* **2.** chocar; agitar.

jargon /'dʒɑrgən/ *n.* jerga *f.*

jasmine /'dʒæzmɪn/ *n.* jazmín *m.*

jaundice /'dʒɔndɪs/ *n.* ictericia *f.*

jaunt /dʒɔnt/ *n.* paseo *m.*

javelin /'dʒævlɪn/ *n.* jabalina *f.*

jaw /dʒɔ/ *n.* quijada *f.*

jay /dʒei/ *n.* grajo *m.*

jazz /dʒæz/ *n.* jazz *m.*

jealous /'dʒɛləs/ *a.* celoso. **to be j.,** tener celos.

jealousy /'dʒɛləsi/ *n.* celos *m.pl.*

jeans /dʒinz/ *n.* vaqueros, tejanos *m.pl.*

jeer /dʒɪər/ *n.* **1.** burla *f.,* mofa *f.* —*v.* **2.** burlar, mofar.

jelly /'dʒɛli/ *n.* jalea *f.*

jellyfish /'dʒɛliˌfɪʃ/ *n.* aguamar *m.*

jeopardize /'dʒɛpərˌdaiz/ *v.* arriesgar.

jeopardy /'dʒɛpərdi/ *n.* riesgo *m.*

jerk /dʒɜrk/ *n.* **1.** sacudida *f.* —*v.* **2.** sacudir.

jerky /'dʒɜrki/ *a.* espasmódico.

Jerusalem /dʒɪ'rusələm/ *n.* Jerusalén *m.*

jest /dʒɛst/ *n.* **1.** broma *f.* —*v.* **2.** bromear.

jester /'dʒɛstər/ *n.* bufón -ona; burlón -ona.

Jesuit /'dʒɛʒuɪt/ *a. & n.* jesuíta *m.*

Jesus Christ /'dʒizəs 'kraist/ *n.* Jesucristo *m.*

jet /dʒɛt/ *n.* chorro *m.;* (gas) mechero *m.*

jet lag *n.* defase horario *m.,* inadaptación horaria *f.*

jetsam /'dʒɛtsəm/ *n.* echazón *f.*

jettison /'dʒɛtəsən/ *v.* echar al mar.

jetty /'dʒɛti/ *n.* muelle *m.*

Jew /dʒu/ n. judío -día.

jewel /'dʒuəl/ n. joya f.

jeweler /'dʒuələr/ n. joyero -ra.

jewelry /'dʒuəlri/ n. joyas f.pl. **j. store,** joyería f.

Jewish /'dʒuɪʃ/ a. judío.

jib /dʒɪb/ n. Naut. foque m.

jiffy /'dʒɪfi/ n. instante m.

jig /dʒɪg/ n. jiga f. **j-saw,** sierra de vaivén f.

jilt /dʒɪlt/ v. dar calabazas.

jingle /'dʒɪŋgəl/ n. **1.** retintín m.; rima pueril f. —v. **2.** retiñir.

jinx /dʒɪŋks/ n. **1.** aojo m. —v. **2.** aojar.

jittery /'dʒɪtəri/ a. nervioso.

job /dʒɒb/ n. empleo m.

jobber /'dʒɒbər/ n. destajista m. & f., corredor m.

jockey /'dʒɒki/ n. jockey m.

jocular /'dʒɒkyələr/ a. jocoso.

jog /dʒɒg/ n. empujoncito m. v. empujar; estimular. **j. along,** ir a un trote corto.

join /dʒɔin/ v. juntar; unir.

joiner /'dʒɔinər/ n. ebanista m.

joint /dʒɔint/ n. juntura f.

jointly /'dʒɔintli/ adv. conjuntamente.

joke /dʒouk/ n. **1.** broma, chanza f.; chiste m. —v. **2.** bromear.

joker /'dʒoukər/ n. bromista m. & f.; comodín m.

jolly /'dʒɒli/ a. alegre, jovial.

jolt /dʒoult/ n. **1.** sacudido m. —v. **2.** sacudir.

jonquil /'dʒɒŋkwɪl/ n. junquillo m.

jostle /'dʒɒsəl/ v. empujar.

journal /'dʒɜrnḷ/ n. diario m.; revista f.

journalism /'dʒɜrnḷ,ɪzəm/ n. periodismo m.

journalist /'dʒɜrnḷɪst/ n. periodista m. & f.

journey /'dʒɜrni/ n. **1.** viaje m.; jornada f. —v. **2.** viajar.

journeyman /'dʒɜrnimən/ n. jornalero m., oficial m.

jovial /'dʒouviəl/ a. jovial.

jowl /dʒaul/ n. carrillo m.

joy /dʒɔi/ n. alegría f.

joyful /'dʒɔifəl/ **joyous** a. alegre, gozoso.

jubilant /'dʒubələnt/ a. jubiloso.

jubilee /'dʒubə,li/ n. jubileo m.

Judaism /'dʒudi,ɪzəm/ n. judaísmo m.

judge /dʒʌdʒ/ n. **1.** juez m. & f. —v. **2.** juzgar.

judgment /'dʒʌddʒmənt/ n. juicio m.

judicial /dʒu'dɪʃəl/ a. judicial.

judiciary /dʒu'dɪʃi,ɛri/ a. judiciario.

judicious /dʒu'dɪʃəs/ a. juicioso.

jug /dʒʌg/ n. jarro m.

juggle /'dʒʌgəl/ v. escamotear.

juice /dʒus/ n. jugo, zumo m.

juicy /'dʒusi/ a. jugoso.

July /dʒu'lai/ n. julio m.

jumble /'dʒʌmbəl/ n. **1.** revoltillo m. —v. **2.** arrebujar, revolver.

jump /dʒʌmp/ n. **1.** salto m. —v. **2.** saltar, brincar.

junction /'dʒʌŋkʃən/ n. confluencia f.; (railway) empalme m.

juncture /'dʒʌŋktʃər/ n. juntura f.; coyuntura f.

June /dʒun/ n. junio m.

jungle /'dʒʌŋgəl/ n. jungla, selva f.

junior /'dʒunyər/ a. menor; más joven. **Jr.,** hijo.

juniper /'dʒunəpər/ n. enebro m.

junk /dʒʌŋk/ n. basura f.

junket /'dʒʌŋkɪt/ n. **1.** leche cuajada f. —v. **2.** festejar.

junkie /'dʒʌŋki/ n. Colloq. yonqui m. & f., toxicómano -na.

junk mail n. porpaganda indeseada f., correo basura m.

jurisdiction /,dʒurɪs'dɪkʃən/ n. jurisdicción f.

jurisprudence /,dʒurɪs'prudns/ n. jurisprudencia f.

jurist /'dʒurɪst/ n. jurista m. & f.

juror /'dʒurər/ n. jurado -da.

jury /'dʒuri/ n. jurado m.

just /dʒʌst/ a. **1.** justo; exacto. —adv. **2.** exactamente; (only) sólo. **j. now,** ahora mismo. **to have j.,** acabar de.

justice /'dʒʌstɪs/ n. justicia f.; (person) juez m. & f.

justifiable /'dʒʌstə,faiəbəl/ a. justificable.

justification /,dʒʌstəfɪ'keiʃən/ n. justificación f.

justify /'dʒʌstə,fai/ v. justificar.

jut /dʒʌt/ v. sobresalir.

jute /dʒut/ n. yute m.

juvenile /'dʒuvənḷ/ a. juvenil.

juvenile delinquency delincuencia de menores, delincuencia juvenil f.

K

kaleidoscope /kə'laidə,skoup/ *n.* calidoscopio *m.*

kangaroo /,kæŋgə'ru/ *n.* canguro *m.*

karakul /'kærəkəl/ *n.* caracul *m.*

karat /'kærət/ *n.* quilate *m.*

karate /kə'rɑti/ *n.* karate *m.*

keel /kil/ *n.* **1.** quilla *f.* —*v.* **2.** to **k. over,** volcarse.

keen /kin/ *a.* agudo; penetrante.

keep /kip/ *v.* mantener, retener; guardar; preservar. **k. on,** seguir, continuar.

keeper /'kipər/ *n.* guardián *m.*

keepsake /'kip,seik/ *n.* recuerdo *m.*

keg /kɛg/ *n.* barrilito *m.*

kennel /'kɛnl/ *n.* perrera *f.*

kerchief /'kɜrtʃif/ *n.* pañuelo *m.*

kernel /'kɜrnl/ *n.* pepita *f.*; grano *m.*

kerosene /'kɛrə,sin/ *n.* kerosén *m.*

ketchup /'kɛtʃəp/ *n.* salsa de tomate *f.*

kettle /'kɛtl/ *n.* caldera, olla *f.*

kettledrum /'kɛtl,drʌm/ *n.* tímpano *m.*

key /ki/ *n.* llave *f.*; (music) clave *f.*; (piano) tecla *f.*

keyboard /'ki,bɔrd/ *n.* teclado *m.*

keyhole /'ki,houl/ *n.* bocallave *f.*

keypad /'ki,pæd/ *n.* teclado *m.*

khaki /'kæki/ *a.* caqui.

kick /kɪk/ *n.* **1.** patada *f.* —*v.* **2.** patear; *Colloq.* quejarse.

kid /kɪd/ *n.* **1.** cabrito *m.*; *Colloq.* niño -ña, chico -ca. —*v.* **2.** *Colloq.* bromear.

kidnap /'kɪdnæp/ *v.* secuestrar.

kidnaper /'kɪdnæpər/ *n.* secuestrador -ora.

kidnaping /'kɪdnæpɪŋ/ *n.* rapto, secuestro *m.*

kidney /'kɪdni/ *n.* riñón *m.*

kidney bean *n.* frijol *m.*

kill /kɪl/ *v.* matar.

killer /'kɪlər/ *n.* matador -ora.

killjoy /'kɪldʒɔi/ *n.* aguafiestas *m.* & *f.*

kiln /kɪl/ *n.* horno *m.*

kilogram /'kɪlə,græm/ *n.* kilogramo *m.*

kilohertz /'kɪlə,hɜrts/ *n.* kilohercio *m.*

kilometer /kɪ'lɒmɪtər/ *n.* kilómetro *m.*

kilowatt /'kɪlə,wɒt/ *n.* kilovatio *m.*

kin /kɪn/ *n.* parentesco *m.*; parientes *m.pl.*

kind /kaind/ *a.* **1.** bondadoso, amable. —*n.* **2.** género *m.*; clase *f.* **k. of,** algo, un poco.

kindergarten /'kɪndər;gɑrtṇ/ *n.* kindergarten *m.*

kindle /'kɪndl/ *v.* encender.

kindling /'kɪndlɪŋ/ *n.* encendimiento *m.* **k.-wood,** leña menuda *f.*

kindly /'kaindli/ *a.* bondadoso.

kindness /'kaindnɪs/ *n.* bondad *f.*

kindred /'kɪndrɪd/ *n.* parentesco *m.*

kinetic /kɪ'nɛtɪk/ *a.* cinético.

king /kɪŋ/ *n.* rey *m.*

kingdom /'kɪŋdəm/ *n.* reino *m.*

king prawn langostino *m.*

kink /kɪŋk/ *n.* retorcimiento *m.*

kinky /'kɪŋki/ *a. Colloq.* pervertidillo; (hair) rizado.

kiosk /'kiosk/ *n.* kiosco *m.*

kiss /kɪs/ *n.* **1.** beso *m.* —*v.* **2.** besar.

kitchen /'kɪtʃən/ *n.* cocina *f.*

kite /kait/ *n.* cometa *f.*

kitten /'kɪtṇ/ *n.* gatito -ta.

kleptomania /,klɛptə'meiniə/ *n.* cleptomanía *f.*

kleptomaniac /,klɛptə'meiniæk/ *n.* cleptómano -na.

klutz /klʌts/ *n. Colloq.* torpe, patoso -sa.

knack /næk/ *n.* don *m.*, destreza *f.*

knapsack /'næp,sæk/ *n.* alforja *f.*

knead /nid/ *v.* amasar.

knee /ni/ *n.* rodilla *f.*

kneecap /'ni,kæp/ *n.* rodillera, rótula *f.*

kneel /nil/ *v.* arrodillarse.

knickers /'nɪkərz/ *n.* calzón corto *m.*, pantalones *m.pl.*

knife /naif/ *n.* cuchillo *m.*

knight /nait/ *n.* caballero *m.*; (chess) caballo *m.*

knit /nɪt/ *v.* tejer.

knob /nɒb/ *n.* tirador *m.*

knock /nɒk/ *n.* **1.** golpe *m.*; llamada *f.* —*v.* **2.** golpear; tocar, llamar.

knot /nɒt/ *n.* **1.** nudo; lazo *m.* —*v.* **2.** anudar.

knotty /'nɒti/ *a.* nudoso.

know /nou/ *v.* saber; (a person) conocer.

knowledge /'nɒlıdʒ/ *n.* conocimiento, saber *m.*

knuckle /'nʌkəl/ *n.* nudillo *m.* **k. bone,** jarrete *m.* **to k. under,** ceder a.

Koran /kə'rɑn/ *n.* Corán *m.*

Korea /ka'riə/ *n.* Corea *f.*

Korean /kə'riən/ *a.* & *n.* coreano.

L

label /'leibəl/ *n.* **1.** rótulo *m.* —*v.* **2.** rotular; designar.

labor /'leibər/ *n.* **1.** trabajo *m.;* la clase obrera. —*v.* **2.** trabajar.

laboratory /'læbrə,tɔri/ *n.* laboratorio *m.*

laborer /'leibərər/ *n.* trabajador, obrero *m.*

laborious /lə'bɔriəs/ *a.* laborioso, difícil.

labor union gremio obrero, sindicato *m.*

labyrinth /'læbərınθ/ *n.* laberinto *m.*

lace /leis/ *n.* **1.** encaje *m.;* (of shoe) lazo *m.* —*v.* **2.** amarrar.

lacerate /'læsə,reit/ *v.* lacerar, lastimar.

laceration /,læsə'reiʃən/ *n.* laceración *f.,* desgarro *m.*

lack /læk/ *n.* **1.** falta *f.* **l. of respect,** desacato *m.* —*v.* **2.** faltar, carecer.

lackadaisical /,lækə'deizıkəl/ *a.* indiferente; soñador.

laconic /lə'kɒnık/ *a.* lacónico.

lacquer /'lækər/ *n.* **1.** laca *f.,* barniz *m.* —*v.* **2.** laquear, barnizar.

lactic /'læktık/ *a.* láctico.

lactose /'læktous/ *n.* lactosa *f.*

ladder /'lædər/ *n.* escalera *f.*

ladle /'leidl/ *n.* **1.** cucharón *m.* —*v.* **2.** servir con cucharón.

lady /'leidi/ *n.* señora, dama *f.*

ladybug /'leidi,bʌg/ *n.* mariquita *f.*

lag /læg/ *n.* **1.** retraso *m.* —*v.* **2.** quedarse atrás.

lagoon /lə'gun/ *n.* laguna *f.*

laid-back /'leid 'bæk/ *a.* de buen talante, ecuánime, pacífico.

laity /'leiıti/ *n.* laicado *m.*

lake /leik/ *n.* lago *m.*

lamb /læm/ *n.* cordero *m.*

lame /leim/ *a.* **1.** cojo; estropeado. —*v.* **2.** estropear, lisiar; incapacitar.

lament /lə'mɛnt/ *n.* **1.** lamento *m.* —*v.* **2.** lamentar.

lamentable /lə'mɛntəbəl/ *a.* lamentable.

lamentation /,læmən'teiʃən/ *n.* lamento *m.;* lamentación *f.*

laminate /'læmə,neit/ *a.* laminado. *v.* laminar.

lamp /læmp/ *n.* lámpara *f.*

lampoon /læm'pun/ *n.* **1.** pasquín *m.* —*v.* **2.** pasquinar.

lance /læns/ *n.* **1.** lanza *f.* —*v.* **2.** *Med.* abrir.

land /lænd/ *n.* **1.** país *m.;* tierra *f.* **native l.,** patria *f.* —*v.* **2.** desembarcar; (plane) aterrizar.

landholder /'lænd,houldər/ *n.* hacendado -da.

landing /'lændıŋ/ *n.* (of stairs) descanso, descansillo *m.;* (ship) desembarcadero *m.;* (airplane) aterrizaje *m.*

landlady /'lænd,leidi/ **landlord** *n.* propietario -ria.

landmark /'lænd,mɑrk/ *n.* mojón *m.,* señal *f.;* rasgo sobresaliente *m.*

landscape /'lænd,skeip/ *n.* paisaje *m.*

landslide /'lænd,slaid/ *n.* derrumbe *m.*

lane /lein/ *n.* senda *f.*

language /'læŋgwıdʒ/ *n.* lengua *f.,* idioma; lenguaje *m.*

languid /'læŋgwıd/ *a.* lánguido.

languish /'læŋgwıʃ/ *v.* languidecer.

languor /'læŋgər/ *n.* languidez *f.*

lanky /'læŋki/ *a.* larguirucho; desgarbado.

lanolin /'lænlın/ *n.* lanolina *f.*

lantern /'læntərn/ *n.* linterna *f.;* farol *m.*

lap /læp/ *n.* **1.** regazo *m.;* falda *f.* —*v.* **2.** lamer.

lapel /lə'pɛl/ *n.* solapa *f.*

lapse /læps/ *n.* **1.** lapso *m.* —*v.* **2.** pasar; decaer; caer en error.

laptop computer /'læp,tɒp/ ordenador portátil *m.*

larceny /'lɑrsəni/ *n.* ratería *f.*

lard /lɑrd/ *n.* manteca de cerdo *f.*

large /lɑrdʒ/ *a.* grande.

largely /'lɑrdʒli/ adv. ampliamente; mayormente; muy.

largo /'lɑrgou/ n. & a. Mus. largo m.

lariat /'læriət/ n. lazo m.

lark /lɑrk/ n. (bird) alondra f.

larva /'lɑrvə/ n. larva f.

laryngitis /,lærən'dʒaitis/ n. laringitis f.

larynx /'læriŋks/ n. laringe f.

lascivious /lə'siviəs/ a. lascivo.

laser /'leizər/ n. láser m.

lash /læʃ/ n. **1.** azote, latigazo m. —v. **2.** azotar.

lass /læs/ n. doncella f.

lassitude /'læsi,tud/ n. lasitud f.

lasso /'læsou/ n. **1.** lazo m. —v. **2.** enlazar.

last /læst/ a. **1.** pasado; (final) último. **at l.,** por fin. **l. but one,** penúltimo. **l. but two,** antepenúltimo. —v. **2.** durar.

lasting /'læstiŋ/ a. duradero.

latch /lætʃ/ n. aldaba f.

late /leit/ a. **1.** tardío; (deceased) difunto. **to be l.,** llegar tarde. —adv. **2.** tarde.

lately /'leitli/ adv. recientemente.

latent /'leitṇt/ a. latente.

lateral /'lætərəl/ a. lateral.

lather /'læðər/ n. **1.** espuma de jabón. —v. **2.** enjabonar.

Latin /'lætṇ/ n. latín m.

Latin America /ə'mɛrikə/ Hispanoamérica, América Latina f.

Latin American hispanoamericano -na.

latitude /'læti,tud/ n. latitud f.

latrine /lə'trin/ n. letrina f.

latter /'lætər/ a. posterior. **the l.,** éste.

lattice /'lætis/ n. celosía f.

laud /lɔd/ v. loar.

laudable /'lɔdəbəl/ a. laudable.

laudanum /'lɔdṇəm/ n. láudano m.

laudatory /'lɔdə,tɔri/ a. laudatorio.

laugh /læf/ n. **1.** risa, risotada f. —v. **2.** reír. **l. at,** reírse de.

laughable /'læfəbəl/ a. risible.

laughter /'læftər/ n. risa f.

launch /lɔntʃ/ n. **1.** Naut. lancha f. —v. **2.** lanzar.

launder /'lɔndər/ v. lavar y planchar la ropa.

laundry /'lɔndri/ n. lavandería f.

laundryman /'lɔndri,mæn/ n. lavandero -ra.

laureate /'lɔriit/ n. & a. laureado -da.

laurel /'lɔrəl/ n. laurel m.

lava /'lɑvə/ n. lava f.

lavatory /'lævə,tɔri/ n. lavatorio m.

lavender /'lævəndər/ n. lavándula f.

lavish /'læviʃ/ a. **1.** pródigo. —v. **2.** prodigar.

law /lɔ/ n. ley f.; derecho m.

lawful /'lɔfəl/ a. legal.

lawless /'lɔlis/ a. sin ley.

lawn /lɔn/ n. césped; prado m.

lawn mower /'mouər/ n. cortacésped m. & f.

lawsuit /'lɔ,sut/ n. pleito m.

lawyer /'lɔyər/ n. abogado m. & f.

lax /læks/ a. flojo, laxo.

laxative /'læksətiv/ n. purgante m.

laxity /'læksiti/ n. laxidad f.; flojedad f.

lay /lei/ a. **1.** secular. —v. **2.** poner.

layer /'leiər/ n. capa f.

layman /'leimən/ n. lego, seglar m.

lazy /'leizi/ a. perezoso.

lead /lɛd , lid/ n. **1.** plomo m.; Theat. papel principal. **to take the l.,** tomar la delantera. —v. **2.** conducir; dirigir.

leaden /'lɛdṇ/ a. plomizo; pesado; abatido.

leader /'lidər/ n. líder m. & f.; jefe m. & f.; director -ora.

leadership /'lidər,ʃip/ n. dirección f.

leaf /lif/ n. hoja f.

leaflet /'liflit/ n. Bot. hojilla f.; folleto m.

league /lig/ n. liga; (measure) legua f.

leak /lik/ n. **1.** escape; goteo m. —v. **2.** gotear; Naut. hacer agua.

leakage /'likidʒ/ n. goteo m., escape m., pérdida f.

leaky /'liki/ a. llovedizo, resquebrajado.

lean /lin/ a. **1.** flaco, magro. —v. **2.** apoyarse, arrimarse.

leap /lip/ n. **1.** salto m. —v. **2.** saltar.

leap year n. año bisiesto m.

learn /lɜrn/ v. aprender; saber.

learned /'lɜrnid/ a. erudito.

learning /'lɜrniŋ/ n. erudición f., instrucción f.

lease /lis/ n. 1. arriendo m. —v. 2. arrendar.
leash /liʃ/ n. 1. correa f. —v. 2. atraillar.
least /list/ a. menor; mínimo. **the l.,** lo menos. **at l.,** por lo menos.
leather /'lɛðər/ n. cuero m.
leathery /'lɛðəri/ a. coriáceo.
leave /liv/ n. 1. licencia f. **to take l.,** despedirse. —v. 2. dejar; (depart) salir, irse. **l. out,** omitir.
leaven /'lɛvən/ n. 1. levadura f. —v. 2. fermentar, imbuir.
lecherous /'lɛtʃərəs/ a. lujurioso.
lecture /'lɛktʃər/ n. conferencia f.
lecturer /'lɛktʃərər/ n. conferencista m. & f.; catedrático -ca.
ledge /lɛdʒ/ n. borde m.; capa f.
ledger /'lɛdʒer/ n. libro mayor m.
lee /li/ n. sotavento m.
leech /litʃ/ n. sanguijuela f.
leek /lik/ n. puerro m.
leer /lɪər/ v. mirar de soslayo.
leeward /'liwərd/ a. sotavento.
left /lɛft/ a. izquierdo. **the l.,** la izquierda. **to be left,** quedarse.
left-handed /'lɛft 'hændɪd/ a. zurdo.
leftist /'lɛftɪst/ n. izquierdista m. & f.
leftovers /'lɛft,ouvərz/ n. sobras f.pl.
leg /lɛg/ n. pierna f.
legacy /'lɛgəsi/ n. legado m., herencia f.
legal /'ligəl/ a. legal.
legalize /'ligə,laiz/ v. legalizar.
legation /lɪ'geiʃən/ n. legación, embajada f.
legend /'lɛdʒənd/ n. leyenda f.
legendary /'lɛdʒən,dɛri/ a. legendario.
legible /'lɛdʒəbəl/ a. legible.
legion /'lidʒən/ n. legión f.
legislate /'lɛdʒɪs,leit/ v. legislar.
legislation /,lɛdʒɪs'leiʃən/ n. legislación f.
legislator /'lɛdʒɪs,leitər/ n. legislador -ra.
legislature /'lɛdʒɪs,leitʃər/ n. legislatura f.
legitimate /lɪ'dʒɪtəmɪt/ a. legítimo.
legume /'lɛgyum/ n. legumbre f.
leisure /'liʒər/ n. desocupación f.; horas libres.
leisurely /'liʒərli/ a. 1. deliberado. —adv. 2. despacio.
lemon /'lɛmən/ n. limón m.

lemonade /,lɛmə'neid/ n. limonada f.
lend /lɛnd/ v. prestar.
length /lɛŋkθ/ n. largo m.; duración f.
lengthen /'lɛŋkθən/ v. alargar.
lengthwise /'lɛŋkθ,waiz/ adv. a lo largo.
lengthy /'lɛŋkθi/ a. largo.
lenient /'liniənt/ a. indulgente.
lens /lɛnz/ n. lente m. or f.
Lent /lɛnt/ n. cuaresma f.
Lenten /'lɛntn̩/ a. cuaresmal.
lentil /'lɛntɪl/ n. lenteja f.
leopard /'lɛpərd/ n. leopardo m.
leotard /'liə,tard/ n. mallas f.pl.
leper /'lɛpər/ n. leproso -sa.
leprosy /'lɛprəsi/ n. lepra f.
lesbian /'lɛzbiən/ n. lesbiana f.
lesion /'liʒən/ n. lesión f.
less /lɛs/ a. & adv. menos.
lessen /'lɛsən/ v. disminuir.
lesser /'lɛsər/ a. menor; más pequeño.
lesson /'lɛsən/ n. lección f.
lest /lɛst/ conj. para que no.
let /lɛt/ v. dejar; permitir; arrendar.
letdown /'lɛt,daun/ n. decepción f.
lethal /'liθəl/ a. letal.
lethargic /lə'θardʒɪk/ a. letárgico.
lethargy /'lɛθərdʒi/ n. letargo m.
letter /'lɛtər/ n. carta; (of alphabet) letra f.
letterhead /'lɛtər,hɛd/ n. membrete m.
lettuce /'lɛtɪs/ n. lechuga f.
leukemia /lu'kimiə/ n. leucemia f.
levee /'lɛvi, lɛ'vi/ n. recepción f.
level /'lɛvəl/ a. 1. llano, nivelado. —n. 2. nivel m.; llanura f. —v. 3. allanar; nivelar.
lever /'lɛvər/ n. palanca f.
levity /'lɛvɪti/ n. levedad f.
levy /'lɛvi/ n. 1. leva f. —v. 2. imponer.
lewd /lud/ a. lascivo.
lexicon /'lɛksɪ,kɒn/ n. léxico m.
liability /,laiə'bɪlɪti/ n. riesgo m.; obligación f.
liable /'laiəbəl/ a. sujeto; responsable.
liaison /li'eizən/ n. vinculación f., enlace m.; concubinaje m.
liar /'laiər/ n. embustero -ra.
libel /'laibəl/ n. 1. libelo m. —v. 2. difamar.
libelous /'laibələs/ a. difamatorio.

liberal /'lɪbərəl/ *a.* liberal; generoso.

liberalism /'lɪbərə,lɪzəm/ *n.* liberalismo *m.*

liberality /,lɪbə'ræləti/ *n.* liberalidad *f.*

liberate /'lɪbə,reit/ *v.* libertar.

liberty /'lɪbərti/ *n.* libertad *f.*

libidinous /lɪ'bɪdṇəs/ *a.* libidinoso.

librarian /lai'brɛəriən/ *n.* bibliotecario -ria.

library /'lai,brɛri/ *n.* biblioteca *f.*

libretto /lɪ'brɛtou/ *n.* libreto *m.*

license /'laisəns/ *n.* licencia *f.;* permiso *m.*

licentious /lai'sɛnʃəs/ *a.* licencioso.

lick /lɪk/ *v.* lamer.

licorice /'lɪkərɪʃ, 'lɪkrɪʃ, 'lɪkərɪs/ *n.* regaliz *m.*

lid /lɪd/ *n.* tapa *f.*

lie /lai/ *n.* **1.** mentira *f.* —*v.* **2.** mentir. **l. down,** acostarse, echarse.

lieutenant /lu'tɛnənt/ *n.* teniente *m.*

life /laif/ *n.* vida *f.*

lifeboat /'laif,bout/ *n.* bote salvavidas *m.*

life buoy boya *f.*

lifeguard /'laif,gɑrd/ socorrista *m.* & *f.*

life insurance seguro de vida *m.*

life jacket chaleco salvavidas *m.*

lifeless /'laiflɪs/ *a.* sin vida.

life preserver /prɪ'zɜrvər/ salvavidas *m.*

lifestyle /'laifstail/ *n.* modo de vida *m.*

lift /lɪft/ *v.* levantar, alzar, elevar.

ligament /'lɪgəmənt/ *n.* ligamento *m.*

ligature /'lɪgətʃər/ *n.* ligadura *f.*

light /lait/ *a.* **1.** ligero; liviano; (in color) claro. —*n.* **2.** luz; candela *f.* —*v.* **3.** encender; iluminar.

light bulb bombilla *f.*

lighten /'laitṇ/ *v.* aligerar; aclarar; iluminar.

lighter /'laitər/ *n.* encendedor *m.*

lighthouse /'lait,haus/ *n.* faro *m.*

lightness /'laitnɪs/ *n.* ligereza; agilidad *f.*

lightning /'laitnɪŋ/ *n.* relámpago *m.*

like /laik/ *a.* **1.** semejante. —*prep.* **2.** como. —*v.* **3. I like...** me gusta, me gustan... **I should like,** quisiera.

likeable /'laikəbəl/ *a.* simpático, agradable.

likelihood /'laikli,hʊd/ *n.* probabilidad *f.*

likely /'laikli/ *a.* probable; verosímil.

liken /'laikən/ *v.* comparar; asemejar.

likeness /'laiknɪs/ *n.* semejanza *f.*

likewise /'laik,waiz/ *adv.* igualmente.

lilac /'lailək/ *n.* lila *f.*

lilt /lɪlt/ *n.* **1.** cadencia alegre *f.* —*v.* **2.** cantar alegremente.

lily /'lɪli/ *n.* lirio *m.*

lily of the valley muguete *m.*

limb /lɪm/ *n.* rama *f.*

limber /'lɪmbər/ *a.* flexible. **to l. up,** ponerse flexible.

limbo /'lɪmbou/ *n.* limbo *m.*

lime /laim/ *n.* cal *f.;* (fruit) limoncito *m.*, lima *f.*

limestone /'laim,stoun/ *n.* piedra caliza *f.*

limewater /'laim,wɔtər/ *n.* agua de cal *f.*

limit /'lɪmɪt/ *n.* **1.** límite *m.* —*v.* **2.** limitar.

limitation /,lɪmɪ'teiʃən/ *n.* limitación *f.*

limitless /'lɪmɪtlɪs/ *a.* ilimitado.

limousine /'lɪmə,zin/ *n.* limusina *f.*

limp /lɪmp/ *n.* **1.** cojera *f.* —*a.* **2.** flojo. —*v.* **3.** cojear.

limpid /'lɪmpɪd/ *a.* límpido.

line /lain/ *n.* **1.** línea; fila; raya *f.;* (of print) renglón *m.* —*v.* **2.** forrar; rayar.

lineage /'lɪnɪdʒ/ *n.* linaje *m.*

lineal /'lɪniəl/ *a.* lineal.

linear /'lɪniər/ *a.* linear, longitudinal.

linen /'lɪnən/ *n.* lienzo, lino *m.;* ropa blanca.

liner /'lainər/ *n.* vapor *m.*

linger /'lɪŋgər/ *v.* demorarse.

lingerie /,lɑnʒə'rei/ *n.* ropa blanca *f.*

linguist /'lɪŋgwɪst/ *n.* lingüista *m.* & *f.*

linguistic /lɪŋ'gwɪstɪk/ *a.* lingüístico.

liniment /'lɪnəmənt/ *n.* linimento *m.*

lining /'lainɪŋ/ *n.* forro *m.*

link /lɪŋk/ *n.* **1.** eslabón; vínculo *m.* —*v.* **2.** vincular.

linoleum /lɪ'nouliəm/ *n.* linóleo *m.*

linseed /'lɪn,sid/ n. linaza f.; simiente de lino f.
lint /lɪnt/ n. hilacha f.
lion /'laɪən/ n. león m.
lip /lɪp/ n. labio m.
liposuction /'lɪpə,sʌkʃən, 'laɪpə-/ n. liposucción f.
lipstick /'lɪp,stɪk/ n. lápiz de labios.
liqueur /lɪ'kɜr/ n. licor m.
liquid /'lɪkwɪd/ a. & n. líquido m.
liquidate /'lɪkwɪ,deit/ v. liquidar.
liquidation /,lɪkwɪ'deiʃən/ n. liquidación f.
liquor /'lɪkər/ n. licor m.
lisp /lɪsp/ n. **1.** ceceo m. —v. **2.** cecear.
list /lɪst/ n. **1.** lista f. —v. **2.** registrar.
listen (to) /'lɪsən/ v. escuchar.
listless /'lɪstlɪs/ a. indiferente.
litany /'lɪtn̩i/ n. letanía f.
liter /'litər/ n. litro m.
literal /'lɪtərəl/ a. literal.
literary /'lɪtə,rɛri/ a. literario.
literate /'lɪtərɪt/ a. alfabetizado.
literature /'lɪtərətʃər/ n. literatura f.
litigant /'lɪtɪgənt/ n. & a. litigante m. & f.
litigation /,lɪtɪ'geiʃən/ n. litigio, pleito m.
litter /'lɪtər/ n. **1.** litera f.; cama de paja. —v. **2.** poner en desorden.
little /'lɪtl̩/ a. pequeño; (quantity) poco.
little finger meñique m.
liturgical /lɪ'tɜrdʒɪkəl/ a. litúrgico.
liturgy /'lɪtərdʒi/ n. liturgia f.
live /a laiv; v lɪv/ a. **1.** vivo. —v. **2.** vivir.
livelihood /'laivli,hʊd/ n. subsistencia f.
lively /'laivli/ a. vivo; rápido; animado.
liver /'lɪvər/ n. hígado m.
livery /'lɪvəri/ n. librea f.
livestock /'laiv,stɒk/ n. ganadería f.
livid /'lɪvɪd/ a. lívido.
living /'lɪvɪŋ/ a. **1.** vivo. —n. **2.** sustento m. **to earn (make) a living,** ganarse la vida.
living room salón m.
lizard /'lɪzərd/ n. lagarto m., lagartija f.
llama /'lɑmə/ n. llama f.
load /loud/ n. **1.** carga f. —v. **2.** cargar.

loaf /louf/ n. **1.** pan m. —v. **2.** holgazanear.
loam /loum/ n. marga f.
loan /loun/ n. **1.** préstamo m. —v. **2.** prestar.
loathe /louð/ v. aborrecer, detestar.
loathsome /'louðsəm/ a. repugnante.
lobby /'lɒbi/ n. vestíbulo m.
lobe /loub/ n. lóbulo m.
lobster /'lɒbstər/ n. langosta f.
local /'loukəl/ a. local.
local area network red local f.
locale /lou'kæl/ n. localidad f.
locality /lou'kælɪti/ n. localidad f., lugar m.
localize /'loukə,laiz/ v. localizar.
locate /'loukeit/ v. situar; hallar.
location /lou'keiʃən/ n. sitio m.; posición f.
lock /lɒk/ n. **1.** cerradura f.; (pl.) cabellos m.pl. —v. **2.** cerrar con llave.
locker /'lɒkər/ n. cajón m.; ropero m.
locket /'lɒkɪt/ n. guardapelo m.; medallón m.
lockjaw /'lɒk,dʒɔ/ n. trismo m.
locksmith /'lɒk,smɪθ/ n. cerrajero -ra.
locomotive /,loukə'moutɪv/ n. locomotora f.
locust /'loukəst/ n. cigarra f., saltamontes m.
locution /lou'kyuʃən/ n. locución f.
lode /loud/ n. filón m., veta f.
lodge /lɒdʒ/ n. **1.** logia; (inn) posada f. —v. **2.** fijar; alojar, morar.
lodger /'lɒdʒər/ n. inquilino m.
lodging /'lɒdʒɪŋ/ n. alojamiento m.
loft /lɔft/ n. desván, sobrado m.
lofty /'lɔfti/ a. alto; altivo.
log /lɔg/ n. tronco de árbol; Naut. barquilla f.
loge /louʒ/ n. palco m.
logic /'lɒdʒɪk/ n. lógica f.
logical /'lɒdʒɪkəl/ a. lógico.
loin /lɔin/ n. lomo m.
loincloth /'lɔin,klɔθ/ n. taparrabos m.
loiter /'lɔitər/ v. haraganear.
lone /loun/ a. solitario.
loneliness /'lounlinɪs/ n. soledad f.
lonely, /'lounli **lonesome** a. solo y triste.

lonesome /'lounsəm/ *a.* solitario, aislado.

long /lɔŋ/ *a.* **1.** largo. **a l. time,** mucho tiempo. —*adv.* **2.** mucho tiempo. **how l.,** cuánto tiempo. **no longer,** ya no. —*v.* **3. l. for,** anhelar.

long-distance call /'lɔŋ 'dɪstəns/ conferencia interurbana *f.*

longevity /lɒn'dʒɛvɪti/ *n.* longevidad *f.*

long-haired /'lɔŋ 'hɛərd/ *a.* melenudo.

longing /'lɔŋɪŋ/ *n.* anhelo *m.*

longitude /'lɒndʒɪ,tud/ *n.* longitud *m.*

look /lʊk/ *n.* **1.** mirada *f.;* aspecto *m.* —*v.* **2.** parecer; mirar. **l. at,** mirar. **l. for,** buscar. **l. like,** parecerse a. **l. out!,** ¡cuidado! **l. up,** buscar; ir a ver, venir a ver.

looking glass /'lʊkɪŋ/ espejo *m.*

loom /lum/ *n.* **1.** telar *m.* —*v.* **2.** asomar.

loop /lup/ *n.* vuelta *f.*

loophole /'lup,houl/ *n.* aspillera *f.; Fig.* callejuela, evasiva *f.,* efugio *m.*

loose /lus/ *a.* suelto; flojo.

loose change suelto *m.*

loosen /'lusən/ *v.* soltar; aflojar.

loot /lut/ *n.* **1.** botín *m.,* saqueo *m.* —*v.* **2.** saquear.

lopsided /'lɒp'saɪdɪd/ *a.* desequilibrado.

loquacious /lou'kweiʃəs/ *a.* locuaz.

lord /lɔrd/ *n.* señor *m.;* (Brit. title) lord *m.*

lordship /'lɔrdʃɪp/ *n.* señorío *m.*

lose /luz/ *v.* perder. **l. consciousness,** perder el conocimiento.

loss /lɔs/ *n.* pérdida *f.*

lost /lɔst/ *a.* perdido.

lot /lɒt/ *n.* suerte *f.* **building l.,** solar *m.* **a lot (of), lots of,** mucho.

lotion /'louʃən/ *n.* loción *f.*

lottery /'lɒtəri/ *n.* lotería *f.*

loud /laud/ *a.* **1.** fuerte; ruidoso. —*adv.* **2.** alto.

loudspeaker /'laud,spikər/ *n.* altavoz *m.*

lounge /laundʒ/ *n.* sofá *m.;* salón de fumar *m.*

louse /laus/ *n.* piojo *m.*

love /lʌv/ *n.* **1.** amor *m.* **in l.,** enamorado. **to fall in l.,** enamorarse. **l. at first sight,** flechazo *m.* —*v.* **2.** querer; amar; adorar.

lovely /'lʌvli/ *a.* hermoso.

lover /'lʌvər/ *n.* amante *m.* & *f.*

low /lou/ *a.* bajo; vil.

low-cut /'lou 'kʌt/ *a.* escotado.

lower /'louər/ *v.* bajar; (in price) rebajar.

lower-case letter /'louər 'keis/ minúscula *f.*

lowly /'louli/ *a.* humilde.

low neckline /'nɛk,lain/ escote *m.*

loyal /'lɔiəl/ *a.* leal, fiel.

loyalist /'lɔiəlɪst/ *n.* lealista *m.* & *f.*

loyalty /'lɔiəlti/ *n.* lealtad *f.*

lozenge /'lɒzɪndʒ/ *n.* pastilla *f.*

lubricant /'lubrɪkənt/ *n.* lubricante *m.*

lubricate /'lubrɪ,keit/ *v.* engrasar, lubricar.

lucid /'lusɪd/ *a.* claro, lúcido.

luck /lʌk/ *n.* suerte; fortuna *f.*

lucky /'lʌki/ *a.* afortunado. **to be l.,** tener suerte.

lucrative /'lukrətɪv/ *a.* lucrativo.

ludicrous /'ludɪkrəs/ *a.* ridículo.

luggage /'lʌgɪdʒ/ *n.* equipaje *m.*

lukewarm /'luk'wɔrm/ *a.* tibio.

lull /lʌl/ *n.* **1.** momento de calma. —*v.* **2.** calmar.

lullaby /'lʌlə,bai/ *n.* arrullo *m.*

lumbago /lʌm'beigou/ *n.* lumbago *m.*

lumber /'lʌmbər/ *n.* madera *f.*

luminous /'lumənəs/ *a.* luminoso.

lump /lʌmp/ *n.* protuberancia *f.;* (of sugar) terrón *m.*

lump sum suma global *f.*

lunacy /'lunəsi/ *n.* locura *f.*

lunar /'lunər/ *a.* lunar.

lunatic /'lunətɪk/ *a.* & *n.* loco -ca.

lunch, luncheon /lʌntʃ; 'lʌnteshən/ *n.* **1.** merienda *f.,* almuerzo *m.* —*v.* **2.** merendar, almorzar.

lunch box /'lʌntʃ,bɒks/ fiambrera *f.*

lung /lʌŋ/ *n.* pulmón *m.*

lunge /lʌndʒ/ *n.* **1.** estocada, arremetida *f.* —*v.* **2.** dar un estocada, arremeter.

lure /lʊr/ *v.* atraer.

lurid /'lʊrɪd/ *a.* sensacional; espeluznante.

lurk /lɜrk/ *v.* esconderse; espiar.

luscious /'lʌʃəs/ *a.* sabroso, delicioso.

lust /lʌst/ *n.* sensualidad; codicia *f.*

luster /'lʌstər/ *n.* lustre *m.*

lustful /'lʌstfəl/ a. sensual, lascivo.

lusty /'lʌsti/ a. vigoroso.

lute /lut/ n. laúd m.

Lutheran /'luθərən/ n. & a. luterano -na.

luxuriant /lʌg'ʒʊriənt/ a. exuberante, frondoso.

luxurious /lʌg'ʒʊriəs/ a. lujoso.

luxury /'lʌkʃəri/ n. lujo m.

lying /'laiiŋ/ a. mentiroso.

lymph /lɪmf/ n. linfa f.

lynch /lɪntʃ/ v. linchar.

lyre /laiər/ n. lira f.

lyric /'lɪrɪk/ a. lírico.

lyricism /'lɪrə,sɪzəm/ n. lirismo m.

M

macabre /mə'kabrə/ a. macabro.

macaroni /,mækə'rouni/ n. macarrones m.

machine /mə'ʃin/ n. máquina f.

machine gun ametralladora f.

machinery /mə'ʃinəri/ n. maquinaria f.

machinist /mə'ʃinɪst/ n. maquinista m. & f., mecánico m.

macho /'matʃou/ a. machista.

mackerel /'mækərəl/ n. escombro m.

macro /'mækrou/ n. (computer) macro m.

mad /mæd/ a. loco; furioso.

madam /'mædəm/ n. señora f.

mafia /'mafiə/ n. mafia f.

magazine /,mægə'zin/ n. revista f.

magic /'mædʒɪk/ a. 1. mágico. —n. 2. magia f.

magician /mə'dʒɪʃən/ n. mágico m.

magistrate /'mædʒə,streit/ n. magistrado -da.

magnanimous /mæg'nænəməs/ a. magnánimo.

magnate /'mægneit/ n. magnate m.

magnesium /mæg'niziəm/ n. magnesio m.

magnet /'mægnɪt/ n. imán m.

magnetic /mæg'nɛtɪk/ a. magnético.

magnificence /mæg'nɪfəsəns/ n. magnificencia f.

magnificent /mæg'nɪfəsənt/ a. magnífico.

magnify /'mægnə,fai/ v. magnificar.

magnifying glass /'mægnə,faiiŋ/ lupa f.

magnitude /'mægnɪ,tud/ n. magnitud f.

magpie /'mæg,pai/ n. hurraca f.

mahogany /mə'hɒgəni/ n. caoba f.

maid /meid/ n. criada f. **old m.,** solterona f.

maiden /'meidn̩/ a. soltera.

mail /meil/ n. **1.** correo m. **air m.,** correo aéreo. **by return m.,** a vuelta de correo. —v. **2.** echar al correo.

mailbox /'meil,bɒks/ n. buzón m.

mailman /'meil,mæn/ n. cartero m.

maim /meim/ v. mutilar.

main /mein/ a. principal.

mainframe /'mein,freim/ n. componente central de una computadora.

mainland /'mein,lænd/ n. continente m.

maintain /mein'tein/ v. mantener; sostener.

maintenance /'meintənəns/ n. mantenimiento; sustento m.; conservación f.

maître d' /,mei'tər di, ,meitrə, ,mɛtrə/ n. jefe de sala m. & f.

maize /meiz/ n. maíz m.

majestic /mə'dʒɛstɪk/ a. majestuoso.

majesty /'mædʒəsti/ n. majestad f.

major /'meidʒər/ a. **1.** mayor. —n. **2.** Mil. comandante m.; (study) especialidad f.

majority /mə'dʒɔrɪti/ n. mayoría f.

make /meik/ n. **1.** marca f. —v. **2.** hacer; fabricar; (earn) ganar.

maker /'meikər/ n. fabricante m.

makeshift /'meik,ʃɪft/ a. provisional.

make-up /'meik,ʌp/ n. cosméticos m.pl.

malady /'mælədi/ n. mal m., enfermedad f.

malaria /mə'lɛəriə/ n. paludismo m.

male /meil/ a. & n. macho m.

malevolent /mə'lɛvələnt/ a. malévolo.

malice /'mælɪs/ n. malicia f.

malicious /mə'lɪʃəs/ a. malicioso.

malign /mə'lain/ v. **1.** difamar.
—a. **2.** maligno.
malignant /mə'lıgnənt/ a.
maligno.
malnutrition /ˌmælnu'trıʃən/ n.
desnutrición f.
malt /mɔlt/ n. malta f.
mammal /'mæməl/ n. mamífero
m.
man /mæn/ n. hombre; varón m.
v. tripular.
manage /'mænıdʒ/ v. manejar;
dirigir; administrar; arreglárselas.
m. to, lograr.
management /'mænıdʒmənt/ n.
dirección, administración f.
manager /'mænıdʒər/ n. director
-ora.
mandate /'mændeit/ n. mandato
m.
mandatory /'mændə,tɔri/ a. obligatorio.
mandolin /'mændlın/ n. man-
dolina f.
mane /mein/ n. crines f.pl.
maneuver /mə'nuvər/ n. **1.**
maniobra f. —v. **2.** maniobrar.
manganese /'mæŋgə,nis, -,niz/ n.
manganeso m.
manger /'meindʒər/ n. pesebre m.
mangle /'mæŋgəl/ n. **1.** rodillo,
exprimidor m. —v. **2.** mutilar.
manhood /'mænhʊd/ n. virilidad
f.
mania /'meiniə/ n. manía f.
maniac /'meini,æk/ a. & n. maniático -ca; maníaco -ca.
manicure /'mænı,kyʊr/ n.
manicura f.
manifest /'mænə,fɛst/ a. & n. **1.**
manifiesto m. —v. **2.** manifestar.
manifesto /ˌmænə'fɛstou/ n.
manifiesto m.
manifold /'mænə,fould/ a. **1.**
muchos. —n. **2.** Auto. tubo múltiple.
manipulate /mə'nıpyə,leit/ v. manipular.
mankind /'mæn'kaind/ n. humanidad f.
manly /'mænli/ a. varonil.
manner /'mænər/ n. manera f.,
modo m. **manners,** modales
m.pl.
mannerism /'mænə,rızəm/ n.
manerismo m.
mansion /'mænʃən/ n. mansión f.
mantel /'mæntl/ n. manto de chimenea.
mantle /'mæntl/ n. manto m.

manual /'mænyuəl/ a. & n. manual m.
manufacture /ˌmænyə'fæktʃər/ v.
fabricar.
manufacturer /ˌmænyə'fæktʃərər/
n. fabricante m.
manufacturing /ˌmænyə-
'fæktʃərıŋ/ n. fabricación f.
manure /mə'nʊr/ n. abono, estiércol m.
manuscript /'mænyə,skrıpt/ n.
manuscrito m.
many /'mɛni/ a. muchos. **how
m.,** cuántos. **so m.,** tantos. **too
m.,** demasiados. **as m. as,** tantos
como.
map /mæp/ n. mapa m.
maple /'meipəl/ n. arce m.
mar /mɑr/ v. estropear; desfigurar.
marble /'mɑrbəl/ n. mármol m.
march /mɑrtʃ/ n. **1.** marcha f.
—v. **2.** marchar.
March /mɑrtʃ/ n. marzo m.
mare /mɛər/ n. yegua f.
margarine /'mɑrdʒərın/ n. mar-
garina f.
margin /'mɑrdʒın/ n. margen m.
or f.
marijuana /ˌmærə'wɑnə/ n. marijuana f.
marine /mə'rin/ a. **1.** marino. —n.
2. soldado de marina.
mariner /'mærənər/ n. marinero m.
marionette /ˌmæriə'nɛt/ n. mario-
neta f.
marital /'mærıtl/ a. marital.
maritime /'mærı,taim/ a. marítimo.
mark /mɑrk/ n. **1.** marca f. —v. **2.**
marcar.
market /'mɑrkıt/ n. mercado m.
meat m., carnicería f. **stock m.,**
bolsa f. v. comercializar.
marmalade /'mɑrmə,leid/ n. mermelada f.
maroon /mə'run/ a. & n. color
rojo oscuro. v. dejar abandonado.
marquis /'mɑrkwıs/ n. marqués
m.
marriage /'mærıdʒ/ n. matrimonio
m.
marriage certificate partida de
matrimonio f.
married /'mærid/ a. casado. **to
get m.,** casarse.
marrow /'mærou/ n. médula f.;
substancia f.
marry /'mæri/ v. casarse con; casar.

marsh /mɑrʃ/ n. pantano m.

marshal /'mɑrʃəl/ n. mariscal m.

marshmallow /'mɑrʃ,mɛlou/ n. malvarisco m.; bombón de altea m.

martial /'mɑrʃəl/ a. marcial. **m. law,** gobierno militar.

martyr /'mɑrtər/ n. mártir m. & f.

martyrdom /'mɑrtərdəm/ n. martirio m.

marvel /'mɑrvəl/ n. **1.** maravilla f. —v. **2.** maravillarse.

marvelous /'mɑrvələs/ a. maravilloso.

mascara /mæ'skærə/ n. rimel m.

mascot /'mæskɒt/ n. mascota f.

masculine /'mæskyəlɪn/ a. masculino.

mash /mæʃ/ v. majar. **mashed potatoes,** puré de papas m.

mask /mæsk/ n. máscara f.

mason /'meisən/ n. albañil m.

masquerade /,mæskə'reid/ n. mascarada f.

mass /mæs/ n. masa f.; Relig. misa f. **to say m.,** cantar misa. **m. production,** producción en serie.

massacre /'mæsəkər/ n. **1.** carnicería, matanza f. —v. **2.** matar atrozmente, destrozar.

massage /mə'sɑʒ/ n. **1.** masaje m.; soba f. —v. **2.** sobar.

masseur /mə'sɜr/ n. masajista m. & f.

massive /'mæsɪv/ a. macizo, sólido.

mast /mæst/ n. palo, árbol m.

master /'mæstər/ n. **1.** amo; maestro m. —v. **2.** domar, dominar.

masterpiece /'mæstər,pis/ n. obra maestra f.

master's degree /'mæstərz/ maestría f.

mastery /'mæstəri/ n. maestría f.

mat /mæt/ n. **1.** estera; palleta f. —v. **2.** enredar.

match /mætʃ/ n. **1.** igual m; fósforo m.; (sport) partida, contienda f.; (marriage) noviazgo; casamiento. —v. **2.** ser igual a; igualar.

matchbox /'mætʃ,bɒks/ caja de cerillas, caja de fósforos f.

mate /meit/ n. **1.** consorte m. & f.; compañero -ra. —v. **2.** igualar; casar.

material /mə'tɪəriəl/ a. & n. material m. **raw materials,** materias primas.

materialism /mə'tɪəriə,lɪzəm/ n. materialismo m.

materialize /mə'tɪəriə,laiz/ v. materializar.

maternal /mə'tɜrnl/ a. materno.

maternity /mə'tɜrnɪti/ n. maternidad f.

maternity hospital maternidad f.

mathematical /,mæθə'mætɪkəl/ a. matemático.

mathematics /,mæθə'mætɪks/ n. matemáticas f.pl.

matinee /,mætn'ei/ n. matiné f.

matrimony /'mætrə,mouni/ n. matrimonio m.

matron /'meitrən/ n. matrona; directora f.

matter /'mætər/ n. **1.** materia f.; asunto m. **what's the m.?,** ¿qué pasa? —v. **2.** importar.

mattress /'mætrɪs/ n. colchón m.

mature /mə'tʃʊr/ a. **1.** maduro. —v. **2.** madurar.

maturity /mə'tʃʊrɪti/ n. madurez f.

maudlin /'mɔdlɪn/ a. sentimental en exceso; sensiblero.

maul /mɔl/ v. aporrear.

maxim /'mæksɪm/ n. máxima f.

maximum /'mæksəməm/ a. & n. máximo.

may /mei/ v. poder.

May /mei/ n. mayo m.

maybe /'meibi/ adv. quizá, quizás, tal vez.

mayonnaise /,meiə'neiz/ n. mayonesa f.

mayor /'meiər/ n. alcalde m. alcaldesa f.

maze /meiz/ n. laberinto m.

me /mi/ pron. mí; me. **with me,** conmigo.

meadow /'mɛdou/ n. prado m.; vega f.

meager /'migər/ a. magro; pobre.

meal /mil/ n. comida; (flour) harina f.

mean /min/ a. **1.** bajo; malo. —n. **2.** medio (see also **means**). —v. **3.** significar; querer decir.

meander /mi'ændər/ v. (river) serpentear; (person) deambular.

meaning /'minɪŋ/ n. sentido, significado m.

meaningless /'minɪŋlɪs/ a. sin sentido.

means /minz/ n.pl. medios, recursos m. **by all m.,** sin falta. **by no**

m., de ningún modo. **by m. of,** por medio de.

meanwhile /'min,wail/ adv. mientras tanto.

measles /'mizəlz/ n. sarampión m.

measure /'mɛʒər/ n. **1.** medida f.; (music) compás m. —v. **2.** medir.

measurement /'mɛʒərmənt/ n. medida, dimensión f.

meat /mit/ n. carne f.

mechanic /mə'kænɪk/ n. mecánico m. & f.

mechanical /mə'kænɪkəl/ a. mecánico.

mechanism /'mɛkə,nɪzəm/ n. mecanismo m.

mechanize /'mɛkə,naiz/ v. mecanizar.

medal /'mɛdl̩/ n. medalla f.

meddle /'mɛdl̩/ v. meterse, entremeterse.

mediate /'midi,eit/ v. mediar.

medical /'mɛdɪkəl/ a. médico.

medicine /'mɛdəsɪn/ n. medicina f.

medicine chest botiquín m.

medieval /,midi'ivəl/ a. medieval.

mediocre /,midi'oukər/ a. mediocre.

mediocrity /,midi'ɒkrɪti/ n. mediocridad f.

meditate /'mɛdɪ,teit/ v. meditar.

meditation /,mɛdɪ'teiʃən/ n. meditación f.

Mediterranean /,mɛdɪtə'reiniən/ n. Mediterráneo m.

medium /'midiəm/ a. **1.** mediano, medio. —n. **2.** medio m.

medley /'mɛdli/ n. mezcla f., ensalada f.

meek /mik/ a. manso; humilde.

meekness /'miknɪs/ n. modestia; humildad f.

meet /mit/ a. **1.** apropiado. —n. **2.** concurso m. —v. **3.** encontrar; reunirse; conocer.

meeting /'mitɪŋ/ n. reunión f.; mitin m.

megahertz /'mɛgə,hɜrts/ n. megahercio m.

megaphone /'mɛgə,foun/ n. megáfono m.

melancholy /'mɛlən,kɒli/ a. **1.** melancólico. —n. **2.** melancolía f.

mellow /'mɛlou/ a. suave; blando; maduro.

melodious /mə'loudiəs/ a. melodioso.

melodrama /'mɛlə,dramə/ n. melodrama m.

melody /'mɛlədi/ n. melodía f.

melon /'mɛlən/ n. melón m.

melt /mɛlt/ v. derretir.

meltdown /'mɛlt,daun/ n. fundición resultante de un accidente en un reactor nuclear.

member /'mɛmbər/ n. socio -ia; miembro m. **m. of the crew,** tripulante m. & f.

membership /'mɛmbər,ʃɪp/ n. número de miembros.

membrane /'mɛmbrein/ n. membrana f.

memento /mə'mɛntou/ n. recuerdo m.

memoir /'mɛmwɑr/ n. memoria f.

memorable /'mɛmərəbəl/ a. memorable.

memorandum /,mɛmə'rændəm/ n. memorándum, volante m.

memorial /mə'mɔriəl/ a. **1.** conmemorativo. —n. **2.** memorial m.

memorize /'mɛmə,raiz/ v. aprender de memoria.

memory /'mɛməri/ n. memoria f.; recuerdo m.

menace /'mɛnɪs/ n. **1.** amenaza f. —v. **2.** amenazar.

mend /mɛnd/ v. reparar, remendar.

menial /'miniəl/ a. **1.** servil. —n. **2.** sirviente -ta.

meningitis /,mɛnɪn'dʒaitɪs/ n. meningitis. f.

menopause /'mɛnə,pɔz/ n. menopausia f.

menstruation /,mɛnstru'eiʃən/ n. menstruación f.

menswear /'mɛnz,wɛər/ n. ropa de caballeros f.

mental /'mɛntl̩/ a. mental.

mental disorder trastorno mental m.

mentality /mɛn'tælɪti/ n. mentalidad f.

menthol /'mɛnθɔl/ n. mentol m.

mention /'mɛnʃən/ n. **1.** mención f. —v. **2.** mencionar.

menu /'mɛnyu/ n. menú m., lista f.

mercantile /'mɜrkən,til/ a. mercantil.

mercenary /'mɜrsə,nɛri/ a. & n. mercenario -ria.

merchandise /'mɜrtʃən,daiz/ n. mercancía f.

merchant /'mɜrtʃənt/ a. **1.** mercante. —n. **2.** comerciante m.

merciful /'mɜrsɪfəl/ a. misericordioso, compasivo.

merciless /'mɜrsɪlɪs/ a. cruel, inhumano.

mercury /'mɜrkyəri/ n. mercurio m.

mercy /'mɜrsi/ n. misericordia; merced f.

mere /mɪər/ a. mero, puro.

merely /'mɪərli/ adv. solamente; simplemente.

merge /mɜrdʒ/ v. unir, combinar.

merger /'mɜrdʒər/ n. consolidación, fusión f.

meringue /mə'ræŋ/ n. merengue m.

merit /'mɛrɪt/ n. **1.** mérito m. —v. **2.** merecer.

meritorious /,mɛrɪ'tɔriəs/ a. meritorio.

mermaid /'mɜr,meid/ n. sirena f.

merriment /'mɛrɪmənt/ n. regocijo m.

merry /'mɛri/ a. alegre, festivo.

merry-go-round /'mɛri gou ,raund/ n. caballitos m. pl.; tíovivo m.

mesh /mɛʃ/ n. malla f.

mess /mɛs/ n. **1.** lío m.; confusión f.; Mil. salón comedor; rancho m. —v. **2. m. up,** ensuciar; enredar.

message /'mɛsɪdʒ/ n. mensaje, recado m.

messenger /'mɛsəndʒər/ n. mensajero -ra.

messy /'mɛsi/ a. confuso; desarreglado.

metabolism /mə'tæbə,lɪzəm/ n. metabolismo m.

metal /'mɛtḷ/ n. metal m.

metallic /mə'tælɪk/ a. metálico.

metaphysics /,mɛtə'fɪzɪks/ n. metafísica f.

meteor /'mitiər/ n. meteoro m.

meteorology /,mitiə'rɒlədʒi/ n. meteorología f.

meter /'mitər/ n. contador, medidor; (measure) metro m.

method /'mɛθəd/ n. método m.

meticulous /mə'tɪkyələs/ a. meticuloso.

metric /'mɛtrɪk/ a. métrico.

metropolis /mɪ'trɒpəlɪs/ n. metrópoli f.

metropolitan /,mɛtrə'pɒlɪtṇ/ a. metropolitano.

Mexican /'mɛksɪkən/ a. & n. mexicano -na.

Mexico /'mɛksɪ,kou/ n. México m.

mezzanine /'mɛzə,nin/ n. entresuelo m.

microbe /'maikroub/ n. microbio m.

microchip /'maikrou,tʃɪp/ n. microchip m.

microfiche /'maikrə,fiʃ/ n. microficha f.

microfilm /'maikrə,fɪlm/ n. microfilm m.

microform /'maikrə,fɔrm/ n. microforma f.

microphone /'maikrə,foun/ n. micrófono m.

microscope /'maikrə,skoup/ n. microscopio m.

microscopic /,maikrə'skɒpɪk/ a. microscópico.

mid /mɪd/ a. medio.

middle /'mɪdḷ/ a. & n. medio m. **in the m. of,** en medio de, a mediados de.

middle-aged /eidʒd/ a. de edad madura.

Middle East Medio Oriente m.

middle finger dedo corazón m.

midget /'mɪdʒɪt/ n. enano -na.

midnight /'mɪd,nait/ n. medianoche f.

midwife /'mɪd,waif/ n. comadrona, partera f.

might /mait/ n. poder m., fuerza f.

mighty /'maiti/ a. poderoso.

migraine /'maigrein/ n. migraña f.; jaqueca f.

migrate /'maigreit/ v. emigrar.

migration /mai'greiʃən/ n. emigración f.

migratory /'maigrə,tɔri/ a. migratorio.

mild /maild/ a. moderado, suave; templado.

mildew /'mɪl,du/ n. añublo m., moho m.

mile /mail/ n. milla f.

mileage /'mailɪdʒ/ n. kilometraje m.

militant /'mɪlɪtənt/ a. militante.

militarism /'mɪlɪtə,rɪzəm/ n. militarismo m.

military /'mɪlɪ,tɛri/ a. militar.

militia /mɪ'lɪʃə/ n. milicia f.

milk /mɪlk/ n. **1.** leche f. —v. **2.** ordeñar.

milk chocolate chocolate con leche m.

milkman /'mɪlk,mæn/ n. lechero m.

milk shake batido m.

milky /'mɪlki/ a. lácteo; lechoso.
mill /mɪl/ n. **1.** molino m.; fábrica f. —v. **2.** moler.
miller /'mɪlər/ n. molinero -ra.
millimeter /'mɪlə,mitər/ n. milímetro m.
milliner /'mɪlənər/ n. sombrerero -ra.
millinery /'mɪlə,nɛri/ n. sombrerería f.
million /'mɪlyən/ n. millón m.
millionaire /,mɪlyə'nɛər/ n. millonario -ria.
mimic /'mɪmɪk/ n. **1.** mimo -ma. —v. **2.** imitar.
mind /maind/ n. **1.** mente; opinión f. —v. **2.** obedecer. **never m.,** no se ocupe.
mindful /'maindfəl/ a. atento.
mine /main/ pron. **1.** mío. —n. **2.** mina f. —v. **3.** minar.
miner /'mainər/ n. minero m.
mineral /'mɪnərəl/ a. & n. mineral m.
mineral water agua mineral f.
mine sweeper /'main,swipər/ dragaminas f.
mingle /'mɪŋgəl/ v. mezclar.
miniature /'mɪniətʃər/ n. miniatura f.
miniaturize /'mɪniətʃə,raiz/ v. miniaturizar.
minibus /'mɪni,bʌs/ n. microbús m.
minicab /'mɪni,kæb/ n. microtaxi m.
minimize /'mɪnə,maiz/ v. menospreciar.
minimum /'mɪnəməm/ a. & n. mínimo m.
mining /'mainɪŋ/ n. minería f.
minister /'mɪnəstər/ n. **1.** ministro -tra; _Relig._ pastor m. —v. **2.** ministrar.
ministry /'mɪnəstri/ n. ministerio m.
mink /mɪŋk/ n. visón m.; (fur) piel de visón m.
minor /'mainər/ a. **1.** menor. —n. **2.** menor de edad.
minority /mɪ'nɔrɪti/ n. minoría f.
minstrel /'mɪnstrəl/ n. juglar m.
mint /mɪnt/ n. **1.** menta f.; casa de moneda. —v. **2.** acuñar.
minus /'mainəs/ prep. menos.
minute /a. mai'nut; n. 'mɪnɪt/ a. **1.** minucioso. —n. **2.** minuto, momento m.
miracle /'mɪrəkəl/ n. milagro m.

miraculous /mɪ'rækyələs/ a. milagroso.
mirage /mɪ'rɑʒ/ n. espejismo m.
mire /maiər/ n. lodo m.
mirror /'mɪrər/ n. espejo m.
mirth /mɜrθ/ n. alegría; risa f.
misbehave /,mɪsbɪ'heiv/ v. portarse mal.
miscellaneous /,mɪsə'leiniəs/ a. misceláneo.
mischief /'mɪstʃɪf/ n. travesura, diablura f.
mischievous /'mɪstʃəvəs/ a. travieso, dañino.
miser /'maizər/ n. avaro -ra.
miserable /'mɪzərəbəl/ a. miserable; infeliz.
miserly /'maizərli/ a. avariento, tacaño.
misfortune /mɪs'fɔrtʃən/ n. desgracia f., infortunio, revés m.
misgiving /mɪs'gɪvɪŋ/ n. recelo m., desconfianza f.
mishap /'mɪshæp/ n. desgracia f., contratiempo m.
mislay /mɪs'lei/ v. perder.
mislead /mɪs'lid/ v. extraviar, despistar; pervertir.
misplaced /mɪs'pleist/ a. extraviado.
mispronounce /,mɪsprə'nouns/ v. pronunciar mal.
miss /mɪs/ n. **1.** señorita f. —v. **2.** perder; echar de menos, extrañar. **be missing,** faltar.
missile /'mɪsəl/ n. proyectil m.
mission /'mɪʃən/ n. misión f.
missionary /'mɪʃə,nɛri/ n. misionero -ra.
mist /mɪst/ n. niebla, bruma f.
mistake /mɪ'steik/ n. equivocación f.; error m. **to make a m.,** equivocarse.
mistaken /mɪ'steikən/ a. equivocado.
mister /'mɪstər/ n. señor m.
mistletoe /'mɪsəl,tou/ n. muérdago m.
mistreat /mɪs'trit/ v. maltratar.
mistress /'mɪstrɪs/ n. ama; señora; concubina f.
mistrust /mɪs'trʌst/ v. desconfiar; sospechar.
misty /'mɪsti/ a. nebuloso, brumoso.
misunderstand /,mɪsʌndər'stænd/ v. entender mal.
misuse /mɪs'yuz/ v. maltratar; abusar.
mite /mait/ n. pizca f., blanca f.

mitten /'mɪtṇ/ n. mitón, confortante m.

mix /mɪks/ v. mezclar. **m. up,** confundir.

mixer /'mɪksər/ (for food), n. batidora f.

mixture /'mɪkstʃər/ n. mezcla, mixtura f.

mix-up /'mɪks,ʌp/ n. confusión f.

moan /moun/ n. **1.** quejido, gemido m. —v. **2.** gemir.

mob /mɒb/ n. muchedumbre f.; gentío m.

mobilization /,moubələ'zeiʃən/ n. movilización f.

mobilize /'moubə,laiz/ v. movilizar.

mock /mɒk/ v. burlar.

mockery /'mɒkəri/ n. burla f.

mod /mɒd/ a. a la última; en boga.

mode /moud/ n. modo m.

model /'mɒdḷ/ n. **1.** modelo m. —v. **2.** modelar.

modem /'moudəm/ n. módem m.

moderate /a 'mɒdərɪt; v -ə,reit/ a. **1.** moderado. —v. **2.** moderar.

moderation /,mɒdə'reiʃən/ n. moderación; sobriedad f.

modern /'mɒdərn/ a. moderno.

modernize /'mɒdər,naiz/ v. modernizar.

modest /'mɒdɪst/ a. modesto.

modesty /'mɒdəsti/ n. modestia f.

modify /'mɒdə,fai/ v. modificar.

modulate /'mɒdʒə,leit/ v. modular.

moist /mɔist/ a. húmedo.

moisten /'mɔisən/ v. humedecer.

moisture /'mɔistʃər/ n. humedad f.

moisturize /'mɔistʃə,raiz/ v. hidratar.

molar /'moulər/ n. molar m.

molasses /mə'læsɪz/ n. melaza f.

mold /mould/ n. **1.** molde; moho m. —v. **2.** moldar, formar; enmohecerse.

moldy /'mouldi/ a. mohoso.

mole /'moulei/ n. lunar m.; (animal) topo m.

molecule /'mɒlɪ,kyul/ n. molécula f.

molest /mə'lɛst/ v. molestar.

mollify /'mɒlə,fai/ v. molificar.

moment /'moumənt/ n. momento m.

momentary /'moumən,tɛri/ a. momentáneo.

momentous /mou'mɛntəs/ a. importante.

monarch /'mɒnərk/ n. monarca m. & f.

monarchy /'mɒnərki/ n. monarquía f.

monastery /'mɒnə,stɛri/ n. monasterio m.

Monday /'mʌndei/ n. lunes m.

monetary /'mɒnɪ,tɛri/ a. monetario.

money /'mʌni/ n. dinero m. **m. order,** giro postal.

mongrel /'mʌŋgrəl/ n. **1.** mestizo m. —a. **2.** mestizo, cruzado.

monitor /'mɒnɪtər/ n. amonestador m.; (computer) consola f., pantalla f.

monk /mʌŋk/ n. monje m.

monkey /'mʌŋki/ n. mono -na.

monocle /'mɒnəkəl/ n. monóculo m.

monologue /'mɒnə,lɔg/ n. monólogo m.

monopolize /mə'nɒpə,laiz/ v. monopolizar.

monopoly /mə'nɒpəli/ n. monopolio m.

monosyllable /'mɒnə,sɪləbəl/ n. monosílabo m.

monotone /'mɒnə,toun/ n. monotonía f.

monotonous /mə'nɒtṇəs/ a. monótono.

monotony /mə'nɒtṇi/ n. monotonía f.

monsoon /mɒn'sun/ n. monzón m.

monster /'mɒnstər/ n. monstruo m.

monstrosity /mɒn'strɒsɪti/ n. monstruosidad f.

monstrous /'mɒnstrəs/ a. monstruoso.

month /mʌnθ/ n. mes m.

monthly /'mʌnθli/ a. mensual.

monument /'mɒnyəmənt/ n. monumento m.

monumental /,mɒnyə'mɛntḷ/ a. monumental.

mood /mud/ n. humor m.; Gram. modo m.

moody /'mudi/ a. caprichoso, taciturno.

moon /mun/ n. luna f.

moonlight /'mun,lait/ n. luz de la luna.

moonlighting /'mun,laitɪŋ/ n. pluriempleo m.

mud

moor /mʊr/ *n.* **1.** párano *m.* —*v.*
2. anclar.

Moor /mʊr/ *n.* moro -ra.

mop /mɒp/ *n.* **1.** fregasuelos *m.*,
fregona *f.*, (*S.A.*) trapeador *m.*
—*v.* **2.** fregar, (*S.A.*) trapear.

moped /ˈmoʊˌpɛd/ *n.* (vehicle)
velomotor *m.*

moral /ˈmɔrəl/ *a.* **1.** moral. —*n.* **2.**
moraleja *f.* **morals,** moralidad *f.*

morale /məˈræl/ *n.* espíritu *m.*

moralist /ˈmɔrəlɪst/ *n.* moralista
m. & f.

morality /məˈræləti/ *n.* moralidad,
ética *f.*

morbid /ˈmɔrbɪd/ *a.* mórbido.

more /mɔr/ *a. & adv.* más. **m.**
and m., cada vez más.

moreover /mɔrˈoʊvər/ *adv.* además.

morgue /mɔrg/ *n.* necrocomio *m.*

morning /ˈmɔrnɪŋ/ *n.* mañana *f.*
good m., buenos días.

Morocco /məˈrɒkoʊ/ *n.* Marruecos
m.

morose /məˈroʊs/ *a.* malhumorado.

morphine /ˈmɔrfin/ *n.* morfina *f.*

morsel /ˈmɔrsəl/ *n.* bocado *m.*

mortal /ˈmɔrtl̩/ *a. & n.* mortal *m.*
& f.

mortality /mɔrˈtæləti/ *n.* mortalidad *f.*

mortar /ˈmɔrtər/ *n.* mortero *m.*

mortgage /ˈmɔrgɪdʒ/ *n.* **1.** hipoteca *f.* —*v.* **2.** hipotecar.

mortify /ˈmɔrtəˌfai/ *v.* mortificar.

mosaic /moʊˈzeiɪk/ *n. & a.* mosaico *m.*

mosque /mɒsk/ *n.* mezquita *f.*

mosquito /məˈskitoʊ/ *n.* mosquito
m.

moss /mɔs/ *n.* musgo *m.*

most /moʊst/ *a.* **1.** más. —*adv.* **2.**
más; sumamente. —*pron.* **3. m.**
of, la mayor parte de.

mostly /ˈmoʊstli/ *adv.* principalmente; en su mayor parte.

motel /moʊˈtɛl/ *n.* motel *m.*

moth /mɔθ/ *n.* polilla *f.*

mother /ˈmʌðər/ *n.* madre *f.*

mother-in-law /ˈmʌðər ɪn ˌlɔ/ *n.*
suegra *f.*

motif /moʊˈtif/ *n.* tema *m.*

motion /ˈmoʊʃən/ *n.* **1.** moción *f.*;
movimiento *m.* —*v.* **2.** hacer
señas.

motionless /ˈmoʊʃənlɪs/ *a.* inmóvil.

motion picture película *f.*

motivate /ˈmoʊtəˌveit/ *v.* motivar.

motive /ˈmoʊtɪv/ *n.* motivo *m.*

motor /ˈmoʊtər/ *n.* motor *m.*

motorboat /ˈmoʊtərˌbout/ *n.*
lancha motora *f.*, autobote, mo-
torbote *m.*, gasolinera *f.*

motorcycle /ˈmoʊtərˌsaikəl/ *n.*
motocicleta *f.*

motorcyclist /ˈmoʊtərˌsaiklɪst/ *n.*
motociclista *m. & f.*

motorist /ˈmoʊtərɪst/ *n.* motorista
m. & f.

motto /ˈmɒtoʊ/ *n.* lema *m.*

mound /maund/ *n.* terrón; montón *m.*

mount /maunt/ *n.* **1.** monte *m.*;
(horse) montura *f.* —*v.* **2.** montar;
subir.

mountain /ˈmauntn̩/ *n.* montaña
f.

mountaineer /ˌmauntn̩ˈɪər/ *n.*
montañés *m.*

mountainous /ˈmauntn̩əs/ *a.*
montañoso.

mourn /mɔrn/ *v.* lamentar, llorar;
llevar luto.

mournful /ˈmɔrnfəl/ *a.* triste.

mourning /ˈmɔrnɪŋ/ *n.* luto; lamento *m.*

mouse /maus/ *n.* ratón, ratoncito
m.

mouth /mauθ/ *n.* boca *f.*; (of
river) desembocadura *f.*

mouthwash /ˈmauθˌwɒʃ/ *n.* enjuague bucal *m.*

movable /ˈmuvəbəl/ *a.* movible,
movedizo.

move /muv/ *n.* **1.** movimiento *m.*;
mudanza *f.* —*v.* **2.** mover; mudarse; emocionar, conmover. **m.**
away, quitar; alejarse; mudarse.

movement /ˈmuvmənt/ *n.* movimiento *m.*

movie /ˈmuvi/ *n.* película *f.* **m.**
theater, movies, cine *m.*

moving /ˈmuvɪŋ/ *a.* conmovedor;
persuasivo.

mow /moʊ/ *v.* guadañar, segar.

Mr. /ˈmɪstər/ *title.* Señor (Sr.).

Mrs. /ˈmɪsəz/ *title.* Señora (Sra.).

much /mʌtʃ/ *a. & adv.* mucho.
how m., cuánto. **so m.,** tanto.
too m., demasiado. **as m. as,**
tanto como.

mucilage /ˈmyusəlɪdʒ/ *n.* mu-
cílago *m.*

mucous /ˈmyukəs/ *a.* mucoso.

mucous membrane *n.* membrana
mucosa *f.*

mud /mʌd/ *n.* fango, lodo *m.*

muddy /'mʌdi/ a. **1.** lodoso; turbio. —v. **2.** ensuciar; enturbiar.

muff /mʌf/ n. manguito m.

muffin /'mʌfɪn/ n. panecillo m.

mug /mʌg/ n. cubilete m.

mugger /'mʌgər/ n. asaltante m. & f.

mulatto /mə'lætou/ n. mulato m.

mule /myul/ n. mula f.

mullah /'mʌlə/ n. mullah m.

multicultural /ˌmʌlti'kʌltʃərəl, ˌmʌltai-/ a. multicultural.

multinational /ˌmʌlti'næʃənļ, ˌmʌltai-/ a. multinacional.

multiple /'mʌltəpəl/ a. múltiple.

multiplication /ˌmʌltəplɪ'keiʃən/ n. multiplicación f.

multiplicity /ˌmʌltə'plɪsɪti/ n. multiplicidad f.

multiply /'mʌltəpli/ v. multiplicar.

multitasking /ˌmʌlti'tæskɪŋ, ˌmʌltai-/ n. multitarea f.

multitude /'mʌltɪˌtud/ n. multitud f.

mummy /'mʌmi/ n. momia f.

mumps /mʌmps/ n. paperas f.pl.

municipal /myu'nɪsəpəl/ a. municipal.

munificent /myu'nɪfəsənt/ a. munífico.

munitions /myu'nɪʃənz/ n. municiones m.pl.

mural /'myurəl/ a. & n. mural m.

murder /'mɜrdər/ n. **1.** asesinato; homicidio m. —v. **2.** asesinar.

murderer /'mɜrdərər/ n. asesino -na.

murmur /'mɜrmər/ n. **1.** murmullo m. —v. **2.** murmurar.

muscle /'mʌsəl/ n. músculo m.

muscular /'mʌskyələr/ a. muscular.

muse /myuz/ n. **1.** musa f. —v. **2.** meditar.

museum /myu'ziəm/ n. museo m.

mushroom /'mʌʃrum/ n. seta f., hongo m.

music /'myuzɪk/ n. música f.

musical /'myuzɪkəl/ a. musical; melodioso.

musician /myu'zɪʃən/ n. músico -ca.

Muslim /'mʌzlɪm/ a. & n. musulmano.

muslin /'mʌzlɪn/ n. muselina f.; percal m.

mussel /'mʌsəl/ n. mejillón m.

must /mʌst/ v. deber; tener que.

mustache /'mʌstæʃ/ n. bigotes m.pl.

mustard /'mʌstərd/ n. mostaza f.

muster /'mʌstər/ n. **1.** Mil. revista f. —v. **2.** reunir, juntar.

mute /myut/ a. & n. mudo -da.

mutilate /'myutļˌeit/ v. mutilar.

mutiny /'myutņi/ n. **1.** motín m. —v. **2.** amotinarse.

mutt /mʌt/ n. Colloq. chucho m.

mutter /'mʌtər/ v. refunfuñar, gruñir.

mutton /'mʌtņ/ n. carnero m.

mutual /'myutʃuəl/ a. mutuo.

muzzle /'mʌzəl/ n. **1.** hocico m.; bozal m. —v. **2.** embozar.

my /mai/ a. mi.

myriad /'mɪriəd/ n. miríada f.

myrtle /'mɜrtļ/ n. mirto m.

myself /mai'sɛlf/ pron. mí, mí mismo; me. **I m.,** yo mismo.

mysterious /mɪ'stɪəriəs/ a. misterioso.

mystery /'mɪstəri/ n. misterio m.

mystic /'mɪstɪk/ a. místico.

mystify /'mɪstəˌfai/ v. confundir.

myth /mɪθ/ n. mito m.

mythical /'mɪθɪkəl/ a. mítico.

mythology /mɪ'θɒlədʒi/ n. mitología f.

N

nag /næg/ n. **1.** jaca f. —v. **2.** regañar; sermonear.

nail /neil/ n. **1.** clavo m.; (finger) uña f. **n. polish,** esmalte para las uñas. —v. **2.** clavar.

naïve /nɑ'iv/ a. ingenuo.

naked /'neikɪd/ a. desnudo.

name /neim/ n. **1.** nombre m.; reputación f. —v. **2.** nombrar, mencionar.

namely /'neimli/ adv. a saber; es decir.

namesake /'neimˌseik/ n. tocayo m.

nanny /'næni/ n. niñera f.

nap /næp/ n. siesta f. **to take a n.,** echar una siesta.

naphtha /'næfθə, 'næp-/ n. nafta f.

napkin /'næpkɪn/ n. servilleta f.

narcissus /nɑr'sɪsəs/ n. narciso m.

narcotic /nɑr'kɒtɪk/ a. & n. narcótico m.

narrate /'næreit/ v. narrar.

narrative /'nærətɪv/ a. **1.** narrativo. —n. **2.** cuento, relato m.

narrow /'nærou/ a. estrecho, angosto. **n.-minded,** intolerante.

nasal /'neizəl/ a. nasal.

nasty /'næsti/ a. desagradable.

nation /'neiʃən/ n. nación f.

national /'næʃənḷ/ a. nacional.

nationalism /'næʃənḷ,ɪzəm/ n. nacionalismo m.

nationality /,næʃə'næliti/ n. nacionalidad f.

nationalization /,næʃənḷə'zeiʃən/ n. nacionalización f.

nationalize /'næʃənḷ,aiz, 'næʃnə,laiz/ v. nacionalizar.

native /'neitɪv/ a. **1.** nativo. —n. **2.** natural; indígena m. & f.

nativity /nə'tɪvɪti/ n. natividad f.

natural /'nætʃərəl/ a. natural.

naturalist /'nætʃərəlɪst/ n. naturalista m. & f.

naturalize /'nætʃərə,laiz/ v. naturalizar.

naturalness /,nætʃərəlnɪs/ n. naturalidad f.

nature /'neitʃər/ n. naturaleza f.; índole f.; humor m.

naughty /'nɔti/ a. travieso, desobediente.

nausea /'nɔziə, -ʒə/ n. náusea f.

nauseous /'nɔʃəs/ a. nauseoso.

nautical /'nɔtɪkəl/ a. náutico.

naval /'neivəl/ a. naval.

nave /neiv/ n. nave f.

navel /'neivəl/ n. ombligo m.

navigable /'nævɪgəbəl/ a. navegable.

navigate /'nævɪ,geit/ v. navegar.

navigation /,nævɪ'geiʃən/ n. navegación f.

navigator /'nævɪ,geitər/ n. navegante m. & f.

navy /'neivi/ n. marina f.

navy blue azul marino m.

near /nɪər/ a. **1.** cercano, próximo. —adv. **2.** cerca. —prep. **3.** cerca de.

nearby /'nɪər'bai/ a. **1.** cercano. —adv. **2.** cerca.

nearly /'nɪərli/ adv. casi.

nearsighted /'nɪər,saitɪd/ a. corto de vista.

neat /nit/ a. aseado; ordenado.

neatness /'nitnɪs/ n. aseo m.

nebulous /'nɛbyələs/ a. nebuloso.

necessary /'nɛsə,sɛri/ a. necesario.

necessity /nə'sɛsɪti/ n. necesidad f.

neck /nɛk/ n. cuello m.

necklace /'nɛklɪs/ n. collar m.

necktie /'nɛk,tai/ n. corbata f.

nectar /'nɛktər/ n. néctar m.

nectarine /,nɛktə'rin/ n. nectarina f.

need /nid/ n. **1.** necesidad; (poverty) pobreza f. —v. **2.** necesitar.

needle /'nidḷ/ n. aguja f.

needless /'nidlɪs/ a. innecesario, inútil.

needy /'nidi/ a. indigente, necesitado, pobre.

nefarious /nɪ'fɛəriəs/ a. nefario.

negative /'nɛgətɪv/ a. negativo. n. negativa f.

neglect /nɪ'glɛkt/ n. **1.** negligencia f.; descuido m. —v. **2.** descuidar.

negligee /,nɛglɪ'ʒei/ n. negligé m., bata de casa f.

negligent /'nɛglɪdʒənt/ a. negligente, descuidado.

negligible /'nɛglɪdʒəbəl/ a. insignificante.

negotiate /nɪ'gouʃi,eit/ v. negociar.

negotiation /nɪ,gouʃi'eiʃən/ n. negociación f.

Negro /'nigrou/ n. negro -ra.

neighbor /'neibər/ n. vecino -na.

neighborhood /'neibər,hʊd/ n. vecindad f.

neither /'niðər, 'nai-/ a. & pron. **1.** ninguno de los dos. —adv. **2.** tampoco. —conj. **3. neither... nor,** ni... ni.

neon /'nibn/ n. neón m. **n. light,** tubo neón m.

nephew /'nɛfyu/ n. sobrino m.

nerve /nɜrv/ n. nervio m.; Colloq. audacia f.

nervous /'nɜrvəs/ a. nervioso.

nervous breakdown /'breik,daun/ crisis nerviosa f.

nest /nɛst/ n. nido m.

net /nɛt/ a. **1.** neto. —n. **2.** red f. **hair n.,** albanega, redecilla f. v. redar; Com. ganar.

netiquette /'nɛtɪkɪt/ n. etiqueta de la red f.

netting /'nɛtɪŋ/ n. red m.; obra de malla f.

network /'nɛt,wɜrk/ n. (radio) red radiodifusora.

neuralgia /nʊ'rældʒə/ n. neuralgia f.

neurology /nʊ'rɒlədʒi/ n. neurología f.

neurotic /nʊ'rɒtɪk/ a. neurótico.

neutral /'nutrəl/ *a.* neutral.

neutrality /nu'træliti/ *n.* neutralidad *f.*

neutron /'nutron/ *n.* neutrón *m.*

neutron bomb bomba de neutrones *f.*

never /'nɛvər/ *adv.* nunca, jamás; **n. mind,** no importa.

nevertheless /ˌnɛvərðə'lɛs/ *adv.* no obstante, sin embargo.

new /nu/ *a.* nuevo.

newbie /'nubi/ *n. Colloq.* novato -ta, inexperto -ta.

news /nuz/ *n.* noticias *f.pl.*

newsboy /'nuz,bɔi/ *n.* vendedor -ra de periódicos.

news bulletin boletín informativo *m.*

news flash *n.* noticia de última hora *f.*

newsgroup /'nuz,grup/ *n.* grupo de discusion *m.*

newsletter /'nuz,lɛtər/ *n.* hoja informativa *f.*

newspaper /'nuz,peipər/ *n.* periódico *m.*

New Testament Nuevo Testamento *m.*

new year *n.* año nuevo *m.*

next /nɛkst/ *a.* **1.** próximo; siguiente; contiguo. —*adv.* **2.** luego, después. **n. door,** al lado. **n. to,** al lado de.

next-to-the-last /'nɛkst tə ðə 'læst/ *a.* penúltimo.

nibble /'nıbəl/ *v.* picar.

nice /nis/ *a.* simpático, agradable; amable; hermoso; exacto.

nick /nık/ *n.* muesca *f.,* picadura *f.* **in the n. of time,** a punto.

nickel /'nıkəl/ *n.* níquel *m.*

nickname /'nık,neim/ *n.* **1.** apodo, mote *m.* —*v.* **2.** apodar.

nicotine /'nıkə,tin/ *n.* nicotina *f.*

niece /nis/ *n.* sobrina *f.*

niggardly /'nıgərdli/ *a.* mezquino.

night /nait/ *n.* noche *f.* **good n.,** buenas noches. **last n.,** anoche. **n. club,** cabaret *m.*

nightclub /'nait,klʌb/ *n.* cabaret *m.*

nightclub owner cabaretero -ra *m. & f.*

nightgown /'nait,gaun/ *n.* camisa de dormir.

nightingale /'naitṇ,geil, 'naitıŋ-/ *n.* ruiseñor *m.*

nightly /'naitli/ *adv.* todas las noches.

nightmare /'nait,mɛər/ *n.* pesadilla *f.*

night school escuela nocturna *f.*

night watchman vigilante nocturno *m.*

nimble /'nımbəl/ *a.* ágil.

nine /nain/ *a. & pron.* nueve.

nineteen /'nain'tin/ *a. & pron.* diecinueve.

ninety /'nainti/ *a. & pron.* noventa.

ninth /nainθ/ *a.* noveno.

nipple /'nıpəl/ *n.* teta *f.;* pezón *m.*

nitrogen /'naitrədʒən/ *n.* nitrógeno *m.*

no /nou/ *a.* **1.** ninguno. **no one,** nadie. —*adv.* **2.** no.

nobility /nou'bıliti/ *n.* nobleza *f.*

noble /'noubəl/ *a. & n.* noble *m.*

nobleman /'noubəlmən/ *n.* noble *m.*

nobody /'nou,bɒdi/ *pron.* nadie.

nocturnal /nɒk'tɜrnḷ/ *a.* nocturno.

nocturne /'nɒktɜrn/ *n.* nocturno *m.*

nod /nɒd/ *n.* **1.** seña con la cabeza. —*v.* **2.** inclinar la cabeza; (doze) dormitar.

no-frills /'nou 'frılz/ *a.* sin extras.

noise /nɔiz/ *n.* ruido *m.*

noiseless /'nɔizlıs/ *a.* silencioso.

noisy /'nɔizi/ *a.* ruidoso.

nominal /'nɒmənḷ/ *a.* nominal.

nominate /'nɒmə,neit/ *v.* nombrar.

nomination /ˌnɒmə'neiʃən/ *n.* nombramiento *m.,* nominación *f.*

nominee /ˌnɒmə'ni/ *n.* candidato -ta.

nonaligned /ˌnɒnə'laind/ (in political sense), *a.* no alineado.

nonchalant /ˌnɒnʃə'lɑnt/ *a.* indiferente.

noncombatant /ˌnɒnkəm'bætnt/ *n.* no combatiente *m.*

noncommittal /ˌnɒnkə'mıtḷ/ *a.* evasivo; reservado.

nondescript /ˌnɒndı'skrıpt/ *a.* difícil de describir.

none /nʌn/ *pron.* ninguno.

nonentity /nɒn'ɛntıti/ *n.* nulidad *f.*

nonpartisan /nɒn'pɑrtəzən/ *a.* sin afiliación.

non-proliferation /ˌnɒnprə,lıfə'reiʃən/ *n.* no proliferación *m.*

nonsense /'nɒnsɛns/ *n.* tontería *f.*

nonsmoker /nɒn'smoukər/ *n.* no fumador -dora.

noodle /'nudḷ/ *n.* fideo *m.*

noon /nun/ *n.* mediodía *m.*

noose /nus/ *n.* lazo corredizo *m.;* dogal *m.*

nor /nɔr; *unstressed* nər/ *conj.* ni.

normal /'nɔrməl/ *a.* normal.

north /nɔrθ/ *n.* norte *m.*

North America /ə'mɛrɪkə/ Norte América *f.*

North American *a. & n.* norteamericano -na.

northeast /,nɔrθ'ist; *Naut.* ,nɔr-/ *n.* nordeste *m.*

northern /'nɔrðərn/ *a.* septentrional.

North Pole *n.* Polo Norte *m.*

northwest /,nɔrθ'wɛst; *Naut.* ,nɔr-/ *n.* noroeste *m.*

Norway /'nɔrwei/ *n.* Noruega *f.*

Norwegian /nɔr'widʒən/ *a. & n.* noruego -ga.

nose /nouz/ *n.* nariz *f.*

nosebleed /'nouz,blid/ *n.* hemorragia nasal *f.*

nostalgia /nɒ'stældʒə/ *n.* nostalgia *f.*

nostril /'nɒstrəl/ *n.* ventana de la nariz; (pl.) narices *f.pl.*

not /nɒt/ *adv.* no. **n. at all,** de ninguna manera. **n. even,** ni siquiera.

notable /'noutəbəl/ *a.* notable.

notary /'noutəri/ *n.* notario *m.*

notation /nou'teiʃən/ *a.* notación *f.*

notch /nɒtʃ/ *n.* muesca *f.;* corte *m.*

note /nout/ *n.* **1.** nota *f.;* apunte *m.* —*v.* **2.** notar.

notebook /'nout,bʊk/ *n.* libreta *f.,* cuaderno *m.*

noted /'noutɪd/ *a.* célebre.

notepaper /'nout,peipər/ *n.* papel de notas *m.*

noteworthy /'nout,wɜrði/ *a.* notable.

nothing /'nʌθɪŋ/ *pron.* nada.

notice /'noutɪs/ *n.* **1.** aviso *m.;* noticia *f.* —*v.* **2.** observar, fijarse en.

noticeable /'noutɪsəbəl/ *a.* notable.

notification /,noutəfɪ'keiʃən/ *n.* notificación *f.*

notify /'noutə,fai/ *v.* notificar.

notion /'nouʃən/ *n.* noción; idea *f.;* (pl.) novedades *f.pl.*

notoriety /,noutə'raiɪti/ *n.* notoriedad *f.*

notorious /nou'tɔriəs/ *a.* notorio.

noun /naun/ *n.* nombre, sustantivo *m.*

nourish /'nɜrɪʃ/ *v.* nutrir, alimentar.

nourishment /'nɜrɪʃmənt/ *n.* nutrimento; alimento *m.*

novel /'nɒvəl/ *a.* **1.** nuevo, original. —*n.* **2.** novela *f.*

novelist /'nɒvəlɪst/ *n.* novelista *m. & f.*

novelty /'nɒvəlti/ *n.* novedad *f.*

November /nou'vɛmbər/ *n.* noviembre *m.*

novena /nou'vinə/ *n.* novena *f.*

novice /'nɒvɪs/ *n.* novicio -cia, novato -ta.

novocaine /'nouvə,kein/ *n.* novocaína *f.*

now /nau/ *adv.* ahora. **n. and then,** de vez en cuando. **by n.,** ya. **from n. on,** de ahora en adelante. **just n.,** ahorita. **right n.,** ahora mismo.

nowadays /'nauə,deiz/ *adv.* hoy día, hoy en día, actualmente.

nowhere /'nou,wɛər/ *adv.* en ninguna parte.

nozzle /'nɒzəl/ *n.* boquilla *f.*

nuance /'nuɑns/ *n.* matiz *m.*

nuclear /'nukliər/ *a.* nuclear.

nuclear energy energía nuclear *f.*

nuclear warhead /'wɔr,hɛd/ cabeza nuclear *f.*

nuclear waste desechos nucleares *m.pl.*

nucleus /'nukliəs/ *n.* núcleo *m.*

nude /nud/ *a.* desnudo.

nuisance /'nusəns/ *n.* molestia *f.*

nuke /nuk/ *n.* bomba atómica *f.*

nullify /'nʌlə,fai/ *v.* anular.

number /'nʌmbər/ *n.* **1.** número *m.;* cifra *f.* **license n.,** matrícula *f.* —*v.* **2.** numerar, contar.

numeric /nu'mɛrɪk/ **numerical** *a.* numérico.

numeric keypad /nu'mɛrɪk/ teclado numérico *m.*

numerous /'numərəs/ *a.* numeroso.

nun /nun/ *n.* monja *f.*

nuptial /'nʌpʃəl/ *a.* nupcial.

nurse /nɜrs/ *n.* **1.** enfermera *f.;* (child's) ama, niñera *f.* —*v.* **2.** criar, alimentar, amamantar; cuidar.

nursery /'nɜrsəri/ *n.* cuarto destinado a los niños; *Agr.* plantel, criadero *m.*

nursery school jardín de infancia *m.*

nurture /'nɜrtʃər/ v. nutrir.

nut /nʌt/ n. nuez f.; *Mech.* tuerca f.

nutcracker /'nʌt,krækər/ n. cas canueces m.

nutrition /nu'trɪʃən/ n. nutrición f.

nutritious /nu'trɪʃəs/ a. nutritivo.

nylon /'nailɒn/ n. nilón m.

nymph /nɪmf/ n. ninfa f.

O

oak /ouk/ n. roble m.

oar /ɔr/ n. remo m.

OAS abbr. (Organization of American States) OEA (Organización de los Estados Americanos) f.

oasis /ou'eisɪs/ n. oasis m.

oat /out/ n. avena f.

oath /ouθ/ n. juramento m.

oatmeal /'out,mil/ n. harina de avena f.

obedience /ou'bidiəns/ n. obediencia f.

obedient /ou'bidiənt/ a. obediente.

obese /ou'bis/ a. obeso, gordo.

obey /ou'bei/ v. obedecer.

obituary /ou'bɪtʃu,eri/ n. obituario m.

object /n 'ɒbdʒɪkt; v əb'dʒɛkt/ n. **1.** objeto m.; *Gram.* complemento m. —v. **2.** oponerse; objetar.

objection /əb'dʒɛkʃən/ n. objeción f.

objectionable /əb'dʒɛkʃənəbəl/ a. censurable.

objective /əb'dʒɛktɪv/ a. & n. objetivo m.

obligation /,ɒblɪ'geiʃən/ n. obligación f.

obligatory /ə'blɪgə,tɔri/ a. obligatorio.

oblige /ə'blaidʒ/ v. obligar; complacer.

oblique /ə'blik/ a. oblicuo.

obliterate /ə'blɪtə,reit/ v. borrar; destruir.

oblivion /ə'blɪviən/ n. olvido m.

oblong /'ɒb,lɔŋ/ a. oblongo.

obnoxious /əb'nɒkʃəs/ a. ofensivo, odioso.

obscene /əb'sin/ a. obsceno, indecente.

obscure /əb'skyʊr/ a. **1.** obscuro. —v. **2.** obscurecer.

observance /əb'zɜrvəns/ n. observancia; ceremonia f.

observation /,ɒbzɜr'veiʃən/ n. observación f.

observatory /əb'zɜrvə,tɔri/ n. observatorio m.

observe /əb'zɜrv/ v. observar; celebrar.

observer /əb'zɜrvər/ n. observador -ra.

obsession /əb'sɛʃən/ n. obsesión f.

obsolete /,ɒbsə'lit/ a. anticuado.

obstacle /'ɒbstəkəl/ n. obstáculo m.

obstetrician /,ɒbstɪ'trɪʃən/ n. obstétrico -ca, tocólogo -ga m. & f.

obstinate /'ɒbstənɪt/ a. obstinado, terco.

obstruct /əb'strʌkt/ v. obstruir, impedir.

obstruction /əb'strʌkʃən/ n. obstrucción f.

obtain /əb'tein/ v. obtener, conseguir.

obtuse /əb'tus/ a. obtuso.

obviate /'ɒbvi,eit/ v. obviar.

obvious /'ɒbviəs/ a. evidente, obvio.

occasion /ə'keiʒən/ n. **1.** ocasión f. —v. **2.** ocasionar.

occasional /ə'keiʒənl/ a. ocasional.

occult /ə'kʌlt/ a. oculto.

occupant /'ɒkyəpənt/ n. ocupante m. & f.; inquilino -na.

occupation /,ɒkyə'peiʃən/ n. ocupación f.; empleo m.

occupy /'ɒkyə,pai/ v. ocupar; emplear.

occur /ə'kɜr/ v. ocurrir.

occurrence /ə'kɜrəns/ n. ocurrencia f.

ocean /'ouʃən/ n. océano m.

o'clock /ə'klɒk/ it's one o., es la una. it's two o., son las dos, etc. at... o., a las...

octagon /'ɒktə,gɒn/ n. octágono m.

octave /'ɒktɪv/ n. octava f.

October /ɒk'toubər/ n. octubre m.

octopus /'ɒktəpəs/ n. pulpo m.

oculist /'ɒkyəlɪst/ n. oculista m. & f.

odd /ɒd/ a. impar; suelto; raro.

odd number número impar m.

odious /'oudiəs/ *a.* odioso.
odor /'oudər/ *n.* olor *m.;* fragancia *f.*
of /əv/ *prep.* de.
off /ɔf/ *adv.* (see under verb: **stop off, take off,** etc.)
offend /ə'fɛnd/ *v.* ofender.
offender /ə'fɛndər/ *n.* ofensor -ra; delincuente *m.* & *f.*
offense /ə'fɛns/ *n.* ofensa *f.;* crimen *m.*
offensive /ə'fɛnsɪv/ *a.* **1.** ofensivo. —*n.* **2.** ofensiva *f.*
offer /'ɔfər/ *n.* **1.** oferta *f.* —*v.* **2.** ofrecer.
offering /'ɔfərɪŋ/ *n.* oferta *f.*
office /'ɔfɪs/ *n.* oficina *f.;* despacho *m.;* oficio, cargo *m.*
officer /'ɔfəsər/ *n.* oficial *m.* & *f.* **police o.,** agente de policía *m.* & *f.*
official /ə'fɪʃəl/ *a.* **1.** oficial. —*n.* **2.** oficial *m.* & *f.,* funcionario -ria.
officiate /ə'fɪʃi,eit/ *v.* oficiar.
officious /ə'fɪʃəs/ *a.* oficioso.
offspring /'ɔf,sprɪŋ/ *n.* hijos *m.pl.;* progenie *f.*
often /'ɔfən/ *adv.* muchas veces, a menudo. **how o.,** con qué frecuencia.
oil /ɔil/ *n.* **1.** aceite; óleo; petróleo *m.* —*v.* **2.** aceitar; engrasar.
oil refinery /rɪ'fainəri/ destilería de petróleo *f.*
oil tanker /'tæŋkər/ petrolero *m.*
oily /'ɔili/ *a.* aceitoso.
ointment /'ɔintmənt/ *n.* ungüento *m.*
okay /'ou'kei, ,ou'kei/ *adv.* bien; de acuerdo.
old /ould/ *a.* viejo; antiguo. **o. man, o. woman,** viejo -ja.
old-fashioned /'ould 'fæʃənd/ *a.* fuera de moda, anticuado.
Old Testament Antiguo Testamento *m.*
olive /'ɒlɪv/ *n.* aceituna, oliva *f.*
ombudsman /'ɒmbədzmən/ *n.* ombudsman *m.*
omelet /'ɒmlɪt/ *n.* tortilla de huevos.
omen /'oumən/ *n.* agüero *m.*
ominous /'ɒmənəs/ *a.* ominoso, siniestro.
omission /ou'mɪʃən/ *n.* omisión *f.;* olvido *m.*
omit /ou'mɪt/ *v.* omitir.
omnibus /'ɒmnə,bʌs/ *n.* ómnibus *m.*

omnipotent /ɒm'nɪpətənt/ *a.* omnipotente.
on /ɒn/ *prep.* **1.** en, sobre, encima de. —*adv.* **2.** adelante.
once /wʌns/ *adv.* una vez. **at o.,** en seguida. **o. in a while,** de vez en cuando.
one /wʌn/ *a.* & *pron.* uno -na.
one-armed bandit /'wʌn ,ɑrmd/ tragaperras *f.*
oneself /wʌn'sɛlf/ *pron.* sí mismo -ma; se. **with o.,** consigo.
onion /'ʌnyən/ *n.* cebolla *f.*
on-line /'ɒn 'lain/ *a.* conectado.
only /'ounli/ *a.* **1.** único, solo. —*adv.* **2.** sólo, solamente.
onward /'ɒnwərd/ *adv.* adelante.
opal /'oupəl/ *n.* ópalo *m.*
opaque /ou'peik/ *a.* opaco.
open /'oupən/ *a.* **1.** abierto; franco. **o. air,** aire libre. —*v.* **2.** abrir.
opening /'oupənɪŋ/ *n.* abertura *f.*
opera /'ɒpərə/ *n.* ópera *f.* **o. glasses,** anteojos de ópera; gemelos *m.pl.*
operate /'ɒpə,reit/ *v.* operar.
operation /,ɒpə'reiʃən/ *n.* operación *f.* **to have an o.,** operarse, ser operado.
operative /'ɒpərətɪv/ *a.* eficaz, operativo.
operator /'ɒpə,reitər/ *n.* operario -ria. **elevator o.,** ascensorista *m.* & *f.* **telephone o.,** telefonista *m.* & *f.*
operetta /,ɒpə'rɛtə/ *n.* opereta *f.*
ophthalmic /ɒf'θælmɪk, ɒp-/ *a.* oftálmico.
opinion /ə'pɪnyən/ *n.* opinión *f.*
opponent /ə'pounənt/ *n.* antagonista *m.* & *f.*
opportunism /,ɒpər'tunɪzəm/ *n.* oportunismo *m.*
opportunity /,ɒpər'tuniti/ *n.* ocasión, oportunidad *f.*
oppose /ə'pouz/ *v.* oponer.
opposite /'ɒpəzɪt/ *a.* **1.** opuesto, contrario. —*prep.* **2.** al frente de. —*n.* **3.** contrario *m.*
opposition /,ɒpə'zɪʃən/ *n.* oposición *f.*
oppress /ə'prɛs/ *v.* oprimir.
oppression /ə'prɛʃən/ *n.* opresión *f.*
oppressive /ə'prɛsɪv/ *a.* opresivo.
optic /'ɒptɪk/ *a.* óptico.
optical disc /'ɒptɪkəl 'dɪsk/ disco óptico *m.*

optical illusion /'ɒptɪkəl/ ilusión de óptica *f.*

optician /ɒp'tɪʃən/ *n.* óptico -ca.

optics /'ɒptɪks/ *n.* óptica *f.*

optimism /'ɒptə,mɪzəm/ *n.* optimismo.

optimistic /,ɒptə'mɪstɪk/ *a.* optimista.

option /'ɒpʃən/ *n.* opción, elección *f.*

optional /'ɒpʃənl/ *a.* discrecional, facultativo.

optometry /ɒp'tɒmɪtri/ *n.* optometría *f.*

opulent /'ɒpyələnt/ *a.* opulento.

or /ɔr/ *conj.* o, (before o-, ho-) u.

oracle /'ɔrəkəl/ *n.* oráculo *m.*

oral /'ɔrəl/ *a.* oral, vocal.

orange /'ɔrɪndʒ/ *n.* naranja *f.*

orange juice jugo de naranja, zumo de naranja *m.*

orange squeezer /'skwizər/ *n.* exprimidora de naranjas *f.*

oration /ɔ'reɪʃən/ *n.* discurso *m.;* oración *f.*

orator /'ɔrətər/ *n.* orador -ra.

oratory /'ɔrə,tɔri/ *n.* oratoria *f.;* (church) oratorio *m.*

orbit /'ɔrbɪt/ *n.* órbita *f.*

orchard /'ɔrtʃərd/ *n.* huerto *m.*

orchestra /'ɔrkəstrə/ *n.* orquesta *f.* **o. seat,** butaca *f.*

orchid /'ɔrkɪd/ *n.* orquídea *f.*

ordain /ɔr'dein/ *v.* ordenar.

ordeal /ɔr'dil/ *n.* prueba *f.*

order /'ɔrdər/ *n.* orden, *m. or f.;* clase *f.;* Com. pedido *m.* **in o. that,** para que. *v.* ordenar; mandar; pedir.

order blank hoja de pedidos *f.*

orderly /'ɔrdərli/ *a.* ordenado.

ordinance /'ɔrdṇəns/ *n.* ordenanza *f.*

ordinary /'ɔrdṇ,eri/ *a.* ordinario.

ordination /,ɔrdṇ'eiʃən/ *n.* ordenación *f.*

ore /ɔr/ *n.* mineral *m.*

organ /'ɔrgən/ *n.* órgano *m.*

organdy /'ɔrgəndi/ *n.* organdí *m.*

organic /ɔr'gænɪk/ *a.* orgánico.

organism /'ɔrgə,nɪzəm/ *n.* organismo *m.*

organist /'ɔrgənɪst/ *n.* organista *m. & f.*

organization /,ɔrgənə'zeiʃən/ *n.* organización *f.*

organize /'ɔrgə,naiz/ *v.* organizar.

orgy /'ɔrdʒi/ *n.* orgía *f.*

orient /'ɔriənt/ *n.* **1.** oriente *m.* —*v.* **2.** orientar.

Orient /'ɔriənt/ *n.* Oriente *m.*

Oriental /,ɔri'ɛntl/ *a.* oriental.

orientation /,ɔriən'teiʃən/ *n.* orientación *f.*

origin /'ɔrɪdʒɪn/ *n.* origen *m.*

original /ə'rɪdʒənl/ *a. & n.* original *m.*

originality /ə,rɪdʒə'næliti/ *n.* originalidad *f.*

ornament /n 'ɔrnəmənt; v -,mɛnt/ *n.* **1.** ornamento *m.* —*v.* **2.** ornamentar.

ornamental /,ɔrnə'mɛntl/ *a.* ornamental, decorativo.

ornate /ɔr'neit/ *a.* ornado.

ornithology /,ɔrnə'θɒlədʒi/ *n.* ornitología *f.*

orphan /'ɔrfən/ *a. & n.* huérfano -na.

orphanage /'ɔrfənɪdʒ/ *n.* orfanato *m.*

orthodox /'ɔrθə,dɒks/ *a.* ortodoxo.

ostentation /,ɒstɛn'teiʃən/ *n.* ostentación *f.*

ostentatious /,ɒstɛn'teiʃəs/ *a.* ostentoso.

ostrich /'ɒstrɪtʃ/ *n.* avestruz *f.*

other /'ʌðər/ *a. & pron.* otro. **every o. day,** un día sí otro no.

otherwise /'ʌðər,waiz/ *adv.* de otra manera.

ought /ɔt/ *v.* deber.

ounce /auns/ *n.* onza *f.*

our /auᵊr; *unstressed* ɑr/ **ours** *a. & pron.* nuestro.

ourselves /ɑr'sɛlvz/ *pron.* nosotros -as; mismos -as; nos.

oust /aust/ *v.* desalojar.

ouster /'austər/ *n.* desahucio *m.*

out /aut/ *adv.* **1.** fuera, afuera. **out of,** fuera de. —*prep.* **2.** por.

outbreak /'aut,breik/ *n.* erupción *f.*

outcast /'aut,kæst/ *n.* paria *m. & f.*

outcome /'aut,kʌm/ *n.* resultado *m.*

outdoors /,aut'dɔrz/ *adv.* fuera de casa; al aire libre.

outer /'autər/ *a.* exterior, externo.

outfit /'aut,fɪt/ *n.* **1.** equipo; traje *m.* —*v.* **2.** equipar.

outgrowth /'aut,grouθ/ *n.* resultado *m.*

outing /'autɪŋ/ *n.* paseo *m.*

outlaw /'aut,lɔ/ *n.* **1.** bandido *m.* —*v.* **2.** proscribir.

outlet /'autlɛt/ *n.* salida *f.*

outline /'aut,lain/ *n.* **1.** contorno;

esbozo *m.*; silueta *f.* —*v.* **2.** esbozar.

outlive /ˌautˈlɪv/ *v.* sobrevivir.

out-of-court settlement /ˈautəvˌkɔrt/ arreglo pacífico *m.*

out-of-date /ˈaut əv ˈdeit/ *a.* anticuado.

out of focus *a.* desenfocado.

outpost /ˈautˌpoust/ *n.* puesto avanzado.

output /ˈautˌput/ *n.* capacidad *f.*; producción *f.*

outrage /ˈautreidʒ/ *n.* **1.** ultraje *m.*; atrocidad *f.* —*v.* **2.** ultrajar.

outrageous /autˈreidʒəs/ *a.* atroz.

outrun /ˌautˈrʌn/ *v.* exceder.

outside /*a, prep, adv* ˌautˈsaid; *n* ˈautˈsaid/ *a. & n.* **1.** exterior *m.* —*adv.* **2.** afuera, por fuera. —*prep.* **3.** fuera de.

outskirt /ˈautˌskərt/ *n.* borde *m.*

outward /ˈautwərd/ *adv.* hacia afuera.

outwardly /ˈautwərdli/ *adv.* exteriormente.

oval /ˈouvəl/ *a.* **1.** oval, ovalado. —*n.* **2.** óvalo *m.*

ovary /ˈouvəri/ *n.* ovario *m.*

ovation /ouˈveiʃən/ *n.* ovación *f.*

oven /ˈʌvən/ *n.* horno *m.*

over /ˈouvər/ *prep.* **1.** sobre, encima de; por. —*adv.* **2. o. here,** aquí. **o. there,** allí, por allí. **to be o.,** estar terminado.

overcoat /ˈouvərˌkout/ *n.* abrigo, sobretodo *m.*

overcome /ˌouvərˈkʌm/ *v.* superar, vencer.

overdose /ˈouvərˌdous/ *n.* sobredosis *f.*

overdue /ˌouvərˈdu/ *a.* retrasado.

overflow /*n* ˈouvərˌflou; *v* ˌouvərˈflou/ *n.* **1.** inundación *f.* —*v.* **2.** inundar.

overhaul /ˌouvərˈhɔl/ *v.* repasar.

overhead /ˈouvərˈhɛd/ *adv.* arriba, en lo alto.

overkill /ˈouvərˌkɪl/ *n.* efecto mayor que el pretendido.

overlook /ˌouvərˈluk/ *v.* pasar por alto.

overnight /ˈouvərˈnait/ *adv.* **to stay or stop o.,** pasar la noche.

overpower /ˌouvərˈpauər/ *v.* vencer.

overrule /ˌouvərˈrul/ *v.* predominar.

overrun /ˌouvərˈrʌn/ *v.* invadir.

oversee /ˌouvərˈsi/ *v.* superentender.

oversight /ˈouvərˌsait/ *n.* descuido *m.*

overt /ouˈvɜrt/ *a.* abierto.

overtake /ˌouvərˈteik/ *v.* alcanzar.

overthrow /*n* ˈouvərˌθrou; *v* ˌouvərˈθrou/ *n.* **1.** trastorno *m.* —*v.* **2.** trastornar.

overture /ˈouvərtʃər/ *n. Mus.* obertura *f.*

overturn /ˌouvərˈtɜrn/ *v.* trastornar.

overview /ˈouvərˌvyu/ *n.* visión de conjunto *f.*

overweight /ˈouvərˌweit/ *a.* demasiado pesado.

overwhelm /ˌouvərˈwɛlm/ *v.* abrumar.

overwork /ˌouvərˈwɜrk/ *v.* trabajar demasiado.

owe /ou/ *v.* deber. **owing to,** debido a.

owl /aul/ *n.* búho *m.*, lechuza *f.*

own /oun/ *a.* **1.** propio. —*v.* **2.** poseer.

owner /ˈounər/ *n.* dueño -ña.

ox /ɒks/ *n.* buey *m.*

oxygen /ˈɒksɪdʒən/ *n.* oxígeno *m.*

oxygen tent tienda de oxígeno *f.*

oyster /ˈɔistər/ *n.* ostra *f.*

P

pace /peis/ *n.* **1.** paso *m.* —*v.* **2.** pasearse. **p. off,** medir a pasos.

pacific /pəˈsɪfɪk/ *a.* pacífico.

Pacific Ocean Océano Pacífico *m.*

pacifier /ˈpæsəˌfaiər/ *n.* pacificador *m.*; (baby p.) chupete *m.*

pacifism /ˈpæsəˌfɪzəm/ *n.* pacifismo *m.*

pacifist /ˈpæsəfɪst/ *n.* pacifista *m. & f.*

pacify /ˈpæsəˌfai/ *v.* pacificar.

pack /pæk/ *n.* **1.** fardo; paquete *m.*; (animals) muta *f.* **p. of cards,** baraja *f.* —*v.* **2.** empaquetar; (baggage) empacar.

package /ˈpækɪdʒ/ *n.* paquete, bulto *m.*

package tour viaje todo incluido *m.*

pact /pækt/ *n.* pacto *m.*

pad /pæd/ *n.* **1.** colchoncillo *m.* **p. of paper,** bloc de papel. —*v.* **2.** rellenar.

paddle /'pædḷ/ n. 1. canalete m. —v. 2. remar.

padlock /'pæd,lɒk/ n. candado m.

pagan /'peigən/ a. & n. pagano -na.

page /peidʒ/ n. página f.; (boy) paje m.

pageant /'pædʒənt/ n. espectáculo m.; procesión f.

pail /peil/ n. cubo m.

pain /pein/ n. dolor m. **to take pains,** esmerarse.

painful /'peinfəl/ a. doloroso; penoso.

pain killer /'pein,kılər/ analgésico m.

paint /peint/ n. 1. pintura f. —v. 2. pintar.

painter /'peintər/ n. pintor -ra.

painting /'peintıŋ/ n. pintura f.; cuadro m.

pair /pɛər/ n. 1. par m.; pareja f. —v. 2. parear. **p. off,** emparejarse.

pajamas /pə'dʒɑməz, -'dʒæməz/ n. pijama m.

palace /'pælıs/ n. palacio m.

palatable /'pælətəbəl/ a. sabroso, agradable.

palate /'pælıt/ n. paladar m.

palatial /pə'leiʃəl/ a. palaciego, suntuoso.

pale /peil/ a. pálido. **to turn pale,** palidecer.

paleness /'peilnıs/ n. palidez f.

palette /'pælıt/ n. paleta f.

pallbearer /'pɔl,bɛərər/ n. portador del féretro, portaféretro m.

pallid /'pælıd/ a. pálido.

palm /pɑm/ n. palma f. **p. tree,** palmera f.

palpitate /'pælpı,teit/ v. palpitar.

paltry /'pɔltri/ a. miserable.

pamper /'pæmpər/ v. mimar.

pamphlet /'pæmflıt/ n. folleto m.

pan /pæn/ n. cacerola f.

panacea /,pænə'siə/ n. panacea f.

Pan-American /,pænə'mɛrıkən/ a. panamericano.

pane /pein/ n. hoja de vidrio f., cuadro m.

panel /'pænḷ/ n. tablero m.

pang /pæŋ/ n. dolor; remordimiento m.

panic /'pænık/ n. pánico m.

panorama /,pænə'ræmə, -'rɑmə/ n. panorama m.

pant /pænt/ v. jadear.

panther /'pænθər/ n. pantera f.

pantomine /'pæntə,maim/ n. pantomima f.; mímica f.

pantry /'pæntri/ n. despensa f.

pants /pænts/ n. pantalones, m.pl.

panty hose /'pænti,houz/ n. pantys, pantimedias f.pl. (medias hasta la cintura).

papal /'peipəl/ a. papal.

paper /'peipər/ n. papel; periódico; artículo m.

paperback /'peipər,bæk/ n. libro en rústica m.

paper clip sujetapapeles m.

paper cup vaso de papel m.

paper hanger /'peipər,hæŋər/ empapelador -ra.

paper money papel moneda m.

paperweight /'peipər,weit/ pisapapeles m.

papier-mâché /,peipərmə'ʃei, pɑ,pyei-/ n. cartón piedra m.

paprika /pæ'prikə, pə-, pɑ-, 'pæprıkə/ n. pimentón m.

par /pɑr/ n. paridad f.; Com. par f.

parable /'pærəbəl/ n. parábola f.

parachute /'pærə,ʃut/ n. paracaídas m.

parade /pə'reid/ n. 1. desfile m., procesión f. —v. 2. desfilar.

paradise /'pærə,dais/ n. paraíso m.

paradox /'pærə,dɒks/ n. paradoja f.

paraffin /'pærəfın/ n. parafina f.

paragraph /'pærə,græf/ n. párrafo m.

parakeet /'pærə,kit/ n. perico m.

parallel /'pærə,lɛl/ a. 1. paralelo. —v. 2. correr parejas con.

paralysis /pə'ræləsıs/ n. parálisis f.

paralyze /'pærə,laiz/ v. paralizar.

paramedic /,pærə'mɛdık/ n. paramédico -ca.

parameter /pə'ræmıtər/ n. parámetro m.

paramount /'pærə,maunt/ a. supremo.

paraphrase /'pærə,freiz/ n. 1. paráfrasis f. —v. 2. parafrasear.

paraplegic /'pærə'plidʒık/ n. parapléjico -ca.

parasite /'pærə,sait/ n. parásito m.

parboil /'pɑr,bɔil/ v. sancochar.

parcel /'pɑrsəl/ n. paquete m. **p. of land,** lote de terreno.

parchment /'pɑrtʃmənt/ n. pergamino m.

335 **patent leather**

pardon /'pardn̩/ *n.* **1.** perdón *m.*
—*v.* **2.** perdonar.
pare /pɛər/ *v.* pelar.
parentage /'pɛərəntɪdʒ, 'pær-/ *n.*
origen *m.*; extracción *f.*
parenthesis /pə'rɛnθəsɪs/ *n.* paréntesis *m.*
parents /'pɛərənts/ *n.* padres
m.pl.
parish /'pærɪʃ/ *n.* parroquia *f.*
Parisian /pə'rɪʒən, -'riʒən,
-'rɪziən/ *a. & n.* parisiense *m. & f.*
parity /'pærɪti/ *n.* igualdad, paridad *f.*
park /park/ *n.* **1.** parque *m.* —*v.*
2. estacionar.
parking lot /'parkɪŋ/ *n.* estacionamiento, aparcamiento *m.*
parking meter /'parkɪŋ/ parquímetro *m.*
parking space /'parkɪŋ/ estacionamiento, aparcamiento *m.*
parkway /'park,wei/ *n.* bulevar
m.; autopista *f.*
parley /'parli/ *n.* conferencia *f.*;
Mil. parlamento *m.*
parliament /'parləmənt/ *n.* parlamento *m.*
parliamentary /,parlə'mɛntəri,
-tri; *sometimes* ,parlyə-/ *a.* parlamentario.
parlor /'parlər/ *n.* sala *f.*, salón *m.*
parochial /pə'roukiəl/ *a.* parroquial.
parody /'pærədi/ *n.* **1.** parodia *f.*
—*v.* **2.** parodiar.
parole /pə'roul/ *n.* **1.** palabra de
honor *f.*; *Mil.* santo y seña. —*v.*
2. poner en libertad bajo palabra.
paroxysm /'pærək,sɪzəm/ *n.*
paroxismo *m.*
parrot /'pærət/ *n.* loro, papagayo
m.
parsimony /'parsə,mouni/ *n.* parsimonia *f.*
parsley /'parsli/ *n.* perejil *m.*
parson /'parsən/ *n.* párroco *m.*
part /part/ *n.* **1.** parte *f.*; *Theat.*
papel *m.* —*v.* **2.** separarse, par-
tirse. **p. with,** desprenderse de.
partake /par'teik/ *v.* tomar parte.
partial /'parʃəl/ *a.* parcial.
participant /par'tɪsəpənt/ *n.* parti-
cipante *m. & f.*
participate /par'tɪsə,peit/ *v.* participar.
participation /par,tɪsə'peiʃən/ *n.*
participación *f.*
participle /'partə,sɪpəl, -səpəl/ *n.*
participio *m.*

particle /'partɪkəl/ *n.* partícula *f.*
particular /pər'tɪkyələr/ *a. & n.*
particular *m.*
parting /'partɪŋ/ *n.* despedida *f.*
partisan /'partəzən, -sən/ *a. & n.*
partidario -ria.
partition /par'tɪʃən, pər-/ *n.* tabique *m. v.* dividir, partir.
partly /'partli/ *adv.* en parte.
partner /'partnər/ *n.* socio -cia;
compañero -ra.
partridge /'partrɪdʒ/ *n.* perdiz *f.*
party /'parti/ *n.* tertulia, fiesta *f.*;
grupo *m.*; (political) partido *m.*
pass /pæs/ *n.* **1.** pase; (mountain)
paso *m.* —*v.* **2.** pasar. **p. away,**
fallecer.
passable /'pæsəbəl/ *a.* transitable;
regular.
passage /'pæsɪdʒ/ *n.* pasaje; (corridor) pasillo *m.*
passé /pæ'sei/ *a.* anticuado.
passenger /'pæsəndʒər/ *n.* pasajero -ra.
passenger ship buque de pasajeros *m.*
passerby /'pæsər'bai/ *n.* transeúnte *m. & f.*
passion /'pæʃən/ *n.* pasión *f.*
passionate /'pæʃənɪt/ *a.* apasionado.
passive /'pæsɪv/ *a.* pasivo.
passport /'pæsport/ *n.* pasaporte
m.
password /'pæs,wɜrd/ *n.* código
m., clave *m.*, contraseña *f.*
past /pæst/ *a. & n.* **1.** pasado *m.*
—*prep.* **2.** más allá de; después
de.
paste /peist/ *n.* **1.** pasta *f.* —*v.* **2.**
empastar; pegar.
pasteurize /'pæstʃə,raiz/ *v.*
pasteurizar.
pastime /'pæs,taim/ *n.* pasatiempo *m.*; diversión *f.*
pastor /'pæstər/ *n.* pastor *m.*
pastrami /pə'strami/ *n.* pastrón
m.
pastry /'peistri/ *n.* pastelería *f.*
pasture /'pæstʃər/ *n.* **1.** pasto *m.*;
pradera *f.* —*v.* **2.** pastar.
pat /pæt/ *n.* **1.** golpecillo *m.* **to
stand p.,** mantenerse firme. —*v.*
2. dar golpecillos.
patch /pætʃ/ *n.* **1.** remiendo *m.*
—*v.* **2.** remendar.
patent /'pætn̩t/ *a. & n.* **1.** patente
m. —*v.* **2.** patentar.
patent leather /'pætnt, 'pætn̩/
charol *m.*

paternal /pə'tɜrnļ/ *a.* paterno, paternal.

paternity /pə'tɜrniti/ *n.* paternidad *f.*

path /pæθ/ *n.* senda *f.*

pathetic /pə'θɛtɪk/ *a.* patético.

pathology /pə'θɒlədʒi/ *n.* patología *f.*

pathos /'peiɒs/ *n.* rasgo conmovedor *m.*

patience /'peiʃəns/ *n.* paciencia *f.*

patient /'peiʃənt/ *a.* **1.** paciente. —*n.* **2.** enfermo -ma, paciente *m.* & *f.*

patio /'pæti,ou/ *n.* patio *m.*

patriarch /'peitri,ɑrk/ *n.* patriarca *m.*

patriot /'peitriət/ *n.* patriota *m.* & *f.*

patriotic /,peitri'ɒtɪk/ *a.* patriótico.

patriotism /'peitriə,tizəm/ *n.* patriotismo *m.*

patrol /pə'troul/ *n.* **1.** patrulla *f.* —*v.* **2.** patrullar.

patrolman /pə'troulmən/ *n.* vigilante *m.*; patrullador *m.*

patron /'peitrən/ *n.* patrón *m.*

patronize /'peitrə,naiz/ *v.* condescender; patrocinar; ser cliente de.

pattern /'pætərn/ *n.* modelo *m.*

pauper /'pɔpər/ *n.* indigente *m.* & *f.*

pause /pɔz/ *n.* **1.** pausa *f.* —*v.* **2.** pausar.

pave /peiv/ *v.* pavimentar. **p. the way,** preparar el camino.

pavement /'peivmənt/ *n.* pavimento *m.*

pavilion /pə'vɪlyən/ *n.* pabellón *m.*

paw /pɔ/ *n.* **1.** pata *f.* —*v.* **2.** patear.

pawn /pɔn/ *n.* **1.** prenda *f.*; (chess) peón de ajedrez *m.* —*v.* **2.** empeñar.

pay /pei/ *n.* **1.** pago; sueldo, salario *m.*; —*v.* **2.** pagar. **p. back,** pagar; vengarse de. **p. cash,** pagar en metálico.

payee /pei'i/ *n.* destinatario -ria *m.* & *f.*

payment /'peimənt/ *n.* pago *m.*; recompensa *f.*

pay phone teléfono público *m.*

pea /pi/ *n.* guisante *m.*

peace /pis/ *n.* paz *f.*

peaceable /'pisəbəl/ *a.* pacífico.

peaceful /'pisfəl/ *a.* tranquilo.

peach /pitʃ/ *n.* durazno, melocotón *m.*

peacock /'pi,kɒk/ *n.* pavo real *m.*

peak /pik/ *n.* pico, cumbre; máximo *m.*

peal /pil/ *n.* repique; estruendo *m.* **p. of laughter,** risotada *f.*

peanut /'pi,nʌt/ *n.* maní, cacahuete *m.*

pear /pɛər/ *n.* pera *f.*

pearl /pɜrl/ *n.* perla *f.*

peasant /'pɛzənt/ *n.* campesino -na.

pebble /'pɛbəl/ *n.* guija *f.*

peck /pɛk/ *n.* **1.** picotazo *m.* —*v.* **2.** picotear.

peckish /'pɛkɪʃ/ *a.* tener un poco de hambre.

peculiar /pɪ'kyulyər/ *a.* peculiar.

pecuniary /pɪ'kyuni,ɛri/ *a.* pecuniario.

pedagogue /'pɛdə,gɒg/ *n.* pedagogo -ga.

pedagogy /'pɛdə,goudʒi, -,gɒdʒi/ *n.* pedagogía *f.*

pedal /'pɛdļ/ *n.* pedal *m.*

pedant /'pɛdņt/ *n.* pedante *m.* & *f.*

peddler /'pɛdlər/ *n.* buhonero *m.*

pedestal /'pɛdəstļ/ *n.* pedestal *m.*

pedestrian /pə'dɛstriən/ *n.* peatón -na.

pedestrian crossing paso de peatones *m.*

pediatrician /,pidiə'trɪʃən/ *n.* pediatra *m.* & *f.*

pediatrics /,pidi'ætrɪks/ *n.* puericultura *f.*

pedigree /'pɛdɪ,gri/ *n.* genealogía *f.*

peek /pik/ *n.* **1.** atisbo *m.* —*v.* **2.** atisbar.

peel /pil/ *n.* **1.** corteza *f.*; (fruit) pellejo *m.* —*v.* **2.** descortezar; pelar.

peep /pip/ *n.* **1.** ojeada *f.* —*v.* **2.** mirar, atisbar.

peer /pɪər/ *n.* **1.** par *m.* —*v.* **2.** mirar fijamente.

peg /pɛg/ *n.* clavija; estaquilla *f.*; gancho *m.*

pelt /pɛlt/ *n.* **1.** pellejo *m.* —*v.* **2.** apedrear; (rain) caer con fuerza.

pelvis /'pɛlvɪs/ *n.* pelvis *f.*

pen /pɛn/ *n.* pluma *f.*; corral *m.* **fountain p.,** pluma fuente.

penalty /'pɛnļti/ *n.* pena; multa *f.*; castigo *m.*

penance /'pɛnəns/ *n.* penitencia *f.* **to do p.,** penar.

penchant /'pɛntʃənt;/ n. propensión f.

pencil /'pɛnsəl/ n. lápiz m.

pencil sharpener /'ʃɑrpənər/ sacapuntas m.

pending /'pɛndɪŋ/ a. pendiente. **to be p.,** pender.

penetrate /'pɛnɪˌtreit/ v. penetrar.

penetration /ˌpɛnɪ'treiʃən/ n. penetración f.

penicillin /ˌpɛnə'sɪlɪn/ n. penicilina f.

peninsula /pə'nɪnsələ, -'nɪnsyələ/ n. península f.

penitent /'pɛnɪtənt/ n. & a. penitente m. & f.

penknife /'pɛnˌnaif/ n. cortaplumas f.

penniless /'pɛnɪlɪs/ a. indigente.

penny /'pɛni/ n. penique m.

pension /'pɛnʃən/ n. pensión f.

pensive /'pɛnsɪv/ a. pensativo.

penultimate /pɪ'nʌltəmɪt/ a. penúltimo.

penury /'pɛnyəri/ n. penuria f.

people /'pipəl/ n. **1.** gente f.; (of a nation) pueblo m. —v. **2.** poblar.

pepper /'pɛpər/ n. pimienta f.; (plant) pimiento m.

per /pər; unstressed pər/ prep. por.

perambulator /pər'æmbyəˌleitər/ n. cochecillo de niño m.

perceive /pər'siv/ v. percibir.

percent /pər'sɛnt/ adv. por ciento.

percentage /pər'sɛntɪdʒ/ n. porcentaje m.

perceptible /pər'sɛptəbəl/ a. perceptible.

perception /pər'sɛpʃən/ n. percepción f.

perch /pɜrtʃ/ n. percha f.; (fish) perca f.

perdition /pər'dɪʃən/ n. perdición f.

peremptory /pə'rɛmptəri/ a. perentorio, terminante.

perennial /pə'rɛniəl/ a. perenne.

perfect /a. 'pɜrfɪkt; v. pər'fɛkt/ a. **1.** perfecto. —v. **2.** perfeccionar.

perfection /pər'fɛkʃən/ n. perfección f.

perfectionist /pər'fɛkʃənɪst/ a. & n. perfeccionista m. & f.

perforation /ˌpɜrfə'reiʃən/ n. perforación f.

perform /pər'fɔrm/ v. hacer; ejecutar; Theat. representar.

performance /pər'fɔrməns/ n. ejecución f.; Theat. representación f.

perfume /n. 'pɜrfyum; v. pər'fyum/ n. **1.** perfume m.; fragancia f. —v. **2.** perfumar.

perfunctory /pər'fʌŋktəri/ a. perfunctorio, superficial.

perhaps /pər'hæps/ adv. quizá, quizás, tal vez.

peril /'pɛrəl/ n. peligro m.

perilous /'pɛrələs/ a. peligroso.

perimeter /pə'rɪmɪtər/ n. perímetro m.

period /'pɪəriəd/ n. período m.; Punct. punto m.

periodic /ˌpɪəri'ɒdɪk/ a. periódico.

periodical /ˌpɪəri'ɒdɪkəl/ n. revista f.

periphery /pə'rɪfəri/ n. periferia f.

perish /'pɛrɪʃ/ v. perecer.

perishable /'pɛrɪʃəbəl/ a. perecedero.

perjury /'pɜrdʒəri/ n. perjurio m.

permanent /'pɜrmənənt/ a. permanente. **p. wave,** ondulado permanente.

permeate /'pɜrmiˌeit/ v. penetrar.

permissible /pər'mɪsəbəl/ a. permisible.

permission /pər'mɪʃən/ n. permiso m.

permit /n. 'pɜrmɪt; v. pər'mɪt/ n. **1.** permiso m. —v. **2.** permitir.

pernicious /pər'nɪʃəs/ a. pernicioso.

perpendicular /ˌpɜrpən'dɪkyələr/ n. & a. perpendicular f.

perpetrate /'pɜrpɪˌtreit/ v. perpetrar.

perpetual /pər'pɛtʃuəl/ a. perpetuo.

perplex /pər'plɛks/ v. confundir.

perplexity /pər'plɛksɪti/ n. perplejidad f.

persecute /'pɜrsɪˌkyut/ v. perseguir.

persecution /ˌpɜrsɪ'kyuʃən/ n. persecución f.

perseverance /ˌpɜrsə'vɪərəns/ n. perseverancia f.

persevere /ˌpɜrsə'vɪər/ v. perseverar.

persist /pər'sɪst/ v. persistir.

persistent /pər'sɪstənt/ a. persistente.

person /'pɜrsən/ n. persona f.

personage /'pɜrsənɪdʒ/ n. personaje m.

personal /'pɜrsənl/ a. personal.

personality /ˌpɜrsə'nælɪti/ n. personalidad f.

personnel /ˌpɜrsə'nɛl/ n. personal m.

perspective /pər'spɛktɪv/ n. perspectiva f.

perspiration /'pɜrspə'reiʃən/ n. sudor m.

perspire /pər'spaiᵊr/ v. sudar.

persuade /pər'sweid/ v. persuadir.

persuasive /pər'sweisɪv/ a. persuasivo.

pertain /pər'tein/ v. pertenecer.

pertinent /'pɜrtn̩ənt/ a. pertinente.

perturb /pər'tɜrb/ v. perturbar.

peruse /pə'ruz/ v. leer con cuidado.

pervade /pər'veid/ v. penetrar; llenar.

perverse /pər'vɜrs/ a. perverso.

perversion /pər'vɜrʒən/ n. perversión f.

pessimism /'pɛsə,mɪzəm/ n. pesimismo m.

pester /'pɛstər/ v. molestar; fastidiar.

pesticide /'pɛstə,said/ n. pesticida m.

pestilence /'pɛstl̩əns/ n. pestilencia f.

pet /pɛt/ n. **1.** favorito -ta.; animal doméstico m. —v. **2.** mimar.

petal /'pɛtl̩/ n. pétalo m.

petition /pə'tɪʃən/ n. **1.** petición, súplica f. —v. **2.** pedir, suplicar.

petrify /'pɛtrə,fai/ v. petrificar.

petroleum /pə'trouliəm/ n. petróleo m.

petticoat /'pɛti,kout/ n. enagua f.

petty /'pɛti/ a. mezquino, insignificante.

petulant /'pɛtʃələnt/ a. quisquilloso.

pew /pyu/ n. banco de iglesia m.

pewter /'pyutər/ n. peltre m.

phantom /'fæntəm/ n. espectro, fantasma m.

pharmacist /'fɑrməsɪst/ n. farmacéutico -ca, boticario -ria.

pharmacy /'fɑrməsi/ n. farmacia, botica f.

phase /feiz/ n. fase f.

pheasant /'fɛzənt/ n. faisán m.

phenomenal /fɪ'nɒmənl̩/ a. fenomenal.

phenomenon /fɪ'nɒmə,nɒn/ n. fenómeno f.

philanthropy /fɪ'lænθrəpi/ n. filantropía f.

philately /fɪ'lætl̩i/ n. filatelia f.

philosopher /fɪ'lɒsəfər/ n. filósofo -fa.

philosophical /ˌfɪlə'sɒfɪkəl/ a. filosófico.

philosophy /fɪ'lɒsəfi/ n. filosofía f.

phlegm /flɛm/ n. flema f.

phlegmatic /flɛg'mætɪk/ a. flemático.

phobia /'foubiə/ n. fobia f.

phone /foun/ n. teléfono m.

phonetic /fə'nɛtɪk/ a. fonético.

phonograph /'founə,græf/ n. fonógrafo m.

phosphorus /'fɒsfərəs/ n. fósforo m.

photocopier /'foutə,kɒpiər/ n. fotocopiadora f.

photocopy /'foutə,kɒpi/ n. **1.** fotocopia f. —v. **2.** fotocopiar.

photoelectric /ˌfoutoʊɪ'lɛktrɪk/ a. fotoeléctrico.

photogenic /ˌfoutə'dʒɛnɪk/ a. fotogénico.

photograph /'foutə,græf/ n. **1.** fotografía f. —v. **2.** fotografiar; retratar.

photography /fə'tɒgrəfi/ n. fotografía f.

phrase /freiz/ n. **1.** frase f. —v. **2.** expresar.

physical /'fɪzɪkəl/ a. físico.

physician /fɪ'zɪʃən/ n. médico m. & f.

physics /'fɪzɪks/ n. física f.

physiology /ˌfɪzi'ɒlədʒi/ n. fisiología f.

physiotherapy /ˌfɪziou'θɛrəpi/ n. fisioterapia f.

physique /fɪ'zik/ n. físico m.

pianist /pi'ænɪst, 'piənɪst/ n. pianista m. & f.

piano /pi'ænou/ n. piano m.

picayune /ˌpɪkə'yun/ a. insignificante.

piccolo /'pɪkə,lou/ n. flautín m.

pick /pɪk/ n. **1.** pico m. —v. **2.** escoger. **p. up,** recoger.

picket /'pɪkɪt/ n. piquete m.

pickle /'pɪkəl/ n. **1.** salmuera f.; encurtido m. —v. **2.** escabechar.

pickpocket /'pɪk,pɒkɪt/ n. cortabolsas m. & f.

picnic /'pɪknɪk/ n. picnic m.

picture /'pɪktʃər/ n. **1.** cuadro; retrato m.; fotografía f. (movie) película f. —v. **2.** imaginarse.

picturesque /ˌpɪktʃə'rɛsk/ a. pintoresco.

pie /pai/ n. pastel m.

piece /pis/ *n.* pedazo *m.;* pieza *f.*
pieceworker /'pis,wɜrkər/ *n.* destajero -ra, destajista *m. & f.*
pier /pɪər/ *n.* muelle *m.*
pierce /pɪərs/ *v.* perforar; pinchar; traspasar.
piety /'paɪɪti/ *n.* piedad *f.*
pig /pɪg/ *n.* puerco, cerdo, lechón *m.*
pigeon /'pɪdʒən/ *n.* paloma *f.*
pigeonhole /'pɪdʒən,houl/ *n.* casilla *f.*
pigment /'pɪgmənt/ *n.* pigmento *m.*
pile /pail/ *n.* **1.** pila *f.;* montón *m.; Med.* hemorroides *f.pl.* —*v.* **2.** amontonar.
pilfer /'pɪlfər/ *v.* ratear.
pilgrim /'pɪlgrɪm/ *n.* peregrino -na, romero -ra.
pilgrimage /'pɪlgrəmɪdʒ/ *n.* romería *f.*
pill /pɪl/ *n.* píldora *f.*
pillage /'pɪlɪdʒ/ *n.* **1.** pillaje *m.* —*v.* **2.** pillar.
pillar /'pɪlər/ *n.* columna *f.*
pillow /'pɪlou/ *n.* almohada *f.*
pillowcase /'pɪlou,keis/ *n.* funda de almohada *f.*
pilot /'pailət/ *n.* **1.** piloto *m. & f.* —*v.* **2.** pilotar.
pimple /'pɪmpəl/ *n.* grano *m.*
pin /pɪn/ *n.* **1.** alfiler; broche *m.; Mech.* clavija *f.* —*v.* **2.** prender. **p. up,** fijar.
pinafore /'pɪnə,fɔr/ *n.* delantal (de niña) *m.*
pinch /pɪntʃ/ *n.* **1.** pellizco *m.* —*v.* **2.** pellizcar.
pine /pain/ *n.* **1.** pino *m.* —*v.* **2.** **p. away,** languidecer. **p. for,** anhelar.
pineapple /'pai,næpəl/ *n.* piña *f.,* ananás *m.pl.*
pink /pɪŋk/ *a.* rosado.
pinky /'pɪŋki/ *n.* meñique *m.*
pinnacle /'pɪnəkəl/ *n.* pináculo *m.;* cumbre *f.*
pint /paint/ *n.* pinta *f.*
pioneer /,paiə'nɪər/ *n.* pionero -ra.
pious /'paiəs/ *a.* piadoso.
pipe /paip/ *n.* pipa *f.;* tubo; (of organ) cañón *m.*
pipeline /'paip,lain/ *n.* oleoducto *m.*
piper /'paipər/ *n.* flautista *m. & f.*
piquant /'pikənt/ *a.* picante.
pirate /'pairət/ *n.* pirata *m.*
pistol /'pɪstl/ *n.* pistola *f.*

piston /'pɪstən/ *n.* émbolo, pistón *m.*
pit /pɪt/ *n.* hoyo *m.;* (fruit) hueso *m.*
pitch /pɪtʃ/ *n.* **1.** brea *f.;* grado de inclinación; (music) tono *m.;* —*v.* **2.** lanzar; (ship) cabecear.
pitchblende /'pɪtʃ,blɛnd/ *n.* pechblenda *f.*
pitcher /'pɪtʃər/ *n.* cántaro *m.;* (baseball) lanzador -ra.
pitchfork /'pɪtʃ,fɔrk/ *n.* horca *f.;* tridente *m.*
pitfall /'pɪt,fɔl/ *n.* trampa *f.,* hoya cubierta *f.*
pitiful /'pɪtɪfəl/ *a.* lastimoso.
pitiless /'pɪtɪlɪs/ *a.* cruel.
pituitary gland /pɪ'tui,teri/ glándula pituitaria *f.*
pity /'pɪti/ *n.* **1.** compasión, piedad *f.* **to be a p.,** ser lástima. —*v.* **2.** compadecer.
pivot /'pɪvət/ *n.* **1.** espiga *f.,* pivote *m.;* punto de partida *m.* —*v.* **2.** girar sobre un pivote.
pizza /'pitsə/ *n.* pizza *f.*
placard /'plækɑrd/ *n.* **1.** cartel *m.* —*v.* **2.** fijar carteles.
placate /'pleikeit/ *v.* aplacar.
place /pleis/ *n.* **1.** lugar, sitio, puesto *m.* —*v.* **2.** colocar, poner.
placid /'plæsɪd/ *a.* plácido.
plagiarism /'pleidʒə,rɪzəm/ *n.* plagio *m.*
plague /pleig/ *n.* **1.** plaga, peste *f.* —*v.* **2.** atormentar.
plain /plein/ *a.* **1.** sencillo; puro; evidente. —*n.* **2.** llano *m.*
plaintiff /'pleintɪf/ *n.* demandante *m. & f.*
plan /plæn/ *n.* **1.** plan, propósito *m.* —*v.* **2.** planear; pensar; planificar. **p. on,** contar con.
plane /plein/ *n.* **1.** plano; (tool) cepillo *m.* —*v.* **2.** allanar; acepillar.
planet /'plænɪt/ *n.* planeta *m.*
planetarium /,plænɪ'tɛəriəm/ *n.* planetario *m.*
plank /plæŋk/ *n.* tablón *m.*
planning /'plænɪŋ/ *n.* planificación *f.*
plant /plænt/ *n.* **1.** mata, planta *f.* —*v.* **2.** sembrar, plantar.
plantation /plæn'teiʃən/ *n.* plantación *f.* **coffee p.,** cafetal *m.*
planter /'plæntər/ *n.* plantador; hacendado *m.*
plasma /'plæzmə/ *n.* plasma *m.*
plaster /'plæstər/ *n.* **1.** yeso; em-

plasto *m.* —*v.* **2.** enyesar; emplastar.

plastic /'plæstɪk/ *a.* plástico.

plate /pleit/ *n.* **1.** plato *m.;* plancha de metal. —*v.* **2.** planchear.

plateau /plæ'tou/ *n.* meseta *f.*

platform /'plætfɔrm/ *n.* plataforma *f.*

platinum /'plætṇəm/ *n.* platino *m.*

platitude /'plætɪ,tud/ *n.* perogrullada *f.*

platter /'plætər/ *n.* fuente *f.*, platel *m.*

plaudit /'plɔdɪt/ *n.* aplauso *m.*

plausible /'plɔzəbəl/ *a.* plausible.

play /plei/ *n.* **1.** juego *m.; Theat.* pieza *f.* —*v.* **2.** jugar; (music) tocar; *Theat.* representar. **p. a part,** hacer un papel.

player /'pleiər/ *n.* jugador -ra; (music) músico -ca.; *Theat.* actor *m.*, actriz *f.*

playful /'pleifəl/ *a.* juguetón.

playground /'plei,graund/ *n.* campo de deportes; patio de recreo.

playmate /'plei,meit/. *n.* compañero -ra de juego.

playwright /'plei,rait/ *n.* dramaturgo -ga.

plea /pli/ *n.* ruego *m.; súplica f.;* (legal) declaración *f.*

plead /plid/ *v.* suplicar; declararse. **p. a case,** defender un pleito.

pleasant /'plɛzənt/ *a.* agradable.

please /pliz/ *v.* **1.** gustar, agradar. **Pleased to meet you,** Mucho gusto en conocer a Vd. —*adv.* **2.** por favor. **Please...** Haga el favor de..., Tenga la bondad de..., Sírvase...

pleasure /'plɛʒər/ *n.* gusto, placer *m.*

pleat /plit/ *n.* **1.** pliegue *m.* —*v.* **2.** plegar.

plebiscite /'plɛbə,sait/ *n.* plebiscito *m.*

pledge /plɛdʒ/ *n.* **1.** empeño *m.* —*v.* **2.** empeñar.

plentiful /'plɛntɪfəl/ *a.* abundante.

plenty /'plɛnti/ *n.* abundancia *f.* **p. of,** bastante. **p. more,** mucho más.

pleurisy /'plʊrəsi/ *n.* pleuritis *f.*

pliable, pliant /'plaiəbəl; 'plaiənt/ *a.* flexible.

pliers /'plaiərz/ *n.pl.* alicates *m.pl.*

plight /plait/ *n.* apuro, aprieto *m.*

plot /plɒt/ *n.* **1.** conspiración; (of a story) trama; (of land) parcela *f.* —*v.* **2.** conspirar; tramar.

plow /plau/ *n.* **1.** arado *m.* —*v.* **2.** arar.

pluck /plʌk/ *n.* **1.** valor *m.* —*v.* **2.** arrancar; desplumar.

plug /plʌg/ *n.* **1.** tapón; *Elec.* enchufe *m.* **spark p.,** bujía *f.* —*v.* **2.** tapar.

plum /plʌm/ *n.* ciruela *f.*

plumage /'plumɪdʒ/ *n.* plumaje *m.*

plumber /'plʌmər/ *n.* fontanero -era, plomero -era.

plume /plum/ *n.* pluma *f.*

plump /plʌmp/ *a.* regordete.

plunder /'plʌndər/ *n.* **1.** botín *m.;* despojos *m.pl.* —*v.* **2.** saquear.

plunge /plʌndʒ/ *v.* zambullir; precipitar.

plural /'plʊrəl/ *a. & n.* plural *m.*

plus /plʌs/ *prep.* más.

plutocrat /'plutə,kræt/ *n.* plutócrata *m. & f.*

pneumatic /nʊ'mætɪk/ *a.* neumático.

pneumonia /nʊ'mounyə/ *n.* pulmonía *f.*

poach /poutʃ/ *v.* (eggs) escalfar; invadir; cazar en vedado.

pocket /'pɒkɪt/ *n.* **1.** bolsillo *m.* —*v.* **2.** embolsar.

pocketbook /'pɒkɪt,bʊk/ *n.* cartera *f.*

podiatry /pə'daiətri/ *n.* podiatría *f.*

poem /'pouəm/ *n.* poema *m.*

poet /'pouɪt/ *n.* poeta *m. & f.*

poetic /pou'ɛtɪk/ *a.* poético.

poetry /'pouɪtri/ *n.* poesía *f.*

poignant /'pɔinyənt/ *a.* conmovedor.

point /pɔint/ *n.* **1.** punta *f.;* punto *m.* —*v.* **2.** apuntar. **p. out,** señalar.

pointed /'pɔintɪd/ *a.* puntiagudo; directo.

pointless /'pɔintlɪs/ *a.* inútil.

poise /pɔiz/ *n.* **1.** equilibrio *m.;* serenidad *f.* —*v.* **2.** equilibrar; estar suspendido.

poison /'pɔizən/ *n.* **1.** veneno *m.* —*v.* **2.** envenenar.

poisonous /'pɔizənəs/ *a.* venenoso.

poke /pouk/ *n.* **1.** empuje *m.*, hurgonada *f.* —*v.* **2.** picar; haronear.

Poland /'poulənd/ *n.* Polonia *f.*

polar /'poulər/ *a.* polar.

pole /poul/ *n.* palo *m.; Geog.* polo *m.*

polemical /pə'lɛmɪkəl/ *a.*
polémico.

police /pə'lis/ *n.* policía *f.*

policeman /pə'lismən/ *n.* policía
m.

policy /'pɒləsi/ *n.* política *f.* **insurance p.,** póliza de seguro.

Polish /'pɒlɪʃ/ *a. & n.* polaco -ca.

polish /'pɒlɪʃ/ *n.* **1.** lustre *m.* —*v.*
2. pulir, lustrar.

polite /pə'lait/ *a.* cortés.

politic /'pɒlɪtɪk/ **political** *a.* político.

politician /ˌpɒlɪ'tɪʃən/ *n.* político
-ca.

politics /'pɒlɪtɪks/ *n.* política *f.*

poll /poul/ *n.* encuesta *f.;* (pl.)
urnas *f.pl.*

pollen /'pɒlən/ *n.* polen *m.*

pollute /pə'lut/ *v.* contaminar.

pollution /pə'luʃən/ *n.* contaminación *f.*

polo /'poulou/ *n.* polo *m.*

polyester /ˌpɒli'ɛstər/ *n.* poliéster
m.

polygamy /pə'lɪgəmi/ *n.* poligamia *f.*

polygon /'pɒliˌgɒn/ *n.* polígono
m.

pomp /pɒmp/ *n.* pompa *f.*

pompous /'pɒmpəs/ *a.* pomposo.

poncho /'pɒntʃou/ *n.* poncho *m.*

pond /pɒnd/ *n.* charca *f.*

ponder /'pɒndər/ *v.* ponderar,
meditar.

ponderous /'pɒndərəs/ *a.*
ponderoso, pesado.

pontiff /'pɒntɪf/ *n.* pontífice *m.*

pontoon /pɒn'tun/ *n.* pontón *m.*

pony /'pouni/ *n.* caballito *m.*

ponytail /'pouniˌteil/ *n.* cola de
caballo *f.*

poodle /'pudl/ *n.* caniche *m.*

pool /pul/ *n.* charco *m.* **swimming p.,** piscina *f.*

poor /pur/ *a.* pobre; (not good)
malo.

pop /pɒp/ *n.* chasquido *m.*

popcorn /'pɒpˌkɔrn/ *n.* rosetas de
maíz, palomitas de maíz *f.pl.*

pope /poup/ *n.* papa *m.*

poppy /'pɒpi/ *n.* amapola *f.*

popsicle /'pɒpsɪkəl/ *n.* polo *m.*

popular /'pɒpyələr/ *a.* popular.

popularity /ˌpɒpyə'lærɪti/ *n.*
popularidad *f.*

population /ˌpɒpyə'leiʃən/ *n.*
población *f.*

porcelain /'pɔrsəlɪn/ *n.* porcelana
f.

porch /pɔrtʃ/ *n.* pórtico *m.;*
galería *f.*

pore /pɔr/ *n.* poro *m.*

pork /pɔrk/ *n.* carne de puerco.

pornography /pɔr'nɒgrəfi/ *n.*
pornografía *f.*

porous /'pɔrəs/ *a.* poroso, esponjoso.

port /pɔrt/ *n.* puerto; *Naut.* babor
m. **p. wine,** oporto *m.*

portable /'pɔrtəbəl/ *a.* portátil.

portal /'pɔrtl/ *n.* portal *m.*

portend /pɔr'tɛnd/ *v.* pronosticar.

portent /'pɔrtɛnt/ *n.* presagio *m.*,
portento *m.*

porter /'pɔrtər/ *n.* portero *m.*

portfolio /pɔrt'fouliˌou/ *n.* cartera
f.

porthole /'pɔrtˌhoul/ *n.* porta *f.*

portion /'pɔrʃən/ *n.* porción *f.*

portly /'pɔrtli/ *a.* corpulento.

portrait /'pɔrtrɪt/ *n.* retrato *m.*

portray /pɔr'trei/ *v.* pintar.

Portugal /'pɔrtʃəgəl/ *n.* Portugal
m.

Portuguese /ˌpɔrtʃə'giz/ *a. & n.*
portugués -esa.

pose /pouz/ *n.* **1.** postura; actitud
f. —*v.* **2.** posar. **p. as,** pretender
ser.

position /pə'zɪʃən/ *n.* posición *f.*

positive /'pɒzɪtɪv/ *a.* positivo.

possess /pə'zɛs/ *v.* poseer.

possession /pə'zɛʃən/ *n.* posesión
f.

possessive /pə'zɛsɪv/ *a.* posesivo.

possibility /ˌpɒsə'bɪlɪti/ *n.* posibilidad *f.*

possible /'pɒsəbəl/ *a.* posible.

post /poust/ *n.* **1.** poste; puesto
m. —*v.* **2.** fijar; situar; echar al
correo.

postage /'poustɪdʒ/ *n.* porte de
correo. **p. stamp,** sello *m.*

postal /'poustl/ *a.* postal.

post card tarjeta postal.

poster /'poustər/ *n.* cartel, letrero
m.

posterior /pɒ'stɪəriər/ *a.* posterior.

posterity /pɒ'stɛrɪti/ *n.* posteridad
f.

postgraduate /poust'grædʒuɪt/ *a.*
& n. postgraduado -da.

postmark /'poustˌmɑrk/ *n.* mata-
sellos *m.*

post office correos *m.pl.*

postpone /poust'poun/ *v.* posponer, aplazar.

postscript /'poust,skrıpt/ *n.* posdata *f.*

posture /'pɒstʃər/ *n.* postura *f.*

pot /pɒt/ *n.* olla, marmita; (marijuana) marijuana, hierba *f.*
flower p., tiesto *m.*

potassium /pə'tæsiəm/ *n.* potasio *m.*

potato /pə'teitou/ *n.* patata, papa *f.* **sweet p.**, batata *f.*

potent /'poutṇt/ *a.* potente, poderoso.

potential /pə'tɛnʃəl/ *a. & n.* potencial *f.*

potion /'pouʃən/ *n.* poción, pócima *f.*

pottery /'pɒtəri/ *n.* alfarería *f.*

pouch /pautʃ/ *n.* saco *m.*; bolsa *f.*

poultry /'poultri/ *n.* aves de corral.

pound /paund/ *n.* **1.** libra *f.* —*v.* **2.** golpear.

pour /pɔr/ *v.* echar; verter; llover a cántaros.

poverty /'pɒvərti/ *n.* pobreza *f.*

powder /'paudər/ *n.* **1.** polvo *m.*; (gun) pólvora *f.* —*v.* **2.** empolvar; pulverizar.

power /'pauər/ *n.* poder *m.*; potencia *f.*

powerful /'pauərfəl/ *a.* poderoso, fuerte.

powerless /'pauərlıs/ *a.* impotente.

practical /'præktıkəl/ *a.* práctico.

practical joke inocentada *f.*

practically /'præktıkli/ *adv.* casi; prácticamente.

practice /'præktıs/ *n.* **1.** práctica; costumbre; clientela *f.* —*v.* **2.** practicar; ejercer.

practiced /'præktıst/ *a.* experto.

practitioner /præk'tıʃənər/ *n.* practicante *m. & f.*

pragmatic /præg'mætık/ *a.* pragmático.

prairie /'prɛəri/ *n.* llanura; *S.A.* pampa *f.*

praise /preiz/ *n.* **1.** alabanza *f.* —*v.* **2.** alabar.

prank /præŋk/ *n.* travesura *f.*

prawn /prɔn/ *n.* gamba *f.*

pray /prei/ *v.* rezar; (beg) rogar.

prayer /'preiər/ *n.* oración; súplica *f.*, ruego *m.*

preach /pritʃ/ *v.* predicar; sermonear.

preacher /'pritʃər/ *n.* predicador *m.*

preamble /'pri,æmbəl/ *n.* preámbulo *m.*

precarious /prı'kɛəriəs/ *a.* precario.

precaution /prı'kɔʃən/ *n.* precaución *f.*

precede /prı'sid/ *v.* preceder, anteceder.

precedent /n. 'prɛsıdənt; a. prı'sidnt/ *n. & a.* precedente *m.*

precept /'prisɛpt/ *n.* precepto *m.*

precinct /'prisıŋkt/ *n.* recinto *m.*

precious /'prɛʃəs/ *a.* precioso.

precipice /'prɛsəpıs/ *n.* precipicio *m.*

precipitate /prı'sıpı,teit/ *v.* precipitar.

precise /prı'sais/ *a.* preciso, exacto.

precision /prı'sıʒən/ *n.* precisión *f.*

preclude /prı'klud/ *v.* evitar.

precocious /prı'kouʃəs/ *a.* precoz.

precooked /pri'kʊkt/ *a.* precocinado.

predatory /'prɛdə,tɔri/ *a.* de rapiña, rapaz.

predecessor /'prɛdə,sɛsər/ *n.* predecesor -ra, antecesor -ra.

predicament /prı'dıkəmənt/ *n.* dificultad *f.*; apuro *m.*

predict /prı'dıkt/ *v.* pronosticar, predecir.

predictable /prı'dıktəbəl/ *a.* previsible.

predilection /,prɛdḷ'ɛkʃən/ *n.* predilección *f.*

predispose /,pridı'spouz/ *v.* predisponer.

predominant /prı'dɒmənənt/ *a.* predominante.

prefabricate /pri'fæbrı,keit/ *v.* fabricar de antemano.

preface /'prefıs/ *n.* prefacio *m.*

prefer /prı'fɜr/ *v.* preferir.

preferable /'prɛfərəbəl/ *a.* preferible.

preference /'prɛfərəns/ *n.* preferencia *f.*

prefix /'prifıks/ *n.* **1.** prefijo *m.* —*v.* **2.** prefijar.

pregnant /'prɛgnənt/ *a.* preñada.

prehistoric /,prihı'stɔrık/ *a.* prehistórico.

prejudice /'prɛdʒədıs/ *n.* prejuicio *m.*

prejudiced /'prɛdʒədıst/ *a.* (*S.A.*) prejuiciado.

preliminary /prı'lımə,nɛri/ *a.* preliminar.

prelude /'prɛlyud/ n. preludio m.

premature /,primə'tʃur/ a. prematuro.

premeditate /prɪ'mɛdɪ,teit/ v. premeditar.

premier /prɪ'mɪər/ n. primer ministro.

première /prɪ'mɪər/ n. estreno m.

premise /'prɛmɪs/ n. premisa f.

premium /'primiəm/ n. premio m.

premonition /,primə'nɪʃən/ n. presentimiento m.

prenatal /pri'neitl/ a. prenatal.

preparation /,prɛpə'reiʃən/ n. preparativo m.; preparación f.

preparatory /prɪ'pærə,tɔri/ a. preparatorio. **p. to,** antes de.

prepare /prɪ'pɛər/ v. preparar.

preponderant /prɪ'pɒndərənt/ a. preponderante.

preposition /,pripə'zɪʃən/ n. preposición f.

preposterous /prɪ'pɒstərəs/ a. prepóstero, absurdo.

prerequisite /pri'rɛkwəzɪt/ n. requisito previo.

prerogative /prɪ'rɒgətɪv/ n. prerrogativa f.

prescribe /prɪ'skraib/ v. prescribir; Med. recetar.

prescription /prɪ'skrɪpʃən/ n. prescripción; Med. receta f.

presence /'prɛzəns/ n. presencia f.; porte m.

present /a, n 'prɛzənt; v prɪ'zɛnt/ a. **1.** presente. **to be present at,** asistir a. —n. **2.** presente; (gift) regalo m. **at p.,** ahora, actualmente. **for the p.,** por ahora. —v. **3.** presentar.

presentable /prɪ'zɛntəbəl/ a. presentable.

presentation /,prɛzən'teiʃən/ n. presentación; introducción f.; Theat. representación f.

presently /'prɛzəntli/ adv. luego; dentro de poco.

preservative /prɪ'zɜrvətɪv/ a. & n. preservativo m.

preserve /prɪ'zɜrv/ n. **1.** conserva f.; (hunting) vedado m. —v. **2.** preservar.

preside /prɪ'zaid/ v. presidir.

presidency /'prɛzɪdənsi/ n. presidencia f.

president /'prɛzɪdənt/ n. presidente -ta.

press /prɛs/ n. **1.** prensa f. —v. **2.** apretar; urgir; (clothes) planchar.

pressing /'prɛsɪŋ/ a. urgente.

pressure /'prɛʃər/ n. presión f.

pressure cooker /'kukər/ cocina de presión f.

prestige /prɛ'stiʒ/ n. prestigio m.

presume /prɪ'zum/ v. presumir, suponer.

presumptuous /prɪ'zʌmptʃuəs/ a. presuntuoso.

presuppose /,prisə'pouz/ v. presuponer.

pretend /prɪ'tɛnd/ v. fingir. **p. to the throne,** aspirar al trono.

pretense /prɪ'tɛns, 'pritɛns/ n. pretensión f.; fingimiento m.

pretension /prɪ'tɛnʃən/ n. pretensión f.

pretentious /prɪ'tɛnʃəs/ a. presumido.

pretext /'pritɛkst/ n. pretexto m.

pretty /'prɪti/ a. **1.** bonito, lindo. —adv. **2.** bastante.

prevail /prɪ'veil/ v. prevalecer.

prevailing /prɪ'veilɪŋ/ **prevalent** a. predominante.

prevent /prɪ'vɛnt/ v. impedir; evitar.

prevention /prɪ'vɛnʃən/ n. prevención f.

preventive /prɪ'vɛntɪv/ a. preventivo.

preview /'pri,vyu/ n. vista anticipada f.

previous /'priviəs/ a. anterior, previo.

prey /prei/ n. presa f.

price /prais/ n. precio m.

priceless /'praislɪs/ a. sin precio.

prick /prɪk/ n. **1.** punzada f. —v. **2.** punzar.

pride /praid/ n. orgullo m.

priest /prist/ n. sacerdote, cura m.

prim /prɪm/ a. estirado, remilgado.

primary /'praimɛri/ a. primario, principal.

prime /praim/ a. **1.** primero. —n. **2.** flor f. —v. **3.** alistar.

prime minister primer ministro m. & f.

primitive /'prɪmɪtɪv/ a. primitivo.

prince /prɪns/ n. príncipe m.

Prince Charming Príncipe Azul m.

princess /'prɪnsɪs/ n. princesa f.

principal /'prɪnsəpəl/ a. **1.** principal. —n. **2.** principal m. & f.; director -ra.

principle /'prɪnsəpəl/ n. principio m.

print /prɪnt/ n. **1.** letra de molde

f.; (art) grabado *m.* —*v.* **2.** imprimir, estampar.

printer /'prɪntər/ *n.* impresora *f.*

printing /'prɪntɪŋ/ *n.* impresión; **p. office,** imprenta *f.*

printing press prensa *f.*

printout /'prɪnt,aut/ *n.* impreso producido por una computadora, impresión *f.*

priority /praɪ'ɔrɪti/ *n.* prioridad, precedencia *f.*

prism /'prɪzəm/ *n.* prisma *m.*

prison /'prɪzən/ *n.* prisión, cárcel *f.*

prisoner /'prɪzənər/ *n.* presidiario -ria, prisionero -ra, preso -sa.

pristine /'prɪstin/ *a.* inmaculado.

privacy /'praivəsi/ *n.* soledad *f.*

private /'praivɪt/ *a.* **1.** particular. —*n.* **2.** soldado raso. **in p.,** en particular.

privation /praɪ'veiʃən/ *n.* privación *f.*

privet /'prɪvɪt/ *n.* ligustro *m.*

privilege /'prɪvəlɪdʒ/ *n.* privilegio *m.*

privy /'prɪvi/ *n.* letrina *f.*

prize /praiz/ *n.* **1.** premio *m.* —*v.* **2.** apreciar, estimar.

probability /,prɒbə'bɪlɪti/ *n.* probabilidad *f.*

probable /'prɒbəbəl/ *a.* probable.

probate /'proubeit/ *a.* testamentario.

probation /prou'beiʃən/ *n.* prueba *f.*; probación *f.*; libertad condicional *f.*

probe /proub/ *n.* **1.** indagación *f.* —*v.* **2.** indagar; tentar.

probity /'proubɪti/ *n.* probidad *f.*

problem /'prɒbləm/ *n.* problema *m.*

procedure /prə'sidʒər/ *n.* procedimiento *m.*

proceed /prə'sid/ *v.* proceder; proseguir.

process /'prɒsɛs/ *n.* proceso *m.*

procession /prə'sɛʃən/ *n.* procesión *f.*

proclaim /prou'kleim/ *v.* proclamar, anunciar.

proclamation /,prɒklə'meiʃən/ *n.* proclamación *f.*; decreto *m.*

procrastinate /prou'kræstə,neit/ *v.* dilatar.

procure /prou'kyur/ *v.* obtener, procurar.

prodigal /'prɒdɪgəl/ *n.* & *a.* pródigo -ga.

prodigy /'prɒdɪdʒi/ *n.* prodigio *m.*

produce /prə'dus/ *v.* producir.

product /'prɒdəkt/ *n.* producto *m.*

production /prə'dʌkʃən/ *n.* producción *f.*

productive /prə'dʌktɪv/ *a.* productivo.

profane /prə'fein/ *a.* **1.** profano. —*v.* **2.** profanar.

profanity /prə'fænɪti/ *n.* profanidad *f.*

profess /prə'fɛs/ *v.* profesar; declarar.

profession /prə'fɛʃən/ *n.* profesión *f.*

professional /prə'fɛʃənl/ *a.* & *n.* profesional *m.* & *f.*

professor /prə'fɛsər/ *n.* profesor -ra; catedrático -ca.

proficient /prə'fɪʃənt/ *a.* experto, proficiente.

profile /'proufail/ *n.* perfil *m.*

profit /'prɒfɪt/ *n.* **1.** provecho *m.*; ventaja *f.*; Com. ganancia *f.* —*v.* **2.** aprovechar; beneficiar.

profitable /'prɒfɪtəbəl/ *a.* provechoso, ventajoso, lucrativo.

profiteer /,prɒfɪ'tɪər/ *n.* **1.** explotador -ra. —*v.* **2.** explotar.

profound /prə'faund/ *a.* profundo, hondo.

profuse /prə'fyus/ *a.* pródigo; profuso.

prognosis /prɒg'nousɪs/ *n.* pronóstico *m.*

program /'prougræm/ *n.* programa *m.*

progress /*n.* 'prɒgrɛs; *v.* prə'grɛs/ *n.* **1.** progresos *m.pl.* **in p.,** en marcha. —*v.* **2.** progresar; marchar.

progressive /prə'grɛsɪv/ *a.* progresivo; progresista.

prohibit /prou'hɪbɪt/ *v.* prohibir.

prohibition /,prouə'bɪʃən/ *n.* prohibición *f.*

prohibitive /prou'hɪbɪtɪv/ *a.* prohibitivo.

project /*n.* 'prɒdʒɛkt; *v.* prə'dʒɛkt/ *n.* **1.** proyecto *m.* —*v.* **2.** proyectar.

projectile /prə'dʒɛktɪl/ *n.* proyectil *m.*

projection /prə'dʒɛkʃən/ *n.* proyección *f.*

projector /prə'dʒɛktər/ *n.* proyector *m.*

proliferation /prə,lɪfə'reiʃən/ *n.* proliferación *f.*

prolific /prə'lɪfɪk/ *a.* prolífico.

prologue /'proulɔg/ *n.* prólogo *m.*

prolong /prə'lɔŋ/ v. prolongar.

prominent /'prɒmənənt/ a. prominente; eminente.

promiscuous /prə'mɪskyuəs/ a. promiscuo.

promise /'prɒmɪs/ n. **1.** promesa f. —v. **2.** prometer.

promote /prə'mout/ v. fomentar; estimular; adelantar; promocionar.

promotion /prə'mouʃən/ n. promoción f.; adelanto m.

prompt /prɒmpt/ a. **1.** puntual. —v. **2.** impulsar; *Theat.* apuntar. —adv. **3.** pronto.

promulgate /'prɒməl,geit/ v. promulgar.

pronoun /'prou,naun/ n. pronombre m.

pronounce /prə'nauns/ v. pronunciar.

pronunciation /prə,nʌnsi'eiʃən/ n. pronunciación f.

proof /pruf/ n. prueba f.

proof of purchase certificado de compra m.

proofread /'pruf,rid/ v. corregir pruebas.

prop /prɒp/ n. **1.** apoyo, m. —v. **2.** sostener.

propaganda /,prɒpə'gændə/ n. propaganda f.

propagate /'prɒpə,geit/ v. propagar.

propel /prə'pɛl/ v. propulsar.

propeller /prə'pɛlər/ n. hélice f.

propensity /prə'pɛnsɪti/ n. tendencia f.

proper /'prɒpər/ a. propio; correcto.

property /'prɒpərti/ n. propiedad f.

prophecy /'prɒfəsi/ n. profecía f.

prophesy /'prɒfə,sai/ v. predecir, profetizar.

prophet /'prɒfɪt/ n. profeta m.

prophetic /prə'fɛtɪk/ a. profético.

propitious /prə'pɪʃəs/ a. propicio.

proponent /prə'pounənt/ n. & a. proponente m.

proportion /prə'pɔrʃən/ n. proporción f.

proportionate /prə'pɔrʃənɪt/ a. proporcionado.

proposal /prə'pouzəl/ n. propuesta; oferta f.; (marriage) declaración f.

propose /prə'pouz/ v. proponer; pensar; declararse.

proposition /,prɒpə'zɪʃən/ n. proposición f.

proprietor /prə'praiitər/ n. propietario -ria, dueño -ña.

propriety /prə'praiiti/ n. corrección f., decoro m.

prosaic /prou'zeiik/ a. prosaico.

proscribe /prou'skraib/ v. proscribir.

prose /prouz/ n. prosa f.

prosecute /'prɒsɪ,kyut/ v. acusar, procesar.

prospect /'prɒspɛkt/ n. perspectiva; esperanza f.

prospective /prə'spɛktɪv/ a. anticipado, presunto.

prosper /'prɒspər/ v. prosperar.

prosperity /prɒ'spɛrɪti/ n. prosperidad f.

prosperous /'prɒspərəs/ a. próspero.

prostate gland /'prɒsteit/ glándula prostática f.

prostitute /'prɒstɪ,tut/ n. **1.** prostituta f. —v. **2.** prostituir.

prostrate /'prɒstreit/ a. **1.** postrado. —v. **2.** postrar.

protect /prə'tɛkt/ v. proteger; amparar.

protection /prə'tɛkʃən/ n. protección f.; amparo m.

protective /prə'tɛktɪv/ a. protector.

protector /prə'tɛktər/ n. protector -ora.

protégé /'proutə,ʒei/ n. protegido -da.

protein /'proutin, -tiin/ n. proteína f.

protest /n. 'proutɛst; v. prə'tɛst, 'proutɛst/ n. **1.** protesta f. —v. **2.** protestar.

Protestant /'prɒtəstənt/ a. & n. protestante m. & f.

protocol /'proutə,kɔl/ n. protocolo m.

proton /'proutɒn/ n. protón m.

protract /prou'trækt/ v. alargar, demorar.

protrude /prou'trud/ v. salir fuera.

protuberance /prou'tubərəns/ n. protuberancia f.

proud /praud/ a. orgulloso.

prove /pruv/ v. comprobar.

proverb /'prɒvərb/ n. proverbio, refrán m.

provide /prə'vaid/ v. proporcionar; proveer.

provided /prə'vaidɪd/ *conj.* con tal que.

providence /'prɒvɪdəns/ *n.* providencia *f.*

province /'prɒvɪns/ *n.* provincia *f.*

provincial /prə'vɪnʃəl/ *a.* **1.** provincial. —*n.* **2.** provinciano -na.

provision /prə'vɪʒən/ *n.* **1.** provisión *f.*; (pl.) comestibles *m.pl.* —*v.* **2.** abastecer.

provocation /,prɒvə'keiʃən/ *n.* provocación *f.*

provoke /prə'vouk/ *v.* provocar.

prowess /'prauɪs/ *n.* proeza *f.*

prowl /praul/ *v.* rondar.

prowler /'praulər/ *n.* merodeador -dora *m. & f.*

proximity /prɒk'sɪmɪti/ *n.* proximidad *f.*

proxy /'prɒksi/ *n.* delegado -da. **by p.,** mediante apoderado.

prudence /'prudns/ *n.* prudencia *f.*

prudent /'prudnt/ *a.* prudente, cauteloso.

prune /prun/ *n.* ciruela pasa *f.*

pry /prai/ *v.* atisbar; curiosear; *Mech.* alzaprimar.

psalm /sɑm/ *n.* salmo *m.*

pseudonym /'sudnɪm/ *n.* seudónimo *m.*

psychedelic /,saikɪ'dɛlɪk/ *a.* psiquedélico.

psychiatrist /sɪ'kaiətrɪst, sai-/ *n.* psiquiatra *m. & f.*

psychiatry /sɪ'kaiətri, sai-/ *n.* psiquiatría *f.*

psychoanalysis /,saikouə'næləsɪs/ *n.* psicoanálisis *m.*

psychoanalyst /,saikou'ænlɪst/ *n.* psicoanalista *m. & f.*

psychological /,saikə'lɒdʒɪkəl/ *a.* psicológico.

psychology /sai'kɒlədʒi/ *n.* psicología *f.*

psychosis /sai'kousɪs/ *n.* psicosis *f.*

ptomaine /'toumein/ *n.* tomaína *f.*

pub /pʌb/ *n.* bar *m.*

public /'pʌblɪk/ *a. & n.* público *m.*

publication /,pʌblɪ'keiʃən/ *n.* publicación; revista *f.*

publicity /pʌ'blɪsɪti/ *n.* publicidad *f.*

publicity agent publicista *m. & f.*

publish /'pʌblɪʃ/ *v.* publicar.

publisher /'pʌblɪʃər/ *n.* editor -ora.

pudding /'pudɪŋ/ *n.* pudín *m.*

puddle /'pʌdl/ *n.* charco, lodazal *m.*

Puerto Rican /'pwɛrtə 'rikən, 'pɔr-/ *a. & n.* puertorriqueño -ña.

Puerto Rico /'pwɛrtə rikou, 'pɔrtə/ Puerto Rico *m.*

puff /pʌf/ *n.* **1.** soplo *m.*; (of smoke) bocanada *f.* **powder p.,** polvera *f.* —*v.* **2.** jadear; echar bocanadas. **p. up,** hinchar; *Fig.* engreír.

pugnacious /pʌg'neiʃəs/ *a.* pugnaz.

puh-lease! /pʌ 'liz/ ¡Favor!

pull /pul/ *n.* **1.** tirón *m.*; *Colloq.* influencia *f.* —*v.* **2.** tirar; halar.

pulley /'puli/ *n.* polea *f.*, motón *m.*

pulmonary /'pʌlmə,nɛri/ *a.* pulmonar.

pulp /pʌlp/ *n.* pulpa *f.*; (of fruit) carne *f.*

pulpit /'pulpɪt, 'pʌl-/ *n.* púlpito *m.*

pulsar /'pʌlsɑr/ *n.* pulsar *m.*

pulsate /'pʌlseit/ *v.* pulsar.

pulse /pʌls/ *n.* pulso *m.*

pump /pʌmp/ *n.* **1.** bomba *f.* —*v.* **2.** bombear. **p. up,** inflar.

pumpkin /'pʌmpkɪn/ *n.* calabaza *f.*

pun /pʌn/ *n.* juego de palabras.

punch /pʌntʃ/ *n.* **1.** puñetazo; *Mech.* punzón; (beverage) ponche *m.* —*v.* **2.** dar puñetazos; punzar.

punch bowl ponchera *f.*

punctual /'pʌŋktʃuəl/ *a.* puntual.

punctuate /'pʌŋktʃu,eit/ *v.* puntuar.

puncture /'pʌŋktʃər/ *n.* **1.** pinchazo *m.*, perforación *f.* —*v.* **2.** pinchar, perforar.

pungent /'pʌndʒənt/ *a.* picante, pungente.

punish /'pʌnɪʃ/ *v.* castigar.

punishment /'pʌnɪʃmənt/ *n.* castigo *m.*

punitive /'pyunɪtɪv/ *a.* punitivo.

puny /'pyuni/ *a.* encanijado.

pupil /'pyupəl/ *n.* alumno -na; *Anat.* pupila *f.*

puppet /'pʌpɪt/ *n.* muñeco *m.*

puppy /'pʌpi/ *n.* perrito -ta.

purchase /'pɜrtʃəs/ *n.* **1.** compra *f.* —*v.* **2.** comprar.

purchasing power /'pɜrtʃəsɪŋ/ poder adquisitivo *m.*

pure /pyur/ *a.* puro.

purée /pyu'rei/ *n.* puré *m.*

purge /pɜrdʒ/ *v.* purgar.

purify /'pyurə,fai/ v. purificar.
puritanical /,pyurɪ'tænɪkəl/ a.
puritano.
purity /'pyurɪti/ n. pureza f.
purple /'pɜrpəl/ a. **1.** purpúreo.
—n. **2.** púrpura f.
purport /n. 'pɜrpɔrt; v. pər'pɔrt/
n. **1.** significación f. —v. **2.** significar.
purpose /'pɜrpəs/ n. propósito m.
on p., de propósito.
purr /pɜr/ v. ronronear.
purse /pɜrs/ n. bolsa f.
pursue /pər'su/ v. perseguir.
pursuit /pər'sut/ n. caza; busca;

ocupación f. **p. plane**, avión de
caza m.
push /pʊʃ/ n. **1.** empuje; impulso
m. —v. **2.** empujar.
put /pʊt/ v. poner, colocar. **p.
away**, guardar. **p. in**, meter. **p.
off**, dejar. **p. on**, ponerse. **p. out**,
apagar. **p. up with**, aguantar.
putrid /'pyutrɪd/ a. podrido.
putt /pʌt/ n. (golf) golpe corto m.
puzzle /'pʌzəl/ n. **1.** enigma; rompecabezas m. —v. **2.** dejar perplejo. **p. out**, descifrar.
pyramid /'pɪrəmɪd/ n. pirámide f.
pyromania /,pairə'meiniə/ n. piro-
manía f.

Q

quack /kwæk/ n. **1.** (doctor) curandero -ra; (duck) graznido m.
—v. **2.** graznar.
quadrangle /'kwɒd,ræŋgəl/ n.
cuadrángulo m.
quadraphonic /,kwɒdrə'fɒnɪk/ a.
cuatrifónico.
quadruped /'kwɒdrʊ,pɛd/ a. & n.
cuadrúpedo m.
quail /kweil/ n. **1.** codorniz f. —v.
2. descorazonarse.
quaint /kweint/ a. curioso.
quake /kweik/ n. **1.** temblor m.
—v. **2.** temblar.
qualification /,kwɒləfɪ'keiʃən/ n.
requisito m.; (pl.) preparaciones
f.pl.
qualified /'kwɒlə,faid/ a. califi-
cado, competente; preparado.
qualify /'kwɒlə,fai/ v. calificar,
modificar; llenar los requisitos.
quality /'kwɒliti/ n. calidad f.
quandary /'kwɒndəri, -dri/ n. incertidumbre f.
quantity /'kwɒntɪti/ n. cantidad f.
quarantine /'kwɔrən,tin, 'kwɒr-,
,kwɔrən'tin, ,kwɒr-/ n. cuarentena f.
quarrel /'kwɔrəl, 'kwɒr-/ n. **1.**
riña, disputa f. —v. **2.** reñir, disputar.
quarry /'kwɔri, 'kwɒri/ n. cantera;
(hunting) presa f.
quarter /'kwɔrtər/ n. cuarto m.;
(pl.) vivienda f.
quarterly /'kwɔrtərli/ a. **1.** trimestral. —adv. **2.** por cuartos.
quartet /kwɔr'tɛt/ n. cuarteto m.
quartz /kwɔrts/ n. cuarzo m.
quasar /'kweizɑr/ n. cuasar m.
quaver /'kweivər/ v. temblar.

queen /kwin/ n. reina f.; (chess)
dama f.
queer /kwɪər/ a. extraño, raro.
quell /kwɛl/ v. reprimir.
quench /kwɛntʃ/ v. apagar.
query /'kwɪəri/ n. **1.** pregunta f.
—v. **2.** preguntar.
quest /kwɛst/ n. busca f.
question /'kwɛstʃən/ n. **1.** pregunta; cuestión f. **q. mark**, signo
de interrogación. —v. **2.** preguntar; interrogar; dudar.
questionable /'kwɛstʃənəbəl/ a.
dudoso.
questionnaire /,kwɛstʃə'nɛər/ n.
cuestionario m.
quiche /kiʃ/ n. quiche f.
quick /kwɪk/ a. rápido.
quicken /'kwɪkən/ v. acelerar.
quicksand /'kwɪk,sænd/ n. arena
movediza.
quiet /'kwaiɪt/ a. **1.** quieto, tranquilo; callado. **be q., keep q.**,
callarse. —n. **2.** calma; quietud f.
—v. **3.** tranquilizar. **q. down**, callarse; calmarse.
quilt /kwɪlt/ n. colcha f.
quinine /'kwainain/ n. quinina f.
quintet /kwɪn'tɛt/ n. Mus. quin-
teto m.
quip /kwɪp/ n. **1.** pulla f. —v. **2.**
echar pullas.
quit /kwɪt/ v. dejar; renunciar a.
q. doing (etc.) dejar de hacer
(etc.).
quite /kwait/ adv. bastante; completamente. **not q.**, no precisa-
mente; no completamente.
quiver /'kwɪvər/ n. **1.** aljaba f.;
temblor m. —v. **2.** temblar.

quixotic /kwɪk'sɒtɪk/ *a.* quijotesco.

quorum /'kwɔrəm/ *n.* quórum *m.*

quota /'kwoutə/ *n.* cuota *f.*

quotation /kwou'teiʃən/ *n.* citación; *Com.* cotización *f.* **q. marks,** comillas *f.pl.*

quote /kwout/ *v.* citar; *Com.* cotizar.

R

rabbi /'ræbai/ *n.* rabí, rabino *m.*

rabbit /'ræbɪt/ *n.* conejo *m.*

rabble /'ræbəl/ *n.* canalla *f.*

rabid /'ræbɪd/ *a.* rabioso.

rabies /'reibiz/ *n.* hidrofobia *f.*

race /reis/ *n.* **1.** raza; carrera *f.* —*v.* **2.** echar una carrera; correr de prisa.

race track /'reis,træk/ hipódromo *m.*

rack /ræk/ *n.* **1.** (cooking) pesebre *m.*; (clothing) colgador *m.* —*v.* **2.** atormentar.

racket /'rækɪt/ *n.* (noise) ruido *m.*; (tennis) raqueta *f.*; (graft) fraude organizado.

radar /'reidɑr/ *n.* radar *m.*

radiance /'reidiəns/ *n.* brillo *m.*

radiant /'reidiənt/ *a.* radiante.

radiate /'reidi,eit/ *v.* irradiar.

radiation /,reidi'eiʃən/ *n.* irradiación *f.*

radiator /'reidi,eitər/ *n.* calorífero *m.*; *Auto.* radiador *m.*

radical /'rædɪkəl/ *a. & n.* radical *m.*

radio /'reidi,ou/ *n.* radio *m. or f.* **r. station,** estación radiodifusora *f.*

radioactive /,reidiou'æktɪv/ *a.* radioactivo.

radio cassette radiocasete *m.*

radish /'rædɪʃ/ *n.* rábano *m.*

radium /'reidiəm/ *n.* radio *m.*

radius /'reidiəs/ *n.* radio *m.*

raffle /'ræfəl/ *n.* **1.** rifa, lotería *f.* —*v.* **2.** rifar.

raft /ræft/ *n.* balsa *f.*

rafter /'ræftər/ *n.* viga *f.*

rag /ræg/ *n.* trapo *m.*

ragamuffin /'rægə,mʌfɪn/ *n.* galopín *m.*

rage /reidʒ/ *n.* **1.** rabia *f.* —*v.* **2.** rabiar.

ragged /'rægɪd/ *a.* andrajoso; desigual.

raid /reid/ *n. Mil.* correría *f.*

rail /reil/ *n.* baranda *f.*; carril *m.* **by r.,** por ferrocarril.

railroad /'reil,roud/ *n.* ferrocarril *m.*

rain /rein/ *n.* **1.** lluvia *f.* —*v.* **2.** llover.

rainbow /'rein,bou/ *n.* arco iris *m.*

raincoat /'rein,kout/ *n.* impermeable *m.*; gabardina *f.*

rainfall /'rein,fɔl/ *n.* precipitación *f.*

rainy /'reini/ *a.* lluvioso.

raise /reiz/ *n.* **1.** aumento *m.* —*v.* **2.** levantar, alzar; criar.

raisin /'reizɪn/ *n.* pasa *f.*

rake /reik/ *n.* **1.** rastro *m.* —*v.* **2.** rastrillar.

rally /'ræli/ *n.* **1.** reunión *f.* —*v.* **2.** reunirse.

ram /ræm/ *n.* carnero *m.*

ramble /'ræmbəl/ *v.* vagar.

ramp /ræmp/ *n.* rampa *f.*

rampart /'ræmpɑrt/ *n.* terraplén *m.*

ranch /ræntʃ/ *n.* rancho *m.*

rancid /'rænsɪd/ *a.* rancio.

rancor /'ræŋkər/ *n.* rencor *m.*

random /'rændəm/ *a.* fortuito. **at r.,** a la ventura.

range /reindʒ/ *n.* **1.** extensión *f.*; alcance *m.*; estufa; sierra *f.*; terreno de pasto. —*v.* **2.** recorrer; extenderse.

rank /ræŋk/ *a.* **1.** espeso; rancio. —*n.* **2.** fila *f.*; grado *m.* —*v.* **3.** clasificar.

ransack /'rænsæk/ *v.* saquear.

ransom /'rænsəm/ *n.* **1.** rescate *m.* —*v.* **2.** rescatar.

rap /ræp/ *n.* **1.** golpecito *m.* —*v.* **2.** golpear.

rapid /'ræpɪd/ *a.* rápido.

rapist /'reipɪst/ *n.* violador -dora *m. & f.*

rapport /ræ'pɔr/ *n.* armonía *f.*

rapture /'ræptʃər/ *n.* éxtasis *m.*

rare /rɛɑr/ *a.* raro; (of food) a medio cocer.

rascal /'ræskəl/ *n.* pícaro, bribón *m.*

rash /ræʃ/ *a.* **1.** temerario. —*n.* **2.** erupción *f.*

raspberry /'ræz,bɛri/ *n.* frambuesa *f.*

rat /ræt/ *n.* rata *f.*

rate /reit/ *n.* **1.** velocidad; tasa *f.*; precio *m.*; (of exchange; of interest) tipo *m.* **at any r.**, de todos modos. —*v.* **2.** valuar.

rather /'ræðər/ *adv.* bastante; más bien, mejor dicho.

ratify /'rætə,fai/ *v.* ratificar.

ratio /'reiʃou/ *n.* razón; proporción *f.*

ration /'ræʃən, 'reiʃən/ *n.* **1.** ración *f.* —*v.* **2.** racionar.

rational /'ræʃənl/ *a.* racional.

rattle /'rætl/ *n.* **1.** ruido *m.*; matraca *f.* **r. snake**, culebra de cascabel, serpiente de cascabel *f.* —*v.* **2.** matraquear; rechinar.

raucous /'rɔkəs/ *a.* ronco.

ravage /'rævidʒ/ *v.* pillar; destruir; asolar.

rave /reiv/ *v.* delirar; entusiasmarse.

ravel /'rævəl/ *v.* deshilar.

raven /'reivən/ *n.* cuervo *m.*

ravenous /'rævənəs/ *a.* voraz.

raw /rɔ/ *a.* crudo; verde.

ray /rei/ *n.* rayo *m.*

rayon /'reiɒn/ *n.* rayón *m.*

razor /'reizər/ *n.* navaja de afeitar. **r. blade**, hoja de afeitar.

reach /ritʃ/ *n.* **1.** alcance *m.* —*v.* **2.** alcanzar.

react /ri'ækt/ *v.* reaccionar.

reaction /ri'ækʃən/ *n.* reacción *f.*

reactionary /ri'ækʃə,nɛri/ *a.* **1.** reaccionario. —*n.* **2.** *Pol.* retrógrado *m.*

read /rid/ *v.* leer.

reader /'ridər/ *n.* lector -ra; libro de lectura *m.*

readily /'rɛdli/ *adv.* fácilmente.

reading /'ridɪŋ/ *n.* lectura *f.*

ready /'rɛdi/ *a.* listo, preparado; dispuesto.

ready-cooked /'rɛdi ,kʊkt/ *a.* precocinado.

real /rei'ɑl/ *a.* verdadero; real.

real estate bienes inmuebles, *m.pl.*

real-estate agent /'riəl ɪ'steit/ agente inmobiliario *m.*, agente inmobiliaria *f.*

realist /'riəlɪst/ *n.* realista *m.* & *f.*

realistic /,riə'lɪstɪk/ *a.* realista.

reality /ri'ælɪti/ *n.* realidad *f.*

realization /,riələ'zeiʃən/ *n.* comprensión; realización *f.*

realize /'riə,laiz/ *v.* darse cuenta de; realizar.

really /'riəli/ *adv.* de veras; en realidad.

realm /rɛlm/ *n.* reino; dominio *m.*

reap /rip/ *v.* segar, cosechar.

rear /riər/ *a.* **1.** posterior. —*n.* **2.** parte posterior. —*v.* **3.** criar; levantar.

reason /'rizən/ *n.* **1.** razón; causa *f.*; motivo *m.* —*v.* **2.** razonar.

reasonable /'rizənəbəl/ *a.* razonable.

reassure /,riə'ʃʊr/ *v.* calmar, tranquilizar.

rebate /'ribeit/ *n.* rebaja *f.*

rebel /*n.* 'rɛbəl; *v.* rɪ'bɛl/ *n.* **1.** rebelde *m.* & *f.* —*v.* **2.** rebelarse.

rebellion /rɪ'bɛlyən/ *n.* rebelión *f.*

rebellious /rɪ'bɛlyəs/ *a.* rebelde.

rebirth /ri'bɜrθ/ *n.* renacimiento *m.*

rebound /rɪ'baund/ *v.* repercutir; resaltar.

rebuff /rɪ'bʌf/ *n.* **1.** repulsa *f.* —*v.* **2.** rechazar.

rebuke /rɪ'byuk/ *n.* **1.** reprensión *f.* —*v.* **2.** reprender.

rebuttal /rɪ'bʌtl/ *n.* refutación *f.*

recalcitrant /rɪ'kælsɪtrənt/ *a.* recalcitrante.

recall /rɪ'kɔl/ *v.* recordar; acordarse de; hacer volver.

recapitulate /,rikə'pɪtʃə,leit/ *v.* recapitular.

recede /ri'sid/ *v.* retroceder.

receipt /rɪ'sit/ *n.* recibo *m.*; (com., pl.) ingresos *m.pl.*

receive /rɪ'siv/ *v.* recibir.

receiver /rɪ'sivər/ *n.* receptor *m.*

recent /'risənt/ *a.* reciente.

recently /'risəntli/ *adv.* recién.

receptacle /rɪ'sɛptəkəl/ *n.* receptáculo *m.*

reception /rɪ'sɛpʃən/ *n.* acogida; recepción *f.*

receptionist /rɪ'sɛpʃənɪst/ *n.* recepcionista *m.* & *f.*

receptive /rɪ'sɛptɪv/ *a.* receptivo.

recess /rɪ'sɛs, 'risɛs/ *n.* nicho; retiro; recreo *m.*

recipe /'rɛsəpi/ *n.* receta *f.*

recipient /rɪ'sɪpiənt/ *n.* recibidor -ra, recipiente *m.* & *f.*

reciprocate /rɪ'sɪprə,keit/ *v.* corresponder; reciprocar.

recite /rɪ'sait/ *v.* recitar.

reckless /'rɛklɪs/ *a.* descuidado; imprudente.

reckon /'rɛkən/ *v.* contar; calcular.

reclaim /rɪ'kleim/ *v.* reformar; *Leg.* reclamar.

recline /rɪ'klain/ *v.* reclinar; recostar.

recognition /ˌrɛkəg'nɪʃən/ n. reconocimiento m.

recognize /'rɛkəgˌnaiz/ v. reconocer.

recoil /n. 'riˌkɔil; v. rɪ'kɔil/ n. **1.** culatada f. —v. **2.** recular.

recollect /ˌrɛkə'lɛkt/ v. recordar, acordarse de.

recommend /ˌrɛkə'mɛnd/ v. recomendar.

recommendation /ˌrɛkəmɛn'deiʃən/ n. recomendación f.

recompense /'rɛkəmˌpɛns/ n. **1.** recompensa f. —v. **2.** recompensar.

reconcile /'rɛkənˌsail/ v. reconciliar.

recondition /ˌrikən'dɪʃən/ v. reacondicionar.

reconsider /ˌrikən'sɪdər/ v. considerar de nuevo.

reconstruct /ˌrikən'strʌkt/ v. reconstruir.

record /n. 'rɛkərd, v. rɪ'kɔrd/ n. **1.** registro; (sports) record m. **phonograph r.,** disco m. —v. **2.** registrar.

record player tocadiscos m.

recount /rɪ'kaunt/ v. relatar; contar.

recover /rɪ'kʌvər/ v. recobrar; restablecerse.

recovery /rɪ'kʌvəri/ n. recobro m.; recuperación f.

recruit /rɪ'krut/ n. **1.** recluta m. —v. **2.** reclutar.

rectangle /'rɛkˌtæŋgəl/ n. rectángulo m.

rectify /'rɛktəˌfai/ v. rectificar.

recuperate /rɪ'kupəˌreit/ v. recuperar.

recur /rɪ'kɜr/ v. recurrir.

recycle /ri'saikəl/ v. reciclar.

red /rɛd/ a. rojo, colorado.

redeem /rɪ'dim/ v. redimir, rescatar.

redemption /rɪ'dɛmpʃən/ n. redención f.

redhead /'rɛdˌhɛd/ n. pelirrojo -ja.

red mullet /'mʌlɪt/ salmonete m.

reduce /rɪ'dus/ v. reducir.

reduction /rɪ'dʌkʃən/ n. reducción f.

reed /rid/ n. caña f., S.A. bejuco m.

reef /rif/ n. arrecife, escollo m.

reel /ril/ n. **1.** aspa f., carrete m. —v. **2.** aspar.

refer /rɪ'fɜr/ v. referir.

referee /ˌrɛfə'ri/ n. árbitro m. & f.

reference /'rɛfərəns/ n. referencia f.

refill /n. 'riˌfɪl; v. ri'fɪl/ n. **1.** relleno m. —v. **2.** rellenar.

refine /rɪ'fain/ n. refinar.

refinement /rɪ'fainmənt/ n. refinamiento m.; cultura f.

reflect /rɪ'flɛkt/ v. reflejar; reflexionar.

reflection /rɪ'flɛkʃən/ n. reflejo m.; reflexión f.

reflex /'riflɛks/ a. reflejo.

reform /rɪ'fɔrm/ n. **1.** reforma f. —v. **2.** reformar.

reformation /ˌrɛfər'meiʃən/ n. reformación f.

refractory /rɪ'fræktəri/ a. refractario.

refrain /rɪ'frein/ n. **1.** estribillo m. —v. **2.** abstenerse.

refresh /rɪ'frɛʃ/ v. refrescar.

refreshment /rɪ'frɛʃmənt/ n. refresco m.

refrigerator /rɪ'frɪdʒəˌreitər/ n. refrigerador m.

refuge /'rɛfyudʒ/ n. refugio m.

refugee /ˌrɛfyu'dʒi/ n. refugiado -da.

refund /n 'rifʌnd; v ri'fʌnd/ n. **1.** reembolso m. —v. **2.** reembolsar.

refusal /rɪ'fyuzəl/ n. negativa f.

refuse /n 'rɛfyus; v rɪ'fyuz/ n. **1.** basura f. —v. **2.** negarse, rehusar.

refute /rɪ'fyut/ v. refutar.

regain /ri'gein/ v. recobrar. **r. consciousness,** recobrar el conocimiento.

regal /'rigəl/ a. real.

regard /rɪ'gard/ n. **1.** aprecio; respeto m. **with r. to,** con respecto a. —v. **2.** considerar; estimar.

regarding /rɪ'gardɪŋ/ prep. en cuanto a, acerca de.

regardless (of) /rɪ'gardlɪs/ a pesar de.

regent /'ridʒənt/ n. regente m. & f.

regime /rə'ʒim, rei-/ n. régimen m.

regiment /n. 'rɛdʒəmənt; v. -ˌmɛnt/ n. **1.** regimiento m. —v. **2.** regimentar.

region /'ridʒən/ n. región f.

register /'rɛdʒəstər/ n. **1.** registro m. **cash r.,** caja registradora f. —v. **2.** registrar; matricularse; (a letter) certificar.

registration /ˌrɛdʒə'streiʃən/ n. registro m.; matrícula f.

regret /rɪ'grɛt/ n. **1.** pena f. —v. **2.** sentir, lamentar.

regular /'rɛgyələr/ a. regular; ordinario.

regularity /ˌrɛgyə'lærɪti/ n. regularidad f.

regulate /'rɛgyə,leit/ v. regular.

regulation /ˌrɛgyə'leiʃən/ n. regulación f.

regulator /'rɛgyə,leitər/ n. regulador m.

rehabilitate /ˌrihə'bɪlɪ,teit, ˌriə-/ v. rehabilitar.

rehearse /rɪ'hɜrs/ v. repasar; Theat. ensayar.

reheat /ri'hit/ v. recalentar.

reign /rein/ n. **1.** reino, reinado m. —v. **2.** reinar.

reimburse /ˌriɪm'bɜrs/ v. reembolsar.

rein /rein/ n. **1.** rienda f. —v. **2.** refrenar.

reincarnation /ˌriɪnkar'neiʃən/ n. reencarnación f.

reindeer /'rein,dɪər/ n. reno m.

reinforce /ˌriɪn'fɔrs, -'fours/ v. reforzar.

reinforcement /ˌriɪn'fɔrsmənt, -'fours-/ n. refuerzo m.; armadura f.

reiterate /ri'ɪtə,reit/ v. reiterar.

reject /rɪ'dʒɛkt/ v. rechazar.

rejoice /rɪ'dʒɔis/ v. regocijarse.

rejoin /rɪ'dʒɔin/ v. reunirse con; replicar.

rejuvenate /rɪ'dʒuvə,neit/ v. rejuvenecer.

relapse /v. rɪ'læps; n. also 'rilæps/ v. **1.** recaer. —n. **2.** recaída f.

relate /rɪ'leit/ v. relatar, contar; relacionar. **r. to,** llevarse bien con.

relation /rɪ'leiʃən/ n. relación f.; pariente m. & f.

relative /'rɛlətɪv/ a. **1.** relativo. —n. **2.** pariente m. & f.

relativity /ˌrɛlə'tɪvɪti/ n. relatividad f.

relax /rɪ'læks/ v. descansar; relajar.

relay /'rilei; v. also rɪ'lei/ n. **1.** relevo m. —v. **2.** retransmitir.

release /rɪ'lis/ n. **1.** liberación f. —v. **2.** soltar.

relent /rɪ'lɛnt/ v. ceder.

relevant /'rɛləvənt/ a. pertinente.

reliability /rɪˌlaiə'bɪliti/ n. veracidad f.

reliable /rɪ'laiəbəl/ a. responsable; digno de confianza.

relic /'rɛlɪk/ n. reliquia f.

relief /rɪ'lif/ n. alivio; (sculpture) relieve m.

relieve /rɪ'liv/ v. aliviar.

religion /rɪ'lɪdʒən/ n. religión f.

religious /rɪ'lɪdʒəs/ a. religioso.

relinquish /rɪ'lɪŋkwɪʃ/ v. abandonar.

relish /'rɛlɪʃ/ n. **1.** sabor; condimento m. —v. **2.** saborear.

reluctant /rɪ'lʌktənt/ a. renuente.

rely /rɪ'lai/ v. **r. on,** confiar en; contar con; depender de.

remain /rɪ'mein/ n. **1.** (pl.) restos m.pl. —v. **2.** quedar, permanecer.

remainder /rɪ'meindər/ n. resto m.

remark /rɪ'mark/ n. **1.** observación f. —v. **2.** observar.

remarkable /rɪ'markəbəl/ a. notable.

remedial /rɪ'midiəl/ a. reparador.

remedy /'rɛmɪdi/ n. **1.** remedio m. —v. **2.** remediar.

remember /rɪ'mɛmbər/ v. acordarse de, recordar.

remembrance /rɪ'mɛmbrəns/ n. recuerdo m.

remind /rɪ'maind/ v. **r. of,** recordar.

reminisce /ˌrɛmə'nɪs/ v. pensar en o hablar de cosas pasadas.

remiss /rɪ'mɪs/ a. remiso; flojo.

remit /rɪ'mɪt/ v. remitir.

remorse /rɪ'mɔrs/ n. remordimiento m.

remote /rɪ'mout/ a. remoto.

remote control mando a distancia m.

removal /rɪ'muvəl/ n. alejamiento m.; eliminación f.

remove /rɪ'muv/ v. quitar; remover.

renaissance /ˌrɛnə'sɑns/ n. renacimiento m.

rend /rɛnd/ v. hacer pedazos; separar.

render /'rɛndər/ v. dar; rendir; Theat. interpretar.

rendezvous /'rɑndə,vu, -dei-/ n. cita f.

rendition /rɛn'dɪʃən/ n. interpretación, rendición f.

renege /rɪ'nɪg, -'nɛg/ v. renunciar; faltar a su palabra, no cumplir una promesa.

renew /rɪ'nu, -'nyu/ v. renovar.

renewal /rɪ'nuəl, -'nyu-/ n. renovación; Com. prórroga f.

renounce /rɪ'nauns/ v. renunciar a.

renovate /'rɛnə,veit/ v. renovar.

renown /rɪ'naun/ n. renombre m., fama f.

rent /rɛnt/ n. **1.** alquiler m. —v. **2.** arrendar, alquilar.

repair /rɪ'pɛər/ n. **1.** reparo m. —v. **2.** reparar.

repairman /rɪ'pɛər,mæn/ n. técnico m.

repatriate /ri'peitri,eit/ v. repatriar.

repay /rɪ'pei/ v. pagar; devolver.

repeat /rɪ'pit/ v. repetir.

repel /rɪ'pɛl/ v. repeler, repulsar.

repent /'ripənt, rɪ'pɛnt/ v. arrepentirse.

repentance /rɪ'pɛntns, -'pɛntəns/ n. arrepentimiento m.

repercussion /,ripər'kʌʃən, ,rɛpər-/ n. repercusión f.

repertoire /'rɛpər,twɑr/ n. repertorio m.

repetition /,rɛpɪ'tɪʃən/ n. repetición f.

replace /rɪ'pleis/ v. reemplazar.

replenish /rɪ'plɛnɪʃ/ v. rellenar; surtir de nuevo.

reply /rɪ'plai/ n. **1.** respuesta f. —v. **2.** replicar; contestar.

report /rɪ'pɔrt, -'pourt/ n. **1.** informe m. —v. **2.** informar, contar; denunciar; presentarse.

reporter /rɪ'pɔrtər, -'pour-/ n. repórter m. & f., reportero -ra.

repose /rɪ'pouz/ n. **1.** reposo m. —v. **2.** reposar; reclinar.

reprehensible /,rɛprɪ'hɛnsəbəl/ a. reprensible.

represent /,rɛprɪ'zɛnt/ v. representar.

representation /,rɛprɪzɛn'teiʃən, -zən-/ n. representación f.

representative /,rɛprɪ'zɛntətɪv/ a. **1.** representativo. —n. **2.** representante m. & f.

repress /rɪ'prɛs/ v. reprimir.

reprimand /'rɛprə,mænd, -,mɑnd/ n. **1.** regaño m. —v. **2.** regañar.

reprisal /rɪ'praizəl/ n. represalia f.

reproach /rɪ'proutʃ/ n. **1.** reproche m. —v. **2.** reprochar.

reproduce /,riprə'dus, -'dyus/ v. reproducir.

reproduction /,riprə'dʌkʃən/ n. reproducción f.

reproof /rɪ'pruf/ n. censura f.

reprove /rɪ'pruv/ v. censurar, regañar.

reptile /'rɛptɪl, -tail/ n. reptil m.

republic /rɪ'pʌblɪk/ n. república f.

republican /rɪ'pʌblɪkən/ a. & n. republicano -na.

repudiate /rɪ'pyudi,eit/ v. repudiar.

repulsive /rɪ'pʌlsɪv/ a. repulsivo, repugnante.

reputation /,rɛpyə'teiʃən/ n. reputación; fama f.

repute /rɪ'pyut/ n. **1.** reputación f. —v. **2.** reputar.

request /rɪ'kwɛst/ n. **1.** súplica f., ruego m. —v. **2.** pedir; rogar; suplicar.

require /rɪ'kwaiər/ v. requerir; exigir.

requirement /rɪ'kwaiərmənt/ n. requisito m.

requisite /'rɛkwəzɪt/ a. **1.** necesario. —n. **2.** requisito m.

requisition /,rɛkwə'zɪʃən/ n. requisición f.

rescind /rɪ'sɪnd/ v. rescindir, anular.

rescue /'rɛskyu/ n. **1.** rescate m. —v. **2.** rescatar.

research /rɪ'sɜrtʃ, 'risɜrtʃ/ n. investigación f.

researcher /rɪ'sɜrtʃər/ n. investigador -dora.

resemble /rɪ'zɛmbəl/ v. parecerse a, asemejarse a.

resent /rɪ'zɛnt/ v. resentirse de.

reservation /,rɛzər'veiʃən/ n. reservación f.

reserve /rɪ'zɜrv/ n. **1.** reserva f. —v. **2.** reservar.

reservoir /'rɛzər,vwɑr, -,vwɔr, -,vɔr, 'rɛzə-/ n depósito; tanque m.

reside /rɪ'zaid/ v. residir, morar.

residence /'rɛzɪdəns/ n. residencia, morada f.

resident /'rɛzɪdənt/ n. residente m. & f.

residue /'rɛzɪ,du/ n. residuo m.

resign /rɪ'zain/ v. dimitir; resignar.

resignation /,rɛzɪg'neiʃən/ n. dimisión; resignación f.

resist /rɪ'zɪst/ v. resistir.

resistance /rɪ'zɪstəns/ n. resistencia f.

resolute /'rɛzə,lut/ a. resuelto.

resolution /,rɛzə'luʃən/ n. resolución f.

resolve /rɪ'zɒlv/ v. resolver.

resonant /'rɛzənənt/ a. resonante.

resort /rɪ'zɔrt/ n. **1.** recurso; expediente *m.* **summer r.,** lugar de veraneo. —*v.* **2.** acudir, recurrir.

resound /rɪ'zaʊnd/ *v.* resonar.

resource /'risɔrs/ *n.* recurso *m.*

respect /rɪ'spɛkt/ *n.* **1.** respeto *m.* **with r. to,** con respecto a. —*v.* **2.** respetar.

respectable /rɪ'spɛktəbəl/ *a.* respetable.

respectful /rɪ'spɛktfəl/ *a.* respetuoso.

respective /rɪ'spɛktɪv/ *a.* respectivo.

respiration /ˌrɛspə'reɪʃən/ *n.* respiración *f.*

respite /'rɛspɪt/ *n.* pausa, tregua *f.*

respond /rɪ'spɒnd/ *v.* responder.

response /rɪ'spɒns/ *n.* respuesta *f.*

responsibility /rɪˌspɒnsə'bɪlɪti/ *n.* responsabilidad *f.*

responsible /rɪ'spɒnsəbəl/ *a.* responsable.

responsive /rɪ'spɒnsɪv/ *a.* sensible *a.*

rest /rɛst/ *n.* **1.** descanso; reposo *m.;* (music) pausa *f.* **the r.,** el resto, lo demás; los demás. —*v.* **2.** descansar; recostar.

restaurant /'rɛstərənt, -tə,rɑnt, -trɑnt/ *n.* restaurante *m.*

restful /'rɛstfəl/ *a.* tranquilo.

restitution /ˌrɛstɪ'tuʃən, -'tyu-/ *n.* restitución *f.*

restless /'rɛstlɪs/ *a.* inquieto.

restoration /ˌrɛstə'reɪʃən/ *n.* restauración *f.*

restore /rɪ'stɔr, -'stoʊr/ *v.* restaurar.

restrain /rɪ'streɪn/ *v.* refrenar.

restraint /rɪ'streɪnt/ *n.* limitación, restricción *f.*

restrict /rɪ'strɪkt/ *v.* restringir, limitar.

rest room aseos *m.pl.*

result /rɪ'zʌlt/ *n.* **1.** resultado *m.* —*v.* **2.** resultar.

resume /rɪ'zum/ *v.* reasumir; empezar de nuevo.

résumé /'rɛzʊ,meɪ/ *n.* resumen *m.*

resurgent /rɪ'sɜrdʒənt/ *a.* resurgente.

resurrect /ˌrɛzə'rɛkt/ *v.* resucitar.

resuscitate /rɪ'sʌsɪ,teɪt/ *v.* resucitar.

retail /'riteɪl/ *n.* **at r.,** al por menor.

retain /rɪ'teɪn/ *v.* retener.

retaliate /rɪ'tæli,eɪt/ *v.* vengarse.

retard /rɪ'tɑrd/ *v.* retardar.

retention /rɪ'tɛnʃən/ *n.* retención *f.*

reticent /'rɛtəsənt/ *a.* reticente.

retire /rɪ'taɪər/ *v.* retirar.

retirement /rɪ'taɪərmənt/ *n.* jubilación *f.*

retort /rɪ'tɔrt/ *n.* **1.** réplica; *Chem.* retorta *f.* —*v.* **2.** replicar.

retreat /rɪ'trit/ *n.* **1.** retiro *m.;* *Mil.* retirada, retreta *f.* —*v.* **2.** retirarse.

retribution /ˌrɛtrə'byuʃən/ *n.* retribución *f.*

retrieve /rɪ'triv/ *v.* recobrar.

return /rɪ'tɜrn/ *n.* **1.** vuelta *f.*, regreso; retorno *m.* **by r. mail,** a vuelta de correo. —*v.* **2.** volver, regresar; devolver.

reunion /ri'yunyən/ *n.* reunión *f.*

rev /rɛv/ *n.* **1.** revolución *f.* —*v.* **2.** (motor) acelerar.

reveal /rɪ'vil/ *v.* revelar.

revelation /ˌrɛvə'leɪʃən/ *n.* revelación *f.*

revenge /rɪ'vɛndʒ/ *n.* venganza *f.* **to get r.,** vengarse.

revenue /'rɛvən,yu, -ə,nu/ *n.* renta *f.*

revere /rɪ'vɪər/ *v.* reverenciar, venerar.

reverence /'rɛvərəns, 'rɛvrəns/ *n.* **1.** reverencia *f.* —*v.* **2.** reverenciar.

reverend /'rɛvərənd, 'rɛvrənd/ *a.* **1.** reverendo. —*n.* **2.** pastor *m.*

reverent /'rɛvərənt, 'rɛvrənt/ *a.* reverente.

reverse /rɪ'vɜrs/ *a.* **1.** inverso. —*n.* **2.** revés, inverso *m.* —*v.* **3.** invertir; revocar.

revert /rɪ'vɜrt/ *v.* revertir.

review /rɪ'vyu/ *n.* **1.** repaso *m.;* revista *f.* —*v.* **2.** repasar; *Mil.* revistar.

revise /rɪ'vaɪz/ *v.* revisar.

revision /rɪ'vɪʒən/ *n.* revisión *f.*

revival /rɪ'vaɪvəl/ *n.* reavivamiento *m.*

revive /rɪ'vaɪv/ *v.* avivar; revivir, resucitar.

revoke /rɪ'voʊk/ *v.* revocar.

revolt /rɪ'voʊlt/ *n.* **1.** rebelión *f.* —*v.* **2.** rebelarse.

revolting /rɪ'voʊltɪŋ/ *a.* repugnante.

revolution /ˌrɛvə'luʃən/ *n.* revolución *f.*

revolutionary /ˌrɛvə'luʃə,nɛri/ *a.* & *n.* revolucionario -ria.

revolve /rɪ'vɒlv/ v. girar; dar vueltas.

revolver /rɪ'vɒlvər/ n. revólver m.

revolving door /rɪ'vɒlvɪŋ/ puerta giratoria f.

reward /rɪ'wɔrd/ n. 1. pago m.; recompensa f. —v. 2. recompensar.

rhetoric /'rɛtərɪk/ n. retórica f.

rheumatism /'rumə,tɪzəm/ n. reumatismo m.

rhinoceros /rai'nɒsərəs/ n. rinoceronte m.

rhubarb /'rubɑrb/ n. ruibarbo m.

rhyme /raim/ n. 1. rima f. —v. 2. rimar.

rhythm /'rɪðəm/ n. ritmo m.

rhythmical /'rɪðmɪkəl/ a. rítmico.

rib /rɪb/ n. costilla f.

ribbon /'rɪbən/ n. cinta f.

rib cage caja torácica f.

rice /rais/ n. arroz m.

rich /rɪtʃ/ a. rico.

rid /rɪd/ v. librar. **get r. of,** deshacerse de, quitarse.

riddle /'rɪdl/ n. enigma; rompecabezas m.

ride /raid/ n. 1. paseo (a caballo, en coche, etc.) m. —v. 2. cabalgar; ir en coche.

ridge /rɪdʒ/ n. cerro m.; arruga f.; (of a roof) caballete m.

ridicule /'rɪdɪ,kyul/ n. 1. ridículo m. —v. 2. ridiculizar.

ridiculous /rɪ'dɪkyələs/ a. ridículo.

riding /'raidɪŋ/ n. equitación f.

riding school picadero m.

rifle /'raifəl/ n. 1. fusil m. —v. 2. robar.

rig /rɪg/ n. 1. aparejo m. —v. 2. aparejar.

right /rait/ a. 1. derecho; correcto. **to be r.,** tener razón. —adv. 2. bien, correctamente. **r. here,** etc., aquí mismo, etc. **all r.,** está bien, muy bien. —n. 3. derecho m.; justicia f. **to the r.,** a la derecha. —v. 4. corregir; enderezar.

righteous /'raitʃəs/ a. justo.

rigid /'rɪdʒɪd/ a. rígido.

rigor /'rɪgər/ n. rigor m.

rigorous /'rɪgərəs/ a. riguroso.

rim /rɪm/ n. margen m. or f.; borde m.

ring /rɪŋ/ n. 1. anillo m.; sortija f.; círculo m.; campaneo m. —v. 2. cercar; sonar; tocar.

ring finger dedo anular m.

rinse /rɪns/ v. enjuagar, lavar.

riot /'raiət/ n. motín; alboroto m.

rip /rɪp/ n. 1. rasgadura f. —v. 2. rasgar; descoser.

ripe /raip/ a. maduro.

ripen /'raipən/ v. madurar.

ripoff /'rɪp,ɔf/ n. robo, atraco m.

ripple /'rɪpəl/ n. 1. onda f. —v. 2. ondear.

rise /raiz/ n. 1. subida f. —v. 2. ascender; levantarse; (moon) salir.

risk /rɪsk/ n. 1. riesgo m. —v. 2. arriesgar.

rite /rait/ n. rito m.

ritual /'rɪtʃuəl/ a. & n. ritual m.

rival /'raivəl/ n. rival m. & f.

rivalry /'raivəlri/ n. rivalidad f.

river /'raivər/ n. río m.

rivet /'rɪvɪt/ n. 1. remache, roblón m. —v. 2. remachar, roblar.

road /roud/ n. camino m.; carretera f.

roadside /'roud,said/ n. borde de la carretera m.

roam /roum/ v. vagar.

roar /rɔr, rour/ n. 1. rugido, bramido m. —v. 2. rugir, bramar.

roast /roust/ n. 1. asado m. —v. 2. asar.

rob /rɒb/ v. robar.

robber /'rɒbər/ n. ladrón -na.

robbery /'rɒbəri/ n. robo m.

robe /roub/ n. manto m.

robin /'rɒbɪn/ n. petirrojo m.

robust /rou'bʌst, 'roubʌst/ a. robusto.

rock /rɒk/ n. 1. roca, peña f.; (music) rock m., música (de) rock f. —v. 2. mecer; oscilar.

rocker /'rɒkər/ n. mecedora f.

rocket /'rɒkɪt/ n. cohete m.

rocking chair /'rɒkɪŋ/ mecedora f.

Rock of Gibraltar /dʒɪ'brɔltər/ Peñón de Gibraltar m.

rocky /'rɒki/ a. pedregoso.

rod /rɒd/ n. varilla f.

rodent /'roudnt/ n. roedor m.

rogue /roug/ n. bribón, pícaro m.

roguish /'rougɪʃ/ a. pícaro.

role /roul/ n. papel m.

roll /roul/ 1. rollo m.; lista f.; panecillo m. **to call the r.,** pasar lista. —v. 2. rodar. **r. up,** enrollar. **r. up one's sleeves,** arremangarse.

roller /'roulər/ n. rodillo, cilindro m.

roller skate patín de ruedas m.

Roman /'roumən/ a. & n. romano -na.

romance /rou'mæns, 'roumæns/ a.

1. románico. *—n.* **2.** romance *m.;*
amorío *m.*
romantic /rou'mæntɪk/ *a.* romántico.
romp /rɒmp/ *v.* retozar; jugar.
roof /ruf, rʊf/ *n.* **1.** techo *m.;*
—v. **2.** techar.
room /rum, rʊm/ *n.* **1.** cuarto *m.,*
habitación *f.;* lugar *m. —v.* **2.** alojarse.
roommate /'rum,meit, 'rʊm-/ *n.*
compañero -ra de cuarto.
rooster /'rustər/ *n.* gallo *m.*
root /rut/ *n.* raíz *f.* **to take r.,**
arraigar.
rootless /'rutlɪs/ *a.* desarraigado.
rope /roup/ *n.* cuerda, soga *f.*
rose /rouz/ *n.* rosa *f.*
rosy /'rouzi/ *a.* róseo, rosado.
rot /rɒt/ *n.* **1.** putrefacción *f. —v.*
2. pudrirse.
rotary /'routəri/ *a.* giratorio; rota-
tivo.
rotate /'routeit/ *v.* girar; alternar.
rotation /rou'teiʃən/ *n.* rotación *f.*
rotten /'rɒtṇ/ *a.* podrido.
rouge /ruʒ/ *n.* colorete *m.*
rough /rʌf/ *a.* áspero; rudo;
grosero; aproximado.
round /raund/ *a.* **1.** redondo. **r.
trip,** viaje de ida y vuelta. *—n.* **2.**
ronda *f.;* (boxing) asalto *m.*
rouse /rauz/ *v.* despertar.
rout /raut, rut/ *n.* **1.** derrota *f.*
—v. **2.** derrotar.
route /rut, raut/ *n.* ruta, vía *f.*
routine /ru'tin/ *a.* **1.** rutinario.
—n. **2.** rutina *f.*
rove /rouv/ *v.* vagar.
rover /'rouvər/ *n.* vagabundo -da.
row /rou/ *n.* **1.** fila *f. —v.* **2.** *Naut.*
remar.
rowboat /'rou,bout/ *n.* bote de
remos.
rowdy /'raudi/ *a.* alborotado.
royal /'rɔiəl/ *a.* real.
royalty /'rɔiəlti/ *n.* realeza *f.;* (pl.)
regalías *f.pl.*
rub /rʌb/ *v.* frotar. **r. against,** rozar. **r. out,** borrar.
rubber /'rʌbər/ *n.* goma *f.;* caucho
m.; (pl.) chanclos *m.pl.,* zapatos
de goma.
rubbish /'rʌbɪʃ/ *n.* basura *f.;*
(nonsense) tonterías *f.pl.*
ruby /'rubi/ *n.* rubí *m.*
rudder /'rʌdər/ *n.* timón *m.*

ruddy /'rʌdi/ *a.* colorado.
rude /rud/ *a.* rudo; grosero; descortés.
rudiment /'rudəmənt/ *n.* rudimento *m.*
rudimentary /ˌrudə'mɛntəri, -tri/
a. rudimentario.
rue /ru/ *v.* deplorar; lamentar.
ruffian /'rʌfiən, 'rʌfyən/ *n.* rufián,
bandolero *m.*
ruffle /'rʌfəl/ *n.* **1.** volante frun-
cido. *—v.* **2.** fruncir; irritar.
rug /rʌg/ *n.* alfombra *f.*
rugged /'rʌgɪd/ *a.* áspero; robusto.
ruin /'ruɪn/ *n.* **1.** ruina *f. —v.* **2.**
arruinar.
ruinous /'ruənəs/ *a.* ruinoso.
rule /rul/ *n.* **1.** regla *f.* **as a r.,** por
regla general. *—v.* **2.** gobernar;
mandar; rayar.
ruler /'rulər/ *n.* gobernante *m. &
f.;* soberano -na; regla *f.*
rum /rʌm/ *n.* ron *m.*
rumble /'rʌmbəl/ *v.* retumbar.
rumor /'rumər/ *n.* rumor *m.*
rumpus /'rʌmpəs/ *n.* lío, jaleo, es-
candalo *m.*
run /rʌn/ *v.* correr; hacer correr. **r.
away,** escaparse. **r. into,** chocar
con.
runner /'rʌnər/ *n.* corredor -ra;
mensajero -ra.
runner-up /'rʌnər 'ʌp/ *n.* subcampeón -ona.
runproof /'rʌnpruf/ *a.* indesmallable.
rupture /'rʌptʃər/ *n.* **1.** rotura;
hernia *f. —v.* **2.** reventar.
rural /'rʊrəl/ *a.* rural, campestre.
rush /rʌʃ/ *n.* **1.** prisa *f.;* *Bot.* junco
m. —v. **2.** ir de prisa.
rush hour hora punta *f.*
Russia /'rʌʃə/ *n.* Rusia *f.*
Russian /'rʌʃən/ *a. & n.* ruso -sa.
rust /rʌst/ *n.* **1.** herrumbre *f. —v.*
2. aherrumbrarse.
rustic /'rʌstɪk/ *a.* rústico.
rustle /'rʌsəl/ *n.* **1.** susurro *m.*
—v. **2.** susurrar.
rusty /'rʌsti/ *a.* mohoso.
rut /rʌt/ *n.* surco *m.*
ruthless /'ruθlɪs/ *a.* cruel, inhumano.
rye /rai/ *n.* centeno *m.*
rye bread pan de centeno *m.*

S

saber /'seibər/ n. sable m.

sable /'seibəl/ n. cebellina f.

sabotage /'sæbə,taʒ/ n. sabotaje m.

sachet /sæ'ʃei/ n. perfumador m.

sack /sæk/ n. **1.** saco m. —v. **2.** Mil. saquear.

sacred /'seikrɪd/ a. sagrado, santo.

sacrifice /'sækrə,fais/ n. **1.** sacrificio m. —v. **2.** sacrificar.

sacrilege /'sækrəlɪdʒ/ n. sacrilegio m.

sad /sæd/ a. triste.

saddle /'sædl/ n. **1.** silla de montar. —v. **2.** ensillar.

sadness /'sædnɪs/ n. tristeza f.

safe /seif/ a. **1.** seguro; salvo. —n. **2.** caja de caudales.

safeguard /'seif,gard/ n. **1.** salvaguardia m. —v. **2.** proteger, poner a salvo.

safety /'seifti/ n. seguridad, protección f.

safety belt cinturón de seguridad m.

safety pin imperdible m.

safety valve /vælv/ válvula de seguridad f.

sage /seidʒ/ a. **1.** sabio, sagaz. —n. **2.** sabio m.; Bot. salvia f.

sail /seil/ n. **1.** vela f.; paseo por mar. —v. **2.** navegar; embarcarse.

sailboat /'seil,bout/ n. barco de vela.

sailor /'seilər/ n. marinero m.

saint /seint/ n. santo -ta.

sake /seik/ n. **for the s. of,** por; por el bien de.

salad /'sæləd/ n. ensalada f. **s. bowl,** ensaladera f.

salad dressing aliño m.

salary /'sæləri/ n. sueldo, salario m.

sale /seil/ n. venta f.

salesman /'seilzmən/ n. vendedor m.; viajante de comercio.

sales tax /seilz/ impuesto sobre la venta.

saliva /sə'laivə/ n. saliva f.

salmon /'sæmən/ n. salmón m.

salt /sɔlt/ a. **1.** salado. —n. **2.** sal f. —v. **3.** salar.

salute /sə'lut/ n. **1.** saludo m. —v. **2.** saludar.

salvage /'sælvɪdʒ/ v. salvar; recobrar.

salvation /sæl'veiʃən/ n. salvación f.

salve /sæv/ n. emplasto, ungüento m.

same /seim/ a. & pron. mismo. **it's all the s.,** lo mismo da.

sample /'sæmpəl/ n. **1.** muestra f. —v. **2.** probar.

sanatorium /,sænə'tɔriəm/ n. sanatorio m.

sanctify /'sæŋktə,fai/ v. santificar.

sanction /'sæŋkʃən/ n. **1.** sanción f. —v. **2.** sancionar.

sanctity /'sæŋktɪti/ n. santidad f.

sanctuary /'sæŋktʃu,ɛri/ n. santuario, asilo m.

sand /sænd/ n. arena f.

sandal /'sændl/ n. sandalia f.

sandpaper /'sænd,peipər/ n. papel de lija m.

sandwich /'sændwɪtʃ, 'sæn-/ n. emparedado, sándwich m.

sandy /'sændi/ a. arenoso; (color) rufo.

sane /sein/ a. cuerdo; sano.

sanitary /'sænɪ,tɛri/ a. higiénico, sanitario. **s. napkin,** toalla sanitaria.

sanitation /,sænɪ'teiʃən/ n. saneamiento m.

sanity /'sænɪti/ n. cordura f.

Santa Claus /'sæntə klɔz/ Papá Noel m.

sap /sæp/ n. **1.** savia f.; Colloq. estúpido, bobo m. —v. **2.** agotar.

sapphire /'sæfaiˀr/ n. zafiro m.

sarcasm /'sarkæzəm/ n. sarcasmo m.

sardine /sar'din/ n. sardina f.

sash /sæʃ/ n. cinta f.

satellite /'sætl,ait/ n. satélite m.

satellite dish antena parabólica f.

satin /'sætn/ n. raso m.

satire /'sætaiˀr/ n. sátira f.

satisfaction /,sætɪs'fækʃən/ n. satisfacción; recompensa f.

satisfactory /,sætɪs'fæktəri/ a. satisfactorio.

satisfy /'sætɪs,fai/ v. satisfacer. **be satisfied that...,** estar convencido de que.

saturate /'sætʃə,reit/ v. saturar.

Saturday /'sætər,dei/ n. sábado m.

sauce /sɔs/ n. salsa; compota f.

saucer /'sɔsər/ n. platillo m.

saucy /'sɔsi/ a. descarado, insolente.

sauna /'sɔnə/ n. sauna f.

sausage /'sɔsɪdʒ/ n. salchicha f.

savage /'sævɪdʒ/ a. & n. salvaje m. & f.

save /seiv/ v. 1. salvar; guardar; ahorrar, economizar. —prep. 2. salvo, excepto.

savings /'seivɪŋz/ n. ahorros m.pl.

savings account cuenta de ahorros m.

savings bank caja de ahorros f.

savior /'seivyər/ n. salvador -ora.

savor /'seivər/ n. 1. sabor m. —v. 2. saborear.

savory /'seivəri/ a. sabroso.

saw /sɔ/ n. 1. sierra f. —v. 2. aserrar.

saxophone /'sæksə,foun/ n. saxofón, saxófono, m.

say /sei/ v. decir; recitar.

saying /'seiɪŋ/ n. dicho, refrán m.

scaffold /'skæfəld/ n. andamio; (gallows) patíbulo m.

scald /skɔld/ v. escaldar.

scale /skeil/ n. 1. escala; (of fish) escama f.; (pl.) balanza f. —v. 2. escalar; escamar.

scalp /skælp/ n. pericráneo m. v. escalpar.

scan /skæn/ v. hojear, repasar; (poetry) escandir; (computer) escanear, digitalizar.

scandal /'skændl/ n. escándalo m.

scanner /'skænər/ n. escáner m.

scant /skænt/ a. escaso.

scar /skɑr/ n. cicatriz f.

scarce /skɛərs/ a. escaso; raro.

scarcely /'skɛərsli/ adv. & conj. apenas.

scare /skɛər/ n. 1. susto m. —v. 2. asustar. **s. away,** espantar.

scarf /skɑrf/ n. pañueleta, bufanda f.

scarlet /'skɑrlɪt/ n. escarlata f.

scarlet fever escarlatina f.

scatter /'skætər/ v. esparcir; dispersar.

scavenger /'skævɪndʒər/ n. basurero m.

scenario /sɪ'nɛəri,ou, -'nɑr-/ n. escenario m.

scene /sin/ n. vista f., paisaje m.; *Theat.* escena f. **behind the scenes,** entre bastidores.

scenery /'sinəri/ n. paisaje m.; *Theat.* decorado m.

scent /sɛnt/ n. 1. olor, perfume; (sense) olfato m. —v. 2. perfumar; *Fig.* sospechar.

schedule /'skɛdʒul, -ʊl, -uəl/ n. 1. programa, horario m. —v. 2. fijar la hora para.

scheme /skim/ n. 1. proyecto; esquema m. —v. 2. intrigar.

scholar /'skɒlər/ n. erudito -ta; becado -da.

scholarship /'skɒlər,ʃɪp/ n. beca; erudición f.

school /skul/ n. 1. escuela f.; colegio m.; (of fish) banco m. —v. 2. enseñar.

sciatica /sai'ætɪkə/ n. ciática f.

science /'saiəns/ n. ciencia f.

science fiction ciencia ficción.

scientific /,saiən'tɪfɪk/ a. científico.

scientist /'saiəntɪst/ n. científico -ca.

scissors /'sɪzərz/ n. tijeras f.pl.

scoff /skɔf, skɒf/ v. mofarse, burlarse.

scold /skould/ v. regañar.

scoop /skup/ n. 1. cucharón m.; cucharada f. —v. 2. **s. out,** recoger, sacar.

scope /skoup/ n. alcance; campo m.

score /skɔr/ n. 1. tantos m.pl.; (music) partitura f. —v. 2. marcar, hacer tantos.

scorn /skɔrn/ n. 1. desprecio m. —v. 2. despreciar.

scornful /'skɔrnfəl/ a. desdeñoso.

Scotland /'skɒtlənd/ n. Escocia f.

Scottish /'skɒtɪʃ/ a. escocés.

scour /skauᵊr/ v. fregar, estregar.

scourge /skɔrdʒ/ n. azote m.; plaga f.

scout /skaut/ n. 1. explorador -ra. —v. 2. explorar, reconocer.

scramble /'skræmbəl/ n. 1. rebatiña f. —v. 2. bregar. **scrambled eggs,** huevos revueltos.

scrap /skræp/ n. 1. migaja f.; pedacito m.; *Colloq.* riña f. **s. metal,** hierro viejo m. **s. paper,** papel borrador. —v. 2. desechar; *Colloq.* reñir.

scrapbook /'skræp,bʊk/ n. álbum de recortes m.

scrape /skreip/ n. 1. lío, apuro m. —v. 2. raspar; (feet) restregar.

scratch /skrætʃ/ n. 1. rasguño m. —v. 2. rasguñar; rayar.

scream /skrim/ n. 1. grito, chillido m. —v. 2. gritar, chillar.

screen /skrin/ n. biombo m.; (for

window) tela metálica; (movie) pantalla f.

screw /skru/ n. **1.** tornillo m. —v. **2.** atornillar.

screwdriver /'skru,draivər/ n. destornillador m.

scribble /'skrɪbəl/ v. hacer garabatos.

scroll /skroul/ n. rúbrica f.; rollo de papel.

scroll bar n. barra de enrollar f.

scrub /skrʌb/ v. fregar, estregar.

scruple /'skrupəl/ n. escrúpulo m.

scrupulous /'skrupyələs/ a. escrupuloso.

scuba diving /'skubə 'daivɪŋ/ submarinismo m.

sculptor /'skʌlptər/ n. escultor -ra.

sculpture /'skʌlptʃər/ n. **1.** escultura f. —v. **2.** esculpir.

scythe /saið/ n. guadaña f.

sea /si/ n. mar m. or f.

seabed /'si,bɛd/ n. lecho marino m.

sea breeze brisa marina f.

seafood /'si,fud/ n. mariscos m.pl.

seal /sil/ n. **1.** sello m.; (animal) foca f. —v. **2.** sellar.

seam /sim/ n. costura f.

seamy /'simi/ a. sórdido.

seaplane /'si,plein/ n. hidroavión m.

seaport /'si,pɔrt/ n. puerto de mar.

search /sɜrtʃ/ n. **1.** registro m. **in s. of,** en busca de. —v. **2.** registrar. **s. for,** buscar.

search engine motor de búsqueda m., buscador m., indexador de información m.

seasick /'si,sɪk/ a. mareado. **to get s.,** marearse.

season /'sizən/ n. **1.** estación; sazón; temporada f. —v. **2.** sazonar.

seasoning /'sizənɪŋ/ n. condimento m.

season ticket abono m.

seat /sit/ n. **1.** asiento m.; residencia, sede f.; Theat. localidad f. **s. belt,** cinturón de seguridad. —v. **2.** sentar. **be seated,** sentarse.

seaweed /'si,wid/ n. alga, alga marina f.

second /'sɪkɒnd/ a. & n. **1.** segundo m. —v. **2.** apoyar, segundar.

secondary /'sɛkən,dɛri/ a. secundario.

secret /'sikrɪt/ a. & n. secreto m.

secretary /'sɛkrɪ,tɛri/ n. secretario -ria; Govt. ministro -tra; (furniture) papelera f.

sect /sɛkt/ n. secta f.; partido m.

section /'sɛkʃən/ n. sección, parte f.

sectional /'sɛkʃənl/ a. regional, local.

secular /'sɛkyələr/ a. secular.

secure /sɪ'kyur/ a. **1.** seguro. —v. **2.** asegurar; obtener; Fin. garantizar.

security /sɪ'kyurɪti/ n. seguridad; garantía f.

sedative /'sɛdətɪv/ a. & n. sedativo m.

seduce /sɪ'dus/ v. seducir.

see /si/ v. ver; comprender. **s. off,** despedirse de. **s. to,** encargarse de.

seed /sid/ n. **1.** semilla f. —v. **2.** sembrar.

seek /sik/ v. buscar. **s. to,** tratar de.

seem /sim/ v. parecer.

seep /sip/ v. colarse.

segment /'sɛgmənt/ n. segmento m.

segregate /'sɛgrɪ,geit/ v. segregar.

seize /siz/ v. agarrar; apoderarse de.

seldom /'sɛldəm/ adv. rara vez.

select /sɪ'lɛkt/ a. **1.** escogido, selecto. —v. **2.** elegir, seleccionar.

selection /sɪ'lɛkʃən/ n. selección f.

selective /sɪ'lɛktɪv/ a. selectivo.

selfish /'sɛlfɪʃ/ a. egoísta.

selfishness /'sɛlfɪʃnɪs/ n. egoísmo m.

sell /sɛl/ v. vender.

semester /sɪ'mɛstər/ n. semestre m.

semicircle /'sɛmi,sɜrkəl/ n. semicírculo m.

semolina /,sɛmə'linə/ n. sémola f.

senate /'sɛnɪt/ n. senado m.

senator /'sɛnətər/ n. senador -ra.

send /sɛnd/ v. mandar, enviar; (a wire) poner. **s. away,** despedir. **s. back,** devolver. **s. for,** mandar buscar. **s. off,** expedir. **s. word,** mandar recado.

senile /'sinail/ a. senil.

senior /'sinyər/ a. mayor; más viejo. **Sr.,** padre.

senior citizen persona de edad avanzada.

sensation /sɛn'seiʃən/ n. sensación f.

sensational /sɛn'seiʃənl̩/ a. sensacional.

sense /sɛns/ n. **1.** sentido; juicio m. —v. **2.** percibir; sospechar.

sensible /'sɛnsəbəl/ a. sensato, razonable.

sensitive /'sɛnsɪtɪv/ a. sensible; sensitivo.

sensual /'sɛnʃuəl/ a. sensual.

sentence /'sɛntn̩s/ n. **1.** frase; *Gram.* oración; *Leg.* sentencia f. —v. **2.** condenar.

sentiment /'sɛntəmənt/ n. sentimiento m.

sentimental /ˌsɛntə'mɛntl̩/ a. sentimental.

separate /a. 'sɛpərɪt; v. -ˌreit/ a. **1.** separado; suelto. —v. **2.** separar, dividir.

separation /ˌsɛpə'reiʃən/ n. separación f.

September /sɛp'tɛmbər/ n. septiembre m.

sequence /'sikwəns/ n. serie f. **in s.,** seguidos.

serenade /ˌsɛrə'neid/ n. **1.** serenata f. —v. **2.** dar serenata a.

serene /sə'rin/ a. sereno; tranquilo.

sergeant /'sɑrdʒənt/ n. sargento m.

serial /'sɪəriəl/ a. en serie, de serie.

series /'sɪəriz/ n. serie f.

serious /'sɪəriəs/ a. serio; grave.

sermon /'sɜrmən/ n. sermón m.

serpent /'sɜrpənt/ n. serpiente f.

servant /'sɜrvənt/ n. criado -da; servidor -ra.

serve /sɜrv/ v. servir.

server /'sɜrvər/ n. servidor m.

service /'sɜrvɪs/ n. **1.** servicio m. **at the s. of,** a las órdenes de. **be of s.,** servir; ser útil. —v. **2.** *Auto.* reparar.

service station estación de servicio f.

session /'sɛʃən/ n. sesión f.

set /sɛt/ a. **1.** fijo. —n. **2.** colección f.; (of a game) juego; *Mech.* aparato; *Theat.* decorado m. —v. **3.** poner, colocar; fijar; (sun) ponerse. **s. forth,** exponer. **s. off, s. out,** salir. **s. up,** instalar; establecer.

settle /'sɛtl̩/ v. solucionar; arreglar; establecerse.

settlement /'sɛtl̩mənt/ n. caserío; arreglo; acuerdo m.

settler /'sɛtlər/ n. poblador -ra.

seven /'sɛvən/ a. & pron. siete.

seventeen /ˈsɛvən'tin/ a. & pron. diecisiete.

seventh /'sɛvənθ/ a. séptimo.

seventy /'sɛvənti/ a. & pron. setenta.

sever /'sɛvər/ v. desunir; romper.

several /'sɛvərəl/ a. & pron. varios.

severance pay /'sɛvərəns/ indemnización de despido.

severe /sə'vɪər/ a. severo; grave.

severity /sə'vɛrɪti/ n. severidad f.

sew /sou/ v. coser.

sewer /'suər/ n. cloaca f.

sewing /'souɪŋ/ n. costura f.

sewing basket costurero m.

sewing machine máquina de coser f.

sex /sɛks/ n. sexo m.

sexism /'sɛksɪzəm/ n. sexismo m.

sexist /'sɛksɪst/ a. & n. sexista m. & f.

sexton /'sɛkstən/ n. sacristán m.

sexual /'sɛkʃuəl/ a. sexual.

shabby /'ʃæbi/ a. haraposo, desaliñado.

shade /ʃeid/ n. **1.** sombra f.; tinte m.; (window) transparente m. —v. **2.** sombrear.

shadow /'ʃædou/ n. sombra f.

shady /'ʃeidi/ a. sombroso; sospechoso.

shaft /ʃæft/ n. (columna) fuste; *Mech.* asta f.

shake /ʃeik/ v. sacudir; agitar; temblar. **s. hands with,** dar la mano a.

shallow /'ʃælou/ a. poco hondo; superficial.

shame /ʃeim/ n. **1.** vergüenza f. **be a s.,** ser una lástima. —v. **2.** avergonzar.

shameful /'ʃeimfəl/ a. vergonzoso.

shampoo /ʃæm'pu/ n. champú m.

shape /ʃeip/ n. **1.** forma f.; estado m. —v. **2.** formar.

share /ʃɛər/ n. **1.** parte; (stock) acción f. **2** —v. **2.** compartir.

shareholder /'ʃɛərˌhouldər/ n. accionista m. & f.

shareware /'ʃɛərˌwɛər/ n. programas compartidos m.pl.

shark /ʃɑrk/ n. tiburón m.

sharp /ʃɑrp/ *a.* agudo; (blade) afilado.

sharpen /'ʃɑrpən/ *v.* aguzar; afilar.

shatter /'ʃætər/ *v.* estrellar; hacer pedazos.

shave /ʃeiv/ *n.* **1.** afeitada *f.* —*v.* **2.** afeitarse.

shawl /ʃɔl/ *n.* rebozo, chal *m.*

she /ʃi/ *pron.* ella *f.*

sheaf /ʃif/ *n.* gavilla *f.*

shear /ʃiər/ *v.* cizallar.

shears /ʃiərz/ *n.* cizallas *f.pl.*

sheath /ʃiθ/ *n.* vaina *f.*

shed /ʃɛd/ *n.* **1.** cobertizo *m.* —*v.* **2.** arrojar, quitarse.

sheep /ʃip/ *n.* oveja *f.*

sheet /ʃit/ *n.* sábana; (of paper) hoja *f.*

shelf /ʃɛlf/ *n.* estante, *m.*, repisa *f.*

shell /ʃɛl/ *n.* **1.** cáscara; (sea) concha *f.*; *Mil.* proyectil *m.* —*v.* **2.** desgranar; bombardear.

shellac /ʃə'læk/ *n.* laca *f.*

shelter /'ʃɛltər/ *n.* **1.** albergue; refugio *m.* —*v.* **2.** albergar; amparar.

shepherd /'ʃɛpərd/ *n.* pastor *m.*

sherry /'ʃɛri/ *n.* jerez *m.*

shield /ʃild/ *n.* **1.** escudo *m.* —*v.* **2.** amparar.

shift /ʃift/ *n.* **1.** cambio; (work) turno *m.* —*v.* **2.** cambiar, mudar. **s. for oneself,** arreglárselas.

shine /ʃain/ *n.* **1.** brillo, lustre *m.* —*v.* **2.** brillar; (shoes) lustrar.

shiny /'ʃaini/ *a.* brillante, lustroso.

ship /ʃip/ *n.* **1.** barco *m.*, nave *f.* —*v.* **2.** embarcar; *Com.* enviar.

shipment /'ʃipmənt/ *n.* envío; embarque *m.*

shirk /ʃɜrk/ *v.* faltar al deber.

shirt /ʃɜrt/ *n.* camisa *f.*

shiver /'ʃivər/ *n.* **1.** temblor *m.* —*v.* **2.** temblar.

shock /ʃɒk/ *n.* **1.** choque *m.* —*v.* **2.** chocar.

shoe /ʃu/ *n.* zapato *m.*

shoelace /'ʃu,leis/ *n.* lazo *m.*; cordón de zapato.

shoemaker /'ʃu,meikər/ *n.* zapatero *m.*

shoot /ʃut/ *v.* tirar; (gun) disparar. **s. away, s. off,** salir disparado.

shop /ʃɒp/ *n.* tienda *f.*

shopping /'ʃɒpiŋ/ *n.* **to go s.,** hacer compras, ir de compras.

shop window escaparate *m.*

shore /ʃɔr/ *n.* orilla; playa *f.*

short /ʃɔrt/ *a.* corto; breve; (in stature) pequeño, bajo. **a s. time,** poco tiempo. **in s.,** en suma.

shortage /'ʃɔrtidʒ/ *n.* escasez; falta *f.*

shorten /'ʃɔrtn/ *v.* acortar, abreviar.

shortly /'ʃɔrtli/ *adv.* en breve, dentro de poco.

shorts /ʃɔrts/ *n.* calzoncillos *m.pl.*

shot /ʃɒt/ *n.* tiro, disparo *m.*

shoulder /'ʃouldər/ *n.* **1.** hombro *m.* —*v.* **2.** asumir; cargar con.

shoulder blade *n.* omóplato *m.*, paletilla *f.*

shout /ʃaut/ *n.* **1.** grito *m.* —*v.* **2.** gritar.

shove /ʃʌv/ *n.* **1.** empujón *m.* —*v.* **2.** empujar.

shovel /'ʃʌvəl/ *n.* **1.** pala *f.* —*v.* **2.** traspalar.

show /ʃou/ *n.* **1.** ostentación *f.*; *Theat.* función *f.*; espectáculo *m.* —*v.* **2.** enseñar, mostrar; verse. **s. up,** destacarse; *Colloq.* asomar.

shower /'ʃauər/ *n.* chubasco *m.*; (bath) ducha *f. v.* ducharse.

shrapnel /'ʃræpnl/ *n.* metralla *f.*

shrewd /ʃrud/ *a.* astuto.

shriek /ʃrik/ *n.* **1.** chillido *m.* —*v.* **2.** chillar.

shrill /ʃril/ *a.* chillón, agudo.

shrimp /ʃrimp/ *n.* camarón *m.*

shrine /ʃrain/ *n.* santuario *m.*

shrink /ʃriŋk/ *v.* encogerse, contraerse. **s. from,** huir de.

shroud /ʃraud/ *n.* **1.** mortaja *f.* —*v.* **2.** *Fig.* ocultar.

shrub /ʃrʌb/ *n.* arbusto *m.*

shudder /'ʃʌdər/ *n.* **1.** estremecimiento *m.* —*v.* **2.** estremecerse.

shun /ʃʌn/ *v.* evitar, huir de.

shut /ʃʌt/ *v.* cerrar. **s. in,** encerrar. **s. up,** *Colloq.* callarse.

shutter /'ʃʌtər/ *n.* persiana *f.*

shy /ʃai/ *a.* tímido, vergonzoso.

sick /sik/ *a.* enfermo. **s. of,** aburrido de, cansado de.

sickness /'siknis/ *n.* enfermedad *f.*

side /said/ *n.* **1.** lado; partido *m.*; parte *f.*; *Anat.* costado *m.* —*v.* **2.** **s. with,** ponerse del lado de.

sidewalk /'said,wɔk/ *n.* acera, vereda *f.*

siege /sidʒ/ *n.* asedio *m.*

sieve /siv/ *n.* cedazo *m.*

sift /sift/ *v.* cerner.

sigh /sai/ *n.* **1.** suspiro *m.* —*v.* **2.** suspirar.

sight /sait/ *n.* **1.** vista *f.;* punto de interés *m.* **lose s. of,** perder de vista. —*v.* **2.** divisar.

sign /sain/ *n.* **1.** letrero; señal, seña *f.* —*v.* **2.** firmar. **s. up,** inscribirse.

signal /'sɪgnl/ *n.* **1.** señal *f.* —*v.* **2.** hacer señales.

signature /'sɪgnətʃər/ *n.* firma *f.*

significance /sɪg'nɪfɪkəns/ *n.* significación *f.*

significant /sɪg'nɪfɪkənt/ *a.* significativo.

significant other pareja *m.* & *f.*

signify /'sɪgnə,faɪ/ *v.* significar.

silence /'saɪləns/ *n.* **1.** silencio *m.* —*v.* **2.** hacer callar.

silent /'saɪlənt/ *a.* silencioso; callado.

silk /sɪlk/ *n.* seda *f.*

silken /'sɪlkən/ **silky** *a.* sedoso.

sill /sɪl/ *n.* umbral de puerta *m.,* solera *f.*

silly /'sɪli/ *a.* necio, tonto.

silo /'saɪlou/ *n.* silo *m.*

silver /'sɪlvər/ *n.* plata *f.*

silver-plated /'sɪlvər 'pleɪtɪd/ *a.* chapado en plata.

silverware /'sɪlvər,wɛər/ *n.* vajilla de plata *f.*

similar /'sɪmələr/ *a.* semejante, parecido.

similarity /,sɪmə'lærɪti/ *n.* semejanza *f.*

simple /'sɪmpəl/ *a.* sencillo, simple.

simplicity /sɪm'plɪsɪti/ *n.* sencillez *f.*

simplify /'sɪmplə,faɪ/ *v.* simplificar.

simulate /'sɪmyə,leɪt/ *v.* simular.

simultaneous /,saɪməl'teɪniəs/ *a.* simultáneo.

sin /sɪn/ *n.* **1.** pecado *m.* —*v.* **2.** pecar.

since /sɪns/ *adv.* **1.** desde entonces. —*prep.* **2.** desde. —*conj.* **3.** desde que; puesto que.

sincere /sɪn'sɪər/ *a.* sincero.

sincerely /sɪn'sɪərli/ *adv.* sinceramente.

sincerity /sɪn'sɛrɪti/ *n.* sinceridad *f.*

sinew /'sɪnyu/ *n.* tendón *m.*

sinful /'sɪnfəl/ *a.* pecador.

sing /sɪŋ/ *v.* cantar.

singe /sɪndʒ/ *v.* chamuscar.

singer /'sɪŋər/ *n.* cantante *m.* & *f.*

single /'sɪŋgəl/ *a.* solo; (room) sencillo; (unmarried) soltero. **s. room,** habitación individual.

singular /'sɪŋgyələr/ *a.* & *n.* singular *m.*

sinister /'sɪnəstər/ *a.* siniestro.

sink /sɪŋk/ *n.* **1.** fregadero *m.* —*v.* **2.** hundir; *Fig.* abatir.

sinner /'sɪnər/ *n.* pecador -ra.

sinuous /'sɪnyuəs/ *a.* sinuoso.

sinus /'saɪnəs/ *n.* seno *m.*

sip /sɪp/ *n.* **1.** sorbo *m.* —*v.* **2.** sorber.

siphon /'saɪfən/ *n.* sifón *m.*

sir /sɜr/ *title.* señor.

siren /'saɪrən/ *n.* sirena *f.*

sirloin /'sɜrlɔɪn/ *n.* solomillo *m.*

sisal /'saɪsəl, 'sɪsəl/ *n.* henequén *m.*

sister /'sɪstər/ *n.* hermana *f.*

sister-in-law /'sɪstərɪn,lɔ/ *n.* cuñada *f.*

sit /sɪt/ *v.* sentarse; posar. **be sitting,** estar sentado. **s. down,** sentarse. **s. up,** incorporarse; quedar levantado.

site /saɪt/ *n.* sitio, local *m.*

sitting /'sɪtɪŋ/ *n.* sesión *f. a.* sentado.

situate /'sɪtʃu,eɪt/ *v.* situar.

situation /,sɪtʃu'eɪʃən/ *n.* situación *f.*

sit-up /'sɪt ,ʌp/ *n.* abdominal *m.*

six /sɪks/ *a.* & *pron.* seis.

sixteen /'sɪks'tin/ *a.* & *pron.* dieciseis.

sixth /sɪksθ/ *a.* sexto.

sixty /'sɪksti/ *a.* & *pron.* sesenta.

size /saɪz/ *n.* tamaño; (of shoe, etc.) número *m.;* talla *f.*

sizing /'saɪzɪŋ/ *n.* upreso *m.;* sisa, cola de retazo *f.*

skate /skeɪt/ *n.* **1.** patín *m.* —*v.* **2.** patinar.

skateboard /'skeɪt,bɔrd/ *n.* monopatín *m.*

skein /skeɪn/ *n.* madeja *f.*

skeleton /'skɛlɪtn/ *n.* esqueleto *m.*

skeptic /'skɛptɪk/ *n.* escéptico -ca.

skeptical /'skɛptɪkəl/ *a.* escéptico.

sketch /skɛtʃ/ *n.* **1.** esbozo *m.* —*v.* **2.** esbozar.

ski /ski/ *n.* **1.** esquí *m.* —*v.* **2.** esquiar.

skid /skɪd/ *v.* **1.** resbalar. —*n.* **2.** varadera *f.*

skill /skɪl/ *n.* destreza, habilidad *f.*

skillful /'skɪlfəl/ *a.* diestro, hábil.

skim /skɪm/ *v.* rasar; (milk) desnatar. **s. over, s. through,** hojear.

skin /skɪn/ *n.* **1.** piel; (of fruit) corteza *f.* —*v.* **2.** desollar.

skin doctor dermatólogo -ga *m.* & *f.*

skip /skɪp/ *n.* **1.** brinco *m.* —*v.* **2.** brincar. **s. over,** pasar por alto.

skirmish /'skɜrmɪʃ/ *n.* escaramuza *f.*

skirt /skɜrt/ *n.* falda *f.*

skull /skʌl/ *n.* cráneo *m.*

skunk /skʌŋk/ *n.* zorrillo *m.*

sky /skai/ *n.* cielo *m.*

skylight /'skai,lait/ *n.* tragaluz *m.*

skyscraper /'skai,skreipər/ *n.* rascacielos *m.*

slab /slæb/ *n.* tabla *f.*

slack /slæk/ *a.* flojo; descuidado.

slacken /'slækən/ *v.* relajar.

slacks /slæks/ *n.* pantalones flojos.

slam /slæm/ *n.* **1.** portazo *m.* —*v.* **2.** cerrar de golpe. **slamming on the brakes,** frenazo *m.*

slander /'slændər/ *n.* **1.** calumnia *f.* —*v.* **2.** calumniar.

slang /slæŋ/ *n.* jerga *f.*

slant /slænt/ *n.* **1.** sesgo *m.* —*v.* **2.** sesgar.

slap /slæp/ *n.* **1.** bofetada, palmada *f.* —*v.* **2.** dar una bofetada.

slash /slæʃ/ *n.* **1.** cuchillada *f.* —*v.* **2.** acuchillar.

slat /slæt/ *n.* **1.** tablilla *f.* —*v.* **2.** lanzar.

slate /sleit/ *n.* **1.** pizarra *f.*; lista de candidatos. —*n.* **2.** destinar.

slaughter /'slɔtər/ *n.* **1.** matanza *f.* —*v.* **2.** matar.

slave /sleiv/ *n.* esclavo -va.

slavery /'sleivəri/ *n.* esclavitud *f.*

Slavic /'slɑvɪk/ *a.* eslavo.

slay /slei/ *v.* matar, asesinar.

sled /slɛd/ *n.* trineo *m.*

sleek /slik/ *a.* liso y brillante.

sleep /slip/ *n.* **1.** sueño *m.* **to get much s.,** dormir mucho. —*v.* **2.** dormir.

sleeping car /'slipɪŋ/ coche cama.

sleeping pill /'slipɪŋ/ pastilla para dormir, somnífero *m.*

sleepy /'slipi/ *a.* soñoliento. **to be s.,** tener sueño.

sleet /slit/ *n.* **1.** cellisca *f.* —*v.* **2.** cellisquear.

sleeve /sliv/ *n.* manga *f.*

slender /'slɛndər/ *a.* delgado.

slice /slais/ *n.* **1.** rebanada; (of meat) tajada *f.* —*v.* **2.** rebanar; tajar.

slide /slaid/ *v.* resbalar, deslizarse.

slide rule regla de cálculo *f.*

slight /slait/ *n.* **1.** desaire *m.* —*a.* **2.** pequeño; leve. —*v.* **3.** desairar.

slim /slɪm/ *a.* delgado.

slime /slaim/ *n.* lama *f.*

sling /slɪŋ/ *n.* **1.** honda *f.*; *Med.* cabestrillo *m.* —*v.* **2.** tirar.

slink /slɪŋk/ *v.* escabullirse.

slip /slɪp/ *n.* **1.** imprudencia; (garment) combinación *f.*; (of paper) trozo *m.*; ficha *f.* —*v.* **2.** resbalar; deslizar. **s. up,** equivocarse.

slipper /'slɪpər/ *n.* chinela *f.*

slippery /'slɪpəri/ *a.* resbaloso.

slit /slɪt/ *n.* **1.** abertura *f.* —*v.* **2.** cortar.

slogan /'slougən/ *n.* lema *m.*

slope /sloup/ *n.* **1.** declive *m.* —*v.* **2.** inclinarse.

sloppy /'slɒpi/ *a.* desaliñado, chapucero.

slot /slɒt/ *n.* ranura *f.*

slot machine tragaperras *f.*

slouch /slautʃ/ *n.* **1.** patán *m.* —*v.* **2.** estar gacho.

slovenly /'slʌvənli/ *a.* desaliñado.

slow /slou/ *a.* **1.** lento; (watch) atrasado. —*v.* **2.** **s. down, s. up,** retardar; ir más despacio.

slowly /'slouli/ *adv.* despacio.

slowness /'slounɪs/ *n.* lentitud *f.*

sluggish /'slʌgɪʃ/ *a.* perezoso, inactivo.

slum /slʌm/ *n.* barrio bajo *m.*

slumber /'slʌmbər/ *v.* dormitar.

slur /slɜr/ *n.* **1.** estigma *m.* —*v.* **2.** menospreciar.

slush /slʌʃ/ *n.* fango *m.*

sly /slai/ *a.* taimado. **on the s.** a hurtadillas.

smack /smæk/ *n.* **1.** manotada *f.* —*v.* **2.** manotear.

small /smɔl/ *a.* pequeño.

small letter minúscula *f.*

smallpox /'smɔl,pɒks/ *n.* viruela *f.*

smart /smɑrt/ *a.* **1.** listo; elegante. —*v.* **2.** escocer.

smash /smæʃ/ *v.* aplastar; hacer pedazos.

smear /smɪər/ *n.* **1.** mancha; difamación *f.* —*v.* **2.** manchar; difamar.

smell /smɛl/ *n.* **1.** olor; (sense) olfato *m.* —*v.* **2.** oler.

smelt /smɛlt/ *n.* **1.** eperlano *m.* —*v.* **2.** fundir.

smile /smail/ *n.* **1.** sonrisa *f.* —*v.* **2.** sonreír.

smite /smait/ *v.* afligir; apenar.

smock /smɒk/ *n.* camisa de mujer *f.*

smoke /smouk/ *n.* **1.** humo *m.*
—*v.* **2.** fumar; (food) ahumar.
smokestack /'smouk,stæk/ *n.* chimenea *f.*
smolder /'smouldər/ *v.* arder sin
llama.
smooth /smuð/ *a.* **1.** liso; suave;
tranquilo. —*v.* **2.** alisar.
smother /'smʌðər/ *v.* sofocar.
smug /smʌg/ *a.* presumido.
smuggle /'smʌgəl/ *v.* pasar de
contrabando.
snack /snæk/ *n.* bocadillo *m.*
snag /snæg/ *n.* nudo; obstáculo
m.
snail /sneil/ *n.* caracol *m.*
snake /sneik/ *n.* culebra, serpiente
f.
snap /snæp/ *n.* **1.** trueno *m.* —*v.*
2. tronar; romper.
snapshot /'snæp,ʃɒt/ *n.* instantánea *f.*
snare /snɛər/ *n.* trampa *f.*
snarl /snɑrl/ *n.* **1.** gruñido *m.* —*v.*
2. gruñir; (hair) enredar.
snatch /snætʃ/ *v.* arrebatar.
sneak /snik/ *v.* ir, entrar, salir
(etc.) a hurtadillas.
sneaker /'snikər/ *n.* sujeto ruín *m.*
zapatilla de tenis.
sneer /snɪər/ *n.* **1.** mofa *f.* —*v.* **2.**
mofarse.
sneeze /sniz/ *n.* **1.** estornudo *m.*
—*v.* **2.** estornudar.
snicker /'snɪkər/ *n.* risita *m.*
snob /snɒb/ *n.* esnob *m.*
snore /snɔr/ *n.* **1.** ronquido *m.*
—*v.* **2.** roncar.
snow /snou/ *n.* **1.** nieve *f.* —*v.* **2.**
nevar.
snowball /'snou,bɔl/ *n.* bola de
nieve *f.*
snowdrift /'snou,drift/ *n.* ventisquero *m.*
snowplow /'snou,plau/ *n.* quitanieves *m.*
snowstorm /'snou,stɔrm/ *n.*
nevasca *f.*
snub /snʌb/ *v.* desairar.
snug /snʌg/ *a.* abrigado y cómodo.
so /sou/ *adv.* **1.** así; (also) también. **so as to,** para. **so that,**
para que. **so... as,** tan... como.
so... that, tan... que. —*conj.* **2.**
así es que.
soak /souk/ *v.* empapar.
soap /soup/ *n.* **1.** jabón *m.* —*v.* **2.**
enjabonar.
soap powder jabón en polvo *m.*

soar /sɔr/ *v.* remontarse.
sob /sɒb/ *n.* **1.** sollozo *m.* —*v.* **2.**
sollozar.
sober /'soubər/ *a.* sobrio; pensativo.
sociable /'souʃəbəl/ *a.* sociable.
social /'souʃəl/ *a.* **1.** social. —*n.* **2.**
tertulia *f.*
socialism /'souʃə,lɪzəm/ *n.* socialismo *m.*
socialist /'souʃəlɪst/ *a. & n.* socialista *m. & f.*
society /sə'saiɪti/ *n.* sociedad;
compañía *f.*
sociological /,sousiə'lɒdʒɪkəl/ *a.*
sociológico.
sociologist /,sousi,ɒlədʒɪst/ *n.* sociólogo -ga *m. & f.*
sociology /,sousi'ɒlədʒi/ *n.* sociología *f.*
sock /sɒk/ *n.* **1.** calcetín; puñetazo
m. —*v.* **2.** dar un puñetazo a.
socket /'sɒkɪt/ *n.* cuenca *f.*; *Elec.*
enchufe *m.*
sod /sɒd/ *n.* césped *m.*
soda /'soudə/ *n.* soda; *Chem.* sosa
f.
sodium /'soudiəm/ *n.* sodio *m.*
sofa /'soufə/ *n.* sofá *m.*
soft /sɔft/ *a.* blando; fino; suave.
soft drink bebida no alcohólica.
soften /'sɔfən/ *v.* ablandar; suavizar.
software /'sɔft,wɛər/ *n.* software
m., programa *m.*
soil /sɔil/ *n.* **1.** suelo *m.* —*v.* **2.**
ensuciar.
sojourn /'soudʒɜrn/ *n.* morada *f.*,
estancia *f.*
solace /'sɒlɪs/ *n.* **1.** solaz *m.* —*v.*
2. solazar.
solar /'soulər/ *a.* solar.
solar system sistema solar *m.*
solder /'sɒdər/ *v.* **1.** soldar. —*n.*
2. soldadura *f.*
soldier /'souldʒər/ *n.* soldado *m.*
& *f.*
sole /soul/ *n.* **1.** suela; (of foot)
planta *f.*; (fish) lenguado *m.* —*a.*
2. único.
solemn /'sɒləm/ *a.* solemne.
solemnity /sə'lɛmnɪti/ *n.* solemnidad *f.*
solicit /sə'lɪsɪt/ *v.* solicitar.
solicitous /sə'lɪsɪtəs/ *a.* solícito.
solid /'sɒlɪd/ *a. & n.* sólido *m.*
solidify /sə'lɪdə,fai/ *v.* solidificar.
solidity /sə'lɪdɪti/ *n.* solidez *f.*
solitary /'sɒlɪ,tɛri/ *a.* solitario.
solitude /'sɒlɪ,tud/ *n.* soledad *f.*

solo /'soulou/ *n.* solo *m.*

soloist /'soulouɪst/ *n.* solista *m.* & *f.*

soluble /'sɒlyəbəl/ *a.* soluble.

solution /sə'luʃən/ *n.* solución *f.*

solve /sɒlv/ *v.* solucionar; resolver.

solvent /'sɒlvənt/ *a.* solvente.

somber /'sɒmbər/ *a.* sombrío.

some /sʌm; *unstressed* səm/ *a.* & *pron.* algo (de), un poco (de); alguno; (pl.) algunos, unos.

somebody, someone /'sʌmbɒdi; 'sʌm,wʌn/ *pron.* alguien.

somehow /'sʌm,hau/ *adv.* de algún modo.

someone /'sʌm,wʌn/ *n.* alguien o alguno.

somersault /'sʌmər,sɔlt/ *n.* salto mortal *m.*

something /'sʌm,θɪŋ/ *pron.* algo, alguna cosa.

sometime /'sʌm,taim/ *adv.* alguna vez.

sometimes /'sʌm,taimz/ *adv.* a veces, algunas veces.

somewhat /'sʌm,wʌt/ *adv.* algo, un poco.

somewhere /'sʌm,wɛər/ *adv.* en (*or* a) alguna parte.

son /sʌn/ *n.* hijo *m.*

song /sɔŋ/ *n.* canción *f.*

son-in-law /'sʌn ɪn ,lɔ/ *n.* yerno *m.*

soon /sun/ *adv.* pronto. **as s. as possible,** cuanto antes. **sooner or later,** tarde o temprano. **no sooner... than,** apenas... cuando.

soot /sʊt/ *n.* hollín *m.*

soothe /suð/ *v.* calmar.

soothingly /'suðɪŋli/ *adv.* tiernamente.

sophisticated /sə'fɪstɪ,keitɪd/ *a.* sofisticado.

sophomore /'sɒfə,mɔr/ *n.* estudiante de segundo año *m.*

soprano /sə'prænou/ *n.* soprano *m.* & *f.*

sorcery /'sɔrsəri/ *n.* encantamiento *m.*

sordid /'sɔrdɪd/ *a.* sórdido.

sore /sɔr/ *n.* **1.** llaga *f.* —*a.* **2.** lastimado; *Colloq.* enojado. **to be s.,** doler.

sorority /sə'rɔrɪti, -'rɒr-/ *n.* hermandad de mujeres *f.*

sorrow /'sɒrou/ *n.* pesar, dolor *m.*, aflicción *f.*

sorrowful /'sɒrəfəl/ *a.* doloroso; afligido.

sorry /'sɒri/ *a.* **to be s.,** sentir, lamentar. **to be s. for,** compadecer.

sort /sɔrt/ *n.* **1.** tipo *m.*; clase, especie *f.* **s. of,** algo, un poco. —*v.* **2.** clasificar.

soul /soul/ *n.* alma *f.*

sound /saund/ *a.* **1.** sano; razonable; firme. —*n.* **2.** sonido *m.* —*v.* **3.** sonar; parecer.

soundproof /'saund,pruf/ *a.* insonorizado. *v.* insonorizar.

soundtrack /'saund,træk/ *n.* banda sonora *f.*

soup /sup/ *n.* sopa *f.*

sour /sauᵊr/ *a.* agrio; ácido; rancio.

source /sɔrs/ *n.* fuente; causa *f.*

south /sauθ/ *n.* sur *m.*

South Africa /'æfrɪkə/ Sudáfrica *f.*

South African *a.* & *n.* sudafricano.

South America /ə'mɛrɪkə/ Sud América, América del Sur.

South American *a.* & *n.* sudamericano -na.

southeast /,sauθ'ist; *Naut.* ,sau-/ *n.* sudeste *m.*

southern /'sʌðərn/ *a.* meridional.

South Pole *n.* Polo Sur *m.*

southwest /,sauθ'wɛst; *Naut.* ,sau-/ *n.* sudoeste *m.*

souvenir /,suvə'nɪər/ *n.* recuerdo *m.*

sovereign /'sɒvrɪn/ *n.* soberano -na.

sovereignty /'sɒvrɪnti/ *n.* soberanía *f.*

Soviet Russia Rusia Soviética *f.*

sow /*n.* sau; *v.* sou/ *n.* **1.** puerca *f.* —*v.* **2.** sembrar.

space /speis/ *n.* **1.** espacio *m.* —*v.* **2.** espaciar.

space out *v.* escalonar.

spaceship /'speis,ʃɪp/ *n.* nave espacial, astronave *f.*

space shuttle /'ʃʌtl/ transbordador espacial *m.*

spacious /'speiʃəs/ *a.* espacioso.

spade /speid/ *n.* **1.** laya; (cards) espada *f.* —*v.* **2.** layar.

spaghetti /spə'gɛti/ *n.* espaguetis *m.pl.*

Spain /spein/ *n.* España *f.*

span /spæn/ *n.* **1.** tramo *m.* —*v.* **2.** extenderse sobre.

Spaniard /'spænyərd/ *n.* español -ola.

Spanish /'spænɪʃ/ *a.* & *n.* español -ola.

spank /spæŋk/ *v.* pegar.
spanking /'spæŋkɪŋ/ *n.* tunda, zumba *f.*
spar /spɑr/ *v.* altercar.
spare /spɛər/ *a.* **1.** de repuesto. —*v.* **2.** perdonar; ahorrar; prestar. **have... to s.,** tener... de sobra.
spare tire neumático de recambio *m.*
spark /spɑrk/ *n.* chispa *f.*
sparkle /'spɑrkəl/ *n.* **1.** destello *m.* —*v.* **2.** chispear. **sparkling wine,** vino espumoso.
spark plug /'spɑrk,plʌg/ *n.* bujía *f.*
sparrow /'spærou/ *n.* gorrión *m.*
sparse /spɑrs/ *a.* esparcido.
spasm /'spæzəm/ *n.* espasmo *m.*
spasmodic /spæz'mɒdɪk/ *a.* espasmódico.
spatter /'spætər/ *v.* salpicar; manchar.
speak /spik/ *v.* hablar.
speaker /'spikər/ *n.* conferencista *m. & f.*
spear /spɪər/ *n.* lanza *f.*
spearmint /'spɪər,mɪnt/ *n.* menta romana *f.*
special /'spɛʃəl/ *a.* especial. **s. delivery,** entrega inmediata, entrega urgente.
specialist /'spɛʃəlɪst/ *n.* especialista *m. & f.*
specialty /'spɛʃəlti/ *n.* especialidad *f.*
species /'spiʃiz, -siz/ *n.* especie *f.*
specific /spɪ'sɪfɪk/ *a.* específico.
specify /'spɛsə,fai/ *v.* especificar.
specimen /'spɛsəmən/ *n.* espécimen *m.;* muestra *f.*
spectacle /'spɛktəkəl/ *n.* espectáculo *m.;* (pl.) lentes, anteojos *m.pl.*
spectacular /spɛk'tækyələr/ *a.* espectacular, aparatoso.
spectator /'spɛkteitər/ *n.* espectador -ra.
spectrum /'spɛktrəm/ *n.* espectro *m.*
speculate /'spɛkyə,leit/ *v.* especular.
speculation /,spɛkyə'leiʃən/ *n.* especulación *f.*
speech /spitʃ/ *n.* habla *f.;* lenguaje; discurso *m.* **part of s.,** parte de la oración.
speechless /'spitʃlɪs/ *a.* mudo.
speed /spid/ *n.* **1.** velocidad; rapidez *f.* —*v.* **2. s. up,** acelerar, apresurar.

speed limit velocidad máxima *f.*
speedometer /spi'dɒmɪtər/ *n.* velocímetro *m.*
speedy /'spidi/ *a.* veloz, rápido.
spell /spɛl/ *n.* **1.** hechizo; rato; *Med.* ataque *m.* —*v.* **2.** escribir; relevar.
spelling /'spɛlɪŋ/ *n.* ortografía *f.*
spend /spɛnd/ *v.* gastar; (time) pasar.
spendthrift /'spɛnd,θrɪft/ *a. & n.* pródigo; manirroto *m.*
sphere /sfɪər/ *n.* esfera *f.*
spice /spais/ *n.* **1.** especia *f.* —*v.* **2.** especiar.
spider /'spaidər/ *n.* araña *f.*
spider web telaraña *f.*
spike /spaik/ *n.* alcayata *f.;* punta *f.,* clavo *m.*
spill /spɪl/ *v.* derramar. *n.* caída *f.,* vuelco *m.*
spillway /'spɪl,wei/ *n.* vertedero *m.*
spin /spɪn/ *v.* hilar; girar.
spinach /'spɪnɪtʃ/ *n.* espinaca *f.*
spine /spain/ *n.* espina dorsal *f.*
spinet /'spɪnɪt/ *n.* espineta *m.*
spinster /'spɪnstər/ *n.* solterona *f.*
spiral /'spairəl/ *a. & n.* espiral *f.*
spire /spaiᵊr/ *n.* caracol *m.,* espiral *f.*
spirit /'spɪrɪt/ *n.* espíritu; ánimo *m.*
spiritual /'spɪrɪtʃuəl/ *a.* espiritual.
spiritualism /'spɪrɪtʃuə,lɪzəm/ *n.* espiritismo *m.*
spirituality /,spɪrɪtʃu'ælɪti/ *n.* espiritualidad *f.*
spit /spɪt/ *v.* escupir.
spite /spait/ *n.* despecho *m.* **in s. of,** a pesar de.
splash /splæʃ/ *n.* **1.** salpicadura *f.* —*v.* **2.** salpicar.
splendid /'splɛndɪd/ *a.* espléndido.
splendor /'splɛndər/ *n.* esplendor *m.*
splice /splais/ *v.* **1.** empalmar. —*n.* **2.** empalme *m.*
splint /splɪnt/ *n.* tablilla *f.*
splinter /'splɪntər/ *n.* **1.** astilla *f.* —*v.* **2.** astillar.
split /splɪt/ *n.* **1.** división *f.* —*v.* **2.** dividir, romper en dos.
splurge /splɜrdʒ/ *v.* **1.** fachendear. —*n.* **2.** fachenda *f.*
spoil /spɔil/ *n.* **1.** (pl.) botín *m.* —*v.* **2.** echar a perder; (a child) mimar.

spoke /spouk/ *n.* rayo (de rueda) *m.*

spokesman /'spouksmən/ *n.* portavoz *m.* & *f.*

spokesperson /'spouks,pɜrsən/ *n.* portavoz *m.* & *f.*

sponge /spʌndʒ/ *n.* esponja *f.*

sponsor /'spɒnsər/ *n.* **1.** patrocinador *m.* —*v.* **2.** patrocinar; costear.

spontaneity /,spɒntə'niɪti, -'nei-/ *n.* espontaneidad *f.*

spontaneous /spɒn'teiniəs/ *a.* espontáneo.

spool /spul/ *n.* carrete *m.*

spoon /spun/ *n.* cuchara *f.*

spoonful /'spunfʊl/ *n.* cucharada *f.*

sporadic /spə'rædɪk/ *a.* esporádico.

sport /spɔrt/ *n.* deporte *m.*

sport jacket chaqueta deportiva *f.*

sports center /spɔrts/ pabellón de deportes, polideportivo *m.*

sportsman /'spɔrtsmən/ *a.* **1.** deportivo. —*n.* **2.** deportista *m.* & *f.*

spot /spɒt/ *n.* **1.** mancha *f.*; lugar, punto *m.* —*v.* **2.** distinguir.

spouse /spaus/ *n.* esposo -sa.

spout /spaut/ *n.* **1.** chorro; (of teapot) pico *m.* —*v.* **2.** correr a chorro.

sprain /sprein/ *n.* **1.** torcedura *f.*, esguince *m.* —*v.* **2.** torcerse.

sprawl /sprɔl/ *v.* tenderse.

spray /sprei/ *n.* **1.** rociada *f.* —*v.* **2.** rociar.

spread /sprɛd/ *n.* **1.** propagación; extensión; (for bed) colcha *f.* —*v.* **2.** propagar; extender.

spreadsheet /'sprɛd,ʃit/ *n.* hoja de cálculo *f.*

spree /spri/ *n.* parranda *f.*

sprig /sprɪg/ *n.* ramita *f.*

sprightly /'spraitli/ *a.* garboso.

spring /sprɪŋ/ *n.* resorte, muelle *m.*; (season) primavera *f.*; (of water) manantial *m.*

springboard /'sprɪŋ,bɔrd/ *n.* trampolín *m.*

spring onion cebolleta *f.*

sprinkle /'sprɪŋkəl/ *v.* rociar; (rain) lloviznar.

sprint /sprɪnt/ *n.* carrera *f.*

sprout /spraut/ *n.* retoño *m.*

spry /sprai/ *a.* ágil.

spun /spʌn/ *a.* hilado.

spur /spɜr/ *n.* **1.** espuela *f.* **on the s. of the moment,** sin pensarlo. —*v.* **2.** espolear.

spurious /'spyʊriəs/ *a.* espurio.

spurn /spɜrn/ *v.* rechazar, despreciar.

spurt /spɜrt/ *n.* **1.** chorro *m.*; esfuerzo supremo. —*v.* **2.** salir en chorro.

spy /spai/ **1.** espía *m.* & *f.* —*v.* **2.** espiar.

squabble /'skwɒblɪŋ/ *n.* **1.** riña *f.* —*v.* **2.** reñir.

squad /skwɒd/ *n.* escuadra *f.*

squadron /'skwɒdrən/ *n.* escuadrón *m.*

squalid /'skwɒlɪd/ *a.* escuálido.

squall /skwɔl/ *n.* borrasca *f.*

squalor /'skwɒlər/ *n.* escualidez *f.*

squander /'skwɒndər/ *v.* malgastar.

square /skwɛər/ *a.* **1.** cuadrado. —*n.* **2.** cuadrado *m.*; plaza *f.*

square dance *n.* contradanza *f.*

squat /skwɒt/ *v.* agacharse.

squeak /skwik/ *n.* **1.** chirrido *m.* —*v.* **2.** chirriar.

squeamish /'skwimɪʃ/ *a.* escrupuloso.

squeeze /skwiz/ *n.* **1.** apretón *m.* —*v.* **2.** apretar; (fruit) exprimir.

squirrel /'skwɜrəl/ *n.* ardilla *f.*

squirt /skwɜrt/ *n.* **1.** chisguete *m.* —*v.* **2.** jeringar.

stab /stæb/ *n.* **1.** puñalada *f.* —*v.* **2.** apuñalar.

stability /stə'bɪlɪti/ *n.* estabilidad *f.*

stabilize /'steibə,laiz/ *v.* estabilizar.

stable /'steibəl/ *a.* **1.** estable, equilibrado. —*n.* **2.** caballeriza *f.*

stack /stæk/ *n.* **1.** pila *f.* —*v.* **2.** apilar.

stadium /'steidiəm/ *n.* estadio *m.*

staff /stæf/ *n.* personal *m.* **editorial s.,** cuerpo de redacción. **general s.,** estado mayor.

stag /stæg/ *n.* ciervo *m.*

stage /steidʒ/ *n.* **1.** etapa; *Theat.* escena *f.* —*v.* **2.** representar.

stagflation /stæg'fleiʃən/ *n.* estagflación.

stagger /'stægər/ *v.* (teeter) tambalear; (space out) escalonar.

stagnant /'stægnənt/ *a.* estancado.

stagnate /'stægneit/ *v.* estancarse.

stain /stein/ *n.* **1.** mancha *f.* —*v.* **2.** manchar.

stainless steel /'steinlɪs/ acero inoxidable *m.*

staircase /'stɛər,keis/ **stairs** n. escalera f.

stake /steik/ n. estaca; (bet) apuesta f. **at s.,** en juego; en peligro.

stale /steil/ a. rancio.

stalemate /'steil,meit/ n. estancación f.; tablas f.pl.

stalk /stɔk/ n. caña f.; (of flower) tallo m. v. acechar.

stall /stɔl/ n. **1.** tenderete; (for horse) pesebre m. —v. **2.** demorar; (motor) atascar.

stallion /'stælyən/ n. S.A. garañón m.

stalwart /'stɔlwərt/ a. fornido.

stamina /'stæmənə/ n. vigor m.

stammer /'stæmər/ v. tartamudear.

stamp /stæmp/ n. **1.** sello m., estampilla f. —v. **2.** sellar.

stamp collecting /kə'lɛktɪŋ/ filatelia f.

stampede /stæm'pid/ n. estampida f.

stand /stænd/ n. **1.** puesto m.; posición; (speaker's) tribuna; (furniture) mesita f. —v. **2.** estar; estar de pie; aguantar. **s. up,** pararse, levantarse.

standard /'stændərd/ a. **1.** normal, corriente. —n. **2.** norma f. **s. of living,** nivel de vida.

standardize /'stændər,daiz/ v. uniformar.

standing /'stændɪŋ/ a. fijo; establecido.

standpoint /'stænd,pɔint/ n. punto de vista m.

staple /'steipəl/ n. materia prima f.; grapa f.

stapler /'steiplər/ n. grapadora f.

star /stɑr/ n. estrella f.

starboard /'stɑrbərd/ n. estribor m.

starch /stɑrtʃ/ n. **1.** almidón m.; (in diet) fécula f. —v. **2.** almidonar.

stare /stɛər/ v. mirar fijamente.

stark /stɑrk/ a. **1.** severo. —adv. **2.** completamente.

start /stɑrt/ n. **1.** susto; principio m. —v. **2.** comenzar, empezar; salir; poner en marcha; causar.

startle /'stɑrtl̩/ v. asustar.

starvation /stɑr'veiʃən/ n. hambre f.

starve /stɑrv/ v. morir de hambre.

state /steit/ n. **1.** estado m. —v. **2.** declarar, decir.

statement /'steitmənt/ n. declaración f.

stateroom /'steit,rum/ n. camarote m.

statesman /'steitsmən/ n. estadista m.

static /'stætɪk/ a. **1.** estático. —n. **2.** estática f.

station /'steiʃən/ n. estación f.

stationary /'steiʃə,nɛri/ a. estacionario, fijo.

stationery /'steiʃə,nɛri/ n. papel de escribir.

statistics /stə'tɪstɪks/ n. estadística f.

statue /'stætʃu/ n. estatua f.

stature /'stætʃər/ n. estatura f.

status /'steitəs, 'stætəs/ n. condición, estado m.

statute /'stætʃut/ n. ley f.

staunch /stɔntʃ/ a. fiel; constante.

stay /stei/ n. **1.** estancia; visita f. —v. **2.** quedar, permanecer; parar, alojarse. **s. away,** ausentarse. **s. up,** velar.

steadfast /'stɛd,fæst/ a. inmutable.

steady /'stɛdi/ a. **1.** firme; permanente; regular. —v. **2.** sostener.

steak /steik/ n. biftec, bistec m.

steal /stil/ v. robar. **s. away,** escabullirse.

stealth /stɛlθ/ n. cautela f.

steam /stim/ n. vapor m.

steamboat /'stim,bout/ **steamer, steamship** n. vapor m.

steel /stil/ n. **1.** acero m. —v. **2.** **s. oneself,** fortalecerse.

steep /stip/ a. escarpado, empinado.

steeple /'stipəl/ n. campanario m.

steer /stɪər/ n. **1.** buey m. —v. **2.** guiar, manejar.

stellar /'stɛlər/ a. astral.

stem /stɛm/ n. **1.** tallo m. —v. **2.** parar. **s. from,** emanar de.

stencil /'stɛnsəl/ n. **1.** estarcido. —v. **2.** estarcir.

stenographer /stə'nɒgrəfər/ n. estenógrafo -fa.

stenography /stə'nɒgrəfi/ n. taquigrafía f.

step /stɛp/ n. **1.** paso m.; medida f.; (stairs) escalón m. —v. **2.** pisar. **s. back,** retirarse.

stepladder /'stɛp,lædər/ n. escalera de mano f.

stereophonic /ˌstɛriə'fɒnɪk/ a. estereofónico.

stereotype /'stɛriə,taip/ *n.* **1.** estereotipo *m.* —*v.* **2.** estereotipar.

sterile /'stɛril/ *a.* estéril.

sterilize /'stɛrə,laiz/ *v.* esterilizar.

sterling /'stɜrliŋ/ *a.* esterlina, genuino.

stern /stɜrn/ *n.* **1.** popa *f.* —*a.* **2.** duro, severo.

stethoscope /'stɛθə,skoup/ *n.* estetoscopio *m.*

stevedore /'stivi,dɔr/ *n.* estibador *m.*

stew /stu/ *n.* **1.** guisado *m.* —*v.* **2.** estofar.

steward /'stuərd/ *n.* camarero.

stewardess /'stuərdɪs/ *n.* azafata *f.*, aeromoza *f.*

stick /stɪk/ *n.* **1.** palo, bastón *m.* —*v.* **2.** pegar; (put) poner, meter.

sticky /'stɪki/ *a.* pegajoso.

stiff /stɪf/ *a.* tieso; duro.

stiffness /'stɪfnɪs/ *n.* tiesura *f.*

stifle /'staifəl/ *v.* sofocar; *Fig.* suprimir.

stigma /'stɪgmə/ *n.* estigma *m.*

still /stɪl/ *a.* **1.** quieto; silencioso. **to keep s.,** quedarse quieto. —*adv.* **2.** todavía, aún; no obstante. —*n.* **3.** alambique *m.*

stillborn /'stɪl,bɔrn/ *n. & a.* nacido -da muerto -ta.

still life *n.* naturaleza muerta *f.*

stillness /'stɪlnɪs/ *n.* silencio *m.*

stilted /'stɪltɪd/ *a.* afectado, artificial.

stimulant /'stɪmyələnt/ *a. & n.* estimulante *m.*

stimulate /'stɪmyə,leit/ *v.* estimular.

stimulus /'stɪmyələs/ *n.* estímulo *m.*

sting /stɪŋ/ *n.* **1.** picadura *f.* —*v.* **2.** picar.

stingy /'stɪndʒi/ *a.* tacaño.

stipulate /'stɪpyə,leit/ *v.* estipular.

stir /stɜr/ *n.* **1.** conmoción *f.* —*v.* **2.** mover. **s. up,** conmover; suscitar.

stitch /stɪtʃ/ *n.* **1.** puntada *f.* —*v.* **2.** coser.

stock /stɒk/ *n.* surtido *f.*; raza *f.*; (finance) acciones. *f.pl.* **in s.,** en existencia. **to take s. in,** tener fe en.

stock exchange bolsa *f.*

stockholder /'stɒk,houldər/ *n.* accionista *m. & f.*

stocking /'stɒkɪŋ/ *n.* media *f.*

stockyard /'stɒk,yɑrd/ *n.* corral de ganado *m.*

stodgy /'stɒdʒi/ *a.* pesado.

stoical /'stouɪkəl/ *a.* estoico.

stole /stoul/ *n.* estola *f.*

stolid /'stɒlɪd/ *a.* impasible.

stomach /'stʌmək/ *n.* estómago *m.*

stomachache /'stʌmək,eik/ *n.* dolor de estómago *m.*

stone /stoun/ *n.* piedra *f.*

stool /stul/ *n.* banquillo *m.*

stoop /stup/ *v.* encorvarse; *Fig.* rebajarse. espaldas encorvadas *f.pl.*

stop /stɒp/ *n.* **1.** parada *f.* **to put a s. to,** poner fin a. —*v.* **2.** parar; suspender; detener; impedir. **s. doing** (etc.), dejar de hacer (etc.).

stopgap /'stɒp,gæp/ *n.* recurso provisional *m.*

stopover /'stɒp,ouvər/ *n.* parada *f.*

stopwatch /'stɒp,wɒtʃ/ *n.* cronómetro *m.*

storage /'stɔrɪdʒ/ *n.* almacenaje *m.*

store /stɔr/ *n.* **1.** tienda; provisión *f.* **department s.,** almacén *m.* —*v.* **2.** guardar; almacenar.

store window escaparate *m.*

stork /stɔrk/ *n.* cigüeña *f.*

storm /stɔrm/ *n.* tempestad, tormenta *f.*

stormy /'stɔrmi/ *a.* tempestuoso.

story /'stɔri/ *n.* cuento; relato *m.*; historia *f.* **short s.,** cuento.

stout /staut/ *a.* corpulento.

stove /stouv/ *n.* hornilla; estufa *f.*

straight /streit/ *a.* **1.** recto; derecho. —*adv.* **2.** directamente.

straighten /'streitn̩/ *v.* enderezar. **s. out,** poner en orden.

straightforward /,streit'fɔrwərd/ *a.* recto, sincero.

strain /strein/ *n.* **1.** tensión *f.* —*v.* **2.** colar.

strainer /'streinər/ *n.* colador *m.*

strait /streit/ *n.* estrecho *m.*

strand /strænd/ *n.* **1.** hilo *m.* —*v.* **2. be stranded,** encallarse.

strange /streindʒ/ *a.* extraño; raro.

stranger /'streindʒər/ *n.* extranjero -ra; forastero -ra; desconocido -da.

strangle /'stræŋgəl/ *v.* estrangular.

strap /stræp/ *n.* correa *f.*

stratagem /'strætədʒəm/ *n.* estratagema *f.*

strategic /strə'tidʒɪk/ *a.* estratégico.

strategy /'strætɪdʒi/ *n.* estrategia *f.*

stratosphere /'strætə,sfɪər/ *n.* estratosfera *f.*

straw /strɔ/ *n.* paja *f.*

strawberry /'strɔ,bɛri/ *n.* fresa *f.*

stray /strei/ *a.* **1.** vagabundo. —*v.* **2.** extraviarse.

streak /strik/ *n.* **1.** racha; raya *f.;* lado *m.* —*v.* **2.** rayar.

stream /strim/ *n.* corriente *f.;* arroyo *m.*

street /strit/ *n.* calle *f.*

streetcar /'strit,kɑr/ *n.* tranvía *m.*

street lamp /'strit,læmp/ *n.* farol *m.*

strength /strɛŋkθ, strɛnθ/ *n.* fuerza *m.*

strengthen /'strɛŋkθən, 'strɛn-/ *v.* reforzar.

strenuous /'strɛnyuəs/ *a.* estrenuo.

streptococcus /ˌstrɛptə'kɒkəs/ *n.* estreptococo *m.*

stress /strɛs/ *n.* **1.** tensión *f.;* énfasis *m.* —*v.* **2.** recalcar; acentuar.

stretch /strɛtʃ/ *n.* **1.** trecho *m.* **at one s.,** de un tirón. —*v.* **2.** tender; extender; estirarse.

stretcher /'strɛtʃər/ *n.* camilla *f.*

strew /stru/ *v.* esparcir.

stricken /'strɪkən/ *a.* agobiado.

strict /strɪkt/ *a.* estricto; severo.

stride /straid/ *n.* **1.** tranco *m.;* (fig., pl.) progresos. —*v.* **2.** andar a trancos.

strife /straif/ *n.* contienda *f.*

strike /straik/ *n.* **1.** huelga *f.* —*v.* **2.** pegar; chocar con; (clock) dar.

striker /'straikər/ *n.* huelguista *m.* & *f.*

string /strɪŋ/ *n.* cuerda *f.;* cordel *m.*

string bean *n.* habichuela *f.*

stringent /'strɪndʒənt/ *a.* estricto.

strip /strɪp/ *n.* **1.** tira *f.* —*v.* **2.** despojar; desnudarse.

stripe /straip/ *n.* raya *f.;* Mil. galón *m.*

strive /straiv/ *v.* esforzarse.

stroke /strouk/ *n.* golpe *m.;* (swimming) brazada *f.;* Med. ataque *m.* **s. of luck,** suerte *f.*

stroll /stroul/ *n.* **1.** paseo *m.* —*v.* **2.** pasearse.

stroller /'stroulər/ *n.* vagabundo *m.;* cochecito (de niño).

strong /strɔŋ/ *a.* fuerte.

stronghold /'strɔŋ,hould/ *n.* fortificación *f.*

structure /'strʌktʃər/ *n.* estructura *f.*

struggle /'strʌgəl/ *n.* **1.** lucha *f.* —*v.* **2.** luchar.

strut /strʌt/ *n.* **1.** pavonada *f.* —*v.* **2.** pavonear.

stub /stʌb/ *n.* **1.** cabo; (ticket) talón *m.* —*v.* **2. s. on one's toes,** tropezar con.

stubborn /'stʌbərn/ *a.* testarudo.

stucco /'stʌkou/ *n.* **1.** estuco *m.* —*v.* **2.** estucar.

student /'studnt/ *n.* alumno -na, estudiante -ta.

studio /'studi,ou/ *n.* estudio *m.*

studious /'studiəs/ *a.* aplicado; estudioso.

study /'stʌdi/ *n.* **1.** estudio *m.* —*v.* **2.** estudiar.

stuff /stʌf/ *n.* **1.** cosas *f.pl.* —*v.* **2.** llenar; rellenar.

stuffing /'stʌfɪŋ/ *n.* relleno *m.*

stumble /'stʌmbəl/ *v.* tropezar.

stump /stʌmp/ *n.* cabo; tocón; muñón *m.*

stun /stʌn/ *v.* aturdir.

stunt /stʌnt/ *n.* **1.** maniobra sensacional *f.* —*v.* **2.** impedir crecimiento.

stupendous /stu'pɛndəs/ *a.* estupendo.

stupid /'stupɪd/ *a.* estúpido.

stupidity /stu'pɪditi/ *n.* estupidez *f.*

stupor /'stupər/ *n.* estupor *m.*

sturdy /'stɜrdi/ *a.* robusto.

stutter /'stʌtər/ *v.* **1.** tartamudear. —*n.* **2.** tartamudeo *m.*

sty /stai/ *n.* pocilga *f.;* Med. orzuelo.

style /stail/ *n.* estilo *m.;* moda *f.*

stylish /'stailɪʃ/ *a.* elegante; a la moda.

suave /swɑv/ *a.* afable, suave.

subconscious /sʌb'kɒnʃəs/ *a.* subconsciente.

subdue /səb'du/ *v.* dominar.

subject /*n.* 'sʌbdʒɪkt; *v.* səb'dʒɛkt/ *n.* **1.** tema *m.;* (of study) materia *f.;* Pol. súbdito -ta; Gram. sujeto *m.* —*v.* **2.** someter.

subjugate /'sʌbdʒə,geit/ *v.* sojuzgar, subyugar.

subjunctive /səb'dʒʌŋktɪv/ *a.* & *n.* subjuntivo *m.*

sublimate /'sʌblə,meit/ *v.* sublimar.

sublime /sə'blaim/ *a.* sublime.

submarine /ˌsʌbməˈrin/ a. & n. submarino m.

submerge /səbˈmɜrdʒ/ v. sumergir.

submission /səbˈmɪʃən/ n. sumisión f.

submit /səbˈmɪt/ v. someter.

subnormal /sʌbˈnɔrməl/ a. subnormal.

subordinate /a, n səˈbɔrdṇɪt; v -dṇˌeit/ a. & n. **1.** subordinado -da. —v. **2.** subordinar.

subscribe /səbˈskraib/ v. aprobar; abonarse.

subscriber /səbˈskraibər/ n. abonado -da m. & f.

subscription /səbˈskrɪpʃən/ n. abono m.

subsequent /ˈsʌbsɪkwənt/ a. subsiguiente.

subservient /səbˈsɜrviənt/ a. servicial.

subside /səbˈsaid/ v. apaciguarse, menguar.

subsidy /ˈsʌbsɪdi/ n. subvención f.

subsoil /ˈsʌbˌsɔil/ n. subsuelo m.

substance /ˈsʌbstəns/ n. substancia f.

substantial /səbˈstænʃəl/ a. substancial; considerable.

substitute /ˈsʌbstɪˌtut/ a. **1.** substitutivo. —n. **2.** substituto -ta. —v. **3.** substituir.

substitution /ˌsʌbstɪˈtuʃən/ n. substitución f.

subterfuge /ˈsʌbtərˌfyudʒ/ n. subterfugio m.

subtitle /ˈsʌbˌtaitḷ/ n. subtítulo m.

subtle /ˈsʌtḷ/ a. sutil.

subtract /səbˈtrækt/ v. substraer.

suburb /ˈsʌbɜrb/ n. suburbio m.; (pl.) afueras f.pl.

subversive /səbˈvɜrsɪv/ a. subversivo.

subway /ˈsʌbˌwei/ n. metro m.

succeed /səkˈsid/ v. lograr, tener éxito; (in office) suceder a.

success /səkˈsɛs/ n. éxito m.

successful /səkˈsɛsfəl/ a. próspero; afortunado.

succession /səkˈsɛʃən/ n. sucesión f.

successive /səkˈsɛsɪv/ a. sucesivo.

successor /səkˈsɛsər/ n. sucesor -ra; heredero -ra.

succor /ˈsʌkər/ n. **1.** socorro m. —v. **2.** socorrer.

succumb /səˈkʌm/ v. sucumbir.

such /sʌtʃ/ a. tal.

suck /sʌk/ v. chupar.

suction /ˈsʌkʃən/ n. succión f.

sudden /ˈsʌdṇ/ a. repentino, súbito. **all of a s.,** de repente.

suds /sʌdz/ n. jabonaduras f.pl.

sue /su/ v. demandar.

suffer /ˈsʌfər/ v. sufrir; padecer.

suffice /səˈfais/ v. bastar.

sufficient /səˈfɪʃənt/ a. suficiente.

suffocate /ˈsʌfəˌkeit/ v. sofocar.

sugar /ˈʃugər/ n. azúcar m.

sugar bowl azucarero m.

suggest /səgˈdʒɛst/ v. sugerir.

suggestion /səgˈdʒɛstʃən/ n. sugerencia f.

suicide /ˈsuəˌsaid/ n. suicidio m.; (person) suicida m. & f. **to commit s.,** suicidarse.

suit /sut/ n. **1.** traje; (cards) palo m. (law) pleito m. —v. **2.** convenir a.

suitable /ˈsutəbəl/ a. apropiado; que conviene.

suitcase /ˈsutˌkeis/ n. maleta f.

suite /swit/ n. serie f., séquito m.

suitor /ˈsutər/ n. pretendiente m.

sullen /ˈsʌlən/ a. hosco.

sum /sʌm/ n. **1.** suma f. —v. **2.** s. **up,** resumir.

summarize /ˈsʌməˌraiz/ v. resumir.

summary /ˈsʌməri/ n. resumen m.

summer /ˈsʌmər/ n. verano m.

summon /ˈsʌmən/ v. llamar; (law) citar.

summons /ˈsʌmənz/ n. citación f.

sumptuous /ˈsʌmptʃuəs/ a. suntuoso.

sun /sʌn/ n. **1.** sol m. —v. **2.** tomar el sol.

sunbathe /ˈsʌnˌbeið/ v. tomar el sol.

sunburn /ˈsʌnˌbɜrn/ n. quemadura de sol.

sunburned /ˈsʌnˌbɜrnd/ a. quemado por el sol.

Sunday /ˈsʌndei/ n. domingo m.

sunken /ˈsʌŋkən/ a. hundido.

sunny /ˈsʌni/ a. asoleado. **s. day,** día de sol. **to be s.,** (weather) hacer sol.

sunshine /ˈsʌnˌʃain/ n. luz del sol.

suntan /ˈsʌnˌtæn/ n. bronceado m. **s. lotion,** loción bronceadora f., bronceador m.

superb /suˈpɜrb/ a. soberbio.

superficial /ˌsupərˈfɪʃəl/ a. superficial.

superfluous /suˈpɜrfluəs/ a. superfluo.

superhuman /ˌsupərˈhyumən/ a. sobrehumano.

superintendent /ˌsupərɪnˈtɛndənt/ n. superintendente m. & f.; (of building) conserje m.; (of school) director -ra general.

superior /səˈpɪəriər/ a. & n. superior m.

superiority /səˌpɪəriˈɔriti/ n. superioridad f.

superlative /səˈpɜrlətɪv/ a. superlativo.

supernatural /ˌsupərˈnætʃərəl/ a. sobrenatural.

supersede /ˌsupərˈsid/ v. reemplazar.

superstar /ˈsupərˌstɑr/ n. superestrella m. & f.

superstition /ˌsupərˈstɪʃən/ n. superstición f.

superstitious /ˌsupərˈstɪʃəs/ a. supersticioso.

supervise /ˈsupərˌvaiz/ v. supervisar.

supper /ˈsʌpər/ n. cena f.

supplement /ˈsʌpləmənt/ n. **1.** suplemento m. —v. **2.** suplementar.

supply /səˈplai/ n. **1.** provisión f.; Com. surtido m.; Econ. existencia f. —v. **2.** suplir; proporcionar.

support /səˈpɔrt/ n. **1.** sustento; apoyo m. —v. **2.** mantener; apoyar.

suppose /səˈpouz/ v. suponer. **be supposed to,** deber.

suppository /səˈpɒzɪˌtɔri/ n. supositorio m.

suppress /səˈprɛs/ v. suprimir.

suppression /səˈprɛʃən/ n. supresión f.

supreme /səˈprim/ a. supremo.

sure /ʃʊr, ʃɜr/ a. seguro, cierto. **for s.,** con seguridad. **to make s.,** asegurarse.

surety /ˈʃʊriti, ˈʃɜr-/ n. garantía f.

surf /sɜrf/ n. **1.** oleaje m. —v. **2.** (Internet) navegar; (sport) surfear.

surface /ˈsɜrfɪs/ n. superficie f.

surfboard /ˈsɜrfˌbɔrd/ n. tabla de surf f.

surfer /ˈsɜrfər/ n. (Internet) usuario -ria, navegante m. & f.; (sport) surfero -ra.

surge /sɜrdʒ/ v. surgir.

surgeon /ˈsɜrdʒən/ n. cirujano -na.

surgery /ˈsɜrdʒəri/ n. cirugía f.

surmise /sərˈmaiz/ v. suponer.

surmount /sərˈmaunt/ v. vencer.

surname /ˈsɜrˌneim/ n. apellido m.

surpass /sərˈpæs/ v. superar.

surplus /ˈsɜrplʌs/ a. & n. sobrante m.

surprise /sərˈpraiz, sə-/ n. **1.** sorpresa —v. **2.** sorprender. **I am surprised...,** me extraña...

surrender /səˈrɛndər/ n. **1.** rendición f. —v. **2.** rendir.

surround /səˈraund/ v. rodear, circundar.

surveillance /sərˈveiləns/ n. vigilancia f.

survey /n. ˈsɜrvei; v. sərˈvei/ n. **1.** examen; estudio m. —v. **2.** examinar; (land) medir.

survival /sərˈvaivəl/ n. supervivencia f.

survive /sərˈvaiv/ v. sobrevivir.

susceptible /səˈsɛptəbəl/ a. susceptible.

suspect /v. səˈspɛkt; n. ˈsʌspɛkt/ v. **1.** sospechar. —n. **2.** sospechoso -sa.

suspend /səˈspɛnd/ v. suspender.

suspense /səˈspɛns/ n. incertidumbre f. **in s.,** en suspenso.

suspension /səˈspɛnʃən/ n. suspensión f.

suspension bridge n. puente colgante m.

suspicion /səˈspɪʃən/ n. sospecha f.

suspicious /səˈspɪʃəs/ a. sospechoso.

sustain /səˈstein/ v. sustentar; mantener.

swallow /ˈswɒlou/ n. **1.** trago m.; (bird) golondrina f. —v. **2.** tragar.

swamp /swɒmp/ n. **1.** pantano m. —v. **2.** Fig. abrumar.

swan /swɒn/ n. cisne m.

swap /swɒp/ n. **1.** trueque m. —v. **2.** cambalachear.

swarm /swɔrm/ n. enjambre m.

swarthy /ˈswɔrði/ a. moreno.

sway /swei/ n. **1.** predominio m. —v. **2.** bambolearse; Fig. influir en.

swear /swɛər/ v. jurar. **s. off,** renunciar a.

sweat /swɛt/ n. **1.** sudor m. —v. **2.** sudar.

sweater /ˈswɛtər/ n. suéter m.

sweatshirt /ˈswɛtˌʃɜrt/ n. sudadera f.

Swede /swid/ n. sueco -ca.

Sweden /ˈswidn̩/ n. Suecia f.

Swedish /'swidɪʃ/ a. sueco.
sweep /swip/ v. barrer.
sweet /swit/ a. **1.** dulce; amable, simpático. —n. **2.** (pl.) dulces m.pl.
sweetheart /'swit,hɑrt/ n. novio -via.
sweetness /'switnɪs/ n. dulzura f.
sweet-toothed /'swit ,tuθt/ a. goloso.
swell /swɛl/ a. **1.** Colloq. estupendo, excelente. —n. **2.** (of the sea) oleada f. —v. **3.** hincharse; aumentar.
swelter /'swɛltər/ v. sofocarse de calor.
swift /swɪft/ a. rápido, veloz.
swim /swɪm/ n. **1.** nadada f. —v. **2.** nadar.
swimming /'swɪmɪŋ/ n. natación f.
swimming pool alberca, piscina f.
swindle /'swɪndḷ/ n. **1.** estafa f. —v. **2.** estafar.
swine /swain/ n. puercos m.pl.
swing /swɪŋ/ n. **1.** columpio m. **in full s.,** en plena actividad. —v. **2.** mecer; balancear.
swirl /swɜrl/ n. **1.** remolino m. —v. **2.** arremolinar.
Swiss /swɪs/ a. & n. suizo -za.
switch /swɪtʃ/ n. **1.** varilla f.; Elec. llave f., conmutador m.; (railway) cambiavía m. —v. **2.** cambiar; trocar.
switchboard /'swɪtʃ,bɔrd/ n. cuadro conmutador m., centralita f.
Switzerland /'swɪtsərlənd/ n. Suiza f.
sword /sɔrd/ n. espada f.
syllable /'sɪləbəl/ n. sílaba f.
symbol /'sɪmbəl/ n. símbolo m.
sympathetic /ˌsɪmpə'θɛtɪk/ a. compasivo. **to be s.,** tener simpatía.
sympathy /'sɪmpəθi/ n. lástima; condolencia f.
symphony /'sɪmfəni/ n. sinfonía f.
symptom /'sɪmptəm/ n. síntoma m.
synagogue /'sɪnə,gɒg/ n. sinagoga f.
synchronize /'sɪŋkrə,naiz/ v. sincronizar.
syndicate /'sɪndɪkɪt/ n. sindicato m.
syndrome /'sɪndroum, -drəm/ n. síndrome m.
synonym /'sɪnənɪm/ n. sinónimo m.
synthetic /sɪn'θɛtɪk/ a. sintético.
syringe /sə'rɪndʒ/ n. jeringa f.
syrup /'sɪrəp, 'sɜr-/ n. almíbar; Med. jarabe m.
system /'sɪstəm/ n. sistema m.
systematic /ˌsɪstə'mætɪk/ a. sistemático.

T

tabernacle /'tæbər,nækəl/ n. tabernáculo m.
table /'teibəl/ n. mesa; (list) tabla f.
tablecloth /'teibəl,klɔθ/ n. mantel m.
table of contents /'kɒntɛnts/ índice de materias m.
tablespoon /'teibəl,spun/ n. cuchara f.
tablespoonful /'teibəlspun,fʊl/ n. cucharada f.
tablet /'tæblɪt/ n. tableta; Med. pastilla f.
tack /tæk/ n. tachuela f.
tact /tækt/ n. tacto m.
tag /tæg/ n. etiqueta f., rótulo m.
tail /teil/ n. cola f., rabo m.
tailor /'teilər/ n. sastre m.
take /teik/ v. tomar; llevar. **t. a bath,** bañarse. **t. a shower,** ducharse. **t. away,** quitar. **t. off,** quitarse. **t. out,** sacar. **t. long,** tardar mucho.
tale /teil/ n. cuento m.
talent /'tælənt/ n. talento m.
talk /tɔk/ n. **1.** plática, habla f.; discurso m. —v. **2.** hablar.
talkative /'tɔkətɪv/ a. locuaz.
tall /tɔl/ a. alto.
tame /teim/ a. **1.** manso, domesticado. —v. **2.** domesticar.
tamper /'tæmpər/ v. **t. with,** entremeterse en.
tampon /'tæmpɒn/ n. tampón m.
tan /tæn/ a. **1.** color de arena. —v. **2.** curtir; tostar. n. bronceado.
tangerine /ˌtændʒə'rin/ n. clementina f.
tangible /'tændʒəbəl/ a. tangible.
tangle /'tæŋgəl/ n. **1.** enredo m. —v. **2.** enredar.
tank /tæŋk/ n. tanque m.
tap /tæp/ n. **1.** golpe ligero. —v. **2.** golpear ligeramente; decantar.
tape /teip/ n. cinta f.

tape recorder /rɪˈkɔrdər/ magnetófono *m.*, grabadora *f.*

tapestry /ˈtæpəstri/ *n.* tapiz *m.*; tapicería *f.*

tar /tɑr/ *n.* **1.** brea *f.* —*v.* **2.** embrear.

target /ˈtɑrgɪt/ *n.* blanco *m.*

tarnish /ˈtɑrnɪʃ/ *n.* **1.** deslustre *m.* —*v.* **2.** deslustrar.

tarpaulin /tɑrˈpɔlɪn, ˈtɑrpəlɪn/ *n.* lona *f.*

task /tæsk/ *n.* tarea *f.*

taste /teist/ *n.* **1.** gusto; sabor *m.* —*v.* **2.** gustar; probar. **t. of,** saber a.

tasty /ˈteisti/ *a.* sabroso.

tattoo /tæˈtu/ *v.* tatuar.

taut /tɔt/ *a.* tieso.

tavern /ˈtævərn/ *n.* taberna *f.*

tax /tæks/ *n.* **1.** impuesto *m.* —*v.* **2.** imponer impuestos.

tax collector *n.* recaudador -ra *m.* & *f.*

taxi /ˈtæksi/ *n.* taxi, taxímetro *m.* **t. driver,** taxista *m.* & *f.*

taxpayer /ˈtæks,peiər/ *n.* contribuyente *m.* & *f.*

tax reform reforma tributaria *f.*

tax return declaración de la renta *f.*

tea /ti/ *n.* té *m.*

teach /titʃ/ *v.* enseñar.

teacher /ˈtitʃər/ *n.* maestro -tra, profesor -ra.

team /tim/ *n.* equipo *m.*; pareja *f.*

tear /tɪər/ *n.* **1.** rasgón *m.*; lágrima *f.* —*v.* **2.** rasgar, lacerar. **t. apart,** separar.

tease /tiz/ *v.* atormentar; embromar.

teaspoon /ˈti,spun/ *n.* cucharita *f.*

technical /ˈtɛknɪkəl/ *a.* técnico.

technician /tɛkˈnɪʃən/ *n.* técnico -ca *m.* & *f.*

technique /tɛkˈnik/ *n.* técnica *f.*

technology /tɛkˈnɒlədʒi/ *n.* tecnología *f.*

teddy bear /ˈtɛdi/ oso de felpa *m.*

tedious /ˈtidiəs/ *a.* tedioso.

telegram /ˈtɛlɪ,græm/ *n.* telegrama *m.*

telegraph /ˈtɛlɪ,græf/ *n.* **1.** telégrafo *m.* —*v.* **2.** telegrafiar.

telephone /ˈtɛlə,foun/ *n.* **1.** teléfono *m.* **t. book,** directorio telefónico. —*v.* **2.** telefonear; llamar por teléfono.

telescope /ˈtɛlə,skoup/ *n.* **1.** telescopio *m.* —*v.* **2.** enchufar.

television /ˈtɛlə,vɪʒən/ *n.* televisión *f.*

tell /tɛl/ *v.* decir; contar; distinguir.

temper /ˈtɛmpər/ *n.* **1.** temperamento, genio *m.* —*v.* **2.** templar.

temperament /ˈtɛmpərəmənt, -prəmənt/ *n.* temperamento.

temperamental /ˌtɛmpərəˈmɛntḷ, -prəˈmɛn-/ *a.* sensitivo, emocional.

temperance /ˈtɛmpərəns/ *n.* moderación; sobriedad *f.*

temperate /ˈtɛmpərɪt/ *a.* templado.

temperature /ˈtɛmpərətʃər/ *n.* temperatura *f.*

tempest /ˈtɛmpɪst/ *n.* tempestad *f.*

tempestuous /tɛmˈpɛstʃuəs/ *a.* tempestuoso.

temple /ˈtɛmpəl/ *n.* templo *m.*

temporary /ˈtɛmpə,rɛri/ *a.* temporal, temporario.

tempt /tɛmpt/ *v.* tentar.

temptation /tɛmpˈteiʃən/ *n.* tentación *f.*

ten /tɛn/ *a.* & *pron.* diez.

tenant /ˈtɛnənt/ *n.* inquilino -na.

tend /tɛnd/ *v.* tender. **t. to,** atender.

tendency /ˈtɛndənsi/ *n.* tendencia *f.*

tender /ˈtɛndər/ *a.* **1.** tierno. —*v.* **2.** ofrecer.

tenderness /ˈtɛndərnɪs/ *n.* ternura *f.*

tennis /ˈtɛnɪs/ *n.* tenis *m.*

tennis court cancha de tenis, pista de tenis *f.*

tenor /ˈtɛnər/ *n.* tenor *m.*

tense /tɛns/ *a.* **1.** tenso. —*n.* **2.** *Gram.* tiempo *m.*

tent /tɛnt/ *n.* tienda, carpa *f.*

tenth /tɛnθ/ *a.* décimo.

term /tɜrm/ *n.* **1.** término; plazo *m.* —*v.* **2.** llamar.

terminal /ˈtɜrmənḷ/ *n.* terminal *f.*

terrace /ˈtɛrəs/ *n.* terraza *f.*

terrible /ˈtɛrəbəl/ *a.* terrible, espantoso; pésimo.

territory /ˈtɛrɪ,tɔri/ *n.* territorio *m.*

terror /ˈtɛrər/ *n.* terror, espanto, pavor *m.*

test /tɛst/ *n.* **1.** prueba *f.*; examen *m.* —*v.* **2.** probar; examinar.

testament /ˈtɛstəmənt/ *n.* testamento *m.*

testify /ˈtɛstə,fai/ *v.* atestiguar, testificar.

testimony /ˈtɛstə,mouni/ *n.* testimonio *m.*

test tube tubo de ensayo *m.*

text /tɛkst/ *n.* texto; tema *m.*

textbook /'tɛkst,bʊk/ *n.* libro de texto.

textile /'tɛkstail/ *a.* **1.** textil. —*n.* **2.** tejido *m.*

texture /'tɛkstʃər/ *n.* textura *f.*; tejido *m.*

than /ðæn, ðɛn; *unstressed* ðən, ən/ *conj.* que; de.

thank /θæŋk/ *v.* agradecer, dar gracias; **thanks, th. you,** gracias.

thankful /'θæŋkfəl/ *a.* agradecido; grato.

that /ðæt; *unstressed* ðət/ *a.* **1.** ese, aquel. —*dem. pron.* **2.** ése, aquél; eso, aquello. —*rel. pron.* & *conj.* **3.** que.

the /*stressed* ði; *unstressed before a consonant* ðə, *unstressed before a vowel* ði/ *art.* el, la, los, las; lo.

theater /'θiətər/ *n.* teatro *m.*

theft /θɛft/ *n.* robo *m.*

their /ðɛər; *unstressed* ðər/ *a.* su.

theirs /ðɛərz/ *pron.* suyo, de ellos.

them /ðɛm; *unstressed* ðəm, əm/ *pron.* ellos, ellas; los, las; les.

theme /θim/ *n.* tema; *Mus.* motivo *m.*

themselves /ðəm'sɛlvz, ˌðɛm-/ *pron.* sí, sí mismos -as. **they th.,** ellos mismos, ellas mismas. **with th.,** consigo.

then /ðɛn/ *adv.* entonces, después; pues.

thence /ðɛns/ *adv.* de allí.

theology /θi'ɒlədʒi/ *n.* teología *f.*

theory /'θiəri/ *n.* teoría *f.*

there /ðɛər; *unstressed* ðər/ *adv.* allí, allá, ahí. **there is, there are,** hay.

therefore /'ðɛər,fɔr/ *adv.* por lo tanto, por consiguiente.

thermometer /θər'mɒmɪtər/ *n.* termómetro *m.*

thermostat /'θɜrmə,stæt/ *n.* termostato *m.*

they /ðei/ *pron.* ellos, ellas.

thick /θɪk/ *a.* espeso, grueso, denso; torpe.

thicken /'θɪkən/ *v.* espesar, condensar.

thief /θif/ *n.* ladrón -na.

thigh /θai/ *n.* muslo *m.*

thimble /'θɪmbəl/ *n.* dedal *m.*

thin /θɪn/ *a.* **1.** delgado; raro; claro; escaso. —*v.* **2.** enrarecer; adelgazar.

thing /θɪŋ/ *n.* cosa *f.*

thingamabob /'θɪŋəmə,bɒb/ *n. Colloq.* chisme *m.*

think /θɪŋk/ *v.* pensar; creer.

thinker /'θɪŋkər/ *n.* pensador -ra.

third /θɜrd/ *a.* tercero.

Third World Tercer Mundo *m.*

thirst /θɜrst/ *n.* sed *f.*

thirsty /'θɜrsti/ *a.* sediento. **to be th.,** tener sed.

thirteen /'θɜr'tin/ *a.* & *pron.* trece.

thirty /'θɜrti/ *a.* & *pron.* treinta.

this /ðɪs/ *a.* **1.** este. —*pron.* **2.** éste; esto.

thoracic cage /θɔ'ræsɪk/ *n.* caja torácica *f.*

thorn /θɔrn/ *n.* espina *f.*

thorough /'θɜrou/ *a.* completo; cuidadoso.

though /ðou/ *adv.* **1.** sin embargo. —*conj.* **2.** aunque. **as th.,** como si.

thought /θɔt/ *n.* pensamiento *m.*

thoughtful /'θɔtfəl/ *a.* pensativo; considerado.

thousand /'θauzənd/ *a.* & *pron.* mil.

thread /θrɛd/ *n.* hilo *m.*; (of screw) rosca *f.*

threat /θrɛt/ *n.* amenaza *f.*

threaten /'θrɛtn̩/ *v.* amenazar.

three /θri/ *a.* & *pron.* tres.

thrift /θrɪft/ *n.* economía, frugalidad *f.*

thrill /θrɪl/ *n.* **1.** emoción *f.* —*v.* **2.** emocionar.

thrive /θraiv/ *v.* prosperar.

throat /θrout/ *n.* garganta *f.*

throne /θroun/ *n.* trono *m.*

through /θru/ *prep.* **1.** por; a través de; por medio de. —*a.* **2.** continuo. **th. train,** tren directo. **to be th.,** haber terminado.

throughout /θru'aut/ *prep.* **1.** por todo, durante todo. —*adv.* **2.** en todas partes; completamente.

throw /θrou/ *n.* **1.** tiro *m.* —*v.* **2.** tirar, lanzar. **th. away,** arrojar. **th. out,** echar.

thrust /θrʌst/ *n.* **1.** lanzada *f.* —*v.* **2.** empujar.

thumb /θʌm/ *n.* dedo pulgar, pulgar *m.*

thumbtack /'θʌm,tæk/ *n.* chincheta *f.*

thunder /'θʌndər/ *n.* **1.** trueno *m.* —*v.* **2.** tronar.

Thursday /'θɜrzdei/ *n.* jueves *m.*

thus /ðʌs/ *adv.* así, de este modo.

thwart /θwɔrt/ *v.* frustrar.

ticket /'tɪkɪt/ *n.* billete, boleto *m.*
t. window, taquilla *f.* **round trip
t.,** billete de ida y vuelta.
tickle /'tɪkəl/ *n.* **1.** cosquilla *f.*
—*v.* **2.** hacer cosquillas a.
ticklish /'tɪklɪʃ/ *a.* cosquilloso.
tide /taid/ *n.* marea *f.*
tidy /'taidi/ *a.* **1.** limpio, ordenado. —*v.* **2.** poner en orden.
tie /tai/ *n.* **1.** corbata *f.;* lazo;
(game) empate *m.* —*v.* **2.** atar;
anudar.
tier /'tɪər/ *n.* hilera *f.*
tiger /'taigər/ *n.* tigre *m.*
tight /tait/ *a.* apretado; tacaño.
tighten /'taitn/ *v.* estrechar, apretar.
tile /tail/ *n.* teja *f.;* azulejo *m.*
till /tɪl/ *prep.* **1.** hasta. —*conj.* **2.**
hasta que. —*n.* **3.** cajón *m.* —*v.*
4. cultivar, labrar.
tilt /tɪlt/ *n.* **1.** inclinación; justa *f.*
—*v.* **2.** inclinar; justar.
timber /'tɪmbər/ *n.* madera *f.;*
(beam) madero *m.*
time /taim/ *n.* tiempo *m.;* vez *f.;*
(of day) hora *f,; v.* cronometrar.
timetable /'taim,teibəl/ *n.* horario, itinerario *m.*
time zone huso horario *m.*
timid /'tɪmɪd/ *a.* tímido.
timidity /tɪ'mɪdɪti/ *n.* timidez *f.*
tin /tɪn/ *n.* estaño *m.;* hojalata *f.*
t. can, lata *f.*
tin foil papel de estaño *m.*
tint /tɪnt/ *n.* **1.** tinte *m.* —*v.* **2.**
teñir.
tiny /'taini/ *a.* chiquito, pequeñito.
tip /tɪp/ *n.* **1.** punta; propina *f.*
—*v.* **2.** inclinar; dar propina a.
tire /taiər/ *n.* **1.** llanta, goma *f.,*
neumático *m.* —*v.* **2.** cansar.
tired /taiərd/ *a.* cansado.
tissue /'tɪʃu/ *n.* tejido *m.* **t. paper,** papel de seda.
title /'taitl/ *n.* **1.** título *m.* —*v.* **2.**
titular.
to /tu; *unstressed* tʊ, tə/ *prep.* a;
para.
toast /toust/ *n.* **1.** tostada *f.;*
(drink) brindis *m.* —*v.* **2.** tostar;
brindar.
toaster /'toustər/ *n.* tostador *m.*
tobacco /tə'bækou/ *n.* tabaco *m.*
t. shop, tabaquería *f.*
toboggan /tə'bɒgən/ *n.* tobogán
m.
today /tə'dei/ *adv.* hoy.
toe /tou/ *n.* dedo del pie.

together /tə'gɛðər/ *a.* **1.** juntos.
—*adv.* **2.** juntamente.
toil /tɔil/ *n.* **1.** trabajo *m.* —*v.* **2.**
afanarse.
toilet /'tɔilɪt/ *n.* tocado; excusado,
retrete *m.* **t. paper,** papel higiénico.
token /'toukən/ *n.* señal *f.*
tolerance /'tɒlərəns/ *n.* tolerancia
f.
tolerate /'tɒlə,reit/ *v.* tolerar.
toll-free number /'toul 'fri/ teléfono gratuito *m.*
tomato /tə'meitou/ *n.* tomate *m.*
tomb /tum/ *n.* tumba *f.*
tomorrow /tə'mɔrou/ *adv.* mañana. **day after t.,** pasado mañana.
ton /tʌn/ *n.* tonelada *f.*
tone /toun/ *n.* tono *m.*
tongue /tʌŋ/ *n.* lengua *f.*
tonic /'tɒnɪk/ *n.* tónico *m.*
tonight /tə'nait/ *adv.* esta noche.
tonsil /'tɒnsəl/ *n.* amígdala *f.*
too /tu/ *adv.* también. **t. much,**
demasiado. **t. many,** demasiados.
tool /tul/ *n.* herramienta *f.*
tooth /tuθ/ *n.* diente *m.;* (back)
muela *f.*
toothache /'tuθ,eik/ *n.* dolor de
muela.
toothbrush /'tuθ,brʌʃ/ *n.* cepillo
de dientes.
toothpaste /'tuθ,peist/ *n.* crema
dentífrica, pasta dentífrica.
top /tɒp/ *n.* **1.** parte de arriba.
—*v.* **2.** cubrir; sobrepasar.
topic /'tɒpɪk/ *n.* S.A. tópico *m.*
topical /'tɒpɪkəl/ *a.* tópico.
torch /tɔrtʃ/ *n.* antorcha *f.*
torment /*n.* 'tɔrmɛnt; *v.* tɔr'mɛnt/
n. **1.** tormento *m.* —*v.* **2.** atormentar.
torrent /'tɔrənt/ *n.* torrente *m.*
torture /'tɔrtʃər/ *n.* **1.** tortura *f.*
—*v.* **2.** torturar.
toss /tɔs/ *v.* tirar; agitar.
total /'toutl/ *a.* **1.** total, entero.
—*n.* **2.** total *m.*
touch /tʌtʃ/ *n.* **1.** tacto *m.* **in t.,**
en comunicación. —*v.* **2.** tocar;
conmover.
tough /tʌf/ *a.* tosco; tieso; fuerte.
tour /tʊr/ *n.* **1.** viaje *m.* —*v.* **2.**
viajar.
tourist /'tʊrɪst/ *n.* turista *m.* & *f.*
a. turístico.
tournament /'tʊrnəmənt/ *n.*
torneo *m.*

tow /tou/ n. 1. remolque m. —v. 2. remolcar.

toward /tɔrd, tə'wɔrd/ prep. hacia.

towel /'tauəl/ n. toalla f.

tower /'tauər/ n. torre f.

town /taun/ n. pueblo m.

town meeting cabildo abierto m.

tow truck grúa f.

toy /tɔi/ n. 1. juguete m. —v. 2. jugar.

trace /treis/ n. 1. vestigio; rastro m. —v. 2. trazar; rastrear; investigar.

track /træk/ n. 1. huella, pista f. **race t.**, hipódromo m. —v. 2. rastrear.

tract /trækt/ n. trecho; tracto m.

tractor /'træktər/ n. tractor m.

trade /treid/ n. 1. comercio, negocio; oficio; canje m. —v. 2. comerciar, negociar; cambiar.

trader /'treidər/ n. comerciante m.

tradition /trə'dɪʃən/ n. tradición f.

traditional /trə'dɪʃənl/ a. tradicional.

traffic /'træfɪk/ n. 1. tráfico m. —v. 2. traficar.

traffic jam atasco, embotellamiento m.

traffic light semáforo m.

tragedy /'trædʒɪdi/ n. tragedia f.

tragic /'trædʒɪk/ a. trágico.

trail /treil/ n. 1. sendero; rastro m. —v. 2. rastrear; arrastrar.

train /trein/ n. 1. tren m. —v. 2. enseñar; disciplinar; (sport) entrenarse.

traitor /'treitər/ n. traidor -ora.

tramp /træmp/ n. 1. caminata f.; vagabundo m. —v. 2. patear.

tranquil /'træŋkwɪl/ a. tranquilo.

tranquilizer /'træŋkwə,laizər/ n. tranquilizante m.

tranquillity /træŋ'kwɪlɪti/ n. tranquilidad f.

transaction /træn'sækʃən/ n. transacción f.

transfer /n. 'trænsfər, v. træns'fɜr/ n. 1. traslado m.; boleto de transbordo. —v. 2. trasladar, transferir.

transform /træns'fɔrm/ v. transformar.

transfusion /træns'fyuʒən/ n. transfusión f.

transistor /træn'zɪstər/ n. transistor m.

transition /træn'zɪʃən/ n. transición f.

translate /træns'leit/ v. traducir.

translation /træns'leiʃən/ n. traducción f.

transmit /træns'mɪt/ v. transmitir.

transparent /træns'pɛərənt/ a. transparente.

transport /n. 'trænspɔrt, v. træns'pɔrt/ n. 1. transporte m. —v. 2. transportar.

transportation /,trænspər'teiʃən/ n. transporte m.

transsexual /træns'sɛkʃuəl/ a. & n. transexual m. & f.

transvestite /træns'vɛstait/ n. travestí m. & f.

trap /træp/ n. 1. trampa f. —v. 2. atrapar.

trash /træʃ/ n. desecho m.; basura f.

trash can cubo de la basura m.

travel /'trævəl/ n. 1. tráfico m.; (pl.) viajes m.pl. —v. 2. viajar.

travel agency agencia de viajes f.

traveler /'trævələr/ n. viajero -ra.

traveler's check /'trævələrz/ cheque de viaje m.

tray /trei/ n. bandeja f.

tread /trɛd/ n. 1. pisada f.; (of a tire) cubierta f. —v. 2. pisar.

treason /'trizən/ n. traición f.

treasure /'trɛʒər/ n. tesoro m.

treasurer /'trɛʒərər/ n. tesorero -ra.

treasury /'trɛʒəri/ n. tesorería f.

treat /trit/ v. tratar; convidar.

treatment /'tritmənt/ n. trato, tratamiento m.

treaty /'triti/ n. tratado, pacto m.

tree /tri/ n. árbol m.

tremble /'trɛmbəl/ v. temblar.

tremendous /trɪ'mɛndəs/ a. tremendo.

trench /trɛntʃ/ n. foso m.; Mil. trinchera f.

trend /trɛnd/ n. 1. tendencia f. —v. 2. tender.

trespass /'trɛspəs, -pæs/ v. traspasar; violar.

triage /tri'ɑʒ/ n. clasificación de los heridos después del combate.

trial /'traiəl/ n. prueba f.; Leg. proceso, juicio m.

triangle /'trai,æŋgəl/ n. triángulo m.

tribulation /,trɪbyə'leiʃən/ n. tribulación f.

tributary /'trɪbyə,tɛri/ a. & n. tributario m.

tribute /'trɪbyut/ n. tributo m.

trick /trɪk/ n. **1.** engaño m.; maña f.; (cards) baza f. —v. **2.** engañar.
trifle /'traifəl/ n. **1.** pequeñez f. —v. **2.** juguetear.
trigger /'trɪgər/ n. gatillo m.
trim /trɪm/ a. **1.** ajustado; acicalado. —n. **2.** adorno m. —v. **3.** adornar; ajustar; cortar un poco.
trinket /'trɪŋkɪt/ n. bagatela, chuchería f.
trip /trɪp/ n. **1.** viaje m. —v. **2.** tropezar.
triple /'trɪpəl/ a. **1.** triple —v. **2.** triplicar.
tripod /'traipɒd/ n. trípode m.
trite /trait/ a. banal.
triumph /'traiəmf/ n. **1.** triunfo m. —v. **2.** triunfar.
triumphant /trai'ʌmfənt/ a. triunfante.
trivial /'trɪviəl/ a. trivial.
trolley /'trɒli/ n. tranvía m.
trombone /trɒm'boun/ n. trombón m.
troop /trup/ n. tropa f.
trophy /'troufi/ n. trofeo m.
tropical /'trɒpɪkəl/ a. trópico.
tropics /'trɒpɪks/ n. trópico m.
trot /trɒt/ n. **1.** trote m. —v. **2.** trotar.
trouble /'trʌbəl/ n. **1.** apuro m.; congoja; aflicción f. —v. **2.** molestar; afligir.
troublesome /'trʌbəlsəm/ a. penoso, molesto.
trough /trɒf/ n. artesa f.
trousers /'trauzərz/ n. pantalones, calzones m.pl.
trout /traut/ n. trucha f.
truce /trus/ n. tregua f.
truck /trʌk/ n. camión m.
true /tru/ a. verdadero, cierto, verdad.
truffle /'trʌfəl/ n. trufa f.
trumpet /'trʌmpɪt/ n. trompeta, trompa f.
trunk /trʌŋk/ n. baúl m.; (of a tree) tronco m.
trust /trʌst/ n. **1.** confianza f. —v. **2.** confiar.
trustworthy /'trʌst,wɜrði/ a. digno de confianza.
truth /truθ/ n. verdad f.
truthful /'truθfəl/ a. veraz.
try /trai/ n. **1.** prueba f.; ensayo m. —v. **2.** tratar; probar; ensayar; Leg. juzgar. **t. on,** probarse.
T-shirt /'ti,ʃɜrt/ n. camiseta f.
tub /tʌb/ n. tina f.
tube /tub/ n. tubo m.

tuberculosis /tʊ,bɜrkyə'lousɪs/ n. tuberculosis f.
tuck /tʌk/ n. **1.** recogido m. —v. **2.** recoger.
Tuesday /'tuzdei/ n. martes m.
tug /tʌg/ n. **1.** tirada f.; (boat) remolcador m. —v. **2.** tirar de.
tuition /tu'ɪʃən/ n. matrícula, colegiatura f.
tumble /'tʌmbəl/ n. **1.** caída f. —v. **2.** caer, tumbar; voltear.
tumult /'tumʌlt/ n. tumulto, alboroto m.
tuna /'tʌni/ n. atún m.
tune /tun/ n. **1.** tono m.; melodía, canción f. —v. **2.** templar.
tunnel /'tʌnl/ n. túnel m.
turf /tɜrf/ n. césped m.
Turkey /'tɜrki/ n. Turquía f.
Turkish /'tɜrkɪʃ/ a. turco.
turmoil /'tɜrmɔil/ n. disturbio m.
turn /tɜrn/ n. **1.** vuelta f.; giro; turno m. —v. **2.** volver, tornear, girar; **t. into,** transformar. **t. around,** volverse. **t. on,** encender; abrir. **t. off, t. out,** apagar.
turnip /'tɜrnɪp/ n. nabo m.
turret /'tɜrɪt/ n. torrecilla f.
turtle /'tɜrtl/ n. tortuga f.
turtleneck sweater /'tɜrtl,nɛk/ jersey de cuello alto m.
tutor /'tutər/ n. **1.** tutor -ra. —v. **2.** enseñar.
tweezers /'twizərz/ n.pl. pinzas f.pl.
twelve /twɛlv/ a. & pron. doce.
twenty /'twɛnti/ a. & pron. veinte.
twice /twais/ adv. dos veces.
twig /twɪg/ n. varita; ramita f.; vástago m.
twilight /'twai,lait/ n. crepúsculo m.
twin /twɪn/ n. gemelo -la.
twine /twain/ n. **1.** guita f. —v. **2.** torcer.
twinkle /'twɪŋkəl/ v. centellear.
twist /twɪst/ v. torcer.
two /tu/ a. & pron. dos.
type /taip/ n. **1.** tipo m. —v. **2.** escribir a máquina.
typewriter /'taip,raitər/ n. máquina de escribir.
typhoid fever /'taifɔid/ fiebre tifoidea.
typical /'tɪpɪkəl/ a. típico.
typist /'taipɪst/ n. mecanógrafo -fa.
tyranny /'tɪrəni/ n. tiranía f.
tyrant /'tairənt/ n. tirano -na.

U

udder /'ʌdər/ *n.* ubre *f.*

UFO *abbr.* (unidentified flying object) OVNI *m.* (objeto volador no identificado).

ugly /'ʌgli/ *a.* feo.

Ukraine /yu'krein/ *n.* Ucrania *f.*

Ukrainian /yu'kreiniən/ *a. & n.* ucranio.

ulcer /'ʌlsər/ *n.* úlcera *f.*

ulterior /ʌl'tɪəriər/ *a.* ulterior.

ultimate /'ʌltəmɪt/ *a.* último.

ultrasonic /,ʌltrə'sɒnɪk/ *a.* ultrasónico.

umbrella /ʌm'brɛlə/ *n.* paraguas *m.* **sun u.,** quitasol *m.*

umpire /'ʌmpaɪər/ *n.* árbitro *m.*

unable /ʌn'eibəl/ *a.* incapaz. **to be u.,** no poder.

unanimous /yu'nænəməs/ *a.* unánime.

uncertain /ʌn'sɜrtn/ *a.* incierto, inseguro.

uncle /'ʌŋkəl/ *n.* tío *m.*

unconscious /ʌn'kɒnʃəs/ *a.* inconsciente; desmayado.

uncover /ʌn'kʌvər/ *v.* descubrir.

undeniable /,ʌndɪ'naiəbəl/ *a.* innegable.

under /'ʌndər/ *adv.* **1.** debajo, abajo. —*prep.* **2.** bajo, debajo de.

underestimate /,ʌndər'ɛstə,meit/ *v.* menospreciar; subestimar.

undergo /,ʌndər'gou/ *v.* sufrir.

underground / 'ʌndər,graund;/ *a.* subterráneo; clandestino.

underline /'ʌndər,lain/ *v.* subrayar.

underneath /,ʌndər'niθ/ *adv.* **1.** por debajo. —*prep.* **2.** debajo de.

undershirt /'ʌndər,ʃɜrt/ *n.* camiseta *f.*

understand /,ʌndər'stænd/ *v.* entender, comprender.

undertake /,ʌndər'teik/ *v.* emprender.

underwear /'ʌndər,wɛər/ *n.* ropa interior.

undo /ʌn'du/ *v.* deshacer; desatar.

undress /ʌn'drɛs/ *v.* desnudar, desvestir.

uneasy /ʌn'izi/ *a.* inquieto.

uneven /ʌn'ivən/ *a.* desigual.

unexpected /,ʌnɪk'spɛktɪd/ *a.* inesperado.

unfair /ʌn'fɛər/ *a.* injusto.

unfit /ʌn'fɪt/ *a.* incapaz; inadecuado.

unfold /ʌn'fould/ *v.* desplegar; revelar.

unforgettable /,ʌnfər'gɛtəbəl/ *a.* inolvidable.

unfortunate /ʌn'fɔrtʃənɪt/ *a.* desafortunado, desgraciado.

unfurnished /ʌn'fɜrnɪʃt/ *a.* desamueblado.

unhappy /ʌn'hæpi/ *a.* infeliz.

uniform /'yunə,fɔrm/ *a. & n.* uniforme *m.*

unify /'yunə,fai/ *v.* unificar.

union /'yunyən/ *n.* unión *f.* **labor u.,** sindicato de obreros.

unique /yu'nik/ *a.* único.

unisex /'yunə,sɛks/ *a.* unisex.

unit /'yunɪt/ *n.* unidad *f.*

unite /yu'nait/ *v.* unir.

United Nations /yu'naitɪd 'neiʃənz/ Naciones Unidas *f.pl.*

United States /yu'naitɪd 'steits/ Estados Unidos *m.pl.*

unity /'yunɪti/ *n.* unidad *f.*

universal /,yunə'vɜrsəl/ *a.* universal.

universe /'yunə,vɜrs/ *n.* universo *m.*

university /,yunə'vɜrsɪti/ *n.* universidad *f.*

unleaded /ʌn'lɛdɪd/ *a.* sin plomo.

unless /ʌn'lɛs/ *conj.* a menos que, si no es que.

unlike /ʌn'laik/ *a.* disímil.

unload /ʌn'loud/ *v.* descargar.

unlock /ʌn'lɒk/ *v.* abrir.

unplug /ʌn'plʌg/ *v.* desenchufar.

unpopular /ʌn'pɒpyələr/ *a.* impopular.

unreasonable /ʌn'rizənəbəl/ *a.* desrazonable.

unscrew /ʌn'skru/ *v.* desatornillar.

untie /ʌn'tai/ *v.* desatar; soltar.

until /ʌn'tɪl/ *prep.* **1.** hasta. —*conj.* **2.** hasta que.

unusual /ʌn'yuʒuəl/ *a.* raro, inusitado.

up /ʌp/ *adv.* **1.** arriba. —*prep.* **2. u. the street,** *etc.* calle arriba, etc.

uphold /ʌp'hould/ *v.* apoyar; defender.

upholster /ʌp'houlstər, ə'poul-/ *v.* entapizar.

upload /'ʌp,loud/ *n.* **1.** ascenso de archivos *m.* —*v.* **2.** subir, cargar.

upon /ə'pɒn/ *prep.* sobre, encima de.

upper /'ʌpər/ *a.* superior.

upper-case letter /'ʌpər 'keis/ mayúscula f.

upright /'ʌp,rait/ a. derecho, recto.

upriver /'ʌp,rɪvər/ adv. río arriba.

uproar /'ʌp,rɔr/ n. alboroto, tumulto m.

upset /n. 'ʌp,sɛt; v. ʌp'sɛt/ n. **1.** trastorno m. —v. **2.** trastornar.

upsetting /ʌp'sɛtɪŋ/ a. inquietante.

upstream /'ʌp'strim/ adv. aguas arriba, contra la corriente, río arriba.

uptight /'ʌp'tait/ a. (psicológicamente) tenso, tieso.

upward /'ʌpwərd/ adv. hacia arriba.

urge /ɜrdʒ/ n. **1.** deseo m. —v. **2.** instar.

urgency /'ɜrdʒənsi/ n. urgencia f.

urgent /'ɜrdʒənt/ a. urgente. **to be u.,** urgir.

us /ʌs/ pron. nosotros -as; nos.

use /n. yus; v. yuz/ n. **1.** uso m. —v. **2.** usar, emplear. **u. up,** gastar, agotar. **be used to,** estar acostumbrado a.

useful /'yusfəl/ a. útil.

useless /'yuslɪs/ a. inútil, inservible.

user-friendly /'yuzər 'frɛndli/ a. amigable.

username /'yuzər'neim/ n. nombre de usuario m.

usher /'ʌʃər/ n. **1.** acomodador -ora. —v. **2.** introducir.

usual /'yuʒuəl/ a. usual.

utensil /yu'tɛnsəl/ n. utensilio m.

utmost /'ʌt,moust/ a. sumo, extremo.

utter /'ʌtər/ a. **1.** completo. —v. **2.** proferir; dar.

utterance /'ʌtərəns/ n. expresión f.

V

vacancy /'veikənsi/ n. vacante f.

vacant /'veikənt/ a. desocupado, libre.

vacation /vei'keiʃən/ n. vacaciones f.pl.

vaccinate /'væksə,neit/ v. vacunar.

vacuum /'vækyum/ n. vacuo, vacío m. **v. cleaner,** aspiradora f.

vagrant /'veigrənt/ a. & n. vagabundo- da.

vague /veig/ a. vago.

vain /vein/ a. vano; vanidoso. **in v.,** en vano.

valiant /'vælyənt/ a. valiente.

valid /'vælɪd/ a. válido.

valley /'væli/ n. valle m.

valor /'vælər/ n. valor m.

valuable /'vælyuəbəl/ a. valioso. **to be v.,** valer mucho.

value /'vælyu/ n. **1.** valor, importe m. —v. **2.** valorar; estimar.

van /væn/ n. furgoneta f.

vandal /'vændļ/ n. vándalo m.

vandalism /'vændļ,ɪzəm/ n. vandalismo m.

vanish /'vænɪʃ/ v. desaparecer.

vanity /'væniti/ n. vanidad f. **v. case,** polvera f.

vanquish /'væŋkwɪʃ/ v. vencer.

vapor /'veipər/ n. vapor m.

variation /,vɛəri'eiʃən/ n. variación f.

varicose vein /'væri,kous/ variz f.

variety /və'raiiti/ n. variedad f.

various /'vɛəriəs/ a. varios; diversos.

varnish /'vɑrnɪʃ/ n. **1.** barniz m. —v. **2.** barnizar.

vary /'vɛəri/ v. variar; cambiar.

vase /veis, veiz, vɑz/ n. florero; jarrón m.

vasectomy /væ'sɛktəmi/ n. vasectomía f.

vassal /'væsəl/ n. vasallo m.

vast /væst/ a. vasto.

vat /væt/ n. tina f., tanque m.

VAT /væt/ n. IVA (impuesto sobre el valor añadido).

vault /vɔlt/ n. bóveda f.

vegetable /'vɛdʒtəbəl/ a. & n. vegetal m.; (pl.) legumbres, verduras f.pl.

vehement /'viəmənt/ a. vehemente.

vehicle /'viikəl/ n. vehículo m.

veil /veil/ n. **1.** velo m. —v. **2.** velar.

vein /vein/ n. vena f.

velocity /və'lɒsiti/ n. velocidad f.

velvet /'vɛlvɪt/ n. terciopelo m.

Venetian /və'niʃən/ a. & n. veneciano.

vengeance /'vɛndʒəns/ n. venganza f.

Venice /'vɛnɪs/ n. Venecia f.

vent /vɛnt/ n. apertura f.

ventilate /'vɛntļ,eit/ v. ventilar.

venture /'vɛntʃər/ *n.* ventura *f.*

verb /vɜrb/ *n.* verbo *m.*

verbose /vər'bous/ *a.* verboso.

verdict /'vɜrdɪkt/ *n.* veredicto, fallo *m.*

verge /vɜrdʒ/ *n.* borde *m.*

verify /'vɛrə,faɪ/ *v.* verificar.

versatile /'vɜrsətl/ *a.* versátil.

verse /vɜrs/ *n.* verso *m.*

version /'vɜrʒən/ *n.* versión *f.*

vertical /'vɜrtɪkəl/ *a.* vertical.

very /'vɛri/ *a.* **1.** mismo. —*adv.* **2.** muy.

vessel /'vɛsəl/ *n.* vasija *f.;* barco *m.*

vest /vɛst/ *n.* chaleco *m.*

veteran /'vɛtərən/ *a. & n.* veterano -na.

veto /'vitou/ *n.* veto *m.*

vex /vɛks/ *v.* molestar.

via /'vaɪə, 'viə/ *prep.* por la vía de; por.

viaduct /'vaɪə,dʌkt/ *n.* viaducto *m.*

vibrate /'vaɪbreɪt/ *v.* vibrar.

vibration /vaɪ'breɪʃən/ *n.* vibración *f.*

vice /vaɪs/ *n.* vicio *m.*

vicinity /vɪ'sɪnɪti/ *n.* vecindad *f.*

vicious /'vɪʃəs/ *a.* vicioso.

victim /'vɪktəm/ *n.* víctima *f.*

victor /'vɪktər/ *n.* vencedor -ora.

victorious /vɪk'tɔriəs/ *a.* victorioso.

victory /'vɪktəri/ *n.* victoria *f.*

video camera /'vɪdi,ou/ videocámara *f.*

videoconference /'vɪdiou,kɒnfərəns/ videoconferencia *f.*

videodisc /'vɪdiou,dɪsk/ *n.* videodisco *m.*

video game /'vɪdi,ou/ videojuego *m.*

videotape /'vɪdiou,teɪp/ *n.* vídeo *m.*, magnetoscopio *m.*

view /vyu/ *n.* **1.** vista *f.* —*v.* **2.** ver.

viewpoint /'vyu,pɔɪnt/ *n.* punto de vista *m.*

vigil /'vɪdʒəl/ *n.* vigilia, vela *f.*

vigilant /'vɪdʒələnt/ *a.* vigilante.

vigor /'vɪgər/ *n.* vigor *m.*

vile /vaɪl/ *a.* vil, bajo.

village /'vɪlɪdʒ/ *n.* aldea *f.*

villain /'vɪlən/ *n.* malvado -da.

vindicate /'vɪndɪ,keɪt/ *v.* vindicar.

vine /vaɪn/ *n.* parra, vid *f.*

vinegar /'vɪnɪgər/ *n.* vinagre *m.*

vintage /'vɪntɪdʒ/ *n.* vendimia *f.*

violate /'vaɪə,leɪt/ *v.* violar.

violation /,vaɪə'leɪʃən/ *n.* violación *f.*

violence /'vaɪələns/ *n.* violencia *f.*

violent /'vaɪələnt/ *a.* violento.

violin /,vaɪə'lɪn/ *n.* violín *m.*

virgin /'vɜrdʒɪn/ *n.* virgen *f.*

virile /'vɪrəl/ *a.* viril.

virtual /'vɜrtʃuəl/ *a.* virtual.

virtual memory memoria virtual *f.*

virtual reality realidad virtual *f.*

virtue /'vɜrtʃu/ *n.* virtud *f.*

virtuous /'vɜrtʃuəs/ *a.* virtuoso.

virus /'vaɪrəs/ *n.* virus *m.*

visa /'vizə/ *n.* visa *f.*

visible /'vɪzəbəl/ *a.* visible.

vision /'vɪʒən/ *n.* visión *f.*

visit /'vɪzɪt/ *n.* **1.** visita *f.* —*v.* **2.** visitar.

visitor /'vɪzɪtər/ *n.* visitante *m. & f.*

visual /'vɪʒuəl/ *a.* visual.

vital /'vaɪtl/ *a.* vital.

vitality /vaɪ'tælɪti/ *n.* vitalidad, energía vital *f.*

vitamin /'vaɪtəmɪn/ *n.* vitamina *f.*

vivacious /vɪ'veɪʃəs/ *a.* vivaz.

vivid /'vɪvɪd/ *a.* vivo; gráfico.

vocabulary /vou'kæbyə,lɛri/ *n.* vocabulario *m.*

vocal /'voukəl/ *a.* vocal.

vodka /'vɒdkə/ *n.* vodca *m.*

vogue /voug/ *n.* boga; moda *f.* **be in vogue** estilarse.

voice /vɔɪs/ *n.* **1.** voz *f.* —*v.* **2.** expresar.

voice mail correo de voz *m.*

voice recognition reconocimiento de voz *m.*

void /vɔɪd/ *a.* **1.** vacío. —*n.* **2.** vacío *m.* —*v.* **3.** invalidar.

voltage /'voultɪdʒ/ *n.* voltaje *m.*

volume /'vɒlyum/ *n.* volumen; tomo *m.*

voluntary /'vɒlən,tɛri/ *a.* voluntario.

volunteer /,vɒlən'tɪər/ *n.* **1.** voluntario -ria. —*v.* **2.** ofrecerse.

vomit /'vɒmɪt/ *v.* vomitar.

vote /vout/ *n.* **1.** voto *m.* —*v.* **2.** votar.

voter /'voutər/ *n.* votante *m. & f.*

vouch /vautʃ/ *v.* **v. for,** garantizar.

vow /vau/ *n.* **1.** voto *m.* —*v.* **2.** jurar.

vowel /'vauəl/ *n.* vocal *f.*

voyage /'vɔɪɪdʒ/ *n.* viaje *m.*

vulgar /'vʌlgər/ *a.* vulgar; común; soez.

vulnerable /'vʌlnərəbəl/ *a.* vulnerable.

W X Y Z

wade /weid/ v. vadear.

wag /wæg/ v. menear.

wage /weidʒ/ n. 1. (pl.) sueldo, salario m. —v. 2. w. war, hacer guerra.

wagon /'wægən/ n. carreta f.

wail /weil/ n. 1. lamento, gemido m. —v. 2. lamentar, gemir.

waist /weist/ n. cintura f.

wait /weit/ n. 1. espera f. —v. 2. esperar. **w. for,** esperar. **w. on,** atender.

waiter /'weitər/ **waitress** n. camarero -ra.

waiting room /'weitɪŋ/ sala de espera.

wake /weik/ v. **w. up,** despertar.

walk /wɔk/ n. 1. paseo m.; vuelta; caminata f.; modo de andar. —v. 2. andar; caminar; ir a pie.

wall /wɔl/ n. pared; muralla f.

wallcovering /'wɔl,kʌvərɪŋ/ n. tapizado de pared m.

wallet /'wɒlɪt/ n. cartera f.

wallpaper /'wɔl,peipər/ n. 1. empapelado m. —v. 2. empapelar.

walnut /'wɔl,nʌt/ n. nuez f.

waltz /wɔlts/ n. vals m.

wander /'wɒndər/ v. vagar.

want /wɒnt/ n. 1. necesidad f. —v. 2. querer.

war /wɔr/ n. guerra f.

ward /wɔrd/ n. 1. Pol. barrio m.; (hospital) cuadra f. —v. 2. **w. off,** parar.

warehouse /'wɛər,haus/ n. almacén m.

wares /wɛərz/ n. mercancías f.pl.

warlike /'wɔr,laik/ a. belicoso.

warm /wɔrm/ a. 1. caliente; Fig. caluroso. **to be w.,** tener calor; (weather) hacer calor. —v. 2. calentar.

warmth /wɔrmθ/ n. calor m.

warn /wɔrn/ v. advertir.

warning /'wɔrnɪŋ/ n. aviso m.

warp /wɔrp/ v. alabear.

warrant /'wɔrənt, 'wɒr-/ v. justificar.

warrior /'wɔriər/ n. guerrero -ra.

warship /'wɔr,ʃɪp/ n. navío de guerra, buque de guerra m.

wash /wɒʃ/ v. lavar.

washing machine /'wɒʃɪŋ/ máquina de lavar, lavadora f.

wasp /wɒsp/ n. avispa f.

waste /weist/ n. 1. gasto m.; desechos m.pl. —v. 2. gastar; perder.

watch /wɒtʃ/ n. 1. reloj m.; Mil. guardia f. —v. 2. observar, mirar. **w. for,** esperar. **w. out for,** tener cuidado con. **w. over,** guardar; velar por.

watchful /'wɒtʃfəl/ a. desvelado.

watchmaker /'wɒtʃ,meikər/ n. relojero -ra.

watchman /'wɒtʃmən/ n. sereno m.

water /'wɔtər/ n. 1. agua f. **w. color,** acuarela f. —v. 2. aguar.

waterbed /'wɔtər,bɛd/ n. cama de agua f.

waterfall /'wɔtər,fɔl/ n. catarata f.

watering can /'wɔtərɪŋ/ regadera f.

waterproof /'wɔtər,pruf/ a. impermeable.

wave /weiv/ n. 1. onda; ola f. —v. 2. ondear; agitar; hacer señas.

waver /'weivər/ v. vacilar.

wax /wæks/ n. 1. cera f. —v. 2. encerar.

way /wei/ n. camino; modo m., manera f. **in a w.,** hasta cierto punto. **a long w.,** muy lejos. **by the w.,** a propósito. **this w.,** por aquí. **that w.,** por allí. **which w.,** por dónde.

we /wi/ pron. nosotros -as.

weak /wik/ a. débil.

weaken /'wikən/ v. debilitar.

weakness /'wiknɪs/ n. debilidad f.

wealth /wɛlθ/ n. riqueza f.

wealthy /'wɛlθi/ a. adinerado.

wean /win/ v. destetar.

weapon /'wɛpən/ n. arma f.

wear /wɛər/ n. 1. uso; desgaste m.; (clothes) ropa f. —v. 2. usar, llevar. **w. out,** gastar; cansar.

weary /'wɪəri/ a. cansado, rendido.

weather /'wɛðər/ n. tiempo m.

weave /wiv/ v. tejer.

weaver /'wivər/ n. tejedor -ra.

web /wɛb/ n. tela f.

Web /wɛb/ n. (Internet) malla f., telaraña f., web m.

wedding /'wɛdɪŋ/ n. boda f.

wedge /wɛdʒ/ n. cuña f.

Wednesday /'wɛnzdei/ n. miércoles m.

weed /wid/ *n.* maleza *f.*

week /wik/ *n.* semana *f.*

weekday /'wik,dei/ *n.* día de trabajo.

weekend /'wik,ɛnd/ *n.* fin de semana.

weekly /'wikli/ *a.* semanal.

weep /wip/ *v.* llorar.

weigh /wei/ *v.* pesar.

weight /weit/ *n.* peso *m.*

weightless /'weitlɪs/ *v.* ingrávido.

weightlessness /'weitlɪsnɪs/ *n.* ingravidez *f.*

weird /wɪərd/ *a.* misterioso, extraño.

welcome /'wɛlkəm/ *a.* **1.** bienvenido. **you're w.,** de nada, no hay de qué. —*n.* **2.** acogida, bienvenida *f.* —*v.* **3.** acoger, recibir bien.

welfare /'wɛl,fɛər/ *n.* bienestar *m.*

well /wɛl/ *a.* **1.** sano, bueno. —*adv.* **2.** bien; pues. —*n.* **3.** pozo *m.*

well-done /'wɛl 'dʌn/ *a.* (food) bien cocido.

well-known /'wɛl 'noun/ *a.* bien conocido.

well-mannered /'wɛl 'mænərd/ *a.* educado.

west /wɛst/ *n.* oeste, occidente *m.*

western /'wɛstərn/ *a.* occidental.

westward /'wɛstwərd/ *adv.* hacia el oeste.

wet /wɛt/ *a.* **1.** mojado. **to get w.,** mojarse. —*v.* **2.** mojar.

whale /weil/ *n.* ballena *f.*

what /wʌt; *unstressed* wət/ *a.* **1.** qué; cuál. —*interrog. pron.* **2.** qué. —*rel. pron.* **3.** lo que.

whatever /wʌt'ɛvər/ *a.* **1.** cualquier. —*pron.* **2.** lo que; todo lo que.

wheat /wit/ *n.* trigo *m.*

wheel /wil/ *n.* rueda *f.* **steering w.,** volante *m.*

when /wɛn; *unstressed* wən/ *adv.* **1.** cuándo. —*conj.* **2.** cuando.

whenever /wɛn'ɛvər/ *conj.* siempre que, cuando quiera que.

where /wɛər/ *adv.* **1.** dónde, adónde. —*conj.* **2.** donde.

wherever /wɛər'ɛvər/ *conj.* dondequiera que, adondequiera que.

whether /'wɛðər/ *conj.* si.

which /wɪtʃ/ *a.* **1.** qué. —*interrog. pron.* **2.** cuál. —*rel. pron.* **3.** que; el cual; lo cual.

whichever /wɪtʃ'ɛvər/ *a. & pron.* cualquiera que.

while /wail/ *conj.* **1.** mientras; mientras que. —*n.* **2.** rato *m.*

whip /wɪp/ *n.* **1.** látigo *m.* —*v.* **2.** azotar.

whipped cream /wɪpt/ nata batida *f.*

whirl /wɜrl/ *v.* girar.

whirlpool /'wɜrl,pul/ *n.* vórtice *m.*

whirlwind /'wɜrl,wɪnd/ *n.* torbellino *m.*

whisk broom /wɪsk/ escobilla *f.*

whisker /'wɪskər/ *n.* bigote *m.*

whiskey /'wɪski/ *n.* whisky *m.*

whisper /'wɪspər/ *n.* **1.** cuchicheo *m.* —*v.* **2.** cuchichear.

whistle /'wɪsəl/ *n.* **1.** pito; silbido *m.* —*v.* **2.** silbar.

white /wait/ *a.* **1.** blanco. —*n.* **2.** (of egg) clara *f.*

who /hu/ **whom** *interrog. pron.* **1.** quién. —*rel. pron.* **2.** que; quien.

whoever /hu'ɛvər/ **whomever** *pron.* quienquiera que.

whole /houl/ *a.* **1.** entero. **the wh.,** todo el. —*n.* **2.** totalidad *f.* **on the wh.,** por lo general.

wholesale /'houl,seil/ *n.* **at wh.,** al por mayor.

wholesaler /'houl,seilər/ *n.* mayorista *m. & f.*

wholesome /'houlsəm/ *a.* sano, saludable.

wholly /'houli/ *adv.* enteramente.

whose /huz/ *interrog. adj.* **1.** de quién. —*rel. adj.* **2.** cuyo.

why /wai/ *adv.* por qué; para qué.

wicked /'wɪkɪd/ *a.* malo, malvado.

wickedness /'wɪkɪdnɪs/ *n.* maldad *f.*

wide /waid/ *a.* **1.** ancho; extenso. —*adv.* **2.** **w. open,** abierto de par en par.

widen /'waidṇ/ *v.* ensanchar; extender.

widespread /'waid'sprɛd/ *a.* extenso.

widow /'wɪdou/ *n.* viuda *f.*

widower /'wɪdouər/ *n.* viudo *m.*

width /wɪdθ/ *n.* anchura *f.*

wield /wild/ *v.* manejar, empuñar.

wife /waif/ *n.* esposa, señora, mujer *f.*

wig /wɪg/ *n.* peluca *f.*

wild /waild/ *a.* salvaje; bárbaro.

wilderness /'wɪldərnɪs/ *n.* desierto *m.*

wildlife /'waild,laif/ *n.* fauna silvestre *f.*

will /wɪl/ *n.* **1.** voluntad *f.*; testamento *m.* —*v.* **2.** querer; determinar; *Leg.* legar.

willful /'wɪlfəl/ *a.* voluntarioso; premeditado.

willing /'wɪlɪŋ/ *a.* **to be w.,** estar dispuesto.

willingly /'wɪlɪŋli/ *adv.* de buena gana.

wilt /wɪlt/ *v.* marchitar.

win /wɪn/ *v.* ganar.

wind /*n.* wɪnd; *v.* waind/ *n.* **1.** viento *m.* —*v.* **2.** torcer; dar cuerda a.

windmill /'wɪnd,mɪl/ *n.* molino de viento *m.*

window /'wɪndou/ *n.* ventana; (of car) ventanilla *f.*; (of shop or store) escaparate *m.*

windshield /'wɪnd,ʃild/ *n.* parabrisas *m.*

windy /'wɪndi/ *a.* ventoso. **to be w.,** (weather) hacer viento.

wine /wain/ *n.* vino *m.*

wing /wɪŋ/ *n.* ala *f.*; *Theat.* bastidor *m.*

wink /wɪŋk/ *n.* **1.** guiño *m.* —*v.* **2.** guiñar.

winner /'wɪnər/ *n.* ganador -ra.

winter /'wɪntər/ *n.* invierno *m.*

wipe /waip/ *v.* limpiar; (dry) secar. **w. out,** destruir.

wire /waiᵊr/ *n.* **1.** alambre; hilo; telegrama *m.* —*v.* **2.** telegrafiar.

wireless /'waiᵊrlɪs/ *n.* telégrafo sin hilos.

wisdom /'wɪzdəm/ *n.* juicio *m.*; sabiduría *f.*

wise /waiz/ *a.* sensato, juicioso; sabio.

wish /wɪʃ/ *n.* **1.** deseo; voto *m.* —*v.* **2.** desear; querer.

wit /wɪt/ *n.* ingenio *m.*, sal *f.*

witch /wɪtʃ/ *n.* bruja *f.*

with /wɪθ, wɪð/ *prep.* con.

withdraw /wɪð'drɔ, wɪθ-/ *v.* retirar.

wither /'wɪðər/ *v.* marchitar.

withhold /wɪθ'hould, wɪð-/ *v.* retener, suspender.

within /wɪð'ɪn, wɪθ-/ *adv.* **1.** dentro, por dentro. —*prep.* **2.** dentro de; en.

without /wɪð'aut, wɪθ-/ *adv.* **1.** fuera, por fuera. —*prep.* **2.** sin.

witness /'wɪtnɪs/ *n.* **1.** testigo; testimonio *m.* & *f.* —*v.* **2.** presenciar; atestar.

witty /'wɪti/ *a.* ingenioso, gracioso, ocurrente.

wizard /'wɪzərd/ *n.* hechicero *m.*

woe /wou/ *n.* dolor *m.*; pena *f.*

wolf /wʊlf/ *n.* lobo -ba.

woman /'wʊmən/ *n.* mujer *f.*

womb /wum/ *n.* entrañas *f.pl.*, matriz *f.*

wonder /'wʌndər/ *n.* **1.** maravilla; admiración *f.* **for a w.,** por milagro. **no w.,** no es extraño. —*v.* **2.** preguntarse; maravillarse.

wonderful /'wʌndərfəl/ *a.* maravilloso; estupendo.

woo /wu/ *v.* cortejar.

wood /wʊd/ *n.* madera; (for fire) leña *f.*

wooden /'wʊdn̩/ *a.* de madera.

wool /wʊl/ *n.* lana *f.*

word /wɜrd/ *n.* **1.** palabra *f.* **the words** (of a song), la letra. —*v.* **2.** expresar.

word processing /'prɒsɛsɪŋ/ procesamiento de textos *m.*

word processor /'prɒsɛsər/ procesador de textos *m.*

work /wɜrk/ *n.* **1.** trabajo *m.*; (of art) obra *f.* —*v.* **2.** trabajar; obrar; funcionar.

worker /'wɜrkər/ *n.* trabajador -ra; obrero -ra.

workman /'wɜrkmən/ *n.* obrero *m.*

work station estación de trabajo *f.*

work week /'wɜrk,wik/ semana laboral *f.*

world /wɜrld/ *n.* mundo *m.* **w. war,** guerra mundial.

worldly /'wɜrldli/ *a.* mundano.

worldwide /'wɜrld'waid/ *a.* mundial.

worm /wɜrm/ *n.* gusano *m.*

worn /wɔrn/ *a.* usado. **w. out,** gastado; cansado; rendido.

worrisome /'wɜrisəm/ *a.* inquietante.

worry /'wɜri/ *n.* **1.** preocupación *f.* —*v.* **2.** preocupar.

worrying /'wɜriɪŋ/ *a.* inquietante.

worse /wɜrs/ *a.* peor. **to get w.,** empeorar.

worship /'wɜrʃɪp/ *n.* **1.** adoración *f.* —*v.* **2.** adorar.

worst /wɜrst/ *a.* peor.

worth /wɜrθ/ *a.* **1.** **to be w.,** valer. —*n.* **2.** valor *m.*

worthless /'wɜrθlɪs/ *a.* sin valor.

worthy /'wɜrði/ *a.* digno.

wound /wund/ *n.* **1.** herida *f.* —*v.* **2.** herir.

wrap /ræp/ *n.* **1.** (pl.) abrigos *m.pl.* —*n.* **2.** envolver.

wrapping /'ræpɪŋ/ *n.* cubierta *f.*

wrath /ræθ/ *n.* ira, cólera *f.*

wreath /riθ/ *n.* guirnalda; corona *f.*

wreck /rɛk/ *n.* **1.** ruina *f.*; accidente *m.* —*v.* **2.** destrozar, arruinar.

wrench /rɛntʃ/ *n.* llave *f.* **monkey w.**, llave inglesa.

wrestle /'rɛsəl/ *v.* luchar.

wretched /'rɛtʃɪd/ *a.* miserable.

wring /rɪŋ/ *v.* retorcer.

wrinkle /'rɪŋkəl/ *n.* **1.** arruga *f.* —*v.* **2.** arrugar.

wrist /rɪst/ *n.* muñeca *f.* **w. watch,** reloj de pulsera.

write /rait/ *v.* escribir. **w. down,** apuntar.

writer /'raitər/ *n.* escritor -ra.

writhe /raið/ *v.* contorcerse.

writing paper /'raitɪŋ/ papel de escribir *m.*

wrong /rɔŋ/ *a.* **1.** equivocado; incorrecto. **to be w.,** equivocarse; no tener razón. —*adv.* **2.** mal, incorrectamente. —*n.* **3.** agravio *m.* **right and w.,** el bien y el mal. —*v.* **4.** agraviar, ofender.

WWW *abbr.* (World Wide Web) malla mundial *f.*

x-ray /'ɛks,rei/ *n.* **1.** rayo X *m.*, radiografía, *f.* —*v.* **2.** radiografiar.

xylophone /'zailə,foun/ *n.* xilófono *m.*

yacht /yɒt/ *n.* yate *m.*

yard /yɑrd/ *n.* patio, corral *m.*; (measure) yarda *f.*

yarn /yɑrn/ *n.* hilo.

yawn /yɔn/ *n.* **1.** bostezo *m.* —*v.* **2.** bostezar.

year /yɪər/ *n.* año *m.*

yearly /'yɪərli/ *a.* anual.

yearn /yɜrn/ *v.* anhelar.

yell /yɛl/ *n.* **1.** grito *m.* —*v.* **2.** gritar.

yellow /'yɛlou/ *a.* amarillo.

yes /yɛs/ *adv.* sí.

yesterday /'yɛstər,dei/ *adv.* ayer.

yet /yɛt/ *adv.* todavía, aún.

Yiddish /'yɪdɪʃ/ *n.* yídish *m.*

yield /yild/ *v.* producir; ceder.

yogurt /'yougərt/ *n.* yogur *m.*

yoke /youk/ *n.* yugo *m.*

yolk /youk/ *n.* yema *f.*

you /yu; *unstressed* yʊ, yə/ *pron.* usted, (pl.) ustedes; lo, la, los, las; le, les; (familiar) tú, (pl.) vosotros -as; ti; te, (pl.) os. **with y.,** contigo, con usted.

young /yʌŋ/ *a.* joven.

youngster /'yʌŋstər/ *n.* muchacho -cha *m. & f.*

your /yʊr, yɔr; *unstressed* yər/ *a.* su; (familiar) tu; (pl.) vuestro.

yours /yʊrz, yɔrz/ *pron.* suyo; (familiar) tuyo; (pl.) vuestro.

yourself -selves /yʊr'sɛlf, yər-yər-/ *pron.* sí; se; (familiar) ti; te. **with y.,** consigo; contigo. **you y.,** usted mismo, ustedes mismos; tú mismo, vosotros mismos.

youth /yuθ/ *n.* juventud *f.*; (person) joven *m. & f.*

youth club club juvenil *m.*

youthful /'yuθfəl/ *a.* juvenil.

yuppie /'yʌpi/ *n.* yuppie *m. & f.*

zap /zæp/ *v.* desintegrar, aniquilar.

zeal /zil/ *n.* celo, fervor *m.*

zealous /'zɛləs/ *a.* celoso, fervoroso.

zero /'zɪərou/ *n.* cero *m.*

zest /zɛst/ *n.* gusto *m.*

zip code /zɪp/ número de distrito postal.

zipper /'zɪpər/ *m.* cremallera *f.*

zone /zoun/ *n.* zona *f.*

zoo /zu/ *n.* jardín zoológico.

Spanish Irregular Verbs

Infinitive	Present	Future	Preterit	Past Part.
andar	ando	andaré	anduve	andado
caber	quepo	cabré	cupe	cabido
caer	caigo	caeré	caí	caído
conducir	conduzco	conduciré	conduje	conducido
dar	doy	daré	di	dado
decir	digo	diré	dije	dicho
estar	estoy	estaré	estuve	estado
haber	he	habré	hube	habido
hacer	hago	haré	hice	hecho
ir	voy	iré	fui	ido
jugar	juego	jugaré	jugué	jugado
morir	muero	moriré	morí	muerto
oir	oigo	oiré	oí	oído
poder	puedo	podré	pude	podido
poner	pongo	pondré	puse	puesto
querer	quiero	querré	quise	querido
saber	sé	sabré	supe	sabido
salir	salgo	saldré	salí	salido
ser	soy	seré	fui	sido
tener	tengo	tendré	tuve	tenido
traer	traigo	traeré	traje	traído
valer	valgo	valdré	valí	valido
venir	vengo	vendré	vine	venido
ver	veo	veré	vi	visto

Las formas del verbo inglés

1. Se forma la 3ª. persona singular del tiempo presente exactamente al igual que el plural de los sustantivos, añadiendo -es o -s a la forma sencilla según las mismas reglas, así:

(1)	teach	pass	wish	fix	buzz	
	teaches	passes	wishes	fixes	buzzes	

(2)	place	change	judge	please	freeze	
	places	changes	judges	pleases	freezes	

(3a)	find	sell	clean	hear	love	buy	know
	finds	sells	cleans	hears	loves	buys	knows

(3b)	think	like	laugh	stop	hope	meet	want
	thinks	likes	laughs	stops	hopes	meets	wants

(4)	cry	try	dry	carry	deny
	cries	tries	dries	carries	denies

Cinco verbos muy comunes tienen 3ª persona singular irregular:

(5)	go	do	say	have	be
	goes	does	says	has	is

2. Se forman el tiempo pasado y el participio de modo igual, añadiendo a la forma sencilla la terminación **-ed** o **-d** según las reglas que siguen:

(1) Si la forma sencilla termina en **-d** o **-t,** se le pone **-ed** como sílaba aparte:

end	fold	need	load
ended	folded	needed	loaded

want	feast	wait	light
wanted	feasted	waited	lighted

(2) Si la forma sencilla termina en cualquier otra consonante, se añade también **-ed** pero sin hacer sílaba aparte:

(2a)	bang	sail	seem	harm	earn	weigh
	banged	sailed	seemed	harmed	earned	weighed

(2b)	lunch	work	look	laugh	help	pass
	lunched	worked	looked	laughed	helped	passed

(3) Si la forma sencilla termina en **-e,** se le pone sólo **-d:**

(3a)	hate	taste	waste	guide	fade	trade
	hated	tasted	wasted	guided	faded	traded

(3b)	free	judge	rule	name	dine	scare
	freed	judged	ruled	named	dined	scared

(3c)	place	force	knife	like	hope	base
	placed	forced	knifed	liked	hoped	based

(4) Una **-y** final que sigue a cualquier consonante se cambia en **-ie** al añadir la **-d** del pasado/participio:

cry	try	dry	carry	deny
cried	tried	dried	carried	denied

3. Varios verbos muy comunes forman el tiempo pasado y el participio de manera irregular. Pertenecen a tres grupos.

(1) Los que tienen una sola forma irregular para tiempo pasado y participio, como los siguientes:

bend	bleed	bring	build	buy	catch	creep	deal
bent	bled	brought	built	bought	caught	crept	dealt

dig	feed	feel	fight	find	flee	get	hang
dug	fed	felt	fought	found	fled	got	hung

have	hear	hold	keep	lead	leave	lend	lose
had	heard	held	kept	led	left	lent	lost

make	mean	meet	say	seek	sell	send	shine
made	meant	met	said	sought	sold	sent	shone

shoot	sit	sleep	spend	stand	strike	sweep	teach
shot	sat	slept	spent	stood	struck	swept	taught

(2) Los que tienen una forma irregular para el tiempo pasado y otra forma irregular para el participio, como los siguientes:

be	beat	become	begin	bite
was	beat	became	began	bit
been	beaten	become	begun	bitten

blow	break	choose	come	do
blew	broke	chose	came	did
blown	broken	chosen	come	done

draw	drink	drive	eat	fall
drew	drank	drove	ate	fell
drawn	drunk	driven	eaten	fallen

fly	forget	freeze	give	go
flew	forgot	froze	gave	went
flown	forgotten	frozen	given	gone

grow	hide	know	ride	ring
grew	hid	knew	rode	rang
grown	hidden	known	ridden	rung

rise	run	see	shake	shrink
rose	ran	saw	shook	shrank
risen	run	seen	shaken	shrunk

sing	sink	speak	steal	swear
sang	sank	spoke	stole	swore
sung	sunk	spoken	stolen	sworn

swim	tear	throw	wear	write
swam	tore	threw	wore	wrote
swum	torn	thrown	worn	written

(3) Los que no varían del todo, la forma sencilla funcionando también como pasado/participio; entre éstos son de mayor frecuencia:

bet	burst	cast	cost	cut
hit	hurt	let	put	quit
read	set	shed	shut	slit
spit	split	spread	thrust	wet

El plural del sustantivo inglés

A la forma singular se añade la terminación -es o -s de acuerdo con las reglas siguientes.

(1) Si el singular termina en -ch, -s, -sh, -x o -z, se le pone -es como sílaba aparte:

match	glass	dish	box	buzz
matches	glasses	dishes	boxes	buzzes

(2) Si el singular termina en -ce, -ge, -se o -ze, se le pone una -s que con la vocal precedente forma sílaba aparte:

face	page	house	size
faces	pages	houses	sizes

(3) Una -y final que sigue a cualquier consonante se cambia en -ie a ponérsele la -s del plural:

sky	city	lady	ferry	penny
skies	cities	ladies	ferries	pennies

(4) Los siguientes sustantivos comunes tienen plural irregular:

man	woman	child	foot	mouse	goose
men	women	children	feet	mice	geese

wife	knife	life	half	leaf	deer
wives	knives	lives	halves	leaves	deer

Weights and Measures/Pesos y Medidas

Spanish/			
English	1 centímetro	=	.3937 inches
	1 metro	=	39.37 inches
	1 kilómetro	=	.621 mile
	1 centigramo	=	.1543 grain
	1 gramo	=	15.432 grains
	1 kilogramo	=	2.2046 pounds
	1 tonelada	=	2.204 pounds
	1 centilitro	=	.338 ounces
	1 litro	=	1.0567 quart (liquid); .908 quart (dry)
	1 kilolitro	=	264.18 gallons

English/			
Spanish	1 inch	=	2.54 centímetros
	1 foot	=	.305 metros
	1 mile	=	1.61 kilómetros
	1 grain	=	.065 gramos
	1 pound	=	.455 kilogramos
	1 ton	=	.907 toneladas
	1 ounce	=	2.96 centilitros
	1 quart	=	1.13 litros
	1 gallon	=	4.52 litros

Days of the Week/Días de la Semana

Sunday	domingo	**Thursday**	jueves
Monday	lunes	**Friday**	viernes
Tuesday	martes	**Saturday**	sábado
Wednesday	miércoles		

Months/Meses

January	enero	**July**	julio
February	febrero	**August**	agosto
March	marzo	**September**	septiembre
April	abril	**October**	octubre
May	mayo	**November**	noviembre
June	junio	**December**	diciembre

Useful Phrases/Locuciones Útiles

Good day, Good morning. Buenos días.
Good afternoon. Buenas tardes.
Good night, Good evening. Buenas noches.
Hello. ¡Hola!
Welcome! ¡Bienvenido!
See you later. Hasta luego.
Goodbye. ¡Adiós!
How are you? ¿Cómo está usted?
I'm fine, thank you. Estoy bien, gracias.
I'm pleased to meet you. Mucho gusto en conocerle.
May I introduce… Quisiera presentar…
Thank you very much. Muchas gracias.
You're welcome. De nada *or* No hay de qué.
Please. Por favor.
Excuse me. Con permiso.
Good luck. ¡Buena suerte!
To your health. ¡Salud!

Please help me. Ayúdeme, por favor.
I don't know. No sé.
I don't understand. No entiendo.
Do you understand? ¿Entiende usted?
I don't speak Spanish. No hablo español.
Do you speak English? ¿Habla usted inglés?
How do you say . . . in Spanish? ¿Cómo se dice . . . en español?
What do you call this? ¿Cómo se llama esto?
Speak slowly, please. Hable despacio, por favor.
Please repeat. Repita, por favor.
I don't like it. No me gusta.
I am lost. Ando perdido; Me he extraviado.

What is your name? ¿Cómo se llama usted?
My name is . . . Me llamo . . .
I am an American. Soy norteamericano.
Where are you from? ¿De dónde es usted?
I'm from… Soy de…

How is the weather?   ¿Qué tiempo hace?
It's cold (hot) today.   Hace frío (calor) hoy.
What time is it?   ¿Qué hora es?

How much is it?   ¿Cuánto es?
It is too much.   Es demasiado.
What do you wish?   ¿Qué desea usted?
I want to buy . . .   Quiero comprar . . .
May I see something better?   ¿Podría ver algo mejor?
May I see something cheaper?   ¿Podría ver algo menos caro?
It is not exactly what I want.   No es exactamente lo que quiero.

I'm hungry.   Tengo hambre.
I'm thirsty.   Tengo sed.
Where is there a restaurant?   ¿Dónde hay un restaurante?
I have a reservation.   Tengo una reservación.
I would like…   Quisiera…; Me gustaría…
Please give me…   Por favor, déme usted…
Please bring me…   Por favor, tráigame usted…
May I see the menu?   ¿Podría ver el menú?
The bill, please.   La cuenta, por favor.
Is service included in the bill?   ¿El servicio está incluido en la cuenta?
Where is there a hotel?   ¿Dónde hay un hotel?
Where is the post office?   ¿Dónde está el correo?
Is there any mail for me?   ¿Hay correo para mí?
Where can I mail this letter?   ¿Dónde puedo echar esta carta al correo?

Take me to…   Lléveme a…
I believe I am ill.   Creo que estoy enfermo.
Please call a doctor.   Por favor, llame al médico.
Please call the police.   Por favor, llame a la policía.
I want to send a telegram.   Quiero poner un telegrama.
As soon as possible.   Cuanto antes.

Round trip.   Ida y vuelta.

Please help me with my luggage.   Por favor, ayúdeme con mi equipaje.

Where can I get a taxi?   ¿Dónde se puede encontrar un taxi?

What is the fare to…   ¿Cuánto es el pasaje hasta…?

Please take me to this address.   Por favor, lléveme a esta dirección.

Where can I change my money?   ¿Dónde puedo cambiar mi dinero?

Where is the nearest bank?   ¿Dónde está el banco más cercano?

Can you accept my check?   ¿Puede aceptar usted mi cheque?

Do you accept traveler's checks?   ¿Aceptan cheques de viaje?

What is the postage?   ¿Cuánto es el franqueo?

Where is the nearest drugstore?   ¿Dónde está la farmacia más cercana?

Where is the men's (women's) room?   ¿Dónde está el servicio de caballeros (de señoras)?

Please let me off at…   Por favor, déjeme bajar en…

Right away.   ¡Pronto!

Help.   ¡Socorro!

Who is it?   ¿Quién es?

Just a minute!   ¡Un momento no más!

Come in.   ¡Pase usted!

Pardon me.   Disculpe usted.

Stop.   ¡Pare!

Look out.   ¡Cuidado!

Hurry.   ¡De prisa! *or* ¡Dése prisa!

Go on.   ¡Siga!

To (on, at) the right.   A la derecha.

To (on, at) the left.   A la izquierda.

Straight ahead.   Adelante.